*The New College*
# ITALIAN & ENGLISH
## Dictionary

### ROBERT C. MELZI
Widener College

*Dedicated to serving*

*our nation's youth*

## AMSCO SCHOOL PUBLICATIONS, INC.
315 Hudson Street / New York, N.Y. 10013

THE NEW COLLEGE ITALIAN & ENGLISH DICTIONARY

ISBN 0-87720-592-2

Published by Amsco School Publications, Inc., by arrangement with the copyright owners.

The cover photograph of Rome, J. Allan Cash/Rapho/Photo Researchers.

Printed in the United States of America

2 3 4 5 6 7 8 9

Robert C. Melzi, D. in L., A.M., Ph.D., was trained in Italy, at the University of Padua, and in the United States, at the University of Pennsylvania. He has done extensive linguistic research, traveling frequently to his native country. Now Professor of Romance Languages at Widener College, he has contributed articles and reviews to many learned journals and is the author of *Castelvetro's Annotations to the Inferno* (1966). Professor Melzi is a Cavaliere in the Order of Solidarity of the Republic of Italy.

Edwin B. Williams (1891–1975), under whose editorship *The New College Italian & English Dictionary* was prepared, was Chairman of the Department of Romance Languages, Dean of the Graduate School, and Provost of the University of Pennsylvania. Among his many works on the Spanish, Portuguese, and French languages are *The Williams Spanish and English Dictionary* and *The New College Spanish & English Dictionary*. He created and coordinated the New College series of original dictionaries—Spanish, French, Italian, Latin, and (forthcoming) German.

*The New College Italian & English Dictionary* is the most modern, authoritative, and usefully organized Italian and English dictionary in print, and the most extensive one in a paperback edition. There are 60,000 entries, based on spoken and written sources and organized to achieve the utmost clarity, precision, and convenience.

Important features:

1. Shows in English which of two or more words is the one you want ⟶

**clutch** [klʌtʃ] *s* presa; (*claw*) grinfia; (*of chickens*) covata; (mach) innesto; (aut) frizione...

**tèmpo** *m* time; weather; age; period, stage; cycle (*of internal combustion engine*); (gram) tense; (mus) tempo, (mus) movement; (sports) period; (theat, mov) part...

2. Transitive verbs translated strictly by transitive verbs and expressions ⟶

**calzare** ...‖ *tr* to wear, put on (*shoes, gloves or socks*)‖ *intr* to fit (*said of any garment*)...

3. Shows quality of stressed e's and o's of first person singular of regular verbs, and of all other parts of speech ⟶

**notare** (nòto) *tr*...
**scodellare** (scodèllo) *tr*...
**famó·so -sa** [s] *adj*...
**bène** ...‖ *adv*...
**giò·co** *m* (-chi)...

4. Shows first person singular of the present indicative of verbs in which the stress falls on the third syllable from the end ⟶

**ricuperare** (ricùpero) *tr*...
**considerare** (consìdero) *tr*...

5. Shows plural endings of nouns and adjectives which are formed irregularly ⟶

**cit·tà** *f* (-tà)...
**laburi·sta** (-sti -ste) *adj*...‖ **mf**...

6. Gender of Italian nouns shown also on English side ⟶

**tool** [tul] *s* utensile *m*...

# Contents

Preface     vii

Labels and Abbreviations     xi
    (Sigle ed abbreviazioni)

## Part One   Italian-English

Italian Spelling and Pronunciation     3

Grammatical Tables     7

Table of Regular Endings of Italian Verbs     15

Model Verbs     17

Italian-English     37–364

## Part Two   Inglese-Italiano

La pronunzia dell'inglese     3

Inglese-Italiano     7–355

v

# *Preface*

A dictionary is not only a link between two languages; it is a bridge across two cultures. This book is really two dictionaries: a dictionary of Italian words with their translations in English and a dictionary of English words with their translations in Italian.

There are six purposes that an Italian and English dictionary must fulfill. It must provide:

1. Italian words which an English-speaking person wishes to use in speaking and writing (by means of the English-Italian part)
2. English meanings of Italian words which an English-speaking person encounters in listening and reading (by means of the Italian-English part)
3. The spelling, pronunciation, and inflection of Italian words and the gender of Italian nouns which an English-speaking person needs in order to use Italian words correctly (by means of the Italian-English part)
4. English words which an Italian-speaking person wishes to use in speaking and writing (by means of the Italian-English part)
5. Italian meanings of English words which an Italian-speaking person encounters in listening and reading (by means of the English-Italian part)
6. The spelling, pronunciation, and inflection of English words which an Italian-speaking person needs in order to use English words correctly (by means of the English-Italian part)

In order to accomplish purpose **6**, International Phonetic Alphabet transcriptions of English words and their inflections are provided in the English-Italian part.

In order to accomplish purposes **1** and **3**, definitions and discriminations are provided in English. Since Italian is an almost perfectly phonetic language, IPA transcription of Italian words has been omitted. The only elements of pronunciation not shown by standard spelling are the values of tonic **e** and **o**, the stress of words stressed on the third syllable from the end, the value of intervocalic **s** when unvoiced, and the value of **z** and **zz** when voiced, which are shown in the entry words themselves.

The gender of Italian nouns is shown on both sides of the Dictionary, except that the gender of masculine nouns ending in -o or modified by an adjective ending in -o and feminine nouns ending in -a and -ione or modified by an adjective ending in -a is not shown on the English-Italian side.

Prepositional phrases and expressions containing a verb and a noun are listed under the noun, e.g.:

> **channel** ['tʃænəl] *s*...; **through channels** per via gerarchica
> **sky** [skaɪ] *s* (**skies**)...; **to praise to the skies** portare al cielo
> **ghiro** *m*...; **dormire come un ghiro** to sleep like a log

Italian expressions consisting of a noun and an adjective or a noun and an adjective phrase are listed under the noun, e.g.:

> **bilànc·ia** *f* (-ce)...; **bilancia commerciale** balance of trade;...
> **orolò·gio** *m* (-gi)...; **orologio a pendolo** clock;...

All words are treated in a fixed order according to the parts of speech and the functions of verbs, as follows: adjective, article, substantive, pronoun, adverb, preposition, conjunction, transitive verb, intransitive verb, reflexive verb, auxiliary verb, impersonal verb, interjection.

Meanings with labels come after more general meanings. Labels (printed in roman and in parentheses) refer to the preceding entry or phrase (printed in boldface).

The centered period is used in vocabulary entries of inflected words to mark off, according to standard orthographic principles in the two languages, the final syllable that has to be detached before the syllable showing the inflection is added:

> **vèc·chio -chia** (-**chi** -**chie**) *adj*...
> **put·ty** ['pʌti] *s* (-**ties**)...‖ *v* (*pret & pp* -**tied**)...
> **hap·py** ['hæpi] *adj* (-**pier**; -**piest**)...

If the entry word cannot be divided by a centered period, the full form is given in parentheses:

> **mouse** [maʊs] *s* (**mice** [maɪs])...
> **mouth** [maʊθ] *s* (**mouths** [maʊðz])...
> **die** [daɪ] *s* (**dice** [daɪs])...‖ *s* (**dies**)...‖ *v* (*pret & pp* **died**; *ger* **dying**) *intr*

Definitions and discriminations are printed in italics and in parentheses and refer to the English word they particularize:

> **porter** ['pɔrtər] *s* (*doorman*) portiere *m*; (*man who carries luggage*) facchino;...
> **órdine** *m* order;...series (*e.g., of years*); college (*e.g., of surgeons*);...

In order to facilitate finding the desired meaning and use, changes within a vocabulary entry in part of speech and function of verb, for an irregular inflection, in the use of an initial capital, in the gender of Italian nouns, and in the pronunciation of English words are marked with parallels, ||, instead of the usual semicolons.

Since vocabulary entries are not determined on the basis of etymology, homographs are included in a single entry. When the pronunciation of an English homograph changes, this is shown in the proper place after parallels:

> **frequent** ['frikwənt] *adj* frequente|| [frɪˈkwɛnt] or ['frikwənt] *tr...*

However, when the pronunciation of an Italian homograph changes, the words are entered separately:

> **retina** *f* small net
> **rètina** *f* (anat) retina
> **tóc·co -ca (-chi -che)** *adj...*|| *m* touch;...
> **tòc·co** *m* (**-chi**) chunk, piece;...

Periods are omitted after labels and grammatical abbreviations and at the end of vocabulary entries.

Proper nouns are listed in their alphabetical position in the main body of the Dictionary. Thus, **Svezia** and **svedese** do not have to be looked up in two different sections of the book. And all subentries are listed in strictly alphabetical order.

English adjectives are always translated by the Italian masculine form regardless of whether the translation of the exemplary noun modified would be masculine or feminine:

> **tough** [tʌf] *adj* duro;...; (*luck*) cattivo;...

The feminine form of an Italian adjective used as a noun (or an Italian feminine noun having identical spelling with the feminine form of an adjective) which falls alphabetically in a separate position from the adjective is treated in that position and is listed again as a cross reference under the adjective:

> **nòta** *f* mark, score,...
> **nò·to -ta** *adj...*|| *m...*|| *f* see **nota**

Many Italian verbs which take an indirect object have, as their equivalent, English verbs which take a direct object. This is shown on both sides of this Dictionary by the insertion of (with *dat*) after the Italian verb, e.g.,

> **ubbidire** §176 *intr...*; (with *dat*) to obey
> **obey** [oˈbe] *tr* ubbidire (with *dat*)

ix

On the Italian-English side inflection is shown by:

*a.* Numbers that refer to the grammatical tables of articles, pronouns, etc., and to the tables of model verbs; they are placed before the abbreviation indicating the part of speech:

> **mì·o -a** §6 *adj & pron poss*
> **lui** §5 *pron pers*
> **congiùngere** §183 *tr & ref*

*b.* The first person singular of the present indicative of verbs in which the stress falls on either an **e** or an **o** not stressed in the infinitive or on the third syllable from the end, whatever the vowel may be:

> **ritornare (ritórno)** *tr* ...
> **visitare (vìsito)** *tr* ...

*c.* The feminine ending of all adjectives which end in **-o** in the singular:

> **laborió·so -sa** [s] *adj* ...

*d.* The plural endings of nouns and adjectives which are formed irregularly:

> **bràc·cio** *m* (**-cia** *fpl*) ... ‖ *m* (**-ci**) ...
> **cit·tà** *f* (**-tà**) ...
> **dià·rio -ria** (**-ri -rie**) *adj* ... ‖ *m* ... ‖ *f* ...
> **fotogram·ma** *m* (**-mi**) ...
> **fràn·gia** *f* (**-ge**) ...
> **laburi·sta** (**-sti -ste**) *adj* ... ‖ *mf* ...
> **la·go** *m* (**-ghi**) ...
> **òr·co** *m* (**-chi**) ...
> **òtti·co -ca** (**-ci -che**) *adj* ... ‖ *m* ... ‖ *f* ...

*e.* The full plural forms of all nouns that cannot be divided by a centered period or whose plural cannot be shown by such division:

> **re** *m* (**re**) ...
> **caporeparto** *m* (**capireparto**) ...

I wish to express my gratitude to the many persons who helped me in the production of this book, and particularly to the late Dr. Edwin B. Williams, who, ever since graduate school, was a constant inspiration and who established the principles upon which this book was compiled; to my wife and children, who patiently aided and abetted me through ten years of research and compilation; to Richard J. Wiezell, Sebastiano DiBlasi, Walter D. Glanze, Miro Dogliotti, Michele Ricciardelli, and the late Giacomo Devoto.

# Labels and abbreviations
# Sigle ed abbreviazioni

*abbr* abbreviation—abbreviazione
(acronym) word formed from the initial letters or syllables of a series of words—parola costituita dalle lettere o sillabe iniziali di una serie di parole
*adj* adjective—aggettivo
*adv* adverb—avverbio
(aer) aeronautics—aeronautica
(agr) agriculture—agricoltura
(alg) algebra—algebra
(anat) anatomy—anatomia
(archaic) arcaico
(archeol) archeology—archeologia
(archit) architecture—architettura
(arith) arithmetic—aritmetica
*art* article—articolo
(astr) astronomy—astronomia
(astrol) astrology—astrologia
(aut) automobile—automobile
*aux* auxiliary verb—verbo ausiliare
(bact) bacteriology—batteriologia
(baseball) baseball
(basketball) pallacanestro
(bb) bookbinding—legatoria
(Bib) Biblical—biblico
(billiards) biliardo
(biochem) biochemistry—biochimica
(biol) biology—biologia
(bot) botany—botanica
(bowling) bowling
(boxing) pugilato
(bridge) bridge
(Brit) British—britannico
(cards) carte da gioco
(carp) carpentry—falegnameria
(checkers) gioco della dama
(chem) chemistry—chimica
(chess) scacchi
(coll) colloquial—familiare
(com) commercial—commerciale
*comb form* elemento di parola composta
*comp* comparative—comparativo
*cond* conditional—condizionale
*conj* conjunction—congiunzione
(cricket) cricket
(culin) cooking—cucina
*dat* dative—dativo
*def* definite—determinativo, definito
*dem* demonstrative—dimostrativo
(dentistry) medicina dentaria
(dial) dialectal—dialettale
(dipl) diplomacy—diplomazia

(disparaging) sprezzante
(eccl) ecclesiastical—ecclesiastico
(econ) economics—economia
(educ) education—istruzione
e.g., or *e.g.*, per esempio
(elec) electricity—elettricità
(electron) electronics—elettronica
(ent) entomology—entomologia
(equit) horseback riding—equitazione
*f* feminine noun—nome femminile
(fa) fine arts—belle arti
*fem* feminine—femminile
(fencing) scherma
(fig) figurative—figurato
(fin) financial—finanziario
(football) football americano
*fpl* feminine noun plural—nome femminile plurale
*fut* future—futuro
(geog) geography—geografia
(geol) geology—geologia
(geom) geometry—geometria
*ger* gerund—gerundio
(golf) golf
(gram) grammar—grammatica
(herald) heraldry—araldica
(hist) history—storia
(hort) horticulture—orticoltura
(hunt) hunting—caccia
(ichth) ichthyology—ittiologia
i.e., cioè
*imperf* imperfect—imperfetto
*impers* impersonal verb—verbo impersonale
*impv* imperative—imperativo
*ind* indicative—indicativo
*indef* indefinite—indefinito, indeterminativo
*inf* infinitive—infinito
(ins) insurance—assicurazione
*interj* interjection—interiezione
*interr* interrogative—interrogativo
*intr* intransitive verb—verbo intransitivo
*invar* invariable—invariabile
(Italian cards) carte italiane
(jewelry) gioielleria
(joc) jocular—faceto
(journ) journalism—giornalismo
(law) diritto, legge
(letterword) word in the form of an abbreviation which is pronounced by sounding the names of its letters in

xi

succession and which functions as a part of speech—parola in forma di abbreviazione che si ottiene pronunziando consecutivamente la denominazione di ciascuna lettera e che funziona come parte del discorso

(lexicography) lessicografia
(ling) linguistics—linguistica
(lit) literary—letterario
(log) logic—logica
*m* masculine noun—nome maschile
(mach) machinery—macchinario
*masc* masculine—maschile
(math) mathematics—matematica
(mech) mechanics—meccanica
(med) medicine—medicina
(metallurgy) metallurgia
(meteor) meteorology—meteorologia
*mf* masculine or feminine noun according to sex—nome maschile o nome femminile secondo il sesso
*m & f* see below between (mythol) and (naut)
(mil) military—militare
(min) mining—lavorazione delle miniere
(mov) moving pictures—cinematografo
*mpl* masculine noun plural—nome maschile plurale
(mus) music—musica
(mythol) mythology—mitologia
*m & f* masculine and feminine noun without regard to sex—nome maschile e femminile senza distinzione di sesso
(naut) nautical—nautico
(nav) naval—navale
*neut* neuter—neutro
*num* number—numero
(obs) obsolete—in disuso
(obstet) obstetrics—ostetricia
(opt) optics—ottica
(orn) ornithology—ornitologia
(painting) pittura
(pathol) pathology—patologia
(pej) pejorative—peggiorativo
*perf* perfect—perfetto, passato
*pers* personal—personale; person—persona
(pharm) pharmacy—farmacia
(philately) filatelia
(philol) philology—filologia
(philos) philosophy—filosofia
(phonet) phonetics—fonetica
(phot) photography—fotografia
(phys) physics—fisica
(physiol) physiology—fisiologia
*pl* plural—plurale
(poet) poetical—poetico
(poker) poker
(pol) politics—politica
*pp* past participle—participio passato
*poss* possessive—possessivo
*pref* prefix—prefisso
*prep* preposition—preposizione

*prep phrase* prepositional phrase—frase preposizionale
*pres* present—presente
*pret* preterit—passato remoto
*pron* pronoun—pronome
(pros) prosody—prosodia
(psychoanal) psychoanalysis—psicanalisi
(psychol) psychology—psicologia
(psychopath) psychopathology—psicopatologia
qlco or *qlco* qualcosa—something
qlcu or *qlcu* qualcuno—someone
(racing) corse
(rad) radio—radio
*ref* reflexive verb—verbo riflessivo o pronominale
*rel* relative—relativo
(rel) religion—religione
(rhet) rhetoric—retorica
(rok) rocketry—studio dei razzi
(rowing) canottaggio
(rr) railroad—ferrovia
(rugby) rugby
*s* substantive—sostantivo
(scornful) sprezzante
(Scot) Scottish—scozzese
(sculp) sculpture—scultura
(sew) sewing—cucito
*sg* singular—singolare
(slang) gergo
s.o. or *s.o.* someone—qualcuno
(soccer) calcio
*spl* substantive plural—sostantivo plurale
(sports) sport
*ssg* substantive singular—sostantivo singolare
s.th or *s.th* something—qualcosa
*subj* subjunctive—congiuntivo
*suf* suffix—suffisso
*super* superlative—superlativo
(surg) surgery—chirurgia
(surv) surveying—agrimensura, topografia
(taur) bullfighting—tauromachia
(telg) telegraphy—telegrafia
(telp) telephone—telefonia
(telv) television—televisione
(tennis) tennis
(tex) textile—tessile
(theat) theater—teatro
(theol) theology—teologia
*tr* transitive verb—verbo transitivo
(trademark) marchio di fabbrica
(typ) printing—tipografia
(U.S.A.) S.U.A.
*v* verb—verbo
var variant—variante
(vet) veterinary medicine—medicina veterinaria
(vulg) vulgar—volgare, ordinario
(wrestling) lotta
(zool) zoology—zoologia

# PART ONE

## *Italian-English*

# Italian Spelling and Pronunciation

**§1. The Italian Alphabet. 1.** The twenty-one letters of the Italian alphabet are listed below with their names and their sounds in terms of approximate equivalent English sounds. Their gender is masculine or feminine.

| LETTER | NAME | APPROXIMATE SOUND |
|---|---|---|
| **a** | a | Like *a* in English *father*, e.g., **facile, padre.** |
| **b** | bi | Like *b* in English *boat*, e.g., **bello, abate.** |
| **c** | ci | When followed by **e** or **i**, like *ch* in English *cherry*, e.g., **cento, cinque;** if the **i** is unstressed and followed by another vowel, its sound is not heard, e.g., **ciarla, cieco.** When followed by **a, o, u,** or a consonant, like *c* in English *cook*, e.g., **casa, come, cura, credere.** The digraph **ch,** which is used before **e** and **i,** has likewise the sound of *c* in English *cook*, e.g., **chiesa, perché.** |
| **d** | di | Like *d* in English *dance*, e.g., **dare, madre.** |
| **e** | e | Has two sounds. One like *a* in English *make*, shown on stressed syllables in this DICTIONARY by the acute accent, e.g., **séra, trénta;** and one like *e* in English *met*, shown on stressed syllables in this DICTIONARY by the grave accent, e.g., **fèrro, fèsta.** |
| **f** | effe | Like *f* in English *fool*, e.g., **farina, efelide.** |
| **g** | gi | When followed by **e** or **i,** like *g* in English *general*, e.g., **gelato, ginnasta;** if the **i** is unstressed and followed by another vowel, its sound is not heard, e.g., **giallo, giorno.** When followed by **a, o, u,** or a consonant, like *g* in English *go*, e.g., **gamba, goccia, gusto, grado.** The digraph **gh,** which is used before **e** and **i,** has likewise the sound of *g* in English *go*, e.g., **gherone, ghisa.** When the combination **gli** (a) is a form of the definite article or the personal pronoun, (b) is final in a word, or (c) is intervocalic, it has the sound of Castilian *ll*, which is somewhat like *lli* in English *million*, e.g., (a) **gli uomini, gli ho parlato ieri,** (b) **battagli,** (c) **figlio, migliore.** When it is (a) initial (except in the word **gli,** above), (b) preceded by a consonant, or (c) followed by a consonant, it is pronounced like *gli* in English *negligence*, e.g., (a) **glioma,** (b) **garglio,** (c) **negligenza.** The combination **gl** followed by **a, e, o,** or **u** is pronounced like *gl* in English *globe*, e.g., **glabro, gleba, globo, gluteo, inglese, poliglotto.** The digraph **gn** has the sound of Castilian *ñ*, which is somewhat like *ni* in English *onion*, e.g., **signore, gnocco.** |
| **h** | acca | Always silent, e.g., **ah, hanno.** See **ch** under **c** above and **gh** under **g** above. |
| **i** | i | Like *i* in English *machine*, e.g., **piccolo, sigla.** When unstressed and followed by another vowel, like *y* in English *yes*, e.g., **piatto, piede, fiore, fiume.** For **i** in **ci,** see **c** above, in **gi,** see **g** above, and in **sci,** see **s** below. |

3

| LETTER | NAME | APPROXIMATE SOUND |
|--------|------|-------------------|
| l | elle | Like *l* in English *lamb*, e.g., **labbro, lacrima.** |
| m | emme | Like *m* in English *money*, e.g., **mano, come.** |
| n | enne | Like *n* in English *net*, e.g., **nome, cane.** |
| o | o | Has two sounds. One like *o* in English *note*, shown on stressed syllables in this DICTIONARY by the acute accent, e.g., **dópo, sóle;** and one like *ou* in English *ought*, shown on stressed syllables in this DICTIONARY by the grave accent, e.g., **còsa, dònna.** |
| p | pi | Like *p* in English *pot*, e.g., **passo, carpa.** |
| q | cu | This letter is always followed by the letter **u** and the combination has the sound of *qu* in English *quart*, e.g., **quanto, questo.** |
| r | erre | Like *r* in English *rubber*, with a slight trill, e.g., **roba, carta.** |
| s | esse | Has two sounds. When initial and followed by a vowel, when preceded by a consonant and followed by a vowel, and when followed by **c** [k] **f, p, q,** or **t,** like *s* in English *see*, e.g., **sale, falso, scappare, spazio, stoffa;** and when standing between two vowels and when followed by **b, d, g** [g], **l, m, n, r** or **v,** like *z* in English *zero*, e.g., **paese, sbaglio, svenire.** However, **s** standing between two vowels in some words and initial **s** followed by **b, d, g** [g], **l, m, n, r,** or **v** in some foreign borrowings are pronounced like *s* in *see*, e.g., **casa\*, tesa, smoking, slam.** In this DICTIONARY this is indicated by the insertion of [s] immediately after the entry word. However, when initial **s** stands between two vowels in a compound, its pronunciation remains that of initial **s,** e.g., **autoservizio** and this is not indicated. The digraph **sc,** when followed by **e** or **i** has the sound of *sh* in English *shall*, e.g., **scelta, scimmia;** if the **i** is unstressed and followed by another vowel, its sound is not heard, e.g., **sciame, sciopero.** The trigraph **sch** has the sound of *sc* in English *scope*, e.g., **scherzo, schiavo.** |
| t | ti | Like *t* in English *table*, e.g., **terra, pasto.** |
| u | u | Like *u* in English *rule*, e.g., **luna, mulo.** When followed by a vowel, like *w* in English *was*, e.g., **quanto, guerra, nuovo.** |
| v | vu | Like *v* in English *vain*, e.g., **vita, uva.** |
| z | zeta | Has two sounds. One like *ts* in English *nuts*, e.g., **grazia, zucchero;** and one like *dz* in English *adze*, e.g., **zero, mezzo.** In this DICTIONARY the sound of *dz* in *adze* is indicated by the insertion of [dz] immediately after the entry word. If the sound is long, [ddzz] is inserted |

\* Intervocalic **s** is generally voiced in the north of Italy.

2. The following five letters are found in borrowings from other languages.

| LETTER | NAME | EXAMPLES |
|--------|------|----------|
| j | i lunga | **jazz, jingo** |
| k | cappa | **kiosco, kodak** |
| w | doppia vu | **water-polo, whisky** |
| x | ics | **xenofobo, xilofono** |
| y | ìpsilon | **yacht, yoghurt** |

3. Consonants written double are longer than consonants written single, that is, it takes a longer time to pronounce them, e.g., **camino** *chimney* and **cam-**

**mino** *road,* **capello** *hair* and **cappello** *hat.* Special attention is called to the following double consonants: **cc** followed by **e** or **i** has the sound of *ch ch* in English *beach chair,* that is, a lengthened *ch* (not the sound of *ks*), *e.g.,* **accento; cch** has the sound of *kk* in English *bookkeeper,* e.g., **becchino; cq** has the sound of *kk* in English *bookkeeper,* e.g., **acqua; gg** followed by **e** or **i** has the sound of *ge j* in English *carriage joiner,* e.g., **peggio; ggh** has the sound of *g g* in English *tag game,* e.g., **agghindare.**

**§2. Division of Syllables.** In the application of the following rules for the syllabic division of words, the digraphs **ch, gh, gl, gn,** and **sc** count as single consonants.

(a) When a single consonant stands between two vowels it belongs to the following syllable, e.g., **ca·sa, fu·mo, ami·che, la·ghi, fi·glio, biso·gno, la·sciare.**

(b) When a consonant group consisting of two consonants of which the second is **l** or **r** stands between two vowels, the group belongs to the following syllable, e.g., **nu·cleo, so·brio, qua·dro.**

(c) When a consonant group consisting of two or more consonants of which the first or the second is **s** stands between two vowels, that part of the group beginning with **s** belongs to the following syllable, e.g., **ta·sca, bo·schi, fine·stra, super·sti·zione, sub·strato.**

(d) When a consonant group consisting of two or three consonants of which the first is **l, m, n,** or **r** stands between two vowels, the **l, m, n,** or **r** belongs to the preceding syllable, the other consonant or consonants to the following syllable, e.g., **al·bero, am·pio, prin·cipe, mor·te, in·flazione, com·pleto.**

(e) When a double consonant stands between two vowels or between a vowel and **l** or **r,** the first belongs to the preceding syllable, the second to the following syllable, e.g., **bab·bo, caval·lo, an·no, car·ro, mez·zo, sup·plica, lab·bro, quat·tro.**

**§3. Stress and Accent Marks.** 1. Whenever stress is shown as part of regular spelling, it is shown on **a, i,** and **u** by the grave accent mark, e.g., **libertà, giovedì, gioventù,** on close **e** and **o** by the acute accent mark, e.g., **perché,** and on open **e** and **o** by the grave accent mark, e.g., **caffè, parlò.** This occurs (a) in words ending in a stressed vowel, as in the above examples, (b) in stressed monosyllables in which the vocalic element is a diphthong of which the first letter is unstressed **i** or **u,** e.g., **già, più, può,** and (c) on the stressed monosyllable of any pair of monosyllables of which one is stressed and the other unstressed, in order to distinguish one from the other, e.g., **dà** *he gives* and **da** *from,* **è** *is* and **e** *and,* **sé** *himself* and **se** *if,* **sì** *yes* and **si** *himself.*

2. Whenever stress is not shown as part of regular spelling, it is often difficult to determine where it falls.

(a) In words of two syllables, the stress falls on the syllable next to the last, e.g., **ca'sa, mu'ro, ter'ra.** If the syllable next to the last contains a diphthong, that is, a combination of a strong vowel (**a, e,** or **o**) and a weak vowel (**i** or **u**), the strong vowel is stressed, regardless of which vowel comes first, e.g., **da'ino, ero'ico, ne'utro, fia'to, dua'le, sie'pe, fio're, buo'no.**

(b) In words of more than two syllables, the stress may fall on the syllable next to the last, e.g., **anda'ta, canzo'ne, pasto're** or on a preceding syllable, e.g., **fis'sile, gon'dola, man'dor.a.** In these positions also the stressed syllable may contain a diphthong, e.g., **inca'uto, idra'ulico, fio'cina.**

(c) If a weak vowel in juxtaposition with a strong vowel is stressed, the two vowels constitute two separate syllables, e.g., **abba·i'no, ero·i'na, pa·u'ra, miri'ade, vi'a.**

(d) Two strong vowels in juxtaposition constitute two separate syllables, e.g., **pa·e'se, aure'ola, ide'a, oce'ano.**

(e) Two weak vowels in juxtaposition generally constitute a diphthong in which the first vowel is stressed in some words, e.g., **flu'ido** and the second vowel in others, e.g., **piu'ma.**

(f) If a word ends in a diphthong, the diphthong is stressed, e.g., **marina'i, parla'i, ero'i.**

3. In this DICTIONARY, stress is understood or shown on all words that do not bear an accent mark as part of regular spelling according to the following principles. In the application of these principles, individual vowels and not diphthongs are counted as units. In some words in which it is not necessary to show stress, an accent mark is used to show the quality of the stressed vowels **e** and **o.**

As in regular Italian spelling, stress is shown on **a, i,** and **u** by the grave accent mark, on close **e** and **o** by the acute accent mark, and on open **e** and **o** by the grave accent mark.

(a) It is understood that in words of more than one syllable in which no accent mark is shown, the stress falls on the vowel next to the last, e.g., **casa,**

5

fiato, duale, abbaino, paura. In such words as sièpe, fióre, buòno, paése, fluènte, eròe, nói, pòi, the accent mark is used to show the quality of the vowel.

(b) An accent mark is placed on the stressed vowel if the word is stressed on the third vowel from the end, e.g., mùsica, sìmbolo, dàino, incàuto, marinàio, contìnuo, infànzia. If this vowel is e or o, the acute or grave accent mark must correspond to the quality of the vowel, e.g., fiòcina, rómpere, nèutro, eròico, assèdio, filatóio.

(c) Contrary to the above-mentioned principle of counting vowels, an accent mark is placed on the strong vowel of a final diphthong, e.g., marinài, assài.

(d) Contrary to the above-mentioned principle of counting vowels, an accent mark is placed on the i of final ia, ie, ii, and io, e.g., farmacìa, scìa, farmacìe, mormorìi, gorgoglìo, fìo.

(e) An accent mark is placed on some borrowings ending in a consonant, e.g., hàrem, revòlver.

(f) The loss of the last vowel or last syllable of a word does not alter the position of the stress of the word, e.g., la maggior parte, in alcun modo, fan bene.

# Grammatical Tables

§4. The Definite Article and Combinations with Prepositions.

| | | MASC BEFORE CONSONANT | MASC BEFORE S IMPURE OR Z[1] | MASC BEFORE VOWEL | FEM BEFORE CONSONANT | FEM BEFORE VOWEL |
|---|---|---|---|---|---|---|
| | SG | il | lo | l' | la | l' |
| | PL | i | gli | gli[2] | le | le[3] |
| WITH a | SG | al | allo | all'[2] | alla | all' |
| | PL | ai | agli | agli[2] | alle | alle[3] |
| WITH di | SG | del | dello | dell'[2] | della | dell' |
| | PL | dei | degli | degli[2] | delle | delle[3] |
| WITH con | SG | col | collo | coll'[2] | colla | coll' |
| | PL | coi | cogli | cogli[2] | colle | colle[3] |
| WITH da | SG | dal | dallo | dall'[2] | dalla | dall' |
| | PL | dai | dagli | dagli[2] | dalle | dalle[3] |
| WITH in | SG | nel | nello | nell'[2] | nella | nell' |
| | PL | nei | negli | negli[2] | nelle | nelle[3] |
| WITH su | SG | sul | sullo | sull'[2] | sulla | sull' |
| | PL | sui | sugli | sugli[2] | sulle | sulle[3] |

[1] Other letters and groups of letters, which occur in a few words, are **gn, pn, ps, sc, x,** and **i** before a vowel, sometimes spelled **j** or **y.**

[2] These forms may drop the **i** before words beginning with **i,** e.g., **gl'inglesi.**
[3] The **e** of these forms is not elided, e.g., **le erbe.**

7

§5. Personal and Reflexive Pronouns.

| PERSONS | SUBJECT | PERSONAL DIRECT OBJECT | PERSONAL INDIRECT OBJECT | REFLEX. & RECIPROCAL DIRECT & INDIRECT OBJECT | PERSONAL PREPOSITIONAL OBJECT | REFLEX. & RECIPROCAL PREPOSITIONAL OBJECT |
|---|---|---|---|---|---|---|
| **SG** | | | | | | |
| 1 | io *I* | mi *me* | mi *to me* | mi *myself; to myself* | me *me* | me *myself* |
| 2 | tu *you* | ti *you* | ti *to you* | ti *yourself; to yourself* | te *you* | te *yourself* |
| 3 MASC | egli, lui *he* | lo *him or it* | gli *to him* | si *himself; to himself* | lui *him* | sé *himself* |
| 3 FEM | lei, essa *she* | la *her or it* | le *to her* | si *herself; to herself* | lei, essa *her* | sé *herself* |
| 2 FORMAL | Lei *you* | La *you* | Le *to you* | si *yourself; to yourself* | Lei *you* | sé *yourself* |
| **PL** | | | | | | |
| 1 | noi *we* | ci *us* | ci *to us* | ci *ourselves; to ourselves; each other; to each other* | noi *us* | noi *ourselves; each other* |
| 2 | voi *you* | vi *you* | vi *to you* | vi *yourself; yourselves; to yourself; to yourselves; each other; to each other* | voi *you* | voi *yourself; yourselves; each other* |
| 3 MASC | loro, essi *they* | li *them* | loro *to them* | si *themselves; to themselves; each other; to each other* | loro, essi *them* | sé *themselves; each other* |
| 3 FEM | loro, esse *they* | le *them* | loro *to them* | si *themselves; to themselves; each other; to each other* | loro, esse *them* | sé *themselves; each other* |
| 2 FORMAL | Loro *you* | Li } Le } *you* | Loro *to you* | si *yourselves; to yourselves; each other; to each other* | Loro *you* | sé *yourselves; each other* |

ci and vi both mean also *here, there, to it, in it, to them, in them, about it.*
ne means *of, from,* or *with him, her, it, them; some, any; from here, from there, thence, about it.*

meco *with me,* teco *with you,* and seco *with him, with himself; with her, with herself; with you, with yourself, with yourselves; with them, with themselves; with each other* may be used instead of con me, con te, and con sé respectively.

COMBINATION OF DIRECT AND INDIRECT OBJECT

| PERSONS | | |
|---|---|---|
| 1 SG & 3 SG | me lo } him, her, it to me<br>me la } |
| 1 SG & 3 PL | me li } them to me<br>me le } |
| 2 SG & 3 SG | te lo } him, her, it to you<br>te la } |
| 2 SG & 3 PL | te li } them to you<br>te le } |
| 3 SG & 3 SG | glielo } him, her, it to him<br>gliela } him, her, it to her |
| 3 SG & 3 PL | glieli } them to him<br>gliele } them to her |
| 2 SG FORMAL & 3 SG | Glielo } him, her, it to you<br>Gliela } |
| 2 SG FORMAL & 3 PL | Glieli } them to you<br>Gliele } |

| PERSONS | | |
|---|---|---|
| 1 PL & 3 SG | ce lo } him, her, it to us<br>ce la } |
| 1 PL & 3 PL | ce li } them to us<br>ce le } |
| 2 PL & 3 SG | ve lo } him, her, it to you<br>ve la } |
| 2 PL & 3 PL | ve li } them to you<br>ve le } |
| 3 SG & 3 PL | lo } VERB loro him, her, it to them<br>la } |
| 3 PL & 3 PL | li } VERB loro them to them<br>le } |
| 3 SG & 2 PL FORMAL | lo } VERB Loro him, her, it to you<br>la } |
| 3 PL & 2 PL FORMAL | li } VERB Loro them to you<br>le } |

The form **si** (third singular and plural reflexive and reciprocal indirect object) changes to **se** before one of the direct objects **lo, la, li,** and **le,** and before **ne,** e.g., **se lo mette** he puts it on; **se n'è andato** he went away.

In combinations, **ne** occupies the same position as **lo, la, li,** and **le,** e.g., **me ne,** and forms one word with **gli,** namely, **gliene.**

## 86 Possessive Adjectives and Pronouns

| PERSON, NUMBER & SEX OF POSSESSOR | GENDER & NUMBER OF POSSESSIVE ADJECTIVE OR PRONOUN ACCORDING TO THE GENDER & NUMBER OF THE PERSON OR THING POSSESSED | | | | MEANING OF ADJECTIVE | MEANING OF PRONOUN |
|---|---|---|---|---|---|---|
| | MSG | MPL | FSG | FPL | | |
| **SG** | | | | | | |
| 1 | il mio | i miei | la mia | le mie | *my* | *mine* |
| 2 | il tuo | i tuoi | la tua | le tue | *your* | *yours* |
| 3 MASC | il suo | i suoi | la sua | le sue | *his* | *his* |
| 3 FEM | il suo | i suoi | la sua | le sue | *her* | *hers* |
| 3 NEUT | il suo | i suoi | la sua | le sue | *its* | *its* |
| 2 FORMAL | il Suo | i Suoi | la Sua | le Sue | *your* | *yours* |
| **PL** | | | | | | |
| 1 | il nostro | i nostri | la nostra | le nostre | *our* | *ours* |
| 2 | il vostro | i vostri | la vostra | le vostre | *your* | *yours* |
| 3 | il loro | i loro | la loro | le loro | *their* | *theirs* |
| 2 FORMAL | il Loro | i Loro | la Loro | le Loro | *your* | *yours* |

The definite article, shown here, is not generally used (a) in direct address, e.g., **mio caro amico** *my dear friend*, (b) after the verb **essere**, e.g., **la casa è nostra** *the house is ours*, and (c) when a singular form modifies the name of a relative, e.g., **sua sorella** *his sister*.

With forms of the indefinite article, the possessive adjective, whether standing before or after the noun, is translated by *of* plus the possessive pronoun, e.g., **un amico mio** *a friend of mine*; **una sua zia** *an aunt of his* (or *of hers*).

The forms of the possessive pronouns also have the force of nouns, e.g., **il mio** *my property, my belongings*; **i suoi** *his people, relatives, followers, troops, retinue,* etc.; **la mia** *my letter*; **la sua** *his opinion*.

10

§7. The Demonstrative Adjective.

|  | MASC<br>BEFORE<br>CONSONANT | MASC<br>BEFORE s<br>IMPURE OR z<br>(see note 1, p. 7) | MASC<br>BEFORE<br>VOWEL | FEM<br>BEFORE<br>CONSONANT | FEM<br>BEFORE<br>VOWEL |
|---|---|---|---|---|---|
| SG<br>PL | quel *that*<br>quei *those* | quello<br>quegli | quell'<br>quegli | quella<br>quelle | quell'<br>quelle |
| SG<br>PL | questo *this*<br>questi *these* | questo<br>questi | questo or quest'<br>questi | questa<br>queste | questa or quest'<br>queste |

11

## §8. The Demonstrative Pronoun.

|      | MASC              | FEM    | MASC                            |
|------|-------------------|--------|---------------------------------|
| SG   | quello *that one* | quella | **quegli** *that one;*          |
| PL   | quelli *those*    | quelle | *the former*                    |
| SG   | questo *this one* | questa | **questi** *this one;*          |
| PL   | questi *these*    | queste | *the latter*                    |

The demonstrative pronoun **quello** is often followed by **che, di,** or **da** and the masculine singular form may be shortened to **quel** before these words.

|      |                    |         |
|------|--------------------|---------|
| SG   | colui *that one*   | colei   |
| PL   | coloro *those*     | coloro  |
| SG   | costui *this one*  | costei  |
| PL   | costoro *these*    | costoro |

**code•sto •sta •sti •ste** and **cote•sto •sta •sti -ste** are demonstrative adjectives and demonstrative pronouns and mean *that (of yours).*

§9. Indefinite Article and Numeral Adjective.

| MASC BEFORE CONSONANT | MASC BEFORE S IMPURE OR Z (see note 1, p. 7) | MASC BEFORE VOWEL | FEM BEFORE CONSONANT | FEM BEFORE VOWEL |
|---|---|---|---|---|
| un *a, an; one* | uno | un | una | un' |

## §10. Indefinite Pronoun uno.

| MASC | FEM |
|------|-----|
| uno *one* | una |

## §11. Correlative Indefinite Pronoun.

| | MASC | FEM |
|------|------|-----|
| SG | l'uno . . . l'altro *one . . . the other* | l'una . . . l'altra |
| PL | gli uni . . . gli altri *some . . . the others* | le une . . . le altre |

## §12. Reciprocal Indefinite Pronoun.

| | MASC | FEM |
|------|------|-----|
| SG | l'un l'altro *each other, one another* | l'una l'altra |
| PL | gli uni gli altri | le une le altre |

# Table of Regular Endings of Italian Verbs

The stem to which the endings of the gerund, past participle, present participle, imperative, present indicative, present subjunctive, imperfect indicative, preterit indicative, and imperfect subjunctive are attached is obtained by dropping the ending of the infinitive, viz., **-are**, **-ere**, **-ire**.

The stem to which the endings of the future indicative and present conditional are attached is obtained by dropping the **-e** of the ending of the infinitive of all conjugations and changing the **a** of the ending of the infinitive of the first conjugation to **e**.

The letters before the names of some of the tenses of this table correspond to the designation of the tenses shown on the following page.

Letters printed in italics have a written accent that is not part of the regular spelling.

| TENSE | FIRST CONJUGATION | SECOND CONJUGATION | THIRD CONJUGATION |
|---|---|---|---|
| *inf* | **-are** | **-ére** (or **-ere**) | **-ire** |
| *ger* | -ando | -èndo | -èndo |
| *pp* | -ato | -uto | -ito |
| *pres part* | -ante | -ènte | -ènte |
| (a) *impv* | -a<br>-ate | -i<br>-éte | -i<br>-ite |
| (b) *pres ind* | -o<br>-i<br>-a<br>-iamo<br>-ate<br>-ano | -o<br>-i<br>-e<br>-iamo<br>-éte<br>-ono | -o<br>-i<br>-e<br>-iamo<br>-ite<br>-ono |
| (c) *pres subj* | -i<br>-i<br>-i<br>-iamo<br>-iate<br>-ino | -a<br>-a<br>-a<br>-iamo<br>-iate<br>-ano | -a<br>-a<br>-a<br>-iamo<br>-iate<br>-ano |
| (d) *imperf ind* | -avo<br>-avi<br>-ava<br>-avamo<br>-avate<br>-àvano | -évo<br>-évi<br>-éva<br>-evamo<br>-evate<br>-évano | -ivo<br>-ivi<br>-iva<br>-ivamo<br>-ivate<br>-ìvano |
| (e) *pret ind* | -ài<br>-asti<br>-ò<br>-ammo<br>-aste<br>-àrono | -éi<br>-ésti<br>-è<br>-émmo<br>-éste<br>-érono | -ìi<br>-isti<br>-ì<br>-immo<br>-iste<br>-ìrono |
| *imperf subj* | -assi<br>-assi<br>-asse<br>-àssimo<br>-aste<br>-àssero | -éssi<br>-éssi<br>-ésse<br>-éssimo<br>-éste<br>-éssero | -issi<br>-issi<br>-isse<br>-ìssimo<br>-iste<br>-ìssero |
| (f) *fut ind* | -er-ò<br>-er-ài<br>-er-à<br>-er-émo<br>-er-éte<br>-er-anno | -ò<br>-ài<br>-à<br>-émo<br>-éte<br>-anno | -ò<br>-ài<br>-à<br>-émo<br>-éte<br>-anno |

| TENSE | FIRST CONJUGATION | SECOND CONJUGATION | THIRD CONJUGATION |
|-------|-------------------|--------------------|--------------------|
| *pres cond* | -er-èi<br>-er-ésti<br>-er-èbbe<br>-er-émmo<br>-er-éste<br>-er-èbbero | -èi<br>-ésti<br>-èbbe<br>-émmo<br>-éste<br>-èbbero | -èi<br>-ésti<br>-èbbe<br>-émmo<br>-éste<br>-èbbero |

# MODEL VERBS
## ORDER OF TENSES

(a) imperative             (d) imperfect indicative
(b) present indicative       (e) preterit indicative
(c) present subjunctive      (f) future indicative

In addition to the infinitive, gerund, and past participle, which are shown in line one of these tables, all simple tenses are shown if they contain at least one irregular form, except (1) the present conditional, which is always formed on the stem of the future indicative, (2) the imperfect subjunctive, which is always formed on the stem of the *2nd sg* of the preterit indicative, and (3) the present participle, which is generally formed by changing the final -do of the gerund to -te (exceptions being shown in parentheses after the gerund).

Letters printed in italics have a written accent that is not part of the regular spelling.

§100 **ACCÈDERE**—accedèndo—acceduto
     (e) accedètti *or* accedéi *or* accèssi; accedésti; accedètte *or* accedé *or* accèsse; accedémmo; accedéste; accedèttero *or* accedérono *or* accèssero

§101 **ACCÈNDERE**—accendèndo—accéso
     (e) accési, accendésti, accése, accendémmo, accendéste, accésero

§102 **ADDURRE**—adducèndo—addótto
     (b) adduco, adduci, adduce, adduciamo, adducéte, addùcono
     (c) adduca, adduca, adduca, adduciamo, adduciate, addùcano
     (d) adducévo, adducévi, adducéva, adducevamo, adducevate, adducévano
     (e) addussi, adducésti, addusse, adducémmo, adducéste, addùssero

§103 **AFFÌGGERE**—affiggèndo—affisso
     (e) affissi, affiggésti, affisse, affiggémmo, affiggéste, affìssero

**§104 AFFLÌGGERE**—affliggèndo—afflitto
(e) afflissi, affliggésti, afflisse, affliggémmo, affliggéste, afflìssero

**§105 ALLÙDERE**—alludèndo—alluso
(e) allusi, alludésti, alluse, alludémmo, alludéste, allùsero

**§106 ANDARE**—andando—andato
(a) va *or* va' *or* vai, andate
(b) vò *or* vado, vai, va, andiamo, andate, vanno
(c) vada, vada, vada, andiamo, andiate, vàdano
(f) andrò, andrài, andrà, andrémo, andréte, andranno

**§107 ANNÈTTERE**—annettèndo—annèsso *or* **annèttere,** annetténdo, annésso
(e) annettéi *or* annèssi *or* annéssi; annettésti; annetté *or* annèsse *or* annésse; annettémmo; annettéste; annettérono *or* annèssero *or* annéssero

**§108 APPARIRE**—apparèndo—apparso
(a) apparisci *or* appari; apparite
(b) apparisco *or* appàio; apparisci *or* appari; apparisce *or* appare; appariamo; apparite; apparìscono *or* appàiono
(c) apparisca *or* appàia; apparisca *or* appàia; apparisca *or* appàia; appariamo; appariate; apparìscano *or* appàiano
(e) apparvi *or* apparìi *or* apparsi; apparisti; apparve *or* apparì *or* apparse; apparimmo; appariste; appàrvero *or* apparìrono *or* appàrsero

**§109 APPÈNDERE**—appendèndo—appéso
(e) appési, appendésti, appése, appendémmo, appendéste, appésero

**§110 APRIRE**—aprèndo—apèrto
(e) aprìi *or* apèrsi; apristi; aprì *or* apèrse; aprimmo; apriste; aprìrono *or* apèrsero

**§111 ÀRDERE**—ardèndo—arso
(e) arsi, ardésti, arse, ardémmo, ardéste, àrsero

**§112 ASPÈRGERE**—aspergèndo—aspèrso
(e) aspèrsi, aspergésti, aspèrse, aspergémmo, aspergéste, aspèrsero

**§113 ASSÌDERE**—assidèndo—assiso
(e) assisi, assidésti, assise, assidémmo, assidéste, assìsero

**§114 ASSÌSTERE**—assistèndo—assistito
(e) assistéi *or* assistètti; assistésti; assisté *or* assistètte; assistémmo; assistéste; assistérono *or* assistèttero

18

**§115 ASSÒLVERE**—assolvèndo—assòlto *or* assoluto
(e) assolvéi *or* assolvètti *or* assòlsi; assolvésti; assolvé *or* assolvètte *or* assòlse; assolvémmo; assolvéste; assolvérono *or* assolvèttero *or* assòlsero

**§116 ASSÙMERE**—assumèndo—assunto
(e) assunsi, assumésti, assunse, assumémmo, assuméste, assùnsero

**§117 ASSÙRGERE**—assurgèndo—assurto
(e) assursi, assurgésti, assurse, assurgémmo, assùrgéste, assùrsero

**§118 AVÈRE**—avèndo—avuto
(a) abbi, abbiate
(b) ho, hai, ha, abbiamo, avete, hanno
(c) àbbia, àbbia, àbbia, abbiamo, abbiate, àbbiano
(e) èbbi, avésti, èbbe, avémmo, avéste, èbbero
(f) avrò, avrài, avrà, avrémo, avréte, avranno

**§119 AVVIARE**—avviando—avviato
(b) avvìo, avvìi, avvìa, avviamo, avviate, avvìano
(c) avvìi, avvìi, avvìi, avviamo, avviate, avvìino

**§120 BÉRE**—bevèndo—bevuto
(a) bévi, bevéte
(b) bévo, bévi, béve, beviamo, bevéte, bévono
(c) béva, béva, béva, beviamo, beviate, bévano
(d) bevévo, bevévi, bevéva, bevevamo, bevevate, bevévano
(e) bévvi *or* bevéi *or* bevètti; bevésti, bévve *or* bevé *or* bevètte; bevémmo; bevéste; bévvero *or* bevérono *or* bevèttero
(f) berrò, berrài, berrà, berrémo, berréte, berranno

**§121 CADÉRE**—cadèndo—caduto
(e) caddi, cadésti, cadde, cadémmo, cadéste, càddero
(f) cadrò, cadrài, cadrà, cadrémo, cadréte, cadranno

**§122 CECARE**—cecando—cecato
(a) cièca *or* cèca; cecate
(b) cièco *or* cèco; cièchi *or* cèchi; cièca *or* cèca; cechiamo; cecate; ciècano *or* cècano
(c) cièchi *or* cèchi; cièchi *or* cèchi; cièchi *or* cèchi; cechiamo; cechiate; cièchino *or* cèchino
(f) cecherò, cecherài, cecherà, cecherémo, cecheréte, cecheranno

**§123 CÈDERE**—cedèndo—ceduto
(e) cedéi *or* cedètti; cedésti; cedé *or* cedètte; cedémmo; cedéste; cedérono *or* cedèttero

19

**§124 CHIÈDERE**—chiedèndo—chièsto
(e) chièsi, chiedésti, chièse, chiedémmo, chiedéste, chièsero

**§125 CHIÙDERE**—chiudèndo—chiuso
(e) chiusi, chiudésti, chiuse, chiudémmo, chiudéste, chiùsero

**§126 CÌNGERE**—cingèndo—cinto
(e) cinsi, cingésti, cinse, cingémmo, cingéste, cìnsero

**§127 CÒGLIERE**—coglièndo—còlto
(a) còly, cogliéte
(b) còlgo, còly, còglie, cogliamo, cogliéte, còlgono
(c) còlga, còlga, còlga, cogliamo, cogliate, còlgano
(e) còlsi, cogliésti, còlse, cogliémmo, cogliéste, còlsero

**§128 COMINCIARE**—cominciando—cominciato
(b) comìncio, cominci, comìncia, cominciamo, cominciate, comìnciano
(c) cominci, cominci, cominci, cominciamo, cominciate, comìncino
(f) comincerò, comincerài, comincerà, comincerémo, cominceréte, cominceranno

**§129 COMPÈTERE**—competèndo—*pp* missing

**§130 CÒMPIERE**—compièndo—compiuto
(a) cómpi, compite
(b) cómpio, cómpi, cómpie, compiamo, compite, cómpiono
(c) cómpia, cómpia, cómpia, compiamo, compiate, cómpiano
(d) compivo, compivi, compiva, compivamo, compivate, compìvano
(e) compiéi *or* compìi; compiésti *or* compisti; compié *or* compì; compiémmo *or* compimmo; compiéste *or* compiste; compiérono *or* compìrono

**§131 COMPRÌMERE**—comprimèndo—comprèsso
(e) comprèssi, comprimésti, comprèsse, comprimémmo, compriméste, comprèssero

**§132 CONCÈDERE**—concedèndo—concèsso
(e) concedéi *or* concèssi *or* concedètti; concedésti; concedé *or* concèsse *or* concedètte; concedémmo; concedéste; concedérono *or* concèssero *or* concedèttero

**§133 CONCÈRNERE**—concernèndo—*pp* missing
(e) concernéi *or* concernètti; concernésti; concerné *or* concernètte; concernémmo; concernéste; concernérono *or* concernèttero

**§134 CONÓSCERE**—conoscèndo—conosciuto
(e) conóbbi, conoscésti, conóbbe, conoscémmo, conoscéste, conóbbero

**§135 CONQUÌDERE**—conquidèndo—conquiso
(e) conquisi, conquidésti, conquise, conquidémmo, conquidéste, conquìsero

**§136 CONSÙMERE**—*ger* missing—consunto
(a) missing
(b) missing
(c) missing
(d) missing
(e) consunsi, consunse, consùnsero
(f) missing

**§137 CONVÈRGERE**—convergèndo—convèrso
(e) convèrsi *or* convergéi; convergésti; convèrse *or* convergé; convergémmo; convergéste; convèrsero *or* convergérono

**§138 CONVERTIRE**—convertèndo—convertito
(e) convertìi *or* convèrsi; convertisti; convertì or convèrse; convertimmo; convertiste; convertìrono *or* convèrsero

**§139 CÓRRERE**—corrèndo—córso
(e) córsi, corrésti, córse, corrémmo, corréste, córsero

**§140 COSTRUIRE**—costruèndo—costruito
(a) costruisci, costruite
(b) costruisco, costruisci, costruisce, costruiamo, costruite, costruìscono
(c) costruisca, costruisca, costruisca, costruiamo, costruiate, costruìscano
(e) costruìi *or* costrussi; costruisti; costruì *or* costrusse; costruimmo; costruiste; costruìrono *or* costrùssero

**§141 CRÉDERE**—credèndo—creduto
(e) credéi *or* credètti; credésti; credé *or* credètte; credémmo; credéste; credérono *or* credèttero

**§142 CRÉSCERE**—crescèndo—cresciuto
(e) crébbi, crescésti, crébbe, crescémmo, crescéste, crébbero

**§143 CUCIRE**—cucèndo—cucito
(b) cùcio, cuci, cuce, cuciamo, cucite, cùciono
(c) cùcia, cùcia, cùcia, cuciamo, cuciate, cùciano

**§144a CUÒCERE**—cuocèndo *or* cocèndo (cocènte)—còtto *or* cociuto

(a) cuòci, cocéte
(b) cuòcio, cuòci, cuòce, cociamo, cocéte, cuòciono
(c) cuòcia, cuòcia, cuòcia, cociamo, cociate, cuòciano
(d) cocévo, cocévi, cocéva, cocevamo, cocevate, cocévano
(e) còssi, cocésti, còsse, cocémmo, cocéste, còssero
(f) cocerò, cocerài, cocerà, cocerémo, coceréte, coceranno

**§144b DARE**—dando—dato
(a) dà *or* dài *or* da'; date
(b) dò *or* dò; dài; dà; diamo; date; danno
(c) dìa, dìa, dìa, diamo, diate, dìano
(e) dièdi *or* dètti; désti; diède *or* dètte *or* diè; démmo; déste; dièdero *or* dèttero
(f) darò, darài, darà, darémo, daréte, daranno

**§145 DECÌDERE**—decidèndo—deciso
(e) decisi, decidésti, decise, decidémmo, decidéste, decìsero

**§146 DELÌNQUERE**—delinquèndo—*pp* missing
(a) missing
(c) missing
(e) missing

**§147 DEVÒLVERE**—devolvèndo—devoluto
(e) devolvéi *or* devolvètti; devolvésti; devolvé *or* devolvètte; devolvémmo; devolvéste; devolvérono *or* devolvèttero

**§148 DIFÈNDERE**—difendèndo—diféso
(e) difési, difendésti, difése, difendémmo, difendéste, difésero

**§149 DILÌGERE**—diligèndo—dilètto
(a) missing
(b) missing
(c) missing
(d) missing
(e) dilèssi, diligésti, dilèsse, diligémmo, diligéste, dilèssero
(f) missing

**§150 DIPÈNDERE**—dipendèndo—dipéso
(e) dipési, dipendésti, dipése, dipendémmo, dipendéste, dipésero

**§151 DIRE**—dicèndo—détto
(a) di' *or* dì; dite
(b) dico, dici, dice, diciamo, dite, dìcono
(c) dica, dica, dica, diciamo, diciate, dìcano
(d) dicévo, dicévi, dicéva, dicevamo, dicevate, dicévano
(e) dissi, dicésti, disse, dicémmo, dicéste, dìssero
(f) dirò, dirài, dirà, dirémo, diréte, diranno

22

**§152  DIRÌGERE**—dirigèndo—dirètto
    (e) dirèssi, dirigésti, dirèsse, dirigémmo, dirigéste, dirèssero

**§153  DISCÈRNERE**—discernèndo—*pp* missing
    (e) discernéi; discernésti; discerné *or* discernètte; discernémmo; discernéste; discernérono *or* discernèttero

**§154  DISCÙTERE**—discutèndo—discusso
    (e) discussi, discutésti, discusse, discutémmo, discutéste, discùssero

**§155  DISSÒLVERE**—dissolvèndo—dissòlto
    (e) dissòlsi *or* dissolvéi *or* dissolvètti; dissolvésti; dissòlse *or* dissolvé *or* dissolvètte; dissolvémmo; dissolvéste; dissòlsero *or* dissolvérono *or* dissolvèttero

**§156  DISTÌNGUERE**—distinguèndo—distinto
    (e) distinsi; distinguésti, distinse, distinguémmo, distinguéste, distìnsero

**§157  DIVÈRGERE**—divergèndo—*pp* missing
    (e) obsolete

**§158  DIVÌDERE**—dividèndo—diviso
    (e) divisi, dividésti, divise, dividémmo, dividéste, divìsero

**§159  DOLÉRE**—dolèndo—doluto
    (a) duòli, doléte
    (b) dòlgo, duòli, duòle, doliamo, doléte, dòlgono
    (c) dòlga, dòlga, dòlga, doliamo, doliate, dòlgano
    (e) dòlsi, dolésti, dòlse, dolémmo, doléste, dòlsero
    (f) dorrò, dorrài, dorrà, dorrémo, dorréte, dorranno

**§160  DOVÉRE**—dovèndo—dovuto
    (b) dèbbo *or* dèvo; dèvi; dève; dobbiamo; dovéte; dèbbono *or* dèvono
    (c) dèva *or* dèbba; dèva *or* dèbba; dèva *or* dèbba; dobbiamo; dobbiate; dèvano *or* dèbbano
    (e) dovéi *or* dovètti; dovésti; dové *or* dovètte; dovémmo; dovéste; dovérono *or* dovèttero

**§161  ELÌDERE**—elidèndo—eliso
    (e) elisi, elidésti, elise, elidémmo, elidéste, elìsero

**§162  EMÈRGERE**—emergèndo—emèrso
    (e) emèrsi, emergésti, emèrse, emergémmo, emergéste, emèrsero

**§163  ÉMPIERE & EMPIRE**—empièndo—empito *or* empiuto
    (a) émpi, empite

(b) émpio, émpi, émpie, empiamo, empite, émpiono
(c) émpia, émpia, émpia, empiamo, empiate, émpiano
(d) empivo, empivi, empiva, empivamo, empivate, em‑
pìvano
(e) empiéi or empìi; empiésti; or empisti; empié or empì;
empiémmo or empimmo; empiéste or empiste;
empiérono or empìrono
(f) empirò, empirài, empirà, empirémo, empiréte, em‑
piranno

§164 ÈRGERE—ergèndo—èrto
(e) èrsi, ergésti, èrse, ergémmo, ergéste, èrsero

§165 ESÌGERE—esigèndo—esatto
(e) esigéi or esigètti; esigésti; esigé or esigètte; esigémmo;
esigéste; esigérono or esigèttero

§166 ESÌMERE—esimèndo—pp missing
(e) esiméi or esimètti; esimésti; esimé or esimètte;
esimémmo; esiméste; esimérono or esimèttero

§167 ESPÀNDERE—espandèndo—espanso
(e) espandéi or espandètti or espansi; espandésti; espandé
or espandètte or espanse; espandémmo; espandéste;
espandérono or espandèttero or espànsero

§168 ESPÈLLERE—espellèndo—espulso
(e) espulsi, espellésti, espulse, espellémmo, espelléste,
espùlsero

§169 ESPLÒDERE—esplodèndo—esplòso
(e) esplòsi, esplodésti, esplòse, esplodémmo, esplodéste,
esplòsero

§170 ÈSSERE—essèndo—stato
(a) sii, siate
(b) sóno, sèi, è, siamo, sièic, sóno
(c) sìa, sìa, sìa, siamo, siate, sìano
(d) èro, èri, èra, eravamo, eravate, èrano
(e) fui, fósti, fu, fummo, fóste, fùrono
(f) sarò, sarài, sarà, sarémo, saréte, saranno

§171 ESTÒLLERE—estollèndo—pp missing
(e) missing

§172 EVÀDERE—evadèndo—evaso
(e) evasi, evadésti, evase, evadémmo, evadéste, evàsero

§173 FARE—facèndo—fatto
(a) fa or fài or fa'; fate

24

(b) fàccio *or* fò; fài; fa; facciamo; fate; fanno
(c) fàccia, fàccia, fàccia, facciamo, facciate; fàcciano
(d) facévo, facévi, facéva, facevamo, facevate, facévano
(e) féci, facésti, féce, facémmo, facéste, fécero
(f) farò, faràii, farà, farémo, faréte, faranno

§174 **FÈNDERE**—fendèndo—fenduto *or* fésso
(e) fendéi *or* fendètti; fendésti; fendé *or* fendètte; fendémmo; fendéste; fendérono *or* fendèttero

§175 **FÈRVERE**—fervèndo—*pp* missing
(e) fervéi *or* fervètti; fervésti; fervé *or* fervètte; fervémmo; fervéste; fervérono *or* fervèttero

§176 **FINIRE**—finèndo—fínito
(a) finisci, finite
(b) finisco, finisci, finisce, finiamo, finite, finìscono
(c) finisca, finisca, finisca, finiamo, finiate, finìscano

§177 **FLÈTTERE**—flettèndo—flèsso
(e) flettéi *or* flèssi; flettésti; fletté *or* flèsse; flettémmo; flettéste; flettérono *or* flèssero

§178 **FÓNDERE**—fondèndo—fuso
(e) fusi, fondésti, fuse, fondémmo, fondéste, fùsero

§179 **FRÀNGERE**—frangèndo—franto
(e) fransi, frangésti, franse, frangémmo, frangéste, frànsero

§180 **FRÌGGERE**—friggèndo—fritto
(e) frissi, friggésti, frisse, friggémmo, friggéste, frìssero

§181 **GIACÉRE**—giacèndo—giaciuto
(b) giàccio; giaci; giace; giacciamo *or* giaciamo; giacete; giàcciono
(c) giàccia, giàccia, giàccia, giacciamo, giacciate, giàcciano
(e) giàcqui, giacésti, giàcque, giacémmo, giacéste, giàcquero

§182 **GIOCARE**—giocando—giocato
(a) giuòca *or* giòca; giocate
(b) giuòco *or* giòco; giuòchi *or* giòchi; giuòca *or* giòca; giochiamo; giocate; giuòcano *or* giòcano
(c) giuòchi *or* giòchi; giuòchi *or* giòchi; giuòchi *or* giòchi; giochiamo; giochiate; giuòchino *or* giòchino
(f) giocherò, giocheràii, giocherà, giocherémo, giocheréte, giocheranno

§183 **GIÙNGERE**—giungèndo—giunto
(e) giunsi, giungésti, giunse, giungémmo, giungéste, giùnsero

25

**§184 GODÉRE**—godèndo—goduto
- (e) godéi *or* godètti; godésti; godé *or* godètte; godémmo; godéste; godérono *or* godèttero
- (f) godrò, godrài, godrà, godrémo, godréte, godranno

**§185 IMBÉVERE**—imbevèndo—imbevuto
- (e) imbévvi, imbevésti, imbévve, imbevémmo, imbevéste, imbévvero

**§186 INCÓMBERE**—incombèndo—*pp* missing
- (e) incombéi *or* incombètti; incombésti; incombé *or* incombètte; incombémmo; incombéste; incombérono *or* incombèttero

**§187 INDÙLGERE**—indulgèndo—indulto
- (e) indulsi, indulgésti, indulse, indulgémmo, indulgéste, indùlsero

**§188a INFERIRE**—inferèndo—inferito *or* infèrto
- (a) inferisci, inferite
- (b) inferisco, inferisci, inferisce, inferiamo, inferite, inferìscono
- (c) inferisca, inferisca, inferisca, inferiamo, inferiate, inferìscano
- (e) inferìi *or* infèrsi; inferisti; inferì *or* infèrse; inferimmo; inferiste; inferìrono *or* infèrsero

**§188b INSTARE**—instando—*pp* missing

**§189 INTRÌDERE**—intridèndo—intriso
- (e) intrisi, intridésti, intrise, intridémmo, intridéste, intrìsero

**§190 INTRÙDERE**—intrudèndo—intruso
- (e) intrusi, intrudésti, intruse, intrudémmo, intrudéste, intrùsero

**§191 IRE**—*ger* missing—ito
- (a) *sg* missing, ite
- (b) missing
- (c) missing
- (d) ivo, ivi, iva, ivamo, ivate, ìvano
- (e) *1st sg* missing, isti, *3rd sg* missing, *1st pl* missing, iste, ìrono

**§192 LÈDERE**—ledèndo—léso *or* lèso
- (e) lési, ledésti, lése, ledémmo, ledéste, lésero

**§193 LÈGGERE**—leggèndo—lètto
- (e) lèssi, leggésti, lèsse, leggémmo, leggéste, lèssero

**§194 LIQUEFARE**—liquefacèndo—liquefatto
- (a) liquefà, liquefate
- (b) liquefò or liquefàccio; liquefài; liquefà liquefacciamo; liquefate; liquefanno
- (c) liquefàccia, liquefàccia, liquefàccia, liquefacciamo, liquefacciate, liquefàcciano
- (d) liquefacévo, liquefacévi, liquefacéva, liquefacevamo, liquefacevate, liquefacévano
- (e) liquefacéci, liquefacésti, liquefacéce, liquefacémmo, liquefacéste, liquefacécero
- (f) liquefarò, liquefaràu, liquefarà, liquefarémo, liquefaréte, liquefaranno

**§195 MALEDIRE**—maledicèndo—maledétto
- (a) maledici, maledite
- (b) maledico, maledici, maledice, malediciamo, maledite, maledìcono
- (c) maledica, maledica, maledica, malediciamo, malediciate, maledìcano
- (d) maledicévo or maledivo; maledicévi or maledivi; maledicéva or malediva; maledicevamo or maledivamo; maledicevate or maledivate; maledicévano or maledìvano
- (e) maledìi or maledissi; maledisti or maledicésti; maledì or maledisse; maledimmo or maledicémmo; malediste or maledicéste; maledìrono or maledìssero
- (f) maledirò, maledirài, maledirà, maledirémo, malediréte, malediranno

**§196 MALVOLÉRE**—*ger* missing—malvoluto
- (a) missing
- (b) missing
- (c) missing
- (d) missing
- (e) missing
- (f) missing

**§197 MANCARE**—mancando—mancato
- (b) manco, manchi, manca, manchiamo, mancate, màncano
- (c) manchi, manchi, manchi, manchiamo, manchiate, mànchino
- (f) mancherò, mancherài, mancherà, mancherémo, mancheréte, mancheranno

**§198 MÉTTERE**—mettèndo—mésso
- (e) misi, mettésti, mise, mettémmo, mettéste, mìsero

**§199 MÌNGERE**—mingèndo—minto
- (e) minsi, mingésti, minse, mingémmo, mingéste, mìnsero

27

§200 **MÒRDERE**—mordèndo—mòrso
(e) mòrsi, mordésti, mòrse, mordémmo, mordéste, mòrsero

§201 **MORIRE**—morèndo—mòrto
(a) muòri, morite
(b) muòio, muòri, muòre, moriamo, morìte, muòiono
(c) muòia. muòia, muòia, moriamo, moriate, muòiano
(f) morrò or morirò; morrài or morirài; morrà or morirà;
morrémo or morirémo; morréte or moriréte; mor-
ranno or moriranno

§202 **MUÒVERE**—muovèndo or movèndo (movènte)—mòsso
(a) muòvi, movéte
(b) muòvo, muòvi, muòve, moviamo, movéte, muòvono
(c) muòva, muòva, muòva, moviamo, moviate, muòvano
(d) movévo, movévi, movéva, movevamo, movevate,
movévano
(e) mòssi, movésti, mòsse, movémmo, movéste, mòssero
(f) moverò, moverài, moverà, moverémo, moveréte, move-
ranno

§203 **NÀSCERE**—nascèndo—nato
(e) nàcqui, nascésti, nàcque, nascémmo, nascéste, nàcquero

§204 **NASCÓNDERE**—nascondèndo—nascósto
(e) nascósi, nascondésti, nascóse, nascondémmo, nas-
condéste, nascósero

§205 **NEGLÌGERE**—negligèndo—neglètto
(a) missing
(b) missing
(c) missing
(e) neglèssi, negligésti, neglèsse, negligémmo, negligéste,
neglèssero

§206 **NUÒCERE**—nuocèndo—nociuto
(a) nuòci, nocéte
(b) nuòccio or nòccio; nuòci; nuòce; nociamo; nocéte;
nuòcciono or nòcciono
(c) nòccia, nòccia, nòccia, nociamo, nociate, nòcciano
(d) nocévo, nocévi, nocéva, nocevamo, nocevate, nocévano
(e) nòcqui, nocésti, nòcque, nocémmo, nocéste, nòcquero
(f) nocerò, nocerài, nocerà, nocerémo, noceréte, noceranno

§207 **OFFRIRE**—offrèndo (offerènte)—offèrto
(e) offrìi or offèrsi; offristi; offrì or offèrse; offrimmo;
offriste; offrìrono or offèrsero

§208 **OTTÙNDERE**—ottundèndo—ottuso
(e) ottusi, ottundésti, ottuse, ottundémmo, ottundéste,
ottùsero

**§209 PAGARE**—pagando—pagato
(b) pago, paghi, paga, paghiamo, pagate, págano
(c) paghi, paghi, paghi, paghiamo, paghiate, pàghino
(f) pagherò, pagherài, pagherà, pagherémo, pagheréte, pagheranno

**§210 PARÉRE**—parèndo (parvènte)—parso
(a) missing
(b) pàio; pari; pare; pariamo *or* paiamo; paréte; pàiono
(c) pàia; pàia; pàia; pariamo *or* paiamo; pariate *or* paiate; pàiano
(e) parvi, parésti, parve, parémmo, paréste, pàrvero
(f) parrò, parrài, parrà, parrémo, parréte, parranno

**§211 PÀSCERE**—pascèndo—pasciuto
(a) pascéi *or* pascètti; pascésti; pascé *or* pascètte; pascémmo; pascéste; pascérono *or* pascèttero

**§212 PÈRDERE**—perdèndo—pèrso *or* perduto
(e) perdéi *or* pèrsi *or* perdètti; perdésti; perdé, *or* pèrse *or* perdètte; perdémmo; perdéste; perdérono *or* pèrsero *or* perdèttero

**§213 PERSUADÉRE**—persuadèndo—persuaso
(e) persuasi, persuadésti, persuase, persuadémmo, persuadéste, persuàsero

**§214 PIACÉRE**—piacèndo—piaciuto
(b) piàccio, piaci, piace, piacciamo, piacéte, piàcciono
(c) piàccia, piàccia, piàccia, piacciamo, piacciate, piàcciano
(e) piàcqui, piacésti, piàcque, piacémmo, piacéste, piàcquero

**§215 PIÀNGERE**—piangèndo—pianto
(e) piansi, piangésti, pianse, piangémmo, piangéste, piànsero

**§216 PIÒVERE**—piovèndo—piovuto
(e) piòvvi, piovésti, piòvve, piovémmo, piovéste, piòvvero

**§217 PÒRGERE**—porgèndo—pòrto
(e) pòrsi, porgésti, pòrse, porgémmo, porgéste, pòrsero

**§218 PÓRRE**—ponèndo—pósto
(a) póni, ponéte
(b) póngo, póni, póne, poniamo, ponéte, póngono
(c) pónga, pónga, pónga, poniamo, poniate, póngano
(d) ponévo, ponévi, ponéva, ponevamo, ponevate, ponévano
(e) pósi, ponésti, póse, ponémmo, ponéste, pósero

**§219 POTÉRE**—potèndo (potènte *or* possènte)—potuto
(a) missing
(b) pòsso, puòi, può, possiamo, potéte, pòssono

    (c) pòssa, pòssa, pòssa, possiamo, possiate, pòssano
    (e) potéi *or* potètti; potésti, poté *or* potètte; potémmo;
         potéste; potérono *or* potèttero
    (f) potrò, potrài, potrà, potrémo, potréte, potranno

**§220 PRÈNDERE**—prendèndo—préso
    (e) prési, prendésti, prése, prendémmo, prendéste, présero

**§221 PROVVEDÉRE**—provvedèndo—provveduto *or* provvisto
    (e) provvidi, provvedésti, provvide, provvedémmo, prov-
        vedéste, provvìdero

**§222 PRÙDERE**—prudèndo—*pp* missing
    (e) *1st sg* missing; *2nd sg* missing; prudé *or* prudètte; *1st*
        *pl* missing; *2nd pl* missing; prudérono *or* prudèttero

**§223 RÀDERE**—radèndo—raso
    (e) rasi, radésti, rase, radémmo, radéste, ràsero

**§224 REDÌGERE**—redigèndo—redatto
    (e) redassi, redigésti, redasse, redigémmo, redigéste, redàs-
        sero

**§225 REDÌMERE**—redimèndo—redènto
    (e) redènsi, redimésti, redènse, redimémmo, rediméste,
        redènsero

**§226 RÈGGERE**—reggèndo—rètto
    (e) rèssi, reggésti, rèsse, reggémmo, reggéste, rèssero

**§227 RÈNDERE**—rendèndo—réso
    (e) rési *or* rendéi *or* rendètti; rendésti; rése *or* rendé *or*
        rendètte; rendémmo; rendéste; résero *or* rendérono
        *or* rendèttero

**§228 RETROCÈDERE**—retrocedèndo—retrocèsso *or* retroceduto
    (e) retrocèssi *or* retrocedéi *or* retrocedètti; retrocedésti;
        retrocèsse *or* retrocedé *or* retrocedètte; retro-
        cedémmo; retrocedéste; retrocèssero *or* retrocedérono
        *or* retrocedèttero

**§229 RIAVÉRE**—riavèndo—riavuto
    (a) riabbi, riabbiate
    (b) riò, riài, rià, riabbiamo, riavéte, rianno
    (c) riàbbia, riàbbia, riàbbia, riabbiamo, riabbiate, riàbbiano
    (e) rièbbi, riavésti, rièbbe, riavémmo, riavéste, rièbbero
    (f) riavrò, riavrài, riavrà, riavrémo, riavréte, riavranno

**§230 RIDARE**—ridando—ridato
    (a) ridài *or* ridà; ridate
    (b) ridò, ridài, ridà, ridiamo, ridate, ridanno
    (c) ridìa, ridìa, ridìa, ridiamo, ridiate, ridìano

(e) ridièdi *or* ridètti; ridésti; ridiède *or* ridètte; ridémmo; ridéste; ridièdero *or* ridèttero

(f) ridarò, ridaràì, ridarà, ridarémo, ridaréte, ridaranno

§231 **RÌDERE**—ridèndo—riso
(e) risi, ridésti, rise, ridémmo, ridéste, rìsero

§232 **RIFLÈTTERE**—riflettèndo—riflèsso *or* riflettuto

§233 **RIFÙLGERE**—rifulgèndo—rifulso
(e) rifulsi, rifulgésti, rifulse rifulgémmo, rifulgéste, rifùlsero

§234 **RILÙCERE**—rilucèndo—*pp* missing

§235 **RIMANÉRE**—rimanèndo—rimasto
(b) rimango, rimani, rimane, rimaniamo, rimanéte, rimàngono
(c) rimanga, rimanga, rimanga, rimaniamo, rimaniate, rimàngano
(e) rimasi, rimanésti, rimase, rimanémmo, rimanéste, rimàsero
(f) rimarrò, rimarràì, rimarrà, rimarrémo, rimarréte, rimarranno

§236 **RINCORARE**—rincorando—rincorato
(a) rincuòra, rincorate
(b) rincuòro, rincuòri, rincuòra, rincoriamo, rincorate, rincuòrano
(c) rincuòri, rincuòri, rincuòri, rincoriamo, rincoriate, rincuòrino

§237 **RISOLARE**—risolando—risolato
(a) risuòla, risolate
(b) risuòlo, risuòli, risuòla, risoliamo, risolate, risuòlano
(c) risuòli, risuòli, risuòli, risoliamo, risoliate, risuòlino

§238 **RISPÓNDERE**—rispondèndo—rispósto
(e) rispósi, rispondésti, rispóse, rispondémmo, rispondéste, rispósero

§239 **RÓDERE**—rodèndo—róso
(e) rósi, rodésti, róse, rodémmo, rodéste, rósero

§240 **RÓMPERE**—rompèndo—rótto
(e) ruppi, rompésti, ruppe, rompémmo, rompéste, rùppero

§241 **ROTARE**—rotando—rotato
(a) ruòta, rotate
(b) ruòto, ruòti, ruòta, rotiamo, rotate, ruòtano
(c) ruòti, ruòti, ruòti, rotiamo, rotiate, ruòtino

**§242 SALIRE**—salèndo—salito
- (b) salgo, sali, sale, saliamo, salite, sàlgono
- (c) salga, salga, salga, saliamo, saliate, sàlgano

**§243 SAPÉRE**—sapèndo (sapiènte)—saputo
- (a) sappi, sappiate
- (b) sò, sai, sa, sappiamo, sapéte, sanno
- (c) sàppia, sàppia, sàppia, sappiamo, sappiate, sàppiano
- (e) sèppi, sapésti, sèppe, sapémmo, sapéste, sèppero
- (f) saprò, saprài, saprà, saprémo, sapréte, sapranno

**§244 SCÉGLIERE**—sceglièndo—scélto
- (a) scégli, scegliéte
- (b) scélgo, scégli, scéglie, scegliamo, scegliéte, scélgono
- (c) scélga, scélga, scélga, scegliamo, scegliate, scélgano
- (e) scélsi, scegliésti, scélse, scegliémmo, scegliéste, scélsero

**§245 SCÉNDERE**—scendèndo—scéso
- (e) scési, scendésti, scése, scendémmo, scendéste, scésero

**§246 SCÈRNERE**—scernèndo—*pp* missing
- (e) scernéi *or* scernètti; scernésti; scerné *or* scernètte; scernémmo; scernéste; scernérono *or* scernèttero

**§247 SCÌNDERE**—scindèndo—scisso
- (e) scissi, scindésti, scisse, scindémmo, scindéste, scìssero

**§248 SCOIARE**—scoiando—scoiato
- (a) scuòia, scoiate
- (b) scuòio, scuòi, scuòia, scoiamo, scoiate, scuòiano
- (c) scuòi, scuòi, scuòi, scoiamo, scoiate, scuòino

**§249 SCÒRGERE**—scorgèndo—scòrto
- (e) scòrsi, scorgésti, scòrse, scorgémmo, scorgéste, scòrsero

**§250 SCRÌVERE**—scrivèndo—scritto
- (e) scrissi, scrivésti, scrisse, scrivémmo, scrivéste, scrìssero

**§251 SCUÒTERE**—scotèndo—scòsso
- (a) scuòti, scotéte
- (b) scuòto, scuòti, scuòte, scotiamo, scotéte, scuòtono
- (c) scuòta, scuòta, scuòta, scotiamo, scotiate, scuòtano
- (d) scotévo, scotévi, scotéva, scotevamo, scotevate, scotévano
- (e) scòssi, scotésti, scòsse, scotémmo, scotéste, scòssero

**§252 SEDÉRE**—sedéndo—seduto
- (a) sièdi, sedéte
- (b) sièdo *or* sèggo; sièdi; sième; sediamo; sedéte; sièdono *or* sèggono
- (c) sièda *or* sègga; sièda *or* sègga; sièda *or* sègga; sediamo; sediate; sièdano *or* sèggano
- (e) sedéi *or* sedètti; sedésti; sedé *or* sedètte; sedémmo; sedéste; sedérono *or* sedèttero

32

§253   **SEPPELLIRE**—seppellèndo—sepólto *or* seppellito
    (a) seppellisci, seppellite
    (b) seppellisco, seppellisci, seppellisce, seppelliamo, seppel-
       lite, seppellìscono
    (c) seppellisca, seppellisca, seppellisca, seppelliamo, seppel-
       liate, seppellìscano

§254   **SODDISFARE**—soddisfacèndo—soddisfatto
    (a) soddisfa *or* soddisfài *or* soddisfa'
    (b) soddisfàccio *or* soddisfò *or* soddisfo; soddisfài *or*
       soddisfi; soddisfà *or* soddisfa; soddisfacciamo; sod-
       disfate; soddisfanno *or* soddìsfano
    (c) soddisfàccia *or* soddisfi; soddisfàccia *or* soddisfi; soddi-
       sfàccia *or* soddisfi; soddisfacciamo; soddisfacciate;
       soddisfàcciano *or* soddìsfino
    (d) soddisfacévo, soddisfacévi, soddisfacéva, soddisface-
       vamo, soddisfacevate, soddisfacévano
    (e) soddisféci, soddisfacésti, soddisféce, soddisfacémmo,
       soddisfacéste, soddisfécero
    (f) soddisfarò, soddisfarài, soddisfarà, soddisfarémo, soddi-
       sfaréte, soddisfaranno

§255   **SOLÉRE**—solèndo—sòlito
    (a) missing
    (b) sòglio, suòli, suòle, sogliamo, soléte, sògliono
    (c) sòglia, sòglia, sòglia, sogliamo, sogliate, sògliano
    (e) missing
    (f) missing

§256   **SÒLVERE**—solvèndo—soluto
    (e) solvéi *or* solvètti; solvésti; solvé *or* solvètte; solvémmo;
       solvéste; solvérono *or* solvèttero

§257   **SONARE**—sonando—sonato
    (a) suòna, sonate
    (b) suòno, suòni, suòna, soniamo, sonate, suònano
    (c) suòni, suòni, suòni, soniamo, soniate, suònino

§258   **SÓRGERE**—sorgèndo—sórto
    (e) sórsi, sorgésti, sórse, sorgémmo, sorgéste, sórsero

§259   **SOSPÈNDERE**—sospendèndo—sospéso
    (e) sospési, sospendésti, sospése, sospendémmo, sospendéste,
       sospésero

§260   **SPÀNDERE**—spandèndo—spanto
    (e) spandéi *or* spandètti *or* spansi; spandésti; spandé *or*
       spandètte *or* spanse; spandémmo; spandéste; spandé-
       rono *or* spandèttero *or* spànsero

§261   **SPÀRGERE**—spargèndo—sparso
    (e) sparsi, spargésti, sparse, spargémmo, spargéste, spàrsero

**§262 SPÈGNERE**—spegnèndo—spènto
- (b) spéngo *or* spèngo; spégni *or* spègni; spégne *or* spègne; spegniamo; spegnéte; spéngono *or* spèngono
- (c) spénga *or* spènga; spénga *or* spènga; spénga *or* spènga; spegniamo; spegniate; spéngano *or* spèngano
- (e) spènsi, spegnésti, spènse, spegnémmo, spegnéste, spènsero

**§263 STARE**—stando—stato
- (a) sta *or* stai *or* sta'; state
- (b) stò, stài, sta, stiamo, state, stanno
- (c) stìa, stìa, stìa, stiamo, stiate, stìano
- (e) stètti, stésti, stètte, stémmo, stéste, stèttero
- (f) starò, starài, starà, starémo, staréte, staranno

**§264 STRÌDERE**—stridèndo—*pp* missing
- (e) stridéi *or* stridètti; stridésti; stridé *or* stridètte; stridémmo; stridéste; stridérono *or* stridèttero

**§265 STRÌNGERE**—stringèndo—strétto
- (e) strinsi, stringésti, strinse, stringémmo, stringéste, strìnsero

**§266 STRÙGGERE**—struggèndo—strutto
- (e) strussi, struggésti, strusse, struggémmo, struggéste, strùssero

**§267 SVÈLLERE**—svellèndo—svèlto
- (b) svèllo *or* svèlgo; svèlli; svèlle; svelliamo; svelléte; svèllono *or* svèlgono
- (c) svèlla *or* svèlga; svèlla *or* svèlga; svèlla *or* svèlga; svelliamo; svelliate; svèllano *or* svèlgano
- (e) svèlsi, svellésti, svèlse, svellémmo, svelléste, svèlsero

**§268 TACÉRE**—tacèndo—taciuto
- (b) tàccio, taci, tace, taciamo, tacéte, tàcciono
- (c) tàccia, tàccia, tàccia, taciamo, taciate, tàcciano
- (e) tàcqui, tacésti, tàcque, tacémmo, tacéste, tàcquero

**§269 TÀNGERE**—tangèndo—pp missing
- (a) missing
- (b) *1st sg* missing; *2nd sg* missing; tange; *1st pl* missing; *2nd pl* missing; tàngono
- (c) *1st sg* missing; *2nd sg* missing; tanga; *1st pl* missing; *2nd pl* missing; tàngano
- (d) *1st sg* missing; *2nd sg* missing; tangéva; *1st pl* missing; *2nd pl* missing; tangévano
- (e) missing
- (f) *1st sg* missing; *2nd sg* missing; tangerà; *1st pl* missing; *2nd pl* missing; tangeranno

§270 **TÈNDERE**—tendèndo—téso
(e) tési, tendésti, tése, tendémmo, tendéste, tésero

§271 **TENÉRE**—tenèndo—tenuto
(a) tièni, tenéte
(b) tèngo, tièni, tiène, teniamo, tenéte, tèngono
(c) tènga, tènga, tènga, teniamo, teniate, tèngano
(e) ténni, tenésti, ténne, tenémmo, tenéste, ténnero
(f) terrò, terrài, terrà, terrémo, terréte, terranno

§272 **TÒRCERE**—torcèndo—tòrto
(e) tòrsi, torcésti, tòrse, torcémmo, torcéste, tòrsero

§273 **TRARRE**—traèndo—tratto
(a) trài, traéte
(b) traggo, trài, trae, traiamo, traéte, tràggono
(c) tragga, tragga, tragga, traiamo, traiate, tràggano
(d) traévo, traévi, traéva, traevamo, traevate, traévano
(e) trassi, traésti, trasse, traémmo, traéste, tràssero

§274 **UCCÌDERE**—uccidèndo—ucciso
(e) uccisi, uccidésti, uccise, uccidémmo, uccidéste, uccìsero

§275 **UDIRE**—udèndo *or* udièndo—udito
(a) òdi, udite
(b) òdo, òdi, òde, udiamo, udite, òdono
(c) òda, òda, òda, udiamo, udiate, òdano
(f) udirò *or* udrò; udirài *or* udrài; udirà *or* udrà; udirémo *or* udrémo; udiréte *or* udréte; udiranno *or* udranno

§276 **ÙRGERE**—urgèndo—*pp* missing
(a) missing
(e) missing

§277 **USCIRE**—uscèndo—uscito
(a) èsci, uscite
(b) èsco, èsci, èsce, usciamo, uscite, èscono
(c) èsca, èsca, èsca, usciamo, usciate, èscano

§278 **VALÉRE**—valèndo—valso
(b) valgo, vali, vale, valiamo, valéte, vàlgono
(c) valga, valga, valga, valiamo, valiate, vàlgano
(e) valsi, valésti, valse, valémmo, valéste, vàlsero
(f) varrò, varrài, varrà, varrémo, varréte, varranno

§279 **VEDÉRE**—vedèndo—veduto *or* visto
(e) vidi, vedésti, vide, vedémmo, vedéste, vìdero
(f) vedrò, vedrài, vedrà, vedrémo, vedréte, vedranno

§280 **VEGLIARE**—vegliando—vegliato
(b) véglio, végli, véglia, vegliamo, vegliate, végliano
(c) végli, végli, végli, vegliamo, vegliate; véglino

§281 **VÉNDERE**—vendèndo—venduto
(e) vendéi *or* vendètti; vendésti; vendé *or* vendètte; vendémmo; vendéste; vendérono *or* vendèttero

§282 **VENIRE**—venèndo (veniènte)—venuto
(a) vièni, venite
(b) vèngo, vièni, viène, veniamo, venite, vèngono
(c) vènga, vènga, vènga, veniamo, veniate, vèngano
(e) vénni, venisti, vénne, venimmo, veniste, vénnero
(f) verrò, verrài, verrà, verrémo, verréte, verranno

§283 **VÈRTERE**—vertèndo—*pp* missing

§284 **VÌGERE**—vigèndo—*pp* missing
(a) missing
(b) *1st sg* missing; *2nd sg* missing; vige; *1st pl* missing; *2d pl* missing; vìgono
(c) *1st sg* missing; *2d sg* missing; viga; *1st pl* missing; *2d pl* missing; vìgano
(d) *1st sg* missing; *2d sg* missing; vigéva; *1st pl* missing; *2d pl* missing; vigévano
(e) missing

§285 **VÌNCERE**—vincèndo—vinto
(e) vinsi, vincésti, vinse, vincémmo, vincéste, vìnsero

§286 **VÌVERE**—vivèndo—vissuto
(e) vissi, vivésti, visse, vivémmo, vivéste, vìssero
(f) vivrò, vivrài, vivrà, vivrémo, vivréte, vivranno

§287 **VIZIARE**—viziando—viziato
(b) vìzio, vizi, vìzia, viziamo, viziate, vìziano
(c) vizi, vizi, vizi, viziamo, viziate, vìzino

§288 **VOLÉRE**—volèndo—voluto
(a) vògli, vogliate
(b) vòglio, vuòi, vuòle, vogliamo, voléte, vògliono
(c) vòglia, vòglia, vòglia, vogliamo, vogliate, vògliano
(e) vòlli, volésti, vòlle, volémmo, voléste, vòllero
(f) vorrò, vorrài, vorrà, vorrémo, vorréte, vorranno

§289 **VÒLGERE**—volgèndo—vòlto
(e) vòlsi, volgésti, vòlse, volgémmo, volgéste, vòlsero

§290 **VOLTEGGIARE**—volteggiando—volteggiato
(b) voltéggio, voltéggi, voltéggia, volteggiamo, volteggiate, voltéggiano
(c) voltéggi, voltéggi, voltéggi, volteggiamo, volteggiate, voltéggino
(f) volteggerò, volteggerài, volteggerà, volteggerémo, volteggeréte, volteggeranno

# ITALIAN-ENGLISH

**A, a** [ɑ] *m & f* first letter of the Italian alphabet

**a** *prep* (**ad** in front of a vowel) to, e.g., **diede il libro a Giovanni** he gave the book to John; in, e.g., **a Milano** in Milan; at, e.g., **a casa** at home; within, e.g., **a tre miglia da qui** within three miles from here; on, e.g., **portare una catena al collo** to wear a chain on one's neck; e.g., **al sabato** on Saturdays; for, e.g., **a vita** for life; by, e.g., **fatto a mano** made by hand; with, e.g., **una gonna a pieghe** a skirt with pleats; as, e.g., **eleggere a presidente** to elect as chairman; into, e.g., **fu gettato a mare** he was thrown into the sea; of, e.g., **un quarto alle due** fifteen minutes of two

**àba·co** *m* (**-chi**) (archit) abacus

**abate** *m* abbot

**abbacchiare** §287 *tr* to knock down (*e.g., olives*); to sell too cheap ‖ *ref* to lose courage; to be dejected

**abbacchia·to -ta** *adj* (coll) dejected

**abbàc·chio** *m* (**-chi**) baby lamb (*slaughtered*)

**abbacinare** (**abbàcino**) *tr* to dazzle; to deceive

**abbadéssa** *f* var of **badessa**

**abbagliante** *adj* dazzling ‖ *m* (aut) bright light, high beam

**abbagliare** §280 *tr* to dazzle; to deceive; to blind (*with the lights of a car*)

**abbà·glio** *m* (**-gli**) error; **prendere abbaglio** to make a mistake

**abbaiaménto** *m* bark (*of dog*)

**abbaiare** §287 *intr* to bark; to yelp

**abbaino** *m* dormer window; skylight; attic

**abbambinare** *tr* to walk (*a heavy piece of furniture*)

**abbandonare** (**abbandóno**) *tr* to abandon; to give up; to let go (*e.g., the reins*); to let fall; (sports) to withdraw from ‖ *ref* to yield; to lose courage

**abbandóno** *m* abandon, abandonment; desertion; neglect; relaxation; renunciation (*of a right*); cession (*of property*); withdrawal (*from a fight*)

**abbarbicare** §197 (**abbàrbico**) *intr & ref* to cling; to hold on

**abbassalin·gua** *m* (**-gua**) tongue depressor

**abbassaménto** *m* lowering; reduction; drop, fall

**abbassare** *tr* to lower; to dim (*lights*); to turn (*the radio*) lower; **abbassare le armi** to surrender; **abbassare la cresta** to yield ‖ *ref* to lower oneself; to drop

**abbas·so** *m* (**-so**) angry shout (*of a crowd*) ‖ *adv* down, below; downstairs ‖ *interj* down with!

**abbastanza** *adj invar* enough ‖ *adv* enough; rather, fairly

**abbàttere** *tr* to demolish; to fell; to shoot down; to refute (*an argument*); to depress ‖ *ref* to be depressed, be downcast

**abbattiménto** *m* demolition; felling; shooting down; chill; (fig) depression; **abbattimento alla base** (econ) basic exemption (*from taxes*)

**abbattu·to -ta** *adj* dejected, downcast ‖ *f* clearing (*of trees*)

**abbazìa** *f* abbey; abbacy

**abbecedà·rio** *m* (**-ri**) speller, primer

**abbelliménto** *m* embellishment, ornamentation

**abbellire** §176 *tr* to embellish, adorn; to landscape

**abbeverare** (**abbévero**) *tr* to water (*animals*) ‖ *ref* to quench one's thirst

**abbevera·tóio** *m* (**-tói**) watering trough

**abbic·cì** *m* (**-cì**) alphabet; speller, primer; ABC's, rudiments

**abbiènte** *adj* well-to-do ‖ *m*—**gli abbienti** the haves; **gli abbienti e nullatenenti** the haves and the have-nots

**abbiettézza** or **abiettézza** *f* abjectness, baseness

**abbièt·to -ta** or **abièt·to -ta** *adj* abject, base, low

**abbiezióne** or **abiezióne** *f* wretchedness, baseness

**abbigliaménto** *m* attire, wear

**abbigliare** §280 *tr & ref* to dress; to dress up

**abbinaménto** *m* coupling; merger

**abbinare** *tr* to couple; to join, merge

**abbindolare** (**abbìndolo**) *tr* to dupe, deceive

**abbiosciare** §128 *ref* to fall down; to lose heart, be downcast

**abbisognare** (**abbisógno**) *intr* to be in need

**abboccaménto** *m* interview, conversation

**abboccare** §197 (**abbócco**) *tr* to swallow (*the hook*); to fit (*pipes*) ‖ *intr* to bite (*said of fish*); to fall; to fit (*said of pipes*) ‖ *ref* to confer

**abbocca·to -ta** *adj* palatable; slightly sweet (*wine*)

**abbonacciare** §128 *ref* to calm down, abate (*said of weather*)

**abbonaménto** *m* subscription; **abbonamento postale** mailing permit

**abbonare** (**abbòno**) *tr* to take out a subscription for (*s.o.*) ‖ *ref* to subscribe ‖ §257 *tr* to remit (*a debt*); to forgive

**abbona·to -ta** *mf* subscriber; commuter

**abbondante** *adj* abundant, plentiful; heavy (*rain*)

**abbondanza** *f* abundance, plenty

**abbondare** (**abbóndo**) *intr* (ESSERE & AVERE) to abound; to exceed; **abbondare di** or **in** to abound in

**abbonire** §176 *tr* to calm; to placate ‖ *ref* to calm down

**abbordàbile** *adj* accessible, approachable; negotiable (*curve*) abbordàg·gio *m* (-gi) boarding (*of an enemy ship*); andare all'abbordaggio di to board

abbordare (abbórdo) *tr* to board (*an enemy ship*); to negotiate (*a curve*); to face (*a problem*); (fig) to button-hole

abborracciare §128 *tr* to botch, bungle

abborracciatura *f* botch, bungle

abbottonare (abbottóno) *tr* to button || *ref* (coll) to keep to oneself

abbottonatura *f* buttoning; row of buttons

abbozzare (abbòzzo) *tr* to sketch; to hew (*e.g., a statue*); (naut) to tie up || *intr* (coll) to take it

abbòzzo *m* sketch, draft

abbracciabò·sco *m* (-schi) (bot) woodbine

abbracciare *m* embrace, embracing || §128 *tr* to embrace, hug; to seize (*an opportunity*); to become converted to (*e.g., Christianity*); to enter (*a profession*); to span, encompass || *ref* to cling; to embrace one another

abbràc·cio *m* (-ci) embrace, hug

abbrancare §197 *tr* to grab; to herd || *ref* to cling; to join a herd

abbreviaménto *m* abbreviation, shortening

abbreviare §287 (abbrèvio) *tr* to abbreviate, shorten, abridge

abbreviatura *f* shortening, abridgment

abbreviazióne *f* abbreviation

abbrivo or abbrivio *m* headway (*of a ship*); prendere l'abbrivio to gather momentum

abbronzante [dz] *adj* suntanning || *m* suntan lotion

abbronzare [dz] (abbrónzo) *tr* & *ref* to bronze; to tan

abbronza·to -ta [dz] *adj* tanned, suntanned

abbronzatura [dz] *f* tan, suntan

abbruciacchiare §287 *tr* to singe

abbrunare *tr* to brown; to hang crepe on || *ref* to wear mourning

abbrunire §176 *tr* to turn brown; to tan; to burnish

abbrustolire §176 *tr* to toast; to singe || *ref* to tan; to become sunburned

abbrutiménto *m* degradation, brutishness

abbrutire §176 *tr* to degrade; to brutalize || *intr* & *ref* to become brutalized

abbuiare §287 *tr* to darken; to hush up, hide || *ref* to grow dark; to become gloomy || *impers*—abbuia it's growing dark

abbuòno *m* allowance, discount; handicap (*in racing*)

abburattaménto *m* sifting

abburattare *tr* to sift, bolt

abdicare §197 (àbdico) *tr* & *intr* to abdicate; abdicare a to give up, renounce; to abdicate (*e.g., the throne*)

abdicazióne *f* abdication

aberrare (abèrro) *intr* to deviate

aberrazióne *f* aberration

abéte *m* fir

abetina *f* forest of fir trees

abiàti·co *m* (-ci) (coll) grandson

abièt·to -ta *adj* abject, base, low

abigeato *m* (law) cattle rustling

àbile *adj* able, clever, capable; (mil) fit

abili·tà *f* (tà) ability, skill

abilitare (abìlito) *tr* to certify (*e.g., a teacher*); to qualify, license

abilita·to -ta *adj* certified (*teacher*)

abilitazióne *f* qualification; certification (*of teachers*)

abissale *adj* abysmal

Abissìnia, l' *f* Abyssinia

abissi·no -na *adj* & *mf* Abyssinian

abisso *m* abyss; fountain (*of knowledge*); slough (*of degradation*)

abitàbile *adj* inhabitable

abitàcolo *m* (aer) cockpit; (aut) cab, interior; (naut) compass bowl; abitacolo eiettabile (aer) ejection capsule

abitante *mf* inhabitant; resident

abitare (àbito) *tr* to inhabit; to occupy || *intr* to dwell, live, reside

abitati·vo -va *adj* living, e.g., condizioni abitative living conditions

abita·to -ta *adj* inhabited, populated || *m* built-up area

abita·tóre -trice *mf* dweller

abitazióne *f* dwelling; housing

àbito *m* suit (*for men*); dress (*for women*); garb, attire; habit; abiti clothes; abito da ballo evening gown; abito da cerimonia formal dress; abito da inverno winter suit; winter clothes; levarsi l'abito to doff the cassock; prender l'abito to enter the Church

abituale *adj* habitual

abituare (abìtuo) *tr* to accustom || *ref* to grow accustomed

abitudinà·rio -ria *adj* (-ri -rie) set in his ways

abitùdine *f* habit, custom

abituro *m* (poet) shanty, hut

abiura *f* abjuration

abiurare *tr* to abjure

ablati·vo -va *adj* & *m* ablative

ablazióne *f* (med) removal; (geol) erosion

abluzióne *f* ablution

abnegare §209 (abnégo & abnègo) *tr* to renounce, abnegate

abnegazióne *f* abnegation, self-denial

abnòrme *adj* abnormal

abolire §176 *tr* to abolish

abolizióne *f* abolition

abominàbile *adj* abominable

abominare (abòmino) *tr* to abominate, detest

abominazióne *f* abomination

abominévole *adj* abominable

aborìge·no -na *adj* aboriginal || *m* aborigine; aborigeni aborigines

aborrire §176 & (abòrro) *tr* to abhor, loathe || *intr*—aborrire da to shun, shrink from

abortire §176 *intr* to abort

abòrto *m* abortion, miscarriage; aborto di natura monstrosity

abrasióne *f* abrasion; erosion

abrasi·vo -va *adj* & *m* abrasive

abrogare §209 (àbrogo) *tr* to abrogate

abrogazióne *f* abrogation

**abruzzése** *adj* of the Abruzzi ‖ *mf* person of the Abruzzi ‖ *m* dialect of the Abruzzi

**àbside** *f* (archit) apse

**abusare** *intr*—**abusare di** to go to excesses in (*e.g., smoking*); to take advantage of; to impose on

**abusi·vo -va** *adj* illegal, abusive; unwarranted

**abuso** *m* abuse, excess

**acà·cia** *f* (-cie) acacia

**acanto** *m* acanthus

**àcaro** *m* (ent) acarus, mite, tick; **acaro della scabbia** itch mite

**ac·ca** *m* & *f* (-ca or -che) h (*letter*); **non valere un'acca** (coll) to not be worth a fig

**accadèmia** *f* academy

**accadèmi·co -ca** (-ci -che) *adj* academic ‖ *mf* academician

**accadére** §121 *intr* (ESSERE) to happen, occur

**accadu·to -ta** *adj* happened, occurred ‖ *m* fact, event; what has taken place

**accagliare** §280 *tr, intr* (ESSERE) & *ref* to curdle, coagulate

**accalappiaca·ni** *m* (-ni) dogcatcher

**accalappiare** §287 *tr* to catch (*a dog*); to snare; (fig) to fool

**accalcare** §197 *tr* to crowd ‖ *ref* to throng

**accaldare** *ref* to get hot; to become flushed

**accalda·to -ta** *adj* hot; perspired

**accalorare** (accalóro) *tr* to excite ‖ *ref* to get excited

**accalora·to -ta** *adj* excited, animated

**accampaménto** *m* encampment, camp; camping

**accampare** *tr* to encamp; to advance, lay (*a claim*) ‖ *ref* to camp, encamp

**accaniménto** *m* animosity, bitterness; obstinacy, stubbornness

**accanire** §176 *ref* to persist; to work doggedly; **accanirsi contro** to harass

**accani·to -ta** *adj* obstinate, persistent; furious; fierce, ruthless, bitter (*fight*)

**accanto** *adv* near, nearby; **accanto a** near

**accantonaménto** *m* tabling (*e.g., of a discussion*); reserve (*of money*); (mil) billeting; (sports) camping

**accantonare** (accantóno) *tr* to set aside (*money*); (mil) to billet

**accaparraménto** *m* cornering (*of market*)

**accaparrare** *tr* to corner (*merchandise*); to hoard; to put a down payment on (*e.g., a house*); (coll) to gain (*somebody's affection*)

**accaparra·tóre -trice** *mf* monopolizer; hoarder

**accapigliare** §280 *ref* to pull each other's hair; to scuffle; to come to blows

**accapo** or **a capo** *m* paragraph

**accappa·tóio** *m* (-tói) bathrobe

**accapponare** (accappóno) *tr* to castrate (*a rooster*) ‖ *ref* to wrinkle; **mi si accappona la pelle** I get gooseflesh

**accarezzare** (accarézzo) *tr* to caress, fondle; to pet; to nurture (*e.g., a*

**hope*); **accarezzare le spalle di** to strike; to club

**accartocciare** §128 (**accartòccio**) *tr* to wrap up in a cone ‖ *ref* to curl up

**accartoccia·to -ta** *adj* curled up

**accasare** [s] *tr* & *ref* to marry

**accasciaménto** *m* dejection

**accasciare** §128 *tr* to weaken, enfeeble; to depress ‖ *ref* to weaken; to lose heart

**accasermare** [s] (**accasèrmo**) *tr* to quarter, billet

**accatastare** *tr* to register (*real estate*); to pile, heap up

**accattabri·ghe** *mf* (-ghe) quarrelsome person, scrapper

**accattare** *tr* to beg for; to borrow (*e.g., ideas*) ‖ *intr* to beg

**accattonàg·gio** *m* (-gi) begging, mendicancy

**accattó·ne -na** *mf* mendicant, beggar

**accavalcare** §197 *tr* to straddle; to go over

**accavalciare** §128 *tr* to bestride

**accavallare** *tr* to superimpose; to cross (*one's legs*) ‖ *ref* to pour forward, run high (*said of waves*)

**accecaménto** *m* blinding

**accecare** §122 *tr* to blind; to countersink ‖ *intr* (ESSERE) to become blind ‖ *ref* to blind oneself

**acceca·tóio** *m* (-tói) countersink

**accèdere** §100 *intr* (ESSERE) to enter, approach; to accede

**acceleraménto** *m* acceleration

**accelerare** (accèlero) *tr* & *intr* to accelerate

**accelera·to -ta** *adj* accelerated; intensive (*course*); local (*train*) ‖ *m* local train

**acceleratóre** *m* accelerator

**accelerazióne** *f* acceleration

**accèndere** §101 *tr* to kindle; to turn on (*e.g., the light*); to light (*e.g., a match, a cigar*) ‖ *ref* to catch fire; to become lit; **accendersi in viso** to become flushed

**accendisìgaro** *m* lighter

**accendi·tóio** *m* (-tói) candle lighter

**accenditóre** *m* lighter

**accennare** (accénno) *tr* to nod; to point at; to sketch ‖ *intr* to refer; to hint

**accénno** *m* nod; sign; allusion

**accensióne** *f* lighting, kindling; (aut) ignition; (law) contraction (*of a debt*); **accensione improvvisa** spontaneous combustion

**accentare** (accènto) *tr* to accent

**accènto** *m* accent; stress; (poet) accent (*word*); **accento tonico** stress accent

**accentraménto** *m* centralization

**accentrare** (accèntro) *tr* to concentrate, centralize

**accentuare** (accèntuo) *tr* to accentuate ‖ *ref* to become aggravated

**accentuazióne** *f* accentuation

**accerchiaménto** *m* encirclement

**accerchiare** §287 (**accérchio**) *tr* to encircle, surround

**accertàbile** *adj* verifiable

**accertaménto** *m* ascertainment, verification; determination (*e.g., of taxes*)

**accertare** (accèrto) *tr* to assure; to ascertain, verify; to determine (*the tax due*) ‖ *ref* to make sure

**accé·so -sa** [s] *adj* lit; turned on; on (*e.g., radio*); excited, aroused; bright (*color*)

**accessìbile** *adj* accessible; moderate (*price*)

**accessióne** *f* accession

**accèsso** *m* access, approach; admittance, entry; fit (*of anger, of coughing*)

**accessò·rio -ria** (**-ri -rie**) *adj* accessory ‖ *m* accessory; (mach) accessory, attachment

**accètta** *f* hatchet, axe, cleaver; **tagliato con l'accetta** rough-hewn

**accettàbile** *adj* acceptable

**accettare** (accètto) *tr* to accept

**accettazióne** *f* acceptance; receiving room; (econ) acceptance

**accèt·to -ta** *adj* agreeable; welcome; **male accetto** unwelcome

**accezióne** *f* meaning, acceptation

**acchiappafarfal·le** *m* (**-le**) butterfly net

**acchiappamó·sche** *m* (**-sche**) fly catcher

**acchiappare** *tr* to grab, seize; (coll) to catch in the act

**acchito** *m* (billiards) break; **di primo acchito** at first

**acciaccare** §197 *tr* to crush; to trample upon; (coll) to lay low (*e.g., by illness*)

**acciac·co** *m* (**-chi**) illness, infirmity, ailment

**acciaiare** §287 *tr* to convert into steel; to strengthen with steel

**acciaierìa** *f* steel mill, steelworks

**ac·ciàio** *m* (**-ciài**) steel; **acciaio inossidabile** stainless steel

**acciaiòlo** *m* whetstone

**acciambellare** (acciambèllo) *tr* to shape in the form of a doughnut ‖ *ref* to curl up

**acciarino** *m* flintlock; linchpin; (nav) war nose (*of a torpedo*)

**accidèmpoli** *interj* (slang) darn it!

**accidentale** *adj* accidental

**accidenta·to -ta** *adj* paralyzed; uneven, rough (*road*); broken (*ground*)

**accidènte** *m* accident; crack-up; (coll) paralytic stroke; (coll) hoot, fig; (coll) pest, menace (*child*); (mus) accidental; **accidenti!** (coll) darn!, damn!; **correre come un accidente** to run like the devil; **mandare un accidente a** to wish ill luck to; **per accidente** perchance

**accìdia** *f* sloth

**accidió·so -sa** [s] *adj* slothful

**accigliare** §280 *ref* to frown, knit one's brow

**accingere** §126 *ref*—**accingersi a** to get ready to

**-àccio -àccia** *suf adj & mf* (**-acci -acce**) no good, e.g., **gentaccia** no good people; good-for-nothing, e.g., **ragazzaccio** good-for-nothing boy

**acciò** or **acciocché** *conj* (poet) so that

**acciottolare** (acciòttolo) *tr* to pave with cobblestones

**acciottola·to -ta** *adj* cobblestone ‖ *m* cobblestone pavement

**acciottolì·o** *m* (**-i**) clatter (*e.g., of dishes*)

**accipicchia** *interj* (coll) darn it!

**acciuffare** *tr* to seize, grab, pinch (*a thief*)

**acciu·ga** *f* (**-ghe**) anchovy

**acclamare** *tr* to acclaim ‖ *intr* to voice one's approval

**acclamazióne** *f* acclamation

**acclimatare** (acclìmato) *tr & ref* to acclimate

**acclimatazióne** *f* acclimatation

**acclive** *adj* (poet) steep

**acclivi·tà** *f* (**-tà**) acclivity

**acclùdere** §105 *tr* to enclose

**acclu·so -sa** *adj* enclosed

**accoccare** §197 (accòcco & accócco) *tr* (poet) to nock (*the arrow*)

**accoccolare** (accòccolo) *ref* to squat down

**accodare** (accódo) *tr* to line up ‖ *ref* to line up, queue

**accogliènte** *adj* cozy, hospitable, inviting

**accogliènza** *f* reception, welcome

**accògliere** §127 *tr* to receive; to welcome; to grant (*a request*) ‖ *ref* (poet) to gather

**accoglitrice** *f* receptionist

**accòlito** *m* acolyte, altar boy; follower

**accollare** (accòllo) *tr* to overload (*a cart*); **accollare qlco a qlcu** to charge s.o. with s.th ‖ *intr* to go up to the neck (*said of a dress*) ‖ *ref* to assume, take upon oneself

**accolla·to -ta** *adj* high-necked (*dress*); high-cut (*shoes*) ‖ *f* accolade

**accollatura** *f* neck, neckhole

**accòlta** *f* (poet) gathering

**accoltellare** (accoltèllo) *tr* to knife

**accomandante** *m* limited partner

**accomandatà·rio** *m* (**-ri**) (law) general partner

**accomàndita** *f* (law) limited partnership

**accomiatare** *tr* to dismiss ‖ *ref* to take leave

**accomodaménto** *m* arrangement; compromise; settlement

**accomodante** *adj* accommodating, obliging

**accomodare** (accòmodo) *tr* to arrange; to fix; to settle ‖ *intr* to be convenient ‖ *ref* to adapt oneself; to agree; to sit down; **si accomodi** have a seat, make yourself comfortable

**accomodatura** *f* arrangement; repair

**accompagnaménto** *m* retinue; cortege; (mus) accompaniment; (law) writ of mandamus; (mil) softening-up (*by gunfire*)

**accompagnare** *tr* to accompany; to escort; to follow; to match ‖ *ref*—**accompagnarsi a** or **con** to join

**accompagna·tóre -trice** *mf* escort; guide; (mus) accompanist

**accomunare** *tr* to mingle, mix; to unite, associate; to share

**acconciaménto** *m* arrangement

**acconciare** §128 (accóncio) *tr* to prepare for use; to arrange; to set (*e.g., the hair*) ‖ *ref* to adorn oneself; to dress one's hair; to adapt oneself

**acconcia·tóre -trice** *mf* hairdresser

**acconciatura** *f* hairdo; headdress

**accón·cio -cia** *adj* (**-ci -ce**) proper, fitting

**accondiscendènte** *adj* acquiescing, acquiescent

**accondiscendènza** *f* acquiescence

**accondiscéndere** §245 *intr* to acquiesce, consent; to yield

**acconsentire** (**acconsènto**) *intr* to consent, acquiesce

**acconsenziènte** *adj* consenting, acquiescing

**accontentare** (**accontènto**) *tr* to satisfy, please ‖ *ref* to be satisfied, be pleased

**accónto** *m* installment

**accoppare** (**accòppo**) *tr* (coll) to kill; (coll) to beat to death ‖ *ref* (coll) to get killed

**accoppiaménto** *m* pairing; mating; (mach) parallel operation

**accoppiare** §287 (**accòppio**) *tr* to couple, pair, cross (*e.g., animals*) ‖ *ref* to mate, copulate

**accoppiata** *f* daily double (*in races*)

**accoraménto** *m* sadness, sorrow

**accorare** (**accòro**) *tr* to stab to death; to sadden ‖ *ref* to sadden, grieve

**accora·to -ta** *adj* saddened, grieving

**accorciare** §128 (**accórcio**) *tr & ref* to shorten; to shrink

**accorciatura** *f* shortening; shrinking

**accordare** (**accòrdo**) *tr* to harmonize (*colors*); to reconcile (*people*); to tune up; to grant; (gram) to make agree ‖ *ref* to agree; to match

**accorda·to -ta** *adj* tuned up ‖ *m* (econ) credit limit

**accorda·tóre -trice** *mf* (mus) tuner

**accordatura** *f* tuning

**accòrdo** *m* agreement, accordance; (law) mutual consent; (mus) harmony; **d'accordo** O.K., agreed; **d'accordo con** in accord with; **di comune accordo** with one accord; **essere d'accordo** to agree; **mettersi d'accordo** to come to an agreement

**accòrgere** §249 *ref* to perceive, notice; **accorgersi di** to become aware of, realize; **senza accorgersi** inadvertently

**accorgiménto** *m* smartness; device, trick

**accórrere** §139 *intr* (ESSERE) to run up, rush up

**accortézza** *f* alertness; shrewdness, perspicacity

**accòr·to -ta** *adj* alert; shrewd, perspicacious

**accosciare** §128 (**accòscio**) *ref* to squat

**accostàbile** *adj* approachable

**accostaménto** *m* approach; combination (*e.g., of colors*)

**accostare** (**accòsto**) *tr* to approach; to bring near; to leave (*a door*) ajar ‖ *intr* to be near; to cling, adhere; (naut) to come alongside; (naut) to maneuver alongside a pier; (naut) to change direction, haul ‖ *ref* to approach, come near; to cling (*e.g., to a faith*)

**accosta·to -ta** *adj* ajar

**accò·sto -sta** *adj* (coll) near ‖ *m* approach; help ‖ **accosto** *adv* near; **accosto a** near, close to

**accovacciare** §128 *ref* to crouch

**accovonare** (**accovóno**) *tr* to sheave

**accozzàglia** *f* hodgepodge; motley crowd

**accozzare** (**accòzzo**) *tr* to jumble up; to collect, gather (*people*) together ‖ *ref* to collect, congregate

**accòzzo** *m* jumble, medley

**accreditàbile** *adj* chargeable (*e.g., account*); creditable

**accreditaménto** *m* crediting

**accreditare** (**accrédito**) *tr* to credit, believe; to accredit (*an ambassador*); to credit (*one's account*)

**accredita·to -ta** *adj* confirmed (*news*); accredited

**accréscere** §142 *tr & ref* to increase

**accresciménto** *m* increase

**accucciare** §128 *ref* to curl up (*said of dogs*)

**accudire** §176 *tr* (coll) to attend (*a sick person*) ‖ *intr*—**accudire a** to take care of

**acculturazióne** *f* acculturation

**accumulare** (**accùmulo**) *tr, intr & ref* to accumulate; to gather

**accumulatóre** *m* storage battery

**accumulazióne** *f* accumulation

**accuratézza** *f* care, carefulness

**accura·to -ta** *adj* careful, painstaking

**accusa** *f* accusation, charge; **pubblica accusa** (law) public prosecutor

**accusare** *tr* to accuse, charge; to betray; to acknowledge (*receipt*); (cards) to declare, bid

**accusati·vo -va** *adj & m* accusative

**accusa·to -ta** *adj* accused ‖ *mf* defendant

**accusató·re -trice** *mf* accuser; **pubblico accusatore** (law) public prosecutor, district attorney

**accusatò·rio -ria** *adj* (**-ri -rie**) accusatory, accusing

**acèfa·lo -la** *adj* headless; without the first page (*said of a manuscript*)

**acèr·bo -ba** *adj* unripe, green, sour

**àcero** *m* maple tree, sugar maple

**acèrri·mo -ma** *adj* bitter, fierce

**acetato** *m* acetate

**acèti·co -ca** *adj* (**-ci -che**) acetic

**acetificare** §197 (**acetìfico**) *tr* to acetify

**acetilène** *m* acetylene

**acéto** *m* vinegar; **aceto aromatico** aromatic spirits; **sotto aceto** pickled

**acetóne** *m* acetone

**acetósa** [s] *f* (bot) sorrel

**acetosèlla** [s] *f* wood sorrel

**acetó·so -sa** [s] *adj* vinegarish ‖ *f* see **acetosa**

**Acherónte** *m* Acheron

**Achille** *m* Achilles

**acidificare** §197 (**acidìfico**) *tr* to acidify

**acidi·tà** *f* (**-tà**) acidity; **acidità di stomaco** heartburn

**àci·do -da** *adj* acid, sour ‖ *m* acid; **sapere d'acido** to taste sour

**acìdu·lo -la** *adj* acidulous

**àcino** *m* berry (*of grapes*); bead (*of rosary*)

**acme** *f* acme; crisis

**acne** *f* acne

**acònito** *m* (bot) monkshood

**àcqua** *f* water; rain; purity (*e.g., of a diamond*); **acqua a catinelle** pouring rain; **acqua alta** high water; **acqua corrente** running water; **acqua dolce** fresh water; drinking water; **acqua in bocca!** mum's the word!; **acqua morta** stagnant water; **acqua ossigenata** hydrogen peroxide; **acqua potabile** drinking water; **acqua salata** salt water; **acqua viva** spring; **all'acqua di rose** very mild; **avere l'acqua alla gola** to be in dire straits; **della più bell'acqua** of the first water; **fare acqua** to leak (*said of a boat*); **fare un buco nell'acqua** to waste one's efforts; **portare acqua al mare** to carry coals to Newcastle; **prendere l'acqua** to get wet; **sott'acqua** (fig) underhand; **tirare l'acqua al proprio mulino** to be grist to one's mill; **versare acqua in un cesto** to waste one's efforts

**acquafòrte** *f* (**acquefòrti**) etching

**acquaforti·sta** *mf* (**-sti -ste**) etcher

**ac·quàio -quàia** (**-quài -quàie**) *adj* watering (*trough*) || *m* sink

**acquaiò·lo -la** *adj* water || *m* water carrier; (sports) water boy

**acquamarina** *f* (**acquemarine**) aquamarine

**acquaplano** *m* aquaplane

**acquaràgia** *f* turpentine

**acquarèllo** *m* var of **acquerello**

**acquà·rio** *m* (**-ri**) aquarium || **Acquario** *m* (astr) Aquarius

**acquartierare** (**acquartièro**) *tr* (mil) to quarter || *ref* to be quartered

**acquasanta** *f* holy water

**acquasantièra** *f* (eccl) stoup

**acquàti·co -ca** *adj* (**-ci -che**) aquatic, water

**acquattare** *ref* to crouch, squat

**acquavite** *f* brandy; liquor, rum

**acquazzóne** *m* downpour, heavy shower

**acquedótto** *m* aqueduct

**àcque·o -a** *adj* aqueous, watery

**acquerelli·sta** *mf* (**-sti -ste**) watercolorist

**acquerèllo** *m* watercolor; watered-down wine

**acquerùgiola** *f* fine drizzle

**acquiescènte** *adj* acquiescent

**acquietare** (**acquièto**) *tr* to pacify, placate || *ref* to quiet down

**acquirènte** *mf* buyer, purchaser; **il miglior acquirente** the highest bidder

**acquisire** §176 *tr* to acquire

**acquisi·tóre -trice** *mf* salesperson, agent || *m* salesman || *f* saleswoman

**acquistare** *tr* to purchase, buy; to acquire; to gain (*e.g., ground*) || *intr* to improve

**acquisto** *m* buy, purchase; acquisition

**acquitrino** *m* marsh

**acquitrinó·so -sa** [s] *adj* marshy

**acquolina** *f*—**far venire l'acquolina in bocca a** to make one's mouth water

**acquó·so -sa** [s] *adj* watery

**acre** *adj* sour; pungent; acrid; bitter (*words*)

**acrèdine** *f* acrimony, sourness

**acrimònia** *f* acrimony

**acro** *m* acre

**acròba·ta** *mf* (**-ti -te**) acrobat

**acrobàti·co -ca** (**-ci -che**) *adj* acrobatic || *f* acrobatics

**acrobatismo** *m* acrobatics

**acrobazìa** *f* acrobatics; stunt, feat

**acrocòro** *m* plateau

**acrònimo** *m* acronym

**acròpo·li** *f* (**-li**) acropolis

**acròsti·co** *m* (**-ci**) acrostic

**acuire** §176 *tr* to sharpen, whet

**acuità** *f* acuity

**acùle·o** *m* (**-i**) quill; prickle, thorn; stinger (*of an insect*)

**acume** *m* acumen

**acuminare** (**acùmino**) *tr* to sharpen, whet

**acumina·to -ta** *adj* pointed, sharp

**acùsti·co -ca** (**-ci -che**) *adj* acoustic(al) || *f* acoustics

**acutézza** *f* acuteness, sharpness

**acutizzare** [ddzz] *tr & ref* to sharpen

**acu·to -ta** *adj* acute, sharp || *m* high note

**ad** *prep* var of **a** before words beginning with a vowel

**adagiare** §290 *tr* to lay down gently; to lower gently || *ref* to lie down; to stretch out

**adà·gio** *m* (**-gi**) adage; (mus) adagio || *adv* slowly; gently; (mus) adagio

**Adamo** *m* Adam

**adattàbile** *adj* adaptable

**adattaménto** *m* adaptation; adaptability

**adattare** *tr* to adapt, fit || *ref* to adapt oneself; to become adapted; **adattarsi a** to go with; to match; to be becoming to

**adat·to -ta** *adj* suitable, adequate

**addebitaménto** *m* debiting

**addebitare** (**addébito**) *tr* to debit; **addebitare una spesa a qlcu** to debit s.o. with an expense

**addébito** *m* charge; (com) debit; **elevare l'addebito di qlco a qlcu** (law) to charge s.o. with s.th

**addènda** *mpl* addenda

**addèndo** *m* (math) addend

**addensare** (**addènso**) *tr* to thicken || *ref* to thicken; to gather, throng

**addentare** (**addènto**) *tr* to bite || *ref* (mach) to mesh

**addentatura** *f* bite; (carp) tongue (*of tongue and groove*)

**addentella·to -ta** *adj* toothed, notched || *m* chance, occasion; (archit) toothing

**addentrare** (**addéntro**) *tr* to penetrate || *ref* to penetrate; to proceed

**addéntro** *adv* inside; **addentro in** into; inside of

**addestraménto** *m* training

**addestrare** (**addèstro**) *tr & ref* to train

**addestra·tóre -trice** *mf* trainer

**addét·to -ta** *adj* assigned; attached; pertaining || *m* attaché; **addetto stampa** press secretary

**addì** *adv* the (+ *a certain date*), e.g., **addì 27 gennaio** the 27th of January

**addiàc·cio** *m* (**-ci**) sheepfold; bivouac

**addiètro** *m* (naut) stern; **per l'addietro** in the past || *adv* behind; ago; **dare**

**addietro** to back up; **lasciarsi addietro** to delay; **tempo addietro** some time ago; **tirarsi addietro** to back away
**addì·o** m (-i) farewell; **dare l'addio** to say good-bye; **dare l'estremo addio** to pay one's last respects; **fare gli addii** to say good-bye || interj farewell!, good-bye!
**addire** §151 tr (poet) to consecrate || ref to be suitable, be becoming; **addirsi a** to be becoming to
**addirittura** adv directly; even, without hesitation; absolutely, positively
**addirizzare** tr to straighten up; **addirizzare le gambe ai cani** to try the impossible
**additare** tr to point out
**additi·vo -va** adj & m additive
**addivenire** §282 intr (ESSERE)—**addivenire a** to come to, reach (e.g., an agreement)
**addizionale** adj additional || f supplementary tax
**addizionare** (**addizióno**) tr & intr to add
**addizionatrice** f adding machine
**addizióne** f addition
**addobbaménto** m adornment, decoration
**addobbare** (**addòbbo**) tr to adorn, bedeck, decorate
**addobba·tóre -trice** mf decorator
**addòbbo** m adornment, decoration; hangings (in a church)
**addocilire** §176 tr to soften up
**addolcire** §176 tr to sweeten; to calm down || ref to mellow, soften
**addolorare** (**addolóro**) tr & ref to grieve; **addolorarsi per** to grieve over, lament
**addolora·to -ta** adj sorrowful || l'**Addolorata** f (eccl) Our Lady of Sorrows
**addòme** m abdomen
**addomesticàbile** adj tamable
**addomesticaménto** m taming
**addomesticare** §197 (**addomèstico**) tr to tame; to accustom || ref to become accustomed
**addomestica·to -ta** adj tame, domesticated
**addominale** adj abdominal
**addormentare** (**addorménto**) tr to put to sleep; to numb || ref to fall asleep; to be asleep (said of a limb)
**addormenta·to -ta** adj asleep; numbed
**addossare** (**addòsso**) tr to put on; **addossare qlco a qlco** to lean s.th against s.th; **addossare qlco a qlcu** to put s.th on s.o.; (fig) to entrust s.o. with s.th || ref to take upon oneself; to crowd together; **addossarsi a** to lean against; to crowd
**addossa·to -ta** adj leaning
**addòsso** adv on; on oneself, on one's back; about oneself; **addosso a** on, upon; against; **avere la sfortuna addosso** to be always unlucky; **dare addosso a qlcu** to assail s.o.; **levarsi d'addosso** to get rid of; **levarsi i panni d'addosso** to take the shirt off one's back
**addót·to -ta** adj adduced, alleged

**addottorare** (**addottóro**) tr to confer the doctor's degree on || ref to receive the doctor's degree
**addurre** §102 tr to adduce; to allege; (poet) to bring
**Ade** m Hades
**adeguare** (**adéguo**) tr to equalize; to bring in line || ref to conform, adapt oneself
**adegua·to -ta** adj adequate
**adeguazióne** f equalization
**adémpiere** §163 tr to fulfill, accomplish || ref to come true
**adempiménto** m fulfillment, discharge (of one's duty)
**adempire** §176 tr to fulfill, accomplish || ref to come true
**adenòide** adj adenoid || **adenoidi** fpl adenoids
**adèpto** m follower; initiate
**aderènte** adj adherent || mf adherent, supporter
**aderènza** f adherence; (mach) friction; (pathol) adhesion; **aderenze** connections
**aderire** §176 intr to adhere; to stick; **aderire a** to grant (e.g., a request); to concur with; to subscribe to
**adescare** §197 (**adésco**) tr to lure, bait, entice; (mach) to prime (a pump)
**adesióne** f adhesion; support; (phys) adherence
**adesi·vo -va** adj & m adhesive
**adèsso** adv now, just now; **da adesso in poi** from now on; **per adesso** for the time being
**adiacènte** adj adjacent
**adiacènza** f adjacency; **adiacenze** vicinity
**adianto** m (bot) maidenhair
**adibire** §176 tr to assign; to use
**àdipe** m fat
**adipó·so -sa** [s] adj adipose
**adirare** ref to get angry
**adira·to -ta** adj angry, mad
**adire** §176 tr to apply to (the court); to enter into possession of (an inheritance)
**adocchiare** §287 (**adòcchio**) tr to eye; to ogle; to spot
**adolescènte** adj & mf adolescent
**adolescènza** f adolescence
**adombrare** (**adómbro**) tr to shade; to hide, veil || ref to shy (said of a horse); (fig) to take umbrage
**Adóne** m Adonis
**adontare** (**adónto**) tr (obs) to offend || ref to take offense
**adoperare** (**adòpero** & **adópero**) tr to use, employ || ref to exert oneself; to do one's best
**adoràbile** adj adorable
**adorare** (**adóro**) tr to adore; to worship || intr (archaic) to pray
**adora·tóre -trice** mf worshiper || m (joc) admirer, suitor
**adorazióne** f adoration, worship
**adornare** (**adórno**) tr to adorn || ref to bedeck oneself
**adór·no -na** adj adorned, bedecked; (poet) fine, beautiful
**adottante** mf (law) adopter

**adottare (adòtto)** *tr* to adopt
**adotti•vo -va** *adj* adoptive; foster *(child)*
**adozióne** *f* adoption
**Adrìàti•co -ca** *adj* (**-ci -che**) Adriatic || **Adriatico** *m* Adriatic
**adulare (àdulo)** *tr* to flatter; to fawn on
**adula•tóre -trice** *mf* flatterer
**adulatò•rio -ria** *adj* (**-ri -rie**) flattering; fawning
**adulazióne** *f* adulation; fawning
**adulterante** *adj & m* adulterant
**adulteri•no -na** *adj* bastard; adulterated
**adultè•rio** *m* (**-ri**) adultery
**adùlte•ro -ra** *adj* adulterous || *m* adulterer || *f* adulteress
**adul•to -ta** *adj & mf* adult
**adunanza** *f* assembly
**adunare** *tr & ref* to assemble, gather
**adunata** *f* reunion, meeting; (mil) muster
**adun•co -ca** *adj* (**-chi -che**) hooked, crooked
**adunghiare §287** *tr* (poet) to claw
**adu•sto -sta** *adj* skinny; (poet) burnt
**aerare (àero)** *tr* to air, ventilate
**aerazióne** *f* aeration; airing
**aère•o -a** *adj* aerial; air; overhead; high, lofty; airy, fanciful || *m* airplane; (rad & telv) aerial
**aerobrigata** *f* (mil) wing
**aerocistèrna** *f* (aer) tanker
**aerodinàmi•co -ca** *adj* (**-ci -che**) aerodynamic(al); streamlined || *f* aerodynamics
**aeròdromo** *m* airfield, airdrome
**aerofaro** *m* airport beacon
**aerofotogram•ma** *m* (**-mi**) aerial photograph
**aerogiro** *m* helicopter
**aerògrafo** *m* spray gun *(for painting)*
**aerolìnea** *f* airline; **aerolinea principale** trunkline
**aeròlito** *m* aerolite, meteorite
**aeromarìtti•mo -ma** *adj* air-sea
**aeròmetro** *m* aerometer
**aeromòbile** *m* aircraft; **aeromobile senza pilota** drone, pilotless aircraft
**aeromodellismo** *m* model-airplane building
**aeromodelli•sta** *mf* (**-sti -ste**) model-airplane builder
**aeromodèllo** *m* model airplane
**aeromotóre** *m* windmill; aircraft motor
**aeronàu•ta** *m* (**-ti**) aeronaut
**aeronàuti•co -ca** (**-ci -che**) *adj* aeronautic(al) || *f* aeronautics
**aeronave** *f* airship, aircraft
**aeroplano** *m* airplane
**aeropòrto** *m* airport, airfield
**aeroportuale** *adj* airport
**aerorazzo** [ddzz] *m* rocket spaceship
**aeroriméssa** *f* hangar
**aerosbar•co** *m* (**-chi**) landing of airborne troops
**aeroservì•zio** [s] *m* (**-zi**) air service
**aerosilurante** [s] *f* torpedo plane
**aerosiluro** [s] *m* aerial torpedo
**aerosòl** [s] *m* aerosol
**aerosostenta•to -ta** [s] *adj* airborne
**aerospaziale** *adj* aerospace
**aerospà•zio** *m* (**-zi**) aerospace

**aerostàti•co -ca** (**-ci -che**) *adj* aerostatic(al) || *f* aerostatics
**aeròstato** *m* aerostat
**aerostazióne** *f* air terminal
**aerotas•sì** *m* (**-sì**) taxiplane
**aerotrasportare (aerotraspòrto)** *tr* to airlift
**aerotrasporta•to -ta** *adj* airlifted; airborne
**aerovìa** *f* (aer) beam *(course indicated by a radio beam)*; (aer) air lane
**afa** *f* sultriness; **fare afa a** (coll) to be a pain in the neck to
**afèresi** *f* apheresis
**affàbile** *adj* affable, agreeable
**affaccendare (affaccèndo)** *tr* to busy || *ref* to busy oneself, bustle
**affaccenda•to -ta** *adj* busy, bustling; occupied with busywork
**affacciare §128** *tr* to show or display at the window; to bring forward *(e.g., an objection)*; to raise *(a doubt)* || *ref* to show oneself *(at the door or window)*; to present itself *(said of a doubt)*
**affaccia•to -ta** *adj* facing
**affagottare (affagòtto)** *tr* to bundle || *ref* to bundle up; to dress sloppily
**affamare** *tr* to starve
**affama•to -ta** *adj* starved, ravenous || *mf* starveling; hungry person; wretch
**affannare** *tr* to worry, to afflict || *intr* to pant; to be out of breath || *ref* to worry; to bustle around
**affanna•to -ta** *adj* panting; out of breath; worried
**affanno** *m* shortness of breath; grief, sorrow
**affannó•so -sa** [s] *adj* panting; wearisome
**affardellare (affardèllo)** *tr* to bundle together; (mil) to pack
**affare** *m* affair, matter; business; condition, quality; deal; **affari** business; **affari esteri** foreign affairs; **un buon affare** a good deal; a bargain
**affarismo** *m* sharp business practice
**affari•sta** *mf* (**-sti -ste**) unscrupulous operator
**affarìsti•co -ca** *adj* (**-ci -che**) sharp
**affascinante** *adj* fascinating, charming
**affascinare (affàscino)** *tr* to fascinate, charm; to seduce; to spellbind || (affàscino) *tr* to bundle, to sheave
**affascina•tóre -trice** *adj* fascinating, charming || *mf* charmer, spellbinder
**affastellare (affastèllo)** *tr* to fagot *(twigs)*: to sheave, bundle *(e.g., hay)*; to pile, heap *(wood, crops, etc)*; (fig) to jumble up
**affaticare §197** *tr* to fatigue, tire, weary || *ref* to get tired; to weary; to toil
**affatica•to -ta** *adj* weary, tired
**affatto** *adv* quite, entirely; **niente affatto** not at all; **non . . . affatto** not at all
**affatturare** *tr* to bewitch; to adulterate *(e.g., food)*
**affermare (affèrmo)** *tr* to affirm, assert || *intr* to nod assent || *ref* to take hold *(said, e.g., of a new product)*
**affermati•vo -va** *adj & f* affirmative
**affermazióne** *f* affirmation; assertion,

statement; success (*e.g., of a new product*); (sports) victory

**afferrare (afferro)** *tr* to grab, grasp; to catch, nab || *ref* to cling

**affettare (affetto)** *tr* to slice; to cut up || (**affetto**) *tr* to affect

**affetta·to -ta** *adj* affected || *m* cold cuts

**affettatrice** *f* slicing machine

**affettazióne** *f* affectation

**affetti·vo -va** *adj* emotional

**affet·to -ta** *adj* afflicted, burdened || *m* affection, love; feeling

**affettuosi·tà** [s] *f* (**-tà**) love, affection

**affettuó·so -sa** [s] *adj* affectionate, loving, tender

**affezionare (affezióno)** *tr* to inspire affection in || *ref*—**affezionarsi a** to become fond of

**affeziona·to -ta** *adj* affectionate, loving; **Suo affezionatissimo** best regards; **tuo affezionatissimo** love, as ever

**affezióne** *f* affection

**affiancare** §197 *tr* to place next; to favor, help; (mil) to flank

**affiatamento** *m* harmony; teamwork

**affiatare** *tr* to harmonize

**affibbiare** §287 *tr* to buckle, fasten; to deliver (*a blow*); to play (*a trick*); to slap (*a fine*)

**affidamento** *m* consignment, delivery; trust, confidence; **dare affidamento** to be trustworthy; **fare affidamento su** to rely upon

**affidare** *tr* to entrust; to commit (*to memory*); **affidare qlco a qlcu** to entrust s.o with s.th || *ref* to trust; **affidarsi a** to trust in

**affievoliménto** *m* weakening

**affievolire** §176 *tr* to weaken || *ref* to grow weaker

**affiggere** §103 *tr* to post; to fix (*one's eyes or glance*) || *ref* to gaze, stare

**affigliare** §280 *tr & ref* var of **affiliare**

**affilacoltèi·li** *m* (**-li**) steel (*for sharpening knives*)

**affilara·sóio** *m* (**-sói**) strop

**affilare** *tr* to sharpen, hone, whet; to make thin || *ref* to become thin

**affila·to -ta** *adj* sharp, sharpened; thin || *f* sharpening

**affila·tóio** *m* (**-tói**) sharpener

**affilatrice** *f* grindstone

**affiliare** §287 *tr* to affiliate || *ref* to become affiliated; **affiliarsi a** to become a member of

**affilia·to -ta** *adj* affiliated || *mf* affiliate; foster child; member of a secret society

**affiliazióne** *f* affiliation

**affinare** *tr* to sharpen; to refine, purify; to improve (*e.g., one's style*) || *ref* to improve

**affinché** *conj* so that, in order that; **affinché non** lest

**affine** *adj* akin, related; similar || *mf* in-law || *m* kinsman || *f* kinswoman || *adv*—**affine di** in order to

**affini·tà** *f* (**-tà**) affinity

**affiochire** §176 *tr* to make hoarse; to weaken || *ref* to become hoarse; to grow dim (*said of a candle*)

**affioraménto** *m* surfacing; (min) outcrop

**affiorare (affióro)** *intr* to surface, emerge; to appear, to show

**affissare** *tr* (poet) to fix || *ref* to concentrate; (poet) to gaze

**affissióne** *f* posting, bill posting

**affis·so -sa** *adj* fixed; posted || *m* bill, poster; door or window; (gram) affix

**affittacàme·re** *m* (**-re**) landlord || *f* landlady

**affittanza** *f* rent

**affittare** *tr* to rent || *ref*—**si affitta** for rent

**affitto** *m* rent, rental; **dare in affitto** to rent (*to grant by lease*); **prendere in affitto** to rent (*to take by lease*)

**affittuà·rio -ria** *mf* (**-ri -rie**) renter; tenant

**affliggènte** *adj* tormenting, distressing

**affliggere** §104 *tr* to afflict, distress || *ref* to grieve

**afflit·to -ta** *adj* afflicted, grieving || *mf* afflicted person, wretch

**afflizióne** *f* affliction, distress

**afflosciare** §128 (**afflòscio**) *tr* to cause to sag; to weaken || *ref* to droop; to sag; to be deflated; to faint

**affloscire** §176 *tr & ref* var of **afflosciare**

**affluènte** *adj & m* confluent

**affluènza** *f* confluence; abundance; crowd

**affluire** §176 *intr* (ESSERE) to flow (*said of river*); to flock (*said of people*); to pour in (*said of earnings*)

**afflusso** *m* flow

**affogaménto** *m* drowning

**affogare** §209 (**affógo**) *tr* to drown; to smother || *intr* (ESSERE) to drown

**affoga·to -ta** *adj* drowned; poached (*egg*)

**affollaménto** *m* crowd, throng

**affollare (affóllo & affòllo)** *tr* to crowd; to overcome || *ref* to crowd

**affolla·to -ta** *adj* crowded

**affondaménto** *m* sinking

**affondami·ne** *m* (**-ne**) mine layer

**affondare (affóndo)** *tr* to sink; to stick || *ref* to sink

**affondata** *f* (aer) nosedive

**affóndo** *m* (fencing) lunge || *adv* deeply

**afforestare (afforèsto)** *tr* to reforest

**affossare (affòsso)** *tr* to ditch; (fig) to table (*e.g., a proposal*); to hollow out || *ref* to become sunken or hollow (*said, e.g., of cheeks*)

**affossatóre** *m* ditchdigger; gravedigger

**affrancare** §197 *tr* to set free; to free; to redeem (*a property*); to stamp || *ref* to free oneself; to take heart

**affrancatrice** *f* postage meter

**affrancatura** *f* stamp, stamping

**affràngere** §179 *tr* to weary; (obs) to break down (*the spirit*)

**affran·to -ta** *adj* weary; broken down, broken-hearted

**affratellaménto** *m* fraternization

**affratellare (affratèllo)** *tr* to bind in brotherly love || *ref* to fraternize

**affrescare** §197 (**affrésco**) *tr* to fresco; to paint in fresco

**affré·sco** *m* (-schi) fresco
**affrettare** (**affrétto**) *tr & ref* to hurry, hasten
**affretta· to -ta** *adj* hurried
**affrontare** (**affrónto**) *tr* to face, confront ‖ *ref* to meet in combat; to come to blows
**affronta·to -ta** *adj—***affrontati** (herald) combattant
**affrónto** *m* affront, offense
**affumicare** §197 (**affùmico**) *tr* to smoke; to blacken; to smoke out; to smoke (*meat or fish*)
**affumica·to -ta** *adj* smoked; dark (*glasses*)
**affusolare** [s] (**affùsolo**) *tr & ref* to taper
**affusola·to -ta** [s] *adj* tapered; slender
**affusto** *m* gun carriage
**afga·no -na** *adj & mf* Afghan
**àfo·no -na** *adj* voiceless
**afori·sma** *m* (-smi) aphorism
**afó·so -sa** [s] *adj* sultry
**Africa, l'** *f* Africa
**africa·no -na** *adj & mf* African
**afrodisìa·co -ca** *adj & m* (-ci -che) aphrodisiac
**afta** *m* mouth ulcer; **afta epizootica** (vet) foot-and-mouth disease
**àgata** *f* agate ‖ **Agata** *f* Agatha
**agènda** *f* notebook; agenda
**agènte** *adj* active ‖ *m* agent; broker; merchant; officer; **agente delle tasse** tax collector; **agente di cambio** stockbroker; money changer; **agente di commercio** broker, commission merchant; **agente di custodia** jailer; **agente di polizia** police officer, policeman; **agente di spionaggio** informer; **agente provocatore** agent provocateur
**agenzìa** *f* agency; office, branch; **agenzia immobiliare** real-estate office
**agevolare** (**agévolo**) *tr* to facilitate, help
**agevolazióne** *f* facility; **agevolazione di pagamento** easy terms
**agévole** *adj* easy
**agevolézza** *f* facility
**aggallare** *intr* to come to the surface
**agganciaménto** *m* docking (*in space*); (rr) coupling
**agganciare** §128 *tr* to hook; (rr) to couple; (mil) to engage (*the enemy*)
**aggàn·cio** *m* (-ci) docking (*in space*); (rr) coupling
**aggég·gio** *m* (-gi) gadget
**aggettivale** *adj* adjectival
**aggettivo** *m* adjective
**agghiacciaménto** *m* freezing
**agghiacciante** *adj* hair-raising, frightful
**agghiacciare** §128 *tr* to freeze ‖ *ref* to freeze; to be horrified
**agghiaccia·to -ta** *adj* frozen, icy
**agghindare** *tr & ref* to preen, primp
**àg·gio** *m* (-gi) agio; **fare aggio** to be at a premium
**aggiogare** §209 (**aggiógo**) *tr* to yoke
**aggiornaménto** *m* adjournment (*e.g., of a meeting*); bringing up to date
**aggiornare** (**aggiórno**) *tr* to bring up to date; to adjourn ‖ *ref* to keep up with the times

**aggiraménto** *m* surrounding, outflanking
**aggirare** *tr* to surround, outflank; to swindle ‖ *ref* to roam, wander; **aggirarsi su** to approximate; to be almost
**aggiudicare** §197 (**aggiùdico**) *tr* to adjudicate, award ‖ *ref* to win
**aggiudicazióne** *f* adjudication, award
**aggiùngere** §183 *tr* to add; to join, connect ‖ *ref* to be added; to join
**aggiunta** *f* addition
**aggiuntare** *tr* to attach, join
**aggiun·to -ta** *adj & m* associate, assistant, deputy ‖ *f* see **aggiunta**
**aggiustàbile** *adj* repairable
**aggiustaménto** *m* settlement; adjustment; (mil) correction (*of fire*)
**aggiustare** *tr* to fix, repair; to adjust; (mil) to correct (*cannon fire*); **aggiustare per le feste** (coll) to fix; (coll) to give a good beating to ‖ *ref* (archaic) to come closer; (coll) to manage; (coll) to come to an agreement
**aggiusta·tóre -trice** *mf* repairer, fixer ‖ *m* repairman
**aggiustatura** *f* fixing, repairing, repair
**agglomerare** (**agglòmero**) *tr & ref* to pile up; to crowd together
**agglomerato** *m* built-up area; **agglomerato urbano** urban center
**agglutinare** (**agglùtino**) *tr & ref* to agglutinate
**agglutinazióne** *f* agglutination
**aggobbire** §176 *tr* to bend, bend over ‖ *intr* (ESSERE) & *ref* to hunch over
**aggomitolare** (**aggomitolo**) *tr* to coil ‖ *ref* to curl up
**aggradare** *intr* (with *dat*) (poet) to please; **come Le aggrada** as you please
**aggradire** §176 *tr* to appreciate ‖ *intr* (poet) (with *dat*) to please
**aggraffare** *tr* to hook; to grab; to join (*metal sheets*) with a double seam; to stitch, staple
**aggraffatrice** *f* folding machine; (mach) can sealer
**aggranchire** §176 *tr* to benumb; to deaden, stupefy ‖ *intr* to become numb
**aggrappare** *tr* to grab; to clamp ‖ *ref* to cling
**aggravaménto** *m* aggravation
**aggravante** *adj* (law) aggravating (*circumstances*)
**aggravare** *tr* to aggravate; to overload (*e.g., one's stomach*) ‖ *ref* to get worse
**aggrà·vio** *m* (-vi) burden (*e.g., of taxes*); **fare aggravio a qlcu di qlco** to impute s.th to s.o.
**aggraziare** §287 *tr* to embellish; to render graceful ‖ *ref* to win, gain; to ingratiate oneself
**aggrazia·to -ta** *adj* graceful; polite
**aggredire** §176 *tr* to assail, attack, assault
**aggregare** §209 (**aggrègo**) *tr & ref* to join, unite
**aggrega·to -ta** *adj* adjunct ‖ *m* aggregation
**aggressióne** *f* aggression

**aggressi·vo -va** *adj* aggressive ‖ *m* (mil) poison gas
**aggressóre** *m* aggressor
**aggricciare** §128 *tr* to wrinkle; (slang) to knit (*e.g., the brow*) ‖ *ref* (poet) to shiver
**aggrinzare** *tr & ref* to wrinkle
**aggrinzire** §176 *tr & ref* var of **aggrinzare**
**aggrondare** (**aggróndo**) *tr* to knit (*the brow*)
**aggrottare** (**aggròtto**) *tr* to knit (*the brow*)
**aggrovigliare** §280 *tr* to tangle, entangle ‖ *ref* to become entangled
**aggrumare** *tr & ref* to clot; to coagulate
**aggruppare** *tr* to group
**agguagliare** §280 *tr* to level; to equalize; to compare
**agguantare** *tr* to grab; to nab; (coll) to hit; **agguantare per il collo** to grab by the neck ‖ *ref*—**agguantarsi a** to get hold of
**agguato** *m* ambush; **cadere in un agguato** to fall into a trap; **stare in agguato** to wait in ambush
**agguerrire** §176 *tr* to train for war; to inure to war; to inure
**aghétto** *m* shoestring; (mil) lanyard
**agiatézza** *f* comfort, wealth; **vivere nell'agiatezza** to live in comfort
**agia·to -ta** *adj* well-to-do, comfortable
**àgile** *adj* agile, nimble; prompt
**agili·tà** *f* (**-tà**) agility, nimbleness; promptness
**à·gio** *m* (**-gi**) comfort; opportunity; ease; **agi** conveniences, comforts; **a Suo agio** at your convenience; **aver agio** to have time; **stare a proprio agio** to feel at ease; to be comfortable; **vivere negli agi** to live comfortably
**agiografia** *f* hagiography
**agiògrafo** *m* hagiographer
**agire** §176 *intr* to act; to work; (theat) to act, perform
**agitare** (**àgito**) *tr* to agitate, shake; to stir; to stir up; to discuss (*e.g., a problem*) ‖ *ref* to toss; to shake; to stir; to get excited
**agita·to -ta** *adj* rough, choppy (*sea*); troubled, upset ‖ *mf* violently insane person
**agita·tóre -trice** *mf* agitator ‖ *m* shaker
**agitazióne** *f* agitation
**agli** §4
**agliàce·o -a** *adj* garlicky
**à·glio** *m* (**-gli**) garlic
**agnellino** *m* little lamb, lambkin
**agnèllo** *m* lamb
**agnizióne** *f* recognition
**agnòsti·co -ca** *adj & mf* (**-ci -che**) agnostic
**a·go** *m* (**-ghi**) needle; pointer (*of scales*); stem (*of valve*)
**agognare** (**agógno**) *tr* to covet
**agóne** *m* contest; arena
**agonìa** *f* agony, death struggle; anguish
**agonìsti·co -ca** *adj* (**-ci -che**) competitive, aggressive (*spirit*); athletic (*competition*) ‖ *f* athletics

**agonizzare** [ddzz] *intr* to agonize, be in agony; (fig) to die out
**agopuntura** *f* acupuncture
**ago·ràio** *m* (**-rài**) needle case
**agosta·no -na** *adj* August, e.g., **pomeriggio agostano** August afternoon
**agostinia·no -na** *adj & m* Augustinian
**agósto** *m* August
**agrà·rio -ria** (**-ri -rie**) *adj & m* agrarian ‖ *m* landlord ‖ *f* agriculture
**agrèste** *adj* country
**agrìco·lo -la** *adj* agricultural
**agricoltóre** *m* farmer; agriculturist
**agricoltura** *f* agriculture
**agrifò·glio** *m* (**-gli**) holly
**agrimensóre** *m* surveyor
**agrimensura** *f* surveying
**a·gro -gra** *adj* sour, bitter ‖ *m* citrus juice; sourness, bitterness; surrounding country
**agrodólce** *adj* sweet and sour; (fig) acidulous (*tone*)
**agronomìa** *f* agronomy
**agrònomo** *m* agronomist
**agrume** *m* citrus (*tree and fruit*); **agrumi** citrus fruit
**agucchiare** §287 *intr* to knit or sew idly
**agùglia** *f* spire; top; (ichth) gar; (poet) eagle; (obs) needle
**aguzzare** *tr* to sharpen; to whet (*the appetite*)
**aguzzino** [ddzz] *m* slave driver; jailer
**aguz·zo -za** *adj* sharp, pointed
**ah** *interj* ah!, aha!; ha!
**ahi** *interj* ouch!
**ahimè** *interj* alas!
**àia** *f* yard, barnyard; threshing floor; governess ‖ **L'Àia** *f* the Hague
**Aiace** *m* Ajax
**àio** *m* (**ài**) tutor
**aiòla** *f* lawn; flower bed
**àire** *m* push; short run (*preparing for a jump*); **dare l'aire a** to start off; **prendere l'aire** to take off
**airóne** *m* heron
**aitante** *adj* robust, stalwart
**aiuòla** *f* (poet) var of **aiola**
**aiutante** *adj* helping ‖ *mf* assistant ‖ *m* (mil) adjutant; **aiutante di campo** aide-de-camp; **aiutante di sanità** orderly
**aiutare** *tr* to help ‖ *ref* to strive; to help oneself; to help one another
**aiutato** *m* first assistant (*e.g., of a surgeon*)
**aiuto** *m* aid, help; assistant; first assistant (*of a surgeon*)
**aizzare** (**aìzzo**) *tr* to incite, to incite to riot; to sic (*a dog*)
**al** §4
**a·la** *f* (**-li & -le**) wing; sail, vane (*of windmill*); blade (*e.g., of fan*); brim (*of hat*); (football) end; **ala a freccia** backswept wing; **ala di popolo** throng; **fare ala a** to line up along
**alabarda** *f* halberd
**alabardière** *m* halberdier
**alabastri·no -na** *adj* alabaster; white as alabaster
**alabastro** *m* alabaster
**àlacre** *adj* eager, lively
**alacrità** *f* alacrity

alàg·gio *m* (-gi) hauling, towing
alamaro *m* braid, gimp
alambic·co *m* (-chi) still
alano *m* Great Dane
alare *adj* wing (*e.g.*, *span*) || *m* andiron || *tr* to haul
Alasca, l' *f* Alaska
ala·to -ta *adj* winged, sublime
alba *f* dawn, daybreak
albagìa *f* haughtiness
albanése [s] *adj* & *mf* Albanian
Albanìa, l' *f* Albania
àlbatro *m* (orn) albatross
albeggiaménto *m* dawning
albeggiare §290 (albéggio) *intr* (ESSERE) to dawn; (poet) to sparkle (*said, e.g., of ice*) || *impers* (ESSERE)—albeggia the day dawns
alberare (àlbero) *tr* to plant (*trees*); to reforest; to hoist (*a mast*); to mast (*a ship*)
albera·to -ta *adj* tree-lined; (naut) masted
alberèllo *m* small tree; apothecary's jar
albergare §209 (albèrgo) *tr* to lodge; to put up at a hotel; (fig) to harbor || *intr* to lodge; to put up
alberga·tóre -trice *mf* hotelkeeper
alberghiè·ro -ra *adj* hotel
albèr·go *m* (-ghi) hotel; refuge; hospitality; albergo diurno day hostel; albergo per la gioventù youth hostel
àlbero *m* tree; poplar; (mach) shaft; (naut) mast; albero a camme (aut) camshaft; albero a gomito (aut) crankshaft; albero di distribuzione (aut) camshaft; albero di Natale Christmas tree; albero di trasmissione (aut) transmission; albero genealogico family tree
albicòc·ca *f* (-che) apricot
albicòc·co *m* (-chi) apricot tree
al·bo -ba *adj* (poet) white || *m* album; bulletin board; (law) roll; comic book; albo d'onore honor roll || *f* see alba
albóre *m* (poet) whiteness; (poet) dawn
album *m* (album) album, scrapbook
albume *m* albumen
albumina *f* albumin
àlca·li *m* (-li) alkali
alcali·no -na *adj* alkaline
alce *m* moose; elk
alchìmia *f* alchemy
alchimi·sta *m* (-sti) alchemist
alcióne *m* halcyon
alciò·nio -nia *adj* (-ni -nie) halcyon
àlco·le *m* alcohol
alcolici·tà *f* (-tà) alcoholic content
alcòli·co -ca *adj* (-ci -che) alcoholic || *m* alcoholic beverage
alcolismo *m* alcoholism
alcolizzare [ddzz] *tr* to intoxicate || *ref* to become intoxicated
alcolizza·to -ta [ddzz] *adj* intoxicated || *mf* alcoholic
alcool *m* (alcool) var of alcole
alcoolici·tà *f* (-tà) var of alcolicità
alcoòli·co -ca (-ci -che) *adj* & *m* var of alcolico
alcoolismo *m* var of alcolismo
alcoolizzare [ddzz] *tr* var of alcolizzare

alcoolizza·to -ta [ddzz] *adj* & *mf* var of alcolizzato
alcòva *f* bedroom; bed; alcove
alcunché *pron* something, anything
alcu·no -na *adj* & *pron* some; alcu·ni -ne some; quite a few, several, a good many
aldilà *m* life beyond, afterlife
àlea *f* chance, hazard; correre l'alea to try one's luck
aleggiare §290 (aléggio) *intr* to flutter; to flap the wings; to hover
aleróne *m* var of alettone
alesàg·gio *m* (-gi) (mach) bore
alesare (alèso) *tr* (mach) to bore
alesatóre *m* reamer
alesatrice *s* boring machine
Alessandria d'Egitto *f* Alexandria
alessandri·no -na *adj* & *mf* Alexandrian || *m* Alexandrine (*verse*)
Alessandro *m* Alexander; Alessandro Magno Alexander the Great
alétta *f* small wing; fin (*of fish*); (aer) tab; aletta di compensazione trim tab; aletta parasole (aut) sun visor
alettóne *m* (aer) aileron, flap
Aleuti·no -na *adj*—Isole Aleutine Aleutian Islands
al·fa *m* (-fa) alpha || *f* esparto
alfabèti·co -ca *adj* (-ci -che) alphabetical
alfabetizzazióne [ddzz] *f* teaching to read; learning to read
alfabèto *m* alphabet; code (*e.g., Morse*)
alfière *m* flagbearer, standardbearer; (chess) bishop
alfine *adv* finally, at last
al·ga *f* (-ghe) alga; alga marina seaweed
àlgebra *f* algebra
algèbri·co -ca *adj* (-ci -che) algebraic
Algèri *f* Algiers
Algerìa, l' *f* Algeria
algeri·no -na *adj* & *mf* Algerian
aliante *m* (aer) glider
alianti·sta *mf* (-sti -ste) glider pilot
àli·bi *m* (-bi) alibi
alice *f* anchovy
alienàbile *adj* alienable
alienare (alièno) *tr* to alienate; to transfer, convey || *ref*—alienarsi dalla ragione to go out of one's mind
aliena·to -ta *adj* alienated || *mf* insane person; dispossessed person
alienazióne *f* alienation
alieni·sta *mf* (-sti -ste) alienist
alièno -na *adj* disinclined; (poet) foreign, alien
alimentare *adj* alimentary || alimentari *mpl* food, foodstuff || *v* (aliménto) *tr* to feed; to fuel
alimentari·sta *m* (-sti) food merchant; food-industry worker
alimenta·tóre -trice *mf* stoker || *m* (mach) stoker, feeder
alimentazióne *f* nourishment; feeding; (mil) loading; alimentazione artificiale intravenous feeding
aliménto *m* food, nourishment; feed; alimenti alimony (*maintenance*)
alimònia *f* alimony
alìnea *f* (law) paragraph, section

**alìquota** f share; parcel, quota
**aliscafo** m hydrofoil
**alisè·o -a** adj trade (wind) ‖ m trade wind
**alitare (àlito)** intr to breathe; to blow gently; **non alitare** to not breathe a word
**àlito** m breath; (fig) breeze
**alìvo·lo -la** adj (poet) winged; (fig) swift
**alla** §4
**allacciaménto** m binding; connection, linking
**allacciare** §128 tr to bind, tie; to connect; to buckle; (fig) to deceive
**allacciatura** f lacing; buckling
**allagare** §209 tr to flood, overflow
**allampana·to -ta** adj tall and lean, lanky
**allargare** §209 tr to broaden, widen; **allargare la mano** to be lenient; to be liberal; **allargare il freno** to give free rein ‖ ref to widen, spread out; **mi si allarga il cuore** I feel relieved
**allargatura** f widening
**allarmante** adj alarming
**allarmare** tr to alarm ‖ ref to worry, become alarmed
**allarme** m alarm; **allarme aereo** air-raid warning; **cessato allarme** all clear; **falso allarme** false alarm; **stare in allarme** to be alarmed
**allascare** §197 tr (naut) to ease, slacken (a rope)
**allato** adv (poet) near; **allato a** near; beside; in comparison with
**allattaménto** m nursing, feeding; **allattamento artificiale** bottle feeding
**allattare** tr to nurse (at the breast); to feed (with a bottle)
**alle** §4
**alleanza** f alliance
**alleare (allèo)** tr to ally ‖ ref to become allied; to be connected
**allea·to -ta** adj allied ‖ mf ally
**allegare** §209 (allégo) tr to enclose; to adduce; to allege; **allegare i denti** to set the teeth on edge ‖ intr (hort) to ripen
**allega·to -ta** adj enclosed ‖ m enclosure
**alleggeriménto** m lightening, easing
**alleggerire** §176 tr to lighten; to alleviate ‖ ref to put on lighter clothes; **alleggerirsi di** (naut) to jettison
**allegoria** f allegory
**allegòri·co -ca** adj (-ci -che) allegorical
**allegraménte** adv cheerfully, merrily; thoughtlessly
**allegrézza** f joy, cheerfulness
**allegrìa** f cheer, gaiety; **stare in allegria** to be merry ‖ interj good cheer!
**allé·gro -gra** adj cheerful, merry, gay ‖ m (mus) allegro
**allelùia** m hallelujah
**allenaménto** m training
**allenare (allèno)** tr & ref to train
**allena·tóre -trice** adj training ‖ mf trainer, coach
**allentare (allènto)** tr to loosen, slacken; to mitigate; (coll) to deliver (a blow); **essere allentato** to have a hernia ‖ ref to slow up; to loosen up; to diminish

**allergìa** f allergy
**allèrgi·co -ca** adj (-ci -che) allergic
**allérta** f alert ‖ adv alert, on the alert
**allessare (allésso)** tr to boil
**allés·so -sa** adj boiled ‖ m boiled meat, boiled beef
**allestire** §176 tr to prepare, make ready; to rig (e.g., a ship); to produce (e.g., a play)
**allettaménto** m allure, fascination
**allettante** adj alluring, enticing
**allettare (allètto)** tr to allure, entice; to confine to bed; to bend (plants) to the ground ‖ ref to be confined to bed
**allevaménto** m raising, breeding; flock
**allevare (allèvo)** tr to raise, breed; to rear
**alleva·tóre -trice** mf raiser, breeder
**alleviare** §287 (allèvio) tr to alleviate, lighten
**allibìre** §176 intr (ESSERE) to turn pale; to be astonished, be dismayed
**allibraménto** m registration, entry; booking (of bets)
**allibrare** tr to register, enter; to book (a bet) on a horse
**allibratóre** m bookmaker (at races)
**allietare (alliéto)** tr to cheer, enliven
**alliè·vo -va** mf pupil, student; follower, disciple ‖ m trainee; **allievo ufficiale** cadet
**alligatóre** m alligator
**allignare** intr to take root; to do well, prosper
**allineaménto** m alignment; falling in line
**allineare (allìneo)** tr to align; (typ) to justify ‖ ref to align oneself, be aligned
**allinea·to -ta** adj aligned; **non allineato** nonaligned, uncommitted
**allitterazióne** f alliteration
**allo** §4
**allòc·co** m (-chi) horned owl; (fig) dolt, nincompoop
**allocu·tóre -trice** mf (poet) speaker
**allocuzióne** f (poet) speech, address
**allòdola** f lark, skylark
**allogare** §209 (allògo) tr to place; to let, lease; to find employment for; to invest (money); to marry off (a daughter)
**allòge·no -na** adj minority ‖ mf member of an ethnic minority
**alloggiaménto** m (mil) lodging, quarters; (carp, mach) housing
**alloggiare** §290 (allòggio) tr to lodge, put up ‖ intr to lodge, stay
**allòg·gio** m (-gi) lodging, living quarters; accommodations
**allontanaménto** m removal; estrangement
**allontanare** tr to remove; to send away; to exonerate; to dismiss; to alienate ‖ ref to go away; to withdraw; to become estranged
**allóra** adj then ‖ adv then; at that time; in that case; **da allora** ever since; **da allora in poi** from that time on; **fino allora** until then; **per allora** at that time

allorché *conj* when

allòro *m* laurel; **riposare sugli allori** to rest on one's laurels

allorquando *conj* (poet) when

àlluce *m* big toe

allucinante *adj* hallucinating; dazzling; deceptive

allucinare (allùcino) *tr* to hallucinate; to dazzle; to deceive

allucinazióne *f* hallucination

allùdere §105 *intr* to allude

allume *m* alum

alluminare (allùmino) *tr* to illuminate (*a manuscript*); (poet) to light

allumìnio *m* aluminum

allunàg·gio *m* (-gi) lunar landing; **allunaggio morbido** soft lunar landing

allunare *intr* to land on the moon

allunga *f* (mach) adapter

allungàbile *adj* extensible; extension (*table*)

allungaménto *m* lengthening

allungare §209 *tr* to lengthen; to stretch out (*e.g., the hand*); to dilute (*e.g., wine*); (coll) to deliver (*e.g., a slap*); (sports) to pass (*the ball*); **allungare il collo** to crane the neck; **allungare il passo** to walk faster || *ref* to grow longer; to stretch; to grow taller

allun·go *m* (-ghi) (sports) sprint; (sports) forward pass

allusióne *f* allusion

alluvióne *m* flood

almanaccare §197 *tr* to dream of || *intr* to dream, muse

almanac·co *m* (-chi) almanac

alméno *adv* at least; if only

alno *m* (bot) alder

àloe *m* & *f* aloe

alògeno *m* halogen

alogenuro *m* halide

alóne *m* halo

alòsa *f* (ichth) shad

alpacca *f* German silver

alpe *f* high mountain, alp || **le Alpi** the Alps

alpèstre *adj* mountainous; (fig) uncouth

alpigia·no -na *adj* mountain, mountainous; (fig) uncouth || *mf* mountaineer

alpinismo *m* mountain climbing

alpini·sta *mf* (-sti -ste) mountain climber

alpinìsti·co -ca *adj* (-ci -che) mountain-climbing

alpi·no -na *adj* alpine; Alpine || *m* alpine soldier

alquan·to -ta *adj* & *pron* some; **alquanti -te** some; quite a few, several, a good many || **alquanto** *adv* somewhat, rather

Alsàzia, l' *f* Alsace

alsazia·no -na *adj* & *mf* Alsacian

alt *m* (alt) halt, stop || *interj* halt!, stop!

altaléna *f* seesaw; swing; (fig) ups and downs; **altalena a bilico** seesaw; **altalena sospesa** swing

altalenare (altaléno) *intr* to seesaw; to swing

altana *f* roof terrace

altare *m* altar

altarino *m* small altar; **svelare gli alta-**rini (joc) to expose the skeleton in the closet

altèa *f* marsh mallow

alterare (àltero) *tr* to alter; to falsify; to adulterate; to anger || *ref* to alter; to become adulterated; to get angry

altera·to -ta *adj* altered; adulterated; feverish; angry

alterazióne *f* change, alteration; adulteration; slight fever

altercare §197 (altèrco) *intr* to dispute, quarrel

altèr·co *m* (-chi) altercation; **venire a un alterco** to get into a quarrel

alterìgia *f* haughtiness

alternare (altèrno) *tr* & *ref* to alternate

alternati·vo -va *adj* alternating || *f* alternative; choice

alterna·to -ta *adj* alternate; alternating (*current*)

alternatóre *m* (elec) alternator

altèr·no -na *adj* alternate

altè·ro -ra *adj* proud, haughty

altézza *f* height; width (*of cloth*); depth (*of water*); pitch (*of sound*); (astr, geom) altitude; (fig) loftiness, nobility; (naut) latitude; (typ) size; **essere all'altezza di** to be up to, be equal to; (naut) to be off || **Altezza** *f* Highness

altezzó·so -sa [s] *adj* haughty

altìc·cio -cia *adj* (-ci -ce) tipsy

altìmetro *m* altimeter

altipiano *m* var of **altopiano**

altisonante [s] *adj* high-sounding

altìssi·mo -ma *adj* very high, highest || **l'Altissimo** *m* the Most High

altitùdine *f* altitude

al·to -ta *adj* high; tall; wide (*cloth*); deep (*water*); upper; full (*day*); late (*e.g., Easter*); deep (*sleep*); early (*Middle Ages*); loud (*voice*); lofty (*peak*) || *m* top; upper part; high quarters; **alti e bassi** ups and downs; **fare alto e basso** to be the undisputed boss; **guardare qlcu dall'alto in basso** to look down one's nose at s.o.; **in alto** up || **alto** *adv* up

altofórno *m* (altifórni) blast furnace

altoloca·to -ta *adj* high-placed, high-ranking

altoparlante *m* loudspeaker

altopiano *m* (altipiani) plateau

altrettan·to -ta *adj* & *pron* as much; the same; **altrettanti -te** as many || **altrettanto** *adv* as much; the same

altri *indef pron invar* someone; someone else; **non altri che** no one else but

altrièri *m* & *adv* day before yesterday

altriménti *adv* otherwise

al·tro -tra *adj* other; next (*world*); **altro ieri** day before yesterday; **chi altro?** who else?; **domani l'altro** the day after tomorrow; **fra l'altro** among other things; **ieri l'altro** the day before yesterday; **l'altro anno** last year; **l'altro giorno** the other day; **noi altri** we; **qualcun altro** somebody else; anybody else; **quest'altro (giorno, mese, anno)** next (day, month, year) || *pron* other; anything else; **altro che!** why yes! ‖ **l'altro** §11 *correlative indef pron* ‖ **l'altro** §12 *reciprocal pron*

**altrónde** *adv* (poet) somewhere else; **d'altronde** besides; on the other hand

**altróve** *adv* elsewhere, somewhere else

**altrui** *adj invar* somebody else's, other people's ‖ *pron invar* somebody else ‖ *m*—**l'altrui** what belongs to someone else

**altrui·sta** (**-sti -ste**) *adj* altruistic ‖ *mf* altruist

**altura** *f* height; (naut) high seas

**alun·no -na** *mf* pupil, student

**alveare** *m* beehive

**àlveo** *m* bed (*of a river*)

**alvèolo** *m* alveolus; socket (*of tooth*); cell (*of honeycomb*)

**alzabandiè·ra** *m* (**-ra**) raising of the flag

**alzacristal·lì** *m* (**-lì**) (aut) crank (*to raise a window*)

**alzàia** *f* tow line; towpath

**alzare** *tr* to lift, raise; to cut (*cards*); to shrug (*one's shoulders*); to set (*sail*); **alzare al cielo** to praise to the sky; **alzare i tacchi** to show a clean pair of heels; **alzare la cresta** to get cocky ‖ *ref* to rise; to get up; **alzarsi in piedi** to stand up

**alzata** *f* raising, lifting; shrugging (*of shoulders*); standing up; riser (*of step*); three-tier candy tray; **alzata di scudi** rebellion; **alzata di testa** whim, caprice

**alzavàlvo·le** *m* (**-le**) (aut) valve lifter

**alzo** *m* gunsight

**amàbile** *adj* amiable; sweetish (*wine*)

**amabili·tà** *f* (**-tà**) amiability, kindness

**ama·ca** *f* (**-che**) hammock

**amàlga·ma** *m* (**-mi**) amalgam

**amalgamare** (**amàlgamo**) *tr* to amalgamate ‖ *ref* to amalgamate; to blend

**amalgamazióne** *f* amalgamation

**amante** *adj* loving, fond ‖ *m* lover ‖ *f* mistress

**amanuènse** *m* amanuensis, scribe

**amare** *tr* to love; to like ‖ *ref* to love one another

**amareggiare** §290 (**amaréggio**) *tr* to make bitter; to sadden ‖ *ref* to become bitter; to sadden

**amarèna** *f* sour cherry

**amarétto** *m* macaroon

**amarézza** *f* bitterness

**ama·ro -ra** *adj* bitter ‖ *m* bitters; bitterness

**amarógno·lo -la** *adj* bitterish

**amarra** *f* (naut) hawser

**amarrare** *tr* & *intr* var of **ammarrare**

**ama·tóre -trice** *mf* lover; amateur

**amató·rio -ria** *adj* (**-ri -rie**) amatory, of love

**amàzzone** [ddzz] *f* horsewoman; female jockey; (obs) riding habit; **cavalcare all'amazzone** to ride sidesaddle ‖ **Amazzone** *f* (myth) Amazon

**ambage** *f* winding path; **ambagi** circumlocutions; **senz'ambagi** without beating about the bush

**ambascerìa** *f* embassy

**ambà·scia** *f* (**-sce**) shortness of breath; grief, sorrow

**ambasciata** *f* embassy; ambassadorship; errand, mission

**ambasciatóre** *m* ambassador

**ambasciatrice** *f* ambassadress

**ambedùe** *adj invar*—**ambedue i** or **le** both ‖ *pron invar* both

**ambiare** §287 *intr* to amble, pace (*said of a horse*)

**ambiatura** *f* pacing (*said of a horse*)

**ambidè·stro -stra** *adj* ambidextrous

**ambidùe** *adj* & *pron invar* var of **ambedue**

**ambientare** (**ambiènto**) *tr* to accustom; to place (*a story in a certain period*) ‖ *ref* to get accustomed to one's surroundings; to orient oneself

**ambienta·tóre -trice** *mf* interior decorator; (theat) decorator

**ambiènte** *adj* room, e.g., **temperatura ambiente** room temperature ‖ *m* environment; habitat; milieu; room; **trovarsi fuori del proprio ambiente** to be out of one's element

**ambigui·tà** *f* (**-tà**) ambiguity

**ambì·guo -gua** *adj* ambiguous

**àm·bio** *m* (**-bi**) amble, pacing

**ambire** §176 *tr* to be eager for ‖ *intr* to be ambitious; **ambire a** to be ambitious for

**àmbito** *m* range, circle; (mus) range; **nell'ambito di** within

**ambizióne** *f* ambition

**ambizióso -sa** [s] *adj* ambitious ‖ *mf* ambitious person

**ambo** or **am·bi -be** *adj* *pl*—**ambo i**, **ambo le**, **ambi i**, **ambe le** both

**ambosèssi** *adj invar* of both sexes, e.g., **giovani ambosessi** young people of both sexes

**ambra** *f* amber; **ambra grigia** ambergris

**ambròsia** *f* ambrosia; (bot) ragweed

**ambulante** *adj* itinerant; circulating; ambulant ‖ *m* mail car

**ambulanza** *f* ambulance

**ambulare** (**àmbulo**) *intr* (coll) to ambulate

**ambulatò·rio -ria** (**-ri -rie**) *adj* ambulatory ‖ *m* clinic, first-aid department

**Amburgo** *m* Hamburg

**amèba** *f* amoeba

**a·men** *m* (**-men**) amen ‖ *interj* amen!

**ameni·tà** *f* (**-tà**) *f* amenity; pleasantry

**amèno -na** *adj* pleasant, agreeable; amusing (*fellow*)

**Amèrica, l'** *f* America; **l'America del Nord** North America; **l'America del Sud** South America

**americana** *f* bicycle race between pairs

**americanismo** *m* Americanism

**americanizzare** [ddzz] *tr* to Americanize ‖ *ref* to become Americanized

**america·no -na** *adj* & *mf* American ‖ *m* vermouth with bitters ‖ *f* see **americana**

**ametista** *f* amethyst

**amianto** *m* asbestos

**amicale** *adj* (poet) friendly

**amichévole** *adj* friendly; (sports) noncompetitive

**amicìzia** *f* friendship; **stringere amicìzia con** to make friends with

**ami·co -ca (-ci -che)** *adj* friendly ‖ *mf* friend; beloved ‖ *m* boy friend; lover, paramour; **amico del cuore** bosom friend ‖ *f* girl friend; mistress

**amidàce·o -a** *adj* starchy

**amidatura** *f* starching

**àmido** *m* starch

**Amlèto** *m* Hamlet

**ammaccare** §197 *tr* to crush; to pound; to bruise; to dent

**ammaccatura** *f* bruise; dent

**ammaestraménto** *m* instruction, teaching; training

**ammaestrare (ammaèstro & ammaéstro)** *tr* to teach, to educate; to train (*animals*)

**ammainare (ammàino)** *tr* to lower (*e.g., a flag*)

**ammalare** *intr* (ESSERE) to fall ill ‖ *ref* to fall ill; **ammalarsi di** to come down with

**ammala·to -ta** *adj* ill, sick ‖ *mf* patient

**ammaliare** §287 *tr* to cast a spell on; to charm, enchant, fascinate; to bewitch

**ammalia·tóre -trice** *adj* charming, enchanting ‖ *mf* charmer ‖ *m* enchanter, sorcerer ‖ *f* enchantress, sorceress

**amman·co** *m* (-chi) shortage

**ammanettare (ammanétto)** *tr* to handcuff

**ammaniglia·to -ta** *adj* shackled; (fig) closely bound, closely tied

**ammannare** *tr* to sheave (*grain*)

**ammannire** §176 *tr* to prepare (*a dish*); to dish up (*a meal*)

**ammansare** *tr & ref* var of **ammansire**

**ammansa·tóre -trice** *mf* (poet) tamer

**ammansire** §176 *tr* to tame; to calm ‖ *ref* to become tamed; to calm down

**ammantare** *tr* to mantle, clothe; to cover; to hide (*the truth*)

**ammanto** *m* mantle, cloak; (fig) authority

**ammaràg·gio** *m* (-gi) landing on water; splashdown (*of a space vehicle*)

**ammaraménto** *m* var of **ammaraggio**

**ammarare** *intr* (aer) to land on water; (rok) to splash down

**ammarrare** *tr* (naut) to moor

**ammassare** *tr* to amass ‖ *ref* to crowd, throng

**ammasso** *m* heap, pile; cluster (*of stars*); government stockpile

**ammattiménto** *m* worry, nuisance

**ammattire** §176 *intr* (ESSERE) to go crazy; **fare ammattire** to drive crazy

**ammattonare (ammattóno)** *tr* to floor with bricks

**ammattona·to -ta** *adj* floored with bricks ‖ *m* brick floor; bricklaying

**ammazzare** *tr* to kill ‖ *ref* to kill oneself; to get killed

**ammazzasèt·te** *m* (-te) braggart

**ammazza·tóio** *m* (-tói) slaughterhouse

**ammènda** *f* fine; satisfaction (*for injury*); **fare ammenda** to make amends

**ammendaménto** *m* emendation: improvement (*of land*)

**ammendare (ammèndo)** *tr* to emendate; to improve (*land*)

**ammennìcolo** *m* excuse; trifle; **ammennicoli** extras

**ammés·so -sa** *adj* admitted; **ammesso che** supposing that; **ammesso e non concesso** for the sake of argument

**amméttere** §198 *tr* to admit; to accept, suppose

**ammezzare [ddzz] (ammèzzo)** *tr* to leave half-finished (*a piece of work*); to fill halfway; to empty halfway

**ammezzato [ddzz]** *m* mezzanine

**ammiccare** §197 *intr* to wink; to cock one's eye

**amministrare** *tr* to administer, manage

**amministra·tóre -trice** *mf* administrator, manager; **amministratore delegato** chairman of the board

**amministrazióne** *f* administration, management: **ordinaria amministrazione** run-of-the-mill business

**ammiràbile** *adj* admirable

**ammiràglia** *f* (nav) flagship

**ammiragliato** *m* admiralty

**ammirà·glio** *m* (-gli) admiral; **ammiraglio d'armata** admiral; **ammiraglio di divisione** rear admiral; **ammiraglio di squadra** vice admiral; **grande ammiraglio** admiral of the fleet

**ammirare** *tr* to admire ‖ *intr* to wonder

**ammirati·vo -va** *adj* admiring; exclamation (*mark*)

**ammira·tóre -trice** *mf* admirer ‖ *m* suitor

**ammirazióne** *f* admiration

**ammirévole** *adj* admirable

**ammissìbile** *adj* admissible; permissible

**ammissióne** *f* admission; (mach) intake; **ammissione comune** consensus

**ammobiliaménto** *m* furnishing; furniture

**ammobiliare** §287 *tr* to furnish

**ammodernare (ammodèrno)** *tr* to modernize

**ammòdo** *adj invar* well-mannered, polite ‖ *adv* properly

**ammogliare** §280 (ammóglio) *tr* to marry, give in marriage ‖ *ref* to marry, get married

**ammoglia·to** *adj* married ‖ *m* married man

**ammollare (ammòllo)** *tr* to soften; to soak; to slacken (*e.g., a hawser*); to deliver (*a slap*) ‖ *ref* to get soaked

**ammollire** §176 *tr* to soften; to weaken ‖ *ref* to soften; to mellow

**ammonìaca** *f* ammonia

**ammoniménto** *m* warning

**ammonire** §176 *tr* to admonish, reprimand

**ammoni·tóre -trice** *adj* warning

**ammonizióne** *f* admonition, warning

**ammontare** *m* amount, total ‖ *v* (ammónto) *tr* to pile up ‖ *intr* (ESSERE) to amount

**ammonticchiare** §287 *tr* to pile up, heap up

**ammorbare (ammòrbo)** *tr* to infect, contaminate

**ammorbidènte** *m* softener

**ammorbidire** §176 *tr* to soften; to mitigate ‖ *ref* to soften

**ammortaménto** *m* amortization; payment, redemption (*of a loan*)

ammortare (ammòrto) tr to amortize

ammortire §176 tr to deaden; to weaken, soften

ammortizzaménto [ddzz] m amortization, amortizement

ammortizzare [ddzz] tr to amortize; (aut) to absorb (shocks)

ammortizzatóre [ddzz] m (aut) shock absorber

ammosciare §128 (ammóscio) tr, intr & ref var of ammoscire

ammoscia‧to -ta adj (coll) downcast

ammoscire §176 tr to make sag; to make flabby ‖ intr & ref to sag; to become flabby; to droop

ammucchiare §287 tr to heap up, pile up ‖ ref to crowd together

ammuffire §176 intr (ESSERE) to become moldy

ammusare tr & intr to nuzzle

ammutinaménto m mutiny, riot

ammutinare (ammùtino & ammutino) tr to incite to riot ‖ ref to mutiny

ammutinato m mutineer

ammutolire §176 intr (ESSERE) to become silent; to be dumfounded

amnesìa f amnesia

amnistìa f amnesty

amnistiare §287 or §119 tr to amnesty

amo m hook; abboccare all'amo to bite, to swallow the hook

amorale adj immoral; amoral

amorali‧tà f (-tà) immorality; amorality

amóre m love; eagerness; amor proprio amour-propre, self-esteem; con amore with pleasure; d'amore e d'accordo in perfect agreement; fare all'amore to make love; fare l'amore to flirt; per amor del cielo for heaven's sake; per amore di for the sake of; un amore di bambino a charming child; un amore di cappello a darling hat

amoreggiare §290 (amoréggio) intr to flirt; to play around

amorévole adj loving; kindly

amòr‧fo -fa adj amorphous; safety (match)

amorino m cupid; cute child; love seat; (bot) mignonette

amoró‧so -sa [s] adj loving; kindly; amorous; love (e.g., life) ‖ mf lover ‖ m fiancé ‖ f fiancée

amovìbile adj removable

amperàg‧gio m (-gi) amperage

ampère m ampere

amperòmetro m ammeter

amperóra m ampere-hour

ampiézza f width, breadth; trajectory (of a missile); amplitude; ampiezza di vedute open-mindedness

àm‧pio -pia adj (-pi -pie) ample; wide; roomy

amplèsso m (poet) embrace

ampliaménto m amplification, extension

ampliare §287 tr to enlarge, widen ‖ ref to widen

amplificare §197 (amplìfico) tr to amplify; to widen; to exaggerate

amplifica‧tóre m (rad & telv) amplifier

amplificazióne f amplification

amplitùdine f amplitude

ampólla f cruet; (eccl) ampulla

ampollièra f cruet stand

ampollosi‧tà [s] f (-tà) grandiloquence, turgidity

ampolló‧so -sa [s] adj grandiloquent, turgid

amputare (àmputo) tr to amputate

amputazióne f amputation

amulèto m amulet, charm

anabbagliante m (aut) low beam; anabbaglianti (aut) dimmers

anacàr‧dio m (-di) cashew

ànace m var of anice

anacorè‧ta m (-ti) anchorite, hermit

anacronismo m anachronism

anacronìsti‧co -ca adj (-ci -che) anachronistic(al)

anàgrafe m bureau of vital statistics; registry of births, deaths, and marriages

anagram‧ma m (-mi) anagram

analcòli‧co -ca (-ci -che) adj nonalcoholic; soft (drink) ‖ m soft drink

analfabè‧ta mf (-ti -te) illiterate

analfabèti‧co -ca adj (-ci -che) unalphabetized, unalphabetic

analfabetismo m illiteracy

analgèsi‧co -ca adj & m (-ci -che) analgesic

anàli‧si f (-si) analysis; breakdown; analisi grammaticale parsing; analisi dell'urina urinalysis

anali‧sta mf (-sti -ste) analyst; analista finanziario financial analyst; analista tempi e metodi efficiency expert, efficiency engineer

analìti‧co -ca adj (-ci -che) analytic(al)

analizzare [ddzz] tr to analyze; to assay (ores); (telv) to scan

analogìa f analogy

anàlo‧go -ga adj (-ghi -ghe) analogous; similar

anamnè‧si f (-si) (med) case history

ananasso m pineapple

anarchìa f anarchy

anàrchi‧co -ca (-ci -che) adj anarchical ‖ m anarchist

anatè‧ma or anàte‧ma m (-mi) anathema

anatomìa f anatomy

anatòmi‧co -ca adj (-ci -che) anatomic(al)

ànatra f duck; drake

anatròccolo m duckling

an‧ca f (-che) hip; (coll) thigh (e.g., of a chicken); dare d'anche to run away; menare anca to walk

ancèlla f maidservant

ancestrale adj ancestral

anche adv also, too; even; (poet) yet; anche a + inf even if + ind

anchilosare (anchilòso) tr to paralyze ‖ ref to become paralyzed

anchilòsto‧ma m (-mi) hookworm

àn‧cia f (-ce) (mus) reed

ancillare adj servant

ancòra adv still, yet; again; more e.g., ancora cinque minuti five minutes more

àncora f anchor; keeper (of magnet); armature (of buzzer or electric bell); ancora di salvezza last hope; gettar l'ancora to cast anchor; salpare or levar l'ancora to weigh anchor

ancoràg‧gio m (-gi) anchorage, berth

**ancorare (àncoro)** *tr* to anchor; to tie (*e.g., a currency to gold*) ‖ *ref* to anchor; to hold fast

**ancorché** *conj* although

**andalu·so -sa** *adj & mf* Andalusian

**andaménto** *m* course, progress

**andante** *adj* ordinary, common; continuous

**andare** *m* going; gait; **a lungo andare** in the long run ‖ §106 *intr* (ESSERE) to go; to spread (*said of news*); to be (*e.g., proud*); to work (*said of machinery*); (with *dat*) to fit, e.g., **quel vestito non gli va** that suit does not fit him; (with *dat*) to please, e.g. **quel vestito non le va** that dress does not please her; **andare a cavallo** to go horseback riding; **andare a finire** to wind up; **andare a male** to spoil; **andare a picco** to sink; **andare d'accordo** to agree; **andare in cerca di** to seek; **andare in macchina** to be in press; **andare in onda** (rad & telv) to go on the air; **andare per i vent'anni** to be bordering on twenty years; **andare pazzo per** to be crazy about; **andare soldato** to be drafted; **andare via** to go away; **come va?** how are things?; **mi va il vino dolce** I like sweet wine; **ne va della vita** life is at stake; **va da sé** it goes without saying ‖ *ref*—**andarsene** to go away, leave

**anda·to -ta** *adj* gone, past; finished; (coll) spoiled (*e.g., meat*) ‖ *f* going; journey, trip; **a lunga andata** in the long run; **andata e ritorno** round trip; **dare l'andata a** to give the go-ahead to

**andatura** *f* gait; pace; **fare l'andatura** to set the pace

**andazzo** *m* bad practice, bad habit; fad

**Ande, le** the Andes

**andicappare** *tr* to handicap

**andi·no -na** *adj* Andean

**andiriviè·ni** *m* (-ni) coming and going; maze; ado

**àndito** *m* corridor, hallway

**andróne** *m* hall, lobby

**aneddòti·co -ca** *adj* (-ci -che) anecdotal

**anèddoto** *m* anecdote

**anelante** *adj* panting

**anelare (anèlo)** *tr* to long for ‖ *intr* to yearn; (poet) to pant

**anèlito** *m* last breath; yearning; (poet) panting; **mandare l'ultimo anelito** to breathe one's last

**anellino** *m* ringlet

**anèllo** *m* ring; link (*of a chain*); traffic circle; segment (*of a worm*); (sports) track; **ad anello** ring-shaped; **anello di congiunzione** (fig) link; **anello di fidanzamento** engagement ring ‖ **anella** *fpl* (poet) ringlets; (archaic) rings

**anemia** *f* anemia

**anèmi·co -ca** *adj* (-ci -che) anemic

**anestesìa** *f* anesthesia

**anestesi·sta** *mf* (-sti -ste) anesthetist

**anestèti·co -ca** *adj & m* (-ci -che) anesthetic

**anestetizzare** [ddzz] *tr* to anesthetize

**aneuri·sma** *m* (-smi) aneurysm

**anfi·bio -bia** (-bi -bie) *adj* amphibian; (fig) ambiguous ‖ *m* amphibian

**anfiteatro** *m* amphitheater

**anfitrióne** *m* (lit) generous host

**anfratto** *m* ravine; narrow, winding, rugged spot

**anfrattuosi·tà** [s] *f* (-tà) rough broken ground; winding, rough spot

**anfrattuó·so -sa** [s] *adj* winding, rough, craggy

**angariare** §287 *tr* to pester, oppress

**angèli·co -ca** *adj* (-ci -che) angelic(al)

**àngelo** *m* angel; **angelo custode** guardian angel

**angherìa** *f* vexation; outrage; imposition

**angina** *f* quinsy; **angina pectoris** angina pectoris

**angipòrto** *m* blind alley; narrow lane

**anglica·no -na** *adj & mf* Anglican

**anglicismo** *m* Anglicism

**anglicizzare** [ddzz] *tr* to Anglicize ‖ *ref* to become Anglicized

**anglòfo·no -na** *adj* English-speaking ‖ *m* English-speaking person

**anglosàssone** *adj & mf* Anglo-Saxon

**angolare** *adj* angular; corner (*stone*) ‖ *m* angle iron ‖ *v* (àngolo) *tr* to take an angle shot of; (sports) to kick (*the ball*) into the corner of the goal

**angolazióne** *f* (mov) angle shot

**angolièra** *f* corner shelving; corner cupboard

**àngolo** *m* angle; corner

**angoló·so -sa** [s] *adj* angular

**àngora** *f* Angora cat; Angora goat

**angò·scia** *f* (-sce) anxiety, distress, anguish

**angosciare** §128 (angòscio) *tr* to distress

**angoscia·to -ta** *adj* tormented, distressed

**angosció·so -sa** [s] *adj* agonizing

**anguilla** *f* eel

**anguillé·sco -sca** *adj* (-schi -sche) as slippery as an eel

**angùria** *f* watermelon

**angùstia** *f* narrowness; scarcity; **stare in angustia** to be worried

**angustiare** §287 *tr* to distress, grieve ‖ *ref* to worry

**angu·sto -sta** *adj* narrow

**ànice** *m* anise

**anicino** *m* anise cookie

**anidride** *f* anhydride

**àni·dro -dra** *adj* anhydrous

**anilina** *f* aniline

**ànima** *f* soul; life (*e.g., of the party*); core; kernel; bore (*of gun*); mold (*of button*); mind; enthusiasm; pith (*of fruit*); sounding post (*of violin*); web (*of rail*); **anima dannata** evil counselor; **anima mia!** darling!; **anima nera** villain; **anima viva** living soul; **buon'anima** late, e.g., **mio padre, buon'anima** my late father; **dannare l'anima** to lose patience; **la buon'anima di** the late; **rompere l'anima a** to annoy

**animale** *adj* animal; (poet) of the soul; (poet) animate ‖ *m* animal; (fig) boor, lout

**animalé·sco -sca** adj (**-schi -sche**) animal, bestial

**animare** (**ànimo**) tr to animate, to enliven; to promote ‖ ref to become lively or heated

**anima·to -ta** adj animated (cartoon); animated, lively; animal

**anima·tóre -trice** adj animating ‖ m moving spirit; (mov) animator

**animazióne** f animation

**animèlla** f sweetbread

**ànimo** m mind; heart, affection; courage; **aprire l'animo** to open one's heart; **avere in animo di** to have a mind to; **mal animo** ill will; **mettersi l'animo in pace** to resign oneself; **perdersi d'animo** to lose heart; **serbare nell'animo** to keep in mind

**animosi·tà** [s] f (**-tà**) animosity, ill will

**animó·so -sa** [s] adj bold; spirited (animal); hostile

**anióne** m anion

**anisétta** f anisette

**ànitra** f var of **anatra**

**anitròccolo** m var of **anatroccolo**

**annacquare** (**annàcquo**) tr to water; to water down

**annaffiare** §287 tr to sprinkle; to water (wine)

**annaffia·tóio** m (**-tói**) sprinkling can

**annaffia·tóre -trice** adj watering, sprinkling

**annali** mpl annals spl

**annaspare** tr to reel ‖ intr to gesticulate; to grope; to flounder

**annata** f year; year's activity; year's rent; year's issues (of a magazine)

**annebbiare** §287 (**annébbio**) tr to befog; to dim ‖ ref to become foggy; to become dim

**annegaménto** m drowning

**annegare** §209 (**annégo**) tr & intr (ESSERE) to drown

**anneriménto** m blackening

**annerire** §176 tr to blacken ‖ ref to turn black

**annessióne** f annexation

**annès·so -sa** adj united, attached ‖ m annex; **con tutti gli annessi e connessi** everything included

**annèttere** §107 tr to annex; to attach, enclose; to unite; to ascribe (importance)

**annichilante** adj annihilating; devastating (e.g., reply)

**annichilare** (**annìchilo**) tr to annihilate ‖ ref to destroy oneself; (fig) to humble oneself

**annichilire** §176 tr & ref var of **annichilare**

**annidare** tr to nest; (fig) to nourish, cherish ‖ ref to nest; to hide; (fig) to settle

**annientaménto** m annihilation

**annientare** (**anniènto**) tr to annihilate; to knock down, demolish; (fig) to crush ‖ ref to humble oneself

**anniversà·rio -ria** adj & m (**-ri -rie**) anniversary

**anno** m year; **anno bisestile** leap year; **anno luce** light-year; **anno nuovo** New Year; **anno scolastico** school year; **avere . . . anni** to be . . . years old; **l'anno che viene** next year; **l'anno corrente** this year; **quest'altr'anno** next year; **un anno dopo l'altro** year in, year out

**annobilire** §176 tr to ennoble

**annodare** (**annòdo**) tr to knot, tie; (fig) to tie up ‖ ref to get entangled

**annoiare** §287 (**annòio**) tr to bore ‖ ref to become bored

**annòna** f food; food-control agency

**annonà·rio -ria** adj (**-ri -rie**) food; rationing (card)

**annó·so -sa** [s] adj old, aged

**annotare** (**annòto**) tr to jot down; to chalk up; to annotate; to comment

**annotazióne** f note; notation, annotation

**annottare** (**annòtta**) impers (ESSERE) & ref to grow dark, e.g., **si annotta** it's growing dark; **è annottato** it grew dark

**annoverare** (**annòvero**) tr to count, number

**annuale** adj annual ‖ m anniversary

**annuà·rio** m (**-ri**) annual, yearbook

**annuire** §176 intr to nod assent; to consent

**annullaménto** m nullification, annulment

**annullare** tr to annul, nullify, cancel; to call off ‖ ref to cancel one another

**annunciare** §128 tr var of **annunziare**

**Annunciazióne** f Annunciation

**annunziare** §287 tr to announce; (fig) to forecast, foreshadow

**annunzia·tóre -trice** mf announcer, newscaster

**annùn·zio** m (**-zi**) announcement, notice; **annunzio economico** classified ad; **annunzio pubblicitario** advertisement; **annunzio pubblicitario radiofonico** (rad) commercial

**ànnu·o -a** adj yearly, annual

**annusare** [s] tr to smell; to snuff (tobacco)

**annuvolaménto** m cloudiness

**annuvolare** (**annùvolo**) tr to cloud, becloud ‖ ref to become cloudy; to turn somber

**anòdi·no -na** adj pain-relieving; ineffective; weak, colorless (person)

**ànodo** m anode

**anomalìa** f anomaly

**anòma·lo -la** adj anomalous

**anonimìa** f anonymity

**anòni·mo -ma** adj anonymous ‖ m anonymous author; **serbare l'anonimo** to preserve one's anonymity

**anormale** adj abnormal ‖ m queer fellow

**anormali·tà** f (**-tà**) abnormality

**ansa** f handle (of vase); pretext; bend (of a river)

**ansante** adj panting

**ansare** intr to pant

**ànsia** f anxiety; **essere in ansia** to be worried

**ansie·tà** f (**-tà**) anxiety

**ansimare** (**ànsimo** ) intr to pant

**ansió·so -sa** [s] adj anxious

**antagonismo** m antagonism

**antagoni·sta** (-sti -ste) *adj* antagonistic || *mf* antagonist, opponent

**antagonisti·co -ca** *adj* (-ci -che) antagonistic

**antàrti·co -ca** *adj* (-ci -che) antarctic || **Antartico** *m* Antarctic

**antecedènte** *adj* preceding || *m* antecedent

**antecedènza** *f* antecedence

**antecessóre** *m* predecessor

**antefatto** *m* background, antecedents

**anteguèr·ra** (-ra) *adj* prewar || *m* prewar period

**anteluca·no -na** *adj* (poet) predawn

**antenato** *m* ancestor

**anténna** *f* lance; (naut) yard; (rad & telv) aerial, antenna; (zool) antenna

**antepórre** §218 *tr* to prefer; to place before

**anteprima** *f* (mov & theat) preview

**anterióre** *adj* fore, front; previous; earlier

**antesignano** [s] *m* forerunner

**anti-** *pref adj* anti-, e.g., **anticomunistico** anticommunist; un-, e.g., **antieconomico** uneconomical || *pref mf* anti-, e.g., **anticomunista** anticommunist

**antiabbagliante** *adj* antiglare || *m* low beam

**antiàci·do -da** *adj* & *m* antacid

**antiaère·o -a** *adj* antiaircraft || *f* antiaircraft defense

**antibattèri·co -ca** (-ci -che) *adj* antibacterial || *m* bactericide

**antibiòti·co -ca** *adj* & *m* (-ci -che) antibiotic

**anticà·glia** *f* (-glie) antique, curio; rubbish, junk

**anticàmera** *f* waiting room, anteroom; **fare anticamera** to cool one's heels

**anticarro** *adj invar* antitank

**antichi·tà** *f* (-tà) antiquity; **antichità** *fpl* antiques

**anticipare** (**antìcipo**) *tr* to advance; to speed up; to pay in advance; to leak (*news*); to expect, anticipate || *intr* to be early

**anticipa·to -ta** *adj* in advance (*e.g., payment*)

**anticipazióne** *f* advance; collateral loan; expectation, anticipation

**antìcipo** *m* advance; loan (*on accounts receivable*); **in anticipo** in advance

**anti·co -ca** *adj* (-chi -che) antique, ancient, old; **all'antica** in the old-fashioned manner; **gli antichi** the ancients; the forefathers; **in antico** in olden times

**anticoncezionale** *adj* & *f* contraceptive

**anticonformi·sta** *mf* (-sti -ste) nonconformist

**anticonformìsti·co -ca** *adj* (-ci -che) unconventional

**anticongelante** *adj* & *m* antifreeze

**anticongiunturale** *adj* crisis, emergency

**anticòrpo** *m* antibody

**anticristo** *m* Antichrist

**antidatare** *tr* to predate

**antiderapante** *adj* nonskid

**antidetonante** *adj* antiknock || *m* antiknock compound

**antidiluvia·no -na** *adj* antediluvian

**antidoto** *m* antidote

**antievanescènza** *f* (rad) antifading device

**antifecondati·vo -va** *adj* & *m* contraceptive

**antìfona** *f* antiphon; **capire l'antifona** (fig) to get the message

**antifurto** *adj invar* antitheft || *m* antitheft device

**antigàs** *adj invar* gas (*e.g., mask*)

**antigièni·co -ca** *adj* (-ci -che) unsanitary

**antìlope** *f* antelope

**antimeridia·no -na** *adj* antemeridian, A.M.

**antimìssile** *adj invar* antimissile

**antimònio** *m* antimony

**antincèndio** *adj invar* fire-fighting; fire, e.g., **scala antincendio** fire escape

**antinéb·bia** *adj invar* fog || *m* (-bia) fog light

**antinéve** *adj invar* snow, e.g., **catena antineve** snow chain

**antiorà·rio -ria** *adj* (-ri -rie) counterclockwise

**antipatìa** *f* antipathy, dislike

**antipàti·co -ca** *adj* (-ci -che) antipathetic; disagreeable; uncongenial

**antipièga** *adj invar* crease-resistant, wrinkle-proof

**antìpodi** *mpl* antipodes

**antipòlio** *adj invar* polio (*e.g., vaccine*)

**antipòrta** *f* stormdoor; corridor

**antiquà·rio -ria** (-ri -rie) *adj* antiquarian || *m* antiquary, antiquarian

**antiqua·to -ta** *adj* obsolete; antiquated

**antireligió·so -sa** [s] *adj* antireligious, irreligious

**antirùggine** *adj invar* antirust

**antirumóre** *adj invar* antinoise

**antisala** [s] *f* anteroom, waiting room

**antisassi** [s] *adj invar* protecting against falling stones

**antischiavi·sta** *adj* & *mf* (-sti -ste) abolitionist

**antisemi·ta** [s] (-ti -te) *adj* anti-Semitic || *mf* anti-Semite

**antisemiti·co -ca** [s] *adj* (-ci -che) anti-Semitic

**antisemitismo** [s] *m* anti-Semitism

**antisètti·co -ca** [s] *adj* & *m* (-ci -che) antiseptic

**antisociale** [s] *adj* antisocial

**antisóle** [s] *adj invar* sun (*glasses*); suntan (*lotion*)

**antisommergìbile** [s] *adj* antisubmarine

**antistatale** *adj* antigovernment

**antitàrmi·co -ca** *adj* (-ci -che) mothproof

**antitèmpo** *adv* early, prematurely

**antìte·si** *f* (-si) antithesis

**antitèti·co -ca** *adj* (-ci -che) antithetic(al)

**antitossina** *f* antitoxin

**antiuòmo** *adj invar* (mil) antipersonnel

**antivigìlia** *f*—**l'antivigilia di** two days before

**antologìa** *f* anthology

**antònimo** *m* antonym

**antrace** *m* anthrax

**antracite** *f* anthracite

**antro** *m* cave; den, hovel
**antròpi·co -ca** *adj* (**-ci -che**) human
**antropofagìa** *f* cannibalism
**antropòfa·go -ga** (**-gi -ghe**) *adj* cannibalistic ‖ *m* cannibal
**antropòide** *adj* anthropoid
**antropologìa** *f* anthropology
**antropomòrfi·co -ca** *adj* (**-ci -che**) anthropomorphic
**antropomòr·fo -fa** *adj* see **scimmia**
**anulare** *adj* ring-shaped, annular ‖ *m* ring finger
**Anvèrsa** *f* Antwerp
**anzi** *adv* on the contrary, rather; **anzi che no** rather ‖ *prep* (poet) before
**anziani·tà** *f* (**-tà**) seniority
**anzia·no -na** *adj* old, elderly; senior ‖ *m* senior
**anziché** *conj* rather than
**anzidét·to -ta** *adj* aforesaid
**anzitutto** *adv* above all, first of all
**apatìa** *f* apathy
**apàti·co -ca** *adj* (**-ci -che**) apathetic
**ape** *f* bee; **ape operaia** worker; **ape regina** queen bee
**aperitivo** *m* apéritif
**apèr·to -ta** *adj* open; frank, candid ‖ *m* open space; **all'aperto** in the open
**apertura** *f* opening; aperture; approach; **ad apertura di libro** at sight; **apertura alare** (*of a bird*) wingspread; (aer) wingspan
**apià·rio** *m* (**-ri**) apiary
**àpice** *m* apex, top; climax
**apicol·tóre -trice** *mf* beekeeper, apiarist
**apicoltura** *f* beekeeping, apiculture
**Apocalisse** *f* Apocalypse, Revelation
**apocalìtti·co -ca** *adj* (**-ci -che**) apocalyptic(al)
**apòcri·fo -fa** *adj* apocryphal
**apofonìa** *f* ablaut
**apogèo** *m* apogee
**apòlide** *adj* stateless ‖ *m* man without a country
**apolìti·co -ca** *adj* (**-ci -che**) nonpolitical, nonpartisan
**apologè·ta** *m* (**-ti**) apologist
**apologèti·co -ca** *adj* (**-ci -che**) apologetic
**apologìa** *f* apology
**apòlo·go** *m* (**-ghi**) apologue
**apoplessìa** *f* apoplexy
**apoplètti·co -ca** *adj* & *m* (**-ci -che**) apoplectic
**apostasìa** *f* apostasy
**apòsta·ta** *mf* (**-ti -te**) apostate
**apostolato** *m* apostolate
**apostòli·co -ca** *adj* (**-ci -che**) apostolic(al)
**apòstolo** *m* apostle
**apostrofare** (**apòstrofo**) *tr* to write with an apostrophe; to apostrophize
**apòstrofe** *f* apostrophe (*to a person*)
**apòstrofo** *m* (gram) apostrophe
**apoteò·si** *f* (**-si**) apotheosis
**appagare** §209 *tr* to satisfy, gratify ‖ *ref*—**appagarsi di** to be content with
**appaiare** §287 *tr* to pair, couple; to match ‖ *ref* to match (*said, e.g., of colors*)
**appallottolare** (**appallòttolo**) *tr* to

crumple into a ball ‖ *ref* to become lumpy
**appaltare** *tr* to contract for
**appalta·tóre -trice** *mf* contractor
**appalto** *m* contract; state monopoly; **appalto di sali e tabacchi** tobacco shop
**appannàg·gio** *m* (**-gi**) appanage; (fig) prerogative
**appannare** *tr* to tarnish; to befog, becloud ‖ *ref* to become clouded (*said, e.g., of one's eyesight*)
**apparato** *m* decoration; display; appliance; leadership (*of political party*); (rad, telv) set
**apparecchiare** §287 (**apparécchio**) *tr* to prepare; to set (*the table*) ‖ *ref* to get ready
**apparecchiatura** *f* sizing (*of paper; of a wall*); preparation (*of a canvas*); apparatus
**apparéc·chio** *m* (**-chi**) apparatus; sizing; preparation; gadget; (rad, telv) set; airplane; **apparecchio da caccia** fighter plane; **apparecchio telefonico** telephone
**apparentare** (**apparènto**) *tr* to tie, unite (*through marriage*) ‖ *ref* to become related; to become intimate; (pol) to form a coalition
**apparènte** *adj* apparent, seeming
**apparènza** *f* appearance; **in apparenza** seemingly
**apparigliare** §280 *tr* to pair, team (*horses*)
**apparire** §108 *intr* (ESSERE) to appear, seem; to look
**appariscènte** *adj* showy, flashy, gaudy
**apparizióne** *f* apparition; appearance
**appartamento** *m* apartment
**appartare** *tr* to set aside ‖ *ref* to withdraw, retire
**apparta·to -ta** *adj* secluded, solitary
**appartenènza** *f* belonging, membership; **appartenenze** accessories; annexes
**appartenére** §271 *intr* (ESSERE & AVERE) to belong; to pertain ‖ *impers* (ESSERE & AVERE)—**appartiene a** it behooves, it is up to
**appassionaménto** *m* excitement, interest, enthusiasm
**appassionare** (**appassióno**) *tr* to move; to interest; to excite ‖ *ref* to be deeply interested
**appassiona·to -ta** *adj* impassioned; deep, ardent ‖ *m* fan, amateur
**appassire** §176 *intr* (ESSERE) to wilt, wither; to decay; to dry up (*said, e.g., of grapes*)
**appellare** (**appèllo**) *tr* (law) to appeal; (poet) to call ‖ *ref* to appeal; **appellarsi da** or **contro** (law) to appeal
**appèllo** *m* call, roll call; **fare appello a** to summon (*e.g., one's strength*); **fare l'appello** to call the roll; **mancare all'appello** to be absent
**appéna** *adv* hardly, scarcely; only; just ‖ *conj* as soon as; **non appena** as soon as, no sooner
**appèndere** §109 *tr* to hang
**appendice** *f* appendix; feuilleton
**appendicectomìa** *f* appendectomy

**appendicite** *f* appendicitis

**Appennino, l'** *m* the Appennines

**appesantire** [s] §176 *tr* to make heavy; to burden, overwhelm ‖ *ref* to get heavy; to get fat

**appestare (appèsto)** *tr* to infect; to stink up

**appesta·to -ta** *adj* plague-ridden ‖ *m* plague victim

**appetire** §176 *tr* to crave, long for ‖ *intr* (ESSERE & AVERE) to be appetizing

**appetito** *m* appetite

**appetitó·so -sa** [s] *adj* appetizing, tempting

**appètto** *adv* opposite; **appetto a** opposite; in comparison with

**appezzaménto** *m* plot, parcel (*of land*)

**appianare** *tr* to smooth, level; to settle (*a dispute*); to get around (*a difficulty*)

**appiana·tóio** *m* (-tói) road grader

**appiattare** *tr* & *ref* to hide

**appiattiménto** *m* leveling; equalization

**appiattire** §176 *tr* & *ref* to flatten, to level

**appiccare** §197 *tr* to hang; **appiccare il fuoco a** to set on fire; **appiccare una lite** to pick a fight

**appicciare** §128 *tr* (coll) to string together; (coll) to kindle, light

**appiccicare** §197 (appiccico) *tr* to stick, glue; **appiccicare uno schiaffo a** to slap ‖ *ref* to stick, adhere

**appiccicatíc·cio -cia** *adj* (-ci -ce) sticky

**appic·co** *m* (-chi) grip; steep wall (*of mountain*); (fig) pretext

**appiè** *adv*—**appiè di** at the foot of; at the bottom of

**appiedare (appièdo)** *tr* to order (*a cavalryman*) off a horse; to order (*e.g., troops*) off a vehicle; to force out of a car (*said, e.g., of motor trouble*)

**appièno** *adv* (poet) fully

**appigionare (appigióno)** *tr* to rent ‖ *ref*—**appigionasi** for rent

**appigiónasi** [s] *m* for-rent sign

**appigliare** §280 *ref* to cling, adhere; **appigliarsi a un pretesto** to seize a pretext

**appì·glio** *m* (-gli) grip; (fig) pretext

**appiómbo** *m* perpendicular ‖ *adv* plumb, perpendicularly

**appioppare (appiòppo)** *tr* to plant with poplar trees; to tie (*a vine*) to a poplar tree; (coll) to deliver (*a blow*); (coll) to pass off (*e.g., inferior goods*)

**appisolare (appìsolo)** *ref* to snooze, doze

**applaudire** §176 & (applàudo) *tr* to applaud ‖ *intr* to applaud, clap the hands; (with *dat*) to applaud

**applàuso** *m* applause; **applausi** applause

**applicàbile** *adj* applicable

**applicare** §197 (àpplico) *tr* to apply; to attach; to give (*e.g., a slap*); to put into effect (*a law*); to assign ‖ *ref* to apply oneself

**applica·to -ta** *adj* applied; appliqué ‖ *m* clerk

**applicazióne** *f* application; appliqué

**applique** *m* (elec) wall fixture

**appoggiaca·po** *m* (-po) headrest; tidy (*on back of chair*)

**appoggiagómi·ti** *m* (-ti) elbowrest

**appoggiama·no** *m* (-no) mahlstick

**appoggiare** §290 (appòggio) *tr* to lean; to rest; to prop, support; to raise (*the tone of voice*); to give (*a slap*); to second (*a motion*); (fig) to back, support ‖ *intr* to lean; to rest ‖ *ref*—**appoggiarsi a** or **su** to lean on

**appoggia·tóio** *m* (-tói) support, rest; banister

**appoggiatura** *f* (mus) grace note

**appòg·gio** *m* (-gi) support, prop; backer; backing, support; grip; (mach) bearing

**appollaiare** §287 *ref* to roost

**appórre** §218 *tr* to affix, append

**apportare (appòrto)** *tr* to cause; to presage; (poet) to carry

**appòrto** *m* carrying; contribution; (law) share

**appositaménte** *adv* expressly, on purpose

**appòsi·to -ta** *adj* proper, fitting

**apposizióne** *f* apposition

**appòsta** *adj* *invar* suitable ‖ *adv* on purpose, expressly, intentionally

**appostaménto** *m* ambush

**appostare (appòsto)** *tr* to ambush ‖ *ref* to lie in ambush

**apprèndere** §220 *tr* to learn ‖ *ref* (poet) to take hold

**apprendi·sta** *mf* (-sti -ste) apprentice

**apprendistato** *m* apprenticeship

**apprensióne** *f* apprehension, fear

**apprensi·vo -va** *adj* apprehensive

**appressare (apprèsso)** *tr* (poet) to approach ‖ *ref* to come near

**appresso** *adj* *invar* next, following ‖ *adv* near; later on; **appresso a** near; after

**apprestare (apprèsto)** *tr* to prepare; to supply, provide (*e.g., help*) ‖ *ref* to prepare, get ready

**apprettare (apprètto)** *tr* to dress (*leather*); to size (*cloth*)

**apprètto** *m* tan (*for leather*); sizing (*for cloth*)

**apprezzàbile** *adj* appreciable

**apprezzaménto** *m* appreciation; estimation

**apprezzare (apprèzzo)** *tr* to appreciate

**apprezza·to -ta** *adj* esteemed

**appròc·cio** *m* (-ci) approach; **approcci** advances

**approdare (appròdo)** *intr* (ESSERE & AVERE) to land; (with *dat*) (poet) to benefit; **approdare a** to come to

**appròdo** *m* landing

**approfittare** *intr*—**approfittare di** to capitalize on ‖ *ref*—**approfittarsi di** to take advantage of

**approfondire** §176 *tr* to make deep; to study thoroughly ‖ *ref*—**approfondirsi in** to go deep into

**approntare (apprónto)** *tr* to prepare, make ready

**appropriare** §287 (appròprio) *tr* to adapt; to bestow ‖ *ref*—**appropriarsi a** to befit; **appropriarsi di** to appropriate; to embezzle

**appropria·to -ta** *adj* appropriate
**appropriazióne** *f* appropriation; **appropriazione indebita** fraudulent conversion, embezzlement
**approssimare** (**appròssimo**) *tr* to bring near || *ref* to approach, come near
**approssimati·vo -va** *adj* approximate
**approssimazióne** *f* approximation
**approvàbile** *adj* laudable
**approvare** (**appròvo**) *tr* to approve, countenance; to subscribe to (*an opinion*); to pass (*a student; a law*); to confirm
**approvazióne** *f* approval; confirmation; passage (*of a law*)
**approvvigionaménto** *m* supply
**approvvigionare** (**approvvigióno**) *tr* to supply || *ref* to be supplied
**appuntaménto** *m* appointment; date; **appuntamento amoroso** assignation
**appuntare** *tr* to sharpen; to fasten, pin; to stick (*a pin*) in; to point; to jot down, take note of; to prick up (*one's ears*); (fig) to reproach || *ref* to be turned; to aim
**appunta·to -ta** *adj* sharpened || *m* corporal (*of Italian police*)
**appuntellare** (**appuntèllo**) *tr* to shore up, prop up
**appuntellatura** *f* shoring up, propping up
**appuntino** *adv* precisely, meticulously
**appuntire** §176 *tr* to sharpen
**appunti·to -ta** *adj* sharp, pointed
**appunto** *m* note; blame, charge; **muovere un appunto a** to blame; **per l'appunto** just, precisely || *adv* exactly, precisely
**appurare** *tr* to ascertain
**appuzzare** *tr* to befoul, pollute
**apribottì·glie** *m* (-**glie**) bottle opener
**apri·co -ca** *adj* (-**chi -che**) (poet) sunny, bright
**aprile** *m* April
**apripi·sta** *m* (-**sta**) blade (*of bulldozer*); bulldozer
**aprire** §110 *tr* to open; to turn on; to dig (*e.g., a grave*) || *ref* to open; to clear up (*said of the weather*); **aprirsi con** to open one's heart to; **aprirsi il varco tra** to press through
**apriscàto·le** *m* (-**le**) can opener
**aquà·rio** *m* (-**ri**) aquarium || **Aquario** *m* (astr) Aquarius
**aquàti·co -ca** *adj* (-**ci -che**) aquatic
**àquila** *f* eagle; genius
**aquili·no -na** *adj* aquiline
**aquilóne** *m* north wind; kite
**aquilòtto** *m* eaglet; cadet (*in Italian Air Force Academy*)
**Aquinate, l'** *m* Saint Thomas Aquinas
**ara** *f* (poet) altar; are (*100 square meters*)
**arabé·sca** *f* (-**sche**) (mus) arabesque
**arabesca·to -ta** *adj* arabesque
**arabé·sco -sca** (-**schi -sche**) *adj* arabesque || *m* arabesque; doodle || *f* see **arabesca**
**Aràbia, l'** *f* Arabia
**aràbi·co -ca** *adj* (-**ci -che**) Arabic
**aràbile** *adj* tillable

**àra·bo -ba** *adj* Arabic, Arabian || *mf* Arab (*person*) || *m* Arabic (*language*)
**aràchide** *f* peanut (*vine*)
**aragonése** [s] *adj* & *mf* Aragonese
**aragósta** *f* (*Palinurus vulgaris*) lobster
**aràldi·co -ca** (-**ci -che**) *adj* heraldic || *f* heraldry
**araldo** *m* herald
**arancéto** *m* orange grove
**aràn·cia** *f* (-**ce**) orange
**aranciata** *f* orangeade
**aràn·cio** *adj invar* orange (*in color*) || *m* (-**ci**) orange tree
**arancióne** *adj* & *m* orange (*color*)
**arare** *tr* to plow; (naut) to drag (*the anchor*)
**aratro** *m* plow
**arazzo** *m* tapestry, arras
**arbitràg·gio** *m* (-**gi**) (sports) umpiring; (com) arbitrage
**arbitrale** *adj* judge's, umpire's
**arbitrare** (**àrbitro**) *tr* to umpire, referee || *intr* to arbitrate || *ref*—**arbitrarsi di** to take the liberty to
**arbitrà·rio -ria** *adj* (-**ri -rie**) arbitrary; wanton
**arbitrato** *m* arbitration
**arbì·trio** *m* (-**tri**) will; abuse, violation; **libero arbitrio** free will
**àrbitro** *m* arbiter; judge, referee, umpire
**arboscèllo** *m* small tree
**arbusto** *m* shrub, bush
**ar·ca** *f* (-**che**) sarcophagus; ark; chest; **arca di Noè** Noah's Ark; **arca di scienza** (fig) fountain of knowledge
**àrcade** *adj* & *m* Arcadian
**Arcàdia** *f* Arcadia, Arcady
**arcài·co -ca** *adj* (-**ci -che**) archaic
**arcaismo** *m* archaism
**arcàngelo** *m* archangel
**arca·no -na** *adj* mysterious, arcane || *m* mystery
**arcata** *f* arch; arcade
**archeologìa** *f* archaeology
**archeològi·co -ca** *adj* (-**ci -che**) archaeological
**archeòlo·go -ga** *mf* (-**gi -ghe**) archaeologist
**archètipo** *m* archetype
**archétto** *m* (archit) small arch; (elec) trolley pole; (mus) bow
**archi-** *pref adj* archi-, e.g., **architettonico** architectonic || *pref m* & *f* archi-, e.g., **architettura** architecture
**archibù·gio** *m* (-**gi**) harquebus
**Archimède** *m* Archimedes
**architettare** (**architétto**) *tr* to plan (*a building*); (fig) to contrive, plot
**architétto** *m* architect
**architettòni·co -ca** *adj* (-**ci -che**) architectural
**architettura** *f* architecture
**architetturale** *adj* architectural
**architrave** *m* architrave; doorhead, lintel
**archiviare** §287 *tr* to file; to lay aside, shelve; (law) to throw out
**archì·vio** *m* (-**vi**) archives; record office; chancery, public records
**archivi·sta** *mf* (-**sti -ste**) archivist, file clerk

**arci-** *pref adj* archi-, e.g., **arcivescovile** archiepiscopal || *pref m & f* arch-, e.g., **arciprete** archpriest

**arcicontèn•to -ta** *adj* (coll) very glad

**arcidiàcono** *m* archdeacon

**arcidu•ca** *m* (-**chi**) archduke

**arciduchéssa** *f* archduchess

**arcière** *m* archer, bowman

**arci•gno -gna** *adj* gruff, surly

**arcióne** *m* saddlebow; **montare in arcioni** to mount, to mount a horse

**arcipèla•go** *m* (-**ghi**) archipelago

**arciprète** *m* archpriest; dean

**arcivescovado** *m* archbishopric

**arcivéscovo** *m* archbishop

**ar•co** *m* (-**chi**) bow; (archít) arch; (geom, elec) arc; **arco rampante** flying buttress

**arcobaléno** *m* rainbow

**arco•làio** *m* (-**lài**) reel; **girare come un arcolaio** to spin like a top

**arcuare (àrcuo)** *tr* to arch; to bend; to camber

**arcua•to -ta** *adj* bent, curved; bow (*e.g., legs*); **avere le gambe arcuate** to be bowlegged

**ardènte** *adj* burning; hot; ardent, impassioned

**àrdere** §111 *tr* to burn || *intr* to burn; to be in full swing (*said, e.g., of a war*)

**ardèsia** *f* slate

**ardiménto** *m* boldness, daring

**ardire** *m* boldness; presumption, impudence || §176 *intr*—**ardire** + *inf* or **ardire di** + *inf* to dare to + *inf*

**arditézza** *f* daring; temerity

**ardi•to -ta** *adj* daring; rash || *m* (hist) shock trooper

**ardóre** *m* intense heat; ardor

**àr•duo -dua** *adj* arduous

**àrea** *f* area, surface; group, camp; **area arretrata** backward area

**àrem** *m* (**àrem**) harem

**arèna** *f* arena; **scendere nell'arena** to throw one's hat in the ring

**aréna** *f* sand

**arenare (aréno)** *intr* (ESSERE) & *ref* to run aground

**arenària** *f* sandstone

**arén•go** *m* (-**ghi**) (hist) town meeting

**arenile** *m* sandy beach

**arenó•so -sa** [*s*] *adj* sandy

**areòmetro** *m* hydrometer

**aeronàuti•co -ca** *adj & f* (-**ci -che**) var of **aeronautico**

**areoplano** *m* var of **aeroplano**

**areopòrto** *m* var of **aeroporto**

**areòstato** *m* var of **aerostato**

**àrgano** *m* winch; (naut) capstan

**argentare (argènto)** *tr* to silver; to silver-plate; to back (*a mirror*) with foil

**argenta•to -ta** *adj* silver; silvery; silver-plated

**argentatura** *f* silver plating; silver plate; foil (*of mirror*)

**argènte•o -a** *adj* silver, silvery

**argenteria** *f* silverware

**argentière** *m* silversmith; jeweler

**argenti•no -na** *adj* silver, silvery; Argentine || *mf* Argentine || *f* high-necked sweater || **l'Argentina** *f* Argentina

**argènto** *m* silver; (archaic) money; **argenti** silverware; **argento vivo** quicksilver

**argentóne** *m* German silver

**argilla** *f* clay

**argilló•so -sa** [*s*] *adj* clayey

**arginare (àrgino)** *tr* to dam, dike; to hold back, check

**àrgine** *m* embankment, dam; (fig) defense

**ar•go** *m* (-**ghi**) (chem) argon; (orn) grouse || **Argo** *m* Argus

**argomentare (argoménto)** *tr & intr* to argue

**argomentazióne** *f* argumentation, discussion

**argoménto** *m* argument; pretext; subject; **fuori dell'argomento** beside the point

**argonàu•ta** *m* (-**ti**) Argonaut

**arguire** §176 *tr* to deduce, infer; (archaic) to denote

**argutézza** *f* wit; witty remark

**argu•to -ta** *adj* keen, acute; witty

**argùzia** *f* keenness; wit

**ària** *f* air; climate; look; mien; aria, tune; poem; **all'aria aperta** in the open air; **a mezz'aria** in midair; halfway; **andare all'aria** to fail; **aria condizionata** air conditioning; **avere l'aria di** to seem to; to look like; **dare aria a** to air; **in aria** in the air; **tira un'aria pericolosa** a mean wind is blowing

**aria•no -na** *adj & mf* Aryan

**aridi•tà** *f* (-**tà**) dryness, aridity; dearth

**àri•do -da** *adj* arid, dry, barren; (fig) dry

**arieggiare** §290 (**ariéggio**) *tr* to air; to imitate || *ref*—**arieggiarsi a** to give oneself the airs of

**ariète** *m* ram; (mil) battering ram || **Ariete** *m* (astr) Aries

**ariétta** *s* breeze; (mus) short aria

**arin•ga** *f* (-**ghe**) herring; **aringa affumicata** kippered herring, kipper

**arin•go** *m* (-**ghi**) assembly; field; joust; **scendere nell'aringo** to throw one's hat in the ring

**arió•so -sa** [*s*] *adj* airy, breezy; (fig) of wide scope

**àrista** *f* loin of pork

**arista** *f* (bot) awn

**aristocràti•co -ca** (-**ci -che**) *adj* aristocratic || *mf* aristocrat

**aristocrazìa** *f* aristocracy

**Aristòtele** *m* Aristotle

**aristotèli•co -ca** *adj & m* (-**ci -che**) Aristotelian

**aritmèti•co -ca** (-**ci -che**) *adj* arithmetical || *m* arithmetician || *f* arithmetic

**arlecchino** *adj invar* harlequin; fiesta (*e.g., dishes*) || **Arlecchino** *m* Harlequin

**ar•ma** *f* (-**mi**) arm, weapon; (fig) army; (mil) corps, service; **alle prime armi** at the beginning; **arma bianca** steel blade; **arma da taglio** cutting weapon; **arma delle trasmissioni** signal corps

**armacòllo** *m*—**ad armacollo** slung across the shoulders (*said of a rifle*)

**armà•dio** *m* (-**di**) cabinet; closet; **armadio a muro** built-in closet; **armadio**

**d'angolo** corner cupboard; **armadio farmaceutico** medicine cabinet; **armadio guardaroba** armoire

**armaiòlo** *m* gunsmith

**armamentà·rio** *m* (**-ri**) outfit, set (*of tools*)

**armaménto** *m* armament; crew; gun crew; crew (*of rowboat*); outfit, equipment

**armare** *tr* to arm; to dub (*s.o. a knight*); to outfit, commission (*a ship*); to cock (*a gun*); to brace, shore up (*a building*); (rr) to furnish with track ‖ *ref* to arm oneself; to outfit oneself

**arma·to -ta** *adj* armed; reinforced (*concrete*) ‖ *m* soldier ‖ *f* army; navy; fleet; (nav) task force

**arma·tóre -trice** *adj* outfitting ‖ *m* shipowner; (min) carpenter; (rr) trackwalker

**armatura** *f* armor; scaffold; framework, support; reinforcement (*for concrete*); (elec) plate (*of condenser*)

**armeggiare** §290 (**arméggio**) *intr* to fumble, fool around; to scheme; (archaic) to handle arms; (archaic) to joust

**armeggì·o** *m* (**-i**) fooling around; scheming, intriguing

**armè·no -na** *adj* & *mf* Armenian

**arménto** *m* herd

**armerìa** *f* armory

**armière** *m* (aer) gunner

**armìge·ro -ra** *adj* warlike, bellicose ‖ *m* warrior; bodyguard

**armistiziale** *adj* armistice

**armistì·zio** *m* (**-zi**) *m* armistice

**armonìa** *f* harmony; **in armonia con** according to

**armòni·co -ca** (**-ci -che**) *adj* harmonic; resonant; harmonious ‖ *f* harmonica; **armonica a bocca** mouth organ

**armonió·so -sa** [s] *adj* harmonious

**armonizzare** [ddzz] *tr* & *intr* to harmonize

**arnése** [s] *m* tool, implement; garb, dress; (coll) gadget; **bene in arnese** well-heeled; **male in arnese** down at the heels

**àrnia** *f* beehive

**arò·ma** *m* (**-mi**) aroma, odor; zest

**aromàti·co -ca** *adj* (**-ci -che**) aromatic

**aromatizzare** [ddzz] *tr* to flavor; to spice

**arpa** *f* harp

**arpeggiare** §290 (**arpéggio**) *intr* to play arpeggios; to play a harp; to strum

**arpég·gio** *m* (**-gi**) arpeggio

**arpìa** *f* Harpy; (coll) harpy

**arpionare** (**arpióno**) *tr* to harpoon

**arpióne** *m* hinge (*of door*); hook; harpoon; spike (*for mountain climbing*)

**arpionismo** *m* ratchet

**arpi·sta** *mf* (**-sti -ste**) harpist

**arrabattare** *ref* to exert oneself, to strive, to endeavor

**arrabbiare** §287 *intr* (ESSERE) to go mad (*said of dogs*) ‖ *ref* to become angry (*said of people*)

**arrabbia·to -ta** *adj* mad (*dog*); angry; obstinate; confirmed

**arrabbiatura** *f* rage; **prendersi un'arrabbiatura** to burn up (*with rage*)

**arraffare** *tr* to snatch

**arrampicare** §197 (**arràmpico**) *ref* to climb, climb up

**arrampicata** *f* climbing

**arrampica·tóre -trice** *mf* climber; mountain climber; **arrampicatore sociale** social climber

**arrancare** §197 *intr* to hobble, limp; to struggle, work hard; to row hard

**arrangiaménto** *m* agreement; (mus) arrangement

**arrangiare** §290 *tr* to arrange; to fix; (coll) to steal ‖ *ref* to manage, get along

**arrecare** §197 (**arrèco**) *tr* to cause; to carry, deliver

**arredaménto** *m* furnishing; furnishings; equipment

**arredare** (**arrèdo**) *tr* to furnish; to equip

**arreda·tóre -trice** *mf* interior decorator; upholsterer; (mov) property man

**arrèdo** *m* furnishings, furniture; piece of furniture; **arredi sacri** church supplies

**arrembàg·gio** *m* (**-gi**) boarding (*of a ship*)

**arrenare** (**arréno**) *tr* to sand

**arrèndere** §227 *tr* (archaic) to surrender ‖ *ref* to surrender; **arrendersi a discrezione** to surrender unconditionally

**arrendévole** *adj* yielding, compliant, flexible

**arrendevolézza** *f* suppleness; compliance

**arrestare** (**arrèsto**) *tr* to stop; to arrest ‖ *ref* to stop, stay

**arrèsto** *m* arrest; stop; pause; (mach) stop, catch; **arresti** (mil) house arrest; **in stato d'arresto** under arrest

**arretrare** (**arrètro**) *tr* to withdraw ‖ *intr* (ESSERE & AVERE) & *ref* to withdraw

**arretra·to -ta** *adj* withdrawn; backward; back (*issue*); overdue ‖ **arretrati** *mpl* arrears

**arricchiménto** *m* enrichment

**arricchire** §176 *tr* to enrich ‖ *intr* (ESSERE) & *ref* to get rich

**arricchi·to -ta** *mf* nouveau riche

**arricciacapél·li** *m* (**-li**) curler

**arricciare** §128 *tr* to curl; to wrinkle; to screw up (*one's nose*); **arricciare il pelo** to bristle (*said of a person*); to bristle up (*said of an animal*) ‖ *ref* to curl up

**arriccia·to -ta** *adj* curled up ‖ *m* first coat (*of cement*)

**arricciatura** *f* curling (*of hair*); pleating (*of a skirt*); kink (*in a rope*)

**arrìdere** §231 *tr* (poet) to grant ‖ *intr* to smile

**arrìn·ga** *f* (**-ghe**) harangue; (law) lawyer's plea

**arringare** §209 *tr* to harangue; (law) to plead

**arrischiare** §287 *tr* to endanger; to risk ‖ *ref* to dare, venture

**arrischia·to -ta** *adj* risky; daring

**arrivare** *tr* to reach ‖ *intr* (ESSERE) to arrive; to happen; to get along, be successful; **arrivare a** to reach; to succeed in

**arriva·to -ta** *adj* arrived; successful; **ben arrivato** welcome

**arrivedér·ci** *m* (**-ci**) good-bye || *interj* good-bye!, so long!

**arrivedéria** *interj* good-bye!

**arrivismo** *m* social climbing, ruthless ambition

**arrivi·sta** *mf* (**-sti -ste**) social climber

**arrivo** *m* arrival; (sports) goal line; (sports) finishing line

**arroccare** §197 (**arrócco**) *tr* to put (*e.g., flax*) on the distaff || §197 (**arròcco**) *tr* to shelter; (chess) to castle || *ref* to seek shelter; (chess) to castle

**arròc·co** *m* (**-chi**) castling

**arrochire** §176 *tr* to make hoarse || *intr* (ESSERE) to become hoarse

**arrogante** *adj* arrogant, insolent

**arroganza** *f* arrogance, insolence

**arrogare** §209 (**arrògo**) *tr*—**arrogare a sé** to arrogate to oneself || *ref* to arrogate to oneself

**arrolare** §237 *tr* var of **arruolare**

**arrossare** (**arrósso**) *tr* to redden

**arrossire** §176 *intr* (ESSERE) to blush; to change color

**arrostire** §176 *tr* to roast; to toast; **arrostire allo spiedo** to barbecue on the spit || *intr* (ESSERE) & *ref* to roast

**arrò·sto** *m* (**-sto** & **-sti**) roast

**arrotare** (**arròto**) *tr* to grind, hone; to smooth; to strike, run over; to grit (*one's teeth*) || *ref* to grind (*to work hard*); to sideswipe

**arrotatrice** *f* floor sander

**arrotatura** *f* sharpening

**arrotino** *m* grinder

**arrotolare** (**arròtolo**) *tr* to roll

**arrotondamento** *m* rounding; rounding out; increase (*in salary*)

**arrotondare** (**arrotóndo**) *tr* to make round; to round out; to supplement (*a salary*) || *ref* to round out, become plump

**arrovellare** (**arrovèllo**) *tr* to vex || *ref* to become angry; to strive, endeavor; **arrovellarsi il cervello** to rack one's brains

**arroventare** (**arrovènto**) *tr* to make red-hot || *ref* to become red-hot

**arroventire** §176 *tr* & *ref* var of **arroventare**

**arruffapòpo·li** *m* (**-li**) rabble-rouser

**arruffare** *tr* to tangle; to muss, rumple; to confuse

**arruf·fio** *m* (**-fii**) tangle; confusion, mess

**arruffó·ne -na** *mf* blunderer; swindler

**arrugginire** §176 *tr*, *intr* (ESSERE) & *ref* to rust

**arruolamento** *m* enlistment; draft

**arruolare** (**arruòlo**) *tr* to recruit; to draft || *ref* to enlist

**arruvidire** §176 *tr* to make rough, roughen || *intr* (ESSERE) to become rough

**arsenale** *m* arsenal; navy yard

**arsèni·co -ca** (**-ci -che**) *adj* arsenic, arsenical || *m* arsenic

**ar·so -sa** *adj* burnt; dry, parched; **arso di** consumed with

**arsura** *f* sultriness; dryness

**arte** *f* art; ability; guile; **ad arte** on purpose; **arti e mestieri** arts and crafts

**artefare** §173 *tr* to adulterate

**artefat·to -ta** *adj* adulterated; artificial

**artéfice** *m* craftsman; creator

**artèria** *f* artery

**arterioscleròsi** *m* arteriosclerosis

**arterió·so -sa** [s] *adj* arterial

**artesia·no -na** *adj* artesian

**àrti·co -ca** *adj* (**-ci -che**) arctic || **Artico** *m* Arctic

**articolare** *adj* articular || *v* (**artìcolo**) *tr* & *ref* to articulate

**articola·to -ta** *adj* articulated; articulate; (gram) combined; jagged (*coastline*)

**articolazióne** *f* articulation

**articoli·sta** *mf* (**-sti -ste**) columnist; feature writer

**artìcolo** *m* article; item; paragraph; **articolo di fondo** editorial; **articolo di spalla** comment

**artificiale** *adj* artificial

**artificière** *m* pyrotechnist; (mil) demolition expert

**artifi·cio** *m* (**-ci**) artifice; sophistication, affectation; **artificio d'illuminazione** (mil) flare

**artificiosi·tà** [s] *f* (**-tà**) artfulness, craftiness; artificiality

**artifició·so -sa** [s] *adj* artful, crafty; artificial, affected

**artigianato** *m* craftsmanship

**artigia·no -na** *adj* of craftsmen || *m* craftsman

**artigliare** §280 *tr* (poet) to claw

**artiglière** *m* artilleryman

**artiglierìa** *f* artillery; **artiglieria a cavallo** mounted artillery

**artì·glio** *m* (**-gli**) claw; **cadere negli artigli di** to fall into the clutches of

**arti·sta** *mf* (**-sti -ste**) artist; actor

**artìsti·co -ca** *adj* (**-ci -che**) artistic

**ar·to -ta** *adj* (poet) narrow || *m* limb

**artrite** *f* arthritis

**artrìti·co -ca** *adj* & *mf* (**-ci -che**) arthritic

**arturia·no -na** *adj* Arthurian

**arzigogolare** [dz] (**arzigògolo**) *intr* to muse; to cavil

**arzigògolo** [dz] *m* fantasy; cavil

**arzil·lo -la** [dz] *adj* lively, sprightly; (coll) sparkling (*wine*)

**arzin·ga** *f* (**-ghe**) tong (*of a blacksmith*)

**asbèsto** *m* asbestos

**ascèlla** *f* armpit

**ascendènte** *adj* ascendant || *m* upper hand, ascendancy; **ascendenti** forefathers

**ascendènza** *f* ancestry, lineage

**ascéndere** §245 *tr* to climb || *intr* (ESSERE & AVERE) to ascend, climb

**ascensionale** *adj* rising; lifting

**ascensióne** *f* ascent, climb || **Ascensione** *f* Ascension, Ascension Day

**ascensóre** *m* elevator

**ascésa** [s] *f* ascent

**ascèsso** *m* abscess

**ascè·ta** *mf* (**-ti -te**) ascetic

**ascèti·co -ca** *adj* (**-ci -che**) ascetic

**ascetismo** *m* asceticism

**à·scia** *f* (**-sce**) adze

asciugacapél·li *m* (-li) hair drier
asciugamano *m* towel; asciugamano spugna Turkish towel
asciugante *adj* drying; blotting; soaking || *m* dryer
asciugare §209 *tr* to dry, dry up; to wipe; to drain (*e.g., a glass of wine*) || *ref* to dry oneself; to dry, dry up
asciuga·tóio *m* (-tói) towel; bath towel
asciugatrice *f* dryer
asciut·to -ta *adj* dry; skinny; blunt (*in speech*) || *m* dry land; dry climate; all'asciutto pennyless
ascoltare (ascólto) *tr* to listen to || *intr* to listen
ascolta·tóre -trice *mf* listener
ascólto *m* listening; stare in ascolto to listen
ascòrbi·co -ca *adj* (-ci -che) ascorbic
ascrit·to -ta *adj* ascribed; belonging || *m* member
ascrìvere §250 *tr* to inscribe, register; to ascribe, attribute
ascultare *tr* to sound (*s.o.'s chest*)
asèpsi [s] *f* asepsis
asètti·co -ca [s] *adj* (-ci -che) aseptic
asfaltare *tr* to tar, pave
asfalto *m* asphalt
asfissìa *f* asphyxia
asfissiante *adj* asphyxiating; poison (*gas*); boring
asfissiare §287 *tr* to asphyxiate; to bore || *intr* (ESSERE) to be asphyxiated
asfodèlo *m* asphodel
Àsia, l' *f* Asia; l'Asia Minore Asia Minor
asiàti·co -ca *adj & mf* (-ci -che) Asian, Asiatic
asilo *m* shelter; asylum; home; asilo di mendicità poorhouse; asilo infantile kindergarten; asilo per i vecchi old-age home, nursing home
asimmetrìa [s] *f* asymmetry
asimmètri·co -ca [s] *adj* (-ci -che) asymmetric(al)
asinàggine [s] *f* stupidity, asininity
asi·nàio [s] *m* (-nài) donkey driver
asinata [s] *f* stupidity, folly
asinerìa [s] *f* asininity
asiné·sco -sca [s] *adj* (-schi -sche) asinine
asini·no -na [s] *adj* asinine
àsino [s] *m* ass, donkey; fare l'asino a (slang) to play up to; qui casca l'asino here is the rub
asma *f* asthma
asmàti·co -ca *adj & mf* (-ci -che) asthmatic
àsola *f* buttonhole; buttonhole hem
aspàra·go *m* (-gi) asparagus; piece of asparagus; asparagi asparagus (*as food*)
aspèrgere §112 *tr* to sprinkle
aspersióne *f* aspersing, sprinkling
aspettare (aspètto) *tr* to wait for, await; to expect; aspettare al varco to be on the lookout for || *intr* to wait; fare aspettare to keep waiting || *ref* to expect
aspettativa *f* expectancy, expectation; leave of absence without pay
aspètto *m* waiting; aspect, look; al primo aspetto at first sight

àspide *m* asp
aspirante *adj* suction (*pump*) || *m* aspirant; applicant, candidate; suitor; upperclassman (*in naval academy*)
aspirapólve·re *m* (-re) vacuum cleaner
aspirare *tr* to inhale, breathe in; to suck (*e.g., air*); (phonet) to aspirate || *intr* to aspire
aspiratóre *m* exhaust fan
aspirazióne *f* aspiration; (aut) intake
aspirina *f* aspirin
aspo *m* reel
asportàbile *adj* removable
asportare (aspòrto) *tr* to remove, take away
asportazióne *f* removal
asprézza *f* sourness; roughness, harshness
a·spro -spra *adj* sour; rough, harsh
assaggiare §290 *tr* to taste; to sample, test; assaggiare il terreno (fig) to see how the land lies
assaggia·tóre -trice *mf* taster
assàg·gio *m* (-gi) taste, sample; tasting; test, trial
assài *adj invar* a lot of || *m* much || *adv* enough; fairly; very
assale *m* axle
assalire §242 *tr* to attack, assail; (fig) to seize
assali·tóre -trice *mf* assailant
assaltare *tr* to assault; assaltare a mano armata to stick up
assalto *m* assault, attack; (law) battery; cogliere d'assalto to catch unawares; prendere d'assalto to assault
assaporare (assapóro) *tr* to taste; to relish, enjoy
assassinare *tr* to assassinate; (fig) to murder
assassì·nio *m* (-ni) assassination, murder
assassi·no -na *adj* murderous || *mf* assassin, murderer
asse *m* axle; shaft, spindle; (geom, phys) axis; asse ereditario estate; asse stradale median strip || *f* plank; asse da stiro ironing board
assecondare (assecóndo) *tr* to help; to second; to uphold
assediante *adj* besieging || *m* besieger
assediare §287 (assèdio) *tr* to lay siege to, besiege
assè·dio *m* (-di) siege; assedio economico economic sanctions; cingere d'assedio to besiege
assegnaménto *m* awarding; allowance; faith, reliance; fare assegnamento su to rely upon
assegnare (asségno) *tr* to assign; to prescribe; to distribute; to award
assegnatà·rio -ria *mf* (-ri -rie) assignee
assegnazióne *f* assignment; awarding
asségno *m* allowance; check; assegni fringe benefits; assegni familiari family allowance; assegno a copertura garantita certified check; assegno a vuoto worthless check; assegno di studio (educ) stipend; assegno turistico traveler's check; assegno vademecum certified check; contro assegno C.O.D.

**assemblàg·gio** *m* (**-gi**) (mach) assembling, assembly

**assemblèa** *f* assembly

**assembraménto** *m* gathering

**assembrare** (**assémbro**) *tr* & *ref* to gather

**assennatézza** *f* good judgment, discretion

**assenna·to -ta** *adj* sensible, prudent

**assènso** *m* approval, consent

**assentare** (**assènto**) *ref* to be absent, to absent oneself

**assènte** *adj* absent || *mf* absentee

**assenteismo** *m* absenteeism

**assentire** (**assènto**) *tr* (poet) to grant || *intr* to assent, acquiesce; **assentire con un cenno** to nod assent

**assènza** *f* absence

**assenziènte** *adj* consenting, approving

**assèn·zio** *m* (**-zi**) absinthe; (bot) wormwood

**asserire** §176 *tr* to affirm, assert

**asserragliare** §280 *tr* to barricade || *ref* to barricade oneself

**assèrto** *m* (poet) assertion

**asser·tóre -trice** *mf* advocate, supporter

**asserviménto** *m* enslavement

**asservire** §176 *tr* to enslave; to subjugate

**asserzióne** *f* assertion

**assessóre** *m* councilman; alderman

**assestaménto** *m* arrangement; settling (*of a building*)

**assestare** (**assèsto**) *tr* to arrange; to adapt, regulate; to deliver, deal (*a blow*) || *ref* to become organized; to settle (*said of a building*)

**assesta·to -ta** *adj* sensible, prudent

**assetare** (**asséto**) *tr* to make thirsty; (fig) to inflame

**asseta·to -ta** *adj* thirsty; parched; eager || *mf* thirsty person

**assettare** (**assètto**) *tr* to tidy, straighten up || *ref* to straighten oneself up

**assetta·to -ta** *adj* tidy

**assètto** *m* arrangement; order; (naut) trim; **assetto longitudinale** (aer) pitch, attitude; **in assetto di guerra** ready for war; **male in assetto** in poor shape

**asseverare** (**assèvero**) *tr* to asseverate, assert

**assicèlla** *f* roofing board, lath; batten

**assicuràbile** *adj* insurable

**assicurare** *tr* to assure; to insure; to protect; to fasten; to deliver (*e.g., a thief*) || *ref* to make sure; to take out insurance

**assicura·to -ta** *adj* & *mf* insured || *f* insured letter

**assicura·tóre -trice** *mf* insurer

**assicurazióne** *f* assurance; insurance; **assicurazione contro gli infortuni sul lavoro** workman's compensation insurance; **assicurazione contro i danni** casualty insurance; **assicurazione incendio** fire insurance; **assicurazione infortuni** accident insurance; **assicurazione per la vecchiaia** old age insurance; **assicurazione sociale** social security; **assicurazione sulla vita** life insurance

**assideraménto** *m* freezing; frostbite

**assiderare** (**assidero**) *ref* to freeze; to become frostbitten

**assidere** §113 *ref* (poet) to take one's seat (*e.g., on the throne*)

**assi·duo -dua** *adj* assiduous, diligent

**assième** *m* ensemble || *adv* together; **assieme a** together with

**assiepare** (**assièpo**) *tr* & *ref* to crowd

**assillante** *adj* disturbing, troublesome

**assillare** *tr* to beset, trouble

**assillo** *m* gadfly; (fig) stimulus, goad

**assimilare** (**assìmilo**) *tr* to assimilate; to compare

**assimilazióne** *f* assimilation

**assiòlo** *m* horned owl

**assiò·ma** *m* (**-mi**) axiom

**assiomàti·co -ca** *adj* (**-ci -che**) axiomatic

**assi·ro -ra** *adj* & *mf* Assyrian

**assisa** *f* (poet) uniform, livery; (geol) layer; (archaic) duty, tax; **assise** criminal court; assembly, session; (hist) assises

**assistènte** *mf* assistant; **assistente sanitario** practical nurse; **assistente sociale** social worker || *m*—**assistente ai lavoro** foreman || *f*—**assistente di volo** (aer) hostess

**assistènza** *f* assistance, help; intervention; **assistenza pubblica** relief

**assistenziale** *adj* welfare, charity

**assistere** §114 *tr* to assist, help || *intr*— **assistere a** to attend, be present at

**assito** *m* flooring, boarding

**assiuòlo** *m* var of **assiolo**

**asso** *m* ace; **asso del volante** speed king; **piantare in asso** to walk out on

**associare** §128 (**assòcio**) *tr* to associate; **associare alle carceri** to take to prison || *ref* to associate; to become a member; to subscribe; to participate

**associa·to -ta** *adj* associate || *mf* associate, partner

**associazióne** *f* association; union; subscription; membership

**assodare** (**assòdo**) *tr* to solidify; to strengthen; to ascertain || *ref* to solidify; to strengthen

**assoggettare** (**assoggètto**) *tr* to subject, subdue || *ref* to submit

**assola·to -ta** *adj* sunny, exposed to the sun

**assolcare** §197 (**assólco**) *tr* to furrow

**assoldare** (**assòldo**) *tr* to hire, recruit

**assólo** *m* (mus) solo

**assolutismo** *m* absolutism

**assolutìsti·co -ca** *adj* (**-ci -che**) absolutist, despotic

**assolu·to -ta** *adj* & *m* absolute

**assoluzióne** *f* absolution

**assòlvere** §115 *tr* to absolve; to fulfill

**assomigliare** §280 *tr* to compare; to make similar, make equal || *intr* (ESSERE & AVERE) (with *dat*) to resemble, to look like; to be like || *ref* to resemble each other, look alike; **assomigliarsi a** to resemble

**assommare** (**assómmo**) *tr* to add; to be the epitome of; (archaic) to complete || *intr* (ESSERE) to amount

**assonna·to -ta** *adj* sleepy

**assopire** §176 *tr* to lull to sleep; to

soothe ‖ *ref* to drowse, to nod; to calm down

**assorbènte** *adj* absorbent ‖ *m* sanitary napkin

**assorbiménto** *m* absorption

**assorbire** §176 & (assòrbo) *tr* to absorb

**assorbi·to -ta** *adj* absorbed; **assorbito da** consumed with

**assordare** (assórdo) *tr* to deafen ‖ *ref* to become deaf; to dim; to lessen

**assortiménto** *m* assortment; **avere in assortimento** (com) to carry, stock

**assortire** §176 *tr* to assort, sort out; to stock

**assorti·to -ta** *adj* assorted; **bene assortito** well matched

**assòr·to -ta** *adj* engrossed, absorbed

**assottigliare** §280 *tr* to thin; to sharpen; to reduce ‖ *ref* to grow thinner

**assuefare** §173 *tr* to accustom ‖ *ref* to become accustomed

**assuefazióne** *f* habit, custom

**assùmere** §116 *tr* to assume; to hire; to raise, elevate; (law) to accept in evidence

**Assunta** *f* Assumption

**assunto** *m* thesis, argument; (poet) task

**assun·tóre -trice** *mf* contractor

**assunzióne** *f* assumption; hiring; (law) examination ‖ **Assunzione** *f* Assumption

**assurdi·tà** *f* (-tà) absurdity

**assur·do -da** *adj* absurd ‖ *m* absurdity

**assùrgere** §117 *intr* (ESSERE) (poet) to rise

**asta** *f* staff; rod; arm (*e.g., of scale*); lance; leg (*of compass*); stroke (*in handwriting*); shaft (*of arrow*); auction; (naut) boom; (naut) mast; (elec) trolley pole; **a mezz'asta** half-mast; **vendere all'asta** to auction, auction off

**astante** *mf* bystander ‖ *m* physician on duty (*in a hospital*)

**astanterìa** *f* receiving ward

**astato** *m* (chem) astatine

**astè·mio -mia** *adj* abstemious, temperate ‖ *mf* teetotaler

**astenére** §271 *ref* to abstain

**astensióne** *f* abstension

**astenuto** *m* person who abstains from voting; abstention (*vote withheld*)

**astèrgere** §164 (*pp* astèrso) *tr* to wipe

**asteri·sco** *m* (-schi) asterisk

**asticcìòla** *f* penholder; rib (*of umbrella*); temple (*of eyeglasses*)

**àstice** *m* (*Hommarus vulgaris*) lobster

**asticèlla** *f* (sports) bar

**astinènte** *adj* abstinent

**astinènza** *f* abstinence

**à·stio** *m* (-sti) grudge, rancor

**astió·so -sa** [s] *adj* full of malice, spiteful

**astóre** *m* goshawk

**astràgalo** *m* astragalus, anklebone

**astrakàn** *m* Persian lamb

**astrarre** §273 *tr* to abstract ‖ *intr—* **astrarre da** to leave aside, overlook

**astrat·to -ta** *adj* abstract ‖ *m* abstract

**astrazióne** *f* abstraction

**astringènte** *adj* & *m* astringent

**-astro -astra** *suf adj* -ish, e.g., **verdastro**

greenish ‖ *suf mf* -aster, e.g., **poe·tastro** poetaster

**astro** *m* star, heavenly body; (bot) aster; (fig) star

**astrologìa** *f* astrology

**astrològi·co -ca** *adj* (-ci -che) astrological

**astròlo·go** *m* (-gi or -ghi) astrologer

**astronàu·ta** *mf* (-ti -te) astronaut

**astronàuti·co -ca** (-ci -che) *adj* astronautic(al) ‖ *f* astronautics

**astronautizzare** [ddzz] *intr* (ESSERE) to be an astronaut

**astronave** *f* spaceship, spacecraft

**astronomìa** *f* astronomy

**astrònomo** *m* astronomer

**astronòmi·co -ca** *adj* (-ci -che) astronomic(al)

**astruserìa** *f* abstruseness

**astrusi·tà** *f* (-tà) abstruseness

**astru·so -sa** *adj* abstruse

**astùc·cio** *m* (-ci) case, box

**astu·to -ta** *adj* astute, crafty

**astùzia** *f* astuteness, craftiness

**àta·vo -va** *mf* ancestor

**ateismo** *m* atheism

**atei·sta** *mf* (-sti -ste) atheist

**Atène** *f* Athens

**atenèo** *m* athenaeum; university

**ateniése** [s] *adj* & *mf* Athenian

**àte·o -a** *adj* atheistic ‖ *mf* atheist

**atlante** *m* atlas ‖ **Atlante** *m* Atlas

**atlànti·co -ca** *adj* (-ci -che) Atlantic ‖ **Atlantico** *m* Atlantic

**atlè·ta** *mf* (-ti -te) athlete

**atletéssa** *f* female athlete

**atlèti·co -ca** (-ci -che) *adj* athletic ‖ *f* athletics; **atletica leggera** track and field

**atmosfèra** *f* atmosphere

**atmosfèri·co -ca** *adj* (-ci -che) atmospheric

**atòllo** *m* atoll

**atòmi·co -ca** *adj* (-ci -che) atomic; (coll) stunning

**atomizzare** [ddzz] *tr* to atomize

**atomizzatóre** [ddzz] *m* atomizer

**àtomo** *m* atom

**atòni·co -ca** *adj* (-ci -che) (pathol) weak

**àto·no -na** *adj* (gram) atonic

**atout** *m* (atouts) trump

**à·trio** *m* (-tri) entrance hall, lobby

**atróce** *adj* atrocious

**atroci·tà** *f* (-tà) atrocity

**atrofìa** *f* atrophy

**atròfi·co -ca** *adj* (-ci -che) atrophied

**atrofizzare** [ddzz] *tr* & *ref* to atrophy

**attaccabottó·ni** *mf* (-ni) bore, pest, buttonholer

**attaccabri·ghe** *mf* (-ghe) (coll) quarrelsome person, scrapper

**attaccaménto** *m* attachment, affection

**attaccapan·ni** *m* (-ni) coathanger

**attaccare** §197 *tr* to attach; to bind, unite; to sew on; to stick; to hitch (*a horse*); to hang; to attack; to strike up (*a conversation*); to begin; to communicate (*a disease*); **attaccare un bottone a** (fig) to buttonhole ‖ *intr* to stick; to gain a foothold, take root; to begin ‖ *ref* to stick; to cling; to spread (*said of a disease*); (fig) to become attached

**attaccatìc·cio -cia** *adj* (**-ci -ce**) sticky

**attacchino** *m* billposter

**attac·co** *m* (**-chi**) attachment; onslaught; fastening; beginning; seizure (*e.g., of epilepsy*); spell (*e.g., of coughing*); (elec) plug; (rad) jack; (sports) forward line; **attacco cardiaco** heart attack

**attagliare** §280 *ref*—**attagliarsi a** to fit, become

**attanagliare** §280 *tr* to grip; to seize; to hold (*e.g., with tongs*)

**attardare** *ref* to tarry, delay

**attecchire** §176 *intr* to take root; to take hold

**atteggiaménto** *m* attitude

**atteggiare** §290 (**attéggio**) *tr* to compose (*e.g., one's face*); to place ‖ *ref* to pose; to strike an attitude

**attempa·to -ta** *adj* elderly

**attendaménto** *m* camping; jamboree (*of Boy Scouts*)

**attendare** (**attèndo**) *ref* to encamp; to pitch one's tent

**attendènte** *m* (mil) orderly

**attèndere** §270 *tr* to await; (archaic) to keep; **attendere l'ora propizia** to bide one's time ‖ *intr*—**attendere a** to attend to

**attendìbile** *adj* reliable

**attendismo** *m* wait-and-see attitude

**attendi·sta** (**-sti -ste**) *adj* wait-and-see ‖ *mf* fence-sitter

**attenére** §271 *tr* (poet) to keep (*a promise*) ‖ *intr*—**attenere** (with *dat*) to concern, e.g., **ciò non gli attiene** this does not concern him ‖ *ref*—**attenersi a** to conform to

**attentare** (**attènto**) *intr*—**attentare a** to attempt (*s.o.'s life*) ‖ *ref* to make an attempt, dare

**attentato** *m* attempt

**attenta·tóre -trice** *mf* would-be murderer; attacker

**attèn·ti** *m* (**-ti**) attention ‖ *interj* (mil) attention!

**attèn·to -ta** *adj* attentive; careful

**attenuare** (**attènuo**) *tr* to extenuate, play down; to attenuate; to mitigate

**attenzióne** *f* attention; **fare attenzione** to take care; **prestare attenzione** to pay attention

**atterràg·gio** *m* (**-gi**) landing; **atterraggio di fortuna** emergency landing; **atterraggio senza carrello** crash-landing

**atterraménto** *m* landing; pinning, pin (*in wrestling*); (boxing) knocking down; **atterramento frenato** (aer) arrested landing

**atterrare** (**attèrro**) *tr* to fell; to knock down; to pin (*in wrestling*); (fig) to humiliate ‖ *intr* to land; **atterrare scassando** or **atterrare senza carrello** to crash-land

**atterrire** §176 *tr* to frighten, terrify ‖ *ref* to become frightened

**atté·so -sa** [s] *adj* awaited, expected; **atteso che** considering that ‖ *f* waiting; expectation; **in attesa (di)** waiting (for)

**attestare** (**attèsto**) *tr* to certify, attest; to prove; to join; (mil) to deploy ‖ *ref* (mil) to take a stand

**attestato** *m* certificate

**attestazióne** *f* testimony; affidavit; attestation, proof

**àtti·co -ca** (**-ci -che**) *adj* & *mf* Attic ‖ *m* attic

**atti·guo -gua** *adj* adjacent, contiguous

**attillare** *tr* & *ref* to preen

**attilla·to -ta** *adj* tight, close-fitting; tidy, all dressed up

**àttimo** *m* moment, split second; **di attimo in attimo** any moment

**attinènte** *adj* related, pertinent

**attinènza** *f* relation; **attinenze** appurtenances; annexes

**attingere** §126 *tr* to draw (*water*); to get; (poet) to attain (*e.g., glory*)

**attingi·tóio** *m* (**-tói**) ladle

**attirare** *tr* to draw, attract

**attitùdine** *f* aptitude; attitude

**attivare** *tr* to activate; to expedite

**attivazióne** *f* activation; reassessment

**attivi·tà** *f* (**-tà**) activity; **attività** *fpl* assets

**atti·vo -va** *adj* active; profit-making ‖ *m* assets

**attizzare** *tr* to stir, poke (*a fire*); (fig) to stir up

**attizza·tóio** *m* (**-tói**) poker

**at·to -ta** *adj* apt, fit ‖ *m* act, action; gesture; (law) instrument; **all'atto pratico** in reality; **atti** proceedings (*of a learned society*); **atti notarili** legal proceedings; **atto di nascita** birth certificate; **fare atto di presenza** to put in a brief formal appearance; **atto di vendita** bill of sale; **nell'atto o sull'atto** in the act

**attòni·to -ta** *adj* astonished

**attorcigliare** §280 *tr* to twist ‖ *ref* to wind; to coil up

**attóre** *m* actor; (law) plaintiff; **attore giovane** (theat) juvenile; **primo attore** (theat) lead

**attorniare** §287 (**attórnio**) *tr* to surround; (fig) to dupe

**attórno** *adv* around; **andare attorno to** walk around; **attorno a** around, near; **darsi d'attorno** to busy oneself; **levarsi qlcu d'attorno** to get rid of s.o.

**attortigliare** §280 *tr* to twist ‖ *ref* to wind; to coil up

**attraccare** §197 *tr* & *intr* to moor, dock

**attrac·co** *m* (**-chi**) mooring, docking

**attraènte** *adj* attractive

**attrarre** §273 *tr* to attract, draw

**attratti·vo -va** *adj* attractive; alluring ‖ *f* attraction, charm

**attraversaménto** *m* crossing; **attraversamento pedonale** pedestrian crossing

**attraversare** (**attravèrso**) *tr* to cross; to go through; to thwart; **attraversare il passo a** to stand in the way of

**attravèrso** *adv* across; crosswise; **andare attraverso** to go down the wrong way (*said of food or drink*); (fig) to go wrong; **attraverso a** through, across ‖ *prep* through, across

**attrazióne** *f* attraction

**attrezzare** (**attrézzo**) *tr* to outfit, equip

**attrezzatura** *f* outfit; gear, equipment; **attrezzatura di una nave** rigging; **attrezzature** facilities

**attrezzi·sta** (-sti -ste) *mf* gymnast || *m* toolmaker; (theat) property man

**attrézzo** *m* tool, utensil; **attrezzi** gymnastic equipment

**attribuire** §176 *tr* to award; to attribute; **attribuire qlco a qlcu** to credit s.o. with s.th || *ref* to ascribe to oneself, claim for oneself

**attributo** *m* attribute

**attribuzióne** *f* attribution

**attrice** *f* actress; (law) plaintiff; **prima attrice** (theat) lead

**attristare** *tr* (poet) to sadden || *ref* to become sad

**attri·to** **-ta** *adj* worn, worn-out || *m* attrition; disagreement

**attruppare** *tr* to band, group || *ref* to mill about, throng

**attuàbile** *adj* feasible

**attuale** *adj* present; present-day, current

**attuali·tà** *f* (-tà) timeliness; reality; **attualità** *fpl* current events; **di viva attualità** newsworthy; timely; **in the news**

**attualizzare** [ddzz] *tr* to bring up to date || *ref* to become a reality

**attuare** (**àttuo**) *tr* to carry out, make come true || *ref* to come true

**attuà·rio** **-ria** (-ri -rie) *adj* (hist) transport (*e.g., ship*) || *m* actuary

**attuazióne** *f* realization

**attutire** §176 *tr* to mitigate; to deaden (*a sound, a blow*) || *ref* to diminish (*said of a sound*)

**audace** *adj* audacious

**audàcia** *f* audacity

**audiofrequènza** *f* audio frequency

**audiovisi·vo** **-va** *adj* audio-visual

**auditi·vo** **-va** *adj* var of **uditivo**

**auditóre** *m* var of **uditore**

**auditò·rio** *m* (-ri) auditorium

**audizióne** *f* program; audition; (law) hearing

**àuge** *f* acme; **essere in auge** to enjoy a great reputation; to be in vogue; to be on top of the world

**augurale** *adj* well-wishing; salutatory

**augurare** (**àuguro**) *tr* to wish; to bid (*good day*) || *intr* to augur || *ref* to hope; to expect

**àugure** *m* augur

**augù·rio** *m* (-ri) wish; augury, omen

**augustè·o** **-a** *adj* Augustan

**augu·sto** **-sta** *adj* august, venerable

**àula** *f* hall; classroom; (poet) chamber (*of a palace*)

**àuli·co** **-ca** *adj* (-ci -che) courtly; noble, elevated

**aumentare** (**auménto**) *tr* to augment, increase || *intr* (ESSERE) to increase, rise

**auménto** *m* increase

**àura** *f* (poet) breeze; (poet) breath

**àure·o** **-a** *adj* golden, gold

**aurèola** *f* halo

**auricolare** *adj* ear; first-hand || *m* (telp) receiver; (rad) earphone

**auròra** *f* dawn; (fig) aurora

**ausiliare** *adj* auxiliary || *m* collaborator, helper

**ausilià·rio** **-ria** (-ri -rie) *adj* auxiliary; (mil) supply || *m* helper; (mil) reserve officer || *f* female member of the armed forces

**ausì·lio** *m* (-li) (poet) help

**auspicare** §197 (**àuspico**) *tr* to wish, augur

**àuspice** *m* sponsor; (hist) augur

**auspì·cio** *m* (-ci) sponsorship; (hist, poet) augury, omen; **sotto gli auspici di** under the auspices of

**austeri·tà** *f* (-tà) austerity

**austè·ro** **-ra** *adj* austere

**australe** *adj* austral, southern

**Austràlia, l'** *f* Australia

**australia·no** **-na** *adj* & *mf* Australian

**Austria, l'** *f* Austria

**austrìa·co** **-ca** *adj* & *mf* (-ci -che) Austrian

**autarchìa** *f* autarky; autonomy (*of an administration*)

**autàrchi·co** **-ca** *adj* (-ci -che) autonomous, independent

**autènti·ca** *f* (-che) authentication of a signature or a document

**autenticare** §197 (**autèntico**) *tr* to authenticate

**autentici·tà** *f* (-tà) authenticity

**autènti·co** **-ca** (-ci -che) *adj* authentic, genuine || *f* see **autentica**

**autière** *m* (mil) driver

**auti·sta** *mf* (-sti -ste) (aut) driver

**au·to** *f* (-to) auto

**autoabbronzante** [dz] *adj* tanning || *m* tanning lotion

**autoaffondaménto** *m* scuttling

**autoambulanza** *f* ambulance

**autobiografìa** *f* autobiography

**autobiogràfi·co** **-ca** *adj* (-ci -che) autobiographical

**autoblinda·to** **-ta** *adj* armored

**autoblin·do** *m* (-do) armored car

**autobótte** *f* tank truck

**àuto·bus** *m* (-bus) bus

**autocarro** *m* truck, motor truck

**autocèntro** *m* (mil) motor pool

**autocistèrna** *f* tank truck

**autocivétta** *f* unmarked police car

**autocolónna** *f* row of cars

**autocombustióne** *f* spontaneous combustion

**autocontròllo** *m* self-control

**autocorrièra** *f* intercity bus, highway bus

**autocrazìa** *f* autocracy

**autocrìti·ca** *f* (-che) self-criticism

**autòcto·no** **-na** *adj* autochthonous, independent

**autodecisióne** *m* free will

**autodeterminazióne** *f* self-determination

**autodidat·ta** *mf* (-ti -te) self-taught person

**autodidàtti·co** **-ca** *adj* (-ci -che) self-instructional

**autodifésa** [s] *f* self-defense

**autodisciplìna** *f* self-discipline

**autòdromo** *m* automobile race track

**autoemotè·ca** *f* (-che) bloodmobile

**autofilettante** *adj* self-threading

**autofurgóne** *m* van; **autofurgone cellu-**

lare police van; **autofurgone funebre** hearse

**autogiro** *m* autogyro

**autogovèrno** *m* self-government

**autògra·fo -fa** *adj* autographic(al) || *m* autograph

**auto·grù** *f* (**-grù**) tow truck

**autolesioni·sta** *mf* (**-sti -ste**) person who wounds himself to avoid the draft or collect insurance

**autoletti·ga** *f* (**-ghe**) ambulance

**autolibro** *m* bookmobile

**autolìnea** *f* bus line

**autò·ma** *m* (**-mi**) automaton, robot

**automàti·co -ca** (**-ci -che**) *adj* automatic || *m* snap

**automatizzare** [ddzz] *tr* to automate

**automazióne** *f* automation

**automèzzo** [ddzz] *m* motor vehicle

**automòbile** *f* automobile, car; **automobile da corsa** racing car; **automobile di serie** stock car; **automobile fuori serie** custom-made car

**automobilismo** *m* motoring

**automobili·sta** *mf* (**-sti -ste**) motorist

**automobilìsti·co -ca** *adj* (**-ci -che**) car, automobile

**automo·tóre -trice** *adj* self-propelled || *f* (rr) automotive rail car

**autonolég·gio** *m* (**-gi**) car rental agency

**autonomìa** *f* autonomy; (aer, naut) cruising radius

**autonomi·sta** *adj* (**-sti -ste**) autonomous

**autòno·mo -ma** *adj* autonomous, independent

**autoparchég·gio** *m* (**-gi**) parking; parking lot

**autopar·co** *m* (**-chi**) parking; parking lot

**autopiano** *m* player piano

**autopilò·ta** *m* (**-ti**) (aer) automatic pilot

**autopómpa** *f* fire engine

**autopsìa** *f* autopsy

**autorà·dio** *f* (**-dio**) car radio

**autóre** *m* author; perpetrator; creator, maker

**autoreattóre** *m* ramjet engine

**autorespiratóre** *m* aqualung

**autorévole** *adj* authoritative

**autoriméssa** *f* garage

**autori·tà** *f* (**-tà**) authority

**autorità·rio -ria** *adj* (**-ri -rie**) authoritarian

**autoritratto** *m* self-portrait

**autorizzare** [ddzz] *tr* to authorize

**autorizzazióne** [ddzz] *f* authorization

**autoscala** *f* hook and ladder; ladder (*of hook and ladder*)

**autoscuòla** *f* driving school

**autoservì·zio** *m* (**-zi**) bus service, bus line; self-service

**autosilo** *m* parking garage

**autostazióne** *f* bus station

**autostèllo** *m* roadside motel

**auto·stòp** *m* (**-stòp**) hitchhiking; **fare l'autostop** to hitchhike

**autostoppi·sta** *mf* (**-sti -ste**) hitchhiker

**autostrada** *f* highway, turnpike

**autosufficiènte** *adj* self-sufficient

**autote·làio** *m* (**-lài**) (aut) frame

**autotrasportare** (**autotraspòrto**) *tr* to truck

**autotrasportatóre** *m* trucker

**autotreni·sta** *m* (**-sti**) truck driver, teamster

**autotrèno** *m* tractor trailer

**autoveicolo** *m* motor vehicle

**autovettura** *f* car, automobile

**autrice** *f* authoress

**autunnale** *adj* autumnal, fall

**autunno** *m* autumn, fall

**avallare** *tr* to endorse (*a promissory note*); to guarantee

**avallo** *m* endorsement (*of a promissory note*)

**avambràc·cio** *m* (**-ci**) forearm

**avampósto** *m* outpost

**avancàrica** *f*—**ad avancarica** muzzleloading

**avanguàrdia** *f* vanguard; avant-garde

**avanguardismo** *m* avant-garde

**avanguardi·sta** *m* (**-sti**) avant-gardist; (hist) member of Fascist youth organization

**avannòtto** *m* small fry (*young freshwater fish*)

**avanti** *adj* preceding || *m* forward || *adv* forward, ahead; **andare avanti** to proceed, to go ahead; **andare avanti negli anni** to be up in years; **avanti a** in front of; **avanti che** rather than; **avanti di** before; **essere avanti** to be advanced (*in work or study*); **in avanti** ahead || *prep*—**avanti Cristo** before Christ; **avanti giorno** before daybreak || *interj* come in!

**avantièri** *adv* day before yesterday

**avantrèno** *m* (aut) front-axle assembly; (mil) limber

**avanzaménto** *m* advancement

**avanzare** *tr* to advance; to overcome; to be creditor for, e.g., **avanza cento dollari da suo fratello** he is his brother's creditor for one hundred dollars; to save || *intr* (mil) to advance || *intr* (ESSERE) to advance; to stick out; to be abundant; to be left over, e.g., **avanzano due polpette** two meatballs are left over; **avanzare negli anni** to grow older || *ref* to advance, come forward

**avanza·to -ta** *adj* advanced; progressive || *f* (mil) advance

**avanzo** *m* remainder; **avanzi** remains

**avarìa** *f* damage, breakdown; (naut) average

**avariare** §287 *tr* to damage, spoil || *intr* to spoil

**avaria·to -ta** *adj* damaged, spoiled

**avarìzia** *f* avarice, greed

**ava·ro -ra** *adj* avaricious, stingy || *mf* miser

**avellana** *f* filbert

**avellano** *m* filbert tree

**avèllo** *m* (poet) tomb

**avéna** *f* oats

**avére** *m* belongings, property; assets, credit; amount due || §118 *tr* to have; to hold; to wear; to receive, get; to stand (*a chance*); to be, e.g., **avere . . . anni** to be . . . years old; **avere caldo** to be hot; to be warm; **avere fame** to be hungry; **avere freddo** to be cold; **avere fretta** to be in a hurry;

avere paura to be afraid; avere ragione to be right; avere sete to be
thirsty; avere sonno to be sleepy;
avere torto to be wrong; avere vergogna to be ashamed; avere voglia di
to be anxious to; avere qlco da + *inf*
to have s.th to + *inf*, e.g., ho molto
lavoro da fare I have a lot of work
to do; averla con to be angry at;
non avere niente a che fare con to
have nothing to do with || *impers*—
v'ha there is || *aux* to have, e.g., ha
letto il giornale he has read the newspaper; avere da + *inf* to have to +
*inf*, e.g., avevo da lavorare I had to
work; to be to + *inf*, e.g., ha da
venire alle cinque he is to arrive at
five o'clock
avià·rio -ria (-ri -rie) *adj* bird || *m*
aviary
avia·tóre -trice *mf* aviator || *f* aviatrix
aviazióne *f* aviation
avicoltóre *m* bird raiser; poultry farmer
avidi·tà *f* (-tà) avidity, greediness
àvi·do -da *adj* avid, greedy
avière *m* airman
aviogètto *m* jet plane
aviolìnea *f* airline
aviopista *f* (aer) airstrip
aviorimèssa *f* (aer) hangar
aviotrasporta·to -ta *adj* airborne
avi·to -ta *adj* ancestral
a·vo -va *mf* grandparent; ancestor || *m*
grandfather || *f* grandmother
avocare §197 (àvoco) *tr* to demand
(*jurisdiction*); to expropriate
avò·rio *m* (-ri) ivory
avul·so -sa *adj* (poet) torn, uprooted;
(poet) separated
avvalére §278 *ref*—avvalersi di to avail
oneself of
avvallaménto *m* sinking, settling
avvallare *tr* (poet) to lower (*e.g., one's
eyes*) || *ref* to sink; (lit) to humiliate
oneself
avvalorare (avvalóro) *tr* to strengthen,
confirm || *ref* to gain strength
avvampare *tr* (poet) to inflame || *intr*
(ESSERE) to burn
avvantaggiare §290 *tr* to be profitable
to; to benefit || *ref* to profit; avvan-
taggiarsi su to overcome; to beat
avvedére §279 *ref*—avvedersi di to
notice, become aware of
avvedutézza *f* discernment; shrewdness
avvedu·to -ta *adj* prudent; shrewd; fare
qlcu avveduto di to inform s.o. of
avvelenaménto *m* poisoning
avvelenare (avveléno) *tr* to poison ||
*ref* to take poison; to be poisoned
avveniménto *m* happening, event
avvenire *adj invar* future, to come || *m*
future; in avvenire in the future ||
§282 *intr* (ESSERE) to happen, occur;
avvenga quel che vuole come what
may
avventare (avvènto) *tr* to hurl; to deliver (*a blow*); to venture (*an opin-
ion*) || *ref* to throw oneself
avventatézza *f* thoughtlessness, heed-
lessness

avventa·to -ta *adj* thoughtless, heedless;
all'avventata heedlessly
avventi·zio -zia *adj* (-zi -zie) outside,
exterior; temporary, occasional
avvènto *m* advent; elevation, rise
avven·tóre -tóra *mf* customer, consumer
avventura *f* adventure
avventuriè·ro -ra *adj* adventurous || *m*
adventurer || *f* adventuress
avventuró·so -sa *adj* adventurous,
adventuresome
avverare (avvéro) *tr* to make true ||
*ref* to come true
avvèr·bio *m* (-bi) adverb
avversà·rio -ria (-ri -rie) *adj* opposing,
contrary || *mf* adversary, opponent
aversióne *f* aversion
avversi·tà *f* (-tà) adversity
avvèr·so -sa *adj* adverse; (obs) opposite
|| avverso *prep* (law) against
avvertènza *f* prudence, caution; advice;
avvertenze instructions, directions
avvertiménto *m* caution, warning; advice
avvertire (avvèrto) *tr* to caution, warn;
to notice
avvezzare (avvézzo) *tr* to accustom; to
inure; to train; avvezzar male to spoil
|| *ref* to get accustomed
avvéz·zo -za *adj* accustomed
avviaménto *m* starting; introduction;
trade school; good shape (*of a business*); (mach) starting; (typ) adjustment (*of printing press*)
avviare §119 *tr* to start, set in motion;
to introduce; to initiate; to begin ||
*ref* to set out
avvia·to -ta *adj* going, thriving (*concern*)
avvicendaménto *m* alteration, rotation
(*of crops*)
avvicendare (avvicèndo) *tr* & *ref* to
alternate
avvicinaménto *m* approach; rapprochement
avvicinare *tr* to bring near or closer; to
approach, go or come near to || *ref*
to approach, come near; avvicinarsi
a to come closer, approach
avviliménto *m* discouragment, dejection
avvilire §176 *tr* to degrade; to deject ||
*ref* to become dejected, become discouraged
avviluppare *tr* to entangle, snarl; to
wrap
avvinazza·to -ta *adj* & *mf* drunk
avvincènte *adj* fascinating
avvìncere §285 *tr* to fascinate, charm;
(poet) to twine
avvinghiare §287 *tr* to claw; to clasp,
clutch || *ref* to grip one another
avvì·o *m* (-i) beginning
avvisàglia *f* skirmish; prime avvisaglie
onset; first signs
avvisare *tr* to inform, advise; (archaic)
to observe, notice
avvisa·tóre -trice *mf* announcer, mes-
senger || *m* alarm; (theat) callboy;
avvisatore acustico (aut) horn; avvisatore d'incendio fire alarm
avviso *m* advise; notice, poster; opinion; avviso di chiamata alle armi

notice of induction; **sull'avviso** on one's guard
**avvistare** *tr* to sight
**avvitaménto** *m* (aer) tailspin
**avvitare** *tr* to screw; to fasten ‖ *ref* (aer) to go into a tailspin
**avviticchiare** §287 *tr* to entwine ‖ *ref* to cling
**avvivare** *tr* to revive; to stir up
**avvizzire** §176 *tr & intr* (ESSERE) to wither
**avvocatéssa** *f* woman lawyer
**avvocato** *m* lawyer, attorney
**avvocatura** *f* law, legal profession
**avvòlgere** §289 *tr* to wind; to wrap up; to spread over, surround ‖ *ref* to wind around; to wrap oneself up
**avvolgiménto** *m* winding; wrapping; (elec) coil; (mil) envelopment
**avvol·tóio** *m* (-tói) vulture
**avvoltolare** (avvòltolo) *tr* to roll up ‖ *ref* to roll around, wallow
**aziènda** [dz] *f* business, firm
**azionare** (azióno) *tr* to start; to drive, propel
**azionà·rio -ria** *adj* (-ri -rie) (com) stock
**azióne** *f* action, act; (law) suit; (com) share (*of stock*); **azione legale** prosecution; **azione privilegiata** preferred stock
**azioni·sta** *mf* (-sti -ste) stockholder, shareholder

**azòto** [dz] *m* nitrogen
**azoturo** [dz] *m* nitride
**aztè·co -ca** *adj & mf* (-chi -che) Aztec
**azzannare** *tr* to seize with the fangs
**azzardare** [ddzz] *tr* to risk; to advance ‖ *ref* to dare
**azzarda·to -ta** [ddzz] *adj* daring
**azzardo** [ddzz] *m* chance, hazard
**azzardó·so -sa** [ddzz] [s] *adj* hazardous, risky
**azzeccagarbu·gli** *m* (-gli) shyster
**azzeccare** §197 (azzécco) *tr* to hit; to deliver; to pass off (*counterfeit money*); **azzeccarla** (coll) to hit the mark
**azzimare** [ddzz] (àzzimo) *tr & ref* to spruce up
**àzzi·mo -ma** [ddzz] *adj* unleavened (*bread*)
**azzittare & azzittire** §176 *tr* to hush ‖ *ref* to keep quiet
**azzoppare** (azzòppo) *tr* to cripple ‖ *ref* to become lame or crippled
**Azzòrre** [ddzz] *fpl* Azores
**azzuffare** *ref* to come to blows; to scuffle
**azzur·ro -ra** [ddzz] *adj* blue ‖ *m* blue; Italian athlete (*in international competition*)
**azzurrógno·lo -la** [ddzz] *adj* bluish

# B

**B, b** [bi] *m & f* second letter of the Italian alphabet
**ba·bàu** *m* (-bàu) bogey, bugbear
**babbè·o -a** *adj* foolish ‖ *mf* fool
**babbo** *m* (coll) daddy, father
**babbù·cia** *f* (-ce) babouche; bedroom slipper
**babbuino** *m* baboon
**babèle** *f* babel ‖ **Babele** *f* Babel
**babilònia** *f* confusion ‖ **Babilònia** *f* Babylon
**babórdo** *m* (naut) port
**bacare** §197 *ref* to become worm-eaten
**baca·to -ta** *adj* worm-eaten; rotten
**bac·ca** *f* (-che) berry
**bacca·là** *m* (-là) dried codfish; (coll) skinny person; (coll) lummox
**baccalaureato** *m* baccalaureate, bachelor's degree
**baccanale** *m* bacchanal
**baccano** *m* noise, hubbub; **fare baccano** to carry on
**baccante** *f* bacchant
**baccellière** *m* (hist) bachelor
**baccèllo** *m* pod
**baccellóne** *m* simpleton, fool
**bacchétta** *f* rod, wand, baton; **bacchetta magica** magic wand; **bacchette del tamburo** drumsticks
**bacchétto** *m* stick; handle (*of a whip*)
**bacchettó·ne -na** *mf* bigot
**bàcchi·co -ca** *adj* (-ci -che) Bacchic
**Bacco** *m* Baccus

**bachè·ca** *f* (-che) showcase
**bachelite** *f* bakelite
**bacheròzzo** *m* worm; earthworm; (coll) cockroach
**bachicoltura** *f* silkworm raising
**baciama·no** *m* (-ni) kissing of the hand
**baciapi·le** *mf* (-le) bigot
**baciare** §128 *tr* to kiss; **baciare la polvere** to bite the dust ‖ *ref* to kiss one another
**bacia·to -ta** *adj* kissed; rhymed (*couplet*)
**bacile** *m* basin
**bacillo** *m* bacillus
**bacinèlla** *f* small basin; (phot) tray
**bacino** *m* basin; reservoir; cove; (anat) pelvis; **bacino carbonifero** coal field; **bacino di carenaggio** drydock; **bacino fluviale** river basin
**bà·cio** *m* (-ci) kiss; **a bacio** with a northern exposure
**baciucchiare** §287 *tr* to keep on kissing ‖ *ref* to pet
**ba·co** *m* (-chi) worm; **baco da seta** silkworm
**bacuc·co -ca** *adj* (-chi -che)—**vecchio bacucco** dotard
**bada** *f*—**tenere a bada** to stave off; to delay
**badare** *tr* to tend, take care of ‖ *intr* to attend; to take care; to pay attention; **badare a** to mind; to watch

over; to attend to; **badare alla salute** to take care of one's health
**badéssa** f abbess
**badìa** f abbey
**badilata** f shovelful
**badile** m shovel
**baffo** m whiskers; whisker; **baffi** mustache; whiskers; **baffo di gatto** (rad) cat's whiskers; **leccarsi i baffi** to lick one's chops; **sotto i baffi** up one's sleeve
**baga·gliàio** m (**-gliài**) (rr) baggage car; (rr) baggage room; (aut) baggage rack
**bagaglièra** f baggage room
**bagaglière** m baggage master
**bagà·glio** m (**-gli**) baggage, luggage; (of knowledge) fund
**bagagli·sta** m (**-sti**) porter (in a hotel)
**bagarinàg·gio** m (**-gi**) profiteering; (theat) scalping
**bagarino** m profiteer; scalper
**bagà·scia** f (**-sce**) harlot, prostitute
**bagattèlla** f trifle, bauble
**baggiano** m nitwit, simpleton
**bà·glio** m (**-gli**) (naut) beam
**baglióre** m shine, gleam
**bagnante** mf bather, swimmer; vacationer at the seashore
**bagnare** tr to bathe; to wet; to soak; to water, sprinkle; to moisten; (fig) to celebrate || ref to bathe; to wet one another
**bagnaròla** f (coll) bathtub
**bagnasciu·ga** f (**-ghe**) (naut) waterline
**bagnino** m lifeguard
**bagno** m bath; bathroom; bathtub; **bagno di luce** diathermy; **bagno di schiuma** bubble bath; **bagno di sole** sun bath; **bagno di vapore** steam bath; **bagno turco** Turkish bath; **essere in un bagno di sudore** to be soaked with perspiration; **fare il bagno** to take a bath
**bagnomarìa** m (**bagnimarìa**) double boiler; bain-marie; **a bagnomaria in** a double boiler
**bagórdo** m carousal, revelry; **far bagordi** to carouse, revel
**bàio bàia** (**bài bàie**) adj & m bay || f bay; jest; trifle; **dare la baia a** to make fun of, tease
**baionétta** f bayonet; **baionetta in canna** with fixed bayonet
**bàita** f mountain hut
**balaustrata** f balustrade
**balaùstro** m baluster
**balbettaménto** m stammering
**balbettare** (**balbétto**) tr to stammer; to speak poorly (a foreign language) || intr to stammer; to babble (said of a baby)
**balbettì·o** m (**-i**) babble (of a baby); stammering
**balbùzie** f stammering
**balbuziènte** adj stammering || mf stammerer
**Balcani, i** the Balkans
**balcàni·co -ca** adj (**-ci -che**) Balkan
**balconata** f balcony; (theat) upper gallery
**balcóne** m balcony

**baldacchino** m canopy, baldachin
**baldanza** f boldness; aplomb, assurance
**baldanzó·so -sa** [s] adj bold; self-assured
**bal·do -da** adj bold; self-assured
**baldòria** f carousal, revelry; **fare baldoria** to carouse, revel
**baldrac·ca** f (**-che**) harlot, prostitute
**baléna** f whale
**balenare** (**baléno**) intr to stagger || intr (ESSERE) to flash, e.g., **gli balena un pensiero** a thought flashes through his mind || impers (ESSERE)—**balena,** it is lightning
**balenièra** f whaler, whaleboat
**baléno** m flash; flash of lightning; **in un baleno** in a flash
**balenòttera** f rorqual
**balèstra** f crossbow; (aut) spring, leaf spring
**balestrière** m crossbowman
**bàlia** f wet nurse; **balia asciutta** dry nurse; **prendere a balia** to wet-nurse
**balìa** f power; **in balia di** at the mercy of
**balìsti·co -ca** (**-ci -che**) adj ballistic || f ballistics
**balla** f bale; (vulg) lie
**ballàbile** adj dance || m dance tune
**ballare** tr to dance || intr to dance; to shake; to be loose; to wobble (said, e.g., of a chair)
**ballata** f ballad; (mus) ballade
**balla·tóio** m (**-tói**) gallery; perch (in birdcage)
**balleri·no -na** adj dancing || m ballet dancer; dancer; dancing partner || f dancing girl; ballerina; chorus girl; ballet slipper; (orn) wagtail
**ballétto** m ballet; chorus
**ballo** m dance; chorus; ball; stake; **ballo di San Vito** Saint Vitus's dance; **ballo in maschera** masked ball; **in ballo** at stake; in question; **tirare in ballo** to drag in
**ballonzolare** (**ballónzolo**) intr to hop around
**ballottàg·gio** m (**-gi**) runoff
**ballottare** (**ballòtto**) tr to ballot (e.g., a candidate)
**balneare** adj bathing; water, watering
**baloccare** §197 (**balòcco**) tr to amuse with toys || ref to play; to trifle, to fool around
**balòc·co** m (**-chi**) toy; hobby
**balordàggine** f silliness
**balór·do -da** adj silly, foolish
**balsàmi·co -ca** adj (**-ci -che**) balmy; antiseptic
**balsamina** f balsam
**bàlsamo** m balm, balsam
**bàlti·co -ca** adj (**-ci -che**) Baltic
**baluardo** m bastion, bulwark
**baluginare** (**balùgino**) intr (ESSERE) to flicker; to flash (through one's mind)
**balza** f crag, cliff; flounce (on dress); fringe (on curtains, bedspreads, etc.)
**balza·no -na** adj white-footed (horse); odd, funny || f flounce; fringe; white mark (on horse's foot)
**balzare** tr to throw (a rider; said of a horse) || intr (ESSERE) to jump, leap;

to bounce; **balzare in mente a** to suddenly dawn on

**balzellare (balzèllo)** *intr* to hop

**balzèllo** *m* hop; tribute; tax; toll; **stare a balzello** to lie in wait

**balzellóni** *adv*—**a balzelloni** leaping, skipping

**balzo** *m* leap; bounce; **pigliare la palla al balzo** to take time by the forelock

**bambàgia** *f* cotton wool

**bambinàggine** *f* childishness

**bambinàia** *f* nursemaid; **bambinaia ad ore** baby sitter

**bambiné·sco -sca** *adj* (**-schi -sche**) childish

**bambi·no -na** *adj* childish ‖ *mf* child

**bambòc·cio** *m* (**-ci**) fat baby; doll; rag doll

**bàmbola** *f* doll; **bambola di pezza** ragdoll

**bam·bù** *m* (**-bù**) bamboo

**banale** *adj* banal, commonplace

**banali·tà** *f* (**-tà**) banality, commonplaceness, triviality

**banana** *f* banana; hair with curls shaped as rolls

**bananièia** *f* banana boat

**banano** *m* banana plant

**ban·ca** *f* (**-che**) bank; embankment

**bancàbile** *adj* negotiable

**bancarèlla** *f* cart, pushcart; stall

**bancà·rio -ria** (**-ri -rie**) *adj* bank, banking ‖ *m* bank clerk

**bancaròtta** *f* bankruptcy; **fare bancarotta** to go bankrupt

**banchettare (banchétto)** *intr* to feast, banquet

**banchétto** *m* banquet

**banchière** *m* banker

**banchina** *f* garden bench; bicycle path; sidewalk; shoulder (*of highway*); dock, pier; (*rr*) platform; (*mil*) banquette

**ban·co** *m* (**-chi**) bench; seat; bank; witness stand; school (*of fish*); **banco di coralli** coral reef; **banco di ghiaccio** ice pack; **banco di nebbia** fog bank; **banco di prova** (*mach*) bench; **banco di sabbia** sandbar; **banco d'ostriche** oyster bed; **banco lotto** lottery office

**bancogiro** *m* (*com*) transfer of funds

**bancóne** *m* counter; bench

**banconòta** *f* banknote

**banda** *f* band; **andare alla banda** (*naut*) to list; **da ogni banda** from every side; **mettere da banda** to put aside

**bandèlla** *f* hinge (*of door or window*); hinged leaf (*of table*)

**banderuòla** *f* banderole; weather vane

**bandièra** *f* flag; banner; **battere la bandiera** (e.g., **italiana**) to fly the (*e.g Italian*) flag; **mutar bandiera** to change sides

**bandierare (bandièro)** *tr* (*aer*) to feather

**bandire** §176 *tr* to announce (*e.g., a competitive examination*); to banish

**bandìsti·co -ca** *adj* (**-ci -che**) (*mus*) band

**bandi·to -ta** *adj* announced; open (*house*) ‖ *m* bandit ‖ *f* preserve (*for hunting or fishing*)

**bandi·tóre -trice** *mf* town crier; auctioneer; barker

**bando** *m* announcement; banishment; **bandi matrimoniali** (*eccl*) banns; **mandare in bando** to exile, banish

**bandolièra** *f* bandoleer; **a bandoliera** slung across the shoulders

**bàndolo** *m* end of a skein; **perdere il bandolo** to lose the thread (*e.g., of a story*)

**bara** *f* bier, coffin

**barac·ca** *f* (**-che**) hut, cabin; (*fig*) household; **fare baracca** to carouse around

**baracca·to -ta** *adj* lodged in a hut or a cabin; slum (*e.g., section*) ‖ *m* dweller in a hut or a cabin; slum dweller

**baraccóne** *m* big circus tent

**baraónda** *f* hubbub; mess

**barare** *intr* to cheat (*e.g., at cards*)

**bàratro** *m* abyss, chasm

**barattare** *tr* to barter; **barattare le carte in mano a uno** to distort someone's words; **barattar parole** to chat, talk ‖ *intr* to barter

**barattière** *m* grafter

**baratto** *m* barter

**baràttolo** *m* can, canister, jar

**barba** *f* beard; whiskers; barb, vane (*of feather*); (*naut*) line; **barba a punta** imperial, goatee; **fare la barba (a)** to shave; **farla in barba a qlcu** to act in spite of s.o.; to dupe s.o.; **mettere barbe** to take root; **radersi la barba** to shave

**barbabiètola** *f* beet; sugar beet

**barbafòrte** *m* horseradish

**barbagian·ni** *m* (**-ni**) owl; (*fig*) jackass

**barbà·glio** *m* (**-gli**) glitter, dazzle

**barbaré·sco -sca** (**-schi -sche**) *adj* Barbary ‖ *m* inhabitant of the Barbary States

**barbàri·co -ca** *adj* (**-ci -che**) barbaric

**barbà·rie** *f* (**-rie**) barbarism, barbarity

**barbarismo** *m* barbarism

**bàrba·ro -ra** *adj* barbarous, barbaric ‖ *m* barbarian

**barbazzale** *m* curb (*of bit*)

**Barberìa, la** Barbary States

**barbétta** *f* fetlock (*tuft of hair on horse*); goatee; (*mil*) barbette; (*naut*) painter

**barbière** *m* barber

**barbierìa** *f* barbershop

**barbì·glio** *m* (**-gli**) barb (*of arrow*)

**barbi·no -na** *adj* shoddy; botched; stingy

**bàr·bio** *m* (**-bi**) (*ichth*) barbel

**barbiturato** *m* barbiturate

**barbitùri·co -ca** (**-ci -che**) *adj* barbituric ‖ *m* barbiturate

**barbo** *m* var of **barbio**

**barbò·gio -gia** *adj* (**-gi -gie**) senile

**barbóne** *m* long beard, thick beard; poodle; (*coll*) bum, hobo

**barbó·so -sa** [*s*] *adj* boring

**barbugliare** §280 *tr* to stutter (*e.g., a word*) ‖ *intr* to stutter; to bubble, gurgle

**barbu·to -ta** *adj* bearded

**bar·ca** *f* (**-che**) boat; heap; (*fig*) family

affairs; **barca a motore** motorboat; **barca da pesca** fishing boat; **barca a remi** rowboat
**barcàc·cia** f (-ce) (theat) stage box
**barcaiòlo** m boatman
**barcamenare** (**barcaméno**) ref to manage, get along
**barcarizzo** m (naut) gangway
**barcaròla** f barcarole
**barcata** f boatful
**barchéssa** f tool shed
**barchétta** f small boat; (naut) log chip
**barcollare** (**barcòllo**) intr to totter, stagger
**barcollóni** adv staggering, tottering
**barcóne** m barge
**bardare** tr to harness ‖ ref to get dressed
**bardatura** f harnessing; harness
**bardo** m bard
**bardòsso** m —**a bardosso** (archaic) bareback
**barèlla** f stretcher
**barellare** (**barèllo**) tr to carry on a stretcher ‖ intr to totter, stagger
**barenatura** f (mach) boring
**bargèllo** m (hist) chief of police; (hist) police headquarters
**bargì·glio** m (-gli) wattle
**baricèntro** m center of gravity; (fig) essence, gist
**barile** m barrel, cask
**barilòtto** m keg
**bàrio** m barium
**bari·sta** mf (-sti -ste) bartender, barkeeper ‖ m barman ‖ f barmaid
**baritonale** adj baritone
**barìto·no -na** adj barytone ‖ m baritone
**barlume** m glimmer, gleam
**baro** m cheat, cardsharp
**baròc·co -ca** adj & m (-chi -che) baroque
**baròmetro** m barometer
**baróne** m baron
**baronéssa** f baroness
**barra** f bar; link; rod; sandbar; **andare alla barra** to plead a case; **barra del timone** (naut) tiller; **barra di torsione** (aut) torsion bar; **barra spaziatrice** space bar (of typewriter)
**barrare** tr to cross, draw lines across (a check)
**barrétta** f bar (e.g., of chocolate)
**barricare** §197 (**bàrrico**) tr to barricade ‖ ref to barricade oneself
**barricata** f barricade
**barrièra** f barrier; bar; **barriera corallina** barrier reef
**barrire** §176 intr to trumpet (said of elephant)
**barrito** m trumpeting, cry of an elephant
**barroc·ciàio** m (-ciài) cart driver
**barròc·cio** m (-ci) cart
**baruffa** f fight, quarrel
**barzellétta** [dz] f joke
**basale** adj basal
**basalto** m basalt
**basaménto** m foundation (of building); baseboard; base (of column)

**basare** tr to base ‖ ref—**basarsi su** to be based on; to rest on
**ba·sco -sca** adj & mf (-schi -sche) Basque
**basculla** f balance, scale
**base** f base, foundation; (fig) basis; **a base di** composed of, made of; **base navale** naval base, naval station; **in base a** according to
**basétta** f sideburns
**bàsi·co -ca** adj (-ci -che) (chem) basic
**basilare** adj basic, fundamental
**Basilèa** f Basel
**basìli·ca** f (-che) basilica
**basìli·co** m (-ci) basil
**basilissa** f (fig) queen bee
**bàsolo** m large paving stone
**bassacórte** f barnyard
**bassézza** f baseness
**bas·so -sa** adj low; shallow; late (e.g., date); (fig) base, vile; **basso di statura** short ‖ m bottom; hovel (in Naples); (mus) basso ‖ **basso** adv low; down; **a basso, da basso** or **in basso** downstairs
**bassofóndo** m (**bassifóndi**) (naut) shallows, shallow water; **bassifondi** underworld, slums
**bassopiano** m lowland
**bassorilièvo** m bas-relief
**bassòt·to -ta** adj stocky ‖ m basset hound
**bassotuba** m bass horn
**bassura** f lowland; (fig) baseness
**basta** f hem; basting (with long stitches) ‖ interj enough!
**bastante** adj sufficient, adequate; comfortable (income)
**bastar·do -da** adj bastard; irregular ‖ m bastard
**bastare** intr to suffice, be enough; **basta!** enough!; **basta che** + subj as long as + ind; **bastare a sé stesso** to be self-sufficient; **non basta che** + subj not only + ind
**bastévole** adj sufficient
**bastiménto** m ship; shipload
**bastióne** m bastion; (fig) defense, rampart
**basto** m packsaddle; (fig) burden
**bastonare** (**bastóno**) tr to club, cudgel; **bastonare di santa ragione** to give a good thrashing to
**bastonata** f clubbing, cudgeling; **darsi bastonate da orbi** to thrash one another soundly
**bastoncino** m small stick; roll; (anat) rod
**bastóne** m stick, cane; pole; club; baton; staff; French bread; **bastone a leva** crowbar; **bastone animato** sword cane; **bastone da golf** club; **bastone da montagna** alpenstock; **bastone da passeggio** walking stick; **bastone da sci** ski pole; **bastoni** suit in Neapolitan cards corresponding to clubs; **mettere il bastone tra le ruote** to throw a monkey wrench into the machinery
**batàc·chio** m (-chi) clapper (of bell); cudgel
**batata** f sweet potato

**batisfèra** *f* bathysphere
**batista** *f* batiste, cambric
**batòsta** *f* blow; (fig) blow
**bàtrace** or **batrace** *m* batrachian
**battà·glia** *f* (**-glie**) battle; campaign
**battagliare** §280 *intr* to fight
**battagliè·ro -ra** *adj* fighting, warlike
**battà·glio** *m* (**-gli**) clapper (*of bell*); knocker
**battaglióne** *m* battalion
**battèllo** *m* boat; **battello di salvataggio** lifeboat; **battello pneumatico** rubber raft
**battènte** *m* leaf (*e.g., of door*); knocker; tapper (*of alarm clock*)
**bàttere** *m*—**in un batter d'occhio** in the twinkling of an eye ‖ *tr* to beat; to hit; to strike (*the hour; said of a clock*); to click (*teeth, heels*); to clap (*hands*); to stamp (*one's foot*); to mint (*coins*); to fly (*a flag*); to beat (*time*); to scour (*the countryside*); to flap (*the wings*); (sports) to bat; (sports) to kick (*a penalty*); **battere a macchina** to type; **battere il naso in** to chance upon; **battere la fiacca** to goof off; **battere la grancassa per** to ballyhoo; **battere la strada** to be a streetwalker; **senza batter ciglio** without batting an eye ‖ *intr* (ESSERE) to beat down (*said, e.g., of rain*); to beat (*said of the heart*); to chatter (*said of teeth*); to knock (*at the door*); **battere in ritirata** to beat a retreat; **battere in testa** (aut) to knock
**batteria** *f* battery; set (*of utensils*); (sports) heat
**batterici·da** (**-di -de**) *adj* bactericidal ‖ *m* bactericide
**battèri·co -ca** *adj* (**-ci -che**) bacterial
**battè·rio** *m* (**-ri**) bacterium
**batteriologìa** *f* bacteriology
**batteriòlo·go -ga** *mf* (**-gi -ghe**) bacteriologist
**batteri·sta** *mf* (**-sti -ste**) jazz drummer
**battesimale** *adj* baptismal
**battésimo** *m* baptism; **tenere a battesimo** to christen
**battezzare** (**battézzo**) [ddzz] *tr* to christen ‖ *ref* to receive baptism; to assume the name of
**battibaléno** *m*—**in un battibaleno** in the twinkling of an eye
**battibéc·co** *m* (**-chi**) squabble
**batticuòre** *m* palpitation; (fig) trepidation
**battilò·ro** *m* (**-ro**) goldsmith; silversmith
**battimano** *m* applause
**battimuro** *m*—**giocare a battimuro** to pitch pennies (against a wall)
**battipalo** *m* pile driver
**battipan·ni** *m* (**-ni**) clothes beater
**battira·me** *m* (**-me**) coppersmith
**battiscó·pa** *m* (**-pa**) washboard, baseboard
**batti·sta** *adj* & *mf* (**-sti -ste**) Baptist
**battistèro** *m* baptistry
**battistra·da** *m* (**-da**) outrider; (sports) leader; (aut) tread
**battitappéto** *m* carpet sweeper
**bàttito** *m* beating; palpitation; ticking;

wink; pitter-patter (*of rain*)
**batti·tóio** *m* (**-tói**) leaf (*e.g., of door*); casement; cotton beater
**battitóre** *m* (hunt) beater; (baseball) batter
**battitrice** *f* threshing machine
**battitura** *f* thrashing, whipping; threshing (*e.g., of wheat*)
**battu·to -ta** *adj* beaten; hammered ‖ *m* pavement ‖ *f* beat; stroke, keystroke; meter (*in poetry*); witticism, quip; (hunt) battue; (tennis) service; (theat) line; (theat) cue; **battuta d'aspetto** (mus) pause; **dare la battuta** to give the cue
**batùffolo** *m* wad; (fig) bundle
**baule** *m* trunk; **baule armadio** wardrobe trunk; **fare i bauli** to be on one's way; **fare il baule** to pack one's trunk
**baulétto** *m* small trunk; handbag; jewel case
**bava** *f* slobber; foam, froth; burr (*on metal edge*); **avere la bava alla bocca** to be frothing at the mouth; **bava di vento** breath of air, soft breeze
**bavaglino** *m* bib
**bavà·glio** *m* (**-gli**) gag
**bavarése** [s] *adj* & *mf* Bavarian ‖ *f* Bavarian cream; chocolate cream
**bàvero** *m* collar
**bavièra** *f* beaver (*of helmet*) ‖ **la Baviera** Bavaria
**bavó·so -sa** [s] *adj* slobbering, slobbery
**bazza** [ddzz] *f* protruding chin; windfall
**bazzana** [ddzz] *f* sheepskin
**bazzècola** [ddzz] *f* trifle, bauble
**bazzicare** §197 (**bàzzico**) *tr* to frequent
**bazzòt·to -ta** [ddzz] *adj* soft-boiled; uncertain (*weather*)
**beare** (**bèo**) *tr* to delight ‖ *ref* to be delighted, be enraptured
**beatificare** §197 (**beatìfico**) *tr* to beatify
**beatitùdine** *f* beatitude, bliss
**bea·to -ta** *adj* blissful, happy; blessed ‖ *mf* blessed
**be·bè** *m* (**-bè**) baby
**beccàc·cia** *f* (**-ce**) woodcock
**beccaccino** *m* snipe
**beccafi·co** *m* (**-chi**) figpecker, beccafico
**bec·càio** *m* (**-cài**) butcher
**beccamòr·ti** *m* (**-ti**) gravedigger
**beccare** §197 (**bécco**) *tr* to peck; to pick; (coll) to catch ‖ *ref* to peck one another; to quarrel
**beccata** *f* peck
**beccheggiare** §290 (**becchéggio**) *intr* (naut) to pitch
**becchég·gio** *m* (**-gi**) (naut) pitching
**beccherìa** *f* butcher shop
**becchime** *m* food for poultry
**becchino** *m* gravedigger
**béc·co** *m* (**-chi**) beak, bill; tip, point; nozzle (*e.g., of teapot*); billy goat; (vulg) cuckold; **bagnarsi il becco** (joc) to wet one's whistle; **mettere il becco in** (coll; joc) to stick one's nose into; **non avere il becco di un quattrino** to not have a red cent
**beccùc·cio** *m* (**-ci**) small bill; lip, spout
**beccuzzare** *tr* to peck ‖ *ref* to bill (*said of doves*)

**béce·ro -ra** *adj* (coll) boorish || *m* (coll) boor

**beduì·no -na** *adj* & *m* Bedouin

**befana** *f* (coll) Epiphany; old hag

**bèffa** *f* jest, mockery; **farsi beffa di** to make fun of

**beffar·do -da** *adj* mocking

**beffare (bèffo)** *tr* to mock, deride || *ref* —**beffarsi di** to make fun of

**beffeggiare §290 (befféggio)** *tr* to scoff at, deride

**bè·ga** *f* (-ghe) quarrel; trouble

**beghina** *f* Beguine; bigoted woman

**begònia** *f* begonia

**bèl** *adj* apocopated form of **bello**, used only before masculine singular nouns beginning with a consonant except impure **s, z, gn, ps,** and **x,** e.g., **bel ragazzo**

**belare (bèlo)** *tr* to croon || *intr* to bleat, baa; to moan

**belato** *m* bleat, baa

**bèl·ga** *adj* & *mf* (-gi -ghe) Belgian

**Bèlgio, il** Belgium

**bèll'** *adj* apocopated form of **bello**, used only before singular nouns of both genders beginning with a vowel, e.g., **bell'amico; bell'epoca**

**bèlla** *adj* *fem* of **bello** || *f* belle; girlfriend; final draft; (sports) final game; (sports) rubber match; **alla bell'e meglio** the best one could; **bella di notte** (bot) four-o'clock

**belladònna** *f* belladonna

**bellétto** *m* rouge, makeup

**bellézza** *f* beauty; **che bellezza!** how lovely!; **la bellezza di** as much as

**bellici·sta** *adj* (-sti -ste) bellicose

**bèlli·co -ca** *adj* (-ci -che) war, warlike

**bellicó·so -sa** [s] *adj* bellicose

**belligerante** *adj* & *m* belligerent

**belligeranza** *f* belligerence

**bellimbusto** *m* fop, dandy, beau

**bèl·lo -la** (declined like **quello §7**) *adj* beautiful; lovely; handsome; good-looking; pleasing; fine; quite a, e.g., **una bella cifra** quite a sum; fair; pretty; **bell'e fatto** ready-made; taken care of; **farla bella** to start trouble; (coll) to do it, e.g., **l'hai fatta bella** you've done it; **farsi bello** to dress up; **farsi bello di** to appropriate || *m* beauty; beautiful; climax; fine weather; beau; **il bello è** the funny thing is; **sul più bello** just then; **sul più bello che** just when || *f* see **bella** || **bello** *adv*—**bel bello** slowly

**bellospìrito** *m* (**begli spiriti**) wit, bel-esprit

**belluì·no -na** *adj* wild, fierce

**bellumóre** *m* (**begli umori**) jolly fellow

**bel·tà** *f* (-tà) beauty (*woman*); (lit) beauty

**bélva** *f* wild beast

**belvedére** *adj* (rr) observation (*car*) || *m* belvedere; (naut) topgallant

**Belzebù** *m* Beelzebub

**bemòlle** *m* (mus) flat

**benama·to -ta** *adj* beloved

**benarriva·to -ta** *adj* welcome

**benché** *conj* although, albeit

**bènda** *f* bandage; band; blindfold; **benda gessata** cast, surgical dressing

**bendàg·gio** *m* (-gi) bandage

**bendare (bèndo)** *tr* to bandage; **bendare gli occhi a** to blindfold

**bendispó·sto -sta** *adj* well-disposed

**bène** *adj* well; well-born || *m* goal, aim; good; love; sake; **bene dell'anima** profound affection; **beni** (econ) assets, goods; **beni di consumo** consumer goods; **beni immobili** real estate; **beni mobili** personal property, chattels; **beni rifugio** hedge (*e.g., against inflation*); **è un bene** it is a blessing; **fare del bene** to do good; **per il Suo bene** for your sake; **voler bene a** to love, like; to care for || *adv* well; all right; properly; **ben bene** quite carefully; **star bene** to be well; **va bene** O.K., all right

**benedetti·no -na** *adj* & *m* Benedictine

**benedét·to -ta** *adj* blessed; holy

**benedire §195** *tr* to bless; to praise; **andare a farsi benedire** (coll) to go to wrack and ruin; **mandare a farsi benedire** (coll) to get rid of, dump

**benedizióne** *f* benediction; boon

**beneduca·to -ta** *adj* well-behaved

**benefattóre** *m* benefactor

**benefattrice** *f* benefactress

**beneficare §197 (benèfico)** *tr* to benefit, help

**beneficènza** *f* welfare; charity, beneficence

**beneficiale** *adj* beneficial

**beneficiare §128** *intr* to benefit

**beneficià·rio -ria** *adj* & *mf* (-ri -rie) beneficiary

**beneficiata** *f* benefit performance; streak of good luck; streak of bad luck

**benefì·cio** *m* (-ci) benefice; profit; favor; benefit

**benèfi·co -ca** *adj* (-ci -che) beneficial; beneficent

**benemerènte** *adj* deserving, well-deserving

**benemèri·to -ta** *adj* worthy, deserving || *m*—**benemerito della patria** national hero || *f*—**la Benemerita** the Carabinieri

**beneplàcito** *m* approval, consent; **a beneplacito di** at the pleasure of

**benèssere** *m* well-being, comfort; prosperity

**benestante** *adj* well-to-do || *mf* well-to-do person

**benestare** *m* approval; prosperity; **dare il benestare a** to approve

**benevolènte** *adj* benevolent

**benevolènza** *f* benevolence

**benèvo·lo -la** *adj* well-meaning; benevolent

**benfat·to -ta** *adj* well-done; well-favored; shapely

**benga·la** *m* (-li & -la) fireworks

**benga·li** *adj* & *m* (-li) Bengalese

**beniami·no -na** *mf* favorite child; favorite

**benigni·tà** *f* (-tà) benignity; graciousness; mildness (*of climate*)

**beni-gno -gna** *adj* benign; gracious; mild (*climate*)

**benintenziona•to -ta** *adj* well-meaning

**benintéso** [s] *adv* of course, naturally

**bènna** *f* bucket, scoop (*e.g., of dredge*)

**benna•to -ta** *adj* (lit) well-born

**benpensante** *m* sensible person; conformist

**benportante** *adj* well-preserved

**benservito** *m* testimonial, recommendation; **dare il benservito a** to dismiss, fire

**bensì** *adv* indeed || *conj* but

**bentorna•to -ta** *adj & m* welcome || *interj* welcome back!

**benvenu•to -ta** *adj & m* welcome; **dare il benvenuto a** to welcome

**benvi•sto -sta** *adj* well-thought-of

**benvolére** *tr*—**farsi benvolere da qlcu** to enter the good graces of s.o.; **prendere a benvolere qlcu** to be well-disposed toward s.o.

**benvolu•to -ta** *adj* liked, loved

**benzina** *f* gasoline, gas; benzine; **far benzina** (coll) to get gas

**benzi•nàio** *m* (**-nài**) gasoline dealer; gas-station attendant

**benzòlo** *m* benzene

**beóne** *m* drunkard, toper

**bequadro** *m* (mus) natural

**berciare** §128 (**bèrcio**) *intr* (coll) to yell

**bére** *m* drink, drinking || §120 *tr* to drink; (fig) to swallow; **bere come una spugna** to drink like a fish; **darla a bere** to make believe

**bergamòt•to -ta** *adj* bergamot || *m* bergamot orange || *f* bergamot pear

**berìllio** *m* beryllium

**berlina** *f* pillory; berlin, coach; (aut) sedan; **mettere alla berlina** to pillory

**berlinése** [s] *adj* Berlin || *mf* Berliner

**Berlino** *m* Berlin

**bermuda** *mpl* Bermuda shorts || **le Bermude** Bermuda

**bernòccolo** *m* bump, protuberance; (fig) knack

**berrétta** *f* biretta

**berrétto** *m* cap; **berretto a sonagli** cap and bells; **berretto da notte** nightcap; **berretto gogliardico** student cap

**bersagliare** §280 *tr* to harass, pursue; to bomb, bombard

**bersà•glio** *m* (**-gli**) target; butt (*of a joke*); target (*of criticism*)

**bèrta** *f* pile driver; **dar la berta a** to ridicule

**bertùc•cia** *f* (**-ce**) Barbary ape; **fare la bertuccia di** to ape

**bestémmia** *f* blasphemy

**bestemmiare** §287 (**bestémmio**) *tr* to blaspheme, curse

**bestemmia•tóre -trice** *adj* blasphemous || *mf* blasphemer

**béstia** *f* beast, animal; **andare in bestia** to fly into a rage; **bestia da soma** beast of burden; **bestia nera** pet aversion, bête noire; **bestie grosse** cattle

**bestiale** *adj* beastly, bestial

**bestiali•tà** *f* (**-tà**) beastliness; blunder

**bestiame** *m* livestock; **bestiame da cortile** barnyard animals; **bestiame grosso** cattle

**bestino** *m* gamy odor; stench of perspiration

**bestiòla** *f* tiny animal; pet

**bestsèl•ler** *m* (**-ler**) best seller

**Betlèmme** *f* Bethlehem

**betonièra** *f* cement mixer

**béttola** *f* tavern

**bettolière** *m* tavern keeper

**bettònica** *f* betony; **conosciuto più della bettonica** very well-known

**betulla** *f* birch

**bèuta** *f* flask

**bevanda** *f* drink, beverage

**beveràg•gio** *m* (**-gi**) beverage, potion

**bevìbile** *adj* drinkable

**bevi•tóre -trice** *mf* drinker

**bevuta** *f* drink, drinking

**bezzicare** §197 (**bézzico**) *tr* to peck; to vex || *ref* to fight one another

**biacca** *f* white lead

**biada** *f* feed; **biade** harvest

**bianca•stro -stra** *adj* whitish

**biancherìa** *f* laundry; linen; underwear; **biancheria da letto** bed linen; **biancheria da tavola** table linen; **biancheria di bucato** freshly laundered clothes; **biancheria intima** underclothes

**bianchézza** *f* whiteness

**bianchire** §176 *tr* to blanch; to bleach; to polish

**bian•co -ca** (**-chi -che**) *adj* white; clean; **bianco come un cencio lavato** as white as a ghost || *m* white; **dare il bianco a** to whitewash; **in bianco** blank (*paper*); **mangiare in bianco** to eat a bland or non-spicy diet; **ricamare in bianco** to embroider

**biancóre** *m* whiteness

**biancospino** *m* hawthorn

**biascicare** §197 (**biàscico**) *tr* to chew with difficulty; to peck at (*one's food*); to mumble

**biasimare** (**biàsimo**) *tr* to blame

**biasimévole** *adj* blamable, censurable

**biàsimo** *m* blame, censure; **dare una nota di biasimo a** to censure

**biauricolare** *adj* binaural

**Bìbbia** *f* Bible

**bibe•rón** *m* (**-rón**) nursing bottle

**bìbita** *f* soft drink

**bìbli•co -ca** *adj* (**-ci -che**) Biblical

**bìblio•bus** *m* (**-bus**) bookmobile

**bibliòfi•lo -la** *mf* bibliophile

**bibliografìa** *f* bibliography

**bibliotè•ca** *f* (**-che**) library; bookshelf, stack; collection (*of books*); **biblioteca ambulante** walking encyclopedia

**bibliotecà•rio -ria** *mf* (**-ri -rie**) librarian

**bìbu•lo -la** *adj* absorbent (*e.g., paper*)

**bi•ca** *f* (**-che**) pile of sheaves

**bicarbonato** *m* bicarbonate; **bicarbonato di soda** bicarbonate of soda, baking soda

**bicchierata** *f* glassful; wine party

**bicchière** *m* glass

**bicchierino** *m* small glass, liquor glass; **bicchierino da rosolio** whiskey glass, jigger

**biciclétta** *f* bicycle

**bicilìndri•co -ca** *adj* (**-ci -che**) two-cylinder

**bicìpite** adj two-headed ‖ m biceps
**bicòc·ca** f (-che) castle built on a hill; shanty, hut
**bicolóre** adj two-color
**bicòrno** m two-cornered hat
**bidèllo** m school janitor, caretaker
**bidènte** m two-pronged pitchfork
**bidimensionale** adj two-dimensional
**bidóne** m can (for milk); drum (for gasoline or oil); jalopy; (slang) fraud
**bidon·ville** f (-ville) shantytown
**biè·co -ca** adj (-chi -che) awry; sullen; cross; fierce; **guardar bieco** to look askance (at)
**bièlla** f connecting rod
**biennale** adj biennial ‖ f biennial show
**biènne** adj biennial
**bièn·nio** m (-ni) biennium
**biètola** f Swiss chard
**biétta** f wedge, chock; (naut) batten
**bifase** adj diphase
**biffa** f (surv) rod
**biffare** tr to cross out; (surv) to level
**bifi·do -da** adj bifurcate
**bifocale** adj bifocal
**bifól·co** m (-chi) ox driver; clodhopper, boor
**biforcaménto** m bifurcation
**biforcare** §197 (bifórco) tr to bifurcate
**biforcazióne** f bifurcation, branching off; fork (of a road)
**biforcu·to -ta** adj forked; cloven (e.g., hoof)
**bifrónte** adj two-faced
**bi·ga** f (-ghe) chariot
**bigamìa** f bigamy
**biga·mo -ma** adj bigamous ‖ mf bigamist
**bighellonare** (bighellóno) intr to idle, dawdle, dally
**bighelló·ne -na** mf idler, dawdler
**bigino** m (slang) pony (used to cheat)
**bi·gio -gia** adj (-gi -gie) gray, grayish; (fig) undecided
**bigiotterìa** f costume jewelry; costume jewelry store
**bigliardo** m billiards
**bigliet·tàio** m (-tài) ticket agent; (rr) conductor
**biglietterìa** f ticket office; (theat) box office
**bigliétto** m note; card; ticket; **biglietto d'abbonamento** commutation ticket; season ticket; **biglietto d'andata e ritorno** round-trip ticket; **biglietto di banca** banknote; **biglietto di lotteria** lottery ticket, chance; **biglietto d'invito** invitation; **biglietto di visita** calling card; business card; **biglietto di Stato** banknote; **mezzo biglietto** half fare
**bigné** m (bigné) puff, creampuff
**bigodino** m curler; roller
**bigón·cia** f (-ce) vat; bucket; **a bigonce** abundantly
**bigón·cio** m (-ci) vat; tub; (theat) ticket box (for stubs)
**bigottismo** m bigotry
**bigòt·to -ta** adj bigoted ‖ mf bigot
**bilàn·cia** f (-ce) balance, scale; **bilancia commerciale** balance of trade; **bilan-**

**cia dei pagamenti** balance of payments ‖ **Bilancia** f (astr) Libra
**bilanciare** §128 tr & ref to balance
**bilancière** m balance; balance wheel; rope-walker's balancing rod
**bilàn·cio** m (-ci) balance; **bilancio consuntivo** balance sheet; **bilancio preventivo** budget; **fare il bilancio** to balance; to strike a balance
**bile** f bile; **rodersi dalla bile** to burn with anger
**bìlia** f billiard ball; marble; (billiards) pocket
**biliardino** m pocket billiards; pinball machine
**biliardo** m billiards
**biliare** adj bile; gall (stone)
**bili·co** m (-chi) balance, equipoise; **in bilico** in balance; **tenere in bilico** to balance
**bilìngue** adj bilingual
**bilióne** m billion; trillion (Brit)
**bilió·so -sa** [s] adj bilious
**bim·bo -ba** mf child
**bimensile** adj bimonthly
**bimèstre** m period of two months
**bimotóre** adj twin-engine ‖ m twin-engine plane
**binà·rio -ria** (-ri -rie) adj binary ‖ m (rr) track; **binario morto** (rr) siding; **uscire dai binari** (rr) to run off the track; (fig) to go astray
**bina·to -ta** adj binary; twin (e.g., guns)
**binda** f (aut) jack
**binòcolo** m binoculars; **binocolo da teatro** opera glasses
**binò·mio -mia** (-mi -mie) adj binomial ‖ m binomial; couple, pair
**biòccolo** m wad (of cotton); flake (of snow); flock (of wool)
**biochìmi·co -ca** (-ci -che) adj biochemical ‖ m biochemist ‖ f biochemistry
**biodegradàbile** adj biodegradable
**biofìsica** f biophysics
**biografìa** f biography
**biogràfi·co -ca** adj (-ci -che) biographic(al)
**biògra·fo -fa** mf biographer
**biologìa** f biology
**biòlo·go** m (-gi) biologist
**biondeggiare** §290 (biondéggio) intr to be or become blond; to ripen (said of grain)
**bión·do -da** adj blond, fair ‖ m blond; blondness ‖ f blonde
**biopsìa** f biopsy
**biòssido** m dioxide
**bipartìti·co -ca** adj (-ci -che) two-party, bipartisan
**biparti·to -ta** adj bipartite ‖ m two-party government
**bìpede** adj & m biped
**bipènne** f double-bitted ax
**biplano** m biplane
**bipósto** adj invar having seats for two ‖ m two-seater
**birba** f rascal, rogue
**birbante** m scoundrel, rascal; (joc) madcap, wild young fellow
**birbanterìa** f knavery; trick
**birbonata** f trick

**birbó·ne -na** *adj* wicked ‖ *mf* rascal, rogue, scoundrel

**bireattóre** *m* twin jet

**birichinata** *f* prank

**birichi·no -na** *adj* prankish; spirited ‖ *mf* rogue; urchin

**birillo** *m* pin; **birilli** ninepins; tenpins

**Birmània, la** Burma

**birra** *f* beer; **birra chiara** light beer; **birra scura** dark beer

**bir·ràio** *m* (-rài) brewer; beer distributor

**birrerìa** *f* brewery; tavern; beer saloon

**bis** *adj invar*—**treno bis** (rr) second section ‖ *m* (bis) encore ‖ *interj* encore!

**bisàc·cia** *f* (-ce) knapsack; saddlebag; bag (*of mendicant friar*)

**Bisànzio** *m* Byzantium

**bisa·vo -va** *mf* great-grandparent; ancestor ‖ *m* great-grandfather ‖ *f* great-grandmother

**bisbèti·co -ca** (-ci -che) *adj* shrewish; crotchety; cantankerous ‖ *f* (fig) shrew

**bisbigliare** §280 *tr & intr* to whisper

**bisbì·glio** *m* (-gli) whisper

**bisbòccia** *f*—**fare bisboccia** to revel

**bisboccióne** *m* reveler

**bis·ca** *f* (-che) gambling house

**Biscàglia** *f* Biscay, e.g., **Baia di Biscaglia** Bay of Biscay; **la Biscaglia** Biscay

**biscaglina** *f* (naut) Jacob's ladder

**biscazzière** *m* gaming-house operator; habitué of a gaming house; marker (*at billiards*)

**bìschero** *m* (mus) peg

**bi·scia** *f* (-sce) snake; **biscia d'acqua** water snake

**biscottare (biscòtto)** *tr* to toast

**biscotterìa** *f* cookie factory; cookie store

**biscottièra** *f* cookie jar

**biscottifi·cio** *m* (-ci) cookie factory

**biscòt·to -ta** *adj* twice-baked ‖ *m* cookie

**biscròma** *f* (mus) demisemiquaver

**bisdòsso** *m*—**a bisdosso** bareback

**bisecare** [s] §197 (**bìseco**) *tr* to bisect

**bisènso** [s] *m* double meaning

**bisessuale** [s] *adj* bisexual

**bisestile** *adj* leap (*year*)

**bisettimanale** [s] *adj* biweekly

**bisettrice** [s] *f* bisector

**bisezióne** [s] *f* bisection

**bisìlla·bo -ba** [s] *adj* disyllabic

**bislac·co -ca** *adj* (-chi -che) queer, extravagant

**bislun·go -ga** *adj* (-ghi -ghe) oblong

**bismuto** *m* bismuth

**bisnòn·no -na** *mf* great-grandparent; **bisnonni** ancestors ‖ *m* great-grandfather ‖ *f* great-grandmother

**bisógna** *f* (lit) task, job

**bisognare (bisógna)** *intr* (with *dat*) to need, e.g., **gli bisognavano tre litri di benzina** he needed three liters of gasoline ‖ *impers*—**bisogna** + *inf* it is necessary to, e.g., **bisogna partire** it is necessary to leave; **bisogna che** + *subj* must, to have to, e.g., **bisogna che me ne vada** I must go,

I have to go; **bisognando** if need be; **non bisogna** one should not; **più che non bisogna** more than necessary

**bisognévole** *adj* needy

**bisógno** *m* need; want, lack; **aver bisogno di** to need; **c'è bisogno di** there is need of; **se ci fosse bisogno** if need be

**bisognó·so -sa** *adj* needy ‖ **i bisognosi** the needy

**bisolfato** [s] *m* bisulfate

**bisolfito** [s] *m* bisulfite

**bisolfuro** [s] *m* bisulfide

**bisónte** *m* bison

**bistec·ca** *f* (-che) beefsteak, steak; **bistecca al sangue** rare steak

**bisticciare** §128 *intr & ref* to quarrel, bicker

**bistìc·cio** *m* (-ci) quarrel, bickering; play on words, pun

**bistrattare** *tr* to mistreat

**bìstu·ri** *m* (-ri) bistouri, surgical knife

**bisul·co -ca** [s] *adj* (-chi -che) cloven

**bisun·to -ta** *adj* greasy

**bitagliènte** *adj* double-edged

**bitórzolo** *m* wart (*on humans, plants, or animals*); pimple (*on human face*)

**bitta** *f* (naut) bollard

**bitume** *m* bitumen, asphalt

**bituminó·so -sa** [s] *adj* bituminous

**bivaccare** §197 *intr* to bivouac; to spend the night

**bivac·co** *m* (-chi) bivouac

**bi·vio** *m* (-vi) fork (*of road*); **essere al bivio** (fig) to be at the crossroads

**bizanti·no -na** [dz] *adj* Byzantine

**bizza** [ddzz] *f* tantrum; **fare le bizze** to go into a tantrum

**bizzarrìa** [ddzz] *f* extravagance, oddity

**bizzar·ro -ra** [ddzz] *adj* bizarre, odd; skittish (*e.g., horse*)

**bizzèffe** [ddzz] *adv*— **a bizzeffe** plenty, in abundance

**bizzó·so -sa** [ddzz] [s] *adj* irritable

**blandire** §176 *tr* to blandish, coax; to soothe, mitigate

**blandìzie** *fpl* blandishment

**blan·do -da** *adj* bland

**blasfemare (blasfèmo)** *tr & intr* to blaspheme

**blasfè·mo -ma** *adj* blasphemous

**blasona·to -ta** *adj* emblazoned

**blasóne** *m* coat of arms, blazon

**blaterare (blàtero)** *intr* to babble

**blatta** *f* water bug, cockroach

**blenoraggìa** *f* gonorrhea

**blè·so -sa** *adj* lisping

**blindàg·gio** *m* (-gi) armor

**blindare** *tr* to armor

**bloccare** §197 (**blòcco**) *tr* to block; to blockade; to stop; to jam; to close up; to freeze (*e.g., prices*); (sports) to block ‖ *intr*—**bloccare su** to vote as a block for ‖ *ref* to stop

**blòc·co** *m* (-chi) block; blockade; notebook, pad; freezing (*e.g., of wages*); **in blocco** in bulk

**bloc-notes** *m* (-notes) notebook

**blu** *adj invar & m* blue

**blua·stro -stra** *adj* bluish

**bluffare** *intr* to bluff

**blusa** *f* blouse; smock

bò•a *m* (-a) boa || *f* buoy
boà•rio -ria *adj* (-ri -rie) cattle
boa•ro -ra *adj* ox || *m* stable boy
boato *m* roar; **boato sonico** sonic boom
bobina *f* spool (*of thread*); coil (*of wire*); reel (*of movie film; of magnetic tape*); roll (*of film*); cylinder, bobbin; (elec) coil; **bobina d'accensione** spark coil
bóc•ca *f* (-che) mouth; nozzle; muzzle (*of gun*); pit (*of the stomach*); opening; straits; pass; **a bocca aperta** agape; **bocca da fuoco** cannon; **di buona bocca** easily pleased; **in bocca al lupo!** good luck!; **per bocca** orally; **rimanere a bocca asciutta** to be foiled; to be left high and dry; **tieni la bocca chiusa!** shut up!
boccaccé•sco -sca *adj* (-schi -sche) written by or in the style of Boccaccio; bawdy, licentious
boccàc•cia *f* (-ce) ugly mouth; grimace; **fare le boccacce** to make faces
boccà•glio *m* (-gli) nozzle (*of hose or pipe*); mouthpiece (*of megaphone*)
boccale *adj* oral || *m* jug, tankard
boccapòrto *m* hatch; port; mouth (*of oven or furnace*); **chiudere i boccaporti** to batten the hatches
boccascè•na *m* (-na) proscenium, front (*of stage*)
boccata *f* mouthful; **andare a prendere una boccata d'aria** to go out for a breath of fresh air
boccétta *f* small bottle, vial; small billiard ball
boccheggiante *adj* gasping; moribund
boccheggiare §290 (bocchéggio) *intr* to gasp
bocchétta *f* nozzle (*of sprinkling can*); mouthpiece (*of wind instrument*); opening (*of drainage or ventilation system*); **bocchetta stradale** manhole
bocchino *m* cigarette holder; mouthpiece (*of cigarette or of musical instrument*)
bòc•cia *f* (-ce) decanter; ball (*for bowling*); **bocce** bowls
bocciare §128 (bòccio) *tr* to score (*at bowling*); to reject (*a proposal*); to flunk (*a student*)
bocciatura *f* failure
boccino *m* jack (*at bowls*)
bocciòlo *m* bud
bóccola *f* buckle; earring; (mach) bushing
bocconcino *m* morsel; (culin) stew
boccóne *m* mouthful; piece; morsel; **buttar giù un boccone amaro** to swallow a bitter pill; **levarsi il boccone di bocca** to take the bread out of one's mouth (to help someone); **mangiare un boccone** to have a bite || **bocconi** *adv* flat on one's face
boè•mo -ma *adj & mf* Bohemian
boè•ro -ra *adj & m* Boer
bofonchiare §287 (bofónchio) *intr* to snort, grumble
bò•ia *m* (-ia) hangman, executioner
boiata *f* (slang) infamy; (slang) trash
boicottàg•gio *m* (-gi) boycott
boicottare (boicòtto) *tr* to boycott

bòl•gia *f* (-ge) pit (*in hell*)
bólide *m* (astr) bolide, fireball; (aut) racer; (joc) lummox; **andare come un bolide** to go like a flash
bolina *f* (naut) bowline; **di bolina** (naut) close-hauled
bolivia•no -na *adj & mf* Bolivian
bólla *f* bubble; blister; ticket; **bolla di consegna** receipt; **bolla di spedizione** delivery ticket; **bolla di sapone** soap bubble; **bolla papale** papal bull
bollare (bóllo) *tr* to stamp; to brand
bolla•to -ta *adj* stamped; sealed
bollatura *f* stamp; brand; postage
bollènte *adj* boiling, scalding hot
bollétta *f* ticket; receipt; bill; **essere in bolletta** (coll) to be broke
bollettà•rio *m* (-ri) receipt book
bollettino *m* bulletin; receipt; **bollettino dei prezzi correnti** price list; **bollettino di versamento** (com) deposit ticket; **bollettino meteorologico** weather forecast
bollire (bóllo) *tr & intr* to boil
bolli•to -ta *adj* boiled || *m* boiled beef
bollitura *f* boiling
bóllo *m* mark, cancellation; revenue stamp; postmark; seal; **bollo a freddo** seal (*embossed*); **bollo postale** cancellation, postmark
bollóre *m* boiling; sultriness; (fig) passion, excitement; **alzare il bollore** to begin to boil
bolló•so -sa [s] *adj* blistery
bolscevì•co -ca *adj & mf* (-chi -che) Bolshevik
bolscevismo *m* Bolshevism
ból•so -sa *adj* broken-winded (*horse*); asthmatic
bòma *f* (naut) boom
bómba *f* bomb; bubble gum; fireworks; (aer) double loop; (journ) scandal; **bomba a idrogeno** hydrogen bomb; **bomba a mano** hand grenade; **bomba antisommergibile** depth charge; **bomba a orologeria** time bomb; **bomba atomica** atom bomb; **bomba H** (acca) H bomb; **tornare a bomba** (fig) to get back to the point
bombàg•gio *m* swelling (*of a spoiled can of food*)
bombardaménto *m* bombing, bombardment
bombardare *tr* to bomb, bombard; to besiege (*with questions*)
bombardière *m* (aer) bomber; (mil) artilleryman
bombétta *f* derby (*hat*)
bómbola *f* bottle, cylinder; **bombola d'ossigeno** oxygen tank
bombonièra *f* candy box
bomprèsso *m* (naut) bowsprit
bonàc•cia *f* (-ce) calm; calm sea; (fig) normalcy; (com) stagnation
bonacció•ne -na *adj* good-hearted, good-natured
bonarie•tà *f* (-tà) kindheartedness, good nature
bonà•rio -ria *adj* (-ri -rie) kindhearted, good-natured
boncinèllo *m* hasp
bonìfi•ca *f* (-che) reclamation; re-

claimed land; improvement (*e.g., of morals*); clearing of mines; (metallurgy) hardening and tempering
**bonificare** §197 (**bonìfico**) *tr* to reclaim; to discount, make a reduction of; to clear of mines
**bonifi·co** *m* (**-ci**) discount
**bonomìa** *f* good nature; simple-heartedness
**bon·tà** *f* (**-tà**) goodness; kindness; **avere la bontà di** to be kind enough to; **bontà mia** (**sua, etc.**) through my (his, her, etc.) kindness; **per mia** (**sua, etc.**) **bontà** through my (his, her, etc.) efforts
**bòra** *f* northeast wind
**borace** *m* borax
**borbogliare** §280 (**borbóglio**) *intr* to gurgle; to rumble
**borbòni·co -ca** (**-ci -che**) *adj* Bourbon ‖ *m* Bourbonist
**borbottare** (**borbòtto**) *tr* to mutter ‖ *intr* to mutter; to gurgle; to rumble (*said, e.g., of thunder*)
**borbottì·o** *m* (**-i**) mutter; gurgle; rumble
**bòrchia** *f* upholsterer's nail; boss, stud
**bordare** (**bórdo**) *tr* to border, hem
**bordata** *f* (naut) tack; (nav) broadside
**bordatura** *f* border, hem
**bordeggiare** §290 (**bordéggio**) *intr* (naut) to tack
**bordèllo** *m* brothel
**borde·rò** *m* (**-rò**) list; note; (theat) box office, receipts
**bórdo** *m* side (*of ship*); border, hem; edge, rim; (naut) tack; (naut) board; **a bordo** on board; **a bordo di** on board; on, in; **bordo d'entrata** (aer) leading edge; **bordo d'uscita** (aer) trailing edge; **d'alto bordo** (naut) big, sea-going; (fig) high-toned; **virare di bordo** (naut) to change course
**bordóne** *m* staff; bass stop (*of organ*); drone (*of insect*); **tener bordone a** (mus) to accompany; (fig) to hold the bag for
**bordura** *f* hem, edge; rim
**boreale** *adj* northern, boreal
**borgata** *f* hamlet, village
**borghése** [*s*] *adj* middle-class ‖ *mf* bourgeois, person of the middle class; civilian; **in borghese** in civilian clothes; in plainclothes
**borghesìa** *f* bourgeoisie, middle class; **alta borghesia** upper middle class
**bór·go** *m* (**-ghi**) borough; small town; suburb
**borgógna** *m* Burgundy (*wine*) ‖ **la Borgogna** Burgundy
**borgognóne** *m* iceberg
**borgomastro** *m* burgomaster
**bòria** *f* haughtiness, vainglory
**bòri·co -ca** *adj* (**-ci -che**) boric
**borió·so -sa** [*s*] *adj* haughty, puffed-up; blustery
**bòro** *m* boron
**borotal·co** *m* (**-chi**) talcum powder
**bórra** *f* flock (*for pillows*); (fig) rubbish, filler
**borràc·cia** *f* (**-ce**) canteen (*e.g., for carrying water*)

**bórro** *m* gully
**bórsa** *f* bag; pouch; bourse, exchange; (sports) purse; **borsa da viaggio** traveling bag; **borsa dell'acqua** hot-water bag; **borsa della spesa** shopping bag; **borsa di ghiaccio** ice bag; **borsa di studio** scholarship; **borsa merci** commodity exchange; **borsa nera** black market; **borsa valori** stock exchange; **essere di borsa larga** to be generous; **o la borsa o la vita!** your money or your life!; **pagare di borsa propria** to pay out of one's own pocket
**borsaiòlo** *m* pickpocket
**borsanéra** *f* black market
**borsaneri·sta** *mf* (**-sti -ste**) black marketeer
**borseggiare** §290 (**borséggio**) *tr* to pick the pocket of; to rob
**borseggia·tóre -trice** *mf* pickpocket
**borség·gio** *m* (**-gi**) theft
**borsellino** *m* purse
**borsétta** *f* handbag, pocketbook
**borsétto** *m* man's purse
**borsi·sta** *mf* (**-sti -ste**) recipient of a scholarship; stockbroker
**borsìsti·co -ca** *adj* (**-ci -che**) stock-exchange
**borsite** *f* bursitis
**boscàglia** *f* thicket, underbrush
**boscaiòlo** *m* woodcutter
**boscheréc·cio -cia** *adj* (**-ci -ce**) wood, woodland; rustic; pastoral
**boschétto** *m* coppice, copse
**boschi·vo -va** *adj* wooded, wood
**bò·sco** *m* (**-schi**) woods, forest; **bosco ceduo** or **da taglio** tree farm
**boscó·so -sa** [*s*] *adj* wooded, woody
**bòsforo** *m* (lit) straits ‖ **Bosforo** *m* Bosphorus
**bòsso** *m* boxwood
**bòssolo** *m* box; cartridge case
**botàni·co -ca** (**-ci -che**) *adj* botanic(al) ‖ *m* botanist ‖ *f* botany
**bòtola** *f* trap door
**bòtolo** *m* small snarling dog
**bòtta** *f* hit; bump; rumble (*e.g., of an explosion*); thrust, lunging (*in fencing*); (fig) disaster; **botta dritta** (fencing) lunge; **botta e risposta** give-and-take; **botte da orbi** severe beating
**bot·tàio** *m* (**-tài**) cooper
**bótte** *f* barrel, cask, casket
**botté·ga** *f* (**-ghe**) store, shop; **chiudere bottega** to close up shop
**botte·gàio -gàia** (**-gài -gàie**) *adj* store, shop ‖ *mf* storekeeper, shopkeeper
**botteghino** *m* box office; lottery agency
**bottiglia** *f* bottle; **bottiglia Molotov** Molotov cocktail
**bottiglierìa** *f* wine store, liquor store
**bottino** *m* booty, spoil; capture; cesspool; sewage
**bòtto** *m* hit, bump; explosion; noise; toll (*of bell*); **di botto** all of a sudden
**bottoncino** *m* small button; cuff button; **bottoncino di rosa** rosebud
**bottóne** *m* button; stud; bud; **attaccare un bottone a** (fig) to buttonhole; **botton d'oro** (bot) buttercup; **bottone automatico** snap; **bottone della**

**luce** (elec) pushbutton; **bottoni gemelli** cuff links; **bottoni gustativi** taste buds

**bottonièra** f row of buttons; buttonhole; (elec) panel (*with buttons*)

**bova·ro -ra** adj & m var of **boaro**

**bovile** m ox stable

**bovi·no -na** adj cattle, cow; bovine ‖ m bovine

**box** m (**box**) locker (*e.g., in a station*); box stall (*for a horse*); pit (*in auto racing*); garage (*on the ground floor of a split-level*); play pen

**boxare** (**bòxo**) intr to box

**boxe** f boxing

**bòzza** f stud, boss; bump (*caused by blow*); rough copy, draft; **bozze** (typ) galleys, galley proof

**bozzèllo** m (mach) block and tackle

**bozzétto** m sketch

**bòzzolo** m cocoon; lump (*of flour*)

**bra·ca** f (**-che**) safety belt; (naut) sling; **brache** (archaic) breeches; (joc) trousers

**braccare** §197 tr to stalk; to hunt out

**braccétto—a braccetto** arm in arm

**bracciale** m armlet, armband; arm rest

**braccialétto** m bracelet

**bracciante** m laborer

**bracciata** f armful; stroke (*in swimming*); **bracciata a rana** breaststroke; **bracciata sul dorso** backstroke

**bràc·cio** m (**-cia** fpl) arm (*of body*); unit of length (*about 60 centimeters*); **a braccia aperte** with open arms; **avere le braccia legate** to have one's hands tied; **braccia** laborers; **braccio destro** right-hand man; **braccio di ferro** Indian wrestling; **fare a braccio di ferro** to play at Indian wrestling; **sentirsi cascare le braccia** to lose courage ‖ m (**-ci**) arm (*e.g., of sea, chair, lamp, etc.*); beam (*of balance*); **braccio diretto** cutoff (*of river*)

**bracciòlo** m arm; arm rest; banister

**brac·co** m (**-chi**) hound, beagle

**bracconàg·gio** m (**-gi**) poaching

**bracconière** m poacher

**brace** f embers; (coll) charcoal; **farsi di brace** to blush

**brachétta** f flap (*of trousers*); (bb) joint; **brachette** shorts

**brachière** m truss (*for hernia*)

**bracière** m brazier

**braciòla** f chop, cutlet

**bra·do -da** adj wild, untamed

**bra·go** m (**-ghi**) (lit) mud, slime

**brama** f ardent desire; covetousness; longing

**bramare** tr to desire intensely; to covet; to long for

**bramino** m Brahmin

**bramire** §176 intr to roar; to bell (*said of a deer*)

**bramito** m bell (*of deer*)

**bramosìa** [s] f covetousness; greed

**bramó·so -sa** [s] adj (lit) covetous, greedy

**bran·ca** f (**-che**) branch (*of tree*); flight (*of stairs*); **branche** (poet) clutches

**brànchia** f gill

**brancicare** §197 (**bràncico**) tr to finger, handle ‖ intr to grope

**bran·co** m (**-chi**) flock, herd; (pej) crowd

**brancolare** (**bràncolo**) intr to grope

**branda** f cot

**brandèllo** m tatter, shred

**brandire** §176 tr to brandish

**brando** m (lit) sword

**brano** m shred, bit; excerpt; **cadere a brani** to fall apart; **fare a brani** to tear apart

**brasare** tr to braze (*to solder with brass*); (culin) to braise

**brasile** m brazil (*nut*) ‖ **il Brasile** Brazil

**brasilia·no -na** adj & mf Brazilian

**bravàc·cio** m (**-ci**) braggart, swaggerer

**bravare** tr to challenge; to threaten ‖ intr to brag

**bravata** f swagger, bluster; boast; stunt

**bra·vo -va** adj good, able; honest; good-hearted; brave; **alla brava** rapidly; **bravo ragazzo** good boy; **fare il bravo** to boast, be a braggart ‖ m mercenary soldier; bravo, hired assassin ‖ **bravo!** interj well done!, bravo!

**bravura** f ability; bravery; bravura

**brèc·cia** f (**-ce**) breach, gap; crushed stone

**brefotrò·fio** m (**-fi**) foundling hospital

**Bretagna, la** Britanny

**bretèlla** f suspenders; strap, shoulder strap

**brètone** adj Breton; Arthurian

**brève** adj brief, short; **in breve** in a nutshell; **per farla breve** in short ‖ m (eccl) brief ‖ adv (lit) in short

**brevettare** (**brevétto** ) tr to patent

**brevétto** m patent; (aer) license; (obs) commission

**brevià·rio** m (**-ri**) compendium; handbook, vade mecum; (eccl) breviary

**brevi·tà** f (**-tà**) brevity

**brézza** [ddzz] f breeze

**brezzare** (**brézzo**) [ddzz] tr to winnow ‖ intr to blow gently

**bricchétta** f briquet

**bric·co** m (**-chi**) kettle, pot

**bricconata** f rascality

**briccó·ne -na** mf rascal

**bricconerìa** f rascality

**brìciola** f crumb; **ridurre in briciole** to crumb, crumble

**brìciolo** m bit, fragment; (fig) least bit; **andare in bricioli** to crumble; **mandare in bricioli** to crumble

**bri·ga** f (**-ghe**) worry, trouble, **attaccar briga** to pick a fight; **darsi la briga di** to worry about; **trovarsi in una briga** to be in trouble

**brigadière** m noncommissioned officer (*in carabinieri*); (hist) brigadier

**brigantàg·gio** m (**-gi**) brigandage

**brigante** m brigand

**brigantino** m (naut) brig, brigantine; **brigantino goletta** (naut) brigantine

**brigare** §209 tr to plot; to scheme to get ‖ intr to plot, scheme

**brigata** f company; (mil) brigade

**brì·glia** f (**-glie**) bridle; harness (*for holding baby*); (naut) bobstay; **a briglia sciolta** at full speed; **tirare le briglie a** to bridle

**brillante** adj brilliant ‖ m cut diamond

**brillare** *tr* to husk, hull (*rice*); to explode (*e.g., a mine*) ‖ *intr* to shine, sparkle; **far brillare** to explode, blow up

**brillì·o** *m* (**-ìi**) shine, sparkle

**bril·lo -la** *adj* tipsy

**brina** *f* frost

**brinare** *tr* to frost; to turn (*e.g., hair*) gray ‖ *impers* (ESSERE)—**è brinato** there was frost; **brina** there is frost

**brinata** *f* frost

**brindare** *intr* to toast; **brindare alla salute di** to toast

**brìndisi** *m* (**-si**) toast; pledge; **fare un brindisi a** to toast

**brì·o** *m* (**-i**) sprightliness, liveliness, verve, spirit

**briò·scia** *f* (**-sce**) brioche

**briò·so -sa** [s] *adj* sprightly, lively

**brìscola** *f* briscola (*game*); trump (*card*)

**britànni·co -ca** *adj* (**-ci -che**) British, Britannic

**britan·no -na** *adj* British ‖ *mf* Briton

**brìvido** *m* shake, shiver; thrill; **brìvido di freddo** chill, shiver

**brizzola·to -ta** *adj* grizzled

**bròc·ca** *f* (**-che**) pitcher; pitcherful; shoot, bud; hobnail

**broccatèllo** *m* brocatel

**broccato** *m* brocade

**bròc·co** *m* (**-chi**) twig; shoot; center pin (*of shield or target*); (coll) nag; **dar nel brocco** to hit the bull's eye

**bròccolo** *m* (bot) broccoli; **bròccoli** broccoli (*as food*)

**bròda** *f* slop, thin or tasteless soup; mud

**brodàglia** *f* slop

**brodétto** *m* fish soup

**bròdo** *m* broth; **andar in brodo di giuggiole** (fig) to swoon with joy; **brodo in dadi** cube bouillon; **brodo ristretto** consommé

**brodó·so -sa** [s] *adj* thin, watery (*soup*)

**brogliàc·cio** *m* (**-ci**) (com) daybook, first draft; (naut) first draft of logbook

**brò·glio** *m* (**-gli**) plot, intrigue; maneuver; **broglio elettorale** political maneuver

**bròlo** *m* (archaic) garden; (lit) garland

**bromìdri·co -ca** *adj* (**-ci -che**) hydrobromic

**bròmo** *m* bromine

**bromuro** *m* bromide

**bronchite** *f* bronchitis

**brón·cio** *m* (**-ci**) pout, pouting; **fare il broncio** to sulk; **tenere il broncio a** to harbor a grudge against

**brón·co** *m* (**-chi**) bronchial tube; thorny branch; ramification (*of antlers*)

**brontolare** (**bróntolo**) *tr* to grumble (*to express with a grumble*); to grumble at ‖ *intr* to grumble, mutter; to rumble; to gurgle (*said of water*)

**brontolì·o** *m* (**-i**) grumble, mutter; rumble; gurgle

**brontoló·ne -na** *mf* grumbler; curmudgeon

**bronzare** [dz] (**brónzo**) *tr* to bronze

**brónze·o -a** [dz] *adj* bronze; tanned

**bronzina** [dz] *f* little bell; (mach) bearing; (mach) bushing

**brónzo** [dz] *m* bronze

**brossura** *f* brochure; **in brossura** paperback

**brucare** §197 *tr* to browse, graze

**bruciacchiare** §287 *tr* to singe

**bruciante** *adj* burning

**bruciapélo** *m*—**a bruciapelo** point-blank

**bruciare** §128 *tr* to burn; to burn down; to singe; to scorch; to cauterize (*a wound*); (sports) to overcome with a burst of speed; **bruciare le tappe** to go straight ahead; to press on ‖ *intr* (ESSERE) to burn; to smart, sting ‖ *ref* to burn (*e.g., one's fingers*); to get burnt; to blow (*one's brains*) out; to burn out (*said of an electric light or fuse*); **bruciarsi i vascelli alle spalle** to burn one's bridges behind one

**bruciatìc·cio** *m* (**-ci**) burnt material; **sapere di bruciaticcio** to taste burnt

**brucia·to -ta** *adj* burnt; burnt out ‖ *m* burnt taste or smell ‖ *f* roast chestnut

**bruciatóre** *m* burner; heater; **bruciatore a gas** gas burner; **bruciatore a nafta** oil burner

**bruciatorì·sta** *m* (**-sti**) oil burner mechanic

**bruciatura** *f* burn

**brucióre** *m* burning; burn; inflammation; **bruciore agli occhi** eye inflammation; **bruciore di stomaco** heartburn

**bru·co** *m* (**-chi**) caterpillar; worm

**brùffolo** *m* (coll) small boil

**brughièra** *f* waste land; heath

**brulicare** §197 (**brùlico**) *intr* to crawl; to swarm (*e.g., with bees*); to teem (*with people*)

**brulichì·o** *m* (**-i**) crawling; swarming; teeming

**brùl·lo -la** *adj* barren, bare

**bruma** *f* shipworm; (lit) fog; (lit) winter

**bruna·stro -stra** *adj* brownish

**brunire** §176 *tr* to burnish

**bru·no -na** *adj* brown; dark (*bread; complexion*) ‖ *m* brown; dark; brunet; **vestire a bruno** to dress in black ‖ *f* brunette

**bru·sca** *f* (**-sche**) horse brush; **con le brusche** curtly

**bruschézza** *f* brusqueness

**bruschino** *m* scrub brush

**bru·sco -sca** (**-schi -sche**) *adj* sour; curt, gruff; sharp (*weather*); dangerous; sudden ‖ *m* twig ‖ *f* see **brusca**

**brùscolo** *m* speck, mote; **fare di un bruscolo una trave** to make a mountain out of a molehill

**brusì·o** *m* (**-i**) buzz, buzzing; (fig) whispering (*gossip*)

**brutale** *adj* brutal

**brutali·tà** *f* (**-tà**) brutality

**brutalizzare** [ddzz] *tr* to brutalize

**bru·to -ta** *adj & m* brute

**brutta** *f* rough copy

**bruttare** *tr* (lit) to soil

**bruttézza** *f* ugliness; (fig) lowliness

**brut·to -ta** *adj* ugly, homely; foul (*weather*); bad (*news*); **alle brutte** at the worst; **con le brutte** harshly; **farla brutta a** to play a mean trick on;

**guardare brutto** to look irritated; **vedersela brutta** to foresee trouble ‖ *m* worst; bad weather ‖ *f* see **brutta**
**bruttura** *f* ugliness
**bùbbola** *f* lie; trifle
**bùbbolo** *m* jingle bell (*on horse*)
**bubbòni·co -ca** *adj* (*-ci -che*) bubonic
**bu·ca** *f* (*-che*) hole; pit; hollow; **buca cieca** trap (*for hunting*); **buca del biliardo** pocket; **buca delle lettere** mailbox; **buca del suggeritore** prompter's box; **buca sepolcrale** grave
**bucané·ve** *m* (*-ve*) snowdrop
**bucanière** *m* buccaneer
**bucare** §197 *tr* to pierce; to prick; to puncture (*a tire*)
**bucato** *m* wash; laundry; **di bucato** freshly laundered; **fare il bucato in famiglia** (fig) to not air one's family affairs, to not wash one's dirty linen in public
**bucatura** *f* piercing; puncturing; puncture; **bucatura di una gomma** flat tire
**bùc·cia** *f* (*-ce*) rind, peel; skin (*of a person; of fruit and vegetables*); tender bark; **fare le bucce a** (coll) to thwart, frustrate
**bucherellare (bucherèllo)** *tr* to riddle
**bu·co** *m* (*-chi*) hole; **fare un buco nell'acqua** to fail miserably
**bucòli·co -ca** *adj* (*-ci -che*) bucolic, pastoral
**Budda** *m* Buddha
**buddismo** *m* Buddhism
**buddi·sta** *mf* (*-sti -ste*) Buddhist
**budèl·lo** *m* (*-la* *fpl*) bowel; **budella** bowels; guts ‖ *m* (*-li*) casing (*for salami*); pipe; blind alley
**budino** *m* pudding
**bùe** *m* (**buòi**) ox (*for draft*); steer (*for meat*); **bue muschiato** musk ox
**bùfalo** *m* buffalo
**bufèra** *f* storm; **bufera di neve** snowstorm; **bufera di pioggia** rainstorm; **bufera di vento** windstorm
**buffa** *f* cowl; gust of wind; (archaic) trick, jest
**buffare** *tr* to huff (*at checkers*) ‖ *intr* to joke; (archaic) to blow
**buffetterìa** *f* (mil) accouterments
**buffétto** *m* tap, slight blow
**buf·fo -fa** *adj* funny, comical ‖ *m* gust of wind; comic ‖ *f* see **buffa**
**buffonata** *f* buffoonery; antics
**buffóne** *m* buffoon, clown; (hist) jester; **buffone di corte** court jester
**buffonerìa** *f* buffoonery
**buffoné·sco -sca** *adj* (*-schi -sche*) clownish
**bugìa** *f* lie; candlestick; **bugia ufficiosa** white lie
**bugiar·do -da** *adj* lying, false ‖ *mf* liar
**bugigàttolo** *m* cubbyhole
**bugna** *f* ashlar; (naut) clew
**bugnato** *m* ashlar; (archit) boss
**bù·io -ia** (*pl -i -ie*) *adj* dark ‖ *m* darkness; **buio pesto** pitch dark
**bulbo** *m* bulb
**bùlga·ro -ra** *adj* & *mf* Bulgarian ‖ *m* Russian leather
**bulinare** *tr* to engrave
**bulino** *m* burin

**bullétta** *f* tack
**bullonare (bullóno)** *tr* to bolt
**bullóne** *m* bolt
**buon** *adj* apocopated form of **buono,** used before masculine singular nouns except those beginning with impure s, z, gn, ps, and x
**buon'** *adj* apocopated form of **buona** used before feminine singular nouns beginning with a vowel, e.g., **buon'ora**
**buonagràzia** *f* (**buonegràzie**) courtesy, good manners; **con Sua buonagrazia** with your permission
**buonamano** *f* (**buonemani**) tip, gratuity
**buonànima** *f* departed; **la buonanima di** the late lamented
**buonavò·glia** *m* (*-glia*) intern (*in a hospital*); (coll) lazybones ‖ *f* good will
**buoncostume** *m* morals
**buongu·stàio** *m* (*-stài*) gourmet; connoisseur
**buò·no -na** *adj* good; kind; high (*society*); cheap (*price*); **alla buona** plainly; without ceremony; **buono a nulla** good-for-nothing; **con le buone** kindly, gently; **che Dio la mandi buona** a may God be kind with; **essere in buona con** to be on good terms with ‖ *m* good person; bond; ticket; **buono a nulla** ne'er-do-well; **buono del tesoro** government bond; **buono di consegna** delivery order; **buono premio** trading stamp
**buonsènso** *m* common sense
**buontempó·ne -na** *adj* jolly ‖ *m* playboy ‖ *f* fun-loving girl; playgirl
**buonumóre** *m* good humor, good cheer
**buonuscìta** *f* indemnity, bonus; severance pay
**burattare** *tr* to sift
**buratti·nàio** *m* (*-nài*) puppeteer; puppet maker
**burattinata** *f* clowning
**burattino** *m* puppet
**buratto** *m* sifter, sifting machine
**burbanza** *f* haughtiness, arrogance
**burbanzó·so -sa** [s] *adj* haughty, arrogant
**bùrbe·ro -ra** *adj* gruff, surly
**bùr·chio** *m* (*-chi*) (naut) lighter
**burgun·do -da** *adj* & *mf* Burgundian
**burla** *f* joke, jest; prank; **mettere in burla** to ridicule; **fuori di burla** joking aside
**burlare** *tr* to ridicule ‖ *intr* to be joking ‖ *ref*—**burlarsi di** to make fun of
**burlé·sco -sca** *adj* (*-schi -sche*) funny; mocking; burlesque; jocose ‖ *m* burlesque; mock-heroic
**burletta** *f* joke, jest; **mettere in burletta** to ridicule
**burló·ne -na** *mf* joker, jester
**buròcrate** *m* bureaucrat
**burocràti·co -ca** *adj* (*-ci -che*) bureaucratic; clerical (*error*)
**burocrazìa** *f* bureaucracy; red tape
**burra·sca** *f* (*-sche*) storm
**burrascó·so -sa** [s] *adj* stormy
**burrièra** *f* butter dish
**burrifi·cio** *m* (*-ci*) butter factory, dairy
**burro** *m* butter
**burróne** *m* canyon, ravine
**burró·so -sa** [s] *adj* buttery

**buscare** §197 *tr* to get; to catch ‖ *intr* to be damaged ‖ *ref*—**buscarsi un malanno** to catch a cold

**busécchia** *f* casing (*for sausage*)

**busillis** *m*—**qui sta il busillis** here's the rub, that's the trouble

**bussa** *f* hit, blow; **venire alle busse** to come to blows

**bussare** *intr* to knock; **bussare a quattrini** (fig) to hit somebody for a loan

**bussata** *f* knock (*at the door*)

**bussa·tòio** *m* (-**tòi**) knocker

**bùssola** *f* sedan chair; door; revolving door; swinging door; ballot box; (mach) bushing; (aer & naut) compass; **perdere la bussola** to lose one's bearings

**bussolòtto** *m* dice box

**busta** *f* envelope; briefcase; **busta a finestrella** window envelope; **busta primo giorno** first-day cover; **in busta a parte** under separate cover

**bustapa·ga** *f* (-**ga**) pay envelope

**bustarèlla** *f* bribery; kickback

**bustina** *f* powder, dose; small envelope; (mil) cap, fatigue cap

**busto** *m* chest, trunk; bust; corset

**butirró·so** -**sa** [s] *adj* buttery

**buttafuò·ri** *m* (-**ri**) bouncer (*in a night club*); (theat) callboy; (naut) outrigger

**buttare** *tr* to throw; to waste (*e.g., time*); to give off (*e.g., smoke*); **buttar giù** to demolish; to swallow; (fig) to discredit; to jot down; **buttar via** to throw away; to cast aside ‖ *intr* to secrete, ooze ‖ *ref* to throw oneself; to let oneself fall; **buttarsi giù** (fig) to become downcast

**butterare** (**bùttero**) *tr* to pock, pit

**bùttero** *m* pockmark; cowboy

**buzzo** [ddzz] *m* (vulg) belly; **di buzzo buono** with energy; willingly

# C

**C, c** [t/ì] *m & f* third letter of the Italian alphabet

**càbala** *f* cabala; cabal, intrigue

**cabina** *f* cabin, stateroom; car, cage (*of elevator*); cockpit (*of airplane*); booth (*of telephone*); cab (*of locomotive*)

**cablàg·gio** *m* (-**gi**) (elec) cable (*in auto or radio*)

**cablare** *tr* to cable

**cablografare** (**cablògrafo**) *tr* to cable

**cablogram·ma** *m* (-**mi**) cablegram, cable

**cabotàg·gio** *m* (-**gi**) coasting trade, coastal traffic

**cabrare** *intr* to zoom

**cabrata** *f* zoom

**cacào** *m* cocoa

**cacasènno** *m* (slang) wiseacre

**cacatò·a** *m* (-**a**) cockatoo

**càc·cia** *m* (-**cia**) pursuit plane, fighter; (nav) destroyer ‖ *f* chase, hunt; pursuit; **caccia alle streghe** witch hunt

**cacciagióne** *f* small game; venison; kill (*e.g., of game birds*)

**cacciapiè·tre** *m* (-**tre**) (rr) cowcatcher

**cacciare** §128 *tr* to hunt; to chase; to rout; to send out; to stick, thrust; to utter (*e.g., a cry*); **cacciar fuori** to pull out; **cacciar via** to chase away ‖ *ref* to hide; to intrude; to get; to wind up; to thrust oneself; **cacciarsi negli affari di** to butt into the affairs of

**cacciasommergìbi·li** *m* (-**li**) subchaser, submarine chaser

**cacciata** *f* hunting party; expulsion

**cacciatóra** *f* hunting jacket; **alla cacciatora** (culin) stewed with herbs

**cacciatóre** *m* hunter; (aer) fighter pilot; **cacciatore di frodo** poacher; **cacciatore di teste** headhunter

**cacciatorpediniè·re** *m* (-**re**) destroyer

**cacciatrice** *f* huntress

**cacciavi·te** *m* (-**te**) screwdriver

**càccola** *f* gum (*on edge of eyelid*); (slang) snot

**caccoló·so** -**sa** [s] *adj* gummy (*eyelid*); (slang) snotty

**ca·chi** (-**chi**) *adj* khaki ‖ *m* Japanese persimmon; khaki

**cacic·co** *m* (-**chi**) Indian chief; boss (*in Latin America*)

**cà·cio** *m* (-**ci**) cheese; **come il cacio sui maccheroni** (coll) at the right moment

**cacofóni·co** -**ca** *adj* (-**ci** -**che**) cacophonous

**cac·tus** *m* (-**tus**) cactus

**cadau·no** -**na** *adj* each ‖ *pron* each one

**cadàvere** *m* corpse, cadaver

**cadavèri·co** -**ca** *adj* (-**ci** -**che**) cadaverous

**cadènte** *adj* falling (*star*); rickety (*house*); run-down, decrepit (*person*)

**cadènza** *f* cadence, rhythm; accent (*peculiar to a region*)

**cadére** §121 *intr* (ESSERE) to fall; to sink; to slough (*said, e.g., of crust*); to fail; (gram) to end; **cadere a proposito** to come in handy; to come at the right moment; **cadere dalle nuvole** to be dumfounded

**cadétto** *m* cadet

**càdmio** *m* cadmium

**caducità** *f* transiency, brevity

**cadu·co** -**ca** *adj* (-**ci** -**che**) fleeting; deciduous

**cadu·no** -**na** *adj & pron* var of **cadauno**

**cadu·to** -**ta** *adj* fallen; lost, gone astray; **i caduti** the fallen, the dead ‖ *f* fall; crash (*of stock market*); slump (*of prices*)

**caf·fè** *m* (-**fè**) coffee; café

**caffeina** *f* caffeine

**caffetteria** *f* cafeteria

**caffettièra** *f* coffeepot

**cafó·ne -na** *adj* loud, gaudy || *m* boor, lout

**cagionare (cagióno)** *tr* to cause, produce

**cagióne** *f* cause, reason; **a cagione di** because of

**cagionévole** *adj* sickly, delicate

**cagliare** §280 *tr, intr* (ESSERE) & *ref* to curdle, curd

**cagliata** *f* curd

**cà·glio** *m* (**-gli**) rennet

**cagna** *f* bitch

**cagnara** *f* barking (*of dogs*); uproar, confusion

**cagné·sco -sca** (**-schi -sche**) *adj* dog-like, doggish || *m*—**guardare in cagnesco** to look askance at; **stare in cagnesco con** to be angry with

**Caino** *m* Cain

**Càiro, il** Cairo

**cala** *f* cove; (naut) hold

**calabrése** [s] *adj* & *mf* Calabrian

**calabróne** *m* hornet

**calafatare** *tr* (naut) to caulk

**cala·màio** *m* (**-mài**) inkwell

**calamaro** *m* squid

**calamita** *f* magnet; (*mineral*) loadstone; (fig) magnet, attraction

**calami·tà** *f* (**-tà**) calamity, disaster

**calamitare** *tr* to magnetize

**calamitó·so -sa** [s] *adj* calamitous

**càlamo** *m* reed, quill

**calandra** *f* calender; (aut) grille

**calandrare** *tr* to calender

**calante** *adj* waning (*moon*)

**calàp·pio** *m* (**-pi**) snare; noose

**calapran·zi** *m* (**-zi**) dumbwaiter

**calare** *tr* to lower; to strike (*sails*) || *intr* (ESSERE) to fall, sag (*said, e.g., of prices*); to grow shorter (*said of days*); to come down; to shrink (*said, e.g., of meat*); to lose weight; to set (*said, e.g., of the sun*); to wane (*said of the moon*); (mus) to drop in pitch || *ref* to let oneself down; to dive

**calata** *f* lowering; descent; invasion; fall; wharf; (coll) intonation; **calata del sole** sunset

**cal·ca** *f* (**-che**) crowd, throng

**calca·gno** *m* (**-gni**) heel || *m* (**-gna** *fpl*) (fig) heel; **alle calcagna di** at the heels of

**calcare** *m* limestone || §197 *tr* to trample; to trace (*on paper*); to tread (*the boards*); to emphasize; **calcare la mano** to exaggerate; **calcare le orme di** to follow in the footsteps of

**calce** *m*—**in calce** at the foot of the page; **in calce a** at the foot of || *f* lime; **calce viva** quicklime

**calcedònio** *m* chalcedony

**calcestruzzo** *m* concrete

**calciare** §128 *tr* & *intr* to kick

**calciatóre** *m* soccer player; football player

**calcificare** §197 (**calcìfico**) *tr* & *ref* to calcify

**calcificazióne** *f* calcification

**calcina** *f* mortar; lime

**calcinàc·cio** *m* (**-ci**) flake of plaster; **calcinacci** ruins, rubble

**calci·nàio** *m* (**-nài**) lime pit

**calcinare** *tr* to calcine; to lime (*e.g., a field*)

**càl·cio** *m* (**-ci**) kick; soccer; calcium; (*e.g., of rifle*) butt; **calcio d'inizio** (sports) kickoff

**calciocianamide** *m* calcium cyanamide

**cal·co** *m* (**-chi**) tracing; cast; imprint

**calcografia** *f* copper engraving

**calcolare** (**càlcolo**) *tr* to calculate; to estimate, reckon; to compute; to consider

**calcola·tóre -trice** *adj* calculating || *m* calculator; computer; schemer || *f* calculating machine, adding machine

**càlcolo** *m* calculation; estimate; planning; calculus; (pathol) calculus, stone; **calcolo biliare** gallstone; **calcolo errato** miscalculation; **fare calcolo su** to count upon

**calcolò·si** *f* (**-si**) (pathol) stones

**calcomanìa** *f* decalcomania

**caldàia** *f* boiler

**cal·dàio** *m* (**-dài**) cauldron, boiler

**caldalléssa** *f* boiled chestnut

**caldana** *f* flush

**caldano** *m* brazier

**caldarròsta** *f* roast chestnut

**caldeggiare** §290 (**caldéggio**) *tr* to favor, support; to recommend

**calde·ràio** *m* (**-rài**) coppersmith; boilermaker

**calderóne** *m* cauldron

**cal·do -da** *adj* warm; hot; rich (*voice*); **caldo, caldo** quite recent || *m* heat; warmth; **aver caldo** to be warm (*said of people*); to be hot (*said of people*); **fa caldo** it is warm; it is hot; **non mi fa nè caldo nè freddo** it leaves me cold, it does not move me

**calefazióne** *f* heating

**caleidoscò·pio** *m* (**-pi**) kaleidoscope

**calendà·rio** *m* (**-ri**) calendar

**calènde** *fpl*—**calende greche** Greek calends

**calendimàggio** *m* May Day

**calèsse** *m* buggy, gig

**calére** *impers*—**non mi cale** (lit) I don't care

**calettare** (**calétto**) *tr* to dovetail, mortise || *intr* to fit

**calibrare** (**càlibro**) *tr* to gauge, calibrate

**càlibro** *m* caliber; (mach) calipers; (fig) quality, importance

**càlice** *m* wine cup; (bot) calyx; (eccl) chalice

**cali·cò** *m* (**-cò**) calico

**califfo** *m* caliph

**calìgine** *f* fog, mist; (fig) darkness

**caliginó·so -sa** [s] *adj* foggy, misty; (fig) dark, gloomy

**calla** *f*—**calla dei fioristi** calla lily

**calle** *f* lane, alley

**callifu·go** *m* (**-ghi**) corn remedy

**calligrafia** *f* penmanship; handwriting

**calli·sta** *mf* (**-sti -ste**) chiropodist

**callo** *m* corn; callus; **fare il callo a** to get used to; **pestare i calli a qlcu** to step on s.o.'s feet

**callosi·tà** [s] *f* (**-tà**) callosity; callus

**calló·so -sa** [s] *adj* corny; callous; hard

**calma** *f* calm, tranquillity

**calmante** *adj* sedative, calming, soothing ‖ *m* sedative

**calmare** *tr* to calm, soothe, appease ‖ *ref* to calm down; to subside, abate

**calmierare (calmièro)** *tr* to fix the price of

**calmière** *m* ceiling price; price control

**cal·mo -ma** *adj* calm, quiet, still ‖ *f* see **calma**

**calo** *m* decrease; shrinkage

**calomelano** *m* calomel

**calóre** *m* heat; warmth; fervor, ardor; (pathol) rash, inflammation; (vet) rut, mating season

**caloria** *f* calorie

**calòri·co -ca** *adj* (**-ci -che**) caloric

**calorìfero** *m* heater, radiator

**caloró·so -sa** [s] *adj* warm; hot; cordial; heated

**calò·scia** *f* (**-sce**) var of **galoscia**

**calòtta** *f* skullcap; case (*e.g., of watch*); (aut) hubcap; (mach) cap; **calotta cranica** skull

**calpestare (calpésto)** *tr* to trample

**calpestì·o** *m* (**-ì**) trampling

**calùgine** *f* down (*of bird*)

**calùnnia** *f* calumny, slander

**calunniare** §287 *tr* to calumniate, slander

**calunnia·tóre -trice** *mf* slanderer

**calunnió·so -sa** [s] *adj* slanderous

**Calvàrio** *m* (Bib) Calvary

**calvìzie** *f* baldness

**cal·vo -va** *adj* bald

**calza** *f* sock; stocking; wick; **calza da donna** stocking; **calze** hose, hosiery; **fare la calza** to knit

**calzamàglia** *f* tights

**calzare** *m* footwear ‖ *tr* to wear, put on (*shoes, gloves, or socks*) ‖ *intr* to fit (*said of any garment*); to suit

**calzascar·pe** *m* (**-pe**) shoehorn

**calza·tóio** *m* (**-tói**) shoehorn

**calzatura** *f* footwear; **calzature** footwear

**calzaturière** *m* shoe manufacturer

**calzaturiè·ro -ra** *adj* shoe (*e.g., industry*) ‖ *m* shoe worker

**calzaturifì·cio** *m* (**-ci**) shoe factory

**calzeròtto** *m* woolen sock

**calzet·tàio** *m* (**-tài**) hosier

**calzettóne** *m* knee-high woolen sock (*for mountain boots*)

**calzifì·cio** *m* (**-ci**) hosiery mill

**calzino** *m* sock; **calzini corti** socks; half hose; **calzini lunghi** knee-high socks

**calzo·làio** *m* (**-lài**) shoemaker; cobbler

**calzolerìa** *f* shoemaker's shop; shoe store

**calzoncini** *mpl* shorts

**calzóne** *m* trouser leg; **calzoni** trousers, pants; slacks; **calzoni a zampe d'elefante** bell-bottom trousers, flares

**camaleònte** *m* chameleon

**camarilla** *f* cabal, clique

**cambiadi·schi** *m* (**-schi**) record changer

**cambiale** *f* promissory note, IOU

**cambiaménto** *m* change, modification

**cambiare** §287 *tr* to change, exchange; to shift (*gears*) ‖ *intr* to change, switch ‖ *ref* to change (*clothing*); **cambiarsi in** to turn into

**cambiavalu·te** *m* (**-te**) moneychanger

**càm·bio** *m* (**-bi**) change; switch; rate of exchange; (mil) relief; **cambio a cloche** shift lever, stick; **cambio di velocità** gearshift; **in cambio di** in exchange for, in place of

**cambrètta** *f* staple (*to hold a wire*)

**cam·brì** *m* (**-brì**) cambric

**cambusa** *f* (naut) galley

**cambusière** *m* steward

**càmera** *f* room; bedroom; chamber; **camera ardente** funeral parlor; **Camera dei comuni** House of Commons; **Camera dei deputati** House of Representatives; **camera d'aria** inner tube; **camera di sicurezza** detention cell; vault (*of bank*)

**camera·ta** *m* (**-ti**) friend, comrade ‖ *f* dormitory; barracks; roomful (*of students or soldiers*)

**cameratismo** *m* comradeship

**camerièra** *f* waitress; maid, chambermaid

**camerière** *m* waiter; steward; valet

**camerino** *m* small room; toilet, lavatory; (nav) noncommissioned officer's quarters; (theat) dressing room

**càmice** *m* gown (*of physician*); smock (*of painter*); (eccl) alb

**camicerìa** *f* shirt store; shirt factory

**camicétta** *f* blouse

**camìcia** *f* shirt; casing, jacket (*e.g., of boiler*); lining (*e.g., of furnace*); vest (*of sailor*); folder; **camicia da giorno** chemise; **camicia da notte** nightgown; **camicia di forza** strait jacket; **camicia di maglia** coat of mail; **camicia nera** black shirt (*Fascist*); **camicia rossa** red shirt (*Garibaldine*); **dare la camicia** to give the shirt off one's back; **essere nato con la camicia** to be born with a silver spoon in one's mouth; **perdere la camicia** to lose one's shirt

**cami·ciàio -ciàia** *mf* (**-ciài -ciàie**) shirtmaker, haberdasher

**camiciòla** *f* sport shirt; undershirt; T-shirt; (obs) vest

**camiciòtto** *m* smock (*of mechanic*); jumper; sport shirt

**caminétto** *m* small fireplace; fireplace

**camino** *m* fireplace; chimney, smokestack; shaft (*in mountain*); mouth (*of volcano*); (naut) funnel

**cà·mion** *m* (**-mion**) truck

**camionale** *f* highway

**camioncino** *m* small truck; panel truck, pickup truck

**camionétta** *f* small truck; van (*e.g., of police*)

**camioni·sta** *m* (**-sti**) truckdriver, teamster

**camma** *f* (mach) cam; (mach) wiper

**cammellière** *m* camel driver

**cammèllo** *m* camel

**cammèo** *m* cameo

**camminaménto** *m* (mil) communication trench

**camminare** *intr* to walk; to go, run

**camminata** *f* walk; gait; (obs) hall with fireplace

**cammina·tóre -trice** *mf* walker; runner

**cammino** *m* road, way, route; path (*e.g., of the moon*); course; journey; **cammin facendo** on the way; **cammino battuto** beaten path; **cammino coperto** (mil) covered way; **mettersi in cammino** to set out, start out

**camomilla** *f* camomile

**camòrra** *f* underworld

**camò·scio** *m* (-**sci**) chamois

**campagna** *f* country; countryside; country property; season (*for harvesting*); campaign; **andare in campagna** to go on vacation (in the country)

**campagnò·lo -la** *adj* country, rural ‖ *mf* peasant

**campale** *adj* field (*artillery*); pitched, decisive (*battle*)

**campana** *f* bell; bell glass, bell jar; lamp shade; (archit) bell; **a campana** bell-bottomed; **campana a martello** alarm bell, tocsin; **campana di vetro** bell glass; **campana pneumatica** caisson

**campanàc·cio** *m* (-**ci**) cowbell

**campanaro** *m* bell ringer; (archaic) bell founder

**campanèlla** *f* small bell; door knocker; curtain ring; (bot) bluebell

**campanèllo** *m* bell; small bell; doorbell, chimes; **campanello d'allarme** alarm bell

**campanile** *m* steeple, belfry; native city or town

**campanilismo** *m* parochialism

**campano** *m* cowbell

**campare** *tr* to keep alive; to save; to bring out the details of ‖ *intr* (ESSERE) to live; to survive; **si campa** one ekes out a living

**campa·to -ta** *adj*—**campato in aria** without any foundation ‖ *f* span

**campeggiare** §290 (**campéggio**) *intr* to camp, encamp; to stand out

**campeggia·tóre -trice** *mf* camper

**campég·gio** *m* (-**gi**) camping, outing; campground; (bot) logwood

**campeggi·sta** *mf* (-**sti -ste**) camper

**campèstre** *adj* field, country; (sports) cross-country

**campidò·glio** *m* (-**gli**) capitol ‖ **Campidoglio** *m* Capitoline (*hill*); Capitol (*temple*)

**campionare** (**campióno**) *tr* to sample

**campionà·rio -ria** (-**ri -rie**) *adj* of samples; trade (*exposition*) ‖ *m* sample book, catalogue, pattern book

**campionato** *m* championship, title

**campióne** *m* champion; sample; specimen; standard; **campione senza valore** uninsured parcel, sample post

**campionéssa** *f* championess

**campionìssimo** *m* world champion, ace

**campo** *m* field; camp; ground; tennis court; golf course; center (*e.g., for refugees*); **campo addestramento** training camp; **campo d'aviazione** airfield, airport; **campo di battaglia** battlefield; **campo petrolifero** oil field; **lasciare il campo** to retreat; **mettere in campo** to bring up, adduce; **piantare il campo** to pitch camp

**camposanto** *m* cemetery, churchyard

**camuffare** *tr* to disguise, mask; to camouflage ‖ *ref* to disguise oneself

**camu·so -sa** *adj* snub-nosed

**Canadà, il** Canada

**canadése** [s] *adj* & *mf* Canadian

**canàglia** *f* scoundrel; rabble

**canagliata** *f* knavery, mean trick

**canale** *m* canal; irrigation ditch; network (*of communications*); pipe, drain; (anat) duct, tract; (rad, telv) channel; (theat) aisle; **Canale della Manica** English Channel; **Canale di Panama** Panama Canal; **Canale di Suez** Suez Canal

**canalizzare** [ddzz] *tr* to channel; to install pipes in; (elec) to wire

**canalizzazióne** [ddzz] *f* channeling; piping; ductwork; (elec) wiring

**canalóne** *m* ravine

**cànapa** *f* hemp

**cana·pè** *m* (-**pè**) sofa, couch; (culin) canapé

**cànapo** *m* rope, cable

**Canàrie, le** the Canaries

**canarino** *m* canary

**cancàn** *m* noise, racket

**cancellare** (**cancèllo**) *tr* to cancel, erase; to obliterate; to write off (*a debt*); to scratch (*a horse*) ‖ *ref* to vanish, fade

**cancellata** *f* railing

**cancellatura** *f* erasure

**cancellazióne** *f* cancellation; erasure (*of a tape*)

**cancellerìa** *f* chancellery; stationery

**cancellière** *m* chancellor; court clerk; registrar, recorder

**cancèllo** *m* gate, railing, grating

**canceró·so -sa** [s] *adj* cancerous ‖ *mf* cancer victim

**cànchero** *m* trouble; troublesome person; (coll) cancer

**cancrèna** *f* gangrene; **andare in cancrena** to become gangrenous

**cancrenó·so -sa** [s] *adj* gangrenous

**cancro** *m* cancer; (bot) canker ‖ **Cancro** *m* (astr) Cancer

**candeggiante** *adj* bleaching ‖ *m* bleaching agent, bleach

**candeggiare** §290 (**candéggio**) *tr* to bleach

**candeggina** *f* bleach

**candég·gio** *m* (-**gi**) bleaching

**candéla** *f* candle; candlestick; candlepower; (aut) spark plug; **studiare a lume di candela** to burn the midnight oil; **tenere la candela a** to favor the love affair of

**candelabro** *m* candelabrum

**candelière** *m* candlestick

**candelòra** *f* Candlemas

**candelòtto** *m* big wax candle; **candelotto lacrimogeno** tear-gas canister

**candida·to -ta** *mf* candidate

**candidatura** *f* candidature, candidacy

**càndi·do -da** *adj* white; candid

**candire** §176 *tr* to candy

**candi·to -ta** *adj* candied ‖ *m* candied fruit

**candóre** *m* whiteness; candor

**cane** *m* dog; hound; hammer, cock (*of gun*); ham actor; **cane barbone**

poodle; **cane bastardo** mongrel; **cane da ferma** setter; **cane da guardia** watchdog; **cane da presa** retriever; **cane da punta** pointer; **cane grosso** big shot; **cane guida per ciechi** seeing eye dog; **cane sciolto** (pol) lone wolf; **come un cane** all alone; **come un cane in chiesa** as an unwelcome guest; **da cani** poorly; **menare il can per l'aia** to beat around the bush; **non c'è un cane** there is nobody there; **raddrizzare le gambe ai cani** to perform an impossible task

**canèstro** m basket

**cànfora** f camphor

**cangiante** adj changeable (color); changing, iridescent

**canguro** m kangaroo

**canìcola** f dog days

**canile** m doghouse, kennel

**canino** adj canine || m canine tooth

**canìzie** f gray hair; head of gray hair; old age

**canna** f cane, reed; rod (for fishing or measuring); pipe (of organ); barrel (of gun); **canna da zucchero** sugar cane; **canna di caduta** disposal chute; **canna fumaria** chimney; **canna della gola** (coll) windpipe

**cannèlla** f small tube; tap (of barrel); cinnamon

**cannèllo** m pipe, tube; stick (e.g., of licorice); (chem) pipette; **cannello ossiacetilenico** acetylene torch; **cannello ossidrico** oxyhydrogen blowpipe

**cannellóni** mpl cannelloni

**cannéto** m cane field

**cannìbale** m cannibal

**cannìc·cio** m (-ci) wicker frame; shade made out of rushes

**cannocchiale** m spyglass; **cannocchiale astronomico** telescope

**cannonata** f cannonade, cannon shot; (slang) hit

**cannoncino** m small gun; **cannoncino antiaereo** antiaircraft gun

**cannóne** m gun, cannon; pipe, stovepipe; box pleat; shin (of cattle); **è un cannone** (coll) he's the tops

**cannoneggiare** §290 (**cannonéggio**) tr to cannonade, shell

**cannonièra** f gunboat

**cannonière** m gunner, artilleryman; kicker (in soccer)

**cannùc·cia** f (-ce) reed; thin tube; stem (e.g., of pipe); straw (for drinking); (chem) pipette

**canòa** f canoe; launch

**canòcchia** f mantis shrimp

**cànone** m canon; rule; rent; fee, charge (for use of radio)

**canonicato** m canonry

**canòni·co -ca** (-ci -che) adj canonical, canon (law) || m canon; priest || f parsonage, rectory

**canonizzare** [ddzz] tr to canonize

**canò·ro -ra** adj song (bird); melodious

**canottàg·gio** m (-gi) boating, rowing

**canottièra** f undershirt, T-shirt; skimmer, boater

**canottière** m oarsman

**canòtto** m skiff, scull, shell

**canovàc·cio** m (-ci) dishcloth; embroidery cloth; plot (of novel or play)

**cantàbile** adj singable; songlike; cantabile || m song

**cantamban·co** m (-chi) jongleur, wandering minstrel; mountebank

**cantante** adj singing, song || mf singer

**cantare** m song; chant; laisse, epic strophe || tr to sing; to chant || intr to sing; to chant; (coll) to squeal

**cantàride** f Spanish fly

**càntaro** m urn

**cantastò·rie** mf (-rie) minstrel

**canta·tóre -trice** adj singing || mf singer

**cantau·tóre -trice** mf singer composer

**canterano** m chest of drawers

**canterellare** (**canterèllo**) tr & intr to sing in a low voice, hum

**canteri·no -na** adj singing, warbling; decoy (bird) || mf songster, singer

**càntero** m urinal

**canticchiare** §287 tr & intr to hum

**cànti·co** m (-ci) canticle

**cantière** m shipyard, dockyard; navy yard; undertaking, work in progress; **avere in cantiere** to have in hand, be working at; **cantiere edile** building site; builder's yard

**cantilèna** f singsong; **la stessa cantilena** the same old tune

**cantimban·co** m (-chi) var of **cantambanco**

**cantina** f cellar; wine cellar; wine shop, canteen

**cantinière** m cellarman; butler; wineshop keeper; sommelier

**canto** m song, singing; chant; canto; crow (of rooster); chirping (of grasshopper); corner, edge; (mus) voice part; **canto del cigno** swan song; **dal canto mio** for my part; **d'altro canto** on the other hand; **da un canto** on the one hand

**cantonata** f corner (of street); **prendere una cantonata** to make a blunder

**cantóne** m corner (of room or building); canton

**cantonièra** f corner cupboard; (rr) section worker's house

**cantonière** m road laborer; (rr) section hand

**cantóre** m choir singer; cantor; (poet) singer

**cantùc·cio** m (-ci) nook, niche

**canutézza** f hoariness

**canutiglia** f gold thread

**canu·to -ta** adj gray-haired; white-haired; (poet) white

**canzonare** (**canzóno**) tr to mock, ridicule

**canzonatò·rio -ria** adj (-ri -rie) mocking

**canzonatura** f mockery, gibe

**canzóne** f song; canzone

**canzonétta** f canzonet; popular song

**canzonetti·sta** mf (-sti -ste) singer (e.g., in a nightclub) || m songster || f songstress

**canzonière** m songbook; collection of poems; song writer

**caolino** m kaolin

caos *m* chaos

caòti·co -ca *adj* (-ci -che) caotic

capace *adj* capacious; capable, intelligent; legally qualified; capace di with a capacity of (*e.g.*, *fifty people*); essere capace di to be able to; fare capace di to convince of

capaci·tà *f* (-tà) capacity; capability

capacitare (capàcito) *tr* to persuade ‖ *ref* to become convinced

capanna *f* hut, cabin; thatched cottage; bathhouse

capannèllo *m* group, crowd

capanno *m* hunting box; cabana, bathhouse

capannóne *m* large shed; hangar

caparbiàggine *f* var of caparbietà

caparbie·tà *f* (-tà) obstinacy, stubborness

capàr·bio -bia *adj* (-bi -bie) stubborn, hard-headed

caparra *f* down payment, deposit; performance bond

capatina *f* short visit

capeggiare §290 (capéggio) *tr* to lead

capeggia·tóre -trice *mf* leader

capellini *mpl* small vermicelli

capéllo *m* hair; averne fin sopra i capelli to have one's fill; capelli hair; capelli a spazzola crew cut; c'è mancato un capello che + *subj* he came close to + *ger*; far rizzare i capelli a qlcu to make s.o.'s hair stand on end

capellóne *m* hippie, beatnik

capellu·to -ta *adj* hairy; long-haired

capelvènere *m* maidenhair

capèstro *m* halter; gallows

capezzale *m* bolster; (fig) bedside

capézzolo *m* nipple, teat; udder

capidò·glio *m* (-gli) var of capodoglio

capiènza *f* capacity (*e.g.*, *of bus*)

capigliatura *f* head of hair

capillare *adj* capillary; (fig) far-reaching

capinéra *f* (orn) blackcap

capintè·sta *m* (-sta) boss; (sports) head, leader

capire §176 *tr* to understand; capire a volo to grasp immediately ‖ *intr*—non capire dalla contentezza to be bursting with joy ‖ *ref* to understand each other; to agree

capitale *adj* capital; mortal (*sin*) ‖ *m* capital; principal; capitale sociale capital stock ‖ *f* capital (*of country*)

capitalismo *m* capitalism

capitali·sta *mf* (-sti -ste) capitalist

capitalìsti·co -ca *adj* (-ci -che) capitalistic

capitalizzare [ddzz] *tr* to capitalize; to compound (*interest*)

capitana *f* flagship

capitanare *tr* to lead, captain

capitanerìa *f* (hist) captaincy; capitaneria di porto harbor-master's office; coast guard office; port authority's office

capitano *m* captain; skipper, master (*of ship*); commander (*in air force*); capitano di corvetta or capitano di fregata (nav) lieutenant commander;

capitano di gran cabotaggio master; capitano di lungo corso master; capitano di porto harbor master; capitano di vascello (nav) commander

capitare (càpito) *intr* (ESSERE) to arrive; to happen, occur; to happen to get, *e.g.*, capitò a casa mia alle tre he happened to get to my house at three; capitare bene to be lucky; dove capita at random

capitazióne *f* poll tax

capitèllo *m* (archit) capital; (bb) headband

capitolare *adj* & *m* capitular ‖ *v* (capìtolo) *intr* to capitulate, surrender

capitolato *m* (com) specifications

capitolazióne *f* capitulation

capitolo *m* chapter; article, paragraph (*of contract*)

capitombolare (capitómbolo) *intr* to tumble

capitómbolo *m* tumble; fare un capitombolo (fig) to collapse

capitóne *m* big eel

capitozzare (capitòzzo) *tr* to poll (*a tree*)

capo *m* head; chief; boss, leader; top; (geog) cape; (nav) chief petty officer; a capo scoperto bareheaded; capo d'accusa (law) charge; capo del governo prime minister; capo dello stato president, chief of state; capo di vestiario garment; capo scarico scatterbrain; col capo nel sacco (fig) heedlessly; da capo all over (again); fare capo a to flow into; in capo a at the end of (*e.g.*, *one month*); in capo al mondo at the end of the world; per sommi capi briefly; rompersi il capo to rack one's brain; scoprirsi il capo to take one's hat off; senza capo né coda without rhyme or reason; venire a capo di to come to the end of

capobanda *m* (capibanda) bandmaster; ringleader

capocamerière *m* headwaiter

capocannonière *m* (capicannonièri) petty gunnery officer; (soccer) leader in number of goals

capòcchia *f* head (*e.g.*, *of a match*)

capòc·cia *m* (-ci & -cia) head of household; foreman, boss (*e.g.*, *of roadworkers or farmers*)

capocòmi·co *m* (-ci) head of dramatic company

capocòr·da *m* (capicòrda) (elec) binding post, terminal

capocrònaca *m* (capicrònaca) leading article

capocronista *m* (capicronisti) city editor

capocuòco *m* (capocuòchi & capicuòchi) chef

capodanno *m* (capodanni & capi d'anno) New Year's Day

capodò·glio *m* (-gli) sperm whale

capofàbbrica *m* (capifàbbrica) foreman, superintendent

capofabbricato *m* (capifabbricato) air-raid warden

capofamìglia *m* (capifamìglia) head of the family

capofila *m* (capifila) head of a line ‖ *f* (capofila) head of a line

capofitto *adj invar*—a capofitto headlong

capogiro *m* vertigo, dizziness; da capogiro dizzying, e.g., prezzi da capogiro dizzying prices

capolavó·ro *m* (-ri) masterpiece

capolèttera *m* (capilèttera) letterhead; (typ) first large bold letter of a paragraph

capolinea *m* (capilìnea) terminal, terminus

capolino *m*—fare capolino to peep

capolista *m* (capilista) first (*of a list*); (sports) leader ‖ *f* (capolista) first (*of a list*)

capoluò·go *m* (-ghi) capital (*of province*); county seat

capomacchini·sta *m* (-sti) chief engineer

capomastro *m* (capomastri & capimastri) foreman; building contractor

capomùsica *m* (capimùsica) bandmaster

capoofficina *m* (capiofficina) superintendent (*of shop*)

capopàgina *m* (capipàgina) heading (*of newspaper*)

capopèzzo *m* (capipèzzo) gunnery sergeant

capopòpolo *m* (capipòpolo) demagogue

caporale *m* corporal

caporeparto *m* (capireparto) department manager, floor walker; shop foreman

caporióne *m* ringleader

caposaldo *m* (capisaldi) (fig) main point, basis; (mil) stronghold; (surv) datum

caposezióne *m* (capisezióne) department head

caposquadra *m* (capisquadra) group leader; (sports) team captain

capostazióne *m* (capistazióne) station master

capostìpite *m* founder (*of family*); prototype, archetype

capotaménto *m* var of cappottamento

capotare (capòto) *intr* var of cappottare

capotasto *m* nut (*of violin*)

capotàvola *m* (capitàvola) head of the table, honored guest

capòte *f* (aut) top

capotrèno *m* (capitrèno & capotrèni) (rr) conductor

capottaménto *m* var of cappottamento

capottare (capòtto) *intr* var of cappottare

capoufficio *m* (capiufficio) office manager

capovèrso *m* paragraph; (typ) indentation

capovòlgere §289 *tr* to overturn; (fig) to upset ‖ *ref* to overturn; (fig) to be or become reversed

capovolgiménto *m* upset; (fig) reversal

capovòlta *f* overturn; turn (*in swimming*)

cappa *f* cape, cloak; mantle; letter K; shroud (*of clouds*); (naut) trysail;

cappa del cielo vault of heaven; navigare alla cappa (naut) to lay to

cappèlla *f* chapel; cappella mortuaria undertaker's parlor ‖ Cappella Sistina Sistine Chapel

cappel·làio *m* (-lài) hatter, hat maker or dealer

cappellano *m* chaplain

cappellata *f* hatful

cappellerìa *f* hat store

cappellièra *f* hatbox

cappèllo *m* hat; bonnet; cap (*of mushroom*); head (*of nail*); cowl (*of chimney*); preamble (*of newspaper article*); cappello a cencio slouch hat; cappello a cilindro top hat; cappello a cono dunce cap; cappello a due punte cocked hat; cappello a tre punte three-cornered hat; cappello del lume lampshade; cappello di feltro felt hat; cappello di paglia straw hat; cappello floscio fedora; fare di cappello to take one's hat off; prendere cappello to take offense

cappellóne *adj invar* Western (*movie*) ‖ *m* big hat; (coll) recruit; (mov) Western character

càppero *m* (bot) caper; capperi! (coll) wow!

càp·pio *m* (-pi) bow; noose; loop

capponàia *f* chicken coop

cappóne *m* capon

cappòtta *f* cape; navy coat; hood (*of car*)

cappottaménto *m* upset, rolling over

cappottare (cappòtto) *intr* to upset, roll over

cappottatura *f* (aer) cowl

cappòtto *m* overcoat; lurch (*at the close of game*); (cards) slam; cappotto da mezza stagione lightweight coat

cappuccino *m* espresso with cream; Capuchin (*friar*)

Cappuccétto *m*—Cappuccetto Rosso Little Red Ridinghood

cappùc·cio *m* (-ci) hood, cowl; cabbage; cap (*of fountain pen*)

capra *f* goat; nanny goat; tripod

ca·pràio -pràia *mf* (-prài -pràie) goatherd

caprét·to -ta *mf* kid

capriata *f* truss (*to support roof*)

caprìc·cio *m* (-ci) whim, fancy, caprice; tantrum; flirting; (mus) capriccio

capricció·so -sa [s] *adj* whimsical, capricious; naughty; fanciful, bizarre

Capricòrno *m* (astr) Capricorn

caprifò·glio *m* (-gli) honeysuckle

caprimul·go *m* (-gi) (orn) goatsucker

capri·no -na *adj* goatlike, goatish ‖ *m* smell of goat

capriòla *f* female roe deer; caper, somersault; fare capriole to cut capers, to caper

capriòlo *m* roe deer; roebuck

capro *m* he-goat, billy goat; capro espiatorio scapegoat

capróne *m* he-goat, billy goat

càpsula *f* capsule; percussion cap; cap (*of bottle*); (rok) capsule

captare *tr* to captivate; to catch, intercept; to harness (a waterfall); (rad, telv) to pick up (a signal)

**captazióne** f undue influence (to secure an inheritance)

**capzió·so -sa** [s] adj insidious, treacherous

**carabàttola** f (coll) trifle

**carabina** f carbine

**carabinière** m carabineer; Italian military policeman, carabiniere; (hist) cavalryman

**caracollare** (**caracòllo**) intr to caracole, caper; (coll) to trot along

**caracòllo** m caracole, caper

**caraffa** f carafe, decanter

**caràmbola** f carom

**carambolare** (**caràmbolo**) intr to carom

**caramèlla** f piece of hard candy; taffy; (coll) monocle; **caramelle** hard candy

**caramellare** (**caramèllo**) tr to caramel; to candy

**caramèllo** m caramel (burnt sugar)

**caraménte** adv affectionately

**carati·sta** m (-sti) shareholder (in ship or business)

**carato** m carat; share (of ship)

**caràttere** m character; type; handwriting; characteristic; disposition; **carattere corsivo** (typ) italic; **carattere maiuscolo** capital; **carattere minuscolo** small letter, lower case; **carattere neretto** or **grassetto** (typ) boldface

**caratteri·sta** m (-sti) character actor || f (-ste) character actress

**caratterìsti·co -ca** (-ci -che) adj & f characteristic

**caratterizzare** [ddzz] tr to characterize

**caratura** f share (in business or ship)

**cara·vàn** m (-vàn) trailer, mobile home

**caravanserrà·glio** m (-gli) caravansary

**caravèlla** f caravel; carpenter's glue

**carbo·nàio -nàia** (-nài -nàie) adj coal || m coal man, coal dealer || f charcoal pit; coalbin, bunker; coal yard

**carbonato** m carbonate

**carbón·chio** m (-chi) (agr) smut (on wheat); (jewelry) carbuncle

**carboncino** m charcoal (pencil and drawing)

**carbóne** m coal; charcoal; carbon (of arc light or primary battery); **carbone bianco** hydroelectric power; **carbone dolce** charcoal; **carbone fossile** coal; **fare carbone** to coal

**carbòni·co -ca** adj (-ci -che) carbonic

**carbonièra** f coal yard; (naut) collier; (rr) tender

**carbonile** m (naut) bunker

**carbònio** m (chem) carbon

**carbonizzare** [ddzz] tr to carbonize; to char

**carbùncolo** m boil, carbuncle; (archaic) ruby

**carburante** m fuel

**carburatóre** m carburetor

**carburazióne** f (aut) mixture

**carburo** m carbide

**carcassa** f carcass; framework; (aut) jalopy; (fig) wreck

**carcerare** (**càrcero**) tr to jail

**carcerà·rio -ria** adj (-ri -rie) jail, prison

**carcera·to -ta** adj imprisoned || mf prisoner

**càrce·re** m (-ri fpl) jail, prison

**carcerière** m jailer, prison guard

**carciòfo** m artichoke

**cardàni·co -ca** adj (-ci -che) universal (e.g., joint)

**cardano** m universal joint

**cardatrice** f carding machine

**cardellino** m goldfinch

**cardìa·co -ca** (-ci -che) adj heart, cardiac || m heart patient

**cardinale** adj cardinal || m (eccl, orn) cardinal

**cardinalì·zio -zia** adj (-zi -zie) cardinal, cardinal's

**càrdine** m hinge; (fig) pivot, mainstay (e.g., of theory)

**càr·dio** m (-di) cockle (mollusk)

**cardiochirurgìa** f heart surgery

**cardiogram·ma** m (-mi) cardiogram

**cardiòlo·go** m (-gi) cardiologist

**cardiopalmo** m tachycardia

**cardiopatìa** f heart disease

**cardo** m (bot) thistle; (bot) cardoon

**carèna** f ship's bottom; (aer) outer cover (of airship); (bot) rib

**carenàg·gio** m (-gi) careening a ship; careen

**carenare** (**carèno**) tr to careen (a ship)

**carenatura** f streamlining; **carenatura di fusoliera** (aer) turtleback

**carènza** f lack, want

**carestìa** f famine; scarcity (e.g., of manpower)

**carézza** f caress; **fare una carezza a** to caress

**carezzare** (**carézzo**) tr to caress

**carezzévole** adj caressing, fondling; sweet, suave; blandishing

**cariare** §287 tr to cause (a tooth) to decay; to corrode || ref to decay; to rot

**cariàtide** f caryatid

**caria·to -ta** adj decayed

**cà·rica** f (-che) office, appointment; charge; (fig) insistence

**caricaménto** m loading

**caricare** §197 (**càrico**) tr to load; to burden; to wind (a watch); to fill (a pipe); to charge (a battery); to deepen (a color); **caricare la mano to** exceed; **caricare le dosi** to exaggerate || ref to burden oneself

**carica·tóre -trice** adj loading || m clip, magazine (for rifle); loader (of gun); cassette (of tape recorder); charger (of battery); longshoreman; (phot) cartridge, cassette

**caricatura** f caricature, cartoon; **mettere in caricatura** to ridicule

**caricaturi·sta** mf (-sti -ste) cartoonist, caricaturist

**càrice** m (bot) sedge

**càri·co -ca** (-chi -che) adj loaded; burdened; vivid (color); strong (tea); charged (battery) || m loading; load, burden; charge; cargo || f see **carica**

**càrie** f caries, decay

**cari·no -na** adj nice, pretty, cute; **questa è carina!** this is funny!

**cari·tà** *f* (-tà) charity; alms; (poet) love; **per carità** please

**caritatévole** *adj* charitable

**caritati·vo -va** *adj* (obs) charitable

**carlin·ga** *f* (-ghe) fuselage

**Carlo** *m* Charles

**Carlomagno** *m* Charlemagne

**carlóna** *f*—**alla carlona** carelessly, haphazardly

**carlòtta** *f* charlotte || **Carlotta** Charlotte

**carme** *m* poem, lyric poem

**carmì·nio** *m* (-ni) carmine

**carnagióne** *f* complexion

**car·nàio** *m* (-nài) carnage; slaughter house; mass of humanity

**carnale** *adj* carnal, sensual; full (*e.g., brother, cousin*)

**carname** *m* carrion

**carne** *f* flesh; meat; **bene in carne** plump; **carne da macello** cannon fodder; **carne suina** pork; **carne viva** open wound; **essere solo carne ed ossa** to be nothing but skin and bones; **in carne ed ossa** in person, in the flesh; **troppa carne al fuoco** too many irons in the fire

**carnéfice** *m* executioner

**carneficina** *f* slaughter, carnage

**càrne·o -a** *adj* fleshy, meaty; flesh-colored

**carnet** *m* (**carnet**) notebook; checkbook; backlog

**carnevale** *m* carnival

**carnièra** *f* hunting jacket; gamebag

**carnière** *m* gamebag

**carnìvo·ro -ra** *adj* carnivorous || *mpl* carnivores; Carnivora

**carnó·so -sa** [s] *adj* fleshy

**ca·ro -ra** *adj* dear (*beloved; high in price*) || **caro** *adv* dear || *m* high price; beloved; **i miei cari** my parents; my relatives; my friends

**carógna** *f* carcass; cad, rotter; **carogne** carrion

**carosèllo** *m* tournament; carousel, merry-go-round

**caròta** *f* carrot; (fig) lie

**caròtide** *f* carotid artery

**carovana** *f* caravan; group, crowd; union of longshoremen; apprenticeship; (naut, nav) convoy; **far carovana** to join a tour; **fare la carovana** to be an apprentice

**carovaniè·ro -ra** *adj* caravan || *f* desert trail

**carovi·ta** *m* (-ta) high cost of living; cost-of-living increase

**carovìve·ri** *m* (-ri) high cost of living; cost-of-living increase

**carpa** *f* (ichth) carp

**carpentière** *m* carpenter

**carpire** §176 *tr* to snatch, seize; to extract, worm (*a secret*)

**carpóni** *adv* on all fours; **avanzare carponi** to crawl

**carradóre** *m* cart maker, wheelwright

**car·ràio -ràia** (-rài -ràie) *adj* passable for vehicles || *f* cart road

**carrarèc·cia** *f* (-ce) country road; rut

**carreggiata** *f* paved road; track (*of vehicles*); (fig) right path

**carrellare** (**carrèllo**) *intr* (mov, telv) to dolly

**carrellata** *f* (mov) dolly shot, tracking shot

**carrèllo** *m* car (*for narrow-gauge track*); carriage (*of typewriter*); cart (*for shopping*); (aer) landing gear; (mach, rr) truck; (mov, telv) dolly; **carrello d'atterraggio** (aer) undercarriage, landing gear; **carrello elevatore** fork-lift truck

**carrétta** *f* cart; tramp steamer

**carrettata** *f* cartful; **a carrettate** abundantly

**carrettière** *m* cart driver, drayman; teamster

**carrétto** *m* small cart; **carretto a mano** pushcart

**carriàg·gio** *m* (-gi) wagon; **carriaggi** (mil) baggage train

**carrièra** *f* career; **di gran carriera** at top speed

**carrieri·sta** *mf* (-sti -ste) unscrupulous go-getter

**carriòla** *f* wheelbarrow

**carro** *m* wagon; cart; wagonload; cartload; carload; (rr) car; (astr) Plough; (poet) chariot; **carri armati** (mil) armor; **carro allegorico** float (*in a pageant*); **carro armato** (mil) tank; **carro attrezzi** (aut) tow truck, wrecker; **carro bestiame** (rr) cattle car; **carro botte** or **carro cisterna** (aut) tank truck; (rr) tank car; **carro di Tespi** traveling show; **carro funebre** hearse; **carro gru** (rr) wrecking crane; **carro marsupio** (rr) double decker (*used to transport automobiles*); **carro merci** (rr) freight car; **Gran Carro** (astr) Big Dipper; **mettere il carro innanzi ai buoi** to put the cart before the horse; **Piccolo Carro** (astr) Little Dipper || *m* (**carra** *fpl*) carload; wagonload; cartload

**carròzza** *f* wagon carriage; **carrozza letti** (rr) sleeping car; **carrozza ristorante** (rr) dining car; **carrozza salone** (rr) club car; **con la carrozza di S. Francesco** on shank's mare; **signori, in carrozza!** (rr) all aboard!

**carrozzàbile** *adj* open to vehicular traffic || *f* road open to vehicular traffic

**carrozzèlla** *f* small wagon; baby carriage; wheelchair; hackney

**carrozzino** *m* baby carriage; sidecar

**carrozzóne** *m* wagon; hearse; caravan (*e.g., of gypsies*); (rr) car

**carruba** *f* carob

**carrubo** *m* carob tree

**carrùcola** *f* pulley

**carta** *f* paper; document (*e.g., of identification*); **alla carta** à la carte; **carta assorbente** blotter; **carta astronomica** astronomical map; **carta bianca** carte blanche; **carta bollata** stamped paper (*for official documents*); **carta carbone** carbon paper; **carta catramata** tar paper; **carta da disegno** drawing paper; **carta da gioco** playing card; **carta da giornale** newsprint; **carta da imballaggio** or **da impacco** wrapping paper; **carta da lettera** or **da lettere** writing paper; **carta geografica** map, chart; **carta igienica** toilet paper; **carta oleata** wax paper; **carta torna-**

sole litmus paper; **carta velina** India paper; tissue paper; **carta vetrata** sandpaper; **carte** papers, writings; **carte francesi** cards in the four suits spades, hearts, diamonds, and clubs; **carte napoletane** cards in the four suits gold coins, cups, swords, and clubs; **fare le carte** to shuffle the cards; **fare le carte a qlcu** to tell s.o.'s fortune with cards

**cartacarbóne** *f* (**cartecarbóne**) carbon paper

**cartàc·cia** *f* (**-ce**) waste paper

**cartàce·o -a** *adj* (**-i -e**) paper

**Cartàgine** *f* Carthage

**car·tàio** *m* (**-tài**) papermaker; paper dealer; (cards) dealer

**cartamonéta** *f* paper money

**cartapècora** *f* parchment

**cartapésta** *f* papier-mâché

**cartà·rio -ria** *adj* (**-ri -rie**) paper

**cartastràccia** *f* (**cartestracce**) wrapping paper; wastepaper

**cartég·gio** *m* (**-gi**) correspondence; (aer, naut) reckoning

**cartèlla** *f* lottery ticket; card (*e.g., of bingo*); page of manuscript; Manila folder; schoolbag; briefcase; binding (*of book*); **cartella clinica** clinical chart; **cartella di rendita** government bond; **cartella esattoriale** tax bill; **cartella fondiaria** bond certificate

**cartellino** *m* label; nameplate (*on door*); file; (sports) contract; **cartellino di presenza** timecard; **cartellino signaletico** criminal record

**cartèllo** *m* poster; sign (*on store*); (com) cartel, trust; **cartello di sfida** challenge; **cartello stradale** traffic sign

**cartellóne** *m* show bill, theater poster; bill (*for advertising*); **tenere il cartellone** to find public favor, make a hit, be the rage

**car·ter** *m* (**-ter**) chain guard (*of bicycle*); (aut) crankcase

**cartièra** *f* papermill

**cartilàgine** *f* cartilage, gristle

**cartina** *f* dose; cigarette paper; small map

**cartòc·cio** *m* (**-ci**) paper cone; charge (*of gun*); cornhusk; (archit) scroll

**cartògrafo** *m* cartographer

**carto·làio** *m* (**-lài**) stationer

**cartolerìa** *f* stationery store

**cartolina** *f* card, post card; **cartolina precetto** induction notice

**cartomante** *mf* fortuneteller

**cartoncino** *m* light cardboard, calling card; **cartoncino natalizio** Christmas card

**cartóne** *m* cardboard, carton; **cartone animato** (mov) animated cartoon

**cartùc·cia** *f* (**-ce**) cartridge; shot, shell; **mezza cartuccia** (fig) half pint

**cartuccièra** *f* cartridge belt

**casa** [s] *f* house; dwelling; home; household; **andare a casa** to go home; **casa base** (baseball) home base; **casa colonica** farm house; **casa da gioco** gambling house; **casa del diavolo** faraway place; **casa di bambole** playhouse, doll's house; **casa di correzione** reform school; **casa di cura** sanatorium, private clinic; **casa di riposo** convalescent home, nursing home; **casa di spedizione** shipping agency; **casa di tolleranza** bawdyhouse; **casa madre** home office, headquarters; **esser di casa** to be intimate; **fuori casa** (sports) away; **in casa** (sports) home; **metter su casa** to set up housekeeping; **sentirsi a casa** to feel at home; **stare a casa** to stay at home; **star di casa** to dwell, live

**casac·ca** *f* (**-che**) coat; **voltar casacca** to be a turncoat

**casàccio** *m*—**a casaccio** at random; heedlessly

**casalin·go -ga** (**-ghi -ghe**) [s] *adj* home, domestic; stay-at-home; homey; home-made || **casalinghi** *mpl* household articles || *f* housewife

**casamatta** [s] *f* casemate, bunker

**casaménto** [s] *m* apartment house, tenement; tenants

**casata** [s] *f* house, lineage

**casato** [s] *m* birth, family; (obs) family name

**cascame** *m* waste; remnants (*e.g., of silk*)

**cascante** *adj* flabby, loose; (poet) languid, dull

**cascare** §197 *intr* (ESSERE) to fall, droop; to fit (*said of clothes*); **cascare dalla noia** to be bored to death; **cascare dal sonno** to be overwhelmed with sleep; **cascare diritto** to escape unscathed; **non casca il mondo** the world is not coming to an end

**cascata** *f* fall, waterfall; necklace (*e.g., of pearls*); **a cascata** flood of, e.g., **telefonate a cascata** flood of telephone calls || **le Cascate del Niagara** Niagara Falls

**cascina** *f* farm house; dairy barn

**ca·sco** *m* (**-schi**) helmet, crash helmet; electric hairdrier; cluster (*e.g., of bananas*)

**caseggiato** [s] *m* built-up zone; block, row of houses; apartment house

**caseifì·cio** *m* (**-ci**) dairy, creamery, cheese factory

**casèlla** [s] *f* pigeonhole; square (*of paper*); **casella postale** post-office box

**casellante** [s] *mf* gatekeeper || *m* (**rr**) trackwalker

**casellà·rio** [s] *m* (**-ri**) filing cabinet; row of post-office boxes; **casellario giudiziale** criminal file

**casèllo** [s] *m* tollgate (*on turnpike*); (rr) trackwalker's house

**casèrma** *f* barracks; fire station

**casino** [s] *m* country house; clubhouse; (slang) whorehouse; (slang) noise, racket

**casìsti·ca** *f* (**-che**) case study; (eccl) casuistry

**caso** *m* case; chance; fate; vicissitude; opportunity; **a caso** inadvertently; **al caso** eventually; **caso fortuito** (law) act of God; **caso mai** assuming that, in the event that; **è il caso** it is the moment; **far caso a qlco** to notice s.th; **in ogni caso** in any event; **mettere il caso che** suppose; **mi fa caso** I am surprised; **non fare caso a** to make nothing of, pay no attention to; **per caso** perchance

**casolare** [s] *m* hut, hovel; isolated farmhouse

**casòtto** [s] *m* cabana, bathhouse; sentry box

**Càspio** *adj* Caspian

**càspita** *interj* you don't say!

**cassa** *f* box; chest; case; stock (*of rifle*); cash; cash register; desk (*e.g., in hotel*); check-out (*in a supermarket*); **a pronta cassa** by cash; **cassa acustica** loudspeaker; **cassa di risparmio** savings bank; **cassa malattia** health insurance; **cassa rurale** farmers' credit cooperative; **in cassa** in hand (*said of money*)

**cassafórma** *f* (**casseforme**) (archit) form (*for cement*)

**cassafòrte** *f* (**casseforti**) safe

**cassapanca** *f* (**cassapanche** & **cassepanche**) wooden chest

**cassare** *tr* to erase, cancel; to cross off; (law) to annull

**cassata** *f* Neapolitan ice cream with soft core; Sicilian cake

**cassazióne** *f* annulment, abolition; cancellation

**casserétto** *m* (naut) poop

**càssero** *m* (naut) quarterdeck; **cassero di poppa** (naut) cockpit

**casseruòla** *f* saucepan

**cassétta** *f* small box; coach box; (theat) box office; **cassetta dei ferri** workbox; **cassetta delle lettere** mail box; **cassetta di cottura** dish warmer; **cassetta di sicurezza** safe-deposit box; **cassetta per ugnature** miter box

**cassettièra** *f* chest of drawers

**cassétto** *m* drawer; **cassetto di distribuzione** (mach) slide valve

**cassettóne** *m* chest of drawers; (archit) coffer, caisson

**cassiè·re -ra** *mf* cashier; teller

**cassóne** *m* large case, large box; chest; caisson (*for underwater construction*); body (*of truck*); (mil) caisson

**cassonétto** *m* cornice

**cast** *m* cast (*of actors*)

**casta** *f* caste

**castagna** *f* chestnut; **castagna d'India** horse chestnut

**castagnéto** *m* chestnut grove

**castagno** *m* chestnut tree; chestnut (*lumber*); **castagno d'India** horse chestnut tree

**casta·no -na** *adj* chestnut (*color*)

**castellana** *f* chatelaine

**castellano** *m* lord of the castle, squire

**castellétto** *m* scaffold; (min) gallows, headframe

**castèl·lo** *m* castle; works (*e.g., of watch*); scaffold; jungle gym; hydraulic boom, bucket lift (*on truck*); (naut) forecastle; **castello di menzogne** pack of lies; **castello in aria** castle in Spain ‖ *m* (-la *fpl*) (archaic) castle

**castigare** §209 *tr* to punish; (poet) to correct, castigate

**castigatézza** *f* purity (*e.g., of style*)

**castiga·to -ta** *adj* decent, modest; pure (*language*)

**Castìglia, la** Castile

**castiglia·no -na** *adj* & *mf* Castilian

**casti·go** *m* (-ghi) punishment; (fig) scourge; **mettere in castigo** (coll) to punish

**casti·tà** *f* (-tà) chastity; (fig) purity

**ca·sto -sta** *adj* chaste; pure, elegant (*language or style*)

**castóne** *m* setting (*of stone*)

**castòro** *m* beaver

**castrare** *tr* to castrate; to spay; (fig) to expurgate

**castra·to -ta** *adj* castrated; spayed; (fig) effeminate ‖ *m* mutton (of castrated sheep); eunuch

**castróne** *m* wether (*sheep*); gelding (*horse*); (fig) nincompoop

**castroneria** *f* (vulg) stupidity

**casuale** *adj* fortuitous, casual; sundry (*e.g., expenses*)

**casuali·tà** *f* (-tà) chance, accident

**casùpola** [s] *f* hut, hovel

**catacli·sma** *m* (-smi) cataclysm

**catacómba** *f* catacomb

**catafal·co** *m* (-chi) catafalque

**catafàscio** *adv*—**a catafascio** topsy-turvy

**catalès·si** *f* (-si) catalepsy

**catàli·si** *f* (-si) catalysis

**catalizza·tóre -trice** [ddzz] *adj* catalytic ‖ *m* catalyst

**catalogare** §209 (**catàlogo**) *tr* to catalogue

**catàlo·go** *m* (-ghi) catalogue

**catapècchia** *f* hovel

**catapla·sma** *m* (-smi) poultice, plaster; (fig) bore

**catapulta** *f* catapult

**catapultare** *tr* to catapult

**cataratta** *f* cataract; sluice (*of canal*)

**catarro** *m* catarrh

**catar·si** *f* (-si) catharsis

**catàrti·co -ca** *adj* (-ci -che) cathartic

**catasta** *f* pile, heap

**catastale** *adj* land (*office*)

**catasto** *m* real-estate register; land office

**catàstrofe** *f* catastrophe; wreck

**catastròfi·co -ca** *adj* (-ci -che) catastrophic

**catechismo** *m* catechism

**catechizzare** [ddzz] *tr* to catechize

**categoria** *f* category; weight (*in boxing*); (sports) class

**categòri·co -ca** *adj* (-ci -che) categorical; classified (*telephone directory*)

**caténa** *f* chain; range (*of mountains*); (archit) tie beam; **catene da neve** tire chains; **mordere la catena** to champ the bit

**catenàc·cio** *m* (-ci) bolt; (fig) jalopy; (journ) giant-size headline

**catenèlla** *f* chain

**cateratta** *f* var of **cataratta**

**catèrva** *f* great quantity, large number

**catetère** *m* catheter

**cateterizzare** [ddzz] *tr* to catheterize

**catinèlla** *f* water basin; **piovere a catinelle** (coll) to rain cats and dogs

**catino** *m* basin

**càtodo** *m* cathode

**Catóne** *m* Cato; **Catone il Maggiore** Cato the Elder

**catòr·cio** *m* (-ci) (coll) piece of junk

**catramàre** *tr* to tar
**catramatrice** *f* asphalt-paving machine
**catrame** *m* tar, coal tar
**càttedra** *f* desk (*of teacher*); chair, professorship
**cattedrale** *adj* & *f* cathedral
**cattedràti·co -ca (-ci -che)** *adj* pedantic || *m* professor
**catte·gù** *m* (**-gù**) catgut
**cattivare** *tr* to captivate
**cattivèria** *f* wickedness; piece of wickedness
**cattivi·tà** *f* (**-tà**) captivity
**catti·vo -va** *adj* bad; wicked; vicious (*animal*); worthless; poor (*reputation; condition*); nasty; naughty; (archaic) cowardly || *mf* wicked person || *m* bad taste; **sapere di cattivo** to taste bad
**cattolicità** *f* catholicity
**cattòli·co -ca (-ci -che)** *adj* catholic || *adj* & *mf* Catholic
**cattura** *f* capture, seizure; arrest
**catturare** *tr* to capture, seize; to arrest
**caucàsi·co -ca** *adj* & *mf* (**-ci -che**) Caucasian
**caucciù** *m* (**cauccù**) rubber
**càusa** *f* cause, motive; fault; lawsuit, action; **a causa di** on account of; **causa civile** civil suit; **causa penale** criminal suit; **fare causa** to take legal action; **intentare causa a** to bring suit against
**causale** *adj* causal || *f* cause
**causare** (**càuso**) *tr* to cause
**causìdi·co** *m* (**-ci**) amicus curiae; (joc) pettifogger
**càusti·co -ca** *adj* (**-ci -che**) caustic
**cautèla** *f* caution; precaution, care
**cautelare** *adj* guaranteeing, protecting || *v* (**cautèlo**) *tr* to guarantee, protect || *ref* to take precautions
**cauterizzare** [ddzz] *tr* to cauterize
**càu·to -ta** *adj* cautious, prudent; cagey
**cauzióne** *f* security, bail; **dare cauzione** to give bail
**cava** *f* quarry, cave; (fig) mine
**cavadènti** *m* (**-ti**) (coll) tooth puller, poor dentist
**cavagno** *m* (coll) basket
**cavalcare** §197 *tr* to ride; to cross over (*e.g., a river*) || *intr* to ride; **cavalcare a bisdosso** to ride bareback; **cavalcare all'amazzone** to ride side-saddle
**cavalcata** *f* ride; cavalcade
**cavalcatura** *f* mount
**cavalca·vìa** *m* (**-vìa**) bridge (*between two buildings*); overpass
**cavalcióni** *adj*—**a cavalcioni (di)** astride
**cavalierato** *m* knighthood
**cavalière** *m* rider (*on horseback*); knight; cavalier; chevalier; **a cavaliere** astride; **cavaliere d'industria** adventurer; **cavaliere errante** knight errant; **essere a cavaliere di** to overlook (*e.g., a valley*); to stretch over (*e.g., two centuries*)
**cavalla** *f* mare
**cavalleggièro** *m* cavalryman
**cavalleré·sco -sca** *adj* (**-schi -sche**) chivalrous, knightly

**cavallerìa** *f* cavalry; chivalry, knighthood; (fig) chivalry
**cavallerizza** *f* manège, riding school; horsemanship; horsewoman
**cavallerizzo** *m* horseman; riding master
**cavallétta** *f* grasshopper
**cavallétto** *m* tripod; easel; trestle (*of ski lift*); scaffold (*e.g., of stonemason*); sawhorse, sawbuck
**cavalli·no -na** *adj* horse, horse-like || *m* foal, colt || *f* foal, filly; **correre la cavallina** to be on the loose; to sow one's wild oats
**cavallo** *m* horse; knight (*in chess*); crotch (*of pants*); **a cavallo** on horseback; **a cavallo di** astride; **andare col cavallo di San Francesco** to ride shank's mare; **cavallo a dondolo** hobbyhorse; **cavallo di battaglia** battle horse; (fig) specialty, forte; **cavallo da corsa** race horse; **cavallo da tiro** draft horse; **cavallo di Frisia** cheval-de-frise; **cavallo di ritorno** confirmed news; **cavallo vapore** metric horsepower; **essere a cavallo** (fig) to have turned the corner
**cavallóne** *m* big horse; billow
**cavallùc·cio** *m* (**-ci**) little horse; **a cavalluccio** on one's shoulders; **cavalluccio marino** (ichth) sea horse
**cavare** *tr* to dig; to extract (*e.g., a tooth*); to pull out (*e.g., money*); to draw; **cavare il cuore a qlcu** to move s.o. to compassion; **cavare una spina dal cuore a qlcu** to ease so.o.'s mind || *ref* to take off (*e.g., one's hat*); **cavarsela** to overcome an obstacle; to get out of trouble; **cavarsi la camicia di dosso** to give the shirt off one's back; **cavarsi la fame** to eat one's fill; **cavarsi la voglia** to satisfy one's wishes
**cavastiva·li** *m* (**-li**) bootjack
**cavatap·pi** *m* (**-pi**) corkscrew
**cavaturàccio·li** *m* (**-li**) corkscrew
**cavèrna** *f* cave, cavern
**cavernó·so -sa** [s] *adj* cavernous; deep (*voice*)
**cavézza** *f* halter; (fig) check
**càvia** *f* guinea pig; **cavia umana** (fig) guinea pig
**caviale** *m* caviar
**cavìc·chio** *m* (**-chi**) peg
**cavì·glia** *f* (**-glie**) ankle; bolt; pin, dowel, peg
**caviglièra** *f* ankle support
**cavillare** *intr* to cavil, quibble
**cavillo** *m* quibble
**cavilló·so -sa** [s] *adj* quibbling, captious
**cavi·tà** *f* (**-tà**) cavity
**ca·vo -va** *adj* hollow || *m* hollow; cable; trough (*between two waves*); (naut) hawser; **cavo di rimorchio** towline; **cavo telefonico** telephone cable || *f* see **cava**
**cavolfióre** *m* cauliflower
**càvolo** *m* cabbage; **cavolo di Bruxelles** Brussels sprouts (*food*); (bot) Brussels sprout; **non capire un cavolo** (vulg) to not understand a blessed thing
**cazzòtto** *m* (vulg) punch, sock
**cazzuòla** *f* trowel

**ce** §5
**cecare** §122 *tr* to blind
**cèc·ca** *f* (-che) magpie; **fare cecca** to misfire
**cecchino** *m* sniper
**céce** *m* chickpea
**ceci·tà** *f* (-tà) blindness
**cè·co** -ca *adj* & *mf* (-chi -che) Czech Cecoslovàcchia, la Czechoslovakia
**cecoslovac·co** -ca *adj* & *mf* (-chi -che) Czechoslovak
**cèdere** §123 *tr* to cede; to give up; to sell at cost; **cedere il passo** to let s.o. through; **cedere la strada** to yield the right of way; **non cederla** to be second to none ‖ *intr* to give in, yield; to give way, succumb; to sag
**cedévole** *adj* yielding; soft; pliable
**cediglia** *f* cedilla
**cediménto** *m* cave-in; (fig) yielding
**cèdola** *f* slip; coupon
**cedri·no** -na *adj* citron; citron-like; cedar, cedar-like
**cédro** *m* (*Citrus medica*) citron; (*Cedrus*) cedar; **cedro del Libano** cedar of Lebanon
**CEE** *m* (letterword) (**Comunità Economica Europea**) EEC (*European Economic Community - Common Market*)
**cefalèa** *f* slight headache; headache
**cèfalo** *m* (ichth) mullet
**cèffo** *m* snout; (pej) face; **brutto ceffo** ugly mug
**ceffóne** *m* slap in the face
**celare** (**cèlo**) *tr* to hide, conceal
**cela·to** -ta *adj* hidden ‖ *f* sallet
**celebèrri·mo** -ma *adj* very famous, renowned
**celebrare** (**cèlebro**) *tr* & *intr* to celebrate
**celebrazióne** *f* celebration
**cèlebre** *adj* famous, renowned, celebrated
**celebri·tà** *f* (-tà) celebrity
**cèlere** *adj* swift, rapid; express (*train*); short, quick; prompt ‖ **Celere** *f* special police
**celeri·tà** *f* (-tà) swiftness, rapidity; speed (*e.g., of a machine gun*)
**celèste** *adj* heavenly, celestial; blue, sky-blue ‖ *m* blue, sky blue; **celesti** heavenly spirits; (mythol) gods
**celestiale** *adj* celestial, heavenly
**cèlia** *f* jest; **mettere in celia** to deride; **per celia** in jest
**celiare** §287 (**cèlio**) *intr* to jest, joke
**celibatà·rio** -ria (-ri -rie) *adj* single ‖ *m* old bachelor
**celibato** *m* celibacy; bachelorhood
**cèlibe** *adj* single, unmarried ‖ *m* bachelor
**cèlla** *f* cell; **cella frigorifera** walk-in refrigerator; **cella campanaria** belfry
**cèllofan** or **cellofàn** *m* cellophane
**cèllula** *f* cell; **cellula fotoelettrica** photoelectric cell
**cellulare** *adj* cellular; ventilated (*fabric*); solitary (*confinement*)
**cellulòide** *f* celluloid
**celluló·so** -sa [s] *adj* cell-like, cellular ‖ *f* cellulose
**cèl·ta** *mf* (-ti -te) Celt

**cèlti·co** -ca *adj* (-ci -che) Celtic; venereal (*disease*)
**cementare** (**ceménto**) *tr* to cement
**ceménto** *m* cement, concrete; **cemento armato** reinforced concrete
**céna** *f* supper; **Ultima Cena** Last Supper
**cenàcolo** *m* cenacle
**cenare** (**céno**) *intr* to sup, have supper
**cenciaiò·lo** -la *mf* ragpicker
**cén·cio** *m* (-ci) rag, duster (*for cleaning*)
**cenció·so** -sa [s] *adj* tattered, ragged
**cénere** *adj* ashen ‖ *f* ash; cinder; **andare in cenere** to go up in smoke; **ceneri** ashes (*of a person*); **ridurre in cenere** to burn to ashes ‖ **le Ceneri** Ash Wednesday
**cenerèntola** *f* (fig) Cinderella ‖ **Cenerèntola** *f* Cinderella (*of the fable*)
**cén·gia** *f* (-ge) ledge (*of a mountain*)
**cénno** *m* sign; wave (*with hand*); nod; wag; wink; gesture; hint; notice; **ai cenni di** at the orders of; **fare cenno a** or **di** to mention; **fare cenno di no** to shake one's head; **fare cenno di sì** to nod assent
**cenò·bio** *m* (-bi) monastery
**cenobi·ta** *m* (-ti) monk, cenobite
**censiménto** *m* census
**censire** §176 *tr* to take the census of
**cènso** *m* wealth, income; census (*in ancient Rome*)
**censóre** *m* censor; faultfinder; (educ) proctor
**censuà·rio** -ria (-ri -rie) *adj* income; tax (*register*) ‖ *m* taxpayer
**censura** *f* censure; censorship; faultfinding
**censurare** *tr* to censure; to criticize, find fault with
**centàuro** *m* centaur
**centellinare** *tr* to sip; to take a nip of
**centellino** *m* sip, nip
**centenà·rio** -ria (-ri -rie) *adj* & *mf* centenary, centennial ‖ *m* centenary, centennial (*anniversary*)
**centèsi·mo** -ma *adj* hundredth ‖ *m* hundredth; centime; cent; penny
**centigrado** *m* centigrade
**centigrammo** *m* centigram
**centimetro** *m* centimeter; tape measure
**cèntina** *f* (archit) centering; (aer) rib
**centi·nàio** *m* hundred; **un centinaio di** about a hundred ‖ *m* (-nàia *fpl*)—a **centinaia** by the hundreds
**cènto** *adj*, *m* & *pron* a hundred, one hundred; **per cento** per cent
**centomila** *adj*, *m* & *pron* a hundred thousand, one hundred thousand
**centóne** *m* cento
**centopiè·di** *m* (-di) centipede
**centrale** *adj* central ‖ *f* headquarters, home office; powerhouse, generating station; telephone exchange; **centrale di conversione** (elec) transformer station; **centrale telefonica** central
**centralini·sta** *mf* (-sti -ste) telephone operator
**centralino** *m* telephone exchange
**centralizzare** [ddzz] *tr* to centralize
**centrare** (**cèntro**) *tr* to center; to hit the center of

**centrattac·co** *m* (**-chi**) (sports) center forward
**centrìfu·go -ga** *adj* (**-ghi -ghe**) centrifugal ‖ *f* centrifuge
**centrino** *m* centerpiece
**centrìpe·to -ta** *adj* centripetal
**centri·sta** *mf* (**-sti -ste**) (pol) centrist
**cèntro** *m* center; **al centro** downtown; **far centro** to hit the mark
**centrocampo** *m* (soccer) midfield
**centuplicare** §197 (**centùplico**) *tr* to multiply a hundredfold
**cèntu·plo -pla** *adj & m* hundredfold
**céppo** *m* trunk, stump; log; block (*for beheading*); brake shoe; stock (*of anchor*); **ceppi** stocks, fetters ‖ **il Ceppo** (coll) Christmas
**céra** *f* wax; face, aspect, air, look; **di cera** waxen; pale; **cera da scarpe** shoe polish; **avere buona cera** to look well; **fare buona cera a** to welcome
**ceralac·ca** *f* (**-che**) sealing wax
**ceràmi·co -ca** (**-ci -che**) *adj* ceramic ‖ *f* ceramics
**cerare** (**céro**) *tr* to wax
**Cèrbero** *m* Cerberus
**cerbiatto** *m* fawn
**cerbottana** *f* blowgun, peashooter
**cer·ca** *f* (**-che**) search, quest; **in cerca di** in search of
**cercare** §197 (**cérco**) *tr* to seek, look for; to desire, yearn for; **cercare il pelo nell'uovo** to be a faultfinder, to nitpick ‖ *intr* to try
**cerca·tóre -trice** *adj* seeking ‖ *mf* seeker; mendicant ‖ *m* prospector
**cérchia** *f* coterie; compass, limits (*of a wall*); circle (*of friends*)
**cerchiare** §287 (**cérchio**) *tr* to hoop (*a barrel*); to circle, encircle
**cér·chio** *m* (**-chi**) circle; hoop; loop; **fare il cerchio della morte** (aer) to loop the loop; **in cerchio** in a circle ‖ *m* (**-chia** *fpl*) (archaic) circle
**cerchióne** *m* rim; tire (*of metal*)
**cereale** *adj & m* cereal
**cerebrale** *adj* cerebral
**cère·o -a** *adj* waxen; wax-colored, pale
**cerfò·glio** *m* (**-gli**) chervil
**cerimònia** *f* ceremony; **fare cerimonie** to stand on ceremony; to make a fuss
**cerimoniale** *adj & m* ceremonial
**cerimonière** *m* master of ceremonies (*at court*)
**cerimonió·so -sa** [*s*] *adj* ceremonious
**cerino** *m* wax match; taper
**cernéc·chio** *m* (**-chi**) tuft (*of hair*)
**cernièra** *f* hinge; clasp (*of handbag*); **a cerniera** hinged; **cerniera lampo** zipper
**cèrnita** *f* sorting, selection, grading
**céro** *m* church candle; **offrire un cero** to light a candle
**ceróne** *m* make-up (*of actor*)
**ceròtto** *m* adhesive tape; (fig) bore; **cerotto per i calli** corn plaster
**certame** *m* (poet) combat; competition, contest (*of poets*)
**certézza** *f* certitude, assurance, conviction, certainty
**certificare** §197 (**certìfico**) *tr* to certify, certificate

**certificato** *m* certificate
**cèr·to -ta** *adj* such, some; convinced; certain; real, positive ‖ *m* certainty; **di certo** or **per certo** for certain ‖ **certi** *pron* some ‖ **certo** *adv* undoubtedly
**certósa** *f* Carthusian monastery, charterhouse
**certosi·no** *m* Carthusian monk; chartreuse (*liquor*); **da certosino** with great patience
**certu·no -na** *adj* (obs) some ‖ **certuni** *pron* some
**cerùle·o -a** *adj* cerulean
**cerume** *m* ear wax
**cervellétto** *m* cerebellum
**cervelli·no -na** *adj & mf* scatterbrain
**cervèllo** *m* (**cervèlli & cervèlla** *fpl*) brain; head; mind; **dare al cervello** to go to one's head
**cervellòti·co -ca** *adj* (**-ci -che**) queer, extravagant
**cervice** *f* (anat) cervix; (poet) nape of the neck
**cerviè·ro -ra** *adj* lynx-like; ‖ *m* lynx
**cervi·no -na** *adj* deer-like; ‖ **Cervino** *m* Matterhorn
**cèrvo** *m* deer; (ent) stag beetle; **cervo volante** kite
**Cèsare** *m* Caesar
**cesàre·o -a** *adj* Caesarean; (poet) courtly
**cesellare** (**cesèllo**) *tr* to chase, chisel; to carve, engrave; to polish (*e.g., a poem*)
**cesella·tóre -trice** *mf* chaser, engraver, chiseler
**cesellatura** *f* chasing, engraving; polished writing
**cesèllo** *m* burin, graver
**cesóia** *f* shears, metal shears; **cesoie** shears (*for gardening*)
**cesoiatrice** *f* shearing machine
**cèspite** *m* source (*of income*); (poet) tuft
**céspo** *m* tuft
**cespù·glio** *m* (**-gli**) bush, shrub, thicket
**cèssa** *f*—**senza cessa** without letup
**cessare** (**cèsso**) *tr* to stop, interrupt ‖ *intr* to cease, stop; **cessare di** + *inf* to stop + *ger*
**cessazióne** *f* cessation, discontinuance; **cessazione d'esercizio** going out of business
**cessionà·rio** *m* (**-ri**) assignee
**cèsso** *m* (vulg) privy, outhouse
**césta** *f* basket, hamper
**cestinare** *tr* to throw into the wastebasket; to reject (*a book, article, etc.*)
**césto** *m* basket; tuft; head (*e.g., of lettuce*)
**cesura** *f* caesura
**cetàceo** *m* cetacean
**cèto** *m* class; **ceto medio** middle class
**cétra** *f* lyre; cither; inspiration
**cetriolino** *m* gherkin
**cetriòlo** *m* cucumber; (fig) dolt
**che** *adj* what; which; what a, e.g., **che bella giornata!** what a beautiful day! ‖ *pron interr* what ‖ *pron rel* who; whom; that; which; (coll) in which ‖ *m*—**essere un gran che** to be a big

shot, to be somebody || *adv* how, e.g., **che bello!** how nice!; **non . . . che** only, e.g., **non venne che Luigi** only Luigi came; no one but, e.g., **non restò che mio cugino** no one but my cousin stayed || *conj* that; (*after comparatives*) than, as

**ché** *adv* (coll) why || *conj* (coll) because; (coll) so that

**checché** *pron* (lit) whatever, no matter what

**checchessìa** *pron* (lit) anything, everything

**chèla** *f* claw

**che·pì** *m* (**-pì**) kepi

**cherubino** *m* cherub

**chetare** (**chéto**) *tr* to quiet; to placate || *ref* to quiet down, become quiet

**chetichèlla** *f*—**alla chetichella** surreptitiously, stealthily

**ché·to -ta** *adj* quiet, still

**chi** *pron interr* who; whom || *pron rel* who; whom; **chi . . . chi** some . . . some

**chiàcchiera** *f* chatter, idle talk; gossip; glibness; **fare quattro chiacchiere** to have a chat

**chiacchierare** (**chiàcchiero**) *intr* to chat; to gossip

**chiacchierata** *f* talk, chat; **fare una chiacchierata** to visit

**chiacchieri·no -na** *adj* talkative, loquacious

**chiacchierì·o** *m* (**-i**) chattering, jabbering (*of a crowd*)

**chiacchieró·ne -na** *adj* talkative, loquacious || *mf* chatterbox

**chiama** *f* roll call; **fare la chiama** to call the roll; **mancare alla chiama** to be absent at the roll call

**chiamare** *tr* to call; to hail (*a cab*); to invoke, call upon; **chiamare al telefono** to call up; **esser chiamato a** to have the vocation for || *ref* to be named; **si chiama Giovanni** his name is John

**chiamata** *f* call; (law) designation (*of an heir*); (telp) ring; (theat) curtain call; (typ) catchword

**chiappa** *f* (vulg) buttock; (slang) catch (*e.g., of fish*)

**chiarét·to -ta** *adj & m* claret

**chiarézza** *f* clarity, clearness

**chiarificare** §197 (**chiarìfico**) *tr* to clarify

**chiarificazióne** *f* clarification

**chiariménto** *m* explanation

**chiarire** §176 *tr* to clear up, explain; to unravel || *intr* (ESSERE) to clear, become clear || *ref* to make oneself clear; to assure oneself

**chia·ro -ra** *adj* clear; bright; light (*color*); honest; clear-cut; plain (*language*); illustrious, famous || *m* light; bright color; brightness; **chiaro di luna** moonlight; **con questi chiari di luna** in these troubled times; **mettere in chiaro** to clarify, explain || **chiaro** *adv* plainly; **chiaro e tondo** bluntly, frankly

**chiaróre** *m* light, glimmer

**chiaroveggènte** *adj & mf* clairvoyant

**chiaroveggènza** *f* clairvoyance

**chiassata** *f* uproar, disturbance, racket; noisy scene

**chiasso** *m* noise; uproar; alley; **fare chiasso** to cause a sensation

**chiassó·so -sa** [s] *adj* noisy; gaudy

**chiatta** *f* barge; pontoon

**chiavarda** *f* bolt

**chiave** *f* key; wrench; (archit) keystone; (mus) clef; **avere le chiavi di** to own; **chiave a rollino** adjustable wrench; **chiave a tubo** socket wrench; **chiave di volta** keystone; **chiave inglese** monkey wrench; **fuori chiave** off key; **sotto chiave** under lock and key

**chiavétta** *f* key; cock; cotter pin

**chiàvi·ca** *f* (**-che**) sewer

**chiavistèllo** *m* bolt

**chiazza** *f* spot, blotch

**chiazzare** *tr* to spot, blotch; to mottle

**chiazza·to -ta** *adj* spotted, mottled

**chic·ca** *f* (**-che**) sweet, candy

**chìcchera** *f* cup

**chicchessìa** *pron indef* anyone, anybody

**chicchirichì** *m* cock-a-doodle-doo

**chic·co** *m* (**-chi**) grain, seed; bead (*of rosary*); bean (*of coffee*); **chicco di grandine** hailstone; **chicco d'uva** grape

**chièdere** §124 *tr* to ask; to ask for; to beg (*pardon*); to require; to sue (*for damages or peace*); **chiedere a qlcu di** + *inf* to ask s.o. to + *inf*; **chiedere in prestito** to borrow; **chiedere qlco a qlcu** to ask s.o. for s.th || *ref* to wonder

**chiéri·ca** *f* (**-che**) tonsure; priesthood

**chiéri·co** *m* (**-ci**) clergyman; altar boy; (archaic) clerk

**chièsa** *f* church

**chiesuòla** *f* small church; clique, set (*e.g., of artists*); (naut) binnacle

**chì·glia** *f* (**-glie**) keel; **chiglia mobile** (naut) centerboard

**chilo** *m* kilo, kilogram; **fare il chilo** to take a siesta

**chilociclo** *m* kilocycle

**chilogrammo** *m* kilogram

**chilohèrtz** *m* kilohertz

**chilometràg·gio** *m* (**-gi**) distance in kilometers

**chilomètri·co -ca** *adj* (**-ci -che**) kilometric; interminable (*e.g., speech*)

**chilòmetro** *m* kilometer

**chilo·watt** *m* (**-watt**) kilowatt

**chimèra** *f* chimera; daydream, utopia

**chimèri·co -ca** *adj* (**-ci -che**) chimerical

**chìmi·co -ca** (**-ci -che**) *adj* chemical || *m* chemist || *f* chemistry

**chimòno** *m* kimono

**china** *f* slope, decline; India ink; cinchona

**chinare** *tr* to bend; to lower (*one's eyes*); **chinare il capo** to nod assent; **chinare la fronte** to yield, give in || *ref* to bend, stoop

**china·to -ta** *adj* bent, lowered; bitter; with quinine, e.g., **vino chinato** wine with quinine

**chincàglie** *fpl* notions, knicknacks, sundries

**chincaglière** *m* notions or knicknack dealer

**chincaglierìa** *f* knicknack; **chincaglierie** knicknacks, notions

**chinina** *f* quinine (*alkaloid*)

**chinino** *m* quinine (*salt of the alkaloid*)

**chi·no -na** *adj* bent, lowered || *f* see **china**

**chiòc·cia** *f* (-ce) brooding hen

**chiocciare** §128 (**chiòccio**) *intr* to cluck; to sit, brood; to crouch

**chiocciata** *f* brood

**chiòc·cio -cia** (-ci -ce) *adj* hoarse || *f* see **chioccia**

**chiòcciola** *f* snail; (anat) cochlea; (mach) nut

**chioccolì·o** *m* (-i) cackle (*of hen*); gurgle (*of water*)

**chiodare** (**chiòdo**) *tr* to nail

**chioda·to -ta** *adj* nailed shut; hobnailed

**chiòdo** *m* nail; spike; obsession; craze; (coll) debt; **chiodi** climbing irons; **chiodo a espansione** expansion bolt; **chiodo da cavallo** horseshoe nail; **chiodo di garofano** clove; **chiodo ribattino** rivet

**chiòma** *f* hair; mane; foliage; (astr) coma

**chioma·to -ta** *adj* hairy, long-haired; leafy

**chiòsa** *f* gloss

**chiosare** (**chiòso**) *tr* to gloss, comment on

**chiò·sco** *m* (-schi) kiosk, stand, newsstand; pavilion, bandstand

**chiòstra** *f* circular range (*of mountains*); (poet) enclosure; (poet) set (*of teeth*); (poet) zone, region

**chiòstro** *m* cloister

**chiòt·to -ta** *adj* quiet, still; **chiotto chiotto** still as a mouse

**chiromante** *mf* palmist

**chiromanzìa** *f* palmistry

**chiropràtica** *f* chiropractice

**chirurgìa** *f* surgery

**chirùrgi·co -ca** *adj* (-ci -che) surgical

**chirur·go** *m* (-ghi & -gi) surgeon

**chissà** *adv* maybe

**chitarra** *f* guitar; **chitarra hawaiana** ukulele

**chitarri·sta** *mf* (-sti -ste) guitar player

**chiùdere** §125 *tr* to shut, close; to lock; to turn off; to fasten; to block (*a road*); to fence in; to nail shut (*a box*); to strike (*a balance*); to conclude, wind up; **chiudere a chiave** to lock; **chiudere bottega** to go out of business; **chiudere il becco** (slang) to shut up || *intr* to shut, close; to lock || *ref* to shut, close; to lock; to withdraw; to cloud over

**chiùnque** *pron indef invar* anybody, anyone || *pron rel invar* whoever, whomever; anyone who, anyone whom

**chiurlo** *m* (orn) curlew

**chiusa** [s] *f* fence; lock (*of canal*); end, conclusion (*e.g., of letter*)

**chiusino** [s] *m* manhole

**chiu·so -sa** [s] *adj* shut, closed, locked; stuffy (*air*); high-bodiced (*dress*);

**close** (*vowel*) || *m* enclosure, corral; **close** || *f* see **chiusa**

**chiusura** [s] *f* closing, end; fastener; lock; **chiusura lampo** zipper, slide fastener

**ci** §5

**ciabatta** *f* slipper; old shoe

**ciabat·tàio** *m* (-tài) cobbler

**ciabattare** *intr* to shuffle along

**ciabattino** *m* cobbler, shoemaker

**ciàc** *f* (mov) clappers

**cialda** *f* wafer; thin waffle

**cialdóne** *m* cone (*for ice cream*)

**cialtró·ne -na** *mf* rogue, scoundrel; slovenly person

**ciambèlla** *f* doughnut; **ciambella di salvataggio** life saver

**ciambellano** *m* chamberlain

**ciampicare** §197 (**ciàmpico**) *intr* to stumble along

**ciana** *f* (slang) fishwife

**cianamide** *f* cyanamide

**ciàn·cia** *f* (-ce) chatter, prattle, idle gossip

**cianciare** §128 (**ciàncio**) *intr* to chatter, prattle

**cianciafrùscola** *f* trifle, bagatelle

**cianfrusà·glia** *f* (-glie) trifle, trinket; rubbish, trash, junk

**cianìdri·co -ca** *adj* (-ci -che) hydrocyanic

**cianògeno** *m* cyanogen

**cianuro** *m* cyanide

**ciao** *interj* (coll) hi!, hello!; (coll) goodbye!, so long!

**ciarla** *f* chatter, prattle, idle talk; gossip

**ciarlare** *intr* to chatter, prattle

**ciarlatanata** *f* charlatanism, quackery

**ciarlatanerìa** *f* charlatanism

**ciarlatané·sco -sca** *adj* (-schi -sche) charlatan

**ciarlatano** *m* charlatan, quack

**ciarliè·ro -ra** *adj* talkative, garrulous

**ciarpame** *m* rubbish, junk

**ciaschedu·no -na** *adj indef* each || *pron indef* each one, everyone

**ciascu·no -na** *adj indef* each || *pron indef* each one, everyone

**cibare** *tr & ref* to feed

**cibà·rio -ria** (-ri -rie) *adj* alimentary || **cibarie** *fpl* foodstuffs, victuals

**cibo** *m* food; meal; (fig) dish

**cicala** *f* cicada; grasshopper; locust; (fig) chatterbox; (naut) anchor ring

**cicalare** *intr* to prattle, babble; to chatter

**cicaléc·cio** *m* (-ci) prattle, babble; chatter

**cicatrice** *f* scar

**cicatrizzare** [ddzz] *tr* to heal (*a wound*) || *intr* (ESSERE) & *ref* to heal, scar

**cicatrizzazióne** [ddzz] *f* closing, healing (*of a wound*)

**cic·ca** *f* (-che) butt (*of cigar or cigarette*); (slang) chewing gum

**ciccare** §197 *intr* to chew tobacco; (coll) to boil with anger

**cicchettare** (**cicchétto**) *tr* (slang) to prime (*a carburetor*); (slang) to dress down, reprimand || *intr* to tipple

**cicchétto** *m* nip (*of liquor*); (slang) dressing down

**cìc·cia** *f* (**-ce**) (joc) flesh; (joc) fat

**cicció·ne -na** *mf* fatty

**ciceróne** *m* guide || **Cicerone** *m* Cicero

**ciclàbile** *adj* open to bicycles; bicycle, e.g., **pista ciclabile** bicycle trail

**cìcli·co -ca** *adj* (**-ci -che**) cyclic(al)

**cicli·sta** *mf* (**-sti -ste**) cyclist, bicyclist

**ciclo** *m* cycle; (coll) bicycle; **ciclo operativo** (econ) turnover

**ciclomotóre** *m* motorbike

**ciclomotori·sta** *mf* (**-sti -ste**) driver of motorbike

**ciclóne** *m* cyclone

**ciclòpe** *m* cyclops

**ciclòpi·co -ca** *adj* (**-ci -che**) cyclopean, gigantic

**ciclopista** *f* bicycle trail

**ciclostilare** *tr* to mimeograph

**ciclostile** or **ciclostilo** *m* mimeograph

**ciclotróne** *m* cyclotron

**cicógna** *f* stork

**cicòria** *f* chicory; endive

**cicuta** *f* hemlock

**ciè·co -ca** (**-chi -che**) *adj* blind; **alla cieca** blindly || *mf* blind person || *m* blind man; **i ciechi** the blind

**cièlo** *m* sky; heaven; weather, climate; roof (*e.g., of wagon*); **a ciel sereno** in the open air; **cielo a pecorelle** mackerel or fleecy sky; **dal cielo** from above; **non stare né in cielo né in terra** to be utterly absurd; **per amor del cielo** for heaven's sake; **portare al cielo** to praise to the skies; **santo cielo!** good heavens!; **volesse il cielo che . . . !** would that . . . !

**cifra** *f* number, figure; Arabic numeral; sum, total; digit; initial, monogram; cipher, code; **cifra d'affari** amount of business, turnover; **cifra tonda** round number

**cifrare** *tr* to cipher, code; to embroider (*a monogram*)

**cifrà·rio** *m* (**-ri**) code, cipher

**cì·glio** *m* (**-glia** *fpl*) eyelash; eyebrow; **a ciglio asciutto** with dry eyes; **ciglia** (zool) cilia; **senza batter ciglio** without batting an eye || *m* (**-gli**) (fig) edge, brow

**ciglóne** *m* bank, embankment

**cigno** *m* swan; cob

**cigolante** *adj* creaky, squeaky

**cigolare** (**cìgolo**) *intr* to squeak, creak

**cigolì·o** *m* (**-i**) squeak, creak

**Cile, il** Chile

**cilécca** *f*—**fare cilecca** to misfire

**cileccare** §197 (**cilécco**) *intr* to goof, blunder; to fail

**cilè·no -na** *adj* & *mf* Chilean

**cilè·stro -stra** *adj* (poet) azure, blue

**cili·cio** *m* (**-ci**) sackcloth

**ciliè·gia** *f* (**-gie** & **-ge**) cherry

**ciliè·gio** *m* (**-gi**) cherry tree

**cilindrare** *tr* to calender (*e.g., paper*); to roll (*a road*)

**cilindrata** *f* (aut) cylinder capacity, piston displacement

**cilìndri·co -ca** *adj* (**-ci -che**) cylindric(al)

**cilindro** *m* cylinder; top hat; roll, roller

**cima** *f* top, summit; tip (*e.g., of a pole*); peak (*of mountain*); edge, end; rope, cable; head (*e.g., of let-*

*tuce*); (coll) genius; **da cima a fondo** from top to bottom

**cimare** *tr* to cut the tip off; to shear; (agr) to prune

**cimasa** *f* (archit) coping

**cimbalo** *m* gong; (obs) cymbal; **in cimbali** tipsy; in a tizzy

**cimè·lio** *m* (**-li**) relic, souvenir, memento

**cimentare** (**ciménto**) *tr* to risk (*e.g., one's life*); to provoke; (archaic) to assay || *ref* to expose oneself; to venture

**ciménto** *m* risk, danger; (archaic) assay

**cimice** *f* bug; bedbug; (coll) thumbtack

**cimièro** *m* crest; (poet) helmet

**ciminièra** *f* chimney (*of factory*); smokestack (*of locomotive*); funnel (*of steamship*)

**cimitèro** *m* cemetery, graveyard; (fig) ghosttown

**cimósa** [s] or **cimóssa** *f* selvage; blackboard eraser

**cimurro** *m* distemper; (joc) cold

**Cina, la** China

**cinabro** *m* cinnabar; crimson; red ink

**cìn·cia** *f* (**-ce**) titmouse

**cinciallégra** *f* great titmouse

**cincilla** *f* chinchilla

**cincischiare** §287 *tr* to shred; to wrinkle, crease; to waste (*time*); to mumble (*words*) || *intr* to wrinkle, crease

**cine** *m* (coll) cinema

**cineamatóre** *m* amateur movie maker

**cine·asta** *m* (**-sti**) motion-picture producer; movie fan; movie actor || *f* movie actress

**cinecàmera** *f* movie camera

**cinedilettante** *mf* amateur movie maker

**cinegiornale** *m* newsreel

**cinelàndia** *f* movieland

**cìne·ma** *m* (**-ma**) movies; movie house

**cinematografare** (**cinematògrafo**) *tr* to film, shoot

**cinematografìa** *f* cinema, motion pictures, movie industry

**cinematogràfi·co -ca** *adj* (**-ci -che**) movie, motion-picture; movie-like

**cinematògrafo** *m* motion picture; movie theater; (fig) hubbub; (fig) funny sight

**cineparchég·gio** *m* (**-gi**) drive-in movie

**cinepar·co** *m* (**-chi**) drive-in movie

**cineprésa** [s] *f* movie camera

**cinère·o -a** *adj* ashen

**cinescò·pio** *m* (**-pi**) kinescope, TV tube

**cinése** [s] *adj* & *mf* Chinese

**cineteatro** *m*: movie house; **cineteatro all'aperto** outdoor movie

**cinetè·ca** *f* (**-che**) film library

**cinèti·co -ca** (**-ci -che**) *adj* kinetic || *f* kinetics

**cingallégra** *f* var of **cinciallegra**

**cìngere** §126 *tr* to surround; to gird (*e.g., the head*); to gird on (*e.g., the sword*); **cingere cavaliere** to dub a knight; **cingere d'assedio** to besiege

**cìnghia** *f* belt, strap; **tirare la cinghia** to tighten one's belt

**cinghiale** *m* wild boar

**cinghiata** *f* lash

**cingola·to -ta** *adj* track-driven, caterpillar

**cìngolo** *m* endless metal belt, track; girdle, belt (*of a priest*)

**cinguettare** (**cinguétto**) *intr* to chirp, twitter; to babble

**cinguettì·o** *m* (**-i**) chirp, twitter; (fig) babble

**cìni·co** **-ca** (**-ci -che**) *adj* cynical || *m* cynic

**cinìglia** *f* chenille

**cinismo** *m* cynicism

**cinòfilo** *m* dog lover

**cinquanta** *adj, m & pron* fifty

**cinquantenà·rio** **-ria** (**-ri -rie**) *adj* fifty-year-old; occurring every fifty years || *m* fiftieth anniversary

**cinquantènne** *adj* fifty-year-old || *mf* fifty-year-old person

**cinquantèn·nio** *m* (**-ni**) period of fifty years, half century

**cinquantèsi·mo** **-ma** *adj, m & pron* fiftieth

**cinquantina** *f* about fifty; **sulla cinquantina** about fifty years old

**cìnque** *adj & pron* five; **le cinque** five o'clock || *m* five; fifth (*in dates*)

**cinquecénté·sco** **-sca** *adj* (**-schi -sche**) sixteenth-century

**cinquecènto** *adj, m & pron* five hundred || *f* small car || **il Cinquecento** the sixteenth century

**cinquina** *f* set of five; five numbers (*drawn at Italian lotto*); (mil) pay

**cinta** *f* fence, wall; circuit, enclosure; circumference (*of a city*)

**cintare** *tr* to surround; to fence in; to hold (*in wrestling*)

**cin·to** **-ta** *adj* surrounded, girded || *m* belt; girdle; **cinto erniario** truss || *f* see **cinta**

**cìntola** *f* waist; belt; **con le mani alla cintola** idling, loafing

**cintura** *f* belt; waist; waistband; lock (*in wrestling*); **cintura di salvataggio** life preserver; **cintura di sicurezza** safety belt

**cinturare** *tr* to surround

**cinturino** *m* strap (*of watch or shoes*); hem (*e.g., of cuffs*)

**cinturóne** *m* belt; Sam Browne belt

**ciò** *pron* this; that; **a ciò** for that purpose; **a ciò che** so that; **ciò nondimeno** or **ciò nonostante** though, nevertheless; **con tutto ciò** in spite of everything; **per ciò** therefore

**ciòc·ca** *f* (**-che**) lock (*of hair*); cluster (*e.g., of cherries*)

**ciòc·co** *m* (**-chi**) log; **dormire come un ciocco** to sleep like a log

**cioccolata** *adj invar* chocolate || *f* chocolate (*beverage*)

**cioccolatino** *m* chocolate candy

**cioccolato** *m* chocolate; **cioccolato al latte** milk chocolate

**cioè** *adv* that is to say, namely; to wit; rather

**ciondolare** (**cióndolo**) *tr* to dangle || *intr* to dawdle; to stroll, saunter

**cióndolo** *m* pendant, charm

**ciondolóne** *m* idler || *adv* dangling

**ciòtola** *f* bowl

**ciòttolo** *m* pebble, small stone; cobblestone

**ciottoló·so** **-sa** [s] *adj* pebbly

**cip** *m* (**cip**) chip (*in gambling*)

**cipì·glio** *m* (**-gli**) frown

**cipólla** *f* onion; bulb (*e.g., of a lamp*); nozzle (*of sprinkling can*)

**cippo** *m* column; bench mark

**ciprèsso** *m* cypress

**cipria** *f* face powder; **cipria compatta** compact

**cipriò·ta** *adj & mf* (**-ti -te**) Cypriot

**Cipro** *m* Cyprus

**circa** *adv* about, nearly || *prep* concerning, regarding, as to

**cir·co** *m* (**-chi**) circus; **circo equestre** circus; **circo glaciale** cirque; **circo lunare** walled plain

**circolante** *adj* circulating; lending (*library*) || *m* available cash (*of a corporation*)

**circolare** *adj* circular; cashier's (*check*) || *f* circular (*letter*); (rr) beltline || *v* (**cìrcolo**) *intr* to circulate

**circolazióne** *f* circulation; traffic; currency; **circolazione sanguigna** bloodstream; circulation of blood

**cìrcolo** *m* circle; circulation (*of blood*); reception (*e.g., at court*); club, set, group

**circoncìdere** §145 *tr* to circumcise

**circoncisióne** *f* circumcision

**circonci·so** **-sa** *adj* circumcised

**circondare** (**circóndo**) *tr* to surround, encircle; to overwhelm (*e.g., with kindness*) || *ref* to surround oneself; to be surrounded

**circondà·rio** *m* (**-ri**) district; surrounding territory

**circonduzióne** *f* rotation (*e.g., of the body in calisthenics*)

**circonferènza** *f* circumference

**circonflès·so** **-sa** *adj* circumflex

**circonlocuzióne** *f* circumlocution

**circonvallazióne** *f* city-line road; (rr) beltline

**circonvenire** §282 *tr* to circumvent; to outwit

**circonvenzióne** *f* circumvention

**circonvici·no** **-na** *adj* neighboring, nearby

**circoscrìt·to** **-ta** *adj* circumscribed

**circoscrìvere** §250 *tr* to circumscribe

**circoscrizióne** *f* district; circuit

**circospèt·to** **-ta** *adj* circumspect, cautious

**circospezióne** *f* circumspection

**circostante** *adj* neighboring, surrounding, nearby || **circostanti** *mpl* neighbors; bystanders, onlookers

**circostanza** *f* circumstance

**circostanziale** *adj* circumstantial

**circostanziare** §287 *tr* to describe in detail; to circumstanciate

**circostanzia·to** **-ta** *adj* detailed, circumstantial

**circuire** §176 *tr* to circumvent

**circùito** *m* circuit; race (*of automobiles or bicycles*); **circuito stampato** (rad, telv) printed circuit

**circumnavigare** §209 (**circumnàvigo**) *tr* to circumnavigate

**circumnavigazióne** *f* circumnavigation

**cirìlli·co** **-ca** *adj* (**-ci -che**) Cyrillic

**Ciro** m Cyrus
**cirro** m cirrus
**cirrò·si** f (-si) cirrhosis
**cispa** f gum (on edge of eyelids)
**cisposità** [s] f gum; gumminess
**cispó·so -sa** [s] adj gummy
**ciste** f cyst
**cistèrna** f cistern; tank
**cisti** f cyst
**cistifèllea** f gall bladder
**citante** mf (law) plaintiff
**citare** tr to cite, quote; to mention; (law) to summon, subpoena
**citazióne** f citation, quotation; mention; (law) summons, subpoena; (mil) commendation
**citillo** m (zool) gopher
**citòfono** m intercom
**citostàti·co -ca** adj (-ci -che) (biochem) cancer-inhibiting
**citrato** m citrate
**cìtri·co -ca** adj (-ci -che) citric
**citrul·lo -la** adj simple, foolish || mf simpleton, fool
**cit·tà** f (-tà) city, town || **Città del Capo** Cape Town; **Città del Messico** Mexico City; **Città del Vaticano** Vatican City; **città fungo** boom town
**cittadèlla** f citadel
**cittadinanza** f citizenship
**cittadi·no -na** adj city, town, civic || mf citizen; city dweller, urbanite || m townsman
**ciù·co** m (-chi) (coll) donkey, ass
**ciuffo** m lock, forelock; tuft; (bot) tassel
**ciuffolòtto** m (orn) bullfinch
**ciurlare** intr—**ciurlare nel manico** to play fast and loose
**ciurma** f crew, gang, mob
**ciurmare** tr (archaic) to charm; (archaic) to trick, inveigle
**ciurmatóre** m swindler, charlatan
**civétta** f barn owl, little owl; unmarked police car; ship used as decoy; (fig) coquette, flirt
**civettare** (civétto) intr to flirt
**civetterìa** f coquettishness, coquetry
**civettuò·lo la** adj coquettish; attractive
**cìvi·co -ca** adj (-ci -che) civic; town, city
**civile** adj civil; civilian || mf civilian
**civili·sta** mf (-sti -ste) attorney, solicitor
**civilizzare** [ddzz] tr to civilize || ref to become civilized
**civilizzazióne** [ddzz] f civilizing (e.g., of barbarians); civilization
**civil·tà** f (-tà) civilization; civility
**civismo** m good citizenship
**clac·son** m (-son) horn (of a car)
**claire** f (claire) grating (in front of a store window)
**clamóre** m clamor, uproar
**clamoró·so -sa** [s] adj noisy; clamorous
**clan** m (clan) clan; clique
**clandestì·no -na** adj clandestine
**clangóre** m clangor, clang
**clarinetti·sta** mf (-sti -ste) clarinet player
**clarinétto** m clarinet
**clarino** m clarion
**classe** f class

**classicheggiante** adj classicistic
**classicismo** m classicism
**classici·sta** mf (-sti -ste) classicist
**classici·tà** f (-tà) classical spirit; classical antiquity
**clàssi·co -ca** (-ci -che) adj classic(al) || m classic
**classìfi·ca** f (-che) rank, rating (in competitive testing); classification; (sports) rating
**classificare** §197 (classìfico) tr to classify; to rate, rank || ref to score
**classificazióne** f classification
**claudicante** adj lame, limping
**claudicare** §197 (clàudico) intr to limp
**clauné·sco -sca** adj (-schi -sche) clownish
**clàusola** f provision, proviso; clause; close, conclusion (e.g., of a speech); **clausola rossa** instructions for payment (in bank-credit documents); **clausola verde** shipping instructions (in bank-credit documents)
**clausura** f (eccl) seclusion; (fig) secluded place
**clava** f club, bludgeon
**clavicémbalo** m harpsichord
**clavìcola** f clavicle, collarbone
**clemàtide** f clematis
**clemènte** adj clement, indulgent; mild (climate)
**clemènza** f clemency; mildness
**cleptòmane** adj & mf kleptomaniac
**clericale** adj clerical || m clericalist
**clericalismo** m clericalism
**clèro** m clergy
**clessidra** f water clock; sandglass
**clicchettì·o** m (-ìi) clicking, click-clack (e.g., of a typewriter)
**cli·ché** m (-ché) cliché; stereotype (plate)
**cliènte** m client, customer, patron
**clientèla** f clientele, customers; practice (of a professional man)
**cli·ma** m (-mi) climate
**climatèri·co -ca** adj (-ci -che) climacteric; crucial
**climatè·rio** m (-ri) climacteric; crucial period
**climàti·co -ca** adj (-ci -che) climatic
**climatizzazióne** [ddzz] f air conditioning
**clìni·co -ca** (-ci -che) adj clinic || m clinician; highly skilled physician || f clinic; private hospital
**cli·sma** m (-smi) enema
**clistère** m enema; **clistere a pera** fountain syringe
**cloa·ca** f (-che) sewer
**cloche** f (cloche) woman's wide-brimmed hat; (aer) stick; (aut) floor gearshift
**clorare** (clòro) tr to chlorinate
**clorato** m chlorate
**clorìdri·co -ca** adj (-ci -che) hydrochloric
**clòro** m chlorine
**clorofilla** f chlorophyll
**cloroför·mio** m (-mi) chloroform
**cloroformizzare** [ddzz] tr to chloroform
**cloruro** m chloride

**coabitare** (coàbito) *intr* to live together; to cohabit

**coabitazióne** *f* sharing (*of an apartment*)

**coaccusa·to -ta** *adj* jointly accused ‖ *m* codefendant

**coacèrvo** *m* accumulation (*e.g., of interest*)

**coadiutóre** *m* coadjutor

**coadiuvante** *adj* helping ‖ *m* helper

**coadiuvare** (coàdiuvo) *tr* to assist, advise

**coagulare** (coàgulo) *tr* & *ref* to coagulate, clot

**coagulazióne** *f* coagulation, clotting

**coàgulo** *m* clot

**coalescènza** *f* coalescence

**coalizióne** *f* coalition

**coalizzare** [ddzz] *tr* & *ref* to unite, rally

**coartare** *tr* to coerce, force

**coartazióne** *f* coercion, forcing

**coatti·vo -va** *adj* forceful, compelling

**coat·to -ta** *adj* coercive

**coautóre** *m* coauthor

**coazióne** *f* coercion

**cobalto** *m* cobalt

**cocaina** *f* cocaine

**cocainòmane** *mf* cocaine addict

**coc·ca** *f* (-che) notch (*of arrow*); corner, edge (*e.g., of a handkerchief*); three-mast galley

**coccarda** *f* cockade

**cocchière** *m* coachman, cab driver

**còc·chio** *m* (-chi) coach; chariot

**cocchiume** *m* bung

**còc·cia** *f* (-ce) sword guard; (coll) head, noggin

**còccige** *m* coccyx

**coccinèlla** *f* ladybug

**cocciniglia** *f* cochineal

**còc·cio** *m* (-ci) earthenware; broken piece of pottery

**cocciutàggine** *m* stubbornness

**cocciu·to -ta** *adj* stubborn

**còc·co** *m* (-chi) coconut (*tree and nut*); (bact) coccus; (coll) egg; (coll) darling, favorite

**cocco·dè** *m* (-dè) cackle

**coccodrillo** *m* crocodile

**còccola** *f* berry (*of cypress*); darling girl

**coccolare** (còccolo) *tr* to fondle, cuddle ‖ *ref* to nestle, cuddle up; to bask

**còcco·lo -la** *adj* (coll) nice, darling ‖ *m* darling boy ‖ *f* see **coccola**

**coccolóne** or **coccolóni** *adv* squatting

**cocènte** *adj* burning

**cocktail** *m* (cocktail) cocktail; cocktail party

**còclea** *f* dredge; (anat) cochlea

**cocómero** *m* watermelon; (coll) simpleton

**cocorita** *f* parakeet

**cocuzza** *f* (coll) pumpkin; (coll) head, noggin

**cocùzzolo** *m* crown (*of hat*); peak (*of mountain*)

**códa** *f* tail; train (*of skirt*); pigtail (*of hair*); **coda di paglia** (coll) uneasy conscience; **con la coda dell'occhio** out of the corner of the eye; **con la coda tra le gambe** with its tail between its legs; (fig) crestfallen; **di**

**coda** last; **fare la coda** to stand in line; **in coda** in a row; **at the tail end**

**codardìa** *f* (lit) cowardice

**codar·do -da** *adj* cowardly ‖ *mf* coward

**codazzo** *m* (pej) trail (*of people*)

**codeina** *f* codein

**codé·sto -sta** §7 *adj* ‖ §8 *pron*

**còdice** *m* code; codex; **codice della strada** traffic laws; **codice di avviamento postale** zip code

**codicillo** *m* codicil

**codificare** §197 (codìfico) *tr* to codify

**codi·no -na** *adj* reactionary; conformist ‖ *m* pigtail (*of a man*); (fig) reactionary; conformist ‖ *f* small tail

**códolo** *m* tang, shank (*e.g., of knife*); handle (*of spoon or knife*); head (*of violin*)

**coeducazióne** *f* coeducation

**coefficiènte** *m* coefficient

**coerciti·vo -va** *adj* coercive

**coercizióne** *f* coercion

**coerède** *mf* coheir

**coerènte** *adj* coherent; consistent

**coerènza** *f* coherence; consistency

**coesióne** *f* cohesion

**coesistènza** *f* coexistence

**coesìstere** §114 *intr* to coexist

**coesi·vo -va** *adj* cohesive

**coetàne·o -a** *adj* & *m* contemporary

**coè·vo -va** *adj* contemporaneous, coeval

**cofanétto** *m* small chest, small coffer

**còfano** *m* chest, coffer; box, case (*for ammunition*); (aut) hood

**còffa** *f* masthead, crow's-nest

**cofirmatà·rio -ria** *adj* & *mf* (-ri -rie) cosigner

**cogitabón·do -da** *adj* (poet & joc) thoughtful, meditative

**cogitare** (cògito) *tr* & *intr* (poet & joc) to cogitate

**cógli** §4

**cògliere** §127 *tr* to gather; to hit (*the target*); to pluck (*flowers*); to grab, seize; (fig) to guess; **cogliere in flagrante** to catch in the act; **cogliere la palla al balzo** to seize time by the forelock; **cogliere nel giusto** to hit the nail on the head; **cogliere qlcu alla sprovvista** to catch s.o. napping; **cogliere sul fatto** to catch in the act

**coglióne** *m* (vulg) testicle; (vulg) simpleton, fool

**coglioneria** *f* (vulg) great stupidity

**cognata** *f* sister-in-law

**cognato** *m* brother-in-law

**cògni·to -ta** *adj* (poet & law) well-known

**cognizióne** *f* cognition, knowledge

**cognóme** *m* surname, family name

**coguaro** *m* cougar

**cói** §4

**coibènte** *adj* nonconducting ‖ *m* nonconductor

**coincidènza** *f* coincidence; harmony, identity; transfer (*from one streetcar or bus to another*); (rr) connection

**coincìdere** §145 *intr* to coincide

**coinquilino** *m* fellow tenant

**cointeressare** (cointerèsso) *tr* to give a share (*of profit*) to

cointeressa·to -ta *adj* jointly interested || *mf* party having a joint interest

cointeressènza *f* interest, share

coinvòlgere §289 *tr* to involve

còito *m* coitus, intercourse

cól §4

colà *adv* over there

colabròdo *m* colander, strainer

colàg·gio *m* (-gi) loss, leak

colapa·sta *m* (-sta) colander

colare (cólo) *tr* to filter, strain; to sift (*wheat*); to cast (*metals*); **colare a picco** to sink || *intr* to leak, drip; to flow (*said of blood*); **colare a picco** to sink

colata *f* casting (*of metal*); stream of lava; slide (*of snow or rocks*)

colatíc·cio *m* (-ci) drip, dripping

cola·tóio *m* (-tói) colander, strainer

colazione *f* breakfast; lunch; **colazione al sacco** picnic; **prima colazione** breakfast; **seconda colazione** lunch

colbac·co *m* (-chi) busby

colèi §8 *pron dem*

colèn·do -da *adj* (archaic) honorable

colè·ra *m* (-ra) cholera

colesterina *f* cholesterol

coli·brì *m* (-brì) hummingbird

còli·co -ca *adj* & *f* (-ci -che) colic

colino *m* strainer

cólla §4

còlla *f* glue; paste; **colla di pesce** ísínglass

collaborare (collàboro) *intr* to collaborate; to contribute (*to newspaper or magazine*)

collaboratóre *m* collaborator; contributor (*to newspaper or magazine*)

collaborazióne *f* collaboration

collaborazioni·sta *mf* (-sti -ste) collaborationist

collana *f* necklace; series, collection (*of literary works*)

collante *adj* & *m* adhesive

collare *m* collar || *v* (còllo) *tr* to lift or lower (*with a rope*)

collasso *m* collapse

collaterale *adj* & *m* collateral

collaudare (collàudo) *tr* to test; to approve; to pass

collauda·tóre -trice *mf* tester

collàudo *m* test

collazionare (collazióno) *tr* to collate

cólle §4

còlle *m* hill; low peak; mountain pass

collè·ga *mf* (-ghi -ghe) colleague, associate

collegaménto *m* connection, telephone connection; contact; (mil) liaison

collegare §209 (collégo) *tr* to join, connect || *intr* to agree, be in harmony || *ref* to become allied; to make contact, make connection (*e.g., by phone*)

collegiale *adj* collegiate || *mf* boardingschool student

collegiata *f* collegiate church

collè·gio *m* (-gi) college (*e.g., of surgeons*); boarding school, academy

còllera *f* anger, wrath; **montare in collera** to become angry

collèri·co -ca *adj* (-ci -che) hot-tempered, choleric

collètta *f* collection; collect (*in church*)

collettivismo *m* collectivism

collettivi·tà *f* (-tà) collectivity, community

colletti·vo -va *adj* collective || *m* party worker (*of leftist party*)

collétto *m* collar; flank (*of a tooth*)

collet·tóre -trice *adj* connecting; collecting (*pipe*) || *m* collector; tax collector; manifold; (elec) commutator (*of D.C. device*); (elec) collector (*of A.C. device*); **collettore d'ammissione** intake manifold; **collettore di scarico** exhaust manifold

collettoria *f* tax office; small post office

collezionare (collezióno) *tr* to collect (*e.g., stamps*)

collezióne *f* collection; collection, series (*of literary works*)

collezioni·sta *mf* (-sti -ste) collector

collìdere §135 *intr* to collide

collimare *tr* to point (*a telescope*) || *intr* to coincide, match; to dovetail

collina *f* hill; **in collina** in the hill country

collinó·so -sa [s] *adj* hilly

colli·rio *m* (-ri) eyewash

collisióne *f* collision; (fig) conflict: **entrare in collisione** to collide

cóllo §4

còllo *m* neck; piece (*of baggage*); package, parcel; **al collo** in a sling; (fig) downhill; **collo del piede** instep; **collo d'oca** crankshaft; **in collo** in one's arms (*said of a baby*)

collocaménto *m* placement, employment; **collocamento a riposo** retirement; **collocamento in aspettativa** leave of absence without pay; **collocamento in malattia** sick leave

collocare §197 (còlloco) *tr* to place; to find employment for; to sell; **collocare a riposo** to retire; **collocare in aspettativa** to give a leave of absence without pay to; **collocare in malattia** to send to sick leave to

collocazióne *f* location (*of a book in a library*); catalogue card

colloidale *adj* colloidal

collòide *m* colloid

colloquiale *adj* colloquial

collò·quio *m* (-qui) talk, conference; colloquy; colloquium, symposium

colló·so -sa [s] *adj* gluey, sticky

collotòrto *m* (collitòrti) bigot, hypocrite

collòttola *f* nape or scruff of the neck

collùdere §105 *intr* to be in collusion

collusióne *f* collusion

collutó·rio *m* (-ri) mouthwash

colluttare *intr* to scuffle, fight

colluttazióne *f* scuffle, fight

cólma *f* high-water level (*during high tide*)

colmare (cólmo) *tr* to fill, fill up; to fill in (*with dirt*); to overwhelm; **colmare una lacuna** to bridge a gap

colmata *f* silting; reclaimed land; sand bank

cól·mo -ma *adj* full, filled up || *m* top, peak, summit; (archit) ridgepole; (fig) acme; **al colmo di** at the height of; **è il colmo** that's the limit ‖ *f* see **colma**

**colofóne** *m* colophon

**colofònia** *f* rosin

**colombàia** *f* dovecot

**colombèlla** *f* ingenue; **a colombella** vertically

**colóm·bo -ba** *mf* pigeon, dove ‖ **Colombo** *m* Columbus

**colònia** *f* colony; cologne; settlement; summer camp; **colonia penale** penal colony; penitentiary ‖ **Colonia** *f* Cologne

**coloniale** *adj* colonial ‖ *m* colonial; colonist; **coloniali** imported foods

**colòni·co -ca** *adj* (**-ci -che**) farm (*e.g., house*)

**colonizzare** [ddzz] *tr* to colonize; to settle

**colonizzazióne** [ddzz] *f* colonization

**colonna** *f* column; row; **colonna sonora** sound track; **Colonne d'Ercole** Pillars of Hercules

**colonnato** *m* colonnade

**colonnèllo** *m* colonel

**colonnétta** *f* small column; gasoline pump

**colò·no -na** *mf* sharecropper; colonist; settler; (*poet*) farmer

**colorante** *adj* coloring ‖ *m* dye; stain

**colorare** (**colóro**) *tr & ref* to color; to stain

**colora·to -ta** *adj* colored; stained (*glass*)

**colorazióne** *f* coloring

**colóre** *m* color; paint; suit (*of cards*); flush (*at poker*); shade; character (*of a deal*); **di colore** colored (*man*); **farne di tutti i colori** to be up to all kinds of deviltry; **farsi di tutti i colori** to change countenance

**colorifi·cio** *m* (**-ci**) paint factory; dye factory

**colorire** §176 *tr* to color

**colori·to -ta** *adj* colored, flushed; expressive ‖ *m* color, complexion; (*fig*) expression

**coloritura** *f* coloring; characteristic; political complexion

**colóro** §8

**colossale** *adj* colossal

**Colossèo** *m* Coliseum

**colòsso** *m* colossus

**cólpa** *f* fault; sin; guilt; (*law*) injury; **avere la colpa** to be guilty; to be wrong; **essere in colpa** to be guilty

**colpévole** *adj* guilty ‖ *mf* guilty person, culprit

**colpevoli·sta** *mf* (**-sti -ste**) person who prejudges s.o. guilty

**colpire** §176 *tr* to hit, strike; to harm; to impress; **colpire nel segno** to hit the mark

**cólpo** *m* hit, blow; strike; tip, rap; knock; shot; round (*of gun*); cut, slash (*of knife*); thrust (*e.g., of spear*); lash (*of animal's tail*); toot (*of car's horn*); **andare a colpo sicuro** to know where to hit; **colpo apoplettico** stroke; **colpo da maestro** master stroke; **colpo d'aria** draft; **colpo d'ariete** water hammer; **colpo di fortuna** stroke of luck; **colpo di fulmine** love at first sight; **colpo di**

**grazia** coup de grâce; **colpo di mano** surprise attack; **colpo di scena** dramatic turn of events; **colpo di sole** sunstroke; **colpo di spugna** wiping the slate clean; **colpo di stato** coup d'état; **colpo di telefono** telephone call; **colpo di testa** sudden decision, inconsiderate action; **colpo di vento** gust of wind; **colpo d'occhio** view; glance, look; **di colpo** at once; **fallire il colpo** to miss the mark; **fare colpo** to make a hit; **sul colpo** then and there; **tutto in un colpo** all at once

**colpó·so -sa** [s] *adj* unpremeditated; involuntary (*e.g., manslaughter*)

**coltèlla** *f* butcher knife; (*elec*) knife switch

**coltellàc·cio** *m* (**-ci**) hunting knife; butcher knife; (*naut*) studding sail

**coltellata** *f* stab, gash, slash; **fare a coltellate** to fight with knives

**coltellerìa** *f* cutlery

**coltelli·nàio** *m* (**-nài**) cutler

**coltèllo** *m* knife; **a coltello** edgewise (*said of bricks*); **avere il coltello per il manico** to have the upper hand; **coltello a serramanico** switchblade knife; pocketknife

**coltivare** *tr* to cultivate

**coltiva·to -ta** *adj* cultivated

**coltivatóre** *m* farmer

**coltivazióne** *f* cultivation

**cól·to -ta** *adj* cultivated; learned (*word*) ‖ *m* garden; (*archaic*) worship

**cóltre** *f* blanket; comforter; (*fig*) pall; **coltri** bedclothes

**coltróne** *m* quilt

**coltura** *f* cultivation; crop; culture (*e.g., of silkworms, bacteria*)

**colubrina** *f* culverin

**colùi** §8 *pron dem*

**comandaménto** *m* commandment

**comandante** *m* commanding officer; commandant; (*nav*) captain; **comandante del porto** harbor master; **comandante in seconda** (*naut*) first mate

**comandare** *tr* to command, order; to direct (*employees*); to register (*a letter*); (*mach*) to regulate; (*mach*) to control; (*poet*) to overlook, command the view of (*e.g., a valley*); **comandare a bacchetta** to command in a dictatorial manner ‖ *intr* to command; **comandi!** (*mil*) at your orders!

**comando** *m* command, order

**comare** *f* godmother; (*coll*) friend, neighbor; (*coll*) gossip

**combaciare** §128 *tr* (*archaic*) to gather ‖ *intr* to fit closely together; to tally, dovetail; to coincide

**combattènte** *adj* fighting ‖ *m* combatant

**combàttere** *tr & intr* to combat ‖ *ref* to fight one another

**combattiménto** *m* combat; fight; battle; **fuori combattimento** knockout, K.O.; **fuori combattimento tecnico** technical knockout, T.K.O.; **mettere fuori combattimento** to knock out; (*fig*) to weaken

**combatti·vo -va** *adj* pugnacious, combative

**combattu·to -ta** *adj* heated (*discussion*); overcome (*by doubt*); torn (*between two opposing feelings*)

**combinare** *tr* to combine; to match (*e.g., colors*); to organize || *intr* to agree; **combinare a** to succeed in || *ref* to agree; to chance, happen; to combine

**combinazióne** *f* combination; chance; coverall (*for mechanics or flyers*)

**combrìccola** *f* gang

**combustìbile** *adj* combustible || *m* fuel, combustible

**combustióne** *f* combustion; (poet) upheaval

**combutta** *f* gang, band; **essere in combutta** to be in cahoots

**cóme** *m* manner, way; **il come e il perchè** the why and the wherefore || *adv* as; like; as for; how; **come mai?** why?; **e come!** and how!; **ma come?** what?, how is it? || *conj* as; as soon as; while; how; because; since; **come se** as if

**comecché** *conj* (lit) although; (poet) wherever

**comedóne** *m* blackhead

**cométa** *f* comet

**comici·tà** *f* (-tà) comicalness

**còmi·co -ca** (-ci -che) *adj* comic(al) || *m* comic; author of comedies; comic actor

**comìgnolo** *m* chimney pot; ridge (*of roof*)

**cominciare** §128 *tr & intr* to begin, start, commence

**comitato** *m* committee

**comitiva** *f* group, party; (poet) retinue

**comi·zio** *m* (-zi) (pol) meeting, rally; (hist) comitia

**còm·ma** *m* (-mi) paragraph, article (*of law or decree*)

**commèdia** *f* comedy; play, drama; (fig) farce; **commedia di carattere** comedy of character; **commedia d'intreccio** comedy of intrigue; **far la commedia** to pretend, feign; **finire in commedia** to end ludicrously; **finire la commedia** to stop faking

**commediante** *mf* actor; comedian (*amusing person*); (fig) hypocrite

**commediògra·fo -fa** *mf* playwright, comedian

**commemorare** (**commèmoro**) *tr* to commemorate

**commemorati·vo -va** *adj* commemorative, memorial

**commemorazióne** *f* commemoration

**commènda** *f* commandership (*of an order*); (eccl) commendam

**commendàbile** *adj* commendable

**commendare** (**commèndo**) *tr* (lit) to commend, praise; (obs) to entrust

**commendati·zio -zia** (-zi -zie) *adj* introductory || *f* letter of introduction; recommendation

**commendatóre** *m* commander (*of an order*)

**commendévole** *adj* commendable

**commensale** *mf* guest; table companion

**commensurare** (**commènsuro & commensuro**) *tr* to compare; to proportion, prorate

**commentare** (**comménto**) *tr* to comment, comment on

**commentà·rio** *m* (-ri) commentary; diary, journal

**commenta·tóre -trice** *mf* commentator

**comménto** *m* comment; **fare commenti** to criticize; **non far commenti!** don't waste your time talking!

**commerciàbile** *adj* marketable

**commerciale** *adj* commercial; common, ordinary

**commerciali·sta** *mf* (-sti -ste) business-administration major; attorney specializing in commercial law

**commerciante** *mf* merchant, dealer

**commerciare** §128 (**commèrcio**) *tr* to deal in; to buy and sell || *intr* to deal

**commèr·cio** *m* (-ci) commerce, trade; illegal traffic; (poet) intercourse; **commercio all'ingrosso** wholesale (trade); **commercio al minuto** retail (trade); **fuori commercio** not for sale; **in commercio** for sale

**commés·so -sa** *adj* committed || *mf* clerk (*in a store*) || *m* salesman; clerk (*in a court*); janitor (*in a school*); **commesso viaggiatore** traveling salesman || *f* saleslady; order (*of merchandise*)

**commestìbile** *adj* edible || **commestibili** *mpl* staples, groceries; foodstuffs

**commèttere** §198 *tr* to join, connect; to commit; to charge, commission; to peg; (poet) to entrust || *intr* to join, fit

**commettitura** *f* joint, seam

**commiato** *m* leave; **dare commiato a** to dismiss; **prender commiato** to take one's leave

**commilitóne** *m* comrade, comrade in arms

**comminare** *tr* (law) to determine, fix (*a penalty*)

**comminatò·rio -ria** *adj* threatening

**commiserare** (**commìsero**) *tr* to pity, feel sorry for

**commiserazióne** *f* commiseration

**commissariale** *adj* commissioner's, e.g., **funzioni commissariali** commissioner's functions; commissar's functions

**commissariato** *m* commissary; inspector's office

**commissà·rio** *m* (-ri) commissary; inspector; commissioner; **commissario del popolo** commissar; **commissario di bordo** purser; **commissario di pubblica sicurezza** police inspector; **commissario tecnico** (sports) soccer commissioner

**commissionare** (**commissióno**) *tr* to commission, order

**commissionà·rio -ria** (-ri -rie) *adj* commission || *m* commission merchant

**commissióne** *f* commission, agency; order (*of merchandise*); committee; errand; commitment (*of an act*)

**commisurare** *tr* to proportion (*e.g., crime to punishment*)

**committènte** *mf* buyer, customer

**commodòro** *m* commodore

**commòs·so -sa** *adj* moved; moving

**commovènte** *adj* moving, touching

**commozióne** *f* commotion; emotion; **commozione cerebrale** (pathol) concussion

**commuòvere** §202 *tr* to move; to touch; to stir || *ref* to be moved; to be touched

**commutare** *tr* to commute; to switch || *ref* to turn

**commuta·tóre -trice** *adj* commutative || *m* (elec) change-over switch; (elec) commutator (*switch*); (telp) plugboard || *f* converter

**commutatori·sta** *mf* (-sti -ste) (telp) operator

**commutazióne** *f* commutation; (telp) selection; (elec) switchover

**co·mò** *m* (-mò) chest; chest of drawers

**còmoda** *f* commode

**comodare** (**còmodo**) *tr* to lend || *intr* (with *dat*) to please, e.g., **non le comoda** it doesn't please her

**comodino** *m* night table; (theat) bit player; **fare il comodino a** (coll) to follow sheepishly

**comodi·tà** *f* (-tà) comfort; convenience; opportunity

**còmo·do -da** *adj* comfortable; convenient; easy; loose-fitting; calm || *m* convenience; ease; advantage; comfort; opportunity; **a Suo comodo** at your convenience; **comodo di cassa** credit (*at the bank*); **con comodo** without hurrying; **fare comodo** to come in handy; (with *dat*) to please, e.g., **non gli fa comodo** it doesn't please him; **fare il proprio comodo** to think only of oneself; **stia comodo!** make yourself at home! || *f* see **comoda**

**compaesa·no -na** *mf* fellow citizen || *m* fellow countryman || *f* fellow countrywoman

**compàgine** *f* strict union; connection; assemblage; (fig) cohesion

**compagna** *f* companion, mate; (archaic) company

**compagnìa** *f* company; **Compagnia di Gesù** Society of Jesus; **compagnia stabile** (theat) stock company

**compa·gno -gna** *adj* like, similar || *m* fellow; companion, comrade; mate; partner; **compagno d'armi** comrade in arms; **compagno di viaggio** fellow traveler || *f* see **compagna**

**companàti·co** *m* (-ci) food to eat with bread

**comparàbile** *adj* comparable

**comparati·vo -va** *adj* & *m* comparative

**compara·to -ta** *adj* comparative

**comparazióne** *f* comparison

**compare** *m* godfather; best man (*at wedding*); fellow; confederate

**comparire** §108 *intr* to appear; to be known; to cut a figure

**comparizióne** *f* appearance (*in court*)

**comparsa** *f* appearance; (theat) extra, supernumerary; (law) petition, brief; **far comparsa** to cut a figure

**compartecipare** (**compartécipo**) *intr* to share

**compartecipazióne** *f* sharing; **compartecipazione agli utili** profit sharing

**compartécipe** *adj* sharing

**compartiménto** *m* circle, clique; district; (naut, rr) compartment

**compartire** §176 & (**comparto**) *tr* to divide up, distribute

**compassa·to -ta** *adj* measured; stiff, formal; reserved; self-controlled

**compassionare** (**compassióno**) *tr* to pity

**compassióne** *f* compassion, pity

**compassionévole** *adj* compassionate; pitiful

**compasso** *m* compass; **compasso a grossezza** calipers

**compatìbile** *adj* excusable; compatible

**compatiménto** *m* compassion; condescension

**compatire** §176 *tr* to pity; to forgive, overlook; to bear with; **farsi compatire** to become an object of ridicule || *intr* to pity

**compatriò·ta** *mf* (-ti -te) compatriot

**compattézza** *f* compactness

**compat·to -ta** *adj* compact, tight

**compendiare** §287 (**compèndio**) *tr* to epitomize, summarize

**compèn·dio** *m* (-di) compendium, summary; **fare un compendio di** to abstract

**compendió·so -sa** [s] *adj* compendious, brief, succinct

**compenetràbile** *adj* penetrable

**compenetrabilità** *f* penetrability

**compenetrare** (**compènetro**) *tr* to penetrate; to permeate; to pervade || *ref* to be overcome; **compenetrarsi di** to be conscious of

**compensare** (**compènso**) *tr* to compensate, pay; to balance, offset; to clear (*checks*)

**compensa·to -ta** *adj* compensated; laminated || *m* laminate; plywood

**compensazióne** *f* compensation; offset; (com) clearing (*of checks*)

**compènso** *m* reward; retribution, pay; **in compenso** on the other hand

**cómpera** *f* var of **compra**

**comperare** (**cómpero**) *tr* & *intr* var of **comprare**

**competènte** *adj* competent

**competènza** *f* competence; jurisdiction; **competenze honoraria**

**compètere** §129 *intr* to compete; to concern; to have jurisdiction

**competiti·vo -va** *adj* competitive

**competi·tóre -trice** *mf* competitor, contender

**competizióne** *f* competition, contest

**compiacènte** *adj* complaisant, obliging

**compiacènza** *f* complaisance, kindness; pleasure

**compiacére** §214 *tr* to gratify || *intr* (with *dat*) to please, e.g., **non posso compiacere a tutti** I cannot please everybody || *ref* to be pleased; **compiacersi con** to congratulate; **compiacersi di** to be kind enough to

**compiaciménto** *m* pleasure; congratulation; approval

**compiaciu·to -ta** *adj* pleased, satisfied
**compiàngere** §215 *tr* to pity ‖ *ref* to feel sorry
**compian·to -ta** *adj* lamented (*departed person*) ‖ *m* sympathy; (poet) sorrow; (poet) lament
**compiegare** §209 (**compiègo**) *tr* to enclose (*in a letter*)
**cómpiere** §130 *tr* to complete, finish; to fulfill, accomplish; **compiere ... anni** to be ... years old; **compiere gli anni** to have a birthday ‖ *ref* to happen; to come true
**compilare** *tr* to compile
**compila·tóre -trice** *mf* compiler
**compilazióne** *f* compilation
**compiménto** *m* fulfillment, accomplishment
**compire** §176 *tr* to complete, finish; to fulfill, accomplish; **per compir l'opera** as if it weren't enough ‖ *ref* to happen; to come true
**compitare** (**cómpito**) *tr* to syllabify; to read poorly; to spell, spell letter by letter
**compitazióne** *f* spelling letter by letter
**compitézza** *f* courtesy, politeness
**cómpito** *m* task; exercise; homework
**compi·to -ta** *adj* courteous, polite; (poet) adequate
**compiu·to -ta** *adj* accomplished
**compleanno** *m* birthday; **buon compleanno** happy birthday
**complementare** *adj* complementary; additional (*tax*) ‖ *f* graduated income tax
**compleménto** *m* complement; (mil, nav) reserve
**complessióne** *f* build, physique
**complessi·tà** *f* (**-tà**) complexity
**complessi·vo -va** *adj* total, aggregate
**complès·so -sa** *adj* complex, complicated; compound (*fracture*) ‖ *m* whole; complex; **in complesso** in general
**completare** (**complèto**) *tr* to complete, carry through; to supplement, round off
**complè·to -ta** *adj* complete, full; overall, thoroughgoing; **al completo** full (*e.g., bus*) ‖ *m* set (*of matching items*); suit of clothes; **completo femminile** lady's tailor-made suit; **completo maschile** suit
**complicare** §197 (**còmplico**) *tr* to complicate ‖ *ref* to become complicated
**complica·to -ta** *adj* complicated, complex
**complicazióne** *f* complication
**còmplice** *mf* accomplice, accessory
**complici·tà** *f* (**-tà**) complicity
**complimentare** (**compliménto**) *tr* to compliment ‖ *ref*—**complimentarsi con** to congratulate
**compliménto** *m* compliment; congratulation; favor; **complimenti** regards; **complimenti!** congratulations!; **fare complimenti** to stand on ceremony; **senza complimenti** without ceremony; without any further ado
**complimentó·so -sa** [s] *adj* ceremonious; complimentary

**complottare** (**complòtto**) *intr* to plot
**complòtto** *m* plot, machination
**complù·vio** *m* (**-vi**) valley (*of roof*)
**componènte** *adj* component ‖ *mf* member ‖ *m* component (*component part*) ‖ *f* component (*force*)
**componìbile** *adj* sectional (*e.g., bookcase*)
**componiménto** *m* composition, settlement (*of a dispute*)
**compórre** §218 *tr* to compose; to arrange; to settle (*a quarrel*); to lay out (*a corpse*); (typ) to set
**comportaménto** *m* behavior
**comportare** (**compòrto**) *tr* to allow, tolerate; to entail ‖ *ref* to behave; to handle (*said, e.g., of a motor*); **comportarsi male** to misbehave
**compòrto** *m* (com) delay
**compòsi·to -ta** *adj* composite ‖ **composite** *fpl* (bot) Compositae
**composi·tóio** *m* (**-tói**) (typ) composing stick
**composi·tóre -trice** *mf* compositor, typesetter; composer ‖ *f* typesetting machine
**composizióne** *f* composition; settlement
**compósta** *f* compote; **composta di frutta** stewed fruit
**compostézza** *f* neatness, tidiness; good behavior; orderliness
**compostièra** *f* compote, compotier
**compó·sto -sta** *adj* compound; neat, tidy; well-behaved ‖ *m* compound ‖ *f* see **composta**
**cómpra** *f* purchase; shopping; **compre** shopping
**comprare** (**cómpro**) *tr* to buy, purchase; to buy off ‖ *intr* to buy, shop; to trade
**compra·tóre -trice** *mf* buyer, purchaser
**compravéndere** §281 *tr* to make a deal in, to transfer (*e.g., a house*)
**compravéndita** *f* transaction; transfer (*e.g., of real estate*)
**comprèndere** §220 *tr* to comprehend, include, comprise; to overwhelm; to understand; to forgive
**comprendò·nio** *m* (**-ni**) (joc) understanding
**comprensìbile** *adj* understandable, comprehensible
**comprensióne** *f* comprehension, understanding
**comprensi·vo -va** *adj* comprehensive; understanding
**comprensò·rio** *m* (**-ri**) land to be reclaimed; area, zone, e.g., **comprensorio turistico** tourist area
**comprè·so -sa** [s] *adj* comprised, included; understood; deeply touched; immersed
**comprèssa** *f* compress
**compressióne** *f* compression
**comprès·so -sa** *adj* compressed; (fig) repressed; (aut) supercharged ‖ *f* see **compressa**
**compressóre** *m* compressor; **compressore stradale** road roller
**comprimà·rio** *m* (**-ri**) (med) associate chief of staff; (theat) second lead

**comprìmere** §131 *tr* to compress; to repress, restrain; to tamp

**compromés·so -sa** *adj* jeopardized, in danger ‖ *m* compromise; referral (*to arbitration*)

**compromettènte** *adj* compromising

**comprométtere** §198 *tr* to compromise; to endanger; to involve, commit; (law) to refer (*to arbitration*)

**comproprie·tà** *f* (-tà) joint ownership

**comproprietà·rio -ria** *mf* (-ri -rie) joint owner

**compròva** *f* confirmation

**comprovare (compròvo)** *tr* to confirm; to circumstantiate

**compulsare** *tr* to consult, peruse; to summon (*to appear in court*)

**compulsi·vo -va** *adj* compulsive

**compun·to -ta** *adj* contrite, repentant

**compunzióne** *f* compunction

**computàbile** *adj* computable

**computare (còmputo)** *tr* to compute

**computi·sta** *mf* (-sti -ste) bookkeeper

**computisterìa** *f* bookkeeping

**còmputo** *m* computation, reckoning

**comunale** *adj* municipal, town (*e.g., hall*); community-owned; (poet) common

**comunanza** *f* community; **in comunanza** in common

**comune** *adj* common ‖ *m* normalcy; commune, municipality, town; town hall; (hist) guild; (nav) common seaman; **in comune** in common ‖ *f* commune (*in communist countries*); (theat) main stage entrance; **andare per la comune** to follow the crowd; **per la comune** commonly

**comunèlla** *f* cabal, clique; passkey (*in a hotel*); (law) mutual insurance (*of cattlemen*); **fare comunella con** to consort with

**comunicàbile** *adj* communicable

**comunicante** *adj* communicant; communicating ‖ *m* priest who gives communion

**comunicare** §197 (**comùnico**) *tr* to communicate; to administer communion to ‖ *intr* to communicate ‖ *ref* to spread; to receive communion, to commune

**comunicati·vo -va** *adj* communicable, spreading; communicative

**comunicato** *m* communiqué; **comunicato commerciale** advertisement, ad; **comunicato stampa** press release

**comunicazióne** *f* communication; statement; (telp) connection; **comunicazioni** communications

**comunióne** *f* community; (law) community property ‖ **Comunione** *f* Communion

**comunismo** *m* communism

**comuni·sta** (-sti -ste) *adj* communist ‖ *mf* communist; (law) joint tenant

**comunìsti·co -ca** *adj* (-ci -che) communistic

**comuni·tà** *f* (-tà) community

**comunità·rio -ria** *adj* (-ri -rie) community, e.g., **interessi comunitari** community interests

**comùnque** *adv* however, nevertheless ‖ *conj* however, no matter how

**cón** §4 *prep* with; by (*e.g., boat*); **con + art + inf** by + ger, e.g., **col leggere** by reading

**conato** *m* effort, attempt

**cón·ca** *f* (-che) washbowl, washbasin; copper water jug; valley, hollow; (poet) shell; **conca idraulica** drydock

**concatenaménto** *m* (poet) concatenation

**concatenare (concaténo)** *tr* to link ‖ *ref* to unfold, ensue

**concatenazióne** *f* concatenation

**concàusa** *f* joint cause; (law) aggravation

**cònca·vo -va** *adj* concave; hollow ‖ *m* hollow

**concèdere** §132 *tr* to grant, concede; to stretch (*a point*) ‖ *ref* to let oneself go, give oneself over

**concènto** *m* harmony; (fig) agreement

**concentraménto** *m* concentration

**concentrare (concèntro)** *tr* to concentrate; to center ‖ *ref* to concentrate, focus; to center

**concentra·to -ta** *adj* concentrated; condensed (*e.g., milk*) ‖ *m* purée (*e.g., of tomatoes*)

**concentrazióne** *f* concentration; (chem) condensation

**concèntri·co -ca** *adj* (-ci -che) concentric

**concepìbile** *adj* conceivable

**concepiménto** *m* conception; (fig) formulation

**concepire** §176 *tr* to conceive; (fig) to nurture

**concerìa** *f* tannery

**concèrnere** §133 *tr* to concern

**concertare (concèrto)** *tr* to scheme, concert; (mus) to orchestrate, arrange ‖ *ref* to agree

**concerta·to -ta** *adj* agreed upon; (mus) with accompaniment ‖ *m* ensemble (*of orchestra, soloists, and chorus*)

**concerta·tóre -trice** *mf* arranger ‖ *m* plotter, schemer

**concertazióne** *f* (mus) arrangement

**concerti·sta** *mf* (-sti -ste) concert performer, soloist

**concèrto** *m* concert; concerto; (fig) choir

**concessionà·rio** *m* (-ri) sole agent, concessionaire; dealer; lessee (*of business establishment*)

**concessióne** *f* concession; dealership; admission

**concessi·vo -va** *adj* concessive

**concès·so -sa** *adj* granted, admitting

**concètto** *m* concept; opinion

**concetto·so -sa** [s] *adj* concise; full of ideas; full of conceits

**concettuale** *adj* conceptual

**concezióne** *f* conception; formulation

**conchìglia** *f* shell, conch; (sports) jock guard, protective cup

**conchiùdere** §125 *tr, intr & ref* var of **concludere**

**cón·cia** *f* (-ce) tanning

**conciapèl·li** *m* (-li) tanner

**conciare** §128 (**cóncio**) *tr* to tan; to cure (*e.g., tobacco*); to arrange; to straighten up; to reduce; to cut (*a precious stone*); **conciare per le feste** (coll) to give a good beating to ‖ *ref* to get messed up, get dirty

**conciatét·ti** *m* (**-ti**) roofer

**conciató·re -trice** *mf* tanner

**conciliàbile** *adj* reconcilable

**conciliàbolo** *m* conventicle, secret meeting

**conciliante** *adj* conciliatory

**conciliare** *adj* council ‖ *m* member of an ecclesiastical council ‖ §287 *tr* to conciliate, reconcile; to settle (*a fine*); to promote (*e.g., sleep*); to obtain (*a favor*) ‖ *ref* to become reconciled

**concilia·tóre -trice** *adj* conciliatory ‖ *mf* conciliator, peacemaker ‖ *m* justice of the peace

**conciliazióne** *f* conciliation ‖ **la Conciliazione** the Concordat (*of 1929 between Italy and the Vatican*)

**concì·lio** *m* (**-li**) council; church council

**concimàia** *f* manure pit

**concimare** *tr* to manure

**concimazióne** *f* spreading of manure; chemical fertilization

**concime** *m* manure; fertilizer

**cón·cio -cia** (**-ci -ce**) *adj* tanned ‖ *m* ashlar; dung, manure; (archaic) agreement; **concio di scoria** cinder block ‖ *f* see **concia**

**conciofossecosaché** *conj* (archaic) since

**concionare** (**concióno**) *intr* (archaic) to harangue

**concióne** *f* (archaic) harangue; (archaic) assembly

**conciossiacosaché** *conj* (archaic) since

**concisióne** *f* concision, brevity

**conci·so -sa** *adj* concise, brief

**concistòro** *m* consistory; (fig) assembly

**concitare** (**còncito**) *tr* to excite, stir up

**concita·to -ta** *adj* excited; (poet) decisive

**concitazióne** *f* impetus; excitement

**concittadi·no -na** *mf* fellow citizen

**conclave** *m* conclave

**conclùdere** §105 *tr* to conclude ‖ *intr* to conclude; to be convincing ‖ *ref* to conclude, end; **concludersi con** to end with; to result in

**conclusionale** *adj* (law) summary

**conclusióne** *f* conclusion; **conclusioni** (law) summation

**conclusi·vo -va** *adj* conclusive

**conclu·so -sa** *adj* concluded; terminated; (poet) closed

**concomitante** *adj* concomitant

**concordanza** *f* concordance, agreement; (gram) concord; **concordanze** concordance (*e.g., to the Bible*)

**concordare** (**concòrdo**) *tr* to agree on; to make agree ‖ *intr* & *ref* to come to an agreement

**concordato** *m* agreement; concordat; settlement (*with creditors*)

**concòrde** *adj* in agreement

**concòrdia** *f* concord, harmony

**concorrènte** *adj* competitive ‖ *m* (com) competitor; (sports) contestant

**concorrènza** *f* competition

**concorrenziale** *adj* competitive (*e.g., price*)

**concórrere** §139 *intr* to converge; to concur; to compete

**concórso** *m* attendance; concurrence; combination (*of circumstances*); competition; competitive examination; contest; **concorso di bellezza** beauty contest; **concorso di pubblico** turnout; **fuori concorso** not entering the competition; in a class by itself

**concretare** (**concrèto**) *tr* to realize (*e.g., a dream*); to conclude, accomplish ‖ *ref* to come true

**concretézza** *f* concreteness, consistency

**concrè·to -ta** *adj* concrete, real; practical ‖ *m* practical matter; **in concreto** really, in reality

**concubina** *f* concubine

**concubinàg·gio** *m* (**-gi**) concubinage

**concubinato** *m* var of **concubinaggio**

**conculcare** §197 *tr* (lit) to trample under foot; (lit) to violate

**concupire** §176 *tr* (poet) to lust for

**concupiscènza** *f* concupiscence, lust

**concussióne** *f* extortion, shakedown; **concussione cerebrale** (pathol) concussion

**condanna** *f* conviction; sentence; (fig) blame, condemnation

**condannare** *tr* to condemn; to find guilty, convict; to sentence; to damn (*to eternal punishment*); to declare incurable; to wall up

**condanna·to -ta** *adj* condemned ‖ *m* convict

**condensare** (**condènso**) *tr* & *ref* to condense

**condensa·to -ta** *adj* condensed (*e.g., milk*)

**condensatóre** *m* condenser

**condensazióne** *f* condensation

**condiménto** *m* condiment, seasoning

**condire** §176 *tr* to season

**condiret·tóre -trice** *mf* associate manager

**condiscendènte** *adj* condescending

**condiscendènza** *f* condescension

**condiscéndere** §245 *intr* to condescend

**condiscépo·lo -la** *mf* schoolmate, school companion

**condivìdere** §158 *tr* to share

**condizionale** *adj* & *m* conditional ‖ *f* (law) suspended sentence

**condizionare** (**condizióno**) *tr* to condition; to treat (*to prevent spoilage*)

**condizionatóre** *m* air conditioner

**condizióne** *f* condition; term (*of sale*); **a condizione che** provided that; **condizioni** condition, shape (*e.g., of a shipment*); **essere in condizione di** to be in a position to

**condoglianza** *f* condolence; **fare le condoglianze a** to extend one's sympathy to

**condolére** §159 *ref* to condole

**condomì·nio** *m* (**-ni**) condominium

**condòmi·no -na** *mf* joint owner (*of real estate*)

**condonare** (**condóno**) *tr* to condone; to remit

**condóno** *m* pardon, parole

**condót·to -ta** *adj* country (*doctor*) ‖ *m* duct, canal; conduit ‖ *f* behavior, conduct; district (*of country doctor*); transportation; pipeline; (theat) baggage; **condotta forzata** flume

**conducènte** *m* driver; bus driver; motorman

**condù·plex** *mf* (**-plex**) (telp) party-line user

**condurre** §102 *tr* to lead; to drive (*a car*); to round up (*cattle*); to pipe (*e.g., gas*); to conduct; to trace (*a line*); to take; to bring; to manage; **condurre a termine** to bring to fruition, realize ‖ *intr* to lead ‖ *ref* to behave; to betake oneself, go; **condursí a** (poet) to be reduced to (*e.g., poverty*)

**conduttivi·tà** *f* (**-tà**) conductivity

**condutti·vo -va** *adj* conductive

**condut·tóre -trice** *adj* guiding, leading ‖ *m* operator (*of a bus*); driver (*of a car*); (rr) engineer; (rr) ticket collector; (phys) conductor

**conduttura** *f* conduit, pipeline

**conduzióne** *f* conduction; leasing

**conestàbile** *m* constable (*keeper of a castle*)

**confabulare** (**confàbulo**) *intr* to confabulate, commune; to connive, scheme

**confacènte** *adj* suitable, appropriate; helpful

**confare** §173 *ref*—**confarsi a** to agree with, e.g., **le uova non gli si confanno** eggs do not agree with him

**confederare** (**confèdero**) *tr & ref* to confederate

**confedera·to -ta** *adj & m* confederate

**confederazióne** *f* confederation

**conferènza** *f* conference; lecture; **conferenza illustrata** chalk talk; **conferenza stampa** press conference

**conferenziè·re -ra** *mf* speaker, lecturer

**conferiménto** *m* conferring, bestowal

**conferire** §176 *tr* to confer, bestow; to add; to contribute ‖ *intr* to confer; to contribute; **conferire alla salute** to be healthful

**confèrma** *f* confirmation; **a conferma di** (com) in reply to, confirming

**confermare** (**confèrmo**) *tr* to confirm; to verify; to retain (*in office*) ‖ *ref* to become more sure of oneself; to prove to be; to remain (*in the conclusion of a letter*)

**confessare** (**confèsso**) *tr & ref* to confess

**confessionale** *adj* confessional; church; church-related, parochial (*e.g., school*) ‖ *m* confessional

**confessióne** *f* confession

**confès·so -sa** *adj* acknowledged, self-admitted; **confesso e comunicato** having made one's confession and taken communion

**confessóre** *m* confessor

**confetteria** *f* candy store, confectioner's shop

**confettièra** *f* candy box

**confettière** *m* candy maker; candy dealer, confectioner

**confètto** *m* sugar-covered nut, sweetmeat; losenge, drop

**confettura** *f* candy; preserves, jam; **confetture** confectionery

**confezionare** (**confezióno**) *tr* to make; to tailor (*a suit*)

**confezióne** *f* preparation, manufacturing; packaging; **confezioni** ready-made clothes

**confezioni·sta** *mf* (**-sti -ste**) ready-made clothier

**conficcare** §197 *tr* to drive (*a nail*); to thrust (*a knife*) ‖ *ref* to become embedded

**confidare** *tr* to trust (*a secret*) ‖ *intr* to trust ‖ *ref* to confide

**confidènte** *adj* confident ‖ *mf* confident; informer

**confidènza** *f* confidence; secret; familiarity

**confidenziale** *adj* confidential; friendly

**confìggere** §104 *tr* to plunge, thrust

**configurazióne** *f* configuration

**confinante** *adj* bordering ‖ *mf* neighbor

**confinare** *tr* to exile; to confine ‖ *intr* to border

**confinà·rio -ria** *adj* (**-ri -rie**) border (*e.g., zone*)

**Confindùstria** *f* (acronym) **Confederazione Nazionale degli Industriali** National Confederation of Industrialists

**confine** *m* border, boundary line; boundary mark, landmark

**confino** *m* exile (*in a different town*)

**confi·sca** *f* (**-sche**) confiscation

**confiscare** §197 *tr* to confiscate

**confit·to -ta** *adj* nailed; bound; tied; **confitto in croce** nailed to the cross

**conflagrazióne** *f* conflagration

**conflitto** *m* conflict

**conflittualità** *f* confrontation; belligerent attitude

**confluènte** *m* confluent

**confluènza** *f* confluence

**confluire** §176 *intr* to flow together, join; to converge

**confóndere** §178 *tr* to confuse; to overwhelm (*with kindness*); to humiliate; **confondere con** to mistake for ‖ *ref* to mix; to become confused

**conformare** (**confórmo**) *tr* to shape; to conform ‖ *ref* to conform

**conformazióne** *f* conformation

**confórme** *adj* faithful, exact; in agreement; true (*copy*)

**conformeménte** *adv* in conformity

**conformi·sta** *mf* (**-sti -ste**) conformist

**conformi·tà** *f* (**-tà**) conformity; **in conformità di** in conformity with, in accord with

**confortante** *adj* comforting

**confortare** (**confòrto**) *tr* to comfort

**confortévole** *adj* comforting, consoling; comfortable

**confòrto** *m* comfort, solace; convenience; corroboration; **conforti religiosi** last rites

**confratèllo** *m* brother, confrere

**confratèrnita** *f* brotherhood

**confricare** §197 *tr* to rub

**confrontare** (**confrónto**) *tr* to compare, confront; to consult ‖ *intr* to correspond

**confrónto** *m* comparison; (law) cross examination; **a confronto di** or **in confronto a** in comparison with; with regard to

**confusaménte** *adv* vaguely, hazily

**confusionale** *adj* confusing; confused

**confusionà·rio -ria (-ri -rie)** *adj* blundering; scatterbrain || *mf* blunderer; scatterbrain

**confusióne** *f* confusion, disorder; noise; error; embarrassment; shambles

**confu·so -sa** *adj* confused, mixed; vague, hazy; **in confuso** indistinctly

**confutare (cònfuto)** *tr* to confute

**confutazióne** *f* confutation

**congedare (congèdo)** *tr* to dismiss; to let (*a tenant*) go; (mil) to discharge || *ref* to take leave

**congeda·to -ta** *adj* discharged || *m* discharged soldier

**congèdo** *m* dismissal; leave; permission to leave; (mil) discharge; envoy, envoi; **congedo per motivi di salute** sick leave; **dare il congedo a** to discharge; **prender congedo** to take leave

**congegnare (congégno)** *tr* to assemble (*machinery*); to contrive, cook up

**congégno** *m* contrivance, gadget; mechanism; design (*of a play*)

**congelaménto** *m* freezing; frostbite

**congelare (congèlo)** *tr & ref* to freeze, congeal

**congela·tóre -trice** *adj* freezing || *m* freezer; freezer unit; freezing compartment (*of a refrigerator*)

**congènere** *adj* similar, alike

**congeniale** *adj* congenial

**congèni·to -ta** *adj* congenital

**congèrie** *f* congeries

**congestionare (congestióno)** *tr* to congest

**congestióne** *f* congestion

**congettura** *f* conjecture

**congetturare** *tr* to conjecture

**congiùngere** §183 *tr & ref* to unite, join

**congiuntiva** *f* (anat) conjunctiva

**congiuntivite** *f* (pathol) conjunctivitis

**congiunti·vo -va** *adj* conjunctive; subjunctive || *m* subjunctive || *f* see **congiuntiva**

**congiun·to -ta** *adj* joined; joint || *m* relative

**congiuntura** *f* juncture; joint; circumstance, situation; **bassa congiuntura** (econ) unfavorable circumstance; (econ) crisis

**congiunzióne** *f* conjunction

**congiura** *f* conspiracy, plot

**congiurare** *intr* to conspire, plot

**congiura·to -ta** *adj & m* conspirator

**conglobare (conglòbo)** *tr* to lump together

**conglomerare (conglòmero)** *tr & ref* to pile up, conglomerate

**conglomera·to -ta** *adj & m* conglomerate

**congratulare (congràtulo)** *intr* to rejoice || *ref*—**congratularsi con** to congratulate

**congratulazióne** *f* congratulation

**congrèga** *f* gang; cabal; religious brotherhood

**congregare** §209 **(congrègo)** *tr & ref* to congregate

**congregazióne** *f* congregation

**congressi·sta** *mf* (-sti -ste) delegate || *m* congressman || *f* congresswoman

**congrèsso** *m* congress, assembly; conference; convention

**congruènte** *adj* congruous

**congruènza** *f* congruence

**còn·gruo -grua** *adj* congruous; congruent

**conguagliare** §280 *tr* to adjust; to make up (*what is owed*)

**conguà·glio** *m* (-gli) balance; adjustment (*of wages*)

**coniare** §287 **(cònio)** *tr* to mint, coin

**coniatura** *f* mintage, coinage

**còni·co -ca (-ci -che)** *adj* conic(al) || *f* conic section

**conìfera** *f* conifer

**coniglièra** *f* warren, rabbit hutch

**conì·glio** *m* (-gli) rabbit

**cò·nio** *m* (-ni) die (*to mint coins*); mintage; wedge; **dello stesso conio** (fig) of the same feather; **di nuovo conio** newly-minted; new-fangled

**coniugale** *adj* conjugal

**coniugare** §209 **(còniugo)** *tr* to conjugate || *ref* to marry, get married

**coniuga·to -ta** *adj* coupled, paired || *mf* spouse, consort

**coniugazióne** *f* conjugation

**còniuge** *mf* spouse; **coniugi** *mpl* husband and wife

**connaturale** *adj* inborn, innate

**connatura·to -ta** *adj* deep-seated, deep-rooted; congenital

**connazionale** *mf* fellow countryman

**connessióne** *f* connection

**connés·so -sa & connès·so -sa** *adj* connected, tied

**connèttere** §107 *tr* to connect, link || *ref* to refer

**connetti·vo -va** *adj* connective  .

**connivènte** *adj* conniving

**connivènza** *f* connivance

**connotare (connòto)** *tr* to connote

**connotato** *m* personal characteristic

**connù·bio** *m* (-bi) wedding, union

**còno** *m* cone

**conòcchia** *f* distaff

**conoscènte** *mf* acquaintance

**conoscènza** *f* knowledge; acquaintance; understanding; consciousness; **conoscenza di causa** full knowledge; **essere a conoscenza di** to be acquainted with; **prendere conoscenza di** to take cognizance of

**conóscere** §134 *tr* to know; to recognize; **conoscere i propri polli** to know one's onions; **conoscere per filo e per segno** to know thoroughly; **conoscere ragioni** to listen to reason; **darsi a conoscere** to make oneself known; to reveal oneself || *intr* to reason || *ref* to acknowledge oneself to be; to know one another

**conoscìbile** *adj* knowable

**conosci·tóre -trice** *mf* connoisseur, expert

**conosciu·to -ta** *adj* known, well-known; proven

**conquìdere** §135 *tr* (poet) to conquer

**conquista** *f* conquest
**conquistare** *tr* to conquer, win
**conquista·tóre -trice** *adj* conquering ‖ *m* conqueror; lady killer
**consacrare** *tr* to consecrate ‖ *ref* to dedicate oneself
**consacrazióne** *f* consecration
**consanguineità** *f* consanguinity
**consanguìne·o -a** *adj* consanguineous; **fratello consanguineo** half brother on the father's side ‖ *m* kin
**consapévole** *adj* aware, conscious
**consapevolézza** *f* awareness, consciousness
**còn·scio -scia** *adj* (**-sci -sce**) conscious
**consecutì·vo -va** *adj* consecutive
**conségna** *f* delivery; (mil) order; (mil) confinement (*to barracks*); **in consegna** (com) on consignment
**consegnare** (**conségno**) *tr* to deliver; to entrust; (mil) to confine (*to barracks*)
**consegnatà·rio** *m* (**-ri**) consignee
**conseguènte** *adj* consequent; consistent; **conseguente a** resulting from; consistent with
**conseguènza** *f* consequence; consistency; **in conseguenza di** as a result of
**conseguìbile** *adj* attainable
**conseguiménto** *m* attainment
**conseguire** (**conséguo**) *tr* to attain; to obtain ‖ *intr* to ensue, result
**consènso** *m* consent, approval; consensus
**consensuale** *adj* mutual-consent (*e.g., agreement*)
**consentiménto** *m* consent
**consentire** (**consènto**) *tr* to allow, permit ‖ *intr* to agree, consent; to yield; to admit
**consenziènte** *adj* consenting
**consèr·to -ta** *adj* intertwined; folded (*arms*); **di conserto** in agreement
**consèrva** *f* preserve; purée (*e.g., of tomatoes*); tank (*for water*); sauce (*e.g., of cranberries*); **conserve alimentari** canned goods; **di conserva** together, in a group; **far conserva di** to preserve
**conservare** (**consèrvo**) *tr* to preserve; to keep; to cure (*e.g., meat*); to cherish (*a memory*) ‖ *ref* to keep; to remain; to keep in good health
**conservatì·vo -va** *adj* preserving; conservative ‖ *m* conservative
**conserva·tóre -trice** *adj* preserving; conservative ‖ *mf* keeper, curator; conservative
**conservatorìa** *f* registrar's office (*in a court house*)
**conservatò·rio** *m* (**-ri**) conservatory; girl's boarding school (*run by nuns*)
**conservatorismo** *m* conservatism
**conservazióne** *f* conservation; preservation; self-preservation; canning
**consèsso** *m* assembly
**consideràbile** *adj* considerable; large, important
**considerare** (**consìdero**) *tr* to consider; to rate; (law) to provide for
**considera·to -ta** *adj* considered; **considerato che** considering that, since;

**tutto considerato** all in all, considering
**considerazióne** *f* consideration
**considerévole** *adj* considerable
**consigliare** *adj* council, councilmanic ‖ §280 *tr* to advise, counsel ‖ *ref* to consult
**consigliè·re -ra** *mf* counselor, advisor ‖ *m* chancellor (*of embassy*); councilman; **consigliere delegato** chairman of the board
**consì·glio** *m* (**-gli**) advice, counsel; will (*of God*); decision, idea; council; **consiglio d'amministrazione** (com) board of directors; **consiglio dei ministri** cabinet; **consiglio municipale** city council; **l'eterno consiglio** the will of God; **venire a più miti consigli** to become more reasonable
**consìmile** *adj* similar
**consistènte** *adj* consistent, solid; trustworthy
**consistènza** *f* consistency, resistance; foundation, grounds
**consistere** §114 *intr* to consist; **consistere in** to consist of
**consociare** §128 (**consòcio**) *tr* to syndicate, unite
**consocia·to -ta** *adj* syndicated, united
**consociazióne** *f* syndicate, association, group
**consò·cio** *mf* (**-ci -cie**) fellow shareholder; associate, partner
**consolare** *adj* consular ‖ *v* (**consólo**) *tr* to console, cheer, comfort ‖ *ref* to rejoice; to take comfort
**consolato** *m* consulate
**consola·tóre -trice** *adj* comforting ‖ *mf* comforter
**consolazióne** *f* consolation
**cònsole** *m* consul
**consò·le** *f* (**-le**) console
**consòlida** *f*—**consolida maggiore** comfrey; **consolida reale** field larkspur
**consolidaménto** *m* consolidation
**consolidare** (**consòlido**) *tr* to consolidate ‖ *ref* to consolidate; to harden
**consolida·to -ta** *adj* consolidated; joint (*e.g., balance sheet*); hardened ‖ *m* funded public debt; government bonds
**consonante** *adj* & *f* consonant
**consonànti·co -ca** *adj* (**-ci -che**) consonant
**consonanza** *f* consonance; agreement; (mus) harmony
**cònso·no -na** *adj* consonant
**consorèlla** *adj* sister (*e.g., company*) ‖ *f* sister of charity; sister branch; sister firm
**consòrte** *adj* (poet) equally fortunate; (poet) united ‖ *mf* consort, mate, spouse
**consorterìa** *f* political clique
**consòr·zio** *m* (**-zi**) syndicate, consortium; (poet) society
**constare** (**cònsto**) *intr* to consist ‖ *impers* to be known; to be proved; to understand, e.g., **gli consta che Lei ha torto** he understands that you are wrong
**constatare** (**constato** & **cònstato**) *tr* to verify, ascertain, establish

constatazióne *f* ascertainment, verification

consuè·to -ta *adj* usual, customary; consueto a accustomed to, used to ‖ *m* manner, custom; di consueto generally

consuetudinà·rio -ria *adj* (-ri -rie) customary; common (*law*)

consuetùdine *f* custom; common law; (poet) familiarity

consulènte *adj* advising, consulting ‖ *mf* adviser, expert

consulènza *f* expert advice

consulta *f* council

consultare *tr* to consult ‖ *ref* to take counsel; to counsel with one another; consultarsi con to take counsel with

consultazióne *f* consultation; reference; consultazione popolare referendum

consulti·vo -va *adj* advisory

consulto *m* consultation (*of physicians*); legal conference

consul·tóre -trice *mf* adviser, expert ‖ *m* councilman

consultò·rio *m* (-ri) clinic, dispensary

consumare *tr* to consume; to perform, to consummate ‖ *ref* to be consumed, to waste away

consuma·to -ta *adj* consummate, accomplished; consummated (*marriage*); consumed, worn out

consuma·tóre -trice *adj* consuming ‖ *mf* consumer; customer (*of a restaurant*)

consumazióne *f* consummation (*e.g., of a crime*); consumption (*of food*); food or drink

consumismo *m* consumerism

consumo *m* consumption; wear

consunti·vo -va *adj* end-of-year (*e.g., report*); (econ) consumption ‖ *m* balance sheet

consun·to -ta *adj* worn-out

consunzióne *f* consumption

contàbile *adj* bookkeeping ‖ *mf* accountant; bookkeeper, clerk; esperto contabile certified public accountant

contabili·tà *f* (-tà) accounting, bookkeeping; accounts

contachilòme·tri *m* (-tri) odometer; (coll) speedometer

contadiné·sco -sca *adj* (-schi -sche) farm, farmer; rustic

contadi·no -na *adj* rustic ‖ *mf* peasant, farmer

contado *m* country, countryside

contagiare §290 *tr* to infect

contà·gio *m* (-gi) contagion

contagió·so -sa [s] *adj* contagious

contagi·ri *m* (-ri) tachometer

contagóc·ce *m* (-ce) dropper, eyedropper

contaminare (contàmino) *tr* to contaminate; to pollute

contaminazióne *f* contamination; pollution

contante *adj* & *m* cash; in contanti cash

contare (cónto) *tr* to count; to limit; to regard, value; to propose; contarle grosse (coll) to tell tall tales ‖ *intr* to count; contare su to count on

contasecón·di *m* (-di) watch with second hand

conta·to -ta *adj* limited; numbered (*e.g., days*)

conta·tóre -trice *adj* counting ‖ *mf* counter ‖ *m* meter; contatore dell'acqua water meter; contatore della luce electric meter

contattare *tr* to contact

contatto *m* contact

cónte *m* count

contèa *f* county

conteggiare §290 (contéggio) *tr* to charge (*e.g., a bill*) ‖ *intr* to count

contég·gio *m* (-gi) reckoning, calculation; (sports) count; conteggio alla rovescia countdown

contégno *m* behavior; reserve, reserved attitude; air

contegnó·so -sa [s] *adj* reserved, dignified

contemperare (contèmpero) *tr* to adapt; to mitigate, moderate

contemplare (contèmplo) *tr* to contemplate

contemplati·vo -va *adj* contemplative

contemplazióne *f* contemplation

contèmpo *m*—nel contempo meanwhile

contemporaneaménte *adv* at the same time

contemporàne·o -a *adj* contemporaneous ‖ *mf* contemporary

contendènte *adj* fighting ‖ *m* contender, fighter; (law) contestant

contèndere §270 *tr* to contest, oppose ‖ *intr* to contend, fight ‖ *ref* to fight

contenére §271 *tr* to contain ‖ *ref* to restrain oneself; to behave

conteniménto *m* containment

contenitóre *m* container

contentare (contènto) *tr* to satisfy, content ‖ *ref* to be satisfied

contentézza *f* gladness, contentedness, contentment

contentino *m* gratuity, makeweight, gift to a customer

contèn·to -ta *adj* contented, glad, happy; satisfied ‖ *m* (poet) happiness, contentedness

contenuto *m* content; contents

contenzióne *f* contention

contenzióso [s] *m* legal matter; legal department (*of a corporation*)

conterìe *fpl* beads, sequins

conterrà·neo -nea *adj* from the same country ‖ *m* fellow countryman ‖ *f* fellow countrywoman

conté·so -sa [s] *adj* coveted ‖ *f* contest; dispute; venire a contesa to dispute

contéssa *f* countess

contestare (contèsto) *tr* to serve (*e.g., a summons*); to deny; to challenge, contest; contestare qlco a qlcu to charge s.o. with s.th

contestazióne *f* notification, summons; dispute, confrontation; challenge

contè·sto -sta *adj* (poet) intertwined ‖ *m* context

contì·guo -gua *adj* contiguous

continentale *adj* continental

continènte *adj* & *m* continent

continènza *f* continence

contingentaménto *m* import quota

contingentare (contingènto) *tr* to assign a quota to (*imports*)

**contingènte** *adj* possible, contingent; (obs) due || *m* contingent; import quota; **contingente di leva** draft quota

**contingènza** *f* contingency

**continuare (contìnuo)** *tr* to continue || *intr* to last, continue; **continuare a** + *inf* to keep on + *ger*

**continuazióne** *f* continuation

**continui·tà** *f* (**-tà**) continuity

**contì·nuo -nua** *adj* continuous; direct (*current*); **di continuo** continuously

**cón·to -ta** *adj* (archaic) well-known; (poet) gentle; (poet) narrated || *m* figuring; account; bill, invoice; check (*in a restaurant*); opinion; worth, value; **a conti fatti** everything considered; **chiedere conto di** to call to account; **conto all'indietro** countdown; **di conto** valuable; **estratto conto** (com) statement; **fare conto di** + *inf* to intend to + *inf*; **fare conto su** to count on; **fare di conto** to count; **fare i conti senza l'oste** to reckon without one's host; **il conto non torna** the sums do not jibe; **in conto** on account; **in conto di** in one's position as; **per conto di** in the name of; **per conto mio** as far as I am concerned; **render conto di** to give an account of; **rendersi conto di** to realize, be aware of; **tener conto di** to reckon with; **tener di conto** to treat with care; **torna conto** it is worthwhile

**contòrcere** §272 *tr* to twist || *ref* to writhe

**contorciménto** *m* contortion, writhing

**contornare (contórno)** *tr* to surround

**contórno** *m* outline; contour; circle (*of people*); side dish (*of vegetables*)

**contorsióne** *f* contorsion; gyration (*e.g., of a dancer*); squirm

**contòr·to -ta** *adj* twisted (*e.g., face*)

**contrabbandare** *tr* to smuggle

**contrabbandiè·re -ra** *adj* smuggling || *mf* smuggler; bootlegger

**contrabbando** *m* contraband; smuggling; **di contrabbando** by smuggling; (fig) without paying

**contrabbasso** *m* contrabass, bass viol

**contraccambiare** §287 *tr* to reciprocate, return || *intr* to reciprocate

**contraccàm·bio** *m* (**-bi**) exchange; **in contraccambio di** in exchange for, in return for

**contraccólpo** *m* shock, rebound; recoil (*of a rifle*); backlash (*of a machine*)

**contrada** *f* road; (poet) region

**contraddire** §151 (*impv sg* **contraddici**) *tr* to contradict || *ref* to contradict oneself; to contradict one another

**contraddistìnguere** §156 *tr* to earmark || *ref* to stand out

**contraddittò·rio -ria** (**-ri -rie**) *adj* contradictory; incoherent || *m* open discussion, debate

**contraddizióne** *f* contradiction

**contraènte** *adj* contracting; acting || *mf* contractor (*person who makes a contract*); (law) party

**contraère·o -a** *adj* antiaircraft

**contraffare** §173 *tr* to counterfeit; to fake, sham || *intr* (archaic) to disobey || *ref* to camouflage oneself, disguise oneself

**contraffat·to -ta** *adj* counterfeit; adulterated; apocryphal

**contraffat·tóre -trice** *mf* counterfeiter; falsifier

**contraffazióne** *f* forgery; fake; imitation; piracy (*of book*); mockery (*of justice*)

**contraffòrte** *m* spur (*of mountain*); crossbar (*to secure door*); (archit) buttress

**contraggènio** *m*—**a contraggenio** against one's will

**contral·to (-to)** *adj* alto || *m* contralto (*voice*) || *f* contralto (*singer*)

**contrammirà·glio** *m* (**-gli**) rear admiral

**contrappasso** *m* retributive justice

**contrappesare** [s] (**contrappéso**) *tr* to counterweight, counterbalance

**contrappéso** [s] *m* counterweight, counterpoise

**contrappórre** §218 *tr* to oppose; to compare || *ref*—**contrapporsi a** to oppose

**contrappó·sto -sta** *adj* opposing || *m* opposite, antithesis

**contrappunto** *m* counterpoint

**contrare (cóntro)** *tr* (boxing) to counter; (bridge) to double

**contrariare** §287 *tr* to oppose, counter; to thwart; to contradict; to bother, vex

**contrarie·tà** *f* (**-tà**) contrariety, vexation; setback

**contrà·rio -ria** (**-ri -rie**) *adj* contrary, opposite || *m* opposite; **al contrario** on the contrary; **al contrario di** unlike; **avere qlco in contrario** to have some objection; **contrarre** §273 *tr & ref* to contract

**contrassegnare (contrasségno)** *tr* to earmark, mark

**contrasségno** *m* earmark; proof

**contrastare** *tr* to oppose; to obstruct; to prevent || *intr* to contrast; to disagree; (poet) to quarrel || *ref* to contend

**contrasto** *m* contrast; fight, dispute; (telv) contrast knob

**contrattàbile** *adj* negotiable

**contrattaccare** §197 *tr* to counterattack

**contrattac·co** *m* (**-chi**) counterattack

**contrattare** *tr* to contract for, negotiate a deal for || *intr* to bargain

**contrattèmpo** *m* mishap

**contrat·to -ta** *adj* contracted || *m* contract

**contrattuale** *adj* contractual

**contravveléno** *m* antidote

**contravvenire** §282 *intr* (with *dat*) to contravene; **contravvenire a** to infringe upon

**contravvenzióne** *f* violation; ticket, fine; **in contravvenzione** in the wrong; **intimare una contravvenzione a** to give a ticket to

**contrazióne** *f* contraction

**contribuènte** *mf* taxpayer

**contribuire** §176 *intr* to contribute

**contributo** *m* contribution

**contribu·tóre -trice** *mf* contributor

**contribuzióne** f contribution
**contristare** tr & ref to sadden
**contri·to -ta** adj contrite
**contrizióne** f contrition
**cóntro** m con, contrary opinion || adv —contro di against, versus; **dar contro a** to oppose; **di contro** opposite, facing; **per contro** on the other hand || prep against, versus; at; **contro pagamento** upon payment; **contro vento** into the wind; **contro voglia** unwillingly
**controbàttere** tr (mil) to counterattack; (fig) to contest
**controbilanciare** §128 tr to counterpoise, counterbalance
**controcanto** m (mus) counterpoint
**controcarro** adj invar antitank
**controchìglia** f keelson
**controcorrènte** f countercurrent; undertow; (fig) undercurrent || adv upstream
**controdado** m lock nut
**controffensiva** f counteroffensive
**controfigura** f (mov) stand-in; (mov) stuntman
**controfilo** m—a **controfilo** against the grain
**controfinèstra** f storm window
**controfirma** f countersign
**controfirmare** tr to countersign
**controfòdera** f inner facing (of a suit, between lining and cloth)
**controfuò·co** m (-chi) backfire (to check the advance of a forest fire)
**controindicare** §197 (controìndico) tr to contraindicate
**controllare** (contròllo) tr to control, check || ref to control oneself
**contròllo** m control, check; restraint; (rad, telv) knob
**controllóre** m (com) comptroller; (rr) ticket collector, conductor
**controluce** f picture taken against the light || adv against the light
**contromano** adv against traffic
**contromar·ca** f (-che) check, stub (e.g., of ticket)
**contromàr·cia** f (-ce) countermarch; (aut) reverse, reverse gear
**contromezzana** [ddzz] f (naut) topsail
**contronòta** f countermanding note
**contropalo** m strut
**controparte** f (law) opponent
**contropedale** m foot brake (of a bicycle)
**contropélo** m close shave (in the opposite direction of hair's growth) || adv against the grain; the wrong way (said of the hair); against the nap; **accarezzare contropelo** to stroke the wrong way
**contropiède** m counterattack; **cogliere in contropiede** to catch off balance
**contropòrta** f storm door
**controproducènte** adj counterproductive, self-defeating
**contropropósta** f counterproposition
**contropròva** f proof; second balloting
**contrórdine** m countermand
**controrèplica** f retort; (law) rejoinder
**controrifórma** f Counter Reformation

**controrivoluzióne** f counterrevolution
**controsènso** m nonsense; mistranslation
**controspallina** f (mil) epaulet
**controspionàg·gio** m (-gi) counterespionage
**controvalóre** m equivalent
**controvènto** m (archit) strut; (archit) crossbrace || adv windward
**controvèrsia** f controversy
**controvèr·so -sa** adj controversial, moot
**controvòglia** adv unwillingly
**contumace** adj (archaic) contumacious; (law) absent from court; (law) guilty of nonappearance
**contumàcia** f quarantine; (archaic) contumacy; (law) nonappearance; **in contumacia** (law) in absentia
**contumèlia** f contumely
**contundènte** adj blunt
**conturbante** adj disturbing, upsetting
**conturbare** tr to disturb, upset || ref to become perturbed
**contusióne** f bruise, contusion
**contu·so -sa** adj bruised
**contuttoché** conj although
**contuttociò** conj although
**convalescènte** adj convalescent
**convalescènza** f convalescence
**convalescenzià·rio** m (-ri) convalescent home
**convàlida** f validation; confirmation
**convalidare** (convàlido) tr to validate; to confirm; to strengthen (e.g., a suspicion)
**convégno** m meeting, convention
**conveniènte** adj convenient; adequate; useful; profitable (business); cheap, reasonable
**conveniènza** f convenience; suitability, fitness; propriety; profit; **convenienze** conventions
**convenire** §282 tr to fix (e.g., a price); (law) to summon || intr (ESSERE) to convene; to agree; to fit, be appropriate; (poet) to flow together || ref to be proper; (with dat) to behoove, befit, e.g., **gli si conviene** it behooves him || impers—**conviene** it is necessary
**convènto** m convent; monastery
**convenu·to -ta** adj agreed upon || m agreement; (law) defendant; **convenuti** conventioners, delegates
**convenzionale** adj conventional
**convenzióne** f convention
**convergènte** adj converging, convergent
**convergènza** f convergence
**convèrgere** §137 intr to converge
**convèrsa** f lay sister; flashing (on a roof)
**conversare** (convèrso) intr to converse
**conversazióne** f conversation
**conversióne** f conversion; change of heart; (mil) wheeling
**convèrso** m lay brother
**convertìbile** adj convertible || m (aer) fighter-bomber || f (aut) convertible
**convertibili·tà** f (-tà) convertibility
**convertire** §138 tr to convert, change; to translate || ref to convert, change; (poet) to address oneself

convèrti·to -ta *adj* converted ‖ *mf* convert
convertitóre *m* converter
convès·so -sa *adj* convex
convincènte *adj* convincing
convìncere §285 *tr* to convince; to convict ‖ *ref* to become convinced
convinciménto *m* conviction
convìn·to -ta *adj* convinced, confirmed; convicted
convinzióne *f* conviction
convita·to -ta *adj* invited ‖ *mf* guest (*at a banquet*)
convìto *m* banquet
convìtto *m* boarding school
convit·tóre -trìce *mf* boarding-school student
convivènte *adj* living together
convivènza *f* living together; **convivenza illecita** cohabitation; **convivenza umana** human society
convìvere §286 *intr* to live together; to cohabit
conviviale *adj* convivial
convì·vio *m* (-vi) banquet
convocare §197 (cònvoco) *tr* to summon, convoke; to convene
convocazióne *f* convocation
convogliare §280 (convòglio) *tr* to convoy, escort; to convey, carry
convò·glio *m* (-gli) convoy; cortege; (rr) train
convolare (convòlo) *intr*—**convolare a nozze** to get married
convòlvolo *m* (bot) morning-glory
convulsióne *f* convulsion
convul·so -sa *adj* convulsive; convulsed; choppy (*style*)
coonestare (coonèsto) *tr* to justify, palliate
cooperare (coòpero) *intr* to cooperate
cooperatì·vo -va *adj & f* cooperative
coopera·tóre -trìce *adj* coadjutant, cooperating ‖ *m* coadjutor
cooperazióne *f* cooperation
coordinaménto *m* coordination
coordinare (coórdino) *tr* to coordinate; to collect (*ideas*)
coordinatì·vo -va *adj* (gram) coordinate
coordina·to -ta *adj & f* coordinate
coordinazióne *f* coordination
coòrte *f* cohort
copèr·chio *m* (-chi) lid, cover; top (*of box*)
copertina *f* small blanket, child's blanket; cover (*of book*)
copèr·to -ta *adj* covered; protected; cloudy; obscure ‖ *m* cover; shelter; **al coperto** under cover; indoors; secure ‖ *f* blanket, cover; seat cover; case, sheath; (naut) deck; **coperta da viaggio** steamer rug, lap robe; **far coperta a** to cover up for
copertóne *m* canvas; casing, shoe (*of tire*); **copertone cinturato** belted tire
copertura *f* covering; cover; coverage; whitewash; (boxing) defensive stance; (archit) roof
cò·pia *f* copy; (poet) abundance; (archaic) opportunity; **brutta copia** first draft; **copia a carbone** carbon copy; **copia dattiloscritta** typescript; **per copia conforme** certified copy (*formula appearing on a document*)
copialètte·re *m* (-re) letter file; copying press
copiare §287 (còpio) *tr* to copy
copiatì·vo -va *adj* indelible; copying
copiatura *f* copying; copy; plagiarism
copìglia *f* cotterpin
copilò·ta *mf* (-ti -te) copilot
copióne *m* (theat) script
copiosi·tà [s] *f* (-tà) copiousness
copió·so -sa [s] *adj* copious
copì·sta *mf* (-sti -ste) scribe; copyist
copisterìa *f* copying office; public typing office
còppa *f* cup, goblet; bowl; pan (*of balance*); trophy; (aut) crankcase; (aut) housing; **coppe** suit of Neapolitan cards corresponding to hearts
coppàia *f* chuck (*of lathe*)
còppia *f* couple; pair; **a coppie** two by two; **far coppia fissa** to go steady
coppière *m* cupbearer
coppìglia *f* var of **copiglia**
cóppo *m* earthenware jar (*for oil*); roof tile
copribu·sto *m* (-sto) bodice
copricapo *m* headgear
copricaté·na *m* (-na) chain guard (*on bicycle or motorcycle*)
coprifuò·co *m* (-chi) curfew
coprinu·ca *m* (-ca) havelock
coprìre §110 *tr* to cover; to occupy (*a position*); to coat (*e.g., a wall*); to drown (*a noise*) ‖ *ref* to cover oneself; (econ) to hedge
copriteiè·ra *m* (-ra) cozy
coprivivan·de *m* (-de) dish cover
cò·pto -pta *adj* Coptic ‖ *mf* Copt
còpula *f* copulation; (gram) copula
coque *f* see **uovo**
coràg·gio *m* (-gi) courage; effrontery; (obs) heart; **fare coraggio a** to hearten, encourage; **prendere il coraggio a quattro mani** to screw up one's courage
coraggió·so -sa [s] *adj* courageous
corale *adj* choral; (archaic) cordial; (fig) unanimous ‖ *m* chorale
coralli·no -na *adj* coral
corallo *m* coral
corame *m* engraved leather
coramèlla *f* razor strop
Corano *m* Koran
corata *f* haslet
coratèlla *f* giblets
corazza *f* breastplate, cuirass; shoulder pad (*in football*); armor plate; carapace, shell
corazzare *tr* to armor ‖ *ref* to armor, protect oneself
corazza·to -ta *adj* armor-plated, armored; plated; protected ‖ *f* battleship, dreadnought
corazzière *m* cuirassier; mounted carabineer
còrba *f* basket
corbellerìa *f* (coll) blunder
corbèllo *m* basket; basketful
corbézzolo *m* (bot) arbutus; **corbezzoli!** gosh!
còrda *f* rope; tightrope; string (*of an*

*instrument*); chord; woof; cord; plumbline; **dare la corda a** to wind (*a clock*); **essere con la corda al collo** to have a rope around one's neck; **mostrare la corda** to be threadbare; **tagliare la corda** to take off, leave; **tenere sulla corda** to keep in suspense

**cordame** *m* cordage

**cordata** *f* group of climbers tied together

**cordellina** *f* (mil) braided cord, braid; (mil) lanyard

**cordiale** *adj & m* cordial

**cordiali·tà** *f* (-tà) cordiality

**cordièra** *f* (mus) tailpiece

**cordò·glio** *m* (-gli) sorrow, grief

**cordonata** *f* gradient

**cordóne** *m* cordon; (anat, elec) cord; curbstone; **cordone litorale** sandbar; **cordone sanitario** sanitary cordon

**corèa** *f* St. Vitus's dance || **Corea** *f* Korea

**corea·no -na** *adj & mf* Korean

**coréggia** *f* leather strap

**coreografia** *f* choreography

**coreògrafo** *m* choreographer

**coriàce·o -a** *adj* tough, leathery

**coriàndolo** *m* (bot) coriander; **coriandoli** confetti

**coricare** §197 (**còrico**) *tr* to put to bed || *ref* to lie down, go to bed

**corindóne** *m* corundum

**corìn·zio -zia** *adj & mf* (-zi -zie) Corinthian

**cori·sta** *mf* (-sti -ste) choir singer, choirmaster || *m* chorus man; (mus) tuning fork; (mus) pitch pipe

**coriza** [dz] or **corizza** [ddzz] *f* coryza

**cormorano** *m* cormorant

**cornàcchia** *f* rook, crow

**cornamusa** *f* bagpipe

**cornata** *f* butt; hook, goring (*by bull*)

**còrne·o -a** *adj* horn, horn-like || *f* cornea

**cornétta** *f* (mus) cornet; (mus) cornet player; (telp) receiver; (hist) pennon (*of cavalry*)

**cornétto** *m* little horn; amulet (*in shape of horn*); crescent (*bread*); ear trumpet

**cornice** *f* cornice; frame; (typ) box; (archit) pediment

**cornicióne** *m* (archit) ledge; (archit) cornice

**cornificare** §197 (**cornìfico**) *tr* (joc) to cuckold

**corniòla** *f* carnelian

**còrniola** *f* (bot) dogberry

**còrniolo** *m* (bot) dogwood

**còrno** *m* horn; wing (*of army*); edge, end; (mus) horn; **corno da caccia** hunting horn; **corno da scarpe** shoe horn; **corno dell'abbondanza** horn of plenty; **corno dogale** (hist) Doge's hat; **corno inglese** (mus) English horn; **non capire un corno** to not understand a blessed thing; **non valere un corno** to not be worth a fig; **un corno!** (slang) heck no! || *m* (**còrna** *fpl*) horn (*of animal*); **alzare le corna** to raise one's head; to become rambunctious; **dire corna di** to speak evil of; **fare le corna** to make horns, to touch wood (*to ward off the evil eye*); **mettere le corna a** to cuckold (*one's husband*); to be unfaithful to (*one's wife*); **portare le corna** to be cuckolded; **rompersi le corna** to get the worst of it

**cornu·to -ta** *adj* horny; horn-shaped; (vulg) cuckolded

**còro** *m* choir; chorus; chancel

**corollà·rio** *m* (-ri) corollary

**coróna** *f* crown; coronet; wreath, garland; range (*of mountains*); collection (*e.g., of sonnets*); stem (*of watch*); felloe (*of wheel*); (astr) corona; (rel) string (*of beads*); (mus) pause; **fare corona a** to surround

**coronaménto** *m* crowning; (archit) capstone; (naut) taffrail

**coronare** (**coróno**) *tr* to crown; to top, surmount

**coronà·rio -ria** *adj* (-ri -rie) coronary; (hist) rewarded with a garland

**corpétto** *m* baby's shirt; waistcoat, vest

**corpino** *m* bodice; vest

**còrpo** *m* body; substance; staff (*of teachers*); (mil) corps; (typ) em quad; **a corpo a corpo** hand-to-hand (*fight*); (sports) in a clinch; **a corpo morto** heavily; doggedly; **andare di corpo** to have a bowel movement; **avere in corpo** (fig) to have inside; **corpo del reato** corpus delicti; **corpo di Bacco!** good Heavens!; **corpo di ballo** ballet; **corpo di commissariato** (mil) supply corps; **corpo di guardia** guard, guardhouse; **corpo semplice** (chem) simple substance; **prendere corpo** to materialize

**corporale** *adj* bodily, body || *m* (eccl) corporal, Communion cloth

**corporativismo** *m* corporatism (*e.g., of Fascist Italy*)

**corporati·vo -va** *adj* corporative, corporate

**corpora·to -ta** *adj* corporate

**corporatura** *f* size, build

**corporazióne** *f* corporation

**corpòre·o -a** *adj* corporeal

**corpó·so -sa** [s] *adj* heavy-bodied

**corpulèn·to -ta** *adj* corpulent

**corpùscolo** *m* particle; (phys) corpuscle

**Corpus Dòmini** *m* (eccl) Corpus Christi

**corredare** (**corrèdo**) *tr* to provide, furnish; to annotate, accompany

**corredino** *m* layette

**corrèdo** *m* trousseau; outfit, garb; actor's kit; furniture; equipment; apparatus (*e.g., footnotes*)

**corrèggere** §226 *tr* to correct; to straighten (*e.g., a road*); to rewrite, revise (*news*); to touch up the flavor of || *ref* to reform

**corrég·gia** *f* (-ge) leather strap

**corregionale** *adj* fellow || *mf* person of the same section of the country

**correità** *f* complicity

**correlare** (**corrèlo**) *tr* to correlate

**correlati·vo -va** *adj* correlative

**correla·tóre -trice** *mf* second reader (*of a doctoral dissertation*)

**correlazióne** *f* correlation; (gram) sequence

**corrènte** *adj* current; running; fluent; recurring; run-of-the-mill || *m*—**essere al corrente di** to be acquainted with; to be abreast of; **mettere al corrente di** to acquaint with || *f* current; draft (*of air*); stream (*of water*); mass (*of lava*); (elec) current; (fig) tide; **contro corrente** upstream; **corrente alternata** (elec) alternating current; **corrente continua** (elec) direct current; **corrente di rete** (elec) house current

**córrere** §139 *tr* to travel; to run (*a risk; a race*); **correre la cavallina** to sow one's wild oats || *intr* (ESSERE & AVERE) to run; to speed; to race; to flow; to fly (*said of time*); to elapse; to be (e.g., *the year 1820*); to be current (*said of coins*); to spread (*said of gossip*); to mature (*said of interest*); to intervene (*said of distance*); to have dealings; **ci corre!** there is quite a difference!; **ci corre poco che cadesse** he narrowly escaped falling; **correre a gambe levate** to run at breakneck speed; **corre l'uso** it is the fashion; **corrono parole grosse** they are having words; **non corre buon sangue fra loro** there is bad blood between them

**corresponsàbile** *adj* jointly responsible

**corresponsióne** *f* payment; (fig) gratitude

**correttézza** *f* correctness

**corretti·vo -va** *adj* corrective || *m* flavoring

**corrèt·to -ta** *adj* correct; flavored; spiked

**corret·tóre -trice** *mf* corrector; **correttore di bozze** proofreader

**correzionale** *adj* correctional

**correzióne** *f* correction

**còrri còrri** *m* rush

**corri·dóio** *m* (-dói) corridor; hallway; (tennis) alley; (theat) aisle

**corridóre** *adj* running || *m* racer; runner (*in baseball*)

**corrièra** *f* mail coach; bus

**corrière** *m* courier; mail; carrier (*of merchandise*)

**corrispetti·vo -va** *adj* equivalent, proportionate || *m* requital, compensation

**corrispondènte** *adj* corresponding, equivalent || *mf* correspondent

**corrispondènza** *f* correspondence

**corrispóndere** §238 *tr* to pay, compensate || *intr* to correspond

**corri·vo -va** *adj* rash; indulgent

**corroborante** *adj* corroborating || *m* tonic

**corroborare** (corròboro) *tr* to corroborate; to invigorate

**corroborazióne** *f* corroboration

**corródere** §239 *tr* to corrode; to erode

**corrómpere** §240 *tr* to spoil; to corrupt; to suborn || *ref* to putrefy, rot

**corrosióne** *f* corrosion

**corrosi·vo -va** *adj* & *m* corrosive

**corró·so -sa** *adj* corroded; eroded

**corrót·to -ta** *adj* corrupted, corrupt; putrefied, rotten || *m* (archaic) lament

**corrucciare** §128 *tr* to anger, vex || *ref* to get angry

**corrùc·cio** *m* (-ci) anger, vexation

**corrugaménto** *m* wrinkling; (geol) fold

**corrugare** §209 *tr* to wrinkle, knit (*one's brow*) || *ref* to frown

**corruscare** §197 *intr* (poet) to shine

**corruttèla** *f* corruption

**corruttìbile** *adj* corruptible

**corrut·tóre -trice** *adj* corrupting, depraving || *m* seducer; briber

**corruzióne** *f* corruption; putrefaction, decomposition

**córsa** *f* race; run; trip; fare; (mach) stroke; (hist) privateering; **a tutta corsa** at full speed; **corsa al galoppo** flat race; **corsa al trotto** harness racing; **corsa semplice** one-way ticket; **corse** horse racing; **da corsa** race, for racing, e.g., **cavallo da corsa** race horse; **di corsa** running, in a hurry; **fare una corsa** to run an errand; **prendere la corsa** to begin to run

**corsalétto** *m* corselet

**corsa·ro -ra** *adj* privateering || *m* privateer, corsair, pirate

**corsétto** *m* corset

**corsìa** *f* aisle; ward (*in hospital*); runner (*of carpet*); lane (*of highway*); **corsia d'accesso** entrance lane; **corsia d'uscita** exit lane

**Còrsica, la** Corsica

**corsivi·sta** *mf* (-sti -ste) (journ) political writer

**corsi·vo -va** *adj* cursive; (poet) running; (poet) current || *m* cursive handwriting; (typ) italics

**córso** *m* course; navigation (*by sea*); path (*of stars*); parade; large street; boulevard; tender (*of currency*); current rate, current price (*of stock at the exchange*); **corso d'acqua** watercourse; **fuori corso** (*coin*) no longer in circulation; **in corso** in circulation; in progress; **in corso di** in the course of; **in corso di stampa** in press

**còr·so -sa** *adj* & *mf* Corsican

**cor·sóio -sóia** (-sói -sóie) *adj* running (*knot*); (mach) on rollers || *m* slide (*of slide rule*); (mach) slide

**córte** *f* court; **corte bandita** open house; **Corte d'appello** appellate court; **Corte di cassazione** Supreme Court; **fare la corte a** to pay court to, woo

**cortéc·cia** *f* (-ce) bark; crust (*of bread*); (fig) appearance; (anat) cortex

**corteggiaménto** *m* courtship

**corteggiatóre** *m* wooer, suitor

**cortég·gio** *m* (-gi) retinue; cortege

**cortèo** *m* procession; parade; funeral train; wedding party

**cortése** *adj* courteous, polite; (lit) liberal; (poet & hist) courtly

**cortesìa** *f* courtesy, politeness; (lit) liberality; (poet & hist) courtliness; **per cortesia** please

**còrtice** *f* cortex

**cortigia·no -na** *adj* flattering; courtly || *mf* courtier; flatterer || *f* courtesan

**cortile** *m* courtyard; barnyard

**cortina** *f* curtain; **cortina di ferro** iron curtain; **cortina di fumo** smoke screen; **oltre cortina** behind the iron curtain

**cortisóne** *m* cortisone

**cór·to -ta** *adj* short; close (*haircut*); **alle corte** in short; **essere a corto di** to be short of; **per farla corta** in short

**cortocircùito** *m* short circuit

**cortometràg·gio** *m* (**-gi**) (*mov*) short

**cor·vè** *f* (**-vè**) tiresome task, drudgery; **corvè di cucina** kitchen police

**corvétta** *f* corvette

**corvi·no -na** *adj* raven-black

**còrvo** *m* raven; crow

**còsa** [s] *f* thing; **belle cose!** or **buone cose!** regards!; **che cosa** what; **cosa da nulla** a mere trifle, nothing at all; **cos'ha?** what's the matter with you (him, her)?; **cosa pubblica** commonweal; **cosa strana** no wonder; **cose belongings**; **per la qual cosa** wherefore; **per prima cosa** first of all; **sopra ogni cosa** above all; **tante belle cose!** best regards!; **una cosa** something; **una cosa nuova** a piece of news

**cosac·co -ca** (**-chi -che**) *adj* Cossack's ‖ *mf* Cossack

**cò·scia** *f* (**-sce**) thigh; haunch; leg (*of gun*); (*archit*) abutment; **coscia di montone** leg of lamb

**cosciènte** *adj* conscious; sensible; aware

**cosciènza** *f* conscience; consciousness; conscientiousness; awareness

**coscienzió·so -sa** [s] *adj* conscientious

**cosciòtto** *m* leg; leg of lamb

**coscrit·to -ta** *adj* conscript ‖ *m* conscript, recruit, draftee

**coscrivere** §250 *tr* to conscript

**coscrizióne** *f* conscription, draft

**così** [s] *adj invar*—**un così... or un... così** such a ‖ *adv* thus; like this; so; **così ... come** as ... as; **così così** so so; **e così via** and so on, and so forth; **per così dire** so to speak

**cosicché** [s] *conj* so that

**cosiddét·to -ta** [s] *adj* so-called

**cosiffat·to -ta** [s] *adj* such, similar

**cosino** [s] *m* (*coll*) little fellow

**cosmèti·co -ca** *adj* & *m* (**-ci -che**) cosmetic

**còsmi·co -ca** *adj* (**-ci -che**) cosmic; outer (*space*)

**còsmo** *m* cosmos; outer space

**cosmòdromo** *m* space center

**cosmologìa** *f* cosmology

**cosmonàu·ta** *mf* (**-ti -te**) cosmonaut, astronaut

**cosmopoli·ta** *adj* & *mf* (**-ti -te**) cosmopolitan

**còso** [s] *m* (*coll*) thing, what-d'you-call-it

**cospàrgere** §261 *tr* to spread; to sprinkle

**cospèrgere** §112 *tr* (*poet*) to wet, sprinkle

**cospètto** *m* presence; **al cospetto di** in the presence of

**cospì·cuo -cua** *adj* distinguished, outstanding; huge, immense; (*poet*) conspicuous

**cospirare** *intr* to conspire, plot

**cospira·tóre -trice** *mf* conspirator

**cospirazióne** *f* conspiracy, plot

**còsta** *f* side; rib; coast, seashore; slope; welt (*along seam*); wale (*in fabric*); (*naut*) frame

**costà** *adv* there; over there

**costaggiù** *adv* down there

**costante** *adj* & *f* constant

**Costantinòpoli** *f* Constantinople

**costanza** *f* constancy ‖ **Costanza** *f* Constance

**costare** (**còsto**) *intr* (ESSERE) to cost; to be expensive; **costare caro** to cost dear; **costare un occhio della testa** to cost a fortune

**costarica·no -na** or **costaricènse** *adj* & *mf* Costa Rican

**costassù** *adv* up there

**costata** *f* rib roast; side

**costeggiare** §290 (**costéggio**) *tr* to sail along; to run along; to border on ‖ *intr* to coast

**costèi** §8 *pron dem*

**costellare** (**costèllo**) *tr* to stud, star

**costellazióne** *f* constellation

**costernare** (**costèrno**) *tr* to dismay, cause consternation to

**costernazióne** *f* consternation

**costì** *adv* there

**costiè·ro -ra** *adj* coast, coastal; offshore ‖ *f* coastline; gentle slope

**costipare** *tr* to constipate; to heap, pile ‖ *ref* to become constipated

**costipazióne** *f* constipation

**costituènte** *adj* constituent; constituting ‖ *m* member of constituent assembly; (*chem*) constituent

**costituire** §176 *tr* to constitute; to form ‖ *ref* to form; to become; to appoint oneself; to give oneself up (*to justice*); **costituirsi in giudizio** (*law*) to sue (*in civil court*); **costituirsi parte civile** (*law*) to appear as a plaintiff (*in civil court*)

**costituto** *m* (*law*) pact, agreement; (*naut*) master's declaration (*to health authorities*)

**costituzionale** *adj* constitutional

**costituzióne** *f* constitution; charter; composition; (*law*) appearance; surrender (*to justice*)

**còsto** *m* cost; **a costo di** at the price of; **ad ogni costo** at any cost; **a nessun costo** by no means; **a tutti i costi** at any cost, in any event; **costo della vita** cost of living; **sotto costo** below cost

**còstola** *f* rib; spine (*of book*); back (*of knife*); **avere qlcu alle costole** to have s.o. at one's heels; **rompere le costole a** (*fig*) to break the bones of; **stare alle costole di** to be at the back of

**costolétta** *f* chop, cutlet

**costolóne** *m* (*archit*) groin

**costóro** §8 *pron dem*

**costó·so -sa** [s] *adj* costly

**costrìngere** §265 *tr* to force, constrain; (*poet*) to compress

**costritti·vo -va** *adj* constrictive

**costrizióne** *f* constriction

**costruire** §140 *tr* to construct, build

**costrut·to -ta** adj constructed ‖ m profit; sense; (gram) construction; **dov'è il costrutto?** what's the point?

**costruttóre** m builder

**costruzióne** f construction; building

**costùi** §8 pron dem

**costumanza** f custom

**costumare** intr (+ inf) to be in the habit of (+ ger) ‖ intr (ESSERE) to be the custom; to be in use

**costumatézza** f good manners

**costuma·to -ta** adj polite, well-bred

**costume** m custom, manner; costume, dress; bathing suit

**costumì·sta** mf (-sti -ste) (theat) costumer

**costura** f seam

**cotale** adj & pron such ‖ adv (archaic) thus

**cotan·to -ta** adj & pron (poet) so much ‖ **cotanto** adv (poet) such a long time

**còte** f flint

**coténna** f pigskin; rind; (coll) hide, skin

**coté·sto -sta** §7 adj dem ‖ §8 pron dem

**cóti·ca** f (-che) (coll) hide, skin (of porker)

**cotógna** f quince (fruit)

**cotognata** f quince jam

**cotógno** m quince (tree)

**cotolétta** f chop, cutlet

**cotóne** m cotton; thread; **cotone fulminante** guncotton; **cotone idrofilo** absorbent cotton; **cotone silicato** mineral wool

**cotonière** m cotton manufacturer

**cotoniè·ro -ra** adj cotton ‖ mf cotton worker

**cotonifì·cio** m adj (-ci) cotton mill

**cotonó·so -sa** [s] adj cotton; cottony

**còtta** f cooking; baking; drying (of bricks); (sports) exhaustion; (coll) drunkenness; (joc) infatuation, love; (eccl) surplice; **cotta d'armi** coat of mail

**cottimi·sta** mf (-sti -ste) pieceworker

**còttimo** m piecework

**còt·to -ta** adj cooked; baked; burnt; suntanned; (joc) half-baked; (joc) in love; (sports) exhausted ‖ m brick ‖ f see **cotta**

**cottura** f cooking; **a punto di cottura** (culin) done just right

**coutènte** mf (law) joint user; (telp) party-line user

**cóva** f brooding; nest

**covare** (cóvo) tr to brood, to hatch; to harbor or nurse (an enmity); to nurture (a disease); **covare con gli occhi** to look fondly at; **covare le lenzuola** to loll around ‖ intr to smolder (said of fire or passion)

**covata** f brood, covey

**covile** m doghouse; den

**cóvo** m shelter; den, lair; **farsi il covo** (fig) to gather a nestegg; **uscire dal covo** to stick one's nose out of the house

**covóne** m sheaf; cock (of hay)

**còzza** f cockle

**cozzare** (còzzo) tr to hit; to butt (one's head) ‖ intr to butt; (fig) to clash;

**cozzare contro** to bump into ‖ ref to hit one another; to fight

**còzzo** m butt; clash, conflict

**crac** m crash

**crampo** m cramp

**crà·nio·co -ca** adj (-ci -che) cranial

**cra·nio** m (-ni) cranium, skull

**cràpula** f excess (in eating and drinking)

**cras·so -sa** adj crass, gross; large (intestine)

**cratère** m crater; bomb crater

**cràuti** mpl sauerkraut

**cravatta** f tie, necktie; **cravatta a farfalla** bow tie; **fare cravatte** to be a usurer

**creanza** f politeness; **buona creanza** good manners

**creare** (crèo) tr to create; to name, elect

**creati·vo -va** adj creative

**crea-to -ta** adj created ‖ m creation, universe

**crea·tóre -trice** adj creative ‖ mf creator

**creatura** f creature; baby; **povera creatura!** poor thing!

**creazióne** f creation; (poet) election

**credènte** adj believing ‖ mf believer

**credènza** f credence, faith, belief; sideboard, buffet; (coll) credit

**credenziale** f letter of credit; **credenziali** credentials

**credenzière** m butler

**crédere** §141 tr to believe; to think; **lo credo bene!** I should say so! ‖ intr to believe; to trust; **credere a** to believe in; **credere in Dio** to believe in God ‖ ref to believe oneself to be

**credìbile** adj credible

**credibilità** f credibility

**crédito** m credit

**credi·tóre -trice** mf creditor

**crèdo** m credo, creed

**credulità** f credulity

**crèdu·lo -la** adj credulous

**crèma** f cream; custard; **crema da scarpe** shoe polish; **crema di bellezza** beauty cream; **crema di pomodoro** cream of tomato soup; **crema evanescente** vanishing cream; **crema per barba** shaving cream

**cremaglièra** f rack; cogway, cograil

**cremare** (crèmo) tr to cremate

**crema·tóio** m (-tói) crematory

**cremató·rio** m (-ri) crematory

**cremazióne** f cremation

**cremerìa** f creamery

**crèmisi** adj & m crimson

**Cremlino** m Kremlin

**cremlinologìa** f Kremlinology

**cremortàrtaro** m cream of tartar

**cremó·so -sa** [s] adj creamy

**crèn** m horseradish

**creolina** f creolin

**crè·o·lo -la** adj & mf Creole

**creosòto** m creosote

**crèpa** f crack, crevice; rift

**crepàc·cio** m (-ci) crevasse; fissure

**crepacuòre** m heartbreak

**crepapància** m—**mangiare a crepapancia** to burst from eating too much

**crepapèlle** m—**ridere a crepapelle** to split one's sides laughing

**crepare** (**crèpo**) *intr* to burst; to crack; to chip; (slang) to croak; **crepare dalla sete** to die of thirst; **crepare dalle risa** to die laughing; **crepare d'invidia** to be green with envy

**crepitare** (**crèpito**) *intr* to crackle (*said of fire or weapons*); to rustle (*said of leaves*)

**crepiti·o** *m* (**-ii**) crackle; rustle; pitter-patter (*of rain*)

**crepuscolare** *adj* twilight; (fig) dim

**crepùscolo** *m* twilight

**crescènte** *adj* rising, growing; crescent (*moon*) ‖ *m* (astr & heral) crescent

**crescènza** *f* growth

**créscere** §142 *tr* to grow, raise; to increase ‖ *intr* (ESSERE) to grow; to increase; to rise (*said, e.g., of prices*); to wax (*said of the moon*); **farsi crescere** to grow (*a beard*)

**crescióne** *m* watercress

**créscita** *f* growth; outgrowth; rise (*of water*)

**crèsima** *f* confirmation

**cresimare** (**crèsimo**) *tr* to confirm

**Crèso** *m* (mythol) Croesus

**cré·spo -spa** *adj* crispy, kinky; (archaic) wrinkled ‖ *m* crepe ‖ *f* wrinkle; ruffle

**crésta** *f* comb (*of chicken*); crest; **abbassare la cresta** to come down a peg or two; **alzare la cresta** to become insolent

**crestàia** *f* (coll) milliner

**créta** *f* clay

**cretése** [s] *adj & mf* Cretan

**cretinerìa** *f* idiocy

**creti·no -na** *adj & mf* idiot, cretin

**cribro** *m* (poet) sieve

**cric·ca** *f* (**-che**) clique, gang; group; crevice

**cric·co** *m* (**-chi**) (aut) jack

**cricéto** *m* hamster

**cri cri** *m* chirping (*of crickets*)

**criminale** *adj* criminal; (law) penal ‖ *mf* criminal

**criminali·sta** *mf* (**-sti -ste**) penal lawyer, criminal lawyer

**criminalità** *f* criminality

**crimine** *m* crime

**criminologìa** *f* criminology

**criminòlo·go** *m* (**-gi**) criminologist

**criminó·so -sa** [s] *adj* criminal

**crinale** *adj* (poet) hair ‖ *m* ridge (*of mountains*)

**crine** *m* horsehair; (poet) hair; (poet) sunbeam

**crinièra** *f* mane

**crinolina** *f* crinoline

**cripta** *f* crypt

**criptocomuni·sta** *mf* (**-sti -ste**) fellow traveler

**crisàlide** *f* chrysalis

**crisantèmo** *m* chrysanthemum

**cri·si** *f* (**-si**) crisis; shortage (*of houses*); attack (*e.g., of fever*); outburst (*of tears*); (econ) slump; **crisi ancillare** or **domestica** servant problem; **in crisi** in difficulties

**cristallerìa** *f* glassware; crystal service; glassware shop; glassworks

**cristallièra** *f* china closet

**cristalli·no -na** *adj* crystalline ‖ *m* crystalline lens

**cristallizzare** [ddzz] *tr & ref* to crystallize

**cristallo** *m* crystal; glass; pane (*of glass*); windshield; **cristallo di rocca** rock crystal; **cristallo di sicurezza** (aut) safety glass

**cristianaménte** *adv* in a Christian manner, like a Christian; (coll) decently; **morire cristianamente** to die in the faith

**cristianésimo** *m* Christianity

**cristianità** *f* Christendom

**cristia·no -na** *adj & mf* Christian

**Cristo** *m* Christ; **avanti Cristo** before Christ (B.C.); **dopo Cristo** after Christ (A.D.); **un povero cristo** (slang) a poor guy

**critè·rio** *m* (**-ri**) criterion; judgment

**crìti·ca** *f* (**-che**) criticism; critique; slur

**criticare** §197 (**crìtico**) *tr* to criticize, censure; to find fault with

**crìti·co -ca** (**-ci -che**) *adj* critical ‖ *mf* critic; (coll) faultfinder ‖ *f* see **critica**

**crittografìa** *f* cryptography

**crittogram·ma** *m* (**-mi**) cryptogram

**crivellare** (**crivèllo**) *tr* to riddle

**crivèllo** *m* sieve, riddle

**croa·to -ta** *adj & mf* Croatian

**Croàzia, la** Croatia

**croccante** *adj* crisp, crunchy ‖ *m* almond brittle, peanut brittle

**crocchétta** *f* croquette

**cròcchia** *f* chignon, topknot

**crocchiare** §287 (**cròcchio**) *intr* to crackle; to sound cracked or broken; to cluck (*said of a hen*); to crack (*said of joints*)

**cròc·chio** *m* (**-chi**) group (*of people*); **far crocchio** to gather around

**cróce** *f* cross; x (*mark made by illiterate person*); tail (*of coin*); (fig) trial; **Croce del Sud** Southern Cross; **croce di Malta** Maltese cross; **Croce Rossa** Red Cross; **croce uncinata** swastika; **fare una croce sopra** to forget about; **gettare la croce addosso** (fig) to put the blame on; **mettere in croce** to crucify

**crocefisso** *m* crucifix

**crocerossina** *f* Red Cross worker

**croceségno** *m* cross, x (*mark made instead of signature*)

**crocétta** *f* (naut) crosstree

**croce·via** *m* (**-via**) crossroads, intersection

**crocia·to -ta** *adj* crossed; crusading; see **parola** ‖ *m* crusader ‖ *f* crusade

**crocièra** *f* cruise; (archit) cross (*vault*); (mach) cross (*of universal joint*)

**crocière** *m* (orn) crossbill

**crocifìggere** §104 *tr* to crucify

**crocifissióne** *f* crucifixion

**crocifis·so -sa** *adj* crucified ‖ *m* crucifix

**crò·co** *m* (**-chi**) crocus

**crogiolare** (**crògiolo**) *tr* to cook on a low fire; to simmer; to temper (*glass*) ‖ *ref* to bask; to snuggle (*e.g., in bed*)

**crogiolo** *m* cooking on a low fire; simmering; tempering (*of glass*)

**crogiòlo** *m* crucible; (fig) melting pot

**crollare** (**cròllo**) *tr* to shake (*e.g., one's head*) ‖ *intr* (ESSERE) to fall down, collapse ‖ *ref* to shake

**cròllo** *m* shake; fall, collapse

**cròma** *f* (mus) quaver

**cromare (cròmo)** *tr* to plate with chromium

**croma·to -ta** *adj* chromium-plated; chrome ‖ *m* chrome yellow

**cromatura** *f* chromium plating

**cròmo** *m* chrome, chromium

**cromosfèra** *f* chromosphere

**cromosò·ma** [s] *m* (-mi) chromosome

**cròna·ca** *f* (-che) chronicle; report, news; **cronaca bianca** news of the day; **cronaca giudiziaria** court news; **cronaca mondana** social column; **cronaca nera** police and accident report; **cronaca rosa** wedding column; stork news

**cròni·co -ca (-ci -che)** *adj* chronic ‖ *mf* incurable

**croni·sta** *mf* (-sti -ste) reporter; chronicler

**cronistòria** *f* chronicle

**cronologìa** *f* chronology

**cronològi·co -ca** *adj* (-ci -che) chronologic(al)

**cronometrare (cronòmetro)** *tr* to time

**cronomètri·co -ca** *adj* (-ci -che) chronometric(al); split-second

**cronometri·sta** *m* (-sti) (sports) timekeeper

**cronòmetro** *m* stopwatch; chronometer

**crosciare §128 (cròscio)** *tr* (archaic) to heave, throw ‖ *intr* to rustle (*said of dry leaves*); to pitter-patter (*said of rain*)

**cròsta** *f* crust; bark (*of tree*); scab; slough; shell (*of crustacean*); poor painting

**crostàceo** *m* crustacean

**crostata** *f* pie

**crostino** *m* toast

**crostó·so -sa** [s] *adj* crusty

**croupier** *m* (**croupier**) croupier

**crucciare §128** *tr* to worry, vex; to chagrin ‖ *ref* to worry; to become angry

**cruccia·to -ta** *adj* afflicted; worried; angry; chagrined

**crùc·cio** *m* (-ci) sorrow; (obs) anger; **darsi cruccio** to fret

**cruciale** *adj* crucial

**crucivèr·ba** *m* (-ba) crossword puzzle

**crudèle** *adj* cruel

**crudel·tà** *f* (-tà) cruelty

**crudézza** *f* crudity; harshness

**cru·do -da** *adj* raw; rare (*meat*); (poet) cruel

**cruèn·to -ta** *adj* (lit) bloody

**crumiro** *m* scab (*in strikes*)

**cruna** *f* eye (*of a needle*)

**cru·sca** *f* (-sche) bran; (coll) freckles

**cruscante** *adj* Della-Cruscan; affected ‖ *m* member of the Accademia della Crusca

**cruschèllo** *m* middlings

**cruscòtto** *m* (aut) dashboard; (aer) instrument panel

**cuba·no -na** *adj* & *mf* Cuban

**cubatura** *f* volume

**cùbi·co -ca** *adj* (-ci -che) cubic; cube (*root*)

**cubitale** *adj* very large (*handwriting or type*)

**cùbito** *m* cubit; (poet) elbow

**cubo** *m* cube

**cuccagna** *f* plenty; windfall; Cockaigne

**cuccétta** *f* berth

**cucchiàia** *f* large spoon; ladle; trowel; bucket (*of power shovel*); **cucchiaia bucata** skimmer

**cucchiaiàta** *f* spoonful; tablespoonful

**cucchiaino** *m* teaspoon; teaspoonful; spoon (*lure*)

**cuc·chiàio** *m* (-chiài) spoon; spoonful; tablespoon; **cucchiaio da minestra** soupspoon

**cucchiaióne** *m* ladle

**cùc·cia** *f* (-ce) dog's bed; **a cuccia!** lie down!

**cucciare §128** *intr* (ESSERE) & *ref* to lie down (*said of a dog*)

**cucciolata** *f* litter (*e.g., of puppies*)

**cùcciolo** *m* puppy; cub; (fig) greenhorn

**cuc·co** *m* (-chi) cuckoo; simpleton; darling (*child*)

**cuccuru·cù** *m* (-cù) cock-a-doodle-doo

**cucina** *f* kitchen; cuisine; kitchen range; **cucina componibile** kitchen with sectional cabinets; **cucina economica** kitchen range; **fare da cucina** to prepare a meal

**cucinare** *tr* to cook; (fig) to fix

**cucinétta** *f* kitchenette

**cuciniè·re -ra** *mf* cook

**cucire §143** *tr* to sew; to stitch ‖ *ref—* **cucirsi la bocca** to keep one's mouth shut

**cucirino** *m* sewing thread

**cuci·tóre -trice** *adj* sewing ‖ *mf* sewing machine operator ‖ *f* seamstress; sewing machine (*for bookbinding*); **cucitrice a grappe** stapler

**cuci·to -ta** *adj* sewn ‖ *m* sewing; needlework

**cucitura** *f* seam; sewing; stitches

**cu·cù** *m* (-cù) cuckoo

**cuculo** or **cùculo** *m* cuckoo

**cùffia** *f* bonnet (*for baby*); coif; (rad) headset; (telp) headpiece; (theat) prompter's box

**cugi·no -na** *mf* cousin

**cui** *pron invar* whose; to which; whom; which; of whom; of which; **per cui** (coll) therefore

**culatta** *f* breech (*of a gun*)

**culinà·rio -ria (-ri -rie)** *adj* culinary ‖ *f* gastronomy

**culla** *f* cradle

**cullare** *tr* to rock (*a baby*); (fig) to delude ‖ *ref* to have delusions

**culminante** *adj* highest; culminating

**culminare (cùlmino)** *intr* to culminate

**cùlmine** *m* top, summit

**culo** *m* (vulg) behind; (slang) bottom (*of glass or bottle*): **culi di bicchiere** (coll) fake diamonds

**cul·to -ta** *adj* cultivated; learned (*e.g., word*) ‖ *m* cult, worship

**cul·tóre -trice** *mf* devotee

**cultura** *f* culture; **cultura fisica** physical culture

**culturale** *adj* cultural

**cumino** *m* (bot) caraway seed; (bot) cumin

**cumulati·vo -va** *adj* cumulative

cùmulo *m* heap, pile; concurrence (*of penal sentences*); cumulus

cuna *f* cradle

cùneo *m* wedge; chock; (archit) voussoir

cunétta *f* ditch; gutter

cunìcolo *m* small tunnel; burrow

cuòcere §144a *tr* to cook; to bake (*bricks*); to burn, dry up; (fig) to stew || *intr* to cook; to burn; to dry up; (with *dat*) to grieve, to pain

cuò·co -ca *mf* (-chi -che) cook

cuòio *m* (cuòi) leather; avere il cuoio duro to have a tough hide; cuoio capelluto scalp || *m* (cuoia *fpl*) (archaic) leather; tirare le cuoia (slang) to croak, to kick the bucket

cuòre *m* heart; avere il cuore da coniglio to be chicken-hearted; avere il cuore da leone to be lion-hearted; cuori (cards) hearts; di cuore gladly; heartily; fare cuore a to encourage; stare a cuore to be important

cupidìgia *f* cupidity, greed, covetousness

Cupido *m* Cupid

cùpi·do -da *adj* greedy, covetous

cu·po -pa *adj* dark; deep (*color, voice*); sad, gloomy

cùpola *f* dome, cupola; crown (*of hat*)

cura *f* care; interest; cure; ministry; (poet) anxiety; a cura di edited by (*e.g., text*)

curare *tr* to take care of; to heed || *intr* to see to it || *ref* to take care of oneself; to care; to deign; curarsi di to care for

curatèla *f* (law) guardianship

curati·vo -va *adj* curative

cura·to -ta *adj* cured; healed || *m* curate

cura·tóre -trice *mf* curator; trustee; editor (*of critical edition*); receiver (*in bankruptcy*)

curculióne *m* (ent) weevil

cur·do -da *adj* & *mf* Kurd

cùria *f* curia; bar

curiale *adj* curia; legal

curialé·sco -sca *adj* (-schi -sche) hairsplitting, legalistic

curiosare [s] (curióso) *intr* to pry around, snoop; to browse around

curiosi·tà [s] *f* (-tà) curiosity; whim; curio

curió·so -sa [s] *adj* curious; bizarre, quaint

curro *m* roller

cursóre *m* process server; court messenger; slide (*of slide ruler*)

curva *f* curve, bend; sweep; curva di livello contour line

curvare *tr* to curve, bend; curvare la fronte to bow down, yield || *intr* to curve (*said of a road*); to take a curve, negotiate a curve || *ref* to curve, bend; to bow; to become bent; to warp

curvatura *f* curving, bending; warp; stoop, curvature; camber

cur·vo -va *adj* bent, curved || *f* see curva

cuscinétto *m* small pillow; pad (*for ink*); buffer (*zone*); (mach) bearing; cuscinetto a rulli roller bearing; cuscinetto a sfere ball bearing

cuscino *m* pillow; cushion

cùspide *f* point (*e.g., of arrow*); (archit) steeple

custòde *adj* guardian (*angel*) || *m* custodian; janitor; warden; guard; (coll) policeman, cop

custòdia *f* safekeeping, custody; case (*e.g., of violin*); trust; (mach) housing

custodire §176 *tr* to keep; to protect, guard; to be in charge of (*prisoners*); to take care of; to cherish (*a memory*)

cutàne·o -a *adj* cutaneous

cute *f* (anat) skin

cuticagna *f* (joc) nape of the neck

cutìcola *f* epidermis; cuticle; dentine

cutireazióne *f* skin test (*for allergic reactions*)

cutréttola *f* (orn) wagtail

# D

D, d [di] *m* & *f* fourth letter of the Italian alphabet

da *prep* from; to; at; on; through; between; since; with; by, e.g., è stato arrestato dalla polizia he was arrested by the police; worth, e.g., un libro da mille lire a book worth a thousand lire; worthy of, e.g., azione da gentiluomo action worthy of a gentleman; at the house, office, shop, etc., of, e.g., dal pittore at the house of the painter; da Giovanni at John's; dall'avvocato at the lawyer's office; d'altro lato on the other hand; d'ora in poi from now on

dabbasso *adv* downstairs; down below

dabbenàggine *f* simplicity, foolishness

dabbène *adj invar* honest, upright, e.g., un uomo dabbene an honest man; simple, foolish, e.g., un dabben uomo a Simple Simon

daccanto *adv* near, nearby

daccapo *adv* again, all over again; andar daccapo to begin a new paragraph; daccapo a piedi from top to bottom

dacché *conj* since

dado *m* cube; pedestal (*of column*); (mach) nut; (mach) die (*to cut threads*); dadi dice; giocare ai dadi to shoot craps; il dado è tratto the die is cast

daffare *m* things to do; bustle; darsi daffare to bustle, bustle about

da·ga *f* (-ghe) dagger

dagli §4 || *interj*—dagli al ladro! stop thief!; e dagli! cut it out!

dài §4

**dài·no -na** *mf* fallow deer ‖ *m* fallow deer; buckskin
**dal** §4
**dàlia** *f* dahlia
**dalla** §4
**dallato** *adv* aside; sideways
**dalle** §4
**dalli** *interj*—**dalli al ladro! stop thief!; e dalli!** cut it out!
**dallo** §4
**dàlma·ta** *adj & mf* (**-ti -te**) Dalmatian
**Dalmàzia, la** Dalmatia
**daltòni·co -ca** *adj* (**-ci -che**) color-blind
**daltonismo** *m* color blindness
**dama** *f* lady; dancing partner; checkers; **andare a dama** (checkers) to be crowned; **dama di compagnia** companion; **dama di corte** lady-in-waiting
**damare** *tr* (checkers) to crown
**damascare** §197 *tr* to damask
**damaschinare** *tr* to damascene
**dama·sco** *m* (**-schi**) damask ‖ **Damasco** *f* Damascus
**damerino** *m* fop, dandy
**damigèlla** *f* (lit) damsel; (orn) demoiselle; **damigella d'onore** bridesmaid
**damigiana** *f* demijohn
**danaro** *m* var of **denaro**
**danaró·so -sa** [s] *adj* wealthy, rich
**dande** *fpl* leading strings
**danése** [s] *adj* Danish ‖ *mf* Dane ‖ *m* Danish (*language*); **Great Dane**
**Danimarca, la** Denmark
**dannare** *tr* to damn; to bedevil ‖ *ref* to be damned; to fret
**danna·to -ta** *adj* damned; wicked; terrible (*e.g., fear*) ‖ *m* damned soul
**dannazióne** *f* damnation
**danneggiare** §290 (**dannéggio**) *tr* to damage; to injure, impair
**danneggia·to -ta** *adj* damaged; injured, impaired ‖ *mf* victim
**danno** *m* damage; injury; (ins) loss; **chiedere i danni** to ask for indemnification; **far danni** to a damage; **rifare i danni a** to indemnify; **tuo danno** so much the worse for you
**danný·so -sa** [s] *adj* damaging, harmful
**dante** *m*—**pelle di dante** buckskin
**danté·sco -sca** *adj* (**-schi -sche**) Dantean, Dantesque
**danti·sta** *mf* (**-sti -ste**) Dante scholar
**Danùbio** *m* Danube
**danza** *f* dance; dancing
**danzare** *tr & intr* to dance
**danza·tóre -trice** *mf* dancer
**dappertutto** *adv* everywhere
**dappiè** *adv*—**dappiè di** at the foot of
**dappiù** *adv*—**dappiù di** more than
**dappòco** *adj invar* worthless
**dappòi** *adv* (obs) afterwards, after
**dapprèsso** *adv* near, nearby, close
**dapprima** *adv* first, in the first place
**dapprincìpio** *adv* first, in the beginning; over again
**dardeggiare** §290 (**dardéggio**) *tr* to hurl darts at; to beat down on; to look daggers at ‖ *intr* to hurl darts; to beat down
**dardo** *m* dart, arrow; tip (*of blowtorch*)
**da·re** *m* (**-re**) (com) debit; **dare e avere**

debit and credit ‖ §144b *tr* to give; to set (*fire*); to hand over; to lay down (*one's life*); to render (*e.g., unto Caesar*); to give away (*a bride*); to take (*an examination*); to tender (*one's resignation*); to say (*good night*); to shed (*tears*); **dare acqua a** to water; **dare alla luce** to give birth to; to bring out (*e.g., a book*); **dare aria a** to air; **dare ... anni a qlcu** to think that s.o. is ... years old; **dare a ridire** to give rise to complaint; **dare da intendere** to lead to believe; **dare fastidio a** to bother, annoy; **dare fondo a** to use up; **dare gli otto giorni a** to dismiss, fire; **dare il benvenuto a** to welcome; **dare il via a** to start (*e.g., a race*); **dare la colpa a** to declare guilty; to put the blame on; **dare la mano a** to shake hands with; **dare l'assalto a** to assault; **dare luogo a** to give rise to; **dare noia a** to bother; **dare per certo a** to assure; **dare ragione a** to agree with; **dare torto a** to disagree with; **dare via** to give away ‖ *intr* to burst; to begin; to beat down (*said of the sun*); **dare a** to verge on; to face, overlook; **dare addosso a** to attack, persecute; **dare ai** or **sui nervi di** to irritate, irk; **dare alla testa a** to go to one's head, e.g., **il vino gli dà alla testa** wine goes to his head; **dare contro a** to disagree with; **dare del ladro a** to call (s.o.) a thief; **dare del Lei a** to address formally; **dare del tu a** to address familiarly; **dare di volta il cervello a** to go raving mad, e.g., **gli ha dato di volta il cervello** he went raving mad; **dare giù** to abate; **dare in** to hit; **dare in affitto** to rent, lease; **dare nell'occhio** to attract attention; to hit the eye; **dare nel segno** to hit the target ‖ *ref* to put on, e.g., **darsi la cipria** to put powder on; **darsela a gambe** to take to one's heels; **darsela per intesa** to become convinced; to take for granted; **darsele** to strike one another; **darsi a** to give oneself over to; **darsi delle arie** to put on airs; **darsi il vanto di** to boast of; **darsi un bacio** to kiss one another; **darsi la mano** to shake hands; **darsi la morte** to commit suicide; **darsi pace** to resign oneself; **darsi pensiero** to worry; **darsi per malato** to declare oneself ill; to fall ill; **darsi per vinto** to give in, submit; **può darsi** it's possible, maybe; **si dà il caso** it happens
**dàrsena** *f* dock; basin
**data** *f* date; deal (*of cards*); **a ... data** (com) ... days hence, on or before ... days; **di fresca data** new (*e.g., friend*); **di vecchia data** old (*e.g., friend*)
**datare** *tr* to date ‖ *intr*—**a datare da** beginning with
**datà·rio** *m* (**-ri**) date stamp
**dati·vo -va** *adj & m* dative
**da·to -ta** *adj* inclined, bent; addicted; given; appointed (*date*); **dato e non concesso** assumed for the sake of

argument; **dato che** since ‖ *m* datum ‖ *f* see **data**

**da·tóre -trice** *mf* giver, donor; **datore di lavoro** employer; **datore di sangue** blood donor; **datori di lavoro** management

**dàttero** *m* date; (zool) date shell

**dattilografare (dattilògrafo)** *tr* to typewrite, type

**dattilografìa** *f* typewriting

**dattilògra·fo -fa** *mf* typist

**dattiloscopìa** *f* examination of fingerprints

**dattiloscrit·to -ta** *adj* typewritten ‖ *m* typescript

**dattórno** *adv* near, nearby; **darsi dattorno** to strive; **stare dattorno a** to cling to; **togliersi dattorno qlcu** to get rid of s.o.

**davanti** *adj invar* fore, front ‖ **davan·ti** *m* (**-ti**) front, face ‖ *adv* ahead, in front; **davanti a** in front of; **levarsi davanti a qlcu** to get out of someone's way; **passare davanti a** to pass, outstrip

**davanzale** *m* window sill

**davanzo** *adv* more than enough

**davvéro** *adv* indeed; **dire davvero** to speak in earnest

**daziare** §287 *tr* to levy a duty on

**dà·zio** *m* (**-zi**) duty, custom; custom office

**dèa** *f* goddess

**debellare (debèllo)** *tr* (lit) to crush

**debilitare (debìlito)** *tr* to debilitate

**debilitazióne** *f* debilitation

**débi·to -ta** *adj* due ‖ *m* debit; debt; **debito pubblico** national debt

**debi·tóre -trice** *mf* debtor

**débole** *adj* weak; faint; gentle (*sex*); **debole di mente** feeble-minded ‖ *m* weakness, weak point; weakness, foible; weakling

**debolézza** *f* weakness, debility

**debordare (debórdo)** *intr* (ESSERE & AVERE) to overflow

**debòscia** *f* debauchery

**deboscia·to -ta** *adj* debauched ‖ *mf* debauchee

**debuttante** *adj* beginning ‖ *mf* beginner ‖ *f* debutante

**debuttare** *intr* to come out, make one's debut; (theat) to perform for the first time; (theat) to open

**debutto** *m* debut; (theat) opening night, opening

**dècade** *f* ten; period of ten days; (mil) ten days' pay

**decadènte** *adj & m* decadent

**decadènza** *f* decadence; lapse (*of insurance policy*); (law) forfeiture

**decadére** §121 *intr* (ESSERE) to decline; to lose one's standing; (ins) to lapse; **decadere da** (law) to forfeit

**decadiménto** *m* decadence; (law) forfeiture

**decadu·to -ta** *adj* fallen upon hard times

**decaffeinizzare** [ddzz] *tr* to decaffeinate

**decalcificatóre** *m* water softener

**decalcomanìa** *f* decalcomania

**decàlo·go** *m* (**-ghi**) decalogue

**decampare** *intr* to decamp; **decampare da** to abandon (*a plan*)

**decano** *m* dean

**decantare** *tr* to praise, extol; to decant; (lit) to purify ‖ *intr* to undergo decantation

**decapàggio** *m* (metallurgy) pickling

**decapitare (decàpito)** *tr* to behead, decapitate

**decapitazióne** *f* beheading

**decappottàbile** *adj & f* (aut) convertible

**decèdere** §123 *intr* (ESSERE) to die; to decease

**decelerare (decèlero)** *tr & intr* to decelerate

**decennale** *adj & m* decennial

**decènne** *adj & mf* ten-year-old

**decèn·nio** *m* (**-ni**) decade

**decènte** *adj* decent; proper

**decentralizzare** [ddzz] *tr* to decentralize

**decentrare (decèntro)** *tr* to decentralize

**decènza** *f* decency; propriety

**decèsso** *m* decease, demise

**decidere** §145 *tr* to decide; to persuade ‖ *intr & ref* to decide; **deciditi!** make up your mind!

**decifràbile** *adj* decipherable

**decifrare** *tr* to decipher, decode; (fig) to puzzle out (*e.g., somebody's intentions*); (mus) to sight-read

**dècima** *f* tithe

**decimale** *adj & m* decimal

**decimare (dècimo)** *tr* to decimate

**decìmetro** *m* decimeter; **doppio decimetro** ruler

**dèci·mo -ma** *adj, m & pron* tenth ‖ *f* see **decima**

**decisionale** *adj* decision-making

**decisióne** *f* decision

**decisi·vo -va** *adj* decisive, conclusive

**deci·so -sa** *adj* determined, resolute; appointed (*time*)

**declamare** *tr* to declaim ‖ *intr* to declaim; to inveigh

**declamazióne** *f* declamation

**declaratò·rio -ria** *adj* (**-ri -rie**) declarative

**declinare** *tr* to decline; to declare, show; (gram) to decline; (lit) to bend ‖ *intr* to set (*said, e.g., of a star*); to slope; to diminish

**declinazióne** *f* declination; (gram) declension

**declino** *m* decline

**declì·vio** *m* (**-vi**) declivity, slope

**decollàg·gio** *m* (**-gi**) take-off; lift-off

**decollare (decòllo)** *tr* to decapitate ‖ *intr* (aer) to take off; (rok) to lift off

**decòllo** *m* take-off; lift-off

**decolorante** *adj* bleaching ‖ *m* bleach

**decompórre** §218 *tr, intr & ref* to decompose

**decomposizióne** *f* decomposition

**decompressióne** *f* decompression

**decongelare (decongèlo)** *tr* to thaw; (com) to unfreeze

**decontaminare (decontàmino)** *tr* to decontaminate

**decorare (decòro)** *tr* to decorate

**decorati·vo -va** *adj* decorative

**decora·tóre -trice** *mf* decorator

**decorazióne** *f* decoration

**decòro** *m* decorum, propriety; decor; dignity; decoration

**decoró·so -sa** [s] *adj* fitting, decorous, proper; dignified

**decorrènza** *f* beginning, effective date; lapse

**decórrere** §139 *intr* (ESSERE) to elapse; to begin; (lit) to run; **a decorrere da** effective, beginning with

**decór·so -sa** *adj* past ‖ *m* period, span; course; development; **nel decorso di** in the course of

**decòt·to -ta** *adj* (com) insolvent ‖ *m* decoction

**decozióne** *f* (com) insolvency

**decrèpi·to -ta** *adj* decrepit

**decréscere** §142 *intr* (ESSERE) to decrease

**decretare** (**decréto**) *tr* to decree

**decréto** *m* decree; **decreto legge** decree law

**decùbito** *m* recumbency

**decuplicare** §197 (**decùplico**) *tr* to multiply tenfold

**dècu·plo -pla** *adj* tenfold ‖ *m* tenfold part

**decurtare** *tr* to diminish, decrease

**decurtazióne** *f* decrease

**dèda·lo -la** *adj* (lit) ingenious ‖ *m* maze, labyrinth

**dèdi·ca** *f* (**-che**) dedication; inscription (*in a book*)

**dedicare** §197 (**dèdico**) *tr* to dedicate; to inscribe (*a book*) ‖ *ref* to devote oneself

**dèdi·to -ta** *adj* devoted; addicted

**dedizióne** *f* devotion; (obs) surrender

**dedurre** §102 *tr* to deduce; to deduct; to derive; (hist) to found (*a colony*)

**deduzióne** *f* deduction

**defalcàbile** *adj* deductible

**defalcare** §197 *tr* to deduct, withhold

**defal·co** *m* (**-chi**) deduction, withholding

**defecare** §197 (**deféco**) *tr* (chem) to purify ‖ *intr* to defecate

**defenestrare** (**defenèstro**) *tr* to throw out of the window; (fig) to fire; (pol) to unseat

**defenestrazióne** *f* defenestration; (fig) firing, dismissal

**deferènte** *adj* deferential; (anat) deferent

**deferènza** *f* deference

**deferire** §176 *tr* to submit; (law) to commit; **deferire il giuramento a qlcu** to put s.o. under oath ‖ *intr* to defer

**defezionare** (**defezióno**) *intr* to desert, defect

**defezióne** *f* defection

**deficiènte** *adj* deficient, lacking ‖ *mf* idiot

**deficiènza** *f* deficiency; idiocy

**dèfi·cit** *m* (**-cit**) deficit

**deficità·rio -ria** *adj* (**-ri -rie**) lacking; deficit (*e.g., budget*)

**defilare** *tr* to defilade ‖ *ref* to protect oneself

**denfinìbile** *adj* definable

**definire** §176 *tr* to define; to settle (*an argument*)

**definiti·vo -va** *adj* definitive; **in definitiva** after all

**defini·to -ta** *adj* definite

**definizióne** *f* definition; settlement (*of an argument*)

**deflagrare** *intr* to burst into flame; (fig) to burst out

**deflazionare** (**deflazióno**) *tr* (com) to deflate

**deflazióne** *f* deflation

**deflèttere** §177 *intr* to deflect

**deflettóre** *m* (aut) vent window; (mach) baffle

**deflorare** (**deflòro**) *tr* to deflower

**defluire** §176 *intr* (ESSERE) to flow down; (fig) to pour out

**deflusso** *m* flow; outflow, outpour; ebbtide

**deformare** (**defórmo**) *tr* to deform; to cripple; to alter (*a word*)

**defórme** *adj* deformed, crippled

**deformi·tà** *f* (**-tà**) deformity

**defraudare** (**defràudo**) *tr* to defraud, bilk

**defun·to -ta** *adj* dead; deceased; defunct; late ‖ *mf* dead person, deceased ‖ *m* deceased; **i defunti** the deceased

**degenerare** (**degènero**) *intr* (ESSERE & AVERE) to degenerate; to worsen

**degenera·to -ta** *adj* degenerate, perverted ‖ *mf* degenerate, pervert

**degenerazióne** *f* degeneracy, degeneration

**degènere** *adj* degenerate

**degènte** *adj* bedridden; hospitalized ‖ *mf* patient; inpatient

**degènza** *f* confinement; hospitalization

**dégli** §4

**deglutire** §176 *tr* to swallow

**degnare** (**dégno**) *tr* to honor ‖ *ref* to deign, condescend

**degnazióne** *f* condescension

**dé·gno -gna** *adj* worthy; **degno di nota** noteworthy

**degradante** *adj* degrading

**degradare** *tr* to degrade; to downgrade; (mil) to break ‖ *ref* to become degraded

**degradazióne** *f* degradation

**degustare** *tr* to taste

**degustazióne** *f* tasting

**dèh** *interj* oh!

**déi** §4

**deiezióne** *f* excrement; (geol) detritus

**deificare** §197 (**deìfico**) *tr* to deify

**dei·tà** *f* (**-tà**) deity

**dél** §4

**dela·tóre -trice** *mf* informer

**delazióne** *f* informing; (law) administration of an oath

**dèle·ga** *f* (**-ghe**) proxy, power of attorney

**delegare** §209 (**dèlego**) *tr* to delegate

**delega·to -ta** *adj* delegated ‖ *m* delegate; (eccl) legate

**delegazióne** *f* delegation

**deletè·rio -ria** *adj* (**-ri -rie**) deleterious

**delfino** *m* dolphin; (hist) dauphin

**delibare** *tr* to relish; to touch on; to ratify (*a foreign decree*)

**delibazióne** f ratification (of a foreign decree)

**deliberare (delìbero)** tr to deliberate; to decide; to award (at auction) ‖ intr to deliberate

**delibera·to -ta** adj deliberate; resolved

**deliberazióne** f deliberation; decision

**delicatézza** f delicacy; gentleness; tactfulness; luxury

**delica·to -ta** adj delicate; gentle; tactful

**delimitare (delìmito)** tr to delimit

**delineare (delìneo)** tr to outline, sketch ‖ ref to take shape; to appear

**delinquènte** m criminal

**delinquènza** f delinquency; **delinquenza minorile** juvenile delinquency

**delinquere** §146 intr to commit a crime

**delì·quio** m (-qui) fainting spell, swoon; **cadere in deliquio** to faint

**delirare** intr to be delirious; to rave; (lit) to stray

**delì·rio** m (-ri) delirium; frenzy; **andare in delirio** to go wild; **cadere in delirio** to become delirious

**delitto** m crime

**delittuó·so -sa** adj criminal

**delìzia** f delight; (hort) Delicious (variety of apple)

**deliziare** §287 tr & ref to delight

**delizió·so -sa** [s] adj delicious; delightful

**délla** §4

**délle** §4

**déllo** §4

**dèl·ta** m (-ta) delta

**delucidare (delùcido)** tr to elucidate; to remove the sheen from

**delucidazióne** f elucidation; removal of sheen

**delùdere** §105 tr to disappoint; to deceive; to foil

**delusióne** f disappointment; deception

**delu·so -sa** adj disappointed; deceived

**demagnetizzare** [ddzz] tr to demagnetize

**demagogìa** f demagogy

**demagò·go** m (-ghi) demagogue

**demandare** tr (law) to commit

**demà·nio** m (-ni) state land, state property

**demarcare** §197 tr to demarcate

**demarcazióne** f demarcation

**demènte** adj demented, crazy; idiotic ‖ mf insane person; idiot

**demènza** f insanity, madness; idiocy

**demèrito** m demerit

**demilitarizzare** [ddzz] tr to demilitarize

**democràti·co -ca** (-ci -che) adj democratic ‖ mf democrat

**democrazìa** f democracy ‖ **Democrazia Cristiana** Christian Democratic Party

**democristia·no -na** adj Christian Democratic ‖ mf Christian Democrat

**demogràfi·co -ca** adj (-ci -che) demographic

**demolire** §176 tr to demolish

**demoli·tóre -trice** adj wrecking; destructive ‖ mf wrecker

**demolizióne** f demolition

**dèmone** m demon

**demonìa·co -ca** adj (-ci -che) fiendish; demoniacal

**demò·nio** m (-ni) demon; **avere il demonio addosso** to be full of the devil

**demoralizzare** [ddzz] tr to demoralize ‖ ref to become demoralized

**demoralizza·to -ta** [ddzz] adj demoralized, dejected

**denaro** m money; denier (of nylon thread); **avere il denaro contato** to be short of money; **denari** suit of Neapolitan cards corresponding to diamonds

**denatura·to -ta** adj denatured

**denegare** §209 (dènego or denégo) tr to deny

**denigrare** tr to denigrate; to backbite

**denominare (denòmino)** tr to call, designate

**denomina·tóre -trice** adj designating ‖ m denominator

**denominazióne** f denomination; designation

**denotare (denòto)** tr to denote

**densi·tà** f (-tà) density

**dèn·so -sa** adj dense, thick

**dentale** adj & f dental

**dentare (dènto)** tr to notch, scallop ‖ intr to teethe

**dentaruòlo** m teething ring

**denta·to -ta** adj toothed

**dentatura** f set of teeth; teeth (of gear)

**dènte** m tooth; peak (of mountain); pang (of jealousy); fluke (of anchor); prong (of fork); **battere i denti** to shiver; **dente canino** canine tooth; **dente del giudizio** wisdom tooth; **dente di latte** baby tooth; **dente di leone** (bot) dandelion; **mettere i denti** to teethe

**dentellare (dentèllo)** tr to notch, scallop; to perforate (stamps)

**dentellatura** f notch; perforation (of postage stamps); (archit) denticulation

**dentèllo** m notch, scallop; lace; (archit) dentil

**dentièra** f denture, plate; cog

**dentifrì·cio -cia** (-ci -cie) adj tooth ‖ m dentifrice

**denti·sta** mf (-sti -ste) dentist

**dentizióne** f teething

**déntro** adv inside, in; **dentro di** inside of; within; **essere dentro** (coll) to be behind bars; **in dentro** inward ‖ prep inside of

**denuclearizzare** [ddzz] tr to denuclearize

**denudare** tr to denude; to strip; (lit) to unveil

**denunciare** §128 tr var of **denunziare**

**denùnzia** f denunciation; announcement; report

**denunziare** §287 tr to denounce; to accuse; to announce; to report

**denutri·to -ta** adj undernourished

**denutrizióne** f undernourishment

**deodorante** adj & m deodorant

**deodorare (deodóro)** tr to deodorize

**depauperare (depàupero)** tr to impoverish

**depennare (depénno)** tr to strike out, expunge

**deperìbile** adj perishable

**deperiménto** *m* deterioration; decline
**deperire** §176 *intr* (ESSERE) to deteriorate; to perish; to decay
**depilatò·rio** -ria *adj & m* (·ri ·rie) depilatory
**deplorare** (deplòro) *tr* to deplore; to reproach
**deplorévole** *adj* deplorable; reproachable
**depolarizzare** [ddzz] *tr* to depolarize
**depórre** §218 *tr* to lay; to lay down (*crown, arms*); to depose (*e.g., a king*); to take off (*clothes*); to give up (*hope*); to renounce; **deporre l'abito talare** to doff the cassock
**deportare** (depòrto) *tr* to deport
**deporta·to** -ta *adj* deported || *mf* deportee
**deportazióne** *f* deportation
**depositare** (depòsito) *tr* to deposit; to register, check || *intr* to settle (*said, e.g., of sand*)
**depositá·rio** -ria (·ri ·rie) *adj* deposit || *mf* depositary
**depòsito** *m* deposit; checking (*e.g., of a suitcase*); registration; heap (*e.g., of refuse*); warehouse; morgue; receiving ward; (mil) depot; **deposito bagagli** baggage room
**deposizióne** *f* deposition; Descent from the Cross
**deprava·to** -ta *adj* depraved
**depravazióne** *f* depravation
**deprecare** §197 (deprèco) *tr* to deprecate
**depredare** (deprèdo) *tr* to plunder
**depredazióne** *f* depredation
**depressióne** *f* depression
**deprès·so** -sa *adj* depressed
**deprezzaménto** *m* depreciation
**deprezzare** (deprèzzo) *tr* to depreciate; to underestimate || *intr* (ESSERE) to depreciate
**deprimènte** *adj* depressing
**deprìmere** §131 *tr* to humble, discourage; to depress
**depurare** *tr* to purify
**deputare** (dèputo) *tr* to deputize, delegate
**deputa·to** -ta *mf* deputy, delegate; representative
**deputazióne** *f* deputation, delegation
**deragliaménto** *m* derailment
**deragliare** §280 *intr* to be derailed, to run off the track
**derapàg·gio** *m* (·gi) skidding
**derapare** *intr* to skid
**derelit·to** -ta *adj & mf* derelict
**derelizióne** *f* dereliction
**dereta·no** -na *adj & m* posterior
**deridere** §231 *tr* to deride, mock
**derisióne** *f* derision, ridicule
**derisò·rio** -ria *adj* (·ri ·rie) derisory, derisive
**deriva** *f* (aer) vertical stabilizer; (aer, naut) leeway; (naut) drift; **alla deriva** adrift
**derivare** *tr* to derive; to branch off (*e.g., a canal*) || *intr* (ESSERE) to be derived, arise; to drift
**deriva·to** -ta *adj* derivative || *m* derivative (*word*) || *f* (math) derivative

**derivazióne** *f* derivation; (elec) shunt; (telp) extension
**dermatòlo·go** *m* (·gi) dermatologist
**dermòide** *f* imitation leather
**dèro·ga** *f* (·ghe) exception; **in deroga a** deviating from
**derogare** §209 (dèrogo) *intr* to transgress; **derogare a** to deviate from
**derrata** *f* foodstuff; **derrate** foodstuff, produce
**derubare** *tr* to rob
**dèr·vis** *m* (·vis) or **dervì·scio** *m* (·sci) dervish
**desalazióne** [s] *f* desalinization
**desalificare** [s] §197 (desalìfico) *tr* to desalt
**dé·sco** *m* (·schi) dinner table; meal
**descritti·vo** -va *adj* descriptive
**descrivere** §250 *tr* to describe
**descrizióne** *f* description
**desegregazióne** [s] *f* desegregation
**desensibilizzare** [s] [ddzz] *tr* to desensitize
**desèrti·co** -ca *adj* (·ci ·che) desert, wild
**desèr·to** -ta *adj* deserted; **andare deserto** to be unattended || *m* desert
**desideràbile** [s] *adj* desirable
**desiderare** (desìdero) [s] *tr* to desire; **farsi desiderare** to make oneself scarce; to be dilatory
**desidè·rio** [s] *m* (·ri) desire; craving; lust; **lasciar desiderio di sé** to be greatly missed
**desideró·so** -sa [s] *adj* desirous
**designare** [s] *tr* to designate
**designazióne** [s] *f* designation
**desinare** *m* dinner || *intr* to dine
**desinènza** *f* (gram) ending
**desì·o** *m* (·i) (lit) desire
**desìstere** [s] §114 *intr* to desist
**desolante** *adj* distressing
**desolare** (dèsolo) *tr* to distress; (lit) to devastate
**desola·to** -ta *adj* desolate; distressed
**desolazióne** *f* desolation; distress
**dèspo·ta** *m* (·ti) despot
**despòti·co** -ca *adj* (·ci ·che) var of dispotico
**despotismo** *m* var of **dispotismo**
**des·sèrt** *m* (·sèrt) dessert
**destare** (dèsto) *tr* to awaken; to stir up || *ref* to wake up
**destinare** *tr* to destine; to assign; to address
**destinatà·rio** -ria *mf* (·ri ·rie) consignee; addressee
**destinazióne** *f* destination; assignment
**destino** *m* destiny; (com) destination
**destituire** §176 *tr* to demote; to dismiss; to deprive
**destituzióne** *f* demotion; dismissal
**dé·sto** -sta *adj* awake; (fig) wide-awake
**dèstra** *f* right, right hand
**destreggiare** §290 (destréggio) *intr* to maneuver || *ref* to manage shrewdly
**destrézza** *f* skill, dexterity
**destrière** or **destrièro** *m* (lit) steed
**dè·stro** -stra *adj* right; skillful || *f* see **destra**
**destròr·so** -sa *adj* clockwise; right-hand; (bot) dextrorse
**destròsio** *m* dextrose

**desùmere** [s] §116 *tr* to obtain; to infer
**detecti·ve** *m* (-ve) detective
**detèc·tor** *m* (-tor) (rad) detector
**detenére** §271 *tr* to hold; to detain
**deten·tóre -trice** *mf* holder; receiver (*of stolen goods*)
**detenu·to -ta** *mf* prisoner
**detenzióne** *f* illegal possession; detention
**detergènte** *adj & m* detergent
**detèrgere** §164 (*pp* **detèrso**) *tr* to cleanse; to wipe
**deterioràbile** *adj* perishable
**deteriorare** (**deterióro**) *tr* to spoil || *intr* (ESSERE) & *ref* to deteriorate, spoil
**determinare** (**detèrmino**) *tr* to determine; to fix; to decide; to cause || *ref* to decide; to happen
**determinatézza** *f* determination; precision
**determinati·vo -va** *adj* (gram) definite
**determina·to -ta** *adj* given; resolved, determined
**determinazióne** *f* determination
**deterrènte** *adj & m* deterrent
**detersi·vo -va** *adj* cleansing || *m* cleanser; detergent
**detestàbile** *adj* detestable
**detestare** (**detèsto**) *tr* to detest
**detettóre** *m* detector; **detettore di bugie** lie detector
**detonare** (**detòno**) *intr* to explode, detonate
**detonatóre** *m* blasting cap, detonator
**detonazióne** *f* detonation; report
**detrarre** §273 *tr* to take away; (lit) to detract
**detrat·tóre -trice** *mf* detractor
**detrazióne** *f* detraction; deduction
**detriménto** *m* detriment
**detrito** *m* debris; detritus; (fig) outcast, outlaw
**detronizzare** [ddzz] *tr* to dethrone
**détta** *f*—a **detta di** according to
**dettagliante** *m* retailer
**dettagliare** §280 *tr* to tell in detail; to itemize; to retail || *intr*—**pregasi dettagliare** please send detailed information
**dettà·glio** *m* (-gli) detail; retail
**dettame** *m* (lit) law, norm
**dettare** (**détto**) *tr* to dictate; (lit) to compose, write; **dettar legge** to impose one's will
**dettato** *m* dictation; (lit) style
**dettatura** *f* dictation
**dét·to -ta** *adj* called, named; **detto** (e) **fatto** no sooner said than done || *m* saying || *f* see **detta**
**deturpare** *tr* to disfigure, mar
**deturpazióne** *f* disfigurement, disfiguration
**devalutazióne** *f* devaluation
**devastare** *tr* to devastate, lay waste; (fig) to disfigure
**devasta·tóre -trice** *adj* devastating || *m* devastator
**devastazióne** *f* devastation
**deviaménto** *m* switching; derailment; (fig) straying
**deviare** §119 *tr* to turn aside; to lead astray; (rr) to switch; (rr) to derail

|| *intr* to deviate; to wander; to go astray; (rr) to run off the track
**deviatóre** *m* (rr) switchman; (elec) two-way switch
**deviazióne** *f* deviation; detour; curvature (*of the spine*); (phys) declination; (phys) deflection; (rr) switching
**deviazionismo** *m* deviationism
**deviazioni·sta** *mf* (-sti -ste) deviationist
**devoluzióne** *f* transfer
**devòlvere** §147 *tr* to transfer || *intr & ref* (lit) to roll down
**devò·to -ta** *adj* devoted; devout, pious || *m* devout person; worshiper
**devozióne** *f* devotion
**di** §4 *prep* of; in, e.g., **la più bella della famiglia** the prettiest one in the family; (*with definite article*) some, e.g., **mi occorrono dei fiammiferi** I need some matches; than, e.g., **più veloce del baleno** faster than lightning; from, e.g., **è di Milano** he is from Milan; off, e.g., **smontare di sella** to get off the saddle; about, e.g., **discutere di politica** to talk about politics; with, e.g., **ornare di fiori** to adorn with flowers; made of, e.g., **una casa di mattoni** a house made of bricks; by, e.g., **di notte** by night; for, e.g., **amor di patria** love for one's country; worth, e.g., **casa di dieci milioni** house worth ten million; in the amount of, e.g., **multa di mille lire** fine in the amount of one thousand lire; son of, e.g., **Carlo Giovannini di Filippo** Carlo Giovannini son of Philip; daughter of, e.g., **Anna Ponti di Antonio** Anna Ponti daughter of Anthony; **di corsa** running; **di gran lunga** greatly; by far; **di . . . in** from . . . to; **di là da** beyond; **di nascosto** stealthily; **di qua da** on this side of; **di quando in quando** from time to time; **di tre metri** three meters long or wide or high
**dì** *m* (**dì**) day; **a dì** (e.g., **ventisei**) this (e.g., twenty-sixth) day; **conciare per il dì delle feste** (coll) to beat up
**diabète** *m* diabetes
**diabèti·co -ca** *adj & mf* (-ci -che) diabetic
**diabòli·co -ca** *adj* (-ci -che) diabolic(al)
**diàcono** *m* deacon
**diadè·ma** *m* (-mi) diadem (*of king*); tiara (*of lady*)
**diàfa·no -na** *adj* diaphanous
**diafonìa** *f* (telp) cross talk
**diafram·ma** *m* (-mi) diaphragm; (fig) partition
**diàgno·si** *f* (-si) diagnosis
**diagnosticare** §197 (**diagnòstico**) *tr* to diagnose
**diagonale** *adj & f* diagonal
**diagram·ma** *m* (-mi) diagram; chart
**diagrammare** *tr* to diagram
**dialettale** *adj* dialectal
**dialètti·co -ca** (-ci -che) *adj* dialectic(al) || *m* dialectician || *f* dialectic; (philos) dialectics
**dialètto** *m* dialect
**dialettòfo·no -na** *adj* dialect-speaking || *m* dialect-speaking person

**dialogare** §209 (**diàlogo**) *intr* to carry on a dialogue

**dialoga·to** -**ta** *adj* written in the form of a dialogue ‖ *m* dialogue

**diàlo·go** *m* (-**ghi**) dialogue

**diamante** *m* diamond; **diamante taglia-vetro** glass cutter

**diametrale** *adj* diametric(al)

**diàmetro** *m* diameter

**diàmine** *interj* good heavens!; the devil!; sure!

**diana** *f* (mil) reveille ‖ **Diana** *f* Diana

**dianzi** *adv* (lit) a short while ago

**diàpa·son** *m* (-**son**) (mus) pitch; (mus) tuning fork

**diapositiva** *f* (phot) slide, transparency

**dià·rio** -**ria** (-**ri** -**rie**) *adj* daily ‖ *m* diary; journal; **diario scolastico** homework book ‖ *f* per diem

**diarrèa** *f* diarrhea

**diascò·pio** *m* (-**pi**) slide projector

**diaspro** *m* jasper

**diàstole** *f* diastole

**diatermìa** *f* diathermy

**diatriba** *f* diatribe

**diavolàc·cio** *m* (-**ci**) devil; **buon dia-volaccio** good fellow

**diavolerìa** *f* deviltry; devilment; evil plot

**diavolè·rio** *m* (-**ri**) hubbub, uproar

**diavoléto** *m* hubbub, uproar

**diavolétto** *m* little devil, imp

**diàvolo** *m* devil; **avere il diavolo in corpo** to be nervous; **avere un dia-volo per capello** to be in a horrible mood; **buon diavolo** good fellow; **essere come il diavolo e l'acqua santa** to be at opposite poles; **fare il dia-volo a quattro** to make a racket; to try very hard

**dibàttere** *tr* to debate ‖ *ref* to struggle; to writhe

**dibattiménto** *m* debate; (law) pleading, trial

**dibàttito** *m* debate

**dicastèro** *m* department, ministry

**dicèmbre** *m* December

**dicerìa** *f* rumor, gossip

**dichiarare** *tr* to declare, state; to find (*guilty*); to proclaim; to nominate, name ‖ *ref* to declare oneself to be; to declare one's love; to plead (*e.g., guilty*)

**dichiarazióne** *f* declaration; avowal (*of love*); return (*of income tax*); **dichia-razioni** representations

**diciannòve** *adj* & *pron* nineteen; **le diciannove** seven P.M. ‖ *m* nineteen; nineteenth (*in dates*)

**diciannovèsi·mo** -**ma** *adj*, *m* & *pron* nineteenth

**diciassètte** *adj* & *pron* seventeen; **le diciassette** five P.M. ‖ *m* seventeen; seventeenth (*in dates*)

**diciassettèsi·mo** -**ma** *adj*, *m* & *pron* seventeen

**diciottèsi·mo** -**ma** *adj*, *m* & *pron* eighteenth

**diciòtto** *adj* & *pron* eighteen; **le diciotto** six P.M. ‖ *m* eighteen; eighteenth (*in dates*)

**dici·tóre** -**trice** *mf* reciter

**dicitura** *f* caption, legend; (lit) word-ing, language

**dicotomìa** *f* dichotomy

**didascalìa** *f* note, notice; caption; legend (*e.g., on coin*); (mov) sub-title

**didascàli·co** -**ca** *adj* (-**ci** -**che**) didactic

**didàtti·co** -**ca** (-**ci** -**che**) *adj* didactic; elementary school (*director, princi-pal*) ‖ *f* didactics

**didéntro** *m* (coll) inside

**didiètro** *m* behind; back (*of house*) ‖ *adv* behind

**dièci** *adj* & *pron* ten; **le dieci** ten o'clock ‖ *m* ten; tenth (*in dates*)

**diecimila** *adj*, *m* & *pron* ten thousand

**diecina** *f* about ten

**dière·si** *f* (-**si**) dieresis

**diè·sis** *m* (-**sis**) (mus) sharp

**dièta** *f* diet; **dieta idrica** fluid diet

**dietèti·co** -**ca** (-**ci** -**che**) *adj* dietetic ‖ *f* dietetics

**dieti·sta** *mf* (-**sti** -**ste**) dietitian

**diètro** *adj invar* back, rear ‖ *m* back, rear ‖ *adv* back, behind; **dal di dietro** from behind; **di dietro** hind (*legs*); back (*side*); behind, back (*e.g., of cupboard*) ‖ *prep* behind; beyond; after; upon; **dietro a** behind; beyond; after; according to; **dietro consegna** on delivery; **dietro domanda** upon application; **dietro versamento** upon payment; **essere dietro a** to be in the process of

**dietrofrónt** *m* (mil) about face

**difatti** *adv* indeed

**difèndere** §148 *tr* to defend, protect ‖ *ref* to protect oneself; (coll) to get along

**difensi·vo** -**va** *adj* & *f* defensive

**difen·sóre** -**sóra** or **difenditrice** *adj* de-fense ‖ *mf* defender

**difésa** [s] *f* defense; bulwark; protec-tion; **legittima difesa** self-defense; **pigliare le difese di** to defend, back up; **venire in difesa di** to go to the defense of

**difettare** (**difètto**) *intr* to be lacking; to be defective; **difettare di** to lack

**difetti·vo** -**va** *adj* defective

**difètto** *m* lack; blemish; fault; defect; **essere in difetto** to be at fault; **far difetto a** to lack, e.g., **gli fa difetto il denaro** he lacks money

**difettó·so** -**sa** [s] *adj* defective

**diffamare** *tr* to defame, slander

**diffama·tóre** -**trice** *mf* defamer, slan-derer

**diffamazióne** *f* defamation, slander

**differènte** *adj* different

**differènza** *f* difference; spread; vari-ance; **a differenza di** unlike; **c'è una bella differenza** it's a horse of an-other color

**differenziale** *adj* & *m* differential

**differenziare** §287 (**differènzio**) *tr* to differentiate

**differiménto** *m* deferment

**differire** §176 *tr* to postpone, defer ‖ *intr* to be different; to differ

**difficile** *adj* hard, difficult; awkward (*situation*); hard-to-please; unlikely

‖ *mf* hard-to-please person ‖ *m*—**fare il difficile** to be hard to please; **qui sta il difficile!** here's the trouble!

**difficol·tà** *f* (-**tà**) difficulty; defect; obstacle; objection

**difficoltó·so -sa** [s] *adj* difficult, troublesome; fastidious

**diffida** *f* notice; warning

**diffidare** *tr* to give notice to; to warn ‖ *intr* to mistrust

**diffidènte** *adj* distrustful

**diffidènza** *f* mistrust

**diffóndere** §178 *tr* to spread; to circulate; to broadcast ‖ *ref* to spread; to dwell at length

**diffórme** *adj* unlike; (obs) deformed

**diffrazióne** *f* diffraction

**diffusióne** *f* spreading; circulation (*of a newspaper*); diffusion; (rad) broadcast

**diffu·so -sa** *adj* diffuse; widespread

**diffusóre** *m* diffuser (*to soften light*); baffle (*of loudspeaker*); (mach) choke

**difilato** *adv* forthwith, right away

**difrónte** *adj invar* in front

**difterite** *f* diphtheria

**di·ga** *f* (-**ghe**) dike; dam

**digerènte** *adj* alimentary (*canal*), digestive (*tube*)

**digeríbile** *adj* digestible

**digerire** §176 *tr* to digest; to tolerate, stand

**digestióne** *f* digestion

**digesti·vo -va** *adj* digestive

**digèsto** *m* digest

**digitale** *adj* digital ‖ *f* (bot) digitalis

**digitalina** *f* (pharm) digitalin

**digiunare** *intr* to fast

**digiu·no -na** *adj* without food; deprived; **digiuno di cognizioni** ignorant; **tenere digiuno** to keep in ignorance ‖ *m* fast; **a digiuno** on an empty stomach; **fare digiuno** to fast

**digni·tà** *f* (-**tà**) dignity; **dignità** *fpl* dignitaries

**dignità·rio** *m* (-**ri**) dignitary

**dignitó·so -sa** [s] *adj* dignified

**digradare** *tr* to shade (*colors*) ‖ *intr* to slope; to fade

**digredire** §176 *intr* to digress

**digressióne** *f* digression

**digrignare** *tr* to show (*one's or its teeth*); to grit (*one's teeth*)

**digrossare** (**digròsso**) *tr* to rough-hew; to whittle down; (fig) to refine ‖ *ref* to become refined

**diguazzare** *tr* to beat (*a liquid*) ‖ *intr* to wallow; to splash

**dilagare** §209 *intr* to flood, to overflow; to spread abroad

**dilaniare** §287 *tr* to tear to pieces ‖ *ref* to slander one another

**dilapidare** (**dilàpido**) *tr* to squander

**dilatare** *tr* to expand; to dilate ‖ *ref* to expand; to spread

**dilatazióne** *f* expansion; dilation

**dilatò·rio -ria** *adj* (-**ri** -**rie**) delaying; dilatory

**dilavare** *tr* to wash away, erode

**dilava·to -ta** *adj* dull, flat; wan

**dilazionare** (**dilazióno**) *tr* to delay, put off; (com) to extend

**dilazióne** *f* delay; (com) extension

**dileggiare** §290 (**diléggio**) *tr* to mock

**dilég·gio** *m* (-**gi**) mockery, scoffing; **mettere in dileggio** to scoff at

**dileguare** (**diléguo**) *tr* to scatter ‖ *intr* (ESSERE) to disappear, vanish; to melt

**dilèm·ma** *m* (-**mi**) dilemma

**dilettante** *mf* amateur; dilettante

**dilettanté·sco -sca** *adj* (-**schi** -**sche**) amateurish

**dilettare** (**dilètto**) *tr* to delight ‖ *ref* to delight; **dilettarsi a** + *inf* to delight in + *ger*; **dilettarsi di** to pursue as a hobby, e.g., **si diletta di pittura** he pursues painting as a hobby

**dilettévole** *adj* delectable, delightful

**dilèt·to -ta** *adj* beloved ‖ *m* loved one; pleasure; hobby

**diligènte** *adj* diligent

**diligènza** *f* diligence; stagecoach

**dilucidare** (**dilùcido**) *tr* to elucidate

**diluire** §176 *tr* to dilute

**dilungare** §209 *tr* (archaic) to stretch ‖ *ref* to expatiate; to be ahead by several lengths (*said of a race horse*)

**dilungo** *m*—**a un dilungo** more or less

**diluviare** §287 *tr* to devour ‖ *intr* (ESSERE & AVERE) to rain (*said, e.g., of bullets*) ‖ *impers* (ESSERE)—**diluvia** it is pouring

**dilù·vio** *m* (-**vi**) deluge, flood; **diluvio universale** Flood

**dimagrante** *adj* reducing

**dimagrare** *tr* to thin down ‖ *intr* (ESSERE) to become thin; to lose weight; to become exhausted (*said of land*); (fig) to become meager

**dimagrire** §176 *intr* (ESSERE) to become thin; to lose weight, reduce

**dimanda** *f* var of **domanda**

**dimane** *adv* (coll) tomorrow

**dimani** *m* & *adv* var of **domani**

**dimenare** (**diméno**) *tr* to wag (*the tail*); to beat (*eggs*); to wave (*one's arms*); to stir up (*a question*) ‖ *ref* to toss; to busy oneself

**dimensióne** *f* dimension; (fig) nature

**dimenticanza** *f* oversight, neglect; **andare in dimenticanza** to be forgotten

**dimenticare** §197 (**diméntico**) *tr* to forget; to forgive ‖ *ref* to forget; **dimenticarsi di** to forget; to neglect

**dimenticatóio** *m*—**mettere nel dimenticatoio** (coll) to forget

**diménti·co -ca** *adj* (-**chi** -**che**) forgetful; neglectful

**dimés·so -sa** *adj* humble, modest (*demeanor*); low (*voice*); shabby (*clothes*)

**dimestichézza** *f* familiarity

**dimèttere** §198 *tr* to dismiss; to release ‖ *ref* to resign

**dimezzare** [ddzz] (**dimèzzo**) *tr* to halve

**diminuire** §176 *tr* to lessen, reduce; to lower (*prices*) ‖ *intr* (ESSERE) to diminish

**diminuti·vo -va** *adj* & *m* diminutive

**diminuzióne** *f* diminution

**dimissionare** (**dimissióno**) *tr* to dismiss, discharge ‖ *ref* to resign

**dimissionà·rio -ria** *adj* (-**ri** -**rie**) resigning, outgoing

**dimissióne** *f* resignation; **dare le dimissioni** to resign

**dimól·to -ta** *adj & m* (coll) much ‖ **dimolto** *adv* (coll) much

**dimòra** *f* stay; residence; (lit) delay; **mettere a dimora** to install; to plant (*trees*); **senza dimora** (lit) without delay; **senza fissa dimora** vagrant

**dimorare (dimòro)** *intr* to stay; to reside; (lit) to delay

**dimostràbile** *adj* demonstrable

**dimostrante** *m* demonstrator

**dimostrare (dimóstro)** *tr* to demonstrate; to register (*e.g., anger*); **dimostrare trent'anni** to look thirty ‖ *intr* to demonstrate ‖ *ref* to prove oneself to be

**dimostrati·vo -va** *adj* demonstrative; (mil) diverting

**dimostra·tóre -trice** *mf* demonstrator

**dimostrazióne** *f* demonstration

**dinàmi·co -ca (-ci -che)** *adj* dynamic ‖ *f* dynamics

**dinamismo** *m* dynamism

**dinamite** *f* dynamite

**dìna·mo** *f* (-mo) generator, dynamo

**dinanzi** *adj invar* front, e.g., **la porta dinanzi** the front door; preceding, e.g., **il mese dinanzi** the preceding month ‖ *adv* ahead; beforehand; (lit) before; **dinanzi a** before, in front of

**dina·sta** *m* (-sti) dynast

**dinastìa** *f* dynasty

**dinàsti·co -ca** *adj* (-ci -che) dynastic

**dindo** *m* (coll) turkey

**dindòn** *m* ding-dong ‖ *interj* ding-dong!

**diniè·go** *m* (-ghi) denial

**dinoccola·to -ta** *adj* gangling; clumsy (*gait*)

**dinosàuro** [s] *m* dinosaur

**dintórno** *m—dintorni* surroundings, neighborhood ‖ *adv* around; **dintorno a** around

**dì·o -a** *adj* (**-ì -e**) (poet) godly ‖ *m* (dèi) god; **gli dei** the gods ‖ **Dio** *m* God; **che Dio la manda** cats and dogs (*said of rain*); **come Dio volle** at long last; **come Dio vuole** botched (*piece of work*); **Dio ci scampi!** God forbid!; **Dio santo!** good heavens!; **grazie a Dio** God willing; thank God; **voglia Dio** God grant

**diòce·si** *f* (-si) diocese

**diòdo** *m* (electron) diode

**diomedèa** *f* (orn) albatross

**diottrìa** *f* (opt) diopter

**dipanare** *tr* to unravel, unwind

**dipartiménto** *m* department

**dipartire** §176 *tr* (archaic) to divide ‖ *intr* (**diparto**) (ESSERE) & *ref* (lit) to depart

**dipartita** *f* (lit) departure; (lit) demise

**dipendènte** *adj* dependent ‖ *mf* employee

**dipendènza** *f* dependence; employment; annex; (com) branch; **in dipendenza di** as a consequence of

**dipèndere** §150 *intr* (ESSERE) to depend; **dipendere da** to depend on

**dipingere** §126 *tr* to paint; **dipingere a olio** to paint in oils; **dipingere a tempera** to distemper ‖ *ref* to paint oneself; to put make-up on; to appear, e.g., **gli si dipinse in volto la paura** fear appeared on his face

**dipin·to -ta** *adj* painted ‖ *m* painting, picture

**diplò·ma** *m* (-mi) diploma, certificate

**diplomare (diplòmo)** *tr* to grant a degree to; to graduate ‖ *ref* to receive a degree; to graduate

**diplomàti·co -ca (-ci -che)** *adj* diplomatic; true, faithful (*copy*) ‖ *m* diplomat ‖ *f* diplomatics

**diploma·to -ta** *adj* graduated ‖ *mf* graduate ‖ *m* alumnus ‖ *f* alumna

**diplomazìa** *f* diplomacy

**dipòi** *adv* after, thereafter

**diportare (dipòrto)** *ref* (lit) to behave; (obs) to have a good time

**dipòrto** *m* recreation; (obs) sport; **andare a diporto** to go on an outing; to go for a walk

**diprèsso** *adv—a un dipresso* about, approximately

**diradare** *tr* to thin out (*vegetation*); to disperse; to space out (*one's visits*) ‖ *intr* (ESSERE) & *ref* to diminish; to disperse

**diramare** *tr* to prune; to circulate (*notices*); to issue (*a communiqué*) ‖ *ref* to branch out; to spread

**diramazióne** *f* branch; ramification; issuance

**dire** *m* talk; **per sentito dire** by hearsay; **stando al dire** according to his words ‖ §151 *tr & intr* to say; to tell; to call (*e.g., s.o. a genius*); to talk; **detto (e) fatto** no sooner said than done; **dica pure!** go ahead!; speak up!; **dire bene di** to speak well of; **dire di no** to say no; **dire di sì** to say yes; **direi quasi** I dare say; **dire la sua** to have one's say; **dire male di** to speak ill of; **dirla grossa** to make a blunder; to tell a tall tale; **dirlo chiaro e tondo** to speak bluntly; **dirne un sacco e una sporta a** to pour insults upon; **è tutto dire** that's all; **non c'è che dire** it's a fact; **non fo per dire** I do not want to boast; **per così dire** so to speak; **per meglio dire** rather; **trovarci a dire** to find fault with; **trovare da dire con** to have words with; **voler ben dire** to be sure; **voler dire** to mean ‖ *ref—dirsela con* to connive with; **sì dice** it is said

**dirètro** *m & adv* (archaic) behind, back

**direttìssima** *f* (rr) high-speed line; **per direttissima** straight up (*in mountain climbing*)

**direttìssimo** *m* express train

**diretti·vo -va** *adj* managerial ‖ *m* board of directors ‖ *f* directive; direction; guideline

**dirèt·to -ta** *adj* direct; **diretto a** addressed to; directed at; bound for ‖ *m* through train

**diret·tóre -trice** *mf* manager; principal ‖ *m* director; **direttore di macchina** (naut, nav) chief engineer; **direttore di tiro** (nav) gunnery officer; **direttore di un giornale** editor; **direttore d'or-**

**chestra** orchestra leader; **direttore responsabile** publisher; **direttore tecnico** (sports) manager ‖ *f* see **direttrice**

**direttò·rio -ria** (-**ri** -**rie**) *adj* directorial ‖ *m* directory

**direttrice** *adj fem* directing; guiding; front (*wheels*) ‖ *f* directress; line of action

**direzionale** *adj* directional; managerial

**direzióne** *f* direction; management; run (*of events*)

**dirigènte** *adj* leading; managerial ‖ *m* employer; boss; leader; executive

**dirìgere** §152 *tr* to direct; to turn; to lead ‖ *ref* to address oneself; **dirigersi verso** to head for

**dirigìbile** *adj* & *m* dirigible

**dirimpètto** *adj invar* & *adv* opposite; **dirimpetto a** opposite to; in comparison with

**dirìt·to -ta** *adj* straight; right; unswerving; (coll) smart ‖ *m* law; obverse, face (*of coin*); fee, dues; (fin) right; **a buon diritto** rightly so; **di diritto** by law; **diritti d'autore** copyright; **diritti di segreteria** registration fee; **diritti doganali** customs duty; **diritti speciali di prelievo** (econ) special drawing rights; **diritto canonico** canon law; **diritto consuetudinario** common law; **diritto internazionale** international law; **in diritto** according to law ‖ *f* right, right hand ‖ **diritto** *adv* straight; **tirare diritto** to go straight ahead

**dirittura** *f* direction; uprightness; (sports) straightaway, home stretch

**dirizzóne** *m* blunder

**diroccare** §197 (**diròcco**) *tr* to knock down ‖ *intr* (ESSERE) (archaic) to fall down

**dirocca·to -ta** *adj* dilapidated, rickety

**dirompènte** *adj* fragmentation (*bomb*)

**dirottaménto** *m* hijacking; skyjacking (*of an airplane*)

**dirottare** (**dirótto**) *tr* to detour (*traffic*); to hijack (*e.g., a ship*); to skyjack (*an airplane*) ‖ *intr* to change course

**dirottatóre** *m* hijacker; skyjacker (*of a plane*)

**dirót·to -ta** *adj* copious, heavy (*rain, tears*); (lit) craggy; **a dirotto** cats and dogs (*said of rain*)

**dirozzare** [ddzz] (**dirózzo**) *tr* to roughhew; to refine ‖ *ref* to become polished

**dirugginire** §176 *tr* to take the rust off; to limber up; to gnash (*one's teeth*); to clear (*one's mind*)

**dirupa·to -ta** *adj* rocky, craggy

**dirupo** *m* rock; crag, cliff

**disabbigliare** §280 *tr* & *ref* to undress, disrobe

**disabita·to -ta** *adj* uninhabited

**disabituare** (**disabìtuo**) *tr* to disaccustom ‖ *ref* to become unaccustomed

**disaccenta·to -ta** *adj* unaccented

**disaccòrdo** *m* disagreement

**disadat·to -ta** *adj* unfit

**disadór·no -na** *adj* unadorned, bare

**disaffezionare** (**disaffezióno**) *tr* to alien-

ate the affection of; to estrange ‖ *ref* to become estranged

**disaffezióne** *f* dislike

**disagévole** *adj* troublesome, uncomfortable

**disagiare** §290 *tr* to trouble, inconvenience

**disagia·to -ta** *adj* uncomfortable; needy

**disà·gio** *m* (-**gi**) discomfort; need

**disalberare** (**disàlbero**) *tr* to dismast

**disambienta·to -ta** *adj* bewildered, strange

**disàmina** *f* examination, scrutiny

**disaminare** (**disàmino**) *tr* to scrutinize; to weigh

**disamorare** (**disamóro**) *tr* to alienate the affection of; to estrange ‖ *ref* to become estranged

**disancorare** (**disàncoro**) *intr* to weigh anchor; to leave port ‖ *ref* to weigh anchor; (fig) to free oneself

**disanimare** (**disànimo**) *tr* to dishearten

**disappetènza** *f* loss of appetite

**disapprovare** (**disappròvo**) *tr* to disapprove

**disapprovazióne** *f* disapproval

**disappunto** *m* disappointment

**disarcionare** (**disarció no**) *tr* to unsaddle, unhorse; to kick out

**disarmare** *tr* to disarm; to dismantle (*a scaffold*); to ship (*oars*); (naut) to unrig ‖ *ref* to disarm; (fig) to give up

**disarma·to -ta** *adj* unarmed, defenseless

**disarmo** *m* disarmament; dismantling; unrigging

**disarmonìa** *f* discord; contrast

**disarmòni·co -ca** *adj* (-**ci** -**che**) discordant

**disarticolare** (**disàrticolo**) *tr* to limber up; to disjoint ‖ *ref* to become dislocated

**disassociare** §128 (**disassòcio**) *tr* to disassociate

**disastra·to -ta** *adj* damaged ‖ *mf* victim

**disastro** *m* disaster, calamity; wreck

**disastró·so -sa** [s] *adj* disastrous

**disattèn·to -ta** *adj* inattentive; careless

**disattenzióne** *f* inattention; carelessness

**disattivare** *tr* to deactivate (*e.g., a mine*)

**disavanzo** *m* (com) deficit

**disavvedu·to -ta** *adj* heedless

**disavventura** *f* misfortune

**disavvertènza** *f* inadvertence

**disavvezzare** (**disavvézzo**) *tr* to break (*s.o.*) of a habit ‖ *ref*—**disavvezzarsi da** to give up or lose the habit of

**disavvéz·zo -za** *adj* unaccustomed

**disbórso** *m* disbursement, outlay

**disboscare** §197 (**disbòsco**) *tr* to deforest

**disbrigare** §209 *tr* to dispatch ‖ *ref* to extricate oneself

**disbrì·go** *m* (-**ghi**) prompt execution, dispatch

**discacciare** §128 *tr* (lit) to chase away

**discanto** *m* (mus) harmonizing

**discàpito** *m* damage; **tornare a discapito di** to be detrimental to

**discàri·ca** *f* (-**che**) discharge (*e.g., of pollutants*); dumping (*of refuse*); unloading (*of a ship*) discàri·co m (-chi) exculpation; a discarico di in defense of

discatóre m hockey player; discus thrower

discendènte adj descending; sloping; down (train) || mf descendant

discendènza f descent; pedigree

discéndere §245 tr to go down || intr (ESSERE & AVERE) to descend, go down; to slope; to fall (said, e.g., of thermometer); to get off; discendere in picchiata (aer) to nose-dive

discènte mf student, pupil

discépo·lo -la mf disciple

discèrnere §153 tr to discern

discernìbile adj discernible

discerniménto m discernment

discésa [s] f descent; slope; drop

discettare (discètto) tr (lit) to discuss

dischiodare (dischiòdo) tr to take the nails out of

dischiùdere §125 tr to open; to reveal

discin·to -ta adj scantily dressed; untidy; in disarray

disciògliere §127 tr to dissolve, melt; (lit) to untie || ref to dissolve, melt

disciplina f discipline; whip, scourge

disciplinare adj disciplinary || m regulation || tr to discipline

disciplina·to -ta adj obedient

di·sco m (-schi) disk; (phonograph) record; bob (of pendulum); (ice hockey) puck; (sports) discus; (rr) signal; (pharm) tablet; disco combinatore (telp) dial; disco microsolco microgroove record; disco volante flying saucer

discòfilo m record lover

discòide m (pharm) tablet, pill

dìsco·lo -la adj undisciplined, wild || m rogue, rascal

discolorare (discolóro) tr to discolor || ref to pale

discolorazióne f discoloration; paleness

discólpa f defense

discolpare (discólpo) tr to defend

disconnèttere §107 tr to disconnect

disconóscere §134 tr to ignore, to disregard; to be ungrateful for

discontinuare (discontìnuo) tr to perform sporadically || intr to lose continuity

discontì·nuo -nua adj uneven

disconvenire §282 intr (ESSERE) (lit) to disagree || impers (ESSERE) (lit) to be improper

discoprire §110 (discòpro) tr to discover

discordante adj discordant

discordare (discòrdo) intr (ESSERE) to disagree, differ

discòrde adj discordant; opposing

discòrdia f discord, dissension

discórrere §139 intr to talk, chat; (coll) to keep company; discorrere del più e del meno to make small talk; e via discorrendo and so forth

discórso m discourse; conversation; speech; pochi discorsi! (coll) cut it out!

discostare (discòsto) tr to remove || ref to withdraw; to differ

discò·sto -sta adj distant || discosto adv far

discotè·ca f (-che) record library; discotheque

discreditare (discrédito) tr to discredit

discrédito m discredit

discrepanza f discrepancy

discretaménte adv rather; fairly well

discré·to -ta adj discreet; fairly large; fair

discrezióne f discretion

discriminante adj discriminatory; extenuating || m (math) discriminant

discriminare (discrìmino) tr to discriminate; to extenuate

discriminazióne f discrimination

discussióne f discussion; argument

discus·so -sa adj controversial

discùtere §154 tr to discuss || intr to discuss; to argue

discutìbile adj moot, debatable

disdegnare (disdégno) tr to disdain, scorn || ref (obs) to be angry

disdégno m disdain, scorn

disdegnó·so -sa [s] adj disdainful

disdétta f ill luck; (law) notice

disdicévole adj unbecoming, unseemly

disdire §151 tr to retract; to belie; to cancel; to countermand; to terminate the contract of || ref to retract; disdire a to be unbecoming to

disdòro m shame; tornare a disdoro di to bring shame on

disegnare [s] (diségno) tr to draw; to sketch; to design; (obs) to elect

disegna·tóre -trice [s] mf cartoonist; designer || m draftsman

diségno [s] m drawing; sketch; outline; plan; design; disegno animato (mov) cartoon; disegno di legge (law) bill

disellare [s] (disèllo) tr var of dissellare

diserbante adj weed-killing || m weed-killer

diseredare (diserèdo) tr to disinherit

diséreda·to -ta adj disinherited || i diseredati the underprivileged

disertare (disèrto) tr to desert; (lit) to lay waste || intr to desert

disertóre m deserter

diserzióne f desertion

disfaciménto m disintegration

disfare §173 tr to undo; to defeat; to melt; to unknit; to break up (housekeeping); disfare il letto to remove the bedclothes || ref to spoil (said, e.g., of meat); disfarsi di to get rid of

disfatta f defeat

disfattismo m defeatism

disfatti·sta mf (-sti -ste) defeatist

disfat·to -ta adj undone; defeated; melted; broken up; ravaged || f see disfatta

disfida f (lit) challenge

disfunzióne f malfunction

disgelare (disgèlo) tr & intr to thaw

disgèlo m thaw

disgiùngere §183 tr & ref to separate

disgiuntì·vo -va adj disjunctive

disgràzia f disfavor; bad luck, misfortune; accident; per disgrazia unfortunately

**disgrazia·to -ta** *adj* unlucky; wretched
**disgregaménto** *m* disintegration
**disgregare** §209 (**disgrègo**) *tr* & *ref* to disintegrate
**disgregazióne** *f* disintegration
**disguido** *m* miscarriage, missending (*of a letter*)
**disgustare** *tr* to disgust, sicken || *ref* to become disgusted, sicken; to have a falling-out, to part company
**disgusto** *m* disgust, repugnance
**disgustó·so -sa** [s] *adj* disgusting
**disidratare** *tr* to dehydrate
**disìlla·bo -ba** *adj* disyllabic || *m* disyllable
**disillùdere** §105 *tr* to delude, deceive || *ref* to become disillusioned
**disillusióne** *f* disillusion
**disimboscare** §197 (**disimbòsco**) *tr* to put back in circulation
**disimparare** *tr* to unlearn, forget
**disimpegnare** (**disimpégno**) *tr* to release; to free, to open; to loosen; to redeem (*a pledge*); to clear; to perform || *ref* to succeed
**disimpégno** *m* release; redemption; performance; disengagement; **di disimpegno** for every day (*e.g., a suit*); main (*e.g., hallway*)
**disimpiè·go** *m* (**-ghi**) unemployment; (mil) withdrawal
**disincagliare** §280 *tr* to set afloat; (fig) to disentangle
**disincantare** *tr* disenchant
**disinfestare** (**disinfèsto**) *tr* to exterminate
**disinfestazióne** *f* extermination
**disinfettante** *adj* & *m* disinfectant
**disinfettare** (**disinfètto**) *tr* to disinfect
**disingannare** (**disinfètto**) *tr* to disillusion || *ref* to become disillusioned
**disinganno** *m* disillusion
**disinnescare** §197 (**disinnésco**) *tr* to defuse
**disinnestare** (**disinnèsto**) *tr* to disconnect; to throw out, disengage
**disinserire** §176 *tr* (elec) to disconnect; (aut) to disengage
**disintasare** [s] *tr* to unclog
**disintegrare** (**disìntegro**) *tr* & *ref* to disintegrate
**disintegrazióne** *f* disintegration
**disinteressare** (**disinterèsso**) *tr* to make (*s.o.*) lose interest || *ref* to lose interest; to take no interest
**disinteressa·to -ta** *adj* selfless, unselfish
**disinterèsse** *m* disinterest; unselfishness
**disintossicare** §197 (**disintòssico**) *tr* to free of poison; (fig) to clean the air in || *ref* to shake the drug habit
**disinvòl·to -ta** *adj* free and easy; fresh, forward
**disinvoltura** *f* naturalness, ease of manners, offhandedness; freshness; impudence
**disì·o** *m* (**-i**) (poet) desire
**disistima** *f* scorn, low regard, disesteem
**disistimare** *tr* to scorn, hold in low regard
**dislivèllo** *m* difference of level; disparity
**dislocaménto** *m* transfer of troops; (naut) displacement

**dislocare** §197 (**dislòco**) *tr* to transfer (*troops*); to post (*sentries*); (naut) to displace
**dislocazióne** *f* (mil) transfer; (geog, naut, psychol) displacement
**dismisura** *f* excess; **a dismisura** excessively
**disobbedire** §176 *intr* var of **disubbidire**
**disobbligare** §209 (**disòbbligo**) *tr* to free from an obligation || *ref* to repay a favor
**disoccupa·to -ta** *adj* unemployed, jobless; idle; unoccupied || *m* unemployed person; **i disoccupati** the jobless
**disoccupazióne** *f* unemployment
**disone·stà** *f* (**-stà**) dishonesty; shamelessness
**disonè·sto -sta** *adj* dishonest; shameless; immoral
**disonorante** *adj* disgraceful
**disonorare** (**disonóro**) *tr* to dishonor, disgrace; to seduce
**disonóre** *m* dishonor, shame
**disonorévole** *adj* dishonorable; shameful
**disoppilare** (**disòppilo**) *tr* to clear of obstructions
**disópra** *adj invar* upper || *m* (**disópra**) upper part, top; **prendere il disopra** to have the upper hand || *adv* above; **al disopra di** above
**disordinare** (**disórdino**) *tr* to cancel, countermand; to confuse; to mess up || *intr* to indulge || *ref* to become disorganized
**disordina·to -ta** *adj* confused; messy; untidy; intemperate
**disórdine** *m* confusion; mess; disarray; disorder; intemperance
**disorganizzare** [ddzz] *tr* to disorganize; to disrupt
**disorganizzazióne** [ddzz] *f* disorganization, disorder; disruption
**disorientaménto** *m* disorientation; confusion, bewilderment
**disorientare** (**disoriènto**) *tr* to cause (*s.o.*) to lose his way; to confuse; to disorient || *ref* to be bewildered; to lose one's bearings
**disorienta·to -ta** *adj* disoriented; confused, bewildered; lost, astray
**disormeggiare** §290 (**disorméggio**) *tr* to unmoor
**disossare** (**disòsso**) *tr* to bone || *ref* (lit) to lose weight
**disótto** [s] *adj invar* below || *m* (**disótto**) lower part, bottom || *adv* below; **al disotto di** below, underneath
**disotturare** *tr* to unclog
**dispàc·cio** *m* (**-ci**) dispatch; urgent letter; **dispaccio telegrafico** telegram
**dispara·to -ta** *adj* disparate
**disparére** *m* disagreement
**dìspari** *adj invar* odd, uneven
**dispari·tà** *f* (**-tà**) disparity
**dispàrte** *adv*—**in disparte** apart, aside; **starsene in disparte** to keep aloof
**dispèn·dio** *m* (**-di**) expenditure; waste
**dispendió·so -sa** [s] *adj* expensive; wasteful

**dispènsa** *f* cupboard; pantry; distribution; number (*of magazine*); installment (*of book*); dispensation; (naut) storeroom; (coll) store

**dispensare** (dispènso) *tr* to exempt, free; to distribute || *ref*—**dispensarsi da** to get out of

**dispensà·rio** *m* (-**ri**) dispensary

**dispensa·tóre** -**tríce** *mf* dispenser

**dispensiè·re** -**ra** *mf* dispenser || *m* steward

**dispepsìa** *f* dyspepsia

**dispèpti·co** -**ca** *adj* & *mf* (-**ci** -**che**) dyspeptic

**disperare** (dispèro) *intr* to despair; **fare disperare** to drive crazy || *ref* to despair

**dispera·to** -**ta** *adj* hopeless || *m* poor wretch; **come un disperato** desperately || *f*—**alla disperata** with all one's might

**disperazióne** *f* desperation, despair

**dispèrdere** §212 *tr* to scatter; to waste || *ref* to disperse; (fig) to waste one's energies

**dispersióne** *f* dispersion; loss; (elec) leakage

**dispersività** *f* tendency toward disorganization

**dispersì·vo** -**va** *adj* dispersive; disorganized

**dispèr·so** -**sa** *adj* scattered; lost; dispersed; missing in action

**dispersóre** *m* (elec) leakage conductor

**dispètto** *m* spite; (lit) haughtiness; **a dispetto di** in spite of; **far dispetto a** to provoke

**dispettó·so** -**sa** [s] *adj* pestiferous; spiteful, resentful

**dispiacènte** *adj* sorry; distressing

**dispiacére** *m* sorrow, displeasure || §214 *intr* (ESSERE) to be displeasing; to be sorry, e.g., **mi dispiace** I am sorry; (with *dat*) to displease; (with *dat*) to dislike, e.g., **le mie parole gli dispiacciono** he dislikes my words; **Le dispiace?** would you please?; **se non Le dispiace** if you don't mind

**dispiegare** §209 (dispiègo) *tr* to manifest; (lit) to unfurl || *ref* to spread out; to flow out

**displù·vio** *m* (-**vi**) divide, watershed; ridge (*of roof*)

**disponìbile** *adj* available; open-minded

**disponibili·tà** *f* (-**tà**) availability; inactive status; **disponibilità** *fpl* available funds

**dispórre** §218 *tr* to dispose; to prepare || *intr* to provide; to dispose; **disporre di** to have (*available*) || *ref* to get ready

**dispositivo** *m* gadget; device; (mil) deployment

**disposizióne** *f* arrangement; inclination, disposition; disposal; instruction; (law) provision

**dispó·sto** -**sta** *adj* arranged; disposed; provided; willing; **ben disposto** disposed || *m* (law) proviso

**dispòti·co** -**ca** *adj* (-**ci** -**che**) despotic

**dispotismo** *m* despotism

**dispregiati·vo** -**va** *adj* disparaging; (gram) pejorative

**disprè·gio** *m* (-**gi**) contempt; disrepute

**disprezzàbile** *adj* contemptible; negligible

**disprezzare** (disprèzzo) *tr* to despise

**disprèzzo** *m* contempt, scorn

**dìsputa** *f* dispute; debate

**disputàbile** *adj* debatable

**disputare** (dìsputo) *tr* to contest; to discuss; to vie for (*victory*) || *intr* to dispute, debate; to vie || *ref* to vie for

**disqualificare** §197 (disqualìfico) *tr* to disqualify

**disquisizióne** *f* disquisition

**dissacrare** *tr* to desecrate

**dissacrazióne** *f* desecration

**dissaldare** *tr* to unsolder

**dissanguare** (dissànguo) *tr* to bleed || *ref* to bleed; to ruin oneself

**dissangua·to** -**ta** *adj* bled white; **morire dissanguato** to bleed to death

**dissapóre** *m* disagreement

**disseccare** §197 (dissécco) *tr* to dry || *ref* to dry; to dry up

**disselciare** §128 (dissélcio) *tr* to remove the cobblestones from

**dissellare** (dissèllo) *tr* to unsaddle

**disseminare** (dissémino) *tr* to disseminate; to scatter

**dissenna·to** -**ta** *adj* foolish, unwise; crazy, mad

**dissensióne** *f* dissension

**dissènso** *m* dissent; disagreement

**dissenterìa** *f* dysentery

**dissentire** (dissènto) *intr* to dissent

**dissenziènte** *adj* dissenting || *mf* dissenter

**disseppellire** §176 *tr* to exhume

**dissertare** (dissèrto) *intr* to discourse

**dissertazióne** *f* dissertation

**disservì·zio** *m* (-**zi**) poor service

**dissestare** (dissèsto) *tr* to unsettle; to disarrange

**dissesta·to** -**ta** *adj* financially embarrassed; mentally deranged

**dissèsto** *m* financial embarrassment; mental derangement

**dissetante** *adj* thirst-quenching

**dissetare** (dissèto) *tr* to quench the thirst of || *ref* to quench one's thirst

**dissezióne** *f* dissection

**dissidènte** *adj* & *m* dissident

**dissidènza** *f* dissent

**dissì·dio** *m* (-**di**) dissent; disagreement

**dissigillare** *tr* to unseal || *ref* (lit) to melt

**dissìmile** *adj* unlike

**dissimulare** (dissìmulo) *tr* to dissimulate, disguise || *intr* to dissimulate

**dissimulazióne** *f* dissimulation

**dissipare** (dìssipo) *tr* to dissipate; to squander; to clear up (*a doubt*) || *ref* to dissipate

**dissipa·to** -**ta** *adj* & *mf* profligate

**dissipa·tóre** -**trice** *mf* squanderer

**dissipazióne** *f* dissipation

**dissociare** §128 (dissòcio) *tr* to dissociate, disassociate || *ref* to dissociate or disassociate oneself

**dissociazióne** *f* dissociation

**dissodare** (dissòdo) *tr* to cultivate
**dissolutézza** *f* profligacy
**dissolu·to -ta** *adj & mf* profligate
**dissoluzióne** *f* dissolution
**dissolvènza** *f* (mov) fade-out; **dissolvenza incrociata** (mov) lap dissolve
**dissòlvere** §155 *tr* to dissolve; to clear up (*a doubt*); (obs) to untie ‖ *ref* to dissolve
**dissomiglianza** *f* dissimilarity
**dissonanza** *f* dissonance
**dissotterrare** (dissottèrro) *tr* to exhume; to unearth
**dissuadére** §213 *tr* to dissuade
**dissuè·to -ta** *adj* (lit) unaccustomed
**dissuggellare** (dissuggèllo) *tr* to unseal
**distaccaménto** *m* (mil) detachment
**distaccare** §197 *tr* to detach; to remove; to transfer; to outdistance ‖ *ref* to stand out; to withdraw, become separated
**distacca·to -ta** *adj* detached; branch (*office*)
**distac·co** *m* (**-chi**) detachment; separation; (sports) spread (*in points*)
**distante** *adj* distant; aloof; different ‖ *adv* far away
**distanza** *f* distance; **mantenere le distanze** to keep one's distance; **tenere a distanza** to keep at arm's length
**distanziare** §287 *tr* to outdistance
**distare** *intr* to be distant
**distèndere** §270 *tr* to stretch; to spread; to unfurl; to relax; to knock down; to write ‖ *ref* to stretch; to spread out; to relax
**distensióne** *f* relaxation; relaxation of tension
**disté·so -sa** [s] *adj* stretched out; full (*voice*); lank (*hair*) ‖ *m*—**per disteso** in full ‖ *f* expanse; row; **a distesa** with full voice; at full peal
**distillare** *tr* to distill; to exude; to pour; to trickle ‖ *intr* (ESSERE) to trickle ‖ *ref*—**distillarsi il cervello** to rack one's brain
**distilla·to -ta** *adj* distilled ‖ *m* distillate
**distilla·tóre -trice** *mf* distiller ‖ *m* still
**distillerìa** *f* distillery
**distinguìbile** *adj* distinguishable
**distìnguere** §156 *tr* to distinguish; to make out; to tell (*one thing from another*); to divide
**distinta** *f* note, list; **distinta di versamento** deposit slip
**distintaménte** *adv* distinctly; sincerely yours
**distinti·vo -va** *adj* distinctive ‖ *m* emblem, insignia, badge
**distin·to -ta** *adj* distinct; distinguished; sincere (*greetings*); reserved (*seat*); **Distinto Signor . . .** (*on an envelope*) Mr. . . . ‖ *f* see **distinta**
**distinzióne** *f* distinction
**distògliere** §127 *tr* to dissuade; to deter; to distract; to turn (*one's eyes*) away
**distòrcere** §272 *tr* to distort; to twist ‖ *ref* to become distorted; to sprain (*e.g., one's ankle*)
**distorsióne** *f* distortion; sprain; **distorsione acustica** wow
**distrarre** §273 *tr* to distract; to divert;

to amuse; to pull (*a muscle*) ‖ *ref* to become distracted; to relax
**distrat·to -ta** *adj* absent-minded
**distrazióne** *f* absent-mindedness; distraction; diversion (*of money*); pull (*of muscle*)
**distrét·to -ta** *adj* (obs) close; (obs) hard-pressed ‖ *m* district; precinct (*of police*); circuit (*of court*); ward (*in city*); **distretto militare** draft board; **distretto postale** postal zone ‖ *f* stricture; necessity
**distrettuale** *adj* district
**distribuire** §176 *tr* to distribute; to pass out; to allot; to deploy (*troops*); (theat) to cast (*roles*); (mov) to release; (mil) to issue (*e.g., clothing*)
**distribu·tóre -trice** *adj* distributing, dispensing ‖ *mf* distributor, dispenser ‖ *m* distributor; **distributore automatico** vending machine; **distributore di benzina** gasoline pump
**distribuzióne** *f* distribution; issue; delivery; (aut) timing gears; (mov) release; (fig) dispensation
**districare** §197 *tr* to unravel ‖ *ref* to extricate oneself
**distrofìa** *f* dystrophy
**distrùggere** §266 *tr* to destroy; to ruin
**distrutti·vo -va** *adj* destructive
**distruzióne** *f* destruction
**disturbare** *tr* to disturb, bother; **disturbo?** may I come in? ‖ *ref* to bother; to go out of one's way
**disturba·tóre -trice** *mf* disturber; **disturbatore della quiete pubblica** disturber of the peace
**disturbo** *m* trouble, bother; disturbance; (rad) interference; **disturbi atmosferici** static, atmospherics; **togliere il disturbo a** to take leave of
**disubbidiènte** *adj* disobedient
**disubbidiènza** *f* disobedience
**disubbidire** §176 *intr* to disobey; (with *dat*) to disobey
**disuguaglianza** *f* inequality; disparity
**disuguale** *adj* uneven; unequal
**disuma·no -na** *adj* inhumane; unbearable
**disunióne** *f* disunion
**disunire** §176 *tr* to disunite
**disusa·to -ta** *adj* obsolete, out of use
**disuso** *m* disuse; **in disuso** obsolete
**disùtile** *adj* useless; burdensome ‖ *m* worthless fellow; (com) loss
**disvì·o** *m* (**-i**) miscarriage, missending (*of a letter*)
**ditale** *m* thimble; fingerstall
**ditata** *f* poke with a finger; finger mark; dab (*with a finger*)
**dito** *m* (**dita** *fpl*) finger; toe; **avere le dita d'oro** to have a magic touch; **dita della mano** fingers; **dita del piede** toes; **legarsela al dito** to never forget ‖ *m* (**diti**) finger, e.g., **dito indice** index finger; **dito anulare** ring finger; **dito medio** middle finger; **dito mignolo** little finger; **dito pollice** thumb
**ditta** *f* firm, house; office
**dittàfono** *m* intercom; dictaphone
**dittatóre** *m* dictator

**dittatura** *f* dictatorship
**dittongare** §209 (**dittòngo**) *tr* to diphthongize
**dittòn·go** *m* (**-ghi**) diphthong
**diurèti·co** **-ca** *adj* & *m* (**-ci** **-che**) diuretic
**diur·no** **-na** *adj* daily; daytime ‖ *f* (theat) matinée
**diutur·no** **-na** *adj* long-lasting
**diva** *f* diva; (mov) star; (lit) goddess
**divagare** §209 *tr* to amuse; to distract ‖ *intr* to digress ‖ *ref* to relax
**divagazióne** *f* distraction; digression; relaxation
**divampare** *intr* (ESSERE & AVERE) to blaze, flare
**divano** *m* divan; couch, sofa
**divaricare** §197 (**divàrico**) *tr* to spread (*one's legs*); to open up (*an incision*)
**divà·rio** *m* (**-ri**) difference
**divèllere** §267 *tr* to eradicate, uproot
**diveni·re** *m* (**-re**) (philos) becoming ‖ §282 *intr* (ESSERE) (lit) to become; (archaic) to come
**diventare** (**divènto**) *intr* (ESSERE) to become; **diventare di tutti i colori** to blush; to be embarrassed; **diventare grande** to grow up; **diventare matto** to go mad; **diventare pallido** to turn pale; **diventare piccolo** to grow smaller; **diventare rosso** to blush
**divèr·bio** *m* (**-bi**) argument; **venire a diverbio** to have an altercation
**divergènza** *f* divergency
**divèrgere** §157 *intr* to diverge
**diversificare** §197 (**diversìfico**) *tr* to diversify ‖ *ref* to be diversified; to differ
**diversióne** *f* diversion
**diversi·tà** *f* (**-tà**) diversity
**diversi·vo** **-va** *adj* diverting ‖ *m* diversion
**diver·so** **-sa** *adj* different; **diver·si** **-se** several, e.g., **diverse ragazze** several girls ‖ **diver·si** **-se** *pron* several
**divertènte** *adj* diverting, amusing
**divertiménto** *m* amusement, pastime; fun; (mus) divertimento
**divertire** (**divèrto**) *tr* to amuse, entertain; (lit) to turn aside ‖ *ref* to have fun, enjoy oneself; (lit) to go away
**diverti·to** **-ta** *adj* amused; amusing
**divétta** *f* starlet
**divezzare** (**divézzo**) *tr* to wean ‖ *ref*—**divezzarsi da** to get out of the habit of
**dividèndo** *m* dividend
**divìdere** §158 *tr* to divide; to partition; to split; to share in (*e.g., s.o.'s grief*) ‖ *ref* to be divided; to become separated; **dividersi fra** to divide one's time between
**divièto** *m* prohibition; **divieto d'affissione** post no bills; **divieto di parcheggio** no parking; **divieto di sosta** no stopping; **divieto di svolta** no turns; **divieto di transito** no thoroughfare
**divinare** *tr* (lit) to divine
**divina·tóre** **-trice** *adj* divining ‖ *m* diviner

**divinazióne** *f* divination
**divincolare** (**divìncolo**) *tr* & *ref* to wriggle
**divini·tà** *f* (**-tà**) divinity
**divinizzare** [ddzz] *tr* to deify
**divi·no** **-na** *adj* divine
**divisa** *f* uniform; motto; part (*in hair*); **divise** foreign exchange
**divisare** *tr* (lit) to intend
**divisìbile** *adj* divisible
**divisióne** *f* division; partition; (sports) league
**divisionismo** *m* (painting) divisionism; (pol) separatism
**divismo** *m* (mov) star system; (mov) adulation of stars
**divisóre** *m* (math) divisor
**divisò·rio** **-ria** (**-ri** **-rie**) *adj* dividing ‖ *m* partition; (math) divisor
**di·vo** **-va** *adj* (lit) divine ‖ *m* (theat, mov) star; (lit) god ‖ *f* see **diva**
**divolgare** §209 (**divólgo**) *tr* & *ref* var of **divulgare**
**divorare** (**divóro**) *tr* to devour; to gulp down; to consume; **divorare la via** to burn up the road
**divora·tóre** **-trice** *adj* consuming ‖ *mf* consumer (*e.g., of food, books*)
**divorziare** §287 (**divòrzio**) *intr* to become divorced; **divorziare da** to divorce
**divorzia·to** **-ta** *adj* divorced ‖ *m* divorcé ‖ *f* divorcée
**divòr·zio** *m* (**-zi**) divorce
**divulgare** §209 *tr* to divulge; to publicize; to popularize ‖ *ref* to spread; to become popular
**divulga·tóre** **-trice** *adj* popularizing ‖ *mf* popularizer; **divulgatore di calunnie** scandalmonger; **divulgatore di notizie** telltale
**divulgazióne** *f* publicizing; popularization
**divulsióne** *f* (surg) dilation
**dizionà·rio** *m* (**-ri**) dictionary; **dizionario geografico** gazetteer
**dizióne** *f* diction; reading (*of poetry*)
**do** [dɔ] *m* (**do**) (mus) do; (mus) C
**dóc·cia** *f* (**-ce**) shower; gutter (*on roof*); spout; (fig) dash of cold water; **fare la doccia** to take a shower
**docciare** §128 (**dóccio**) *tr*, *intr* (ESSERE) & *ref* to shower
**doccióne** *m* trough, gutter; gargoyle
**docènte** *adj* teaching ‖ *m* teacher; **libero docente** certified university teacher
**docènza** *f* teaching post; **libera docenza** lectureship
**dòcile** *adj* docile; tame; amenable (*person*); workable (*material*)
**documentare** (**documénto**) *tr* to document ‖ *ref* to gather information
**documentà·rio** **-ria** *adj* & *m* (**-ri** **-rie**) documentary
**documénto** *m* document; paper; **documenti di bordo** ship's papers
**dodecafonìa** *f* twelve-tone system
**dodecasìlla·bo** **-ba** *adj* twelve-syllable, dodecasyllable
**dodicèsi·mo** **-ma** *adj*, *m* & *pron* twelfth
**dódici** *adj* & *pron* twelve; **le dodici**

twelve o'clock ‖ *m* twelve; twelfth (*in dates*)

**dó·ga** *f* (-ghe) stave

**dogale** *adj* (hist) of the doge

**dogana** *f* duty; customs; custom house

**doganière** *m* customs officer

**dòge** *m* (hist) doge

**dò·glia** *f* (-glie) (lit) pain, pang; **doglie** labor pains

**dò·glio** *m* (-gli) barrel; (lit) large jar

**doglió·so -sa** [s] *adj* (lit) sorrowful

**dòg·ma** *m* (-mi) dogma

**dogmàti·co -ca** (-ci -che) *adj* dogmatic ‖ *mf* dogmatist

**dogmatismo** *m* dogmatism

**dólce** *adj* sweet; soft; gentle; fresh (*water*); mild (*climate*); delicate (*feet*); **dolce far niente** sweet idleness ‖ *m* sweet; sweet dish; **dolci** candy

**dolceama·ro -ra** *adj* bittersweet

**dolcézza** *f* sweetness; mildness; gentleness

**dolcia·stro -stra** *adj* sweetish

**dolcière** *m* candy maker; pastry baker

**dolcificare** §197 (**dolcìfico**) *tr* to sweeten

**dolciume** *m* sweet; **dolciumi** candy

**dolènte** *adj* aching; sorrowful; sorry

**dolére** §159 *intr* (ESSERE & AVERE) to ache, e.g., **gli dolgono i denti** his teeth ache ‖ *ref* to grieve ‖ *impers* (ESSERE) to be sorry, e.g., **mi duole che Lei non possa venire** I am sorry that you won't be able to come

**dolicònice** *m* bobolink

**dòllaro** *m* dollar

**dòlo** *m* fraud, malice, guile

**dolomite** *f* dolomite ‖ **Dolomiti** *fpl* Dolomites

**dolorante** *adj* aching

**dolorare** (**dolóro**) *intr* (lit) to ache

**dolóre** *m* ache; sorrow; contrition

**doloró·so -sa** [s] *adj* painful; sorrowful

**doló·so -sa** [s] *adj* intentional, fraudulent; (law) felonious

**domàbile** *adj* tamable

**domanda** *f* question; application; appeal; (econ) demand; **domanda suggestiva** (com) leading question; **fare una domanda** to ask a question

**domandare** *tr* to ask; to ask for; **domandare la parola** to ask for the floor ‖ *intr* to inquire ‖ *ref* to wonder; (lit) to be called

**doma·ni** *m* (-ni) tomorrow ‖ *adv* tomorrow; **a domani** until tomorrow; **domani a otto** a week from tomorrow; **domani l'altro** the day after tomorrow

**domare** (**dómo**) *tr* to tame; to extinguish; to quell

**doma·tóre -trice** *mf* tamer

**domattina** *adv* tomorrow morning

**domèni·ca** *f* (-che) Sunday

**domenicale** *adj* Sunday (*e.g., rest*)

**domenica·no -na** *adj & m* Dominican (*e.g., order*)

**domesticare** §197 (**domèstico**) *tr* to domesticate

**domèsti·co -ca** (-ci -che) *adj* family; household; familiar; domestic ‖ *mf* domestic, servant ‖ *f* maid; **alla**

**domestica** family style; **domestica a mezzo servizio** part-time domestic

**domiciliare** *adj* house ‖ §287 *tr* (com) to draw ‖ *ref* to dwell; to settle

**domicilia·to -ta** *adj* residing

**domicì·lio** *m* (-li) domicile, residence; principal office; **domicilio coatto** imprisonment; **franco domicilio** free delivery

**dominare** (**dòmino**) *tr* to dominate, rule; to master; to overlook ‖ *intr* to prevail; to reign ‖ *ref* to control oneself

**domina·tóre -trice** *mf* ruler

**dominazióne** *f* domination; rule

**domineddìo** *m* *invar* (coll) the Lord God

**dominica·no -na** *adj & mf* Dominican (*e.g., Republic*)

**domì·nio** *m* (-ni) dominion; domain

**dòmi·no** *m* (-no) domino (*cloak*); dominoes (*game*)

**dòn** *m* (used only before singular Christian name) don (*Spanish title*); Don (*priest*); uncle (*familiar title of elderly man*)

**donare** (**dóno**) *tr* to donate; to give as a present ‖ *intr*—**donare a** to be becoming to

**dona·tóre -trice** *mf* donor; **donatore di sangue** blood donor

**donazióne** *f* gift, donation

**donchisciotté·sco -sca** *adj* (-schi -sche) quixotic

**dónde** *adv* wherefrom, whence

**dondolare** (**dóndolo**) *tr* to swing, rock ‖ *ref* to swing, rock; to loaf around

**dondolì·o** *m* (-i) swinging, rocking

**dóndolo** *m*—**a dondolo** rocking (*chair, horse*); **andare a dondolo** to loaf around

**dondoló·ne -na** *mf* idler, loafer

**dongiovan·ni** *m* (-ni) Don Juan

**dònna** *f* woman; ladyship; (lit) lady; (coll) Mrs.; (coll) maid; (cards) queen; **da donna** woman's, e.g., **scarpe da donna** woman's shoes; **donna cannone** fat lady (*of circus*); **donna di casa** housewife; **Nostra Donna** Our Lady

**donnaiòlo** *m* ladies' man, philanderer

**donné·sco -sca** *adj* (-schi -sche) womanly, feminine

**dònnola** *f* weasel

**dóno** *m* gift; **in dono** as a gift

**donzèlla** [dz] *f* (lit) damsel

**donzèllo** [dz] *m* (coll) doorman; (lit) page

**dópo** *adv* afterwards, later; **dopo che** after; **dopo di** after ‖ *prep* after; **dopo + pp** after having + *pp*

**dopobar·ba** *adj invar* after-shaving ‖ *m* (-ba) after-shaving lotion

**dopodomani** *m & adv* the day after tomorrow

**dopoguèr·ra** *m* (-ra) postwar era

**dopolavóro** *m* government office designed to organize workers' leisure time

**dopopranzo** *m* afternoon ‖ *adv* in the afternoon

**doppiàg·gio** *m* (-gi) (mov) dubbing

**doppiare** §287 (dóppio) *tr* to double; (mov) to dub

**doppière** *m* candelabrum

**doppiétta** *f* double-barreled shotgun; (aut) double shift

**doppiézza** *f* duplicity

**dóp·pio -pia (-pi -pie)** *adj* double; coupled; double-dealing ‖ *adv* twice, twofold ‖ *m* double; twice as much; (tennis) doubles; (theat) understudy

**doppióne** *m* duplicate; (philol) doublet

**doppiopèt·to** *adj invar* double-breasted ‖ *m* (-to) double-breasted suit

**dorare** (dòro) *tr* to gild; (culin) to brown; **dorare la pillola** to sugar-coat the pill

**dora·to -ta** *adj* gilt, golden

**doratura** *f* gilding

**dormicchiare** §287 *intr* to doze

**dormiènte** *adj* sleeping ‖ *mf* sleeper

**dormiglió·ne -na** *mf* sleepyhead

**dormire** (dòrmo) *tr & intr* to sleep; **dormire a occhi aperti** to be overcome with sleep; **dormire della grossa** to sleep profoundly; **dormire tra due guanciali** to be safe and secure

**dormita** *f* long sleep; **fare una bella dormita** to have a long sleep

**dormitò·rio** *m* (-ri) dormitory

**dormivé·glia** *m* (-glia) drowsiness

**dorsale** *adj* dorsal; back (*bone*) ‖ *m* head (*of bed*); back (*of chair*) ‖ *f* (geog) ridge

**dòrso** *m* back; (sports) backstroke

**dosàg·gio** *m* (-gi) dosage

**dosare** (dòso) *tr* to dose

**dosatura** *f* dosage

**dòse** *f* dose

**dòsso** *m* back; (lit) summit; **levarsi di dosso** to take off; **mettersi in dosso** to put on

**dotare** (dòto) *tr* to provide with a dowry; to endow; to bless

**dotazióne** *f* dowry; endowment; supply

**dòte** *f* dowry; gift; endowment

**dòt·to -ta** *adj* learned, erudite ‖ *m* scholar; (anat) duct

**dottorale** *adj* doctoral

**dottó·re -réssa** *mf* doctor

**dottrina** *f* doctrine; Christian doctrine

**dóve** *m* where; **per ogni dove** everywhere ‖ *adv* where; **da dove** or **di dove** from where; which way; **fin dove** up to what point; **per dove** which way ‖ *conj* where; whereas

**dovére** *m* duty, obligation; homework; **a dovere** properly; **doveri** regards; **farsi un dovere di** to feel duty-bound to; **mettere qlcu a dovere** to put s.o. in his place; **più del dovere** more than one should; **sentirsi in dovere di** to feel duty-bound to ‖ §160 *tr & intr* to owe ‖ *aux* (ESSERE & AVERE) must, e.g., **deve farlo** you must do it; to have to, e.g., **dovei partire** I had to leave; ought to, e.g., **dovrebbe lucidare la macchina** he ought to polish the car; should, e.g., **dovresti immaginarti** you should imagine; to be to, e.g., **il treno doveva arrivare alle sei** the train was to arrive at six; to be supposed to, e.g., **deve aver**

**fatto un lungo viaggio** he is supposed to have taken a long journey

**doveró·so -sa** [s] *adj* proper, right

**dovìzia** *f* (lit) abundance, wealth

**dovunque** *adv* wherever, anywhere; everywhere

**dovu·to -ta** *adj & m* due

**dozzina** [ddzz] *f* dozen; room and board; **da** or **di dozzina** common, ordinary; **tenere a dozzina** to board

**dozzinale** [ddzz] *adj* common, ordinary

**dozzinante** [ddzz] *mf* boarder

**dra·ga** *f* (-ghe) dredge

**dragàg·gio** *m* (-gi) dredging

**dragami·ne** *m* (-ne) minesweeper

**dragare** §209 *tr* to dredge

**dràglia** *f* (naut) stay

**dra·go** *m* (-ghi) dragon; **drago volante** kite

**dragóna** *f* sword strap

**dragoncèllo** *m* (bot) tarragon

**dragóne** *m* dragon; dragoon

**dram·ma** *m* (-mi) drama, play; **dramma musicale** (hist) melodrama ‖ *f* drachma; dram

**drammàti·co -ca (-ci -che)** *adj* dramatic ‖ *f* drama, dramatic art

**drammatizzare** [ddzz] *tr* to dramatize

**drammatur·go** *m* (-ghi) playwright, dramatist

**drappég·gio** *m* (-gi) drape; pleats

**drappeggiare** §290 (drappéggio) *tr* to drape ‖ *ref* to be draped

**drappèlla** *f* pennon (*on bugler's trumpet*)

**drappèllo** *m* squad, platoon

**drapperìa** *f* dry goods; dry-goods store

**drappo** *m* cloth, silk cloth; (billiards) green cloth, baize

**dràsti·co -ca** *adj* (-ci -che) drastic

**drenàg·gio** *m* (-gi) drainage

**drenare** (drèno) *tr* to drain

**dressàg·gio** *m* (-gi) *m* training (*of animals*)

**dribblare** *tr & intr* (sports) to dribble

**drit·to -ta** *adj* straight; (lit) correct; **dritto come un fuso** straight as a ramrod ‖ *m* (fig) old fox ‖ *f* right; (naut) starboard

**drizza** *f* (naut) halyard

**drizzare** *tr* to straighten; to address; to erect; to cock (*the head*); to direct (*a blow*); **drizzare le gambe ai cani** to do the impossible; **drizzare le orecchie** to prick up one's ears ‖ *intr* (naut) to hoist the halyard ‖ *ref* to stand erect

**drò·ga** *f* (-ghe) drug; spice; seasoning

**drogare** §209 (drògo) *tr* to drug; to spice, season

**drogherìa** *f* grocery (store)

**droghière** *m* grocer

**dromedà·rio** *m* (-ri) dromedary

**dru·do -da** *adj* (archaic) faithful; (lit) strong ‖ *m* (obs) vassal; (lit) lover

**drùi·da** *m* (-di) druid

**drupa** *f* (bot) drupe, stone fruit

**duale** *adj & m* dual

**dualismo** *m* dualism

**duali·tà** *f* duality

**dùb·bio -bia (-bi -bie)** *adj* doubtful ‖ *m* doubt; misgiving; **mettere in dub-**

**bio** to question; to risk; **senza dubbio** no doubt
**dubbió·so -sa** [s] *adj* dubious; doubtful; (lit) dangerous
**dubitare** (**dùbito**) *intr* to doubt; to suspect; **dubitare di** to mistrust; to doubt; **non dubitare!** don't worry!
**du·ca** *m* (**-chi**) duke; (lit) leader
**ducato** *m* duchy; ducat
**duce** *m* leader; duce
**duchéssa** *f* duchess
**duchessina** *f* young duchess
**duchino** *m* young duke
**due** *adj & pron* two; **le due** two o'clock ‖ *m* two; second (*in dates*) ‖ *f*—**fra le due** between two alternatives
**duecenté·sco -sca** *adj* (**-schi -sche**) thirteenth-century
**duecentèsi·mo -ma** *adj, m & pron* two hundredth
**duecènto** *adj, m & pron* two hundred ‖ **il Duecento** the thirteenth century
**duellante** *adj* dueling ‖ *m* duelist
**duellare** (**duèllo**) *intr* to duel
**duèllo** *m* duel; contest; debate; **sfidare a duello** to challenge to a duel
**duemila** *adj, m & pron* two thousand ‖ **Duemila** *m* twenty-first century
**duepèz·zi** *m* (**-zi**) two-piece bathing suit
**duétto** *m* (mus) duet
**dulcamara** *f* (bot) bittersweet
**dulcina** *f* artificial sweetening
**duna** *f* dune
**dunque** *m*—**venire al dunque** to come

to the point ‖ *adv* then ‖ *conj* therefore, hence ‖ *interj* well!
**duodèno** *m* (anat) duodenum
**duòlo** *m* (lit) grief
**duòmo** *m* cathedral; dome (*e.g., of a boiler*)
**du·plex** *m* (**-plex**) (telp) party line
**duplicare** §197 (**dùplico**) *tr* to duplicate
**duplica·to -ta** *adj & m* duplicate
**duplicatóre** *m* duplicator
**dùplice** *adj* twofold, double ‖ *f* (racing) daily double
**duplici·tà** *f* (**-tà**) duplicity
**duràbile** *adj* durable, lasting
**duràci·no -na** *adj* clingstone ‖ *f* clingstone peach
**duralluminìo** *m* duralumin
**durare** *tr* to endure, bear ‖ *intr* to last; **durare a** + *inf* to keep on + *ger*; **durare in carica** to remain in office
**durata** *f* duration; lasting quality; **di lunga durata** long-lasting
**durante** *prep* during; throughout
**duratu·ro -ra** *adj* enduring, lasting
**durévole** *adj* lasting, durable
**durézza** *f* hardness; toughness; rigidity
**du·ro -ra** *adj* hard; hard-boiled (*egg*); durum (*wheat*); tough (*skin*); harsh; (phonet) voiceless ‖ *m* hard part; hard floor; hard soil; **il duro sta che . . .** the trouble is that . . . ˙ **tener duro** to hold out
**duróne** *m* callousness, callosity
**dùttile** *adj* ductile; tractable

**E**

**E, e** [e] *m & f* fifth letter of the Italian alphabet
**e** *conj* and
**ebani·sta** *m* (**-sti**) cabinetmaker
**ebanisterìa** *f* cabinetmaking; cabinetmaker's shop
**ebanite** *f* ebonite, vulcanite
**èbano** *m* ebony
**ebbène** *interj* well!
**ebbrézza** *f* intoxication, drunkenness
**èb·bro -bra** *adj* intoxicated ‖ *mf* drunk
**ebdomadà·rio -ria** *adj & m* (**-ri -rie**) weekly
**èbete** *adj* stupid, dull, dumb
**ebollizióne** *f* boil, boiling
**ebrài·co -ca** (**-ci -che**) *adj* Hebrew, Hebraic ‖ *m* Hebrew (*language*)
**ebrè·o -a** *adj & mf* Hebrew ‖ *m* Hebrew (*language*); Jew; **ebreo errante** Wandering Jew
**è·bro -bra** *adj & mf* var of **ebbro**
**ebùrne·o -a** *adj* (lit) ivory
**ecatòmbe** *f* hecatomb, slaughter
**eccedènte** *adj* exceeding ‖ *m* excess
**eccedènza** *f* excess, surplus
**eccèdere** §123 *tr* to exceed ‖ *intr* to go too far
**eccellènte** *adj* excellent
**eccellènza** *f* excellence ‖ **Eccellenza** *f* Excellency

**eccèllere** §162 *intr* (ESSERE) to excel
**eccèl·so -sa** *adj* unexcelled; very high ‖ —**l'Eccelso** *m* the Most High
**eccentrici·tà** *f* (**-tà**) eccentricity
**eccèntri·co -ca** (**-ci -che**) *adj* eccentric; suburban ‖ *mf* vaudeville performer ‖ *m* (mach) eccentric
**eccepìbile** *adj* objectionable
**eccepire** §176 *tr* (law) to take exception to ‖ *intr* (law) to object
**eccessi·vo -va** *adj* excessive; overweening (*opinion*)
**eccèsso** *m* excess; **all'eccesso** excessively; **andare agli eccessi** to go to extremes; **dare in eccessi** to fly into a rage; **eccesso di peso** excess weight
**eccètera** *adv* and so forth, et cetera
**eccètto** *prep* except, but; **eccetto che** except that; unless
**eccettuare** (**eccèttuo**) *tr* to except
**eccettua·to -ta** *adj* excepted ‖ **eccettuato** *prep* except
**eccezionale** *adj* exceptional
**eccezióne** *f* exception; objection; **ad eccezione di** with the exception of; **d'eccezione** extraordinary; **sollevare un'eccezione** (law) to take exception
**ecchimò·si** *f* (**-si**) bruise
**ecci·dio** *m* (**-di**) massacre
**eccitàbile** *adj* excitable

**eccitaménto** *m* instigation; excitement
**eccitante** *adj* stimulating ‖ *m* stimulant
**eccitare** (**èccito**) *tr* to excite ‖ *ref* to become excited or aroused; (sports) to warm up
**eccitazióne** *f* excitement; (elec) excitation
**ecclesiàsti·co -ca** (**-ci -che**) *adj* ecclesiastical ‖ *m* clergyman
**ècco** *tr invar* here is (are), there is (are); **ecco che** here, e.g., **ecco che viene** here he comes; **eccoci** here we are; **ecco fatto** that's it; **eccola** here she is; here it is; **eccomi** here I am; **eccone** here are some ‖ *intr invar* here I am; here it is; **quand'ecco** suddenly ‖ *interj* look!
**eccóme** *interj* and how!, indeed!
**echeggiare** §290 (**echéggio**) *intr* (ESSERE & AVERE) to echo
**eclètti·co -ca** *adj & mf* (**-ci -che**) eclectic
**eclissare** *tr* to eclipse ‖ *ref* to be eclipsed; (coll) to vanish, sneak away
**eclis·si** *f* (**-si**) eclipse
**eclìtti·ca** *f* (**-che**) ecliptic
**èclo·ga** *f* (**-ghe**) var of **egloga**
**è·co** *m & f* (**-chi** *mpl*) echo; **far eco a** to echo
**ecogonìòmetro** *m* sonar
**ecologìa** *f* ecology
**economato** *m* comptroller's or administrator's office
**economìa** *f* administration; management; economy; economics; **economia aziendale** business management; **economia di mercato** free enterprise; **economia domestica** home economics; **economia politica** political economy; economics; **economie** savings; **fare economia** to save
**econòmi·co -ca** *adj* (**-ci -che**) economic(al); cheap
**economi·sta** *mf* (**-sti -ste**) economist
**economizzare** [ddzz] *tr & intr* to economize, save
**econo·mo -ma** *adj* thrifty ‖ *m* comptroller; administrator
**ecosistè·ma** [s] *m* (**-mi**) ecosystem
**ecumèni·co -ca** *adj* (**-ci -che**) ecumenical
**eczè·ma** [dz] *m* (**-mi**) eczema
**édera** *f* ivy
**edìcola** *f* shrine; newsstand
**edificante** *adj* edifying
**edificare** §197 (**edìfico**) *tr* to build; to edify ‖ *intr* to build
**edifica·tóre -trice** *adj* building ‖ *mf* builder
**edificazióne** *f* building; edification
**edifì·cio** *m* (**-ci**) building, edifice; pack (*e.g., of lies*); structure
**edile** *adj* building, construction ‖ *m* builder, construction worker
**edilì·zio -zia** (**-zi -zie**) *adj* building, construction ‖ *f* building trade
**edìpi·co -ca** *adj* (**-ci -che**) Oedipus (*e.g., complex*)
**Edipo** *m* Oedipus
**èdi·to -ta** *adj* published
**edi·tóre -trice** *adj* publishing ‖ *mf* publisher; editor (*e.g., of a text*)
**editorìa** *f* publishing; publishers

**editoriale** *adj* editorial; publishing ‖ *m* editorial
**editoriali·sta** *mf* (**-sti -ste**) editorial writer
**editto** *m* edict
**edizióne** *f* edition; performance; (fig) vintage
**edonismo** *m* hedonism
**edoni·sta** *mf* (**-sti -ste**) hedonist
**edòt·to -ta** *adj* (lit) informed, acquainted; **rendere qlcu edotto su qlco** (lit) to inform s.o. of s.th
**edredóne** *m* eider, eider duck
**educanda** *f* boarding-school girl; convent-school girl
**educandato** *m* (convent) boarding school for girls
**educare** §197 (**èduco**) *tr* to educate; to rear, bring up; to train; to accustom, inure; (lit) to grow
**educati·vo -va** *adj* educational
**educa·to -ta** *adj* educated; polite, well-bred
**educa·tóre -trice** *mf* educator
**educazióne** *f* education; breeding, manners; **educazione civica** civics
**edule** *adj* edible
**efèbo** *m* (coll) sissy
**efèlide** *f* freckle
**effeminatézza** *f* effeminacy
**effemina·to -ta** *adj* effeminate; frivolous
**efferatézza** *f* savagery
**effervescènte** *adj* effervescent
**effervescènza** *f* effervescence
**effettivaménte** *adv* really
**effetti·vo -va** *adj* real, true; effective; full (*e.g., member*); regular (*e.g., army officer*) ‖ *m* effective; total amount; (mil) manpower
**effètto** *m* effect, result; (com) promissory note; (billiards) English; (sports) spin; **a questo effetto** for this purpose; **effetti** effects, belongings; **effetto di luce** play of light; **effetto ottico** optical illusion; **fare effetto** to make a sensation; **fare l'effetto di** to give the impression of; **in effetto** in fact; **mandare a effetto** to carry out; **porre in effetto** to put into effect
**effettuàbile** *adj* feasible
**effettuare** (**effèttuo**) *tr* to bring about; to contrive; to actuate; **effettuare** (**una corsa, un servizio**) to run, e.g., **l'autobus effettua una corsa ogni mezz'ora** the bus runs every half hour
**efficace** *adj* effective; forceful (*writer*)
**efficà·cia** *f* (**-cie**) effectiveness, efficacy; (law) validity
**efficiènte** *adj* efficient
**efficiènza** *f* efficiency; **in piena efficienza** in full working order; in top condition
**effigiare** §290 *tr* to portray, represent
**effì·gie** *f* (**-gie** or **-gi**) effigy; image
**effìme·ro -ra** *adj* ephemeral
**efflusso** *m* flow, outflow
**efflù·vio** *m* (**-vi**) effluvium; emanation (*e.g., of light*)
**effrazióne** *f* (law) burglary
**effusióne** *f* effusion; outflow; shedding (*of blood*); effusiveness
**egemonìa** *f* hegemony

**egè·o -a** *adj* Aegean
**ègida** *f* aegis
**Egitto, l'** *m* Egypt
**egizia·no -na** *adj & mf* Egyptian
**eglantina** *f* sweetbrier
**eglefino** *m* haddock
**égli** §5 *pron pers* he
**èglo·ga** *f* (-ghe) eclogue
**egocèntri·co -ca** *adj & mf* (-ci -che) egocentric
**egoismo** *m* egoism, selfishness
**egoi·sta** (-sti -ste) *adj* selfish ‖ *mf* egoist
**egoìsti·co -ca** *adj* (-ci -che) egoistic(al)
**egotismo** *m* egotism
**egoti·sta** (-sti -ste) *adj* egotistic ‖ *mf* egotist
**egrè·gio -gia** *adj* (-gi -gie) (lit) outstanding; **Egregio Signore** Mr. (*before a man's name in an address on a letter*); Dear Sir
**eguaglianza** *f* equality
**eguale** *adj* var of **uguale**
**egualità·rio -ria** *adj & m* (-ri -rie) equalitarian
**éhi** *interj* hey!
**éi** *pron* (lit) he; (archaic) they
**eiaculazióne** *f* ejaculation
**eiettàbile** *adj* ejection (*seat*)
**eiezióne** *f* ejection
**él** *pron* (archaic) he
**elaborare (elàboro)** *tr* to elaborate; to digest; to secrete
**elabora·to -ta** *adj* elaborate ‖ *m* written exercise
**elaboratóre** *m* computer
**elaborazióne** *f* elaboration; data processing
**elargire** §176 *tr* to donate
**elargizióne** *f* donation
**elastici·tà** *f* (-tà) elasticity; agility; (com) oscillation; (com) range
**elàsti·co -ca** *adj* (-ci -che) elastic ‖ *m* rubber band; bedspring
**élce** *m & f* holm oak
**elefante** *m* elephant; **elefante marino** sea elephant
**elefantéssa** *f* female elephant
**elegante** *adj* elegant, fashionable
**elegantó·ne -na** *mf* fashion plate ‖ *m* dandy, dude
**eleganza** *f* elegance, stylishness
**elèggere** §193 *tr* to elect
**eleggìbile** *adj* eligible
**elegìa** *f* elegy
**elegìa·co -ca** *adj* elegiac
**elementare** *adj* elementary ‖ **elementari** *fpl* elementary schools
**eleménto** *m* element; rudiment; member; cell (*of battery*); **elementi personali**, e.g., **elementi femminili** female personnel
**elemòsina** *f* alms; (eccl) collection; **chiedere l'elemosina** to beg; **vivere d'elemosina** to live on charity
**elemosinare (elemòsino)** *intr* to beg
**Èlena** *f* Helen
**elencare** §197 (**elènco**) *tr* to list; to enumerate
**elèn·co** *m* (-chi) list; **elenco telefonico** telephone directory
**eletti·vo -va** *adj* elective
**elèt·to -ta** *adj* elect; distinguished

(*audience*); precious (*metal*); chosen (*people*) ‖ *mf* elect
**elettorato** *m* electorate, constituency
**elet·tóre -trice** *mf* voter; elector
**elettràuto** *m* automobile electrician; automotive electric shop
**elettrici·sta** *mf* (-sti -ste) electrician
**elettrici·tà** *f* (-tà) electricity
**elèttri·co -ca** (-ci -che) *adj* electrical ‖ *m* electrical worker
**elettrificare** §197 (**elettrìfico**) *tr* to electrify
**elettrizzare** [ddzz] *tr* to electrify (*e.g., a person*) ‖ *ref* to become electrified
**ellètro** *m* amber
**elettrocalamita** *f* electromagnet
**elettrocardiògrafo** *m* electrocardiograph
**elettrocardiogram·ma** *m* (-mi) electrocardiogram
**elettrodinàmi·co -ca** (-ci -che) *adj* electrodynamic ‖ *f* electrodynamics
**elèttrodo** *m* electrode
**elettrodomèsti·co -ca** (-ci -che) *adj* electric household ‖ *m* electric household appliance
**elettroesecuzióne** *f* electrocution
**elettròge·no -na** *adj* generating (*unit*)
**elettròli·si** *f* (-si) electrolysis
**elettroliti·co -ca** *adj* (-ci -che) electrolytic
**elettròlito** *m* electrolyte
**elettromagnèti·co -ca** *adj* (-ci -che) electromagnetic
**elettromo·tóre -trice** *adj* electromotive ‖ *m* electric motor ‖ *f* electric train; electric railcar
**elettróne** *m* electron
**elettróni·co -ca** (-ci -che) *adj* electronic ‖ *f* electronics
**elettropómpa** *f* electric pump
**elettrosquasso** *m* electroshock
**elettrostàti·co -ca** (-ci -che) *adj* electrostatic ‖ *f* electrostatics
**elettrotècni·co -ca** (-ci -che) *adj* electrotechnical ‖ *m* electrician; electrical engineer ‖ *f* electrical engineering
**elettrotrèno** *m* electric train
**elevaménto** *m* elevation
**elevare (èlevo & elèvo)** *tr* to lift, elevate; (math) to raise ‖ *ref* to rise
**elevatézza** *f* loftiness, dignity
**eleva·to -ta** *adj* high, lofty
**eleva·tóre -trice** *adj* elevating ‖ *m* elevator
**elevazióne** *f* elevation; (sports) jump; (math) raising
**elezióne** *f* election; choice
**èlfo** *m* elf
**èli·ca** *f* (-che) propeller; (geom) helix
**elicoidale** *adj* helicoidal
**elicòttero** *m* helicopter
**elìdere** §161 *tr* to annul; to elide ‖ *ref* to neutralize one another
**eliminare (elìmino)** *tr* to eliminate
**eliminatò·rio -ria** (-ri -rie) *adj* eliminating ‖ *f* (sports) heat
**eliminazióne** *f* elimination; extermination
**èlio-** *comb form adj* helio-, e.g., **eliocentrico** heliocentric ‖ *comb form*

*m* & *f* helio-, e.g., **elioterapìa** helio-
therapy
**èlio** *m* helium
**eliocèntri·co -ca** *adj* (**-ci -che**) heliocentric
**eliògrafo** *m* heliograph
**elioteràpi·co -ca** *adj* (**-ci -che**) sunshine
(*treatment*); sunbathing (*establishment*)
**eliotrò·pio** *m* (**-pi**) heliotrope; blood-
stone
**elipòrto** *m* heliport
**elisabettìa·no -na** *adj* Elizabethan
**elì·sio -sia** *adj* (**-si -sie**) Elysian
**elisióne** *f* elision
**eli·sir** *m* (**-sìr**) elixir
**èlitra** *f* elytron, shard
**élla** *pron* (lit) she || **Ella** *pron* (lit) you
**ellèboro** *m* hellebore
**ellèni·co -ca** *adj* (**-ci -che**) Hellenic
**ellisse** *f* ellipse
**ellis·si** *f* (**-si**) (gram) ellipsis
**ellìtti·co -ca** *adj* (**-ci -che**) elliptical
**-èllo -èlla** *suf adj* little, e.g., **poverello**
poor little
**elmétto** *m* helmet; tin hat
**élmo** *m* helmet
**elogiare** §290 (**elògio**) *tr* to praise
**elò·gio** *m* (**-gi**) praise, encomium;
write-up; **elogio funebre** eulogy
**eloquènte** *adj* eloquent
**eloquènza** *f* eloquence
**elò·quio** *m* (**-qui**) (lit) speech, dìction
**élsa** *f* hilt
**elucidare** (**elùcido**) *tr* to elucidate
**elùdere** §105 *tr* to elude, evade
**elusì·vo -va** *adj* elusive
**elvèti·co -ca** *adj* & *mf* (**-ci -che**)
Helvetian
**elzevì·ro -ra** [dz] *adj* Elzevir || *m*
Elzevir book; (journ) literary article
**emacia·to -ta** *adj* emaciated, lean
**emanare** *tr* to send forth; to issue ||
*intr* (ESSERE) to emanate; to come
forth
**emanazióne** *f* emanation; issuance
**emancipare** (**emàncipo**) *tr* to emanci-
pate || *ref* to become emancipated
**emancipazióne** *f* emancipation
**emarginare** (**emàrgino**) *tr* to note in
the margin; (fig) to put aside, neglect
**emarginato** *m* marginal note
**emàti·co -ca** *adj* (**-ci -che**) blood,
hematic
**ematite** *f* hematite
**embar·go** *m* (**-ghi**) embargo
**emblè·ma** *m* (**-mi**) emblem
**emblemàti·co -ca** *adj* (**-ci -che**) em-
blematic
**embolìa** *f* embolism
**èmbrice** *m* flat roof tile; shingle
**embriologìa** *f* embryology
**embrionale** *adj* embryonic
**embrióne** *m* embryo
**emendaménto** *m* emendation (*of a
text*); amendment (*to a law*)
**emendare** (**emèndo**) *tr* to correct; to
emend; to amend (*a law*) || *ref* to
reform
**emergènza** *f* emergence; emergency
**emèrgere** §162 *intr* (ESSERE) to emerge;

to surface (*said of a submarine*); to
loom; to stand out
**emèri·to -ta** *adj* emeritus (*professor*);
famous
**emerotè·ca** *f* (**-che**) periodical library
**emersióne** *f* emersion; surfacing
**emèr·so -sa** *adj* emergent
**emèti·co -ca** *adj* & *m* (**-ci -che**) emetic
**eméttere** §198 *tr* to emit, send forth;
to utter (*a statement*); (com) to issue
**emiciclo** *m* hemicycle; floor (*of legislative body*)
**emicrània** *f* migraine, headache
**emigrante** *adj* & *mf* emigrant
**emigrare** *intr* (ESSERE & AVERE) to emigrate
**emigra·to -ta** *adj* & *mf* emigrant
**emigrazióne** *f* emigration; migration
(*e.g., of birds*)
**eminènte** *adj* eminent
**eminènza** *f* eminence; (eccl) Eminence
**emisfèro** *m* hemisphere
**emissà·rio** *m* (**-ri**) emissary; outlet
(*river or lake*); drain
**emissióne** *f* emission; issuance; (rad)
broadcast
**emistì·chio** *m* (**-chi**) hemistich
**emittènte** *adj* emitting; issuing; (rad)
broadcasting || *f* (rad) transmitting
set; broadcasting station
**emofilìa** *f* hemophilia
**emoglobina** *f* hemoglobin
**emolliènte** *adj* & *m* emollient
**emoluménto** *m* fee, emolument
**emorragìa** *f* hemorrhage
**emorròidi** *fpl* hemorrhoids, piles
**emostàti·co -ca** (**-ci -che**) *adj* hemo-
static || *m* hemostat
**emotè·ca** *f* (**-che**) blood bank
**emotivi·tà** *f* (**-tà**) emotionalism
**emotì·vo -va** *adj* emotional || *mf* emo-
tional person
**emottisi** *f* (pathol) hemoptysis
**emozionante** *adj* emotional, moving
**emozionare** (**emozióno**) *tr* to move,
stir; to thrill
**emozióne** *f* emotion
**empiastro** *m* var of **impiastro**
**émpiere** §163 *tr* & *ref* var of **empire**
**empie·tà** *f* (**-tà**) impiety; cruelty
**ém·pio -pia** *adj* (**-pi -pie**) impious;
pitiless, wicked
**empire** §163 *tr* to fill; (lit) to fulfill;
**empire qlcu di insulti** to heap insults
on s.o. || *ref* to get full
**empìre·o -a** *adj* heavenly, sublime ||
*m* empyrean
**empìri·co -ca** (**-ci -che**) *adj* empirical ||
*mf* empiricist
**empirismo** *m* empiricism
**empiri·sta** *mf* (**-sti -ste**) empiricist
**émpito** *m* (lit) rush; fury
**empò·rio** *m* (**-ri**) emporium, mart
**emulare** (**èmulo**) *tr* to emulate
**emulazióne** *f* emulation, rivalry; (law)
evil intent
**èmu·lo -la** *adj* emulous || *mf* emulator
**emulsionare** (**emulsióno**) *tr* to emulsify
**emulsióne** *f* emulsion
**encefalite** *f* encephalitis
**encìcli·ca** *f* (**-che**) encyclical
**enciclopedìa** *f* encyclopedia

**enciclopèdi·co -ca** *adj* (**-ci -che**) encyclopedic
**enclave** *f* enclave
**enclìti·co -ca** *adj & f* (**-ci -che**) enclitic
**encomiàbile** *adj* praiseworthy
**encomiare** §287 (**encòmio**) *tr* to praise
**encò·mio** *m* (**-mi**) encomium, praise
**endecasìlla·bo -ba** *adj* hendecasyllabic || *m* hendecasyllable
**endemìa** *f* endemic
**endèmi·co -ca** *adj* (**-ci -che**) endemic
**èndice** *m* nest egg; (obs) souvenir
**endocàr·dio** *m* (**-di**) (anat) endocardium
**endocarpo** *m* (bot) endocarp
**endòcri·no -na** *adj* endocrine
**endourba·no -na** *adj* inner-city
**endovenó·so -sa** [s] *adj* intravenous
**energèti·co -ca** (**-ci -che**) *adj* energy (*e.g., crisis*); (med) tonic || *m* (med) tonic
**energìa** *f* energy, power
**enèrgi·co -ca** *adj* (**-ci -che**) energetic
**energùme·no -na** *mf* wild or mad person
**ènfa·si** *f* (**-si**) emphasis; forcefulness
**enfàti·co -ca** *adj* (**-ci -che**) emphatic
**enfiare** §287 (**énfio**) *tr & ref* to swell
**enfisè·ma** *m* (**-mi**) emphysema
**enfitèu·si** *f* (**-si**) lease (*of land*)
**enìg·ma** *m* (**-mi**) enigma, riddle, puzzle
**enigmàti·co -ca** *adj* (**-ci -che**) enigmatic, puzzling
**-ènne** *suf adj* -year-old, e.g., **ragazzo diciassettenne** seventeen-year-old boy || *suf mf* -year-old person, e.g., **diciassettenne** seventeen-year-old person
**ennèsi·mo -ma** *adj* nth
**-èn·nio** *suf m* (**-ni**) period of . . . years, e.g., **ventennio** period of twenty years
**enòlo·go -ga** *mf* (**-gi -ghe**) oenologist
**enórme** *adj* enormous
**enormeménte** *adv* enormously
**enormi·tà** *f* (**-tà**) enormity; outrage; absurdity
**Enrico** *m* Henry
**ènte** *m* being; entity; corporation; agency, body
**enterocli·sma** *m* (**-smi**) enema
**enti·tà** *f* (**-tà**) entity; value, importance
**entomologìa** *f* entomology
**entram·bi -be** *adj*—**entrambi i** both || *pron* both
**entrante** *adj* next (*e.g., week*)
**entrare** (**éntro**) *intr* (ESSERE) to enter; to go (*said of numbers*); to set (*into one's head*); **entrarci** to make it, e.g., **con questi soldi non c'entro** I can't make it with this money; **entrarci come i cavoli a merenda** to be completely out of line; **entrare a** to begin to; **entrare in** to enter (*e.g., a room*); to fit in; to go in (*said of a number*); to get into (*one's head*); **entrare in amore** to be in heat (*said of animals*); **entrare in ballo** to come into play; **entrare in carica** to take up one's duties; **entrare in collera** to get angry; **entrare in collisione** to collide; **entrare in contatto** to establish contact; **entrare in gioco** to come into play; **entrare in guerra** to go to war; **entrare in società** to make one's debut; **entrare nella parte di** (theat)

to play the role of; **entrare in vigore** to become effective; **Lei non c'entra** this is none of your business; **questo non c'entra** this is beside the point
**entrata** *f* entry; entrance; **entrata di favore** (theat) complimentary ticket; **entrate** income
**entratura** *f* entry; entrance; assumption (*of a position*); familiarity
**éntro** *adv* inside || *prep* within; **entro di** within, inside of
**entrobórdo** *m* inboard motorboat
**entrotèrra** *f* inland, hinterland
**entusiasmare** *tr* to carry away, enthuse || *ref* to be carried away, to become enthused
**entusiasmo** *m* enthusiasm
**entusia·sta -sti -ste** *adj* enthusiastic || *mf* enthusiast, devotee
**entusiàsti·co -ca** *adj* (**-ci -che**) enthusiastic
**enucleare** (**enùcleo**) *tr* to elucidate; (surg) to remove
**enumerare** (**enùmero**) *tr* to enumerate
**enumerazióne** *f* enumeration
**enunciare** §128 *tr* to enunciate, state
**enunciati·vo -va** *adj* (gram) declarative
**enunciazióne** *f* enunciation, statement
**enzi·ma** [dz] *m* (**-mi**) enzyme
**èpa** *f* (lit) belly, paunch
**epàti·co -ca** *adj* (**-ci -che**) hepatic, liver
**epatite** *f* (pathol) hepatitis
**epènte·si** *f* (**-si**) epenthesis
**eperlano** *m* (ichth) smelt
**èpi·co -ca** *adj & f* (**-ci -che**) epic
**epicurè·o -a** *adj & m* epicurean
**epidemìa** *f* epidemic
**epidèmi·co -ca** *adj* (**-ci -che**) epidemic (al)
**epidèrmi·co -ca** *adj* (**-ci -che**) epidermal; (fig) superficial, skin-deep
**epidèrmide** *f* epidermis
**Epifanìa** *f* Epiphany
**epiglòttide** *f* (anat) epiglottis
**epigono** *m* follower; descendant
**epigrafe** *f* epigraph
**epigram·ma** *m* (**-mi**) epigram
**epigrammàti·co -ca** *adj* (**-ci -che**) epigrammatic
**epilessìa** *f* (pathol) epilepsy
**epilètti·co -ca** *adj & m* (**-ci -che**) epileptic
**epìlo·go** *m* (**-ghi**) epilogue; conclusion
**episcopale** *adj* episcopal
**episcopalia·no -na** *adj & mf* Episcopalian
**episcopato** *m* episcopate, bishopric
**episòdi·co -ca** *adj* (**-ci -che**) episodic
**episò·dio** *m* (**-di**) episode
**epìstola** *f* epistle
**epistolà·rio** *m* (**-ri**) letters, correspondence
**epitàf·fio** *m* (**-fi**) epitaph
**epitè·lio** *m* (**-li**) epithelium
**epìteto** *m* epithet; insult
**epitomare** (**epìtomo**) *tr* to epitomize
**epìtome** *f* epitome
**èpo·ca** *f* (**-che**) epoch; period; moment; **fare epoca** to be epoch-making
**epopèa** *f* epic
**eppure** *conj* yet, and yet
**epsomite** *f* Epsom salt

**epurare** *tr* to cleanse; to purge
**epurazióne** *f* purification; purge
**equànime** *adj* calm, composed; impartial
**equanimità** *f* equanimity; impartiality
**equatóre** *m* equator
**equatoriale** *adj & m* equatorial
**equazióne** *f* equation
**equèstre** *adj* equestrian
**equilàte·ro -ra** *adj* equilateral
**equilibrare** *tr* to balance; (aer) to trim ‖ *ref* to balance one another
**equilibra·to -ta** *adj* level-headed
**equilibra·tóre -trice** *adj* stabilizing ‖ *m* (aer) horizontal stabilizer
**equili·brio** *m* (-bri) equilibrium, balance; (fig) proportion; **equilibrio politico** balance of power
**equilibri·sta** *mf* (-sti -ste) acrobat, equilibrist
**equi·no -na** *adj & m* equine
**equinoziale** *adj* equinoctial
**equinò·zio** *m* (-zi) equinox
**equipaggiaménto** *m* equipment, outfit
**equipaggiare** §290 *tr* to equip, outfit; (naut) to fit out; (naut) to man
**equipàg·gio** *m* (-gi) equipage; (naut) crew, complement; (sports) team; (rowing) crew
**equiparare** *tr* to equalize (*e.g., salaries*)
**équipe** *f* team
**equipollènte** *adj* equivalent
**equi·tà** *f* (-tà) equity, fair-mindedness
**equitazióne** *f* horsemanship
**equivalènte** *adj & m* equivalent
**equivalére** §278 *intr* (ESSERE & AVERE) —**equivalere a** to be equivalent to ‖ *ref* to be equal
**equivocare** §197 (equìvoco) *intr*—**equivocare su** to mistake, misunderstand
**equìvo·co -ca** (-ci -che) *adj* equivocal; ambiguous ‖ *m* misunderstanding
**è·quo -qua** *adj* equitable, fair
**èra** *f* era, age; **era spaziale** space age
**erà·rio** *m* (-ri) treasury
**èrba** *f* grass; **erba limoncina** lemon verbena; **erba medica** alfalfa; **erbe** vegetables; **erbe aromatiche** herbs; **far l'erba** to cut the grass; **in erba** (fig) budding; **metter a erba** to put to pasture
**erbàc·cia** *f* (-ce) weed
**erbaggi** *mpl* vegetables
**erbaiò·lo -la** *mf* fresh vegetable retailer
**erbici·da** *m* (-di) weed-killer
**erbivéndo·lo -la** *mf* fresh fruit and vegetable retailer
**erbìvo·ro -ra** *adj* herbivorous
**erbori·sta** *mf* (-sti -ste) herbalist
**erbó·so -sa** [s] *adj* grassy
**Èrcole** *m* Hercules
**ercùle·o -a** *adj* Herculean
**erède** *m* heir ‖ *f* heiress
**eredi·tà** *f* (-tà) inheritance; heredity
**ereditare** (erèdito) *tr* to inherit
**eredità·rio -ria** *adj* (-ri -rie) hereditary; crown (*prince*)
**ereditièra** *f* heiress
**eremi·ta** *m* (-ti) hermit
**eremitàg·gio** *m* (-gi) hermitage
**èremo** *m* hermitage
**eresìa** *f* heresy

**eresiar·ca** *m* (-chi) heretic
**erèti·co -ca** (-ci -che) *adj* heretical ‖ *mf* heretic
**erèt·to -ta** *adj* erect, straight
**erezióne** *f* erection
**ergastola·no -na** *mf* lifer
**ergàstolo** *m* life imprisonment; prison for persons sentenced to life imprisonment
**èrgere** §164 *tr* (lit) to erect; (lit) to lift ‖ *ref* to rise (*said, e.g., of a mountain*)
**èrgo** *m* *invar*—**venire all'ergo** to come to a conclusion ‖ *adv* thus, hence
**èri·ca** *f* (-che) heather
**erìgere** §152 *tr* to erect, build ‖ *ref* to rise; **erigersi a** to set oneself up as
**eritrè·o -a** *adj & mf* Eritrean
**ermafrodi·to -ta** *adj & m* hermafrodite
**ermellino** *m* ermine
**ermèti·co -ca** *adj* (-ci -che) airtight; watertight; hermetic
**èrnia** *f* hernia; **ernia del disco** (pathol) herniated disk
**eródere** §239 *tr* to erode
**eròe** *m* hero
**erogare** §209 (èrogo) *tr* to distribute; to bestow
**erogazióne** *f* distribution; bestowal
**eròi·co -ca** *adj* (-ci -che) heroic
**eroicòmi·co -ca** *adj* (-ci -che) mock-heroic
**eroina** *f* heroine; (pharm) heroin
**eroismo** *m* heroism
**erómpere** §240 *intr* to erupt, burst out
**erosióne** *f* erosion
**eròti·co -ca** *adj* (-ci -che) erotic
**erotismo** *m* eroticism
**èrpete** *m* (pathol) herpes, shingles
**erpicare** §197 (érpico) *tr* to harrow
**érpice** *m* harrow
**errabón·do -da** *adj* (lit) wandering
**errante** *adj* errant; wandering
**errare** (èrro) *intr* to wander; to err; (lit) to stray
**erra·to -ta** *adj* mistaken, wrong
**erròne·o -a** *adj* erroneous
**erróre** *m* error, mistake; fault; (lit) wandering; **errore di lingua** slip of the tongue; **errore di scrittura** slip of the pen; **errore di stampa** misprint; **errore giudiziario** miscarriage of justice; **salvo errore od omissione** barring error or omission
**ér·to -ta** *adj* arduous, steep; erect ‖ *f* arduous ascent; **all'erta** on the alert
**erudire** §176 *tr* to educate, instruct
**erudi·to -ta** *adj* erudite, learned ‖ *m* scholar, savant
**erudizióne** *f* erudition, learning
**eruttare** *tr* to belch forth (*e.g., lava*); to utter (*obscenities*) ‖ *intr* to belch
**erutti·vo -va** *adj* eruptive
**eruzióne** *f* eruption
**esacerbare** (esacèrbo) *tr* to embitter; to exacerbate ‖ *ref* to become embittered
**esagerare** (esàgero) *tr & intr* to exaggerate
**esagera·to -ta** *adj* exaggerated, excessive ‖ *mf* exaggerator
**esagerazióne** *f* exaggeration

esagitare (esàgito) *tr* to perturb
esàgono *m* hexagon
esalare *tr* to exhale; esalare l'ultimo respiro to breathe one's last || *intr* to spread (*said of odors*)
esalazióne *f* exhalation; fume, vapor
esaltare *tr* to exalt; to excite || *ref* to glorify oneself; to become excited
esalta•to -ta *adj* frenzied, excited || *mf* hothead
esame *m* examination; checkup, test; dare gli esami to take an examination; esame attitudinale aptitude test; esame del sangue blood test; esame di riparazione make-up test; fare gli esami to prepare a test (*for a student*); prendere in esame to take in consideration
esàmetro *m* hexameter
esaminan•do -da *mf* candidate; examinee
esaminare (esàmino) *tr* to examine; to test
esamina•tóre -trice *mf* examiner
esàngue *adj* bloodless; (fig) pale
esànime *adj* lifeless
esasperante *adj* exasperating
esasperare (esàspero) *tr* to exasperate || *ref* to become exasperated
esasperazióne *f* exasperation
esattézza *f* exactness; punctuality
esat•to -ta *adj* exact; punctual
esattóre *m* tax collector; bill collector
esattorìa *f* tax collector's office; bill collector's office
esaudire §176 *tr* to grant
esauriènte *adj* exhaustive; convincing
esauriménto *m* depletion (*e.g., of merchandise*); (pathol) exhaustion; (naut) drainage
esaurire §176 *tr* to exhaust; to play out (*e.g., a hooked fish*); to use up || *ref* to be exhausted; to be depleted; to be sold out
esauri•to -ta *adj* exhausted; depleted; sold out; out of print
esau•sto -sta *adj* exhausted; empty
esautorare (esàutoro) *tr* to deprive of authority; to discredit (*a theory*)
esazióne *f* exaction; collection
é•sca *f* (-sche) bait; punk (*for lighting fireworks*); tinder (*for lighting powder*): dare esca a to foment
escandescènza *f*—dare in escandescenze to fly off the handle
escava•tóre -trice *mf* excavator, digger || *m* excavator; escavatore a vapore steam shovel || *f* (mach) excavator
escavazióne *f* excavation
eschimése [s] *adj & mf* Eskimo
esclamare *tr & intr* to exclaim
esclamati•vo -va *adj* exclamatory; exclamation (*mark*)
esclùdere §105 *tr* to exclude; to keep or shut out
esclusióne *f* exclusion; a esclusione di with the exception of
esclusiva *f* sole right, monopoly; (journ) scoop
esclusivi•sta (-sti -ste) *adj* clannish; bigoted || *mf* bigot; (com) sole agent
esclusi•vo -va *adj* exclusive; intolerant, bigoted || *f* see esclusiva

esclu•so -sa *adj* excluded, excepted
escogitare (escògito) *tr* to think up, invent; to think out
escoriare §287 (escòrio) *tr & ref* to skin
escoriazióne *f* abrasion
escreménto *m* excrement
escrescènza *f* excrescence
escrè•to -ta *adj* excreted || *m* excreta
escursióne *f* excursion; (mach) sweep; (mil) transfer; escursione termica (meteor) temperature range
escursioni•sta *mf* (-sti -ste) excursionist, sightseer
escussióne *f* (law) examination, cross-examination
esecrare (esècro) *tr* to execrate
esecrazióne *f* execration
esecuti•vo -va *adj & m* executive
esecu•tóre -trice *mf* (mus) performer || *m* executor; esecutore di giustizia executioner || *f* executrix
esecuzióne *f* accomplishment, completion; performance; execution; esecuzione capitale capital punishment
esegè•si *f* (-si) exegesis
eseguire (eséguo) & §176 *tr* to execute, carry out; to perform
esèm•pio *m* (-pi) example; a mo' d'esempio as an illustration; dare il buon esempio to set a good example; per esempio for instance
esemplare *adj* exemplary || *m* copy; specimen || *v* (esèmpio) *tr* (lit) to copy
esemplificare §197 (esemplìfico) *tr* to exemplify
esentare (esènto) *tr* to exempt
esènte *adj* exempt, free
esenzióne *f* exemption
esèquie *fpl* obsequies, funeral rites
esercènte *adj* practicing || *mf* dealer, merchant
esercire §176 *tr* to practice; to run (*a store*)
esercitare (esèrcito) *tr* to exercise; to tax (*e.g., s.o.'s patience*); to practice, ply (*a trade*); to wield (*e.g., power*) || *ref* to practice
esercitazióne *f* exercise, training; esercitazioni militari drilling
esèrcito *m* army; (fig) flock; Esercito della Salvezza Salvation Army
esercì•zio *m* (-zi) exercise; practice; training; homework; occupation; drill; d'esercizio (com) administrative (*expenses*); esercizio finanziario fiscal year; esercizio provvisorio (law) emergency appropriation; esercizio pubblico establishment open to the public; esercizio spirituale (eccl) retreat
esibire §176 *tr* to exhibit || *ref* to show oneself, appear; esibirsi di to offer to
esibizióne *f* exhibition
esigènte *adj* demanding, exigent
esigènza *f* demand, requirement, exigency
esìgere §165 *tr* to demand; to require; to exact; to collect
esigìbile *adj* due; collectable
esigui•tà *f* (-tà) meagerness, scantiness
esì•guo -gua *adj* meager, scanty

**esilarante** *adj* exhilarating; laughing (gas)

**esilarare (esìlaro)** *tr* to amuse ‖ *ref* to be amused

**èsile** *adj* slender, thin; weak

**esiliare** §287 *tr* to exile ‖ *ref* to go into exile; to withdraw

**esilia·to -ta** *adj* exiled ‖ *m* exile (*person*)

**esì·lio** *m* (-**li**) exile, banishment

**esìmere** §166 *tr* to exempt ‖ *ref*—**esimersi da** to avoid (*an obligation*)

**esì·mio -mia** *adj* (-**mi -mie**) distinguished, eminent

**-èsi·mo -ma** *suf adj & pron* -eth, e.g., **ventesimo** twentieth; -th, e.g., **diciannovesimo** nineteenth

**esistènte** *adj* existent; extant

**esistènza** *f* existence

**esistenzialismo** *m* existentialism

**esìstere** §114 *intr* (ESSERE) to exist

**esitante** *adj* hesitant

**esitare (èsito)** *tr* to retail ‖ *intr* to hesitate; (med) to resolve itself

**esitazióne** *f* hesitation; haw (*in speech*)

**èsito** *m* result, outcome; sale; outlet; (philol) late form; **dare esito a** (com) to reply

**esiziale** *adj* ruinous, fatal

**èsodo** *m* exodus, flight

**esòfa·go** *m* (-**gi**) esophagus

**esonerare (esònero)** *tr* to exempt, release

**esònero** *m* exemption, release

**Esòpo** *m* Aesop

**esorbitante** *adj* exorbitant

**esorbitare (esòrbito)** *intr*—**esorbitare da** to go beyond

**esorcismo** *m* exorcism

**esorcizzare** [ddzz] *tr* to exorcise

**esordiènte** *adj* beginning, budding ‖ *mf* beginner ‖ *f* debutante

**esòr·dio** *m* (-**di**) beginning

**esordire** §176 *intr* to make a start; (theat) to debut; (theat) to open

**esortare (esòrto)** *tr* to exhort

**esortazióne** *f* exhortation

**esò·so -sa** *adj* greedy, avaricious; hateful; exorbitant (*price*)

**esòti·co -ca** *adj* (-**ci -che**) exotic

**esotismo** *m* exoticism; borrowing (*from a foreign language*)

**espàndere** §167 *tr* to expand ‖ *ref* to spread out; to confide

**espansióne** *f* expansion; effusiveness

**espansionismo** *m* expansionism

**espansivi·tà** *f* (-**tà**) effusiveness

**espansi·vo -va** *adj* expansive; effusive

**espan·so -sa** *adj* flared; expanded, dilated

**espatriare** §287 *intr* to emigrate

**espà·trio** *m* (-**tri**) emigration

**espediènte** *m* expedient, makeshift; ruse; **vivere di espedienti** to live by one's wits

**espedire** §176 *tr* to expedite ‖ *ref*—**espedirsi di** to get rid of

**espèllere** §168 *tr* to expel, eject

**esperiènza** *f* experience; experiment

**esperiménto** *m* experiment; test

**espèr·to -ta** *adj & m* expert

**espettorare (espèttoro)** *tr & intr* to expectorate

**espiare** §119 *tr* to expiate; to placate (*the gods*); **espiare una pena** to serve a sentence

**espiató·rio -ria** *adj* (-**ri -rie**) expiatory

**espiazióne** *f* expiation

**espirare** *tr & intr* to breath out, to exhale

**espirazióne** *f* exhaling

**espletare (esplèto)** *tr* to dispatch, complete

**esplicare** §197 (**èsplico**) *tr* to carry out; (lit) to explain

**esplicati·vo -va** *adj* explanatory

**esplici·to -ta** *adj* explicit

**esplòdere** §169 *tr* to shoot; to fire (*a shot*) ‖ *intr* (ESSERE & AVERE) to explode; to burst forth

**esploditóre** *m* blasting machine

**esplorare (esplòro)** *tr* to explore; to search, probe; (telv) to scan

**esplora·tóre -trice** *mf* explorer ‖ *m* (nav) gunboat; **giovane esploratore** boy scout

**esplorazióne** *f* exploration; (telv) scanning

**esplosióne** *f* explosion, blast; (fig) outburst

**esplosi·vo -va** *adj & m* explosive

**esponènte** *adj* (typ) superior ‖ *m* spokesman; dictionary entry; catchword (*of dictionary*); (math) exponent; (naut) net weight

**espórre** §218 *tr* to expose, show; to expound; to abandon (*a baby*); to lay out (*a corpse*); to lay open (*to danger*) ‖ *intr* to show, exhibit ‖ *ref* to expose oneself

**esportare (espòrto)** *tr* to export

**esporta·tóre -trice** *mf* exporter

**esportazióne** *f* export, exportation

**esposìmetro** *m* exposure meter

**esposi·tóre -trice** *mf* commentator; exhibitor

**esposizióne** *f* exposition; abandonment (*of a baby*); exhibit, fair; line (*of credit*); exposure (*of a house*); (phot) exposure

**espó·sto -sta** *adj* exposed; aforementioned ‖ *m* petition, brief; foundling

**espressióne** *f* expression; feeling

**espressi·vo -va** *adj* expressive

**esprès·so -sa** *adj* manifest; express; prepared on the spot ‖ *m* espresso; messenger; special-delivery letter; special-delivery stamp

**esprìmere** §131 *tr* to express; to convey (*an opinion*); (lit) to squeeze ‖ *ref* to express oneself

**espropriare** §287 (**espròprio**) *tr* to expropriate ‖ *ref* to deprive onself; **espropriarsi di** to divest oneself of

**esprò·prio** *m* (-**pri**) expropriation

**espugnare** *tr* to take by storm

**espulsióne** *f* expulsion; (mach) ejection

**espulsóre** *m* ejector

**espurgare** §209 *tr* to expurgate

**éssa** §5 *pron pers* she; it

**ésse** §5 *pron pers* they

**essènza** *f* essence

**essenziale** *adj* essential ‖ *m* main point

**èssere** *m* being; existence; condition; (coll) character; **in essere** in good shape ‖ §170 *intr* (ESSERE) to be;

c'è there is; **ci sono** there are; **ci sono! I** get it!; **come sarebbe a dire?** what do you mean?; **come se nulla fosse** as if nothing had happened; **esserci** to have arrived, to be there; **essere di** to belong to; **essere per** to be about to; **può essere** maybe; **sarà** maybe; **sia . . . sia** both . . . and; whether . . . or ‖ *aux* (ESSERE) (to form passive) to be, e.g., **fu investito da un tassametro** he was run over by a taxi; (to form the compound tenses of certain intransitive verbs and all reflexive verbs) to have, e.g., **sono arrivati** they have arrived; **mi sono appena alzato** I have just got up ‖ *impers* (ESSERE) to be, e.g., **è giusto** it is fair

**éssi** §5 *pron pers* they
**essiccare** §197 *tr* to dry ‖ *ref* to dry up
**essicca·tóio** *m* (-tói) drier
**essiccazióne** *f* drying
**èsso** §5 *pron pers* he; it; **chi per esso** his representative
**essudare** *intr* to exude
**èst** *m* east
**èsta·si** *f* (-si) ecstasy; **andare in estasi** to become enraptured
**estasiare** §287 *tr* to enrapture, delight ‖ *ref* to become enraptured
**estate** *f* summer
**estàti·co** -ca *adj* (-ci -che) ecstatic, enraptured
**estemporàne·o** -a *adj* extemporaneous
**estèndere** §270 *tr* to extend; to broaden (*e.g., one's knowledge*); to draw up (*a document*) ‖ *ref* to extend
**estensìbile** *adj* applicable; **inviare saluti estensibili a** to send greetings to be extended to (*e.g., another person*)
**estensióne** *f* extension; extent; expanse (*e.g., of water*); (mus) compass, range
**estensi·vo** -va *adj* extensive
**estèn·so** -sa *adj*—**per esteso** fully
**estensóre** *adj* extensible ‖ *m* compiler (*e.g., of a dictionary*); (sports) exerciser, chest expander
**estenuante** *adj* exhausting
**estenuare** (estènuo) *tr* to exhaust ‖ *ref* to become exhausted
**esterióre** *adj* exterior ‖ *m* outside appearance
**esteriori·tà** *f* (-tà) appearance
**esternare** (estèrno) *tr* to reveal, manifest ‖ *ref* to confide
**estèr·no** -na *adj* external; outside; day (*student*) ‖ *m* exterior, outside; (baseball) outfielder; **all'esterno** outside; **in esterno** (mov) on location
**èste·ro** -ra *adj* foreign ‖ *m* foreign countries; **all'estero** abroad
**esterrefat·to** -ta *adj* terrified
**esté·so** -sa [s] *adj* extended, wide; **per esteso** in full
**estè·ta** *mf* (-ti -te) aesthete
**estèti·co** -ca (-ci -che) *adj* aesthetic ‖ *f* aesthetics
**esteti·sta** *mf* (-sti -ste) beautician
**estima·tóre** -trice *mf* appraiser; admirer
**èstimo** *m* appraisal; assessment
**estìnguere** §156 *tr* to extinguish; to quench (*thirst*); to pay off (*a debt*) ‖ *ref* to die out

**estinguìbile** *adj* extinguishable; payable
**estìn·to** -ta *adj* extinguished; extinct ‖ *m* deceased, dead person
**estintóre** *m* fire extinguisher
**estirpare** *tr* to uproot; to eradicate; to pull (*a tooth*)
**estirpa·tóre** -trice *mf* eradicator ‖ *m* (agr) weeder
**estivare** *tr* & *intr* to summer
**esti·vo** -va *adj* summer; summery
**estòllere** §171 *tr* to extol
**èstone** *adj* & *mf* Estonian
**estòrcere** §272 *tr* to extort; **estorcere qlco a qlcu** to extort s.th from s.o.
**estorsióne** *f* extortion
**estradare** *tr* (law) to extradite
**estradizióne** *f* extradition
**estràne·o** -a *adj* extraneous, foreign; aloof ‖ *mf* outsider
**estrapolare** (estràpolo) *tr* to extrapolate
**estrarre** §273 *tr* to extract, draw; to pull (*a tooth*)
**estrat·to** -ta *adj* extracted ‖ *m* extract; abstract; certified copy; (typ) offprint; **estratto conto** bank statement; **estratto dell'atto di nascita** copy of one's birth certificate
**estrazióne** *f* extraction; drawing (*of lottery*)
**estrèma** *f* (sports) wing, end
**estremi·sta** *adj* & *mf* (-sti -ste) extremist
**estremi·tà** *f* (-tà) end; tip, top; extremity; **le estremità** the extremities
**estrè·mo** -ma *adj* extreme; **esalare l'estremo respiro** to breath one's last ‖ *m* extremity; end, extreme; **essere agli estremi** to be near the end; **estremi** essentials ‖ *f* see **estrema**
**estrìnse·co** -ca *adj* (-ci -che) extrinsic
**èstro** *m* horsefly; whim, fancy; inspiration; **estro venereo** heat (*of female animal*)
**estromèttere** §198 *tr* to oust, expel
**estró·so** -sa [s] *adj* fanciful, whimsical; inspired
**estrovèr·so** -sa or **estroverti·to** -ta *adj* & *mf* extrovert
**estrùdere** §190 *tr* to extrude
**estuà·rio** *m* (-ri) estuary
**esuberante** *adj* exuberant; buoyant
**esuberanza** *f* exuberance; buoyancy; **a esuberanza** abundantly
**esulare** (èsulo) *intr* (ESSERE & AVERE) to go into exile; **esulare da** to be alien to
**esulcerare** (esùlcero) *tr* to ulcerate on the surface; (fig) to exacerbate
**esulcerazióne** *f* superficial ulceration; (fig) exasperation, exacerbation
**èsule** *mf* exile (*person*)
**esultante** *adj* exultant, jubilant
**esultare** *intr* to exult
**esumare** *tr* to exhume; to revive (*e.g., a custom*)
**esumazióne** *f* exhumation; revival
**e·tà** *f* (-tà) age; **che età ha?** how old is he (or she)?; **ha la sua età** he (or she) is no longer a youngster; **l'età di mezzo** Middle Ages; **maggiore età** majority; **mezza età** middle age; **minore età** minority
**etamine** *f* cheesecloth
**ètere** *m* ether

etère·o -a *adj* ethereal
eternare (etèrno) *tr* to immortalize ‖ *ref* to become immortal
eterni·tà *f* (-tà) eternity
etèr·no -na *adj* eternal, everlasting ‖ *m* eternity; **in eterno** forever
eterodòs·so -sa *adj* heterodox
eterogène·o -a *adj* heterogeneous
èti·ca *f* (-che) ethics
etichétta *f* label; card (*e.g., of a library*); etiquette; **etichetta gommata** sticker
etichettare (etichétto) *tr* to label
èti·co -ca (-ci -che) *adj* ethical; consumptive ‖ *m* consumptive ‖ *f* see etica
etile *m* ethyl
etilène *m* ethylene
etìli·co -ca *adj* (-ci -che) ethyl
ètimo *m* etymon
etimologìa *f* etymology
etìope *adj & mf* Ethiopian
Etiòpia, l' *f* Ethiopia
etiòpi·co -ca *adj* (-ci -che) Ethiopian
etisìa *f* tuberculosis
ètni·co -ca *adj* (-ci -che) ethnic(al)
etnografìa *f* ethnography
etnologìa *f* ethnology
etru·sco -sca *adj & mf* (-schi -sche) Etruscan
ettàgono *m* heptagon
èttaro *m* hectare
ètte *m* (coll) particle, jot, whit, tittle
ètto or ettogrammo *m* hectogram
-étto -étta *suf adj* rather, e.g., **piccoletto** rather small; -ish, e.g., **rotondetto** roundish
ettòlitro *m* hectoliter
eucalipto *m* eucalyptus
eucaristìa *f* Eucharist
eufemismo *m* euphemism
eufonìa *f* euphony
eufòni·co -ca *adj* (-ci -che) euphonic
euforìa *f* euphoria
eufòri·co -ca *adj* (-ci -che) euphoric
eufuismo *m* euphuism
eugenèti·co -ca (-ci -che) *adj* eugenic ‖ *f* eugenics
eunu·co *m* (-chi) eunuch
europè·o -a *adj & mf* European
Euròpa, l' *f* Europe
eurovisióne *f* European television chain
eutanasìa *f* euthanasia
Èva *f* Eve
evacuaménto *m* evacuation
evacuare (evàcuo) *tr* to evacuate ‖ *intr* to evacuate; to have a bowel movement
evacuazióne *f* evacuation; bowel movement

evàdere §172 *tr* to evade; to complete (*a deal*); to answer (*a letter*); to execute (*orders*) ‖ *intr* (ESSERE) to flee, escape
evanescènza *f* evanescence; (rad) fading
evanescènte *adj* evanescent; vanishing
evangèli·co -ca *adj* (-ci -che) evangelic (al)
evangeli·sta *m* (-sti) evangelist
evangelizzare [ddzz] *tr* to evangelize; to campaign for; to subject to political propaganda
evaporare (evapóro) *tr & intr* to evaporate
evaporatóre *m* evaporator; humidifier
evaporazióne *f* evaporation
evasióne *f* evasion, escape; (com) reply; **dare evasione a** to complete (*an administrative matter*)
evasi·vo -va *adj* evasive
eva·so -sa *adj* escaped ‖ *m* escapee
evasóre *m* tax dodger
evenènza *f* eventuality, contingency; **nell'evenienza che** in the event (that); **per ogni evenienza** just in case
evènto *m* event; **eventi correnti** current events; **fausto** or **lieto evento** happy event
eventuale *adj* contingent
eventuali·tà *f* (-tà) eventuality
eversi·vo -va *adj* upsetting; destructive
evidènte *adj* evident; clear
evidènza *f* evidence; clearness; **mettersi in evidenza** to make oneself conspicuous; **tenere in evidenza** (com) to keep active
evirare *tr* to emasculate
evitare (èvito) *tr* to avoid, shun; **evitare qlco a qlcu** to spare s.o. s.th, to save s.o. from s.th
èvo *m* age, era; **evo antico** ancient times; **evo moderno** modern times; **medio evo** Middle Ages
evocare §197 (èvoco) *tr* to evoke
evoluire §176 *intr* (aer, nav) to maneuver
evolu·to -ta *adj* developed; progressive; modern
evoluzióne *f* evolution
evòlvere §115 *tr* to develop ‖ *ref* to evolve
evvi·va *m* (-va) cheer ‖ *interj* long live!, hurrah for!
èx *adj invar* ex-, e.g., **la sua ex moglie** his ex-wife; ex, e.g., **ex dividendo** ex dividend
ex li·bris *m* (-bris) bookplate
extraconiugale *adj* extramarital
extraeuropè·o -a *adj* non-European
ex vó·to *m* (-to) votive offering
eziologìa *f* etiology

# F

F, f ['effe] *m & f* sixth letter of the Italian alphabet
fa *m* (fa) (mus) F, fa
fabbisógno *m invar* need; requirement
fàbbri·ca *f* (-che) building, construction; factory, plant

fabbricante *mf* builder, manufacturer
fabbricare §197 (fàbbrico) *tr* to manufacture; to fabricate
fabbrica·to -ta *adj* built ‖ *m* building
fabbricazióne *f* building; erection; manufacturing; fabrication (*invention*)

**fabbro** *m* blacksmith; locksmith; (fig) master; **fabbro ferraio** blacksmith
**faccènda** *f* business, matter; **faccende domestiche** household chores
**faccendiè·re -ra** *mf* operator, schemer
**faccétta** *f* small face; face, facet
**facchinàg·gio** *m* (-gi) porterage; (fig) drudgery
**facchino** *m* porter; **lavorare come un facchino** to work like a slave
**fàc·cia** *f* (-ce) face; countenance; **avere la faccia di** to have the gall to; **di faccia a** opposite; **faccia da galeotto** (coll) gallows bird; **faccia tosta** cheek, gall; **in faccia a** in front of
**facciale** *adj* facial
**facciata** *f* façade; page; (fig) surface appearance
**face** *f* (lit) torch
**facè·to -ta** *adj* facetious
**facèzia** *f* pleasantry, banter; **scambiar facezie** to banter with each other
**fachiro** *m* fakir
**fàcile** *adj* easy; inclined; loose (*morals*); glib (*tongue*); **è facile** it is probable ‖ *m* something easy
**facili·tà** *f* (-tà) facility, ease; inclination; **facilità di pagamento** easy payments, easy terms; **facilità di parola** glibness
**facilitare** (**facìlito**) *tr* to facilitate; to grant (*credit*); to give (*easy terms*)
**facilitazióne** *f* facilitation; easy terms; cut rate
**facinoró·so -sa** [s] *adj* criminal ‖ *m* hoodlum, thug
**facoltà** *f* (-tà) faculty; power; school (*of a university*); **facoltà** *fpl* means, wealth
**facoltati·vo -va** *adj* optional
**facoltó·so -sa** [s] *adj* wealthy, affluent
**facóndia** *f* loquacity, gift of gab
**facón·do -da** *adj* loquacious
**facsìmi·le** *m* (-le) facsimile
**faènza** *f* faïence ‖ **Faenza** *f* Faenza
**fàg·gio** *m* (-gi) (bot) beech
**fagia·no -na** *mf* pheasant
**fagiolino** *m* string bean
**fagiòlo** *m* bean; (coll) sophomore; **andare a fagiolo a** (coll) to fit perfectly; **fagiolo bianco** lima bean
**fà·glia** *f* (-glie) (geol) fault
**fagòtto** *m* bundle; (mus) bassoon; **far fagotto** (coll) to pack up
**fàida** *f* vengeance, vendetta
**faìna** *f* stone marten
**falange** *f* phalanx
**fal·bo -ba** *adj* tawny
**falcata** *f* step, stride; bucking
**falce** *f* scythe; crescent (*of moon*); **falce messoria** sickle
**falcétto** *m* sickle
**falciare** §128 *tr* to mow
**falcia·tóre -trice** *mf* mower ‖ *f* mowing machine
**falcidiare** §287 *tr* to reduce; to cut down
**fal·co** *m* (-chi) hawk; **falco pescatore** osprey
**falcóne** *m* falcon
**falconerìa** *f* falconry

**falconière** *m* falconer
**falda** *f* band, strip; flake (*of snow*); gable (*of roof*); brim (*of hat*); foot (*of mountain*); slab (*of stone*); waist plate (*of armor*); hem (*of suit*); flounce (*of dress*); layer (*of rock*); flap, coattail; **falda della camicia** shirttail; **falde** straps (*to hold a baby*); **mettersi in falde** to wear tails
**falegname** *m* carpenter; cabinetmaker
**falegnamerìa** *f* carpentry; cabinetmaking; carpenter shop; woodworker shop
**falèna** *f* moth
**falla** *f* hole, leak; (archaic) fault
**fallace** *adj* fallacious, deceptive
**fallà·cia** *f* (-cie) fallacy
**fallare** *intr* & *ref* (lit) to be mistaken
**fallìbile** *adj* fallible
**fallimentare** *adj* bankrupt; ruinous
**falliménto** *m* bankruptcy; (fig) collapse, failure
**fallire** §176 *tr* to miss (*the target*) ‖ *intr* (ESSERE) to go bankrupt; to fail ‖ *intr* (AVERE) to be mistaken
**falli·to -ta** *adj* & *mf* bankrupt
**fallo** *m* error, fault; sin; flaw; phallus; (sports) penalty; (sports) foul; **cadere in fallo** to make the wrong move; to be mistaken; **cogliere in fallo** to catch in the act; **far fallo a** to fail, e.g., **gli faccio fallo** I fail him; **senza fallo** without fail
**fa·lò** *m* (-lò) bonfire
**falpa·là** *f* (-là) flounce, furbelow
**falsare** *tr* to falsify, alter; (lit) to forge
**falsari·ga** *f* (-ghe) guideline (*for writing*); model, pattern; **seguire la falsariga di** to follow in the footsteps of
**falsà·rio** *m* (-ri) forger; counterfeiter
**falsétto** *m* falsetto
**falsificare** §197 (**falsìfico**) to falsify; to forge, fake
**falsificazióne** *f* falsification; forgery; misrepresentation
**falsi·tà** *f* (-tà) falsehood; falsity
**fal·so -sa** *adj* false; wrong (*step*); assumed (*name*); bogus, counterfeit, fake (*money*); phony ‖ *m* falsehood; perjury; forgery; **commettere un falso** to perjure oneself; to commit forgery; **giurare il falso** to bear false witness; to perjure oneself
**fama** *f* fame; reputation; **cattiva fama** notoriety
**fame** *f* hunger; dearth; **aver fame** to be hungry; **avere una fame da lupo** to be as hungry as a wolf, to be as hungry as a bear; **morire di fame** to starve to death; to be ravenous
**famèli·co -ca** *adj* (-ci -che) starving, famished
**famigera·to -ta** *adj* notorious
**famìglia** *f* family; community; **di famiglia** intimate; **in famiglia** at home
**famì·glio** *m* (-gli) beadle, usher; hired man
**familiare** *adj* family; familiar, intimate; homelike ‖ *m* member of the family
**familiari·tà** *f* (-tà) familiarity; **avere familiarità con** to be familiar with

**familiarizzare** [ddzz] *tr* to familiarize
**famó·so -sa** [s] *adj* famous, illustrious
**fanale** *m* lamp, lantern; (rr) headlight;
  **fanale di coda** taillight
**fanalino** *m* small light; (aut) parking
  light; (aut) tail light
**fanàti·co -ca (-ci -che)** *adj* fanatic,
  fanatical ‖ *mf* fanatic
**fanatismo** *m* fanaticism
**fanatizzare** [ddzz] *tr* to make a fanatic
  of
**fanciulla** *f* girl; spinster; bride
**fanciullè·sco -sca** *adj* **(-schi -sche)**
  childish; children's
**fanciullézza** *f* childhood; (fig) infancy
**fanciulo·lo -la** *adj* childish; childlike
  ‖ *mf* child ‖ *m* boy ‖ *f* see **fanciulla**
**fandònia** *f* fib, tale, yarn
**fanèllo** *m* (orn) linnet; (orn) finch
**fanfara** *f* military band; fanfare
**fanfaróne** *m* braggart
**fangatura** *f* mud bath
**fanghìglia** *f* mud, slush
**fan·go** *m* **(-ghi)** mud; **fare i fanghi** to
  take mud baths
**fangó·so -sa** [s] *adj* muddy
**fannullo·ne -na** *mf* idler, loafer
**fanóne** *m* whalebone
**fantaccino** *m* infantryman, foot soldier
**fantascientìfi·co -ca** *adj* **(-ci -che)**
  science-fiction
**fantasciènza** *f* science fiction
**fantasìa** *f* fantasy, fancy, whim; (mus)
  fantasia; **di fantasia** fancy
**fantasió·so -sa** [s] *adj* fanciful; imaginative
**fanta·sma** *m* **(-smi)** ghost, spirit; phantom; **fantasma poetico** poetic fancy
**fantasticare** §197 **(fantàstico)** *tr* to
  imagine, dream up ‖ *intr* to daydream
**fantasticherìa** *f* imagination, daydream-
  ing
**fantàsti·co -ca** *adj* **(-ci -che)** fantastic ‖
  **fantastico** *interj* unbelievable!
**fante** *m* infantryman, foot soldier;
  (cards) jack; (obs) youth
**fanterìa** *f* infantry
**fantè·sca** *f* **(-sche)** (joc, lit) housemaid
**fantino** *m* jockey
**fantòc·cio** *m* **(-ci)** puppet
**fantomàti·co -ca** *adj* **(-ci -che)** ghostly;
  mysterious
**farabutto** *m* scoundrel, heel
**faraóna** *f* guinea fowl
**faraóne** *m* Pharaoh; (cards) faro
**farcire** §176 *tr* to stuff
**fardèllo** *m* bundle; burden; **far fardello**
  to pack one's bags
**fare** *m* doing; break *(of day)*; way *(of
  acting)*; **sul far della sera** at nightfall
  ‖ §173 *tr* to do; to make; to work;
  to take (*e.g., a walk, a step*); to take
  *(a sigh)*; to deal *(cards)*; to suffer
  *(hunger)*; to lead *(a good or bad life)*;
  to render *(service)*; to log (*e.g., 15
  m.p.h.*); to be, e.g., **tre volte tre fa
  nove** three times three is nine; to
  build (*e.g., a house*); to put together
  *(a collection)*; to prepare *(dinner)*;
  to say, utter *(a word)*; to have *(a
  dream)*; to give *(fruit)*; to pay *(atten-*

*tion)*; to play *(a role)*; to stir up
*(pity)*; to mention *(a name)*; **fare
il (or la)** to be a (*e.g., carpenter*);
**fare + inf** to have + *inf*, e.g., **gli
ho fatto . . .** I had him . . . ; to
make + *inf*, e.g., **il medico mi
fece . . .** the doctor made me . . .; to
have + *pp*, e.g., **farò fare . . .** I shall
have . . . done; **fare acqua** to leak,
to take in water; to get a supply of
water; (coll) to urinate; **fare a metà**
to divide in half; **fare a pugni** to come
to blows; **fare a tempo** to be on time;
**fare benzina** to buy gasoline; **fare
caldo a** to keep warm, e.g., **questa
coperta gli fa caldo** this blanket keeps
him warm; **fare carbone** to coal; **fare
. . . che** to have been . . . since, e.g.,
**fanno tre mesi che siamo in questa
città** it has been three months since
we have been in this city; **fare che +
subj** to see to it that + *ind*, e.g.,
**faccia che comincino a lavorare su-
bito** see to it that they begin to work
at once; **fare colpo** to make an impression; **fare corona a** to crown;
**fare cuore a** to encourage; **fare del
male a** to harm; **fare di + inf** to see
to it that + *ind;* **fare di tutto** to do
one's best; **fare festa a** to cheer; **fare
fiasco** to fail; **fare finta di** to pretend
to; **fare fronte a** to face, meet; **fare
fuoco su** to fire upon; **fare il gioco di**
to play into the hands of; **fare il
pappagallo** to parrot, ape; **fare il
pieno** to fill up *(with gasoline)*; **fare
la bocca a** to get used to; **fare la
calza** to knit; **fare la coda** to queue
up, line up; **fare la festa a** to kill;
**fare la guardia** to stand guard; **fare
la mano a** to get used to; **fare le cose
in famiglia** to wash one's dirty linen
at home; **fare le cose in grande stile**
to splurge; **fare legna** to gather firewood; **fare l'occhio** to become accustomed; **fare mente** to pay attention;
**fare onore a** to do honor to; **fare
paura a** to frighten; **fare sangue** to
bleed; **fare sapere a qlcu** to let s.o.
know; **fare scalo** (aer, naut) to make
a call; **fare sì che** to act in such a
way that; to see to it that; **fare silenzio** to keep silent; **fare specie a** to
amaze, e.g., **il tuo comportamento
gli fa specie** your behavior amazes
him; **fare tesoro di** to prize; **fare una
bella figura** to look good; to make a
fine appearance; **fare una mala figura**
to look bad; to make a bad showing;
**fare una malattia** (coll) to get sick;
**fare vela** to set sail; **fare venire** to
send for; **fare vigilia** to fast; **farla
corta** to cut it short; **farla franca**
to get off scot-free; **farla grossa** to
commit a blunder; **farne di cotte e di crude**,
to outwit; **farne di cotte e di crude**,
**farne di tutti i colori**, or **farne più
di Carlo in Francia** to engage in all
sorts of mischief; to paint the town
red; **non fare che + ind** to do nothing
but + *inf* ‖ *intr*—**averla a che fare
con** to have words with; to have to

deal with; **fare a coltellate** to have a fight with knives; **fare a girotondo** to play ring-around-the-rosy; **fare al caso di** to fit; to suit; **fare a meno di** to do without; **fare da** to serve as, e.g., **fare da cuscino** to serve as a pillow; **fare da cena** to fix dinner; **fare di cappello** to take one's hat off; **fare presto** to hurry; **fare per** to be just the thing for; **fare tardi** to be late || *ref* to become; to cut (*e.g.*, *one's hair*); to move, e.g., **farsi in là** to move farther; **farsi avanti** to come forward; **farsi beffe di** to make fun of; **farsi bello** to bedeck oneself; to dress up; **farsi bello di** to boast about; to appropriate; **farsi gioco di** to make fun of; **farsi le labbra** to put lipstick on; **farsi strada** to make one's way; **farsi una ragione di** to rationalize, explain to oneself; **farsi un baffo** to not give a hoot; **si fa giorno** it is getting light; **si fa tardi** it is getting late || *impers*—**che tempo fa?** what's the weather like?; **fa** ago, e.g., **alcune settimane fa** a few weeks ago; **fa estate** it is like summer; **fa fino** it is smart; **fa freddo** it is cold; **fa luna** there is moonlight, the moon is out; **fa nebbia** it is foggy; **fa notte** it is nighttime; it is dark; it is getting dark; **fa sole** it is sunny, the sun is out; **fa tipo** or **fa tono!** that's classy!; **non fa nulla** it doesn't matter, never mind
**farètra** *f* quiver
**farfalla** *f* butterfly; bow tie; (mach) butterfly valve; (coll) promissory note
**farfallóne** *m* large butterfly; blunder; Don Juan
**farfugliare** §280 *intr* to mumble, mutter
**farina** *f* flour; **farina d'avena** oatmeal; **farina di legno** sawdust; **farina di ossa** bone meal; **farina gialla** yellow corn meal
**farinàce·o -a** *adj* farinaceous || **farinacei** *mpl* flour-yielding cereals
**farinata** *f* porridge
**faringe** *f* pharynx
**faringite** *f* pharingitis
**farinó·so -sa** [s] *adj* floury; powdery (*snow*); crumbly, friable
**farisèo** *m* Pharisee; (fig) pharisee
**farmacèuti·co -ca** *adj* (**-ci -che**) pharmaceutical, drug
**farmacìa** *f* pharmacy; drugstore; medicine cabinet; **farmacia di guardia** or **di turno** drugstore open all night and Sunday
**farmaci·sta** *mf* (**-sti -ste**) pharmacist, druggist
**fàrma·co** *m* (**-ci** or **-chi**) remedy, medicine
**farneticare** §197 (**farnètico**) *intr* to rave
**farnèti·co -ca** (**-chi -che**) *adj* raving || *m* delirium; craze
**faro** *m* lighthouse, beacon; (aut) headlight; **faro retromarcia** (aut) back-up light
**farràgine** *f* hodgepodge
**farraginó·so -sa** [s] *adj* confused, mixed

**farsa** *f* farce; burlesque
**farsè·sco -sca** *adj* (**-schi -sche**) farcical, ludicrous
**farsétto** *m* sweater; (hist) doublet
**fascétta** *f* girdle; band; wrapper; clamp; **fascetta editoriale** advertising band (*of book*)
**fà·scia** *f* (**-sce**) band; belt; bandage; newspaper wrapper; **fascia del cappello** hatband; **fascia di garza** gauze bandage; **fascia elastica** abdominal supporter; (aut) piston ring; **fasce del neonato** swaddling clothes; **in fasce** newborn; **sotto fascia** in a wrapper
**fasciame** *m* (naut) planking; (naut) plating
**fasciare** §128 to bind; to bandage; to wrap; to surround
**fasciatura** *f* bandaging, dressing
**fascìcolo** *m* number, issue; pamphlet; file, dossier; (bb) fasciculus
**fascina** *f* fagot
**fascina·tóre -trice** *mf* charmer
**fàscino** *m* fascination, charm
**fà·scio** *m* (**-sci**) bundle; sheaf; bunch (*of flowers*); pencil or beam (*of rays*); fascist party
**fascismo** *m* fascism
**fasci·sta** *adj & mf* (**-sti -ste**) fascist
**fase** *f* phase, stage; (aut) cycle; (astr, elec, mach) phase
**fastèllo** *m* bundle, fagot
**fasti** *mpl* records, annals; notable events; (hist) Roman calendar
**fastì·dio** *m* (**-di**) annoyance; (coll) loathing, nausea; **avere in fastidio** to loathe; **dar fastidio a** to annoy; **fastidi** troubles, worries
**fastidió·so -sa** [s] *adj* annoying, irksome; irritable; (obs) disgusting
**fastì·gio** *m* (**-gi**) top, summit
**fa·sto -sta** *adj* (lit) propitious || *m invar* pomp, display || *mpl* see **fasti**
**fastó·so -sa** [s] *adj* pompous, ostentatious
**fata** *f* fairy; **buona fata** fairy godmother; **Fata Morgana** Fata Morgana (*mirage; Morgan le Fay*)
**fatale** *adj* fatal; inevitable; irresistible (*woman*)
**fatalismo** *m* fatalism
**fatali·sta** *mf* (**-sti -ste**) fatalist
**fatali·tà** *f* (**-tà**) fatality, fate
**fatalóna** *f* vamp
**fata·to -ta** *adj* fairy, enchanted; (lit) predestined
**fatì·ca** *f* (**-che**) fatigue, weariness; labor; **a fatica** with difficulty; **da fatica** draft (*e.g.*, *horse*); of burden (*beast*); **durar fatica a** + *inf* to have trouble in + *ger*
**faticare** §197 *intr* to toil; **faticare a** to be hardly able to
**faticó·so -sa** [s] *adj* burdensome, heavy; (lit) weary
**fatìdi·co -ca** *adj* (**-ci -che**) fatal
**fato** *m* fate, destiny
**fatta** *f* kind, sort; **essere sulla fatta di** to be on the trail of
**fattàc·cio** *m* (**-ci**) (coll) crime
**fattézze** *fpl* features

**fattìbile** *adj* feasible, possible

**fattispècie** *f*—**nella fattispecie** in this particular case

**fat·to -ta** *adj* made, e.g., **fatto a mano** handmade; broad (*daylight*); deep (*night*); ready-made (*e.g., suit*); **ben fatto** well-done; shapely; **esser fatto per** to be cut out for; **fatto di** made of; **venir fatto a** to happen, chance, e.g., **gli venne fatto d'incontrarmi** he happened to meet me || *m* fact; act, deed; feat; action; business, affair; **badare ai fatti propri** to mind one's own business; **cogliere sul fatto** to catch in the act; **dire a qlcu il fatto suo** to give s.o. a piece of one's mind; **fatto compiuto** fait accompli; **fatto d'arme** feat of arms; **fatto si è** the fact remains that; **in fatto di** concerning; as of; **sapere il fatto proprio** to know one's business; **venire al fatto** to come to the point || *f* see **fatta**

**fat·tóre -tóra** or **-toréssa** *mf* farm manager || *m* maker; factor; steward || *f* stewardess; manager's wife

**fattorìa** *f* farm; stewardship

**fattorino** *m* delivery boy, messenger boy; conductor (*of streetcar*)

**fattrice** *f* (zool) dam

**fattucchiè·re -ra** *mf* magician || *m* sorcerer || *f* sorceress, witch

**fattura** *f* preparation; workmanship; bill, invoice; (coll) witchcraft; (lit) creature

**fatturare** *tr* to adulterate; to invoice, bill

**fattura·to -ta** *adj* adulterated || *m* (com) turnover

**fatturi·sta** *mf* (**-sti -ste**) billing clerk

**fà·tuo -tua** *adj* fatuous

**fàuci** *fpl* jaws; (fig) mouth

**fàuna** *f* fauna

**fàuno** *m* faun

**fàu·sto -sta** *adj* propitious, lucky

**fau·tóre -trice** *mf* supporter, promoter

**fava** *f* broad bean; **pigliare due piccioni con una fava** to catch two birds with one stone

**favèlla** *f* speech; (lit) tongue

**favilla** *f* spark; **far** or **mandare faville** to sparkle

**favo** *m* honeycomb

**fàvola** *f* fable; tale; **favola del paese** talk of the town

**favoló·so -sa** [s] *adj* fabulous; mythical

**favóre** *m* favor; help; cover (*e.g., of night*); **a favore di** for the benefit of; **di favore** special (*price*); complimentary (*ticket*); **favore politico** patronage; **per favore** please; **per favore di** courtesy of

**favoreggiaménto** *m* abetting, support

**favoreggiare** §290 (**favoréggio**) *tr* to abet, support

**favoreggia·tóre -trice** *mf* abettor, supporter, backer

**favorévole** *adj* favorable; propitious

**favorire** §176 *tr* to favor; to accept; to oblige, accommodate; **favorire qlcu di qlco** to oblige s.o. with s.th; **favorisca** + *inf* please + *inf*, be kind

enough to + *inf;* **favorisca alla cassa** please pay the cashier; **favorisca uscire!** please leave!; **tanto per favorire** just to keep you company; **vuol favorire?** won't you please join us (*at a meal*)?; please help yourself!

**favorita** *f* royal mistress

**favoritismo** *m* favoritism

**favori·to -ta** *adj* & *mf* favorite || *m* protegé; **favoriti** sideburns || *f* see **favorita**

**fazióne** *f* faction; **essere di fazione** to be on guard duty

**fazió·so -sa** [s] *adj* factious || *m* partisan

**fazzolétto** *m* handkerchief; **fazzoletto da collo** neckerchief

**fé** *f* var of **fede**

**feb·bràio** *m* (**-brài**) February

**fèbbre** *f* fever; fever blister; **febbre da cavallo** (coll) very high fever; **febbre da fieno** hay fever; **febbre dell'oro** gold fever

**febbricitante** *adj* feverish

**febbrile** *adj* feverish

**Fèbo** *m* Phoebus

**féc·cia** *f* (**-ce**) dregs; (fig) dregs (*of society*); **fino alla feccia** to the bitter end

**fèci** *fpl* feces

**fècola** *f* starch

**fecondare** (**fecóndo**) *tr* to fecundate

**fecondazióne** *f* fecundation; **fecondazione artificiale** artificial insemination

**fecondi·tà** *f* (**-tà**) fecundity

**fecón·do -da** *adj* fecund, prolific

**féde** *f* faith; certificate; wedding ring; faithfulness; **far fede** to bear witness; **in fede di che** in testimony whereof; **in fede mia!** upon my word! **prestar fede a** to put one's faith in; **tener fede alla parola data** to keep one's word

**fedecommésso** *m* fideicommissum; trusteeship

**fedéle** *adj* faithful, devoted || *mf* faithful person; **i fedeli** the faithful

**fedel·tà** *f* (**-tà**) faithfulness, allegiance; fidelity; **ad alta fedeltà** hi-fi

**fèdera** *f* pillowcase

**federale** *adj* federal

**federali·sta** *mf* (**-sti -ste**) federalist

**federati·vo -va** *adj* federative

**federa·to -ta** *adj* federate, federated

**federazióne** *f* federation; (sports) league

**Federico** *m* Frederick

**fedìfra·go -ga** *adj* (**-ghi -ghe**) unfaithful, treacherous

**fedina** *f* police record; **avere la fedina sporca** to have a bad record; **fedine** sideburns

**fégato** *m* liver; courage; **fegato d'oca** pâté de foie gras; **rodersi il fegato** to be consumed with rage

**félce** *f* fern

**feldspato** *m* feldspar

**felice** *adj* happy; blissful; glad; felicitous

**felici·tà** *f* (**-tà**) happiness; bliss

**felicitare** (**felìcito**) *tr* to make happy; **che Dio vi feliciti!** God bless you! ||

*ref* to rejoice; **felicitarsi con qlcu per qlco** to congratulate s.o. for or on s.th
**felicitazióne** *f* congratulation
**feli·no -na** *adj & m* feline
**fellóne** *m* (lit) traitor
**félpa** *f* plush
**felpa·to -ta** *adj* covered with plush; soft (*e.g., step*)
**féltro** *m* felt; felt hat
**felu·ca** *f* (-che) two-cornered hat; (naut) felucca
**fémmina** *adj & f* female
**femminile** *adj* feminine, female ‖ *m* feminine gender
**femminili·tà** *f* (-tà) femininity, womanliness
**femminismo** *m* feminism
**fèmore** *m* femur; thighbone
**fendènte** *m* slash with a sword
**fèndere** §174 *tr* to split, cleave; to plow (*water*); to rend (*air*); to make one's way through (*a crowd*) ‖ *ref* to split; to come apart
**fenditura** *f* split, breach, fissure
**fenice** *f* phoenix
**fení·cio -cia** (-ci -cie) *adj & mf* Phoenician ‖ **la Fenicia** Phoenicia
**fèni·co -ca** *adj* (-ci -che) carbolic
**fenicòttero** *m* flamingo
**fenòlo** *m* phenol
**fenomenale** *adj* phenomenal
**fenòmeno** *m* phenomenon; freak, monster; **essere un fenomeno** to be unbelievable
**ferace** *adj* (lit) fertile
**ferale** *adj* (lit) mortal, deadly
**fèretro** *m* bier, coffin
**feriale** *adj* working (*day*); weekday
**fèrie** *fpl* vacation; **ferie retribuite** vacation with pay
**ferire** §176 *tr* to wound; to strike; **senza colpo ferire** without striking a blow ‖ *ref* to wound oneself
**feri·to -ta** *adj* wounded, injured ‖ *m* wounded person; injured person; **i feriti** the wounded; the injured ‖ *f* wound, injury
**feritóia** *f* loophole; embrasure
**feri·tóre -trice** *mf* assailant
**férma** *f* setting (*of setter or pointer*); (mil) service; (mil) enlistment
**fermacarro** *m* (rr) buffer
**fermacar·te** *m* (-te) paperweight; large paper clip
**fermacravat·ta** *m* (-ta) tiepin
**fermà·glio** *m* (-gli) clasp; buckle; clip; brooch
**fermare** (**férmo**) *tr* to stop; to pay (*attention*); to fasten; to close, shut; to detain (*in police station*); to set (*game*); to reserve (*seats*) ‖ *ref* to stop; to stay
**fermata** *f* stop; **fermata a richiesta** or **facoltativa** stop on signal
**fermentare** (**ferménto**) *tr & intr* to ferment
**fermentazióne** *f* fermentation
**ferménto** *m* ferment
**fermézza** *f* firmness; steadfastness
**fér·mo -ma** *adj* firm; stopped; quiet (*water*); (fig) steadfast; **fermo in**

posta general delivery; **fermo restando che** seeing that; **stare fermo** to be quiet ‖ *m* stop; detention; **mettere il fermo a** to stop (*a check*)
**fermopòsta** *m* general delivery ‖ *adv* care of general delivery
**feróce** *adj* fierce; wild
**feró·cia** *f* (-cie) ferocity, ferociousness, fierceness
**feròdo** *m* (aut) brake lining
**ferragósto** *m* Assumption; mid-August holiday
**ferrame** *m* ironware
**ferramén·to** *m* (-ti) iron or metal bracket; iron or metal trimming ‖ *m* (-ta *fpl*)—**ferramenta** hardware
**ferrare** (**fèrro**) *tr* to shoe (*a horse*); to hoop (*a barrel*)
**ferra·to -ta** *adj* iron; ironclad; shod (*horse*); spiked (*shoe*); well-versed ‖ *f* pressing, ironing; mark or burn (*caused by ironing*); (coll) iron grate
**ferravèc·chio** *m* (-chi) scrap-iron dealer, junkman
**fèrre·o -a** *adj* iron; ironclad
**ferrièra** *f* ironworks; (obs) iron mine
**fèrro** *m* iron; tool; anchor; sword; **ai ferri** on the grill, broiled (*e.g., steak*); **essere sotto i ferri del chirurgo** to go under the knife; **ferri** shackles; **ferri del mestiere** tools of the trade; **ferro battuto** wrought iron; **ferro da arricciare** curling iron; **ferro da calza** knitting needle; **ferro da cavallo** horseshoe; **ferro da stiro** iron, flatiron; **ferro fuso** cast iron; **ferro grezzo** pig iron; **mettere a ferro e fuoco** to put to fire and sword; **venire ai ferri corti** to get into close quarters
**ferromodellismo** *m* hobby of model railroads
**ferrotranvièri** *mpl* transport workers
**ferrovia** *f* railroad; **ferrovia a dentiera** rack railway; **ferrovia sopraelevata** elevated railroad
**ferrovià·rio -ria** *adj* (-ri -rie) railroad
**ferrovière** *m* railroader
**fèrtile** *adj* fertile
**fertilizzante** [ddzz] *adj* fertilizing ‖ *m* fertilizer
**fertilizzare** [ddzz] *tr* to fertilize
**fervènte** *adj* fervent
**fèrvere** §175 *intr* to be fervent; to rage (*said, e.g., of a battle*); to go full blast
**fèrvi·do -da** *adj* fervent
**fervóre** *m* fervor; (fig) heat
**fervorino** *m* lecture, sermon
**fesserìa** *f* (slang) stupidity, nonsense; (slang) trifle
**fés·so -sa** *adj* cracked; cleft; (slang) dumb ‖ *m* (lit) cranny; **fare fesso qlcu** (slang) to play s.o. for a sucker
**fessura** *f* crack; cranny
**fèsta** *f* feast; holiday; birthday; saint's day; **a festa** festively; **buone feste!** happy holiday!; **conciare per le feste** to drub the daylights out of; **fare festa a** to welcome; **fare le feste** to spend the holidays; **far festa** to celebrate; to take the day off; **far la festa**

**a** to do in, kill; **festa del ceppo** Christmas; **festa da ballo** or **danzante** dancing party; **festa della mamma** Mother's Day; **festa del papà** Father's Day; **festa di precetto** (eccl) day of obligation; **festa nazionale** national holiday; **mezza festa** half holiday

**festante** *adj* cheerful

**festeggiaménto** *m* celebration

**festeggiare** §290 (**festéggio**) *tr* to celebrate, fete; to cheer

**festi·no -na** *adj* (lit) rapid || *m* party

**festivi·tà** *f* (-**tà**) festivity

**festi·vo -va** *adj* festive, holiday

**festóne** *m* festoon

**festó·so -sa** [s] *adj* cheerful, merry

**festu·ca** *f* (-**che**) straw; (fig) mote

**fetènte** *adj* stinking; stink (*bomb*) || *mf* (fig) stinker, louse

**fetíc·cio** *m* (-**ci**) fetish

**feticismo** *m* fetishism

**fèti·do -da** *adj* stinking, fetid

**fèto** *m* fetus

**fetóre** *m* stench

**fétta** *f* slice; **tagliare a fette** to slice

**fettina** *f* thin slice; twist (*of lemon*); **fettina di vitello** veal cutlet

**fettùc·cia** *f* (-**ce**) tape, ribbon

**fettuccine** *fpl* noodles

**feudale** *adj* feudal

**feudalismo** *m* feudalism

**feudatà·rio -ria** (-**ri -rie**) *adj* feudatory || *m* feudal vassal

**fèudo** *m* fief

**fiaba** *f* fairy tale; tale, yarn

**fiacca** *f* tiredness; sluggishness; **batter la fiacca** to loaf, to goof off

**fiaccare** §197 *tr* to weaken; to weary; to break || *ref* to weaken; to break (*e.g., one's neck*)

**fiacche·ràio** *m* (-**rài**) (coll) hackman, cabman

**fiacchézza** *f* weakness; sluggishness

**fiac·co -ca** *adj* (-**chi -che**) weak; sluggish; slack || *f* see **fiacca**

**fiàccola** *f* torch; **fiaccola della discordia** firebrand

**fiaccolata** *f* torchlight procession

**fiala** *f* vial, phial

**fiamma** *f* flame; blaze; (mil) insignia; (nav) pennant; **alla fiamma** (culin) flaming; **dare alle fiamme** to set on fire; **diventare di fiamma** to blush; **in fiamme** afire

**fiammante** *adj* blazing; **nuovo fiammante** brand-new

**fiammata** *f* blaze; flare-up

**fiammeggiante** *adj* flaming, blazing; (archit) flamboyant

**fiammeggiare** §290 (**fiamméggio**) *tr* to singe || *intr* to flame, blaze

**fiammìfero** *m* match

**fiammin·go -ga** (-**ghi -ghe**) *adj* Flemish; Dutch (*e.g., master*) || *mf* Fleming || *m* Flemish (*language*); (orn) flamingo

**fiancata** *f* blow with one's hip; dig, sarcastic remark; side, flank; (nav) broadside

**fiancheggiare** §290 (**fianchéggio**) *tr* to flank; to border (*a road*); to support

**fiancheggia·tóre -trice** *mf* supporter, backer

**fian·co** *m* (-**chi**) flank, side; hip; **di fianco** sideways; **fianco a fianco** side by side; **fianco destr'!** (mil) right face!; **fianco destro** (naut) starboard; **fianco sinistr'!** (mil) left face!; **fianco sinistro** (naut) port; **prestare il fianco a** to leave oneself wide open to; **tenersi i fianchi dal ridere** to split one's sides laughing

**Fiandre, le** *fpl* Flanders

**fia·sca** *f* (-**sche**) flask

**fiaschetterìa** *f* tavern, wine shop

**fia·sco** *m* (-**schi**) straw-covered wine bottle; flask; fiasco

**fiata** *f* (archaic) time

**fiatare** *intr* to breathe; **senza fiatare** without breathing a word

**fiato** *m* breath; (archaic) stench; **avere il fiato grosso** to be out of breath; **bere d'un fiato** to gulp down; **col fiato sospeso** holding one's breath; **dare fiato a** to blow, sound (*a trumpet*); **d'un fiato** or **in un fiato** without interruption; in one gulp; **fiati** (mus) winds; **senza fiato** out of breath

**fiatóne** *m*—**avere il fiatone** to be out of breath

**fibbia** *f* clasp, buckle

**fibra** *f* fiber

**fibró·so -sa** [s] *adj* fibrous

**ficcana·so** [s] *mf* (-**si** *mpl* -**so** *fpl*) (coll) busybody, meddler; nosy person

**ficcare** §197 *tr* to stick; to drive (*e.g., a nail*); to push; **ficcare gli occhi addosso a** to gaze at, stare at; **ficcare il naso negli affari degli altri** to poke one's nose in other people's business || *ref* to hide; to butt in; to get involved

**fi·co** *m* (-**chi**) fig; fig tree

**ficodìndia** *m* (*pl* **fichidindia**) prickly pear

**fidanzaménto** *m* engagement, betrothal

**fidanzare** *tr* to betroth || *ref* to become engaged

**fidanza·to -ta** *adj* engaged || *m* fiancé || *f* fiancée

**fidare** *tr* to entrust || *intr* to trust || *ref* to have confidence; **fidarsi a** (coll) to dare to; **fidarsi di** to trust, rely on

**fida·to -ta** *adj* trustworthy, reliable

**fi·do -da** *adj* (lit) faithful, trusted || *m* loyal follower; credit; **far fido to** extend credit

**fidùcia** *f* faith, confidence; (com) credit; **di fiducia** trustworthy

**fiducià·rio -ria** (-**ri -rie**) *adj* fiduciary || *mf* fiduciary, trustee

**fiducíó·so -sa** [s] *adj* confident, hopeful

**fièle** *m invar* gall, bile; acrimony

**fienile** *m* hayloft

**fièno** *m* hay

**fierìsti·co -ca** *adj* (-**ci -che**) of a fair, *e.g.,* **attività fieristica** activity of a fair

**fiè·ro -ra** *adj* fierce; dignified; proud || *f* fair; exhibit; wild beast

**fièvole** _adj_ feeble, weak

**fifa** _f_ (coll) scare; **avere la fifa** (coll) to be chicken; **avere una fifa blu** (coll) to be scared stiff

**fifó·ne -na** _mf_ (coll) scaredy-cat

**figgere** §104 _tr_ (lit) to drive, thrust ‖ _ref_—**figgersi in capo** to get into one's head

**figlia** _f_ daughter; (com) stub; **figlia consanguinea** stepdaughter on the father's side

**figliare** §280 _tr_ & _intr_ to whelp (_said of animals_)

**figlia·stro -stra** _mf_ stepchild ‖ _m_ stepson ‖ _f_ stepdaughter

**figliata** _f_ litter (_e.g., of pigs_)

**fi·glio -glia** _mf_ child, offspring ‖ _m_ son; **figli** children; **figlio consanguineo** stepson on the father's side ‖ _f_ see **figlia**

**figliòc·cio (-ci -ce)** _mf_ godchild ‖ _m_ godson ‖ _f_ goddaughter

**figliolanza** _f_ children, offspring

**figliò·lo -la** _mf_ child ‖ _m_ son, boy ‖ _f_ daughter, girl

**figura** _f_ figure; illustration; figurehead; face card; **far bella figura** to make a good showing; **far cattiva figura** to make a poor showing; **far figura** to look good; **figura retorica** figure of speech

**figurante** _mf_ (theat) extra, super

**figurare** _tr_ to feign; to represent ‖ _intr_ to figure; to appear; to make a good showing ‖ _ref_ to imagine; **si figuri!** imagine!

**figurati·vo -va** _adj_ (fa) figurative

**figura·to -ta** _adj_ figurative (_speech_); transcribed (_pronunciation_); illustrated (_book_)

**figurina** _f_ figurine; card, picture (_of a series of athletes or entertainment celebrities_)

**figurini·sta** _mf_ (-sti -ste) dress designer; costume designer

**figurino** _m_ fashion plate; fashion magazine

**figuro** _m_ scoundrel; gangster

**figuróne** _m_—**fare un figurone** to make a very good showing

**fila** _f_ row; file, line; series; **di fila in a row**; **fare la fila** to wait in line; **file ranks**

**filàc·cia** _f_ (-ce) lint

**filaccicó·so -sa** [s] or **filacció·so -sa** [s] _adj_ thready, stringy

**filaménto** _m_ filament

**filamentó·so -sa** [s] _adj_ thready, stringy; thread-like

**filanda** _f_ spinning mill; silk spinning mill

**filante** _adj_ spinning; shooting (_star_); thready; flowing (_e.g., line_)

**filantropía** _f_ philanthropy

**filantròpi·co -ca** _adj_ (-ci -che) philanthropic

**filàntro·po -pa** _mf_ philanthropist

**filare** _m_ row, line ‖ _tr_ to spin; to drip, ooze; to rest on (_one's oars_); to make (_e.g., ten knots_); (naut) to pay out; (mus) to hold (_a note_); **filare l'amore** to be in love ‖ _intr_ to spin (_said of a spider_); to rope, thread (_said of wine_

_or syrup_); to make sense; to drip; **fare filare dritto qlcu** to keep s.o. in line; **filare a to do** (_e.g., twenty miles an hour_); **filare all'inglese** to take French leave; **fila via!** (coll) get out!

**filarmòni·co -ca** (-ci -che) _adj_ philharmonic ‖ _f_ philharmonic society

**filastròc·ca** _f_ (-che) rigmarole; nursery rhyme

**filatelìa** _f_ philately

**filatèli·co -ca** (-ci -che) _adj_ philatelic(al) ‖ _mf_ philatelist

**fila·to -ta** _adj_ spun; well-constructed (_speech_) ‖ _m_ yarn

**fila·tóio** _m_ (-tói) spinning wheel

**filatura** _f_ spinning; spinning mill

**filettare (filétto)** _tr_ to fillet; (mach) to thread

**filettatura** _f_ stripe (_on a cap_); (mach) thread

**filétto** _m_ fillet; stripe; snaffle (_on a horse's bit_); fine stroke (_in handwriting_); (mach) thread; (typ) ornamental line, headband; (typ) rule

**filiale** _adj_ filial ‖ _f_ branch office

**filiazióne** _f_ filiation

**filibustière** _m_ filibuster, buccaneer; adventurer

**filièra** _f_ (mach) drawplate; (mach) die (_to cut threads_)

**filigrana** _f_ filigree; watermark (_in paper_)

**filippi·no -na** _adj_ Philippine ‖ _m_ Filipino ‖ **le Filippine** the Philippines

**Filippo** _m_ Philip

**filistè·o -a** _adj_ & _m_ philistine; Philistine

**Fìllide** _f_ Phyllis

**film** _m_ (film) film; movie, motion picture; **film parlato** or **sonoro** talking picture

**filmare** _tr_ to film

**filmina** _f_ filmstrip

**filmìsti·co -ca** _adj_ (-ci -che) movie, motion-picture

**filmotè·ca** _f_ (-che) film library

**fi·lo** _m_ (-li) thread; wire; yarn; blade (_of grass_); breath (_of air_); string (_of pearls_); edge (_of razor_); **dare del filo da torcere** to cause trouble; **essere ridotto a un filo** to be only skin and bones; **fil di voce** thin voice; **filo a piombo** plumb line; **filo d'acqua** thin stream; **filo della schiena** or **delle reni** spine; **filo spinato** barbed wire; **passare a fil di spada** to put to the sword; **per filo e per segno** in detail; from beginning to end; **senza fili** wireless; **stare a filo** to stand upright; **tenere i fili** (fig) to pull wires; **tenere in filo** to keep in line; **un filo di** a bit of ‖ _m_ (-la _fpl_) string (_e.g., of cooked cheese_); (archaic) file, row

**fìlo·bus** _m_ (-bus) trolley bus

**filodiffusióne** _f_ wired wireless; cable TV

**filodrammàti·co -ca** _adj_ & _mf_ (-ci -che) (theat) amateur

**filogovernati·vo -va** _adj_ on the government side

**filologìa** _f_ philology

**filòlo·go -ga** (-gi -ghe) _adj_ philologic(al) ‖ _m_ philologist

**filóne** _m_ vein (_of ore_); ripple (_of a cur-_

rent); stream; loaf (*of bread*); (lit) mainstream; **filone d'oro** gold lode

**filó·so -sa** [s] *adj* stringy

**filosofia** *f* philosophy

**filosòfi·co -ca** *adj* (**-ci -che**) philosophic(al)

**filòso·fo -fa** *mf* philosopher

**filovìa** *f* trolley bus line

**filtrare** *tr* to filter; to percolate (*coffee*) || *intr* to filter, permeate

**filtrazióne** *f* filtering, filtration

**filtro** *m* filter; philter

**filugèllo** *m* silkworm

**filza** *f* string (*of pearls*); series (*of errors*); row; dossier, file; basting (*of dress*)

**finale** *adj* final, last; consumer (*goods*) || *m* end, ending; (mus) finale; (sports) finish || *f* end, ending; (sports) finals

**finali·sta** *mf* (**-sti -ste**) finalist

**finali·tà** *f* (**-tà**) end, purpose

**finanche** *adv* even

**finanza** *f* finance

**finanziaménto** *m* financing

**finanziare** §287 *tr* to finance

**finanzià·rio -ria** (**-ri -rie**) *adj* finance, financial || *f* (com) holding company

**finanzia·tóre -trice** *mf* financial backer

**finanzièra** *f* frock coat; **alla finanziera** with giblet gravy

**finanzière** *m* financier; (coll) customs officer

**fin·ca** *f* (**-che**) column, row (*of ledger*)

**finché** *conj* until, as long as; **finché non** until

**fine** *adj* fine, thin; choice, nice || *m* end, purpose; conclusion; (lit) limit, border; **a fin di bene** to good purpose, for the best; **secondo fine** ulterior motive || *f* end, conclusion; **condurre a fine** to bring to fruition; **fine di settimana** weekend; **in fin dei conti** after all; **senza fine** endless

**fine-settima·na** *m* or *f* (**-na**) weekend

**finèstra** *f* window; (lit) gash, wound; **finestra a gangheri** casement window; **finestra a ghigliottina** sash window; **finestra panoramica** picture window; **finestre** (lit) eyes

**finestrino** *m* (aut, rr) window

**finézza** *f* thinness; delicacy; finesse; kindness

**fìngere** §126 *tr* to feign, pretend; (lit) to invent || *intr* to feign, pretend || *ref* to pretend to be

**finiménto** *m* finishing touch; **finimenti** harness

**finimóndo** *m* fracas, uproar

**finire** §176 *tr* to end; to put an end to; **finiscila!** cut it out! || *intr* (ESSERE) to end, to be over; to abut; to wind up; **finire con** + *inf* to wind up + *ger*; **finire di** + *inf* to finish + *ger*, e.g., **ho finito di farmi la barba** I have finished shaving

**fini·to -ta** *adj* finished; accomplished; finite; exhausted; **aver finito** to be through; **falla finita!** cut it out!; **farla finita con** to be through with; **farla finita con la vita** to end one's life

**finitura** *f* finish, finishing touch

**finlandése** [s] *adj* Finnish || *mf* Finlander, Finn || *m* Finnish (*language*)

**Finlàndia, la** Finland

**finni·co -ca** *adj & mf* (**-ci -che**) Finnic

**fi·no -na** *adj* fine, thin; refined; pure; sheer; **fare fino** (coll) to be refined || *adv* even; **fin a quando?** till when?; **fin da domani** beginning tomorrow; **fin da ora** beginning right now; **fin dove?** how far?; **fin in cima** up to the top; **fino a** until; down to; up to; as far as; **fin qui** up to now; up to this point

**finòc·chio** *m* (**-chi**) fennel; (vulg) fairy, queer

**finóra** *adv* up to now, heretofore

**finta** *f* pretense; fly (*of trousers*); (sports) feint; **far finta di** + *inf* to pretend to + *inf*, to feign + *ger*

**fintantoché** *conj* until

**fin·to -ta** *adj* false (*teeth*); fake; fictitious; sham (*battle*) || *mf* hypocrite || *f* see **finta**

**finzióne** *f* pretense; fiction; figment

**fio** *m*—**pagare il fio** to pay the piper; **pagare il fio di** to pay the penalty for

**fioccare** §197 (**fiòcco**) *intr* (ESSERE) to fall (*said of snow*); to flow (*said, e.g., of complaints*) || *impers* (ESSERE) —**fiocca** it is snowing

**fiòc·co** *m* (**-chi**) bow, knot; flake (*of snow*); flock, tuft (*of wool*); (naut) jib; **coi fiocchi** excellent; made to perfection; **fiocco pallone** (naut) spinnaker

**fioccó·so -sa** [s] *adj* flaky

**fiòcina** *f* harpoon

**fiò·co -ca** *adj* (**-chi -che**) feeble, faint

**fiónda** *f* sling; slingshot

**fio·ràio -ràia** (**-rài -ràie**) *mf* florist || *f* flower girl

**fiorami** *mpl*—**a fiorami** with flower design

**fiordaliso** *m* fleur-de-lis; (bot) iris; (lit) lily

**fiòrdo** *m* fjord

**fióre** *m* flower; prime (*of life*); best, pick; bloom; **a fior d'acqua** on the surface; skimming the water; **a fior di labbra** in a low tone, sottovoce; **a fior di pelle** skin-deep, superficial; **fior di** (coll) a lot of; **fiore di latte** cream; **fiori** (cards) clubs; **primo fiore** down (*soft hairy growth*)

**fiorènte** *adj* flourishing, thriving

**fiorenti·no -na** *adj & mf* Florentine

**fiorettare** (**fiorétto**) *tr* (fig) to overembellish

**fiorétto** *m* little flower; choice, pick; overembellishment; choice passage (*from life of saint*); foil; button of foil

**fioricoltóre** *m* var of **floricoltore**

**fioricoltura** *f* var of **floricoltura**

**fiorino** *m* florin

**fiorire** §176 *tr* to cause to flower; to adorn with flowers || *intr* (ESSERE) to flower, bloom; to flourish; to break out (*said of skin eruption*); to get moldy

**fiori·sta** *mf* (**-sti -ste**) florist

**fiori·to -ta** *adj* flowering; flowery;

mottled; moldy; studded (*e.g.*, *with errors*)

**fioritura** *f* flowering; flourish; mold; (pathol) eruption

**fiorrancino** *m* (orn) kinglet, firecrest

**fiorràn·cio** *m* (-ci) marigold

**fiòtto** *m* gush, surge; (obs) wave

**Firènze** *f* Florence

**firma** *f* signature; power of attorney; good reputation; (mil) enlisted man; **buona firma** famous writer; **farci la firma** (coll) to accept quite willingly; **firma di favore** guarantor's signature

**firmaiòlo** *m* (mil) enlisted man

**firmaménto** *m* firmament

**firmare** *tr* to sign

**firmatà·rio -ria (-ri -rie)** *adj* signatory || *mf* signer, signatory

**fisarmòni·ca** *f* (-che) accordion

**fiscale** *adj* fiscal, tax

**fischiare** §287 *tr* to whistle; to boo || *intr* to whistle; to ring (*said of ears*); to blow (*said, e.g., of a factory whistle*)

**fischiettare (fischiétto)** *tr* & *intr* to whistle

**fischiétto** *m* whistle (*instrument*)

**fì·schio** *m* (-schi) whistle; hiss, boo; blow (*of whistle*); ringing (*in the ears*)

**fì·sciù** *m* (-sciù) kerchief, fichu

**fisco** *m* *invar* treasury; internal revenue service

**fìsi·co -ca (-ci -che)** *adj* physical; bodily || *m* physicist; physique; (obs) physician || *f* physics

**fìsima** *f* whim, fancy, caprice

**fisiologìa** *f* physiology

**fisiològi·co -ca** *adj* (-ci -che) physiological

**fisionomìa** or **fisonomìa** *f* physiognomy; countenance, face; appearance

**fisionomì·sta** *mf* (-sti -ste) person good at faces; physiognomist

**fì·so -sa** *adj* (lit) fixed

**fissàg·gio** *m* (-gi) (phot) fixing

**fissare** *tr* to fix; to fasten; to gaze at; to reserve; to hire; **fissare lo sguardo** to gaze || *ref* to gaze, stare; to become obsessed; to settle down

**fissati·vo -va** *adj* fixing

**fissa·to -ta** *adj* fixed; (coll) cracked || *mf* (coll) crackpot

**fissa·tóre -trice** *adj* (phot) fixing || *m* fixer; **fissatore per capelli** hair spray; hair dressing

**fissazióne** *f* fixation; fixed idea

**fìssile** *adj* fissionable

**fissionàbile** *adj* fissionable

**fissióne** *f* fission

**fis·so -sa** *adj* fixed; regular || *m* pay

**fistola** *f* (pathol) fistula; (lit) pipe

**fitta** *f* pang, stitch; crowd; great amount; (coll) blow; (obs) quagmire

**fittàvolo** *m* tenant farmer

**fittì·zio -zia** *adj* (-zi -zie) fictitious

**fìt·to -ta** *adj* fixed, dug in; thick, dense; pitch (*dark*) || *m* thick; rent; tenancy || *f* see **fitta**

**fittóne** *m* (bot) taproot

**fiuma·no -na** *adj* river; from Fiume || *m* person from Fiume || *f* flood, stream

**fiumara** *f* torrent

**fiume** *m* river; **a fiumi** like a river

**fiutare** *tr* to snuff, sniff; to smell

**fiutata** *f* snuff, sniff

**fiuto** *m* sense of smell; snuff; flair

**flàcci·do -da** *adj* flabby

**flacóne** *m* flacon

**flagellare (flagèllo)** *tr* to scourge, lash, flagellate

**flagèllo** *m* whip, scourge; pest, plague; (coll) mess

**flagrante** *adj* flagrant; **in flagrante** (*delitto*) in the act

**flan** *m* (flan) pudding; (typ) mat

**flanèlla** *f* flannel

**flàn·gia** *f* (-ge) flange

**flato** *m* gas, flatus

**flatulènza** *f* flatulence

**flautino** *m* flageolet

**flautì·sta** *mf* (-sti -ste) flutist

**flàuto** *m* flute; **flauto diritto** or **dolce** (mus) recorder

**fla·vo -va** *adj* (lit) blond, golden

**flèbile** *adj* mournful

**flebite** *f* phlebitis

**flèmma** *f* apathy; coolness; phlegm

**flemmàti·co -ca** *adj* (-ci -che) phlegmatic(al)

**flessìbile** *adj* flexible, pliable

**flessióne** *f* bending; (com) fall, drop; (gram) inflection

**flessuó·so -sa** [s] *adj* lithe, willowy; winding; flowing (*style*)

**flèttere** §177 *tr* to flex; (gram) to inflect

**flirtare** *intr* to flirt

**flòra** *f* flora

**floreale** *adj* floral

**floricoltóre** *m* floriculturist

**floricoltura** *f* floriculture

**flòri·do -da** *adj* florid; flourishing

**flò·scio -scia** *adj* (-sci -sce) flabby; soft (*hat*)

**flòtta** *f* fleet

**flottante** *adj* floating || *m* (com) floating stock

**flottare (flòtto)** *tr* & *intr* to float

**flottìglia** *f* flottilla

**fluènte** *adj* flowing

**fluidità** *f* fluidity

**flùi·do -da** *adj* & *m* fluid; fluent (*style*)

**fluire** §176 *intr* (ESSERE) to flow; to pour

**fluitazióne** *f* log driving

**fluorescènte** *adj* fluorescent

**fluorescènza** *f* fluorescence

**fluorìdri·co -ca** *adj* (-ci -che) hydrofluoric

**fluorite** *f* fluor, fluorite

**fluorizzazióne** [ddzz] *f* fluoridation

**fluòro** *m* fluorine

**fluoruro** *m* fluoride

**flusso** *m* flow; flood (*of tide*); high tide; (pathol) flow (*e.g., of blood*); (phys) flux

**flutto** *m* (lit) wave

**fluttuare (flùttuo)** *intr* to fluctuate; to bob, toss; to waver; to surge, stream

**fluviale** *adj* fluvial, river

**fobìa** *f* phobia

**fò·ca** *f* (-che) seal; sealskin

**focàc·cia** *f* (-ce) flat, rounded loaf; cake

**focaccina** *f* bun

fo·càia *adj fem* (-càie) flint

focale *adj* focal

fóce *f* mouth (*of river*)

focèna *f* porpoise

fochi·sta *m* (-sti) fireman, stoker; fire-works manufacturer

foco·làio *m* (-lài) (pathol) focus; (fig) hotbed

focolare *m* hearth; firebox; fireside, home

focó·so -sa [s] *adj* fiery, high-spirited

fòdera *f* lining (*of suit*); cover, case

foderare (fòdero) *tr* to line; to cover

fòdero *m* sheath, scabbard; raft

fó·ga *f* (-ghe) ardor, impetus

fòg·gia *f* (-ge) fashion, shape; a foggia di shaped like

foggiare §290 (fòggio) *tr* to shape, fashion

fòglia *f* leaf; petal; foil (*of gold*); mangiare la foglia (fig) to get wise, catch on

fogliame *m* foliage

fò·glio *m* (-gli) sheet; bill, banknote; folio; newspaper; permit; foglio d'avviso notice; foglio di congedo (mil) discharge; foglio d'iscrizione application; foglio di via (mil) travel orders; foglio modello blank form; foglio rosa (aut) permit; foglio volante flier, handbill

fógna *f* sewer, drain

fognatura *f* sewerage

fòla *f* tale, fable

fola·ga *f* (-ghe) (zool) coot

folata *f* gust; (lit) flight (*of birds*)

folclóre *m* folklore

folgorante *adj* striking; flashing; meteoric (*career*)

folgorare (fólgoro) *tr* to strike (with lightning) || *intr* to flash by || *impers* —folgora it is thundering

fólgore *m* (lit) thunderbolt || *f* flash of lightning; thunderbolt

fólla *f* crowd; (fig) flock

follare (fóllo) *tr* to full

fòlle *adj* mad, crazy; (aut) neutral; (mach) loose (*pulley*)

folleggiare §290 (folléggio) *intr* to act foolishly; to frolic

folleménte *adv* desperately, madly

follétto *m* elf; little imp

follìa *f* madness, lunacy; folly; alla follia madly; far follie per to be crazy about

follìcolo *m* follicle

fól·to -ta *adj* thick; beetle (*brow*); deep (*night*) || *m* depth (*e.g., of the night*); thick (*e.g., of the battle*)

fomentare (foménto) *tr* to foment

fòmite *m* (lit) instigation; impetus

fónda *f* anchorage; lowland; saddlebag; alla fonda at anchor

fónda·co *m* (-chi) (hist) warehouse

fondale *m* depth (*of river, sea*); (theat) backdrop

fondamentale *adj* fundamental, basic

fondamén·to *m* (-ti) ground, foundation; basis; fare fondamento su to count on; fondamenti elements; senza fondamento baseless; without getting anywhere || *m* (-ta *fpl*)—fondamenta foundations (*of a building*)

fondare (fóndo) *tr* to found; to build; to charter || *ref*—fondarsi su to rely on; to be based upon

fondatézza *f* basis, ground, foundation

fonda·to -ta *adj* well-founded

fonda·tóre -trice *mf* founder

fondazióne *f* foundation

fondèllo *m* bottom, base

fondènte *m* flux

fóndere §178 *tr* to smelt; to melt; to blow (*a fuse*); to cast (*a statue*); to blend (*colors*) || *intr* to melt; to blend || *ref* to melt; to blend; to burn out

fonderìa *f* foundry

fondià·rio -ria (-ri -rie) *adj* real-estate, land || *f* real-estate tax

fondina *f* holster; (coll) soup dish

fondi·sta *mf* (-sti -ste) editorialist; (sports) long-distance runner

fóndita *f* (typ) font

fonditóre *m* smelter, founder

fón·do -da *adj* deep || *m* bottom; fund; innermost nature; seat; end; background; land, property; a doppio fondo with a false bottom; a fondo thoroughly; a fondo perduto as an outright grant; dar fondo (naut) to cast anchor; dar fondo a to exhaust; di fondo (journ) editorial; (sports) long-distance; fondi funds; lees; fondi di bottega remnants; fondi di caffè coffee grounds; fondo comune d'investimento mutual fund; fondo d'ammortamento sinking fund; fondo di beneficenza community chest; fondo tinta foundation (*in make-up*); in fondo in the end; at the bottom; after all

fonè·ma *m* (-mi) phoneme

fonèti·co -ca (-ci -che) *adj* phonetic || *f* phonetics

fonògeno *m* pickup (*of record player*)

fonògrafo *m* phonograph, Gramophone

fonogram·ma *m* (-mi) telegram delivered by telephone

fonologìa *f* phonology

fonorivelatóre *m* pickup (*of record player*)

fonovalìgia *f* portable phonograph

fontana *f* fountain; spring; source

fónte *m* (lit) spring, source; fonte battesimale font || *f* spring; fountain; source; da fonte autorevole on good authority

foraggiare §290 *tr* to subsidize || *intr* to forage

foràg·gio *m* (-gi) forage, provender, fodder

foràne·o -a *adj* rural; outer; (naut) outer (*dock*)

forare (fóro) *tr* to pierce; to bore; to puncture || *intr* to have a flat tire || *ref* to be punctured

foratura *f* puncture

fòrbice *f*—a forbice (sports) scissors (*e.g., kick*); forbici scissors; clippers; forbici per le unghie nail clippers

forbire §176 *tr* to wipe; to polish; to shine

fór·ca *f* (-che) fork; pitchfork; gallows; mountain pass; fare la forca a qlcu (slang) to betray s.o.; (slang) to do s.o. dirt; fatto a forca V-shaped

**forcèlla** *f* fork (*of bicycle or motorcycle*); mountain pass; fork-shaped pole; hairpin; cradle (*of handset*); (coll) wishbone (*of chicken*)

**forchétta** *f* fork; (coll) wishbone (*of chicken*); **alla forchetta** (culin) cold (*e.g., lunch*)

**forchettata** *f* forkful; blow with a fork

**forchettóne** *m* carving fork

**forcina** *f* hairpin

**fòrcipe** *m* forceps

**forcóne** *m* pitchfork

**forellino** *m* pinhole

**forèsta** *f* forest

**forestale** *adj* forest, park

**foresterìa** *f* guest quarters (*in college or monastery*)

**forestierismo** *m* borrowing (*from another language*)

**forestiè·ro -ra** *adj* foreign ‖ *mf* foreigner; stranger; outsider

**forfettà·rio -ria** *adj* (**-ri -rie**) job, e.g., **contratto forfettario** job contract; all-inclusive, e.g., **combinazione forfettaria** all-inclusive price agreement

**fórfora** *f* dandruff

**fòr·gia** *f* (**-ge**) forge; smithy

**forgiare** §290 (**fòrgio**) *tr* to forge

**foriè·ro -ra** *adj* forerunning ‖ *mf* forerunner, harbinger

**fórma** *f* shape; form; mold (*e.g., for cakes*); wheel (*of cheese*); (typ) form; **forma da cappelli** hat block; **forma da scarpe** shoe tree; shoe last (*used by shoemaker*); **forme** shape, body; good manners; **salvare le forme** to save face

**formaggièra** *f* dish for grated cheese

**formàg·gio** *m* (**-gi**) cheese

**formaldèide** *f* formaldehyde

**formale** *adj* formal; prim

**formalismo** *m* formality

**formali·tà** *f* (**-tà**) formality

**formalizzare** [ddzz] *tr* to scandalize ‖ *ref* to be shocked

**formare** (**fórmo**) *tr & ref* to form

**forma·to -ta** *adj* formed ‖ *m* format

**formazióne** *f* formation

**fòrmica** *f* (trademark) Formica

**formi·ca** *f* (**-che**) ant

**formi·càio** *m* (**-cài**) anthill; (fig) swarm

**formichière** *m* anteater

**formicolare** (**formìcolo**) *intr* to swarm; to crawl ‖ *intr* (ESSERE) to creep (*said, e.g., of a leg*)

**formicolì·o** *m* (**-i**) swarm; creeping sensation, numbness

**formidàbile** *adj* formidable

**formó·so -sa** [s] *adj* shapely, buxom

**fòrmula** *f* formula; (aut) category, class; **formula dubitativa** (law) lack of evidence; **formula piena** (law) acquittal

**formulare** (**fòrmulo**) *tr* to formulate

**formulà·rio** *m* (**-ri**) formulary; form

**fornace** *f* furnace, kiln

**for·nàio -nàia** *mf* (**-nài -nàie**) baker

**fornèllo** *m* stove, range; (*of boiler*) firebox; bowl (*of pipe*); (min) shaft; **fornello a gas** gas range; **fornello a spirito** kerosene stove; chafing dish

**fornire** §176 *tr* to furnish, supply

**forni·tóre -trice** *mf* supplier, purveyor

**fornitura** *f* supply; order; delivery

**fórno** *m* oven; furnace; kiln; bakery; (theat) empty house; **al forno** or **in forno** baked; **alto forno** blast furnace; **forno crematorio** crematorium; **far forno** (theat) to play before an empty house

**fóro** *m* hole

**fòro** *m* forum; (law) bar

**forosétta** [s] *f* (lit) peasant girl

**fórse** *m* doubt; **mettere in forse** to endanger; to put in doubt ‖ *adv* perhaps, maybe

**forsenna·to -ta** *adj* mad, insane ‖ *mf* lunatic

**fòrte** *adj* strong; firm; bad (*cold*); fat, hefty; fast (*color*); offensive (*joke*); hard (*smoker*); main (*dish*); (lit) thick ‖ *m* strong person; fortress; bulk, main body; forte; (lit) thick; **sapere di forte** to have a strong flavor; **farsi forte** to bear up; **farsi forte di** to appropriate, use; to be cocksure of ‖ *adv* hard, strong; much; loud; openly; a lot; fast; swiftly

**fortézza** *f* fortress; strength; fortitude

**fortificare** §197 (**fortìfico**) *tr* to fortify ‖ *ref* to be strengthened; to dig in

**fortificazióne** *f* fortification

**fortino** *m* blockhouse, redoubt

**fortùi·to -ta** *adj* fortuitous

**fortuna** *f* fortune; luck; good luck; fate, destiny; (lit) storm; **avere fortuna** to be lucky; to be a hit; **buona fortuna!** good luck!; **di fortuna** makeshift, emergency; **non aver la fortuna di** to not be fortunate enough to; **per fortuna** luckily

**fortunale** *m* storm, tempest

**fortuna·to -ta** *adj* fortunate, lucky

**fortunó·so -sa** [s] *adj* eventful

**forùncolo** *m* boil; pimple

**forviare** §119 *tr* to mislead, lead astray ‖ *intr* to go astray

**fòrza** *f* strength; force; power; police; (phys) force; **a forza di** by dint of; **a tutta forza** at full speed; **bassa forza** (mil) enlisted personnel; **di forza** by force; **di prima forza** first-rate; **far forza a** to encourage; to force; **fare forza a sé stesso** to restrain oneself; **forza!** courage!; **forza di corpo** (typ) height-to-paper; **forza maggiore** force majeure, act of God; **forza muscolare** brawn; **forza pubblica** police; **forza viva** kinetic energy; **per forza** of course; under duress

**forzare** (**fòrzo**) *tr* to force; to strain; to rape; to tamper with (*a lock*); **forzare il passo** to hasten one's step; **forzare la consegna** (mil) to violate orders

**forza·to -ta** *adj* forced; force (*e.g., feed*) ‖ *m* convict

**forzière** *m* chest, coffer

**forzó·so -sa** [s] *adj* compulsory; imposed by law

**forzu·to -ta** *adj* husky, robust

**foschìa** *f* smog; mist; haze

**fó·sco -sca** *adj* (**-schi -sche**) dark; gloomy; misty

**fosfato** *m* phosphate

**fosforeggiare** §290 (**fosforéggio**) *intr* to phosphoresce; to glow

**fosforescènte** *adj* phosphorescent

**fòsforo** *m* phosphorus

**fòssa** *f* grave; hollow; hole, ditch; moat; pit; den (*of lions*); **fossa biologica** sewage-treatment plant; **fossa di riparazione** (aut) pit; **fossa settica** septic tank

**fossato** *m* ditch; moat

**fossétta** *f* dimple

**fòssile** *adj* & *m* fossil

**fossilizzare** [ddzz] *tr* to fossilize ‖ *ref* to become fossilized

**fòsso** *m* ditch; moat

**fò·to** *f* (**-to**) photo

**fotocòpia** *f* photocopy

**fotocopiare** §287 (**fotocòpio**) *tr* to photocopy

**fotoelèttri·co -ca** (**-ci -che**) *adj* photo-electric ‖ *f* (mil) searchlight

**fotogèni·co -ca** *adj* (**-ci -che**) photo-genic

**fotogiornale** *m* pictorial magazine

**fotografare** (**fotògrafo**) *tr* to photo-graph

**fotografìa** *f* photography; photograph

**fotogràfi·co -ca** *adj* (**-ci -che**) photo-graphic

**fotògrafo** *m* photographer

**fotogram·ma** *m* (**-mi**) (phot) frame

**fotoincisióne** *f* photoengraving

**fotolampo** *m* flashlight

**fotòmetro** *m* exposure meter

**fotomontàg·gio** *m* (**-gi**) photomontage

**fototubo** *m* phototube

**fra** *m* *invar* brother, e.g., **fra Cristoforo** Brother Christopher ‖ *prep* among; between; in, within

**frac** *m* (**frac**) swallow-tailed coat

**fracassare** *tr* to crash, smash ‖ *ref* to crash

**fracasso** *m* crash; uproar; (coll) slew

**fràdi·cio -cia** (**-ci -cie**) *adj* rotten; soaked ‖ *m* rotten part; decay; wet ground

**fràgile** *adj* fragile; brittle; frail

**fragilità** *f* fragility, frailty

**fràgola** *f* strawberry

**fragóre** *m* din; peal; roar

**fragoró·so -sa** [s] *adj* noisy

**fragrante** *adj* fragrant

**fraintèndere** §270 *tr* to misunderstand

**frammassóne** *m* Freemason

**frammassonerìa** *f* Freemasonry

**frammentare** (**framménto**) *tr* to frag-ment

**frammentà·rio -ria** *adj* (**-ri -rie**) frag-mentary

**framménto** *m* fragment

**framméttere** §198 *tr* to interpose ‖ *ref* to meddle; **frammettersi in** to intrude in, to butt into

**frammèzzo** [ddzz] *adv* in the middle ‖ *prep* in the midst of

**frammischiare** §287 *tr* to mix ‖ *ref* to concern oneself

**frana** *f* landslide; (fig) collapse

**franare** *intr* to slide; to collapse

**francesca·no -na** *adj* & *mf* Franciscan

**francé·sco -sca** *adj* (**-schi -sche**) *adj* (ar-chaic) French ‖ **Francesco** *m* Francis ‖ **Francesca** *f* Frances

**francése** *adj* French ‖ *m* French (*lan-guage*); Frenchman (*person*); **i fran-cesi** the French ‖ *f* Frenchwoman

**francesismo** *m* gallicism

**francesizzare** [ddzz] *tr* to Frenchify

**franchézza** *f* frankness

**franchì·gia** *f* (**-gie**) franchise; exemp-tion; deductible insurance; (naut) shore leave; **franchigia postale** frank-ing privilege

**Frància, la** France

**fran·co -ca** (**-chi -che**) *adj* free; frank; Frankish; **farla franca** to get off scot free; **franco di porto** prepaid, post-paid; **franco domicilio** home delivery, free delivery ‖ *m* franc ‖ **Franco** *m* Frank

**francobóllo** *m* postage stamp, stamp

**frangènte** *m* breaker, surf; **essere nei frangenti** to be in bad straits

**fràngere** §179 *tr* to crush; (lit) to break ‖ *ref* to break, comb (*said of waves*)

**frangétta** *f* bangs

**fràn·gia** *f* (**-ge**) fringe; embellishment; shoreline; bangs; **frangia di corallo** coral reef

**frangìbile** *adj* breakable

**frangiflut·ti** *m* (**-ti**) breakwater

**frangi·vènto** *m* (**-vènto**) windbreak

**frangizòl·le** *m* (**-le**) disc harrow

**Frankfur·ter** *m* (**-ter**) hot dog

**fran·tóio** *m* (**-tói**) crusher; **frantoio a mascelle** jawbreaker

**frantumare** *tr* to crush; to break to pieces ‖ *ref* to be crushed; to go to pieces

**frantume** *m* fragment; **andare in fran-tumi** to go to pieces

**frappé** *m* (**frappé**) shake; frappé; **frappé alla menta** mint julep; **frappé di latte** milk shake

**frappórre** §218 *tr* to interpose ‖ *ref* to interfere; to intervene

**frasà·rio** *m* (**-ri**) language, speech

**fra·sca** *f* (**-sche**) branch; bush; orna-ment; whim; frivolous woman, flirt

**frase** *f* sentence; (mus) phrase; **frase fatta** cliché; **frase idiomatica** idiom; **frasi** words; **frasi di commiserazione** condolences

**fraseggiare** §290 (**fraséggio**) *intr* to use phrasing; to use big words; (mus) to phrase

**fraseologìa** *f* phraseology

**fràssino** *m* ash tree

**frastagliare** §280 *tr* to cut out (*e.g., paper*)

**frastaglia·to -ta** *adj* indented, jagged; ornamented

**frastornare** (**frastórno**) *tr* to disturb; (lit) to prevent

**frastuòno** *m* din, roar

**frate** *m* friar, monk, brother

**fratellanza** *f* brotherhood

**fratellastro** *m* stepbrother; half brother

**fratèllo** *m* brother; **fratelli** brothers and sisters; **fratello consanguineo** half brother on the father's side; **fratello**

di latte foster brother; **fratello ge- mello** twin

**fraterni·tà** *f* (**-tà**) fraternity

**fraternizzare** [ddzz] *intr* to fraternize

**fratèr·no -na** *adj* fraternal, brotherly

**fratrici·da** (**-di -de**) *adj* fratricidal || *mf* fratricide

**fratrici·dio** *m* (**-di**) fratricide

**fratta** *f* brushwood; (coll) hedge

**frattàglie** *fpl* giblets, chitterlings, offal

**frattanto** *adv* meantime, meanwhile

**frattèmpo** *m*—**nel frattempo** meanwhile

**frattura** *f* fracture; break; breach

**fratturare** *tr* & *ref* to fracture, break

**fraudolènto** *adj* fraudulent

**frazionare** (**frazióno**) *tr* to fractionate; to break up

**frazionà·rio -ria** *adj* (**-ri -rie**) fractional

**frazióne** *f* fraction; hamlet; (eccl) breaking of the host

**fréc·cia** *f* (**-ce**) arrow, bolt; steeple, spire; clock (*on hosiery*); (archit) rise; (fig) aspersion; **freccia consensiva** arrow (*on traffic light*); **freccia direzionale** (aut) turn signal

**frecciata** *f* arrow shot; taunt, gibe; **dare una frecciata a** to hit for a loan

**freddare** (**fréddo**) *tr* to chill; to kill

**freddézza** *f* chill; cold, coldness; coolness, cold shoulder; sang-froid

**fréd·do -da** *adj* cold; cool, chilly; frigid || *m* cold, coid weather; chill; **a freddo** cold; cooly; **avere freddo** to be cold (*said of people*); **fare freddo** to be cold (*said of weather*); **freddo cane** biting cold; **sentire freddo** to feel cold; **sudare freddo** to be in a cold sweat

**freddoló·so -sa** [s] *adj* chilly (*person*)

**freddura** *f* joke, pun; cold weather

**fredduri·sta** *mf* (**-sti -ste**) punster

**fregagióne** *f* rubbing, rubdown, massage

**fregare** §209 (**frégo**) *tr* to rub; to strike (*a match*); (slang) to steal; (slang) to cheat, dupe; (vulg) to make love with || *ref* to rub (*e.g., one's hands*); **fregarsene di** (vulg) to not give a hoot about

**fregata** *f* rubbing; (nav) frigate; (orn) frigate bird; (slang) cheating

**fregatura** *f* (slang) cheating; (slang) hitch, halt

**fregiare** §290 (**frégio**) *tr* to decorate; to fret

**fré·gio** *m* (**-gi**) decoration; insignia (*on cap of officer*); (archit) frieze

**fré·go** *m* (**-ghi**) line, stroke

**frégola** *f* rut, heat; (slang) mania, craze

**fremènte** *adj* throbbing; thrilling

**frèmere** §123 *tr* (lit) to beg insistently || *intr* to throb; to be thrilled; to shake, tremble, rustle; to shudder (*with horror*); (fig) to boil; (fig) to fret

**frèmito** *m* throb; thrill; shudder; roar; quiver

**frenare** (**fréno**) *tr* to brake, stop; to bridle (*a horse*); to curb (*passions*); to restrain (*e.g., laughter*); **frenare la corsa** to slow down || *intr* to put the brakes on || *ref* to control oneself

**frenatóre** *m* (**rr**) brakeman

**frenesìa** *f* frenzy; (fig) craze, fever; (lit) thought

**frenèti·co -ca** *adj* (**-ci -che**) frenzied; frantic; crazy, enthusiastic

**fréno** *m* bit, bridle; brake; (fig) check; (mach) lock; **freno ad aria compressa** air brake; **mordere il freno** to champ the bit; **senza freno** wild, unbridled; **tenere a freno** to keep in check

**frenologìa** *f* phrenology

**frequentare** (**frequènto**) *tr* to frequent; to attend || *intr* to associate

**frequenta·tóre -trice** *mf* patron, customer; frequenter, habitué

**frequènte** *adj* frequent; rapid (*pulse*); (lit) crowded

**frequènza** *f* frequency; attendance; **frequenza ultraelevata** ultrahigh frequency

**frèsa** *f* milling cutter; burr (*of dentist's drill*)

**fresatrice** *f* milling machine

**fresatura** *f* (mach) milling

**freschézza** *f* freshness; coolness

**fré·sco -sca** (**-schi -sche**) *adj* fresh; cool; **fresco di malattia** just recovered; **fresco di stampa** fresh off the press; **fresco di studi** fresh out of school; **star fresco** to be in a fix; to be all wrong || *m* cool weather; tropical fabric; **di fresco** recently; **fare fresco** to be cool (*said of weather*); **mettere al fresco** (coll) to put in the clink; **per il fresco** in cool weather

**frescó·ne -na** *mf* (slang) dumbell

**frescura** *f* coolness, freshness

**frétta** *f* hurry, haste; **avere fretta** to be in a hurry; **in fretta** in a hurry; **in fretta e furia** in a rush

**frettazzo** *m* plasterer's wooden trowel; steel brush

**frettoló·so -sa** [s] *adj* hurried, hasty

**freudismo** *m* Freudianism

**friàbile** *adj* friable, crumbly

**friabilità** *f* friableness

**fricassèa** *f* fricassee

**friggere** §180 *tr* to fry; **mandare qlcu a farsi friggere** to tell s.o. to go to the devil || *intr* to fry; to sizzle; to fret

**friggitoria** *f* fried-food shop

**frigidézza** *f* frigidity

**frigidi·tà** *f* (**-tà**) coldness; frigidity

**frigi·do -da** *adj* cold; frigid

**frì·gio -gia** *adj* (**-gi -gie**) Phrygian

**frignare** *intr* to whimper

**frigorìfe·ro -ra** *adj* refrigerating || *m* refrigerator; (journ) morgue

**fringuèl·lo -la** *mf* chaffinch, finch

**frinire** §176 *intr* to chirp

**frisata** *f* gunnel

**frittata** *f* omelet; **fare la frittata** (coll) to make a mess of it

**frittèlla** *f* fritter; pancake; (coll) grease spot

**frit·to -ta** *adj* fried; cooked, ruined || *m* fry, fried platter

**frittura** *f* frying; fry, fried platter

**frivolézza** *f* frivolity

**frìvo·lo -la** *adj* frivolous; flighty

**frizionare** (**frizióno**) *tr* to massage

**frizióne** *f* friction; massage; (aut) clutch

**frizzante** [ddzz] *adj* crisp, brisk (*weather*); sparkling (*wine*)

**frizzare** [ddzz] *intr* to tingle; to sparkle, fizz (*said of wine*); (fig) to sting

**frizzo** [ddzz] *m* jest, witticism; gibe, dig

**frodare** (**fròdo**) *tr* to cheat, swindle

**fròde** *f* fraud; **frode fiscale** tax evasion or fraud

**fròdo** *m invar* customs evasion; **di frodo** smuggled

**frò·gia** *f* (**-ge** or **-gie**) nostril (*of horse*)

**fròl·lo -la** *adj* high (*meat*); soft, tender; (fig) weak

**frónda** *f* branch, bough; political opposition; **fronde** foliage; ornaments

**frondó·so -sa** [s] *adj* leafy

**frontale** *adj* front; frontal

**frónte** *m* (mil, pol) front; **far fronte a** to face; to face up to; to meet (*expenses*); **tenere fronte a** to face, resist || *f* forehead, brow; countenance; title page; headline; (fig) face; **a fronte** opposite, facing; **a fronte di** (com) in reference to; **dietro front!** (mil) about face!; **di fronte a** in the face of; facing; **di fronte a tutti** in plain view; **fronte destr'!** (mil) right face!; **mettere a fronte** to compare; **tenere a fronte** to have in front of one's eyes

**fronteggiare** §290 (**frontéggio**) *tr* to face, front || *ref* to face one another

**frontespì·zio** *m* (**-zi**) title page

**frontièra** *f* border, frontier

**frontóne** *m* (archit) pediment; (archit) gable

**frónzolo** *m* bauble, gewgaw; **fronzoli** finery, frippery

**fròtta** *f* crowd; swarm; flock

**fròttola** *f* fib; popular poem; **frottole** humbug

**frugale** *adj* frugal (*meal; life*); temperate (*in eating or drinking*)

**frugare** §209 *tr* to rummage through; to search (*a person*) || *intr* to rummage, poke around

**frùgo·lo -la** *mf* restless child, imp

**fruire** §176 *tr* to enjoy || *intr*—**fruire di** to enjoy

**fruitóre** *m* user

**frullare** *tr* to beat, whip || *intr* to flutter; to spin; **frullare per il capo a** to get into the head of, e.g., **cosa gli è frullato per il capo?** what got into his head?

**frulla·to -ta** *adj* whipped || *m* shake (*drink*)

**frullatóre** *m* electric beater

**frullino** *m* egg beater

**fruménto** *m* wheat

**frumentóne** *m* corn

**frusciare** §128 *intr* to rustle

**fruscì·o** *m* (**-i**) rustle, rustling

**frusta** *f* whip; egg beater

**frustare** *tr* to whip, lash; (fig) to censure; (coll) to wear out (*clothes*)

**frustata** *f* lash; (fig) censure

**frustino** *m* whip, crop

**fru·sto -sta** *adj* worn out, threadbare || *f* see **frusta**

**frustrare** *tr* to frustrate, baffle; to discomfit

**frut·ta** *f* (**-ta** & **-te**) fruit; **essere alle frutta** to be at the end of the meal, to be having one's dessert

**fruttare** *tr* & *intr* to yield

**fruttéto** *m* orchard

**frutticoltóre** *m* fruit grower

**fruttièra** *f* fruit dish

**fruttìfe·ro -ra** *adj* fruit-bearing; fruitful, profitable; (lit) fecund

**fruttificare** §197 (**fruttìfico**) *intr* to fructify; to yield

**fruttivéndo·lo -la** *mf* fruit dealer

**frutto** *m* fruit; **frutti di mare** shellfish; **mettere a frutto** to make yield

**fruttuó·so -sa** [s] *adj* fruitful, profitable

**fu** *adj invar* late (*deceased*); son of the late . . . ; daughter of the late . . .

**fucilare** *tr* to shoot

**fucilata** *f* rifle shot

**fucilazióne** *f* execution by a firing squad

**fucile** *m* rifle, gun; **fucile ad aria compressa** air gun; **fucile da caccia** shotgun; **un buon fucile** a good shot

**fuclerìa** *f* fusillade

**fucilière** *m* rifleman

**fucina** *f* forge, smithy

**fu·co** *m* (**-chi**) (bot) rockweed; (zool) drone

**fùcsia** *f* fuchsia

**fu·ga** *f* (**-ghe**) flight; leak; row (*e.g., of rooms*); spurt (*in bicycle race*); (mus) fugue; **di fuga** hastily; **prendere la fuga** to take flight; **volgere in fuga** to put to flight; to take flight

**fugace** *adj* passing, fleeting

**fugare** §209 *tr* (lit) to avoid; (lit) to put to flight; (lit) to dispel

**fuggènte** *adj* passing, fleeting

**fuggévole** *adj* fleeting

**fuggia·sco -sca (-schi -sche)** *adj* fleeing, fugitive || *mf* fugitive; refugee

**fuggi fug·gi** *m* (**-gi**) stampede

**fuggire** *tr* to flee; to avoid || *intr* (ESSERE) to flee, run away; (sports) to take the lead; **fuggire a** to flee from

**fuggiti·vo -va** *adj* & *mf* fugitive

**fulcro** *m* fulcrum; (fig) pivot

**fulgènte** *adj* (lit) resplendent

**fùlgi·do -da** *adj* resplendent

**fulgóre** *m* resplendency, radiance

**fulìggine** *f* soot

**fuligginó·so -sa** [s] *adj* sooty

**fulmicotóne** *m* guncotton

**fulminante** *adj* crushing (*illness*); withering (*look*); explosive || *m* exploding cap; (coll) match

**fulminare** (**fùlmino**) *tr* to strike by lightning; to strike down; to confound, dumfound || *ref* (elec) to burn out, to blow out || *impers* (ESSERE)—**fulmina** it is lightning

**fùlmine** *m* lightning, thunderbolt; **fulmine a ciel sereno** bolt out of the blue

**fulmìne·o -a** *adj* swift, instant

**ful·vo -va** *adj* tawny

**fumaiòlo** *m* chimney; smokestack; (naut) funnel

**fumante** *adj* smoking; steaming; dusty
**fumare** *tr* to smoke; (lit) to exhale ‖ *intr* to smoke; to steam; to fume; **fumare come un turco** to smoke like a chimney
**fumata** *f* smoking; smoke signal; **fare una fumata** to have a smoke
**fuma·tóre -trice** *mf* smoker
**fumetti·sta** *mf* (**-sti -ste**) cartoonist
**fumétto** *m* cartoon; **fumetti** comics
**fumigare** §209 (**fùmigo**) *tr* (obs) to fumigate ‖ *intr* to steam, smoke
**fumigazióne** *f* fumigation
**fumi·sta** *m* (**-sti**) heater man; joker, hoaxer
**fumisterìa** *f* fondness for practical jokes; bamboozling
**fumo** *m* smoke; vapor, steam; smoking; (coll) hot air; **andare in fumo** to go up in smoke; **fumi** vapors, fumes; **mandare in fumo** to squander; to thwart; **sapere di fumo** to taste smoky; **vedere qlcu come il fumo negli occhi** to not be able to stand s.o.; **vender fumo** to peddle influence
**fumòge·no -na** *adj* smoke, e.g., **cortina fumogena** smoke curtain
**fumó·so -sa** [s] *adj* smoky; obscure
**funambolismo** *m* tightrope walking; (fig) acrobatics
**funàmbo·lo -la** *mf* tightrope walker; (fig) acrobat
**fune** *f* rope, cable; **fune portante** suspension cable
**fùnebre** *adj* funeral; funereal, gloomy
**funerale** *adj & m* funeral
**funerà·rio -ria** *adj* (**-ri -rie**) funeral
**funère·o -a** *adj* funereal; funeral
**funestare** (**funèsto**) *tr* to afflict
**funè·sto -sta** *adj* baleful; mournful
**fungàia** *f* mushroom farm; mushroom bed; flock, swarm
**fùngere** §183 *intr*—**fungere da** to act as
**fun·go** *m* (**-ghi**) mushroom; fungus; **fungo atomico** mushroom cloud; **venir su come i funghi** to mushroom
**fungó·so -sa** [s] *adj* fungous
**funicolare** *adj* cable, cable-driven ‖ *f* funicular railway
**funivìa** *f* cableway
**funzionale** *adj* functional
**funzionalità** *f* functionalism
**funzionaménto** *m* working order; functioning
**funzionare** (**funzióno**) *intr* to work; to function; **funzionare da** to act as
**funzionà·rio -ria** *mf* (**-ri -rie**) functionary, official; public official
**funzióne** *f* function; office; duty; (eccl) service; **facente funzione** acting; **mettere in funzione** to make (*s.th*) work
**fuò·co** *m* (**-chi**) fire; burner (*of gas range*); focus; (fig) home; (lit) thunderbolt; **al fuoco!** fire! (*warning*); **andare per il fuoco** (culin) to boil over; **cuocere a fuoco lento** (culin) to simmer; **dar fuoco a** to set fire to; **di fuoco** fiery; blushing; **far fuoco** to fire; **fuochi artificiali** fireworks; **fuoco di fila** enfilade; **fuoco!** (mil) fire!; **fuoco di paglia** (fig) flash in the pan; **fuoco di segnalazione** flare; **fuoco fatuo** will-o'-the-wisp; **fuoco**

**incrociato** cross fire; **fuoco nutrito** drumfire; **mettere a fuoco** to focus; **mettere una mano sul fuoco** to be absolutely sure, to swear by it
**fuorché** *prep* except; **fuorché di** except to
**fuòri** *adv* outside, out; aside; e.g., **lasciar fuori** to leave aside; **andar di fuori** (culin) to boil over; **dar fuori** to do away with; to squander; **di fuori** outside; **far fuori** to publish; **fuori di** out of; outside of; beyond (*a doubt*); off (*the road*); beside (*oneself*); **fuori d'uso** out of style; obsolete; **il di fuori** the outside; in **fuori** protruding; forward; **mettere fuori** to throw out; to spread; to exhibit ‖ *prep* beyond; out of; outside; **fuori commercio** not for sale; **fuori concorso** in a class by itself (himself, etc.); **fuori luogo** untimely, out of place; **fuori (di) mano** far away; solitary; **fuori testo** inserted, tipped in
**fuoribór·do** *m* (**-do**) outboard; outboard motor
**fuoricombattimén·to** (**-to**) *adj* knocked out ‖ *m* knockout
**fuorigiò·co** *m* (**-co**) (sports) offside
**fuorilég·ge** *mf* (**-ge**) outlaw
**fuorisè·rie** (**-rie**) *adj* custom-built ‖ *m & f* custom model ‖ *f* custom-built car
**fuoristra·da** *m* (**-da**) land rover
**fuoriusci·to -ta** *adj* exiled ‖ *mf* political exile ‖ *f* leak; flow; protrusion
**fuorvia·to -ta** *adj* mislead, misguided
**furbacchió·ne -na** *mf* slippery person
**furberìa** *f* slyness, cunning
**fur·bo -ba** *adj* sly, cunning ‖ *mf* knave; **furbo di tre cotte** slicker
**furènte** *adj* furious
**furerìa** *f* (mil) company headquarters
**furétto** *m* ferret
**furfante** *m* sharper, scoundrel
**furfanterìa** *f* rascality
**furgoncino** *m* small delivery van
**furgóne** *m* truck; patrol wagon; hearse; **furgone cellulare** prison van
**furgoni·sta** *mf* (**-sti -ste**) truck driver, teamster
**fùria** *f* fury; strength, violence; hurry; **a furia di** by dint of; **con furia** in a hurry; **far furia a** to urge; **montare in furia** to go berserk; to fly off the handle
**furibón·do -da** *adj* furious, wild
**furière** *m* soldier attached to company headquarters
**furió·so -sa** [s] *adj* furious; fierce; mad
**furóre** *m* furor, frenzy; violence; longing; **far furore** to be a hit, to be all the rage
**furoreggiare** §290 (**furoréggio**) *intr* to be a hit, be all the rage
**furti·vo -va** *adj* stealthy; furtive; stolen (*e.g., goods*)
**furto** *m* theft; stolen goods; **di furto** stealthily; **furto con scasso** burglary
**fusa** [s] *fpl*—**fare le fusa** to purr
**fuscèllo** *m* twig
**fusciac·ca** *f* (**-che**) sash (*around the waist*)

**fusèllo** [s] _m_ spindle; axle, shaft
**fusìbile** _adj_ fusible ‖ _m_ (elec) fuse
**fusióne** _f_ fusion; melting; merger; blending (_of colors_)
**fu•so -sa** _adj_ melted; molten
**fuso** [s] _m_ spindle; shank (_of anchor_); shaft (_of column_); (aut) axle; **fuso orario** time zone
**fusolièra** _f_ (aer) fuselage
**fustagno** _m_ fustian
**fustàia** _f_ adult forest, full-grown forest
**fustèlla** _f_ (perforating) punch; (pharm) price stub

**fustigare** §209 (**fùstigo**) _tr_ to whip
**fusto** _m_ trunk (_of tree_); stalk; stem (_of key_); beam (_of balance_); butt (_of gun_); trunk, body; frame (_of armchair_); tank (_for holding liquids_); drum (_metal receptacle_); holding stick (_of umbrella_); shaft (_of column_); **d'alto fusto** full-grown (_tree_)
**fùtile** _adj_ futile, trifling
**futilità** _f_ futility
**futurismo** _m_ futurism
**futuri•sta** _mf_ (**-sti -ste**) futurist
**futu•ro -ra** _adj_ & _m_ future

# G

**G, g** [dʒi] _m_ & _f_ seventh letter of the Italian alphabet
**gabardi•ne** _f_ (**-ne**) gabardine; gabardine raincoat or topcoat
**gabbamón•do** _m_ (**-do**) cheat, sharper
**gabbanèlla** _f_ gown (_of physician or patient_); robe
**gabbano** _m_ cloak; frock; **mutare gabbano** to be a turncoat
**gabbare** _tr_ to dupe, cheat ‖ _ref_—**gabbarsi di** to make fun of
**gàbbia** _f_ cage; ox muzzle; dock (_in courtroom_); (mach) housing; (naut) top; (naut) topsail; **gabbia d'imballaggio** crate; **gabbia toracica** rib cage
**gabbiano** _m_ sea gull
**gabbo** _m_—**farsi gabbo di** to make fun of; **prendere a gabbo** to make light of
**gabèlla** _f_ (obs) customs, duty
**gabellare** (**gabèllo**) _tr_ to palm off; to swallow (_e.g., a tall story_); (obs) to tax
**gabinétto** _m_ office (_of doctor, dentist, lawyer_); cabinet; chamber (_of judge_); toilet; closet; laboratory; **gabinetto da bagno** bathroom; **gabinetto di decenza** toilet, bathroom
**ga•gà** _m_ (**gà**) fop, dandy; lounge lizard
**gaggìa** _f_ acacia
**gagliardétto** _m_ pennon; pennant
**gagliardìa** _f_ (lit) vigor; (lit) prowess
**gagliar•do -da** _adj_ vigorous; stalwart; hearty (_e.g., voice_)
**gagliòf•fo -fa** _adj_ loutish; rascal ‖ _mf_ lout; rascal
**gaiézza** _f_ gaiety, vivacity
**gàio gàia** _adj_ (**gài gàie**) gay, vivacious
**gala** _m_ & _f_ gala; gala affair; **di gala** formal; **mettersi in gala** to dress up ‖ _f_ frill; bow tie (_for formal attire_); (naut) bunting
**galalite** _f_ casein plastic, galalith
**galante** _adj_ gallant, courtly; amorous; pretty, graceful
**galanterìa** _f_ gallantry, courtliness
**galantuò•mo** _m_ (**-mini**) honest man; (coll) my good fellow
**galàssia** _f_ galaxy
**galatèo** _m_ good manners
**galèna** _f_ (min) galena
**galeóne** _m_ galleon
**galeòt•to -ta** _adj_ (archaic) intermediary

(_in love affairs_) ‖ _m_ galley slave; convict; (archaic) procurer
**galèra** _f_ galley; forced labor
**gali•lèo -lèa** (**-lèi -lèe**) _adj_ & _m_ Galilean
**galla** _f_ (bot) gall; (pathol) blister; **a galla** afloat; **tenersi a galla** (fig) to keep alive; to manage; **venire a galla** to come to the surface
**galleggiante** _adj_ floating ‖ _m_ float
**galleggiare** §290 (**galléggio**) _intr_ to float
**gallerìa** _f_ tunnel; gallery; balcony; mall, arcade; wind tunnel
**Galles, il** Wales
**gallése** [s] _adj_ Welsh ‖ _m_ Welshman; Welsh (_language_) ‖ _f_ Welsh woman
**gallétta** _f_ cracker; hardtack; (naut) ball on top of flagpole
**gallétto** _m_ cockerel; (fig) gallant; (fig) whippersnapper; (mach) wing nut; **fare il galletto** to swagger
**gàlli•co -ca** _adj_ & _m_ (**-ci -che**) Gallic
**gallina** _f_ hen; **gallina faraona** guinea fowl
**gal•lo -la** _adj_ Gallic; (sports) Bantam (_weight_) ‖ _m_ rooster, cock; weathercock; Gaul; Gallic (_language_); **fare il gallo** to strut; **gallo cedrone** wood grouse; **gallo d'India** turkey
**gallòc•cia** _f_ (**-ce**) (naut) cleat
**gallóne** _m_ braid; stripe; chevron; gallon
**galoppare** (**galòppo**) _intr_ to gallop; (fig) to rush around
**galoppata** _f_ gallop
**galoppa•tóio** _m_ (**-tói**) bridle path
**galoppino** _m_ errand boy; **galoppino elettorale** ward heeler
**galòppo** _m_ gallop; **andare al piccolo galoppo** to canter; **di gran galoppo** at full speed; **piccolo galoppo** canter
**galò•scia** _f_ (**-sce**) overshoe, rubber
**galvanizzare** [ddzz] _tr_ to electroplate; (fig) to galvanize
**galvanoplàsti•ca** _f_ (**-che**) electroplating
**gamba** _f_ leg; stem; (aer) shock strut; **a gambe all'aria** upside down; **a gambe levate** at top speed; upside down; **darsela a gambe** to take to one's heels; **essere in gamba** to be in good shape; to be on the ball; **essere male in gamba** to be in bad shape; **gamba di legno** peg leg; **gambe a ciambella** bowlegs; **le gambe mi fanno giacomo** my knees shake;

**prendere qlcu sotto gamba** to make light of s.o.; **raddrizzare le gambe ai cani** to try the impossible

**gambale** *m* legging, gaiter; boot last; leg (*of boot*)

**gamberétto** *m* shrimp

**gàmbero** *m* (*Astacus, Cambarus*) crawfish

**gambétto** *m* stumble; trip; (chess) gambit

**gambo** *m* stem

**gamèlla** *f* (mil) mess kit, mess tin

**gamma** *f* gamut; range; **gamma d'onda** (rad) wave band

**ganà·scia** *f* (-sce) jaw; (aut) brake shoe; **mangiare a quattro ganasce** to eat like a horse

**gàn·cio** *m* (-ci) hook; clasp; hanger

**gan·ga** *f* (-ghe) gang; (min) gangue

**gànghero** *m* hinge; clasp; **uscire dai gangheri** to fly off the handle

**gàn·glio** *m* (-gli) ganglion

**ganzo** [dz] *m* (slang) lover; (coll) slicker

**gara** *f* competition, match; **fare a gara** to compete; **gara d'appalto** competitive bidding

**garagi·sta** *m* (-sti) garage man

**garante** *adj* responsible ‖ *m* guarantor; **farsi garante per** to vouch for

**garantire** §176 *tr* to guarantee; to secure (*a mortgage*)

**garanti·to -ta** *adj* guaranteed, warranted; downright, absolute (*liar*)

**garanzìa** *f* guarantee, warranty; insurance, assurance

**garbare** *tr* (naut) to shape (*a hull*) ‖ *intr* (ESSERE) (with *dat*) to like, e.g., **non gli garbano le Sue parole** he does not like your words

**garbatézza** *f* politeness, courtesy

**garba·to -ta** *adj* polite, courteous

**garbo** *m* politeness, good manners; gesture; act; shape (*of a hull*); good cut (*of clothes*); elegance (*in painting or writing*); **a garbo** correctly

**garbù·glio** *m* (-gli) tangle, confusion; mess

**gardènia** *f* gardenia

**gareggiare** §290 (**garéggio**) *intr* to compete, vie

**garétta** *f* var of **garitta**

**garétto** *m* var of **garretto**

**garganèlla** *f*—**bere a garganella** to gulp down

**gargarismo** *m* gargling; gargle

**gargarizzare** [ddzz] *intr & ref* to gargle

**gargaròzzo** *m* throat, gullet

**garitta** *f* railroad-crossing box; (mil) sentry box; (rr) brakeman's box

**garòfano** *m* carnation, pink

**garrése** [s] *m* withers

**garrétto** *m* ankle (*of man*); hock (*of horse*)

**garrire** §176 *intr* to chirp, twitter; to flap; (archaic) to quarrel

**garrito** *m* chirp, twitter

**garròtta** *f* garrote

**gàrru·lo -la** *adj* garrulous

**garza** [dz] *f* gauze

**garzonato** [dz] *m* apprenticeship

**garzó·ne -na** [dz] *mf* helper ‖ *m*

helper, boy; apprentice; (archaic) bachelor; **garzone di stalla** stableboy

**gas** *m* (gas) gas; gasoline; **gas asfissiante** poison gas; **gas delle miniere** firedamp; **gas esilarante** laughing gas; **gas illuminante** illuminating gas; **gas lacrimogeno** tear gas

**gasdótto** *m* gas pipeline

**gasificare** §197 (**gasìfico**) *tr* var of **gassificare**

**gasòlio** *m* Diesel oil

**gasòmetro** *m* var of **gassometro**

**gassificare** §197 (**gassìfico**) *tr* to gasify

**gassi·sta** *m* (-sti) gasworker; gas fitter; gas-meter reader

**gassòmetro** *m* gasholder, gas tank

**gassó·so -sa** [s] *adj* gaseous, gassy ‖ *f* soda, pop

**gastronomìa** *f* gastronomy

**gatta** *f* she-cat, tabby; **comprare la gatta nel sacco** to buy a pig in a poke; **gatta ci cova** something is rotten in Denmark; **pigliare una gatta da pelare** to take on a heavy burden, to get a tiger by the tail

**gattabùia** *f* (coll) clink, lockup

**gattamòrta** *f* (**gattemòrte**) hypocrite

**gattino** *m* kitten; (bot) catkin

**gat·to -ta** *mf* cat ‖ *m* tomcat; tamper, pile driver; **gatto a nove code** cat-o'-nine-tails; **gatto soriano** tortoise-shell cat; **quattro gatti** a handful of people ‖ *f* see **gatta**

**gattóni** *adv* on all fours

**gattopardo** *m* (zool) serval; **gattopardo americano** ocelot

**gattùc·cio** *m* (-ci) compass saw; (ichth) small dotted dogfish

**gaudènte** *adj* jovial ‖ *m* bon vivant

**gàu·dio** *m* (-di) joy, happiness

**gavazzare** *intr* (lit) to revel

**gavétta** *f* mess kit, mess gear; **venire dalla gavetta** to come up through the ranks

**gavitèllo** *m* buoy

**gazza** [ddzz] *f* magpie

**gazzarra** [ddzz] *f* racket, uproar

**gazzèlla** [ddzz] *f* gazelle

**gazzétta** [ddzz] *f* newspaper; gazette; newsmonger, gossip; **Gazzetta Ufficiale** Official Gazette (*in Italy*); Congressional Record (*U.S.A.*)

**gazzettino** [ddzz] *m* small newspaper; column, e.g., **gazzettino rosa** social column; newsmonger, gossip

**gazzósa** [ddzz] *f* var of **gassosa**

**gèl** *m* gel

**gelare** (**gèlo**) *tr* to freeze; to nip ‖ *intr* (ESSERE) & *ref* to freeze ‖ *impers* (ESSERE & AVERE)—**gela** it is freezing

**gelata** *f* frost

**gela·tàio -tàia** *mf* (-tài -tàie) ice-cream dealer

**gelaterìa** *f* ice-cream parlor

**gelatièra** *f* ice-cream freezer

**gelatière** *m* ice-cream dealer

**gelatina** *f* gelatin; jelly; **gelatina di frutta** fruit jelly; gum drop

**gelatinizzare** [ddzz] *tr & ref* to gelatinize; to jell

**gela·to -ta** *adj* frozen ‖ *m* ice-cream;

**gelato da passeggio** ice cream on a stick, popsicle

**gèli·do -da** adj icy, ice-cold

**gèlo** m frost; ice; cold; **diventare di gelo** to remain dumfounded; **farsi di gelo** to be cold or aloof; **sentirsi il gelo addosso** to get a chill

**gelóne** m chilblain

**gelosìa** [s] f jealousy; great care; shutter

**geló·so -sa** [s] adj jealous; solicitous

**gèlso** m mulberry

**gelsomino** m jasmine

**gemebón·do -da** adj (lit) moaning

**gemellàggio** m sisterhood (of two cities)

**gemèl·lo -la** adj twin; sister (ship) || mf twin || **gemelli** mpl cufflinks || **Gemelli** mpl (astr) Gemini

**gèmere** §123 tr (lit) to lament || intr (ESSERE & AVERE) to moan, groan; to suffer; to squeak (said of a wheel); to ooze; to coo (said of a dove)

**gèmito** m moan; howl (of wind)

**gèmma** f gem; (bot) bud

**gemma·to -ta** adj gemmate; jeweled

**gendarme** m gendarme, policeman

**genealogìa** f genealogy

**generalato** m generalship

**generale** adj general || m general; **generale d'armata** (mil) general; **generale di brigata** brigadier general; **generale di corpo d'armata** lieutenant general; **generale di divisione** major general || f (mil) assembly; **stare sulle generali** to speak in vague generalities

**generali·tà** f (-tà) generality; majority; **generalità** fpl personal data

**generalizzare** [ddzz] tr to generalize; to bring into general use || intr to generalize, deal in generalities

**generare** (**gènero**) tr to beget; to generate || ref to occur

**genera·tóre -trice** adj generating || m generator || f generatrix

**generazióne** f generation

**gènere** m genus; kind, type; genre; (gram) gender; **del genere** similar, alike; **farne di ogni genere** to commit all sorts of mischief; **genere umano** mankind; **generi alimentari** foodstuffs; **generi diversi** sundries, assorted articles; **in genere** generally

**genèri·co -ca** (**-ci -che**) adj generic; vague; all-round; general (e.g., practitioner) || mf (theat) actor playing bit parts || m vagueness, imprecision

**gènero** m son-in-law

**generosi·tà** [s] f (-tà) generosity

**generó·so -sa** [s] adj generous; rich (wine)

**gène·si** f (-si) genesis || **il Genesi** Genesis

**genèti·co -ca** (**-ci -che**) adj genetic(al) || f genetics

**genetlìa·co -ca** (**-ci -che**) adj birth || m birthday

**gengiva** f (anat) gum

**genìa** f set, gang; (lit) breed

**geniale** adj clever; genial; inspired, genius-like

**geniali·tà** f (-tà) cleverness, ingeniousness; genius; (lit) geniality

**genière** m (mil) engineer

**gè·nio** m (-ni) genius; (mil) corps of engineers; **andare a genio** (with dat) to like, e.g., **la musica moderna non gli va a genio** he does not like modern music; **fare qlco di genio** to do s.th willingly

**genitale** adj genital || **genitali** mpl genitals

**geniti·vo -va** adj & m genitive

**geni·tóre -trice** mf parent

**gen·nàio** m (-nài) January

**genocìdio** m genocide

**Gènova** f Genoa

**genovése** [s] adj & mf Genoese

**gentàglia** f riffraff, rabble, scum

**gènte** adj (archaic) gentle || f people; nation; family; (nav) crew; **gente d'arme** soldiers; **gente di mal affare** riffraff; **gente di mare** sailors

**gentildònna** f gentlewoman

**gentile** adj gentle; nice; genteel || **Gentili** mpl heathen

**gentilézza** f gentleness; kindness; **per gentilezza** kindly, please

**gentili·zio -zia** adj (**-zi -zie**) of noble family; (lit) ancestral

**gentiluò·mo** m (**-mini**) gentleman, nobleman

**genuflèttere** §177 ref to kneel down

**genui·no -na** adj genuine

**genziana** f gentian

**geofìsi·co -ca** (**-ci -che**) adj geophysical || f geophysics

**geografìa** f geography

**geogràfi·co -ca** adj (**-ci -che**) geographic(al)

**geògra·fo -fa** mf geographer

**geologìa** f geology

**geòlo·go -ga** mf (**-gi -ghe**) geologist

**geòme·tra** m (**-tri**) geometrician; land surveyor

**geometrìa** f geometry

**gerà·nio** m (**-ni**) geranium

**gerar·ca** m (**-chi**) leader

**gerarchìa** f hierarchy

**geràrchi·co -ca** adj (**-ci -che**) hierarchical; **per via gerarchica** through proper channels

**Geremìa** f Jeremiah

**geremìade** f jeremiad

**gerènte** m manager, director; **gerente responsabile** (journ) managing editor

**gèr·go** m (**-ghi**) jargon

**geriatrìa** f geriatrics

**Gèrico** f Jericho

**gèrla** f pannier (carried on the back)

**Germània, la** Germany

**germàni·co -ca** adj (**-ci -che**) Germanic

**germànio** m germanium

**germanizzare** [ddzz] tr to Germanize

**germa·no -na** adj german, e.g., **fratello germano** brother-german; Germanic || m (lit) brother-german; **germano nero** (orn) coot; **germano reale** (orn) mallard

**gèrme** m germ; (lit) offspring

**germici·da** (**-di**) adj germicidal || m germicide

**germinare** (gèrmino) *intr* (ESSERE & AVERE) to germinate

**germogliare** §280 (germóglio) *tr* to put forth ‖ *intr* (ESSERE & AVERE) to bud, sprout

**germó·glio** *m* (-gli) bud, sprout

**geroglìfi·co** -ca *adj* & *m* (-ci -che) hieroglyphic

**Geròlamo** *m* Jerome

**gerontocò·mio** *m* (-mi) or **gerotrò·fio** *m* (-fi) old people's home, nursing home

**gerùn·dio** *m* (-di) gerund

**Gerusalèmme** *f* Jerusalem

**gessare** (gèsso) *tr* to plaster; to lime (*a field*)

**gèsso** *m* gypsum; plaster; chalk; (sculp) plaster cast

**gessó·so** -sa [s] *adj* plastery, chalky; chalklike

**gèsta** *f* (archaic) army; **gesta** *fpl* deeds, exploits

**gestante** *f* pregnant woman

**gestazióne** *f* gestation

**gesticolare** (gestìcolo) *intr* to gesticulate

**gestióne** *f* management, operation; data processing

**gestire** §176 *tr* to manage, operate ‖ *intr* to gesticulate; (theat) to make gestures

**gèsto** *m* gesture; attitude; act, deed

**ge·stóre** -strice *mf* manager, operator; **gestore di stazione** (rr) station agent

**gestualità** *f* bodily movements (*e.g., of an actor*)

**Gesù** *m* Jesus; **Gesù Cristo** Jesus Christ

**gesuì·ta** *m* (-ti) Jesuit

**gesuìti·co** -ca *adj* (-ci -che) Jesuitic(al)

**gettare** (gètto) *tr* to throw; to cast; to pour; to lay (*e.g., a floor*); to send forth; to yield; to broadcast (*seed*); to risk (*one's life*); **gettare la colpa addosso a qlcu** to lay the blame on s.o.; **gettare le armi** to lay down one's arms; **gettar giù** to fell, knock down; **gettar sangue** to bleed ‖ *ref* to throw oneself; to plunge; to flow, empty (*said of a river*)

**gettata** *f* pour, pouring; jetty; shoot, sprout; cast; range (*of a gun*); **gettata cardiaca** (med) rate of flow of blood

**gèttito** *m* yield; waste; **far gettito di** to waste

**gètto** *m* throw; gush; shoot, sprout; cast; precast concrete slab; (aer) jet; **a getto** (aer) jet; **a getto continuo** continuously; **di getto** spontaneously; **far getto di** to waste; **primo getto** first draft

**gettonare** (gettóno) *tr* (coll) to call up from a pay station; (coll) to make the selection of (*a record in a jukebox*)

**gettóne** *m* counter, token; attendance fee; (cards) chip

**gettopropulsióne** *f* jet propulsion

**ghepardo** *m* cheetah

**ghép·pio** *m* (-pi) kestrel

**gherì·glio** *m* (-gli) kernel, meat (*of nut*)

**gherlino** *m* (naut) warp, line

**gherminèlla** *f* trick, sleight of hand· trickery

**ghermire** §176 *tr* to claw; to seize

**gheróne** *m* gusset

**ghétta** *f* gaiter; **ghette** spats

**ghétto** *m* ghetto

**ghiacciàia** *f* icebox, cooler

**ghiac·ciàio** *m* (-ciài) glacier; **ghiacciaio continentale** polar ice cap

**ghiacciare** §128 *tr* to freeze ‖ *intr* (ESSERE) to freeze ‖ *impers* (ESSERE) —**ghiaccia** it is freezing

**ghiaccia·to** -ta *adj* iced; ice-cold; frozen ‖ *f* flavored crushed ice

**ghiàc·cio** -cia (-ci -ce) *adj* icy, ice-cold ‖ *m* ice; **ghiaccio secco** dry ice

**ghiacciò·lo** -la *adj* crumbly, breakable ‖ *m* icicle; popsicle

**ghiàia** *f* gravel, crushed stone

**ghianda** *f* fringe (*on a curtain*); (bot) acorn; **ghiande** mast (*for swine*)

**ghiandàia** *f* (orn) jay

**ghiàndola** *f* gland

**ghibelli·no** -na *adj* & *m* Ghibelline

**ghièra** *f* ferrule; ring

**ghigliottina** *f* guillotine; **a ghigliottina** sash (*window*)

**ghigliottinare** *tr* to guillotine

**ghigna** *f* (coll) grimace

**ghignare** *intr* to grimace; to sneer

**ghigno** *m* sneer, smirk; grin

**ghinèa** *f* guinea

**ghìngheri** *m invar*—**in ghingheri** dressed up

**ghiót·to** -ta *adj* fond; gluttonous; eager; dainty (*food*) ‖ *f* dripping pan

**ghiottó·ne** -na *mf* glutton; (zool) glutton, wolverine

**ghiottonerìa** *f* gluttony; tidbit; (fig) rarity

**ghiòzzo** [ddzz] *m* dolt; (ichth) gudgeon

**ghirba** *f* jar; (coll) skin, life

**ghiribizzo** [ddzz] *m* (coll) whim, caprice

**ghirigòro** *m* doodle, curlicue

**ghirlanda** *f* garland, wreath

**ghiro** *m* dormouse; **dormire come un ghiro** to sleep like a log

**ghisa** *f* cast iron

**già** *adv* already; once upon a time; formerly ‖ *interj* indeed!

**giac·ca** *f* (-che) jacket, coat; **giacca a due petti** double-breasted coat; **giacca a vento** windbreaker

**giacché** *conj* since

**giacènte** *adj* lying; idle (*capital*); unclaimed (*letter*); in abeyance

**giacènza** *f* lying; stay, abeyance; **giacenze di capitali** idle capital; **giacenze di magazzino** unsold stock of merchandise

**giacére** §181 *intr* (ESSERE) to lie; to be in abeyance; (lit) to be prostrate

**giacì·glio** *m* (-gli) pallet, cot

**giaciménto** *m* field, bed; **giacimento petrolifero** oil field

**giacinto** *m* hyacinth

**Giàcomo** *m* James

**giaculatòria** *f* ejaculation (*prayer*); litany (*monotonous account*); curse

**giada** *f* jade

**giaggiòlo** *m* (bot) iris

**giaguaro** *m* jaguar

**giaiétto** *m* jet (*black coal*)

**gialappa** *f* (pharm) jalap

**gialla·stro -stra** *adj* yellowish

**gial·lo -la** *adj* yellow; detective (*book or picture*); white (*with fear*) ‖ *m* yellow; detective story, whodunit; suspense movie; **giallo dell'uovo** egg yolk

**giamaica·no -na** *adj & mf* Jamaican

**giàmbi·co -ca** *adj* (**-ci -che**) iambic

**giambo** *m* iamb

**giammài** *adv* never

**giansenismo** *m* Jansenism

**Giappóne, il** Japan

**giapponése** [s] *adj & mf* Japanese

**giara** *f* crock, jar

**giardinàg·gio** *m* (**-gi**) gardening

**giardinétta** *f* station wagon

**giardiniè·re -ra** *mf* gardener ‖ *f* jardiniere; mixed pickles; mixed salad; wagonette; station wagon

**giardino** *m* garden; **giardino d'infanzia** kindergarten; **giardino pensile** roof garden; **giardino zoologico** zoological garden

**giarrettièra** *f* garter

**Giasóne** *m* Jason

**giavanése** [s] *adj & mf* Javanese

**giavellòtto** *m* javelin

**gibbó·so -sa** [s] *adj* gibbous, humped; humpbacked; rough (*ground*)

**gibèrna** *f* cartridge box; cartridge belt

**gi·bus** *m* (**-bus**) opera hat

**gi·ga** *f* (**-ghe**) gigue, jig

**gigante** *adj & m* giant

**giganté·sco -sca** *adj* (**-schi -sche**) gigantic

**gigantéssa** *f* giantess

**gigióne** *m* ham actor

**gi·glio** *m* (**-gli**) Madonna lily; fleur-de-lys

**gilda** *f* guild

**gi·lè** *f* (**-lè**) vest, waistcoat

**gimnòto** *m* electric eel

**ginecologìa** *f* gynecology

**ginecòlo·go -ga** *mf* (**-gi -ghe**) gynecologist

**gine·pràio** *m* (**-prài**) juniper thicket; (fig) mess

**ginépro** *m* juniper

**ginèstra** *f* (bot) Spanish broom

**Ginèvra** *f* Geneva

**ginevri·no -na** *adj & mf* Genevan

**gingillare** *ref* to trifle; to idle

**gingillo** *m* trifle, bauble

**ginnà·sio** *m* (**-si**) secondary school; gymnasium

**ginna·sta** *mf* (**-sti -ste**) gymnast

**ginnàsti·co -ca** *adj* (**-ci -che**) gymnastic ‖ *f* gymnastics; **ginnastica a corpo libero** or **ginnastica da camera** calisthenics

**gìnni·co -ca** *adj* (**-ci -che**) gymnastic

**ginocchiata** *f* blow with the knee; blow on the knee

**ginocchièra** *f* kneepad; elastic bandage (*for knee*); kneepiece (*of armor*)

**ginòc·chio** *m* (**-chi**) knee; **avere il ginocchio valgo** to be bowlegged; **avere il ginocchio varo** to be knock-kneed; **in ginocchio** on one's knees

‖ *m* (**-chia** *fpl*) knee; **fino alle ginocchia** knee-deep; **gettarsi alle ginocchia di** to go down on one's knees to; **mettere qlcu in ginocchio** to bring s.o. to his knees

**ginocchióni** *adv* on one's knees

**giocare** §182 *tr* to play; to stake, bet, risk, gamble; to make a fool of ‖ *intr* to play; to gamble; to circulate (*said of air*); (fig) to play a role; **giocare a** to play; to wager; **giocare a mosca cieca** to play blindman's buff; **giocare con** to risk; **giocare d'armi** to fence; **giocare d'azzardo** to gamble; **giocare di** to use (*e.g., one's wits*); **giocare di gomiti** to elbow one's way; **giocare di mano** to steal; **giocare sulle parole** to play on words; to pun ‖ *ref* to risk (*e.g., one's life*); to gamble away

**giocata** *f* wager, stake; game, play

**gioca·tóre -trice** *mf* player; gambler; speculator

**giocàttolo** *m* toy, plaything

**giocherellare (giocherèllo)** *intr* to play, trifle

**giochétto** *m* children's game; child's play; dirty trick

**giò·co** *m* (**-chi**) game; gambling; play; wager, stake; set; joke; (cards) hand; **entrare in gioco** to come into play; **fare gioco a** to come in handy to; **fare il doppio gioco** to be guilty of duplicity; **fare il gioco di** to play into the hands of; **giochi di equilibrio** balancing act; **gioco da ragazzi** child's play; **gioco d'azzardo** gambling; game of chance; **gioco dei bussolotti** (fig) jugglery; **gioco di destrezza** game of skill; **gioco di parole** play on words, pun; **gioco di prestigio** sleight of hand; **gioco di società** parlor game; **metter in gioco** to risk; to stake; **per gioco** for fun; **prendersi gioco di** to make fun of

**giocofòrza** *m*—**è giocoforza** + *inf* it is necessary + *inf*

**giocolière** *m* juggler

**giocón·do -da** *adj* merry, joyful

**giocó·so -sa** [s] *adj* jocose, jolly

**giogàia** *f* dewlap; chain of mountains

**gió·go** *m* (**-ghi**) yoke; beam (*of balance*); rounded peak; pass

**gìoia** *f* joy, happiness; darling; jewel; **darsi alla pazza gioia** to have a wild time

**gioiellerìa** *f* jewelry; jewelry store

**gioiellière** *m* jeweler

**gioièllo** *m* jewel

**gioió·so -sa** [s] *adj* joyful

**gioire** §176 (*pres part* missing) *intr* to rejoice

**Gióna** *m* Jonas

**Giordània, la** Jordan (*country*)

**giorda·no -na** *adj & mf* Jordanian ‖ **Giordano** *m* Jordan (*river*)

**Giórgio** *m* George

**giorna·làio -làia** *mf* (**-lài -làie**) newsdealer

**giornale** *m* newspaper; magazine; (com) journal; **giornale di bordo** log, logbook; **giornale murale** poster; **giornale radio** newscast

**giornaliè·ro -ra** *adj* daily ‖ *mf* day laborer

**giornalismo** *m* journalism

**giornali·sta** *mf* (**-sti -ste**) journalist; **giornalista pubblicista** free-lance writer ‖ *m* newspaperman ‖ *f* newspaperwoman

**giornalménte** *adv* daily

**giornata** *f* day; day's work; birthday; pay, salary; battle; day's march; **giornata campale** pitched battle; **giornata della mamma** Mother's Day; **giornata lavorativa** workday; **vivere alla giornata** to live from hand to mouth

**giórno** *m* day; **a giorni** within the next few days; **a giorni . . . a giorni** some days . . . others; **a giorno** open, openwork (*needlework*); full (*light*); **ai giorni nostri** nowadays; **al giorno d'oggi** nowadays; **buon giorno** good day; good morning; good-bye; **dare gli otto giorni a** to dismiss, fire; **di ogni giorno** everyday (*e.g., clothes*); **essere a giorno** to be up to date; **giorno dei morti** All Souls' Day; **giorno di lavoro** workday; **giorno di paga** payday; **giorno fatto** broad daylight; **giorno feriale** weekday; **giorno festivo** holiday; **mettere a giorno** to bring up to date; **otto giorni oggi** one week from today; **passare un brutto giorno** to have a bad time; **un giorno o l'altro** one of these days

**giòstra** *f* joust; merry-go-round

**giostrare** (**giòstro**) *intr* to joust; to get along, manage; to idle, loiter

**Giosuè** *m* Joshua

**Giotté·sco -sca** *adj* (**-schi -sche**) of the school of Giotto

**giovaménto** *m* benefit, advantage

**gióvane** *adj* young; youthful; fresh (*e.g., cheese*); Younger, e.g., **Plinio il Giovane** Pliny the Younger ‖ *m* young man; boy, apprentice; **i giovani** the young ‖ *f* young woman

**giovanile** *adj* youthful

**Giovanni** *m* John; **Giovanni Battista** John the Baptist

**giovanòtta** *f* young woman

**giovanòtto** *m* young man; (coll) bachelor

**giovare** (**gióvo**) *tr* (lit) to help ‖ *intr* (with *dat*) to help, to be of use to ‖ *ref* to avail oneself ‖ *impers* (ESSERE) —**non giova** it's no use

**Giòve** *m* Jupiter

**giove·dì** *m* (**-dì**) Thursday; **giovedì santo** Maundy Thursday

**giovèn·ca** *f* (**-che**) heifer

**gioventù** *f* youth

**giovévole** *adj* helpful, beneficial

**gioviale** *adj* jovial

**giovinézza** *f* youth

**gip** *f* (**gip**) jeep

**gippóne** *m* large jeep, panel truck

**giràbile** *adj* endorsable

**giradi·schi** *m* (**-schi**) record player

**giradito** *m* (pathol) felon

**giraffa** *f* giraffe; (mov, telv) boom, crane

**girafilièra** *f* diestock

**giramà·schio** *m* (**-schi**) tap wrench

**giraménto** *m*—**giramento di testa** vertigo, dizziness

**giramón·do** *m* (**-do**) globetrotter

**giràndola** *f* girandole; pinwheel; (fig) weathercock

**girandolare** (**giràndolo**) *intr* to stroll, saunter

**girante** *mf* endorser ‖ *f* blade (*e.g., of fan*)

**girare** *tr* to turn; to tour; to go around, travel over; to switch (*the conversation*); to film, shoot; to transfer (*a phone call*); to endorse; (mil) to surround ‖ *intr* to turn; to circulate; to spin (*said of one's head*) ‖ *ref* to turn; to toss and turn

**girarrósto** *m* turnspit; **girarrosto a motore** rotisserie

**girasóle** *m* sunflower

**girata** *f* turn; walk, ramble; (com) endorsement; (cards) deal; (coll) tongue-lashing

**giratà·rio -ria** *mf* (**-ri -rie**) endorsee

**giravòlta** *f* turn, pirouette; bend; sudden change of mind

**girellare** (**girèllo**) *intr* to stroll, wander around

**girèllo** *m* rump; go-cart, walker

**girévole** *adj* revolving

**girino** *m* tadpole; bicycle rider competing on the Tour of Italy

**giro** *m* periphery; turn, revolution; ride; size (*of hat*); edge (*of glass*); round (*of a doctor*); (sports) tour; (sports) lap; (com) transfer; (cards) hand; (theat) tour; **a giro di posta** by return mail; **andare in giro** to poke along; **giro collo** neckline; **giro d'affari** volume of business, turnover; **giro di parole** circumlocution; **fare il giro di** to tour; **mettere in giro** to spread (*news, gossip*); **nel giro di** within (*a period*); **prendere in giro** to poke fun at

**girobùssola** *f* gyrocompass

**girondolare** (**giróndolo**) *intr* var of **girandolare**

**giróne** *m* (sports) conference; (sports) division; (sports) league; (archaic) circle

**gironzolare** [dz] (**girónzolo**) *intr* to stroll, saunter

**giropilò·ta** *m* (**-ti**) gyropilot

**giroscò·pio** *m* (**-pi**) gyroscope

**girotóndo** *m* ring-around-a-rosy

**giròtta** *f* weather vane

**girovagare** §209 (**giròvago**) *intr* to roam, wander

**giròva·go -ga** (**-ghi -ghe**) *adj* wandering; strolling (*player*) ‖ *m* vagrant, hobo

**gita** *f* trip, excursion, outing

**gita·no -na** *adj* & *mf* Gypsy

**gitante** *mf* excursionist, vacationist

**gittata** *f* range (*of gun*)

**giù** *adv* down; **andar giù** to go down; to deteriorate; to get worse; **buttar giù** to throw down; (culin) to start to cook, e.g., **buttar giù gli spaghetti** to start to cook the spaghetti; (fig) to jot down; **da . . . in giù** for the past . . . ; **dar giù** to look worse (*said* *of a sick person*); **esser giù** to be downcast; **giù di lì** thereabouts; **in giù** down; downstream; **mandar giù** to swallow; **non andar giù** to not be able to stomach or swallow, e.g., **non gli vanno giù i bugiardi** he cannot stomach liars; **venire giù** to come down; to crumble; to collapse

**giubba** *f* coat, jacket; mane

**giubbétto** *m* small coat; bodice; jerkin

**giubbòtto** *m* jacket (*e.g., of a motorcyclist*); **giubbotto salvagente** (aer, naut) life jacket

**giubilare** (giùbilo) *tr* to retire, to pension || *intr* to rejoice

**giubiléo** *m* jubilee

**giùbilo** *m* jubilation, exultation

**giuda** *m* Judas || **Giuda** *m* Judas

**giudài·co -ca** *adj* (-ci -che) Judaic

**giudaismo** *m* Judaism

**giudè·o -a** *adj* Judean; Jewish || *mf* Judean; Jew

**giudicare** §197 (giùdico) *tr* to judge; to find (*e.g., s.o. innocent*); to try (*a case*) || *intr* to judge, deem

**giudicato** *m* (hist) Sardinian region; **passare in giudicato** (law) to become final

**giùdice** *m* judge; magistrate, justice; **giudice conciliatore** justice of the peace; **giudice popolare** member of the jury

**giudizià·rio -ria** *adj* (-ri -rie) judicial, judiciary

**giudì·zio** *m* (-zi) judgment; wisdom; trial; sentence; **giudizio di Dio** (hist) ordeal; **giudizio finale** Last Judgment; **metter giudizio** to mend one's ways

**giudizió·so -sa** [s] *adj* judicious, wise

**giùggiola** *f* jujube; (joc) trifle; **andare in brodo di giuggiole** to swoon, become ecstatic

**giugno** *m* June

**giugulare** *adj* jugular || *v* (giùgolo) *tr* to cut the throat of

**giulèbbe** *m* julep

**giuliana** *f* (culin) julienne || **Giuliana** Juliana

**giuli·vo -va** *adj* gay

**giullare** *m* jongleur; (pej) mountebank

**giumén·to -ta** *mf* beast of burden || *f* female saddle horse

**giun·ca** *f* (-che) (naut) junk

**giunchìglia** *f* (bot) jonquil

**giun·co** *m* (-chi) (bot) rush

**giùngere** §183 *tr* to join (*e.g., one's hands*) || *intr* (ESSERE) to arrive; **giungere a** or **in** to arrive at, reach; **giungere a** + *inf* to succeed in + *ger*; **mi giunge nuovo** it's news to me

**giungla** *f* jungle

**Giunóne** *f* Juno

**giunòni·co -ca** *adj* (-ci -che) Junoesque

**giunta** *f* addition; makeweight; strip (*of cloth*); junta; committee; **di prima giunta** at the very beginning; **per giunta** in addition

**giuntare** *tr* to join

**giuntatrice** *f* (mov) splicer

**giunto** *m* (mach) joint, coupling;

**giunto a sfere** ball-and-socket joint; **giunto cardanico** universal joint

**giuntura** or **giunzióne** *f* joint; juncture, seam

**giuò·co** *m* (-chi) var of **gioco**

**giuraménto** *m* oath; **deferire il giuramento a** to put under oath

**giurare** *tr* to swear, pledge || *intr* to swear

**giura·to -ta** *adj* sworn || *m* juror

**giurìa** *f* committee; jury

**giurìdi·co -ca** *adj* (-ci -che) juridical

**giurisdizióne** *f* jurisdiction

**giurisprudènza** *f* jurisprudence

**giurì·sta** *mf* (-sti -ste) jurist

**Giusèppe** *m* Joseph

**Giuseppina** *f* Josephine

**giusta** *prep* according to; in accordance with

**giustappórre** §218 *tr* to juxtapose

**giustézza** *f* correctness, justness; (typ) measure

**giustificàbile** *adj* justifiable

**giustificare** §197 (giustìfico) *tr* to justify || *ref* to excuse oneself

**giustificazióne** *f* justification

**giustìzia** *f* justice; **far giustizia a** to execute; **farsi giustizia da sé** to take the law into one's own hands; **render giustizia a** to do justice to

**giustiziare** §287 *tr* to execute

**giustizière** *m* executioner; (obs) judge

**giu·sto -sta** *adj* just; opportune || *m* just man; just price; rights, due || **giusto** *adv* just, justly

**gla·bro -bra** *adj* smooth (*face*)

**glaciale** *adj* glacial; (fig) icy

**gladiatóre** *m* gladiator

**gladiòlo** *m* gladiolus

**glàndola** *f* var of **ghiandola**

**glassa** *f* glaze, icing

**glassare** *tr* to glaze, ice

**glèba** *f* clod, lump of earth

**gli** §4 *art* || §5 *pers pron*

**glicerina** *f* glycerin

**glìcine** *m* wistaria

**gliéla; gliéle; gliéli; gliélo; gliéne** §5

**globale** *adj* total, aggregate

**glòbo** *m* globe; **globo oculare** eyeball

**globulare** *adj* globular, global

**glòbulo** *m* globule; (physiol) corpuscle

**gloglottare** (gloglòtto) *intr* to gobble; to gurgle

**gloglottì·o** *m* (-i) gobble, gobbling; gurgle

**glòria** *f* glory

**gloriare** §287 (glòrio) *tr* (lit) to exalt || *ref* to boast; to glory

**glorificare** §197 (glorìfico) *tr* to glorify

**glorió·so -sa** [s] *adj* glorious; proud

**glòssa** *f* gloss

**glossà·rio** *m* (-ri) glossary

**glòttide** *f* glottis

**glottòlo·go -ga** *mf* (-gi -ghe) linguist

**glucòsio** *m* glucose

**glùtine** *m* gluten

**gnòc·co** *m* (-chi) potato dumpling

**gnòmo** *m* gnome

**gnòrri** *m invar*—**fare lo gnorri** to feign ignorance

**gòb·bo -ba** *adj* hunchbacked || *mf*

hunchback || *f* hump; hunch; hump (*of gibbous moon*); hook (*of nose*)

**góc·cia** *f* (**-ce**) drop; bead; **avere la goccia al naso** to have a runny nose; **goccia d'acqua** raindrop

**góc·cio** *m* (**-ci**) drop, swallow

**gócciola** *f* drop; bead

**gocciolare** (**gócciolo**) *tr & intr* to drip

**gocciola·tóio** *m* (**-tói**) dripstone

**gocciolì·o** *m* (**-i**) drip, trickle

**godére** §184 *tr* to enjoy || *intr* to take pleasure; to revel; to profit || *ref* to enjoy; **godersela** to have a good time

**godìbile** *adj* enjoyable

**godiménto** *m* enjoyment, pleasure

**goffàggine** *f* clumsiness

**gòf·fo -fa** *adj* awkward; ill-fitting

**gógna** *f* pillory; **mettere alla gogna** to pillory

**góla** *f* throat; neck; gluttony; gorge (*of mountain*); mouth (*of cannon*); flue (*of chimney*); (archit) ogee; **far gola a** to tempt; **mentire per la gola** to lie shamelessly; **tornare a gola** to repeat (*said of food*)

**golétta** *f* neck (*of shirt*); (naut) schooner

**gòlf** *m* (**gòlf**) sweater, cardigan; (sports) golf

**gólfo** *m* gulf; **golfo mistico** orchestra pit || **Golfo Persico** Persian Gulf

**Gòlgota, il** Golgotha

**goliardo** *m* goliard; university student

**golosi·tà** [s] *f* (**-tà**) gluttony; tidbit

**golo·so -sa** [s] *adj* gluttonous; appetizing

**gómena** *f* hawser

**gomitata** *f* blow with the elbow; nudge

**gómito** *m* elbow; bend; **alzare il gomito** to crook the elbow; **dare di gomito a** to nudge

**gomìtolo** *m* skein, clew

**gómma** *f* gum; rubber; eraser; tire; **bucare una gomma** to have a flat tire; **gomma arabica** gum arabic; **gomma a terra** flat tire; **gomma da masticare** chewing gum; **gomma lacca** shellac

**gommapiuma** *f* foam rubber

**gomma·to -ta** *adj* gummed; with tires

**gommatura** *f* gumming; (aut) tires

**gommi·sta** *m* (**-sti**) tire dealer; tire repairman

**gommó·so -sa** [s] *adj* gummy

**góndola** *f* gondola; (aer) pod

**gonfalóne** *m* gonfalon

**gonfiare** §287 (**gónfio**) *tr* to inflate, blow up; to bloat; to swell; to exaggerate; to puff up || *intr* (ESSERE) to swell || *ref* to swell; to puff up; to bulge, balloon

**gonfiatura** *f* inflation; exaggeration

**gonfiézza** *f* swelling; grandiloquence

**gón·fio -fia** (**-fi -fie**) *adj* inflated, swollen; conceited || *m* swelling, bulge

**gonfióre** *m* swelling

**gongolare** (**góngolo**) *intr* to rejoice; to be elated

**goniòmetro** *m* goniometer; protractor

**gònna** *f* skirt; **gonna pantaloni** culottes

**gonnèlla** *f* skirt; (fig) petticoat

**gonnellino** *m* kilt; ballerina skirt

**gón·zo -za** [dz] *mf* simpleton, fool

**gòra** *f* millpond; marsh; (coll) spot

**górbia** *f* tip (*of umbrella*)

**gorgheggiare** §290 (**gorghéggio**) *tr & intr* to warble; to trill

**gorghég·gio** *m* (**-gi**) warbling; trill

**gór·go** *m* (**-ghi**) whirlpool; (lit) river

**gorgogliare** §280 (**gorgóglio**) *intr* to gurgle

**gorgó·glio** *m* (**-gli**) gurgle

**gorgoglì·o** *m* (**-i**) gurgling

**goril·la** *m* (**-la**) gorilla

**gòta** *f* cheek; (lit) side

**gòti·co -ca** *adj & m* (**-ci -che**) Gothic

**Gòto** *m* Goth

**gótta** *f* (pathol) gout

**gottazza** *f* (naut) scoop

**gottó·so -sa** [s] *adj* gouty

**governale** *m* fin (*of bomb*); (obs) rudder

**governante** *adj* governing || *m* ruler || *f* governess; housekeeper

**governare** (**govèrno**) *tr* to rule, govern; to steer (*a ship*); to tend (*animals*); to wash and dry (*dishes*); to run (*e.g., a bank*) || *intr* to steer

**governati·vo -va** *adj* government

**govèrno** *m* government; tending (*e.g., of animals*); running (*of household*); cleaning (*of house*); blending (*of wine*); (archaic) steering

**gózzo** *m* crop, craw (*of bird*); (pathol) goiter

**gozzovigliare** §280 *intr* to go on a spree

**gracchiare** §287 *intr* to caw

**gràc·chio** *m* (**-chi**) caw; (orn) chough

**gracidare** (**gràcido**) *intr* to croak; to honk (*said, e.g., of a goose*)

**gràcile** *adj* weak, frail; thin, delicate

**gradasso** *m* swaggerer, braggadocio

**grada·to -ta** *adj* graded; gradual

**gradazióne** *f* gradation; alcoholic proof; **gradazione vocalica** (phonet) ablaut

**gradévole** *adj* pleasant

**gradiménto** *m* pleasure; acceptance (*of a product*); liking

**gradinata** *f* steps; tier (*of seats*)

**gradino** *m* step; (fig) stepping stone

**gradire** §176 *tr* to like; to welcome

**gradi·to -ta** *adj* agreeable; welcome (*guest*); kind (*letter*)

**grado** *m* degree; rank; (nav) rating; (archaic) step; **a buon grado o a mal grado** willy-nilly; **a grado a grado** little by little; **a Suo grado** according to your wishes; **di buon grado** willingly; **di secondo grado** secondary (*school*); **essere in grado di** to be in a position to; **saper grado a** (lit) to be grateful to

**graduale** *adj & m* gradual

**graduare** (**gràduo**) *tr* to graduate

**gradua·to -ta** *adj* graduated || *m* noncommissioned officer

**graduatòria** *f* ranking; rank

**graffa** *f* clamp; brace, bracket

**graffiare** §287 *tr* to scratch; (coll) to swipe

**graffiétto** *m* tiny scratch; marking gage

**gràf·fio** *m* (**-fi**) scratch

**grafìa** *f* writing, spelling; (gram) graph

**gràfi·co -ca (-ci -che)** *adj* graphic ‖ *m* graph, diagram; designer (*for printing industry*); member of printers' union ‖ *f* graphic arts

**grafite** *f* graphite

**grafologìa** *f* graphology

**gragnòla** *f* hail

**gramàglia** *f* crepe; widow's weeds; **in gramaglie** in mourning

**gramigna** *f* couch grass; weed

**grammàti·co -ca (-ci -che)** *adj* grammatical ‖ *m* grammarian ‖ *f* grammar

**grammo** *m* gram

**grammofòni·co -ca** *adj* **(-ci -che)** phonograph, recording

**grammòfono** *m* phonograph, record player

**gra·mo -ma** *adj* poor, sad; wretched, miserable; frail, sickly

**gran** *adj* apocopated form of **grande**, used before singular and plural nouns beginning with a consonant sound other than *gn, pn, ps*, impure *s, x,* and *z*

**gra·na** *m* **(-na)** Parmesan cheese ‖ *f* **(-ne)** cochineal; grain (*of wood, metal, etc*); (slang) dough; (coll) trouble

**granàglie** *fpl* grain, cereals

**gra·nàio** *m* **(-nài)** granary, barn

**granata** *adj invar* & *m* garnet (*color*) ‖ *f* pomegranate (*fruit*); garnet; broom; grenade

**granatière** *m* grenadier

**granatina** *f* grenadine

**Gran Bretagna, la** Great Britain

**grancassa** *f* bass drum

**grancèvola** *f* spider crab

**gràn·chio** *m* **(-chi)** crab; claw (*of hammer*); (coll) cramp; **prendere un granchio** to make a blunder

**grandangolare** *adj* wide-angle

**grande** *adj* big, large; great; tall; high (*mass; voice*); long (*time*); capital (*letter*); full (*speed*); grown-up ‖ *m* grownup; grandeur; grandee; **fare il grande** to show off; **i grandi** the great; **in grande** on a large scale; lavishly

**grandézza** *f* size; enormity; greatness; quantity; **in grandezza naturale** life-size; **grandezze** ostentatiousness

**grandezzó·so -sa** [s] *adj* ostentatious

**grandiloquènza** *f* grandiloquence

**grandinare (gràndino)** *tr* (obs) to hail ‖ *intr* to hail ‖ *impers* (ESSERE & AVERE)—**grandina** it is hailing

**grandinata** *f* hailstorm

**gràndine** *f* hail

**grandiosi·tà** [s] *f* **(-tà)** grandeur, magnificence

**grandió·so -sa** [s] *adj* grandiose, grand

**grandu·ca** *m* **(-chi)** grand duke

**granduchéssa** *f* grand duchess

**granèllo** *m* grain, seed; speck

**grànfia** *f* clutch

**granico·lo -la** *adj* grain, wheat

**granire §176** *tr* to grain; to stipple; (mus) to make (*the notes*) clear-cut ‖ *intr* to teethe

**granita** *f* sherbet, water ice

**granito** *m* granite

**granitura** *f* knurl, milled edge

**grano** *m* wheat; grain of wheat; grain; speck; **grano duro** durum wheat; **grano saraceno** buckwheat; **grano turco** corn

**granturco** *m* corn

**granulare** *adj* granular ‖ *v* **(grànulo)** *tr* to granulate

**granulatóre** *m* crusher

**grànulo** *m* granule, pellet, bud

**granuló·so -sa** [s] *adj* granular; lumpy; gritty; friable, crumbly

**grappa** *f* eau de vie; clamp, brace

**grappétta** *f* staple; crampon

**grappino** *m* (naut) grapnel

**gràppolo** *m* bunch, cluster

**grassàg·gio** *m* **(-gi)** (aut) lubrication

**grassatóre** *m* highwayman

**grassazióne** *f* holdup

**grassétto** *m* boldface

**grassézza** *f* fatness; richness

**gras·so -sa** *adj* fat; rich; greasy; risqué ‖ *m* fat, suet; grease; shortening

**grassòc·cio -cia** *adj* **(-ci -ce)** pudgy, plump

**grata** *f* grate, grating

**gratèlla** *f* strainer; sieve; broiler

**gratìc·cia** *f* **(-ce)** (theat) gridiron

**gratìc·cio** *m* **(-ci)** lattice, trellis

**graticola** *f* gridiron; grating; graticule

**gratìfi·ca** *f* **(-che)** bonus

**gratificare §197 (gratìfico)** *tr* to give a bonus to; (fig) to pelt (*with insults*)

**gratificazióne** *f* bonus

**gratis** *adv* gratis, free, for nothing

**gratitùdine** *f* gratitude

**gra·to -ta** *adj* grateful, appreciative ‖ *f* see **grata**

**grattacapo** *m* trouble, worry

**grattacièlo** *m* skyscraper

**grattare** *tr* to scratch; to scrape; to grate; (slang) to snitch ‖ *intr* to scratch; to grate

**grattùgia** *f* grater

**grattugiare §290** *tr* to grate

**gratùi·to -ta** *adj* gratuitous, free

**gravame** *m* burden; tax; (law) appeal; **fare gravame a qlcu di qlco** to impute s.th to s.o.

**gravare** *tr* to burden, oppress; (obs) to seize ‖ *intr* (ESSERE & AVERE) to weigh; to lie; to be sorry, e.g., **gli grava d'avermi disturbato** he is sorry to have bothered me ‖ *ref*—**gravarsi di** to take upon oneself

**grave** *adj* heavy; burdensome; grave, serious ‖ *m* (phys) body; **stare sul grave** to put on airs

**graveolènte** *adj* stinking

**gravézza** *f* heaviness; burden; oppression; (obs) taxation

**gravidanza** *f* pregnancy

**gràvi·do -da** *adj* pregnant; fraught

**gravi·tà** *f* **(-tà)** gravity

**gravitare (gràvito)** *intr* to gravitate; to weigh, lie

**gravitazióne** *f* gravitation

**gravó·so -sa** [s] *adj* heavy; hard; burdensome; oppressive

**gràzia** *f* grace; pardon, mercy; delicacy; kindness; **di grazia!** please!;

**essere nelle grazie di qlcu** to be in s.o.'s good graces; **fare grazia di qlco a qlcu** to spare s.o. s.th; **grazia di Dio** abundance, bounty; **grazie!** thank you!; **grazie tante!** thanks a lot!; **in grazia di** thanks to; **male grazie** bad manners; **per grazie** as a favor; **render grazia a** to thank; **saper grazia a** to be thankful to

**graziare** §287 *tr* to pardon; **graziare qlcu di qlco** to grant s.th to s.o.

**grazió·so -sa** [s] *adj* graceful, pretty; gracious; (lit) free, gratuitous

**Grècia, la** Greece

**grè·co -ca** (-ci -che) *adj & mf* Greek ‖ *f* fret, fretwork; bullion (*on Italian general's hat*); tunic

**gregà·rio -ria** (-ri -rie) *adj* gregarious ‖ *m* private; follower

**grég·ge** *m* (-gi or -ge *fpl*) flock, herd

**grég·gio -gia** (-gi -ge) *adj* coarse; raw, unrefined ‖ *m* crude oil

**gregoria·no -na** *adj* Gregorian

**grembiale** *m* var of **grembiule**

**grembiule** *m* apron; frock; smock

**grembiulino** *m* pinafore

**grèmbo** *m* lap; womb; bosom

**gremire** §176 *tr* to crowd ‖ *ref* to become crowded

**gremi·to -ta** *adj* overcrowded

**gréppia** *f* manger, crib

**gréto** *m* dry gravel bed of a river

**grettézza** *f* stinginess; narrow-mindedness

**grét·to -ta** *adj* stingy; narrow-minded

**grève** *adj* heavy; uncouth; (lit) grievous

**gréz·zo -za** [ddzz] *adj* raw, crude; coarse

**gridare** *tr* to cry out; to cry for (*help*); (coll) to scold ‖ *intr* to cry out, shout

**grido** *m* cry (*of animal*) ‖ *m* (**grida** *fpl*) cry; scream; shout; yell; fame; **di grido** famous; **grido di guerra** war cry; **ultimo grido** latest fashion

**grifa·gno -gna** *adj* rapacious, fierce

**griffa** *f* hobnail; (mov, phot) sprocket

**grifo** *m* snout (*of pig*); (pej) snoot; (lit) griffin

**grifóne** *m* vulture; (mythol) griffin

**grigia·stro -stra** *adj* grayish

**grì·gio -gia** *adj & m* (-gi -gie) grey

**grigiovérde** *adj invar* olive-drab ‖ *m* olive-drab uniform

**gríglia** *f* gridiron, broiler; grate, grille; (elec) grid (*of vacuum tube*)

**grillare** *tr* to grill, broil ‖ *intr* to sizzle; to bubble (*said of fermenting wine*); to have a sudden whim

**grillétto** *m* trigger

**grillo** *m* cricket; whim, fancy

**grimaldèllo** *m* picklock

**grìnfia** *f* claw, clutch; **grinfie** clutches

**grinta** *f* grim or forbidding face

**grinza** *f* wrinkle; crease; **non fare una grinza** to be perfect

**grinzó·so -sa** [s] *adj* wrinkled; creased

**grippare** *intr & ref* to bind, jam

**grisèlla** *f* (naut) ratline

**gri·sou** *m* (-sou) firedamp

**grissino** *m* breadstick

**Groenlàndia, la** Greenland

**grómma** *f* incrustation, deposit

**grónda** *f* eaves; slope (*of ground*)

**grondàia** *f* gutter (*of roof*)

**grondare** (**gróndo**) *tr* to drip ‖ *intr* (ESSERE) to ooze (*said, e.g., of perspiration*); to drip; **grondare di sangue** to stream with blood

**gròppa** *f* back (*of animal*); top (*of mountain*); **restare sulla groppa a** to be stuck with, e.g., **gli sono restati sulla groppa cento esemplari** he is stuck with one hundred copies

**groppata** *f* bucking (*of horse*)

**gróppo** *m* knot, tangle; lump (*in throat*); squall

**groppóne** *m* back, rump

**gròssa** *f* gross; **dormire della grossa** to sleep like a log

**grossézza** *f* bigness; thickness; density; swelling (*of river*); (fig) coarseness; **grossezza d'udito** hardness of hearing

**grossi·sta** *mf* (-sti -ste) wholesaler

**gròs·so -sa** *adj* big, large; thick; heavy (*seas*); swollen (*river*); hard (*breathing*); offensive (*words*); coarse (*e.g., salt*); pregnant; deep (*voice*); (coll) important; **alla grossa** approximately; **di grosso** a lot, very much; **dirla grossa** to talk nonsense; **farla grossa** to make a blunder; **grosso d'udito** hard of hearing; **in grosso** wholesale; **spararle grosse** to tell tall tales ‖ *m* bulk; main body (*e.g., of an army*) ‖ *f* see **grossa**

**grossola·no -na** *adj* coarse; boorish, uncouth; big (*blunder*)

**gròtta** *f* grotto; (coll) inn

**grotté·sco -sca** (-schi -sche) *adj & m* grotesque ‖ *f* (hist) grotesque painting

**grovièra** *f* Gruyère cheese

**grovì·glio** *m* (-gli) tangle, snarl

**gru** *f* (gru) (orn, mach) crane

**grùc·cia** *f* (-ce) crutch; clothes hanger; (obs) wooden leg

**grufolare** (**grùfolo**) *intr* to nuzzle ‖ *ref* to wallow (*in mud*)

**grugnire** §176 *tr & intr* to grunt

**grugnito** *m* grunt

**grugno** *m* snout; (pej) snoot; **fare il grugno** to sulk

**grui·sta** *m* (-sti) crane operator

**grulleria** *f* foolishness

**grul·lo -la** *adj* silly, simple

**gruma** *f* deposit, incrustation

**grumo** *m* lump; clot

**grùmolo** *m* heart (*e.g., of lettuce*); small lump

**grumó·so -sa** [s] *adj* lumpy; incrusted, scaly

**gruppo** *m* group; main body (*e.g., of runners*); club; **gruppo elettrogeno** generating unit; **gruppo motore** (aut) power plant

**gruzzolo** *m* hoard, pile; **farsi il gruzzolo** to feather one's nest

**guadagnare** *tr* to earn; to win; to gain; to pick up (*speed*); to reach (*port*) ‖ *intr* to win; to look better ‖ *ref* to win; to win over; **guadagnarsi il pane** or **la vita** to earn one's living

**guadagno** *m* earnings; profit; **a basso**

guadagno (rad, telv) low-gain; **ad alto guadagno** (rad, telv) high-gain
guadare *tr* to wade, ford
guado *m* ford; (bot) woad; **passare a guado** to ford
guài *interj* woe!
guaina *f* case; scabbard, sheath; corset; (aut) seat cover
guàio *m* (guài) trouble || *interj* see **guài**
guaire §176 *intr* to yelp; to whine
guaito *m* yelp, whine
gualcire §176 *tr* to crumple
gualdrappa *f* saddlecloth
Gualtièro *m* Walter
guàn•cia *f* (-ce) cheek; moldboard; cheek side (*of gunstock*)
guanciale *m* pillow; **dormire tra due guanciali** to sleep safe and sound
guan•tàio -tàia *mf* (-tài -tàie) glove maker; glove merchant
guanteria *f* glove factory
guantièra *f* glove case; tray
guanto *m* glove; **gettare il guanto** to fling down the gauntlet; **raccogliere il guanto** to take up the gauntlet; **trattare con i guanti gialli** to handle with kid gloves
guantóne *m* big glove; **guantoni da pugilato** boxing gloves
guardabarriè•re *m* (-re) (rr) gatekeeper, crossing watchman
guardabò•schi *m* (-schi) forester
guardacàc•cia *m* (-cia) gamekeeper
guardacò•ste *m* (-ste) coast guard; coast-guard cutter
guardafi•li *m* (-li) (elec) lineman
guardalì•nee *m* (-nee) (rr) trackwalker; (sports) linesman
guardama•no *m* (-no) guard (*of sabre or rifle*); work glove; (naut) handrail
guardaportó•ne *m* (-ne) doorman
guardare *tr* to look at; to protect, watch; to pay attention to; to face, overlook; (obs) to keep to (*one's bed*); (obs) to keep (*a holiday*); **guardare a vista** to keep under close watch; **guardare dall'alto in basso** to look down one's nose at; **guardare di sotto in su** to leer at || *intr* to look; to pay attention; **Dio guardi!** God forbid!; **guardare a** to face (*said, e.g., of a room*); **guardare di non + inf** to be careful not to + *inf;* **guardare in faccia** to face (*e.g., danger*); **stare a guardare** to keep on the sidelines || *ref* to look at one another; to look at oneself; **guardarsi da** to keep from; to guard against
guardarò•ba *m* (-ba) wardrobe; linen closet; checkroom, cloakroom
guardarobiè•re -ra *mf* checkroom attendant || *f* hatcheck girl
guardasigil•li *m* (-li) minister of justice (*in Italy*); (Brit) Lord Privy Seal; (U.S.A.) attorney general; (hist) keeper of the seals
guardaspal•le *m* (-le) bodyguard
guardata *f* quick look, glance
guarda•vìa *m* (-vìa) guardrail; median strip
guàrdia *f* watch; guard; top water level; flyleaf; **di guardia** on duty;

fare la guardia a to watch; **guardia campestre** forester; **guardia carceraria** prison guard; **guardia del corpo** guard, body guard; **guardia di finanza** customs officer; **guardia d'onore** honor guard; **guardia forestale** forester; park guard; **guardia giurata** private policeman; **guardia medica** emergency clinic; **guardia municipale** police officer; **guardia notturna** night watch; **mettere qlcu in guardia** to warn s.o.; **montare la guardia** to be on guard duty, keep guard; **stare in guardia** to be on one's guard
guardiamari•na *m* (-na) (nav) ensign
guardiano *m* keeper; warden; watchdog; (eccl) superior; **guardiano notturno** night watchman
guardina *f* lockup; **in guardina** in jail
guardinfante *m* bustle (*worn under the back of a woman's skirt*)
guardin•go -ga *adj* (-ghi -ghe) wary
guàrdolo *m* welt (*in shoe*)
guardóne *m* peeping tom
guarentì•gia *f* (-gie) guarantee
guarìbile *adj* curable
guarigióne *f* cure, recovery
guarire §176 *tr* to cure; to heal || *intr* (ESSERE) to recover; to heal
guaritóre *m* healer; quack
guarnigióne *f* (mil) garrison
guarnire §176 *tr* to equip; to rig; to trim; (naut) to rig; (culin) to garnish || *intr* to add beauty
guarnizióne *f* decoration; trimming; lining; (culin) garniture; (mach) gasket; (mach) washer
Guascógna, la Gascony
guascó•ne -na *adj & mf* Gascon
guastafè•ste *mf* (-ste) kill-joy
guastare *tr* to ruin, spoil; to undo; to wreck; (obs) to lay waste; **guastare le uova nel paniere a** to spoil the plans of || *ref* to spoil; to worsen (*said, e.g., of the weather*); (mach) to break down; **guastarsi con qlcu** to quarrel with s.o.; **guastarsi il sangue** to blow one's top
guastatóre *m* commando
gua•sto -sta *adj* ruined, spoiled; wrecked || *m* breakdown; corruption; discord
guatare *tr* (lit) to look askance or with fear at
Guayana, la Guyana
guazza *f* dew
guazzabù•glio *m* (-gli) muddle, mess
guazzare *tr* to make (*an animal*) wade in a river || *intr* to wallow
guazzétto *m* stew, ragout
guazzo *m* puddle, pool; gouache
guèl•fo -fa *adj & mf* Guelph
guèr•cio -cia (-ci -ce) *adj* cross-eyed; one-eyed; almost blind || *mf* cross-eyed person; one-eyed person
guèrra *f* war; warfare; **guerra a coltello** internecine feud; **guerra di Troia** Trojan war; **guerra fredda** cold war; **guerra lampo** blitzkrieg; **guerra mondiale** world war

**guerrafon·dàio -dàia (-dài -dàie)** *adj*
warmongering ‖ *mf* warmonger
**guerreggiare** §290 **(guerréggio)** *tr* to
fight, war against ‖ *intr* to fight ‖
*ref* to make war on one another
**guerré·sco -sca** *adj* **(-schi -sche)** warlike
**guerriè·ro -ra** *adj* war, warlike ‖ *mf*
fighter ‖ *m* warrior
**guerrìglia** *f* guerrilla
**guerriglièro** *m* guerrilla (*soldier*)
**gufo** *m* misanthrope; (orn) horned owl
**gùglia** *f* spire; peak
**gugliata** *f* needleful
**Guglièlmo** *m* William
**guida** *f* guide; guidance; driving; runner (*rug*); guidebook; manual (*of instruction*); (aut) steering; **guida a
destra** right-hand drive; **guide** reins
(*of horse*); (mach) slide
**guidaiòlo** *m* leader (*among animals*)
**guidare** *tr* to guide, lead; to steer; to
drive ‖ *intr* to drive ‖ *ref* to restrain
oneself
**guida·tóre -trice** *mf* driver
**guiderdóne** *m* (lit) premium, prize
**guidóne** *m* pennant, pennon
**guidoslitta** *f* bobsled
**guidovìa** *f* ski lift

**Guinèa, la** Guinea
**guinzà·glio** *m* **(-gli)** leash; (fig) fetter,
shackle
**guisa** *f* way, manner; **in guisa che** so
that; **in guisa di** under the guise of
**guit·to -ta** *adj* miserly, niggardly ‖ *m*
strolling player
**guizzare** *intr* to dart; to wriggle; to
flash (*said of lightning*); (naut) to
yaw ‖ *intr* (ESSERE) to slip away
**guizzo** *m* dart; wriggle; flash
**gù·scio** *m* **(-sci)** shell; pod (*of pea*); tick
(*of mattress*); **guscio di noce** nutshell; **guscio d'uovo** eggshell
**gustare** *tr* to taste; to relish ‖ *intr*
(ESSERE & AVERE) to please; to like,
e.g., **gli gustano le gite in barca** he
likes boat rides
**gusto** *m* taste; pleasure, fun; whim;
style; **di cattivo gusto** tasteless; **di
gusto** gladly, with gusto; **prendere
gusto per** to take a liking for; **prendersi il gusto di** to relish; **provar
gusto** to have fun
**gustó·so -sa** [s] *adj* tasty
**guttapèrca** *f* gutta-percha
**gutturale** *adj* & *f* guttural

# H

**H, h** [ˈakka] *m* & *f* eighth letter of the
Italian alphabet
**handicappare** *tr* var of **andicappare**
**hangar** *m* **(hangar)** hangar
**havaia·no -na** *adj* & *mf* Hawaiian
**henné** *m* henna
**hertz** *m* hertz

**hertzia·no -na** *adj* Hertzian
**hi-fi** *f* (coll) hi-fi
**hockei·sta** *m* **(-sti)** hockey player
**hollywoodia·no -na** *adj* Hollywood,
Hollywood-like
**hurrà** *interj* hurrah!

# I

**I, i,** [i] *m* & *f* ninth letter of the Italian
alphabet
**i** §4 *def art* the
**iarda** *f* yard
**iato** *m* hiatus
**iattanza** *f* boasting, bragging
**iattura** *f* misfortune, calamity
**ibèri·co -ca** *adj* **(-ci -che)** Iberian
**ibernare (ibèrno)** *intr* to hibernate
**ibi·sco** *m* **(-schi)** hibiscus
**ibridare (ìbrido)** *tr* & *intr* to hybridize
**ìbri·do -da** *adj* & *m* hybrid
**icàsti·co -ca** *adj* **(-ci -che)** figurative;
realistic
**-ìccio -ìccia** *suf adj* -ish, e.g., **gialliccio**
yellowish
**iconocla·sta** *mf* **(-sti -ste)** iconoclast
**iconografia** *f* iconography
**iconoscò·pio** *m* **(-pi)** iconoscope
**iddì·o** *m* **(-i)** god ‖ **Iddio** *m* God
**idèa** *f* idea; goal, purpose; bit, touch;
**avere idea di** to have a mind to; **dare
l'idea di** to seem; **farsi un'idea di** to

grasp the notion of; **idea fissa** fixed
idea; **neanche per idea** not in the
least
**ideale** *adj* & *m* ideal
**idealismo** *m* idealism
**ideali·sta** *mf* **(-sti -ste)** idealist
**idealìsti·co -ca** *adj* **(-ci -che)** idealistic
**idealizzare** [ddzz] *tr* to idealize
**ideare (idèo)** *tr* to conceive
**idea·tóre -trice** *mf* inventor
**idem** *adv* ditto
**idènti·co -ca** *adj* **(-ci -che)** identical
**identificare** §197 **(idèntifico)** *tr* to identify ‖ *ref* to resemble each other;
**identificarsi con** to identify with
**identificazióne** *f* identification
**identi·tà** *f* **(-tà)** identity
**ideologìa** *f* ideology
**idi** *mpl* & *fpl* ides
**idillìa·co -ca** *adj* **(-ci -che)** idyllic
**idìl·lio** *m* **(-li)** idyll; romance
**idiò·ma** *m* **(-mi)** language, idiom
**idiomàti·co -ca** *adj* **(-ci -che)** idiomatic

**idiosincrasìa** *f* aversion; (med) idiosyncrasy
**idiò·ta** (**-ti -te**) *adj* idiotic ǀǀ *mf* idiot
**idiotismo** *m* idiom; idiocy
**idiozìa** *f* idiocy
**idolatrare** *tr & intr* to idolize
**idolatrìa** *f* idolatry
**ìdolo** *m* idol
**idonei·tà** *f* (**-tà**) fitness, aptitude; qualification
**idòne·o -a** *adj* fit; qualified; opportune
**idra** *f* hydra
**idrante** *m* hydrant, fireplug
**idratante** *adj* moisturizing
**idratare** *tr & ref* to hydrate
**idrato** *m* hydrate
**idràuli·co -ca** (**-ci -che**) *adj* hydraulic ǀǀ *m* plumber ǀǀ *f* hydraulics
**idri·co -ca** *adj* (**-ci -che**) water, e.g., **forza idrica** water power
**idrocarburo** *m* hydrocarbon
**idroelèttri·co -ca** *adj* (**-ci -che**) hydroelectric
**idròfi·lo -la** *adj* absorbent
**idrofobìa** *f* hydrophobia, rabies
**idròfo·bo -ba** *adj* hydrophobic, rabid
**idròfu·go -ga** *adj* (**-ghi -ghe**) waterproof
**idrogenare** (**idrògeno**) *tr* to hydrogenate
**idrògeno** *m* hydrogen
**idròpi·co -ca** (**-ci -che**) *adj* dropsical ǀǀ *mf* patient suffering from dropsy
**idropisìa** *f* dropsy
**idroplano** *m* hydroplane (*boat*)
**idropòrto** *m* seaplane airport
**idrorepellènte** *adj* water-repellent
**idroscalo** *m* seaplane airport
**idro·scì** *m* (**-scì**) water ski
**idroscivolante** *m* (naut) hydroplane
**idrosilurante** *m* torpedo plane
**idròssido** *m* hydroxide
**idroterapìa** *f* hydrotherapy
**idrovìa** *f* inland waterway
**idrovolante** *m* seaplane, hydroplane
**idròvo·ro -ra** *adj* suction (*pump*) ǀǀ *f* suction pump
**ièna** *f* hyena
**ièri** *m & adv* yesterday; **ieri l'altro** the day before yesterday; **ieri notte** last night; **ieri sera** last evening, last night, yesterday evening
**ietta·tóre -trice** *mf* hoodoo
**iettatura** *f* evil eye; bad luck, jinx
**igiène** *f* hygiene; sanitation
**igièni·co -ca** *adj* (**-ci -che**) hygienic, sanitary
**igname** *m* yam
**igna·ro -ra** *adj* unaware; inexperienced
**igna·vo -va** *adj* (lit) slothful
**ignizióne** *f* ignition
**ignòbile** *adj* (lit) ignoble
**ignominìa** *f* ignominy; outrage
**ignominió·so -sa** [s] *adj* ignominious
**ignorante** *adj* ignorant; illiterate ǀǀ *mf* ignoramus
**ignoranza** *f* ignorance
**ignorare** (**ignòro**) *tr* to not know; to ignore
**ignò·to -ta** *adj & m* unknown
**ignu·do -da** *adj* (lit) naked ǀǀ *m* (lit) naked person
**il** §4 *def art* the
**ìlare** *adj* cheerful

**ilari·tà** *f* (**-tà**) cheerfulness; laughter
**ìlice** *f* (lit) ilex, holm oak
**ìlio** *m* (anat) ilium
**illanguidire** §176 *tr* to weaken ǀǀ *intr* (ESSERE) to get weak
**illazióne** *f* inference
**illéci·to -ta** *adj* illicit, unlawful ǀǀ *m* unlawful act
**illegale** *adj* illegal
**illeggiadrire** §176 *tr* to embellish
**illeggìbile** *adj* illegible
**illegìtti·mo -ma** *adj* illegitimate
**illé·so -sa** *adj* unhurt, unharmed
**illettera·to -ta** *adj & mf* illiterate
**illiba·to -ta** *adj* spotless, pure
**illimita·to -ta** *adj* unlimited
**illìri·co -ca** *adj* (**-ci -che**) Illyrian
**illògi·co -ca** *adj* (**-ci -che**) illogical
**illùdere** §105 *tr* to delude
**illuminare** (**illùmino**) *tr* to illuminate; to brighten; to enlighten ǀǀ *ref* to grow bright
**illumina·to -ta** *adj* illuminated; enlightened; educated
**illuminazióne** *f* illumination; enlightenment
**illuminismo** *m* Age of Enlightenment
**illusióne** *f* illusion; delusion; **farsi illusioni** to indulge in wishful thinking
**illusionismo** *m* sleight of hand; magic
**illusioni·sta** *mf* (**-sti -ste**) magician
**illu·so -sa** *adj* deluded ǀǀ *mf* deluded person
**illusò·rio -ria** *adj* (**-ri -rie**) illusory, illusive
**illustrare** *tr* to illustrate; to explain, elucidate ǀǀ *ref* to become famous
**illustra·to -ta** *adj* illustrated, pictorial
**illustra·tóre -trice** *mf* illustrator
**illustrazióne** *f* illustration; illustrious person
**illustre** *adj* illustrious, famous
**illustrissi·mo -ma** *adj* distinguished; honorable; **Illustrissimo Signore** Dear Sir; Mr. (*addressing a letter*)
**imbacuccare** §197 *tr & ref* to muffle up; to wrap up
**imbaldanzire** §176 *tr* to embolden ǀǀ *intr* (ESSERE) & *ref* to grow bold
**imballàg·gio** *m* (**-gi**) wrapping, packaging
**imballare** *tr* to wrap up, package; to bale; to race (*the motor*); **imballare in una gabbia** to crate ǀǀ *ref* to race (*said of a motor*)
**imballa·tóre -trice** *mf* packer
**imballo** *m* packing; packaging, wrapping; racing (*of motor*)
**imbalsamare** (**imbàlsamo**) *tr* to embalm; to stuff (*animals*)
**imbambola·to -ta** *adj* gazing, staring; stunned, dumfounded; sleepy-eyed; sluggish
**imbandierare** (**imbandièro**) *tr* to bedeck with flags
**imbandire** §176 *tr* to prepare (*food, a meal, a table*) lavishly
**imbarazzante** *adj* embarrassing, awkward
**imbarazzare** *tr* to embarrass; to encumber, hamper; to upset (*the stomach*)

imbarazza•to -ta *adj* embarrassed, perplexed; upset (*stomach*); ill-at-ease
imbarazzo *m* embarrassment; annoyance; imbarazzo di stomaco upset stomach
imbarbarire §176 *tr & ref* to make barbarous; to corrupt (*a language*)
imbarcadèro *m* landing pier
imbarcare §197 *tr* to ship; to load, embark; to ship (*water*) || *ref* to sail; to embark; to curve (*said of furniture*)
imbarca•tóio *m* (-tói) landing pier
imbarcazióne *f* boat; imbarcazione di salvataggio lifeboat
imbar•co *m* (-chi) embarkation; port of embarkation
imbardare *intr & ref* (aer) to yaw; (aut) to swerve, lurch
imbardata *f* (aer) yaw; (aut) swerve, lurch
imbarilare *tr* to barrel
imbastardire §176 *tr* to corrupt || *ref* to become corrupt
imbastire §176 *tr* (sew) to baste; (fig) to sketch out
imbastitura *f* (sew) basting
imbàttere *ref*—imbattersi bene to be lucky; imbattersi in to come across; imbattersi male to have bad luck
imbattìbile *adj* unbeatable
imbavagliare §280 *tr* to gag
imbeccare §197 (imbécco) *tr* to feed (*a fledgling*); (fig) to prompt
imbeccata *f* beakful; (fig) prompting
imbecillàggine *f* imbecility
imbecille *adj & mf* imbecile
imbecilli•tà *f* (-tà) imbecility
imbèlle *adj* unwarlike; cowardly
imbellettare (imbellétto) *tr* to apply rouge to, apply make-up on || *ref* to put on make-up
imbellire §176 *tr* to embellish
imbèrbe *adj* beardless; callow
imbestialire §176 *tr* to enrage || *intr* (ESSERE) & *ref* to become enraged
imbévere §185 *tr* to soak; to soak up; to imbue || *ref* to become soaked; to become imbued
imbiancare §197 *tr* to whiten; to bleach; to whitewash || *intr* (ESSERE) & *ref* to turn white (*said, e.g., of hair*); to clear up (*said of weather*)
imbiancatura *f* bleaching (*of laundry*); whitening; whitewashing
imbianchiménto *m* bleaching
imbianchino *m* whitewasher; house painter; (pej) dauber
imbianchire §176 *tr* to whiten; to bleach || *ref* to turn white
imbiondire §176 *tr* to bleach (*hair*) || *intr* to become blond; to ripen (*said of wheat*)
imbizzarrire [ddzz] *intr* (ESSERE) & *ref* to become skittish (*said of a horse*); to become infuriated
imbizzire [ddzz] §176 *intr* (ESSERE) to get angry
imboccare §197 (imbócco) *tr* to feed by mouth; to put (*an instrument*) in one's mouth; to take, enter (*a road*); to prompt || *intr* (ESSERE) to

flow; to open (*said of a road*); (mach) to fit
imboccatura *f* entrance (*of street*); inlet; opening, top (*e.g., of bottle*); bit (*of bridle*); (mus) mouthpiece; avere l'imboccatura a to be experienced in
imbóc•co *m* (-chi) entrance; inlet; opening
imboniménto *m* claptrap
imbonire §176 *tr* to lure, entice (*s.o. to buy or enter*)
imbonitóre *m* barker
imborghesire §176 *tr* to render middle-class || *intr* (ESSERE) to become middle-class
imboscare §197 (imbòsco) *tr* to hide; to hide (*s.o.*) underground || *ref* to shirk; to be a slacker
imbosca•to -ta *adj* (mil) shirking, draft-dodging || *m* (mil) slacker; (mil) goldbrick || *f* ambush; tendere un'imboscata to set an ambush
imboscatóre *m* accomplice of a draft dodger; hoarder (*of scarce items*)
imboschire §176 *tr* to forest
imbottare (imbótto) *tr* to barrel
imbottigliare §280 *tr* to bottle; to bottle up || *ref* to get bottled up (*said of traffic*)
imbottire §176 *tr* to pad, fill; to stuff; to pad (*a speech*)
imbottita *f* bedspread, quilt
imbottitura *f* padding
imbra•ca *f* (-che) breeching strap (*of harness*); safety belt; (naut) sling
imbracare §197 *tr* to sling
imbracciare §128 *tr* to fasten (*shield*); to level (*gun*)
imbrancare §197 *tr & ref* to herd
imbrattacar•te *mf* (-te) scribbler
imbrattamu•ri *mf* (-ri) dauber
imbrattare *tr* to soil, dirty; to smudge, smear
imbrattaté•le *mf* (-le) dauber
imbratto *m* dirt; smudge, smear; daub; scribble; swill
imbrigliare §280 *tr* to bridle
imbroccare §197 (imbròcco) *tr* to hit (*the target*); to guess right
imbrodare (imbròdo) *tr* to soil
imbrogliare §280 (imbròglio) *tr* to cheat; to mix up; to tangle; to confuse; imbrogliare le vele (naut) to take in the reef || *ref* to get tangled up; to get confused; to turn bad (*said of weather*)
imbrò•glio *m* (-gli) cheat; tangle; (naut) reef; cacciarsi in un imbroglio to get involved in a mess
imbroglió•ne -na *mf* swindler
imbronciare §128 (imbróncio) *intr* (ESSERE) & *ref* to pout, sulk || *ref* to lower (*said of the weather*)
imbroncia•to -ta *adj* sulky, surly; cloudy, overcast
imbrunire *m*—sull'imbrunire at nightfall || §176 *intr* (ESSERE) to turn brown || *impers* (ESSERE)—imbrunisce it is growing dark
imbruttire §176 *tr* to mar; to make ugly || *intr* (ESSERE) & *ref* to grow ugly
imbucare §197 *tr* to mail; to put in a hole || *ref* to hide

imburrare *tr* to butter
imbuto *m* funnel
imène *m* (anat) hymen, maidenhead
imitare (ìmito) *tr* to imitate
imita·tóre -trice *mf* imitator; (theat) mimic
imitazióne *f* imitation
immacola·to -ta *adj* immaculate
immagazzinare [ddzz] *tr* to store, store up
immaginare (immàgino) *tr* to imagine; to guess; to invent ‖ *ref*—si immagini! of course!; not at all!
immaginà·rio -ria *adj* (-ri -rie) imaginary
immaginativa *f* imagination
immaginazióne *f* imagination
immàgine *f* image; picture
immaginó·so -sa [s] *adj* imaginative
immalinconire §176 *tr* to sadden ‖ *intr* (ESSERE) & *ref* to become melancholy
immancàbile *adj* unfailing; certain
immane *adj* monstrous; gigantic
immangiàbile *adj* uneatable, inedible
immantinènte *adv* (lit) immediately
immarcescìbile *adj* incorruptible
immateriale *adj* immaterial
immatricolare (immatrìcolo) *tr* to matriculate
immatricolazióne *f* matriculation
immatu·ro -ra *adj* immature; premature
immedesimare (immedésimo) *tr* to identify; to blend ‖ *ref* to identify oneself
immediataménte *adv* immediately
immediatézza *f* immediacy
immedia·to -ta *adj* immediate
immemoràbile *adj* immemorial
immèmore *adj* forgetful
immèn·so -sa *adj* immense, huge
immèrgere §162 *tr* to immerse; to plunge ‖ *ref* to plunge; to become absorbed
immerita·to -ta *adj* undeserved
immeritévole *adj* undeserving
immersióne *f* immersion; submersion (*of a submarine*); (naut) draft
imméttere §198 *tr* to let in; immettere qlcu nel possesso di (law) to grant s.o. possession of
immigrante *adj* & *mf* immigrant
immigrare *intr* (ESSERE) to immigrate
immigrazióne *f* immigration; (biol) migration
imminènte *adj* imminent
imminènza *f* imminence
immischiare §287 *tr* to involve ‖ *ref* to meddle; to become involved
immiserire §176 *tr* to impoverish ‖ *intr* (ESSERE) & *ref* to become impoverished; to become debased
immissà·rio *m* (-ri) tributary
immissióne *f* letting in, introduction; intake; insertion (*in lunar orbit*)
immòbile *adj* motionless, immobile; real (*property*) ‖ immobili *mpl* real estate
immobiliare *adj* real, e.g., proprietà immobiliare real estate; real-estate, e.g., imposta immobiliare real-estate tax
immobilizzare [ddzz] *tr* to immobilize; to pin down; to tie up (*capital*)

immodè·sto -sta *adj* indecent; immodest
immolare (immòlo) *tr* to immolate
immondézza *f* filth; impurity
immondez·zàio *m* (-zài) rubbish heap, dump; garbage can
immondìzia *f* trash; garbage; filth
immón·do -da *adj* filthy, dirty; unclean
immorale *adj* immoral
immorali·tà *f* (-tà) immorality
immortalare *tr* to immortalize
immortale *adj* immortal
immortalità *f* immortality
immò·to -ta *adj* (lit) motionless
immune *adj* immune
immunizzare [ddzz] *tr* to immunize
immutàbile *adj* immutable
immuta·to -ta *adj* unchanged
i·mo -ma *adj* (lit) bottom, lowest ‖ *m* (lit) bottom; (lit) depth
impaccare §197 *tr* to pack, wrap up
impacchettare (impacchétto) *tr* to pack, bundle
impacciare §128 *tr* to hamper; to embarrass ‖ *ref* to meddle
impaccia·to -ta *adj* hampered; clumsy
impàc·cio *m* (-ci) embarrassment; hindrance; trouble; essere d'impaccio to be in the way
impac·co *m* (-chi) wrapping; (med) compress
impadronire §176 *ref*—impadronirsi di to seize; to take possession of; to master (*a language*)
impagàbile *adj* invaluable, priceless
impaginare (impàgino) *tr* (typ) to make up (*in pages*), paginate
impaginato *m* (typ) page proof
impagliare §280 *tr* to cane (*a chair*); to stuff (*an animal; a doll*); to pack in straw
impalare *tr* to impale; to tie to a pole or stake ‖ *ref* to stiffen up
impala·to -ta *adj* stiff, rigid
impalcatura *f* scaffold; frame, framework
impallidire §176 *intr* to turn pale; to blanch; to grow dim (*said of a star*); (fig) to wane
impalmare *tr* (lit) to wed
impalpàbile *adj* impalpable
impaludare *tr* to make swampy or marshy ‖ *intr* to become marshy
impanare *tr* to bread; to thread (*a screw*) ‖ *intr* to screw in
impaniare §287 *tr* to trap, ensnare ‖ *ref* to fall into the trap
impantanare *tr* to turn into a swamp ‖ *ref* to get stuck, to sink (*in vice*)
impaperare (impàpero) *ref* to fluff, make a slip
impappinare *tr* to confuse ‖ *ref* to blunder; to stammer
imparare *tr* to learn; imparare a memoria to learn by heart ‖ *intr* imparare a to learn to, to learn how to
impareggiàbile *adj* peerless, unmatched
imparentare (imparènto) *tr* to bring into the family ‖ *ref*—imparentarsi con to marry into
ìmpari *adj* odd, uneven
imparrucca·to -ta *adj* bewigged
impartire §176 *tr* to impart
imparziale *adj* impartial

**impasse** *f* blind alley; deadlock; (cards) finesse

**impassìbile** *adj* impassible, impassive

**impastare** *tr* to knead; to mix; to smear with paste

**impasta·to -ta** *adj* kneaded; smeared; **impastato di** tainted with; overwhelmed with (*sleep*)

**impasto** *m* paste; pastiche

**impastoiare** §287 (**impastóio**) *tr* to fetter, hamstring

**impataccare** §197 *tr* to besmear, soil

**impattare** *tr* to even up; to tie (*a game*); **impattarla con** to tie (*a person*)

**impatto** *m* impact

**impaurire** §176 *tr* to scare || *ref* to get scared

**impàvi·do -da** *adj* fearless

**impaziènte** *adj* impatient

**impazientire** §176 *intr* (ESSERE) & *ref* to get impatient

**impaziènza** *f* impatience

**impazzare** *intr* (ESSERE) to be wild with excitement; to go mad; (culin) to curdle

**impazzata** *f*—**all'impazzata** at top speed; berserk

**impazzire** §176 *intr* (ESSERE) to go crazy; **fare impazzire** to drive crazy

**impeccàbile** *adj* impeccable

**impeciare** §128 (**impécio**) *tr* to tar

**impedènza** *f* impedance

**impediménto** *m* hindrance, obstacle, impediment

**impedire** §176 *tr* to impede, hinder; to obstruct || *intr* to prevent; **impedire** (with *dat*) **di** + *inf* or **che** + *subj* to prevent from + *ger*

**impegnare** (**impégno**) *tr* to pawn; to reserve (*a room*); to engage (*the enemy*); to keep occupied; to pledge || *ref* to obligate oneself; to go all out; to become entangled

**impegnati·vo -va** *adj* demanding (*activity*); binding (*promise*)

**impegna·to -ta** *adj* pawned; pledged; occupied; committed

**impégno** *m* commitment; obligation; task; zeal; **senza impegno** without promising

**impegolare** (**impégolo**) *tr* to tar || *ref* to become entangled

**impelagare** §209 (**impèlago**) *ref* to bog down; to become entangled

**impellicciare** §128 *tr* to fur; to veneer

**impenetràbile** *adj* impenetrable

**impenitènte** *adj* impenitent; confirmed

**impennàg·gio** *m* (-gi) (aer) empennage

**impennare** (**impénno**) *tr* to feather; (fig) to give wings to || *ref* to rear (*said of a horse*); to take umbrage; (aer) to zoom

**impennata** *f* rearing (*of horse*); (aer) zoom

**impensàbile** *adj* unthinkable

**impensa·to -ta** *adj* unexpected

**impensierire** §176 *tr* & *ref* to worry

**imperante** *adj* prevailing

**imperare** (**impèro**) *intr* to rule, reign; to prevail; **imperare su** to rule over

**imperati·vo -va** *adj* & *m* imperative

**imperatóre** *m* emperor

**imperatrice** *f* empress

**impercettìbile** *adj* imperceptible

**imperdonàbile** *adj* unforgivable

**imperfèt·to -ta** *adj* & *m* imperfect

**imperfezióne** *f* imperfection

**imperiale** *adj* imperial || *m* upper deck (*of bus or coach*); **imperiali** imperial troops

**imperiali·sta** *adj* & *mf* (-sti -ste) imperialist

**impè·rio** *m* (-ri) empire; rule

**imperió·so -sa** [s] *adj* imperious; imperative

**imperi·to -ta** *adj* (lit) inexperienced

**imperitu·ro -ra** *adj* immortal; everlasting, imperishable

**imperizia** *f* inexperience

**imperlare** (**impèrlo**) *tr* to bead; to cover with beads (*of perspiration*)

**impermalire** §176 *tr* to provoke || *ref* to become provoked

**impermeàbile** *adj* waterproof || *m* raincoat

**imperniare** §287 (**impèrnio**) *tr* to pivot; (fig) to base

**impèro** *adj invar* Empire || *m* empire; control, sway

**imperscrutàbile** *adj* inscrutable

**impersonale** *adj* impersonal

**impersonare** (**impersóno**) *tr* to impersonate || *ref*—**impersonarsi in** to be the embodiment of; (theat) to impersonate

**impertèrri·to -ta** *adj* undaunted

**impertinènte** *adj* impertinent, pert

**impertinènza** *f* impertinence

**imperturbàbile** *adj* imperturbable

**imperturba·to -ta** *adj* unperturbed

**imperversare** (**impervèrso**) *intr* to storm, rage; to be the rage

**impèr·vio -via** *adj* (-vi -vie) impassable

**ìmpeto** *m* impetus; onslaught; violence; outburst; **d'impeto** rashly

**impetrare** (**impètro**) *tr* to beg for; to obtain by entreaty || *intr* (ESSERE) (lit) to turn to stone

**impetti·to -ta** *adj* puffed up with pride

**impetuó·so -sa** [s] *adj* impetuous

**impiallacciare** §128 *tr* to veneer

**impiallacciatura** *f* veneer, veneering

**impiantare** *tr* to install (*a machine*); to set up (*a business*); to open (*an account*)

**impiantito** *m* floor, flooring

**impianto** *m* installation; plant; system

**impiastrare** *tr* to plaster; to dirty

**impiastricciare** §128 *tr* to plaster; to daub; to soil

**impiastro** *m* (med) plaster; (fig) bore

**impiccagióne** *f* hanging

**impiccare** §197 *tr* to hang

**impicciare** §128 *tr* to hinder; to bother || *ref* to meddle, butt in; **impicciarsi degli affari propri** to mind one's own business

**impìc·cio** *m* (-ci) hindrance; trouble; **essere d'impiccio** to be in the way

**impicció·ne -na** *mf* meddler

**impiccolire** §176 *tr* to reduce in size || *ref* to shrink in size

**impiegare** §209 (**impiègo**) *tr* to employ;

to use; to devote (*one's energies*); to spend (*time*); to invest (*capital*); to take (*time*) || *ref* to have a job

**impiegatì·zio -zia** *adj* (**-zi -zie**) employee, white-collar

**impiega·to -ta** *mf* employee; clerk

**impiè·go** *m* (**-ghi**) employment; use; job; place of business; investment

**impietosire** [s] §176 *tr* to move to pity || *ref* to be moved to pity

**impietrire** §176 *tr*, *intr* (ESSERE) & *ref* to turn to stone

**impigliare** §280 *tr* to entangle || *ref* to become entangled

**impigrire** §176 *tr* to make lazy || *intr* (ESSERE) & *ref* to get lazy

**impinguare** (**impìnguo**) *tr* & *ref* to fatten

**impinzare** *tr* to stuff || *ref* to stuff oneself; **impinzarsi il cervello** to stuff one's brain (*with knowledge*)

**impiombare** (**impiómbo**) *tr* to lead; to plumb, seal with lead; to fill (*a tooth*); (naut) to splice (*a cable*)

**impiombatura** *f* seal; filling (*of tooth*); (naut) splicing

**impipare** *ref*—**impiparsi di** (slang) to not give a hoot about

**implacàbile** *adj* implacable

**implicare** §197 (**ìmplico**) *tr* to implicate; to imply

**implìci·to -ta** *adj* implicit, implied

**implorare** (**implòro**) *tr* to implore

**implume** *adj* unfledged, featherless

**impolìti·co -ca** *adj* (**-ci -che**) unpolitical; impolitic, injudicious

**impollinare** (**impòllino**) *tr* to pollinate

**impoltronire** §176 *tr* to make lazy || *ref* to get lazy

**impolverare** (**impólvero**) *tr* to cover with dust || *ref* to get covered with dust

**impomatare** *tr* to pomade; to smear with pomade

**imponderàbile** *adj* imponderable; weightless

**imponderabilità** *f* imponderability; weightlessness

**imponènte** *adj* imposing; stately

**imponìbile** *adj* taxable || *m* taxable income

**impopolare** *adj* unpopular

**impopolarità** *f* unpopularity

**impórre** §218 *tr* to place, put; to impose; to order; to compel; to give (*a name*) || *intr* (ESSERE) to be imposing; (with *dat*) to order, command || *ref* to command respect; to win favor; to be necessary

**importante** *adj* important; sizable || *m* important thing

**importanza** *f* importance; size; **darsi importanza** to assume an air of importance

**importare** (**impòrto**) *tr* to import; to imply, to involve || *intr* (ESSERE) to be of consequence || *impers* (ESSERE) —**importa** it matters; **non importa** never mind

**importa·tóre -trice** *mf* importer

**importazióne** *f* importation; import

**impòrto** *m* amount

**importunare** *tr* to bother, importune

**importu·no -na** *adj* importunate, bothersome || *mf* bore

**imposizióne** *f* imposition; giving (*of a name*); order, command; taxation

**impossessare** (**impossèsso**) *ref*—**impossessarsi di** to seize; to master (*a language*)

**impossìbile** *adj* & *m* impossible

**impossibili·tà** *f* (**-tà**) impossibility

**impossibilitare** (**impossibìlito**) *tr* to make impossible; to make unable or incapable

**impossibilita·to -ta** *adj* unable

**impòsta** *f* tax; shutter; (archit) impost; **imposta complementare** surtax; **imposta sul valore aggiunto** value-added tax

**impostare** (**impòsto**) *tr* to start, begin; to state (*a problem*); to mail; to lay (*a stone*); to open (*an account*); to attune (*one's voice*); to lay the keel of (*a ship*) || *ref* to take one's position, get ready

**impostazióne** *f* beginning, starting; laying; mail, mailing; (com) posting

**impo·stóre -stóra** *mf* impostor

**impostura** *f* imposture

**impotènte** *adj* weak; impotent

**impotènza** *f* impotence

**impoverimén to** *m* impoverishment

**impoverire** §176 *tr* to impoverish || *intr* (ESSERE) & *ref* to become impoverished

**impraticàbile** *adj* impracticable; impassable

**impratichire** §176 *tr* to train, familiarize || *ref* to become familiar (*e.g., with a task*)

**imprecare** §197 (**imprèco**) *tr* to wish (*e.g., s.o.'s death*) || *intr* to curse

**imprecazióne** *f* imprecation, curse

**imprecisàbile** *adj* undefinable

**imprecisióne** *f* inexactness, inaccuracy

**impreci·so -sa** *adj* vague, inexact

**impregnare** (**imprégno**) *tr* to impregnate

**impremedita·to -ta** *adj* unpremeditated

**imprendìbile** *adj* impregnable

**imprendi·tóre -trice** *mf* contractor || *m*—**imprenditore di pompe funebri** undertaker

**imprenditoriale** *adj* managerial

**imprepara·to -ta** *adj* unprepared

**impreparazióne** *f* unpreparedness

**imprésa** [s] *f* enterprise; undertaking; achievement; firm, concern; (theat) management; **impresa (di) pompe funebri** undertaking establishment

**impresà·rio** [s] *m* (**-ri**) manager; (theat) impresario

**imprescindìbile** *adj* essential, indispensable; unavoidable

**impresentàbile** *adj* unpresentable

**impressionàbile** *adj* impressionable

**impressionante** *adj* striking, impressive; frightening

**impressionare** (**impressióno**) *tr* to impress; (phot) to expose || *ref* to become frightened; (phot) to be exposed

**impressióne** *f* impression

**imprestare** (**imprèsto**) *tr* (coll) to lend

imprèstito *m* (philol) borrowing
imprevedìbile *adj* unforeseeable
imprevedu·to -ta *adj* unforeseen
imprevidènte *adj* improvident
imprevi·sto -sta *adj* unforeseen, unexpected ‖ imprevisti *mpl* unforeseen events
imprigionare (imprigióno) *tr* to imprison
imprìmere §131 *tr* to impress; to imprint; to impart (*e.g., motion*)
improbàbile *adj* improbable, unlikely
ìmpro·bo -ba *adj* dishonest; laborious
improdutti·vo -va *adj* unproductive
imprónta *f* print, imprint; mark; **impronta digitale** fingerprint
improntare (imprónto) *tr* to impress, imprint; to mark
improntitùdine *f* audacity, impudence
impronunziàbile *adj* unpronounceable
impropè·rio *m* (-ri) insult
improprie·tà *f* (-tà) impropriety; error
immrò·prio -pria *adj* (-pri -prie) improper, inappropriate; (math) improper
improrogàbile *adj* unextendible
immròvvi·do -da *adj* improvident
improvvisare *tr* to improvise ‖ *ref* to suddenly decide to become
improvvisa·to -ta *adj* improvised; impromptu ‖ *f* surprise; surprise party
improvvisazióne *f* improvisation
improvvi·so -sa *adj* sudden ‖ *m* (mus) impromptu; **all'improvviso** or **d'improvviso** suddenly
imprudènte *adj* imprudent; rash
imprudènza *f* imprudence; rashness
impudènte *adj* shameless; brazen; impudent
impudènza *f* shamelessness; impudence
impudicìzia *f* immodesty
impudi·co -ca *adj* (-chi -che) immodest, indecent
impugnare *tr* to grip, seize; to take up (*arms*); to impugn, contest
impugnatura *f* handle; grip, hold; hilt, haft
impulsi·vo -va *adj* impulsive
impulso *m* impulse; **dare impulso a** to promote, foment
impuneménte *adv* with impunity
impunità *f* impunity
impuni·to -ta *adj* unpunished
impuntare *intr* to stumble, trip; to stutter ‖ *ref* to stutter; to balk; to be stubborn; **impuntarsi a** or **di** + *inf* to stubbornly insist on + *ger*
impuntigliare §280 *ref* to persist, insist
impuntire §176 *tr* to tuft (*e.g., a pillow*)
impuntura *f* backstitch
impuri·tà *f* (-tà) impurity; unchastity
impu·ro -ra *adj* impure; unchaste
imputàbile *adj* attributable
imputare (ìmputo) *tr* to impute; to charge, accuse; (com) to post
imputa·to -ta *mf* accused, defendant
imputazióne *f* imputation; charge, accusation; (com) posting
imputridire §176 *tr* & *intr* (ESSERE) to rot
in *prep* in; at; into; to; on, upon; through; during; married to, e.g.,

Maria **Roberti in** Bianchi Marie Roberti married to Bianchi; as, e.g., **in premio** as a prize; by, e.g., **in automobile** by car; of, e.g., **studente in legge** student of law; **essere in quattro** to be four; **in alto** up; **in breve** soon; in a word; **in giù** down; **in là** there; **in qua** here; **in realtà** really; **in seguito a** because of
-ina *suf fem* about, e.g., **cinquantina** about fifty
inabbordàbile *adj* unapproachable
inàbile *adj* unfit; ineligible; awkward
inabili·tà *f* (-tà) unfitness; awkwardness; inability
inabilitare (inabìlito) *tr* to incapacitate; to render unfit; to disqualify
inabilitazióne *f* disqualification
inabissare *tr* to plunge ‖ *ref* to sink
inabitàbile *adj* uninhabitable
inabita·to -ta *adj* uninhabited
inaccessìbile *adj* inaccessible; unfathomable
inaccettàbile *adj* unacceptable
inacerbire §176 *tr* to exacerbate ‖ *ref* to grow bitter
inacidire §176 *tr* & *ref* to sour
inadattàbile *adj* unadaptable; maladjusted
inadat·to -ta *adj* inadequate
inadegua·to -ta *adj* inadequate
inadempiènte *adj* not fulfilling; **inadempiente agli obblighi di leva** draft-dodging
inafferràbile *adj* that cannot be caught or captured; incomprehensible; elusive
inalare *tr* to inhale
inalatóre *m* inhaler
inalberare (inàlbero) *tr* to hoist ‖ *ref* to rear; to fly into a rage
inalteràbile *adj* unalterable
inamidare (inàmido) *tr* to starch
inamida·to -ta *adj* starched; pompous, starchy
inammissìbile *adj* inadmissible
inamovìbile *adj* irremovable
inamovibili·tà *f* (-tà) irremovability; tenure
inane *adj* inane; futile
inanella·to -ta *adj* curly; beringed
inanima·to -ta *adj* inanimate; lifeless
inanizióne *f* starvation
inappagàbile *adj* unquenchable
inappaga·to -ta *adj* unsatisfied
inappellàbile *adj* definitive, final
inappetènza *f* lack of appetite
inapprezzàbile *adj* inappreciable, imperceptible; inestimable
inappuntàbile *adj* faultless, impeccable
inarcare §197 *tr* to arch; to raise (*one's eyebrows*)
inargentare (inargènto) *tr* to silver
inaridire §176 *tr* to dry; to parch ‖ *ref* to dry up
inarrestàbile *adj* irresistible
inarrivàbile *adj* unattainable; inimitable
inarticola·to -ta *adj* indistinct, inarticulate
inascolta·to -ta *adj* unheeded
inaspetta·to -ta *adj* unexpected
inasprimènto *m* exacerbation

**inasprire** §176 *tr* to aggravate ‖ *ref* to sour; to become embittered; to become sharper; to become fierce or furious

**inastare** *tr* to hoist (*flag*); to fix (*bayonets*)

**inattaccàbile** *adj* unattackable; unassailable; **inattaccabile da** resistant to

**inattendìbile** *adj* unreliable

**inatté·so -sa** [s] *adj* unexpected

**inatti·vo -ta** *adj* inactive

**inaudi·to -ta** *adj* unheard-of

**inaugurale** *adj* inaugural; maiden (*voyage*)

**inaugurare** (**inàuguro**) *tr* to inaugurate; to usher in (*the New Year*); to open (*e.g., an exhibit*); to unveil (*a statue*); to sport for the first time

**inaugurazióne** *f* inauguration

**inauspica·to -ta** *adj* (lit) inauspicious

**inavvedu·to -ta** *adj* careless, rash

**inavvertènza** *f* inadvertence, oversight

**inavverti·to -ta** *adj* unnoticed; inadvertent, thoughtless

**inazióne** *f* inaction

**incagliare** §280 *tr* to hamper; to run aground ‖ *intr* (ESSERE) & *ref* to run aground; (fig) to get stuck

**incà·glio** *m* (-gli) running aground; hindrance, obstacle

**incalcinare** *tr* to whitewash; to lime (*a field*)

**incalcolàbile** *adj* incalculable

**incallire** §176 *tr* to make callous ‖ *intr* (ESSERE) to become callous; to become inured

**incalli·to -ta** *adj* callous; inveterate

**incalzante** *adj* pressing

**incalzare** *tr* to press, pursue ‖ *intr* to be imminent; to be pressing ‖ *ref* to follow one another in rapid succession

**incamerare** (**incàmero**) *tr* to confiscate

**incamminare** *tr* to launch; to guide, direct ‖ *ref* to set out; to be on one's way

**incanagli·to -ta** *adj* vile, despicable

**incanalare** *tr* to channel ‖ *ref* to flow

**incancrenire** §176 *tr* to affect with gangrene ‖ *ref* to become gangrenous; (fig) to become callous

**incandescènte** *adj* incandescent; (fig) red-hot

**incandescènza** *f* incandescence

**incannare** *tr* to reel, wind

**incantare** *tr* to bewitch; to auction off ‖ *ref* to become enraptured; to be spellbound; to jam, get stuck (*said of machinery*)

**incanta·tóre -trice** *adj* enchanting ‖ *m* enchanter ‖ *f* enchantress

**incantésimo** *m* enchantment, spell

**incantévole** *adj* enchanting, charming

**incanto** *m* enchantment; bewitchery; auction; **d'incanto** marvelously well

**incanutire** §176 *tr*, *intr* (ESSERE) & *ref* to turn gray-headed, to turn gray (*said of a person*)

**incanuti·to -ta** *adj* hoary

**incapace** *adj* incapable; (law) incompetent ‖ *mf* oaf; (law) incompetent

**incapaci·tà** *f* (-tà) incapacity; (law) incompetence

**incaparbire** §176 *intr* (ESSERE) & *ref* to be obstinate; to be determined

**incaponire** §176 *ref* to get stubborn; to be determined

**incappare** *intr* (ESSERE) to stumble

**incappottare** (**incappòtto**) *tr* to cover with a coat ‖ *ref* to wrap oneself in a coat

**incappucciare** §128 *tr* to cover with a hood

**incapricciare** §128 *ref*—**incapricciarsi di** to take a fancy to; to become infatuated with

**incapsulare** (**incàpsulo**) *tr* to encapsulate; to cap

**incarcerare** (**incàrcero**) *tr* to jail, incarcerate; (fig) to confine

**incaricare** §197 (**incàrico**) *tr* to charge ‖ *ref*—**incaricarsi di** to take charge of; to take care of

**incarica·to -ta** *adj* in charge; visiting (*professor*) ‖ *mf* deputy; **incaricato d'affari** chargé d'affaires

**incàri·co** *m* (-chi) task; appointment, position; **per incarico di** on behalf of

**incarnare** *tr* to incarnate, embody

**incarna·to -ta** *adj* incarnate ‖ *m* pink complexion

**incarnazióne** *f* incarnation

**incarnire** §176 *intr* (ESSERE) & *ref* to grow in (*said of a toenail*)

**incarni·to -ta** *adj* ingrown (*toenail*)

**incartaménto** *m* file, dossier

**incartapecori·to -ta** *adj* shriveled up

**incartare** *tr* to wrap up (*in paper*)

**incasellare** [s] (**incasèllo**) *tr* to file; to sort out

**incasellatóre** [s] *m* post-office file clerk

**incassare** *tr* to box up; to put (*a watch*) in a case; to mortise (*a lock*); to channel (*a river*); to cash (*a check*); (fig) to take (*e.g., blows*) ‖ *intr* to fit; to take it

**incasso** *m* receipts

**incastellatura** *f* scaffolding

**incastonare** (**incastóno**) *tr* to set, mount (*a gem*); **incastonare citazioni in un discorso** to stud a speech with quotations

**incastrare** *tr* to insert; to mortise; (fig) to corner ‖ *intr* to fit ‖ *ref* to fit; to become imbedded; to telescope (*said, e.g., of a train in a collision*)

**incastro** *m* joint; insertion; (carp) tenon; (carp) mortise

**incatenare** (**incaténo**) *tr* to chain, put in chains; to tie down, restrain

**incatramare** *tr* to tar

**incàu·to -ta** *adj* unwary, careless

**incavallatura** *f* truss (*to support roof*)

**incavare** *tr* to hollow out; to groove

**incava·to -ta** *adj* hollow

**incavatura** *f* hollow

**incavicchiare** §287 *tr* to peg

**incavigliare** §280 *tr* to peg

**incavo** *m* hollow; cavity; **incavo dell'ascella** armpit

**incazzottare** (**incazzòtto**) *tr* (naut) to furl

**incèdere** m stately walk || §123 intr to walk stately

**incendiare** §287 (**incèndio**) tr to set on fire; (fig) to inflame || ref to catch fire

**incendià·rio -ria** adj & mf (**-ri -rie**) incendiary

**incèn·dio** m (**-di**) fire; **incendio doloso** arson

**incenerire** §176 tr to reduce to ashes; to wither (e.g., with a look) || ref to turn to ashes

**inceneritóre** m incinerator

**incensare** (**incènso**) tr (eccl) to incense; (fig) to flatter

**incensa·tóre -trice** mf incense burner; (fig) flatterer

**incensière** m incense burner

**incènso** m incense

**incensura·to -ta** adj uncensured; (law) having no previous record

**incentivo** m incentive

**inceppare** (**incéppo**) tr to hinder; to shackle || ref to jam (said of firearm)

**incerare** (**incéro**) tr to wax

**incerata** f oilcloth; (naut) raincoat

**incernierare** (**incernièro**) tr to hinge

**incertézza** f uncertainty, incertitude

**incèr·to -ta** adj uncertain; irresolute || m uncertainty; **incerti** extras; **incerti del mestiere** cares of office, occupational annoyances, occupational hazards

**incespicare** §197 (**incéspico**) intr to stumble

**incessàbile** adj (lit) ceaseless

**incessante** adj unceasing, incessant

**incèsto** m incest

**incestuó·so -sa** [s] adj incestuous

**incètta** f cornering (of market)

**incettare** (**incètto**) tr to corner (market)

**incetta·tóre -trice** mf monopolizer

**inchiavardare** tr to key, bolt

**inchièsta** f probe, inquest; (journ) inquiry

**inchinare** tr to bend; to bow (the head) || intr (lit) to go down (said of stars) || ref to bow; to yield

**inchi·no -na** adj bent; bowing || m bow; curtsy

**inchiodare** (**inchiòdo**) tr to nail; to spike; to rivet; to tie, bind; to stop (a car) suddenly; to transfix || ref to freeze (said, e.g., of brakes); (fig) to be tied down; (fig) to go into debt

**inchiostrare** (**inchiòstro**) tr (typ) to ink

**inchiòstro** m ink; **inchiostro di china** India ink, Chinese ink

**inciampare** intr to trip, stumble

**inciampo** m stumbling block, obstacle; **essere d'inciampo a** to be in the way of

**incidentale** adj incidental

**incidènte** adj incidental || m incident; accident; argument, question

**incidènza** f incidence

**incìdere** §145 tr to engrave; to cut; to record (a record, a tape; a song); **incidere all'acqua forte** to etch || intr—**incidere su** to weigh heavily on (expenses, a budget); to leave a mark on

**incinerazióne** f incineration; cremation

**incinta** adj fem pregnant

**incipiènte** adj incipient

**incipriare** §287 tr to powder || ref to powder oneself

**incirca** adv about; **all'incirca** more or less

**incisióne** f engraving; cutting (of a record); recording (of a tape; of a song); incision; **incisione all'acqua-forte** etching

**incisi·vo -va** adj incisive; sharp (photo-graph || m incisor

**inciso** m (gram) parenthetical clause; (mus) theme; **per inciso** incidentally

**incisóre** m engraver, etcher

**incitare** tr to incite, provoke

**incivile** adj uncivilized; uncouth

**incivilire** §176 tr to civilize || ref to become civilized

**inclemènte** adj inclement, harsh

**inclemènza** f inclemency, harshness

**inclinare** tr to tilt; to bow, bend; to incline || intr (fig) to lean || ref to bend

**inclinazióne** f inclination; slope; **in-clinazione laterale** (aer) bank; **incli-nazione magnetica** magnetic dip

**incline** adj inclined

**incli·to -ta** adj famous; noble

**inclùdere** §105 tr to enclose, include

**inclusi·vo -va** adj including; **inclusivo di** including

**inclu·so -sa** adj enclosed; included; in-clusive || f enclosed letter

**incoerènte** adj incoherent

**incògliere** §127 tr (lit) to catch in the act || intr—**incogliere a** to happen to

**incògni·to -ta** adj unknown || m incog-nito; unknown; **in incognito** incog-nito || f (math) unknown quantity; (fig) puzzle

**incollare** (**incòllo**) tr to glue, paste; to size (paper) || intr to stick || ref to stick; to take on one's shoulders

**incollatura** f neck (of horse); glueing, sticking

**incollerire** §176 intr & ref to get angry

**incolloca·to -ta** adj unemployed

**incolonnare** (**incolónno**) tr to set up in columns

**incolonnatóre** m tabulator

**incolóre** adj colorless

**incolpàbile** adj blamable; (lit) guiltless

**incolpare** (**incólpo**) tr—**incolpare di** to charge with

**incól·to -ta** adj uncultivated; unkempt

**incòlume** adj unharmed, unhurt

**incolumità** f safety, security

**incombènte** adj (danger) impending; (duty) incumbent

**incombènza** f task, charge, incumbency

**incómbere** §186 intr (ESSERE) to be im-pending; to be incumbent

**incombustibile** adj incombustible

**incominciare** §128 tr & intr (ESSERE) to begin

**incommensuràbile** adj immeasurable; (math) incommensurable

**incomodare** (**incòmodo**) tr to bother, disturb || ref to bother; **non s'inco-modi!** don't bother!

**incòmo·do -da** adj bothersome, incon-venient || m inconvenience; ailment;

levare l'incomodo a to get out of the way of
incomparàbile *adj* incomparable
incompatìbile *adj* incompatible; unforgivable
incompetènte *adj & mf* incompetent
incompiu·to -ta *adj* unfinished
incomplè·to -ta *adj* incomplete
incompó·sto -sta *adj* untidy; unkempt; unbecoming (*behavior*)
incomprensìbile *adj* incomprehensible
incomprensióne *f* lack of understanding
incompré·so -sa [s] *adj* misunderstood
incomprimìbile *adj* irrepressible; incompressible
inconcepìbile *adj* inconceivable
inconciliàbile *adj* irreconcilable
inconcludènte *adj* inconclusive; insignificant
inconcus·so -sa *adj* (lit) unshaken
incondiziona·to -ta *adj* unconditional
inconfessàbile *adj* unspeakable, vile
inconfessa·to -ta *adj* unavowed
inconfondìbile *adj* unmistakable
inconfutàbile *adj* irrefutable
incongruènte *adj* inconsistent
incòn·gruo -grua *adj* incongruous
inconoscìbile *adj* unknowable
inconsapèvole *adj* unaware, unconscious
incòn·scio -scia *adj & m* (-sci -sce) unconscious
inconseguènte *adj* inconsistent, inconsequential
inconsidera·to -ta *adj* inconsiderate
inconsistènte *adj* flimsy; inconsistent
inconsistènza *f* flimsiness; inconsistency
inconsolàbile *adj* inconsolable
inconsuè·to -ta *adj* unusual
inconsul·to -ta *adj* ill-advised, rash
incontamina·to -ta *adj* uncontaminated
incontenìbile *adj* irrepressible
incontentàbile *adj* insatiable; hard to please; exacting
incontinènza *f* incontinence
incontrare (incóntro) *tr* to meet; to encounter, meet with || *intr* (ESSERE) to catch on (*said, e.g., of fashions*) || *ref* to meet; to agree || *impers* (ESSERE) to happen
incontrastàbile *adj* indisputable
incontrasta·to -ta *adj* undisputed
incóntro *m* meeting; encounter; success; meet; game, fight, match; occasion, opportunity; all'incontro on the other hand; opposite; andare incontro a to go towards; to go to meet; to face; to meet (*expenses*); to accommodate; farsi incontro a to advance toward
incontrollàbile *adj* uncontrollable
incontrolla·to -ta *adj* unchecked
incontrovertìbile *adj* incontrovertible
inconveniènte *adj* inconvenient || *m* inconvenience, disadvantage
incoraggiante *adj* encouraging
incoraggiare §290 *tr* to encourage
incorare §257 (incuòro) *tr* to hearten
incordare (incòrdo) *tr* to string (*e.g., a racket*); to tie up (*with a cord*) || *ref* to stiffen (*said of a muscle*)
incornare (incòrno) *tr* (taur) to gore

incorniciare §128 *tr* to frame; (journ) to border; (slang) to cuckold
incoronare (incoróno) *tr* to crown
incoronazióne *f* coronation
incorporàbile *adj* absorbable; adaptable
incorporare (incòrporo) *tr* to incorporate; to absorb || *ref* to incorporate
incorpòre·o -a *adj* incorporeal
incorreggìbile *adj* incorrigible
incórrere §139 *intr* (ESSERE)—incorrere in to incur
incorròt·to -ta *adj* uncorrupt
incosciènte *adj* unconscious; unaware; irresponsible || *mf* irresponsible person
incosciènza *f* unconsciousness; irresponsibility; madness
incostante *adj* inconstant, fickle
incredìbile *adj* incredible, unbelievable
incrèdu·lo -la *adj* incredulous || *mf* disbeliever; doubter
incrementare (increménto) *tr* to increase, boost
increménto *m* increase, increment, boost
incresció·so -sa [s] *adj* disagreeable, unpleasant
increspare (incréspo) *tr* to ripple; to wrinkle; to knit (*the brow*); to pleat || *ref* to ripple
incretinire §176 *tr* to make stupid; (fig) to deafen || *intr* (ESSERE) to become stupid; to lose one's mind
incriminare (incrìmino) *tr* to incriminate
incrinare *tr* to flaw; to ruin
incrinatura *f* crack, flaw
incrociare §128 (incròcio) *tr* to cross || *intr* (naut) to cruise || *ref* to cross one another; to interbreed
incrociatóre *m* (nav) cruiser
incró·cio *m* (-ci) crossing; cross; crossroads; crossbreed
incrollàbile *adj* unshakable
incrostare (incròsto) *tr* to incrust; to inlay (*e.g., with mosaic*) || *ref* to become incrusted
incrostazióne *f* incrustation
incrudelire §176 *tr* to enrage || *intr* to commit cruelties || *intr* (ESSERE) to become cruel; incrudelire su to commit cruelties upon
incruèn·to -ta *adj* bloodless
incubare (ìncubo & incubo) *tr* to incubate
incubatrice *f* incubator; brooder
incubazióne *f* incubation; in incubazione brewing (*said of an infectious disease*)
ìncubo *m* nightmare
incùdine *f* anvil; essere tra l'incudine e il martello to be between the devil and the deep blue sea
inculcare §197 *tr* to inculcate
incunàbolo *m* incunabulum
incuneare (incùneo) *tr & ref* to wedge
incuràbile *adj & mf* incurable
incurante *adj* careless, indifferent
incùria *f* malpractice; neglect
incuriosire [s] §176 *tr* to intrigue || *ref* to be intrigued
incursióne *f* incursion; incursione aerea air raid

**incurvare** *tr* to bend; (lit) to lower || *intr* (ESSERE) & *ref* to bend; to warp

**incurvatura** *f* bend, curve

**incustodì·to -ta** *adj* unguarded, unwatched

**incùtere** §154 *tr* to inspire; **incutere terrore a** to strike with terror

**indaco** *adj* & *m* indigo

**indaffarà·to -ta** *adj* busy

**indagare** §209 *tr* & *intr* to investigate; **indagare su** to investigate

**indaga·tóre -trice** *adj* probing, searching || *mf* investigator

**indàgine** *f* investigation, inquiry

**indarno** *adv* (lit) in vain

**indebitare (indébito)** *tr* to burden with debts || *ref* to run into debt

**indebità·to -ta** *adj* indebted

**indébi·to -ta** *adj* undue; unjust; fraudulent (*conversion*) || *m* what one does not owe; excess payment

**indeboliménto** *m* weakening

**indebolire** §176 *tr, intr* (ESSERE) & *ref* to weaken

**indecènte** *adj* indecent

**indecènza** *f* indecency; outrage

**indecifràbile** *adj* indecipherable

**indecisióne** *f* indecision

**indecì·so -sa** *adj* uncertain; undecided; indecisive

**indecoró·so -sa** [s] *adj* indecorous, unseemly

**indefès·so -sa** *adj* indefatigable

**indefinìbile** *adj* indefinable

**indefinì·to -ta** *adj* indefinite; undefined

**indegnì·tà** *f* (-tà) indignity

**indé·gno -gna** *adj* unworthy; disgraceful

**indelèbile** *adj* indelible

**indelicà·to -ta** *adj* indelicate

**indemagliàbile** *adj* runproof

**indemonià·to -ta** *adj* possessed by the devil; restless

**indènne** *adj* undamaged, unscathed; **tener indenne** to guarantee against harm or damage

**indennì·tà** *f* (-tà) indemnity; indemnification; **indennità di carica** special emolument; bonus; **indennità di carovita** cost-of-living allowance; **indennità di preavviso** severance pay; **indennità di trasferta** per diem

**indennizzare** [ddzz] *tr* to indemnify

**indennizzo** [ddzz] *m* indemnification; indemnity

**inderogàbile** *adj* inescapable

**indescrivìbile** *adj* indescribable

**indesideràbile** *adj* undesirable

**indesiderà·to -ta** *adj* unwished-for; undesirable

**indeterminatì·vo -va** *adj* indefinite

**indeterminà·to -ta** *adj* indeterminate; (gram) indefinite

**indi** *adv* (lit) then; (lit) thence; **da indi innanzi** (lit) from that moment on

**India, l'** *f* India; **le Indie Occidentali** the West Indies; **le Indie Orientali** the East Indies

**india·no -na** *adj* & *mf* Indian; **fare l'indiano** to feign ignorance || *f* printed calico

**indiavolà·to -ta** *adj* devilish, fierce; impish (*child*)

**indicare** §197 (**ìndico**) *tr* to indicate; to show

**indicatì·vo -va** *adj* & *m* indicative

**indica·to -ta** *adj* appropriate, fitting; recommended, advisable

**indica·tóre -trice** *adj* indicating, pointing || *m* indicator; **indicatore di direzione** (aut) turn signal; **indicatore di livello** gauge; **indicatore di pressione** pressure gauge; **indicatore di velocità** (aut) speedometer; **indicatore stradale** road sign; **indicatore telefonico** telephone directory

**indicazióne** *f* indication; direction; **indicazioni per l'uso** instructions

**ìndice** *m* index finger; pointer, gauge; indicator; sign, indication; index; (typ) fist; **indice delle materie** table of contents || **Indice** *m* Index; **mettere all'Indice** to put on the Index; to ban, index

**indicìbile** *adj* inexpressible, unspeakable

**indietreggiare** §290 (**indietréggio**) *intr* (ESSERE & AVERE) to withdraw

**indiètro** *adv* back; behind; **all'indietro** backwards; **dare indietro** to return, give back; **domandare indietro** to ask back; **essere indietro** to be slow (*said of a watch*); to be behind; to be backward, be slow; **tirarsi indietro** to withdraw; to step back

**indifendìbile** *adj* indefensible

**indifé·so -sa** [s] *adj* defenseless

**indifferènte** *adj* indifferent; **essere indifferente a** to be the same to; **lasciare indifferente** to leave cold

**indifferènza** *f* indifference

**indìge·no -na** *adj* indigenous || *m* native

**indigènte** *adj* indigent, poor

**indigestìbile** *adj* indigestible

**indigestióne** *f* indigestion

**indigè·sto -sta** *adj* indigestible; (fig) dull, boring

**indignare** *tr* to anger, shock || *ref* to be aroused, be indignant

**indignà·to -ta** *adj* indignant, outraged

**indignazióne** *f* indignation

**indignì·tà** *f* (-tà) indignity

**indimenticàbile** *adj* unforgettable

**indipendènte** *adj* & *m* independent

**indipendènza** *f* independence

**indire** §151 *tr* to announce publicly; (lit) to declare (*war*)

**indirèt·to -ta** *adj* indirect

**indirizzare** *tr* to direct; to address

**indirizzà·rio** *m* (-ri) mailing list

**indirizzo** *m* address; direction

**indiscernìbile** *adj* indiscernible

**indisciplina** *f* lack of discipline

**indisciplinà·to -ta** *adj* undisciplined

**indiscré·to -ta** *adj* indiscreet; tactless

**indiscrezióne** *f* indiscretion; gossip; news leak

**indiscus·so -sa** *adj* unquestioned

**indiscutìbile** *adj* indisputable

**indispensàbile** *adj* indispensable || *m* essential

**indispettire** §176 *tr* to annoy || *ref* to get annoyed

**indisponènte** *adj* vexing, irritating

**indispórre** §218 *tr* to indispose; to disgust
**indisposizióne** *f* indisposition
**indispó·sto -sta** *adj* indisposed
**indissolùbile** *adj* indissoluble
**indistin·to -ta** *adj* indistinct
**indistruttìbile** *adj* indestructible
**indisturba·to -ta** *adj* undisturbed
**indìvia** *f* endive
**individuàbile** *adj* distinguishable
**individuale** *adj* individual
**individuali·tà** *f* (-tà) individuality
**individuare (individuo)** *tr* to individuate; to outline; to single out
**indivìduo** *m* individual; fellow
**indivisìbile** *adj* indivisible
**indivi·so -sa** *adj* undivided
**indiziare** §287 *tr* to cast suspicion on
**indizià·rio -ria** *adj* (-ri -rie) circumstancial
**indì·zio** *m* (-zi) clue; token; symptom
**indòcile** *adj* indocile, unteachable
**Indocina, l'** *f* Indochina
**indocinése** [s] *adj & mf* Indochinese
**indoeuropè·o -a** *adj & m* Indo-European
**indolcire** §176 *tr* to sweeten || *ref* to become sweet
**ìndole** *f* temper, disposition; nature
**indolènte** *adj* indolent
**indolenziménto** *m* soreness, stiffness; numbness
**indolenzire** §176 *tr* to make sore or stiff; to benumb || *ref* to become sore or stiff
**indolenzi·to -ta** *adj* sore, stiff; numb
**indolóre** *adj* painless
**indomàbile** *adj* indomitable
**indoma·ni** *m* (-ni) morrow, next day; **l'indomani di ...** the day after ...
**indoma·to -ta** *adj* (lit) indomitable, untamed
**indòmi·to -ta** *adj* (lit) indomitable, untamed
**Indonèsia l'** *f* Indonesia
**indonesia·no -na** *adj & mf* Indonesian
**indorare (indòro)** *tr* to gild; (culin) to brown; (fig) to sugar-coat
**indoratura** *f* gilding
**indossare (indòsso)** *tr* to wear; to put on
**indossatrice** *f* mannequin, model
**indòsso** *adv* on, on one's back; **avere indosso** to have on, wear
**Indostàn, l'** *m* Hindustan
**indosta·no -na** *adj & mf* Hindustani
**indòtto** *m* (elec) armature (*of motor*)
**indottrinare** *tr* to indoctrinate
**indovinare** *tr* to guess; **indovinarla** to guess right; **non indovinarne una** to never hit the mark
**indovina·to -ta** *adj* felicitous
**indovinèllo** *m* puzzle, riddle
**indovi·no -na** *mf* soothsayer, fortune-teller
**indù** *adj invar & mf* Hindu
**indùb·bio -bia** *adj* (-bi -bie) undoubted, undisputed
**indubita·to -ta** *adj* undeniable
**indugiare** §290 *tr* to delay || *intr* to linger; to hesitate || *ref* to linger
**indù·gio** *m* (-gi) delay; **rompere gli**

**indugi** to come to a decision; **senza ulteriore indugio** without further delay
**indulgènte** *adj* indulgent
**indulgènza** *f* indulgence
**indùlgere** §187 *tr* to grant; to forgive || *intr* to be indulgent; **indulgere a** to indulge; to yield to
**indulto** *m* (law) pardon
**induménto** *m* garment; **indumenti intimi** undergarments, unmentionables
**indurire** §176 *tr* to harden || *intr* (ESSERE) to harden; to get stiff
**indurre** §102 *tr* to induce
**indùstria** *f* industry; **grande industria** heavy industry
**industriale** *adj* industrial || *m* industrialist
**industrializzare** [ddzz] *tr* to industrialize
**industriare** §287 *ref* to try, try hard; **industriarsi a** or **per** + *inf* to try to + *inf*, to do one's best to + *inf*
**industrió·so -sa** [s] *adj* industrious
**indut·tóre -trice** *adj* inducing, provoking || *m* (elec) field (*of motor*)
**induzióne** *f* induction
**inebetire** §176 *tr* to dull; to stun || *intr* (ESSERE) & *ref* to become dull; to be stunned
**inebriare** §287 (**inèbrio**) *tr* to intoxicate || *ref* to get drunk
**inebriante** *adj* intoxicating
**ineccepìbile** *adj* unexceptionable
**inèdia** *f* starvation, inanition; boredom
**inèdi·to -ta** *adj* unpublished; new, novel
**ineduca·to -ta** *adj* uneducated; ill-mannered
**ineffàbile** *adj* ineffable
**inefficace** *adj* ineffectual, ineffective
**inefficàcia** *f* inefficacy
**inefficiènte** *adj* inefficient
**ineguale** *adj* unequal; uneven
**ineleganto** *adj* inelegant; shabby
**ineleggìbile** *adj* ineligible
**ineluttàbile** *adj* inevitable, inescapable
**inenarràbile** *adj* unspeakable
**inerènte** *adj* inherent
**inèrme** *adj* unarmed, defenseless
**inerpicare** §197 (**inérpico**) *ref* to clamber
**inèrte** *adj* inert
**inèrzia** *f* inertia; inactivity
**inesattézza** *f* inaccuracy
**inesat·to -ta** *adj* inaccurate, inexact; uncollected
**inesaudi·to -ta** *adj* unanswered
**inesaurìbile** *adj* inexhaustible
**inescusàbile** *adj* inexcusable
**inesigìbile** *adj* uncollectable
**inesistènte** *adj* inexistent
**inesoràbile** *adj* inexorable
**inesperiènza** *f* inexperience
**inespèr·to -ta** *adj* inexperienced; unskilled
**inesplicàbile** *adj* inexplicable
**inesplica·to -ta** *adj* unexplained
**inesplora·to -ta** *adj* unexplored
**inesplò·so -sa** *adj* unexploded
**inespressi·vo -va** *adj* inexpressive
**inesprimìbile** *adj* inexpressible**

**inespugnàbile** *adj* impregnable; incorruptible

**inespugna·to -ta** *adj* unconquered

**inestimàbile** *adj* priceless, invaluable

**inestinguìbile** *adj* inextinguishable

**inestirpàbile** *adj* ineradicable

**inestricàbile** *adj* inextricable

**inèt·to -ta** *adj* inept

**ineva·so -sa** *adj* unfinished (*business*); unanswered (*mail*)

**inevitàbile** *adj* unavoidable, inevitable

**inèzia** *f* trifle, bagatelle

**infagottare** (**infagòtto**) *tr* & *ref* to bundle up

**infallìbile** *adj* infallible

**infamante** *adj* shameful, disgraceful

**infamare** *tr* to disgrace; to slander

**infame** *adj* infamous; villainous; (coll) horrible || *mf* villain

**infàmia** *f* infamy; (coll) botch, bungle

**infangare** §209 *tr* to splash with mud; (fig) to stain, spot

**infante** *adj* & *mf* infant, baby || *m* infante || *f* infanta

**infantile** *adj* infantile, childish

**infànzia** *f* infancy, childhood

**infarcire** §176 *tr* to cram; (culin) to stuff

**infarinare** *tr* to sprinkle with flour; to powder; (fig) to cram || *ref* to be covered with flour

**infarinatura** *f* sprinkling with flour; (fig) smattering

**infastidire** §176 *tr* to annoy || *ref* to be annoyed, lose one's patience

**infaticàbile** *adj* indefatigable, tireless

**infatti** *adv* indeed; really

**infatuare** (**infàtuo**) *tr* to infatuate || *ref* to become infatuated

**infatua·to -ta** *adj* infatuated

**infàu·sto -sta** *adj* unlucky, fatal

**infecón·do -da** *adj* barren

**infedéle** *adj* unfaithful; inaccurate || *mf* infidel

**infedel·tà** *f* (**-tà**) unfaithfulness; inaccuracy; infidelity

**infelice** *adj* unhappy, unfortunate; unfavorable || *mf* wretch

**infelici·tà** *f* (**-tà**) unhappiness

**inferióre** *adj* inferior; lower; **inferiore a** lower than; less than; smaller than

**inferiorità** *f* inferiority

**inferire** §188a *tr* to inflict; to infer; (naut) to bend (*a sail*)

**infermare** (**inférmo**) *tr* (lit) to weaken || *intr* (ESSERE) to get sick

**infermerìa** *f* infirmary

**infermiè·re -ra** *adj* nursing || *m* male nurse || *f* nurse; **infermiera diplomata** trained nurse

**infermierìsti·co -ca** *adj* (**-ci -che**) nursing

**infermi·tà** *f* (**-tà**) infirmity

**infér·mo -ma** *adj* infirm; sick || *m* patient

**infernale** *adj* infernal

**infèr·no -na** *adj* (lit) lower (*region*) || *m* hell; inferno

**inferocire** §176 *tr* to infuriate || *intr*—**inferocire su** to be pitiless to || *intr* (ESSERE) to become infuriated

**inferriata** *f* grating, grill

**infervorare** (**infèrvoro** & **infervóro**) *tr* to excite, stir up || *ref* to get excited; to become absorbed

**infestare** (**infèsto**) *tr* to infest

**infettare** (**infètto**) *tr* to infect

**infetti·vo -va** *adj* infectious

**infèt·to -ta** *adj* infected; corrupted

**infezióne** *f* infection

**infiacchire** §176 *tr* to weaken || *intr* (ESSERE) & *ref* to grow weak

**infiammàbile** *adj* inflammable

**infiammare** *tr* to inflame; to ignite l' *ref* to catch fire, ignite

**infiamma·to -ta** *adj* burning; aflame; inflamed, excited

**infiammazióne** *f* inflammation

**infi·do -da** *adj* untrustworthy

**infierire** §176 *intr* to become cruel; to be merciless to; to rage (*said, e.g., of a disease*)

**infievolire** §176 *tr* to weaken

**infìggere** §103 *tr* to thrust, stick, sink || *ref*—**infiggersi in** to creep in; to work in

**infilare** *tr* to thread (*a needle*); to insert (*a key*); to transfix (*with a sword*); to put on (*e.g., a coat*); to pull on (*one's pants*); to slip on (*a dress*); to slip (*e.g., one's arm into a sleeve*); to string (*beads*); to hit (*the target*); to take (*a road*); to enter through (*a door*); **infilare l'uscio** to slip away; **infilarle tutte** to succeed all the time; **non infilarne mai una** to never succeed || *ref* to slip; to sink; to slide (*e.g., through a crowd*)

**infilata** *f* row; string (*e.g., of insults*); (mil) enfilade; **d'infilata** lengthwise

**infiltrare** *ref* to infiltrate; to seep; (fig) to creep

**infilzare** *tr* to pierce; to string; (sew) to baste

**infilzata** *f* string (*of pearls, of lies, etc.*)

**infi·mo -ma** *adj* lowest, bottom

**infine** *adv* finally

**infingar·do -da** *adj* lazy, slothful

**infini·tà** *f* (**-tà**) infinity

**infinitèsi·mo -ma** *adj* & *m* infinitesimal

**infiniti·vo -va** *adj* (gram) infinitive

**infini·to -ta** *adj* infinite || *m* infinite; infinity; (gram) infinitive; (math) infinity; **all'infinito** ad infinitum

**infino** *adv* (lit)—**infino a** until; as far as; **infino a che** as long as

**infinocchiare** §287 (**infinòcchio**) *tr* (coll) to fool, bamboozle

**infioccare** §197 (**infiòcco**) *tr* to adorn with tassels

**infiorare** (**infióro**) *tr* to adorn with flowers; (fig) to sprinkle; (fig) to embellish || *ref* to be covered with flowers

**infiorescènza** *f* inflorescence

**infirmare** *tr* to weaken; to invalidate

**infischiare** §287 *ref*—**infischiarsi di** to not care a hoot about

**infisso** *m* frame (*e.g., of door*); fixture

**infittire** §176 *tr, intr* (ESSERE) & *ref* to thicken

**inflazionare** (**inflazióno**) *tr* to inflate

**inflazióne** *f* inflation

**inflessìbile** *adj* inflexible

**inflessióne** f inflection
**inflèttere** §177 tr (lit) to inflect
**inflìggere** §104 tr to inflict
**influènte** adj influential
**influènza** f influence; (pathol) influenza
**influenzare (influènzo)** tr to influence, sway
**influire** §176 intr to have an influence; **influire su** to influence || intr (ESSERE) —**influire in** to flow into
**influsso** m influence; (lit) plague
**infocare** §182 tr to make glow with heat || ref to catch fire; to get excited
**infoca·to -ta** adj red-hot; sultry
**infognare (infógno)** ref (coll) to sink (e.g., in vice); (coll) to get stuck (e.g., in debt)
**infoltire** §176 tr & intr (ESSERE) to thicken
**infonda·to -ta** adj unfounded, groundless
**infóndere** §178 tr to infuse, instill
**inforcare** §197 (infórco) tr to pitch (hay); to bestride; to mount (a horse or bicycle); to put on (one's eyeglasses)
**inforcatura** f pitching with a fork; crotch
**informare (infórmo)** tr to inform; (fig) to mold || ref to conform; to inquire; **informarsi da** to seek or get information from; **informarsi di** or **su** to inquire about; to find out about
**informati·vo -va** adj informative, informational
**informa·tóre -trice** adj underlying || mf informer; (journ) reporter || m informant (of a foreign language)
**informazióne** f piece of information; **chiedere informazioni sul conto di** to inquire about; **informazioni** information
**infórme** adj shapeless
**informicolire** §176 ref to tingle; **informicolirsi a** to go to sleep, e.g., **gli si è informicolita la gamba** his leg went to sleep
**infornare (infórno)** tr to put in the oven; to bake
**infornata** f batch (of bread); (coll) flock
**infortunare** ref to get hurt
**infortuna·to -ta** adj injured || mf casualty, victim
**infortù·nio** m (-ni) accident, mishap; **infortunio sul lavoro** job-connected injury
**infossare (infòsso)** tr to bury || ref to cave in, settle; to become sunken (said of eyes or cheeks)
**infracidare (infràcido)** tr var of **infradiciare**
**infracidire** §176 intr to rot
**infradiciare** §128 (infràdicio) tr to drench || ref to get drenched; to rot (said of fruit)
**inframmettènza** f interference, meddling
**inframméttere** §198 tr to interpose || ref to meddle, interfere
**inframmezzare** [ddzz] (inframmèzzo) tr to intersperse

**infràngere** §179 tr & ref to break
**infrangìbile** adj unbreakable
**infran·to -ta** adj broken, shattered
**infrarós·so -sa** adj & m infrared
**infrascrit·to -ta** adj mentioned below
**infrastruttura** f underpinning; infrastructure; (rr) roadbed
**infrazióne** f infraction, breach
**infreddatura** f mild cold
**infreddolire** §176 ref to feel cold, to be chilled
**infrenàbile** adj irrepressible
**infrequènte** adj infrequent
**infrollire** §176 tr to make (meat) high || intr (ESSERE) & ref to get high (said of meat); (fig) to soften
**infruttuó·so -sa** [s] adj unprofitable
**infuòri** adv out; **all'infuori** outward; **all'infuori di** except
**infuriare** §287 tr to infuriate, enrage || intr to get blustery; to rage || intr (ESSERE) to lose one's temper
**infusióne** f infusion; sprinkling (of holy water)
**infuso** m infusion
**ingabbiare** §287 tr to cage; to jail; to corner; to build the framework of
**ingabbiatura** f frame, framework
**ingaggiare** §290 tr to hire; to engage || ref to sign up; to get tangled up
**ingàg·gio** m (-gi) engagement; (sports) bonus (for signing up)
**ingagliardire** §176 tr to strengthen || ref to become strong
**ingannare** tr to deceive; to cheat; to elude; to beguile || ref to be mistaken
**inganna·tóre -trice** adj deceptive || mf impostor
**ingannévole** adj deceitful; deceptive
**inganno** m deception; illusion
**ingarbugliare** §280 tr to entangle; to jumble || ref to get mixed up; to become embroiled
**ingegnare (ingégno)** ref to manage; to scheme
**ingegnère** m engineer
**ingegneria** f engineering; **ingegneria civile** civil engineering; **ingegneria meccanica** mechanical engineering
**ingégno** m brain, intelligence; talent; genius; expediency; (lit) machinery
**ingegnosità** [s] f ingeniousness
**ingegnó·so -sa** [s] adj ingenious; euphuistic
**ingelosire** [s] §176 tr to make jealous || intr (ESSERE) & ref to become jealous
**ingemmare (ingèmmo)** tr to adorn or stud with gems
**ingenerare (ingènero)** tr to engender
**ingèni·to -ta** adj inborn
**ingènte** adj huge, vast
**ingentilire** §176 tr to refine
**ingenui·tà** f (-tà) ingenuousness; ingenuous act
**ingè·nuo -nua** adj ingenuous, artless || m (theat) artless character || f (theat) ingénue
**ingerènza** f interference
**ingerire** §176 tr to ingest, swallow || ref to meddle

ingessare (ingèsso) *tr* to put in a plaster cast; to plaster up

ingessatura *f* (surg) plaster cast

inghiaiare §287 *tr* to gravel, cover with gravel

Inghilterra, l' *f* England; la Nuova Inghilterra New England

inghiottire (inghiótto) & §176 *tr* to swallow; to swallow up; to pocket (*one's pride*)

inghirlandare *tr* to bedeck with garlands; (lit) to encircle

ingiallire §176 *tr* & *intr* (ESSERE) to turn yellow

ingigantire §176 *tr* to exaggerate ‖ *intr* (ESSERE) to grow larger, increase

inginocchiare §287 (inginòcchio) *ref* to kneel down

inginocchia·tóio *m* (-tói) prie-dieu

ingioiellare (ingioièllo) *tr* to bejewel; (fig) to stud

ingiù *adv* down; all'ingiù downwards

ingiùngere §183 *tr* to order, command ‖ *intr* (with *dat*) to order, command, e.g., il giudice ingiunse all'imputato di rispondere the judge ordered the accused to answer

ingiunzióne *f* order; (law) injunction

ingiùria *f* insult, abuse; damage, wear

ingiuriare §287 *tr* to insult

ingiurió·so -sa [s] *adj* insulting

ingiustificàbile *adj* unjustifiable

ingiustifica·to -ta *adj* unjustified

ingiustìzia *f* injustice

ingiu·sto -sta *adj* unjust, unfair ‖ *m* unjust person

inglése [s] *adj* English; all'inglese in the English fashion; andarsene all'inglese to take French leave ‖ *m* Englishman; English (*language*) ‖ *f* Englishwoman

ingoiare §287 (ingóio) *tr* to swallow; to gulp down; ingoiare un rospo (fig) to swallow one's pride

ingolfare (ingólfo) *tr* (aut) to flood ‖ *ref* to form a gulf; to get involved; (aut) to flood

ingollare (ingóllo) *tr* to swallow, gulp down

ingolosire [s] §176 *tr* to make the mouth of (*s.o.*) water ‖ *intr* (ESSERE) & *ref* to have a craving

ingombrante *adj* cumbersome

ingombrare (ingómbro) *tr* to clutter

ingóm·bro -bra *adj* encumbered, cluttered ‖ *m* encumbrance; essere d'ingombro to be in the way

ingommare (ingómmo) *tr* to glue

ingordìgia *f* greed

ingór·do -da *adj* greedy, covetous

ingorgare §209 (ingórgo) *ref* to get clogged up

ingór·go *m* (-ghi) blocking, congestion; ingorgo stradale traffic jam

ingovernàbile *adj* uncontrollable

ingozzare (ingózzo) *tr* to gobble, gulp down; to swallow; to cram (*e.g., a goose for fattening*)

ingranàg·gio *m* (-gi) gear, gearwheel; (fig) meshes; ingranaggio di distribuzione (aut) timing gear; ingranaggio elicoidale worm gear

ingranare *tr* to engage (*a gear*); ingranare la marcia to throw into gear ‖ *intr* to be in gear; to succeed

ingrandiménto *m* enlargement; increase

ingrandire §176 *tr* to enlarge; to increase; ‖ *intr* (ESSERE) & *ref* to increase, get larger

ingrassare *tr* to fatten; to lubricate ‖ *intr* (ESSERE) & *ref* to get fat; to get rich

ingrassa·tóre -trice *mf* greaser, lubricator ‖ *f* grease gun; lubricating machine

ingratitùdine *f* ingratitude

ingra·to -ta *adj* ungrateful; thankless ‖ *mf* ingrate

ingraziare §287 *ref* to ingratiate oneself with

ingrediènte *m* ingredient

ingrèsso *m* entrance; admittance, entry; ingressi hallway furniture; primo ingresso debut

ingrossaménto *m* enlargement; swelling

ingrossare (ingròsso) *tr* to enlarge; to swell; to make bigger; to dull (*the mind*); to raise (*one's voice*) ‖ *intr* (ESSERE) & *ref* to swell; to thicken; to become fat; to become pregnant; to become important

ingròsso *m*—all'ingrosso wholesale; approximately, more or less

ingrullire §176 *tr* to drive crazy ‖ *intr* (ESSERE) & *ref* to become silly; fare ingrullire to drive crazy

inguadàbile *adj* not fordable

inguainare (inguaìno) *tr* to sheathe

ingualcibile *adj* wrinkle-free, wrinkle-proof

inguanta·to -ta *adj* with gloves on; con le mani inguantate with gloves on

inguarìbile *adj* incurable

inguine *f* (anat) groin

ingurgitare (ingùrgito) *tr* to swallow, gulp down

inibire §176 *tr* to inhibit

inibi·tóre -trice *adj* inhibiting ‖ *m* inhibitor

inidòne·o -a *adj* unfit, unqualified

iniettare (iniètto) *tr* to inject ‖ *ref* to become bloodshot; iniettarsi di sangue to become bloodshot

iniezióne *f* injection

inimicare §197 *tr* to make an enemy of; to alienate ‖ *ref*—inimicarsi con to fall out with

inimicìzia *f* enmity

inimitàbile *adj* inimitable, matchless

ininterrót·to -ta *adj* uninterrupted

iniquì·tà *f* (-tà) injustice; iniquity

inì·quo -qua *adj* unjust; wicked

iniziale *adj* & *f* initial

iniziare §287 *tr* to initiate ‖ *ref* to begin

iniziativa *f* initiative; sponsorship; iniziativa privata private enterprise

inizia·tóre -trice *adj* initiating ‖ *mf* initiator, promoter

iniziazióne *f* initiation

inì·zio *m* (-zi) beginning, start

innaffiare §287 *tr* var of annaffiare

innaffia·tóio *m* (-tói) var of annaffiatoio

innalzaménto *m* elevation

**innalzare** *tr* to raise; to elevate; **innalzare al cielo** to praise to the sky ‖ *ref* to rise; to tower

**innamorare (innamóro)** *tr* to charm, fascinate; to inspire with love ‖ *ref* to fall in love

**innamora·to -ta** *adj* in love, enamored; fond ‖ *mf* sweetheart ‖ *m* boyfriend ‖ *f* girl friend

**innanzi** *adj invar* previous, prior (*e.g., day*) ‖ *adv* ahead, before; **innanzi a** in front of; **innanzi di** + *inf* before + *ger;* **mettere innanzi** to prefer; to place before; to advance (*an excuse*); **per l'innanzi** before, in the past; **tirare innanzi** to get along ‖ *prep* before; above; **innanzi tempo** ahead of time; **innanzi tutto** above all

**innà·rio** *m* (**-ri**) hymnal

**inna·to -ta** *adj* inborn, innate

**innegàbile** *adj* undeniable

**inneggiare** §290 (**innéggio**) *intr*—**inneggiare a** to sing the praises of

**innervosire** [s] §176 *tr* to make nervous

**innescare** §197 (**innésco**) *tr* to bait (*a hook*); to prime (*a bomb*)

**inné·sco** *m* (**-schi**) primer; detonator

**innestare (innèsto)** *tr* (hort & surg) to graft; (surg) to implant; (med) to inoculate (*a vaccine*); (mach) to engage; (elec) to plug in (*e.g., a plug*); **innestare la marcia** (aut) to throw into gear ‖ *ref* to be grafted; **innestarsi in** to merge with; **innestarsi su** to connect with

**innèsto** *m* (hort & surg) graft; (surg) implant; (med) inoculation; (mach) engagement; (mach) coupling; (elec) plug

**inno** *m* hymn; **inno nazionale** national anthem

**innocènte** *adj* innocent ‖ *m* innocent; **innocenti** foundlings

**innocènza** *f* innocence

**innò·cuo -cua** *adj* innocuous, harmless

**innominàbile** *adj* unmentionable

**innomina·to -ta** *adj* unnamed

**innovare (innòvo)** *tr* to innovate

**innovazióne** *f* innovation

**innumerévole** *adj* countless, innumerable

**-ino -ina** *suf adj* little, e.g., **poverino** poor little; hailing from, e.g., **fiorentino** hailing from Florence, Florentine ‖ *suf f* see **-ina**

**inoccupa·to -ta** *adj* unoccupied ‖ *m* person looking for his first job

**inoculare (inòculo)** *tr* to inoculate

**inoculazióne** *f* inoculation

**inodó·ro -ra** *adj* odorless

**inoffensi·vo -va** *adj* inoffensive

**inoltrare (inóltro)** *tr* (com) to forward (*e.g., a request*) ‖ *ref* to advance

**inóltre** *adv* besides, in addition

**inóltro** *m* (com) forwarding

**inondare (inóndo)** *tr* to inundate, flood; to swamp

**inondazióne** *f* flood, inundation

**inoperosità** [s] *f* idleness

**inoperó·so -sa** [s] *adj* idle

**inopina·to -ta** *adj* (lit) unexpected

**inopportu·no -na** *adj* inopportune, untimely

**inoppugnàbile** *adj* incontestable; indisputable

**inorgàni·co -ca** *adj* (**-ci -che**) inorganic

**inorgoglire** §176 *tr* to make proud ‖ *intr* (ESSERE) & *ref* to grow proud

**inorridire** §176 *tr* to horrify ‖ *intr* (ESSERE) to be horrified

**inospitale** *adj* inhospitable

**inosservante** *adj* unobservant

**inosserva·to -ta** *adj* unnoticed; unperceived

**inossidàbile** *adj* stainless

**inquadrare** *tr* to frame; to arrange

**inquadratura** *f* framing; (mov, phot) frame

**inqualificàbile** *adj* unspeakable

**inquietante** *adj* disquieting

**inquietare (inquièto)** *tr* to worry ‖ *ref* to worry; to get angry

**inquiè·to -ta** *adj* worried; restless; angry; (lit) stormy

**inquietùdine** *f* worry; restlessness; preoccupation

**inquili·no -na** *mf* tenant

**inquinaménto** *m* pollution

**inquinare** *tr* to pollute

**inquirènte** *adj* investigating

**inquisi·tóre -trice** *adj* inquiring ‖ *m* inquisitor

**inquisizióne** *f* inquisition

**insabbiare** §287 *tr* to cover with sand; to pigeonhole; to shelve ‖ *ref* to get covered with sand; to bury oneself in sand; to get stuck

**insaccare** §197 *tr* to bag; to stuff (*e.g., salami*); (mil) to hem in; (fig) to bundle up; (coll) to gulp down ‖ *ref* to be packed in; to crumple up; to disappear behind a thick bank of clouds (*said, e.g., of the sun*)

**insaccato** *m* participant in a sack race; **insaccati** cold cuts, lunch meat

**insalata** *f* salad; (fig) mess

**insalatièra** *f* salad bowl

**insalubre** *adj* unhealthy

**insaluta·to -ta** *adj* unsaluted; **andarsene insalutato ospite** to take French leave

**insanàbile** *adj* incurable; implacable

**insanguinare (insànguino)** *tr* to bloody; to cover with blood; to bathe in blood

**insa·no -na** *adj* insane

**insaponare (insapóno)** *tr* to soap; to lather; (fig) to soft-soap

**insaporire** §176 *tr* to flavor ‖ *intr* (ESSERE) to become tasty

**insaputa** *f*—**all'insaputa di** without the knowledge of, unbeknown to

**insaziàbile** *adj* insatiable

**insazia·to -ta** *adj* insatiate, unsatisfied

**inscatolare (inscàtolo)** *tr* to can

**inscenare (inscèno)** *tr* to stage

**inscindìbile** *adj* inseparable

**inscrìvere** §250 *tr* (geom) to inscribe

**inscrutàbile** *adj* inscrutable

**inscurire** §176 *tr, intr* (ESSERE) & *ref* to darken

**insecchire** §176 *tr* to dry ‖ *intr* (ESSERE) & *ref* to dry up

**insediaménto** *m* installation (*into an office*); assumption (*of an office*)

**insediare** §287 (**insèdio**) *tr* to install || *ref* to be installed; to take one's seat; to settle

**inségna** *f* badge, insignia, emblem; ensign, flag; coat of arms; motto; sign (*e.g., on a restaurant*); traffic sign

**insegnaménto** *m* education, instruction

**insegnante** *adj* teaching || *mf* teacher

**insegnare** (**inségno**) *tr* to teach; to show || *intr* to teach

**inseguiménto** *m* pursuit

**inseguire** (**inséguo**) *tr* to pursue, chase; to chase after

**insellare** (**insèllo**) *tr* to saddle; to put on (*e.g., one's glasses*); to bend

**insellatura** *f* saddling; bending

**insenatura** *f* inlet, cove

**insensatézza** *f* nonsense, folly

**insensa·to -ta** *adj* nonsensical, foolish || *mf* scatterbrain

**insensìbile** *adj* insensible; unresponsive; insensitive

**inseparàbile** *adj* inseparable || *m* (orn) lovebird

**insepól·to -ta** *adj* unburied

**inserire** §176 *tr* to insert; to plug in || *ref* to slip in; to butt in

**inseri·tóre -trice** *adj* (elec) connecting || *m* (elec) connector, plug || *f* sorter (*of punch cards*)

**insèrto** *m* file, folder; insert; spliced film

**inservìbile** *adj* useless, worthless

**inserviènte** *m* attendant, porter; (eccl) server

**inserzionare** (**inserzióno**) *intr* to advertise

**inserzióne** *f* insertion; advertisement

**inserzioni·sta** (**-sti -ste**) *adj* advertising || *mf* advertiser

**insettici·da** *adj* & *m* (**-di -de**) insecticide

**insettìfu·go** *m* (**-ghi**) insect repellent

**insètto** *m* insect; **insetti** vermin

**insidia** *f* trap, ambush; **insidie** lure

**insidiare** §287 *tr* to ensnare; to try to trap; to try to seduce; to attempt (*someone's life*)

**insidió·so -sa** [s] *adj* insidious

**insième** *m* whole, entirety; harmony; ensemble; set; **d'insieme** general, comprehensive; **nell'insieme** as a whole || *adv* together

**insigne** *adj* famous; notable; arrant (*knave*)

**insignificante** *adj* insignificant; petty

**insignire** §176 *tr* to decorate; **insignire qlcu di un titolo** to bestow a title upon s.o.

**insignorire** §176 *tr* (lit) to invest with a fief || *intr* (ESSERE) to enrich oneself || *ref* to enrich oneself; **insignorirsi di** to seize; to take possession of

**insilare** *tr* to silo, ensile

**insilato** *m* ensilage

**insincè·ro -ra** *adj* insincere

**insindacàbile** *adj* final, indisputable

**insino** *adv* (lit)—**insino a** until; as far as; **insino a che** as long as

**insinuante** *adj* insinuating

**insinuare** (**insìnuo**) *tr* to stick, thrust;

to insinuate; (law) to register || *ref* to creep, filter; to ingratiate oneself; **insinuarsi in** to worm one's way into

**insinuazióne** *f* insinuation, hint

**insìpi·do -da** *adj* insipid, vapid

**insistènte** *adj* insistent

**insistere** §114 *intr* to insist

**insi·to -ta** *adj* inborn, inherent

**insociévole** *adj* unsociable

**insoddisfat·to -ta** *adj* dissatisfied

**insofferènte** *adj* intolerant

**insoffrìbile** *adj* unbearable, insufferable

**insolazióne** *f* sunning; sun bath; sunstroke; sunny exposure

**insolènte** *adj* insolent

**insolentire** §176 *tr* to insult, abuse || *intr* to be insolent

**insolènza** *f* insolence; insult

**insòli·to -ta** *adj* unusual

**insolùbile** *adj* insoluble

**insolu·to -ta** *adj* unsolved; not dissolved; unpaid

**insolvènza** *f* insolvency

**insolvìbile** *adj* insolvent; bad (*debt*)

**insómma** *adv* in conclusion || *interj* well!

**insommergìbile** *adj* unsinkable

**insondàbile** *adj* unfathomable

**insònne** *adj* sleepless

**insònnia** *f* insomnia

**insonnoli·to -ta** *adj* sleepy, drowsy

**insonorizzazióne** [ddzz] *f* soundproofing

**insopportàbile** *adj* unbearable

**insorgènte** *adj* appearing || *mf* insurgent

**insorgènza** *f* appearance (*of illness*)

**insórgere** §258 *intr* (ESSERE) to rise up, revolt; to appear

**insormontàbile** *adj* unsurmountable, insurmountable

**insór·to -ta** *adj* & *m* insurgent

**insospettàbile** *adj* above suspicion; unexpected

**insospetta·to -ta** *adj* not suspect; unexpected

**insospettire** §176 *tr* to make suspicious || *intr* (ESSERE) & *ref* to become suspicious

**insostenìbile** *adj* indefensible; unbearable

**insostituìbile** *adj* irreplaceable

**insozzare** (**insózzo**) *tr* to soil, sully

**inspera·to -ta** *adj* unexpected; unhoped-for

**inspiegàbile** *adj* unexplainable

**inspirare** *tr* to inhale, breathe in

**inspirazióne** *f* inhalation

**instàbile** *adj* unstable

**installare** *tr* to install; to set up, settle; to induct (*in an office*) || *ref* to settle

**installatóre** *m* plumber; erector

**installazióne** *f* installation; plumbing

**instancàbile** *adj* untiring

**instante** *adj* insistent; impending || *m* petitioner

**instare** (*pp* missing) *intr* to insist; to threaten, be imminent

**instaurare** (**instàuro**) *tr* to establish

**instaurazióne** *f* establishment

**instigare** §209 *tr* var of **istigare**

**instillare** *tr* var of **istillare**

**instituire** §176 *tr* var of **istituire**

**instruire** §176 *tr* var of **istruire**
**instrumento** *m* var of **istrumento**
**instupidire** §176 *tr* var of **istupidire**
**insù** *adv* up; **all'insù** up
**insubordina·to -ta** *adj* insubordinate
**insuccèsso** *m* failure
**insudiciare** §128 (**insùdicio**) *tr* to soil, dirty; to sully ‖ *ref* to get dirty
**insufficiènte** *adj* insufficient; failing (*in school*)
**insufficiènza** *f* insufficiency; failure (*in school*)
**insulare** *adj* insular
**insulina** *f* insulin
**insulsàggine** *f* silliness, nonsense
**insul·so -sa** *adj* insipid; simple, silly
**insultante** *adj* insulting
**insultare** *tr* to insult ‖ *intr* (with *dat*) to insult
**insulto** *m* insult; (pathol) attack
**insuperàbile** *adj* insuperable; unparalleled
**insupera·to -ta** *adj* unsurpassed
**insuperbire** §176 *tr, intr* (ESSERE) & *ref* to swell with pride
**insurrezióne** *f* insurrection
**insussistènte** *adj* nonexistent, unfounded
**intabarrare** *tr* to wrap up
**intaccare** §197 *tr* to notch; to corrode; to scratch; to attack (*said of a disease*); to damage (*e.g., a reputation*); to cut into (*capital*) ‖ *intr* to stutter
**intaccatura** *f* notch; (carp) mortise
**intagliare** §280 *tr* to carve; to engrave
**intà·glio** *m* (-**gli**) carving; intaglio
**intanare** *ref* to hide
**intangìbile** *adj* intangible; inviolable
**intanto** *adv* meanwhile; (coll) yet; (coll) finally; **intanto che** while; **per intanto** at present; in the meantime
**intarsiare** §287 *tr* to inlay; (fig) to stud
**intarsia·to -ta** *adj* inlaid
**intàr·sio** *m* (-**si**) inlay; inlaid work
**intasare** [s] *tr* to clog; to tie up (*traffic*); to stop up ‖ *ref* to be clogged up; to be tied up; to be stopped up (*said of nose*)
**intascare** §197 *tr* to pocket
**intat·to -ta** *adj* intact, untouched
**intavolare** (**intàvolo**) *tr* to start (*a conversation*); to broach (*a subject*); to launch (*negotiations*)
**intavolato** *m* boarding, planking
**integèrri·mo -ma** *adj* of the utmost honesty
**integrale** *adj* integral; whole; wholewheat (*bread*); built-in ‖ *m* integral
**integralismo** *m* policy of the complete absorption of the body politic by an ideology
**integrante** *adj* constituent, integral
**integrare** (**ìntegro**) *tr* to integrate ‖ *ref* to complement each other
**integrazióne** *f* integration
**integrità** *f* integrity
**ìnte·gro -gra** *adj* whole, complete; honest, upright; intact
**intelaiatura** *f* frame; framework
**intellètto** *m* intellect, mind; understanding
**intellettuale** *adj* & *mf* intellectual

**intellettuali·tà** *f* (-**tà**) intellectuality; intelligentsia
**intellettualòide** *mf* highbrow
**intelligènte** *adj* intelligent; clever
**intelligènza** *f* intelligence; understanding; **essere d'intelligenza con** to be in collusion with
**intellighènzia** *f* intelligentsia
**intelligìbile** *adj* intelligible
**intemera·to -ta** *adj* pure, spotless ‖ *f* reprimand, scolding; long, boring speech
**intemperante** *adj* intemperate
**intemperanza** *f* intemperance
**intempèrie** *fpl* inclement weather
**intempesti·vo -va** *adj* untimely
**intendènte** *m* district director; **intendente di finanza** director of customs office; **intendente militare** commissary, quartermaster
**intendènza** *f* office of the district director; intendance; **intendenza militare** quartermaster corps
**intèndere** §270 *tr* to understand; to hear; to intend; to turn (*e.g., one's eyes*); to mean; **dare ad intendere a** to lead (*s.o.*) to believe (*s.th*); **far intendere** to give to understand; **farsi intendere** to force obedience; to make oneself understood; **intender dire che** to hear that; **intèndere a rovescio** to misunderstand; **intèndere a volo** to catch on quickly (to); **intèndere ragione** to listen to reason; **lasciare intendere** to give to understand ‖ *intr* to aim (*toward a goal*) ‖ *ref* to come to an agreement; **intèndersela con** to be in collusion with; to have an affair with; **intèndersi di** to be a good judge of; to be an expert in
**intendiménto** *m* understanding, comprehension; aim, goal
**intendi·tóre -trice** *mf* connoisseur, expert; **a buon intenditore poche parole** a word to the wise is sufficient
**intenerire** §176 *tr* to soften; (fig) to move ‖ *ref* to soften; (fig) to be moved
**intensificare** §197 (**intensìfico**) *tr* & *ref* to intensify
**intensi·tà** *f* (-**tà**) intensity
**intensi·vo -va** *adj* intensive
**intèn·so -sa** *adj* intense
**intentare** (**intènto**) *tr* (law) to bring (*action*)
**intenta·to -ta** *adj* unattempted
**intèn·to -ta** *adj* intent ‖ *m* intent, goal; **coll'intento di** with the purpose of
**intenzionale** *adj* intentional
**intenziona·to -ta** *adj*—**bene intenzionato** well-meaning; **essere intenzionato di** to intend to
**intenzióne** *f* intention; purpose; **con intenzione** on purpose
**intepidire** §176 *tr* & *ref* var of **intiepidire**
**interbase** *f* (baseball) shortstop
**intercalare** *m* refrain; pet word or phrase ‖ *tr* to intercalate; to inset
**intercalazióne** *f* intercalation; inset
**intercapèdine** *f* air space
**intercèdere** §123 *tr* to seek, get (*a par-*

don *for s.o.*) || *intr* to intercede || *intr* (ESSERE)—**intercedere tra** to intervene or elapse between; to extend between; to exist between

**intercettare (intercètto)** *tr* to intercept; to tap (*a phone*)

**intercetta·tóre -trice** *mf* interceptor

**intercettóre** *m* (aer) interceptor

**intercomunale** *adj* long-distance (*call*)

**intercórrere** §139 *intr* (ESSERE) to elapse; to happen; to be, to stand

**interdét·to -ta** *adj* dumfounded; forbidden || *m* interdict; (coll) dumbell

**interdire** §151 *tr* to prohibit; (eccl) to interdict; (law) to disqualify

**interessaménto** *m* interest, concern

**interessante** *adj* interesting; **in stato interessante** in the family way

**interessare (interèsso)** *tr* to interest; to concern || *intr* to be of interest || *ref*—**interessarsi a** to take an interest in; **interessarsi di** to concern oneself with

**interessa·to -ta** *adj* interested; selfish || *m* interested party

**interèsse** *m* interest; self-interest

**interessènza** *f* (com) share, interest

**interferènza** *f* interference

**interferire** §176 *intr* to interfere

**interfogliare** §280 **(interfòglio)** *tr* to interleave

**interiezióne** *f* interjection

**interinato** *m* temporary office or tenure

**interi·no -na** *adj* acting || *m* temporary appointee

**interióra** *fpl* entrails

**interióre** *adj* interior || **interiori** *mpl* entrails

**interlìnea** *f* interlining; (typ) leading

**interlineare** *adj* interlinear || *v* **(interlìneo)** *tr* (typ) to lead

**interlocu·tóre -trice** *mf* participant (*in a discussion*); person speaking

**interloquire** §176 *intr* to take part in a discussion; to chime in

**interlù·dio** *m* **(-di)** interlude

**intermedià·rio -ria (-ri -rie)** *adj & mf* intermediary || *m* middleman

**intermè·dio -dia (-di -die)** *adj* intermediate || *mf* supervisor

**intermèzzo** [ddzz] *m* intermezzo; entr'acte; interval

**interminàbile** *adj* interminable, endless

**intermissióne** *f* intermission

**intermittènte** *adj* intermittent

**internaménto** *m* internment

**internare (intèrno)** *tr* to intern; to confine; to commit (*an insane person*) || *ref* to go deep (*into a problem*)

**interna·to -ta** *adj* interned || *m* internee; inmate; boarder; boarding school

**internazionale** *adj* international

**internazionalizzare** [ddzz] *tr* to internationalize

**interni·sta** *mf* **(-sti -ste)** internist

**intèr·no -na** *adj* inside, internal; inland; interior; boarding (*student*) || *m* inside; interior; (med) intern; lining (*of coat*); **all'interno** inside; **interni** (mov) indoor shots || **gli Interni** the Italian Ministry of Internal Affairs

**inté·ro -ra** *adj* entire, whole; full (*price*); (lit) upright, honest || *m* whole; **per intero** completely

**interpellare (interpèllo)** *tr* to interpellate; to question; to consult

**interpetrare (intèrpetro)** *tr* var of interpretare

**interplanetà·rio -ria (-ri -rie)** interplanetary

**interpolare (intèrpolo)** *tr* to interpolate

**interpolazióne** *f* interpolation

**interpónte** *m* (naut) between-deck

**interpórre** §218 *tr* to interpose || *ref* to intervene

**interpretare (intèrpreto)** *tr* to interpret

**interpretazióne** *f* interpretation

**intèrprete** *mf* interpreter

**interpunzióne** *f* punctuation

**interrare (intèrro)** *tr* to bury, inter; to fill in (*e.g., a marsh*) || *ref* to become silted

**interra·to -ta** *adj* underground; **piano interrato** basement

**interrogare** §209 **(intèrrogo)** *tr* to question; to interrogate

**interrogati·vo -va** *adj* interrogative || *m* why; question

**interrogatò·rio -ria (-ri -rie)** *adj* questioning || *m* (law) interrogatory; **interrogatorio di terzo grado** third degree

**interrogazióne** *f* interrogation; quiz, examination; **interrogazione retorica** rhetorical question

**interrómpere** §240 *tr* to interrupt

**interruttóre** *m* (elec) switch; **interruttore di linea** (elec) controller

**interruzióne** *f* interruption

**interscàm·bio** *m* **(-bi)** interchange

**interscolàsti·co -ca** *adj* **(-ci -che)** interscholastic; intercollegiate

**intersecare** §197 **(intèrseco)** *tr & ref* to intersect

**intersezióne** *f* intersection

**interstellare** *adj* interstellar

**interstì·zio** *m* **(-zi)** interstice

**interurba·no -na** *adj* interurban, intercity; (telp) long-distance || *f* (telp) long-distance call

**intervallo** *m* interval; pause; (educ) recess; (theat) intermission

**intervenire** §282 *intr* (ESSERE) to intervene; (surg) to operate; **intervenire a** to take part in

**interventi·sta** *mf* **(-sti -ste)** interventionist

**intervènto** *m* intervention; attendance; (surg) operation

**intervenzióne** *f* intervention

**intervista** *f* interview; **fare un'intervista a** to interview

**intervistare** *tr* to interview

**inté·so -sa** [s] *adj* understood; intended, designed; **bene inteso** of course; **non darsene per inteso** to not pay attention; **rimanere inteso** to agree || *f* understanding, agreement; entente

**intèssere (intèsso)** *tr* to interweave; to wreathe (*a garland*)

**intestardire** §176 *ref* to get obstinate; to be determined

**intestare** (intèsto) *tr* to caption; to label; (typ) to head (*a page*); **intestare qlco a qlcu** to register s.th in the name of s.o.; **intestare una fattura a** to issue a bill in the name of ‖ *ref* to become obstinate; to take it into one's head

**intesta·to -ta** *adj* headed; registered (*stock*); obstinate; (law) intestate

**intestazióne** *f* heading; registration (*of stock*)

**intestinale** *adj* intestinal

**intesti·no -na** *adj* & *m* intestine; **intestino crasso** large intestine; **intestino tenue** small intestine

**intiepidire** §176 *tr* & *ref* to warm up; to cool off

**intiè·ro -ra** *adj* & *m* var of **intero**

**intimare** (ìntimo & intìmo) *tr* to intimate; to order, command; to declare (*war*); to impose (*a fine*); (law) to enjoin

**intimazióne** *f* intimation; order; (law) injunction

**intimidazióne** *f* intimidation

**intimidire** §176 *tr* to intimidate; to threaten ‖ *ref* to become bashful

**intimi·tà** *f* (-tà) intimacy; privacy

**inti·mo -ma** *adj* intimate; inmost; **biancheria intima** underwear, lingerie ‖ *m* intimate friend; depth (*of one's heart*)

**intimorire** §176 *tr* to frighten

**intìngere** §126 *tr* to dip ‖ *intr*—**intingere in** to dip in ‖ *ref*—**intingersi in un affare** to have a finger in the pie

**intìngolo** *m* sauce, gravy; fancy dish

**intirizzire** [ddzz] §176 *tr* to benumb ‖ *intr* (ESSERE) & *ref* to become numb or stiff; to become stiff and frostbitten

**intirizzi·to -ta** [ddzz] *adj* numb

**intisichire** §176 *tr* to make tubercular; (fig) to weaken ‖ *intr* (ESSERE) to become tubercular; to wither

**intitolare** (intìtolo) *tr* to title; to dedicate ‖ *ref* to be named; to assume the title of

**intoccàbile** *adj* & *m* untouchable

**intollceràbile** *adj* intolerable

**intollerante** *adj* intolerant

**intonacare** §197 (intònaco) *tr* to plaster; to whitewash; to cover (*e.g.*, *with tar*) ‖ *ref*—**intonacarsi la faccia** (joc) to put on one's warpaint

**intòna·co** *m* (-chi) plaster; roughcast

**intonare** (intòno) *tr* to intone; to harmonize; (mus) to tune ‖ *ref* to harmonize, go

**intonazióne** *f* intonation; harmony

**intòn·so -sa** *adj* uncut; (lit) unsheared

**intontire** §176 *tr* to stun ‖ *intr* (ESSERE) & *ref* to become stunned

**intoppare** (intòppo) *tr* to stumble upon ‖ *intr* (ESSERE) & *ref* to stumble

**intòppo** *m* obstacle, hindrance

**intorbidare** (intórbido) *tr* to cloud; to muddy; to obfuscate; to upset (*friendship*); to stir up (*passions*) ‖ *ref* to become cloudy or muddy; to become obfuscated

**intorbidire** §176 *tr* & *ref* to cloud; to muddy

**intormentire** §176 *tr* to benumb ‖ *intr* (ESSERE) to become numb

**intórno** *adv* around, about; **all'intorno** all around; **intorno a** around; about; **levarsi qlcu d'intorno** to get rid of s.o.

**intorpidire** §176 *tr* to benumb ‖ *ref* to become numb

**intossicare** §197 (intòssico) *tr* to poison, intoxicate

**intossicazióne** *f* poisoning, intoxication

**intraducìbile** *adj* untranslatable; inexpressible

**intrafèrro** *m* spark gap; air gap

**intralciare** §128 *tr* to hamper; to intertwine ‖ *ref* to become hampered

**intràl·cio** *m* (-ci) hindrance; **essere d'intralcio** to be in the way; **intralcio del traffico** traffic congestion

**intralicciatura** *f* lattice truss (*of high-tension tower*)

**intrallazzare** *intr* to deal in the black market

**intrallazza·tóre -trice** *mf* black marketeer

**intrallazzo** *m* black-market dealing; kickback

**intramezzare** [ddzz] (intramèzzo) *tr* to alternate

**intramontàbile** *adj* undying, immortal

**intransigènte** *adj* & *mf* intransigent, die-hard

**intransitàbile** *adj* impassable

**intransiti·vo -va** *adj* intransitive

**intrappolare** (intràppolo) *tr* to entrap

**intraprendènte** *adj* enterprising

**intraprendènza** *f* enterprise, initiative

**intraprèndere** §220 *tr* to undertake

**intrattàbile** *adj* unmanageable, intractable

**intrattenére** §271 *tr* to entertain ‖ *ref* to linger; **intrattenersi su** to dwell upon

**intrattenimento** *m* entertainment

**intravedére** §279 *tr* to glimpse, catch a glimpse of; to foresee

**intravenó·so -sa** [s] *adj* intravenous

**intrecciare** §128 (intréccio) *tr* to braid; to twine; to cross (*one's fingers*); (fig) to weave; to begin (*a dance*) ‖ *ref* to become embroiled; to become intertwined; to crisscross

**intréc·cio** *m* (-ci) knitting; intertwining; plot (*of novel*); (theat) intrigue

**intrepidézza** *f* intrepidness, intrepidity

**intrèpi·do -da** *adj* intrepid

**intricare** §197 *tr* (lit) to entangle

**intrica·to -ta** *adj* tangled; intricate

**intri·co** *m* (-chi) tangle, jumble

**intrìdere** §189 *tr* to soak; to knead

**intrigante** *adj* intriguing ‖ *mf* schemer

**intrigare** §209 *tr* to tangle ‖ *intr* to intrigue ‖ *ref* (coll) to meddle

**intrì·go** *m* (-ghi) intrigue; trouble

**intrìnse·co -ca** (-ci -che) *adj* intrinsic; intimate ‖ *m* intimate nature, core

**intrì·so -sa** *adj* soaked ‖ *m* mash

**intristìre** §176 *intr* (ESSERE) to wither; to waste away introdót•to -ta *adj* introduced; well-known; knowledgeable, expert

introdurre §102 *tr* to introduce; to insert; to open (*a speech*); to show in || *ref* to slip in

introdutti•vo -va *adj* introductory

introduzióne *f* introduction

introitare (intròito) *tr* to collect, take in

intròito *m* receipts, collection; (eccl) introit

introméttere §198 *tr* to insert; to introduce; to involve || *ref* to meddle; to pry

intromissióne *f* meddling; intrusion; intervention

intronare (intròno) *tr* to deafen; to stun

intronizzare [ddzz] *tr* to enthrone

introspetti•vo -va *adj* introspective

introspezióne *f* introspection

introvàbile *adj* unobtainable; inaccessible

introvèr•so -sa *adj & mf* introvert

intrùdere §190 *tr* (lit) to slip in || *ref* to intrude; to trespass

intrufolare (intrùfolo) *tr* (coll) to slip (*e.g., one's hand into somebody's pocket*) || *ref* to slip in, intrude

intrù•glio *m* (-gli) concoction, brew; hodgepodge; imbroglio; mess

intrusióne *f* intrusion

intru•so -sa *adj* intrusive || *mf* intruder

intuire §176 *tr* to know by intuition; to guess; to sense

intuiti•vo -va *adj* intuitive; obvious

intùito *m* intuition; insight

intuizióne *f* intuition

inturgidire §176 *intr* (ESSERE) & *ref* to swell

inuma•no -na *adj* inhuman; inhumane

inumare *tr* to bury, inhume

inumazióne *f* burial, inhumation

inumidire §176 *tr* to moisten || *ref* to get wet

inurbaménto *m* migration to the city

inurba•no -na *adj* uncouth, unmannerly

inurbare *ref* to move into the city; to become citified

inusa•to -ta *adj* unused; unusual

inusita•to -ta *adj* unusual; out-of-the-way

inùtile *adj* useless; worthless

inutilizzàbile [ddzz] *adj* unusable

inutilizzare [ddzz] *tr* to waste (*e.g., time*)

inutilizza•to -ta [ddzz] *adj* unused

inutilménte *adv* needlessly, to no purpose || *interj* no use!

invadènte *adj* meddlesome, intrusive

invàdere §172 *tr* to invade; to encroach on; to spread over; to overcome

invaghire §176 *tr* to charm || *ref* to fall in love

invalére §278 *intr* (ESSERE) to become established; to prevail

invalicàbile *adj* impassable, unsurmountable

invalidàbile *adj* voidable

invalidaménto *m* invalidity; invalidation

invalidare (invàlido) *tr* to void, invalidate; to negate (*e.g., evidence*)

invalidi•tà *f* (-tà) invalidity; invalidation; sickness, disability

invàli•do -da *adj* void, invalid; sick, disabled || *m* disabled person; invalid

inval•so -sa *adj* prevailing

invano *adv* in vain, vainly

invariàbile *adj* invariable

invaria•to -ta *adj* unchanging; unchanged

invasare *tr* to pot (*a plant*); to fill up (*a reservoir*); to possess, obsess

invasa•to -ta *adj* possessed, obsessed

invasióne *f* invasion

inva•so -sa *adj* invaded || *m* potting (*of plant*); capacity (*of reservoir*)

inva•sóre -ditrice *adj* invading || *m* invader

invecchiaménto *m* aging

invecchiare §287 (invècchio) *tr & intr* (ESSERE) to age

invéce *adv* on the contrary, instead; invece di instead of

inveire §176 *intr* to inveigh, rail

invelenire §176 *tr* to envenom; to embitter || *intr* (ESSERE) & *ref* to grow bitter

invendibile *adj* unsalable

invendica•to -ta *adj* unavenged

invendu•to -ta *adj* unsold

inventare (invènto) *tr* to invent

inventariare §287 *tr* to inventory

inventà•rio *m* (-ri) inventory

inventi•vo -va *adj* inventive || *f* inventiveness

inven•tóre -trice *adj* inventive || *mf* inventor

invenzióne *f* invention; (lit) find

inverdire §176 *intr* (ESSERE) to turn green

inverecóndia *f* immodesty

inverecón•do -da *adj* immodest

invernale *adj* winter; wintry

inverniciare §128 *tr* to paint; to varnish

invèrno *m* winter

invéro *adv* (lit) truly, indeed

inverosimiglianza [s] *f* unlikelihood

inverosìmile [s] *adj* unlikely

inversióne *f* inversion

invèr•so -sa *adj* inverse, opposite; (coll) cross || *m* inverse

inversóre *m* inverter; inversore di spinta (aer) thrust reverser

invertebra•to -ta *adj & m* invertebrate

invertire §176 & (invèrto) *tr* to invert; to reverse

inverti•to -ta *adj* inverted || *m* invert

investigare §209 (invèstigo) *tr* to investigate

investiga•tóre -trice *adj* investigating || *mf* investigator; detective

investigazióne *f* investigation

investiménto *m* investment; collision

investire (invèsto) *tr* to invest; to collide with; investire di insulti to cover with insults || *ref*—investirsi di to become conscious of (*e.g., one's authority*); (theat) to become identified with (*a character*)

investi•tóre -trice *mf* investor

investitura *f* investiture

invetera•to -ta *adj* inveterate, confirmed

**invetria·to -ta** *adj* glazed || *f* window; window pane
**invettiva** *f* invective
**inviare** §119 *tr* to send
**invia·to -ta** *mf* envoy; correspondent
**invidia** *f* envy
**invidiàbile** *adj* enviable
**invidiare** §287 *tr* to envy; to begrudge; **non aver niente da invidiare a** to be just as good as
**invidió·so -sa** [s] *adj* envious
**invigorire** §176 *tr* to strengthen, invigorate || *intr* (ESSERE) & *ref* to grow stronger
**invilire** §176 *tr* to dishearten; to vilify; to lower (*prices*) || *intr* (ESSERE) & *ref* to lose heart; to lose one's reputation
**inviluppare** *tr* to envelop; to wrap up
**invincìbile** *adj* invincible
**invì·o** *m* (**-i**) dispatch; shipment; remittance; envoy (*of a poem*)
**inviolàbile** *adj* inviolable
**inviperire** §176 *ref* to become enraged
**invischiare** §287 *tr* to smear with birdlime; to ensnare || *ref* to become ensnared
**invisìbile** *adj* invisible
**invi·so -sa** *adj* disliked, hated
**invitante** *adj* attractive, inviting
**invitare** *tr* to invite; to summon; (*cards*) to bid; (*cards*) to open; (*mach*) to screw (*e.g., a light bulb*) in; to screw (*e.g., a lid*) on
**invita·to -ta** *adj* invited || *m* guest
**invito** *m* invitation; inducement; bottom of stairway; (*cards*) opening
**invit·to -ta** *adj* unvanquished
**invocare** §197 (invòco) *tr* to invoke
**invocazióne** *f* invocation
**invogliare** §280 (invòglio) *tr* to induce, entice || *ref* to yearn, long
**involare** (invólo) *tr* to steal; to abduct || *intr* (ESSERE) (aer) to take off || *ref* to disappear; to fly away
**invòlgere** §289 *tr* to wrap, envelop; to involve || *ref* to become entangled
**invólo** *m* (aer) take-off
**involontà·rio -ria** *adj* (**-ri -rie**) involuntary
**invòlto** *m* bundle; wrapper
**invòlucro** *m* wrapping; shell (*of boiler*); (aer) envelope
**involu·to -ta** *adj* (fig) involved; (lit) enveloped
**invòlvere** §147 (*pret* missing; *pp* also invòlto) *tr* (lit) to envelop
**invulneràbile** *adj* invulnerable
**inzaccherare** (inzàcchero) *tr* to bespatter
**inzeppare** (inzéppo) *tr* to cram, stuff
**inzuccherare** (inzùcchero) *tr* to sweeten
**inzuppare** *tr* to soak || *ref* to get drenched
**ìo** *m* ego; self || §5 *pron pers*
**iòdio** *m* iodine
**iodidri·co -ca** *adj* (**-ci -che**) hydriodic
**ioduro** *m* iodide
**iògurt** *m* yogurt
**iò·le** *f* (**-le**) (naut) yawl; (sports) shell
**ióne** *m* ion
**iòni·co -ca** *adj* & *m* (**-ci -che**) Ionic

**ionizzare** [ddzz] *tr* to ionize
**iòsa** [s] *f*—**a iosa** in abundance
**iperacidità** *f* hyperacidity
**ipèrbole** *f* (geom) hyperbola; (rhet) hyperbole
**iperbòli·co -ca** *adj* (**-ci -che**) hyperbolic(al)
**ipereccita·to -ta** *adj* overexcited
**ipermercato** *m* shopping center
**ipersensìbile** *adj* hypersensitive; supersensitive
**ipersostentatóre** *m* landing flap
**ipertensióne** *f* hypertension
**ipnò·si** *f* (**-si**) hypnosis
**ipnòti·co -ca** *adj* & *m* (**-ci -che**) hypnotic
**ipnotismo** *m* hypnotism
**ipnotizzare** [ddzz] *tr* to hypnotize
**ipnotizza·tóre -trice** [ddzz] *adj* hypnotizing || *m* hypnotizer
**ipocondrìa·co -ca** *adj* & *mf* (**-ci -che**) hypochondriac
**ipocrisìa** *f* hypocrisy
**ipòcri·ta** (**-ti -te**) *adj* hypocritical || *mf* hypocrite
**ipodèrmi·co -ca** *adj* (**-ci -che**) hypodermic
**iposolfito** [s] *m* hyposulfite
**ipotè·ca** *f* (**-che**) mortgage
**ipotecare** §197 (ipotèco) *tr* to mortgage
**ipotecà·rio -ria** *adj* (**-ri -rie**) mortgage
**ipotenusa** *f* hypotenuse
**ipòte·si** *f* (**-si**) hypothesis; **nella miglior delle ipotesi** at best; **nell'ipotesi che** in the event; **per ipotesi** by supposition
**ipotèti·co -ca** *adj* (**-ci -che**) hypothetic(al)
**ipotizzare** [ddzz] *tr* to hypothesize
**ìppi·co -ca** (**-ci -che**) *adj* horse, horseracing || *f* horse racing
**ippocampo** *m* sea horse
**ippocastano** *m* horse chestnut tree
**ippòdromo** *m* race track
**ippoglòsso** *m* (ichth) halibut
**ippopòtamo** *m* hippopotamus
**iprite** *f* mustard gas
**ira** *f* wrath, anger, ire
**irachè·no -na** *adj* & *mf* Iraqi
**iracóndia** *f* wrath, anger
**iracón·do -da** *adj* wrathful
**irania·no -na** *adj* & *mf* Iranian
**irascìbile** *adj* irascible
**ira·to -ta** *adj* irate, angry
**ire** §191 *intr* (ESSERE) (lit) to go
**irida·to -ta** *adj* rainbow-hued || *m* world bicycle champion
**ìride** *f* rainbow; (anat, bot) iris
**Irlanda, l'** *f* Ireland
**irlandése** [s] *adj* Irish || *m* Irishman; Irish (*language*) || *f* Irishwoman
**ironìa** *f* irony
**iròni·co -ca** *adj* (**-ci -che**) ironic(al)
**iró·so -sa** [s] *adj* angry, wrathful
**irradiare** §287 *tr* to illuminate; to irradiate, radiate; to brighten; (rad) to broadcast || *intr* to radiate || *ref* to radiate; to spread
**irraggiare** §290 *tr* to illuminate; to irradiate, radiate, beam; to brighten; (rad) to broadcast || *intr* to radiate || *ref* to radiate; to spread

**irraggiungìbile** *adj* unattainable
**irragionévole** *adj* unreasonable
**irrancidire** §176 *intr* (ESSERE) & *ref* to get rancid
**irrazionale** *adj* irrational
**irreale** *adj* unreal
**irreconciliàbile** *adj* irreconcilable
**irrecuperàbile** *adj* irretrievable, irrecoverable
**irredentismo** *m* irredentism
**irredenti·sta** *mf* (-sti -ste) irredentist
**irredèn·to -ta** *adj* not yet redeemed
**irredimìbile** *adj* irredeemable
**irrefrenàbile** *adj* unrestrainable
**irrefutàbile** *adj* irrefutable
**irregimentare** (**irregiménto**) *tr* to regiment
**irregolare** *adj* irregular
**irregolari·tà** *f* (-tà) irregularity
**irreligió·so -sa** [s] *adj* irreligious
**irremovìbile** *adj* irremovable; obstinate
**irreparàbile** *adj* irreparable; unavoidable
**irreperìbile** *adj* not to be found; unaccounted for (*e.g., soldier*)
**irreprensìbile** *adj* irreproachable
**irreprimìbile** *adj* irrepressible
**irrequiè·to -ta** *adj* restless, restive
**irresistìbile** [s] *adj* irresistible
**irresolùbile** [s] *adj* unbreakable (*bond; contract*); insoluble; unsolvable
**irresolu·to -ta** [s] *adj* irresolute
**irrespiràbile** *adj* unbreathable
**irresponsàbile** *adj* irresponsible
**irrestringìbile** *adj* unshrinkable
**irretire** §176 *tr* to ensnare, entrap
**irrevocàbile** *adj* irrevocable
**irriconoscìbile** *adj* unrecognizable
**irriducìbile** *adj* irreducible; stubborn
**irriflessi·vo -va** *adj* thoughtless, rash
**irrigare** §209 *tr* to irrigate
**irrigazióne** *f* irrigation
**irrigidire** §176 *tr* to chill ‖ *intr* & *ref* to stiffen, harden; to get cool
**irrì·guo -gua** *adj* well-watered; irrigating
**irrilevante** *adj* irrelevant
**irrilevanza** *f* irrelevance
**irrimediàbile** *adj* irremediable
**irripetìbile** *adj* unrepeatable
**irrisióne** *f* (lit) derision, mockery
**irrisò·rio -ria** *adj* (-ri -rie) mocking; paltry
**irritàbile** *adj* peevish; irritable
**irritante** *adj* irritating ‖ *m* irritant
**irritare** (**ìrrito**) *tr* to irritate; to anger; to chafe ‖ *ref* to become irritated
**irritazióne** *f* irritation
**irriverènte** *adj* irreverent
**irrobustire** §176 *tr* & *ref* to strengthen
**irrómpere** §240 (*pp* missing) *intr* to burst
**irrorare** (**irròro**) *tr* to sprinkle; to bathe, wet; to spray
**irroratrice** *f* sprayer; **irroratrice a zaino** portable sprayer
**irruènte** *adj* impetuous, rash
**irruzióne** *f* foray, raid; irruption
**irsu·to -ta** *adj* hairy, bristling
**ir·to -ta** *adj* prickly; shaggy (*hair*); **irto di** bristling with
**iscrìvere** §250 *tr* to inscribe; to register ‖ *ref* to register; to sign up

**iscrizióne** *f* inscription; registration
**Islam, l'** *m* Islam
**Islanda, l'** *f* Iceland
**islandése** [s] *adj* Icelandic ‖ *mf* Icelander ‖ *m* Icelandic (*language*)
**ìsola** *f* island; block; **isola spartitraffico** traffic island
**isolaménto** *m* isolation; (elec) insulation
**isola·no -na** *adj* island ‖ *mf* islander
**isolante** *adj* insulating ‖ *m* (elec) insulation
**isolare** (**ìsolo**) *tr* to isolate; (elec) to insulate ‖ *ref* to keep apart
**isola·to -ta** *adj* isolated; (elec) insulated ‖ *m* city block; (sports) independent
**isolatóre** *m* (elec) insulator
**isolazionismo** *m* isolationism
**isolazioni·sta** *mf* (-sti -ste) isolationist
**isolétta** *f* isle
**isòscele** *adj* isosceles
**isòto·po -pa** *adj* isotopic ‖ *m* isotope
**ispani·sta** *mf* (-sti -ste) Hispanist
**ispa·no -na** *adj* Hispanic
**ispanoamerica·no -na** *adj* & *mf* Spanish-American
**ispessire** §176 *tr* & *ref* to thicken
**ispettorato** *m* inspectorship
**ispet·tóre -trice** *mf* inspector; **ispettore di produzione** (mov) production manager
**ispezionare** (**ispezióno**) *tr* to inspect
**ispezióne** *f* inspection
**ispi·do -da** *adj* bristly
**ispirare** *tr* to inspire ‖ *ref* to be inspired
**ispirazióne** *f* inspiration
**Israèle** *m* Israel
**israelia·no -na** *adj* & *mf* Israeli
**israeli·ta** *adj* & *mf* (-ti -te) Israelite
**issare** *tr* to hoist
**issòpo** *m* hyssop
**istallare** *tr* & *ref* var of **installare**
**istantàne·o -a** *adj* instantaneous ‖ *f* snapshot
**istante** *m* instant, moment; petitioner
**istanza** *f* petition; request, application; (law) instance; **in ultima istanza** as a final decision
**istèri·co -ca** (-ci -che) *adj* hysteric(al) ‖ *mf* hysteric
**isterilire** §176 *tr* to make barren ‖ *ref* to become barren
**isterismo** *m* hysteria, hysterics
**istigare** §209 *tr* to instigate, prompt
**istiga·tóre -trice** *mf* instigator
**istillare** *tr* to instill, implant; **istillare il collirio negli occhi** to put drops in the eyes
**istinti·vo -va** *adj* instinctive
**istinto** *m* instinct
**istituire** §176 *tr* to institute, found; (lit) to decide
**istituto** *m* institute; institution; bank; **istituto di bellezza** beauty parlor
**istitu·tóre -trice** *mf* founder; teacher, instructor ‖ *m* tutor ‖ *f* governess; nurse
**istituzionalizzare** [ddzz] *tr* to institutionalize
**istituzióne** *f* institution
**istmo** *m* isthmus
**istologìa** *f* histology

**istoriare** §287 (istòrio) *tr* to adorn with historical figures

**istradare** *tr* to direct || *ref* to wend one's way

**istrice** *m & f* (European) porcupine

**istrióne** *m* ham actor; buffoon

**istriòni·co -ca** *adj* (**-ci -che**) histrionic

**istrionismo** *m* histrionics

**istruire** §176 *tr* to instruct; to train; (law) to draw up, prepare (*a case*) || *ref* to learn

**istrui·to -ta** *adj* learned, educated

**istruménto** *m* (law) instrument

**istrutti·vo -va** *adj* instructive

**istrut·tóre -trice** *mf* instructor; (sports) coach

**istruttò·rio -ria** (**-ri -rie**) *adj* investigating, preliminary || *f* (law) preliminary investigation

**istruzióne** *f* instruction; (law) prelimi-

nary investigation; **istruzioni** instructions; directions

**istupidire** §176 *tr* to make dull; to stupefy

**Itàlia, l'** *f* Italy

**italia·no -na** *adj & mf* Italian

**itàli·co -ca** *adj* (**-ci -che**) italic; Italic; (lit) Italian || *m* italics

**italòfo·no -na** *adj* Italian-speaking || *m* Italian-speaking person

**itinerante** *adj* itinerant

**itinerà·rio** *m* (**-ri**) itinerary

**ittèri·co -ca** *adj* (**-ci -che**) jaundiced

**itterìzia** *f* jaundice

**ittiologìa** *f* ichthiology

**Iugoslàvia, la** Yugoslavia

**iugosla·vo -va** *adj & mf* Yugoslav

**iugulare** *adj & tr* var of **giugulare**

**iuta** *f* jute

**ivi** *adv* (lit) there

# L

**L, l** ['εlle] *m & f* tenth letter of the Italian alphabet

**la** §4 *def art* the || *m* (mus) la, A; **dare il la** to set the tone || §5 *pers pron*

**là** *adv* there; **al di là da venire** to come, future; **al di là (di)** beyond; **andare di là** to go in the next room; **andare troppo in là** to go too far; **farsi in là** to move aside; **in là con gli anni** advanced in years; **l'al di là** the life beyond; **più in là** further; **più in là di** beyond; **va' là!** come on!

**làb·bro** *m* (**-bri**) edge (*of wound*); (lit) lip || *m* (**-bra** *fpl*) lip; **labbro leporino** harelip

**labiale** *adj & f* labial

**làbile** *adj* (coll) weak; (lit) fleeting

**labiolettura** *f* lip reading

**labirinto** *m* labyrinth, maze

**laboratò·rio** *m* (**-ri**) laboratory; workshop; **laboratorio linguistico** language laboratory

**laborió·so -sa** [s] *adj* hard-working, laborious; labored (*e.g., digestion*)

**laburi·sta** (**-sti -ste**) *adj* Labour || *mf* Labourite

**lac·ca** *f* (**-che**) lacquer

**laccare** §197 *tr* to lacquer; to japan; to polish (*nails*)

**lac·chè** *m* (**-chè**) lackey

**lac·cio** *m* (**-ci**) lasso; snare; noose; string; (fig) bond; **laccio delle scarpe** shoelace; **laccio emostatico** tourniquet

**lacciòlo** *m* snare

**lacerare** (**làcero**) *tr* to lacerate; to tear || *ref* to tear

**làce·ro -ra** *adj* torn; tattered

**lacèrto** *m* (lit) shred of flesh; (lit) biceps

**lacòni·co -ca** *adj* (**-ci -che**) laconic

**làcrima** *f* tear; drop

**lacrimare** (**làcrimo**) *tr* (lit) to weep

over || *intr* to water (*said of the eyes*); (lit) to weep

**lacrima·to -ta** *adj* (lit) lamented

**lacrimévole** *adj* pitiful

**lacrimòge·no -na** *adj* tear (*e.g., gas*)

**lacrimó·so -sa** [s] *adj* teary, watery (*eyes*); tearful; lachrymose

**lacuna** *f* gap, lacuna; blank (*in one's mind*); **colmare una lacuna** to bridge a gap

**lacustre** *adj* lake

**laddóve** *conj* while, whereas

**ladré·sco -sca** *adj* (**-schi -sche**) thievish

**la·dro -dra** *adj* thieving; foul (*weather*); bewitching (*eyes*) || *mf* thief; **ladro di strada** highwayman || *f* inside pocket (*of suit*)

**ladróne** *m* thief; highwayman; **ladrone di mare** pirate

**ladrùncolo** *m* petty thief, pilferer

**laggiù** *adv* down there

**lagnanza** *f* complaint

**lagnare** *ref* to complain; to moan

**lagno** *m* complaint, lament

**la·go** *m* (**-ghi**) lake; pool (*of blood*)

**làgrima** *f* var of **lacrima**

**laguna** *f* lagoon

**lai** *m* (lai) lay; **lai** *mpl* (lit) lamentations

**laicato** *m* laity

**lài·co -ca** *adj* (**-ci -che**) lay || *m* layman

**lài·do -da** *adj* foul; obscene

**la·ma** *m* (**-ma**) llama; lama || *f* (**-me**) blade (*of knife*); marsh; (lit) lowland

**lambiccare** §197 *tr* to distill || *ref* to strive; **lambiccarsi il cervello** to rack one's brains

**lambìc·co** *m* (**-chi**) still

**lambire** §176 *tr* to lap; to graze, to touch lightly

**lamèlla** *f* thin sheet

**lamentare** (**laménto**) *tr* to bemoan, lament || *ref* to moan; to complain

**lamentazióne** *f* lamentation

**lamentévole** *adj* plaintive; lamentable

**laménto** *m* complaint, lament; moan

**lamentó·so -sa** [s] *adj* plaintive, doleful

**lamétta** *f* razor blade

**lamièra** *f* plate; armor plate

**lamierino** *m* sheet metal, lamina

**làmina** *f* sheet, lamina

**laminare (làmino)** *tr* to laminate; to roll (*steel*)

**lamina·tóio** *m* (**-tói**) rolling mill

**làmpada** *f* lamp, light; **lampada al neon** neon lamp; **lampada a petrolio** oil lamp; **lampada a stelo** pole lamp; **lampada di sicurezza** (min) safety lamp; **lampada fluorescente** fluorescent lamp; **lampada lampo** (phot) flash bulb

**lampadà·rio** *m* (**-ri**) chandelier

**lampadina** *f* bulb; **lampadina tascabile** flashlight

**lampante** *adj* shiny; clear; lamp (*oil*)

**lampeggiare** §290 (**lampéggio**) *tr* (lit) to flash (*a smile*) ‖ *intr* to flash; (aut) to blink; (coll) to flash the turn signals ‖ *impers* (ESSERE & AVERE)— **lampeggia** it lightens, it is lightning

**lampeggiatóre** *m* (aut) turn signal; (phot) flashlight

**lampio·nàio** *m* (**-nài**) lamplighter

**lampióne** *m* street lamp

**lampìride** *f* glowworm

**lampo** *m* lightning; flash of lightning; (fig) flash

**lampóne** *m* raspberry

**lana** *f* wool; **buona lana** (coll) rogue, rascal; **lana d'acciaio** steel wool; **lana di vetro** fiberglass, glass wool

**lancétta** *f* lancet; hand (*of watch*); pointer (*of instrument*)

**làn·cia** *f* (**-ce**) lance, spear; nozzle (*of fire hose*); launch; **lancia di salvataggio** lifeboat

**lanciabóm·be** *m* (**-be**) trench mortar

**lanciafiam·me** *m* (**-me**) flamethrower

**lanciamissi·li** (**-li**) *adj* missile-launching ‖ *m* missile launcher

**lanciaraz·zi** [ddzz] *m* (**-zi**) rocket launcher

**lanciare** §128 *tr* to throw, hurl; to drop (*from an airplane*); to launch (*e.g., an advertising campaign*) ‖ *ref* to hurl oneself; (rok) to blast off; **lanciarsi col paracadute** to parachute, bail out

**lanciasilu·ri** *m* (**-ri**) torpedo tube

**lancia·to -ta** *adj* hurled, flung; flying, e.g., **partenza lanciata** flying start

**lancia·tóre -trice** *mf* hurler, thrower; (baseball) pitcher

**lancière** *m* lancer

**lancinante** *adj* piercing

**làn·cio** *m* (**-ci**) throw; publicity campaign; (aer) drop; (aer) release (*of bombs*); (baseball) pitch; (rok) launch; **lancio del peso** shot put

**landa** *f* moor; wasteland

**lanerìe** *fpl* woolens

**languidézza** *f* languidness, languor

**làngui·do -da** *adj* languid; sad (*eyes*)

**languire (lànguo)** & §176 *intr* to languish

**languóre** *m* languor; languishing; weakness; tenderness

**lanziè·ro -ra** *adj* wool (*industry*)

**lanifi·cio** *m* (**-ci**) woolen mill

**lanó·so -sa** [s] *adj* woolly; kinky (*hair*); bushy (*face*)

**lantèrna** *f* lantern

**lanùgine** *f* down

**lanzichenéc·co** *m* (**-chi**) landsknecht

**laónde** *conj* (lit) wherefore

**laotia·no -na** *adj* & *mf* Laotian

**lapalissia·no -na** *adj* self-evident

**lapidare (làpido)** *tr* to stone (to death); (fig) to pick to pieces

**làpide** *f* stone tablet; tombstone

**lapillo** *m* lapillus

**là·pis** *m* (**-pis**) pencil

**lappare** *intr* to lap

**làppola** *f* (bot) burdock; (bot) bur

**lappóne** *adj* Lappish ‖ *mf* Lapp ‖ *m* Lapp (*language*)

**Lappónia, la** Lapland

**lardellare (lardèllo)** *tr* to lard; to stuff with bacon

**lardo** *m* lard; **nuotare nel lardo** to live on easy street

**largheggiare** §290 (**larghéggio**) *intr* to be liberal; to be lavish

**larghézza** *f* width; liberality; abundance; **larghezza di vedute** broadmindedness

**largire** §176 *tr* (lit) to bestow liberally

**largizióne** *f* bestowal; donation

**lar·go -ga** (**-ghi -ghe**) *adj* broad, wide; ample; liberal; abundant; (phonet) open; **prenderla larga** to keep away ‖ *m* width; open sea; square; (mus) largo; **al largo di** (naut) off; **fare largo a** to open the way to; **farsi largo** to elbow one's way; **prendere il largo** to run away; (naut) to put to sea; **tenersi al largo** to keep at a distance ‖ *f*—**alla larga!** keep away! ‖ *largo adv*—**girare largo** to keep away

**làrice** *m* larch

**laringe** *f* larynx

**laringite** *f* laryngitis

**laringoia·tra** *mf* (**-tri -tre**) laryngologist

**laringoscò·pio** *m* (**-pi**) laryngoscope

**larva** *f* (ent) larva; (lit) ghost; (lit) skeleton; (lit) sham

**lasagne** *fpl* lasagne

**lasciapassa·re** *m* (**-re**) safe-conduct; permit

**lasciare** §128 *tr* to leave; to let; to let go of; **lasciar cadere** to drop; **lasciarci le penne** (coll) to die; (coll) to be skinned alive; **lasciar correre** to let go; **lasciar detto** to leave word; **lasciar fare** to leave alone; **lasciare in pace** to leave alone; **lasciare libero** to let go; **lasciare scritto** to leave in writing ‖ *ref* to abandon oneself; to abandon one another

**làscito** *m* (law) bequest

**lascivia** *f* lasciviousness

**lasci·vo -va** *adj* lascivious

**lassati·vo -va** *adj* mildly laxative ‖ *m* mild laxative

**lassismo** *m* laxity

**las·so -sa** *adj* lax ‖ *m* lasso; **lasso di tempo** period of time

**lassù** *adv* up there, up above

**lastra** *f* slab; paving stone; (phot)

plate; exposed X-ray film; **farsi le lastre** (coll) to be X-rayed
**lastricare** §197 (**làstrico**) *tr* to pave
**lastricato** *m* paving, pavement
**làstri·co** *m* (**-ci** or **-chi**) pavement; roadway; **ridursi sul lastrico** to fall into abject poverty
**lastróne** *m* slab; plate glass
**latènte** *adj* latent
**laterale** *adj* lateral ‖ *m* (soccer) halfback
**laterì·zio -zia** (**-zi -zie**) *adj* brick ‖ **laterizi** *mpl* bricks, tiles
**làtice** *m* latex
**latifondi·sta** *mf* (**-sti -ste**) rich landowner
**latifóndo** *m* large landed estate
**lati·no -na** *adj* Latin; lateen (*sail*) ‖ *m* Latin
**latitante** *adj* hiding ‖ *mf* fugitive
**latitanza** *f* flight from justice
**latitùdine** *f* latitude
**la·to -ta** *adj* wide; broad (*meaning*) ‖ *m* side; **d'altro lato** on the other hand
**la·tóre -trice** *mf* bearer
**latrare** *intr* to bark
**latrato** *m* bark
**latrina** *f* toilet, lavatory, washroom
**latta** *f* tin; can
**lattàia** *f* milkmaid
**lat·tàio** *m* (**-tài**) milkman, dairyman
**lattante** *adj & m* suckling
**latte** *m* milk; **latte detergente** cleansing cream; **latte di gallina** flip; (bot) star-of-Bethlehem; **latte in polvere** powdered milk; **latte magro** or **scremato** skim milk
**lattemièle** *m* whipped cream
**làtte·o -a** *adj* milky
**latterìa** *f* dairy; creamery
**làttice** *m* var of **latice**
**latticèllo** *m* buttermilk
**lattici·nio** *m* (**-ni**) dairy product
**lattiginó·so -sa** [*s*] *adj* milky
**lattonière** *m* tinsmith
**lattu·ga** *f* (**-ghe**) lettuce; head of lettuce; frill
**làudano** *m* paregoric, laudanum
**laudati·vo -va** *adj* laudatory
**làurea** *f* wreath; doctorate; doctoral examination
**laurean·do -da** *mf* candidate for the doctorate
**laureare** (**làureo**) *tr* to confer the doctorate on; to award (*s.o.*) the title of; (lit) to wreathe ‖ *ref* to receive the doctorate; (sports) to get the tile of
**laurea·to -ta** *adj* laureate ‖ *m* alumnus, graduate
**làuro** *m* laurel
**làu·to -ta** *adj* sumptuous, rich
**lava** *f* lava
**lavabianche·rìa** *f* (**-rìa**) washing machine
**lavàbile** *adj* washable
**lavabo** *m* washstand; lavatory
**lavacristallo** *m* windshield washer
**lavacro** *m* washing; font; purification; **santo lavacro** baptism
**lavàg·gio** *m* (**-gi**) washing; **lavaggio a secco** dry cleaning; **lavaggio del cervello** brainwashing

**lavagna** *f* slate; blackboard; **lavagna di panno** felt board; **lavagna luminosa** overhead projector
**lavama·no** *m* (**-no**) washstand
**lavanda** *f* washing; pumping (*of stomach*); lavender
**lavandàia** *f* laundrywoman; **lavandaia stiratrice** laundress (*woman who washes and irons*)
**lavan·dàio** *m* (**-dài**) laundryman; **lavandaio stiratore** launderer
**lavanderìa** *f* laundry; **lavanderia a gettone** laundromat; **lavanderia a secco** dry-cleaning establishment
**lavandino** *m* sink
**lavapiat·ti** *mf* (**-ti**) dishwasher (*person*)
**lavare** *tr* to wash; to cleanse; **lavare a secco** to dry-clean; **lavare il capo a** to scold ‖ *ref* to wash oneself; **lavarsi le mani** to wash one's hands
**lavastovì·glie** *mf* (**-glie**) dishwasher ‖ *m & f* dishwasher (*machine*)
**lavata** *f* washing; **lavata di capo** scolding
**lavativo** *m* (coll) enema; (coll) bore; (coll) goldbricker
**lava·tóio** *m* (**-tói**) laundry room; washtub
**lava·tóre -trice** *mf* washer ‖ *m* washerman; (mach) purifier ‖ *f* washerwoman; washing machine
**lavatura** *f* washing; **lavatura a secco** dry cleaning; **lavatura di piatti** dishwater; washing of dishes; (fig) watery soup
**lavèllo** *m* wash basin; sink
**lavoràbile** *adj* workable
**lavorante** *mf* helper, apprentice
**lavorare** (**lavóro**) *tr* to work; to till ‖ *intr* to work; to perform; to be busy; to trade; **lavorare ai ferri** to knit; **lavorare di fantasia** to daydream; **lavorare di ganasce** to eat voraciously; **lavorare di gomiti** to elbow one's way; **lavorare di mano** to pilfer; **lavorare di traforo** to work with a jig saw
**lavorati·vo -va** *adj* working; workable
**lavora·to -ta** *adj* wrought; tilled
**lavora·tóre -trice** *mf* worker ‖ *m* workman; workingman ‖ *f* workingwoman
**lavorazióne** *f* working; manufacturing; tilling
**lavorì·o** *m* (**-ì**) bustle; steady work; scheming
**lavóro** *m* work; labor; steady work; homework; piece of work; (coll) trouble; **a lavori ultimati** when the work is finished; **lavori forzati** hard labor; **lavori in economia** time and material contract work; **lavori teatrali** theatrical productions; **lavoro a cottimo** piecework; **lavoro a maglia** knitting; **lavoro di cucito** needlework; **mettere al lavoro** to press into service
**lazzarétto** [*ddzz*] *m* lazaretto
**lazzaróne** [*ddzz*] *m* cad; (coll) goldbricker
**le** §4 *def art* the ‖ §5 *pers pron*
**leale** *adj* loyal; sincere
**leali·sta** *mf* (**-sti -ste**) loyalist
**leal·tà** *f* (**-tà**) loyalty; sincerity

**lébbra** *f* leprosy
**lebbró•so -sa** [s] *adj* leprous ‖ *mf* lèper
**lécca-léc•ca** *m* (**-ca**) (coll) lollypop
**leccapiat•ti** *m* (**-ti**) glutton; sponger
**leccapiè•di** *mf* (**-di**) bootlicker
**leccarda** *f* dripping pan
**leccare** §197 (**lécco**) *tr* to lick; to fawn on; (fig) to polish ‖ *ref* to make oneself up
**lecca•to -ta** *adj* affected; polished ‖ *f* licking
**léc•cio** *m* (**-ci**) holm oak
**leccornìa** *f* dainty morsel, delicacy
**léci•to -ta** *adj* licit, permissible; **mi sia lecito** may I ‖ *m* right
**lèdere** §192 *tr* to damage, injure
**lé•ga** *f* (**-ghe**) league; alloy; **di bassa lega** poor, in poor taste; **fare lega** to unite
**legale** *adj* legal; lawyer's; official ‖ *m* lawyer
**legali•tà** *f* (**-tà**) legality, lawfulness
**legalità•rio -ria** *adj* (**-ri -rie**) (pol) observing the rule of law
**legalizzare** [ddzz] *tr* to legalize; to authenticate
**legame** *m* bond; connection; relationship
**legaménto** *m* tie, bond; ligament; (phonet) liaison
**legare** §209 (**légo**) *tr* to tie; to bind; to unite; to set (*a stone*); to bequeath; to alloy; (bb) to bind ‖ *intr* to bond; to mix (*said of metals*); to go together ‖ *ref* to unite; **legarsela al dito** to never forget
**legatà•rio -ria** *mf* (**-ri -rie**) legatee
**lega•to -ta** *adj* muscle-bound ‖ *m* legate; bequest; (mus) legato
**lega•tóre -trice** *mf* bookbinder
**legatorìa** *f* bookbindery
**legatura** *f* typing; binding; ligature; bookbinding; (mus) tie
**legazióne** *f* legation
**légge** *f* law; act; **dettar legge** to lay down the law; **è fuori della legge** he is an outlaw; **legge stralcio** emergency law
**leggènda** *f* legend; story, tall tale; (journ) caption
**leggendà•rio -ria** *adj* (**-ri -rie**) legendary
**lèggere** §193 *tr, intr & ref* to read
**leggerézza** *f* lightness; nimbleness; thoughtlessness; fickleness
**leggè•ro -ra** *adj* light; nimble; thoughtless; slight; fickle; **alla leggera** lightly ‖ **leggero** *adv* lightly
**leggia•dro -dra** *adj* graceful, lovely
**leggìbile** *adj* legible, readable
**leggì•o** *m* (**-i**) lectern; music stand
**legiferare** (**legìfero**) *intr* to legislate
**legionà•rio -ria** *adj & m* (**-ri -rie**) legionary
**legióne** *f* legion
**legislati•vo -va** *adj* legislative
**legisla•tóre -trice** *mf* legislator
**legislatura** *f* legislature
**legittimare** (**legìttimo**) *tr* to legitimize
**legittimi•tà** *f* (**-tà**) legitimacy
**legìtti•mo -ma** *adj* legitimate; pure; just, right ‖ *f* (law) legitim
**lé•gna** *f* (**-gna & -gne**) firewood; (fig) fuel

**legnàia** *f* woodpile; woodshed
**legname** *m* timber, lumber
**legnata** *f* clubbing, thrashing
**légno** *m* wood; stick; ship; coach; timber; **legno compensato** plywood; **legno dolce** softwood; **legno forte** hardwood
**legnòlo** *m* ply (*e.g., of a cable*)
**legnó•so -sa** [s] *adj* wooden; tough (*meat*); dry (*style*)
**legu•lèio** *m* (**-lèi**) pettifogger
**legume** *m* legume; **legumi** vegetables; legumes
**leguminósa** [s] *f* leguminous plant; **leguminose** legumes
**lèi** §5 *pron pers;* **dare del Lei a** to address formally
**lémbo** *m* edge, border; patch (*of land*)
**lèm•ma** *m* (**-mi**) entry (*in a dictionary*)
**lèmme lèmme** *adv* (coll) slowly
**léna** *f* energy; enthusiasm; (lit) breath
**lèndine** *m* nit
**lène** *adj* (lit) light, soft, gentle; (phonet) voiced
**lenire** §176 *tr* to soothe, assuage
**lenóne** *m* panderer, procurer
**lenóna** *f* procuress
**lènte** *f* lens; bob, pendulum bob; **lente d'ingrandimento** magnifying glass; **lenti** glasses
**lentézza** *f* slowness
**lentìcchia** *f* lentil
**lentìggine** *f* freckle
**lentigginó•so -sa** [s] *adj* freckly
**lèn•to -ta** *adj* slow; slack; (lit) loose (*hair*); (lit) loose-fitting (*garment*) ‖ **lento** *adv* slowly
**lènza** *f* fishline
**lenzuò•lo** *m* (**-li**) sheet; (fig) blanket; **lenzuolo a due piazze** double sheet; **lenzuolo funebre** winding sheet, shroud ‖ *m* (**-la** *fpl*) sheet; **lenzuola** pair of sheets (*in a bed*)
**leoncino** *m* lion cub
**leóne** *m* lion; **leone d'America** cougar; **leone marino** sea lion ‖ **Leone** *m* (astr) Leo
**leonéssa** *f* lioness
**leopardo** *m* leopard
**lepidézza** *f* wit; witticism
**lèpi•do -da** *adj* witty, facetious
**lepisma** *f* (ent) silverfish
**lèpre** *adj invar* rendezvous, e.g., **razzo lepre** rendezvous rocket ‖ *f* hare
**lepròtto** *m* leveret, young hare
**lèr•cio -cia** *adj* (**-ci -ce**) filthy
**lerciume** *m* filth, dirt
**lèsbi•co -ca** (**-ci -che**) *adj & mf* Lesbian ‖ *f* Lesbian (*female homosexual*)
**lésina** *f* awl; stinginess; miser
**lesinare** (**lésino & lèsino**) *tr* to begrudge ‖ *intr* to be miserly
**lesionare** (**lesióno**) *tr* to damage; to crack open
**lesióne** *f* damage; injury; lesion
**lé•so -sa** *adj* damaged; injured
**lessare** (**lésso**) *tr* to boil
**lessicale** *adj* lexical
**lèssi•co** *m* (**-ci**) lexicon
**lessicografìa** *f* lexicography
**lessicogràfi•co -ca** *adj* (**-ci -che**) lexicographic(al)
**lessicògrafo** *m* lexicographer

**lessicologìa** *f* lexicology
**lés·so -sa** *adj* boiled ‖ *m* boiled meat; soup meat
**lè·sto -sta** *adj* swift; nimble; quick; **alla lesta** hastily; **lesto di lìngua** ready-tongued; **lesto di mano** light-fingered
**lestofante** *m* swindler
**letale** *adj* lethal, deadly
**leta·màio** *m* (**-mài**) dunghill
**letame** *m* manure, dung
**letàrgi·co -ca** *adj* (**-ci -che**) lethargic
**letàr·go** *m* (**-ghi**) lethargy; hibernation
**letizia** *f* happiness, joy
**lèttera** *f* letter; **alla lettera** literally; **lettera morta** unheeded, e.g., **le sue parole rimasero lettera morta** his words remained unheeded; **lettere** literature; **lettere credenziali** credentials; **scrivere in tutte lettere** to spell out
**letterale** *adj* literal
**letterà·rio -ria** *adj* (**-ri -rie**) literary; learned (*word*)
**lettera·to -ta** *adj* literary; literate ‖ *m* man of letters; (coll) literate, learned person
**letteratura** *f* literature
**lettièra** *f* litter, bedding
**letti·ga** *f* (**-ghe**) sedan chair; stretcher
**lètto** *m* bed; bedding; **di primo letto** born of the first marriage; **letti gemelli** twin beds; **letto a castello** bunk bed; **letto a due piazze** double bed; **letto a scomparsa** Murphy bed; **letto a una piazza** single bed; **letto bastardo** oversize bed; **letto caldo** hot-bed; **letto di morte** deathbed; **letto operatorio** operating table
**lèttone** or **lettóne** *adj* Lettish ‖ *mf* Lett ‖ *m* Lett, Lettish (*language*)
**Lettónia, La** Latvia
**let·tóre -trice** *mf* reader; lecturer; meter reader ‖ *m* reader (*e.g., for microfilm*); **lettore perforatore** reader (*of punch cards*)
**lettura** *f* reading; lecture; **lettura del pensiero** mind reading
**letturi·sta** *m* (**-sti**) meter reader
**leucemìa** *f* leukemia
**leucorrèa** *f* leucorrhea
**lèva** *f* lever; (mil) draft; (mil) class; **essere di leva** to be of draft age; **fare leva su** to use (*s.o.'s emotions*)
**levachio·di** *m* (**-di**) claw hammer
**levante** *adj* rising ‖ *m* east; Levant
**levanti·no -na** *adj* & *mf* Levantine
**levare (lèvo)** *tr* to lift, raise; to weigh (*anchor*); to pull (*a tooth*); to break (*camp*); to collect (*mail*); to remove, take away; to subtract; **levare alle stelle** to praise to the sky; **levare il disturbo a** to take leave of ‖ *ref* to arise; to get up; to take off; to satisfy (*e.g., one's hunger*); to rise (*said of wind*); **levarsi dai piedi** to get out of the way; **levarsi dai piedi** or **di mezzo qlcu** to get rid of s.o.
**levata** *f* rise; reveille; collection (*of mail*); withdrawal (*of merchandise from warehouse*); **levata di scudi** uprising
**levatàc·cia** *f* (**-ce**) getting up at an im-

possible hour; **ho dovuto fare una levataccia** I had to get up way too early
**leva·tóio -tóia** *adj* (**-tói -tóie**)—**ponte levatoio** drawbridge
**levatrice** *f* midwife
**levatura** *f* intellectual breadth
**leviatano** *m* leviathan
**levigare §209 (lèvigo)** *tr* to polish
**levigatrice** *f* sander; buffer
**levi·tà** *f* (**-tà**) (lit) levity
**levitazióne** *f* levitation
**levrière** *m* greyhound
**lezióne** *f* lesson; lecture; reading
**lezió·so -sa** [s] *adj* affected, mincing
**lézzo** [ddzz] *m* stench; filth
**li** *def art masc plur* (obs) the; **li tre novembre** the third of November (*in official documents*) ‖ §5 *pers pron*
**lì** *adv* there; **di lì** that way; **di lì a un anno** a year hence; **essere lì lì per** to be about to; **fin lì** up to that point; **giù di lì** more or less; **lì per lì** on the spot
**libanése** [s] *adj* & *mf* Lebanese
**Lìbano, il** Lebanon
**libare** *tr* to toast; to taste ‖ *intr* to toast
**libazióne** *f* libation
**lìbbra** *f* pound
**libéc·cio** *m* (**-ci**) southwest wind
**libèllo** *m* libel; (law) brief
**libèllula** *f* dragonfly
**liberale** *adj* & *m* liberal
**liberali·tà** *f* (**-tà**) liberality
**liberare (lìbero)** *tr* to free; to pay in full for; to open into (*said, e.g., of a hall opening into a room*); to clear, empty (*a room*) ‖ *ref*—**liberarsi da** or **di** to get rid of
**libera·tóre -trice** *adj* liberating ‖ *mf* liberator
**liberismo** *m* free trade
**lìbe·ro -ra** *adj* free; vacant; without a revenue stamp (*document*); open (*syllable; heart*); outspoken
**liber·tà** *f* (**-tà**) freedom; release (*e.g., from mortgage*); **libertà provvisoria** bail, parole; **libertà vigilata** probation; **mettersi in libertà** to put comfortable house clothes on; **rimettere in libertà** to set free
**liberti·no -na** *adj* & *mf* libertine
**Lìbia, la** Libya
**lìbi·co -ca** *adj* & *mf* (**-ci -che**) Libyan
**libìdine** *f* lust; greed
**libidinó·so -sa** [s] *adj* lustful
**libido** *f* libido
**li·bràio** *m* (**-brài**) bookseller
**librare** *ref* to balance; to soar; (aer) to glide
**libratóre** *m* (aer) glider
**librerìa** *f* bookstore; library (*room*); bookshelf; book collection
**libré·sco -sca** *adj* (**-schi -sche**) bookish
**librétto** *m* booklet; card; (mus) libretto; **libretto di banca** passbook; **libretto degli assegni** checkbook; **libretto di circolazione** car registration; **libretto ferroviario** railroad pass; **libretto di risparmio** passbook (*of savings bank*)
**libro** *m* book; ledger; register (*e.g., of births*); **a libro** folding; **libro di**

**bordo** log; **libro in brossura** paperback; **libro mastro** ledger; **libro paga** (com) payroll

**liceale** *adj* high-school ǁ *mf* high-school student

**licènza** *f* permit; license; diploma; (mil) leave; **con licenza parlando!** excuse my language!; **dar licenza a** to dismiss; **prender licenza da** to take leave of

**licenziaménto** *m* dismissal; **licenziamento in tronco** firing on the spot

**licenziare** §287 (**licènzio**) *tr* to dismiss; to O.K. (*a book to be published*); to graduate ǁ *ref* to take leave; to give notice, resign; to graduate

**licenzió·so -sa** [s] *adj* licentious

**licèo** *m* high school; lycée

**lichène** *m* lichen

**licitazióne** *f* auction; (bridge) bidding

**lido** *m* shore; sand bar

**lièto -ta** *adj* glad; blessed (*event*)

**lième** *adj* light; slight

**lievitare** (**lièvito**) *tr* to leaven ǁ *intr* (ESSERE & AVERE) to rise; to ferment

**lièvito** *m* yeast; leaven; **lievito in polvere** baking powder

**lì·gio -gia** *adj* (**-gi -gie**) devoted

**lignàg·gio** *m* (**-gi**) ancestry, lineage

**ligustro** *m* privet

**lìl·la** (**-la**) *adj invar & m* lilac

**lillipuzia·no -na** *adj & mf* Lilliputian

**lima** *f* file; **lima per le unghie** nail file

**limaccló·so -sa** [s] *adj* miry, muddy

**limare** *tr* to file; to polish (*e.g., a speech*); to gnaw, plague

**limatura** *f* filing; filings

**limbo** *m* (lit) edge; (fig) limbo ǁ **Limbo** *m* (theol) Limbo

**limétta** *f* nail file; (bot) lime

**limitare** *m* threshold ǁ *v* (**lìmito**) *tr* to limit; to bound

**limitazióne** *f* limitation

**lìmite** *m* limit; boundary; check; (soccer) penalty line; **limite di carico** maximum weight; **limite di età** retirement age; **limite di velocità** speed limit; **senza limiti** limitless

**limìtro·fo -fa** *adj* neighboring (*country*)

**limo** *m* mud, mire

**limonare** (**limóno**) *intr* (coll) to spoon

**limonata** *f* lemonade; (med) citrate of magnesia

**limóne** *m* lemon tree; lemon

**limó·so -sa** [s] *adj* slimy

**lìmpi·do -da** *adj* limpid, clear

**lince** *f* lynx, wildcat

**lincià·gio** *m* (**-gi**) lynching

**linciare** §128 *tr* to lynch

**lìn·do -da** *adj* neat; clean

**lìnea** *f* line; degree (*of temperature*); **conservare la linea** to keep one's figure; **in linea** abreast; (telp) connected; **in linea d'aria** as the crow flies; **linea del fuoco** firing line; **lìnea del cambiamento di data** international date line; **linea di circonvallazione** (rr) beltline; **linea di condotta** policy; **linea di partenza** starting line; **linea laterale** (sports) side line

**lineaménti** *mpl* lineaments; elements

**lineare** *adj* linear ǁ *v* (**lìneo**) *tr* to delineate

**lineétta** *f* dash; hyphen

**linfa** *f* (anat) lymph; (bot) sap; **dar linfa** (bot) to bleed

**lingòtto** *m* (metallurgy) pig, ingot; **lingotto d'oro** bullion

**lìngua** *f* tongue; language; strip (*of land*); **essere di due lingue** to speak with a forked tongue; **in lingua** in the correct language; **lingua di gatto** ladyfinger; **lingua lunga** backbiter; **lingua sciolta** glib tongue; **mala lingua** wicked tongue

**linguacciu·to -ta** *adj* talkative; sharp-tongued

**linguàg·gio** *m* (**-gi**) language

**linguèlla** *f* (philately) gummed strip

**linguétta** *f* tongue (*of shoe*); (mach) pin; (mus) reed

**linguìsti·co -ca** (**-ci -che**) *adj* linguistic ǁ *f* linguistics

**linifì·cio** *m* (**-ci**) flax-spinning mill

**liniménto** *m* liniment

**lino** *m* flax; linen

**linósa** [s] *f* flaxseed, linseed

**linotipi·sta** *mf* (**-sti -ste**) linotypist

**liocòrno** *m* unicorn

**liofilizzare** [ddzz] *tr* to freeze-dry

**liquefare** §194 *tr & ref* to liquefy

**liquefazióne** *f* liquefaction

**liquidare** (**lìquido**) *tr* to liquidate; to close out; to dismiss; to settle

**liquidazióne** *f* liquidation; clearance; **liquidazione del danno** (ins) adjustment

**lìquidità** *f* liquidity

**lìqui·do -da** *adj* liquid; (com) due ǁ *m* liquid; cash ǁ *f* liquid

**lìqui·gàs** *m* (**-gàs**) liquid gas

**liquirìzia** *f* licorice

**liquóre** *m* liqueur; (pharm) liquor

**liquori·sta** *mf* (**-sti -ste**) liqueur manufacturer or dealer

**lira** *f* lira; pound; (mus) lyre ǁ **Lira** *f* (astr) Lyra

**lìri·co -ca** (**-ci -che**) *adj* lyric; (mus) operatic ǁ *m* lyric poet ǁ *f* lyric; lyric poetry; opera

**lirismo** *m* lyricism

**Lisbóna** *f* Lisbon

**lì·sca** *f* (**-sche**) fishbone; lisp

**lisciare** §128 *tr* to smooth; **lisciare il pelo a** to butter up, flatter; to beat up ǁ *ref* to preen

**lì·scio -scia** *adj* (**-sci -sce**) smooth; straight (*drink*); black (*coffee*); **passarla liscia** to get away scot-free

**liscìvia** *f* lye; bleach

**lisciviatrice** *f* washing machine

**lì·so -sa** *adj* worn-out, threadbare

**lista** *f* list; strip, band; stripe; **lista delle spese** shopping list; **lista delle vivande** bill of fare; **lista elettorale** slate (*of candidates*)

**listare** *tr* to border; to stripe

**listèllo** *m* lath; (archit) listel

**listino** *m* price list; market quotation

**litanìa** *f* litany

**lite** *f* quarrel; lawsuit

**litigante** *adj* quarreling ǁ *mf* quarreler; (law) litigant

**litigare** §209 (lìtigo) *tr*—**litigare qlco a qlcu** to fight with s.o. for s.th ‖ *intr* to quarrel; **to litigate** ‖ *ref*—**litigarsi qlco** to strive for s.th
**lìti·gio** *m* (-gi) quarrel, litigation
**litigió·so -sa** [s] *adj* quarrelsome
**lìtio** *m* lithium
**litografìa** *f* lithography
**litògrafo** *m* lithographer
**litorale** *adj* littoral ‖ *m* seashore, coastline
**litro** *m* liter
**Lituània, la** Lithuania
**litua·no -na** *adj* & *mf* Lithuanian ‖ *m* Lithuanian (*language*)
**liturgìa** *f* liturgy
**litùrgi·co -ca** *adj* (-ci -che) liturgical
**liu·tàio** *m* (-tài) lute maker
**liuto** *m* lute
**livèlla** *f* level; **livella a bolla d'aria** spirit level
**livellaménto** *m* leveling; equalization
**livellare** (livèllo) *tr* to level; to equalize; to survey ‖ *intr* (ESSERE) & *ref* to become level
**livella·tóre -trice** *adj* leveling ‖ *mf* surveyor ‖ *f* bulldozer
**livellazióne** *f* leveling
**livèllo** *m* level; **livello delle acque** sea level
**lìvi·do -da** *adj* livid, black-and-blue ‖ *m* bruise
**lividóre** *m* bruise
**livóre** *m* grudge; hatred
**Livórno** *f* Leghorn
**livrèa** *f* livery
**lizza** *f* tilting ground; **entrare in lizza** to enter the lists
**lo** §4 *def art* the ‖ §5 *pers pron*
**lòb·bia** *m* & *f* (-bia *mpl* & *fpl*) homburg
**lòbo** *m* lobe
**locale** *adj* local ‖ *m* room; place (*of business*); (naut) compartment; **locale notturno** night spot
**locali·tà** *f* (-tà) locality, spot
**localizzare** [ddzz] *tr* to localize; to locate ‖ *ref* to become localized
**localizzazióne** [ddzz] *f* localization; **localizzazione dei guasti** troubleshooting
**locanda** *f* inn
**locandiè·re -ra** *mf* innkeeper
**locandina** *f* playbill; flyer; small poster
**locare** §197 (lòco) *tr* to rent, lease
**locatà·rio -ria** *mf* (-ri -rie) lessee, renter
**loca·tóre -trice** *mf* lessor
**locazióne** *f* rent; lease; **dare in locazione** to rent
**locomotiva** *f* locomotive, engine
**locomo·tóre -trice** *adj* locomotive ‖ *m* & *f* (rr) electric locomotive
**locomotorì·sta** *m* (-sti) (rr) engineer
**locomozióne** *f* locomotion; transportation
**lòculo** *m* burial niche
**locusta** *f* locust
**locuzióne** *f* locution, expression; phrase; idiom
**lodàbile** *adj* praiseworthy
**lodare** (lòdo) *tr* to praise ‖ *ref* to praise oneself, brag; **lodarsi di** (poet) to be pleased with

**lodati·vo -va** *adj* laudatory
**lòde** *f* praise; **con la lode** cum laude; **con lode** plus (*on a report card*)
**lodévole** *adj* praiseworthy, commendable
**lòdo** *m* arbitration
**logaritmo** *m* logarithm
**lòg·gia** *f* (-ge) lodge; (archit) loggia
**loggióne** *m* (theat) upper gallery
**lògi·co -ca** (-ci -che) *adj* logical; **esser logico** to think logically ‖ *m* logician ‖ *f* logic
**logìsti·co -ca** (-ci -che) *adj* logistic ‖ *f* logistics
**lò·glio** *m* (-gli) cockle
**logoraménto** *m* wear; attrition
**logorare** (lógoro) *tr* to wear out; to fray ‖ *ref* to wear away; to become threadbare
**logorì·o** *m* (-i) wear and tear
**lógo·ro -ra** *adj* worn out; threadbare
**lòlla** *f* chaff
**lombàggine** *f* lumbago
**lombar·do -da** *adj* & *mf* Lombard
**lombata** *f* loin, sirloin
**lómbo** *m* loin; hip; (lit) ancestry
**lombrì·co** *m* (-chi) earthworm
**londinése** [s] *adj* London ‖ *mf* Londoner
**Londra** *f* London
**longànime** *adj* patient, forbearing
**longanimi·tà** *f* (-tà) patience, forbearance
**longevità** *f* longevity
**longè·vo -va** *adj* long-lived
**longherina** *f* beam, girder
**longheróne** *m* (aer) longeron; (aer) spar; (aut) main frame member
**longitùdine** *f* longitude
**longobar·do -da** *adj* & *mf* Lombard
**lontananza** *f* distance
**lonta·no -na** *adj* distant, remote; vague; indirect ‖ *m* (lit) far-away place ‖ *f*—**alla lontana** from a distance; vaguely; distant (*e.g., relative*) ‖ **lontano** *adv* far; **da lontano** from afar; **lontano da** away from; far from; **rifarsi da lontano** to start from the very beginning
**lóntra** *f* otter
**lónza** *f* pork loin; (poet) leopard
**lòppa** *f* chaff; skin (*of plant*); slag, dross
**loquace** *adj* loquacious; (fig) eloquent
**loquèla** *f* (lit) tongue; (lit) style
**lordare** (lórdo) *tr* to soil, dirty
**lór·do -da** *adj* soiled, dirty; gross (*weight*)
**lordume** *m* dirt, filth
**lordura** *f* dirt, filth; soil
**lóro** §5 *pron pers* ‖ §6 *adj poss* & *pron*
**losan·ga** *f* (-ghe) rhombus; (herald) lozenge
**ló·sco -sca** *adj* (-schi -sche) squint-eyed; cross-eyed; (fig) shady
**lóto** *m* mud
**lòto** *m* lotus
**lòtta** *f* fight; struggle; wrestling; **essere in lotta** to be at war; **lotta libera** catch-as-catch-can
**lottare** (lòtto) *intr* to fight; to quarrel; to struggle; to wrestle

**lotta·tóre -trice** *mf* fighter; wrestler
**lottería** *f* lottery
**lottizzare** [ddzz] *tr* to divide into lots
**lòtto** *m* lotto; parcel, lot
**lozióne** *f* lotion
**lùbri·co -ca** *adj* (**-ci -che**) lewd; (lit) slippery
**lubrificante** *adj & m* lubricant
**lubrificare** §197 (**lubrìfico**) *tr* to lubricate
**lucchétto** *m* padlock
**luccicare** §197 (**lùccico**) *intr* to sparkle; to shine
**luccichi·o** *m* (**-i**) glittering; shining; sparkle
**luccicóne** *m* big tear
**lùc·cio** *m* (**-ci**) pike
**lùcciola** *f* firefly; usherette (*in movie*); **prendere lucciole per lanterne** to make a blunder; to be seeing things
**luce** *f* light; sunlight; opening; glass (*of mirror*); leaf (*e.g., of door*); (archit) span; (coll) electricity; **alla luce del sole** in plain view; **fare luce** to shed light; **luce degli occhi** eyesight; **luce del giorno** daylight; **luce della luna** moonlight; **luce di arresto** (aut) stoplight; **luce di incrocio** (aut) dimmer, low beam; **luce di posizione** (aut) parking light; **luce di profondità** (aut) high beam; **luci** (poet) eyes; **luci della ribalta** (fig) stage, boards; **mettere alla luce** to give birth to; **mettere in luce** to reveal; to publish; **venire alla luce** to be born; to come to light
**lucènte** *adj* shiny, shining
**lucentézza** *f* brightness; sheen
**lucèrna** *f* lamp; light; **lucerne** (lit) eyes ‖ **Lucerna** *f* Lucerne
**lucernà·rio** *m* (**-ri**) skylight
**lucèrtola** *f* lizard
**lucherino** *m* (orn) siskin
**Lucìa** *f* Lucy
**lucidare** (**lùcido**) *tr* to shine, polish; to trace (*a figure*)
**lucida·tóre -trice** *mf* polisher (*person*) ‖ *f* (mach) floor polisher
**lucidatura** *f* polish; tracing (*on paper*)
**lucidi·tà** *f* (**-tà**) polish; lucidity
**lùci·do -da** *adj* bright; lucid ‖ *m* shine; tracing; **lucido per le scarpe** shoe polish
**lucìfe·ro -ra** *adj* (poet) light-bringing ‖ **Lucìfero** *m* Lucifer, morning star
**lucìgnolo** *m* wick
**lucrare** *tr* to win, acquire
**lucratì·vo -va** *adj* lucrative
**lucro** *m* gain, earnings, lucre; **lucro cessante** (law) loss of earnings
**lucró·so -sa** [s] *adj* lucrative
**ludì·brio** *m* (**-bri**) mockery; laughingstock
**lù·glio** *m* (**-gli**) July
**lùgubre** *adj* gloomy, dismal
**lui** §5 *pron pers*
**luìgi** *m* louis ‖ **Luìgi** *m* Louis
**luma·ca** *f* (**-che**) snail
**lume** *m* light; lamp; **lume degli occhi** eyesight; **lume delle stelle** starlight; **lumi** eyesight; **lumi di luna** hard times; **perdere il lume degli occhi**

to lose one's self-control; **reggere il lume a** to close one's eyes to; **studiare al lume di candela** to burn the midnight oil
**lumeggiare** §290 (**luméggio**) *tr* to illuminate, to shed light on
**lumicino** *m* faint light; **essere al lumicino** to be on one's last legs
**luminare** *m* star; luminary
**luminària** *f* illumination
**lumino** *m* night light; votive light; rush light
**luminó·so -sa** [s] *adj* luminous; bright (*idea*)
**luna** *f* moon; **andare a lune** to be fickle; **avere la luna di traverso** to be in a bad mood; **luna calante** waning moon; **luna crescente** crescent moon; **luna di miele** honeymoon
**lunare** *adj* lunar, moon
**lunària** *f* (min) moonstone; (bot) honesty
**lunà·rio** *m* (**-ri**) almanac; **sbarcare il lunario** to live from hand to mouth
**lunàti·co -ca** *adj* (**-ci -che**) moody; whimsical
**lune·dì** *m* (**-dì**) Monday
**lunétta** *f* lunette; fanlight
**lunga** *f*—**alla lunga** in the long run; **alla più lunga** at the latest; **andare per le lunghe** to last a long time, drag on; **di gran lunga** by far; **farla lunga** to dillydally
**lungàggine** *f* delay, procrastination
**lunghézza** *f* length; **lunghezza d'onda** wave length; **prendere la lunghezza di** to measure
**lungi** *adv* (lit) far
**lungimirante** *adj* (fig) far-sighted
**lun·go -ga** (**-ghi -ghe**) *adj* long; sharp (*tongue*); nimble (*fingers*); tall; thin (*soup*); (coll) slow; **a lungo** for a long time; at length; **a lungo andare** in the long run; **lungo disteso** sprawling ‖ *m* length; **in lungo e in largo** far and wide; **per il lungo** lengthwise ‖ *f* see **lunga** ‖ **lungo** *prep* along; during
**lungofiume** *m* river road
**lungola·go** *m* (**-ghi**) lakeshore road
**lungomare** *m* seashore road
**lungometràg·gio** *m* (**-gi**) full-length movie, feature film
**lunòtto** *m* (aut) rear window
**luò·go** *m* (**-ghi**) place; passage; site; (geom) locus; **aver luogo** to take place; **aver luogo in** to be laid in (*e.g., a certain place*); **dar luogo a** to give rise to; **del luogo** local; **far luogo** to make room; **fuori luogo** inopportune(ly); **in alto luogo** high-placed; **in luogo di** instead of; **luogo comune** commonplace; **luogo di decenza** toilet; **luogo di nascita** birthplace; **luogo di pena** penitentiary; **non luogo a procedere** (law) no ground for prosecution; (law) nolle prosequi; **sul luogo** on the spot; on the premises
**luogotenènte** *m* lieutenant
**lupa** *f* she-wolf
**lupanare** *m* (lit) brothel

**lupé·sco -sca** *adj* (**-schi -sche**) wolfish
**lupétto** *m* young wolf; cub (*in Boy Scouts*)
**lupinèlla** *f* sainfoin
**lupi·no -na** *adj* wolfish
**lu·po -pa** *mf* wolf; **lupo cerviero** lynx; **lupo di mare** seadog; **lupo mannaro** werewolf ‖ *f* see **lupa**
**lùppolo** *m* hops
**lùri·do -da** *adj* filthy, dirty
**lusco** *m*—**tra il lusco e il brusco** at twilight
**lusin·ga** *f* (**-ghe**) flattery; illusion
**lusingare** §209 *tr* to flatter ‖ *ref* to be flattered; to hope
**lusinghiè·ro -ra** *adj* flattering; promising
**lussare** *tr* to dislocate
**lussazióne** *f* dislocation

**lusso** *m* luxury; **di lusso** de luxe; **lusso di** abundance of
**lussuó·so -sa** [s] *adj* luxurious, sumptuous
**lussureggiante** *adj* luxuriant
**lussùria** *f* lust
**lussurió·so -sa** [s] *adj* lustful, lecherous
**lustrare** *tr* to polish, shine; to lick (*s.o.'s boots*) ‖ *intr* to shine, be shiny
**lustrascar·pe** *m* (**-pe**) bootblack
**lustrino** *m* sequin; tinsel
**lu·stro -stra** *adj* shiny, polished ‖ *m* shine, polish; period of five years; **dare il lustro a** to shine, polish
**lutto** *m* mourning; bereavement; **a lutto** black-edged (*e.g., stationery*); **lutto stretto** deep mourning
**luttuó·so -sa** [s] *adj* mournful

# M

**M, m** [ˈɛmme] *m & f* eleventh letter of the Italian alphabet
**ma** *m* but; **ma e se** ifs and buts ‖ *conj* but; yet ‖ *interj* who knows?; too bad!
**màca·bro -bra** *adj* macabre
**maca·co** *m* (**-chi**) macaque; (fig) dumbell
**macadàm** *m* macadam
**macadamizzare** [ddzz] *tr* to macadamize
**mac·ca** *f* (**-che**) abundance; **a macca** (coll) abundantly; (coll) without paying
**maccarèllo** *m* mackerel
**maccheróni** *mpl* macaroni
**màcchia** *f* spot, stain; brushwood; thicket; (fig) blot; **alla macchia** clandestinely; (painting) done in pointillism; **darsi alla macchia** to join the underground; to escape the law; **macchia solare** sunspot; **senza macchia** spotless
**macchiare** §287 *tr* to stain, soil ‖ *ref* to become stained; **macchiarsi d'infamia** to soil one's reputation
**macchiétta** *f* caricature; comedian; **fare la macchietta di** to impersonate, to parody
**macchiettare** (**macchiétto**) *tr* to speckle
**macchietti·sta** *mf* (**-sti -ste**) cartoonist; comedian; impersonator
**màcchina** *f* machine; engine; car, automobile; machination; **andare in macchina** to go to press; **fatto a macchina** machine-made; **macchina da presa** (mov) camera; **macchina da proiezione** projector; **macchina fotografica** camera; **macchina per** or **da cucire** sewing machine; **macchina per** or **da scrivere** typewriter; **scrivere a macchina** to typewrite
**macchinale** *adj* mechanical
**macchinare** (**màcchino**) *tr* to plot
**macchinà·rio** *m* (**-ri**) machinery
**macchinazióne** *f* machination

**macchinétta** *f* gadget; **macchinetta del caffè** coffee maker
**macchini·sta** *m* (**-sti**) engineer; (theat) stagehand
**macchinó·so -sa** [s] *adj* heavy, ponderous; complicated
**macedònia** *f* fruit salad, fruit cup
**macel·làio** *m* (**-lài**) butcher
**macellare** (**macèllo**) *tr* to butcher
**macellerìa** *f* butcher shop
**macèllo** *m* slaughterhouse; butchering; carnage; disaster
**macerare** (**màcero**) *tr* to soak; to mortify (*the flesh*) ‖ *ref* to waste away
**macèria** *f* low wall; **macerie** ruins
**màce·ro -ra** *adj* emaciated; skinny ‖ *m* soaking vat (*for papermaking*)
**machiavèlli·co -ca** *adj* (**-ci -che**) Machiavellian
**macigno** *m* boulder
**macilèn·to -ta** *adj* emaciated, pale, wan
**màcina** *f* millstone; (coll) grind
**macinacaf·fè** *m* (**-fè**) coffee grinder
**macinapé·pe** *m* (**-pe**) pepper mill
**macinare** (**màcino**) *tr* to grind, mill; to burn up (*e.g., the road*)
**macina·to -ta** *adj* ground ‖ *m* grindings; ground meat ‖ *f* grinding
**macinino** *m* grinder; (coll) jalopy
**mà·cis** *m & f* (**-cis**) mace (*spice*)
**maciste** *m* strong man (*in circus*)
**maciullare** *tr* to brake (*flax or hemp*); to crush
**macrocòsmo** *m* macrocosm
**màdia** *f* bread bin; kneading trough
**màdi·do -da** *adj* wet, perspiring
**madònna** *f* lady ‖ **Madonna** *f* Madonna
**madornale** *adj* huge; gross (*error*)
**madre** *f* mother; stub; mold; **madre nubile** unwed mother
**madreggiare** §290 (**madréggio**) *intr* to take after one's mother
**madrelìngua** *f* mother tongue
**madrepàtria** *f* mother country
**madrepèrla** *f* mother-of-pearl
**madresélva** *f* (coll) honeysuckle

**madrevite** *f* (mach) nut; die; **madrevite ad alette** wing nut

**madrigna** *f* stepmother

**madrina** *f* godmother; **madrina di guerra** war mother

**mae·stà** *f* (-stà) majesty; **lesa maestà** lese majesty

**maestó·so -sa** [s] *adj* majestic, stately

**maèstra** *f* teacher; (fig) master; **maestra giardiniera** kindergarten teacher

**maestrale** *m* northwest wind (*in Mediterranean*)

**maestranze** *fpl* workmen

**maestrìa** *f* skill, mastery

**maè·stro -stra** *adj* masterly; main ǁ *m* teacher; master; instructor; northwester (*in Mediterranean*); **maestro di cappella** choirmaster ǁ *f* see **maestra**

**mafió·so -sa** [s] *adj* Mafia ǁ *mf* member of the Mafia; gaudy dresser

**ma·ga** *f* (-ghe) sorceress

**magagna** *f* fault, weak spot

**magagna·to -ta** *adj* spoiled (*fruit*)

**magari** *adv* even, maybe ǁ *conj* even if ǁ *interj* would that . . . !

**magazzinàg·gio** [ddzz] *m* (-gi) storage

**magazziniè·re -ra** [ddzz] *mf* stockroom attendant ǁ *m* warehouseman

**magazzino** [ddzz] *m* warehouse; store; inventory; (phot, journ) magazine; **grandi magazzini** department store

**maggése** [s] *adj* May ǁ *m* (agr) fallow

**màg·gio** *m* (-gi) May; May Day

**maggiolino** *m* cockchafer

**maggiorana** *f* sweet marjoram

**maggioranza** *f* majority

**maggiorare** (**maggióro**) *tr* to increase

**maggiorazióne** *f* increase, appreciation

**maggiordòmo** *m* butler; majordomo

**maggióre** *adj* bigger, greater; major; main; higher (*bidder*); older, elder; (mil) master (*e.g., sergeant*); biggest, greatest; highest; oldest, eldest; **andare per la maggiore** to be all the rage; **maggiore età** majority ǁ *m* (mil) major; oldest one; **maggiori** ancestors

**maggiorènne** *adj* of age ǁ *mf* grown-up, adult

**maggiorènte** *mf* notable

**maggiori·tà** *f* (-tà) (mil) C.O.'s office

**maggiorità·rio -ria** *adj* (-ri -rie) majority

**magìa** *f* magic

**màgi·co -ca** *adj* (-ci -che) magic

**Magi** *mpl* Magi, Wise Men

**magióne** *f* (lit) home, dwelling

**magistèro** *m* education, teaching; mastery; (chem) precipitation

**magistrale** *adj* teacher's; masterly ǁ *f* teacher's college

**magistrato** *m* magistrate

**magistratura** *f* judiciary

**màglia** *f* knitting; stitch; link; undershirt; sports shirt; (hist) mail; (fig) web; **lavorare a maglia** to knit

**maglierìa** *f* knitting mill; yarn shop; knitwear store

**magliétta** *f* polo shirt, T-shirt; buckle (*to secure rifle strap*); picture hook; buttonhole

**maglifì·cio** *m* (-ci) knitwear factory

**mà·glio** *m* (-gli) sledge hammer; mallet; drop hammer

**maglióne** *m* heavy sweater, jersey

**magnàni·mo -ma** *adj* magnanimous

**magnano** *m* (coll) locksmith

**magnate** *m* (lit) magnate, tycoon

**magnèsio** *m* magnesium

**magnète** *m* magnet; magneto

**magnèti·co -ca** *adj* (-ci -che) magnetic

**magnetismo** *m* magnetism

**magnetite** *f* loadstone

**magnetizzare** [ddzz] *tr* to magnetize

**magnetòfono** *m* tape recorder

**magnificare** §197 (**magnifico**) *tr* to extol, praise; to magnify (*to exaggerate*)

**magnificènza** *f* magnificence

**magnìfi·co -ca** *adj* (-ci -che) magnificent; munificent; wonderful; splendid

**ma·gno -gna** *adj* (lit) great; the Great, e.g., **Alessandro Magno** Alexander the Great

**magnòlia** *f* magnolia

**ma·go** *m* (-ghi) magician; wizard

**magóne** *m* (coll) gizzard; (coll) grief; **avere il magone** (coll) to be in the dumps

**magra** *f* low water; (fig) dearth, want

**magrézza** *f* leanness; scarcity

**ma·gro -gra** *adj* lean, thin; meager ǁ *m* lean meat; meatless day ǁ *f* see **magra**

**mài** *adv* never; ever; **non . . . mai** never, not ever; **come mai?** how come?

**maia·le -la** *mf* pig; hog ǁ *m* pork ǁ *f* sow

**maialé·sco -sca** *adj* (-schi -sche) piggish

**maiòli·ca** *f* (-che) majolica

**maionése** [s] *f* mayonnaise

**mà·is** *m* (-is) corn, maize

**maiuscolétto** *m* (typ) small capital

**maiùsco·lo -la** *adj* capital ǁ *m*—**scrivere in maiuscolo** to capitalize ǁ *f* capital letter

**Malacca, la** Malay Peninsula

**malaccèt·to -ta** *adj* unwelcome

**malaccòr·to -ta** *adj* imprudent; awkward

**malacreanza** *f* (**malecreanze**) instance of bad manners; **malecreanze** bad manners

**malafatta** *f* (**malefatte**) defect; **malefatte** evildoings

**malaféde** *f* (**malefédi**) bad faith

**malaffare** *m*—**donna di malaffare** prostitute; **gente di malaffare** underworld

**malagévole** *adj* rough (*road*); hard (*work*)

**malagràzia** *f* (**malegràzie**) rudeness, uncouthness

**malalìngua** *f* (**malelìngue**) slanderer, backbiter

**malanda·to -ta** *adj* run-down; shabby

**malandri·no -na** *adj* dishonest; bewitching (*eyes*) ǁ *m* highwayman

**malànimo** *m* ill will; **di malanimo** reluctantly

**malanno** *m* misfortune; illness; (joc) menace

**malaparata** *f* (coll) danger, dangerous situation

**malapéna** *f*—**a malapena** hardly

malària f malaria
malatìc·cio -cia adj (-ci -ce) sickly
mala·to -ta adj sick, ill; essere malato agli occhi to have sore eyes; fare il malato to play sick || mf patient; i malati the sick
malattìa f sickness; illness; disease; malattie del lavoro occupational diseases
malaugura·to -ta adj unfortunate; ill-omened
malaugù·rio m (-ri) ill omen
malavita f underworld
malavòglia f (malevòglie) unwillingness; di malavoglia reluctantly
malcapita·to -ta adj unlucky || m unlucky person
malcàu·to -ta adj rash, heedless
malcón·cio -cia adj (-ci -ce) battered
malcontèn·to -ta adj dissatisfied, malcontent || mf malcontent || m dissatisfaction
malcostume m immorality; bad practice
malcrea·to -ta adj ill-bred
maldè·stro -stra adj clumsy, awkward
maldicènte adj gossipy, slanderous || mf gossip, slanderer, backbiter
maldicènza f gossip, slander
male m evil; ill; trouble; andare a male to go to pot; aversela a male to take offense; di male in peggio from bad to worse, worse and worse; fare del male to do ill; fare male to be in error; fare male a to hurt; farsi male to get hurt; to hurt oneself; far venire il mal di mare a to make seasick; (fig) to nauseate; Lei fa male you should not; mal d'aereo airsickness; mal di capo headache; mal di cuore heart disease; mal di denti toothache; mal di gola sore throat; mal di mare sea-sickness; mal di montagna mountain sickness; mal di pancia bellyache; mal di schiena backache; mandare a male to spoil; mettere male to sow discord; prendere a male to take amiss; voler male a to bear a grudge against || adv badly, poorly; male educato ill-bred; meno male! fortunately!; restar male to be disappointed; sentirsi male to feel sick; stare male to be ill; star male a to not fit, e.g., questo vestito gli sta male this suit does not fit him; veder male qlco to disapprove of s.th; veder male qlcu to dislike s.o.
maledettaménte adv (coll) damned
maledét·to -ta adj cursed, damned
maledire §195 tr to curse
maledizióne f malediction, curse || interj damn it!, confound it!
maleduca·to -ta adj ill-bred || mf boor
malefatta f var of malafatta
malefì·cio m (-ci) curse, spell; witchcraft; wickedness
malèfi·co -ca adj (-ci -che) maleficent
maleolènte adj (lit) malodorous
malèrba f weed, weeds
malése adj & mf Malay
Malésia, la Malaysia
malèssere m malaise; uneasiness; worry

malevolènza f malevolence; malice
malèvo·lo -la adj malevolent; malicious
malfama·to -ta adj ill-famed; notorious
malfat·to -ta adj botched; misshapen || m misdeed
malfat·tóre -trice mf malefactor
malfér·mo -ma adj wobbly, unsteady
malfì·do -da adj untrustworthy
malgarbo m bad manners, rudeness
malgovèrno m misrule; mismanagement; neglect
malgrado prep in spite of; mio malgrado in spite of me || conj although
malìa f spell, charm
maliar·do -da adj enchanting, charming || mf magician || f enchantress, witch
malignare intr to gossip
maligni·tà f (-tà) maliciousness; malevolence; malignancy
mali·gno -gna adj malicious, evil; unhealthy; malignant || il Maligno the Evil One
malinconìa f melancholy; melancholia
malincòni·co -ca adj (-ci -che) melancholy, wistful
malincuòre m—a malincuore unwillingly, against one's will
malintenziona·to -ta adj evil-minded || mf evildoer
malinté·so -sa [s] adj misunderstood; misapplied || m misunderstanding
maliò·so -sa [s] adj malicious; cunning; mischievous; bewitching
malizia f malice; trick; mischief
maliziò·so -sa [s] adj malicious; clever, artful; mischievous
malleàbile adj malleable; manageable
malleva·dóre -drice mf guarantor
malleverìa f surety
mallo m hull, husk
mallòppo m bundle; (aer) trail cable; (coll) lump (in one's throat); (slang) swag, booty
malmenare (malméno) tr to manhandle
malmés·so -sa adj shabby, seedy; tasteless
malna·to -ta adj uncouth; unfortunate; harmful
malnutri·to -ta adj undernourished
malnutrizióne f malnutrition
ma·lo -la adj (lit) bad
malòc·chio m (-chi) evil eye
malóra f ruin; mandare in malora to ruin; va in malora! go to the devil!
malóre m malaise; fainting spell
malpràti·co -ca adj (-ci -che) inexperienced
malsa·no -na adj unhealthy; unsound
malsicu·ro -ra adj unsafe; insecure
malta f mortar; plaster; (obs) mud
maltèmpo m bad weather
malto m malt
maltòlto m ill-gotten gains
maltrattaménto m mistreatment
maltrattare tr to mistreat, maltreat
malumóre m bad humor; di malumore in a bad mood
malva f mallow
malvà·gio -gia (-gi -gie) adj wicked || mf wicked person || il Malvagio the Evil One

**malversare (malvèrso)** *tr* to embezzle; to misappropriate

**malversazióne** *f* embezzlement; misappropriation

**malvestì·to -ta** *adj* shabby, seedy

**malvi·sto -sta** *adj* disliked; unpopular

**malvivènte** *mf* criminal; (lit) profligate

**malvolentièri** *adv* unwillingly

**malvolére** *m* malevolence; indolence || §196 *tr* to dislike

**mamma** *f* mother, mom; (lit) breast; **mamma mia** dear me!

**mammaluc·co** *m* (**-chi**) simpleton

**mammèlla** *f* breast; udder

**mammìfe·ro -ra** *adj* mammalian || *m* mammal

**màmmola** *f* violet; (fig) shrinking violet

**mam·mùt** *m* (**-mut**) mammoth

**manata** *f* slap; handful; **dare una manata a** to slap

**man·ca** *f* (**-che**) left hand, left

**mancante** *adj* missing, lacking; unaccounted for

**mancanza** *f* lack; absence; defect; mistake; **in mancanza di** for lack of

**mancare** §197 *tr* to miss || *intr* (AVERE) to be at fault; **mancare a** to break (*e.g., one's word*); **mancare di** to be wanting; to lack; **mancare di parola** to break one's word || *intr* (ESSERE) to faii (*said, e.g., of electric power*); to be lacking, e.g., **manca il sale nell'arrosto** salt is lacking in the roast; to be missing; to be absent, e.g., **mancano tre soci** three members are absent; to be, e.g., **mancano dieci minuti alle quattro** it is ten minutes to four; (with *dat*) to lack, e.g., **gli mancano le forze** he lacks the strength; to miss, e.g., **mi manca la sua compagnia** I miss his company; **mancare a** to be absent from (*e.g., the roll call*); to be . . . from, e.g., **mancano dieci chilometri all'arrivo** we are ten kilometers from the journey's end; **mancare ai vivi** (lit) to pass away; **sentirsi mancare** to feel faint || *impers*—**mancare poco che** + *subj* to narrowly miss + *ger*, e.g., **ci mancò poco che fosse investito da un'automobile** he narrowly missed being hit by a car; **non ci mancherebbe altro!** that would be the last straw!, I should say not!

**manca·to -ta** *adj* unsuccessful; missed (*opportunity*); abortive (*attempt*), e.g., **omicidio mancato** abortive attempt to murder; manqué, e.g., **un poeta mancato** a poet manqué

**manchévole** *adj* faulty

**manchevolézza** *f* fault, shortcoming

**màn·cia** *f* (**-ce**) tip, gratuity; **mancia competente** reward

**manciata** *f* handful

**manci·no -na** *adj* left-handed; underhanded || *mf* left-handed person || *f* left hand, left; (mach) floating crane

**man·co -ca** (**-chi -che**) *adj* left; (lit) sinister, ill-omened; (lit) lacking || *m* (lit) lack; **senza manco** (coll) without fail || **manco** *adv*—**manco male!**

(coll) at least!; **manco per idea!** (coll) not at all! || *f* see **manca**

**mandaménto** *m* jurisdiction

**mandante** *m* (law) principal

**mandare** *tr* to send; to condemn (*to death*); to commit (*to memory*); to send forth (*e.g., smoke, buds*); to operate (*a machine*); **che Dio ce la mandi buona!** may God help us!; **mandare ad effetto** to carry out; **mandare all'altro mondo** to dispatch, kill; **mandare a monte** to ruin; **mandare a picco** to sink; **mandare a quel paese** to send to the devil; **mandare a spasso** to fire, dismiss; to get rid of; **mandar giù** to swallow; **mandare in malora** to ruin; **mandare in pezzi** to break to pieces; **mandare per le lunghe** to delay || *intr*—**mandare a chiamare** to send for; **mandare a dire** to send word

**mandarino** *m* mandarin; (*Citrus nobilis*) tangerine; (*Citrus reticulata*) mandarin orange

**mandata** *f* sending; delivery (*of merchandise*); group; gang (*e.g., of thieves*); turn (*of key*); **chiudere a doppia mandata** to double-lock

**mandatà·rio** *m* (**-ri**) mandatary, trustee

**mandato** *m* mandate; order; **mandato di cattura** arrest warrant; **mandato di comparizione** subpoena; **mandato di perquisizione** search warrant

**mandìbola** *f* jaw

**mandolino** *m* mandolin

**màndorla** *f* almond; kernel (*of fruit*)

**mandorla·to -ta** *adj* almond || *m* nougat

**màndorlo** *m* almond tree

**mandràgola** *f* mandrake

**màndria** *f* herd

**mandriano** *m* herdsman

**mandrillo** *m* mandrill

**mandrino** *m* (mach) mandrel; (mach) driftpin

**mandritta** *f*—**a mandritta** to the right

**mane** *f*—**da mane a sera** from morning till night

**maneggévole** *adj* usable; manageable; accessible to small craft (*sea*)

**maneggiare** §290 (**manéggio**) *tr* to work (*e.g., clay*); to handle; to wield (*a sword*); to knead (*dough*); to manage; (equit) to train

**manég·gio** *m* (**-gi**) handling; intrigue; horsemanship; management; riding school; manège

**mané·sco -sca** *adj* (**-schi -sche**) readyfisted; hand (*e.g., weapons*)

**manetta** *f* throttle (*on a motorcycle*); **manette** handcuffs, manacles

**manfòrte** *f*—**dar manforte a** to help

**manganèllo** *m* bludgeon, cudgel

**manganése** [s] *m* manganese

**màngano** *m* calender; mangle

**mangeréc·cio -cia** *adj* (**-ci -ce**) edible

**mangerìa** *f* graft, peculation

**mangiàbile** *adj* edible

**mangiana·strì** *m* (**-stri**) tape recorder

**mangia-pane** *m* (**-pane**) idler

**mangia-prèti** *m* (**-prèti**) priest hater

**mangiare** *m* eating; food || *v* §290 *tr*

to eat; to bite, gnaw; to erode; to embezzle, graft; (cards, chess) to take; **mangiar la foglia** to get wise || *intr* to eat; **mangiare alle spalle di qlcu** to eat at the expense of s.o. || *ref* to eat up; **mangiarsi il fegato** to be green with envy; **mangiarsi la parola** to break one's promise; **mangiarsi le unghie** to bite one's nails; **mangiarsi una promessa** to break one's promise

**mangiasòldi** *adj invar* money-eating, e.g., **macchina mangiasoldi** money-eating contraption

**mangiata** *f* (coll) fill, hearty meal, bellyful

**mangia·tóre -trice** *mf* eater

**mangime** *m* fodder; feed; poultry feed

**mangimìsti·co -ca** *adj* (-ci -che) feed, e.g., **attrezzature mangimistiche** feed machinery

**mangió·ne -na** *mf* great eater, glutton

**mangiucchiare** §287 (**mangiùcchio**) *tr* to nibble

**mangusta** *f* mongoose

**mania** *f* mania, craze; complex; whim; **mania di grandezza** delusions of grandeur

**mania·co -ca** (-ci -che) *adj* maniacal; enthusiastic || *m* maniac; fan, enthusiast

**màni·ca** *f* (-che) sleeve; hose; (coll) crowd, bunch; **essere di manica larga** to be broad-minded; **essere nelle maniche di qlcu** to be in the favor of s.o.; **è un altro paio di maniche** this is a horse of another color; **in maniche di camicia** in shirt sleeves; **manica a vento** air sleeve, windsock; **manica per l'acqua** hose || **la Manica** the English Channel

**manicarétto** *m* dainty, delicacy

**manichino** *m* mannequin; cuff; (obs) handcuff; **fare il manichino** to model

**màni·co** *m* (-chi & -ci) handle; stock (*of rifle*); shaft (*of golf club*); stem (*of spoon*); (mus) neck; **manico di scopa** broomstick

**manicò·mio** *m* (-mi) insane asylum, madhouse

**manicòtto** *m* muff; (mach) collar; (mach) nipple; (mach) sleeve

**manicu·re** *mf* (-re) manicure, manicurist (*person*) || *f* (-re) manicure (*treatment*)

**manicuri·sta** *mf* (-sti -ste) manicurist

**manièra** *f* manner, fashion, way; **belle maniere** good manners; **di maniera** (lit, painting) Manneristic; **di maniera che** so that; **in nessuna maniera** by no means; **maniere** bad manners

**maniera·to -ta** *adj* mannered, affected; genteel

**maniè·ro -ra** *adj* tame, gentle || *m* manor house, mansion || *f* see **maniera**

**manieró·so -sa** [s] *adj* genteel; mannered

**manifattura** *f* manufacture; factory; product; ready-made wear

**manifestare** (**manifèsto**) *tr* to manifest

|| *intr* to demonstrate || *ref* to turn out to be

**manifestazióne** *f* manifestation; demonstration

**manifestino** *m* leaflet, handbill

**manifè·sto -sta** *adj* manifest, clear || *m* poster, placard; manifest; (pol) manifesto; **manifesto di carico** (naut) manifest

**maniglia** *f* handle; knob; (naut) link (*of chain*)

**manigóldo** *m* criminal; scoundrel

**manipolare** (**manìpolo**) *tr* to concoct; to adulterate; (telg) to transmit

**manipola·tóre -trice** *mf* schemer || *m* telegraph key

**manìpolo** *m* sheaf; (eccl; hist) maniple; (fig) handful

**maniscal·co** *m* (-chi) blacksmith

**manna** *f* manna; godsend

**mannàia** *f* axe; knife (*of guillotine*)

**mano** *f* hand; way (*in traffic*); coat (*of paint*); (lit) handful; (fig) finger; fingertip; **alla mano** plain, affable; **a mani nude** barehanded; **a mano** by hand; **a mano a mano** little by little; **a mano armata** armed (*e.g., robbery*); at gunpoint; **andare contro mano** to buck traffic; **a quattro mani** four-handed; **avere le mani bucate** to be a spendthrift; **avere le mani in pasta** to have one's fingers in the pie; **avere le mani lunghe** to be light-fingered; **battere le mani** to clap; **con le mani in mano** idle; **dare la mano a** to shake hands with; **dare man forte a** to help; **dare una mano** to pitch in; **dare una mano a** to lend a hand to; **di lunga mano** beforehand; **essere colto con le mani nel sacco** to be caught red-handed; **essere svelto di mano** to be light-fingered; **far man bassa** (su) to plunder; **fuori mano** out of the way; **mani di burro** butterfingers; **mani in alto!** hands up!; **man mano** (**che**) as; **mettere mano a** to begin; **mettere le mani sul fuoco** to guarantee; to swear; **per mano di** at the hands of; **prendere la mano** to balk; to get out of hand; **tenere la mano a** to abet; **venire alle mani** to come to blows

**manodòpera** *f* labor, manpower; **manodopera qualificata** skilled labor

**manòmetro** *m* manometer

**manométtere** §198 *tr* to tamper with

**manomissióne** *f* tampering

**manomòrta** *f* (law) mortmain

**manòpola** *f* mitten; handgrip; strap (*to hold on to*); (rad, telv) knob; (hist) gauntlet

**manoscrit·to -ta** *adj & m* manuscript

**manoscrìvere** §250 *intr* to write in one's own handwriting

**manovale** *m* laborer, helper; hod carrier

**manovèlla** *f* handle, crank; lever

**manòvra** *f* maneuver; (rr) shifting; **fare manovra** to maneuver; (rr) to shift

**manovrare** (**manòvro**) *tr* to maneuver; to handle, drive; (rr) to shift || *intr* to maneuver; (rr) to shunt, shift; (fig) to plot

**manovratóre** *m* motorman; driver; (rr) brakeman; (rr) flagman

**manrovè·scio** *m* (-sci) backhanded slap

**mansalva** *f*—**rubare a mansalva** to help oneself freely (*e.g., to the till*)

**mansarda** *f* mansard

**mansióne** *f* duty, function

**mansuè·to -ta** *adj* tame; meek

**mansuetùdine** *f* tameness; meekness

**mantèlla** *f* coat; (mil) cape

**mantellina** *f* (mil) cape

**mantèllo** *m* woman's coat; coat (*of animal*); (fig) cloak; (mil) cape; (mach) casing

**mantenére** §271 *tr* to keep; to maintain; to hold (*e.g., a position*) || *ref* to stay alive; to last; to remain, stay, continue

**mantenimento** *m* keeping; maintenance

**mantenu·to -ta** *adj* kept || *m* gigolo || *f* kept woman

**màntice** *m* bellows; folding top (*of carriage*); (aut) convertible top

**manto** *m* mantle; coat; cloak

**Màntova** *f* Mantua

**mantovana** *f* valance

**manuale** *adj* & *m* manual

**manualizzare** [ddzz] *tr* to make (*e.g., a machine*) hand-operated; to include in a manual; to prepare a manual of

**manù·brio** *m* (-bri) handlebar; handle; dumbbell

**manufat·to -ta** *adj* manufactured || *m* manufactured product; manufacture

**manutèngolo** *m* accomplice

**manutenzióne** *f* maintenance, upkeep

**manza** [dz] *f* heifer

**manzo** [dz] *m* steer; beef

**maometta·no -na** *adj* & *mf* Mahometan, Mohammedan

**maomettismo** *m* Mahometanism, Mohammedanism

**Maométto** *m* Mahomet

**maóna** *f* barge

**mappa** *f* map; bit (*of key*)

**mappamóndo** *m* globe; map of the world

**marachèlla** *f* mischief

**maramèo** *m*—**fare marameo** to thumb one's nose

**mara·sma** *m* (-smi) utter confusion; (pathol) decreptitude, feebleness

**maratóna** *f* marathon

**maratonè·ta** *m* (-ti) Marathon runner

**mar·ca** *f* (-che) mark, label; make, brand; token; ticket; (hist, geog) march; **di marca** of quality; **marca da bollo** revenue stamp; **marca di fabbrica** trademark

**marcare** §197 *tr* to mark; to label; to brand; to keep the score of; to score (*e.g., a goal*); to accentuate

**marcatèm·po** *m* (-po) timekeeper

**marca·to -ta** *adj* marked, pronounced

**marchésa** *f* marchioness, marquise

**marchése** *m* marquess, marquis

**marchia·no -na** *adj* gross (*error*)

**marchiare** §287 *tr* to brand

**màr·chio** *m* (-chi) brand; initials; characteristic; trademark

**màr·cia** *f* (-ce) march; operation; pus; (aut) gear, speed; (mil) hike; (sports)

walk; **far marcia indietro** to back up; (naut) to back water; **marcia indietro** (aut) reverse; **marcia nuziale** wedding march

**marciapiède** *m* sidewalk; (rr) platform

**marciare** §128 *intr* to march; (mil) to advance; (sports) to walk; (coll) to function; **far marciare qlcu** to keep s.o. in line

**màr·cio -cia** (-ci -ce) *adj* rotten; infected; corrupt || *m* rotten part; decayed part; corruption || *f* see **marcia**

**marcire** §176 *intr* (ESSERE) to rot

**marciume** *m* rot; pus; decay

**mar·co** *m* (-chi) mark

**marconigram·ma** *m* (-mi) radiogram

**marconi·sta** *mf* (-sti -ste) radio operator

**mare** *m* sea; bunch, heap; **al mare** at the seashore; **alto mare** high sea; **fa mare** the sea is rough; **gettare a mare** to throw overboard; **mare grosso** rough sea; **mare territoriale** territorial waters; **promettere mari e monti** to promise the moon; **tenere il mare** to be seaworthy

**marèa** *f* tide; sea (*e.g., of mud*); **alta marea** high tide; **bassa marea** low tide; **marea di quadratura** neap tide; **marea di sizigia** spring tide

**mareggiata** *f* coastal storm

**maremòto** *m* seaquake

**mareògrafo** *m* tide-level gauge

**maresciallo** *m* marshall; warrant officer

**marétta** *f* choppy sea; instability

**margarina** *f* margarine

**margherita** *f* daisy; **margherite** beads

**marginale** *adj* marginal

**marginatóre** *m* margin stop (*of typewriter*); (typ) try square

**màrgine** *m* margin; edge; **margine a scaletta** thumb index

**marijuana** *f* marijuana, marihuana

**marina** *f* seashore; seascape; navy; **marina mercantile** merchant marine

**mari·nàio** *m* (-nài) seaman, sailor

**marinara** *f* middy blouse

**marinare** *tr* to marinate; **marinare la scuola** to cut school, play truant

**marinaré·sco -sca** *adj* (-schi -sche) sailor, seamanlike

**marina·ro -ra** *adj* sea, sailor; seaman-like; nautical || *m* (coll) sailor || *f* see **marinara**

**mari·no -na** *adj* marine, nautical || *f* see **marina**

**mariòlo** *m* rascal

**marionétta** *f* puppet, marionette

**maritale** *adj* marital

**maritare** *tr* to marry || *ref* to get married

**marito** *m* husband

**marìtti·mo -ma** *adj* maritime, sea || *m* merchant seaman

**marmàglia** *f* riffraff, rabble

**marmellata** *f* jam, preserves; **marmellata di arancia** orange marmalade

**marmi·sta** *m* (-sti) marble worker; marble cutter

**marmitta** *f* pot, kettle; (aut) muffler

**marmittóne** *m* (coll) sad sack

**marmo** *m* marble

**marmòc·chio** *m* (-chi) brat

**marmòre·o -a** *adj* marble
**marmorizzare** [ddzz] *tr* to marble
**marmòtta** *f* marmot; woodchuck; (fig) sluggard; (rr) switch signal
**marmottina** *f* salesman's sample case
**marna** *f* marl
**marnare** *tr* to marl
**marocchi·no -na** *adj* & *mf* Moroccan ‖ *m* morocco leather
**Maròcco, il** Morocco
**maróso** [s] *m* billow, surge
**marra** *f* hoe; fluke (*of anchor*)
**marrano** *m* Marrano; (fig) scoundrel; (lit) traitor
**marronata** *f* (coll) blunder, boner
**marróne** *adj invar* maroon, tan ‖ *m* chestnut; (coll) blunder
**Marsìglia** *f* Marseille
**marsigliése** [s] *adj* Marseilles ‖ *m* native or inhabitant of Marseilles ‖ *f* Marseillaise
**marsina** *f* swallow-tailed coat
**Marte** *m* Mars
**marte·dì** *m* (**-dì**) Tuesday; **martedì grasso** Shrove Tuesday
**martellare** (**martèllo**) *tr* to hammer; to pester (*with questions*) ‖ *intr* to throb; (fig) to insist
**martellata** *f* hammer blow
**martellétto** *m* hammer (*of piano or bell*); lever (*of typewriter*)
**martèllo** *m* hammer; **martello dell'uscio** knocker; **martello perforatore** jack-hammer
**martinétto** *m* jack; **martinetto a vite** screw jack
**martingala** *f* half belt (*sewn in back of sports jacket*); martingale (*of harness*)
**martinic·ca** *f* (**-che**) wagon brake
**martìn pescatóre** *m* kingfisher
**màrtire** *m* martyr
**martì·rio** *m* (**-ri**) martyrdom
**martirizzare** [ddzz] *tr* to martyrize
**màrtora** *f* marten
**martoriare** §287 (**martòrio**) *tr* to torment
**marxi·sta** *adj* & *mf* (**-sti -ste**) Marxist
**marzapane** *m* marzipan
**marziale** *adj* martial
**marzia·no -na** *adj* & *mf* Martian
**marzo** *m* March
**mas** *m* (**mas**) torpedo boat
**mascalzóne** *m* cad, rascal
**mascèlla** *f* jaw; jawbone
**màschera** *mf* usher ‖ *f* mask; masque; **maschera antigas** gas mask; **maschera di bellezza** beauty pack; **maschera respiratoria** oxygen mask; **maschera subacquea** diving helmet
**mascheraménto** *m* camouflage
**mascherare** (**màschero**) *tr, intr* & *ref* to mask; to camouflage
**mascherata** *f* masquerade
**mascherina** *f* little mask, loup; tip (*of shoe*); (aut) grille; (phot) mask
**maschiare** §287 *tr* (mach) to tap
**maschiétta** *f* tomboy; **alla maschietta** bobbed (*hair*); **tagliare i capelli alla maschietta** to bob the hair
**maschiétto** *m* baby boy; pintle
**maschile** *adj* masculine; manly; men's;

**male** (*sex*); boys' (*school*) ‖ *m* masculine
**mà·schio -schia** *adj* manly, virile; male ‖ *m* male; keep, donjon; tenon; (mach) tap; (carp) tongue
**mascolinizzare** [ddzz] *tr* to make masculine or mannish ‖ *ref* to act like a man
**mascoli·no -na** *adj* masculine; mannish (*woman*)
**masnada** *f* mob, gang; (obs) group
**masnadière** *m* highwayman
**massa** *f* mass; body (*of water*); (elec) ground; **mettere a massa** (elec) to ground; **in massa** in a body; **massa ereditaria** (law) estate
**massacrante** *adj* killing, fatiguing
**massacrare** *tr* to massacre; to ruin; to wear out, fatigue
**massacro** *m* massacre
**massaggiare** §290 *tr* to massage
**massaggiatóre** *m* masseur
**massaggiatrice** *f* masseuse
**massàg·gio** *m* (**-gi**) massage
**massàia** *f* housewife
**massèllo** *m* block (*of stone*); (metallurgy) pig, ingot
**masseria** *f* farm
**masserìzie** *fpl* household goods
**massicciata** *f* roadbed; (rr) ballast
**massic·cio -cia** (**-ci -ce**) *adj* massive; bulky; heavy; (fig) gross ‖ *m* massif
**màssi·mo -ma** *adj* maximum; top ‖ *m* maximum; limit; **al massimo** at the most ‖ *f* maxim; maximum temperature
**massi·vo -va** *adj* massive
**masso** *m* rock, boulder
**Massóne** *m* Mason
**Massoneria** *f* Masonry
**mastèllo** *m* washtub
**masticare** §197 (**màstico**) *tr* to chew, masticate; to mumble (*words*); to speak (*a language*) poorly; **masticare amaro** to grumble
**masticazióne** *f* mastication
**màstice** *m* mastic; glue; putty
**mastino** *m* mastiff
**mastodònti·co -ca** *adj* (**-ci -che**) mammoth
**ma·stro -stra** *adj* master ‖ *m* ledger; master, e.g., **mastro meccanico** master mechanic
**masturbare** *tr* & *ref* to masturbate
**matassa** *f* skein; trouble
**matemàti·co -ca** (**-ci -che**) *adj* mathematical ‖ *m* mathematician ‖ *f* mathematics
**materassino** *m* (sports) mat; **materassino pneumatico** air mattress
**materasso** *m* mattress; (boxing) sparring partner
**matèria** *f* matter; substance; subject; (coll) pus; **dare materia a** to give ground for; **materia grigia** gray matter; **materie coloranti** dyestuffs; **materie prime** raw materials
**materiale** *adj* material; rough, bulky ‖ *m* material; equipment, supplies; (fig) makings, stuff; **materiale ferroviario** (rr) rolling stock; **materiale stabile** (rr) permanent way

**materni·tà** *f* (**-tà**) maternity; maternity hospital; maternity ward

**matèr·no** **-na** *adj* maternal; mother (*tongue, country*)

**matita** *f* pencil; **matita per gli occhi** eye-shadow pencil; **matita per le labbra** lipstick; cosmetic pencil

**matrice** *f* matrix; stub

**matrici·da** *mf* (**-di** **-de**) matricide

**matricì·dio** *m* (**-di**) matricide

**matrìcola** *f* register, roll; registration (*number*); registry; beginner, novice; freshman (*in university*); **far la matricola a** to haze

**matricola·to** **-ta** *adj* notorious, arrant

**matrigna** *f* stepmother

**matrimoniale** *adj* matrimonial; double (*bed*); married (*life*)

**matrimonialménte** *adv* as husband and wife

**matrimò·nio** *m* (**-ni**) matrimony, marriage; wedding

**matròna** *f* matron

**matronale** *adj* matronly

**matta** *f* joker, wild card

**mattacchió·ne** **-na** *mf* jester, prankster

**mattana** *f* tantrum; fit of laughter

**matta·tóio** *m* (**-tói**) slaughterhouse

**matterèllo** *m* rolling pin

**mattina** *f* morning; **di prima mattina** early in the morning; **la mattina** in the morning

**mattinale** *adj* morning ‖ *m* morning report

**mattinata** *f* morning; (*theat*) matinée

**mattiniè·ro** **-ra** *adj* early-rising

**mattino** *m* morning; **di buon mattino** early in the morning

**mat·to** **-ta** *adj* crazy; whimsical; dull; false (*jewelry*); wild (*desire*); **andare matto per** to be crazy about; **da matti** unbelievable; **fare il matto** to cut a caper; **matto da legare** raving mad ‖ *f* see **matta**

**mattòide** *adj* & *mf* madcap

**mattonare** (**mattóno**) *tr* to pave with bricks

**mattonato** *m* brick floor; **restare sul mattonato** to be utterly destitute

**mattóne** *m* brick; (fig) bore

**mattonèlla** *f* tile; cushion (*of billiard table*)

**mattuti·no** **-na** *adj* morning ‖ *m* matins

**maturan·do** **-da** *mf* lycée student who has to take the baccalaureate examination

**maturare** *tr* to ripen; to ponder; to pass (*a lycée pupil*) ‖ *intr* (ESSERE) to ripen, mature; to fall due

**maturazióne** *f* ripening

**maturi·tà** *f* (**-tà**) maturity; ripening; lycée final

**matu·ro** **-ra** *adj* ripe; mature; due

**Matusalèmme** *m* Methuselah

**mausolèo** *m* mausoleum

**mazza** *f* club; mallet; sledge hammer; cane; mace; golf club; (baseball) bat

**mazzacavallo** *m* well sweep

**mazzapìc·chio** *m* (**-chi**) mallet; sledge

**mazzata** *f* heavy blow, wallop (*with club*)

**mazzeran·ga** *f* (**-ghe**) (mach) tamper

**mazzière** *m* macer; (cards) dealer

**mazzo** *m* bunch; bouquet; deck (*of cards*); **fare il mazzo** to shuffle the cards

**mazzuòla** *f* sledge hammer

**mazzuòlo** *m* sledge; mallet; wedge (*of golf club*); drumstick (*for bass drum*)

**me** §5 *pron pers*

**meandro** *m* meander; labyrinth

**MEC** *m* (letterword) (**Mercato Europeo Comune**) European Economic Community, Common Market

**Mècca, la Mecca**; (fig) the Mecca

**meccàni·co** **-ca** (**-ci** **-che**) *adj* mechanical ‖ *m* mechanic ‖ *f* mechanics; process (*e.g., of digestion*); machinery

**meccanismo** *m* machinery; mechanism; movement (*of watch*)

**meccanizzare** [ddzz] *tr* to mechanize ‖ *ref* to become mechanized

**mecenate** *m* patron (*of the arts*)

**méco** §5 *prep phrase* (lit) with me

**medàglia** *f* medal

**medaglióne** *m* medallion; locket; biographical sketch

**medési·mo** **-ma** *adj* & *pron* same; -self, e.g., **egli medesimo** he himself; very e.g., **la verità medesima** the very truth

**mèdia** *f* average; secondary school, middle school; (math) mean; **media oraria** average speed ‖ **mèdia** *mpl* media (*of communication*)

**mediana** *f* median; (soccer) middle line

**mediàni·co** **-ca** *adj* (**-ci** **-che**) medium

**media·no** **-na** *adj* median ‖ *m* (sports) halfback ‖ *f* see **mediana**

**mediante** *prep* by means of

**mediare** §287 (**mèdio**) *tr* & *intr* (ESSERE) to mediate

**media·to** **-ta** *adj* indirect

**media·tóre** **-trice** *adj* mediating ‖ *mf* mediator; broker; commission merchant

**mediazióne** *f* mediation; brokerage; broker's fee, commission

**medicaménto** *m* medicine

**medicamentó·so** **-sa** [s] *adj* medicinal

**medicare** §197 (**mèdico**) *tr* to medicate; to treat

**medicastro** *m* quack

**medicazióne** *f* medication; dressing

**medichéssa** *f* (pej) lady doctor

**medicina** *f* medicine

**medicinale** *adj* medicinal ‖ *m* medicine

**mèdi·co** **-ca** (**-ci** **-che**) *adj* medical ‖ *m* doctor, physician; healer; **fare il medico** to practice medicine; **medico chirurgo** surgeon; **medico condotto** board-of-health doctor; country doctor; **medico curante** family physician

**medievale** *adj* medieval

**medievali·sta** *mf* (**-sti** **-ste**) medievalist

**mè·dio** **-dia** (**-di** **-die**) *adj* average; median; middle; secondary (*school*); medium ‖ *m* middle finger ‖ *f* see **media**

**mediòcre** *adj* mediocre

**mediocri·tà** *f* (**-tà**) mediocrity

**medioèvo** *m* Middle Ages

**medioleggèro** *m* welterweight

**mediomàssimo** *m* light heavyweight
**meditabón·do -da** *adj* meditative
**meditare** (**mèdito**) *tr & intr* to meditate
**medita·to -ta** *adj* considered
**meditazióne** *f* meditation
**mediterrà·neo -nea** *adj* inland (*sea*) ‖
  **Mediterraneo** *adj & m* Mediterranean
**mè·dium** *mf* (**-dium**) medium
**medusa** *f* jellyfish
**mefistofèli·co -ca** *adj* (**-ci -che**) Mephistophelian
**mefiti·co -ca** *adj* (**-ci -che**) mephitic
**megaciclo** *m* megacycle
**megàfono** *m* megaphone
**megalomanìa** *f* megalomania
**megalòpo·li** *f* (**-li**) megalopolis
**mega·òhm** *m* (**-òhm**) megohm
**megèra** *f* hag, termagant, vixen
**mèglio** *adj invar* better; (coll) best ‖
  *m*—**il meglio** the best; **nel meglio di**
  (coll) in the middle of ‖ *f*—**avere la**
  **meglio** to get the upper hand; **avere**
  **la meglio di** to get the better of
  ‖ *adv* better; best; rather; **stare**
  **meglio** to feel better; to be becoming; to fit better; **stare meglio a** to
  be becoming to; to fit; **tanto meglio!**
  so much the better!
**méla** *f* apple; nozzle (*of sprinkling*
  *can*); **mela cotogna** quince (*fruit*);
  **mela renetta** pippin
**melagrana** *f* pomegranate
**melanzana** [dz] *f* eggplant
**melassa** *f* molasses, treacle
**mela·to -ta** *adj* honey, honeyed
**melèn·so -sa** *adj* dull, silly
**melissa** *f* (bot) balm
**mellìflu·o -a** *adj* mellifluous
**mélma** *f* mud, slime
**melmó·so -sa** [s] *adj* muddy, slimy
**mélo** *m* apple tree
**melodìa** *f* melody
**melòdi·co -ca** *adj* (**-ci -che**) melodic
**melodió·so -sa** [s] *adj* melodious
**melodram·ma** *m* (**-mi**) melodrama;
  lyric opera; (fig) melodrama
**melodrammàti·co -ca** *adj* (**-ci -che**)
  melodramatic
**melograno** *m* pomegranate tree
**melóne** *m* melon; cantaloupe; **melone**
  **d'acqua** watermelon
**membrana** *f* membrane; parchment;
  diaphragm (*of telephone*); (zool) web
**membratura** *f* frame
**mèm·bro** *m* (**-bri,** *considered individ-*
  *ually*) limb; member; penis ‖ *m*
  (**-bra** *fpl, considered collectively*)
  limb (*of human body*)
**membru·to -ta** *adj* burly, husky
**memoràbile** *adj* memorable
**memoràn·dum** *m* (**-dum**) memorandum;
  agenda, calendar; note; note paper
**mèmore** *adj* (lit) mindful, grateful
**memòria** *f* memory; souvenir; memoir;
  dissertation; (law) brief
**memoriale** *m* memoir; memorial
**memorizzare** [ddzz] *tr* to memorize
**ména** *f* intrigue
**mena·bò** *m* (**-bò**) (typ) layout, dummy
**menadito** *m*—**a menadito** at one's
  fingertips; perfectly
**menare** (**méno**) *tr* to lead; to bring

(*luck*); to wag (*the tail*); to deliver
(*a blow*); (coll) to hit; **menare a**
**effetto** to carry out; **menare buono di**
to approve of; **menare il can per l'aia**
to beat around the bush; **menare per**
**le lunghe** to delay; **menare vanto** to
boast
**mènda** *f* (lit) fault, flaw
**mendace** *adj* lying, false, mendacious
**mendà·cio** *m* (**-ci**) (law) falsehood
**mendicante** *adj & m* mendicant
**mendicare** §197 (**méndico**) *tr & intr* to
beg
**mendici·tà** *f* (**-tà**) indigence, poverty
**mendi·co -ca** *adj & mf* (**-chi -che**)
mendicant
**menefreghismo** *m* I-don't-care attitude
**menestrèllo** *m* minstrel
**méno** *adj invar* less ‖ *m* less; least;
minus (*sign*); **i meno** the few; **per lo**
**meno** at least ‖ *adv* less; least;
minus; **a meno che** unless; **da meno**
inferior; **fare a meno di** to do without; to spare; **meno . . . di** less . . .
than; **meno male** fortunately; **meno**
**. . . meno** the less . . . the less; **non**
**poter fare a meno di** + *inf* to not be
able to help + *ger*, e.g., **la confe-**
**renza non poteva fare a meno di**
**essere un successo** the conference
could not help being a success;
**quanto meno** at least; **senza meno**
without fail; **venir meno** to swoon,
pass out; to fail; to lose, e.g., **gli**
**venne meno il cuore** he lost his
courage; **venir meno di** to break
(*one's word*) ‖ *prep* except; less,
minus; of, e.g., **le sette meno dieci**
ten minutes of seven
**menomare** (**mènomo**) *tr* to lessen, diminish; (fig) to hurt, damage
**mèno·mo -ma** *adj* least
**menopàusa** *f* menopause
**mènsa** *f* (prepared) table; mess, mess
hall; (eccl) altar; communion table;
(poet) mass; (poet) altar; **mensa**
**aziendale** company cafeteria
**mensile** *adj* monthly ‖ *m* monthly salary or allowance
**mensili·tà** *f* (**-tà**) monthly installment
**mènsola** *f* bracket; corner shelf; neck
(*of harp*); mantel (*of chimney*); console
**ménta** *f* mint
**mentale** *adj* mental; (anat) chin
**mentali·tà** *f* (**-tà**) mentality, mind
**ménte** *f* mind; **a mente di** according to;
**avere in mente** to mean; to intend;
**di mente** mental; **mente direttiva**
mastermind; **scappare di mente a**
**qlcu** to escape s.o.'s mind, e.g., **gli è**
**scappato di mente** it escaped his
mind; **uscire di mente** to go out of
one's mind; **venire in mente a qlcu**
to remember, e.g., **non gli è venuto**
**in mente di spedire la lettera** he did
not remember to mail the letter
**mentecat·to -ta** *adj & mf* lunatic
**mentina** *f* mint; **mentina digestiva**
after-dinner mint
**mentire** §176 & (**mènto**) *intr* to lie;

**mentire per la gola** to lie through one's teeth

**menti·to -ta** *adj* false; disguised

**menti·tóre -trice** *adj* lying || *mf* liar

**ménto** *m* chin

**mentòlo** *m* menthol

**méntre** *m*—**in quel mentre** at that very moment; **nel mentre che** at the time when || *conj* while; whereas

**me·nù** *m* (-**nù**) menu

**menzionare** (**menzióno**) *tr* to mention

**menzióne** *f* mention

**menzógna** *f* lie

**menzognè·ro -ra** *adj* false, deceptive; lying, untruthful

**meraviglia** *f* marvel, wonder; **a meraviglia** wonderfully; **destare le meraviglie di** to amaze; **dire meraviglie di** to praise to the skies; **fare meraviglia** (with *dat*) to amaze; **far meraviglie** to work wonders

**meravigliare** §280 (**meraviglio**) *tr* to amaze; to astonish || *ref* to be astonished

**meraviglió·so -sa** [s] *adj* marvelous, wonderful || *m* (lit) supernatural

**mercan·te -téssa** *mf* merchant, dealer

**mercanteggiare** §290 (**mercantéggio**) *tr* to sell || *intr* to deal; to haggle

**mercantile** *adj* mercantile; merchant (*marine*) || *m* cargo boat, freighter

**mercanzìa** *f* merchandise; (coll) junk

**mercato** *m* market; trafficking; **a buon mercato** cheap; **far mercato di** to traffic in; **sopra mercato** besides; into the bargain

**mèrce** *f* merchandise, goods; commodity

**mercé** *f* favor, grace; mercy; **alla mercé di** at the mercy of; **mercé a** thanks to; **mercé sua** thanks to him (her, etc.)

**mercéde** *f* pay; (lit) reward

**mercenà·rio -ria** *adj & m* (-**ri** -**rie**) mercenary

**mercerìa** *f* notions store; **mercerìe** notions

**mercerizzare** [ddzz] *tr* to mercerize

**mèr·ci** *adj invar* freight (*train, car, etc.*) || *m* (-**ci**) freight train

**mer·ciàio -ciàia** *mf* (-**ciài** -**ciàie**) notions store owner

**merciaiòlo** *m* small businessman; **merciaiolo ambulante** peddler

**mercole·dì** *m* (-**dì**) Wednesday

**mercuriale** *f* market report; price ceiling

**mercùrio** *m* mercury || **Mercùrio** *m* Mercury

**merènda** *f* afternoon snack, bite

**meretrice** *f* harlot

**meridia·no -na** *adj & m* meridian || *f* sundial

**meridionale** *adj* meridional, southern || *mf* southerner

**meridióne** *m* south; South

**merìg·gio** *m* (-**gi**) noon

**merin·ga** *f* (-**ghe**) meringue

**meritare** (**mèrito**) *tr* to deserve; to win || *intr* (eccl) to merit; **bene meritare di** to deserve the gratitude of || *impers*—**merita** it is worth while to

**meritévole** *adj* deserving, worthy

**mèrito** *m* merit; **in merito a** concerning; **per merito di** thanks to; **render merito a** to reward

**meritò·rio -ria** *adj* (-**ri** -**rie**) meritorious

**merlan·go** *m* (-**ghi**) whiting

**merlatura** *f* battlement

**merlétto** *m* lace, needlepoint

**mèrlo** *m* blackbird; merlon; (fig) simpleton

**merluzzo** *m* cod

**mè·ro -ra** *adj* bare, mere; (poet) pure

**merovìngi·co -ca** (-**ci** -**che**) *adj* Merovingian || *f* Merovingian script

**mesata** [s] *f* month's wages

**méscere** (*pp* **mesciuto**) *tr* to pour (*e.g., wine*); (poet) to mix

**meschini·tà** *f* (-**tà**) pettiness; narrowmindedness; meanness, stinginess

**meschi·no -na** *adj* petty; narrowminded; wretched; puny || *mf* wretch

**méscita** *f* pouring; counter; bar

**mescolanza** *f* mixture, blend

**mescolare** (**méscolo**) *tr* to mix, blend; to shuffle (*cards*); to stir (*e.g., coffee*) || *ref* to mix, blend; to mingle; to consort; **mescolarsi in** to mind (*somebody else's business*)

**mescolatrice** *f* mixer, blender

**mése** [s] *m* month; month's pay

**mesétto** [s] *m* short month

**mesóne** *m* (phys) meson

**méssa** *f* (eccl & mus) Mass; **messa a fuoco** (phot) focusing; **messa a punto** adjustment; clear statement, outline of a problem; (aut) tune-up; **messa a terra** (elec) grounding; **messa cantata** high mass; **messa in marcia** or **in moto** (mach) starting; **messa in orbita** (rok) orbiting; **messa in piega** waving (*of hair*); **messa in scena** staging; **messa in vendita** putting up for sale

**messaggerìe** *fpl* delivery service

**messaggè·ro -ra** *mf* messenger; postal clerk

**messàg·gio** *m* (-**gi**) message

**messale** *m* missal

**mèsse** *f* harvest; crop

**Messìa** *m* Messiah

**messiàni·co -ca** *adj* (-**ci** -**che**) Messianic

**messica·no -na** *adj & mf* Mexican

**Mèssico, il** Mexico

**messinscèna** *f* staging; faking

**mésso** *m* clerk; (poet) messenger

**mestare** (**mésto**) *tr* to stir || *intr* to intrigue

**mesta·tóre -trice** *mf* ringleader; schemer

**mèstica** *f* (painting) filler

**mesticare** §197 (**mèstico**) *tr* to prime (*a canvas*); to mix (*colors*)

**mestierante** *mf* potboiler (*person*); tradesman, craftsman

**mestière** *m* trade, craft; (archaic) task; **di mestiere** by trade; habitual; **essere del mestiere** to be up in one's line

**mestièri** *m*—**essere di** or **far mestièri** to be necessary

**mestìzia** *f* sadness

**mè·sto -sta** *adj* sad

**méstola** *f* ladle; trowel

**méstolo** *m* kitchen spoon; **avere il mestolo in mano** to be the boss

**mèstruo** *m* menses, menstruation

**mèta** f goal, aim; (rugby) goal line
**méta** f heap, stack (*e.g., of hay*)
**me·tà** f (**-tà**) half; middle; halfway; better half; **a metà** halfway, in the middle; **aver qlco a metà con qlcu** to go half and half with s.o.
**metabolismo** m metabolism
**metafìsi·co -ca** (**-ci -che**) *adj* metaphysical || m metaphysician || f metaphysics
**metafonèsi** f umlaut, metaphony
**metafonìa** f umlaut, metaphony
**metàfora** f metaphor
**metafòri·co -ca** *adj* (**-ci -che**) metaphoric(al)
**metàlli·co -ca** *adj* (**-ci -che**) metallic
**metallizzare** [ddzz] *tr* to cover with metal
**metallo** m metal; timbre (*of voice*); (poet) metal object; **il vile metallo** filthy lucre
**metallòide** m nonmetal
**metallurgìa** f metallurgy
**metallùrgi·co -ca** (**ci -che**) *adj* metallurgic(al) || m metalworker
**metalmeccàni·co -ca** (**-ci -che**) *adj* metallurgic(al) and mechanical || m metalworker
**metamòrfo·si** f (**-si**) metamorphosis
**metanizzare** [ddzz] *tr* to provide with methane
**metano** m methane
**metanodótto** m natural gas pipeline
**metàte·si** f (**-si**) metathesis
**metèora** f meteor; atmospheric phenomenon
**meteorite** m & f meteorite
**meteorologìa** f meteorology
**meteorològi·co -ca** *adj* (**-ci -che**) meteorologic(al); weather (*forecast*)
**meteoròlo·go -ga** mf (**-gi -ghe**) meteorologist
**metìc·cio -cia** *adj* & mf (**-ci -ce**) half-breed
**meticoló·so -sa** [s] *adj* meticulous
**metìli·co -ca** *adj* (**-ci -che**) methyl
**metòdi·co -ca** (**-ci -che**) *adj* methodical; subject (*e.g., index*) || mf methodical person || f methodology
**metodi·sta** *adj* & mf (**-sti -ste**) Methodist
**mètodo** m method
**metràg·gio** m (**-gi**) length in meters; **corto metraggio** short; **lungo metraggio** full-length movie, feature film
**metratura** f length in meters
**mètri·co -ca** *adj* (**-ci -che**) metric(al) || f metrics, prosody
**mètro** m meter; (fig) yardstick; (lit) words
**métro** m (coll) subway
**metrònomo** m (mus) metronome
**metronòt·te** m (**-te**) night watchman
**metròpo·li** f (**-li**) metropolis
**metropolita·no -na** *adj* metropolitan || m policeman, traffic cop || f subway
**metrovìa** f subway
**méttere** §198 *tr* to put, place; to set (*e.g., foot*); to run (*e.g., a nail into a board*); to cause (*fear; fever*); to employ; to admit; to put forth; to give out; (coll) to charge; (coll) to install; (aut) to engage (*a gear*); **metterci**

to take (*e.g., an hour*); **mettere a confronto** to compare; **mettere a freno** to check; **mettere a fuoco** (phot) to focus; **mettere al bando** to banish; **mettere all'asta** to auction off; **mettere al mondo** to give birth to; **mettere a nudo** to lay bare; **mettere fuori** to pull out; to give out (*news*); to throw (*s.o.*) out; **mettere giù** to lower; **mettere in onda** to broadcast; **mettere in pericolo** to endanger; **mettere la pulce nell'orecchio a** to put a bug in the ear of; **mettere qlcu alla porta** to show s.o. the door; **mettere su** to set up; (coll) to put (*e.g., a coat*) on; **mettere su qlcu contro qlcu** to excite s.o. against s.o. || *intr* to sprout; to lead (*said, e.g., of a road*) || *ref* to put on, to don; to place oneself, put oneself; to take shape; **mettersi a** to begin to; **mettersi al bello** to clear up (*said of weather*); **mettersi a letto** to go to bed; **mettersi a sedere** to sit down; **mettersi con** to start to work with; **mettersi in ferie** to take one's vacation; **mettersi in malattia** to fall ill; **mettersi in mare** to put to sea; **mettersi in maschera** to wear a masked costume; **mettersi in salvo** to get out of danger; to save oneself; **mettersi in viaggio** to set out on a journey; **mettersi in vista** to make oneself conspicuous || *impers*—**mette conto** it is worth while
**mettima·le** mf (**-le**) troublemaker
**mezzadrìa** [ddzz] f sharecropping
**mezza·dro -dra** [ddzz] mf sharecropper
**mezzaluna** [ddzz] f (**mezzelune**) half-moon; crescent (*symbol of Turkey and Islam*); curved chopping knife; lunette (*of fortification*)
**mezzana** [ddzz] f procuress; (naut) mizzen
**mezzanave** [ddzz] f—**a mezzanave** amidships
**mezzanino** [ddzz] m mezzanine
**mezza·no -na** [ddzz] *adj* median; medium; middle || m procurer || f see mezzana
**mezzanòtte** [ddzz] f (**mezzenòtti**) midnight
**mezzatinta** [ddzz] f (**mezzetinte**) halftone
**méz·zo -za** *adj* overripe, rotten
**mèz·zo -za** [ddzz] *adj* half; middle || m half; middle; medium; means; vehicle; **a mezzo (di)** by (*e.g., messenger*); **andar di mezzo** to suffer the consequences; to be the loser; **entrare di mezzo** to interpose oneself; **esserci di mezzo** to be present; to be at stake; **giusto mezzo** happy medium; **in mezzo a** among; in the lap of, e.g., **in mezzo alle delicatezze** in the lap of luxury; **in quel mezzo** meanwhile; **levar di mezzo** to get rid of; **mezzi** means; facilities; **mezzi di comunicazione di massa** mass media; **per mezzo di** by means of
**mezzobusto** [ddzz] m (**mezzibusti**) (sculp) bust; **a mezzobusto** half-length (*e.g., portrait*)

**mezzo·dì** [ddzz] *m* (**-dì**) noon; south; South

**mezzogiórno** [ddzz] *m* noon; south; South

**mezzùc·cio** [ddzz] *m* (**-ci**) expedient

**mi** §5 *pron*

**miagolare** (**miàgolo**) *intr* to meow

**miagolì·o** *m* (**-i**) meow, mew

**mi·ca** *f* (**-che**) mica; (obs) crumb ‖ *adv*—**mica male** (coll) not too·bad!; **non ... mica** not ... ever; not at all

**mìc·cia** *f* (**-ce**) fuse

**michelàc·cio** *m* (**-ci**) (coll) lazy bum

**micidiale** *adj* deadly; (fig) unbearable

**mì·cio** **-cia** *mf* (**-ci** **-cie**) (coll) pussy cat

**micrò·bio** *m* (**-bi**) microbe

**microbiologìa** *f* microbiology

**mìcrobo** *m* microbe

**microfà·rad** *m* (**-rad**) microfarad

**microferrovìa** *f* model railroad

**micro·film** *m* (**-film**) microfilm

**microfilmare** *tr* to microfilm

**micròfono** *m* microphone

**microlettóre** *m* microfilm reader

**micromotóre** *m* small motor; motor-cycle

**microónda** *f* microwave

**microschèda** *f* microcard

**microscòpi·co** **-ca** *adj* (**-ci** **-che**) microscopic(al)

**microscò·pio** *m* (**-pi**) microscope

**microsól·co** *adj invar* microgroove ‖ *m* (**-chi**) microgroove; microgroove, long-playing record

**microtelèfono** *m* French telephone, handset

**midólla** *f* crumb; (coll) marrow

**midól·lo** *m* (**-la** *fpl*) marrow; (bot & fig) pith; **midollo spinale** (anat) spinal cord

**mièle** *m* honey

**miètere** (**mièto**) *tr* to reap; (lit) to kill

**mietitrebbiatrice** *f* combine

**mieti·tóre** **-trice** *mf* reaper, harvester

**mietitura** *f* harvesting

**mi·gliàio** *m* (**-gliàia** *fpl*) thousand

**mì·glio** *m* (**-glia** *fpl*) mile; milestone; **miglio marino** nautical mile; **miglio terrestre** mile ‖ *m* (**-gli**) millet

**miglioraménto** *m* improvement

**migliorare** (**miglióro**) *tr, intr* (ESSERE & AVERE) & *ref* to improve

**miglióre** *adj* better; best

**migliorìa** *f* improvement (*e.g., of real estate*)

**mignatta** *f* leech

**mìgnolo** *adj masc* little (*finger or toe*) ‖ *m* little finger; little toe

**migrare** *intr* to migrate

**migra·tóre** **-trice** *adj* & *m* migrant

**migrazióne** *f* migration

**Milano** *f* Milan

**miliardà·rio** **-ria** *adj* & *mf* (**-ri** **-rie**) billionaire

**miliardo** *m* billion

**milionà·rio** **-ria** *adj* & *mf* (**-ri** **-rie**) millionaire

**milióne** *m* million

**milionèsi·mo** **-ma** *adj* & *m* millionth

**militante** *adj* & *m* militant

**militare** *adj* military ‖ *m* soldier ‖ *v* (**mìlito**) *intr* to be a member; to mili-

tate; to be in the armed forces; **militare in** to be a member of (*e.g., a party*)

**militaré·sco** **-sca** *adj* (**-schi** **-sche**) military, soldierly

**militarismo** *m* militarism

**militari·sta** (**-sti** **-ste**) *adj* militaristic ‖ *mf* militarist

**militarizzare** [ddzz] *tr* to militarize; to fortify

**mìlite** *m* militiaman; soldier; **milite del fuoco** fireman; **Milite Ignoto** Unknown Soldier

**militesènte** *adj* exempt from military service ‖ *m* man exempt from military service

**milìzia** *f* militia; (mil) service; struggle; **milizie celesti** heavenly host

**miliziano** *m* militiaman

**millantare** *tr* to boast of ‖ *ref* to brag, boast

**millanta·tóre** **-trice** *mf* braggart

**millanterìa** *f* bragging

**mille** *adj*, *m* & *pron* (**mila**) thousand, a thousand, one thousand ‖ **il Mille** the eleventh century; the year one thousand

**millecènto** *m* eleven hundred ‖ *f* car with a 1100 cc. motor

**millefò·glie** *m* (**-glie**) puff-paste cake

**millenà·rio** **-ria** *adj* (**-ri** **-rie**) millennial ‖ *m* millennium

**millèn·nio** *m* (**-ni**) millennium

**millepiè·di** *m* (**-di**) millipede

**millèsi·mo** **-ma** *adj* & *m* thousandth

**milliam·père** *m* (**-père**) milliampere

**milligrammo** *m* milligram

**millimetra·to** **-ta** *adj* divided into squares of one millimeter square

**millìmetro** *m* millimeter

**milli·vòlt** *m* (**-vòlt**) millivolt

**milza** *f* spleen

**mimare** *tr* & *intr* to mime

**mimetizzare** [ddzz] *tr* (mil) to camouflage

**mimetizzazióne** [ddzz] *f* (mil) camouflage

**mìmi·co** **-ca** (**-ci** **-che**) *adj* mimic; sign (*language*) ‖ *f* mimicry; (theat) gestures; (theat) miming

**mì·mo** **-ma** *mf* mime ‖ *m* (orn) mockingbird

**mina** *f* lead (*of pencil*); (mil) mine; **mina anticarro** antitank mine; **mina antiuomo** antipersonnel mine

**minaccévole** *adj* (lit) threatening

**minàc·cia** *f* (**-ce**) threat, menace

**minacciare** §128 *tr* to threaten, menace

**minacció·so** **-sa** [s] *adj* threatening

**minare** *tr* to mine; to undermine

**minaréto** *m* minaret

**minatóre** *m* miner

**minatò·rio** **-ria** *adj* (**-ri** **-rie**) threatening

**minchionare** (**minchióno**) *tr* (slang) to make a sucker of

**minchióne** *m* (slang) sucker

**minerale** *adj* mineral ‖ *m* mineral; ore

**mineralogìa** *f* mineralogy

**minerà·rio** **-ria** *adj* (**-ri** **-rie**) mining

**minèr·va** *m* (**-va**) safety match

**minèstra** *f* vegetable soup

**minestróne** *m* minestrone; hodgepodge

mìngere §199 *intr* to urinate
mingherli·no -na *adj* frail, thin
miniare §287 *tr* to paint in miniature; to illuminate
miniatura *f* miniature
miniaturizzare [ddzz] *tr* to miniaturize
miniaturizzazióne [ddzz] *f* miniaturization
minièra *f* mine
mini·gòlf *m* (-gòlf) miniature golf
minigònna *f* miniskirt
mìnima *f* lowest temperature; (mus) minim
minimizzare [ddzz] *tr* to minimize
mìni·mo -ma *adj* smallest, least; minimum || *m* minimum; al minimo at the least; girare al minimo or tenere il minimo (aut) to idle || *f* see minima
mìnio *m* red lead; rouge
ministeriale *adj* ministerial
ministèro *m* ministry; cabinet; department; pubblico ministero public prosecutor
ministra *f* (joc) wife of minister; (joc) female minister; (poet) minister
ministro *m* minister; secretary; administrator; ministro degli Esteri foreign minister; (U.S.A.) Secretary of State
minoranza *f* minority
minorare (minóro) *tr* to lessen; to disable
minora·to -ta *adj* disabled || *mf* disabled person
minorazióne *f* reduction; disability
minóre *adj* smaller, lesser; minor; smallest, least; younger; youngest || *m* minor
minorènne *adj* underage || *mf* minor
minorile *adj* juvenile (*e.g., court*)
minori·tà *f* (-tà) minority
minuétto *m* minuet
minù·gia *f* (-gia & -gie) (mus) catgut
minùsco·lo -la *adj* small (*letter*); diminutive || *m & f* small letter
minuta *f* first draft, rough copy
minutàglia *f* trifles; small fry
minutante *m* secretary; retailer
minuterìa *f* trinkets, notions
minu·to -ta *adj* minute; small (*change*); common (*people*) || *m* minute; al minuto retail; di minuto in minuto at any moment; minuto secondo second; nel minuto in detail; per minuto minutely || *f* see minuta
minùzia *f* trifle; minuzie minutiae
minuzió·so -sa [s] *adj* meticulous
minùzzolo *m* scrap, crumb; small boy
mìo mìa §6 *adj & pron poss* (mièi mìe)
mìope *adj* nearsighted || *mf* nearsighted person
miopìa *f* nearsightedness
mira *f* aim; sight; target, goal; prendere di mira to aim at; to torment
miràbile *adj* admirable || *m* wonder
mirabìlia *fpl* wonders; far mirabilia to perform wonders; dir mirabilia di to speak highly of
mirabolante *adj* amazing, astonishing
miracola·to -ta *adj* miraculously cured || *mf* miraculously cured person
miràcolo *m* miracle; wonder; dir mira-

coli di to praise to the skies; per miracolo by mere chance
miracoló·so -sa [s] *adj* miraculous; wonderful
miràg·gio *m* (-gi) mirage
mirare *tr* (lit) to look at; (lit) to aim at || *intr* to aim; mirare a to aim at; mirare a + *inf* to aim to + *inf;* to intend to + *inf*
miriade *f* myriad
mirino *m* sight (*of gun*); (phot) finder
mirra *f* myrrh
mirtillo *m* blueberry; whortleberry, huckleberry
mirto *m* myrtle
misantropìa *f* misanthropy
misàntro·po -pa *adj* misanthropic || *mf* misanthrope
miscèla *f* mixture, blend
miscelare (miscèlo) *tr* to mix, blend
miscellàne·o -a *adj* miscellaneous || *f* miscellany
mischia *f* fight; (sports) scrimmage
mischiare §287 *tr* to mix, blend; to shuffle (*cards*) || *ref* to mix
misconóscere §134 *tr* to not appreciate, undervalue
miscredènte *adj* misbelieving || *mf* misbeliever
miscù·glio *m* (-gli) mixture, blend
miseràbile *adj* pitiful, miserable; poor, wretched
miseran·do -da *adj* pitiable
miserère *m* Miserere; essere al miserere to be in one's last hours
miserévole *adj* pitiful; pitiable
misèria *f* destitution, misery; wretchedness; lack, want; trifle; piangere miseria to cry poverty
misericòrdia *f* mercy
misericordió·so -sa [s] *adj* merciful
mìse·ro -ra *adj* unhappy, wretched; poor; meager; mean; too small, too short
misfatto *m* misdeed, misdoing
misiriz·zi [s] *m* (-zi) tumbler (*toy*); (fig) chameleon
misògi·no -na *adj* misogynous || *m* misogynist
mìssile *adj & m* missile; missile antimissile antimissile missile; missile intercontinentale I.C.B.M.; missile teleguidato guided missile
missillìsti·co -ca *adj* (-ci -che) missile
missionà·rio -ria *adj & m* (-ri -rie) missionary
missióne *f* mission
missiva *f* missive
misterió·so -sa [s] *adj* mysterious
mistèro *m* mystery
mìstica *f* mysticism; mystical literature
misticismo *m* mysticism
mìsti·co -ca (-ci -che) *adj & mf* mystic || *f* see mistica
mistificare §197 (mistìfico) *tr* to hoax
mistificazióne *f* hoax
mi·sto -sta *adj* mixed || *m* mixture; mixed train
mistura *f* mixture
misura *f* measure; size; bounds; fitting; a misura che in proportion as; di

**misura** (sports) with a narrow margin; **su misura** made-to-order
**misuràbile** *adj* measurable
**misurare** *tr* to measure; to deliver (*e.g.*, *a slap*); to budget (*expenses*); to try on (*clothes*); to weigh (*the outcome*) || *intr* to measure || *ref* to compete; to limit oneself; **misurarsi con** to try conclusions with
**misura·to -ta** *adj* moderate; scanty
**misurino** *m* measuring spoon or cup
**mite** *adj* mild; tame; low (*price*)
**mìti·co -ca** *adj* (-**ci** -**che**) mythical
**mitigare** §209 (**mìtigo**) *tr* to mitigate; to assuage, allay || *ref* to abate
**mìtilo** *m* mussel
**mito** *m* myth
**mitologìa** *f* mythology
**mitològi·co -ca** *adj* (-**ci** -**che**) mythologic(al)
**mitòmane** *mf* compulsive liar
**mi·tra** *m* (-**tra**) submachine gun || *f* miter
**mitràglia** *f* grapeshot; scrap iron; (coll) machine gun
**mitragliare** §280 (**mitràglio**) *tr* to machine-gun
**mitragliatrice** *f* machine gun
**mitraglièra** *f* heavy machine gun
**mitraglière** *m* machine gunner
**mittènte** *mf* sender; shipper
**mo'** *m*—apocopated form of **modo** by way of; **a mo' d'esempio** as an illustration
**mòbile** *adj* movable; personal (*property*); (fig) fickle; (rr) rolling (*stock*) || *m* piece of furniture; cabinet; (phys) body; **mobili** furniture
**mobìlia** *f* furniture
**mobiliare** *adj* (fin) security; (law) movable || §287 (**mobìlio**) *tr* to furnish
**mobilière** *m* furniture maker; furniture dealer
**mobilità** *f* mobility
**mobilitare** (**mobìlito**) *tr* & *intr* to mobilize
**mobilitazióne** *f* mobilization
**mò·ca** *m* (-**ca**) mocha; **caffè moca** Mocha coffee
**mocassino** *m* mocassin
**moccicare** §197 (**móccico**) *intr* (slang) to snivel; (slang) to run (*said of the nose*); (slang) to whimper
**moccicó·so -sa** [s] *adj* (slang) snotty
**móc·cio** *m* (-**ci**) snot, snivel
**mocció·so -sa** [s] *adj* snotty || *m* brat
**mòccolo** *m* end of candle, snuff; (joc) snot; (slang) curse word; **reggere il moccolo a qlcu** to be a third party to a couple's necking
**mòda** *f* fashion, vogue; **andar di moda** to be fashionable; to be all the rage; **fuori moda** outdated
**modali·tà** *f* (-**tà**) modality; method
**modanatura** *f* molding
**mòdano** *m* mold
**modèlla** *f* model
**modellare** (**modèllo**) *tr* to model; to mold || *ref* to pattern oneself
**modella·tóre -trice** *mf* pattern maker; molder

**modellino** *m* (archit) model, maquette
**modèllo** *adj* *invar* model || *m* model; fashion; style; pattern
**moderare** (**mòdero**) *tr* to moderate, control
**moderatézza** *f* moderation
**modera·to -ta** *adj* moderate; (mus) moderato || *m* middle-of-the-roader
**modera·tóre -trice** *adj* moderating || *m* moderator
**modernizzare** [ddzz] *tr* & *ref* to modernize
**modèr·no -na** *adj* & *m* modern
**modèstia** *f* modesty; scantiness, meagerness
**modè·sto -sta** *adj* modest; humble
**mòdi·co -ca** *adj* (-**ci** -**che**) reasonable
**modìfi·ca** *f* (-**che**) modification; alteration
**modificare** §197 (**modìfico**) *tr* to modify; to change; to alter
**modiglióne** *m* (archit) modillion
**modista** *f* milliner
**modisterìa** *f* millinery; millinery shop
**mòdo** *m* manner, mode, way; custom; idiom; (gram) mood; (mus) mode; **ad ogni modo** anyhow; nevertheless; **ad un modo** equally; **a modo** proper; properly; **a suo modo** in his own way; **bei modi** good manners; **di modo che** so that; **in malo modo** poorly; **in modo da** so as to; **in nessun modo** by no means; **in ogni modo** anyhow; **in qualche modo** somehow; **modo di dire** idiom; turn of phrase; **modo di fare** behavior; **modo di vedere** opinion; **per modo di dire** so to speak
**modulare** (**mòdulo**) *tr* to modulate
**modulazióne** *f* modulation; **modulazione d'ampiezza** amplitude modulation; **modulazione di frequenza** frequency modulation
**mòdulo** *m* module; blank, form
**moffétta** *f* skunk
**mògano** *m* mahogany
**mòg·gio** *m* (-**gi**) bushel
**mò·gio -gia** *adj* (-**gi** -**gie**) downcast, crestfallen
**mó·glie** *f* (-**gli**) wife
**moìne** *fpl* blandishments
**mòla** *f* grindstone; (coll) millstone
**molare** *adj* grinding; molar || *m* molar || *v* (**mòlo**) *tr* to grind
**molassa** *f* molasse, sandstone
**molatóre** *m* grinder (*person*); sander (*person*)
**molatrice** *f* grinder (*machine*); sander (*machine*); **molatrice di pavimenti** floor sander
**mòle** *f* size; pile; bulk, mass; huge structure
**molècola** *f* molecule
**molestare** (**molèsto**) *tr* to bother, annoy
**molèstia** *f* bother, trouble, annoyance
**molè·sto -sta** *adj* bothersome, troublesome
**molibdèno** *m* molybdenum
**molinétto** *m* (naut) winch
**mòlla** *f* spring; (fig) mainspring; **molla a balestra** leaf spring; **molle** tongs; **molle del letto** bedspring; **prendere**

qlco con le molle to keep at a reasonable distance from s.th

**mollare** (**mòllo**) *tr* to let go; to slacken; to drop (*anchor*); (coll) to soak || *intr* to give up; (coll) to soak; **molla!** (coll) cut it out!

**mòlle** *adj* wet, soaked; soft; mild; easy (*life*); weak (*character*); flexible || *m* softness; soft ground; **tenere a molle** to soak

**mollécca** *f* soft-shell crab

**molleggiaménto** *m* suspension; springiness

**molleggiare** §290 (**molléggio**) *tr* to provide with springs, to make elastic; (aut) to provide with suspension || *intr* to be springy, to have bounce || *ref* to bounce along

**mollég·gio** *m* (**-gi**) springs; (aut) suspension; springiness

**mollétta** *f* hairpin; clothespin; **mollette** sugar tongs

**mollettièra** *f* puttee

**mollettóne** *m* swansdown

**mollézza** *f* softness

**molli·ca** *f* (**-che**) crumb (*soft inner portion of bread*); **molliche** crumbs

**mollificare** §197 (**mollìfico**) *tr* & *ref* to mollify; to soften

**mòl·lo -la** *adj* soft || *m*—**mettere a mollo** to soak || *f* see **molla**

**mollu·sco** *m* (**-schi**) mollusk

**mòlo** *m* pier, wharf

**moltéplice** *adj* multiple, mánifold

**moltilaterale** *adj* multilateral, many-sided

**moltìpli·ca** *f* (**-che**) front sprocket (*of bicycle*)

**moltiplicare** §197 (**moltìplico**) *tr* & *ref* to multiply

**moltitùdine** *f* multitude, crowd

**mól·to -ta** *adj* much, a lot of; very, e.g., **ho molta sete** I am very thirsty || *pron* much; a lot; **a dir molto** mostly; **ci corre molto** there is a great difference || **mol·ti -te** *adj* & *pron* many || **molto** *adv* very; quite; much; a lot; widely; long; **fra non molto** before long; **non . . . molto** (coll) not . . . at all

**momentàne·o -a** *adj* momentary

**moménto** *m* moment; opportune time; (slang) trifle; (phys) momentum; **dal momento che** since; **per il momento** for the time being; **sul momento** this very moment

**mòna·ca** *f* (**-che**) nun

**monacale** *adj* monachal, conventual

**monacato** *m* monkhood

**monachésimo** *m* monachism, monasticism

**monachina** *f* little nun; **monachine** sparks

**mòna·co** *m* (**-ci**) monk; (archit) king post || **Monaco** *m* Monaco || *f* Munich

**monar·ca** *m* (**-chi**) monarch

**monarchìa** *f* monarchy

**monàrchi·co -ca** *adj* (**-ci -che**) monarchical; monarchist(ic) (*advocating a monarch*) || *mf* monarchist

**monastèro** *m* monastery

**monàsti·co -ca** *adj* (**-ci -che**) monastic(al)

**moncherino** *m* stump (*without hand*)

**món·co -ca** (**-chi -che**) *adj* one-handed; one-armed; incomplete || *mf* cripple

**moncóne** *m* stump

**mondana** *f* prostitute

**mondani·tà** *f* (**-tà**) worldliness

**monda·no -na** *adj* mundane; worldly; society; fashionable || *m* playboy || *f* see **mondana**

**mondare** (**móndo**) *tr* to peel, pare; to thresh; to weed; to prune; (fig) to cleanse

**mondari·so** *mf* (**-so**) rice weeder

**mondez·zàio** *m* (**-zài**) dump

**mondiale** *adj* world, world-wide; (coll) stupendous

**mondìglia** *f* chaff; trash; refuse

**mondina** *f* rice weeder

**món·do da** *adj* clean-peeled; (lit) pure || *m* world; hopscotch; (coll) heap, bunch; **bel mondo** smart set; **cascasse il mondo!** (coll) come what may!; **da che mondo è mondo** since the world began; **essere nel mondo della luna** to be absent-minded; **mandare all'altro mondo** (coll) to send packing; **mettere al mondo** to give birth to; **mondo della luna** world of fancy; **un mondo** a lot; **venire al mondo** to be born || **Mondo** *m*—**Terzo Mondo** Third World

**monega·sco -sca** *adj* & *mf* (**-schi -sche**) Monacan

**monellerìa** *f* prank

**monèl·lo -la** *mf* urchin, brat || *f* romp

**monéta** *f* money; coin; piece of money; purse (*in horse races*); change; **batter moneta** to mint money; **moneta sonante** cash

**monetà·rio -ria** (**-ri -rie**) *adj* monetary || *m*—**falso monetario** counterfeiter

**monetizzare** [ddzz] *tr* to express in money; to transform into cash

**mòngo·lo -la** *adj* & *mf* Mongolian

**monile** *m* necklace; jewel

**mònito** *m* admonition, warning

**monitóre** *m* monitor

**mònna** *f* (obs) lady; (coll) monkey

**monoàlbero** *adj* *invar* (aut) single-camshaft, valve-in-head (*distribution*)

**monoaurale** *adj* monaural

**monoblòc·co** (**-co**) *adj* single-block || *m* (aut) cylinder block

**monocilìndri·co -ca** *adj* (**-ci -che**) (mach) single-cylinder

**monòco·lo -la** *adj* one-eyed || *m* monocle

**monocolóre** *adj* *invar* one-color; one-party

**monofa·se** *adj* (**-si** & **-se**) single-phase

**monogamìa** *f* monogamy

**monòga·mo -ma** *adj* monogamous || *m* monogamist

**monografìa** *f* monograph

**monogram·ma** *m* (**-mi**) monogram

**monolìti·co -ca** *adj* (**-ci -che**) monolithic

**monolito** *m* monolith

**monòlo·go** *m* (**-ghi**) monologue

**monomanìa** *f* monomania

**monò·mio** m (-mi) monomial
**monopàttino** m scooter
**monopèt·to** (-to) adj single-breasted ‖ m single-breasted suit
**monopiano** m (aer) monoplane
**monopò·lio** m (-li) monopoly
**monopolizzare** [ddzz] tr to monopolize
**monopósto** adj invar one-man ‖ m single-seater
**monorotàia** adj invar single-track ‖ f monorail
**monoscò·pio** m (-pi) (telv) test pattern
**monosìlla·bo -ba** adj monosyllabic ‖ m monosyllable
**monòssido** m monoxide
**monoteìsti·co -ca** adj (-ci -che) monotheistic
**monotipìa** f monotype
**monotipo** m monotype
**monotonìa** f monotony
**monòto·no -na** adj monotonous
**monsignóre** m monsignor
**monsóne** m monsoon
**mónta** f horseback riding; stud; jockey
**montacàri·chi** m (-chi) freight elevator
**montàg·gio** m (-gi) (mach) assembly; (mov) editing; (mov) montage
**montagna** f mountain; **montagna di ghiaccio** iceberg; **montagne russe** roller coaster
**montagnó·so -sa** [s] adj mountainous
**montana·ro -ra** adj mountain ‖ mf mountaineer
**monta·no -na** adj mountain
**montante** adj rising ‖ m riser, upright; (football) goal post; (aer) strut; (boxing) uppercut; (com) aggregate amount
**montare** (**mónto**) tr to mount; to go up (the stairs); to set (jewels); to frame (a painting); to whip (e.g., eggs); to excite; to exaggerate (news); to decorate (a house); to cover (said of a male animal); (mach) to assemble; (mov) to edit; **montare la testa a** to excite; to give a swell head to ‖ intr (ESSERE) to jump; to climb; to go up; to rise; to swell; **montare alla testa a** to go to the head of; **montare in collera** to get angry ‖ impers—**non monta** it doesn't matter, never mind
**monta·tóre -trice** mf (mach) assembler; (mov) editor
**montatura** f assembly; frame (of glasses); appliqué; setting (of gem); (journ) ballyhoo; (mov) editing; **montatura pubblicitaria** publicity stunt
**montavivan·de** m (-de) dumbwaiter
**mónte** m mountain; bank; mount (in palmistry); (cards) discard; **a monte** uphill; upstream; **andare a monte** to fail; **mandare a monte** to cause to fail; **monte di pietà** pawnbroker's; **monte di premi** pot (in a lottery)
**montenegri·no -na** adj & mf Montenegrin
**montessoria·no -na** adj Montessori
**montóne** m ram; mutton; rounded stone
**montuó·so -sa** [s] adj mountainous
**montura** f uniform

**monumentale** adj monumental
**monuménto** m monument
**moquètte** f (**moquètte**) wall-to-wall carpeting
**mòra** f mulberry; blackberry; brunette; Moorish woman; arrears; penalty (for arrears); (archaic) heap of stones
**morale** adj moral ‖ m morale; **giù di morale** downcast; **su di morale** in high spirits ‖ f morals, ethics; moral (of a fable)
**moraleggiare** §290 (**moraléggio**) intr to moralize
**moralismo** m moralism
**morali·tà** f (-tà) morality; morals
**moralizzare** [ddzz] tr & intr to moralize
**moratòria** f moratorium
**morbidézza** f softness
**mòrbi·do -da** adj soft; sleek; pliable ‖ m soft ground
**morbillo** m measles
**mòrbo** m disease; plague
**morbó·so -sa** [s] adj morbid
**mòrchia** f sediment; dregs of oil
**mordace** adj biting, mordacious
**mordènte** adj biting; (chem) mordant; (mach) interlocking ‖ s strength; (chem) mordant
**mòrdere** §200 tr to bite; to grab; to corrode; **mordere il freno** to champ the bit
**mordicchiare** §287 (**mordìcchio**) tr to nibble
**morèl·lo -la** adj blackish; black (horse) ‖ m black horse
**morènte** adj dying ‖ mf dying person
**moré·sco -sca** (-schi -sche) adj Moresque, Moorish ‖ f Moorish dance
**morét·to -ta** adj brunet ‖ m Negro boy; dark-skinned boy; chocolate-covered ice-cream bar ‖ f Negro girl; dark-skinned girl; mask; (orn) scaup duck
**morfè·ma** m (-mi) morpheme
**morfina** f morphine
**morfinòmane** mf morphine addict
**morfologìa** f morphology
**morìa** f pestilence; high mortality
**moribón·do -da** adj moribund
**morigera·to -ta** adj temperate, moderate
**morire** §201 intr (ESSERE) to die; to die out; to end (said of a street); **morire di noia** to be bored to death
**moritu·ro -ra** adj about to die, doomed
**mormóne** mf Mormon
**mormorare** (**mórmoro**) tr to murmur; to whisper ‖ intr to murmur; to whisper; to babble (said of a brook); to rustle; to gossip
**mormorì·o** m (-i) whisper; murmur
**mò·ro -ra** adj Moorish; dark-skinned; dark-brown ‖ mf Moor ‖ m mulberry tree ‖ f see **mora**
**morosi·tà** [s] f (-tà) delinquency (in paying one's bills)
**moró·so -sa** [s] adj delinquent (in paying one's bills) ‖ m (coll) boyfriend; **i morosi** (coll) the lovers ‖ f (coll) girl friend
**mòrsa** f vise; (archit) toothing
**morsétto** m clamp; (elec) binding post

morsicare §197 (mòrsico) *tr* to bite

morsicatura *f* bite

morsicchiare §287 (morsìcchio) *tr* to nibble

mòrso *m* bite; bit

mor·tàio *m* (-tài) mortar

mortale *adj* mortal; deadly || *m* mortal

mortali·tà *f* (-tà) mortality

mortarétto *m* firecracker

mòrte *f* death; end; averla a morte con to harbor hatred for; morte civile (law) attainder, loss of civil rights

mortèlla *f* myrtle

mortificare §197 (mortìfico) *tr* to mortify || *ref* to feel ashamed

mòr·to -ta *adj* dead; still (*life*); morto di fame dying of hunger; morto di paura scared to death || *mf* dead person, deceased || *m* hidden treasure; (cards) dummy, widow; fare il morto to float on one's back; to play possum; morto di fame ne'er-do-well, good-for-nothing; suonare a morto to toll

mortò·rio *m* (-ri) funeral

mortuà·rio -ria *adj* (-ri -rie) mortuary

mosài·co -ca (-ci -che) *adj* Mosaic || *m* mosaic

mó·sca *f* (-sche) fly; imperial (*beard*); mosca bianca one in a million; mosca cieca blindman's buff; fare venire la mosca al naso a to make angry || Mosca *f* Moscow

moscaiòla *f* fly netting; flytrap

moscardino *m* dandy; (zool) dormouse

moscatèl·lo -la *adj* muscat || *m* muscatel

moscato *m* muscat grape; muscat wine

moscerino *m* gnat

moschèa *f* mosque

moschettière *m* musketeer; Italian National soccer player

moschétto *m* musket

moschettóne *m* snap hook

moschici·da *adj* (-di -de) fly-killing

mó·scio -scia *adj* (-sci -sce) flabby, soft

moscóne *m* big fly; pesky suitor

moscovi·ta *adj* & *mf* (-ti -te) Muscovite

Mosè *m* Moses

mòssa *f* gesture; movement; move; fake; post; fare la mossa to sprout (*said of plants*); mossa di corpo bowel movement; prendere le mosse to begin; stare sulle mosse to be about to begin; to be eager to take off (*said of a horse*)

mossière *m* starter (*in a race*)

mòs·so -sa *adj* moved; in motion; plowed; rough (*sea*); blurred (*picture*); wavy (*hair; ground*) || *f* see mossa

mostarda *f* mustard; candied fruit

mósto *m* must

móstra *f* show; pretense, simulation; exhibit; display window; lapel; face (*of watch*); sample; (mil) insignia; (obs) military parade; far mostra di sé to show off; mettersi in mostra to show off

mostrare (móstro) *tr* to show; to put on; mostrare a dito to point to;

mostrare la corda to be threadbare || *ref* to show up; to show oneself

mostreggiatura *f* lapel; cuff

mostrina *f* (mil) insignia

móstro *m* monster

mostruó·so -sa [s] *adj* monstruous

mòta *f* mud, mire

mo·tèl *m* (-tèl) motel

motivare *tr* to cause; to justify

motivazióne *f* justification, reason

motivo *m* motive, reason; motif; theme; (coll) tune; a motivo di because of; motivo per cui wherefore

mò·to *m* (-ti) motion; movement; emotion; riot; mettere in moto to start || *f* (-to) (coll) motorcycle

motobar·ca *f* (-che) motorboat

motocannonièra *f* gunboat

motocarro *m* three-wheeler (*truck*)

motocarrozzétta *f* three-wheeler (*vehicle with sidecar*)

motociclétta *f* motorcycle

motocicli·sta *mf* (-sti -ste) motorcyclist

motocorazza·to -ta *adj* armored, panzer

motofalciatrice *f* power mower

motofurgóne *m* delivery truck

motolàn·cia *f* (-ce) motorboat, speedboat

motonàuti·co -ca (-ci -che) *adj* motorboat || *f* motorboating

motonave *f* motor ship

motopescheréc·cio *m* (-ci) motor fishing boat

mo·tóre -trice *adj* motive (*power*); (mach) drive || *m* motor; engine; car; a motore motorized, motor; motore rotativo (aut) rotary engine; primo motore prime mover || *f* see motrice

motorétta *f* motor scooter

motorino *m* small motor; motor bicycle; motorino d'avviamento (aut) starter

motori·sta *m* (-sti) mechanic

motoristi·co -ca *adj* (-ci -che) motor

motorizzare [ddzz] *tr* to motorize

motoscafo *m* motorboat; motoscafo da corsa speedboat

motosé·ga *f* (-ghe) chain saw

motosilurante *f* torpedo boat

motoveìcolo *m* motor vehicle

motovelièro *m* motor sailer

motrice *f* (rr) engine, motor; (aut) tractor; motrice a vapore steam engine

motteggiare §290 (mottéggio) *tr* to mock, jeer at || *intr* to jest

mottég·gio *m* (-gi) mockery, jest

mòtto *m* witticism; motto; (lit) word

movènte *m* stimulus, motive

movènza *f* bearing, carriage; flow (*of a sentence*); cadence

movìbile *adj* movable

movimenta·to -ta *adj* lively; eventful

moviménto *m* motion, movement; traffic; movimento di cassa cash turnover

moviòla *f* (mov) viewer and splicer

mozióne *f* motion; (lit) movement

mozzare (mózzo) *tr* to lop off; to sever; mozzare la testa a to cut off the head of

**mozzicóne** *m* stump; butt (*e.g., of cigar*)

**móz·zo -za** *adj* cut off; truncated; cropped (*ears*); docked (*tail*); hard (*breathing*) ‖ *m* cabin boy; **mozzo di stalla** stable boy

**mòzzo** [ddzz] *m* hub

**muc·ca** *f* (**-che**) milch cow

**mùc·chio** *m* (**-chi**) pile, heap; bunch

**mucillàgine** *f* mucilage

**mu·co** *m* (**-chi**) mucus, phlegm

**mucó·so -sa** [s] *adj* mucous ‖ *f* mucous membrane

**muda** *f* molt

**muffa** *f* mold; mildew; **fare la muffa** to be musty

**muffire** §176 *intr* (ESSERE) to be musty

**mùffola** *f* mitten; muffle (*of furnace*)

**muflóne** *m* mouflon

**mugghiare** §287 (**mùgghio**) *intr* to bellow; to roar

**mùggine** *m* (ichth) mullet

**muggire** §176 & (**muggo**) *intr* to moo, low; to roar; to howl

**muggito** *m* bellow; moo, low; roar

**mughétto** *m* lily of the valley

**mu·gnàio -gnàia** *mf* (**-gnài -gnàie**) miller

**mugolare** (**mùgolo**) *intr* to yelp; to moan

**mugolì·o** *m* (**-ì**) yelp; moan

**mugò·lio** *m* (**-li**) pine tar

**mugugnare** *intr* (coll) to mumble; (coll) to grumble

**mugugno** *m* (coll) grumble

**mulattière** *m* mule driver, muleteer

**mulattiè·ro -ra** *adj* mule ‖ *f* mule track

**mulat·to -ta** *adj & mf* mulatto

**muliebre** *adj* womanly, feminine

**mulinare** *tr* to twirl; to scheme ‖ *intr* to whirl; to muse; to buzz (*in the mind*)

**mulinèllo** *m* twirl; whirlpool; whirlwind; fishing reel; whirligig; **fare mulinello con** to twirl

**mulino** *m* mill; **mulino ad acqua** water mill; **mulino a vento** windmill

**mu·lo -la** *mf* mule; (slang) bastard

**multa** *f* penalty, fine

**multare** *tr* to fine

**multilaterale** *adj* multilateral, many-sided

**mùlti·plo -pla** *adj & m* multiple

**mùmmia** *f* mummy

**mummificare** §197 (**mummìfico**) *tr* to mummify

**mùngere** §183 *tr* to milk

**mungi·tóre -trice** *mf* milker ‖ *f* milking machine; milk maid

**mungitura** *f* milking

**municipale** *adj* municipal, city

**municipalizzazióne** [ddzz] *f* municipalization; city management

**munici·pio** *m* (**-pi**) municipality; city council; city hall

**munificènza** *f* munificence

**munifi·co -ca** *adj* (**-ci -che**) munificent

**munire** §176 *tr* to fortify; to provide; **munire di** to equip with ‖ *ref* to provide oneself

**munizióne** *f* (obs) fortification; **munizioni** ammunition; building supplies

**muòvere** §202 *tr* to move; to wag; to propel, run; to lift (*one's finger*); to take (*a step*); to pose (*a question*); to stir up (*laughter*); to institute (*a lawsuit*); **muovere accusa a** to reproach ‖ *intr* (ESSERE) to begin; to move, start ‖ *ref* to move; to travel; to stir; to set out; to be moved; **muoviti!** hurry up!

**mura** *fpl* see **muro**

**muràglia** *f* wall; (fig) obstacle; **muraglia cinese** Chinese Wall

**muraglióne** *m* high wall, rampart

**murale** *adj & m* mural

**murare** *tr* to wall; to wall in ‖ *intr* to build a wall; **murare a secco** to build a dry wall ‖ *ref* to close oneself in

**murata** *f* (naut) bulwark

**muratóre** *m* bricklayer, mason

**muratura** *f* bricklaying, stonework

**muriàti·co -ca** *adj* (**-ci -che**) muriatic

**mu·ro** *m* (**-ri**) wall; **muro del pianto** Wailing Wall; **muro del suono** sound barrier ‖ *m* (**-ra** *fpl*)—**mura** walls (*of a city*)

**musa** *f* muse

**muschia·to -ta** *adj* musk (*e.g., ox*)

**mù·schio** *m* (**-schi**) musk; (coll) moss

**mu·sco** *m* (**-schi**) moss

**mùscolo** *m* muscle; (fig) sinew; (coll) mussel

**muscoló·so -sa** [s] *adj* muscular

**muscó·so -sa** [s] *adj* (lit) mossy

**musèo** *m* museum

**museruòla** *f* muzzle

**musétta** *f* nose bag

**mùsi·ca** *f* (**-che**) music; band; **cambiare musica** to change one's tune

**musicale** *adj* musical

**musicante** *adj* music-playing (*angels*) ‖ *mf* band player; second-rate musician

**musicare** §197 (**mùsico**) *tr* to set to music

**musicassétta** *f* cassette, tape cartridge

**music-hall** *m* (**-hall**) *m* vaudeville, burlesque

**musici·sta** *mf* (**-sti -ste**) musician

**musicologìa** *f* musicology

**musicòlo·go** *m* (**-gi**) musicologist

**muso** *m* muzzle, snout; (coll) mug; (fig) nose; **avere il muso lungo** to make a long face; **mettere il muso** to pout

**musó·ne -na** *mf* pouter, sulker

**mussare** *tr* to publish with great fanfare (*a piece of news*) ‖ *intr* to foam (*said of wine*)

**mùssola** or **mussolina** *f* muslin

**mussolinia·no -na** *adj* of Mussolini

**mùssolo** *m* mussel

**mustàc·chio** *m* (**-chi**) shroud (*of bowsprit*); **mustacchi** moustache

**musulma·no -na** [s] *adj & mf* Moslem

**muta** *f* change; shift; molt; set (*of sails*); pack (*of hounds*); (mil) watch

**mutàbile** *adj* changeable

**mutande** *fpl* shorts, briefs, drawers

**mutandine** *fpl* panties; **mutandine da bagno** trunks

**mutare** *tr, intr* (ESSERE) & *ref* to change

**mutazióne** *f* mutation; (biol) mutation, sport

**mutévole** *adj* changeable; fickle

**mutilare** (mùtilo) *tr* to mutilate, maim
**mutila·to -ta** *adj* mutilated ‖ *mf* cripple; amputee; **mutilato di guerra** disabled veteran
**mutismo** *m* silence, willful silence; (pathol) dumbness
**mu·to -ta** *adj* mute; dumb; silent (*movie*); unexpressed ‖ *mf* mute ‖ *f* see **muta**
**mùtria** *f* sulking attitude; proud demeanor

**mùtua** *f* mutual benefit society; medical insurance; **mettersi in mutua** to go on sick leave
**mutuali·tà** *f* (-tà) mutuality; mutual benefit institutions
**mutuare** (mùtuo) *tr* to borrow; to lend
**mutua·to -ta** *mf* person insured by mutual benefit society; person insured by medical insurance
**mù·tuo -tua** *adj* mutual; borrowing ‖ *m* loan ‖ *f* see **mutua**

# N

**N, n** ['ɛnne] *m & f* twelfth letter of the Italian alphabet
**nababbo** *m* nabob
**Nabucodònosor** *m* Nebuchadnezzar
**nàcchera** *f* castanet
**nafta** *f* crude oil; naphta; Diesel oil
**naftalina** *f* naphthalene
**nàia** *f* cobra; (slang) army discipline; (slang) military service
**nàiade** *f* naiad
**nàilon** *m* nylon
**nanna** *f* sleep (*of child*); **fare la nanna** to sleep (*said of child*)
**na·no -na** *adj & mf* dwarf
**nàpalm** *m* napalm
**napoleòne** *m* napoleon (*gold coin*) ‖ **Napoleone** *m* Napoleon
**napoleòni·co -ca** *adj* (-ci -che) Napoleonic
**napoleta·no -na** *adj & mf* Neapolitan ‖ *f* espresso coffee machine
**Nàpoli** *f* Naples
**nappa** tassel; tuft; kid (*leather*)
**narciso** *m* narcissus
**narcòti·co -ca** *adj & m* (-ci -che) narcotic
**narcotizzare** [ddzz] *tr* to drug, dope; to anesthetize
**narghi·lè** *m* (-lè) hookah
**narice** *f* nostril
**narrare** *tr* to narrate, tell, recount
**narrati·vo -va** *adj* narrative; fictional ‖ *f* narrative; fiction
**narra·tóre -trice** *mf* narrator, storyteller
**narrazióne** *f* narration; tale, story; narrative
**nasale** [s] *adj & f* nasal
**nascènte** *adj* nascent; budding; rising (*sun*); dawning (*day*)
**nàscere** *m* beginning, origin ‖ §203 *intr* (ESSERE) to be born; to bud; to shoot; to dawn; to rise; to spring up; **nascere con la camicia** to be born with a silver spoon in one's mouth
**nàscita** *f* birth; birthday; origin
**nascitu·ro -ra** *adj* unborn, future ‖ *mf* unborn child
**nascóndere** §204 *tr* to hide; **nascondere a** to hide from ‖ *ref* to hide; to lurk
**nascondì·glio** *m* (-gli) hiding place; hideout; cache
**nascondino** *m* hide-and-seek; **giocare a nascondino** to play hide-and-seek
**nascó·sto -sta** *adj* hidden, concealed; secret; **di nascosto** secretly

**nasèllo** [s] *m* catch (*of latch*); (ichth) hake
**nasièra** [s] *f* nose ring
**naso** [s] *m* nose; (fig) face; **aver buon naso** to have a keen sense of smell; **ficcare il naso negli affari degli altri** to pry into the affairs of others; **menare per il naso** to lead by the nose; **naso adunco** hooknose; **restare con un palmo di naso** to be duped
**nassa** *f* pot (*for fishing*); **nassa per aragoste** lobster pot
**nastrino** *m* ribbon; badge
**nastro** *m* ribbon; band; tape; streamer; tape measure; **nastro del cappello** hatband; **nastro isolante** friction tape; **nastro per capelli** hair ribbon
**nastùr·zio** *m* (-zi) nasturtium
**natale** *adj* native, natal ‖ **natali** *mpl* birth; birthday; **dare i natali a** to be the birthplace of ‖ **Natale** *m* Christmas
**natali·tà** *f* (-tà) birth rate
**natalì·zio -zia** (-zi -zie) *adj* natal; Christmas ‖ *m* birthday
**natante** *adj* swimming; floating ‖ *m* craft
**natató·rio -ria** *adj* (-ri -rie) swimming
**nàti·ca** *f* (-che) buttock
**nati·o -a** *adj* (-i -e) (poet) native
**nativi·tà** *f* (-tà) birth, nativity ‖ **Natività** *f* Nativity
**nati·vo -va** *adj* native; natural, inborn ‖ *mf* native
**N.A.T.O.** *f* (acronym) (**North Atlantic Treaty Organization**)—**la N.A.T.O.** NATO
**na·to -ta** *adj* born; **nata** née; **nato e sputato** the spit and image of; **nato morto** stillborn ‖ *mf* child
**natura** *f* nature; **natura morta** still life; **in natura** in kind
**naturale** *adj* natural ‖ *m* nature, disposition; **al naturale** life-size
**naturalézza** *f* naturalness; spontaneity
**naturalismo** *m* naturalism
**naturali·sta** *mf* (-sti -ste) naturalist
**naturali·tà** *f* (-tà) naturalization
**naturalizzare** [ddzz] *tr* to naturalize ‖ *ref* to become naturalized
**naturalizzazióne** [ddzz] *f* naturalization
**naturalménte** *adv* naturally; of course
**naufragare** §209 (nàufrago) *intr* (ESSERE

**& AVERE)** to be shipwrecked; to sink, to fail

**naufrà·gio** *m* (**-gi**) shipwreck; failure

**nàufra·go -ga** (**-ghi -ghe**) *adj* shipwrecked || *mf* shipwrecked person; (fig) outcast

**nàusea** *f* nausea; disgust; **avere la nausea** to be sick at one's stomach

**nauseabón·do -da** *adj* sickening, nauseating; (fig) unsavory

**nauseante** *adj* sickening, nauseous

**nauseare** (**nàuseo**) *tr* to nauseate, sicken

**nausea·to -ta** *adj* sickened, disgusted

**nàuti·co -ca** (**-ci -che**) *adj* nautical || *f* sailing, navigation

**navale** *adj* naval, navy, sea

**navata** *f* nave; **navata centrale** nave; **navata laterale** aisle

**nave** *f* ship, vessel, boat; craft; **nave ammiraglia** flagship; **nave a motore** motorboat; **nave appoggio** tender; **nave a vela** sailboat; **nave da carico** freighter; **nave da guerra** warship; **nave petroliera** tanker; **nave portaerei** aircraft carrier; **nave rompighiaccio** icebreaker; **nave traghetto** ferryboat

**navétta** *f* shuttle; **fare la navetta to** shuttle

**navicèlla** *f* nacelle, cabin (*of airship*); car (*of balloon*)

**navigàbile** *adj* navigable

**navigabili·tà** *f* (**-tà**) navigability; seaworthiness

**navigante** *adj* sailing || *m* sailor

**navigare** §209 (**nàvigo**) *tr & intr* to navigate, to sail

**naviga·to -ta** *adj* seawise; wordly-wise

**naviga·tóre -trice** *mf* navigator

**navigazióne** *f* navigation

**navì·glio** *m* (**-gli**) ship, craft, boat; fleet; navy; canal; **naviglio mercantile** merchant marine

**nazionale** *adj* national || *f* national team

**nazionalismo** *m* nationalism

**nazionali·sta** *mf* (**-sti -ste**) nationalist

**nazionalìsti·co -ca** *adj* (**-ci -che**) nationalistic

**nazionali·tà** *f* (**-tà**) nationality

**nazionalizzare** [ddzz] *tr* to nationalize

**nazionalizzazióne** [ddzz] *f* nationalization

**nazióne** *f* nation

**nazi·sta** *adj & mf* (**-sti -ste**) Nazi

**nazzarè·no -na** [ddzz] *adj & mf* Nazarene || **il Nazzareno** the Nazarene

**ne** §5 *pron & adv*

**né** *conj* neither, nor; **né . . . né** neither . . . nor

**neanche** *adv* not even; nor; not . . . either

**nébbia** *f* fog, haze, mist; **fa nebbia** it is foggy; **nebbia artificiale** smoke screen

**nebbióne** *m* thick fog, pea soup

**nebbió·so -sa** [s] *adj* foggy, hazy, misty

**nebulare** *adj* nebular

**nebulizzare** [ddzz] *tr* to atomize

**nebulizzatóre** [ddzz] *m* atomizer

**nebulósa** [s] *f* nebula

**nebulosi·tà** [s] *f* (**-tà**) fogginess, haziness, mistiness

**nebuló·so -sa** [s] *adj* foggy, hazy, misty || *f* see **nebulosa**

**néces·saire** *m* (**-saire**) vanity case; sewing kit

**necessariaménte** *adv* necessarily

**necessà·rio -ria** (**-ri -rie**) *adj* necessary, needed; essential || *m* necessity; necessities (*of life*)

**necessi·tà** *f* (**-tà**) necessity; need, want; **di necessità** necessarily

**necessitare** (**necèssito**) *tr* to require; to force || *intr* to be in want; to be necessary; **necessitare di** to need

**necrologìa** *f* necrology, obituary

**necrològi·co -ca** *adj* (**-ci -che**) obituary

**necromanzìa** *f* necromancy

**necròsi** *f* necrosis, gangrene

**nefan·do -da** *adj* heinous, nefarious

**nefa·sto -sta** *adj* ill-fated; ominous

**nefrite** *f* nephritis

**negare** §209 (**négo & nègo**) *tr* to deny, negate; to refuse

**negati·vo -va** *adj & f* negative

**nega·to -ta** *adj* unfit, unsuited

**negazióne** *f* negation, denial; (gram) negative

**neghittó·so -sa** [s] *adj* lazy, slothful

**neglèt·to -ta** *adj* neglected; untidy

**négli** §4

**negligènte** *adj* negligent, careless

**negligènza** *f* negligence, carelessness; dereliction (*of duty*)

**neglìgere** §205 *tr* to neglect

**negoziàbile** *adj* negotiable

**negoziante** *mf* merchant, shopkeeper; dealer; **negoziante all'ingrosso** wholesaler; **negoziante al minuto** retailer; shopkeeper, storekeeper

**negoziare** §287 (**negòzio**) *tr* to negotiate, transact || *intr* to negotiate, deal

**negoziati** *mpl* negotiations

**negozia·tóre -trice** *mf* negotiator

**negò·zio** *m* (**-zi**) business; transaction; store, shop; **negozio di cancelleria** stationery store

**negrière** *m* slave trader; slave driver

**negriè·ro -ra** *adj* slave || *m* slave trader; slave driver

**né·gro -gra** *adj & mf* Negro

**negromante** *m* sorcerer

**néi** §4

**nél** §4

**nélla** §4

**nélle** §4

**néllo** §4

**némbo** *m* rain cloud; cloud (*e.g., of dust*)

**Nembròd** *m* Nimrod

**nèmesi** *f invar* nemesis || **Nemesi** *f* Nemesis

**nemi·co -ca** (**-ci -che**) *adj* inimical, hostile, unfriendly; enemy; (fig) adverse || *mf* enemy, foe; **Il Nemico** the Evil One

**nemméno** *adv* not even; nor; not . . . either

**nènia** *f* funeral dirge; lamentation

**nenùfaro** *m* water lily

**nèo** *m* mole (*on the skin*); flaw, blemish; neon; beauty spot

**neoclassicheggiante** *adj* in the direction of the neoclassical

**neòfi·ta** *mf* (**-ti -te**) neophite
**neolati·no -na** *adj* Neo-Latin, Romance
**neologismo** *m* neologism
**neomicina** *f* neomycin
**nèon** *m* neon
**neona·to -ta** *adj* newborn ‖ *mf* infant, baby; newborn child
**neozelandése** [dz] [s] *adj* New Zealand ‖ *mf* New Zealander
**nepènte** *f* nepenthe
**Nepóte** *m* Nepos
**neppure** *adv* not even; nor; not . . . either
**nequìzia** *f* iniquity, wickedness
**nera·stro -stra** *adj* blackish
**nerbata** *f* heavy blow
**nèrbo** *m* whip; sinew; bulk; strength (*of an opposing force*)
**nerboru·to -ta** *adj* muscular, sinewy
**nereggiare** §290 (**neréggio**) *intr* to look black; to be blackish
**nerétto** *m* (*typ*) boldface
**né·ro -ra** *adj* black; dark; gloomy; dark-red (*wine*) ‖ *mf* black; Negro ‖ *m* black
**nerofumo** *m* lampblack
**Neróne** *m* Nero
**nervatura** *f* ribbing
**nervi·no -na** *adj* nerve (*gas*); nervine (*medicine*)
**nèrvo** *m* nerve; sinew; **avere i nervi** to be in a bad mood
**nervosismo** [s] *m* nervousness, irritability
**nervó·so -sa** [s] *adj* nervous, irritable; sinewy, vigorous (*style*) ‖ *m* bad mood; **avere il nervoso** to be in a bad mood
**nèsci** *m*—**fare il nesci** to feign ignorance
**nèspola** *f* medlar; **nespole** (coll) blows
**nèspolo** *m* medlar tree
**nèsso** *m* connection, link; **avere nesso** to cohere
**nessu·no -na** *adj* no, not any ‖ **nessuno** *pron* nobody, no one; none; not anybody; not anyone; **nessuno dei due** neither one
**nettapén·ne** *m* (**-ne**) penwiper
**nettare** (**nétto**) *tr* to clean, to cleanse
**nèttare** *m* nectar
**nettézza** *f* cleanness, cleanliness; neatness; **nettezza urbana** department of sanitation; garbage collection
**nét·to -ta** *adj* clean; clear; sharp; net ‖ **netto** *adv* clearly, distinctly
**nettùnio** *m* neptunium
**Nettuno** *m* Neptune
**netturbino** *m* street cleaner
**neurologìa** *f* neurology
**neuró·si** *f* (**-si**) neurosis
**neuròti·co -ca** *adj* (**-ci -che**) neurotic
**neutrale** *adj* & *mf* neutral
**neutrali·sta** *adj* & *mf* (**-sti -ste**) neutralist
**neutrali·tà** *f* (**-tà**) neutrality
**neutralizzare** [ddzz] *tr* to neutralize
**nèu·tro -tra** *adj* neuter; neutral
**neutróne** *m* neutron
**ne·vàio** *m* (**-vài**) snowfield; snowdrift
**néve** *f* snow; **neve carbonica** dry ice
**nevicare** §197 (**névica**) *impers* (ESSERE) —**nevica** it is snowing

**nevicata** *f* snowfall
**nevìschio** *m* sleet
**nevó·so -sa** [s] *adj* snowy
**nevralgìa** *f* neuralgia
**nevrastèni·co -ca** *adj* & *mf* (**-ci -che**) neurasthenic
**nevvéro** (i.e., **n'è vero** for **non è vero**) see **non**
**niacina** *f* niacin
**nìb·bio** *m* (**-bi**) (orn) kite
**nìcchia** *f* niche; nook, recess
**nicchiare** §287 (**nìcchio**) *intr* to waver
**nìc·chio** *m* (**-chi**) shell; nook
**nichel** *m* nickel
**nichelare** (**nìchelo**) *tr* to nickel, to nickel-plate
**nichelatura** *f* nickel-plating
**nichelino** *m* nickel (*coin*)
**nichèlio** *m* var of **nichel**
**Nicòla** *m* Nicholas
**nicotina** *f* nicotine
**nidiata** *f* nestful; brood
**nidificare** §197 (**nidìfico**) *intr* to build a nest, to nest
**nido** *m* nest; home; nursery; den (*of thieves*)
**niènte** *m* nothing; nothingness; **dal niente** from scratch; **di niente** you're welcome ‖ *pron* nothing; not . . . anything; **quasi niente** next to nothing
**nientediméno** *adv* no less, nothing less
**Nilo** *m* Nile
**ninfa** *f* nymph
**ninfèa** *f* white water lily
**ninnananna** *f* lullaby, cradlesong
**nìnnolo** *m* toy; trinket
**nipóte** *mf* grandchild ‖ *m* grandson; nephew; **nipoti** descendants ‖ *f* granddaughter; niece
**nippòni·co -ca** *adj* (**-ci -che**) Nipponese
**nirvana, il** nirvana
**nìti·do -da** *adj* clear, distinct
**nitóre** *m* brightness; elegance
**nitrato** *m* nitrate
**nitrire** §176 *intr* to neigh
**nitrito** *m* neigh; (chem) nitrite
**nitro** *m* niter; **nitro del Cile** Chile saltpeter
**nitroglicerina** *f* nitroglycerin
**nitruro** *m* nitride
**niu·no -na** *adj* (poet) var of **nessuno**
**nìve·o -a** *adj* snow-white
**Nizza** *f* Nice
**no** *adv* no; not; **come no?** why not; certainly; **dire di no** to say no; **no?** is it not so?; **non dir di no** to consent; **proprio no** certainly not
**nòbile** *adj* noble; second (*floor*) ‖ *m* nobleman ‖ *f* noblewoman
**nobiliare** *adj* noble, of nobility
**nobilitare** (**nobìlito**) *tr* to ennoble
**nobil·tà** *f* (**-tà**) nobility
**nòc·ca** *f* (**-che**) knuckle
**nocchière** *m* or **nocchièro** *m* petty officer; (poet) pilot, helmsman
**nocchieru·to -ta** *adj* knotty
**nòc·chio** *m* (**-chi**) knot (*in wood*)
**nocciòla** *adj invar* hazel (*in color*) ‖ *f* hazelnut; filbert
**nocciolina** *f* little nut; **nocciolina americana** peanut; roasted peanut
**nòcciolo** *m* stone, pit, kernel; **il noc-**

**ciolo della questione** the crux of the matter

**nocciòlo** m hazel (tree); filbert (tree)

**nóce** m walnut tree ‖ f walnut (fruit); **noce del collo** Adam's apple; **noce di cocco** coconut; **noce di vitello** filet of veal; **noce moscata** nutmeg

**nocévole** adj harmful

**noci·vo -va** adj harmful, detrimental

**nòdo** m knot; crux, gist (of a question); junction; lump (in one's throat); (naut) knot; (phys) node; **lì è il nodo** there's the rub; **nodo d'amore** true-love knot; **nodo ferroviario** rail center, junction; **nodo scorsoio** noose; **nodo stradale** highway center, crossroads

**nodó·so -sa** [s] adj knotty

**Noè** m Noah

**noi** §5 pron pers we; us; **noi altri we,** e.g., **noi altri italiani** we Italians

**nòia** f boredom; bother, trouble; bug (in a motor); **venire a noia** (with dat) to weary; **dar noia** (with dat) to bother

**noial·tri -tre** pron we; us; **noialtri italiani** we Italians

**noió·so -sa** [s] adj boring, annoying

**noleggiare** §290 (**noléggio**) tr to rent; to hire, to charter ‖ ref—**si noleggia, si noleggiano** for rent

**noleggiatóre** m hirer; lessor (e.g., of a car)

**nolég·gio** m (-gi) rent, lease; car rental; chartering; freightage

**nolènte** adj unwilling

**nòlo** m rent, hire; **a nolo** for hire

**nòmade** adj nomad, nomadic ‖ mf nomad

**nóme** m name; fame; reputation; (gram) noun; **a nome di** on behalf of; **in nome di** in the name of; **nome commerciale** firm name; **nome depositato** registered name; **nome di battesimo** Christian name; **nome e cognome** full name

**nomèa** f name, reputation; notoriety

**nomìgnolo** m nickname; **affibbiare un nomignolo a** to nickname

**nòmina** f appointment; **di prima nomina** newly appointed

**nominale** adj nominal; noun

**nominare** (**nòmino**) tr to name, call; to mention; to elect; to appoint

**nominati·vo -va** adj nominative; with names in alphabetical order; (fin) registered ‖ m nominative; name; model number

**non** adv no, not; none, e.g., **non troppo presto** none too soon; **non appena** as soon as; **non c'è di che** you are welcome; **non . . . che** but, only; **non è vero?** is it not so?, isn't it so? La traduzione in inglese di questa domanda dipende generalmente dalla proposizione che la precede. Se la proposizione è affermativa, l'interrogazione sarà negativa, p.es. **Lei mi scriverà, non è vero?** You will write me. Won't you? Se la proposizione è negativa, l'interrogazione sarà positiva, p.es. **Lei non beve birra, non è**

**vero?** You do not drink beer. Do you? Se il soggetto della proposizione è un nome sostantivo, sarà rappresentato nell'interrogazione da un pronome personale, p.es. **Giovanni ha finito, non è vero?** John has finished. Hasn't he?

**nonagenà·rio -ria** adj & mf (-ri -rie) nonagenarian

**nonagèsi·mo -ma** adj, pron & m ninetieth

**nonconformi·sta** mf (-sti -ste) nonconformist

**noncurante** adj careless, indifferent

**noncuranza** f carelessness, indifference

**nondiméno** conj yet, nevertheless

**nòn·no -na** mf grandparent ‖ m grandfather ‖ f grandmother

**nonnulla** m invar nothing, trifle

**nò·no -na** adj, m & pron ninth

**nonostante** prep in spite of, notwithstanding; **nonostante che** although, even though

**nonpertanto** adv nevertheless, still, yet

**non plus ultra** m ne plus ultra, acme

**nonsènso** m nonsense

**non so ché** adj invar indefinable ‖ m invar something indefinable

**nontiscordardi·mé** m (-mé) forget-me-not

**nòrd** m north

**nòrdi·co -ca** (-ci -che) adj Nordic; northern, north ‖ mf northerner

**nòrma** f rule, regulation; **a norma di legge** according to law; **per Sua norma** for your guidance

**normale** adj normal; normative; perpendicular ‖ f perpendicular line

**normali·tà** f (-tà) normality, normalcy

**normalizzare** [ddzz] tr to normalize, to standardize

**Normandìa, la** Normandy

**norman·no -na** adj & mf Norman ‖ m Norseman

**normati·vo -va** adj normative ‖ f normativeness

**normògrafo** m stencil

**norvegése** [s] adj & mf Norwegian

**Norvègia, la** Norway

**nosocò·mio** m (-mi) hospital

**nossignóra** (i.e., no signora) adv no, Madam

**nossignóre** (i.e., no signore) adv no, Sir

**nostalgìa** f nostalgia, longing; homesickness

**nostàlgi·co -ca** (-ci -che) adj nostalgic; homesick ‖ m worshiper of the good old days (esp. of Fascism)

**nostra·no -na** adj domestic, national; home-grown; regional

**nò·stro -stra** §6 adj & pron poss

**nostròmo** m boatswain

**nòta** f mark; score; memorandum; list; bill, invoice; report (on a subordinate); (mus) note; **note caratteristiche** personal folder, efficiency report (of an employee); **prender nota di** to take down

**notàbile** adj notable, noteworthy ‖ m notable

**no·tàio** m (-tài) notary (public); lawyer

**notare** (nòto) *tr* to mark, check; to note, to jot down; to observe; to bring out; **farsi notare** to attract attention, make oneself conspicuous; **nota bene** note well, take notice

**notariale** or **notarile** *adj* notarial

**notazióne** *f* notation; annotation; observation

**nò·tes** *m* (-tes) notebook

**notévole** *adj* noteworthy, remarkable

**notìfi·ca** *f* (-che) notification, notice; service (*e.g., of a summons*)

**notificare** §197 (**notìfico**) *tr* to report; to serve (*a summons*); to declare ..(*e.g., one's income*)

**notificazióne** *f* notification, notice; service (*e.g., of a summons*)

**notìzia** *f* knowledge; report; piece of news; **aver notizie di** to hear from; **notizie** news; **una notizia** a news item

**notizià·rio** *m* (-ri) news; news report, news bulletin; (rad) newscast; **notiziario sportivo** sports page; (rad, telv) sports news

**nò·to** -ta *adj* known, well-known ‖ *m* south wind; (coll) swimming ‖ *f* see **nota**

**notorie·tà** *f* (-tà) general knowledge; affidavit; notoriety

**notò·rio** -ria *adj* (-ri -rie) well-known

**nottàmbu·lo** -la *adj* nighttime; night-wandering ‖ *mf* nightwalker; night owl

**nottata** *f* night; **far nottata bianca** to spend a sleepless night

**nòtte** *f* night; **buona notte** good night; **di notte** at night, by night, in the nighttime; **la notte di lunedì** Sunday night; Monday night; **lunedì notte** Monday night; **notte bianca** sleepless night; **notte di San Silvestro** New Year's Eve; watch night

**nottetèmpo** *adv*—**di nottetempo** at night, in the nighttime

**nòttola** *f* wooden latch; (zool) bat

**nottolino** *m* small wooden latch; ratchet, catch

**nottur·no** -na *adj* nocturnal, night ‖ *m* nocturne

**novanta** *adj, m & pron* ninety

**novantènne** *adj* ninety-year-old ‖ *mf* ninety-year-old person

**novantèsi·mo** -ma *adj, m & pron* ninetieth

**novantina** *f* about ninety; **sulla novantina** about ninety years old

**nòve** *adj & pron* nine; **le nove** nine o'clock ‖ *m* nine; ninth (*in dates*)

**novecentismo** *m* twentieth-century arts and letters

**novecenti·sta** (-sti -ste) *adj* twentieth-century ‖ *mf* artist of the twentieth century

**novecènto** *adj, m & pron* nine hundred ‖ **il Novecento** the twentieth century

**novèlla** *f* short story; (poet) news

**novelliè·re** -ra *mf* storyteller; short-story writer

**novelli·no** -na *adj* early, tender; inexperienced, green

**novellìstica** *f* storytelling; fiction

**novèl·lo** -la *adj* fresh, young, tender; new ‖ *f* see **novella**

**novèmbre** *m* November

**novenà·rio** -ria *adj* (-ri -rie) nine-syllable

**noverare** (nòvero) *tr* to count; to enumerate; (poet) to remember

**nòvero** *m* number; class

**novilù·nio** *m* (-ni) new moon

**novìssi·mo** -ma *adj* (lit) last, newest

**novi·tà** *f* (-tà) newness, originality; novelty, innovation; latest idea; late news

**noviziato** *m* novitiate; apprenticeship

**novì·zio** -zia (-zi -zie) *mf* novice; apprentice ‖ *f* novice (*in a convent*)

**novocaina** *f* novocaine

**nozióne** *f* notion, conception

**nòzze** *fpl* wedding, marriage; **nozze d'argento** silver wedding; **nozze d'oro** golden wedding

**nube** *f* cloud

**nubifrà·gio** *m* (-gi) cloudburst

**nùbile** *adj* unmarried, single (*woman*); marriageable ‖ *f* unmarried girl

**nu·ca** *f* (-che) nape of the neck, scruff

**nucleare** *adj* nuclear

**nùcleo** *m* nucleus; group; (elec) core

**nudismo** *m* nudism

**nudi·sta** *adj & mf* (-sti -ste) nudist

**nudi·tà** *f* (-tà) nudity, nakedness

**nu·do** -da *adj* naked, bare; barren; simple; **mettere a nudo** to lay bare; **nudo e crudo** stark-naked; destitute ‖ *m* nude

**nùgolo** *m* cloud; throng, swarm

**nulla** *pron* nothing ‖ *m invar* nothing; nothingness

**nulla òsta** *m* permission; visa

**nullatenènte** *adj* poor ‖ *mf* have-not

**nullificare** §197 (**nullìfico**) *tr* to nullify

**nulli·tà** *f* (-tà) nothingness; nonentity; invalidity (*of a document*)

**nul·lo** -la *adj* void, worthless ‖ **nullo** *pron* (poet) none, no one ‖ **nulla** *m & pron* see **nulla**

**nume** *m* divinity, deity

**numerare** (**nùmero**) *tr* to number

**numeratóre** *m* numerator; numbering machine

**numèri·co** -ca *adj* (-ci -che) numerical

**nùmero** *m* number; lottery ticket; size (*of shoes*); **numero dispari** odd number; **numero legale** quorum; **numero pari** even number

**numeró·so** -sa [s] *adj* numerous, large; harmonious

**nùn·zio** *m* (-zi) nuncio; (poet) news

**nuòcere** §206 *intr* to be harmful; (with *dat*) to harm

**nuòra** *f* daughter-in-law

**nuotare** (nuòto) *intr* to swim; to float; to wallow (*in wealth*)

**nuotata** *f* swim, dip, plunge

**nuota·tóre** -trice *mf* swimmer

**nuòto** *m* swimming; **gettarsi a nuoto** to jump into the water; **traversare a nuoto** to swim across

**nuòva** *f* news; late news

**Nuòva York** *f* New York
**Nuova Zelanda, la** [dz] New Zealand
**nuòvo** **-va** *adj* new; **di nuovo** again; **nuovo di zecca** brand-new; **nuovo fiammante** brand-new; **nuovo venuto** new arrival || *m*—**il nuovo** the new || *f* see **nuova**
**nùtria** *f* coypu
**nutrice** *f* wet nurse; (lit) provider
**nutriènte** *adj* nourishing
**nutriménto** *m* nourishment
**nutrire** §176 & (**nutro**) *tr* to nourish;

to nurture; to harbor (*e.g.*, *hatred*) || *ref*—**nutrirsi di** to feed on or upon
**nutriti·vo** **-va** *adj* nutritious, nutritive
**nutri·to** **-ta** *adj* well-fed; strong; rich (*food*); brisk, heavy (*gunfire*)
**nutrizióne** *f* nutrition; food
**nùvo·lo** **-la** *adj* cloudy || *m* cloudy weather; (lit) cloud; (fig) swarm || *f* cloud
**nuvoló·so** **-sa** [s] *adj* cloudy
**nuziale** *adj* wedding, nuptial
**nuzialità** *f* marriage rate

# O

**O, o** [o] *m* & *f* thirteenth letter of the Italian alphabet
**o** *conj* or; now; **o . . . o** either . . . or; whether . . . or || *interj* oh!
**ò·si** *f* (**-si**) oasis
**obbediènte** *adj* var of **ubbidiente**
**obbediènza** *f* obedience
**obbedire** §176 *tr & intr* var of **ubbidire**
**obbiettare** (**obbiètto**) *tr & intr* var of **obiettare**
**obbligare** §209 (**òbbligo**) *tr* to oblige; to compel, to force || *ref* to obligate oneself
**obbligatìssi·mo** **-ma** *adj* much obliged
**obbligatò·rio** **-ria** *adj* (**-ri** **-rie**) compulsory, obligatory
**obbligazióne** *f* obligation; burden; (com) debenture, bond
**obbligazioni·sta** *mf* (**-sti** **-ste**) bondholder
**òbbli·go** *m* (**-ghi**) obligation; duty; **d'obbligo** obligatory, mandatory; **fare d'obbligo a qlcu** + *inf* to be necessary for s.o. to + *inf*, *e.g.*, **gli fa d'obbligo lavorare** it is necessary for him to work
**obbrò·brio** *m* (**-bri**) opprobrium, disgrace; **obbrobri** insults
**obbrobrió·so** **-sa** [s] *adj* opprobrious, disgraceful
**obeli·sco** *m* (**-schi**) obelisk
**obera·to** **-ta** *adj* overburdened
**obesità** *f* obesity
**obè·so** **-sa** *adj* obese, stout
**òbice** *m* howitzer
**obiettare** (**obiètto**) *tr & intr* to argue; to object
**obietti·vo** **-va** *adj & m* objective
**obiettóre** *m* objector; **obiettore di coscienza** conscientious objector
**obiezióne** *f* objection
**obitò·rio** *m* (**-ri**) morgue
**oblare** (**òblo**) *tr* to willingly pay (*a fine*)
**obla·tóre** **-trice** *mf* donor
**oblazióne** *f* donation; (eccl) oblation; (law) payment of a fine
**obliare** §119 *tr* (lit) to forget
**oblì·o** *m* (**-i**) (lit) oblivion
**oblì·quo** **-qua** *adj* oblique
**obliterare** (**oblìtero**) *tr to* obliterate, cancel
**o·blò** *m* (**-blò**) (naut) porthole; **oblò di accesso** door (*of space capsule*)

**oblun·go** **-ga** *adj* (**-ghi** **-ghe**) oblong
**òbo·e** *m* (**-e**) oboe
**oboi·sta** *mf* (**-sti** **-ste**) oboist
**òbolo** *m* mite
**ò·ca** *f* (**-che**) goose; gander
**ocarina** *f* ocarina, sweet potato
**occasionale** *adj* chance; immediate (*cause*)
**occasionare** (**occasióno**) *tr* to occasion
**occasióne** *f* occasion; opportunity; ground, pretext; bargain; **all'occasione** on occasion; **d'occasione** second-hand; occasional (*verses*)
**occhiàia** *f* eye socket; **occhiaie** rings under the eyes
**occhia·làio** *m* (**-lài**) optician
**occhiale** *adj* eye, ocular || **occhiali** *mpl* glasses; goggles; **occhiali antisole** sunglasses; **occhiali a stringinaso** nose glasses
**occhialétto** *m* lorgnon; monocle
**occhiata** *f* glance
**occhieggiare** §290 (**occhiéggio**) *tr* to eye || *intr* to peep
**occhièllo** *m* buttonhole; boutonniere; eyelet; half title; subhead
**occhièra** *f* eyecup
**òc·chio** *m* (**-chi**) eye; speck of grease (*in soup*); handle (*of scissors*); ring (*of stirrup*); (typ) face; (fig) bit; **a occhio e croce** at a rough guess; **a quattr'occhi** in private; **battere gli occhi** to blink; **cavarsi gli occhi** to strain one's eyes; **dar nell'occhio** to attract attention; **di buon occhio** favorably; **fare l'occhio a** to get used to; **fare tanto d'occhi** to be amazed, to open one's eyes wide; **lasciare gli occhi su** to covet; **non chiudere un occhio** not to sleep a wink; **occhio!** watch out!; **occhio della testa** outrageous price; **occhio di bue** (naut) porthole; **occhio di cubia** (naut) hawsehole; **occhio di pavone** (zool) peacock butterfly; **occhio di triglia** sheep's eyes; **occhio pesto** black eye; **occhio pollino** corn (*on toes*); **tenere d'occhio** to keep an eye on
**occhiolino** *m* small eye; **far l'occhiolino** to wink
**occidentale** *adj* western, occidental
**occidènte** *adj* (poet) setting (*sun*) || *m* west, occident

occìpite *m* occipital bone
occlusióne *f* occlusion
occlusi·vo -va *adj & f* occlusive
occlu·so -sa *adj* occluded
occorrènte *adj* necessary ‖ *m* necessary; (lit) occurrence
occorrènza *f* necessity; all'occorrenza if need be
occórrere §139 *intr* (ESSERE) to happen; (with *dat*) to need, e.g., gli occorre dell'olio he needs oil ‖ *impers* (ESSERE)—occorre it is necessary
occultaménto *m* concealment
occultare *tr & ref* to hide
occul·to -ta *adj* occult; (lit) hidden
occupante *adj* occupying ‖ *m* occupant
occupare (òccupo) *tr* to occupy; to employ ‖ *ref* to take employment; occuparsi di to busy oneself with, to mind; to attend to
occupa·to -ta *adj* occupied; busy
occupazionale *adj* occupational
occupazióne *f* occupation
oceàni·co -ca *adj* (-ci -che) oceanic
ocèano *m* ocean
òcra *f* ocher
oculare *adj* ocular; see testimone ‖ *m* eyepiece
oculatézza *f* circumspection, prudence
ocula·to -ta *adj* circumspect, prudent
oculi·sta *mf* (-sti -ste) oculist
od *conj* or
odali·sca *f* (-sche) odalisque
òde *f* ode
odepòri·co -ca (-ci -che) *adj* (lit) travel ‖ *m* (lit) travelogue
odiare §287 (òdio) *tr* to hate
odièr·no -na *adj* today's, current
ò·dio *m* (-di) hatred; avere in odio to hate; essere in odio a to be hated by
odió·so -sa [s] *adj* hateful, odious
odissèa *f* odyssey ‖ Odissèa *f* Odyssey
Odissèo *m* Odysseus
odontoia·tra *mf* (-tri -tre) doctor of dental surgery, dentist
odontoiatrìa *f* odontology, dentistry
odorare (odóro) *tr & intr* to smell
odora·to -ta *adj* (poet) fragrant ‖ *m* smell
odóre *m* smell, odor, scent; cattivo odore bad odor; odori herbs, spice
odoró·so -sa [s] *adj* odorous, fragrant
offèndere §148 *tr & intr* to offend ‖ *ref* to take offense
offensi·vo -va *adj & f* offensive
offensóre *m* offender
offerènte *mf* bidder; miglior offerente highest bidder
offèrta *f* offer; offering, donation; (at an auction) bid; (com) supply
offésa [s] *f* offense; wrongdoing; ravage (*of time*); da offesa (mil) offensive; recarsi a offesa qlco to regard s.th as offensive
officina *f* shop, workshop; officina meccanica machine shop
offició·so -sa [s] *adj* helpful, obliging
offrire §207 *tr* to offer; to sponsor (*a radio or TV program*); to dedicate (*a book*); to bid (*at an auction*); (com) to tender ‖ *ref* to offer oneself, to volunteer

offuscare §197 *tr* to darken, obscure; to obfuscate; to dim (*mind; eyes*) ‖ *ref* to grow dark; to grow dim
oftàlmi·co -ca *adj* (-ci -che) opthalmic
oftalmòlo·go -ga *mf* (-gi -ghe) ophthalmologist
oggettività *f* objectivity
oggetti·vo -va *adj & m* objective
oggètto *m* object; subject, argument; article; oggetti preziosi valuables
òggi *m* today; dall'oggi al domani suddenly; overnight ‖ *adv* today; d'oggi in poi henceforth; oggi a otto a week hence; oggi come oggi at present; oggi è un anno one year ago
oggidì *m invar & adv* nowadays
oggigiórno *m invar & adv* nowadays
ogiva *f* ogive, pointed arch; nose cone
ógni *adj indef invar* each; every, e.g., ogni due giorni every two days; ogni cosa everything; ogni tanto every now and then; per ogni dove (lit) everywhere
ogniqualvòlta *conj* whenever
Ognissan·ti *m* (-ti) All Saints' Day
ognitèmpo *adj invar* all-weather
-ógno·lo -la *suf adj* -ish, e.g., giallognolo yellowish
ognóra *adv* (lit) always
ognu·no -na *adj* (obs) each ‖ *pron* each one, everyone
oh *interj* oh!
òhi *interj* ouch!
ohibò *interj* fie!
ohimè *interj* alas!
ohm *m* (ohm) ohm
olanda *f* Dutch linen ‖ l'Olanda *f* Holland
olandése [s] *adj* Dutch ‖ *m* Dutch (*language*); Dutchman; Dutch cheese ‖ *f* Dutch woman
oleandro *m* oleander
oleà·rio -ria *adj* (-ri -rie) oil
olea·to -ta *adj* oiled
oleifì·cio *m* (-ci) oil mill
oleodótto *m* pipeline
oleó·so -sa [s] *adj* oily
olezzare [ddzz] (olézzo) *intr* (lit) to smell sweet
olézzo [ddzz] *m* perfume, fragrance
olfatto *m* smell
oliare §287 (òlio) *tr* to oil
oliatóre *m* oiler, oil can
olìbano *m* frankincense
olièra *f* cruet
oligarchìa *f* oligarchy
olimpìade *f* Olympiad
olìmpi·co -ca *adj* (-ci -che) Olympic; Olympian
olimpiòni·co -ca *adj* (-ci -che) Olympic ‖ *mf* Olympic athlete
ò·lio *m* (-li) oil; ad olio oil, e.g., quadro ad olio oil painting; olio di fegato di merluzzo cod-liver oil; olio di lino linseed oil; olio di ricino castor oil; olio solare sun-tan lotion
oliva *f* olive
oliva·stro -stra *adj* livid; swarthy ‖ *m* wild olive (*tree*)
olivéto *m* olive grove
Olivièro *m* Oliver
olivo *m* olive tree

**ólmo** *m* elm tree

**olocàu·sto -sta** *adj* (lit) burnt; (lit) sacrificed ‖ *m* holocaust; sacrifice

**ològra·fo -fa** *adj* holographic

**olóna** *f* sailcloth, canvas

**oltracciò** *adv* besides

**oltraggiare** §290 *tr* to outrage; to insult

**oltràg·gio** *m* (**-gi**) outrage; offense; ravages (*of time*); **oltraggio al pudore** offense to public morals; **oltraggio al tribunale** contempt of court

**oltraggió·so -sa** [s] *adj* outrageous

**oltranza** *f*—**a oltranza** to the bitter end

**oltranzi·sta** *mf* (**-sti -ste**) (pol) extremist

**óltre** *adv* beyond; ahead; further; **oltre a** apart from; in addition to; **troppo oltre** too far ‖ *prep* beyond; past; more than

**oltrecortina** *adj invar* beyond-the-iron-curtain ‖ *m* country beyond the iron curtain

**oltremare** *m invar* country overseas ‖ *adv* overseas

**oltremisura** *adv* (lit) beyond measure

**oltremòdo** *adv* (lit) exceedingly

**oltrepassare** *tr* to overstep; to cross (*a river*); to be beyond (. . . *years old*); (sports) to overtake

**oltretómba** *m*—**l'oltretomba** the life beyond

**omàg·gio** *m* (**-gi**) homage; compliment; **in omaggio** complimentary; **rendere omaggio a** to pay tribute to

**òmaro** *m* Norway lobster

**ombeli·co** *m* (**-chi**) navel

**ómbra** *f* shade; shadow; umbrage; form, mass; **nemmeno per ombra** not in the least

**ombreggiare** §290 (**ombréggio**) *tr* to shade

**ombrèlla** *f* shade (*of trees*); (bot) umbel; (coll) umbrella

**ombrel·làio** *m* (**-lài**) umbrella maker

**ombrellino** *m* parasol

**ombrèllo** *m* umbrella

**ombrellóne** *m* beach umbrella

**ombró·so -sa** [s] *adj* shady; touchy; skittish (*horse*)

**omelette** *f* (**omelette**) omelet

**omelìa** *f* homily

**omeopàti·co -ca** (**-ci -che**) *adj* homeopathic ‖ *m* homeopathist

**omèri·co -ca** *adj* (**-ci -che**) Homeric

**òmero** *m* (anat) humerus; (lit) shoulder

**omertà** *f* code of silence of underworld

**ométtere** §198 *tr* to omit

**ométto** *m* little man; (coll) clothes hanger; (billiards) pin; (archit) king post

**omici·da** (**-di -de**) *adj* homicidal, murderous ‖ *mf* homicide, murderer

**omicì·dio** *m* (**-di**) homicide, murder; **omicidio colposo** (law) manslaughter; **omicidio doloso** (law) first-degree murder

**ominó·so -sa** [s] *adj* (lit) ominous

**omissióne** *f* omission

**òmni·bus** *m* (**-bus**) omnibus; way train

**omnisciènte** *adj* all-knowing, omniscient

**omogène·o -a** *adj* homogeneous

**omologare** §209 (**omòlogo**) *tr* to con-

firm, ratify; to probate (*a will*); (sports) to validate

**omòni·mo -ma** *adj* of the same name ‖ *m* namesake; homonym

**omosessuale** [s] *adj & mf* homosexual

**ón·cia** *f* (**-ce**) ounce; **oncia a oncia** little by little

**ónda** *f* wave; **a onde** wavy; wavily; **essere in onda** (rad, telv) to be on the air; **farsi le onde** to have one's hair waved; **mettere in onda** (rad, telv) to put on the air; **onda crespa** whitecap; **onda portante** (rad, telv) carrier wave

**ondata** *f* wave, billow; gust (*e.g., of smoke*); rush (*of blood*); wave (*of cold weather*)

**ondatra** *f* muskrat

**ónde** *pron* from which; of which ‖ *adv* whereof; hence; (poet) wherefrom ‖ *prep* **onde** + *inf* in order to ‖ *conj* **onde** + *subj* so that

**ondeggiante** *adj* waving, swaying

**ondeggiare** §290 (**ondéggio**) *intr* to wave, sway; to waver

**ondina** *f* mermaid; (mythol) undine; (mythol) mermaid

**ondó·so -sa** [s] *adj* wavy

**ondulare** (**óndulo & òndulo**) *tr* to wave; to corrugate (*e.g., metal*) ‖ *intr* to sway

**ondula·to -ta** *adj* wavy (*hair*); corrugated (*e.g., metal*); bumpy (*road*)

**ondulazióne** *f* undulation; **ondulazione permanente** permanent wave

**-óne -óna** *suf mf* big, e.g., **librone** big book; **dormigliona** big sleeper ‖ **-óne** *suf m* (applies to both sexes) big, e.g., **donnone** *m* big woman

**ònere** *m* (lit) onus, burden

**oneró·so -sa** [s] *adj* onerous, burdensome

**onestà** *f* honesty; (poet) modesty

**onè·sto -sta** *adj* honest; fair; (poet) modest ‖ *m* moderate amount; honest gain; honest person

**ònice** *m* onyx

**onnipossènte & onnipotènte** *adj* almighty, omnipotent

**onnisciènte** *adj* omniscient

**onniveggènte** *adj* all-seeing

**onnìvo·ro -ra** *adj* omnivorous

**onomàsti·co -ca** (**-ci -che**) *adj* onomastic ‖ *m* name day ‖ *f* study of proper names

**onomatopèi·co -ca** (**-ci -che**) *adj* onomatopeic

**onoràbile** *adj* honorable

**onoranza** *f* honor; **onoranze** homage; **onoranze funebri** obsequies

**onorare** (**onóro**) *tr* to honor ‖ *ref* to deem it an honor

**onorà·rio -ria** (**-ri -rie**) *adj* honorary ‖ *m* fee, honorarium

**onora·to -ta** *adj* honored; honest; honorable

**onóre** *m* honor; **d'onore** honest, e.g., **uomo d'onore** honest man; **estremi onori** last rites; **fare gli onori di casa** to receive guests; **fare onore a** to honor; **onore al merito** credit where

credit is due; **onor del mento** (lit)
beard

**onorévole** *adj* honorable ‖ *m* honorable member (*of parliament*)

**onorificènza** *f* dignity; decoration

**onorìfi·co -ca** *adj* (**-ci -che**) honorific; honorary (*e.g., title*)

**ónta** *f* dishonor, shame; **a onta di** in spite of; **avere onta** to be ashamed; **fare onta a** to bring shame upon; **in onta a** against

**ontano** *m* alder

**O.N.U.** (acronym) *f* (**Organizzazione delle Nazioni Unite**) United Nations, U.N.

**onu·sto -sta** *adj* (poet) laden

**opa·co -ca** *adj* (**-chi -che**) opaque

**opale** *m* opal

**opali·no -na** *adj* opaline ‖ *f* shiny cardboard; luster (*fabric*)

**òpera** *f* work; organization, foundation; day's work; (mus) opera; **mettere in opera** to install; to start work on; to make ready; to begin using; **opera di consultazione** reference work; **opera morta** (naut) upper works; **opera viva** (naut) quickwork; **per opera di** thanks to

**ope·ràio -ràia (-rài -ràie)** *adj* workman's, worker's; working ‖ *m* workman, worker; **operaio a cottimo** pieceworker; **operaio a giornata** day laborer; **operaio specializzato** craftsman, skilled workman ‖ *f* workwoman

**operante** *adj* actively engaged; operative

**operare (òpero)** *tr* to operate; to work (*a miracle*); (surg) to operate on ‖ *intr* to operate; to be actively engaged ‖ *ref* to be operated on; to occur, take place

**operati·vo -va** *adj* operative; operations, e.g., **ricerca operativa** operations research

**opera·to -ta** *adj* operated; embossed ‖ *m* behavior; patient operated on

**opera·tóre -trice** *mf* operator ‖ *m* (mov) cameraman

**operatò·rio -ria** *adj* (**-ri -rie**) surgical (*operation*); operating (*room*); (math) operational

**operazióne** *f* operation; transaction

**operétta** *f* short work; (mus) operetta

**operìsti·co -ca** *adj* (**-ci -che**) operatic

**operosi·tà** [s] *f* (**-tà**) industry

**operó·so -sa** [s] *adj* industrious; active

**opi·mo -ma** *adj* (lit) fat; rich, fertile

**opinare** *intr* to opine, deem

**opinióne** *f* opinion

**opòs·sum** *m* (**-sum**) opossum

**oppia·to -ta** *adj* opiate (*mixed with opium*); dulled by drugs ‖ *m* opiate (*medicine containing opium*)

**òppio** *m* opium

**oppiòmane** *adj* opium-eating; opium-smoking ‖ *mf* opium addict

**oppórre** §218 *tr* to oppose; to offer, put up (*resistance*) ‖ *ref* to be opposite; **opporsi a** to oppose, to be against

**opportuni·sta** *mf* (**-sti -ste**) opportunist

**opportuni·tà** *f* (**-tà**) opportunity; opportuneness

**opportu·no -na** *adj* opportune

**opposi·tóre -trice** *mf* opponent

**opposizióne** *f* opposition; (law) appeal; **fare opposizione a** to object to

**oppó·sto -sta** *adj* opposite; contrary ‖ *m* opposite; **all'opposto** on the contrary

**oppressióne** *f* oppression

**oppressi·vo -va** *adj* oppressive

**opprès·so -sa** *adj* oppressed; overcome, overwhelmed ‖ **oppressi** *mpl* oppressed people

**oppressóre** *m* oppressor

**opprimènte** *adj* oppressive

**opprìmere** §131 *tr* to oppress; to overcome, overwhelm; to weigh down

**oppugnare** *tr* to refute, contradict

**oppure** *adv* otherwise ‖ *conj* or else; or rather

**optare (òpto)** *intr* to choose; (com) to exercise an option

**optometri·sta** *mf* (**-sti -ste**) optometrist

**opulèn·to -ta** *adj* opulent

**opùscolo** *m* booklet, brochure, pamphlet; **opuscolo d'informazioni** instruction manual

**opzióne** *f* option

**ór** *adv* now; **or ora** right now; **or sono** ago

**óra** *f* hour; time; period (*in school*); **alla buon'ora!** finally!; **a ore** by the hour; **a tarda ora** late; **che ora è?** or **che ore sono?** what time is it?; **da un'ora all'altra** from one moment to the next; **dell'ultima ora** up-to-date (*news*); **di buon'ora** early; early in the morning; **di ora in ora** at any moment; **d'ora in avanti** from this moment on; **d'ora in poi** from now on; **far l'ora** to kill time; **fin ora** until now; **non vedere l'ora di** + *inf* to be hardly able to wait until + *ind;* **ora di cena** suppertime; **ora di punta** rush hour, peak hour; **ora legale** daylight-saving time; **ore piccole** late hours; **un'ora di orologio** one full hour ‖ *adv* now

**oràcolo** *m* oracle

**òra·fo -fa** *adj* goldsmith's ‖ *m* goldsmith

**orale** *adj* & *m* oral

**oralménte** *adv* orally; by word of mouth

**oramài** *adv* now; already

**oran·go** *m* (**-ghi**) orangutan

**orà·rio -ria (-ri -rie)** *adj* hourly; per hour; clockwise ‖ *m* timetable; schedule; roster; **essere in orario** to be on time; **orario di lavoro** working hours; **orario d'ufficio** office hours

**ora·tóre -trice** *mf* orator

**oratò·rio -ria (-ri -rie)** *adj* oratorical ‖ *m* (eccl) oratory; (mus) oratorio ‖ *f* oratory, public speaking

**orazióne** *f* oration; prayer; **orazione domenicale** Lord's Prayer

**orbare (òrbo)** *tr* (lit) to bereave; (lit) to deprive

**òrbe** *f* (lit) orb; (lit) world

**orbène** *adv* well

**òrbita** f orbit; (fig) sphere
**orbitare (òrbito)** intr to orbit
**orbitazióne** f orbiting
**òr•bo -ba** adj bereaved; deprived; blind || m blind man
**òrca** f killer whale
**Òrcadi** fpl Orkney Islands
**orchèstra** f orchestra; band; orchestra pit
**orchestrale** adj orchestral || mf orchestra player, orchestra performer
**orchestrare (orchèstro)** tr to orchestrate; (fig) to organize
**orchestrina** f dance band; dance-band music
**orchidèa** f orchid
**ór•cio** m (-ci) jar, jug, crock
**orciòlo** m—a orciolo puckered up (lips)
**òr•co** m (-chi) ogre
**òrda** f horde
**ordàlia** f (hist) ordeal
**ordigno** m gadget, contrivance; tool; ordigno esplosivo infernal machine
**ordinale** adj & m ordinal
**ordinaménto** m disposition; regulation
**ordinanza** f ordinance; (mil) orderly; d'ordinanza regulation (e.g., uniform); in ordinanza (mil) in formation
**ordinare (órdino)** tr to order; to straighten up; to range; to regulate; to ordain; to trim
**ordinà•rio -ria (-ri -rie)** adj ordinary; plain; inferior; workday (suit) || m ordinary; full professor; d'ordinario ordinarily, usually
**ordina•to -ta** adj orderly, tidy; ordained || f ordinate; straightening up; (aer) frame; (naut) bulkhead
**ordinazióne** f order; ordination
**órdine** m order; row; tier; series (e.g., of years); college (e.g., of surgeons); nature (of things); (law) warrant, writ; in ordine a concerning; ordine del giorno order of the day; ordine d'idee train of thought
**ordire** §176 tr to warp (cloth); to hatch (a plot)
**ordi•to -ta** adj plotted || m warp (of fabric)
**orécchia** f ear; dog-ear; con le orecchie tese all ears
**orecchiale** m earphone (of sonar equipment)
**orecchiétta** f (anat) auricle
**orecchino** m earring
**oréc•chio** m (-chi) ear; hearing; dog-ear; moldboard; fare orecchio da mercante to turn a deaf ear || m (orécchia fpl) (archaic) ear
**orecchióne** m long-eared bat; (mil) trunnion; orecchioni (pathol) mumps
**oréfice** m goldsmith; jeweler
**oreficerìa** f goldsmith shop; jewelry shop
**orfanézza** f orphanage (condition)
**òrfa•no -na** adj orphaned || mf orphan
**orfanotrò•fio** m (-fi) orphanage (institution)
**Orfèo** m Orpheus
**organdi** m organdy
**organétto** m hand organ; mouth organ; organetto di Barberia hand organ

**orgàni•co -ca (-ci -che)** adj organic || m personnel, staff || f (mil) organization
**organigram•ma** m (-mi) organization chart
**organino** m hand organ, barrel organ
**organismo** m organism
**organi•sta** mf (-sti -ste) organist
**organizzare** [ddzz] tr to organize
**organizza•tóre -trice** [ddzz] mf organizer
**organizzazióne** [ddzz] f organization; Organizzazione delle Nazioni Unite United Nations
**òrgano** m organ; part (of a machine); organo di stampa mouthpiece
**orgasmo** m orgasm; agitation, excitement
**òr•gia** f (-ge) orgy
**orgó•glio** m (-gli) pride
**orgoglió•so -sa** [s] adj proud
**orientale** adj & mf oriental; Oriental
**orientaménto** m orientation; bearing; trend; trim (of sail); orientamento scolastico e professionale aptitude test; vocational guidance
**orientare (oriènto)** tr to orient; to guide; to trim (a sail) || ref to find one's bearings
**oriènte** m orient; grand'oriente grand lodge || Oriente m Orient, East; Estremo Oriente Far East; Medio Oriente Middle East; Vicino Oriente Near East
**orifì•zio** m (-zi) orifice, opening
**orìgano** m wild marjoram
**originale** adj original; odd || mf queer character, odd person || m original; copy (for printer)
**originare (orìgino)** tr to originate || intr (ESSERE) & ref to originate
**originà•rio -ria** adj (-ri -rie) originating; native; original
**orìgine** f origin; source; extraction
**origliare** §280 intr to eavesdrop
**origlière** m (lit) pillow
**orina** f var of urina
**orinale** m chamber pot, urinal
**orinare** tr & intr to urinate
**orina•tóio** m (-tói) urinal, comfort station
**oriòlo** m (orn) oriole
**oriun•do -da** adj native || m (sports) native son
**orizzontale** [ddzz] adj horizontal || orizzontali fpl horizontal words (in crossword puzzle)
**orizzontare** [ddzz] (orizzónto) tr to orient || ref to get one's bearings
**orizzónte** [ddzz] m horizon
**Orlando** m Roland
**orlare (órlo)** tr to hem, border; orlare a zigzag to pink
**òrlo** m edge; brim; hem, border; (fig) brink; orlo a giorno hemstitch
**órma** f footprint; orme remains, vestiges; calcare le orme di to follow the footsteps of
**ormeggiare** §290 (orméggio) tr & ref (naut) to moor
**ormég•gio** m (-gi) mooring; mollare gli ormeggi (naut) to cast off
**ormóne** m hormone

**ornamentale** *adj* ornamental
**ornaménto** *m* ornament
**ornare (órno)** *tr* to adorn
**orna·to -ta** *adj* adorned; ornate ‖ *m* ornament; ornamental design
**ornitòlo·go -ga** *mf* (-gi -ghe) ornithologist
**òro** *m* gold; (fig) money; **d'oro** gold, golden; **ori** gold objects; jewels; suit of Neapolitan cards corresponding to diamonds; **oro zecchino** pure gold; **per tutto l'oro del mondo** for all the world
**orologerìa** *f* watchmaking; clockmaking; watchmaker's shop
**orolo·giàio** *m* (-giài) watchmaker; clockmaker
**orolò·gio** *m* (-gi) watch; clock; **orologio a pendolo** clock; **orologio a polvere** sandglass; **orologio a scatto** digital clock; **orologio da polso** wristwatch; **orologio della morte** deathwatch; **orologio solare** sundial
**oròscopo** *m* horoscope
**orpèllo** *m* Dutch gold; (fig) tinsel
**orrèndo** *m* horrible
**orrìbile** *adj* horrible
**òrri·do -da** *adj* horrid ‖ *m* horridness; gorge, ravine
**orripilante** *adj* bloodcurdling, hair-raising
**orróre** *m* horror; awe; **aver in** or **per orrore** to loath; **fare orrore a** to horrify
**órsa** *f* she-bear ‖ **Orsa** *f*—**Orsa maggiore** Great Bear; **Orsa minore** Little Bear
**orsacchiòtto** *m* bear cub; Teddy bear
**ór·so -sa** *mf* bear; **orso bianco** polar bear; **orso grigio** grizzly bear ‖ *f* see **orsa**
**orsù** *interj* come on!
**ortàg·gio** *m* (-gi) vegetable
**ortàglia** *f* vegetable garden; vegetable
**ortènsia** *f* hydrangea
**orti·ca** *f* (-che) nettle; hives
**orticària** *f* hives, nettle rash
**orticoltóre** *m* truck gardener; horticulturist
**òrto** *m* garden, vegetable garden; (lit) sunrise; **orto botanico** botanical garden; **orto di guerra** Victory garden
**ortodòs·so -sa** *adj* orthodox ‖ *m* Greek Catholic
**ortografìa** *f* orthography; spelling
**ortola·no -na** *adj* garden ‖ *m* truck farmer; gardener
**ortopèdi·co -ca** (-ci -che) *adj* orthopedic ‖ *m* orthopedist
**òrza** *f* bowline; windward; **andare all'orza** to sail close to the wind
**orzaiòlo** [dz] *m* (pathol) sty
**orzare (òrzo)** *intr* to sail close to the wind; to luff
**orzata** [dz] *f* orgeat
**orzata** *f* (naut) luff
**òrzo** [dz] *m* barley
**osannare** *intr* to cry or sing hosanna; **osannare a** to acclaim, applaud
**osare (òso)** *intr* to dare
**osceni·tà** *f* (-tà) obscenity
**oscè·no -na** *adj* obscene; (coll) horrible
**oscillante** *adj* oscillating

**oscillare** *intr* to oscillate; to swing; to wobble; to waver, hesitate
**oscillazióne** *f* oscillation; fluctuation
**oscuraménto** *m* darkening, dimming; blackout
**oscurare** *tr* to darken; to blot out; to dim ‖ *ref* to get dark; **oscurarsi in volto** to frown
**oscuri·tà** *f* (-tà) obscurity; darkness; ignorance
**oscu·ro -ra** *adj* obscure, dark; opaque (*style*) ‖ *m* obscurity, darkness; **essere all'oscuro di** to be in the dark about
**osmòsi** *f* osmosis
**ospedale** *m* hospital
**ospedalière** *m* hospital worker
**ospedaliè·ro -ra** *adj* hospital ‖ *m* hospitaler
**ospedalizzare** [ddzz] *tr* to hospitalize
**ospitale** *adj* hospitable ‖ *m* hospital
**ospitali·tà** *f* (-tà) hospitality
**ospitare (òspito)** *tr* to lodge, shelter, accommodate; to entertain; (sports) to play (*an opposing team*) at home
**òspite** *mf* host; guest; **andarsene insalutato ospite** to take French leave; **ospiti** company (*guests at home*)
**ospì·zio** *m* (-zi) hospice; hostel; (lit) hospitality; **ospizio dei vecchi** nursing home; **ospizio di mendicità** poorhouse
**ossatura** *f* frame, framework; skeleton
**òsse·o -a** *adj* bony
**ossequènte** *adj* (lit) respectful; (lit) reverent
**ossequiare** §287 (**ossèquio**) *tr* to pay one's respects to; to honor
**ossè·quio** *m* (-qui) respect; reverence; **i miei ossequi** my best regards; **in ossequio a** in conformity with; **porgere i propri ossequi a** to pay one's respects to
**ossequió·so -sa** [s] *adj* obsequious; respectful
**osservante** *adj* & *m* observant
**osservanza** *f* observance; deference
**osservare (ossèrvo)** *tr* to observe
**osserva·tóre -trice** *adj* observing, observant ‖ *mf* observer
**osservatò·rio** *m* (-ri) observatory
**osservazióne** *f* observation; rebuke
**ossessionare (ossessióno)** *tr* to obsess; to harass, bedevil
**ossessióne** *f* obsession
**ossès·so -sa** *adj* possessed ‖ *mf* person possessed
**ossìa** *conj* or; to wit
**ossidante** *adj* oxidizing ‖ *m* oxidizer
**ossidare (òssido)** *tr* & *ref* to oxidize
**òssido** *m* oxide; **ossido di carbone** carbon monoxide
**ossìdulo** *m* protoxide; **ossidulo di azoto** nitrous oxide
**ossificare** §197 (**ossìfico**) *tr* & *ref* to ossify
**ossigenare (ossìgeno)** *tr* to oxygenate; to bleach (*the hair*); to infuse strength into ‖ *ref* to bleach (*the hair*)
**ossìgeno** *m* oxygen; (fig) transfusion, shot in the arm
**ossìto·no -na** *adj* & *m* oxytone

**òs·so** *m* (**-si**) bone (*of animal*); stone (*of fruit*); **osso di balena** whalebone; **osso di seppia** cuttlebone; **osso duro da rodere** hard nut to crack; **osso sacro** sacrum; **rimetterci l'osso del collo** to be thoroughly ruined; **rompersi l'osso del collo** to break one's neck ‖ *m* (**-sa** *fpl*) bone (*of a person*); **avere le ossa rotte** to be dead-tired

**ossu·to -ta** *adj* bony; scrawny

**ostacolare** (**ostàcolo**) *tr* to hinder; to obstruct; **ostacolare l'azione** (sports) to interfere

**ostàcolo** *m* obstacle; obstruction; (golf) hazard; (sports) hurdle

**ostàg·gio** *m* (**-gi**) hostage

**ostare** (**òsto**) *intr* (lit) to be in the way; (with *dat*) to hinder; **nulla osta** no objection, permission granted

**òste ostéssa** *mf* innkeeper ‖ **oste** *m* & *f* (lit) army in the field ‖ *m* (poet) enemy

**ostèllo** *m* hostel; (poet) abode

**ostentare** (**ostènto**) *tr* to show, display; to affect, feign

**ostenta·to -ta** *adj* affected, ostentatious

**ostentazióne** *f* show, ostentation

**osteopatìa** *f* osteopathy

**osterìa** *f* tavern, inn, taproom

**ostéssa** *f* see **oste**

**ostètri·ca** *f* (**-che**) midwife

**ostetrìcia** *f* obstetrics

**ostètri·co -ca** (**-ci -che**) *adj* obstetrical ‖ *m* obstetrician ‖ *f* see **ostetrica**

**òstia** *f* wafer; Host; sacrificial victim

**òsti·co -ca** *adj* (**-ci -che**) hard; (lit) repugnant, distasteful

**ostile** *adj* hostile

**ostili·tà** *f* (**-tà**) hostility

**ostinare** *ref* to be stubborn; to persist

**ostina·to -ta** *adj* obstinate; persistent

**ostinazióne** *f* obstinacy

**ostracismo** *m* ostracism; **dare l'ostracismo a** to ostracize

**ostracizzare** [ddzz] *tr* (poet) to ostracize

**òstri·ca** *f* (**-che**) oyster; **ostrica perlifera** pearl oyster

**ostri·càio** *m* (**-cài**) oyster bed; oyster-man

**ostruire** §176 *tr* to obstruct; to stop up

**ostruzióne** *f* obstruction

**Otèllo** *m* Othello

**otorinolaringoia·tra** *mf* (**-tri -tre**) ear, nose, and throat specialist, otorhinolaryngologist

**ótre** *f* wineskin; **otre di vento** windbag (*person*)

**ottàni·co -ca** *adj* (**-ci -che**) octane

**ottano** *m* octane

**ottanta** *adj*, *m* & *pron* eighty

**ottantènne** *adj* eighty-year-old ‖ *mf* eighty-year-old person

**ottantèsi·mo -ma** *adj*, *m* & *pron* eightieth

**ottantina** *f* about eighty; **essere sull'ottantina** to be about eighty years old

**ottava** *f* octave

**Ottaviano** *m* Octavian

**ottavino** *m* (mus) piccolo; (com) commission of ⅛ of 1%

**otta·vo -va** *adj* & *pron* eighth ‖ *m* eighth; octavo ‖ *f* see **ottava**

**ottemperare** (**ottèmpero**) *intr* (with *dat*) to obey; **ottemperare a** to comply with

**ottenebrare** (**ottènebro**) *tr* to becloud

**ottenére** §271 *tr* to obtain, get

**ottétto** *m* octet

**òtti·co -ca** (**-ci -che**) *adj* optic(al) ‖ *m* optician ‖ *f* optics

**ottimismo** *m* optimism

**ottimi·sta** *mf* (**-sti -ste**) optimist

**ottimìsti·co -ca** *adj* (**-ci -che**) optimistic

**òtti·mo -ma** *adj* very good, excellent ‖ *m* best; highest rating

**òtto** *adj* & *pron* eight; **le otto** eight o'clock ‖ *m* eight; eighth (*in dates*); (sports) racing shell with eight oarsmen; **otto giorni** a week; **otto volante** roller coaster

**ottóbre** *m* October

**ottocenté·sco -sca** *adj* (**-schi -sche**) nineteenth-century

**ottocènto** *adj*, *m* & *pron* eight hundred ‖ **l'Ottocento** the nineteenth century

**ottoma·no -na** *adj* & *m* Ottoman ‖ *m* ottoman (*fabric*) ‖ *f* ottoman (*sofa*)

**ottomila** *adj*, *m* & *pron* eight thousand

**ottoname** *m* brassware

**ottonare** (**ottóno**) *tr* to coat with brass

**ottóne** *m* brass; **ottoni** (mus) brasses ‖ **Ottone** *m* Otto

**ottuagenà·rio -ria** *adj* & *mf* (**-ri -rie**) octogenerian

**ottùndere** §208 *tr* (fig) to deaden; (lit) to blunt

**otturare** *tr* to fill; to plug; to stop; to obstruct, stop up (*e.g., a channel*) ‖ *ref* to clog up

**otturatóre** *m* breechblock; (phot, mov) shutter; (mach) cutoff (*of cylinder*)

**otturazióne** *f* filling (*of tooth*)

**ottu·so -sa** *adj* obtuse; blunt

**ovàia** *f* ovary

**ovale** *adj* oval ‖ *m* oval; oval face

**ovatta** *f* wadding; absorbent cotton

**ovattare** *tr* to pad, wad; to muffle

**ovazióne** *f* ovation

**óve** *adv* (lit) where ‖ *conj* (lit) if; (poet) while

**òvest** *m* west

**Ovìdio** *m* Ovid

**ovile** *m* sheepcote, fold

**ovi·no -na** *adj* ovine ‖ **ovini** *mpl* sheep

**òvo** *m* var of **uovo**

**ovoidale** *adj* egg-shaped

**òvulo** *m* pill shaped like an egg; (biol) ovum; (bot) ovule

**ovùnque** *adv* (lit) wherever; (lit) everywhere

**ovvéro** *conj* or; to wit

**ovvìa** *interj* come on!

**ovviare** §119 *intr*—(with *dat*) to obviate

**òv·vio -via** *adj* (**-vi -vie**) obvious

**oziare** §287 (**òzio**) *intr* to idle, loiter

**ò·zio** *m* (**-zi**) idleness; leisure

**oziosi·tà** [s] *f* (**-tà**) idleness

**ozió·so -sa** [s] *adj* idle; useless, vain

**ozòno** [dz] *m* ozone

**P**

**P, p** [pi] *m & f* fourteenth letter of the Italian alphabet
**pacare** §197 *tr* (poet) to placate
**pacatézza** *f* tranquillity, serenity
**paca·to -ta** *adj* serene, tranquil
**pac·ca** *f* (-che) slap
**pacchétto** *m* parcel, package; book (*of matches*); pack (*of cigarettes*)
**pàcchia** *f* (coll) hearty meal; (coll) godsend, windfall
**pacchia·no -na** *adj* boorish, uncouth ‖ *mf* boor
**pacciamantura** *f* mulching
**pacciame** *m* mulch
**pac·co** *m* (-chi) package; **pacchi postali** parcel post (*service*); **pacco dono** gift package; **pacco postale** parcel by mail
**paccottìglia** *f* shoddy goods, junk; trinkets
**pace** *f* peace; **lasciare in pace** to leave alone; **mettersi il cuore in pace** to resign oneself
**pachidèr·ma** *m* (-mi) pachyderm
**pachista·no -na** *adj & mf* Pakistani
**paciè·re -ra** *mf* peacemaker
**pacificare** §197 (pacìfico) *tr* to pacify; to appease; to mediate ‖ *ref* to make one's peace
**pacifica·tóre -trice** *adj* pacifying ‖ *mf* peacemaker
**pacificazióne** *f* pacification; appeasement
**pacìfi·co -ca** (-ci -che) *adj* peaceful, pacific; **è pacifico che** it goes without saying that ‖ *m* peaceable person ‖ **Pacifico** *adj & m* Pacific
**pacifismo** *m* pacifism
**pacifi·sta** *mf* (-sti -ste) pacifist
**pacioccó·ne -na** *mf* chubby, easygoing person
**padèlla** *f* frying pan; bedpan; **cadere dalla padella nella brace** to jump from the frying pan into the fire
**padiglióne** *m* pavilion; hunting lodge; roof (*of car*); ward (*of a hospital*); (naut) rigging, tackle; **padiglione auricolare** (anat) auricle of the ear
**Pàdova** *f* Padua
**padre** *m* father; sire; **padre di famiglia** provider; (law) head of household; **Padre Eterno** Heavenly Father
**padreggiare** §290 (padréggio) *intr* to resemble one's father
**padrino** *m* godfather; second (*in duel*)
**padrona** *f* owner, boss, mistress; **padrona di casa** lady of the house
**padronale** *adj* proprietary; private (*e.g., car*)
**padronanza** *f* command; **padronanza di sé stesso** self-control
**padróne** *m* owner, boss, master; **essere padrone di** + *inf* to have the right to + *inf*; **padrone di casa** landlord; **padrone di sé** cool and collected
**padroneggiare** §290 (padronéggio) *tr* to master, control
**paesàg·gio** *m* (-gi) landscape
**paesaggi·sta** *mf* (-sti -ste) landscapist

**paesa·no -na** *adj* country ‖ *mf* villager ‖ *m* countryman ‖ *f* countrywoman; **alla paesana** according to local tradition
**paése** *m* country; village; **i Paesi Bassi** the Netherlands; (hist) the Low Countries; **mandare a quel paese** to send to blazes
**paesi·sta** *mf* (-sti -ste) landscapist
**paffu·to -ta** *adj* chubby, plump
**pa·ga** *f* (-ghe) salary; wages; repayment; **mala paga** poor pay (*person*)
**pagàbile** *adj* payable
**pagàia** *f* paddle
**pagaménto** *m* payment; **pagamento alla consegna** c.o.d.
**paganésimo** *m* paganism
**paga·no -na** *adj & mf* pagan, heathen
**pagare** §209 *tr* to pay; to pay for; **far pagare** to charge; **pagare di egual moneta** to repay in kind; **pagare il fio per** to pay (the penalty) for; **pagare in natura** to pay in kind; **pagare salato** to pay dearly; **pagare un occhio della testa** to pay through the nose ‖ *intr* to pay
**paga·tóre -trice** *mf* payer
**pagèlla** *f* report card
**pàg·gio** *m* (-gi) page (*boy attendant*)
**paghe·rò** *m* (-rò) promissory note, I.O.U.
**pàgina** *f* page (*e.g., of book*)
**paginatura** *f* pagination
**pàglia** *f* straw; thatch (*for roof*); **paglia di ferro** steel wool; **paglia di legno** excelsior
**pagliaccé·sco -sca** *adj* (-schi -sche) clownish
**pagliaccétto** *m* rompers
**pagliacciata** *f* buffoonery, antics
**pagliàc·cio** *m* (-ci) clown, buffoon; **fare il pagliaccio** to clown
**pa·gliàio** *m* (-gliài) heap of straw; haystack
**paglieríc·cio** *m* (-ci) straw mattress
**paglieri·no -na** *adj* straw-colored
**pagliétta** *f* skimmer, boater; steel wool; (coll) pettifogger
**pagnòtta** *f* loaf of bread; (coll) bread
**pa·go -ga** *adj* (-ghi -ghe) satisfied ‖ *f* see paga
**paguro** *m* (zool) hermit crab
**pà·io** *m* (-ia *fpl*) pair, couple; **è un altro paio di maniche** this is a horse of another color; **fare il paio** to match perfectly
**paiòlo** *m* caldron, kettle; (mil) platform
**Pakistan, il** Pakistan
**pala** *f* shovel; blade (*e.g., of turbine*); paddle (*of waterwheel*); peel (*of baker*); **pala d'altare** altarpiece
**paladi·no -na** *mf* champion ‖ *m* paladin; **farsi paladino di** to champion
**palafitta** *f* pile dwelling; piles (*to support a structure*)
**palafronière** *m* groom
**palafréno** *m* palfrey
**palan·ca** *f* (-che) beam, board; (naut)

gangplank; copper coin; **palanche** (coll) money

**palanchino** *m* palanquin; (naut) pulley

**palandrana** *f* (joc) long, full coat

**palata** *f* shovelful; stroke (*of oar*); **a palate** by the bucketful

**palatale** *adj* & *f* palatal

**palati·no -na** *adj* palatine; (anat) palatal

**palato** *m* palate

**palazzina** *f* villa

**palazzo** *m* palace; large office or government building; mansion; **palazzo dello sport** sports arena; **palazzo di città** city hall; **palazzo di giustizia** courthouse

**palchetti·sta** (-sti -ste) *mf* (theat) box-holder ‖ *m* person who lays floors

**palchétto** *m* shelf; (theat) small box; (journ) box

**pal·co** *m* (-chi) flooring; scaffold; stand, platform; (theat) box; (theat) stage

**palcoscèni·co** *m* (-ci) (theat) stage

**palesare** (paléso) *tr* to reveal, manifest ‖ *ref* to show oneself

**palése** *adj* plain, manifest; **fare palese** to manifest, reveal

**palèstra** *f* gymnasium; palestra

**palétta** *f* small shovel, scoop; blade (*of turbine*)

**palettata** *f* shovelful

**palétto** *m* stake; bolt (*of door*)

**palificazióne** *f* pile work (*in the ground for foundation*); line of telephone poles

**pà·lio** *m* (-lii) embroidered cloth (*given as prize*); **metter in palio** to offer as a prize; **palio di Siena** colorful horse-race at Siena

**palissandro** *m* Brazilian rosewood

**palizzata** *f* palisade; picket fence

**palla** *f* ball; bullet; sphere; **dar palla nera a** to blackball; **palla da cannone** cannon ball; **palla di neve** snowball; **prendere la palla al balzo** to seize the opportunity

**pallabase** *f* baseball

**pallacanè·stro** *f* (-stro) basketball

**pallamuro** *m* handball

**pallanuòto** *f* water polo

**pallavó·lo** *f* (-lo) volleyball

**palleggiare** §290 (palléggio) *tr* to toss (*e.g., a javelin*); to shift from one hand to another ‖ *intr* (tennis) to knock a few balls; (soccer) to dribble ‖ *ref*—**palleggiarsi la responsabilità** to shift the responsibility

**pallég·gio** *m* (-gi) (tennis) knocking back and forth; (soccer) dribbling

**palliati·vo -va** *adj* & *m* palliative

**pallidézza** *f* paleness

**pàlli·do -da** *adj* pale; faint

**pallina** *f* marble; small ball; **pallina antitarmica** mothball

**pallino** *m* little ball; (bowling) jack; bullet; **a pallini** polka-dot; **avere il pallino di** to be crazy about; **pallini** buckshot; polka dots

**palloncino** *m* child's balloon; Chinese lantern

**pallóne** *m* (soccer) ball; (aer) balloon

**pallone di sbarramento** barrage balloon; **pallone gonfiato** (fig) stuffed shirt; **pallone sonda** trial balloon

**pallonétto** *m* (tennis) lob

**pallóre** *m* pallor, paleness

**pallòttola** *f* pellet; ball; bullet

**pallottolière** *m* abacus

**pallovale** *f* rugby

**palma** *f* palm; **tenere in palma di mano** to hold in the highest esteem

**palmare** *adj* evident, plain

**palménto** *m* millstone; **mangiare a quattro palmenti** (coll) to stuff oneself eating

**palméto** *m* palm grove

**palmipede** *adj* palmate, web-footed

**palmì·zio** *m* (-zi) palm

**palmo** *m* span; palm (*of hand*); foot (*measure*); **a palmo a palmo** little by little; **restare con un palmo di naso** to be disappointed

**palo** *m* pole (*of wood or metal*); beam; pile; (soccer, football) goal post; **fare il palo** to be on the lookout (*said of thieves*); **palo indicatore** signpost; **saltare di palo in frasca** to digress

**palombaro** *m* diver

**palómbo** *m* dogfish

**palpàbile** *adj* palpable

**palpare** *tr* to touch; to palpate

**pàlpebra** *f* eyelid; **battere le palpebre** to blink

**palpeggiare** §290 (palpéggio) *tr* to finger, touch repeatedly

**palpitante** *adj* throbbing; burning (*question*); fluttering (*e.g., with love*)

**palpitare** (pàlpito) *intr* to palpitate, pulsate; (fig) to pine

**palpitazióne** *f* palpitation

**pàlpito** *m* heartbeat; (fig) throb

**pal·tò** *m* (-tò) overcoat

**paltoncino** *m* child's winter coat; lady's topcoat

**paludaménto** *m* (joc) array, attire

**palude** *f* marsh, bog

**paludó·so -sa** [s] *adj* marshy

**palustre** *adj* marshy

**pàmpino** *m* grape leaf

**panacèa** *f* panacea, cure-all

**pàna·ma** *m* (-ma) Panama hat

**panamé·gno -gna** *adj* & *mf* Panamenian

**panamènse** *adj* & *mf* Panamenian

**panare** *tr* (culin) to bread

**pan·ca** *f* (-che) bench; **scaldare le panche** (coll) to loaf around; (coll) to waste one's time at school

**pancétta** *f* potbelly; bacon

**panchétto** *m* footstool

**panchina** *f* bench

**pàn·cia** *f* (-ce) belly; **a pancia all'aria** on one's back; **mangiare a crepa pancia** to stuff oneself like a pig; **mettere su pancia** to grow a pot-belly; **salvar la pancia per i fichi** to not take any chances; **tenersi la pancia dalle risate** to split one's side laughing

**panciata** *f* belly flop

**pancièra** *f* bellypiece; body girth

**panciòlle** *m*—**in panciolle** frittering one's time away

**pancìotto** *m* waistcoat; vest; **panciotto a maglia** cardigan

**panciu·to -ta** *adj* potbellied

**pàncre·as** *m* (-as) pancreas

**pandemò·nio** *m* (-ni) pandemonium

**pane** *m* bread; thread (*of screw*); cake (e.g., *of butter*); loaf (*of sugar*); (metallurgy) pig; **a pane di zucchero** conic(al); **dire pane al pane e vino al vino** to call a spade a spade; **essere come pane e cacio** to be hand and glove; **essere pane per i propri denti** to be a match for s.o.; **guadagnarsi il pane** to earn one's living; **pane a cassetta** sandwich bread; **pane azzimo** unleavened bread, matzoth; **pan di Spagna** angel food cake, sponge cake; **pane integrale** graham bread; **render pan per focaccia** to give tit for tat

**panegìri·co** *m* (-ci) panegyric

**panetterìa** *f* bakery

**panettière** *m* baker

**panétto** *m* pat (e.g., *of butter*)

**pànfilo** *m* yacht

**panfrutto** *m* plum cake

**pangrattato** *m* bread crumbs

**pània** *f* birdlime; **cadere nella pania** to fall into the trap

**pàni·co -ca** (-ci -che) *adj* panicky ‖ *m* panic

**pani·co** *m* (-chi) (bot) Italian millet

**panièra** *f* basket; basketful

**panière** *m* basket; basketful

**panificazióne** *f* breadmaking

**panifi·cio** *m* (-ci) bakery

**panino** *m* roll, bun; **panino imbottito** sandwich

**panna** *f* cream, heavy cream; **essere in panna** (naut) to lie to; (aut) to have a breakdown; **mettere in panna** (naut) to heave to; **panna montata** whipped cream

**panne** *f* (aut) breakdown; **essere in panne** (aut) to have a breakdown

**pannèllo** *m* linen cloth; pane; panel (*of machine*); (archit; elec) panel

**pannìcolo** *m* (anat) membrane, tissue

**panno** *m* cloth; woolen cloth; film, membrane; **bianco come un panno** as white as a ghost; **mettersi nei panni di** to put oneself in the boots of; **non stare più nei propri panni** to be beside oneself with joy; **panni** clothes; **panno verde** baize

**pannòcchia** *f* ear (*of corn*)

**pannolino** *m* linen cloth; diaper; sanitary napkin

**panòplia** *f* panoply

**panora·ma** *m* (-mi) panorama

**panoràmi·co -ca** *adj* (-ci -che) panoramic ‖ *f* panoramic view; (mov) panoramic scene

**pantaloncini** *mpl* trunks

**pantalóni** *mpl* trousers; **pantaloni da donna** slacks

**pantano** *m* bog, quagmire

**panteismo** *m* pantheism

**pànteon** *m* pantheon

**pantèra** *f* panther; (slang) police car

**pantòfola** *f* slipper

**pantomima** *f* pantomine, mimicry

**panzana** *f* (lit) fib, lie

**Pàolo** *m* Paul

**paonaz·zo -za** *adj* & *m* purple

**pa·pa** *m* (-pi) pope; **ad ogni morte di papa** once in a blue moon; **morto un papa se ne fa un altro** nobody is indispensable

**pa·pà** *m* (-pà) daddy, papa

**papàbile** *adj* likely to be elected ‖ *mf* front runner ‖ *m* cardinal likely to be elected to the papacy

**papale** *adj* papal (e.g., *benediction*); Papal (*States*)

**papali·no -na** *adj* papal ‖ *m* advocate of papal temporal power ‖ *f* skullcap

**paparazzo** *m* freelance photographer

**papato** *m* papacy

**papàvero** *m* poppy; **alto papavero** (fig) big shot

**pàpera** *f* young goose; slip of the tongue; spoonerism; **fare una papera** to make a boner

**pàpero** *m* gander

**papiro** *m* papyrus

**pappa** *f* bread soup, farina, pap; **pappa molla** (fig) jellyfish

**pappafi·co** *m* (-chi) (naut) topgallant; (slang) goatee

**pappagallo** *m* parrot; bedpan; (slang) masher

**pappagòr·gia** *f* (-ge) double chin, jowl

**pappare** *tr* (coll) to gulp; (fig) to gobble up fraudulently

**pappata·ci** *m* (-ci) gnat

**pappina** *f* light pap; poultice

**pàpri·ca** *f* (-che) paprika

**para** *f* crepe rubber

**paràbola** *f* parable; (geom) parabola

**parabórdo** *m* (naut) fender

**parabréz·za** [ddzz] *m* (-za) windshield

**paracadutare** *tr* to parachute, airdrop ‖ *ref* to parachute

**paracadu·te** *m* (-te) parachute

**paracadutismo** *m* parachute jumping; (sports) sky diving

**paracaduti·sta** *mf* (-sti -ste) parachutist; skydiver ‖ *m* paratrooper

**paracarro** *m* spur stone

**paracól·pi** *m* (-pi) doorstop

**paràcqua** *m* (paràcqua) umbrella

**paradèn·ti** *m* (-ti) (sports) mouthpiece

**paradisìa·co -ca** *adj* (-ci -che) heavenly

**paradiso** *m* paradise

**paradossale** *adj* paradoxical

**paradòsso** *m* paradox

**parafa** *f* initials

**parafan·go** *m* (-ghi) fender, mudguard

**parafare** *tr* to initial

**paraffina** *f* paraffin

**parafiam·ma** *m* (-ma) fire-proof partition

**parafrasare** (paràfraso) *tr* to paraphrase

**paràfra·si** *f* (-si) paraphrase

**parafùlmine** *m* lightning rod

**parafuò·co** *m* (-co) screen, fender (*in front of fireplace*)

**paràg·gio** *m* (-gi) lineage; **paraggi** neighborhood, vicinity

**paragonàbile** *adj* comparable

**paragonare** (paragóno) *tr* to compare

**paragóne** *m* comparison; **a paragone di**

in comparison with; **mettere a paragone** to compare; **senza paragone** beyond compare

**paragrafare** (paràgrafo) *tr* to paragraph

**paràgrafo** *m* paragraph

**paraguaia·no** -na *adj* & *mf* Paraguayan

**paràli·si** *f* (-si) paralysis

**paralìti·co** -ca *adj* & *mf* (-ci -che) paralytic

**paralizzare** [ddzz] *tr* to paralyze

**parallè·lo** -la *adj* & *m* parallel ‖ *f* (geom) parallel line; **parallele** (sports) parallel bars

**paralume** *m* lamp shade

**paramano** *m* cuff, wristband; (archit) facing brick

**paraménto** *s* facing (*of a wall*); (eccl) vestment

**parami·ne** *m* (-ne) (nav) paravane

**paramó·sche** *m* (-sche) fly net

**paran·co** *m* (-chi) tackle

**paranin·fo** -fa *mf* matchmaker

**paranòi·co** -ca *adj* & *mf* (-ci -che) paranoiac

**paraòc·chi** *m* (-chi) blinker (*on horse*)

**parapètto** *m* parapet

**parapì·glia** *m* (-glia) hubbub

**parapiòg·gia** *m* (-gia) umbrella

**parare** *tr* to adorn; to hang; to protect; to parry (*a thrust*); to offer; to drive (*e.g., cattle*) ‖ *intr*—**dove va a parare?** what are you driving at? ‖ *ref* to protect oneself; (eccl) to don the vestments; **pararsi dinanzi a** to loom up in front of

**parasóle** *m* parasol; (aut) sun visor

**paraspal·le** *m* (-le) (sports) shoulder pad

**parassi·ta** (-ti -te) *adj* parasitic ‖ *m* parasite

**parassità·rio** -ria *adj* (-ri -rie) parasitic(al)

**parassìti·co** -ca *adj* (-ci -che) parasitic(al)

**parastatale** *adj* government-controlled ‖ *mf* employee of government-controlled agency

**parastin·chi** *m* (-chi) (sports) shin guard

**parata** *f* fence, bar; (fencing) parry; (soccer) catch; (mil) parade; **mala parata** dangerous situation

**paratìa** *f* bulkhead

**parato** *m* hangings; **parati** hangings; (naut) bilgeways

**paratóia** *f* sluice gate

**paraur·ti** *m* (-ti) (aut) bumper; (rr) buffer

**paravènto** *m* screen

**Par·ca** *f* (-che) Fate

**parcare** §197 *tr* & *intr* to park

**parcèlla** *f* bill, fee, honorarium; parcel, lot (*of land*)

**parcheggiare** §290 (parchéggio) *tr* & *intr* to park

**parchég·gio** *m* (-gi) parking; parking lot

**parchìmetro** *m* parking meter

**par·co** -ca (-chi -che) *adj* frugal; parsimonious ‖ *m* park; parking; parking lot; **parco dei divertimenti** amusement park

**paréc·chio** -chia (-chi -chie) *adj indef*

a good deal of, a lot of; **parecchi** several ‖ *pron* a good deal, a lot; **parecchi** several ‖ **parecchio** *adv* a lot; rather

**pareggiare** §290 (paréggio) *tr* to level; to equal; to match; to balance; to recognize ‖ *intr* (sports) to tie

**pareggia·to** -ta *adj* accredited (*school*)

**parég·gio** *m* (-gi) leveling; matching; (sports) tie; **pareggio del bilancio** balancing of the budget

**parentado** *m* kinsfolk, kindred; relationship; **concludere il parentado di** to arrange for the wedding of

**parènte** *mf* relative; (lit) parent; **parenti** kin

**parentèla** *f* relationship; relations

**parènte·si** *f* (-si) parenthesis; break, interval; **fra parentesi** parenthetically; in parentheses; **parentesi quadra** bracket

**parére** *m* opinion, mind; advice; **a mio parere** in my opinion ‖ §210 *intr* (ESSERE) to seem; **che Le pare?** what is your opinion?; **ma Le pare!** not at all!; **mi pare che** + *subj* it seems to me that + *ind*; I guess that + *ind*; **non Le pare?** don't you think so?; **non mi pare vero** I can't believe it

**paréte** *f* wall; **tra le pareti domestiche** within the four walls of the home

**pargolét·to** -ta *adj* (poet) infantile ‖ *mf* (poet) child

**pàrgo·lo** -la *adj* (poet) infantile ‖ *mf* (poet) child

**pari** *adj invar* equal, even; **camminare di pari passo** to walk at the same rate; **essere pari** to be quits; **essere pari al proprio compito** to be equal to the task; **fare un salto a piè pari** to jump with feet together; **pari pari** verbatim; **rimanere pari con** (sports) to be tied with; **saltare a piè pari** to skip (*e.g., a page*); to dodge (*a difficulty*); **trattare da pari a pari** to treat as an equal ‖ *m* peer; **al pari di** as, like; **del pari** also; **in pari** even, leveled; **senza pari** matchless, peerless ‖ *f*—**stare alla pari con** to be an even match for

**parìa** *f* peerage

**pà·ria** *m* (-ria) pariah

**parificare** §197 (parìfico) *tr* to level; to match; to accredit (*a school*); to balance

**Parigi** *f* Paris

**parigi·no** -na *adj* & *mf* Parisian ‖ *f* slow-burning stove; Parisian woman; (rr) switching spur

**pariglia** *f* pair, couple; team (*of horses*); (cards) two of a kind; **rendere la pariglia** to give tit for tat

**pariménti** *adv* likewise

**pari·tà** *f* (-tà) parity

**paritèti·co** -ca *adj* (-ci -che) joint (*e.g., committee*)

**parlamentare** *adj* parliamentary ‖ *mf* member of parliament ‖ *m* (mil) envoy ‖ *v* (parlaménto) *intr* to parley

**parlaménto** *m* parliament

**parlante** *adj* talking; life-like ‖ *mf* speaker

**parlantina** *f* glibness

**parlare** *m* talk, speech; dialect ‖ *tr* to speak (*a language*) ‖ *intr* to speak, talk; to discuss; **chi parla?** (telp) hello!; **far parlare di sé** to be talked about; **parlare chiaro** to speak bluntly; **parlare del più e del meno** to make small talk; **parlare tra sé e sé** to talk to oneself ‖ *ref* to talk to one another

**parla·to -ta** *adj* spoken; current (*speech*); talking (*movie*) ‖ *m* talkie; (mov) sound track; (theat) dialogue ‖ *f* speech, talk; dialect

**parla·tóre -trice** *mf* speaker

**parlatò·rio** *m* (**-ri**) visting room (*e.g., in jail*)

**parlottare (parlòtto)** *intr* to whisper in secret

**parmigia·no -na** *adj & mf* Parmesan ‖ *m* Parmesan cheese

**parnaso** *m* Parnassus (*poetry, poets*) ‖ **il Parnaso** Mount Parnassus

**paro** *m*—**in un par d'ore** in a couple of hours ‖ *adv*—**andare a paro** to keep abreast; **mettere a paro** to compare

**parodìa** *f* parody; **fare la parodia di** to parody

**parodiare** §287 **(paròdio)** *tr* to parody

**paròla** *f* word; speech; **avere parole con** to have words with; **buttare la mezza parola** to make an allusion; **dare la parola a** to give the floor to; **di poche parole** of few words; **domandare la parola a** to ask for the floor; **essere di parola** to keep one's word; **essere in parola con** to have dealings with; **mangiarsi la parola** to break one's word; **mangiarsi le parole** to slur one's words; **non far parola** to not breathe a word; **parola crociata** crossword puzzle; **parola d'ordine** password; **parola macedonia** acronym **parola sdrucciola** proparoxytone; **parole** lyrics; **parole di circostanza** occasional words; **prendere la parola** to take the floor; **rivolgere la parola a** to address; **venire a parole** to begin to quarrel

**parolàc·cia** *f* (**-ce**) dirty word; swearword

**paro·làio -làia (-lài -làie)** *adj* wordy, verbose ‖ *mf* windbag

**parolière** *m* lyricist

**parossismo** *m* paroxysm; climax

**parossìto·no -na** *adj* paroxytone

**parotite** *f* (pathol) parotitis; **parotite epidemica** (pathol) mumps

**parrici·da** *mf* (**-di -de**) patricide

**parrocchétto** *m* parakeet; (naut) foretopsail; (naut) fore-topmast

**parròcchia** *f* parish

**parrocchia·no -na** *mf* parishioner

**pàrro·co** *m* (**-ci**) rector, parson

**parruc·ca** *f* (**-che**) wig; (fig) old fogey

**parsimònia** *f* parsimony

**parsimonió·so -sa** [s] *adj* parsimonious

**partàc·cia** *f*—**fare una partaccia** to break one's word; **fare una partaccia a** to make a scene in front of; to rebuke loudly

**parte** *f* part; share; section; side; party; partiality; (theat) role; **a parte** separately; (theat) aside; **d'altra parte** on the other hand; **da parte** aside; **da parte mia** as for me; **fare le parti** to divide in shares; **gran parte di** a great deal of; **in parte** partially; **la maggior parte di** most of; **parte civile** (law) plaintiff; **parte ... parte** some ... some; **part ... part; prendere in mala parte** to take amiss

**partecipante** *adj* participating ‖ *mf* participant; (sports) contestant

**partecipare (partécipo)** *tr* to announce; (lit) to share in ‖ *intr*—**partecipare a** to share in; to participate in; **partecipare di** to partake of (*e.g., the nature of an animal*)

**partecipazióne** *f* announcement; card; announcement (*of a wedding*); share (*in a business*); participation (*in some action*)

**partécipe** *adj* sharing, partaking

**parteggiare** §290 **(partéggio)** *intr* to side; **parteggiare per** to side with

**Partenóne** *m* Parthenon

**partènte** *adj* departing ‖ *mf* person departing, traveler; (sports) starter

**partènza** *f* departure; sailing; (sports) start; **di partenza** or **in partenza** about to leave; **partenza lanciata** (sports) running start

**particèlla** *f* particle

**particì·pio** *m* (**-pi**) participle

**particolare** *adj* particular; private; **in particolare** especially ‖ *m* detail

**particolareggiare** §290 **(particolaréggio)** *tr* to detail

**particolarismo** *m* regionalism, particularism

**particolarìsti·co -ca** *adj* (**-ci -che**) particularistic; individualistic

**particolari·tà** *f* (**-tà**) peculiarity; detail

**partigianerìa** *f* partisanship, factionalism

**partigia·no -na** *adj & mf* partisan

**partire** §176 *tr* (lit) to divide ‖ *v* (**parto**) *intr* to depart; (fig) to arise; **a partire da** beginning with; **far partire** to start (*e.g., a car*) ‖ *ref* to depart, leave

**parti·to -ta** *adj* parted ‖ *m* match (*in marriage*); (pol) party; **ridotto a mal partito** in bad shape; **mettere la testa a partito** to reform; **partito preso** parti pris; **prendere partito** to take sides; to make up one's mind; **trarre il miglior partito da** to make the best of ‖ *f* panel (*e.g., of door*); lot (*of goods*); game; match; party; round (*of golf*); (com) entry; **partita di caccia** hunting party; **partita doppia** (com) double entry; **partita semplice** (com) single entry

**partitura** *f* (mus) score

**partizióne** *f* partition, division

**parto** *m* birth, childbirth

**partorire** §176 *tr* to bear, bring forth

**parvènza** *f* (lit) appearance

**parziale** *adj* partial, one-sided

**parziali·tà** *f* (**-tà**) partiality

**pàscere** §211 *tr, intr & ref* to pasture, graze

**pa·scià** *m* (**-scià**) pasha

**pasciu·to -ta** *adj* well-fed

**pascolare** (pàscolo) *tr & intr* to pasture

**pàscolo** *m* pasture

**Pàsqua** *f* Easter; **contento come una Pasqua** as happy as a lark; **Pasqua fiorita** Palm Sunday

**pasquale** *adj* paschal (*e.g., lamb*)

**passàbile** *adj* passable, tolerable

**passàg·gio** *m* (-gi) passage; transfer; crossing; traffic; passageway; ride; promotion; (sports) pass; **aprirsi il passaggio** to make one's way; **di passaggio** in passing; transient (*visitor*); **essere di passaggio** to be passing by; **passaggio a livello** railroad crossing; **passaggio zebrato** zebra crossing; **vietato il passaggio** no thoroughfare

**passamano** *m* passing from hand to hand; ribbon; (coll) railing, handrail

**passante** *adj* passing (*shot*) ‖ *mf* passer-by ‖ *m* strap

**passapòrto** *m* passport

**passare** *tr* to cross; to pass; to undergo (*a medical examination*); to move; to hand; to pay; to send (*word*); to pierce; to spend (*time*); to strain; to go over; to let have (*e.g., a slap*); to overstep (*the bounds*); **passare in rassegna** to pass in review; **passare per le armi** to execute; **passare un brutto quarto d'ora** to have a bad ten minutes; **passare un guaio** to have a hard time; **passarla a qlcu** (coll) to forgive s.o.; **passarla liscia** (coll) to get off unscathed; **passarsela bene** (coll) to have a good time ‖ *intr* (ESSERE) to pass; to go; to filter (*said of air, light*); to move; to spoil (*said of food*); to be overcooked; to be promoted; to become; to enter; (lit) to be over; **fare passare qlcu** to let s.o. come in; **passare a nozze** to get married; **passare a seconde nozze** to remarry; **passare avanti a** to overcome; **passare di mente** to forget, e.g., **gli è passata di mente la riunione** he forgot the meeting; **passare di moda** to go out of style; **passare in giudicato** (law) to be no longer appealable; **passare per** to pass as; **passare per il rotto della cuffia** to barely make it; **passare sopra qlco** to overlook s.th; **passi!** come in!; **passo!** (rad) over!; **passo** (cards) pass

**passata** *f* purée; **dare una passata a** to glance at; **dare una passata di straccio a** to rub lightly with a rag; to give a lick and a promise to; **di passata** hurriedly

**passatèmpo** *m* pastime; hobby

**passati·sta** *mf* (-sti -ste) traditionalist

**passa·to -ta** *adj* past; last; overcooked; **essere passato** (coll) to be no longer in one's prime; **passato di moda** out of fashion ‖ *m* past; purée; **passato prossimo** present perfect; **passato remoto** preterit ‖ *f* see **passata**

**passatóia** *f* runner (*rug*)

**passa·tóio** *m* (-tói) stepping stone

**passeggè·ro -ra** *adj* passing ‖ *mf* passenger; **passeggero clandestino** stowaway

**passeggiare** §290 (passéggio) *tr* to walk (*e.g., a horse*) ‖ *intr* to walk, promenade

**passeggiata** *f* promenade; walk; drive, ride; drive, road; **fare una passeggiata** to take a walk; to take a ride

**passeggiatrice** *f* streetwalker

**passég·gio** *m* (-gi) walk; promenade; **andare a passeggio** to take a walk

**passerèlla** *f* gangway; catwalk; footbridge

**pàsse·ro -ra** *mf* sparrow ‖ *f*—**passera di mare** (ichth) flounder

**passìbile** *adj*—**passibile di** subject to, liable to

**passiflòra** *f* passionflower

**passino** *m* colander, strainer

**passióne** *f* passion

**passivi·tà** *f* (-tà) passivity; (com) deficit

**passi·vo -va** *adj* passive ‖ *m* (com) liabilities; (com) debit side; (gram) passive

**pas·so -sa** *adj*—see **uva** ‖ *m* step; passage; pass (*in mountain*); pace; footstep; pitch (*of screw, helix, etc.*); (aut) wheelbase; (phot) tread; (phot) size (*of roll*); **a grandi passi** with great strides; **andare al passo** to march in step; to walk (*said of a horse*); **a passi di gigante** by leaps and bounds; **a passo di corsa** running; **a passo d'uomo** walking, at a walk; **aprire il passo** to open the way; **di buon passo** at a good clip; **di pari passo** at the same rate; **fare quattro passi** to take a stroll; **passo doppio** paso doble; **passo d'uomo** manhole; step; **passo falso** misstep; (fig) stumble; **sbarrare il passo** to block the way; **seguire i passi di** to walk in the footsteps of ‖ *interj* (cards) pass!; over!

**pasta** *f* paste; dough; **di pasta grossa** uncouth, coarse; **pasta alimentare** pasta, macaroni products; **pasta all'uovo** egg noodles; **pasta asciutta** pasta with sauce and cheese; **pasta dentifricia** toothpaste; **una pasta d'uomo** a good-natured man

**pastasciutta** *f* pasta with sauce and cheese

**pasteggiare** §290 (pastéggio) *intr* to dine

**pastèllo** *adj invar & m* pastel ‖ *m* crayon

**pastétta** *f* batter; (coll) trickery

**pastìc·ca** *f* (-che) lozenge, tablet; **pasticche per la tosse** cough drops

**pasticcerìa** *f* pastrymaking; pastry; pastry shop

**pasticciare** §128 (pasticcio) *tr & intr* to bungle; to scribble

**pasticciè·re -ra** *mf* pastry cook; confectioner

**pasticcino** *m* cookie; patty

**pastìc·cio** *m* (-ci) pie (*of meat, macaroni, etc*); bungle; mess; **cacciarsi nei pasticci** to wind up in the soup

**pasticció·ne -na** *mf* bungler

**pastifì·cio** *m* (-ci) spaghetti and macaroni factory

**pastìglia** *f* lozenge, tablet; **pastiglia per la tosse** cough drop

pastina·ca *f* (-che) parsnip
pa·sto -sta *adj* (archaic) fed || *m* meal;
  pasto a prezzo fisso table d'hôte ||
  *f* see pasta
pastóia *f* hobble; (fig) shackle
pastóne *m* mash
pastóra *f* shepherdess
pastorale *adj* pastoral
pastóre *m* shepherd; pastor
pastorì·zio -zia (-zi -zie) *adj* shepherd
  || *f* sheep raising
pastorizzare [ddzz] *tr* to pasteurize
pastó·so -sa [s] *adj* pasty; mellow
pastrano *m* overcoat
pastura *f* pasture; hay; fodder
patac·ca *f* (-che) large, worthless coin;
  fake; (coll) medal; (coll) spot
patata *f* potato
patatràc *m* (patatràc) crash
patèlla *f* kneecap; (zool) limpet
patè·ma *m* (-mi) affliction; patema
  d'animo anxiety
patenta·to -ta *adj* licensed; (coll) well-
  known
patènte *adj* patent || *f* license; driver's
  license; patente sanitaria (naut) bill
  of health
patentino *m* (aut) permit
paterèc·cio *m* (-ci) whitlow
paternale *adj* (obs) paternal || *f* repri-
  mand
paterni·tà *f* (-tà) paternity; authorship
patèr·no -na *adj* paternal; fatherly
paternòstro *m* Lord's Prayer; è vero
  come il paternostro it is the gospel
  truth
patèti·co -ca (-ci -che) *adj* pathetic;
  mawkish || *m* pathos; mawkishness
pathos *m* pathos
patibile *adj* endurable
patibolare *adj* gallows
patibolo *m* executioner's instrument;
  scaffold
patiménto *m* suffering
pàtina *f* patina; coating (*on paper*);
  varnish; fur (*on tongue*)
patinare (pàtino) *tr* to gloss, glaze (*e.g.*,
  *paper*)
patire §176 *tr* to suffer; (gram) to be
  the recipient of (*an action*) || *intr* to
  suffer
pati·to -ta *adj* suffering, sickly || *mf* fan
  || *m* boyfriend || *f* girlfriend
patòge·no -na *adj* pathogenic
patologìa *f* pathology
patològi·co -ca *adj* (-ci -che) patho-
  logic(al)
patos *m* var of pathos
patrasso *m*—andare a patrasso to die;
  to go to ruin; mandare a patrasso
  to kill; to ruin
pàtria *f* fatherland, native land
patriar·ca *m* (-chi) patriarch
patriarcale *adj* patriarchal
patrigno *m* stepfather
patrimoniale *adj* patrimonial; property
  (*tax*); capital (*e.g.*, *transaction*)
patrimò·nio *m* (-ni) patrimony; estate;
  fortune; (fig) heritage
pà·trio -tria (-tri -trie) *adj* paternal; of
  one's country (*e.g.*, *love*) || *f* see
  patria

patriò·ta *mf* (-ti -te) patriot; (coll) fellow citizen
patriòtti·co -ca *adj* (-ci -che) patriotic
patriottismo *m* patriotism
patri·zio -zia (-zi -zie) *adj* & *m* patri-
  cian || Patrizio *m* Patrick
patrocinante *adj* pleading (*lawyer*)
patrocinare *tr* to favor, sponsor; to
  plead
patrocina·tóre -trice *mf* defender;
  pleader
patroci·nio *m* (-ni) support; sponsorship; (law) defense; patrocinio gratuito public defense
patronato *m* patronage; charitable institution, foundation; patronato scolastico state aid fund
patronéssa *f* sponsor; trustee (*of charitable institution*)
patròno *m* patron saint; patron; sponsor; trustee (*of charitable institution*); (law) counsel
patta *f* flap (*of garment*); bill (*of
  anchor*); (coll) potholder; essere or
  far patta to be even, tie
patteggiaménto *m* negotiation
patteggiare §290 (pattéggio) *tr* & *intr*
  to negotiate
pattinàggio *m* skating
pattinare (pàttino) *intr* to skate; to
  skid (*said of a car*)
pattina·tóio *m* (-tói) skating rink
pattina·tóre -trice *mf* skater
pàttino *m* skate; guide block (*of an
  elevator*); (aer) skid, runner; pattino
  a rotelle roller skate
pattino *m* racing shell with outrigger
  floats
patto *m* pact; a nessun patto by no
  means; a patto che provided (that);
  patto sociale social contract; venire a
  patti to come to terms
pattùglia *f* patrol
pattugliare §280 *tr* & *intr* to patrol
pattuire §176 *tr* & *intr* to negotiate
pattui·to -ta *adj* agreed || *m* agreement
pattume *m* litter, garbage
pattumièra *f* dustpan; trash bin
patùrnie *fpl*—avere le paturnie (coll)
  to be in the dumps
paura *f* fear; aver paura di to be afraid
  of; da far paura frightful; dar or
  metter paura a to frighten; per paura
  che for fear that, lest
pauró·so -sa [s] *adj* fearful
pàusa *f* pause
pausare (pàuso) *tr* (lit) to interrupt ||
  *intr* (lit) to pause
paventare (pavènto) *tr* & *intr* to fear
pavesare (pavéso) *tr* to deck with flags;
  to dress (*a ship*)
pavése [s] *adj*—see zuppa || *m* pavis
  (*shield*); (naut) bunting
pàvi·do -da *adj* cowardly, timid
pavimentare (paviménto) *tr* to pave
pavimentazióne *f* paving, pavement
paviménto *m* floor; bottom (*of sea*);
  paving (*of street*)
pavoncèlla *f* lapwing
pavó·ne -na or -néssa *mf* peacock
pavoneggiare §290 (pavonéggio) *ref* to
  swagger, strut
pazientare (paziènto) *intr* to be patient

paziènte *adj & mf* patient
paziènza *f* patience; **fare scappare la pazienza a** to drive mad; **pazienza!** too bad!
pazzé·sco -sca *adj* (-schi -sche) crazy, wild
pazzìa *f* madness, insanity; folly; **fare pazzie** to act like a fool
paz·zo -za *adj* crazy, insane; **andar pazzo per** to be crazy about || *mf* crazy person
pèc·ca *f* (-che) imperfection
peccaminó·so -sa [s] *adj* sinful
peccare §197 (pècco) *intr* to sin; to be lacking; to be at fault
peccato *m* sin; **che peccato!** what a pity!; **è un peccato** it's a shame
pecca·tóre -trice *mf* sinner
pécchia *f* bee
pecchióne *m* drone
péce *f* pitch; **pece greca** rosin
pechinése [s] *adj & mf* Pekingese
Pechino *f* Peking
pècora *f* sheep
peco·ràio *m* (-rài) shepherd
pecorèlla *f* small sheep, lamb
pecori·no -na *adj* sheep; sheepish || *m* sheep-milk cheese || *f* sheep manure
peculato *m* embezzlement, peculation
peculiare *adj* peculiar
peculiari·tà *f* (-tà) peculiarity
pecù·lio *m* (-li) nest egg, savings; (obs) cattle
pecùnia *m* (lit) money
pecunià·rio -ria *adj* (-ri -rie) pecuniary
pedàg·gio *m* (-gi) toll
pedagogìa *f* pedagogy, pedagogics
pedagògi·co -ca *adj* (-ci -che) pedagogic(al)
pedagò·go -ga *mf* (-ghi -ghe) pedagogue
pedalare *intr* to pedal
pedale *m* trunk (*of tree*); pedal; treadle (*e.g., of sewing machine*)
pedalièra *f* pedals, pedal keyboard; (aer) rudder bar
pedalino *m* (coll) sock, short stocking
pedana *f* footrest; platform; bedside rug; hem (*of skirt*); (aut) running board; (sports) springboard
pedante *adj* pedantic || *m* pedant
pedanterìa *f* pedantry
pedanté·sco -sca *adj* (-schi -sche) pedantic
pedata *f* kick; footprint; tread (*of step*)
pedèstre *adj* pedestrian
pedia·tra *mf* (-tri -tre) pediatrician
pediatrìa *f* pediatrics
pedicu·re *mf* (-re) pedicure
pedicu·ro -ra *mf* var of **pedicure**
pedilù·vio *m* (-vi) foot bath
pedina *f* (checkers) checker, man; (chess) pawn
pedinare *tr* to shadow, follow about
pedìsse·quo -qua *adj* servile
pedivèlla *f* pedal crank
pedóne *m* pedestrian; (chess) pawn
pedule *m* stocking foot || *fpl* climbing shoes, sneakers
pedùncolo *m* (anat, bot, zool) peduncle
pegamòide *f* imitation leather
pèggio *adj invar* worse; **il peggio** the worst, e.g., **il peggio ragazzo** the

worst boy; || *m* worst; **andare per il peggio** to be getting worse || *f* worst; **alla peggio** if worst comes to worst; **averne la peggio** to get the worst of it || *adv* worse; worst; at worst; **peggio + pp** less + *pp;* least + *pp;* **tanto peggio** so much the worse
peggioraménto *m* deterioration, worsening
peggiorare (peggióro) *tr & intr* to worsen
peggió·re (-ri) *adj* worse; worst || *m* worst
pégli §4
pégno *m* pledge, pawn
pégola *f* pitch; (coll) bad luck
péi §4
pél §4
pèla·go *m* (-ghi) (poet) open sea; (coll) mess; **pelago di guai** sea of trouble
pelame *m* hair, coat
pelandróne *m* (coll) shirker, do-nothing
pelapata·te *m* (-te) potato peeler
pelare (pélo) *tr* to fleece; to pluck; to pare, peel; to clear (*land*); (fig) to strip; to scald, burn || *ref* (coll) to shed; to become bald
pela·to -ta *adj* peeled; hairless, bald; barren || *m* (coll) baldy; **pelati** peeled tomatoes || *f* fleecing, plucking; (joc) baldness, bald spot
pélla §4
pellàc·cia *f* (-ce) tough hide
pellame *m* skins, hides
pèlle *f* skin, hide; **a fior di pelle** slightly, superficially; **essere nella pelle di** to be in the boots of; **fare la pelle a** to bump off; **non stare più nella pelle** to be beside oneself with joy; **pelle di dante** buckskin; **pelle d'oca** goose skin, goose flesh; **pelle d'uovo** mull; **pelle pelle** skin-deep, superficial
pélle §4
pellegrinàg·gio *m* (-gi) pilgrimage
pellegrinare *intr* (lit) to go on a pilgrimage
pellegri·no -na *adj* wandering; (lit) foreign; (lit) strange, quixotic || *mf* pilgrim, traveler
pelleróssa *mf* (pellirosse) redskin
pelletterìa *f* leather goods; leather goods store
pellicano *m* pelican
pelliccerìa *f* furrier's store; furrier's trade, fur industry
pellic·cia *f* (-ce) fur
pellic·ciàio -ciàia *mf* (-ciài -ciàie) furrier
pelliccióne *m* fur jacket
pellìcola *f* film; **pellicola in rotolo** roll film; **pellicola piana** film pack; **pellicola sonora** sound film; **pellicola vergine** unexposed film
pellirós·sa *mf* (-se) var of **pellerossa**
pélo *m* hair (*of beard*); pile (*of carpet*); fur; **avere pelo sul cuore** not to be easily moved; **cercare il pelo nell'uovo** to split hairs; **di primo pelo** green, inexperienced; **non avere peli sulla lingua** to not mince one's words; **pelo dell'acqua** water surface; **per un pelo** by a hair's breadth

**peloponnesìa·co** **-ca** *adj* (**-ci** **-che**) Peloponnesian

**pelό·so** **-sa** [s] *adj* hairy; self-serving (*e.g.*, *charity*)

**péltro** *m* pewter

**pelùria** *f* down, soft hair

**péna** *f* penalty; concern; compassion; pain, suffering; grief; **a mala pena** barely; **essere in pena per** to worry about; **fare pena** to arouse compassion; **pena infamante** degrading punishment; loss of civil rights; **sotto pena di** under penalty of; **valere la pena** to be worthwhile

**penale** *adj* penal || *f* penalty

**penali·sta** *mf* (**-sti** **-ste**) criminal lawyer

**penali·tà** *f* (**-tà**) penalty

**penalizzare** [ddzz] *tr* (sports) to penalize

**penare** (**péno**) *intr* to suffer; to find it difficult

**pencolare** (**pèncolo**) *intr* to totter; to waver

**pendà·glio** *m* (**-gli**) pendant; **pendaglio da forca** gallows bird

**pendènte** *adj* leaning; hanging; pending || *m* pendant

**pendènza** *f* inclination, pitch; controversy; balance; **in pendenza** pending

**pèndere** §123 *intr* to hang; to lean; to slope; to pitch

**pendice** *f* slope, declivity

**pen·dìo** *m* (**-dìi**) slant; slope

**pèndola** *f* clock

**pendolare** *adj* pendulum-like; commuting; transient (*tourist*) || *mf* commuter || *v* (**pèndolo**) *intr* to sway back and forth; to waver; (nav) to cruise back and forth

**pèndolo** *m* pendulum; clock

**pèndu·lo** **-la** *adj* (lit) hanging

**penetrante** *adj* penetrating, piercing

**penetrare** (**pènetro**) *tr* to penetrate, pierce || *intr* to penetrate || *ref*; **penetrarsi di** to be convinced of; to become aware of

**penicillina** *f* penicillin

**peninsulare** *adj* peninsular

**penìsola** *f* peninsula

**penitènte** *adj & mf* penitent

**penitènza** *f* penitence; punishment

**penitenzià·rio** **-ria** *adj & mf* (**-ri** **-rie**) penitentiary

**pénna** *f* feather; pen; peen (*of hammer*); (mus) plectrum; **penna a sfera** ball-point pen; **penna d'oca** quill; **penna stilografica** fountain pen

**pennàc·chio** *m* (**-chi**) panache; plume, tuft; cloud (*of smoke*)

**pennaiòlo** *m* hack writer

**pennarèllo** *m* felt-tip pen

**pennellare** (**pennèllo**) *intr* to brush; (med) to pencil

**pennellata** *f* brush stroke

**pennèllo** *m* brush; (naut) signal flag; (naut) kedge; **pennello per la barba** shaving brush; **stare a pennello** to fit to a T

**pennino** *m* pen; penpoint, nib

**pennόne** *m* flagpole; (naut) yard; (mil) pennant

**pennu·to** **-ta** *adj* feathered || **pennuti** *mpl* birds

**penόmbra** *f* penumbra; semidarkness; faint light; **vivere in penombra** to live in obscurity

**penό·so** **-sa** [s] *adj* painful

**pensàbile** *adj* thinkable

**pensante** *adj* thinking

**pensare** (**pènso**) *tr* to think; to think of || *intr* to think; to worry; **dar da pensare a** to cause worry to, e.g., **suo figlio gli dà da pensare** his son causes him worry; **pensa ai fatti tuoi** (coll) mind your own business; **pensa alla salute** (coll) don't worry!; **pensare a** to think of; **pensare di** to plan, intend to

**pensata** *f* bright idea, brainstorm

**pensa·tόre** **-trice** *mf* thinker

**pensièro** *m* thought; **dare pensiero a** to cause worry to; **darsi pensiero per** to worry about; **essere sopra pensiero** to be absorbed in thought

**pensieró·so** **-sa** [s] *adj* thoughtful, pensive

**pènsile** *adj* hanging, overhead

**pensilina** *f* marquee

**pensionaménto** *m* retirement

**pensionante** *mf* boarder, paying guest

**pensionare** (**pensiόno**) *tr* to pension

**pensiona·to** **-ta** *adj* pensioned || *mf* pensioner || *m* boarding school

**pensiόne** *f* pension; boarding house; **in pensione** retired; **tenere a pensione** to board (*a lodger*); **vivere a pensione** to board (*said of a lodger*)

**pensό·so** **-sa** [s] *adj* thoughtful, pensive

**pentàgono** *m* pentagon

**pentagram·ma** *m* (**-mi**) (mus) staff, stave

**pentàmetro** *m* pentameter

**Pentecòste, la** Pentecost, Whitsunday

**pentiménto** *m* repentance; correction (*e.g.*, *in a manuscript*); change of heart

**pentire** (**pènto**) *ref* to repent; to change one's mind; **pentirsi di** to repent

**penti·to** **-ta** *adj* repentant, repenting; **pentito e contrito** in sackcloth and ashes

**péntola** *f* pot, kettle; potful; **pentola a pressione** pressure cooker

**penùlti·mo** **-ma** *adj* next to the last || *f* penult

**penùria** *f* shortage, scarcity

**penzolare** (**pènzolo**) [dz] *intr* to dangle, hang down

**penzolόni** [dz] *adv* dangling

**peònia** *f* peony

**pepaiòla** *f* pepper shaker; pepper mill

**pepare** (**pépo**) *tr* to pepper

**pepa·to** **-ta** *adj* peppered; peppery

**pépe** *m* pepper; **pepe della Giamaica** allspice; **pepe di Caienna** red pepper, cayenne pepper

**peperόne** *m* (bot) pepper

**pepita** *f* nugget

**per** *prep* by; through; throughout; for; because of; to, in order to; in favor of; considering; **essere per** to be about to; **per + *adj* or *adv* + che + *subj*** however + *adj* or *adv* + *ind*, e.g., **per intelligente che sia** however intelligent he is; **per caso** perchance; **per che cosa?** what for?; **per l'appunto** exactly, just; **per lungo** lengthwise; **per me** as for me; **per ora** now; **per parte mia** as for me; **per poco** hardly, scarcely, **per quanto** + *adj* or *adv* + *subj* however + *adj* or *adv* + *pres ind,* e.g., **per quanto disperatamente provi** however desperately he attempts; **per tempo** early; **per traverso** diagonally; **per via che** (coll) because; **stare per** to be about to

**péra** *f* pear (*fruit*); bulb, light bulb; (joc) head

**peraltro** *adv* besides, moreover

**peranco** *adv* yet

**perbacco** *interj* by Jove!

**perbène** *adj invar* nice, well brought up

**percalle** *m* percale

**percènto** *m* percent; percentage

**percentuale** *adj* percentage || *f* percent; commission, bonus

**percepìbile** *adj* collectable

**percepire** §176 *tr* to perceive; to receive (*a salary*)

**percettìbile** *adj* perceptible

**percetti·vo -va** *adj* perceptive

**percezióne** *f* perception

**perché** *m* why, reason; **il perché e il percome** the why and the wherefore || *pron rel* for which || *adv* why || *conj* because; so that

**perciò** *conj* therefore, accordingly

**percóme** *m & conj* wherefore

**percorrènza** *f* stretch, distance

**percórrere** §139 *tr* to cross; to cover, go through

**percórso** *m* crossing, distance

**percòssa** *f* hit, blow; contusion

**percuòtere** §251 *tr* to hit, beat; (fig) to shake || *intr* to strike

**percussióne** *f* percussion

**percussóre** *m* firing pin

**perdènte** *adj* losing || *mf* loser

**pèrdere** §212 *tr* to lose; to waste; to miss (*e.g., a train*); to ruin; to leak || *intr* to lose; to leak; to be inferior || *ref* to get lost; to waste one's time; **perdersi d'animo** to lose heart; **perdersi in un bicchier d'acqua** to become discouraged for nothing

**perdifiato** *m*—**a perdifiato** at the top of one's lungs

**perdigiór·no** *mf* (-no) idler

**perdinci** *interj* good Heavens!

**pèrdita** *f* loss; leak; **a perdita d'occhio** as far as the eye can see; **perdite** (mil) casualties

**perditèm·po** *mf* (-po) idler || *m* waste of time

**perdizióne** *f* perdition

**perdonàbile** *adj* pardonable

**perdonare** (**perdóno**) *tr* to forgive; to spare; **perdonare a qlcu qlco** or **perdonare qlcu di qlco** to forgive s.o. for s.th || *intr* (with *dat*) to pardon

**perdóno** *m* forgiveness, pardon

**perdurare** *intr* (ESSERE & AVERE) to last; to persevere

**perdu·to -ta** *adj* lost; **andar perduto** to be desperately in love; to get lost

**peregrinare** *intr* to wander

**peregrinazióne** *f* wandering

**peregri·no -na** *adj* far-fetched, outlandish

**perènne** *adj* everlasting; perennial

**perentò·rio -ria** *adj* (-ri -rie) peremptory

**perequare** (**perèquo**) *tr* to equalize

**perequazióne** *f* equalization

**perfèt·to -ta** *adj & m* perfect

**perfezionaménto** *m* improvement; (educ) specialization

**perfezionare** (**perfezióno**) *tr* to improve, polish up; to perfect || *ref* to improve; (educ) to specialize

**perfezióne** *f* perfection; **a** or **alla perfezione** to perfection

**perfidia** *f* perfidy

**pèrfi·do -da** *adj* perfidious, treacherous; (coll) foul, nasty

**perfini·re** *m* (-re) punch line

**perfino** *adv* even

**perforante** *adj* piercing, perforating

**perforare** (**perfóro**) *tr* to pierce; to perforate; to punch; to bore

**perfora·tóre -trice** *mf* key-punch operator || *m* drill || *f* punch; drill; pneumatic drill, rock drill

**perforazióne** *f* perforation

**pergamèna** *f* parchment, vellum

**pèrgamo** *m* (lit) pulpit

**pèrgola** *f* bower, pergola

**pergolato** *m* arbor, pergola; grape arbor

**pericolante** *adj* tottering, unsafe

**perìcolo** *m* danger; **non c'è pericolo** don't worry

**pericoló·so -sa** [s] *adj* dangerous

**periferìa** *f* periphery; suburbs

**perifèri·co -ca** *adj* (-ci -che) peripheral

**perìfra·si** *f* (-si) periphrasis

**perìmetro** *m* perimeter

**periodare** *m* writing style || *v* (**perìodo**) *intr* to turn a phrase

**periòdi·co -ca** (-ci -che) *adj* periodic(al) || *m* periodical

**perìodo** *m* period; age; (gram) sentence; (phys) cycle; **il periodo delle feste** holiday time

**peripezìa** *f* vicissitude

**pèriplo** *m* circumnavigation

**perire** §176 *intr* (ESSERE) to perish

**periscò·pio** *m* (-pi) periscope

**peritale** *adj* expert

**peritare** (**pèrito**) *ref* (lit) to hesitate

**peri·to -ta** *adj* expert, skilled || *mf* expert; **perito agrario** land surveyor; **perito calligrafo** handwriting expert; **perito chimico** chemist; **perito industriale** industrial engineer

**peritonèo** *m* peritoneum

**perìzia** *f* skill; survey; appraisal

**periziare** §287 (**perìzio**) *tr* to estimate, appraise

**pèrla** *f* pearl; (med) capsule

**perlàce·o -a** *adj* pearly

**perla·to -ta** *adj* pearly, smooth

**perlìfe·ro -ra** *adj* pearl-producing

**perlina** *f* bead

**perloméno** *adv* at least

**perlopiù** *adv* mostly, generally

**perlustrare** *tr* to patrol

**perlustrazióne** *f* patrol, patrolling

**permaló·so -sa** [s] *adj* touchy, grouchy
**permanènte** *adj* permanente ‖ *f* permanent wave
**permanènza** *f* permanence; stay; continuance (*in office*); duration (*of a disease*); **in permanenza** permanent (*employee*); **buona permanenza!** may your stay be happy!
**permanére** §235 (*pp* **permaso**) *intr* (ESSERE) to remain, stay
**permeàbile** *adj* permeable
**permeare** (**pèrmeo**) *tr* to permeate
**permés·so -sa** *adj* permitted, allowed; **è permesso?** may I come in? ‖ *m* permit; (mil) pass, leave
**perméttere** §198 *tr* to permit, allow, let; **permette?** do you mind? ‖ *ref* to take the liberty; to afford
**permissibile** *adj* permissible
**pèrmuta** *f* barter; exchange
**permutàbile** *adj* tradable, exchangeable
**permutare** (**pèrmuto**) *tr* to barter; (math) to permute
**pernàcchia** *f* (vulg) raspberry
**pernice** *f* partridge
**pernició·so -sa** [s] *adj* pernicious ‖ *f* pernicious malaria
**pèr·nio** *m* (-ni) var of **perno**
**pèrno** *m* pivot; pin; kingbolt; swivel; heart (*of the matter*); kernel (*of the story*); support (*of the family*); (mach) journal; **fare perno** to pivot
**pernottare** (**pernòtto**) *intr* to spend the night, stay overnight
**péro** *m* pear tree
**però** *conj* but, yet; however, nevertheless; **e però** (lit) therefore
**peróne** *m* fibula
**peronòspora** *f* downy mildew
**perorare** (**pèroro**) *tr & intr* to perorate; (law) to plead
**perorazióne** *f* peroration; (law) pleading
**peròssido** *m* peroxide; **perossido d'idrogeno** hydrogen peroxide
**perpendicolare** *adj & f* perpendicular
**perpendìcolo** *m* plumb line; **a perpendicolo** perpendicularly
**perpetrare** (**pèrpetro & perpètro**) *tr* (lit) to perpetrate
**perpètua** *f* priest's housekeeper
**perpetuare** (**perpètuo**) *tr* to perpetuate
**perpè·tuo -tua** *adj* perpetual, life ‖ *f* see **perpetua**
**perplessi·tà** *f* (-tà) perplexity
**perplès·so -sa** *adj* perplexed; (lit) ambiguous
**perquisire** §176 *tr* to search
**perquisizióne** *f* search
**persecu·tóre -trice** *mf* persecutor, oppressor
**persecuzióne** *f* persecution
**perseguire** (**perséguo**) *tr* to pursue; to persecute; to pester
**perseguitare** (**perséguito**) *tr* to persecute; to pursue; to pester
**perseveranza** *f* perseverance
**perseverare** (**persèvero**) *intr* to persevere
**persia·no -na** *adj* Persian ‖ *m* Persian; Persian lamb ‖ *f* slatted shutter; **persiana avvolgibile** Venetian blind

**pèrsi·co -ca** (**-ci -che**) *adj* Persian ‖ *m* (ichth) perch; (obs) peach ‖ *f* (coll) peach
**persino** *adv* var of **perfino**
**persistènte** *adj* persistent
**persistènza** *f* persistence
**persistere** §114 *intr* to persist
**pèr·so -sa** *adj* lost, wasted; (archaic) reddish-brown; **a tempo perso** in one's spare time
**persóna** *f* person; **per persona** apiece; **per capita; persona di servizio** servant; **persone** people
**personàg·gio** *m* (-gi) personage; character
**personale** *adj* personal ‖ *m* figure, body; personnel, staff; crew ‖ *f* one-man show
**personali·tà** *f* (-tà) personality; personage
**personificare** §197 (**personìfico**) *tr* to personify
**perspicace** *adj* perspicacious; far-sighted
**perspicàcia** *f* perspicacity
**perspì·cuo -cua** *adj* perspicuous
**persuadére** §213 *tr* to persuade ‖ *ref* to become convinced
**persuasióne** *f* persuasion
**persuasì·vo -va** *adj* persuasive; pleasing ‖ *f* persuasiveness
**persua·so -sa** *adj* convinced; resigned
**pertanto** *conj* therefore; **non pertanto** nevertheless
**pèrti·ca** *f* (-che) perch; pole
**pertinace** *adj* pertinacious, persistent
**pertinà·cia** *f* (-cie) pertinacity, obstinacy
**pertinènte** *adj* pertinent, relevant
**pertinènza** *f* pertinence; competence
**pertósse** *f* whooping cough
**pertù·gio** *m* (-gi) hole
**perturbare** *tr* to perturb ‖ *ref* to be perturbed
**perturbazióne** *f* perturbation; disturbance
**Perù**, **il** Peru; **valere un Perù** to be worth a king's ransom
**peruvia·no -na** *adj & mf* Peruvian
**pervàdere** §172 *tr* (lit) to pervade
**pervenire** §282 *intr* (ESSERE) to arrive; to come; **pervenire a** to reach
**perversióne** *f* perversion
**perversi·tà** *f* (-tà) perversity
**pervèr·so -sa** *adj* perverse; wicked
**pervertiménto** *m* perversion
**pervertire** (**pervèrto**) *tr* to pervert ‖ *ref* to become perverted
**perverti·to -ta** *adj* perverted ‖ *mf* pervert
**pervicace** *adj* (lit) obstinate
**pervin·ca** *f* (-che) periwinkle
**pésa** [s] *f* weighing; scale
**pesage** *m* (pesage) weigh-in; place for weighing in jockeys
**pesalètte·re** [s] *m* (-re) postal scale
**pesante** [s] *adj* heavy
**pesantézza** [s] *f* heaviness; weight
**pesare** (**péso**) [s] *tr* to weigh ‖ *intr* to weigh; **pesare a qlcu** to weigh upon s.o.
**pesa·tóre -trice** [s] *mf* scale or weigh-

bridge operator; **pesatore pubblico** inspector for the department of weights and measures

**pesatura** [s] *f* weighing

**pé·sca** *f* (-sche) fishing; catch (*of fish*); **pesca alla traina** trawling; **pesca d'altura** deep-sea fishing; **pesca di beneficenza** benefit lottery

**pè·sca** *f* (-sche) peach

**pescàg·gio** *m* (-gi) (naut) draft

**pescàia** *f* dam, weir

**pescare** §197 (pésco) *tr* to fish; to draw (*a card*); to dig up (*a piece of news*); to dive for (*pearls*); **pescare con la lenza** to angle for (*fish*) ǁ *intr* to fish; (naut) to displace; **pescare con la lenza** to angle; **pescare di frodo** to poach; **pescare nel torbido** to fish in troubled waters

**pesca·tóre -trice** *mf* fisher; **pescatore di canna** angler; **pescatore di frodo** poacher

**pésce** *m* fish; (typ) omission; (coll) biceps; **a pesce** headlong; **non sapere che pesci pigliare** to not know which way to turn; **pesce d'aprile** April fool; **pesce gatto** catfish; **pesce martello** hammerhead ǁ **Pesci** *mpl* (astr) Pisces

**pescecane** *m* (**pescecani & pescicani**) shark; (fig) war profiteer

**pescheréc·cio -cia** (-ci -ce) *adj* fishing ǁ *m* fishing boat

**pescherìa** *f* fish market

**peschièra** *f* fishpond; fishpound (*net*)

**pescivéndo·lo -la** *mf* fishmonger, fish dealer ǁ *f* fishwife, fishwoman

**pè·sco** *m* (-schi) peach tree

**pesi·sta** [s] *m* (-sti) (sports) weight lifter

**péso -sa** [s] *adj* (coll) heavy ǁ *m* weight; burden; bob (*of clock*); (racing) weigh-in; (sports) shot; **di peso** bodily; **peso lordo** gross weight; **peso massimo** (sports) heavyweight; **peso specifico** specific gravity; **rubare sul peso** to give short weight; **usare due pesi e due misure** to have a double standard ǁ *f* see **pesa**

**pessimismo** *m* pessimism

**pessimi·sta** *mf* (-sti -ste) pessimist

**pessimìsti·co -ca** *adj* (-ci -che) pessimistic

**pèssi·mo -ma** *adj* very bad, very poor

**pésta** *f* track, footprint; **lasciar nelle peste** to leave in the lurch; **seguir le peste di** to follow in the footsteps of

**pestàggio** *m* beating, clubbing

**pestare** (pésto) *tr* to pound; to trample; to step on; **pestare le orme di** to follow in the footsteps of; **pestare i piedi** to stamp the feet; **pestare sodo** to beat up

**pèste** *f* plague, pest

**pestèllo** *m* pestle

**pestìfe·ro -ra** *adj* pestiferous

**pestilènza** *f* pestilence; stench

**pestilenziale** *adj* pestilential; pernicious

**pé·sto -sta** *adj* crushed; thick (*darkness*) ǁ *m* Genoese sauce ǁ *f* see **pesta**

**pètalo** *m* petal

**petardo** *m* petard, firecracker

**petènte** *mf* petitioner

**petizióne** *f* petition; **petizione di principio** begging the question

**péto** *m* wind, gas

**Petrarca** *m* Petrarch

**petrarché·sco -sca** *adj* (-schi -sche) Petrarchan

**petrolièra** *f* (naut) tanker

**petrolière** *adj* incendiary ǁ *m* petroleum-industry worker; incendiary; oilman (*producer*)

**petrolìfe·ro -ra** *adj* oil-yielding

**petrò·lio** *m* (-li) petroleum; coal oil, kerosene

**petró·so -sa** [s] *adj* (lit) stony

**pettegolare** (pettégolo) *intr* to gossip

**pettegolézzo** [ddzz] *m* gossip, rumor

**pettégo·lo -la** *adj* gossipy ǁ *mf* gossip

**pettinare** (pèttino) *tr* to comb; to card; (coll) to scold

**pettinatóre** *m* carder

**pettinatrice** *f* hairdresser; carding machine

**pettinatura** *f* coiffure, hairstyling

**pèttine** *m* comb; (zool) scallop; **a pettine** perpendicular (*parking*)

**pettino** *m* dickey; bib (*of an apron*); plastron

**pettirósso** *m* robin redbreast

**pètto** *m* breast, chest; bust; bosom; **a un petto** single-breasted; **avere al petto** to feed at the breast; **a due petti** or **a doppio petto** double-breasted; **stare a petto** to be equal

**pettorale** *adj* pectoral ǁ *m* pectoral; breast collar (*of horse*)

**pettorina** *f* var of **pettino**

**pettoru·to -ta** *adj* strutting, haughty

**petulante** *adj* importunate; impertinent

**petulanza** *f* importunity; impertinence

**petùnia** *f* petunia

**pèzza** *f* piece (*of cloth*); diaper; patch (*in suit or tire*); bolt (*of paper or cloth*); **pezza d'appoggio** supporting document, voucher; **trattare come una pezza da piedi** to wipe one's boots on

**pezza·to -ta** *adj* spotted, dappled

**pezzatura** *f* dapple (*on a horse*); size (*e.g., of a loaf of bread*)

**pezzènte** *mf* beggar

**pezzétto** *m* little bit; scrap, snip

**pèzzo** *m* piece; cut (*of meat*); coin; (journ) article; **andare** or **cadere a pezzi** to fall apart; **a pezzi e bocconi** by fits and starts; **fare a pezzi** to break to pieces; to blow to bits; **pezzo di ricambio** spare part; **pezzo d'uomo** hunk of a man; **pezzo duro** brick ice cream; **pezzo forte** forte; **pezzo fuso** cast, casting; **un bel pezzo** a good while; **un pezzo grosso** a big shot

**pezzuòla** *f* small piece of cloth; (coll) handkerchief

**phy·lum** *m* (-lum) phylum

**piacènte** *adj* attractive, pleasant

**piacére** *m* pleasure; **a piacere** at will; **a Suo piacere** as you please; **fare piacere a** to do a favor for; to please; **per piacere** please; **piacere!**

pleased to meet you! || §214 *intr* (ESSERE) to please; to be pleasing; (with *dat*) to please, e.g., **come piace a Dio** as it pleases God; to like, e.g., **gli piace il ballo** he likes dancing

**piacévole** *adj* pleasant, pleasing

**piacevolézza** *f* pleasantness; off-color joke

**pià·ga** *f* (**-ghe**) sore; ulcer; wound; plague; (joc) bore; **piaga di decubito** bedsore

**piagare** §209 *tr* to make sore, injure

**pià·gia** *f* (**-ge**) (archaic) declivity; (lit) clime, country

**piaggiare** §290 *tr* (lit) to flatter, blandish || *intr* (archaic) to coast

**piagnistèo** *m* whining

**piagnó·ne -na** *mf* (coll) weeper, crybaby

**piagnucolare** (**piagnùcolo**) *intr* to whimper, whine

**piagnucoló·ne -na** *mf* whimperer, crybaby

**piagnucoló·so -sa** [s] *adj* whimpering, whining

**pialla** *f* (carp) plane

**piallàc·cio** *m* (**-ci**) veneer

**piallare** *tr* (carp) to plane

**piallatrice** *f* (carp) planer

**piallatura** *f* (carp) planing

**piana** *f* plain; wide table

**pianale** *m* plain; platform; (rr) flatcar, platform car

**pianeggiante** *adj* plane, level

**pianèlla** *f* mule (*slipper*); tile

**pianeròttolo** *m* landing (*of stairs*); ledge

**piané·ta** *m* (**-ti**) planet; horoscope || *f* (eccl) chasuble

**piàngere** §215 *tr* to shed (*tears*); to mourn, lament; **piangere miseria** to cry poverty || *intr* to cry, weep

**piangimisè·ria** *mf* (**-ria**) poverty-crying penny pincher

**piangiucchiare** §287 *intr* to whimper

**pianificare** §197 (**pianìfico**) *tr* to level; (econ) to plan

**pianifica·tóre -trice** *mf* planner

**pianino** *m* (coll) barrel organ

**piani·sta** *mf* (**-sti -ste**) pianist

**pià·no -na** *adj* plane; plain, flat || *m* plain; plane; floor; plateau; plan; map; (mus) piano; **di primo piano** first-class; **in piano** horizontal; **piano di coda** (aer) tail assembly; **piano di studio** curriculum; **piano regolatore** building plan; **piano terra** ground floor; **primo piano** (phot) close-up; (theat) foreground || *f* see **piana** || **piano** *adv* slowly; softly

**pianofòrte** *m* piano; **pianoforte a coda** grand piano

**pianòla** *f* player piano

**pianòro** *m* plateau

**pianotèr·ra** *m* (**-ra**) ground floor

**pianta** *f* plant; sole (*of foot*); plan; map; floor plan; **di sana pianta** wholly; **in pianta stabile** permanent (*employee*); **pianta rampicante** (bot) climber

**piantagióne** *f* plantation

**piantana** *f* scaffolding

**piantare** *tr* to plant; to set up (*e.g., a gun emplacement*); to pitch (*a tent*); **piantala!** (slang) cut it out!; **piantare baracca e burattini** (coll) to clear out; **piantar chiodi** (coll) to go into debt; **piantare gli occhi addosso a** to stare at; **piantare in asso** to leave in the lurch || *ref* to place oneself; to abandon one another

**pianta·to -ta** *adj* planted; stuck; driven; **bien piantato** well-built (*person*)

**pianta·tóre -trice** *mf* planter

**pianterréno** *m* ground floor

**piantito** *m* (coll) floor

**pianto** *m* weeping, tears; sadness; (bot) sap; (coll) sight, mess

**piantonare** (**piantóno**) *tr* to watch, guard

**piantóne** *m* watchman; (mil) orderly; (mil) sentry; (bot) cutting, shoot; **piantone di guida** (aut) steering wheel column

**pianura** *f* plain

**piastra** *f* plate; piaster (*coin*)

**piastrèlla** *f* tile; small flat stone; bounce (*of an airplane on landing*)

**piastrellaménto** *m* bump, bounce (*of motorboat or airplane*)

**piastrelli·sta** *m* (**-sti**) tiler, tile layer

**piastrina** *f* or **piastrino** *m* small plate; (mil) dog tag; (biol) platelet

**piatire** §176 *intr* (lit) to argue; (coll) to beg insistently

**piattafórma** *f* platform; roadbed (*of highway*); (rr) turntable; (pol) plank; **piattaforma di lancio** launching pad

**piattèllo** *m* small dish; bobêche; clay pigeon

**piattina** *f* electric cord; metal band; (min) wagon

**piattino** *m* saucer

**piat·to -ta** *adj* flat || *m* dish, plate; pan (*of scale*); pot (*in gambling*); course (*of meal*); cover (*of book*); flat (*e.g., of blade*); **piatti** (mus) cymbals; **piatto del grammofono** turntable; **piatto del giorno** plat du jour; **piatto di lenticchie** (Bib & fig) mess of pottage; **piatto fondo** soup dish; **piatto forte** pièce de résistance

**piàttola** *f* (zool) crab louse; (coll) cockroach; (vulg) bore

**piazza** *f* square; plaza; crowd; market; fortress; **andare in piazza** (coll) to become bald; **da piazza** common, ordinary; **di piazza** for hire (*e.g., cab*); **fare la piazza** (com) to canvass for customers; **far piazza pulita di** to get rid of; to clean out; **mettere in piazza** to noise abroad; **piazza d'armi** parade ground; **scendere in piazza** to take to the streets

**piazzafòrte** *f* (**piazzefòrti**) stronghold, fortress

**piazzale** *m* large square, esplanade, plaza

**piazzaménto** *m* placement; (sports) position (*of a team*)

**piazzare** *tr* to place; to sell || *ref* to place; to show (*said of a racing horse*)

**piazza·to -ta** *adj* placed; arrived (*at a high position*) ‖ *f* row, brawl
**piazzi·sta** *m* (-sti) salesman; traveling salesman
**piazzòla** *f* court, place; rest area (*off a highway*); (mil) emplacement; **piazzola di partenza** (golf) tee
**pi·ca** *f* (-che) (orn) magpie
**picaré·sco -sca** *adj* (-schi -sche) picaresque
**pic·ca** *f* (-che) pike; pique; **per picca** out of spite; **picche** (cards) spades; **rispondere picche** (fig) to answer no
**piccante** *adj* piquant, racy
**piccare** §197 *tr* (obs) to prick ‖ *ref* to become angry; **piccarsi di** to pride oneself on
**pic·chè** *f* (-chè) piqué
**picchettaménto** *m* picketing
**picchettare (picchétto)** *tr* to stake out; to picket
**picchétto** *m* stake; picket; (mil) detail
**picchiare** §287 *tr* to hit, strike ‖ *intr* to knock; to strike; to tap (*said, e.g., of rain*); (aer) to nose-dive; **picchiare in testa** (aut) to knock ‖ *ref* to hit one another
**picchiata** *f* hit, blow; (aer) nose dive
**picchia·tóre -trice** *mf* hitter ‖ *m* (boxing) puncher
**picchierellare (picchierèllo)** *tr & intr* to tap
**picchiettare (picchiétto)** *tr* to tap; to scrape; to speckle ‖ *intr* to tap
**picchiet·tìo** *m* (-tìi) patter (*e.g., of rain*)
**pic·chio** *m* (-chi) knock; (orn) woodpecker; **di picchio** all of a sudden
**picchiòtto** *m* knocker (*on door*)
**piccinerìa** *f* pettiness
**picci·no -na** *adj* little, tiny; petty ‖ *mf* child; baby
**picciòlo** *m* stem (*e.g., of cherry*); leafstalk, petiole
**piccionàia** *f* dovecote; loft; attic; (theat) upper gallery
**piccióne -na** *mf* pigeon; **pigliare due piccioni con una fava** to hit two birds with one stone
**pic·co** *m* (-chi) peak; (naut) gaff; **andare a picco** to sink; to go to ruin; **a picco** vertically; **picco di carico** (naut) derrick
**piccolézza** *f* smallness; trifle
**pìcco·lo -la** *adj* small; low (*speed*); short (*distance*); young; petty; **da piccolo** when young; **in piccolo** on a small scale; **nel mio piccolo** with my modest abilities ‖ *mf* child
**piccóne** *m* pick
**piccòzza** *f* mattock (*for mountain climbing*)
**pidocchierìa** *f* stinginess; meanness
**pidòc·chio** *m* (-chi) louse; **pidocchio rifatto** (slang) parvenu
**pidocchió·so -sa** [s] *adj* lousy; stingy
**piè** *m* (piè) (lit) foot; **ad ogni piè sospinto** on every occasion; **saltare a piè pari** to skip with the feet together; (fig) to skip over
**piède** *m* foot; leg (*of table*); stalk (*of salad*); bottom (*of column*); trunk (*of tree*); footing; **alzarsi in piedi** to stand up; **a piede libero** free; **a piedi** on foot; **a piedi nudi** barefooted; **con i piedi di piombo** cautiously; **essere in piedi** to be up and around; **fare con i piedi** to botch; **mettere un piede in fallo** to stumble; **piede di porco** crowbar; **prendere piede** to take hold; **puntare i piedi** to balk; **su due piedi** offhand; **tenere il piede in due staffe** to carry water on both shoulders
**piedestallo** or **piedistallo** *m* pedestal
**piedritto** *m* buttress
**piè·ga** *f* (-ghe) bend; crease; pleat; crimp; wrinkle; (fig) turn; **prendere una cattiva piega** to take a turn for the worse
**piegare** §209 **(piègo)** *tr* to bend; to wave (*hair*); to fold; to pleat; to bow (*head*) ‖ *intr* to turn ‖ *ref* to bow; to bend; to buckle; to yield
**piega·tóre -trice** *mf* folder ‖ *f* folding machine
**piegatura** *f* fold, crease
**pieghettare (pieghétto)** *tr* to pleat
**pieghévole** *adj* folding; pliant; (fig) versatile ‖ *m* folder
**pieghevolézza** *f* flexibility
**piè·go** *m* (-ghi) folder; bundle of papers
**pièna** *f* flood; rise (*of river*); crowd; (fig) overflow; **in piena** overflowing
**pienézza** *f* plenitude, fullness
**piè·no -na** *adj* full; solid; broad (*daylight*); full (*honors*); **a pieno** or **in pieno** to the full; **colpire nel pieno** to hit the bull's eye; **pieno di** alive with; **pieno di sé** conceited; **pieno zeppo** replete, chock-full ‖ *m* fullness; height (*e.g., of winter*); **fare il pieno** (aut) to fill up ‖ *f* see **piena**
**pie·tà** *f* (-tà) mercy; pity; (lit) piety
**pietanza** *f* main course
**pietó·so -sa** [s] *adj* pitiful, piteous; merciful
**piètra** *f* stone; rock; **pietra angolare** cornerstone; **pietra da affilare** whetstone; **pietra da sarto** French chalk; **pietra dello scandalo** source of scandal; **pietra di paragone** touchstone; **pietra focaia** flint; **pietra miliare** milestone; **pietra tombale** tombstone; **posare la prima pietra** to lay the cornerstone
**pietrificare** §197 **(pietrìfico)** *tr & ref* to petrify
**pietrina** *f* flint (*for lighter*)
**pietri·sco** *m* (-schi) rubble; (rr) ballast
**Pìetro** *m* Peter
**pietró·so -sa** [s] *adj* (lit) stony
**pievano** *m* parish priest
**pìffero** *m* pipe, fife
**pìgia** *m*—**pigia pigia** crowd, throng
**pigia·ma** *m* (-ma & -mi) pajamas
**pigiare** §290 *tr* to squeeze, press ‖ *intr* to insist ‖ *ref* to squeeze
**pigia·tóre -trice** *mf* presser (*of grapes*) ‖ *f* wine press
**pigiatura** *f* pressing, squeezing
**pigionante** *mf* tenant
**pigióne** *f* rent, rental; **dare a pigione** to rent; to grant the possession of; **prendere a pigione** to rent; to hold for payment

**pigliamó·sche** *m* (**-sche**) flypaper; fly-trap; (orn) flycatcher
**pigliare** §280 *tr* to take, catch; to mistake; **che Le piglia?** what's the matter with you? || *ref*—**pigliarsela (con)** to get angry (at)
**pì·glio** *m* (**-gli**) hold; countenance; **dar di piglio a** to grab
**pigménto** *m* pigment
**pigmè·o -a** *adj & mf* pygmy; Pygmy
**pigna** *f* strainer (*at the end of a suction pipe*); bunch (*of grapes*); (bot) pine cone
**pignatta** *f* pot
**pignò·lo -la** *adj* finicky, fussy || *m* pine nut
**pignóne** *m* pinion; embankment
**pignoraménto** *m* (law) seizure
**pignorare (pìgnoro)** *tr* (law) to seize
**pigolare (pìgolo)** *intr* to peep (*said, e.g., of young birds*)
**pigolì·o** *m* (**-i**) peep (*e.g., of a young bird*)
**pigrìzia** *f* laziness
**pì·gro -gra** *adj* lazy; (lit) sluggish
**pila** *f* pier; buttress (*of bridge*); heap; sink; font; (elec) cell; (elec) battery; **pila atomica** atomic pile
**pilastro** *m* pier, pillar
**pillàcchera** *f* mud splash; (fig) fault
**pìllola** *f* pill; (slang) bullet; **addolcire la pillola** to sugar-coat the pill
**pilóne** *m* pier; pylon
**pilò·ta (-ti -te)** *adj* pilot || *mf* pilot; (aut) driver
**pilotàg·gio** *m* (**-gi**) piloting; steering
**pilotare (pilòto)** *tr* to pilot; to drive
**pilotina** *f* (naut) pilot boat
**piluccare** §197 *tr* to pluck (*e.g., grapes one by one*); to nibble, pick at; to scrounge; (lit) to consume
**piménto** *m* allspice
**pinacotè·ca** *f* (**-che**) picture gallery
**pinéta** *f* pine grove
**pìngue** *adj* fat; rich
**pinguèdine** *f* fatness, corpulence
**pinguino** *m* penguin
**pinna** *f* fin (*of fish*); flipper; (zool) pen shell (*mussel*)
**pinnàcolo** *m* pinnacle
**pino** *m* pine tree; **pino marittimo** pinaster; **pino silvestre** Scotch fir
**pinòlo** *m* pine nut
**pinta** *f* pint
**pinza** *f* claw (*of lobster*); **pinza emostatica** hemostat; **pinza tagliafili** wire cutter; **pinze** clippers; pliers; pincers
**pinzatrice** *f* stapler
**pinzétte** *fpl* tweezers, pliers
**pinzòche·ro -ra** *mf* bigot
**pì·o -a** *adj* (**-i -e**) pious; charitable || **Pio** *m* Pius
**piòg·gia** *f* (**-ge**) rain
**piòlo** *m* peg; rung (*of ladder*); picket, stake
**piombàggine** *f* graphite
**piombare (piómbo)** *tr* to lead; to seal; to knock down; to fill (*a tooth*) || *intr* to fall; to swoop down
**piombatura** *f* leading; filling (*of tooth*)
**piombino** *m* weight; seal; plumb; plumb bob

**piómbo** *m* lead; **a piombo** perpendicularly; **di piombo** suddenly
**pionerìsti·co -ca** *adj* (**-ci -che**) pioneering
**pionière** *m* pioneer
**piòppo** *m* poplar; **pioppo tremolo** aspen
**piorrèa** *f* pyorrhea
**piotare (piòto)** *tr* to sod
**piova·no -na** *adj* rain (*water*)
**piova·sco** *m* (**-schi**) rain squall
**piovènte** *m* pitch, slope
**piòvere** §216 *intr* (ESSERE) to rain; to pour; to flock (*said of people*); **piovere addosso a** to rain down on; **piovere su** to flow down over || *impers* (ESSERE & AVERE)—**piove** it is raining; it is leaking (*from rain*); **piove a catinelle** or **a dirotto** it is raining cats and dogs
**piovigginare (piovìggina)** *impers* (ESSERE & AVERE)—**pioviggina** it is drizzling
**piovigginó·so -sa** [*s*] *adj* drizzling, drizzly
**piovór·no -na** *adj* (lit) var of **piovoso**
**piovosi·tà** [*s*] *f* (**-tà**) raininess; rainfall
**piovó·so -sa** [*s*] *adj* rainy
**piòvra** *f* octopus; (fig) leech
**pipa** *f* pipe; **non valere una pipa di tabacco** to not be worth a tinker's dam
**pipare** *intr* to smoke a pipe
**pipata** *f* pipe, pipeful
**pipistrèllo** *m* (zool) bat
**pipita** *f* hangnail; (vet) pip
**pira** *f* (lit) pyre
**piràmide** *f* pyramid
**pira·ta** *adj invar* pirate || *m* (**-ti**) pirate; **pirata dell'aria** skyjacker; **pirata della strada** hit-and-run driver
**pirateggiare** §290 (**piratéggio**) *intr* to pirate
**piraterìa** *f* piracy; **pirateria letteraria** piracy of literary works
**Pirenèi** *mpl* Pyrenees
**pìri·co -ca** *adj* (**-ci -che**) fireworks; **polvere pirica** gunpowder
**pirite** *f* pyrite
**piroétta** *f* pirouette
**pirò·ga** *f* (**-ghe**) pirogue
**pirolisi** *f* (chem) cracking
**piróne** *m* (mus) tuning pin
**piròscafo** *m* steamship; **piroscafo da carico** (naut) freighter; **piroscafo da passeggeri** passenger ship
**piroscissióne** *f* (chem) cracking
**pirotècni·co -ca** (**-ci -che**) *adj* pyrotecnic || *m* pyrotecnist || *f* fireworks, pyrotechnics
**pisciare** §128 *intr* (vulg) to urinate
**piscia·tóio** *m* (**-tói**) (vulg) street urinal
**piscina** *f* swimming pool
**pisèllo** [*s*] *m* pea; **pisello odoroso** sweet pea
**pisolare (pìsolo)** *intr* (coll) to doze
**pìsolo** *m* (coll) nap; **schiacciare un pisolo** (coll) to take a nap
**pìsside** *f* (eccl) pyx; (bot) pyxidium
**pista** *f* track; ring (*of circus*); race track, speedway (*for car races*); ski run; (aer) runway; **pista ciclabile** bicycle trail; **pista da ballo** dance

floor; **seguire una pista** to follow a clue

**pistàc·chio** *m* (**-chi**) pistachio

**pistillo** *m* (bot) pistil

**pistòla** *f* pistol

**pistolettata** *f* pistol shot

**pistolòtto** *m* lecture, talking-to; theatrical peroration

**pistóne** *m* piston; plunger

**pitagòri·co -ca** *adj & m* (**-ci -che**) Pythagorean

**pitale** *m* (coll) chamber pot

**pitoccare** §197 (**pitòcco**) *intr* to beg

**pitòc·co** *m* (**-chi**) beggar; miser

**pitóne** *m* python

**pìttima** *f* plaster; (fig) bore

**pit·tóre -trice** *mf* painter

**pittoré·sco -sca** *adj* (**-schi -sche**) picturesque

**pittòri·co -ca** *adj* (**-ci -che**) pictorial

**pittura** *f* painting; picture; (coll) paint

**pitturare** *tr* to paint; to varnish || *ref* to put on make-up

**più** *adj invar* more; several || *m* (**più**) plus; most; **credersi da più** to believe oneself superior; **dal più al meno** about, more or less; **i più** most, the majority; **parlare del più e del meno** (coll) to make small talk || *adv* more; again; **a più non posso** to the very utmost; **in più** besides; **mai più** never again; **non poterne più** to be exhausted; **per di più** besides; **per lo più** for the most part; **più o meno** more or less; **tanto più** moreover; **tutt'al più** mostly

**piuma** *f* feather, plume; **piume** (fig) bed

**piumàc·cio** *m* (**-ci**) feather pillow

**piumàg·gio** *m* (**-gi**) plumage

**piumino** *m* down; comforter; puff; powder puff; feather duster

**piuttòsto** *adv* rather; somewhat

**piva** *f* bagpipe; **tornare con le pive nel sacco** to return bitterly disappointed

**pivèllo** *m* greenhorn; whippersnapper

**pivière** *m* (orn) plover

**pizza** *f* pizza; (mov) canister; (coll) bore

**pizzaiò·lo -la** *mf* owner of pizzeria || *m* pizza baker || *f*—**alla pizzaiola** prepared with tomato and garlic sauce

**pizzardóne** *m* (coll) cop, officer

**pizzicàgno·lo -la** *mf* grocer; sausage dealer

**pizzicare** §197 (**pìzzico**) *tr* to pinch; to pluck; to bite, burn; (mus) to pick, twang

**pizzicherìa** *f* delicatessen, grocery

**pìzzi·co** *m* (**-chi**) pinch

**pizzicóre** *m* itch

**pizzicòtto** *m* pinch; **dar pizzicotti** to pinch

**pizzo** *m* peak (*of mountain*); goatee; lace

**placare** §197 *tr* to placate || *ref* to calm down

**plac·ca** *f* (**-che**) plate; plaque; tag, badge; (elec, rad) plate; (pathol) blotch, spot

**placcare** §197 *tr* to plate; (sports) to tackle

**plàci·do -da** *adj* placid

**plafond** *m* (**plafond**) ceiling; (aer) ceiling; (com) top credit

**pla·ga** *f* (**-ghe**) (lit) clime, region

**plagiare** §290 *tr* to plagiarize

**plagià·rio -ria** (**-ri -rie**) *adj* plagiaristic || *mf* plagiarist

**plà·gio** *m* (**-gi**) plagiarism

**planare** *intr* (aer) to glide

**planata** *f* (aer) gliding

**plàn·cia** *f* (**-ce**) (naut) gangplank; (naut) bridge

**planetà·rio -ria** (**-ri -rie**) *adj* planetary || *m* planetarium; (aut) planetary gear

**plantare** *m* arch support

**pla·sma** *m* (**-smi**) plasma

**plasmare** *tr* to mold, shape

**plàsti·ca** *f* (**-che**) plastic art; plastics; plastic surgery; plastic

**plasticare** §197 (**plàstico**) *tr* to mold, shape; to cover with plastic

**plàsti·co -ca** (**-ci -che**) *adj* plastic || *m* relief map; maquette; plastic bomb || *f* see **plastica**

**plastilina** *f* modeling clay

**plastron** *m* (**plastron**) ascot

**plàtano** *m* plane tree; **platano americano** buttonwood tree

**platèa** *f* audience; (theat) orchestra; (archit) foundation

**plateale** *adj* obvious; plebeian

**plàtina** *f* (typ) platen

**platinare** (**plàtino**) *tr* to platinize; **to bleach** (*hair*)

**plàtino** *m* platinum

**Platóne** *m* Plato

**plaudènte** *adj* enthusiastic

**plàudere** (**plàudo**) & **plaudire** (**plàudo**) *intr* to applaud; (with *dat*) to applaud, e.g., **plaudere alla generosità** to applaud the generosity

**plausìbile** *adj* plausible

**plàuso** *m* (lit) applause, praise

**plebàglia** *f* rabble

**plèbe** *f* populace; (lit) crowd

**plebè·o -a** *adj & mf* plebeian

**plebiscito** *m* plebiscite

**plenà·rio -ria** *adj* (**-ri -rie**) plenary

**plenilù·nio** *m* (**-ni**) full moon

**plenipotenzià·rio -ria** *adj & m* (**-ri -rie**) plenipotentiary

**plètora** *f* plethora

**plèttro** *m* (mus) pick, plectrum

**pleurite** *f* (pathol) pleurisy

**pli·co** *m* (**-chi**) sealed document; bundle of papers; **in plico a parte** or **in plico separato** under separate cover

**plotóne** *m* platoon; **plotone d'esecuzione** firing squad

**plùmbe·o -a** *adj* lead, leaden

**plurale** *adj & m* plural; **al plurale** in the plural

**plurilìngue** *adj* multilingual

**plurimotóre** *adj* multimotored || *m* multimotor

**pluristàdio** *adj invar* (rok) multistage

**plusvalènza** *f* unearned increment

**plusvalóre** *m;* surplus value (*in Marxist economics*)

**Plutarco** *m* Plutarch

**plutocrazìa** *f* plutocracy

**Plutóne** *m* Pluto

**plutònio** *m* plutonium
**pluviale** *adj* rain ‖ *m* waterspout
**pneumàti·co -ca** (**-ci -che**) *adj* pneumatic, air ‖ *m* tire; **pneumatico da neve** snow tire
**po'** *m* see **poco**
**pochézza** *f* lack, scarcity
**pò·co -ca** (**-chi -che**) *adj* little; short (*distance*); poor (*health*; *memory*); (*with collective nouns*) few, e.g., **poca gente** few people; (*with plural nouns*) a few, e.g., **fra pochi mesi** in a few months; (*with plural nouns having singular meaning in English*) little, e.g., **pochi quattrini** little money ‖ *m invar* little; short distance; short time; **a ogni poco** often; **da poco** a little while ago; of no account; **da un bel po'** quite a while; quite a while ago; **fra poco** in a little while; **manca poco a** it won't be long till; **manca poco che** (*e.g., il ragazzo*) **non** + *subj* (e.g., the boy) almost + *ind*; **per poco non** almost; **poco di buono** good-for-nothing; **poco fa** a little while ago; **saper di poco** to taste flat; **un poco di** or **un po' di** a little ‖ *f*—**poca di buono** hussy ‖ **poco** *adv* little; **poco bene** poorly; **poco dopo** shortly after; **poco male** not too poorly
**podagra** *f* gout
**podére** *m* farm, country property
**poderó·so -sa** [s] *adj* powerful
**pode·stà** *m* (**-stà**) (hist) mayor; (hist) podesta
**podia·tra** *mf* (**-tri -tre**) chiropodist
**pò·dio** *m* (**-di**) podium; platform; (archit) base
**podismo** *m* foot racing
**podi·sta** *mf* (**-sti -ste**) foot racer
**poè·ma** *m* (**-mi**) long poem
**poesìa** *f* poetry; poem
**poè·ta** *m* (**-ti**) poet
**poetéssa** *f* poetess
**poèti·co -ca** (**-ci -che**) *adj* poetic(al) ‖ *f* poetics
**pòg·gia** *f* (**-ge**) leeward
**poggiare** §290 (**pòggio**) *tr* to lean ‖ *intr* to be based; (mil) to move; (naut) to sail before the wind; (archaic) to rise
**poggiatè·sta** *m* (**-sta**) headrest; (aut) head restrainer
**pòg·gio** *m* (**-gi**) hillock, knoll
**poggiòlo** *m* balcony
**pòi** *m* future ‖ *adv* then; later; **a poi** until later; **poi dopo** later on
**poiana** *f* buzzard
**poiché** *conj* since, as; (lit) after
**pòker** *m* poker (*game*); four of a kind; **poker di re** four kings
**polac·co -ca** (**-chi -che**) *adj* Polish ‖ *mf* Pole ‖ *f* (mus) polonaise
**polare** *adj* pole, polar
**polarizzare** [ddzz] *tr* to polarize
**pòl·ca** *f* (**-che**) polka
**polèmi·co -ca** (**-ci -che**) *adj* polemical ‖ *f* polemics
**polemizzare** [ddzz] *intr* to engage in polemics
**polèna** *f* (naut) figurehead
**polènta** *f* corn mush

**polentina** *f* poultice
**poliambulanza** *f* clinic, emergency ward
**policlìni·co** *m* (**-ci**) polyclinic
**polifonìa** *f* polyphony
**polìga·mo -ma** *adj* polygamous ‖ *m* polygamist
**poliglòt·ta** *adj* & *mf* (**-ti -te**) polyglot
**poliglòt·to** *adj* & *mf* polyglot
**polìgono** *m* polygon; **poligono di tiro** shooting range
**polìgrafo** *m* author skilled in many subjects; multigraph
**polinesia·no -na** *adj* & *mf* Polynesian
**polinò·mio** *m* (**-mi**) polynomial
**pòlio** *f* (coll) polio
**poliomielite** *f* poliomielitis, infantile paralysis
**pòlipo** *m* (pathol, zool) polyp
**polisìlla·bo -ba** *adj* polysyllabic ‖ *m* polysyllable
**poli·sta** *m* (**-sti**) polo player
**politea·ma** *m* (**-mi**) theater
**politècni·co -ca** (**-ci -che**) *adj* polytechnic ‖ *m* polytechnic institute
**politei·sta** (**-sti -ste**) *adj* polytheistic ‖ *mf* polytheist
**politeisti·co -ca** *adj* (**-ci -che**) polytheistic
**politézza** *f* smoothness
**polìti·ca** *f* (**-che**) politics; policy
**politicante** *mf* petty politician
**polìti·co -ca** (**-ci -che**) *adj* political ‖ *m* politician ‖ *f* see **politica**
**polìtti·co** *m* (**-ci**) polyptych
**polizìa** *f* police; **polizia sanitaria** health department; **polizia stradale** highway patrol; **polizia tributaria** income-tax investigation department
**polizié·sco -sca** *adj* (**-schi -sche**) police (*car*); detective (*story*)
**poliziòtto** *adj masc* police (*dog*) ‖ *m* policeman; detective; **poliziotto in borghese** plain-clothes man
**pòlizza** *f* policy; ticket (*e.g., of pawnbroker*); **polizza di carico** bill of lading
**pólla** *f* spring (*of water*)
**pol·làio** *m* (**-lài**) chicken coop
**pollaiò·lo -la** *mf* chicken dealer
**pollame** *m* poultry
**pollastra** *f* pullet; (coll) chick
**pollerìa** *f* poultry shop
**pòllice** *m* thumb; big toe; inch
**pollicoltura** *f* poultry raising
**pòlline** *m* pollen
**pollivéndo·lo -la** *mf* poultry dealer
**póllo** *m* chicken; (fig) sucker; **conoscere i propri polli** (fig) to know one's onions; **pollo d'India** turkey
**pollóne** *m* (bot) shoot; (fig) offspring
**polmóne** *m* lung; **a pieni polmoni** at the top of one's lungs; **polmone d'acciaio** iron lung
**polmonite** *f* pneumonia
**pòlo** *m* pole; polo shirt; (sports) polo
**Polònia, la** Poland
**pólpa** *f* meat; pulp; flesh (*of fruit*); (fig) gist; **in polpe** (hist) in knee breeches
**polpàc·cio** *m* (**-ci**) calf (*of leg*); cut of meat; ball of thumb

**polpastrèllo** *m* finger tip
**polpétta** *f* meat ball; meat patty, cutlet
**polpettóne** *m* meat loaf; (fig) hash
**pólpo** *m* (zool) octopus
**polpó·so -sa** [s] *adj* pulpy, fleshy
**polpu·to -ta** *adj* meaty
**polsino** *m* cuff
**pólso** *m* pulse; wrist; cuff, wristband; strong hand, energy; **di polso** energetic
**poltiglia** *f* mash; slush
**poltrire** §176 *intr* to idle; to loll in bed
**poltróna** *f* armchair; (theat) orchestra seat; **poltrona a orecchioni** wing chair; **poltrona a sdraio** chaise longue; **poltrona letto** day bed
**poltroncina** *f* parquet-circle seat
**poltró·ne -na** *mf* lazybones, sluggard ‖ *f* see **poltrona**
**poltronerìa** *f* laziness
**poltronìssima** *f* (theat) first-row seat
**pólvere** *f* dust; powder; **in polvere** powdered; **polvere da sparo** gunpowder; **polvere di stelle** stardust; **polvere nera** or **pirica** gunpowder; **polveri** gunpowder
**polverièra** *f* powder magazine; (fig) tinderbox, trouble spot
**polverifi·cio** *m* (-ci) powder works
**polverina** *f* (pharm) powder
**polverino** *m* pounce, sand
**polverizzare** [ddzz] *tr* to crush, powder; to atomize; to pulverize
**polverizza·to -ta** [ddzz] *adj* powdered (*sugar*)
**polverizzatóre** [ddzz] *m* atomizer
**polveróne** *m* dust cloud
**polveró·so -sa** [s] *adj* dusty; powdery (*snow*)
**pomata** *f* ointment; pomade
**pomella·to -ta** *adj* dapple-grey
**pomèllo** *m* cheek; cheekbone; pommel, knob
**pomeridia·no -na** *adj* afternoon, P.M.
**pomerig·gio** *m* (-gi) afternoon
**pomiciare** §128 (**pómicio**) *tr* to pumice ‖ *intr* (slang) to spoon
**pomicióne** *m* (slang) spooner
**pomidòro** *m* var of **pomodoro**
**pómo** *m* apple; knob; pommel (*of saddle*); **pomo della discordia** apple of discord; **pomo di Adamo** Adam's apple; **pomo di terra** potato
**pomodòro** *m* tomato; **pomodoro di mare** (zool) sea anemone
**pómolo** *m* (coll) knob, handle
**pómpa** *f* pump; pomp; state; **in pompa magna** all dressed up; **pompa aspirante** suction pump; **pompa premente** force pump; see **imprenditore** and **impresa**
**pompare** (**pómpo**) *tr* to pump; to pump up
**pompèlmo** *m* grapefruit
**pompière** *m* fireman
**pompó·so -sa** [s] *adj* pompous
**pòn·ce** *m* (-ci) punch
**ponderare** (**pòndero**) *tr* to weigh, ponder; to weight ‖ *intr* to think it over
**pondera·to -ta** *adj* considerate, careful
**ponderó·so -sa** [s] *adj* ponderous

**ponènte** *m* west; west wind; West; West Wind
**pónte** *m* bridge; metal scaffolding; (aut) axle; (naut) deck; **fare il ponte** to take the day off between two holidays; **fare ponti d'oro a** to offer a good way out to; **ponte aereo** airlift; **ponte delle segnalazioni** (rr) gantry; **ponte di chiatte** pontoon bridge; **ponte di comando** (naut) bridge; **ponte di volo** flight deck; **ponte levatoio** drawbridge; **ponte radio** radio communication; **ponte sospeso** suspension bridge
**pontéfice** *m* pontiff; (hist) pontifex
**pontéggio** *m* scaffolding
**ponticèllo** *m* small bridge; nosepiece (*of eyeglasses*); (mus) bridge
**pontière** *m* (mil) engineer
**pontificale** *adj* pontifical ‖ *m* pontifical mass
**pontifi·cio -cia** *adj* (-ci -cie) papal
**pontile** *m* pier
**pontóne** *m* pontoon, barge
**ponzare** (**pónzo**) *tr* (coll) to strain to accomplish ‖ *intr* (coll) to rack one's brains
**popeli·ne** *f* (-ne) broadcloth
**popola·no -na** *adj* popular ‖ *mf* commoner
**popolare** *adj* popular ‖ *v* (**pòpolo**) *tr* to people, populate ‖ *ref* to be inhabited
**popolarità** *f* popularity
**popola·to -ta** *adj* peopled; crowded
**popolazióne** *f* population
**pòpolo** *m* people; crowd; **popolo grasso** (hist) rich bourgeoisie; **popolo minuto** (hist) artisans, common people
**popoló·so -sa** [s] *adj* populous
**popóne** *m* (coll) melon
**póppa** *f* breast; (naut) stern; (lit) ship; **a poppa** astern, aft
**poppante** *adj* & *mf* suckling
**poppare** (**póppo**) *tr* to suckle
**poppa·tóio** *m* (-tói) nursing bottle
**poppavìa** *f*—**a poppavia** astern, aft
**pòr·ca** *f* (-che) ridge (*between furrows*); sow
**porcacció·ne -na** *m* cad, rake ‖ *f* slut
**por·càio** *m* (-cài) swineherd; pigsty
**porcellana** *f* porcelain, china; (bot) purslane
**porcellino** *m* piggy; **porcellino d'India** guinea pig
**porcherìa** *f* dirt; (coll) dirty trick; (coll) botch
**porchétta** *f* roast suckling pig
**porcile** *m* pigsty
**porci·no -na** *adj* pig ‖ *m* (bot) boletus
**pòr·co -ca** *mf* (-ci -che) pig, hog, swine; pork; **porco mondo!** (slang) heck! ‖ *f* see **porca**
**porcospino** *m* porcupine
**pòrfido** *m* porphyry
**pòrgere** §217 *tr* to hand, offer; to relate; **porgere l'orecchio** to lend an ear ‖ *intr* to declaim ‖ *ref* to appear, show up
**pornografìa** *f* pornography
**pòro** *m* pore
**poró·so -sa** [s] *adj* porous
**pórpora** *f* purple

**porpora·to -ta** *adj* purple ‖ *m* purple; cardinal

**porpori·no -na** *adj* purple

**pórre** §218 *tr* to put; to repose (*trust*); to set (*a limit; one's foot*); to lay (*a stone*); to pose (*a question*); to pay (*attention*); to suppose; to advance (*the candidacy*); **porre gli occhi addosso a** to lay one's eyes on; **porre in dubbio** to cast doubt on; **porre mano a** to set to work at; **porre termine a** to put an end to; **posto che** since, provided ‖ *ref* to place oneself; **porsi in cammino** to set out or forth; **porsi in salvo** to reach safety

**pòrro** *m* wart; (bot) leek

**pòrta** *f* door; gate; (cricket) wicket; (sports) goal; **di porta in porta** door-to-door; **fuori porta** outside the city limits; **mettere alla porta** to dismiss, fire; **porta di servizio** delivery entrance; **porta scorrevole** sliding door; **porta stagna** (naut; theat) safety door

**portabagà·gli** *m* (-gli) porter; baggage rack

**portabandiè·ra** *m* (-ra) standard-bearer

**portàbile** *adj* portable

**portàbi·ti** *m* (-ti) coat hanger

**portabottì·glie** *m* (-glie) bottle rack

**portacar·te** *adj invar & m* (-te) folder

**portacati·no** *adj invar* washstand-supporting ‖ *m* (-no) washstand

**portacéne·re** *m* (-re) ashtray

**portachia·vi** *m* (-vi) key ring

**portaci·pria** *m* (-pria) compact

**portadi·schi** *m* (-schi) record cabinet, record rack; turntable

**portadól·ci** *m* (-ci) candy dish

**portaère·i** *f* (-i) aircraft carrier

**portaferi·ti** *m* (-ti) (mil) stretcher bearer

**portafinèstra** *f* (**portefinèstre**) French window

**portafió·ri** *m* (-ri) flower vase

**portafò·gli** *m* (-gli) or **portafò·glio** *m* (-gli) billfold, wallet; pocketbook; portfolio

**portafortu·na** *m* (-na) charm, amulet

**portafrut·ta** *m* (-ta) fruit dish

**portafusìbi·li** *m* (-li) fuse box

**portagiò·ie** *m* (-ie) jewel box

**portaimmondì·zie** *m* (-zie) trash can, garbage can

**portainsé·gna** *m* (-gna) standard-bearer

**portalàmpa·da** *m* (-da) (elec) socket

**portale** *m* portal

**portalètte·re** (-re) *mf* letter carrier ‖ *m* postman, mailman

**portamaz·ze** *m* (-ze) caddie

**portaménto** *m* posture; gait; (fig) behavior

**portami·na** *m* (-na) mechanical pencil

**portamìssi·li** (-li) *adj invar* missile-carrying ‖ *m* missile carrier

**portamoné·te** *m* (-te) purse

**portamùsi·ca** *m* (-ca) music stand

**portante** *adj* carrying; (architt) weight-bearing; (aer) lifting; (rad) carrier ‖ *m* amble

**portantina** *f* sedan chair; stretcher

**portantino** *m* bearer (*of sedan chair*); stretcher bearer

**portanza** *f* (architt) capacity; (aer) lift

**portaombrèl·li** *m* (-li) umbrella stand

**portaórdi·ni** *m* (-ni) (mil) messenger

**portapac·chi** *m* (-chi) parcel delivery man; basket (*on bicycle*)

**portapén·ne** *m* (-ne) penholder

**portapiat·ti** *m* (-ti) dish rack

**portaposa·te** [s] *m* (-te) silverware chest

**portapran·zi** [dz] *m* (-zi) dinner pail

**portaraz·zi** (-zi) [ddzz] *adj invar* missile-carrying ‖ *m* missile carrier

**portare** (pòrto) *tr* to carry; to bring; to take; to carry along; to lead; to herald; to praise; to wear; to drive (*car*); to run (*a candidate*); to adduce; to nurture (*hatred*); (aut) to hold (*e.g., five people*); **portare a conoscenza di** to let know; **portare avanti** to carry forward; **portare in alto** to lift; **portare via** to steal; to take away ‖ *intr* to carry (*said of a gun*) ‖ *ref* to move; to behave; to be (*a candidate*)

**portaritrat·ti** *m* (-ti) picture frame

**portasapó·ne** *m* (-ne) soap dish

**portasigarét·te** *m* (-te) cigarette case

**portasiga·ri** *m* (-ri) cigar case; humidor

**portaspil·li** *m* (-li) pincushion

**portata** *f* course (*of a meal*); capacity; flow (*of river*); compass (*of voice*); range (*of voice or gun*); importance; (naut) burden; (naut) tonnage; **a portata di mano** within reach; **a portata di voce** within call, within earshot

**portatèsse·re** *m* (-re) card case

**portàtile** *adj* portable

**porta·to -ta** *adj* worn; **portato a** leaning toward ‖ *m* result, effect ‖ *f* see **portata**

**porta·tóre -trice** *mf* bearer

**portatovagliòlo** *m* napkin ring

**portauò·vo** *m* (-vo) eggcup

**portavó·ce** *m* (-ce) megaphone; (fig) mouthpiece

**porte-enfant** *m* (**porte-enfant**) baby bunting

**portèllo** *m* wicket; leaf (*of cabinet door*); (naut) porthole

**portènto** *m* portent

**portica·to -ta** *adj* arcaded ‖ *m* arcade

**pòrti·co** *m* (-ci) portico, arcade, colonnade; shed

**portiè·re -ra** *mf* concierge ‖ *m* janitor, doorman; (sports) goalkeeper ‖ *f* portiere (*in church door*); (aut) door

**porti·nàio -nàia** (-nài -nàie) *adj* door, door-keeping ‖ *mf* doorkeeper, concierge

**portinerìa** *f* janitor's quarters

**pòrto** *m* port, harbor; transportation charge; port wine; goal; **condurre a buon porto** to carry to fruition; **franco di porto** prepaid, postpaid; **porto a carico del mittente** postage prepaid; **porto assegnato** charges to be paid by addressee; **porto d'armi** permit to carry arms; **porto franco** free port

**Portogallo, il** Portugal

**portoghése** [s] *adj & mf* Portuguese;

**fare il portoghese** (theat) to crash the gate

**portóne** *m* portal

**portorica·no -na** *adj & mf* Puerto Rican

**Portorico** *m* Puerto Rico

**portuale** *adj* port, harbor || *m* dock worker, longshoreman

**porzióne** *f* portion

**pòsa** [s] *f* laying (*e.g., of cornerstone*); posing (*for portrait*); posture, affectation, pose; dregs; (phot) exposure; (lit) rest; **senza posa** relentless; relentlessly

**posami·ne** (-ne) [s] *adj invar* minelaying || *f* minelayer

**posare** [s] (**pòso**) *tr* to lay, put down || *intr* to lie; to settle; to pose; **posare a** to pose as || *ref* to settle; to alight; (lit) to rest

**posata** [s] *f* cover, place (*at table*); table utensil (*knife, fork or spoon*); **posate** knife, fork and spoon

**posateria** [s] *f* service (*of knives, forks, and spoons*)

**posa·to -ta** [s] *adj* sedate, quiet; placed || *f* see **posata**

**posa·tóre -trice** [s] *mf* poseur || *m* layer, installer (*of cables or pipes*)

**pòscia** *adv* then, afterwards; **poscia che** after

**poscritto** *m* postscript

**posdatare** *tr* var of **postdatare**

**posdomani** *adv* (lit) day after tomorrow

**positivaménte** *adv* for sure

**positi·vo -va** *adj* positive || *f* (phot) positive, print

**posizióne** *f* position; status; (fig) stand

**pospórre** §218 *tr* to put off, postpone; to put last; **posporre qlco a qlco** to put or place s.th after s.th

**pòssa** *f* (lit) strength, vigor

**possanza** *f* (lit) power

**possedére** §252 *tr* to possess; to own; to master (*a language*); **essere posseduto da** to be enthralled with; to be possessed by

**possediménto** *m* possession, property

**posseditrice** *f* owner, possessor

**possènte** *adj* (lit) powerful

**possessióne** *f* possession

**possessi·vo -va** *adj* possessive

**possèsso** *m* possession

**possessóre** *m* owner, possessor

**possìbile** *adj* possible || *m*—**fare il possibile** to do one's best

**possibili·sta** (-sti -ste) *adj* pragmatically flexible || *mf* pragmatically flexible person, possibilist

**possibili·tà** *f* (-tà) possibility; opportunity; **possibilità** *fpl* means

**possidènte** *mf* proprietor, owner; **possidente terriero** landowner

**pòsta** *f* post; mail; post office; box (*in stable*); ambush; bet; **a giro di posta** by return mail; **a posta** on purpose; **darsi la posta** to set up an appointment; **fare la posta a** to have under surveillance; **fermo in posta** general delivery; **levare la posta** to pick up the mail; **posta aerea** air mail; **posta dei lettori** (journ) letters to the editor; **poste** postal department

**pósta** *f* (archaic) planting; (archaic) footprint

**postagi·ro** *m* (-ro & -ri) postal transfer of funds

**postale** *adj* postal, mail || *m* mail; mail train (boat, bus, or plane)

**postare** (**pòsto**) *tr* (mil) to post || *ref* (mil) to take a position

**postazióne** *f* (mil) emplacement

**postbèlli·co -ca** *adj* (-ci -che) postwar

**postbruciatóre** *m* (aer) afterburner

**postdatare** *tr* to postdate

**posteggiare** §290 (**postéggio**) *tr & intr* to park

**posteggia·tóre -trice** *mf* parking-lot attendant; customer (*in a parking lot*); (coll) outdoor merchant; **posteggiatore abusivo** parking violator

**postég·gio** *m* (-gi) parking lot; stand (*in outdoor market*); **posteggio di tassì** cabstand

**posterióre** *adj* back; subsequent, later

**posteri·tà** *f* (-tà) posterity

**pòste·ro -ra** *adj* later, subsequent || **posteri** *mpl* posterity, descendants

**postic·cio -cia** (-ci -ce) *adj* artificial; false (*e.g., tooth*); temporary || *m* wiglet, ponytail || *f* row of trees

**posticipare** (**postìcipo**) *tr* to postpone

**posticipa·to -ta** *adj* deferred

**postièrla** *f* postern

**postiglióne** *m* postilion

**postilla** *f* marginal note

**postillare** *tr* to annotate

**posti·no -na** *mf* letter carrier || *m* mailman, postman

**pósto** *m* place; room; seat; job; position; spot; (mil) post; **a posto in** order; orderly; **al posto di** instead of; **essere a posto** to have a good job; **mettere a posto** to find a good job for; (coll) to keep quiet; **quel posto** (coll) seat of the pants; (coll) toilet; **posto a sedere** seat; **posto di blocco** road block; (rr) signal tower; **posto di guardia** (mil) guardhouse; **posto di medicazione** or **di pronto soccorso** first-aid station; **posto in piedi** standing room; **posto letto** bed (*e.g., in hospital*); **posto telefonico pubblico** public telephone, pay station; **rimettere a posto** to fix, repair; **saper stare al proprio posto** to know one's place; **sul posto** on the spot

**postrè·mo -ma** *adj* (lit) last

**postrìbolo** *m* (lit) brothel

**postulante** *adj* petitioning || *mf* petitioner, applicant; (eccl) postulant

**postulare** (**pòstulo**) *tr* to postulate

**pòstu·mo -ma** *adj* posthumous || **postumi** *mpl* sequel; (pathol) sequelae

**potàbile** *adj* drinkable

**potare** (**póto**) *tr* to trim, prune

**potassa** *f* potash

**potàssio** *m* potassium

**potatura** *f* pruning, polling

**potentato** *m* (lit) potentate

**potènte** *adj* powerful; influential || **i potenti** the powers that be

**potènza** *f* power, might; (math) power; **all'ennesima potenza** (math) to the nth power; (fig) to the nth degree; **in potenza** potential; potentially

**potenziale** _adj_ & _m_ potential
**potére** _m_ ability; authority, power; **in potere di** in the hands of; **potere d'acquisto** purchasing power; **potere esecutivo** executive; **potere giudiziario** judiciary; **quarto potere** fourth estate ‖ §219 _intr_ to be powerful; **non ne posso più** I am at the end of my rope; **si può?** may I come in? ‖ _aux_ (ESSERE & AVERE) to be able; **non posso fare a meno di** + _inf_ I can't help + _ger;_ **non potere fare a meno di** to not be able to do without; **posso,** etc. I can; I may, etc.; **potrei,** etc. I could; I might, etc.
**pote∙stà** _f_ (-**stà**) power, authority
**poveràc∙cio -cia** _mf_ (-**ci -ce**) poor guy, poor soul
**pòve∙ro -ra** _adj_ poor; needy, wretched; lean (_gasoline mixture_); **povero in canna** as poor as a church mouse ‖ _mf_ pauper; beggar; poor devil ‖ **i poveri** the poor
**pover∙tà** _f_ (-**tà**) poverty; paucity, scantiness
**poveruòmo** _m_ (used only in _sg_) poor devil
**pozióne** _f_ potion, brew
**pózza** _f_ pool, puddle
**pozzànghera** _f_ puddle
**pozzétto** _m_ small well; manhole; forecastle (_in small boat_)
**pózzo** _m_ well; shaft; **pozzo artesiano** artesian well; **pozzo delle catene** (naut) chain locker; **pozzo di scienza** fountain of knowledge; **pozzo di ventilazione** (min) air shaft; **pozzo nero** cesspool; **pozzo petrolifero** oil well; **pozzo trivellato** deep well; **un pozzo di** (fig) a barrel of
**Praga** _f_ Prague
**prammàti∙co -ca** (-**ci -che**) _adj_ pragmatic ‖ _f_ social custom; **di prammatica** obligatory, de rigueur
**pranzare** [dz] _intr_ to dine
**pranzo** [dz] _m_ dinner; **dopo pranzo** afternoon
**pras∙si** _f_ (-**si**) practice, praxis
**pratería** _f_ prairie
**pràti∙ca** _f_ (-**che**) practice; knowledge; matter; file, dossier; business; experience; (naut) pratique; **aver pratica con** to be familiar with (_people_); **aver pratica di** to be familiar with (_things_); **far pratica** to be an apprentice; **fare le pratiche** to make an application; **in pratica** practically; **insabbiare una pratica** to pigeonhole a matter
**praticàbile** _adj_ practicable; passable ‖ _m_ (theat) raised platform
**praticante** _adj_ practicing ‖ _mf_ apprentice; novice; churchgoer
**praticare** §197 (**pràtico**) _tr_ to practice; to frequent; to be familiar with; to make (_e.g., a hole_); to grant (_a discount_) ‖ _intr_ to practice; **praticare in** to frequent
**pratici∙tà** _f_ (-**tà**) utility; practicality
**pràti∙co -ca** (-**ci -che**) _adj_ practical; experienced ‖ _f_ see **pratica**
**praticó∙ne -na** _mf_ (pej) old hand
**prato** _m_ meadow

**pratolina** _f_ daisy
**pra∙vo -va** _adj_ (lit) wicked
**preaccennare** (**preaccénno**) _tr_ to mention in advance
**preaccenna∙to -ta** _adj_ aforementioned
**preallarme** _m_ early warning
**Prealpi** _fpl_ foothills of the Alps
**preàmbolo** _m_ preamble
**preannunziare** §287 (**preannùnzio**) _tr_ to foretell, forebode
**preannùn∙zio** _m_ (-**zi**) advance information; foreboding
**preautunnale** _adj_ pre-fall
**preavvertire** (**preavvèrto**) _tr_ to forewarn
**preavvisare** _tr_ to give advance notice to; to forewarn
**preavviso** _m_ forewarning; notification of dismissal
**prebèlli∙co -ca** _adj_ (-**ci -che**) prewar
**prebènda** _f_ prebend; (fig) easy money, sinecure
**precà∙rio -ria** _adj_ (-**ri -rie**) precarious
**precauzióne** _f_ precaution
**precedènte** _adj_ preceding ‖ _m_ precedent; **precedenti** background; **precedenti penali** previous offenses, record
**precedènza** _f_ precedence; (aut) right of way; (fig) priority
**precèdere** §123 _tr_ & _intr_ to precede
**precettare** (**precètto**) _tr_ (mil) to call back from furlough
**precètto** _m_ precept; (eccl) obligation
**precettore** _m_ tutor
**precipitare** (**precìpito**) _tr_ to precipitate; to hasten; (chem) to precipitate ‖ _intr_ (ESSERE) to fall; to fail; to rush (_said of events_); (chem) to precipitate ‖ _ref_ to rush
**precipitó∙so -sa** [s] _adj_ hasty, headlong
**precipì∙zio** _m_ (-**zi**) precipice, cliff; ruin; **a precipizio** headlong
**precì∙puo -pua** _adj_ chief, principal, primary
**precisare** _tr_ to say exactly, specify, clarify; to fix (_a date_)
**precisazióne** _f_ clarification
**precisióne** _f_ precision
**preci∙so -sa** _adj_ precise, exact; punctilious; identical, same; sharp, e.g., **alle sette precise** at seven o'clock sharp
**precla∙ro -ra** _adj_ (lit) illustrious
**preclùdere** §105 _tr_ to preclude
**precòce** _adj_ precocious, premature
**preconcèt∙to -ta** _adj_ preconceived ‖ _m_ preconception; prejudice, bias
**preconizzare** [ddzz] _tr_ to foretell, forecast; (eccl) to preconize
**precórrere** §139 _tr_ (lit) to precede ‖ _intr_ (lit) to occur before
**precursóre** _m_ precursor
**prèda** _f_ booty, prize; prey
**predace** _adj_ (lit) preying, predatory
**predare** (**prèdo**) _tr_ to pillage; to prey upon
**preda∙tóre -trice** _adj_ predacious, rapacious ‖ _mf_ plunderer
**predecessóre** _m_ predecessor
**predèlla** _f_ dais; altar step; platform
**predellino** _m_ footboard
**predestinare** (**predestino** & **predèstino**) _tr_ to predestine

predét·to -ta *adj* aforementioned
prediale *adj* field, rural ‖ *f* land tax
prèdi·ca *f* (-che) sermon
predicare §197 (prèdico) *tr & intr* to preach
predicato *m* predicate; essere in predicato di + *inf* to be rumored to + *inf;* essere predicato per to be considered for
predica·tóre -trice *mf* preacher
predicazióne *f* preaching; sermon
predicòzzo *m* (coll) lecture, scolding
predilèt·to -ta *adj & m* favorite
predilezióne *f* predilection
prediligere §149 (*pres part* missing) *tr* to prefer; to like best
predire §151 *tr* to foretell
predispórre §218 *tr* to predispose, prearrange ‖ *ref* to prepare oneself
predisposizióne *f* predisposition
predizióne *f* prediction
predominare (predòmino) *tr* to overcome ‖ *intr* to predominate; to prevail
predomì·nio *m* (-ni) predominance
predóne *m* marauder; predone del mare pirate
preesìstere §114 *intr* (ESSERE) to pre-exist
prefabbricare §197 (prefàbbrico) *tr* to prefabricate
prefazióne *f* preface
preferènza *f* preference; a preferenza rather; usar preferenze a to favor
preferìbile *adj* preferable
preferire §176 *tr* to prefer
preferi·to -ta *adj* preferred, favored ‖ *mf* favorite; pet
prefètto *m* prefect
prefettura *f* prefecture
prèfi·ca *f* (-che) professional mourner, paid mourner; (coll) crybaby
prefiggere §103 *tr* to set, fix; (gram) to prefix ‖ *ref* to plan
prefis·so -sa *adj* appointed; prefixed ‖ *m* (gram) prefix; (telp) area code
prefissòide *m* prefixed combining form
pregare §209 (prègo) *tr* to beg, pray; to ask, request; farsi pregare to take a lot of asking; La prego please; prego! please!; beg your pardon!; you are welcome!
pregévole *adj* valuable
preghièra *f* entreaty; prayer
pregiare §290 (prègio) *tr* (lit) to praise, esteem ‖ *ref* to be honored, to have the pleasure
pregia·to -ta *adj* precious; esteemed; la Sua pregiata (lettera) your favor, your kind letter; pregiatissimo Signore (com) dear Sir; pregiato Signore (com) dear Sir
prè·gio *m* (-gi) value, worth; esteem; avere in pregio to value
pregiudicare §197 (pregiùdico) *tr* to damage, harm, jeopardize
pregiudica·to -ta *adj* prejudged; prejudiced; compromised; bound to fail ‖ *m* previous offender
pregiudiziale *adj* (law) pretrial; (pol) essential ‖ *f* (law) pretrial
pregiudiziévole *adj* prejudicial, detrimental

pregiudì·zio *m* (-zi) prejudice, bias; harm, damage
pregnante *adj* pregnant
pré·gno -gna *adj* pregnant; saturated
prè·go *m* (-ghi) (lit) prayer ‖ *interj* please!; beg your pardon!; you are welcome!
pregustare *tr* to foretaste, anticipate with pleasure
preistòri·co -ca *adj* (-ci -che) prehistoric(al)
prelato *m* prelate
prelazióne *f* (law) preemption; (obs) privilege
prelevaménto *m* (com) withdrawal
prelevare (prelèvo) *tr* to withdraw (*money*); to capture
preliba·to -ta *adj* excellent, delicious
prelièvo *m* withdrawal; (med) specimen
preliminare *adj* preliminary ‖ preliminari *mpl* preliminary negotiations
prelùdere §105 *intr* to make an introductory statement; (with *dat*) to precede, usher in
prelù·dio *m* (-di) prelude; (*of an opera*) overture
prematu·ro -ra *adj* premature
premeditare (premèdito) *tr* to premeditate
premeditazióne *f* premeditation; con premeditazione (law) with malice prepense
prèmere §123 *tr* to press; to push; to squeeze ‖ *intr* (ESSERE & AVERE) to press; to be urgent; premere a to matter to, e.g., gli preme it matters to him; premere su to press, put pressure on
preméssa *f* premise; introduction (*to a book*)
preméttere §198 *tr* to state at the onset; to place at the beginning
premiare §287 (prèmio) *tr* to award a prize to, reward
premiazióne *f* awarding of prizes
preminènte *adj* prominent, preeminent
prè·mio *m* (-mi) prize; premium; bonus; award
prèmito *m* straining (*to defecate*)
premolare *adj & m* premolar
premonire §176 *tr* (lit) to foretell
premonizióne *f* premonition
premorire §201 *intr* (ESSERE) (with *dat*) to predecease
premunire §176 *tr* to fortify ‖ *ref*— premunirsi contro to provide against; premunirsi di to provide oneself with
premura *f* haste; attention, care; aver premura (di) to be in a hurry (to); di premura hastily; far premura (with *dat*) to urge
premuró·so -sa [s] *adj* attentive, careful
prèndere §220 *tr* to take; to catch; to lift; to pick up; to fetch; to get; to receive; prendere a calci to kick; prendere a pugni to punch; prendere a servizio to employ, hire; prendere commiato to take leave; prendere con le buone to treat with kid gloves; prendere in castagna to catch in the act; prendere il sole to sun oneself; prendere la fuga to take flight;

**prendere la mano** to run away (*said of a horse*); **prendere le mosse** to begin (*said, e.g., of a story*); **prendere lucciole per lanterne** to commit a gross error; **prender paura** to get scared; **prendere per** to take for; **prendere per il naso** to lead by the nose; **prendere quota** (aer) to gain altitude; **prendere sonno** to fall asleep; **prendere un granchio** to make a blunder || *intr* to take root; to set (*said of cement*); to catch (*said of fire*); to turn (*left or right*); **prendere a** + *inf* to begin to + *inf* || *ref* to grab one another; to get along together; **prendersela con** to become angry with; to lay the blame on; **prendersi a** to take hold of

**prendi·tóre -trice** *mf* receiver; payee (*of a note*); margin buyer || *m* (baseball) catcher

**prenóme** *m* first name, given name

**prenotare (prenòto)** *tr* to reserve, book || *ref* to register

**prenotazióne** *f* reservation, booking

**preoccupante** *adj* worrisome

**preoccupare (preòccupo)** *tr* to preoccupy; **preoccupare la mente di** to win the favor of || *ref* to worry

**preoccupazióne** *f* preoccupation, worry

**preordinare (preórdino)** *tr* to foreordain; to prearrange

**preparare** *tr* to prepare; to prime; to steep, brew || *ref* to be prepared; to brew (*said, e.g., of a storm*)

**preparati·vo -va** *adj* preparatory || **preparativi** *mpl* preparations

**prepara·to -ta** *adj* prepared; well-equipped || *m* patent medicine; (med) preparation; **preparato anatomico** dissection, anatomical specimen

**preparatò·rio -ria** *adj* (**-ri -rie**) preparatory

**preparazióne** *f* preparation

**preponderante** *adj* preponderant, prevailing

**preponderanza** *f* preponderance

**prepórre §218** *tr* to prefix; to place before; to prefer; **preporre (qlcu) a** to place (*s.o.*) at the head of

**preposizióne** *f* preposition

**prepósto** *m* chief; (eccl) provost

**prepotènte** *adj* arrogant, overbearing; urgent (*desire*) || *m* bully

**prepotènza** *f* arrogance; outrage; **di prepotenza** by force

**prerogativa** *f* prerogative

**présa** [s] *f* hold, grip; handle; potholder; capture; pinch (*e.g., of salt*); setting (*of cement*); intake; (cards) trick; (elec) jack; (mov) take; **a pronta presa** quick-setting (*cement*); **dar presa a** to give rise to; **essere alle prese** to come to grips; **far presa** to stick (*said of glue*); to set (*said of cement*); to take root; **far presa su** to impress; **mettere alle prese** to pit (*e.g., animals*); **presa d'acqua** spigot, faucet; **presa d'aria** outlet (*of air hose*); air shaft; **presa di corrente** (elec) wall socket, outlet, receptacle; **presa di terra** (elec) ground; **presa**

**in giro** kidding, joke; **venire alle prese** to come to grips

**presà·gio** *m* (**-gi**) forecast; portent

**presagire §176** *tr* to forecast; to portend

**presalà·rio** [s] *m* (**-ri**) (educ) stipend

**prèsbite** *adj* far-sighted || *mf* far-sighted person

**presbiteria·no -na** *adj* & *mf* Presbyterian

**prescégliere §244** *tr* to choose, select

**prescindere §247** (*pret* **prescindéi** & **prescissi**) *intr*—**a prescindere da** except for; **prescindere da** to leave out

**prescolàsti·co -ca** *adj* (**-ci -che**) preschool

**prescrit·to -ta** *adj* prescribed

**prescrìvere §250** *tr* to prescribe || *intr* (ESSERE) (law) to prescribe, to lapse

**prescrizióne** *f* prescription; (law) extinctive prescription

**presegnale** [s] *m* warning sign

**presentàbile** *adj* presentable

**presentare (presènto)** *tr* to present; to introduce; **presentare la candidatura di** to nominate; **presentat'arm!** present arms! || *ref* to show up, appear; to come, arise (*said, e.g., of an opportunity*)

**presenta·tóre -trice** *mf* presenter; (rad, telv) announcer || *m* master of ceremonies

**presentazióne** *f* presentation; introduction

**presènte** *adj* present; **avere presente** to have in mind; **fare presente qlco a qlcu** to bring s.th to s.o.'s attention; **tenere presente** to keep in mind || *m* present; bystander, onlooker; **al presente** at present; **di presente** immediately || *interj* here!

**presentiménto** [s] *m* presentiment, foreboding

**presentire** [s] (**presènto**) *tr* to have a presentiment of

**presènza** *f* presence; attendance; **di presenza** in person; **presenza di spirito** presence of mind

**presenziare §287 (presènzio)** *tr* to attend; to witness || *intr*—**presenziare a** to be present at; to witness

**presè·pio** *m* (**-pi**) Nativity, crèche

**preservare** [s] (**presèrvo**) *tr* to preserve, protect

**preservati·vo -va** [s] *adj* & *m* prophylactic

**prèside** [s] *m* principal (*of secondary school*); **preside di facoltà** dean

**presidènte** [s] *m* president; chairman; **presidente del Consiglio** premier

**presidentéssa** [s] *f* president; chairwoman

**presidènza** [s] *f* presidency; chairmanship

**presi·dio** [s] *m* (**-di**) garrison; (fig) defense, help; **presidi medical aids

**presièdere §141 (presièdo)** *tr* to preside over || *intr* to preside; **presiedere a** to preside over

**prèssa** *f* crowd; haste; (mach) press; **far pressa** (poet) to urge

**pressacar·te** *m* (**-te**) paperweight

**pressaforàg·gio** *m* (**-gio**) baler, hay baler

**pressante** *adj* pressing, urgent
**pressappòco** *adv* more or less
**pressare** (**prèsso**) *tr* to press; to urge
**pressióne** *f* pressure; **far pressione su** to put pressure on; **pressione sanguigna** blood pressure; **sotto pressione** under steam
**prèsso** *m*—**nei pressi di** in the neighborhood of ‖ *adv* near, nearby; **a un di presso** approximately; **da presso** close; **press'a poco** more or less ‖ *prep* near; about; at; according to; at the house of; at the office of; care of; with, e.g., **godere fama presso** to enjoy popularity with
**pressoché** *adv* almost, about, nearly
**pressurizzare** [ddzz] *tr* to pressurize
**prestabilire** §176 *tr* to preestablish
**prestabili·to -ta** *adj* appointed
**prestanó·me** *m* (**-me**) straw man, figurehead
**prestante** *adj* strong, vigorous; comely
**prestanza** *f* vigor; (lit) comeliness
**prestare** (**prèsto**) *tr* to lend; to loan; to give (*ear; help*); to pay (*attention*); to render (*obedience*); to take (*oath*); to keep (*faith*); **prestar man forte** to give aid; **prestar servizio** to work ‖ *ref* to lend oneself; to be suitable; to be willing; to volunteer
**presta·tóre -trice** *mf* lender; **prestatore d'opera** worker; **prestatori d'opera** labor
**prestazióne** *f* service; performance
**prestigia·tóre -trice** *mf* magician, juggler
**presti·gio** *m* (**-gi**) prestige; spell, influence; ledgerdemain
**prestigió·so -sa** [s] *adj* captivating, spellbinding; illusory
**prèstito** *m* loan; (philol) borrowing; **dare a prestito** to lend; **prendere a prestito** to borrow
**prè·sto -sta** *adj* (archaic) quick ‖ *m* (mus) presto ‖ **presto** *adv* soon; fast; quick, quickly; early; **al più presto** at the earliest possible time; **ben presto** soon; **far presto** to hurry; **più presto che può** as soon as you can; **presto detto** easy to say
**presùmere** §116 *tr* & *intr* to presume
**presunti·vo -va** *adj* presumptive; budgeted, estimated (*expenditure*)
**presun·to -ta** *adj* alleged, supposed; estimated (*expenditure*)
**presuntuó·so -sa** [s] *adj* presumptuous; bumptious
**presunzióne** *f* presumption; conceit
**presuppórre** [s] §218 *tr* to presuppose
**presuppósto** [s] *m* assumption
**prète** *m* priest; minister; wooden frame (*to hold bed warmer*)
**pretendènte** *m* suitor; pretender
**pretèndere** §270 *tr* to demand, claim; **pretenderla a** to pretend to be ‖ *intr*—**pretendere a** to be a suitor for; to claim (e.g., *a throne*)
**pretensióne** *f* demand; pretention; pretense
**pretensió·so -sa** [s] or **pretenzió·so -sa** [s] *adj* pretentious
**preterintenzionale** *adj* (law) unintentional; (law) justifiable

**pretèri·to -ta** *adj* & *m* preterit
**preté·so -sa** [s] *adj* alleged, ostensible; assumed (*name*) ‖ *f* pretense; pretension
**pretèsto** *m* pretext, excuse; **sotto il pretesto di** under pretense of
**pretòni·co -ca** *adj* (**-ci -che**) pretonic
**pretóre** *m* judge, magistrate (*of lower court*)
**prèt·to -ta** *adj* pure, genuine
**pretura** *f* lower court
**prevalènte** *adj* prevalent, prevailing
**prevalènza** *f* prevalence; **essere in prevalenza** to be in the majority; **in prevalenza** for the most part
**prevalére** §278 *intr* (ESSERE & AVERE) to prevail ‖ *ref* to take advantage
**prevaricare** §197 (**prevàrico**) *intr* to transgress; to graft
**prevarica·tóre -trice** *mf* grafter
**prevedére** §279 *tr* to foresee; to provide for (*said of a statute*)
**prevedìbile** *adj* foreseeable
**prevenire** §282 *tr* to precede; to anticipate; to forewarn; to prejudice
**preventivi·sta** *mf* (**-sti -ste**) estimator
**preventi·vo -va** *adj* preventive; prior; estimated (*budget*) ‖ *m* estimate
**prevenu·to -ta** *adj* forewarned; biased, prejudiced ‖ *m* defendant
**prevenzióne** *f* prevention; prejudice, bias
**previdènte** *adj* provident, prudent
**previdènza** *f* providence; foresight; **previdenza sociale** social security
**previdenziale** *adj* social (e.g., *responsibility*); social-security (e.g., *contribution*)
**prè·vio -via** *adj* (**-vi -vie**) with previous, e.g., **previo accordo** with previous agreement
**previsióne** *f* foresightedness; **in previsione di** anticipating; **previsioni del tempo** weather forecast
**previ·sto -sta** *adj* foreseen, expected ‖ *m* expected time; estimated amount
**prezió·so -sa** [s] *adj* precious, valuable; affected; **fare il prezioso** (coll) to play hard to get ‖ **preziosi** *mpl* valuables, jewels
**prezzare** (**prèzzo**) *tr* to care about; to price
**prezzémolo** *m* parsley
**prèzzo** *m* price; cost; **mettere a prezzo** (fig) to sell; **prezzo di favore** special price; **prezzo d'ingresso** admission; **tenere in gran prezzo** to value highly, to esteem highly; **ultimo prezzo** rock-bottom price
**prezzolare** (**prèzzolo**) *tr* to hire (e.g., *a gunman*); to bribe
**prigióne** *f* prison, jail; (naut) brig
**prigionìa** *f* imprisonment; bondage
**prigioniè·ro -ra** *adj* imprisoned ‖ *mf* prisoner ‖ *m* stud bolt
**prillare** *intr* to spin, whirl
**prima** *f* first grade (*in school*); (rr) first class; (theat) first night; (aut) first (gear); **alla prima** or **sulle prime** at the outset ‖ *adv* before; first; prior; ahead; **di prima** previous; **prima che** before; **prima di** ahead of; before;

**prima o poi** sooner or later; **quanto prima** as soon as possible

**primàrio -ria (-ri -rie)** *adj* primary ‖ *m* (elec) primary; (med) chief of staff

**primati·sta** *mf* (-sti -ste) (sports) record holder

**primato** *m* primacy; (sports) record

**primavèra** *f* spring; springtime; (bot) primrose

**primaverile** *adj* spring; spring-like

**primeggiare §290 (priméggio)** *intr* to excel

**primiè·ro -ra** *adj* (lit) prior; (lit) pristine ‖ *f* (cards) meld

**primiti·vo -va** *adj & m* primitive

**primìzia** *f* first fruits; scoop, beat

**pri·mo -ma** *adj* first; early (*dawn*); prime (*cost*); raw (*material*); **sulle prime** at first ‖ *m* first; minute; **primo arrivato** first comer ‖ *f* see **prima**

**primogèni·to -ta** *adj* first-born; (fig) beloved ‖ *mf* first-born child

**primòrdi** *mpl* beginning, origin

**primordiale** *adj* primordial, primeval

**prìmula** *f* primrose ‖ **Primula** *f*—**la Primula Rossa** the Scarlet Pimpernel

**principale** *adj* principal, main ‖ *m* (coll) boss, chief

**principalménte** *adv* chiefly, mainly

**principato** *m* principality

**prìncipe** *adj* princeps ‖ *m* prince; **il principe di Galles** the Prince of Wales; **principe ereditario** crown prince

**principé·sco -sca** *adj* (-schi -sche) princely

**principéssa** *f* princess

**principiante** *adj* beginning ‖ *mf* beginner

**principiare §287** *tr & intr* (ESSERE & AVERE) to begin; **a principiare da** beginning with

**princì·pio** *m* (-pi) beginning; principle; **in principio** at the beginning, at first

**princisbécco** *m* pinchbeck; **restare or rimanere di princisbecco** to be dumfounded

**prióre** *m* prior

**priori·tà** *f* (-tà) priority

**priorità·rio -ria** *adj* (-ri -rie) priority, e.g., **progetto prioritario** priority project

**pri·sma** *m* (-smi) prism

**privare** *tr* to deprive; to remove

**privativa** *f* government monopoly; salt and tobacco store; patent

**priva·to -ta** *adj* private ‖ *m* private individual

**privazióne** *f* privation, loss

**privilegiare §290 (privilègio)** *tr* to privilege; (fig) to endow

**privilegia·to -ta** *adj* privileged; preferred (*stock*) ‖ *m* privileged person

**privilè·gio** *m* (-gi) privilege

**pri·vo -va** *adj* deprived; **privo di** lacking

**prò** *m* (pro) profit, advantage; **a che pro?** what's the use?; **buon pro!** good appetite!; **far pro** to be good for the health; **il pro e il contro** the pros and the cons ‖ *prep* pro, in favor of

**probàbile** *adj* probable

**probabili·tà** *f* (-tà) probability; chance; odds

**probante** *adj* proving; evidential

**probatò·rio -ria** *adj* (-ri -rie) probative, evidential

**problè·ma** *m* (-mi) problem

**prò·bo -ba** *adj* (lit) honest

**procàc·cia** *mf* (-cia) messenger; mail carrier

**procacciare §128** *tr* to get, procure ‖ *ref* to eke out (*a living*); to get into (*trouble*)

**procace** *adj* buxom, sexy; saucy, petulant

**procèdere §123 (procèdo)** *intr* to proceed, take action ‖ *intr* (ESSERE) to proceed, go ahead

**procediménto** *m* procedure; behavior

**procedura** *f* procedure

**procèlla** *f* (lit) storm, tempest

**procellària** *f* (orn) petrel

**processare (procèsso)** *tr* to try, prosecute

**processióne** *f* procession

**procèsso** *m* process; trial; **processo verbale** minutes

**processuale** *adj* trial

**procinto** *m*—**in procinto di** on the point of

**procióne** *m* raccoon

**procla·ma** *m* (-mi) proclamation

**proclamare** *tr* to proclaim

**proclamazióne** *f* proclamation

**proclìti·co -ca** *adj & f* (-ci -che) proclitic

**proclive** *adj* inclined, disposed

**proclivi·tà** *f* (-tà) proclivity

**procrastinare (procràstino)** *tr* to procrastinate, put off ‖ *intr* to procrastinate

**procreare (procrèo)** *tr* to procreate

**procura** *f* agency; power of attorney; **Procura della Repubblica** attorney general's office; district attorney's office

**procurare** *tr* to procure, to get; to cause; **procurare che** to see to it that; **procurare di** to try to ‖ *ref* to get, acquire

**procura·tóre -trice** *mf* proxy; agent; attorney-at-law; (sports) manager; **Procuratore della Repubblica** district attorney

**pròda** *f* shore, bank; (archaic) prow

**pròde** *adj* brave ‖ *m* brave person, hero

**prodézza** *f* prowess; accomplishment

**prodiè·ro -ra** *adj* prow, e.g., **cannone prodiero** prow gun; preceding (*in a row of ships*)

**prodigare §209 (pròdigo)** *tr* to squander, lavish ‖ *ref* to do one's best

**prodì·gio** *m* (-gi) prodigy; wonder

**prodigió·so -sa [s]** *adj* prodigious; wonderful

**pròdi·go -ga** *adj* (-ghi -ghe) lavish, prodigal; **prodigo di** profuse in

**prodito·rio -ria** *adj* (-ri -rie) traitorous

**prodótto** *m* product; result; **prodotti in scatola** canned goods; **prodotti (orto-frutticoli)** produce

**produrre §102** *tr* to produce; to turn out; to yield; to breed; to cause; (lit)

to prolong; (law) to exhibit ‖ *ref*
(theat) to perform, appear
**produtti·vo -va** *adj* productive
**produttivìsti·co -ca** *adj* (**-ci -che**) productivity, e.g., **fine produttivístico**
productivity policy
**produt·tóre -trice** *adj* producing ‖ *mf*
producer; agent; manufacturer's representative ‖ *m* salesman ‖ *f* sales-
woman
**produzióne** *f* production; output; **produzione in massa** or **in serie** mass
production
**proè·mio** *m* (**-mi**) preamble, proem
**profanare** *tr* to profane, desecrate
**profanazióne** *f* profanation, desecration
**profa·no -na** *adj* profane; lay, unin-
formed ‖ *m* layman; **il profano** the
profane
**proferire** §176 *tr* (lit) to utter; (lit) to
proffer
**professare (profèsso)** *tr* to profess; to
practice (*e.g., law*) ‖ *intr* to practice
‖ *ref* to profess oneself to be
**professionale** *adj* professional; occupational (*disease*); trade (*school*)
**professióne** *f* profession; **fare il ladro
di professione** to be a confirmed
thief; **fare qlco di professione** to pursue the trade of s.th, e.g., **fa il falegname di professione** he pursues the
trade of carpenter
**professioni·sta** *mf* (**-sti -ste**) professional
**professorale** *adj* professorial; pedantic
**profes·sóre -soréssa** *mf* professor;
teacher; **professore d'orchestra** orchestra member
**profè·ta** *m* (**-ti**) prophet
**profetéssa** *f* prophetess
**profèti·co -ca** *adj* (**-ci -che**) prophetic
**profetizzare** [ddzz] *tr* to prophesy
**profezìa** *f* prophecy
**profferire** §176 (*pp* **profferto;** *pret* **prof-
ferii & proffersi**) *tr* to offer; (lit) to
utter
**profi·cuo -cua** *adj* profitable
**profilare** *tr* to outline; to sketch; to
hem; (mach) to shape ‖ *ref* to be
outlined; to loom
**profilas·si** *f* (**-si**) prophylaxis
**profila·to -ta** *adj* outlined; hemmed;
(mach) shaped ‖ *m* structural piece
**profilàtti·co -ca** *adj* (**-ci -che**) prophylactic
**profilatura** *f* hemming; (mach) shaping
**profilo** *m* profile; sketch; outline
**profittare** *intr* to profit, benefit
**profitta·tóre -trice** *mf* profiteer
**profittévole** *adj* (lit) profitable
**profitto** *m* profit; progress; **profitti e
perdite** profit and loss
**proflù·vio** *m* (**-vi**) overflow; (pathol)
discharge
**profondare (profóndo)** *tr & intr* to sink
**profóndere** §178 *tr* to squander, lavish
‖ *ref* to be profuse
**profondi·tà** *f* (**-tà**) depth
**profón·do -da** *adj* deep; profound;
searching (*e.g., investigation*) ‖ *m*
bottom; depth; subconscious
**pro fórma** *adj invar* pro forma; perfunctory ‖ *m* (coll) formality

**pròfu·go -ga** (**-ghi -ghe**) *adj* fugitive ‖
*mf* refugee
**profumare** *tr* to perfume ‖ *intr* to smell
**profumataménte** *adv* lavishly
**profuma·to -ta** *adj* perfumed, fragrant
**profumerìa** *f* perfumery; perfume shop
**profumo** *m* perfume; bouquet (*of wine*)
**profusióne** *f* profusion; **a profusione**
in profusion
**profu·so -sa** *adj* profuse
**progè·nie** *f* (**-nie**) progeny, offspring;
(pej) breed
**progeni·tóre -trice** *mf* ancestor
**progettare (progètto)** *tr* to plan; to
design
**progetti·sta** *mf* (**-sti -ste**) planner; designer; wild dreamer
**progètto** *m* project; plan; draft (*of
law*); **far progetti** to plan; **progetto
di scala reale** (cards) possible
straight flush
**prògno·si** *f* (**-si**) prognosis
**program·ma** *m* (**-mi**) program; plan;
curriculum; cycle (*of washing machine*); (mov) feature; (theat) playbill; **programma politico** platform
**programmare** *tr* to program; to plan
**programma·tóre -trice** *mf* programmer
**programmazióne** *f* programming
**progredire** §176 *intr* (ESSERE & AVERE)
to progress, advance
**progredi·to -ta** *adj* advanced
**progressióne** *f* progression
**progressi·sta** *adj & mf* (**-sti -ste**) progressive
**progressi·vo -va** *adj* progressive
**progrèsso** *m* progress; progression, advance; **fare progressi** to progress
**proibire** §176 *tr* to prohibit; to prevent
**proibi·to -ta** *adj* forbidden; **è proibito
entrare** no admission; **è proibito fumare** no smoking
**proibizióne** *f* prohibition
**proibizionismo** *m* prohibition
**proiettare (proiètto)** *tr* to project; to
cast (*a shadow*) ‖ *intr* to project ‖
*ref* to be projected, project
**proièttile** *m* projectile, missile
**proiettóre** *m* projector, projection machine; searchlight; (aut) headlight;
**proiettore acustico** sonar projector
**proiezióne** *f* projection; **proiezione ral-
lentata** slow motion
**pròle** *f invar* offspring, progeny
**proletariato** *m* proletariat
**proletà·rio -ria** *adj & mf* (**-ri -rie**)
proletarian
**proliferare (prolìfero)** *intr* to proliferate
**prolificare** §197 (**prolìfico**) *intr* to proliferate
**prolìfi·co -ca** *adj* (**-ci -che**) prolific
**prolis·so -sa** *adj* prolix, long-winded;
long (*e.g., beard*)
**pròlo·go** *m* (**-ghi**) prologue; preface
**prolun·ga** *f* (**-ghe**) extension
**prolungaménto** *m* prolongation, extension
**prolungare** §209 *tr* to prolong, extend
‖ *ref* to extend; to speak at great
length
**prolunga·to -ta** *adj* extended, protracted
**prolusióne** *f* inaugural lecture

**promemò·ria** or **pro memò·ria** *m* (**-ria**) reminder

**promés·so -sa** *adj* promised ‖ *mf* betrothed ‖ *f* promise; promising individual

**promettènte** *adj* promising

**prométtere** §198 *tr* to promise; to threaten (*e.g., a storm*) ‖ *intr* to promise; **promettere bene** to be very promising ‖ *ref*—**promettersi a Dio** to make a vow to God; **promettersi in matrimonio** to become engaged

**prominènte** *adj* prominent

**promì·scuo -scua** *adj* promiscuous; coeducational; mixed (*marriage; races*); (gram) epicene

**promontò·rio** *m* (**-ri**) promontory, cliff

**promo·tóre -trice** *adj* promoting ‖ *mf* promoter

**promozióne** *f* promotion

**promulgare** §209 *tr* to promulgate

**promuòvere** §202 *tr* to promote; to pass (*a student*); to initiate (*legal suit*); to induce (*e.g., perspiration*)

**pronipóte** *mf* great-grandchild ‖ *m* great-grandson; grandnephew; **pronipoti** descendants ‖ *f* great-granddaughter; grandniece

**prò·no -na** *adj* (lit) prone

**pronóme** *m* pronoun

**pronominale** *adj* (gram) pronominal; (gram) reflexive (*verb*)

**pronosticare** §197 (**pronòstico**) *tr* to prognosticate, forecast

**pronòsti·co** *m* (**-ci**) prognostication, forecast; sign, omen

**prontézza** *f* readiness; quickness, promptness

**prón·to -ta** *adj* ready; first (*aid*); quick; prompt; ready (*cash*) ‖ **pronto** *interj* (telp) hello!

**prontuà·rio** *m* (**-ri**) handbook

**pronùn·cia** *f* (**-cie**) or **pronunzia** *f* pronunciaton; (law) judgment

**pronunziare** §287 *tr* to pronounce; to utter; to pass (*sentence*); to make (*a speech*) ‖ *ref* to pass judgment

**pronunzia·to -ta** *adj* pronounced, marked; prominent (*nose, chin, beard*) ‖ *m* (law) sentence

**propaganda** *f* propaganda; advertisement; advertising

**propagandi·sta** *mf* (**-sti -ste**) propagandist; advertiser; agent; detail man

**propagandìsti·co -ca** *adj* (**-ci -che**) advertising

**propagare** §209 *tr* to propagate; to spread ‖ *ref* to spread

**propàggine** *f* offspring; (geog) spur, counterfort; (hort) layer

**propalare** *tr* (lit) to spread, divulge

**propellènte** *adj & m* propellent

**propèllere** §168 *tr* to propel

**propèndere** §123 (*pp* **propènso**) *intr* to incline, tend

**propensióne** *f* propensity, inclination

**propèn·so -sa** *adj* inclined, bent

**propinare** *tr* to administer (*e.g., poison*); **propinare qlco a qlcu** to put s.th over on s.o.

**propìn·quo -qua** *adj* (lit) near; (lit) related

**propiziare** §287 *tr* to propitiate, appease

**propì·zio -zia** *adj* (**-zi -zie**) propitious, favorable

**proponiménto** *m* intention, plan

**propórre** §218 *tr* to propose, present; to propound; **proporre come candidato** to nominate ‖ *ref*—**proporsi di** to propose to, resolve to

**proporzionare** (**proporzióno**) *tr* to proportion, prorate

**proporzióne** *f* proportion

**propòsito** *m* purpose; **a proposito** opportune; opportunely; proper; by the way; **a proposito di** on the subject of; **di proposito** deliberately; **fuor di proposito** out of place; **parlare a proposito** to speak to the point

**proposizióne** *f* proposition; (gram) clause; **proposizione subordinata** dependent clause

**propósta** *f* proposal; **proposta di legge** bill

**propriaménte** *adv* exactly; properly

**proprie·tà** *f* (**-tà**) propriety; ownership; property; **la proprietà** property owners; **proprietà immobiliare** real estate; **proprietà letteraria** copyright; **sulla proprietà** on the premises

**proprietà·rio -ria** *mf* (**-ri -rie**) owner, proprietor

**prò·prio -pria** (**-pri -prie**) *adj* peculiar, characteristic; proper (*e.g., name*); own, e.g., **il mio proprio libro** my own book ‖ *m* one's own; **i propri** one's folks; **lavorare in proprio** to work for oneself ‖ **proprio** *adv* just, really, exactly; **non . . . proprio** not . . . at all; **proprio adesso** just, just now

**propugnare** *tr* to advocate; (lit) to fight for

**propugna·tóre -trice** *mf* (lit) advocate

**propulsare** *tr* to propel; (lit) to repulse

**propulsióne** *f* propulsion

**propulsóre** *m* propeller, motor

**pròra** *f* prow, bow

**proravìa** *f*—**a proravia** (naut) fore

**pròro·ga** *f* (**-ghe**) delay, extension

**prorogare** §209 (**pròrogo**) *tr* to extend; to put off, delay

**prorómpere** §240 *intr* to overflow; to burst (*into tears*)

**prosa** *f* prose

**prosài·co -ca** *adj* (**-ci -che**) prose; prosaic

**prosàpia** *f* (lit) ancestry

**prosa·tóre -trice** *mf* prose writer

**proscè·nio** *m* (**-ni**) forestage

**prosciògliere** §127 *tr* to free; to exonerate

**prosciugare** §209 *tr* to drain, reclaim ‖ *ref* to dry up

**prosciutto** *m* ham; **prosciutto cotto** boiled ham; **prosciutto crudo** prosciutto

**proscrìvere** §250 *tr* to proscribe, outlaw

**prosecuzióne** [s] *f* prosecution, pursuit

**proseguiménto** [s] *m* prosecution, pursuit

**proseguire** [s] (**proséguo**) *tr* to follow, pursue ‖ *intr* (ESSERE & AVERE) to continue

**prosèlito** *m* proselyte
**prosodìa** *f* prosody
**prosopopèa** *f* conceit
**prosperare (pròspero)** *intr* to prosper, thrive
**prosperi·tà** *f* (**-tà**) prosperity ‖ *interj* gesundheit!
**pròspe·ro -ra** *adj* prosperous, thriving; flourishing; successful ‖ *m* (coll) match
**prosperó·so -sa** [s] *adj* flourishing; healthy; buxom
**prospettare (prospètto)** *tr* to face, overlook; to outline ‖ *intr*—**prospettare su** to face ‖ *ref* to look; to appear; to loom up
**prospetti·vo -va** *adj* prospective ‖ *f* perspective; prospect; view
**prospètto** *m* prospect, view; front (*of building*); diagram; outline; prospectus
**prospettóre** *m* prospector
**prospiciènte** *adj* facing
**prossimaménte** *adv* shortly
**prossimi·tà** *f* -tà proximity, nearness; **in prossimità di** near
**pròssi·mo -ma** *adj* near, close; next; immediate (*cause*) ‖ *m* neighbor, fellow man
**pròstata** *f* prostate
**prosternare (prostèrno)** *ref* to prostrate oneself
**prostituire** §176 *tr* to prostitute
**prostituta** *f* prostitute
**prostituzióne** *f* prostitution
**prostrare (pròstro)** *ref* to prostrate oneself
**prostrazióne** *f* prostration
**protagoni·sta** *mf* (-sti -ste) protagonist
**protèggere** §193 *tr* to protect; to help, defend; to favor, promote
**proteìna** *f* protein
**protèndere** §270 *tr* & *ref* to stretch
**pròte·si** *f* (-si) (philol) prothesis; (surg) prosthesis
**protèsta** *f* protest, protestation
**protestante** *adj* & *mf* protestant; Protestant
**protestare (protèsto)** *tr* to protest; to reject (*faulty merchandise*) ‖ *intr* & *ref* to protest
**protestatà·rio -ria** (-ri -rie) *adj* protesting ‖ *m* protester
**protèsto** *m* (com) protest
**protèt·to -ta** *adj* protected ‖ *m* protegé ‖ *f* protegée
**protettorato** *m* protectorate
**protet·tóre -trice** *adj* patron ‖ *mf* protector, guardian ‖ *m* patron ‖ *f* patroness
**protezióne** *f* protection; patronage
**pròto** *m* (typ) foreman
**protocòllo** *adj invar* commercial (*size*) ‖ *m* protocol; **mettere a protocollo** to register, record
**protopla·sma** *m* (-smi) protoplasm
**protòtipo** *m* prototype; (fig) epitome
**protozòi** [dz] *mpl* protozoa
**protrarre** §273 *tr* to protract, extend ‖ *ref* to continue
**protrùdere** §190 *intr* to protrude (*said, e.g., of a broken bone*)

**protuberante** *adj* protruding, bulging
**pròva** *f* test, examination; proof; try, attempt; probationary period (*of employment*); trial; token (*e.g., of friendship*); (sports) competition, event; (theat) rehearsal; **a prova di bomba** bombproof; foolproof; **a tutta prova** thoroughly tested; **in prova** on approval; **mettere a dura prova** to test (*e.g., one's patience*); **mettere alla prova** to test (*e.g., one's ability*); **mettere in prova** to fit (*a suit*); **prova del fuoco** trial by fire; **prova dell'acido** acid test; **prova generale** dress rehearsal; **prova indiziaria** circumstantial evidence
**provare (pròvo)** *tr* to test; to try; to try on; to try out; to taste; to prove; to feel (*e.g., anger*); (theat) to rehearse ‖ *intr* to try ‖ *ref* to compete
**proveniènza** *f* origin
**provenire** §282 *intr* (ESSERE) to stem, originate
**provènto** *m* income, proceeds
**provenzale** *adj* & *mf* Provençal
**provèr·bio** *m* (-bi) proverb; byword
**provétta** *f* test tube
**provèt·to -ta** *adj* (lit) masterful
**provìn·cia** *f* (-ce) province; **in provincia** outside of the big cities
**provinciale** *adj* provincial ‖ *mf* small-town person ‖ *f* provincial highway, state highway
**provino** *m* gauge; (mov) screen test
**provocare** §197 (**pròvoco**) *tr* to provoke; to bring about, cause; to arouse; to entice
**provoca·tóre -trice** *adj* provoking ‖ *mf* provoker
**provocatò·rio -ria** *adj* (-ri -rie) provoking, provocative
**provocazióne** *f* provocation; challenge
**provvedére** §221 *tr* to prepare; to supply; **provvedere che** to see to it that ‖ *intr* to take the necessary steps; **provvedere a** to provide for; **provvedere a** + *inf* to provide for + *ger;* **provvedere nei confronti di** to take steps against
**provvediménto** *m* measure, step
**provvedi·tóre -trice** *mf* provider ‖ *m* superintendent; **provveditore agli studi** superintendent of schools
**provvedu·to -ta** *adj* supplied; careful
**provvidènza** *f* providence; windfall; **provvidenze** provisions, help
**provvidenziale** *adj* providential
**pròvvi·do -da** *adj* (lit) provident
**provvigióne** *f* (com) commission
**provvisò·rio -ria** *adj* (-ri -rie) provisional, temporary
**provvi·sto -sta** *adj* supplied ‖ *f* supply, provision; **fare le provviste** to shop
**prozìa** *f* grandaunt
**prozì·o** *m* (-i) granduncle
**prua** *f* bow, prow
**prudènte** *adj* prudent, cautious
**prudènza** *f* prudence, discretion
**prùdere** §222 *intr* to itch; **sentirsi prudere le mani** to feel like giving s.o. a beating
**prugna** *f* plum; **prugna secca** prune

**prugno** *m* plum tree
**prùgnola** *f* sloe
**prùgnolo** *m* sloe, blackthorn
**pruno** *m* thorn
**prurito** *m* itch
**pseudònimo** *m* pseudonym; alias; pen name
**psicanàlisi** *f* psychoanalysis
**psicanali·sta** *mf* (-sti -ste) psychoanalyst
**psicanalizzare** [ddzz] *tr* to psychoanalyze
**psiche** *f* psyche; cheval glass
**psichia·tra** *mf* (-tri -tre) psychiatrist
**psichiatrìa** *f* psychiatry
**psìchi·co -ca** *adj* (-ci -che) psychic
**psicologìa** *f* psychology
**psicològi·co -ca** *adj* (-ci -che) psychological
**psicòlo·go -ga** *mf* (-gi -ghe) psychologist
**psicopàti·co -ca** (-ci -che) *adj* psychopathic || *mf* psychopath
**psicò·si** *f* (-si) psychosis
**psicosomàti·co -ca** *adj* (-ci -che) psychosomatic
**psicotècni·co -ca** (-ci -che) *adj* psychotechnical || *m* industrial psychologist || *f* industrial psychology
**psicòti·co -ca** *adj* (-ci -che) psychotic
**pubblicare** §197 (pùbblico) *tr* to publish
**pubblicazióne** *f* publication; **pubblicazioni di matrimonio** marriage banns
**pubblicismo** *m* communications; advertising
**pubblici·sta** *mf* (-sti -ste) free-lance newspaper writer; publicist
**pubblicìsti·co -ca** (-ci -che) *adj* advertising; political-science || *f* newspaper business
**pubblicità** *f* publicity; advertising
**pubblicità·rio -ria** (-ri -rie) *adj* advertising || *mf* advertising agent
**publicizzare** [ddzz] *tr* to publicize
**publicizzazióne** [ddzz] *f* publicizing
**pùbbli·co -ca** *adj* & *m* (-ci -che) public; **mettere in pubblico** to publish
**pubertà** *f* puberty
**pudibón·do -da** *adj* (lit) modest, bashful; (lit) prudish
**pudicìzia** *f* modesty; prudery
**pudi·co -ca** *adj* (-chi -che) modest, chaste; bashful; (lit) reserved
**pudóre** *m* modesty; decency; shame
**puericoltóre** *m* pediatrician
**puerile** *adj* puerile, childish
**puerili·tà** *f* (-tà) puerility, childishness
**puèrpera** *f* lying-in patient
**pugilato** *m* boxing
**pugilatóre** *m* boxer, prize fighter
**pùgile** *m* boxer, prize fighter
**pugili·sta** *m* (-sti) boxer, prize fighter
**pù·glia** *f* (-glie) stake (in gambling)
**pugnace** *adj* (lit) pugnacious
**pugnalare** *tr* to stab
**pugnalata** *f* stab
**pugnale** *m* dagger
**pugno** *m* fist; fistful; punch; **avere in pugno** to have in one's grasp; **di proprio pugno** in one's own hand; **fare a pugni** to fight; to clash

**pula** *f* chaff
**pulce** *f* flea; **mettere una pulce nell'orecchio di** to put a bug in the ear of; **pulce tropicale** jigger, chigger
**pulcèlla** *f* maid, maiden
**pulcinèlla** *f*—**pulcinella di mare** (orn) Atlantic puffin || **Pulcinel·la** *m* (-la) buffoon; Punch, Punchinello
**pulcino** *m* chick
**pulédra** *f* filly
**pulédro** *m* colt, foal
**pu-lég·gia** *f* (-ge) pulley
**pulire** §176 *tr* to clean; to shine (shoes); to wipe; to polish
**puliscipiè·di** *m* (-di) doormat
**puli·to -ta** *adj* clean; polished; clear (conscience) || *f*—**dare una pulita a** to give a lick and a promise to
**pulitura** *f* cleaning; **pulitura a secco** dry cleaning
**pulizìa** *f* cleaning; cleanliness; **fare le pulizie** to clean house
**pullulare** (pùllulo) *intr* to swarm
**pùlpito** *m* pulpit
**pulsante** *m* knob; push button
**pulsare** *intr* to throb; to pulsate
**pulvìscolo** *m* fine dust; haze
**pulzèlla** *f* var of **pulcella**
**pu·ma** *m* (-ma) cougar
**pungènte** *adj* pungent; bitter (cold)
**pùngere** §183 *tr* to sting; (fig) to goad
**pungiglióne** *m* stinger (of bee); (fig) sting; (obs) goad
**pungitòpo** *m* (bot) butcher's broom
**pungolare** (pùngolo) *tr* to goad, prod
**punire** §176 *tr* to punish
**punizióne** *f* punishment; penalty
**punta** *f* point, tip; prong; brad; bit, trifle; needle (of phonograph); avantgarde; point (of dog); (lit) wound; (fig) peak; (mach) broach; **averne fino alla punta dei capelli** to be sick and tired; **fare la punta a** to sharpen; **in punta di penna** elegantly; **prendere di punta** to treat roughly; to face up to; **punta delle dita** fingertip; **punta di piedi** tiptoe
**puntale** *m* tip, ferrule
**puntaménto** *m* aiming
**puntare** *tr* to aim; to aim at; to point; to thrust; to dot; to bet; to stare at; to fix (one's eyes); **puntare i piedi** to stiffen up; (fig) to balk || *intr* to aim; to point; to pin; to bet; **puntare su** to count on; **puntare verso** march on; to sail toward
**puntaspil·li** *m* (-li) pincushion
**puntata** *f* jab (with weapon); excursion; bet; issue, number (of magazine); installment (of story); (mil) incursion
**punteggiare** §290 (puntéggio) *tr* to dot; (gram) to punctuate
**punteggiatura** *f* dotting; punctuation
**puntég·gio** *m* (-gi) score
**puntellare** (puntèllo) *tr* to prop, brace; to support
**puntèllo** *m* prop, brace; support
**punterìa** *f* aiming; aiming gear; (aut) tappet
**punteruòlo** *m* punch; awl
**puntì·glio** *m* (-gli) obstinacy, stubbornness; punctilio

**puntiglió·so -sa** [s] *adj* punctilious, scrupulous; obstinate, stubborn
**puntina** *f* brad; needle; thumbtack
**puntino** *m* small dot; G-string; **a pun·tino** to a T
**punto** *m* point; period; dot; place, spot; extent; stitch; **dare dei punti a** to be superior to; **di punto in bianco** all of a sudden; **di tutto punto** thoroughly; **due punti** colon; **essere a buon punto** to be well advanced; **essere sul punto di** + *inf* to be about to + *inf*; **fare il punto** (fig; naut) to take one's bearings; **in punto** on the dot; **in punto franco** in bond; **in un punto** together; **mettere a punto** to get in working order; (aut) to tune up; **mettere i punti sulle i** to dot one's i's; **punto assistenza** service agency; **punto di partenza** starting point; **punto di vista** viewpoint; **punto esclamativo** exclamation point; **punto e virgola** semicolon; **punto fermo** full stop; **punto interrogativo** question mark; **punto morto** (mach) dead center; **punto stimato** (naut) dead reckoning; **qui sta il punto!** here's the rub!; **vincere ai punti** (boxing) to win by points, win by decision ‖ *adv*—**né punto né poco** not at all; **non . . . punto** not at all
**puntóne** *m* rafter
**puntuale** *adj* punctual, prompt
**puntuali·tà** *f* (**-tà**) punctuality, promptness
**puntura** *f* sting; stitch (*sharp pain*); (coll) injection; **puntura lombare** spinal anesthesia
**punzecchiare** §287 (**punzécchio**) *tr* to keep on stinging; to tease, torment
**punzecchiatura** *f* sting, bite
**punzonare** (**punzóno**) *tr* to mark or stamp with a punch
**punzonatrice** *f* punch press
**punzóne** *m* punch; nailset
**pupa** *f* doll; (zool) pupa
**pupazzetti·sta** *mf* (**-sti -ste**) cartoonist
**pupazzétto** *m* caricature; cartoon; **pupazzetto di carta** paper doll
**pupazzo** *m* puppet; **pupazzo di stoffa** rag doll

**pupil·lo -la** *mf* pupil; ward, protégé ‖ *f* pupil (*of eye*); protégée
**pupo** *m* (coll) baby
**purché** *conj* provided, providing
**pure** *adv* too, also; indeed; (lit) only; **pur** *il* only in order to; **quando pure** even if; **se pure** even if ‖ *conj* though, although; but, yet
**pu·rè** *m* (**-rè**) purée; **purè di patate** mashed potatoes
**purézza** *f* purity
**pur·ga** *f* (**-ghe**) laxative; purification; purge
**purgante** *adj* purging ‖ *m* laxative
**purgare** §209 *tr* to purge; to purify; to expurgate ‖ *ref* to take a laxative
**purgati·vo -va** *adj* laxative
**purgatò·rio** *m* (**-ri**) purgatory
**purificare** §197 (**purìfico**) *tr* to purify
**purismo** *m* purism
**purità** *f* purity
**purita·no -na** *adj* & *m* puritan; Puritan
**pu·ro -ra** *adj* pure; clear; simple, mere
**purosàn·gue** *adj invar* & *m* (**-gue**) thoroughbred
**purpùre·o -a** *adj* (lit) purple
**purtròppo** *adv* unfortunately
**purulèn·to -ta** *adj* purulent
**pus** *m* pus
**pusillànime** *adj* pusillanimous
**pùstola** *f* pustule; pimple
**puta caso** *adv* possibly, maybe
**putifè·rio** *m* (**-ri**) hubbub
**putrefare** §173 *intr* (ESSERE) & *ref* to putrefy, rot
**putrefazióne** *f* putrefaction
**putrèlla** *f* I beam
**pùtri·do -da** *adj* putrid ‖ *m* corruption
**putta** *f* (coll) girl; (lit) prostitute
**puttana** *f* (vulg) whore
**put·to -ta** *adj* (archaic) meretricious ‖ *m* figure of a child ‖ *f* see **putta**
**puzza** *f* var of **puzzo**
**puzzare** *intr* to stink, smell
**puzzo** *m* stench, smell, bad odor
**pùzzola** *f* polecat, skunk
**puzzolènte** *adj* stinking, smelly
**puzzonata** *f* (coll) contemptible action; (coll) botch, bungle
**puzzóne** *m* (coll) skunk (*person*)

# Q

**Q, q** [ku] *m* & *f* fifteenth letter of the Italian alphabet
**qua** *adv* here; **da un (giorno, mese, anno) in qua** for the past (day, month, year); **di qua da** on this side of; **in qua** on this side; here
**quàcche·ro -ra** or **quàcque·ro -ra** *adj* & *mf* Quaker; **alla quacquera** in a plain fashion
**quadèrno** *m* copybook; **quaderno di cassa** cash book
**quadràngo·lo -la** *adj* quadrangular ‖ *m* quadrangle
**quadrante** *m* quadrant; dial; face (*of watch*); **quadrante solare** sundial

**quadrare** *tr* to square ‖ *intr* (ESSERE & AVERE) to square; **quadrare a** to be satisfactory to; **quadrare con** to fit
**quadra·to -ta** *adj* square; sound (*mind*) ‖ *m* square; diaper; (boxing) ring; (nav) wardroom
**quadratura** *f* squaring; concreteness; (astr) quadrature
**quadrèl·lo** *m* (**-li**) square ruler; square tile ‖ *m* (**-la** *fpl*) (lit) bolt, arrow
**quadreria** *f* picture gallery; collection
**quadretta·to -ta** *adj* checkered
**quadrétto** *m* small painting; checker, small square; (fig) picture

**quadriennale** *adj* four-year ‖ *f* quadrennial

**quadrifò·glio** *m* (-**gli**) four-leaf clover; **a quadrifoglio** cloverleaf

**quadrì·glio** *m* (-**gli**) (cards) quadrille

**quadrimensionale** *adj* four-dimensional

**quadrimestrale** *adj* four-month

**quadrimèstre** *m* four-month period; four-month payment

**quadrimotóre** *adj* four-motor ‖ *m* four-motor plane

**quadrireattóre** *m* four-motor jet

**qua·dro -dra** *adj* square; (fig) solìd ‖ *m* picture; painting; sight; square; table, summary; panel, switchboard; (theat) scene; **quadri** bulletin board; (mil) cadres; (cards) diamonds

**quadrùmane** *adj* quadrumanous ‖ *m* monkey; ape

**quadruplicare** §197 (**quadrùplico**) *tr* & *ref* to quadruple

**quadrùplice** *adj* quadruple; **in quadruplice copia** in four copies

**quàdru·plo -pla** *adj* & *m* quadruple

**quaggiù** *adv* down here

**quàglia** *f* quail

**quagliare** §280 *tr, intr* (ESSERE) & *ref* var of **cagliare**

**qualche** *adj* *invar* some, e.g., **qualche giorno** some day; some, e.g., **qualche elefante è bianco** some elephants are white; any, e.g., **ha qualche libro da vendere?** do you have any books to sell?; a few, e.g., **qualche giorno** a few days

**qualchedu·no -na** *pron* *indef* var of **qualcuno**

**qualcòsa** [s] *m* (fig) something; (fig) somebody ‖ *pron* *indef* something; anything; **qualcosa di buono** something good

**qualcu·no -na** *pron* *indef* some; any; somebody; anybody ‖ *m* somebody

**quale** *adj* which, what; what a, e.g., **quale onore!** what an honor!; as, e.g., **il pane, quale vedi, è fresco** the bread, as you can see, is fresh; **quale che sia** regardless of ‖ *pron* which; what; (archaic) who; **il quale** who, whom; **per la quale** o.k.; well-bred; commendable; terrific; **quale . . . quale** some . . . some ‖ *prep* as, e.g., **quale ministro** as a minister

**qualìfi·ca** *f* (-**che**) rating; position; quality, qualification

**qualificare** §197 (**qualìfico**) *tr* to qualify; to classify; to rate, give a rating to ‖ *ref* to introduce oneself; to qualify

**qualifica·to -ta** *adj* aggravated (*assault*); qualified (*personnel*); specialized (*worker*)

**quali·tà** *f* (-**tà**) quality; capacity

**qualóra** *conj* if; (lit) whenever

**qualsìasi** [s] *adj* *invar* any; whatever; ordinary

**qualunque** *adj* *invar* any; whatever; common, ordinary; **in qualunque modo** anyway, anyhow; **qualunque altro** anybody else; **qualunque cosa** anything; no matter what

**qualvòlta** *conj* (lit) whenever

**quando** *m* when ‖ *adv* when; **di quando** in quando from time to time; **quando . . . quando** sometimes . . . sometimes ‖ *conj* when; whenever; while; **da quando** since

**quantìsti·co -ca** *adj* (-**ci -che**) quantum

**quanti·tà** *f* (-**tà**) quantity; number

**quantitativo** *m* quantity

**quan·to -ta** *adj* how much; as much; how great; how great a; what a; **quan·ti -te** how many; as many ‖ *m* quantum ‖ *pron* how much; as much; how great; how long; that which; what; whatever; **a quanto si dice** according to what is rumored; **da quanto** from what; for how long; **fra quanto** how soon; **per quanto io ne sappia** as far as I know; **quanto più** (or **meno**) **. . . tanto più** (or **meno**) the more (or the less) . . . the more (or the less); **quan·ti -te** how many; all those; as many as; **quanti ne abbiamo?** what's the date? ‖ **quanto** *adv* how much; as much as; **in quanto** as; **in quanto che** inasmuch as; **per quanto** although; no matter; nevertheless; **quanto a** as to, as for; **quanto mai** as never before; **quanto meno** at least; **quanto prima** as soon as possible

**quantunque** *conj* although, though

**quaranta** *adj, m* & *pron* forty; **gli anni quaranta** the forties; **i quaranta** the forties (*in age*)

**quarantèna** *f* quarantine

**quarantènne** *adj* forty-year-old ‖ *mf* forty-year-old person

**quarantèsi·mo -ma** *adj, m* & *pron* fortieth

**quarantina** *f* about forty; **essere sulla quarantina** to be about forty years old

**quarantòtto** *adj* forty-eight ‖ *m* forty-eight; (coll) hubbub, uproar

**quarésima** *f* Lent

**quartabuòno** *m* triangle (*in drafting*); **tagliare a quartabuono** to miter

**quartétto** *m* quartet; **quartetto d'archi** string quartet

**quartière** *m* quarter, district; (mil) quarters; (coll) apartment; **quartier generale** headquarters; **senza quartiere** (*fight*) without quarter

**quar·to -ta** *adj* & *pron* fourth ‖ *m* fourth; quarter; quarter of a kilo; quarter of a liter; (naut) watch; **l'una e un quarto** a quarter after one; **l'una meno un quarto** a quarter to one

**quarzo** *m* quartz

**quasi** *adv* almost, nearly; **quasi che** as if; **quasi mai** hardly ever; **senza quasi** without any ifs and buts

**quassù** *adv* up here

**quat·to -ta** *adj* crouching; squatting; **quatto quatto** stealthy, silent; **starsene quatto quatto** to not make a sound

**quattordicènne** *adj* fourteen-year-old ‖ *mf* fourteen-year-old person

**quattordicèsi·mo -ma** *adj, m* & *pron* fourteenth

**quattórdici** *adj* & *pron* fourteen; **le**

**quattordici** two P.M. ‖ *m* fourteen; fourteenth (*in dates*)

**quattrino** *m* penny; (fig) bit; **quattrini** money

**quattro** *adj* four; a few, e.g., **quattro gatti** a few people; **a quattro mani** (mus) for four hands ‖ *pron* four; **dirne quattro a** to upbraid; **farsi in quattro** to go all out; **in quattro e quatt'otto** in a few minutes; **le quattro** four o'clock ‖ *m* four; fourth (*in dates*); racing shell with four oarsmen

**quattrocènto** *adj, m & pron* four hundred ‖ **il Quattrocento** the fifteenth century

**quattromila** *adj, m & pron* four thousand

**quégli** §7 *adj* ‖ §8 *pron*

**quéi** §7 *adj*

**quél** §7 *adj* ‖ §8 *pron*

**quéll'** §7 *adj*

**quél·lo -la** §7 *adj* ‖ §8 *pron*—**per quello che so io** as far as I know

**quèr·cia** *f* (-ce) oak tree

**querci·no -na** *adj* oaken

**querèla** *f* complaint

**querelante** *adj* complaining ‖ *mf* plaintiff

**querelare** (**querèlo**) *tr* to sue ‖ *ref* (law) to sue; (lit) to complain

**querela·to -ta** *adj* accused ‖ *mf* defendant

**quèru·lo -la** *adj* (lit) plaintive

**quesito** *m* question; problem; (lit) request

**quésti** §7 *pron*

**questionare** (**questióno**) *intr* to quarrel

**questionà·rio** *m* (-ri) questionnaire

**questióne** *f* question; (coll) quarrel; **questione di gabinetto** call for a vote of confidence; **venire a questione** to quarrel

**qué·sto -sta** §7 *adj* ‖ §8 *pron*—**e con questo?** so what?; **per questo** therefore; **questa** this matter; **questo ... quello** the former ... the latter

**questóre** *m* police commissioner; sergeant at arms (*of congress*)

**quèstua** *f* begging; collection of alms; **andare alla questua** to go begging; **vietata la questua** no begging

**questura** *f* police department; police headquarters

**questurino** *m* (coll) policeman

**què·to -ta** *adj* var of **quieto**

**qui** *adv* here; **di qui** hence, from here; this way; **di qui a un anno** one year hence; **di qui in avanti** from now on; **qui vicino** nearby

**quiescènza** *f* quiescence; retirement

**quietanza** *f* receipt

**quietanzare** *tr* to receipt

**quietare** (**quièto**) *tr* to quiet, calm; to satisfy (*e.g., thirst*) ‖ *ref* to quiet down

**quiète** *f* quiet, calmness

**quiè·to -ta** *adj* quiet, calm; still; **stia quieto!** don't worry! ‖ *m* quiet life

**quindi** *adv* then; therefore; (archaic) thence, from there

**quindicènne** *adj* fifteen-year-old ‖ *mf* fifteen-year-old person

**quindicèsi·mo -ma** *adj, m & pron* fifteenth

**quìndici** *adj & pron* fifteen; **le quindici** three P.M. ‖ *m* fifteen; fifteenth (*in dates*)

**quindicina** *f* about fifteen; two weeks, fortnight; semimonthly pay

**quindicinale** *adj* fortnightly

**quinquennale** *adj* five-year

**quinta** *f* (theat) wing; (mus) fifth; **dietro le quinte** behind the scenes

**quintale** *m* quintal (*100 kilos*)

**quintèrno** *m* signature of five sheets; (bb) quire

**quintessènza** *f* quintessence

**quintétto** *m* quintet

**quin·to -ta** *adj, m & pron* fifth ‖ *f* see **quinta**

**quisquìlia** *f* trifle

**quivi** *adv* (lit) over there; (lit) then

**quòrum** *m* quorum

**quòta** *f* quota; share; altitude; elevation; level (*of stock market*); market average; odds (*in betting*); subscription (*to club*); **quota zero** (fig) point of departure

**quotare** (**quòto**) *tr* to quote (*a price*); to value, esteem ‖ *ref* to sign up for, e.g., **si quotò duemila lire** he signed up for two thousand lire

**quotazióne** *f* quotation

**quotidia·no -na** *adj & m* daily

**quoziènte** *m* quotient; (sports) percentage; **quoziente d'intelligenza** I.Q.

# R

**R, r** ['erre] *m & f* sixteenth letter of the Italian alphabet

**rabàrbaro** *m* rhubarb

**rabberciare** §128 (**rabbèrcio**) *tr* (coll) to patch up

**ràbbia** *f* rage, anger; rabies

**rabbino** *m* rabbi

**rabbió·so -sa** [s] *adj* furious; rabid

**rabbonire** §176 *tr* to pacify ‖ *ref* to calm down

**rabbrividire** §176 *intr* (ESSERE) to shiver, shudder

**rabbuffare** *tr* to rebuke; to dishevel

**rabbuffo** *m* rebuke; **fare un rabbuffo a** to rebuke

**rabbuiare** §287 *ref* to darken, turn dark

**rabdomante** *m* dowser, diviner

**rabé·sco** *m* (-schi) arabesque; scrawl, scribble

**ràbi·do -da** *adj* rabid

**raccapezzare** (**raccapézzo**) *tr* to put together; to gather (*news*); to find (*one's way*); to make out (*what is* *meant*) ‖ *ref*—**non raccapezzarsi** to not be able to get one's bearings

**raccapricciante** *adj* bloodcurdling

**raccapric•cio** *m* (**-ci**) horror

**raccartocciare** §128 (**raccartòccio**) *tr & ref* to shrivel

**raccattare** *tr* to pick up; to gather

**racchétta** *f* racket; **racchetta da neve** snowshoe; **racchetta da sci** ski pole

**ràc•chio -chia** *adj* (**-chi -chie**) (coll) ugly, homely

**racchiùdere** §125 *tr* to contain, hold

**raccògliere** §127 *tr* to pick up; to gather; to collect (*e.g., stamps*); to take up (*the gauntlet*); to receive; to reap; to furl (*sail*); to draw in (*a net*); to fold (*the wings*); to shelter (*e.g., foundlings*); **raccogliere i passi** to stop walking ‖ *ref* to gather; to concentrate

**raccogliménto** *m* concentration; meditation

**raccogli•tóre -trice** *mf* collector, compiler ‖ *m* folder

**raccòl•to -ta** *adj* crouched; collected; engrossed; snug, intimate ‖ *m* harvest ‖ *f* harvest; collection; **chiamare a raccolta** to rally

**raccomandàbile** *adj* recommendable; **poco raccomandabile** unreliable

**raccomandare** *tr* to recommend; to secure (*e.g., a boat*); to register (*mail*); to exhort ‖ *ref* to recommend oneself; to entreat; **mi raccomando** please; **raccomandarsi a** to beg, implore; **raccomandarsi alle gambe** to take to one's heels

**raccomanda•to -ta** *adj* recommended; registered ‖ *m* protégé ‖ *f* protégée; registered letter

**raccomandazióne** *f* recommendation; registration (*of mail*); exhortation

**raccomodare** (**raccòmodo**) *tr* to fix; to mend

**racconciare** §128 (**raccóncio**) *tr* to fix; to mend ‖ *ref* to clear up (*said of the weather*); to tidy oneself up

**raccontare** (**raccónto**) *tr* to tell; **raccontarla bene** to be good at telling lies

**raccónto** *m* tale; story; narrative

**raccorciaménto** *m* shortening

**raccorciare** §128 (**raccòrcio**) *tr* to shorten

**raccordare** (**raccòrdo**) *tr* to link, connect

**raccòrdo** *m* link, connection; **raccordo a circolazione rotatoria** traffic circle; **raccordo anulare** (rr) belt line; **raccordo ferroviario** junction; spur; siding; **raccordo stradale** connecting road

**raccostare** (**raccòsto**) *tr & ref* to draw near

**raccozzare** (**raccòzzo**) *tr* to scrape together

**ràchide** *m & f* backbone; midrib (*of leaf*); shaft (*of feather*)

**rachiti•co -ca** *adj* (**-ci -che**) stunted; weak; (pathol) rickety

**rachitismo** *m* rickets

**racimolare** (**racìmolo**) *tr* to glean; to scrape together

**rada** *f* roadstead; cove

**ràdar** *m* radar

**addobbare** (**raddòbbo**) *tr* (naut) to refit

**raddolcire** §176 *tr & ref* to sweeten; to mellow

**raddoppiare** §287 (**raddóppio**) *tr, intr* (ESSERE) *& ref* to double, redouble

**raddrizzare** *tr* to straighten; (elec) to rectify ‖ *ref* to straighten up

**raddrizzatóre** *m* (elec) rectifier

**ràdere** §223 *tr* to shave; to raze; to graze, skim ‖ *ref* to shave

**radézza** *f* rarity, rareness; thinness; sparsity (*of vegetation*); space, distance (*e.g., between trees*)

**radiante** *adj* radiating

**radiare** §287 *tr* to strike off; to expel; to condemn (*a ship*); **radiare dall'albo degli avvocati** to disbar

**radiatóre** *m* radiator

**radiazióne** *f* radiation; expulsion

**ràdi•ca** *f* (**-che**) brier; (coll) root

**radicale** *adj & mf* radical ‖ *m & f* (philol) radical, root ‖ *m* (chem, math) radical

**radicare** §197 (**ràdico**) *tr & intr* to root

**radice** *f* root; base or foot (*e.g., of a mountain or tower*); **mettere radice** to take root; **svellere dalle radici** to pull up by the roots; to eradicate

**rà•dio** *adj invar* radio ‖ *m* (**-di**) (anat) radius; (chem) radium ‖ *f* (**-dio**) radio; **radio fante** (mil) grapevine

**radioabbonato** *m* (rad) subscriber (*to radio broadcasting*)

**radioama•tóre -trice** *mf* radio fan; radio ham

**radioannunciatóre** *m* radio announcer

**radioascolta•tóre -trice** *mf* radio listener

**radioatti•vo -va** *adj* radioactive

**radiobùssola** *f* radio compass

**radiocanale** *m* radio channel

**radiocomanda•to -ta** *adj* radio-controlled

**radiocròna•ca** *f* (**-che**) newscast

**radiocroni•sta** *mf* (**-sti -ste**) newscaster

**radiodiffóndere** §178 *tr* to broadcast

**radiodiffusióne** *f* broadcasting

**radiofaro** *m* radio beacon

**radiofòni•co -ca** *adj* (**-ci -che**) radio

**radiofonògrafo** *m* radiophonograph

**radiofò•to** *f* (**-to**) radiophoto

**radiofrequènza** *f* radiofrequency

**radiologìa** *f* radiology

**radiomontatóre** *m* radio assembler

**radioónda** *f* radio wave; **radioonde** airwaves

**radioricevènte** *adj* radio ‖ *f* radio set; radio station

**radioriparatóre** *m* radio repairman

**radiosegnale** *m* radio signal

**radiosentièro** *m* range of a radio beacon

**radió•so -sa** [s] *adj* radiant

**radiosorgènte** *f* quasar

**radiostazióne** *f* radio station

**radiostélla** *f* quasar

**radiotas•sì** *m* (**-sì**) radio-dispatched taxi

**radiotelescò•pio** *m* (**-pi**) radiotelescope

**radiotrasméttere** §198 *tr & intr* to broadcast, radio

**radiotrasmissióne** *f* broadcast

**radiotrasmittènte** *adj* broadcasting ‖ *f* broadcasting station

**ra·do -da** *adj* rare; thin; sheer; sparse, scattered; **di rado** seldom, rarely

**radunare** *tr* & *ref* to assemble, gather

**radunata** *f* gathering; (mil) assembly; **radunata sediziosa** unlawful assembly

**raduno** *m* assembly, gathering

**radura** *f* clearing, glade

**ràfano** *m* (bot) radish

**raffazzonare (raffazzóno)** *tr* to mend, patch up

**raffazzonatura** *f* patchwork, hodgepodge

**rafférma** *f* confirmation; stay (*in office*); return to office; (mil) reenlistment

**raffermare (rafférmo)** *tr* to reaffirm; to secure; (coll) to reconfirm; to reappoint, reelect; to return (*e.g., a mayor*) to office ‖ *intr* (ESSERE) & *ref* to reenlist; (coll) to harden

**raffér·mo -ma** *adj* stale (bread) ‖ *f* see **rafferma**

**ràffi·ca** *f* (-che) gust; blast; burst (*e.g., of machine gun*); **a raffiche** gusty

**raffigurare** *tr* to represent; to symbolize

**raffinare** *tr* to refine; to polish ‖ *intr* (ESSERE) to become refined

**raffinatézza** *f* refinement, polish

**raffinatura** *f* refinement (*of oil*)

**raffinazióne** *f* refining

**raffinerìa** *f* refinery

**ràf·fio** *m* (-fi) hook; grappling iron

**rafforzare (rafförzo)** *tr* to strengthen

**raffreddaménto** *m* cooling

**raffreddare (rafféddo)** *tr* to make cold; to cool; **raffreddare gli spiriti di qlcu** to dampen s.o.'s enthusiasm ‖ *intr* (ESSERE) & *ref* to get cold; to cool

**raffreddóre** *m* cold

**raffrontare (raffrónto)** *tr* to compare; (law) to bring face to face

**raffrónto** *m* comparison; confrontation

**ràfia** *f* raffia

**raganèlla** *f* rattle; (zool) tree frog

**ragazza** *f* girl; spinster; (coll) girl friend; **ragazza copertina** cover girl; **ragazza squillo** call girl

**ragazzata** *f* boyish prank

**ragaz·zo -za** *mf* youth, young person ‖ *m* boy; (coll) boyfriend ‖ *f* see **ragazza**

**raggelare (raggèlo)** *intr* (ESSERE) to freeze

**raggiante** *adj* radiant; beaming

**raggiare** §290 *tr* & *intr* to radiate

**raggièra** *f* rayed halo; **a raggiera** radially

**ràg·gio** *m* (-gi) ray; beam; spoke; (geom) radius; **raggio d'azione** radius, range of action; **raggio di sole** sunbeam

**raggiornare (raggiórno)** *tr* (coll) to bring up to date ‖ *intr* (ESSERE) to dawn ‖ *impers* (ESSERE)—**raggiorna** it is dawning

**raggirare** *tr* to trick, swindle ‖ *ref* to roam, wander; **raggirarsi su** to turn on (*e.g., a certain subject*)

**raggiro** *m* trickery, swindle

**raggiungere** §183 *tr* to reach; to catch up with, rejoin

**raggiungìbile** *adj* attainable

**raggomitolare (raggomìtolo)** *tr* to roll up ‖ *ref* to curl up; to cuddle

**raggranellare (raggranèllo)** *tr* to gather; to scrape together

**raggrinzire** §176 *tr* & *ref* to crease, wrinkle

**raggrumare** *tr* & *ref* to clot, coagulate

**raggruppaménto** *m* grouping; group

**raggruppare** *tr* & *ref* to group, assemble

**ragguagliare** §280 *tr* to compare; to balance; to inform in detail; to level

**ragguà·glio** *m* (-gli) comparison; detailed report

**ragguardévole** *adj* considerable, notable

**ragionaménto** *m* reasoning; discussion

**ragionare (ragióno)** *intr* to reason; to discuss ‖ *impers ref*—**si ragiona** it is rumored

**ragióne** *f* reason; account; rate; justice; (math) ratio; **a maggior ragione** with all the more reason; **a ragione** within reason; **aver ragione** to be right; **aver ragione di** to get the best of; **dar ragione a qlcu** to admit that s.o. is right; **di santa ragione** hard, a great deal; **farsi ragione** to be resigned; **in ragione di** at the rate of; **ragion per cui** and therefore; **ragione sociale** (com) trade name; **rendere di pubblica ragione** to publicize

**ragionerìa** *f* accounting; bookkeeping

**ragionévole** *adj* reasonable

**ragioniè·re -ra** *mf* accountant; bookkeeper

**ragliare** §280 *intr* to bray

**rà·glio** *m* (-gli) bray

**ragnatéla** *f* spider web

**ragno** *m* spider

**ra·gù** *m* (-gù) meat gravy; stew

**ràion** *m* rayon

**rallegraménto** *m* congratulation, act of congratulating; **rallegramenti** congratulations

**rallegrare (rallégro)** *tr* to cheer up; to rejoice, gladden ‖ *ref* to cheer up; to rejoice; **rallegrarsi con** to congratulate

**rallentare (rallènto)** *tr*, *intr* & *ref* to slow down; to lessen

**rallentatóre** *m* slow-motion projector; **al rallentatore** slow-motion

**ra·màio** *m* (-mài) tinker, coppersmith

**ramaiòlo** *m* ladle

**ramanzina** [dz] *f* reprimand

**ramare** *tr* to copperplate; (agr) to spray with copper sulfate

**ramarro** *m* green lizard

**ramazza** *f* broom; (mil) cleaning detail; (mil) soldier on cleaning detail

**rame** *m* copper; etching

**ramerino** *m* (coll) rosemary

**ramificare** §197 (**ramìfico**) *intr* & *ref* to branch; to branch off; to branch out, ramify

**ramin·go -ga** *adj* (-ghi -ghe) wandering

**ramino** *m* copper pot; rummy (*card game*)

**rammagliare** §280 *tr* to reknit; to mend a run in (*a stocking*)

**rammaricare** §197 (**rammàrico**) *tr* to afflict ‖ *ref* to be sorry, regret; **rammaricarsi di** to be sorry for

**rammàri·co** *m* (**-chi**) regret
**rammendare** (**rammèndo**) *tr* to darn
**rammèndo** *m* darn
**rammentare** (**ramménto**) *tr* to remember; to remind || *ref*—**rammentarsi di** to remember
**rammenta·tóre -trice** *mf* prompter
**rammollire** §176 *tr* & *ref* to soften
**rammolli·to -ta** *adj* soft; soft-headed || *m* dodo, jellyfish
**ramo** *m* branch; bough; point (*of antler*); **ramo di pazzia** streak of madness
**ramoscèllo** *m* twig; **ramoscello d'olivo** olive branch
**rampa** *f* ramp; flight (*of stairs*); launching platform
**rampicante** *adj* climbing || *m* (ichth) perch; (orn) climber
**rampino** *m* hook; tine, prong; pretext
**rampógna** *f* (lit) reprimand
**rampóllo** *m* spring (*of water*); scion; shoot (*of a plant*); (joc) offspring
**rampóne** *m* harpoon; crampon
**rana** *f* frog
**rànci·do -da** *adj* rancid
**ràn·cio -cia** (**-ci -ce**) *adj* (poet) orange || *m* (mil) mess
**rancóre** *m* rancor; grudge; **serbar rancore** to bear malice
**randa** *f* (naut) spanker; (obs) edge
**randà·gio -gia** *adj* (**-gi -gie**) wandering; stray
**randellare** (**randèllo**) *tr* to cudgel; to bludgeon; to blackjack
**randèllo** *m* cudgel; bludgeon
**ran·go** *m* (**-ghi**) rank; station
**rannicchiare** §287 *tr* to cause to curl up || *ref* to crouch; to cower; to cuddle up
**ranno** *m* lye; **buttar via il ranno e il sapone** to waste one's time and effort
**rannuvolare** (**rannùvolo**) *tr* & *ref* to cloud; to darken
**ranòcchia** *f* frog
**ranòc·chio** *m* (**-chi**) frog
**rantolare** (**ràntolo**) *intr* to wheeze
**ràntolo** *m* wheezing; death rattle
**ranùncolo** *m* buttercup
**rapa** *f* turnip; **valere una rapa** to be not worth a fig
**rapace** *adj* rapacious || **rapaci** *mpl* birds of prey
**rapare** *tr* to shave (*s.o.'s head*) || *ref* to shave one's head; to have one's head shaved
**rapidi·tà** *f* (**-tà**) rapidity, swiftness
**ràpi·do -da** *adj* rapid, swift || *m* (rr) express || **rapide** *fpl* rapids
**rapiménto** *m* rape, abduction; rapture
**rapina** *f* pillage, plunder; misappropriation; prey; (lit) fury; **rapina a mano armata** armed robbery
**rapinare** *tr* to rob, plunder; to hold up; **rapinare qlco a qlcu** to rob s.o. of s.th
**rapina·tóre -trice** *mf* robber, plunderer
**rapire** §176 *tr* to rape, abduct; to kidnap; to enrapture
**rapi·tóre -trice** *mf* kidnaper
**rappacificare** §197 (**rappacìfico**) *tr* to reconcile || *ref* to become reconciled
**rappezzare** (**rappèzzo**) *tr* to patch; to

piece; **rappezzarla** to get out of trouble
**rappèzzo** *m* patch; patchwork
**rapportare** (**rappòrto**) *tr* to report; to transfer (*a design*) || *ref* to refer
**rapporta·tóre -trice** *mf* reporter || *m* protractor
**rappòrto** *m* report; relation; relationship; (math) ratio; **chiamare a rapporto** to summon; **chiedere di mettersi a rapporto** to ask for a hearing; **fare rapporto** to report; **in rapporto a** concerning; **mettersi a rapporto** to report; **sotto ogni rapporto** in every respect
**rapprèndere** §220 *tr* & *ref* to coagulate
**rappresàglia** [s] *f* reprisal; retaliation
**rappresentante** *adj* representing; representative || *mf* representative; agent; **rappresentante di commercio** agent
**rappresentanza** *f* delegation; proxy; agency; representation
**rappresentare** (**rappresènto**) *tr* to represent; to play; to portray
**rappresentati·vo -va** *adj* representative
**rappresentazióne** *f* representation; description; (theat) performance; **rappresentazione teatrale diurna** matinée; **sacra rappresentazione** (theat) mystery, miracle play
**rapsodìa** *f* rhapsody
**raraménte** *adv* seldom, rarely
**rarefare** §173 *tr* to rarefy || *ref* to become rarefied
**rari·tà** *f* (**-tà**) rarity
**ra·ro -ra** *adj* rare; **di raro** seldom
**rasare** [s] *tr* to shave; to mow; to trim; to smooth || *ref* to shave
**raschiare** §287 (**ràschio**) *tr* to scrape; to scratch || *intr* to clear one's throat
**raschiétto** *m* scraper; erasing knife; footscraper
**rà·schio** *m* (**-schi**) clearing one's throat; hoarseness; frog in the throat
**rasentare** (**rasènto**) *tr* to graze; to scrape; to border on; to come close to
**rasènte** *adv* close; **rasente a** close to || *prep* close to
**ra·so -sa** [s] *adj* shaved; trimmed; brimful; disreputable (*clothes*); flush || *m* satin || *adv*—**raso terra** down-to-earth; **volare raso terra** to skim the ground; to hedgehop
**ra·sóio** [s] *m* (**-sói**) razor; **rasoio a mano libera** straight razor; **rasoio di sicurezza** safety razor
**raspa** *f* rasp
**raspare** *tr* to rasp; to irritate; to stamp, paw; (coll) to steal || *intr* to rasp; to scratch (*said of a chicken*); to scrawl
**raspo** *m* grape stalk; scraper; (vet) mange
**rasségna** *f* review; exposition
**rassegnare** (**rasségno**) *tr* to resign; **rassegnare le dimissioni** to resign || *ref* to resign oneself; to submit
**rassegnazióne** *f* resignation
**rasserenare** (**rasseréno**) *tr* & *ref* to brighten; to cheer up
**rassettare** (**rassètto**) *tr* & *ref* to tidy up

**rassicurare** *tr* to reassure ‖ *ref* to be reassured

**rassodare (rassòdo)** *tr* to harden; to strengthen ‖ *intr* (ESSERE) & *ref* to harden

**rassomigliare** §280 **(rassomìglio)** *tr* to compare ‖ *intr* (ESSERE) (with *dat*) to resemble ‖ *ref* to resemble each other

**rastrellaménto** *m* roundup; mop-up operation

**rastrellare (rastrèllo)** *tr* to rake; to round up; to mop up; to drag (*e.g., the bottom*)

**rastrellièra** *f* rack; crib

**rastrèllo** *m* rake

**rastremare (rastrèmo)** *tr* to taper

**rata** *f* installment; quota; **a rate** on time; by installments

**rateale** *adj* installment

**rateizzare** [ddzz] *tr* to prorate; to divide (*a payment*) into installments

**ratìfi·ca** *f* (**-che**) ratification

**ratificare** §197 **(ratìfico)** *tr* to ratify

**rat·to -ta** *adj* (lit) swift ‖ *m* rat; (lit) rape ‖ **ratto** *adv* (lit) swiftly

**rattoppare (rattòppo)** *tr* to patch, patch up

**rattrappire** §176 *tr* to cramp; to make numb, benumb ‖ *ref* to become cramped; to become numb

**rattristare** *tr* & *ref* to sadden

**raucèdine** *f* hoarseness

**ràu·co -ca** *adj* (**-chi -che**) hoarse, raucous

**ravanèllo** *m* radish

**ravizzóne** *m* (bot) rape

**ravvedére** §279 (*fut* **ravvedrò** & **ravvederò**; *pp* **ravveduto**) *ref* to repent; to mend one's ways

**ravvedu·to -ta** *adj* repentant; reformed

**ravviare** §119 *tr* to arrange, adjust; to poke (*fire*) ‖ *ref* to tidy up; (lit) to reform

**ravvicinaménto** *m* approach; reconciliation; rapprochement

**ravvicinare** *tr* to bring up; to reconcile ‖ *ref* to approach; to become reconciled; **ravvicinarsi a** to approach

**ravviluppare** *tr* to wrap up; to wind up; to bamboozle ‖ *ref* to become tangled

**ravvisare** *tr* to recognize

**ravvivare** *tr* to revive; to enliven; to brighten; to stir (*fire*) ‖ *ref* to revive

**ravvòlgere** §289 *tr* to wrap up

**raziocì·nio** *m* (**-ni**) reasoning; reason; common sense

**razionale** *adj* rational

**razionalizzare** [ddzz] *tr* (com, math) to rationalize

**razionaménto** *m* rationing

**razionare (razióno)** *tr* to ration

**razióne** *f* ration; portion

**razza** *f* race; breed; kind; **di razza** purebred; **far razza** to reproduce; **passare a razza** to go to stud

**razza** [ddzz] *f* (ichth) ray; **razza cornuta** manta ray

**razzìa** *f* raid; foray; insect powder

**razziale** *adj* racial

**razziare** §119 *tr* & *intr* to foray

**razzismo** *m* racism

**razzi·sta** *mf* (**-sti -ste**) racist

**razzo** [ddzz] *m* rocket; (coll) spoke; (mil) flare

**razzolare (ràzzolo)** *intr* to scratch (*said of chickens*); (coll) to rummage

**re** [e] *m* (re) king

**re** [ε] *m* (re) (mus) re

**reagènte** *m* reagent

**reagire** §176 *intr* to react

**reale** *adj* real, actual; royal, regal

**realismo** *m* realism; royalism

**reali·sta** *mf* (**-sti -ste**) realist; royalist

**realìsti·co -ca** *adj* (**-ci -che**) realistic

**realizzare** [ddzz] *tr* to carry out; to realize; to build ‖ *ref* to come true

**realizzazióne** [ddzz] *f* realization; **realizzazione scenica** production

**realizzo** [ddzz] *m* conversion into cash; profit taking; forced sale

**realménte** *adv* really, indeed

**real·tà** *f* (**-tà**) reality; actuality; **realtà romanzesca** truth stranger than fiction

**reato** *m* crime

**reatti·vo -va** *adj* reactive

**reattóre** *m* reactor; jet plane; jet engine

**reazionà·rio -ria** (**-ri -rie**) *adj* & *mf* reactionary

**reazióne** *f* reaction; (mach) backlash; **a reazione** jet-propelled

**réb·bio** *m* (**-bi**) prong

**recalcitrante** *adj* balky, restive; **essere recalcitrante a** to be opposed to, to resist

**recalcitrare (recàlcitro)** *intr* to be balky; to kick; (with *dat*) to buck, resist

**recapitare (recàpito)** *tr* to deliver

**recàpito** *m* address; delivery; **far recapito in** to be domiciled in; **recapiti** (com) notes

**recare** §197 **(rèco)** *tr* to bring; to cause; **recare ad effetto** to carry out; **recare qlco alla memoria di qlcu** to remind s.o. of s.th; **recare qlco a lode di qlcu** to praise s.o. for s.th ‖ *ref* to go, betake oneself

**recèdere** §123 *intr* (ESSERE & AVERE) to recede

**recensióne** *f* book review; collation

**recensire** §176 *tr* to review; to collate

**recensóre** *m* reviewer

**recènte** *adj* recent; **di recente** recently

**recessióne** *f* recession

**recèsso** *m* recess; subsiding (*of fever*); ebb tide

**recìdere** §145 *tr* to cut off; to chop off

**recidiva** *f* relapse; second offense

**recìngere** §126 *tr* to enclose, pen in

**recinto** *m* enclosure; pen, yard; compound; playpen; paddock; **recinto delle grida** floor of the exchange

**recipiènte** *m* container

**reciprocità** *f* reciprocity

**recìpro·co -ca** *adj* (**-ci -che**) reciprocal

**reci·so -sa** *adj* cut off; abrupt

**rècita** *f* show, performance

**recitare (rècito)** *tr* to recite; to portray, play; **recitare la commedia** to put on an act ‖ *intr* to perform, play; **recitare a soggetto** (theat) to improvise

**recitazióne** *f* recitation; diction; acting

**reclamare** *tr* to claim, demand ‖ *intr* to complain

**récla·me** *f* (-me) advertising; advertisement; **fare réclame a** to advertise; to boost

**reclami·sta** *mf* (-sti -ste) advertising agent; show-off ‖ *m* advertising man

**reclamìsti·co -ca** *adj* (-ci -che) advertising

**reclamo** *m* complaint; **fare reclamo** to complain

**reclinare** *tr* to bow ‖ *intr* to recline

**reclusióne** *f* seclusion; imprisonment

**reclu·so -sa** *adj* recluse ‖ *mf* recluse; prisoner

**reclusò·rio** *m* (-ri) penitentiary

**rècluta** *f* recruit; rookie

**reclutaménto** *m* recruitment

**reclutare** (rècluto) *tr* to recruit

**recòndi·to -ta** *adj* concealed; inmost; recondite

**recriminare** (recrìmino) *intr* to recriminate

**recuperare** (recùpero) *tr* see **ricuperare**

**redarguire** §176 *tr* to berate

**redat·tóre -trice** *mf* compiler; newspaper editor; **redattore capo** managing editor; **redattore pubblicitario** copywriter; **redattore responsabile** publisher; **redattore viaggiante** correspondent

**redazionale** *adj* editorial, editor's (*e.g.*, *policy*)

**redazióne** *f* writing; draft; version; (journ) city room

**redazza** *f* mop; (naut) swab

**redditì·zio -zia** *adj* (-zi -zie) lucrative

**rèddito** *m* income, revenue; yield; **reddito nazionale** gross national product

**redèn·to -ta** *adj* redeemed, set free

**reden·tóre -trice** *mf* redeemer ‖ **Redentore** *m*—**il Redentore** the Redeemer

**redenzióne** *f* redemption

**redìgere** §224 *tr* to compile; to write up, compose

**redìmere** §225 *tr* to redeem; to ransom; to save

**rèdine** *f* rein

**redivì·vo -va** *adj* come back to life

**rèduce** *adj* back (*from war*) ‖ *mf* veteran

**réfe** *m* thread

**referèn·dum** *m* (-dum) referendum; **referendum postale** mail questionnaire

**referènza** *f* reference

**referenziare** (referènzio) *tr* to give references to; to write references for ‖ *intr* to have good references

**referenzia·to -ta** *adj* with good references, e.g., **impiegato referenziato** employee with good references

**refèrto** *m* report (*of a physician*)

**refettò·rio** *m* (-ri) refectory

**refezióne** *f* lunch, light meal; **refezione scolastica** school lunch

**refrattà·rio -ria** *adj* (-ri -rie) refractory

**refrigerante** *adj* cooling ‖ *m* refrigerator; (chem) condenser

**refrigerare** (refrìgero) *tr* to refrigerate; to cool ‖ *ref* to cool off

**refrigè·rio** *m* (-ri) relief, comfort

**refurtiva** *f* stolen goods

**refuso** *m* misprint

**regalare** *tr* to present; to deliver (*a slap*); to throw away (*money*); **è regalato** it's a steal

**regale** *adj* regal; royal; imposing

**regalìa** *f* gratuity; bonus

**regalità** *f* regality, royalty

**regalo** *m* present, gift

**regata** *f* regatta

**reggènte** *adj & m* regent

**reggènza** *f* regency

**règgere** §226 *tr* to hold, hold up; to stand, withstand; to guide; (gram) to govern; **reggere il sacco a** to connive with; **reggere l'animo di** + *inf* to bear or stand + *ger*, e.g., **non gli regge l'animo di vederla piangere** he cannot stand seeing her cry ‖ *intr* to hold; to be valid; to last, hold out (*said of weather*); **reggere** (with *dat*) to withstand (*e.g., the cold*); **reggere al paragone** to bear comparison ‖ *ref* to stand up; to hold; to be ruled; **reggersi a** to hold on to; to be governed as (*e.g., a republic*); **reggersi a galla** to float

**règ·gia** *f* (-ge) royal palace

**reggical·ze** *m* (-ze) girdle

**reggilibro** *m* book end

**reggimentale** *adj* regimental

**reggiménto** *m* regiment

**reggipètto** *m* brassiere

**reggisé·no** *m* (-ni & -no) brassiere

**regìa** *f* monopoly; (mov) direction; (theat) production

**regici·da** *mf* (-di -de) regicide

**regicì·dio** *m* (-di) regicide

**regime** *m* regime; diet; flow (*e.g., of river*); government; authoritarian government; (mach) rate; **regime secco** total abstinence

**regina** *f* queen; **regina claudia** greengage; **regina madre** queen mother

**reginétta** *f* young queen; queen (*of a beauty contest*)

**rè·gio -gia** *adj* (-gi -gie) royal ‖ **i regi** the king's soldiers

**regióne** *f* region

**regi·sta** *mf* (-sti -ste) coordinator; (theat) producer; (mov) director

**registrare** *tr* to register, record; to enter; to tally, log; to adjust; to tune up (*a musical instrument*) ‖ *ref* to register

**registra·tóre -trice** *mf* registrar ‖ *m* recorder; **registratore di cassa** cash register

**registrazióne** *f* registration; record, entry; adjustment; (aut) tune-up; (telv) videotaping; (telv) video-taping studio; (telv) video-taped program

**registro** *m* register; registration; classbook; regulator (*of watch*); stop (*of organ*); **cambiar registro** to change one's tune; **dar registro a** to regulate (*a watch*)

**regnante** *adj* reigning; prevailing ‖ **i regnanti** the rulers

**regnare** (régno) *intr* to reign, rule; to prevail; to take hold (*said of a root*)

**régno** *m* kingdom; reign

**règola** *f* rule; regulation; moderation; **a regola d'arte** to a T; **di regola** as a rule; **in regola** in good order; **mettere in regola** to put in order; **regole** menstruation; **secondo le regole** by the book

**regolamentare** *adj* regulation ‖ *v* (**regolaménto**) *tr* to regulate

**regolaménto** *m* regulation; settlement; **regolamento edilizio** building code

**regolare** *adj* regular; steady (*employment*); stock (*material*) ‖ *v* (**règolo**) *tr* to regulate; to adjust; to set (*a watch*); to focus (*a lens*); to settle (*an account*) ‖ *ref* to behave; to control oneself

**regolari·tà** *f* (**-tà**) regularity

**regolarizzare** [ddzz] *tr* to regularize

**regolatézza** *f* regularity; moderation

**regola·to -ta** *adj* regular, orderly

**regola·tóre -trice** *adj* regulating; see **piano** ‖ *m* ruler; regulator (*of watch*); (mach) governor; **regolatore dell'aria** register; **regolatore di volume** (rad, telv) volume control

**regolazióne** *f* regulation

**regolìzia** *f* (coll) licorice

**règolo** *m* ruler; slat; (orn, hist) kinglet; **regolo calcolatore** slide rule

**regredire** §176 (*pres participle* **regrediènte**; *pp* **regredito & regrèsso**) *intr* (ESSERE & AVERE) to retrogress

**regrèsso** *m* regression; abatement (*of fever*); (com) recourse

**reièt·to -ta** *adj* rejected ‖ *mf* outcast

**reimbarcare** §197 *tr* & *ref* to reship; to transship

**reimbar·co** *m* (**-chi**) reshipment; transshipment

**reincarnare** *tr* to reincarnate ‖ *ref* to become reincarnated

**reincarnazióne** *f* reincarnation

**reinseriménto** *m* integration

**reintegrare** (**reìntegro**) *tr* to restore; to reinstate; to indemnify

**reità** *f* guilt

**reiterare** (**reìtero**) *tr* to reiterate

**relativi·tà** *f* (**-tà**) relativity

**relati·vo -va** *adj* relative

**rela·tóre -trice** *adj* reporting ‖ *mf* relator (*of proceedings*); presenter (*of a bill*); dissertation supervisor

**relazióne** *f* relation; relationship; report; **relazione amorosa** affair; **relazioni** relations; connections

**re·lè** *m* (**-lè**) (elec) relay

**relegare** §209 (**rèlego**) *tr* to banish; to store away

**religióne** *f* religion

**religió·so -sa** [s] *adj* religious ‖ *m* clergyman ‖ *f* nun

**relìquia** *f* relic

**relit·to -ta** *adj* residual ‖ *m* shipwreck; air crash; derelict; shoal, bar

**remare** (**rèmo & rémo**) *intr* to row

**rema·tóre -trice** *mf* rower ‖ *m* oarsman

**reminiscènza** *f* reminiscence

**remissióne** *f* submissiveness; remission

**remissi·vo -va** *adj* submissive

**rèmo** *m* oar; **remo alla battana** paddle

**rèmora** *f* hindrance; (lit) delay

**remò·to -ta** *adj* remote; **passato remoto** (gram) preterit

**réna** *f* sand

**Renània, la** the Rhineland

**Renata** *f* Renée

**rèndere** §227 *tr* to return, give back; to give (*thanks*); to render (*justice*); to yield; to translate; to make (*known*); **render conto di** to give an account of; **rendere di pubblica ragione** to publicize; **rendere l'anima a Dio** to give up the ghost; **rendere pan per focaccia** to give tit for tat ‖ *intr* to pay, yield ‖ *ref* to make oneself; to betake oneself; to become; (lit) to surrender; **rendersi conto di** to realize

**rendicónto** *m* account; report; **rendiconti** proceedings

**rendiménto** *m* rendering; yield; output; (mech) efficiency

**rèndita** *f* private income; yield; Italian Government bond

**rène** *m* kidney

**renèlla** *f* (pathol) gravel

**renétta** *f* pippin

**réni** *fpl* loins; **spezzare le reni a** to break the back of

**renitènte** *adj* opposed ‖ *m*—**renitente alla leva** draft dodger

**rènna** *f* reindeer; reindeer skin

**Rèno** *m* Rhine

**rè·o -a** *adj* guilty; (lit) wicked ‖ *m* guilty person; accused

**reòstato** *m* (elec) rheostat

**reparto** *m* department; (mil) unit; **reparto d'assalto** shock troops

**repèllere** §168 *tr* to repel

**repentàglio** *m* jeopardy; **mettere a repentaglio** to jeopardize

**repènte** *adj*—**di repente** suddenly

**repenti·no -na** *adj* sudden

**reperìbile** *adj* available

**reperiménto** *m* finding

**reperire** §176 *tr* to find

**repèrto** *m* (archeol) find; (law) evidence; (law) exhibit; (med) report

**repertò·rio** *m* (**-ri**) repertory; catalogue

**rèpli·ca** *f* (**-che**) repetition; replica; (law) rebuttal; (theat) repeat performance; **in replica** in reply

**replicare** §197 (**rèplico**) *tr* to repeat; to reply, answer; (theat) to repeat (*a performance*)

**reportàg·gio** *m* (**-gi**) news coverage; reporting

**repòr·ter** *m* (**-ter**) reporter

**repressióne** *f* repression; constraint

**repressi·vo -va** *adj* repressive; controlling, checking (*e.g., a disease*)

**reprìmere** §131 *tr* to repress; to hold back (*tears*) ‖ *ref* to restrain oneself

**rèpro·bo -ba** *adj* & *m* reprobate

**repùbbli·ca** *f* (**-che**) republic

**repubblica·no -na** *adj* & *mf* republican

**repulisti** *m*—**fare repulisti** (coll) to make a clean sweep

**repulsióne** *f* repulsion

**repulsi·vo -va** *adj* var of **ripulsivo**

**reputare** (**rèputo**) *tr* to think, esteem, repute

**reputazióne** *f* reputation

**rèquie** *m* & *f* (eccl) requiem ‖ *f* rest, respite

**Rèquiem** *m* & *f* Requiem

**requisire** §176 *tr* to requisition, commandeer

**requisito** *m* requisite, requirement

**requisitòria** *f* scolding, reproach; (law) summation

**requisizióne** *f* requisition

**résa** [s] *f* surrender; rendering (*of an account*); delivery (*of merchandise*); return (*e.g., of newspapers*); yield; **resa a discrezione** unconditional surrender

**rescìndere** §247 *tr* to rescind

**resezióne** [s] *f* (surg) resection

**residènte** [s] *adj & mf* resident

**residènza** [s] *f* residence

**residenziale** [s] *adj* residential

**residua·to -ta** [s] *adj* residual

**resì·duo -dua** [s] *adj* residual ‖ *m* residue; remainder; balance

**rèsina** *f* resin

**resipiscènza** [s] *f* (lit) repentance

**resistènte** [s] *adj* resistant; strong; fast (*color*) ‖ *mf* member of the Resistance

**resistènza** [s] *f* resistance ‖ **Resistenza** *f* Resistance

**resìstere** [s] §114 *intr* to resist; (with *dat*) to withstand; (with *dat*) to endure; (with *dat*) to resist

**rèso** [s] *m* rhesus

**resocónto** [s] *m* report, relation

**respingènte** *m* (rr) bumper, buffer

**respìngere** §126 *tr* to drive back, beat off; to reject; to fail (*a student*); to vote down

**respin·to -ta** *adj* rejected ‖ *mf* failure (*pupil*)

**respirare** *tr & intr* to breathe, respire

**respiratò·rio -ria** *adj* (-ri -rie) respiratory

**respirazióne** *f* breathing

**respiro** *m* breath; breathing; respite

**responsàbile** *adj* responsible; **responsabile di** responsible for

**responsabili·tà** *f* (-tà) responsibility

**respònso** *m* decision (*of an oracle*); report (*of a physician*); return (*of an election*); (lit) response

**rèssa** *f* crowd; **far ressa** to crowd

**rèsta** *f* string (*of garlic or onions*); awn (*e.g., of wheat*); (coll) fishbone; (*for a lance*) (hist) rest

**restante** *adj* remaining ‖ *m* remainder

**restare (rèsto)** *intr* (ESSERE) to remain; to stay; to be located; (lit) to stop; **non restare a...che** to have no alternative but to, e.g., **non gli resta che andarsene** he has no alternative but to go; **non restare a qlcu qlco da +** *inf* to not have s.th + to + *inf*, e.g., **non gli resta molto da finire** he does not have much to finish; **resta a vedere** it remains to be seen; **restare qlco a qlcu** to have s.th left, e.g., **gli restano tre dollari** he has three dollars left; **restare sul colpo** to die on the spot; **resti comodo** please don't get up!

**restaurare (restàuro)** *tr* to restore, renovate

**restaurazióne** *f* restoration

**restàuro** *m* restoration (*of a building*)

**restì·o -a** (**-i -e**) *adj* balky, restive ‖ *m* balkiness

**restituire** §176 *tr* to give back, return; (lit) to restore ‖ *ref* (lit) to return

**restituzióne** *f* restitution, return

**rèsto** *m* remainder; change; balance; **del resto** besides, after all; **resti** remains

**restrìngere** §265 (*pp* **ristrétto**) *tr* to narrow down; to shrink; to take in (*a suit*); to limit (*expenses*); to tighten (*a knot*); to bind (*the bowels*); to restrict ‖ *ref* to contract; to narrow

**restrizióne** *f* restriction

**retàg·gio** *m* (-gi) (lit) heritage

**retata** *f* haul; (fig) roundup

**réte** *f* net; network; (soccer) goal; **rete a strascico** trawl; **rete da pesca** fishing net; **rete del letto** bedspring; **rete metallica** wire mesh; window screen; **rete per i capelli** hair net; **rete viaria** highway network

**reticèlla** *f* small net; hair net; mantle (*of gas jet*)

**reticènte** *adj* secretive, dissembling; evasive, noncommittal

**reticènza** *f* secretiveness; evasiveness

**reticolato** *m* grid (*on map*); wire entanglement

**retìcolo** *m* grid

**retina** *f* small net

**rètina** *f* (anat) retina

**retino** *m* small net; (typ) screen

**retòri·co -ca** (**-ci -che**) *adj* rhetorical ‖ *m* rhetorician ‖ *f* rhetoric

**retràttile** *adj* retractile

**retribuire** §176 *tr* to remunerate

**retributi·vo -va** *adj* retributive; salary (*e.g., conditions*)

**retri·vo -va** *adj* backward

**rètro** *m* back; verso; back of store ‖ *adv* (lit) behind; **retro a** (lit) behind

**retroatti·vo -va** *adj* retroactive

**retrobottè·ga** *m & f* (**-ga** *mpl* **-ghe** *fpl*) back of store

**retrocàmera** *f* back room

**retrocàrica** *f*—**a retrocarica** breech-loading

**retrocèdere** §228 *tr* to demote; (com) to return; (com) to give a discount to ‖ *intr* (ESSERE & AVERE) to retreat

**retrocessióne** *f* demotion; (sports) assignment to a lower division

**retrodatare** *tr* to antedate, predate

**retrògra·do -da** *adj* backward; retrograde

**retroguàrdia** *f* rearguard

**retromàr·cia** *f* (-ce) (aut) reverse

**retrorazzo** [ddzz] *m* retrorocket

**retrosapóre** *m* aftertaste

**retroscè·na** *m* (-na) intrigue, maneuver ‖ *f* backstage

**retrospetti·vo -va** *adj* retrospective

**retrotèr·ra** *m* (-ra) hinterland; (fig) background

**retrotrèno** *m* rear end (*of vehicle*); (aut) rear assembly

**retroversióne** *f* retroversion; retranslation

**retrovìe** *fpl* zone behind the front

**retrovisi·vo -va** *adj* rear-view, e.g., **specchietto retrovisivo** rear-view mirror

**retrovisóre** *m* rear-view mirror

**rètta** *f* board and lodging; straight line; **dar retta a** to pay attention to

**rettangolare** *adj* rectangular

**rettàngolo** *m* rectangle

**rettìfi·ca** *f* (-che) straightening; rectification; (mach) grinding; (mach) reboring

**rettificare** §197 (**rettìfico**) *tr* to straighten; to rectify; (mach) to grind; (mach) to rebore

**rettifica·tóre -trice** *adj* rectifying || *mf* rectifier (*person*) || *m* rectifier (*apparatus*)

**rettifilo** *m* straightaway

**rèttile** *m* reptile

**rettilì·neo -nea** *adj* rectilinear || *m* straightaway || *f* straight line

**rettitùdine** *f* straightness; uprightness, rectitude

**rèt·to -ta** *adj* straight; correct; upright; (geom) right || *m* right; recto; (anat) rectum || *f* see **retta**

**rettóre** *m* rector; president (*of university*)

**reumàti·co -ca** *adj* (-ci -che) rheumatic

**reumatismo** *m* rheumatism

**reverèn·do -da** *adj & m* reverend

**reverènte** *adj* var of **riverente**

**reverènza** *f* var of **riverenza**

**revisióne** *f* revision; (mach) overhaul

**revisionismo** *m* revisionism

**revisóre** *m* inspector; **revisore dei conti** auditor; **revisore di bozze** proofreader

**reviviscènza** *f* rebirth

**rèvo·ca** *f* (-che) revocation; recall; repeal

**revocare** §197 (**rèvoco**) *tr* to revoke; to recall; to repeal

**revòl·ver** *m* (-ver) revolver

**revolverata** *f* gun shot

**revulsióne** *f* (med) revulsion

**ri-** *pref* re-, e.g., **rivivere** to relive; again, e.g., **rifare** to do again; back, e.g., **riandare** to go back

**riabbonare** (**riabbòno**) *tr* to renew the subscription of || *ref* to renew one's subscription

**riabbracciare** §128 (**riabbràccio**) *tr* to embrace again; to greet again

**riabilitare** (**riabìlito**) *tr* to rehabilitate || *ref* to reestablish one's good name

**riaccèndere** §101 *tr* to rekindle || *ref* to become rekindled

**riaccompagnare** *tr* to take home

**riaccostare** (**riaccòsto**) *tr* to bring near; to bring together || *ref* to draw near

**riacquistare** *tr* to buy back; to recover

**riaddormentare** (**riaddorménto**) *tr* to put back to sleep || *ref* to go back to sleep

**riaffacciare** §128 (**riaffàccio**) *tr* to present again || *ref* to reappear

**riaffermare** (**riaffèrmo**) *tr* to reaffirm

**riaggravare** *tr* to make worse || *ref* to get worse again

**rialesare** (**rialèso**) *tr* to rebore

**riallacciare** §128 (**riallàccio**) *tr* to tie again || *ref* to be tied or connected

**rialto** *m* knoll, height; **fare rialto** (coll) to eat better than usual

**rialzare** *tr* to lift, raise; to increase || *ref* to rise

**rialzi·sta** *mf* (-sti -ste) bull (*in stock market*)

**rialzo** *m* rise; raise; knoll, height; **giocare al rialzo** to bull the market

**riammobiliare** §287 *tr* to refurnish

**rianimare** (**riànimo**) *tr* to revive; to encourage || *ref* to revive; to recover one's spirits, to rally

**riapertura** *f* reopening

**riapparire** §108 *intr* (ESSERE) to reappear

**riapparizióne** *f* reappearance

**riaprire** §110 *tr & ref* to reopen

**riarmare** *tr* to rearm; to reinforce; to refit || *intr & ref* to rearm

**riarmo** *m* rearmament

**riar·so -sa** *adj* dry, parched

**riassaporare** (**riassapóro**) *tr* to relish again

**riassettare** (**riassètto**) *tr* to tidy up

**riassicurare** *tr* to reinsure; to fasten again; to reassure

**riassorbire** §176 & (**riassòrbo**) *tr* to reabsorb

**riassùmere** §116 *tr* to hire again; to summarize, sum up

**riassunto** *m* précis, abstract; résumé

**riassunzióne** *f* rehiring; resumption

**riattaccare** §197 *tr* to attach again; (coll) to begin again; (telp) to hang up

**riattare** *tr* to repair, fix

**riattivare** *tr* to reactivate

**riavére** §229 *tr* to get again; to recover; to get back || *ref* to recover

**riavvicinaménto** *m* var of **ravvicinamento**

**riavvicinare** *tr & ref* var of **ravvicinare**

**ribadire** §176 *tr* to clinch (*a nail*); to rivet; to drive home (*an idea*); to back up (*a statement*)

**ribaldo** *m* scoundrel, rogue

**ribalta** *f* lid with hinge; trap door; (theat) footlights; (theat) forestage; (fig) limelight; **a ribalta** hinged

**ribaltàbile** *adj* collapsable (*e.g., seat*) || *m* dump-truck lift; dump truck

**ribaltare** *tr & ref* to upset, turn over

**ribassare** *tr & intr* (ESSERE) to lower

**ribassi·sta** *mf* (-sti -ste) bear (*in stock market*)

**ribasso** *m* fall, decline; discount, rebate; **giocare al ribasso** to be a bear

**ribàttere** *tr* to clinch (*a nail*); to return (*a ball*); to iron smooth; to belabor (*a point*) || *intr* to answer back

**ribattezzare** [ddzz] (**ribattézzo**) *tr* to rebaptize

**ribattino** *m* rivet

**ribellare** (**ribèllo**) *tr* to rouse to rebellion || *ref* to rebel; **ribellarsi a** to rebel against

**ribèlle** *adj* rebellious || *mf* rebel

**ribellióne** *f* rebellion

**ri·bes** *m* (-bes) currant; gooseberry

**ribobinazióne** *f* rewind (*of a tape*)

**riboccare** §197 (**ribócco**) *intr* (ESSERE & AVERE) to overflow

**ribollire** (**ribóllo**) *tr* to boil again ||

**intr** to boil over; to simmer; to ferment

**ribrézzo** [ddzz] *m* repugnance, disgust

**ributtare** *tr* to return (*a ball*); to throw up; to reject; to push back ‖ *intr* to sprout; (with *dat*) to disgust, nauseate

**ricacciare** §128 *tr* to drive back ‖ *intr* to sprout ‖ *ref* to sneak away, disappear

**ricadére** §121 *intr* (ESSERE) to fall back; to fall down; to relapse; **ricadere su** to devolve upon

**ricaduta** *f* relapse

**ricalcare** §197 *tr* to transfer (*a design*); to imitate; **ricalcare le orme di** follow in the footsteps of

**rical·co** *m* (-**chi**) copy, copying; **a ricalco** multiple-copy

**ricamare** *tr* to embroider

**ricambiare** §287 *tr* to return; to repay ‖ *ref* to change clothes

**ricàm·bio** *m* (-**bi**) exchange; spare part; refill; metabolism; **di ricambio** spare (*part*)

**ricamo** *m* embroidery; needlework; **ricami** (*fig*) embellishments

**ricapitolare** (**ricapìtolo**) *tr* to recapitulate

**ricaricare** §197 (**ricàrico**) *tr* to reload; to wind (*a watch*); to charge (*a battery*)

**ricattare** *tr* to blackmail

**ricatta·tóre -trice** *mf* blackmailer

**ricatto** *m* blackmail

**ricavare** *tr* to draw, extract; to obtain, derive

**ricavato** *m* proceeds; (fig) fruit, yield

**ricavo** *m* proceeds

**ricchézza** *f* wealth; **ricchezza mobile** income from personal property; **ricchezze** riches

**rìc·cio -cia** (-**ci** -**ce**) *adj* curly ‖ *m* curl; shaving; burr; scroll (*of violin*); crook (*of crozier*); (zool) hedgehog; **riccio di mare** (zool) sea urchin

**rìcciolo** *m* curl

**ricciolu·to -ta** *adj* curly

**ricciu·to -ta** *adj* curly

**rìc·co -ca** *adj* (-**chi** -**che**) rich ‖ **i ricchi** the rich

**ricér·ca** *f* (-**che**) search; research; **ricerca operativa** operations research

**ricercare** §197 (**ricérco**) *tr* to search for again; to seek; to investigate; (poet) to pluck (*a musical instrument*)

**ricercatézza** *f* affectation; sophistication

**ricerca·to -ta** *adj* sought after, wanted; affected; sophisticated

**ricetrasmettitóre** *m* two-way radio

**ricètta** *f* prescription; recipe

**ricettàcolo** *m* receptacle; depository

**ricettare** (**ricètto**) *tr* to receive (*stolen goods*); to prescribe

**ricettà·rio** *m* (-**ri**) recipe book; prescription pad

**ricetta·tóre -trice** *mf* fence, receiver of stolen goods

**ricetti·vo -va** *adj* receptive

**ricètto** *m* (poet) refuge

**ricévere** §141 *tr* to receive; to get; to contain; to withstand

**riciménto** *m* reception; receipt

**ricevi·tóre -trice** *mf* addressee ‖ *m* receiver; collector; registrar of deeds; **ricevitore postale** postmaster

**ricevitorìa** *f* collection office; **ricevitoria postale** post office

**ricevuta** *f* receipt; **accusare ricevuta di** to acknowledge receipt of

**ricezióne** *f* (rad, telv) reception; **accusare ricezione** to acknowledge receipt

**richiamare** *tr* to call back; to recall; to call (*e.g.*, *attention*); to quote; to chide ‖ *ref* to refer

**richiamato** *m* soldier recalled to active duty

**richiamo** *m* call; recall; admonition; cross reference; advertisement

**richièdere** §124 *tr* to ask again; to demand; to require; to apply for ‖ *ref* to be required

**richiè·sto -sta** *adj*—**essere richiesto** to be in demand ‖ *f* request; demand; petition, application

**richiùdere** §125 *tr* & *ref* to shut again

**riciclare** *tr* to recycle (*e.g.*, *in the chemical industry*)

**rìcino** *m* castor-oil plant

**ricognitóre** *m* scout; reconnaissance plane; (law) recognition

**ricognizióne** *f* recognition; (mil) reconnaissance

**ricollegare** §209 (**ricollégo**) *tr* to connect ‖ *ref* to be connected; to refer

**ricolmare** (**ricólmo**) *tr* to fill to the brim; to overwhelm

**ricominciare** §128 *tr* & *intr* (ESSERE) to begin again, resume

**ricomparire** §108 *intr* (ESSERE) to reappear

**ricomparsa** *f* reappearance

**ricompènsa** *f* compensation, recompense; reward; (mil) award

**ricompensare** (**ricompènso**) *tr* to compensate, recompense; to reward

**ricomperare** (**ricómpero**) *tr* var of **ricomprare**

**ricompórre** §218 *tr* to recompose; to plan again ‖ *ref* to regain one's composure

**ricomprare** (**ricómpro**) *tr* to buy again; to buy back

**riconcentrare** (**riconcèntro**) *tr* to concentrate again; to gather (*one's thoughts*) ‖ *ref* to be withdrawn

**riconciliare** §287 (**riconcìlio**) *tr* to reconcile ‖ *ref* to become reconciled

**ricondurre** §102 *tr* to bring back; to take back ‖ *ref* to go back

**riconfermare** (**riconférmo**) *tr* to reconfirm

**riconfortare** (**riconfòrto**) *tr* to comfort

**ricongiùngere** §183 *tr* & *ref* to reunite

**riconoscènte** *adj* grateful

**riconoscènza** *f* gratitude

**riconóscere** §134 *tr* to recognize; (mil) to reconnoiter

**riconosciménto** *m* recognition; **in riconoscimento di** in recognition of

**riconquistare** *tr* to reconquer

**riconsegnare** (**riconségno**) *tr* to give back, to return

**riconsiderare (riconsìdero)** *tr* to reconsider

**ricontare (ricónto)** *tr* to recount, count again

**riconversióne** *f* reconversion

**riconvertire** §138 *tr* to reconvert; to recycle

**ricopèr·to -ta** *adj* covered; coated

**ricopertura** *f* covering; seat cover

**ricopiare** §287 **(ricòpio)** *tr* to make a fair copy of; to recopy; to copy

**ricoprire** §110 *tr* to cover; to coat; to hide ‖ *ref* to become covered

**ricordanza** *f* (poet) memory

**ricordare (ricòrdo)** *tr* to remember; to remind; to mention ‖ *ref* to remember; **ricordarsi di** to remember

**ricòrdo** *m* memory; souvenir; **ricordo marmoreo** marble statue

**ricorrènte** *adj* recurrent, recurring

**ricorrènza** *f* recurrence; anniversary

**ricórrere** §139 *intr* (ESSERE & AVERE) to run again; to run back; to resort; to recur; (law) to appeal; **ricorrere a** to have recourse to

**ricórso** *m* recurrence; recourse; appeal

**ricostituènte** *adj* invigorating ‖ *m* tonic

**ricostituire** §176 *tr* to reconstitute, to reform; to reinvigorate

**ricostruire** §140 *tr* to rebuild; to reconstruct

**ricostruzióne** *f* rebuilding; reconstruction

**ricòtta** *f* Italian cottage cheese; **di ricotta** weak

**ricoverare (ricóvero)** *tr* to shelter ‖ *ref* to take shelter

**ricóvero** *m* shelter; nursing home; (med) admission; **ricovero antiaereo** air-raid shelter

**ricreare (ricrèo)** *tr* to recreate; to refresh ‖ *ref* to relax

**ricreati·vo -va** *adj* refreshing; recreational

**ricreatò·rio -ria (-ri -rie)** *adj* recreation, recreational ‖ *m* recreation room; playground

**ricreazióne** *f* recreation; recess

**ricrédere** §141 *intr*—**far ricredere qlcu** to make s.o. change his mind ‖ *ref* to change one's mind

**ricréscere** §142 *intr* (ESSERE) to grow again; to swell

**ricucire** §143 *tr* to sew up

**ricuòcere** §144a *tr* to cook again; to anneal

**ricuperare (ricùpero)** *tr* to recover; (naut) to salvage; (sports) to make up for (*rained-out game*)

**ricùpero** *m* recovery; salvage; rally; making up for (*for lost time or postponed game*)

**ricur·vo -va** *adj* bent; bent over

**ricusare** *tr* to refuse

**ridacchiare** §287 *intr* to titter, giggle

**ridancia·no -na** *adj* prone to laughter; amusing

**ridare** §230 (*1st sg pres ind* **ridò**) *tr* to give back; to give again; **ridare fuori** to vomit ‖ *intr* (coll) to reappear, e.g., **gli ha ridato il foruncolo** his boil has reappeared ‖ *intr*

(ESSERE)—**ridare giù** to have a relapse

**ridda** *f* round; confusion; throng

**ridènte** *adj* laughing; bright, pleasant

**ridere** §231 *tr* (poet) to laugh at ‖ *intr* to laugh; (poet) to shine; **far ridere i polli** to be utterly ridiculous; **ridere sotto i baffi** to laugh up one's sleeve ‖ *ref*—**ridersi di** to laugh at

**ridestare (ridésto)** *tr* & *ref* to reawaken

**ridicolizzare** [ddzz] *tr* to ridicule; to twit

**ridìco·lo -la** *adj* ridiculous ‖ *m* ridicule; ridiculousness

**ridipìngere** §126 *tr* to paint again

**ridire** §151 *tr* to tell again; to repeat; to tell (*to express*); **avere** or **trovare a** or **da ridire (su)** to find fault (with)

**ridistribuzióne** *f* redistribution

**ridivenire** §282 or **ridiventare (ridivènto)** *intr* (ESSERE) to become again

**ridonare (ridóno)** *tr* to give back

**ridondante** *adj* redundant

**ridondare (ridóndo)** *intr* (ESSERE & AVERE) (fig) to overflow; **ridondare a** or **in** to redound to

**ridòsso** *m* back; shelter; **a ridosso** sheltered; as a shelter; behind, close behind

**ridót·to -ta** *adj* reduced; **mal ridotto** down at the heel ‖ *m* lounge; (theat) foyer ‖ *f* (mil) redoubt

**ridurre** §102 *tr* to reduce; to adapt; to translate; to lead; to curtail; (mus) to arrange ‖ *ref* to be reduced; to retire

**riduttóre** *m* (mach) reduction gear

**riduzióne** *f* reduction; (mus) arrangement

**riecheggiare** §290 **(riechéggio)** *tr* & *intr* to echo

**riedificare** §197 **(riedìfico)** *tr* to rebuild

**rieducare** §197 **(rièduco)** *tr* to reeducate

**rielèggere** §193 *tr* to reelect

**rielezióne** *f* reelection

**riemèrgere** §162 *intr* to resurface

**riempiménto** *m* fill

**riempire** §163 *tr* to fill; to stuff

**riempiti·vo -va** *adj* expletive ‖ *m* expletive; fill-in

**rientrante** *adj* hollow (*cheeks*); (mil) reentrant

**rientranza** *f* recess

**rientrare (rièntro)** *intr* (ESSERE) to reenter; to come back; to recede; (coll) to shrink; **rientrare in** to recover (*one's expenses*); **rientrare in sé** to come to one's senses

**rièntro** *m* reentry

**riepilogare** §209 **(riepìlogo)** *tr* to sum up, recapitulate

**riepìlo·go** *m* (-**ghi**) recapitulation

**riesame** *m* reexamination

**riesaminare (riesàmino)** *tr* to reexamine

**riesumare** *tr* to exhume; (fig) to dig up; (fig) to bring back

**rievocare** §197 **(rièvoco)** *tr* to recall

**rifaciménto** *m* adaptation; recasting

**rifare** §173 (*3d sg* **rifà**) *tr* to do again, redo; to remake; to imitate; to indemnify; to prepare again; to repeat;

to make (*a bed*) ‖ *ref* to recover; to become again; to recoup one's losses; to begin; **rifarsi con** to get even with; **rifarsi da** to begin with

**rifasciare** §128 *tr* to rebind

**riferiménto** *m* reference

**riferire** §176 *tr* to wound again; to refer; to relate ‖ *ref*—**riferirsi a** to refer to; to concern

**riffa** *f* raffle; lottery; (coll) violence; **di riffa o di raffa** by hook or crook

**rifilare** *tr* to clip; (coll) to reel off (*a list of names*); (coll) to deal (*a blow*); (coll) to palm off

**rifinire** §176 *tr* to give the finishing touch to; to wear out ‖ *intr* to stop ‖ *ref* to wear oneself out

**rifiorire** §176 *tr* (lit) to revive ‖ *intr* to bloom again ‖ *intr* (ESSERE) to flourish; to grow better; to reappear

**rifischiare** §287 *tr* to whistle again; (coll) to report ‖ *intr* to talk, gossip

**rifiutare** *tr* to refuse; (lit) to reject ‖ *intr* (cards) to renege, renounce ‖ *ref* to refuse, deny

**rifiuto** *m* refusal; refuse, rubbish; rejection; rebuff, spurn; (fig) wreck; (cards) renege; **di rifiuto** waste, e.g., **materiale di rifiuto** waste material

**riflessióne** *f* reflexion

**riflessi·vo -va** *adj* thoughtful; (gram) reflexive

**riflès·so -sa** *adj* reflex, e.g., **azione riflessa** reflex action ‖ *m* reflection; (physiol) reflex; **di riflesso** vicarious

**riflèttere** §177 (*pp* **riflettuto** & **riflèsso**) *tr* & *intr* to reflect ‖ *ref* to be reflected

**riflettóre** *m* searchlight; reflector

**rifluire** §176 *intr* (ESSERE & AVERE) to flow; to flow back

**riflusso** *m* flow; ebb, ebb tide

**rifocillare** *tr* to refresh (*with food*) ‖ *ref* to take refreshment

**rifóndere** §178 *tr* to melt again; to recast; to refund; to reedit

**rifórma** *f* reform; (mil) rejection ‖ **Riforma** *f*—**la Riforma** the Reformation

**riformare** (**rifórmo**) *tr* to reform; to amend; (mil) to reject

**riformati·vo -va** *adj* reformatory

**riforma·tóre -trice** *adj* reforming ‖ *mf* reformer

**riformatò·rio** *m* (**-ri**) reform school, reformatory

**riforniménto** *m* supply; refueling; **fare rifornimento di** to fill up with; **rifornimenti** supplies

**rifornire** §176 *tr* to supply; to restock; **rifornire di benzina** to refuel

**rifràngere** §179 *tr* to crush ‖ *ref* to break (*said of waves*) ‖ §179 (*pp* **rifratto**) *tr* to refract ‖ *ref* to be refracted

**rifrat·tóre -trice** *adj* refracting ‖ *m* refractor

**rifrazióne** *f* refraction

**rifrìggere** §180 *tr* to fry again; to rehash ‖ *intr* to fry too long or in too much oil

**rifrit·to -ta** *adj* fried again; (fig) hackneyed ‖ *m* taste of stale fat; (fig) rehash

**rifuggire** *tr* to avoid ‖ *intr*—**rifuggire da** to abhor ‖ *intr* (ESSERE) to take refuge

**rifugiare** §290 *ref* to take refuge, take shelter

**rifugiato** *m* refugee

**rifù·gio** *m* (**-gi**) refuge; **rifugio alpino** mountain hut; **rifugio antiaereo** air-raid shelter; **rifugio antiatomico** fallout shelter

**rifùlgere** §233 *intr* (ESSERE & AVERE) to shine

**rifusióne** *f* recast; refund, reimbursement

**ri·ga** *f* (**-ghe**) line; row; rank; ruler; part (*in hair*); stripe; (fig) quality

**rigàglie** *fpl* giblets

**rigàgnolo** *m* rivulet; gutter (*at the side of a road*)

**rigare** §209 *tr* to rule, line; to stripe; to mark; to rifle (*gun*) ‖ *intr*—**rigare diritto** to toe the line

**rigatino** *m* gingham

**rigattière** *m* second-hand dealer

**rigatura** *f* ruling; rifling (*of gun*)

**rigenerare** (**rigènero**) *tr* to regenerate; to reclaim; to recycle ‖ *ref* to become regenerate

**rigeneratóre** *m*—**rigeneratore per i capelli** hair restorer

**rigettare** (**rigètto**) *tr* to throw back; to reject; to recast; (slang) to throw up ‖ *intr* to sprout

**rigètto** *m* rejection

**righèllo** *m* ruler

**rigidi·tà** *f* (**-tà**) rigidity; rigor; stiffness; **rigidità cadaverica** rigor mortis

**rìgi·do -da** *adj* rigid, stiff; severe

**rigirare** *tr* to keep turning; to dupe; to invest; to encircle ‖ *intr* to ramble ‖ *ref* to turn around; to tumble

**ri·go** *m* (**-ghi**) line; **rigo musicale** (mus) staff

**rigò·glio** *m* (**-gli**) luxuriance; bloom; gurgling

**rigonfiare** §287 (**rigónfio**) *tr* to inflate ‖ *intr* (ESSERE) & *ref* to swell up

**rigóre** *m* rigor; severity; precision; **a rigor di termini** strictly speaking; **di rigore** de rigueur; (sports) penalty (*e.g., kick*)

**rigorismo** *m* rigorism, strictness, severity

**rigori·sta** *mf* (**-sti -ste**) rigorist ‖ *m* (soccer) kicker of penalty goal

**rigoró·so -sa** [*s*] *adj* rigorous, strict

**rigovernare** (**rigovèrno**) *tr* to clean, wash (*dishes*); to groom, tend (*animals*)

**riguadagnare** *tr* to regain

**riguardare** *tr* to look again; to look back; to examine; to consider; to take care of; to concern ‖ *intr*—**riguardare a** to look out for; to face (*said of a window*) ‖ *ref* to take care of oneself; **riguardarsi da** to keep away from

**riguardo** *m* care; esteem; regard; **a questo riguardo** in this regard; **ri-**

guardo a as far as . . . is concerned; senza **riguardo a** irrespective of

**riguardó·so -sa** [s] adj considerate

**rigurgitare (rigùrgito)** tr & intr to regurgitate

**rilanciare** §128 tr to toss back; to reestablish (e.g., fashions); (poker) to raise

**rilasciare** §128 tr to free, let go; to relax; to grant || ref to relax

**rilà·scio** m (-sci) release; delivery; granting, issue (of a document)

**rilassante** adj relaxing

**rilassare** tr & ref to relax

**rilassatézza** f laxity

**rilegare** §209 (rilégo) tr to tie again; to bind, rebind (a book); to set (a stone)

**rilega·tóre -trice** mf binder

**rilegatura** f binding

**rilèggere** §193 tr to reread

**rilènto** m—a rilento slowly

**rilevaménto** m survey; (naut) bearing

**rilevare (rilèvo)** tr to lift again; to observe; to draw; to bring out; to survey; to take over; to pick up; (mil) to relieve || intr to be delineated; to be of import || ref to rise again; to recover

**rilevatà·rio** m (-ri) successor; (law) assignee

**rilièvo** m relief; survey; remark; assumption (of debts); taking over (of business); **mettere in rilievo** to bring out; to set off

**rilò·ga** f (-ghe) traverse rod

**rilucènte** adj shiny, shining

**rilùcere** §234 intr to shine

**riluttante** adj reluctant

**riluttanza** f reluctance

**rima** f rhyme; slit; crevice; **rispondere per le rime** to answer in kind, to retort

**rimandare** tr to send back; to refer; to dismiss; to put off, postpone; to refer; **rimandare a ottobre** to condition (a student)

**rimando** m delay; reference; footnote; repartee; postponement; (sports) return

**rimaneggiare** §290 (rimanéggio) tr to rearrange; to reshuffle; to shake up (personnel); to rewrite (news)

**rimanènte** adj remaining || m remainder; remnant; **i rimanenti** the rest

**rimanènza** f remainder

**rimanére** §235 intr (ESSERE) to remain, stay; to be in agreement; to have left, e.g., **mi sono rimasti solo tre dollari** I only have three dollars left; to be located; (poet) to stop; **rimanerci** (coll) to be killed; (coll) to be duped; **rimanere da** to depend on, e.g., **questo rimane da Lei** this depends on you

**rimangiare** §290 tr to eat again || ref— **rimangiarsi la parola** to go back on one's word

**rimarcare** §197 tr to mark again; to point out

**rimar·co** m (-chi) remark, notice

**rimare** tr & intr to rhyme

**rimarginare (rimàrgino)** tr, intr & ref to heal

**rimaritare** tr & ref to marry again

**rimasù·glio** m (-gli) leftover

**rima·tóre -trice** mf poet; rhymster

**rimbalzare** intr (ESSERE & AVERE) to bounce back, rebound

**rimbalzo** m rebound

**rimbambire** §176 intr (ESSERE) & ref to become feeble-minded (from old age)

**rimbambi·to -ta** adj feeble-minded || mf dotard

**rimbeccare** §197 (rimbécco) tr to peck; to retort

**rimbecilli·to -ta** adj feeble-minded

**rimboccare** §197 (rimbócco) tr to tuck up; to tuck in; to fill to the brim

**rimbombare (rimbómbo)** intr (ESSERE & AVERE) to thunder, boom

**rimbómbo** m thunder, boom

**rimborsare (rimbórso)** tr to reimburse, pay back

**rimbórso** m repayment

**rimboscare** §197 (rimbòsco) tr to reforest || ref to take to the woods

**rimboschiménto** m reforestation

**rimboschire** §176 tr to reforest || intr (ESSERE) to become wooded

**rimbrottare (rimbròtto)** tr to scold

**rimbròtto** m scolding

**rimediare** §287 (rimèdio) tr (coll) to scrape together; (coll) to patch up || intr (with dat) to remedy; to make up (lost time)

**rimè·dio** m (-di) remedy

**rimembranza** f remembrance

**rimeritare (rimèrito)** tr to reward

**rimescolare (riméscolo)** tr to stir; to shuffle (cards)

**riméssa** f remittance; shipment; harvest; store; loss; sprout; carriage house; garage; (sports) return; (sports) putting in play; **rimessa del tram** carbarn

**rimestare (rimésto)** tr to stir

**riméttere** §198 tr to remit; to put back; to set back; to sprout; to postpone, defer; to ship; to vomit; to recover; to deliver; to straighten up; (sports) to return; **rimetterci** to lose; **rimettere a nuovo** to renovate; **rimettere in ordine** to tidy up; **rimettere in piedi** to rebuild, restore || intr (coll) to sprout; (coll) to grow; (lit) to abate || ref to recover; to quiet down; to defer; to be clearing (said of weather); **rimettersi a** to go back to (e.g., bed); **rimettersi a** + inf to start + ger + again; **rimettersi in cammino** to start off again

**rimirare** tr to stare at

**rìmmel** m mascara

**rimodellare (rimodèllo)** tr to remodel

**rimodernare (rimodèrno)** tr to modernize; to remodel; to bring up to date || ref to become modern

**rimónta** f reassembly; return (of migratory birds); revamping (of shoes); (mil) remount

**rimontare (rimónto)** tr to rewind; to go up (a stream); to vamp (shoes); to renovate; to regain; to reassemble (*a machine*); (mil) to remount || *intr* (ESSERE & AVERE) to climb again; to go back (*in time*)

**rimorchiare** §287 (**rimòrchio**) *tr* to tow; to drag along

**rimorchiatóre** *m* tugboat; tow car

**rimòr·chio** *m* (**-chi**) tow; trailer; **prendere a rimorchio** to take in tow

**rimòrdere** §200 *tr* to bite again; to prick (*said, e.g., of conscience*)

**rimòrso** *m* remorse

**rimostranza** *f* remonstrance

**rimostrare** (**rimóstro**) *tr* to show again || *intr* to remonstrate; **rimostrare a** to remonstrate with

**rimozióne** *f* removal; demotion

**rimpannucciare** §128 *tr* to outfit better || *ref* to be better dressed; to be better off

**rimpastare** *tr* to knead again; to reshuffle, remake

**rimpasto** *m* reshuffling, rearrangement

**rimpatriare** §287 *tr* to repatriate || *intr* to be repatriated

**rimpà·trio** *m* (**-tri**) repatriation

**rimpètto** *adv* opposite; **di rimpetto a** opposite to; in comparison with

**rimpiàngere** §215 *tr* to regret; to mourn

**rimpianto** *m* regret

**rimpiattare** *tr* & *ref* to hide; **giocare a rimpiattarsi** to play hide-and-seek

**rimpiattino** *m* hide-and-seek

**rimpiazzare** *tr* to replace

**rimpiazzo** *m* replacement, substitute

**rimpiccolire** §176 *tr* to make smaller || *intr* (ESSERE) to get smaller

**rimpinzare** *tr* to stuff, cram

**rimproverare** (**rimpròvero**) *tr* to chide, reproach; **rimproverare qlcu di qlco** or **rimproverare qlco a qlcu** to reproach s.o. for s.th

**rimpròvero** *m* reproach, rebuke

**rimuginare** (**rimùgino**) *tr* & *intr* to rummage; to stir; to ruminate

**rimunerare** (**rimùnero**) *tr* to reward || *intr* to pay

**rimunerati··vo -va** *adj* remunerative; rewarding

**rimunerazióne** *f* remuneration

**rimuòvere** §202 *tr* to remove; to demote; to move

**rinàscere** §203 *intr* (ESSERE) to be born again; to grow again; to revive; **far rinascere** to revive

**rinasciménto** *m* rebirth || **Rinascimento** *m* Renaissance

**rinàscita** *f* rebirth

**rincagna·to -ta** *adj* snub (*nose*)

**rincalzare** *tr* to hill (*plants*); to underpin; to tuck in

**rincalzo** *m* reinforcement; support

**rincantucciare** §128 *tr* & *ref* to hide in a corner

**rincarare** *tr* to raise the price of; to raise; **rincarare la dose** to add insult to injury || *intr* (ESSERE) to rise, go up (*said of prices*)

**rincasare** [s] *intr* (ESSERE) to return home

**rinchiùdere** §125 *tr* to enclose, shut in

**rinchiu·so -sa** [s] *adj* shut in; musty || *m*—**saper di rinchiuso** to smell musty

**rincitrullire** §176 *intr* (ESSERE) to grow stupid

**rincóntro** *m*—**a rincontro** opposite

**rincorare** §236 *tr* to encourage || *ref* to take heart

**rincórrere** §139 *tr* to pursue, chase

**rincórsa** *f*—**prendere la rincorsa** to take off (*for a jump*); to get a running start

**rincréscere** §142 *intr* (ESSERE) (with *dat*) to displease; to be sorry, e.g., **gli rincresce** he is sorry; to mind, **Le rincresce? do you mind?**

**rincresciménto** *m* regret

**rincrudire** §176 *tr* to sharpen; to embitter || *intr* (ESSERE) to become bitter; to get worse

**rinculare** *intr* (ESSERE & AVERE) to back up; to recoil

**rinculo** *m* recoil

**rinfacciare** §128 *tr* to throw in one's face

**rinfarcire** §176 *tr* to stuff

**rinfiancare** §197 *tr* to support

**rinfocolare** (**rinfòcolo**) *tr* to rekindle; to revive

**rinfoderare** (**rinfòdero**) *tr* sheathe

**rinforzare** (**rinfòrzo**) *tr* to reinforce; strengthen || *intr* (ESSERE) & *ref* to become stronger

**rinfòrzo** *m* reinforcement

**rinfrancare** §197 *tr* to reassure || *ref* to buck up

**rinfrescante** *adj* refreshing || *m* mild laxative

**rinfrescare** §197 (**rinfrésco**) *tr* to refresh; to restore; to renew || *intr* (ESSERE & AVERE) to cool off (*said of the weather*) || *ref* to have some refreshments; to cool off

**rinfré·sco** *m* (**-schi**) refreshment

**rinfusa** *f*—**alla rinfusa** at random; pell-mell; in bulk

**ringalluzzire** §176 *tr* & *ref* to perk up

**ringhiare** §287 *intr* to growl, to snarl

**ringhièra** *f* railing

**rìn·ghio** *m* (**-ghi**) growl, snarl

**ringiovaniménto** *m* rejuvenation

**ringiovanire** §176 *tr* to rejuvenate || *intr* (ESSERE) to grow or look younger

**ringraziaménto** *m* thanks

**ringraziare** §287 *tr* to thank; to dismiss

**ringuainare** (**ringuaìno**) *tr* to sheathe

**rinnegare** §209 (**rinnègo** & **rinnégo**) *tr* to forswear; to repudiate

**rinnega·to -ta** *adj* & *m* renegade

**rinnovaménto** *m* renewal; reawakening

**rinnovare** (**rinnòvo**) *tr* to renew; to renovate; to restore; to replace || *ref* to occur again; to renew

**rinnovellare** (**rinnovèllo**) *tr* to repeat; (poet) to renew || *intr* (ESSERE) & *ref* to change; to renew

**rinnòvo** *m* renewal

**rinocerónte** *m* rhinoceros

**rinomanza** *f* renown

**rinoma·to -ta** *adj* renowned, famous

**rinsaldare** *tr* to starch; (fig) to strengthen || *ref* to become confirmed (*in one's opinion*)

**rinsanguare (rinsànguo)** *tr* to give new strength to ‖ *ref* to regain strength; to recover

**rinsavire** §176 *intr* (ESSERE) to return to reason

**rintanare** *ref* to burrow; to hide

**rintóc·co** *m* (**-chi**) toll (*of bell*)

**rintontire** §176 *tr* to stun, to daze

**rintracciare** §128 *tr* to track down

**rintronare (rintròno)** *tr* to deafen; to make rumble ‖ *intr* (ESSERE & AVERE) to thunder; to rumble

**rintuzzare** *tr* to dull, blunt; to repel; to repress

**rinùn·cia** *f* (**-ce**) or **rinùnzia** *f* renunciation

**rinunziare** §287 *tr* to renounce ‖ *intr* (with *dat*) to give up, renounce, e.g., **rinunziò al trono** he renounced the throne

**rinvangare** §209 *tr* & *intr* var of **rivangare**

**rinvenire** §282 *tr* to find ‖ *intr* (ESSERE) to come to; **far rinvenire** to bring to, revive

**rinviare** §119 *tr* to send back; to postpone; to refer; to adjourn; to remit (*to a lower court*)

**rinvigorire** §176 *tr* to strengthen ‖ *intr* (ESSERE) & *ref* to regain strength

**rinvì·o** *m* (**-i**) return; postponement; adjournment; reference; (law) continuance

**rì·o** *m* (**-i**) (lit) sin; (lit) brook; (coll) canal

**rioccupare (riòccupo)** *tr* to reoccupy

**rioccupazióne** *f* reoccupation

**rionale** *adj* neighborhood

**rióne** *m* district; neighborhood

**riordinare (riórdino)** *tr* to rearrange; to reorganize; to order again

**riorganizzare** [ddzz] *tr* to reorganize

**riottó·so -sa** [s] *adj* (lit) quarrelsome; (lit) unruly, rebellious

**ripa** *f* (lit) bank (*of river*); (lit) escarpment

**ripagare** §209 *tr* to repay; to pay again

**riparare** *tr* to protect; to mend, fix, repair; to make up (*an exam*) ‖ *intr* —**riparare a** to make up for ‖ *intr* (ESSERE) & *ref* to take refuge; to betake oneself

**riparazióne** *f* repair; reparation; redress; (educ) make-up

**riparlare** *intr* to speak again; **ne riparleremo!** you will see!

**riparo** *m* repair; shelter

**ripartire** §176 *tr* to divide; to distribute; to share ‖ (**riparto**) *intr* (ESSERE) to leave again; to start again ‖ §176 *ref* to split up

**ripartizióne** *f* division; distribution

**riparto** *m* division; distribution; allotment

**ripassare** *tr* to cross again; to brush up, review; to repass; to sift again; to check; to read over; (mach) to overhaul ‖ *intr* (ESSERE) to go by; to come by

**ripassata** *f* checkup; review; (coll) rebuke

**ripassa·tóre -trice** *mf* checker

**ripasso** *m* return (*of birds*); (coll) review

**ripensare (ripènso)** *intr* to keep thinking; **ripensare a** to think of again; to think over again

**ripentire (ripènto)** *ref* to repent; **ripentirsi di** to repent

**ripercórrere** §139 *tr* to retrace

**ripercuòtere** §251 *tr* to reflect; to strike again ‖ *ref* to reverberate

**ripescare** §197 (**ripésco**) *tr* to fish again; (fig) to dig up

**ripètere** *tr* & *intr* to repeat ‖ *ref* to be repeated

**ripeti·tóre -trice** *mf* repeater; coach; tutor ‖ *m* (rad, telv) rebroadcasting station; (rad) relay

**ripetizióne** *f* repetition; review; tutoring; **a ripetizione** repeating (*firearm*)

**ripiano** *m* terrace; ledge; shelf; landing; (com) balancing

**ripìc·co** *m* (**-chi**) pique; spite

**ripì·do -da** *adj* steep

**ripiegaménto** *m* bend; (mil) withdrawal, retreat

**ripiegare** §209 (**ripiègo**) *tr* to fold, fold over ‖ *intr* to do better; (mil) to fall back ‖ *ref* to bend over; to withdraw into oneself

**ripiè·go** *m* (**-ghi**) expedient

**ripiè·no -na** *adj* full; stuffed ‖ *m* stuffing; (culin) filling

**ripigliare** §280 *tr* to reacquire; to catch again; to begin again ‖ *intr* to recover ‖ *ref* to renew a quarrel

**ripiombare (ripiómbo)** *tr* to make plumb; (fig) to plunge back ‖ *intr* (ESSERE) (fig) to plunge back

**ripopolare (ripòpolo)** *tr* to repopulate; to restock (*e.g., a pond*)

**ripórre** §218 *tr* to put back; to place (*one's hope*); to repose (*one's trust*) ‖ *ref* to back down; **riporsi a** + *inf* to start + *ger* again

**riportare (ripòrto)** *tr* to bring back; to report; to get; to transfer (*a design*); (com) to carry forward; (hunt) to retrieve; (math) to carry ‖ *ref* to go back

**ripòrto** *m* filler; retrieving; (com) balance carried forward; (math) number carried

**riposante** [s] *adj* restful

**riposare** [s] (**ripòso**) *tr, intr* & *ref* to rest

**ripòso** [s] *m* rest; repose; Requiem; retirement; **buon riposo!** sleep well!; **mettere a riposo** to retire; **riposo!** (mil) at ease

**ripostì·glio** *m* (**-gli**) closet

**ripó·sto -sta** *adj* innermost ‖ *m* (coll) pantry

**riprèndere** §220 *tr* to take back; to take up again; to get back; to take in (*a garment*); to catch (*s.th thrown in the air*); to take up (*arms*); to get; to reconquer; to start again, resume; to reprehend; to recover; (mov, telv) to shoot; **riprendere moglie** to remarry ‖ *intr* to start again; to recover, improve; to pick up (*said of a* *motor*) ‖ *ref* to recover; to catch oneself up

**riprésa** [s] *f* resumption; (aut) pickup; (theat) revival; (mov) shooting, take; (boxing) round; (soccer) second half; (mus, pros) refrain; **a più riprese** several times

**ripresentare** (**ripresènto**) *tr* to present again

**ripristinare** (**riprìstino**) *tr* to restore; to reestablish

**ripristino** *m* revival, restoration

**riprodurre** §102 *tr* to reproduce; to express ‖ *ref* to reproduce; to occur

**riprodut•tóre -trice** *adj* reproducing ‖ *mf* reproducer ‖ *m* reproducer (*e.g., of sound*)

**riproduzióne** *f* reproduction; playback (*e.g., of tape*)

**riprométtere** §198 *tr* to promise again ‖ *ref* to hope; to propose; to hope for

**ripròva** *f* new proof; confirmation

**riprovare** (**ripròvo**) *tr* to try again; to try on again; to feel, experience again; to flunk; to censure ‖ *ref* to try again

**riprovazióne** *f* disapproval

**ripudiare** §287 *tr* to repudiate

**ripugnante** *adj* repugnant, repulsive

**ripugnanza** *f* repugnance; aversion

**ripugnare** *intr* (with *dat*) to disgust, revolt, be repugnant to

**ripulire** §176 *tr* to clean again; to tidy up; to clean up; to polish ‖ *ref* to be dressed up; to become polished

**ripulita** *f*—**dare una ripulita a** to give a lick and a promise to; **fare una ripulita** (fig) to clean house

**ripulsi•vo -va** *adj* repulsive

**riquadrare** *tr* to square; to decorate (*a room*) ‖ *intr* to measure; to square

**riquadro** *m* square

**risac•ca** [s] *f* (**-che**) undertow; backwash

**risàia** [s] *f* rice field

**risalire** [s] §242 *tr* to go up again; to stem (*the tide*); **risalire la corrente** to go upstream ‖ *intr* (ESSERE) to climb again; to reascend; (com) to appreciate; to date back

**risaltare** [s] *tr* to jump again ‖ *intr* (ESSERE & AVERE) to rebound ‖ *intr* to stand out; **far risaltare** to emphasize

**risalto** [s] *m* emphasis; prominence; relief; foil

**risanare** [s] *tr* to heal; to reclaim (*land*); to redevelop (*urban areas*); to reorganize ‖ *intr* (ESSERE) to heal; to improve

**risapére** [s] §243 *tr* to find out

**risapu•to -ta** [s] *adj* well-known

**risarciménto** [s] *m* indemnification, redress

**risarcire** [s] §176 *tr* to indemnify; to compensate

**risata** [s] *f* outburst of laughter

**risatina** [s] *f* chuckle

**riscaldaménto** *m* heating; inflammation

**riscaldare** *tr* to heat; to warm up; to inflame ‖ *ref* to warm up; to go in heat; to perspire; to get excited

**riscaldo** *m* inflammation; prickly heat; padding (*for clothes*)

**riscattare** *tr* to ransom; to redeem ‖ *intr* (ESSERE) to click again (*said, e.g., of a ratchet*)

**riscatto** *m* ransom; redemption

**rischiarare** *tr, intr* (ESSERE) & *ref* to clear, clear up

**rischiare** §287 *tr* to risk ‖ *intr* to run a risk

**rì•schio** *m* (**-schi**) risk

**rischió•so -sa** [s] *adj* risky

**risciacquare** (**risciàcquo**) *tr* to rinse

**risciacquatura** *f* rinse; swill

**risciàcquo** *m* rinsing (*of mouth*); mouthwash

**riscónto** *m* (com) discount

**riscontrare** (**riscóntro**) *tr* to compare, collate; to check; to reply to ‖ *intr* to reply; to tally ‖ *ref* to tally

**riscóntro** *m* comparison; check, control; draft; correspondence; reply; **far riscontro** to correspond; **far riscontro con** to correspond to; **far riscontro di** to check; **mettere a riscontro** to compare; **riscontri** drafts (*of air*); parts (*that fit together*)

**riscoprire** §110 *tr* to rediscover

**riscòssa** *f* insurrection; recovery, reconquest; (mil) counterattack

**riscossióne** *f* collection

**riscrìvere** §250 *tr* to rewrite; to write back

**riscuòtere** §251 *tr* to shake; to wake up; to collect; to get; to redeem ‖ *ref* to wake up; to come to one's senses

**riseccare** [s] §197 (**risécco**) *tr, intr* (ESSERE) & *ref* to dry up

**risecchire** [s] §176 *intr* (ESSERE) & *ref* to dry up

**risentiménto** [s] *m* resentment, pique

**risentire** [s] (**risènto**) *tr* to hear again; to feel ‖ *intr*—**risentire di** to feel the effects of ‖ *ref* to take offense; to wake up; to come to one's senses; (telp) to talk again; **a risentirci!** (telp) until we talk again!; **risentirsi con** to resent (*a person*); **risentirsi di** to feel the effects of; **risentirsi per** to resent (*an act*)

**risenti•to -ta** [s] *adj* heard again; resentful; strong; swift; incisive

**riserbare** [s] (**risèrbo**) *tr* var of **riservare**

**risèrbo** [s] *m* var of **risèrvo**

**risèrva** [s] *f* preservation; exclusive rights; preserve; reserve; supply; backlog; reservation; circumspection; vintage

**riservare** [s] (**risèrvo**) *tr* to reserve

**riservatézza** [s] *f* reservedness

**riserva•to -ta** [s] *adj* reserved; private; classified

**riservista** [s] *m* (**-sti**) reservist

**risèrvo** [s] *m* discretion

**risguardo** *m* end paper

**risièdere** [s] *intr* to reside

**risma** *f* ream; (fig) type

**riso** [s] *m* rice ‖ *m* (**risa** *fpl*) laugh; laughter; jest; cheer; (lit) smile

**risolare** [s] §257 *tr* to resole

**risolino** [s] *m* smile; giggle

risollevare [s] (risollèvo) *tr* to raise again; to lift || *ref* to rise
risolutézza [s] *f* resoluteness
risolu·to -ta [s] *adj* resolved, determined
risoluzióne [s] *f* resolution; resolve; dissolution
risòlvere [s] §256 (*pret ind* risolvéi or risolvètti or risòlsi; *pp* risòlto) *tr* to resolve; to solve; to dissolve; to persuade || *ref* to dissolve; to resolve
risolvìbile [s] *adj* solvable
risonante [s] *adj* resounding
risonanza [s] *f* resonance; (fig) sensation
risonare [s] §257 *tr* to ring again; (lit) to repeat || *intr* (ESSERE & AVERE) to resonate; to resound; to ring again; to echo
risórgere [s] §258 *intr* (ESSERE) to rise again; to revive, to come back to life; to recover
risorgiménto [s] *m* renaissance; resurgence || Risorgimento *m* Risorgimento
risórsa [s] *f* resource
risór·to -ta [s] *adj* arisen; reborn
risòtto [s] *m* risotto, rice cooked with broth
risparmiare §287 *tr* to save; to spare
rispàr·mio *m* (-mi) saving; sparing; savings; risparmi savings; senza risparmio lavishly
rispecchiare §287 (rispècchio) *tr* to reflect
rispedire §176 *tr* to send back; to forward; to reship
rispedizióne *f* reshipment
rispettàbile *adj* respectable
rispettare (rispètto) *tr* to respect; farsi rispettare to command respect; rispettare sé stesso to have self-respect
rispetti·vo -va *adj* respective
rispètto *m* respect; observance; restriction (*e.g.*, *in building*); comparison; regard; con rispetto parlando excuse the word; di rispetto (naut) spare (*e.g.*, *parts*); rispetti regards; rispetto di sé medesimo self-respect; rispetto umano fear of what people will say
rispettó·so -sa [s] *adj* respectful; respectable (*distance*)
risplendènte *adj* resplendent
risplèndere §281 *intr* (ESSERE & AVERE) to shine
rispóndere §238 *tr* to answer; risponder picche (coll) to say no || *intr* to answer; rispondere a to answer (*e.g.*, *a letter*); rispondere con un cenno del capo to nod assent; rispondere di to be responsible for; rispondere in to face, overlook
risposare (rispòso) *tr* & *ref* to marry again, remarry
rispósta *f* answer, reply, response
rissa *f* scuffle, brawl
rissó·so -sa [s] *adj* quarrelsome
ristabilire §176 *tr* to reestablish || *ref* to recover
ristagnare *tr* to tin; to solder || *intr* to stagnate
ristampa *f* reprint

ristampare *tr* to reprint
ristorante *m* restaurant
ristorare (ristòro) *tr* & *ref* to refresh
ristora·tóre -trice *adj* refreshing || *m* restaurant
ristòro *m* refreshment; compensation
ristrettézza *f* narrowness; scarcity; ristrettezza d'idee narrow-mindedness
ristrét·to -ta *adj* narrow; limited; in straitened circumstances; concentrated, condensed (*e.g.*, *broth*)
ristrutturazióne *f* restructuring
risùc·chio [s] *m* (-chi) whirlpool
risultante [s] *adj* resulting || *m* & *f* resultant; (phys) resultant
risultare [s] *intr* (ESSERE) to result; to prove to be, turn out to be; to appear
risultato [s] *m* result
risurrezióne [s] *f* resurrection
risuscitare [s] (risùscito) *tr* to resurrect; to revive || *intr* to be resurrected; to be revived
risvegliare §280 (risvéglio) *tr* & *ref* to awaken; to reawaken
risvé·glio *m* (-gli) awakening, reawakening
risvòlto *m* cuff; lapel; inside flap (*of book*); minor aspect (*of a question*)
ritagliare §280 *tr* to cut again; to clip; to trim
rità·glio *m* (-gli) clipping (*of paper*); scrap (*of meat*); cutting (*of fabric*); bit (*of time*); al ritaglio retail
ritappezzare (ritappézzo) *tr* to repaper
ritardare *tr* to delay; to slow down, retard; || *intr* to tarry; to be late; to be slow (*said of a watch*)
ritardatà·rio -ria *mf* (-ri -rie) latecomer; (com) delinquent
ritardo *m* delay; retard; lateness; essere in ritardo to be late
ritégno *m* reservation; discretion; senza ritegno shamelessly
ritemprare (ritèmpro) *tr* to temper again; to invigorate || *ref* to harden
ritenére §271 *tr* to retain; to hold; to withhold; to believe, think || *ref* to restrain oneself; to consider oneself; to be considered
ritentare (ritènto) *tr* to try again; (law) to retry
ritirare *tr* to withdraw; to pay (*a note*); to throw back; to shoot again; to accept delivery of; to take back (*a promise*) || *intr* to shrink || *ref* to shrink; to withdraw; to fall back, retreat; to retire
ritirata *f* toilet; (mil) retreat
ritiro *m* withdrawal; retreat; retirement; shrinkage; (metallurgy) shrinking
ritma·to -ta *adj* measured (*step*)
ritmi·co -ca *adj* (-ci -che) rhythmic(al)
ritmo *m* rhythm; a ritmo serrato at a quick pace
rito *m* rite; (fig) ritual, ceremony; di rito customary
ritoccare §197 (ritócco) *tr* to retouch; to brush up
ritóc·co *m* (-chi) retouch; improvement; change

**ritòrcere** §272 *tr* to twist, twine; to wring; to retort

**ritornare (ritórno)** *tr* to return, give back ‖ *intr* (ESSERE) to return, go back, come back; **ritornare in sé** to come back to one's senses

**ritornèllo** *m* refrain; chorus (*of song*)

**ritórno** *m* return; reoccurrence; **di ritorno** reoccurring; **essere di ritorno** to be back; **far ritorno** to return; **ritorno di fiamma** backfire

**ritòr·to -ta** *adj* twisted ‖ *m* twist

**ritrarre** §273 *tr* to retract; to draw; to portray ‖ *intr*—**ritrarre da** to look like ‖ *ref* to retreat; to portray oneself

**ritrasméttere** §198 *tr* (rad, telv) to retransmit, rebroadcast

**ritrattare** *tr* to treat again; to retract; (coll) to portray ‖ *ref* to recant

**ritrattazióne** *f* retraction

**ritratti·sta** *mf* (-sti -ste) portrait painter

**ritratto** *m* portrait, picture; photograph; **ritratto parlante** spit and image

**ritri·to -ta** *adj* (fig) stale, trite

**ritrósa** [s] *f* (coll) cowlick

**ritrosìa** [s] *f* coyness, shyness

**ritró·so -sa** [s] *adj* coy, shy; **a ritroso** backwards ‖ *f* see **ritrosa**

**ritrovare (ritròvo)** *tr* to discover; to find; to regain; to meet again ‖ *ref* to meet again; to find oneself; to find one's bearings; **non ritrovarcisi** to be out of sorts

**ritrovato** *m* discovery, find

**ritròvo** *m* meeting; nightspot; **ritrovo estivo** summer resort; **ritrovo notturno** night club

**rìt·to -ta** *adj* upright; straight; right ‖ *m* face (*of medal*); prop; (sports) post ‖ *f* (lit) right hand

**rituale** *adj* & *m* ritual

**riunióne** *f* reunion; meeting; assembly; **riunione alla sommità** summit conference

**riunire** §176 *tr* to assemble; to reunite; to reconcile ‖ *ref* to gather together; to meet; to be reunited; to rally

**riuscire** §277 *intr* (ESSERE) to go out again; to turn out, turn out to be; to lead (*said, e.g., of a door*); to succeed; **riuscire a** + *inf* to succeed in + *ger* ‖ *impers*—**riesce** (with *dat*) **di** + *inf* to succeed in + *ger*, e.g., **non gli è riuscito di farsi ricevere** he did not succeed in being received

**riuscita** *f* success; result; outlet

**riva** *f* shore; bank; (naut) board

**rivale** *adj* & *mf* rival

**rivaleggiare** §290 (**rivaléggio**) *intr* to compete; **rivaleggiare con** to rival

**rivalére** §278 *ref*—**rivalersi di** to use; **rivalersi su qlcu** to resort to s.o. for compensation; to fall back on s.o., to have recourse to s.o.

**rivali·tà** *f* (-tà) rivalry

**rivalsa** *f* compensation; revenge; (com) recourse

**rivalutare (rivàluto** & **rivaluto)** *tr* to revalue

**rivalutazióne** *f* reassessment

**rivangare** §209 *tr* to rake up; to mull over ‖ *intr* to reminisce

**rivedére** §279 *tr* to see again; to review; to check; to reread; to revise; to read (*proof*) ‖ *ref* to see one another; **a rivederci!** good-bye!, au revoir!

**rivedìbile** *adj* deferred (*for draft*)

**rivelare (rivélo)** *tr* to reveal; to detect; (phot) to develop

**rivela·tóre -trice** *adj* revealing ‖ *m* (phot) developer; (rad) detector; **rivelatore di mine** mine detector

**rivelazióne** *f* revelation

**rivéndere** §281 *tr* to resell; (fig) to surpass

**rivendicare** §197 (**rivéndico**) *tr* to demand; to claim

**rivendicazióne** *f* demand; claim

**rivéndita** *f* resale; shop; **rivendita sali e tabacchi** cigar store

**rivendi·tóre -trice** *mf* seller, dealer, retailer

**rivendùgliolo** *m* peddler; huckster

**rivèrbero** *m* reverberation; reflection; glare; echo

**riverènte** *adj* reverent

**riverènza** *f* reverence; curtsy, bow

**riverire** §176 *tr* to revere; to pay one's respects to

**riversare (rivèrso)** *tr* to pour again; to transfer ‖ *ref* to overflow

**rivèr·so -sa** *adj* on one's back

**rivestiménto** *m* coating; covering; lining

**rivestire (rivèsto)** *tr* to dress again; to coat; to line; to cover; to wear; to have (*importance*); to hold (*a rank*) ‖ *ref* to get dressed again; to wear; to be covered

**rivièra** *f* coast ‖ **Riviera** *f* Riviera

**riviera·sco -sca** *adj* (-schi -sche) coastal; riverside

**rivìncere** §285 *tr* to win back

**rivìncita** *f* revenge; return match; **prendersi la rivincita** to get even

**rivista** *f* review; parade; magazine, journal; revue; proofreading

**rivivere** §286 *tr* to relive ‖ *intr* (ESSERE) to live again; to revive

**rivo** *m* (lit) rivulet, brook

**rivolare (rivólo)** *intr* (ESSERE & AVERE) to fly again

**rivolére** §288 *tr* to want back

**rivòlgere** §289 *tr* to turn again; to revolve; to overturn; to train (*a weapon*); to address; to deter ‖ *ref* to turn; to turn around; **rivolgersi a** to apply to

**rivolgiménto** *m* turn; revolution; upheaval

**rivòlta** *f* revolt; cuff

**rivoltante** *adj* revolting

**rivoltare (rivòlto)** *tr* to overturn; to turn inside out; to toss (*salad*); to upset ‖ *ref* to turn around; to revolt; to toss

**rivoltèlla** *f* revolver; spray gun

**rivoltellata** *f* revolver shot

**rivoltó·so -sa** [s] *adj* rebellious ‖ *m* rioter; rebel

**rivoluzionare (rivoluzióno)** *tr* to revolutionize

**rivoluzionà·rio** *-ria adj & mf* (*-ri -rie*) revolutionary
**rivoluzióne** *f* revolution
**rizza** *f* (naut) rigging
**rizzare** *tr* to raise; to hoist; to pay (*attention*); to build; (naut) to lash || *ref* to rise; to bristle (*said of hair*); to rear up (*said of a horse*)
**ròba** *f* things, stuff; property
**robìnia** *f* locust tree
**robivèc·chi** *m* (-chi) junk dealer
**robu·sto** *-sta adj* robust; burly
**róc·ca** *f* (-che) distaff
**ròc·ca** *f* (-che) fortress
**roccafòrte** *f* (rocchefòrti) stronghold
**rocchétto** *m* spool; reel; coil; roll (*of film*); pinion, rear sprocket wheel; (eccl) rochet; **rocchetto d'accensione** ignition coil; **rocchetto d'induzione** induction coil
**ròc·cia** *f* (-ce) rock; crag; cliff
**rocció·so** *-sa* [s] *adj* rocky
**ròco** *-ca adj* (-chi -che) hoarse; (poet) faint
**rodàg·gio** *m* (-gi) breaking in, running in; adjustment period (*to a new situation*); **in rodaggio** (aut) being run in
**Ròdano** *m* Rhone
**rodare** (**ròdo**) *tr* to break in; (aut) to run in
**ródere** §239 *tr* to gnaw; to bite; to corrode || *ref* to worry, to fret
**Ròdi** *f* Rhodes
**rodì·o** *m* (-i) gnawing
**rodi·tóre** *-trice adj* gnawing || *mf* rodent
**rodomónte** *m* braggart
**rogare** §209 (**rògo**) *tr* to draw up (*a contract*); (law) to request
**rògito** *m* (law) instrument, deed
**rógna** *f* mange; itch
**rognóne** *m* (culin) kidney
**rognó·so** *-sa* [s] *adj* scabby, mangy
**rò·go** *m* (-ghi) pyre; stake
**rollì·o** *m* (-i) roll (*of ship*)
**Róma** *f* Rome
**romané·sco** *-sca adj* (-schi -sche) Roman (*dialect*)
**Romanìa, la** Rumania
**romàni·co** *-ca adj & m* (-ci -che) Romanesque
**roma·no** *-na adj & mf* Roman; **pagare alla romana** to go Dutch
**romanticismo** *m* romanticism
**romànti·co** *-ca* (-ci -che) *adj* romantic || *mf* romanticist
**romanza** *f* romance; ballad
**romanzare** *tr* to fictionalize
**romanzé·sco** *-sca adj* (-schi -sche) romantic; of chivalry; novelistic
**romanzière** *m* novelist
**roman·zo** *-za adj* Romance (*language*) || *m* novel; story; romance; fiction; **romanzi** fiction; **romanzo a fumetti** comic strip; comic book; **romanzo d'appendice** serial story, feuilleton; **romanzo giallo** whodunit; **romanzo rosa** love story
**rombare** (**rómbo**) *intr* to thunder
**rómbo** *m* thunder, roar
**romè·no** *-na adj & mf* Rumanian

**romì·to** *-ta adj* (lit) lonely || *m* (coll) hermit
**rómpere** §240 *tr* to break; to bust; **rompere la testa a** to annoy, pester || *intr* to overflow; to be wrecked; to break; **rompere in pianto** to burst out crying || *ref* to fly to pieces; **rompersi la testa** to rack one's brains
**rompicapo** *m* annoyance; puzzle; jigsaw puzzle
**rompicòllo** *m* madcap; **a rompicollo** headlong, rashly; at breakneck speed
**rompighiàc·cio** *m* (-cio) icebreaker; ice pick
**rompiscàto·le** *m* (-le) bore, pest
**roncì·glio** *m* (-gli) (poet) hook
**róncola** *f* pruning hook
**rónda** *f* patrol; beat (*of policeman*)
**rondèlla** *f* (mach) washer
**róndine** *f* swallow
**rondóne** *m* European swift
**ronfare** (**rónfo**) *intr* (coll) to snore; (coll) to purr
**ronzare** [dz] (**rónzo**) *intr* to buzz; to hum
**ronzino** [dz] *m* jade, nag
**ronzì·o** [dz] *m* (-i) buzzing; humming
**ròsa** *adj invar & m* pink || *f* rose; group; rosette; **rosa dei venti** compass card; **rosa del Giappone** (bot) camelia; **rosa delle Alpi** (bot) rhododendron; **rosa di tiro** (mil) dispersion
**ro·sàio** *m* (-sài) rosebush
**rosà·rio** *m* (-ri) rosary; **recitare il rosario** to count one's beads
**rosa·to** *-ta adj* rosy
**ròse·o** *-a adj* rosy
**roséto** *m* rose garden
**rosétta** *f* rosette; hard roll; (mach) washer
**rosicanti** [s] *mpl* rodents
**rosicchiare** [s] §287 *tr* to gnaw; to pick (*a bone*); to bite (*one's fingernails*)
**rosmarino** *m* (bot) rosemary
**rosolare** (**ròsolo**) *tr* (culin) to brown
**rosolìa** *f* German measles
**rosóne** *m* (archit) rosette; (archit) rose window
**ròspo** *m* toad; ugly person; unsociable person; **ingoiare un rospo** to swallow a bitter pill
**rossa·stro** *-stra adj* reddish
**rossétto** *m* rouge; **rossetto per le labbra** lipstick
** rós·so** *-sa adj* red; red-headed; Red; **diventare rosso** to blush || *mf* redhead; Red (*Communist*) || *m* red
**rossóre** *m* redness; blush
**rosticcerìa** *f* grill; rotisserie
**rotàbile** *adj* open to vehicular traffic (*road*); (rr) rolling (*stock*) || *f* road open to vehicular traffic
**rotàia** *f* rail; rut; **uscire dalle rotaie** to jump the track; (fig) to go astray
**rotare** §257 *tr & intr* to rotate; to circle
**rotativa** *f* (typ) rotary press
**rotazióne** *f* rotation
**roteare** (**ròteo**) *tr* to roll (*the eyes*); to flourish (*a sword*) || *intr* to circle
**rotèlla** *f* small wheel; caster; roller; kneecap; disk (*of ski pole*); **gli**

manca una rotella he has a screw loose

**rotocal·co** m (-chi) rotogravure

**rotolare** (ròtolo ) tr & intr (ESSERE) to roll || ref to turn over; to wallow

**ròtolo** m roll; bolt; coil; **a rotoli** to rack and ruin

**rotolóne** m tumble; **a rotoloni** falling down; to rack and ruin

**rotón·do** -da adj round; rotund || f rotunda; terrace

**rótta** f break; rout; (aer, naut) course; **a rotta di collo** at breakneck speed; **mettere in rotta** to rout

**rottame** m fragment; wreck; **rottami** scraps, debris; wreckage; **rottami di ferro** scrap iron

**rót·to** -ta adj broken; shattered; inured || m break, tear; **e rotti** odd, e.g., **duecento e rotti** two hundred odd; **per il rotto della cuffia** hardly; just about || f see **rotta**

**rottura** f break; breakage; rupture; breakdown (of relations); crack

**ròtula** f kneecap

**rovèllo** m (lit) anger

**rovènte** adj red-hot

**róvere** m & f oak tree || m oak (lumber)

**rovè·scia** f (-sce) cuff; **alla rovescia** inside out; upside down; the wrong way

**rovesciaménto** m upset; overturn

**rovesciare** §128 (rovèscio) tr to overturn; to upset; to throw back (one's head); to spill (liquid); to pour; to hurl (insults); to turn inside out || intr to throw up || ref to spill; to pour; to upset

**rovè·scio** -scia (-sci -sce) adj reverse; inverse; inside out; upside down; backwards || m reverse; wrong side; downpour; upset; (com) crash; (tennis) backhand; **a rovescio** upside down; backwards || f see **rovescia**

**rovéto** m bramble; brier patch

**rovina** f ruin; blight; **andare in rovina** to go to ruin; **mandare in rovina** to ruin; **rovine** ruins

**rovinare** tr to ruin || intr (ESSERE) to collapse || ref to go to ruin

**rovinì·o** m (-i) clatter; crash

**rovinó·so** -sa [s] adj ruinous

**rovistare** tr to rummage through

**róvo** m bramble

**ròzza** [ddzz] f nag

**róz·zo** -za [ddzz] adj rough; coarse

**ruba** f—**andare a ruba** to sell like hotcakes; **mettere a ruba** to plunder

**rubacchiare** §287 tr to pilfer

**rubacuò·ri** (-ri) adj ravishing || m ladykiller || f vamp

**rubare** tr to steal; **rubare a man salva** to pillage, loot || intr to steal; **rubare sul peso** to give short measure

**ruberìa** f thieving, stealing

**rubicón·do** -da adj rubicund

**rubinétto** m faucet; cock

**rubino** m ruby; jewel (of watch)

**rubiz·zo** -za adj well-preserved (person)

**rubri·ca** f (-che) title, heading; directory; (journ) section

**rude** adj (lit) rough; (lit) rude

**rùdere** m ruin

**rudimentale** adj rudimentary

**rudiménto** m rudiment

**ruffia·no** -na mf go-between || m pimp, panderer || f bawd, procuress

**ru·ga** f (-ghe) wrinkle; (bot) rocket

**rùggine** f rust; ill-will; (bot) blight

**rugginó·so** -sa [s] adj rusty

**ruggire** §176 tr & intr to roar

**ruggito** m roar

**rugiada** f dew

**rugó·so** -sa [s] adj wrinkled, wrinkly

**rullàg·gio** m (-gi) (aer) taxiing

**rullare** tr to roll || intr to roll; to taxi

**rullì·o** m (-i) roll; rub-a-dub

**rullo** m roll; platen (of typewriter); pin (in tenpins); **rullo compressore** road roller

**rumè·no** -na adj & mf var of **romeno**

**ruminare** (rùmino) tr & intr to ruminate

**rumóre** m noise; rumor; ado; **far molto rumore** to create a stir

**rumoreggiare** §290 (rumoréggio) intr to rumble

**rumoró·so** -sa [s] adj noisy; rumbling; controversial

**ruolino** m roster

**ruòlo** m roll; role; list; **di ruolo** regular, full-time; **fuori ruolo** temporary, part-time

**ruòta** f wheel; paddle wheel; revolving server (in convent); **a quattro ruote** four-wheel; **dar la ruota** to sharpen; **esser l'ultima ruota del carro** to be the fifth wheel to a wagon; **fare la ruota** to spread its tail, strut (said, e.g., of a peacock); to turn cartwheels (said, e.g., of an acrobat); **ruota dentata** cog, cogwheel; **ruota idraulica** water wheel; **seguire a ruota** to follow closely

**rupe** f cliff

**rurale** adj rural, farm, farmer

**ruscèllo** m brook

**ruspa** f road grader

**ruspante** m barnyard chicken

**russare** intr to snore

**Rùssia, la** Russia

**rus·so** -sa adj & mf Russian

**rustica·no** -na adj rustic, boorish

**rùsti·co** -ca (-ci -che) adj rustic; coarse || m tool shed; cottage; (lit) peasant

**rutilante** adj (lit) shiny

**ruttare** tr (lit) to belch || intr (vulg) to belch

**rutto** m (vulg) belch

**ruttóre** m (elec) contact breaker

**ruvidézza** f or **ruvidi·tà** f (-tà) coarseness; roughness

**rùvi·do** -da adj coarse; rough

**ruzzare** [ddzz] intr to romp

**ruzzolare** (rùzzolo) tr to roll || intr (ESSERE) to tumble down; to roll

**ruzzolóne** m tumble; **a ruzzoloni** tumbling down

**S**

**S, s** [ˈɛsse] *m & f* seventeenth letter of the Italian alphabet

**s-** *pref* dis-, e.g., **sleale** disloyal; e.g., **sconto** discount; un-, e.g., **scatenare** to unchain, unleash

**sàbato** *m* Saturday; (*of Jews*) Sabbath; **sabato inglese** Saturday afternocn off

**sabbàti·co -ca** *adj* (*-ci -che*) sabbatical

**sàbbia** *f* sand; **sabbia mobile** quicksand

**sabbiatura** *f* sand bath; sandblast

**sabbièra** *f* (rr) sandbox

**sabbió·so -sa** [s] *adj* sandy

**sabotàg·gio** *m* (*-gi*) sabotage

**sabotare** (**sabòto**) *tr* to sabotage

**sac·ca** *f* (*-che*) bag; satchel; (mil) pocket; **sacca d'aria** (aer) air pocket; **sacca da viaggio** traveling bag; duffel bag

**saccarina** *f* saccharine

**saccènte** *mf* wiseacre, know-it-all

**saccheggiare** §290 (**sacchéggio**) *tr* to pillage, plunder

**sacchég·gio** *m* (*-gi*) pillage, plunder

**sacchétto** *m* little bag, pouch

**sac·co** *m* (*-chi*) bag; sack; sackcloth; pouch; (boxing) punching bag; (fig) heap, lot; **fare sacco** to sag; **mettere a sacco** to sack; **mettere nel sacco** to outwit; **sacco alpino** knapsack; **sacco a pelo** or **a piuma** sleeping bag; **sacco postale** mailbag

**saccòc·cia** *f* (*-ce*) (coll) pocket

**sacerdòte** *m* priest; (fig) devotee

**sacerdotéssa** *f* priestess

**sacerdòzio** *m* priesthood; ministry

**sacramentale** *adj* sacramental; (joc) habitual, ritual

**sacraménto** *m* sacrament

**sacrà·rio** *m* (*-ri*) memorial; sanctuary, shrine

**sacrestìa** *f* var of **sagrestìa**

**sacrificare** §197 (**sacrìfico**) *tr* to sacrifice; to waste; to force ‖ *ref* to sacrifice oneself

**sacrifì·cio** *m* (*-ci*) sacrifice

**sacrilè·gio** *m* (*-gi*) sacrilege

**sacrìle·go -ga** *adj* (*-ghi -ghe*) sacrilegious

**sacri·sta** *m* (*-sti*) sexton

**sacristìa** *f* var of **sagrestìa**

**sa·cro -cra** *adj* sacred

**sacrosan·to -ta** *adj* sacrosanct; sacred (*truth*)

**sàdi·co -ca** (*-ci -che*) *adj* sadistic ‖ *mf* sadist

**sadismo** *m* sadism

**saétta** *f* stroke of lightning; hand (*of watch*); (mach) bit; (lit) arrow

**saettare** (**saétto**) *tr* to shoot; **saettare sguardi a** to look daggers at

**saettóne** *m* (archit) strut

**sagace** *adj* sagacious, shrewd

**sagà·cia** *f* (*-cie*) sagacity

**saggézza** *f* wisdom

**saggiare** §290 *tr* to assay; to test; (dial) to taste

**saggia·tóre -trice** *mf* assayer ‖ *m* assay balance

**saggina** *f* sorghum

**sàg·gio -gia** (*-gi -ge*) *adj* wise ‖ *m* sage; assay; sample; proof; theme; test; rate (*of interest*); display; **di saggio** examination (*copy*)

**saggi·sta** *mf* (*-sti -ste*) essayist

**sagittària** *f* (bot) arrowhead

**sagittà·rio** *m* (*-ri*) (obs) archer ‖ **Sagittario** *m* Sagittarius

**sàgola** *f* (naut) halyard

**sàgoma** *f* outline; target; model, pattern; (joc) character

**sagomare** (**sàgomo**) *tr* to outline; to mold; to shape

**sagomato** *m* billboard

**sagra** *f* anniversary consecration (*of church*); festival

**sagrato** *m* elevated square in front of a church; churchyard; (coll) curse

**sagrestano** *m* sexton, sacristan

**sagrestìa** *f* sacristy, vestry

**sàia** *f* serge

**sàio** *m* (**sài**) habit (*of monk or nun*); doublet; frock coat

**sala** *f* axletree; hall, room; (bot) cattail, reed mace; **sala da ballo** dance hall; **sala da pranzo** dining room; **sala d'aspetto** waiting room; anteroom; **sala operatoria** operating room

**salac·ca** *f* (*-che*) (coll) sardine; (coll) shad

**salace** *adj* salacious; pungent

**salamandra** *f* salamander

**salame** *m* salami

**salamelèc·co** *m* (*-chi*) salaam

**salamòia** *f* brine

**salare** *tr* to salt; (coll) to cut (*school*)

**salaria·to -ta** *adj* wage-earning ‖ *m* wage earner

**salà·rio** *m* (*-ri*) pay, wages

**salassare** *tr* to bleed

**salasso** *m* bloodletting

**sala·to -ta** *adj* salted; salty; dear, expensive; (fig) sharp ‖ *m* salt pork; cold cuts ‖ *f* salting

**salda** *f* starch solution (*used in laundering*)

**saldacón·ti** *m* (*-ti*) bookkeeping department; credit department; ledger; bookkeeping machine

**saldare** *tr* to solder; to set (*a bone*); to weld; to pay, settle ‖ *ref* to knit (*said of a bone*); (lit) to heal

**saldatóre** *m* solderer; welder; soldering iron

**saldatura** *f* soldering; setting (*of bones*); joint; continuity; **saldatura autogena** welding

**saldézza** *f* firmness

**sal·do -da** *adj* firm; valid (*reason*); flawless ‖ *m* balance; clearance sale; job lot; payment; **saldi** remnants ‖ *f* see **salda**

**saldobrasatura** *f* soldering

**sale** *m* salt; wit; (lit) sea; **restare di sale** to be dumbfounded; **sale inglese** Epsom salts; **sali aromatici** smelling salts; **sali da bagno** bath salts

**salgèmma** *f* rock salt

sàlice *m* willow tree; **salice piangente** weeping willow

**salicilato** *m* salicylate

**saliènte** *adj* projecting; (fig) salient ‖ *m* projection

**salièra** *f* saltcellar, salt shaker

**salini·tà** *f* (**-tà**) salinity

**sali·no -na** *adj* saline; salty ‖ *f* salt bed

**salire** §242 *tr* to climb ‖ *intr* (ESSERE) to climb; to go up; to rise; **salire in** or **su** to get on (*e.g., a train*)

**saliscén·di** *m* (**-di**) latch; **saliscendi** *mpl* ups and downs

**salita** *f* climbing; ascent, rise; slope; **in salita** uphill

**saliva** *f* saliva

**salma** *f* corpse, body

**salma·stro -stra** *adj* briny; saltish ‖ *m*— **sapere di salmastro** to smell or taste salty

**salmerìe** *fpl* wagon train; (mil) supplies

**salmì** *m*—**in salmì** (culin) in a stew

**salmo** *m* psalm

**salmodiare** §287 (**salmòdio**) *intr* to chant, sing hymns, intone

**salmóne** *m* salmon

**salnitro** *m* saltpeter

**Salomóne** *m* Solomon

**salóne** *m* hall; salon, drawing room; (naut) saloon; **salone da barbiere** barber shop; **salone dell'automobile** auto show

**salòtto** *m* drawing room; living room, parlor; reception room

**salpare** *tr* to weigh (*anchor*) ‖ *intr* (ESSERE) to weigh anchor

**salsa** *f* sauce

**salsapariglia** *f* sarsaparilla

**salsèdine** *f* saltiness

**salsìc·cia** *f* (**-ce**) sausage

**salsièra** *f* gravy boat

**sal·so -sa** *adj* salty; saline ‖ *m* saltiness ‖ *f* see **salsa**

**saltabeccare** §197 (**saltabécco**) *intr* to hop

**saltaleóne** *m* coil spring

**saltare** *tr* to jump; to skip; to sauté; (sports) to vault, hurdle; **far saltare** to kick out; to blow up (*e.g., a mine*); **saltare la sbarra** (coll) to go A.W.O.L. ‖ *intr* (ESSERE & AVERE) to jump; to pop off, e.g., **mi è saltato un bottone** one of my buttons has popped off; to blow out (*said of a fuse*); **saltare agli occhi** to be self-evident; **saltare a piè pari** to skip with both feet; **saltar fuori** to pop out (*said of the eyes*); to appear suddenly; **saltare in mente a** to come to the mind of; **saltare il ticchio a** (qlcu) **di** to feel like + *ger*, e.g., **gli è saltato il ticchio di cantare** he felt like singing; **saltare la mosca al naso a** (qlcu) to blow one's top, e.g., **le è saltata la mosca al naso** she blew her top; **saltare per aria** to blow up; **saltare su** to start (*to make a sudden jerk*); **saltare su a** + *inf* to begin suddenly to + *inf*

**salta·tóre -trice** *mf* jumper, hurdler

**saltellare** (**saltèllo**) *intr* to skip, hop

**saltellóni** *adv*—**a saltelloni** skipping, hopping

**saltimban·co** *m* (**-chi**) acrobat, tumbler; mountebank

**salto** *m* jump; leap; fall; skip; (*of animals*) mating; (fig) step; **a salti** skipping, jumping; **al salto** sauté; **fare quattro salti** to dance; **fare un salto** to hop, hurry; **salto a pesce** jackknife (*dive*); **salto coll'asta** pole vaulting; **salto in altezza** high jump; **salto in lunghezza** broad jump; **salto mortale** somersault; **salto nel vuoto** leap in the dark

**saltuà·rio -ria** *adj* (**-ri -rie**) desultory, occasional

**salubre** *adj* salubrious, healthy, healthful

**salume** *m* pork product

**salumerìa** *f* pork butcher shop

**salumiè·re -ra** *mf* pork butcher

**salutare** *adj* healthful ‖ *tr* to greet; to salute; (lit) to proclaim

**salute** *f* health; salvation; safety ‖ *interj* good luck; to your health!; gesundheit!

**saluto** *m* salute; greeting; salutation; **distinti saluti** sincerely yours

**salva** *f* salvo; outburst; **a salve** with blank cartridges, with blanks

**salvacondótto** *m* safe-conduct

**salvada·nàio** *m* (**-nài**) piggy bank

**salvagèn·te** *m* (**-te** & **-ti**) life preserver; fender (*of trolley car*) ‖ *m* (**-te**) safety island

**salvaguardare** *tr* to safeguard

**salvaguàrdia** *f* safeguard

**salvaménto** *m* safety

**salvamotóre** *m* circuit breaker; fuse box

**salvapun·te** *m* (**-te**) pencil cap; tap (*on sole of shoe*)

**salvare** *tr* to save; to spare (*a life*); to rescue ‖ *ref* to save oneself; to be rescued; **si salvi chi può!** every man for himself!

**salvatàg·gio** *m* (**-gi**) rescue

**salvatóre** *m* savior, rescuer ‖ **il Salvatore** the Saviour

**salvazióne** *f* salvation

**salve** *interj* hello!, hail!

**salvézza** *f* salvation; safety

**sàlvia** *f* (bot) sage

**salviétta** *f* napkin; paper napkin; paper towel

**sal·vo -va** *adj* safe; saved; secure ‖ *m*—**mettere in salvo** to put in a safe place; **mettersi in salvo** to reach safety ‖ *f* see **salva** ‖ **salvo** *prep* except; **salvo che** unless; **salvo il vero** unless I am mistaken

**samarita·no -na** *adj* & *mf* Samaritan

**sambu·co** *m* (**-chi**) elder tree

**san** *adj* apocopated and unstressed form of **santo**

**sanàbile** *adj* curable

**sanare** *tr* to heal; to remedy; to reclaim (*land*); to normalize

**sanatò·rio** *m* (**-ri**) sanatorium

**sancire** §176 *tr* to ratify, sanction; to establish

**sàndalo** *m* sandal; sandalwood; flat-bottom boat

**sandolino** *m* canoe, skiff, kayak
**sangue** *m* blood; **agitarsi il sangue** to fret; **all'ultimo sangue** (*duel*) to the death; **al sangue** rare (*meat*); **a sangue freddo** in cold blood; coldblooded; **cavar sangue da una rapa** to draw blood from a stone; **farsi cattivo sangue** to get angry; **il sangue non è acqua** blood is thicker than water; **puro sangue** thoroughbred; **sangue dal naso** nosebleed; **sangue freddo** calmness, composure
**sangui·gno -gna** *adj* blood (*circulation*); bloody; sanguine, ruddy || *m* (lit) color of blood
**sanguinante** *adj* bloody, bleeding
**sanguinare** (**sànguino**) *intr* to bleed; to be rare (*said of meat*)
**sanguinà·rio -ria** *adj* (**-ri -rie**) sanguinary
**sanguinó·so -sa** [s] *adj* bloody; bleeding; (fig) stinging
**sanguisu·ga** [s] *f* (**-ghe**) leech
**sani·tà** *f* (**-tà**) health; healthfulness; soundness (*of body*); sanity; health department
**sanità·rio -ria** (**-ri -rie**) *adj* health; sanitary || *m* physician
**sa·no -na** *adj* healthy; sound; **sano e salvo** safe and sound
**sant'** *adj* apocopated form of **santo** and **santa**
**santa** *f* saint
**santabàrbara** *f* (**santebàrbare**) (nav) powder magazine
**santarellina** *f* goody-goody girl
**santificare** §197 (**santìfico**) *tr* to sanctify
**santìssi·mo -ma** *adj* most holy || *m* Eucharist
**santi·tà** *f* (**-tà**) sanctity, holiness; sainthood, saintliness
**san·to -ta** *adj* saintly, holy; sacred; blessed, livelong, e.g., **tutto il santo giorno** all the livelong day || *m* saint; name day; (fig) someone || *f* see **santa**
**santorég·gia** *f* (**-ge**) (bot) savory
**santuà·rio** *m* (**-ri**) sanctuary
**sanzionare** (**sanzióno**) *tr* to sanction; to ratify
**sanzióne** *f* sanction
**sapére** *m* knowledge; **sapere fare** savoirfaire || §243 *tr* to know; to find out; to know how to; **far sapere** to let know; **saperla lunga** to know a thing or two; **un certo non so che** a certain something, something vague || *intr*— **sapere di** to know; to taste; to smell; to smack of; **mi sa che** I think that; **non voler più saperne di** to not want to have anything to do with; **sapere male** (with *dat*) to feel sorry, e.g., **gli sa male** he feels sorry || *ref*—**che io mi sappia** as far as I know
**sàpido -da** *adj* savory; witty
**sapiènte** *adj* wise; talented; trained (*dog*) || *m* wise man
**sapientó·ne -na** *mf* wiseacre, know-it-all
**sapiènza** *f* wisdom; knowledge
**saponària** *f* (bot) soapwort

**saponata** *f* soapsuds; lather; (fig) soft soap
**sapóne** *m* soap; **sapone da toletta** toilet soap; **sapone per la barba** shaving soap
**saponétta** *f* cake of soap
**saponière** *m* soap maker
**saponifi·cio** *m* (**-ci**) soap factory
**saponó·so -sa** [s] *adj* soapy
**sapóre** *m* taste; savor; flavor
**saporire** §176 *tr* to savor
**saporitaménte** *adv* heartily; soundly
**sapori·to -ta** *adj* tasty; flavorful; salty; expensive
**saporó·so -sa** [s] *adj* savory; witty
**saputèl·lo -la** *adj* cocksure || *m* smart aleck
**sarac·co** *m* (**-chi**) hand saw
**saracè·no -na** *adj* Saracen, Saracenic || *m* Saracen; quintain
**saraciné·sca** *f* (**-sche**) metal shutter (*of store*); sluice gate; (hist) portcullis
**sarcasmo** *m* sarcasm
**sarcàsti·co -ca** *adj* (**-ci -che**) sarcastic
**sarchiare** §287 *tr* to weed
**sarchia·tóre -trice** *mf* weeder || *f* (agr) cultivator
**sarchièllo** *m* weeding hoe
**sàr·chio** *m* (**-chi**) hoe
**sarcòfa·go** *m* (**-gi** & **-ghi**) sarcophagus
**sarcràuti** *mpl* sauerkraut
**Sardégna, la** Sardinia
**sardèlla** *f* pilchard; sardine
**sardina** *f* pilchard; sardine
**sar·do -da** *adj* & *mf* Sardinian
**sardòni·co -ca** *adj* (**-ci -che**) sardonic
**sarménto** *m* vine shoot, running stem
**sarta** *f* dressmaker
**sàrtie** *fpl* (naut) shrouds
**sarto** *m* tailor
**sartorìa** *f* dressmaker's shop; tailor shop; dressmaking; tailoring
**sassaiòla** *f* shower of stones
**sassata** *f* blow with a stone
**sasso** *m* stone, rock; pebble; (poet) tombstone; **di sasso** stony; **restare di sasso** to be taken aback; **tirare sassi in colombaia** to cut one's nose to spite one's face
**sassòfono** *m* saxophone
**sàssone** *adj* & *mf* Saxon
**sassó·so -sa** [s] *adj* stony
**Sàtana** *m* Satan
**satanasso** *m* Satan; devil
**satèllite** *m* satellite
**sa·tin** *m* (**-tin**) sateen
**satinare** *tr* to gloss
**sàtira** *f* satire
**satireggiare** §290 (**satiréggio**) *tr* to satirize, lampoon || *intr* to compose satires
**satìri·co -ca** *adj* (**-ci -che**) satiric(al) || *m* satirist
**sàtiro** *m* satyr
**satól·lo -la** *adj* sated, full
**saturare** *tr* (**sàturo**) *tr* to saturate; to steep; (fig) to fill; (com) to glut (*a market*)
**saturni·no -na** *adj* Saturnian; saturnine
**Saturno** *m* (astr) Saturn
**sàtu·ro -ra** *adj* saturated; (fig) full; (lit) sated

sàu·ro -ra *adj & m* sorrel (*horse*)
Savèrio *m* Xavier
sà·vio -via (-vi -vie) *adj* wise ‖ *m* wise man, sage
savoiar·do -da *adj & mf* Savoyard ‖ *m* ladyfinger
saxòfono *m* saxophone
saziare §287 *tr* to satisfy; to cloy, satiate
sazietà *f* satiety, surfeit; **mangiare a sazietà** to eat one's fill
sà·zio -zia *adj* (-zi -zie) sated; full; satisfied
sbaciucchiare §287 (sbaciùcchio) *tr* to kiss again and again ‖ *ref* to neck
sbadatàggine *f* carelessness; oversight
sbada·to -ta *adj* careless; heedless
sbadigliare §280 *intr* to yawn
sbadì·glio *m* (-gli) yawn
sbafa·tóre -trice *mf* sponger
sbafo *m*—a sbafo sponging; **mangiare a sbafo** to sponge
sbagliare §280 *tr* to miss; to mistake; **sbagliarla** to be sadly mistaken ‖ *intr & ref* to be mistaken; to make a mistake
sbaglia·to -ta *adj* wrong; mistaken
sbà·glio *m* (-gli) error, mistake
sbalestrare (sbalèstro) *tr* to fling with the crossbow; to send (*an employee*) far away ‖ *intr* to speak amiss; to ramble; to blunder
sbalestra·to -ta *adj* unbalanced; ill-at-ease
sballare *tr* to unpack; **sballarle grosse** to tell tall tales ‖ *intr* to overbid
sballa·to -ta *adj* unpacked; absurd, wild
sballottare (sballòtto) *tr* to toss
sbalordire §176 *tr* to stun; to amaze; to bewilder ‖ *intr* to lose consciousness; to be dumfounded
sbalorditi·vo -va *adj* amazing
sbalzare *tr* to upset; to send far away; to overthrow; to emboss ‖ *intr* (ESSERE) to bounce
sbalzo *m* leap, jump; climb; embossment, relief; **a sbalzi** by leaps and bounds; **di sbalzo** all of a sudden
sbancare §197 *tr* to clear (*ground*) of rocks; to ruin; (cards) to break (*the bank*)
sbandaménto *m* skid; swerve; disbandment; breaking up; (naut) list
sbandare *tr* to disband; (naut) to cause to list ‖ *intr* to list; to skid; to swerve; to deviate ‖ *ref* to disband; to break up
sbanda·to -ta *adj* disbanded; stray; alienated ‖ *mf* alienated person ‖ *m* straggler ‖ *f* listing (*of ship*); skidding (*of vehicle*); **prendere una sbandata per** to get a crush on
sbandierare (sbandièro) *tr* to wave (*a flag*); to display
sbaragliare §280 *tr* to rout; to crush
sbarà·glio *m*—mettere allo sbaraglio to endanger
sbarazzare *tr* to clear out; to free ‖ *ref*—sbarazzarsi di to get rid of
sbarazzi·no -na *adj* mischievous ‖ *mf* scamp; **alla sbarazzina** cocked, at an angle (*said of a hat*)

sbarbare *tr* to shave; to uproot ‖ *ref* to shave
sbarbatèllo *m* greenhorn, fledgling
sbarcare §197 *tr* to unload; to discharge; to disembark; to pass; to strew (*fodder*); **sbarcare il lunario** to make ends meet ‖ *intr* (ESSERE) to come ashore, land
sbarca·tóio *m* (-tói) landing pier
sbar·co *m* (-chi) unloading; landing
sbarra *f* bar; (typ) dash
sbarraménto *m* barrage; obstacle
sbarrare *tr* to bar; to block (*the way*); to open (*one's eyes*) wide, e.g., **sbarrò gli occhi** he opened his eyes wide
sbarrétta *f* bar; **sbarrette verticali** (typ) parallels
sbatacchiare §287 *tr* to slam; to flap ‖ *intr* to slam
sbatàc·chio *m* (-chi) shore, prop
sbàttere *tr* to flap; to fling; to slam; to beat; to toss; to send away; to make pale; **sbatter fuori** to throw out ‖ *intr* to flap; to slam
sbattighiàc·cio *m* (-cio) cocktail shaker
sbattitóre *m* electric mixer
sbattiuò·va *m* (-va) egg beater
sbattu·to -ta *adj* haggard, downcast
sbavare *tr* to slobber over; (mach) to trim ‖ *intr* to drivel, slobber; to run (*said of colors*)
sbavatura *f* drivel; run (*of colors*); burr (*of metal*); deckle edge; verbosity
sbeccare §197 (sbécco) *tr & ref* to chip
sbeffeggiare §290 (sbefféggio) *tr* to make fun of
sbellicare §197 *ref*—sbellicarsi dalle risa to burst with laughter
sbèrla *f* (coll) slap
sberlèffo *m* scar; grimace; **fare gli sberleffi a** to make faces at
sbevazzare *intr* to guzzle
sbevucchiare §287 *intr* to tipple
sbiadire §176 *tr & intr* (ESSERE) to fade
sbiadi·to -ta *adj* faded; dull
sbiancare §197 *tr* to whiten ‖ *ref* to become white; to pale
sbianchire §176 *tr* (culin) to blanch
sbiè·co -ca (-chi -che) *adj* oblique; **di sbieco** on the bias; **guardare di sbieco** to look askance at ‖ *m* cloth cut diagonally
sbigottire §176 *tr* to terrify, dismay ‖ *intr* (ESSERE) & *ref* to be dismayed
sbilanciare §128 *tr* to unbalance; to upset ‖ *intr* to lose one's balance ‖ *ref* to commit oneself
sbilàn·cio *m* (-ci) disequilibrium; (com) deficit
sbilèn·co -ca *adj* (-chi -che) twisted, crooked
sbirciare §128 *tr* to leer at, ogle; to eye closely
sbir·ro -ra *adj* (coll) smart ‖ *m* (pej) cop
sbizzarrire [ddzz] §176 *tr* to cure the whims of ‖ *ref* to indulge one's whims
sbloccare §197 (sblòcco) *tr* to unblock; to raise the blockade of; to free
sbòbba *f* slop, dishwater
sboccare §197 (sbócco) *tr* to break the

mouth of (*a bottle*); to remove a few drops from (*a bottle*) ‖ *intr* (ESSERE) to flow; to open (*said of a street*); **sboccare in** to turn out to be

**sbocca·to -ta** *adj* foulmouthed; foul (*language*); chipped at the mouth (*said of a bottle*)

**sbocciare** §128 (sbòccio) *intr* (ESSERE) to bud, burgeon, bloom

**sbóc·co** *m* (-chi) outlet; **avere uno sbocco di sangue** to spit blood

**sbocconcellare** (sbocconcèllo) *tr* to nibble at; to chip, nick

**sbollentare** (sbollènto) *tr* to blanch

**sbollire** §176 *intr* to stop boiling; to calm down

**sbolognare** (sbológno) *tr* (coll) to palm off; (coll) to get rid of

**sbòrnia** *f* (coll) drunk, jag; **smaltire la sbornia** to sober up

**sborsare** (sbórso) *tr* to pay out, disburse

**sbórso** *m* disbursement, outlay

**sbottare** (sbòtto) *intr*—**sbottare a + *inf*** to burst out + *ger*

**sbottonare** (sbottóno) *tr* to unbutton ‖ *ref* (fig) to unbosom oneself

**sbozzare** (sbòzzo) *tr* to rough-hew; to sketch, outline

**sbraca·to -ta** *adj* without pants; slovenly; vulgar

**sbracciare** §128 *intr* to gesticulate ‖ *ref* to roll up one's sleeves; to wear sleeveless clothes; to gesticulate; to do one's best

**sbraccia·to -ta** *adj* bare-armed

**sbraitare** (sbràito) *intr* to scream

**sbraitó·ne -na** *mf* bigmouth

**sbranare** *tr* to tear to pieces

**sbrano** *m* tear, rent

**sbrattare** *tr* to clean; to clear

**sbreccare** §197 (sbrécco) *tr* to chip, nick

**sbrecciare** §128 (sbréccio) *tr* to open a gap in

**sbréndolo** *m* tatter, rag

**sbriciolare** (sbrìciolo) *tr* to crumb ‖ *ref* to crumble

**sbrigare** §209 *tr* to transact; to take care of ‖ *ref* to hasten, hurry; **sbrigarsela** to get out of trouble; **sbrigarsi di** to get rid of; **sbrigati!** make it snappy!, hurry up!

**sbrigativ·o -va** *adj* quick, brisk; businesslike

**sbrigliare** §280 *tr* to unbridle; to reduce (*a hernia*); to lance (*an infected wound*) ‖ *ref* to cut loose

**sbrinare** *tr* to defrost

**sbrindella·to -ta** *adj* tattered

**sbrodolare** (sbròdolo) *tr* to soil; (fig) to drag out ‖ *ref* to slobber

**sbrogliare** §280 (sbròglio) *tr* to untangle; to clean up ‖ *ref* to extricate oneself; **sbrogliarsela** to get out of a tight spot

**sbronzare** (sbrónzo) *ref* (coll) to get drunk

**sbruffare** *tr* to squirt out of the mouth; to spatter; to bribe ‖ *intr* to tell tall tales

**sbruffo** *m* sprinkle, squirt; bribe

**sbruffó·ne -na** *mf* braggart

**sbucare** §197 *intr* (ESSERE) to pop out, come out

**sbucciare** §128 *tr* to peel; to skin ‖ *ref* to slough (*said of snakes*); **sbucciarsela** (coll) to goldbrick

**sbucciatura** *f* slight abrasion

**sbudellare** (sbudèllo) *tr* to disembowel ‖ *ref*—**sbudellarsi dalle risa** to burst with laughter, split one's sides laughing

**sbuffare** *tr* & *intr* to puff

**sbuffo** *m* puff; gust (*of wind*); **a sbuffo** puffed (*sleeve*)

**sbullonare** (sbullóno) *tr* to unbolt

**sc-** *pref* dis-, e.g., **sconto** discount; es-, e.g., **scalare** to escalate; ex-, e.g., **scusare** to excuse

**scàbbia** *f* scabies

**sca·bro -bra** *adj* rough; stony; tight (*style*)

**scabró·so -sa** [s] *adj* scabrous

**scacchièra** *f* checkerboard; chessboard

**scacchière** *m* (mil) sector; (obs) checkerboard; exchequer

**scacciaca·ni** *m* & *f* (-ni) toy gun; gun shooting only blanks

**scacciamó·sche** *m* (-sche) fly swatter

**scacciapensiè·ri** *m* (-ri) jew's-harp

**scacciare** §128 *tr* to chase away, drive away; to expel

**scaccino** *m* sexton, sacristan

**scac·co** *m* (-chi) chessman; checker; check; square; **a scacchi** checkered; **dare scacco matto a** to checkmate; **in scacco** or **sotto scacco** in check; **scacchi** chess; **scacco matto** checkmate

**scàccoli** *mpl* cement piles

**scaccomatto** *m* checkmate

**scadènte** *adj* inferior, poor, shoddy

**scadènza** *f* term, maturity; obligation; **a breve scadenza** short-term; **a lunga scadenza** long-term

**scadére** §121 *intr* (ESSERE) to decay, to decline; to fall due; to expire; (naut) to drift

**scafandro** *m* diving suit; **scafandro astronautico** space suit

**scaffale** *m* bookcase; shelf

**scafo** *m* hull

**scagionare** (scagióno) *tr* to exonerate, exculpate

**scàglia** *f* scale (*of fish*); chip; plate (*of medieval armor*); flake (*of soap*); tile (*of slate roof*)

**scagliare** §280 *tr* to hurl, fling, throw; to scale (*fish*) ‖ *ref* to dash, to rush; to flake

**scaglionare** (scaglióno) *tr* to echelon; to stagger (*e.g., payments*)

**scaglióne** *m* terrace (*of mountain*); echelon; scale; **a scaglioni** graded (*e.g., income tax*)

**scala** *f* stairs; ladder; scale; (cards) straight; (rad) dial; **a scale** scaled, graded; **fare le scale** to climb the stairs; **scala a chiocciola** spiral stairway; **scala a gradini** or **a libretto** stepladder; **scala mobile** escalator; (econ) sliding scale; **scala porta** aerial ladder; **scala reale** (poker) straight flush; **su larga scala** large-scale; **su scala nazionale** on a national scale

**scalandróne** *m* (naut) gangway

**scalare** *adj* graded, scaled; gradual ‖ *m* (com) running balance ‖ *tr* to climb, ascend; to scale, grade; to reduce

**scalata** *f* climb, ascent; **dar la scalata a** to climb; to climb up to

**scalcagna•to -ta** *adj* down-at-the-heel

**scalcare** §197 *tr* to slice, carve

**scalciare** §128 *intr* to kick

**scalcina•to -ta** *adj* (*wall or plaster*) that is peeling off; worn-out; down-at-the-heels

**scalda•acqua** *m* (**-acqua**) hot-water heater

**scaldaba•gno** *m* (**-gno**) hot-water heater; **scaldabagno a gas** gas heater

**scaldalèt•to** *m* (**-ti & -to**) bedwarmer

**scaldare** *tr* to warm, warm up; to heat, heat up ‖ *intr* (mach) to become hot ‖ *ref* to warm up; to heat up; **scaldarsi la testa** to get excited

**scaldavivan•de** *m* (**-de**) hot plate

**scaldino** *m* hand warmer

**scalèa** *f* flight of stairs, stairway

**scalèo** *m* stepladder

**scalétta** *f* small ladder; small stairs; (mov) rough draft

**scalfire** §176 *tr* to graze, scratch; to cut (*e.g., glass*)

**scalfittura** *f* graze, scratch

**scalinata** *f* stairway, perron

**scalino** *m* step (*of a stair*); (fig) ladder

**scalmana** *f* chill; flush; **prendere una scalmana per** to take a fancy to

**scalmanare** *ref* to hustle, bustle; to fuss

**scalmana•to -ta** *adj* panting; hotheaded

**scalmo** *m* (naut) oarlock

**scalo** *m* pier, dock; (naut) ways; (naut) port of call; **fare scalo** (naut) to call, stop; (aer) to land; **scalo di alaggio** (naut) slip; **scalo merci** (rr) freight yard; **senza scalo** (aer, naut) nonstop

**scalógna** *f* (coll) bad luck

**scalógno** *m* (bot) scallion

**scalòppa** *f* veal chop

**scaloppina** *f* veal cutlet, scallop

**scalpellare** (**scalpèllo**) *tr* to chisel

**scalpellino** *m* stone cutter

**scalpèllo** *m* chisel; (surg) scalpel; **scalpello a taglio obliquo** skew chisel

**scalpicciare** §128 *tr & intr* to shuffle

**scalpitare** (**scàlpito**) *intr* to paw the ground

**scalpóre** *m* scene; **fare scalpore** to raise a fuss

**scaltrézza** *f* shrewdness, cunning

**scaltrire** §176 *tr* to polish, refine; to sharpen the wits of ‖ *ref* to catch on; to improve

**scal•tro -tra** *adj* shrewd, smart

**scalzare** *tr* to take the shoes or stockings off of; to undermine ‖ *ref* to take off one's shoes or stockings

**scal•zo -za** *adj* barefoot

**scambiare** §287 *tr* to exchange; to mistake ‖ *ref* to exchange (*presents*)

**scambiévole** *adj* mutual

**scàm•bio** *m* (**-bi**) exchange; (rr) switch;

**libero scambio** free trade; **scambio di persona** mistaken identity

**scamicia•to -ta** *adj* in shirt sleeves; extremist ‖ *m* extremist; tunic, waist

**scamoscia•to -ta** *adj* chamois, suede

**scampagnata** *f* excursion, outing

**scampanare** *intr* to peal, chime; to flare (*said of a garment*)

**scampanellare** (**scampanèllo**) *intr* to ring loud and clear

**scampanì•o** *m* (**-i**) toll, peal

**scampare** *tr* to save, rescue; **scamparla bella** to have a narrow escape ‖ *intr* (ESSERE)—**scampare a** to escape from; to take refuge in

**scampo** *m* escape; safety; (zool) Norway lobster; **non c'è scampo** there is no way out

**scàmpolo** *m* remnant; **scampoli di tempo** free moments

**scanalare** *tr* to channel, groove, rabbet ‖ *intr* to overflow

**scanalatura** *f* channel, groove, rabbet

**scandagliare** §280 *tr* to sound

**scandà•glio** *m* (**-gli**) sounding lead; **fare uno scandaglio** to make a sounding or survey

**scandalismo** *m* scandalmongering, yellow journalism

**scandalizzare** [ddzz] *tr* to scandalize, shock ‖ *ref* to be scandalized

**scàndalo** *m* scandal

**scandaló•so -sa** [s] *adj* scandalous

**scandina•vo -va** *adj & mf* Scandinavian

**scandire** §176 *tr* to scan; to syllabize; (telv) to scan

**scàndola** *f* wood shingle

**scannare** *tr* to slaughter, butcher

**scanna•tóio** *m* (**-tói**) slaughterhouse; gyp joint

**scanno** *m* bench; seat; sand bar

**scansafati•che** *mf* (**-che**) loafer

**scansare** *tr* to move; to avoid ‖ *ref* to get out of the way

**scansìa** *f* shelf; bookcase

**scansióne** *f* scansion; (telv) scanning

**scanso** *m*—**a scanso di** in order to avoid

**scantinare** *intr* to make a blunder; (mus) to be out of tune

**scantinato** *m* basement

**scantonare** (**scantóno**) *tr* to round (*a corner*) ‖ *intr* to duck around the corner

**scanzona•to -ta** *adj* flippant; unconventional

**scapaccióne** *m* clout; **dare uno scapaccione a** to clout, slap

**scapa•to -ta** *adj* scatterbrained ‖ *m* scatterbrain

**scapestra•to -ta** *adj & m* libertine

**scapigliare** §280 *tr* to dishevel ‖ *ref* to be disheveled

**scapiglia•to -ta** *adj* disheveled; libertine; unconventional; free and easy

**scapitare** (**scàpito**) *intr* to lose

**scàpito** *m* damage; loss; **a scapito di** to the detriment of

**scàpola** *f* shoulder blade

**scapolare** *m* scapular ‖ *v* (**scàpolo**) *tr* (coll) to escape, avoid ‖ *intr*—**scapolare da** to get out of (*danger*)

**scàpo·lo -la** *adj* unmarried ‖ *m* bachelor ‖ *f* see **scapola**

**scappaménto** *m* escapement (*of watch, of piano*); (aut) exhaust

**scappare** *tr*—**scapparla bella** to have a narrow escape ‖ *intr* (ESSERE) to flee; to abscond; to run; to get away; to escape; to stick out; to burst out (*said, e.g., of sun*); **far scappare la pazienza a qlcu** to make s.o. lose his patience, to tax s.o.'s patience; **scappare a gambe levate** to run away, beat it; **scappare da** to burst out, e.g., **gli è scappato da ridere** he burst out laughing; **scappar detto di** to blurt out that, e.g., **gli scappò detto di non poterne più** he blurted out that he could not hold out; **scappare di mente** to escape one's mind; **scappar fuori con** to come out with

**scappata** *f* excursion; sally; escapade; bolt (*of horse*); **fare una scappata** to take a run; **scappata spiritosa** witticism

**scappatóia** *f* subterfuge; loophole

**scappellare** (**scappèllo**) *ref* to tip one's hat

**scappellòtto** *m* smack, slap (on the head); **entrare a scappellotto** (coll) to squeeze in; **passare a scappellotto** (coll) to squeeze through with influence

**scapricciare** §128 *tr* to satisfy the whims of

**scarabèo** *m* beetle; scarab (*stone*); **scarabeo sacro** scarab; **scarabeo stercorario** dung beetle

**scarabocchiare** §287 (**scarabòcchio**) *tr* to scribble; to blot (*with ink*)

**scaraboc·chio** *m* (-chi) ink blot; scribble; scrawl

**scarafàg·gio** *m* (-gi) cockroach

**scaramanzìa** *f* exorcism; **per scaramanzia** to ward off the evil eye, for good luck

**scaramazza** *adj fem* irregular (*pearl*)

**scaramùc·cia** *f* (-ce) skirmish

**scaraventare** (**scaravènto**) *tr* to hurl, chuck; to transfer suddenly

**scarcerare** (**scàrcero**) *tr* to release from jail

**scardinare** (**scàrdino**) *tr* to unhinge

**scàri·ca** *f* (-che) discharge; volley; evacuation; (elec) discharge; (fig) shower

**scaricabarili** *m*—**giocare a scaricabarili** (fig) to pass the buck

**scaricare** §197 (**scàrico**) *tr* to unload; to discharge; to hurl (*insults*); to wreak (*anger*); to free (*from responsibility*) ‖ *ref* to unburden oneself; to flow (*said of a river*); to discharge; to run down (*said of a battery or a watch*)

**scaricatóre** *m* longshoreman; (elec) lightning arrester

**scàri·co -ca** (-chi -che) *adj* empty, unloaded; discharged; clear (*sky*); free; run-down (*e.g., a clock*) ‖ *m* unloading; discharge; exhaust; waste, refuse; **a mio** (**tuo, etc.**) **scarico** in my (your, etc.) defense ‖ *f* see **scarica**

**scarlattina** *f* scarlet fever

**scarlat·to -ta** *adj & m* scarlet

**scarmigliare** §280 *tr* to dishevel

**scarnificare** §197 (**scarnifico**) or **scarnire** §176 *tr* to bone, take the flesh off; to make thin; to wear down to the bone

**scarni·to -ta** or **scar·no -na** *adj* boned; meager; skinny

**scaròla** *f* escarole, endive

**scarpa** *f* shoe; wedge, skid; scarp; **fare le scarpe a** to undercut; **scarpe al sole** violent death; **scarpe da sci** ski boots

**scarpata** *f* escarp, escarpment; slope (*of embankment*); blow with a shoe; **scarpata continentale** continental slope

**scarpétta** *f* small shoe; low shoe; **scarpette chiodate** spikes; **scarpette da ginnastica** gym shoes

**scarpinare** *intr* to trudge

**scarpóne** *m* heavy boot; clodhopper

**scarròc·cio** *m* (-ci) (aer, naut) leeway

**scarrozzare** (**scarròzzo**) *tr* to take for a ride ‖ *intr* to go for a ride; to go for a walk

**scarrozzata** *f* ride, drive

**scarseggiare** §290 (**scarséggio**) *intr* (ESSERE) to be scarce, be in short supply; **scarseggiare di** to be short of

**scarsèlla** *f* pocket; (obs) purse

**scarsézza** *f* or **scarsi·tà** *f* (-tà) scarcity, dearth, lack

**scar·so -sa** *adj* short; scarce; scanty, scant; weak (*wind*); **scarso a** short of

**scartabellare** (**scartabèllo**) *tr* to leaf through (*a book*)

**scartafàc·cio** *m* (-ci) note pad, notebook; poorly-bound copybook

**scartaménto** *m* (rr) gauge; **a scartamento ridotto** narrow-gauge; small-size; small-scale

**scartare** *tr* to unpack, unwrap; to discard (*cards*); to remove; to scrap (*e.g., a machine*); (mil) to reject ‖ *intr* to swerve; to side-step

**scartata** *f* unwrapping; side step; swerving; (fig) scolding

**scartina** *f* discard

**scarto** *m* discard; reject; swerve; (mil) rejected soldier; (sports) difference; **di scarto** inferior

**scartocciare** §128 (**scartòccio**) *tr* to unwrap; to unfold; to husk (*corn*)

**scartòffie** *fpl* old papers, trash

**scassare** *tr* to uncrate; to plow up; (coll) to ruin, bust ‖ *ref* (coll) to break down

**scassinare** *tr* to pick (*a lock*); to burglarize; to break open

**scassina·tóre -trice** *mf* burglar; **scassinatore di casseforti** safe-cracker

**scasso** *m* plowing, tilling; burglary

**scatenare** (**scaténo**) *tr* to unchain; to trigger; to excite, stir up ‖ *ref* to break loose

**scàtola** *f* box; can; **a scatola chiusa** sight unseen; **in scatola** canned; **rompere le scatole a** (vulg) to bug, pester; **scatola armonica** music box; **scatola a sorpresa** jack-in-the-box;

**scatola cranica** cranium, skull; **scatola del cambio** (aut) transmission, gear box

**scatolame** m boxes; canned food

**scatolifi·cio** m (-ci) box factory

**scattare** tr to take (a picture) ‖ intr (ESSERE & AVERE) to jump, spring; to go off (said of a trap); to go up (said of the cost of living); to go into action, begin

**scatto** m click (of camera, gun); outburst; sprint; automatic increase (in salary); shutter release; **a scatti** in jerks; **di scatto** suddenly

**scaturire** §176 intr (ESSERE) to spring; to pour, gush; to stem

**scavalcare** §197 tr to jump over; to pass over; to unsaddle; to skip (a stitch) ‖ intr (ESSERE) to dismount ‖ ref (coll) to rush

**scavallare** intr to caper, cavort

**scavare** tr to dig; to dig up, unearth

**scava·tóre -trice** adj excavating ‖ m digger ‖ f digger, excavator

**scavezzacòllo** m scamp; daredevil; **a scavezzacollo** headlong, at breakneck speed

**scavezzare** (scavézzo) tr to lop; to burst; to break; to take the halter off (a horse)

**scavo** m digging, excavation

**scazzottare** (scazzòtto) tr to beat up

**scégliere** §244 tr to choose; to pick out

**sceic·co** m (-chi) sheik

**scellerataggine** f or **scelleratézza** f wickedness, villainy

**scellera·to -ta** adj wicked ‖ m villain

**scellino** m shilling

**scél·to -ta** adj choice; selected; (mil) first-class ‖ f choice; pick; selection; **di prima scelta** choice

**scemare** (scémo) tr to diminish, reduce; to lower the level of ‖ intr (ESSERE) & ref to lessen, diminish

**scemènza** f foolishness, stupidity

**scé·mo -ma** adj silly, foolish ‖ mf simpleton, fool

**scempiàggine** f silliness, foolishness

**scém·pio -pia** (-pi -pie) adj simple; single; (lit) wicked ‖ m ruination; (lit) slaughter; **fare scempio di** to ruin, (lit) to slaughter

**scèna** f scene; stage; acting; scenery; **esser di scena** (theat) to be on; **mettere in scena** (theat) to stage; **scene di prossima programmazione** (mov) coming attractions

**scenà·rio** m (-ri) scenery; scenario, setting

**scenari·sta** mf (-sti -ste) scenarist; script writer

**scenata** f scene (outbreak of anger)

**scéndere** §245 tr to descend, go down; to bring down ‖ intr (ESSERE) to descend, go down; to get off; to come (to an agreement); to step (into the ring); to put up (at a hotel); to check in (at a hotel)

**scendilèt·to** m (-to) scatter rug; bathrobe

**sceneggiare** §290 (scenéggio) tr to write a scenario for; to adapt for the stage

**sceneggia·tóre -trice** mf scenarist

**sceneggiatura** f (mov) screenplay; (rad, telv) continuity

**scenètta** f (theat) sketch

**scenògrafo** m scene designer

**scenotècni·ca** f (-che) stagecraft

**sceriffo** m sheriff

**scèrnere** §246 tr to discern; to distinguish; to select

**scervellare** (scervèllo) ref to rack one's brains

**scervella·to -ta** adj scatterbrained

**scésa** [s] f discent; slope

**scespiria·no -na** adj Shakesperean

**scetticismo** m skepticism

**scètti·co -ca** (-ci -che) adj skeptic(al) ‖ m skeptic

**scèttro** m scepter

**sceverare** (scévero) tr (lit) to distinguish

**scé·vro -vra** adj (lit) free, exempt

**schèda** f card; slip, form; **scheda elettorale** ballot; **scheda perforata** punch card

**schedare** (schèdo) tr to file

**schedà·rio** m (-ri) card index, card catalogue; file cabinet

**schég·gia** f (-ge) splinter; chip

**scheggiare** §290 (schéggio) tr & ref to splinter

**schelètri·co -ca** adj (-ci -che) skeleton, skeletal; succint

**schèletro** m skeleton

**schè·ma** m (-mi) diagram; draft; model; scheme; **schema di montaggio** (electron) hookup

**schérma** f fencing

**schermàglia** f argument

**schermare** (schérmo) tr to screen; (elec) to shield

**schermire** §176 tr to protect; (obs) to fence with ‖ ref—**schermirsi da** to ward off, parry; to protect oneself from

**schermi·tóre -trice** mf fencer

**schérmo** m screen; protection; (elec) shield; **farsi schermo di** to use as protection; **farsi schermo delle mani** to ward off a blow with one's hands

**schernire** §176 tr to deride

**schérno** m derision, ridicule, mockery

**scherzare** (schérzo) tr (coll) to mock ‖ intr to play; to joke, trifle

**schérzo** m play; joke, jest; freak (of nature); child's play; trick; **neppure per scherzo** under no circumstances; **per scherzo** in jest; **stare allo scherzo** to take a joke

**scherzó·so -sa** [s] adj joking; playful

**schiacciaménto** m crushing; flattening

**schiacció·ci** m (-ci) nutcracker

**schiacciante** adj crushing

**schiacciapata·te** m (-te) ricer

**schiacciare** §128 tr to crush; to take (a nap); to squelch (a rumor); to subdue (the details of a painting); to mash (potatoes); to tread on, step on (s.o.'s foot); to flatten; to run (s.o.) over; to make (s.o.'s figure) look squatty; to crack (nuts); to flunk; (tennis) to smash

**schiacciata** f hot cake; (tennis) smash

**schiaffare** *tr* (coll) to fling, clap
**schiaffeggiare** §290 (**schiafféggio**) *tr* to slap; to buffet
**schiaffo** *m* slap, box
**schiamazzare** *intr* to squawk, cackle; to honk; to make a racket
**schiamazzo** *m* squawking, cackle; honk; hubbub
**schiantare** *tr* to crush, burst || *intr* (ESSERE) (coll) to burst; (coll) to croak || *ref* to break, crack, split
**schianto** *m* break, crack; crash; bang; knockout (*extraordinary, attractive person or thing*); **di schianto** all of a sudden; **schianto al cuore** heartache
**schiappa** *f* splinter; (coll) good-for-nothing
**schiarimento** *m* elucidation
**schiarire** §176 *tr* to make clearer; to make (*the hair*) light; to clear; to explain; to elucidate || *intr* (ESSERE) to become light || *ref* to clear up (*said of the weather*); to clear (*one's throat*); to fade || *impers* (ESSERE) —**schiarisce** it is getting light
**schiarita** *f* clearing (*of weather*); improvement (*in relations*)
**schiatta** *f* race, stock
**schiattare** *intr* (ESSERE) to burst
**schiavi·sta** (**-sti -ste**) *adj* slave (*e.g., state*) || *mf* antiabolitionist
**schiavi·tù** *f* (**-tù**) slavery; bondage
**schia·vo -va** *adj* enslaved || *mf* slave
**schiccherare** (**schìcchero**) *tr* to scribble; to soil; to sketch; to dash off; to blurt out; (coll) to clean out
**schidionare** (**schidióno**) *tr* to put on the spit
**schidióne** *m* spit
**schièna** *f* back; divide; crown (*of road*); **giocare di schiena** to buck
**schienale** *m* back (*of chair; cut of meat*)
**schièra** *f* crowd; flock; herd; (mil) rank
**schieraménto** *m* alignment
**schierare** (**schièro**) *tr* to line up || *ref* to line up; **schierarsi dalla parte di** to side with
**schièt·to -ta** *adj* pure; frank, honest
**schifare** *tr* to loathe; to disgust || *ref*—**schifarsi di** to feel disgusted with
**schifa·to -ta** *adj* disgusted
**schifiltó·so -sa** [s] *adj* fastidious; squeamish
**schifo** *m* disgust, loathing; skiff; shell; **fare schifo a** to disgust; to make sick
**schifó·so -sa** [s] *adj* disgusting; sickening; (slang) tremendous
**schioccare** §197 (**schiocco**) *tr* to snap (*the fingers*); to click (*the tongue*); to smack (*the lips*); to crack (*a whip*) || *intr* to crack
**schiòc·co** *m* (**-chi**) crack, snap; click; smack
**schiodare** (**schiòdo**) *tr* to take the nails out of
**schioppettata** *f* gunshot; earshot
**schiòppo** *m* gun, shotgun; **a un tiro di schioppo** within earshot
**schiùdere** §125 *tr* & *ref* to open
**schiuma** *f* foam, froth; lather; head (*of beer*); dregs, scum; meerschaum;

**avere la schiuma alla bocca** to froth at the mouth
**schiumaiòla** *f* skimmer
**schiumare** *tr* to scum; to skim || *intr* to foam, froth; to lather
**schiumó·so -sa** [s] *adj* foamy
**schivare** *tr* to avoid; to avert || *ref* to shy
**schi·vo -va** *adj* averse; bashful, shy
**schizzare** *tr* to spray; to sprinkle; to ooze (*venom*); to sketch; **schizzare fuoco dagli occhi** to have fire in one's eyes || *intr* (ESSERE) to gush; to squirt; to dart; **gli occhi gli schizzano dall'orbita** his eyes are popping out of his head
**schizzétto** *m* sprayer; syringe; water pistol
**schizzinó·so -sa** [s] *adj* finicky, fastidious
**schizzo** *m* spray; splash; sketch; survey (*e.g., of literature*)
**sci** *m* (**sci**) ski
**scia** *f* wake; track; trail; **scia di condensazione** contrail
**sciàbola** *f* saber
**sciabordare** (**sciabórdo**) *tr* to shake, agitate || *intr* to break (*said of waves*)
**sciacallo** *m* jackal
**sciacquadì·ta** *m* (**-ta**) finger bowl
**sciacquare** (**sciàcquo**) *tr* to rinse
**sciacquatura** *f* rinse
**sciacquì·o** *m* (**-i**) splash, dash
**sciàcquo** *m* rinsing (*of the mouth*); mouthwash
**sciagura** *f* calamity, misfortune
**sciagura·to -ta** *adj* unfortunate; wretched
**scialacquare** (**scialàcquo**) *tr* to squander
**scialare** *tr* to squander || *intr* to be well off; to live it up
**scial·bo -ba** *adj* pale, faded; wan
**scialle** *m* shawl; **scialle da viaggio** traveling blanket
**scialo** *m* squandering; opulence; **a scialo** lavishly
**scialuppa** *f* launch; lifeboat
**sciamanna·to -ta** *adj* slovenly
**sciamannó·ne -na** *mf* slovenly person || *f* slattern
**sciamare** *intr* (ESSERE & AVERE) to swarm
**sciame** *m* swarm; flock
**sciampagna** *f* champagne
**scianca·to -ta** *adj* cripple, lame; wobbly (*table*)
**sciangài** *m* pick-up-sticks || **Sciangai** *f* Shanghai
**sciarada** *f* charade
**sciare** §119 *intr* to ski; to back water
**sciarpa** *f* scarf; sash (*e.g., of an officer or of a mayor*)
**scias·sì** *m* (**-sì**) chassis
**sciàtica** *f* (pathol) sciatica
**scia·tóre -trice** *mf* skier
**sciatterìa** *f* or **sciattézza** *f* slovenliness
**sciat·to -ta** *adj* slovenly, sloppy
**scìbile** *m* knowledge
**sciènte** *adj* conscious; knowing
**scientìfi·co -ca** *adj* (**-ci -che**) scientific
**sciènza** *f* science; knowledge

scienzia·to -ta *mf* scientist
scilinguàgnolo *m* frenum (*of tongue*); avere lo scilinguagnolo sciolto to have a loose tongue
Scilla *f* Scylla; fra Scilla e Cariddi between Scylla and Charibdis
scimitarra *f* scimitar
scìmmia *f* monkey; (coll) drunk; fare la scimmia a to ape; scimmia antropomorfa anthropoid ape
scimmié·sco -sca *adj* (-schi -sche) monkeyish; apish
scimmiottare (scimmiòtto) *tr* to ape
scimpan·zé *m* (-zé) chimpanzee
scimuni·to -ta *adj* idiotic || *mf* idiot
scìndere §247 *tr* (lit) to split; to separate
scintilla *f* spark; sparkle; (fig) scintilla; scintilla elettrica jump spark
scintillare *intr* to spark; to sparkle
scintillì·o *m* (-i) sparkle, brilliance
scioccare §197 *tr* to shock
sciocchézza *f* silliness; trifle
sciòc·co -ca (-chi -che) *adj* silly, foolish || *mf* fool, blockhead
sciògliere §127 *tr* to loosen; to release; to unfasten, untie; to solve; to disperse; to dissolve; to limber; to fulfill (*a promise*); to unfurl (*sails*) || *ref* to loosen up; to get loose; to dissolve; to melt (*into tears*)
scioglilìn·gua *m*(-gue) tongue twister
sciogliménto *m* melting; dissolution; fulfillment; denouement
sciolina *f* ski wax
scioltézza *f* nimbleness, agility; freedom (*of movement*); ease
sciòl·to -ta *adj* loose; glib; free; blank (*verse*)
scioperante *adj* striking || *mf* striker
scioperare (sciòpero) *intr* to strike
sciopera·to -ta *adj* loafing; lazy || *m* loafer
sciòpero *m* strike; walkout; sciopero a singhiozzo slowdown strike; sciopero bianco sit-down strike; sciopero della fame hunger strike; sciopero di solidarietà sympathy strike; sciopero pignolo slowdown
sciorinare *tr* to display; to tell (*lies*); to air (*laundry*)
sciovìa *f* ski lift
sciovinismo *m* chauvinism, jingoism
scipi·to -ta *adj* insipid
scippo *m* snatching (*e.g., of a bag*)
sciròc·co *m* (-chi) sirocco; southeast
sciròppo *m* syrup
sci·sma *m* (-smi) schism
scismàti·co -ca *adj* (-ci -che) schismatic
scissióne *f* split; (biol, phys) fission
scis·so -sa *adj* split, rent
scisto *m* schist
sciupare *tr* to spoil; to wear out; to waste; to rumple || *ref* to wear; to run down (*said of health*); to get rumpled
sciupa·to -ta *adj* ruined; worn out; wasted; run down
sciupì·o *m* (-i) waste
sciupó·ne -na *mf* waster, squanderer
sciu·scià *m* (-scià) bootblack; urchin
scìvola *f* chute

scivolare (scìvolo) *intr* (ESSERE & AVERE) to slide, glide; to steal; scivolare d'ala (aer) to sideslip
scivolata *f* slide, glide; scivolata d'ala (aer) sideslip
scìvolo *m* chute; (aer) slip (*for seaplanes*)
scivolóne *m* slip, slide
scivoló·so -sa [s] *adj* slippery
scoccare §197 (scòcco) *tr* to shoot (*an arrow*); to give (*a buss*); to strike (*the hour*) || *intr* (ESSERE) to dart; to spring; to strike (*said of a clock*); to shoot
scocciare §128 (scòccio) *tr* (coll) to break; (coll) to bother; (naut) to unhook || *ref* to be bored
scoccia·tóre -trice *mf* (coll) nuisance
scocciatura *f* (coll) bother, annoyance
scòc·co *m* (-chi) darting; stroke (*e.g., of three*); (naut) hook; scocco di baci bussing, kissing
scodella *f* bowl; soup plate
scodellare (scodèllo) *tr* to dish out
scodellino *m* small bowl; (mil) pan (*of musket lock*)
scodinzolare (scodìnzolo) *intr* to wag its tail; to waddle (*said of a woman*)
scoglièra *f* reef (*of rocks*); scogliera corallina coral reef
scò·glio *m* (-gli) rock; reef; cliff; stumbling block
scoiare §248 *tr* to skin
scoiàttolo *m* squirrel
scolabrò·do *m* (-do) colander, strainer
scolafrit·to *m* (-to) strainer
scolapa·sta *m* (-sta) (coll) colander
scolare (scólo) *tr* to drain; (fig) to polish off || *intr* (ESSERE) to drip || *ref* to melt
scolaré·sco -sca (-schi -sche) *adj* school || *f* schoolchildren; student body
scola·ro -ra *mf* pupil; student
scolàsti·co -ca (-ci -che) *adj* school; scholastic || *m* scholastic, schoolman || *f* scholasticism
scola·tóio *m* (-tói) drain; strainer
scolatura *f* drip, drippings; dregs
scollaccia·to -ta *adj* low-necked; wearing a low-cut dress; dirty, obscene
scollare (scòllo) *tr* to cut off at the neck; to unglue || *ref* to wear a low-necked dress; to come unglued
scollatura *f* neckline; ungluing; scollatura a barchetta low neck; scollatura a punta V neck
scòllo *m* neck, neckline
scólo *m* drain; drainage; (slang) clap
scolopèndra *f* centipede
scolorare (scolóro) *tr*, *intr* (ESSERE), & *ref* to fade, discolor; to pale
scolorire §176 *tr*, *intr* (ESSERE), & *ref* to fade, discolor
scolpare (scólpo) *tr* to excuse
scolpire §176 *tr* to sculpture; to engrave; to emphasize
scòlta *f* (lit) sentry; fare la scolta to stand guard
scombaciare §128 *tr* to pull apart, separate
scombinare *tr* to disarrange; to upset
scómbro *m* mackerel

**scombù·glio** m (-gli) (coll) disorder

**scombussolare (scombùssolo)** tr to upset

**scomméssa** f bet, wager

**scomméttere** §198 tr to bet; to separate

**scommetti·tóre -trice** mf bettor

**scomodare (scòmodo)** tr to trouble, disturb || ref to take the trouble

**scomodi·tà** f (-tà) trouble, inconvenience

**scòmo·do -da** adj awkward, unwieldy; uncomfortable || m inconvenience

**scompaginare (scompàgino)** tr to upset; (typ) to pi

**scompagna·to -ta** adj odd

**scomparire** §108 intr (ESSERE) to disappear; to make a bad showing

**scompar·so -sa** adj disappeared; extinct || mf deceased || f disappearance; death

**scompartiménto** m compartment; partition

**scompènso** m lack of compensation; imbalance

**scompigliare** §280 tr to disarray; to trouble, upset

**scompì·glio** m (-gli) disarray; upset

**scompisciare** §128 tr (vulg) to piss on || ref (vulg) to wet oneself; **scompisciarsi dalle risa** (coll) to split one's sides laughing

**scomplè·to -ta** adj incomplete

**scompórre** §218 tr to decompose, disintegrate; to rumple; to dishevel; to upset; to dismantle, take apart; (typ) to pi || ref to lose one's composure

**scompó·sto -sta** adj unseemly

**scomùni·ca** f (-che) excommunication

**scomunicare** §197 (scomùnico) tr to excommunicate; (joc) to ostracize

**sconcertare (sconcèrto)** tr to upset; to disconcert || ref to become disconcerted

**sconcézza** f obscenity, indecency

**scón·cio -cia** (-ci -ce) adj dirty, filthy, obscene || m obscenity; shame

**sconclusiona·to -ta** adj inconsequential; incoherent; rambling

**sconcordanza** f disagreement; (gram) lack of agreement

**scondi·to -ta** adj unseasoned

**sconfessare (sconfèsso)** tr to disavow; to retract

**sconfessióne** f disavowal

**sconfiggere** §104 tr to defeat, rout; to pull (a nail); to unfasten

**sconfinare** intr to cross the border; **sconfinare da** to stray from

**sconfina·to -ta** adj boundless, unlimited

**sconfitta** f defeat, rout

**sconfortante** adj discouraging

**sconfortare (sconfòrto)** tr to discourage; to distress || ref to become discouraged

**sconfòrto** m depression; distress

**scongelare (scongèlo)** tr to thaw

**scongiurare** tr to conjure; to implore

**scongiuro** m conjuration; entreaty

**sconnès·so -sa** adj disconnected; incoherent

**sconnèttere** §107 tr to disconnect; to take apart || intr to be incoherent

**sconoscènte** adj unappreciative

**sconosciu·to -ta** adj unknown || mf stranger

**sconquassare** tr to smash, shatter

**sconquassa·to -ta** adj broken-down; upset

**sconquasso** m destruction; confusion; smash-up

**sconsacrare** tr to desecrate

**sconsideratézza** f thoughtlessness

**sconsidera·to -ta** adj inconsiderate

**sconsigliare** §280 tr to dissuade, discourage

**sconsiglia·to -ta** adj thoughtless

**sconsola·to -ta** adj disconsolate

**scontare (scónto)** tr to expiate; to discount; to serve (time in jail)

**scontentare (scontènto)** tr to dissatisfy

**scontèn·to -ta** adj & m discontent

**scónto** m discount; part payment; (fig) partial remission

**scontrare (scóntro)** tr to meet; (naut) to turn (the wheel) sharply || ref to clash; to collide; to come to blows

**scontrino** m check, ticket

**scóntro** m collision; battle, encounter; clash; ward (of key)

**scontró·so -sa** [s] adj peevish, cross

**sconveniènte** adj unfavorable; unseemly, unbecoming; indecent

**sconvenire** §282 intr (ESSERE) to be unseemly or unbecoming

**sconvòlgere** §289 tr to upset; to disconcert

**sconvolgiménto** m upsetting; **sconvolgimento di stomaco** stomach upset; **sconvolgimento tellurico** upheaval

**sconvòl·to -ta** adj upset; disconcerted; distracted

**scópa** f broom; **scopa per lavaggio** mop

**scopare (scópo)** tr to sweep

**scopata** f sweep

**scoperchiare** §287 (scopèrchio) tr to uncover; to take the lid off

**scopèr·to -ta** adj uncovered; open; bare; exposed; unpaid || m open ground; open air; overdraft; (econ) short sale; (com) balance; **allo scoperto** in the open; overdrawn (check); short (sale) || f discovery; **alla scoperta** openly

**scòpo** m purpose, goal, aim

**scoppiare** §287 (scòppio) tr to uncouple || intr (ESSERE) to burst; to blow; to explode; to break (said, e.g., of news); (fig) to die (e.g., of overeating); **scoppiare a** to burst out (laughing or crying)

**scoppiettare (scoppiétto)** intr to crackle

**scoppietti·o** m (-i) crackle

**scòp·pio** m (-pi) burst; explosion; outbreak; outburst; blowout (of tire); **a scoppio** internal-combustion (engine); **scoppio di tuono** clap of thunder

**scòppola** f drop (of plane in air pocket); (coll) rabbit punch

**scopriménto** m uncovering; unveiling

**scoprire** §110 tr to uncover; to unveil; to discover; to expose || ref to take off one's clothes; to take one's hat off; to reveal oneself

**scopri·tóre -trice** *mf* discoverer
**scoraggiaménto** *m* discouragement
**scoraggiante** *adj* discouraging
**scoraggiare** §290 *tr* to discourage, dishearten ‖ *ref* to be or become discouraged
**scoraménto** *m* (lit) discouragement
**scorbuto** *m* scurvy
**scorciare** §128 **(scórcio)** *tr* to shorten; to foreshorten ‖ *intr* (ESSERE) to shorten, grow shorter; to look foreshortened ‖ *ref* to shorten, grow shorter
**scorciatóla** *f* shortcut, cutoff
**scór·cio** *m* (-ci) foreshortening; end, close (*of a period*); **di scorcio** foreshortened
**scordare (scòrdo)** *tr* to forget; to put out of tune ‖ *ref* to forget; to get out of tune
**scorég·gia** *f* (-ge) (vulg) fart
**scoreggiare** §290 **(scoréggio)** *intr* (vulg) to fart
**scòrgere** §249 *tr* to perceive, to discern
**scòria** *f* slag, dross; (fig) scum, dregs; **scorie atomiche** atomic waste
**scorna·to -ta** *adj* humiliated, ridiculed; hornless
**scòrno** *m* humiliation, ridicule
**scorpacciata** *f* bellyful; **fare una scorpacciata di** to stuff oneself with
**scorpióne** *m* scorpion ‖ **Scorpione** *m* (astrol) Scorpio
**scorrazzare** *tr* to wander over ‖ *intr* to run around; to move about; (fig) to ramble; (mil) to raid
**scórrere** §139 *tr* to raid; to glance over ‖ *intr* (ESSERE) to flow; to run; to glide
**scorrerìa** *f* raid, foray, incursion
**scorrettézza** *f* imprecision; impropriety
**scorrèt·to -ta** *adj* incorrect; improper
**scorrévole** *adj* sliding; flowing, fluent ‖ *m* slide (*of slide rule*)
**scorribanda** *f* raid, foray, incursion
**scór·so -sa** *adj* past, last ‖ *m* error, slip ‖ *f* glance; short stay
**scor·sóio -sóia** *adj* (-sói -sóie) slip (*knot*)
**scòrta** *f* escort; provision, stock; **di scorta** spare (*tire*); **fare di scorta a** to escort; **scorta d'onore** (mil) honor guard; **scorte** (com) stockpile; (com) supplies; **scorte morte** agricultural supplies; **scorte vive** livestock
**scortare (scòrto)** *tr* to escort; to foreshorten
**scortecciare** §128 **(scortéccio)** *tr* to strip the bark from; to peel off; to scrape ‖ *ref* to peel off
**scortése** *adj* discourteous, impolite
**scortesìa** *f* discourtesy, impoliteness
**scorticare** §197 **(scórtico)** *tr* to skin; to be overdemanding with (*students*); to fleece ‖ *ref* to skin (*e.g., one's arm*)
**scòrza** *f* bark; skin, hide; (fig) appearance; **scorza di limone** lemon peel
**scoscendiménto** *m* landslide; cliff
**scoscé·so -sa** [s] *adj* sloping, steep
**scòssa** *f* shake; jerk; **scossa di pioggia**

downpour; **scossa di terremoto** earth tremor; **scossa elettrica** electric shock; **scossa tellurica** earthquake
**scossóne** *m* jolt, jerk
**scostaménto** *m* removal; separation
**scostare (scòsto)** *tr* to move away; to try to avoid ‖ *intr* (ESSERE) to stand away ‖ *ref* to step aside; to stray
**scostuma·to -ta** *adj* dissolute, debauched
**scotennare (scoténno)** *tr* to scalp; to skin (*an animal*)
**scòtta** *f* whey; (naut) sheet
**scottante** *adj* burning (*question*); outrageous (*offense*)
**scottare (scòtto)** *tr* to burn; to scald; to sear; to boil (*eggs*); (fig) to sting ‖ *intr* to burn; to be hot (*said of stolen goods*) ‖ *ref* to get burnt
**scottatura** *f* burn; (fig) blow, jolt
**scòt·to -ta** *adj* overcooked, overdone ‖ *m*—**pagare lo scotto** to foot the bill; **pagare lo scotto di** to expiate ‖ *f* see **scotta**
**scoutismo** *m* scouting
**scovare (scóvo)** *tr* to rouse (*game*); to find, discover
**scovolino** *m* pipe cleaner; (mil) small swab
**scóvolo** *m* (mil) swab
**scòzia** *f* (archit) scotia ‖ **la Scozia** Scotland
**scozzése** [s] *adj* Scotch, Scottish ‖ *m* Scotch, Scottish (*language*); Scotchman ‖ *f* Scotchwoman
**scozzonare (scozzóno)** *tr* to break in (*a horse*); to train
**scranna** *f* (hist) seat
**screanza·to -ta** *adj* ill-mannered, rude
**screditare (scrédito)** *tr* to discredit
**scremare (scrèmo)** *tr* to cream
**scrematrice** *f* cream separator
**screpolare (scrèpolo)** *tr, intr* (ESSERE), & *ref* to crack; to chap
**screpolatura** *f* crack; chap (*of skin*)
**screziare** §287 **(scrèzio)** *tr* to mottle, variegate
**scrè·zio** *m* (-zi) tiff
**scri·ba** *m* (-bi) scribe (*Jewish scholar*)
**scribacchiare** §287 *tr* to scribble, scrawl
**scribacchino** *m* scribbler; hack
**scricchiolare (scrìcchiolo)** *intr* to crack, creak
**scricchiolì·o** *m* (-i) crack, creak
**scrìcciolo** *m* wren
**scrigno** *m* jewel box
**scriminatura** *f* part (*in hair*)
**scrit·to -ta** *adj* written ‖ *m* writing ‖ *f* sign; inscription; contract; **scritta luminosa** electric sign
**scrit·tóio** *m* (-tói) writing desk
**scrit·tóre -trice** *mf* writer
**scrittura** *f* handwriting; penmanship; writing; contract; entry; (theat) booking; **Sacra Scrittura** Holy Scripture; **scrittura privata** contract; **scrittura pubblica** deed, indenture; **scrittura a macchina** typing
**scritturale** *adj* scriptural ‖ *m* clerk; copyist; fundamentalist
**scritturare** *tr* (theat) to book, engage
**scrivanìa** *f* desk

**scrivano** *m* clerk, copyist, typist

**scrìvere** §250 *tr* & *intr* to write; **scrivere a macchina** to type

**scroccare** §197 (**scròcco**) *tr* to sponge (*a meal*); to manage to get (*a prize*) || *intr* to sponge

**scrocca·tóre -trice** *mf* sponger

**scròc·co** *m* (-**chi**) sponging; creaking; **a scrocco** sponging; spring (*lock*); switchblade (*knife*)

**scroccó·ne -na** *mf* sponger

**scròfa** *f* sow; slut

**scrollare** (**scròllo**) *tr* to shake; to shrug (*one's shoulders*) || *ref* to get into action; to pull oneself together

**scrollata** *f* shake; **scrollata di spalle** shrug

**scrosciare** §128 (**scròscio**) *intr* (ESSERE & AVERE) to pelt down; (fig) to thunder

**scrò·scio** *m* (-**sci**) thunder, roar; **scroscio di pioggia** downpour; **scroscio di tuono** thunderclap

**scrostare** (**scròsto**) *tr* to pick (*a scab*); to scrape; to peel off || *ref* to peel off

**scrosta·to -ta** *adj* peeling; scaly

**scròto** *m* scrotum

**scrùpolo** *m* scruple; scrupulousness

**scrupoló·so -sa** [s] *adj* scrupulous

**scrutare** *tr* to scan, scrutinize

**scruta·tóre -trice** *adj* inquisitive || *mf* teller (*of votes*)

**scrutina·tóre -trice** *mf* teller (*of votes*)

**scrutì·nio** *m* (-**ni**) poll, vote; evaluation (*of an examination*); count (*of votes*); **scrutinio segreto** secret ballot

**scucire** §143 *tr* to unstitch; (coll) to cough up || *ref* to come unstitched

**scucitura** *f* unstitching; rip

**scuderìa** *f* stable

**scudétto** *m* badge; escutcheon; (sports) badge of victory

**scudièro** *m* esquire

**scudisciare** §128 *tr* to whip

**scudì·scio** *m* (-**sci**) whip

**scudo** *m* shield; escutcheon; **far scudo a** to shield

**scùffia** *f* (coll) load (*intoxication*); **fare scuffia** to capsize; **prendersi una scuffia per** to fall for, to fall in love with

**scugnizzo** *m* Neapolitan urchin

**sculacciare** §128 *tr* to spank

**sculacciata** *f* spank, spanking

**sculaccióne** *m* spank, spanking

**sculettare** (**sculétto**) *intr* to waddle

**scul·tóre -trice** *mf* sculptor || *f* sculptress

**scultura** *f* sculpture

**scuòla** *f* school; **scuola allievi ufficiali** military academy; officers' candidate school; **scuola dell'obbligo** mandatory education; **scuola di danza** dancing school; **scuola di dressaggio** obedience school (*for dogs*); **scuola di guerra** war college; **scuola di guida** driving school; **scuola di perfezionamento per laureati** postgraduate school; **scuola di taglio** sewing school; **scuola materna** kindergarten; **scuola mista** coeducational school

**scuòla·bus** *m* (-**bus**) school bus

**scuòtere** §251 *tr* to shake; to shake up; **scuotere di dosso** to shake off

**scure** *f* ax; cleaver

**scurire** §176 *tr*, *intr* (ESSERE), & *ref* to darken

**scu·ro -ra** *adj* dark || *m* darkness; dark; shutter; **essere allo scuro** to be in the dark

**scurrile** *adj* scurrilous

**scusa** *f* excuse; apology; pretext; **chiedere scusa** to apologize

**scusare** *tr* to excuse; to pardon; to apologize for; **scusi!** pardon me! || *ref* to apologize; to beg off

**sdaziare** §287 *tr* to clear through customs

**sdebitare** (**sdébito**) *tr* to free from debt || *ref* to become free of debt; **sdebitarsi con** to repay a favor to

**sdegnare** (**sdégno**) *tr* to scorn; to arouse, enrage || *ref* to get mad

**sdégno** *m* indignation, anger; (lit) scorn

**sdegnó·so -sa** [s] *adj* indignant; haughty

**sdenta·to -ta** *adj* toothless

**sdilinquire** §176 *tr* to weaken || *intr* (ESSERE) & *ref* to swoon; to become mawkish

**sdoganare** *tr* to clear through customs

**sdolcina·to -ta** *adj* mawkish

**sdolcinatura** *f* mush, slobber

**sdoppiare** §287 (**sdóppio**) *tr* & *ref* to split

**sdoppiaménto** *m* splitting

**sdottoreggiare** §290 (**sdottoréggio**) *intr* to pontificate

**sdràia** *f* chaise longue; deck chair

**sdraiare** §287 *tr* to lay down || *ref* to stretch out (*e.g., on the ground*)

**sdràio** *m* (**sdrài**) stretching out; **mettersi a sdraio** to lie down

**sdrucciolare** (**sdrùcciolo**) *intr* (ESSERE & AVERE) to slip, slide

**sdrucciolévole** *adj* slippery

**sdrùccio·lo -la** *adj* proparoxytone || *m* slip; slope; proparoxytone

**sdrucciolóni** *adv* slipping, sliding

**sdrucire** (**sdrùcio**) & §176 *tr* to tear, rend, rip

**sdrucitura** *f* tear, rend, rip

**se** *m* (**se**) if || §5 *pron* || *conj* if; whether; **se mai** in the event; **se no** otherwise; **se non tu** (lui, lei, etc.), nobody else but you (him, her, etc.), e.g., **non puoi essere stato se non tu** it could not have been anyone else but you; **se non altro** at least; **se non che** but; **se pure** even if

**sé** §5 *pron* himself; herself; itself; yourself; themselves; yourselves; oneself; **di per sé stesso** by itself; **fuori di sé** beside oneself; **rientrare in sé** to come back to one's senses; **uscire di sé** to be beside oneself

**sebbène** *conj* although, though

**sèbo** *m* sebum, tallow

**séc·ca** *f* (-**che**) sand bank, shoal; drought; **dare in secca** to run aground; **in secca** hard up

**seccante** *adj* drying; annoying

**seccare** §197 (**sécco**) *tr* to dry; to bore;

to bother, annoy ‖ *intr* (ESSERE) to dry up ‖ *ref* to dry up; to be annoyed

**secca·tóio** *m* (**-tói**) drying room; squeegee (*to remove water from wet decks*)

**secca·tóre -trice** *mf* bore, pest

**seccatura** *f* drying; trouble, nuisance

**sécchia** *f* bucket, pail; **piovere a secchie** to rain cats and dogs

**secchièllo** *m* little bucket

**séc·chio** *m* (**-chi**) bucket, pail; bucketful; **secchio dell'immondezza** trash can

**séc·co -ca** (**-chi -che**) *adj* dry; lanky; sharp ‖ *m* dryness; dry land; drought; **a secco** dry (*cleaning*); **dare in secco** to run aground; **in secco** hard up; **lavare a secco** to dry-clean ‖ *f* see **secca**

**secenté·sco -sca** *adj* (**-schi -sche**) seventeenth-century

**secentèsi·mo -ma** *adj, m & pron* six hundredth

**secèrnere** §153 (*pp* **secrèto**) *tr* to secrete

**secessióne** *f* secession

**séco** §5 *prep phrase* (lit) with oneself; along, e.g., **portare seco** to bring along

**secolare** *adj* secular; century-old; worldly ‖ *m* layman

**sècolo** *m* century; age; world

**secónda** *f* second; second-year class; **a seconda** with the wind; **a seconda di** according to; **in seconda** (aut) in second; (mil) second in command

**secondare** (**secóndo**) *tr* to second

**secondà·rio -ria** *adj* (**-ri -rie**) secondary

**secondino** *m* prison guard, turnkey

**secón·do -da** *adj* second; (lit) favorable ‖ *m* second; second course; (nav) executive officer ‖ *f* see **seconda** ‖ *pron* second ‖ **secondo** *prep* according to; **secondo me** (**te, etc.**) in my (your, etc.) opinion

**secondogèni·to -ta** *adj* second-born

**secrezióne** *f* secretion

**sèdano** *m* celery

**sedare** (**sèdo**) *tr* to calm, placate

**sedati·vo -va** *adj & m* sedative

**sède** *f* seat; branch; residence; period; (gram) syllable; (rr) right of way; **in separata sede** in private; (lbb) with change of venue; **Santa Sede** Holy See; **sede centrale** main office, home office

**sedentà·rio -ria** (**-ri -rie**) *adj* sedentary ‖ *m* sedentary person

**sedére** *m* sitting; rear, backside ‖ *v* §252 *intr* (ESSERE) to sit, to be seated; to be in session; to be located ‖ *ref* to sit down

**sèdia** *f* chair; seat; see; **sedia a braccioli** armchair; **sedia a dondolo** rocking chair; **sedia a pozzetto** bucket seat; **sedia a sdraio** deck chair; **sedia da posta** (hist) mail coach; **sedia di vimini** wicker chair; **sedia elettrica** electric chair; **sedia girevole** swivel chair

**sedicènne** *adj* sixteen-year-old ‖ *mf* sixteen-year-old person

**sedicènte** *adj* so-called, self-styled

**sedicèsi·mo -ma** *adj, m & pron* sixteenth

**sédici** *adj & pron* sixteen; **le sedici** four P.M. ‖ *m* sixteen; sixteenth (*in dates*)

**sedile** *m* seat; bench; bottom (*of chair*); (aut) bucket seat

**sediménto** *m* sediment

**sediòlo** *m* sulky

**sedizióne** *f* sedition

**sedizió·so -sa** [s] *adj* seditious

**seducènte** *adj* seductive; alluring

**sedurre** §102 *tr* to seduce; to allure; to lead astray; to charm, captivate

**seduta** *f* sitting; session, meeting; **seduta fiume** (pol) uninterrupted session; **seduta stante** on the spot

**sedut·tóre -trice** *adj* seductive; alluring; charming ‖ *mf* seducer

**seduzióne** *f* seduction; allurement; charm

**sefardi·ta** (**-ti -te**) *adj* Sephardic ‖ *mf* Sephardi

**sé·ga** *f* (**-ghe**) saw; **a sega** serrated; **sega a nastro** band saw; **sega circolare** buzz saw; **sega da carpentiere** lumberman's saw; **sega intelaiata a lama** bucksaw; **sega meccanica** power saw

**ségala** *f* rye

**segali·gno -gna** *adj* rye; lean, wiry

**segare** §209 (**ségo**) *tr* to saw; to cut

**segatrice** *f* power saw; **segatrice a disco** circular saw; **segatrice a nastro** band saw

**segatura** *f* cutting; sawdust

**seggétta** *f* commode

**sèg·gio** *m* (**-gi**) seat (*e.g., in congress*); **seggio elettorale** voting commission

**sèggiola** *f* chair; **seggiola a sdraio** deck chair

**seggiolino** *m* child's chair; stool; bucket seat; **seggiolino eiettabile** (aer) ejection seat

**seggiolóne** *m* highchair; easy chair

**seggiovìa** *f* chair lift

**segheria** *f* sawmill

**seghetta·to -ta** *adj* serrated

**seghétto** *m* hacksaw; **seghetto da traforo** coping saw

**segménto** *m* segment; **segmento elastico** (aut) piston ring

**segnaccènto** *m* accent mark

**segnàcolo** *m* (lit) symbol, sign

**segnalare** *tr* to signal; to point out ‖ *ref* to distinguish oneself

**segnalazióne** *f* signaling; sign, signal; nomination; recommendation; **dare la segnalazione a** to notify; **fare segnalazioni** to signal; **segnalazioni stradali** road signs

**segnale** *m* sign; signal; bookmark; **segnale di allarme** (mil) alarm; **segnale di occupato** (telp) busy signal; **segnale di via libera** (telp) dial tone; **segnale orario** (rad, telv) time signal; **segnali stradali** road signs

**segnalèti·co -ca** *adj* (**-ci -che**) identification (*mark*) ‖ *f* road signs

**segnalibro** *m* bookmark

**segnalìne·e** *m* (**-e**) lineman

**segnapósto** *m* place card

**segnapun·ti** *m* (**-ti**) scorekeeper

**segnare** (ségno) *tr* to mark; to under-score, underline; to jot down; to say (*e.g., five o'clock, said of a watch*); to brand; (sports) to score; **segnare a dito** to point to || *ref* to cross one-self

**segnatas·se** *m* (**-se**) postage-due stamp

**segnatura** *f* signing; signature; library number; (eccl) chancery; (sports) final score; (typ) signature

**segnavèn·to** *m* (**-to**) weather vane

**ségno** *m* mark; bookmark; symbol; sign; signal; boundary; (mus) signa-ture; **a segno che** so that; **a tal segno** to such a point; **essere fatto segno di** to be the target of; **in segno di** as a token of; **mettere a segno** to check, control; **segno della Croce** sign of the Cross; **segno di croce** cross (*mark*); **segno d'interpunzione**, or **di punteggiatura**, or **grafico** punctuation mark; **segno di riconoscimento** identification mark

**ségo** *m* tallow, suet

**segregare** §209 (sègrego) *tr* to segre-gate; to secrete || *ref* to withdraw

**segregazióne** *f* segregation; **segregazione cellulare** solitary confinement

**segregazioni·sta** *mf* (**-sti -ste**) segrega-tionist

**segretariato** *m* secretariat

**segretà·rio -ria** *mf* secretary; clerk

**segreterìa** *f* secretary's office; secretary-ship

**segretézza** *f* secrecy

**segré·to -ta** *adj* secret; secretive || *m* secret; secrecy; **segreto d'alcova** boudoir secret; **segreto di Pulcinella** open secret

**seguace** *mf* follower

**seguènte** *adj* following, next

**segù·gio** *m* (**-gi**) bloodhound; (fig) pri-vate eye

**seguire** (séguo) *tr* to follow; to attend || *intr* (ESSERE) to continue; to follow, ensue; (with *dat*) to follow

**seguitare** (séguito) *intr*—**seguitare a +** *inf* to keep on + *ger*, e.g., **seguitare a parlare** to keep on talking; **seguiti!** go ahead!

**séguito** *m* following; retinue; follow-ers; sequence; sequel; pursuit; **di seguito** in succession; **far seguito a** to refer to; in **seguito** thereafter; **in seguito a** as a consequence of

**sèi** *adj & pron* six; **le sei** six o'clock || *m* six; sixth (*in dates*)

**seicènto** *adj, m & pron* six hundred || *f* car with a motor displacing 600 cubic centimeters || **il Seicento** the seventeenth century

**seimila** *adj, m, & pron* six thousand

**sélce** *f* silica; flint; (lit) stone; **selci** paving blocks

**selciare** §128 (sélcio) *tr* to pave

**selcia·to -ta** *adj* paved || *m* paving

**seletti·vo -va** *adj* selective

**selezionare** (selezióno) *tr* to select, sort out

**selezióne** *f* selection; choice

**sèlla** *f* saddle

**sel·làio** *m* (**-lài**) saddler

**sellare** (sèllo) *tr* to saddle

**sellerìa** *f* saddler's shop; saddlery; (aut) upholstery

**sélva** *f* woods, forest

**selvaggina** *f* game

**selvàg·gio -gia** (**-gi -ge**) *adj* savage; vicious (*horse*) || *m* savage; unsocia-ble person

**selvàti·co -ca** *adj* (**-ci -che**) wild

**selvicoltura** *f* forestry

**sèlz** *m* (sèlz) seltzer, club soda

**semàforo** *m* traffic light; semaphore

**semànti·co -ca** (**-ci -che**) *adj* semantic || *f* semantics

**sembiante** *m* (lit) look; **fare sembianti di** to pretend

**sembianza** *f* look; (lit) similarity

**sembrare** (sémbro) *intr* (ESSERE) to seem, look, appear || *impers*—**sembra** it seems

**séme** *m* seed; stone (*of fruit*); (cards) suit

**seménta** *f* sowing season; (lit) seed

**seménte** *f* seed

**semènza** *f* seed; brads (*used in uphol-stery*)

**semenzà·io** *m* (**-zài**) hotbed, seedbed

**semestrale** *adj* semiannual, semiyearly

**semèstre** *m* semester; half year

**sèmi-** *pref adj* semi-, e.g., **semicircolare** semicircular; half-, e.g., **semichiuso** half-closed || *pref mf* semi-, e.g., **semicerchio** semicircle; half, e.g., **semitono** half tone; demi-, e.g., **semidio** demigod

**semiapèr·to -ta** *adj* half-open; ajar

**semiasse** *m* (mach) axle (*on each side of differential*)

**semicér·chio** *m* (**-chi**) semicircle

**semichiu·so -sa** [s] *adj* half-closed

**semicingola·to -ta** *adj & m* half-track

**semicircolo** *m* semicircle

**semiconduttóre** *m* semiconductor

**semiconvit·tóre -trice** *mf* day student

**semicù·pio** *m* (**-pi**) sitz bath

**semi·dìo** *m* (**-dèi**) demigod

**semidòt·to -ta** *adj* semilearned

**semifinale** *f* semifinal

**sémina** *f* sowing; sowing season

**seminare** (sémino) *tr* to sow, seed; to plant; (coll) to leave behind

**seminà·rio** *m* (**-ri**) seminary; seminar

**seminari·sta** *mf* (**-sti**) seminarian

**semina·to -ta** *adj* sown, seeded || *m* sown land; **uscire dal seminato** to digress

**semina·tóre -trice** *mf* sower || *f* (mach) seeder, seeding machine

**seminterrato** *m* basement

**seminu·do -da** *adj* half-naked

**semioscurità** *f* partial darkness

**semirìgi·do -da** *adj* semirigid; inelastic

**semirimòr·chio** *m* (**-chi**) semitrailer

**semisè·rio -ria** [s] *adj* (**-ri -rie**) serio-comic

**semisfèra** *f* (geom) hemisphere

**semi·ta** (**-ti -te**) *adj* Semitic || *mf* Semite

**semitòno** *m* (mus) semitone, half tone

**semmài** *conj* if ever; in the event that

**sémola** *f* bran; (coll) freckles

**semolino** *m* semolina

**semovènte** *adj* self-propelled

**sempitèr·no -na** *adj* (lit) everlasting
**sémplice** *adj* simple; single; plain; mere; (mil) private; (nav) ordinary ‖ *m* medicinal herb; **semplici** simple folk
**semplició·ne -na** *adj* simple ‖ *mf* simpleton
**semplici·tà** *f* (**-tà**) simplicity
**semplificare** §197 (**semplìfico**) *tr* to simplify ‖ *ref* to become easier or simpler
**sèmpre** *adv* always; ever; yet; **da sempre** from time immemorial; **di sempre** same, same old; **e poi sempre** ever and ever; **ma sempre** but only; **per sempre** forever; **sempre che** provided; **sempre meglio** better and better; **sempre meno** less and less; **sempre però** but only; **sempre vostro** very truly yours
**semprevérde** *adj, m & f* evergreen
**sènape** *f* mustard
**senapismo** *m* mustard plaster
**senato** *m* senate
**sena·tóre -trice** *mf* senator
**senése** [s] *adj & mf* Sienese
**senile** *adj* old; of old age
**senilismo** *m* (pathol) senility
**senilità** *f* old age
**senióre** *adj & m* elder, senior
**Sènna** *f* Seine
**sénno** *m* wisdom; **far senno** to come back to one's senses; **senno di poi** hindsight; **uscir di senno** to go out of one's mind
**séno** *m* chest; breast, bosom; cove; (anat) sinus; (math) sine; (fig) heart; **in seno a** within
**senonché** or **se non che** *conj* but
**sensale** *m* broker; commission merchant
**sensa·to -ta** *adj* sensible, reasonable; sane
**sensazionale** *adj* sensational
**sensazióne** *f* sensation
**sensìbile** *adj* sensible; perceptible; appreciable; sensitive; responsive (*e.g., to affection*) ‖ *m* world of the senses
**sensibili·tà** *f* (**-tà**) sensitivity; sensibility
**sensibilizzare** [ddzz] *tr* to sensitize
**sensiti·vo -va** *adj* sensitive ‖ *m* medium
**sènso** *m* sense; feeling; meaning; aspect; tone, fashion; direction; **ai sensi di legge** according to law; **a senso** free (*translation*); **doppio senso** double entendre; **in senso contrario** in the opposite direction; **perdere i sensi** to lose consciousness; **riprendere i sensi** to come to; **sensi** carnal appetite, flesh; **senso unico** one-way; **senso vietato** no entry, one-way
**sensò·rio -ria** *adj* (**-ri -rie**) sensory
**sensuale** *adj* sensual, carnal; sensuous
**sensualità** *f* sensuality
**sentènza** *f* sentence; maxim
**sentenziare** §287 (**sentènzio**) *tr* to pass sentence upon, sentence ‖ *intr* to pontificate
**sentenziò·so -sa** [s] *adj* sententious
**sentièro** *m* path, pathway
**sentimentale** *adj* sentimental; mawkish
**sentimentalismo** *m* sentimentalism
**sentiménto** *m* feeling; sentiment; sense;

**uscire di sentimento** (coll) to go out of one's mind
**sentina** *f* bilge; sink (*of vice*)
**sentinèlla** *f* sentry, sentinel
**sentire** *m* feeling ‖ *v* (**sènto**) *tr* to feel; to hear; to listen to; to consult (*a doctor*); to smell; to taste **farsi sentire** to make oneself heard ‖ *intr* to feel; to listen; to smell; to taste; **non sentirci di quell'orecchio** to turn a deaf ear; **sentirci bene** to have keen hearing ‖ *ref* to feel; **non sentirsela di** to not have the courage to; **sentirsela** to feel up to it
**senti·to -ta** *adj* heartfelt
**sentóre** *m* inkling, feeling; sign; (lit) smell
**sènza** *prep* without; beyond (*e.g., comparison*); **senza + inf** without + *ger;* **senza che + subj** without + *ger;* **senza di + pron** without + *pron,* e.g., **senza di lui** without him; **senz'altro** without any doubt, of course
**senza·dìo** *m* (**-dìo**)—**i senzadio** the godless
**senzapà·tria** *m* (**-tria**) man without a country; renegade
**senzatét·to** *m* (**-to**) homeless person; **i senzatetto** the homeless
**separare** *tr & ref* to separate
**separazióne** *f* separation
**sepolcrale** *adj* sepulchral
**sepolcréto** *m* cemetery
**sepólcro** *m* sepulcher, grave
**sepoltura** *f* burial; grave
**seppellire** §253 *tr* to bury
**séppia** *adj invar* sepia ‖ *f* cuttlefish
**seppure** *conj* even if
**sè·psi** *f* (**-psi**) sepsis
**sequèla** *f* series
**sequènza** *f* sequence
**sequestrare** (**sequèstro**) *tr* to seize, confiscate; to kidnap; to confine; to quarantine; (law) to attach, sequester
**sequèstro** *m* seizure; attachment; **sequestro di persona** unlawful detention
**séra** *f* evening; night; **da mezza sera** cocktail (*dress*); dark (*suit*); **da sera** evening (*gown*); formal (*attire*)
**serac·co** *m* (**-chi**) serac
**serafino** *m* seraph
**serale** *adj* evening; night
**seralménte** *adv* in the evening; every evening
**serata** *f* evening; soiree, evening party; **serata d'addio** (theat) farewell performance; **di beneficenza** benefit performance
**serbare** (**sèrbo**) *tr* to keep; to save (*e.g., a place*); to bear (*a grudge*) ‖ *ref* to keep oneself; to stay
**serba·tóio** *m* (**-tói**) tank; reservoir; cartridge clip
**sèr·bo -ba** *adj & mf* Serbian ‖ *m*—**in serbo** in store
**serbocroa·to -ta** *adj & mf* Serbo-Croatian
**serenata** *f* serenade
**serenìssi·mo -ma** *adj* Serene (*Highness*)
**sereni·tà** *f* (**-tà**) serenity

seré·no -na *adj* serene; clear, fair (*weather*)

sergènte *m* sergeant; carpenter's clamp; sergente maggiore first sergeant

sèri·co -ca *adj* (-ci -che) silk

sè·rie *f* (-rie) series; (sports) division; fuori serie (aut) custom-built; in serie (aut) standard; (elec) in series

serietà *f* seriousness; gravity

serigrafia *f* silkscreen process

sè·rio -ria (-ri -rie) *adj* serious; stern; poco serio unreliable (*man*); loose (*woman*) || *m* seriousness; sul serio in earnest; really, e.g., bello sul serio really beautiful

sermonare (sermóno) *tr & intr* (lit) to sermonize

sermóne *m* sermon

sermoneggiare §290 (sermonéggio) *intr* to preach; to lecture

seròti·no -na *adj* late; (lit) evening

sèrpa *f* coach box

sèrpe *f* snake, serpent; a serpe coiled, in a coil; nutrirsi or scaldarsi la serpe in seno to nourish a viper in one's bosom

serpeggiare §290 (serpéggio) *intr* to zigzag; to wind; to creep, spread

serpènte *m* snake, serpent; serpente a sonagli rattlesnake

serpenti·no -na *adj* serpentine || *m* serpentine; coil (*of pipe*) || *f* zigzag, turn (*of winding road*); coil (*of pipe*)

sérqua *f* dozen; lot, large number

sèrra *f* dike, levee; hothouse; sierra; un serra serra a milling crowd

serrafi·la *m* (-le) rear-guard soldier || *f* rear ship (*of convoy*)

serrafilo *m* electrician's pliers; (elec) binding post

serrà·glio *m* (-gli) menagerie; seraglio

serramànico *m*—a serramanico clasp (*knife*); switchblade (*knife*)

serrame *m* lock

serraménto *m* closing, bolting || serra-mén·ti & -ta *fpl* closing devices, doors, windows, and shutters

serranda *f* shutter (*of store*)

serrare (sèrro) *tr* to shut, close; to pursue (*the enemy*); to increase (*tempo*); to furl (*sails*); to lock; to clench (*one's teeth, one's fists*); to shake (*hands*) || *intr* to shut; to be tight || *ref* to be wrenched, e.g., gli si serrò il cuore his heart was wrenched (*the enemy*); serrarsi addosso a to press (*the enemy*)

serrata *f* lockout

serrate *m*—serrate finale (sports) finish

serra·to -ta *adj* shut (*e.g., door*); concise (*style*); tight (*game*); rapid (*gallop*); closed (*ranks*); thick (*crowd*) || *f* see serrata

serratura *f* lock

sèrto *m* (poet) crown, wreath

sèrva *f* (pej) maidservant, maid

servènte *adj* (*gentleman*) in waiting || *m* gunner; (obs) servant

servibile *adj* usable

serviènte *m* (eccl) server

servì·gio *m* (-gi) service; favor

servile *adj* servile; menial; modal (*auxiliary*)

servire (sèrvo) *tr* to serve; to wait on; in che posso servirLa? what can I do for you?; may I help you?; per ser-virLa at your service || *intr* to serve || *intr* (ESSERE & AVERE) to serve; to answer the purpose; to last; (with *dat*) (coll) to need, e.g., gli serve il martello he needs the hammer; non servire a nulla to be of no use; ser-vire da to act as || *ref* to help oneself; servirsi da to patronize, deal with; servirsi di to avail oneself of, use

servitóre *m* servant; tea wagon; servitor suo umilissimo your humble servant

servi·tù *f* (-tù) servitude; captivity; servants, help; servitù di passaggio (law) easement

serviziévole *adj* obliging, accommodating

servi·zio *m* (-zi) service; favor; turn; a mezzo servizio part-time (*domestic help*); di servizio delivery (*entrance*); for hire (*car*); domestic (*help*); fuori servizio out of commission; in ser-vizio in commission; servizi kitchen and bath; facilities; servizi pubblici public services; public works; ser-vizio attivo active duty; servizio per-manente effettivo service in the regular army

sèr·vo -va *adj* (lit) enslaved || *m* slave; servant; servo della gleba serf || *f* see serva

servoassisti·to -ta *adj* servocontrolled

servofréno *m* (aut) power brake

servomotóre *m* servomotor

servostèrzo *m* (aut) power steering

sèsamo *m* sesame; apriti sesamo! open sesame!

sessanta *adj, m & pron* sixty

sessantènne *adj* sixty-year-old || *mf* sixty-year-old person

sessantèsi·mo -ma *adj, m & pron* six-tieth

sessantina *f* about sixty

sessióne *f* session

sèsso *m* sex; il sesso debole the fair sex

sessuale *adj* sexual

sestante *m* sextant

sestétto *m* sextet

sestière *m* district, section

sè·sto -sta *adj & pron* sixth || *m* sixth; curve (*of an arch*); fuori sesto out of sorts; mettere in sesto to arrange; to set in order; sesto acuto (archit) ogive

sèt *m* (sèt) set; set all'aperto (mov) location

séta *f* silk; seta artificiale rayon

setacciare §128 *tr* to sift, sieve

setàc·cio *m* (-ci) sieve

setàce·o -a *adj* silky

séte *f* thirst; aver sete to be thirsty; to lust after; sete di thirst for

seterìa *f* silk mill; seterie silk goods

setifì·cio *m* (-ci) silk mill

sétola *f* bristle; (joc) stubble

sètta *f* sect

settanta *adj, m & pron* seventy

settantènne *adj* seventy-year-old || *mf* seventy-year-old person

settantèsi·mo -ma *adj, m & pron* seven-tieth

**settantina** *f* about seventy

**settà·rio -ria** *adj & mf* (**-ri -rie**) sectarian

**sètte** *adj & pron* seven; **le sette** seven o'clock ‖ *m* seven; seventh (*in dates*); V-shaped tear (*in clothing*)

**settecentèsi·mo -ma** *adj, m & pron* seven hundredth

**settecènto** *adj, m & pron* seven hundred ‖ **il Settecento** the eighteenth century

**settèmbre** *m* September

**settennale** *adj* seven-year (*e.g., plan*)

**settènne** *adj* seven-year-old ‖ *mf* seven-year-old child

**settentrionale** *adj* northern ‖ *mf* northerner

**settentrióne** *m* north; (astr) Little Bear

**setticemìa** *f* septicemia

**sètti·co -ca** *adj* (**-ci -che**) septic

**settimana** *f* week; week's wages; **settimana corta** five-day week

**settimanale** *adj & m* weekly

**settimi·no -na** *adj* premature (*baby*) ‖ *m* (mus) septet

**sètti·mo -ma** *adj, m & pron* seventh

**sètto** *m* septum

**settóre** *m* sector; section, branch; dissector, anatomist; coroner's pathologist

**sevè·ro -ra** *adj* severe, stern

**seviziare** §287 *tr* to torture

**sevìzie** *fpl* cruelty

**sezionale** *adj* sectional

**sezionare** (**seziòno**) *tr* to cut up; to divide up; to dissect

**sezióne** *f* section; dissection; chapter (*of club*); department (*of agency*); (geom) cross section

**sfaccenda·to -ta** *adj* loafing ‖ *mf* loafer

**sfaccettare** (**sfaccétto**) *tr* to facet

**sfacchinare** *intr* (coll) to toil, drudge

**sfacchinata** *f* (coll) drudgery, grind

**sfacciatàggine** *f* brazenness, impudence

**sfaccia·to -ta** *adj* brazen, impudent; loud, gaudy; **fare lo sfacciato** to be fresh

**sfacèlo** *m* breakdown, collapse

**sfà·glio** *m* (**-gli**) swerve (*e.g., of horse*); (cards) discard

**sfaldare** *tr* to exfoliate; to cut into slices ‖ *ref* to flake, scale; (fig) to collapse, crumble

**sfamare** *tr* to feed (*the hungry; the family*) ‖ *ref* to get enough to eat

**sfare** §173 *tr* to undo ‖ *ref* to spoil (*said, e.g., of meat*)

**sfarzo** *m* pomp, display; luxury

**sfarzó·so -sa** [s] *adj* sumptuous, luxurious

**sfasare** *tr* to throw out of phase; (coll) to depress ‖ *intr* (ESSERE) (aut) to misfire; (elec) to be out of phase

**sfasciare** §128 *tr* to remove the bandage from; to unswathe; to smash, shatter ‖ *ref* to go to pieces; to lose one's figure

**sfatare** *tr* to discredit; to unmask

**sfatica·to -ta** *adj* lazy ‖ *mf* loafer

**sfat·to -ta** *adj* overdone; overripe; undone (*bed*); ravaged (*by age*)

**sfavillare** *intr* to spark, sparkle

**sfavóre** *m* disfavor

**sfavorévole** *adj* unfavorable

**sfebbra·to -ta** *adj* free of fever

**sfegata·to -ta** *adj* (coll) rabid, fanatical

**sfèra** *f* sphere; (coll) hand (*of clock*); **a sfera** ball-point (*pen*); **a sfere** ball (*bearing*); **sfera di cuoio** (sports) pigskin

**sfèri·co -ca** *adj* (**-ci -che**) spherical

**sferrare** (**sfèrro**) *tr* to unshoe (*a horse*); to unchain; to draw (*a weapon from a wound*); to deliver (*a blow*) ‖ *ref* to hurl oneself

**sfèrza** *f* whip, scourge

**sferzare** (**sfèrzo**) *tr* to whip, scourge

**sfiancare** §197 *tr* to break open; to tire out; to fit (*clothes*) too tight ‖ *ref* to burst open; to get worn out

**sfiatare** *intr* to leak (*said, e.g., of a tire*) ‖ *intr* (ESSERE) to leak (*said of air or gas*) ‖ *ref* to waste one's breath

**sfiata·tóio** *m* (**-tói**) vent

**sfibbiare** §287 *tr* to unbuckle, unfasten; to untie (*a knot*)

**sfibrante** *adj* exhausting

**sfibrare** *tr* to grind (*wood*) into fibers; to shred (*rags*) into fibers; to weaken, wear out

**sfida** *f* challenge

**sfidare** *tr* to challenge, dare; to brave, defy; to endure (*the challenge of time*); **sfidare che** to bet that

**sfidù·cia** *f* (**-cie**) mistrust; (pol) no confidence

**sfiducia·to -ta** *adj* downcast, depressed

**sfigurare** *tr* to disfigure ‖ *intr* to make a bad impression; to lose face

**sfilacciare** §128 *tr & ref* to ravel, fray

**sfilare** *tr* to unstring; to take off (*one's shoes*); to count (*beads*); to unthread; to dull (*a blade*); to ravel ‖ *intr* (ESSERE) to march, parade; to follow one another ‖ *ref* to become unthreaded; to become frayed; to run (*said of knitted work*); to break one's back

**sfilata** *f* parade; row; **sfilata di moda** fashion show

**sfilza** *f* row, sequence

**sfinge** *f* sphinx

**sfiniménto** *m* exhaustion

**sfinire** §176 *tr* to exhaust, wear out ‖ *ref* to be worn out

**sfintère** *m* sphincter

**sfiorare** (**sfióro**) *tr* to graze; to barely touch (*a subject*); to skim; (lit) to barely reach

**sfioratóre** *m* spillway

**sfiorire** §176 *intr* (ESSERE) to wither, fade

**sfit·to -ta** *adj* not rented

**sfocare** §197 (**sfòco**) *tr* to put out of focus; to blur

**sfociare** §128 (**sfócio**) *tr* to dredge (*the mouth of a river*) ‖ *intr* (ESSERE) to flow; **sfociare in** (fig) to lead to

**sfoderare** (**sfòdero**) *tr* to unsheathe; to show off, sport, display; to take the cover or lining off ‖ *intr* to be drawn out

**sfogare** §209 (**sfógo**) *tr* to vent, give vent to ‖ *intr* (ESSERE) to flow; to pour out; **sfogare in** to turn into ‖ *ref—***sfogarsi a** + *inf* to have one's

fill of + *ger;* **sfogarsi con** to unburden oneself to; **sfogarsi su qlcu**
to take it out on s.o.
**sfoga·tóio** *m* (-tói) vent
**sfoggiare** §290 (sfòggio) *tr* to display,
sport; to show off
**sfòg·gio** *m* (-gi) display, ostentation
**sfòglia** *f* foil; skin (*of onion*); layer of
puff paste; (ichth) sole
**sfogliare** §280 (sfòglio) *tr* to pluck (*a
flower*); to defoliate (*a tree*); to leaf
through (*a book*); to deal (*cards*);
to husk (*corn*); to press (*dough*) into
layers ‖ *ref* to shed its leaves; to
flake
**sfogliata** *f* defoliation; puff paste; **dare
una sfogliata a** to glance through
**sfó·go** *m* (-ghi) exhaust; outlet; vent;
(coll) eruption (*of skin*)
**sfolgorare** (sfólgoro) *intr* (ESSERE &
AVERE) to shine, blaze
**sfolgorì·o** *m* (-i) glittering, blazing
**sfollagèn·te** *m* (-te) billy
**sfollaménto** *m* evacuation; layoff
**sfollare** (sfòllo) *tr* to clear; to cut the
staff of ‖ *intr* (ESSERE & AVERE) to
disperse, evacuate; to cut down the
staff
**sfolla·to -ta** *adj* driven from home ‖
*mf* evacuee
**sfoltire** §176 *tr* to thin out
**sfondare** (sfóndo) *tr* to stave in; to
break through; to be heavy on (*the
stomach*) ‖ *intr* to give ‖ *ref* to
break open
**sfóndo** *m* background
**sfondóne** *m* (coll) blunder, error
**sforbiciare** §128 (sfòrbicio) *tr* to clip,
shear
**sforbiciata** *f* clipping; (sports) scissors;
(sports) scissors kick
**sformare** (sfórmo) *tr* to pull out of
shape; to take out of the mold ‖
*intr* to get mad
**sforma·to -ta** *adj* out of shape ‖ *m*
pudding
**sfornare** (sfórno) *tr* to take out of the
oven
**sfornire** §176 *tr* to deprive; to strip
**sfortuna** *f* bad luck, misfortune
**sfortuna·to -ta** *adj* unsuccessful; unlucky, unfortunate
**sforzare** (sfòrzo) *tr* to strain; to force
‖ *ref* to strive, endeavor
**sforza·to -ta** *adj* forced, unnatural
**sfòrzo** *m* effort; strain; stretch (*of
imagination*); **senza sforzo** effort-
lessly
**sfóttere** *tr* (vulg) to make fun of
**sfracassare** *tr* to smash, crash
**sfracellare** (sfracèllo) *tr* & *ref* to shatter, smash
**sfrangiare** §290 *tr* to ravel
**sfrattare** *tr* to evict; to deport ‖ *intr*
to be evicted
**sfratto** *m* eviction; notice of eviction
**sfrecciare** §128 (sfréccio) *intr* (ESSERE
& AVERE) to speed by
**sfregaménto** *m* rubbing
**sfregare** §209 (sfrégo) *tr* to rub; to
scrape; to strike (*a match*)
**sfregiare** §290 (sfrégio & sfrègio) *tr* to
disfigure, slash

**sfregia·to -ta** *adj* disfigured, slashed ‖
*m* scarface
**sfré·gio** or **sfrè·gio** *m* (-gi) slash, scar,
gash; insult
**sfrenare** (sfréno & sfrèno) *tr* to take
the brake off; to give free rein to ‖
*ref* to kick over the traces
**sfrìggere** §180 *intr* to sizzle
**sfrigolì·o** *m* (-i) sizzle
**sfrondare** (sfróndo) *tr* to defoliate; to
lop off; to trim down ‖ *ref* to lose
leaves
**sfrontatézza** *f* effrontery, impudence
**sfronta·to -ta** *adj* brazen, impudent
**sfrusciare** §128 *intr* to rustle
**sfruttare** *tr* to exploit; to exhaust (*e.g.,
a mine*); to take advantage of
**sfrutta·tóre -trice** *mf* exploiter, developer (*e.g., of an invention*)
**sfuggènte** *adj* fleeting; receding (*forehead*); shifty (*glance*)
**sfuggire** *tr* to avoid, flee ‖ *intr* (ESSERE)
to flee, escape, get away; (with *dat*)
to escape, e.g., **nulla gli sfugge** nothing escapes him; to break, e.g.,
**sfuggì a una promessa** he broke a
promise; **lasciarsi sfuggire** to let slip
**sfuggita** *f*—**di sfuggita** hastily; incidentally; **dare una sfuggita** to run
down (*e.g., to the post office*)
**sfumare** *tr* to shade down; to tone
down; to trim (*hair*) ‖ *intr* (ESSERE)
to vanish; to shade
**sfumatura** *f* nuance, shade; razor clipping
**sfumino** *m* stump (*in drawing*)
**sfuriare** §287 *tr* to vent (*one's anger*) ‖
*intr* to rave
**sfuriata** *f* outburst of anger; gust (*of
wind*); **fare una sfuriata a** to give a
scolding to
**sgabèllo** *m* stool, footstool
**sgabuzzino** *m* cubbyhole
**sgambettare** (sgambétto) *tr* to trip ‖
*intr* to toddle; to kick (*said of a
baby*); to scamper
**sgambétto** *m* trip, stumble; **dare lo
sgambetto a** to trip
**sganasciare** §128 *tr* to dislocate the jaw
of; to break the jaw of; to tear apart
‖ *intr* to steal right and left ‖ *ref* to
break one's jaw; **sganasciarsi dalle
risa** to split one's sides laughing
**sganciare** §128 *tr* to unhook; to lay out
(*money*); to drop (*bombs*) ‖ *intr* to
drop bombs; (coll) to go away ‖ *ref*
to get unhooked; (mil) to disengage
oneself; **sganciarsi da** to get rid of
**sgangherare** (sgànghero) *tr* to unhinge;
to burst ‖ *ref*—**sgangherarsi dalle
risa** to split one's sides laughing
**spanghera·to -ta** *adj* unhinged; broken
down; rickety; coarse (*laughter*)
**sgarbatéz·za** *f* rudeness, incivility;
clumsiness
**sgarba·to -ta** *adj* rude; clumsy
**sgarberìa** *f* var of sgarbatezza
**sgarbo** *m*—**fare uno sgarbo a** to be rude
to
**sgargiante** *adj* loud, flashy, showy
**sgarrare** *intr* to go wrong
**sgattaiolare** (sgattàiolo) *intr* (ESSERE)
to slip away; to wriggle out

sgelare (sgèlo) *tr & intr* to thaw, melt
sgèlo *m* thaw
sghém·bo -ba *adj* crooked; a sghembo askew || sghembo *adv* askew; sideways
sghèrro *m* hired assassin; gendarme
sghiacciare §128 *tr* to thaw
sghignazzare *intr* to guffaw
sghignazzata *f* guffaw
sghimbè·scio -scia *adj*—a or di sghimbescio askew, crooked
sghiribizzo [ddzz] *m* whim, fancy
sgobbare (sgòbbo) *intr* to drudge, plod, plug
sgobbó·ne -na *mf* plugger, plodder, drudge
sgocciolare (sgócciolo) *tr* to let drip || *intr* to drip (*said of container*) || *intr* (ESSERE) to drip (*said of liquid*)
sgocciola·tóio *m* (-tói) dish rack; drip pan
sgocciolatura *f* dripping; drippings
sgócciolo *m* last drop; essere agli sgoccioli to be coming to an end
sgolare (sgólo) *ref* to shout oneself hoarse
sgomberare (sgómbero) *tr & intr* var of sgombrare
sgómbero *m* moving
sgombrané·ve *m* (-ve) snowplow (*truck*)
sgombrare (sgómbro) *tr* to clear; to vacate || *intr* to move, vacate
sgóm·bro -bra *adj* clear || *m* moving; (ichth) mackerel
sgomentare (sgoménto) *tr* to frighten; to dismay
sgomén·to -ta *adj* dismayed || *m* dismay; rimanere di sgomento to be dismayed
sgominare (sgòmino) *tr* to rout
sgomma·to -ta *adj* unglued; without tires; with poor tires
sgonfiare §287 (sgónfio) *tr* to deflate; to damn with faint praise (*e.g., a play*); (coll) to bore || *intr* (ESSERE) to boast; to balloon || *ref* to go down (*said of swelling*); to go flat (*said of a tire*); (fig) to collapse
sgón·fio -fia *adj* deflated, flat
sgonfiòtto *m* jelly doughnut; puff (*in clothing*)
sgórbia *f* (carp) gouge
sgorbiare §287 (sgòrbio) *tr* to scribble; (carp) to gouge
sgòr·bio *m* (-bi) ink spot; scribble, scrawl
sgorgare §209 (sgórgo) *tr* to unclog || *intr* (ESSERE) to gush
sgottare (sgótto) *tr* to bail out (*a boat*)
sgozzare (sgózzo) *tr* to slaughter; to slit the throat of; (fig) to bleed, fleece
sgradévole *adj* disagreeable, unpleasant
sgradire §176 *tr* to refuse || *intr* to be displeasing
sgradi·to -ta *adj* unpleasant; unwelcome
sgraffignare *tr* to snitch, snatch
sgrammatica·to -ta *adj* ungrammatical
sgranare *tr* to shell (*e.g., peas*); to count (*one's beads*); to seed (*grapes*); to open (*one's eyes*) wide; (mach) to disengage || *ref* to crumble; to scratch oneself

sgranchire §176 *tr* to stretch (*e.g., one's legs*)
sgranocchiare §287 (sgranòcchio) *tr* to crunch, munch
sgrassare *tr* to remove the grease from; to skim (*broth*); to scour (*wool*)
sgravare *tr* to relieve, lighten || *ref* to be relieved; to give birth
sgrà·vio *m* (-vi) lightening, lessening; a sgravio di coscienza to ease one's conscience
sgrazia·to -ta *adj* gawky, clumsy
sgretolare (sgrétolo) *tr & ref* to crumble
sgretola·to -ta *adj* crumbling, falling down
sgridare *tr* to scold, chide
sgridata *f* scolding, reprimand
sgrondare (sgróndo) *tr* to cause to drip || *intr* to drip, trickle
sgroppare (sgròppo) *tr* to wear (*a horse*) out || *intr* to buck (*said of a horse*)
sgroppare (sgróppo) *tr* to untie
sgrossare (sgròsso) *tr* to rough-hew; (fig) to refine
sgrovigliare §280 *tr* to untangle
sguaiatàggine *f* uncouthness
sguaia·to -ta *adj* crude, vulgar; uncouth || *mf* vulgar person; uncouth person
sguainare *tr* to unsheathe; to show (*one's nails*)
sgualcire §176 *tr* to crumple || *ref* to become crumpled
sgualdrina *f* trollop, strumpet
sguardo *m* glance, look; eyes
sguarnire §176 *tr* to untrim; (mil) to strip, dismantle
sguàtte·ro -ra *mf* dishwasher, scullion || *f* kitchenmaid, scullery maid
sguazzare *tr* to waste, squander || *intr* to splash; to wallow; to be lost (*in shoes too big or clothes too loose*)
sguinzagliare §280 *tr* to unleash, let loose
sgusciare §128 *tr* to shell, hull || *intr* (ESSERE) to slip; sgusciare di soppiatto to slip away
shòp·ping *m* (-ping) shopping; shopping bag; fare lo shopping to go shopping
shràpnel *m* (shràpnel) shrapnel
si *m* (-si) (mus) si || §5 *pron*
sì *m* (sì) yes; yea; stare tra il sì e il no to not be able to make up one's mind; un . . . sì e l'altro no every other (*e.g., day*)
sìa *conj* see essere
siamése [s] *adj & mf* Siamese
siberia·no -na *adj & mf* Siberian
sibilante *adj & f* sibilant
sibilare (sìbilo) *intr* to hiss
sibilla *f* sibyl
sìbilo *m* hiss, hissing
sicà·rio *m* (-ri) hired assassin
sicché *conj* so that
siccità *f* drought
siccóme *adv* as || *conj* since; as; how
Sicìlia, la Sicily
sicilia·no -na *adj & mf* Sicilian
sicomòro *m* sycamore
sicumèra *f* cocksureness, overconfidence
sicura *f* safety lock (*on gun*)

**sicurézza** *f* security; assurance; safety; certainty; reliability; **di sicurezza** safety; **sicurezza sociale** social security

**sicu·ro -ra** *adj* sure; safe; steady; **di sicuro** certainly || *m* safety; **camminare sul sicuro** to take no chances || **sicuro** *adv* certainly || *f* see **sicura**

**sicur·tà** *f* (**-tà**) insurance

**siderale** *adj* sidereal

**sidère·o -a** *adj* sidereal

**siderùrgi·co -ca** (**-ci -che**) *adj* iron-and-steel || *m* iron-and-steel worker

**sidro** *m* cider, hard cider

**sièpe** *f* hedge; (fig) wall

**sièro** *m* serum

**sièsta** *f* siesta; **fare la siesta** to take a nap, take a siesta

**siffat·to -ta** *adj* such

**sifilide** *f* syphilis

**sifóne** *m* siphon; siphon bottle; trap

**siga·ràio -ràia** (**-rài -ràie**) *mf* cigar maker || *m* (ent) grape hopper; || *f* cigarette girl

**sigarétta** *f* cigarette

**sìgaro** *m* cigar

**sigillare** *tr* to seal

**sigillo** *m* seal; **avere il sigillo alle labbra** to have one's lips sealed; **sigillo sacramentale** seal of confession

**sigla** *f* acronym; initials; abbreviation; letterword; **sigla musicale** theme song

**siglare** *tr* to initial

**significare** §197 (**signìfico**) *tr* to mean; to signify; **significare qlco a qlcu** to inform s.o. of s.th

**significati·vo -va** *adj* significant; meaningful

**significato** *m* meaning; **senza significato** meaningless

**signóra** *f* Madam, Mrs.; lady; mistress, owner; wife || **Nostra Signora** Our Lady

**signóre** *m* sir, Mr.; gentleman; rich man; lord, master, owner; man; **il signore desidera?** what is your pleasure?; **per signori** stag || **Signore** *m* Lord

**signoreggiare** §290 (**signoréggio**) *tr* to rule over; to master; to tower over; to overshadow || *intr* to be the master

**signorìa** *f* seigniory; rule; **La Signoria Vostra** your Honor; **Sua Signoria** his Lordship; your Lordship

**signorile** *adj* seigniorial; gentlemanly; ladylike; elegant, refined

**signorìna** *f* miss; Miss; young lady; spinster

**signorino** *m* master, young gentleman

**signornò** *adv* no, Sir

**signoró·ne -na** *mf* (coll) rich person

**signoròtto** *m* lordling

**signorsì** *adv* yes, Sir

**silenziatóre** *m* silencer (*of firearm*); (aut) muffler

**silèn·zio** *m* (**-zi**) silence; (mil) taps; **fare silenzio** to be silent; **ridurre al silenzio** (mil) to silence

**silenzió·so -sa** [s] *adj* silent; noiseless

**sìlfide** *f* sylphid

**silfo** *m* sylph

**silhouèt·te** *f* (**-te**) silhouette

**sìlice** *f* silica

**sìlicio** *m* silicon

**silicóne** *m* silicone

**siliquastro** *m* redbud

**sillaba** *f* syllable

**sillabare** (**sìllabo**) *tr* to syllabify; to spell

**sillabà·rio** *m* (**-ri**) reader, primer

**sìllabo** *m* syllabus

**silo** *m* silo

**silòfono** *m* xylophone

**siluétta** *f* silhouette

**silurante** *adj* torpedoing, torpedo || *f* destroyer; torpedo boat

**silurare** *tr* to torpedo; (fig) to fire, dismiss; (fig) to undermine

**siluro** *m* torpedo

**silva·no -na** *adj* sylvan

**silvèstre** *adj* (lit) sylvan; (lit) wild; (lit) hard, arduous

**simboleggiare** §290 (**simboléggio**) *tr* to symbolize

**simbòli·co -ca** *adj* (**-ci -che**) symbolic

**simbolismo** *m* symbolism

**sìmbolo** *m* symbol

**similari·tà** *f* (**-tà**) similarity

**sìmile** *adj* similar; such || *m* like; **i propri simili** fellow men

**similòro** *m* tombac

**simmetrìa** *f* symmetry

**simmètri·co -ca** *adj* (**-ci -che**) symmetrical

**simonìa** *f* simony

**simpamina** *f* benzedrine

**simpatèti·co -ca** *adj* (**-ci -che**) sympathetic

**simpatìa** *f* like, liking; **cattivarsi la simpatia di** to make oneself well liked by

**simpàti·co -ca** (**-ci -che**) *adj* nice, pleasant, congenial || *m* (anat) sympathetic system

**simpatizzante** [ddzz] *adj* sympathizing || *mf* sympathizer

**simpatizzare** [ddzz] *intr* to sympathize; to become friends

**simpò·sio** *m* (**-si**) symposium

**simulare** (**sìmulo**) *tr* to simulate

**simula·tóre -trice** *mf* faker, impostor || *m* simulator

**simultàne·o -a** *adj* simultaneous

**sin-** *pref adj* syn-, e.g., **sinonimo** synonymous || *pref m & f* syn-, e.g., **sinonimo** synonym

**sin** *adv*—**sin da** ever since

**sinagò·ga** *f* (**-ghe**) synagogue

**sincerare** (**sincèro**) *tr* (lit) to convince || *ref*—**sincerarsi di** to ascertain

**sincè·ro -ra** *adj* sincere; pure

**sinché** *conj* until

**sìncope** *f* fainting spell; (phonet) syncope; (mus) syncopation

**sincronismo** *m* synchronism; **sincronismo orizzontale** (telv) horizontal hold; **sincronismo verticale** (telv) vertical hold

**sincronizzare** [ddzz] *tr* to syncronize

**sìncro·no -na** *adj* syncronous

**sindacale** *adj* mayoral; union

**sindacalismo** *m* trade unionism

**sindacali·sta** *mf* (**-sti -ste**) union member; union leader

**sindacare** §197 (sìndaco) *tr* to criticize; to scrutinize

**sindaca·to -ta** *adj* controlled, scrutinized ‖ *m* control; labor union; syndicate; **sindacato giallo** company union

**sìnda·co** *m* (-ci) mayor; controller; auditor

**sinecura** *f* sinecure

**sinfonìa** *f* symphony; (*of an opera*) overture; (coll) racket (*noise*)

**sinfòni·co -ca** *adj* (-ci -che) symphonic

**singhiozzare** (singhiózzo) *intr* to sob; to hiccup; to jerk

**singhiózzo** *m* sob; hiccups; **a singhiozzo** in jerks; by fits and spurts

**singolare** *adj* singular ‖ *m* singular; (tennis) singles

**singo·lo -la** *adj* single ‖ *m* individual; shell for one oarsman; (rr) roomette; (telp) private line; (tennis) singles

**singulto** *m* hiccups; sob

**sinistra** *f* left hand; left

**sinistrare** *tr* to ruin; to damage

**sinistra·to -ta** *adj* injured, damaged, ruined ‖ *mf* victim (*of bombing or flood*)

**sinistrismo** *m* leftism

**sinistri·sta** *adj* (-sti -ste) leftish, leftist

**sini·stro -stra** *adj* left; sinister ‖ *m* accident; (boxing) left ‖ *f* see **sinistra**

**sinistròide** *adj & mf* leftist

**sino** *adv* var of **fino**

**sinologìa** *f* Sinology

**sinòni·mo -ma** *adj* synonymous ‖ *m* synonym

**sinò·psi** *f* (-psi) (mov) synopsis

**sinóra** *adv* var of **finora**

**sinòs·si** *f* (-si) synopsis

**sinòtti·co -ca** *adj* (-ci -che) synoptic(al)

**sintas·si** *f* (-si) syntax

**sìnte·si** *f* (-si) synthesis

**sintèti·co -ca** *adj* (-ci -che) synthetic(al); concise

**sintetizzare** [ddzz] *tr* to synthesize

**sintogram·ma** *m* (-mi) (rad) dial

**sìntomo** *m* symptom

**sintonìa** *f* harmony; (rad) tuning

**sintonizzare** [ddzz] *tr* (rad) to tune

**sintonizzatóre** [ddzz] *m* (rad) tuner

**sinuó·so -sa** [s] *adj* sinuous, winding

**sionismo** *m* Zionism

**sipà·rio** *m* (-ri) curtain; **sipario di ferro** iron curtain

**sirèna** *f* siren; mermaid; **sirena da nebbia** foghorn

**Sìria, la** Syria

**siria·no -na** *adj & mf* Syrian

**sirin·ga** *f* (-ghe) panpipe; syringe; catheter; grease gun; (orn) syrinx

**siringare** §209 *tr* to catheterize

**siròcchia** *f* (obs) sister

**si·sma** *m* (-smi) earthquake

**sismògrafo** *m* seismograph

**sismologìa** *f* seismology

**sissignóre** *adv* yes, Sir!

**sistè·ma** *m* (-mi) system

**sistemare** (sistèmo) *tr* to arrange; to put in order; to systematize; to settle; to find a job for; to find a husband for; (coll) to fix ‖ *ref* to settle; to get married

**sistemazióne** *f* arrangement; settlement; job, position

**sìstole** *f* systole

**sitibón·do -da** *adj* (lit) thirsty

**si·to -ta** *adj* (lit) located ‖ *m* (lit) site, spot, location; (mil) sight; (coll) musty odor

**situare** (sìtuo) *tr* to locate, place, situate

**situazióne** *f* situation; condition

**slabbrare** *tr* to chip; to open (*a wound*) ‖ *intr* to overflow ‖ *ref* to become chipped; to reopen (*said of a cut*)

**slacciare** §128 *tr* to untie; to unfasten; to unbutton ‖ *ref* to get undone; to get unbuttoned

**sladinare** *tr* (sports) to train; (mach) to run in, break in

**slanciare** §128 *tr* to hurl, throw ‖ *ref* to hurl oneself; to rise (*said, e.g., of a tower*)

**slancia·to -ta** *adj* slender; soaring

**slàn·cio** *m* (-ci) leap; outburst (*of feeling*); momentum; **di slancio** with a rush; **prendere lo slancio** to get a running start

**slargare** §209 *tr* to widen; to warm (*the heart*) ‖ *ref* to widen, spread out

**slattare** *tr* to wean

**slava·to -ta** *adj* pale, washed out

**sla·vo -va** *adj* Slav, Slavic ‖ *mf* Slav ‖ *m* Slavic (*language*)

**sleale** *adj* disloyal; unfair (*competition*)

**sleal·tà** *f* (-tà) disloyalty

**slegare** §209 (slégo) *tr* to untie

**slega·to -ta** *adj* untied; disconnected

**slip** *m* (slip) briefs; tank suit, bathing suit (*for men*)

**slitta** *f* sled, sleigh; (mach) carriage

**slittaménto** *m* skid; slide

**slittare** *intr* to sled; to skid; to slide

**slogare** §209 (slògo) *tr* to dislocate ‖ *ref* to become dislocated; to dislocate (*e.g., an arm*)

**slogatura** *f* dislocation

**sloggiare** §290 (slòggio) *tr* to dislodge; to evict ‖ *intr* to vacate

**slòg·gio** *m* (-gi) moving; eviction

**slovac·co -ca** *adj & mf* (-chi -che) Slovak

**smacchiare** §287 *tr* to clean; to deforest

**smacchia·tóre -trice** *mf* cleaner ‖ *m* cleaning fluid; spot remover

**smac·co** *m* (-chi) letdown; slap in the face

**smagliante** *adj* dazzling, shining

**smagliare** §280 *tr* to break the links of; to undo the meshes of; to remove (*a fish*) from the net ‖ *intr* to shine, dazzle ‖ *ref* to run (*said, e.g., of knitted fabric*); to free itself from the net

**smagliatura** *f* run (*in stockings*); (fig) break

**smagrire** §176 *tr* to impoverish ‖ *intr* (ESSERE) & *ref* to become thin or lean

**smaliziare** §287 *tr* to make wiser ‖ *ref* to get wiser

**smaltare** *tr* to enamel; to glaze

**smaltire** §176 *tr* to digest; to sleep off (*a drunk*); to swallow (*an offense*);

to sell off; to get rid of; to drain off (*water*)

**smalti·tóio** *m* (-tói) drain, sewer

**smalto** *m* enamel; **smalto per le unghie** nail polish

**smancerìe** *fpl* affectation; mawkishness

**smanceró·so -sa** [s] *adj* prissy

**smangiare** §290 *tr* to erode, eat away ‖ *ref* to be consumed (*e.g., by hatred*)

**smània** *f* frenzy; craze, yearning; **dare in smanie** to be in a frenzy

**smaniare** §287 *intr* to be delirious; to yearn, crave

**smanió·so -sa** [s] *adj* eager; disturbing

**smantellare** (**smantèllo**) *tr* to dismantle; to demolish; to disable (*a ship*)

**smargias·so -sa** *mf* braggart, boaster

**smarriménto** *m* loss; bewilderment; discouragement

**smarrire** §176 *tr* to lose ‖ *ref* to get lost; to get discouraged

**smascellare** (**smascèllo**) *ref*—**smascellarsi dalle risa** to split one's sides laughing

**smascherare** (**smàschero**) *tr* & *ref* to unmask

**smazzata** *f* (cards) deal; (cards) hand

**smembraménto** *m* dismemberment

**smembrare** (**smèmbro**) *tr* to dismember

**smemoratàggine** *f* forgetfulness

**smemora·to -ta** *adj* absent-minded; forgetful ‖ *mf* absent-minded or forgetful person

**smentire** §176 *tr* to belie; to refute; to retract; to be untrue to ‖ *ref* to not be consistent, to contradict oneself

**smentita** *f* denial; retraction

**smeraldo** *m* emerald

**smerciare** §128 (**smèrcio**) *tr* to sell, sell out

**smèr·cio** *m* (-ci) sale

**smèr·go** *m* (-ghi) (zool) merganser

**smerigliare** §280 *tr* to grind, polish; to sand

**smeriglia·to -ta** *adj* polished; sand (*paper*); emery (*cloth*); frosted (*glass*)

**smeri·glio** *m* (-gli) emery; (orn) merlin; (ichth) porbeagle

**smerlare** (**smèrlo**) *tr* to scallop

**smèrlo** *m* scallop (*along the edge of a garment*)

**smés·so -sa** *adj* hand-me-down, castoff

**sméttere** §198 *tr* to stop; to stop wearing; to break up (*housekeeping*); **smetterla** to cut it out ‖ *intr*—**smettere di** + *inf* to stop + *ger*

**smezzare** [ddzz] (**smèzzo**) *tr* to halve

**smidollare** (**smidóllo**) *tr* to remove the marrow from; (fig) to emasculate

**smilitarizzare** [ddzz] *tr* to demilitarize

**smil·zo -za** *adj* slender; poor, worthless

**sminare** *tr* to remove mines from

**sminuire** §176 *tr* to belittle

**sminuzzare** *tr* to crumble; to mince; to expatiate on ‖ *ref* to crumble

**smistaménto** *m* sorting (*of mail*); (rr) shunting, shifting

**smistare** *tr* to sort; (rr) to shift; (soccer) to pass; (rad) to unscramble

**smisura·to -ta** *adj* immense, huge

**smitizzante** [ddzz] *adj* debunking, demythologizing

**smitizzare** [ddzz] *tr* to debunk; to demythologize

**smobiliare** §287 *tr* to remove the furniture from

**smobilitare** (**smobìlito**) *tr* to demobilize

**smobilitazióne** *f* demobilization

**smoccolare** (**smòccolo** & **smóccolo**) *tr* to snuff (*a candle*) ‖ *intr* (slang) to swear, curse

**smoda·to -ta** *adj* excessive, immoderate

**smòg** *m* smog

**smóking** *m* (**smóking**) dinner jacket, tuxedo

**smontàbile** *adj* dismountable

**smontàg·gio** *m* (-gi) disassembling, dismantling

**smontare** (**smónto**) *tr* to take apart; to dismantle; to cause (*e.g., whipped cream*) to fall; to take (*a precious stone*) out of its setting; to dishearten; to dissuade; to drop (*s.o.*) off; **smontare la guardia** to come off guard duty ‖ *intr* (ESSERE) to dismount; to get off or out (*of a conveyance*); to fade; to drop (*said, e.g., of beaten eggs*) ‖ *ref* to become downcast

**smòrfia** *f* grimace; mawkishness; **fare le smorfie a** to make faces at

**smorfió·so -sa** [s] *adj* mawkish, prissy

**smòr·to -ta** *adj* pale, wan; faded

**smorzare** (**smòrzo**) *tr* to attenuate; to lessen; to tone down; to turn off (*light*); (phys) to dampen

**smorzatóre** *m* (mus) damper

**smòs·so -sa** *adj* moved; loose

**smottaménto** *m* mud slide

**smozzicare** §197 (**smózzico**) *tr* to crumble; to mince; to clip, mince (*one's words*)

**smun·to -ta** *adj* emaciated, pale, wan

**smuòvere** §202 *tr* to budge; to till; (fig) to move ‖ *ref* to budge; to move away; **smuoviti!** get going!

**smussare** *tr* to blunt; to bevel; (fig) to soften

**snaturalizzare** [ddzz] *tr* to denaturalize; to denationalize

**snaturare** *tr* to change the nature of; to distort, misrepresent

**snatura·to -ta** *adj* distorted; monstrous, unnatural

**snebbiare** §287 (**snébbio**) *tr* to drive the fog from; to clear (*e.g., one's mind*)

**snellézza** *f* slenderness; nimbleness

**snellire** §176 *tr* & *ref* to slenderize

**snèl·lo -la** *adj* slender; nimble; lively

**snervante** *adj* enervating

**snervare** (**snèrvo**) *tr* to enervate, prostrate ‖ *ref* to become enervated

**snidare** *tr* to drive out, flush

**snòb** *adj invar* snobbish ‖ *mf* (**snòb**) snob

**snobbare** (**snòbbo**) *tr* to snub, slight

**snobismo** *m* snobbishness, snobbery

**snobìsti·co -ca** *adj* (-ci -che) snobbish

**snocciolare** (**snòcciolo**) *tr* to spill (*a secret*); to peel off (*sums of money*); to pit, stone (*fruit*)

**snodare** (**snòdo**) *tr* to untie; to limber up; to exercise; to loosen up (*e.g.,* *s.o.'s tongue*) ‖ *ref* to become loose; to wind (*said, e.g., of a road*)

**snòdo** *m* (mach) joint; **a snodo** flexible

**soave** *adj* sweet, gentle

**sobbalzare** *intr* to jerk, jolt

**sobbalzo** *m* jerk, jolt; **di sobbalzo** with a jolt

**sobbarcare** §197 *tr* to overburden ‖ *ref* —**sobbarcarsi a** to take it upon oneself to

**sobbór·go** *m* (**-ghi**) suburb

**sobillare** *tr* to instigate, stir up

**sobilla·tóre -trice** *mf* instigator

**sobrietà** *f* sobriety, temperance

**sò·brio -bria** *adj* sober, temperate; plain

**socchiùdere** §125 *tr* to half-shut; to leave ajar

**socchiu·so -sa** [s] *adj* ajar

**soccómbere** §186 *intr* to succumb

**soccórrere** §139 *tr* to help ‖ *intr* (lit) to occur

**soccórso** *m* help, succor; **mancato soccorso** failure to render assistance; hit-and-run driving

**sociale** *adj* social; company (*e.g., outing*)

**socialismo** *m* socialism

**sociali·sta** (**-sti -ste**) *adj* socialístic ‖ *mf* socialist

**sociali·tà** *f* (**-tà**) gregariousness; social responsibility

**socie·tà** *f* (**-tà**) society; company; **in società** in partnership; **società anonima** corporation; **società a responsabilità limitata** limited company; **Società delle Nazioni** League of Nations; **società finanziaria** holding company; **società in accomandita** limited partnership; **società per azioni** corporation

**sociévole** *adj* sociable; gregarious

**sò·cio** *m* (**-ci**) member; cardholder; partner; shareholder; **socio fondatore** charter member; **socio sostenitore** patron, sustaining member

**sociologìa** *f* sociology

**sociòlo·go -ga** *mf* (**-gi -ghe**) sociologist

**sòda** *f* soda

**sodali·zio** *m* (**-zi**) society; brotherhood, fraternity; friendship

**soddisfacènte** *adj* satisfying, satisfactory

**soddisfare** §173 (*2d sg pres ind* **soddisfài** or **soddisfi**; *3d pl pres* **soddisfanno** or **soddìsfano**; *1st, 2d & 3d sg pres subj* **soddisfaccia** or **soddisfi**; *3d pl pres subj* **soddisfàcciano** or **soddìsfino**) *tr* to satisfy ‖ *intr* (with *dat*) to satisfy ‖ *ref* to be satisfied

**soddisfat·to -ta** *adj* satisfied

**soddisfazióne** *f* satisfaction

**sòdi·co -ca** *adj* (**-ci -che**) sodium

**sòdio** *m* sodium

**sò·do -da** *adj* hard; hard-boiled; stubborn; solid; **prenderle sode** to get a good thrashing ‖ *m* hard ground; untilled soil; solid foundation; **venire al sodo** to come to the point; **mettere in sodo** to ascertain ‖ *f* see **soda** ‖ **sodo** *adv* hard

**sodomìa** *f* sodomy

**so·fà** *m* (**-fà**) couch, sofa; **sofà a letto** sofa bed

**sofferènte** *adj* sickly, aíling; (lit) long-suffering

**sofferènza** *f* suffering, pain; bad debt; **in sofferenza** overdue

**soffermare** (**sofférmo**) *tr*—**soffermare il passo** to come to a stop ‖ *ref* to linger, pause

**soffiare** §287 (**sóffio**) *tr* to blow; to whisper; (checkers) to huff; (coll) to steal ‖ *intr* to blow; to bellow; (slang) to squeal (*about somebody's offense*); **soffiare sul fuoco** to stir up trouble ‖ *ref* to blow (*one's nose*)

**soffia·to -ta** *adj* blown ‖ *m* soufflé ‖ *f* (slang) squealing, **darsi una soffiata di naso** to blow one's nose

**soffiatóre** *m* glass blower

**sòffice** *adj* soft

**soffierìa** *f* glass factory; blower

**soffiétto** *m* bellows; hood (*of carriage*); (journ) puff, ballyhoo

**sóf·fio** *m* (**-fi**) blow; breath; **in un soffio** in a jiffy; **soffio al cuore** heart murmur

**soffióne** *m* blowpipe; fumarole; (bot) dandelion; (coll) spy

**soffitta** *f* attic, garret

**soffitto** *m* ceiling

**soffocaménto** *m* choking

**soffocante** *adj* stifling; oppressive

**soffocare** §197 (**sòffoco**) *tr* to choke; to stifle; to suffocate; to smother; to repress

**sòffo·co** *m* (**-chi**) sultriness

**soffóndere** §178 *tr* (lit) to suffuse

**soffregare** §209 (**soffrégo**) *tr* to rub lightly

**soffrìggere** §180 *tr* to fry lightly ‖ *intr* to mutter

**soffrire** §207 *tr* to suffer; to endure; **non poter soffrire** to not be able to stand ‖ *intr* to suffer; to ail; **soffrire di** to be troubled with

**soffritto** *m* fried onions and bacon

**sofistica·to -ta** *adj* adulterated; sophisticated, studied

**sofisti·co -ca** *adj* (**-ci -che**) sophistic; faultfinding ‖ *f* sophistry

**soggetti·sta** *mf* (**-sti -ste**) scriptwriter

**soggetti·vo -va** *adj* subjective

**soggèt·to -ta** *adj* subject ‖ *m* subject; (coll) character; (law) person; **cattivo soggetto** hoodlum; **recitare a soggetto** to improvise

**soggezióne** *f* subjection; awe, embarrassment; **mettere a soggezione** to awe

**sogghignare** *intr* to sneer

**soggiacére** §181 *intr* (ESSERE & AVERE) to be subject; to succumb

**soggiogare** §209 (**soggiógo**) *tr* to subjugate, subdue

**soggiornare** (**soggiórno**) *intr* to sojourn, stay

**soggiórno** *m* sojourn, stay; living room; sitting room (*in hotel*)

**soggiùngere** §183 *tr* to add

**soggólo** *m* wimple (*of nun*); throatlatch (*on horse*); (mil) chin strap

**sòglia** *f* doorsill; threshhold

**sògliola** *f* sole

**sognare** (**sógno**) *tr* to dream of ‖ *intr*

to dream; **sognare ad occhi aperti** to daydream

**sogna·tóre -trice** *adj* dreaming ‖ *mf* dreamer

**sógno** *m* dream; **nemmeno per sogno** (coll) by no means

**sòia** *f* (bot) soy

**sòl** *m* (sòl) (mus) sol

**so·làio** *m* (-lài) attic, loft; (agr) crib

**solare** *adj* solar; bright; clear ‖ *v* §257 *tr* to sole

**solàr·rio** *m* (-ri) solarium

**solatì·o -a** (-i -e) *adj* sunny ‖ *m*—a **solatio** with a southern exposure

**solcare** §197 (sólco) *tr* to furrow; to plow (*the waves*)

**sól·co** *m* (-chi) furrow; rut; groove (*of phonograph record*); (fig) path; (naut) wake

**solcòmetro** *m* (naut) log

**soldaté·sco -sca** (-schi -sche) *adj* soldier ‖ *f* soldiery; soldiers; undisciplined troops

**soldatino** *m* toy soldier

**soldato** *m* soldier; **andare soldato** to enlist; **soldato di ventura** soldier of fortune; **soldato scelto** private first class; **soldato semplice** private

**sòldo** *m* soldo (*Italian coin*); coin; money; (mil) pay; (fig) penny; **a soldo a soldo** a penny at a time; **al soldo di** in the pay of; **tirare al soldo** to be a tightwad

**sóle** *m* sun; sunshine; (fig) day, daytime; **sole artificiale** sun lamp; **sole a scacchi** (joc) hoosegow, calaboose

**soleggia·to -ta** *adj* sunny

**solènne** *adj* solemn; (joc) first-class

**solenni·tà** *f* (-tà) solemnity

**solennizzare** [ddzz] *tr* to solemnize

**solére** §255 *intr* (ESSERE) + *inf* to be accustomed to + *inf*, *e.g.*, **suole arrivare alle sette** he is accustomed to arrive at seven ‖ *impers* (ESSERE) —**suole** + *inf* it generally + *3d sg ind*, *e.g.*, **suole nevicare** it generally snows

**solèrte** *adj* (lit) diligent, industrious

**solèrzia** *f* (lit) diligence

**solét·to -ta** *adj* (lit) alone, lonely ‖ *f* sole; inner sole; (archit) slab, cement slab

**sòlfa** *f* (mus) solfeggio; **la solita solfa** the same old story

**solfanèllo** *m* var of **zofanello**

**solfara** *f* sulfur mine

**solfato** *m* sulfate

**solfeggiare** §290 (solféggio) *tr* to sol-fa

**solfiè·ro -ra** *adj* sulfur

**solfito** *m* sulfite

**sólfo** *m* var of **zolfo**

**solfòri·co -ca** *adj* (-ci -che) sulfuric

**solforó·so -sa** [s] *adj* sulfurous

**solfuro** *m* sulfide

**solidale** *adj* solidary; (law) joint; (law) jointly responsible; (mach) built-in; **solidale con** integral with

**solidarie·tà** *f* (-tà) solidarity; (law) joint liability

**solidarizzare** [ddzz] *intr* to make common cause, become united

**solidificare** §197 (solidìfico) *tr* to solidify; to settle

**solidi·tà** *f* (-tà) solidity; (fig) soundness

**sòli·do -da** *adj* solid; (law) joint ‖ *m* solid; **in solido** jointly

**solilò·quio** *m* (-qui) soliloquy

**solin·go -ga** *adj* (-ghi -ghe) (lit) lonely; (lit) solitary (*enjoying solitude*)

**solino** *m* detachable collar; **solino duro** stiff collar

**soli·sta** *mf* (-sti -ste) soloist

**solità·rio -ria** (-ri -rie) *adj* solitary, lonely ‖ *m* solitaire; solitary

**sòli·to -ta** *adj* usual, customary; **esser solito** to be accustomed to ‖ *m* habit, custom; **come il solito** as usual; **di solito** usually

**solitùdine** *f* solitude, loneliness

**sollazzare** *tr* to amuse ‖ *ref* to have a good time, amuse oneself

**sollazzo** *m* (lit) amusement; **essere il sollazzo di** to be the laughingstock of

**sollecitare** (sollécito) *tr* to solicit; to urge; to induce; (mach) to stress ‖ *intr & ref* to hasten

**sollecitazióne** *f* solicitation; urging; (mach) stress

**solléci·to -ta** *adj* quick, prompt; diligent; solicitous, anxious ‖ *m* (com) solicitation, urging

**sollecitùdine** *f* solicitude; promptness; diligence; **cortese sollecitudine** (com) prompt attention

**solleóne** *m* dog days

**solleticare** §197 (sollético) *tr* to tickle; (fig) to flatter

**solléti·co** *m* (-chi) tickling; stimulation; **fare il solletico a** to tickle

**sollevaménto** *m* lifting; **sollevamento di pesi** weight lifting

**sollevare** (sollèvo) *tr* to lift; to relieve; to pick up; to raise (*e.g., a question*); to excite; to elevate ‖ *ref* to rise; to lift oneself; to pick up (*said of courage or health*)

**sollevazióne** *f* uprising

**sollièvo** *m* relief

**sollùchero** *m*—**andare in solluchero** to become ecstatic; **mandare in solluchero** to thrill

**só·lo -la** *adj* lone, lonely, alone; only; single; **fare da solo** to operate all by oneself; **solo soletto** all by myself (yourself, himself, etc.); within oneself; **un solo** only one ‖ *m* (mus) solo ‖ **solo** *adv* only ‖ **solo** *conj* only; **solo che** provided that

**solstì·zio** *m* (-zi) solstice

**soltanto** *adv* only

**solùbile** *adj* soluble

**soluzióne** *f* solution; installment; **soluzione di comodo** compromise; **soluzione provvisoria** stopgap

**solvènte** *adj & m* solvent

**solvènza** *f* solvency

**solvìbile** *adj* collectable; solvent

**sòma** *f* burden, load

**Somàlia, la** Somaliland

**sòma·lo -la** *adj & mf* Somali

**soma·ro -ra** *mf* donkey, ass

**someggia·to -ta** *adj* carried by pack animal; carried on mule back

**somigliante** *adj* similar; **essere somigliante a** to look like ‖ *m* same thing

**somiglianza** *f* similarity, resemblance

**somigliare** §280 *tr* to resemble; (lit) to compare ‖ *intr* (ESSERE & AVERE) (with *dat*) to resemble; to seem to be ‖ *ref* to resemble each other

**sómma** *f* addition; sum; summary

**sommare** (sómmo) *tr* to add; to consider; **tutto sommato** all in all ‖ *intr* to amount

**sommà·rio -ria (-ri -rie)** *adj* summary ‖ *m* summary; abstract; (journ) subheading

**sommèrgere** §162 *tr* to submerge; (fig) to plunge; (fig) to flood (*with insults*) ‖ *ref* to submerge

**sommergìbile** *adj & m* submarine

**sommés·so -sa** *adj* submissive; subdued (*voice*)

**somministrare** *tr* to administer; to provide; to deliver (*a blow*); to adduce (*proof*)

**somministrazióne** *f* administration; provision

**sommi·tà** *f* (**-tà**) summit

**sóm·mo -ma** *adj* highest; supreme ‖ *m* top; peak, summit ‖ *f* see **somma**

**sommòssa** *f* insurrection, riot

**sommoviménto** *m* tremor (*of earth*); arousal (*of passions*); riot

**sommozzatóre** *m* skin diver; (nav) frogman

**sommuòvere** §202 *tr* (lit) to agitate; (lit) to stir up, excite

**sonaglièra** *f* collar with bells

**sonà·glio** *m* (**-gli**) bell; rattle; raindrop; pitter-patter (*of the rain*)

**sonante** *adj* ringing, sounding; ready (*cash*)

**sonare** §257 *tr* to sound; to play; to strike (*the hour*); to ring (*a bell*); (coll) to dupe, cheat; (coll) to give a sound thrashing to; **sonare le campane a distesa** to ring a full peal ‖ *intr* (ESSERE & AVERE) to play; to ring (*said of a bell*); to sound; (lit) to spread (*said of reputation*)

**sona·to -ta** *adj* played; past, e.g., **le tre sonate** past three o'clock; **cinquant'anni sonati** past fifty years of age ‖ *f* ring (*of bell*); (mus) sonata; (coll) thrashing; (coll) cheating

**sona·tóre -trice** *mf* (mus) player

**sónda** *f* sound; probe; drill

**sondàg·gio** *m* (**-gi**) sounding; probe; drilling; **sondaggio d'opinioni** opinion survey, public opinion poll

**sondare** (sóndo) *tr* to sound; to probe; to drill; to survey (*public opinion*)

**sonerìa** *f* alarm (*of clock*)

**sonétto** *m* sonnet

**sonnacchió·so -sa** [s] *adj* sleepy, drowsy

**sonnàmbu·lo -la** *mf* sleepwalker

**sonnecchiare** §287 (sonnécchio) *intr* to drowse, take a nap; to nap, nod

**sonnellino** *m* nap

**sonnìfe·ro -ra** *adj* soporific; narcotic ‖ *m* sleeping medicine; narcotic

**sónno** *m* sleep; (lit) dream; **aver sonno** to be sleepy; **far venir sonno a** to bore; **prender sonno** to fall asleep

**sonnolèn·to -ta** *adj* sleepy; lazy

**sonnolènza** *f* drowsiness; laziness

**sonori·tà** *f* (**-tà**) sonority; acoustics

**sonorizzare** [ddzz] *tr* to voice; (mov) to dub ‖ *ref* to voice

**sonò·ro -ra** *adj* sound (*wave*); sonorous; (phonet) sonant, voiced

**sontuó·so -sa** [s] *adj* sumptuous

**sopèr·chio -chia** *adj & m* (**-chi -chie**) var of **soverchio**

**sopire** §176 *tr* to appease, calm

**sopóre** *m* drowsiness

**soporìfe·ro -ra** *adj* soporific

**soppanno** *m* interlining; lining (*of shoes*)

**sopperire** §176 *intr*—**sopperire a** to provide for; to make up for

**soppesare** [s] (soppéso) *tr* to heft; (fig) to weigh

**soppiantare** *tr* to supplant by scheming; to kick out; to replace; to trick

**soppiatto** *m*—**di soppiatto** stealthily

**sopportàbile** *adj* bearable, tolerable

**sopportare** (soppòrto) *tr* to bear, support; to suffer, endure

**sopportazióne** *f* forbearance, endurance

**soppressióne** *f* suppression, abolition

**sopprìmere** §131 *tr* to suppress, do away with

**sópra** *adj invar* upper; above, preceding ‖ *m* upper, upper part; **al di sopra** above; **al di sopra di** above, over; beyond; **di sopra** upper ‖ *adv* above; up; on top ‖ *prep* on; upon; on top of; over; beyond; above; versus; **sopra pensiero** absorbed in thought

**sopràbito** *m* overcoat, topcoat

**sopraccàri·co -ca (-chi -che)** *adj* overburdened ‖ *m* overload; overweight; (naut) supercargo

**sopraccenna·to -ta** *adj* above-mentioned

**sopraccì·glio** *m* (**-gli** & **-glia** *fpl*) brow, eyebrow; window frame

**sopraccita·to -ta** *adj* above-mentioned

**sopraccopèrta** *f* bedspread; book jacket, dust jacket ‖ *adv* (naut) on deck

**sopraddét·to -ta** *adj* above-mentioned

**sopraffare** §173 *tr* to overcome, overpower

**sopraffazióne** *f* overpowering; abuse

**sopraffinèstra** *f* transom window

**sopraffi·no -na** *adj* first-class; superfine

**sopraggitto** *m* (sew) overcasting

**sopraggiùngere** §183 *intr* (ESSERE) to arrive; to happen

**sopraintèndere** §270 *tr* var of **soprintendere**

**sopralluò·go** *m* (**-ghi**) inspection, investigation on the spot

**sopralzo** *m* var of **soprelevazione**

**soprammercato** *m*—**per soprammercato** in addition, to boot

**soprammòbile** *m* knickknack

**soprannaturale** *adj & m* supernatural

**soprannóme** *m* nickname

**soprannominare** (soprannòmino) *tr* to nickname

**soprannùmero** *adj invar* in excess; overtime ‖ *m*—**in soprannumero** extra; in excess

**sopra·no -na** *adj* upper; (lit) supreme

|| **sopra·no** *mf* (**-ni -ne**) soprano (*person*) || *m* soprano (*voice*)

**soprappensièro** *adj invar* & *adv* immersed in thought

**soprappéso** [s] *m*—**per soprappeso** besides, into the bargain

**soprap·più** *m* (**-più**) plus, extra; **in soprappiù** besides, into the bargain

**soprapprèzzo** *m* extra charge, surcharge

**soprascarpa** *f* overshoe

**soprascrit·to -ta** *adj* written above || *f* address

**soprassalto** *m* start, jump; **di soprassalto** with a start

**soprassedére** §252 *intr* to wait; (with *dat*) to postpone

**soprassòldo** *m* extra pay; (mil) war-zone indemnity

**soprastare** §263 *intr* (ESSERE) to be the boss

**soprattac·co** *m* (**-chi**) rubber heel

**soprattassa** *f* surtax; surcharge

**soprattutto** *adv* above all, especially

**sopravanzare** *tr* to overcome || *intr* (ESSERE) to be left over

**sopravanzo** *m* surplus

**sopravvalutare** *tr* to overrate

**sopravvenire** §282 *tr* (lit) to overrun || *intr* (ESSERE) to arrive; to happen, occur; (with *dat*) to befall

**sopravvènto** *m* windward; **avere il sopravvento** to have the upper hand || *adv* windward

**sopravvissu·to -ta** *adj* surviving || *mf* survivor

**sopravvivènza** *f* survival

**sopravvìvere** §286 *intr* (ESSERE) to survive; (with *dat*) to survive, to outlive

**soprelevare** (**soprelèvo**) *tr* to elevate (*e.g., a railroad*); to increase the height of (*building*)

**soprelevazióne** *f* elevation; addition of one or more floors

**soprintendènte** *m* superintendent

**soprintendènza** *f* superintendency

**soprintèndere** §270 *tr* to oversee

**sopròsso** *m* (coll) bony outgrowth

**sopruso** *m* abuse of power

**soqquadro** *m*—**a soqquadro** upside down, topsy-turvy

**sòrba** *f* sorb apple; (coll) hit, blow

**sorbettièra** *f* ice-cream freezer

**sorbétto** *m* ice cream; sherbet

**sorbire** §176 *tr* to sip; (fig) to swallow, endure

**sòrbo** *m* sorb; service tree

**sór·cio** *m* (**-ci**) mouse

**sòrdi·do -da** *adj* sordid; dirty

**sordina** *f* (mus) sordino, mute; (mus) soft pedal; **in sordina** quietly; stealthily; **mettere in sordina** (mus) to muffle

**sór·do -da** *adj* deaf; dull (*pain*); deep-seated (*hatred*); hollow (*sound*); (phonet) surd, voiceless; **sordo come una campana** stone-deaf || *mf* deaf person

**sordomu·to -ta** *adj* deaf and dumb || *mf* deafmute

**sorèlla** *f* sister

**sorellastra** *f* stepsister

**sorgènte** *adj* rising || *f* spring; well (*of oil*); (fig) source; **sorgente del fiume** riverhead

**sórgere** §258 *intr* (ESSERE) to rise; to arise; to spring forth; **sorgere su un'ancora** (naut) to lie at anchor

**sorgi·vo -va** *adj* spring (*water*)

**sór·go** *m* (**-ghi**) sorghum

**sormontare** (**sormónto**) *tr* to surmount; to overcome || *intr* to fit

**sornió·ne -na** *adj* cunning, sly || *m* sneak

**sorpassare** *tr* to get ahead of; to surpass; to overstep; to go above

**sorpasso** *m* (aut) passing

**sorprendènte** *adj* surprising, astonishing

**sorprèndere** §220 *tr* to surprise; to catch; **sorprendere la buona fede di** to take advantage of || *ref* to be surprised

**sorprésa** [s] *f* surprise; surprise investigation; **di sorpresa** suddenly; unprepared; by surprise

**sorrèggere** §226 *tr* to sustain, support; to bolster

**sorrìdere** §231 *tr* (lit) to say with a smile || *intr* to smile; **sorridere a** to appeal to, e.g., **le sorride l'idea di questa gita** the idea of this trip appeals to her; to smile upon, e.g., **gli sorrideva la vita** life was smiling upon him

**sorriso** [s] *m* smile

**sorsata** *f* gulp, draught

**sorseggiare** §290 (**sorséggio**) *tr* to sip

**sórso** *m* sip; **a sorso a sorso** sipping

**sòrta** *f* kind, sort

**sòrte** *f* luck, lot, fate; chance; kind; (com) principal; **per sorte** of each kind; by chance; **tirare a sorte** to cast lots

**sorteggiare** §290 (**sortéggio**) *tr* to choose by lot; to raffle; **sorteggiare un premio** to draw a prize

**sortég·gio** *m* (**-gi**) drawing

**sortilè·gio** *m* (**-gi**) sortilege; sorcery, magic

**sortire** §176 *tr* (lit) to get by lot; (lit) to have (*results*); (lit) to allot || (**sòrto**) *intr* (ESSERE) to come out (*said, e.g., of a newspaper*); (coll) to be drawn (*by lot*); (coll) to go out; (mil) to make a sally

**sortita** *f* witticism; (mil) sally, sortie; (theat) appearance

**sorvegliante** *adj* watchful || *mf* overseer, caretaker; guardian || *m* watchman; foreman

**sorveglianza** *f* surveillance; supervision

**sorvegliare** §280 (**sorvéglio**) *tr* to oversee, watch over; to check, control

**sorvolare** (**sorvólo**) *tr* to fly over; to overfly; (fig) to avoid, skip

**sorvólo** *m* overflight

**sò·sia** *m* (**-sia**) double, counterpart

**sospèndere** §259 *tr* to hang; to suspend; (chem) to prepare a suspension of; (law) to stay

**sospensióne** *f* suspension; suspense; (law) stay; **sospensione cardanica** gimbals

sospensò•rio *m* (-ri) jockstrap, supporter
sospé•so -sa [s] *adj* suspended; suspension (*bridge*); in sospeso in suspense; in abeyance ‖ *m* employee who has been disciplined by suspension; (com) pending item
sospettare (sospètto) *tr* to suspect ‖ *intr*—sospettare di to suspect; to fear
sospèt•to -ta *adj* suspected; suspicious ‖ *m* dash; suspicion
sospettó•so -sa [s] *adj* suspicious
sospingere §126 *tr* (fig) to drive; (lit) to push
sospirare *tr* to long for, crave; fare sospirare to keep waiting ‖ *intr* to sigh
sospiro *m* sigh; longing; (lit) breath; a sospiri little by little
sossópra *adv* upside down
sòsta *f* stop; reprieve; (rr) demurrage
sostanti•vo -va *adj* & *m* substantive
sostanza *f* substance; sostanza grigia gray matter
sostanziale *adj* substantial
sostanzió•so -sa [s] *adj* substantial
sostare (sòsto) *intr* to stop, pause
sostégno *m* prop; (fig) support
sostenére §271 *tr* to support; to sustain; to take (*an examination*); to defend (*a thesis*); to prop up; to stand (*alcohol*); to play (*a role*) ‖ *ref* to support oneself; to hold up (*said, e.g., of a theory*); to take nourishment
sosteni•tóre -trice *mf* backer, supporter
sostentaménto *m* sustenance, support
sostentare (sostènto) *tr* to support, keep ‖ *ref* to feed, eat
sostenu•to -ta *adj* reserved, austere; rising (*prices*); bullish (*market*); starchy (*manner*)
sostituíbile *adj* replaceable
sostituire §176 *tr* to replace, substitute for, take the place of; sostituire (*qlco* or *qlcu*) a to substitute (*s.th* or *s.o.*) for
sostitu•to -ta *adj* acting; associate, assistant ‖ *m* replacement, substitute
sostituzióne *f* replacement, substitution
sostrato *m* substratum
sottàbito *m* slip
sottacére §268 *tr* (lit) to withhold
sottacéto *adj invar* pickled ‖ sottaceti *mpl* pickles
sott'àcqua *adv* underwater
sotta•no -na *adj* lower (*town*) ‖ *f* skirt; petticoat; (eccl) cassock; gettare la sottana alle ortiche to doff the cassock
sottécchi *adv*—di sottecchi stealthily, secretly; guardare di sottecchi to peep, look furtively (at)
sottentrare (sottèntro) *intr* (ESSERE) (with *dat*) to replace
sotterfù•gio *m* (-gi) subterfuge
sottèrra *adv* underground
sotterrràne•o -a *adj* subterranean, underground; secret, clandestine ‖ *m* cave, vault; dungeon; underground passage ‖ *f* (rr) subway, underground

sotterrare (sottèrro) *tr* to bury
sottigliézza *f* thinness; subtlety
sottile *adj* thin; subtle; (naut) light-weight ‖ *m*—guardare troppo per il sottile to split hairs
sottilizzare [ddzz] *intr* to quibble
sottintèndere §270 *tr* to understand ‖ *ref* to be understood, be implied
sottinté•so -sa [s] *adj* understood, implied ‖ *m* innuendo
sótto *adj invar* lower ‖ *m* lower part ‖ *adv* under; underneath; al di sotto below; al di sotto di under, below; di sotto lower; underneath; downstairs; di sotto a under, below; farsi sotto to sneak up; metter sotto to run over (*with a vehicle*); sotto a under; sotto di under ‖ *prep* under; beneath; below; just before; prendere sotto gamba to underestimate; sotto braccio arm in arm; sotto carico (naut) being loaded; sotto i baffi up one's sleeve; sotto le armi in the service; sotto mano within reach; sotto voce under one's breath, sottovoce
sottoascèl•la *m* (-la) underarm pad
sottobanco *adv* under the counter
sottobicchière *m* coaster
sottobò•sco *m* (-schi) underbrush, thicket
sottobràccio *adv* arm in arm
sottòcchio *adv* under one's eyes
sottoccupa•to -ta *adj* underemployed
sottochiave *adv* under lock and key
sottocó•da *m* (-da) crupper
sottocommissióne *f* subcommittee
sottocopèrta *adv* (naut) below decks
sottocóp•pa *m* (-pa) mat; coaster; (aut) oil pan
sottocòsto *adj invar* & *adv* below cost
sottocutàne•o -a *adj* subcutaneous
sottofà•scia *m* (-scia) wrapper; spedire sottofascia to mail (*a newspaper*) in a wrapper ‖ *f* (-sce) wrapper (*for cigars*)
sottogamba *adv* lightly; prendere sottogamba to underestimate
sottogó•la *m* & *f* (-la) chin strap; throatlatch (*of harness*)
sottolineare (sottolíneo) *tr* to underline, underscore; to emphasize
sott'òlio *adv* in oil
sottomano *m* writing pad ‖ *adv* underhand; within reach
sottomari•no -na *adj* & *m* submarine
sottomés•so -sa *adj* conquered; subdued; submissive
sottométtere §198 *tr* to subdue, crush; to defer, postpone; to present (*a bill*); to subject ‖ *ref* to submit, yield
sottomissióne *f* submission
sottopan•cia *m* (-cia) bellyband, girth
sottopassàg•gio *m* (-gi) underpass; lower level (*of highway*)
sottopiatto *m* saucer
sottopórre §218 *tr* to subject; to submit ‖ *ref* to submit; sottoporsi a to submit to; to undergo (*e.g., an operation*)
sottopó•sto -sta *adj* subject; exposed ‖ *m* subordinate

**sottoprèzzo** *adj invar* cut-rate ‖ *adv* at a cut rate

**sottoprodótto** *m* by-product

**sottórdine** *m* suborder; **in sottordine** secondary

**sottosca·la** *m* (**-la**) space under the stairs; closet under the stairs

**sottoscrit·to -ta** *adj & mf* undersigned

**sottoscrit·tóre -trice** *mf* subscriber

**sottoscrìvere** §250 *tr* to subscribe; to sign, undersign; to underwrite ‖ *intr* to subscribe

**sottoscrizióne** *f* subscription

**sottosegretà·rio** *m* (**-ri**) undersecretary

**sottosópra** *adj invar* upset; **mettere sottosopra** to upset; to turn upside down ‖ *m* confusion, disorder ‖ *adv* upside down

**sottostante** *adj* lower; subordinate ‖ *m* subordinate

**sottostare** §263 *intr* (ESSERE) to be located below; to be subject; to yield, submit; (with *dat*) to undergo (*e.g., an examination*)

**sottosuòlo** *m* subsoil; cellar

**sottosviluppa·to -ta** *adj* underdeveloped

**sottotenènte** *m* second lieutenant; **sottotenente di vascello** (nav) lieutenant j.g.

**sottotèr·ra** *m* (**-ra**) basement ‖ *adv* underground

**sottotétto** *m* attic, garret

**sottotìtolo** *m* subtitle; (mov) caption

**sottovalutare** *tr* to underrate

**sottovènto** *m & adv* leeward

**sottovèste** *f* slip (*undergarment*)

**sottovóce** *adv* sotto voce, under one's breath

**sottrarre** §273 *tr* to subtract; **sottrarre a** to take away from, steal from ‖ *ref*—**sottrarsi a** to avoid; to escape from

**sottrazióne** *f* subtraction

**sottufficiale** *m* noncommissioned officer

**sovènte** *adv* often

**soverchiante** *adj* overwhelming

**soverchiare** §287 (sovèrchio) *tr* to overwhelm; to excel; to bully; (lit) to overflow ‖ *intr* to be in excess

**soverchia·tóre -trice** *adj* overbearing ‖ *mf* overbearing person, oppressor

**sovèr·chio -chia** (**-chi -chie**) *adj* excessive; overbearing ‖ *m* overbearing action

**sovè·scio** *m* (**-sci**) plowing under (*of green manure*)

**sovièti·co -ca** (**-ci -che**) *adj* Soviet ‖ *mf* Soviet citizen

**sovrabbondante** *adj* superabundant

**sovrabbondare** (sovrabbóndo) *intr* (ESSERE & AVERE) to be superabundant; to go to excesses

**sovraccaricare** §197 (sovraccàrico) *tr* to overload

**sovraccàri·co -ca** (**-chi -che**) *adj* overburdened ‖ *m* overload; overweight

**sovraespó·sto -sta** *adj* overexposed

**sovraggiùngere** §183 *intr* (ESSERE) var of **sopraggiungere**

**sovralimentazióne** *f* (aut) supercharging

**sovrani·tà** *f* (**-tà**) sovereignty

**sovra·no -na** *adj & mf* sovereign

**sovrappopolare** (sovrappòpolo) *tr* to overpopulate

**sovrappórre** §218 *tr* to overlay; to superimpose; **sovrapporre qlco a** to lay s.th on ‖ *ref* to be superimposed; to be added; **sovrapporsi a** to put oneself above

**sovrapproduzióne** *f* overproduction

**sovrastampa** *f* overprint

**sovrastante** *adj* overlooking, overhanging; impending

**sovrastare** *tr* to tower over; to hang over; to surpass; to excel ‖ *intr* (ESSERE & AVERE)—**sovrastare a** to tower over; to overlook; to hang over; to surpass; to excel

**sovratensióne** *f* (elec) surge

**sovreccitare** (sovrèccito) *tr* to overexcite

**sovrespórre** §218 *tr* to overexpose

**sovrimpòsta** *f* surtax

**sovrimpressióne** *f* double exposure

**sovruma·no -na** *adj* superhuman

**sovvenire** §282 *tr* (lit) to help ‖ *intr* (with *dat*) to help ‖ *impers* (ESSERE)—**sovviene** (with *dat*) **di** remember, e.g., **gli sovviene spesso dei suoi cari** he often remembers his dear ones ‖ *ref*—**sovvenirsi di** to remember

**sovvenzionare** (sovvenzióno) *tr* to subsidize, grant a subvention to

**sovvenzióne** *f* subsidy, subvention

**sovversi·vo -va** *adj & m* subversive

**sovvertire** (sovvèrto) *tr* to subvert

**sóz·zo -za** *adj* dirty, filthy, foul

**sozzura** *f* dirt, filth

**spaccalé·gna** *m* (**-gna**) woodcutter

**spaccamón·ti** *m* (**-ti**) braggart

**spaccaòs·sa** *m* (**-sa**) butcher's cleaver

**spaccare** §197 *tr* to break, burst; to crack; to unpack; to chop; to split ‖ *ref* to crack; to break; to split

**spacca·to -ta** *adj* broken; split; (coll) identical; (coll) true ‖ *f* (sports, theat) splits

**spaccatura** *f* break; crack; cleavage; split

**spacchétto** *m* vent (*in jacket*)

**spacciare** §128 *tr* to sell out; to palm off; to spread (*reports*); to expedite; to abandon (*as hopeless*); (slang) to push (*e.g., dope*) ‖ *ref*—**spacciarsi per** to pretend to be, pass oneself off as

**spaccia·to -ta** *adj* (coll) cooked, done for; (coll) hopeless

**spaccia·tóre -trice** *mf* passer (*of bad currency or stolen goods*); **spacciatore di notizie false** gossipmonger

**spàc·cio** *m* (**-ci**) sale; passing (*of counterfeit money*); spreading (*of false news*); post exchange; tobacco shop

**spac·co** *m* (**-chi**) break; split; tear; crack; vent (*in jacket*)

**spacconata** *f* brag, braggadocio

**spaccó·ne -na** *mf* braggart, braggadocio

**spada** *f* sword; **a spada tratta** doggedly; **spade** suit of Neapolitan cards corresponding to spades

**spadaccino** *m* swordsman; swash-buckler

**spadóne** *m* two-handed sword

**spadroneggiare** §290 (**spadronéggio**) *intr* to be domineering or bossy

**spaesa·to -ta** *adj* out-of-place

**spaghétto** *m* (coll) fear, jitters; **avere lo spaghetto** (coll) to be scared stiff; **spaghetti** spaghetti

**Spagna, la** Spain

**spagnòla** *f* Spanish woman; Spanish influenza

**spagnolétta** *f* espagnolette; spool; (coll) cigarette; (coll) peanut

**spagnò·lo -la** *adj* Spanish || *m* Spaniard (*individual*); Spanish (*language*); **gli spagnoli** the Spanish || *f* see **spagnola**

**spa·go** *m* (**-ghi**) string, twine; (coll) fear, jitters

**spaiare** §287 *tr* to break a pair of

**spaia·to -ta** *adj* unmatched

**spalancare** §197 *tr* to open wide || *ref* to open up; to gape

**spalare** *tr* to shovel; to feather (*oar*)

**spalla** *f* shoulder; back; abutment (*of bridge*); (theat) stooge, straight man; **alle spalle di qlcu** behind s.o.'s back; **a spalla** on one's back; **fare spalla a** to help; **lavorare di spalle** to elbow one's way; (fig) to worm one's way up; **vivere alle spalle di** to sponge on

**spallàrm** *interj* (mil) shoulder arms!

**spallata** *f* push with the shoulder; shrug of the shoulders

**spalleggiare** §290 (**spalléggio**) *tr* to back, support; (mil) to carry on one's back

**spallétta** *f* parapet, retaining wall; jamb

**spallièra** *f* back (*of chair*); head (*of bed*); foot (*of bed*); espalier

**spallina** *f* epaulet; shoulder strap

**spallùccia** *f*—**fare spallucce** to shrug one's shoulders

**spalmare** *tr* to spread; to smear

**spalto** *m* glacis; **spalti** seats (*of a stadium*)

**spanare** *tr* to strip the thread of || *ref* to be stripped (*said, e.g., of the thread of a nut*)

**spanciare** §128 *tr* to disembowel, gut || *intr* to belly-flop; to bulge (*said of a wall*) || *ref*—**spanciarsi dalle risa** to split one's sides laughing

**spanciata** *f* belly flop; bellyful; **fare una spanciata** to stuff oneself

**spàndere** §260 *tr* to spread; to spill; to shed (*tears*); to squander || *ref* to spread

**spanna** *f* span

**spannare** *tr* to skim (*milk*)

**spannocchiare** §287 (**spannòcchio**) *tr* to husk (*corn*)

**spappolare** (**spàppolo**) *tr* to crush, squash || *ref* to become mushy

**sparadrappo** *m* adhesive tape; (obs) plaster, poultice

**sparagnare** *tr* (coll) to save

**sparare** *tr* to gut, disembowel; to shoot; to let go with (*a kick*); to remove

the hangings from; **spararne delle grosse** to tell tall tales

**sparato** *m* shirt front, dickey

**sparatòria** *f* shooting

**sparecchiare** §287 (**sparécchio**) *tr* to clear (*the table*); to clear away (*one's tools*); to eat up

**sparég·gio** *m* (**-gi**) disparity; deficit; (sports) play-off

**spàrgere** §261 *tr* to spread; to shed; to spill || *ref* to spread

**spargiménto** *m* spreading; **spargimento di sangue** bloodshed

**spargisa·le** [s] *m* (**-le**) salt shaker

**sparigliare** §280 *tr* to break a pair of; to break (*a set*)

**spariglia·to -ta** *adj* unmatched

**sparire** §176 *intr* (ESSERE) to disappear

**sparlare** *intr* to backbite; **sparlare di** to backbite, slander

**sparo** *m* shot

**sparpagliare** §280 *tr* & *intr* to scatter

**spar·so -sa** *adj* scattered; dotted; speckled; hanging loosely (*e.g., hair*)

**sparta·no -na** *adj* & *mf* Spartan

**spartiàc·que** *m* (**-que**) watershed

**spartiné·ve** *m* (**-ve**) snowplow

**spartire** §176 *tr* to divide, share; to separate; **non aver nulla da spartire con** to have nothing to do with

**spartito** *m* (mus) score; (mus) arrangement

**spartitràffi·co** *m* (**-co**) median strip

**spar·to -ta** *adj* (lit) spread || *m* esparto grass

**sparu·to -ta** *adj* lean, wan; meager

**sparvière** *m* sparrow hawk; mortar-board

**spasimante** *m* (joc) lover, wooer

**spasimare** (**spàsimo**) *intr* to writhe; **spasimare per** to long for; to be madly in love with

**spàsimo** *m* pang; severe pain; longing

**spasmo** *m* spasm

**spasmòdi·co -ca** *adj* (**-ci -che**) spasmodic

**spassare** *tr* to amuse || *ref*—**spassarsela** to have a good time

**spassiona·to -ta** *adj* dispassionate, unbiased

**spasso** *m* fun, amusement; walk; (coll) funny guy; **andare a spasso** to go out for a walk; **essere a spasso** to be out of a job; **mandare a spasso** to fire, dismiss; to get rid of; **per spasso** for fun; **portare a spasso** to lead by the nose; **prendersi spasso di** to make fun of

**spassó·so -sa** [s] *adj* amusing, droll

**spàsti·co -ca** *adj* & *mf* spastic

**spato** *m* spar

**spàtola** *f* spatula; putty knife; slapstick (*of harlequin*)

**spauràc·chio** *m* (**chi**) scarecrow; buga-boo, bugbear

**spaurare** *tr* & *ref* (lit) var of **spaurire**

**spaurire** §176 *tr* to frighten || *ref* to be scared

**spaval·do -da** *adj* bold, swaggering

**spaventapàs·seri** *m* (**-ri**) scarecrow

**spaventare** (spavènto) *tr* to scare, frighten || *ref* to be scared

**spaventévole** *adj* frightening, dreadful

**spavènto** *m* fright, fear

**spaventó·so -sa** [s] *adj* frightful, fearful

**spaziale** *adj* space

**spaziare** §287 *tr* (typ) to space || *intr* to soar; to range, rove (*said, e.g., of eye*)

**spazia·tóre -trice** *adj* spacing || *f* space bar (*of typewriter*)

**spaziatura** *f* spacing

**spazientire** §176 *tr* to make (*s.o.*) lose his patience || *intr* (ESSERE) & *ref* to lose patience

**spà·zio** *m* (-zi) space; (fig) room; **spazio aereo** air space; **spazio cosmico** outer space

**spazió·so -sa** [s] *adj* spacious, roomy; wide

**spazzacamino** *m* chimney sweep

**spazzami·ne** *m* (-ne) mine sweeper

**spazzané·ve** *m* (-ve) snowplow

**spazzare** *tr* to sweep; to plow (*snow*); to clean up

**spazzata** *f*—**dare una spazzata a** to give a lick and a promise to

**spazzatrice** *f* street sweeper

**spazzatura** *f* sweeping; sweepings; rubbish, trash

**spazzatu·ràio** *m* (-rài) or **spazzino** *m* street cleaner; trashman, garbage collector, trash collector

**spàzzola** *f* brush; **capelli a spazzola** crew cut

**spazzolare** (spàzzolo) *tr* to brush

**spazzolino** *m* little brush; (elec) brush; **spazzolino da denti** toothbrush; **spazzolino per le unghie** nailbrush

**spazzolóne** *m* push broom

**specchiare** §287 (spècchio) *tr* (lit) to reflect || *ref* to look at oneself (*in a mirror*); to be reflected; **specchiarsi in qlcu** to model oneself on s.o.

**specchièra** *f* mirror; dressing table; full-length mirror

**specchiétto** *m* mirror; synopsis; **specchietto retrovisivo** (aut) rear-view mirror

**spèc·chio** *m* (-chi) mirror; synopsis; shore (*of lake or river*); panel (*of door or window*); sheet (*of water*); (sports) goal line; (sports) board; **specchio di poppa** (naut) transom; **specchio ustorio** burning glass

**speciale** *adj* special

**speciali·sta** *mf* (-sti -ste) specialist

**speciali·tà** *f* (-tà) specialty; (mil) special services; **specialità farmaceutica** patent or proprietary medicine

**specializzare** [ddzz] *tr* & *ref* to specialize

**spè·cie** *f* (-cie) species; kind, sort; appearance, semblance; **fare specie** (with *dat*) (coll) to be surprised, e.g., **gli fa specie** he is surprised; **in specie** especially; **sotto specie di** under pretext of

**specifi·ca** *f* (-che) itemized list; specification

**specificare** §197 (specìfico) *tr* to specify; to itemize

**specìfi·co -ca** (-ci -che) *adj* & *m* specific || *f* see **specifica**

**specillo** *m* (med) probe

**speció·so -sa** [s] *adj* specious

**spè·co** *m* (-chi) (lit) cave

**spècola** *f* observatory

**spècolo** *m* (med, surg) speculum

**speculare** (spèculo) *tr* to observe; to meditate on || *intr* to speculate

**specula·tóre -trice** *adj* speculating || *mf* speculator; **speculatore al rialzo** bull; **speculatore al ribasso** bear

**speda·to -ta** *adj* footworn

**spedire** §176 *tr* to expedite; to prepare; to ship, send, forward; (law) to deliver

**spedi·to -ta** *adj* rapid; free, easy

**spedi·tóre -trice** *mf* shipper, sender; shipping clerk

**spedizióne** *f* shipment, shipping; sending, forwarding; expedition; (naut) papers; **di spedizione** expeditionary

**spedizionière** *m* shipper, forwarder, forwarding agent

**spègnere** §262 *tr* to extinguish, put out; to turn off; to slake (*lime*); to kill; to mix (*flour*) with water or milk; to quench; to obliterate (*a memory*) || *ref* to burn out; to go out (*said of a light*); to fade, die away; to die

**spegni·tóio** *m* (-tói) snuffer

**spegnitura** *f* (theat) blackout

**spelacchiare** §287 *tr* to strip of hair || *ref* to shed hair or fur

**spelacchia·to -ta** *adj* mangy; (pej) baldy

**spelare** (spélo) *tr* to strip of hair; to pluck (*e.g., a chicken*); (fig) to fleece || *ref* to shed hair or fur; to get bald

**spellare** (spèllo) *tr* to skin; (fig) to skin, fleece

**spelón·ca** *f* (-che) cave; hovel, den

**spème** *f* (poet) hope

**spendacció·ne -na** *mf* spendthrift

**spèndere** §220 *tr* to spend

**spenderéc·cio -cia** *adj* (-ci -ce) spendthrift, prodigal

**spennacchiare** §287 *tr* to pluck; (fig) to fleece || *ref* to lose its feathers

**spennare** (spénno) *tr* & *ref* var of **spennacchiare**

**spennellare** (spennèllo) *tr* to dab

**spensieratézza** *f* thoughtlessness

**spensiera·to -ta** *adj* thoughtless, careless; carefree, happy-go-lucky

**spèn·to -ta** *adj* extinguished; turned off; slaked (*lime*); dull (*color*); low (*tone*)

**spenzolare** [dz] (spènzolo) *tr* & *intr* to hang || *ref*—**spenzolarsi da** to hang out of

**speranza** *f* hope; prospect, expectation

**speranzó·so -sa** [s] *adj* hopeful

**sperare** (spèro) *tr* to candle (*eggs*); to hope for; to expect || *intr* to hope; to trust

**spèrdere** §212 *tr* (lit) to scatter; (lit) to lose (*one's way*) || *ref* to lose one's way, get lost

**sperdu·to -ta** *adj* lost, astray; godforsaken (*place*)

**sperequazióne** *f* disproportion; inequality; unjust distribution spergiurare *tr* & *intr* to swear falsely; giurare e spergiurare to swear over and over again

spergiu•ro -ra *adj* perjured || *mf* perjurer || *m* perjury

spericola•to -ta *adj* reckless, daring

sperimentale *adj* experimental

sperimentare (speriménto) *tr* to test, try out; to experience

sperimenta•to -ta *adj* experienced

spèr•ma *m* (-mi) sperm

speronare (speróno) *tr* (naut) to ram

speróne *m* spur; abutment; (nav) ram

sperperare (spèrpero) *tr* to squander

spèrpero *m* squandering

spèr•so -sa *adj* lost, stray

spertica•to -ta *adj* too long; too tall; exaggerated, excessive

spésa [s] *f* expense; shopping; buy, purchase; fare la spesa to shop; fare le spese di to be the butt of; lavorare per le spese to work for one's keep; pagare le spese to bear the charges; spese expenses; room and board; spese di manutenzione upkeep; spese minute petty expenses; spese processuali (law) costs

spesare [s] (spéso) *tr* to support

spesa•to -ta [s] *adj* with all expenses paid

spés•so -sa *adj* thick; many (*times*) || spesso *adv* often; spesso spesso again and again

spessóre *m* thickness

spettàbile *adj* esteemed; Spettabile Ditta (com) Gentlemen

spettàcolo *m* spectacle, show; sight; dar spettacolo di sé to make a show of oneself; spettacolo all'aperto outdoor performance

spettacoló•so -sa [s] *adj* spectacular; (coll) exceptional; (coll) sensational

spettanza *f* concern; pay

spettare (spètto) *intr* (ESSERE)—spettare a to belong to || *impers* (ESSERE) —spetta a it behooves, it is up to

spetta•tóre -trice *mf* spectator, bystander; spettatori public, audience

spettegolare (spettégolo) *intr* to gossip

spettinare (spèttino) *tr* to muss the hair of

spettrale *adj* ghost-like; spectral

spèttro *m* specter, ghost; spectrum

speziale *m* dealer in spices; (coll) pharmacist

spèzie *fpl* spices

spezieria *f* grocery; (coll) drug store, pharmacy; spezierie spices

spezzare (spèzzo) *tr* to break; to smash; to interrupt || *ref* to break

spezzatino *m* stew; spezzatini change

spezza•to -ta *adj* broken; fragmentary; interrupted || *m* stew; (theat) set piece; spezzati change

spezzettare (spezzétto) *tr* to mince

spezzóne *m* small aerial bomb; fragmentation bomb; fragment

spia *f* spy; indication; peephole; (aut) gauge; (aut) pilot light; fare la spia to be an informer

spiaccicare §197 (spiàccico) *tr* to squash, crush || *ref* to be squashed

spiacènte *adj* sorry; (lit) disliked

spiacére §214 *intr* (ESSERE) (with *dat*) to dislike, e.g., queste parole gli spiacciono he dislikes these words; to mind, e.g., se non Le spiace if you don't mind || *ref*—spiacersi di to be sorry for || *impers* (ESSERE) (with *dat*)—gli spiace he is sorry

spiacévole *adj* unpleasant

spiàg•gia *f* (-ge) beach, shore

spianare *tr* to grade (*land*); to roll (*dough*); to pave (*the way*); to iron (*pleats*); to raze, demolish; to level (*a gun*); spianare la fronte to smooth one's brow || *intr* (ESSERE) to be level

spianata *f* esplanade; dare una spianata a to level

spianatóia *f* board (*for rolling dough*)

spiana•tóio *m* (-tói) rolling pin

spianatrice *f* grader

spiano *m* leveling; esplanade; a tutto spiano at full blast; continuously

spiantare *tr* to uproot; to raze, level; to ruin (*financially*) || *ref* to ruin oneself

spianta•to -ta *adj* ruined || *m* pauper

spiare §119 *tr* to spy on; to keep an eye on

spiattellare (spiattèllo) *tr* to blurt out

spiazzo *m* square; plain; clearing

spiccare §197 *tr* to detach; to pick; to enunciate; to begin; to draw up (*a commercial paper*); to issue (*a warrant*); spiccare il volo (aer) to take off || *intr* to stand out || *ref* to separate (*said, e.g., of the stone of a peach*)

spicca•to -ta *adj* clear, distinct; typical; outstanding

spìc•chio *m* (-chi) section (*of fruit*); clove (*of garlic*); slice (*e.g., of apple*); arm (*of cross*)

spicciare §128 *tr* to clear up; to wait on; to dispatch (*business*) || *intr* (ESSERE) to flow forth, gush out || *ref* to hurry up, make haste

spicciati•vo -va *adj* expeditious, quick; straightforward; gruff

spiccicare §197 (spiccico) *tr* to unglue; to enunciate; to utter || *ref* to come unglued; spiccicarsi di to get rid of

spìc•cio -cia (-ci -ce) *adj* expeditious, quick; unhampered; small (*change*) || spicci *mpl* change

spicciolata *adj* *fem*—alla spicciolata little by little; a few at a time

spiccio•lo -la *adj* small (change); (coll) plain || spiccioli *mpl* small change

spìc•co -ca (-chi -che) *adj* freestone (*e.g., peach*) || *m*—fare spicco to stand out

spidocchiare §287 (spidòcchio) *tr* to delouse

spièdo *m* spit; allo spiedo barbecued

spiegàbile *adj* explainable

spiegaménto *m* (mil) array; (mil) deployment

spiegare §209 (spiègo) *tr* to unfold; to let go (*with one's voice*); to unfurl; to spread (*wings*); to deploy (*troops*); to explain; to show, demonstrate; spiegare il volo (aer) to take off || *ref* to become unfurled or unfolded;

to make oneself understood; to come to an understanding; to realize

**spiega·to -ta** *adj* open; full (*voice*)

**spiegazióne** *f* explanation

**spiegazzare** *tr* to crumple, rumple

**spieta·to -ta** *adj* pitiless, ruthless

**spifferare (spiffero)** *tr* (coll) to blurt out ‖ *intr* to blow in (*said of wind*)

**spìffero** *m* (coll) draft

**spi·ga** *f* (**ghe**) panicle (*of oats*); (bot) ear, spike; **a spiga** herringbone

**spiga·to -ta** *adj* herringbone

**spighétta** *f* braid; (bot) spikelet

**spigionare (spigióno)** *ref* to be or become vacant

**spiglia·to -ta** *adj* easy, free and easy

**spi·go** *m* (**-ghi**) lavender

**spigolare (spìgolo)** *tr* to glean

**spigola·tóre -trice** *mf* gleaner

**spìgolo** *m* corner; edge; (archit) arris

**spilla** *f* brooch, pin; **spilla da cravatta** tiepin; **spilla di sicurezza** safety pin

**spillare** *tr* to draw off, tap; to wheedle, worm (*money*) ‖ *intr* to leak (*said of container*) ‖ *intr* (ESSERE) to leak (*said of liquid*)

**spillàti·co** *m* (**-ci**) (law) pin money (*for one's wife*)

**spillo** *m* pin; gimlet; trifle; **a spillo** spikelike; **spillo da balia** or **di sicurezza** safety pin

**spillóne** *m* hatpin; bodkin

**spilluzzicare** §197 (**spillùzzico**) *tr* to pick at, nibble; to scrape together

**spilorcerìa** *f* stinginess

**spilòr·cio -cia** (**-ci -ce**) *adj* stingy ‖ *mf* miser, tightwad

**spilungó·ne -na** *mf* lanky person

**spina** *f* thorn; quill, spine (*of porcupine*); bone (*of fish*); (fig) preoccupation, worry; **alla spina** (*beer*) on tap; **a spina di pesce** herringbone (*fabric*); **con una spina nel cuore** sick at heart; **essere sulle spine** to be on pins and needles; **spina della botte** tap; bunghole; **spina dorsale** spinal column; (fig) backbone; **spina elettrica** plug

**spinà·cio** *m* (**-ci**) spinach (*plant*); **spinaci** spinach (*as food*)

**spinapésce** *m*—**a spinapesce** herringbone

**spina·to -ta** *adj* barbed (*wire*); herringbone (*fabric*)

**spìngere** §126 *tr* to push, press; to prod, goad ‖ *ref* to push; to reach

**spi·no -na** *adj* thorny ‖ *m* thorn ‖ *f* see **spina**

**spinóne** *m* griffon

**spinó·so -sa** [s] *adj* thorny

**spinòtto** *m* wrist pin

**spinta** *f* push; pressure; poke, prod; stress

**spinterògeno** *m* (aut) distributor unit, ignition system

**spin·to -ta** *adj* pushed; bent, inclined; (coll) risqué; (coll) far-out, offbeat ‖ *f* see **spinta**

**spintóne** *m* (coll) push, shove

**spionàg·gio** *m* (**-gi**) espionage, spying

**spioncino** *m* peephole

**spió·ne -na** *mf* spy, stool pigeon

**spiovènte** *adj* drooping; sloping; falling ‖ *m* slope; drainage area (*of a mountain*)

**spiòvere** §216 *intr* to fall, to hang down (*said, e.g., of hair*); to flow down ‖ *impers* (ESSERE)—**è spiovuto** it stopped raining

**spira** *f* turn (*of a coil*); coil (*of serpent*); **a spire** spiral

**spirà·glio** *m* (**-gli**) small opening; gleam (*of light or hope*)

**spirale** *adj* spiral ‖ *f* spiral; hairspring; wreath (*of smoke*); **spirale di fumo** smoke ring

**spirare** *tr* to send forth; (lit) to inspire, infuse; (lit) to show (*kindness*) ‖ *intr* to blow; to emanate; to die; to expire

**spirita·to -ta** *adj* possessed; wild, mad

**spiríti·co -ca** *adj* (**-ci -che**) spiritual; spiritualistic

**spiritismo** *m* spiritualism

**spirito** *m* spirit; wit; mind; spirits, alcohol; sprite; **bello spirito** wit (*person*); **fare dello spirito** to be witty; to crack jokes; **l'ultimo spirito** (lit) one's last breath; **spirito di corpo** esprit de corps; **spirito di parte** partisanship; **spirito sportivo** sportsmanship

**spiritosàggine** [s] *f* witticism

**spiritó·so -sa** [s] *adj* witty; alcoholic

**spirituale** *adj* spiritual

**spizzi·co** *m* (**-chi**)—**a spizzico** or **a spizzichi** little by little; a little at a time

**splendènte** *adj* resplendent, shining

**splèndere** §281 *intr* (ESSERE & AVERE) to shine

**splèndi·do -da** *adj* splendid; gorgeous; bright ‖ *m*—**fare lo splendido** to be a big spender

**splendóre** *m* splendor; brightness; beauty

**splène** *m* (anat) spleen

**spòcchia** *f* haughtiness

**spodestare (spodèsto)** *tr* to dispossess; to dethrone; to oust

**spoetizzare** [ddzz] *tr* to disillusion

**spòglia** *f* slough (*of snake*); skin (*of onion*); husk (*of corn*); (lit) body; (lit) outer garment; **sotto mentite spoglie** under false pretense; **spoglie** spoils

**spogliare** §280 (**spòglio**) *tr* to undress, strip; to strip of armor; to defraud, deprive; to free; to check, examine; to husk (*corn*); to go through (*e.g., correspondence*) ‖ *ref* to undress; to slough (*said, e.g., of a snake*); **spogliarsi di** to get rid of; to divest oneself of; to shake (*a habit*)

**spogliarelli·sta** *f* (**-ste**) stripteaser

**spogliarèllo** *m* striptease

**spoglia·tóio** *m* (**-tói**) dressing room; locker room

**spò·glio -glia** (**-gli -glie**) *adj* stripped, bare; free ‖ *m* cast-off clothing; sorting; scrutiny; counting (*of votes*); **di spoglio** second-hand (*material*) ‖ *f* see **spoglia**

**spòla** *f* bobbin; shuttle; **fare la spola** to shuttle

**spolétta** f bobbin, spool; (mil) fuse

**spolmonare (spolmóno)** ref (coll) to talk, sing, or shout oneself hoarse

**spolpare (spólpo)** tr to gnaw (a bone); to eat up (fruit); (fig) to fleece

**spolverare (spólvero)** tr to dust off, whisk; to powder, dust; to pounce

**spolveratura** f dusting; powdering; sprinkling, smattering (of knowledge); **dare una spolveratura a** to brush up on

**spolverina** f (coll) duster

**spolverino** m duster, smock; powder-sugar duster; pounce; (coll) whisk broom

**spolverizzaménto** [ddzz] m sprinkling (with powder)

**spolverizzare** [ddzz] tr to dust, powder, pounce

**spólvero** m dusting; powdering; pounce; smattering, sprinkling (of knowledge); display

**spónda** f bank (of river); side; cushion (of billiard table)

**sponsale** adj (lit) wedding ‖ **sponsali** mpl (lit) wedding

**spontàne·o -a** adj spontaneous; artless

**spopolare (spòpolo)** tr to depopulate ‖ intr to be a hit; to become depopulated or deserted

**spoppare (spóppo)** tr to wean

**sporàdi·co -ca** adj (-ci -che) sporadic

**sporcaccló·ne -na** adj filthy ‖ mf filthy person; (fig) dirty mouth

**sporcare §197 (spòrco)** tr to dirty; to soil ‖ ref to get dirty; to soil oneself; **sporcarsi la fedina** (coll) to get a black mark on one's record

**sporcizia** f dirt, filth

**spòr·co -ca (-chi -che)** adj dirty, filthy; foul; **farla sporca** to pull a dirty trick ‖ m dirt, filth

**sporgènte** adj leaning; protruding; beetle (brow)

**sporgènza** f prominence, projection

**spòrgere §217** tr to stick out; to stretch out; to lodge (a complaint) ‖ intr (ESSERE) to project, jut out ‖ ref to lean out

**spòrt** m (spòrt) sport; game; **per sport** for fun, for pleasure

**spòrta** f shopping bag; bagful; basket; basketful; shopping; **a sporta** wide-brimmed (hat)

**sportèllo** m door; panel; window (in bank, station, etc.); wicket; branch (of a bank); (theat) box office

**sportivi·tà** f (-tà) sportsmanship

**sporti·vo -va** adj sporting; sportsman-like; athletic ‖ m sportsman

**spòr·to -ta** adj projecting; jutting out ‖ m projection; removable shutter (on store door or window) ‖ f see **sporta**

**spòsa** f bride; wife; **andare in sposa a** to get married to; **sposa promessa** fiancée

**sposalí·zio -zia (-zi -zie)** adj (lit) nuptial ‖ m wedding

**sposare (spòso)** tr to marry; to unite; to embrace (a cause); to fit perfectly; to give in marriage ‖ ref to get married, marry

**spòso** m bridegroom; **sposi** newlyweds

**spossare (spòsso)** tr to exhaust ‖ ref to become worn out

**spossatézza** f exhaustion

**spostaménto** m shift; movement; displacement; change

**spostare (spòsto)** tr to move; to change, shift; to upset ‖ ref to move; to shift; to get out of place; to be upset

**sposta·to -ta** adj ill-adjusted, out of place ‖ mf misfit

**spran·ga** f (-ghe) bar, crossbar

**sprangare §209** tr to bar, bolt

**sprazzo** m spray; flash; burst

**sprecare §197 (sprèco)** tr to waste; to miss (an opportunity) ‖ ref to waste one's efforts

**sprè·co** m (-chi) waste; squandering

**sprecó·ne -na** adj & mf spendthrift

**spregévole** adj contemptible, despicable

**spregiare §290 (sprègio)** tr to despise

**sprè·gio** m (-gi) contempt, scorn

**spregiudica·to -ta** adj open-minded, un-biased ‖ m open-minded person

**sprèmere §123** tr to squeeze, press; **spremere le lacrime a** to move to tears ‖ ref—**spremersi il cervello** to rack one's brain

**spremifrut·ta** m (-ta) squeezer

**spremilimó·ni** m (-ni) lemon squeezer

**spremuta** f squeezing; **spremuta d'arancia** orange juice

**spretare (sprèto)** ref to doff the cassock

**sprezzante** adj contemptuous, haughty

**sprezzare (sprèzzo)** tr (lit) to despise

**sprèzzo** m disdain, contempt

**sprigionare (sprigióno)** tr to exhale, emit; to free from prison ‖ ref to free oneself; to escape, come forth, issue (said, e.g., of steam)

**sprimacciare §128** tr to beat, fluff (e.g., a pillow)

**sprizzare** tr to spout; to sparkle with (joy, health) ‖ intr (ESSERE) to spurt; to fly (said of sparks); to sparkle

**sprizzo** m sprinkle; spurt; spark

**sprofondare (sprofóndo)** tr to send to the bottom; to destroy, ruin; to sink ‖ intr (ESSERE) to sink; to founder; to cave in; to be sunk (e.g., in meditation)

**sprolò·quio** m (-qui) long rigmarole

**spronare (spróno)** tr to spur, goad

**spróne** m spur; prodding; example; guimpe; buttress; abutment (of bridge); **a sprone battuto** at full speed; at once; **dar di sprone a** to spur on; **sprone di cavaliere** (bot) rocket larkspur

**sproporziona·to -ta** adj out of proportion, disproportionate

**sproporzióne** f disproportion

**sproposita·to -ta** adj out of proportion; excessive; gross (error)

**spropòsito** m blunder, gross error; excessive amount; **a sproposito** out of place; inopportunely

**sprovvedu·to -ta** adj deprived; brainless, witless

**sprovvi·sto -sta** adj deprived; devoid, lacking; **alla sprovvista** suddenly; unawares, off guard

**spruzzabianche·rìa** *m* (**-rìa**) sprinkler (*to sprinkle clothes*)

**spruzzare** *tr* to sprinkle, spray; to powder (*sugar*)

**spruzzatóre** *m* sprayer; (aut) nozzle (*of carburetor*)

**spruzzo** *m* spray; splash (*of mud*)

**spudora·to -ta** *adj* shameless; impudent

**spugna** *f* sponge; **dare un colpo di spugna** to wipe the slate clean; **gettare la spugna** to throw in the towel

**spugnare** *tr* to sponge; to swab

**spugnatura** *f* sponge bath

**spugnó·so -sa** [s] *adj* spongy

**spulciare** §128 *tr* to pick the fleas off; to scrutinize, examine minutely

**spuma** *f* foam, froth

**spumante** *adj* sparkling || *m* sparkling wine; champagne

**spumare** *intr* to froth

**spumeggiante** *adj* sparkling; vaporous; foamy

**spumeggiare** §290 (**spuméggio**) *intr* to foam

**spumóne** *m* spumoni

**spumó·so -sa** [s] *adj* foamy, frothy

**spunta** *f* check; check list; check mark

**spuntare** *tr* to blunt; to unpin; to overcome; to clip, trim; to check off; **spuntarla** to come out on top; to overcome || *intr* (ESSERE) to appear; to sprout; to rise; to well up (*said of tears*); to pop out; to break through || *ref* to become blunt; to die down

**spuntino** *m* bite, snack; **fare uno spuntino** to have a bite

**spunto** *m* sourness (*of wine*); (theat) cue; (sports) sprint; (fig) starting point, impetus

**spuntóne** *m* spike; pike; crag

**spurgare** §209 *tr* to purge, clear; to clean up || *ref* to expectorate

**spur·go** *m* (**-ghi**) discharge; reject (*e.g., book*)

**spù·rio -ria** *adj* (**-ri -rie**) spurious

**sputacchiare** §287 *tr* to spit upon || *intr* to sputter

**sputacchièra** *f* spittoon, cuspidor

**sputare** *tr* to spit; to cough up; (fig) to spew (*venom*); **sputare sangue** to spit blood; (fig) to sweat blood || *intr* to spit

**sputasentènze** *mf* (**-ze**) wiseacre

**sputo** *m* spit, sputum; spitting

**squadernare** (**squadèrno**) *tr* to leaf through; **squadernare qlco a qlcu** to put s.th under the nose of s.o. || *ref* to come apart (*said of a book*)

**squadra** *f* square (*for measuring right angles*); squad, group; (mil) squadron; (sports) team; **a squadra** at right angles; **fuori squadra** out of kilter; **squadra di pompieri** fire company; **squadra mobile** flying squad

**squadrare** *tr* to square; (fig) to examine, study

**squadrìglia** *f* (aer, nav) squadron

**squadróne** *m* squadron (*of cavalry*)

**squagliare** §280 *tr* to melt || *ref* to melt; **squagliarsela** to take French leave

**squalifi·ca** *f* (**-che**) disqualification

**squalificare** §197 (**squalìfico**) *tr* to disqualify || *ref* to disqualify oneself; to prove to be unqualified

**squalli·do -da** *adj* wretched, dreary, gloomy; faint (*smile*); (lit) emaciated

**squallóre** *m* wretchedness, dreariness, gloominess

**squalo** *m* shark

**squama** *f* scurf (*shed by the skin*); (bot, pathol, zool) scale

**squamare** *tr* & *ref* to scale

**squamó·so -sa** [s] *adj* scaly

**squarciagóla** *adv*—**a squarciagola** at the top of one's voice

**squarciare** §128 *tr* to rend, tear apart; to dispel (*a doubt*) || *ref* to become torn; to open

**squàr·cio** *m* (**-ci**) tear, rip; passage (*of book*)

**squartare** *tr* to quarter

**squartatura** *f* quartering

**squassare** *tr* to shake violently; to wreck

**squattrina·to -ta** *adj* penniless || *m* pauper

**squilibra·to -ta** *adj* unbalanced, deranged || *mf* mad or insane person

**squili·brio** *m* (**-bri**) lack of balance; **squilibrio mentale** insanity; unbalanced mental condition

**squillante** *adj* ringing, shrill; sharp

**squillare** *intr* to ring; to ring out; to blare

**squillo** *m* ring; peal; blare, blast (*of horn*); || *f* call girl

**squinternare** (**squintèrno**) *tr* to tear (*a book*) to pieces; (fig) to upset

**squisi·to -ta** *adj* exquisite

**squittire** §176 *intr* to squeak; to squeal

**sradicare** §197 (**sràdico**) *tr* to uproot; to eradicate; to pull (*a tooth*)

**sragionare** (**sragióno**) *intr* to talk nonsense

**sregola·to -ta** *adj* intemperate; dissolute

**srotolare** (**sròtolo**) *tr* to unroll

**stàb·bio** *m* (**-bi**) pen; manure, dung

**stabbiòlo** *m* pigpen

**stàbile** *adj* stable; real (*estate*); permanent; stock (*company*) || *m* building

**stabiliménto** *m* plant, factory; establishment; settlement, colony; conclusion (*of a deal*)

**stabilire** §176 *tr* to establish; to decide || *ref* to settle

**stabili·tà** *f* (**-tà**) stability, steadiness

**stabilito** *m* (law) agreement of sale (*drawn up by a broker*)

**stabilizzare** [ddzz] *tr* & *ref* to stabilize

**stabilizza·tóre -trice** [ddzz] *mf* stabilizing person || *m* (aer) stabilizer; (elec) voltage stabilizer

**staccare** §197 *tr* to detach; to unhitch; to outdistance; to draw (*a check*); to tear off; to take (*one's eyes*) away; to begin; to enunciate (*words*) || *intr* to stand out; (coll) to stop working || *ref* to come off; **staccarsi da** to come off (*e.g., the wall*); to leave (*one's home; the shore*); (aer) to take off from

**stacciare** §128 *tr* to sift, sieve

**stàc·cio** *m* (**-ci**) sieve

**staccionata** *f* fence; hurdle; stockade

**stac·co** *m* (**-chi**) tearing off; cut of cloth (*for a suit*); interval; **fare stacco** to stand out

**stadèra** *f* steelyard; **stadera a ponte** weighbridge

**stàdia** *f* leveling rod

**stà·dio** *m* (**-di**) stadium; stage

**staffa** *f* stirrup; heel (*of sock*); gaiter strap; clamp; (mach) bracket; **perdere le staffe** to lose one's nerve

**staffétta** *f* courier, messenger; pilot (*car*); **a staffetta** relay

**staffière** *m* groom, footman; servant

**staffilare** *tr* to whip, belt, lash

**staffilata** *f* lash

**staffile** *m* stirrup strap; whip

**stàg·gio** *m* (**-gi**) stay, upright

**stagionale** *adj* seasonal ‖ *mf* seasonal worker

**stagionare** (**stagióno**) *tr* to season, cure

**stagiona·to -ta** *adj* seasoned, ripe

**stagióne** *f* season; **da mezza stagione** spring-and-fall (*coat*); **di fine stagione** year-end (*sale*)

**stagliare** §280 *tr* to hack ‖ *ref* to stand out

**staglia·to -ta** *adj* sheer (*cliff*)

**sta·gnàio** *m* (**-gnài**) tinsmith; plumber

**stagnante** *adj* stagnant

**stagnare** *tr* to tin; to solder; to stanch ‖ *intr* to stagnate

**stagnaro** *m* var of **stagnaio**

**stagnina** *f* tin can

**stagnino** *m* (coll) var of **stagnaio**

**sta·gno -gna** *adj* watertight; airtight ‖ *m* tin; pond, pool

**stagnòla** *f* tin foil; tin can

**stàio** *m* (**stài**) bushel (*container*); **a staio** (coll) top (*hat*) ‖ *m* (**stàia** *fpl*) bushel (*measure*); **a staia** in abundance

**stalla** *f* stable

**stallìa** *f* (com) lay day

**stallière** *m* stableman, stableboy

**stallo** *m* seat; stall; (chess) stalemate

**stallóne** *m* stallion

**stamane, stamani** or **stamattina** *adv* this morning

**stambéc·co** *m* (**-chi**) ibex

**stambèr·ga** *f* (**-ghe**) hovel

**stambù·gio** *m* (**-gi**) hole, hovel

**stamburare** *tr* to puff up, to boast about ‖ *intr* to drum

**stame** *m* (bot) stamen; thread, yarn

**stamigna** *f* cheesecloth

**stampa** *f* printing; print; (fig) print; (fig) mold; **stampe** printed matter

**stampàg·gio** *m* (**-gi**) (mach) stamping

**stampare** *tr* to stamp; to print; to impress; to publish ‖ *ref* (fig) to be ingraved

**stampatèllo** *m*—**in stampatello** in block letters; **scrivere in stampatello** to print (*with pen or pencil*)

**stampa·to -ta** *adj* printed; impressed ‖ *m* printed form; **stampati** printed matter

**stampa·tóre -trice** *mf* printer

**stampèlla** *f* crutch

**stamperìa** *f* print shop

**stampìglia** *f* rubber stamp; billboard; overprint

**stampigliare** §280 *tr* to stamp; to overprint

**stampinare** *tr* to stencil

**stampino** *m* stencil

**stampo** *m* mold; stencil; stamp, kind; decoy

**stanare** *tr* to flush (*game*); (fig) to dig up

**stancare** §197 *tr* to tire, fatigue; to bore ‖ *ref* to tire, weary

**stanchézza** *f* tiredness, weariness

**stan·co -ca** *adj* (**-chi -che**) tired; tired out; (lit) left (*hand*)

**standardizzare** [ddzz] *tr* to standardize

**stan·ga** *f* (**-ghe**) bar; shaft (*of cart*); beam (*of plow*)

**stangata** *f* blow

**stanghétta** *f* small bar; bolt (*of lock*); temple (*of spectacles*); (mus) bar

**stanòtte** *adv* tonight; last night

**stante** *adj* being; standing; **a sé stante** by itself, independent ‖ *prep* because of; **stante che** since

**stan·tìo -tìa** *adj* (**-tìi; -tìe**) stale; musty

**stantuffo** *m* piston; plunger

**stanza** *f* room; stanza; **essere di stanza** (mil) to be stationed; **stanza da bagno** bath room; **stanza di compensazione** clearing house; **stanza di soggiorno** living room

**stanziare** §287 *tr* to allocate; to appropriate; to budget ‖ *ref* to settle

**stanzino** *m* small room; closet

**stappare** *tr* to uncork

**stare** §263 *intr* (ESSERE) to stay; to stand; to live; to be; to be located; to linger; to last; to stick (*e.g., to a rule*); (poker) to stand pat; **come sta?** how are you?; **lasciar stare** to leave alone; **lasciar stare che** to leave aside that; **non stare in sé dalla gioia** to be beside oneself with joy; **sta bene!** O.K.!; **starci** to fit, e.g., **ci stanno trecento persone** three hundred people fit there; **starci di** to be in favor of, e.g., **io ci starei d'andare al cine** I would be in favor of going to the movies; **stare + ger** to be + ger, e.g., **stava leggendo** he was reading; **stare a** to be up to; to stand on (*ceremony*); to base oneself on; to take (*a joke*); to cost, e.g., **a quanto sta il prosciutto?** how much does the ham cost?; **stare a + inf** to keep + ger, e.g., **stai sempre a sognare** you always keep dreaming; to take + inf, e.g., **stette poco a decidere** he took little time to decide; **stare a cuore** (with *dat*) to deem important, e.g., **gli sta a cuore il lavoro** he deems his work important; **stare a pancia all'aria** to not do a stroke of work; **stare al proprio posto** to keep one's place; **stare a segno** to behave properly; **stare a vedere** to be possible, e.g., **sta a vedere che non viene?** could it be possible that he won't come?; **stare bene** to be well; to be well-off; (with *dat*) to fit, to become, e.g., **questo vestito gli sta**

**bene** this suit fits him well, this suit becomes him; to serve right, e.g., **gli sta bene!** it serves him right!; **stare comodo** to be at ease; to remain seated; **stare con** (fig) to be on the side of; **starsene** to stay apart, e.g., **se ne sta solo soletto** he stays apart or all alone; **stare fermo** to be quiet; to not move; **stare in forse** to doubt; to be doubtful; **stare sulle proprie** to stand aloof; **stare su** to stand erect; **stare su tardi** to stay up late; **stia comodo!** remain seated!

**starna** f gray partridge
**starnazzare** intr to flap its wings; to flutter; to cackle
**starnutare** intr to sneeze
**starnuto** m sneeze
**stasare** [s] tr to unplug, unblock
**staséra** [s] adv tonight, this evening
**sta·si** f (-si) (com) stagnation; (pathol) stasis
**statale** adj government; state || mf government employee
**stàti·co -ca** (-ci -che) static || f statics
**stati·no -na** adj (coll) migratory || m itemized list; (educ) registration form
**stati·sta** m (-sti) statesman
**statisti·co -ca** (-ci -che) adj statistical || m statistician || f statistics; **fare una statistica (di)** to survey; **statistiche** statistics (data)
**stati·vo -va** adj nonmigratory; permanent || m stand (of microscope)
**stato** m state; condition; plight; frame (of mind); status; estate (social class); **di stato** public (e.g., school); **essere in stato di arresto** to be under arrest; **stati** extracts from vital statistics; **Stati Pontifici** Papal States; **Stati Uniti** United States; **stato civile** marital status; vital statistics; **stato confessionale** state under ecclesiastical rule; **stato cuscinetto** buffer state; **stato di preallarme** state of emergency; **stato di previsione** preliminary budget; **stato interessante** pregnancy; **stato maggiore** (mil) general staff
**statoreattóre** m ramjet engine
**stàtua** f statue
**statuà·rio -ria** (-ri -rie) adj statuary; statuesque || m sculptor
**statunitènse** adj & mf American (U.S.A.)
**statura** f stature; height
**statuto** m statute
**stavòlta** adv (coll) this time
**stazionaménto** m parking; **stazionamento vietato** no parking
**stazionare** (stazióno) intr to park
**stazionà·rio -ria** adj (-ri -rie) stationary
**stazióne** f station; bearing; posture; **stazione balneare** shore resort; **stazione climatica** health resort, spa; **stazione di rifornimento** service station; **stazione di tassametri** cab stand; **stazione estiva** summer resort; **stazione generatrice** power plant; **stazione orbitale** orbiting station; **stazione sanitaria** clinic

**stazza** f tonnage; (naut) displacement
**stazzare** tr (naut) to gauge; (naut) to displace
**stazzonare** (stazzóno) tr to crumple
**steatite** f French chalk
**stéc·ca** f (-che) small stick; slat (of shutter); rib (of umbrella); bone (of whale); carton (of cigarettes); rail (of fence); letter opener; chisel (of sculptor); (billiards) cue; (billiards) miscue; (surg) splint; **fare una stecca** (billiards) to miscue; (mus) to sing or play a sour note
**steccadèn·ti** m (-ti) (coll) toothpick
**steccare** §197 (stécco) tr to fence; to put in a splint || intr to play or sing a sour note; (billiards) to miscue
**steccato** m fence; (racing) inside track
**stecchétto** m small stick; **tenere a stecchetto** to keep on a strict diet; to keep short of money
**stecchino** m toothpick
**stecchi·to -ta** adj stiff; lean, lank; dry (twig); dumfounded
**stéc·co** m (-chi) stick, twig
**stecconata** f stockade; fence
**stélla** f star; rowel (of spur); speck of fat (in soup); (fig) sky; **a stella** star-shaped; stellar; **montare alle stelle** to be sky-high (said, e.g., of prices); **portare alle stelle** to praise to the skies; **stella alpina** edelweiss; **stella cadente** shooting star; **stella di mare** starfish; **stella filante** shooting star; confetti; **stella polare** polestar, lodestar
**stellare** adj stellar; (mach) radial || v (stéllo) tr to spangle with stars; to stud
**stella·to -ta** adj starry; star-spangled; star-shaped; studded
**stellétta** f (mil) star; (typ) asterisk; **guadagnarsi le stellette** (mil) to earn a promotion; **portare le stellette** (mil) to be in the service
**stellina** f starlet
**stelloncino** m (journ) short paragraph
**stèlo** m stem, stalk
**stèm·ma** m (-mi) coat of arms; genealogy (of a manuscript)
**stemperare** (stèmpero) tr to dilute; to blunt; to untemper; (lit) to waste || ref to melt; to become dull or blunt
**stendardo** m banner, standard
**stèndere** §270 tr to stretch; to hang up (laundry); to spread; to draw up (a document); to deploy; **stendere a terra** to knock down || ref to stretch out
**stendibianche·rìa** m (-rìa) clothes rack, clotheshorse
**stenodattilògra·fo -fa** mf shorthand typist
**stenografare** (stenògrafo) tr to take down in shorthand
**stenografìa** f shorthand, stenography
**stenogràfi·co -ca** adj (-ci -che) stenographic, shorthand
**stenògra·fo -fa** mf stenographer
**stenòsi** f (pathol) stricture
**stenotipìa** f stenotypy
**stentare** (stènto) tr to eke out (a living)

‖ *intr* to barely make ends meet; **stentare a** to hardly be able to; to find it hard to

**stenta·to -ta** *adj* hard; stunted; strained (*smile*)

**stènto** *m* privation; hardship; **a stento** hardly; with difficulty; **senza stento** without any trouble

**stèr·co** *m* (*-chi*) dung

**stereofòni·co -ca** *adj* (*-ci -che*) stereo, stereophonic

**stereoscòpi·co -ca** *adj* (*-ci -che*) stereoscopic

**stereoscò·pio** *m* (*-pi*) stereoscope

**stereotipa·to -ta** *adj* stereotyped

**sterilizzare** [ddzz] *tr* to sterilize

**sterlina** *f* pound sterling

**sterminare** (**stèrmino**) *tr* to exterminate

**stermina·to -ta** *adj* immense, boundless

**stermì·nio** *m* (*-ni*) extermination; (coll) large amount, lots

**stèrno** *m* breastbone

**sterpàglia** *f* brushwood; undergrowth

**stèrpo** *m* dry twig; bramble

**sterrare** (**stèrro**) *tr* to excavate

**sterratóre** *m* digger

**sterzare** (**stèrzo**) *tr* to diminish by one third; to thin out (*woodland*); (aut) to steer ‖ *intr* to swerve

**sterzata** *f* swerve

**stèrzo** *m* handle bar; (aut) steering gear; (aut) steering wheel

**stésa** [s] *f* coat (*of paint*); string (*of clothes on line*)

**stés·so -sa** *adj* same, e.g., **lo stesso mese** the same month; very, e.g., **tuo fratello stesso** your very brother; **essere alle stesse** to be just the same; **io stesso** I myself; **lui stesso** he himself, etc.; **per sé stesso** by himself; by itself ‖ *pron* same; same thing; **fa lo stesso** it's all the same, it makes no difference

**stesura** [s] *f* drawing up (*of a contract*); **prima stesura** first draft

**stetoscò·pio** *m* (*-pi*) stethoscope

**stìa** *f* chicken coop

**Stige** *m* Styx

**stì·gio -gia** *adj* (*-gi -gie*) Stygian

**stìgmate** *fpl* stigmata

**stilare** *tr* to draft properly

**stile** *m* style

**stilè** *adj invar* stylish

**stilétto** *m* dagger, stiletto

**stilizzare** [ddzz] *tr* to stylize

**stilla** *f* (lit) drop, droplet

**stillare** *tr* to exude; to distill ‖ *intr* (ESSERE) to ooze, drip, exude ‖ *ref*— **stillarsi il cervello** to rack one's brains

**stillici·dio** *m* (*-di*) dripping; repetition

**stilo** *m* stylus; arm (*of steelyard*); dagger; gnomon (*of sundial*); (poet) style ‖ *f* (coll) fountain pen

**stilogràfi·ca** *f* (*-che*) fountain pen

**stima** *f* appraisal; esteem; (naut) dead reckoning; **a stima d'occhio** more or less

**stimare** *tr* to estimate; to deem; to esteem ‖ *ref* (coll) to think a lot of oneself

**stima·tóre -trice** *mf* appraiser; admirer

**stìmmate** *fpl* var of **stigmate**

**stimolante** *adj & m* stimulant

**stimolare** (**stìmolo**) *tr* to stimulate

**stìmolo** *m* influence; stimulus

**stin·co** *m* (*-chi*) shinbone; shin; **stinco di santo** saintly person, saint; **rompere gli stinchi a** to annoy

**stingere** §126 *tr*, *intr* (ESSERE) & *ref* to fade

**stipa** *f* kindling wood, brushwood

**stipare** *tr & ref* to crowd, jam

**stipendiare** §287 (**stipèndio**) *tr* to employ, hire; to pay a salary to

**stipendia·to -ta** *adj* salaried ‖ *mf* salaried person

**stipèn·dio** *m* (*-di*) pay, salary

**stipétto** *m* (naut) closet, cabinet

**stìpite** *m* jamb; stock, family; (bot) trunk (*of palm tree*)

**stipo** *m* cabinet

**stipulare** (**stìpulo**) *tr* to draw up (*a contract*); to stipulate

**stiracchiare** §287 *tr* to stretch; to eke out (*a living*); to twist (*a meaning*); to haggle over ‖ *intr* to haggle; to economize ‖ *ref* to stretch out

**stirare** *tr* to stretch; to iron, press ‖ *intr* to iron ‖ *ref* to stretch out

**stira·tóre -trice** *mf* ironer, presser

**stiratura** *f* ironing; stretching

**stireria** *f* ironing shop

**stiro** *m*—**ferro da stiro** see **ferro**

**stirpe** *f* family; birth, origin

**stitichézza** *f* constipation

**stìti·co -ca** *adj* (*-ci -che*) constipated; (fig) tight

**stiva** *f* (naut) hold; (lit) beam (*of plow*)

**stivàg·gio** *m* (*-gi*) stowage

**stivale** *m* boot; **dei miei stivali** good-for-nothing; **lustrare gli stivali a qlcu** to lick s.o.'s boots

**stivalétto** *m* high shoe

**stivalóne** *m* boot; **stivaloni da equitazione** riding boots; **stivaloni da palude** hip boots

**stivare** *tr* to stow

**stivatóre** *m* stevedore

**stizza** *f* anger; irritation

**stizzire** §176 *tr* to anger, vex ‖ *ref* to get angry

**stizzó·so -sa** [s] *adj* peevish, irritable

**stoccafisso** *m* stockfish

**stoccata** *f* thrust (*with dagger or rapier*); dig, sarcastic remark; touch (*for money*)

**stòc·co** *m* (*-chi*) dagger; rapier; stalk (*of corn*)

**Stoccólma** *f* Stockholm

**stòffa** *f* cloth, material; (fig) stuff, makings

**stoicismo** *m* stoicism

**stòi·co -ca** (*-ci -che*) *adj* stoic, stoical ‖ *m* stoic; Stoic

**stoino** *m* doormat

**stòla** *f* stole

**stòli·do -da** *adj* foolish, silly

**stoltézza** *f* foolishness, silliness

**stól·to -ta** *adj* silly ‖ *mf* fool

**stomacare** §197 (**stòmaco**) *tr* to disgust; to nauseate

**stomachévole** *adj* disgusting, sickening

**stòma·co** *m* (**-ci** or **-chi**) stomach; maw (*of animal*); **dare di stomaco** to vomit

**stonare** (**stòno**) *tr* to sing or play out of tune; to upset || *intr* to sing or play out of tune; to be out of place; to not harmonize

**stona·to** **-ta** *adj* out-of-tune; upset; clashing (*color*)

**stonatura** *f* jarring sound; clash (*of colors*); lack of harmony

**stóppa** *f* tow; oakum; **di stoppa** flaxen; weak, trembling; **stoppa incatramata** oakum

**stoppàc·cio** *m* (**-ci**) wad

**stóppie** *fpl* stubble

**stoppino** *m* wick

**stoppó·so** **-sa** [s] *adj* stubby; stringy

**stórcere** §272 *tr* to twist; to twitch; to wrench (*one's ankle*); to roll (*one's eyes*) || *ref* to twist; to writhe; to bend

**stordiménto** *m* bewilderment; dizziness

**stordire** §176 *tr* to bewilder; to daze || *intr* to be bewildered || *ref* to dull one's senses

**storditàggine** *f* carelessness; mistake, blunder

**stordi·to** **-ta** *adj* careless; bewildered; amazed; dizzy || *mf* scatterbrain

**stòria** *f* history; story; tale; fact; **fare storie** to stand on ceremony; **un'altra storia** a horse of another color

**stòri·co** **-ca** (**-ci** **-che**) *adj* historical || *m* historian

**storièlla** *f* tale, short story; joke

**storiografìa** *f* historiography

**storióne** *m* sturgeon

**stormire** §176 *intr* to rustle

**stórmo** *m* swarm, flock; (aer) group

**stornare** (**stórno**) *tr* to ward off; to dissuade; to divert (*funds*); to write off (*as noncollectable*)

**stornèllo** *m* Italian folksong; (orn) starling

**stór·no** **-na** *adj* dapple-gray || *m* (com) transfer; (orn) starling

**storpiare** §287 (**stòrpio**) *tr* to cripple; to clip (*one's words*)

**stòr·pio** **-pia** (**-pi** **-pie**) *adj* crippled || *m* cripple

**stòr·to** **-ta** *adj* twisted; crooked; crippled || *f* twist; dislocation; retort

**stovìglie** *fpl* dishes; **lavare le stoviglie** to wash the dishes

**stra-** *pref adj* extra-, e.g., **straordinario** extraordinary; over-, e.g., **stracarico** overloaded

**stràbi·co** **-ca** *adj* (**-ci** **-che**) crosseyed

**strabiliante** *adj* astonishing, amazing

**strabiliare** §287 *tr* to amaze || *intr* & *ref* to be amazed

**strabismo** *m* strabismus, squint

**straboccare** §197 (**strabócco**) *intr* to overflow

**strabocchévole** *adj* overflowing

**strabuzzare** [ddzz] *tr* (coll) to roll (*one's eyes*)

**stracàri·co** **-ca** *adj* (**-chi** **-che**) overloaded, overburdened

**stracca** *f*—**pigliare una stracca** to be dead tired

**straccale** *m* breeching (*of harness*); **straccali** (coll) suspenders

**straccare** §197 *tr* (coll) to tire

**stracciaiò·lo** **-la** *mf* ragpicker

**stracciare** §128 *tr* to tear, rend; to comb (*natural silk*)

**stràc·cio** **-cia** (**-ci** **-ce**) *adj* torn, in rags; waste (*paper*) || *m* rag, tatter; tear, rend; combed silk

**stracció·ne** **-na** *mf* tatterdemalion

**straccivéndo·lo** **-la** *mf* ragpicker; rag dealer

**strac·co** **-ca** *adj* (**-chi** **-che**) tired; worn-out; **alla stracca** lazily || *f* see **stracca**

**stracòt·to** **-ta** *adj* overcooked, overdone || *m* stew

**stracuòcere** §144a *tr* to overcook, overdo

**strada** *f* roadway; street; **da strada** vulgar, common; **divorare la strada** to burn up the road; **essere in mezzo a una strada** to be in a bad way; **fare strada a** to pave the way for; **farsi strada** to make one's way; **prender la strada** to set forth; **strada carrozzabile** carriage road; **strada dell'orto** easy way out; **strada ferrata** railroad; **strada maestra** main road; **tagliare la strada a** to stand in the way of; (aut) to cut in front of

**stradale** *adj* road; street; traffic (*e.g., accident*); highway (*police*) || *m* avenue || *f* highway patrol

**stradà·rio** *m* (**-ri**) street directory

**strafalcióne** *m* blunder, gross error

**strafare** §173 *tr* to overdo; to overcook

**strafóro** *m* drilled hole; **di straforo** stealthily

**strafottènte** *adj* unconcerned, nonchalant; arrogant, impudent

**strafottènza** *f* nonchalance, unconcern; arrogance, impudence

**strage** *f* butchery, massacre, carnage; (coll) multitude, lot

**stragrande** *adj* enormous, huge

**stralciare** §128 *tr* to prune, trim (*grapevines*); to eliminate, remove; (com) to liquidate

**stràl·cio** *adj invar* interim; emergency (*e.g., law*); liquidating || *m* (**-ci**) excerpt; clearance sale; **a stralcio** at a bargain

**strale** *m* (lit) arrow

**strallo** *m* (naut) stay

**stralunare** *tr* to roll (*one's eyes*)

**straluna·to** **-ta** *adj* upset; wild-eyed

**stramazzare** *tr* to fell || *intr* (ESSERE) to fall down

**stramazzo** *m* sluice; (coll) straw mattress

**stramberìa** *f* eccentricity

**stram·bo** **-ba** *adj* odd, queer, eccentric; crooked (*legs*); squint (*eyes*)

**strame** *m* litter; fodder

**strampala·to** **-ta** *adj* strange; preposterous, absurd

**stranézza** *f* strangeness; oddity

**strangolare** (**stràngolo**) *tr* to strangle; (naut) to furl

**strangola·tóre** **-trice** *mf* strangler

**straniare** §287 *tr* (lit) to draw away || *ref* to become estranged

**straniè·ro -ra** *adj* foreign, alien; (lit) strange ‖ *mf* foreigner, alien

**stra·no -na** *adj* strange, odd; (lit) estranged

**straordinà·rio -ria (-ri -rie)** *adj* extraordinary; extra ‖ *mf* temporary employee ‖ *m* overtime

**strapagare** §209 *tr* to overpay; to pay too much for

**strapazzare** *tr* to rebuke, upbraid; to mishandle; to bungle ‖ *ref* to overwork oneself

**strapazza·to -ta** *adj* crumpled; bungled; scrambled (*eggs*); overworked ‖ *f* upbraiding, rebuke; fatigue

**strapazzo** *m* misuse; fatigue; excess; **da strapazzo** working (*clothes*); hackneyed, second-rate

**strapèrdere** §212 *tr & intr* to lose hopelessly ‖ *intr* to be wiped out

**strapiè·no -na** *adj* chock-full

**strapiombare (strapiómbo)** *intr* to overhang, jut out

**strapiómbo** *m* overhang; **a strapiombo** sheer (*cliff*)

**strapotènte** *adj* overpowerful

**strappare** *tr* to pull; to tear, rend; to wring (*s.o.'s heart*); **strappare le lacrime a qlcu** to move s.o. to tears; **strappare qlco a qlcu** to pry s.th out of s.o.; to snatch s.th from s.o. ‖ *ref* to tear (*e.g., one's hair*)

**strappata** *f* pull, tug, snatch

**strappo** *m* pull; tear, rip; infraction, breach; pulling away (*on a bicycle*); patch (*of sky*); **a strappi** in jerks; **strappo muscolare** pulled muscle; sprain

**strapuntino** *m* folding seat, jump seat; bucket seat; (naut) mattress

**straric·co -ca** *adj* (-chi -che) (coll) immensely rich

**straripare** *intr* (ESSERE & AVERE) to overflow

**strascicare** §197 (stràscico) *tr* to drag; to shuffle; **strascicare le parole** to drawl

**strascichì·o** *m* (-i) shuffle (*of feet*)

**stràsci·co** *m* (-chi) train (*of skirt*); trail; sequel, aftermath; **a strascico** dragging

**strascinare (stràscino)** *tr* to drag ‖ *ref* to drag oneself, drag

**strascinì·o** *m* (-i) shuffle

**stràscino** *m* dragnet, trawl

**stratagèm·ma** *m* (-mi) stratagem

**strategìa** *f* strategy

**stratègi·co -ca** *adj* (-ci -che) strategic

**stratè·go** *m* (-ghi) strategist; general, commander

**stratificare** §197 (stratìfico) *tr* to stratify

**strato** *m* layer; coat, coating; stratum; (meteor) stratus

**stratosfèra** *f* stratosphere

**strattóne** *m* jerk, tug

**stravagante** *adj* extravagant; whimsical, capricious ‖ *mf* eccentric

**stravèc·chio -chia** *adj* (-chi -chie) aged (*cheese, wine, etc.*); very old

**stravìncere** §285 *tr* to overpower

**straviziare** §287 *intr* to be intemperate

**stravì·zio** *m* (-zi) intemperance, excess

**stravòlgere** §289 *tr* to roll (*the eyes*); to distort; to derange

**straziante** *adj* heartbreaking; excruciating (*pain*); horrible

**straziare** §287 *tr* to torture; to dismay; to mangle; to murder (*a language*)

**strazia·to -ta** *adj* torn, stricken

**strà·zio** *m* (-zi) suffering, pain; torture; shame; boredom; **fare strazio di** to squander

**stré·ga** *f* (-ghe) witch; sorceress

**stregare** §209 (strégo) *tr* to bewitch

**stregóne** *m* sorcerer; witch doctor

**stregonerìa** *f* witchcraft; sorcery

**strègua** *f* standard, criterion; **alla strègua di** on the basis of

**strema·to -ta** *adj* exhausted

**strènna** *f* Christmas gift, New Year's gift; special New Year's issue

**strè·nuo -nua** *adj* strenuous

**strepitare (strèpito)** *intr* to make a noise; to shout, make a racket

**strèpito** *m* noise, racket; **fare strepito** to make a hit

**strepitó·so -sa** [s] *adj* loud, noisy; resounding (*success*)

**streptomicina** *f* streptomycin

**stressa·to -ta** *adj* under stress

**strétta** *f* grasp, clench; tightening (*of brakes*); hold; press, crush; pang; mountain pass; **mettere alle strette** to drive into a corner; **stretta dei conti** rendering of accounts; **stretta di mano** handshake; **stretta finale** climax

**strettézza** *f* narrowness; **strettezze** straits, hardship

**strét·to -ta** *adj* narrow; tight; bare (*necessities*); pure (*e.g., dialect*); strict; clenched (*fist*); heavy (*heart*); minimum (*price*); (phonet) close ‖ *m* straits, narrows ‖ *f* see **stretta** ‖ **stretto** *adv* tightly

**strettóia** *f* narrow stretch; hardship; bandage

**strìa** *f* stripe, streak

**striare** §119 *tr* to stripe, streak

**stricnina** *f* strychnine

**stridènte** *adj* jarring; clashing (*colors*); strident (*sound*)

**strìdere** §264 *tr* to grit (*one's teeth*) ‖ *intr* to shriek; to squeak; to creak; to clash (*said of colors*); to croak (*said of raven*); to hoot (*said of owl*); to howl (*said of wind*) ‖ *ref* (coll) to be resigned

**strido** *m* (-di & -da *fpl*) shriek; squeak

**stridóre** *m* shriek; creak, squeak; gnashing (*of teeth*)

**strìdu·lo -la** *adj* shrill

**strigare** §209 *tr* to disentangle ‖ *ref* to extricate oneself

**strìglia** *f* currycomb

**strigliare** §280 *tr* to curry; to upbraid ‖ *ref* to groom oneself

**strillare** *tr* to shout; (coll) to scold; (coll) to hawk (*newspapers*) ‖ *intr* to scream

**strillo** *m* shriek; shout, scream

**strilló·ne -na** *mf* loud-mouthed person ‖ *m* newsdealer; newsboy, paperboy

**striminzi·to -ta** *adj* shrunken; tight; stunted; skinny

**strimpellare (strimpèllo)** *tr* to thrum; to thrum on

**strinare** *tr* to singe; to burn (*with a flatiron*)

**strin·ga** *f* (-ghe) lace; shoelace

**stringa·to -ta** *adj* terse, concise

**stringere** §265 *tr* to tighten; to grip; to shake, clasp (*a hand*); to drive into a corner; to squeeze; to embrace; to close (*an alliance, a deal*); to wring (*one's heart*); to clench (*the fist*); (lit) to gird (*a sword*); (mus) to accelerate; **stringere d'assedio** to besiege; **stringere i freni** to put the brakes on || *intr* to be tight; **il tempo stringe** time is running short; **stringi, stringi** at the very end, in conclusion || *ref* to squeeze close together; to shrink; to coagulate; to draw close; **stringersi a** to snuggle up to; **stringersi addosso a** to attack; **stringersi nelle spalle** to shrug one's shoulders

**stringina·so** [s] *m* (-so) pince-nez

**stri·scia** *f* (-sce) strip, band; trail; stripe; line; **a strisce** striped; **striscia d'atterramento** airstrip; **striscia di cuoio** strop

**strisciante** *adj* crawling; (fig) fawning

**strisciare** §128 *tr* to shuffle (*feet*); to graze; **strisciare una riverenza** to curtsy || *intr* to creep, crawl; to graze by || *ref* to fawn; **strisciarsi a** to rub one's back against

**strisciata** or **strisciatura** *f* sliding; trail

**strì·scio** *m* (-sci) rubbing; shuffling; **ballare di striscio** to shuffle; **da** or **di striscio** superficial (*wound*)

**striscióne** *m* festoon; festooned sign; flatterer; **striscione d'arrivo** landing (*in gymnastics*); **striscione del traguardo** (sports) tape

**striscióni** *adv* crawling

**stritolare (strìtolo)** *tr* to crush, smash

**strizzalimó·ni** *m*(-ni) lemon squeezer

**strizzare** *tr* to squeeze, press; to wink (*the eye*); **strizzare l'occhio** to wink

**strizza·tóio** *m* (-tói) wringer

**strò·fa** or **strò·fe** *f* (-fe) strophe

**strofinàc·cio** *m* (-ci) dust cloth

**strofinare** *tr* to rub; to polish || *ref* to rub oneself; to fawn

**strofinata** *f*—**dare una strofinata a** to give a lick and a promise to

**strofinì·o** *m* (-i) rubbing; wiping

**stròla·ga** *f* (-ghe) (orn) loon

**strombatura** *f* embrasure

**strombazzare** *tr* to glorify; **strombazzare i propri meriti** to toot one's own horn || *intr* to blast away on the trumpet

**strombazza·tóre -trice** *mf* show-off

**strombettare (strombétto)** *tr* to trumpet, toot

**stroncare** §197 **(strónco)** *tr* to break off; to break down; to eliminate; (fig) to criticize severely

**stroncatura** *f* devastating criticism

**strònzio** *m* strontium

**strónzo** *m* (vulg) turd

**stropicciare** §128 *tr* to rub (*hands*); to

drag, shuffle (*feet*); (coll) to crumple || *ref*—**stropicciarsene** (coll) to not give a hoot

**stropiccì·o** *m* (-i) rubbing; shuffling

**stròzza** *f* (coll) gullet, throat

**strozzare (stròzzo)** *tr* to strangle; to stop up; to fleece, swindle || *ref* to choke; to narrow

**strozza·to -ta** *adj* choked; choking; strangulated (*hernia*)

**strozzatura** *f* narrowing

**strozzinàg·gio** *m* (-gi) usury

**strozzino** *m* usurer, loan shark

**strùggere** §266 *tr* to melt; to consume || *ref* to melt; to pine away; to be upset; **struggersi di** to be consumed by

**struggiménto** *m* melting; longing; torment

**strumentale** *adj* instrument (*flying*); capital (*goods*); instructional (*language, in multi-lingual regions*); (gram, mus) instrumental

**strumentali·sta** *mf* (-sti -ste) instrumentalist

**strumentalizzare** [ddzz] *tr* to use, take advantage of

**strumentare (struménto)** *tr* to orchestrate

**struménto** *m* instrument; tool, implement; **strumento a corda** stringed instrument; **strumento a fiato** wind instrument; **strumento di bordo** (aer) flight recorder

**strusciare** §128 *tr* to rub; to shuffle (*feet*); to crumple; to wear out || *ref*—**strusciarsi a** to fawn on

**strutto** *m* lard, shortening

**struttura** *f* structure

**strutturare** *tr* to organize, structure

**struzzo** *m* ostrich

**stuccare** §197 *tr* to putty; to stucco; to surfeit || *ref* to grow weary

**stucchévole** *adj* sickening

**stuc·co -ca** (-chi -che) *adj* bored; **stucco e ristucco** sick and tired || *m* putty; stucco; plaster of Paris; **rimanere di stucco** to be taken aback

**studèn·te -téssa** *mf* student

**studentésco -sca** (-schi -sche) *adj* student; student-like || *f* student body

**studiare** §287 *tr* to study; **studiarle tutte** to consider every angle || *intr* to study; to try || *ref* to try; to gaze at oneself

**studia·to -ta** *adj* affected, studied

**stù·dio** *m* (-di) study; school district; office (*of professional man*); studio; (hist) university; (lit) wish; (mus) étude; **a studio** on purpose; **essere allo studio** to be under consideration

**studió·so -sa** [s] *adj* studious || *m* scholar

**stufa** *f* stove, heater; hothouse

**stufare** *tr* to warm up, heat up; to stew; (coll) to bore

**stufato** *m* stew

**stu·fo -fa** *adj* (coll) bored, sick and tired || *f* see **stufa**

**stuòia** *f* mat; matting

**stuòlo** *m* throng, crowd; flock; (lit) army

**stupefacènte** *adj* amazing; habit-forming ‖ *m* dope

**stupefare** §173 *tr* to amaze, astonish

**stupefazióne** *f* amazement, astonishment; stupefaction

**stupèn·do -da** *adj* stupendous

**stupidàggine** *f* stupidity; silliness; child's play, cinch

**stùpi·do -da** *adj* stupid; silly; (lit) amazed

**stupire** §176 *tr* to amaze ‖ *ref* to be amazed

**stupóre** *m* amazement

**stuprare** *tr* to rape

**stura** *f* tapping; uncorking; **dar la stura a** to begin (*a speech*)

**sturabottì·glie** *m* (-glie) bottle opener

**sturalavandi·ni** *m* (-ni) plunger (*to open up clogged sink*)

**sturare** *tr* to uncork; to take the wax out of (*ears*); to open up (*clogged line*)

**stuzzicadèn·ti** *m* (-ti) toothpick

**stuzzicare** §197 (stùzzico) *tr* to pick (*e.g., one's teeth*); to bother; to excite, arouse; to tease; to sharpen (*appetite*)

**su** *adv* up; on top; upstairs; **da . . . in su** from . . . on, e.g., **dal mese scorso in su** from last month on; **di su** from upstairs; **in su** up; **metter su** to put on the fire; to instigate; **metter su bottega** to set up shop; **metter su casa** to set up housekeeping; **più su** higher; further up; **su!** come on!; let's go!; **su di** on; **su e giù** back and forth; up and down; **su per giù** more or less; **tirarsi su** to lift oneself up; to sit up; to get better, recover; **tirar su** to pick up; to grow, raise; **venir su** to grow; to come up ‖ §4 *prep* on, upon; up; towards; over, above; onto; against; at, e.g., **sul far del giorno** at daybreak; on top of; out of, e.g., **due volte su tre** two times out of three; **mettere su superbia** to become proud; **stare sulle sue** to be reserved; **sul serio** in earnest; **su misura** made to order

**suaccenna·to -ta** *adj* above-mentioned

**sub** *m* (sub) (coll) skindiver

**subàcque·o -a** *adj* submarine

**subaffittare** *tr* to sublet

**subaffitto** *m* subletting, sublet; **prendere in subaffitto** to sublet

**subaltèr·no -na** *adj & m* subaltern; subordinate

**subastare** *tr* to auction off

**sùbbia** *f* stonecutter's chisel

**subbù·glio** *m* (-gli) turmoil, hubbub

**subcosciènte** *adj & m* subconscious

**sùbdo·lo -la** *adj* treacherous, deceitful

**subentrare** (subéntro) *intr* (ESSERE) (with *dat*) to succeed, follow

**subire** §176 *tr* to suffer; to undergo

**subissare** *tr* to ruin; to sink; to overwhelm ‖ *intr* (ESSERE) to sink; to go to rack and ruin

**subisso** *m* ruin; (coll) lots, plenty

**subitàne·o -a** *adj* sudden

**sùbi·to -ta** *adj* (lit) sudden ‖ *m—d'un subito* all of a sudden ‖ **subito** *adv*

rapidly; immediately; right away; **subito al principio** at the very beginning; **subito dopo** right after; **subito prima** right before ‖ *interj* right away!

**sublima·to -ta** *adj* sublimated ‖ *m* **sublimato corrosivo** corrosive sublimate

**sublime** *adj & m* sublime

**subodorare** (subodóro) *tr* to suspect; to get wind of

**subordinare** (subórdino) *tr* to subordinate

**subordina·to -ta** *adj & m* subordinate ‖ *f* subordinate clause

**subornare** (subórno) *tr* to bribe

**substrato** *m* substratum

**suburba·no -na** *adj* suburban

**subùr·bio** *m* (-bi) suburb

**succedàne·o -a** *adj & m* substitute

**succèdere** §132 (*pp* succeduto or succèsso) *intr* (ESSERE) (with *dat*) to succede, to follow ‖ *ref* to follow one another, follow one after the other ‖ (*pret* succèssi; *pp* succèsso) *intr* (ESSERE) to happen, to come to pass; (with *dat*) to happen to, to come over, e.g., **che gli è successo?** what happened to him?

**successióne** *f* succession; **in successione** in succession; in a row

**successì·vo -va** *adj* successive; next

**succèsso** *m* success; outcome

**successóre** *m* successor

**successò·rio -ria** *adj* (-ri -rie) inheritance (*tax*)

**succhiare** §287 *tr* to suck

**succhièllo** *m* gimlet

**succhiétto** *m* pacifier

**sùc·chio** *m* (-chi) suck, sucking; (bot) sap; (coll) gimlet

**succiaca·pre** *m* (-pre) goatsucker, whippoorwill

**succin·to -ta** *adj* scanty (*clothing*); succinct, concise

**suc·co** *m* (-chi) juice; (fig) gist

**succó·so -sa** [s] *adj* juicy; pithy

**succursale** *f* branch, branch office

**sud** *m* south

**sudafrica·no -na** *adj & mf* South African

**sudamerica·no -na** *adj & mf* South American

**sudàmina** *f* prickly heat

**sudare** *tr* to sweat; to ooze; **sudare il pane** to earn one's living by the sweat of one's brow; **sudare sette camicie** to toil very hard ‖ *intr* to perspire, sweat; to reek

**sudà·rio** *m* (-ri) shroud

**suda·to -ta** *adj* wet with perspiration; hard-earned ‖ *f* sweat, sweating

**suddét·to -ta** *adj* aforesaid, above

**sùddi·to -ta** *adj & mf* subject

**suddivìdere** §158 *tr* to subdivide

**sud-èst** *m* southeast

**sudicerìa** *f* filth, filthiness; smut

**sùdi·cio -cia** (-ci -cie) *adj* dirty, filthy ‖ *m* dirt, filth

**sudiciume** *m* dirt, filth

**sudi·sta** *mf* (-sti -ste) Southerner

**sudóre** *m* sweat, perspiration

**sud-òvest** *m* southwest
**sufficiènte** *adj* sufficient, adequate; self-sufficient ‖ *m* sufficient
**sufficiènza** *f* sufficiency; self-sufficiency; (educ) minimum passing grade
**suffisso** *m* suffix
**suffragare** §209 *tr* to support; to pray for
**suffragétta** *f* suffragette
**suffrà·gio** *m* (-gi) suffrage
**suffumicare** §197 (**suffùmico**) *tr* to fumigate
**suffumi·gio** *m* (-gi) treatment by inhalation; fumigation
**suggellare** (**suggèllo**) *tr* to seal
**suggèllo** *m* seal
**suggeriménto** *m* suggestion
**suggerire** §176 *tr* to suggest; to prompt
**suggeri·tóre** -**trice** *mf* prompter ‖ *m* (baseball) coach
**suggestionàbile** *adj* suggestible
**suggestionare** (**suggestióno**) *tr* to influence by suggestion ‖ *ref*—**suggestionarsi a** + *inf* to talk oneself into + *ger*
**suggestióne** *f* suggestion; fascination
**suggesti·vo** -**va** *adj* suggestive; fascinating; (law) leading (*question*)
**sùghero** *m* cork
**sugli** §4
**sugna** *f* fat; lard
**su·go** *m* (-ghi) juice; gravy; gist, pith; **non c'è sugo** it's no fun; there's nothing to it; **senza sugo** pointless, dull
**sugó·so** -**sa** [s] *adj* juicy
**sui** §4
**suicì·da** (-**di** -**de**) *adj* suicidal ‖ *mf* suicide (*person*)
**suicidare** *ref* to commit suicide
**suicì·dio** *m* (-di) suicide (*act*)
**sui·no** -**na** *adj* swinish; see **carne** ‖ *m* swine
**sul** §4
**sulfamìdi·co** -**ca** (-**ci** -**che**) *adj* sulfa ‖ *m* sulfa drug
**sulla** §4
**sulle** §4
**sulli** §4
**sullo** §4
**sulloda·to** -**ta** *adj* above-mentioned
**sultano** *m* sultan
**summentova·to** -**ta**, **summenziona·to** -**ta**, **sunnomina·to** -**ta** *adj* above-mentioned
**sunteggiare** §290 (**suntéggio**) *tr* to summarize
**sunto** *m* résumé, summary
**suo sua** §6 *adj* & *pron poss* (**suòi sue**)
**suòcera** *f* mother-in-law
**suòcero** *m* father-in-law; **i suoceri** the in-laws
**suòla** *f* sole (*of shoe*); share (*of plow*); (naut) sliding ways; (rr) flange (*of rail*)
**suòlo** *m* ground; soil; floor ‖ *m* (**suola** *fpl*) (coll) layer; (coll) sole (*of shoe*)
**suonare** (**suòno**) *tr* & *intr* var of **sonare**
**suòno** *m* sound; (fig) ring; **a suon di bastonate** with a sound thrashing; **a suon di fischi** with loud boos; **suono armonico** (mus) overtone

**suòno·stère·o** *m* (-o) stereo tape player
**suòra** *f* nun, sister
**super-** *pref adj* & *mf* super-, e.g., **supersonico** supersonic; over-, e.g., **superallenamento** overtraining
**superaffollaménto** *m* overcrowding
**superare** (**sùpero**) *tr* to surpass; to cross; to overcome; to pass; to exceed; (cards) to trump
**supera·to** -**ta** *adj* out-of-date, passé
**supèrbia** *f* pride, haughtiness; **montare in superbia** to get a swelled head
**superbió·so** -**sa** [s] *adj* proud, haughty
**supèr·bo** -**ba** *adj* proud, haughty; superb; spirited ‖ **i superbi** the haughty ones
**supercarburante** *m* high-octane gas
**supercolòsso** *m* supercolossal film
**superdònna** *f*—**si da arie di superdonna** she thinks she's hot stuff
**supereterodina** *f* superheterodyne
**superficiale** *adj* superficial; surface; cursory, perfunctory ‖ *m* superficial fellow
**superfi·cie** *f* (-ci & **cie**) surface; area; **superficie portante** airfoil
**supèr·fluo** -**flua** *adj* superfluous ‖ *m* surplus
**super-ìo** *m* (-ìo) superego
**superióra** *f* (eccl) mother superior
**superióre** *adj* superior; upper; higher; above; **superiore a** higher than; more than; larger than ‖ *m* superior
**superlati·vo** -**va** *adj* & *m* superlative
**superlavóro** *m* overwork
**supermercato** *m* supermarket
**supersòni·co** -**ca** *adj* (-**ci** -**che**) supersonic
**supèrstite** *adj* surviving; remaining ‖ *mf* survivor
**superstizióne** *f* superstition
**superstizió·so** -**sa** [s] *adj* superstitious
**superstrada** *f* superhighway
**superuòmo** *m* superman
**supervisióne** *f* supervision
**supervisóre** *m* supervisor; (mov) director
**supi·no** -**na** *adj* supine; on one's back
**suppellèttile** *f* furnishings; equipment; fixtures; fund (*of knowledge*)
**supplementare** *adj* supplementary
**suppleménto** *m* supplement; (mil) reinforcement
**supplènte** *adj* & *mf* substitute
**supplènza** *f* substitute assignment
**suppleti·vo** -**va** *adj* additional; (gram) suppletive
**sùppli·ca** *f* (-**che**) supplication; plea; petition
**supplicante** *mf* supplicant
**supplicare** §197 (**sùpplico**) *tr* to beseech; to plead with; to appeal to
**supplichévole** *adj* beseeching, imploring
**supplire** §176 *tr* to replace ‖ *intr* (with *dat*) to supplement, make up for
**suppliziare** §287 *tr* to torture; to execute
**supplì·zio** *m* (-zi) torture, torment; **estremo supplizio** capital punishment
**suppórre** §218 *tr* to suppose
**suppòrto** *m* support, prop
**suppositò·rio** *m* (-ri) suppository

**supposizióne** *f* supposition; presumption

**suppó·sto -sta** *adj* alleged ‖ *m* supposition ‖ *f* suppository

**suppurare** *intr* (ESSERE & AVERE) to suppurate

**supremazìa** *f* supremacy

**suprè·mo -ma** *adj* supreme

**surclassare** *tr* to outclass

**surgelare (surgèlo)** *tr* to quick-freeze

**surreali·sta** *mf* (-sti -ste) surrealist

**surrenale** *adj* adrenal (*gland*)

**surrène** *m* (anat) adrenal gland

**surriscaldare** *tr* to overheat

**surrogare** §209 (surrògo) *tr* to replace

**surroga·to -ta** *adj* replaceable ‖ *m* makeshift, substitute, ersatz

**suscettìbile** *adj* susceptible; touchy

**suscitare (sùscito)** *tr* to rouse; to give rise to; to provoke

**susina** *f* plum

**susino** *m* plum tree

**susseguènte** *adj* subsequent, following

**susseguire (susséguo)** *intr* (ESSERE) (with *dat*) to follow ‖ *ref* to follow one after the other

**sussidiare** §287 *tr* to subsidize

**sussidià·rio -ria** (-ri -rie) *adj* subsidiary; (nav) auxiliary ‖ *m* supplementary text book; subsidiary

**sussì·dio** *m* (-di) subsidy; assistance, relief; **sussidi audiovisivi** audio-visual aids; **sussidi didattici** teaching aids; **sussidio di disoccupazione** unemployment compensation

**sussiè·go** *m* (-ghi) stiffness, haughtiness

**sussistènza** *f* substance; subsistence; (mil) quartermaster corps

**sussìstere** §114 *intr* (ESSERE & AVERE) to subsist; to be, exist

**sussultare** *intr* to start, jump; to quake

**sussulto** *m* start, jump; **sussulto di terremoto** earth tremor

**sussurrare** *tr* to whisper; to murmur, mutter ‖ *intr* to whisper; to rustle ‖ *ref—*si **sussurra** it is rumored

**sussurra··tóre -trice** *mf* whisperer; grumbler

**sussurrì·o** *m* (-i) whispering; murmur; rustle

**sussurro** *m* whisper; murmur

**susta** *f* temple (*of spectacles*); (coll) spring

**suvvìa** *interj* come!, come on!

**svagare** §209 *tr* to entertain; to distract ‖ *ref* to have a good time; to relax

**svaga·to -ta** *adj* absent-minded; inattentive

**sva·go** *m* (-ghi) entertainment, diversion; avocation, hobby

**svaligiare** §290 *tr* to ransack; to rob; to pirate

**svaligia·tóre -trice** *mf* thief, robber

**svalutare (svàluto & svaluto)** *tr* to devaluate; to depreciate; to belittle ‖ *ref* to depreciate

**svalutazióne** *f* depreciation

**svanire** §176 *intr* (ESSERE) to evaporate; to vanish

**svani·to -ta** *adj* faded, evaporated; vanished; enfeebled

**svantàg·gio** *m* (-gi) disadvantage

**svantaggió·so -sa** [s] *adj* disadvantageous

**svaporare (svapóro)** *intr* (ESSERE) to evaporate; to vanish

**svaria·to -ta** *adj* varied; **svaria·ti -te** several

**svarióne** *m* blunder, gross error

**svasare** *tr* to transplant from a pot; to make (*e.g., a gown*) flare

**svasa·to -ta** *adj* bell-mouthed, flaring

**svecchiare** §287 (svècchio) *tr* to renew; to rejuvenate; to modernize

**svedése** [s] *adj* Swedish; safety (*match*) ‖ *mf* Swede ‖ *m* Swedish

**svéglia** *f* awakening; reveille; alarm clock; **dare la sveglia a** to wake up

**svegliare** §280 *tr* & *ref* to wake up

**svegliarino** *m* alarm clock; (coll) rebuke

**své·glio -glia** *adj* (-gli -glie) awake; alert ‖ *f* see **sveglia**

**svelare (svélo)** *tr* to reveal; to unveil ‖ *ref* to reveal oneself; **svelarsi per** to reveal oneself to be

**svèllere** §267 *tr* (lit) to eradicate

**sveltézza** *f* quickness; slenderness

**sveltire** §176 *tr* to make shrewd; to quicken, accelerate ‖ *ref* to become smart

**svèl·to -ta** *adj* quick; slender; brisk; quick-witted; **alla svelta** quickly; **svelto di lingua** loose-tongued; **svelto di mano** light-fingered ‖ **svelto** *interj* quick!

**svenare (svéno)** *tr* to bleed to death; (fig) to bleed ‖ *ref* to bleed to death; (fig) to bleed oneself white

**svéndere** §281 *tr* to sell below cost; to undersell

**svéndita** *f* clearance sale

**svenévole** *adj* maudlin, mawkish

**svenevolézza** *f* maudlinness, mawkishness

**sveniménto** *m* faint, swoon

**svenire** §282 *intr* (ESSERE) to faint

**sventagliare** §280 *tr* to fan; to flash, display

**sventagliata** *f* blow with a fan; volley

**sventare (svènto)** *tr* to foil, thwart; (naut) to spill (*a sail*)

**sventa·to -ta** *adj* careless, thoughtless

**svèntola** *f* fan (*to kindle fire*); (coll) box, slap; **a sventola** (*ears*) that stick out

**sventolare (svèntolo)** *tr* to wave; to fan; to winnow ‖ *intr* to flutter ‖ *ref* to fan oneself

**sventolì·o** *m* (-i) fluttering, flutter

**sventraménto** *m* demolition; disembowelment; hernia

**sventrare (svèntro)** *tr* to demolish; to disembowel; to draw (*a fowl*)

**sventura** *f* misfortune, mishap; bad luck

**sventura·to -ta** *adj* unfortunate, unlucky

**sverginare (svérgino)** *tr* to deflower

**svergognare (svergógno)** *tr* to put to shame; to unmask

**svergogna·to -ta** *adj* shameless

**svergolare** (svérgolo) *tr & ref* to warp; (mach) to twist

**svernare** (svèrno) *intr* to winter

**svérza** [dz] *f* big splinter

**sverzino** [dz] *m* lash, whipcord

**svestire** (svèsto) *tr* to undress; to hull (*rice*); (fig) to strip || *ref* to undress; **svestirsi di** to shed (*e.g., leaves*)

**svettare** (svétto) *tr* to pollard, top || *intr* to stand out; to sway (*said of a tree*)

**Svè·vo -va** *adj & m* Swabian

**Svèzia, la** Sweden

**svezzaménto** *m* weaning

**svezzare** (svézzo) *tr* to wean; **svezzare da** to break (*s.o.*) of (*e.g., a habit*)

**sviare** §119 *tr* to turn aside; to lead astray || *intr & ref* to go astray; to straggle; (rr) to run off the track

**svignare** *intr* (ESSERE) to slip away || *ref*—**svignarsela** to sneak away

**svilire** §176 *tr* to devaluate

**svillaneggiare** §290 (svillanéggio) *tr* to insult, abuse

**sviluppare** *tr* to develop; to cause; (lit) to uncoil || *intr* (ESSERE & AVERE) & *ref* to develop; to break out (*said of fire*)

**sviluppo** *m* development; puberty

**svincolare** (svìncolo) *tr* to free; to clear (*at customs*)

**svìncolo** *m*—**svincolo autostradale** interchange; **svincolo doganale** customs clearance

**svirilizzare** [ddzz] *tr* (fig) to emasculate

**svisare** *tr* to alter, distort

**sviscerare** (svìscero) *tr* to eviscerate; to examine thoroughly || *ref*—**sviscerarsi per** to be crazy about; to bow and scrape to

**sviscera·to -ta** *adj* ardent, passionate; obsequious

**svista** *f* slip, error, oversight

**svitare** *tr* to unscrew

**svìzze·ro -ra** *adj & mf* Swiss || **la Svizzera** Switzerland

**svocia·to -ta** *adj* hoarse

**svogliatézza** *f* laziness; listlessness

**svoglia·to -ta** *adj* lazy; listless

**svolazzare** *intr* to flutter, flit

**svolazzo** *m* flutter; short flight; curlicue, flourish

**svòlgere** §289 *tr* to unwrap; to unfold; to unwind; to develop; to pursue (*an activity*); to dissuade || *ref* to unwind; to free oneself; to develop; to take place; to unfold

**svolgiménto** *m* development; composition

**svòlta** *f* turn; curve; turning point

**svoltare** (svòlto) *tr* to unwrap || *intr* to turn

**svotare** §257 or **svuotare** (svuòto) *tr* to empty

## T

**T, t** [ti] *m & f* eighteenth letter of the Italian alphabet

**tabac·càio -càia** *mf* (-cài -càie) tobacconist

**tabaccare** §197 *intr* to take snuff

**tabaccherìa** *f* cigar store

**tabacchièra** *f* snuffbox

**tabac·co** *m* (-chi) tobacco; **tabacco da fiuto** snuff

**tabarro** *m* winter coat; cloak

**tabèlla** *f* tablet; list; schedule; (coll) clapper, noisemaker; **tabella di marcia** timetable

**tabellare** *adj* (typ) on wooden blocks; scheduled

**tabellóne** *m* board; bulletin board; (basketball) backboard

**tabernàcolo** *m* tabernacle

**ta·bù** *adj invar & m* (-bù) taboo

**tàbula** *f*—**far tabula rasa di** to make a clean sweep of

**tabulare** (tàbulo) *tr* to tabulate

**tabulatóre** *m* tabulator

**tabulatrice** *f* printer (*of computer*)

**tac·ca** *f* (-che) notch; size; kind; tally; blemish; (typ) nick; **di mezza tacca** middle-sized; mediocre; **tacca di mira** rear sight (*of firearm*)

**tacca·gno -gna** *adj* stingy, closefisted || *mf* miser

**taccheggia·tóre -trice** *mf* shoplifter || *f* prostitute, streetwalker

**taccheggiatura** *f* or **tacchég·gio** *m* (-gi) shoplifting

**tacchétto** *m* high heel; cleat (*on soccer or football shoe*)

**tacchina** *f* turkey hen

**tacchino** *m* turkey

**tàc·cia** *f* (-ce) notoriety

**tacciare** §128 *tr*—**tacciare di** to accuse of, charge with

**tac·co** *m* (-chi) heel; block; (typ) underlay; **battere i tacchi** to take to one's heels

**taccóne** *m* (coll) patch; (coll) hobnail; **battere il taccone** to take to one's heels

**taccuino** *m* pocketbook; notebook

**tacére** *m* silence; **mettere a tacere** to silence || §268 *tr* to conceal, withhold; to imply, understand || *intr* to keep quiet; to stop playing; to quiet down; to be silent; **far tacere** to silence; **taci!** (coll) shut up!

**tachìmetro** *m* tachometer; (aut) speedometer

**tacitare** (tàcito) *tr* to silence, satisfy (*a creditor*); to pay off

**tàci·to -ta** *adj* silent; tacit

**tacitur·no -na** *adj* taciturn

**tafano** *m* horsefly, gadfly

**tafferù·glio** *m* (-gli) scuffle

**taffe·tà** *m* (-tà) taffeta; **taffetà adesivo**

or **inglese** adhesive plaster, court plaster

**tàglia** *f* ransom, reward; size; build; tally; (mach) tackle

**tagliabór·se** *m* (-se) pickpocket

**tagliabò·schi** *m* (-schi) woodcutter, woodsman

**tagliacar·te** *m* (-te) letter opener, paper knife

**tagli·àcque** *m* (-àcque) cutwater (*of bridge*)

**tagliaèrba** *adj invar* grass-cutting

**tagliafèr·ro** *m* (-ro) cold chisel

**taglialé·gna** *m* (-gna) woodcutter

**tagliama·re** *m* (-re) cutwater (*of ship*)

**tagliando** *m* coupon

**tagliapiè·tre** *m* (-tre) stonecutter

**tagliare** §280 *tr* to cut; to cut down; to cut off; to pick (*a pocket*); to cross (*finish line*); to tailor (*a suit*); to blend (*wine*); to turn off (*e.g., water*); **tagliare a fette** to slice; **tagliare in due** to split; **tagliare i panni addosso a qlcu** to slander s.o.; **tagliare i ponti con** to sever relations with; **tagliare i viveri a** to cut off supplies from; **tagliare la corda** to run away; **tagliare la strada a** to stand in the way of; (aut) to cut in front of; **tagliare le gambe a** to make wobbly (*said of wine*) ‖ *intr* to cut; to bite (*said of cold*); **tagliare per una scorciatoia** to take a shortcut ‖ *ref* to cut oneself; to tear (*said of material*)

**tagliasìga·ri** *m* (-ri) cigar cutter

**tagliata** *f* cut; clearing; (mil) abatis; **tagliata ai capelli** haircut

**tagliatèlle** *fpl* noodles

**taglia·to -ta** *adj* cut; fashioned; **essere tagliato per** to be cut out for; **tagliato all'antica** old-fashioned; **tagliato con l'accetta** rough-hewn ‖ *f* see tagliata

**taglia·tóre -trice** *mf* cutter

**tagliènte** *adj* cutting ‖ *m* edge

**taglière** *m* carving board

**taglierina** *f* paper cutter

**tà·glio** *m* (-gli) cut; cutting; dressmaking; cutting edge; sharpness; blending (*of wines*); size; denomination (*of paper money*); crossing (*of t*); (bb) fore edge; **a due tagli** double-edged; **a tagli** by the slice; **dare un taglio a** to chop; **di taglio** edgewise; **rifare il taglio a** to sharpen; **taglio cesareo** Caesarean section; **taglio d'abito** suiting; **taglio dei capelli** haircut; **venire in taglio** to come in handy

**tagliòla** *f* trap

**tagliuzzare** *tr* to shred, cut into shreds

**tailandése** [s] *adj & mf* Thai

**Tailàndia, la** Thailand

**tailleur** *m* (tailleur) woman's tailored costume

**talal·tro -tra** *pron indef* another, some other

**tàlamo** *m* (lit) nuptial bed

**talare** *adj* ankle-length ‖ *f* soutane, cassock

**talché** *conj* so that

**talco** *m* talcum; talcum powder

**tale** *adj* such; such a; that; **il tale** such and such a; **un tale** such a; a certain; **un tal quale** such a; a certain ‖ *pron* so-and-so; **il tal dei tali** so-and-so; Mr. so-and-so; **il tale** that fellow; that guy; **quel tale** that fellow, that guy; **tale e quale** like; **tali e quali** exactly, word for word; **un tale** someone, a certain person

**talèa** *f* (hort) cutting

**talènto** *m* talent; inclination; **a proprio talento** gladly, willingly; **di mal talento** grudgingly; **andare a talento a** to suit, e.g., **non gli va a talento nulla** nothing suits him

**talismano** *m* talisman

**tallire** §176 *intr* (ESSERE & AVERE) to sprout

**tallonare (tallóno)** *tr* (sports) to be at the heels of

**talloncino** *m* coupon, stub

**tallóne** *m* heel; coupon, stub; tang (*of knife*); **tallone d'Achille** Achilles heel

**talménte** *adv* so, so much

**talóra** *adv* sometimes

**talpa** *f* mole

**talu·no -na** *pron indef* some; someone, somebody ‖ **talu·ni -ne** *adj & pron indef* some

**talvòlta** *adv* sometimes

**tamarindo** *m* tamarind

**tambureggiare** §290 (tamburéggio) *intr* to drum; to beat down (*said, e.g., of hail*)

**tamburèllo** *m* tambour (*for embroidering*); (mus) tambourine

**tamburino** *m* drummer

**tamburo** *m* drum; barrel (*of watch; of windlass*); **a tamburo battente** on the spot

**tamerice** *f* tamarisk

**Tamigi** *m* Thames

**tampòco** *adv*—**né tampoco** (archaic) nor ... either

**tamponaménto** *m* stopping, plugging; rear-end collision

**tamponare (tampóno)** *tr* to tampon, plug; to collide with; to hit from the rear; (surg) to tampon

**tampóne** *m* plug, tampon; pad; (mus) drumstick; (rr) buffer; (surg) tampon; **tampone di vapore** vapor lock

**tana** *f* burrow; den; hole; hovel; base (*in children games*)

**tanàglie** *fpl* var of **tenaglie**

**tan·ca** *f* (-che) can, jerry can; tank

**tanfo** *m* musty or stuffy smell

**tangènte** *adj* tangent ‖ *f* tangent; (com) commission

**tàngere** §269 *tr* (lit) to touch

**Tàngeri** *f* Tangier

**tànghero** *m* boor, lout

**tangìbile** *adj* tangible

**tàni·ca** *f* (-che) var of **tanca**

**tantino** *m*—**un tantino** a little, e.g., **è un tantino arrabbiato** he is a little angry; a little bit, e.g., **un tantino di dolce** a little bit of cake

**tan·to -ta** *adj & pron indef* such, such a; so much; as much; **a dir tanto** or **a far tanto** at the most; **ai tanti**

(*del mese*) on such and such a day (*of the month*); **a tanto** to such a point; to such a level; **e tanto** odd, e.g., **mille dollari e tanto** a thousand odd dollars; **è tanto** it has been a long time, e.g., **è tanto che lo conosco** it has been a long time since I made his acquaintance; **fra tanto** meanwhile; **senza tanto chiasso** without any noise; **tan·ti -te** many; so many; as many; a lot, e.g., **grazie tante!** thanks a lot! **tanti ... che** so many ... that; **tanti ... quanti** as many ... as; **tanto di guadagnato** so much the better || **tanto** *adv* so much; so; only, e.g., **tanto per passare il tempo** only to pass the time; anyhow; anyway; **nè tanto nè quanto** at all; **tant'è** it's the same; **tanto che** so much that, e.g., **mi ha annoiato tanto che l'ho mandato via** he bothered me so much that I dismissed him; **tanto ... che** both ... and, e.g., **tanto Maria che Roberto** both Mary and Robert; so much ... that; **tanto fa** or **vale** it's all the same; **tanto meglio** so much the better; **tanto meno** so much the less; **tanto per cambiare** as usual; **tanto più ... quanto più** the more ... the more; **tanto ... quanto** as ... as || *s—* **ascoltare con tanto d'orecchie** to be all ears; **di tanto in tanto** from time to time

**tapi·no -na** *adj* (lit) wretched || *mf* (lit) wretch

**tappa** *f* stopping place; stop; stage, leg; (sports) lap; **bruciare le tappe** to press on, keep going; **fare tappa** to stop

**tappabu·chi** *mf* (-chi) makeshift, pinch hitter, substitute

**tappare** *tr* to cork, plug; to shut up tight || *ref* to shut oneself in; to plug (*e.g., one's ears*)

**tapparèlla** *f* (coll) inside rolling shutter

**tappéto** *m* rug, carpet; (sports) canvas, mat; **mettere al tappeto** (boxing) to knock out; **tappeto erboso** lawn, green; **tappeto verde** gambling table

**tappezzare** (**tappèzzo**) *tr* to paper (*a wall*); to upholster

**tappezzerìa** *f* wallpaper; upholstery; upholsterer's shop; tapestry; wallflower

**tappezzière** *m* paperhanger; upholsterer

**tappo** *m* cork, stopper; cap; plug; **tappo a corona** bottle cap; **tappo a vite** screw cap

**tara** *f* tare

**taràntola** *f* tarantula

**tarare** *tr* to tare; to set, adjust

**tara·to -ta** *adj* net (*weight*); calibrated (*instrument*); sickly, weak

**tarchia·to -ta** *adj* stocky, sturdy

**tardare** *tr* to delay || *intr* to delay; to be late

**tardi** *adv* late; **al più tardi** at the latest; **a più tardi!** so long!; **fare tardi** to be late; **più tardi** later; later on; **sul tardi** in the late afternoon

**tardi·vo -va** *adj* late; retarded, slow; belated

**tar·do -da** *adj* slow; late; **di età tarda** of advanced years; **tardo d'ingegno** slow-witted

**tardó·ne -na** *adj* slow-moving || *mf* slowpoke || *f* old dame, middle-aged vamp

**tar·ga** *f* (-ghe) plate; nameplate; shield; (aut) license plate; (sports) trophy

**targare** §209 *tr* (aut) to register

**targatura** *f* (aut) registration

**targhétta** *f* nameplate

**tariffa** *f* tariff; rate; rates

**tariffà·rio -ria** (-ri -rie) *adj* tariff; rate || *m* price list; rate book

**tarlare** *tr* to eat (*said of woodworms or moths*) || *intr* (ESSERE) & *ref* to become worm-eaten; to become moth-eaten

**tarlo** *m* woodworm; moth; bookworm; (fig) gnawing

**tarma** *f* moth; clothes moth

**tarmare** *tr* to eat (*said of moths*) || *intr* (ESSERE) & *ref* to become moth-eaten

**tarmici·da (-di -de)** *adj* moth-repelling || *m* moth repellent

**taròc·co** *m* (-chi) tarot; tarok

**tarpare** *tr* to clip; **tarpare le ali a** to clip the wings of

**tartagliare** §280 *tr* & *intr* to stutter, stammer

**tàrta·ro -ra** *adj* Tartar || *m* tartar; Tartar || **Tartaro** *m* Tartarus

**tartaru·ga** *f* (-ghe) turtle, tortoise; tortoise shell

**tartassare** *tr* to ill-treat; to harass

**tartina** *f* slice of bread and butter; canapé

**tartufo** *m* truffle; (fig) tartuffe, hypocrite

**ta·sca** *f* (-sche) pocket; briefcase; **aver le tasche piene di** to be sick and tired of; **da tasca** pocket; **rompere le tasche a** (vulg) to bother, annoy; **tasca in petto** inside pocket

**tascàbile** *adj* pocket; vest-pocket

**tascapane** *m* knapsack, rucksack

**tascata** *f* pocketful

**taschino** *m* vest pocket, small pocket

**tassa** *f* tax; (coll) duty, fee; **tassa complementare** surtax; **tassa di circolazione** road-use tax; **tassa di registro** registration fee; **tassa scolastica** tuition

**tassàbile** *adj* taxable

**tassàmetro** *m* taximeter; **tassametro di parcheggio** parking meter

**tassare** *tr* to tax; to assess || *ref* to pledge money

**tassati·vo -va** *adj* positive; specific; peremptory

**tassazióne** *f* taxation; tax

**tassèllo** *m* dowel; inlay; plug; patch; reinforcement

**tas·sì** *m* (-sì) taxi, taxicab

**tassi·sta** *m* (-sti) taxi driver

**tasso** *m* stake (*anvil*); yew tree; (com) rate (*e.g., of interest*); (zool) badger; **tasso valutario fluttuante** (econ) fluctuation of currency rate

**tastare** *tr* to touch; to feel; to probe; **tastare il terreno** (fig) to see how the land lies

**tastièra** *f* keyboard; manual (*of organ*)

**tasto** m touch, feeling, feel; plug (e.g., in watermellon); key (of piano or typewriter); sample (in drilling); **tasto bianco** white key, natural; **toccare un tasto falso** to strike a sour note

**tastóni** adv—**a tastoni** gropingly

**tàtti·co -ca** (-ci -che) adj tactical; tactful ‖ m tactician ‖ f tactics; prudence; tactfulness

**tatto** m touch; tact

**tatuàg·gio** m (-gi) tattoo

**tatuare** (tàtuo) tr to tattoo

**taumatur·go** m (-gi & -ghi) wonderworker

**tauri·no -na** adj taurine, bull-like; bull

**tavèrna** f tavern, inn

**tavernière** m tavernkeeper

**tàvola** f board, plank; slab; table; tablet; bookplate; list; **tavola a ribalta** drop-leaf table; **tavola armonica** (mus) sound board; **tavola calda** cafeteria, snack bar; **tavola da stirare** ironing board; **tavola di salvezza** (fig) last recourse, lifesaver; **tavola imbandita** open house; **tavola nera** blackboard; **tavola operatoria** operating table; **tavola pitagorica** multiplication table; **tavola reale** backgammon; **tavole di fondazione** charter (of a charitable institution)

**tavolàc·cio** m (-ci) wooden board (on which soldiers on guard and prisoners used to sleep)

**tavolare** (tàvolo) tr to board up

**tavolata** f tableful

**tavolato** m planking; plateau

**tavolétta** f small table; tablet; bar (e.g., of chocolate)

**tavolière** m chessboard table; card table; plateau, tableland

**tavolino** m small table; desk

**tàvolo** m table; desk; **tavolo di gioco** gambling table; **tavolo d'ufficio** office desk

**tavolòzza** f palette

**tazza** f cup; bowl

**tazzina** f demitasse

**tazzóna** f mug

**te** §5 pron pers

**tè** m (tè) tea; **tè danzante** tea dance, thé dansant

**tèa** adj fem—**rosa tea** tea rose

**teatrale** adj theatrical

**teatro** m theater; performance; drama; stage; (fig) scene; **che teatro!** what fun!; **teatro dell'opera** or **teatro lirico** opera house; **teatro di posa** (mov) studio; **teatro di prosa** legitimate theater

**teatróne** m large theater; (coll) excellent box office

**Tèbe** f Thebes

**tè·ca** f (-che) case; (eccl) reliquary

**tecnicismo** m technicality

**tècni·co -ca** (-ci -che) adj technical ‖ m technician; engineer ‖ f technique; technics

**téco** §5 prep phrase (lit) with you

**tedé·sco -sca** adj & mf (-schi -sche) German

**tediare** §287 (tèdio) tr to bore ‖ ref to get bored

**tè·dio** m (-di) dullness, tedium, boredom; **recare tedio a** to annoy, bother

**tedió·so -sa** [s] adj dull, tedious

**tegame** m pan; **al tegame** fried (e.g., eggs)

**tegamino** m small pan; **uova al tegamino** fried eggs

**téglia** f pan; baking pan

**tégola** f tile; (fig) blow

**tégolo** m tile

**teièra** f teapot, teakettle

**tèk** m teak

**téla** f linen; cloth; material; canvas, oil painting; (fig) plot, trap; (lit) weft; (theat) curtain; **far tela** (coll) to beat it; **tela batista** batiste; **tela cerata** oilcloth; **tela da imballaggio** burlap; **tela di ragno** cobweb; **tela di sacco** sackcloth; **tela greggia** gunny, burlap; **tela smeriglio** emery cloth

**te·làio** m (-lài) loom; frame; embroidery frame; sash; stretcher (for oil painting); (aut) chassis; **telaio di finestra** window sash

**teleama·tóre -trice** mf TV viewer

**telear·ma** f (-mi) guided missile

**telecabina** f cable car

**telecàmera** f TV camera

**telecomanda·to -ta** adj remote-control

**telecomando** m remote control

**telecommentatóre** m TV newscaster

**telecròna·ca** f (-che) TV broadcast; **telecronaca diretta** live broadcast

**telecroni·sta** mf (-sti -ste) TV news announcer, TV newscaster

**telediffusióne** f TV broadcasting

**teledram·ma** m (-mi) teleplay

**telefèri·ca** f (-che) cableway, telpherage

**telefonare** (telèfono) tr & intr to telephone ‖ ref to call one another

**telefonata** f telephone call

**telefòni·co -ca** adj (-ci -che) telephone

**telefoni·sta** mf (-sti -ste) telephone operator, central; telephone installer

**telèfono** m telephone; **telefono a gettone** pay telephone (operated by tokens); **telefono a moneta** pay telephone; **telefono interno** intercommunication system, intercom

**telegèni·co -ca** adj (-ci -che) telegenic, videogenic

**telegiornale** m TV newscast

**telegrafare** (telègrafo) tr & intr to telegraph

**telegràfi·co -ca** adj (-ci -che) telegraphic

**telegrafi·sta** mf (-sti -ste) telegrapher; telegraph installer

**telègrafo** m telegraph; **telegrafo di macchina** (naut) engine-room telegraph; **telegrafo ottico** heliograph; wigwag; **telegrafo senza fili** wireless

**telegram·ma** m (-mi) telegram

**teleguida** f remote control

**teleguidare** tr to control from a distance, to operate by remote control

**Telèmaco** m Telemachus

**telèmetro** m telemeter; range finder

**teleobbiettivo** m (phot) telephoto lens

**telepatìa** f telepathy

**teleproiètto** m guided missile

**telericévere** §141 tr to receive by TV; to teleview

**teleschérmo** m television screen

telescò·pio *m* (-pi) telescope
telescrivènte *f* teletypewriter; ticker
telescriventi·sta *mf* (-sti -ste) teletype operator
teleselezióne *f* (telp) direct distance dialing
telespetta·tóre -trice *mf* televiewer
teletrasméttere §198 *tr* to televise, telecast
teletrasmissióne *f* telecast
televisióne *f* television, TV
televisi·vo -va *adj* television, TV
televisóre *m* television set
tellina *f* sunset shell or clam
télo *m* piece of cloth; yardage, length of material; (mil) side (*of tent*)
tèlo *m* (lit) dart, arrow
telóne *m* canvas; (theat) curtain
tè·ma *m* (-mi) theme; (gram) stem
téma *f* (lit) fear; **per tema di** (lit) for fear of
temerarie·tà *f* (-tà) recklessness, rashness
temerà·rio -ria *adj* (-ri -rie) reckless, rash; ill-founded
temére (témo & tèmo) *tr* to fear; to respect || *intr* to fear; **temere di** to be afraid to
temeri·tà *f* (-tà) temerity
temìbile *adj* frightening
tèmpera *f* tempera, distemper
temperala·pis *m* (-pis) or **temperamati·te** *m* (-te) pencil sharpener
temperaménto *m* middle course, compromise; temper, temperament
temperante *adj* temperate, moderate
temperanza *f* temperance
temperare (tèmpero) *tr* to mitigate; to temper; to sharpen (*a pencil*)
tempera·to -ta *adj* temperate; tempered (*metal*); watered (*wine*)
temperatura *f* temperature; **temperatura ambiente** room temperature
temperino *m* penknife, pocketknife
tempèsta *f* tempest, storm; **tempesta in un bicchier d'acqua** tempest in a teapot
tempestare (tempèsto) *tr* to pound; to pepper, pelt; to pester || *intr* to storm
tempesta·to -ta *adj* studded, spangled
tempesti·vo -va *adj* timely
tempestó·so -sa [s] *adj* stormy, tempestuous
tèmpia *f* temple (*side of forehead*); **tempie** (lit) head
tempiale *m* temple (*in loom; of spectacles*)
tempière *m* Templar
tèm·pio *m* (-pi & -pli) temple (*edifice*)
tempi·sta *mf* (-sti -ste) person or athlete showing good timing; (mus) rhythmist
tèmpo *m* time; weather; age; period, stage; cycle (*of internal-combustion engine*); (gram) tense; (mus) tempo, (mus) movement; (sports) period; (theat, mov) part; **ad un tempo** at the same time; **al tempo che Berta filava** long ago; **a suo tempo** in due time; long ago; **a tempo debito** in due time; **a tempo e luogo** at the opportune time; **a tempo perso** in

one's spare time; **aver fatto il proprio tempo** to be outdated; **c'è sempre tempo** we are still in time; **col tempo** in time; **dare tempo al tempo** to allow time to heal things; **darsi del bel tempo** to have a good time; **da tempo** for a long time; **del tempo di** from the time of; **è scaduto il tempo utile** the time is up; **è tanto tempo** it's been a long time; **fa bel tempo** the weather is fine; **il Tempo** Father Time; **lasciare il tempo che trova** to have no effect; **molto tempo dopo** long afterward; **nel tempo che** while; **per tempo** early; **prima del tempo** formerly; **quanto tempo** how long; **sentire il tempo** to feel the weather in one's bones; **senza por tempo in mezzo** without any delay; **tempi che corrono** present times; **tempo fa** some time ago; **tempo legale** legal time limit; **tempo libero** leisure time; **tempo supplementare** (sports) overtime; **tempo un . . .** within (*e.g., one month*); **un tempo** long ago
temporale *adj* temporal || *m* storm
temporàne·o -a *adj* temporary, provisional
temporeggiare §290 (temporéggio) *intr* to temporize
tèmpra *f* (metallurgy) tempering, temper; (mus) timbre; (fig) fiber, timber
temprare (tèmpro) *tr* to temper (*metal*); to harden, inure || *ref* to become hardened or inured
tenace *adj* tenacious; tough
tenàcia *f* tenacity
tenaci·tà *f* (-tà) strength, resistance; tenacity
tenàglie *fpl* nippers, pincers, pliers; tongs; **a tenaglie** (mil) pincers (*e.g., action*)
tènda *f* curtain; awning; tent
tendènza *f* tendency; trend
tendenzió·so -sa [s] *adj* tendentious
tèn·der *m* (-der) (rr) tender
tèndere §270 *tr* to stretch; to tighten; to draw (*a bow*); to cast (*nets*); to lay (*snares*); to reach out (*one's hand*); to prick up (*one's ears*); to draw (*s.o.'s attention*); to set (*sail*) || *intr* to aim; to lean; to tend; to tend to be
tendina *f* curtain, blind
tèndine *m* (anat) tendon
tendiscar·pe *m* (-pe) shoetree
tenditóre *m* turnbuckle; **tenditore della racchetta** (tennis) press
tendóne *m* big curtain; canvas; tent (*of circus*); (theat) curtain
tendòpo·li *f* (-li) tent city
tènebre *fpl* darkness
tenebró·so -sa [s] *adj* dark, gloomy
tenènte *m* lieutenant; (mil) first lieutenant; (nav) lieutenant junior grade; **tenente colonnello** (mil) lieutenant colonel; **tenente di vascello** (nav) lieutenant senior grade
tenére §271 *tr* to hold; to have; to keep; to stand (*e.g., rough sea*); to wear; to make (*a speech*); to follow

(*a course*); **tenere a battesimo** to stand for, sponsor; **tenere al corrente** to keep informed; **tenere a memoria** to remember; **tenere da conto** to hold in high esteem; to take good care of (*s.th*); **tenere d'occhio** to keep an eye on; **tenere la destra** to keep to the right; **tenere la strada** (aut) to hug the road; **tenere la testa a partito** to mend one's ways; **tenere le distanze** to keep aloof; **tenere mano a** to connive with; **tenere presente** to bear in mind; **tenere qlco a conto** to take good care of s.th || *intr* to hold; to take root; **tenerci che** to be anxious for, e.g., **ci tengo che vinca le elezioni** I am anxious for him to win the elections; **tenere a destra** to keep to the right; **tenere alle apparenze** to stand on ceremony; to keep up appearances; **tenere da** to hail from; to take after; **tenere dietro a** to follow; to keep abreast of; **tenere duro** to keep fast; **tenere per** (sports) to be a fan of || *ref* to hold; to hold on; to keep; to keep (*e.g.*, *ready*); to regard oneself; **tenersi a** to adhere to (*e.g.*, *a treaty*); to hold on to; to stick to; to follow; **tenersi a galla** to stay afloat; **tenersi al largo** (naut) to keep to the open sea; **tenersi al vento** (naut) to sail to leeward; (fig) to follow a safe course; **tenersi in piedi** to stand up; **tenersi per mano** to hold hands; **tenersi sulle proprie** to keep aloof

**tenerézza** *f* tenderness; fondness, endearment

**tène·ro -ra** *adj* tender || *m* tender portion

**tènia** *f* tapeworm

**teni·tóre -trice** *mf* keeper

**tènnis** *m* tennis; **tennis da tavolo** table tennis, ping-pong

**tenni·sta** *mf* (-sti -ste) tennis player

**tennisti·co -ca** *adj* (-ci -che) tennis

**tenóne** *m* tenon

**tenóre** *m* character, tone; tenor; alcoholic content; manner (*of living*); **tenore di vita** way of life; standard of living

**tensióne** *f* tension; **alta tensione** high tension; **tensione sanguigna** blood pressure

**tentàcolo** *m* tentacle

**tentare** (**tènto**) *tr* to try, attempt; to assay; to tempt; (lit) to touch

**tentativo** *m* attempt; **tentativo di furto** attempted robbery

**tenta·tóre -trice** *adj* tempting || *m* tempter || *f* temptress

**tentazióne** *f* temptation

**tentennare** (**tenténno**) *tr* to shake; to rock || *intr* to shake; to wobble; to hesitate; to stagger

**tentóne** or **tentóni** *adv* blindly; gropingly; at random

**tènue** *adj* small (*intestine*); (lit) tenuous, thin

**tenu·to -ta** *adj* bound, obliged || *f* capacity, volume; estate, farm; uniform; outfit; (sports) endurance,

resistance; **a tenuta d'acqua** watertight; **a tenuta d'aria** airtight; **tenuta dei libri** bookkeeping; **tenuta di gala** (mil, nav) full-dress uniform; **tenuta di servizio** (mil) fatigues; **tenuta di strada** (aut) roadability

**tenzóne** *f* combat; poetic contest

**teologìa** *f* theology

**teòlo·go** *m* (-gi) theologian

**teorè·ma** *m* (-mi) theorem

**teorèti·co -ca** *adj* (-ci -che) theoretic(al)

**teorìa** *f* theory; (lit) series, row

**teòri·co -ca** (-ci -che) *adj* theoretical || *m* theoretician

**tèpi·do -da** *adj* var of **tiepido**

**tepóre** *m* warmth

**téppa** *f* underworld, rabble

**teppi·sta** *m* (-sti) hoodlum, hooligan

**terapèuti·co -ca** (-ci -che) *adj* therapeutic || *f* therapeutics

**terapìa** *f* therapy; **terapia convulsivante** or **terapia d'urto** shock therapy

**Terèsa** *f* Theresa

**tèrgere** §162 *tr* (lit) to wipe

**tergicristallo** *m* windshield wiper

**tergiversare** (**tergivèrso**) *intr* to stall; to beat around the bush

**tèr·go** *m* (-ghi) back (*of a coin*); **a tergo** on the reverse side || *m* (-ga *fpl*) (lit) back; **volgere le terga** (lit) to turn one's back

**termale** *adj* thermal (*e.g.*, *waters*)

**tèrme** *fpl* spa, hot spring

**tèrmi·co -ca** *adj* (-ci -che) thermal; heat, heating

**terminale** *adj & m* terminal

**terminare** (**tèrmino**) *tr* to border; to end, terminate || *intr* (ESSERE) to end, terminate

**terminazióne** *f* termination; completion; (gram) ending

**tèrmine** *m* border; marker; term; deadline; end; goal; boundary, bounds; (fig) point; **a termini di legge** according to law; **avere termine** to end; **in altri termini** in other words; **mezzo termine** half measure; **porre termine a** to put an end to; **portare a termine** to put through

**terminologìa** *f* terminology

**termistóre** *m* (elec) thermistor

**tèrmite** *f* termite

**termoconvettóre** *m* baseboard radiator

**termocòppia** *f* thermocouple

**termodinàmi·co -ca** (-ci -che) *adj* thermodynamic || *f* thermodynamics

**termòforo** *m* heating pad

**termòmetro** *m* thermometer

**termonucleare** *adj* thermonuclear

**tèr·mos** *m* (-mos) thermos bottle

**termosifóne** *m* radiator; hot-water heating system; steam heating system

**termòstato** *m* thermostat

**termovisièra** *f* electric defroster

**tèrno** *m* tern (*in lotto*); **vincere un terno al lotto** to hit the jackpot

**tèrra** *f* earth; land; ground; world; city, town; dirt, soil; clay; **essere a terra** to be downcast; to be broke; to be flat (*said of a tire*); **rimanere a terra** to miss the boat; **sotto terra** underground; **terra bruciata** scorched earth; **terra di nessuno** no man's land; **terra di Siena** sienna; **terra ferma** terra firma; mainland; **terra** skimming the ground; (naut) close to the shore; (fig) mediocre, second-rate

**terracòtta** *f* (**terrecòtte**) terra cotta; earthenware

**terraférma** *f* mainland (*as distinguished from adjacent islands*); terra firma (*dry land, not air or water*)

**terràglia** *f* crockery; **terraglie** earthenware

**terranò·va** *m* (**-va**) Newfoundland (*dog*) || **Terranova** *f* Newfoundland

**terrapièno** *m* embankment

**terrazza** *f* terrace; **a terrazza** terraced

**terrazza·no -na** *mf* villager

**terrazzo** *m* balcony; terrace; ledge, shelf; terrazzo

**terremota·to -ta** *adj* hit by an earthquake || *mf* earthquake victim

**terremòto** *m* earthquake

**terré·no -na** *adj* terrestrial, earthly; ground-floor; first-floor || *m* ground floor; first floor; ground; soil; land, plot of ground; combat zone, terrain; **preparare il terreno** to work the soil; (fig) to pave the way; **scendere sul terreno** to fight a duel; **tastare il terreno** to feel one's way; **terreno di gioco** (sports) field

**tèrre·o -a** *adj* wan, sallow

**terrèstre** *adj* terrestrial; ground, land || *m* earthling

**terrìbile** *adj* terrible; awesome, awful

**terrìc·cio** *m* (**-ci**) soil; top soil

**terriè·ro -ra** *adj* land; landed

**terrificare** §197 (**terrìfico**) *tr* to terrify

**terrina** *f* tureen

**territò·rio** *m* (**-ri**) territory

**terróre** *m* terror

**terrorismo** *m* terrorism

**terrori·sta** *mf* (**-sti -ste**) terrorist

**terrorizzare** [ddzz] *tr* to terrorize

**terró·so -sa** [s] *adj* dirty (*e.g., spinach*); dirty-earth (*color*); (chem) rare-earth (*metal*)

**tèr·so -sa** *adj* clear

**tèrza** *f* third grade; (aut) third; (eccl) tierce; (rr) third class

**terzaforzì·sta** (**-sti -ste**) *adj* of the third force || *m* partisan of the third force

**terzaròlo** *m* (naut) reef

**terzétto** *m* trio

**terzià·rio -ria** *adj* (**-ri -rie**) tertiary

**terzina** *f* tercet

**terzino** *m* (soccer) back

**tèr·zo -za** *adj & pron* third || *m* third; third party || *f* see **terza**

**terzùlti·mo -ma** *adj* third from the end

**tésa** [s] *f* brim (*of hat*); snare, net

**tesare** [s] (**téso**) *tr* to pull taut

**tè·schio** *m* (**-schi**) skull

**tè·si** *f* (**-si**) thesis; dissertation

**té·so -sa** [s] *adj* taut, tight; strained; outstretched (*hand*); **con le orecchie tese** all ears || *f* see **tesa**

**tesorerìa** *f* treasury; liquid assets

**tesorière** *m* treasurer

**tesòro** *m* treasure; treasury; thesaurus; bank vault; **far tesoro di** to treasure, prize; **tesoro mio!** my darling!

**Tèspi** *m* Thespis

**tèssera** *f* card; domino (*piece*); tessera (*of mosaic*)

**tessera·to -ta** *adj* card-carrying; rationed || *mf* card-carrying member; holder of ration card

**tèssere** *tr* to weave; to spin

**tèssile** *adj* textile || *m* textile; **tessili** textile workers

**tessilsac·co** *m* (**-chi**) garment bag

**tessi·tóre -trice** *mf* weaver

**tessitura** *f* weaving; spinning mill; (mus) range; (fig) plot

**tessuto** *m* cloth, fabric; tissue

**tèsta** *f* head; mind; bulb (*of garlic*); spindle (*of wheel*); warhead (*of torpedo*); row (*of bricks*); **a testa** apiece; per capita; **a testa a testa** neck and neck; **fare di testa propria** to act on one's own; **fare la testa grossa a** to stun; to annoy; **levarsi di testa** to forget about; **mettersi in testa di** to get it into one's head to; **non avere testa di** + *inf* to not feel like + *ger*; **non sapere dove battere la testa** to not know which way to turn; **per una corta testa** by a neck; **rompersi la testa** to rack one's brains; **tenere testa a** to face up to; **testa coda** (aut) spin; **testa di ponte** (mil) bridgehead; **testa di sbarco** beachhead; **testa e croce** head or tails

**testaménto** *m* will, testament || **Antico** or **Vecchio Testamento** Old Testament; **Nuovo Testamento** New Testament

**testardàggine** *f* stubborness

**testar·do -da** *adj* stubborn

**testata** *f* headboard (*of bed*); top; end (*e.g., of beam*); heading (*of newspaper*); butt with the head; nose (*of rocket*)

**tèste** *m* witness

**testé** *adv* (lit) a short time ago; (lit) presently, in a little while

**testicolo** *m* testicle

**testièra** *f* headboard; crown (*of harness*); battering ram

**testimòne** *m* witness; **testimone di nozze** best man; **testimone di veduta** or **testimone oculare** eyewitness

**testimonianza** *f* testimony

**testimoniare** §287 (**testimònio**) *tr* to attest; to depose, testify; **testimoniare il falso** to bear false witness || *intr* to bear witness

**testimò·nio** *m* (**-ni**) (coll) witness

**testina** *f* small head; whimsical person; boiled head of veal; head (*e.g., of tape recorder*)

**tèsto** *m* text; pie dish; (coll) flower vase; **fare testo** to serve as a model

**testó·ne -na** *mf* dolt; stubborn person

**testuale** *adj* textual; word-for-word

**testùggine** *f* turtle; tortoise

**tètano** *m* tetanus

**tè·tro -tra** *adj* (lit) gloomy, dark

**tétta** *f* (coll) teat

**tettarèlla** *f* nipple

**tétto** *m* roof; ceiling price; home; **senza tetto** homeless; **tetto a capanna** gable roof; **tetto a padiglione** hip roof; **tetto a una falda** lean-to roof; **tetto di paglia** thatched roof

**tettóia** *f* shed; pillared roof

**tettóia-garage** *f* (**tettóie-garage**) carport

**tettùc·cio** *m* (**-ci**) (aut) roof; (aut) top; **tettuccio a bulbo** dome; **tettuccio rigido** (aut) convertible top

**ti** §5 *pron*

**tìbia** *f* tibia, shinbone

**tic** *m* (**tic**) twitch; habit

**ticchettì·o** *m* (**-i**) click (*of typewriter*); patter (*of rain*); tick (*of clock*)

**tìc·chio** *m* (**-chi**) whim; tic; viciousness (*of animal*); blemish

**tièpi·do -da** *adj* tepid, lukewarm

**tifo** *m* typhus; **fare il tifo per** to root for; to be a fan of

**tifoidèa** *f* typhoid fever

**tifóne** *m* typhoon

**tifó·so -sa** [s] *adj* rooting ‖ *mf* fan, rooter

**tì·glio** *m* (**-gli**) linden, lime; bast; fiber

**tigliό·so -sa** [s] *adj* tough, fibrous

**tigna** *f* ringworm; (coll) tightwad

**tignòla** *f* clothes moth

**tigra·to -ta** *adj* striped; tabby

**tigre** *f* tiger

**timballo** *m* pie, meat pie; timbale; (lit) drum

**timbrare** *tr* to stamp; to cancel (*stamps*)

**timbro** *m* stamp; character (*of a writer*); (mus) timbre; **timbro di gomma** rubber stamp; **timbro postale** postmark

**timidézza** *f* shyness, bashfulness; timidity

**tìmi·do -da** *adj* shy, bashful; timid ‖ *mf* shy person

**timo** *m* (anat) thymus; (bot) thyme

**timóne** *m* rudder, helm; shaft, pole (*of cart*); **timone di direzione** (aer) rudder; **timone di profondità** (aer) elevator; (nav) diving plane (*of submarine*)

**timonièra** *f* (naut) pilot house

**timonière** *m* helmsman, steersman; coxswain

**timoniè·ro -ra** *adj* rudder; tail (*feather*) ‖ *f* see **timoniera**

**timora·to -ta** *adj* conscientious; **timorato di Dio** God-fearing

**timóre** *m* fear; awe; **avere timore di** to fear

**timoró·so -sa** [s] *adj* timorous

**tìmpano** *m* (archit) tympanum; (anat) eardrum; (mus) kettledrum; **rompere i timpani a** to deafen

**tin·ca** *f* (**-che**) (ichth) tench

**tinèllo** *m* pantry; breakfast room

**tìngere** §126 *tr* to dye; to dirty, soil; to color ‖ *ref* to dye (*e.g., one's hair*); to put on make-up; to become colored

**tino** *m* tub, vat

**tinòzza** *f* tub, washtub

**tinta** *f* paint; color; dye; shade; stain; **calcare le tinte** to exaggerate; **mezza tinta** halftone, shade; **vedere qlco a fosche tinte** to take a dim view of s.th; **vedere qlco a tinte rosee** to see s.th through rose-colored glasses

**tintarèlla** *f* (coll) suntan

**tinteggiare** §290 (**tintéggio**) *tr* to calci-

mine; to whitewash; to tint; to paint (*e.g., a house*)

**tintinnare** *intr* (ESSERE & AVERE) to jingle; to clink

**tintinnì·o** *m* (**-i**) jingling; clink

**tin·to -ta** *adj* dyed; tinged; soiled; (lit) dark ‖ *f* see **tinta**

**tintó·re -ra** *mf* dyer; dry cleaner

**tintorìa** *f* dyeworks; dry cleaning establishment; dyeing

**tintura** *f* dyeing; dyestuff; tincture; smattering; **tintura di iodio** iodine

**tìpi·co -ca** *adj* (**-ci -che**) typical

**tipificare** §197 (**tipìfico**) *tr* to standardize

**tipizzare** [ddzz] *tr* to standardize

**tipo** *adj invar* typical, e.g., **famìglia tipo** typical family ‖ *m* type; standard, model; fellow, guy; phylum (*in taxonomy*); **bel tipo** (coll) character, card; **coi tipi di** printed in the shop of; **sul tipo di** similar to; **vero tipo** prototype, epitome

**tipografìa** *f* typography; print shop

**tipogràfi·co -ca** *adj* (**-ci -che**) typographical

**tipògrafo** *m* typographer; owner of print shop, printer

**tipòmetro** *m* (typ) line gauge

**tiptologìa** *f* table rapping (*during séance*); tapping in code (*among jailbirds*)

**tiraba·ci** *m* (**-ci**) (coll) spitcurl

**tiràg·gio** *m* (**-gi**) draft; **a tiraggio forzato** forced-draft

**tiralìne·e** *m* (**-e**) ruling pen

**tirannìa** *f* tyranny

**tirànni·co -ca** *adj* (**-ci -che**) tyrannical

**tiran·no -na** *adj* tyrannical ‖ *mf* tyrant

**tirante** *m* brace; rod; strap; trace (*of harness*); **tirante degli stivali** bootstrap

**tirapiè·di** *m* (**-di**) hangman's assistant; underling

**tirapu·gni** *m* (**-gni**) brass knuckles

**tirare** *tr* to pull; to draw; to tug; to suck; to haul in (*nets*); to deserve (*a slap*); to pluck; to throw; to give (*blows*); to utter (*oaths*); to shoot (*arrows, bullets*); to stretch; to tighten (*one's belt*); to print; to make (*an addition*); (sports) to force (*the pace*); **tirare a lucido** to polish; **tirare a sé** to attract; **tirare a sorte** to draw lots for; **tirare fuori** to draw out; to pull out; to get out; **tirare giù** to lower; to jot down; (coll) to gulp down; **tirare gli orecchi a** to punish by yanking the ears of; **tirare il collo a** to wring the neck of; **tirare in ballo** to bring up (*a subject*); **tirare l'acqua al proprio mulino** to look out for number one; **tirare l'anima coi denti** to be at the end of one's rope; **tirare l'aria** to draw (*said of a chimney*); **tirare le cuoia** (slang) to kick the bucket; **tirare per i capelli** to drag by the hair; to drag in; to push, coerce; **tirare per le lunghe** to stretch out; **tirare su** to lift; to raise (*children*); to pull up ‖ *intr* to be too tight (*said of clothes*); to shoot; to blow (*said of wind*); to draw (*said, e.g., of chimney*); **tirare a** to tend toward, lean toward; **tirare a** + *inf* to try to + *inf;* **tirare a campare** (coll) to goldbrick; **tirare avanti** to go ahead; to manage to get along; **tirare di boxe** to box; **tirare diritto** to go straight ahead; **tirare di scherma** to fence; **tirare in lungo** to delay, linger; to dillydally; **tirare innanzi** to keep on going; to go ahead; **tirare sul prezzo** to haggle; **tirare via** to hurry along || *ref*—**tirarsi addosso** (coll) to bring upon oneself; **tirarsi dietro** to drag along; **tirarsi fuori da** to get out of (*e.g., trouble*); **tirarsi gente in casa** to keep open house; **tirarsi indietro** to move back; **tirarsi in là** to move aside; **tirarsi su** to get up; to recover; to roll up (*one's sleeves*); **tirarsi un colpo di rivoltella** to shoot oneself

**tirastiva·li** *m* (-li) bootjack

**tirata** *f* pull; stretch; tirade

**tirati·ra** *m* (-ra) (coll) yen; **fare a tiratira per** (coll) to scramble for

**tira·to -ta** *adj* taut; forced (*smile*); drawn (*face*); tight, closefisted; **tirato con** short of || *f* see **tirata**

**tira·tóre -trice** *mf* shot; **tiratore scelto** sharpshooter; **franco tiratore** sniper

**tiratura** *f* printing

**tirchierìa** *f* stinginess

**tìr·chio -chia** (-chi -chie) *adj* stingy, closefisted || *mf* miser

**tirèlla** *f* trace (*of harness*)

**tirétto** *m* (coll) drawer

**tiritèra** *f* rigmarole

**tiro** *m* pull; pair, brace (*e.g., of oxen*); throw; fire, shot; trick; **a tiro** within reach; **a un tiro di schioppo** within gunshot; **da tiro** draft; **fuori del tiro dell'orecchio** out of earshot; **tiro alla fune** tug of war; **tiro al piattello** trapshooting; **tiro a quattro** four-in-hand; **tiro a segno** rifle range; shooting gallery

**tiroci·nio** *m* (-ni) apprenticeship; internship; **tirocinio didattico** practice teaching

**tiròide** *f* thyroid

**tirolése** [s] *adj & mf* Tyrolean

**tirrèni·co -ca** *adj* (-ci -che) Tyrrhenian **Tirrèno** *m* Tyrrhenian Sea

**tisana** *f* tea, infusion

**tisi** *f* consumption, tuberculosis

**tìsi·co -ca** (-ci -che) *adj* consumptive; stunted || *mf* consumptive

**titàni·co -ca** *adj* (-ci -che) titanic

**titànio** *m* titanium

**titillare** *tr* to tickle

**titolare** *adj* titular; regular, full-time || *m* owner, boss; incumbent || *v* (tìtolo) *tr* to name, call

**titolo** *m* title; heading; name; caption; entry (*in dictionary*); grade; fineness (*of gold*); (chem) titer; (educ) credit; **avere titolo a** to have a right to; **a titolo di** as, by way of; **titoli di testa** (mov) credits; **titolo al portatore** security payable to bearer; **titolo azionario** share; **titolo corrente** subtitle; **titolo di credito** instrument of credit; certificate; deed; conveyance; **titolo di studio** degree, diploma; credits; **titolo di trasporto** travel document

**titubare** (tìtubo) *intr* to hesitate; to waver

**tiziané·sco -sca** *adj* (-schi -sche) titian; Titian

**tì·zio** *m* (-zi) fellow, guy

**tizzo** or **tizzóne** *m* brand, firebrand

**to'** *interj* here!; well!

**tobò·ga** *m* (-ga) toboggan

**toccafèrro** *m* tag (*game*)

**toccamano** *m* handshake (*to close a deal*); bribe, under-the-table tip

**toccante** *adj* touching, moving

**toccare** §197 (tócco) *tr* to touch; to reach; to concern; to push (*a button*); to play (*an instrument*); to feel; to hit (*the target*); to border on (*e.g., the age of forty*); **toccare con mano** to make sure of; **toccare il cielo col dito** to be in seventh heaven; **toccare nel vivo** to touch to the quick; **toccare terra** to land; **toccarne molte** to get a good thrashing; **toccato!** touché! || *intr* (ESSERE) to be touching; **toccare a** to be up to, e.g., **tocca a lui** it's up to him; to have to, e.g., **le tocca partire domani** she has to leave tomorrow; to deserve, e.g., **gli è toccato il premio** he deserved the prize || *ref* to meet, e.g., **gli estremi si toccano** extremes meet

**toccasa·na** [s] *m* (-na) cure-all, panacea

**tocca·to -ta** *adj* touché; touched in the head, nutty; **già toccato** abovementioned || *f* (mus) toccata

**tóc·co -ca** (-chi -che) *adj* touched, nutty; spoiled (*fruit*) || *m* touch; knock; one o'clock (*P.M.*); (coll) stroke

**tòc·co** *m* (-chi) chunk, piece; mortarboard; toque; **un bel tocco di ragazza** a buxom lass

**tò·ga** *f* (-ghe) gown, academic gown; (hist) toga

**tògliere** §127 *tr* to remove, take away; to take; to cut (*telephone connection*); to deduct; to take off; to preclude, prevent; **togliere a** to take away from; **togliere al cielo** (lit) to praise to the skies; **togliere di mezzo** to remove; to do away with; **togliere la parola a** to take the floor from; **togliere l'onore a** to dishonor; **togliere una spina dal cuore a** to relieve the heart and mind of || *intr*— **tolga Dio!** God forbid! || *ref* to take off (*e.g., one's coat*); to have (*e.g., a tooth*) pulled; to satisfy (*a whim*); **togliersi di mezzo** to get out of the way; **togliersi la vita** to take one's life; **togliersi qlcu dai piedi** to get rid of s.o.

**tòlda** *f* (naut) deck

**tolemài·co -ca** *adj* (-ci -che) Ptolemaic

**tolétta** *f* dressing table; dressing room; toilet, washroom; dress, gown; **fare toletta** or **farsi la toletta** to make one's toilet

**tolleràbile** *adj* tolerable

**tollerante** *adj* tolerant; liberal

**tolleranza** *f* tolerance; leeway

**tollerare** (**tòllero**) *tr* to tolerate; to bear, stand

**tòl·to** **-ta** *adj* taken; except, leaving out, e.g., **tolta sua figlia** leaving his daughter out ‖ *m*—**il mal tolto** ill-gotten goods

**to·màio** *m* (**-mài** & **-màia** *fpl*) or **to·màia** *f* (**-màie**) upper (*of shoe*)

**tómba** *f* tomb, grave

**tombale** *adj* grave (*e.g., stone*)

**tombino** *m* sewer inlet

**tómbola** *f* bingo; (coll) tumble

**tombolare** (**tómbolo**) *tr* (coll) to tumble down (*the steps*) ‖ *intr* (ESSERE) to fall headlong; (coll) to go to rack and ruin; (aer) to tumble

**tómbolo** *m* fall, tumble; bolster; lace pillow; (coll) fatso; **fare un tombolo** to go to rack and ruin; to lose one's position

**Tommaso** *m* Thomas

**tòmo** *m* volume; (coll) character

**tòna·ca** *f* (**-che**) (eccl) frock; (eccl) soutane; **gettare la tonaca alle ortiche** to doff the cassock

**tonare** §257 *intr* to peal; to thunder ‖ *impers* (ESSERE & AVERE)—**tuona** it is thundering

**tondeggiante** *adj* round; rounded; chubby; curvaceous

**tondino** *m* coaster; iron rod (*for reinforced concrete*); (archit) molding (*at top or bottom of column*); (archit) astragal

**tón·do** **-da** *adj* round; (typ) roman ‖ *m* round; circle; plate, dish; (typ) roman; **in tondo** around

**tónfo** *m* splash; thump

**tòni·co** **-ca** (**-ci** **-che**) *adj* tonic ‖ *m* tonic (*medicine*) ‖ *f* (mus) tonic

**tonificare** §197 (**tonìfico**) *tr* to invigorate

**tonnara** *f* tuna nets

**tonnellàg·gio** *m* (**-gi**) tonnage

**tonnellata** *f* ton; **tonnellata di stazza** displacement ton

**tónno** *m* tuna

**tòno** *m* tone; tune; hue; style; (mus) pitch; (mus) key; **darsi tono** to put on airs; **di tono** stylish; **fuori di tono** out of tune

**tonsilla** *f* tonsil

**tonsura** *f* tonsure

**tón·to** **-ta** *adj* (coll) dumb, stupid

**topàia** *f* rat's nest; hovel

**topà·zio** *m* (**-zi**) topaz

**tòpi·co** **-ca** (**-ci** **-che**) *adj* topical ‖ *f* topic; (coll) blunder

**tòpo** *m* mouse; rat; **topo campagnolo** field mouse; **topo d'acqua** water rat; **topo d'albergo** hotel thief; **topo d'auto** car thief; **topo di biblioteca** bookworm

**topografia** *f* topography

**topolino** *m* little mouse ‖ **Topolino** *m* Mickey Mouse

**toporagno** *m* shrew

**tòppa** *f* patch; keyhole

**tòppo** *m* stump; headstock (*of lathe*)

**torace** *m* thorax

**tórba** *f* peat

**tórbi·do** **-da** *adj* cloudy; murky ‖ *m* trouble; **pescare nel torbido** to fish in troubled waters; **torbidi** disorder

**torbièra** *f* peatbog

**tòrcere** §272 *tr* to twist; to wring; to bend, curve; to curl (*the lips*); to lead astray ‖ *intr* (ESSERE) to bend, curve ‖ *ref* to writhe; to bend over; **torcersi dalle risa** to split with laughter

**torchiare** §287 (**tòrchio**) *tr* to press

**tòr·chio** *m* (**-chi**) press; printing press

**tòr·cia** *f* (**-ce**) torch

**torcicòllo** *m* stiff neck; (orn) wryneck

**torcinaso** [s] *m* (vet) twitch

**tórdo** *m* thrush; simpleton

**torèllo** *m* young bull; (naut) garboard

**torèro** *m* bullfighter

**tórlo** *m* yolk

**tórma** *f* crowd, throng; herd

**torménta** *f* blizzard

**tormentare** (**torménto**) *tr* to torture, torment; to pester, nag ‖ *ref* to worry

**torménto** *m* torture, torment; pang; bore, pest, annoyance

**tornacónto** *m* interest, advantage

**tornante** *m* curve

**tornare** (**tórno**) *tr* (lit) to restore; (obs) to turn ‖ *intr* (ESSERE) to return; to go back; (coll) to jibe, agree, square; **tornare a** to be profitable to; **tornare a** + *inf* verb + again, e.g., **tornare a essere** to become again; **tornare a fare** to do again; **tornare a bomba** to return to the point; **tornare a galla** to come back to the surface; **tornare a gola** to repeat (*said of food*); **tornare a onore a qlcu** to do credit to s.o.; **tornare a pennello** to fit to a T; **tornare in sé** to come to; **tornare opportuno** or **utile a** to suit, e.g., **non gli tornó opportuno vendere la casa** it did not suit him to sell the house; **tornare utile** to come in handy; **tornare sulle proprie decisioni** to change one's mind

**tornasóle** *m* litmus

**tornèllo** *m* turnstile

**tornèo** *m* tournament, tourney

**tór·nio** *m* (**-ni**) lathe

**tornire** §176 *tr* to turn, turn up (*on a lathe*); to polish

**tornitóre** *m* lathe operator

**tórno** *m* turn; period (*of time*); **levarsi di torno** to get rid of; **torno torno** all around

**tòro** *m* bull; (archit, geom) torus; (lit) marital bed ‖ **Toro** *m* (astrol) Taurus

**torpèdine** *f* torpedo

**torpedinièra** *f* destroyer escort; torpedo-boat destroyer

**torpè·do** *f* (**-do**) (aut) touring car

**torpedóne** *m* bus, motor coach

**tòrpi·do** **-da** *adj* torpid, sluggish; numb

**torpóre** *m* torpor, sluggishness; numbness

**tórre** *f* tower; (chess) castle; (nav) turret; **torre campanaria** bell tower; **torre d'avorio** ivory tower; **torre di**

**lancio** (rok) gantry; **torre pendente** leaning tower

**torrefare** §173 *tr* to roast (*coffee*)

**torreggiante** *adj* towering

**torreggiare** §290 (**torréggio**) *intr* to tower

**torrènte** *m* torrent

**torrenziale** *adj* torrential

**torrétta** *f* turret; (nav) conning tower (*of submarine*); (archit) bartizan

**tòrri·do -da** *adj* torrid

**torrióne** *m* donjon; (nav) conning tower (*of battleship*)

**torróne** *m* nougat

**torsióne** *f* torsion

**tórso** *m* stalk; core (*of fruit*); torso, trunk; **a torso nudo** bare-chested

**tórsolo** *m* core; stalk; stem; **non vale un torsolo** it's not worth a fig

**tórta** *f* pie; cake, tart; **torta di mele** apple pie

**tòrta** *f* twist

**tortièra** *f* baking pan

**tòr·to -ta** *adj* twisted; crooked; gloomy (*face*) ‖ *m* wrong; **a torto** unjustly; **avere torto** to be wrong; **avere torto marcio** to be dead wrong; **dar torto a** to lay the blame on; **fare torto a** to wrong, e.g., **fece torto al proprio fratello** he wronged his own brother; to bring discredit upon ‖ *f* see **tòrta** ‖ **torto** *adv* askance

**tórtora** *f* turtledove

**tortuó·so -sa** [s] *adj* winding; ambiguous; (fig) devious

**tortura** *f* torture

**torturare** *tr* to torture; to pester ‖ *ref* to torment oneself; **torturarsi il cervello** to rack one's brain

**tosare** (**tóso**) *tr* to clip, crop; to shear; (fig) to fleece

**tosa·tóre -trice** *mf* clipper, shearer ‖ *f* clippers; lawn mower

**tosatura** *f* sheepshearing; clip (*of wool*)

**tosca·no -na** *adj* & *mf* Tuscan ‖ *m* stogy ‖ **Toscana, la** Tuscany

**tósse** *f* cough; **tosse asinina** or **canina** whooping cough

**tòssi·co -ca** (**-ci -che**) toxic ‖ *m* (archaic) poison

**tossicòmane** *mf* drug addict

**tossicomanìa** *f* drug addiction

**tossina** *f* toxin

**tossire** (**tósso**) & §176 *intr* to cough

**tostapa·ne** *m* (**-ne**) toaster

**tostare** (**tòsto**) *tr* to toast; to roast (*e.g., coffee*)

**tò·sto -sta** *adj* (lit) prompt; (lit) impudent; (lit) brazen (*face*) ‖ **tosto** *adv* soon; **ben tosto** (lit) very soon; **tosto che** (lit) as soon as

**tòt** *adj pl invar* so many, that many ‖ *pron invar* so much, that much

**totale** *adj* & *m* total

**totalità·rio -ria** *adj* (**-ri -rie**) total, complete; totalitarian

**totalizzare** [ddzz] *tr* to add up; to make (*so many points*)

**totalizzatóre** [ddzz] *m* pari-mutuel; betting window; (mach) totalizator

**tòtano** *m* squid; (orn) tattler

**totocàlcio** *m* soccer pool

**tovàglia** *f* tablecloth

**tovaglìolo** *m* napkin

**tòz·zo -za** *adj* stubby, stocky ‖ *m* piece (*of fresh bread*); crust (*of bread*)

**tra** *prep* among; between

**trabàccolo** *m* small fishing boat

**traballare** *intr* to shake; to totter; to wobble; to stagger; to toddle

**trabìccolo** *m* frame for bedwarmer; jalopy; hulk

**traboccante** *adj* overflowing

**traboccare** §197 (**trabócco**) *tr* to knock down ‖ *intr* to overflow (*said of container*) ‖ *intr* (ESSERE) to overflow (*said of liquid*) ‖ *intr* (ESSERE & AVERE) to tip (*said of scales*); **far traboccare** to make (*the scales*) tip

**trabocchétto** *m* pitfall; trapdoor

**trabóc·co** *m* (**-chi**)—**trabocco di sangue** internal hemorrhage

**tracagnòt·to -ta** *adj* stubby, stocky ‖ *mf* stocky person

**tracannare** *tr* to gulp down

**tracchég·gio** *m* (**-gi**) delay; (fencing) feint

**tràc·cia** *f* (**-ce**) track; trace, clue; trail; outline, plan; (lit) line, row; **buona traccia** right track; **fare la traccia a** to open the way for; **in** or **sotto traccia** concealed (*e.g., wiring*); **tracce** tinge; (chem) traces

**tracciante** *adj* tracer (*bullet*)

**tracciare** §128 *tr* to trace; to pave (*the way*); to outline; (lit) to track

**tracciato** *m* tracing, drawing; outline; map; layout

**trachèa** *f* trachea, windpipe

**tracòlla** *f* baldric; shoulder strap; **a tracolla** slung across the shoulders

**tracòllo** *m* collapse, debacle

**tracotanza** *f* arrogance

**tradiménto** *m* treason; treachery; **a tradimento** unawares, unexpectedly; treacherously

**tradire** §176 *tr* to betray; to fail (*a person; said of memory*) ‖ *ref* to give oneself away

**tradi·tóre -trice** *adj* charming, seductive; treacherous; deceitful, faithless ‖ *mf* traitor; betrayer ‖ *f* traitress

**tradizionale** *adj* traditional

**tradizióne** *f* tradition

**tradótta** *f* military train

**tradurre** §102 *tr* to translate

**tradut·tóre -trice** *mf* translator

**traduzióne** *f* translation

**traènte** *mf* (com) drawer

**trafela·to -ta** *adj* breathless, out of breath

**traferro** *m* (elec) air gap; (elec) spark gap

**trafficante** *m* dealer, trader; trafficker

**trafficare** §197 (**tràffico**) *tr* to sell; to traffic in ‖ *intr* to trade, deal; to hustle

**tràffi·co** *m* (**-ci**) traffic

**trafficó·ne -na** *mf* hustler

**trafiggere** §104 *tr* to pierce, stab, transfix; to wound

**trafila** *f* routine; red tape; (mach) drawplate

**trafilare** *tr* to wiredraw

**trafilétto** *m* (journ) short feature, special item; (journ) notice

**trafitta** *f* stab wound; shooting pain

**trafittura** *f* stab; shooting pain

**traforare** (**trafòro** & **trafóro**) *tr* to bore; to pierce; to carve (*wood*); to pink (*leather*); to embroider with open work

**trafóro** *m* boring; tunnel; open work

**trafugare** §209 *tr* to purloin; to sneak off with

**tragèdia** *f* tragedy; **far tragedie** (coll) to make a fuss

**traghettare** (**traghétto**) *tr* to ferry

**traghétto** *m* ferry; **traghetto spaziale** space shuttle

**tràgi·co -ca** (**-ci -che**) *adj* tragic ‖ *m* tragedian; **il tragico** (fig) the tragic

**tragitto** *m* journey; (obs) ferry

**traguardo** *m* sight; aim; goal; finish line; (phot) viewfinder; (sports) tape

**traiettòria** *f* trajectory; path

**tràina** *f* towline; **pescare alla traina** to troll

**trainare** (**tràino**) *tr* to drag, tug, pull

**tràino** *m* drag; load; trailer

**tralasciare** §128 *tr* to interrupt; to omit; **non tralasciare di** to not fail to

**tràl·cio** *m* (**-ci**) stem (*of vine*)

**tralìc·cio** *m* (**-ci**) ticking, bedtick; trellis; tower (*of high-tension line*)

**tralice** *m*—**in tralice** askance

**tralignare** *intr* (ESSERE & AVERE) to degenerate

**tram** *m* (**tram**) streetcar

**trama** *f* woof, weft; plot (*of play*); texture (*of cloth*)

**tramà·glio** *m* (**-gli**) trammel net

**tramandare** *tr* to hand down

**tramare** *tr* & *intr* to weave; to plot

**trambusto** *m* bustle

**tramestì·o** *m* (**-i**) bustle, confusion

**tramèzza** [ddzz] *f* partition

**tramezzare** (**tramèzzo**) [ddzz] *tr* to interpose; to partition

**tramezzino** [ddzz] *m* small partition; sandwich; sandwich man

**tramèzzo** [ddzz] *m* partition; side dish; (sew) insertion ‖ *adv* in between; **tramezzo a** among

**tràmite** *m* intermediary; (lit) pass; **per tramite di** through ‖ *prep* (coll) by; by means of

**tramòg·gia** *f* (**-ge**) hopper

**tramontana** *f* north wind; **perdere la tramontana** to lose one's bearings

**tramontare** (**tramónto**) *intr* (ESSERE) to set (*said, e.g., of sun*); to end

**tramónto** *m* setting; sunset; decline

**tramortire** §176 *tr* to stun ‖ *intr* (ESSERE) to faint, swoon

**trampolière** *m* wading bird; (orn) stilt

**tràmpoli** *mpl* stilts

**trampolino** *m* diving board; springboard; ski jump; (fig) springboard

**tramutare** *tr* to transfer; to transform

**tràn·cia** *f* (**-ce**) slice; (mach) shears

**tranèllo** *m* trap, snare

**trangugiare** §290 *tr* to swallow; to gulp down

**tranne** *prep* except, save; **tranne che** unless

**tranquillante** *m* tranquilizer

**tranquillare** *tr* & *ref* (lit) to tranquilize; to calm down

**tranquilli·tà** *f* (**-tà**) tranquillity

**tranquillizzare** [ddzz] *tr* to tranquilize; to reassure ‖ *ref* to become reassured

**tranquil·lo -la** *adj* tranquil, calm; clear (*conscience*)

**transatlànti·co -ca** *adj* & *m* (**-ci -che**) transatlantic

**transazióne** *f* compromise

**transènna** *f* bar, barrier

**transètto** *m* (archit) transept

**trànsfu·ga** *m* (**-ghi**) (lit) deserter

**transìgere** §165 *tr* to settle ‖ *intr* to compromise

**transistóre** *m* transistor

**transitàbile** *adj* passable

**transitare** (**trànsito**) *intr* to move; to walk

**transiti·vo -va** *adj* transitive

**trànsito** *m* passage; traffic; (lit) passing; **di transito** transient

**transitò·rio -ria** *adj* (**-ri -rie**) temporary; transitory; transitional

**transizióne** *f* transition

**transoceàni·co -ca** *adj* (**-ci -che**) transoceanic

**transòni·co -ca** *adj* (**-ci -che**) transonic

**transunto** *m* abstract, summary (*of a document*)

**trantràn** *m* routine

**tran·vài** *m* (**-vài**) (coll) streetcar

**tranvìa** *f* streetcar line

**tranvià·rio -ria** *adj* (**-ri -rie**) streetcar

**tranvière** *m* streetcar conductor; motorman

**trapanare** (**tràpano**) *tr* to drill; (surg) to trephine

**tràpano** *m* drill; (surg) trephine; **trapano a vite** automatic drill

**trapassare** *tr* to pierce; (fig) to grieve; (poet) to cross; (lit) to pass, spend ‖ *intr* (ESSERE) to go through; to pass (*said of an inheritance*); (lit) to pass away; **trapassare da, per** or **al di là di** to come through (*said, e.g., of a nail, light*)

**trapassato** *m* (lit) deceased; **trapassato prossimo** past perfect

**trapasso** *m* crossing; transfer; transition; (lit) passing, death

**trapelare** (**trapélo**) *intr* (ESSERE) to ooze; to trickle out; to leak through; (fig) to leak out

**trapè·zio** *m* (**-zi**) trapeze; (geom) trapezoid

**trapezòide** *adj* trapezoidal ‖ *m* trapezoid

**trapiantare** *tr* to transplant ‖ *ref* to transfer

**trapianto** *m* transplantation; transplant; **trapianto cardiaco** heart transplant

**tràppola** *f* trap; (coll) gadget; (fig) lie; **trappola esplosiva** booby trap

**trapunta** *f* quilt

**trapuntare** *tr* to quilt; to embroider

**trapun·to -ta** *adj* quilted; embroidered; studded ‖ *m* embroidery ‖ *f* see **trapunta**

**trarre** §273 *tr* to pull; to drag; to draw; to bring; to deduct; to lead; to unsheathe (*a sword*); to heave (*a sigh*); to spin (*silk, wool,* etc.); **il dado è tratto** the die is cast; **trarre dalla prigione** to free from prison; **trarre d'impaccio** to get (*s.o.*) out of trouble; **trarre fuori** to extract; **trarre in inganno** to deceive; **trarre in rovina** to ruin; **trarre per mano** to lead by the hand ‖ *intr* to kick (*said of a mule*); (lit) to run; (lit) to blow (*said of the wind*) ‖ *ref* to take off (*e.g., one's hat*); **trarsi d'impaccio** to get out of trouble; **trarsi indietro** to pull back; **trarsi in disparte** to move aside

**trasalire** [s] §176 *intr* (ESSERE & AVERE) to start, jump

**trasanda·to -ta** *adj* untidy, slovenly

**trasbordare (trasbórdo)** *tr* to transfer, transship

**trasbórdo** *m* transfer, transshipment

**trascéndere** §245 *tr* to transcend ‖ *intr* (ESSERE) to go to excesses

**trascinare** *tr* to drag; to stir; to enthrall; to lead astray; **trascinare la vita** to barely make ends meet ‖ *ref* to drag oneself; to drag on

**trascolorare (trascolóro)** *tr* to discolor; to change the color of ‖ *intr* (ESSERE) & *ref* to discolor; to change color

**trascórrere** §139 *tr* to pass (*time*); to skim through (*e.g., a book*); (lit) to go through ‖ *intr* to go to excesses ‖ *intr* (ESSERE) to elapse, pass

**trascórso** *m* slip (*e.g., of pen*); peccadillo

**trascrivere** §250 *tr* to transcribe

**trascrizióne** *f* transcription; registration (*e.g., of a deed*)

**trascuràbile** *adj* negligible

**trascurare** *tr* to neglect; to fail; to disregard ‖ *ref* to not take care of oneself

**trascuratézza** *f* negligence, neglect; carelessness; slovenliness

**trascura·to -ta** *adj* neglected; careless; slovenly

**trasecolare (trasècolo)** [s] *intr* (ESSERE & AVERE) to marvel, be astonished

**trasferìbile** *adj* transferable

**trasferiménto** *m* transfer; conveyance

**trasferire** §176 *tr* to transfer; to assign, convey ‖ *ref* to move

**trasfèrta** *f* business trip; traveling expenses, per diem

**trasfigurare** *tr* to transfigure; to distort (*the truth*) ‖ *ref* to be transfigured; to change countenance

**trasfocatóre** *m* (phot) zoom lens

**trasfóndere** §178 *tr* to transfuse; (fig) to instill

**trasformàbile** *adj* transformable; (aut) convertible

**trasformare (trasfórmo)** *tr* to transform; to alter ‖ *ref* to transform oneself; to be converted

**trasformati·vo -va** *adj* (gram) transformational

**trasformatóre** *m* transformer

**trasformazióne** *f* transformation

**trasformi·sta** *mf* (-sti -ste) quick-change artist

**trasfusióne** *f* transfusion

**trasgredire** §176 *tr* & *intr* to transgress

**trasgressióne** *f* transgression

**trasgressóre** *m* transgressor

**trasla·to -ta** *adj* figurative; metaphorical; (lit) transferred ‖ *m* figure of speech; metaphor

**traslitterare (traslìttero)** *tr* to transliterate

**traslocare** §197 (traslòco) *tr* to transfer; to move ‖ *intr* & *ref* to move

**traslò·co** *m* (-chi) moving

**traslùci·do -da** *adj* translucent

**trasméttere** §198 *tr* to transmit; (rad) to broadcast

**trasmetti·tóre -trice** *mf* transmitter ‖ *m* (naut) engine-room telegraph; (telg) sender

**trasmigrare** *intr* (ESSERE & AVERE) to transmigrate ‖ *intr* (ESSERE) to pass, pass on

**trasmissióne** *f* transmission; conveyance; broadcast; telecast; **trasmissione del pensiero** thought transference

**trasmittènte** *adj* transmitting; broadcasting ‖ *f* broadcasting station

**trasmutare** *tr* to transmute; to change

**trasogna·to -ta** [s] *adj* dreamy; day-dreaming; dazed

**trasparènte** *adj* transparent ‖ *m* transparency

**trasparènza** *f* transparence; **in trasparenza** against the light

**trasparire** §108 *intr* (ESSERE) to appear; to shine; to show through; to show, be revealed (*said of feelings*); **far trasparire** to reveal

**traspirare** *intr* to perspire ‖ *intr* (ESSERE) to show, be revealed

**traspirazióne** *f* perspiration

**traspórre** §218 *tr* to transpose

**trasportare (traspòrto)** *tr* to transport; to carry away; to transfer; to translate; to postpone; (mus) to transpose; **lasciarsi trasportare** to be carried away ‖ *ref* to move; (fig) to go back

**trasporta·tóre -trice** *mf* carrier ‖ *m* (mach) conveyor belt; (phot) sprocket

**traspòrto** *m* transportation; transport; transfer; eagerness; moving; (mus) transposition; **trasporto funebre** funeral procession

**trasposi·tóre -trice** *mf* (mus) transposer

**trassa·to -ta** *adj* paying ‖ *m* drawee

**trastullare** *tr* to amuse; to entice ‖ *ref* to have a good time; to loiter

**trastullo** *m* play, game; fun; plaything

**trasudare** [s] *tr* to ooze; (fig) to exude ‖ *intr* to ooze (*said of a wall*) ‖ *intr* (ESSERE) to drip (*said of perspiration*)

**trasversale** *adj* transverse, cross ‖ *f* crossroad

**trasvèr·so -sa** *adj* transverse ‖ *m* transverse beam

**trasvolare (trasvólo)** *tr* to fly over, cross by air ‖ *intr*—**trasvolare su** to skip over

**trasvolata** *f* non-stop flight

**tratta** *f* tug, pull; (rr) stretch; (com)

draft; (lit) crowd; **tratta dei neri** slave trade; **tratta delle bianche** white slavery

**trattàbile** *adj* negotiable; friendly, sociable

**trattaménto** *m* treatment; working conditions; food, spread; reception, welcome; **trattamento di favore** special treatment; **trattamento di quiescenza** retirement benefits

**trattare** *tr* to treat; to deal with; to transact; to wield; to play (*an instrument*); to work (*e.g., iron*); to deal in; **trattare qlcu da bugiardo** to call s.o. a liar; **trattare da cane** to treat like a dog || *intr* to bargain; **trattare di** to deal with; to take care of; to treat, handle || *ref* to take good care of oneself || *impers* (ESSERE) **si tratta di** it's question of

**trattà·rio -ria** *mf* (**-ri -rie**) drawee

**trattativa** *f* negotiation

**trattato** *m* treatise; treaty

**trattazióne** *f* treatment

**tratteggiare** §290 (**trattéggio**) *tr* to sketch; to outline; to hatch

**trattég·gio** *m* (**-gi**) hatching

**trattenére** §271 *tr* to keep; to entertain; to withhold; to hold back; to detain || *ref* to stop; to refrain; to remain

**tratteniménto** *m* entertainment, party; delay

**trattenuta** *f* withholding; checkoff

**trattino** *m* dash; hyphen

**trat·to -ta** *adj* drawn, extracted || *m* stretch; span; passage; tract; gesture; throw (*of dice*); stroke (*of pen*); bearing; section; (chess) move; **a larghi tratti** in broad outline; **a tratti** from time to time; **a un tratto** all of a sudden; at the same time; **dare un tratto alla bilancia** to tip the scales; **tratti** features; **tratti del volto** features; **tratto di corda** strappado; **tratto di unione** hyphen; **tutto d'un tratto** all of a sudden; **un bel tratto** quite a while

**trat·tóre -trice** *mf* innkeeper; restaurateur || *m* tractor; **trattore a cingoli** caterpillar tractor || *f* tractor (*vehicle*)

**trattoría** *f* inn, restaurant

**tratturo** *m* cow path

**traumatizzare** [ddzz] *tr* to traumatize

**travagliare** §280 *tr* to torment; to molest || *intr & ref* to toil, labor

**travà·glio** *m* (**-gli**) suffering; toil; trave (*to inhibit horse being shod*); **travaglio di parto** labor pains; **travaglio di stomaco** upset stomach

**travasare** *tr* to pour off; to decant; to transfer || *ref* to spill

**travaso** *m* pouring off; transfer; **travaso di bile** gall bladder attack; **travaso di sangue** hemorrhage

**travatura** *f* roof timbers; **travatura maestra** ridgepole

**trave** *f* beam; joist; **fare una trave d'un fuscello** to make a mountain out of a molehill

**travedére** §279 *tr* to glimpse || *intr* to be mistaken

**travéggole** *fpl*—**avere le traveggole** to see things; to see one thing for another

**travèrsa** *f* crossbar; crossroad; crosspiece; rung; bar (*of goalpost*); dam; rail (*of fence*); transom; slat (*to hold bedspring*); rubber pad; (rr) tie

**traversare** (**travèrso**) *tr* to cross

**traversata** *f* passage, crossing

**traversìa** *f* strong wind; **traversie** misfortunes

**traversina** *f* (rr) tie

**travèr·so -sa** *adj* cross; devious || *m* width; crossbar; (naut) beam; (naut) side; **a traverso** (naut) on the beam; **capire a traverso** to misunderstand; **di traverso** askance; crosswise; the wrong way || *f* see **traversa**

**traversóne** *m* large crossbar; westerly gale; side blow with saber

**travestiménto** *m* disguise; travesty

**travestire** (**travèsto**) *tr* to disguise; to travesty, parody || *ref* to disguise oneself

**traviare** §119 *tr* to lead astray || *intr & ref* to go astray

**travicèllo** *m* joist

**travisare** *tr* to distort

**travolgènte** *adj* impetuous; fascinating; sweeping

**travòlgere** §289 *tr* to overwhelm; to overturn; to sweep away

**trazióne** *f* traction

**tre** [e] *adj & pron* three; **le tre** three o'clock || *m* three; third (*in dates*)

**trébbia** *f* thresher; threshing

**trebbiare** §287 (**trébbio**) *tr & intr* to thresh

**trebbiatrice** *f* thresher, threshing machine

**trebbiatura** *f* threshing

**tréc·cia** *f* (**-ce**) plait; braid; **treccia a ciambella** bun, knot

**trecentèsi·mo -ma** *adj, m & pron* three hundredth

**trecènto** *adj, m & pron* three hundred || **il Trecento** the fourteenth century

**tredicèsi·mo -ma** *adj, m & pron* thirteenth || *f* Xmas bonus

**trédici** *adj & pron* thirteen; **le tredici** one P.M. || *m* thirteen; thirteenth (*in dates*)

**trégua** *f* truce; respite; **tregua atomica** nuclear test ban; **senza tregua** without letup

**tremare** (**trèmo**) *intr* to shake, tremble; to quiver; **far tremare** to shake

**tremarèlla** *f*—**avere la tremarella** (coll) to shake in one's boots

**tremebón·do -da** *adj* (lit) shaky

**tremèn·do -da** *adj* tremendous

**trementina** *f* turpentine

**tremila** *adj, m & pron* three thousand

**trèmito** *m* trembling; quivering

**tremolare** (**trèmolo**) *intr* to shake; to quiver; to flicker

**trèmo·lo -la** *adj* tremulous || *m* (bot) aspen; (mus) tremolo

**trèno** *m* train; quarter (*of animal*); set (*of tires*); threnody, lamentation; **treno accelerato** local; **treno di lusso** Pullman train; **treno direttissimo** express; **treno di vita** mode of life; mode of living; **treno merci** freight train; **treno stradale** tractor-trailer

**trenodìa** *f* threnody

**trénta** *adj & pron* thirty ‖ *m* thirty; thirtieth (*in dates*)

**trentèsi·mo -ma** *adj, m & pron* thirtieth

**trentina** *f* about thirty

**Trènto** *f* Trent

**trepidare (trèpido)** *intr* to fear; to worry

**trepidazióne** *f* fear, trepidation

**treppiède** *m* tripod; trivet

**tré·sca** *f* (**-sche**) intrigue; liaison

**tréspolo** *m* stool; pedestal; stand, perch; (coll) jalopy

**triàngolo** *m* triangle; **triangolo rettangolo** right triangle

**tribolare (tribolo)** *tr* to torment, afflict ‖ *intr* to suffer

**tribolazióne** *f* tribulation, ordeal

**tribórdo** *m* (naut) starboard

**tri·bù** *f* (**-bù**) tribe

**tribuna** *f* rostrum, platform; (sports) grandstand; **tribuna stampa** press box

**tribunale** *m* court, tribunal; courthouse; **tribunale dei minorenni** juvenile court; **tribunale di prima istanza** court of first instance

**tributare** *tr* to bestow

**tributà·rio -ria (-ri -rie)** *adj* tributary; tax ‖ *m* tributary

**tributo** *m* tribute; tax

**trichè·co** *m* (**-chi**) walrus

**triciclo** *m* tricycle

**tricolóre** *adj & m* tricolor

**tricòrno** *m* cocked hat, tricorn

**tricromìa** *f* three-color printing; three-color print

**tridènte** *m* trident

**trifase** *adj* three-phase

**trifocale** *adj* trifocal

**trifò·glio** *m* (**-gli**) clover; three-leaf clover

**trifola** *f* (coll) truffle

**trìglia** *f* red mullet

**trigonometrìa** *f* trigonometry

**trilióne** *m* trillion

**trillare** *intr* to trill; to vibrate

**trillo** *m* trill; ringing

**trilogìa** *f* trilogy

**trimestrale** *adj* quarterly

**trimèstre** *m* quarter; quarterly dues; quarterly payment; (educ) quarter, trimester

**trimotóre** *m* three-engine plane

**trina** *f* lace

**trin·ca** *f* (**-che**) (naut) gammoning; **di trinca** clearly, cleanly; **nuovo di trinca** brand-new

**trincare** §197 *tr* (coll) to gulp down, swill

**trincèa** *f* trench

**trincerare (trincèro)** *tr* to dig trenches in ‖ *ref* to entrench oneself

**trincétto** *m* shoemaker's blade

**trinchétto** *m* (naut) foremast; (naut) foresail

**trinciante** *adj* cutting ‖ *m* carving knife

**trinciapòllo** *m* meat shears

**trinciare** §128 *tr* to carve; to shred; to advance (*rash opinions*); to cut up

**trinciato** *m* smoking tobacco

**trinciatrice** *f* shredder; slicer

**Trinità** *f* Trinity

**trionfale** *adj* triumphal

**trionfante** *adj* triumphant

**trionfare (triónfo)** *intr* to triumph

**triónfo** *m* triumph; center piece; tidbit dish with three or four tiers; trump (*in game of tarot*)

**triparti·to -ta** *adj* tripartite

**triplicare** §197 (**triplico**) *tr & ref* to triple

**triplice** *adj* threefold

**tri·plo -pla** *adj & m* triple

**tripode** *m* tripod

**trippa** *f* tripe; (coll) belly

**tripudiare** §287 *intr* to exult

**tripù·dio** *m* (**-di**) exultation

**tris** *m* (tris) (poker) three of a kind

**trisàvola** *f* great-great-grandmother

**trisàvolo** *m* great-great-grandfather; **trisavoli** great-great-grandparents

**trisma** *m* lockjaw

**triste** *adj* sad; gloomy, bleak

**tristézza** *f* sadness

**tri·sto -sta** *adj* wicked; wretched; poor (*figure*); (lit) sad

**tritacar·ne** *m* (**-ne**) meat grinder

**tritaghiàc·cio** *m* (**-cio**) ice crusher

**tritare** *tr* to chop; to grind; to mince, hash; to pound

**tri·to -ta** *adj* minced, hashed; worn, trite

**tritòlo** *m* T.N.T.

**tritóne** *m* (zool) newt; (fig) merman ‖ **Tritone** *m* Triton

**trìtti·co** *m* (**-ci**) triptych; export document in triplicate; trilogy

**trittòn·go** *m* (**-ghi**) triphthong

**triturare** *tr* to mince, hash

**trivèlla** *f* auger, drill; post-hole digger

**trivellare (trivèllo)** *tr* to drill, bore

**triviale** *adj* vulgar

**triviali·tà** *f* (**-tà**) vulgarity

**tri·vio** *m* (**-vi**) crossroads; trivium; **da trivio** vulgar

**trofèo** *m* trophy; (mil) insignia (*on headpiece*)

**trògolo** *m* trough

**tròia** *f* sow; slut ‖ **Troia** *f* Troy

**troia·no -na** *adj & m* Trojan

**trómba** *f* trumpet; bugle, clarion; trunk (*of elephant*); leg (*of boot*); (anat) tube; (aut, rad) horn; **con le trombe nel sacco** crestfallen, dejected; **tromba d'aria** whirlwind; tornado; **tromba marina** waterspout; **tromba delle scale** stairwell

**trombétta** *f* trumpet

**trombettière** *m* (mil) trumpeter

**trombetti·sta** *m* (**-sti**) trumpet player

**trombóne** *m* trombone; blunderbuss

**trombò·si** *f* (**-si**) thrombosis

**troncare** §197 (**trónco**) *tr* to chop; to cut off; to clip (*words*); to break, sever; to block (*s.o.'s progress*); to apocopate

**tronchése** [s] *m* wire cutter

**trón·co -ca (-chi -che)** *adj* truncate; oxytone; apocopated; exhausted, dead-tired; incomplete; **in tronco** in the middle; (*dismissal*) on the spot ‖ *m* trunk; stub (*of receipt book*);

section (*of highway*); log; strain (*of a family*); (rr) branch; **tronco di cono** truncated cone; **tronco maggiore** (naut) lower mast

**troncóne** *m* stump

**troneggiare** §290 (**tronéggio**) *intr* to tower; to hold forth; **troneggiare su** to lord it over

**trón·fio -fia** *adj* (**-fi -fie**) haughty; bombastic

**tròno** *m* throne

**tropicale** *adj* tropical

**tròpi·co** *m* (**-ci**) tropic

**troposfèra** *f* troposphere

**tròp·po -pa** *adj* & *pron* too much; **trop·pi -pe** too many ‖ *m* too much; **questo è troppo!** enough is enough! ‖ **troppo** *adv* too; too much; **essere di troppo** to be in the way

**tròta** *f* trout

**trottare** (**tròtto**) *intr* to trot

**trotterellare** (**trotterèllo**) *intr* to trot along; to toddle

**tròtto** *m* trot; **piccolo trotto** jog trot

**tròttola** *f* top

**trovare** (**tròvo**) *tr* to find; to visit; **trovare a** or **da ridire** (**su**) to find fault (with); **trovi?** don't you think so? ‖ *ref* to find oneself; to meet; to be; to be located; to happen, e.g., **mi trovai a passare di fronte a casa sua** I happened to pass in front of his house

**trovarò·be** *m* (**-be**) (theat) property man ‖ *f* (theat) dresser

**trovata** *f* find; trick, gimmick

**trovatèl·lo -la** *mf* foundling, waif

**trovatóre** *m* troubadour

**trovièro** *m* trouvère

**truccare** §197 *tr* to make up; to falsify; (aut) to soup up ‖ *ref* to put on make-up

**truccatura** *f* make-up; trick, gimmick

**truc·co** *m* (**-chi**) make-up; trick, gimmick

**truce** *adj* fierce, cruel; menacing

**trucidare** (**trùcido**) *tr* to massacre

**trùciolo** *m* chip, shaving

**truculènto** *adj* truculent

**truffa** *f* cheat, fraud, swindle; **truffa all'americana** confidence game

**truffare** *tr* to cheat, swindle

**truffa·tóre -trice** *mf* cheat, swindler

**truismo** *m* truism

**truògolo** *m* var of **trogolo**

**truppa** *f* troop; soldiers; **di truppa** (mil) enlisted (*man or woman*); **in truppa** in a flock

**tu** §5 *pron pers*; **a tu per tu** face to face; **dare del tu a** to address in the familiar form

**tuba** *f* tuba; (hist) horn, trumpet; (joc) top hat, stovepipe; (anat) tube

**tubare** *intr* to coo

**tubatura** *f* piping, tubing; pipe, tube; pipeline

**tubazióne** *f* tubes, pipes

**tubèrcolo** *m* tubercle

**tubercolosà·rio** [s] *m* (**-ri**) tuberculosis sanitarium

**tubercolò·si** *f* (**-si**) tuberculosis

**tubercoló·so -sa** [s] *adj* tuberculous ‖ *mf* T.B. patient

**tùbero** *m* tuber

**tubétto** *m* tube (*for pills or toothpaste*); spool

**tubino** *m* small tube; derby (hat)

**tubo** *m* tube; pipe; (anat) canal, duct; **a tubo** tubular; **tubo di scarico** exhaust pipe; **tubo di troppopieno** overflow; **tubo di ventilazione** air shaft

**tubolare** *adj* tubular ‖ *m* tire (*for racing bicycle*)

**tuffare** *tr* to dip; to plunge ‖ *ref* to plunge; to dive

**tuffa·tóre -trice** *mf* diver ‖ *m* dive bomber

**tuffétto** *m* (orn) dabchick, grebe

**tuffo** *m* dive; plunge; throb; **a tuffo** (aer) diving; **scendere a tuffo** (aer) to dive; **tuffo ad angelo** (sports) swan dive; **tuffo d'acqua** downpour

**tufo** *m* tufa

**tu·ga** *f* (**-ghe**) (naut) deckhouse

**tugù·rio** *m* (**-ri**) hovel

**tulipano** *m* tulip

**tumefare** §173 *tr* & *ref* to swell

**tumefazióne** *f* swelling

**tùmi·do -da** *adj* tumid

**tumóre** *m* tumor

**tùmulo** *m* tomb; tumulus

**tumulto** *m* tumult, riot; commotion

**tumultuó·so -sa** [s] *adj* tumultuous

**tungstèno** *m* tungsten

**tùni·ca** *f* (**-che**) tunic

**Tùnisi** *f* Tunis

**Tunisìa, la** Tunisia

**tunisi·no -na** *adj* & *mf* Tunisian

**tuo tua** §6 *adj* & *pron poss* (**tuòi tue**)

**tuòno** *m* thunder

**tuòrlo** *m* yolk

**turàcciolo** *m* cork, stopper

**turare** *tr* to plug, stop; to cork

**turba** *f* crowd; mob; (pathol) upset

**turbaménto** *m* commotion, perturbation; disturbance, breach (*of law and order*)

**turbante** *m* turban

**turbare** *tr* to muddy; to disturb; to upset ‖ *ref* to become cloudy; to become upset

**turba·to -ta** *adj* upset; disturbed; distracted

**tùrbi·do -da** *adj* turbid

**turbina** *f* turbine

**turbinare** (**tùrbino**) *tr* to separate in a centrifuge ‖ *intr* to whirl

**tùrbine** *m* whirlwind; swarm; tumult

**turbinó·so -sa** [s] *adj* whirling; tumultuous

**turboèli·ca** *m* (**-ca**) turboprop

**turbogètto** *m* turbojet

**turbolèn·to -ta** *adj* turbulent

**turbolènza** *f* turbulence

**turbomotrice** *f* (rr) turbine engine

**turboreattóre** *m* turbojet

**turcasso** *m* quiver

**turchése** [s] *m* turquoise

**Turchìa, la** Turkey

**turchinétto** *m* bluing

**turchi·no -na** *adj* dark-blue ‖ *m* dark blue

**tur·co -ca** (**-chi -che**) *adj* Turkish; **sedere alla turca** to sit cross-legged ‖ *mf* Turk ‖ *m* Turkish (*language*); **bestemmiare come un turco** to swear

like a trooper; **fumare come un turco** to smoke like a steam engine
**tùrgi·do -da** *adj* turgid
**turìbolo** *m* thurible, censer
**turismo** *m* tourism
**turi·sta** *mf* (**-sti -ste**) tourist
**turìsti·co -ca** *adj* (**-ci -che**) tourist; travel (*e.g.*, *bureau*); traveler's (*check*)
**turlupinare** *tr* to hoodwink, swindle
**turlupinatura** *f* swindle, confidence game
**turno** *m* turn; shift; **a turno** in turn; **di turno** on duty; **fare a turno** to take turns
**turpe** *adj* base, abject; (lit) ugly
**turpilò·quio** *m* (**-qui**) foul language
**turpitùdine** *f* turpitude
**tuta** *f* overalls; **tuta antigravità** anti-G suit; **tuta da bambini** jumpers; **tuta spaziale** spacesuit
**tutèla** *f* guardianship; defense, protection
**tutelare** *adj* tutelary ‖ *v* (**tutèlo**) *tr* to protect, defend

**tùtolo** *m* corncob
**tu·tóre -trice** *mf* guardian; protector
**tuttavìa** *adv* yet, nevertheless; (lit) always, continuously
**tut·to -ta** *adj* whole; all; full; **con tutto** in spite of, e.g., **con tutto quello che ho fatto per lui** in spite of all I have done for him; **del tutto** fully, completely; **è tutt'uno** it's all the same; **tutt'altro** completely different; on the contrary; **tutt'altro che** anything but; **tutti** every, e.g., **tutti gli scolari** every pupil; **tutti e due** both ‖ *m* everything; whole; **con tutto che** although; **fare di tutto** to do everything possible; **in tutto** altogether ‖ *pron* **tut·ti -te** all, everybody (*of a group*); **tutti** everybody ‖ **tutto** *adv* quite; **tutt'a un tratto** all of a sudden; **tutto al contrario** quite the opposite
**tuttofa·re** *adj invar* of all trades; of all work ‖ *m* (**-re**) factotum, jack-of-all-trades ‖ *f* (**-re**) maid of all work
**tuttóra** *adv* yet, still
**tziga·no -na** *adj & mf* var of **zigano**

# U

**U, u** [u] *m & f* nineteenth letter of the Italian alphabet
**ubbìa** *f* prejudice, bias; complex; whim
**ubbidiènte** *adj* obedient
**ubbidire** §176 *tr* to obey ‖ *intr* to obey; to respond (*said of a car*); (with *dat*) to obey, e.g., **gli ubbedì** he obeyed him
**ubertó·so -sa** [s] *adj* fruitful; fertile
**ubicazióne** *f* location
**ubiquità** *f* ubiquity; **non ho il dono dell'ubiquità** I can't be everywhere at the same time
**ubì·quo -qua** *adj* ubiquitous
**ubriacare** §197 *tr* to make drunk, intoxicate ‖ *ref* to get drunk
**ubriacatura** or **ubriachézza** *f* drunkenness, intoxication
**ubria·co -ca** (**-chi -che**) *adj* drunk; **ubriaco fradicio** dead drunk ‖ *mf* drunkard
**ubriacó·ne -na** *mf* drunkard
**uccellare** (**uccèllo**) *tr* to take in, cajole ‖ *intr* to snare; to fowl; to hunt birds
**uccèllo** *m* bird; **uccello di bosco** fugitive; **uccello di galera** gallows bird; **uccello di passo** bird of passage
**uccella·tóre -trice** *mf* live-bird catcher
**uccellièra** *f* aviary; large birdcage
**uccìdere** §274 *tr* to kill ‖ *ref* to kill oneself; to get killed; to kill one another
**-ùccio -ùccia** (**-ucci -ucce**) *suf adj* not very, e.g., **calduccio** not very hot; rather, e.g., **magruccio** rather thin; poor little, e.g., **caruccio** poor little darling ‖ *suf m & f* small e.g., **cappelluccio** small hat
**uccisióne** *f* killing; murder
**ucci·so -sa** *adj* killed ‖ *mf* victim

**ucci·sóre -ditrice** *mf* killer
**ucrai·no -na** *adj & mf* Ukrainian ‖ **l'Ucraina** *f* the Ukraine
**udìbile** *adj* audible
**udiènza** *f* audience; hearing; **l'udienza è aperta!** the court is now in session!
**udire** §275 *tr* to hear; to listen to
**udito** *m* hearing
**uditòfono** *m* hearing aid
**udi·tóre -trice** *adj* hearing ‖ *mf* (educ) auditor ‖ *m* magistrate
**uditò·rio -ria** (**-ri -rie**) *adj* auditory ‖ *m* audience
**ufficiale** *adj* official ‖ *m* official; officer; **primo ufficiale** (naut) first officer, mate; **ufficiale di giornata** (mil) officer of the day; **ufficiale di rotta** (aer, naut) navigator; **ufficiale giudiziario** clerk of the court; process server, bailiff; **ufficiale medico** (mil) medical officer
**ufficiare** §128 *tr* to officiate
**uffi·cio** *m* (**-ci**) duty; office; bureau; department (*of agency*); **d'ufficio** ex-officio; public, e.g., **avvocato d'ufficio** public defender; **ufficio di collocamento** placement bureau; **ufficio di compensazione** clearing house; **ufficio d'igiene** board of health
**uffició·so -sa** [s] *adj* unofficial; kindly; white (*lie*)
**uffi·zio** *m* (**-zi**) (eccl) office
**ufo** *m*—**a ufo** gratis, without paying
**ugèllo** *m* nozzle
**ùg·gia** *f* (**-ge**) darkness; gloom; dislike; **avere in uggia** to dislike
**uggiolare** (**ùggiolo**) *intr* to whine (*said of a dog*)
**uggió·so -sa** [s] *adj* gloomy; boring
**ugnare** *tr* to bevel; to miter

**ugnatura** f bevel; miter

**ùgola** f uvula; **bagnarsi l'ugola** (coll) to wet one's whistle

**ugonòtto** m Huguenot

**uguaglianza** f equality

**uguagliare** §280 tr to equal; to make equal; to equalize; to level; to compare || ref to compare oneself; to be equal; to be compared

**uguale** adj equal; same; even; level; **per me è uguale** it's the same to me || m equal; (math) equal sign

**ùlcera** f ulcer; sore

**ulcerare** (**ùlcero**) tr & ref to ulcerate

**uliva** f var of **oliva**

**ulterióre** adj further, subsequent, ulterior

**ùltima** f latest news; last straw

**ultimare** (**ùltimo**) tr to complete, finish

**ultimato** m ultimatum

**ultimìssima** f latest edition (of newspaper); **ultimissime** late news

**ùlti·mo- ma** adj last; final; latest; latter; farthest; ultimate; least; top (floor); **all'ultimo, dall'ultimo, nell'ultimo** or **sull'ultimo** lately; finally, at the end || f see **ultima**

**ultimogèni·to -ta** adj last-born || mf last-born child

**ultra-** pref adj and m & f ultra-, e.g., **ultraelevato** ultrahigh; super-, e.g., **ultrasonico** supersonic (speed)

**ultracór·to -ta** adj ultrashort

**ultrarós·so -sa** adj & m infrared

**ultraterré·no -na** adj ultramundane; unearthly

**ultraviolét·to -ta** adj & m ultraviolet

**ululare** (**ùlulo**) intr to howl

**ululato** m howl

**umanésimo** m humanism

**umani·sta** mf (**-sti -ste**) humanist

**umani·tà** f (**-tà**) humanity; **umanità** fpl humanities

**umanità·rio -ria** adj & mf (**-ri -rie**) humanitarian

**uma·no -na** adj human; humane || m human nature; **umani** human beings

**um·bro -bra** adj & m Umbrian

**umettare** (**umétto**) tr to moisten, dampen

**umidìc·cio -cia** adj (**-ci -ce**) dampish

**umidi·tà** f (**-tà**) humidity, dampness

**ùmi·do -da** adj humid, damp || m humidity, dampness; **in umido** stewed (e.g., meat)

**ùmile** adj humble || **gli umili** mpl the meek

**umiliare** §287 tr to humiliate, humble || ref to humble oneself

**umiliazióne** f humiliation

**umiltà** f humility

**umóre** m humor, mood, temper; whim; (bot) sap; **un bell'umore** (coll) quite a character

**umorismo** m humor

**umori·sta** mf (**-sti -ste**) humorist

**umorìsti·co -ca** adj (**-ci -che**) humorous; amusing, comic, funny

**un** (apocopated form of **uno**) §9 indef art a, an || §9 numeral adj one || §12 reciprocal indef pron—**l'un l'altro** each other, one another

**unànime** adj unanimous

**unanimità** f unanimity

**unàni·mo -ma** adj unanimous

**uncinare** tr to hook, grapple

**uncinétto** m small hook; crochet hook

**uncino** m hook; grapnel; clasp; pothook; (fig) pretext; **a uncino** hooked

**undicèsi·mo -ma** adj, m & pron eleventh

**ùndici** adj & pron eleven; **le undici** eleven o'clock || m eleven; eleventh (in dates); (soccer) squad

**ùngere** §183 tr to grease; to oil; to smear; to anoint; to flatter || ref to smear oneself

**Ungherìa, l'** f Hungary

**ungherése** [s] adj & mf Hungarian

**ùnghia** f nail; fingernail; claw; hoof; fluke (of anchor); (fig) hairbreadth; **avere le unghie lunghe** to be light-fingered; **unghia del piede** toenail; **unghie** (fig) clutches

**unghiata** f nail scratch

**unguènto** m unguent, ointment

**ùni·co -ca** adj (**-ci -che**) only, sole; unique; single (copy); complete (text) || f—**l'unica** the only solution

**unicòrno** m unicorn

**unificare** §197 (**unìfico**) tr to unify; to standardize

**unificazióne** f unification; standardization

**uniformare** (**unifórmo**) tr to make uniform, standardize || ref—**uniformarsi a** to conform to; to comply with

**unifórme** adj uniform; standard || f uniform; **alta uniforme** (mil) full dress

**unilaterale** adj unilateral

**unióne** f union; agreement; **unione libera** free love

**unire** §176 tr & ref to unite

**unìsono** [s] m unison; **all'unisono** in unison

**uni·tà** f (**-tà**) unity; unit; **unità di misura** unit of measurement

**unità·rio -ria** (**-ri -rie**) adj unit (e.g., price); united || m Unitarian

**uni·to -ta** adj united; joined; compact; plain (color); consolidated

**universale** adj universal; last (judgment)

**universi·tà** f (**-tà**) university

**università·rio -ria** (**-ri -rie**) adj university; college || mf university or college student; university or college professor

**univer·so -sa** adj universal || m universe

**unno** m Hun

**u·no -na** §9 indef art a, an || §9 numeral adj one || m one || §10 pron indef one; **le una, la una,** or **l'una** one o'clock; **l'uno e l'altro** both; **l'uno o l'altro** either, either one; **per uno** in single file; **uno per uno** one by one; each other || §11 correlative pron one

**un·to -ta** adj greasy || m grease, fat; flattery; anointed one

**untuosità** [s] f greasiness; unction, unctuousness

**untuó·so -sa** [s] adj greasy; unctuous

unzióne *f* unction

uò·mo *m* (-mini) man; **come un sol uomo** to a man; **uomo d'affari** businessman; **uomo del giorno** man of the hour; **uomo della strada** man of the street; **uomo di chiesa** churchman; **uomo di fatica** laborer; **uomo di fiducia** trusted man; **uomo di mare** seaman; **uomo di paglia** straw man; **uomo di parola** man of his word; **uomo in mare!** man overboard!; **uomo meccanico** automaton; **uomo morto** (rr) deadman brake; **uomo nuovo** nouveau riche; **uomo rana** frogman

uòpo *m*—**all'uopo** if need be; **essere d'uopo** (lit) to be necessary

uòse [s] *fpl* leggings

uò·vo *m* (-va *fpl*) egg; **meglio un uovo oggi che una gallina domani** a bird in a hand is worth two in the bush; **rompere le uova nel paniere a qlcu** to spoil s.o.'s plans; **uovo affogato** poached egg; **uovo alla coque** softboiled egg; **uovo all'occhio di bue** fried egg; **uovo da tè** tea ball; **uovo strapazzato** scrambled egg

uragano *m* hurricane; storm (*of applause*); **uragano di neve** blizzard

Urali *mpl* Ural Mountains

uranìfe·ro -ra *adj* uranium-bearing

urànio *m* uranium

urbanésimo *m* urbanization, migration toward the cities

urbanìsti·co -ca (-ci -che) *adj* city-planning ‖ *f* city planning

urbani·tà *f* (-tà) urbanity, civility; city population

urbanizzare [ddzz] *tr* to urbanize

urba·no -na *adj* urban; urbane

urètra *f* urethra

urgènte *adj* urgent, pressing

urgènza *f* urgency; **d'urgenza** urgent; emergency (*e.g., operation*); **fare urgenza a** to urge

ùrgere §276 *tr* to urge, press ‖ *intr* to be urgent

urina *f* urine

urinà·rio -ria *adj* (-ri -rie) urinary

urlare *tr* to shout; to shout down ‖ *intr* to howl; to shout, yell

urla·tóre -trice *adj* screaming ‖ *mf* screamer; loud singer

ur·lo *m* howl ‖ *m* (-la *fpl*) yell, scream

urna *f* urn; ballot box; (poet) grave; **urne** polls

-uro *suf m* (chem) -ide, e.g., **cloruro** chloride

urologìa *f* urology

urrà *interj* hurrah!

ursóne *m* Canada porcupine

urtare *tr* to hit; to bump; to annoy ‖ *intr*—**urtare contro** to hit, strike against; **urtare in** to hit; to stumble into ‖ *ref* to get annoyed; to clash; to bump into one another

urto *m* hit; bump; collision; onslaught; clash, disagreement; **urto di nervi** huff

Uruguai, l' *m* Uruguay

uruguaia·no -na *adj* & *mf* Uruguayan

usanza *f* usage, custom; habit, practice

usare *tr* to use, employ; to wear out; (lit) to frequent; **usare + inf** to be accustomed to + *ger* ‖ *intr* to be fashionable; **usare di** to use, employ ‖ *ref* to become accustomed; **si usa + inf** it is customary to + *inf*

usa·to -ta *adj* used, second-hand; worn; worn-out; (lit) usual ‖ *m* usage, custom; norm; second-hand goods

usbèr·go *m* (-ghi) hauberk; (fig) shield, protection

uscènte *adj* ending, terminating; retiring

uscière *m* receptionist; office boy, errand boy; (coll) court clerk; (coll) bailiff; tipstaff

ù·scio *m* (-sci) door; **infilar l'uscio** to take French leave; **metter tra l'uscio e il muro** (fig) to corner

uscire §277 *intr* (ESSERE) to go out, leave; to come out; to flow out; to escape; to turn out, ensue; **essere uscito** to be out; **uscire da** to leave; to run off (*the track*); **uscire dai gangheri** to get mad; **uscire dal comune** to be out of the ordinary; **uscire dal segno** to go too far; **uscire dal seminato** to go astray; **uscire di mente a** to escape one's mind, e.g., **gli è uscito di mente** it escaped his mind; **uscire di sentimento** to pass out; **uscire di vita** to die; **uscire in** to lead into; **uscire per il rotto della cuffia** to barely make it

uscita *f* exit; outlay; quip, sally; gate (*e.g., in an airport*); (gram) ending; **all'uscita** on the way out; **buona uscita** severance pay; bonus; **libera uscita** day off (*of servants*); (mil) pass; **uscita di sicurezza** emergency exit

usignòlo *m* nightingale

u·so -sa *adj* (lit) accustomed ‖ *m* practice; usage; use; wear; faculty; power (*e.g., of hearing*); (lit) intimate relations; **all'uso di** in the fashion of; **avere per uso di** to be wont to; **come d'uso** as usual; **farci l'uso** to get used to it!; **fuori d'uso** worn-out, out of commission; **uso esterno!** (pharm) not to be taken internally!

ustionare (ustióno) *tr* to burn, scorch

ustióne *f* burn

usuale *adj* usual; ordinary, common

usufruire §176 *intr*—**usufruire di** to have the use of; to enjoy

usura *f* usury; (mach) wear and tear; **ad usura** abundantly

usu·ràio -ràia (-rài -ràie) *adj* usurious ‖ *mf* usurer, loanshark

usurpare *tr* to usurp

utensile *adj* tool, e.g., **macchina utensile** machine tool ‖ *m* utensil; tool

utènte *m* user; customer, consumer

ùtero *m* uterus, womb

ùtile *adj* useful; usable; workable; legal, prescribed (*e.g., time*); **essere utile a** to help; **venire utile** to come in handy ‖ *m* usefulness; profit, gain

utili·tà *f* (-tà) utility, usefulness; profit, gain

utilitària *f* economy car, compact

utilizzare [ddzz] *tr* to utilize

**utopìa** *f* utopia
**utopì·sta** *mf* (**-sti -ste**) utopian
**utopìstì·co -ca** *adj* (**-ci -che**) utopian
**uva** *f* grapes; **un grano di uva passa** a raisin; **uva passa** raisins

**uxorici·da** *m* (**-di**) uxoricide ‖ *f* (**-de**) murderer of one's husband
**uxorici·dio** *m* (**-di**) uxoricide; murder of one's husband
**ùzzolo** [ddzz] *m* whim, fancy, caprice

## V

**V, v** [vu] *m & f* twentieth letter of the Italian alphabet
**V.** *abbr* (**vostro**) your
**vacante** *adj* vacant
**vacanza** *f* vacancy; vacation; **fare vacanza** to be on vacation; **vacanze** vacation
**vacanzière** *m* vacationer
**vac·ca** *f* (**-che**) cow
**vac·càio** *m* (**-cài**) cowboy; stable boy
**vaccherìa** *f* dairy farm
**vacchétta** *f* cowhide
**vaccina** *f* cow manure; cow
**vaccinare** *tr* to vaccinate
**vaccinazióne** *f* vaccination
**vacci·no -na** *adj* cow; bovine ‖ *m* vaccine ‖ *f* see **vaccina**
**vacillante** *adj* vacillating
**vacillare** *intr* to totter; to vacillate; to shake; to flicker; to fail, e.g., **la memoria gli vacilla** his memory is failing; **far vacillare** to rock
**vacui·tà** *f* (**-tà**) vacuity
**và·cuo -cua** *adj* empty ‖ *m* vacuum
**vademè·cum** *m* (**-cum**) almanac, ready-reference handbook
**vagabondàg·gio** *m* (**-gi**) vagrancy; wandering; rambling
**vagabondare** (**vagabóndo**) *intr* to wander, rove
**vagabón·do -da** *adj* wandering; vagabond ‖ *mf* vagrant, bum, tramp; rover
**vagare** §209 *intr* to wander, ramble, rove
**vagheggiare** §290 (**vaghéggio**) *tr* to gaze fondly at; to cherish
**vagire** §176 *intr* to cry, whimper
**vagito** *m* cry, whimper
**và·glia** *m* (**-glia**) money order ‖ *f—di* **vaglia** worthy, capable
**vagliare** §280 *tr* to sift, bolt
**và·glio** *m* (**-gli**) sieve; **mettere al vaglio** to scrutinize
**va·go -ga** (**-ghi -ghe**) *adj* vague; vacant (*stare*); (lit) beautiful; (lit) roving; (poet) desirous ‖ *m* vagueness; (lit) rover; (anat) vagus
**vagonata** *f* carload
**vagóne** *m* (rr) car; **vagone frigorifero** (rr) refrigerator car; **vagone letto** (rr) sleeping car, sleeper; **vagone ristorante** (rr) dining car; **vagone volante** (aer) flying boxcar
**vàio vàia** (**vài vàie**) *adj* dark-grey ‖ *m* dark grey; (heral) vair; (zool) Siberian squirrel
**vaiòlo** *m* smallpox
**valan·ga** *f* (**-ghe**) avalanche
**valènte** *adj* capable, skillful; clever
**valentìa** *f* skill; cleverness

**valentino** *m* Valentine (*sweetheart*)
**valènza** *f* (chem) valence
**valére** §278 *tr* to win, get (*e.g., an honor for s.o.*); **che vale?** what's the use?; **valere la pena** to be worthwhile; **valere un Perù** to be worth a king's ransom ‖ *intr* (ESSERE & AVERE) to be worth: to be of avail; to be valid; to mean; to be the equivalent; **far valere** to enforce; **farsi valere** to assert oneself; **tanto vale** it's all the same; **vale a dire** that is to say; **valere meglio** to be better ‖ *ref—* **valersi di** to avail oneself of; to play on; to employ
**valévole** *adj* valid, good
**valicare** §197 (**vàlico**) *tr* to cross, pass
**vàli·co** *m* (**-chi**) mountain pass; passage; opening (*in a hedge*)
**validi·tà** *f* (**-tà**) validity
**vàli·do -da** *adj* valid; able, able-bodied; strong
**valigerìa** *f* luggage; luggage store
**valigétta** *f* valise; **valigetta diplomatica** attaché case
**valì·gia** *f* (**-ge**) suitcase; traveling bag; **fare le valige** to pack one's bags; **valigia diplomatica** diplomatic pouch; attaché case; **valigia per abiti** suit carrier
**vallata** *f* valley
**valle** *f* valley; **a valle** downhill; downstream
**vallétta** *f* (telv) assistant
**vallétto** *m* valet; page; (telv) assistant
**valló·ne -na** *adj & mf* Walloon ‖ *m* narrow valley
**valóre** *m* value; valor, bravery; force; (fig) jewel; (math) variable; **mettere in valore** to raise the value of; **valore di mercato** market value; **valore facciale** face value; **valore locativo** rental value; **valori** valuables; securities; **valori mobiliari** securities
**valorizzare** [ddzz] *tr* to enhance the value of
**valoró·so -sa** [s] *adj* brave, valiant
**valuta** *f* currency; (com) effective date; (com) value (*of promissory note*)
**valutare** *tr* to estimate, appraise; to value, prize; to count, reckon; to take into consideration
**valutazióne** *f* estimation, appraisal; evaluation
**valva** *f* (bot, zool) valve
**vàlvola** *f* (anat, mach) valve; (elec) fuse; (rad, telv) tube, valve; **valvola a galleggiante** ball cock; **valvola di sicurezza** safety valve; **valvola in testa** overhead valve
**vàl·zer** *m* (**-zer**) waltz

**vamp** *f* (**vamp**) vamp

**vampa** *f* flame; blaze; flash; flush

**vampata** *f* burst (*of heat*); blast (*of hot air*); flash, flush

**vampiro** *m* vampire

**vanàdio** *m* vanadium

**vanaglòria** *f* vainglory, boastfulness

**vanaglorió·so -sa** [s] *adj* vainglorious

**vandalismo** *m* vandalism

**vànda·lo -la** *adj & m* vandal || **Vandalo** *m* Vandal

**vaneggiare** §290 (**vanéggio**) *intr* to rave; to be delirious; (lit) to open, yawn

**vanè·sio -sia** *adj* (**-si -sie**) vain

**van·ga** *f* (**-ghe**) spade

**vangare** §209 *tr* to spade up; to dig with a spade

**vangèlo** *m* gospel || **Vangelo** *m* Gospel

**vanghétto** *m* spud

**vaniglia** *f* vanilla

**vanilò·quio** *m* (**-qui**) empty talk

**vani·tà** *f* (**-tà**) vanity

**vanitó·so -sa** [s] *adj* vain, conceited

**va·no -na** *adj* vain; (lit) empty, hollow; **in vano** in vain || *m* empty space; room

**vantàg·gio** *m* (**-gi**) advantage; profit; odds, handicap; discount; (coll) extra; (typ) galley; **a vantaggio di** on behalf of

**vantaggió·so -sa** [s] *adj* advantageous

**vantare** *tr* to boast of; to set up (*a claim*) || *ref* to boast; **vantarsi di** to brag about, vaunt

**vanteria** *f* brag, boast, vaunt

**vanto** *m* brag, boast; **aver vanto su** (lit) to overcome

**vànvera** *f*—**a vanvera** at random

**vapóre** *m* vapor; steam; locomotive; steamship; **a tutto vapore** at full speed

**vaporétto** *m* small river boat; vaporetto (*in Venice*)

**vaporizzare** [ddzz] *tr* to vaporize; to spray || *intr* (ESSERE) & *ref* to evaporate

**vaporizzatóre** [ddzz] *m* vaporizer; sprayer

**vaporó·so -sa** [s] *adj* vaporous

**varaménto** *m* assemblage (*of prefab pieces*)

**varano** *m* monitor lizard

**varare** *tr* to launch; to pass (*a law*); (coll) to back, promote (*a candidate*)

**varcare** §197 *tr* to cross || *intr* (poet) to pass (*said of time*)

**var·co** *m* (**-chi**) opening; mountain pass; breach; **attendere al varco** to lie in wait for; **cogliere al varco** to catch unawares; **fare varco in** to breach

**varechina** *f* (laundry) bleach

**variàbile** *adj & f* variable

**variante** *f* variant; detour; (aut) model

**variare** §287 *tr & intr* (ESSERE & AVERE) to vary

**variazióne** *f* variation

**varicèlla** *f* chicken pox

**varicó·so -sa** [s] *adj* varicose

**variega·to -ta** *adj* variegated

**varie·tà** *m* (**-tà**) (theat) vaudeville || *f* variety

**và·rio -ria** (**-ri -rie**) *adj* varied; various; variable; different; **va·ri -rie** several || *m* variety || **varie** *fpl* miscellanies || **va·ri -rie** *pron indef* several

**variopìn·to -ta** *adj* multicolored

**varo** *m* (naut) launch

**vas** *m* (**vas**) subchaser

**va·sàio** *m* (**-sài**) potter

**va·sca** *f* (**-sche**) tub; basin; pool; **vasca da bagno** bathtub; **vasca dei pesci** aquarium; **vasca navale** (naut) basin

**vascèllo** *m* vessel, ship

**vaselina** or **vasellina** *f* vaseline

**vasellame** *m* dishes; set of dishes; **vasellame da cucina** kitchen ware; **vasellame d'argento** silverware; **vasellame di porcellana** chinaware

**vasèllo** *m* (lit) vessel

**vasi·stas** [s] *m* (**-stas**) transom

**vaso** *m* vase; vessel; jar, pot; nave (*of church*); hall (*of building*); (naut) shipway; (poet) cup; **vasi vinari** wine containers; **vaso da fiori** flowerpot; **vaso da notte** chamber pot; **vaso d'elezione** (eccl) chosen vessel (*viz., Saint Paul*)

**vassallo** *m* vassal; (obs) helper

**vas·sóio** *m* (**-sói**) tray; mortarboard

**vasti·tà** *f* (**-tà**) vastness

**va·sto -sta** *adj* spacious; vast; (fig) deep

**vate** *m* (lit) prophet, poet

**vatica·no -na** *adj* Vatican || **Vaticano** *m* Vatican

**vaticinare** (**vatìcino** & **vaticìno**) *tr* to prophesy

**vaticì·nio** *m* (**-ni**) prophecy

**ve** §5 *pron*

**V.E.** *abbr* (**Vostra Eccellenza**) Your Excellency

**vècchia** *f* old woman

**vecchiàia** *f* old age

**vecchiézza** *f* old age

**vèc·chio -chia** (**-chi -chie**) *adj* old; elder; **vecchio come il cucco** as old as the hills || *m* old man; **vecchi** old people; **vecchio del mestiere** old hand || *f* see **vecchia**

**véc·cia** *f* (**-ce**) vetch

**véce** *f* stead, e.g., **in vece mia** in my stead; (lit) vicissitude; **fare le veci di** to act for or as

**vedére** *m* seeing; looks; view, opinion || §279 *tr* to see; to review; to look over; **chi s'è visto s'è visto!** good-by and good luck!; **dare a vedere** to make believe; **stare a vedere** to watch; observe; **non poter vedere** to not be able to stand; **non vedere l'ora di** to be hardly able to wait for; **vedere male qlcu** to be ill-disposed toward s.o. || *intr*—**stare a vedere** to wait and see; **vederci bene** to see (*e.g., in the dark*); **vederci chiaro** to look into it; **vedere di** to try to || *ref* to see oneself; to see each other; **vedersela brutta** to anticipate trouble

**vedétta** *f* lookout; (nav) vedette

**védova** *f* widow

**vedovanza** *f* widowhood

**vedovile** *adj* widow's; widower's || *m* dower

**védo·vo -va** *adj* widowed || *m* widower || *f* see **vedova**

**veduta** *f* view; (lit) eyesight; **di corte vedute** narrowminded; **di larghe vedute** broadminded

**veemènte** *adj* vehement; violent; impassioned

**veemènza** *f* vehemence; violence

**vegetale** *adj* vegetable || *m* plant, vegetable

**vegetare (vègeto)** *intr* to vegetate

**vegetaria·no -na** *adj & mf* vegetarian

**vegetazióne** *f* vegetation

**vège·to -ta** *adj* vigorous, spry

**veggènte** *adj* (obs) seeing || *mf* fortuneteller || *m* seer, prophet; **i veggenti** people having eyesight || *f* seeress, prophetess

**véglia** *f* vigil, watch; wakefulness; evening party, soirée; party, crowd; **a veglia** unbelievable (*tale*); **veglia danzante** dance; **veglia funebre** wake

**vegliardo** *m* old man

**vegliare** §280 (**véglio**) *tr* to keep watch over || *intr* to stay awake; to keep watch; to stay up

**veglióne** *m* masked ball

**veìcolo** *m* vehicle; carrier (*of disease*)

**véla** *f* sail; sailing; **alzare le vele** to set sail; **ammainare le vele** to take in sail; **a vela** under sail; **far vela** to set sail; **vela aurica** lugsail; **vela bermudiana** or **Marconi** jib; **vela maestra** mainsail

**ve·làio** *m* (**-lài**) sailmaker

**velare** *adj & f* (phonet) velar || *v* (**vélo**) *tr* to veil; to cover; to muffle (*sound*); to attenuate, reduce (*a shock*); to dim, cloud; to conceal; (phot) to fog || *ref* to cover oneself with a veil; to take the veil; to get dim, e.g., **gli si è velata la vista** his eyesight got dim

**velà·rio** *m* (**-ri**) (hist) velarium; (theat) curtain

**vela·to -ta** *adj* veiled; sheer (*hosiery*)

**velatura** *f* coating; (aer) airfoil; (naut) sails

**veleggiare** §290 (**veléggio**) *tr* (lit) to sail over (*the sea*) || *intr* to sail; (aer) to glide

**veleggiatóre** *m* sailboat; (aer) glider

**veléno** *m* poison; (fig) venom

**velenó·so -sa** [s] *adj* poisonous; (fig) venomous

**velétta** *f* veil; (naut) topgallant

**vèli·co -ca** *adj* (**-ci -che**) sail, sailing

**velièro** *m* sailing ship

**veli·no -na** *adj* thin (*paper*) || *f* carbon copy; onionskin; slant (*given to a news item*)

**velìvo·lo -la** *adj* (lit) gliding; (lit) sailing || *m* (lit) airplane, aircraft

**vellei·tà** *f* (**-tà**) wild ambition, dream

**vellicare** §197 (**vèllico**) *tr* to tickle

**vèllo** *m* (lit) fleece; **vello d'oro** Golden Fleece

**velló·so -sa** [s] *adj* hairy

**velluta·to -ta** *adj* velvety

**vellutino** *m* thin velvet; velvet ribbon; **vellutino di cotone** velveteen

**vellu·to -ta** *adj* (lit) hairy || *m* velvet; **velluto a coste** corduroy

**vélo** *m* veil; coating; film; skin (*e.g., of onion*); (anat, bot) velum; (fig) body; **fare velo a** to becloud; to fog

**velóce** *adj* speedy, quick, fast; fleeting

**velocipedastro** *m* poor or reckless bicycle rider

**veloci·sta** *mf* (**-sti -ste**) (sports) sprinter

**veloci·tà** *f* (**-tà**) velocity; speed; (aut) speed; **a grande velocità** by express; **a piccola velocità** by freight; **velocità di crociera** cruising speed; **velocità di fuga** (rok) escape velocity

**velòdromo** *m* bicycle ring or track

**véna** *f* vein; grain (*in wood or stone*); mood; streak (*of madness*); **di vena** willingly; **essere in vena di** to be in the mood to

**venale** *adj* venal

**venare (véno)** *tr* to vein

**vena·to -ta** *adj* veined; streaked; suffused; **venato di sangue** bloodshot

**venatura** *f* veining; (fig) streak

**vendémmia** *f* vintage

**vendemmiare** §287 (**vendémmio**) *tr* to harvest (*grapes*) || *intr* to gather grapes; (fig) to make a killing

**vendemmia·tóre -trice** *mf* vintager

**véndere** §281 *tr* to sell; **da vendere** plenty, more than enough; **vendere allo scoperto** (fin) to sell short; **vendere fumo** to peddle influence || *intr* to sell; **vendere allo scoperto** (fin) to sell short || *ref* to sell; **si vende** for sale

**vendétta** *f* vengeance; revenge; **gridare vendetta** to cry out for retribution

**vendicare** §197 (**véndico**) *tr* to avenge || *ref* to get revenge

**vendicati·vo -va** *adj* vengeful, vindictive

**vendica·tóre -trice** *adj* avenging || *mf* avenger

**vendifu·mo** *mf* (**-mo**) influence peddler

**véndita** *f* sale; shop; **in vendita** for sale; **vendita allo scoperto** (fin) short sale; **vendita per corrispondenza** catalogue sale

**vendi·tóre -trice** *mf* seller; clerk (*in store*) || *m* salesman; **venditore ambulante** peddler; **venditore di fumo** influence peddler || *f* saleslady

**veneràbile** or **venerando** *adj* venerable

**venerare (vènero)** *tr* to venerate, revere; to worship

**venerazióne** *f* veneration; worship

**vener·dì** *m* (**-dì**) Friday || **Venerdì Santo** Good Friday

**Vènere** *m* (astr) Venus || *f* (mythol & fig) Venus

**venè·reo -rea** *adj* (**-rei -ree**) venereal

**Venèzia** *f* Venice; Venetia (*province*)

**venezia·no -na** *adj & mf* Venetian || *f* Venetian blind

**venezola·no -na** *adj & mf* Venezuelan

**vènia** *f* (lit) forgiveness, pardon

**venire** §282 *intr* (ESSERE) to come; to turn out (*well or badly*); to turn out to be; **che viene** next, e.g., **il mese che viene** next month; **come viene** as it is; **far venire** to send for; to give, cause; **un va e vieni** a backward-and-forward motion; **venire** + *ger;* to keep + *ger;* **venire** + *pp* to be + *pp, e.g.,* **il portone viene aperto alle tre** the gate is opened at three; **venire a capo di** to solve; **venire ai ferri corti** to come into open conflict; **venire al dunque** or **al fatto** to come to the point; **venire alle corte** to get down to brass tacks; **venire alle mani** or **alle prese** to come to blows; **venire a parole** to have words; **venire a patti con** to come to terms with; **venire a proposito** to come in handy; **venire incontro a** to go to meet; **venire in possesso di** to come into possession of (*s.th*); **venire in mano** to come into the hands of (*s.o.*); **venire meno** to faint; **venir meno a** to fail to keep (*one's word*); **venir su** to grow, come up; **venire via** to give way ‖ *ref*—**venirsene** to stroll along ‖ *impers* (with *dat*)—**viene da** feel the urge to, e.g., **gli venne da starnutire** he felt the urge to sneeze; **gli è venuto da ridere** he felt the urge to laugh; **viene detto** blurt out, e.g., **gli è venuto detto che non gli piaceva quel tipo** he blurted out that he did not like that fellow; **viene fatto di**+*inf* succeed in+*ger*, e.g., **le venne fatto di convincerli** she succeeded in convincing them; happen to + *inf*, e.g., **gli venne fatto di incontrarmi per istrada** he happened to meet me on the way

**ventà·glio** *m* (**-gli**) fan; (fig) spread; **a ventaglio** fanlike; **diramarsi a ventaglio** to fan out

**ventaròla** *f* weather vane

**ventata** *f* gust of wind; (fig) wave

**ventènne** *adj* twenty-year-old ‖ *mf* twenty-year-old person

**ventèsi·mo -ma** *adj, m & pron* twentieth

**vénti** *adj & pron* twenty; **le venti** eight P.M. ‖ *m* twenty; twentieth (*in dates*)

**ventidue** *adj & pron* twenty-two **le ventidue** ten P.M. ‖ *m* twenty-two; twenty-second (*in dates*)

**ventilare** (**vèntilo**) *tr* to air, ventilate; to winnow (*grain*); to discuss minutely; to air (*a subject*); to broach (*a subject*); to unfurl (*a flag*) ‖ *ref* to fan oneself

**ventilatóre** *m* fan, ventilator; vent; (min) ventilation shaft; (naut) funnel

**ventilazióne** *f* ventilation; winnowing

**ventina** *f* score; **una ventina (di)** twenty, about twenty

**ventino** *m* twenty-cent coin

**ventiquattro** *adj & pron* twenty-four; **le ventiquattro** twelve P.M. ‖ *m* twenty-four; twenty-fourth (*in dates*)

**ventiquattró·re** *f* (**-re**) overnight bag; twenty-four-hour race; **ventiquattrore** *fpl* period of twenty-four hours

**ventitré** *adj & pron* twenty-three; **le ventitré** eleven P.M.; **portare il cappello alle ventitré** to wear one's hat cocked ‖ *m* twenty-three; twenty-third (*in dates*)

**vènto** *m* wind; air; guy wire; **presentarsi al vento** to sail into the wind; **farsi vento** to fan oneself; **a vento** windproof; wind-propelled; **col vento in prora** downwind; **col vento in poppa** upwind; favorably, famously

**vèntola** *f* fireside fan; lampshade; candle sconce; blade (*of fan*)

**ventó·so -sa** [s] *adj* windy ‖ *f* cupping glass; suction cup; (zool) sucker

**vèntre** *m* belly; **a ventre a terra** on one's belly; on one's face; at full speed (*said of a horse*)

**ventrìcolo** *m* ventricle

**ventrièra** *f* abdominal band or belt

**ventrilòquia** *f* ventriloquism

**ventrìlo·quo -qua** *mf* ventriloquist

**ventuno** *adj & pron* twenty-one; **le ventuno** nine P.M. ‖ *m* twenty-one; twenty-first (*in dates*); (cards) blackjack

**ventu·ro -ra** *adj* next ‖ *f* (lit) luck, fortune; (lit) good fortune; **alla ventura** at random, at a venture; **di ventura** of fortune, e.g., **soldato di ventura** soldier of fortune

**venustà** *f* (lit) pulchritude

**venu·to -ta** *mf*—**nuovo venuto** newcomer; **primo venuto** firstcomer ‖ *f* coming, arrival

**véra** *f* curbstone (*of well*); (coll) wedding ring

**verace** *adj* true; truthful, veracious

**veraci·tà** *f* (**-tà**) veracity, truthfulness

**veranda** *f* veranda; porch

**verbale** *adj* verbal ‖ *m* minutes; ticket (*given by a policeman*); **mettere a verbale** to enter into the record

**verbèna** *f* verbena

**vèrbo** *m* verb; (lit) word ‖ **Verbo** *m* (theol) Word

**verbosità** [s] *f* verbiage, verbosity

**verbó·so -sa** [s] *adj* windy, long-winded, verbose

**verda·stro -stra** *adj* greenish

**vérde** *adj* green; young, youthful ‖ *m* green; **al verde** (coll) broke, penniless; **nel verde degli anni** in the prime of life

**verdeggiante** *adj* verdant

**verderame** *m* blue vitriol; verdigris

**verdét·to -ta** *adj* greenish ‖ *m* verdict

**verdógno·lo -la** *adj* greenish; sallow (*face*)

**verdura** *f* vegetables

**verecóndia** *f* modesty, bashfulness

**verecón·do -da** *adj* modest, bashful

**vér·ga** *f* (**-ghe**) switch; rod; ingot, bar; pole; penis; (eccl) staff, crosier; (naut) yard; **tremare a verga a verga** to shake like a leaf

**vergare** §209 (**vérgo**) *tr* to switch; to rule (*paper*); to stripe; to write

**vergati·no -na** *adj* thin (*paper*) ‖ *m* striped cloth

**verga·to -ta** *adj* striped; watermarked with stripes ‖ *m* (obs) serge

**verginale** *adj* maidenly, virginal

**vérgine** *adj & f* virgin ‖ **Vergine** *f* (eccl) Virgin; (astr) Virgo

**verginità** *f* virginity, maidenhood

**vergógna** *f* shame; **aver vergogna** to be

ashamed; **vergogne** privates ‖ *interj* for shame!

**vergognare** (**vergógno**) *ref* to be ashamed; to feel cheap; **vergognati!** shame on you!

**vergognó·so -sa** [s] *adj* ashamed; bashful; shameful

**veridici·tà** *f* (**-tà**) veracity

**verìdi·co -ca** *adj* (**-ci -che**) veracious

**verifi·ca** *f* (**-che**) verification; control; **verifica fiscale** auditing (*of tax return*)

**verificare** §197 (**verìfico**) *tr* to verify; to control, check; to audit ‖ *ref* to come true; to happen

**verifica·tóre -trice** *mf* checker, inspector

**verismo** *m* verism (*as developed in Italy*)

**veri·sta** *adj & mf* (**-sti -ste**) verist

**veri·tà** *f* (**-tà**) truth; **in verità** truthfully, verily

**veritiè·ro -ra** *adj* truthful

**vèrme** *m* worm; (mach) thread; **verme solitario** tapeworm

**vermì·glio -glia** (**-gli -glie**) *adj* vermilion; ruby (*lips*) ‖ *m* vermilion

**vèr·mut** *m* (**-mut**) vermouth

**vernàcolo** *m* vernacular

**vernice** *f* varnish; paint; polish; patina; (painting) private viewing; (fig) veneer; **scarpe di vernice** patent-leather shoes; **vernice a olio** oil paint; **vernice a spruzzo** spray paint; **vernice da scarpe** shoe polish

**verniciare** §128 *tr* to varnish; to paint

**vé·ro -ra** *adj* true; real; right; pure; **non è vero?** isn't that so? La traduzione precedente è generalmente rimpiazzata da molte altre frasi. Se la prima espressione è negativa, la domanda equivalente a **non è vero?** sarà affermativa, per esempio, **Lei non lavora, non è vero?** You are not working, are you? Se la prima espressione è affermativa, la domanda sarà negativa, per esempio, **Lei lavora, non è vero?** You are working, are you not? or aren't you? Se la prima espressione contiene un ausiliare, la domanda conterrà l'ausiliare stesso senza infinito o senza participio passato, per esempio, **Arriveranno domani, non è vero?** They will arrive tomorrow, won't they? **Ha finito il compito, non è vero?** He has finished his homework, hasn't he? Se la prima espressione non contiene né un ausiliare, né una delle forme del verbo "to be" in funzione di copula, la domanda conterrà l'ausiliare "do" o "did" senza l'infinito del verbo, per esempio, **Lei è vissuto a Milano, non è vero?** You lived in Milano, did you not? **Lei non va mai al parco, non è vero?** You never go to the park, do you?; **non mi par vero** it seems unbelievable ‖ *m* truth; actuality; **a dire il vero** to tell the truth, as a matter of fact; **dal vero** from nature; **salvo il vero** if I am not mistaken ‖ *f* see **vera**

**veróne** *m* (lit) balcony

**verosimiglianza** *f* verisimilitude; probability, likelihood

**verosìmile** *adj* verisimilar; probable, likely

**verricèllo** *m* winch, windlass

**vèrro** *m* boar

**verru·ca** *f* (**-che**) wart

**versaménto** *m* spilling; payment; deposit

**versante** *m* depositor; slope, side

**versare** (**vèrso**) *tr* to pour; to spill; to shed; to pay; to deposit ‖ *intr* to overflow; **versare in gravi condizioni** to be in a bad way ‖ *ref* to spill; to pour (*said of people*); to empty (*said of a river*)

**versàtile** *adj* versatile; fickle

**versa·to -ta** *adj* versed; gifted; fully subscribed to (*e.g., stock of a corporation*)

**verseggia·tóre -trice** *mf* verse writer

**versétto** *m* verse (*of Bible*)

**versificare** §197 (**versìfico**) *tr & intr* to versify

**versificazióne** *f* versification

**versióne** *f* version; translation

**vèrso** *adj invar*—**pollice verso** (hist) thumbs down ‖ *m* verse; local accent; voice, cry; reverse (*of coin*); verso (*of page*); line (*of poetry*); singsong; gesture; direction, way, manner; respect; **andare a verso** (with *dat*) to suit, e.g., **le sue maniere non gli vanno a verso** her manners do not suit him; **a verso** properly; **contro verso** against the grain; **fare un verso** to make faces; **per un verso** on one hand; **rifare il verso** (with *dat*) to mimick; **senza verso** without rhyme or reason; **verso sciolto** blank verse ‖ *prep* toward; near, around; about; for, toward; upon, in return for; as compared with; **verso di** toward

**vèrtebra** *f* vertebra

**vertebrale** *adj* vertebral; spinal

**vertebra·to -ta** *adj & m* vertebrate

**vertènza** *f* quarrel, dispute; **vertenza sindacale** labor dispute

**vèrtere** §283 *intr*—**vertere su** to deal with, to turn on

**verticale** *adj & f* vertical

**vèrtice** *m* top, summit; vertex; **summit conference**

**vertìgine** *f* vertigo, dizziness; **avere le vertigini** to feel dizzy

**vertiginó·so -sa** [s] *adj* dizzy; breathtaking

**vérza** [dz] *f* cabbage

**verzière** [dz] *m* (lit) fruit, vegetable, and flower garden; (coll) produce market

**verzura** [dz] *f* verdure

**vesci·ca** *f* (**-che**) bladder; blister; **vescica di vento** (fig) windbag; **vescica gonfiata** swellhead; **vescica natatoria** air bladder

**vescichétta** *f* blister; vescicle; **vescichetta biliare** gall bladder

**vescìcola** *f* blister

**vescovado** *m* bishopric

**véscovo** *m* bishop

**vè·spa** f wasp, yellowjacket ‖ f (-spe & -spa) motor scooter

**ve·spàio** m (-spài) wasp's nest; (fig) hornet's nest

**vespasiano** m public urinal

**Vèspero** m Vesper

**vesperti·no -na** adj (lit) evening

**vèspro** m (eccl) vespers; (lit) vespertide

**vessare (vèsso)** tr (lit) to oppress

**vessatò·rio -ria** adj (-ri -rie) vexatious

**vessazióne** f oppression

**vessillo** m flag

**vestàglia** f negligee, dressing gown; **vestaglia da bagno** bathrobe

**vèste** f dress; cover; (lit) body; **in veste di** in the quality of; as; in the guise of; **veste da camera** negligee, dressing gown; bathrobe; **veste talare** (eccl) long vestment; **vesti** clothes

**vestià·rio** m (-ri) wardrobe

**vestibolo** m vestibule, lobby

**vestì·gio** m (-gi & -gia fpl) vestige, trace; (lit) footprint

**vestire (vèsto)** tr to dress; to don; to wear; to clothe; to cover, bedeck ‖ intr to dress; to fit ‖ ref to get dressed; to dress; to dress oneself; to buy one's own clothes

**vestì·to -ta** adj dressed; covered ‖ m dress; suit; clothing; **vestiti** clothes; **vestito da donna** dress; **vestito da festa** Sunday best; **vestito da sera** evening clothes, formal suit; evening gown; **vestito da uomo** suit

**Vesùvio, il** Vesuvius

**vetera·no -na** adj & mf veteran

**veterinà·rio -ria (-ri -rie)** adj veterinary ‖ m veterinarian ‖ f veterinary medicine

**vèto** m veto; **porre il veto a** to veto

**ve·tràio** m (-trài) glass manufacturer; glass dealer; glass blower

**vetra·to -ta** adj glass, glass-enclosed; sand (paper) ‖ m glare ice, glaze ‖ f glass door; glass window; glass enclosure; **vetrata a colori** or **vetrata istoriata** stained-glass window

**vetrerìa** f glassworks; **vetrerie** glassware

**vetria·to -ta** adj glassy; glass-covered

**vetrificare** §197 (vetrifico) tr to vitrify ‖ ref to become vitrified

**vetrina** f show window; showcase, glass cabinet; **mettersi in vetrina** to show off; **vetrine** (coll) eyeglasses

**vetrini·sta** mf (-sti -ste) window dresser

**vetri·no -na** adj glass-like; brittle, fragile ‖ m slide (of microscope) ‖ f see **vetrina**

**vetriòlo** m vitriol

**vétro** m glass; glassware; window pane; piece of glass; **vetro aderente** contact lens; **vetro infrangibile** (aut) safety glass; **vetro smerigliato** ground glass, frosted glass

**vetrorèsina** f fiberglass

**vetró·so -sa** [s] adj vitreous, glassy

**vétta** f peak; top, tip; limb (of tree); (naut) end (of hawser); **tremare come una vetta** to shake like a leaf

**vet·tóre -trice** adj leading, guiding; spreading, carrying ‖ m carrier; (math, phys) vector

**vettovagliare** §280 tr to supply with food

**vettovàglie** fpl victuals, food; supplies

**vettura** f forwarding; coach; car; freight; **in vettura!** (rr) all aboard!; **prendere in vettura** to hire (a conveyance); **vettura belvedere** (rr) observation car; **vettura da turismo** (aut) pleasure car; **vettura di piazza** hack, hackney; **vettura letto** (rr) sleeping car; **vettura ristorante** (rr) diner

**vetturétta** f economy car, compact

**vetturino** m hackman, cab driver

**vetu·sto -sta** adj old, ancient

**vezzeggiare** §290 (vezzéggio) tr to coddle ‖ intr (lit) to strut

**vezzeggiati·vo -va** adj endearing ‖ m endearing expression; diminutive

**vézzo** m habit; caress; necklace; bad habit; **vezzi** fondling, petting; mawkish behavior; charms

**vezzó·so -sa** [s] adj graceful, charming; affected, mincing

**vi** §5

**vìa** m (vìa) starting signal; **dare il via a** to give the go-ahead to ‖ f street; road, way; route; career; **dare la via a** to open the way to; **in via confidenziale** in confidence; **in via eccezionale** as an exception; **per via di** via, through; (coll) because of; **per via gerarchica** through administrative channels; **per via orale** orally; **per via rettale** rectally; **prendere la via** to be on one's way; **venire a vie di fatto** to come to blows; **Via Crucis** Way of the Cross; **via d'acqua** waterway; **via di scampo** (fig) way out; **via d'uscita** way out; **Via Lattea** Milky Way; **vie di fatto** assault and battery; **vie legali** legal steps ‖ adv away; (math) times, by; **e così via** and so on; **e via dicendo** and so on; **tirar via** to hurry along; **via via che** as ‖ prep via, by way of

**viadótto** m viaduct

**viaggiare** §290 intr to travel; (com) to deal

**viaggia·tóre -trice** adj traveling; homing (pigeon) ‖ mf traveler ‖ m traveling salesman

**vìàg·gio** m (-gi) travel; journey, trip; **buon viaggio!** bon voyage!; **viaggio d'andata e ritorno** round trip; **viaggio di prova** (naut) trial run, shakedown cruise

**viale** m boulevard

**viandante** mf (lit) wayfarer

**vià·rio -ria** adj (-ri -rie) road, highway

**viàti·co** m (-ci) viaticum

**viavài** m coming and going; hustle and bustle

**vibrante** adj vibrant; wiry; (phonet) vibrant ‖ f (phonet) trill, vibrant

**vibrare** tr to jar; to deliver (a blow); to vibrate; (lit) to hurl ‖ intr to vibrate

**vibra·to -ta** adj vibrant; resolute, vigorous ‖ m vibrating sound

**vibrazióne** f vibration

**vicariato** m vicarage

**vicà·rio** m (-ri) vicar

**vice-** *pref adj* vice-, e.g., **vicereale** viceroyal ‖ *pref m & f* vice-, e.g., **viceammiraglio** vice-admiral; assistant, e.g., **vicegovernatore** assistant governor; deputy, e.g., **vicesindaco** deputy mayor

**vicediret·tóre -trice** *mf* assistant manager

**vicènda** *f* vicissitude; rotation (*of crops*); **a vicenda** in turn

**vicendévole** *adj* mutual, reciprocal

**vicepresidènte** [s] *mf* vice president

**vice·ré** *m* (**-ré**) viceroy

**vicevèrsa** *adv* vice versa; (coll) instead, on the contrary

**vichin·go -ga** *adj & mf* (**-ghi -ghe**) Viking

**vicinanza** *f* nearness; **in vicinanza di** in the neighborhood of; **vicinanze** vicinity, neighborhood

**vicinato** *m* neighborhood

**vici·no -na** *adj* near; neighboring; next; close (*relative*) ‖ *mf* neighbor ‖ **vicino** *adv* nearby, near; **da vicino** closely; at close quarters; **vicino a** near; next to, close to

**vicissitùdine** *f* vicissitude

**vi·co** *m* (**-chi**) alley, lane; village; (lit) region

**vìcolo** *m* alley, court, place; **vicolo cieco** blind alley, dead end

**videocassétta** *f* video cassette

**vidimare** (**vìdimo**) *tr* to validate, visa; to sign

**vidimazióne** *f* validation, visa; signature

**viennése** [s] *adj & mf* Viennese

**viepiù** *adv* (lit) more and more

**vietare** (**vièto**) *tr* to forbid, prohibit

**vieta·to -ta** *adj* forbidden; **senso vietato** one way; **sosta vietata** no parking; no stopping; **vietato fumare** no smoking

**Vietnam, il** Vietnam

**vietnami·ta** *adj & mf* (**-ti -te**) Vietnamese

**viè·to -ta** *adj* (lit) old-fashioned; (coll) musty-smelling, rancid

**vigènte** *adj* current, in force

**vigere** §284 *intr* to be in force

**vigèsi·mo -ma** *adj* twentieth

**vigilante** *adj* watchful, vigilant ‖ *m* watchman

**vigilanza** *f* vigilance; surveillance

**vigilare** (**vìgilo**) *tr* to watch; to watch over; to police ‖ *intr* to watch; **vigilare che** to see to it that

**vigila·tóre -trice** *mf* inspector ‖ *f* camp counselor; **vigilatrice sanitaria** child health inspector

**vìgile** *adj* (lit) watchful ‖ *m* watch; **vigile del fuoco** fireman; **vigile urbano** policeman

**vigìlia** *f* fast; vigil; **la vigilia di** on the eve of, the night before

**vigliaccherìa** *f* cowardice

**vigliac·co -ca** (**-chi -che**) *adj* cowardly ‖ *m* coward

**vigna** *f* vineyard

**vignaiòlo** *m* vine dresser

**vignéto** *m* vineyard

**vignétta** *f* vignette; **vignetta umoristica** cartoon

**vignetti·sta** *mf* (**-sti -ste**) cartoonist

**vigógna** *f* vicuña

**vigóre** *m* vigor; **in vigore** in force

**vigoria** *f* vigor

**vigoró·so -sa** [s] *adj* vigorous

**vile** *adj* cowardly; vile, low, cheap; base (*metal*)

**vilificare** §197 (**vilìfico**) *tr* to vilify

**vilipèndere** §148 *tr* to despise; to show scorn for

**villa** *f* villa; country house; one-family detached house; (lit) country

**villàg·gio** *m* (**-gi**) village; **villaggio del fanciullo** boys' town

**villanata** *f* boorishness

**villania** *f* boorishness, rudeness; insult

**villa·no -na** *adj* rude, churlish ‖ *mf* boor, churl; (lit) peasant

**villanzó·ne -na** *mf* boor, uncouth person

**villeggiante** *mf* vacationist

**villeggiare** §290 (**villéggio**) *intr* to vacation

**villeggiatura** *f* vacation, summer vacation

**villétta** *f* or **villino** *m* bungalow

**villó·so -sa** [s] *adj* hairy

**vil·tà** *f* (**-tà**) baseness; cowardice

**viluppo** *m* tangle, twist

**vìmine** *m* withe, wicker, osier

**vinàcce** *fpl* pressed grapes

**vi·nàio** *m* (**-nài**) wine merchant

**vincènte** *adj* winning ‖ *mf* winner

**vincere** §285 *tr* to overcome; to win; to convince; to check; to defeat; **vincere per un pelo** to nose out; **vincerla** to come out on top ‖ *ref* to control oneself

**vincetòssi·co** *m* (**-ci**) swallowwort, tame poison

**vincipèr·di** *m* (**-di**) giveaway

**vìncita** *f* gain; winnings

**vinci·tóre -trice** *adj* conquering, victorious ‖ *mf* winner; conqueror; victor

**vincolare** *adj* binding; bound ‖ *v* (**vìncolo**) *tr* to tie; to bind, obligate; to restrict the use of (*real-estate property*)

**vìncolo** *m* tie, bond; (law) entail; (law) restriction (*in a real-estate deed*)

**vinìco·lo -la** *adj* wine, wine-producing

**vinile** *m* vinyl

**vino** *m* wine; **vin caldo** mulled wine; **vino da pasto** table wine; **vino di marca** vintage wine; **vino di mele** cider

**vin·to -ta** *adj* vanquished, overcome, defeated; victorious (*battle*); **averla vinta su** to overcome; **darla vinta a qlcu** to let s.o. get away with murder; **darsi per vinto** to give in, yield ‖ *m* vanquished person; **i vinti** the vanquished

**viò·la** *adj invar* violet ‖ *m* (**-la**) violet (*color*) ‖ *f* violet; (mus) viola; **viola del pensiero** pansy; **viola mammola** sweet violet

**violacciò·ca** *f* (**-che**) (bot) wallflower

**violà·ceo -cea** *adj* violet

**violare** (**vìolo**) *tr* to violate; to run (*a blockade*)

**violazióne** *f* violation; **violazione di**

**domicilio** housebreaking, burglary; **violazione di proprietà** trespass
**violentare (violènto)** *tr* to violate, force; to do violence to; to rape
**violèn·to -ta** *adj* violent ‖ *m* violent person
**violènza** *f* violence; **violenza carnale** rape
**violét·to -ta** *adj* & *m* violet ‖ *f* (bot) violet
**violini·sta** *mf* (-sti -ste) violinist
**violino** *m* violin; **primo violino** concertmaster
**violoncelli·sta** *mf* (-sti -ste) violoncellist
**violoncèllo** *m* violoncello, cello
**viòttolo** *m* path
**vìpera** *f* viper, adder
**viràg·gio** *m* (-gi) turn; (aer) banking; (naut) tacking; (phot) toning
**virare** *tr* to veer; to turn (*a winch*); (aer) to bank; (phot) to tone ‖ *intr* to veer, steer; **virare di bordo** (naut) to put about; (naut) to tack
**virata** *f* turn, veer; (aer) banking; (naut) tacking
**virginale** *adj* var of **verginale**
**virgi·nia** *m* (-nia) Virginia tobacco ‖ *f* (-nia) Virginia cigarette
**vìrgola** *f* comma; (*used in Italian to set off the decimal fraction from the integer*) decimal point; **doppia virgola** quotation mark
**virgolétta** *f* quotation mark
**virgulto** *m* (lit) shoot; (lit) shrub
**virile** *adj* virile
**virilità** *f* virility
**viròla** *f* (mach) male piece
**virologìa** *f* virology
**vir·tù** *f* (-tù) virtue; (lit) valor
**virtuale** *adj* virtual
**virtualménte** *adv* virtually, to all intents and purposes
**virtuosismo** [s] *m* virtuosity; showing off
**virtuosità** [s] *f* virtuosity
**virtuó·so -sa** [s] *adj* virtuous ‖ *mf* virtuoso
**virulèn·to -ta** *adj* virulent
**virulènza** *f* virulence
**vi·rus** *m* (-rus) virus
**vìsce·re** *m* (-ri) internal organ; **visceri** entrails, viscera ‖ **viscere** *fpl* entrails, viscera; (fig) heart, feeling; (fig) bowels (*of the earth*)
**vì·schio** *m* (-schi) mistletoe; birdlime; (fig) trap
**vischió·so -sa** [s] *adj* sticky, viscous; (com) steady
**vìsci·do -da** *adj* viscid; clammy; (fig) unctuous
**vìsciola** *f* sour cherry
**vìsciolo** *m* sour cherry tree
**viscónte** *m* viscount
**viscontéssa** *f* viscountess
**viscó·so -sa** [s] *adj* viscous, sticky ‖ *f* viscose
**visétto** *m* small face; baby face
**visìbile** *adj* visible; obvious
**visibi·lio** *m* (-li) (coll) crowd; (coll) bunch; **andare in visibilio** to become ecstatic; **mandare in visibilio** to throw into ecstasy, enrapture

**visibilità** *f* visibility
**visièra** *f* visor; fencing mask; eyeshade; **visiera termica** (aut) electric defroster
**visigò·to -ta** *adj* Visigothic ‖ *mf* Visigoth
**visionà·rio ·ria** *adj* & *mf* (-ri -rie) visionary
**visióne** *f* vision; sight; (mov, telv) showing; **in visione gratuita** for free examination; **mandare qlco a qlcu in visione** to send s.th to s.o. for his (or her) opinion; **prendere visione di** to examine; to peruse
**vi·sìr** *m* (-sìr) vizier
**visita** *f* visit; visitation; **fare una visita** to pay a visit; **marcare visita** (mil) to report sick; **visita doganale** customs inspection
**visitare (vìsito)** *tr* to visit; to inspect
**visita·tóre -trice** *mf* visitor ‖ *f* social worker
**visitazióne** *f* visitation
**visi·vo -va** *adj* visual
**viso** *m* face; **far buon viso a cattivo gioco** to grin and bear it
**visóne** *m* mink
**visóre** *m* (phot) viewer; (phot) viewfinder
**vi·spo -spa** *adj* brisk, lively
**vissu·to -ta** *adj* wordly-wise
**vista** *f* sight, eyesight; view; vista; glance; (poet) window; **a vista** exposed, visible; **a vista d'occhio** as far as the eye can see; **essere in vista** to be expected; to be imminent; to be in the limelight; **far vista di** to pretend to; **in vista di** in view of; **mettere in vista** to show off; **vista a volo d'uccello** bird's-eye view; **vista corta** poor eyesight
**vistare** *tr* to validate, visa
**vi·sto -sta** *adj*—**visto che** seeing that, inasmuch as ‖ *m* visa; approval ‖ *f* see vista
**vistó·so -sa** [s] *adj* showy, flashy; (fig) considerable
**visuale** *adj* visual ‖ *f* view; line of sight
**visualizzare** [ddzz] *tr* to visualize
**vita** *f* life; livelihood; living; waist; **avere breve vita** to be short-lived; **fare la vita** to be a prostitute; **vita natural durante** for life; during one's lifetime
**vitaiòlo** *m* man about town; playboy, bon vivant
**vitale** *adj* vital
**vitalità** *f* vitality
**vitali·zio -zia** (-zi -zie) *adj* life, lifetime ‖ *m* life annuity
**vitamina** *f* vitamin
**vite** *f* (bot) grapevine; (mach) screw; **a vite** threaded; (aer) in a tailspin; **vite autofilettante** self-tapping screw; **vite del Canadà** woodbine, Virginia creeper; **vite per legno** wood screw; **vite per metallo** machine screw; **vite perpetua** (mach) endless screw, worm gear; **vite prigioniera** stud bolt
**vitèllo** *m* calf; veal
**vitìc·cio** *m* (-ci) tendril
**vìtre·o -a** *adj* vitreous; glassy (*eyes*)

vìttima *f* victim

vitto *m* food; diet; **vitto e alloggio** room and board

vittòria *f* victory; **cantar vittoria** to crow; to crow too soon

vittorió·so -sa [s] *adj* victorious

vituperare (vitùpero) *tr* to vituperate

vituperévole *adj* contemptible, shameful

vitupè·rio *m* (-ri) shame, infamy; insult; (lit) blame

viuzza *f* narrow street, lane

viva *interj* long live!

vivacchiare §287 *intr* (coll) to get along || *ref*—si **vivacchia** (coll) so, so

vivace *adj* lively, brisk; brilliant; vivacious

vivacità *f* liveliness, briskness; brilliancy, brightness; vivacity

vivaddìo *interj* yes, of course!; by Jove!

vivagno *m* selvage; edge

vi·vàio *m* (-vài) fishpond; fish tank; tree nursery; (fig) seedbed

vivanda *f* food

vivandiè·re -ra *mf* (mil) sutler

vìvere *m* life; living; cost of living; **viveri** food, provisions; allowance || §286 *tr* to live; **vivere un brutto momento** to spend an uncomfortable moment || *intr* (ESSERE) to live; **vive** (typ) stet; **vivere alla giornata** to live from hand to mouth

vivézza *f* liveliness

vìvi·do -da *adj* vivid, lively

vivificare §197 (vivìfico) *tr* to vivify

visezionare (visezióno) *tr* to visect; to scrutinize

visezióne *f* vivisection

vi·vo -va *adj* alive; living; live, vivacious; lively; vivid; high (*flame*); bright (*light*); raw (*flesh*); sharp, acute (*pain*); hearty (*thanks*); outright (*expense*); gross (*weight*); brute (*strength*); modern (*language*); kinetic (*energy*); running (*water*) || *m* living being; heart (*of a question*); **al vivo** lively; lifelike; **i vivi e i morti** the quick and the dead; **toccare nel vivo** to sting to the quick || **viva** *interj* see **viva**

viziare §287 *tr* to spoil; to ruin; (law) to vitiate || *ref* to become spoiled

vizia·to -ta *adj* spoiled; ruined; stale (*air*)

vì·zio *m* (-zi) vice; defect; flaw; (law) vitiation

vizió·so -sa [s] *adj* vicious; defective || *mf* profligate

vìz·zo -za *adj* withered

vocabolà·rio *m* (-ri) dictionary; vocabulary

vocàbolo *m* word

vocale *adj* vocal; (lit) sonorous || *f* vowel

vocalizzare [ddzz] *tr & ref* to vocalize

vocativo *m* vocative

vocazióne *f* vocation

vóce *f* voice; noise, roar; word; rumor; entry; tone; **ad alta voce** aloud; **a bassa voce** in a low voice; **a viva voce** by word of mouth; **a voce** orally; **dare una voce a** (coll) to call; **dare sulla voce a** to rebuke; to con-

tradìct; **fare la voce grossa** to raise one's voice; **non avere voce in capitolo** to have no say; **schiarirsi la voce** to clear one's throat; **senza voce** hoarse; **sotto voce** in a low tone; **voce bianca** child's voice (*in singing*)

vociare *m* bawl || §128 (vócio) *intr* to bawl

vociferare (vocìfero) *intr* to vociferate, shout || *ref*—**si vocifera** it is rumored

vó·ga *f* (-ghe) fashion, vogue; energy, enthusiasm; rowing

vogare §209 (vógo) *tr & intr* to row

voga·tóre -trice *mf* rower || *m* oarsman; rowing machine

vòglia *f* wish; whim, fancy; willingness; birthmark; **aver voglia di** to feel like, have a notion to; **di buona voglia** willingly; **di mala voglia** unwillingly

voglió·so -sa [s] *adj* fanciful; (lit) desirous

vói §5 *pron pers* you; **voi altri** you, e.g., **voi altri americani** you Americans

voial·tri -tre *pron pl* you, e.g., **voialtri americani** you Americans

volano *m* shuttlecock; (mach) flywheel

volante *adj* flying; loose (*sheet*); free (*agent*) || *m* steering wheel; (mach) hand wheel; shuttlecock

volantino *m* leaflet; fringe; (mach) hand wheel

volare (vólo) *tr* (soccer) to overthrow || *intr* (ESSERE & AVERE) to fly

volata *f* flight; sprint; run; mouth (*of gun*); (tennis) volley; **di volata** in a hurry

volàtile *adj* volatile; flying (*animal*) || **volatili** *mpl* birds

volatilizzare [ddzz] *tr & intr* (ESSERE) to volatilize

volènte *adj*—**Dio volente** God willing; **volente o nolente** willy-nilly

volentièri *adv* gladly, willingly

volére *m* will, wish; **al volere di** at the bidding of || §288 *tr* to will; to want, desire; (lit) to believe, affirm; **l'hai voluto tu** it's your fault; **non vuol dire!** never mind!; **qui ti voglio** here's the rub, that's the trouble; **senza volere** without meaning to; **voglia Dio!** may God grant!; **voler bene** (with *dat*) to like; **volerci** to take, e.g., **ci vorranno due anni per finire questo palazzo** it will take two years to complete this building; **ce ne vogliono ancora tre** it takes three more of them; **voler dire** to mean; to try, e.g., **vuole piovere** it is trying to rain; **volere che** + *subj* to want + *inf*, e.g., **vuole che vengano** he wants them to come; **volere piuttosto** to prefer; **volere è potere** where there is a will there is a way; **voler male** (with *dat*) to dislike; **volerne a** to bear a grudge against; **vorrei** I should like, I'd like; **vuoi . . . vuoi** either . . . or

volgare *adj* vernacular, popular, common; vulgar || *m* vernacular

volgari·tà *f* (-tà) vulgarity

**volgarizzare** [ddzz] *tr* to popularize
**vòlgere** §289 *tr* to turn; (lit) to translate ‖ *intr* to turn; (lit) to go by; **volgere a** to turn toward; to draw near, to approach; **volgere in fuga** to take to flight ‖ *ref* to turn; to devote oneself
**vól·go** *m* (-ghi) (lit) crowd, mob
**volièra** *f* aviary
**voliti·vo** -**va** *adj* volitional; strong-minded, strong-willed
**vólo** *m* flight; fall; **al volo** on the spot; on the wing; **a volo d'uccello** as the crow flies; bird's-eye (*e.g., view*); **di volo** at top speed, immediately; **in volo** aloft, in the air; **prendere il volo** to take flight; **volo a vela** or **volo planato** gliding; **volo strumentale** instrument flying; **volo veleggiato** gliding
**volon·tà** *f* (-tà) will; **di spontanea volontà** of one's own volition; **pieno di buona volontà** eager to please; **ultime volontà** last will and testament
**volontariato** *m* volunteer work; apprenticeship without pay; (mil) volunteer service
**volontà·rio** -**ria** (-ri -rie) *adj* voluntary ‖ *m* volunteer
**volonteró·so** -**sa** [s] *adj* willing, well-disposed
**volpacchiòtto** *m* fox cub; (fig) sly fox
**vólpe** *f* fox; (agr) smut; **volpe argentata** silver fox
**volpi·no** -**na** *adj* fox; fox-colored; foxy ‖ *m* Pomeranian
**volpó·ne** -**na** *mf* sly fox
**vòlt** *m* (vòlt) (elec) volt
**vòl·ta** *m* (-ta) (elec) volt ‖ *f* turn; time; vault; roof (*of mouth*); **alla volta di** toward; **a volta di corriere** by return mail; **a volte** sometimes; **c'era una volta** once upon a time there was; **certe volte** sometimes; **dare di volta il cervello a** to go crazy, e.g., **gli ha dato di volta il cervello** he went crazy; **dar la volta** to turn sour (*said of wine*); **due volte** twice; **molte volte** often; **per una volta tanto** only once; **poche volte** seldom; **tante volte** often; **tutto in una volta** at one swoop, at one stroke; in one gulp, in one swallow; **una volta** once; **una volta che** (coll) inasmuch as; **una volta per sempre** once and for all; **una volta tanto** for once; **volta a crociera** cross vault; **volta per volta** little by little; **volte** (math) times, e.g., **cinque volte cinque** five times five
**voltafàc·cia** *m* (-cia) volte-face; **fare voltafaccia** to wheel around (*said of a horse*)
**voltagabba·na** *mf* (-na) turncoat
**voltàg·gio** *m* (-gi) voltage
**voltài·co** -**ca** *adj* (-ci -che) voltaic
**voltare** (vòlto) *tr, intr & ref* to turn
**voltastòma·co** *m* (-chi) (coll) nausea; **fare venire il voltastomaco a qlcu** (coll) to turn s.o.'s stomach
**voltata** *f* turn; curve

**volteggiare** §290 (**voltéggio**) *tr* to put (*a horse*) through its paces ‖ *intr* to hover; to flit, flutter; (sports) to vault (*e.g., on horseback or trapeze*)
**voltég·gio** *m* (-gi) (sports) vaulting
**vòltmetro** *m* voltmeter
**vólto** *m* (lit) face
**voltura** *f* (com, law) transfer
**volùbile** *adj* fickle
**volubilità** *f* fickleness
**volume** *m* volume; bulk; mass
**voluminó·so** -**sa** [s] *adj* voluminous, bulky
**volu·to** -**ta** *adj* desired; intentional ‖ *f* (archit) volute, scroll
**volut·tà** *f* (-tà) pleasure, enjoyment; voluptuousness
**voluttuà·rio** -**ria** *adj* (-ri -rie) luxury (*goods*)
**voluttuó·so** -**sa** [s] *adj* voluptuous, sensuous
**vòmere** *m* plowshare; trail spade (*of gun*)
**vòmi·co** -**ca** *adj* (-ci -che) emetic
**vomitare** (vòmito) *tr & intr* to vomit
**vomitati·vo** -**va** *adj & m* emetic
**vòmito** *m* vomit
**vóngola** *f* clam
**vorace** *adj* voracious
**voraci·tà** *f* (-tà) voracity
**voràgine** *f* chasm, gulf, abyss
**vòrtice** *m* vortex, whirlpool; whirlwind
**verticó·so** -**sa** [s] *adj* whirling, swirling
**vò·stro** -**stra** §6 *adj & pron poss*
**votare** (vóto) *tr* to devote; to vote ‖ *intr* to vote ‖ *ref* to devote oneself
**votazióne** *f* vote, voting, poll; (educ) grades
**voti·vo** -**va** *adj* votive
**vóto** *m* vow; wish; votive offering; vote, ballot; grade, mark; **a pieni voti** with highest honors; **fare un voto** to make a vow; **pronunciare i voti** to take vows; **voto di fiducia** vote of confidence; **voto preferenziale** write-in vote; preferential ballot
**vudù** *m* voodoo
**vudui·sta** *mf* (-sti -ste) voodoo (*person*)
**vulcàni·co** -**ca** *adj* (-ci -che) volcanic
**vulcanizzare** [ddzz] *tr* to vulcanize
**vulcano** *m* volcano
**vulga·to** -**ta** *adj* disseminated ‖ **Vulgata** *f* Vulgate
**vulneràbile** *adj* vulnerable
**vuotare** (vuòto) *tr* to empty; **vuotare il sacco** to speak one's mind, unburden oneself ‖ *ref* to empty
**vuò·to** -**ta** *adj* empty; devoid ‖ *m* vacuum; emptiness; empty space; empty seat; empty feeling; empty (*e.g., container*); **a vuoto** in vain; wide of the mark; (*check*) without sufficient funds; **andare a vuoto** to fail; (mach) to idle; **cadere nel vuoto** to fall on deaf ears; **mandare a vuoto** to thwart; **sotto vuoto** in a vacuum; **vuoto d'aria** (aer) air pocket; **vuoto di cassa** deficit; **vuoto di potere** power vacuum

# W

**W, w** ['doppjo 'vu] *m & f*
**wà·fer** *m* (**-fer**) wafer
**water-clòset** *m* (**-clòset**) flush toilet
**watt** *m* (**watt**) watt

**watt·óra** *m* (**-óra**) watt-hour
**wèstern** *m* (**wèstern**) (mov) western
**whisky** *m* (**whisky**) whiskey
**wìgwam** *m* (**wìgwam**) wigwam

# X

**X, x** [ɪks] *m & f*
**xèno** *m* xenon
**xenòfo·bo -ba** *mf* xenophobe

**xè·res** *m* (**-res**) sherry
**xerografìa** *f* xerography
**xerófito** *m* xerophyte

# Y

**Y, y** ['ɪpsɪlon] *m & f*
**yacht** *m* (**yachts**) yacht
**yak** *m* (**yak**) yak

**yànkee** *m* (**yànkees**) Yankee
**yìddish** *adj invar & m* Yiddish

# Z

**Z, z** ['dzɛtɑ] *m & f* twenty-first letter
    of the Italian alphabet
**zabaióne** [dz] *m* eggnog
**zàcchera** *f* splash of mud
**zaffare** *tr* to plug; to bung
**zaffata** *f* unpleasant whiff, stench; gust
**zafferano** [dz] *m* saffron
**zaffiro** [dz] *m* sapphire
**zaffo** *m* plug; bung; tampon
**zàgara** [dz] *f* orange blossom
**zàino** [dz] *m* knapsack; (mil) pack
**zampa** *f* paw; (culin) leg; **a quattro
    zampe** on all fours; **zampa di gallina**
    crow's-foot; illegible scrawl; **zampa
    di porco** crowbar
**zampare** *intr* to paw; to stamp
**zampettare** (**zampétto**) *intr* to toddle;
    to scamper
**zampillare** *intr* (ESSERE & AVERE) to
    spurt, gush, spring
**zampillo** *m* spurt, gush, spring
**zampino** *m* little paw; **metterci lo zam-
    pino** to put one's finger in the pie
**zampiróne** *m* slow-burning mosquito
    repellent; foul-smelling cigarette
**zampógna** *f* bagpipe
**zampognare** (**zampógno**) *intr* to pipe,
    play the bagpipe
**zampóne** *m* Modena salami (*stuffed
    forepaw of a hog*)
**zanèlla** *f* gully
**zàngola** *f* butter churn
**zanna** *f* tusk; fang; **mostrare le zanne**
    to show one's teeth
**zanzara** [dz] [dz] *f* mosquito
**zanzarièra** [dz] [dz] *f* mosquito net;
    window screen
**zappa** *f* hoe; **darsi la zappa sui piedi**

to cut one's nose off to spite one's
    face
**zappare** *tr* to hoe
**zappatóre** *m* hoer, digger; (mil) sapper
**zar** *m* (**zar**) czar
**zàttera** *f* raft; **zattera di salvataggio** life
    raft
**zatterière** *m* log driver
**zavòrra** [dz] *f* ballast; (fig) deadwood
**zavorrare** [dz] (**zavòrro**) *tr* to ballast
**zàzzera** *f* mop (*of hair*)
**zèbra** [dz] *f* zebra; **zebre** zebra cross-
    ing
**zebra·to -ta** [dz] *adj* zebra-striped
**ze·bù** [dz] *m* (**-bù**) zebu
**zéc·ca** *f* (**-che**) mint; (ent) tick; **nuovo
    di zecca** brand-new
**zecchino** *m* sequin, gold coin
**zèfiro** [dz] *m* zephyr
**zelante** [dz] *adj* zealous; studious ‖ *mf*
    zealot; eager beaver
**zèlo** [dz] *m* zeal; **zelo pubblico** public
    spirit
**zènit** [dz] *m* zenith
**zénzero** [dz] [dz] *m* ginger
**zép·po -pa** *adj* crammed, jammed ‖ *f*
    wedge; (fig) padding
**zerbino** [dz] *m* doormat; dandy
**zerbinòtto** [dz] *m* dandy, sporty fellow
**zèro** [dz] *m* zero
**zìa** *f* aunt
**zibaldóne** [dz] *m* notebook; collection
    of thoughts; (pej) hodgepodge
**zibellino** [dz] *m* sable
**zibétto** [dz] *m* civet cat; civet (*sub-
    stance used in perfumery*)
**zibibbo** [dz] *m* raisin
**ziga·no -na** *adj & mf* gypsy
**zìgomo** [dz] *m* cheekbone

**zigrinare** [dz] *tr* to grain (*leather*); to mill, knurl (*metal*)

**zigrina·to -ta** [dz] *adj* shagreened, grained (*leather*); knurled

**zigzàg** [dz] [dz] *m* (**zigzàg**) zigzag; **andare a zigzag** to zigzag

**zigzagare** §209 [dz] [dz] *intr* to zigzag

**zimarra** [dz] *f* cassock; (obs) overcoat

**zimbèllo** *m* decoy (*bird*); laughingstock

**zincare** §197 *tr* to zinc

**zinco** *m* zinc

**zingaré·sco -sca** (**-schi -sche**) *adj & mf* gypsy

**zìnga·ro -ra** *mf* gypsy

**zìnnia** [dz] *f* zinnia

**zìo** *m* uncle; **zio d'America** rich uncle

**zìpolo** *m* peg, bung

**zircóne** [dz] *m* zircon

**zircònio** [dz] *m* zirconium

**zirlare** *intr* to warble; to squeak (*said of mouse*)

**zitèlla** *f* old maid

**zittire** §176 *tr & intr* to hoot, hiss

**zit·to -ta** *adj* silent; **far stare zitto** to hush up; **stare zitto** to keep quiet || *m* whisper || **zitto** *interj* quiet!; hush!; shut up!

**zizzània** [dz] [ddzz] *f* (bot) darnel; **seminar zizzania** to sow discord

**zòccolo** *m* clog, sabot; clump, clod; clodhopper; base (*of column*); pedestal; wide baseboard; (zool) hoof

**zodìaco** [dz] *m* zodiac

**zolfanèllo** *m* sulfur match

**zolfara** *f* var of **solfara**

**zólfo** *m* sulfur

**zòlla** *f* clod, clump; turf; lump, cube (*of sugar*)

**zollétta** *f* lump, cube (*of sugar*)

**zòna** [dz] *f* zone; area; girdle; band, stripe; ticker tape; (pathol) shingles; (telg) tape; **zona glaciale** frigid zone; **zona tropicale** tropics, tropical zone

**zónzo** [dz] [dz] *m*—**andare a zonzo** to stroll, loiter along

**zoòfito** [dz] *m* zoophite

**zoologìa** [dz] *f* zoology

**zoològi·co -ca** [dz] *adj* (**-ci -che**) zoological

**zoòlo·go -ga** [dz] *mf* (**-gi -ghe**) zoologist

**zootecnìa** [dz] *f* animal husbandry

**zootècni·co -ca** [dz] (**-ci -che**) *adj* livestock || *m* livestock specialist

**zoppicante** *adj* limping; halting; shaky

**zoppicare** §197 (**zòppico**) *intr* to limp; to be shaky (*in one's studies*); to wobble

**zoppicatura** *f* limp; wobble

**zòp·po -pa** *adj* crippled; lame; wobbly || *mf* cripple; lame person

**zòti·co -ca** [dz] *adj* (**-ci -che**) uncouth, boorish || *m* churl, boor

**zuc·ca** *f* (**-che**) pumpkin; (joc) pate; (coll) empty head

**zuccata** *f* bump with the head

**zuccherare** (**zùcchero**) *tr* to sweeten, sugar

**zuccherièra** *f* sugar bowl

**zuccherifì·cio** *m* (**-ci**) sugar refinery

**zuccheri·no -na** *adj* sugary || *m* candy; sugar plum; sugar-coated pill

**zùcchero** *m* sugar; **zucchero filato** cotton candy; **zucchero in polvere** powdered sugar

**zuccheró·so -sa** [s] *adj* sugary

**zucchétto** *m* scull cap; zucchetto

**zucchi·no -na** *m & f* zucchini

**zuccó·ne -na** *mf* dunce, dumbbell

**zuffa** *f* brawl, fight

**zufolare** (**zùfolo**) *tr & intr* to whistle

**zùfolo** *m* (mus) whistle, pipe

**zu·lù** (**-lù**) [dz] *adj & mf* Zulu

**zumare** [dz] *tr & intr* (mov, telv) to zoom

**zumata** [dz] *f* (mov, telv) zoom

**zuppa** *f* soup; (fig) mess; **zuppa inglese** cake with brandy and whipped cream; **zuppa pavese** consommé with toast and eggs

**zuppièra** *f* tureen

**zup·po -pa** *adj* drenched, soaked || *f* see **zuppa**

**Zurigo** *f* Zurich

**zuzzurulló·ne -na** [dz] [ddzz] *mf* overgrown child, just a big kid

# PART TWO

## Inglese–Italiano

# La pronunzia dell'inglese

I simboli seguenti rappresentano approssimativamente tutti i suoni della lingua inglese.

## VOCALI

| SIMBOLO | SUONO | ESEMPIO |
|---------|-------|---------|
| [æ] | Più chiuso della a in **caso.** | **hat** [hæt] |
| [ɑ] | Come la a in **basso.** | **father** [ˈfɑðər]<br>**proper** [ˈprɑpər] |
| [ɛ] | Come la e in **sella.** | **met** [mɛt] |
| [e] | Più chiuso della e in **ché**. Specialmente in posizione finale, si pronunzia come se fosse seguita da [ɪ]. | **fate** [fet]<br>**they** [ðe] |
| [ə] | Come la seconda e nella parola francese **gouvernement.** | **heaven** [ˈhɛvən]<br>**pardon** [ˈpɑrdən] |
| [i] | Come la i in **nido.** | **she** [ʃi]<br>**machine** [məˈʃin] |
| [ɪ] | Come la i in **ritto.** | **fit** [fɪt]<br>**beer** [bɪr] |
| [o] | Più chiuso della o in **sole**. Specialmente in posizione finale, si pronunzia come se fosse seguito da [ʊ]. | **nose** [noz]<br>**road** [rod]<br>**row** [ro] |
| [ɔ] | Meno chiuso della o in **torre.** | **bought** [bɔt]<br>**law** [lɔ] |
| [ʌ] | Piuttosto simile alla **eu** nella parola francese **peur** | **cup** [kʌp]<br>**come** [kʌm]<br>**mother** [ˈmʌðər] |
| [ʊ] | Meno chiuso della u in **insulto.** | **pull** [pʊl]<br>**book** [bʊk]<br>**wolf** [wʊlf] |
| [u] | Come la u in **acuto.** | **rude** [rud]<br>**move** [muv]<br>**tomb** [tum] |

## DITTONGHI

| SIMBOLO | SUONO | ESEMPIO |
|---------|-------|---------|
| [aɪ] | Come **ai** in **laico.** | **night** [naɪt]<br>**eye** [aɪ] |
| [aʊ] | Come **au** in **causa.** | **found** [faʊnd]<br>**cow** [kaʊ] |
| [ɔɪ] | Come **oi** in **poi.** | **voice** [vɔɪs]<br>**oil** [ɔɪl] |

3

| SIMBOLO | SUONO | ESEMPIO |
|---------|-------|---------|
| [b] | Come la **b** in **bambino**. Suono bilabiale occlusivo sonoro. | **bed** [bɛd] <br> **robber** ['rɑbər] |
| [d] | Come la **d** in **caldo**. Suono dentale occlusivo sonoro. | **dead** [dɛd] <br> **add** [æd] |
| [dʒ] | Come la **g** in **gente**. Suono palatale affricato sonoro. | **gem** [dʒɛm] <br> **jail** [dʒel] |
| [ð] | Come la **d** nella pronuncia castigliana di **nada**. Suono interdentale fricativo sonoro. | **this** [ðɪs] <br> **father** ['fɑðər] |
| [f] | Come la **f** in **fare**. Suono labiodentale fricativo sordo. | **face** [fes] <br> **phone** [fon] |
| [g] | Come la **g** in **gatto**. Suono velare occlusivo sonoro. | **go** [go] <br> **get** [gɛt] |
| [h] | Come la **c** aspirata nella pronuncia toscana di **casa**. | **hot** [hɔt] <br> **alcohol** ['ælkə,hɔl] |
| [j] | Come la **i** in **ieri** o la **y** in **yo-yo**. Semiconsonante di suono palatale sonoro. | **yes** [jɛs] <br> **unit** ['junɪt] |
| [k] | Come la **c** in **casa** ma accompagnato da un'aspirazione. Suono velare occlusivo sordo. | **cat** [kæt] <br> **chord** [kɔrd] <br> **kill** [kɪl] |
| [l] | Come la **l** in **latino**. Suono alveolare fricativo laterale sonoro. | **late** [let] <br> **allow** [ə'lau] |
| [m] | Come la **m** in **madre**. Suono bilabiale nasale sonoro. | **more** [mor] <br> **command** [kə'mænd] |
| [n] | Come la **n** in **notte**. Suono alveolare nasale sonoro. | **nest** [nɛst] <br> **manner** ['mænər] |
| [ŋ] | Come la **n** in **manca**. Suono velare nasale sonoro. | **king** [kɪŋ] <br> **conquer** ['kɑŋkər] |
| [p] | Come la **p** in **patto** ma accompagnato da un'aspirazione. Suono bilabiale occlusivo sordo. | **pen** [pɛn] <br> **cap** [kæp] |
| [r] | La **r** più comune in molte parti dell'Inghilterra e nella maggior parte degli Stati Uniti e del Canadà è un suono semivocalico articolato con la punta della lingua elevata verso la volta del palato. Questa consonante è debolissima in posizione intervocalica o alla fine di una sillaba, e può appena percepirsi. L'articolazione di questa consonante ha la tendenza di influenzare il suono delle vocali contigue. La **r**, preceduta dai suoni [ʌ] o [ə], dà il proprio colorito a questi suoni e sparisce completamente come suono consonantico. | **run** [rʌn] <br> **far** [fɑr] <br> **art** [ɑrt] <br> **carry** ['kæri] <br><br><br><br><br><br> **burn** [bʌrn] <br> **learn** [lʌrn] <br> **weather** ['wɛðər] |
| [s] | Come la **s** in **sette**. Suono alveolare fricativo sordo. | **send** [sɛnd] <br> **cellar** ['sɛlər] |
| [ʃ] | Come **sc** in **lasciare**. Suono palatale fricativo sordo. | **shall** [ʃæl] <br> **machine** [mə'ʃin] |
| [t] | Come la **t** in **tavolo** ma accompagnato da un'aspirazione. Suono dentale occlusivo sordo. | **ten** [tɛn] <br> **dropped** [drɑpt] |
| [tʃ] | Come **c** in **cibo**. Suono palatale affricato sordo. | **child** [tʃaɪld] <br> **much** [mʌtʃ] <br> **nature** ['netʃər] |
| [θ] | Come la **z** castigliana in **zapato**. Suono interdentale fricativo sordo. | **think** [θɪŋk] <br> **truth** [truθ] |
| [v] | Come la **v** in **vento**. Suono labiodentale fricativo sonoro. | **vest** [vɛst] <br> **over** ['ovər] <br> **of** [ɑv] |

4

| SIMBOLO | SUONO | ESEMPIO |
|---------|-------|---------|
| [w] | Come la **u** in **quadro**. Suono labiovelare fricativo sonoro. | **work** [wʌrk] **tweed** [twid] **queen** [kwin] |
| [z] | Come la **s** in **asilo**. Suono alveolare fricativo sonoro. | **zeal** [zil] **busy** [ˈbɪzi] **his** [hɪz] |
| [ʒ] | Come la seconda **g** nella parola francese **garage**. Suono palatale fricativo sonoro. | **azure** [ˈeʒər] **measure** [ˈmɛʒər] |

## ACCENTO

L'accento tonico principale, indicato col segno grafico ˈ, e l'accento secondario, indicato col segno grafico ˌ precedono la sillaba sulla quale cadono, per es., **fascinate** [ˈfæsɪ ˌnet].

## La pronunzia delle parole composte

Nella parte inglese-italiano di questo Dizionario la pronunzia figurata di tutte le parole inglesi semplici è indicata in parentesi quadre che seguono immediatamente l'esponente, secondo un nuovo adattamento dell'alfabeto fonetico internazionale.

Vi sono tre generi di parole composte in inglese: (1) le parole in cui gli elementi componenti si sono uniti per formare una parola solida, come per es., **steamboat** vapore; (2) la parole in cui gli elementi componenti sono uniti da un trattino, come per es., **high′-grade′** di qualità superiore; (3) le parole in cui gli elementi componenti rimangono graficamente indipendenti gli uni da gli altri, per es., **post card** cartolina postale. La pronunzia delle parole inglesi composte non è indicata in questo Dizionario qualora gli elementi componenti appaiono come esponenti indipendenti nella loro normale posizione alfabetica e mostrano quindi la loro pronunzia figurata. Solo gli accenti principali e secondari di tali parole sono indicati, come per es., **steam′boat′, high′-grade′, post′ card′.** Se i due membri di una parola composta inglese solida non sono separati da un accento grafico, si usa un punto leggermente elevato sopra il rigo per indicarne la divisione, come per es., **la′dy·like′.**

Nei nomi in cui l'accento secondario cade sul membro **-man** o **-men,** le vocali di tali membri si pronunziano come nelle parole semplici **man** e **men,** come per es., **mailman** [ˈmel ˌmæn] e **mailmen** [ˈmel ˌmɛn]. Nei nomi in cui tali membri componenti non sono accentati, le loro vocali si pronunziano come se fossero un'e muta francese, come per es., **policeman** [pəˈlismən] e **policemen** [pəˈlismən]. In questo Dizionario la trascrizione fonetica di tali nomi non è stata indicata qualora il primo membro componente appaia come esponente con la sua pronunzia in alfabeto fonetico internazionale. Gli accenti sono ciò nondimeno indicati:

mail′man′ *s* (-men′)
police′man *s* (-men)

### La pronunzia dei participi passati

La pronunzia di una parola la cui desinenza è **-ed** (o **-d** dopo una e muta) non è indicata nel presente Dizionario, purché la pronunzia della parola stessa senza tale suffisso appaia con il suo esponente nella sua posizione alfabetica. In tale caso la pronunzia segue le regole indicate qui sotto. Si osservi che il raddoppiamento della vocale finale dopo una semplice vocale tonica non muta la pronunzia del suffisso **-ed,** per es.: **batted** [ˈbætɪd], **dropped** [drɑpt], **robbed** [rɑbd].

La desinenza **-ed** (o **-d** dopo una e muta) del preterito, del participio passato e di certi aggettivi ha tre pronunzie differenti, che dipendono dal suono in cui il tema termina:

1) Se il tema termina in suono consonantico sonoro (che non sia [d]), cioè [b], [g], [l], [m], [n], [ŋ], [r], [v], [z], [ð], [ʒ] o [dʒ] o in un suono vocalico, l'**-ed** è pronunziato [d]:

| SUONO IN CUI TERMINA IL TEMA | INFINITO | PRETERITO E PARTICIPIO PASSATO |
|---|---|---|
| [b] | **ebb** [ɛb] **rob** [rɑb] **robe** [rob] | **ebbed** [ɛbd] **robbed** [rɑbd] **robed** [robd] |

5

| SUONO IN CUI TERMINA IL TEMA | INFINITO | PRETERITO E PARTICIPIO PASSATO |
|---|---|---|
| [g] | egg [ɛg]<br>sag [sæg] | egged [ɛgd]<br>sagged [sægd] |
| [l] | mail [mel]<br>scale [skel] | mailed [meld]<br>scaled [skeld] |
| [m] | storm [stɔrm]<br>bomb [bɑm]<br>name [nem] | stormed [stɔrmd]<br>bombed [bɑmd]<br>named [nemd] |
| [n] | tan [tæn]<br>sign [saɪn]<br>mine [maɪn] | tanned [tænd]<br>signed [saɪnd]<br>mined [maɪnd] |
| [ŋ] | hang [hæŋ] | hanged [hæŋd] |
| [r] | fear [fɪr]<br>care [kɛr] | feared [fɪrd]<br>cared [kɛrd] |
| [v] | rev [rɛv]<br>save [sev] | revved [rɛvd]<br>saved [sevd] |
| [z] | buzz [bʌz]<br>fuze [fjuz] | buzzed [bʌzd]<br>fuzed [fjuzd] |
| [ð] | smooth [smuð]<br>bathe [beð] | smoothed [smuðd]<br>bathed [beðd] |
| [ʒ] | massage [məˈsɑʒ] | massaged [məˈsɑʒd] |
| [dʒ] | page [pedʒ] | paged [pedʒd] |
| suono vocalico | key [ki]<br>sigh [saɪ]<br>paw [pɔ] | keyed [kid]<br>sighed [saɪd]<br>pawed [pɔd] |

2) Se il tema termina in un suono consonantico sordo (che non sia [t]), cioè [f], [k], [p], [s], [θ], [ʃ] o [tʃ], l'**-ed** si pronunzia [t]:

| SUONO IN CUI TERMINA IL TEMA | INFINITO | PRETERITO E PARTICIPIO PASSATO |
|---|---|---|
| [f] | loaf [lof]<br>knife [naɪf] | loafed [loft]<br>knifed [naɪft] |
| [k] | back [bæk]<br>bake [bek] | backed [bækt]<br>baked [bekt] |
| [p] | cap [kæp]<br>wipe [waɪp] | capped [kæpt]<br>wiped [waɪpt] |
| [s] | hiss [hɪs]<br>mix [mɪks] | hissed [hɪst]<br>mixed [mɪkst] |
| [θ] | lath [læθ] | lathed [læθt] |
| [ʃ] | mash [mæʃ] | mashed [mæʃt] |
| [tʃ] | match [mætʃ] | matched [mætʃt] |

3) Se il tema termina in un suono dentale, cioè [t] o [d], l'**-ed** si pronunzia [ɪd] o [əd]:

| SUONO IN CUI TERMINA IL TEMA | INFINITO | PRETERITO E PARTICIPIO PASSATO |
|---|---|---|
| [t] | wait [wet]<br>mate [met] | waited [ˈwetɪd]<br>mated [ˈmetɪd] |
| [d] | mend [mend]<br>wade [wed] | mended [ˈmendɪd]<br>waded [ˈwedɪd] |

L'**-ed** di alcuni aggettivi aggiunto ad un tema che termina in suono consonantico (oltre a quelli che terminano in [d] o [t]), è ciò nonostante talvolta pronunziato [ɪd] e tale fenomeno è idicato con la piena pronunzia della parola in simboli dell'alfabeto fonetico internazionale, per es., **blessed** [ˈblɛsɪd], **crabbed** [ˈkræbɪd].

6

# INGLESE-ITALIANO

**A, a** [e] *s* prima lettera dell'alfabeto inglese

**a** [e] *art indef* un, uno, una, un'

**aback** [ə'bæk] *adv* all'indietro; **taken aback** colto alla sprovvista, sconcertato

**aba·cus** ['æbəkəs] *s* (**-cuses** or **-ci** [,saɪ]) pallottoliere *m;* (archit) abaco

**abaft** [ə'bæft] or [ə'baft] *adv* a poppa ‖ *prep* dietro a

**abandon** [ə'bændən] *s* disinvoltura ‖ *tr* abbandonare

**abase** [ə'bes] *tr* umiliare, degradare

**abash** [ə'bæʃ] *tr* imbarazzare; sconcertare

**abate** [ə'bet] *tr* ridurre; omettere; (law) terminare ‖ *intr* diminuire, calmarsi

**aba·tis** ['æbətɪs] or [ə'bætɪs] *s* (**-tis** or **-tises**) (mil) tagliata

**abattoir** ['æbə,twɑr] *s* macello

**abba·cy** ['æbəsi] *s* (**-cies**) abbazia

**abbess** ['æbɪs] *s* badessa

**abbey** ['æbi] *s* badia, abbazia

**abbot** ['æbət] *s* abate *m*

**abbreviate** [ə'brivɪ,et] *tr* abbreviare, raccorciare

**abbreviation** [ə,brivɪ'eʃən] *s* (*abbreviated form*) abbreviazione; (*shortening*) abbreviamento

**A B C** [,e,bi'si] *s* (letterword) abbicci *m;* **A B C's** abbecedario

**abdicate** ['æbdɪ,ket] *tr* abdicare a ‖ *intr* abdicare

**abdomen** ['æbdəmən] or [æb'domən] *s* addome *m*

**abduct** [æb'dʌkt] *tr* rapire

**abed** [ə'bed] *adv* a letto

**abet** [ə'bet] *v* (*pret & pp* **abetted;** *ger* **abetting**) *tr* favoreggiare

**abeyance** [ə'be·əns] *s* sospensione; **in abeyance** in sospeso

**ab·hor** [æb'hɔr] *v* (*pret & pp* **-horred;** *ger* **-horring**) *tr* aborrire

**abhorrent** [æb'hɑrənt] or [æb'hɔrənt] *adj* detestabile

**abide** [ə'baɪd] *v* (*pret & pp* **abode** or **abided**) *tr* aspettare; tollerare ‖ *intr* —**to abide by** attenersi a; rimanere fedele a

**abili·ty** [ə'bɪlɪti] *s* (**-ties**) abilità *f,* bravura

**abject** ['æbdʒɛkt] or [æb'dʒɛkt] *adj* abietto, turpe

**abjure** [æb'dʒur] *tr* abiurare

**ablative** ['æblətɪv] *adj & s* ablativo

**ablaut** ['æblaut] *s* apofonia

**ablaze** [ə'blez] *adj* in fiamme; risplendente

**able** ['ebəl] *adj* abile, esperto; **to be able to** + *inf* potere + *inf*

**able-bodied** ['ebəl'bɑdid] *adj* sano; forte

**abloom** [ə'blum] *adj & adv* in fiore

**abnormal** [æb'nɔrməl] *adj* anormale

**aboard** [ə'bord] *adv* a bordo; **all aboard!** (rr) signori, in vettura!; **to go aboard** imbarcarsi; **to take aboard** imbarcare ‖ *prep* a bordo di; (*a bus, train, etc.*) in, su

**abode** [ə'bod] *s* abitazione, dimora

**abolish** [ə'balɪʃ] *tr* abolire

**A-bomb** ['e,bam] *s* bomba atomica

**abominable** [ə'bamənəbəl] *adj* abominevole

**abomination** [ə,bamɪ'neʃən] *s* abominazione

**aborigenes** [,æbə'rɪdʒɪ,niz] *spl* aborigeni *mpl*

**abort** [ə'bɔrt] *tr* terminare prematuramente; provocare un aborto in ‖ *intr* abortire

**abortion** [ə'bɔrʃən] *s* aborto

**abound** [ə'baund] *intr* abbondare; **to abound in** or **with** abbondare di

**about** [ə'baut] *adv* circa, press'a poco; qua intorno; qua e là; in direzione opposta; (coll) quasi; **to be about to** star sul punto di ‖ *prep* intorno a; circa a; addosso a; tutt'intorno a; riguardo a

**about'-face'** *interj* (mil) dietro front!

**about'-face'** or **about'-face'** *s* voltafaccia; (mil) dietro front *m* ‖ **about'-face'** *intr* fare dietro front

**above** [ə'bʌv] *adj* soprammenzionato; superiore ‖ *s*—**from above** dal cielo; dall'alto ‖ *adv* in alto; su; più sopra ‖ *prep* sopra, sopra a; più di; al di là di, oltre; **above all** soprattutto

**above-mentioned** [ə'bʌv'menʃənd] *adj* summenzionato, sunnominato

**abrasive** [ə'bresɪv] or [ə'brezɪv] *adj & s* abrasivo

**abreast** [ə'brest] *adj & adv* in fila, in linea; **to keep abreast of** tenersi alla pari con; essere al corrente di

**abridge** [ə'brɪdʒ] *tr* compendiare; ridurre

**abroad** [ə'brɔd] *adv* all'estero; all'aria aperta; **to be abroad** (*said of news*) circolare

**abrupt** [ə'brʌpt] *adj* brusco, improvviso; (*very steep*) scosceso

**abscess** ['æbses] *s* ascesso

**abscond** [æb'skand] *intr* scappare; **to abscond with** svignarsela con

**absence** ['æbsəns] *s* assenza; **in the absence of** in mancanza di

**absent** ['æbsənt] *adj* assente ‖ [æb,sent] *tr*—**to absent oneself** assentarsi

**absentee** [,æbsən'ti] *s* assente *mf*

**absent-minded** ['æbsənt'maɪndɪd] *adj* distratto, assente

**absinth** ['æbsɪnθ] *s* assenzio

**absolute** ['æbsə,lut] *adj & s* assoluto

**absolutely** ['æbsə,lutli] *adv* assolutamente, certamente ‖ [,æbsə'lutli] *interj* certamente!

**absolve** [æb'salv] *tr* assolvere

**absorb** [æb'sɔrb] *tr* assorbire; **to be** or **become absorbed** essere assorto

**absorbent** [æb'sɔrbənt] *adj* assorbente; (*cotton*) idrofilo ‖ *s* sostanza assorbente

**absorbing** [æb'sɔrbɪŋ] *adj* interessantissimo

**abstain** [æb'sten] *intr* astenersi

**abstemious** [æb'stimɪ·əs] *adj* astemio

**abstention** [æb'stenʃən] *s* astensione; astenuto (*vote withheld*)

**abstinent** ['æbstɪnənt] *adj* astinente
**abstract** ['æbstrækt] *adj* astratto || *s* compendio, sommario || *tr* compendiare || (æb'strækt) *tr* astrarre; (*to steal*) sottrarre
**abstruse** [æb'strus] *adj* astruso
**absurd** [æb'sʌrd] *or* [æb'zʌrd] *adj* assurdo
**absurdi·ty** [æb'sʌrdɪti] *or* [æb'zʌrdɪti] *s* (-ties) assurdità *f*
**abundant** [ə'bʌndənt] *adj* abbondante
**abuse** [ə'bjus] *s* (*misuse*) abuso; maltrattamento; insulto || [ə'bjuz] *tr* (*to misuse, take unfair advantage of*) abusare di; maltrattare; insultare
**abusive** [ə'bjusɪv] *adj* abusivo; insultante
**abut** [ə'bʌt] *v* (*pret & pp* **abutted;** *ger* **abutting**) *intr*—to abut on confinare con
**abutment** [ə'bʌtmənt] *s* rinfianco; (*at either end of bridge*) spalla; (*of buttresses of bridge*) sprone *m*
**abysmal** (ə'bɪzməl] *adj* abissale; (*e.g., ignorance*) spropositato
**abyss** [ə'bɪs] *s* abisso
**academic** [,ækə'dɛmɪk] *adj* accademico
**ac′ademic cos′tume** *s* toga accademica
**academician** [ə,kædə'mɪʃən] *s* accademico
**ac′adem′ic year′** *s* anno scolastico
**acade·my** [ə'kædəmi] *s* (-mies) accademia
**accede** [æk'sid] *intr* accedere; **to accede** to salire a; accedere a
**accelerate** [æk'sɛlə,ret] *tr & intr* accelerare
**accelerator** [æk'sɛlə,retər] *s* acceleratore *m*
**accent** ['æksɛnt] *s* accento || ['æksɛnt] *or* [æk'sɛnt] *tr* accentare; (*to accentuate*) accentuare
**ac′cent mark′** *s* segnaccento, accento grafico
**accentuate** [æk'sɛntʃʊ,et] *tr* accentuare
**accept** [æk'sɛpt] *tr* accettare
**acceptable** [æk'sɛptəbəl] *adj* accettabile
**acceptance** [æk'sɛptəns] *s* accettazione
**access** ['ækses] *s* accesso
**accessible** [æk'sɛsɪbəl] *adj* accessibile; (*person*) abbordabile
**accession** [æk'sɛʃən] *s* accessione, acquisto; (*e.g., to the throne*) adito
**accesso·ry** [æk'sɛsəri] *adj* accessorio || *s* (-ries) accessorio; (*to a crime*) complice *m*
**accident** ['æksɪdənt] *s* accidente *m;* **by accident** accidentalmente, per caso
**accidental** [,æksɪ'dɛntəl] *adj* accidentale || *s* (mus) accidente *m*
**acclaim** [ə'klem] *s* acclamazione, applauso || *tr & intr* acclamare, applaudire
**acclimate** ['æklɪ,met] *tr* acclimatare || *intr* acclimatarsi
**accolade** [,ækə'led] *s* accollata; (fig) elogio
**accommodate** [ə'kɑmə,det] *tr* (*to adjust, make fit*) accomodare; (*to pro-*

*vide with a loan*) venire incontro a; (*to supply with lodging*) alloggiare; (*to oblige*) favorire; (*to have room for*) aver posto per
**accommodating** [ə'kɑmə,detɪŋ] *adj* servizievole, compiacente
**accommodation** [ə,kɑmə'deʃən] *s* (*favor*) favore *m;* (*loan*) prestito; (*adaptation*) adattamento; (*reconciliation*) conciliazione; (*compromise*) accomodamento; **accommodations** (*traveling space*) posto; (*in a hotel*) alloggio
**accommoda′tion train′** *s* treno accelerato
**accompaniment** [ə'kʌmpənɪmənt] *s* accompagnamento
**accompanist** [ə'kʌmpənɪst] *s* accompagnatore *m*
**accompa·ny** [ə'kʌmpəni] *v* (*pret & pp* -nied) *tr* accompagnare
**accomplice** [ə'kɑmplɪs] *s* complice *mf*
**accomplish** [ə'kɑmplɪʃ] *tr* compiere
**accomplished** [ə'kɑmplɪʃt] *adj* (*completed*) compiuto, terminato; (*skilled*) finito, compiuto
**accomplishment** [ə'kɑmplɪʃmənt] *s* (*completion*) esecuzione, realizzazione; (*something accomplished*) opera; (*acquired ability*) talento; (*military achievement*) prodezza; (*social skill*) compitezza
**accord** [ə'kɔrd] *s* accordo; **in accord with** in conformità con; **of one's own accord** spontaneamente; **with one accord** di comune accordo || *tr* concedere || *intr* accordarsi
**accordance** [ə'kɔrdəns] *s* accordo; **in accordance with** in conformità con
**according** [ə'kɔrdɪŋ] *adv*—**according as** a seconda che; **according to** secondo, a seconda di
**accordingly** [ə'kɔrdɪŋli] *adv* per conseguenza, perciò; in conformità
**accordion** [ə'kɔrdɪ·ən] *s* fisarmonica
**accost** [ə'kɔst] *or* [ə'kɑst] *tr* accostare, abbordare
**accouchement** [ə'kuʃmənt] *s* parto
**account** [ə'kaʊnt] *s* (*explanation*) versione; (*report*) resoconto; conto; (*statement*) estratto conto; **by all accounts** secondo la voce comune; **of account** d'importanza; **of no account** senza importanza; **on account** in conto; **on account of** a causa di; per l'amor di; **on all accounts** in ogni modo; **on no account** in nessuna maniera; **to call to account** chiedere conto di; **to give a good account of oneself** comportarsi bene; **to take account of** prendere in considerazione; **to turn to account** trarre profitto da || *intr*—**to account for** render conto di; essere responsabile per
**accountable** [ə'kaʊntəbəl] *adj* responsabile; (*explainable*) spiegabile
**accountant** [ə'kaʊntənt] *s* contabile *mf;* ragioniere *m*
**accounting** [ə'kaʊntɪŋ] *s* contabilità *f,* ragioneria
**accouterments** [ə'kutərmənts] *spl* (mil)

buffetterie *fpl*; (*trappings*) ornamenti *mpl*

**accredit** [ə'krɛdɪt] *tr* accreditare; **to accredit s.o. with s.th** ascrivere qlco a credito di qlcu

**accrue** [ə'kru] *intr* accumularsi; (*said of interest*) maturare

**acculturation** [əˌkʌltʃə'reʃən] *s* acculturazione

**accumulate** [ə'kjumjəˌlet] *tr* accumulare || *intr* accumularsi

**accuracy** ['ækjərəsi] *s* esattezza, precisione; fedeltà *f*

**accurate** ['ækjərɪt] *adj* esatto, preciso; fedele

**accursed** [ə'kʌrsɪd] or [ə'kʌrst] *adj* maledetto

**accusation** [ˌækjə'zeʃən] *s* accusa

**accusative** [ə'kjuzətɪv] *adj* & *s* accusativo

**accuse** [ə'kjuz] *tr* accusare

**accustom** [ə'kʌstəm] *tr* abituare

**ace** [es] *s* asso; **to be within an ace of** essere quasi sul punto di

**ace' in the hole'** *s* asso nella manica

**acetate** ['æsɪˌtet] *s* acetato

**ace'tic ac'id** [ə'sitɪk] *s* acido acetico

**aceti·fy** [ə'setɪˌfaɪ] *v* (*pret* & *pp* **-fied**) *tr* acetificare || *intr* acetificarsi

**acetone** ['æsɪˌton] *s* acetone *m*

**acetylene** [ə'setɪˌlin] *s* acetilene *m*

**acet'ylene torch'** *s* cannello ossiacetilenico

**ache** [ek] *s* dolore *m* || *intr* dolere, e.g., **my tooth aches** mi duole il dente

**Acheron** ['ækəˌrɑn] *s* Acheronte *m*

**achieve** [ə'tʃiv] *tr* compiere, conseguire

**achievement** [ə'tʃivmənt] *s* compimento; successo; (*exploit*) impresa, prodezza

**Achil'les heel'** [ə'kɪliz] *s* tallone *m* d'Achille

**acid** ['æsɪd] *adj* & *s* acido

**acidi·fy** [ə'sɪdɪˌfaɪ] *v* (*pret* & *pp* **-fied**) *tr* & *intr* acidificare

**acidity** [ə'sɪdɪti] *s* acidità *f*

**acid' test'** *s* prova del fuoco

**ack-ack** ['æk'æk] *s* (slang) cannone antiaereo

**acknowledge** [æk'nɑlɪdʒ] *tr* riconoscere; (*receipt of a letter*) accusare; (*a claim*) ammettere; mostrare la gratitudine per; (law) certificare

**acknowledgment** [æk'nɑlɪdʒmənt] *s* riconoscimento; (*of receipt of a letter*) accusa, cenno

**acme** ['ækmi] *s* acme *f*

**acolyte** ['ækəˌlaɪt] *s* accolito

**acorn** ['ekɔrn] or ['ekərn] *s* ghianda

**acoustic** [ə'kustɪk] *adj* acustico || **acoustics** *s* acustica

**acquaint** [ə'kwent] *tr* mettere al corrente; **to be acquainted with** conoscere; essere al corrente di; **to become acquainted** (*with each other*) conoscersi

**acquaintance** [ə'kwentəns] *s* conoscenza; (*person*) conoscente *mf*, conoscenza

**acquiesce** [ˌækwɪ'ɛs] *intr* acconsentire, accondiscendere

**acquiescence** [ˌækwɪ'ɛsəns] *s* accondiscendenza

**acquire** [ə'kwaɪr] *tr* acquistare

**acquisition** [ˌækwɪ'zɪʃən] *s* acquisto

**acquit** [ə'kwɪt] *v* (*pret* & *pp* **acquitted;** *ger* **acquitting**) *tr* (*to pay*) ripagare; (*to declare not guilty*) assolvere; **to acquit oneself** condursi

**acquittal** [ə'kwɪtəl] *s* assoluzione

**acre** ['ekər] *s* acro

**acrid** ['ækrɪd] *adj* acrido, pungente

**acrobat** ['ækrəˌbæt] *s* acrobata *mf*

**acrobatic** [ˌækrə'bætɪk] *adj* acrobatico || **acrobatics** *ssg* (*e.g., of a stunt pilot*) acrobazie *fpl*; **acrobatics** *spl* (*gymnastics*) acrobatica

**acronym** ['ækrənɪm] *s* acronimo, parola macedonia

**acropolis** [ə'krɑpəlɪs] *s* acropoli *f*

**across** [ə'krɔs] or [ə'krɑs] *adv* dall'altra parte; **to get an idea across to** farsi capire da || *prep* attraverso; (*on the other side of*) al di là di, dall'altra parte di; **to come across** (*a person*) imbattersi in; **to go across** attraversare

**across'-the-board'** *adj* generale

**act** [ækt] *s* atto; legge *f*; rappresentazione; **in the act** in flagrante || *tr* (*a drama*) rappresentare; (*a role*) recitare || *intr* (*on the stage*) recitare; (*to behave*) comportarsi; (*to perform special duties; to reach a decision*) agire; (*to have an effect*) reagire; **to act as** fungere da; **to act for** rimpiazzare; **to act on** eseguire; **to act up** (coll) fare il matto; non funzionare bene (*said, e.g., of a motor*); **to act up** (coll) fare festa a

**acting** ['æktɪŋ] *adj* facente funzione, interino || *s* recita

**action** ['ækʃən] *s* azione; (*moving parts*) meccanismo; **to take action** iniziare azione; (law) intentare causa

**activate** ['æktɪˌvet] *tr* attivare

**active** ['æktɪv] *adj* & *s* attivo

**activi·ty** [æk'tɪvɪti] *s* (**-ties**) attività *f*

**act' of God'** *s* forza maggiore

**actor** ['æktər] *s* attore *m*

**actress** ['æktrɪs] *s* attrice *f*

**actual** ['æktʃu·əl] *adj* reale

**actually** ['æktʃu·əli] *adv* realmente, in realtà

**actuar·y** ['æktʃuˌɛri] *s* (**-ies**) attuario

**actuate** ['æktʃuˌet] *tr* attuare, mettere in azione; (*to motivate*) stimulare

**acuity** [ə'kju·ɪti] *s* acuità *f*

**acumen** [ə'kjumən] *s* acume *m*

**acupuncture** ['ækjuˌpʌŋktʃər] *s* agopuntura

**acute** [ə'kjut] *adj* acuto

**ad** [æd] *s* (coll) inserzione pubblicitaria

**Adam** ['ædəm] *s* Adamo; **not to know from Adam** non conoscere affatto

**adamant** ['ædəmənt] *adj* saldo, inflessibile

**Ad'am's ap'ple** *s* pomo d'Adamo

**adapt** [ə'dæpt] *tr* adattare

**adaptation** [ˌædæp'teʃən] *s* adattamento; (*e.g., of a play*) rifacimento

**add** [æd] *tr* aggiungere; (*numbers*)

sommare || *intr* aggiungere; far di conto; **to add up to** ammontare a; (coll) voler dire

**adder** [ˈædər] *s* vipera

**addict** [ˈædɪkt] *s* (*to drugs*) tossicomane *mf*; (*to a sport*) tifoso || [əˈdɪkt] *tr* abituare; rendere propenso alla tossicomania; **to addict oneself to** darsi a, abbandonarsi a

**addiction** [əˈdɪkʃən] *s* dedizione; (*to drugs*) tossicomania; (*to sports*) tifo

**add'ing machine'** *s* calcolatrice *f*

**addition** [əˈdɪʃən] *s* addizione; (*building*) annessi *mpl;* **in addition** inoltre, per di più; **in addition to** oltre a

**additive** [ˈædɪtɪv] *adj & s* additivo

**address** [əˈdrɛs] *or* [ˈædrɛs] *s* (*speech*) discorso; (*place and destination of mail*) indirizzo; (*skill*) destrezza; (*formal request*) petizione; **to deliver an address** pronunciare un discorso || [əˈdrɛs] *tr* indirizzare; (*to speak to*) rivolgere la parola a

**addressee** [ˌædrɛˈsi] *s* destinatario

**address'ing machine'** *s* macchina per indirizzi

**adduce** [əˈdjus] *or* [əˈdus] *tr* addurre

**adenoids** [ˈædəˌnɔɪds] *spl* vegetazioni *fpl* adenoidi, adenoidi *fpl*

**adept** [əˈdɛpt] *adj & s* esperto

**adequate** [ˈædɪkwɪt] *adj* sufficiente; (*suitable*) conveniente

**adhere** [ædˈhɪr] *intr* aderire

**adherence** [ædˈhɪrəns] *s* aderenza

**adherent** [ædˈhɪrənt] *adj & s* aderente *m*

**adhesion** [ædˈhiʒən] *s* adesione; (pathol) aderenza

**adhesive** [ædˈhisɪv] *or* [ædˈhizɪv] *adj & s* adesivo

**adhe'sive tape'** *s* tela adesiva, cerotto

**adieu** [əˈdju] *or* [əˈdu] *s* (**adieus** *or* **adieux**) addio || *interj* addio!

**adjacent** [əˈdʒesənt] *adj* adiacente

**adjective** [ˈædʒɪktɪv] *adj* aggettivale; accessorio, secondario || *s* aggettivo

**adjoin** [əˈdʒɔɪn] *tr* confinare con || *intr* essere confinanti

**adjoining** [əˈdʒɔɪnɪŋ] *adj* confinante; vicino, attiguo

**adjourn** [əˈdʒʌrn] *tr* aggiornare, rinviare || *intr* rinviarsi

**adjournment** [əˈdʒʌrnmənt] *s* aggiornamento, rinvio

**adjust** [əˈdʒʌst] *tr* accomodare; regolare; (ins) liquidare || *intr* abituarsi

**adjustable** [əˈdʒʌstəbəl] *adj* regolabile

**adjustment** [əˈdʒʌstmənt] *s* aggiustamento; accomodamento; (ins) liquidazione del danno

**adjutant** [ˈædʒətənt] *s* aiutante *mf*

**ad-lib** [ˌædˈlɪb] *v* (*pret & pp* **-libbed;** *ger* **-libbing**) *tr & intr* improvvisare

**administer** [ædˈmɪnɪstər] *tr* amministrare; (*medicine*) somministrare; (*an oath*) dare || *intr*—**to administer to** ministrare, prestare aiuto a

**administrator** [ædˈmɪnɪsˌtretər] *s* amministratore *m*

**admirable** [ˈædmɪrəbəl] *adj* ammirabile, ammirevole

**admiral** [ˈædmɪrəl] *s* ammiraglio

**admiral·ty** [ˈædmɪrəlti] *s* (**-ties**) ammiragliato

**admire** [ædˈmaɪr] *tr* ammirare

**admirer** [ædˈmaɪrər] *s* ammiratore *m*

**admissible** [ædˈmɪsɪbəl] *adj* ammissibile

**admission** [ædˈmiʃən] *s* ammissione; confessione; (*entrance fee*) prezzo d'ingresso; **to gain admission** arrivare a entrare

**ad·mit** [ædˈmɪt] *v* (*pret & pp* **-mitted;** *ger* **-mitting**) *tr* ammettere; confessare || *intr* dare l'ingresso; **to admit of** permettere, ammettere; consentire

**admittance** [ædˈmɪtəns] *s* ammissione; permesso di entrare; **no admittance** divieto d'ingresso

**admonish** [ædˈmɑnɪʃ] *tr* ammonire

**ado** [əˈdu] *s* confusione, trambusto; **much ado about nothing** molto rumore per nulla; **to make a big ado** fare cerimonie

**adobe** [əˈdobi] *s* mattone crudo

**adolescence** [ˌædəˈlɛsəns] *s* adolescenza

**adolescent** [ˌædəˈlɛsənt] *adj & s* adolescente *mf*

**adopt** [əˈdɑpt] *tr* adottare

**adoption** [əˈdɑpʃən] *s* adozione

**adorable** [əˈdorəbəl] *adj* adorabile

**adore** [əˈdor] *tr* adorare

**adorn** [əˈdɔrn] *tr* adornare

**adornment** [əˈdɔrnmənt] *s* ornamento

**adre'nal gland'** [ædˈrinəl] *s* glandola surrenale

**Adriatic** [ˌedriˈætɪk] *or* [ˌædriˈætɪk] *adj* adriatico || *adj & s* Adriatico

**adrift** [əˈdrɪft] *adj & adv* alla deriva

**adroit** [əˈdrɔɪt] *adj* destro

**adult** [əˈdʌlt] *or* [ˈædʌlt] *adj & s* adulto

**adulterate** [əˈdʌltəˌret] *tr* adulterare

**adulterer** [əˈdʌltərər] *s* adultero

**adulteress** [əˈdʌltərɪs] *s* adultera

**adulter·y** [əˈdʌltəri] *s* (**-ies**) adulterio

**advance** [ædˈvæns] *or* [ædˈvɑns] *adj* avanzato || *s* avanzata; (*increase in price*) aumento; (*of money*) anticipo; **advances** approcci *mpl;* **in advance** in anticipo || *tr* avanzare; aumentare; (*to make earlier*) anticipare; (*money*) anticipare; (*a clock*) mettere avanti || *intr* avanzare; (*said, e.g., of prices*) aumentare

**advanced** [ædˈvænst] *or* [ædˈvɑnst] *adj* avanzato, progredito

**advanced' stand'ing** *s* trasferimento di voti scolastici

**advancement** [ædˈvænsmənt] *or* [ædˈvɑnsmənt] *s* progresso; promozione; (mil) avanzata

**advance' public'ity** *s* pubblicità *f* di lancio

**advantage** [ædˈvæntɪdʒ] *or* [ædˈvɑntɪdʒ] *s* vantaggio; **to advantage in** maniera favorevole; **to take advantage of** approfittarsi di; abusare di || *tr* avantaggiare

**advantageous** [ˌædvənˈtedʒəs] *adj* vantaggioso

**advent** [ˈædvɛnt] *s* avvento

**adventure** [æd'vɛntʃər] *s* avventura ‖ *tr* avventurare ‖ *intr* avventurarsi
**adventurer** [æd'vɛntʃərər] *s* avventuriero
**adventuresome** [æd'vəntʃərsəm] *adj* avventuroso
**adventuress** [æd'vɛntʃɛrɪs] *s* avventuriera
**adventurous** [æd'vɛntʃərəs] *adj* avventuroso
**adverb** ['ædvʌrb] *s* avverbio
**adversar·y** ['ædvər ˌsɛri] *s* (-ies) avversario
**adverse** [æd'vʌrs] or ['ædvʌrs] *adj* avverso, contrario
**adversi·ty** [æd'vʌrsɪti] *s* (-ties) avversità *f*
**advertise** ['ædvər ˌtaɪz] or [ ˌædvər'taɪz] *tr* propagandare; reclamizzare ‖ *intr* fare la pubblicità; inserire un annunzio; inserzionare
**advertisement** [ ˌædvər'taɪzmənt] or [æd'vʌrtɪsmənt] *s* annuncio pubblicitario, inserzione
**advertiser** ['ædvər ˌtaɪzer] or [ ˌædvər'taɪzər] *s* inserzionista *mf*
**advertising** ['ædvər ˌtaɪzɪŋ] *s* pubblicità *f*, pubblicismo
**ad'vertising a'gent** *s* pubblicista *mf*
**ad'vertising campaign'** *s* campagna pubblicitaria
**ad'vertising man'** *s* agente *m* di pubblicità, reclamista *m*
**advice** [æd'vaɪs] *s* consiglio; **a piece of advice** un consiglio
**advisable** [æd'vaɪzəbəl] *adj* consigliabile
**advise** [æd'vaɪz] *tr* consigliare; informare ‖ *intr*—**to advise with** chiedere il consiglio di; avere una conferenza con
**advisement** [æd'vaɪzmənt] *s* considerazione; **to take under advisement** prendere in considerazione
**adviser** [æd'vaɪzər] *s* consigliere *m*
**advisory** [æd'vaɪzəri] *adj* consultivo
**advocate** ['ædvə ˌket] *s* difensore *m; (lawyer)* avvocato ‖ *tr* sostenere, propugnare
**adze** [ædz] *s* ascia
**Aege'an Sea'** [ɪ'dʒi·ən] *s* mare Egeo
**aegis** ['idʒɪs] *s* egida
**Aeneid** [i'ni·ɪd] *s* Eneide *f*
**aerate** ['ɛret] or ['e·ə ˌret] *tr* aerare
**aerial** ['ɛri·əl] or [e'ɪri·əl] *adj* aereo ‖ ['ɛri·əl] *s* (rad & telv) antenna
**aer'ial pho'tograph** *s* aerofotogramma *m*
**aerodrome** ['ɛrə ˌdrom] *s* aerodromo
**aerodynamic** [ ˌɛrodaɪ'næmɪk] *adj* aerodinamico ‖ **aerodynamics** *ssg* aerodinamica
**aeronaut** ['ɛrə ˌnɔt] *s* aeronauta *m*
**aeronautic** [ ˌɛrə'nɔtɪk] *adj* aeronautico ‖ **aeronautics** *ssg* aeronautica
**aerosol** ['ɛrə ˌsol] *s* aerosol *m*
**aerospace** ['ɛro ˌspes] *adj* aerospaziale ‖ *s* aerospazio
**Aesop** ['isɑp] *s* Esopo
**aesthete** ['ɛsθit] *s* esteta *mf*
**aesthetic** [ɛs'θɛtɪk] *adj* estetico ‖ **aesthetics** *ssg* estetica

**afar** [ə'fɑr] *adv* lontano; **from afar** da lontano
**affable** ['æfəbəl] *adj* affabile
**affair** [ə'fɛr] *s* affare *m; (romance)* relazione amorosa
**affect** [ə'fɛkt] *tr* influenzare; *(to touch the heart of)* commuovere; *(to pretend to have)* affettare
**affectation** [ ˌæfɛk'teʃən] *s* affettazione
**affected** [ə'fɛktɪd] *adj* affettato
**affection** [ə'fɛkʃən] *s* affezione
**affectionate** [ə'fɛkʃənɪt] *adj* affettuoso, affezionato
**affidavit** [ ˌæfɪ'devɪt] *s* affidavit *m*, dichiarazione sotto giuramento
**affiliate** [ə'fɪlɪ ˌet] *adj & s* affiliato ‖ *tr* affiliare ‖ *intr* affiliarsi
**affini·ty** [ə'fɪnɪti] *s* (-ties) affinità *f*
**affirm** [ə'fʌrm] *tr* affermare; confermare
**affirmative** [ə'fʌrmətɪv] *adj* affermativo ‖ *s* affermativa
**affix** ['æfɪks] *s* affisso ‖ [ə'fɪks] *tr* affiggere; *(a signature)* apporre; *(e.g., blame)* attribuire
**afflict** [ə'flɪkt] *tr* affliggere
**affliction** [ə'flɪkʃən] *s* afflizione
**affluence** ['æflʊ·əns] *s* opulenza, abbondanza
**affluent** ['æflʊ·ənt] *adj* opulento, abbondante; ricco ‖ *s* affluente *m*
**afford** [ə'fɔrd] *tr* permettersi il lusso di; *(to furnish)* provvedere; *(to give)* dare
**affray** [ə'fre] *s* rissa
**affront** [ə'frʌnt] *s* affronto ‖ *tr* fare un affronto a
**afghan** ['æfgən] or ['æfgæn] *s* coperta di lana all'uncinetto ‖ **Afghan** *adj & s* afgano
**afield** [ə'fild] *adv* sul campo; **far afield** lontano
**afire** [ə'faɪr] *adj* ardente; in fuoco, in fiamme
**aflame** [ə'flem] *adj* in fiamme
**afloat** [ə'flot] *adj & adv* a galla; a bordo; *(drifting)* alla deriva; *(said of a rumor)* in circolazione
**afoot** [ə'fʊt] *adj & adv* a piedi; in movimento, in moto
**aforementioned** [ə'fɔr ˌmɛnʃənd] or **aforesaid** [ə'fɔr ˌsɛd] *adj* suddetto
**afoul** [ə'faʊl] *adj & adv* in collisione; **to run afoul of** finire nelle mani di, impigliarsi con
**afraid** [ə'fred] *adj* impaurito, spaventato; **to be afraid (of)** aver paura (di)
**African** ['æfrɪkən] *adj & s* africano
**aft** [æft] or [ɑft] *adv* a poppa; indietro
**after** ['æftər] or ['ɑftər] *adj* seguente; di poppa ‖ *adv* dopo; che ‖ *prep* dopo; dopo di; *(in the manner of)* secondo; *(behind)* dietro a ‖ *conj* dopo che
**afterburner** ['æftər ˌbʌrnər] or ['ɑftər ˌbʌrnər] *s* (aer) postbruciatore *m*
**af'ter-din'ner** *adj* dopo la cena
**aftereffect** ['æftərɪ ˌfɛkt] or ['ɑftərɪ ˌfɛkt] *s* conseguenza
**af'ter-hours'** *adj* dopo le ore di ufficio
**af'ter·life'** *s* aldilà *m*; vita susseguente

**aftermath** ['æftər ˌmæθ] or ['ɑftər- ˌmæθ] *s* conseguenze *fpl;* gravi conseguenze *fpl*
**af'ter·noon'** *adj* pomeridiano ‖ *s* pomeriggio
**after-shaving** ['æftər ˌʃevɪŋ] or ['ɑftər- ˌʃevɪŋ] *adj* dopobarba
**af'ter·taste'** *s* retrosapore *m*
**af'ter·thought'** *s* pensiero tardivo
**afterward** ['æftərwərd] or ['ɑftərwərd] *adv* dopo; **long afterward** molto tempo dopo
**af'ter·while'** *adv* fra un po'
**again** [ə'gen] *adv* di nuovo; ancora; un'altra volta; **again and again** ripetutamente; **as much again** due volte tanto, altrettanto; **to** + *inf* + **again** tornare a + *inf,* e.g., **to cook again** tornare a cuocere
**against** [ə'genst] *prep* contro; (*opposite*) in faccia a; **to be against** opporsi a; **to go against the grain** ripugnare
**agape** [ə'gep] *adj & adv* a bocca aperta
**age** [edʒ] *s* età *f;* (*old age*) vecchiaia; (*full term of life*) vita; (*historical or geological period*) evo; generazione; **of age** maggiorenne; **to come of age** diventare maggiorenne; **under age** minorenne ‖ *tr & intr* invecchiare
**aged** [edʒd] *adj* dell'età di ‖ ['edʒɪd] *adj* vecchio, invecchiato
**ageless** ['edʒlɪs] *adj* eternamente giovane, che non invecchia mai
**agen·cy** ['edʒənsɪ] *s* (**-cies**) azione; agenzia; mediazione; (*of government*) ente *m*
**agenda** [ə'dʒɛndə] *s* agenda, ordine *m* del giorno
**agent** ['edʒənt] *s* agente *m;* (coll) commesso viaggiatore, agente *m* di commercio; (rr) gestore *m*
**Age' of Enlight'enment** *s* illuminismo
**agglomeration** [ə ˌglɑmə'reʃən] *s* agglomerazione
**aggrandizement** [ə'grændɪzmənt] *s* aumento, innalzamento
**aggravate** ['ægrə ˌvet] *tr* aggravare; (coll) irritare, esasperare
**aggregate** ['ægrɪ ˌget] *adj & s* aggregato, totale *m;* **in the aggregate** nel complesso ‖ *tr* aggregare; ammontare a
**aggression** [ə'greʃən] *s* aggressione
**aggressive** [ə'gresɪv] *adj* aggressivo, attivo
**aggressor** [ə'gresər] *s* aggressore *m*
**aggrieve** [ə'griv] *tr* affliggere
**aghast** [ə'gæst] or [ə'gɑst] *adj* atterrito
**agile** ['ædʒɪl] *adj* agile
**agitate** ['ædʒɪ ˌtet] *tr* agitare ‖ *intr* agitarsi
**agitator** ['ædʒɪ ˌtetər] *s* agitatore *m*
**aglow** [ə'glo] *adj* splendente
**agnostic** [æg'nɑstɪk] *adj & s* agnostico
**ago** [ə'go] *adv* fa, e.g., **a year ago** un anno fa; **long ago** molto tempo fa
**agog** [ə'gɑg] *adj & adv* ansioso; **to set agog** riempire di ansietà
**agonize** ['ægə ˌnaɪz] *intr* soffrire straziantemente; (*to struggle*) dibattersi
**ago·ny** ['ægənɪ] *s* (**-nies**) agonia

**agrarian** [ə'grerɪ·ən] *adj* agrario ‖ *s* membro del partito agrario
**agree** [ə'gri] *intr* aderire, andar d'accordo; (*to consent*) acconsentire; (gram) concordare; **to agree with** confarsi a, e.g., **eggs do not agree with him** le uova non gli si confanno
**agreeable** [ə'gri·əbəl] *adj* gentile; gradevole; (*willing to agree*) consenziente
**agreement** [ə'grimənt] *s* accordo; **in agreement** d'accordo
**agriculture** ['ægrɪ ˌkʌltʃər] *s* agricoltura
**agriculturist** [ ˌægrɪ'kʌltʃərɪst] *s* (*farmer*) agricoltore *m;* perito in agricoltura, agronomo
**agronomy** [ə'grɑnəmɪ] *s* agronomia
**aground** [ə'graund] *adv* alla riva; **to run aground** andare or dare in secca
**ague** ['egju] *s* (*chill*) brivido; febbre *f*
**ahead** [ə'hɛd] *adv* davanti, avanti; **to get ahead** (coll) andare avanti, aver successo; **to get ahead of** sorpassare; **to go ahead** avanzare; continuare
**ahoy** [ə'hɔɪ] *interj*—**ship ahoy!** ehi della barca!
**aid** [ed] *s* aiuto; assistente *m;* (mil) aiutante *m* di campo ‖ *tr* aiutare; **to aid and abet** essere complice di
**aide** [ed] *s* assistente *m*
**aide-de-camp** ['eddə'kæmp] *s* (**aides-de-camp**) aiutante *m* di campo
**ail** [el] *tr* affliggere; **what ails you?** che ha? ‖ *intr* soffrire, essere malato
**aileron** ['elə ˌrɑn] *s* alerone *m*
**ailing** ['elɪŋ] *adj* ammalato
**ailment** ['elmənt] *s* malattia, indisposizione; (*chronic*) acciacco
**aim** [em] *s* mira; intento ‖ *tr* (*a gun*) puntare; (*words*) dirigere ‖ *intr* mirare; **to aim to** cercare di, aver l'intenzione di
**air** [er] *adj* (*e.g., pocket*) d'aria; (*e.g., show*) aeronautico ‖ *s* aria; **by air** per via aerea; **in the open air** all'aria aperta; **to be in the air** circolare; **to be on the air** (rad, telv) essere in onda; **to go on the air** (rad, telv) andare in onda; **to put on airs** darsi delle arie; **to take the air** andar fuori; **up in the air** incerto; (slang) arrabbiato ‖ *tr* aerare, ventilare
**airborne** ['er ˌbɔrn] or ['er ˌborn] *adj* aerosostentato; aerotrasportato
**air' brake'** *s* freno ad aria compressa
**air' cas'tle** *s* castello in aria
**air'-condi'tion** *tr* climatizzare
**air' condi'tioner** *s* condizionatore *m*
**air' condi'tioning** *s* aria condizionata, climatizzazione
**air-'cool'** *tr* raffreddare con aria
**air' corps'** *s* aviazione, arma aeronautica
**air'craft'** *s* (**-craft**) aeromobile *m*
**air'craft car'rier** *s* portaerei *f*
**airdrome** ['er ˌdrom] *s* aerodromo
**air'drop'** *tr* paracadutare
**air'field'** *s* campo d'aviazione
**air'foil'** *s* superficie *f* portante, velatura
**air' force'** *s* forza aerea
**air' gap'** *s* (elec) intraferro

**airing** ['erɪŋ] *s* aerazione; passeggiata all'aria aperta; pubblica discussione
**air' jack'et** *s* (aer, naut) giubbotto salvagente
**air' lane'** *s* aerovia
**air'lift'** *s* ponte aereo, aerotrasporto ‖ *tr* aerotrasportare
**air'line'** *s* linea aerea; tubo dell'aria
**air' mail'** *s* posta aerea
**air'-mail'** *adj* per via aerea ‖ *s* lettera per posta aerea ‖ *adv* per posta aerea ‖ *tr* spedire per posta aerea
**air'-mail let'ter** *s* lettera per posta aerea
**air'-mail stamp'** *s* francobollo posta aerea
**air'man** *s* (-men) aviatore *m*, aviere *m*
**air' mat'tress** *s* materassino pneumatico
**air'plane'** *s* aeroplano, aereo
**air'plane car'rier** *s* portaerei *f*
**air' pock'et** *s* vuoto d'aria
**air' pollu'tion** *s* contaminazione atmosferica, inquinamento atmosferico
**air' port'** *s* aeroporto
**air' pump'** *s* pompa pneumatica
**air' raid'** *s* incursione aerea
**air'-raid shel'ter** *s* rifugio antiaereo
**air'-raid warn'ing** *s* allerta
**air' ri'fle** *s* fucile *m* ad aria compressa
**air' serv'ice** *s* aeroservizio
**air' shaft'** *s* tubo di ventilazione
**air'ship'** *s* aeronave *f*
**airsickness** ['ɛr ˌsɪknɪs] *s* male *m* d'aria
**air' sleeve'** *s* manica a vento
**airspace** ['ɛr ˌspes] *s* aerospazio
**air'strip'** *s* aviopista
**air' ter'minal** *s* aerostazione
**air'tight'** *adj* impermeabile all'aria, ermetico
**air'waves'** *spl* onde *fpl*, radioonde *fpl*
**air'way'** *s* aerovia; **airways** (rad) onda, onde *fpl*
**air·y** ['ɛri] *adj* (-ier; -iest) arioso; leggero; aereo
**aisle** [aɪl] *s* (*between rows of seats*) corsia; (*of a church*) navata laterale; (theat) canale *m*
**ajar** [ə'dʒɑr] *adj* socchiuso; in disaccordo
**akimbo** [ə'kɪmbo] *adj* & *adv*—**with arms akimbo** con le mani sui fianchi
**akin** [ə'kɪn] *adj* affine; congiunto
**alabaster** ['ælə ˌbæstər] *or* ['ælə-ˌbɑstər]*s* alabastro
**à la carte** [ ˌalə 'kɑrt] *adv* alla carta
**à la mode** [ ˌalə 'mod] *or* [ ˌælə 'mod] *adv* alla moda; servito con gelato
**alarm** [ə'lɑrm] *s* allarme *m* ‖ *tr* allarmare
**alarm' clock'** *s* sveglia
**alas** [ə'læs] *or* [ə'lɑs] *interj* ahimé!; povero me!
**Albanian** [æl'benɪ·ən] *adj* & *s* albanese *mf*
**albatross** ['ælbə ˌtrɔs] *or* ['ælbə ˌtrɑs] *s* albatro, diomedea
**album** ['ælbəm] *s* album *m*
**albumen** [æl'bjumən] *s* albume *m*
**alchemy** ['ælkəmi] *s* alchimia
**alcohol** ['ælkə ˌhɔl] *or* ['ælkə ˌhɑl] *s* alcole *m*
**alcoholic** [ ˌælkə 'hɔlɪk] *or* [ ˌælkə 'hɑlɪk] *adj* alcolico ‖ *s* alcolizzato

**alcove** ['ælkov] *s* (*recess*) alcova; (*in a garden*) chiosco, padiglione *m;* cameretta attigua
**alder** ['ɔldər] *s* ontano, alno
**al'der·man** *s* (-men) assessore *m* municipale, consigliere *m* municipale
**ale** [el] *s* birra amara
**alembic** [ə'lɛmbɪk] *s* alambicco
**alert** [ə'lʌrt] *adj* attento; vispo ‖ *s* allerta; **to be on the alert** stare allerta ‖ *tr* dare l'allerta a
**Aleu'tian Is'lands** [ə'luʃən] *spl* Isole Aleutine
**Alexander** [ ˌælɪg'zændər] *or* [ ˌælɪg-'zɑndər] *s* Alessandro
**Alexan'der the Great'** *s* Alessandro Magno
**Alexandrine** [ ˌælɪg'zændrɪn] *adj* & *s* alessandrino
**alfalfa** [æl'fælfə] *s* (bot) erba medica
**algae** ['ældʒi] *spl* alghe *fpl*
**algebra** ['ældʒɪbrə] *s* algebra
**algebraic** [ ˌældʒɪ'bre·ɪk] *adj* algebrico
**Algeria** [æl'dʒɪrɪ·ə] *s* l'Algeria
**Algerian** [æl'dʒɪrɪ·ən] *adj* & *s* algerino
**Algiers** [æl'dʒɪrz] *s* Algeri *f*
**alias** ['elɪ·əs] *s* pseudonimo ‖ *adv* alias
**ali·bi** ['ælɪ ˌbaɪ] *s* (-bis) alibi *m*
**alien** ['eljən] *or* ['elɪ·ən] *adj* straniero; (*strange*) strano ‖ *s* straniero; (*outsider*) estraneo
**alienate** ['eljə ˌnet] *or* ['elɪ·ə ˌnet] *tr* alienare
**alight** [ə'laɪt] *v* (*pret & pp* **alighted** or **alit** [ə'lɪt]) *intr* scendere; **to alight on** or **upon** posarsi su
**align** [ə'laɪn] *tr* allineare ‖ *intr* allinearsi
**alike** [ə'laɪk] *adj* uguali; **to look alike** assomigliarsi ‖ *adv* nello stesso modo
**alimen'tary canal'** [ ˌælɪ'mɛntəri] *s* tubo digestivo
**alimony** ['ælɪ ˌmoni] *s* alimonia
**alive** [ə'laɪv] *adj* vivo, in vita; (*lively*) vivace; **alive to** conscio di; **alive with** brulicante di, pieno zeppo di; **look alive!** fa presto!
**alka·li** ['ælkə ˌlaɪ] *s* (-lis or -lies) alcali *m*
**alkaline** ['ælkə ˌlaɪn] *or* ['ælkəlɪn] *adj* alcalino
**all** [ɔl] *adj indef* tutto, tutto il, ogni ‖ *s* tutto ‖ *pron* tutto; tutti; **all of** tutti ‖ *adv* completamente; **all but** quasi; **all in** (slang) stanco morto; **all in all** tutto considerato; **all the better** tanto meglio; **all the worse** tanto peggio; **far all that** per quello che, e.g., **for all that I know** per quello che io ne sappia; **in all** tutto contato; **it's all right!** va bene!; **not at all** niente affatto; prego
**allay** [ə'le] *tr* calmare, mitigare
**all' clear'** *s* fine *f* dell'allarme, cessato allarme
**allegation** [ ˌælɪ'geʃən] *s* asserzione, affermazione
**allege** [ə'lɛdʒ] *tr* asserire, affermare; addurre
**allegiance** [ə'lidʒəns] *s* fedeltà *f*, lealtà *f*

**allegoric(al)** [ˌælɪˈgɑrɪk(əl)] or [ˌælɪˈgɔrɪk(əl)] *adj* allegorico
**allego·ry** [ˈælɪˌgori] *s* (**-ries**) allegoria
**aller·gy** [ˈælərdʒi] *s* (**-gies**) allergia
**alleviate** [əˈliviˌet] *tr* alleviare
**alley** [ˈæli] *s* vicolo, calle *f;* (*for bowling*) pista; (*tennis*) corridoio
**All' Fools' Day'** *s* primo d'aprile
**all' fours'** *spl*—**on all fours** a quattro gambe
**alliance** [əˈlaɪ·əns] *s* alleanza
**alligator** [ˈælɪˌgetər] *s* alligatore *m*
**alliteration** [əˌlɪtəˈreʃən] *s* allitterazione
**all-knowing** [ˈɔlˈno·ɪŋ] *adj* onnisciente
**allocate** [ˈæləˌket] *tr* assegnare; (*funds*) stanziare; (*to fix the place of*) allogare
**allot** [əˈlɑt] *v* (*pret & pp* **allotted;** *ger* **allotting**) *tr* distribuire, assegnare
**all'-out'** *adj* completo; (*ruthless*) acerrimo
**allow** [əˈlaʊ] *tr* permettere; ammettere; concedere ‖ *intr* **to allow for** prendere in considerazione
**allowance** [əˈlaʊ·əns] *s* (*limited share*) assegno; concessione; (*reduction in price*) sconto; tolleranza; **to make allowance for** prendere in considerazione
**alloy** [ˈælɔɪ] or [əˈlɔɪ] *s* lega; impurezza ‖ [əˈlɔɪ] *tr* far lega di, legare; adulterare
**all-powerful** [ˈɔlˈpaʊ·ərfəl] *adj* onnipotente
**all' right'** *adj* esatto; bene; in buona salute; (slang) dabbene
**All' Saints'' Day'** *s* Ognissanti *m*
**All' Souls'' Day'** *s* giorno dei morti
**all'spice'** *s* pimento, pepe *m* della Giamaica
**all'-star game'** *s* partita sportiva in cui tutti i giocatori sono scelti fra i migliori
**allude** [əˈlud] *intr* alludere
**allure** [əˈlʊr] *s* fascino, incanto ‖ *tr* affascinare, incantare
**alluring** [əˈlʊrɪŋ] *adj* affascinante, seducente
**allusion** [əˈluʃən] *s* allusione
**al·ly** [ˈælaɪ] or [əˈlaɪ] *s* (**-lies**) alleato ‖ [əˈlaɪ] *v* (*pret & pp* **-lied**) *tr* alleare; associare; **to become allied** allearsi; imparentarsi ‖ *intr* allearsi
**almanac** [ˈɔlməˌnæk] *s* almanacco
**almighty** [ɔlˈmaɪti] *adj* onnipotente
**almond** [ˈɑmənd] or [ˈæmənd] *s* (*nut*) mandorla; (*tree*) mandorlo
**al'mond brittle'** *s* croccante *m*
**almost** [ˈɔlmost] or [ɔlˈmost] *adv* quasi
**alms** [ɑmz] *s* elemosina
**aloe** [ˈælo] *s* aloe *m*
**aloft** [əˈlɔft] or [əˈlɑft] *adv* in alto, sopra; (aer) in volo; (naut) nell'alberatura
**alone** [əˈlon] *adj* solo; **let alone** senza menzionare; **to leave alone** non disturbare ‖ *adv* solo, solamente
**along** [əˈlɔŋ] or [əˈlɑŋ] *adv* (*lengthwise*) per il lungo; (*onward*) avanti; **all along** tutto il tempo; **along with**

con; **to get along** andar d'accordo; andarsene; avanzare; aver successo; **to take along** prendere con sè ‖ *prep* lungo
**along'side'** *adv* a lato; **alongside of** a lato di ‖ *prep* a lato di, vicino a
**aloof** [əˈluf] *adj* riservato, freddo; **to keep** or **stand aloof from** tenersi a distanza da ‖ *adv* lontano; da solo
**aloud** [əˈlaʊd] *adv* ad alta voce
**alphabet** [ˈælfəˌbet] *s* alfabeto
**alpine** [ˈælpaɪn] *adj* alpino
**Alps** [ælps] *spl* Alpi *fpl*
**already** [ɔlˈredi] *adv* già
**Alsace** [ælˈses] or [ˈælsæs] *s* l'Alsazia
**Alsatian** [ælˈseʃən] *adj & s* alsaziano
**also** [ˈɔlso] *adv* anche
**altar** [ˈɔltər] *s* altare *m*
**al'tar boy'** *s* accolito, chierico
**al'tar-piece'** *s* pala d'altare
**alter** [ˈɔltər] *tr* alterare; (*a male animal*) castrare ‖ *intr* diventare differente, cambiare
**alteration** [ˌɔltəˈreʃən] *s* alterazione, modifica
**alternate** [ˈɔltərnɪt] or [ˈæltərnɪt] *s* sostituto, supplente *mf* ‖ [ˈɔltərˌnet] or [ˈæltərˌnet] *tr* alternare ‖ *intr* alternarsi, avvicendarsi
**al'ternating cur'rent** *s* corrente alternata
**alternator** [ˈɔltərˌnetər] or [ˈæltərˌnetər] *s* alternatore *m*
**although** [ɔlˈðo] *conj* benchè, per quanto, malgrado
**altimeter** [ælˈtɪmɪtər] or [ˈæltəˌmitər] *s* altimetro
**altitude** [ˈæltɪˌtjud] or [ˈæltɪˌtud] *s* altitudine *f*
**al·to** [ˈælto] *s* (**-tos**) contralto
**altogether** [ˌɔltəˈgeðər] *adv* completamente, affatto, tutt'insieme
**altruist** [ˈæltru·ɪst] *s* altruista *mf*
**altruistic** [ˌæltruˈɪstɪk] *adj* altruistico
**alum** [ˈæləm] *s* allume *m*
**aluminum** [əˈlumɪnəm] *s* alluminio
**alum·na** [əˈlʌmnə] *s* (**-nae** [ni]) diplomata, laureata
**alum·nus** [əˈlʌmnəs] *s* (**-ni** [naɪ]) diplomato, laureato
**always** [ˈɔlwɪz] or [ˈɔlwez] *adv* sempre
**amalgam** [əˈmælgəm] *s* amalgama *m*
**amalgamate** [əˈmælgəˌmet] *tr* amalgamare ‖ *intr* amalgamarsi
**amass** [əˈmæs] *tr* ammassare
**amateur** [ˈæmətˌər] *adj* da dilettante ‖ *s* amatore *m*, dilettante *mf*
**amaze** [əˈmez] *tr* stupire, meravigliare
**amazing** [əˈmezɪŋ] *adj* straordinario
**Amazon** [ˈæməˌzɑn] or [ˈæməzən] *s* rio delle Amazzoni; (myth) Amazzone *f*
**ambassador** [æmˈbæsədər] *s* ambasciatore *m*
**ambassadress** [æmˈbæsədrɪs] *s* ambasciatrice *f*
**amber** [ˈæmbər] *s* ambra
**ambigui·ty** [ˌæmbɪˈgju·ɪti] *s* (**-ties**) ambiguità *f*
**ambiguous** [æmˈbɪgju·əs] *adj* ambiguo

**ambition** [æm'bɪʃən] *s* ambízione
**ambitious** [æm'bɪʃəs] *adj* ambizioso
**amble** ['æmbəl] *s* ambio ‖ *intr* ambiare
**ambulance** ['æmbjələns] *s* ambulanza
**ambush** ['æmbʊʃ] *s* imboscata; **to lie in ambush** tendere un'imboscata ‖ *tr* appostare ‖ *intr* appostarsi
**amelioration** [ə‚miljə're/ən] *s* miglioramento
**amen** ['e'men] or ['ɑ'men] *s* amen *m* ‖ *interj* amen!
**amenable** [ə'minəbəl] or [ə'menəbəl] *adj* docile, aperto; (*accountable*) responsabile
**amend** [ə'mend] *tr* emendare ‖ **amends** *spl* ammenda, contravvenzione; **to make amends for** fare ammenda per
**amendment** [ə'mendmənt] *s* emendamento
**ameni·ty** [ə'minɪti] or [ə'menɪti] *s* (**-ties**) amenità *f*
**American** [ə'merɪkən] *adj* & *s* americano
**Americanize** [ə'merɪkə‚naɪz] *tr* americanizzare
**amethyst** ['æmɪθɪst] *s* ametista
**amiable** ['emɪ·əbəl] *adj* amabile
**amicable** ['æmɪkəbəl] *adj* amichevole
**amid** [ə'mɪd] *prep* in mezzo a, fra, tra
**amidship** [ə'mɪd/ɪp] *adv* a mezzanave
**amiss** [ə'mɪs] *adj* erroneo, sbagliato ‖ *adv* erroneamente; **to take amiss** offendersi, prendere in mala parte
**ami·ty** ['æmɪti] *s* (**-ties**) amicizia
**ammeter** ['æm‚mitər] *s* amperometro
**ammonia** [ə'monɪ·ə] *s* ammoniaca; acqua ammoniacale
**ammunition** [‚æmjə'nɪʃən] *s* munizione, munizioni *fpl*
**amnes·ty** ['æmnɪsti] *s* (**-ties**) amnistia ‖ *v* (*pret* & *pp* **-tied**) *tr* amnistiare
**amoeba** [ə'mibə] *s* ameba
**among** [ə'mʌŋ] *prep* fra, tra, in mezzo a
**amorous** ['æmərəs] *adj* amoroso; erotico
**amortize** ['æmər‚taɪz] *tr* ammortare
**amount** [ə'maʊnt] *s* ammontare *m* ‖ *intr*—**to amount to** ammontare a
**ampere** ['æmpɪr] *s* ampere *m*
**am'pere-hour'** *s* amperora *m*
**amphibious** [æm'fɪbɪ·əs] *adj* anfibio
**amphitheater** ['æmfɪ‚θi·ətər] *s* anfiteatro
**ample** ['æmpəl] *adj* ampio
**amplifier** ['æmplɪ‚faɪ·ər] *s* amplificatore *m*
**ampli·fy** ['æmplɪ‚faɪ] *v* (*pret* & *pp* **-fied**) *tr* amplificare
**amplitude** ['æmplɪ‚tjud] or ['æmplɪ‚tud] *s* ampiezza
**am'plitude modula'tion** *s* modulazione d'ampiezza
**amputate** ['æmpjə‚tet] *tr* amputare
**amputee** [‚æmpjə'ti] *s* chi ha subito l'amputazione di un arto
**amuck** [ə'mʌk] *adv* freneticamente; **to run amuck** dare in un accesso di pazzia; attaccare alla cieca
**amulet** ['æmjəlɪt] *s* amuleto
**amuse** [ə'mjuz] *tr* divertire

**amusement** [ə'mjuzmənt] *s* divertimento
**amuse'ment park'** *s* parco dei divertimenti, luna park *m*
**amusing** [ə'mjuzɪŋ] *adj* divertente
**an** [æn] or [ən] *art indef* var of **a**, used before words beginning with vowel or mute *h*
**anachronism** [ə'nækrə‚nɪzəm] *s* anacronismo
**anaemia** [ə'nimɪ·ə] *s* var of **anemia**
**anaesthesia** [‚ænɪs'θiʒə] *s* anestesia
**anaesthetic** [‚ænɪs'θetɪk] *adj* & *s* anestetico
**anaesthetize** [æ'nesθɪ‚taɪz] *tr* anestetizzare
**analogous** [ə'næləgəs] *adj* analogo
**analo·gy** [ə'nælədʒi] *s* (**-gies**) analogia
**analy·sis** [ə'nælɪsɪs] *s* (**-ses** [‚siz]) analisi *f*
**analyst** ['ænəlɪst] *s* analista *mf*
**analytic(al)** [‚ænə'lɪtɪk(əl)] *adj* analitico
**analyze** ['ænə‚laɪz] *tr* analizzare
**anarchist** ['ænərkɪst] *s* anarchico
**anarchy** ['ænərki] *s* anarchia
**anathema** [ə'næθɪmə] *s* anatema *m*
**anatomic(al)** [‚ænə'tɑmɪk(əl)] *adj* anatomico
**anato·my** [ə'nætəmi] *s* (**-mies**) anatomia
**ancestor** ['ænsestər] *s* antenato
**ances·try** ['ænsestri] *s* (**-tries**) lignaggio, prosapia
**anchor** ['æŋkər] *s* ancora; **to cast anchor** gettare l'ancora; **to ride at anchor** stare all'ancora; **to weigh anchor** salpare l'ancora, salpare ‖ *tr* ancorare ‖ *intr* ancorarsi, stare all'ancora
**ancho·vy** ['ænt/ovi] *s* (**-vies**) acciuga
**ancient** ['en/ənt] *adj* antico ‖ *s* vecchio, anziano; **the ancients** gli antichi
**ancillary** ['ænsɪ‚leri] *adj* dipendente; ausiliario, ausiliare
**and** [ænd] or [ənd] *conj* e, ed; **and so on, and so forth** e così via
**Andean** [æn'di·ən] or ['ændɪ·ən] *adj* andino ‖ *s* abitante *mf* della regione andina
**Andes** ['ændiz] *spl* Ande *fpl*
**andiron** ['ænd‚aɪ·ərn] *s* alare *m*
**anecdote** ['ænɪk‚dot] *s* aneddoto
**anemia** [ə'nimɪ·ə] *s* anemia
**anemic** [ə'nimɪk] *adj* anemico
**an'eroid barom'eter** ['ænə‚rɔɪd] *s* barometro aneroide
**anesthesia** [‚ænɪs'θiʒə] *s* anestesia
**anesthetic** [‚ænɪs'θetɪk] *adj* & *s* anestetico
**anesthetize** [æ'nesθɪ‚taɪz] *tr* anestetizzare
**aneurysm** ['ænjə‚rɪzəm] *s* aneurisma *m*
**anew** [ə'nju] or [ə'nu] *adv* di nuovo, nuovamente
**angel** ['endʒəl] *s* angelo; (*financial backer*) (coll) finanziatore *m*
**angelic(al)** [æn'dʒelɪk(əl)] *adj* angelico
**anger** ['æŋgər] *s* ira, collera ‖ *tr* adirare ‖ *intr* adirarsi, incollerirsi
**angle** ['æŋgəl] *s* angolo; punto di vista

|| *intr* intrigare; **to angle for** darsi da fare per

**an'gle i'ron** *s* cantonale *m*, angolare *m*

**angler** ['æŋglər] *s* pescatore *m* alla lenza; (fig) intrigante *m*

**Anglo-Saxon** ['æŋglo'sæksən] *adj* & *s* anglosassone *mf*

**an·gry** ['æŋgri] *adj* (**-grier; -griest**) arrabbiato; (pathol) infiammato; **to become angry at** incollerirsi per; **to become angry with** adirarsi con

**anguish** ['æŋgwɪʃ] *s* angoscia, pena

**angular** ['æŋgjələr] *adj* angolare

**anhydrous** [æn'haɪdrəs] *adj* anidro

**aniline** ['ænɪlɪn] or ['ænɪ,laɪn] *s* anilina

**animal** ['ænɪməl] *adj* & *s* animale *m*

**an'imated cartoon'** ['ænɪ,metɪd] *s* cartone animato

**animation** [,ænɪ'meʃən] *s* animazione

**animosi·ty** [,ænɪ'masɪti] *s* (**-ties**) animosità *f*

**animus** ['ænɪməs] *s* odio, malanimo

**anion** ['æn,aɪ·ən] *s* anione *m*

**anise** ['ænɪs] *s* anice *f*

**anisette** [,ænɪ'zɛt] *s* anisetta

**ankle** ['æŋkəl] *s* caviglia

**an'kle·bone'** *s* malleolo

**an'kle support'** *s* cavigliera

**anklet** ['æŋklɪt] *s* calzino corto; bracciale *m* da caviglia

**annals** ['ænəlz] *spl* annali *mpl*

**annex** ['ænɛks] *s* annesso, dipendenza || [ə'nɛks] *tr* annettere, appropriarsi di

**annihilate** [ə'naɪ·ɪ,let] *tr* annientare

**anniversa·ry** [,ænɪ'vʌrsəri] *adj* anniversario || *s* (**-ries**) anniversario

**annotate** ['ænə,tet] *tr* annotare

**announce** [ə'naʊns] *tr* annunciare

**announcement** [ə'naʊnsmənt] *s* annuncio, partecipazione

**announcer** [ə'naʊnsər] *s* annunziatore *m*

**annoy** [ə'nɔɪ] *tr* annoiare, seccare

**annoyance** [ə'nɔɪ·əns] *s* fastidio, seccatura

**annoying** [ə'nɔɪ·ɪŋ] *adj* noioso

**annual** ['ænju·əl] *adj* annuale || *s* annuario; pianta annuale

**annui·ty** [ə'nju·ɪti] or [ə'nu·ɪti] *s* (**-ties**) annualità *f*; (for life) vitalizio

**an·nul** [ə'nʌl] *v* (*pret* & *pp* **-nulled;** *ger* **-nulling**) *tr* annullare, cassare

**annunciation** [ə,nʌnsɪ'eʃən] *s* annunzio || **Annunciation** *s* Annunciazione

**anode** ['ænod] *s* anodo

**anoint** [ə'nɔɪnt] *tr* ungere

**anomalous** [ə'namələs] *adj* anomalo

**anoma·ly** [ə'naməli] *s* (**-lies**) anomalia

**anonymi·ty** [,ænə'nɪmɪti] *s* (**-ties**) anonimia; **to preserve one's anonymity** serbare l'anonimo

**anonymous** [ə'nanɪməs] *adj* anonimo

**another** [ə'nʌðər] *adj* & *pron indef* un altro

**answer** ['ænsər] or ['ansər] *s* risposta; (to a problem) soluzione || *tr* rispondere a; **this will answer your purpose** questo fa per Lei; **to answer back** (slang) dare una rispostaccia a; **to answer the door** andare a rispondere

|| *intr* rispondere; corrispondere; essere responsabile; **to answer back** (slang) dare una rispostaccia

**ant** [ænt] *s* formica

**antagonism** [æn'tægə,nɪzəm] *s* antagonismo

**antagonize** [æn'tægə,naɪz] *tr* opporsi a; creare antagonismo in

**antarctic** [ænt'arktɪk] *adj* antartico || **the Antarctic** la regione antartica

**anteater** ['ænt,itər] *s* formichiere *m*

**antecedent** [,æntɪ'sidənt] *adj* & *s* antecedente *m;* **antecedents** antenati *mpl*

**antechamber** ['æntɪ,tʃembər] *s* anticamera

**antedate** ['æntɪ,det] *tr* antidatare; (to happen before) antecedere

**antelope** ['æntɪ,lop] *s* antilope *f*

**anten·na** [æn'tɛnə] *s* (**-nae** [ni]) (of insect) antenna || *s* (**-nas**) (rad, telv) antenna

**antepenult** [,æntɪ'pinʌlt] *s* terzultima sillaba

**anteroom** ['æntɪ,rum] or ['æntɪ,rʊm] *s* anticamera, sala d'aspetto

**anthem** ['ænθəm] *s* inno

**ant'hill'** *s* formicaio

**antholo·gy** [æn'θalədʒi] *s* (**-gies**) antologia

**anthracite** ['ænθrə,saɪt] *s* antracite *f*

**anthrax** ['ænθræks] *s* antrace *m*

**anthropoid** ['ænθrə,pɔɪd] *adj* antropoide, antropomorfo

**anthropology** [,ænθrə'palədʒi] *s* antropologia

**antiaircraft** [,æntɪ'ɛr,kræft] or [,æntɪ'ɛr,kraft] *adj* antiaereo

**antibiotic** [,æntɪbaɪ'atɪk] *adj* & *s* antibiotico

**antibod·y** ['æntɪ,badi] *s* (**-ies**) anticorpo

**anticipate** [æn'tɪsɪ,pet] *tr* anticipare, prevedere; ripromettersi

**anticipation** [æn,tɪsɪ'peʃən] *s* anticipazione, previsione

**antics** ['æntɪks] *spl* pagliacciate *fpl*, buffonate *fpl*

**antidote** ['æntɪ,dot] *s* antidoto

**antifreeze** ['æntɪ,friz] *s* anticongelante *m*

**antiglare** [,æntɪ'glɛr] *adj* antiabbagliante

**anti-G' suit'** *s* tuta antigravità

**antiknock** [,æntɪ'nak] *adj* antidetonante

**antimissile** [,æntɪ'mɪsɪl] *adj* antimissile

**antimony** ['æntɪ,moni] *s* antimonio

**antinoise** [,æntɪ'nɔɪz] *adj* antirumore

**antipa·thy** [æn'tɪpəθi] *s* (**-thies**) antipatia

**antipersonnel** [,æntɪ,pʌrsə'nɛl] *adj* (e.g., mine) antiuomo

**antiquarian** [,æntɪ'kwɛrɪ·ən] *adj* & *s* antiquario

**antiquar·y** ['æntɪ,kwɛri] *s* (**-ies**) antiquario

**antiquated** ['æntɪ,kwetɪd] *adj* antiquato

**antique** [æn'tik] *adj* antico, vecchio; antiquato || *s* oggetto d'epoca, antichità *f*

**antique' deal'er** *s* antiquario
**antique' store'** *s* negozio d'antiquariato
**antiqui·ty** [æn'tıkwıti] *s* (**-ties**) antichità *f*
**anti-Semitic** [ˌæntısı'mıtık] *adj* antisemita
**antiseptic** [ˌæntı'septık] *adj & s* antisettico
**antislavery** [ˌæntı'sleveri] *adj* antischiavista
**antitank** [ˌæntı'tæŋk] *adj* anticarro
**antitheft** [ˌæntı'θeft] *adj* antifurto
**antithe·sis** [æn'tıθısıs] *s* (**-ses** [ˌsiz]) antitesi *f*
**antitoxin** [ˌæntı'taksın] *s* antitossina
**antitrust** [ˌæntı'trʌst] *adj* antitrust
**antler** ['æntlər] *s* corno di cervo
**antonym** ['æntənım] *s* antonimo
**Antwerp** ['æntwərp] *s* Anversa
**anvil** ['ænvıl] *s* incudine *m*
**anxie·ty** [æŋ'zaı·əti] *s* (**-ties**) ansietà *f; (psychol)* angoscia
**anxious** ['æŋkʃəs] *adj* ansioso; **anxious about** sollecito di; **anxious for** desideroso di
**any** ['eni] *adj indef* ogni, qualunque, qualsiasi; qualche, e.g., **do you know any boy who could help me?** conosce qualche ragazzo che possa aiutarmi?; di + *art*, e.g., **do you want any cheese?** vuole del formaggio?; **not . . . any** non . . . nessuno, e.g., **he does not read any newspaper** non legge nessun giornale ‖ *adv* un po', e.g., **do you want any?** ne vuole un po'?; **not . . . any longer** non . . . più; **not . . . any more** non . . . più ‖ *pron* ne, e.g., **do you want any?** ne vuole?
**an'y·bod'y** *pron indef* chiunque; *(in interrogative sentences)* qualcuno; **not . . . anybody** non . . . nessuno
**an'y·how'** *adv* in qualunque modo, comunque; in ogni caso; *(haphazardly)* alla rinfusa
**an'y·one'** *pron indef* chiunque; *(in interrogative sentences)* qualcuno; **not . . . anyone** non . . . nessuno
**an'y·thing'** *s* qualunque cosa ‖ *pron indef* qualcosa; qualunque cosa; tutto quanto; checchessia; **anything at all** qualunque cosa; **not . . . anything** non . . . niente; **not . . . anything at all** non . . . niente affatto, non . . . nulla; **not . . . anything else** non . . . nient'altro
**an'y·way'** *adv* in qualunque modo, comunque; in ogni caso; *(haphazardly)* alla rinfusa
**an'y·where'** *adv* dovunque, in qualsiasi luogo; **not . . . anywhere** non . . . in nessun luogo
**apace** [ə'pes] *adv* presto, rapidamente
**apart** [ə'part] *adv* a parte, a pezzi; separatamente; **apart from** a parte da; oltre a; **to come apart** andare a pezzi, cadere a pezzi; **to set apart** mettere in disparte; **to take apart** smontare; **to tear apart** fare a pezzi; **to tell apart** distinguere
**apartment** [ə'partmənt] *s* appartamento; *(single room)* stanza

**apart'ment house'** *s* casa d'appartamenti
**apathetic** [ˌæpə'θetık] *adj* apatico
**apathy** ['æpəθi] *s* apatia
**ape** [ep] *s* scimmia antropomorfa; scimmia ‖ *tr* imitare, scimmiottare
**Apennines** ['æpəˌnaınz] *spl* Appennini *mpl*
**aperture** ['æpərtʃər] *s* apertura
**apex** ['epeks] *s* (**apexes** or **apices** ['æpıˌsiz]) apice *m*
**apheresis** [ə'ferısıs] *s* aferesi *f*
**aphorism** ['æfəˌrızəm] *s* aforisma *m*
**aphrodisiac** [ˌæfrə'dızıˌæk] *adj & s* afrodisiaco
**apiar·y** ['epiˌeri] *s* (**-ies**) apiario
**apiece** [ə'pis] *adv* a testa, per persona; ciascuno
**apish** ['epıʃ] *adj* scimmiesco; da scimmia
**aplomb** [ə'plam] *s* disinvoltura, baldanza
**apocalypse** [ə'pakəˌlıps] *s* apocalisse *f*
**apogee** ['æpəˌdʒi] *s* apogeo
**apologetic** [əˌpalə'dʒetık] *adj* pieno di scuse
**apologize** [ə'paləˌdʒaız] *intr* chiedere scusa, scusarsi
**apolo·gy** [ə'palədʒi] *s* (**-gies**) scusa; *(makeshift)* surrogato
**apoplectic** [ˌæpə'plektık] *adj & s* apoplettico
**apoplexy** ['æpəˌpleksi] *s* apoplessia
**apostle** [ə'pasəl] *s* apostolo
**apostrophe** [ə'pastrəfi] *s (mark)* apostrofo; *(rhet)* apostrofe *f*
**apothecar·y** [ə'paθıˌkeri] *s* (**-ies**) farmacista *mf*
**appall** [ə'pɔl] *tr* sgomentare, sbigottire
**appalling** [ə'pɔlıŋ] *adj* sconcertante
**appara·tus** [ˌæpə'retəs] or [ˌæpə'rætəs] *s* (**-tus** or **-tuses**) apparato
**apparel** [ə'pærəl] *s* confezioni *fpl*, vestiario
**apparent** [ə'pærənt] or [ə'perənt] *adj* apparente; chiaramente visibile
**apparition** [ˌæpə'rıʃən] *s* apparizione
**appeal** [ə'pil] *s* appello; *(attraction)* attrattiva, fascino ‖ *tr (a sentence)* appellare contro ‖ *intr* dare nell'occhio; **to appeal from** *(law)* appellarsi contro; **to appeal to** supplicare, pregare; piacere a, e.g., **his idea appeals to me** la sua idea mi piace
**appear** [ə'pır] *intr* apparire; *(to seem)* sembrare; *(said of a book)* uscire; *(before the public)* presentarsi; *(law)* comparire
**appearance** [ə'pırəns] *s* apparizione; *(of a book)* pubblicazione; *(outward look)* apparenza; *(law)* comparizione; **to keep up appearances** salvare le apparenze
**appease** [ə'piz] *tr* pacificare, placare; *(a desire)* soddisfare
**appeasement** [ə'pizmənt] *s* pacificazione, tranquillizzazione
**appel'late court'** [ə'pelıt] *s* corte *f* d'appello
**appellation** [ˌæpə'leʃən] *s* denominazione, nome *m*
**append** [ə'pend] *tr* allegare, aggiungere

**appendage** [ə'pendɪdʒ] *s* appendice *f*
**appendicitis** [ə‚pendɪ'saɪtɪs] *s* appendicite *f*
**appen·dix** [ə'pendɪks] *s* (**-dixes** or **-dices** [dɪ‚siz]) appendice *f*
**appertain** [‚æpər'ten] *intr* spettare, riferirsi
**appetite** ['æpɪ‚taɪt] *s* appetito
**appetizer** ['æpɪ‚taɪzər] *s* (*drink*) aperitivo; (*food*) stimulante *m* dell'appetito
**appetizing** ['æpɪ‚taɪzɪŋ] *adj* appetitoso
**applaud** *tr* applaudire, applaudire (with *dat*) || *intr* applaudire
**applause** [ə'plɔz] *s* applauso, applausi *mpl*
**apple** ['æpəl] *s* mela, pomo; (*tree*) melo, pomo
**ap'plejack'** *s* acquavite *f* di mele
**ap'ple of dis'cord** *s* pomo della discordia
**ap'ple of one's eye'** *s* pupilla degli occhi di qlcu, beniamino di qlcu
**ap'ple pie'** *s* torta di mele
**ap'ple pol'isher** *s* leccapiedi *mf*
**ap'ple·sauce'** *s* marmellata di mele; (slang) scemenza
**appliance** [ə'plaɪ·əns] *s* apparecchio, apparato; (*complicated instrument*) congegno; (*for domestic chores*) utensile *m;* (*act of applying*) applicazione
**applicant** ['æplɪkənt] *s* postulante *mf,* aspirante *m,* candidato
**application** [‚æplɪ'keʃən] *s* applicazione; uso; richiesta, domanda
**ap·ply** [ə'plaɪ] *v* (*pret & pp* **-plied**) *tr* applicare; (*the brakes*) mettere; (*e.g.,* *a nickname*) affibbiare || *intr* (*said of a rule*) essere applicabile; fare richiesta; **to apply for** sollecitare
**appoint** [ə'pɔɪnt] *tr* nominare; assegnare; (*to furnish*) ammobiliare
**appointee** [‚æpɔɪn'ti] *s* persona nominata a una carica
**appointive** [ə'pɔɪntɪv] *adj* a nomina
**appointment** [ə'pɔɪntmənt] *s* nomina; (*position*) ufficio; (*agreement to meet*) appuntamento; **appointments** mobilia, arredamento; **by appointment** previo appuntamento
**apportion** [ə'porʃən] *tr* spartire, dividere proporzionatamente
**appraisal** [ə'prezəl] *s* stima, valutazione; (*of real estate*) estimo
**appraise** [ə'prez] *tr* stimare, valutare
**appreciable** [ə'priʃɪ·əbəl] *adj* apprezzabile, notevole
**appreciate** [ə'priʃɪ‚et] *tr* apprezzare, valutare; (*to be grateful for*) gradire; (*to be aware of*) rendersi conto di; (*to raise in value*) valorizzare || *intr* aumentare di valore
**appreciation** [ə‚priʃɪ'eʃən] *s* apprezzamento, valutazione; (*grateful recognition*) gradimento, riconoscenza; valorizzazione
**appreciative** [ə'priʃɪ‚etɪv] *adj* grato, riconoscente
**apprehend** [‚æprɪ'hend] *tr* (*to fear*) temere; (*to understand*) comprendere; (*to arrest*) arrestare

**apprehension** [‚æprɪ'henʃən] *s* timore *m,* apprensione; comprensione; arresto
**apprehensive** [‚æprɪ'hensɪv] *adj* apprensivo
**apprentice** [ə'prentɪs] *s* apprendista *mf,* novizio || *tr* mettere in apprendistato; accettare in apprendistato
**apprenticeship** [ə'prentɪs‚ʃɪp] *s* apprendistato, carovana
**apprise** or **apprize** [ə'praɪz] *tr* avvertire, avvisare; stimare, valutare
**approach** [ə'protʃ] *s* (*a coming near*) avvicinamento; (*of night*) avvicinarsi *m,* far *m;* approssimazione; (*access*) via d'accesso; (*to a problem*) impostazione; **approaches** approcci *mpl* || *tr* avvicinarsi a, avvicinare; fare approcci con || *intr* avvicinarsi, approssimarsi
**approbation** [‚æprə'beʃən] *s* approvazione
**appropriate** [ə'proprɪ·ɪt] *adj* appropriato, acconcio || [ə'proprɪ‚et] *tr* (*to take*) appropriarsi di; (*to set aside for some specific use*) stanziare
**approval** [ə'pruvəl] *s* approvazione, consenso; **on approval** in prova
**approve** [ə'pruv] *tr & intr* approvare
**approximate** [ə'praksɪmɪt] *adj* approssimato, approssimativo || [ə'praksɪ‚met] *tr* approssimarsi a || *intr* approssimarsi
**apricot** ['eprɪ‚kat] or ['æprɪ‚kat] *adj* color albicocca || *s* (*fruit*) albicocca; (*tree*) albicocco
**April** ['eprɪl] *s* aprile *m*
**A'pril fool'** *s* pesce *m* d'aprile
**A'pril Fools'' Day'** *s* primo d'aprile
**apron** ['eprən] *s* grembiale *m,* grembiule *m;* **tied to the apron strings of** attaccato alle sottane di
**apropos** [‚æprə'po] *adj* opportuno || *adv*—**apropos of** a proposito di
**apse** [æps] *s* abside *f*
**apt** [æpt] *adj* atto, appropriato; (*quick*) pronto; **to be apt to** essere propenso a, portato a
**aptitude** ['æptɪ‚tjud] or ['æptɪ‚tud] *s* attitudine *f*
**ap'titude test'** *s* esame *m* attitudinale
**Apulia** [ə'pjulɪ·ə] *s* la Puglia
**aqualung** ['ækwə‚lʌŋ] *s* autorespiratore *m*
**aquamarine** [‚ækwəmə'rin] *s* acquamarina
**aquaplane** ['ækwə‚plen] *s* acquaplano || *intr* andare in acquaplano
**aquari·um** [ə'kwerɪ·əm] *s* (**-ums** or **-a** [ə]) acquario, vasca dei pesci
**Aquarius** [ə'kwerɪ·əs] *s* (astr) Acquario
**aquatic** [ə'kwætɪk] or [ə'kwatɪk] *adj* acquatico || *s* animale acquatico; pianta acquatica; **aquatics** sport acquatici
**aqueduct** ['ækwə‚dʌkt] *s* acquedotto
**aqueous** ['ekwɪ·əs] or ['ækwɪ·əs] *adj* acquoso
**aq'uiline nose'** ['ækwɪ‚laɪn] *s* naso aquilino
**Arab** ['ærəb] *adj & s* arabo
**Arabic** ['ærəbɪk] *adj & s* arabo

**arbiter** ['ɑrbɪtər] s arbitro
**arbitrary** ['ɑrbɪ‚treri] adj arbitrario
**arbitrate** ['ɑrbɪ‚tret] tr arbitrare ‖ intr fare l'arbitro
**arbitration** [‚ɑrbɪ'treʃən] s arbitrato
**arbitrator** ['ɑrbɪ‚tretər] s arbitro
**arbor** ['ɑrbər] s pergola, pergolato; (mach) albero, asse m
**arbore·tum** [‚ɑrbə'ritəm] s (-tums or -ta [tə]) arboreto
**arbutus** [ɑr'bjutəs] s (Arbutus unedo) corbezzolo
**arc** [ɑrk] s arco; (elec) arco voltaico ‖ intr (elec) formare un arco
**arcade** [ɑr'ked] s arcata, portico
**arch** [ɑrtʃ] adj malizioso ‖ s arco; (anat) arco del piede ‖ tr attraversare; arcuare ‖ intr inarcarsi
**archaeology** [‚ɑrkɪ'alədʒi] s archeologia
**archaic** [ɑr'ke·ɪk] adj arcaico
**archaism** ['ɑrke‚ɪzəm] or ['ɑrki‚ɪzəm] s arcaismo
**archangel** ['ɑrk‚endʒəl] s arcangelo
**archbishop** ['ɑrtʃ'bɪʃəp] s arcivescovo
**archduke** ['ɑrtʃ'djuk] or ['ɑrtʃ'duk] s arciduca m
**archene·my** ['ɑrtʃ'ɛnɪmi] s (-mies) nemico giurato
**archer** ['ɑrtʃər] s arciere m
**archery** ['ɑrtʃəri] s tiro con l'arco
**archetype** ['ɑrkɪ‚taɪp] s archetipo, prototipo
**archipela·go** [‚ɑrkɪ'pɛləgo] s (-gos or -goes) arcipelago
**architect** ['ɑrkɪ‚tɛkt] s architetto
**architectural** [‚ɑrkɪ'tɛkt/ərəl] adj architetturale, architettonico
**architecture** ['ɑrkɪ‚tɛktʃər] s architettura
**archives** ['ɑrkaɪvz] spl archivio
**arch'way'** s arcata
**arc' lamp'** s lampada ad arco
**arctic** ['ɑrktɪk] adj artico ‖ the Arctic la regione artica
**arc' weld'ing** s saldatura ad arco
**ardent** ['ɑrdənt] adj ardente
**ardor** ['ɑrdər] s ardore m
**arduous** ['ɑrdʒʊ·əs] or ['ɑrdjʊ·əs] adj arduo
**area** ['ɛrɪ·ə] s area
**ar'ea code'** s prefisso
**Argentina** [‚ɑrdʒən'tinə] s l'Argentina
**Argentine** ['ɑrdʒən‚tin] or ['ɑrdʒən‚taɪn] adj & s argentino ‖ the Argentine l'Argentina
**Argonaut** ['ɑrgə‚nɔt] s argonauta m
**argue** ['ɑrgju] tr dibattere; (to indicate) indicare, provare; **to argue out of** dissuadere da; **to argue s.o. into s.th** persuadere qlcu di qlco ‖ intr argomentare, discutere
**argument** ['ɑrgjəmənt] s discussione, argomentazione; (theme) argomento
**argumentative** [‚ɑrgjə'mɛntətɪv] adj litigioso
**aria** ['ɑrɪ·ə] or ['ɛrɪ·ə] s aria
**arid** ['ærɪd] adj arido
**aridity** [ə'rɪdɪti] s aridità f
**Aries** ['ɛriz] or ['ɛri‚iz] s (astr) Ariete m

**aright** [ə'raɪt] adv correttamente; **to set aright** rettificare
**arise** [ə'raɪz] v (pret **arose** [ə'roz]; pp **arisen** [ə'rɪzən]) intr alzarsi; (to originate) provenire, trarre origine; (to occur) succedere, avvenire; (to be raised, as objections) avanzarsi
**aristocra·cy** [‚ærɪs'takrəsi] s (-cies) aristocrazia
**aristocrat** [ə'rɪstə‚kræt] s aristocratico
**aristocratic** [ə‚rɪstə'krætɪk] adj aristocratico
**Aristotelian** [‚ærɪstə'tilɪ·ən] adj & s aristotelico
**Aristotle** ['ærɪ‚statəl] s Aristotele m
**arithmetic** [ə'rɪθmətɪk] s aritmetica
**arithmetical** [‚ærɪθ'mɛtɪkəl] adj aritmetico
**arithmetician** [‚ærɪθmə'tɪʃən] or [ə‚rɪθmə'tɪʃən] s aritmetico
**ark** [ɑrk] s arca
**ark' of the cov'enant** s arca dell'alleanza
**arm** [ɑrm] s braccio; (e.g., of a bear) zampa; (of a chair) bracciolo; (weapon) arma; **arm in arm** a braccetto; **to be up in arms** essere in armi; essere indignato; **to lay down one's arms** deporre le armi; **to rise up in arms** levarsi in armi; **with open arms** a braccia aperte ‖ tr armare ‖ intr armarsi
**armament** ['ɑrməmənt] s armamento
**armature** ['ɑrmə‚tʃər] s (of an animal) corazza; (of motor or dynamo) indotto; (of a buzzer or electric bell) ancora
**arm'chair'** s poltrona
**Armenian** [ɑr'minɪ·ən] adj & s armeno
**armful** ['ɑrm‚fʊl] s bracciata
**arm'hole'** s giro manica
**armistice** ['ɑrmɪstɪs] s armistizio
**armlet** ['ɑrmlɪt] s bracciale m
**armor** ['ɑrmər] s armatura, corazza ‖ tr corazzare, blindare
**ar'mored car'** s carro armato
**ar'mor plate'** s lamiera di corazza
**armor·y** ['ɑrməri] s (-ies) armeria; arsenale m
**arm'pit'** s ascella
**arm'rest'** s bracciolo
**ar·my** ['ɑrmi] adj dell'esercito, militare ‖ s (-mies) esercito; (two or more army corps) armata
**ar'my corps'** s corpo d'armata
**aromatic** [‚ærə'mætɪk] adj aromatico
**around** [ə'raʊnd] adv intorno; all'intorno; dappertutto; **to turn around** voltarsi ‖ prep intorno a; (coll) vicino a; (approximately) (coll) circa
**arouse** [ə'raʊz] tr eccitare, incitare; svegliare
**arpeg·gio** [ɑr'pɛdʒo] s (-gios) arpeggio
**arraign** [ə'ren] tr citare, portare in giudizio; accusare
**arrange** [ə'rendʒ] tr disporre, sistemare; (a dispute) comporre, accomodare; (mus) ridurre, arrangiare
**arrangement** [ə'rendʒmənt] s disposizione, sistemazione; composizione, accomodamento; (mus) riduzione,

arrangiamento; **arrangements** preparazione, preparativi *mpl*
**array** [ə'reɪ] *s* ordine *m;* (*clothes*) abbigliamento; (mil) spiegamento, schiera ‖ *tr* disporre; abbigliare, adornare; (mil) spiegare, schierare
**arrears** [ə'rɪrz] *spl* arretrati *mpl;* **in arrears** in arretrato
**arrest** [ə'rest] *s* arresto; **under arrest** in arresto ‖ *tr* arrestare; (*the attention*) attrarre
**arresting** [ə'restɪŋ] *adj* interessante, che fa colpo
**arrival** [ə'raɪvəl] *s* arrivo; persona arrivata
**arrive** [ə'raɪv] *intr* arrivare
**arrogance** ['ærəgəns] *s* arroganza
**arrogant** ['ærəgənt] *adj* arrogante
**arrogate** ['ærə,get] *tr* (*to take without right*) arrogare per sé, arrogarsi; (*to claim for another*) attribuire ingiustamente
**arrow** ['æro] *s* freccia, saetta
**ar'row·head'** *s* punta di freccia; (bot) sagittaria
**arsenal** ['ɑrsənəl] *s* arsenale *m*
**arsenic** ['ɑrsɪnɪk] *s* arsenico
**arson** ['ɑrsən] *s* incendio doloso
**art** [ɑrt] *s* arte *f*
**arter·y** ['ɑrtəri] *s* (-ies) arteria
**artful** ['ɑrtfəl] *adj* artificioso; (*clever*) destro; (*crafty*) astuto
**arthritic** [ɑr'θrɪtɪk] *adj & s* artritico
**arthritis** [ɑr'θraɪtɪs] *s* artrite *f*
**artichoke** ['ɑrtɪ,tʃok] *s* carciofo
**article** ['ɑrtɪkəl] *s* articolo
**articulate** [ɑr'tɪkjəlɪt] *adj* articolato; facile di parola ‖ ['ɑrtɪkjə,let] *tr* articolare ‖ *intr* pronunziare in modo articolato
**articulation** [ɑr,tɪkjə'leʃən] *s* articolazione
**artifact** ['ɑrtɪ,fækt] *s* manufatto
**artifice** ['ɑrtɪfɪs] *s* artificio
**artificial** [,ɑrtɪ'fɪʃəl] *adj* artificiale
**artillery** [ɑr'tɪləri] *s* artiglieria
**artil'lery·man** *s* (-men) artigliere *m*, cannoniere *m*
**artisan** ['ɑrtɪzən] *s* artigiano
**artist** ['ɑrtɪst] *s* artista *mf*
**artistic** [ɑr'tɪstɪk] *adj* artistico
**artistry** ['ɑrtɪstri] *s* abilità artistica
**artless** ['ɑrtlɪs] *adj* ingenuo, naturale; ignorante; (*clumsy*) grossolano
**arts' and crafts'** *spl* arti *fpl* e mestieri *mpl*
**art·y** ['ɑrti] *adj* (-ier; -iest) (coll) interessato nell'arte con ostentazione
**Aryan** ['erɪ·ən] *or* ['ɑrjən] *adj & s* ariano
**as** [æz] *or* [əz] *pron rel* che; **the same as** lo stesso che ‖ *adv* come; per esempio; **as . . . as** così . . . come; **as far as** fino a; **as far as I know** per quanto mi consta; **as for** in quanto a, per quanto concerne; **as is** (slang) com'è, nelle condizioni in cui si trova; **as long as** tanto che, mentre che; **as per** secondo; **as soon as** appena, non appena, non appena che; **as to** per quanto concerne; **as well** pure, anche; **as yet** ancora ‖ *prep* come; da; **as a rule** come regola ‖

*conj* come; mentre; dato che; per quanto; **as if** come se; **as it were** per così dire; **as though** come se
**asbestos** [æs'bestəs] *s* asbesto, amianto
**ascend** [ə'send] *tr* ascendere, scalare ‖ *intr* ascendere, salire
**ascension** [ə'senʃən] *s* ascensione, scalata ‖ **Ascension** *s* Ascensione
**ascent** [ə'sent] *s* scalata; salita; (*slope*) erta
**ascertain** [,æsər'ten] *tr* sincerarsi di, verificare
**ascertainable** [,æsər'tenəbəl] *adj* verificabile
**ascetic** [ə'setɪk] *adj* ascetico ‖ *s* asceta *m*
**ascor'bic ac'id** [ə'skɔrbɪk] *s* acido ascorbico
**ascribe** [ə'skraɪb] *tr* attribuire, imputare
**aseptic** [ə'septɪk] *or* [e'septɪk] *adj* asettico
**ash** [æʃ] *s* cenere *f;* (bot) frassino
**ashamed** [ə'ʃemd] *adj* vergognoso; **to be** *or* **feel ashamed** vergognarsi
**ash'can'** *s* pattumiera; (coll) bomba antisommergibile
**ashen** ['æʃən] *adj* cinereo
**ashlar** ['æʃlər] *s* bugna, bugnato
**ashore** [ə'ʃor] *adv* a terra; **to come ashore** andare a terra, sbarcare; **to run ashore** arenarsi
**ash'tray'** *s* portacenere *m*
**Ash' Wednes'day** *s* le Ceneri
**Asia** ['eʒə] *or* ['eʃə] *s* l'Asia *f*
**A'sia Mi'nor** *s* l'Asia *f* Minore
**Asian** ['eʒən] *or* ['eʃən] *or* **Asiatic** [,eʒɪ'ætɪk] *or* [,eʃɪ'ætɪk] *adj & s* asiatico
**aside** [ə'saɪd] *s* parola detta a parte; (theat) a parte *m* ‖ *adv* da parte; a parte; **aside from** (coll) eccetto; separato da; **to step aside** farsi da un lato
**asinine** ['æsɪnaɪn] *adj* (*like an ass*) asinino; (*stupid*) asinesco
**ask** [æsk] *or* [ɑsk] *tr* chiedere (with *dat*), domandare (with *dat*); invitare; (*a question*) fare; **to ask s.o. for s.th** chiedere *or* domandare qlco a qlcu; **to ask s.o. to** + *inf* chiedere a qlcu di + *inf* ‖ *intr* chiedere; **to ask about** chiedere informazioni di; **to ask for** chiedere, domandare; **to ask for it** (coll) andare in cerca di disgrazie; (coll) volerlo, e.g., **he asked for it** l'ha voluto
**askance** [ə'skæns] *adv* di traverso, di sbieco; (fig) con sospetto
**asleep** [ə'slip] *adj* addormentato; **to fall asleep** addormentarsi
**asp** [æsp] *s* aspide *m*
**asparagus** [ə'spærəgəs] *s* asparago; (*as food*) asparagi *mpl*
**aspect** ['æspekt] *s* aspetto; (*direction anything faces*) esposizione
**aspen** ['æspən] *s* pioppo tremolo, tremolo
**aspersion** [ə'spʌrʒən] *or* [ə'spʌrʃən] *s* diffamazione, calunnia; (eccl) aspersione
**asphalt** ['æsfɔlt] *or* ['æsfælt] *s* asfalto ‖ *tr* asfaltare

asphyxiate [æs'fɪksɪ ,et] *tr* asfissiare
aspirant [ə'spaɪrənt] or ['æspɪrənt] *s* aspirante *mf*
aspire [ə'spaɪr] *intr* aspirare
aspirin ['æspɪrɪn] *s* aspirina
ass [æs] *s* asino
assail [ə'sel] *tr* assalire, assaltare
assassin [ə'sæsɪn] *s* assassino
assassinate [ə'sæsɪ ,net] *tr* assassinare
assassination [ə ,sæsɪ'neʃən] *s* assassinio
assault [ə'sɔlt] *s* assalto ‖ *tr* assaltare
assault' and bat'tery *s* vie *fpl* di fatto
assay [ə'se] or ['æse] *s* saggio, esame *m* ‖ [ə'se] *tr* saggiare
assemblage [ə'sɛmblɪdʒ] *s* assemblea; (mach) montaggio
assemble [ə'sɛmbəl] *tr* riunire; (mach) montare, mettere insieme ‖ *intr* assembrarsi, riunirsi
assembler [ə'sɛmblər] *s* montatore *m*
assem•bly [ə'sɛmbli] *s* (-blies) assemblea, riunione; (mach) montaggio
assem'bly hall' *s* sala di riunioni
assem'bly line' *s* catena di montaggio
assem'bly•man *s* (-men) membro dell'assemblea legislativa
assent [ə'sɛnt] *s* assenso ‖ *intr* assentire
assert [ə'sʌrt] *tr* asserire; to assert oneself far valere i propri diritti
assertion [ə'sʌrʃən] *s* asserzione
assess [ə'sɛs] *tr* stimare, valutare; (for taxation or fine) tassare
assessment [ə'sɛsmənt] *s* valutazione; tassazione
assessor [ə'sɛsər] *s* agente *m* delle tasse
asset ['æsət] *s* vantaggio; persona di valore; assets (com) attivo; (law) beni *mpl*
assiduous [ə'sɪdʒʊ•əs] or [ə'sɪdju•əs] *adj* assiduo
assign [ə'saɪn] *s* cessionario ‖ *tr* assegnare; (e.g., a date) fissare; (a right) trasferire
assignation [ ,æsɪg'neʃən] *s* assegnazione; trasferimento; (date) appuntamento amoroso
assignment [ə'saɪnmənt] *s* assegnamento; (of rights) trasferimento; (schoolwork) compito
assimilate [ə'sɪmɪ ,let] *tr* assimilare ‖ *intr* essere assimilato; assimilarsi
assist [ə'sɪst] *s* aiuto ‖ *tr* aiutare, assistere
assistance [ə'sɪstəns] *s* assistenza, aiuto
assistant [ə'sɪstənt] *adj* & *s* assistente
associate [ə'soʃɪ•ɪt] or [ə'soʃɪ ,et] *adj* associato ‖ *s* associato; membro limitato ‖ [ə'soʃɪ ,et] *tr* associare ‖ *intr* associarsi
association [ə ,soʃɪ'eʃən] *s* associazione
assort [ə'sɔrt] *tr* assortire ‖ *intr* associarsi
assortment [ə'sɔrtmənt] *s* assortimento
assuage [ə'swedʒ] *tr* alleviare
assume [ə'sum] or [ə'sjum] *tr* assumere; (to appropriate) usurpare; (to pretend) fingere; (to suppose) supporre
assumed [ə'sumd] or [ə'sjumd] *adj* supposto, immaginario

assumption [ə'sʌmpʃən] *s* (arrogance) aria, arroganza; (thing taken for granted) supposizione; (of an undertaking) assunzione
assurance [ə'ʃʊrəns] *s* assicurazione, certezza; baldanza, fiducia in sè; (too much boldness) sicumera
assure [ə'ʃʊr] *tr* assicurare
assuredly [ə'ʃʊrɪdli] *adv* sicuramente
astatine ['æstə ,tin] *s* astato
asterisk ['æstə ,rɪsk] *s* asterisco, stelloncino
astern [ə'stʌrn] *adv* a poppa, a poppavia
asthma ['æzmə] or ['æsmə] *s* asma
astonish [ə'stɑnɪʃ] *tr* meravigliare, stupefare
astonishing [ə'stɑnɪʃɪŋ] *adj* stupefacente, sorprendente
astound [ə'staund] *tr* stupefare, sbalordire
astounding [ə'staundɪŋ] *adj* stupefacente
astraddle [ə'strædəl] *adv* a cavaliere, a cavalcioni
astray [ə'stre] *adv* sulla cattiva via; to go astray traviarsi; to lead astray traviare
astride [ə'straɪd] *adj* & *adv* a cavaliere; (said of a person) a cavalcioni ‖ *prep* a cavaliere di; a cavalcioni di
astrology [ə'strɑlədʒi] *s* astrologia
astronaut ['æstrə ,nɔt] *s* astronauta *mf*
astronautic [ ,æstrə'nɔtɪk] *adj* astronautico ‖ astronautics *ssg* astronautica
astronomer [ə'strɑnəmər] *s* astronomo
astronomic(al) [ ,æstrə'nɑmɪk(əl)] *adj* astronomico
astronomy [ə'strɑnəmi] *s* astronomia
astute [ə'stjut] or [ə'stut] *adj* astuto
asunder [ə'sʌndər] *adv* a pezzi; to tear asunder separare, fare a pezzi
asylum [ə'saɪləm] *s* asilo
asymmetry [ə'sɪmɪtri] *s* asimmetria
at [æt] or [ət] *prep* a; in; a casa di, e.g., at John's a casa di Giovanni; da, e.g., at Mary's da Maria; di, e.g., to be surprised at essere sorpreso di; to laugh at ridersi di
atheist ['eθi•ɪst] *s* ateista *mf*
Athenian [ə'θini•ən] *adj* & *s* ateniese *mf*
Athens ['æθɪnz] *s* Atene *f*
athirst [ə'θʌrst] *adj* assetato
athlete ['æθlit] *s* atleta *mf*
athletic [æθ'lɛtɪk] *adj* atletico ‖ athletics *ssg* & *spl* atletica
Atlantic [æt'læntɪk] *adj* atlantico ‖ *adj* & *s* Atlantico
atlas ['ætləs] *s* atlante *m* ‖ Atlas *s* Atlante *m*
atmosphere ['ætməs ,fɪr] *s* atmosfera
atmospheric [ ,ætməs'fɛrɪk] *adj* atmosferico ‖ atmospherics *spl* disturbi atmosferici
atom ['ætəm] *s* atomo
at'om bomb' *s* bomba atomica
atomic [ə'tɑmɪk] *adj* atomico
atom'ic age' *s* era atomica
atom'ic sub'marine *s* sommergibile *m* nucleare
atomize ['ætə ,maɪz] *tr* atomizzare

**atomizer** ['ætə ,maɪzər] *s* nebulizzatore *m*

**at'om smash'er** *s* acceleratore *m* di particelle

**atone** [ə'ton] *intr*—**to atone for** espiare

**atonement** [ə'tonmənt] *s* riparazione; espiazione

**atop** [ə'tap] *adv* in cima ǁ *prep* in cima a

**atrocious** [ə'troʃəs] *adj* atroce

**atroci·ty** [ə'trɑsɪti] *s* (-**ties**) atrocità *f*

**atro·phy** ['ætrəfi] *s* atrofia ǁ *v* (*pret* & *pp* -**phied**) *tr* atrofizzare ǁ *intr* atrofizzarsi

**attach** [ə'tætʃ] *tr* attaccare; (*to affix*) apporre; (*to attribute*) attribuire; (*law*) sequestrare; **to be attached to** essere legato a; **fare parte di** ǁ *intr*—**to attach to** essere pertinente a

**attaché** [ ,ætə'ʃe] or [ə'tæʃe] *s* attaché *m.*, addetto

**attaché' case'** *s* valigetta diplomatica

**attachment** [ə'tætʃmənt] *s* attacco, unione; affezione; (mach) accessorio; (law) sequestro

**attack** [ə'tæk] *s* attacco ǁ *tr* & *intr* attaccare

**attain** [ə'ten] *tr* raggiungere ǁ *intr*—**to attain to** raggiungere, conseguire

**attainder** [ə'tendər] *s* morte *f* civile

**attainment** [ə'tenmənt] *s* raggiungimento, realizzazione; (*accomplishment*) dote *f*

**attempt** [ə'tempt] *s* tentativo; (*attack*) attentato ǁ *tr* tentare; (*s.o.'s life*) attentare a

**attend** [ə'tend] *tr* (*to be present at*) presenziare, presenziare a, assistere a; (*to accompany*) accompagnare; (*to take care of; to pay attention to*) assistere ǁ *intr*—**to attend to** occuparsi di, attendere a

**attendance** [ə'tendəns] *s* (*attending*) presenza; (*company present*) concorso; **to dance attendance** essere al servizio completo

**attendant** [ə'tendənt] *adj* assistente; (*accompanying*) concomitante ǁ *s* (*servant*) inserviente *mf*; presente *m*

**attention** [ə'tenʃən] *s* attenzione; (mil) attenti *m*; **attentions** attenzioni *fpl*; **to call s.o.'s attention to s.th** fare presente qlco a qlcu; **to stand at attention** stare sull'attenti ǁ *interj* attenti!

**attentive** [ə'tentɪv] *adj* attento, premuroso

**attenuate** [ə'tenju ,et] *tr* attenuare

**attest** [ə'test] *tr* attestare ǁ *intr*—**to attest to** attestare, testimoniare

**attic** ['ætɪk] *s* attico, solaio ǁ **Attic** *adj* & *s* attico

**attire** [ə'taɪr] *s* vestiti *mpl*, vestiario ǁ *tr* vestire

**attitude** ['ætɪ ,tjud] or ['ætɪ ,tud] *s* atteggiamento, attitudine *f*; **to strike an attitude** atteggiarsi

**attorney** [ə'tʌrni] *s* avvocato; (*proxy*) procuratore *m*

**attor'ney gen'eral** *s* (**attor'neys gen'eral** or **attor'ney gen'erals**) procuratore *m* generale ǁ **Attorney General** *s* (U.S.A.) ministro di grazia e giustizia

**attract** [ə'trækt] *tr* attrarre; (*attention*) chiamare

**attraction** [ə'trækʃən] *s* attrazione

**attractive** [ə'træktɪv] *adj* attrattivo

**attribute** ['ætrɪ ,bjut] *s* attributo ǁ [ə'trɪbjut] *tr* attribuire

**attrition** [ə'trɪʃən] *s* attrito; diminuzione di numero

**auburn** ['ɔbərn] *adj* & *s* biondo fulvo, rosso tizianesco

**auction** ['ɔkʃən] *s* asta, incanto ǁ *tr* vendere all'asta

**auctioneer** [ ,ɔkʃə'nɪr] *s* banditore *m* ǁ *tr* & *intr* vendere all'asta

**audacious** [ɔ'deʃəs] *adj* audace

**audaci·ty** [ɔ'dæsɪti] *s* (-**ties**) audacia

**audience** ['ɔdɪ·əns] *s* (*hearing*) udienza; uditorio, pubblico

**au'dio fre'quency** ['ɔdɪ ,o] *s* audiofrequenza

**au'dio-vis'ual aids'** *spl* sussidi audiovisivi

**audit** ['ɔdɪt] *s* verifica or esame *m* dei conti ǁ *tr* esaminare i conti di; (*a class*) assistere a, come uditore ǁ *intr* assistere a una classe come uditore

**audition** [ɔ'dɪʃən] *s* audizione ǁ *tr* dare un'audizione a

**auditor** ['ɔdɪtər] *s* revisore *m* dei conti; (educ) uditore *m*

**auditorium** [ ,ɔdɪ'torɪ·əm] *s* auditorio

**auger** ['ɔgər] *s* succhiello, trivella

**aught** [ɔt] *s* zero; **for aught I know** per quanto ne so ǁ *adv* affatto

**augment** [ɔg'ment] *tr* & *intr* aumentare

**augur** ['ɔgər] *s* augure *m* ǁ *tr* & *intr* vaticinare

**augu·ry** ['ɔgəri] *s* (-**ries**) augurio

**august** [ɔ'gʌst] *adj* augusto ǁ **August** ['ɔgəst] *s* agosto

**aunt** [ænt] or [ɑnt] *s* zia

**aurora** [ə'rorə] *s* aurora

**auspice** ['ɔspɪs] *s* auspicio; **under the auspices of** sotto gli auspici di

**austere** [ɔs'tɪr] *adj* austero

**Australia** [ɔ'streljə] *s* l'Australia *f*

**Australian** [ɔ'streljən] *adj* & *s* australiano

**Austria** ['ɔstrɪ·ə] *s* l'Austria *f*

**Austrian** ['ɔstrɪ·ən] *adj* & *s* austriaco

**authentic** [ɔ'θentɪk] *adj* autentico

**authenticate** [ɔ'θentɪ ,ket] *tr* autenticare

**author** ['ɔθər] *s* autore *m*

**authoress** ['ɔθərɪs] *s* autrice *f*

**authoritarian** [ɔ ,θɑrɪ'terɪ·ən] or [ə- ,θɑrɪ'terɪ·ən] *adj* autoritario ǁ *s* persona autoritaria

**authoritative** [ɔ'θɑrɪ ,tetɪv] or [ɔ'θɔrɪ- ,tetɪv] *adj* autorevole; autoritario

**authori·ty** [ɔ'θɑrɪti] or [ɔ'θɔrɪti] *s* (-**ties**) autorità *f*; **on good authority** da buona fonte, da fonte autorevole

**authorize** ['ɔθə ,raɪz] *tr* autorizzare

**authorship** ['ɔθər ,ʃɪp] *s* paternità letteraria

**au·to** ['ɔto] *s* (-**tos**) (coll) auto *f*

**autobiogra·phy** [ ,ɔtobaɪ'ɑgrəfi] or [ ,ɔtobɪ'ɑgrəfi] *s* (-**phies**) autobiografia

**autobus** ['ɔto ,bʌs] *s* autobus *m*
**autocratic(al)** [,ɔtə'krætɪk(əl)] *adj* autocratico
**autograph** ['ɔtə ,græf] or ['ɔtə ,grɑf] *adj & s* autografo ‖ *tr* porre l'autografo su, firmare con firma autografa
**automat** ['ɔtə ,mæt] *s* ristorante *m* self-service a distribuzione automatica
**automate** ['ɔtə ,met] *tr* automatizzare
**automatic** [,ɔtə'mætɪk] *adj* automatico ‖ *s* pistola automatica
**automat'ic transmis'sion** *s* trasmissione automatica
**automation** [,ɔtə'meʃən] *s* automazione
**automa·ton** [ɔ'tɑmə ,tɑn] *s* (**-tons** or **-ta** [tə]) automa *m*
**automobile** [,ɔtəmo'bil] or [,ɔtə'mo-bil] *adj & s* automobile *f*
**automobile' show'** *s* salone *m* dell'automobile
**automotive** [,ɔtə'motɪv] *adj* (*self-propelled*) automotore; automobilistico
**autonomous** [ɔ'tɑnəməs] *adj* autonomo
**autonomy** [ɔ'tɑnəmi] *s* autonomia
**autop·sy** ['ɔtɑpsi] *s* (**-sies**) autopsia
**au'to trans'port rig'** *s* autotreno per trasporto di automobili
**autumn** ['ɔtəm] *s* autunno
**autumnal** [ɔ'tʌmnəl] *adj* autunnale
**auxilia·ry** [ɔg'zɪljəri] *adj & s* (**-ries**) ausiliare *m*
**avail** [ə'vel] *s* utilità *f;* **of no avail** che non serve a nulla ‖ *tr* servire (*with dat*); **to avail oneself of** servirsi di; approfittare di ‖ *intr* servire
**available** [ə'veləbəl] *adj* disponibile; **to make available to** mettere alla disposizione di
**avalanche** ['ævə ,læntʃ] or ['ævə ,lɑntʃ] *s* valanga
**avant-garde** [əvɑ'gɑrd] *adj* d'avanguardia
**avant-gardism** [ə'vɑ'gɑrdɪzəm] *s* avanguardismo
**avarice** ['ævərɪs] *s* avarizia
**avaricious** [,ævə'rɪʃəs] *adj* avaro
**avenge** [ə'vendʒ] *tr* vendicare; **to avenge oneself on** vendicarsi di
**avenue** ['ævə ,nju] or ['ævənu] *s* viale *m,* corso
**aver** [ə'vʌr] *v* (*pret & pp* **averred;** *ger* **averring**) *tr* asserire, affermare
**average** ['ævərɪdʒ] *adj* medio ‖ *s* media; (*naut*) avaria; (*e.g., of goals*) (sports) quoziente *m;* **on the average** di media ‖ *tr* fare la media di; fare . . . di media, e.g., **he averages one hundred dollars a week** fa cento dollari di media alla settimana
**averse** [ə'vʌrs] *adj* avverso
**aversion** [ə'vʌrʒən] *s* avversione
**avert** [ə'vʌrt] *tr* (*to ward off*) evitare; (*to turn away*) distogliere
**aviar·y** ['ævɪ ,eri] *s* (**-ies**) aviario, voliera
**aviation** [,evɪ'eʃən] *s* aviazione
**aviator** ['evɪ ,etər] *s* aviatore *m*
**avid** ['ævɪd] *adj* avido
**avidity** [ə'vɪdɪti] *s* avidità *f*

**avocation** [,ævə'keʃən] *s* svago, passatempo
**avoid** [ə'vɔɪd] *tr* evitare
**avoidable** [ə'vɔɪdəbəl] *adj* evitabile
**avow** [ə'vau] *tr* confessare, ammettere
**avowal** [ə'vau·əl] *s* confessione, ammissione
**await** [ə'wet] *tr* aspettare, attendere
**awake** [ə'wek] *adj* sveglio ‖ *v* (*pret & pp* **awoke** [ə'wok] or **awaked**) *tr* svegliare ‖ *intr* svegliarsi
**awaken** [ə'wekən] *tr* svegliare ‖ *intr* svegliarsi
**awakening** [ə'wekənɪŋ] *s* risveglio
**award** [ə'wɔrd] *s* (*prize*) premio; (*decision by judge*) sentenza ‖ *tr* aggiudicare
**aware** [ə'wer] *adj* conscio, consapevole; **to become aware of** rendersi conto di
**awareness** [ə'wernɪs] *s* coscienza
**awash** [ə'wɑʃ] or [ə'wɔʃ] *adj & adv* a fior d'acqua
**away** [ə'we] *adj* distante, assente ‖ *adv* lontano; via; continuamente; **away back** (coll) molto tempo fa; **away from** lontano da; **to do away with** disfarsi di, sopprimere; **to get away** scappare, sfuggire; **to go away** andarsene; **to run away** fuggire; **to send away** mandar via; **to take away** portar via
**awe** [ɔ] *s* estremo rispetto; sacro timore ‖ *tr* infondere rispetto a; infondere un sacro timore a
**aweigh** [ə'we] *adj* (*anchor*) levato
**awesome** ['ɔsəm] *adj* grandioso, imponente
**awestruck** ['ɔ ,strʌk] *adj* pieno di sacro timore
**awful** ['ɔfəl] *adj* terribile; imponente ‖ *adv* (coll) terribilmente
**awfully** ['ɔfəli] *adv* tremendamente, terribilmente; (coll) molto
**awhile** [ə'hwaɪl] *adv* un po', un po' di tempo
**awkward** ['ɔkwərd] *adj* (*clumsy*) goffo, maldestro; (*unwieldly*) scomodo; (*embarrassing*) imbarazzante
**awl** [ɔl] *s* punteruolo
**awning** ['ɔnɪŋ] *s* tenda; (*in front of a store*) tendone *m*
**A.W.O.L.** ['ewəl] (acronym) or ['e-'dʌbəl ,ju'o'el] (letterword) *adj* (mil) assente al contrappello
**awry** [ə'raɪ] *adv*—**to go awry** andare a capovescio; **to look awry** guardare di sbieco
**ax** or **axe** [æks] *s* scure *f;* **to have an axe to grind** (coll) avere un interesse speciale
**axiom** ['æksɪ·əm] *s* assioma *m*
**axiomatic** [,æksɪ·ə'mætɪk] *adj* assiomatico
**axis** ['æksɪs] *s* (**axes** ['æksiz]) asse *m*
**axle** ['æksəl] *s* assale *m,* asse *m*
**ax'le·tree'** *s* assale *m*
**ay** [aɪ] *s & adv* sì *m*
**Azores** [ə'zorz] or ['ezorz] *spl* Azzorre *fpl*
**azure** ['æʒər] or ['eʒər] *adj & s* azzurro, blu *m*

# B

**B, b** [bi] *s* seconda lettera dell'alfabeto inglese

**baa** [ba] *s* belato || *intr* belare

**babble** ['bæbəl] *s* (*murmuring sound*) mormorio; (*senseless prattle*) balbettio || *tr* (*e.g., a secret*) divulgare || *intr* mormorare; balbettare; (*to talk idly*) parlare a vanvera

**babe** [beb] *s* bebè *m*, bambino; persona inesperta; (slang) ragazza

**baboon** [bæ'bun] *s* babbuino

**ba·by** ['bebi] *s* (**-bies**) bebè *m*, neonato; bambino; (*the youngest child*) piccolo || *v* (*pret & pp* **-bied**) *tr* coccolare, ninnare

**ba'by car'riage** *s* carrozzella

**ba'by grand'** *s* piano a mezza coda

**babyhood** ['bebi‚hʊd] *s* infanzia

**babyish** ['bebi‚ɪʃ] *adj* infantile

**Babylon** ['bæbɪlən] or ['bæbɪ‚lan] *s* Babilonia

**ba'by sit'ter** *s* bambinaia ad ore

**ba'by teeth'** *spl* denti *mpl* di latte

**baccalaureate** [‚bækə'lɔrɪ·ɪt] *s* baccalaureato; servizio religioso prima del baccalaureato

**bacchanal** ['bækənəl] *adj* bacchico || *s* baccanale *m;* (*person*) ubriacone *m*, bisboccione *m*

**bachelor** ['bætʃələr] *s* (*unmarried man*) scapolo, celibe *m;* (*holder of bachelor's degree*) diplomato; (*apprentice knight*) baccelliere *m*

**bachelorhood** ['bætʃələr‚hʊd] *s* celibato

**bacil·lus** [bə'sɪləs] *s* (**-li** [laɪ]) bacillo

**back** [bæk] *adj* di dietro, posteriore; arretrato; contrario || *s* dorso, schiena; parte *f* posteriore, didietro; (*of a sheet or coin*) tergo; (*of a knife*) costola; (*of a room*) fondo; (*of a book*) fine *f;* (*of a chair*) schienale *m;* **behind one's back** dietro le spalle di uno; **to turn one's back on** volgere la schiena a || *adv* dietro; indietro; **a few weeks back** alcune settimane fa; **as far back as** sino da; **back of** dietro, dietro a; **to go back on one's word** mancare di parola; **to go back to** ritornare a; **to back** ripagare; **to send back** restituire || *tr* appoggiare; far indietreggiare || *intr* indietreggiare; rinculare; **to back down** rinunciarci; **to back off** or **out** ritirarsi; **to back up** (*said of a car*) fare marcia indietro

**back'ache'** *s* mal *m* di schiena

**back'bite'** *v* (*pret* **-bit;** *pp* **-bitten** or **-bit**) *tr* sparlare di || *intr* sparlare

**back'bit'er** *s* maldicente *mf*

**back'board'** *s* (basketball) tabellone *m*

**back'bone'** *s* spina dorsale; (*of a book*) costola, dorso; (fig) fermezza

**back'break'ing** *adj* sfiancante

**back'door'** *adj* segreto, clandestino

**back' door'** *s* porta di dietro; (fig) mezzo clandestino

**back'drop'** *s* (theat) fondale *m*

**backer** ['bækər] *s* sostenitore *m*, difensore *m;* (com) finanziatore *m*

**back'fire'** *s* (*for firefighting*) controfuoco; (aut) ritorno di fiamma || *intr* (aut) avere un ritorno di fiamma; (fig) raggiungere l'effetto opposto

**back'ground'** *s* fondo, sfondo; precedenti *mpl;* origine *f*

**back'ground mu'sic** *s* musica di fondo

**backhand** ['bæk‚hænd] *adj* obliquo || *s* scrittura inclinata a sinistra; (tennis) rovescio

**back'hand'ed** *adj* obliquo; sarcastico; insincero

**backing** ['bækɪŋ] *s* appoggio; sostegno; (bb) dorso

**back'ing light'** *s* (aut) faro retromarcia; (theat) luce *f* per il fondale

**back'lash'** *s* reazione; contraccolpo; (mach) gioco

**back'log'** *s* ceppo; (fig) riserva

**back' num'ber** *s* numero arretrato; (coll) persona all'antica

**back' pay'** *s* paga arretrata, arretrati *mpl*

**back' scratch'er** *s* manina per grattare la schiena; (coll) leccapiedi *m*

**back' seat'** *s* (aut) sedile *m* posteriore; (fig) posizione secondaria

**back'side'** *s* dorso; didietro

**back'slide'** *v* (*pret & pp* **-slid** [‚slɪd]) *intr* ricadere

**back'spac'er** *s* tasto ritorno

**back'spin'** *s* effetto

**back'stage'** *adj* dietro alle quinte || *s* retroscena *m* || *adv* a retroscena, dietro alle quinte

**back'stairs'** *adj* indiretto, segreto

**back' stairs'** *spl* scala di servizio

**back'stitch'** *s* impuntura || *tr & intr* impunturare

**back'stroke'** *s* (swimming) bracciata sul dorso

**back'swept wing'** *s* ala a freccia

**back' talk'** *s* risposta impertinente

**back'track'** *intr* ritornare sulle proprie tracce; (fig) fare macchina indietro

**back'up light'** *s* (aut) faro retromarcia

**backward** ['bækwərd] *adj* ritroso; poco progredito, retrogrado || *adv* a ritroso, all'indietro; verso il passato; alla rovescia; **backward and forward** (coll) completamente, perfettamente; **to go backward and forward** andare avanti e indietro

**back'wash'** *s* risacca

**back'wa'ter** *s* gora, ristagno; (fig) eremo

**back'woods'** *spl* zona boscosa lontana dai centri popolati

**back'yard'** *s* cortile *m* posteriore

**bacon** ['bekən] *s* pancetta

**bacteria** [bæk'tɪrɪ·ə] *spl* batteri *mpl*

**bacterial** [bæk'tɪrɪ·əl] *adj* batterico

**bacteriologist** [bæk‚tɪrɪ'alədʒɪst] *s* batteriologo

**bacteriology** [bæk‚tɪrɪ'alədʒi] *s* batteriologia

**bad** [bæd] *adj* (**worse** [wʌrs]; **worst** [wʌrst]) cattivo; (*coin*) falso; (*weather*) brutto; (*debt*) insolvibile; severo || *s* male *m;* **from bad to**

**worse** da male in peggio ‖ *adv* male; **to be too bad** essere peccato; **to feel bad** esser spiacente; sentirsi male; **to look bad** aver brutta cera

**bad' breath'** *s* fiato cattivo

**bad' egg'** *s* (slang) cattivo soggetto

**badge** [bædʒ] *s* divisa; decorazione; simbolo, placca

**badger** ['bædʒər] *s* tasso ‖ *tr* molestare

**badly** ['bædlɪ] *adv* male; gravemente; molto

**bad'ly off'** *adj* in cattive condizioni

**badminton** ['bædmɪntən] *s* badminton *m*

**baffle** ['bæfəl] *s* (mach) deflettore *m*; (rad) schermo acustico ‖ *tr* frustrare, confondere

**baffling** ['bæflɪŋ] *adj* sconcertante

**bag** [bæg] *s* sacco; borsetta; (*of a marsupial*) borsa; (hunt) presa; **bag and baggage** con armi e bagagli; **to be in the bag** (slang) averlo nel sacco; **to be left holding the bag** (coll) essere piantato in asso ‖ *v* (*pret & pp* **bagged**; *ger* **bagging**) *tr* insaccare; (hunt) pigliare ‖ *intr* (*to hang loosely*) far pieghe

**baggage** ['bægɪdʒ] *s* bagaglio

**bag'gage car'** *s* bagagliaio

**bag'gage check'** *s* scontrino del bagaglio

**bag'gage room'** *s* deposito bagagli

**bag·gy** ['bægi] *adj* (**-gier**; **-giest**) come un sacco

**bag'pipe'** *s* cornamusa, zampogna

**bag'pip'er** *s* zampognaro

**bail** [bel] *s* cauzione; libertà provvisoria sotto cauzione; (*bucket*) sassola ‖ *tr* liberare sotto cauzione; **to bail out** (*a boat*) sgottare ‖ *intr*—**to bail out** (aer) gettarsi col paracadute

**bailiwick** ['belɪwɪk] *s* (fig) sfera di competenza

**bait** [bet] *s* esca; (fig) allettamento ‖ *tr* adescare; (fig) allettare

**baize** [bez] *s* panno verde

**bake** [bek] *tr* cuocere al forno ‖ *intr* cuocersi al forno; abbrustolirsi

**bakelite** ['bekə‚laɪt] *s* bachelite *f*

**baker** ['bekər] *s* fornaio, panettiere *m*

**bak'er's doz'en** *s* tredici per ogni dozzina

**baker·y** ['bekəri] *s* (**-ies**) panetteria

**bak'ing pan'** ['bekɪŋ] *s* tortiera

**bak'ing pow'der** *s* lievito in polvere

**bak'ing so'da** *s* bicarbonato di soda

**balance** ['bæləns] *s* (*scales*) bilancia; equilibrio; armonia; (*of watch*) bilanciere *m*; (*remainder; amount due*) resto; (*of budget*) pareggio; **in the balance** in bilico; **to lose one's balance** perdere l'equilibrio; **to strike a balance** fare il bilancio ‖ *tr* bilanciare, pesare; (com) bilanciare, pareggiare ‖ *intr* bilanciarsi

**bal'ance of pay'ments** *s* bilancia dei pagamenti

**bal'ance of pow'er** *s* equilibrio politico

**bal'ance of trade'** *s* bilancia commerciale

**bal'ance sheet'** *s* bilancio

**balco·ny** ['bælkəni] *s* (**-nies**) balcone *m*; (theat) galleria

**bald** [bɔld] *adj* calvo; (*bare*) nudo; (*unadorned*) semplice

**bald' ea'gle** *s* aquila col capo bianco dell'America del Nord

**baldness** ['bɔldnɪs] *s* calvizie *f*

**baldric** ['bɔldrɪk] *s* tracolla

**bale** [bel] *s* balla; collo ‖ *tr* imballare

**baleful** ['belfəl] *adj* minaccioso, funesto

**balk** [bɔk] *tr* ostacolare ‖ *intr* intestarsi, impuntarsi

**Balkan** ['bɔlkən] *adj* balcanico ‖ **the Balkans** i Balcani

**balk·y** ['bɔki] *adj* (**-ier; -iest**) caparbio, ostinato

**ball** [bɔl] *s* palla; pallone *m*; sfera; (*of the thumb*) polpastrello; (*of wool*) gomitolo; (*projectile*) palla, pallottola; (*dance*) ballo; **on the ball** (slang) capace, efficiente; (slang) in gamba; **to play ball** giocare alla palla; **to play ball with** essere in cooperazione con ‖ *tr*—**to ball up** (slang) confondere

**ballad** ['bæləd] *s* ballata

**ball' and chain'** *s* palla di piombo; (fig) impedimento; (slang) moglie *f*

**ball'-and-sock'et joint'** ['bɔlən'sɑkɪt] *s* giunto a sfere

**ballast** ['bæləst] *s* zavorra; (rr) pietrisco ‖ *tr* zavorrare

**ball' bear'ing** *s* cuscinetto a sfere

**ballet** ['bæle] *s* balletto

**ballistic** [bə'lɪstɪk] *adj* balistico ‖ **ballistics** *ssg* balistica

**balloon** [bə'lun] *s* pallone *m*; (*for children*) palloncino; (*in comic strip*) fumetto

**ballot** ['bælət] *s* scheda elettorale; voto ‖ *intr* votare, ballottare

**bal'lot box'** *s* bussola, urna

**ball'play'er** *s* giocatore *m* di palla, giocatore *m* di baseball

**ball'-point pen'** *s* penna a sfera

**ball'room'** *s* salone *m* da ballo

**ballyhoo** ['bælɪ‚hu] *s* chiasso; montatura ‖ *tr* far chiasso a favore di

**balm** [bɑm] *s* balsamo

**balm·y** ['bɑmi] *adj* (**-ier; -iest**) balsamico; salubre; (slang) pazzo

**balsam** ['bɔlsəm] *s* balsamo; (*plant*) balsamina

**Baltic** ['bɔltɪk] *adj* baltico

**baluster** ['bæləstər] *s* balaustro

**balustrade** [‚bæləs'tred] *s* balaustrata

**bamboo** [bæm'bu] *s* bambù *m*

**bamboozle** [bæm'buzəl] *tr* ingannare, raggirare

**bamboozler** [bæm'buzlər] *s* raggiratore *m*

**ban** [bæn] *s* bando; (*of marriage*) pubblicazione matrimoniale; (eccl) interdetto, scomunica ‖ *v* (*pret & pp* **banned**; *ger* **banning**) *tr* proibire

**banal** ['benəl] or [bə'næl] *adj* banale

**banana** [bə'nænə] *s* banana, (*tree*) banano

**band** [bænd] *s* banda, striscia; (*of thin cloth*) benda; (*of metal, rubber*) fascia, nastro; (*of hat*) nastro; (mus) banda, fanfara; **to beat the band** fortemente; abbondantemente ‖ *tr* unire ‖ *intr*—**to band together** unirsi

**bandage** ['bændɪdʒ] *s* benda, bendaggio ‖ *tr* fasciare

**bandanna** [bæn'dænə] *s* fazzolettone colorato

**band'box'** *s* cappelliera

**bandit** ['bændɪt] *s* bandito

**band'mas'ter** *s* capomusica *m*

**bandoleer** [ˌbændə'lɪr] *s* bandoliera

**band' saw'** *s* sega a nastro

**band'stand'** *s* chiosco della banda

**band'wag'on** *s* carrozzone *m* da circo; **to jump on the bandwagon** prendere le parti del vincitore

**baneful** ['benfəl] *adj* nocivo; funesto

**bang** [bæŋ] *s* rumore *m*, scoppio; (*coll*) energia; (*pleasure*) (slang) piacere *m*, eccitazione; **bangs** frangetta ‖ *adv* tutto d'un colpo ‖ *tr* sbattere ‖ *intr* rimbombare ‖ *interj* bum!

**bang'-up'** *adj* (slang) eccellente, di prim'ordine

**banish** ['bænɪʃ] *tr* sbandire, mettere al bando

**banishment** ['bænɪʃmənt] *s* bando, esilio

**banister** ['bænɪstər] *s* balaustra; **banisters** balaustrata

**bank** [bæŋk] *s* (*of fish; of fog*) banco; (*of a river*) sponda; (*for coins*) salvadanaio; (*financial institution*) banca, banco; (*of earth, snow*) mucchio, banco; (*of clouds*) cumulo; (aer) inclinazione laterale; (billiards) sponda ‖ *tr* (*a fire*) coprire di cenere; (*to pile up*) ammonticchiare; (*a curve*) sopraelevare; (*money*) depositare ‖ *intr* depositare denaro; (aer) inclinarsi lateralmente; **to bank on** (coll) contare su (di)

**bank'book'** *s* libretto bancario, libretto di deposito

**banker** ['bæŋkər] *s* banchiere *m*

**banking** ['bæŋkɪŋ] *adj* bancario ‖ *s* attività bancaria; professione di banchiere

**bank' note'** *s* biglietto di banca

**bank'roll'** *s* rotolo di carta moneta; soldi *mpl* ‖ *tr* (slang) finanziare

**bankrupt** ['bæŋkrʌpt] *adj* & *s* fallito; **to go bankrupt** andare in fallimento ‖ *tr* dichiarare in fallimento; far fallire

**bankrupt·cy** ['bæŋkrʌptsi] *s* (-cies) fallimento

**banner** ['bænər] *adj* importante ‖ *s* bandiera, stendardo; (journ) titolo in grassetto

**banns** [bænz] *spl* bandi *mpl* matrimoniali

**banquet** ['bæŋkwɪt] *s* banchetto ‖ *tr* dar un banchetto a ‖ *intr* banchettare

**bantam** ['bæntəm] *adj* piccolo ‖ *s* pollo nano

**ban'tam·weight'** *s* peso gallo, bantam *m*

**banter** ['bæntər] *s* scherzo, facezia ‖ *intr* scherzare, celiare

**baptism** ['bæptɪzəm] *s* battesimo

**baptismal** [bæp'tɪzməl] *adj* battesimale; (*certificate*) di battesimo

**Baptist** ['bæptɪst] *adj* & *s* battista *mf*

**baptister·y** ['bæptɪstəri] *s* (-ies) battistero

**baptize** [bæp'taɪz] *or* ['bæptaɪz] *tr* battezzare

**bar** [bɑr] *s* barra; sbarra; (*of soap*) saponetta; (*of chocolate*) tavoletta; (*of sand*) banco; (*obstacle*) barriera; bar *m*; (*of public opinion*) tribunale *m*; (*legal profession*) avvocatura; (*of door or window*) spranga; (*of lead*) (typ) lingotto; (mus) battuta; **behind bars** in guardina; **to be admitted to the bar** diventare avvocato; **to tend bar** fare il barista ‖ *prep* eccetto, salvo; **bar none** senza eccezione ‖ *v* (*pret* & *pp* **barred;** *ger* **barring**) *tr* sbarrare; sprangare; bloccare; escludere

**bar' associa'tion** *s* associazione dell'ordine degli avvocati

**barb** [bɑrb] *s* (*of arrow*) barbiglio

**barbarian** [bɑr'berɪ·ən] *s* barbaro

**barbaric** [bɑr'bærɪk] *adj* barbaro

**barbarism** ['bɑrbəˌrɪzəm] *s* barbarismo

**barbari·ty** [bɑr'bærɪti] *s* (-ties) barbarie *f*

**barbarous** ['bɑrbərəs] *adj* barbaro, crudele

**Bar'bary ape'** ['bɑrbəri] *s* bertuccia

**barbecue** ['bɑrbɪˌkju] *s* arrosto allo spiedo ‖ *tr* arrostire allo spiedo

**barbed** [bɑrbd] *adj* irto di punte; mordace, pungente

**barbed' wire'** *s* filo spinato

**barber** ['bɑrbər] *s* barbiere *m*; (*who cuts and styles hair*) parrucchiere *m*

**bar'ber·shop'** *s* barbieria, negozio di barbiere; negozio di parrucchiere

**barbiturate** [bɑr'bɪtʃəˌret] *s* barbiturato, barbiturico

**bard** [bɑrd] *s* bardo, poeta *m*

**bare** [ber] *adj* nudo; (*head*) a capo scoperto; (*unconcealed*) palese; (*empty*) vuoto; (*wire*) senza isolante; (*unadorned*) semplice; **to lay bare** mettere a nudo ‖ *tr* denudare, scoprire

**bare'back'** *adj* & *adv* senza sella

**barefaced** ['ber ˌfest] *adj* impudente, sfacciato, spudorato

**bare'foot'** *adj* scalzo

**barehanded** ['ber ˌhændɪd] *adj* & *adv* a mani nude

**bareheaded** ['ber ˌhedɪd] *adj* a capo scoperto

**barelegged** ['ber ˌlegɪd] *adj* a gambe nude

**barely** ['berli] *adv* appena, soltanto

**bargain** ['bɑrgɪn] *s* affare *m*, buon affare *m*; contrattazione; **at a bargain** a buon prezzo; **into the bargain** in soprappiù ‖ *tr*—**to bargain away** vendere a buonissimo prezzo ‖ *intr* contrattare, mercanteggiare; **to bargain for** aspettarsi

**bar'gain sale'** *s* vendita sottoprezzo

**barge** [bɑrdʒ] *s* barcone *m*, chiatta ‖ *intr*—**to barge in** entrare senza chiedere permesso

**baritone** ['bærɪˌton] *adj* di baritono ‖ *s* baritono *m*

**barium** ['berɪ·əm] *s* bario

**bark** [bɑrk] *s* corteccia, scorza; (*of dog*) abbaiamento, latrato ‖ *tr* (e.g., *insults)* lanciare ‖ *intr* abbaiare, latrare

**bar'keep'er** *s* barista *mf*

**barker** ['bɑrkər] *s* banditore *m*, imbonitore *m*

**barley** ['bɑrli] *s* orzo

**bar' mag'net** *s* calamita a forma di barra allungata

**bar'maid'** *s* barista *f*

**bar'man** *s* (-men) barista *m*

**barn** [bɑrn] *s* granaio; *(for hay)* fienile *m; (for livestock)* stalla

**barnacle** ['bɑrnəkəl] *s* cirripede *m*

**barn' owl'** *s* civetta

**barn'yard'** *s* bassacorte *f*, aia

**barn'yard fowl'** *s* animale *m* da cortile ‖ *spl* animali *mpl* da cortile

**barometer** [bə'rɑmɪtər] *s* barometro

**baron** ['bærən] *s* barone *m; (industrialist)* cavaliere *m* d'industria

**baroness** ['bærənɪs] *s* baronessa

**baroque** [bə'rok] *adj & s* barocco

**bar'rack-room'** *adj* da caserma ‖ *s* camerata

**barracks** ['bærəks] *spl* caserma; camerata

**barrage** [bə'rɑʒ] *s* (mil) fuoco di sbarramento

**barrel** ['bærəl] *s* barile *m*, botte *f; (of gun)* canna; (mach) cilindro

**bar'rel or'gan** *s* organetto di Barberia

**barren** ['bærən] *adj* sterile; *(without vegetation)* brullo

**barricade** [‚bærɪ'ked] *s* barricata ‖ *tr* barricare

**barrier** ['bærɪ‑ər] *s* barriera

**bar'rier reef'** *s* barriera corallina

**barring** ['bɑrɪŋ] *prep* eccetto, salvo

**barrister** ['bærɪstər] *s* (Brit) avvocato

**bar'room'** *s* bar *m*, cantina, mescita

**bar'tend'er** *s* barista *mf*, barman *m*

**barter** ['bɑrtər] *s* baratto ‖ *tr & intr* barattare, permutare

**basalt** [bə'sɔlt] *s* basalto

**base** [bes] *adj* basale; basso; servile; *(morally low)* turpe; *(metal)* vile, non prezioso ‖ *s* base *f; (in children's games)* tana; *(of a word)* radice *f* basale ‖ *tr* basare

**base'ball'** *s* baseball *m*, pallabase *f*

**base'board'** *s* basamento; *(of wall)* zoccolo

**Basel** ['bazəl] *s* Basilea

**baseless** ['beslɪs] *adj* infondato

**basement** ['besmənt] *s* scantinato, piano interrato

**bashful** ['bæ/fəl] *adj* timido

**basic** ['besɪk] *adj* fondamentale; (chem) basico

**ba'sic commod'ities** *spl* articoli *mpl* di prima necessità

**basilica** [bə'sɪlɪkə] *s* basilica

**basin** ['besɪn] *s* catino; vasca; *(of balance)* piatto; *(of river)* bacino; *(of harbor)* darsena

**ba·sis** ['besɪs] *s* (-ses [siz]) base *f*

**bask** [bæsk] *or* [bɑsk] *intr* crogiolarsi

**basket** ['bæskɪt] *or* ['bɑskɪt] *s* cesta; (sports) cesto

**bas'ket·ball'** *s* pallacanestro *f*

**Basque** [bæsk] *adj & s* basco

**bas-relief** [‚bɑrɪ'lif] *or* [‚bærɪ'lif] *s* bassorilievo

**bass** [bes] *adj & s* (mus) basso ‖ [bæs] *s* (ichth) pesce persico

**bass' drum'** *s* grancassa

**bass' horn'** *s* bassotuba *m*

**bassinet** ['bæsə‚nɛt] *or* [‚bæsə'nɛt] *s* culla a forma di cesto; carrozzina a forma di cesto

**bas·so** ['bæso] *or* ['bɑso] *s* (-sos *or* -si [si]) basso

**bassoon** [bə'sun] *s* fagotto

**bass' vi'ol** ['vaɪ‑əl] *s* contrabbasso

**bastard** ['bæstərd] *adj & s* bastardo

**baste** [best] *tr (to sew)* imbastire; *(meat)* inumidire con acqua o grasso

**bastion** ['bæst/ən] *or* ['bæstɪ‑ən] *s* bastione *m*

**bat** [bæt] *s* mazza; *(in cricket)* maglio; (coll) colpo; (zool) pipistrello ‖ *v* *(pret & pp* **batted;** *ger* **batting)** *tr* colpire con la mazza; **without batting an eye** (coll) senza batter ciglio

**batch** [bæt/] *s (of bread)* infornata; gruppo, numero

**bath** [bæθ] *or* [bɑθ] *s* bagno; **to take a bath** fare il bagno

**bathe** [beð] *tr* bagnare, lavare ‖ *intr* bagnarsi, fare il bagno

**bather** ['beðər] *s* bagnante *mf*

**bath'house'** *s (individual)* cabina; spogliatoio

**bath'ing beau'ty** *s* bellezza in costume da bagno

**bath'ing cap'** *s* cuffia da bagno

**bath'ing resort'** *s* stazione balneare

**bath'ing suit'** *s* costume *m* da bagno

**bath'ing trunks'** *spl* mutandine *fpl* da bagno

**bath'robe'** *s* accappatoio

**bath'room'** *s* stanza da bagno

**bath' salts'** *spl* sali *mpl* da bagno

**bath'tub'** *s* bagno, vasca da bagno

**baton** [bæ'tɑn] *or* ['bætən] *s* bastone *m; (mus)* bacchetta

**battalion** [bə'tæljən] *s* battaglione *m*

**batten** ['bætən] *tr* assicella; piccola traversa; (naut) bietta ‖ *tr*—**to batten down the hatches** chiudere ermeticamente i boccaporti

**batter** ['bætər] *s* pasta, farina pastosa; (baseball) battitore *m* ‖ *tr* battere, tempestare di colpi; *(to wear out)* logorare

**bat'tering ram'** *s* ariete *m*

**batter·y** ['bætəri] *s* (-ies) *(primary cell)* pila; *(secondary cell)* accumulatore *m; (group of batteries)* batteria; (law) assalto; (mil & mus) batteria

**battle** ['bætəl] *s* battaglia; **to do battle** dar battaglia ‖ *tr* combattere contro ‖ *intr* combattere

**bat'tle cry'** *s* grido di guerra

**battledore** ['bætəl‚dor] *s* racchetta; **battledore and shuttlecock** gioco del volano

**bat'tle·field'** *s* campo di battaglia

**bat'tle·front'** *s* fronte *m* di combattimento

**battlement** ['bætəlmənt] *s* merlatura

**bat'tle roy'al** *s* baruffa generale, zuffa generale

**bat'tle·ship'** *s* corazzata

**battue** [bæ'tu] *or* [bæ'tju] *s* (hunt) battuta

**bat·ty** [ˈbæti] *adj* (**-tier; -tiest**) (slang) pazzo, eccentrico

**bauble** [ˈbɔbəl] *s* bazzecola, gingillo

**Bavaria** [bəˈvɛrɪ·ə] *s* la Baviera

**Bavarian** [bəˈvɛrɪ·ən] *adj* & *s* bavarese *mf*

**bawd** [bɔd] *s* ruffiano; ruffiana

**bawd·y** [ˈbɔdi] *adj* (**-ier; -iest**) indecente, osceno

**bawd'y·house'** *s* casa di malaffare

**bawl** [bɔl] *s* grido; (coll) pianto ‖ *tr*— **to bawl out** (slang) fare una ramanzina a ‖ *intr* strillare; (coll) piangere

**bay** [be] *adj* baio ‖ *s* baia; vano, alcova; (*recess in wall*) apertura nel muro; finestra sporgente; (*of dog*) latrato; cavallo baio; (bot) lauro; **at bay** in una posizione disperata ‖ *intr* latrare

**bayonet** [ˈbe·ənɪt] *s* baionetta ‖ *tr* dare baionettate a ‖ *intr* dare baionettate

**bay' win'dow** *s* finestra sporgente; (slang) pancia

**bazooka** [bəˈzukə] *s* bazooka *m*

**be** [bi] *v* (*pres* **am** [æm], **is** [ɪz], **are** [ɑr]; *pret* **was** [wɑz] or [wʌz], **were** [wʌr]; *pp* **been** [bɪn]) *intr* essere; fare, e.g., **to be a mason** fare il muratore; fare, e.g., **3 times 3 is 9** tre volte tre fa nove; **be as it may be** comunque sia; **here is** or **here are** ecco; **there are** ci sono; **there is** c'è; **to be** futuro, e.g., **my wife to be** la mia futura sposa; **to be ashamed** aver vergogna; **to be cold** aver freddo; **to be hot** aver caldo; **to be hungry** aver fame; **to be in** stare a casa; **to be in a hurry** aver fretta; **to be in with** (coll) essere amico intimo di; **to be off** andarsene; **to be out** essere fuori; **to be out of** (coll) non aver più; **to be right** aver ragione; **to be sleepy** aver sonno; **to be thirsty** avere sete; **to be up** essere alzato; **to be up to** essere all'altezza di; toccare, e.g., **it's up to you** tocca a Lei; **to be warm** avere caldo; **to be wrong** avere torto; sbagliarsi; **to be . . . years old** avere . . . anni ‖ *aux* stare, e.g., **to be waiting** stare aspettando; essere, e.g., **the murder has been committed** l'omicidio è stato commesso; dovere, e.g., **he is to clean the stables tomorrow** domani deve pulire la stalla ‖ *impers* essere, e.g., **it is necessary** è necessario; fare, e.g., **it is cold** fa freddo; **it is hot** fa caldo

**beach** [bitʃ] *s* spiaggia ‖ *tr* (*a boat*) arenare ‖ *intr* arenarsi

**beach'comb'** *intr* raccogliere relitti sulla spiaggia

**beach'comb'er** *s* girellone *m* di spiaggia

**beach'head'** *s* testa di sbarco

**beach' robe'** *s* accappatoio

**beach' shoe'** *s* sandalo da spiaggia

**beach' umbrel'la** *s* ombrellone *m* da spiaggia

**beacon** [ˈbikən] *s* faro ‖ *tr* rischiarare; fare da guida a ‖ *intr* brillare

**bead** [bid] *s* perlina; grano, chicco; (*drop*) goccia; **beads** (*in a necklace or rosary*) conterie *fpl;* **to count one's beads** recitare il rosario

**beagle** [ˈbigəl] *s* segugio, bracco

**beak** [bik] *s* becco; promontorio

**beam** [bim] *s* trave *f;* (*of balance*) braccio; (*of light*) raggio; (*ship's breadth*) larghezza; (*smile*) sorriso; (*radio signal*) fascio direttore; (*course indicated by radio beam*) aerovia; (naut) traverso ‖ *tr* (*a radio signal*) dirigere; (e.g., *light*) irraggiare ‖ *intr* raggiare

**bean** [bin] *s* fagiolo; (*of coffee*) chicco; (slang) testa

**beaner·y** [ˈbinəri] *s* (**-ies**) (slang) gargotta, taverna di secondo ordine

**bean'pole'** *s* puntello per i fagioli; (coll) palo del telegrafo

**bear** [bɛr] *s* orso; (astr) orsa; (com) ribassista *m*, giocatore *m* al ribasso ‖ *v* (*pret* **bore** [bor]; *pp* **borne** [born]) *tr* (*to carry*) portare; (*to give birth to*) partorire; (*to sustain*) sostenere; (*to withstand*) sopportare; (*a grudge*) serbare; (*in mind*) tenere; (*interest*) produrre; (*to pay*) pagare; **to bear the date** aver la data; **to bear out** confermare; **to bear witness** testimoniare ‖ *intr* (*to be productive*) fruttificare; (*to move*) dirigersi; (*to be oppressive*) fare pressione; **to bear down on** fare pressione su; avvicinarsi a; **to bear up** resistere; **to bear with** tollerare

**bearable** [ˈbɛrəbəl] *adj* tollerabile

**beard** [bɪrd] *s* barba; (e.g., *in wheat*) arista

**bearded** *adj* barbuto

**beardless** [ˈbɪrdlɪs] *adj* imberbe

**bearer** [ˈbɛrər] *s* portatore *m*

**bearing** [ˈbɛrɪŋ] *s* portamento; relazione; importanza; (mach) bronzina, cuscinetto; **bearings** orientamento; **to lose one's bearings** perdere la bussola; perdere l'orientamento

**bearish** [ˈbɛrɪʃ] *adj* (*like a bear*) orsino; (e.g., *prices*) in ribasso; (*market*) al ribasso; (*speculator*) ribassista

**bear'skin'** *s* pelle *f* dell'orso; (mil) colbacco

**beast** [bist] *s* bestia

**beast·ly** [ˈbistli] *adj* (**-lier; -liest**) bestiale ‖ *adv* (coll) malissimo

**beast' of bur'den** *s* bestia da soma

**beast' of prey'** *s* animale *m* da rapina

**beat** [bit] *s* (*of heart*) battito; (*of policeman*) ronda; (*stroke*) colpo; (*habitual route*) cammino battuto; (mus) tempo; (phys) battimento ‖ *v* (*pret* **beat;** *pp* **beat** or **beaten**) *tr* battere; percuotere; (*eggs*) frullare; (*to whip*) frustare; (coll) confondere; **beat it!** (slang) vattene!; **to beat a retreat** battere in ritirata; **to beat back** respingere; **to beat down** sopprimere; **to beat off** respingere; **to beat up** (*eggs*) frullare; (*people*) dargliene a ‖ *intr* battere; pulsare; **to beat around the bush** (coll) menare il can per l'aia

**beat'en path'** [ˈbitən] *s* cammino battuto

**beater** [ˈbitər] *s* frullino

**beati·fy** [bɪˈætɪ ˌfaɪ] *v* (*pret* & *pp* **-fied**) *tr* beatificare

**beating** ['bitɪŋ] *s* battitura; (*whipping*) frustatura; (*throbbing*) pulsazione, battito; (*defeat*) sconfitta

**beau** [bo] *s* (**beaus** or **beaux** [boz]) (*dandy*) bellimbusto; (*girl's sweetheart*) spasimante *m*

**beautician** [bju'tɪʃən] *s* estetista *mf*

**beautiful** ['bjutɪfəl] *adj* bello

**beauti·fy** ['bjutɪ ,faɪ] *v* (*pret & pp* -**fied**) *tr* abbellire

**beau·ty** ['bjuti] *s* (-**ties**) bellezza

**beau'ty con'test** *s* concorso di bellezza

**beau'ty par'lor** *s* istituto di bellezza

**beau'ty sleep'** *s* primo sonno

**beau'ty spot'** *s* neo; posto pittoresco

**beaver** ['bivər] *s* castoro; pelle *f* di castoro; cappello a cilindro

**because** [bɪ'kɔz] *conj* perchè; **because of** a causa di

**beck** [bɛk] *s* gesto; **at the beck and call of** agli ordini di

**beckon** ['bɛkən] *s* gesto ‖ *tr* fare gesto a ‖ *intr* fare gesto

**becloud** [bɪ'klaʊd] *tr* annebbiare; oscurare

**be·come** [bɪ'kʌm] *v* (*pret* -**came**; *pp* -**come**) *tr* convenire a; stare bene a, e.g., **this hat becomes you** questo cappello Le sta bene ‖ *intr* diventare; farsi; convertirsi, e.g., **water became wine** l'acqua si convertì in vino; succedere, e.g., **what became of my coat?** che è successo del mio pastrano?; essere, e.g., **what will become of me?** che sarà di me?; **to become accustomed** abituarsi; **to become angry** entrare in collera; **to become crazy** impazzire; **to become ill** ammalarsi

**becoming** [bɪ'kʌmɪŋ] *adj* conveniente; appropriato; acconcio; **this is very becoming to you** questo Le sta molto bene

**bed** [bɛd] *s* letto; (*layer*) strato; giacimento; **to go to bed** andare a letto; **to take to one's bed** mettersi a letto

**bed' and board'** *s* vitto e alloggio; pensione completa

**bed'bug'** *s* cimice *f*

**bed'clothes'** *spl* lenzuola *fpl* e coperte *fpl*, biancheria da letto

**bed'cov'er** *s* coperta da letto

**bedding** ['bɛdɪŋ] *s* lenzuola *fpl* e coperte *fpl; (litter)* lettiera; (*foundation*) fondamenta *fpl*

**bedeck** [bɪ'dɛk] *tr* ornare, adornare

**bedev·il** [bɪ'dɛvɪl] *v* (*pret & pp* -**iled** or -**illed**; *ger* -**iling** or -**illing**) *tr* tormentare diabolicamente; confondere

**bed'fast'** *adj* confinato a letto

**bed'fel'low** *s* compagno di letto; compagno di stanza; compagno

**bedlam** ['bɛdləm] *s* manicomio; pandemonio

**bed' lin'en** *s* biancheria da letto

**bed'pan'** *s* padella

**bedridden** ['bɛd ,rɪdən] *adj* degente a letto

**bed'room'** *s* stanza da letto, camera da letto

**bed'room slip'per** *s* babbuccia, pantofola

**bed'side'** *s* capezzale *m*

**bed'side man'ner** *s* maniera di fare coi pazienti

**bed'sore'** *s* piaga da decubito

**bed'spread'** *s* coperta da letto

**bed'spring'** *s* rete *f* del letto; molla del letto

**bed'stead'** *s* fusto del letto

**bed'tick'** *s* traliccio

**bed'time'** *s* ora di coricarsi

**bed'warm'er** *s* scaldaletto

**bee** [bi] *s* ape *f*

**beech** [bitʃ] *s* faggio

**beech'nut'** *s* faggiola

**beef** [bif] *s* bue *m*, manzo; carne *f* di manzo; (*coll*) forza; (*slang*) lamentela ‖ *tr*—**to beef up** (*coll*) rinforzare ‖ *intr* (*slang*) lamentarsi

**beef' cat'tle** *s* manzi *mpl* da carne

**beef'steak'** *s* bistecca

**beef' stew'** *s* stufato di manzo

**bee'hive'** *s* alveare *m*

**bee'keep'er** *s* apicoltore *m*

**bee'line'** *s*—**to make a beeline for** (*coll*) andare direttamente verso

**beer** [bɪr] *s* birra

**beer' saloon'** *s* birreria

**beeswax** ['biz ,wæks] *s* cera d'api

**beet** [bit] *s* barbabietola

**beetle** ['bitəl] *adj* sporgente, folto ‖ *s* scarafaggio

**bee'tle-browed'** *adj* dalle sopracciglia folte

**beet' su'gar** *s* zucchero di barbabietola

**be·fall** [bɪ'fɔl] *v* (*pret* -**fell** ['fɛl]; *pp* -**fallen** ['fɔlən]) *tr* succedere a ‖ *intr* succedere

**befitting** [bɪ'fɪtɪŋ] *adj* appropriato

**before** [bɪ'for] *adv* prima, prima d'ora ‖ *prep* (*in time*) prima di; (*in place*) dinnanzi a, davanti a; **before Christ** avanti Cristo ‖ *conj* prima che

**before'hand'** *adv* in anticipo; precedentemente

**befriend** [bɪ'frɛnd] *tr* diventare amico di, proteggere, favorire; aiutare

**befuddle** [bɪ'fʌdəl] *tr* confondere

**beg** [bɛg] *v* (*pret & pp* **begged;** *ger* **begging**) *tr* chiedere; implorare; (*alms*) mendicare; **I beg your pardon** Le chiedo scusa; **to beg s.o. for s.th** chiedere qlco a qlcu ‖ *intr* chiedere la carità; **to beg for** sollecitare; **to beg off** scusarsi; **to go begging** rimanere invenduto

**be·get** [bɪ'gɛt] *v* (*pret* -**got** ['gɑt]; *pp* -**gotten** or -**got;** *ger* -**getting**) *tr* generare

**beggar** ['bɛgər] *s* accattone *m*, mendicante *m*

**be·gin** [bɪ'gɪn] *v* (*pret* -**gan** ['gæn]; *pp* -**gun** ['gʌn]; *ger* -**ginning**) *tr & intr* cominciare, iniziare; **beginning with** a partire da; **to begin with** per cominciare

**beginner** [bɪ'gɪnər] *s* principiante *mf*

**beginning** [bɪ'gɪnɪŋ] *s* inizio, origine *f*, principio, esordio

**begrudge** [bɪ'grʌdʒ] *tr* invidiare; concedere con riluttanza

**beguile** [bɪ'gaɪl] *tr* ingannare; sedurre; (*to delight*) divertire

**behalf** [bɪ'hæf] or [bɪ'hɑf] *s*—**on behalf of** nell'interesse di; a nome di behave [bɪ'hev] *intr* comportarsi; comportarsi bene

behavior [bɪ'hevjər] *s* comportamento, condotta; funzionamento

behead [bɪ'hɛd] *tr* decapitare

behest [bɪ'hɛst] *s* ordine *m*, comando

behind [bɪ'haɪnd] *s* didietro; (slang) sedere *m* ‖ *adv* dietro; (*in arrears*) in arretrato; **from behind** dal didietro ‖ *prep* dietro a, dietro di; **behind time** in ritardo

be·hold [bɪ'hold] *v* (*pret & pp* -**held** ['hɛld]) *tr* contemplare; ammirare ‖ *interj* guarda!

behoove [bɪ'huv] *impers*—**it behooves him to** gli conviene di

being ['bi·ɪŋ] *adj* esistente; **for the time being** per ora ‖ *s* essere *m*, ente *m*

belabor [bɪ'lebər] *tr* attaccare; (fig) ribattere, confutare; (fig) insistere su

belated [bɪ'letɪd] *adj* tardivo

belch [bɛltʃ] *s* rutto ‖ *tr* eruttare, vomitare ‖ *intr* ruttare

beleaguer [bɪ'ligər] *tr* assediare

bel·fry ['bɛlfri] *s* (-**fries**) (*tower*) campanile *m*; (*site of bell*) cella campanaria; (slang) testa

Belgian ['bɛldʒən] *adj & s* belga *mf*

Belgium ['bɛldʒəm] *s* il Belgio

be·lie [bɪ'laɪ] *v* (*pret & pp* -**lied** ['laɪd]; *ger* -**lying** ['laɪ·ɪŋ]) *tr* (*to misrepresent*) tradire; (*to prove false*) smentire

belief [bɪ'lif] *s* fede *f*, credenza

believable [bɪ'livəbəl] *adj* credibile

believe [bɪ'liv] *tr* credere ‖ *intr* credere, aver fede; **to believe in** credere in

believer [bɪ'livər] *s* credente *mf*

belittle [bɪ'lɪtəl] *tr* menomare

bell [bɛl] *s* campana; (*for a door*) campanello; (*sound*) rintocco; (*on cattle*) campanaccio; (*of deer*) bramito ‖ *intr* bramire

belladonna [,bɛlə'dɑnə] *s* belladonna

bell'-bot'tom *adj* a campana

bell'boy' *s* cameriere *m*, ragazzo

belle [bɛl] *s* bella

belles-lettres [,bɛl'lɛtrə] *spl* belle lettere

bell' glass' *s* campana di vetro

bell'hop' *s* cameriere *m*, ragazzo

bellicose ['bɛlɪ,kos] *adj* bellicoso

belligerent [bə'lɪdʒərənt] *adj & s* belligerante *m*

bellow ['bɛlo] *s* muggito; **bellows** mantice *m*; (*of camera*) soffietto ‖ *tr* gridare ‖ *intr* muggire

bell' ring'er *s* campanaro

bellwether ['bɛl,wɛðər] *s* pecora guida

bel·ly ['bɛli] *s* (-**lies**) ventre *m*, pancia ‖ *v* (*pret & pp* -**lied**) *tr* far pancia

bel'ly·ache' *s* (coll) mal *m* di pancia ‖ *intr* (slang) lamentarsi

bel'ly·but'ton *s* (coll) ombelico

bel'ly dance' *s* (coll) danza del ventre

bel'ly flop' *s* panciata

bellyful ['bɛli,ful] *s*—**to have a bellyful** (slang) averne fino agli occhi

bel'ly·land' *intr* (aer) atterrare sul ventre

belong [bɪ'lɔŋ] or [bɪ'lɑŋ] *intr* appartenere; stare bene, e.g., **this chair belongs in this room** questa sedia sta bene in questa stanza

belongings [bɪ'lɔŋɪŋz] or [bɪ'lɑŋɪŋz] *spl* effetti *mpl* personali

beloved [bɪ'lʌvɪd] or [bɪ'lʌvd] *adj & s* diletto, amato

below [bɪ'lo] *adv* sotto; più sotto; **ten below** dieci gradi sotto zero ‖ *prep* sotto, sotto di

belt [bɛlt] *s* cintura, cinghia; (mach) nastro; (mil) cinturone *m*; (geog) fascia, zona; **to tighten one's belt** far cintura ‖ *tr* cingere; (slang) staffilare

belt'ed tire' *s* copertone cinturato

belt' line' *s* linea di circonvallazione

beltway ['bɛlt,we] *s* raccordo anulare

bemoan [bɪ'mon] *tr* lamentare; compiangere

bench [bɛntʃ] *s* banco, panca; tribunale *m*; (mach) banco di prova; **to be on the bench** (law) essere giudice

bend [bɛnd] *s* curva; (*e.g., of pipe*) gomito, angolo ‖ *v* (*pret & pp* **bent** [bɛnt]) *tr* curvare; piegare; far piegare ‖ *intr* deviare; piegare, piegarsi; **to bend over** inchinarsi

beneath [bɪ'niθ] *adv* sotto; più sotto ‖ *prep* sotto, sotto di

benediction [,bɛnɪ'dɪkʃən] *s* benedizione

benefactor ['bɛnɪ,fæktər] or [,bɛnɪ'fæktər] *s* benefattore *m*

benefactress ['bɛnɪ,fæktrɪs] or [,bɛnɪ'fæktrɪs] *s* benefattrice *f*

beneficence [bɪ'nɛfɪsəns] *s* beneficenza

beneficent [bɪ'nɛfɪsənt] *adj* caritatevole; benefico

beneficial [,bɛnɪ'fɪʃəl] *adj* benefico

beneficiar·y [,bɛnɪ'fɪʃɪ,ɛri] *s* (-**ies**) beneficiario

benefit ['bɛnɪfɪt] *s* beneficio; festa di beneficenza; **for the benefit of** a beneficio di ‖ *tr & intr* beneficiare

ben'efit perfor'mance *s* beneficiata

benevolence [bɪ'nɛvələns] *s* benevolenza; carità *f*

benevolent [bɪ'nɛvələnt] *adj* benevolo; (*institution*) benefico

benign [bɪ'naɪn] *adj* benigno

bent [bɛnt] *adj* curvo; **bent on** deciso a ‖ *s* curva; tendenza, propensità *f*

Benzedrine ['bɛnzɪ,drin] (trademark) *s* benzedrina

benzene ['bɛnzin] *s* benzolo

benzine [bɛn'zin] *s* benzina

bequeath [bɪ'kwiθ] or [bɪ'kwið] *tr* legare, lasciare in eredità

bequest [bɪ'kwɛst] *s* legato, lascito

berate [bɪ'ret] *tr* redarguire

be·reave [bɪ'riv] *v* (*pret & pp* -**reaved** or -**reft** ['rɛft]) *tr* spogliare

bereavement [bɪ'rivmənt] *s* lutto, perdita

beret [bə're] or ['bɛre] *s* berretto

Berlin [bər'lɪn] *adj* berlinese ‖ *s* Berlino

Berliner [bər'lɪnər] *s* berlinese *mf*

Bermuda [bər'mjudə] *s* le Bermude

ber·ry ['bɛri] *s* (-**ries**) (*dry seed*) chicco; (*fruit*) bacca

**berserk** [bʌr'sʌrk] *adj* infuriato ‖ *adv*
—**to go berserk** impazzire
**berth** [bʌrθ] *s* (*for a ship*) posto di
ormeggio; (*bed*) cuccetta; (coll)
posto
**beryllium** [bə'rɪlɪ·əm] *s* berillio
**be·seech** [bɪ'sitʃ] *v* (*pret & pp* **-sought**
['sɔt] or **-seeched**) *tr* supplicare
**be·set** [bɪ'sɛt] *v* (*pret & pp* **-set;** *ger*
**-setting**) *tr* assediare, circondare;
(*e.g., with problems*) assillare
**beside** [bɪ'saɪd] *adv* oltre, inoltre ‖
*prep* vicino a; in confronto di; oltre
a; **beside oneself** fuori di sé; **beside
the point** fuori del seminato
**besides** [bɪ'saɪdz] *adv* inoltre; d'altronde ‖ *prep* oltre a
**besiege** [bɪ'sidʒ] *tr* assediare; (*with
questions*) bombardare
**besmear** [bɪ'smɪr] *tr* imbrattare, sgorbiare; sporcare
**besmirch** [bɪ'smʌrtʃ] *tr* insudiciare
**bespatter** [bɪ'spætər] *tr* inzaccherare
**be·speak** [bɪ'spik] *v* (**-spoke** ['spok];
**-spoken**) *tr* chiedere anticipatamente
a; (*to show*) dimostrare
**best** [bɛst] *adj super* (il) migliore; ottimo ‖ *s* meglio; **at best** nella miglior
delle ipotesi; **to do one's best** fare
del proprio meglio; **to get the best of**
avere la meglio di; **to make the best
of** adattarsi a ‖ *adv super* meglio;
**had best,** e.g., **I had best** dovrei ‖ *tr*
battere, riuscire superiore a
**bestial** ['bɛstjəl] or ['bɛstʃəl] *adj* bestiale
**be·stir** [bɪ'stʌr] *v* (*pret & pp* **-stirred;**
*ger* **-stirring**) *tr* eccitare; **to bestir
oneself** darsi da fare
**best' man'** *s* testimone *m* di nozze
**bestow** [bɪ'sto] *tr* accordare; conferire
**best' sell'er** *s* best-seller *m*
**bet** [bɛt] *s* scommessa ‖ *v* (*pret & pp*
**bet** or **betted;** *ger* **betting**) *tr & intr*
scommettere; **I bet** ci scommetto;
**you bet** (coll) evidentemente
**be·take** [bɪ'tek] *v* (*pret* **-took** ['tʊk];
*pp* **-taken**) *tr*—**to betake oneself**
andare, dirigersi
**be·think** [bɪ'θɪŋk] *v* (*pret & pp*
**-thought** ['θɔt]) *tr* **to bethink oneself**
pensare; ricordarsi
**Bethlehem** ['bɛθlɪ·əm] or ['bɛθlɪ‚hɛm]
*s* Betlemme *f*
**betide** [bɪ'taɪd] *tr* accadere a ‖ *intr*
accadere
**betoken** [bɪ'tokən] *tr* indicare, presagire
**betray** [bɪ'tre] *tr* tradire, ingannare;
(*to reveal*) rivelare
**betroth** [bɪ'troð] or [bɪ'trɔθ] *tr* promettere in matrimonio a
**betrothal** [bɪ'troðəl] or [bɪ'trɔθəl] *s*
fidanzamento
**betrothed** [bɪ'troðd] or [bɪ'trɔθt] *adj*
fidanzato ‖ *s* promesso sposo, fidanzato
**better** ['bɛtər] *adj comp* migliore; **to
grow better** migliorare ‖ *s*—**betters**
superiori *mpl;* ottimati *mpl;* **to get
the better of** avere la meglio di ‖ *adv*
meglio; **had better** dovere, e.g., **I had**

**better** dovrei; **to be better off** stare
meglio; **to think better of** riconsiderare; **you ought to know better** dovrebbe vergognarsi ‖ *tr* sorpassare;
migliorare; **to better oneself** migliorare la propria situazione
**bet'ter half'** *s* metà *f*
**betterment** ['bɛtərmənt] *s* miglioramento
**bettor** ['bɛtər] *s* scommettitore *m*
**between** [bɪ'twin] *adv* in mezzo; **in between** in mezzo, fra i piedi ‖ *prep*
fra, tra
**between'-decks'** *s* interponte *m*
**bev·el** ['bɛvəl] *s* (*instrument*) falsa
squadra; (*sloping part*) augnatura ‖
*v* (*pret & pp* **-eled** or **-elled;** *ger* **-eling**
or **-elling**) *tr* augnare
**beverage** ['bɛvərɪdʒ] *s* bevanda
**bev·y** ['bɛvi] *s* (**-ies**) (*of women*)
gruppo; (*of birds*) stormo
**bewail** [bɪ'wel] *tr* lamentare
**beware** [bɪ'wer] *tr* fare attenzione a,
guardarsi da ‖ *intr* fare attenzione,
guardarsi
**bewilder** [bɪ'wɪldər] *tr* lasciar perplesso, confondere, disorientare
**bewilderment** [bɪ'wɪldərmənt] *s* perplessità *f*, disorientamento
**bewitch** [bɪ'wɪtʃ] *tr* stregare
**beyond** [bɪ'jand] *s*—**the beyond** l'aldilà *m* ‖ *adv* più lontano ‖ *prep* al
di là di; oltre a; più tardi di; **beyond
a doubt** fuori dubbio; **beyond repair**
irreparabile
**bias** ['baɪ·əs] *s* linea diagonale; pregiudizio; **on the bias** diagonalmente
‖ *tr* prevenire
**bib** [bɪb] *s* bavaglino
**Bible** ['baɪbəl] *s* Bibbia
**Biblical** ['bɪblɪkəl] *adj* biblico
**bibliogra·phy** [‚bɪblɪ'agrəfɪ] *s* (**-phies**)
bibliografia
**bibliophile** ['bɪblɪ·ə‚faɪl] *s* bibliofilo
**bicarbonate** [baɪ'karbə‚net] *s* bicarbonato
**biceps** ['baɪsɛps] *s* bicipite *m*
**bicker** ['bɪkər] *s* bisticcio, disputa ‖
*intr* bisticciare, disputare
**bicycle** ['baɪsɪkəl] *s* bicicletta
**bid** [bɪd] *s* offerta; (cards) dichiarazione; (coll) invito ‖ *v* (*pret* **bade**
[bæd] or **bid;** *pp* **bidden** ['bɪdən] or
**bid;** *ger* **bidding**) *tr & intr* offrire;
comandare; (cards) dichiarare
**bidder** ['bɪdər] *s* offerente *mf;* (cards)
dichiarante *mf;* **the highest bidder** il
miglior offerente
**bidding** ['bɪdɪŋ] *s* ordine *m;* offerte
*fpl;* (cards) dichiarazione
**bide** [baɪd] *tr*—**to bide one's time** attendere l'ora propizia
**biennial** [baɪ'ɛnɪ·əl] *adj* biennale
**bier** [bɪr] *s* catafalco
**bifocal** [baɪ'fokəl] *adj* bifocale ‖ **bifo-
cals** *spl* occhiali *mpl* bifocali
**big** [bɪg] *adj* (**bigger; biggest**) grande;
(coll) importante; (coll) stravagante;
**big with child** incinta ‖ *adv*—**to talk
big** (coll) parlare con iattanza
**bigamist** ['bɪgəmɪst] *s* bigamo
**bigamous** ['bɪgəməs] *adj* bigamo

**big-bellied** ['bɪg ˌbɛlɪd] *adj* panciuto
**Big' Dip'per** *s* Gran Carro
**big' game'** *s* caccia grossa
**big-hearted** ['bɪg ˌhɑrtɪd] *adj* magnanimo, generoso
**big' mouth'** *s* (slang) sbraitone *m*
**bigot** ['bɪgət] *s* bigotto, bacchettone *m*
**bigoted** ['bɪgətɪd] *adj* (*in religion*) bigotto; intransigente
**bigot·ry** ['bɪgətri] *s* (-**ries**) bigottismo; intransigenza
**big' shot'** *s* (slang) pezzo grosso, (un) qualcuno
**big' slam'** *s* (bridge) grande slam *m*
**big'-time op'erator** *s* (slang) grosso trafficante
**big' toe'** *s* alluce *m*
**big' wheel'** *s* (slang) pezzo grosso
**bike** [baɪk] *s* (coll) bicicletta
**bile** [baɪl] *s* bile *f*
**bilge** [bɪldʒ] *s* sentina; (*of barrel*) ventre *m*
**bilge'ways'** *spl* parati *mpl*
**bilingual** [baɪ'lɪŋgwəl] *adj* bilingue
**bilious** ['bɪljəs] *adj* bilioso
**bilk** [bɪlk] *tr* defraudare
**bill** [bɪl] *s* (*of bird*) becco; (*statement of charges*) conto; (*e.g., for electricity*) bolletta; (*menu*) lista; (*money*) biglietto; (*proposed law*) disegno di legge; (*handbill*) annunzio; (law) atto; (theat) cartellone *m;* **to fill the bill** (coll) riempire i requisiti; **to foot the bill** (coll) pagare lo scotto ‖ *tr* fare una lista di; mettere in conto a ‖ *intr* (*said of doves*) beccuzzarsi; (*said of lovers*) baciucchiarsi
**bill'board'** *s* cartellone *m;* (rad, telv) titolo di testa
**billet** ['bɪlɪt] *s* (mil) alloggiamento; (mil) ordine *m* d'alloggiamento ‖ *tr* (mil) alloggiare, accasermare
**bill'fold'** *s* portafoglio
**bill'head'** *s* intestazione di fattura
**billiards** ['bɪljərdz] *s* bigliardo
**bil'ling clerk'** *s* fatturista *mf*
**billion** ['bɪljən] *s* (U.S.A.) miliardo; (Brit) bilione *m*
**bill' of exchange'** *s* tratta
**bill' of fare'** *s* menu *m,* lista delle vivande
**bill' of lad'ing** ['ledɪŋ] *s* polizza di carico
**bill' of rights'** *s* dichiarazione dei diritti
**bill' of sale'** *s* atto di vendita
**billow** ['bɪlo] *s* ondata, cavallone *m*
**bill'post'er** *s* attacchino
**bil·ly** ['bɪli] *s* (-**lies**) manganello
**bil'ly goat'** *s* capro, caprone *m*
**bimonthly** [baɪ'mʌnθli] *adj* (*occurring every two months*) bimestrale; (*occurring twice a month*) bimensile
**bin** [bɪn] *s* cassone *m;* (*for bread*) madia; (*e.g., for coal*) deposito
**binaural** [baɪ'nɔrəl] *adj* biauricolare
**bind** [baɪnd] *v* (*pret & pp* **bound** [baʊnd]) *tr* legare; allacciare; (*to bandage*) fasciare; (*to constipate*) costipare; (*a book*) rilegare; (*to oblige*) obbligare; (mach) grippare
**binder** ['baɪndər] *s* rilegatore *m;* (*cover*) cartella

**binder·y** ['baɪndəri] *s* (-**ies**) rilegatoria
**binding** ['baɪndɪŋ] *adj* obbligatorio ‖ *s* (*of book*) rilegatura; legatura; fasciatura
**bind'ing post'** *s* (elec) capocorda; (*e.g., of battery*) (elec) serrafilo
**binge** [bɪndʒ] *s*—**to go on a binge** (coll) far baldoria
**bingo** ['bɪŋgo] *s* tombola
**binnacle** ['bɪnəkəl] *s* abitacolo
**binoculars** [bɪ'nɑkjələrz] or [baɪ'nɑkjələrz] *spl* binocolo
**biochemical** [ˌbaɪ·ə'kɛmɪkəl] *adj* biochimico
**biochemist** [ˌbaɪ·ə'kɛmɪst] *s* biochimico
**biochemistry** [ˌbaɪ·ə'kɛmɪstri] *s* biochimica
**biodegradable** [ˌbaɪ·odɪ'gredəbəl] *adj* biodegradabile
**biographer** [baɪ'ɑgrəfər] *s* biografo
**biographic(al)** [ˌbaɪ·ə'græfɪk(əl)] *adj* biografico
**biogra·phy** [baɪ'ɑgrəfi] *s* (-**phies**) biografia
**biologist** [baɪ'ɑlədʒɪst] *s* biologo
**biology** [baɪ'ɑlədʒi] *s* biologia
**biophysics** [ˌbaɪ·ə'fɪzɪks] *s* biofisica
**biop·sy** ['baɪ ˌɑpsi] *s* (-**sies**) biopsia
**bipartisan** [baɪ'pɑrtɪzən] *adj* (*system*) bipartitico; (*government*) bipartito
**biped** ['baɪpɛd] *adj & s* bipede *m*
**birch** [bʌrtʃ] *s* betulla ‖ *tr* scudisciare
**bird** [bʌrd] *s* uccello; **a bird in the hand is worth two in the bush** un uovo oggi vale meglio di una gallina domani; **birds of a feather** gente *f* della stessa risma; **to kill two birds with one stone** pigliare due piccioni con una fava
**bird' cage'** *s* gabbia
**bird' call'** *s* richiamo
**birdie** ['bʌrdi] *s* uccellino; (golf) giocata di un colpo sotto la media
**bird'lime'** *s* pania
**bird' of pas'sage** *s* uccello di passo
**bird' of prey'** *s* uccello da preda
**bird'seed'** *s* becchime *m*
**bird's'-eye view'** *s* vista a volo d'uccello
**bird' shot'** *s* pallini *mpl* da caccia
**birth** [bʌrθ] *s* nascita; **to give birth to** dare i natali a; mettere alla luce
**birth' certif'icate** *s* certificato di nascita
**birth' control'** *s* limitazione delle nascite
**birth'day'** *s* natalizio, compleanno; (*of an event*) anniversario
**birth'mark'** *s* voglia
**birth'place'** *s* patria; (*e.g., city*) luogo di nascita; **to be the birthplace of** dare i natali a
**birth' rate'** *s* natalità *f*
**birth'right'** *s* diritto acquisito sin dalla nascita
**biscuit** ['bɪskɪt] *s* panino soffice; (Brit) biscotto
**bisect** [baɪ'sɛkt] *tr* bisecare ‖ *intr* (*said of roads*) incrociarsi
**bisection** [baɪ'sɛkʃən] *s* bisezione
**bishop** ['bɪʃəp] *s* vescovo; (chess) alfiere *m*
**bishopric** ['bɪʃəprɪk] *s* vescovado

**bismuth** ['bɪzməθ] s bismuto
**bison** ['baɪsən] or ['baɪzən] s bisonte m
**bisulfate** [baɪ'sʌlfet] s bisolfato
**bisulfite** [baɪ'sʌlfaɪt] s bisolfito
**bit** [bɪt] s (of bridle) morso; (of key) mappa; (tool) punta, trivella; (small piece) briciolo; **a bit** un po'; (coll) un momento; **a good bit** una buona quantità; **bit by bit** poco a poco; **to blow to bits** fare a pezzi; **to champ the bit** mordere il freno; **two bits** (slang) quarto di dollaro, cinque soldi
**bitch** [bɪtʃ] s cagna; (vulg) donnaccia || intr (slang) lamentarsi
**bite** [baɪt] s morso; (mouthful) boccone m; **to take a bite** fare uno spuntino; mangiare un boccone || v (pret bit [bɪt]; pp bit or bitten ['bɪtən]) tr mordere, addentare; pungere; (the dust) baciare || intr mordere; (said of insects) pungere; (said of fish) abboccare
**biting** ['baɪtɪŋ] adj mordace; pungente
**bitter** ['bɪtər] adj amaro; (e.g., fight) accanito; (cold) pungente || s amaro; **bitters** amaro
**bit'ter end'** s—**to the bitter end** fino alla fine; fino alla morte
**bit'ter·en'der** s (coll) intransigente mf
**bitterness** ['bɪtərnɪs] s amarezza
**bit'ter·sweet'** adj dolceamaro; (fig) agrodolce || s dulcamara
**bitumen** [bɪ'tjumən] or [bɪ'tumən] s bitume m
**bivou·ac** ['bɪvʊ ,æk] or ['bɪvwæk] s bivacco || v (pret & pp -acked; ger -acking) intr bivaccare
**biweekly** [baɪ'wikli] adj bisettimanale; quindicinale || adv ogni due settimane
**biyearly** [baɪ'jɪrli] adj semestrale || adv semestralmente
**bizarre** [bɪ'zɑr] adj bizzarro
**blab** [blæb] s chiacchierone m || v (pret & pp blabbed; ger blabbing) tr rivelare || intr chiacchierare
**black** [blæk] adj nero; (without light) buio || s nero; **to wear black** vestire a lutto, vestire di nero || intr—**to black out** perdere i sensi
**black'-and-blue'** adj livido e pesto
**black'-and-white'** adj in bianco e nero
**black'ball'** s palla nera, voto contrario || tr dare la palla nera a
**black'ber'ry** s (-ries) mora
**black'bird'** s merlo
**black'board'** s lavagna, tavola nera
**black'cap'** s capinera
**black'damp'** s putizza
**Black' Death'** s peste bubbonica
**blacken** ['blækən] tr annerire; (shoes) lucidare; (reputation) sporcare
**black' eye'** s occhio pesto; (fig) cattiva reputazione
**blackguard** ['blægɑrd] s canaglia
**black'head'** s comedone m
**blackish** ['blækɪʃ] adj nerastro
**black'jack'** s randello; (cards) ventuno || tr randellare
**black' mag'ic** s magia nera

**black'mail'** s ricatto || tr ricattare
**blackmailer** ['blæk ,melər] s ricattatore m
**Black' Mari'a** [mə'raɪ·ə] s (coll) furgone m cellulare
**black' mar'ket** s borsa nera
**black' marketeer'** [ ,mɑrkɪ'tɪr] s borsanerista mf
**blackness** ['blæknɪs] s nerezza
**black'out'** s oscuramento; (theat) spegnitura; (pathol) svenimento passeggero
**black' sheep'** s (fig) pecora nera
**black'smith'** s fabbro
**black' tie'** s cravatta da smoking; smoking m
**bladder** ['blædər] s vescica
**blade** [bled] s (of a leaf) pagina; (of grass) stelo, filo; (of oar) pala; (of turbine) paletta; (of fan) ventola; (of knife) lama; (coll) caposcarico
**blame** [blem] s colpa; **to be to blame for** aver la colpa di; **to put the blame on s.o. for s.th** attribuire a qlcu la colpa di qlco; **you are to blame** è colpa Sua || tr biasimare, incolpare
**blameless** ['blemlɪs] adj innocente, senza colpa
**blanch** [blæntʃ] or [blɑntʃ] tr bianchire || intr impallidire
**bland** [blænd] adj blando; (weather) mite
**blandish** ['blændɪʃ] tr blandire
**blank** [blæŋk] adj (not written on) in bianco; (e.g., stare) vuoto; (utter) completo || s (printed form) modulo; (cartridge) cartuccia a salve; (of the mind) lacuna; **to draw a blank** (coll) non avere alcun successo || tr—**to blank out** cancellare
**blank' check'** s assegno in bianco; (fig) carta bianca
**blanket** ['blæŋkɪt] adj generale, combinato || s coperta; (of snow) cappa || tr coprire con una coperta; oscurare
**blank' verse'** s verso sciolto
**blare** [blɛr] s squillo || tr proclamare; fare echeggiare || intr squillare; echeggiare
**blaspheme** [blæs'fim] tr & intr bestemmiare
**blasphemous** ['blæsfɪməs] adj bestemmiatore
**blasphe·my** ['blæsfɪmi] s (-mies) bestemmia
**blast** [blæst] or [blɑst] s (of air) raffica; (of a horn) squillo; (blight) rovina; scoppio, esplosione; **at full blast** a piena velocità || tr rovinare; fare scoppiare, far saltare || intr —**to blast off** (rok) lanciarsi
**blast' fur'nace** s altoforno
**blast'off'** s lancio di missile or di nave spaziale
**blatant** ['bletənt] adj (noisy) rumoroso; (obtrusive) palmare; (flashy) chiassoso
**blaze** [blez] s fiammata; splendore m; (on a horse's head) stella; **in a blaze** in fiamme || tr proclamare; **to blaze a**

**trail** marcare il cammino || *intr* divampare

**bleach** [blitʃ] *s* candeggio, candeggina || *tr* imbiancare, candeggiare

**bleachers** ['blitʃərz] *spl* posti *mpl* allo scoperto or di gradinata

**bleak** [blik] *adj* nudo, deserto; *(cold)* freddo; *(gloomy)* triste

**blear·y** ['blɪri] *adj* (-ier; iest) *(sight)* cisposo; confuso; offuscato

**bleat** [blit] *s* belato || *intr* belare

**bleed** [blid] *v (pret & pp* **bled** [blɛd]) *tr (to draw blood from)* salassare; *(a tree)* estrare linfa da; *(coll)* sfruttare || *intr* sanguinare; *(said of a tree)* dar linfa; **to bleed to death** morire dissanguato

**blemish** ['blemɪʃ] *s* difetto; macchia || *tr* danneggiare; macchiare

**blend** [blɛnd] *s* mescolanza, miscuglio; *(of gasoline)* miscela || *v (pret & pp* **blended** or **blent** [blɛnt]) *tr* mescolare, miscelare || *intr* mescolarsi, miscelarsi; armonizzare; fondersi

**bless** [blɛs] *tr* benedire; *(to endow)* dotare; *(to make happy)* allietare

**blessed** ['blɛsɪd] *adj* benedetto; beato; fortunato; dotato

**bless'ed event'** *s* lieto evento

**blessing** ['blɛsɪŋ] *s* benedizione

**blight** [blaɪt] *s (insect; disease)* piaga, rovina; *(fungus)* ruggine *f* || *tr* rovinare, guastare

**blimp** [blɪmp] *s* piccolo dirigibile

**blind** [blaɪnd] *adj* cieco; (slang) ubriaco || *s* persiana; tendina; *(decoy)* mascheratura; pretesto || *adv* alla cieca || *tr* accecare

**blind' al'ley** *s* vicolo cieco

**blinder** ['blaɪndər] *s* paraocchi *m*

**blind' fly'ing** *s* (aer) volo senza visibilità

**blind'fold'** *adj* bendato, cogli occhi bendati || *s* benda || *tr* bendare gli occhi a

**blindly** ['blaɪndli] *adv* alla cieca

**blind' man'** *s* cieco

**blind'man's buff'** *s* mosca cieca

**blindness** ['blaɪndnɪs] *s* cecità *f*

**blind' spot'** *s* (anat) punto cieco; (rad) zona di silenzio; (fig) debole *m*

**blink** [blɪŋk] *s* batter *m* di ciglio; *(glimpse)* occhiata; *(glimmer)* barlume *m;* **on the blink** (slang) fuori servizio || *tr*—**to blink one's eyes** batter il ciglio || *intr* occhieggiare; *(to wink)* ammiccare; *(to flash on and off)* lampeggiare; **to blink at** ignorare; far finta di non vedere

**blinker** ['blɪŋkər] *s (at a crossing)* luce *f* intermittente; *(on a horse)* paraocchi *m*

**blip** [blɪp] *s* guizzo sullo schermo radar

**bliss** [blɪs] *s* beatitudine *f,* felicità *f*

**blissful** ['blɪsfəl] *adj* beato, felice

**blister** ['blɪstər] *s* vescica, bolla || *tr* coprire di vesciche; (fig) bollare || *intr* coprirsi di vesciche

**blithe** [blaɪð] *adj* gaio, giocondo

**blitzkrieg** ['blɪts ˌkrig] *s* guerra lampo

**blizzard** ['blɪzərd] *s* tormenta, ventoneve *m*

**bloat** [blot] *tr* gonfiare || *intr* gonfiarsi

**blob** [blɑb] *s (lump)* zolla; *(of liquid)* macchia

**block** [blɑk] *s (e.g., of wood)* blocco; *(for chopping)* ceppo; *(pulley)* puleggia; ostacolo; *(of houses)* isolato; (typ) cliché *m* || *tr* bloccare; *(a hat)* mettere in forma; **to block up** tappare

**blockade** [blɑ'ked] *s* blocco; **to run a blockade** forzare il blocco || *tr* bloccare

**block' and tack'le** *s* bozzello

**block'bust'er** *s* (coll) superbomba

**block'head'** *s* imbecille *mf*

**block' let'ter** *s* carattere *m* stampatello

**block' sig'nal** *s* (rr) segnale di blocco

**blond** [blɑnd] *adj* & *s* biondo

**blonde** [blɑnd] *s* bionda

**blood** [blʌd] *s* sangue *m;* **in cold blood** a sangue freddo; **to draw blood** ferire, fare sanguinare

**blood' bank'** *s* emoteca

**bloodcurdling** ['blʌd ˌkʌrdlɪŋ] *adj* orripilante

**blood' do'nor** *s* donatore *m* di sangue

**blood'hound'** *s* segugio

**bloodless** ['blʌdlɪs] *adj* esangue; *(e.g., revolution)* senza effusione di sangue

**blood'mobile'** [mo ˌbil] *s* autoemoteca

**blood' poi'soning** *s* avvelenamento del sangue

**blood' pres'sure** *s* pressione sanguigna

**blood' rela'tion** *s* consanguineo

**blood'shed'** *s* spargimento di sangue, carneficina

**blood'shot'** *adj* iniettato di sangue

**blood'stained'** *adj* macchiato di sangue

**blood'stream'** *s* circolazione sanguigna

**blood'suck'er** *s* sanguisuga

**blood' test'** *s* esame *m* del sangue

**blood'thirst'y** *adj* assetato di sangue

**blood' transfu'sion** *s* trasfusione di sangue

**blood' type'** *s* gruppo sanguigno

**blood' ves'sel** *s* vaso sanguigno

**blood·y** ['blʌdi] *adj* (-ier; -iest) sanguinoso; *(bloodthirsty)* avido di sangue || *v (pret & pp* -ied) *tr* macchiare di sangue

**bloom** [blum] *s* fiore *m; (state of having open buds)* sboccio; *(youthful glow)* incarnato || *intr* fiorire; sbocciare

**bloomers** ['blumərz] *spl* pantaloni *mpl* femminili larghi fermati sotto il ginocchio

**blossom** ['blɑsəm] *s* fiore *m;* sboccio || *intr* sbocciare

**blot** [blɑt] *s* macchia || *v (pret & pp* **blotted;** *ger* **blotting)** *tr* macchiare; *(with blotting paper)* asciugare; **to blot out** cancellare; oscurare || *intr* macchiarsi; *(to be absorbent)* essere assorbente; *(said of a pen)* fare macchie

**blotch** [blɑtʃ] *s* chiazza, macchia || *tr* chiazzare

**blotter** ['blɑtər] *s* carta asciugante, carta assorbente; *(book)* registro

**blouse** [blaʊs] *s* blusa

**blow** [blo] *s* colpo; *(blast)* folata; *(of*

*horn)* squillo; *(sudden reverse)* batosta; **at one blow** d'un sol colpo; **to come to blows** venire alle mani; **without striking a blow** senza colpo ferire ‖ *v (pret* **blew** [blu]; *pp* **blown)** *tr* soffiare, soffiare su; *(an instrument)* suonare; *(one's nose)* soffiarsi; **to blow in** sfondare; **to blow one's brains out** bruciarsi le cervella; **to blow open** aprire completamente; **to blow out** *(e.g., a candle)* spegnere; *(a fuse)* fondere; **to blow up** *(e.g., a mine)* far brillare; *(phot)* ingrandire ‖ *intr* soffiare; *(to pant)* ansimare; *(with an instrument)* suonare; *(to puff)* sbuffare; *(slang)* andarsene; **to blow hot and cold** cambiare d'opinione ogni cinque minuti; **to blow in** (coll) arrivare inaspettatamente; **to blow out** *(said, e.g., of a candle)* spegnersi; *(said of a fuse)* saltare, fondersi; *(said of a tire)* scoppiare; **to blow over** passare; **to blow up** saltar per aria; *(said of a storm)* scoppiare; (coll) perdere la pazienza, scoppiare d'ira

**blow'out'** *s* scoppio di un pneumatico
**blow'pipe'** *s (tube)* soffione *m;* *(peashooter)* cerbottana
**blow'torch'** *s* saldatrice *f* a benzina
**blubber** ['blʌbər] *s* grasso di balena ‖ *intr* piangere, lamentarsi
**bludgeon** ['blʌdʒən] *s* randello ‖ *tr* randellare
**blue** [blu] *adj* blu, azzurro; *(gloomy)* triste; *(e.g., laws)* puritanico ‖ *s* blu *m,* azzurro; **out of the blue** inaspettatamente; **the blues** la malinconia; (mus) blues *m;* **to have the blues** essere giù di morale ‖ *tr* tingere di azzurro; *(a metal)* brunire
**blue'ber'ry** *s* (-ries) mirtillo
**blue'bird'** *s* uccello azzurro
**blue' blood'** *s* sangue *m* blu
**blue' cheese'** *s* gorgonzola americano
**blue' chip'** *s* (fin) azione di prim'ordine
**blue' jay'** *s* ghiandaia azzurra
**blue' moon'** *s*—**once in a blue moon** ad ogni morte di papa
**blue'-pen'cil** *v (pret & pp* -**ciled** or -**cilled;** *ger* -**ciling** or -**cilling)** *tr* correggere col lapis blu
**blue'print'** *s* riproduzione cianografica; *(plan)* piano ‖ *tr* riprodurre in cianografia; preparare dettagliatamente
**blue'stock'ing** *s* saccente *f,* sapientona
**blue' streak'** *s*—**like a blue streak** (coll) come un razzo
**bluff** [blʌf] *adj* scosceso; brusco, burbero ‖ *s* promontorio scosceso; bluff *m;* bluffatore *m* ‖ *intr* bluffare
**bluing** ['bluɪŋ] *s* turchinetto
**bluish** ['blu·ɪʃ] *adj* bluastro
**blunder** ['blʌndər] *s* errore *m* madornale ‖ *intr* pigliare un granchio
**blunt** [blʌnt] *adj* ottuso; *(plain-spoken)* franco ‖ *tr* rendere ottuso
**bluntness** ['blʌntnɪs] *s* ottusità *f;* franchezza
**blur** [blʌr] *s* macchia; offuscamento; confusione ‖ *v (pret & pp* **blurred;**

*ger* **blurring)** *tr* macchiare; *(the view)* offuscare
**blurb** [blʌrb] *s* annuncio pubblicitario
**blurt** [blʌrt] *tr*—**to blurt out** prorompere a dire, lasciarsi sfuggire
**blush** [blʌʃ] *s* rossore *m;* *(pinkish natural tinge)* incarnato ‖ *intr* arrossire; **to blush at** vergognarsi di
**bluster** ['blʌstər] *s* frastuono; (fig) boria ‖ *intr* *(said of the wind)* infuriare; fare il bravaccio
**blustery** ['blʌstəri] *adj* tempestuoso; violento; *(swaggering)* borioso
**boar** [bor] *s* verro; *(wild hog)* porco selvatico, cinghiale *m*
**board** [bord] *s* asse *m;* *(notice)* cartello; *(pasteboard)* cartone *m;* *(table)* tavola; *(meals)* vitto; *(group of administrators)* consiglio; (naut) bordo; **above board** franco; **in boards** rilegato; **on board** a bordo; (rr) in vettura; **to go by the board** andare in rovina; **to tread the boards** fare l'attore ‖ *tr* chiudere con assi; *(to provide with meals)* dare pensione a, tenere a dozzina; *(a ship)* salire a bordo di; *(a train)* salire su; (naut) abbordare ‖ *intr* essere a pensione
**board' and lodg'ing** *s* pensione completa
**boarder** ['bordər] *s* pensionante *mf*
**board'ing house'** *s* pensione di famiglia
**board'ing school'** *s* collegio di pensionanti
**board' of direc'tors** *s* consiglio d'amministrazione
**board' of health'** *s* ufficio d'igiene
**board' of trade'** *s* camera di commercio
**board'walk'** *s* passeggiata a mare
**boast** [bost] *s* millanteria, vanteria ‖ *intr* vantarsi
**boastful** ['bostfəl] *adj* millantatore
**boat** [bot] *s* nave *f,* battello; *(small ship)* barca, imbarcazione; *(dish)* salsiera; **in the same boat** nella stessa situazione
**boat' hook'** *s* alighiero
**boat'house'** *s* capannone *m* per i canotti
**boating** ['botɪŋ] *s* escursione in barca
**boat'man** *s* (-men) barcaiolo
**boat' race'** *s* regata
**boatswain** ['bosən] or ['bot‚swen] *s* nostromo
**bob** [bab] *s* *(plumb)* piombino; *(short haircut)* taglio alla bebè; coda mozza (di cavallo); *(jerky motion)* strattone *m;* *(on pendulum of clock)* lente *f;* *(on fishing line)* sughero ‖ *v (pret & pp* **bobbed;** *ger* **bobbing)** *tr* tagliare alla bebè; far muovere a scatti ‖ *intr* muoversi a scatti; fare mossa; **to bob up** apparire
**bobbin** ['babɪn] *s* bobina
**bob'by pin'** ['babi] *s* forcina
**bob'by-socks'** *spl* (coll) calzini *mpl* da ragazza
**bobbysoxer** ['babi ‚saksər] *s* (coll) ragazzina
**bobolink** ['babə ‚lɪŋk] *s* doliconice *m*
**bob'sled'** *s* guidoslitta
**bode** [bod] *tr & intr* presagire
**bodice** ['badɪs] *s* giubbetto, copribusto

**bodily** ['bɑdɪli] *adj* fisico, corporeo ‖ *adv* fisicamente, corporeamente; di persona; in massa

**bodkin** ['bɑdkɪn] *s* punteruolo; *(for lady's hair)* spillone *m*

**bod·y** ['bɑdi] *s* (**-ies**) corpo; *(corpse)* cadavere *m; (of water)* massa; *(of people)* gruppo; *(of a liquid)* sostanza; *(of truck)* cassone *m; (of car)* carrozzeria; *(of tree)* tronco; *(coll)* persona; **in a body** in massa

**bod'y·guard'** *s (of a high official)* guardia del corpo; *(e.g., of a movie star)* guardaspalle *m*

**bod'y suit'** *s* calzamaglia

**bog** [bɑg] *s* pantano, palude *m* ‖ *(pret & pp* **bogged**; *ger* **bogging**) *intr*—**to bog down** impelagarsi

**bogey·man** ['bogi ,mæn] *s* (**-men** [men]) babau *m*

**bogus** ['bogəs] *adj* (coll) falso, finto

**Bohemian** [bo'himɪ·ən] *adj* boemo; da bohémien ‖ *s* boemo; (fig) bohémien *m*

**boil** [bɔɪl] *s* bollore *m*, ebollizione; (pathol) foruncolo; **to come to a boil** cominciare a bollire ‖ *tr* bollire; **to boil down** condensare ‖ *intr* bollire; **to boil away** evaporare completamente; **to boil down** condensarsi; **to boil over** andare per il fuoco

**boiled' ham'** *s* prosciutto cotto

**boiler** ['bɔɪlər] *s* caldaia; *(for cooking)* caldaio

**boil'er·mak'er** *s* calderaio

**boiling** ['bɔɪlɪŋ] *adj* bollente ‖ *s* bollore *m*, ebollizione

**boisterous** ['bɔɪstərəs] *adj (storm)* violento; *(loud)* rumoroso

**bold** [bold] *adj (daring)* coraggioso; *(impudent)* sfacciato; *(steep)* scosceso; *(clear, sharp)* netto

**bold'face'** *s* (typ) neretto, grassetto

**boldness** ['boldnɪs] *s* coraggio, audacia; sfacciataggine *f*, impudenza

**boll' wee'vil** [bol] *s* antonomo del cotone

**bologna** [bə'lonə] or [bə'lonjə] *s* mortadella

**Bolshevik** ['bɑlʃəvɪk] or ['bolʃəvɪk] *adj & mf* bolscevico

**bolster** ['bolstər] *s* cuscino; cuscinetto; *(support)* sostegno ‖ *tr* sorreggere; **to bolster up** sostenere

**bolt** [bolt] *s (arrow)* freccia; *(of lightning)* fulmine *m; (sliding bar)* chiavistello; *(threaded rod)* bullone *m; (of paper or cloth)* pezza, rotolo ‖ *adv*—**bolt upright** dritto come un fuso ‖ *tr (to swallow hurriedly)* ingollare; *(to fasten, e.g., a door)* sprangare; *(to fasten, e.g., two metal parts)* bullonare; *(e.g., a political party)* abbandonare ‖ *intr (said of people)* spiccare un salto; *(said of a horse)* prendere la mano; precipitarsi

**bolt' from the blue'** *s* fulmine *m* a ciel sereno

**bomb** [bɑm] *s* bomba; *(e.g., for spraying)* bombola ‖ *tr* bombardare

**bombard** [bɑm'bɑrd] *tr* bombardare; *(with questions)* bersagliare

**bombardment** [bɑm'bɑrdmənt] *s* bombardamento

**bombast** ['bɑmbæst] *s* ampollosità *f*

**bombastic** [bɑm'bæstɪk] *adj* ampolloso

**bomb' cra'ter** *s* cratere *m*

**bomber** ['bɑmər] *s* bombardiere *m*

**bomb'proof'** *adj* a prova di bomba

**bomb'shell'** *s* bomba; (fig) colpo di bomba, colpo di sorpresa

**bomb' shel'ter** *s* rifugio antiaereo

**bomb'sight'** *s* traguardo aereo

**bona fide** ['bonə ,faɪdə] *adj* sincero ‖ *adv* in buona fede

**bonanza** [bə'nænzə] *s* (min) ricca vena; (coll) fortuna

**bond** [bɑnd] *s* legame *m*, vincolo; *(contractual obligation)* obbligazione; *(interest-bearing certificate)* buono, obbligazione; *(surety)* cauzione; **bonds** catene *fpl;* **in bond** sotto cauzione; *(said of goods)* in punto franco ‖ *tr* unire, connettere

**bondage** ['bɑndɪdʒ] *s* schiavitù *f*

**bond'ed ware'house** *s* deposito in punto franco

**bond'hold'er** *s* obbligazionista *mf*

**bonds'man** *s* (**-men**) garante *m*

**bone** [bon] *s* osso; *(of fish)* spina; *(of whale)* stecca; **bones** ossa *fpl;* **to have a bone to pick with** avere un conto da regolare con; **to make no bones about** (coll) ammettere; (coll) parlare esplicitamente ‖ *tr* disossare; cavare le spine a ‖ *intr*—**to bone up on** (coll) ripassare

**bone'head'** *s* (coll) testa dura

**boneless** ['bonlɪs] *adj* senz'osso; *(fish)* senza spine

**boner** ['bonər] *s* (slang) errore *m* madornale

**bonfire** ['bɑn ,faɪr] *s* falò *m*

**bonnet** ['bɑnɪt] *s* cappello da donna; *(of child)* berrettino

**bonus** ['bonəs] *s* gratifica; indennità *f; (to an outgoing employee)* buonuscita

**bon·y** ['boni] *adj* (**-ier; -iest**) *(having bones)* osseo; *(emaciated)* scarno; *(fish)* spinoso

**boo** [bu] *s* fischio, urlaccio ‖ *tr & intr* fischiare, disapprovare

**boo·by** ['bubi] *s* (**-bies**) stupido

**boo'by hatch'** *s* (naut) portello; (slang) manicomio; (slang) prigione *f*

**boo'by prize'** *s* premio dato al peggior giocatore

**boo'by trap'** *s* (mil) trappola esplosiva; (fig) tranello

**boogie-woogie** ['bugi'wugi] *s* bughi-bughi *m*

**book** [bʊk] *s* libro; *(e.g., of matches)* pacchetto; (mus) libretto; (fig) regole *fpl;* **the Book** la Bibbia; **to be in one's book** essere nelle grazie di; **to bring s.o. to book** fare una ramanzina a ‖ *tr* registrare; *(e.g., on a horse)* allibrare; *(e.g., a room)* prenotare; *(an actor)* scritturare

**book'bind'er** *s* rilegatore *m*

**book'bind'er·y** *s* (**-ies**) rilegatoria

**book'bind'ing** *s* rilegatura

**book'case'** *s* scaffale *m*

**book' end'** *s* reggilibri *m*

**bookie** ['bʊki] s (coll) allibratore m
**booking** ['bʊkɪŋ] s (of a trip) prenotazione; (of an actor) scrittura
**book'ing clerk'** s impiegato alla biglietteria
**bookish** ['bʊkɪʃ] adj studioso; libresco
**book'keep'er** s contabile mf
**booklet** ['bʊklɪt] s libretto; (pamphlet) opuscolo
**book'keep'ing** s contabilità f
**book'mak'er** s (one who accepts bets) allibratore m
**book'mark'** s segnalibro
**bookmobile** ['bʊkmo ,bil] s bibliobus m
**book'plate'** s ex libris m
**book' review'** s rassegna, recensione
**book'sell'er** s libraio
**book'shelf'** s (-shelves) scaffale m
**book'stand'** s (rack) scansia; (stall) edicola
**book'store'** s libreria
**book'worm'** s (zool) tarlo dei libri; (fig) topo da biblioteca
**boom** [bum] s (of crane) braccio; (barrier) barriera galleggiante; (noise) bum m; (fin) boom m; (naut) boma; (mov, telv) giraffa || intr rimbombare; essere in condizioni floride
**boomerang** ['bumə ,ræŋ] s bumerang m
**boom' town'** s città f fungo
**boon** [bun] s fortuna, benedizione
**boon' compan'ion** s compagnone m
**boor** [bʊr] s bifolco, zotico
**boorish** ['bʊrɪʃ] adj grossolano
**boost** [bust] s aumento; (coll) spinta || tr spingere in su; sostenere; (prices) alzare; parlare a favore di
**booster** ['bustər] s (backer) sostenitore m; propulsore m a razzo; (rok) propulsore m del primo stadio; (med) seconda iniezione
**boot** [but] s stivale m; (kick) calcio; (patch) (aut) pezza; **the boot is on the other foot** la situazione è rovesciata; **to be in the boots of** essere nella pelle di; **to boot per di più; to get the boot** (coll) essere messo sulla strada; **to lick the boots of** leccare i piedi a; **to wipe one's boots on** trattare come una pezza da piedi || tr dare un calcio a; **to boot out** (slang) buttar fuori
**boot'black'** s lustrascarpe m
**booth** [buθ] s (stall) banco da mercato; (for telephoning, voting) cabina
**boot'jack'** s tirastivali m
**boot'leg'** adj di contrabbando || s liquore m di contrabbando || v (pret & pp -legged) ger -legging) tr vendere di contrabbando || intr vendere alcol di contrabbando
**bootlegger** ['but ,legər] s contrabbandiere m di liquori
**boot'lick'er** [ ,lɪkər] s (coll) leccapiedi mf
**boot'strap'** s tirante m degli stivali
**boo•ty** ['buti] s (-ties) bottino
**booze** [buz] s (coll) bevanda alcolica || intr (coll) ubriacarsi
**borax** ['boræks] s borace m
**border** ['bɔrdər] adj confinario, con-

finante || s bordo, margine m; (between two countries) confine m || tr bordare; confinare con || intr confinare
**bor'der clash'** s incidente m ai confini
**bor'der-line'** adj incerto || s frontiera
**bore** [bor] s (drill hole) buco, foro; (hollow part of gun) anima; (caliber) calibro; (dull person) seccatore m; (annoyance) seccatura; (mach) alesaggio || tr bucare, forare; seccare; (mach) alesare
**boredom** ['bordəm] s noia, tedio
**boring** ['borɪŋ] adj noioso || s trivellazione
**born** [bɔrn] adj nato, partorito; **to be born again** rinascere; **to be born with a silver spoon in one's mouth** nascere con la camicia
**borough** ['bʌro] s borgata, comune m
**borrow** ['bʌro] or ['bɔro] tr chiedere a or in prestito; prendere a or in prestito; ricevere a or in prestito; (to adopt) adottare; **to borrow trouble** preoccuparsi per nulla
**borrower** ['bʌro•ər] or ['bɔro•ər] s chi riceve a prestito; (law) comodatario, prestatario
**borrowing** ['bʌro•ɪŋ] or ['bɔro•ɪŋ] s prestito; prestito linguistico, forestierismo
**bosom** ['buzəm] s petto, seno; (e.g., of the family) grembo, seno; (of shirt) pettorina
**bos'om friend'** s amico del cuore
**Bosporus** ['bʌspərəs] s Bosforo
**boss** [bɔs] or [bas] s (coll) padrone m; (coll) direttore m; (coll) capintesta m; (coll) principale m; (archit) bugna, bozza || tr fare da padrone a || intr fare da padrone
**boss•y** ['bɔsi] or ['basi] adj (-ier; -iest) autoritario
**botanical** [bə'tænɪkəl] adj botanico
**botanist** ['batənɪst] s botanico
**botany** ['batəni] s botanica
**botch** [batʃ] s abborracciatura || tr abborracciare
**both** [boθ] adj entrambi i, tutti e due i || pron entrambi, tutti e due || conj del pari, al medesimo tempo; **both ... and** tanto ... quanto
**bother** ['baðər] s (worry) noia, seccatura; (person) seccatore m || tr dar noia a, seccare || intr preoccuparsi; **to bother about** or **with** occuparsi di; **to bother to** + inf molestarsi di + inf
**bothersome** ['baðərsəm] adj incomodo
**bottle** ['batəl] s bottiglia, fiasco || tr imbottigliare; **to bottle up** imbottigliare
**bot'tle cap'** s tappo a corona
**bot'tle•neck'** s collo di bottiglia; (of traffic) congestione, imbottigliamento
**bot'tle o'pener** ['opənər] s apribottiglie m
**bottom** ['batəm] adj basso; (price, dollar) ultimo; infimo || s fondo; (of chair) sedile m; base f; (of bottle) culo; (of ship) scafo; **at bottom** in realtà; **to begin at the bottom** comin-

ciare dalla gavetta; **to get at the bottom of** andare a fondo di; **to go to the bottom** andare a picco
**bottomless** ['bɑtəmlɪs] *adj* senza fondo
**boudoir** [bu'dwɑr] *s* gabinetto di toletta (da signora)
**bough** [bau] *s* ramo
**bouillon** ['bujɑn] *s* brodo schietto
**boulder** ['boldər] *s* masso, roccia
**boulevard** ['bulə‚vɑrd] *s* corso
**bounce** [bauns] *s* balzo; salto; elasticità *f*; (*of boat or plane*) piastrellamento; (fig) spirito; **to get the bounce** (slang) essere licenziato ‖ *tr* far balzare; (slang) buttar fuori ‖ *intr* rimbalzare; saltare; (aer, naut) piastrellare
**bouncer** ['baunsər] *s* (*in night club*) (slang) buttafuori *m*
**bouncing** ['baunsɪŋ] *adj* forte, vigoroso; grande, rumoroso
**bound** [baund] *adj* legato; collegato; obbligato; (bb) rilegato; (coll) risoluto; **bound for** destinato a, diretto per; **bound up in** or **with** in strette relazioni con; assorto in ‖ *s* salto; rimbalzo; limite *m*; **bounds** zona limitrofa; **out of bounds** fuori limiti; al di là delle convenienze ‖ *tr* delimitare
**bounda·ry** ['baundəri] *s* (**-ries**) confine *m*, limite *m*
**bound'ary stone'** *s* pietra di confine
**boundless** ['baundlɪs] *adj* illimitato, sconfinato
**bountiful** ['bauntɪfəl] *adj* generoso; abbondante
**boun·ty** ['baunti] *s* (**-ties**) dono generoso; generosità *f*, abbondanza; (*reward*) premio
**bouquet** [bu'ke] or [bo'ke] *s* mazzo, mazzolino; profumo, aroma *m*
**bourgeois** ['burʒwɑ] *adj & s* borghese *mf*
**bourgeoisie** [‚burʒwɑ'zi] *s* borghesia
**bout** [baut] *s* lotta, contesa; (*of illness*) attacco
**bow** [bau] *s* inchino, riverenza; (naut) prua; **to take a bow** ricevere gli applausi ‖ *tr* chinare, piegare ‖ *intr* inchinarsi; sottomettersi; **to bow and scrape** fare riverenze ‖ [bo] *s* (*weapon*) arco; (*knot*) nodo; (mus) archetto; (*stroke of bow*) (mus) arcata ‖ *tr & intr* (mus) suonare con l'archetto
**bowdlerize** ['baudlə‚raɪz] *tr* espurgare
**bowel** ['bau·əl] *s* budello; **bowels** viscere *fpl*
**bow'el move'ment** *s* evacuazione; **to have a bowel movement** andar di corpo
**bower** ['bau·ər] *s* pergolato
**bowery** ['bau·əri] *adj* frondoso
**bowknot** ['bo‚nɑt] *s* nodo scorsoio
**bowl** [bol] *s* (*dish*) ciotola; (*cup*) tazza; (*of pipe*) fornello; (*basin*) catino; (*amphitheater*) arena; (*ball*) boccia; (*delivery of ball*) bocciata; **bowls** bocce *fpl* ‖ *tr* bocciare; **to bowl down** or **over** abbattere ‖ *intr* giocare alle bocce

**bowlegged** ['bo‚lɛgd] or ['bo‚lɛgɪd] *adj* con le gambe storte
**bowler** ['bolər] *s* giocatore *m* di bocce
**bowling** ['bolɪŋ] *s* bocce *fpl*; bowling *m*, birilli *mpl*
**bowl'ing al'ley** *s* pista per il bowling; bowling *m*
**bowl'ing green'** *s* campo di bocce erboso
**bowshot** ['bo‚ʃɑt] *s* tiro d'arco
**bowsprit** ['bausprit] or ['bosprit] *s* (naut) bompresso
**bow' tie'** [bo] *s* cravatta a farfalla
**bowwow** ['bau‚wau] *interj* bau bau!
**box** [bɑks] *s* scatola; cassa; (*for jury*) banco; (*for sentry*) garitta; (*on coach*) cassetta; (*in stable*) posta; (*slap*) ceffone *m*; (*with fist*) pugno; (bot) bosso; (theat) palco, barcaccia; (baseball) posto del battitore; (typ) riquadratura ‖ *tr* mettere in scatola; (*to slap*) schiaffeggiare; (*to hit with fist*) fare a pugilato con; **to box in** or **up** rinchiudere ‖ *intr* fare a pugni; combattere
**box'car'** *s* vagone *m* merci coperto
**boxer** ['bɑksər] *s* pugile *m*
**box'hold'er** *s* palchettista *mf*
**boxing** ['bɑksɪŋ] *s* pugilato
**box'ing gloves'** *spl* guantoni *mpl* da pugilato
**box' of'fice** *s* sportello, biglietteria; (theat) incasso; (theat) successo
**box'-of'fice hit'** *s* grande successo
**box' pleat'** *s* (*of skirt*) cannone *m*
**box' seat'** *s* posto in palco
**box'wood'** *s* bosso
**boy** [bɔɪ] *s* ragazzo, giovane *m* ‖ *interj* accidempoli!
**boycott** ['bɔɪkɑt] *s* boicottaggio ‖ *tr* boicottare
**boy'friend'** *s* innamorato, amico
**boyhood** ['bɔɪhud] *s* fanciullezza
**boyish** ['bɔɪ·ɪʃ] *adj* giovanile
**boy' scout'** *s* giovane esploratore *m*
**bra** [brɑ] *s* (coll) reggiseno
**brace** [bres] *s* (*couple*) paio; (*device for maintaining tension*) tirante *m*; (*prop*) sostegno; (*tool*) trapano; (typ) graffa; **braces** (Brit) bretelle *fpl* ‖ *tr* legare; serrare; puntellare; sostenere; invigorare; **to brace oneself** pigliare animo ‖ *intr*—**to brace up** (coll) pigliare animo
**brace' and bit'** *s* menarola, trapano
**bracelet** ['breslɪt] *s* braccialetto
**bracer** ['bresər] *s* (coll) bicchierino
**bracket** ['brækɪt] *s* mensola; (*for lamp*) braccio; angolo; classifica; (typ) parentesi quadra ‖ *tr* sostenere con mensola; mettere tra parentesi quadra; classificare
**brackish** ['brækɪʃ] *adj* salmastro
**brad** [bræd] *s* chiodino, punta
**brag** [bræg] *s* vanto ‖ *v* (*pret & pp* **bragged**; *ger* **bragging**) *intr* vantare
**braggart** ['brægərt] *s* millantatore *m*
**Brah·man** ['brɑmən] *s* (**-mans**) bramino
**braid** [bred] *s* treccia; (*strip of cloth*) spighetta; (mil) cordellina ‖ *tr* intrecciare; decorare con spighette

**brain** [bren] *s* cervello; **brains** cervello, intelligenza; **to rack one's brains** rompersi la testa ‖ *tr* far saltare le cervella di
**brain'child'** *s* (coll) parto dell'ingegno, idea geniale
**brain' drain'** *s* (coll) fuga di cervelli
**brainless** ['brenlɪs] *adj* senza testa
**brain' pow'er** *s* intelligenza
**brain'storm'** *s* (coll) ispirazione
**brain' trust'** *s* consiglio d'esperti
**brain'wash'ing** *s* lavaggio del cervello
**brain' wave'** *s* onda encefalica; (coll) idea geniale
**brain'work'** *s* lavoro intellettuale
**brain·y** ['breni] *adj* (-ier; -iest) intelligente
**braise** [brez] *tr* (culin) brasare
**brake** [brek] *s* freno; (*thicket*) macchia ‖ *tr & intr* frenare
**brake' drum'** *s* tamburo del freno
**brake' lin'ing** *s* ferodo
**brake'man** *s* (-men) frenatore *m*
**brake' shoe'** *s* ganascia
**bramble** ['bræmbəl] *s* rovo
**bran** [bræn] *s* crusca
**branch** [bræntʃ] *s* (*of tree*) branca, ramo; (*of river*) braccio; (*of a family*) ramo; (*of business*) filiale *f*; (rr) diramazione ‖ *intr* biforcarsi; **to branch off** or **out** ramificarsi, diramarsi
**branch' line'** *s* ferrovia di diramazione
**branch' of'fice** *s* succursale *f*
**brand** [brænd] *s* (*burning stick*) tizzone *m*; (*mark; stigma*) marchio; (*label; make*) marca ‖ *tr* (*to mark with a brand*) marchiare; (*to put a stigma on*) bollare; **to brand as** tacciare di
**brandied** ['brændid] *adj* conservato in acquavite
**brand'ing i'ron** *s* ferro da marchio
**brandish** ['brændɪʃ] *tr* brandire
**brand'-new'** *adj* nuovo fiammante
**bran·dy** ['brændi] *s* (-dies) cognac *m*, acquavite *f*
**brash** [bræʃ] *adj* (*too hasty*) avventato; (*insolent*) impudente ‖ *s* frammenti *mpl;* attacco (di malattia), indigestione
**brass** [bræs] or [brɑs] *s* ottone *m;* (coll) faccia tosta; (slang) alti ufficiali; **brasses** (mus) ottoni *mpl*
**brass' band'** *s* fanfara
**brassiere** [brə'zir] *s* reggiseno
**brass' knuck'les** *spl* tirapugni *m*
**brass' tack'** *s* chiodino or borchia d'ottone; **to get down to brass tacks** (coll) venire al sodo
**brass·y** ['bræsi] or ['brɑsi] *adj* (-ier; -iest) fatto d'ottone; sfacciato, impudente
**brat** [bræt] *s* marmocchio, monello
**brava·do** [brə'vɑdo] *s* (-does or -dos) bravata
**brave** [brev] *adj* coraggioso ‖ *s* persona coraggiosa; guerriero indiano ‖ *tr* (*to defy*) sfidare; (*to meet with courage*) affrontare
**bravery** ['brevəri] *s* coraggio
**bra·vo** ['brɑvo] *s* (-vos) bravo; applauso ‖ *interj* bravo!

**brawl** [brɔl] *s* zuffa, rissa ‖ *intr* azzuffarsi, rissare
**brawn** [brɔn] *s* forza muscolare
**brawn·y** ['brɔni] *adj* (-ier; -iest) muscoloso
**bray** [bre] *s* raglio ‖ *intr* ragliare
**braze** [brez] *s* brasatura ‖ *tr* brasare
**brazen** ['brezən] *adj* d'ottone; (*shameless*) sfrontato; (*sound*) penetrante ‖ *tr*—**to brazen out** or **through** affrontare sfacciatamente
**brazier** ['breʒər] *s* caldano, braciere *m;* (*workman*) ottonaio
**Brazil** [brə'zɪl] *s* il Brasile
**Brazilian** [brə'zɪljən] *adj & s* brasiliano
**Brazil' nut'** *s* noce *f* del Brasile
**breach** [britʃ] *s* (*gap*) breccia; (*failure to observe a law*) infrazione ‖ *tr* fare breccia su, fare varco in
**breach' of faith'** *s* abuso di confidenza
**breach' of prom'ise** *s* rottura di promessa di matrimonio
**breach' of the peace'** *s* violazione dell'ordine pubblico
**bread** [bred] *s* pane *m;* **to break bread with** sedersi a tavola con ‖ *tr* impannare
**bread' and but'ter** *s* pane *m* e burro; (coll) pane quotidiano
**bread' crumbs'** *spl* pangrattato
**breaded** ['bredɪd] *adj* impannato
**bread' knife'** *s* coltello da pane
**bread' line'** *s* coda del pane
**bread' stick'** *s* grissino
**breadth** [brɛdθ] *s* (*width*) larghezza; (*scope*) ampiezza
**bread'win'ner** *s* sostegno della famiglia
**break** [brek] *s* interruzione; intervallo; omissione; (*breaking*) rottura; (*of bones*) frattura; (*of day*) fare *m*, spuntare *m;* (*sudden change*) mutamento; (*from jail*) evasione; (*luck*) (coll) fortuna; **to give s.o. a break** dare a qlcu l'opportunità ‖ *v* (*pret* **broke** [brok]; *pp* **broken**) *tr* (*to smash*) rompere, spezzare; (*to tame*) domare; (*to demote*) destituire; (*a record*) superare; (*to violate*) violare; (*to make bankrupt*) mandare al fallimento; (*to interrupt*) interrompere; (*to reduce the effects of*) attutire; (*to disclose*) rivelare; (*to bring to an end by force*) battere; (*a banknote*) cambiare; (*one's word*) mancare (with *dat*); (*a law*) rompere; **to break asunder** separare; **to break down** analizzare; **to break in** forzare; **to break open** forzare, scassinare; **to break up** dissolvere ‖ *intr* (*to divide*) rompersi; (*to burst*) scoppiare; (*said of voice of youngster*) cambiare; (*said of voice*) indebolirsi; (*said of a crowd*) disperdersi; (*said of weather*) rischiararsi; (*said of prices*) ribassare; (*to come into being*) scoppiare; (boxing) separarsi; **to break asunder** separarsi; **to break away** scappare; **to break down** abbattersi; (aut) essere or rimanere in panna; **to break even** fare patta; **to break in** irrompere; interrompere; **to break into** forzare; **to break into a run** inco-

minciare a correre; **to break loose** liberarsi; (*said of a storm*) scatenarsi; **to break off** interrompere; **to break out** (*said of the skin*) avere un'eruzione; (*said, e.g., of war*) scoppiare; **to break through** aprirsi il varco; **to break up** disperdersi; **to break with** rompere le relazioni con

**breakable** ['brekəbəl] *adj* fragile

**breakage** ['brekɪdʒ] *s* rottura

**break′down′** *s* (*in negotiations*) rottura; (aut) panna; (chem) analisi *f*; (pathol) colasso

**breaker** ['brekər] *s* (*wave*) frangente *m*

**breakfast** ['brɛkfəst] *s* prima colazione ‖ *intr* fare prima colazione

**break′neck′** *adj* pericoloso; **at breakneck speed** a rotta di collo, a rompicollo

**break′ of day′** *s* alba

**break′through′** *s* (mil) penetrazione; (fig) scoperta sensazionale

**break′up′** *s* dispersione; dissoluzione; (*of a friendship*) rottura

**break′wa′ter** *s* diga, frangiflutti *m*

**breast** [brɛst] *s* petto; (*of female*) seno; (*source of emotions*) animo; **to make a clean breast of** fare una piena confessione di

**breast′bone′** *s* sterno

**breast′ drill′** *s* trapano da petto

**breast′feed′** *v* (*pret & pp* -fed [fɛd]) *tr* allattare

**breast′pin′** *s* spilla

**breast′stroke′** *s* bracciata a rana

**breath** [brɛθ] *s* respiro, respirazione; (*odor*) alito; (*breeze*) soffio; (*whisper*) sussurro; (fig) vita; **out of breath** ansimante; **short of breath** corto di respiro; **to gasp for breath** respirare affannosamente; **under one's breath** sottovoce

**breathe** [brið] *tr* respirare; (*to whisper*) sussurrare; **to breathe one's last** esalare l'ultimo sospiro; **to not breathe a word** non dire una parola ‖ *intr* respirare; **to breathe in** inspirare; **to breathe out** espirare

**breath′ing spell′** *s* attimo di respiro

**breathless** ['brɛθlɪs] *adj* senza fiato, ansimante; soffocante

**breath′tak′ing** *s* emozionante, commovente

**breech** [britʃ] *s* (*buttocks*) natiche *fpl*; (*rear part*) parte *f* posteriore; (*of gun*) culatta; **breeches** ['brɪtʃɪz] pantaloni *mpl* al ginocchio; pantaloni *mpl* da cavallo; **to wear the breeches** (coll) portare le brache

**breed** [brid] *s* razza; tipo; (*stock*) origine *f* ‖ *v* (*pret & pp* bred [brɛd]) *tr* produrre; (*to raise*) allevare

**breeder** ['bridər] *s* allevatore *m*; riproduttore *m*

**breeding** ['bridɪŋ] *s* (*e.g., of livestock*) allevamento; educazione

**breeze** [briz] *s* brezza

**breez·y** ['brizi] *adj* (-ier; -iest) ventilato; (*brisk*) vivace, brioso

**brethren** ['brɛðrɪn] *spl* fratelli *mpl*

**brevi·ty** ['brɛvɪti] *s* (-ties) brevità *f*

**brew** [bru] *s* pozione; bevanda ‖ *tr* (*beer*) fabbricare; (*to steep*) preparare; (*to plot*) complottare ‖ *intr* (*said of beer*) fermentare; (*said of a storm*) prepararsi

**brewer** ['bru·ər] *s* birraio

**brew′er's yeast′** *s* lievito di birra

**brewer·y** ['bru·əri] *s* (-ies) birreria, fabbrica di birra

**bribe** [braɪb] *s* subornazione, bustarella ‖ *tr* subornare, dare la bustarella a

**briber·y** ['braɪbəri] *s* (-ies) subornazione, corruzione

**bric-a-brac** ['brɪkə‚bræk] *s* bric-a-brac *m*, cianfrusaglia, cianfrusaglie *fpl*

**brick** [brɪk] *s* mattone *m* ‖ *tr* mattonare

**brick′bat′** *s* pezzo di mattone; (coll) insulto

**brick′kiln′** *s* fornace *f* per mattoni

**bricklayer** ['brɪk‚le·ər] *s* muratore *m*

**brick′yard′** *s* deposito di mattoni

**bridal** ['braɪdəl] *adj* nuziale, da sposa

**brid′al wreath′** *s* serto nuziale

**bride** [braɪd] *s* sposa

**bride′groom′** *s* sposo

**bridesmaid** ['braɪdz‚med] *s* damigella d'onore

**bridge** [brɪdʒ] *s* ponte *m*; (*of violin*) ponticello; (*on a ship*) ponte *m* di comando ‖ *tr* gettare un ponte su; congiungere; **to bridge a gap** colmare una lacuna

**bridge′head′** *s* testa di ponte

**bridle** ['braɪdəl] *s* briglia ‖ *tr* mettere la briglia a; (fig) frenare ‖ *intr* drizzare il capo, insuperbirsi

**bri′dle path′** *s* strada cavalcabile

**brief** [brif] *adj* breve ‖ *s* sommario; (law) esposto; (eccl) breve *m*; **briefs** slip *m* ‖ *tr* dare istruzioni a, mettere al corrente

**brief′ case′** *s* cartella, borsa d'avvocato

**brier** ['braɪ·ər] *s* radica; pipa di radica

**brig** [brɪg] *s* (naut) brigantino; (naut) prigione

**brigade** [brɪ'ged] *s* brigata

**brigadier** [‚brɪgə'dir] *s* (coll) brigadier generale *m*, generale *m* di brigata

**brigand** ['brɪgənd] *s* brigante *m*

**brigantine** ['brɪgən‚tin] *or* ['brɪgən‚taɪn] *s* (naut) brigantino goletta

**bright** [braɪt] *adj* (*shining*) lucido; (*light*) brillante; (*lively*) vivo; intelligente; famoso; (*idea*) luminoso

**brighten** ['braɪtən] *tr* illuminare; ravvivare ‖ *intr* illuminarsi; ravvivarsi; rischiararsi

**bright′ lights′** *spl* luci *fpl* abbaglianti; (aut) fari *mpl* abbaglianti

**brilliance** ['brɪljəns] *or* **brilliancy** ['brɪljənsi] *s* splendore *m*, scintillio

**brilliant** ['brɪljənt] *adj* brillante

**brim** [brɪm] *s* (*e.g., of cup*) orlo, bordo; (*of hat*) ala, tesa ‖ *v* (*pret & pp* brimmed; *ger* brimming) *intr* essere pieno sino all'orlo

**brim′stone′** *s* zolfo

**brine** [braɪn] *s* salamoia; acqua di mare

**bring** [brɪŋ] *v* (*pret & pp* brought

[brɔt]) *tr* far venire; provocare; (*to carry along*) portare con sè; **to bring about** causare; **to bring around** persuadere; **to bring back** restituire; **to bring down** far abbassare; (fig) umiliare; **to bring forth** dare alla luce; **to bring forward** (*an excuse*) addurre; (math) riportare; **to bring in** introdurre; far entrare; **to bring off** compiere; **to bring on** causare; **to bring oneself to** rassegnarsi a; **to bring out** (*to expose*) rivelare; (*to offer to the public*) presentare al pubblico; (*a book*) far uscire; **to bring to** far rinvenire; (*a ship*) fermare; **to bring together** riunire; **to bring up** (*children*) allevare, tirar su; (*to introduce*) allegare; (*to cough up*) rigettare

**bringing-up** ['brɪŋɪŋ'ʌp] *s* educazione
**brink** [brɪŋk] *s* orlo
**briquet** [brɪ'kɛt] *s* bricchetta
**brisk** [brɪsk] *adj* (*quick*) svelto; (*sharp*) acuto; (*invigorating*) frizzante; (*gunfire*) nutrito
**bristle** ['brɪsəl] *s* setola ‖ *intr* (*to be stiff*) irrigidirsi; (*said of hair*) rizzarsi; (*with anger*) adirarsi
**bris·tly** ['brɪsli] *adj* (-**tlier; -tliest**) irto di setole
**British** ['brɪtɪʃ] *adj* britannico ‖ **the British** i britannici, gl'inglesi
**Britisher** ['brɪtɪʃər] *s* britannico
**Briton** ['brɪtən] *s* britannico
**Brittany** ['brɪtəni] *s* la Bretagna
**brittle** ['brɪtəl] *adj* fragile, friabile; (*crisp*) croccante
**broach** [brotʃ] *s* (*pin*) spilla; (*spit*) spiedo; (mach) alesatore *m* ‖ *tr* perforare; (*a subject*) intavolare
**broad** [brɔd] *adj* largo; tollerante, liberale; (*daylight*) pieno; (*story*) grossolano; (*extensive*) lato; (*accent*) pronunciato
**broad'cast'** *s* disseminazione; (rad) radiodiffusione ‖ *v* (*pret & pp* -**cast**) *tr* disseminare, diffondere ‖ (*pret & pp* -**cast** or -**casted**) *tr* radiodiffondere
**broad'casting sta'tion** *s* stazione radiotrasmittente
**broad'cloth'** *s* (*wool*) panno di lana; (*cotton*) popeline *f*
**broaden** ['brɔdən] *tr* allargare, estendere ‖ *intr* allargarsi, estendersi
**broad' jump'** *s* salto in lunghezza
**broadloom** ['brɔd,lum] *adj* tessuto su telaio largo
**broad-minded** ['brɔd'maɪndɪd] *adj* di ampie vedute, liberale
**broad-shouldered** ['brɔd'ʃoldəred] *adj* largo di spalle
**broad'side'** *s* (nav) bordo; (nav) bordata; (*verbal criticism*) (coll) sfuriata; (*written criticism*) (coll) attacco violento
**broad'sword'** *s* spada da taglio
**brocade** [bro'ked] *s* broccato
**broccoli** ['brɑkəli] *s* broccolo; (*as food*) broccoli *mpl*
**brochure** [bro'ʃur] *s* opuscolo, libriccino

**brogue** [brog] *s* accento irlandese; scarpa forte e comoda
**broil** [brɔɪl] *s* cottura alla graticola; carne *f* cotta alla graticola; (*quarrel*) rissa, zuffa ‖ *tr* cucinare alla graticola; bruciare ‖ *intr* cucinare alla graticola; (*to quarrel*) rissare, azzuffarsi
**broiler** ['brɔɪlər] *s* graticola, gratella; (*chicken*) pollo da cucinare alla gratella or allo spiedo
**broke** [brok] *adj* (coll) al verde
**broken** ['brokən] *adj* rotto; fratturato; (*e.g., English*) parlato male; (*tamed*) domato
**bro'ken-down'** *adj* avvilito; rovinato
**broken-hearted** ['brokən'hɑrtɪd] *adj* affranto
**broker** ['brokər] *s* sensale *m;* (*on the stock exchange*) agente *m* di cambio
**brokerage** ['brokərɪdʒ] *s* mediazione
**bromide** ['bromaɪd] *s* bromuro; (coll) banalità *f*
**bromine** ['bromin] *s* bromo
**bronchitis** [brɑŋ'kaɪtɪs] *s* bronchite *f*
**bron·co** ['brɑŋko] *s* (-**cos**) puledro brado
**broncobuster** ['brɑŋko,bʌstər] *s* domatore *m* di puledri bradi
**bronze** [brɑnz] *adj* bronzeo ‖ *s* bronzo ‖ *tr* bronzare ‖ *intr* abbronzarsi
**brooch** [brotʃ] or [brutʃ] *s* spilla
**brood** [brud] *s* covata, nidiata ‖ *tr* covare ‖ *intr* chiocciare; meditare; **to brood on** or **over** meditare con tristezza (su)
**brook** [bruk] *s* ruscello ‖ *tr*—**to brook no** non sopportare
**broom** [brum] or [brum] *s* scopa; (*shrub*) saggina
**broom'corn'** *s* sorgo
**broom'stick'** *s* manico di scopa
**broth** [brɔθ] or [brɑθ] *s* brodo
**brothel** ['brɑθəl] or ['brɑðəl] *s* postribolo, bordello
**brother** ['brʌðər] *s* fratello
**brotherhood** ['brʌðər,hud] *s* fratellanza; (*association*) confraternita
**broth'er-in-law'** *s* (**brothers-in-law**) cognato
**brotherly** ['brʌðərli] *adj* fraterno ‖ *adv* fraternamente
**brow** [brau] *s* ciglio; (*forehead*) fronte *f;* **to knit one's brow** aggrottare la fronte
**brow'beat'** *v* (*pret* -**beat;** *pp* -**beaten**) *tr* intimidire, intimorire
**brown** [braun] *adj* bruno; (*tanned*) abbronzato ‖ *s* color bruno ‖ *tr* colorare di bruno; abbronzare; (*metal*) brunire; (culin) dorare ‖ *intr* colorarsi di bruno; abbronzarsi; brunirsi; (culin) dorarsi
**brownish** ['braunɪʃ] *adj* brunastro
**brown' stud'y** *s*—**in a brown study** assorto in fantasticherie
**brown' sug'ar** *s* zucchero greggio
**browse** [brauz] *intr* (*said of cattle*) brucare; sfogliare; **to browse around** curiosare
| **bruise** [bruz] *s* ammaccatura, contu-

sione || *tr* ammaccare || *intr* ammaccarsi

**brunet** [bru'nɛt] *adj* bruno

**brunette** [bru'nɛt] *adj & s* bruna

**brunt** [brʌnt] *s* forza; scontro; peso

**brush** [brʌʃ] *s* pennello; spazzola; (*stroke*) pennellata; (*light touch*) tocco; (*brushwood*) macchia; (*brief encounter*) scaramuccia; (elec) spazzola || *tr* spazzolare; pennellare; **to brush aside** rigettare; **to brush up** ritoccare || *intr*—**to brush by** passar vicino; **to brush up on** ripassare

**brush'-off'** *s* (slang) scortesia; **to give the brush-off to** (slang) snobbare

**brush'wood'** *s* macchia, fratta

**brusque** [brʌsk] *adj* brusco

**brusqueness** ['brʌsknɪs] *s* bruschezza

**Brussels** ['brʌsəlz] *s* Bruxelles *f*

**Brus'sels sprouts'** *spl* cavolini *mpl*

**brutal** ['brutəl] *adj* brutale

**brutali·ty** [bru'tælɪti] *s* (**-ties**) brutalità *f*

**brute** [brut] *adj & s* bruto

**brutish** ['brutɪʃ] *adj* bruto

**bubble** ['bʌbəl] *s* bolla; (fig) chimera || *intr* bollire; (*to make a bubbling sound*) barbugliare; **to bubble over** traboccare

**bub'ble bath'** *s* bagno di schiuma

**buccaneer** [ˌbʌkə'nɪr] *s* bucaniere *m*

**buck** [bʌk] *s* (*deer*) cervo; (*goat*) caprone *m*; (*sawhorse*) cavalletto; (*rabbit*) coniglio maschio; (*bucking*) groppata; (*dandy*) damerino; (slang) dollaro; **to pass the buck** (coll) giocare a scaricabarile || *tr* resistere accanitamente || *intr* (*said of a horse*) fare salti da caprone; **to buck for** (slang) cercare di ottenere; **to buck up** (coll) rianimarsi, prender animo

**bucket** ['bʌkɪt] *s* secchio; bigoncia; (*e.g., of dredge*) benna; **to kick the bucket** (slang) tirare le cuoia

**buck'et seat'** *s* sedile *m*, strapuntino

**buckle** ['bʌkəl] *s* (*clasp*) fibbia, boccola; piega || *tr* affibbiare || *intr* piegarsi, curvarsi; **to buckle down to** (coll) mettersi di buzzo buono a

**buck' pri'vate** *s* (slang) soldato semplice

**buckram** ['bʌkrəm] *s* tela da fusto

**buck'saw'** *s* cavalletto

**buck'shot'** *s* pallini *mpl* da caccia

**buck'tooth'** *s* (**-teeth**) dente *m* in fuori, dente *m* sporgente

**buck'wheat'** *s* grano saraceno

**bud** [bʌd] *s* bocciolo, gemma; **to nip in the bud** troncare sul nascere || *v* (*pret & pp* **budded;** *ger* **budding**) *intr* sbocciare; nascere

**Buddhism** ['budɪzəm] *s* buddismo

**bud·dy** ['bʌdi] *s* (**-dies**) (coll) amico, compare *m*

**budge** [bʌdʒ] *tr* smuovere || *intr* muoversi

**budget** ['bʌdʒɪt] *s* bilancio || *tr* stanziare, preventivare; (*to schedule*) anticipare; (*time*) calcolare in anticipo

**budgetary** ['bʌdʒɪˌtɛri] *adj* preventivo, di bilancio

**buff** [bʌf] *adj* bruno giallastro; di pelle || *s* (*leather*) pelle gialla; dilet-

tante *m;* (mil) giacca di pelle gialla; (coll) pelle nuda || *tr* lucidare; (*to reduce the force of*) ammortizzare

**buffa·lo** ['bʌfəˌlo] *s* (**-loes** or **-los**) bufalo || *tr* (coll) intimidire

**buffer** ['bʌfər] *s* ammortizzatore *m;* cuscinetto; (*worker*) lucidatore *m;* (mach) lucidatrice *f;* (rr) respingente *m*

**buff'er state'** *s* stato cuscinetto

**buffet** [bu'fe] *s* (*piece of furniture*) credenza; (*counter*) buffet *m* || ['bʌfɪt] *s* pugno; schiaffo || *tr* dar pugni a; schiaffeggiare; lottare con; (*to push about*) sballottare

**buffet' car'** [bu'fe] *s* vagone *m* ristorante

**buffoon** [bə'fun] *s* buffone *m*

**buffoner·y** [bə'funəri] *s* (**-ies**) buffoneria

**bug** [bʌg] *s* insetto; (coll) germe *m;* (*in motor*) (slang) noia; (slang) pazzo; **to put a bug in the ear of** mettere una pulce nell'orecchio di || *v* (*pret & pp* **bugged;** *ger* **bugging**) *tr* (slang) installare un sistema d'ascolto nel telefono di; (*to annoy*) (slang) seccare || *intr*—**to bug out** (slang) andarsene

**bug'bear'** *s* spauracchio

**bug·gy** ['bʌgi] *adj* (**-gier; -giest**) pieno di cimici; (slang) pazzo || *s* (**-gies**) carrozzino

**bug'house'** *adj* (slang) pazzo || *s* (slang) manicomio

**bugle** ['bjugəl] *s* tromba, cornetta

**bugler** ['bjuglər] *s* trombettiere *m*

**build** [bɪld] *s* corporatura, taglia || *v* (*pret & pp* **built** [bɪlt]) *tr* costruire, edificare; fondare, basare; **to build up** sviluppare

**builder** ['bɪldər] *s* costruttore *m;* costruttore *m* edile

**building** ['bɪldɪŋ] *s* edificio, stabile *m;* costruzione; edilizia

**build'ing and loan' associa'tion** *s* società *f* di credito fondiario

**build'ing lot'** *s* (coll) terreno da costruzioni

**build'ing trades'** *spl* edilizia

**build'-up'** *s* concentrazione; sviluppo; processo di preparazione; propaganda favorevole

**built'-in'** *adj* (*in a wall*) murato; (*in a cabinet*) incassato, incorporato

**built'-in clos'et** *s* armadio a muro

**built'-up'** *adj* armato; popolato

**bulb** [bʌlb] *s* bulbo; (*lamp*) lampadina; (*of a lamp*) globo, cipolla

**Bulgarian** [bʌl'gɛrɪən] *adj & s* bulgaro

**bulge** [bʌldʒ] *s* protuberanza, sporgenza || *intr* sporgere, gonfiarsi

**bulk** [bʌlk] *s* volume *m*, massa; **in bulk** in blocco; sciolto || *intr* avere importanza; aumentare d'importanza

**bulk'head'** *s* diga; (naut) paratia

**bulk·y** ['bʌlki] *adj* (**-ier; -iest**) voluminoso

**bull** [bul] *s* toro; (*in the stockmarket*) rialzista *mf;* (slang) scemenza; (eccl) bulla || *tr*—**to bull the market** giocare al rialzo

**bull'dog'** *s* molosso

**bulldoze** ['bʊl͵doz] *tr* intimidire; (*land*) livellare
**bulldozer** ['bʊl͵dozər] *s* livellatrice *f*, apripista *m*
**bullet** ['bʊlɪt] *s* palla, pallottola
**bulletin** ['bʊlətɪn] *s* bollettino; (*of a school*) albo; (journ) comunicato
**bul'letin board'** s tabellone *m*
**bul'let·proof'** *adj* blindato
**bull'fight'** *s* corrida
**bull'fight'er** *s* torero
**bull'finch'** *s* (orn) ciuffolotto
**bull'frog'** *s* rana americana
**bull·headed** ['bʊl͵hɛdɪd] *adj* testardo
**bullion** ['bʊljən] *s* lingotti *mpl* d'oro or d'argento; frangia d'oro; (*on an Italian general's hat*) greca
**bullish** ['bʊlɪʃ] *adj* ostinato; (*market*) al rialzo; (*speculator*) rialzista
**bullock** ['bʊlək] *s* manzo
**bull'ring'** *s* arena
**bull's-eye** ['bʊlz͵aɪ] *s* centro, tiro in pieno sul bersaglio; **to hit the bull's-eye** fare centro
**bul·ly** ['bʊli] *adj* (coll) eccellente ‖ *s* (-lies) bravaccio ‖ *v* (*pret & pp* -lied) *tr* intimidire
**bulrush** ['bʊl͵rʌʃ] *s* giunco; (Bibl) papiro
**bulwark** ['bʊlwərk] *s* baluardo; protezione ‖ *tr* proteggere
**bum** [bʌm] *adj* (slang) pessimo ‖ *s* (slang) vagabondo; **on the bum** (slang) rotto, fuori servizio ‖ *v* (*pret & pp* **bummed**; *ger* **bumming**) *tr* (slang) scroccare ‖ *intr* (slang) oziare; (slang) vivere d'elemosina; (slang) fare lo scroccatore
**bumble** ['bʌmbəl] *tr* abborracciare ‖ *intr* abborracciare; (*to stagger*) barcollare; (*to stumble*) balbettare; (*said of a bee*) ronzare
**bum'blebee'** *s* calabrone *m*
**bump** [bʌmp] *s* botta, botto; (*collision*) colpo, urto; (*swelling*) bernoccolo ‖ *tr* urtare; **to bump off** (slang) uccidere ‖ *intr* urtare, cozzare; **to bump into** incontrarsi con; cozzare contro
**bumper** ['bʌmpər] *adj* (coll) abbondante ‖ *s* bicchiere pieno fino all'orlo; (aut) paraurti *m;* (rr) respingente *m*
**bumpkin** ['bʌmpkɪn] *s* beota *m*
**bumptious** ['bʌmpʃəs] *adj* vanitoso, presuntuoso
**bump·y** ['bʌmpi] *adj* (-ier; -iest) (*road*) irregolare, ondulato; (*air*) agitato
**bun** [bʌn] *s* panino; (*of hair*) crocchia, treccia a ciambella
**bunch** [bʌntʃ] *s* (*of grapes*) grappolo; (*of keys*) mazzo; (*of grass*) ciuffo; (*of people*) gruppo; (*of twigs*) fastello; (*of animals*) branco ‖ *tr* (*things*) ammonticchiare; (*people*) raggruppare ‖ *intr* raggrupparsi
**bundle** ['bʌndəl] *s* fascio, fastello; (*package*) pacco; (*large package*) collo; (*bunch*) mucchio ‖ *tr* affastellare; impacchettare; ammucchiare; **to bundle off** or **out** cacciare precipitosamente; **to bundle up** infagottare ‖ *intr*—**to bundle up** infagottarsi
**bung** [bʌŋ] *s* spina, cannella

**bungalow** ['bʌŋgə͵lo] *s* casetta, villino, bungalow *m*
**bung'hole'** *s* spina, foro della botte
**bungle** ['bʌŋgəl] *s* abborracciatura ‖ *tr* abborracciare ‖ *intr* lavorare alla carlona
**bungler** ['bʌŋglər] *s* abborraccione *m*
**bungling** ['bʌŋglɪŋ] *adj* goffo; mal fatto ‖ *s* abborracciatura
**bunion** ['bʌnjən] *s* gonfiore *m* dell'alluce
**bunk** [bʌŋk] *s* letto a castello; (nav) cuccetta; (slang) sciocchezza ‖ *intr* dormire in cuccetta
**bunk' bed'** *s* letto a castello
**bunker** ['bʌŋkər] *s* (bin) carbonile *m;* (mil) casamatta; (golf) ostacolo
**bun·ny** ['bʌni] *s* (-nies) coniglietto
**bunting** ['bʌntɪŋ] *s* ornamento di bandiere; (nav) gala; (orn) zigolo
**buoy** [bɔɪ] or ['bu·i] *s* boa; (*life preserver*) salvagente *m* ‖ *tr*—**to buoy up** tenere a galla; (fig) rincuorare
**buoyancy** ['bɔɪ·ənsi] or ['bujənsi] *s* galleggiabilità *f;* (*cheerfulness*) allegria, esuberanza
**buoyant** ['bɔɪ·ənt] or ['bujənt] *adj* galleggiante; allegro, esuberante
**bur** [bʌr] *s* riccio, aculeo
**burble** ['bʌrbəl] *s* gorgoglio ‖ *intr* gorgogliare
**burden** ['bʌrdən] *s* carico, peso, fardello; (*of a speech*) tema *m;* (*chorus*) ritornello; (naut) portata ‖ *tr* caricare
**bur'den of proof'** *s* onere *m* della prova
**burdensome** ['bʌrdənsəm] *adj* oneroso
**burdock** ['bʌrdak] *s* lappa, lappola
**bureau** ['bjuro] *s* comò *m;* (*agency*) ufficio, servizio
**bureaucra·cy** [bju'rakrəsi] *s* (-cies) burocrazia
**bureaucrat** ['bjurə͵kræt] *s* burocrate *m*
**burglar** ['bʌrglər] *s* scassinatore *m*
**bur'glar alarm'** *s* campanello antifurto
**burglarize** ['bʌrglə͵raɪz] *tr* scassinare
**bur'glar·proof'** *adj* a prova di furto
**burgla·ry** ['bʌrgləri] *s* (-ries) furto con scasso, scassinatura
**Burgundy** ['bʌrgəndi] *s* la Borgogna; (*wine*) borgogna *m*
**burial** ['bɛrɪ·əl] *s* sepoltura
**bur'ial ground'** *s* cimitero
**burin** ['bjurɪn] *s* burino, cesello
**burlap** ['bʌrlæp] *s* tela di iuta
**burlesque** [bʌr'lɛsk] *adj* burlesco ‖ *s* farsa, burlesque *m* ‖ *tr* parodiare
**burlesque' show'** *s* spettacolo di varietà, music-hall *m*
**bur·ly** ['bʌrli] *adj* (-lier; -liest) membruto, robusto
**Burma** ['bʌrmə] *s* la Birmania
**burn** [bʌrn] *s* bruciatura, scottatura ‖ *v* (*pret & pp* **burned** or **burnt** [bʌrnt]) *tr* bruciare; (*to set on fire*) dar fuoco a; (*bricks*) cuocere; **to burn down** radere al suolo; **to burn up** consumare; (*the road*) divorare; (coll) fare arrabbiare ‖ *intr* bruciare, bruciarsi; (*said of lights*) essere acceso, e.g., **the lights were burning** la luce era accesa; **to burn out** (*said of an electric bulb or a fuse*) bruciarsi;

**to burn to** (fig) agognare di; **to burn up** (coll) essere arrabiato; **to burn with** (*e.g., envy*) ardere di

**burner** ['bʌrnər] *s* (*of gas fixture or lamp*) becco; (*of furnace*) bruciatore *m*

**burning** ['bʌrnɪŋ] *adj* bruciante, scottante || *s* incendio; (*ceramic*) cottura finale

**burn'ing ques'tion** *s* questione di attualità palpitante

**burnish** ['bʌrnɪʃ] *s* lucidatura || *tr* brunire

**burnt' al'mond** [bʌrnt] *s* mandorla tostata

**burp** [bʌrp] *s* (coll) rutto || *intr* (coll) ruttare

**burr** [bʌr] *s* riccio, aculeo; (*rough edge*) bava; (*dentist's drill*) fresa

**burrow** ['bʌro] *s* tana, buca || *intr* imbucarsi, rintanarsi

**bursar** ['bʌrsər] *s* tesoriere universitario

**burst** [bʌrst] *s* esplosione; (*e.g., of machine gun*) raffica; (*break*) crepa; (*of passion*) accesso; (*of speed*) slancio || *tr* far scoppiare || *intr* scoppiare, esplodere; **to burst into** (*e.g., a room*) irrompere in; (*e.g., angry words*) esplodere in; **to burst out crying** scoppiare in lacrime; **to burst with laughter** scoppiare dalle risa

**bur·y** ['beri] *v* (*pret & pp* **-ied**) *tr* sotterrare; **to be buried in thought** essere immerso nel pensiero; **to bury the hatchet** fare la pace

**bus** [bʌs] *s* (**buses** or **busses**) bus *m*, autobus *m* || *v* (*pret & pp* **bused** or **bussed**; *ger* **busing** or **bussing**) *tr* trasportare con autobus

**bus'boy'** *s* secondo cameriere

**bus·by** ['bʌzbi] *s* (**-bies**) colbacco

**bus' driv'er** *s* conducente *mf* di autobus

**bush** [buʃ] *s* cespuglio, arbusto; **to beat around the bush** menare il can per l'aia

**bushed** [buʃt] *adj* (coll) stanco morto

**bushel** ['buʃəl] *s* staio

**bushing** ['buʃɪŋ] *s* (mach) bronzina

**bush·y** ['buʃi] *adj* (**-ier; -iest**) ricco di arbusti; (*face*) barbuto

**business** ['bɪznɪs] *adj* commerciale || *s* occupazione; commercio; affare *m*, negozio; faccenda; impiego; **it is not your business** non è affare Suo; **to know one's business** sapere il fatto proprio; **to make it one's business to** proporsi di; **to mean business** (coll) farla sul serio; **to mind one's own business** impicciarsi degli affari propri

**businesslike** ['bɪznɪs,laɪk] *adj* metodico; serio; efficace

**busi'ness·man'** *s* (**-men'**) commerciante *m*, uomo d'affari

**busi'ness suit'** *s* abito da passeggio

**busi'ness·wom'an** *s* (**wom'en**) commerciante *f*

**bus'man** *s* (**-men**) guidatore *m* d'autobus

**buss** [bʌs] *s* (coll) bacione sonoro || *tr* (coll) baciare sonoramente

**bus' stop'** *s* fermata degli autobus

**bust** [bʌst] *s* busto; petto; (slang) fallimento; (slang) pugno || *tr* (slang) rompere; (slang) far fallire; (slang) colpire, dare pugni a; (mil) degradare

**buster** ['bʌstər] *s* (coll) ragazzo; (coll) rompitore *m*

**bustle** ['bʌsəl] *s* (*on a dress*) guardinfante *m*; attività *f* || *intr* affrettarsi

**bus·y** ['bɪzi] *adj* (**-ier; -iest**) occupato || *v* (*pret & pp* **-ied**) *tr* occupare, tenere occupato; **to busy oneself with** occuparsi di

**bus'y·bod'y** *s* (**-ies**) ficcanaso

**bus'y sig'nal** *s* (telp) segnale *m* d'occupato

**but** [bʌt] *s* ma *m* || *adv* solo, solamente; **but for** se non . . . per || *prep* eccetto, ad eccezione di, meno, se non; **all but** quasi || *conj* ma; che non, e.g., **I never go out in the rain but I catch a cold** non esco mai con la pioggia che non mi pigli un raffreddore

**butcher** ['butʃər] *s* macellaio || *tr* macellare; massacrare

**butch'er knife'** *s* coltello da cucina, coltella

**butch'er shop'** *s* macelleria

**butcher·y** ['butʃəri] *s* (**-ies**) macello; carneficina

**butler** ['bʌtlər] *s* cantiniere *m*, credenziere *m*

**butt** [bʌt] *s* (*butting*) cornata; (*of rifle or gun*) calcio; (*of cigar*) mozzicone *m*; (*target*) bersaglio; (*end*) estremità *f*; (*of ridicule*) zimbello; (*cask*) botte *f* || *tr* dare cornate a; cozzare contro || *intr*—**to butt into** (slang) intromettersi in

**butter** ['bʌtər] *s* burro || *tr* imburrare; **to butter up** (coll) adulare

**but'ter·cup'** *s* (bot) bottone *m* d'oro, ranuncolo

**but'ter dish'** *s* piattino per il burro, burriera

**but'ter·fat'** *s* grasso nel latte

**but'ter·fly'** *s* (**-flies**) farfalla

**but'ter knife'** *s* coltello per il burro

**but'ter·milk'** *s* latticello

**but'ter sauce'** *s* burro fuso

**but'ter·scotch'** *s* caramella al burro

**buttocks** ['bʌtəks] *spl* chiappe *fpl*, natiche *fpl*

**button** ['bʌtən] *s* bottone *m* || *tr* abbottonare

**but'ton·hole'** *s* occhiello, asola || *tr* attaccare un bottone a

**but'ton·hook'** *s* allacciabottoni *m*

**buttress** ['bʌtrɪs] *s* contrafforte *m*; piedritto || *tr* rinforzare

**buxom** ['bʌksəm] *adj* avvenente, procace

**buy** [baɪ] *s* compra || *v* (*pret & pp* **bought** [bɔt]) *tr* comprare; **to buy off** corrompere; **to buy out** comprare la parte di

**buyer** ['baɪ·ər] *s* compratore *m*

**buzz** [bʌz] *s* brusio, ronzio || *tr* volare a bassa quota sopra; (coll) fare una telefonata a || *intr* ronzare

**buzzard** ['bʌzərd] *s* (*hawk*) poiana; avvoltoio americano

**buzzer** ['bʌzər] *s* suoneria ronzante

**buzz' saw'** *s* sega circolare, segatrice *f* a disco

**by** [baɪ] *adv* oltre, e.g., **to speed by** correre velocemente oltre; **by and by** fra poco; **by and large** generalmente || *prep* vicino a; di, durante, e.g., **by night** di notte, durante la notte; a, e.g., **they work by the hour** lavorano all'ora; (*not later than, through*) per; (*past*) in fronte a; (*through the agency of*) da; (*according to*) secondo; (*math*) per, volte; **by far** di molto; **by the way** a proposito

**bygone** ['baɪ,gɔn] *or* ['baɪ,gɑn] *adj & s* passato; **to let bygones be bygones** dimenticare il passato

**bylaw** ['baɪ,lɔ] *s* legge *f* locale, regolamento di una società

**by'-line'** *s* (journ) firma

**by'pass'** *s* linea secondaria; (*detour*) deviazione || *tr* fare una deviazione oltre a; (*a difficulty*) evitare

**by'path'** *s* sentiero secondario; sentiero privato

**by'prod'uct** *s* sottoprodotto

**bystander** ['baɪ,stændər] *s* astante *m*, spettatore *m*

**byway** ['baɪ,we] *s* via traversa

**byword** ['baɪ,wʌrd] *s* proverbio; oggetto di obbrobrio

**Byzantium** [bɪ'zænʃɪ·əm] *or* [bɪ-'zæntɪ·əm] *s* Bisanzio

# C

**C, c** [si] *s* terza lettera dell'alfabeto inglese

**cab** [kæb] *s* vettura di piazza; tassì *m;* (*of truck or locomotive*) cabina

**cabbage** ['kæbɪdʒ] *s* cavolo, verza

**cab' driv'er** *s* autista *m* di piazza; (*of horse-drawn cab*) vetturino

**cabin** ['kæbɪn] *s* (*shed*) capanna; (*hut*) baracca; (aer, naut) cabina

**cab'in boy'** *s* mozzo

**cabinet** ['kæbɪnɪt] *s* (*piece of furniture*) vetrina; (*for a radio*) armadietto; (*small room; ministry of a government*) gabinetto

**cab'inet·mak'er** *s* ebanista *m*

**cab'inet·mak'ing** *s* ebanisteria

**cable** ['kebəl] *s* cavo; cablogramma; (elec) cablaggio || *tr* cablare, mandare un cablogramma a

**ca'ble address'** *s* indirizzo telegrafico

**ca'ble car'** *s* funicolare *f*, teleferica

**cablegram** ['kebel,græm] *s* cablogramma *m*

**caboose** [kə'bus] *s* (rr) vagone *m* di coda

**cab'stand'** *s* stazione di tassametri

**cache** [kæʃ] *s* nascondiglio || *tr* mettere in un nascondiglio

**cachet** [kæ'ʃe] *s* sigillo; (*distinguishing feature*) impronta

**cackle** ['kækəl] *s* (*of chickens*) coccodè *m;* (*of people*) chiaccherio || *intr* fare coccodè; ciarlare

**cac·tus** ['kæktəs] *s* (-tuses *or* -ti [taɪ]) cactus *m*

**cad** [kæd] *s* mascalzone *m*

**cadaver** [kə'dævər] *s* cadavere *m*

**cadaverous** [kə'dævərəs] *adj* cadaverico

**caddie** ['kædi] *s* portamazze *m*

**cadence** ['kedəns] *s* cadenza

**cadet** [kə'dɛt] *s* cadetto

**cadmium** ['kædmɪ·əm] *s* cadmio

**cadres** ['kædriz] *spl* (mil) quadri *mpl*

**Caesar'ean sec'tion** [sɪ'zɛrɪ·ən] *s* taglio cesareo

**café** [kæ'ʃe] *s* caffè *m*, bar *m*, ristorante *m*

**ca'fé soci'ety** *s* bel mondo

**cafeteria** [,kæfə'tɪrɪ·ə] *s* mensa, tavola calda, caffetteria

**caffeine** [kæ'fin] *or* ['kæfi·ɪn] *s* caffeina

**cage** [kedʒ] *s* gabbia; (*of elevator*) cabina || *tr* ingabbiare

**ca·gey** ['kedʒi] *adj* (-gier; -giest) (coll) astuto, cauto

**cahoots** [kə'huts] *s*—**to be in cahoots** (slang) far lega, essere in combutta; **to go cahoots** (slang) dividere in parti eguali

**Cain** [ken] *s* Caino; **to raise Cain** (slang) arrabbiarsi; (slang) fare una sfuriata

**Cairo** ['kaɪro] *s* il Cairo

**caisson** ['kesən] *s* cassone *m;* (archit) cassettone *m*

**cajole** [kə'dʒol] *tr* lusingare; persuadere con lusinghe

**cajoler·y** [kə'dʒoləri] *s* (-ies) lusinga

**cake** [kek] *s* dolce *m;* torta, pasta; (*with bread-like dough*) focaccia; (*of soap*) saponetta; (*of earth*) zolla; **to take the cake** (coll) essere il colmo || *tr* incrostare || *intr* indurirsi; incrostarsi

**calabash** ['kælə,bæʃ] *s* zucca a fiasca

**calaboose** ['kælə,bus] *s* (coll) gattabuia

**calamitous** [kə'læmɪtəs] *adj* calamitoso

**calami·ty** [kə'læmɪti] *s* (-ties) calamità *f*

**calci·fy** ['kælsɪ,faɪ] *v* (pret & pp -fied) *tr* calcificare || *intr* calcificarsi

**calcium** ['kælsɪ·əm] *s* calcio

**calculate** ['kælkjə,let] *tr* calcolare || *intr* calcolare; **to calculate on** contare su

**cal'culating machine'** *s* (macchina) calcolatrice

**calcu·lus** ['kælkjələs] *s* (-luses *or* -li [,laɪ]) (math, pathol) calcolo

**calendar** ['kæləndər] *s* calendario; (*agenda*) ordine *m* del giorno

**calf** [kæf] *or* [kɑf] *s* (calves [kævz] *or* [kɑvz]) vitello; (*of shoes or binding*) pelle *f* di vitello; (*of the leg*) polpaccio

**calf'skin'** *s* pelle *f* di vitello

caliber ['kælɪbər] s calibro
calibrate ['kælɪ‚bret] tr calibrare
cali·co ['kælɪ‚ko] s (-coes or -cos) cotone stampato, calico
California [‚kælɪ'fɔrnɪ·ə] s la California
calipers ['kælɪpərz] spl compasso a grossezze, calibro
caliph ['kelɪf] or ['kælɪf] s califfo
calisthenic [‚kælɪs'θɛnɪk] adj ginna· stico || calisthenics spl ginnastica a corpo libero
calk [kɔk] tr var of caulk
call [kɔl] s chiamata; visita; (shout) grido, richiamo; (of bugle) squillo; (of telephone) colpo; (of ship) scalo; obbligo; vocazione; (com) richiesta; on call disponibile; within call a portata di voce || tr chiamare; convocare; (to awaken) svegliare; to call back richiamare; to call in (e.g., an expert) fare venire; (e.g., currency) domandare, esigere; to call off annullare; to call out chiamare; to call together convocare; to call up chiamare per telefono || intr chiamare; visitare; to call at passare per la casa di; (naut) fare scalo a; to call for venire a prendere; to call out gridare; to go calling andare a fare visite
cal'la lil'y ['kælə] s (Zantedeschia aethiopica) calla dei fioristi
call'boy' s (in a hotel) fattorino; (theat) buttafuori m
caller ['kɔlər] s visitatore m
call' girl' s ragazza squillo
calling ['kɔlɪŋ] s appello; professione
call'ing card' s biglietto da visita
call' num'ber s numero telefonico; numero di biblioteca
callous ['kæləs] adj calloso; insensibile
callow ['kælo] adj inesperto, immaturo
call' to arms' s chiamata alle armi
call' to the col'ors s chiamata sotto la bandiera
callus ['kæləs] s callo
calm [kɑm] adj calmo, tranquillo || calma || tr calmare, tranquillizzare || intr—to calm down calmarsi; (said of weather) abbonacciarsi
calmness ['kɑmnɪs] s calma, placidità f, tranquillità f
calomel ['kælə‚mɛl] s calomelano
calorie ['kæləri] s caloria
calum·ny ['kæləmnɪ] s (-nies) calunnia
Calvary ['kælvəri] s (Bib) Calvario
cam [kæm] s camma
camber ['kæmbər] s curvatura; convessità f || tr arcuare || intr curvarsi
cambric ['kembrɪk] s cambrì m
camel ['kæməl] s cammello
came·o ['kæmi‚o] s (-os) cammeo
camera ['kæmərə] s macchina fotografica; (mov) cinepresa
cam'era·man' s (-men') operatore m
camomile ['kæmə‚maɪl] s camomilla
camouflage ['kæmə‚flɑʒ] s mascheramento || tr mascherare, camuffare
camp [kæmp] s accampamento, campo || intr accamparsi
campaign [kæm'pen] s campagna || intr fare una campagna

campaigner [kæm'penər] s veterano; (pol) propagandista mf
camp' bed' s letto da campo, branda
camper ['kæmpər] s campeggiatore m, campeggista mf
camp'fire' s fuoco di accampamento
camp'ground' s terreno per campeggio
camphor ['kæmfər] s canfora
camp'stool' s seggiolino pieghevole
campus ['kæmpəs] s campo, terreno dell'università
cam'shaft' s albero di distribuzione, albero a camme
can [kæn] s lattina, barattolo; (of gasoline or oil) bidone m || v (pret & pp canned; ger canning) tr inscatolare; (slang) licenziare || v (pret & cond could) aux I can speak English so parlare inglese; can he go now? se ne può andare ora?
Canada ['kænədə] s il Canadà
Canadian [kə'nedɪ·ən] adj & s canadese mf
canal [kə'næl] s canale m
canar·y [kə'neri] s (-ies) canarino || Canaries spl Canarie fpl
can·cel ['kænsəl] v (pret & pp -celed or -celled; ger -celing or -celling) tr cancellare; annullare; revocare; (stamps) timbrare, annullare
cancellation [‚kænsə'leʃən] s cancellazione, annullamento; cassazione; (of a stamp) bollo
cancer ['kænsər] s cancro || Cancer s Cancro
cancerous ['kænsərəs] adj canceroso
candela·brum [‚kændə'labrəm] s (-bra [brə] or -brums) candelabro
candid ['kændɪd] adj candido; sincero, franco
candida·cy ['kændɪdəsi] s (-cies) candidatura
candidate ['kændɪ‚det] s candidato; (for a degree) laureando
can'did cam'era s camera fotografica indiscreta
candied ['kændɪd] adj candito
candle ['kændəl] s candela || tr (eggs) sperare
can'dle·hold'er s var of candlestick
can'dle·light' s luce f or lume m di candela
can'dle·pow'er s (phys) candela
can'dle·stick' s (ornate) candeliere m; (plain) bugia
candor ['kændər] s candore m; ingenuità f
can·dy ['kændi] s (-dies) dolciumi mpl; a piece of candy un bombon || v (pret & pp -died) tr candire
can'dy box' s bomboniera
can'dy dish' s bomboniera; (three-tier-high) alzata
can'dy store' s confetteria
cane [ken] s canna, giunco; (for walking) bastone m || tr bastonare; (chairs) impagliare
cane' seat' s sedia impagliata
cane' sug'ar s zucchero di canna
canine ['kenaɪn] adj canino || s (tooth) canino; (dog) cane m
canister ['kænɪstər] s barattolo

**canned' goods'** *spl* conserve *fpl* alimentari; prodotti *mpl* in scatola

**canned' mu'sic** *s* (slang) musica su dischi

**canner·y** ['kænəri] *s* (**-ies**) fabbrica di conserve alimentari

**cannibal** ['kænɪbəl] *adj* & *s* cannibale *mf*, antropofago

**canning** ['kænɪŋ] *s* conservazione

**cannon** ['kænən] *s* cannone *m*

**cannonade** [ ˌkænəˈned] *s* cannonata ‖ *tr* cannoneggiare

**can'non·ball'** *s* palla da cannone

**can'non fod'der** *s* carne *f* da cannone

**can·ny** ['kæni] *adj* (**-nier; -niest**) astuto, fino; malizioso

**canoe** [kəˈnu] *s* canoa, piroga

**canon** ['kænən] *s* canone *m; (priest)* canonico

**canonical** [kəˈnɑnɪkəl] *adj* canonico ‖ **canonicals** *spl* paramenti liturgici

**canonize** ['kænəˌnaɪz] *tr* canonizzare

**can'on law'** *s* diritto canonico

**canon·ry** ['kænənri] *s* (**-ries**) canonicato

**can' o'pener** ['opənər] *s* apriscatole *m*

**cano·py** ['kænəpi] *s* (**-pies**) tenda; baldacchino; *(of sky)* (fig) volta

**cant** [kænt] *adj* ipocrita ‖ *s* linguaggio ipocrita; gergo; *(slope)* inclinazione

**cantaloupe** ['kæntəˌlop] *s* melone *m*

**cantankerous** [kænˈtæŋkərəs] *adj* bisbetico, attaccabrighe

**canteen** [kænˈtin] *s* cantina, spaccio; *(metal bottle)* borraccia

**canter** ['kæntər] *s* piccolo galoppo ‖ *intr* andare al piccolo galoppo

**cantiliver** ['kæntɪˌlivər] *adj* a cantiliver ‖ *s* trave *f* a sbalzo; (archit) trave *f* a mensola

**cantle** ['kæntəl] *s* arcione *m* posteriore

**canton** ['kænˈtɑn] *s* cantone *m; region* ‖ *tr* accantonare

**cantonment** [kænˈtɑnmənt] *s* accantonamento

**cantor** ['kæntər] or ['kæntɔr] *s* cantore *m*

**canvas** ['kænvəs] *s* *(cloth)* olona; *(e.g. on open truck)* copertone *m; (painting)* tela; (naut) vela; **under canvas** (naut) a vele spiegate

**canvass** ['kænvəs] *s* discussione; dibattito; (pol) sollecitazione di voti ‖ *tr* discutere; *(votes)* sollecitare; *(to investigate)* indagare; (com) fare la piazza a ‖ *intr* discutere; sollecitare voti; indagare; (com) fare la piazza

**canyon** ['kænjən] *s* cañon *m*

**cap** [kæp] *s* berretto; cuffia; *(of academic costume)* berrettone *m; (of bottle)* tappo, capsula; *(e.g., of fountain pen)* cappuccio ‖ *v* (*pret* & *pp* **capped**); *ger* **capping**) *tr* (*a person*) coprire il capo di; (*s.o.'s head*) coprire con il berretto; (*a bottle*) mettere il tappo a; terminare; **to cap the climax** essere il colmo

**capabili·ty** [ ˌkepəˈbɪlɪti] *s* (**-ties**) capacità *f*, abilità *f*

**capable** ['kepəbəl] *adj* capace, abile

**capacious** [kəˈpeʃəs] *adj* ampio, capace

**capaci·ty** [kəˈpæsɪti] *s* (**-ties**) capacità *f;* **filled to capacity** pieno zeppo; **in the capacity of** in veste di

**cap' and bells'** *spl* berretto a sonagli; scettro di buffone

**cap' and gown'** *s* costume accademico, toga e tocco

**caparison** [kəˈpærɪsən] *s* bardatura ‖ *tr* bardare

**cape** [kep] *s* cappa, mantello; (mil) mantella; (geog) capo

**Cape' of Good' Hope'** *s* Capo di Buona Speranza

**caper** ['kepər] *s* capriola; (bot) cappero; **to cut capers** far capriole; (fig) fare monellerie ‖ *intr* fare capriole; saltellare

**Cape' Town'** *s* Città *f* del Capo

**capital** ['kæpɪtəl] *adj* capitale ‖ *s* *(money)* capitale *m; (city)* capitale *f; (of column)* capitello

**cap'ital expen'ditures** *spl* spese *fpl* d'impianto

**cap'ital goods'** *spl* beni *mpl* strumentali

**capitalism** ['kæpɪtəˌlɪzəm] *s* capitalismo

**capitalize** ['kæpɪtəˌlaɪz] *tr* capitalizzare; scrivere con la maiuscola ‖ *intr*—**to capitalize on** approfittare di

**cap'ital let'ter** *s* lettera maiuscola

**cap'ital pun'ishment** *s* pena capitale

**cap'ital stock'** *s* capitale *m* sociale

**capitol** ['kæpɪtəl] *s* campidoglio

**capitulate** [kəˈpɪtʃəˌlet] *intr* capitolare

**capon** ['kepɑn] *s* cappone *m*

**caprice** [kəˈpris] *s* capriccio, ghiribizzo

**capricious** [kəˈprɪʃəs] *adj* capriccioso, estroso

**Capricorn** ['kæprɪˌkɔrn] *s* Capricorno

**capsize** ['kæpsaɪz] *tr* capovolgere ‖ *intr* capovolgersi

**capstan** ['kæpstən] *s* argano

**cap'stone'** *s* (archit) coronamento

**capsule** ['kæpsəl] *adj* in miniatura; riassuntivo ‖ *s* capsula

**captain** ['kæptən] *s* capitano; (naut) comandante *m;* ‖ *tr* capitanare

**caption** ['kæpʃən] *s* titolo; (mov) didascalia; (journ) leggenda

**captivate** ['kæptɪˌvet] *tr* cattivare, affascinare

**captive** ['kæptɪv] *adj* & *s* prigioniero

**captivi·ty** ['kæpˈtɪvɪti] *s* (**-ties**) cattività *f*, prigionia

**captor** ['kæptər] *s* persona che cattura

**capture** ['kæptʃər] *s* cattura, presa; *(person)* prigioniero; *(thing)* bottino ‖ *tr* catturare; prendere

**car** [kɑr] *s* *(of train)* vagone *m*, vettura; *(automobile)* automobile *m* & *f*, macchina, vettura; *(of elevator)* cabina; *(of balloon)* navicella; *(for narrow-gauge track)* carrello

**carafe** [kəˈræf] *s* caraffa

**caramel** ['kærəməl] or ['kɑrməl] *s* *(burnt sugar)* caramello; *(candy)* caramella appiccicaticcia

**carat** ['kærət] *s* carato

**caravan** ['kærəˌvæn] *s* carovana; *(covered vehicle)* furgone *m*

**caravansa·ry** [ ˌkærəˈvænsəri] *s* (**-ries**) caravanserraglio

**caraway** ['kærəˌwe] *s* cumino

**car'barn'** *s* rimessa del tram

**carbide** ['karbaɪd] s carburo
**carbine** ['karbaɪn] s carabina
**carbol'ic ac'id** [kar'balɪk] s acido fenico
**carbon** ['karbən] s (in arc light, battery, auto cylinder) carbone m; carta carbone; (chem) carbonio
**car'bon cop'y** s copia a carbone, velina
**car'bon diox'ide** s anidride carbonica
**car'bon monox'ide** s ossido di carbonio, monossido di carbonio
**car'bon pa'per** s carta carbone
**carbuncle** ['karbʌŋkəl] s (stone; boil) carbonchio; (boil) foruncolo
**carburetor** ['karbə‚retər] or ['karbjə‚retər] s carburatore m
**carcass** ['karkəs] s carcassa; (in state of decay) carogna
**card** [kard] s (file) scheda; (post card) cartolina; (personal card) biglietto; (announcement) partecipazione; (playing card) carta da gioco; (coll) tipo divertente, bel tipo
**card'board'** s cartone m
**card'-car'rying mem'ber** s tesserato
**card' case'** s portatessere m
**card' cat'alogue** s schedario
**card'hold'er** s socio, tesserato
**cardiac** ['kardɪ‚æk] adj & s cardiaco
**cardigan** ['kardɪgən] s panciotto a maglia
**cardinal** ['kardɪnəl] adj cardinale, fondamentale || s cardinale m
**card' in'dex** s schedario
**cardiogram** ['kardɪ‚o‚græm] s cardiogramma m
**card' par'ty** s riunione per giocare a carte
**card'sharp'** s baro
**card' ta'ble** s tavoliere m, tavolino da gioco
**card' trick'** s gioco di prestigio colle carte
**care** [ker] s cura, custodia; inquietudine f, preoccupazione; cautela; **care of** presso, e.g., **R. Smith care of Jones** R. Smith presso Jones; **to take care** fare attenzione; **to take care of** prendersi cura di, badare a; **to take care of oneself** badare alla salute || intr curarsi, badare; **I don't care** non m'importa; **to care about** preoccuparsi di; **to care for** voler bene a; curarsi di; **to care to** volere
**careen** [kə'rin] s carenaggio || intr sbandare
**career** [kə'rir] adj di carriera || s carriera
**care'free'** adj spensierato
**careful** ['kerfəl] adj attento; diligente; premuroso; **careful!** faccia attenzione!
**careless** ['kerlɪs] adj trascurato; imprudente; indifferente
**carelessness** ['kerlɪsnɪs] s trascuratezza; imprudenza; indifferenza
**caress** [kə'res] s carezza || tr carezzare, accarezzare
**caretaker** ['ker‚tekər] adj interinale, provvisorio || s custode m; guardiano; (of school) bidello
**care'taker gov'ernment** s governo interinale

**care'worn'** adj accasciato dalle preoccupazioni
**car'fare'** s passaggio, denaro per il tram; (small sum of money) spiccioli mpl
**car·go** ['kargo] s (-goes or -gos) carico mercantile
**car'go boat'** s battello da carico
**Caribbean** [‚kærɪ'bi·ən] or [kə'rɪbɪ·ən] s Mare m dei Caraibi
**caricature** ['kærɪkətʃər] s caricatura || tr mettere in caricatura
**carillon** ['kærɪ‚lan] or [kə'rɪljən] s carillon m || intr suonare il carillon
**car'load'** s vagone completo, vagonata
**carnage** ['karnɪdʒ] s carnaio, carneficina
**carnal** ['karnəl] adj carnale
**carnation** [kar'neʃən] adj incarnato || s garofano; (color) incarnato
**carnival** ['karnɪvəl] adj carnevalesco || s carnevale m; festa, spettacolo all'aperto
**carob** ['kærəb] s (fruit) carruba; (tree) carrubo
**car·ol** ['kærəl] s canzone f popolare; pastorella di Natale || v (pret & pp -oled or -olled; ger -oling or -olling) tr cantare
**carom** ['kærəm] s carambola || intr carambolare
**carousal** [kə'rauzəl] s baldoria, gozzoviglia
**carouse** [kə'rauz] intr fare baldoria, gozzovigliare
**carousel** [‚kærə'zel] or [‚kæru'zel] s giostra, carosello
**carp** ['karp] s carpa || intr lagnarsi, criticare
**carpenter** ['karpəntər] s falegname m
**carpentry** ['karpəntri] s falegnameria
**carpet** ['karpɪt] s tappeto || tr coprire con un tappeto, tappetare
**carpetbagger** ['karpɪt‚bægər] s avventuriero; (hist) politicante m
**car'pet sweep'er** s spazzolone elettrico per tappeti
**car'port'** s tettoia-garage f
**car'-ren'tal serv'ice** s servizio di autonoleggi
**carriage** ['kærɪdʒ] s carrozza; (of gun) affusto; (of typewriter) carrello; (bearing) portamento; (mach) slitta
**carrier** ['kærɪ·ər] s portatore m; (person or organization in business of carrying goods) spedizioniere m; (of mail) postino; (e.g., on top of station wagon) portabagagli m; (of a disease) veicolo
**car'rier pig'eon** s piccione m viaggiatore
**car'rier wave'** s (rad) onda portante
**carrion** ['kærɪ·ən] s carogne fpl
**carrot** ['kærət] s carota
**car·ry** ['kæri] v (pret & pp -ried) tr portare; trasportare; (a burden) sopportare; (an election) guadagnare; (to keep in stock) avere in assortimento; **to carry along** portare con sé; **to carry away** trasportare; entusiasmare; **to carry forward** riportare; **to carry out** eseguire; **to carry**

**through** completare; **to carry weight** aver importanza ‖ *intr* avere la portata (di), e.g., **this gun carries two miles** questo cannone ha la portata di due miglia; **to carry on** continuare; (coll) fare baccano

**cart** [kɑrt] *s* carro, carretto; (*for shopping*) carrello; **to put the cart before the horse** mettere il carro davanti ai buoi ‖ *tr* trasportare col carro

**carte blanche** ['kɑrt'blɑnʃ] *s* carta bianca

**cartel** [kɑr'tɛl] *s* cartello

**Carthage** ['kɑrθɪdʒ] *s* Cartagine *f*

**cart' horse'** *s* cavallo da tiro

**cartilage** ['kɑrtɪlɪdʒ] *s* cartilagine *f*

**carton** ['kɑrtən] *s* cartone *m;* scatola di cartone; (*of cigarettes*) stecca

**cartoon** [kɑr'tun] *s* disegno; caricatura; (*comic strip*) fumetto; (mov) disegno animato ‖ *tr* fare caricature di

**cartoonist** [kɑr'tunɪst] *s* disegnatore *m;* caricaturista *mf*

**cartridge** ['kɑrtrɪdʒ] *s* cartuccia; (*e.g., of camera*) caricatore *m*

**car'tridge belt'** *s* cartucciera; (mil) giberna

**car'tridge clip'** *s* serbatoio

**cart'wheel'** *s* ruota di carro; **to turn cartwheels** fare la ruota

**carve** [kɑrv] *tr* (*meats*) trinciare; scolpire, intagliare

**carv'ing knife'** *s* trinciante *m*

**car' wash'er** *s* lavamacchine *m*

**cascade** [kæs'ked] *s* cascata ‖ *intr* cadere a mo' di cascata

**case** [kes] *s* (*box*) cassetta; (*of watch*) calotta; (*outer covering*) astuccio; (*instance*) caso; (gram) caso; (law) causa; (typ) cassa; **in case** in caso, nel caso; **in no case** in nessun modo ‖ *tr* rinchiudere; (*to package*) impaccare; (slang) ispezionare

**casement** ['kesmənt] *s* telaio di finestra; finestra a gangheri

**case' stud'y** *s* casistica

**cash** [kæʃ] *s* contante *m;* **cash on delivery** spedizione contro assegno; **for cash** in contanti; a pronta cassa ‖ *tr* (*a check*) cambiare, incassare ‖ *intr* —**to cash in on** (coll) trarre profitto da

**cash' box'** *s* cassa

**cashew** ['kæʃu] *s* (*tree*) anacardio; (*nut*) mandorla indiana

**cashier** [kæ'ʃɪr] *s* cassiere *m* ‖ *tr* (*to dismiss*) silurare

**cashier's' check'** *s* assegno circolare

**cash' reg'ister** *s* registratore *m* cassa

**casing** ['kesɪŋ] *s* rivestimento; tubo di rivestimento; (*for salami*) budello; (*of tire*) copertone *m*

**cask** [kæsk] or [kɑsk] *s* barile *m*, botte *f*

**casket** ['kæskɪt] or ['kɑskɪt] *s* scrigno, cofanetto; (*coffin*) bara, cassa da morto

**casserole** ['kæsə,rol] *s* tegame *m* di terracotta or vetro; (*food*) pasticcio, timballo

**cassette** [kə'sɛt] *s* (mus) musicassetta; (mus & phot) caricatore *m*

**cassock** ['kæsək] *s* sottana, tonaca; **to doff the cassock** gettar la tonaca alle ortiche

**cast** [kæst] or [kɑst] *s* getto; lancio; forma; (mach) pezzo fuso; (surg) gesso; (theat) complesso artistico; **cast** *m* ‖ *v* (*pret & pp* **cast**) *tr* gettare; fondere; (*a ballot*) dare; (*the roles*) distribuire; (*actors*) scegliere; **to cast aside** abbandonare; **to cast down** deprimere; **to cast lots** tirare a sorte; **to cast off** abbandonare; **to cast out** buttar fuori ‖ *intr* tirare i dadi; **to cast off** (naut) mollare gli ormeggi

**castanets** [,kæstə'nɛts] *spl* nacchere *fpl*

**cast'a·way'** *adj & s* naufrago; (fig) reprobo

**caste** [kæst] or [kɑst] *s* casta; **to lose caste** perdere prestigio

**caster** ['kæstər] or ['kɑstər] *s* ampollina, saliera, pepaiola; (*roller*) rotella per i mobili

**castigate** ['kæstɪ,get] *tr* castigare, punire; correggere

**Castile** [kæs'til] *s* (la) Castiglia

**Castilian** [kæs'tɪljən] *adj & s* castigliano

**casting** ['kæstɪŋ] or ['kɑstɪŋ] *s* getto, getto fuso; (*in fishing*) pesca a getto

**cast' i'ron** *s* ghisa

**cast'-i'ron** *adj* fatto di ghisa; (*e.g., stomach*) fatto d'acciaio, di struzzo

**castle** ['kæsəl] or ['kɑsəl] *s* castello; (chess) torre *f* ‖ *tr & intr* (chess) arroccare

**cas'tle in Spain'** or **cas'tle in the air'** *s* castello in aria

**cast'off'** *adj* abbandonato ‖ *s* rigetto; persona abbandonata; (typ) stima

**cas'tor oil'** ['kæstər] or ['kɑstər] *s* olio di ricino

**castrate** ['kæstret] *tr* castrare

**casual** ['kæʒʊ·əl] *adj* casuale, fortuito; (*clothing*) semplice, sportivo

**casually** ['kæʒʊ·əli] *adv* con disinvoltura; (*by chance*) fortuitamente

**casual·ty** ['kæʒʊ·əlti] *s* (**-ties**) accidente *m*, disastro; vittima; **casualties** (*in war*) perdite *fpl*

**casuist·ry** ['kæʃʊ·ɪstri] *s* (**-ries**) (*specious reasoning*) speciosità *f;* (philos) casistica

**cat** [kæt] *s* gatto; donna perfida; **to let the cat out of the bag** lasciarsi scappare il segreto

**cataclysm** ['kætə,klɪzəm] *s* cataclisma *m*

**catacomb** ['kætə,kom] *s* catacomba

**catalogue** ['kætə,lɔg] or ['kætə,lɑg] *s* catalogo ‖ *tr* catalogare

**cat'alogue sale'** *s* vendita per corrispondenza

**catalyst** ['kætəlɪst] *s* catalizzatore *m*

**catapult** ['kætə,pʌlt] *s* catapulta ‖ *tr* catapultare

**cataract** ['kætə,rækt] *s* cataratta

**catarrh** [kə'tɑr] *s* catarro

**catastrophe** [kə'tæstrəfi] *s* catastrofe *f*, disastro

**cat'call'** s urlo di disapprovazione
**catch** [kætʃ] s presa; cattura; (of door) paletto; (in marriage) partito; (trick) inganno; (of fish) pesca; (mach) nottolino ‖ v (pret & pp **caught** [kɔt]) tr prendere, acchiappare; (a cold) pigliare, buscarsi; **to catch hold of** afferrare; **to catch it** (coll) prendersele; **to catch oneself** contenersi; **to catch up** sorprendere sul fatto ‖ intr agganciarsi; (said of a disease) trasmettersi; **to catch on** capire l'antifona; **to catch up** mettersi al corrente; **to catch up with** raggiungere
**catch'-as-catch'-can'** s lotta libera americana
**catch' ba'sin** s ricettacolo di fogna
**catcher** ['kætʃər] s ricevitore m, catcher m
**catching** ['kætʃɪŋ] adj (alluring) seducente; (infectious) contagioso
**catch'word'** s slogan m; (typ) chiamata; (typ) esponente m in testa di pagina
**catch·y** ['kætʃi] adj (-ier; -iest) attraente, vivo; (tricky) insidioso
**catechism** ['kætɪ,kɪzəm] s catechismo
**catego·ry** ['kætɪ,gori] s (-ries) categoria
**cater** ['ketər] intr provvedere cibo; **to cater to** servire
**cater-cornered** ['kætər,kɔrnərd] adj diagonale ‖ adv diagonalmente
**caterer** ['ketərər] s provveditore m
**caterpillar** ['kætər,pɪlər] s bruco
**cat'erpillar trac'tor** s trattore m a cingoli
**cat'fish'** s pesce m gatto
**cat'gut'** s (mus) corda di minugia; (surg) catgut m, cattegù m
**cathartic** [kə'θɑrtɪk] adj & s catartico
**cathedral** [kə'θidrəl] s cattedrale f
**catheter** ['kæθɪtər] s catetere m
**catheterize** ['kæθɪtə,raɪz] tr cateterizzare
**cathode** ['kæθod] s catodo
**catholic** ['kæθəlɪk] adj cattolico; (e.g., mind) liberale ‖ **Catholic** adj & s cattolico
**catkin** ['kætkɪn] s (bot) amento, gattino
**cat'nap'** s corta siesta, sonnellino
**cat-o'-nine-tails** [,kætə'naɪn,telz] s gatto a nove code
**cat's'-paw'** s gonzo; (breeze) brezzolina
**catsup** ['kætsəp] or ['ketʃəp] s salsa piccante di pomodoro, ketchup m
**cat'tail'** s stiancia
**cattle** ['kætəl] s bestiame grosso
**cat'tle·man** s (-men) allevatore m di bestiame
**cat·ty** ['kæti] adj (-tier; -tiest) malizioso, maligno; felino, gattesco
**cat'walk'** s passerella, ballatoio
**Caucasian** [kɔ'keʒən] or [kɔ'keʃən] adj & s caucasico
**caucus** ['kɔkəs] s comitato elettorale; conciliabolo politico
**cauldron** ['kɔldrən] s calderone m
**cauliflower** ['kɔlɪ,flau·ər] s cavolfiore m
**caulk** [kɔk] tr calafatare, stoppare
**cause** [kɔz] s causa, cagione ‖ tr causare, cagionare; **to cause to** + inf

fare + inf, e.g., **she caused him to fall** l'ha fatto cadere
**cause'way'** s strada rialzata, scarpata
**caustic** ['kɔstɪk] adj caustico
**cauterize** ['kɔtə,raɪz] tr cauterizzare
**caution** ['kɔʃən] s cautela, prudenza; ammonizione ‖ tr ammonire
**cautious** ['kɔʃəs] adj prudente
**cavalcade** ['kævəl,ked] or [,kævəl'ked] s cavalcata
**cavalier** [,kævə'lir] or ['kævə,lir] adj altero, sdegnoso; disinvolto ‖ s cavaliere m
**caval·ry** ['kævəlri] s (-ries) cavalleria
**cav'alry·man'** or **cav'alry·man** s (-men' or -men) cavalleggero, soldato di cavalleria
**cave** [kev] s caverna, grotta ‖ intr— **to cave in** sprofondarsi; (to give in) (coll) cedere; (to become exhausted) (coll) diventare spossato
**cave'-in'** s sprofondamento
**cave' man'** s troglodita m
**cavern** ['kævərn] s caverna
**caviar** ['kævɪ,ɑr] or [,kævɪ'ɑr] s caviale m
**cav·il** ['kævɪl] v (pret & pp **-iled** or **-illed**; ger **-iling** or **-illing**) intr cavillare
**cavi·ty** ['kævɪti] s (-ties) cavità f; (in tooth) carie f
**cavort** [kə'vɔrt] intr far capriole
**caw** [kɔ] s gracchiamento ‖ intr gracchiare
**cease** [sis] tr cessare, interrompere ‖ intr cessare, interrompersi; **to cease** + ger cessare di + inf
**cease'-fire'** s sospensione delle ostilità
**ceaseless** ['sislɪs] adj incessante
**cedar** ['sidər] s cedro; legno di cedro
**cede** [sid] tr cedere, trasferire
**ceiling** ['silɪŋ] s soffitto; (aer) altezza massima; **to hit the ceiling** (slang) uscire dai gangheri
**ceil'ing price'** s calmiere m, tetto
**celebrate** ['selɪ,bret] tr celebrare ‖ intr celebrare; far festa
**celebrated** ['selɪ,bretɪd] adj celebre, famoso
**celebration** [,selɪ'breʃən] s celebrazione
**celebri·ty** [sɪ'lebrɪti] s (-ties) celebrità f
**celery** ['seləri] s sedano
**celestial** [sɪ'lestʃəl] adj celestiale, celeste
**celibacy** ['seləbəsi] s celibato
**celibate** ['selə,bet] or ['seləbɪt] adj & s celibe m; nubile f
**cell** [sel] s (e.g., of jail) cella; (of electric battery) elemento; (biol, phys, pol) cellula
**cellar** ['selər] s cantina; (partly above ground) seminterrato
**cellist** or **'cellist** ['tʃelɪst] s violoncellista mf
**cel·lo** or **'cel·lo** ['tʃelo] s (-los) violoncello
**cellophane** ['selə,fen] s cellofan m
**celluloid** ['seljə,lɔɪd] s celluloide f
**Celtic** ['seltɪk] or ['keltɪk] adj celtico ‖ s lingua celtica

**cement** [sɪ'mɛnt] *s* cemento || *tr* cementare

**cemete·ry** ['sɛmɪ ˌtɛri] *s* (**-ries**) cimitero

**censer** ['sɛnsər] *s* turibolo

**censor** ['sɛnsər] *s* censore *m* || *tr* censurare

**censure** ['sɛnʃər] *s* censura, critica || *tr* censurare, criticare

**census** ['sɛnsəs] *s* censo, censimento

**cent** [sɛnt] *s* centesimo di dollaro, cent *m;* **not to have a red cent to one's name** non avere il becco di un quattrino

**centaur** ['sɛntɔr] *s* centauro

**centennial** [sɛn'tɛnɪ·əl] *adj & s* centenario

**center** ['sɛntər] *s* centro || *tr* centrare, concentrare || *intr*—**to center on** concentrarsi su

**cen'ter·board'** *s* chiglia mobile

**cen'ter·piece'** *s* centro tavola

**cen'ter punch'** *s* punzone *m*, punteruolo

**centigrade** ['sɛntɪ ˌgred] *adj* centigrado

**centimeter** ['sɛntɪ ˌmitər] *s* centimetro

**centipede** ['sɛntɪ ˌpid] *s* centopiedi *m*

**cento** ['sɛnto] *s* centone *m*

**central** ['sɛntrəl] *adj* centrale || *s* centrale *f*, centrale telefonica; (*operator*) telefonista *mf*

**Cen'tral Amer'ica** *s* l'America Centrale

**centralize** ['sɛntrə ˌlaɪz] *tr* centralizzare || *intr* centralizzarsi

**centu·ry** ['sɛntʃəri] *s* (**-ries**) secolo

**ceramic** [sɪ'ræmɪk] *adj* ceramico || **ceramics** *ssg* ceramica; *spl* oggetti *mpl* di ceramica

**cereal** ['sɪrɪ·əl] *adj* cerealicolo || *s* (*grain*) cereale *m;* (*uncooked breakfast food, e.g., cornflakes*) fiocchi *mpl;* (*breakfast food to be cooked*) farina

**cerebral** ['sɛrɪbrəl] *adj* cerebrale

**ceremonious** [ ˌsɛrɪ'moni·əs] *adj* cerimonioso

**ceremo·ny** ['sɛrɪ ˌmoni] *s* (**-nies**) cerimonia; **to stand on ceremony** fare cerimonie

**certain** ['sʌrtən] *adj* certo; **for certain** di or per certo; **to be certain to** + *inf* non mancare di + *inf*

**certainly** ['sʌrtənli] *adv* certamente; (*gladly*) con piacere

**certain·ty** ['sʌrtənti] *s* (**-ties**) certezza

**certificate** [sər'tɪfɪkɪt] *s* certificato; (com) titolo || [sər'tɪfɪ ˌket] *tr* certificare

**cer'tified check'** *s* assegno a copertura garantita

**cer'tified cop'y** *s* estratto; (*as a formula on a document*) per copia conforme

**cer'tified pub'lic account'ant** *s* esperto contabile

**certi·fy** ['sʌrtɪ ˌfaɪ] *v* (*pret & pp* **-fied**) *tr* certificare, garantire

**cervix** ['sʌrvɪks] *s* (**cervices** (sər'vaɪsiz) *cervice f*

**cessation** [sɛ'seʃən] *s* cessazione

**cesspool** ['sɛs ˌpul] *s* pozzo nero

**Ceylo·nese** [ ˌsilə'niz] *adj & s* (**-nese**) singalese *mf*

**chafe** [tʃef] *s* irritazione || *tr* (*the hands*) strofinare; irritare; (*to wear away*) logorare || *intr* irritarsi; logorarsi

**chaff** [tʃæf] or [tʃɑf] *s* lolla; pula; (*joke*) burla; (fig) loppa

**chaf'ing dish'** *s* fornello a spirito

**cha·grin** [ʃə'grɪn] *s* cruccio, dispiacere *m* || *v* (*pret* **-grined** or **-grinned;** *ger* **-grining** or **-grinning**) *tr* crucciare, affliggere

**chain** [tʃen] *s* catena; (*e.g., for necklace*) catenella || *tr* incatenare

**chain' gang'** *s* catena di forzati

**chain' reac'tion** *s* reazione a catena

**chain' saw'** *s* motosega

**chain'-smoke'** *intr* fumare come un turco

**chain' store'** *s* negozio a catena

**chair** [tʃɛr] *s* sedia, seggiola; (*of important person*) seggio; (*at a university*) cattedra; (*chairman*) presidente *m*, presidenza; **to take the chair** cominciare una riunione || *tr* (*a meeting*) presiedere

**chair' lift'** *s* seggiovia

**chair'man** *s* (**-men**) presidente *m*

**chair'man·ship'** *s* presidenza

**chair'wom'an** *s* (**-wom'en**) presidentessa

**chalice** ['tʃælɪs] *s* calice *m*

**chalk** [tʃɔk] *s* gesso || *tr* marcare or scrivere col gesso; **to chalk up** prendere appunti di; attribuire

**chalk' talk'** *s* conferenza illustrata

**chalk·y** ['tʃɔki] *adj* (**-ier; -iest**) gessoso

**challenge** ['tʃælɪndʒ] *s* sfida; (law) ricusazione; (mil) chi va là *m* || *tr* sfidare; (*a juror*) (law) ricusare; (mil) dare il chi va là a

**chamber** ['tʃembər] *s* camera, stanza; (*of a palace*) aula; (*of a judge*) gabinetto

**chamberlain** ['tʃembərlɪn] *s* ciambellano

**cham'ber·maid'** *s* cameriera

**cham'ber of com'merce** *s* camera di commercio

**cham'ber pot'** *s* orinale *m*

**chameleon** [kə'mil·ən] *s* camaleonte *m*

**cham·ois** ['ʃæmi] *s* (**-ois**) camoscio

**champ** [tʃæmp] *s* (slang) campione *m* || *tr* masticare rumorosamente; (*the bit*) mordere || *intr* masticare rumorosamente

**champagne** [ʃæm'pen] *s* champagne *m*, spumante *m*

**champion** ['tʃæmpɪ·ən] *s* campione *m* || *tr* difendere; farsi paladino di

**championship** ['tʃæmpɪ·ən ˌʃɪp] *s* campionato

**chance** [tʃæns] or [tʃɑns] *adj* casuale, fortuito || *s* occasione; caso; probabilità *f*; rischio; biglietto di lotteria; **by chance** per caso; **not to stand a chance** non avere la probabilità di riuscita; **to take one's chances** arrischiarsi; **to wait for a chance** attendere l'opportunità || *intr* succedere; **to chance upon** imbattersi in

**chancel** ['tʃænsəl] or ['tʃɑnsəl] *s* presbiterio, coro

**chanceller·y** ['tʃænsələri] or ['tʃɑnsələri] *s* (**-ies**) cancelleria

**chancellor** ['tʃænsələr] or ['tʃɑnsələr] s cancelliere m

**chandelier** [,ʃændə'lir] s lampadario

**change** [tʃendʒ] s cambiamento; (of clothes) muta; (of currency) cambio; (coins) spiccioli mpl; **for a change** tanto per cambiare; **to keep the change** tenere il resto ‖ tr cambiare, rimpiazzare; (clothes) cambiare, cambiarsi di ‖ intr cambiare, mutare

**changeable** ['tʃendʒəbəl] adj mutevole, variabile, incostante

**change' of heart'** s pentimento, conversione

**change' of life'** s menopausa

**chan·nel** ['tʃænəl] s canale m; tubo, passaggio; stretto; (of river) alveo; (groove) solco; (rad, telv) canale m; **through channels** per via gerarchica ‖ v (pret & pp **-neled** or **-nelled;** ger **-neling** or **-nelling**) tr incanalare; (a river) incassare ‖ **the Channel** il Canale della Manica

**chant** [tʃænt] or [tʃɑnt] s canto; salmodia; canzone f ‖ tr & intr cantare

**chanticleer** ['tʃæntɪ,klɪr] s il gallo

**chaos** ['ke·ɑs] s caos m

**chaotic** [ke'ɑtɪk] adj caotico

**chap** [tʃæp] s (fellow) individuo, tipo; (of skin) screpolatura; **chaps** pantaloni mpl di cuoio ‖ v (pret & pp **chapped;** ger **chapping**) tr screpolare ‖ intr screpolarsi

**chapel** ['tʃæpəl] s cappella

**chaperon** or **chaperone** ['ʃæpə,ron] s accompagnatrice f (di signorina) ‖ tr accompagnare

**chaplain** ['tʃæplɪn] s cappellano

**chaplet** ['tʃæplɪt] s (wreath) corona, ghirlanda; rosario

**chapter** ['tʃæptər] s capitolo; (of a club) sezione

**chap'ter and verse'** s—**to give chapter and verse** citare le autorità

**char** [tʃɑr] v (pret & pp **charred;** ger **charring**) tr carbonizzare; bruciare

**character** ['kærɪktər] s carattere m; lettera, scrittura; indole f; (theat) personaggio; (coll) tipo; **in character** caratteristico di lui (lei, loro, etc.)

**char'acter ac'tor** s caratterista m

**char'acter ac'tress** s caratterista f

**char'acter assassina'tion** s linciaggio morale

**characteristic** [,kærɪktə'rɪstɪk] adj caratteristico ‖ s caratteristica

**characterize** ['kærɪktə,raɪz] tr caratterizzare

**char'coal'** s carbone m di legna, carbone m dolce; (for sketching) carboncino; (sketch) disegno al carboncino

**charge** [tʃɑrdʒ] s carica; incarico; responsabilità f; (indictment) accusa; costo; prezzo; debito; **in charge** in comando; **in charge of** a cura di; **to take charge of** prendersi cura di ‖ tr caricare; comandare; accusare; (a price) fare pagare; mettere in conto; **to charge s.o. with s.th** addebitare qlco a qlcu; accusare qlcu di qlco ‖ intr fare una carica

**charge' account'** s conto corrente

**chargé d'affaires** [ʃɑr'ʒe də'fɛr] s (chargés d'affaires) incaricato d'affari

**charger** ['tʃɑrdʒər] s cavallo di battaglia; (of a battery) caricatore m

**chariot** ['tʃærɪ·ət] s cocchio

**charioteer** [,tʃærɪ·ə'tɪr] s auriga m

**charis·ma** [kə'rɪzmə] s (-mata [mətə]) fascino personale; (theol) carisma m

**charitable** ['tʃærɪtəbəl] adj (person) caritatevole; (institution) caritativo

**chari·ty** ['tʃærɪti] s (-ties) carità f; associazione di beneficenza

**charlatan** ['ʃɑrlətən] s ciarlatano

**charlatanism** ['ʃɑrlətən,ɪzəm] s ciarlataneria

**Charlemagne** ['ʃɑrlə,men] s Carlomagno

**Charles** [tʃɑrlz] s Carlo

**char'ley horse'** ['tʃɑrli] s (coll) crampo

**charlotte** ['ʃɑrlət] s charlotte f ‖ **Charlotte** s Carlotta

**charm** [tʃɑrm] s fascino; amuleto; portafortuna m ‖ tr incantare, stregare

**charming** ['tʃɑrmɪŋ] adj affascinante

**charnel** ['tʃɑrnəl] adj orribile ‖ s ossario

**chart** [tʃɑrt] s carta geografica; lista; diagramma m ‖ tr tracciare

**charter** ['tʃɑrtər] s statuto; privilegio ‖ tr (a company) fondare; (a conveyance) noleggiare

**char'ter mem'ber** s socio fondatore

**char'wom'an** s (-wom'en) domestica per la pulizia

**chase** [tʃes] s inseguimento; caccia; (typ) telaio ‖ tr inseguire; cacciare; (to chisel) cesellare; **to chase away** scacciare ‖ intr—**to chase after** inseguire

**chaser** ['tʃesər] s cacciatore m; (coll) bibita da bersi dopo un liquore

**chasm** ['kæzəm] s abisso, baratro

**chas·sis** ['tʃæsi] s (-sis [siz]) telaio

**chaste** [tʃest] adj casto

**chasten** ['tʃesən] tr castigare

**chastise** [tʃæs'taɪz] tr castigare

**chastity** ['tʃæstɪti] s castità f

**chat** [tʃæt] s chiacchierata ‖ v (pret & pp **chatted;** ger **chatting**) intr chiacchierare

**chatelaine** ['ʃætə,len] s castellana

**chattels** ['tʃætəlz] spl beni mpl mobili

**chatter** ['tʃætər] s cicaleccio; balbettio; (of teeth) battito ‖ intr cicalare; balbettare; (said of teeth) battere

**chat'ter·box'** s chiacchierone m

**chauffeur** ['ʃofər] or [ʃo'fʌr] s autista mf ‖ intr fare l'autista

**cheap** [tʃip] adj a buon mercato, economico; (of poor quality) scadente; **to feel cheap** vergognarsi ‖ adv a buon mercato

**cheapen** ['tʃipən] tr deprezzare; avvilire; rendere di cattivo gusto

**cheapness** ['tʃipnəs] s buon mercato, prezzo basso

**cheat** [tʃit] s truffa; truffatore m ‖ tr imbrogliare, truffare ‖ intr truffare; (at cards) barare

**check** [tʃɛk] s arresto, pausa; ostacolo;

esame *m;* verifica, controllo; (*of bank*) assegno; (*for baggage*) tagliando, scontrino; (*square pattern*) quadretto; (*fabric in squares*) tessuto a scacchi; (*in a restaurant*) conto; **in check** controllato, sotto controllo; (chess) sotto scacco ‖ *tr* fermare; confrontare; ispezionare; marcare; (*e.g., a coat*) depositare; disegnare a quadretti; (chess) dare scacco a; **to check off** controllare marcando; **to check on** controllare, verificare ‖ *intr* fermarsi; corrispondere perfettamente; **to check in** scendere (a un albergo); **to check out** andar via; pagare il conto; **to check up on** controllare

**check'book'** s libretto d'assegni

**checker** ['tʃɛkər] s ispettore *m;* quadretto; (*in game of checkers*) pedina; **checkers** dama ‖ *tr* variegare; marcare a quadretti

**check'er·board'** s scacchiera

**check'ered** *adj* (*e.g., career*) pieno di vicissitudini; (*marked with squares*) a scacchi; (*in color*) variegato

**check'ing account'** s conto corrente

**check'mate'** s scacco matto ‖ *tr* dare scacco matto a ‖ *interj* scacco matto!

**check'off'** **dues'** *spl* trattenute *fpl* sindacali

**check'-out'** s (*from hotel room*) partenza; (*time*) ora della partenza; (*examination*) esame *m* di controllo; (*in a supermarket*) cassa

**check'point'** s punto di ispezione

**check'room'** s guardaroba *m*

**check'up'** s (*of car*) ispezione; (*of patient*) esame *m* (fisico)

**cheek** [tʃik] s guancia, gota; (coll) faccia tosta

**cheek'bone'** s zigomo

**cheek·y** ['tʃiki] *adj* (**-ier; -iest**) (coll) impudente, sfacciato

**cheer** [tʃɪr] s gioia, allegria; applauso; **of good cheer** di buon umore ‖ *tr* riempire di gioia, rallegrare; applaudire; ricevere con applausi ‖ *intr* rallegrarsi; **cheer up!** animo!, coraggio!

**cheerful** ['tʃɪrfəl] *adj* allegro, di buon umore; (*willing*) volonteroso

**cheerless** ['tʃɪrlɪs] *adj* tetro, triste

**cheese** [tʃiz] s formaggio ‖ *intr*— **cheese it!** (slang) scappa via!

**cheese'** **cake'** s torta di formaggio; (slang) pin-up girl *f*

**cheese'cloth'** s etamine *f*, stamigna

**chees·y** [tʃizi] *adj* (**-ier; -iest**) di formaggio; come il formaggio; (slang) meschino, di cattiva qualità

**chef** [ʃɛf] s chef *m*, capocuoco

**chemical** ['kɛmɪkəl] *adj* chimico ‖ *s* prodotto chimico

**chemise** [ʃə'miz] s sottoveste *f*

**chemist** ['kɛmɪst] s chimico

**chemistry** ['kɛmɪstri] s chimica

**cherish** ['tʃɛrɪʃ] *tr* accarezzare; (*a memory*) custodire; (*a hope*) nutrire

**cher·ry** ['tʃɛri] s (**-ries**) (*tree*) ciliegio; (*fruit*) ciliegia

**cher·ub** ['tʃɛrəb] s (**-ubim** [əbɪm] & **-ubs**) cherubino

**chess** [tʃɛs] s scacchi *mpl*

**chess'board'** s scacchiera

**chess'man'** or **chess'man** s (**-men'** or **-men**) scacco

**chest** [tʃɛst] s petto; (*box*) cassapanca; (*furniture with drawers*) cassettone *m;* (*for money*) forziere *m*

**chestnut** ['tʃɛsnət] s (*tree, wood, color*) castagno; (*nut*) castagna

**chest'** **of drawers'** s cassettone *m*

**cheval'** **glass'** [ʃə'væl] s psiche *f*

**chevalier** [ˌʃɛvə'lɪr] s cavaliere *m*

**chevron** ['ʃɛvrən] s gallone *m*

**chew** [tʃu] *tr* masticare; **to chew the cud** ruminare; **to chew the rag** (slang) chiacchierare ‖ *intr* masticare

**chew'ing gum'** s gomma da masticare

**chic** [ʃik] *adj* & s chic

**chicaner·y** [ʃɪ'kɛnəri] s (**-ies**) trucco, rigiro

**chick** [tʃɪk] s pulcino; (slang) ragazza

**chicken** ['tʃɪkən] s pollo, pollastro; (coll) giovane *mf;* **to be chicken** (slang) avere la fifa ‖ *intr*—**to chicken out** (coll) indietreggiare

**chick'en coop'** s pollaio

**chick'en feed'** s (slang) spiccioli *mpl*

**chicken-hearted** ['tʃɪkən,hɑrtɪd] *adj* timido, fifone

**chick'en pox'** s varicella

**chick'en store'** s polleria

**chick'en wire'** s rete metallica esagonale

**chick'pea'** s cece *m*

**chico·ry** ['tʃɪkəri] s (**-ries**) cicoria

**chide** [tʃaɪd] *v* (*pret* **chided** or **chid** [tʃɪd]; *pp* **chided, chid,** or **chidden** ['tʃɪdən]) *tr* & *intr* rimproverare, correggere

**chief** [tʃif] *adj* principale, sommo, supremo ‖ s capo, comandante supremo; (slang) padrone *m*

**chief'** **exec'utive** s capo del governo

**chief'** **jus'tice** s presidente *m* di una corte; presidente *m* della corte suprema

**chiefly** ['tʃifli] *adv* principalmente

**chief'** **of staff'** s capo di stato maggiore

**chief'** **of state'** s capo dello stato

**chieftain** ['tʃiftən] s capo

**chiffon** [ʃɪ'fɑn] s velo trasparente, chiffon *m;* **chiffons** trine *fpl*

**chiffonier** [ˌʃɪfə'nɪr] s mobile *m* a cassettini, chiffonier *m*

**chilblain** ['tʃɪl,blen] s gelone *m*

**child** [tʃaɪld] s (**children** ['tʃɪldrən]) bebè *mf,* bambino; figlio; discendente *mf;* **with child** incinta

**child'birth'** s parto

**childhood** ['tʃaɪldhʊd] s infanzia

**childish** ['tʃaɪldɪʃ] *adj* infantile

**childishness** ['tʃaɪldɪʃnɪs] s puerilità *f,* infanzia

**child'** **la'bor** s lavoro dei minorenni

**childless** ['tʃaɪldlɪs] *adj* senza figli

**child'like'** *adj* infantile, innocente

**child's'** **play'** s un gioco

**child'** **wel'fare** s protezione dell'infanzia

**Chile** ['tʃɪli] s il Cile

**Chilean** ['tʃɪlɪ·ən] *adj* cileno

**chil′i sauce′** [′tʃɪli] *s* salsa di pomodoro con peperoni

**chill** [tʃɪl] *adj* freddo ‖ *s* freddo; brivido di freddo; freddezza; (*depression*) abbattimento ‖ *tr* raffreddare; (*a metal*) temprare; (fig) scoraggiare ‖ *intr* raffreddarsi

**chill·y** [′tʃɪli] *adj* (**-ier; -iest**) fresco, freddiccio; (*reception*) freddo

**chime** [tʃaɪm] *s* scampanio; **chimes** campanello ‖ *intr* scampanare; **to chime in** cominciare a cantare all'unisono; (coll) intromettersi

**chime′ clock′** *s* orologio con carillon

**chimney** [′tʃɪmni] *s* camino; (*of factory*) ciminiera; **to smoke like a chimney** fumare come un turco

**chim′ney flue′** *s* tubo di stufa, canna del camino

**chim′ney pot′** *s* testa della canna fumaria, comignolo

**chim′ney sweep′** *s* spazzacamino

**chimpanzee** [tʃɪm′pænzi] or [ˌtʃɪmpænˈzi] *s* scimpanzé *m*

**chin** [tʃɪn] *s* mento; **to keep one's chin up** (coll) non perdersi di coraggio; **to take it on the chin** (slang) subire una sconfitta ‖ *v* (*pret & pp* **chinned;** *ger* **chinning**) *tr*—**to chin oneself** sollevarsi fino al mento (ai manubri) ‖ *intr* (slang) chiacchierare

**china** [′tʃaɪnə] *s* porcellana ‖ **China** *s* la Cina

**chi′na clos′et** *s* armadio per le stoviglie

**chi′na·ware′** *s* porcellana, stoviglie *fpl*

**Chi·nese** [tʃaɪ′niz] *adj* cinese ‖ *s* (**-nese**) cinese *mf*

**Chi′nese lan′tern** *s* lampioncino alla veneziana

**Chi′nese puz′zle** *s* rebus *m*

**chink** [tʃɪŋk] *s* fessura

**chin′ strap′** *s* sottogola

**chintz** [tʃɪnts] *s* chintz *m*

**chip** [tʃɪp] *s* scheggia; frammento; (*in card games*) gettone *m*; (*of wood*) truciolo; **chip off the old block** vero figlio di suo padre (di sua madre); **chip on one's shoulder** propensità *f* a attaccar brighe ‖ *v* (*pret & pp* **chipped;** *ger* **chipping**) *tr* scheggiare; **to chip in** contribuire ‖ *intr* scheggiarsi

**chipmunk** [′tʃɪpˌmʌŋk] *s* tamia

**chipper** [′tʃɪpər] *adj* (coll) allegro, vivo

**chiropodist** [kaɪ′rɑpədɪst] or [kɪ′rɑpədɪst] *s* callista *mf*, pedicure *mf*

**chiropractice** [′kaɪrəˌpræktɪs] *s* chiropratica

**chirp** [tʃʌrp] *s* (*of birds*) cinguettio; (*of crickets*) cri cri *m* ‖ *intr* cinguettare; fare cri cri

**chis·el** [′tʃɪzəl] *s* (*for wood and metal*) scalpello; (*for metal*) cesello ‖ *v* (*pret & pp* **-eled** or **-elled;** *ger* **-eling** or **-elling**) *tr* scalpellare; cesellare; (slang) imbrogliare ‖ *intr* (slang) imbrogliare, fare l'imbroglione

**chiseler** [′tʃɪzələr] *s* scalpellino; cesellatore *m*; (slang) imbroglione *m*

**chit-chat** [′tʃɪt ˌtʃæt] *s* chiacchierata

**chivalrous** [′ʃɪvəlrəs] *adj* cavalleresco

**chivalry** [′ʃɪvəlri] *s* cavalleria

**chive** [tʃaɪv] *s* cipolla porraia

**chloride** [′klɔraɪd] *s* cloruro

**chlorine** [′klorɪn] *s* cloro

**chloroform** [′klɔrəˌfɔrm] *s* cloroformio ‖ *tr* cloroformizzare

**chlorophyll** [′klorəfɪl] *s* clorofilla

**chock** [tʃɑk] *s* (*wedge*) bietta, cuneo

**chock-full** [′tʃɑk′fʊl] *adj* colmo, pieno zeppo

**chocolate** [′tʃɔkəlɪt] or [′tʃɑkəlɪt] *s* (*candy*) cioccolato; (*drink*) cioccolata

**choc′olate bar′** *s* barretta di cioccolato

**choice** [tʃɔɪs] *adj* di prima scelta, superiore ‖ *s* scelta; (*variety*) assortimento

**choir** [kwaɪr] *s* coro

**choir′boy′** *s* ragazzo cantore

**choir′ loft′** *s* coro

**choir′mas′ter** *s* maestro di cappella

**choke** [tʃok] *s* strozzatura; (aut) farfalla del carburatore ‖ *tr* strozzare; ostruire; (*an internal-combustion engine*) arricchire la miscela di; **to choke back** trattenere; **to choke up** tappare, ostruire ‖ *intr* soffocarsi; **to choke up** tapparsi; (coll) soffocarsi

**choker** [′tʃokər] *s* (*necklace*) (coll) collana; (*scarf*) (coll) foulard *m*

**cholera** [′kɑlərə] *s* colera *m*

**choleric** [′kɑlərɪk] *adj* collerico

**cholesterol** [kə′lɛstəˌrol] or [kə′lɛstəˌral] *s* colesterina

**choose** [tʃuz] *v* (*pret* **chose** [tʃoz]; *pp* **chosen** [′tʃozən]) *tr* scegliere ‖ *intr*—**to choose to** decidere di

**choos·y** [′tʃuzi] *adj* (**-ier; -iest**) (coll) di difficile contentatura

**chop** [tʃɑp] *s* colpo; (*of meat*) cotoletta; **chops** labbra *fpl*, bocca ‖ *v* (*pret & pp* **chopped;** *ger* **chopping**) *tr* tagliare; (*meat*) tritare; **to chop off** troncare; **to chop up** sminuzzare

**chopper** [′tʃɑpər] *s* (*man*) tagliatore *m*; interruttore automatico; coltello da macellaio; (slang) elicottero; **choppers** (slang) i denti

**chop′ping block′** *s* tagliere *m*

**chop·py** [′tʃɑpi] *adj* (**-pier; -piest**) (*wind*) variabile; (*sea*) agitato; (*style*) instabile

**choral** [′korəl] *adj & s* corale *m*

**chorale** [ko′ral] *s* corale *m*

**chord** [kord] *s* corda; (mus) accordo

**chore** [tʃor] *s* lavoro; lavoro spiacevole; **chores** faccende domestiche

**choreography** [ˌkori′ɑgrəfi] *s* coreografia

**chorine** [ko′rin] *s* (slang) ballerina

**chorus** [′korəs] *s* coro; (*group of dancers*) corpo di ballo; (*of a song*) ritornello

**cho′rus girl′** *s* ballerina

**cho′rus man′** *s* (**men′**) corista *m*

**chow** [tʃaʊ] *s* (*dog*) chow chow *m*; (slang) cibo, pappa

**chowder** [′tʃaʊdər] *s* zuppa di vongole; zuppa di pesce

**Christ** [kraɪst] *s* Cristo

**christen** [′krɪsən] *tr* battezzare

**Christendom** [′krɪsəndəm] *s* cristianità *f*

**christening** ['krɪsənɪŋ] s battesimo
**Christian** ['krɪstʃən] adj & s cristiano
**Christianity** [,krɪstʃɪ'ænɪti] s (Christendom) cristianità f; (religion) cristianesimo
**Chris'tian name'** s nome m di battesimo
**Christmas** ['krɪsməs] adj natalizio ‖ s Natale m; **Merry Christmas!** Buon Natale!
**Christ'mas card'** s cartoncino natalizio
**Christ'mas car'ol** s pastorella di Natale
**Christ'mas Eve'** s vigilia di Natale
**Christ'mas gift'** s strenna natalizia
**Christ'mas tree'** s albero di Natale
**chrome** [krom] adj cromato ‖ s cromo ‖ tr cromare
**chromium** ['kromɪ·əm] s cromo
**chromosome** ['kromə,som] s cromosoma m
**chronic** ['krɑnɪk] adj cronico
**chronicle** ['krɑnɪkəl] s cronaca ‖ tr fare la storia di
**chronicler** ['krɑnɪklər] s cronista mf
**chronolo·gy** [krə'nɑlədʒi] s (-gies) cronologia
**chronometer** [krə'nɑmɪtər] s cronometro
**chrysanthemum** [krɪ'sænθɪməm] s crisantemo
**chub·by** ['tʃʌbi] adj (-bier; -biest) paffuto
**chuck** [tʃʌk] s buffetto sotto il mento; (cut of meat) reale m; (of lathe) coppaia ‖ tr accarezzare sotto il mento; (to throw) (coll) gettare
**chuckle** ['tʃʌkəl] s risatina ‖ intr ridacchiare
**chum** [tʃʌm] s (coll) amico intimo; (coll) compagno di stanza ‖ v (pret & pp chummed; ger chumming) intr (coll) essere amico intimo; essere compagno di stanza
**chum·my** ['tʃʌmi] adj (-mier; -miest) (coll) intimo, amicone
**chump** [tʃʌmp] s ciocco, ceppo; (coll) sciocco
**chunk** [tʃʌŋk] s grosso pezzo
**church** [tʃʌrtʃ] s chiesa
**churchgoer** ['tʃʌrtʃ,go·ər] s praticante mf
**church'man** s (-men) parrocchiano; (clergyman) sacerdote m
**Church' of Eng'land** s chiesa anglicana
**church'yard'** s camposanto
**churl** [tʃʌrl] s zotico, villano
**churlish** ['tʃʌrlɪʃ] adj villano
**churn** [tʃʌrn] s zangola ‖ tr agitare violentemente, sbattere ‖ intr (said of water) ribollire
**chute** [ʃut] s piano inclinato, canna; (in a river) cascata, rapida; (paracadute m; (into a swimming pool) toboga m
**Cicero** ['sɪsə,ro] s Cicerone m
**cider** ['saɪdər] s sidro
**cigar** [sɪ'gɑr] s sigaro
**cigar' case'** s portasigari m
**cigar' cut'ter** s tagliasigari m
**cigarette** [,sɪgə'rɛt] s sigaretta
**cigarette' butt'** s cicca
**cigarette' case'** s portasigarette m
**cigarette' hold'er** s bocchino

**cigarette' light'er** s accendisigaro, accendino
**cigarette' pa'per** s cartina da sigarette
**cigar' store'** s tabaccheria, rivendita di sali e tabacchi
**cinch** [sɪntʃ] s (on a horse) sottopancia m; (hold) (coll) presa; (slang) giochetto ‖ tr legare con una cinghia; (slang) agguantare
**cinder** ['sɪndər] s tizzone m; (slag) scoria; **cinders** cenere f
**cin'der block'** s concio di scoria
**Cinderella** [,sɪndə'rɛlə] s (la) Cenerentola
**cinema** ['sɪnəmə] s cine m, cinema m
**cinnabar** ['sɪnə,bɑr] s cinabro
**cinnamon** ['sɪnəmən] s cannella
**cipher** ['saɪfər] s zero; cifra; codice m; monogramma m ‖ tr calcolare; (to write in code) cifrare
**circle** ['sʌrkəl] s cerchio; (of theater) prima galleria; (of friends) cerchia ‖ tr cerchiare, compiere una rotazione intorno a
**circuit** ['sʌrkɪt] s circuito; (district) circoscrizione
**cir'cuit break'er** s salvamotore m, interruttore automatico
**circuitous** [sər'kju·ɪtəs] adj tortuoso
**circuitry** ['sʌrkɪtri] s (plan) schema m di montaggio; (components) elementi mpl di un circuito
**circular** ['sʌrkjələr] adj & s circolare f
**circulate** ['sʌrkjə,let] tr mettere in circolazione, diffondere ‖ intr circolare
**cir'culating li'brary** s biblioteca circolante
**circulation** [,sʌrkjə'leʃən] s circolazione; (of newspaper) diffusione
**circumcise** ['sʌrkəm,saɪz] tr circoncidere
**circumference** [sər'kʌmfərəns] s circonferenza
**circumflex** ['sʌrkəm,flɛks] adj circonflesso ‖ s accento circonflesso
**circumscribe** [,sʌrkəm'skraɪb] tr circoscrivere
**circumspect** ['sʌrkəm,spɛkt] adj circospetto
**circumstance** ['sʌrkəm,stæns] s circostanza; (fact) dettaglio; solennità f; **circumstances** condizioni fpl; dettagli mpl; condizioni economiche; **under no circumstances** a nessuna condizione; **under the circumstances** le cose essendo come sono
**circumstantial** [,sʌrkəm'stænʃəl] adj circostanziale, indiziario; (incidental) secondario; (complete) circostanziato
**cir'cumstan'tial ev'idence** s prova indiziaria
**circumstantiate** [,sʌrkəm'stænʃɪ,et] tr (to support with particulars) comprovare; (to describe in detail) circonstanziare
**circumvent** [,sʌrkəm'vɛnt] tr (to surround) accerchiare; (to outwit) circuire; (a difficulty) eludere, scansare
**circus** ['sʌrkəs] s circo equestre
**cistern** ['sɪstərn] s cisterna, serbatoio
**citadel** ['sɪtədəl] s cittadella
**citation** [saɪ'teʃən] s citazione

**cite** [saɪt] *tr* citare
**cither** ['sɪðər] *s* cetra
**citizen** ['sɪtɪzən] *s* cittadino; (*civilian*) civile *mf*
**citizenship** ['sɪtɪzən‚ʃɪp] *s* cittadinanza
**citric** ['sɪtrɪk] *adj* citrico
**citron** ['sɪtrən] *s* cedro; cedro candito
**cit'rus fruit'** ['sɪtrəs] *s* agrumi *mpl*
**cit·y** ['sɪti] *s* (**-ies**) città *f*
**cit'y counc'il** *s* consiglio municipale
**cit'y ed'itor** *s* capocronista *m*
**cit'y fa'thers** *spl* maggiorenti *mpl;* consiglieri *mpl* municipali
**cit'y hall'** *s* municipio
**cit'y plan'ning** *s* urbanistica
**cit'y room'** *s* (journ) redazione
**civic** ['sɪvɪk] *adj* civico || **civics** *s* educazione civica
**civil** ['sɪvɪl] *adj* civile
**civ'il engineer'ing** *s* genio civile
**civilian** [sɪ'vɪljən] *adj* & *s* civile *mf*, borghese *mf*
**civili·ty** [sɪ'vɪlɪti] *s* (**-ties**) cortesia; civilities ossequi *mpl*
**civilization** [‚sɪvɪlɪ'zeʃən] *s* civilizzazione, civiltà *f*
**civilize** ['sɪvɪ‚laɪz] *tr* civilizzare
**civ'il law'** *s* diritto civile
**civ'il serv'ant** *s* impiegato statale
**civ'il war'** *s* guerra civile || **Civil War** *s* (*of the U.S.A.*) guerra di secessione
**claim** [klem] *s* pretesa; richiesta; (min) concessione || *tr* (*one's rights*) rivendicare; (*one's property*) richiedere; dichiarare; **to claim to be** pretendere d'essere
**claim' check'** *s* tagliando
**clairvoyance** [kler'vɔɪ·əns] *s* chiaroveggenza
**clairvoyant** [kler'vɔɪ·ənt] *adj* chiaroveggente || *s* veggente *mf*, chiaroveggente *mf*
**clam** [klæm] *s* vongola || *intr*—**to clam up** (coll) essere muto come un pesce
**clamber** ['klæmər] *intr* arrampicarsi
**clam·my** ['klæmi] *adj* (**-mier; -miest**) coperto di sudore freddo; morbido
**clamor** ['klæmər] *s* clamore *m* || *intr* fare clamore
**clamorous** ['klæmərəs] *adj* clamoroso
**clamp** [klæmp] *s* graffa, morsetto; (*e.g., to hold a hose*) fascetta || *tr* assicurare con graffa, aggrappare; (*a tool*) montare || *intr*—**to clamp down on** (coll) fare pressione su, mettere i freni a
**clan** [klæn] *s* clan *m*
**clandestine** [klæn'dɛstɪn] *adj* clandestino
**clang** [klæŋ] *s* clangore *m* || *intr* risonare con clangore
**clannish** ['klænɪʃ] *adj* esclusivista, partigiano
**clap** [klæp] *s* applauso; (*of thunder*) scoppio || *v* (*pret* & *pp* **clapped;** *ger* **clapping**) *tr* (*the hands*) battere; (*e.g., in jail*) schiaffare; **to clap shut** sbattere || *intr* applaudire
**clapper** ['klæpər] *s* applauditore *m*; (*of bell*) batacchio
**clap'trap'** *s* imbonimento
**claret** ['klærɪt] *adj* & *s* chiaretto

**clari·fy** ['klærɪ‚faɪ] *v* (*pret* & *pp* **-fied**) *tr* chiarificare, chiarire
**clarinet** [‚klærɪ'nɛt] *s* clarinetto
**clarion** ['klærɪ·ən] *adj* chiaro e metallico || *s* tromba, clarino
**clash** [klæʃ] *s* cozzo, urto; conflitto di opinioni || *intr* cozzare, urtarsi; essere in conflitto
**clasp** [klæsp] *or* [klɑsp] *s* gancio, fermaglio; (*hold*) presa; (*grip*) stretta || *tr* agganciare; (*to hold in the arms*) abbracciare; (*to grip*) stringere
**class** [klæs] *or* [klɑs] *s* classe *f* || *tr* classificare
**class'book'** *s* registro
**classic** ['klæsɪk] *adj* & *s* classico
**classical** ['klæsɪkəl] *adj* classico
**classicism** ['klæsɪ‚sɪzəm] *s* classicismo
**classicist** ['klæsɪsɪst] *s* classicista *mf*
**classified** ['klæsɪ‚faɪd] *adj* segreto
**clas'sified ad'** *s* annunzio economico
**classi·fy** ['klæsɪ‚faɪ] *v* (*pret* & *pp* **-fied**) *tr* classificare
**class'mate'** *s* compagno di scuola
**class'room'** *s* aula scolastica
**class' strug'gle** *s* lotta di classe
**class·y** ['klæsi] *adj* (**-ier; -iest**) (slang) di lusso, di prim'ordine
**clatter** ['klætər] *s* (*of dishes*) acciottolio; vocio, schiamazzo || *tr* acciottolare || *intr* fare schiamazzo
**clause** [klɔz] *s* clausola; (gram) proposizione
**clavicle** ['klævɪkəl] *s* clavicola
**claw** [klɔ] *s* artiglio; (*of lobster*) pinza; (*tool*) raffio; (*of hammer*) granchio; (coll) dita *fpl* || *tr* aggraffiare; artigliare
**claw' ham'mer** *s* levachiodi *m*
**clay** [kle] *s* argilla, creta
**clay' pipe'** *s* pipa di terracotta
**clean** [klin] *adj* pulito; (*precise*) netto; (*e.g., break*) completo || *adv* completamente || *tr* pulire; **to clean out** pulire, fare repulisti di; (slang) ripulire; **to clean up** pulire completamente; mettere in ordine || *intr* pulirsi, fare pulizia
**clean' bill' of health'** *s* patente sanitaria; (fig) esonero completo
**clean'-cut'** *adj* ben delineato, deciso
**cleaner** ['klinər] *s* pulitore *m*, smacchiatore *m*; (*machine*) pulitrice *f*, smacchiatrice *f*; **to send to the cleaners** (slang) spolpare
**clean'ing fluid'** *s* smacchiatore *m*
**clean'ing wom'an** *s* donna di servizio per fare la pulizia
**clean·ly** ['klɛnli] *adj* (**-lier; -liest**) pulito, netto
**cleanse** [klɛnz] *tr* pulire; detergere; purificare
**cleanser** ['klɛnzər] *s* detergente *m*
**clean'-sha'ven** *adj* sbarbato di fresco
**clean'up'** *s* pulizia; (slang) guadagno enorme
**clear** [klɪr] *adj* chiaro; evidente; completo; innocente; (*profit*) netto; **clear of** libero da || *s* posto libero; **in the clear** libero; esonerato; non in codice || *adv* chiaramente; completamente || *tr* (*e.g., trees*) rischiarare; (*e.g., peo-*

*ple*) sgombrare; (*the table*) sparecchiare; (*an obstacle*) superare; (*from guilt*) discolpare; (*a profit*) guadagnare; (*goods at customs*) svincolare; (*a ship through customs*) dichiarare il carico di; (*checks*) compensare; **to clear away** or **off** liberare; **to clear out** sgomberare, sbarazzare; **to clear up** spiegare; (*a doubt*) dissipare || *intr* rasserenarsi; (*said of a ship*) partire; **to clear away** or **off** sparire; **to clear out** (coll) andarsene; **to clear up** rasserenarsi

**clearance** ['klɪrəns] *s* liberazione; (*of a ship*) partenza; (*of goods through customs*) sdoganamento; (*of checks*) compensazione; (*of goods*) liquidazione; (mach) gioco

**clear'ance sale'** *s* liquidazione

**clear'-cut'** *adj* chiaro, distinto

**clearing** ['klɪrɪŋ] *s* (*open space*) radura; (*of checks*) compensazione

**clear'ing house'** *s* stanza di compensazione

**cleat** [klit] *s* bietta, cuneo; (*on the sole of shoe*) tacchetto; (naut) galloccia

**cleavage** ['klivɪdʒ] *s* divisione; fessura

**cleave** [kliv] *v* (*pret & pp* **cleft** [klɛft] or **cleaved**) *tr* dividere, fendere || *intr* aderire, essere fedele

**cleaver** ['klivər] *s* scure *f*, accetta; (*of butcher*) spaccaossa *m*, fenditoio

**clef** [klɛf] *s* (mus) chiave *f*

**cleft** [klɛft] *adj* diviso, fesso || *s* fessura, crepaccio

**cleft' pal'ate** *s* palato spaccato, gola lupina

**clematis** ['klɛmətɪs] *s* clematide *f*

**clemen·cy** ['klɛmənsi] *s* (**-cies**) clemenza

**clement** ['klɛmənt] *adj* clemente

**clench** [klɛntʃ] *s* stretta || *tr* stringere; afferrare

**clergy** ['klɛrdʒi] *s* clero

**cler'gy·man** *s* (**-men**) ecclesiastico

**cleric** ['klɛrɪk] *s* ecclesiastico, sacerdote *m*

**clerical** ['klɛrɪkəl] *adj* da impiegato; (*error*) burocratico; (*of clergy*) clericale || *s* ecclesiastico; **clericals** abiti ecclesiastici

**cler'ical work'** *s* lavoro d'ufficio

**clerk** [klʌrk] *s* impiegato, commesso; (*accountant*) contabile *mf*; (*e.g., in a record office*) ufficiale *m*; cancelliere *m*; (*copyist, typist*) scrivano

**clever** ['klɛvər] *adj* intelligente; bravo, abile; destro

**cleverness** ['klɛvərnɪs] *s* intelligenza; bravura, abilità *f*

**clew** [klu] *s* indizio, traccia; (*of yarn*) gomitolo; (naut) bugna

**cliché** [kli'ʃe] *s* cliché *m*, luogo comune

**click** [klɪk] *s* (*of camera or gun*) scatto; (*of typewriter*) battito, ticchettio || *tr* (*the tongue*) schioccare; (*the heels*) battere || *intr* ticchettare; (slang) andare d'accordo; (slang) avere fortuna

**client** ['klaɪ·ənt] *s* cliente *mf*

**clientele** [ˌklaɪ·ən'tɛl] *s* clientela

**cliff** [klɪf] *s* rupe *f*, precipizio

**climate** ['klaɪmɪt] *s* clima *m*

**climax** ['klaɪmæks] *s* apice *m*; (*acute phase*) parossismo

**climb** [klaɪm] *s* salita; (*of a mountain*) scalata, ascensione || *tr* (*the stairs*) salire; (*a mountain*) scalare, ascendere || *intr* salire, arrampicarsi; **to climb down** discendere a carponi; (coll) ritirarsi

**climber** ['klaɪmər] *s* scalatore *m*; pianta rampicante; (*ambitious person*) (coll) arrampicatore *m*

**clinch** [klɪntʃ] *s* stretta, presa; (*boxing*) corpo a corpo *m* || *tr* (*nails*) ribattere, ribadire

**clincher** ['klɪntʃər] *s* chiodo per ribaditura; argomento decisivo

**cling** [klɪŋ] *v* (*pret & pp* **clung** [klʌŋ]) *intr* avviticchiare, attaccarsi; aderire, rimanere attaccato

**cling'stone' peach'** *s* pesca duracino

**clinic** ['klɪnɪk] *s* clinica

**clinical** ['klɪnɪkəl] *adj* clinico

**clinician** [klɪ'nɪʃən] *s* clinico

**clink** [klɪŋk] *s* tintinnio; (slang) gattabuia || *tr* (*glasses*) toccare || *intr* tintinnare

**clinker** ['klɪŋkər] *s* clinker *m*; mattone vetrificato; (slang) sbaglio

**clip** [klɪp] *s* (*of hair*) taglio; (*of wool*) tosatura; (*speed*) passo rapido; clip *f*, fermaglio; (*large clip*) fermacarte *m*; (*for cartridges*) caricatore *m*; (coll) colpo || *v* (*pret & pp* **clipped;** *ger* **clipping**) *tr* tagliare, tosare; (*words*) mangiare, storpiare; (*paper*) ritagliare; ritenere; (coll) battere || *intr* andare di buon passo

**clipper** ['klɪpər] *s* tagliatore *m*; (aer, naut) clipper *m*; **clippers** (*for hair*) tosatrice *f*; (*for nails*) pinze *fpl* per le unghie

**clipping** ['klɪpɪŋ] *s* taglio; (*from newspaper*) ritaglio

**clique** [klik] *s* cricca, chiesuola

**cloak** [klok] *s* mantello, manto; (fig) velo, maschera || *tr* ammantare, velare

**cloak'-and-dag'ger** *adj* d'avventura

**cloak'-and-sword'** *adj* di cappa e spada

**cloak'room'** *s* guardaroba *m*

**clock** [klɑk] *s* orologio; (*with pendulum*) pendolo, pendola; (*on stocking*) freccia || *tr* registrare, cronometrare

**clock'mak'er** *s* orologiaio

**clock' tow'er** *s* torre *f* dell'orologio

**clock'wise'** *adj & adv* nella direzione delle lancette dell'orologio

**clock'work'** *s* movimento d'orologeria; **like clockwork** come un orologio

**clod** [klɑd] *s* zolla; (fig) tonto

**clod'hop'per** *s* (*shoe*) scarpone *m*; (fig) villano, bifolco

**clog** [klɑg] *s* intoppo; (*to impede movement*) pastoia; scarpone *m*, zoccolo || *v* (*pret & pp* **clogged;** *ger* **clogging**) *tr* intoppare; (*to hold back*) impastoiare || *intr* otturarsi, ostruirsi

**cloister** ['klɔɪstər] *s* chiostro || *tr* rinchiudere in un chiostro

**close** [klos] *adj* vicino; (*translation*)

fedele; (*air in room*) male arieggiato; (*weather*) soffocante; (*stingy*) avaro; limitato, senza gioco; (*haircut*) corto; (*friend*) intimo; (*hit*) preciso; (*enclosed*) chiuso; (*narrow*) stretto || *adv* da vicino; **close to** vicino a || [kloz] *s* fine *f*, conclusione; **to bring to a close** concludere || *tr* chiudere; otturare; concludere; **to close down** chiudere completamente; **to close out** vendere in liquidazione; **to close up** bloccare || *intr* chiudersi; serrarsi; **to close down** chiudersi completamente; **to close in on** venire alle prese con; **to close up** bloccarsi; (*said of a wound*) rimarginarsi

**close' call'** [klos] *s* rischio scampato per miracolo

**closed' chap'ter** *s* affare chiuso

**closed' cir'cuit** *s* circuito chiuso

**closed' sea'son** *s* periodo di caccia o pesca vietata

**closefisted** ['klos'fɪstɪd] *adj* taccagno

**close'-fit'ing** [klos] *adj* attillato

**close-lipped** ['klos'lɪpt] *adj* riservato

**closely** ['klosli] *adv* da vicino; strettamente; fedelmente; attentamente

**close' quar'ters** [klos] *spl* (*cramped space*) pigia pigia *m*; **at close quarters** a corpo a corpo

**close' quote'** [kloz] *s* fine *f* della citazione

**close' shave'** [klos] *s*—**to have a close shave** farsi fare la barba a contropelo; (coll) scamparla per un pelo

**closet** ['klɑzɪt] *s* armadio a muro; (*small private room*) gabinetto; (*for keeping clothing*) ripostiglio || *tr*—**to be closeted with** essere in conciliabolo con

**close'-up'** [klos] *s* (mov) primo piano

**closing** ['klozɪŋ] *s* fine *f*, conclusione

**clos'ing price'** *s* ultimo corso

**clot** [klɑt] *s* grumo, coagulo || *v* (*pret & pp* **clotted;** *ger* **clotting**) *intr* raggrumarsi, coagularsi

**cloth** [klɔθ] *or* [klɑθ] *s* panno, tessuto, stoffa; abito; (*for binding books*) tela; **the cloth** il clero

**clothe** [kloð] *v* (*pret & pp* **clothed** *or* **clad** [klæd]) *tr* vestire, rivestire, coprire

**clothes** [kloz] *or* [kloðz] *spl* vestiti *mpl*, abiti *mpl*; (*for a bed*) coltre *f*; **to change clothes** cambiarsi

**clothes'bas'ket** *s* cesto della biancheria

**clothes'brush'** *s* spazzola per vestiti

**clothes' dry'er** *s* asciugatrice *f*

**clothes' hang'er** *s* attaccapanni *m*

**clothes'horse'** *s* cavalletto per stendere il bucato; elegantone *m*

**clothes'line'** *s* corda per stendere il bucato

**clothes' moth'** *s* tarma, tignola

**clothes'pin'** *s* molletta

**clothes' tree'** *s* attaccapanni *m*

**clothier** ['kloðjər] *s* negoziante *m* di confezioni; mercante *m* di panno

**clothing** ['kloðɪŋ] *s* vestiti *mpl*, vestiario

**cloud** [klaʊd] *s* nuvola, nube *f*; (*great number*) nuvolo; macchia; sospetto || *tr* annuvolare; offuscare || *intr* annuvolarsi; offuscarsi

**cloud' bank'** *s* banco di nubi

**cloud'burst'** *s* acquazzone *m*, nubifragio

**cloud'-capped'** *adj* coperto di nubi

**cloudless** ['klaʊdlɪs] *adj* senza nubi

**cloud·y** ['klaʊdi] *adj* (**-ier; -iest**) nuvoloso, annuvolato; confuso; tenebroso

**clout** [klaʊt] *s* (coll) schiaffo || *tr* (coll) schiaffeggiare

**clove** [klov] *s* chiodo di garofano; (*of garlic*) spicchio

**cloven-hoofed** ['klovən'huft] *adj* dal piede biforcuto; demoniaco

**clover** ['klovər] *s* trifoglio; **in clover** come un papa

**clo'ver-leaf'** *s* (**-leaves** [ ,livz]) foglia di trifoglio; incrocio stradale a quadrifoglio

**clown** [klaʊn] *s* pagliaccio, buffone *m* || *intr* fare il pagliaccio

**clownish** ['klaʊnɪʃ] *adj* buffonesco, clownesco, claunesco

**cloy** [klɔɪ] *tr* saziare fino alla nausea

**club** [klʌb] *s* bastone *m*; circolo, società *f*; (*playing card*) fiore *m* || *v* (*pret & pp* **clubbed;** *ger* **clubbing**) *tr* bastonare || *intr*—**to club together** unirsi

**club' car'** *s* vagone *m* con servizio di buffet

**club'house'** *s* sede *f* di un circolo

**club'man** *s* (**-men'**) frequentatore *m* di circoli

**club'room'** *s* sala delle riunioni

**club' sand'wich** *s* sandwich *m* a tre fette di pane con insalata

**club'wom'an** *s* (**-wom'en**) frequentatrice *f* di circoli

**cluck** [klʌk] *s* (il) chiocciare || *intr* chiocciare

**clue** [klu] *s* traccia, indizio

**clump** [klʌmp] *s* gruppo, massa; (*of earth*) zolla || *intr* camminare con passo pesante

**clum·sy** ['klʌmzi] *adj* (**-sier; -siest**) goffo, malaccorto, sgraziato

**cluster** ['klʌstər] *s* gruppo; (*of grapes*) grappolo; (*of bees*) sciame *m*; (*of stars*) ammasso; (*of people*) folla || *tr* raggruppare || *intr* raggrupparsi

**clutch** [klʌtʃ] *s* presa; (*claw*) grinfia; (*of chickens*) covata; (mach) innesto; (aut) frizione; **clutches** grinfie *fpl*; **to throw the clutch** in innestare la marcia; **to throw the clutch out** disinnestare la marcia || *tr* afferrare, aggrappare || *intr*—**to clutch at** aggrapparsi a

**clutter** ['klʌtər] *tr*—**to clutter up** ingombrare alla rinfusa

**coach** [kotʃ] *s* carrozza, vettura; vagone *m*; (*automobile*) berlina; autobus *m*; (*trainer*) allenatore *m*; (*teacher*) ripetitore *m* || *tr* allenare; preparare

**coach' house'** *s* rimessa

**coaching** ['kotʃɪŋ] *s* suggerimento; (*in school*) ripetizione; (sports) allenamento

**coach'man** *s* (**-men**) cocchiere *m*

**coagulate** [koˈægjəˌlet] *tr* coagulare ‖ *intr* coagularsi

**coal** [kol] *s* carbone *m;* (*piece of burning wood*) tizzone *m;* **to call** or **haul over the coals** rimproverare ‖ *tr* rifornire di carbone ‖ *intr* rifornirsi di carbone; (*naut*) fare carbone

**coal′bin′** *s* carbonaia

**coal′ deal′er** *s* (*wholesale*) negoziante *m* di carbone; (*retail*) carbonaio

**coal′ field′** *s* bacino carbonifero

**coal′ gas′** *s* gas *m* illuminante

**coalition** [ˌko·əˈlɪʃən] *s* coalizione

**coal′ mine′** *s* miniera di carbone

**coal′ oil′** *s* cherosene *m*

**coal′ scut′tle** *s* secchio del carbone

**coal′ tar′** *s* catrame *m*

**coal′ yard′** *s* carbonaia, carboniera

**coarse** [kors] *adj* (*manners*) volgare, ordinario; (*unrefined*) greggio; (*lacking refinement in manners*) rozzo, grossolano

**coast** [kost] *s* costa; discesa a ruota libera; **the coast is clear** la via è libera ‖ *tr* costeggiare ‖ *intr* costeggiare; scendere a ruota libera

**coastal** [ˈkostəl] *adj* costiero

**coaster** [ˈkostər] *s* nave *f* di cabotaggio; (*amusement*) otto volante, montagna russa; (*small tray*) sottobicchiere *m*

**coast′er brake′** *s* freno a contropedale

**coast′ guard′** *s* guardacoste *m*

**coast′-guard cut′ter** *s* guardacoste *m*

**coast′ing trade′** *s* cabotaggio

**coast′land′** *s* costa

**coast′line′** *s* linea costiera, litorale *m*

**coast′wise′** *adv* lungo la costa

**coat** [kot] *s* soprabito; cappotto; (*jacket*) giacca; (*hide of man and animals*) mantello; (*of paint*) mano *f;* (*layer*) strato ‖ *tr* vestire, proteggere; ricoprire, coprire

**coat′ed** [ˈkotɪd] *adj* rivestito; (*tongue*) patinato

**coat′ hang′er** *s* attaccapanni *m*

**coating** [ˈkotɪŋ] *s* rivestimento; (*of paint*) mano *f;* (*of cement*) strato; (*cloth*) tessuto per abiti

**coat′ of arms′** *s* scudo, stemma *m*

**coat′room′** *s* guardaroba *m*

**coat′tail′** *s* falda

**coax** [koks] *tr* blandire; ottenere con lusinghe

**cob** [kab] *s* spiga di granturco; (*horse*) cavallo da tiro; (*swan*) cigno maschio

**cobalt** [ˈkobɔlt] *s* cobalto

**cobble** [ˈkabəl] *s* ciottolo ‖ *tr* acciottolare; (*to mend*) raccomodare, riparare

**cobbler** [ˈkablər] *s* calzolaio, ciabattino; (*pie*) torta di frutta

**cob′ble·stone′** *s* ciottolo

**cob′web′** *s* tela di ragno, ragnatela

**cocaine** [koˈken] *s* cocaina

**cock** [kak] *s* gallo; (*faucet*) rubinetto; (*of gun*) cane *m;* (*of the eye*) ammicco; (*of nose*) angolo (del naso) rivolto all′insù; (*of hay*) covone *m* ‖ *tr* (*a gun*) armare; (*the head*) drizzare

**cockade** [kaˈked] *s* coccarda

**cock-a-doodle-doo** [ˈkakəˌdudəlˈdu] *s* chicchirichì *m*

**cock′-and-bull′ sto′ry** *s* racconto incredibile

**cocked′ hat′** *s* tricorno, cappello tricorno; **to knock into a cocked hat** (*slang*) distruggere completamente

**cockeyed** [ˈkakˌaɪd] *adj* strabico; (*slang*) sbilenco; (*slang*) sciocco, scemo

**cockle** [ˈkakəl] *s* (*mollusk*) cardio; (*weed*) loglio; (*boat*) barchetta; (*wrinkle*) grinza; **to warm the cockles of one′s heart** far bene al cuore ‖ *intr* raggrinzirsi

**cock′ of the walk′** *s* gallo del pollaio

**cock′pit′** *s* (*of boat*) cabina; (*aer*) carlinga; (*naut*) cassero di poppa

**cock′roach′** *s* scarafaggio, blatta

**cocks′comb′** *s* cresta di gallo; berretto da buffone

**cock′sure′** *adj* ostinato; troppo sicuro di sé stesso

**cock′tail′** *s* cocktail *m*

**cock′tail par′ty** *s* cocktail *m*

**cock·y** [ˈkaki] *adj* (**-ier; -iest**) impudente, presuntuoso

**cocoa** [ˈkoko] *s* (*bean*) cacao; (*drink*) cioccolata; (*tree*) cocco

**coconut** [ˈkokəˌnʌt] *s* noce *f* di cocco

**co′conut palm′** or **tree′** *s* cocco

**cocoon** [kəˈkun] *s* bozzolo

**cod** [kad] *s* merluzzo

**C.O.D.** [ˈsiˈoˈdi] *s* (letterword) (**Collect on Delivery**) contro assegno

**coddle** [ˈkadəl] *tr* vezzeggiare

**code** [kod] *s* codice *m*, cifra; **in code** in codice, in cifra ‖ *tr* mettere in codice or in cifra; cifrare

**codex** [ˈkodɛks] *s* (**codices** [ˈkodɪˌsiz] or [ˈkadɪˌsiz]) codice *m*

**cod′fish′** *s* merluzzo

**codger** [ˈkadʒər] *s*—**old codger** (coll) vecchietto

**codicil** [ˈkadɪsɪl] *s* codicillo

**codi·fy** [ˈkadɪˌfaɪ] or [ˈkodɪˌfaɪ] *v* (*pret & pp* **-fied**) *tr* codificare

**cod′-liver oil′** *s* olio di fegato di merluzzo

**coed** [ˈcoˌɛd] *s* studentessa di scuola mista

**coeducation** [ˌkoˌɛdʒəˈkeʃən] *s* coeducazione

**co′educa′tional school′** [ˌko·ɛdʒəˈkeʃənəl] *s* scuola mista

**coefficient** [ˌko·ɪˈfɪʃənt] *s* coefficiente *m*

**coerce** [koˈʌrs] *tr* forzare, costringere

**coercion** [koˈʌrʃən] *s* coercizione

**coexist** [ˌko·ɪgˈzɪst] *intr* coesistere

**coffee** [ˈkɔfi] or [ˈkafi] *s* caffè *m;* **ground coffee** caffè macinato; **roasted coffee** caffè torrefatto

**cof′fee bean′** *s* chicco di caffè

**cof′fee·cake′** *s* pasticcino (da mangiarsi con il caffè)

**cof′fee grind′er** *s* macinino da caffè, macinacaffè *m*

**cof′fee grounds′** *spl* fondi *mpl* di caffè

**cof′fee house′** *s* caffè *m*

**cof′fee mak′er** *s* macchinetta del caffè

**cof'fee mill'** s macinino del caffè, macinacaffè m
**cof'fee-pot'** s caffettiera
**cof'fee shop'** s caffè m
**coffer** ['kɔfər] or ['kɑfər] s forziere m; (ceiling) soffitto a cassettoni; (archit) cassettone m; **coffers** tesoro
**coffin** ['kɔfɪn] or ['kɑfɪn] s bara
**cog** [kɑg] s dente m d'ingranaggio; ruota dentata; **to slip a cog** fare un errore
**cogent** ['kodʒənt] adj convincente, persuasivo
**cogitate** ['kɑdʒɪ,tet] tr & intr cogitare, ponzare
**cognac** ['konjæk] or ['kɑnjæk] s cognac m
**cognate** ['kɑgnet] adj consanguineo, parente, affine || s parola dello stesso ceppo linguistico; consanguineo, parente mf
**cognizance** ['kɑgnɪzəns] or ['kɑnɪzəns] s conoscenza; **to take cognizance of** prendere conoscenza di
**cognizant** ['kɑgnɪzənt] or ['kɑnɪzənt] adj informato, al corrente
**cog'wheel'** s ruota dentata
**cohabit** [ko'hæbɪt] intr convivere; (archaic) coabitare
**coheir** [ko'ɛr] s coerede mf
**cohere** [ko'hɪr] intr aderire; (fig) avere nesso
**coherent** [ko'hɪrənt] adj coerente
**coiffeur** [kwɑ'fʌr] s parrucchiere m per signora; (Brit) parrucchiere m
**coiffure** [kwɑ'fjur] s pettinatura || tr pettinare
**coil** [kɔɪl] s (of rope) rotolo; (of pipe) serpentino; (of wire) bobina, avvolgimento || tr arrotolare || intr arrotolarsi
**coil' spring'** s molla a spirale, molla elicoidale
**coin** [kɔɪn] s moneta; **to pay back in one's own coin** pagare della stessa moneta; **to toss a coin** giocare a testa o croce || tr (money) coniare, battere; (words) inventare, creare; **to coin money** battere moneta; (coll) fare soldoni
**coincide** [,ko·ɪn'saɪd] intr coincidere
**coincidence** [ko'ɪnsɪdəns] s coincidenza
**coke** [kok] s coke m, carbone m coke
**colander** ['kʌləndər] or ['kɑləndər] s colabrodo, colapasta m
**cold** [kold] adj freddo; **it is cold** (said of weather) fa freddo; **to be cold** (said of a person) avere freddo || s freddo; (ailment) raffreddore m; **out in the cold** solo soletto; **to catch cold** pigliare freddo, pigliarsi un raffreddore
**cold' blood'** s—**in cold blood** a sangue freddo
**cold'-blood'ed** adj insensibile; (sensitive to cold) freddoloso; (animal) a sangue freddo
**cold' chis'el** s tagliaferro
**cold' com'fort** s magra consolazione
**cold' cream'** s crema emolliente
**cold' cuts'** spl salumi mpl, affettato

**cold' feet'** spl—**to get cold feet** (coll) perdersi d'animo
**cold'-heart'ed** adj—**to be coldhearted** avere il cuore duro
**coldness** ['koldnɪs] s freddezza
**cold' shoul'der** s—**to get the cold shoulder** (coll) essere trattato con freddezza; **to turn a cold shoulder on** (coll) trattare con freddezza
**cold' snap'** s freddo breve e improvviso
**cold' stor'age** s conservazione a freddo
**cold' war'** s guerra fredda
**cold' wave'** s ondata di freddo
**coleslaw** ['kol,slɔ] s insalata di cavolo cappuccio
**colic** ['kɑlɪk] adj colico || s colica
**coliseum** [,kɑlɪ'si·əm] s stadio, arena || **Coliseum** s Colosseo
**collaborate** [kə'læbə,ret] intr collaborare
**collaborationist** [kə,læbə're/ənɪst] s collaborazionista mf
**collaborator** [kə'læbə,retər] s collaboratore m
**collapse** [kə'læps] s (of business) fallimento; (e.g., of a roof) caduta; (of a person) collasso || tr piegare || intr (to shrink) restringersi, sgonfiarsi; (said of a business) fallire; (said of health) venir meno; (said, e.g., of a roof) cadere, crollare
**collapsible** [kə'læpsɪbəl] adj pieghevole, smontabile
**collar** ['kɑlər] s (of shirt) colletto; (for dog or horse) collare m; (ring) anello; (short piece of pipe) manicotto || tr afferrare per il collo, catturare
**col'lar-band'** s cinturino della camicia
**col'lar-bone'** s clavicola
**collate** [kə'let] or ['kɑlet] tr collazionare, confrontare
**collateral** [kə'lætərəl] adj collaterale; accessorio, addizionale || s collaterale m
**colleague** ['kɑlig] s collega mf
**collect** ['kɑlɛkt] s (eccl) colletta || [kə'lɛkt] adv contro assegno; (telp) pagamento all'abbonato chiamato || tr raccogliere, riunire; (e.g., stamps) collezionare; (mail) levare; (bills) incassare; (ideas) coordinare; (thoughts) riordinare; (e.g., classroom papers) raccogliere; (taxes) riscuotere; **to collect oneself** riprendersi, riprendere il controllo di sé stesso || intr (for the poor) fare la colletta; riunirsi, raccogliersi
**collected** [kə'lɛktɪd] adj raccolto; equilibrato, padrone di sè
**collection** [kə'lɛkʃən] s collezione; (for the poor) colletta; (of mail) levata; (heap) deposito; (of taxes) esazione; (of bills) riscossione
**collec'tion a'gency** s agenzia di riscossione
**collective** [kə'lɛktɪv] adj collettivo
**collector** [kə'lɛktər] s (of stamps) collezionista mf; (of taxes) esattore m; (of tickets) controllore m
**college** ['kɑlɪdʒ] s scuola superiore,

università *f; (e.g., of medicine)* facoltà *f; (electoral)* collegio

**collide** [kə'laɪd] *intr* collidere, scontrarsi

**collie** ['kɑli] *s* collie *m*

**collier** ['kɑljər] *s (ship)* carboniera; *(min)* minatore *m* di carbone

**collier·y** ['kɑljəri] *s (-ies)* miniera di carbone

**collision** [kə'lɪʒən] *s* collisione

**colloid** ['kalɔɪd] *adj* colloidale ‖ *s* colloide *m*

**colloquial** [kə'lokwɪ·əl] *adj* familiare, colloquiale

**colloquialism** [kə'lokwɪ·ə‚lɪzəm] *s* espressione familiare

**collo·quy** ['kɑləkwi] *s (-quies)* colloquio

**collusion** [kə'luʒən] *s* collusione; **to be in collusion with** essere d'intelligenza con

**cologne** [kə'lon] *s* acqua di colonia, colonia ‖ **Cologne** *s* Colonia

**colon** ['kolən] *s (anat)* colon *m; (gram)* due punti *mpl*

**colonel** ['kʌrnəl] *s* colonnello

**colonist** ['kɑlənɪst] *s* colono, coloniale *m*

**colonize** ['kɑlə‚naɪz] *tr & intr* colonizzare

**colonnade** [‚kɑlə'ned] *s* colonnato

**colo·ny** ['kɑləni] *s (-nies)* colonia

**color** ['kʌlər] *s* colore *m; off color* sbiadito, scolorito; *(slang)* sporco, volgare; **the colors** i colori, la bandiera; **to call to the colors** chiamare in servizio militare; **to change color** cambiar colore; arrossire; impallidire; **to give or lend color to** far parere probabile; **to lose color** impallidire; **to show one's colors** mostrarsi come si è; **under color of** sotto il pretesto di ‖ *tr* colorare; *(fig)* colorire ‖ *intr* arrossire

**col′or-blind′** *adj* daltonico

**colored** ['kʌlərd] *adj* colorato; *(person)* di colore; esagerato

**colorful** ['kʌlərfəl] *adj* colorito, espressivo

**col′or guard′** *s* guardia d'onore alla bandiera

**coloring** ['kʌlərɪŋ] *s* colorazione; colore *m;* pigmento; *(fig)* specie *f*

**colorless** ['kʌlərlɪs] *adj* incolore, incoloro

**col′or photog′raphy** *s* fotografia a colori

**col′or ser′geant** *s* sergente *m* portabandiera

**col′or tel′evision** *s* televisione a colori

**colossal** [kə'lɑsəl] *adj* colossale

**colossus** [kə'lɑsəs] *s* colosso

**colt** [kolt] *s* puledro

**Columbus** [kə'lʌmbəs] *s* Colombo

**column** ['kɑləm] *s* colonna

**columnist** ['kɑləmɪst] *s* giornalista incaricato di una colonna speciale; articolista *mf*

**coma** ['komə] *s* coma *m*

**comb** [kom] *s* pettine *m; (for horse)* striglia; *(of hen or wave)* cresta; *(honeycomb)* favo ‖ *tr* pettinare;

*(fig)* esaminare minuziosamente ‖ *intr (said of waves)* frangersi

**com·bat** ['kɑmbæt] *s* combattimento ‖ ['kɑmbæt] or [kəm'bæt] *v (pret & pp -bated* or *-batted; ger -bating* or *-batting) tr & intr* combattere

**combatant** ['kɑmbətənt] *s* combattente *mf*

**com′bat du′ty** *s* servizio in zona di guerra

**combination** [‚kɑmbɪ'neʃən] *s* combinazione

**combine** ['kɑmbaɪn] *s* consorzio; *(pol)* coalizione; mieto-trebbiatrice *f* ‖ [kəm'baɪn] *tr* combinare ‖ *intr* combinarsi

**combin′ing form′** *s* membro di parola composta

**combo** ['kɑmbo] *s* orchestrina

**combustible** [kəm'bʌstɪbəl] *adj & s* combustibile *m*

**combustion** [kəm'bʌstʃən] *s* combustione

**come** [kʌm] *v (pret came* [kem]; *pp come) intr* venire; arrivare; *(to become)* diventare; *(to amount)* ammontare; **come!** macchè!; **come along!** andiamo!; **come in!** avanti!, entri!; **come on!** andiamo!; avanti!, coraggio!; **to come about** accadere, succedere; **to come across** incontrarsi con; *(slang)* pagare; **to come around** cedere; mettersi d'accordo; *(said of health)* rimettersi; **to come at** raggiungere; *(to attack)* attaccare; **to come back** ritornare; **to come between** mettersi fra; **to come by** ottenere; **to come down** scendere; decadere; essere trasmesso; **to come down with** ammalarsi di; **to come forward** farsi avanti; **to come in** entrare, passare; **to come in for** ricevere; **to come into** ricevere; ereditare; **to come off** succedere; riuscire; **to come on** mostrarsi; migliorare; incontrarsi; **to come out** uscire; debuttare in società; andare a finire; **to come out with** uscire con; mostrare; **to come over** succedere a, *e.g., what came over him?* che gli è successo?; **to come through** riuscire; **to come to** riprendere i sensi; **to come under** essere di competenza di; appartenere a; **to come up** salire; **to come up to** salire fino a; avvicinarsi a; **to come up with** raggiungere; produrre, fornire; proporre

**come′back′** *s (coll)* ritorno; *(slang)* pronta risposta; **to stage a comeback** *(coll)* ritornare in auge

**comedian** [kə'midɪ·ən] *s* attore comico; *(author)* commediografo; *(amusing person)* commediante *mf*

**comedienne** [kə‚midɪ'ɛn] *s* attrice comica

**come′down′** *s (coll)* rovescio di fortuna

**come·dy** ['kɑmədi] *s (-dies)* commedia

**come·ly** ['kʌmli] *adj (-lier; -liest)* bello, grazioso

**comet** ['kɑmɪt] *s* cometa

**comfort** ['kʌmfərt] *s* conforto, sollievo;

(*ease*) benessere *m* ‖ *tr* confortare, alleviare

**comfortable** ['kʌmfərtəbəl] *adj* comodo, agiato; (*e.g., income*) (coll) bastante ‖ *s* coltre *f*

**comforter** ['kʌmfərtər] *s* consolatore *m;* (*bedcover*) coltre *f;* sciarpa di lana ‖ **the Comforter** lo Spirito Santo, lo Spirito Consolatore

**comforting** ['kʌmfərtɪŋ] *adj* confortante

**com'fort sta'tion** *s* latrina pubblica

**comic** ['kɑmɪk] *adj* comico ‖ *s* (*actor*) comico; comicità *f;* **comics** fumetti *mpl*

**comical** ['kɑmɪkəl] *adj* comico

**com'ic book'** *s* libretto a fumetti

**com'ic op'era** *s* opera buffa

**com'ic strip'** *s* racconto umoristico a fumetti

**coming** ['kʌmɪŋ] *adj* venturo, prossimo; promettente ‖ *s* venuta

**com'ing out'** *s* debutto in società; (*e.g., of stock*) emissione

**comma** ['kɑmə] *s* virgola

**command** [kə'mænd] or [kə'mɑnd] *s* comando; (*e.g., of a language*) padronanza ‖ *tr* comandare, ordinare; (*to overlook*) dominare; (*to be able to have*) disporre di ‖ *intr* avere il comando

**commandant** [‚kɑmən'dænt] or [‚kɑmən'dɑnt] *s* comandante *m*

**commandeer** [‚kɑmən'dɪr] *tr* requisire

**commander** [kə'mændər] or [kə'mɑndər] *s* (*of knighthood*) commendatore *m;* (mil) comandante *m;* (nav) capitano di vascello

**command'er in chief'** *s* comandante *m* in capo

**command'ing of'ficer** *s* comandante *m*

**commandment** [kə'mændmənt] or [kə'mɑndmənt] *s* comandamento

**command' mod'ule** *s* (rok) modulo di comando

**commando** [kə'mændo] *s* guastatore *m*

**commemorate** [kə'mɛmə‚ret] *tr* commemorare, celebrare

**commence** [kə'mɛns] *tr & intr* cominciare

**commencement** [kə'mɛnsmənt] *s* inizio, esordio; (*in a school*) cerimonia per la distribuzione dei diplomi

**commend** [kə'mɛnd] *tr* lodare; (*to entrust*) raccomandare, affidare

**commendable** [kə'mɛndəbəl] *adj* (*person*) lodevole; (*act*) commendevole

**commendation** [‚kɑmən'defən] *s* lode *f;* raccomandazione; (mil) citazione

**comment** ['kɑment] *s* commento ‖ *tr* commentare ‖ *intr* fare commenti; **to comment on** fare commenti su

**commentar·y** ['kɑmən‚tɛri] *s* (**-ies**) commentario

**commentator** ['kɑmən‚tetər] *s* commentatore *m*

**commerce** ['kɑmərs] *s* commercio

**commercial** [kə'mɛrʃəl] *adj* commerciale ‖ *s* (rad, telv) programma *m* di pubblicità; (rad, telv) annunzio pubblicitario

**commiserate** [kə'mɪzə‚ret] *intr—to*

**commiserate with** commiserare, compiangere

**commissar** ['kɑmɪ‚sɑr] or [‚kɑmɪ'sɑr] *s* commissario del popolo

**commissar·y** ['kɑmɪ‚seri] *s* (**-ies**) (*store*) economato; (*deputy*) commissario; (*in army*) intendente *m*

**commission** [kə'mɪʃən] *s* commissione; (*e.g., in army*) nomina, brevetto; autorità *f;* (*of a crime*) perpetrazione; (il) fare; **in commission** in servizio, in uso; **out of commission** fuori servizio ‖ *tr* nominare, dare un brevetto a; autorizzare; (*a ship*) armare

**commis'sioned of'ficer** *s* (mil, nav) ufficiale *m*

**commissioner** [kə'mɪʃənər] *s* commissario; membro di una commissione

**commis'sion mer'chant** *s* sensale *m*

**com·mit** [kə'mɪt] *v* (*pret & pp* **-mitted;** *ger* **-mitting**) *tr* commettere, perpetrare; (*to deliver*) affidare, consegnare; (*to imprison*) mandare in prigione; (*an insane person*) internare; (*to refer*) rinviare; (*to involve*) compromettere; **to commit oneself** compromettersi; **to commit to memory** imparare a memoria; **to commit to writing** mettere in iscritto

**commitment** [kə'mɪtmənt] *s* (*act of committing*) commissione; (*to an asylum*) internamento; promessa; (law) mandato

**committal** [kə'mɪtəl] *s* consegna; promessa

**committee** [kə'mɪti] *s* comitato, commissione

**commode** [kə'mod] *s* (*chest of drawers*) cassettone *m;* (*washstand*) lavabo; seggetta, comoda

**commodious** [kə'modɪ·əs] *adj* spazioso; conveniente

**commodi·ty** [kə'mɑdɪti] *s* (**-ties**) merce *f;* articolo di prima necessità

**commod'ity exchange'** *s* borsa merci

**common** ['kɑmən] *adj* comune ‖ *s* fondo comunale; pascolo comune; **commons** gente *f* non nobile; refettorio; **in common** in comune ‖ **the Commons** la Camera dei Comuni

**com'mon car'rier** *s* impresa di trasporti pubblici

**commoner** ['kɑmənər] *s* plebeo, borghese *m;* membro della Camera dei Comuni

**com'mon law'** *s* consuetudine *f,* diritto consuetudinario

**com'mon-law mar'riage** *s* matrimonio basato sulla mera convivenza

**commonly** ['kɑmənli] *adv* generalmente

**com'mon·place'** *adj* banale, ordinario ‖ *s* banalità *f,* cosa ordinaria

**com'mon sense'** *s* senso comune

**com'mon-sense'** *adj* giudizioso

**com'mon stock'** *s* azione ordinaria; azioni ordinarie

**commonweal** ['kɑmən‚wil] *s* bene pubblico

**com'mon·wealth'** *s* (*citizens of a state*) cittadinanza; repubblica; (*one of the*

*50 states of the U.S.A.*) stato; comunità *f*, federazione
**commotion** [kə'moʃən] *s* agitazione
**commune** [kə'mjun] *s* comune *m* ‖ *intr* confabulare; (*eccl*) comunicarsi
**communicate** [kə'mjunɪ ˌket] *tr & intr* comunicare
**communicating** [kə'mjunɪ ˌketɪŋ] *adj* comunicante
**communication** [kə ˌmjunɪ'keʃən] *s* comunicazione; **communications** sistema *m* di comunicazione; mezzi *mpl* di comunicazione
**communicative** [kə'mjunɪ ˌketɪv] *adj* comunicativo
**Communion** [kə'mjunjən] *s* Comunione; **to take Communion** comunicarsi
**communiqué** [kə ˌmjunɪ'ke] *or* [kə'mjunɪ ˌke] *s* comunicato
**communism** ['kɑmjə ˌnɪzəm] *s* comunismo
**communist** ['kɑmjənɪst] *s* comunista *mf*
**communi•ty** [kə'mjunɪti] *s* (**-ties**) (*people living together*) comunità *f*; (*sharing together*) comunanza; (*neighborhood*) circondario
**commu'nity cen'ter** *s* centro sociale
**commu'nity chest'** *s* fondo di beneficenza
**commuta'tion tick'et** [ ˌkɑmjə'teʃən] *s* biglietto d'abbonamento
**commutator** [ 'kɑmjə ˌtetər] *s* (*switch*) commutatore *m*; (*of dynamo or motor*) collettore *m*
**commute** [kə'mjut] *tr* commutare ‖ *intr* commutare; fare il pendolare
**commuter** [kə'mjutər] *s* pendolare *mf*
**compact** [kəm'pækt] *adj* compatto ‖ ['kɑmpækt] *s* (*small case for face powder*) portacipria *m*; (*agreement*) accordo; (*small car*) utilitaria
**companion** [kəm'pænjən] *s* compagno; (*one of two items*) pendant *m*; (*lady*) dama di compagnia
**compan'ion•ship'** *s* cameratismo
**compan'ion•way'** *s* (naut) scaletta per andare sottocoperta
**compa•ny** ['kʌmpəni] *s* (**-nies**) compagnia; (*coll*) ospite *m* or ospiti *mpl*; (naut) equipaggio; **to bear company** accompagnare; **to be good company** essere simpatico; **to keep company** (*said of a couple*) andare insieme; **to keep company with** accompagnare; (*coll*) fare la corte a; **to part company** separarsi
**comparable** [ 'kɑmpərəbəl] *adj* comparabile, paragonabile
**comparative** [kəm'pærətɪv] *adj* comparativo; (*e.g., anatomy*) comparato ‖ *s* (gram) comparativo
**compare** [kəm'pɛr] *s*—**beyond compare** incomparabile ‖ *tr* confrontare; **compared to** a confronto di, in confronto a
**comparison** [kəm'pærɪsən] *s* confronto; (gram) comparazione; **in comparison with** in confronto a, a confronto di
**compartment** [kəm'pɑrtmənt] *s* com-

partimento; (naut) compartimento stagno; (rr) compartimento
**compass** ['kʌmpəs] *s* (*instrument for showing direction*) bussola; (*boundary*) limite *m*; (*range*) ambito; (*range of voice*) portata; (*of a wall*) cerchia; (*circuit*) circuito; (*drawing instrument*) compasso; **compasses** (*drawing instrument*) compasso ‖ *tr* girare intorno a; comprendere; **to compass about** accerchiare
**com'pass card'** *s* rosa dei venti
**compassion** [kəm'pæʃən] *s* compassione
**compassionate** [kəm'pæʃənɪt] *adj* compassionevole
**com'pass saw'** *s* gattuccio
**com•pel** [kəm'pɛl] *v* (*pret & pp* **-pelled;** *ger* **-pelling**) *tr* forzare, obbligare
**compelling** [kəm'pɛlɪŋ] *adj* imperioso, coercitivo
**compendious** [kəm'pɛndɪ•əs] *adj* compendioso, conciso
**compensate** ['kɑmpən ˌset] *tr & intr* compensare
**compensation** [ ˌkɑmpən'seʃən] *s* compensazione; (*pay*) pagamento; (*something given to offset a loss*) risarcimento, indennità *f*
**compete** [kəm'pit] *intr* competere
**competence** ['kɑmpɪtəns] *or* **competency** [ 'kɑmpɪtənsi] *s* (*fitness*) abilità *f*; (*money*) agiatezza; (*authority*) competenza
**competent** ['kɑmpɪtənt] *adj* abile; competente
**competition** [ ˌkɑmpɪ'tɪʃən] *s* competizione, gara; (*in business*) concorrenza
**competitive** [kəm'pɛtɪtɪv] *adj* competitivo; (*based on competition*) di concorso
**compet'itive pric'es** *spl* prezzi *mpl* di concorrenza
**competitor** [kəm'pɛtɪtər] *s* competitore *m*, concorrente *mf*; rivale *mf*
**compilation** [ ˌkɑmpɪ'leʃən] *s* compilazione
**compile** [kəm'paɪl] *tr* compilare
**complacence** [kəm'plesəns] *or* **complacency** [kəm'plesənsi] *s* compiacenza; compiacenza di sé stesso
**complacent** [kəm'plesənt] *adj* compiaciuto or soddisfatto con sé stesso
**complain** [kəm'plen] *intr* lagnarsi
**complainant** [kəm'plenənt] *s* (law) querelante *mf*
**complaint** [kəm'plent] *s* lagnanza, reclamo; (*sickness*) malattia; (law) querela
**complaisance** [kəm'plezəns] *or* ['kɑmplɪ ˌzæns] *s* compiacenza
**complaisant** [kəm'plezənt] *or* ['kɑmplɪ ˌzænt] *adj* compiacente, cortese
**complement** ['kɑmplɪmənt] *s* complemento; (naut) equipaggio ‖ ['kɑmplɪ ˌment] *tr* completare
**complete** [kəm'plit] *adj* completo; (*done*) finito ‖ *tr* completare, finire
**completion** [kəm'pliʃən] *s* completamento, compimento
**complex** [kəm'plɛks] *or* ['kɑmplɛks]

*adj* complesso, complicato ‖ ['kɑmplɛks] *s* complesso

**complexion** [kəm'plɛkʃən] *s* (*of skin*) carnagione; (*appearance*) aspetto; (*viewpoint*) punto di vista

**compliance** [kəm'plaɪ·əns] *s* condiscendenza, arrendevolezza; **in compliance with** in conformità di

**complicate** ['kɑmplɪ‚ket] *tr* complicare

**complicated** ['kɑmplɪ‚ketɪd] *adj* complicato

**complici·ty** [kəm'plɪsɪti] *s* (*-ties*) complicità *f*

**compliment** ['kɑmplɪmənt] *s* complimento, omaggio ‖ ['kɑmplɪ‚ment] *tr*—**to compliment s.o. on s.th** felicitarsi con qlcu per qlco; **to compliment s.o. with s.th** regalare qlco a qlcu

**complimentary** [‚kɑmplɪ'mentəri] *adj* complimentoso, lusinghiero; (*free*) in omaggio, gratis; (*ticket*) di favore

**com·ply** [kəm'plaɪ] *v* (*pret & pp -plied*) *intr* acconsentire, accondiscendere; **to comply with** accedere a

**component** [kəm'ponənt] *adj* componente, costituente ‖ *s* (*component part*) componente *m*; (*force*) componente *f*

**compose** [kəm'poz] *tr* comporre; **to be composed of** essere composto di; **to compose oneself** calmarsi

**composed** [kəm'pozd] *adj* calmo, tranquillo

**composer** [kəm'pozər] *s* (*peacemaker*) conciliatore *m*; (mus) compositore *m*

**compos'ing stick'** *s* (typ) compositoio

**composite** [kəm'pɑzɪt] *adj & s* composto, composito

**composition** [‚kɑmpə'zɪʃən] *s* composizione; (*agreement*) compromesso

**compositor** [kəm'pɑzɪtər] *s* compositore *m*

**compost** ['kɑmpost] *s* concime *m* naturale

**composure** [kəm'poʒər] *s* calma

**compote** ['kɑmpot] *s* (*stewed fruit*) composta; (*dish*) compostiera

**compound** ['kɑmpaʊnd] *adj* composto; (*fracture*) complesso; (archit, bot) composito ‖ *s* composto; parola composta; (*yard*) recinto ‖ [kɑm'paʊnd] *tr* (*to mix*) combinare; (*to settle*) comporre; (*interest*) capitalizzare

**comprehend** [‚kɑmprɪ'hend] *tr* comprendere

**comprehensible** [‚kɑmprɪ'hensɪbəl] *adj* comprensibile

**comprehension** [‚kɑmprɪ'henʃən] *s* comprensione

**comprehensive** [‚kɑmprɪ'hensɪv] *adj* comprensivo

**compress** ['kɑmprɛs] *s* compressa ‖ [kəm'prɛs] *tr* comprimere

**compressed' air'** *s* aria compressa

**compression** [kəm'prɛʃən] *s* compressione

**comprise** [kəm'praɪz] *tr* comprendere, includere; **to be comprised of** consistere di

**compromise** ['kɑmprə‚maɪz] *s* com-

promesso ‖ *tr* (*a dispute*) transigere, comporre; (*to put in danger*) compromettere ‖ *intr* transigere, fare un compromesso

**comptroller** [kən'trolər] *s* economo, amministratore *m*, controllore *m*

**compulsive** [kəm'pʌlsɪv] *adj* obbligatorio, coercitivo; (psychol) compulsivo

**compulsory** [kəm'pʌlsəri] *adj* obbligatorio

**compute** [kəm'pjut] *tr & intr* computare, calcolare

**computer** [kəm'pjutər] *s* calcolatore *m;* elaboratore *m*

**comrade** ['kɑmræd] or ['kɑmrɪd] *s* camerata *m*, compagno

**com'rade in arms'** *s* compagno d'armi

**con** [kɑn] *s* contro ‖ *v* (*pret & pp conned; ger conning*) *tr* imparare a memoria; (slang) imbrogliare

**concave** ['kɑnkev] or [kɑn'kev] *adj* concavo

**conceal** [kən'sil] *tr* nascondere; (*to keep secret*) celare

**concealment** [kən'silmənt] *s* occultamento; (*place*) nascondiglio

**concede** [kən'sid] *tr* concedere

**conceit** [kən'sit] *s* (*high opinion of oneself*) presunzione; (*fanciful notion*) concetto sottile

**conceited** [kən'sitɪd] *adj* vanitoso

**conceivable** [kən'sivəbəl] *adj* concepibile

**conceive** [kən'siv] *tr & intr* concepire

**concentrate** ['kɑnsən‚tret] *s* concentrato ‖ *tr* concentrare ‖ *intr* concentrarsi; **to concentrate on** concentrarsi in

**concentra'tion camp'** [‚kɑnsən'treʃən] *s* campo di concentrazione

**concept** ['kɑnsept] *s* concetto

**conception** [kən'sepʃən] *s* concezione

**concern** [kən'sʌrn] *s* interesse *m;* (*worry*) ansietà *f;* (*firm*) ditta, compagnia; **of concern** d'interesse ‖ *tr* concernere; **as concerns** circa; **to concern oneself** interessarsi; **to whom it may concern** a chiunque possa averne interesse

**concerning** [kən'sʌrnɪŋ] *prep* riguardo a

**concert** ['kɑnsərt] *s* concerto ‖ [kən'sʌrt] *tr & intr* concertare

**con'cert·mas'ter** *s* primo violino

**concer·to** [kən'tʃerto] *s* (*-tos* or *-ti* [ti]) concerto

**concession** [kən'seʃən] *s* concessione

**conciliate** [kən'sɪlɪ‚et] *tr* conciliare, conciliarsi con

**concise** [kən'saɪs] *adj* conciso

**conclude** [kən'klud] *tr* concludere ‖ *intr* concludersi, terminare

**conclusion** [kən'kluʒən] *s* conclusione; **in conclusion** per finire; **to try conclusions with** misurarsi con

**conclusive** [kən'klusɪv] *adj* decisivo, convincente

**concoct** [kən'kɑkt] *tr* preparare, confezionare; (*a story*) inventare

**concoction** [kɑn'kɑkʃən] *s* preparazione, mescolanza; (unpleasant in taste) intruglio

**concomitant** [kən'kɑmɪtənt] adj concomitante || s fatto or sintomo concomitante

**concord** ['kɑŋkɔrd] s concordia, armonia; (treaty) accordo; (gram) concordanza

**concourse** ['kɑŋkors] s confluenza; (crowd) affluenza, concorso; (boulevard) viale m; (rr) salone m principale

**concrete** ['kɑnkrit] or [kɑn'krit] adj concreto; fatto di cemento; solido || s cemento, calcestruzzo || tr (e.g., a sidewalk) cementare

**con'crete mix'er** s betoniera

**con·cur** [kən'kʌr] v (pret & pp -curred; ger -curring) intr (to work together) concorrere; (to agree) essere d'accordo, aderire

**concurrence** [kən'kʌrəns] s concorso; (agreement) accordo

**concurrent** [kən'kʌrənt] adj concomitante, simultaneo; cooperante; armonioso

**concussion** [kən'kʌʃən] s scossa, urto; (of brain) commozione cerebrale

**condemn** [kən'dɛm] tr condannare; (to take for public use) espropriare

**condemnation** [,kɑndɛm'neʃən] s condanna

**condense** [kən'dɛns] tr condensare || intr condensarsi

**condescend** [,kɑndɪ'sɛnd] intr condiscendere, degnarsi

**condescending** [,kɑndɪ'sɛndɪŋ] adj condiscendente

**condescension** [,kɑndɪ'sɛnʃən] s condiscendenza, degnazione

**condiment** ['kɑndɪmənt] s condimento

**condition** [kən'dɪʃən] s condizione; clausola; **on condition that** a condizione che || tr condizionare; mettere in buone condizioni fisiche

**conditional** [kən'dɪʃənəl] adj & s condizionale m

**condole** [kən'dol] intr condolersi

**condolence** [kən'doləns] s condoglianza

**condone** [kən'don] tr condonare

**conduce** [kən'djus] or [kən'dus] intr contribuire, indurre

**conducive** [kən'djusɪv] or [kən'dusɪv] adj contribuente

**conduct** ['kɑndʌkt] s condotta; direzione || [kən'dʌkt] tr condurre; (an orchestra) dirigere; **to conduct oneself** condursi, comportarsi || intr dirigere

**conductor** [kən'dʌktər] s direttore m; (of a streetcar) fattorino, conduttore m; (phys) conduttore m; (rr) capotreno

**conduit** ['kɑndɪt] or ['kɑndu·ɪt] s condotto

**cone** [kon] s cono; (bot) pigna

**Con'estoga wag'on** ['kɑnɪ'stogə] s carriaggio coperto

**confectioner** [kən'fɛkʃənər] s confettiere m, pasticcere m

**confec'tioners' sug'ar** s zucchero in polvere finissimo

**confectioner·y** [kən'fɛkʃə,neri] s (-ies) confetteria, pasticceria; (candies) confetture fpl

**confedera·cy** [kən'fɛdərəsi] s (-cies) confederazione; lega

**confederate** [kən'fɛdərɪt] s alleato; (in crime) complice mf || [kən'fɛdə,ret] tr confederare || intr confederarsi

**con·fer** [kən'fʌr] v (pret & pp -ferred; ger -ferring) tr conferire || intr conferire, abboccarsi

**conference** ['kɑnfərəns] s conferenza

**confess** [kən'fɛs] tr confessare, ammettere || intr confessare, confessarsi

**confession** [kən'fɛʃən] s confessione

**confessional** [kən'fɛʃənəl] s confessionale m

**confes'sion of faith'** s professione di fede

**confessor** [kən'fɛsər] s confessore m

**confetti** [kən'fɛti] s coriandoli mpl

**confide** [kən'faɪd] tr confidare; (to entrust) affidare || intr confidarsi

**confidence** ['kɑnfɪdəns] s fiducia, sicurezza di sé; (boldness) baldanza; (secrecy) confidenza

**confident** ['kɑnfɪdənt] adj fiducioso; baldanzoso || s confidente mf

**confidential** [,kɑnfɪ'dɛnʃəl] adj confidenziale

**confine** ['kɑnfaɪn] s confine m || [kən'faɪn] tr limitare; confinare; **to be confined** essere in altro stato; **to be confined to bed** dover stare a letto

**confinement** [kən'faɪnmənt] s confino; (childbirth) parto; (imprisonment) prigionia

**confirm** [kən'fʌrm] tr confermare; (eccl) cresimare

**confirmed** [kən'fʌrmd] adj (e.g., piece of news) confermato; (bachelor; drunkard) impenitente; inveterato; (e.g., invalid) cronico

**confiscate** ['kɑnfɪs,ket] tr confiscare

**conflagration** [,kɑnflə'greʃən] s conflagrazione

**conflict** ['kɑnflɪkt] s conflitto || [kən'flɪkt] intr lottare; essere in conflitto

**conflicting** [kən'flɪktɪŋ] adj contrastante; contraddittorio

**confluence** ['kɑnflu·əns] s confluenza

**conform** [kən'fɔrm] tr conformare || intr conformarsi

**conformi·ty** [kən'fɔrmɪti] s (-ties) conformità f; **in conformity with** in conformità di

**confound** [kɑn'faʊnd] tr confondere || ['kɑn'faʊnd] tr maledire; **confound it!** accidenti!

**confounded** [kɑn'faʊndɪd] or ['kɑn'faʊndɪd] adj maledetto; (hateful) odioso

**confront** [kən'frʌnt] tr affrontare, opporsi a; (to bring face to face) raffrontare; (to compare) confrontare

**confrontation** [,kɑnfrən'teʃən] s contestazione

**confuse** [kən'fjuz] tr confondere; **to get confused** confondersi

**confusion** [kən'fjuʒən] s confusione

**congeal** [kən'dʒil] *tr* congelare; coagulare || *intr* congelarsi; (*said, e.g., of blood*) coagularsi

**congenial** [kən'dʒinjəl] *adj* (*agreeable*) simpatico; (*having similar tastes*) affine; (*suited to one's needs or tastes*) congeniale

**congenital** [kən'dʒɛnɪtəl] *adj* congenito

**con'ger eel'** ['kaŋgər] *s* grongo

**congest** [kən'dʒɛst] *tr* congestionare || *intr* essere congestionato

**congestion** [kən'dʒɛstʃən] *s* congestione

**conglomerate** [kən'glamərɪt] *adj* & *s* conglomerato || [kən'glamə‚ret] *tr* conglomerare || *intr* conglomerarsi

**congratulate** [kən'grætʃə‚let] *tr* congratularsi con

**congratulation** [kən‚grætʃə'leʃən] *s* congratulazione, felicitazione

**congregate** ['kaŋgrɪ‚get] *intr* congregarsi

**congregation** [‚kaŋgrɪ'geʃən] *s* congregazione; fedeli *mpl* di una chiesa

**congress** ['kaŋgrɪs] *s* parlamento; congresso

**con'gress·man** *s* (**-men**) deputato al congresso degli S.U.

**con'gress·wom'an** *s* (**-wom'en**) deputatessa al congresso degli S.U.

**conical** ['kanɪkəl] *adj* conico

**conjecture** [kən'dʒɛktʃər] *s* congettura || *tr* & *intr* congetturare

**conjugate** ['kandʒə‚get] *tr* coniugare

**conjugation** [‚kandʒə'geʃən] *s* coniugazione

**conjunction** [kən'dʒʌŋkʃən] *s* congiunzione

**conjure** [kən'dʒur] *tr* (*to entreat*) scongiurare || ['kandʒər] or ['kʌndʒər] *tr* evocare, stregare; **to conjure up** evocare || *intr* fare delle stregonerie

**conk** [kaŋk] *intr*—**to conk out** (slang) essere in panna; (slang) svenire

**connect** [kə'nɛkt] *tr* connettere, unire || *intr* connettersi, essere associato; (*said of public conveyances*) operare in coincidenza

**connect'ing rod'** [kə'nɛktɪŋ] *s* (mach) biella

**connection** [kə'nɛkʃən] *s* connessione, unione, associazione; (*of trains*) coincidenza; (*relative*) parente *mf*; (*e.g., of a water pipe*) allacciamento; **in connection with** rispetto a

**con'ning tow'er** ['kanɪŋ] *s* (nav) torretta

**conniption** [kə'nɪpʃən] *s* (slang) attacco di rabbia

**connive** [kə'naɪv] *intr* essere connivente; **to connive at** chiudere un occhio su

**connote** [kə'not] *tr* indicare, suggerire

**conquer** ['kaŋkər] *tr* & *intr* conquistare

**conqueror** ['kaŋkərər] *s* conquistatore *m*

**conquest** ['kaŋkwɛst] *s* conquista

**conscience** ['kanʃəns] *s* coscienza; **in all conscience** a prezzo onesto; certamente

**conscientious** [‚kanʃɪ'ɛnʃəs] *adj* coscienzoso

**conscien'tious objec'tor** [əb'dʒɛktər] *s* obiettore *m* di coscienza

**conscious** ['kanʃəs] *adj* (*aware of one's existence*) cosciente; (*aware*) conscio, consapevole; (*lie*) consapevole; **to become conscious** riprendere i sensi

**consciousness** ['kanʃəsnɪs] *s* coscienza, conoscenza; **to lose consciousness** perdere la conoscenza

**conscript** ['kanskrɪpt] *s* coscritto || [kən'skrɪpt] *tr* coscrivere, arruolare

**conscription** [kən'skrɪpʃən] *s* coscrizione

**consecrate** ['kansɪ‚kret] *tr* consacrare

**consecutive** [kən'sɛkjətɪv] *adj* consecutivo; di seguito

**consensus** [kən'sɛnsəs] *s* consenso

**consent** [kən'sɛnt] *s* consenso; **by common consent** per comune consenso || *intr* consentire

**consequence** ['kansɪ‚kwɛns] *s* conseguenza

**consequential** [‚kansɪ'kwɛnʃəl] *adj* conseguente; importante, d'importanza; pomposo, pieno di sé

**consequently** ['kansɪ‚kwɛntli] *adv* conseguentemente, per conseguenza

**conservation** [‚kansər'veʃən] *s* conservazione; preservazione delle foreste

**conservatism** [kən'sʌrvə‚tɪzəm] *s* conservatorismo

**conservative** [kən'sʌrvətɪv] *adj* conservatore; (*cautious*) cauto; (*preserving*) conservativo; (*free from fads*) tradizionale || *s* conservatore *m*

**conserva·to·ry** [kən'sʌrvə‚tori] *s* (**-ries**) (*greenhouse*) serra; (mus) conservatorio

**conserve** [kən'sʌrv] *tr* conservare

**consider** [kən'sɪdər] *tr* considerare

**considerable** [kən'sɪdərəbəl] *adj* (*fairly large*) considerevole; (*worth thinking about*) considerabile

**considerate** [kən'sɪdərɪt] *adj* riguardoso, premuroso

**consideration** [kən‚sɪdə'reʃən] *s* considerazione; (*reason*) motivo; (*money*) pagamento; **in consideration of** a cagione di; in cambio di; **on no consideration** in nessuna maniera, mai; **under consideration** in considerazione, sotto esame; **without due consideration** senza riflessione, alla leggera

**considering** [kən'sɪdərɪŋ] *adv* tutto considerato || *prep* per, visto || *conj* considerando che, visto che

**consign** [kən'saɪn] *tr* consegnare; (*to send*) inviare; (*to set apart*) assegnare

**consignee** [‚kansaɪ'ni] *s* consegnatario

**consignment** [kən'saɪnmənt] *s* consegna; **on consignment** in consegna

**consist** [kən'sɪst] *intr*—**to consist in** consistere in; **to consist of** consistere in, constare di

**consisten·cy** [kən'sɪstənsi] *s* (**-cies**) (*firmness, amount of firmness*) consistenza; (*logical connection*) coerenza

**consistent** [kən'sɪstənt] *adj* (*holding firmly together*) consistente; (*agree-*

*ing with itself or oneself*) conseguente, coerente; compatibile

**consolation** [ˌkɑnsəˈleʃən] *s* consolazione

**console** [ˈkɑnsol] *s* (*table*) console *f;* (rad, telv) mobile *m;* (mus) console *f* ‖ [kənˈsol] *tr* consolare

**consonant** [ˈkɑnsənənt] *adj* consonante, armonioso; (gram) consonantico ‖ *s* consonante *f*

**consort** [ˈkɑnsɔrt] *s* consorte *mf* ‖ [kənˈsɔrt] *intr* associarsi; (*to agree*) concordarsi

**conspicuous** [kənˈspɪkju·əs] *adj* visibile, manifesto; notevole; (*too noticeable*) appariscente; **to make oneself conspicuous** farsi notare

**conspira·cy** [kənˈspɪrəsi] *s* (-cies) cospirazione, congiura

**conspire** [kənˈspaɪr] *intr* cospirare, congiurare; (*to act together*) cooperare

**constable** [ˈkɑnstəbəl] or [ˈkʌnstəbəl] *s* poliziotto; (*keeper of a castle*) conestabile *m*

**constancy** [ˈkɑnstənsi] *s* costanza

**constant** [ˈkɑnstənt] *adj & s* costante *f*

**constellation** [ˌkɑnstəˈleʃən] *s* costellazione

**constipate** [ˈkɑnstɪˌpet] *tr* costipare

**constipation** [ˌkɑnstɪˈpeʃən] *s* costipazione

**constituen·cy** [kənˈstɪtʃu·ənsi] *s* (-cies) (*voters*) elettorato; (*district*) circoscrizione elettorale

**constituent** [kənˈstɪtʃu·ənt] *adj* costituente ‖ *s* (*component*) parte *f* costituente; (*voter*) elettore *m;* (*of a chemical substance*) costituente *m*

**constitute** [ˈkɑnstɪˌtjut] or [ˈkɑnstɪˌtut] *tr* costituire

**constitution** [ˌkɑnstɪˈtjuʃən] or [ˌkɑnstɪˈtuʃən] *s* costituzione

**constrain** [kənˈstren] *tr* (*to force*) costringere; (*to restrain*) restringere, comprimere

**constrict** [kənˈstrɪkt] *tr* stringere, comprimere

**construct** [kənˈstrʌkt] *tr* costruire

**construction** [kənˈstrʌkʃən] *s* costruzione; (*meaning*) interpretazione

**construe** [kənˈstru] *tr* (*to interpret*) interpretare; (*to translate*) tradurre; (gram) analizzare

**consul** [ˈkɑnsəl] *s* console *m*

**consular** [ˈkɑnsələr] or [ˈkɑnsjələr] *adj* consolare

**consulate** [ˈkɑnsəlɪt] or [ˈkɑnsjəlɪt] *s* consolato

**consult** [kənˈsʌlt] *tr* consultare ‖ *intr* consultarsi

**consultation** [ˌkɑnsəlˈteʃən] *s* consultazione, conferenza

**consume** [kənˈsum] or [kənˈsjum] *tr* consumare; distruggere; **consumed with** (*passion*) arso di; (*curiosity*) assorbito da

**consumer** [kənˈsumər] or [kənˈsjumər] *s* consumatore *m*

**consum'er goods'** *spl* beni *mpl* di consumo

**consumerism** [kənˈsumərˌɪzem] *s* consumismo

**consummate** [kənˈsʌmɪt] *adj* consumato ‖ [ˈkɑnsəˌmet] *tr* consumare

**consumption** [kənˈsʌmpʃən] *s* (*decay*) consunzione; (*using up*) consumo; (pathol) consunzione

**consumptive** [kənˈsʌmptɪv] *adj* tubercolotico, tisico; (*wasteful*) logorante ‖ *s* tisico, etico

**contact** [ˈkɑntækt] *s* contatto; (elec) contatto; (elec) presa di corrente ‖ *tr* (coll) mettersi in contatto con ‖ *intr* (coll) mettersi in contatto

**con'tact break'er** *s* ruttore *m*

**con'tact lens'** *s* lente *f* a contatto

**contagion** [kənˈtedʒən] *s* contagio

**contagious** [kənˈtedʒəs] *adj* contagioso

**contain** [kənˈten] *tr* contenere; **to contain oneself** frenarsi

**container** [kənˈtenər] *s* recipiente *m*, contenitore *m*

**contaminate** [kənˈtæmɪˌnet] *tr* contaminare

**contamination** [kənˌtæmɪˈneʃən] *s* contaminazione

**contemplate** [ˈkɑntəmˌplet] *tr* contemplare; (*to think about*) meditare; (*to have in mind*) progettare, avere in mente ‖ *intr* meditare

**contemplation** [ˌkɑntəmˈpleʃən] *s* contemplazione; (*intention*) intenzione

**contemporaneous** [kənˌtempəˈreni·əs] *adj* contemporaneo, coevo

**contemporar·y** [kənˈtempəˌreri] *adj* contemporaneo, coevo ‖ *s* (-ies) contemporaneo

**contempt** [kənˈtempt] *s* (*despising*) disprezzo; (*condition of being despised*) dispregio; (*of the law*) disprezzo

**contemptible** [kənˈtemptɪbəl] *adj* disprezzabile, spregevole

**contempt' of court'** *s* (law) offesa alla magistratura, oltraggio al tribunale

**contemptuous** [kənˈtemptʃu·əs] *adj* sprezzante, sdegnoso

**contend** [kənˈtend] *tr* dichiarare ‖ *intr* (*to argue*) disputare, contendere; (*to fight*) lottare

**contender** [kənˈtendər] *s* competitore *m*, concorrente *m*

**content** [kənˈtent] *adj* contento; (*willing*) pronto ‖ *s* contentezza ‖ [ˈkɑntent] *s* contenuto; **contents** contenuto ‖ [kənˈtent] *tr* contentare

**contented** [kənˈtentɪd] *adj* soddisfatto

**contention** [kənˈtenʃən] *s* disputa, litigio; contenzione

**contentious** [kənˈtenʃəs] *adj* litigioso

**contentment** [kənˈtentmənt] *s* contentezza

**contest** [ˈkɑntest] *s* contesa, controversia; (*game*) gara ‖ [kənˈtest] *tr* disputare, contestare ‖ *intr* combattere, fare resistenza

**contestant** [kənˈtestənt] *s* concorrente *m;* (law) contendente *m*

**context** [ˈkɑntekst] *s* contesto

**contiguous** [kənˈtɪgju·əs] *adj* contiguo

**continence** [ˈkɑntɪnəns] *s* continenza

**continent** [ˈkɑntɪnənt] *adj & s* conti-

nente *m;* **on the Continent** nel continente europeo
**continental** [ˌkɑntɪ'nɛntəl] *adj & s*
continentale *mf*
**contingen·cy** [kən'tɪndʒənsi] *s* **(-cies)**
contingenza, congiuntura; *(chance)*
eventualità *f*
**contingent** [kən'tɪndʒənt] *adj* eventuale; imprevisto; (philos) contingente; **to be contingent upon** dipendere da
**continual** [kən'tɪnjʊ·əl] *adj* continuo
**continuance** [kən'tɪnjʊəns] *s* continua-
zione; *(in office)* permanenza; (law)
rinvio
**continue** [kən'tɪnjʊ] *tr* continuare; *(to
cause to remain)* mantenere; (law)
rinviare ‖ *intr* continuare; rimanere
**continui·ty** [ˌkɑntɪ'nju·ɪti] or [ˌkɑntɪ-
'nu·ɪti] *s* **(-ties)** continuità *f;* (mov &
telv) sceneggiatura; (rad) copione *m*
**continuous** [kən'tɪnjʊ·əs] *adj* continuo
**contin'uous show'ing** *s* (mov) spettacolo permanente
**contortion** [kən'tɔrʃən] *s* contorsione;
*(of facts)* distorsione
**contour** ['kɑntur] *s* contorno
**con'tour line'** *s* curva di livello, isoipsa
**contraband** ['kɑntrəˌbænd] *adj* di contrabbando ‖ *s* contrabbando
**contrabass** ['kɑntrəˌbes] *s* contrabasso
**contraceptive** [ˌkɑntrə'sɛptɪv] *adj & s*
antifecondativo
**contract** ['kɑntrækt] *s* contratto ‖
['kɑntrækt] or [kən'trækt] *tr (a
business deal)* contrattare; *(marriage)* contrarre ‖ *intr (to shrink)*
contrarsi; **to contract for** contrattare,
appaltare
**contraction** [kən'trækʃən] *s* contra-
zione
**contractor** [kən'træktər] *s (person who
makes a contract)* contraente *m;
(person who contracts to supply material)* appaltatore *m,* imprenditore
*m; (in building)* capomastro
**contradict** [ˌkɑntrə'dɪkt] *tr* contraddire
**contradiction** [ˌkɑntrə'dɪkʃən] *s* con-
traddizione
**contradictory** [ˌkɑntrə'dɪktəri] *adj*
contraddittorio
**contrail** ['kɑnˌtrel] *s* (aer) scia di condensazione
**contral·to** [kən'trælto] *s* **(-tos)** *(person)*
contralto *mf; (voice)* contralto *m*
**contraption** [kən'træpʃən] *s* (coll) aggeggio
**contra·ry** ['kɑntreri] *adj* contrario ‖
[kən'treri] *adj* ostinato, caparbio ‖
['kɑntreri] *s* **(-ries)** contrario; **on
the contrary** al contrario ‖ *adv* contrariamente
**contrast** ['kɑntræst] *s* contrasto ‖
[kən'træst] *tr* confrontare ‖ *intr*
contrastare
**contravene** [ˌkɑntrə'vin] *tr* contraddire; *(a law)* contravvenire (with
*dat)*
**contribute** [kən'trɪbjut] *tr* contribuire
‖ *intr* contribuire; *(to a newspaper)*
collaborare

**contribution** [ˌkɑntrɪ'bjuʃən] *s* contribuzione; *(to a newspaper)* collaborazione
**contributor** [kən'trɪbjutər] *s* contribu-
tore *m; (to a newspaper)* collaboratore *m*
**contrite** [kən'traɪt] *adj* contrito
**contrition** [kən'trɪʃən] *s* contrizione
**contrivance** [kən'traɪvəns] *s* dispositivo, congegno; *(faculty)* invenzione;
*(scheme)* artificio, piano
**contrive** [kən'traɪv] *tr* inventare; *(to
scheme up)* macchinare; *(to bring
about)* effettuare; **to contrive to** trovare il modo di
**con·trol** [kən'trol] *s* controllo; *(check)*
freno; **controls** comandi *mpl;* **to get
under control** riuscire a controllare ‖
*v (pret & pp* **-trolled;** *ger* **-trolling)** *tr*
controllare
**controller** [kən'trolər] *s* controllore *m;*
analista *mf* di gestione; economo;
(mach) regolatore *m;* (elec) interruttore *m* di linea
**control'ling in'terest** *s* maggioranza
delle azioni
**control' stick'** *s* leva di comando
**controversial** [ˌkɑntrə'vɑrʃəl] *adj* controverso, polemico, discusso
**controver·sy** ['kɑntrəˌvɑrsi] *s* **(-sies)**
controversia
**controvert** ['kɑntrəˌvɑrt] or [ˌkɑntrə-
'vɑrt] *tr* contraddire
**contumacious** [ˌkɑntjʊ'meʃəs] or
[ˌkɑntu'meʃəs] *adj* ribelle, contumace
**contuma·cy** ['kɑntjuməsi] or ['kɑn-
tuməsi] *s* **(-cies)** contumacia
**contusion** [kən'tjuʒən] or [kən'tuʒən]
*s* contusione
**conundrum** [kə'nʌndrəm] *s* indovinello
**convalesce** [ˌkɑnvə'lɛs] *intr* essere convalescente
**convalescence** [ˌkɑnvə'lɛsəns] *s* con-
valescenza
**convalescent** [ˌkɑnvə'lɛsənt] *adj & s*
convalescente *mf*
**con'vales'cent home'** *s* convalescenziario
**convene** [kən'vin] *tr* convocare ‖ *intr*
convenire
**convenience** [kən'vinjəns] *s* convenienza; *(comfort)* agio; *(anything
that saves work)* conforto; **at your
earliest convenience** quanto prima
**convenient** [kən'vinjənt] *adj* conveniente, adatto; comodo; **convenient
to** *(near)* (coll) vicino a
**convent** ['kɑnvɛnt] *s* convento di re-
ligiose
**convention** [kən'vɛnʃən] *s* convenzione,
assemblea; **conventions** *(customs)*
convenzioni *fpl*
**conventional** [kən'vɛnʃənəl] *adj* convenzionale
**converge** [kən'vɑrdʒ] *intr* convergere
**conversant** [kən'vɑrsənt] *adj* versato,
esperto, dotto
**conversation** [ˌkɑnvər'seʃən] *s* conversazione
**converse** ['kɑnvʌrs] *adj & s* contrario
‖ [kən'vʌrs] *intr* conversare

**conversion** [kən'vʌrʒən] *s* conversione; (*unlawful appropriation*) malversazione

**convert** ['kɑnvʌrt] *s* convertito ‖ [kən'vʌrt] *tr* convertire; misappropriare ‖ *intr* convertirsi

**convertible** [kən'vʌrtɪbəl] *adj & s* convertibile *f;* (aut) trasformabile *f*, decappottabile *f*

**convex** ['kɑnvɛks] or [kɑn'vɛks] *adj* convesso

**convey** [kən've] *tr* (*to carry*) trasportare; (*liquids*) convogliare; (*sounds*) trasmettere; (*to express*) esprimere; (*e.g., property*) trasferire

**conveyance** [kən've·əns] *s* trasporto; veicolo; comunicazione; (*of property*) trasferimento; (*deed*) titolo di proprietà

**convey'or belt'** [kən've·ər] *s* trasportatore *m*

**convict** ['kɑnvɪkt] *s* condannato ‖ [kən'vɪkt] *tr* convincere, condannare

**conviction** [kən'vɪkʃən] *s* condanna; (*belief*) convinzione, convincimento

**convince** [kən'vɪns] *tr* convincere

**convincing** [kən'vɪnsɪŋ] *adj* convincente

**convivial** [kən'vɪvɪ·əl] *adj* (*festive*) conviviale; gioviale, bonaccione

**convocation** [ˌkɑnvə'keʃən] *s* convocazione, assemblea

**convoke** [kən'vok] *tr* convocare

**convoy** ['kɑnvɔɪ] *s* (*of ships*) convoglio; (*of vehicles*) carovana ‖ *tr* convogliare

**convulse** [kən'vʌls] *tr* (*to shake*) scuotere; (*to throw into convulsions*) mettere in convulsioni; (*to cause to shake with laughter*) far torcere dalle risa

**coo** [ku] *intr* tubare, gemere

**cook** [kʊk] *s* cuoco ‖ *tr* cuocere; **to cook up** (coll) preparare, macchinare ‖ *intr* (*said of food*) cuocere; (*said of a person*) fare il cuoco

**cook'book'** *s* libro di cucina

**cookie** ['kʊki] *s* var of **cooky**

**cooking** ['kʊkɪŋ] *s* culinaria

**cook'out'** *s* picnic *m*, spuntino all'aperto

**cook'stove'** *s* cucina economica

**cook·y** ['kʊki] *s* (**-ies**) pasticcino, biscotto

**cool** [kul] *adj* fresco; calmo; (*not cordial*) freddo; (*bold*) sfacciato ‖ *s* fresco ‖ *tr* rinfrescare; **to cool one's heels** fare anticamera ‖ *intr* rinfrescarsi; **to cool off** rinfrescarsi; calmarsi

**coolant** ['kulənt] *s* miscela refrigerante

**cooler** ['kulər] *s* ghiacciaia; (slang) prigione

**cool'-head'ed** *adj* calmo, imperturbabile

**coolish** ['kulɪʃ] *adj* freschetto

**coon** [kun] *s* procione *m*

**coop** [kʊp] *s* pollaio; cconigliera; **to fly the coop** (slang) scapparsene ‖ *tr—* **to coop up** rinchiudere tra quattro mura

**cooper** ['kupər] *s* bottaio

**cooperate** [ko'ɑpəˌret] *intr* cooperare

**cooperation** [koˌɑpə're ʃən] *s* cooperazione

**cooperative** [ko'ɑpəˌretɪv] *adj* cooperativo ‖ *s* cooperativa

**coordinate** [ko'ɔrdɪnɪt] *adj* coordinato; (gram) coordinativo ‖ *s* (math) coordinata ‖ [ko'ɔrdɪˌnet] *tr & intr* coordinare

**coot** [kut] *s* (zool) folaga; (slang) vecchio pazzo

**cootie** ['kuti] *s* (slang) pidocchio

**cop** [kɑp] *s* (slang) poliziotto ‖ *v* (*pret & pp* **copped**; *ger* **copping**) *tr* (slang) rubare

**copartner** [ko'pɑrtnər] *s* consocio, socio

**cope** [kop] *intr—***to cope with** tener testa a

**cope'stone'** *s* pietra da cimasa

**copier** ['kɑpɪ·ər] *s* (*person*) copista *mf;* imitatore *m;* (*machine*) duplicatore *m*

**copilot** ['koˌpaɪlət] *s* copilota *mf*

**coping** ['kopɪŋ] *s* coronamento, cimasa

**cop'ing saw'** *s* seghetto da traforo

**copious** ['kopɪ·əs] *adj* copioso

**copper** [kɑp'ər] *s* rame *m;* (*coin*) soldo; (*boiler*) calderone *m;* (slang) poliziotto

**cop'per·head'** *s* vipera (*Ancistrodon contortrix*)

**cop'per·smith'** *s* battirame *m*, calderaio

**coppice** ['kɑpɪs] or **copse** [kɑps] *s* boschetto

**copulate** ['kɑpjəˌlet] *intr* copularsi, congiungersi carnalmente

**cop·y** ['kɑpi] *s* (**-ies**) copia; modello; manoscritto ‖ *v* (*pret & pp* **-ied**) *tr* copiare, imitare ‖ *intr* copiare; **to copy after** imitare

**cop'y·book'** *s* quaderno

**copyist** ['kɑpɪ·ɪst] *s* copista *mf;* imitatore *m*

**cop'y·right'** *s* copyright *m*, diritto di proprietà letteraria ‖ *tr* registrare; proteggere con copyright

**cop'y·writ'er** *s* copy-writer *m*, redattore *m* pubblicitario

**coquet·ry** ['kokətri] or [ko'ketri] *s* (**-ries**) civetteria

**coquette** [ko'ket] *s* civetta

**coquettish** [ko'ketɪʃ] *adj* civettuolo

**coral** ['kɑrəl] or ['kɔrəl] *adj* corallino ‖ *s* corallo

**cor'al reef'** *s* banco di coralli

**cord** [kɔrd] *s* corda, fune *f;* (*corduroy*) tessuto cordonato; (elec) cordone *m* ‖ *tr* legare con corda

**cordial** ['kɔrdʒəl] *adj & s* cordiale *m*

**corduroy** ['kɔrdəˌrɔɪ] *s* velluto a coste; **corduroys** pantaloni *mpl* alla cacciatora

**core** [kor] *s* (*of fruit*) torsolo; (*central part*) centro; (*of problem*) nocciolo; (*of earth*) barisfera, nucleo centrale; (phys) nucleo; **rotten to the core** guasto nelle ossa

**corespondent** [ˌkorɪs'pɑndənt] *s* coimputato in un processo di divorzio

**cork** [kɔrk] *s* (*bark*) sughero; (*stopper*) tappo, tappo di sughero ‖ *tr* tappare

**cork' oak'** *s* sughero

**cork'screw'** s cavatappi m
**cormorant** ['kɔrmərənt] s cormorano
**corn** [kɔrn] s granturco, mais m; (ker-nel) chicco; (thickening of skin) callo; (whiskey) whisky m di gran-turco; (Brit) grano; (Scot) avena; (slang) banalità f
**corn' bread'** s pane m di farina gialla
**corn' cake'** s omelette f di granturco
**corn'cob'** s tutolo
**corn'cob pipe'** s pipa fatta di un tutolo di pannocchia
**corn'crib'** s granaio per le pannocchie
**corn' cure'** s callifugo
**cornea** ['kɔrnɪ-ə] s cornea
**corner** ['kɔrnər] s angolo; (of street) cantonata; situazione difficile; (of the eye) coda dell'occhio; (com) acca-parramento, incetta, bagarinaggio; to cut corners tagliare le spese; to turn the corner passare il punto più peri-coloso || tr mettere in una situazione difficile; (the market) incettare, acca-parrare
**cor'ner cup'board** s cantoniera, arma-dio d'angolo
**cor'ner stone'** s pietra angolare; (of new building) prima pietra
**cornet** [kɔr'nɛt] s cornetta
**corn' exchange'** s borsa dei cereali
**corn'field'** s (in U.S.A.) campo di gran-turco; (in England) campo di grano; (in Scotland) campo di avena
**corn'flakes'** spl fiocchi mpl di granturco
**corn' flour'** s farina di granturco
**corn'flow'er** s fiordaliso
**corn'husk'** s brattea, cartoccio
**cornice** ['kɔrnɪs] s (of house) corni-cione m; (of room) cornice f
**corn' liq'uor** s whisky m di granturco
**corn' meal'** s farina di granturco
**corn' on the cob'** s granturco servito in pannocchia
**corn' plas'ter** s cerotto per i calli
**corn' silk'** s barba del granturco
**corn'stalk'** s fusto di granturco
**corn'starch'** s amido di granturco
**corn·y** ['kɔrnɪ] adj (-ier; -iest) (slang) banale, trito, triviale
**coronation** [ˌkɑrə'neʃən] or [ˌkɔrə-'neʃən] s incoronazione
**coroner** ['kɑrənər] or ['kɔrənər] s magistrato inquirente
**cor'oner's in'quest** s inchiesta giudi-ziaria dinanzi a giuria
**coronet** ['kɑrə ˌnɛt] or ['kɔrə ˌnɛt] s corona (non reale); diadema m
**corporal** ['kɔrpərəl] adj caporalesco || s caporale m
**corporation** [ˌkɔrpə'reʃən] s società anonima
**corps** [kor] s (corps [korz]) corpo
**corps' de bal'let** s corpo di ballo
**corpse** [kɔrps] s cadavere m
**corpulent** ['kɔrpjələnt] adj corpulento
**corpuscle** ['kɔrpəsəl] s (anat) globulo; (phys) corpuscolo
**cor·ral** [kə'ræl] s recinto per bestiame || v (pret & pp -ralled; ger -ralling) tr mettere in un recinto; catturrare
**correct** [kə'rɛkt] adj corretto || tr cor-reggere
**correction** [kə'rɛkʃən] s correzione

**corrective** [kə'rɛktɪv] adj & s corret-tivo
**correctness** [kə'rɛktnɪs] s correttezza
**correlate** ['kɑrə ˌlet] or ['kɔrə ˌlet] tr correlare || intr essere in correlazione
**correlation** [ˌkɑrə'leʃən] or [ˌkɔrə-'leʃən] s correlazione
**correspond** [ˌkɑrɪ'spɑnd] or [ˌkɔrɪ-'spɑnd] intr corrispondere
**correspondence** [ˌkɑrɪ'spɑndəns] or [ˌkɔrɪ'spɑndəns] s corrispondenza
**correspond'ence school'** s scuola per corrispondenza
**correspondent** [ˌkɑrɪ'spɑndənt] or [ˌkɔrɪ'spɑndənt] adj & s corrispon-dente mf
**corridor** ['kɑrɪdər] or ['kɔrɪdər] s corridoio
**corroborate** [kə'rɑbə ˌret] tr corrobo-rare
**corrode** [kə'rod] tr corrodere || intr corrodersi
**corrosion** [kə'roʒən] s corrosione
**corrosive** [kə'rosɪv] adj & s corrosivo
**corrugated** ['kɑrə ˌgetɪd] or ['kɔrə-ˌgetɪd] adj ondulato
**corrupt** [kə'rʌpt] adj corrotto || tr cor-rompere; (a language) imbarbarire || intr corrompersi
**corruption** [kə'rʌpʃən] s corruzione
**corsage** [kɔr'sɑʒ] s (bodice) corpetto; (bouquet) mazzolino di fiori da ap-puntarsi al vestito
**corsair** ['kɔr ˌser] s corsaro
**corset** ['kɔrsɪt] s corsetto
**Corsican** ['kɔrsɪkən] adj & s corso
**cortege** [kɔr'teʒ] s corteggio
**cor·tex** ['kɔr ˌtɛks] s (-tices [tɪ ˌsiz]) cortice f
**cortisone** ['kɔrtɪ ˌson] s cortisone m
**corvette** [kɔr'vɛt] s corvetta
**cosmetic** [kaz'mɛtɪk] adj & s cosme-tico
**cosmic** ['kazmɪk] adj cosmico
**cosmonaut** ['kazmə ˌnɔt] s cosmonauta mf
**cosmopolitan** [ˌkazmə'palɪtən] adj & s cosmopolita mf
**cosmos** ['kazməs] s cosmo
**cost** [kɔst] or [kast] s costo, prezzo; at all costs or at any cost ad ogni costo; costs (law) spese fpl proces-suali || v (pret & pp cost) intr costare
**cost·ly** ['kɔstli] or ['kastli] adj (-lier; -liest) costoso; (sumptuous) lussuoso
**cost' of liv'ing** s costo della vita
**costume** ['kastjum] or ['kastum] s costume m
**cos'tume ball'** s ballo in costume
**cos'tume jew'elry** s gioielli falsi
**cot** [kat] s (narrow bed) branda; (cot-tage) capanna, cabina
**coterie** ['kotəri] s gruppo; (clique) chiesuola
**cottage** ['katɪdʒ] s casetta, villino
**cot'tage cheese'** s ricotta americana
**cot'ter pin'** ['katər] s copiglia, coppi-glia
**cotton** ['katən] s cotone m || intr—to cotton up to (coll) cominciare a pro-vare della simpatia per; (coll) andare d'accordo con
**cot'ton can'dy** s zucchero filato

**cot'ton gin'** *s* sgranatrice *f*
**cot'ton pick'er** ['pɪkər] *s* chi raccoglie il cotone; macchina che raccoglie il cotone
**cot'tonseed oil'** *s* olio di semi di cotone
**cot'ton waste'** *s* cascame *m* di cotone
**cot'ton·wood'** *s* pioppo deltoide
**couch** [kautʃ] *s* canapè *m*, sofà *m*, divano ‖ *tr* esprimere
**couch' grass'** *s* gramigna
**cougar** ['kugər] *s* puma *m*
**cough** [kɔf] or [kaf] *s* tosse *f* ‖ *tr*—**to cough up** sputare, sputare tossendo; (slang) dare, pagare ‖ *intr* tossire
**cough' drop'** *s* pastiglia per la tosse
**cough' syr'up** *s* sciroppo per la tosse
**could** [kud] *v aux*—**I could not come yesterday** non ho potuto venire ieri; **I could not see you tomorrow** non potrei vederLa domani; **it could not be so** non potrebbe essere così
**council** ['kaunsəl] *s* consiglio; (eccl) concilio
**coun'cil·man** *s* (-men) consigliere *m* or assessore *m* municipale
**coun·sel** ['kaunsəl] *s* consiglio; (lawyer) avvocato; **to keep one's counsel** essere riservato; **to take counsel with** consultarsi con ‖ *v* (pret & pp -seled or -selled; ger -seling or -selling) *tr* consigliare ‖ *intr* consigliare; consigliarsi
**counselor** ['kaunsələr] *s* consigliere *m*; avvocato
**count** [kaunt] *s* conto; (nobleman) conte *m*; (law) capo d'accusa ‖ *tr* contare; **to count off by** (twos, threes) contare per (due, tre); **to count out** escludere; (boxing) contare ‖ *intr* contare; (to be worth) valere; **to count on** contare su
**count'down'** *s* conteggio alla rovescia
**countenance** ['kauntɪnəns] *s* espressione; (face) faccia; (approval) approvazione ‖ *tr* approvare, incoraggiare
**counter** ['kauntər] *adj* contrario ‖ *s* contatore *m*; (token) gettone *m*; (table in store) banco; (opposite) contrario ‖ *adv* contro, contrariamente ‖ *tr* contrariare, opporre ‖ *intr* (boxing) rispondere
**coun'ter·act'** *tr* contrariare, neutralizzare
**coun'ter·attack'** *s* contrattacco ‖ **coun'ter·attack'** *tr & intr* contrattaccare
**coun'ter·bal'ance** *s* contrappeso ‖ **coun'ter·bal'ance** *tr* controbilanciare
**coun'ter·clock'wise'** *adj* antiorario ‖ *adv* in senso antiorario
**coun'ter·es'pionage'** *s* controspionaggio
**counterfeit** ['kauntərfɪt] *adj* contraffatto ‖ *s* contraffazione; moneta falsa ‖ *tr & intr* contraffare
**counterfeiter** ['kauntər͵fɪtər] *s* contraffattore *m*
**coun'ter·feit mon'ey** *s* moneta falsa
**countermand** ['kauntər͵mænd] or ['kauntər͵mand] *tr* (troops) dare un contrordine a; (an order; a payment) cancellare

**coun'ter·march'** *s* contromarcia ‖ *intr* fare contromarcia
**coun'ter·offen'sive** *s* controffensiva
**coun'ter·pane'** *s* sopraccoperta
**coun'ter·part'** *s* copia; (person) sosia
**coun'ter·point'** *s* (mus) contrappunto; (mus) controcanto
**Coun'ter Reforma'tion** *s* controriforma
**coun'ter·rev'olu'tion** *s* controrivoluzione
**coun'ter·sign'** *s* (password) parola d'ordine; (signature) controfirma ‖ *tr* controfirmare
**coun'ter·sink'** *v* (pret & pp -sunk) *tr* incassare, accecare
**coun'ter·spy'** *s* (-spies) membro del controspionaggio
**coun'ter·stroke'** *s* contraccolpo
**coun'ter·weight'** *s* contrappeso
**countess** ['kauntɪs] *s* contessa
**countless** ['kauntlɪs] *adj* innumerevole
**countrified** ['kʌntrɪ͵faɪd] *adj* rustico, rurale
**coun·try** ['kʌntri] *s* (-tries) (land) terreno; (nation) paese *m*; (land of one's birth) patria; (rural region) campagna
**coun'try club'** *s* circolo privato sportivo situato nei sobborghi
**coun'try cous'in** *s* campagnolo
**coun'try estate'** *s* tenuta
**coun'try·folk'** *s* campagnoli *mpl*
**coun'try gen'tleman** *s* proprietario terriero, signorotto di campagna
**coun'try house'** *s* casa di campagna
**coun'try jake'** *s* (coll) zoticone *m*
**coun'try life'** *s* vita rustica
**coun'try·man** *s* (-men) paesano, compaesano
**coun'try·peo'ple** *s* gente *f* di campagna
**coun'try·side'** *s* campagna
**coun'try-wide'** *adj* nazionale
**coun'try·wom'an** *s* (-wom'en) *s* paesana, compaesana
**coun·ty** ['kaunti] *s* (-ties) contea, distretto
**coun'ty seat'** *s* capoluogo di contea
**coup** [ku] *s* colpo; colpo di stato
**coup de grâce** [ku də 'gras] *s* colpo di grazia
**coup d'état** [ku de'ta] *s* colpo di stato
**coupe** [kup] or **coupé** [ku'pe] *s* coupé *m*
**couple** ['kʌpəl] *s* (of people or animals) paio, coppia; (of things) paio; (link) unione ‖ *tr* accoppiare; (to link) unire, agganciare ‖ *intr* accoppiarsi
**couplet** ['kʌplɪt] *s* coppia di versi; (mus) couplet *m*
**coupling** ['kʌplɪŋ] *s* unione; (mach) giunto
**coupon** ['kupan] or ['kjupan] *s* coupon *m*, tagliando
**courage** ['kʌrɪdʒ] *s* coraggio; **to have the courage of one's convictions** avere il coraggio delle proprie opinioni
**courageous** [kə'redʒəs] *adj* coraggioso
**courier** ['kʌrɪ·ər] or ['kurɪ·ər] *s* corriere *m*
**course** [kors] *s* corso; (part of meal) portata; (place for games) campo;

(*row*) fila; **in due course** a tempo debito; **in the course of** durante, nel corso di; **of course** certamente, senza dubbio

**court** [kort] *s* (*uncovered place surrounded by walls*) corte *f*, cortile *m*; (*royal residence; courtship*) corte *f*; (*short street*) vicolo; (*playing area*) campo; (law) corte *f* || *tr* corteggiare; (*e.g., disaster*) andare in cerca di

**courteous** ['kʌrtɪ·əs] *adj* cortese

**courtesan** ['kʌrtɪzən] or ['kortɪzən] *s* cortigiana, meretrice *f*

**courte·sy** ['kʌrtɪsi] *s* (-**sies**) cortesia, gentilezza; **through the courtesy of** con il gentile permesso di

**court'house'** *s* palazzo di giustizia

**courtier** ['kortɪ·ər] *s* cortigiano

**court' jest'er** *s* buffone *m* di corte

**court·ly** ['kortli] *adj* (-**lier**; -**liest**) cortese, cortigiano; ossequioso

**court'-mar'tial** *s* (**courts-martial**) corte *f* marziale || *v* (*pret & pp* -**tialed** or -**tialled**; *ger* -**tialing** or -**tialling**) *tr* sottomettere a corte marziale

**court' plas'ter** *s* taffettà *m*

**court'room'** *s* aula di giustizia

**courtship** ['kortʃɪp] *s* corte *f*, corteggiamento

**court'yard'** *s* corte *f*, cortile *m*

**cousin** ['kʌzɪn] *s* cugino

**cove** [kov] *s* piccola baia, cala

**covenant** ['kʌvənənt] *s* convenzione, patto || *tr* promettere solennemente

**cover** ['kʌvər] *s* (*lid*) coperchio; (*tablecloth; shelter*) coperto; (*of book*) copertina; **to take cover** nascondersi; **under cover** in segreto, segretamente; **under cover of** sotto la protezione di; **under separate cover** in busta a parte, in plico a parte || *tr* coprire; puntare un'arma verso; (journ) riferire, riportare; **to cover up** coprire completamente || *intr* (*said of paint*) spandersi

**coverage** ['kʌvərɪdʒ] *s* copertura; (journ) servizio giornalistico; (rad, telv) raggio di udibilità

**coveralls** ['kʌvər‚ɔlz] *spl* tuta

**cov'er charge'** *s* coperto

**cov'ered wag'on** *s* carro coperto da tendone

**cov'er girl'** *s* ragazza-copertina

**covering** ['kʌvərɪŋ] *s* copertura; involucro

**covert** ['kʌvərt] *adj* nascosto, segreto

**cov'er-up'** *s* dissimulazione; sotterfugio

**covet** ['kʌvɪt] *tr* desiderare, agognare

**covetous** ['kʌvɪtəs] *adj* cupido

**covey** ['kʌvi] *s* covata

**cow** [kau] *s* vacca; (*of seal, elephant, etc.*) femmina || *tr* spaventare, intimidire

**coward** ['kau·ərd] *s* codardo, vile *m*

**cowardice** ['kau·ərdɪs] *s* codardia, viltà *f*

**cowardly** ['kau·ərdli] *adj* codardo, vile || *adv* vilmente

**cow'bell'** *s* campano, campanaccio

**cow'boy'** *s* cowboy *m*

**cow'catch'er** *s* (rr) cacciapietre *m*

**cower** ['kau·ər] *intr* rannicchiarsi

**cow'herd'** *s* guardiano d'armenti

**cow'hide'** *s* pelle *f* di vacca

**cowl** [kaul] *s* (*hood*) cappuccio; (*monk's cloak*) cappa; (*of car*) sostegno del cofano; (*of chimney*) cappello; (aer) cappottatura

**cow'lick'** *s* ritrosa

**cow'pox'** *s* (vet) vaiolo bovino

**coxcomb** ['kaks‚kom] *s* zerbinotto

**coxwain** ['kaksən] or ['kak‚swen] *s* timoniere *m*

**coy** [kɔɪ] *adj* timido, ritroso

**co·zy** ['kozi] *adj* (-**zier**; -**ziest**) comodo || *s* (-**zies**) copriteiera *m*

**C.P.A.** ['si'pi'e] *s* (letterword) (**certified public accountant**) esperto contabile

**crab** [kræb] *s* granchio; (aer) scarroccio; (*complaining person*) (coll) scontroso || *v* (*pret & pp* **crabbed**; *ger* **crabbing**) *intr* (coll) lamentarsi

**crab' apple'** *s* mela selvatica; (*tree*) melo selvatico

**crabbed** ['kræbɪd] *adj* sgarbato; (*handwriting*) da gallina; (*style*) oscuro, ermetico

**crab' louse'** *s* piattola

**crab·by** ['kræbi] *adj* (-**bier**; -**biest**) scontroso, sgarbato

**crack** [kræk] *adj* (slang) di prim'ordine, eccellente || *s* (*noise*) schiocco; (*break*) rottura, screpolatura, crepa; (*opening*) fessura; (slang) tentativo; (slang) barzelletta || *tr* (*e.g., a whip*) schioccare; (*to break*) rompere, screpolare; (*oil*) ridurre con distillazione; (coll) risolvere; (*a safe*) (slang) forzare; (*a joke*) (slang) dire; **cracked up to be** (slang) avendo fama di || *intr* (*to make a noise*) scricchiolare; (*to break*) rompersi, screpolarsi; (*said of voice*) diventare fesso; (slang) avere un esaurimento nervoso; **to crack down** (slang) essere severo; **to crack up** (slang) andare a pezzi

**cracked** [krækt] *adj* rotto, spezzato; (*voice*) fesso; (coll) pazzo

**cracker** ['krækər] *s* cracker *m*, galletta

**crack'er·bar'rel** *adj* in piccolo, alla buona

**crack'er·jack'** *adj* (slang) di prim'ordine || *s* (slang) persona di prim'ordine

**cracking** ['krækɪŋ] *s* piroscissione

**crackle** ['krækəl] *s* crepitio, crepito || *intr* crepitare

**crack'pot'** *adj & s* (coll) mattoide *mf*

**crack'-up'** *s* accidente *m*; collisione; (*breakdown in health or in relations*) (coll) colasso; (aer) accidente *m* d'atterraggio

**cradle** ['kredəl] *s* culla; (*of handset*) forcella || *tr* cullare

**crad'le·song'** *s* ninnananna

**craft** [kræft] or [kraft] *s* (*skill*) abilità *f*; (*trade*) mestiere *m*; (*guile*) astuzia, furberia; (*ship*) nave *f*; aeronave

**craftiness** ['kræftɪnɪs] or ['kraftɪnɪs] *s* astuzia, furberia

**crafts'man** *s* (-**men**) operaio specializzato, artigiano

**craft' un'ion** s artigianato, sindacato artigiano
**craft·y** ['kræfti] or ['krɑfti] adj (-ier; -iest) astuto, furbo
**crag** [kræg] s roccia scoscesa, rupe f
**cram** [kræm] v (pret & pp **crammed;** ger **cramming**) tr (to pack full) riempire fino all'orlo; (to stuff with food) rimpinzare || intr rimpinzarsi; (coll) preparare un esame alla svelta
**cramp** [kræmp] s (painful contraction) crampo; (bar with hooks) grappa; (fig) ostacolo || tr ostacolare, restringere
**cranber·ry** ['kræn‚bɛri] s (-ries) mirtillo
**crane** [kren] s (orn, mach) gru f; (boom) (telv, mov) giraffa || tr (one's neck) allungare || intr allungare il collo
**crani·um** ['krenɪ·əm] s (-a [ə]) cranio
**crank** [kræŋk] s manovella; (aut) alzacristalli m; (coll) eccentrico || tr girare con la manovella; mettere in moto con la manovella
**crank'case'** s coppa dell'olio, carter m
**crank'shaft'** s albero a gomito
**crank·y** ['kræŋki] adj (-ier; -iest) irritabile; eccentrico
**cran·ny** ['kræni] s (-nies) (crevice) crepaccio; (crack) fessura
**crape** [krep] s crespo
**crape'hang'er** s (slang) pessimista uggioso, guastafeste mf
**craps** [kræps] s gioco dei dadi; **to shoot craps** giocare ai dadi
**crash** [kræʃ] adj (coll) d'emergenza || s (noise) scoppio, schianto; accidente m; (collapse of business) crac m, rovescio; (bad landing) atterraggio senza carrello || tr fracassare; **to crash the gate** (coll) entrare senza invito || intr fracassarsi; (com) fallire; **to cash into** investire, cozzare contro; **to cash through** sfondare
**crash' dive'** s immersione rapida di un sottomarino
**crash' hel'met** s casco
**crass** [kræs] adj crasso
**crate** [kret] s gabbia d'imballaggio || tr imballare in una gabbia
**crater** ['kretər] s cratere m
**cravat** [krə'væt] s cravatta
**crave** [krev] tr anelare; (to beg) implorare || intr—**to crave for** desiderare ardentemente
**craven** ['krevən] adj & s codardo
**craving** ['krevɪŋ] s anelito, desiderio
**craw** [krɔ] s gozzo
**crawl** [krɔl] s strisciamento, avanzata striscioni; (sports) crawl m || intr strisciare, avanzare striscioni; (said of worms) brulicare; (said of insects) formicolare; (to feel creepy) sentirsi il formicolio
**crayfish** ['krefɪʃ] s (Palinurus vulgaris) aragosta; (Astacus; Cambarus) gambero
**crayon** ['kre·ən] s pastello; disegno a pastello || tr disegnare a pastello
**craze** [krez] s mania, moda || tr fare impazzire

**cra·zy** ['krezi] adj (-zier; -ziest) pazzo, matto; **to be crazy about** (coll) esser matto per; **to drive crazy** fare impazzire
**cra'zy bone'** s osso rabbioso (del gomito)
**creak** [krik] s scricchiolio, cigolio || intr scricchiolare, cigolare
**creak·y** ['kriki] adj (-ier; -iest) stridente, cigolante
**cream** [krim] s crema, panna; (finest part) fior fiore m || tr rendere di consistenza cremosa; (to remove cream from) scremare; prendere il meglio di
**creamer·y** ['kriməri] s (-ies) (factory) caseificio; (store) cremeria
**cream' puff'** s bignè m
**cream·y** ['krimi] adj (-ier; -iest) cremoso; butirroso
**crease** [kris] s piega, grinza || tr piegare, raggrinzire || intr piegarsi, raggrinzirsi, far pieghe
**crease'-resis'tant** adj antipiega
**create** [kri'et] tr creare
**creation** [kri'eʃən] s creazione; **the Creation** il creato
**creative** [kri'etɪv] adj creativo
**creator** [kri'etər] s creatore m
**creature** ['kritʃər] s creatura
**credence** ['kridəns] s credenza
**credentials** [krɪ'dɛnʃəlz] spl lettere fpl credenziali; documento d'autorizzazione
**credible** ['krɛdɪbəl] adj credibile
**credit** ['krɛdɪt] s credito; (in a school) unità f di promozione; (com) avere m; **credits** (mov, telv) titoli mpl di testa || tr accreditare; **to credit s.o. with s.th** attribuire qlco a qlcu
**creditable** ['krɛdɪtəbəl] adj lodevole
**cred'it card'** s carta di credito
**creditor** ['krɛdɪtər] s creditore m
**cre·do** ['krido] or ['kredo] s (-dos) credo
**credulous** ['krɛdʒələs] adj credulo
**creed** [krid] s credo
**creek** [krik] s fiumicello
**creep** [krip] v (pret & pp **crept** [krɛpt]) intr strisciare, avanzare striscioni; (to grow along a wall) arrampicarsi; (to feel creepy) sentirsi il formicolio
**creeper** ['kripər] s strisciante m; (plant) rampicante f
**creeping** ['kripɪŋ] adj lento; (plant) rampicante
**cremate** ['krimet] tr cremare
**cremato·ry** ['krimə‚tori] adj crematorio || s (-ries) forno crematorio
**Creole** ['kri·ol] adj & s creolo
**crescent** ['krɛsənt] s (of Islam) mezzaluna; (of moon) crescente m; (roll) cornetto
**cress** [krɛs] s crescione m
**crest** [krɛst] s cresta; (heral) stemma m, insegna
**crestfallen** ['krɛst‚fɔlən] adj depresso
**Cretan** ['kritən] adj & s cretese mf
**cretin** ['kritən] s cretino
**crevice** ['krɛvɪs] s fessura, fenditura
**crew** [kru] s (group working together) personale m; (group of workmen;

*mob*) ciurma; (*of a ship or racing boat*) equipaggio; (sports) canottaggio

**crew' cut'** *s* capelli *mpl* a spazzola

**crib** [krɪb] *s* (*bed*) lettino; (*rack*) rastrelliera; (*building*) capanna, granaio; (coll) bigino ‖ *v* (*pret & pp* **cribbed**) *ger* **cribbing**) *tr* (coll) usare un bigino in ‖ *intr* (coll) usare un bigino; (coll) commettere un plagio

**cricket** [ˈkrɪkɪt] *s* grillo; (sports) cricket *m*, palla a spatola

**crier** [ˈkraɪ·ər] *s* banditore *m*

**crime** [kraɪm] *s* delitto, crimine *m*

**criminal** [ˈkrɪmɪnəl] *adj* criminale; (*code*) penale ‖ *s* delinquente *mf*

**crimp** [krɪmp] *s* piega, pieghettatura; **to put a crimp in** (slang) mettere i bastoni fra le ruote a ‖ *tr* pieghettare; (*the hair*) arricciare

**crimson** [ˈkrɪmzən] *adj & s* cremisi *m* ‖ *intr* imporporarsi

**cringe** [krɪndʒ] *intr* rannicchiarsi; (*to fawn*) umiliarsi

**crinkle** [ˈkrɪŋkəl] *tr* arricciare ‖ *intr* (*to rustle*) sfrusciare

**cripple** [ˈkrɪpəl] *s* zoppo, sciancato ‖ *tr* storpiare; (*e.g., business*) paralizzare

**cri·sis** [ˈkraɪsɪs] *s* (**-ses** [siz]) crisi *f*

**crisp** [krɪsp] *adj* (*brittle*) croccante, friabile; (*air*) frizzante; (*sharp and clear*) acuto

**criteri·on** [kraɪˈtɪrɪ·ən] *s* (**-a** [ə] or **-ons**) criterio

**critic** [ˈkrɪtɪk] *s* critico

**critical** [ˈkrɪtɪkəl] *adj* critico

**criticism** [ˈkrɪtɪˌsɪzəm] *s* critica

**criticize** [ˈkrɪtɪˌsaɪz] *tr & intr* criticare

**critique** [krɪˈtik] *s* critica

**croak** [krok] *s* (*of frogs*) gracidio; (*of crows*) gracchiamento ‖ *intr* gracidare; gracchiare; (slang) crepare

**Croat** [ˈkro·æt] *s* croato

**Croatian** [kroˈeʃən] *adj & s* croato

**cro·chet** [kroˈʃe] *s* lavoro all'uncinetto ‖ *v* (*pret & pp* **-cheted** [ˈʃed]) *ger* **-cheting** [ˈʃe·ɪŋ]) *tr & intr* lavorare all'uncinetto

**crock** [krak] *s* vaso di terracotta, giara, orcio

**crockery** [ˈkrakəri] *s* vasellame *m* di terracotta, terracotta

**crocodile** [ˈkrakəˌdaɪl] *s* coccodrillo

**croc'odile tears'** *spl* lacrime *fpl* di coccodrillo

**crocus** [ˈkrokəs] *s* croco

**crone** [kron] *s* vecchia incartapecorita

**cro·ny** [ˈkroni] *s* (**-nies**) amicone *m*, compare *m*

**crook** [kruk] *s* (*hook*) uncino; (*staff*) pastorale *m*; (*bend*) curva; (*bend of pipe*) gomito; (coll) imbroglione *m* ‖ *tr* piegare ‖ *intr* piegarsi

**crooked** [ˈkrukɪd] *adj* uncinato; curvo, piegato; (coll) disonesto

**croon** [krun] *intr* canterellare; cantare in modo sentimentale

**crop** [krap] *s* (*of bird*) gozzo; (*agricultural product, growing or harvested*) messe *f*; (*agricultural product harvested*) raccolto; (*riding whip*) fru-

stino; (*hair cut close*) capelli corti; gruppo ‖ *v* (*pret & pp* **cropped**) *ger* **cropping**) *tr* (*to cut the ends off of*) spuntare; (*to reap*) raccogliere; (*to cut short*) tosare ‖ *intr*—**to crop out** or **up** apparire inaspettatamente

**crop'-dust'ing** *s* fumigazione aerea

**cropper** [ˈkrapər] *s* mietitore *m*; (*sharecropper*) mezzadro; **to come a cropper** (coll) fare una cascataccia; (coll) andare in rovina

**croquet** [kroˈke] *s* croquet *m*, pallamaglio *m & f*

**croquette** [kroˈket] *s* crocchetta

**crosier** [ˈkroʒər] *s* pastorale *m*

**cross** [krɔs] or [kras] *adj* trasversale, contrario, obliquo; (*irritable*) bisbetico, di cattivo umore; (*of mixed breed*) incrociato ‖ *s* croce *f*; (*crossing of breeds*) incrocio; **to take the cross** farsi crociato ‖ *tr* crociare, segnare con una croce; (*the street*) attraversare; (*e.g., the legs*) incrociare; (*to draw a line across*) barrare; (*to thwart*) ostacolare; **to cross oneself** farsi il segno della croce; **to cross one's mind** venire in mente a uno; **to cross out** cancellare ‖ *intr* incrociarsi

**cross'bones'** *spl* teschio e tibie incrociate (*simbolo della morte*)

**cross'bow'** *s* balestra

**cross'breed'** *v* (*pret & pp* **-bred** [ˌbred]) *tr* incrociare, ibridare

**cross'-coun'try** *adj* campestre; attraverso il paese

**cross'-examina'tion** *s* (law) confronto, interrogatorio in contraddittorio

**cross-eyed** [ˈkrɔsˌaɪd] or [ˈkrasˌaɪd] *adj* guercio, strabico

**crossing** [ˈkrɔsɪŋ] or [ˈkrasɪŋ] *s* incrocio; ostacolo; (*of the sea*) traversata; (*of a river*) guado; (rr) passaggio a livello

**cross'patch'** *s* (coll) bisbetico

**cross'piece'** *s* traversa

**cross' ref'erence** *s* richiamo, rimando

**cross'road'** *s* strada trasversale; **at the crossroads** al bivio; **crossroads** crocicchio

**cross' sec'tion** *s* sezione trasversale

**cross' street'** *s* traversa

**cross' talk'** *s* conversazione; (telp) diafonia

**cross'word puz'zle** *s* cruciverba *m*, parole incrociate

**crotch** [kratʃ] *s* inforcatura; (*of pants*) cavallo

**crotchety** [ˈkratʃɪti] *adj* bisbetico

**crouch** [krautʃ] *intr* accoccolarsi

**croup** [krup] *s* (pathol) crup *m*

**crouton** [ˈkrutan] *s* crostino

**crow** [kro] *s* corvo, cornacchia; (*cry of rooster*) chicchirichì *m*; **as the crow flies** in linea retta, a volo d'uccello; **to eat crow** (coll) rimangiarsi le parole ‖ *intr* fare chicchirichì; **to crow over** vantarsi di, esultare per

**crow'bar'** *s* bastone *m* a leva

**crowd** [kraud] *s* folla; (*common people*) masse *fpl*; (coll) gruppo ‖ *tr* affollare; (*to push*) spingere ‖ *intr* affollarsi; (*to press forward*) spingersi

**crowded** ['kraʊdɪd] *adj* affollato

**crown** [kraʊn] *s* corona; (*of hat*) cupola; (*highest point*) sommo ‖ *tr* coronare; (*checkers*) damare; **to crown s.o.** (coll) battere qlcu sulla testa

**crown' prince'** *s* principe ereditario

**crown' prin'cess** *s* principessa ereditaria

**crow's'-foot'** *s* (**-feet**) zampa di gallina

**crow's'-nest'** *s* coffa, gabbia

**crucial** ['kruʃəl] *adj* cruciale, critico

**crucible** ['krusɪbəl] *s* crogiolo

**crucifix** ['krusɪfɪks] *s* crocefisso

**crucifixion** [,krusɪ'fɪkʃən] *s* crocifissione

**cruci·fy** ['krusɪ,faɪ] *v* (*pret & pp* **-fied**) *tr* crocifiggere

**crude** [krud] *adj* (*raw*) grezzo; (*unripe*) acerbo; (*roughly made; uncultured*) rozzo

**crudi·ty** ['krudɪti] *s* (**-ties**) rozzezza

**cruel** ['kru·əl] *adj* crudele

**cruel·ty** ['kru·əlti] *s* (**-ties**) crudeltà *f*

**cruet** ['kru·ɪt] *s* oliera

**cruise** [kruz] *s* crociera ‖ *tr* navigare ‖ *intr* andare in crociera; andare avanti e indietro

**cruiser** ['kruzər] *s* (nav) incrociatore *m*

**cruising** ['kruzɪŋ] *adj* di crociera

**cruis'ing ra'dius** *s* autonomia di crociera

**cruller** ['krʌlər] *s* frittella

**crumb** [krʌm] *s* briciola ‖ *tr* sbriciolare; (*e.g., a cutlet*) impannare ‖ *intr* sbriciolarsi

**crumble** ['krʌmbəl] *tr* sbriciolare, polverizzare ‖ *intr* andare a pezzi, polverizzarsi, sbriciolarsi

**crum·my** ['krʌmi] *adj* (**-mier; -miest**) (slang) sporco; (*miserable*) (slang) schifoso; (*e.g., joke*) (slang) povero

**crumple** ['krʌmpəl] *tr* sgualcire, spiegazzare; **to crumple into a ball** appallottolare ‖ *intr* spiegazzarsi

**crunch** [krʌntʃ] *s* crocchio; (coll) stretta, morsa ‖ *tr* sgranocchiare ‖ *intr* crocchiare

**crusade** [kru'sed] *s* crociata ‖ *intr* crociarsi; (*to take up a cause*) farsi paladino

**crusader** [kru'sedər] *s* crociato; (*of a cause*) paladino

**crush** [krʌʃ] *s* pigiatura, schiacciatura; (*crowd*) calca; (coll) infatuazione ‖ *tr* schiacciare; (*to grind*) frantumare; (*to subdue*) sottomettere; (*to extract by squeezing*) pigiare

**crust** [krʌst] *s* crosta; (slang) faccia tosta ‖ *tr* incrostare ‖ *intr* incrostare, incrostarsi

**crustacean** [krʌs'teʃən] *s* crostaceo

**crust·y** ['krʌsti] *adj* (**-ier; -iest**) crostoso; duro; rude

**crutch** [krʌtʃ] *s* gruccia, stampella; (fig) sostegno

**crux** [krʌks] *s* difficoltà *f*, busillis *m;* (*crucial point*) punto cruciale

**cry** [kraɪ] *s* (**cries**) (*shout*) grido; (*fit of weeping*) pianto; (*entreaty*) richiamo; (*of animal*) urlo; **a far cry** ben lontano, ben distinto; **to have a good cry** sfogarsi, piangere a calde lacrime ‖ *tr* gridare; (*to proclaim*) bandire; **to cry down** disprezzare; **to cry one's heart out** piangere a calde lacrime; **to cry out** proclamare; **to cry up** elogiare ‖ *intr* gridare, urlare; piangere; **to cry for** implorare

**cry'ba'by** *s* (**-bies**) piagnucolone *m*

**crypt** [krɪpt] *s* cripta

**cryptic(al)** ['krɪptɪk(əl)] *adj* segreto, occulto, misterioso

**crystal** ['krɪstəl] *s* cristallo

**crys'tal ball'** *s* globo di cristallo

**crystalline** ['krɪstəlɪn] or ['krɪstə,laɪn] *adj* cristallino

**crystallize** ['krɪstə,laɪz] *tr* cristallizzare ‖ *intr* cristallizzarsi

**cub** [kʌb] *s* cucciolo; (*of lion*) leoncino; (*of fox*) volpicino, volpacchiotto

**cubbyhole** ['kʌbɪ,hol] *s* sgabuzzino, bugigattolo

**cube** [kjub] *adj* cubico ‖ *s* cubo; (*of sugar*) zolla ‖ *tr* elevare al cubo; (*to shape*) tagliare in quadretti

**cubic** ['kjubɪk] *adj* cubico

**cub' report'er** *s* giornalista novello

**cuckold** ['kʌkəld] *adj & s* cornuto, becco ‖ *tr* cornificare

**cuckoo** ['kuku] *adj* (slang) pazzo ‖ *s* cuculo

**cuck'oo clock'** *s* orologio a cucù

**cucumber** ['kjukʌmbər] *s* cetriolo

**cud** [kʌd] *s* mangime masticato; **to chew the cud** ruminare

**cuddle** ['kʌdəl] *tr* abbracciare affettuosamente ‖ *intr* (*to lie close*) giacere vicino; (*to curl up*) rannicchiarsi, raggomitolarsi

**cudg·el** ['kʌdʒəl] *s* manganello, randello; **to take up the cudgels for** farsi paladino di ‖ *v* (*pret & pp* **-eled** or **-elled;** *ger* **-eling** or **-elling**) *tr* bastonare, randellare; **to cudgel one's brains** rompersi la testa

**cue** [kju] *s* suggerimento, imbeccata; (billiards) stecca; **to miss a cue** (theat) mancare la battuta; (coll) non capire l'antifona ‖ *tr*—**to cue s.o. (in) on** (coll) dare a qlcu informazioni su

**cuff** [kʌf] *s* (*of shirt*) polsino; (*of trousers*) risvolto; (*slap*) schiaffo ‖ *tr* schiaffeggiare

**cuff' links'** *spl* bottoni doppi, gemelli *mpl*

**cuirass** [kwɪ'ræs] *s* corazza

**cuisine** [kwɪ'zin] *s* cucina

**culinary** ['kjulɪ,neri] *adj* culinario

**cull** [kʌl] *s* scarto ‖ *tr* (*to gather, pluck*) cogliere; selezionare, scegliere

**culminate** ['kʌlmɪ,net] *intr* culminare

**culottes** [ku'lɑts] *spl* gonna pantalone

**culpable** ['kʌlpəbəl] *adj* colpevole

**culprit** ['kʌlprɪt] *s* colpevole *m*, imputato

**cult** [kʌlt] *s* culto

**cultivate** ['kʌltɪ,vet] *tr* coltivare

**cultivated** ['kʌltɪ ,vetɪd] *adj* colto, coltivato

**cultivation** [ ,kʌltɪ've∫ən] *s* coltivazione, cultura

**culture** ['kʌlt∫ər] *s* cultura

**cultured** ['kʌlt∫ərd] *adj* colto

**cul'tured pearl'** *s* perla coltivata

**culvert** ['kʌlvərt] *s* chiavica

**cumbersome** ['kʌmbərsəm] *adj* ingombrante, incomodo; (*clumsy*) goffo

**cumulative** ['kjumjə,letɪv] *adj* cumulativo

**cunning** ['kʌnɪŋ] *adj* (*sly*) astuto; (*skillful*) abile; (*pretty*) bello; (*created with skill*) ben fatto, fine || *s* astuzia; abilità *f*, destrezza

**cup** [kʌp] *s* tazza; (mach, sports) coppa; (eccl) calice *m;* **in one's cups** ubriaco || *v* (*pret & pp* **cupped;** *ger* **cupping**) *tr* mettere ventose a; **to cup one's hands** foggiare le mani a mo' di conca

**cupboard** ['kʌbərd] *s* armadio a muro, dispensa; (*buffet*) credenza

**Cupid** ['kjupɪd] *s* Cupido

**cupidity** [kju'pɪdɪti] *s* cupidigia

**cup' of tea'** *s* tazza di tè; (coll) forte *m,* e.g., **physics is not my cup of tea** la fisica non è il mio forte

**cupola** ['kjupələ] *s* cupola

**cur** [kʌr] *s* cane bastardo; (*despicable fellow*) canaglia, gaglioffo

**curate** ['kjurɪt] *s* curato

**curative** ['kjurətɪv] *adj* curativo

**curator** [kju'retər] *s* conservatore *m*

**curb** [kʌrb] *s* (*of bit*) barbazzale *m;* (*of pavement*) orlo del marciapiede; (*check*) freno || *tr* frenare

**curb'stone'** *s* cordone *m;* (*of well*) sponda del pozzo

**curd** [kʌrd] *s* cagliata || *tr* cagliare || *intr* cagliarsi

**curdle** ['kʌrdəl] *tr* cagliare; (*the blood*) far gelare || *intr* cagliarsi; (*said of custard*) impazzare

**cure** [kjur] *s* cura || *tr* curare; (*e.g., meat*) conservare; (*wood*) stagionare

**cure'-all'** *s* panacea

**curfew** ['kʌrfju] *s* coprifuoco

**curi·o** ['kjurɪ,o] *s* (**-os**) curiosità *f*

**curiosi·ty** [ ,kjurɪ'ɑsɪti] *s* (**-ties**) curiosità *f*

**curious** ['kjurɪ·əs] *adj* curioso

**curl** [kʌrl] *s* (*of hair*) ricciolo; (*anything curled*) rotolo, spirale *f* || *tr* arricciare; arrotolare; (*the lips*) torcere || *intr* arricciarsi; arrotolarsi; **to curl up** raggomitolarsi

**curlicue** ['kʌrlɪ ,kju] *s* ghirigoro

**curl'ing i'ron** *s* ferro da arricciare

**curl'pa'per** *s* bigodino

**curl·y** ['kʌrli] *adj* (**-ier; -iest**) ricciuto

**curmudgeon** [kər'mʌdʒən] *s* bisbetico

**currant** ['kʌrənt] *s* (*seedless raisin*) uva passa di Corinto, uva sultanina; (*shrub and berry of genus Ribes*) ribes *m*

**curren·cy** ['kʌrənsi] *s* (**-cies**) (*circulation*) circolazione; (*money*) denaro circolante; (*general use*) corso

**current** ['kʌrənt] *adj & s* corrente *f*

**cur'rent account'** *s* conto corrente

**cur'rent events'** *spl* attualità *fpl,* eventi *mpl* correnti

**curricu·lum** [kə'rɪkjələm] *s* (**-lums** or **-la** [lə]) programma *m;* piano educativo

**cur·ry** ['kʌri] *s* (**-ries**) (*spice*) curry *m* || *v* (*pret & pp* **-ried**) *tr* (*a horse*) strigliare; (*leather*) conciare; **to curry favor** cercare di compiacere

**cur'ry·comb'** *s* striglia || *tr* strigliare

**curse** [kʌrs] *s* maledizione; bestemmia || *tr* maledire || *intr* imprecare, bestemmiare

**cursed** ['kʌrsɪd] or [kʌrst] *adj* maledetto; (*hateful*) odiato

**cursive** ['kʌrsɪv] *adj & s* corsivo

**cursory** ['kʌrsəri] *adj* rapido, superficiale

**curt** [kʌrt] *adj* (*rude*) brusco, sgarbato; (*short*) breve, conciso

**curtail** [kər'tel] *tr* ridurre, restringere

**curtain** ['kʌrtən] *s* (*in front of stage*) sipario; (*for window*) tendina; (fig) cortina || *tr* coprire con tenda; separare con tenda; coprire, nascondere

**cur'tain call'** *s* (theat) chiamata

**cur'tain rais'er** ['rezər] *s* (theat) avanspettacolo; (sports) incontro preliminare

**cur'tain ring'** *s* campanella

**cur'tain rod'** *s* bastone *m* su cui si fissano le tende

**curt·sy** ['kʌrtsi] *s* (**-sies**) riverenza, inchino || *v* (*pret & pp* **-sied**) *intr* fare la riverenza, inchinarsi

**curve** [kʌrv] *s* curva || *tr* curvare || *intr* curvarsi

**curved** [kʌrvd] *adj* curvo, curvato

**cushion** ['ku∫ən] *s* cuscino; (*of billiard table*) mattonella || *tr* proteggere, ammortizzare, attutire

**cuspidor** ['kʌspɪ ,dɔr] *s* sputacchiera

**cuss** [kʌs] *s* (coll) bestemmia; (coll) tipo perverso || *tr* maledire || *intr* bestemmiare

**custard** ['kʌstərd] *s* crema

**custodian** [kəs'todɪ·ən] *s* (*caretaker*) custode *m,* guardiano *m;* (*person who is entrusted with s.th*) conservatore *m;* (*janitor of school*) bidello

**custo·dy** ['kʌstədi] *s* (**-dies**) custodia; (*imprisonment*) arresto; **in custody** in prigione; **to take into custody** arrestare

**custom** ['kʌstəm] *s* costume *m;* (*customers*) clientela; **customs** dogana; diritti *mpl* doganali

**customary** ['kʌstə ,meri] *adj* consueto, abituale

**custom-built** ['kʌstəm'bɪlt] *adj* fatto su misura; (*car*) fuori serie

**customer** ['kʌstəmər] *s* cliente *mf*

**cus'tom·house'** *adj* doganale || *s* dogana

**custom-made** ['kʌstəm'med] *adj* fatto su misura

**cus'toms inspec'tion** *s* visita doganale

**cus'toms of'ficer** *s* doganiere *m*

**cus'tom work'** *s* lavoro fatto su misura

**cut** [kʌt] *adj* (*prices*) ridotto; **to be cut out for** essere tagliato per || *s* taglio; (*reduction*) ribasso; (typ) cliché *m;*

(*snub*) (coll) affronto; (coll) assenza non autorizzata; (coll) parte *f;* **a cut above** (coll) un po' meglio di ‖ *tr* tagliare; (*cards*) alzare; (*prices*) ridurre; (coll) far finta di non riconoscere; (coll) marinare; **cut it out!** basta!; **to cut back** ridurre; **to cut off** tagliare; diseredare; (surg) amputare; **to cut short** interrompere; **to cut teeth** fare i denti; **to cut up** sminuzzare; criticare ‖ *intr* tagliare, tagliarsi; **to cut across** attraversare; **to cut in** interrompere; **to cut under** vendere sottoprezzo; **to cut up** (slang) fare il pagliaccio

**cut-and-dried** ['kʌtən'draɪd] *adj* monotono, stantio; bell'e fatto, fatto in anticipo

**cutaneous** [kju'tenɪ·əs] *adj* cutaneo

**cut'away' coat'** ['kʌtə,we] *s* marsina da giorno

**cut'back'** *s* riduzione; eliminazione; (mov) ritorno dell'azione a un'epoca anteriore

**cute** [kjut] *adj* (coll) carino, grazioso; (*shrewd*) (coll) furbo

**cut' glass'** *s* cristallo intagliato

**cuticle** ['kjutɪkəl] *s* cuticola

**cutlass** ['kʌtləs] *s* sciabola

**cutler** ['kʌtlər] *s* coltellinaio

**cutlery** ['kʌtləri] *s* coltelleria

**cutlet** ['kʌtlɪt] *s* cotoletta; (*flat croquette*) polpetta

**cut'off'** *s* taglio; (*road*) scorciatoia; (*of cylinder*) otturatore *m*, chiusura dell'ammissione; (*of river*) braccio diretto

**cut'out'** *s* ritaglio; (aut) valvola di scappamento libero

**cut'-rate'** *adj* a prezzo ridotto

**cutter** ['kʌtər] *s* tagliatore *m;* (naut) cutter *m*

**cut'throat'** *adj* spietato; (*relentless*) senza posa ‖ *s* assassino

**cutting** ['kʌtɪŋ] *adj* tagliente ‖ *s* taglio; (*from a newspaper*) ritaglio;

(*e.g., of prices*) riduzione; (hort) talea

**cut'ting board'** *s* tagliere *m;* (*of dishwasher*) piano d'appoggio

**cut'ting edge'** *s* taglio

**cuttlefish** ['kʌtəl,fɪʃ] *s* seppia

**cut'wat'er** *s* (*of bridge*) tagliacque *m;* (*of boat*) tagliamare *m*

**cyanamide** [saɪ'ænə,maɪd] *s* cianamide *f;* cianamide *f* di calcio

**cyanide** ['saɪ·ə,naɪd] *s* cianuro

**cycle** ['saɪkəl] *s* ciclo; bicicletta; (*of internal combustion engine*) tempo; (phys) periodo ‖ *intr* andare in bicicletta

**cyclic(al)** ['saɪklɪk(əl)] or ['sɪklɪk(əl)] *adj* ciclico

**cyclone** ['saɪklon] *s* ciclone *m*

**cyclops** ['saɪklɑps] *s* ciclope *m*

**cyclotron** ['saɪklo,trɑn] or ['sɪklo-,trɑn] *s* ciclotrone *m*

**cylinder** ['sɪlɪndər] *s* cilindro; (*container*) bombola

**cyl'inder block'** *s* monoblocco

**cyl'inder bore'** *s* alesaggio

**cyl'inder head'** *s* testa

**cylindric(al)** [sɪ'lɪndrɪk(əl)] *adj* cilindrico

**cymbals** ['sɪmbəls] *spl* piatti *mpl*

**cynic** ['sɪnɪk] *adj & s* cinico

**cynical** ['sɪnɪkəl] *adj* cinico

**cynicism** ['sɪnɪ,sɪzəm] *s* cinismo

**cynosure** ['saɪnə,ʃur] or ['sɪnə,ʃur] *s* centro dell'attenzione

**cypress** ['saɪprəs] *s* cipresso

**Cyprus** ['saɪprəs] *s* Cipro

**Cyrus** ['saɪrəs] *s* Ciro

**cyst** [sɪst] *s* ciste *f*, cisti *f*

**czar** [zɑr] *s* zar *m*

**czarina** [zɑ'rinə] *s* zarina

**Czech** [tʃɛk] *adj & s* ceco

**Czecho-Slovak** ['tʃɛko'slovæk] *adj & s* cecoslovacco

**Czecho-Slovakia** [,tʃɛkoslo'vækɪ·ə] *s* la Cecoslovacchia

# D

**D, d** [di] *s* quarta lettera dell'alfabeto inglese

**dab** [dæb] *s* tocco; (*of mud*) schizzo; (*e.g., of butter*) spalmata ‖ *v* (*pret & pp* **dabbed;** *ger* **dabbing**) *tr* toccare leggermente; (*to apply a substance to*) spennellare

**dabble** ['dæbəl] *tr* spruzzare ‖ *intr* diguazzare; **to dabble in** occuparsi di; (*stocks*) speculare in

**dad** [dæd] *s* (coll) papà *m*

**dad·dy** ['dædi] *s* (**-dies**) (coll) papà *m*

**daffodil** ['dæfədɪl] *s* trombone *m*

**daff·y** ['dæfi] *adj* (**-ier; -iest**) (coll) pazzo

**dagger** ['dægər] *s* daga, pugnale *m;* (typ) croce *f;* **to look daggers at** fulminare con lo sguardo

**dahlia** ['dæljə] *s* dalia

**dai·ly** ['deli] *adj* quotidiano, diurno ‖ *s* (**-lies**) quotidiano ‖ *adv* giornalmente

**dai'ly dou'ble** *s* duplice *f*, accoppiata

**dain·ty** ['denti] *adj* (**-tier; -tiest**) delicato ‖ *s* (**-ties**) manicaretto

**dair·y** ['deri] *s* (**-ies**) (*store*) latteria; (*factory*) caseificio

**dair'y farm'** *s* vaccheria

**dair'y·man** *s* (**-men**) lattaio

**dais** ['de·ɪs] *s* predella

**dai·sy** ['dezi] *s* (**-sies**) margherita

**dal·ly** ['dæli] *v* (*pret & pp* **-lied**) *intr* (*to loiter*) bighellonare; (*to trifle*) scherzare

**dam** [dæm] *s* diga; (*for fishing*) pescaia; (zool) fattrice *f* ‖ *v* (*pret & pp* **dammed;** *ger* **damming**) *tr* arginare; ostruire; tappare

**damage** ['dæmɪdʒ] *s* danno, scapito; (fig) menomazione; (com) avaria; **damages** danni *mpl* || *tr* danneggiare, ledere; sinistrare

**damascene** ['dæmə,sin] or [,dæmə-'sin] *adj* damasceno || *s* damaschinatura || *tr* damaschinare

**dame** [dem] *s* dama, signora; (slang) donna

**damn** [dæm] *s*—**I don't give a damn** (slang) me ne impipo; **that's not worth a damn** (slang) non vale un fico || *tr* dannare, condannare || *intr* maledire || *interj* maledizione!

**damnation** [dæm'neʃən] *s* dannazione; (theol) condanna

**damned** [dæmd] *adj* dannato, maledetto || **the damned** i dannati || *adv* maledettamente

**damp** [dæmp] *adj* umido || *s* umidità *f*; (firedamp) grisou *m* || *tr* inumidire; umettare; (to muffle) smorzare; (waves) (elec) smorzare; **to damp s.o.'s enthusiasm** raffreddare gli spiriti di qlcu; scoraggiare qlcu

**dampen** ['dæmpən] *tr* inumidire; umettare; smorzare; (s.o.'s enthusiasm) raffreddare

**damper** ['dæmpər] *s* (of chimney) valvola di tiraggio; (fig) doccia fredda; (mus) smorzatore *m*; (mus) sordina

**damsel** ['dæmzəl] *s* damigella

**dance** [dæns] or [dɑns] *s* ballo, danza || *tr* & *intr* ballare, danzare

**dance' band'** *s* orchestrina

**dance' floor'** *s* pista da ballo

**dance' hall'** *s* sala da ballo

**dancer** ['dænsər] or ['dɑnsər] *s* danzatore *m*; (expert or professional) ballerino

**danc'ing part'ner** *s* cavaliere *m*; dama

**danc'ing par'ty** *s* festa da ballo

**dandelion** ['dændɪ,laɪ·ən] *s* dente *m* di leone, soffione *m*

**dandruff** ['dændrəf] *s* forfora

**dan·dy** ['dændi] *adj* (-dier; -diest) (coll) eccellente, magnifico || *s* (-dies) damerino, elegantone *m*

**Dane** [den] *s* danese *mf*

**danger** ['dendʒər] *s* pericolo

**dangerous** ['dendʒərəs] *adj* pericoloso

**dangle** ['dæŋgəl] *tr* dondolare || *intr* penzolare, ciondolare

**Danish** ['denɪʃ] *adj* & *s* danese *m*

**dank** [dæŋk] *adj* umido

**Danube** ['dænjub] *s* Danubio

**dapper** ['dæpər] *adj* azzimato

**dapple** ['dæpəl] *adj* pezzato || *tr* chiazzare

**dap'ple-gray'** *adj* storno

**dare** [der] *s* sfida || *tr* sfidare || *intr* osare; **I dare say** oserei dire; forse, e.g., **I dare say we will be done at seven** forse avremo finito alle sette; **to dare to** (to have the courage to) osare di, fidarsi a

**dare'dev'il** *s* scavezzacollo

**daring** ['derɪŋ] *adj* temerario, spericolato || *s* audacia, temerarietà *f*

**dark** [dɑrk] *adj* scuro; (complexion) bruno; oscuro, segreto; (gloomy) tetro, fosco || *s* oscurità *f*, scuro; tenebre *fpl*; **in the dark** al buio

**Dark' Ag'es** *spl* alto medio evo

**dark-complexioned** ['dɑrkkəm'plɛk-ʃənd] *adj* bruno

**darken** ['dɑrkən] *tr* scurire, oscurare || *intr* scurirsi, oscurarsi

**dark' horse'** *s* vincitore imprevisto, outsider *m*

**darkly** ['dɑrkli] *adv* oscuramente; segretamente

**dark' meat'** *s* gamba o anca (di pollo o tacchino)

**darkness** ['dɑrknɪs] *s* oscurità *f*

**dark'room'** *s* camera oscura

**darling** ['dɑrlɪŋ] *adj* & *s* caro, amato

**darn** [dɑrn] *s* rammendo || *tr* rammendare || *interj* (coll) accidenti!

**darned** [dɑrnd] *adj* (coll) maledetto || *adv* maledettamente; (coll) tremendamente

**darnel** ['dɑrnəl] *s* zizzania

**darning** ['dɑrnɪŋ] *s* rammendo

**darn'ing nee'dle** *s* ago da rammendo

**dart** [dɑrt] *s* freccia, dardo; (game) frecciolo || *intr* dardeggiare; lanciarsi, precipitarsi

**dash** [dæʃ] *s* sciacquio; piccola quantità, sospetto; (spirit) brio; (typ, telg) trattino, lineetta || *tr* lanciare; mescolare; (s.o.'s hopes) frustrare; deprimere; **to dash off** gettar giù; **to dash to pieces** fare a pezzi || *intr* precipitarsi; **to dash against** gettarsi contro; **to dash by** passare a gran velocità; **to dash in** entrare come un razzo; **to dash off** or **out** andarsene in fretta; lanciarsi fuori

**dash'board'** *s* cruscotto; (in an open carriage) parafango

**dashing** ['dæʃɪŋ] *adj* impetuoso; vistoso || *s* (of waves) sciacquio

**dastard** ['dæstərd] *adj* & *s* vile *mf*, codardo

**da'ta proc'essing** *s* elaborazione

**date** [det] *s* (time) data; (palm) palma da datteri; (fruit) dattero; (appointment) (coll) appuntamento; **out of date** fuori moda; **to date** sinora; **up to date** a giorno || *tr* datare; (coll) avere un appuntamento con || *intr*— **to date from** partire da

**date' line'** *s* linea del cambiamento di data

**dative** ['detɪv] *adj* & *s* dativo

**datum** ['detəm] or ['dætəm] *s* (data ['detə] or ['dætə]) dato

**daub** [dɔb] *s* imbratto || *tr* imbrattare

**daughter** ['dɔtər] *s* figlia, figliola

**daughter-in-law** ['dɔtərɪn,lɔ] *s* (daughters-in-law) nuora

**daunt** [dɔnt] *tr* spaventare; intimidire

**dauntless** ['dɔntlɪs] *adj* intrepido

**dauphin** ['dɔfɪn] *s* delfino

**davenport** ['dævən,port] *s* sofà *m*, sofà *m* letto

**davit** ['dævɪt] *s* gru *f* per lancia

**daw** [dɔ] *s* cornacchia

**dawdle** ['dɔdəl] *intr* bighellonare

**dawn** [dɔn] *s* alba || *intr* (said of the day) farsi, nascere, spuntare; **to dawn on** cominciare a apparire nella mente di

**day** [de] *adj* diurno; (student) esterno || *s* giorno; (of travel, work, etc.)

giornata; **a few days ago** giorni fa; **any day now** da un giorno all'altro; **by day** di giorno; **the day after** il giorno dopo; **the day after tomorrow** dopodomani; **the day before yesterday** ieri l'altro; **to call it a day** (coll) finire di lavorare

**day' bed'** s sofà m letto

**day'book'** s brogliaccio

**day'break'** s far m del giorno

**day'dream'** s fantasticheria || *intr* fantasticare

**day' la'borer** s giornaliero

**day'light'** s luce f del giorno; alba; **in broad daylight** alla luce del sole; **to see daylight** comprendere; vedere la fine

**day'light-sav'ing time'** s ora legale, ora estiva

**day' nurs'ery** s asilo infantile

**day' off'** s giorno di vacanza; (*of servant*) libera uscita

**day' of reck'oning** s giorno di rendiconto; (*last judgment*) giorno del giudizio

**day' shift'** s turno diurno

**day'time'** adj diurno || s giornata

**daze** [dez] s stordimento; **in a daze** stordito || *tr* stordire

**dazzle** ['dæzəl] s abbagliamento || *tr* abbagliare

**dazzling** ['dæzlɪŋ] adj abbagliante

**deacon** ['dikən] s diacono

**dead** [dɛd] adj morto || s—**in the dead of** (*e.g., night*) nel pieno di; **the dead** i morti || *adv* (coll) completamente; (*abruptly*) (coll) di colpo

**dead' beat'** adj (coll) stanco morto

**dead'beat'** s (coll) scroccone m

**dead' cen'ter** s punto morto

**dead'drunk'** adj ubriaco fradicio

**deaden** ['dɛdən] *tr* attutire; (*e.g., s.o.'s senses*) ottundere

**dead' end'** s vicolo cieco

**dead' let'ter** s lettera morta; lettera non reclamata

**dead'line'** s termine m

**dead'lock'** s punto morto || *tr* portare al punto morto || *intr* giungere al punto morto

**dead·ly** ['dɛdli] adj (**-lier; -liest**) mortale; insopportabile

**dead' pan'** s (slang) faccia senza espressione

**dead'pan'** adj senza espressione

**dead' reck'oning** s (naut) stima

**dead'wood'** s legna secca; (fig) zavorra

**deaf** [dɛf] adj sordo; **to turn a deaf ear** fare orecchio di mercante

**deaf'-and-dumb'** adj sordomuto

**deafen** ['dɛfən] *tr* assordare, intronare

**deafening** ['dɛfənɪŋ] adj assordante

**deaf'-mute'** s sordomuto

**deafness** ['dɛfnɪs] s sordità f

**deal** [dil] s accordo; quantità f; (cards) mano, girata; (coll) affare m; (coll) trattamento; **a good deal (of) or a great deal (of)** moltissimo || v (*pret & pp* dealt [dɛlt]) *tr* (*a blow*) menare; (cards) fare, sfogliare; **to deal s.o. in** (coll) includere || *intr* mercanteggiare, commerciare; fare le

carte; **to deal with** trattare con; trattare di

**dealer** ['dilər] s commerciante mf, esercente mf; (cards) mazziere m

**dean** [din] s decano

**dear** [dir] adj (*beloved; expensive*) caro; **dear me!** povero me!; **Dear Sir** egregio Signore || s caro

**dearie** ['dɪri] s (coll) caro

**dearth** [dʌrθ] s scarsezza; insufficienza

**death** [dɛθ] s morte f; **to bleed to death** morire dissanguato; **to burn to death** morire bruciato; **to choke to death** morire di soffocazione; **to freeze to death** morire di gelo; **to put to death** dare la morte a; **to shoot to death** uccidere a fucilate; **to stab to death** scannare; **to starve to death** far morire di fame; morire di fame

**death'bed'** s letto di morte

**death'blow'** s colpo mortale

**deathless** ['dɛθlɪs] adj immortale, eterno

**deathly** ['dɛθli] adj mortale || adv mortalmente; assolutamente

**death' pen'alty** s pena di morte

**death' rate'** s mortalità f

**death' rat'tle** s rantolo della morte

**death' ray'** s raggio della morte

**death' sen'tence** s pena di morte

**death' war'rant** s pena di morte; fine f di ogni speranza

**death'watch'** s veglia mortuaria; (zool) orologio della morte

**debacle** [de'bakəl] s disastro; (*downfall*) tracollo; (*in a river*) sgelo repentino

**de-bar** [dɪ'bar] v (*pret & pp* **-barred**; *ger* **-barring**) *tr* escludere; proibire (with *dat*)

**debark** [dɪ'bark] *tr & intr* sbarcare

**debarkation** [ˌdibar'keʃən] s sbarco

**debase** [dɪ'bes] *tr* degradare; adulterare

**debatable** [dɪ'betəbəl] adj discutibile

**debate** [dɪ'bet] s discussione || *tr & intr* discutere

**debauch** [dɪ'bɔtʃ] s dissolutezza, corruzione || *tr* corrompere

**debauchee** [ˌdɛbɔ'i] or [ˌdɛbɔ'tʃi] s degenerato, vizioso

**debaucher·y** [dɪ'bɔtʃəri] s (**-ies**) dissolutezza, corruzione

**debenture** [dɪ'bɛntʃər] s (*bond*) obbligazione; (*voucher*) buono

**debilitate** [dɪ'bɪlɪˌtet] *tr* debilitare

**debili·ty** [dɪ'bɪlɪti] s (**-ties**) debolezza

**debit** ['dɛbɪt] s debito; (*debit side*) (com) dare m || *tr* addebitare

**debonair** [ˌdɛbə'nɛr] adj gioviale; cortese

**debris** [de'bri] s detrito, rottami mpl

**debt** [dɛt] s debito; **to run into debt** indebitarsi

**debtor** ['dɛtər] s debitore m

**debut** [de'bju] or ['debju] s debutto; **to make one's debut** debuttare || *intr*

**debutante** [ˌdɛbju'tant] or ['dɛbjəˌtænt] s debuttante f, esordiente f

**decade** ['dɛked] s decennio

**decadence** [dɪ'kedəns] s decadenza

**decadent** [dɪ'kedənt] *adj & s* decadente *mf*

**decanter** [dɪ'kæntər] *s* boccia

**decapitate** [dɪ'kæpɪ‚tet] *tr* decapitare

**decay** [dɪ'ke] *s* (*decline*) decadimento; (*rotting*) marciume *m*, putredine *f*; (*of teeth*) carie *f* || *tr* imputridire || *intr* imputridire, marcire; (*said of teeth*) cariarsi

**decease** [dɪ'sis] *s* decesso || *intr* decedere

**deceased** [dɪ'sist] *adj & s* defunto

**deceit** [dɪ'sit] *s* inganno, frode *f*

**deceitful** [dɪ'sitfəl] *adj* ingannatore, menzognero, subdolo

**deceive** [dɪ'siv] *tr & intr* ingannare

**decelerate** [dɪ'sɛlə‚ret] *tr & intr* decelerare

**December** [dɪ'sɛmbər] *s* dicembre *m*

**decen·cy** ['disənsi] *s* (**-cies**) decenza, pudore *m*; **decencies** convenienze *fpl*

**decent** ['disənt] *adj* decente; (*proper*) conveniente

**decentralize** [dɪ'sɛntrə‚laɪz] *tr* decentrare

**deception** [dɪ'sɛpʃən] *s* inganno

**deceptive** [dɪ'sɛptɪv] *adj* ingannevole

**decide** [dɪ'saɪd] *tr* decidere || *intr* decidere, decidersi

**decimal** ['dɛsɪməl] *adj & s* decimale *m*

**dec'imal point'** *s* (*in Italian the comma is used to separate the decimal fraction from the integer*) virgola

**decimate** ['dɛsɪ‚met] *tr* decimare

**decipher** [dɪ'saɪfər] *tr* decifrare

**decision** [dɪ'sɪʒən] *s* decisione

**decisive** [dɪ'saɪsɪv] *adj* decisivo; (*resolute*) fermo

**deck** [dɛk] *s* (*of cards*) mazzo; (naut) coperta, tolda, ponte *m*; **on deck** (coll) pronto; (coll) prossimo || *tr*— **to deck out** adornare; (*with flags*) imbandierare

**deck' chair'** *s* sedia a sdraio

**deck' hand'** *s* marinaio di coperta

**deck'house'** *s* (naut) tuga

**deck'le edge'** ['dɛkəl] *s* sbavatura

**declaim** [dɪ'klem] *tr & intr* declamare

**declaration** [‚dɛklə'reʃən] *s* dichiarazione

**declarative** [dɪ'klærətɪv] *adj* declaratorio; (gram) enunciativo

**declare** [dɪ'klɛr] *tr* dichiarare || *intr* dichiararsi

**declension** [dɪ'klɛnʃən] *s* declinazione

**declination** [‚dɛklɪ'neʃən] *s* declinazione

**decline** [dɪ'klaɪn] *s* decadenza; (*in prices*) ribasso; (*in health*) deperimento; (*of sun*) tramonto || *tr* declinare || *intr* declinare; decadere, scadere

**declivi·ty** [dɪ'klɪvɪti] *s* (**-ties**) declivio, pendice *f*

**decode** [di'kod] *tr* decifrare

**décolleté** [‚dekɑl'te] *adj* scollato

**decompose** [‚dɪkəm'poz] *tr* decomporre || *intr* decomporsi

**decomposition** [‚dikɑmpə'zɪʃən] *s* decomposizione

**décor** [de'kɔr] *s* decorazione; (*of a room*) stile *m*; (theat) scenario

**decorate** ['dɛkə‚ret] *tr* decorare

**decoration** [‚dɛkə're{ʃ}ən] *s* decorazione

**decorator** ['dɛkə‚retər] *s* decoratore *m*

**decorous** ['dɛkərəs] *or* [dɪ'korəs] *adj* corretto, decoroso

**decorum** [dɪ'korəm] *s* decoro, correttezza

**decoy** [dɪ'kɔɪ] *or* ['dikɔɪ] *s* richiamo; (*for birds*) zimbello; (*person*) adescatore *m* || *tr* (*to lure*) adescare; (*to deceive*) abbindolare

**decrease** ['dikris] *or* [dɪ'kris] *s* diminuzione; (*of salary*) decurtazione || [dɪ'kris] *tr* decurtare || *intr* diminuire

**decree** [dɪ'kri] *s* decreto || *tr* decretare

**de·cry** [dɪ'kraɪ] *v* (*pret & pp* **-cried**) *tr* denigrare, screditare

**dedicate** ['dɛdɪ‚ket] *tr* dedicare

**dedication** [‚dɛdɪ'keʃən] *s* dedizione; (*inscription in a book*) dedica

**deduce** [dɪ'djus] *or* [dɪ'dus] *tr* dedurre

**deduct** [dɪ'dʌkt] *tr* dedurre, defalcare

**deductible** [dɪ'dʌktɪbəl] *adj* defalcabile || *s* (ins) franchigia

**deduction** [dɪ'dʌkʃən] *s* deduzione

**deed** [did] *s* fatto; (*exploit*) prodezza; (law) titolo || *tr* trasferire legalmente

**deem** [dim] *tr & intr* credere, giudicare

**deep** [dip] *adj* profondo; basso; (*woods*) folto; (*friendship*) intimo; **deep in debt** carico di debiti; **deep in thought** assorto in pensieri || *adv* profondamente; **deep into the night** a notte fatta; **to go deep into** approfondirsi in

**deepen** ['dipən] *tr* approfondire || *intr* approfondirsi

**deep'-freeze'** *tr* (*pret* **-froze** [froz]; *pp* **-frozen** [frozən]) *tr* surgelare

**deep-laid** ['dip‚led] *adj* preparato astutamente

**deep' mourn'ing** *s* lutto stretto

**deep-rooted** ['dip‚rutɪd] *adj* profondo

**deep'-sea' fish'ing** *s* pesca d'alto mare or d'altura

**deep-seated** ['dip‚sitɪd] *adj* profondo, connaturato

**Deep' South'** *s* Profondo Sud

**deer** [dɪr] *s* cervo

**deer'skin'** *s* pelle *f* di daino

**deface** [dɪ'fes] *tr* sfigurare

**defamation** [‚dɛfə'meʃən] *or* [‚difə'meʃən] *s* diffamazione

**defame** [dɪ'fem] *tr* diffamare

**default** [dɪ'fɔlt] *s* mancanza; (*failure to act*) inadempienza; **in default of** per mancanza di; **to lose by default** dichiarare forfeit || *tr* essere inadempiente a || *intr* essere inadempiente; (sports) dichiarare forfeit

**defeat** [dɪ'fit] *s* sconfitta, disfatta || *tr* sconfiggere, vincere

**defeatism** [dɪ'fitɪzəm] *s* disfattismo

**defeatist** [dɪ'fitɪst] *adj & s* disfattista *mf*

**defecate** ['dɛfɪ‚ket] *intr* defecare

**defect** [dɪ'fɛkt] *or* ['difɛkt] *s* vizio, difetto || [dɪ'fɛkt] *intr* defezionare

**defection** [dɪ'fɛkʃən] *s* defezione

**defective** [dɪ'fɛktɪv] *adj* difettivo, difettoso

**defend** [dɪ'fɛnd] *tr* difendere, proteggere

**defendant** [dɪ'fɛndənt] *s* (law) imputato, querelato

**defender** [dɪ'fɛndər] *s* difensore *m*

**defense** [dɪ'fɛns] *s* difesa

**defenseless** [dɪ'fɛnslɪs] *adj* indifeso

**defensive** [dɪ'fɛnsɪv] *adj* difensivo ‖ *s* difensiva

**de·fer** [dɪ'fʌr] *v* (*pret* & *pp* **-ferred**; *ger* **-ferring**) *tr* differire, rinviare ‖ *intr* rimettersi

**deference** ['dɛfərəns] *s* deferenza

**deferential** [ˌdɛfə'rɛnʃəl] *adj* deferente

**deferment** [dɪ'fʌrmənt] *s* differimento

**defiance** [dɪ'faɪ·əns] *s* opposizione; sfida; **in defiance of** a dispetto di

**defiant** [dɪ'faɪ·ənt] *adj* provocante, ostile

**deficien·cy** [dɪ'fɪʃənsi] *s* (**-cies**) deficienza; (com) ammanco

**deficient** [dɪ'fɪʃənt] *adj* deficiente

**deficit** ['dɛfɪsɪt] *adj* deficitario ‖ *s* deficit *m*, disavanzo

**defile** [dɪ'faɪl] *or* ['difaɪl] *s* gola, passo ‖ [dɪ'faɪl] *tr* profanare ‖ *intr* marciare in fila

**define** [dɪ'faɪn] *tr* definire

**definite** ['dɛfɪnɪt] *adj* definito; (gram) determinativo, determinato

**definition** [ˌdɛfɪ'nɪʃən] *s* definizione

**definitive** [dɪ'fɪnɪtɪv] *adj* definitivo

**deflate** [dɪ'flet] *tr* sgonfiare; (*s.o.'s hopes*) deprimere; (*e.g., currency*) deflazionare

**deflation** [dɪ'fleʃən] *s* sgonfiamento; (*of prices*) deflazione

**deflect** [dɪ'flɛkt] *tr* far deflettere ‖ *intr* deflettere

**deflower** [di'flaʊ·ər] *tr* privare dei fiori; (*a woman*) deflorare

**deforest** [di'fɑrɛst] *or* [di'fɔrɛst] *tr* disboscare, smacchiare

**deform** [dɪ'fɔrm] *tr* deformare

**deformed** [dɪ'fɔrmd] *adj* deforme

**deformi·ty** [dɪ'fɔrmɪti] *s* (**-ties**) deformità *f*

**defraud** [dɪ'frɔd] *tr* defraudare

**defray** [dɪ'fre] *tr* pagare

**defrost** [di'frɔst] *or* [di'frɑst] *tr* sgelare, sbrinare

**defroster** [di'frɔstər] *or* [di'frɑstər] *s* (aut) visiera termica

**deft** [dɛft] *adj* destro, lesto

**defunct** [dɪ'fʌŋkt] *adj* defunto

**de·fy** [dɪ'faɪ] *v* (*pret* & *pp* **-fied**) *tr* sfidare, provocare

**degeneracy** [dɪ'dʒɛnərəsi] *s* degenerazione

**degenerate** [dɪ'dʒɛnərɪt] *adj* & *s* degenerato ‖ [dɪ'dʒɛnəˌret] *intr* degenerare, tralignare

**degrade** [dɪ'gred] *tr* degradare

**degrading** [dɪ'gredɪŋ] *adj* degradante

**degree** [dɪ'gri] *s* grado; titolo accademico; **by degrees** a grado a grado; **to a degree** fino a un certo punto; troppo; **to take a degree** ricevere un titolo di studio

**dehydrate** [di'haɪdret] *tr* disidratare

**deice** [di'aɪs] *tr* sgelare

**dei·fy** ['di·ɪ ˌfaɪ] *v* (*pret* & *pp* **-fied**) *tr* deificare

**deign** [den] *intr* degnarsi

**dei·ty** ['di·ɪti] *s* (**-ties**) deità *f*; **the Deity** Dio

**dejected** [dɪ'dʒɛktɪd] *adj* demoralizzato

**dejection** [dɪ'dʒɛkʃən] *s* (*in spirits*) demoralizzazione; (*evacuation*) deiezione

**delay** [dɪ'le] *s* ritardo, proroga; dilazione; **without further delay** senza ulteriore indugio ‖ *tr* tardare; (*to put off*) differire ‖ *intr* tardare, ritardare

**delayed'-ac'tion** *adj* a azione differita

**delectable** [dɪ'lɛktəbəl] *adj* dilettevole

**delegate** ['dɛlɪ ˌget] *or* ['dɛlɪgɪt] *s* delegato, incaricato; (*to a convention*) congressista *mf* ‖ ['dɛlɪ ˌget] *tr* delegare, incaricare

**delegation** [ˌdɛlɪ'geʃən] *s* delegazione

**delete** [dɪ'lit] *tr* cancellare, sopprimere

**deletion** [dɪ'liʃən] *s* cancellazione

**deliberate** [dɪ'lɪbərɪt] *adj* meditato; (*slow in deciding*) cauto; (*slow in moving*) lento ‖ [dɪ'lɪbəˌret] *tr* & *intr* deliberare

**deliberately** [dɪ'lɪbərɪtli] *adv* (*on purpose*) deliberatamente; (*without hurrying*) con ponderatezza

**delica·cy** ['dɛlɪkəsi] *s* (**-cies**) delicatezza; (*choice food*) leccornia

**delicatessen** [ˌdɛlɪkə'tɛsən] *s* negozio di salumerie ‖ *spl* salumerie *fpl*, articoli alimentari scelti

**delicious** [dɪ'lɪʃəs] *adj* delizioso

**delight** [dɪ'laɪt] *s* gioia, delizia ‖ *tr* dilettare ‖ *intr* dilettarsi

**delightful** [dɪ'laɪtfəl] *adj* delizioso

**delinquen·cy** [dɪ'lɪŋkwənsi] *s* (**-cies**) colpa; (*offense*) delinquenza; (*in payment of a debt*) morosità *f*

**delinquent** [dɪ'lɪŋkwənt] *adj* colpevole; (*in payment*) moroso; non pagato ‖ *s* delinquente *m*; debitore moroso

**delirious** [dɪ'lɪrɪ·əs] *adj* in delirio

**deliri·um** [dɪ'lɪrɪ·əm] *s* (**-ums** *or* **-a** [ə]) delirio

**deliver** [dɪ'lɪvər] *tr* consegnare; (*a blow*) affibbiare; (*a speech*) fare; (*a letter*) recapitare; (*electricity or gas*) erogare; (*said of a pregnant woman*) partorire; (*said of a doctor*) assistere durante il parto

**deliver·y** [dɪ'lɪvəri] *s* (**-ies**) consegna; (*of mail*) distribuzione; (*of merchandise*) fornitura; (*of a speech*) dizione; (*childbirth*) parto; (sports) lancio

**deliv'ery·man'** *s* (**-men'**) fattorino

**deliv'ery room'** *s* sala parto

**deliv'ery truck'** *s* furgoncino

**dell** [dɛl] *s* valletta

**delouse** [di'laʊs] *or* [di'laʊz] *tr* spidocchiare

**delude** [dɪ'lud] *tr* illudere, ingannare

**deluge** ['dɛljudʒ] *s* diluvio, inondazione ‖ **the Deluge** il diluvio universale ‖ *tr* inondare

**delusion** [dɪ'luʒən] *s* illusione, inganno; (psychopath) allucinazione;

(psychopath) idea fissa; **delusions of grandeur** mania di grandezza

**de luxe** [dɪˈlʊks] or [dɪˈlʌks] *adj* di lusso || *adv* in gran lusso

**delve** [dɛlv] *intr* frugare; **to delve into** approfondirsi in

**demagnetize** [diˈmægnɪ ˌtaɪz] *tr* smagnetizzare

**demagogue** [ˈdɛmə ˌgɑg] *s* demagogo

**demand** [dɪˈmænd] or [dɪˈmɑnd] *s* esigenza; (com) richiesta, domanda; **to be in demand** essere in richiesta || *tr* esigere

**demanding** [dɪˈmændɪŋ] or [dɪˈmɑndɪŋ] *adj* esigente, impegnativo

**demarcate** [dɪˈmɑrket] or [ˈdimɑrˌket] *tr* demarcare

**démarche** [deˈmɑrʃ] *s* progetto, piano

**demean** [dɪˈmin] *tr* degradare; **to demean oneself** comportarsi; degradarsi

**demeanor** [dɪˈminər] *s* condotta, contegno

**demented** [dɪˈmentɪd] *adj* demente

**demigod** [ˈdɛmɪ ˌgɑd] *s* semidio

**demijohn** [ˈdɛmɪ ˌdʒɑn] *s* damigiana

**demilitarize** [diˈmɪlɪtə ˌraɪz] *tr* smilitarizzare

**demimonde** [ˈdɛmɪ ˌmɑnd] *s* donne *fpl* della società equivoca

**demise** [dɪˈmaɪz] *s* decesso

**demitasse** [ˈdɛmɪ ˌtæs] or [ˈdɛmɪ ˌtɑs] *s* tazzina da caffè; (*contents*) caffè nero

**demobilize** [diˈmobɪ ˌlaɪz] *tr* smobilitare

**democra·cy** [dɪˈmɑkrəsi] *s* (**-cies**) democrazia

**democrat** [ˈdɛmə ˌkræt] *s* democratico

**democratic** [ ˌdɛməˈkrætɪk] *adj* democratico

**demolish** [dɪˈmɑlɪʃ] *tr* demolire

**demolition** [ ˌdɛməˈlɪʃən] or [ ˌdiməˈlɪʃən] *s* demolizione

**demon** [ˈdimən] *s* demonio

**demoniacal** [ ˌdiməˈnaɪ·əkəl] *adj* demoniaco

**demonstrate** [ˈdɛmən ˌstret] *tr* & *intr* dimostrare

**demonstration** [ ˌdɛmənˈstreʃən] *s* dimostrazione

**demonstrative** [dɪˈmɑnstrətɪv] *adj* dimostrativo; (*giving open exhibition of emotion*) espansivo

**demonstrator** [ˈdɛmən ˌstretər] *s* (*of a product*) dimostratore *m*; (*in a public gathering*) dimostrante *m*; (*product*) prodotto usato da dimostratori

**demoralize** [dɪˈmɑrə ˌlaɪz] or [dɪˈmɔrə ˌlaɪz] *tr* demoralizzare

**demote** [dɪˈmot] *tr* retrocedere

**demotion** [dɪˈmoʃən] *s* retrocessione

**de·mur** [dɪˈmʌr] *v* (*pret* & *pp* **-murred**; *ger* **-murring**) *intr* sollevare obiezioni

**demure** [dɪˈmjʊr] *adj* modesto; sobrio

**demurrage** [dɪˈmʌrɪdʒ] *s* (com) controstallie *fpl*; (rr) sosta

**den** [dɛn] *s* (*of animals, thieves*) tana; (*little room*) bugigattolo; (*little room for studying or writing*) studiolo; (*of lions*) (Bib) fossa

**denaturalize** [diˈnætʃərə ˌlaɪz] *tr* snaturare; privare della nazionalità

**dena'tured al'cohol** [diˈnetʃərd] *s* alcole denaturato

**denial** [dɪˈnaɪ·əl] *s* diniego; (*disavowal*) smentita

**denim** [ˈdɛnɪm] *s* tessuto di cotone per tuta; **denims** tuta; (*trousers*) jeans *mpl*

**denizen** [ˈdɛnɪzən] *s* abitante *mf*

**Denmark** [ˈdɛnmɑrk] *s* la Danimarca

**denomination** [dɪ ˌnɑmɪˈneʃən] *s* denominazione; categoria; (com) taglio; (eccl) confessione

**denote** [dɪˈnot] *tr* denotare, significare

**denouement** [denuˈmɑ] *s* scioglimento

**denounce** [dɪˈnaʊns] *tr* denunziare

**dense** [dɛns] *adj* denso; stupido

**densi·ty** [ˈdɛnsɪti] *s* (**-ties**) densità *f*

**dent** [dɛnt] *s* ammaccatura; (*in a gearwheel*) tacca, dente *m*; **to make a dent** fare progresso; fare impressione || *tr* ammaccare; (fig) ferire

**dental** [ˈdɛntəl] *adj* dentale, dentario || *s* dentale *f*

**den'tal floss'** *s* filo cerato dentario

**dentifrice** [ˈdɛntɪfrɪs] *s* dentifricio

**dentist** [ˈdɛntɪst] *s* dentista *mf*

**dentistry** [ˈdɛntɪstri] *s* odontoiatria

**denture** [ˈdɛntʃər] *s* dentiera

**denunciation** [dɪ ˌnʌnsɪˈeʃən] or [dɪ ˌnʌnʃɪˈeʃən] *s* denunzia

**de·ny** [dɪˈnaɪ] *v* (*pret* & *pp* **-nied**) *tr* (*to declare not to be true*) negare; (*to refuse*) rifiutare; **to deny oneself to callers** sottrarsi alle visite || *intr* negare; rifiutare

**deodorant** [diˈodərənt] *adj* & *s* deodorante *m*

**deo'dorant spray'** *s* deodorante *m* spray

**deodorize** [diˈodə ˌraɪz] *tr* deodorare

**depart** [dɪˈpɑrt] *intr* partire, andarsene; (*to diverge*) dipartire

**departed** [dɪˈpɑrtɪd] *adj* morto, defunto || **the departed** i defunti

**department** [dɪˈpɑrtmənt] *s* dipartimento; (*of government*) ministero; (*e.g., of a hospital*) reparto; (*of agency*) sezione, ufficio

**depart'ment store'** *s* grandi magazzini *mpl*

**departure** [dɪˈpɑrtʃər] *s* partenza; divergenza, deviazione

**depend** [dɪˈpend] *intr* dipendere; **to depend on** (*to rely on*) contare su; dipendere da

**dependable** [dɪˈpendəbəl] *adj* sicuro, fidato

**dependence** [dɪˈpendəns] *s* dipendenza; (*trust*) fiducia

**dependen·cy** [dɪˈpendənsi] *s* (**-cies**) dipendenza; (*territory*) possessione

**dependent** [dɪˈpendənt] *adj* dipendente; a carico; **to be dependent on** dipendere da || *s* persona a carico

**depend'ent clause'** *s* proposizione subordinata

**depict** [dɪˈpɪkt] *tr* descrivere, dipingere

**deplete** [dɪˈplit] *tr* esaurire

**depletion** [dɪˈpliʃən] *s* esaurimento

**deplorable** [dɪˈplorəbəl] *adj* deplorevole

**deplore** [dɪˈplor] *tr* deplorare

**deploy** [dɪˈplɔɪ] *tr* (mil) spiegare, stendere

deployment [dɪ'plɔɪmənt] s (mil) dispositivo, spiegamento

depolarize [di'polə,raɪz] tr depolarizzare

depopulate [di'papjə,let] tr spopolare

deport [dɪ'port] tr deportare; to deport oneself comportarsi

deportation [,dipor'teʃən] s deportazione

deportee [,dipor'ti] s deportato

deportment [dɪ'portmənt] s condotta, comportamento

depose [dɪ'poz] tr & intr deporre

deposit [dɪ'pazɪt] s deposito; (down payment) caparra || tr depositare || intr depositarsi

depos'it account' s conto corrente

depositor [dɪ'pazɪtər] s versante mf; (to the credit of an established account) correntista mf

deposito·ry [dɪ'pazɪ,tori] s (-ries) deposito; (person) depositario

depos'it slip' s distinta di versamento

depot ['dipo] or ['depo] s magazzino; (mil) deposito; (rr) stazione

depraved [dɪ'prevd] adj depravato

depravi·ty [dɪ'prævɪti] s (-ties) depravazione

deprecate ['depri,ket] tr deprecare

depreciate [dɪ'priʃɪ,et] tr svalutare, deprezzare || intr deprezzarsi

depreciation [dɪ,priʃɪ'eʃən] s (drop in value) deprezzamento; (disparagement) disprezzo

depredation [,depri'deʃən] s depredazione

depress [dɪ'pres] tr deprimere; avvilire; (prices) far abbassare

depression [dɪ'preʃən] s depressione; (gloom) sconforto; (slump) crisi f

deprive [dɪ'praɪv] tr privare; to deprive oneself espropriarsi

depth [depθ] s profondità f; (of a house or room) lunghezza; (of sea) fondale m; (fig) vastità f; in the depth of nel cuor di; to go beyond one's depth non toccare più; (fig) andare oltre le proprie possibilità

depth' bomb' s (aer) bomba antisommergibile

depth' charge' s (nav) granata antisommergibile

depth' of hold' s (naut) puntale m

deputation [,depjə'teʃən] s deputazione

deputize ['depjə,taɪz] tr deputare

depu·ty ['depjəti] s (-ties) deputato

derail [dɪ'rel] tr far deragliare || intr deragliare, deviare

derailment [dɪ'relmənt] s deragliamento, deviamento

derange [dɪ'rendʒ] tr (to disarrange) dissestare; (to make insane) squilibrare, render pazzo

derangement [dɪ'rendʒmənt] s (disorder) disordine m; (insanity) squilibrio mentale, pazzia

der·by ['dɑrbi] s (-bies) bombetta; (race) derby m

derelict ['derɪlɪkt] adj derelitto; negligente || s derelitto; (naut) relitto

dereliction [,derɪ'lɪkʃən] s (in one's duty) negligenza; (law) derelizione

deride [dɪ'raɪd] tr deridere, schernire, farsi beffe di

derision [dɪ'riʒən] s derisione, scherno

derisive [dɪ'raɪsɪv] adj derisorio

derivation [,derɪ'veʃən] s derivazione

derivative [dɪ'rɪvətɪv] adj & s derivato

derive [dɪ'raɪv] tr & intr derivare

dermatology [,dʌrmə'talədʒi] s dermatologia

derogatory [dɪ'ragə,tori] adj dispregiativo

derrick ['derɪk] s gru f; (naut) picco di carico

dervish ['dʌrvɪʃ] s dervis m

desalinization [di,selɪnɪ'zeʃən] s desalazione

desalt [di'sɔlt] tr desalificare

descend [dɪ'send] tr discendere || intr discendere; to descend on calare su, gettarsi su

descendant [dɪ'sendənt] adj & s discendente mf

descendent [dɪ'sendənt] adj discendente

descent [dɪ'sent] s (slope) china; (decline) declino; discesa; (lineage) stirpe f, discendenza; (sudden raid) calata

Descent' from the Cross' s Deposizione dalla Croce

describe [dɪ'skraɪb] tr descrivere

description [dɪ'skrɪpʃən] s descrizione

descriptive [dɪ'skrɪptɪv] adj descrittivo

de·scry [dɪ'skraɪ] v (pret & pp -scried) tr avvistare

desecrate ['desɪ,kret] tr profanare, dissacrare

desecration [,desɪ'kreʃən] s profanazione, dissacrazione

desegregate [di'segrɪ,get] intr sopprimere la segregazione razziale

desegregation [di,segrɪ'geʃən] s desegregazione

desensitize [di'sensɪ,taɪz] tr desensibilizzare

desert ['dezərt] adj & s deserto || [dɪ'zʌrt] s merito; he received his just deserts ricevette quanto meritava || tr & intr disertare

deserter [dɪ'zʌrtər] s disertore m

deserted [dɪ'zʌrtɪd] adj (person) abbandonato; (place) deserto

desertion [dɪ'zʌrʃən] s diserzione; abbandono del coniuge

deserve [dɪ'zʌrv] tr & intr meritare

deservedly [dɪ'zʌrvɪdli] adv meritatamente, meritevolmente

design [dɪ'zaɪn] s disegno; (of a play) congegno; to have designs on aver mire su || tr disegnare; progettare || intr disegnare; designed for destinato a

designate ['dezɪg,net] tr designare

designer [dɪ'saɪnər] s disegnatore m

designing [dɪ'zaɪnɪŋ] adj intrigante, macchinatore || s disegnazione

desirable [dɪ'zaɪrəbəl] adj desiderabile

desire [dɪ'zaɪr] s desiderio || tr desiderare

desirous [dɪ'zaɪrəs] adj desideroso

desist [di'zɪst] intr desistere

desk [desk] s scrittoio; tavolo d'ufficio;

(*lectern*) leggio; (*of professor*) cattedra; (*of pupil*) banco; (com) cassa
**desk'bound'** *adj* sedentario; legato al tavolino
**desk' pad'** *s* blocco da tavolo; blocco per appunti
**desolate** ['desəlɪt] *adj* desolato, deserto; (*hopeless*) disperato; (*dismal*) lugubre || ['desə,let] *tr* desolare; devastare
**desolation** [,desə'leʃən] *s* desolazione; devastazione
**despair** [dɪ'sper] *s* disperazione; **to be in despair** disperarsi || *intr* disperare, disperarsi
**despairing** [dɪ'sperɪŋ] *adj* disperato
**despera·do** [,despə'redo] *or* [,despə-'rɑdo] *s* (**-does** *or* **-dos**) fuorilegge disposto a tutto
**desperate** ['despərɪt] *adj* disposto a tutto; (*hopeless*) disperato; (*very bad*) atroce, terribile; (*bitter, excessive*) accanito; (*remedy*) estremo
**desperation** [,despə'reʃən] *s* disperazione
**despicable** ['despɪkəbəl] *adj* spregevole, incanaglito
**despise** [dɪ'spaɪz] *tr* sprezzare, disprezzare, vilipendere
**despite** [dɪ'spaɪt] *prep* malgrado
**despoil** [dɪ'spɔɪl] *tr* spogliare
**desponden·cy** [dɪ'spandənsi] *s* (**-cies**) scoraggiamento, abbattimento
**despondent** [dɪ'spandənt] *adj* scoraggiato, abbattuto
**despot** ['despat] *s* despota *m*
**despotic** [des'patɪk] *adj* dispotico
**despotism** ['despə,tɪzəm] *s* dispotismo
**dessert** [dɪ'zʌrt] *s* dessert *m*
**dessert' spoon'** *s* cucchiaio *or* cucchiaino da dessert
**destination** [,destɪ'neʃən] *s* destinazione
**destine** ['destɪn] *tr* destinare
**desti·ny** ['destɪni] *s* (**-nies**) destino
**destitute** ['destɪ,tjut] *or* ['destɪ,tut] *adj* (*poverty-stricken*) indigente; (*lacking*) privo
**destitution** [,destɪ'tjuʃən] *or* [,destɪ-'tuʃən] *s* indigenza, miseria
**destroy** [dɪ'strɔɪ] *tr* distruggere
**destroyer** [dɪ'strɔɪ·ər] *s* (nav) caccia-torpediniere *m*
**destruction** [dɪ'strʌkʃən] *s* distruzione
**destructive** [dɪ'strʌktɪv] *adj* distruttivo
**desultory** ['desəl,tori] *adj* saltuario, sconnesso
**detach** [dɪ'tætʃ] *tr* staccare, distaccare; (mil) distaccare
**detachable** [dɪ'tætʃəbəl] *adj* staccabile; separabile
**detached** [dɪ'tætʃt] *adj* (*e.g., stub*) staccato; (*e.g., house*) discosto; (*aloof*) riservato, freddo; imparziale
**detachment** [dɪ'tætʃmənt] *s* distacco; imparzialità *f;* (mil) distaccamento
**detail** [dɪ'tel] *or* ['ditel] *s* dettaglio, ragguaglio; (mil) distaccamento || [dɪ'tel] *tr* dettagliare; (mil) distaccare
**detain** [dɪ'ten] *tr* detenere, trattenere
**detect** [dɪ'tekt] *tr* scoprire, discernere; (rad) rivelare

**detection** [dɪ'tekʃən] *s* scoperta; (rad) rivelazione
**detective** [dɪ'tektɪv] *s* detective *m*
**detec'tive sto'ry** *s* romanzo poliziesco, romanzo giallo
**detector** [dɪ'tektər] *s* (rad) detector *m*, rivelatore *m*
**detention** [dɪ'tenʃən] *s* detenzione
**de·ter** [dɪ'tʌr] *v* (*pret* & *pp* **-terred;** *ger* **-terring**) *tr* distogliere, impedire
**detergent** [dɪ'tʌrdʒənt] *adj* & *s* detergente *m*
**deteriorate** [dɪ'tɪrɪ·ə,ret] *tr* deteriorare || *intr* deteriorarsi, andar giù
**determination** [dɪ,tʌrmɪ'neʃən] *s* determinazione
**determine** [dɪ'tʌrmɪn] *tr* determinare
**determined** [dɪ'tʌrmɪnd] *adj* determinato, risoluto
**deterrent** [dɪ'tʌrənt] *s* deterrente *m*
**detest** [dɪ'test] *tr* detestare, odiare
**dethrone** [dɪ'θron] *tr* detronizzare
**detonate** ['detə,net] *or* ['dɪtə,net] *tr* far scoppiare || *intr* detonare
**detonator** ['detə,netər] *s* innesco
**detour** ['ditur] *or* [dɪ'tur] *s* deviazione || *tr* far deviare || *intr* deviare
**detract** [dɪ'trækt] *tr* detrarre || *intr—* **to detract from** diminuire
**detractor** [dɪ'træktər] *s* detrattore *m*
**detriment** ['detrɪmənt] *s* detrimento; **to the detriment of** a danno di
**detrimental** [,detrɪ'mentəl] *adj* pregiudizievole
**deuce** [djus] *or* [dus] *s* (cards) due *m;* **the deuce!** diavolo!
**devaluate** [di'vælju,et] *tr* svalutare
**devaluation** [di,vælju'eʃən] *s* devalutazione, svalutazione
**devastate** ['devəs,tet] *tr* devastare
**devastating** ['devəs,tetɪŋ] *adj* devastatore, devastante; (*e.g., reply*) schiacciante, annichilante
**devastation** [,devəs'teʃən] *s* devastazione
**develop** [dɪ'veləp] *tr* sviluppare; (phot) sviluppare, rivelare || *intr* svilupparsi; manifestarsi
**developer** [dɪ'veləpər] *s* (*e.g., of a new engine*) sfruttatore *m;* (*in real estate*) specialista *mf* in lottizzazione; (phot) sviluppatore *m*, rivelatore *m*
**development** [dɪ'veləpmənt] *s* sviluppo; valorizzazione; sfruttamento; (phot) rivelazione
**deviate** ['divi,et] *tr* sviare || *intr* deviare, sviarsi
**deviation** [,divi'eʃən] *s* deviazione
**deviationism** [,divi'eʃə,nɪzəm] *s* deviazionismo
**deviationist** [,divi'eʃənɪst] *s* deviazionista *mf*
**device** [dɪ'vaɪs] *s* dispositivo, congegno; (*trick*) stratagemma *m;* (*motto*) divisa, emblema *m;* **to leave s.o. to his own devices** lasciare che qlcu faccia come gli pare e piace
**dev·il** ['devəl] *s* diavolo; **between the devil and the deep blue sea** fra l'incudine e il martello; **to raise the devil** (slang) fare diavolo a quattro || *v* (*pret* & *pp* **-iled** *or* **-illed;** *ger*

-iling or -illing) *tr* condire con spezie or con pepe; (coll) infastidire

**devilish** ['dɛvəlɪʃ] *adj* diabolico

**devilment** ['dɛvəlmənt] *s* (*mischief*) diavoleria; (*evil*) cattiveria

**devil·try** ['dɛvəltri] *s* (**-tries**) malvagità *f*, crudeltà *f;* (*mischief*) diavoleria

**devious** ['divɪ·əs] *adj* (*tricky*) traverso; (*roundabout*) tortuoso

**devise** [dɪ'vaɪz] *tr* ideare, inventare; (law) legare, disporre per testamento

**devoid** [dɪ'vɔɪd] *adj* sprovvisto

**devolve** [dɪ'vɑlv] *intr*—**to devolve on** ricadere su

**devote** [dɪ'vot] *tr* dedicare

**devoted** [dɪ'votɪd] *adj* devoto; dedito, dedicato

**devotee** [,dɛvə'ti] *s* devoto; (*fan*) fanatico, tifoso, entusiasta *mf*

**devotion** [dɪ'voʃən] *s* devozione; (*e.g., to work*) dedizione; **devotions** orazioni *mpl*, preghiere *fpl*

**devour** [dɪ'vaʊr] *tr* divorare

**devout** [dɪ'vaʊt] *adj* devoto; sincero

**dew** [dju] or [du] *s* rugiada

**dew'drop'** *s* goccia di rugiada

**dew'lap'** *s* giogaia

**dew·y** ['dju·i] or ['du·i] *adj* (**-ier; -iest**) rugiadoso

**dexterity** [dɛks'tɛrɪti] *s* destrezza

**diabetes** [,daɪ·ə'bitɪs] or [,daɪ·ə'bitɪz] *s* diabete *m*

**diabetic** [,daɪ·ə'bɛtɪk] or [,daɪ·ə-'bitɪk] *adj & s* diabetico

**diabolic(al)** [,daɪ·ə'bɑlɪk(əl)] *adj* diabolico

**diadem** ['daɪ·ə,dɛm] *s* diadema *m*

**diaere·sis** [daɪ'ɛrɪsɪs] *s* (**-ses** [,siz]) dieresi *f*

**diagnose** [,daɪ·əg'nos] or [,daɪ·əg-'noz] *tr* diagnosticare

**diagno·sis** [,daɪ·əg'nosɪs] *s* (**-ses** [siz]) diagnosi *f*

**diagonal** [daɪ'ægənəl] *adj & s* diagonale *f*

**dia·gram** ['daɪ·ə,græm] *s* diagramma *m;* (*drawing*) schema *m;* (*plan*) prospetto ǁ *v* (*pret & pp* **-gramed** or **-grammed;** *ger* **-graming** or **-gramming**) *tr* diagrammare

**dial** ['daɪ·əl] *s* (*of watch*) quadrante *m;* (rad) tabella graduata, sintogramma *m;* (telp) disco combinatore ǁ *tr* (rad) sintonizzare; (*a person*) (telp) chiamare; (*a number*) (telp) comporre; (*the phone*) (telp) comporre il numero di ǁ *intr* (telp) comporre il numero

**dialect** ['daɪ·ə,lɛkt] *s* dialetto

**dialing** ['daɪ·əlɪŋ] *s* composizione del numero

**dialogue** ['daɪ·ə,lɔg] or ['daɪ·ə,lɑg] *s* dialogo

**di'al tel'ephone** *s* telefono automatico

**di'al tone'** *s* (telp) segnale *m* di via libera

**diameter** [daɪ'æmɪtər] *s* diametro

**diametric(al)** [,daɪ·ə'mɛtrɪk(əl)] *adj* diametrico, diametrale

**diamond** ['daɪmənd] *s* diamante *m;* (*figure of a rhombus*) losanga; (baseball) diamante *m;* **diamonds** (cards) quadri *mpl*

**diaper** ['daɪ·pər] *s* pannolino

**diaphanous** [daɪ'æfənəs] *adj* diafano

**diaphragm** ['daɪ·ə,fræm] *s* diaframma *m;* (telp) membrana

**diarrhea** [,daɪ·ə'ri·ə] *s* diarrea

**dia·ry** ['daɪ·əri] *s* (**-ries**) diario

**diastole** [daɪ'æstəli] *s* diastole *f*

**diathermy** ['daɪ·ə,θʌrmi] *s* diatermia

**dice** [daɪs] *spl* dadi *mpl;* (*small cubes*) cubetti *mpl;* **no dice** (slang) niente da fare; (slang) risposta a picche

**dice' cup'** *s* bussolotto

**dichloride** [daɪ'klɔraɪd] *s* bicloruro

**dichoto·my** [daɪ'kɑtəmi] *s* (**-mies**) dicotomia

**dickey** ['dɪki] *s* camiciola; (*starched insert*) sparato; (*bib*) bavaglino

**dictaphone** ['dɪktə,fon] *s* dittafono

**dictate** ['dɪktet] *s* dettato ǁ ['dɪktet] or [dɪk'tet] *tr* dettare

**dictation** [dɪk'teʃən] *s* dettato; (*act of ordering*) ordine *m;* **to take dictation** scrivere sotto dettatura

**dictator** ['dɪktetər] or [dɪk'tetər] *s* dittatore *m*

**dictatorship** ['dɪktetər,ʃɪp] or [dɪk-'tetər/ɪp] *s* dittatura

**diction** ['dɪkʃən] *s* dizione

**dictionar·y** ['dɪkʃən,ɛri] *s* (**-ies**) dizionario, vocabolario

**dic·tum** ['dɪktəm] *s* (**-ta** [tə]) detto, sentenza

**didactic(al)** [daɪ'dæktɪk(əl)] or [dɪ-'dæktɪk(əl)] *adj* didattico

**die** [daɪ] *s* (**dice** [daɪs]) dado; **the die is cast** il dado è tratto ǁ *s* (**dies**) (*for stamping coins, medals, etc.*) stampo; (*for cutting threads*) filiera ǁ *v* (*pret & pp* **died;** *ger* **dying**) *intr* morire; **to die hard** morire lentamente; morire lottando; **to die laughing** morire dalle risa; **to die off** morire uno per uno

**die'-hard'** *adj & s* intransigente *m*

**die'sel oil'** ['dizəl] *s* nafta, gasolio

**die'stock'** *s* girafiliera

**diet** ['daɪ·ət] *s* dieta, regime *m* ǁ *intr* stare a dieta

**dietetic** [,daɪ·ə'tɛtɪk] *adj* dietetico ǁ **dietetics** *ssg* dietetica

**dietitian** [,daɪ·ə'tɪʃən] *s* dietista *mf*

**differ** ['dɪfər] *intr* (*to be different*) differire, differenziarsi; **to differ with** dissentire da

**difference** ['dɪfərəns] *s* differenza; **to make no difference** fare lo stesso; **to split the difference** dividere la differenza; (fig) venire a un compromesso

**different** ['dɪfərənt] *adj* differente

**differential** [,dɪfə'rɛnʃəl] *adj & s* differenziale *m*

**differentiate** [,dɪfə'rɛnʃɪ,et] *tr* differenziare ǁ *intr* differenziarsi

**difficult** ['dɪfɪ,kʌlt] *adj* difficile

**difficul·ty** ['dɪfɪ,kʌlti] *s* (**-ties**) difficoltà *f*

**diffident** ['dɪfɪdənt] *adj* timido, imbarazzato

**diffuse** [dɪ'fjus] *adj* diffuso ǁ [dɪ'fjuz] *tr* diffondere ǁ *intr* diffondersi

**dig** [dɪg] *s* (*poke*) botta, spintone *m;* (*jibe*) stoccata, fiancata ǁ *v* (*pret & pp* **dug** [dʌg];* ger* **digging**) *tr* scavare, sterrare; **to dig up** dissodare; (*to uncover*) dissotterrare ‖ *intr* scavare; **to dig in** (mil) fortificarsi; **to dig into** (coll) sprofondarsi in

**digest** ['daɪdʒɛst] *s* compendio; (law) digesto ‖ [dɪ'dʒɛst] or [daɪ'dʒɛst] *tr & intr* digerire

**digestible** [dɪ'dʒɛstɪbəl] or [daɪ'dʒɛstɪbəl] *adj* digeribile, digestibile

**digestion** [dɪ'dʒɛstʃən] or [daɪ'dʒɛstʃən] *s* digestione

**digestive** [dɪ'dʒɛstɪv] or [daɪ'dʒɛstɪv] *adj* (*tube*) digerente ‖ *s* digestivo

**digit** ['dɪdʒɪt] *s* cifra, unità *f;* (*finger*) dito; (*toe*) dito del piede

**dig'ital clock'** *s* orologio a scatto

**digitalis** [ˌdɪdʒɪ'tælɪs] or [ˌdɪdʒɪ'telɪs] *s* (bot) digitale *f;* (pharm) digitalina

**dignified** ['dɪgnɪ ˌfaɪd] *adj* dignitoso, fiero, contegnoso

**digni·fy** ['dɪgnɪ ˌfaɪ] *v* (*pret & pp* **-fied**) *tr* (*to ennoble*) nobilitare; onorare, esaltare; dare la dignità a

**dignitar·y** ['dɪgnɪ ˌtɛri] *s* (**-ies**) dignitario; **dignitaries** dignità *fpl*

**digni·ty** ['dɪgnɪti] *s* (**-ties**) dignità *f,* decoro; **to stand on one's dignity** mantenere la propria dignità

**digress** [dɪ'grɛs] or [daɪ'grɛs] *intr* digredire, divagare

**digression** [dɪ'grɛʃən] or [daɪ'grɛʃən] *s* digressione, divagazione

**dike** [daɪk] *s* diga; (*in a river*) argine *m;* (*ditch*) fosso; scarpata

**dilapidated** [dɪ'læpɪ ˌdetɪd] *adj* dilapidato, decrepito

**dilate** [daɪ'let] *tr* dilatare ‖ *intr* dilatarsi

**dilatory** ['dɪlə ˌtori] *adj* lento, tardivo; (*e.g., strategy*) dilatorio

**dilemma** [dɪ'lɛmə] *s* dilemma *m*

**dilettan·te** [ˌdɪlə'tænti] *adj* dilettantesco ‖ *s* (**-tes** or **-ti** [ti]) dilettante *mf*

**diligence** ['dɪlɪdʒəns] *s* diligenza

**diligent** ['dɪlɪdʒənt] *adj* diligente

**dill** [dɪl] *s* (bot) aneto

**dillydal·ly** ['dɪlɪ ˌdæli] *v* (*pret & pp* **-lied**) *intr* farla lunga

**dilute** [dɪ'lut] or [daɪ'lut] *adj* diluito ‖ [dɪ'lut] *tr* diluire ‖ *intr* diluirsi

**dilution** [dɪ'luʃən] *s* diluizione

**dim** [dɪm] *adj* (**dimmer; dimmest**) (*light*) fioco; (*sight*) debole; (*memory*) vago; (*color*) smorzato; (*sound*) sordo; **to take a dim view of** avere una visione pessimistica di ‖ *v* (*pret & pp* **dimmed;** *ger* **dimming**) *tr* (*lights*) smorzare; **to dim the headlights** abbassare i fari

**dime** [daɪm] *s* moneta di dieci centesimi di dollaro

**dimension** [dɪ'mɛnʃən] *s* dimensione

**diminish** [dɪ'mɪnɪʃ] *tr & intr* diminuire, scemare

**diminutive** [dɪ'mɪnjətɪv] *adj* (*tiny*) minuscolo; (gram) diminutivo ‖ *s* diminutivo

**dimly** ['dɪmli] *adv* indistintamente

**dimmer** ['dɪmər] *s* smorzatore *m;* (aut) luce *f* di incrocio; **dimmers** fari *mpl* antiabbaglianti

**dimple** ['dɪmpəl] *s* fossetta

**dimwit** ['dɪm ˌwɪt] *s* (slang) stupido, cretino

**din** [dɪn] *s* fragore *m,* frastuono ‖ *v* (*pret & pp* **dinned;** *ger* **dinning**) *tr* assordare; **to din s.th into s.o.'s ears** rintronare qlco nelle orecchie di qlcu

**dine** [daɪn] *tr* offrire un pranzo a; offrire una cena a ‖ *intr* pasteggiare; cenare; **to dine out** mangiare fuori di casa

**diner** ['daɪnər] *s* commensale *m;* (rr) vettura ristorante; (U.S.A.) ristorante *m* a forma di vagone

**ding-dong** ['dɪŋ ˌdɒŋ] or ['dɪŋ ˌdɑŋ] *s* dindon *m*

**din·gy** ['dɪndʒi] *adj* (**-gier; -giest**) sporco, sbiadito

**din'ing car'** *s* vagone *m* ristorante

**din'ing room'** *s* sala da pranzo

**dinner** ['dɪnər] *s* cena; pranzo; (*formal meal*) banchetto

**din'ner coat'** or **jack'et** *s* smoking *m*

**din'ner knife'** *s* coltello da tavola

**din'ner set'** *s* servizio da tavola

**din'ner ta'ble** *s* desco

**din'ner time'** *s* ora di pranzo or di cena

**dinosaur** ['daɪnə ˌsɔr] *s* dinosauro

**dint** [dɪnt] *s* tacca, ammaccatura; **by dint of** a forza di ‖ *tr* ammaccare

**diocese** ['daɪə ˌsis] or ['daɪəsɪs] *s* diocesi *f*

**diode** ['daɪod] *s* diodo

**dioxide** [daɪ'ɑksaɪd] *s* biossido

**dip** [dɪp] *s* immersione; (*brief swim*) tuffo, nuotata; (*in a road*) depressione; inclinazione magnetica ‖ *v* (*pret & pp* **dipped;** *ger* **dipping**) *tr* immergere, tuffare; (*the flag*) abbassare; (*bread*) inzuppare ‖ *intr* immergersi, tuffarsi; inclinarsi; (*to drop down*) sparire subitamente; **to dip into** (*a book*) sfogliare; (*business*) mettersi in; (*a container of liquids*) intingere; **to dip into one's purse** spendere soldi

**diphtheria** [dɪf'θɪrɪ·ə] *s* difterite *f*

**diphthong** ['dɪfθɒŋ] or ['dɪfθɑŋ] *s* dittongo

**diphthongize** ['dɪfθɒŋ ˌgaɪz] or ['dɪfθɑŋ ˌgaɪz] *tr & intr* dittongare

**diploma** [dɪ'plomə] *s* diploma *m*

**diploma·cy** [dɪ'ploməsi] *s* (**-cies**) diplomazia

**diplomat** ['dɪplə ˌmæt] *s* diplomatico

**diplomatic** [ˌdɪplə'mætɪk] *adj* diplomatico

**dip'lomat'ic pouch'** *s* valigia diplomatica

**dipper** ['dɪpər] *s* mestolo

**dip'stick'** *s* asta di livello

**dire** [daɪr] *adj* terribile, orrendo

**direct** [dɪ'rɛkt] or [daɪ'rɛkt] *adj* diretto; sincero ‖ *tr* dirigere; ordinare

**direct' cur'rent** *s* corrente continua

**direct' dis'course** *s* discorso diretto

**direct' dis'tance di'aling** *s* (telp) teleselezione *f*

**direct' hit'** *s* colpo centrato

**direction** [dɪ'rɛkʃən] or [daɪ'rɛkʃən] *s* direzione; **directions** istruzioni *fpl;* (*for use*) indicazioni *fpl* per l'uso

**directional** [dɪ'rɛkʃənəl] or [daɪ-'rɛkʃənəl] *adj* direzionale

**directive** [dɪ'rɛktɪv] or [daɪ'rɛktɪv] *s* direttiva

**direct' ob'ject** *s* (gram) complemento diretto, complemento oggetto

**director** [dɪ'rɛktər] or [daɪ'rɛktər] *s* direttore *m*, gerente *m*; (*member of a governing body*) consigliere *m*

**directorship** [dɪ'rɛktər‚ʃɪp] or [daɪ-'rɛktər‚ʃɪp] *s* direzione; amministrazione

**directo·ry** [dɪ'rɛktəri] or [daɪ'rɛktəri] *s* (**-ries**) (*board of directors*) direzione, direttorio; (*list of names and addresses*) rubrica, elenco; (telp) elenco dei telefoni, guida telefonica

**dirge** [dʌrdʒ] *s* canto funebre

**dirigible** ['dɪrɪdʒɪbəl] *adj* & *s* dirigibile *m*

**dirt** [dʌrt] *s* (*soil*) terra, suolo; (*dust*) polvere *m*; (*mud*) fango; (*accumulation of dirt*) sudiciume *m*, lerciume *m*; (*moral filth*) porcheria, sozzura; (*gossip*) pettegolezzi *mpl*; **to do s.o. dirt** (slang) calunniare qlcu

**dirt'-cheap'** *adj* a prezzo bassissimo

**dirt' road'** *s* strada di terra battuta

**dirt·y** ['dʌrti] *adj* (**-ier; -iest**) sporco, sudicio; fangoso; polveroso; (*e.g., spinach*) terroso; (*obscene*) sconcio, lurido; immondo ‖ *v* (*pret* & *pp* (**-ied**) *tr* sporcare, insudiciare, imbrattare

**dir'ty lin'en** *s* roba sporca; **to air one's dirty linen in public** mettere i panni al sole

**dir'ty trick'** *s* brutto tiro

**disabili·ty** [‚dɪsə'bɪlɪti] *s* (**-ties**) incapacità *f*, invalidità *f*

**disabil'ity insur'ance** *s* assicurazione invalidità

**disable** [dɪs'ebəl] *tr* mutilare, storpiare; (*a ship*) smantellare; (law) invalidare

**disabuse** [‚dɪsə'bjuz] *tr* disingannare

**disadvantage** [‚dɪsəd'væntɪdʒ] or [‚dɪsəd'vɑntɪdʒ] *s* svantaggio

**disadvantageous** [dɪs‚ædvən'tedʒəs] *adj* svantaggioso

**disagree** [‚dɪsə'gri] *intr* discordare, disconvenire; (*to quarrel*) litigare, altercare; **to disagree with** non essere del parere di

**disagreeable** [‚dɪsə'gri·əbəl] *adj* sgradevole

**disagreement** [‚dɪsə'grimənt] *s* sconcordanza, dissidio, dissenso

**disallow** [‚dɪsə'lau] *tr* non permettere, rifiutare

**disappear** [‚dɪsə'pɪr] *intr* sparire, scomparire

**disappearance** [‚dɪsə'pɪrəns] *s* scomparsa

**disappoint** [‚dɪsə'pɔɪnt] *tr* deludere, disilludere; **to be disappointed** rimanere deluso

**disappointment** [‚dɪsə'pɔɪntmənt] *s* delusione, disinganno, disappunto

**disapproval** [‚dɪsə'pruvəl] *s* disapprovazione, riprova

**disapprove** [‚dɪsə'pruv] *tr* & *intr* disapprovare

**disarm** [dɪs'ɑrm] *tr* disarmare ‖ *intr* disarmare, disarmarsi

**disarmament** [dɪs'ɑrməmənt] *s* disarmo

**disarming** [dɪs'ɑrmɪŋ] *adj* ingraziante, simpatico

**disarray** [‚dɪsə're] *s* disordine *m*, scompiglio; (*of apparel*) sciatteria ‖ *tr* scomporre, scompigliare

**disassemble** [‚dɪsə'sɛmbəl] *tr* smontare, sconnettere

**disassociate** [‚dɪsə'soʃɪ‚et] *tr* dissociare, disassociare

**disaster** [dɪ'zæstər] or [dɪ'zɑstər] *s* disastro, sinistro

**disastrous** [dɪ'zæstrəs] or [dɪ'zɑstrəs] *adj* disastroso

**disavow** [‚dɪsə'vau] *tr* sconfessare

**disavowal** [‚dɪsə'vau·əl] *s* sconfessione

**disband** [dɪs'bænd] *tr* (*an assembly*) sciogliere; (*troops*) congedare; (*any group*) sbandare ‖ *intr* sbandarsi

**dis·bar** [dɪs'bɑr] *v* (*pret* & *pp* **-barred;** *ger* **-barring**) *tr* (law) radiare dall'albo degli avvocati

**disbelief** [‚dɪsbɪ'lif] *s* incredulità *f*

**disbelieve** [‚dɪsbɪ'liv] *tr* rifiutarsi di credere a ‖ *intr* rifiutarsi di credere

**disburse** [dɪs'bʌrs] *tr* sborsare

**disbursement** [dɪs'bʌrsmənt] *s* sborso, disborso

**discard** [dɪs'kɑrd] *s* scarto, scartina; **to put into the discard** scartare ‖ *tr* scartare

**discern** [dɪ'zʌrn] or [dɪ'sʌrn] *tr* scernere, discernere, sceverare

**discernible** [dɪ'zʌrnɪbəl] or [dɪ'sʌrnɪbəl] *adj* discernibile

**discerning** [dɪ'zʌrnɪŋ] or [dɪ'sʌrnɪŋ] *adj* perspicace, oculato

**discernment** [dɪ'zʌrnmənt] or [dɪ-'sʌrnmənt] *s* discernimento

**discharge** [dɪs't'ʃɑrdʒ] *s* (*of a load*) scarico; (*of a gun; of electricity*) scarica; (*of a prisoner*) liberazione; (*of a duty*) adempimento; (*of a debt*) pagamento; (*from a job*) licenziamento; (mil) foglio di congedo; (pathol) spurgo ‖ *tr* scaricare; (a *duty*) adempiere; (*a prisoner*) liberare; (*a debt*) pagare; (*an employee*) licenziare; (*a patient*) lasciar uscire; (*a passenger from a ship*) sbarcare; (*a battery*) scaricare; (mil) congedare ‖ *intr* (said, *e.g., of a liquid*) sboccare; (*said of a gun or a battery*) scaricarsi

**disciple** [dɪ'saɪpəl] *s* discepolo

**disciplinarian** [‚dɪsɪplɪ'nɛrɪ·ən] *s* disciplinatore *m*; partigiano di una forte disciplina

**disciplinary** ['dɪsɪplɪ‚nɛri] *adj* disciplinare

**discipline** ['dɪsɪplɪn] *s* disciplina; castigo ‖ *tr* disciplinare; castigare

**disclaim** [dɪs'klem] *tr* non riconoscere, negare

**disclose** [dɪs'kloz] *tr* rivelare, scoprire

**disclosure** [dɪs'kloʒər] *s* rivelazione, scoperta; divulgazione

**discolor** [dɪs'kʌlər] *tr* scolorare, scolorire ‖ *intr* scolorirsi

**discoloration** [dɪs‚kʌlə'reʃən] *s* discolorazione

**discomfit** [dɪs'kʌmfɪt] *tr* sconcertare, turbare; frustrare, battere, mettere in fuga

**discomfiture** [dɪs'kʌmfɪtʃər] *s* sconcerto, turbamento; frustrazione; disfatta

**discomfort** [dɪs'kʌmfərt] *s* disagio ‖ *tr* incomodare

**disconcert** [ˌdɪskən'sʌrt] *tr* sconcertare

**disconnect** [ˌdɪskə'nɛkt] *tr* sconnettere; (elec) disinserire

**disconsolate** [dɪs'kɑnsəlɪt] *adj* sconsolato, desolato

**discontent** [ˌdɪskən'tɛnt] *adj* & *s* scontento ‖ *tr* scontentare

**discontented** [ˌdɪskən'tɛntɪd] *adj* scontento

**discontinue** [ˌdɪskən'tɪnjʊ] *tr* cessare, interrompere

**discord** ['dɪskɔrd] *s* discordia, dissidio

**discordance** [dɪs'kɔrdəns] *s* discordanza

**discotheque** [ˌdɪsko'tɛk] *s* discoteca

**discount** ['dɪskaʊnt] *s* sconto ‖ ['dɪskaʊnt] or [dɪs'kaʊnt] *tr* scontare; (news) fare la tara a

**dis'count rate'** *s* tasso di sconto

**discourage** [dɪs'kʌrɪdʒ] *tr* scoraggiare, sconfortare; (to dissuade) sconsigliare

**discouragement** [dɪs'kʌrɪdʒmənt] *s* scoraggiamento; disapprovazione

**discourse** ['dɪskors] or [dɪs'kors] *s* discorso ‖ [dɪs'kors] *intr* discorrere

**discourteous** [dɪs'kʌrtɪ·əs] *adj* scortese

**discourte·sy** [dɪs'kʌrtəsi] *s* (-sies) scortesia

**discover** [dɪs'kʌvər] *tr* scoprire

**discoverer** [dɪs'kʌvərər] *s* scopritore *m*

**discover·y** [dɪs'kʌvəri] *s* (-ies) scoperta

**discredit** [dɪs'krɛdɪt] *s* discredito ‖ *tr* screditare

**discreditable** [dɪs'krɛdɪtəbəl] *adj* indegno, disonorevole

**discreet** [dɪs'krit] *adj* discreto

**discrepan·cy** [dɪs'krɛpənsi] *s* (-cies) discrepanza, divario

**discretion** [dɪs'krɛʃən] *s* discrezione

**discriminate** [dɪs'krɪmɪˌnet] *tr* discriminare ‖ *intr*—**to discriminate against** fare delle discriminazioni contro

**discrimination** [dɪsˌkrɪmɪ'neʃən] *s* discriminazione

**discriminatory** [dɪs'krɪmɪnəˌtori] *adj* discriminante

**discuss** [dɪs'kʌs] *tr* & *intr* discutere

**discussion** [dɪs'kʌʃən] *s* discussione

**discus thrower** ['dɪskəs 'θro·ər] *s* discobolo

**disdain** [dɪs'den] *s* disdegno ‖ *tr* disdegnare, sdegnare

**disdainful** [dɪs'denfəl] *adj* sdegnoso

**disease** [dɪ'ziz] *s* malattia

**diseased** [dɪ'zizd] *adj* malato

**disembark** [ˌdɪsɛm'bɑrk] *tr* & *intr* sbarcare

**disembarkation** [dɪsˌɛmbɑr'keʃən] *s* sbarco

**disembowel** [ˌdɪsɛm'bau·əl] *tr* sbudellare, sventrare

**disenchant** [ˌdɪsɛn'tʃænt] or [ˌdɪsɛn'tʃɑnt] *tr* disincantare

**disenchantment** [ˌdɪsɛn'tʃæntmənt] or [ˌdɪsɛn'tʃɑntmənt] *s* disinganno

**disengage** [ˌdɪsɛn'gedʒ] *tr* (from a pledge) svincolare; (to disconnect) sgranare, disinnestare; (mil) sganciare

**disengagement** [ˌdɪsɛn'gedʒmənt] *s* liberazione; disinnesto; svincolamento

**disentangle** [ˌdɪsɛn'tæŋgəl] *tr* disincagliare, districare

**disentanglement** [ˌdɪsɛn'tæŋgəlmənt] *s* districamento

**disestablish** [ˌdɪsɛs'tæblɪʃ] *tr* (the Church) separare dallo Stato

**disfavor** [dɪs'fevər] *s* disfavore *m*

**disfigure** [dɪs'fɪgjər] *tr* sfigurare, deturpare

**disfigurement** [dɪs'fɪgjərmənt] *s* deturpazione

**disfranchise** [dɪs'fræntʃaɪz] *tr* privare dei diritti civili

**disgorge** [dɪs'gɔrdʒ] *tr* vomitare; (something illicitly obtained) restituire; (said of a river) scaricare ‖ *intr* vomitare; scaricarsi

**disgrace** [dɪs'gres] *s* vergogna; disgrazia ‖ *tr* disonorare; privare del favore

**disgraceful** [dɪs'gresfəl] *adj* infamante, disonorante

**disgruntle** [dɪs'grʌntəl] *tr* scontentare, irritare

**disgruntled** [dɪs'grʌntəld] *adj* irritato, di cattivo umore

**disguise** [dɪs'gaɪz] *s* travestimento ‖ *tr* travestire, dissimulare

**disgust** [dɪs'gʌst] *s* disgusto, schifo ‖ *tr* disgustare, fare schifo a

**disgusting** [dɪs'gʌstɪŋ] *adj* disgustoso, schifoso

**dish** [dɪʃ] *s* piatto, **dishes** vasellame *m;* **to wash the dishes** fare i piatti ‖ *tr* scodellare; (to defeat) (slang) sconfiggere; **to dish out** (slang) distribuire

**dish'cloth'** *s* canovaccio, strofinaccio

**dishearten** [dɪs'hɑrtən] *tr* scoraggiare, disanimare, desolare

**dishev·el** [dɪ'ʃɛvəl] *v* (pret & pp **-eled** or **-elled**; ger **-eling** or **-elling**) *tr* scomporre, scarmigliare, scapigliare

**dishonest** [dɪs'ɑnɪst] *adj* disonesto

**dishones·ty** [dɪs'ɑnɪsti] *s* (-ties) disonestà *f*

**dishonor** [dɪs'ɑnər] *s* disonore *m* ‖ *tr* disonorare; (com) rifiutare di pagare

**dishonorable** [dɪs'ɑnərəbəl] *adj* disonorevole, disonorante

**dish'pan'** *s* bacinella per lavare i piatti

**dish'rack'** *s* portapiatti *m,* sgocciolatoio

**dish'rag'** *s* canovaccio, strofinaccio

**dish'towel'** *s* canovaccio per le stoviglie

**dish'wash'er** *s* (person) sguattero, lavapiatti *m;* (machine) lavastoviglie *m* & *f*

**dish'wa'ter** *s* lavatura di piatti

**disillusion** [ˌdɪsɪ'luʒən] *s* disillusione ‖ *tr* disilludere

**disillusionment** [ˌdɪsɪ'luʒənmənt] *s* disillusione

**disinclination** [dɪsˌɪnklɪ'neʃən] *s* riluttanza, avversione

**disinclined** [ˌdɪsɪn'klaɪnd] *adj* riluttante, avverso

**disinfect** [ˌdɪsɪn'fɛkt] *tr* disinfettare
**disinfectant** [ˌdɪsɪn'fɛktənt] *adj & s* disinfettante *m*
**disingenuous** [ˌdɪsɪn'dʒɛnjʊ·əs] *adj* poco schietto, insincero
**disinherit** [ˌdɪsɪn'hɛrɪt] *tr* diseredare
**disintegrate** [dɪs'ɪntɪ ˌgret] *tr* disintegrare, disgregare || *intr* disintegrarsi, disgregarsi
**disintegration** [dɪs ˌɪntɪ'greʃən] *s* disintegrazione, disgregamento
**disin·ter** [ˌdɪsɪn'tʌr] *v* (*pret & pp* -terred; *ger* -terring) *tr* dissotterrare
**disinterested** [dɪs'ɪntə ˌrɛstɪd] or [dɪs-'ɪntrɪstɪd] *adj* disinteressato
**disjunctive** [dɪs'dʒʌŋktɪv] *adj* disgiuntivo
**disk** [dɪsk] *s* disco; (*of ski pole*) rotella
**disk' jock'ey** *s* presentatore *m* di un programma radiodiffuso di dischi
**dislike** [dɪs'laɪk] *s* antipatia, avversione; **to take a dislike for** prendere in uggia || *tr* non piacere (with *dat*), e.g., **he dislikes wine** non gli piace il vino
**dislocate** ['dɪslo ˌket] *tr* spostare, mettere fuori posto; (*a bone*) slogare
**dislodge** [dɪs'lɑdʒ] *tr* sloggiare
**disloyal** [dɪs'lɔɪ·əl] *adj* sleale
**disloyal·ty** [dɪs'lɔɪ·əlti] *s* (-ties) slealtà *f*
**dismal** ['dɪzməl] *adj* tetro, triste; cattivo, orribile
**dismantle** [dɪs'mæntəl] *tr* smontare, smantellare; (*a fortress*) sguarnire
**dismay** [dɪs'me] *s* costernazione || *tr* costernare
**dismember** [dɪs'mɛmbər] *tr* smembrare
**dismiss** [dɪs'mɪs] *tr* congedare; (*to fire*) licenziare; (*a subject*) scartare; (*from the mind*) scacciare
**dismissal** [dɪs'mɪsəl] *s* congedo; licenziamento
**dismount** [dɪs'maʊnt] *tr* disarcionare || *intr* scendere, smontare
**disobedience** [ˌdɪsə'bidɪ·əns] *s* disubbidienza
**disobedient** [ˌdɪsə'bidɪ·ənt] *adj* disubbidiente
**disobey** [ˌdɪsə'be] *tr* disubbidire (with *dat*) || *intr* disubbidire
**disorder** [dɪs'ɔrdər] *s* disordine *m* || *tr* disordinare, confondere
**disorderly** [dɪs'ɔrdərli] *adj* disordinato, confuso; (*unruly*) turbolento
**disor'derly con'duct** *s* contegno contrario all'ordine pubblico
**disor'derly house'** *s* bordello, lupanare *m*
**disorganize** [dɪs'ɔrgə ˌnaɪz] *tr* disorganizzare
**disoriented** [dɪs'ɔrɪ ˌɛntɪd] *adj* disorientato
**disown** [dɪs'on] *tr* disconoscere
**disparage** [dɪs'pærɪdʒ] *tr* svilire, deprezzare
**disparagement** [dɪs'pærɪdʒmənt] *s* discredito, deprezzamento
**disparate** ['dɪspərɪt] *adj* disparato
**dispari·ty** [dɪs'pærɪti] *s* (-ties) disparità *f*, spareggio
**dispassionate** [dɪs'pæʃənɪt] *adj* spassionato

**dispatch** [dɪs'pætʃ] *s* dispaccio || *tr* spedire; (*to dismiss*) congedare; uccidere; (*a meal*) (coll) liquidare
**dis·pel** [dɪs'pɛl] *v* (*pret & pp* -pelled; *ger* -pelling) *tr* dissipare
**dispensa·ry** [dɪs'pɛnsəri] *s* (-ries) dispensario
**dispensation** [ˌdɪspɛn'seʃən] *s* (*dispensing*) distribuzione, dispensa; (*exemption*) dispensa
**dispense** [dɪs'pɛns] *tr* (*medicines*) distribuire; (*justice*) amministrare; (*to distribute*) dispensare; (*to exempt*) esimere || *intr*—**to dispense with** fare a meno di; esimersi da
**dispenser** [dɪ'spɛnsər] *s* dispensatore *m*; (*automatic*) distributore *m*
**disperse** [dɪs'pʌrs] *tr* disperdere || *intr* disperdersi
**dispersion** [dɪ'spʌrʒən] or [di'spɛrʃən] *s* dispersione
**dispersive** [dɪ'spʌrsɪv] *adj* dispersivo
**dispirit** [dɪ'spɪrɪt] *tr* scoraggiare
**displace** [dɪs'ples] *tr* muovere; costringere a lasciare il proprio paese; (*to supplant*) rimpiazzare; (naut) dislocare
**displaced' per'son** *s* rifugiato politico
**displacement** [dɪs'plesmənt] *s* spostamento; sostituzione; (*of a piston*) cilindrata; (naut) dislocamento
**display** [dɪs'ple] *s* sfoggio, mostra || *tr* mostrare; (e.g., *in a store window*) mettere in mostra; (*to unfold*) spiegare; (*to show ostentatiously*) sfoggiare, ostentare; (*ignorance*) rivelare
**display' cab'inet** *s* bacheca
**display' win'dow** *s* mostra, vetrina
**displease** [dɪs'pliz] *tr* dispiacere (with *dat*)
**displeasing** [dɪs'plizɪŋ] *adj* spiacevole
**displeasure** [dɪs'plɛʒər] *s* dispiacere *m*; sfavore *m*
**disposable** [dɪs'pozəbl] *adj* (*available*) disponibile; (*made to be thrown away after use*) scartabile, da gettarsi via, usa e getta
**disposal** [dɪs'pozəl] *s* disposizione; eliminazione; **to have at one's disposal** disporre di
**dispose** [dɪs'poz] *tr* disporre; **to dispose of** disporre di; (*to get rid of*) sbarazzarsi di; vendere
**disposed** [dɪ'spozd] *adj*—**to be disposed to** essere disposto a
**disposition** [ˌdɪspə'zɪʃən] *s* disposizione; (*mental outlook*) indole *f*; tendenza; (mil) ordinamento
**dispossess** [ˌdɪspə'zɛs] *tr* spodestare, bandire; (*to evict*) sfrattare
**disproof** [dɪs'pruf] *s* confutazione
**disproportionate** [ˌdɪsprə'porʃənɪt] *adj* sproporzionato
**disprove** [dɪs'pruv] *tr* confutare
**dispute** [dɪs'pjut] *s* disputa; **beyond dispute** incontestabile; **in dispute** in discussione || *tr & intr* disputare
**disquali·fy** [dɪs'kwɑlɪ ˌfaɪ] *v* (*pret & pp* -fied) *tr* squalificare
**disquiet** [dɪs'kwaɪ·ət] *s* inquietudine *f* || *tr* inquietare, turbare
**disquisition** [ˌdɪskwɪ'zɪʃən] *s* disquisizione

**disregard** [ˌdɪsrɪˈgɑrd] *s (of a rule)* inosservanza; *(of danger)* disprezzo, noncuranza ‖ *tr* non fare attenzione a

**disrepair** [ˌdɪsrɪˈpɛr] *s* cattivo stato, rovina

**disreputable** [dɪsˈrɛpjətəbəl] *adj* malfamato; disonorevole; *(in bad condition)* raso, logoro

**disrepute** [ˌdɪsrɪˈpjut] *s* cattiva fama; **to bring into disrepute** rovinare la reputazione di

**disrespect** [ˌdɪsrɪˈspɛkt] *s* mancanza di rispetto ‖ *tr* mancare di rispetto a

**disrespectful** [ˌdɪsrɪˈspɛktfəl] *adj* non rispettoso, irriverente

**disrobe** [dɪsˈrob] *tr* svestire ‖ *intr* svestirsi, spogliarsi

**disrupt** [dɪsˈrʌpt] *tr* disorganizzare; interrompere

**disruption** [dɪsˈrʌpʃən] *s* rottura; disorganizzazione

**dissatisfaction** [ˌdɪssætɪsˈfækʃən] *s* scontento, malcontento

**dissatisfied** [dɪsˈsætɪsˌfaɪd] *adj* scontento, malcontento; insoddisfatto

**dissatis·fy** [dɪsˈsætɪsˌfaɪ] *v (pret & pp -fied) tr* scontentare

**dissect** [dɪˈsɛkt] *tr* sezionare

**dissemble** [dɪˈsɛmbəl] *tr & intr* dissimulare

**disseminate** [dɪˈsɛmɪˌnet] *tr* disseminare, divulgare

**dissension** [dɪˈsɛnʃən] *s* dissensione

**dissent** [dɪˈsɛnt] *s* dissenso; *(nonconformity)* dissidio ‖ *intr* dissentire

**dissenter** [dɪˈsɛntər] *s* dissenziente *m*

**dissertation** [ˌdɪsərˈteʃən] *s* dissertazione

**disservice** [dɪˈsʌrvɪs] *s* danno; cattivo servizio

**dissidence** [ˈdɪsɪdəns] *s* dissidenza

**dissident** [ˈdɪsɪdənt] *adj & s* dissidente *m*

**dissimilar** [dɪˈsɪmɪlər] *adj* dissimile

**dissimilate** [dɪˈsɪmɪˌlet] *tr* dissimilare ‖ *intr* dissimilarsi

**dissimulate** [dɪˈsɪmjəˌlet] *tr & intr* dissimulare

**dissipate** [ˈdɪsɪˌpet] *tr* dissipare ‖ *intr* dissiparsi; *(to indulge oneself)* darsi alla dissipatezza

**dissipated** [ˈdɪsɪˌpetɪd] *adj* dissipato

**dissipation** [ˌdɪsɪˈpeʃən] *s* dissipazione

**dissociate** [dɪˈsoʃɪˌet] *tr* dissociare ‖ *intr* dissociarsi

**dissolute** [ˈdɪsəˌlut] *adj* dissoluto

**dissolution** [ˌdɪsəˈluʃən] *s* dissoluzione

**dissolve** [dɪˈzɑlv] *tr* sciogliere, disciogliere ‖ *intr* sciogliersi, disciogliersi

**dissonance** [ˈdɪsənəns] *s* dissonanza

**dissuade** [dɪˈswed] *tr* dissuadere

**dissyllabic** [ˌdɪsɪˈlæbɪk] *adj* disillabo

**dissyllable** [dɪˈsɪləbəl] *s* disillabo

**distaff** [ˈdɪstæf] or [ˈdɪstɑf] *s* rocca

**dis'taff side'** *s* ramo femminile di una famiglia

**distance** [ˈdɪstəns] *s* distanza; **a long distance** (fig) moltissimo; **in the distance** in lontananza; **to keep at a distance** or **to keep one's distance** mantenere le distanze ‖ *tr* distanziare

**distant** [ˈdɪstənt] *adj* distante; *(relative)* lontano; *(aloof)* freddo, riservato

**distaste** [dɪsˈtest] *s* ripugnanza

**distasteful** [dɪsˈtestfəl] *adj* ripugnante, sgradevole

**distemper** [dɪsˈtɛmpər] *s* cimurro; *(painting)* tempera ‖ *tr* dipingere a tempera

**distend** [dɪsˈtɛnd] *tr* stendere, distendere; gonfiare ‖ *intr* stendersi, distendersi; gonfiarsi

**distension** [dɪsˈtɛnʃən] *s* distensione; gonfiamento

**distill** [dɪsˈtɪl] *tr* distillare

**distillation** [ˌdɪstɪˈleʃən] *s* distillazione

**distiller·y** [dɪsˈtɪləri] *s (-ies)* distilleria

**distinct** [dɪsˈtɪŋkt] *adj* distinto, chiaro; *(not blurred)* nitido

**distinction** [dɪsˈtɪŋkʃən] *s* distinzione

**distinctive** [dɪsˈtɪŋktɪv] *adj* distintivo

**distinguish** [dɪsˈtɪŋgwɪʃ] *tr* distinguere

**distinguished** [dɪsˈtɪŋgwɪʃt] *adj* distinto

**distort** [dɪsˈtɔrt] *tr* distorcere; *(the truth)* svisare, snaturare

**distortion** [dɪsˈtɔrʃən] *s* deformazione; *(of the truth)* alterazione, svisamento; (rad) distorsione

**distract** [dɪsˈtrækt] *tr* distrarre

**distracted** [dɪsˈtræktɪd] *adj* distratto; *(irrational)* turbato, sconvolto

**distraction** [dɪsˈtrækʃən] *s* distrazione

**distraught** [dɪsˈtrɔt] *adj* turbato, stordito

**distress** [dɪsˈtrɛs] *s* pena, dispiacere *m;* pericolo; (naut) difficoltà *f* ‖ *tr* sconfortare, affliggere

**distressing** [dɪsˈtrɛsɪŋ] *adj* penoso

**distress' mer'chandise** *s* merce *f* sotto costo

**distress' sig'nal** *s* segnale *m* di soccorso

**distribute** [dɪsˈtrɪbjut] *tr* distribuire

**distribution** [ˌdɪstrɪˈbjuʃən] *s* distribuzione, erogazione

**distributor** [dɪsˈtrɪbjətər] *s* distributore *m;* (aut) distributore *m* d'accensione

**district** [ˈdɪstrɪkt] *s* regione; *(of a city)* rione *m*, quartiere *m;* *(administrative division)* distretto ‖ *tr* dividere in distretti

**dis'trict attor'ney** *s* procuratore *m* generale

**distrust** [dɪsˈtrʌst] *s* diffidenza ‖ *tr* diffidare di

**distrustful** [dɪsˈtrʌstfəl] *adj* diffidente

**disturb** [dɪsˈtʌrb] *tr* disturbare, turbare; disordinare

**disturbance** [dɪsˈtʌrbəns] *s* disturbo, turbamento, perturbazione; disordine *m*

**disuse** [dɪsˈjus] *s* disuso

**ditch** [dɪtʃ] *s* fossa, fossato ‖ *tr* scavare un fosso in; (rr) far deragliare; (slang) piantare in asso ‖ *intr* fare un ammaraggio forzato

**dither** [ˈdɪðər] *s* agitazione; **to be in a dither** (coll) essere agitato

**dit·to** [ˈdɪto] *s (-tos)* lo stesso; *(ditto symbol)* virgolette *fpl* ‖ *adv* ugualmente, idem ‖ *tr* copiare, duplicare

**dit'to marks'** *spl* virgolette *fpl*

**dit·ty** ['dɪti] s (-ties) canzonetta
**diva** ['divɑ] s (mus) diva
**divan** ['daɪvæn] or [dɪ'væn] s divano
**dive** [daɪv] s tuffo; (of a submarine) immersione; (aer) picchiata; (coll) taverna; (com) discesa ‖ v (pret & pp dived or dove [dov]) intr tuffarsi; (said of submarine) immergersi; (to plunge) lanciarsi; (aer) scendere in picchiata; **to dive for** (e.g., pearls) pescare
**dive'-bomb'** tr bombardare in picchiata ‖ intr scendere a tuffo
**dive' bomb'ing** s bombardamento in picchiata
**diver** ['daɪvər] s tuffatore m; (person who works under water) palombaro; (orn) tuffetto
**diverge** [dɪ'vʌrdʒ] or [daɪ'vʌrdʒ] intr divergere
**divers** ['daɪvərz] adj diversi, vari
**diverse** [dɪ'vʌrs], [daɪ'vʌrs] or ['daɪvʌrs] adj (different) diverso; (of various kinds) multiforme
**diversification** [dɪ,vʌrsɪfɪ'keʃən] or [daɪ,vʌrsɪfɪ'keʃən] s diversificazione
**diversi·fy** [dɪ'vʌrsɪ,faɪ] or [daɪ'vʌrsɪ,faɪ] v (pret & pp -fied) tr diversificare ‖ intr diversificarsi
**diversion** [dɪ'vʌrʒən] or [daɪ'vʌrʒən] s diversione; (pastime) svago
**diversi·ty** [dɪ'vʌrsɪti] or [daɪ'vʌrsɪti] s (-ties) diversità f
**divert** [dɪ'vʌrt] or [daɪ'vʌrt] tr deviare; (to entertain) divertire; (money) stornare, distrarre
**diverting** [dɪ'vʌrtɪŋ] or [daɪ'vʌrtɪŋ] adj divertente
**divest** [dɪ'vest] or [daɪ'vest] tr spogliare; spossessare; **to divest oneself of** spogliarsi di, espropriarsi di
**divide** [dɪ'vaɪd] s spartiacque m ‖ tr dividere ‖ intr dividersi
**dividend** ['dɪvɪ,dend] s dividendo
**dividers** [dɪ'vaɪdərz] spl compasso a punte fisse
**divination** [,dɪvɪ'neʃən] s divinazione
**divine** [dɪ'vaɪn] adj divino ‖ s sacerdote m, prete m ‖ tr divinare
**diviner** [dɪ'vaɪnər] s divinatore m
**diving** ['daɪvɪŋ] s tuffo, immersione
**div'ing bell'** s campana da palombaro
**div'ing board'** s trampolino
**div'ing suit'** s scafandro
**divin'ing rod'** [dɪ'vaɪnɪŋ] s bacchetta rabdomantica
**divini·ty** [dɪ'vɪnɪti] s (-ties) divinità f; teologia; **the Divinity** Dio
**divisible** [dɪ'vɪsɪbəl] adj divisibile
**division** [dɪ'vɪʒən] s divisione
**divisor** [dɪ'vaɪzər] s divisore m
**divorce** [dɪ'vors] s divorzio; **to get a divorce** divorziare ‖ tr (a married couple) divorziare; (one's spouse) divorziare da ‖ intr divorziare
**divorcé** [dɪvor'se] s divorziato
**divorcee** [dɪvor'si] s divorziata
**divulge** [dɪ'vʌldʒ] tr divulgare
**dizziness** ['dɪzɪnɪs] s vertigine f, stordimento; confusione
**diz·zy** ['dɪzi] adj (-zier; -ziest) (causing dizziness) vertiginoso; (suffering diz-

ziness) preso da vertigine, stordito; (coll) stupido
**do** [du] v (3rd pers does [dʌz]; pret did [dɪd]; pp done [dʌn]; ger doing ['du·ɪŋ]) tr fare; (a problem) risolvere; (a distance) percorrere; (to study) studiare; (to explore) attraversare; (to tire) stancare; **to do one's best** fare del proprio meglio; **to do over** tornare a fare; ripetere; **to do right by** trattare bene; **to do s.o. out of s.th** (coll) portare via qlco a qlcu; **to do to death** mettere a morte; **to do up** (coll) impacchettare; stancare; (one's hair) farsi; vestire; (a shirt) lavare e stirare; **to have done** far fare ‖ intr fare; agire; comportarsi; servire; bastare; stare; succedere; **how do you do?** come sta?; **that will do** basta; è sufficiente; **to have done with** non aver più nulla a che fare con; **to have nothing to do with** non aver nulla a che vedere con; **to have to do with** aver a che fare con, trattarsi di; **to do away with** togliere di mezzo; **to do for** servire da; **to do well** crescere bene; **to do without** fare a meno di ‖ v aux used 1) in interrogative sentences: **Do you speak Italian?** Parla italiano?; 2) in negative sentences: **I do not speak Italian** Non parlo italiano; 3) to avoid repetition of a verb or full verbal expression: **Did you go to church this morning? Yes, I did.** È stato in chiesa questa mattina? Sì, ci sono stato; 4) to lend emphasis to a principal verb: **I do believe what you told me** Ci credo a quello che mi ha detto; 5) in inverted constructions after certain adverbs: **Seldom does he come to see me** Mi viene a vedere di raro; 6) in a supplicating tone with imperatives: **Do come in** entri per favore
**docile** ['dɑsɪl] adj docile
**dock** [dɑk] s (wharf) molo; (waterway between two piers) darsena; (area including piers and waterways) scalo portuario; (law) gabbia degli imputati ‖ tr (to deduct from the wages of) fare una deduzione a; (to deduct s.o.'s salary) dedurre da; (an animal) scodare; (naut) attraccare ‖ intr (aer) agganciarsi; (naut) attraccare
**dockage** ['dɑkɪdʒ] s attracco; (charges) diritti mpl di porto
**docket** ['dɑkɪt] s ordine m del giorno; (law) ruolo delle sentenze; **on the docket** (coll) pendente, in sospeso
**dock' hand'** s portuale m
**docking** ['dɑkɪŋ] s (aer) aggancio; (naut) attracco
**dock'yard'** s cantiere m navale
**doctor** ['dɑktər] s dottore m; (physician) medico ‖ tr curare; aggiustare; falsificare; adulterare ‖ intr esercitare la medicina; (coll) curarsi, prendere medicine
**doctorate** ['dɑktərɪt] s dottorato
**doctrine** ['dɑktrɪn] s dottrina
**document** ['dɑkjəmənt] s documento ‖ ['dɑkjə,ment] tr documentare

**documenta·ry** [ ˌdɑkjə'mɛntəri] *adj &*
*s* (**-ries**) documentario
**documentation** [ ˌdɑkəmɛn'teʃən] *s* do-
cumentazione
**doddering** ['dɑdərɪŋ] *adj* tremante,
rimbambito
**dodge** [dɑdʒ] *s* scarto, schivata; (fig)
stratagemma *m* ‖ *tr* schivare, evitare
‖ *intr* schivarsi; (fig) rispondere eva-
sivamente; **to dodge around the corner** scantonare
**do·do** ['dodo] *s* (**-dos** or **-does**) (coll)
rimbecillito
**doe** [do] *s* (*of deer*) cerva; (*of goat*)
capretta; (*of rabbit*) coniglia
**doeskin** ['do ˌskɪn] *s* pelle *f* di daino,
pelle *f* di dante; lana finissima
**doff** [dɑf] or [dɔf] *tr* (*one's hat*) togliersi; (*clothing*) deporre
**dog** [dɔg] or [dɑg] *s* cane *m;* **to go to
the dogs** (coll) andare in malora; **to
put on the dog** (coll) darsi delle arie
‖ *v* (*pret & pp* **dogged;** *ger* **dogging**)
*tr* seguire; perseguitare
**dog'catch'er** *s* accalappiacani *m*
**dog' days'** *s* solleone *m,* canicola
**doge** [dodʒ] *s* doge *m*
**dog'-ear'** *s* orecchia, orecchio
**dog'fight'** *s* duello aereo
**dogged** ['dɔgɪd] or ['dɑgɪd] *adj* accanito
**doggerel** ['dɔgərəl] or ['dɑgərəl] *s*
versi *mpl* da colascione
**dog·gy** ['dɔgi] or ['dɑgi] *adj* (**-gier;
-giest**) vistoso; canino ‖ *s* (**-gies**)
cagnolino
**dog'house'** *s* canile *m;* **to be in the doghouse** (slang) essere in disgrazia
**dog' Lat'in** *s* latino maccheronico
**dogma** ['dɔgmə] or ['dɑgmə] *s* dogma
*m*
**dogmatic** [dɔg'mætɪk] or [dɑg'mætɪk]
*adj* dogmatico
**dog' rac'ing** *s* corse *fpl* dei cani
**dog' show'** *s* mostra canina
**dog's' life'** *s* vita da cani
**Dog' Star'** *s* canicola
**dog' tag'** *s* (mil) piastrina, piastrino
**dog'-tired'** *adj* (coll) stanco morto
**dog'tooth'** *s* (**-teeth** [ ˌtiθ]) canino
**dog' track'** *s* cinodromo
**dog'watch'** *s* (naut) quarto di solo due
ore, gaettone *m*
**dog'wood'** *s* corniolo
**doi·ly** ['dɔɪli] *s* (**-lies**) centrino
**doings** ['du·ɪŋz] *spl* azioni *fpl,* fatti
*mpl*
**do'-it-your·self'** *s* il fare tutto da sé
**doldrums** ['dɑldrəmz] *spl* calma equatoriale; inattività *f;* depressione
**dole** [dol] *s* elemosina; (*to the jobless*)
sussidio di disoccupazione ‖ *tr*—**to
dole out** distribuire parsimoniosa-
mente
**doleful** ['dolfəl] *adj* lugubre, triste
**doll** [dɑl] *s* bambola ‖ *intr*—**to doll up**
(slang) agghindarsi
**dollar** ['dɑlər] *s* dollaro
**dol'lar·wise'** *adv* in termini finanziari
**dol·ly** ['dɑli] *s* (**-lies**) pupattola; (*low,
wheeled frame for moving heavy
loads*) carrello; (mov, telv) carrello

‖ *v* (*pret & pp* **-lied**) *intr* (mov, telv)
carrellare
**dol'ly shot'** *s* (mov, telv) carrellata
**dolphin** ['dɑlfɪn] *s* delfino
**dolt** [dolt] *s* gonzo, balordo
**doltish** ['doltɪʃ] *adj* gonzo, balordo
**domain** [do'men] *s* dominio; (law) proprietà *f;* (fig) campo, orbita
**dome** [dom] *s* cupola
**dome' light'** *s* lampadario
**domestic** [də'mɛstɪk] *adj & s* domestico
**domesticate** [də'mɛstɪ ˌket] *tr* domesticare
**domicile** ['dɑmɪsɪl] or ['dɑmɪ ˌsaɪl] *s*
domicilio ‖ *tr* domiciliare
**dominance** ['dɑmɪnəns] *s* dominio
**dominant** ['dɑmɪnənt] *adj & s* domi-
nante *f*
**dominate** ['dɑmɪ ˌnet] *tr & intr* dominare
**domination** [ ˌdɑmɪ'neʃən] *s* domina-
zione
**domineer** [ ˌdɑmɪ'nɪr] *intr* spadroneggiare
**domineering** [ ˌdɑmɪ'nɪrɪŋ] *adj* dispotico, tirannico
**Dominican** [də'mɪnɪkən] *adj & s* do-
minicano; (eccl) domenicano
**dominion** [də'mɪnjən] *s* dominio
**domi·no** ['dɑmɪ ˌno] *s* (**-noes** or **-nos**)
(*costume and person*) domino;
(*piece*) tessera di domino; **dominoes**
(*game*) domino
**don** [dɑn] *s* signore *m;* don *m;* membro
di un collegio universitario inglese ‖
*v* (*pret & pp* **donned;** *ger* **donning**)
*tr* (*clothes*) mettersi, vestire
**donate** ['donet] *tr* donare, dare
**donation** [do'neʃən] *s* donazione
**done** [dʌn] *adj* fatto; finito; stanco;
(culin) ben cotto, ben rosolato
**done' for'** *adj* (coll) stanco morto;
(coll) rovinato; (coll) fuori combattimento; (coll) morto
**donjon** ['dʌndʒən] or ['dɑndʒən] *s* torrione *m,* maschio
**Don Juan** [dɑn 'wɑn] or [dɔn 'hwɑn]
*s* Don Giovanni
**donkey** ['dɑŋki] or ['dʌŋki] *s* asino,
somaro
**donnish** ['dɑnɪʃ] *adj* pedante
**donor** ['donər] *s* donatore *m*
**doodle** ['dudəl] *tr & intr* scarabocchiare, riempire di ghirigori
**doom** [dum] *s* destino; morte *f,* rovina;
sentenza di morte; giudizio finale ‖
*tr* destinare; condannare; condannare
a morte
**doomsday** ['dumz ˌde] *s* giorno del
giudizio
**door** [dor] *s* porta; (*of a carriage or
automobile*) portiera, sportello; (*one
part of a double door*) battente *m;*
**behind closed doors** a porte chiuse;
**to see to the door** accompagnare alla
porta; **to show s.o. the door** mettere
qlcu alla porta
**door'bell'** *s* campanello della porta
**door' check'** *s* chiusura automatica di
porta, scontro
**door'frame'** *s* cornice *f*

**door'head'** s architrave m
**door'jamb'** s stipite m
**door'keep'er** s portinaio
**door'knob'** s maniglia della porta
**door' knock'er** s battente m
**door' latch'** s paletto
**door'man'** s (-men') portiere m, portinaio; (of large apartment house) guardaportone m
**door'mat'** s stoino, zerbino
**door'nail'** s borchione m; **dead as a doornail** morto e ben morto
**door'post'** s stipite m
**door' scrap'er** s raschietto
**door'sill'** s soglia
**door'step'** s gradino davanti la porta
**door'stop'** s paracolpi m
**door'-to-door'** adj (shipment) diretto; (selling) di porta in porta
**door'way'** s vano della porta; porta
**dope** [dop] s lubrificante m; (aer) vernice f; (slang) stupido, scemo; (slang) informazioni fpl; (slang) narcotico || tr (slang) narcotizzare; **to dope out** (slang) indovinare, decifrare, immaginare
**dope' fiend'** s (slang) tossicomane mf
**dope'sheet'** s giornaletto con le previsioni della corse ippiche
**dormant** ['dɔrmənt] adj dormente; latente
**dor'mer win'dow** ['dɔrmər] s abbaino
**dormito·ry** ['dɔrmɪˌtori] s (-ries) dormitorio
**dor·mouse** ['dɔrˌmaʊs] s (-mice [ˌmaɪs]) ghiro
**dosage** ['dosɪdʒ] s dosatura
**dose** [dos] s dose f; (coll) boccone amaro || tr dosare; somministrare
**dossier** ['dɑsɪˌe] s incartamento
**dot** [dɑt] s punto; **on the dot** (coll) in punto || v (pret & pp **dotted;** ger **dotting**) tr punteggiare; **to dot one's i's** mettere i punti sulle i
**dotage** ['dotɪdʒ] s rimbecillimento; **to be in one's dotage** essere rimbambito
**dotard** ['dotərd] s vecchio rimbambito
**dote** [dot] intr rimbambirsi; **to dote on** essere pazzo per
**doting** ['dotɪŋ] adj che ama alla follia; (from old age) rimbambito, rimbecillito
**dots' and dash'es** spl (telg) punti mpl e tratti mpl
**dot'ted line'** s linea punteggiata; **to sign on the dotted line** firmare inconsideratamente
**double** ['dʌbəl] adj doppio || s doppio; (bridge) contre m; **doubles** (tennis) doppio || tr raddoppiare; (bridge) contrare || intr raddoppiarsi; (bridge) contrare; (mov, theat) sostenere due ruoli; (mov) doppiare; **to double up** (said of two people) dividere la stessa camera, dividere lo stesso letto; piegarsi in due
**double-barreled** ['dʌbəl'bærəld] adj a due canne; (fig) a doppio fine
**dou'ble bass'** s contrabbasso
**dou'ble bed'** s letto matrimoniale
**dou'ble boil'er** s bagnomaria m

**double-breasted** ['dʌbəl'brestɪd] adj a doppio petto, doppiopetto
**dou'ble chin'** s pappagorgia
**dou'ble-cross'** tr (coll) tradire
**dou'ble date'** s (coll) appuntamento amoroso di due coppie
**dou'ble-deal'ing** adj doppio
**dou'ble-deck'er** s (bed) letto a castello; (sandwich) tramezzino doppio; autobus m a due piani; (naut) nave f due ponti; (aer) aereo due ponti
**double-edged** ['dʌbəl'edʒd] adj a due tagli, a doppio taglio
**dou'ble en'try** s (com) partita doppia
**dou'ble fea'ture** s (mov) programma m di due lungometraggio
**double-header** ['dʌbəl'hedər] s treno con due locomotive; due partite di baseball giocate successivamente
**double-jointed** ['dʌbəl'dʒɔɪntɪd] adj snodato
**dou'ble-park'** tr & intr parcheggiare in doppia fila
**dou'ble-quick'** adj & adv a passo di carica
**dou'ble stand'ard** s—**to have a double standard** usare due pesi e due misure
**doublet** ['dʌblɪt] s (close-fitting jacket) farsetto; (philol) doppione m
**dou'ble-talk'** s discorso incomprensibile; **to give s.o. double-talk** parlare evasivamente a qlcu || intr parlare evasivamente
**dou'ble time'** s paga doppia; (mil) passo di carica
**doubleton** ['dʌbəltən] s doppio
**doubly** ['dʌbli] adv doppiamente
**doubt** [daʊt] s dubbio; **beyond doubt** senza dubbio; **if in doubt** in caso di dubbio; **no doubt** senza dubbio || tr dubitare di || intr dubitare
**doubter** ['daʊtər] s incredulo
**doubtful** ['daʊtfəl] adj incerto; dubbioso
**doubtless** ['daʊtlɪs] adj indubitabile || adv senza dubbio; probabilmente
**douche** [duʃ] s irrigazione f; (instrument) irrigatore m || tr irrigare || intr fare irrigazioni
**dough** [do] s pasta di pane; (money) (slang) soldi mpl, quattrini mpl
**dough'boy'** s fantaccino americano
**dough'nut'** s ciambella; (with filling) sgonfiotto
**dough·ty** ['daʊti] adj (-tier; -tiest) forte, coraggioso
**dough·y** ['do·i] adj (-ier; -iest) pastoso, molle
**dour** [daʊr] or [dʊr] adj triste, severo
**douse** [daʊs] tr immergere; bagnare; (the light) (coll) spegnere
**dove** [dʌv] s colomba, tortora
**dovecote** ['dʌvˌkot] s piccionaia
**dove'tail'** s coda di rondine || tr calettare a coda di rondine; (to make fit) adattare, far combaciare || intr (to fit) combaciare; corrispondere
**dowager** ['daʊ·ədʒər] s vedova titolata; vecchia signora austera; **queen dowager** regina madre
**dow·dy** ['daʊdi] adj (-dier; -diest) trasandato

**dow·el** ['dau·əl] *s* caviglia, tassello ‖ *v* (*pret* & *pp* **-eled** or **-elled; ger -eling** or **-elling**) *tr* tassellare

**dower** ['dau·ər] *s* (*widow's portion*) legittima, vedovile *m;* (*marriage portion; natural gift*) dote *f* ‖ *tr* dotare; assegnare un vedovile a

**down** [daun] *adj* che discende; basso; (*train*) che va al centro; depresso; finito; (*money, payment*) anticipato; (*storage battery*) esaurito ‖ *s* (*of fruit and human body*) lanugine *f;* (*of birds*) piumino; (*upset*) rovescio; discesa; (*sandhill*) duna ‖ *adv* giù; all'ingiù, in giù; dabbasso; a terra; al sud; (*in cash*) a contanti; **down and out** rovinato; senza una soldo; **down from** da; **down on one's knees** in ginocchio; **down to** fino a; **down under** agli antipodi; **down with . . . !** abasso . . . !; **to get down to work** mettersi seriamente al lavoro; **to go down** scendere; **to lie down** sdraiarsi; andare a letto; **to sit down** sedersi ‖ *prep* giù per; **down the river** a valle; **down the street** giù per la strada ‖ *tr* abbattere; (coll) buttar giù, tracannare

**down'cast'** *adj* mogio, sfiduciato

**down'fall'** *s* rovina, rovescio

**down'grade'** *adj* & *adv* in declivio, a valle ‖ *s* discesa; **to be on the downgrade** essere in declino ‖ *tr* attribuire minor importanza a; degradare

**downhearted** ['daun ,hartɪd] *adj* scoraggiato, abbattuto

**down'hill'** *adj* & *adv* in declivio; **to go downhill** declinare

**down' pay'ment** *s* acconto

**down'pour'** *s* acquazzone *m*, rovescio

**down'right'** *adj* assoluto; completo; franco, diretto ‖ *adv* completamente

**down'stairs'** *adj* del piano di sotto ‖ *s* il piano di sotto; i piani di sotto ‖ *adv* dabbasso, di sotto, giù

**down'stream'** *adv* a valle

**down'stroke'** *s* corsa discendente

**down'town'** *adj* centrale ‖ *s* centro della città ‖ *adv* al centro della città

**down' train'** *s* treno discendente, treno che va al centro

**down'trend'** *s* tendenza al ribasso

**downtrodden** ['daun ,tradən] *adj* calpestato, oppresso

**downward** ['daunwərd] *adj* & *adv* all'ingiù

**down·y** ['dauni] *adj* (**-ier; -iest**) piumoso, lanuginoso; (*soft*) molle, morbido

**dow·ry** ['dauri] *s* (**-ries**) dote *f*

**doze** [doz] *s* pisolo ‖ *intr* dormicchiare; **to doze off** appisolarsi

**dozen** ['dʌzən] *s* dozzina

**dozy** ['dozi] *adj* sonnolento

**drab** [dræb] *adj* (**drabber; drabbest**) grigiastro; (*dull*) scialbo ‖ *s* colore grigiastro; (*fabric*) tela naturale; donna di malaffare

**drach·ma** ['drækmə] *s* (**-mas** or **-mae** [mi]) dramma

**draft** [dræft] or [draft] *s* corrente *f* d'aria; (*pulling*) tiro; (*in a chimney*) tiraggio; (*sketch, outline*) schizzo; (*first form of a writing*) prima stesura; (*drink*) sorso, bicchiere *m;* (com) tratta, lettera di credito; (law) progetto, disegno; (naut) pesca; (mil) coscrizione *f*, leva; **on draft** alla spina ‖ *tr* disegnare; fare uno schizzo di; (*a document*) stendere; (mil) coscrivere; **to be drafted** essere di leva, andar coscritto

**draft' age'** *s* età *f* di leva

**draft' beer'** *s* birra alla spina

**draft' board'** *s* consiglio di leva

**draft' dodg'er** ['dadʒər] *s* renitente *m* alla leva, imboscato

**draftee** [ ,dræf'ti] or [ ,draf'ti] *s* coscritto

**draft' horse'** *s* cavallo da tiro

**drafts'man** *s* (**-men**) disegnatore *m;* (*man who draws up documents*) redattore *m*

**draft' trea'ty** *s* progetto di trattato

**draft·y** ['dræfti] or ['drafti] *adj* (**-ier; -iest**) pieno di correnti d'aria

**drag** [dræg] *s* (*sledge for conveying heavy bodies*) traino, treggia; (*on a cigarette*) boccata; (aer) resistenza aerodinamica; (naut) pressione idrostatica; (naut) draga; (fig) noia; (*influence*) (slang) aderenze *fpl;* (*a bore*) (slang) rompiscatole *m* ‖ *v* (*pret* & *pp* **dragged; ger dragging**) *tr* strascinare, strascicare; (naut) rastrellare ‖ *intr* strascicare, strascicarsi; dilungarsi; **to drag on** andare per le lunghe

**drag'net'** *s* paranza; (fig) retata

**dragon** ['drægən] *s* drago, dragone *m*

**drag'on·fly'** *s* (**-flies**) libellula

**dragoon** [drə'gun] *s* (mil) dragone *m* ‖ *tr* forzare, costringere

**drain** [dren] *s* scolo; prosciugamento; (geog) spiovente *m;* (surg) drenaggio; (fig) salasso ‖ *tr* (*a liquid*) scolare; prosciugare; (*humid land; a wound*) drenare ‖ *intr* scolare; prosciugarsi; (geog) defluire

**drainage** ['drenɪdʒ] *s* drenaggio; (geog) displuvio, spartiacque *m*

**drain'board'** *s* scolatoio per le stoviglie

**drain' cock'** *s* rubinetto di scarico

**drain'pipe'** *s* tubo di scarico

**drake** [drek] *s* anatra maschio

**dram** [dræm] *s* dramma; bicchierino di liquore

**drama** ['dramə] or ['dræmə] *s* dramma *m;* (*art and genre*) drammatica

**dramatic** [drə'mætɪk] *adj* drammatico ‖ **dramatics** *ssg* drammatica; *spl* rappresentazione dilettantesca; comportamento drammatico

**dramatist** ['dræmətɪst] *s* drammaturgo

**dramatize** ['dræmə ,taɪz] *tr* drammatizzare

**drape** [drep] *s* tenda, cortina; (*of a curtain*) drappeggio; (*of a skirt*) taglio ‖ *tr* drappeggiare

**draper·y** ['drepəri] *s* (**-ies**) drapperia; negozio di tessuti; **draperies** tendaggi *mpl*

**drastic** ['dræstɪk] *adj* drastico

**draught** [dræft] or [drɑft] *s & tr* var of **draft**

**draught' beer'** *s* birra alla spina

**draw** [drɔ] *s* (*in a game*) patta; (*in a lottery*) sorteggio; (*act of drawing*) tiro; (*of chimney*) tiraggio; (*attraction*) attrazione; (*of a drawbridge*) ala ‖ *v* (*pret* **drew** [dru]; *pp* **drawn** [drɔn]) *tr* (*a line*) tirare; (*to attract*) richiamare; (*butter*) fondere; (*a sword*) sguainare; (*a nail*) estrarre; (*people*) attrarre; (*a sigh*) emettere; (*a curtain*) far scorrere; (*a salary*) pigliare; (*a prize*) ricevere; (*a game*) impattare; (*in card games*) pescare; (*a drawbridge*) sollevare; (*said of a ship*) pescare; (*a comparison*) fare; (*a profit*) ricavare; (*a chicken*) sventrare; (*e.g., a picture*) disegnare, ritrarre; (*to sketch in words*) descrivere; (*a contract*) stipulare; (*interest*) ricevere; (com) spiccare, staccare; **to draw forth** far uscire; **to draw off** estrarre; (*a liquid*) spillare; **to draw** (*shoes*) **on** mettersi; **to draw** (*money*) **on** ritirare da; **to draw** (*a draft*) **on** domiciliare presso; **to draw oneself up** raddrizzarsi; **to draw out** (*to persuade to talk*) far parlare, tirar fuori le parole a; **to draw up** (*a document*) estendere; (mil) schierare ‖ *intr* (*said of chimney*) tirare; impattare; sorteggiare un premio; aver attrazione; disegnare; **to draw aside** scostarsi; **to draw back** retrocedere, ritirarsi; **to draw near** avvicinarsi; volgere a; **to draw to a close** essere quasi finito; **to draw together** unirsi

**draw'back'** *s* inconveniente *m*

**draw'bridge'** *s* ponte levatoio

**drawee** [ˌdrɔ'i] *s* trattario, trassato

**drawer** ['drɔ·ər] *s* disegnatore *m*; (com) traente *m* ‖ [drɔr] *s* cassetto; **drawers** mutande *fpl*

**drawing** ['drɔ·ɪŋ] *s* disegno; (*in a lottery*) sorteggio

**draw'ing board'** *s* tavolo da disegno

**draw'ing card'** *s* attrazione

**draw'ing room'** *s* salotto, salottino

**draw'knife'** *s* (-**knives** [ˌnaɪvz]) coltello a petto

**drawl** [drɔl] *s* accento strascicato ‖ *tr* dire con accento strascicato ‖ *intr* strascicare le parole

**drawn' but'ter** *s* burro fuso

**drawn' work'** *s* lavoro a giorno

**dray** [dre] *s* carro pesante; slitta, treggia; autocarro

**drayage** ['dre·ɪdʒ] *s* carreggio

**dray'man** *s* (-**men**) carrettiere *m*

**dread** [drɛd] *adj* spaventoso, terribile ‖ *s* spavento, terrore *m* ‖ *tr & intr* temere

**dreadful** ['drɛdfəl] *adj* spaventevole, terribile; (coll) orribile

**dread'nought'** *s* corazzata

**dream** [drim] *s* sogno; illusione, fantasticheria; **dream come true** sogno fatto realtà ‖ *v* (*pret & pp* **dreamed** or **dreamt** [drɛmt]) *tr* sognare; **to dream up** (coll) immaginare, fantasticare ‖ *intr* sognare

**dreamer** ['drimər] *s* sognatore *m*

**dream'land'** *s* paese *m* dei sogni

**dream·y** ['drimi] *adj* (**-ier**; **-iest**) sognante; (*visionary*) trasognato; vago

**drear·y** ['drɪri] *adj* (**-ier**; **-iest**) squallido; triste; (*boring*) noioso

**dredge** [drɛdʒ] *s* draga ‖ *tr* dragare; (culin) infarinare

**dredger** ['drɛdʒər] *s* (*boat*) draga; (*container*) spolverino

**dredging** ['drɛdʒɪŋ] *s* dragaggio

**dregs** [drɛgz] *spl* feccia

**drench** [drɛntʃ] *tr* infradiciare, inzuppare

**dress** [drɛs] *s* vestito; vestiti *mpl*; vestito da donna; abito; abito da cerimonia; (*of a bird*) piumaggio ‖ *tr* vestire; adornare, decorare; (*hair*) pettinare; (*a wound*) medicare; (*leather*) conciare; (*food*) condire; (*a boat*) pavesare; **to dress down** (coll) rimproverare; **to get dressed** vestirsi ‖ *intr* vestire; vestirsi; (mil) schierarsi; **to dress up** vestirsi da sera; farsi bello, mettersi in gala

**dress' ball'** *s* ballo di gala

**dress' coat'** *s* frac *m*

**dresser** ['drɛsər] *s* toletta; (*sideboard*) credenza; **to be a good dresser** vestire con eleganza

**dress' goods'** *spl* stoffa per abiti

**dressing** ['drɛsɪŋ] *s* ornamento; (*for food*) condimento, salsa; (*stuffing for fowl*) ripieno; (*fertilizer*) concime *m*; (*for a wound*) medicazione

**dress'ing down'** *s* ramanzina

**dress'ing gown'** *s* vestaglia

**dress'ing room'** *s* spogliatoio, toletta; (theat) camerino

**dress'ing sta'tion** *s* posto di pronto soccorso

**dress'ing ta'ble** *s* toletta, specchiera

**dress'mak'er** *s* sarta, sarto per donna

**dress'mak'ing** *s* taglio, sartoria

**dress' rehears'al** *s* prova generale

**dress' shirt'** *s* camicia inamidata

**dress' suit'** *s* marsina

**dress' u'niform** *s* (mil) alta uniforme

**dress·y** ['drɛsi] *adj* (**-ier**; **iest**) (coll) elegante, ricercato

**dribble** ['drɪbəl] *s* goccia ‖ *tr* (sports) palleggiare, dribblare ‖ *intr* gocciolare; (*at the mouth*) sbavare; (sports) dribblare

**driblet** ['drɪblɪt] *s* piccola quantità; **in driblets** col contagocce

**dried' beef'** [draɪd] *s* carne seccata

**dried' fruit'** *s* frutta secca

**drier** ['draɪ·ər] *s* (*for hair*) asciugacapelli *m*; (*for clothes*) asciugatrice *f*

**drift** [drɪft] *s* movimento; (*of sand, snow, etc.*) cumulo; (*snowdrift*) neve accumulata dal vento; tendenza, corrente *f*; intenzione; (aer, naut) deriva; (rad, telv) deviazione ‖ *intr* andare alla deriva; (*said of snow*) accumularsi; (aer, naut) derivare, scadere

**drift' ice'** *s* ghiaccio alla deriva

**drift'pin'** *s* (mach) mandrino

**drift'wood'** *s* legname andato alla deriva

**drill** [drɪl] *s* esercizio; (*fabric*) tela cruda; (agr) seminatrice *f;* (mach) trapano, trivella; (mil) esercitazioni *fpl* militari ‖ *tr* trivellare; istruire; (mil) insegnare gli esercizi militari a ‖ *intr* addestrarsi; (mil) fare gli esercizi militari
**drill'mas'ter** *s* istruttore *m*
**drill' press'** *s* trapano a colonna
**drink** [drɪŋk] *s* bevanda; **the drinks are on the house!** paga il proprietario! ‖ *v* (*pret* **drank** [dræŋk]; *pp* **drunk** [drʌŋk]) *tr* bere; assorbire; **to drink down** tracannare; **to drink in** bere, assorbire; (*air*) aspirare ‖ *intr* bere; **to drink out of** bere da; **to drink to the health of** bere alla salute di
**drinkable** ['drɪŋkəbəl] *adj* bevibile, potabile
**drinker** ['drɪŋkər] *s* bevitore *m*
**drinking** ['drɪŋkɪŋ] *s* (il) bere
**drink'ing foun'tain** *s* fontanella pubblica
**drink'ing song'** *s* canzone bacchica
**drink'ing straw'** *s* cannuccia
**drink'ing trough'** *s* abbeveratoio
**drink'ing wa'ter** *s* acqua potabile
**drip** [drɪp] *s* sgocciolo, sgocciolatura ‖ *v* (*pret & pp* **dripped**; *ger* **dripping**) *intr* sgocciolare, stillare; (*said of perspiration*) trasudare
**drip' cof'fee** *s* caffè fatto con la macchinetta
**drip'-dry'** *adj* non-stiro
**drip' pan'** *s* (culin) ghiotta; (mach) coppa
**dripping** ['drɪpɪŋ] *s* gocciolio; **drippings** grasso che cola dall'arrosto
**drive** [draɪv] *s* scarrozzata; strada; passeggiata; impulso; forza, iniziativa; urgenza; spinta; campagna; (aut) trazione; (mach) trasmissione ‖ *v* (*pret* **drove** [drov]; *ger* **driven** ['drɪvən]) *tr* (*a nail*) ficcare, piantare; (*e.g., cattle*) condurre, parare; (*s.o. in a carriage or auto*) condurre, portare; spingere; stimulare; forzare; spingere a lavorare; (sports) colpire molto forte; **to drive away** scacciare; **to drive back** respingere; **to drive mad** far impazzire; **to drive out** scacciare ‖ *intr* fare una scarrozzata; **to drive in** entrare in automobile; (*a place*) entrare in automobile in; **to drive on the right** guidare a destra; **to drive out** uscire in macchina; **to drive up** arrivare in macchina
**drive'-in' mov'ie the'ater** *s* cineparco
**drive'-in' res'taurant** *s* ristorante *m* con servizio alla portiera
**driv•el** ['drɪvəl] *s* (*slobber*) bava; (*nonsense*) scemenza ‖ *v* (*pret* **-eled** or **-elled**; *ger* **-eling** or **-elling**) *intr* sbavare; dire scemenze
**driver** ['draɪvər] *s* guidatore *m;* (*of a carriage*) cocchiere *m;* (*of a locomotive*) macchinista *m;* (*of pack animals*) carrettiere *m,* mulattiere *m*
**driv'er's li'cense** *s* patente automobilistica
**driv'er's seat'** *s* posto di guida

**drive' shaft'** *s* albero motore
**drive'way'** *s* strada privata d'accesso; carrozzabile *f*
**drive' wheel'** *s* ruota motrice
**driv'ing school'** ['draɪvɪŋ] *s* autoscuola, scuola guida
**drizzle** ['drɪzəl] *s* pioviggine *f* ‖ *intr* piovigginare
**droll** [drol] *adj* buffo, spassoso
**dromedar•y** ['draməˌdɛri] *s* (**-ies**) dromedario
**drone** [dron] *s* fuco, pecchione *m;* (*hum*) ronzio; (*of bagpipe*) bordone *m;* areoplano teleguidato ‖ *tr* dire in tono monotono ‖ *intr* (*to live in idleness*) fare il fannullone; (*to buzz, hum*) ronzare
**drool** [drul] *s* (*slobber*) bava; (slang) scemenza ‖ *intr* sbavare; (slang) dire scemenze
**droop** [drup] *s* accasciamento ‖ *intr* (*to sag*) pendere; (*to lose spirit*) accasciarsi; (*said, e.g., of wheat*) avvizzire
**drooping** ['drupɪŋ] *adj* (*eyelid*) abbassato; (*shoulder*) spiovente; (fig) accasciato
**drop** [drɑp] *s* goccia; (*slope*) pendenza; (*earring*) pendente *m;* (in *temperature*) discesa; (*from an airplane*) lancio; (*trap door*) botola; (*gallows*) trabocchetto della forca; (*lozenge*) pastiglia; (*slit for letters*) buca; (*curtain*) tela; (*in prices*) calo; **a drop in the bucket** una goccia nell'oceano ‖ *v* (*pret & pp* **dropped**; *ger* **dropping**) *tr* lasciar cadere; (*a letter*) imbucare; (*a curtain*) abbassare; (*a remark*) lasciar scappare; (*a note*) scrivere; omettere; abbandonare; (*anchor*) gettare; (*from an airplane*) lanciare; (*from an automobile*) lasciare; (*from a list*) cancellare ‖ *intr* cadere; lasciarsi cadere; terminare; **to drop dead** cader morto; **to drop in** entrare un momento; **to drop off** sparire; addormentarsi; morire improvvisamente; **to drop out** scomparire; ritirarsi; dare le dimissioni
**drop' cur'tain** *s* telone *m*
**drop' ham'mer** *s* maglio
**drop'-leaf' ta'ble** *s* tavola a ribalta
**drop'light'** *s* lampada sospesa
**drop'out'** *s* studente *m* che abbandona permanentemente la scuola media
**dropper** ['drɑpər] *s* contagocce *m*
**dropsical** ['drɑpsɪkəl] *adj* idropico
**dropsy** ['drɑpsi] *s* idropisia
**dross** [drɔs] or [drɑs] *s* scoria; (fig) feccia
**drought** [draʊt] *s* siccità *f;* (*shortage*) mancanza
**drove** [drov] *s* branco; folla; **in droves** in massa
**drover** ['drovər] *s* mandriano
**drown** [draʊn] *tr & intr* affogare, annegare
**drowse** [draʊz] *intr* sonnecchiare
**drow•sy** ['draʊzi] *adj* (**-sier; -siest**) sonnolento, insonnolito
**drub** [drʌb] *v* (*pret & pp* **drubbed;** *ger* **drubbing**) *tr* bastonare; battere

**drudge** [drʌdʒ] s sgobbone m ‖ intr sgobbare, sfacchinare
**drudger·y** ['drʌdʒəri] s (-ies) lavoro ingrato, sfacchinata
**drug** [drʌg] s droga, medicina; narcotico; **drug on the market** merce f invendibile ‖ v (pret & pp **drugged;** ger **drugging**) tr drogare, narcotizzare
**drug' ad'dict** s tossicomane mf
**drug' addic'tion** s tossicomania
**druggist** ['drʌgɪst] s farmacista mf
**drug' hab'it** s tossicomania
**drug'store'** s farmacia
**drug' traf'fic** s traffico in stupefacenti
**druid** ['dru·ɪd] s druida m
**drum** [drʌm] s (cylinder; instrument) tamburo; (container) fusto ‖ v (pret & pp **drummed;** ger **drumming**) tr stamburare; **to drum up** (customers) farsi; (enthusiasm) creare ‖ intr tambureggiare; (with the fingers) tamburellare
**drum'beat'** s rullo di tamburi
**drum' corps'** s banda di tamburi
**drum'fire'** s fuoco nutrito
**drum'head'** s membrana del tamburo
**drum' ma'jor** s tamburo maggiore
**drummer** ['drʌmər] s (salesman) agente m viaggiatore; (mus) tamburo; (mil) tamburino
**drum'stick'** s bacchetta del tamburo; (of cooked fowl) coscia
**drunk** [drʌŋk] adj ubriaco; **to get drunk** ubriacarsi ‖ s ubriaco; (spree) sbornia; **to go on a drunk** (coll) ubriacarsi
**drunkard** ['drʌŋkərd] s ubriacone m
**drunken** ['drʌŋkən] adj ubriaco
**drunk'en driv'ing** s—**to be arrested for drunken driving** esser arrestato per aver guidato in stato di ubriachezza
**drunkenness** ['drʌŋkənnɪs] s ubriachezza, ebbrezza
**dry** [draɪ] adj (drier; driest) secco; (boring) arido; **to be dry** aver sete ‖ s (drys) abolizionista mf ‖ v (pret & pp **dried**) tr seccare; (to wipe dry) asciugare ‖ intr seccarsi; **to dry up** prosciugarsi, essiccarsi; (slang) star zitto
**dry' bat'tery** s pila a secco; (group of dry cells) batteria a secco
**dry' cell'** s pila a secco
**dry'-clean'** tr lavare a secco, pulire a secco
**dry' clean'er** s tintore m
**dry' clean'ing** s lavaggio a secco, pulitura a secco
**dry'-clean'ing estab'lishment** s tintoria
**dry' dock'** s bacino di carenaggio
**dryer** ['draɪ·ər] s var of drier
**dry'-eyed'** adj a occhi asciutti
**dry' farm'ing** s coltivazione di terreno arido
**dry' goods'** spl tessuti mpl; aridi mpl
**dry'-goods store'** s drapperia, negozio di tessuti
**dry' ice'** s neve carbonica, ghiaccio secco
**dry' law'** s legge f proibizionista
**dry' meas'ure** s misura per solidi
**dryness** ['draɪnɪs] s siccità f; (e.g., of a speaker) aridità f

**dry' nurse'** s balia asciutta
**dry' run'** s esercizio di prova; (mil) esercitazione senza munizioni
**dry' sea'son** s stagione arida
**dry' wash'** s roba lavata e asciugata ma non stirata
**dual** ['dju·əl] or ['du·əl] adj & s duale m
**duali·ty** [dju'ælɪti] or [du'ælɪti] s (-ties) dualità f
**dub** [dʌb] s (slang) giocatore inesperto ‖ v (pret & pp **dubbed;** ger **dubbing**) tr chiamare, affibbiare il nome di; (a knight) armare; (mov) doppiare
**dubbing** ['dʌbɪŋ] s doppiaggio
**dubious** ['djubɪ·əs] or ['dubɪ·əs] adj dubbioso; incerto
**ducat** ['dʌkət] s ducato
**duchess** ['dʌtʃɪs] s duchessa
**duch·y** ['dʌtʃi] s (-ies) ducato
**duck** [dʌk] s anatra; mossa rapida; (in the water) tuffo; (dodge) schivata; **ducks** pantaloni mpl di tela cruda ‖ tr (one's head) abbassare rapidamente; (in water) tuffare; (a blow) schivare ‖ intr tuffarsi; **to duck out** (coll) svignarsela
**duckling** ['dʌklɪŋ] s anatroccolo
**ducks' and drakes'** s—**to play ducks and drakes with** buttar via, sperperare
**duck' soup'** s (slang) cosa facilissima
**duct** [dʌkt] s tubo, condotto
**ductile** ['dʌktɪl] adj duttile
**duct'less gland'** ['dʌktlɪs] s ghiandola a secrezione interna
**duct'work'** s condotto, canalizzazione
**dud** [dʌd] s (slang) bomba inesplosa; (person) (slang) fallito; (enterprise) (slang) fallimento; **duds** (coll) vestito; roba
**dude** [djud] or [dud] s elegantone m
**due** [dju] or [du] adj dovuto; atteso, debito; pagabile; **due to** dovuto a; **to fall due** scadere; **when is the train due?** a che ora arriva il treno? ‖ s spettanza; debito; **dues** (of a member) quota sociale; **to get one's due** ricevere quanto uno merita; **to give the devil his due** trattare ognuno con giustizia ‖ adv in direzione, e.g., **due north** in direzione nord
**duel** ['dju·əl] or ['du·əl] s duello; **to fight a duel** battersi a duello ‖ v (pret & pp **dueled** or **duelled;** ger **dueling** or **duelling**) intr duellare
**duelist** or **duellist** ['dju·əlɪst] or ['du·əlɪst] s duellante mf
**dues-paying** ['djuz,pe·ɪŋ] or ['duz,pe·ɪŋ] adj regolare, effettivo
**duet** [dju'ɛt] or [du'ɛt] s duetto
**duf'fel bag'** ['dʌfəl] s sacca da viaggio
**duke** [djuk] or [duk] s duca m
**dukedom** ['djukdəm] or ['dukdəm] s ducato
**dull** [dʌl] adj (not sharp) spuntato, senza filo; (color) spento, sbiadito; (sound, pain) sordo; (stupid) ebete, tonto; (business) inattivo; (boring) noioso, melenso; (flat) opaco, appannato ‖ tr spuntare; indebolire; inebetire; ottundere; (enthusiasm) raffreddare; (pain) alleviare ‖ intr

spuntarsi; sbiadirsi; inebetirsi; raf-freddarsi

**dullard** ['dʌlərd] *s* stupido

**duly** ['djuli] *or* ['duli] *adv* debitamente

**dumb** [dʌm] *adj (lacking the power to speak)* muto; (coll) tonto, stupido

**dumb'bell'** *s* manubrio; (slang) zuccone *m*, stupido

**dumb' crea'ture** *s* animale *m*, bruto

**dumb' show'** *s* pantomima

**dumb'wai'ter** *s* montavivande *m*

**dumfound** [,dʌm'faund] *tr* interdire, lasciare esterrefatto

**dum·my** ['dʌmi] *adj* copiato; falso ‖ *s* (-mies) *(dress form)* manichino; *(in card games)* morto; *(figurehead)* uomo di paglia, prestanome *m;* *(skeleton copy of a book)* menabò *m;* copia; (slang) stupido, tonto

**dump** [dʌmp] *s* immondezzaio; mucchio di spazzature; (mil) deposito munizioni; (min) montagnetta di scarico; **to be down in the dumps** (coll) avere le paturnie ‖ *tr* scaricare; *(to tip over)* rovesciare; (com) scaricare sul mercato; (com) vendere sottocosto

**dumping** ['dʌmpɪŋ] *s* scarico; (com) dumping *m*

**dumpling** ['dʌmplɪŋ] *s* gnocco

**dump' truck'** *s* ribaltabile *m*

**dump·y** ['dʌmpi] *adj* (-ier; -iest) grassoccio, tarchiato

**dun** [dʌn] *adj* bruno grigiastro ‖ *s* creditore importuno; *(demand for payment)* sollecitazione di pagamento ‖ *v* (pret & pp **dunned;** ger **dunning**) *tr* sollecitare

**dunce** [dʌns] *s* ignorante *mf*, zuccone *m*

**dunce' cap'** *s* berretto d'asino

**dune** [djun] *or* [dun] *s* duna

**dung** [dʌŋ] *s* sterco, letame *m* ‖ *tr* concimare con il letame

**dungarees** [,dʌŋgə'riz] *spl* tuta di cotone blu

**dungeon** ['dʌndʒən] *s* carcere sotterraneo; *(fortified tower)* torrione *m*, maschio

**dung'hill'** *s* letamaio

**dunk** [dʌŋk] *tr* inzuppare

**du·o** ['dju·o] *or* ['du·o] *s* (-os) duo

**duode·num** [,dju·ə'dinəm] *or* [,du·ə'dinəm] *s* (-na [nə]) duodeno

**dupe** [djup] *or* [dup] *s* gonzo ‖ *tr* gabbare, ingannare

**du'plex house'** ['djuplɛks] *or* ['dupleks] *s* casa di due appartamenti

**duplicate** ['djuplɪkɪt] *or* ['duplɪkɪt] *adj & s* duplicato ‖ ['djuplɪ,ket] *or* ['duplɪ,ket] *tr* duplicare

**du'plicating machine'** *s* duplicatore *m*

**duplici·ty** [dju'plɪsɪti] *or* [du'plɪsɪti] *s* (-ties) duplicità *f*, doppiezza

**durable** ['djurəbəl] *or* ['durəbəl] *adj* durabile, duraturo

**du'rable goods'** *spl* beni *mpl* durevoli

**duration** [dju're/ən] *or* [du're/ən] *s* durata

**during** ['djurɪŋ] *or* ['durɪŋ] *prep* durante

**du'rum wheat'** ['durəm] *or* ['djurəm] *s* grano duro

**dusk** [dʌsk] *s* crepuscolo

**dust** [dʌst] *s* polvere *f* ‖ *tr (to free of dust)* spolverare; *(to sprinkle with dust)* spolverizzare; **to dust off** (slang) rimettere in uso; (slang) spolverare le spalle a

**dust' bowl'** *s* regione polverosissima

**dust'cloth'** *s* strofinaccio

**dust' cloud'** *s* polverone *m*

**duster** ['dʌstər] *s (cloth)* cencio; *(light overgarment)* spolverino

**dust' jack'et** *s* sopraccoperta

**dust'pan'** *s* pattumiera

**dust' rag'** *s* strofinaccio

**dust·y** ['dʌsti] *adj* (-ier; -iest) polveroso; grigiastro

**Dutch** [dʌt/] *adj* olandese; (slang) tedesco ‖ *s (language)* olandese *m;* *(language)* (slang) tedesco; **in Dutch** (slang) in disgrazia; (slang) nei pasticci; **the Dutch** gli olandesi; (slang) i tedeschi; **to go Dutch** (coll) pagare alla romana

**Dutch'man** *s* (-men) olandese *m;* (slang) tedesco

**Dutch' treat'** *s* invito alla romana

**dutiable** ['djuti·əbəl] *or* ['duti·əbəl] *adj* soggetto a dogana

**dutiful** ['djutɪfəl] *or* ['dutɪfəl] *adj* obbediente, doveroso

**du·ty** ['djuti] *or* ['duti] *s* (-ties) dovere *m; (task)* funzione; dazio, dogana; **off duty** libero; in libera uscita; **on duty** in servizio; di guardia; **to do one's duty** fare il proprio dovere; **to take up one's duties** entrare in servizio

**du'ty-free'** *adj* esente da dogana

**dwarf** [dwɔrf] *adj & s* nano ‖ *tr* rimpiccolire ‖ *intr* rimpiccolire; apparire più piccolo

**dwarfish** ['dwɔrfɪ/] *adj* nano, da nano

**dwell** [dwel] *v* (pret & pp **dwelled** or **dwelt** [dwelt]) *intr* dimorare, abitare; **to dwell on** or **upon** intrattenersi su

**dwelling** ['dwɛlɪŋ] *s* abitazione, residenza

**dwell'ing house'** *s* casa d'abitazione

**dwindle** ['dwɪndəl] *intr* diminuire; restringersi, consumarsi

**dye** [dai] *s* tinta, colore *m* ‖ *v* (pret & pp **dyed;** ger **dyeing**) *tr* tingere

**dyed-in-the-wool** ['daɪdɪnðə,wul] *adj* tinto prima della tessitura; completo, intransigente

**dyeing** ['daɪ·ɪŋ] *s* tintura

**dyer** ['daɪ·ər] *s* tintore *m*

**dye'stuff'** *s* tintura, materia colorante

**dying** ['daɪ·ɪŋ] *adj* morente

**dynamic** [daɪ'næmɪk] *or* [dɪ'næmɪk] *adj* dinamico

**dynamite** ['daɪnə,maɪt] *s* dinamite *f* ‖ *tr* far saltare con la dinamite

**dyna·mo** ['daɪnə,mo] *s* (-mos) dinamo *f*

**dynast** ['daɪnæst] *s* dinasta *m*

**dynas·ty** ['daɪnəsti] *s* (-ties) dinastia *f*

**dysentery** ['dɪsən,tɛri] *s* dissenteria

**dyspepsia** [dɪs'pɛpsi·ə] *or* [dɪs'pɛp/ə] *s* dispepsia

**E**

**E, e** [i] *s* quinta lettera dell'alfabeto inglese

**each** [itʃ] *adj indef* ogni ‖ *pron indef* ognuno, ciascuno; **each other** ci; vi; si; l'un l'altro ‖ *adv* l'uno; a testa

**eager** ['igər] *adj* (*enthusiastic*) ardente; **eager for** avido di; **eager to** + *inf* desideroso di + *inf*

**ea'ger bea'ver** *s* zelante *mf*

**eagerness** ['igərnɪs] *s* ardore *m;* brama

**eagle** ['igəl] *s* aquila

**ea'gle owl'** *s* gufo reale

**eaglet** ['iglɪt] *s* aquilotto

**ear** [ir] *s* orecchio; (*of corn*) pannocchia; (*of wheat*) spiga; **to be all ears** essere tutt'orecchi; **to prick up one's ears** tendere l'orecchio; **to turn a deaf ear** far l'orecchio da mercante

**ear'ache'** *s* mal *m* d'orecchi

**ear'drop'** *s* pendente *m*

**ear'drum'** *s* timpano

**ear'flap'** *s* paraorecchi *m*

**earl** [ʌrl] *s* conte *m*

**earldom** ['ʌrldəm] *s* contea

**ear·ly** ['ʌrli] (**-lier; -liest**) *adj* (*occurring before customary time*) di buon'ora; (*first in a series*) primo; (*far back in time*) remoto, antico; (*occurring in near future*) prossimo ‖ *adv* presto; per tempo, di buon'ora; **as early as** (*a certain time of day*) già a; (*a certain time or date*) fin da, già in; **as early as possible** quanto prima possibile; **early in** (*e.g., the month*) all'inizio di; **early in the morning** di mattina presto, di buon mattino; **early in the year** all'inizio dell'anno

**ear'ly bird'** *s* persona mattiniera

**ear'ly mass'** *s* prima messa

**ear'ly ris'er** *s* persona mattiniera

**ear'mark'** *s* contrassegno ‖ *tr* contrassegnare; assegnare a scopo speciale

**ear'muff'** *s* paraorecchi *m*

**earn** [ʌrn] *tr* guadagnare, guadagnarsi; (*to get one's due*) meritarsi; (*interest*) (com) produrre ‖ *intr* trarre profitto, rendere

**earnest** ['ʌrnɪst] *adj* serio; fervente; **in earnest** sul serio ‖ *s* caparra

**ear'nest mon'ey** *s* caparra

**earnings** ['ʌrnɪŋz] *s* guadagno; salario

**ear'phone'** *s* (*of sonar*) orecchiale *m;* (rad, telp) cuffia

**ear'piece'** *s* (*of eyeglasses*) susta; (telp) ricevitore *m*

**ear'ring'** *s* orecchino

**ear'shot'** *s* tiro dell'orecchio; **within earshot** a portata di voce

**ear'split'ting** *adj* assordante

**earth** [ʌrθ] *s* terra; **to come back to or down to earth** scendere dalle nuvole

**earthen** ['ʌrθən] *adj* di terra; di terracotta

**ear'then·ware'** *s* coccio, terraglie *fpl,* terracotta

**earthling** ['ʌrθlɪŋ] *s* terrestre *mf*

**earthly** ['ʌrθli] *adj* terreno, terrestre;

**to be of no earthly use** non servire assolutamente a niente

**earthmover** ['ʌrθ ˌmuvər] *s* ruspa

**earth'quake'** *s* terremoto

**earth'work'** *s* terrapieno

**earth'worm'** *s* lombrico

**earth·y** ['ʌrθi] *adj* (**-ier; -iest**) terroso; (*coarse*) rozzo; pratico; sincero, diretto

**ear' trum'pet** *s* corno acustico

**ear'wax'** *s* cerume *m*

**ease** [iz] *s* facilità *f;* (*naturalness*) spigliatezza, disinvoltura; (*comfort*) benestare *m;* tranquillità *f;* **at ease!** (mil) riposo!; **with ease** con facilità ‖ *tr* facilitare; (*a burden*) alleggerire; (*to let up on*) rallentare; mitigare; **to ease out** licenziare con le buone maniere ‖ *intr* alleviarsi, mitigarsi, diminuire; rallentare

**easel** ['izəl] *s* cavalletto

**easement** ['izmənt] *s* attenuamento; (law) servitù *f*

**easily** ['izɪli] *adv* facilmente; senza dubbio; probabilmente

**easiness** ['izɪnɪs] *s* facilità *f;* disinvoltura; grazia, agilità *f;* indifferenza

**east** [ist] *adj* orientale, dell'est ‖ *s* est *m* ‖ *adv* verso l'est

**Easter** ['istər] *s* Pasqua

**East'er egg'** *s* uovo di Pasqua

**East'er Mon'day** *s* lunedì *m* di Pasqua

**eastern** ['istərn] *adj* orientale

**East'er·tide'** *s* tempo pasquale

**eastward** ['istwərd] *adv* verso l'est

**eas·y** ['izi] *adj* (**-ier; -iest**) facile; (*conducive to ease*) comodo, agiato; (*free from worry*) tranquillo; (*easygoing*) disinvolto, spigliato; (*not tight*) ampio; (*not hurried*) lento, moderato ‖ *adv* (coll) facilmente; (coll) tranquillamente; **to take it easy** (coll) riposarsi; (coll) non prendersela; (coll) andar piano

**eas'y chair'** *s* poltrona

**eas'y·go'ing** *adj* (*person*) comodone; (*horse*) sciolto nell'andatura

**eas'y mark'** *s* (coll) gonzo

**eas'y mon'ey** *s* denaro fatto senza fatica; soldi rubati

**eas'y terms'** *spl* facilitazioni *fpl* di pagamento

**eat** [it] *v* (*pret* **ate** [et]; *pp* **eaten** ['itən]) *tr* mangiare; **to eat away** smangiare; **to eat up** mangiarsi ‖ *intr* mangiare

**eatable** ['itəbəl] *adj* mangiabile ‖ **eatables** *spl* commestibili *mpl*

**eaves** [ivz] *spl* gronda

**eaves'drop'** *v* (*pret & pp* **-dropped;** *ger* **-dropping**) *intr* origliare

**ebb** [ɛb] *s* riflusso; decadenza ‖ *intr* (*said of the tide*) ritirarsi; decadere

**ebb' and flow'** *s* flusso e riflusso

**ebb' tide'** *s* riflusso, deflusso

**ebon·y** ['ɛbəni] *s* (**-ies**) ebano

**ebullient** [ɪ'bʌljənt] *adj* bollente

**eccentric** [ɛk'sɛntrɪk] *adj & s* eccentrico

**eccentrici·ty** [ˌɛksɛn'trɪsɪti] *s* (**-ties**) eccentricità *f*, originalità *f*

**ecclesiastic** [ɪˌklizɪ'æstɪk] *adj & s* ecclesiastico

**echelon** ['ɛʃəˌlɑn] *s* scaglione *m;* (mil) scaglione *m* ‖ *tr* scaglionare

**ech·o** ['ɛko] *s* (**-oes**) eco ‖ *tr* far eco a ‖ *intr* echeggiare, riecheggiare

**éclair** [e'klɛr] *s* dolce ripieno di crema

**eclectic** [ɛk'lɛktɪk] *adj & s* eclettico

**eclipse** [ɪ'klɪps] *s* eclisse *f,* eclissi *f* ‖ *tr* eclissare

**eclogue** ['ɛklɔg] *or* ['ɛklɑg] *s* egloga

**ecology** [ɪ'kɑlədʒi] *s* ecologia

**economic(al)** [ˌikə'nɑmɪk(əl)] *or* [ˌɛkə'nɑmɪk(əl)] *adj* economico

**economics** [ˌikə'nɑmɪks] *or* [ˌɛkə'nɑmɪks] *s* economia (politica)

**economist** [ɪ'kɑnəmɪst] *s* economista *mf*

**economize** [ɪ'kɑnəˌmaɪz] *tr & intr* economizzare

**econo·my** [ɪ'kɑnəmi] *s* (**-mies**) economia

**ecosystem** ['ɛkoˌsɪstəm] *s* ecosistema *m*

**ecsta·sy** ['ɛkstəsi] *s* (**-sies**) estasi *f*

**ecstatic** [ɛk'stætɪk] *adj* estatico

**ecumenic(al)** [ˌɛkjə'mɛnɪk(əl)] *adj* ecumenico

**eczema** ['ɛksɪmə] *or* [ɛg'zimə] *s* eczema *m*

**ed·dy** ['ɛdi] *s* (**-dies**) turbine *m* ‖ *v* (*pret & pp* **-died**) *tr & intr* turbinare

**edelweiss** ['edəlˌvaɪs] *s* stella alpina

**edge** [ɛdʒ] *s* (*of knife, sword, etc*) filo, tagliente *m;* (*border at which a surface terminates*) orlo, bordo; (*of a wound*) labbro, margine *m;* (*of a book*) taglio; (*of a tumbler*) giro; (*of clothing*) vivagno; (*of a table*) spigolo; (slang) vantaggio; **on edge** nervoso; **to have the edge on** (coll) avere il vantaggio su; **to set the teeth on edge** far allegare i denti ‖ *tr* affilare, aguzzare; orlare, bordare; **to edge out** riuscire ad eliminare ‖ *intr* avanzare lentamente

**edgeways** ['ɛdʒˌwez] *adv* di taglio; **to not let s.o. get a word in edgeways** non lasciar dire una parola a qlcu

**edging** ['ɛdʒɪŋ] *s* orlo, bordo

**edg·y** ['ɛdʒi] *adj* (**-ier; -iest**) acuto, angolare; nervoso, ansioso

**edible** ['ɛdɪbəl] *adj* mangereccio, mangiabile ‖ **edibles** *spl* commestibili *mpl*

**edict** ['idɪkt] *s* editto

**edification** [ˌɛdɪfɪ'keʃən] *s* edificazione

**edifice** ['ɛdɪfɪs] *s* edificio

**edi·fy** ['ɛdɪˌfaɪ] *v* (*pret & pp* **-fied**) *tr* edificare

**edifying** ['ɛdɪˌfaɪ·ɪŋ] *adj* edificante

**edit** ['ɛdɪt] *tr* redigere; (*e.g., a manuscript*) correggere; (*an edition*) curare; (*a newspaper*) dirigere; (mov) montare

**edition** [ɪ'dɪʃən] *s* edizione

**editor** ['ɛdɪtər] *s* (*of a newspaper or magazine*) direttore *m*, gerente *mf;* (*of an editorial*) redattore *m*, cronista *mf;* (*of a critical edition*) editore *m;* (*of a manuscript*) revisore *m*

**editorial** [ˌɛdɪ'torɪ·əl] *adj* editoriale ‖ *s* capocronaca *m*, articolo di fondo

**ed'ito'rial staff'** *s* redazione

**ed'itor in chief'** *s* gerente *mf* responsabile

**educate** ['ɛdʒuˌket] *tr* educare, erudire

**education** [ˌɛdʒu'keʃən] *s* educazione; istruzione, insegnamento

**educational** [ˌɛdʒu'keʃənəl] *adj* educativo

**educa'tional institu'tion** *s* istituto di magistero

**educator** ['ɛdʒuˌketər] *s* educatore *m*

**eel** [il] *s* anguilla; **to be as slippery as an eel** guizzare di mano come un'anguilla

**ee·rie** *or* **ee·ry** ['ɪri] *adj* (**-rier; -riest**) spettrale, pauroso

**efface** [ɪ'fes] *tr* cancellare; **to efface oneself** eclissarsi, mettersi in disparte

**effect** [ɪ'fɛkt] *s* effetto; (*main idea*) tenore *m;* **in effect** in vigore; in realtà; **to go into effect** *or* **to take effect** andare in vigore; **to put into effect** mandare ad effetto ‖ *tr* effettuare

**effective** [ɪ'fɛktɪv] *adj* efficace; (*actually in effect*) effettivo; (*striking*) che colpisce; **to become effective** entrare in vigore

**effectual** [ɪ'fɛktʃu·əl] *adj* efficace

**effectuate** [ɪ'fɛktʃuˌet] *tr* effettuare

**effeminacy** [ɪ'fɛmɪnəsi] *s* effemminatezza

**effeminate** [ɪ'fɛmɪnɪt] *adj* effemminato

**effervesce** [ˌɛfər'vɛs] *intr* essere in effervescenza

**effervescence** [ˌɛfər'vɛsəns] *s* effervescenza

**effervescent** [ˌɛfər'vɛsənt] *adj* effervescente

**effete** [ɪ'fit] *adj* esausto, sterile

**efficacious** [ˌɛfɪ'keʃəs] *adj* efficace

**effica·cy** [ˈɛfɪkəsi] *s* (**-cies**) efficacia

**efficien·cy** [ɪ'fɪʃənsi] *s* (**-cies**) efficienza; (mech) rendimento, efficienza

**effi'ciency engineer'** *s* analista *mf* tempi e metodi

**efficient** [ɪ'fɪʃənt] *adj* efficiente; (*person*) abile; (mech) efficiente

**effi·gy** ['ɛfɪdʒi] *s* (**-gies**) effigie *f*

**effort** ['ɛfərt] *s* sforzo

**effronter·y** [ɪ'frʌntəri] *s* (**-ies**) sfrontatezza, sfacciataggine *f*

**effusion** [ɪ'fjuʒən] *s* effusione

**effusive** [ɪ'fjusɪv] *adj* espansivo

**egg** [ɛg] *s* uovo; (slang) bravo ragazzo ‖ *tr*—**to egg on** incitare

**egg'beat'er** *s* frullino, sbattiuova *m*

**egg'cup'** *s* portauovo

**egg'head'** *s* (coll) intellettuale *mf*

**eggnog** ['ɛgˌnɑg] *s* zabaione *m*

**egg'plant'** *s* melanzana, petonciano

**egg'shell'** *s* guscio d'uovo

**egoism** ['ɛgoˌɪzəm] *or* ['igoˌɪzəm] *s* egoismo

**egoist** ['ɛgo·ɪst] *or* ['igo·ɪst] *s* egoista *mf*

**egotism** ['ɛgoˌtɪzəm] *or* ['igoˌtɪzəm] *s* egotismo

**egotist** ['ɛgotɪst] *or* ['igotɪst] *s* egotista *mf*

**egregious** [ɪˈgridʒəs] *adj* gigantesco, tremendo, marchiano
**egress** [ˈigres] *s* uscita
**Egypt** [ˈidʒɪpt] *s* l'Egitto
**Egyptian** [ɪˈdʒɪpʃən] *adj & s* egiziano
**ei'der down'** [ˈaɪdər] *s* piumino
**ei'der duck'** *s* edredone *m*
**eight** [et] *adj & pron* otto ‖ *s* otto; **eight o'clock** le otto
**eighteen** [ˈetˈtin] *adj, s & pron* diciotto
**eighteenth** [ˈetˈtinθ] *adj, s & pron* diciottesimo ‖ *s* (*in dates*) diciotto
**eighth** [etθ] *adj & s* ottavo ‖ *s* (*in dates*) otto
**eight' hun'dred** *adj, s & pron* ottocento
**eightieth** [ˈetɪ·ɪθ] *adj, s & pron* ottantesimo
**eight·y** [ˈeti] *adj & pron* ottanta ‖ *s* (**-ies**) ottanta *m*; **the eighties** gli anni ottanta
**either** [ˈiðər] or [ˈaɪðər] *adj* l'uno o l'altro; l'uno e l'altro; ciascuno; entrambi i, tutti e due i ‖ *pron* l'uno o l'altro; l'uno e l'altro; entrambi ‖ *adv*—**not either** nemmeno ‖ *conj*—**either . . . or** o . . . o
**ejaculate** [ɪˈdʒækjəˌlet] *tr* esclamare; (physiol) emettere ‖ *intr* esclamare; (physiol) avere un'eiaculazione
**eject** [ɪˈdʒɛkt] *tr* espellere, gettar fuori; (*to evict*) sfrattare
**ejection** [ɪˈdʒɛkʃən] *s* espulsione; (*of a tenant*) sfratto
**ejec'tion seat'** *s* sedile *m* eiettabile
**eke** [ik] *tr*—**to eke out a living** sbarcare il lunario
**elaborate** [ɪˈlæbərɪt] *adj* (*done with great care*) elaborato; (*detailed*) minuzioso; (*ornate*) ornato ‖ [ɪˈlæbəˌret] *tr* elaborare ‖ *intr*—**to elaborate on** or **upon** circonstanziare, particolareggiare
**elapse** [ɪˈlæps] *intr* passare, trascorrere
**elastic** [ɪˈlæstɪk] *adj & s* elastico
**elasticity** [ɪˌlæsˈtɪsɪti] or [ˌilæsˈtɪsɪti] *s* elasticità *f*
**elated** [ɪˈletɪd] *adj* esultante, gongolante
**elation** [ɪˈleʃən] *s* esultanza, gaudio
**elbow** [ˈɛlbo] *s* gomito; (*in a river*) ansa; (*of a chair*) braccio; **at one's elbow** sotto mano; **out at the elbows** coi gomiti logori; **to crook the elbow** alzare il gomito; **to rub elbows** stare gomito a gomito; **up to the elbows** fino al collo ‖ *tr*—**to elbow one's way** aprirsi il passo a gomitate ‖ *intr* dar gomitate
**el'bow grease'** *s* (coll) olio di gomiti
**el'bow patch'** *s* toppa al gomito
**el'bow rest'** *s* bracciolo
**el'bow·room'** *s* spazio sufficiente; libertà *f* d'azione
**elder** [ˈɛldər] *adj* seniore, maggiore ‖ *s* (bot) sambuco; (eccl) maggiore *m*
**el'der·ber'ry** *s* (**-ries**) sambuco; (*fruit*) bacca del sambuco
**elderly** [ˈɛldərli] *adj* attempato, anziano
**eld'er states'man** *s* uomo di stato esperto
**eldest** [ˈɛldɪst] *adj* (il) maggiore; (il) più vecchio

**elect** [ɪˈlɛkt] *adj & s* eletto; **the elect** gli eletti ‖ *tr* eleggere
**election** [ɪˈlɛkʃən] *s* elezione
**electioneer** [ɪˌlɛkʃəˈnɪr] *intr* fare una campagna elettorale
**elective** [ɪˈlɛktɪv] *adj* elettivo ‖ *s* corso facoltativo
**electorate** [ɪˈlɛktərɪt] *s* elettorato
**electric(al)** [ɪˈlɛktrɪk(əl)] *adj* elettrico
**elec'tric blend'er** *s* frullatore *m*
**elec'tric chair'** *s* sedia elettrica
**elec'tric cord'** *s* piattina, filo elettrico
**elec'tric eel'** *s* gimnoto
**elec'tric eye'** *s* occhio elettrico
**electrician** [ɪˌlɛkˈtrɪʃən] or [ˌɛlɛkˈtrɪʃən] *s* elettricista *m*
**electricity** [ɪˌlɛkˈtrɪsɪti] or [ˌɛlɛkˈtrɪsɪti] *s* elettricità *f*
**elec'tric me'ter** *s* contatore *m* della luce
**elec'tric per'cola'tor** *s* caffettiera elettrica
**elec'tric shav'er** *s* rasoio elettrico
**elec'tric shock'** *s* scossa elettrica, elettroscuasso
**elec'tric tape'** *s* nastro isolante
**elec'tric train'** *s* elettrotreno
**electri·fy** [ɪˈlɛktrɪˌfaɪ] *v* (*pret & pp* **-fied**) *tr* (*to provide with electric power*) elettrificare; (*to communicate electricity to; to thrill*) elettrizzare
**electrocute** [ɪˈlɛktrəˌkjut] *tr* fulminare con la corrente; far morire sulla sedia elettrica
**electrode** [ɪˈlɛktrod] *s* elettrodo
**electrolysis** [ɪˌlɛkˈtrɑlɪsɪs] or [ˌɛlɛkˈtrɑlɪsɪs] *s* elettrolisi *f*
**electrolyte** [ɪˈlɛktrəˌlaɪt] *s* elettrolito
**electromagnet** [ɪˌlɛktrəˈmægnɪt] *s* elettrocalamita
**electromagnetic** [ɪˌlɛktrəmægˈnɛtɪk] *adj* elettromagnetico
**electromotive** [ɪˌlɛktrəˈmotɪv] *adj* elettromotore
**electron** [ɪˈlɛktrɑn] *s* elettrone *m*
**electronic** [ɪˌlɛkˈtrɑnɪk] or [ˌɛlɛkˈtrɑnɪk] *adj* elettronico ‖ **electronics** *s* elettronica
**electroplating** [ɪˈlɛktrəˌpletɪŋ] *s* galvanostegia
**electrostatic** [ɪˌlɛktrəˈstætɪk] *adj* elettrostatico
**electrotype** [ɪˈlɛktrəˌtaɪp] *s* stereotipia ‖ *tr* stereotipare
**eleemosynary** [ˌɛlɪˈmɑsɪˌnɛri] *adj* caritatevole, di beneficenza
**elegance** [ˈɛlɪgəns] *s* eleganza
**elegant** [ˈɛlɪgənt] *adj* elegante
**elegiac** [ˌɛlɪˈdʒaɪˌæk] *adj* elegiaco
**ele·gy** [ˈɛlɪdʒi] *s* (**-gies**) elegia
**element** [ˈɛlɪmənt] *s* elemento; **to be out of one's element** essere fuori del proprio ambiente
**elementary** [ˌɛlɪˈmɛntəri] *adj* elementare
**elephant** [ˈɛlɪfənt] *s* elefante *m*
**elevate** [ˈɛlɪˌvet] *tr* elevare, innalzare
**elevated** [ˈɛlɪˌvetɪd] *adj* elevato ‖ *s* ferrovia soprelevata, metropolitana soprelevata
**elevation** [ˌɛlɪˈveʃən] *s* elevazione; (surv) quota
**elevator** [ˈɛlɪˌvetər] *s* ascensore *m*;

*(for freight)* montacarichi *m; (for hoisting grain)* elevatore *m* di grano; *(warehouse for storing grain)* deposito granaglie; *(aer)* timone *m* di profondità

**eleven** [ɪ'lɛvən] *adj & pron* undici ǁ *s* undici *m; eleven o'clock* le undici

**eleventh** [ɪ'lɛvənθ] *adj, s & pron* undicesimo ǁ *s (in dates)* undici *m*

**elev'enth hour'** *s* ultimo momento

**elf** [ɛlf] *s* **(elves** [ɛlvz]) elfo

**elicit** [ɪ'lɪsɪt] *tr* cavare, sottrarre

**elide** [ɪ'laɪd] *tr* elidere

**eligible** ['ɛlɪdʒɪbəl] *adj* eleggibile; accettabile

**eliminate** [ɪ'lɪmɪ,net] *tr* eliminare

**elision** [ɪ'lɪʒən] *s* elisione

**elite** [e'lit] *adj* eletto, scelto ǁ *s—the elite* l'élite *f*

**elk** [ɛlk] *s* alce *m*

**ellipse** [ɪ'lɪps] *s* (geom) ellisse *f*

**ellip·sis** [ɪ'lɪpsɪs] *s* **(-ses** [siz]) (gram) ellissi *f*

**elliptic(al)** [ɪ'lɪptɪk(əl)] *adj* ellittico

**elm** [ɛlm] *s* olmo

**elongate** [ɪ'lɔŋget] or [ɪ'laŋget] *tr* allungare, prolungare

**elope** [ɪ'lop] *intr* fuggire con un amante

**elopement** [ɪ'lopmənt] *s* fuga con un amante

**eloquence** ['ɛləkwəns] *s* eloquenza

**eloquent** ['ɛləkwənt] *adj* eloquente

**else** [ɛls] *adj—nobody else* nessun altro; **nothing else** nient'altro; **somebody else** qualcun altro; **something else** qualcosa d'altro; **what else** che altro; **who else** chi altro; **whose else** di che altra persona ǁ *adv—how else* in che altra maniera; **or else** se no; altrimenti; **when else** in che altro momento; **in che** altro periodo; **where else** dove mai, da che parte

**else'where'** *adv* altrove

**elucidate** [ɪ'lusɪ,det] *tr* dilucidare

**elude** [ɪ'lud] *tr* eludere

**elusive** [ɪ'lusɪv] *adj* elusivo; *(evasive)* fugace, sfuggente

**emaciated** [ɪ'meʃɪ,etɪd] *adj* smunto, emaciato, macilento

**emanate** ['ɛmə,net] *tr & intr* emanare

**emancipate** [ɪ'mænsɪ,pet] *tr* emancipare

**embalm** [ɛm'bam] *tr* imbalsamare

**embankment** [ɛm'bæŋkmənt] *s* terrapieno

**embar·go** [ɛm'bargo] *s* **(-goes)** embargo ǁ *tr* mettere l'embargo a

**embark** [ɛm'bark] *intr* imbarcarsi

**embarkation** [,ɛmbar'keʃən] *s* imbarco

**embarrass** [ɛm'bærəs] *tr* imbarazzare, mettere a disagio; *(to impede)* imbarazzare, impacciare; mettere in difficoltà economiche

**embarrassing** [ɛm'bærəsɪŋ] *adj* sconcertante; imbarazzante

**embarrassment** [ɛm'bærəsmənt] *s* imbarazzo, disagio, confusione; impaccio; difficoltà finanziaria, dissesto

**embas·sy** ['ɛmbəsi] *s* **(-sies)** ambasciata

**em·bed** [ɛm'bɛd] *s* *(pret & pp* **-bedded;** *ger* **-bedding)** *tr* incastrare, incassare

**embellish** [ɛm'bɛlɪʃ] *tr* imbellire

**embellishment** [ɛm'bɛlɪʃmənt] *s* abbellimento; *(fig)* fioretto

**ember** ['ɛmbər] *s* brace *f;* **embers** braci *fpl*

**Em'ber days'** *spl* tempora *fpl*

**embezzle** [ɛm'bɛzəl] *tr* appropriare, malversare ǁ *intr* appropriarsi

**embezzlement** [ɛm'bɛzəlmənt] *s* appropriazione indebita, malversazione; *(of public funds)* peculato

**embezzler** [ɛm'bɛzlər] *s* malversatore *m*

**embitter** [ɛm'bɪtər] *tr* amareggiare

**emblazon** [ɛm'blezən] *tr* blasonare; celebrare

**emblem** ['ɛmbləm] *s* emblema *m*

**emblematic(al)** [,ɛmblə'mætɪk(əl)] *adj* emblematico

**embodiment** [ɛm'badɪmənt] *s* incarnazione, personificazione

**embod·y** [ɛm'badi] *v (pret & pp* **-ied)** *tr* incarnare, personificare; incorporare

**embolden** [ɛm'boldən] *tr* imbaldanzire

**embolism** ['ɛmbə,lɪzəm] *s* embolia

**emboss** [ɛm'bɔs] or [ɛm'bas] *tr* *(metal)* sbalzare; *(paper)* goffrare

**embrace** [ɛm'bres] *s* abbraccio ǁ *tr* abbracciare ǁ *intr* abbracciarsi

**embrasure** [ɛm'breʒər] *s* *(archit)* strombatura; *(mil)* feritoia

**embroider** [ɛm'brɔɪdər] *tr* ricamare, trapuntare

**embroider·y** [ɛm'brɔɪdəri] *s* **(-ies)** ricamo, trapunto

**embroil** [ɛm'brɔɪl] *tr* ingarbugliare; *(to involve in contention)* coinvolgere

**embroilment** [ɛm'brɔɪlmənt] *s* imbroglio; *(in contention)* disaccordo

**embry·o** ['ɛmbrɪ,o] *s* **(-os)** embrione *m*

**embryology** [,ɛmbrɪ'alədʒi] *s* embriologia

**embryonic** [,ɛmbrɪ'anɪk] *adj* embrionale

**emcee** ['ɛm'si] *s* presentatore *m* ǁ *tr* presentare

**emend** [ɪ'mɛnd] *tr* emendare

**emendation** [,imɛn'deʃən] *s* emendamento

**emerald** ['ɛmərəld] *s* smeraldo

**emerge** [ɪ'mʌrdʒ] *intr* emergere

**emergence** [ɪ'mʌrdʒəns] *s* emergenza

**emergen·cy** [ɪ'mʌrdʒənsi] *s* **(-cies)** emergenza

**emer'gency brake'** *s* freno a mano

**emer'gency ex'it** *s* uscita di sicurezza

**emer'gency land'ing** *s* atterragio di fortuna

**emer'gency ward'** *s* sala d'urgenza

**emeritus** [ɪ'mɛrɪtəs] *adj* emerito

**emersion** [ɪ'mʌrʒən] or [ɪ'mʌrʃən] *s* emersione

**emery** ['ɛməri] *s* smeriglio

**em'ery cloth'** *s* tela smeriglio

**em'ery wheel'** *s* mola a smeriglio

**emetic** [ɪ'mɛtɪk] *adj & s* emetico

**emigrant** ['ɛmɪgrənt] *adj & s* emigrante *mf*

**emigrate** ['ɛmɪ,gret] *intr* emigrare

**émigré** [emi'gre] or ['ɛmɪ,gre] *s* emigrato

**eminence** ['emɪnəns] *s* eminenza; (eccl) Eminenza

**eminent** ['emɪnənt] *adj* eminente

**emissar·y** ['emɪ,seri] *s* (**-ies**) emissario

**emission** [ɪ'mɪʃən] *s* emissione

**emit** [ɪ'mɪt] *v* (*pret & pp* **emitted;** *ger* **emitting**) *tr* emettere

**emolument** [ɪ'mɑljəmənt] *s* emolumento

**emotion** [ɪ'moʃən] *s* emozione

**emotional** [ɪ'moʃənəl] *adj* emotivo

**emperor** ['empərər] *s* imperatore *m*

**empha·sis** ['emfəsɪs] *s* (**-ses** [,sɪz]) enfasi *f*. risalto

**emphasize** ['emfə,saɪz] *tr* dar rilievo a, sottolineare

**emphatic** [em'fætɪk] *adj* enfatico

**emphysema** [,emfɪ'simə] *s* enfisema *m*

**empire** ['empaɪr] *s* impero

**empiric(al)** [em'pɪrɪk(əl)] *adj* empirico

**empiricist** [em'pɪrɪsɪst] *s* empirista *mf*

**emplacement** [em'plesmənt] *s* piazzola, postazione

**employ** [em'plɔɪ] *s* impiego || *tr* impiegare, usare; valersi di

**employee** [em'plɔɪ·i] or [,emplɔɪ'i] *s* impiegato, dipendente *mf*

**employer** [em'plɔɪ·ər] *s* dirigente *mf*, datore *m* di lavoro

**employment** [em'plɔɪmənt] *s* impiego, occupazione

**employ'ment a'gency** *s* agenzia di collocamento

**empower** [em'pau·ər] *tr* autorizzare; permettere

**empress** ['emprɪs] *s* imperatrice *f*

**emptiness** ['emptɪnɪs] *s* vuoto

**emp·ty** ['empti] *adj* (**-tier; -tiest**) vuoto; (*gun*) scarico; (*hungry*) (coll) digiuno; (fig) esausto || *v* (*pret & pp* **-tied**) *tr* vuotare || *intr* vuotarsi

**empty-handed** ['empti'hændɪd] *adj* a mani vuote

**empty-headed** ['empti'hedɪd] *adj* dalla testa vuota, balordo

**empyrean** [,empɪ'ri·ən] *adj & s* empireo

**emulate** ['emjə,let] *tr* emulare

**emulator** ['emjə,letər] *s* emulo

**emulous** ['emjələs] *adj* emulo

**emulsi·fy** [ɪ'mʌlsɪ,faɪ] *v* (*pret & pp* **-fied**) *tr* emulsionare

**emulsion** [ɪ'mʌlʃən] *s* emulsione

**enable** [en'ebəl] *tr* abilitare; permettere (*with dat*)

**enact** [en'ækt] *tr* decretare; (*a role*) rappresentare

**enactment** [en'æktmənt] *s* legge *f*; (*of a law*) promulgazione; (*of a play*) rappresentazione

**enam·el** [ɪn'æməl] *s* smalto || *v* (*pret & pp* **-eled** or **-elled;** *ger* **-eling** or **-elling**) *tr* smaltare

**enam'el·ware'** *s* utensili *mpl* di cucina di ferro smaltato

**enamor** [en'æmər] *tr* innamorare; **to become enamored of** innamorarsi di

**encamp** [en'kæmp] *tr* accampare || *intr* accamparsi

**encampment** [en'kæmpmənt] *s* campeggio; (mil) accampamento

**encase** [en'kes] *tr* incassare

**encephalitis** [en,sefə'laɪtɪs] *s* encefalite *f*

**enchain** [en'tʃen] *tr* incatenare

**enchant** [en'tʃænt] or [en'tʃɑnt] *tr* incantare

**enchantment** [en'tʃæntmənt] or [en'tʃɑntmənt] *s* incanto, malia

**enchanting** [en'tʃæntɪŋ] or [en'tʃɑntɪŋ] *adj* incantatore, incantevole

**enchantress** [en'tʃæntrɪs] or [en'tʃɑntrɪs] *s* incantatrice *f*, maliarda

**enchase** [en'tʃes] *tr* incastonare

**encircle** [en'sʌrkəl] *tr* rigirare, girare intorno a; (mil) circondare

**enclave** ['enklev] *s* enclave *f*

**enclitic** [en'klɪtɪk] *adj* enclitico || *s* enclitica

**enclose** [en'kloz] *tr* rinchiudere; (*in a letter*) accludere, includere; **to enclose herewith** accludere alla presente

**enclosure** [en'kloʒər] *s* (*land surrounded by fence*) recinto, chiuso; (*e.g., letter*) allegato

**encomi·um** [en'komi·əm] *s* (**-ums** or **-a** [ə]) encomio, elogio

**encompass** [en'kʌmpəs] *tr* circondare; racchiudere, contenere

**encore** ['aŋkor] *s* bis *m* || *tr* (*a performance*) chiedere il bis di; (*a performer*) chiedere il bis a || *interj* bis!

**encounter** [en'kauntər] *s* (*casual meeting*) incontro; (*combat*) scontro || *tr* incontrare || *intr* scontrarsi

**encourage** [en'kʌrɪdʒ] *tr* incoraggiare; (*to foster*) favorire

**encouragement** [en'kʌrɪdʒmənt] *s* incoraggiamento; favoreggiamento

**encroach** [en'krotʃ] *intr*—**to encroach on** or **upon** invadere; usurpare; occupare il territorio di

**encumber** [en'kʌmbər] *tr* imbarazzare; ingombrare; (*to load with debts, etc*) gravare

**encumbrance** [en'kʌmbrəns] *s* imbarazzo; ingombro; gravame *m*

**encyclical** [en'sɪklɪkəl] or [en'saɪklɪkəl] *s* enciclica

**encyclopedia** [en,saɪklə'pidɪ·ə] *s* enciclopedia

**encyclopedic** [en,saɪklə'pidɪk] *adj* enciclopedico

**end** [end] *s* (*extremity; concluding part*) fine *f*; (*e.g., of the week*) fine *f*; (*purpose*) fine *m*; (*part adjacent to an extremity*) lembo; (*small piece*) pezza, avanzo; (*of a beam*) testata; (sports) estrema; **at the end of** in capo a; in fondo a; **in the end** alla fine, all'ultimo; **no end** (coll) moltissimo; **no end of** (coll) un mucchio di; **to make both ends meet** sbarcare il lunario; **to no end** senza effetto; **to stand on end** mettere in piedi, drizzare; mettersi diritto; (*said of hair*) drizzarsi; **to the end that** affinché || *tr* finire, terminare; **to end up** andare a finire || *intr* finire, terminare; **to end up** finire

**endanger** [en'dendʒər] *tr* mettere in pericolo

**endear** [ɛn'dɪr] *tr* affezionare; **to endear oneself to** rendersi caro a

**endeavor** [ɛn'dɛvər] *s* tentativo, sforzo || *intr* tentare, sforzarsi

**endemic** [ɛn'dɛmɪk] *adj* endemico || *s* endemia

**ending** ['ɛndɪŋ] *s* fine *f*, conclusione; (gram) terminazione, desinenza

**endive** ['ɛndaɪv] *s* indivia

**endless** ['ɛndlɪs] *adj* interminabile; sterminato; (mach) senza fine

**end'most'** *adj* estremo, ultimo

**endorse** [ɛn'dɔrs] *tr* girare; (fig) approvare, confermare

**endorsee** [ˌɛndɔr'si] *s* giratario

**endorsement** [ɛn'dɔrsmənt] *s* girata; approvazione, conferma

**endorser** [ɛn'dɔrsər] *s* girante *mf*

**endow** [ɛn'dau] *tr* dotare

**endowment** [ɛn'daumənt] *adj* dotale || *s* (*of an institution*) dotazione; (*gift, talent*) dote *f*

**end' pap'er** *s* risguardo

**endurance** [ɛn'djurəns] or [ɛn'durəns] *s* sopportazione, tolleranza; (*ability to hold out*) resistenza, forza; (*lasting time*) durata

**endure** [ɛn'djur] or [ɛn'dur] *tr* sopportare, tollerare; resistere (**with** *dat*) || *intr* durare, resistere

**enduring** [ɛn'djurɪŋ] or [ɛn'durɪŋ] *adj* duraturo, durevole; paziente

**enema** ['ɛnəmə] *s* clistere *m*

**ene·my** ['ɛnəmi] *adj* nemico || *s* (**-mies**) nemico

**en'emy al'ien** *s* straniero nemico

**energetic** [ˌɛnər'dʒɛtɪk] *adj* energetico, vigoroso

**ener·gy** ['ɛnərdʒi] *s* (**-gies**) energia

**enervate** ['ɛnər ˌvet] *tr* snervare

**enfeeble** [ɛn'fibəl] *tr* indebolire

**enfold** [ɛn'fold] *tr* avvolgere; abbracciare

**enforce** [ɛn'fors] *tr* far osservare; ottenere per forza; (*e.g., obedience*) imporre; (*an argument*) far valere

**enforcement** [ɛn'forsmənt] *s* imposizione; (*of a law*) esecuzione

**enfranchise** [ɛn'fræntʃaɪz] *tr* liberare; concedere il diritto di voto a

**engage** [ɛn'gedʒ] *tr* occupare; riservare; (*s.o.'s attention*) attrarre; (*a gear*) ingranare; (*the enemy*) ingaggiare; (*to hire*) assumere; (theat) scritturare; **to be engaged, to be engaged to be married** essere fidanzato; **to engage s.o. in conversation** intavolare una conversazione con qlcu || *intr* essere occupato; essere impiegato; assumere un'obbligazione; (mil) impegnarsi; (mach) ingranare, incastrarsi

**engaged** [ɛn'gedʒd] *adj* fidanzato; occupato, impegnato; (*column*) murato

**engagement** [ɛn'gedʒmənt] *s* accordo; fidanzamento; impegno, contratto; (*appointment*) appuntamento; (mil) azione; (mach) innesto

**engage'ment ring'** *s* anello di fidanzamento

**engaging** [ɛn'gedʒɪŋ] *adj* attrattivo

**engender** [ɛn'dʒɛndər] *tr* ingenerare

**engine** ['ɛndʒɪn] *s* macchina; (aut) motore *m*; (rr) locomotiva, motrice *f*

**engineer** [ˌɛndʒə'nɪr] *s* ingegnere *m*; (rr) macchinista *m*; (mil) zappatore *m*, geniere *m* || *tr* costruire; progettare

**engineering** [ˌɛndʒə'nɪrɪŋ] *s* ingegneria

**en'gine house'** *s* stazione dei pompieri

**en'gine·man'** *s* (**-men**) (rr) macchinista *m*

**en'gine room'** *s* sala macchine

**en'gine-room' tel'egraph** *s* (naut) telegrafo di macchina, trasmettitore *m*

**England** ['ɪŋglənd] *s* l'Inghilterra

**Englander** ['ɪŋgləndər] *s* nativo dell'Inghilterra

**English** ['ɪŋglɪʃ] *adj* inglese || *s* inglese *m*; (billiards) effetto; **the English** gli inglesi

**Eng'lish Chan'nel** *s* Canale *m* della Manica

**Eng'lish dai'sy** *s* margherita

**Eng'lish horn'** *s* (mus) corno inglese

**Eng'lish·man** *s* (**-men**) inglese *m*

**Eng'lish-speak'ing** *adj* di lingua inglese, anglofono

**Eng'lish·wom'an** *s* (**-wom'en**) inglese *f*

**engraft** [ɛn'græft] or [ɛn'graft] *tr* (hort) innestare; (fig) inculcare

**engrave** [ɛn'grev] *tr* incidere

**engraver** [ɛn'grevər] *s* incisore *m*

**engraving** [ɛn'grevɪŋ] *s* incisione

**engross** [ɛn'gros] *tr* preoccupare, assorbire; redigere ufficialmente, scrivere a grandi caratteri; monopolizzare

**engrossing** [ɛn'grosɪŋ] *adj* assorbente

**engulf** [ɛn'gʌlf] *tr* sommergere, inondare

**enhance** [ɛn'hæns] or [ɛn'hans] *tr* valorizzare; far risaltare

**enigma** [ɪ'nɪgmə] *s* enigma *m*

**enigmatic(al)** [ˌɪnɪg'mætɪk(əl)] *adj* enigmatico

**enjambment** [ɛn'dʒæmmənt] or [ɛn'dʒæmbmənt] *s* inarcatura

**enjoin** [ɛn'dʒɔɪn] *tr* ingiungere, intimare

**enjoy** [ɛn'dʒɔɪ] *tr* godere; **to enjoy +** *ger* provar piacere in + *inf*; **to enjoy oneself** divertirsi

**enjoyable** [ɛn'dʒɔɪ·əbəl] *adj* gradevole

**enjoyment** [ɛn'dʒɔɪmənt] *s* (*pleasure*) piacere *m*; (*pleasurable use*) godimento

**enkindle** [ɛn'kɪndəl] *tr* infiammare

**enlarge** [ɛn'lɑrdʒ] *tr* aumentare; ingrossare; (phot) ingrandire || *intr* aumentare; **to enlarge on** or **upon** dilungarsi su

**enlargement** [ɛn'lɑrdʒmənt] *s* aumento; ingrossamento; (phot) ingrandimento

**enlighten** [ɛn'laɪtən] *tr* illustrare, illuminare

**enlightenment** [ɛn'laɪtənmənt] *s* spiegazione, schiarimento || **Enlightenment** *s* illuminismo

**enlist** [ɛn'lɪst] *tr* (*e.g., s.o.'s favor*) guadagnarsi; (*the help of a person*) ottenere; (mil) ingaggiare || *intr* (mil) ingaggiarsi, arruolarsi; **to enlist**

**in** (*a cause*) dare il proprio appoggio a

**enlistment** [ɛn'lɪstmənt] *s* arruolamento, ingaggio

**enliven** [ɛn'laɪvən] *tr* ravvivare

**enmesh** [ɛn'mɛʃ] *tr* irretire

**enmi·ty** ['ɛnmɪti] *s* (**-ties**) inimicizia

**ennoble** [ɛn'nobəl] *tr* nobilitare

**ennui** ['ɑnwi] *s* noia, tedio

**enormous** [ɪ'nɔrməs] *adj* enorme

**enormously** [ɪ'nɔrməsli] *adv* enormemente

**enough** [ɪ'nʌf] *adj* abbastanza || *s* il sufficiente || *adv* abbastanza || *interj* basta!

**enounce** [ɪ'naʊns] *tr* enunciare; (*to declare*) affermare

**enrage** [ɛn'redʒ] *tr* infuriare, irritare

**enrapture** [ɛn'ræptʃər] *tr* mandare in visibilio, estasiare

**enrich** [ɛn'rɪtʃ] *tr* arricchire

**enroll** [ɛn'rol] *tr* arruolare, ingaggiare; (*a student*) iscrivere || *intr* arruolarsi, ingaggiarsi; (*said of a student*) iscriversi

**enrollment** [ɛn'rolmənt] *s* arruolamento, ingaggio; (*of a student*) iscrizione

**en route** [ɑn 'rut] *adv* in cammino; **en route to** in via per

**ensconce** [ɛn'skɑns] *tr* nascondere; **to esconce oneself** rannicchiarsi, istallarsi comodamente

**ensemble** [ɑn'sɑmbəl] *s* insieme *m*; (*mus*) concertato

**ensign** ['ɛnsaɪn] *s* (*standard*) bandiera, insegna; (*badge*) distintivo || ['ɛnsən] *or* ['ɛnsaɪn] *s* guardamarina *m*

**ensilage** ['ɛnsəlɪdʒ] *s* (*preservation of fodder*) insilamento; (*preserved fodder*) insilato

**ensile** ['ɛnsaɪl] *or* [ɛn'saɪl] *tr* insilare

**enslave** [ɛn'slev] *tr* fare schiavo, asservire

**enslavement** [ɛn'slevmənt] *s* asservimento

**ensnare** [ɛn'snɛr] *tr* irretire

**ensue** [ɛn'su] *or* [ɛn'sju] *intr* risultare; seguire, conseguire

**ensuing** [ɛn'su·ɪŋ] *or* [ɛn'sju·ɪŋ] *adj* risultante, conseguente; seguente

**ensure** [ɛn'ʃʊr] *tr* assicurare, garantire

**entail** [ɛn'tel] *s* (law) obbligo || *tr* provocare, comportare; (law) obbligare

**entangle** [ɛn'tæŋgəl] *tr* intricare, imbrogliare, impigliare

**entanglement** [ɛn'tæŋgəlmənt] *s* groviglio, garbuglio

**enter** ['ɛntər] *tr* (*a house*) entrare in; (*in the customhouse*) dichiarare; (*to make a record of*) registrare; (*a student*) iscrivere; iscriversi a; fare membro; (*to undertake*) intraprendere; **to enter s.o.'s head** passare per la testa a qlcu || *intr* entrare; (theat) entrare in scena; **to enter into** entrare in; (*a contract*) impegnarsi in; **to enter on** or **upon** intraprendere

**enterprise** ['ɛntər‚praɪz] *s* (*undertak-*

*ing*) impresa; (*spirit, push*) intraprendenza

**enterprising** ['ɛntər‚praɪzɪŋ] *adj* intraprendente

**entertain** [‚ɛntər'ten] *tr* divertire, intrattenere; (*guests*) ospitare; (*a hope*) accarezzare; (*a proposal*) considerare || *intr* ricevere

**entertainer** [‚ɛntər'tenər] *s* (*host*) ospite *mf*; (*in public*) attore *m*, cantante *mf*, fine dicitore *m*

**entertaining** [‚ɛntər'tenɪŋ] *adj* divertente

**entertainment** [‚ɛntər'tenmənt] *s* trattenimento, svago; spettacolo, attrazione; buon trattamento

**enthrall** [ɛn'θrɔl] *tr* affascinare, incantare; (*to subjugate*) asservire, soggiogare

**enthrone** [ɛn'θron] *tr* mettere sul trono, intronizzare; esaltare, innalzare

**enthuse** [ɛn'θuz] *or* [ɛn'θjuz] *tr* (coll) entusiasmare || *intr* (coll) entusiasmarsi

**enthusiasm** [ɛn'θuzɪ‚æzəm] *or* [ɛn'θjuzɪ‚æzəm] *s* entusiasmo

**enthusiast** [ɛn'θuzɪ‚æst] *or* [ɛn'θjuzɪ‚æst] *s* entusiasta *mf*, maniaco

**enthusiastic** [ɛn‚θuzɪ'æstɪk] *or* [ɛn‚θjuzɪ'æstɪk] *adj* entusiastico

**entice** [ɛn'taɪs] *tr* attrarre, provocare; tentare

**enticement** [ɛn'taɪsmənt] *s* attrazione, provocazione; tentazione

**entire** [ɛn'taɪr] *adj* intero

**entirely** [ɛn'taɪrli] *adv* interamente; (*solely*) solamente

**entire·ty** [ɛn'taɪrti] *s* (**-ties**) interezza; totalità *f*

**entitle** [ɛn'taɪtəl] *tr* dar diritto a; (*to give a name to*) intitolare

**enti·ty** ['ɛntɪti] *s* (**-ties**) (*something real; organization, institution*) ente *m*; (*existence*) entità *f*

**entomb** [ɛn'tum] *tr* seppellire

**entombment** [ɛn'tummənt] *s* sepoltura

**entomology** [‚ɛntə'mɑlədʒi] *s* entomologia

**entourage** [‚ɑntu'rɑʒ] *s* seguito

**entrails** ['ɛntrelz] *or* ['ɛntrəlz] *spl* visceri *mpl*

**entrain** [ɛn'tren] *tr* far salire sul treno || *intr* imbarcarsi sul treno

**entrance** ['ɛntrəns] *s* entrata, ingresso || [ɛn'træns] *or* [ɛn'trɑns] *tr* ipnotizzare, incantare

**en'trance exam'ina'tion** *s* esame *m* d'ammissione

**entrancing** [ɛn'trænsɪŋ] *or* [ɛn'trɑnsɪŋ] *adj* incantatore

**entrant** ['ɛntrənt] *s* nuovo membro; (sports) concorrente *mf*

**en·trap** [ɛn'træp] *v* (*pret* & *pp* **-trapped;** *ger* **-trapping**) *tr* intrappolare, irretire

**entreat** [ɛn'trit] *tr* implorare

**entreat·y** [ɛn'triti] *s* (**-ies**) implorazione, supplica

**entree** ['ɑntre] *s* entrata, ingresso; (culin) prima portata

**entrench** [ɛn'trɛntʃ] *tr* trincerare || *intr* —**to entrench on** or **upon** violare

**entrust** [ɛn'trʌst] *tr* affidare, confidare

**en·try** ['ɛntri] *s* (**-tries**) entrata; (*item*) partita, registrazione; (*in a dictionary*) lemma, esponente *m;* (sports) concorrente *mf*

**entwine** [ɛn'twaɪn] *tr* intrecciare ‖ *intr* intrecciarsi

**enumerate** [ɪ'njumə‚ret] or [ɪ'numə‚ret] *tr* enumerare

**enunciate** [ɪ'nʌnsɪ‚et] or [ɪ'nʌnʃɪ‚et] *tr* enunciare, staccare

**envelop** [ɛn'vɛləp] *tr* involgere

**envelope** ['ɛnvə‚lop] or ['ɑnvə‚lop] *s* (*for a letter*) busta; (*wrapper*) involucro

**envenom** [ɛn'vɛnəm] *tr* avvelenare

**enviable** ['ɛnvɪ·əbəl] *adj* invidiabile

**envious** ['ɛnvɪ·əs] *adj* invidioso

**environment** [ɛn'vaɪrənmənt] *s* ambiente *m;* condizioni *fpl* ambientali

**environs** [ɛn'vaɪrənz] *spl* dintorni *mpl,* sobborghi *mpl*

**envisage** [ɛn'vɪzɪdʒ] *tr* considerare, immaginare

**envoi** ['ɛnvɔɪ] *s* (pros) congedo

**envoy** ['ɛnvɔɪ] *s* inviato; (mil) parlamentare *m;* (pros) congedo

**en·vy** ['ɛnvi] *s* (**-vies**) invidia ‖ *v* (*pret* & *pp* **-vied**) *tr* invidiare

**enzyme** ['ɛnzaɪm] or ['ɛnzɪm] *s* enzima *m*

**epaulet** or **epaulette** ['ɛpə‚lɛt] *s* spallina

**epenthe·sis** [ɛ'pɛnθɪsɪs] *s* (**-ses** [‚siz]) epentesi *f*

**ephemeral** [ɪ'fɛmərəl] *adj* effimero

**epic** ['ɛpɪk] *adj* epico ‖ *s* epica

**epicure** ['ɛpɪ‚kjʊr] *s* epicureo

**epicurean** [‚ɛpɪkjuˈri·ən] *adj* & *s* epicureo

**epidemic** [‚ɛpɪ'dɛmɪk] *adj* epidemico ‖ *s* epidemia

**epidermis** [‚ɛpɪ'dʌrmɪs] *s* epidermide *f*

**epiglottis** [‚ɛpɪ'glɑtɪs] *s* epiglottide *f*

**epigram** ['ɛpɪ‚græm] *s* epigramma *m*

**epilepsy** ['ɛpɪ‚lɛpsi] *s* epilessia

**epileptic** [‚ɛpɪ'lɛptɪk] *adj* & *s* epilettico

**epilogue** ['ɛpɪ‚lɔg] or ['ɛpɪ‚lɑg] *s* epilogo

**Epiphany** [ɪ'pɪfəni] *s* Epifania

**Episcopalian** [ɪ‚pɪskə'peli·ən] *adj* & *s* episcopaliano

**episode** ['ɛpɪ‚sod] *s* episodio

**epistle** [ɪ'pɪsəl] *s* epistola

**epitaph** ['ɛpɪ‚tæf] *s* epitaffio

**epithet** ['ɛpɪ‚θɛt] *s* epiteto

**epitome** [ɪ'pɪtəmi] *s* epitome *f;* (fig) prototipo, personificazione

**epitomize** [ɪ'pɪtə‚maɪz] *tr* epitomare; (fig) incarnare, personificare

**epoch** ['ɛpək] or ['ipɑk] *s* epoca

**epochal** ['ɛpəkəl] *adj* memorabile

**ep'och-mak'ing** *adj*—**to be epoch-making** fare epoca

**Ep'som salt'** ['ɛpsəm] *s* sale *m* inglese

**equable** ['ɛkwəbəl] or ['ikwəbəl] *adj* uniforme; tranquillo

**equal** ['ikwəl] *adj* uguale; **equal to** pari a, all'altezza di ‖ *s* uguale *m* ‖ *v* (*pret* & *pp* **equaled** or **equalled;** *ger* **equaling** or **equalling**) *tr* uguagliare

**equali·ty** [ɪ'kwɑlɪti] *s* (**-ties**) uguaglianza

**equalize** ['ikwə‚laɪz] *tr* uguagliare; (*to make uniform*) perequare, pareggiare

**equally** ['ikwəli] *adv* ugualmente

**equanimity** [‚ikwə'nɪmɪti] *s* equanimità *f*

**equate** [i'kwet] *tr* mettere in forma di equazione; considerare uguale or uguali

**equation** [i'kweʒən] or [i'kweʃən] *s* equazione

**equator** [i'kwetər] *s* equatore *m*

**equatorial** [‚ikwə'torɪ·əl] *adj* equatoriale

**equer·ry** ['ɛkwəri] or [ɪ'kwɛri] *s* (**-ries**) scudiero

**equestrian** [ɪ'kwɛstrɪ·ən] *adj* equestre ‖ *s* cavallerizzo

**equilateral** [‚ikwɪ'lætərəl] *adj* equilatero

**equilibrium** [‚ikwɪ'lɪbrɪ·əm] *s* equilibrio

**equinoctial** [‚ikwɪ'nɑkʃəl] *adj* equinoziale

**equinox** ['ikwɪ‚nɑks] *s* equinozio

**equip** [ɪ'kwɪp] *v* (*pret* & *pp* **equipped;** *ger* **equipping**) *tr* equipaggiare; **to equip** (*e.g., a ship*) **with** munire di

**equipment** [ɪ'kwɪpmənt] *s* equipaggiamento; (*skill*) attitudine *f,* capacità *f*

**equipoise** ['ikwɪ‚pɔɪz] or ['ɛkwɪ‚pɔɪz] *s* equilibrio ‖ *tr* equilibrare

**equitable** ['ɛkwɪtəbəl] *adj* equo

**equi·ty** ['ɛkwɪti] *s* (**-ties**) (*fairness*) equità *f;* valore *m* al netto; (*in a corporation*) interessenza azionaria

**equivalent** [ɪ'kwɪvələnt] *adj* equivalente ‖ *s* equivalente *m;* (com) controvalore *m*

**equivocal** [ɪ'kwɪvəkəl] *adj* equivoco

**equivocate** [ɪ'kwɪvə‚ket] *intr* giocare sulle parole, parlare in maniera equivoca

**equivocation** [ɪ‚kwɪvə'keʃən] *s* equivocità *f;* equivoco

**era** ['ɪrə] or ['irə] *s* era, evo

**eradicate** [ɪ'rædɪ‚ket] *tr* sradicare

**erase** [ɪ'res] *tr* cancellare

**eraser** [ɪ'resər] *s* gomma da cancellare; (*for blackboard*) spugna

**erasure** [ɪ'reʃər] or [ɪ'reʒər] *s* cancellatura; (*of a tape*) cancellazione

**ere** [ɛr] *prep* (lit) prima di ‖ *conj* (lit) prima che

**erect** [ɪ'rɛkt] *adj* dritto, eretto; (*hair*) irto ‖ *tr* (*to set in upright position*) drizzare; (*a building*) erigere, costruire; (*a machine*) montare

**erection** [ɪ'rɛkʃən] *s* erezione

**ermine** ['ʌrmɪn] *s* ermellino; (fig) carica di giudice, toga, magistratura

**erode** [ɪ'rod] *tr* erodere ‖ *intr* corrodersi, consumarsi

**erosion** [ɪ'roʒən] *s* erosione

**erotic** [ɪ'rɑtɪk] *adj* erotico

**err** [ʌr] *intr* errare; (*to be incorrect*) sbagliarsi

**errand** ['ɛrənd] *s* corsa, commissione; **to run an errand** fare una commissione

**er'rand boy'** *s* fattorino, galoppino

**erratic** [ɪ'rætɪk] *adj* erratico; strano, eccentrico

**erra·tum** [ɪ'retəm] *or* [ɪ'ratəm] *s* (**-ta** [tə]) errore *m* di stampa

**erroneous** [ɪ'ronɪ·əs] *adj* erroneo

**error** ['ɛrər] *s* errore *m*, sbaglio

**erudite** ['ɛrʊ ˌdaɪt] *or* ['ɛrjʊ ˌdaɪt] *adj* erudito, dotto

**erudition** [ ˌɛrʊ'dɪʃən] *or* [ ˌɛrjʊ'dɪʃən] *s* erudizione

**erupt** [ɪ'rʌpt] *intr* (*said of a volcano*) eruttare; (*said of a skin rash*) fiorire; (*said of a tooth*) spuntare; (fig) erompere

**eruption** [ɪ'rʌpʃən] *s* eruzione

**escalate** ['ɛskə ˌlet] *tr & intr* aumentare

**escalation** [ ˌɛskə'leʃən] *s* aumento

**escalator** ['ɛskə ˌletər] *s* scala mobile

**escallop** [ɛs'kæləp] *s* (*on edge of cloth*) dentellatura, festone *m;* (*mollusk*) pettine *m* ‖ *tr* cuocere in conchiglia; cuocere al forno con salsa e pane grattugiato

**escapade** [ ˌɛskə'ped] *s* scappatella

**escape** [ɛs'kep] *s* (*getaway*) fuga; (*from responsibility, duties, etc.*) scampo ‖ *tr* sottrarsi a, eludere; **to escape s.o.** scappare da qlcu; scappar di mente a qlcu ‖ *intr* scappare; sprigionarsi; **to escape from** (*a person*) sfuggire a; (*jail*) evadere da

**escapee** [ ˌɛskə'pi] *s* evaso

**escape' lit'erature'** *s* letteratura di evasione

**escapement** [ɛs'kepmənt] *s* scappamento

**escape' veloc'ity** *s* (rok) velocità *f* di fuga

**escarpment** [ɛs'karpmənt] *s* scarpata

**eschew** [ɛs't/u] *tr* evitare, rifuggire da

**escort** ['ɛskɔrt] *s* scorta; (*of a woman or girl*) compagno, cavaliere *m* ‖ [ɛs'kɔrt] *tr* scortare

**escutcheon** [ɛs'kʌtʃən] *s* scudo; (*plate in front of lock on door*) bocchetta

**Esk·imo** ['ɛskɪ ˌmo] *adj* eschimese ‖ (**-mos** *or* **-mo**) eschimese *mf*

**esopha·gus** [i'safəgəs] *s* (**-gi** [ ˌdʒaɪ]) esofago

**espalier** [ɛs'pæljər] *s* spalliera

**especial** [ɛs'pɛʃəl] *adj* speciale

**espionage** ['ɛspɪ·ənɪdʒ] *or* [ ˌɛspɪ·ə-'naʒ] *s* spionaggio

**esplanade** [ ˌɛsplə'ned] *or* [ ˌɛsplə'nad] *s* spianata, piazzale *m*

**espousal** [ɛs'paʊzəl] *s* sposalizio; (*of a cause*) adozione

**espouse** [ɛs'paʊz] *tr* sposare; (*to advocate*) abbracciare, adottare

**esquire** [ɛs'kwaɪr] *or* ['ɛskwaɪr] *s* scudiero ‖ **Esquire** *s* titolo di cortesia usato generalmente con persone di riguardo

**essay** ['ɛse] *s* saggio

**essayist** ['ɛse·ɪst] *s* saggista *mf*

**essence** ['ɛsəns] *s* essenza

**essential** [ɛ'sɛnʃəl] *adj & s* essenziale *m*

**establish** [ɛs'tæblɪʃ] *tr* stabilire

**establishment** [ɛs'tæblɪʃmənt] *s* stabilimento; fondazione; **the Establishment** l'autorità costituita

**estate** [ɛs'tet] *s* stato; condizione sociale; (*landed property*) tenuta; (*a*

*person's possessions*) patrimonio; (*left by a decedent*) massa ereditaria

**esteem** [ɛs'tim] *s* stima ‖ *tr* stimare

**esthete** ['ɛsθit] *s* esteta *mf*

**esthetic** [ɛs'θɛtɪk] *adj* estetico ‖ **esthetics** *ssg* estetica

**estimable** ['ɛstɪməbəl] *adj* stimabile

**estimate** ['ɛstɪ ˌmet] *or* ['ɛstɪmɪt] *s* stima, valutazione; (*statement of cost of work to be done*) preventivo ‖ ['ɛstɪ ˌmet] *tr* stimare, valutare; preventivare

**estimation** [ ˌɛstɪ'meʃən] *s* stima; **in my estimation** a mio parere

**estimator** ['ɛstɪ ˌmetər] *s* preventivista *mf*

**estrangement** [ɛs'trendʒmənt] *s* alienazione, disaffezione

**estuar·y** ['ɛst/ʊ ˌɛri] *s* (**-ies**) estuario

**etch** [ɛtʃ] *tr & intr* incidere all'acquaforte

**etcher** ['ɛtʃər] *s* acquafortista *mf*

**etching** ['ɛtʃɪŋ] *s* acquaforte *f*

**eternal** [ɪ'tʌrnəl] *adj* eterno

**eterni·ty** [ɪ'tʌrnɪti] *s* (**-ties**) eternità *f*

**ether** ['iθər] *s* etere *m*

**ethereal** [ɪ'θɪrɪ·əl] *adj* etereo

**ethical** ['ɛθɪkəl] *adj* etico

**ethics** ['ɛθɪks] *ssg* etica

**Ethiopian** [ ˌiθɪ'opɪ·ən] *adj & s* etiope *mf*

**ethnic(al)** ['ɛθnɪk(əl)] *adj* etnico

**ethnography** [ɛθ'nagrəfi] *s* etnografia

**ethnology** [ɛθ'nalədʒi] *s* etnologia

**ethyl** ['ɛθɪl] *s* etile *m*

**ethylene** ['ɛθɪ ˌlin] *s* etilene *m*

**etiquette** ['ɛtɪ ˌket] *s* etichetta

**étude** [e'tjud] *s* (mus) studio

**etymology** [ ˌɛtɪ'malədʒi] *s* etimologia

**ety·mon** ['ɛtɪ ˌman] *s* (**-mons** *or* **-ma** [mə]) etimo

**eucalyp·tus** [ ˌjukə'lɪptəs] *s* (**-tuses** *or* **-ti** [taɪ]) eucalipto

**Eucharist** ['jukərɪst] *s* Eucaristia

**eugenics** [jʊ'dʒɛnɪks] *ssg* eugenetica

**eulogistic** [ ˌjulə'dʒɪstɪk] *adj* elogiativo

**eulogize** ['julə ˌdʒaɪz] *tr* elogiare

**eulo·gy** ['julədʒi] *s* (**-gies**) elogio; elogio funebre

**eunuch** ['junək] *s* eunuco

**euphemism** ['jufɪ ˌmɪzəm] *s* eufemismo

**euphemistic** [ ˌjufɪ'mɪstɪk] *adj* eufemistico

**euphonic** [ju'fanɪk] *adj* eufonico

**eupho·ny** ['jufəni] *s* (**-nies**) eufonia

**euphoria** [ju'forɪ·ə] *s* euforia

**euphuism** ['jufju ˌɪzəm] *s* eufuismo

**Europe** ['jʊrəp] *s* l'Europa

**European** [ ˌjʊrə'pi·ən] *adj & s* europeo

**euthanasia** [ ˌjuθə'neʒə] *s* eutanasia

**evacuate** [ɪ'vækju ˌet] *tr & intr* evacuare

**evacuation** [ɪ ˌvækju'eʃən] *s* evacuazione

**evacuee** [ɪ'vækju ˌi] *or* [ɪ ˌvækju'i] *s* sfollato

**evade** [ɪ'ved] *tr* eludere ‖ *intr* evadere

**evaluate** [ɪ'vælju ˌet] *tr* valutare

**evaluation** [ɪ ˌvælju'eʃən] *s* valutazione

**Evangel** [ɪ'vændʒəl] *s* Vangelo

**evangelic(al)** [ ˌivæn'dʒɛlɪk(əl)] *or* [ ˌɛvən'dʒɛlɪk(əl)] *adj* evangelico

**Evangelist** [ɪ'vændʒəlɪst] *s* evangelista *m*

**evaporate** [ɪ'væpə͵ret] *tr* & *intr* evaporare

**evasion** [ɪ'veʒən] *s* evasione; (*subterfuge*) scappatoia

**evasive** [ɪ'vesɪv] *adj* evasivo

**eve** [iv] *s* vigilia; **on the eve of** la vigilia di

**even** ['ivən] *adj* (*smooth*) piano, regolare; (*number*) pari; uguale, uniforme; (*temperament*) calmo, placido; **even with** a livello di; **to be even** mettersi in pari; **to get even** prendersi la rivincita ‖ *adv* anche; fino, perfino; pure; esattamente; magari; **even as** proprio mentre; **even if** anche se, quando pure; **even so** anche se così; **even though** quantunque; **even when** anche quando; **not even** neppure, nemmeno; **to break even** impattare ‖ *tr* spianare; **to even up** bilanciare

**evening** ['ivnɪŋ] *adj* serale ‖ *s* sera, serata; **all evening** tutta la sera; **every evening** tutte le sere; **in the evening** la sera

**eve′ning clothes′** *spl* vestito da sera

**eve′ning gown′** *s* vestito da sera da signora

**eve′ning star′** *s* espero

**e′ven·song′** *s* (eccl) vespro

**event** [ɪ'vɛnt] *s* avvenimento; (*outcome*) evenienza; (*public function*) manifestazione; (sports) prova; **at all events** or **in any event** in ogni caso; **in the event that** in caso che, se mai

**eventful** [ɪ'vɛntfəl] *adj* ricco di avvenimenti; movimentato

**eventual** [ɪ'vɛntʃʊ·əl] *adj* finale

**eventuali·ty** [ɪ͵vɛntʃʊ'ælɪti] *s* (**-ties**) eventualità *f*, evenienza

**eventually** [ɪ'vɛntʃʊ·əli] *adv* finalmente, alla fine

**eventuate** [ɪ'vɛntʃʊ͵et] *intr* risultare; accadere

**ever** ['ɛvər] *adv* (*at all times*) sempre; (*at any time*) mai; **as ever** come sempre; **as much as ever** tanto come prima; **ever since** (*since that time*) sin da; da allora in poi; **ever so** molto; **ever so much** moltissimo; **hardly ever** or **scarcely ever** quasi mai; **not . . . ever** non . . . mai

**ev′er·glade′** *s* terreno paludoso coperto di erbe

**ev′er·green′** *adj* & *s* sempreverde *m* & *f;* **evergreens** decorazione di sempreverdi

**ev′er·last′ing** *adj* eterno; incessante; (*lasting indefinitely*) duraturo; (*wearisome*) noioso ‖ *s* eternità *f;* (bot) semprevivo

**ev′er·more′** *adv* eternamente; **for evermore** per sempre

**every** ['ɛvri] *adj* tutti i; (*each*) ogni, ciascuno; (*being each in a series*) ogni, e.g., **every three days** ogni tre giorni; **every bit** (coll) in tutto e per tutto, e.g., **every bit a man** un uomo in tutto e per tutto; **every now and then** di quando in quando; **every once in a while** una volta ogni tanto;

**every other day** ogni secondo giorno; **every which way** (coll) da tutte le parti; (coll) in disordine

**ev′ery·bod′y** *pron indef* ognuno, tutti

**ev′ery·day′** *adj* di ogni giorno; quotidiano; ordinario

**ev′ery·man′** *s* l'uomo qualunque ‖ *pron* chiunque

**ev′ery·one′** or **ev′ery one′** *pron indef* ciascuno, tutti

**ev′ery·thing′** *pron indef* tutto, ogni cosa, tutto quanto

**ev′ery·where′** *adv* dappertutto, dovunque

**evict** [ɪ'vɪkt] *tr* sfrattare, sloggiare

**eviction** [ɪ'vɪkʃən] *s* sfratto, sloggio

**evidence** ['ɛvɪdəns] *s* evidenza; (law) prova

**evident** ['ɛvɪdənt] *adj* evidente

**evil** ['ivəl] *adj* cattivo, malvagio ‖ *s* male *m;* disgrazia

**evildoer** ['ivəl͵du·ər] *s* malfattore *m*, malvagio

**e′vil·do′ing** *s* malafatta, malvagità *f*

**e′vil eye′** *s* iettatura, malocchio

**evil-minded** ['ivəl'maɪndɪd] *adj* malintenzionato

**e′vil one′, the** il nemico

**evince** [ɪ'vɪns] *tr* mostrare, manifestare

**evoke** [ɪ'vok] *tr* evocare

**evolution** [͵ɛvə'luʃən] *s* evoluzione

**evolve** [ɪ'vɑlv] *tr* sviluppare ‖ *intr* evolversi

**ewe** [ju] *s* pecora

**ewer** ['ju·ər] *s* brocca

**ex** [ɛks] *prep* senza includere

**exacerbation** [ɪg͵zæsər'beʃən] *s* esulcerazione, esacerbazione

**exacerbate** [ɪg'zæsər͵bet] *tr* esacerbare, esulcerare

**exact** [ɛg'zækt] *adj* esatto ‖ *tr* esigere

**exacting** [ɛg'zæktɪŋ] *adj* esigente

**exaction** [ɛg'zækʃən] *s* esazione

**exactly** [ɛg'zæktli] *adv* esattamente; (*sharp, on the dot*) in punto

**exactness** [ɛg'zæktnɪs] *s* esattezza

**exaggerate** [ɛg'zædʒə͵ret] *tr* esagerare

**exalt** [ɛg'zɔlt] *tr* elevare, esaltare

**exam** [ɛg'zæm] *s* (coll) esame *m*

**examination** [ɛg͵zæmɪ'neʃən] *s* esame *m;* **to take an examination** sostenere un esame

**examine** [ɛg'zæmɪn] *tr* esaminare

**examiner** [ɛg'zæmɪnər] *s* esaminatore *m*

**example** [ɛg'zæmpəl] or [ɛg'zampəl] *s* esempio; (*precedent*) precedente *m;* (*of mathematics*) problema *m;* **for example** per esempio

**exasperate** [ɛg'zæspə͵ret] *tr* esasperare

**excavate** ['ɛkskə͵vet] *tr* scavare

**exceed** [ɛk'sid] *tr* eccedere

**exceedingly** [ɛk'sidɪŋli] *adv* estremamente, sommamente

**ex·cel** [ɛk'sɛl] *v* (*pret* & *pp* **-celled;** *ger* **-celling**) *tr* sorpassare ‖ *intr* eccellere

**excellence** ['ɛksələns] *s* eccellenza

**excellen·cy** ['ɛksələnsi] *s* (**-cies**) eccellenza; **Your Excellency** Sua Eccellenza

**excelsior** [ɛk'sɛlsɪ·ər] *s* trucioli *mpl* per imballaggio

**except** [ɛk'sɛpt] *prep* eccetto; **except**

**for** tranne, ad eccezione di; **except that** eccetto che ‖ *tr* eccettuare

**exception** [ɛk'sɛpʃən] *s* eccezione; **to take exception** obiettare; scandalizzarsi; **with the exception of** a esclusione di, eccetto

**exceptional** [ɛk'sɛpʃənəl] *adj* eccezionale

**excerpt** ['ɛksʌrpt] or [ɛk'sʌrpt] *s* brano, selezione ‖ [ɛk'sʌrpt] *tr* scegliere, selezionare

**excess** ['ɛksɛs] or [ɛk'sɛs] *adj* eccedente ‖ [ɛk'sɛs] *s* (*amount or degree by which one thing exceeds another*) eccedente *m*, eccedenza; (*excessive amount; immoderate indulgence; unlawful conduct*) eccesso; **in excess of** più di

**ex'cess bag'gage** *s* bagaglio eccedente

**ex'cess fare'** *s* (rr) supplemento

**excessive** [ɛk'sɛsɪv] *adj* eccessivo

**ex'cess-prof'its tax'** *s* tassa sui sopraprofitti

**exchange** [ɛks'tʃendʒ] *s* scambio; (*place for buying and selling*) borsa; (*transactions in the currencies of two different countries*) cambio; (telp) centrale *f*, centralino; **in exchange for** in cambio di ‖ *tr* scambiare, scambiarsi; **to exchange blows** venire alle mani; **to exchange greetings** salutarsi

**exchequer** [ɛks'tʃɛkər] or ['ɛkstʃɛkər] *s* erario, tesoro

**ex'cise tax'** [ɛk'saɪz] or ['ɛksaɪz] *s* imposta sul consumo

**excitable** [ɛk'saɪtəbəl] *adj* eccitabile

**excite** [ɛk'saɪt] *tr* eccitare

**excitement** [ɛk'saɪtmənt] *s* eccitazione

**exciting** [ɛk'saɪtɪŋ] *adj* emozionante; (*stimulating*) eccitante

**exclaim** [ɛks'klem] *tr & intr* esclamare

**exclamation** [ˌɛksklə'meʃən] *s* esclamazione

**exclama'tion mark'** or **point'** *s* punto esclamativo

**exclude** [ɛks'klud] *tr* escludere

**excluding** [ɛks'kludɪŋ] *prep* a esclusione di, senza contare

**exclusion** [ɛks'kluʒən] *s* esclusione; **to the exclusion of** tranne, salvo

**exclusive** [ɛks'klusɪv] *adj* esclusivo; **exclusive of** escluso, senza contare ‖ *s* (journ) esclusiva

**excommunicate** [ˌɛkskə'mjunɪˌket] *tr* scomunicare

**excommunication** [ˌɛkskəˌmjunɪ'keʃən] *s* scomunica

**excoriate** [ɛks'korɪˌet] *tr* criticare aspramente, vituperare

**excrement** ['ɛkskrəmənt] *s* escremento

**excruciating** [ɛks'kruʃɪˌetɪŋ] *adj* (*e.g., pleasure*) estremo; (*e.g., pain*) atroce, lancinante, straziante

**exculpate** ['ɛkskʌlˌpet] or [ɛks'kʌlpet] *tr* scolpare, scagionare

**excursion** [ɛks'kʌrʒən] or [ɛks'kʌrʃən] *s* escursione, gita

**excursionist** [ɛks'kʌrʒənɪst] or [ɛks'kʌrʃənɪst] *s* escursionista *mf*

**excusable** [ɛks'kjuzəbəl] *adj* scusabile

**excuse** [ɛks'kjus] *s* scusa ‖ [ɛks'kjuz] *tr* scusare; esentare; (*a debt*) rimettere

**execute** ['ɛksɪˌkjut] *tr* (*to carry out; to produce*) eseguire; (*to put to death*) giustiziare; (law) rendere esecutorio

**execution** [ˌɛksɪ'kjuʃən] *s* esecuzione; (*e.g., of a criminal*) esecuzione capitale

**executioner** [ˌɛksɪ'kjuʃənər] *s* giustiziere *m*, boia *m*, carnefice *m*

**executive** [ɛg'zɛkjətɪv] *adj* esecutivo ‖ *s* esecutivo; (*of a school, business, etc.*) dirigente *mf*

**Exec'utive Man'sion** *s* palazzo del governatore; residenza del capo del governo statunitense

**executor** [ɛg'zɛkjətər] *s* (law) esecutore testamentario

**executrix** [ɛg'zɛkjətrɪks] *s* (law) esecutrice testamentaria

**exemplary** [ɛg'zɛmpləri] or ['ɛgzəmˌpleri] *adj* esemplare

**exempli•fy** [ɛg'zɛmplɪˌfaɪ] *v* (*pret & pp* -fied) *tr* esemplificare

**exempt** [ɛg'zɛmpt] *adj* esente ‖ *tr* esimere, esentare

**exemption** [ɛg'zɛmpʃən] *s* esenzione

**exercise** ['ɛksərˌsaɪz] *s* esercizio; cerimonia; **to take exercise** fare del moto ‖ *tr* esercitare; (*care*) usare; (*to worry*) preoccupare ‖ *intr* esercitarsi

**exert** [ɛg'zʌrt] *tr* (*e.g., power*) esercitare; **to exert oneself** sforzarsi

**exertion** [ɛg'zʌrʃən] *s* sforzo, tentativo; (*active use*) uso, esercizio

**exhalation** [ˌɛks·hə'leʃən] *s* (*of gas, vapors*) esalazione; (*of air from lungs*) espirazione

**exhale** [ɛks'hel] or [ɛg'zel] *tr* (*gases, vapors, etc.*) esalare; (*air from lungs*) espirare ‖ *intr* esalare; espirare

**exhaust** [ɛg'zɔst] *s* scarico, scappamento; tubo di scarico or scappamento ‖ *tr* (*to wear out*) spossare, finire; (*to use up*) esaurire, dar fondo a; vuotare

**exhaust' fan'** *s* aspiratore *m*

**exhaustion** [ɛg'zɔstʃən] *s* esaurimento; estenuazione; (sports) cotta

**exhaustive** [ɛg'zɔstɪv] *adj* esauriente

**exhaust' man'ifold** *s* collettore *m* di scarico

**exhaust' pipe'** *s* tubo di scarico

**exhaust' valve'** *s* valvola di scappamento

**exhibit** [ɛg'zɪbɪt] *s* esposizione; (law) documento in giudizio ‖ *tr* esibire

**exhibition** [ˌɛksɪ'bɪʃən] *s* esibizione

**exhibitor** [ɛg'zɪbɪtər] *s* espositore *m*

**exhilarating** [ɛg'zɪləˌretɪŋ] *adj* esilarante

**exhort** [ɛg'zɔrt] *tr* esortare

**exhume** [ɛks'hjum] or [ɛg'zjum] *tr* esumare, dissotterrare

**exigen•cy** ['ɛksɪdʒənsi] *s* (-cies) esigenza

**exigent** ['ɛksɪdʒənt] *adj* esigente

**exile** ['ɛgzaɪl] or ['ɛksaɪl] *s* esilio; (*person*) esule *mf* ‖ *tr* esiliare

**exist** [ɛg'zɪst] *intr* esistere

**existence** [ɛg'zɪstəns] *s* esistenza

**existing** [ɛg'zɪstɪŋ] *adj* esistente

**exit** ['ɛgzɪt] or ['ɛksɪt] *s* uscita ‖ *intr* uscire

**exodus** ['ɛksədəs] *s* esodo
**exonerate** [ɛg'zɑnə,ret] *tr (from an obligation)* esonerare; *(from blame)* scagionare
**exorbitant** [ɛg'zɔrbɪtənt] *adj* esorbitante
**exorcise** ['ɛksɔr,saɪz] *tr* esorcizzare
**exotic** [ɛg'zɑtɪk] *adj* esotico
**expand** [ɛks'pænd] *tr (a metal)* dilatare; *(gas)* espandere; *(to enlarge)* allargare, ampliare; *(to unfold)* spiegare; (math) svolgere, sviluppare ‖ *intr* dilatarsi; espandersi; allargarsi, ampliarsi; spiegarsi, estendersi
**expanse** [ɛks'pæns] *s* vastità *f*
**expansion** [ɛks'pænʃən] *s* espansione
**expansive** [ɛks'pænsɪv] *adj* espansivo
**expatiate** [ɛks'peʃɪ,et] *intr* dilungarsi
**expatriate** [ɛks'petrɪ,ɪt] *adj* esiliato ‖ *s* esule *mf* ‖ [ɛks'petri,et] *tr* esiliare; **to expatriate oneself** espatriare
**expect** [ɛks'pɛkt] *tr* aspettare, attendere; (coll) credere, supporre; **to expect it** aspettarselo, aspettarsela
**expectan·cy** [ɛks'pɛktənsi] *s* **(-cies)** aspettativa, aspettazione
**expect'ant moth'er** [ɛks'pɛktənt] *s* futura madre
**expectation** [,ɛkspɛk'teʃən] *s* aspettativa
**expectorate** [ɛks'pɛktə,ret] *tr & intr* espettorare
**expedien·cy** [ɛks'pidɪ·ənsi] *s* **(-cies)** industria, ingegno; opportunismo, vantaggio personale
**expedient** [ɛks'pidɪ·ənt] *adj* conveniente; vantaggioso; *(acting with self-interest)* opportunista ‖ *s* espediente *m*
**expedite** ['ɛkspɪ,daɪt] *tr* sbrigare, accelerare; *(a document)* dar corso a
**expedition** [,ɛkspɪ'dɪʃən] *s* spedizione; *(speed)* celerità *f*
**expeditionary** [,ɛkspɪ'dɪʃən,ɛri] *adj (e.g., corps)* di spedizione
**expeditious** [,ɛkspɪ'dɪʃəs] *adj* spicciativo, spiccio
**ex·pel** [ɛks'pɛl] *v (pret & pp* **-pelled;** *ger* **-pelling)** *tr* espellere, scacciare
**expend** [ɛks'pɛnd] *tr* spendere, consumare
**expendable** [ɛks'pɛndəbəl] *adj* spendibile; da buttarsi via; (mil) da sacrificare
**expenditure** [ɛks'pɛndɪtʃər] *s* spesa
**expense** [ɛks'pɛns] *s* spesa; **at the expense of** al costo di; **expenses** spese *fpl;* **to meet expenses** far fronte alle spese
**expense' account'** *s* conto delle spese risarcibili
**expensive** [ɛks'pɛnsɪv] *adj* caro, costoso
**experience** [ɛks'pɪrɪ·əns] *s* esperienza ‖ *tr* sperimentare, provare
**experienced** [ɛks'pɪrɪ·ənst] *adj* esperto, sperimentato
**experiment** [ɛks'pɛrɪmənt] *s* esperimento ‖ [ɛks'pɛrɪ,mɛnt] *intr* sperimentare
**expert** ['ɛkspərt] *adj & s* esperto
**expertise** [,ɛkspər'tiz] *s* maestria

**expiate** ['ɛkspɪ,et] *tr* espiare
**expiation** [,ɛkspɪ'eʃən] *s* espiazione
**expire** [ɛks'paɪr] *tr* espirare ‖ *intr (to breathe out)* espirare; *(said of a contract)* scadere; *(to die)* morire
**explain** [ɛks'plen] *tr* spiegare; **to explain away** giustificare; dar ragione di ‖ *intr* spiegare, spiegarsi
**explainable** [ɛks'plenəbəl] *adj* spiegabile
**explanation** [,ɛksplə'neʃən] *s* spiegazione, delucidazione
**explanatory** [ɛks'plænə,tori] *adj* esplicativo
**explicit** [ɛks'plɪsɪt] *adj* esplicito
**explode** [ɛks'plod] *tr* far scoppiare; *(a theory)* smontare ‖ *intr* scoppiare
**exploit** [ɛks'plɔɪt] *or* ['ɛksplɔɪt] *s* impresa, prodezza ‖ [ɛks'plɔɪt] *tr* utilizzare, sfruttare
**exploitation** [,ɛksplɔɪ'teʃən] *s* utilizzazione, sfruttamento
**exploration** [,ɛksplə'reʃən] *s* esplorazione
**explore** [ɛks'plor] *tr* esplorare
**explorer** [ɛks'plorər] *s* esploratore *m*
**explosion** [ɛks'ploʒən] *s* esplosione, scoppio; *(of a theory)* confutazione
**explosive** [ɛks'plosɪv] *adj & s* esplosivo
**exponent** [ɛks'ponənt] *s* esponente *m*
**export** ['ɛksport] *adj* di esportazione ‖ *s* esportazione, articolo di esportazione ‖ [ɛks'port] *or* ['ɛksport] *tr & intr* esportare
**exportation** [,ɛkspor'teʃən] *s* esportazione
**exporter** ['ɛksportər] *or* [ɛks'portər] *s* esportatore *m*
**expose** [ɛks'poz] *tr* esporre; *(to unmask)* smascherare
**exposé** [,ɛkspo'ze] *s* rivelazione scandalosa, smascheramento
**exposition** [,ɛkspə'zɪʃən] *s* esposizione; interpretazione, commento
**expostulate** [ɛks'pɑstʃə,let] *intr* protestare; **to expostulate with** lagnarsi con
**exposure** [ɛks'poʒər] *s (disclosure)* rivelazione; *(situation with regard to sunlight)* esposizione; (phot) esposizione
**expo'sure me'ter** *s* (phot) fotometro, esposimetro
**expound** [ɛks'paʊnd] *tr* esporre
**express** [ɛks'prɛs] *adj* espresso ‖ *s* (rr) celere *m*, rapido, direttissimo; **by express** per espresso, a grande velocità ‖ *adv* per espresso, a grande velocità ‖ *tr* esprimere; mandare per espresso; *(to squeeze out)* spremere; **to express oneself** esprimersi
**ex'press com'pany** *s* servizio corriere
**expression** [ɛks'prɛʃən] *s* espressione
**expressive** [ɛks'prɛsɪv] *adj* espressivo
**expressly** [ɛks'prɛsli] *adv* espressamente
**express'man** *s* **(-men)** fattorino di servizio corriere
**express'way'** *s* autostrada
**expropriate** [ɛks'propri,et] *tr* espropriare
**expulsion** [ɛks'pʌlʃən] *s* espulsione

**expunge** [ɛks'pʌndʒ] *tr* espungere
**expurgate** ['ɛkspər‿get] *tr* espurgare
**exquisite** ['ɛkskwɪzɪt] or [ɛks'kwɪzɪt] *adj* squisito; intenso
**ex'serv'ice-man'** *s* (**-men'**) ex combattente *m*
**extant** ['ɛkstənt] or [ɛks'tænt] *adj* ancora esistente
**extemporaneous** [ɛks‿tɛmpə'rɛnɪ‿əs] *adj* estemporaneo; (*made for the occasion*) improvvisato
**extempore** [ɛks'tɛmpəri] *adj* improvvisato || *adv* senza preparazione
**extemporize** [ɛks'tɛmpə‿raɪz] *tr & intr* improvvisare
**extend** [ɛks'tɛnd] *tr* allungare; estendere; (*e.g., aid*) offrire; (*payment of a debt*) dilazionare || *intr* estendersi
**extended** [ɛks'tɛndɪd] *adj* esteso; prolungato
**extension** [ɛks'tɛnʃən] *s* estensione; prolungamento; (com) proroga; (telp) derivazione
**exten'sion lad'der** *s* scala porta, scala a prolunga
**exten'sion ta'ble** *s* tavola allungabile
**exten'sion tel'ephone'** *s* telefono interno
**extensive** [ɛks'tɛnsɪv] *adj* (*wide*) vasto; (*lengthy*) lungo; (*characterized by extention*) estensivo
**extent** [ɛks'tɛnt] *s* estensione; **to a certain extent** fino a un certo punto; **to a great extent** in larga misura; **to the full extent** all'estremo limite
**extenuate** [ɛks'tɛnju‿et] *tr* (*to make seem less serious*) attenuare; (*to underrate*) sottovalutare
**exterior** [ɛks'tɪrɪ‿ər] *adj & s* esteriore *m*
**exterminate** [ɛks'tʌrmɪ‿net] *tr* sterminare
**external** [ɛks'tʌrnəl] *adj* esterno || **externals** *spl* esteriorità *f*, di fuori *m*
**extinct** [ɛks'tɪŋkt] *adj* estinto
**extinction** [ɛks'tɪŋkʃən] *s* estinzione
**extinguish** [ɛks'tɪŋgwɪʃ] *tr* estinguere
**extinguisher** [ɛks'tɪŋgwɪʃər] *s* estintore *m*
**extirpate** ['ɛkstər‿pet] or [ɛks'tʌrpet] *tr* estirpare
**ex•tol** [ɛks'tol] or [ɛks'tal] *v* (*pret & pp* **-tolled;** *ger* **-tolling**) *tr* inneggiare
**extort** [ɛks'tɔrt] *tr* estorcere
**extortion** [ɛks'tɔrʃən] *s* estorsione
**extra** ['ɛkstrə] *adj* extra; (*spare*) di scorta || *s* (*of a newspaper*) edizione straordinaria; (*something additional*) soprappiù *m*; (theat) figurante *mf* || *adv* straordinariamente
**ex'tra charge'** *s* supplemento
**extract** ['ɛkstrækt] *s* estratto || [ɛks'trækt] *tr* (*to pull out*) estrarre; (*to take from a book*) scegliere, selezionare
**extraction** [ɛks'trækʃən] *s* estrazione
**extracurricular** [‿ɛkstrəkə'rɪkjələr] *adj* fuori del programma normale
**extradition** [‿ɛkstrə'dɪʃən] *s* estradizione
**ex'tra•dry'** *adj* molto secco, brut
**ex'tra fare'** *s* supplemento al biglietto

**ex'tra•mar'ital** *adj* extraconiugale
**extramural** [‿ɛkstrə'mjʊrəl] *adj* fuori della scuola, interscolastico; fuori delle mura
**extraneous** [ɛks'trɛnɪ‿əs] *adj* estraneo
**extraordinary** [‿ɛkstrə'ɔrdɪ‿nɛri] or [ɛks'trɔrdɪ‿nɛri] *adj* straordinario
**extrapolate** [ɛks'træpə‿let] *tr & intr* estrapolare
**extrasensory** [‿ɛkstrə'sɛnsəri] *adj* extrasensoriale
**extravagance** [ɛks'trævəgəns] *s* prodigalità *f*; (*wildness, folly*) stravaganza
**extravagant** [ɛks'trævəgənt] *adj* prodigo; (*wild, foolish*) stravagante
**extreme** [ɛks'trim] *adj & s* estremo; **in the extreme** in massimo grado; **to go to extremes** andare agli estremi
**extremely** [ɛks'trimli] *adv* estremamente, in sommo grado
**extreme' unc'tion** *s* Estrema Unzione
**extremist** [ɛks'trimɪst] *adj & s* estremista *mf*
**extremi•ty** [ɛks'trɛmɪti] *s* (**-ties**) estremità *f*; (*great want*) estrema necessità; **extremities** estremi *mpl*; (*hands and feet*) estremità *fpl*
**extricate** ['ɛkstrɪ‿ket] *tr* districare
**extrinsic** [ɛks'trɪnsɪk] *adj* estrinseco
**extrovert** ['ɛkstrə‿vʌrt] *s* estroverso
**extrude** [ɛks'trud] *tr* estrudere || *intr* protrudere
**exuberant** [ɛg'zubərənt] or [ɛg'zjubərənt] *adj* esuberante
**exude** [ɛg'zud] or [ɛk'sud] *tr & intr* trasudare, stillare
**exult** [ɛg'zʌlt] *intr* esultare, tripudiare
**exultant** [ɛg'zʌltənt] *adj* esultante
**eye** [aɪ] *s* occhio; (*of hook and eye*) occhiello; **to catch one's eye** attirare l'attenzione di qlcu; **to feast one's eyes on** deliziarsi la vista con; **to lay eyes on** riuscire a vedere; **to make eyes at** fare gli occhi dolci a; **to roll one's eyes** stralunare gli occhi; **to see eye to eye** andare perfettamente d'accordo; **to shut one's eyes to** chiudere un occhio a; far finta di non vedere; **without batting an eye** senza batter ciglio || *v* (*pret & pp* **eyed;** *ger* **eying** or **eyeing**) *tr* occhieggiare; **to eye up and down** guardare da capo a piedi
**eye'ball'** *s* globo oculare
**eye'bolt'** *s* bullone *m* ad anello
**eye'brow'** *s* sopracciglio; **to raise one's eyebrows** inarcare le sopracciglia
**eye'cup'** *s* occhiera
**eye'drop'per** *s* contagocce *m*
**eyeful** ['aɪ‿fʊl] *s* vista, colpo d'occhio; (coll) bellezza
**eye'glass'** *s* (*of optical instrument*) lente *f*, oculare *m*; (*eyecup*) occhiera; **eyeglasses** occhiali *mpl*
**eye'lash'** *s* ciglio
**eyelet** ['aɪlɪt] *s* occhiello, maglietta, asola; (*hole to look through*) feritoia
**eye'lid'** *s* palpebra
**eye' o'pener** ['opənər] *s* affare *m* che apre gli occhi; (coll) bicchierino bevuto di mattina presto

**eye'piece'** *s* oculare *m*
**eye'shade'** *s* visiera
**eye' shad'ow** *s* rimmel *m*
**eye'shot'** *s*—**within eyeshot** a portata di vista
**eye'sight'** *s* vista; *(range)* capacità visiva
**eye' sock'et** *s* occhiaia, orbita
**eye'sore'** *s* pugno in un occhio

**eye'strain'** *s* vista affaticata
**eye'-test chart'** *s* tabella optometrica
**eye'tooth'** *s* (-**teeth**) dente canino; **to cut one's eyeteeth** (coll) fare esperienza; **to give one's eyeteeth for** (coll) dare un occhio della testa per
**eye'wash'** *s* (*flattery*) burro, lusinga; (pharm) collirio; (slang) balla
**eye' wit'ness** *s* testimone *m* oculare

# F

**F, f** [ɛf] *s* sesta lettera dell'alfabeto inglese
**fable** ['febəl] *s* favola
**fabric** ['fæbrɪk] *s* stoffa, tessuto; fabbrica, struttura
**fabricate** ['fæbrɪ‚ket] *tr* fabbricare
**fabrication** [‚fæbrɪ'keʃən] *s* fabbricazione; falsificazione, invenzione
**fabulous** ['fæbjələs] *adj* favoloso
**façade** [fə'sɑd] *s* facciata
**face** [fes] *s* volto, viso, faccia; (*surface*) superficie *f*; (*of coin*) diritto; (*of precious stone*) faccetta; (*of watch*) mostra; (*grimace*) smorfia; (*of building*) facciata; (typ) occhio; **in the face of** di fronte a; **to have a long face** fare il muso lungo; **to keep a straight face** contenere le risa; **to show one's face** farsi vedere ‖ *tr* far fronte a, fronteggiare; (*a wall*) ricoprire; (*a suit*) foderare; **facing** di fronte a ‖ *intr*—**to face about** voltarsi, fare dietro front; **to face on** dare a; **to face up to** guardare in faccia
**face' card'** *s* figura
**face' lift'ing** *s* plastica facciale
**face' pow'der** *s* cipria
**facet** ['fæsɪt] *s* faccetta; (fig) faccia
**facetious** [fə'siʃəs] *adj* faceto
**face' val'ue** *s* valore *m* facciale
**facial** ['feʃəl] *adj* facciale ‖ *s* massaggio facciale
**fa'cial tis'sue** *s* velina detergente
**facilitate** [fə'sɪlɪ‚tet] *tr* facilitare
**facili·ty** [fə'sɪlɪti] *s* (-**ties**) facilità *f*; **facilities** (*installations*) attrezzature *fpl*; (*for transportation*) mezzi *mpl*; (*services*) servizi *mpl*
**facing** ['fesɪŋ] *s* rivestimento
**facsimile** [fæk'sɪmɪli] *s* facsimile *m*
**fact** [fækt] *s* fatto; **in fact** in realtà; **the fact is that** il fatto si è che
**faction** ['fækʃən] *s* fazione; discordia
**factional** ['fækʃənəl] *adj* fazioso; (*partisan*) partigiano
**factionalism** ['fækʃənə‚lɪzəm] *s* partigianeria; parzialità *f*
**factor** ['fæktər] *s* fattore *m* ‖ *tr* scomporre in fattori
**facto·ry** ['fæktəri] *s* (-**ries**) fabbrica
**factual** ['fæktʃʊ·əl] *adj* effettivo, reale
**facul·ty** ['fækəlti] *s* (-**ties**) facoltà *f*
**fad** [fæd] *s* moda passeggera
**fade** [fed] *tr* stingere ‖ *intr* (*said of colors*) stingersi, sbiadire; (*said of*

*sounds, sight, radio signals, memory, etc.*) svanire, affievolirsi; (*said of beauty*) sfiorire
**fade'-out'** *s* affievolimento, affievolirsi *m*; (mov) chiusura in dissolvenza; (rad, telv) evanescenza
**fading** ['fedɪŋ] *s* affievolimento; (mov) dissolvenza; (rad, telv) evanescenza
**fag** [fæg] *s* schiavo del lavoro; (coll) sigaretta ‖ *tr*—**to fag out** stancare
**fagot** ['fægət] *s* fascina, fastello
**fail** [fel] *s*—**without fail** senza meno ‖ *tr* mancare (with *dat*); (*a student*) riprovare; (*an examination*) farsi bocciare in ‖ *intr* fallire, venire a meno; (*said of a student*) farsi riprovare; (*said of a motor*) rompersi, fermarsi; (com) cadere in fallimento; **to fail to** mancare di
**failure** ['feljər] *s* insuccesso; insufficienza; (*student*) bocciato; (com) fallimento
**faint** [fent] *adj* debole; **to feel faint** sentirsi mancare ‖ *s* svenimento ‖ *intr* svenire
**faint-hearted** ['fent'hɑrtɪd] *adj* codardo, timido
**fair** [fer] *adj* giusto, onesto; (*moderately large*) discreto; (*even*) liscio; (*civil*) gentile; (*hair*) biondo; (*complexion*) chiaro; (*sky, weather*) sereno ‖ *s* (*exhibition*) fiera; (*carnival*) sagra ‖ *adv* direttamente; **to play fair** agire onestamente
**fair'ground'** *s* terreno dell'esposizione, campo della fiera
**fairly** ['ferli] *adv* giustamente, imparzialmente; discretamente, abbastanza; completamente
**fair-minded** ['fer'maɪndɪd] *adj* equanime, equo, giusto
**fairness** ['fernɪs] *s* giustizia, imparzialità *f*; bellezza; (*of complexion*) bianchezza
**fair' play'** *s* comportamento leale
**fair' sex'** *s* bel sesso
**fair'-weath'er** *adj*—**a fair-weather friend** un amico del tempo felice
**fair·y** ['feri] *adj* fatato ‖ *s* (-**ies**) fata; (slang) finocchio
**fair'y god'mother** *s* buona fata
**fair'y·land'** *s* terra delle fate
**fair'y tale'** *s* fiaba, racconto delle fate
**faith** [feθ] *s* fede *f*; **to break faith with** venir meno alla parola data a; **to keep faith with** tener fede alla parola

data a; **to pin one's faith on** porre tutte le proprie speranze su; **upon my faith!** in fede mia!

**faithful** ['feθfəl] *adj* fedele || **the faithful** i fedeli

**faithless** ['feθlɪs] *adj* infedele, sleale

**fake** [fek] *adj* falso, finto || *s* contraffazione; (*person*) imbroglione *m* || *tr & intr* contraffare, falsificare

**faker** ['fekər] *s* (coll) imbroglione *m*

**falcon** ['fɔkən] or ['fɔlkən] *s* falcone *m*

**falconer** ['fɔkənər] or ['fɔlkənər] *s* falconiere *m*

**falconry** ['fɔkənri] or ['fɔlkənri] *s* falconeria

**fall** [fɔl] *adj* autunnale || *s* caduta; (*of water*) cataratta, cascata; (*of prices*) ribasso; (*autumn*) autunno; **falls** cataratta, cascate *fpl* || *v* (*pret* **fell** [fɛl]; *pp* **fallen** ['fɔlən]) *intr* cadere; discendere; **to fall apart** farsi a pezzi; **to fall back** (mil) ripiegare; **to fall behind** rimanere indietro; **to fall down** cadere; stramazzare; **to fall due** scadere; **to fall flat** stramazzare; essere un insuccesso; **to fall for** (slang) lasciarsi abbindolare da; (slang) innamorarsi di; **to fall in** (*said of a building*) crollare; (mil) allinearsi; **to fall in with** imbattersi in; mettersi d'accordo con; **to fall off** ritirarsi; diminuire; **to fall out** accadere; essere in disaccordo; (mil) rompere i ranghi; **to fall out of** cadere da; **to fall out with** inimicarsi con; **to fall over** cadere; (coll) adulare; **to fall through** fallire; **to fall to** cominciare; (coll) cominciare a mangiare; (*said, e.g., of an inheritance*) ricadere su; **to fall under** rientrare in

**fallacious** [fə'leʃəs] *adj* fallace

**falla·cy** ['fæləsi] *s* (**-cies**) fallacia

**fall' guy'** *s* (slang) testa di turco

**fallible** ['fælɪbəl] *adj* fallibile

**fall'ing star'** *s* stella cadente

**fall'out'** *s* pulviscolo radioattivo

**fall'out shel'ter** *s* rifugio antiatomico

**fallow** ['fælo] *adj* incolto; **to lie fallow** rimanere incolto || *s* maggese *m* || *tr* maggesare

**false** [fɔls] *adj* falso; (*hair, teeth, etc.*) posticcio, finto || *adv* falsamente; **to play false** tradire

**false' bot'tom** *s* doppio fondo

**false' col'ors** *spl* apparenze mentite

**false' face'** *s* maschera; (*ugly false face*) mascherone *m*

**false'-heart'ed** ['fɔls'hɑrtɪd] *adj* perfido

**falsehood** ['fɔls·hʊd] *s* falsità *f*, falso

**false' pretens'es** *spl* falso, impostura; **under false pretenses** allegando ragioni false

**falset·to** [fɔl'seto] *s* (**-tos**) (*voice*) falsetto; (*person*) cantante *m* in falsetto

**falsi·fy** ['fɔlsɪ,faɪ] *v* (*pret & pp* **-fied**) *tr* falsificare; (*to disprove*) smentire || *intr* mentire

**falsi·ty** ['fɔlsɪti] *s* (**-ties**) falsità *f*

**falter** ['fɔltər] *s* vacillamento; (*in speech*) balbettio || *intr* vacillare; balbettare

**fame** [fem] *s* fama

**famed** [femd] *adj* famoso

**familiar** [fə'mɪljər] *adj* familiare; intimo; **to be familiar with** (*people*) aver pratica con; (*things*) aver pratica di

**familiari·ty** [fə,mɪlɪ'ærɪti] *s* (**-ties**) familiarità *f*, dimestichezza

**familiarize** [fə'mɪljə,raɪz] *tr* far conoscere

**fami·ly** ['fæmɪli] *adj* familiare; **in the family way** (coll) in altro stato || *s* (**-lies**) famiglia

**fam'ily man'** *s* (**men'**) padre *m* di famiglia

**fam'ily name'** *s* cognome *m*

**fam'ily tree'** *s* albero genealogico

**famine** ['fæmɪn] *s* carestia

**famished** ['fæmɪʃt] *adj* famelico; **to be famished** avere una fame da lupo

**famous** ['feməs] *adj* famoso; (coll) eccellente

**fan** [fæn] *s* ventaglio; (elec) ventilatore *m*; (coll) tifoso, patito || *v* (*pret & pp* **fanned**; *ger* **fanning**) *tr* sventagliare; (*to winnow*) vagliare; (*fire, passions*) attizzare || *intr* sventagliarsi; **to fan out** (*said of a road*) diramarsi a ventaglio

**fanatic** [fə'nætɪk] *adj & s* fanatico

**fanatical** [fə'nætɪkəl] *adj* fanatico

**fanaticism** [fə'nætɪ,sɪzəm] *s* fanatismo

**fan' belt'** *s* (aut) cinghia del ventilatore

**fancied** ['fænsid] *adj* immaginario

**fancier** ['fænsɪ·ər] *s* maniaco, tifoso; (*of animals*) conoscitore *m*, allevatore *m*

**fanciful** ['fænsɪfəl] *adj* fantasioso, estroso; immaginario

**fan·cy** ['fænsi] *adj* (**-cier; -ciest**) immaginario; immaginativo; ornamentale; di lusso; fantasioso, estroso || *s* fantasia; (*whim*) grillo, estro; **to take a fancy to** prendere una passione per || *v* (*pret & pp* **-cied**) *tr* immaginare

**fan'cy ball'** *s* ballo in costume

**fan'cy dress'** *s* costume *m*

**fan'cy foods'** *spl* cibi *mpl* di lusso

**fan'cy-free'** *adj* libero dai lacci dell'amore

**fan'cy skat'ing** *s* pattinaggio artistico

**fan'cy·work'** *s* (sew) ricamo ornamentale

**fanfare** ['fænfɛr] *s* fanfara

**fang** [fæŋ] *s* zanna; (*of reptile*) dente velenoso

**fan'light'** *s* lunetta

**fantastic(al)** [fæn'tæstɪk(əl)] *adj* fantastico

**fanta·sy** ['fæntəzi] or ['fæntəsi] *s* (**-sies**) fantasia

**far** [fɑr] *adj* distante; **on the far side of** dall'altra parte di || *adv* lontano; **as far as** fino a; **as far as I am concerned** per quanto mi riguardi; **as far as I know** per quanto io sappia; **by far** di gran lunga; **far and near** in lungo e in largo; **far away** molto lontano; **far be it from me** Dio me ne scampi e liberi; **far better** molto meglio; molto migliore; **far different** molto differente; **far from** lontano da; **far from it** tutto al contrario; **far into** fino al fondo di; **far into the night** fino a tarda ora; **far more** molto più; **far off** lontanissimo; **how far** quanto lontano; **how far is it?** a che distanza è da qui?; **in so far as** in quanto; **thus far** sinora; **to go far towards** contribuire molto a

**faraway** ['fɑrə,we] adj distante, lontano; distratto

**farce** [fɑrs] s farsa

**farcical** ['fɑrsɪkəl] adj farsesco

**fare** [fer] s prezzo della corsa; passeggero; (food) vitto || intr andare, e.g., **how did you fare?** come Le è andata?

**Far' East'** s Estremo Oriente

**fare'well'** s congedo, commiato; **to bid farewell to** or **to take farewell of** prender commiato da || interj addio!

**far-fetched** ['fɑr'fɛtʃt] adj peregrino, campato in aria

**far-flung** ['fɑr'flʌŋ] adj ampio; d'ampia distribuzione

**farm** [fɑrm] adj agricolo || s fattoria, tenuta || tr (land) coltivare || intr fare l'agricoltore or l'allevatore

**farmer** ['fɑrmər] s agricoltore m, contadino

**farm' hand'** s bracciante m

**farm'house'** s casa colonica, masseria

**farming** ['fɑrmɪŋ] s agricoltura, coltivazione

**farm'yard'** s aia

**far'-off'** adj lontano

**far-reaching** ['fɑr'ritʃɪŋ] adj di grande portata

**far-sighted** ['fɑr'saɪtɪd] adj lungimirante; perspicace; presbite

**farther** ['fɑrðər] adj più lontano; addizionale || adv più lontano, più in là; inoltre; **farther on** più oltre

**farthest** ['fɑrðɪst] adj (il) più lontano; ultimo || adv al massimo

**farthing** ['fɑrðɪŋ] s (Brit) quarto di centesimo

**Far' West'** s (U.S.A.) lontano Occidente

**fascinate** ['fæsɪ,net] tr affascinare

**fascinating** ['fæsɪ,netɪŋ] adj incantatore, affascinante

**fascism** ['fæʃɪzəm] s fascismo

**fascist** ['fæʃɪst] adj & s fascista mf

**fashion** ['fæʃən] s voga, moda, foggia, maniera; alta società; **after a fashion** in certo modo; **in fashion** di moda; **out of fashion** fuori moda; **to go out of fashion** passare di moda || tr fare, foggiare

**fashionable** ['fæʃənəbəl] adj elegante, alla moda

**fash'ion design'ing** s alta moda

**fash'ion plate'** s figurino

**fash'ion show'** s sfilata di moda

**fast** [fæst] or [fɑst] adj veloce; (clock) che corre, in anticipo; dissoluto; ben legato; (color) solido; (friend) fedele || s digiuno; **to break fast** rompere il digiuno || adv rapidamente; forte-mente; (asleep) profondamente; **to hold fast** tenersi saldo; **to live fast**

condurre una vita dissoluta || intr digiunare, fare vigilia

**fast'** day' s giorno di magro

**fasten** ['fæsən] or ['fɑsən] tr fissare; attaccare; (a door) sbarrare; (a nickname; blows) affibbiare; (a dress) allacciarsi || intr attaccarsi

**fastener** ['fæsənər] or ['fɑsənər] s legaccio, laccio; (snap, clasp) ferma-glio; (for papers) fermacarte m

**fastidious** [fæs'tɪdɪ·əs] adj schizzinoso; meticoloso

**fasting** ['fæstɪŋ] or ['fɑstɪŋ] s digiuno

**fat** [fæt] adj (fatter; fattest) grasso; (productive) forte, ricco, pingue; **to get fat** ingrassare || s grasso, unto; (of pork) sugna

**fatal** ['fetəl] adj fatale

**fatalism** ['fetə,lɪzəm] s fatalismo

**fatalist** ['fetəlɪst] s fatalista mf

**fatali·ty** [fə'tælɪti] s (-ties) (in an accident) morte f; accidente m mortale; fatalità f

**fate** [fet] s fato; **the Fates** le Parche || tr predestinare

**fated** ['fetɪd] adj destinato

**fateful** ['fetfəl] adj fatidico, fatale

**fat'head'** s (coll) zuccone m

**father** ['fɑðər] s padre m; (male ancestor) antenato || tr procreare; creare; assumere la paternità di

**fatherhood** ['fɑðər,hud] s paternità f

**fa'ther-in-law'** s (fathers-in-law) suocero

**fa'ther·land'** s patria

**fatherless** ['fɑðərlɪs] adj orfano di padre; senza padre

**fatherly** ['fɑðərli] adj paterno

**Fa'ther's Day'** s festa del papà

**Fa'ther Time'** s il Tempo

**fathom** ['fæðəm] s braccio || tr sondare

**fathomless** ['fæðəmlɪs] adj senza fondo; imponderabile

**fatigue** [fə'tig] s fatica, strapazzo; (mil) comandata || tr stancare, affaticare

**fatigue' clothes'** spl (mil) tenuta di servizio, tenuta di fatica

**fatten** ['fætən] tr & intr ingrassare

**fat·ty** ['fæti] adj (-tier; -tiest) grasso; (pathol) adiposo || s (-ties) (coll) tombolo

**fatuous** ['fætʃu·əs] adj fatuo

**faucet** ['fɔsɪt] s rubinetto

**fault** [fɔlt] s (misdeed, blame) colpa; (defect) difetto, magagna; (geol) faglia; (sports) fallo; **it's your fault** è colpa Sua; **to a fault** all'eccesso; **to find fault with** trovare a ridire sul conto di

**fault'find'er** s ipercritico, criticone m

**fault'find'ing** adj criticone || s ipercritica

**faultless** ['fɔltlɪs] adj perfetto, inappuntabile

**fault·y** ['fɔlti] adj (-ier; -iest) manchevole, difettoso

**faun** [fɔn] s fauno

**fauna** ['fɔnə] s fauna

**favor** ['fevər] s favore m; (letter) pregiata; **do me the favor to** mi faccia il piacere di; **by your favor** col Suo permesso; **favors** regali *mpl* di festa; **to be in favor with** essere nelle grazie di; **to be out of favor** cadere in disgrazia || *tr* favorire; (coll) assomigliare (with *dat*)

**favorable** ['fevərəbəl] *adj* favorevole

**favorite** ['fevərɪt] *adj & s* favorito

**favoritism** ['fevərɪ,tɪzəm] *s* favoritismo

**fawn** [fɔn] *s* cerbiatto || *intr*—**to fawn on** adulare, strusciarsi a

**faze** [fez] *tr* (coll) perturbare

**fear** [fɪr] *s* paura; **for fear of** per paura di; **for fear that** per paura che; **no fear** non c'è pericolo; **to be in fear of** aver timore di || *tr & intr* temere

**fearful** ['fɪrfəl] *adj* pauroso, timorato; (coll) spaventoso

**fearless** ['fɪrlɪs] *adj* impavido

**feasible** ['fizɪbəl] *adj* fattibile, possibile

**feast** [fist] *s* festa; (*sumptuous meal*) festino, banchetto || *tr* intrattenere || *intr* banchettare; **to feast on** rallegrarsi alla vista di

**feat** [fit] *s* fatto, prodezza

**feather** ['fɛðər] *s* penna; (*soft and fluffy structure covering bird*) piuma; (*type*) qualità *f*, conio; (*tuft*) pennacchio; **in fine feather** di buon umore; in buona salute || *tr* impennare; coprire di piume; (naut) spalare; (aer) bandierare; **to feather one's nest** arricchirsi

**feath'er bed'** *s* letto di piume

**feath·er·bed·ding** *s* impiego di mano d'opera non necessaria richiesto da un sindacato operaio

**feath'er·brain'** *s* cervello di gallina

**feath'er·edge'** *s* (*of board*) augnatura; (*of sharpened tool*) filo morto

**feath'er·weight'** *s* peso piuma

**feathery** ['fɛðərɪ] *adj* piumato; leggero

**feature** ['fitʃər] *s* fattezza; caratteristica; (journ) articolo principale; (mov) attrazione; **features** fattezze *fpl* || *tr* caratterizzare; mettere in evidenza; (coll) immaginare

**fea'ture film'** *s* lungometraggio

**fea'ture sto'ry** *s* articolo di spalla

**February** ['fɛbru,ɛri] *s* febbraio

**feces** ['fisiz] *spl* feci *fpl*

**feckless** ['fɛklɪs] *adj* debole; inetto

**federal** ['fɛdərəl] *adj* federale || *s* federalista *mf*

**federate** ['fɛdə,ret] *adj* federato || *tr* federare || *intr* federarsi

**federation** [,fɛdə'reʃən] *s* federazione

**federative** ['fɛdə,retɪv] or ['fɛdərətɪv] *adj* federativo

**fedora** [fɪ'dorə] *s* cappello floscio di feltro

**fed' up'** [fɛd] *adj* stanco e stufo; **to be fed up with** averne fin sopra gli occhi di

**fee** [fi] *s* onorario; (*charge allowed by law*) diritto; (*tip*) mancia; (*for tuition*) tassa; (*for admission*) ingresso || *tr* pagare

**feeble** ['fibəl] *adj* debole, fievole

**feeble-minded** ['fibəl'maɪndɪd] *adj* rimbecillito; debole, vacillante

**feed** [fid] *s* mangime *m*; (coll) mangiata; (mach) dispositivo d'alimentazione || *v* (*pret & pp* **fed** [fɛd]) *tr* nutrire; (*a machine*) alimentare; (*cattle*) pascere; (theat) imbeccare || *intr* mangiare; **to feed upon** nutrirsi di

**feed'back'** *s* (*of a computer*) ritorno d'informazioni; (electron) reazione

**feed' bag'** *s* musetta

**feed' pump'** *s* pompa di alimentazione

**feed' trough'** *s* (*for cattle*) vasca; (*for hogs*) trogolo

**feed' wire'** *s* cavo di alimentazione

**feel** [fil] *s* sensazione; (*touch*) tocco; (*vague mental impression*) senso || *v* (*pret & pp* **felt** [fɛlt]) *tr* sentire; (*e.g., with the hands*) palpare, toccare; (*s.o.'s pulse*) tastare || *intr* (*sick, tired, etc.*) sentirsi; **to feel bad** sentirsi male; (*to be unhappy*) essere spiacente; **to feel cheap** vergognarsi; **to feel comfortable** sentirsi a proprio agio; **to feel for** cercare di toccare; avere compassione per; **to feel like** aver voglia di; **to feel safe** sentirsi al sicuro; **to feel sorry** essere spiacente; **to feel sorry for** aver compassione di; pentirsi di

**feeler** ['filər] *s* (*hint*) sondaggio; **feelers** (*of insect*) antenne *fpl*; (*of mollusk*) tentacoli *mpl*; **to put out feelers** (fig) tastare il terreno

**feeling** ['filɪŋ] *s* (*with senses*) senso; (*impression, emotion*) sentimento, sensazione; opinione

**feign** [fen] *tr* fingere; inventare; imitare || *intr* far finta; **to feign to be** fingersi

**feint** [fent] *s* finta || *intr* fare una finta

**feldspar** ['fɛld,spar] *s* feldspato

**felicitate** [fə'lɪsɪ,tet] *tr* felicitarsi con

**felicitous** [fə'lɪsɪtəs] *adj* felice, indovinato; eloquente

**fell** [fɛl] *adj* crudele, mortale || *tr* (*trees*) abbattere

**felloe** ['fɛlo] *s* cerchione *m*; (*part of the rim*) gavello

**fellow** ['fɛlo] *s* compagno; collega *m*; (*of a society*) membro, socio; (*holder of fellowship*) borsista *mf*; (coll) tipo, tizio; (coll) innamorato; **good fellow** buon diavolo; galantuomo

**fel'low cit'izen** *s* concittadino

**fel'low coun'try·man** *s* (**-men**) concittadino

**fel'low crea'ture** *s* prossimo

**fel'low-man'** *s* (**-men'**) prossimo

**fel'low mem'ber** *s* consocio

**fellowship** ['fɛlo,ʃɪp] *s* compagnia; (*for study*) borsa di studio

**fel'low trav'eler** *s* simpatizzante *mf*; criptocomunista *mf*; compagno di viaggio

**felon** ['fɛlən] *s* criminale *mf*; (pathol) patereccio, giradito

**felo·ny** ['fɛləni] *s* (**-nies**) delitto doloso

**felt** [fɛlt] *s* feltro

**felt' board'** *s* lavagna di panno

**felt'-tip pen'** *s* pennarello

**female** ['fimel] *adj* (*sex*) femminile;

(*animal, plant, piece of a device*) femmina || *s* femmina

**feminine** ['fɛmɪnɪn] *adj & s* femminile *m*

**feminism** ['fɛmɪ ˌnɪzəm] *s* femminismo

**fence** [fɛns] *s* steccato, staccionata; (*for stolen goods*) ricettatore *m;* (carp) squadra di guida; (sports) scherma; **on the fence** (coll) indeciso || *tr* recingere || *intr* tirare di scherma

**fencing** ['fɛnsɪŋ] *s* scherma; (fig) schermaglia

**fenc'ing mask'** *s* visiera

**fend** [fɛnd] *tr*—**to fend off** parare || *intr*—**to fend for oneself** (coll) badare a sé stesso

**fender** ['fɛndər] *s* (*of trolley car*) salvagente *m;* (*of fireplace*) parafuoco; (aut) parafango; (naut) parabordo

**fennel** ['fɛnəl] *s* finocchio

**ferment** ['fʌrment] *s* fermento || [fər-'ment] *tr & intr* fermentare

**fern** [fʌrn] *s* felce *f*

**ferocious** [fə'roʃəs] *adj* feroce

**ferocity** [fə'rasɪti] *s* ferocia

**ferret** ['fɛrɪt] *s* furetto || *tr*—**to ferret out** scovare || *intr* indagare

**Fer'ris wheel'** ['fɛrɪs] *s* ruota (del parco dei divertimenti)

**fer·ry** ['fɛri] *s* (**-ries**) traghetto; nave *f* traghetto || *v* (*pret & pp* **-ried**) *tr* traghettare || *intr* attraversare

**fer'ry·boat'** *s* nave *f* traghetto, ferryboat *m*

**fertile** ['fʌrtɪl] *adj* fertile

**fertilize** ['fʌrtɪ ˌlaɪz] *tr* fertilizzare; (*to impregnate*) fecondare

**fertilizer** ['fʌrtɪ ˌlaɪzər] *s* fertilizzante *m;* (*e.g., of flowers*) fecondatore *m*

**fervent** ['fʌrvənt] *adj* fervente, fervido

**fervid** ['fʌrvɪd] *adj* fervido

**fervor** ['fʌrvər] *s* fervore *m*

**fester** ['fɛstər] *s* ulcera, piaga || *tr* corrompere || *intr* suppurare; (fig) corrompersi

**festival** ['fɛstɪvəl] *adj* festivo || *s* festa; (*of music*) festival *m*

**festive** ['fɛstɪv] *adj* festivo

**festivi·ty** [fɛs'tɪvɪti] *s* (**-ties**) festività *f*

**festoon** [fɛs'tun] *s* festone *m* || *tr* ornare di festoni

**fetch** [fɛtʃ] *tr* andare a prendere; (*a price*) fruttare, vendersi per

**fetching** ['fɛtʃɪŋ] *adj* (coll) cattivante, attraente

**fete** [fɛt] *s* festa || *tr* festeggiare

**fetid** ['fɛtɪd] *or* ['fitɪd] *adj* fetido

**fetish** ['fitɪʃ] *or* ['fɛtɪʃ] *s* feticcio

**fetlock** ['fɛtlɑk] *s* nocca; (*tuft of hair*) barbetta

**fetter** ['fɛtər] *s* ceppo, catena || *tr* mettere ai ceppi, incatenare

**fettle** ['fɛtəl] *s* stato, condizione; **in fine fettle** in buone condizioni

**fetus** ['fitəs] *s* feto

**feud** [fjud] *s* antagonismo; odio ereditario || *intr* essere in lotta

**feudal** ['fjudəl] *adj* feudale

**feudalism** ['fjudə ˌlɪzəm] *s* feudalismo

**fever** ['fivər] *s* febbre *f*

**feverish** ['fivərɪʃ] *adj* febbrile

**few** [fju] *adj & pron* pochi; **a few** alcuni; **quite a few** molti

**fiancé** [ ˌfi·ɑn'se] *s* fidanzato

**fiancée** [ ˌfi·ɑn'se] *s* fidanzata

**fias·co** [fɪ'æsko] *s* (**-cos** *or* **-coes**) fiasco

**fib** [fɪb] *s* menzogna, frottola || *v* (*pret & pp* fibbed*;* *ger* fibbing) *intr* raccontar frottole

**fiber** ['faɪbər] *s* fibra; (fig) tempra

**fi'ber·glass'** *s* vetroresina

**fibrous** ['faɪbrəs] *adj* fibroso

**fickle** ['fɪkəl] *adj* volubile, incostante, mobile

**fiction** ['fɪkʃən] *s* (*invention*) finzione; (*branch of literature*) novellistica

**fictional** ['fɪkʃənəl] *adj* immaginario

**fictionalize** ['fɪkʃənə ˌlaɪz] *tr* romanzare

**fictitious** [fɪk'tɪʃəs] *adj* fittizio

**fiddle** ['fɪdəl] *s* violino; **fit as a fiddle** in perfetta salute || *tr* (coll) suonare sul violino; **to fiddle away** (coll) sprecare || *intr* (coll) suonare il violino; **to fiddle with** (coll) giocherellare con

**fiddler** ['fɪdlər] *s* (coll) violinista *mf*

**fiddling** ['fɪdlɪŋ] *adj* triviale, futile, insignificante

**fideli·ty** [faɪ'dɛlɪti] *or* [fɪ'dɛlɪti] *s* (**-ties**) fedeltà *f*

**fidget** ['fɪdʒɪt] *intr* agitarsi; **to fidget with** giocherellare con

**fidgety** ['fɪdʒɪti] *adj* irrequieto

**fiduciar·y** [fɪ'djuʃɪ ˌɛri] *or* [fɪ'duʃɪ ˌɛri] *adj* fiduciario || *s* (**-ies**) fiduciario

**fie** [faɪ] *interj* vergogna!

**fief** [fif] *s* feudo

**field** [fild] *adj* (mil) da campagna || *s* campo; (sports) terreno; (min) giacimento; (*of motor or dynamo*) (elec) induttore *m;* (phys) campo

**fielder** ['fildər] *s* (*outfielder*) giocatore *m* del campo esterno

**field' glass'es** *spl* binocolo

**field' hock'ey** *s* hockey *m* su prato

**field' mag'net** *s* induttore *m,* calamita induttrice

**field' mar'shal** *s* (mil) maresciallo di campo

**field' mouse'** *s* topo di campagna

**field'piece'** *s* pezzo da campagna

**fiend** [find] *s* diavolo; (coll) addetto, tifoso

**fiendish** ['findɪʃ] *adj* diabolico

**fierce** [fɪrs] *adj* fiero, feroce; (*wind*) furioso; (coll) maledetto

**fierceness** ['fɪrsnɪs] *s* ferocia

**fier·y** ['faɪri] *or* ['faɪ·əri] *adj* (**-ier;** **-iest**) ardente, focoso

**fife** [faɪf] *s* piffero

**fifteen** ['fɪf'tin] *adj, s & pron* quindici *m*

**fifteenth** ['fɪf'tinθ] *adj, s & pron* quindicesimo || *s* (*in dates*) quindici *m*

**fifth** [fɪfθ] *adj, s & pron* quinto || *s* (*in dates*) cinque *m*

**fifth' col'umn** *s* quinta colonna

**fiftieth** ['fɪftɪ·ɪθ] *adj, s & pron* cinquantesimo

**fif·ty** ['fɪfti] *adj & pron* cinquanta || *s* (**-ties**) cinquanta *m;* **the fifties** gli anni cinquanta

**fif'ty-fif'ty** *adv*—**to go fifty-fifty** fare a metà

**fig** [fɪg] *s* fico

**fight** [faɪt] *s* lotta; baruffa; combattimento; spirito combattivo; (sports) incontro; **to pick a fight with** attaccar briga con ‖ *v* (*pret & pp* **fought** [fɔt]) *tr* lottare con; combattere contro; opporsi a ‖ *intr* lottare; combattere; **to fight shy of** cercar di evitare

**fighter** ['faɪtər] *s* lottatore *m;* (*warrior*) combattente *m;* (aer) caccia *m*

**fig' leaf'** *s* foglia di fico

**figment** ['fɪgmənt] *s* finzione

**figurative** ['fɪgjərətɪv] *adj* (fa) figurativo; (rhet) figurato

**figure** ['fɪgjər] *s* figura; numero; prezzo; **to be good at figures** far bene di conto; **to cut a figure** fare una buona figura; **to keep one's figure** conservare la linea ‖ *tr* figurare; immaginare; raffigurare; supporre, calcolare; **to figure out** calcolare; decifrare ‖ *intr* apparire; **to figure on** (coll) contare su

**fig'ure-head'** *s* uomo di paglia, prestanome *m;* (naut) polena

**fig'ure of speech'** *s* figura retorica

**fig'ure skat'ing** *s* pattinaggio artistico

**figurine** [ˌfɪgjə'rin] *s* figurina

**filament** ['fɪləmənt] *s* filamento

**filbert** ['fɪlbərt] *s* (*tree*) nocciolo, avellano; (*nut*) nocciola, avellana

**filch** [fɪltʃ] *tr* rubacchiare

**file** [faɪl] *s* (*row*) fila; (*tool*) lima; (*folder*) filza; (*room*) archivio; (*of cards*) schedario ‖ *tr* mettere in fila; limare; archiviare, schedare; (journ) trasmettere ‖ *intr* sfilare; **to file for** fare domanda di

**file' clerk'** *s* schedarista *mf*

**filet** [fɪ'le] or ['fɪle] *s* filetto ‖ *tr* tagliare in filetti

**filial** ['fɪlɪ·əl] *adj* filiale

**filiation** [ˌfɪlɪ'eʃən] *s* filiazione

**filibuster** ['fɪlɪˌbʌstər] *s* (*tactics*) ostruzionismo; (*speech*) discorso ostruzionista; (*person making such a speech*) ostruzionista *mf;* (*buccaneer*) filibustiere *m* ‖ *tr* fare ostruzionismo contro ‖ *intr* fare dell'ostruzionismo

**filigree** ['fɪlɪˌgri] *adj* filigranato ‖ *s* filigrana ‖ *tr* lavorare in filigrana

**filing** ['faɪlɪŋ] *s* (*of documents*) schedatura; limatura; **filings** limatura

**fil'ing cab'inet** *s* schedario

**fil'ing card'** *s* cartellino, scheda

**fill** [fɪl] *s* sazietà *f;* (*place filled with earth*) terrapieno; **to have** or **get one's fill** mangiare a sazietà ‖ *tr* riempire; (*an order*) eseguire; (*a hole*) otturare; (*a tooth*) piombare; (*a tire*) gonfiare; (*a place*) occupare; (*with sand*) interrare; **to fill out** (*a form*) riempire; **to fill up** (aut) fare il pieno di ‖ *intr* riempirsi; **to fill in** prendere il posto; **to fill up** riempirsi

**filler** ['fɪlər] *s* ripieno; (*person*) riempitore *m;* (painting) mestica; (journ) articolo riempitivo

**fillet** ['fɪlɪt] *s* nastro, fascia; (*for hair*) nastro; (archit) listello ‖ *tr* filettare

‖ ['fɪle] or ['fɪlɪt] *s* (*of meat or fish*) filetto ‖ *tr* tagliare a filetti

**filling** ['fɪlɪŋ] *s* (*of a tooth*) impiombatura; (*of turkey*) ripieno

**fill'ing sta'tion** *s* stazione di rifornimento

**fillip** ['fɪlɪp] *s* stimolo; colpetto col dito ‖ *tr* dare un colpetto col dito a; (fig) stimulare

**fil·ly** ['fɪli] *s* (**-lies**) puledra

**film** [fɪlm] *s* pellicola; (mov, phot) pellicola, film *m* ‖ *tr* filmare

**film' li'brary** *s* cineteca, filmoteca

**film'strip'** *s* filmina

**film·y** ['fɪlmi] *adj* (**-ier; -iest**) sottile, delicato; (*look*) annebbiato

**filter** ['fɪltər] *s* filtro ‖ *tr & intr* filtrare

**filtering** ['fɪltərɪŋ] *s* filtrazione

**fil'ter pa'per** *s* carta da filtro

**fil'ter tip'** *s* filtro, bocchino filtro

**filth** [fɪlθ] *s* sporco, sporcizia

**filth·y** ['fɪlθi] *adj* (**-ier; -iest**) sporco, sudicio

**filth'y lu'cre** ['lukər] *s* il vile metallo

**filtrate** ['fɪltret] *s* liquido filtrato ‖ *tr & intr* filtrare

**fin** [fɪn] *s* pinna; (slang) biglietto da cinque dollari

**final** ['faɪnəl] *adj* finale; (*last in a series*) ultimo; definitivo, insindacabile ‖ *s* esame *m* finale; **finals** (sports) finale *f*

**finale** [fɪ'nɑli] *s* (mus) finale *m*

**finalist** ['faɪnəlɪst] *s* finalista *mf*

**finally** ['faɪnəli] *adv* finalmente

**finance** [fɪ'næns] or ['faɪnæns] *s* finanza; **finances** finanze *fpl* ‖ *tr* finanziare

**financial** [fɪ'nænʃəl] or [faɪ'nænʃəl] *adj* finanziario

**financier** [ˌfɪnən'sɪr] or [ˌfaɪnən'sɪr] *s* finanziere *m*

**financing** [fɪ'nænsɪŋ] or ['faɪnænsɪŋ] *s* finanziamento

**finch** [fɪntʃ] *s* fringuello

**find** [faɪnd] *s* trovata ‖ *v* (*pret & pp* **found** [faʊnd]) *tr* trovare; rinvenire; (*s.o. innocent or guilty*) dichiarare; **to find out** venire a sapere ‖ *intr* (law) sentenziare; **to find out about** informarsi su

**finder** ['faɪndər] *s* (phot) mirino; (astr) cannochiale cercatore

**finding** ['faɪndɪŋ] *s* scoperta; (law) sentenza

**fine** [faɪn] *adj* buono; bello; fino, fine ‖ *s* multa ‖ *adv* (coll) benissimo; **to feel fine** (coll) sentirsi benissimo ‖ *tr* multare

**fine' arts'** *spl* belle arti

**fineness** ['faɪnnɪs] *s* finezza; (*of metal*) titolo

**fine' print'** *s* testo in caratteri minuti

**finer·y** ['faɪnəri] *s* (**-ies**) ornamenti *mpl*, fronzoli *mpl;* abito vistoso

**fine-spun** ['faɪnˌspʌn] *adj* sottile

**finesse** [fɪ'nes] *s* finezza; (bridge) impasse *f* ‖ *tr* fare l'impasse a ‖ *intr* fare l'impasse

**fine'-tooth comb'** *s* pettine fitto; **to go over with a fine-tooth comb** esaminare minuziosamente

**finger** ['fɪŋgər] s dito; **to have a finger in the pie** avere le mani in pasta; **to put one's finger on the spot** mettere il dito nella piaga; **to slip between the fingers** sfuggire di tra le dita; **to snap one's fingers at** infischiarsi di; **to twist around one's little finger** fare ciò che si vuole di ‖ tr toccare con le dita; (to pilfer) rubacchiare; (slang) mostrare a dito

**fin'ger board'** s (mus) tastiera

**fin'ger bowl'** s sciacquadita m

**fingering** ['fɪŋgərɪŋ] s palpeggiamento; (mus) diteggiatura

**fin'ger mark'** s ditata

**fin'ger·nail'** s unghia

**fin'ger·print'** s impronta digitale ‖ tr prendere le impronte digitali di

**fin'ger·tip'** s polpastrello; **to have at one's fingertips** avere sulla punta delle dita, sapere a menadito

**finical** ['fɪnɪkəl] or **finicky** ['fɪnɪki] adj pignolo, schizzinoso

**finish** ['fɪnɪʃ] s fine f; finitura; (sports) finale m ‖ tr finire; **to finish off** distruggere ‖ intr finire; **to finish + ger** finire di + inf; **to finish by + ger** finire per + inf

**fin'ishing school'** s scuola di perfezionamento per signorine

**fin'ishing touch'** s ultimo tocco

**finite** ['faɪnaɪt] adj finito

**Finland** ['fɪnlənd] s la Finlandia

**Finlander** ['fɪnləndər] s finlandese mf

**Finn** [fɪn] s (member of a Finnish-speaking group of people) finnico; (native or inhabitant of Finland) finlandese mf

**Finnic** ['fɪnɪk] adj & s finnico

**Finnish** ['fɪnɪʃ] adj finlandese ‖ s (language) finlandese m

**fir** [fʌr] s abete m

**fire** [faɪr] s fuoco; (destructive burning) incendio; **to be on fire** ardere; **to be under enemy fire** essere sotto tiro nemico; **to catch fire** infiammarsi; **to hang fire** essere in sospeso; **to open fire** aprire il fuoco; **to set on fire, to set fire to** dar fuoco a; **under fire** sotto fuoco nemico; accusato ‖ tr accendere; (an oven) scaldare; (bricks) cuocere; (a weapon) sparare; (the imagination) riscaldare; (an employee) (coll) licenziare ‖ intr accendersi; **to fire on** far fuoco su; **to fire up** attivare una caldaia

**fire' alarm'** s avvisatore m d'incendio

**fire'arm'** s arma da fuoco

**fire'ball'** s palla da cannone esplosiva; (lightning) lampo a forma di globo infocato; meteorite m a forma di globo infocato; globo infocato

**fire'boat'** s lancia dei pompieri

**fire'box'** s (of a boiler) fornello; (to give alarm) stazione d'allarme

**fire'brand'** s tizzone m; (fig) fiaccola della discordia

**fire'brick'** s mattone refrattario

**fire' brigade'** s corpo di pompieri volontari

**fire'bug'** s (coll) incendiario

**fire' com'pany** s corpo dei pompieri; compagnia d'assicurazioni contro gli incendi

**fire'crack'er** s mortaretto

**fire'damp'** s grisou m

**fire' depart'ment** s corpo dei pompieri

**fire'dog'** s alare m

**fire' drill'** s esercitazione in caso d'incendio

**fire' en'gine** s autopompa

**fire' escape'** s scala di sicurezza

**fire' extin'guisher** s estintore m

**fire'fly'** s (-flies) lucciola

**fire'guard'** s parafuoco

**fire' hose'** s manichetta

**fire'house'** s caserma dei pompieri

**fire' hy'drant** s bocca d'incendi

**fire' insur'ance** s assicurazione contro gli incendi

**fire' i'rons** spl arnesi mpl del camino

**fire'man** s (-men) (man who extinguishes fires) pompiere m, vigile m del fuoco; (stoker) fochista m

**fire'place'** s camino

**fire'plug'** s bocca da incendio, idrante m

**fire'proof'** adj incombustibile ‖ tr rendere incombustibile

**fire' sale'** s vendita di merce avariata dal fuoco

**fire' screen'** s parafuoco

**fire' ship'** s brulotto

**fire'side'** s focolare m

**fire'trap'** s edificio senza mezzi adeguati per combattere incendi

**fire' wall'** s paratia antincendio

**fire'wa'ter** s (coll) acquavite f

**fire'wood'** s legna

**fire'works'** spl fuochi mpl artificiali

**firing** ['faɪrɪŋ] s (of furnace) alimentazione; (of bricks) cottura; (of a gun) sparo; (of soldiers) tiro; (of an internal-combustion engine) accensione; (of an employee) (coll) licenziamento

**fir'ing line'** s linea del fuoco

**fir'ing or'der** s (aut) ordine m d'accensione

**fir'ing pin'** s percussore m

**fir'ing squad'** s (for saluting at a burial) plotone m d'onore; (for executing) plotone m d'esecuzione

**firm** [fʌrm] adj forte, fermo ‖ s ditta, compagnia

**firmament** ['fʌrməmənt] s firmamento

**firm' name'** s ragione f sociale

**firmness** ['fʌrmnɪs] s fermezza

**first** [fʌrst] adj primo ‖ s primo; (aut) prima; (mus) voce f principale; **at first** sulle prime; **from the first** da bel principio ‖ adv prima; **first of all** per prima cosa

**first' aid'** s pronto soccorso

**first'-aid' kit'** s cassetta farmaceutica d'urgenza

**first'-aid' sta'tion** s posto di pronto soccorso

**first'-born'** adj & s primogenito

**first'-class'** adj di prim'ordine, sopraffino ‖ adv in prima classe

**first' cous'in** s cugino primo

**first'-day cov'er** s busta primo giorno

**first' draft'** s brutta copia

**first' fin'ger** s dito indice
**first' floor'** s pianoterra m
**first' fruits'** spl primizie fpl
**first' lieuten'ant** s tenente m
**firstly** ['fʌrstli] adv in primo luogo
**first' mate'** s (naut) primo ufficiale, comandante m in seconda, secondo
**first' name'** s nome m di battesimo
**first' night'** s (theat) prima
**first' of'ficer** s (naut) primo ufficiale, comandante m in seconda, secondo
**first'-rate'** adj di prima forza; eccellente || adv (coll) benissimo
**first'-run'** adj di prima visione
**fiscal** ['fɪskəl] adj (pertaining to public treasury) fiscale; finanziario || s avvocato fiscale
**fis'cal year'** s esercizio finanziario
**fish** [fɪʃ] s pesce m; **to be like a fish out of water** essere come un pesce fuor d'acqua; **to be neither fish nor fowl** non essere né carne né pesce; **to drink like a fish** bere come una spugna || tr pescare || intr pescare; **to fish for compliments** cercare di farsi fare dei complimenti; **to go fishing** andare alla pesca; **to take fishing** portare con sé alla pesca
**fish'bone'** s lisca, spina di pesce
**fish'bowl'** s vaschetta per i pesci rossi
**fisher** ['fɪʃər] s pescatore m; (zool) martora canadese
**fish'er·man** s (-men) pescatore m; (boat) peschereccio
**fisher·y** ['fɪʃəri] s (-ies) (activity) pesca; (business) pescheria; (grounds) riserva di pesca, luogo dove si pesca
**fish' glue'** s colla di pesce
**fish'hook'** s amo
**fishing** ['fɪʃɪŋ] adj da pesca || s pesca
**fish'ing reel'** s mulinello
**fish'ing rod'** s canna da pesca
**fish'ing tack'le** s attrezzatura da pesca
**fish'line'** s lenza
**fish' mar'ket** s pescheria
**fish'pool'** s peschiera
**fish' spear'** s fiocina
**fish' sto'ry** s (coll) fandonia; **to tell fish stories** spararle grosse
**fish'tail'** s (aut) imbardata (aer) spedalata || intr (aut) imbardare; (aer) compiere una spedalata
**fish'wife'** s (-wives') pescivendola; (foul-mouthed woman) ciana
**fish'worm'** s lombrico
**fish·y** ['fɪʃi] adj (-ier; -iest) che sa di pesce; (coll) dubbioso, inverosimile
**fission** ['fɪʃən] s (biol) scissione; (phys) fissione
**fissionable** ['fɪʃənəbəl] adj fissionabile
**fissure** ['fɪʃər] s fenditura; (in rock) crepaccio
**fist** [fɪst] s pugno; (typ) indìce m; **to shake one's fist at** mostrare i pugni a
**fist'fight'** s scontro a pugni
**fist'ful'** s pugno, manciata
**fisticuff** ['fɪstɪ,kʌf] s pugno; **fisticuffs** scontro a pugni
**fit** [fɪt] adj (fitter; fittest) indicato; idoneo, adatto; in buona salute; **fit to be tied** (coll) infuriato, arrabbia-

tissimo; **fit to eat** mangiabile; **to feel fit** sentirsi in buona salute; **to see fit** giudicare conveniente || s equipaggiamento; (of a suit) taglio; (of one piece with another) incastro; (of coughing) accesso; (of anger) attacco; **by fits and starts** a pezzi e a bocconi || v (pret & pp **fitted**; ger **fitting**) tr adattare; quadrare a; andar bene a; equipaggiare; preparare; servire a; esser d'accordo con; **to fit out** or **up** attrezzare, equipaggiare || intr stare; incastrare; (said of clothes) cascare; entrare; **to fit in** entrarci
**fitful** ['fɪtfəl] adj capriccioso; incostante, irregolare
**fitness** ['fɪtnɪs] s convenienza; idoneità f; buona salute
**fitter** ['fɪtər] s aggiustatore m; (of machinery) montatore m; (of clothing) sarto che mette in prova
**fitting** ['fɪtɪŋ] adj appropriato, adatto, conveniente || s adattamento; (of a garment) prova; tubo adattabile; (carp) incastro; **fittings** accessori mpl; utensili mpl; (iron trimmings) ferramenta fpl
**five** [faɪv] adj & pron cinque || s cinque m; **five o' clock** le cinque
**five' hun'dred** adj, s & pron cinquecento
**five'-year plan'** s piano quinquennale
**fix** [fɪks] s—**in a tight fix** (coll) nei pasticci; **to be in a fix** (coll) star fresco, essere nei guai || tr riparare; fissare; (a meal) preparare; (a bayonet) inastare; (attention) attrarre, fermare; (hair) mettere a posto; (coll) arrangiare || intr fissarsi, stabilirsi; **to fix on** scegliere
**fixed** [fɪkst] adj fisso; (time) improrogabile; (coll) arrangiato
**fixing** ['fɪksɪŋ] adj fissativo || s (fastening) attacco; (phot) fissaggio; **with all the fixings** (coll) con tutti i contorni
**fix'ing bath'** s bagno di fissaggio
**fixture** ['fɪkstʃər] s infisso; accessorio; (of a lamp) guarnizione; **fixtures** (e.g., of a store) suppellettili fpl
**fizz** [fɪz] s effervescenza; gazosa; (Brit) spumante m || intr frizzare
**fizzle** ['fɪzəl] s (coll) fiasco || intr crepitare; (coll) fare fiasco
**flabbergast** ['flæbər,gæst] tr (coll) sbalordire, lasciare stupefatto
**flab·by** ['flæbi] adj (-bier; -biest) floscio, flaccido, cascante
**flag** [flæg] s bandiera || v (pret & pp **flagged**; ger **flagging**) tr imbandierare; segnalare; (rr) far fermare || intr ammosciarsi, afflosciarsi
**flageolet** [,flædʒə'lɛt] s flautino
**flag'man** s (-men) (rr) manovratore m
**flag' of truce'** s bandiera parlamentaria
**flag'pole'** s pennone m
**flagrant** ['flegrənt] adj flagrante; scandaloso
**flag'ship'** s nave ammiraglia
**flag'staff'** s pennone m
**flag' sta'tion** s (rr) stazione facoltativa
**flag'stone'** s lastra di pietra

**flag' stop'** s (rr) fermata facoltativa
**flail** [flel] s correggiato || tr battere col correggiato; battere
**flair** [fler] s fiuto, istinto
**flak** [flæk] s fuoco antiaereo
**flake** [flek] s falda; (of snow) fiocco, falda; (of cereal) fiocco; || tr sfaldare; (fish) scagliare || intr sfaldarsi
**flak·y** ['fleki] adj (-ier; -iest) a falde, faldoso
**flamboyant** [flæm'bɔɪ·ənt] adj sgargiante; (architt) fiammeggiante
**flame** [flem] s fiamma || tr & intr fiammeggiare
**flamethrower** ['flem,θro·ər] s lanciafiamme m
**flaming** ['flemɪŋ] adj fiammeggiante; appassionato; (culin) alla fiamma
**flamin·go** [flə'mɪŋgo] s (-gos or -goes) fenicottero, fiammingo
**flammable** ['flæməbəl] adj infiammabile
**Flanders** ['flændərz] s le Fiandre
**flange** [flændʒ] s (e.g., on a pipe) flangia; (on I beam) bordo; (of a wheel) cerchione m
**flank** [flæŋk] s fianco || tr fiancheggiare
**flannel** ['flænəl] s flanella
**flap** [flæp] s (in clothing) falda; (of hat) tesa; (of book) risvolto; (of pocket) patta; (of shoe) linguetta; (blow) colpo; (of a table) pannello; (of the counter in a store) ribalta; (of wings) alata || v (pret & pp **flapped;** ger **flapping**) tr battere, sbattere; (to move violently) sbatacchiare || intr penzolare
**flare** [fler] s vampa; scintillio; (of a dress) svasatura; (mil) fuoco di segnalazione; **flares** (trousers) calzoni mpl a zampe d'elefante || tr svasare || intr scintillare; (said of a garment) scampanare; **to flare up** divampare; (said of an illness) aggravarsi, infiammarsi
**flare'-up'** s vampa, fiammata; (of an illness) recrudescenza; scoppio d'ira, accesso di collera
**flash** [flæʃ] s (of light) sprazzo; (of lightning) lampo, baleno; (of hope) raggio; (of joy) accesso; (journ, phot) flash m; (fig) lampo; **flash in the pan** fuoco di paglia || tr (powder) accendere; (a sword) brandire; (journ) diffondere; (e.g., money) (coll) ostentare || intr lampeggiare, balenare, folgorare; **to flash by** passare come un lampo
**flash'back'** s flashback m
**flash' bulb'** s lampada lampo
**flash' cube'** s cuboflash m
**flash' flood'** s inondazione torrenziale
**flashing** ['flæʃɪŋ] s metallo per coprire la conversa; commessura metallica fra tetto e comignolo
**flash'light'** s lampadina tascabile; (of a lighthouse) luce f intermittente; (phot) fotolampo, lampeggiatore m
**flash'light bulb'** s lampada per fotolampo
**flash·y** ['flæʃi] adj (-ier; -iest) sgargiante, chiassoso, vistoso

**flask** [flæsk] or [flɑsk] s fiasco, fiasca; (for laboratory use) beuta
**flat** [flæt] adj (**flatter; flattest**) piano; (nose) camuso; (boat) a fondo piatto; (surface) liscio; (beer) svanito; (tire) sgonfio; (denial) deciso; (mus) bemolle; (coll) al verde || s (flat surface) piatto; (flat area) piano; (apartment) appartamento; (mus) bemolle m; (coll) gomma a terra || adv—**to fall flat** fallire
**flat'boat'** s chiatta
**flat'car'** s (rr) pianale m
**flat-footed** ['flæt,futɪd] adj dai piedi piatti; (coll) inflessibile
**flat'head'** s (of a bolt) testa piatta; (coll) testa di legno
**flat'i'ron** s ferro da stiro
**flat' race'** s corsa piana
**flatten** ['flætən] tr schiacciare; distendere || intr appiattirsi; indebolirsi; **to flatten out** appiattirsi; (aer) porsi in linea orizzontale di volo
**flatter** ['flætər] tr adulare, lusingare; (to make seem more attractive) favorire || intr adulare
**flatterer** ['flætərər] s adulatore m, lusingatore m
**flattering** ['flætərɪŋ] adj lusinghiero
**flatter·y** ['flætəri] s (-ies) lusinga
**flat' tire'** s gomma a terra
**flat'top'** s portaerei f
**flatulence** ['flætʃələns] s flatulenza
**flat'ware'** s argenteria, vasellame m
**flaunt** [flɔnt] or [flɑnt] tr sfoggiare, ostentare
**flautist** ['flɔtɪst] s flautista mf
**flavor** ['flevər] s sapore m, gusto; condimento || tr insaporire; condire; aromatizzare, profumare
**flavoring** ['flevərɪŋ] s condimento, sapore m
**flaw** [flɔ] s difetto, menda, fallo; (crack) incrinatura
**flawless** ['flɔlɪs] adj senza difetti
**flax** [flæks] s lino
**flaxen** ['flæksən] adj di lino; biondo
**flax'seed'** s linosa
**flay** [fle] tr scorticare, scoiare
**flea** [fli] s pulce f
**flea'bite'** s morso di pulce; (fig) inezia, seccatura secondaria
**fleck** [flɛk] s macchia; efelide f || tr chiazzare, macchiare
**fledgling** ['flɛdʒlɪŋ] s uccellino appena nato; (fig) pivello
**flee** [fli] v (pret & pp **fled** [flɛd]) tr & intr fuggire, sfuggire
**fleece** [flis] s vello; (e.g., of clouds) bioccolo || tr tosare; (fig) pelare
**fleec·y** ['flisi] adj (-ier; -iest) lanoso; (sky) a pecorelle
**fleet** [flit] adj rapido || s flotta
**fleeting** ['flitɪŋ] adj fugace, passeggero
**Fleming** ['flɛmɪŋ] s fiammingo
**Flemish** ['flɛmɪʃ] adj & s fiammingo
**flesh** [flɛʃ] s carne f; (of fruit) polpa; **in the flesh** in carne ed ossa; **to lose flesh** dimagrire; **to put on flesh** ingrassare
**flesh' and blood'** s (relatives) carne f della carne, i miei, i suoi, etc.; il corpo umano

**flesh-colored** ['flɛʃ ˌkʌlərd] *adj* color carne

**fleshiness** ['flɛʃɪnɪs] *s* carnosità *f*

**fleshless** ['flɛʃlɪs] *adj* scarno

**flesh'pot'** *s* piatto di carne; locale *m* di dissoluzione; **fleshpots** vita dissoluta

**flesh' wound'** *s* ferita superficiale

**flesh•y** ['flɛʃi] *adj* (-ier; -iest) carnoso; polposo

**flex** [flɛks] *tr* piegare ‖ *intr* piegarsi

**flexible** ['flɛksɪbəl] *adj* flessibile; (*joint*) a snodo

**flick** [flɪk] *s* schiocco; (slang) pellicola cinematografica ‖ *tr* schioccare

**flicker** ['flɪkər] *s* fiamma tremolante; (*of eyelids*) battito; (*of hope*) bagliore *m* ‖ *intr* tremolare; vacillare

**flier** ['flaɪ·ər] *s* aviatore *m;* (*venture*) (coll) impresa rischiosa; (coll) foglio volante

**flight** [flaɪt] *s* fuga; (*of an airplane*) volo; (*of birds*) stormo; (*of stairs*) rampa; (*of fancy*) slancio; **to put to flight** mettere in fuga; **to take flight** prendere la fuga

**flight' deck'** *s* ponte *m* di volo

**flight•y** ['flaɪti] *adj* (-ier; -iest) frivolo; volubile

**flim-flam** ['flɪm ˌflæm] *s* (coll) imbroglio, truffa ‖ *v* (*pret & pp* -flammed; *ger* -flamming) *tr* (coll) imbrogliare, truffare

**flim•sy** ['flɪmzi] *adj* (-sier; -siest) leggero; (*material*) di scarsa consistenza; (*excuse*) inconsistente

**flinch** [flɪntʃ] *intr* indietreggiare; **without flinching** senza scomporsi

**fling** [flɪŋ] *s* tiro; ballo scozzese; **to go on a fling** darsi alla pazza gioia; **to have a fling** at tentare di fare; **to have one's fling** correre la cavallina ‖ *v* (*pret & pp* flung [flʌŋ]) *tr* sbattere, scagliare; (*e.g., in jail*) schiaffare; **to fling open** spalancare; **to fling shut** chiudere improvvisamente

**flint** [flɪnt] *s* selce *f*, pietra focaia

**flint'lock'** *s* fucile *m* a pietra focaia

**flint•y** ['flɪnti] *adj* (-ier; -iest) pietroso; (*unmerciful*) spietato; duro come un macigno

**flip** [flɪp] *adj* (flipper; flippest) impertinente ‖ *s* buffetto; salto mortale ‖ *v* (*pret & pp* flipped; *ger* flipping) *tr* sbattere in aria; muovere d'un tratto **to flip a coin** giocare a testa e croce; **to flip shut** (*e.g., a fan*) chiudere improvvisamente

**flippancy** ['flɪpənsi] *s* leggerezza

**flippant** ['flɪpənt] *adj* scanzonato, leggero

**flirt** [flʌrt] *s* (*woman*) civetta; (*man*) vagheggino ‖ *intr* (*said of a woman*) civettare; (*said of a man*) fare il damerino; **to flirt with** flirtare con; (*an idea*) accarezzare; (*death*) giocare con

**flit** [flɪt] *v* (*pret & pp* flitted; *ger* flitting) *intr* svolazzare, volteggiare; passare rapidamente, volare

**flitch** [flɪtʃ] *s* fetta di pancetta

**float** [flot] *s* (*raft*) galleggiante *m;* (*of mason*) cazzuola; carro allegorico ‖ *tr* far galleggiare; (*a business*) lanciare; (*stocks, bonds*) emettere ‖ *intr* galleggiare, tenersi a galla

**floating** ['flotɪŋ] *adj* galleggiante

**flock** [flɑk] *s* (*of birds*) stormo; (*of sheep*) gregge *m;* (*of people*) stuolo; (*of wool*) fiocco; (fig) mucchio ‖ *intr* affollarsi, riunirsi, radunarsi

**floe** [flo] *s* tavola di ghiaccio

**flog** [flɑg] *v* (*pret & pp* flogged; *ger* flogging) *tr* battere, fustigare

**flood** [flʌd] *s* (*caused by rain*) diluvio; (*sudden rise of river*) piena, fiumana; (*of tide*) flusso ‖ *tr* inondare; (aut) ingolfare ‖ *intr* straripare; (aut) ingolfarsi ‖ **the Flood** il diluvio universale

**flood'gate'** *s* (*of a canal*) chiusa; (*of a dam*) saracinesca

**flood'light'** *s* riflettore *m*

**flood' tide'** *s* flusso

**floor** [flor] *s* (*inside bottom surface of room*) pavimento; (*story of building*) piano; (*of the sea, a swimming pool, etc.*) fondo; (*of the exchange*) recinto delle grida; (*of an assembly hall*) emiciclo; (naut) madiere *m;* **to ask for the floor** chiedere la parola; **to have the floor** avere la parola; **to take the floor** prendere la parola ‖ *tr* pavimentare; abbattere, gettare al suolo; (coll) confondere; (coll) vincere

**flooring** ['florɪŋ] *s* palco, impiantito

**floor' mop'** *s* redazza

**floor' plan'** *s* pianta

**floor' show'** *s* spettacolo di caffè concerto

**floor'walk'er** *s* direttore *m* di sezione

**floor' wax'** *s* cera da pavimenti

**flop** [flɑp] *s* (coll) fiasco ‖ *v* (*pret & pp* flopped; *ger* flopping) *tr* lasciar cadere; sbattere ‖ *intr* lasciarsi cadere; (coll) fare fiasco; **to flop over** (*to change sides*) cambiare casacca

**flora** ['florə] *s* flora

**floral** ['florəl] *adj* floreale

**Florence** ['florəns] or ['flɑrəns] *s* Firenze *f*

**Florentine** ['florən ˌtin] or ['flɑrən- ˌtin] *adj & s* fiorentino

**florescence** [flo'rɛsəns] *s* inflorescenza

**florid** ['flɑrɪd] or ['flɔrɪd] *adj* florido

**florist** ['florɪst] *s* fiorista *mf*, fioraio

**floss** [flɔs] or [flɑs] *s* lanugine *f;* (*of corn*) barba

**floss•y** ['flɔsi] or ['flɑsi] *adj* (-ier; -iest) serico; (*downy*) lanuginoso; (coll) vistoso

**flotsam** ['flɑtsəm] *s* relitti gettati a mare

**flot'sam and jet'sam** *s* relitti *mpl* di naufragio; (*trifles*) cianfrusaglie *fpl;* gentaglia, vagabondi *mpl*

**flounce** [flauns] *s* balza, falda, falpalà *m* ‖ *tr* ornare di falpalà ‖ *intr*—**to flounce out** andarsene irosamente

**flounder** ['flaundər] *s* (ichth) passera ‖ *intr* dibattersi

**flour** [flaur] *adj* farinoso ‖ *s* farina ‖ *tr* infarinare

**flourish** ['flʌrɪʃ] *s* (*with the sword*) mulinello; (*with the pen*) ghirigoro; (*as part of signature*) svolazzo; (mus)

fioritura || *tr (one's sword)* roteare ||
*intr* rifiorire, prosperare
**flourishing** ['flʌrɪʃɪŋ] *adj* prosperoso
**flour' mill'** *s* mulino per grano
**floury** ['flauri] *adj* farinoso; infarinato
**flout** [flaut] *tr* burlarsi di || *intr* bur-
lare, motteggiare
**flow** [flo] *s* flusso; *(of a river)* regime
*m* || *intr* fluire; *(said of tide)* mon-
tare; *(said of hair in the air)* ondeggiare; **to flow into** gettarsi in, sfociare in; **to flow over** traboccare; **to
flow with** abbondare di
**flower** ['flau·ər] *s* fiore *m* || *tr* infio-
rare || *intr* fiorire
**flow'er bed'** *s* aiola fiorita
**flow'er gar'den** *s* giardino
**flow'er girl'** *s* fioraia; *(at a wedding)*
damigella d'onore
**flow'er·pot'** *s* vaso da fiori
**flow'er shop'** *s* negozio di fiori
**flow'er show'** *s* esposizione di fiori
**flow'er·stand'** *s* portafiori *m*
**flowery** ['flau·əri] *adj* fiorito
**flowing** ['flo·ɪŋ] *adj (water)* corrente;
*(language)* scorrevole; *(e.g., hair)*
fluente; *(e.g., lines of a dress)* filante
**flu** [flu] *s* influenza
**fluctuate** ['flʌktʃu‚et] *intr* fluttuare,
ondeggiare; *(said of prices)* oscillare
**flue** [flu] *s* gola, fumaiolo
**fluency** ['flu·ənsi] *s* facilità *f* di parola
**fluent** ['flu·ənt] *adj (speaker)* facondo;
*(style)* fluido
**fluently** ['flu·əntli] *adv* correntemente
**fluff** [flʌf] *s* lanugine *f*; vaporosità *f*;
*(of an actor)* papera || *tr* sprimac-
ciare || *intr* sprimacciarsi; *(coll)* im-
paperarsi
**fluff·y** ['flʌfi] *adj* (-**ier**; -**iest**) lanuginoso; vaporoso
**fluid** ['flu·ɪd] *adj & s* fluido
**flu'id drive'** *s* trasmissione idraulica
**fluidity** [flu'ɪdɪti] *s* fluidità *f*
**fluke** [fluk] *s (of anchor)* marra, dente
*m*; *(in billiards)* colpo fortunato;
(ichth) passera
**flume** [flum] *s* gora; condotta forzata
**flunk** [flʌŋk] *s* (coll) bocciatura || *tr*
(coll) bocciare; *(a course)* (coll)
farsi bocciare in || *intr* (coll) fare
fiasco; **to flunk out** (coll) farsi bocciare
**flunk·y** ['flʌŋki] *s* (-**ies**) valletto; parassita *m*
**fluor** ['flu·ər] *s* fluorite *f*
**fluorescence** [‚flu·ə'rɛsəns] *s* fluore-
scenza
**fluorescent** [‚flu·ə'rɛsənt] *adj* fluorescente
**fluoridation** [‚flu·ərɪ'deʃən] *s* fluoriz-
zazione
**fluoride** ['flu·ə‚raɪd] *s* fluoruro
**fluorine** ['flu·ə‚rin] *s* fluoro
**fluoroscope** ['flu·ərə‚skop] *s* schermo
fluorescente
**fluorspar** ['flu·er‚spɑr] *s* spatofluore *m*
**flur·ry** ['flʌri] *s* (-**ries**) agitazione; *(of
wind)* raffica; *(of rain)* acquazzone
*m*; *(of snow)* turbine *m* || *v* (*pret &
pp* -**ried**) *tr* agitare
**flush** [flʌʃ] *adj* livellato; contiguo; pro-

spero, ben provvisto; abbondante;
vigoroso; *(full to overflowing)* rigur-
gitante; arrossito; **flush with** allo
stesso livello che || *s (of water)*
flusso improvviso; *(in the cheeks)*
caldana, scalmana; *(of spring)* germogliare *m*; *(of joy)* ebbrezza; *(of
youth)* rigoglio; *(in poker)* colore *m*
|| *adv* rasente, raso || *tr (to cause to
blush)* far arrossire; lavare con un
getto d'acqua; *(e.g., a rabbit)* snidare
|| *intr* essere accaldato; *(to blush)*
arrossire; *(to gush)* zampillare
**flush' tank'** *s* sciacquone *m*
**flush' toi'let** *s* gabinetto a sciacquone
**fluster** ['flʌstər] *s* nervosismo, eccita-
zione || *tr* innervosire, eccitare
**flute** [flut] *s (of a column)* scanala-
tura; (mus) flauto || *tr* scanalare
**flutist** ['flutɪst] *s* flautista *mf*
**flutter** ['flʌtər] *s* svolazzo; agitazione;
sensazione || *intr* frullare; svolaz-
zare; agitarsi; *(said of the heart)* palpitare; *(said of the heartbeat)* essere
irregolare
**flux** [flʌks] *s (flow)* flusso; *(for fusing
metals)* fondente *m*
**fly** [flaɪ] *s (flies)* mosca; *(of trousers)*
finta; *(for fishing)* mosca artificiale
|| *v (pret* flew [flu]; *pp* flown [flon])
*tr (an airplane)* pilotare, far volare;
trasportare a volo; *(e.g., an ocean)*
trasvolare; *(a flag)* battere || *intr*
volare; fuggire, scappare; *(said of a
flag)* ondeggiare; **to fly away** invo-
larsi; **to fly into a rage** andare in
eccessi; **to fly off** volare via; scappare; **to fly over** trasvolare; **to fly
shut** chiudersi improvvisamente
**fly'blow'** *s* uovo di mosca
**fly'-by-night'** *adj* poco raccomandabile;
di breve durata
**fly'catch'er** *s* (orn) pigliamosche *m*
**flyer** ['flaɪ·ər] *s* var of **flier**
**fly'-fish'** *intr* pescare con le mosche
artificiali
**flying** ['flaɪ·ɪŋ] *adj* volante; rapido; in
fuga; *(start)* lanciato || *s* volo
**fly'ing boat'** *s* idrovolante *m* a scafo
centrale
**fly'ing but'tress** *s* contrafforte *m*
**fly'ing col'ors** *spl* successo; **with flying
colors** a bandiere spiegate
**fly'ing field'** *s* campo d'aviazione
**fly'ing sau'cer** *s* disco volante
**fly'ing sick'ness** *s* male *m* d'aria
**fly'ing squad'** *s* squadra mobile
**fly'ing time'** *s* ore *fpl* di volo
**fly'leaf'** *s* (-**leaves**) (bb) guardia
**fly' net'** *s (for a bed)* moschettiera;
*(for a horse)* scacciamosche *m*
**fly'pa'per** *s* carta moschicida
**fly'speck'** *s* macchia di mosca; mac-
chiolina
**fly' swat'ter** ['swɑtər] *s* scacciamosche
*m*
**fly'trap'** *s* pigliamosche *m*
**fly'wheel'** *s* volano *m*
**foal** [fol] *s* puledro || *intr (said of a
mare)* figliare
**foam** [fom] *s* schiuma || *intr* schiumare
**foam' rub'ber** *s* gommapiuma

**foam·y** ['fomi] *adj* (**-ier; -iest**) spumoso, schiumeggiante

**fob** [fɑb] *s* taschino per l'orologio; (*chain*) catenina per l'orologio || *v* (*pret & pp* **fobbed;** *ger* **fobbing**) *tr—* **to fob off** *s.th* **on** *s.o.* rifilare qlco a qlcu

**f.o.b.** or **F.O.B.** [ˌɛf ˌoˈbi] *adv* (letter-word) (**free on board**) franco

**focal** ['fokəl] *adj* focale

**fo·cus** ['fokəs] *s* (**-cuses** or **-ci** [saɪ]) fuoco; (*of a disease*) focolaio || *v* (*pret & pp* **-cused** or **-cussed;** *ger* **-cusing** or **-cussing**) *tr* mettere a fuoco; (*attention*) concentrare || *intr* convergere

**fodder** ['fɑdər] *s* foraggio

**foe** [fo] *s* nemico

**fog** [fɑg] or [fɔg] *s* nebbia; (*phot*) velo || *v* (*pret & pp* **fogged;** *ger* **fogging**) *tr* annebbiare; (*phot*) velare || *intr* annebbiarsi; (*phot*) velarsi

**fog' bank'** *s* banco di nebbia

**fog'bound'** *adj* avvolto nella nebbia

**fog·gy** ['fɑgi] or ['fɔgi] *adj* (**-gier; -giest**) annebbiato; nebbioso; (*idea*) vago; (*phot*) velato; **it is foggy** fa nebbia

**fog'horn'** *s* sirena da nebbia

**foible** ['fɔɪbəl] *s* debolezza, debole *m*

**foil** [fɔɪl] *s* (*thin sheet of metal*) foglia; (*of mirror*) argentatura; contrasto, risalto; (*sword*) fioretto || *tr* sventare; (*a mirror*) argentare

**foist** [fɔɪst] *tr—***to foist** *s.th* **on** *s.o.* rifilare qlco a qlcu

**fold** [fold] *s* piega; drappeggio; (*for sheep*) ovile *m*; (*of sheep; of the faithful*) gregge *m*; (*geol*) corrugamento || *tr* piegare; (*the arms*) incrociare; **to fold up** ripiegare || *intr* piegarsi; **to fold up** (*coll*) fare fallimento

**folder** ['foldər] *s* (*pamphlet*) pieghevole *m*; (*cover*) portacarte *m*

**folding** ['foldɪŋ] *adj* pieghevole

**fold'ing cam'era** *s* macchina fotografica a soffietto

**fold'ing chair'** *s* sedia pieghevole

**fold'ing cot'** *s* branda

**fold'ing door'** *s* porta a libro

**fold'ing seat'** *s* strapuntino

**foliage** ['folɪ·ɪdʒ] *s* fogliame *m*

**foli·o** ['folɪ ˌo] *adj* in-folio || *s* (**-os**) foglio; (*book*) in-folio || *tr* numerare

**folk** [fok] *adj* popolare || *s* (**folk** or **folks**) gente *f*; **your folks** i Suoi

**folk'lore'** *s* folclore *m*

**folk' mu'sic** *s* musica folcloristica

**folk' song'** *s* canzone *f* tradizionale

**folk·sy** ['foksi] *adj* (**-sier; -siest**) socievole; alla buona, alla mano

**folk'ways'** *spl* costumi *mpl* tradizionali

**follicle** ['fɑlɪkəl] *s* follicolo

**follow** ['fɑlo] *tr* seguire; (*to keep up with*) interessarsi di; **to follow suit** seguire l'esempio; (*cards*) rispondere al colore || *intr* seguire; derivare; **as follows** come segue; **it follows** ne risulta

**follower** ['fɑlo·ər] *s* seguace *m;* discepolo; partigiano

**following** ['fɑlo·ɪŋ] *adj* susseguente || *s* seguito; aderenti *mpl*

**fol'low-up'** *adj* susseguente; ricordativo; da continuarsi || *s* prosecuzione; lettera ricordativa

**fol·ly** ['fɑli] *s* (**-lies**) follia; **follies** rivista di varietà

**foment** [fo'ment] *tr* fomentare

**fond** [fɑnd] *adj* appassionato; (*of food*) ghiotto; **to become fond of** appassionarsi di

**fondle** ['fɑndəl] *tr* accarezzare, vezzeggiare

**fondness** ['fɑndnɪs] *s* tenerezza; passione

**font** [fɑnt] *s* acquasantiera, pila; fonte *f* battesimale; (*typ*) fondita

**food** [fud] *adj* alimentare || *s* cibo, vitto; (*for animals*) mangiare *m;* **food for thought** materia di che pensare

**food' store'** *s* negozio di commestibili

**food'stuffs'** *spl* commestibili *mpl*

**fool** [ful] *s* scemo, sciocco; (*jester*) buffone *m;* (*person imposed on*) vittima, zimbello; **to make a fool of** beffarsi di; **to play the fool** fare lo stupido || *tr* infinocchiare, ingannare; **to fool away** sprecare || *intr* giocare, fare per gioco; **to fool around** perdere il proprio tempo; **to fool with** giocherellare con

**fooler·y** ['fuləri] *s* (**-ies**) pazzia, buffonata

**fool'har'dy** *adj* (**-dier; -diest**) temerario

**fooling** ['fulɪŋ] *s* scherzo; **no fooling** senza scherzi, parlando sul serio

**foolish** ['fulɪʃ] *adj* sciocco; matto

**fool'proof'** *adj* a tutta prova; infallibile

**fools'cap'** *s* berretto a sonagli; carta formato protocollo

**fool's' er'rand** *s* impresa inutile

**fool's' par'adise** *s* felicità immaginaria

**foot** [fʊt] *s* (**feet** [fit]) piede *m;* (*of an animal*) zampa; (*of horse*) zoccolo; **to drag one's feet** procedere a passo di lumaca; **to put one's best foot forward** fare del proprio meglio; **to put one's foot down** farsi valere, imporsi; **to put one's foot in it** (*coll*) fare una topica; **to stand on one's own two feet** agire indipendentemente; **to tread under foot** calcare || *tr* (*the bill*) pagare; **to foot it** andare a piedi; ballare

**footage** ['fʊtɪdʒ] *s* distanza or lunghezza in piedi; (*of film measured in meters*) metraggio

**foot'-and-mouth' disease'** *s* (*vet*) afta epizootica

**foot'ball'** *s* (*ball*) pallone *m;* (*game*) pallovale *f;* (*soccer*) calcio, football *m*

**foot'board'** *s* (*support for foot*) predellino; (*of bed*) spalliera

**foot' brake'** *s* freno a pedale

**foot'bridge'** *s* passerella, ponte riservato ai pedoni

**foot'fall'** *s* passo

**foot'hill'** *s* collina ai piedi di una montagna

**foot'hold'** *s* stabilità *f;* **to gain a foot-hold** prender piede

**footing** ['futɪŋ] *s* piede *m,* e.g., **he lost his footing** perse piede; **on a friendly footing** in relazioni amichevoli; **on an equal footing** su un piede di parità; **on a war footing** su un piede di guerra

**foot'lights'** *spl* luci *fpl* della ribalta; (fig) ribalta, scena

**foot'loose'** *adj* completamente libero

**foot'man** *s* (-men) staffiere *m*

**foot'mark'** *s* orma

**foot'note'** *s* rimando, rinvio

**foot'path'** *s* sentiero

**foot'print'** *s* orma, pesta

**foot' race'** *s* corsa podistica

**foot'rest'** *s* pedana

**foot' rule'** *s* regolo di un piede

**foot' soldier'** *s* fante *m,* fantaccino

**foot'sore'** *adj* coi piedi stanchi

**foot'step'** *s* passo; **to follow in the footsteps of** seguire le orme di

**foot'stone'** *s* pietra tombale a piè di un sepolcro; (archit) pietra di sostegno

**foot'stool'** *s* sgabello

**foot' warm'er** *s* scaldino

**foot'wear'** *s* calzature *fpl*

**foot'work'** *s* allenamento delle gambe; (fig) manovra delicata

**foot'worn'** *adj* (road) battuto; (person) spedato

**foozle** ['fuzəl] *s* schiappinata ‖ *tr & intr* mancare completamente

**fop** [fɑp] *s* bellimbusto, gagà *m*

**for** [fɔr] *prep* per; malgrado, e.g., **for all his wealth** malgrado tutta la sua ricchezza; come, e.g., **he uses his house for an office** adopera la casa come ufficio; di, e.g., **time for bed** ora di andare a letto; da, e.g., **he has been here for three days** è qui da tre giorni; per amor di; **to go for a walk** andare a fare una passeggiata ‖ *conj* perchè, poichè

**forage** ['fɑrɪdʒ] or ['fɔrɪdʒ] *adj* foraggero ‖ *s* foraggio ‖ *tr* foraggiare ‖ *intr* andare in cerca di foraggio

**foray** ['fɑre] or ['fɔre] *s* razzia, scorreria ‖ *intr* razziare

**for·bear** [fɔr'ber] *v* (pret -bore ['bor]; pp -borne ['born]) *tr* astenersi da ‖ *intr* essere longanime

**forbearance** [fɔr'berəns] *s* longanimità *f,* tolleranza; astensione

**for·bid** [fɔr'bɪd] *v* (pret -bade ['bæd] or -bad ['bæd]; pp -bidden ['bɪdən]; ger -bidding) *tr* proibire, vietare ‖ *intr*—**God forbid!** Dío ci scampi!

**forbidding** [fɔr'bɪdɪŋ] *adj* severo, sinistro

**force** [fɔrs] *s* forza; (staff of workers) forza, personale *m;* (phys) forza; **by force of** a forza di; **by main force** con tutte le sue forze; **in force** vigente; in gran numero; **to join forces** allearsi ‖ *tr* forzare; obbligare; **to force back** respingere; **to force open** forzare; **to force s.th on s.o.** obbligare qlcu a accettare qlco

**forced** [fɔrst] *adj* forzato; studiato

**forced' air'** *s* aria sotto pressione

**forced' draft'** *s* tiraggio forzato

**forced' land'ing** *s* atterraggio forzato

**forced' march'** *s* marcia forzata

**forceful** ['fɔrsfəl] *adj* vigoroso, energico

**for·ceps** ['fɔrsəps] *s* (-ceps or -cipes [sɪ‚piz]) (dent, surg) pinze *fpl;* (obstet) forcipe *m*

**force' pump'** *s* pompa premente

**forcible** ['fɔrsɪbəl] *adj* impetuoso, energico; efficace

**ford** [fɔrd] *s* guado ‖ *tr* guadare

**fore** [for] *adj* davanti; (naut) prodiero ‖ *s* davanti *m;* (naut) prua; **to the fore** alla ribalta; d'attualità ‖ *adv* prima; (naut) a proravia ‖ *interj* attenzione!

**fore' and aft'** *adv* a poppa e a prua

**fore'arm'** *s* avambraccio ‖ **fore·arm'** *tr* premunire; prevenire

**fore'bears'** *spl* antenati *mpl*

**forebode** [for'bod] *tr* (to portend) preannunziare; (to have a presentiment of) presentire

**foreboding** [for'bodɪŋ] *s* preannunzio; presentimento

**fore'cast'** *s* pronostico ‖ *v* (pret & pp -cast or -casted) *tr* pronosticare

**forecastle** ['foksəl], ['for‚kæsəl] or ['for‚kɑsəl] *s* castello, pozzetto

**fore·close'** *tr* escludere, precludere; (a mortgage) (law) precludere il riscatto di

**fore·doom'** *tr* condannare all'insuccesso

**fore' edge'** *s* (bb) taglio

**fore'fa'ther** *s* antenato

**fore'fin'ger** *s* dito indice

**fore'front'** *s*—**in the forefront** all'avanguardia

**fore·go'** *v* (pret -went'; pp -gone') *tr & intr* precedere

**fore·go'ing** *adj* precedente, anteriore

**fore'gone' conclu'sion** *s* conclusione inevitabile; decisione già scontata

**fore'ground'** *s* primo piano

**forehanded** ['for‚hændɪd] *adj* previdente; (thrifty) risparmiatore

**forehead** ['fɑrɪd] or ['fɔrɪd] *s* fronte *f*

**foreign** ['fɑrɪn] or ['fɔrɪn] *adj* straniero; (product; affairs) estero; **foreign to** estraneo a

**for'eign affairs'** *spl* affari esteri

**for'eign-born'** *adj* nato all'estero

**foreigner** ['fɑrɪnər] or ['fɔrɪnər] *s* straniero, forestiero

**for'eign exchange'** *s* divise *fpl;* (money) valuta

**for'eign min'ister** *s* ministro degli affari esteri

**for'eign of'fice** *s* ministero degli affari esteri

**for'eign serv'ice** *s* servizio diplomatico e consolare; (Brit) servizio militare in paesi d'oltremare

**fore'leg'** *s* zampa anteriore

**fore'lock'** *s* ciuffo sulla fronte; **to take time by the forelock** acchiappare l'occasione

**fore'man** *s* (-men) sorvegliante *m,* capomastro; presidente *m* dei giurati

**foremast** ['forməst], ['for‚mæst] or ['for‚mɑst] *s* trinchetto

**foremost** ['for‚most] *adj* primo, principale, più importante

**fore'noon'** *adj* mattinale ‖ *s* mattina
**fore'part'** *s* parte *f* anteriore; prima parte
**fore'paw'** *s* zampa anteriore
**fore'quar'ter** *s* quarto anteriore
**fore'run'ner** *s* precursore *m*, predecessore *m*, foriero
**fore·sail** ['fɔrsəl] or ['fɔr,sel] *s* trinchetto
**fore·see'** *v* (*pret* -saw'; *pp* -seen') *tr* prevedere
**foreseeable** [for'si·əbəl] *adj* prevedibile
**fore·shad'ow** *tr* presagire
**fore·short'en** *tr* scorciare
**fore'sight'** *s* (*prudence*) previdenza; (*foreknowledge*) previsione
**fore'sight'ed** *adj* previdente
**fore'skin'** *s* prepuzio
**forest** ['fɑrɪst] or ['fɔrɪst] *adj* forestale ‖ *s* foresta, bosco
**fore·stall'** *tr* prevenire; anticipare; (*to buy up*) accaparrare
**for'est rang'er** ['rendʒər] *s* guardaboschi *m*, guardia forestale
**forestry** ['fɑrɪstri] or ['fɔrɪstri] *s* selvicoltura
**fore'taste'** *s* pregustazione ‖ *tr* pregustare
**fore·tell'** *v* (*pret* & *pp* -told') *tr* predire, presagire, preannunziare
**fore'thought'** *s* premeditazione; previdenza
**forever** [fɔr'ɛvər] *adv* per sempre; continuamente
**fore·warn'** *tr* prevenire, preavvertire
**fore'word'** *s* avvertenza, prefazione
**forfeit** ['fɔrfɪt] *adj* perduto ‖ *s* perdita, confisca; multa; (*article deposited*) pegno; **forfeits** (*game*) pegni *mpl* ‖ *tr* decadere da
**forfeiture** ['fɔrfɪtʃər] *s* perdita di un pegno
**forgather** [fɔr'gæðər] *intr* riunirsi; incontrarsi
**forge** [fɔrdʒ] *s* fucina, forgia ‖ *tr* forgiare; (*a lie*) inventare; (*e.g., handwriting*) falsificare ‖ *intr* forgiare; commettere un falso; **to forge ahead** farsi strada
**forger·y** ['fɔrdʒəri] *s* (-ies) falsificazione, falso, contraffazione
**for·get** [fɔr'gɛt] *v* (*pret* -got ['gɑt]; *pp* -got or -gotten ['gɑtən]) *tr* dimenticare; **forget it!** non si preoccupi!; **to forget oneself** venir meno alla propria dignità; **to forget to** passare di mente a (qlcu) di, e.g., **he forgot to turn off the lights** gli è passato di mente di spegnere la luce
**forgetful** [fɔr'gɛtfəl] *adj* (*apt to forget*) smemorato; (*neglectful*) dimentico, immemore
**forgetfulness** [fɔr'gɛtfəlnɪs] *s* (*inability to recall*) smemorataggine *f*; (*neglectfulness*) dimenticanza
**for·get'-me-not'** *s* nontiscordardimé *m*
**forgivable** [fɔr'gɪvəbəl] *adj* perdonabile
**for·give** [fɔr'gɪv] *v* (*pret* -gave'; *pp* -giv'en) *tr* perdonare
**forgiveness** [fɔr'gɪvnɪs] *s* perdono
**forgiving** [fɔr'gɪvɪŋ] *adj* clemente
**for·go** [fɔr'go] *v* (*pret* -went; *pp* -gone) *tr* rinunciare (with *dat*)

**fork** [fɔrk] *s* (*pitchfork*) forca, forcone *m*; (*of a bicycle*) forcella; (*for eating*) forchetta; (*of a tree or road*) biforcazione, diramazione ‖ *tr* muovere col forcone; inforcare; **to fork out** (slang) cacciar fuori ‖ *intr* biforcarsi, diramarsi
**forked** [fɔrkt] *adj* biforcuto
**fork'-lift truck'** *s* carrello elevatore a forca
**forlorn** [fɔr'lɔrn] *adj* abbandonato; disperato; miserabile
**forlorn' hope'** *s* impresa disperata
**form** [fɔrm] *s* forma; (*paper to be filled out*) formulario; (*construction to give shape to cement*) cassaforma ‖ *tr* formare ‖ *intr* formarsi
**formal** ['fɔrməl] *adj* formale; di gala, da sera, da etichetta
**for'mal attire'** *s* vestito da cerimonia
**for'mal call'** *s* visita di prammatica
**formali·ty** [fɔr'mælɪti] *s* (-ties) formalità *f*; (*excessive adherence to rules*) formalismo
**for'mal par'ty** *s* ricevimento di gala
**for'mal speech'** *s* discorso ufficiale
**format** ['fɔrmæt] *s* formato
**formation** [fɔr'meʃən] *s* formazione
**former** ['fɔrmər] *adj* (*preceding*) anteriore; (*long past*) passato, antico; (*having once been*) già, ex; (*of two*) primo; **the former** quello
**formerly** ['fɔrmərli] *adv* già, prima, in tempi passati
**form'fit'ting** *adj* aderente al corpo
**formidable** ['fɔrmɪdəbəl] *adj* formidabile
**formless** ['fɔrmlɪs] *adj* informe
**form' let'ter** *s* lettera a formulario, stampato
**formu·la** ['fɔrmjələ] *s* (-las or -lae [,li]) formula
**formulate** ['fɔrmjə,let] *tr* formulare
**for·sake** [fɔr'sek] *v* (*pret* -sook ['suk]; *pp* -saken ['sekən]) *tr* abbandonare
**fort** [fɔrt] *s* forte *m*, fortezza
**forte** [fɔrt] *s* forte *m*
**forth** [fɔrθ] *adv* avanti; **and so forth** e così via; **from this day forth** da oggi in poi; **to go forth** uscire
**forth'com'ing** *adj* prossimo; immediatamente disponibile
**forth'right'** *adj* diretto ‖ *adv* direttamente; senza ambagi; immediatamente
**forth'with'** *adv* immediatamente
**fortieth** ['fɔrti·ɪθ] *adj*, *s* & *pron* quarantesimo
**fortification** [,fɔrtɪfɪ'keʃən] *s* fortificazione
**forti·fy** ['fɔrtɪ,faɪ] *v* (*pret* & *pp* -fied) *tr* fortificare; aumentare il livello alcolico di
**fortitude** ['fɔrtɪ,tjud] or ['fɔrtɪ,tud] *s* fortezza, fermezza
**fortnight** ['fɔrtnaɪt] or ['fɔrtnɪt] *s* quindicina, due settimane
**fortress** ['fɔrtrɪs] *s* fortezza, forte *m*
**fortuitous** [fɔr'tju·ɪtəs] or [fɔr'tu·ɪtəs] *adj* fortuito, occasionale
**fortunate** ['fɔrtʃənɪt] *adj* fortunato
**fortune** ['fɔrtʃən] *s* fortuna; **to make a fortune** farsi un patrimonio; **to tell**

**s.o. his fortune** leggere il futuro a qlcu

**for'tune hunt'er** *s* cacciatore *m* di dote

**for'tune·tel'ler** *s* indovino, cartomante *mf*

**for·ty** ['fɔrti] *adj & pron* quaranta || *s* (**-ties**) quaranta *m;* **the forties** gli anni quaranta

**fo·rum** ['forəm] *s* (**-rums or -ra** [rə]) foro

**forward** ['fɔrwərd] *adj* avanzato; precoce; impertinente || *s* (soccer) avanti *m* || *adv* avanti; **to bring forward** mettere in luce; riportare; **to come forward** avanzare; **to look forward to** anticipare il piacere di || *tr* inoltrare, trasmettere; promuovere

**fossil** ['fɑsɪl] *adj & s* fossile *m*

**foster** ['fɑstər] or ['fɔstər] *adj* adottivo; di latte || *tr* allevare; promuovere

**fos'ter home'** *s* famiglia adottiva

**foul** [faʊl] *adj* sporco; (*air*) viziato; (*wind*) contrario; (*weather; breath*) cattivo; (baseball) fuori linea di gioco || *s* (*of boats*) urto, collisione; (baseball) palla colpita fuori linea di gioco; (boxing) colpo basso; (sports) fallo || *adv* slealmente; (baseball) fuori linea di gioco; **to fall foul of** entrare in collisione con; urtarsi con; **to run foul of** avere una controversia con || *tr* sporcare; otturare; (baseball) colpire fuori linea di gioco || *intr* (*said of two boats*) entrare in collisione; (*said, e.g., of a rope*) imbrogliarsi

**foul-mouthed** ['faʊl'maʊðd] or ['faʊl-'maʊθt] *adj* sboccato, osceno

**foul' play'** *s* reato; (sports) gioco sleale

**found** [faʊnd] *tr* fondare; (*to melt, to cast*) fondere

**foundation** [faʊn'deʃən] *s* fondazione; (*endowment*) dotazione; (*charitable*) patronato; (*masonry support*) platea, fondamenta *fpl;* (*make-up*) fondo tinta; (fig) fondatezza

**founder** ['faʊndər] *s* fondatore *m;* (*of family*) capostipite *m;* (*of metals*) fonditore *m* || *intr* (*said of a ship*) affondare; (*said of a horse*) azzopparsi; (*to fail*) fare fiasco

**foundling** ['faʊndlɪŋ] *s* trovatello

**found'ling hos'pital** *s* brefotrofio

**found·ry** ['faʊndri] *s* (**-ries**) fonderìa

**found'ry·man** *s* (**-men**) fonditore *m*

**fount** [faʊnt] *s* fonte *f*

**fountain** ['faʊntən] *s* fonte *f*, fontana; (*of knowledge*) pozzo

**foun'tain·head'** *s* sorgente *f*

**foun'tain pen'** *s* penna stilografica

**foun'tain syringe'** *s* clistere *m* a pera

**four** [for] *adj & pron* quattro || *s* quattro; **four o'clock** le quattro; **on all fours** gattoni, carponi

**four'-cy'cle** *adj* a quattro tempi

**four'-cyl'inder** *adj* a quattro cilindri

**four'-flush'** *intr* (coll) millantarsi

**fourflusher** ['for ˌflʌʃər] *s* (coll) millantatore *m*

**four-footed** ['for'fʊtɪd] *adj* quadrupede

**four' hun'dred** *adj, s & pron* quattro-cento || **the Four Hundred** l'alta società

**four'-in-hand'** *s* cravatta a cappio; tiro a quattro

**four'-lane'** *adj* a quattro corsie

**four'-leaf clo'ver** *s* quadrifoglio

**four-legged** ['for'lɛgɪd] or ['for'lɛgd] *adj* a quattro zampe; (*schooner*) (coll) a quattro alberi

**four'-letter word'** *s* parolaccia di quattro lettere

**four'-mo'tor plane'** *s* quadrimotore *m*

**four'-o'clock'** *s* (bot) bella di notte

**four' of a kind'** *s* (cards) poker *m*

**four'post'er** *s* letto a baldacchino

**four'score'** *adj* ottanta

**foursome** ['forsəm] *s* gruppo di quattro giocatori

**fourteen** ['for'tin] *adj, s & pron* quattordici *m*

**fourteenth** ['for'tinθ] *adj, s & pron* quattordicesimo || *s* (*in dates*) quattordici *m*

**fourth** [forθ] *adj, s & pron* quarto || *s* (*in dates*) quattro

**fourth' estate'** *s* quarto potere

**four'-way'** *adj* a quattro orifizi; fra quattro persone; quadruplice

**fowl** [faʊl] *s* pollo || *intr* uccellare

**fowl'ing piece'** *s* fucile *m* da caccia

**fox** [fɑks] *s* volpe *f* || *tr* (coll) ingannare

**fox'glove'** *s* digitale *f*

**fox'hole'** *s* buca ricovero

**fox'hound'** *s* segugio

**fox' hunt'** *s* caccia alla volpe

**fox' ter'rier** *s* fox-terrier *m*

**fox'-trot'** *s* (*of a horse*) piccolo trotto; (*dance*) fox-trot *m*

**fox·y** ['fɑksi] *adj* (**-ier; -iest**) volpino, astuto

**foyer** ['fɔɪ·ər] *s* (*of a private house*) ingresso, vestibolo; (theat) ridotto

**fracas** ['frekəs] *s* lite *f*, tumulto

**fraction** ['frækʃən] *s* frazione; frammento

**fractional** ['frækʃənəl] *adj* frazionario; insignificante

**fractious** ['frækʃəs] *adj* litigioso, permaloso; indisciplinato

**fracture** ['fræktʃər] *s* frattura || *tr* fratturare; (*e.g., an arm*) fratturarsi, rompersi || *intr* fratturarsi

**fragile** ['frædʒɪl] *adj* fragile

**fragment** ['frægmənt] *s* frammento; (*e.g., of a movie*) spezzone *m* || *tr* frammentare, spezzare

**fragmenta'tion bomb'** [ˌfrægmən'teʃən] *s* bomba dirompente

**fragrant** ['fregrənt] *adj* fragrante

**frail** [frel] *adj* (*not robust*) gracile; (*easily broken*) fragile; (*morally weak*) debole || *s* canestro di giunco

**frail·ty** ['frelti] *s* (**-ties**) fragilità *f;* (*of a person*) debolezza

**frame** [frem] *s* (*of picture*) cornice *f;* (*of glasses*) montatura; (*structure*) ossatura; (*of a building*) ingabbiatura, impalcatura; (*for embroidering*) telaio; (*of a window*) intelaiatura; (*of mind*) stato; (mov) inquadratura; (phot) fotogramma *m;* (aer) ordinata;

(naut) costa ‖ *tr* (*to put in a frame*) incorniciare; montare; costruire; inventare; esprimere; (slang) architettare un' accusa contro

**frame' house'** *s* casa con l'ossatura di legno

**frame'-up'** *s* (slang) complotto per incriminare un innocente

**frame'work'** *s* intelaiatura, impalcatura; palificazione

**franc** [fræŋk] *s* franco

**France** [fræns] or [frɑns] *s* la Francia

**Frances** ['frænsɪs] or ['frɑnsɪs] *s* Francesca

**franchise** ['fræntʃaɪz] *s* diritto di voto; concessione; (*privilege*) franchigia

**Francis** ['frænsɪs] or ['frɑnsɪs] *s* Francesco

**Franciscan** [fræn'sɪskən] *adj* & *s* francescano

**frank** [fræŋk] *adj* sincero, schietto ‖ *s* affrancatura postale; lettera affrancata; (*franking privilege*) franchigia postale ‖ *tr* affrancare ‖ **Frank** *s* (*member of Frankish tribe*) franco; (*masculine name*) Franco

**frankfurter** ['fræŋkfərtər] *s* salsiccia di Francoforte, Frankfurter *m*

**frankincense** ['fræŋkɪn,sɛns] *s* olibano

**Frankish** ['fræŋkɪʃ] *adj* & *s* franco

**frankness** ['fræŋknɪs] *s* franchezza

**frantic** ['fræntɪk] *adj* frenetico

**frappé** [fræ'pe] *adj* & *s* frappé *m*

**frat** [fræt] *s* (slang) associazione di studenti

**fraternal** [frə'tʌrnəl] *adj* fraterno

**fraterni·ty** [frə'tʌrnɪti] *s* (**-ties**) (*brotherliness*) fraternità *f;* sodalizio; (eccl) confraternita; (U.S.A.) associazione di studenti

**fraternize** ['frætər,naɪz] *intr* fraternizzare

**fraud** [frɔd] *s* truffa, frode *f;* (*person*) (coll) truffatore *m*

**fraudulent** ['frɔdjələnt] *adj* fraudolento; (*conversion*) indebito

**fraught** [frɔt] *adj*—**fraught with** carico di, gravido di

**fray** [fre] *s* zuffa, rissa, lotta ‖ *intr* sfilacciarsi, logorarsi

**freak** [frik] *s* (*sudden fancy*) capriccio, ticchio; (*person, animal*) fenomeno

**freakish** ['frikɪʃ] *adj* capriccioso; strano, grottesco

**freckle** ['frɛkəl] *s* lentiggine *f,* efelide *f*

**freckle-faced** ['frɛkəl,fest] *adj* lentigginoso

**freckly** ['frɛkli] *adj* lentigginoso

**Frederick** ['frɛdərɪk] *s* Federico

**free** [fri] *adj* (**freer** ['fri·ər]; **freest** ['fri·ɪst]) libero; gratis; franco; sciolto; esente; generoso; **to be free with** essere prodigo di; **to set free** liberare ‖ *adv* liberamente; in libertà; gratis ‖ *v* (*pret* & *pp* **freed** [frid]; *ger* **freeing** ['fri·ɪŋ]) *tr* liberare; (*from customs*) svincolare; esimere

**freebooter** ['fri,butər] *s* pirata *m*

**free'born'** *adj* nato in libertà; proprio di un popolo libero

**freedom** ['fridəm] *s* libertà *f*

**free'dom of speech'** *s* libertà *f* di parola

**free'dom of the press'** *s* libertà *f* di stampa

**free'dom of the seas'** *s* libertà *f* di navigazione

**free'dom of wor'ship** *s* libertà religiosa

**free' en'terprise** *s* economia libera

**free'-for-all'** *s* rissa, tafferuglio

**free' hand'** *s* libertà assoluta

**free'-hand'** *adj* a mano libera

**freehanded** ['fri'hændɪd] *adj* liberale, generoso

**free' lance'** *s* giornalista *mf* pubblicista; scrittore *m* che lavora senza contratto; soldato di ventura

**free'load'er** ['lodər] *s* (coll) mangiatore *m* a sbafo

**free'man** *s* (**-men**) uomo libero; cittadino

**Free'ma'son** *s* frammassone *m*

**Free'ma'sonry** *s* frammassoneria

**free' of charge'** *adj* gratis, senza spese

**free' port'** *s* porto franco

**free' serv'ice** *s* manutenzione gratuita

**free'-spo'ken** *adj* franco, aperto

**free'stone'** *adj* spiccagnolo ‖ *s* pesca spicca

**free'think'er** *s* libero pensatore

**free' thought'** *s* libero pensiero

**free' trade'** *s* libero scambio

**free'trad'er** *s* liberoscambista *mf*

**free'way'** *s* autostrada

**free' will'** *s* libero arbitrio

**freeze** [friz] *s* gelo, gelata; (*e.g., of prices*) blocco ‖ *v* (*pret* **froze** [froz]; *pp* **frozen**) *tr* gelare; (*credits, rentals, etc.*) bloccare ‖ *intr* gelarsi; (*said of brakes*) inchiodarsi; morire assiderato; (*to become immobilized*) irrigidirsi

**freeze'-dry'** *v* (*pret* & *pp* **-dried'**) *tr* liofilizzare

**freezer** ['frizər] *s* congelatore *m;* (*for making ice cream*) sorbettiera

**freight** [fret] *s* carico; (*charge*) porto; (naut) nolo; **by freight** come carico mercantile; (rr) a piccola velocità ‖ *tr* spedire come carico

**freight' car'** *s* vagone *m* or carro merci

**freighter** ['fretər] *s* speditore *m;* nave *f* da carico

**freight' plat'form** *s* (rr) banchina adibita al traffico merci

**freight' sta'tion** *s* (rr) stazione merci

**freight' train'** *s* treno merci, merci *m*

**freight' yard'** *s* (rr) scalo merci

**French** [frɛntʃ] *adj* & *s* francese *m;* **the French** i francesi

**French' bread'** *s* pane *m* a bastone

**French' chalk'** *s* pietra da sarto

**French' door'** *s* porta a vetri

**French' dress'ing** *s* salsa verde con aceto

**French' fried' pota'toes** *spl* patate fritte affettate

**French' horn'** *s* (mus) corno

**French' leave'**—**to take French leave** andarsene all'inglese, filare all'inglese

**French'man** *s* (**-men**) francese *m*

**French' tel'ephone** *s* microtelefono

**French' toast'** *s* pane dorato al salto

**French' win'dow** *s* portafinestra

**French'wom'an** *s* (**-wom'en**) francese *f*

**frenzied** ['frɛnzid] *adj* frenetico

**fren·zy** ['frɛnzi] *s* (**-zies**) frenesia

**frequen·cy** ['frikwənsi] *s* (**-cies**) frequenza

**fre'quency modula'tion** *s* modulazione di frequenza

**frequent** ['frikwənt] *adj* frequente || [fri'kwɛnt] or ['frikwənt] *tr* frequentare, praticare

**frequently** ['frikwəntli] *adv* frequentemente

**fres·co** ['frɛsko] *s* (**-coes** or **-cos**) affresco || *tr* affrescare

**fresh** [frɛʃ] *adj* fresco; (*water*) dolce; (*new*) nuovo; (*wind*) moderato; (*inexperienced*) novizio; (*cheeky*) (slang) sfacciato || *adv* recentemente, di recente; **fresh in** (coll) appena arrivato; **fresh out** (coll) appena esaurito

**freshen** ['frɛʃən] *tr* rinfrescare || *intr* rinfrescarsi

**freshet** ['frɛʃɪt] *s* piena, crescita

**fresh'man** *s* (**-men**) (*newcomer*) novizio; (educ) matricola

**freshness** ['frɛʃnɪs] *s* freschezza; (*of air*) frescura; (*cheek*) (slang) sfacciataggine *f*

**fresh'-wa'ter** *adj* d'acqua dolce; poco conosciuto; piccolo

**fret** [frɛt] *s* (*interlaced design*) fregio, greca; irritazione; (mus) tasto || *v* (*pret* & *pp* **fretted**; *ger* **fretting**) *tr* fregiare || *intr* fremere, trepidare, agitarsi

**fretful** ['frɛtfəl] *adj* irritabile, permaloso

**fret'work'** *s* greca

**Freudianism** ['frɔɪdɪ·ə ˌnɪzəm] *s* freudismo

**friar** ['fraɪ·ər] *s* frate *m*

**friar·y** ['fraɪ·əri] *s* (**-ies**) convento di frati

**fricassee** [ˌfrɪkə'si] *s* fricassea

**friction** ['frɪkʃən] *s* frizione; disaccordo, dissenso

**fric'tion tape'** *s* nastro isolante

**Friday** ['fraɪdi] *s* venerdì *m*

**fried** [fraɪd] *adj* fritto

**fried' egg'** *s* uovo al tegame, uovo occhio di manzo

**friend** [frɛnd] *s* amico; **to be friends with** essere amico di; **to make friends** allacciare amicizie; **to make friends with** fare l'amicizia di

**friend·ly** ['frɛndli] *adj* (**-lier**; **-liest**) amico, amichevole

**friendship** ['frɛndʃɪp] *s* amicizia

**frieze** [friz] *s* (archit) fregio

**frigate** ['frɪgɪt] *s* fregata

**fright** [fraɪt] *s* spavento; **to take fright at** spaventarsi di

**frighten** ['fraɪtən] *tr* intimorire, spaventare; **to frighten away** mettere in fuga, sgomentare || *intr* spaventarsi

**frightful** ['fraɪtfəl] *adj* spaventevole, orribile; (coll) enorme

**frightfulness** ['fraɪtfəlnɪs] *s* spavento; terrorismo

**frigid** ['frɪdʒɪd] *adj* freddo; (*zone*) glaciale

**frigidity** [frɪ'dʒɪdɪti] *s* (fig) frigidezza; (pathol) frigidità *f*

**frill** [frɪl] *s* pieghettatura; (*of birds and other animals*) collarino; (*in dress, speech, etc.*) affettazione

**fringe** [frɪndʒ] *s* frangia; (*in dressmaking*) volantino; (*on curtains*) balza; **on the fringe of** all'orlo di || *tr* orlare

**fringe' ben'efits** *spl* assegni *mpl*, benefici *mpl* marginali

**fripper·y** ['frɪpəri] *s* (**-ies**) (*finery*) fronzoli *mpl*; ostentazione; (*trifles*) cianfrusaglie *fpl*

**frisk** [frɪsk] *tr* perquisire; (slang) derubare || *intr* fare capriole

**frisk·y** ['frɪski] *adj* (**-ier**; **-iest**) gaio, vivace

**fritter** ['frɪtər] *s* frittella; frammento || *tr*—**to fritter away** sprecare

**frivolous** ['frɪvələs] *adj* frivolo

**friz** [frɪz] *s* (**frizzes**) ricciolo || *v* (*pret* & *pp* **frizzed**; *ger* **frizzing**) *tr* arricciare

**frizzle** ['frɪzəl] *s* ricciolo || *tr* arricciare || *intr* arricciarsi

**friz·zly** ['frɪzli] *adj* (**-zlier**; **-zliest**) crespo, riccio

**fro** [fro] *adv*—**to and fro** avanti e indietro; **to go to and fro** andare e venire

**frock** [frɑk] *s* gabbano; (*smock*) grembiule *m*; blusa; (*of priest*) tonaca

**frock' coat'** *s* finanziera

**frog** [frɑg] or [frɔg] *s* rana; (*button and loop on a garment*) alamaro; (*in throat*) raschio

**frog'man'** *s* (**-men'**) sommozzatore *m*, uomo rana

**frol·ic** ['frɑlɪk] *s* scherzo, monelleria || *v* (*pret* & *pp* **-icked**; *ger* **-icking**) *intr* scherzare, folleggiare

**frolicsome** ['frɑlɪksəm] *adj* scherzoso

**from** [frʌm], [frɑm] or [frəm] *prep* da; di, e.g., **I am from New York** sono di New York; da parte di, a, e.g., **to take s.th away from s.o.** portar via qlco a qlcu

**front** [frʌnt] *adj* frontale, anteriore; di fronte || *s* fronte *m* & *f*; (*of a building*) prospetto; (*of a book*) principio; (*of a shirt*) sparato; (*e.g., of wealth*) apparenza; (theat) boccascena *m*; (mil) fronte *m*; **in front of** dinanzi a; **to put on a front** (coll) fare ostentazione; **to put up a bold front** (coll) farsi coraggio || *tr* (*to face*) fronteggiare; (*to confront*) affrontare; (*to supply with a front*) coprire; servire da facciata a || *intr*—**to front on** dare su

**frontage** ['frʌntɪdʒ] *s* facciata, veduta; terreno di fronte alla casa

**front' door'** *s* porta d'entrata

**front' drive'** *s* (aut) trazione anteriore

**frontier** [frʌn'tɪr] *adj* limitrofo || *s* frontiera

**fron'tiers'man** *s* (**-men**) pioniere *m*

**frontispiece** ['frʌntɪs ˌpis] *s* (*of book*) pagina illustrata di fronte al frontispizio; (*of building*) facciata

**front' mat'ter** *s* (*of book*) parte *f* preliminare

**front'-page'** *tr* stampare in prima pagina

**front' porch'** *s* porticato

**front' room'** s stanza con vista sulla strada

**front' row'** s prima fila

**front' seat'** s posto in una delle file davanti; (aut) sedile m anteriore

**front' steps'** spl scalinata d'ingresso

**front' view'** s vista sulla strada

**frost** [frɔst] or [frɑst] s gelo, brina, gelata; (fig) freddezza; (slang) fiasco || tr agghiacciare; (with sugar) glassare; (glass) smerigliare

**frost'bite'** s congelamento

**frost'ed glass'** s vetro smerigliato

**frosting** ['frɔstɪŋ] or ['frɑstɪŋ] s glassatura; (of glass) smerigliatura

**frost·y** ['frɔsti] or ['frɑsti] adj (-ier; -iest) brinato; (hair) canuto; (fig) gelido

**froth** [frɔθ] or [frɑθ] s schiuma; (fig) frivolezza || intr schiumare; (at the mouth) avere la schiuma

**froth·y** ['frɔθi] or ['frɑθi] adj (-ier; -iest) spumoso; frivolo

**froward** ['frowərd] adj indocile

**frown** [fraun] s aggrottare m delle ciglia; (of disapproval) cipiglio || intr aggrottare le ciglia; **to frown at** or **on** disapprovare

**frows·y** or **frowz·y** ['frauzi] adj (-ier; -iest) sporco; puzzolente

**fro'zen foods'** ['frozən] spl cibi congelati; cibi surgelati

**frugal** ['frugəl] adj parsimonioso; (in food and drink) frugale

**fruit** [frut] adj (tree) fruttifero; (dish) da frutta || s (such as apple) frutto; (collectively) frutta, e.g., **I like fruit** mi piace la frutta; (fig) frutto

**fruit' cake'** s torta con noci e canditi

**fruit' cup'** s macedonia di frutta

**fruit' dish'** s fruttiera, portafrutta m

**fruit' fly'** s moscerino del vino

**fruitful** ['frutfəl] adj fruttuoso

**fruition** [fru'ɪʃən] s realizzazione; **to come to fruition** giungere a buon fine

**fruit' jar'** s vaso da frutta

**fruit' juice'** s sugo or spremuta di frutta

**fruitless** ['frutlɪs] adj infruttuoso

**fruit' sal'ad** s macedonia di frutta

**fruit' stand'** s bancarella da fruttivendolo

**fruit' store'** s negozio di frutta

**frumpish** ['frʌmpɪʃ] adj trasandato

**frustrate** ['frʌstret] tr frustrare

**fry** [fraɪ] s (fries) fritto || v (pret & pp fried) tr & intr friggere

**fry'ing pan'** s padella; **out of the frying pan into the fire** dalla padella nella brace

**fudge** [fʌdʒ] s dolce m di cioccolato

**fuel** ['fju·əl] s combustibile m; (fig) cibo || v (pret & pp fueled or fuelled; ger fueling or fuelling) tr rifornire di carburante || intr rifornirsi di carburante

**fuel' cell'** s cellula elettrogena

**fu'el oil'** s nafta, olio pesante

**fu'el tank'** s serbatoio del carburante

**fugitive** ['fjudʒɪtɪv] adj & s fuggiasco, fuggitivo

**fugue** [fjug] s (mus) fuga

**ful·crum** ['fʌlkrəm] s (-crums or -cra [krə]) fulcro

**fulfill** [ful'fɪl] tr (to carry out) eseguire; (an obligation) mantenere; (to bring to an end) completare

**fulfillment** [ful'fɪlmənt] s adempimento; realizzazione

**full** [ful] adj pieno; (speed) tutto; (garment) ampio; (voice) spiegato; (of food) sazio; (member) effettivo; **full of aches and pains** pieno d'acciacchi; **full of fun** divertentissimo; **full of play** pieno di vita || s pieno; colmo; in full per esteso, in pieno; **to the full** completamente || adv completamente; **full many (a)** moltissimi; **full well** perfettamente || tr follare

**full-blooded** ['ful'blʌdɪd] adj vigoroso; purosangue

**full-blown** ['ful'blon] adj completamente sbocciato; maturo

**full-bodied** ['ful'bɑdɪd] adj forte, ricco

**full' dress'** s vestito da sera; (mil) tenuta di gala, alta uniforme

**full-faced** ['ful'fest] adj paffuto; (view) intero; (typ) grassetto

**full-fledged** ['ful'fledʒd] adj completamente sviluppato; vero, autentico

**full-grown** ['ful'gron] adj completamente sviluppato, adulto

**full' house'** s (theat) piena; (poker) full m

**full'-length' mir'ror** s specchiera

**full'-length mo'vie** s lungometraggio

**full' moon'** s luna piena

**full' name'** s nome m e cognome m

**full'-page'** adj di tutta una pagina

**full' pow'ers** spl pieni poteri

**full' sail'** adv a vele spiegate

**full'-scale'** adj in grandezza naturale; completo

**full-sized** ['ful'saɪzd] adj in grandezza naturale

**full' speed'** adv a tutta velocità

**full' stop'** s fermata; (gram) punto

**full' swing'** s piena attività

**full' tilt'** adv a tutta forza

**full'-time'** adj a orario completo

**fully** ['fuli] or ['fulli] adv completamente, del tutto

**fulsome** ['fulsəm] or ['fʌlsəm] adj basso, volgare; nauseante

**fumble** ['fʌmbəl] tr (a ball) lasciar cadere || intr titubare; andare a tentoni; (in one's pocket) cercare alla cieca

**fume** [fjum] s fumo, vapore m, esalazione || tr affumicare || intr fumare, esalare fumo; (to show anger) irritarsi

**fumigate** ['fjumɪ‚get] tr fumigare

**fumigation** [‚fjumɪ'geʃən] s fumigazione

**fun** [fʌn] s divertimento, spasso; **to be fun** essere divertente; **to have fun** divertirsi; **to make fun of** prendersi gioco di

**function** ['fʌŋkʃən] s funzione || intr funzionare, marciare, camminare

**functional** ['fʌŋkʃənəl] adj funzionale

**functionalism** ['fʌŋkʃənəl‚ɪzəm] s funzionalismo

**functionar·y** ['fʌŋkʃə‚nɛri] s (-ies) funzionario

**fund** [fʌnd] s fondo; (of knowledge) suppellettile f || tr (debts) consolidare
**fundamental** [ˌfʌndə'mentəl] adj fondamentale || s fondamento
**fundamentalist** [ˌfʌndə'mentəlɪst] adj & s scritturale m
**funeral** ['fjunərəl] adj funebre, funerario || s funerale m, trasporto funebre; **it's not my funeral** (slang) non sono affari miei
**fu'neral direc'tor** s imprenditore m di pompe funebri
**fu'neral home'** or **par'lor** s impresa di pompe funebri
**fu'neral serv'ice** s ufficio dei defunti
**funereal** [fju'nɪrɪ-əl] adj funebre
**fungous** ['fʌŋgəs] adj fungoso
**fungus** ['fʌŋgəs] s (funguses or fungi ['fʌndʒaɪ]) fungo
**funicular** [fju'nɪkjələr] adj & s funicolare f
**funk** [fʌŋk] s (coll) paura; (coll) codardo; **in a funk** (coll) con una paura matta
**fun•nel** ['fʌnəl] s imbuto; (smokestack) fumaiolo; (for ventilation) manica a vento || v (pret & pp -neled or -nelled; ger -neling or -nelling) tr incanalare
**funnies** ['fʌniz] spl pagine fpl fumetti
**fun•ny** ['fʌni] adj (-nier; -niest) comico, buffo; (coll) strano; **to strike as funny** parere strano or buffo a
**fun'ny bone'** s osso rabbioso (del gomito); **to strike s.o.'s funny bone** far ridere qlcu
**fur** [fʌr] s pelo; (garment) pelliccia; (on the tongue) patina
**furbelow** ['fʌrbə‚lo] s falpalà m
**furbish** ['fʌrbɪʃ] tr lustrare; mettere a nuovo; **to furbish up** rinfrescare
**furious** ['fjurɪ-əs] adj furioso
**furl** [fʌrl] tr (a flag) incazzottare; (naut) raccogliere, strangolare
**fur-lined** ['fʌr‚laɪnd] adj foderato di pelliccia
**furlong** ['fʌrlɔŋ] or ['fʌrlɑŋ] s un ottavo di miglio terrestre
**furlough** ['fʌrlo] s licenza || tr licenziare
**furnace** ['fʌrnɪs] s fornace f; (to heat a house) caldaia del calorifero
**furnish** ['fʌrnɪʃ] tr fornire; ammobiliare
**furnishings** ['fʌrnɪʃɪŋz] spl mobilia; (things to wear) accessori mpl da uomo
**furniture** ['fʌrnɪtʃər] s mobili mpl, mobilia; (naut) attrezzatura; **a piece of furniture** un mobile

**fur'ni•ture deal'er** s mobiliere m
**furor** ['fjurɔr] s furore m
**furrier** ['fʌrɪ-ər] s pellicciaio
**furrier•y** ['fʌrɪ-əri] s (-ies) pellicceria
**furrow** ['fʌro] s solco || tr solcare
**further** ['fʌrðər] adj più lontano; ulteriore || adv oltre; più; inoltre || tr favorire, incoraggiare
**furtherance** ['fʌrðərəns] s avanzamento, incoraggiamento
**furthermore** ['fʌrðər‚mor] adv inoltre
**furthest** ['fʌrðɪst] adj (il) più lontano || adv al massimo
**furtive** ['fʌrtɪv] adj furtivo
**fu•ry** ['fjuri] s (-ries) furia
**furze** [fʌrz] s ginestra spinosa
**fuse** [fjuz] s (for igniting an explosive) miccia; (for detonating an explosive) spoletta; (elec) fusibile m; **to burn out a fuse** bruciare un fusibile || tr fondere; (elec) saltare
**fuse' box'** s valvoliera
**fuselage** ['fjuzəlɪdʒ] or [ˌfjuzə'laʒ] s fusoliera
**fusible** ['fjuzɪbəl] adj fusibile
**fusillade** [ˌfjuzɪ'led] s fucileria; (fig) gragnola || tr attaccare con fuoco di fucileria
**fusion** ['fjuʒən] s fusione
**fuss** [fʌs] s agitazione inutile; (coll) alterco per nulla; **to make a fuss** accogliere festosamente; fare molte storie; **to make a fuss over** aver un alterco su || tr disturbare || intr agitarsi per un nonnulla
**fuss•y** ['fʌsi] adj (-ier; -iest) (person) pignolo, meticoloso; (object) carico di fronzoli; (writing) complicato
**fustian** ['fʌstʃən] s fustagno; (fig) verbosità f, magniloquenza
**fust•y** ['fʌsti] adj (-ier; -iest) ammuffito, che sa di muffa; antico, sorpassato
**futile** ['fjutɪl] adj (unproductive) sterile; (unimportant) futile
**futili•ty** [fju'tɪlɪti] s (-ties) sterilità f; futilità f
**future** ['fjutʃər] adj futuro || s futuro; **futures** contratto con consegna a termine; **in the near future** nel prossimo avvenire
**fuze** [fjuz] s (for igniting an explosive) miccia; (for detonating an explosive) spoletta; (elec) fusibile m || tr innestare la spoletta a
**fuzz** [fʌz] s lanugine f, peluria; (in corners) polvere f; (slang) poliziotto; (slang) polizia
**fuzz•y** ['fʌzi] adj (-ier; -iest) lanuginoso; coperto di polvere; (indistinct) confuso

# G

**G, g** [dʒi] s settima lettera dell'alfabeto inglese
**gab** [gæb] s (coll) parlantina || v (pret & pp gabbed; ger gabbing) intr (coll) chiacchierare
**gabardine** ['gæbər‚din] s gabardine f
**gabble** ['gæbəl] s barbugliamento || intr barbugliare

**gable** ['gebəl] s (archit) timpano
**ga'ble roof'** s tetto a due falde, tetto a capanna
**gad** [gæd] v (pret & pp gadded; ger gadding) intr bighellonare
**gad'about'** adj ozioso || s vagabondo, bighellone m; fannullone m
**gad'fly'** s (-flies) tafano, moscone m

**gadget** ['gædʒɪt] *s* congegno, dispositivo, macchinetta

**Gaelic** ['gelɪk] *adj & s* gaelico

**gaff** [gæf] *s* arpione *m;* (naut) picco; **to stand the gaff** (slang) aver pazienza

**gag** [gæg] *s* bavaglio; (*joke*) barzelletta; (theat) battuta improvvisata ‖ *v* (*pret & pp* **gagged;** *ger* **gagging**) *tr* imbavagliare; soffocare ‖ *intr* sentirsi venire la nausea

**gage** [gedʒ] *s* (*pledge*) pegno; (*challenge*) sfida

**gaie·ty** ['ge·ɪti] *s* (**-ties**) gaiezza

**gaily** ['geli] *adv* allegramente

**gain** [gen] *s* profitto; (*increase*) aumento ‖ *tr* guadagnare; (*to reach*) raggiungere; (*altitude*) prendere ‖ *intr* (*said of a patient*) migliorare; (*said of a watch*) correre; **to gain on** guadagnar terreno su; sorpassare

**gainful** ['genfəl] *adj* rimunerativo

**gain'say'** *v* (*pret & pp* **-said** [,sed] or [,sed]) *tr* disdire, misconoscere; negare

**gait** [get] *s* portamento, andatura

**gaiter** ['getər] *s* ghetta

**gala** ['gælə] or ['gelə] *adj* di gala ‖ *s* gala *m & f,* festa

**galax·y** ['gæləksi] *s* (**-ies**) galassia

**gale** [gel] *s* (*of wind*) bufera; (*of laughter*) scoppio; **to weather the gale** resistere alla tempesta

**gall** [gɔl] *s* fiele *m;* bile *f;* cistifellea; scorticatura; (*gallnut*) galla; (*audacity*) (coll) faccia tosta ‖ *tr* irritare ‖ *intr* irritarsi; (naut) logorarsi

**gallant** ['gælənt] or [gə'lænt] *adj* galante ‖ ['gælənt] *adj* (*brave*) valoroso; (*grand*) magnifico; (*showy*) festivo ‖ *s* prode *m;* (*man attentive to women*) galante *m*

**gallant·ry** ['gæləntri] *s* (**-ries**) galanteria; valore *m*

**gall' blad'der** *s* vescichetta biliare

**gall'-blad'der attack'** *s* travaso di bile

**galleon** ['gæli·ən] *s* galeone *m*

**galler·y** ['gæləri] *s* (**-ies**) galleria; tribuna; (*cheapest seats in theater*) loggione *m*

**galley** ['gæli] *s* (*vessel*) galera; (*kitchen*) (aer) cucina; (*kitchen*) (naut) cambusa; (*galley proof*) (typ) bozza in colonna; (*tray*) (typ) vantaggio

**gal'ley proof'** *s* bozza in colonna

**gal'ley slave'** *s* galeotto

**Gallic** ['gælɪk] *adj* gallo, gallico

**galling** ['gɔlɪŋ] *adj* irritante

**gallivant** ['gælɪ,vænt] *intr* andare a spasso; fare il galante

**gall'nut'** *s* galla

**gallon** ['gælən] *s* gallone *m*

**galloon** [gə'lun] *s* gallone *m,* nastro

**gallop** ['gæləp] *s* galoppo; **at a gallop** al galoppo ‖ *tr* far galoppare ‖ *intr* galoppare

**gal·lows** ['gæloz] *s* (**-lows** or **-lowses**) forca; (min) castelletto

**gal'lows bird'** *s* (coll) remo di galera, pendaglio da forca

**gall'stone'** *s* calcolo biliare

**galore** [gə'lor] *adv* in abbondanza

**galosh** [gə'lɑʃ] *s* stivaletto di gomma

**galvanize** ['gælvə,naɪz] *tr* galvanizzare

**gal'vanized i'ron** *s* ferro zincato

**gambit** ['gæmbɪt] *s* gambetto

**gamble** ['gæmbəl] *s* azzardo; (*game*) gioco d'azzardo ‖ *tr* giocare; **to gamble away** giocarsi ‖ *intr* giocare d'azzardo; (com) speculare

**gambler** ['gæmblər] *s* giocatore *m;* speculatore *m*

**gambling** ['gæmblɪŋ] *s* gioco (d'azzardo)

**gam'bling den'** *s* bisca

**gam'bling house'** *s* casa da gioco

**gam·bol** ['gæmbəl] *s* salto, capriola ‖ *v* (*pret & pp* **-boled** or **-bolled;** *ger* **-boling** or **-bolling**) *intr* saltare, far capriole

**gambrel** ['gæmbrəl] *s* garretto

**gam'brel roof'** *s* tetto a mansarda

**game** [gem] *adj* da caccia; coraggioso; (*leg*) (coll) zoppo; (coll) pronto ‖ *s* (*amusement*) gioco; (*contest*) partita; (*any sport*) sport *m;* (*wild animals hunted*) selvaggina; (*any pursuit*) attività *f;* (*object of pursuit*) bersaglio; (bridge) manche *f;* **the game is up** il gioco è fallito; **to make game of** farsi gioco di; **to play the game** giocare onestamente

**game' bag'** *s* carniere *m*

**game'cock'** *s* gallo da combattimento

**game'keep'er** *s* guardacaccia *m*

**game' of chance'** *s* gioco d'azzardo

**game' preserve'** *s* bandita di caccia

**game' war'den** *s* guardacaccia *m*

**gamut** ['gæmət] *s* (mus, fig) gamma

**gam·y** ['gemi] *adj* (**-ier; -iest**) coraggioso; (culin) che sa di selvatico

**gander** ['gændər] *s* papero, oca

**gang** [gæŋ] *adj* multiplo ‖ *s* (*of workers*) banga; (*of thugs*) cricca ‖ *intr*—**to gang up** riunirsi; **to gang up against** or **on** (coll) gettarsi insieme contro

**gangling** ['gæŋglɪŋ] *adj* dinoccolato

**gangli·on** ['gæŋglɪ·ən] *s* (**-ons** or **-a** [ə]) ganglio

**gang'plank'** *s* palanca, plancia

**gangrene** ['gæŋgrin] *s* cancrena ‖ *tr* far andare in cancrena ‖ *intr* andare in cancrena

**gangster** ['gæŋstər] *s* gangster *m*

**gang'way'** *s* (*passageway*) corridoio; (*gangplank*) passerella, scalandrone *m;* (*in ship's side*) barcarizzo ‖ *interj* lasciar passare!

**gan·try** ['gæntri] *s* (**-tries**) (*of crane*) cavalletto; (rr) ponte *m* delle segnalazioni; (rok) piattaforma verticale, torre *f* di lancio

**gap** [gæp] *s* (*pass*) passo; (*in a wall*) breccia; (*interval*) lacuna; (*between two points of view*) abisso; (mach) gioco

**gape** [gep] or [gæp] *s* apertura; (*yawn*) sbadiglio; sguardo di meraviglia ‖ *intr* stare a bocca aperta; **to gape at** guardare a bocca aperta

**garage** [gə'rɑʒ] *s* rimessa

**garb** [gɑrb] *s* veste *f* ‖ *tr* vestire

**garbage** ['gɑrbɪdʒ] *s* pattume *m,* immondizia, immondizie *fpl*

**gar'bage can'** *s* portaimmondizie *m*

**gar'bage collec'tor** *s* spazzaturaio, spazzino, netturbino

**garble** ['gɑrbəl] *tr* falsare, mutilare

**garden** ['gɑrdən] *s* (*of vegetables*) orto; (*of flowers*) giardino

**gardener** ['gɑrdnər] *s* (*of vegetables*) ortolano; (*of flowers*) giardiniere *m*

**gardenia** [gɑr'dinɪ·ə] *s* gardenia

**gardening** ['gɑrdnɪŋ] *s* orticoltura; giardinaggio

**gar'den par'ty** *s* trattenimento in giardino

**gargle** ['gɑrgəl] *s* gargarismo ‖ *intr* gargarizzare

**gargoyle** ['gɑrgɔɪl] *s* doccione *m*, gargolla

**garish** ['gerɪʃ] or ['gærɪʃ] *adj* appariscente; abbagliante

**garland** ['gɑrlənd] *s* ghirlanda ‖ *tr* inghirlandare

**garlic** ['gɑrlɪk] *s* aglio

**garment** ['gɑrmənt] *s* capo di vestiario

**gar'ment bag'** *s* tessilsacco

**garner** ['gɑrnər] *tr* mettere in granaio; (*to get*) acquistarsi; (*to hoard*) incettare

**garnet** ['gɑrnɪt] *adj* & *s* granata

**garnish** ['gɑrnɪʃ] *s* guarnizione; ‖ *tr* guarnire; (law) sequestrare

**garret** ['gærɪt] *s* sottotetto, soffitta

**garrison** ['gærɪsən] *s* guarnigione, presidio ‖ *tr* presidiare

**garrote** [gə'rɑt] or [gə'rot] *s* strangolamento; garrotta ‖ *tr* strangolare; giustiziare con la garrotta

**garrulous** ['gærələs] or ['gærjələs] *adj* garrulo, loquace

**garter** ['gɑrtər] *s* giarrettiera

**gas** [gæs] *s* gas *m*; (coll) benzina; (slang) successo; (slang) chiacchiere *fpl* ‖ *v* (*pret* & *pp* **gassed**; *ger* **gassing**) *tr* fornire di gas; (mil) gassare; (slang) divertire ‖ *intr* emettere gas; (slang) chiacchierare; **to gas up** fare il pieno

**gas'bag'** *s* involucro per il gas; (coll) chiacchierone *m*

**gas' burn'er** *s* becco a gas; (*on a stove*) fornello a gas

**Gascony** ['gæskəni] *s* la Guascogna

**gaseous** ['gæsɪ·əs] *adj* gassoso

**gas' fit'ter** *s* gassista *m*

**gash** [gæʃ] *s* sfregio ‖ *tr* sfregiare

**gas' heat'** *s* calefazione a gas

**gas'hold'er** *s* gassometro

**gasi·fy** ['gæsɪ,faɪ] *v* (*pret* & *pp* **-fied**) *tr* gassificare ‖ *intr* gassificarsi

**gas' jet'** *s* fornello a gas; fiamma

**gasket** ['gæskɪt] *s* guarnizione

**gas'light'** *s* luce *f* del gas

**gas' main'** *s* tubatura principale del gas

**gas' mask'** *s* maschera antigas

**gas' me'ter** *s* contatore *m* del gas

**gasoline** ['gæsə,lin] or [,gæsə'lin] *s* benzina

**gas'oline' deal'er** *s* benzinaio

**gas'oline' pump'** *s* colonnetta, distributore *m* di benzina

**gasp** [gæsp] or [gɑsp] *s* respirazione affannosa; (*of death*) rantolo ‖ *tr* dire affannosamente ‖ *intr* boccheggiare

**gas' range'** *s* cucina a gas, fornello a gas

**gas'-sta'tion attend'ant** *s* benzinaio

**gas' stove'** *s* cucina a gas

**gas' tank'** *s* gassometro; (aut) serbatoio di benzina

**gastric** ['gæstrɪk] *adj* gastrico

**gastronomy** [gæs'trɑnəmi] *s* gastronomia

**gas' works'** *s* officina del gas

**gate** [get] *s* porta; (*in fence or wall*) cancello; (*of sluice*) saracinesca; (*in an airport or station*) uscita; (rr) barriera; (sports, theat) incasso totale; **to crash the gate** (coll) fare il portoghese

**gate'keep'er** *s* portiere *m*; (rr) guardiabarriere *m*

**gate'way'** *s* passaggio, entrata

**gather** ['gæðər] *tr* raccogliere, cogliere; (*news*) raccapezzare; (*dust*) coprirsi di; (*e.g., a shawl*) avvolgere; (*speed*) aumentare (di); concludere, dedurre; (*signatures*) (bb) riunire; (sew) increspare ‖ *intr* riunirsi; raccogliersi; accumularsi

**gathering** ['gæðərɪŋ] *s* riunione; (bb) raccolta e piegatura; (pathol) ascesso; (sew) pieghettatura

**gaud·y** ['gɔdi] *adj* (**-ier; -iest**) chiassoso, vistoso

**gauge** [gedʒ] *s* misura; calibro; (*for liquids*) indicatore *m* di livello; (*of carpenter*) graffietto; indice *m*; diametro; (aut) spia; (rr) scartamento ‖ *tr* misurare; calibrare; (naut) stazzare

**Gaul** [gɔl] *s* gallo

**gaunt** [gɔnt] or [gɑnt] *adj* magro, emaciato; (*e.g., landscape*) desolato

**gauntlet** ['gɔntlɪt] or ['gɑntlɪt] *s* guanto; guanto di ferro; guantone *m*, manopola; **to run the gauntlet** (fig) esporsi alla critica; **to take up the gauntlet** raccogliere il guanto; **to throw down the gauntlet** gettare il guanto

**gauze** [gɔz] *s* garza

**gavel** ['gævəl] *s* martello, martelletto

**gavotte** [gə'vɑt] *s* gavotta

**gawk** [gɔk] *s* sciocco ‖ *intr* guardare a bocca aperta

**gawk·y** ['gɔki] *adj* (**-ier; -iest**) sgraziato, goffo

**gay** [ge] *adj* gaio; brillante; dissipato; (slang) omosessuale

**gaye·ty** ['ge·ɪti] *s* (**-ties**) gaiezza

**gaze** [gez] *s* sguardo fisso ‖ *intr* fissare lo sguardo

**gazelle** [gə'zɛl] *s* gazzella

**gazette** [gə'zɛt] *s* gazzetta

**gazetteer** [,gæzə'tɪr] *s* dizionario geografico

**gear** [gɪr] *s* utensili *mpl*, attrezzi *mpl*; (*mechanism*) meccanismo, dispositivo; (aut) marcia; (mach) ingranaggio **out of gear** disingranato; (fig) disturbato; **to throw into gear** ingranare; **to throw out of gear** disingranare; (fig) disturbare ‖ *tr* adattare ‖ *intr* adattarsi

**gear' box'** *s* scatola del cambio

**gear'shift'** *s* cambio di velocità

**gear'shift lev'er** *s* leva del cambio
**gear'wheel'** *s* ruota dentata
**gee** [dʒi] *interj* oh!; che bellezza!; **gee up!** (*command to a draft animal*) arri!
**Gei'ger count'er** ['gaɪgər] *s* contatore *m* Geiger
**gel** [dʒɛl] *s* gel *m* ‖ *v* (*pret & pp* **gelled;** *ger* **gelling**) *intr* gelatinizzarsi
**gelatine** ['dʒɛlətɪn] *s* gelatina
**geld** [gɛld] *v* (*pret & pp* **gelded** or **gelt** [gɛlt]) *tr* castrare
**gem** [dʒɛm] *s* gemma, gioia
**Gemini** ['dʒɛmɪ ˌnaɪ] *spl* i Gemelli
**gender** ['dʒɛndər] *s* (gram) genere *m;* (coll) sesso
**gene** [dʒin] *s* (biol) gene *m*
**genealo·gy** [ ˌdʒɛnɪ'ælədʒi] or [ ˌdʒini-'ælədʒi] *s* (**-gies**) genealogia
**general** ['dʒɛnərəl] *adj & s* generale *m*
**gen'eral deliv'ery** *s* fermo in posta, fermo posta *m*
**generalissi·mo** [ ˌdʒɛnərə'lɪsɪmo] *s* (**-mos**) generalissimo
**generali·ty** [ ˌdʒɛnə'rælɪti] *s* (**-ties**) generalità *f*
**generalize** ['dʒɛnərə ˌlaɪz] *tr & intr* generalizzare
**generally** ['dʒɛnərəli] *adv* in genere, generalmente
**gen'eral part'ner** *s* accomandatario
**gen'eral practi'tioner** *s* medico generico
**generalship** ['dʒɛnərəl ˌʃɪp] *s* generalato; strategia, abilità *f* militare; abilità amministrativa
**gen'eral staff'** *s* stato maggiore
**generate** ['dʒɛnə ˌret] *tr* (*offspring; electricity*) generare; (math) originare
**gen'erat'ing sta'tion** *s* centrale elettrica
**generation** [ ˌdʒɛnə're ʃən] *s* generazione
**generative** ['dʒɛnə ˌretɪv] *adj* generativo
**gen'erative gram'mar** *s* grammatica generativa
**generator** ['dʒɛnə ˌretər] *s* generatore *m;* (elec) generatrice *f*
**generic** [dʒɪ'nɛrɪk] *adj* generico
**generous** ['dʒɛnərəs] *adj* generoso; abbondante, copioso
**gene·sis** ['dʒɛnɪsɪs] *s* (**-ses** [ ˌsiz]) genesi *f* ‖ **Genesis** *s* (Bib) Genesi *m*
**genetic** [dʒɪ'nɛtɪk] *adj* genetico ‖ **genetics** *ssg* genetica
**Geneva** [dʒɪ'nivə] *s* Ginevra
**Genevan** [dʒɪ'nivən] *adj & s* ginevrino
**genial** ['dʒinɪ·əl] *adj* affabile, geniale
**genie** ['dʒini] *s* genio
**genital** ['dʒɛnɪtəl] *adj* genitale ‖ **genitals** *spl* genitali *mpl*
**genitive** ['dʒɛnɪtɪv] *adj & s* genitivo
**genius** ['dʒinjəs] or ['dʒini·əs] *s* (**geniuses**) genio ‖ *s* (**genii**) ['dʒini- ˌaɪ] (*spirit; deity*) genio
**Genoa** ['dʒɛno·ə] *s* Genova
**genocide** ['dʒɛnə ˌsaɪd] *s* (*act*) genocidio; (*person*) genocida *mf*
**Geno·ese** [ ˌdʒɛno'iz] *adj* genovese ‖ *s* (**-ese**) genovese *mf*
**genre** ['ʒɑnrə] *adj* (*e.g., painting*) di genere ‖ *s* genere *m*

**genteel** [dʒɛn'til] *adj* (*well-bred*) beneducato; (*affectedly polite*) manieroso, manierato
**gentian** ['dʒɛnʃən] *s* genziana
**gentile** ['dʒɛntɪl] or ['dʒɛntaɪl] *adj* gentilizio ‖ ['dʒɛntaɪl] *adj & s* non circonciso; non ebreo; cristiano; (*pagan*) gentile
**gentili·ty** [dʒɛn'tɪlɪti] *s* (**-ties**) distinzione, raffinatezza
**gentle** ['dʒɛntəl] *adj* (*e.g., manner*) gentile; (*e.g., wind*) dolce, soave; (*wellborn*) bennato; (*tap*) leggero
**gen'tle·folk'** *s* gente *f* per bene
**gen'tle·man** *s* (**-men**) signore *m;* (*attendant to a person of high rank*) gentiluomo; (*well-mannered man*) gentleman *m*
**gen'tleman in wait'ing** *s* gentiluomo di camera
**gentlemanly** ['dʒɛntəlmənli] *adj* signorile
**gen'tleman of the road'** *s* brigante *m;* vagabondo
**gen'tlemen's agree'ment** *s* accordo fondato sulla buona fede
**gen'tle sex'** *s* gentil sesso
**gentry** ['dʒɛntri] *s* gente *f* per bene
**genuine** ['dʒɛnju·ɪn] *adj* genuino
**genus** ['dʒinəs] *s* (**genera** ['dʒɛnərə] or **genuses**) genere *m*
**geographer** [dʒɪ'ɑgrəfər] *s* geografo
**geographic(al)** [ ˌdʒɪ·ə'græfɪk(əl)] *adj* geografico
**geogra·phy** [dʒɪ'ɑgrəfi] *s* (**-phies**) geografia
**geologic(al)** [ ˌdʒɪ·ə'lɑdʒɪk(əl)] *adj* geologico
**geologist** [dʒɪ'ɑlədʒɪst] *s* geologo
**geolo·gy** [dʒɪ'ɑlədʒi] *s* (**-gies**) geologia
**geometric(al)** [ ˌdʒɪ·ə'mɛtrɪk(əl)] *adj* geometrico
**geometrician** [dʒɪ ˌɑmɪ'trɪʃən] *s* geometra *mf*
**geome·try** [dʒɪ'ɑmɪtri] *s* (**-tries**) geometria
**George** [dʒɔrdʒ] *s* Giorgio
**geranium** [dʒɪ'renɪ·əm] *s* geranio
**geriatrics** [ ˌdʒɛrɪ'ætrɪks] *ssg* geriatria
**germ** [dʒʌrm] *s* germe *m*
**German** ['dʒʌrmən] *adj & s* tedesco
**germane** [dʒər'men] *adj* pertinente
**Germanize** ['dʒʌrmə ˌnaɪz] *tr* germanizzare
**Ger'man mea'sles** *s* rosolia, rubeola
**Ger'man sil'ver** *s* alpacca
**Germany** ['dʒʌrməni] *s* la Germania
**germ' car'rier** *s* portatore *m* di germi
**germ' cell'** *s* cellula germinale
**germicidal** [ ˌdʒʌrmɪ'saɪdəl] *adj* germicida
**germicide** ['dʒʌrmɪ ˌsaɪd] *s* germicida *m*
**germinate** ['dʒʌrmɪ ˌnet] *intr* germinare
**germ' war'fare** *s* guerra batteriologica
**gerontology** [ ˌdʒɛrɑn'tɑlədʒi] *s* gerontologia
**gerund** ['dʒɛrənd] *s* gerundio
**gestation** [dʒɛs'teʃən] *s* gestazione
**gesticulate** [dʒɛs'tɪkjə ˌlet] *intr* gesticolare

**gesticulation** [dʒɛs͵tɪkjə'leʃən] *s* gesticolazione

**gesture** ['dʒɛstʃər] *s* gesto || *intr* gestire, gesticolare

**get** [gɛt] *v* (*pret* **got** [gɑt]; *pp* **got** or **gotten** ['gɑtən]; *ger* **getting**) *tr* ottenere; ricevere; prendere; andare a comprare; procacciare; riportare; procurarsi; riscuotere; guadagnare; **to get across** far capire; **to get back** riacquistare; **to get down** staccare; (*to swallow*) tranguggiare; **to get off** togliere, cavare; **to get s.o. to** + *inf* indurre che qlcu + *subj*; **to get done** far fare; **to have got** (coll) avere; **to have got to** + *inf* (coll) dovere + *inf* || *intr* (*to become*) diventare, farsi; (*to arrive*) arrivare, venire; **to get out** (*said of a convalescent*) alzarsi; **to get along** andarsene; andare avanti; tirare avanti, giostrare; aver successo; **to get along in years** essere avanti con gli anni; **to get along with** andare d'accordo con; **to get angry** arrabbiarsi; **to get around** uscire; divulgarsi; rigirare; **to get away** scappare, darsela a gambe; **to get away with s.th** scappare con qlco; (coll) farla franca; **to get back** ritornare; ricuperare; **to get back at** (coll) vendicarsi di; **to get behind** rimanere indietro; (*to support*) appoggiare, patrocinare; **to get better** migliorare; **to get by** passare oltre; (*to succeed*) arrivare a farcela; passare inosservato; **to get even with** rifarsi con, prendersi la rivincita con; **to get going** mettersi in moto; **to get in** entrare; rientrare; arrivare; **to get in deeper and deeper** cacciarsi nei pasticci; **to get in with** diventare amico di; **to get married** sposarsi; **to get off** andarsene; smontare da; **to get old** invecchiare; **to get on** andare avanti; andare d'accordo; **to get out** uscire; propagarsi; **to get out of** (*a car*) uscire da; (*trouble*) trarsi di; **to get out of the way** togliersi di mezzo; **to get run over** essere investito; **to get through** finire; arrivare; farsi capire; **to get to be** finire per essere; **to get under way** mettersi in cammino; **to get up** alzarsi; **to not get over it** (coll) non arrivare a rassegnarsi

**get'a·way'** *s* fuga; (sports) partenza

**get'-to·geth'er** *s* riunione, crocchio

**get'up'** *s* (coll) stile *m*, presentazione; (coll) costume *m*, abbigliamento

**gewgaw** ['gjugɔ] *s* cianfrusaglia

**geyser** ['gaɪzər] *s* geyser *m*

**ghast·ly** ['gæstli] or ['gɑstli] *adj* (**-lier**; **-liest**) orribile, orrendo; spettrale

**gherkin** ['gʌrkɪn] *s* cetriolino

**ghet·to** ['gɛto] *s* (**-tos** or **-toes**) ghetto

**ghost** [gost] *s* spettro, fantasma *m*; **not a ghost of** nemmeno l'ombra di; **to give up the ghost** rendere l'anima

**ghost·ly** ['gostli] *adj* (**-lier**; **-liest**) spettrale, fantomatico

**ghost' sto'ry** *s* storia di fantasmi

**ghost' town'** *s* città morta

**ghost' writ'er** *s* collaboratore anonimo

**ghoul** [gul] *s* spirito necrofago; ladro di tombe

**ghoulish** ['gulɪʃ] *adj* demoniaco, macabro

**GI** ['dʒi'aɪ] (letterword) (**General Issue**) *s* (**GI's**) soldato degli Stati Uniti

**giant** ['dʒaɪ·ənt] *adj* & *s* gigante *m*

**giantess** ['dʒaɪ·əntɪs] *s* gigantessa

**gibberish** ['dʒɪbərɪʃ] or ['gɪbərɪʃ] *s* linguaggio inintelligibile

**gibbet** ['dʒɪbɪt] *s* forca || *tr* impiccare sulla forca; (*to hold up to scorn*) mettere alla berlina

**gibe** [dʒaɪb] *s* scherno, frecciata || *intr* schernire; **to gibe at** beffarsi di

**giblets** ['dʒɪblɪts] *spl* rigaglie *fpl*

**giddiness** ['gɪdɪnɪs] *s* vertigine *f*; frivolezza

**gid·dy** ['gɪdi] *adj* (**-dier**; **-diest**) vertiginoso; preso dalle vertigini; frivolo

**gift** [gɪft] *s* regalo; (*natural ability*) dono, dote *f*; (*for Christmas*) strenna

**gifted** ['gɪftɪd] *adj* dotato

**gift' horse' s**—**never look a gift horse in the mouth** a caval donato non si guarda in bocca

**gift' of gab'** *s* (coll) facondia; **to have the gift of gab** (coll) avere la lingua sciolta

**gift' pack'age** *s* pacco-dono

**gift' shop'** *s* negozio di regali

**gift'-wrap'** *v* (*pret* & *pp* **-wrapped;** *ger* **-wrapping**) *tr* incartare in carta speciale per regali

**gigantic** [dʒaɪ'gæntɪk] *adj* gigantesco

**giggle** ['gɪgəl] *s* risolino || *intr* ridere scioccamente, ridacchiare

**gigo·lo** ['dʒɪgə͵lo] *s* (**-los**) gigolo

**gild** [gɪld] *v* (*pret* & *pp* **gilded** or **gilt** [gɪlt]) *tr* dorare, indorare

**gilding** ['gɪldɪŋ] *s* doratura

**gill** [gɪl] *s* (*of fish*) branchia || [dʒɪl] *s* quarto di pinta

**gilt** [gɪlt] *adj* & *s* dorato

**gilt-edged** ['gɪlt͵ɛdʒd] *adj* a bordo dorato; di primissima qualità

**gimcrack** ['dʒɪm͵kræk] *adj* di nessun valore || *s* cianfrusaglia

**gimlet** ['gɪmlɪt] *s* succhiello

**gimmick** ['gɪmɪk] *s* (slang) trucco

**gin** [dʒɪn] *s* (*liquor*) gin *m*; (*trap*) trappola; (mach) arganello; (tex) sgranatrice *f* di cotone || *v* (*pret* & *pp* **ginned;** *ger* **ginning**) *tr* ginnare, sgranare

**ginger** ['dʒɪndʒər] *s* zenzero; (coll) energia, vivacità *f*

**gin'ger ale'** *s* gazosa allo zenzero

**gin'ger·bread'** *s* pan di zenzero; ornamento di cattivo gusto

**gingerly** ['dʒɪndʒərli] *adj* cauto || *adv* con cautela

**gin'ger·snap'** *s* biscotto allo zenzero

**gingham** ['gɪŋəm] *s* rigatino

**giraffe** [dʒɪ'ræf] or [dʒɪ'rɑf] *s* giraffa

**girandole** ['dʒɪrən͵dol] *s* girandola

**gird** [gʌrd] *v* (*pret* & *pp* **girt** [gʌrt] or **girded**) *tr* cingere; (*to equip*) dotare; (*to prepare*) preparare; (*to surround*) circondare

**girder** ['gʌrdər] *s* longherina

**girdle** ['gʌrdəl] s reggicalze m, zona, fascetta ‖ tr fasciare; circondare
**girl** [gʌrl] s fanciulla; ragazza
**girl' friend'** s amica, innamorata
**girlhood** ['gʌrlhʊd] s adolescenza, giovinezza
**girlish** ['gʌrlɪʃ] adj fanciullesco; da ragazza
**girl' scout'** s giovane esploratrice f
**girth** [gʌrθ] s circonferenza; fascia; (to hold a saddle) sottopancia m
**gist** [dʒɪst] s sugo, nocciolo, essenza
**give** [gɪv] s elasticità f ‖ v (pret gave [gev]; pp given ['gɪvən]) tr dare; (trouble) causare; (a play) rappresentare; (a speech; fruit; a sigh) fare; to give away distribuire gratuitamente; (to reveal) lasciarsi sfuggire; (a bride) accompagnare all'altare; (coll) tradire; to give back restituire; to give forth (odors) emettere; to give oneself up darsi; to give up cedere; (a position) abbandonare ‖ intr dare; cedere; (said, e.g., of a rope) rompersi; to give in cedere; darsi per vinto; to give out esaurirsi; venir meno; to give up darsi per vinto
**give'-and-take'** s compromesso; conversazione briosa
**give'a·way'** s premio gratuito; rivelazione involontaria; (game) vinciperdi m; (rad, telv) programma m a premi
**given** ['gɪvən] adj dato; **given that** dato che, concesso che
**giv'en name'** s nome m di battesimo
**giver** ['gɪvər] s donatore m; dispensatore m
**gizzard** ['gɪzərd] s magone m
**glacial** ['gleʃəl] adj glaciale
**glacier** ['gleʃər] s ghiacciaio
**glad** [glæd] adj (**gladder; gladdest**) felice, lieto, contento; **to be glad (to)** essere felice (di)
**gladden** ['glædən] tr rallegrare
**glade** [gled] s radura
**glad' hand'** s (coll) accoglienza calorosa
**gladiator** ['glædɪˌetər] s gladiatore m
**gladiola** [ˌglædɪ'olə] or [glə'daɪ·ələ] s gladiolo
**gladly** ['glædli] adv volentieri, di buon grado
**gladness** ['glædnɪs] s contentezza
**glad' rags'** s (coll) panni mpl da festa; (coll) vestito da sera
**glamorous** ['glæmərəs] adj affascinante, attraente
**glamour** ['glæmər] s fascino, malia
**glam'our girl'** s ragazza sci-sci
**glance** [glæns] or [glɑns] s occhiata, guardata; **at first glance** a prima vista ‖ intr lanciare uno sguardo; **to glance at** dare un'occhiata a; **to glance off** sorvolare su; deviare da; **to glance over** dare una scorsa a
**gland** [glænd] s ghiandola
**glanders** ['glændərz] spl morva
**glare** [gler] s splendore m, luce f abbagliante; sguardo minaccioso ‖ intr risplendere; lanciare occhiatacce; **to glare at** fare la faccia feroce a
**glare' ice'** s vetrato

**glaring** ['glerɪŋ] adj risplendente, abbagliante; (look) torvo; evidente
**glass** [glæs] or [glɑs] s vetro; (tumbler) bicchiere m; (mirror) specchio; (glassware) cristalleria; **glasses** occhiali mpl
**glass' blow'er** ['blo·ər] s vetraio
**glass' case'** s vetrinetta
**glass' cut'ter** s tagliatore m di cristallo; (tool) diamante m tagliavetro
**glass' door'** s porta a vetri
**glassful** ['glæsfʊl] or ['glɑsfʊl] s bicchiere m
**glass'house'** s vetreria; (fig) casa di vetro
**glass'ware'** s vetreria, cristalleria
**glass' wool'** s vetro filato
**glass'work'er** s vetraio
**glass'works'** s vetreria, cristalleria
**glass·y** ['glæsi] or ['glɑsi] adj (**·ier; -iest**) vetriato, vetroso
**glaze** [glez] s vernice vitrea; smalto; (of ice) superficie invetriata; (culin) glassa ‖ tr smaltare; invetriare; (culin) glassare
**glazier** ['gleʒər] s vetraio
**gleam** [glim] s barlume m, raggio ‖ intr baluginare
**glean** [glin] tr spigolare, racimolare; (to gather facts) raccogliere
**glee** [gli] s gioia, esultanza
**glee' club'** s società f corale
**glib** [glɪb] adj (**glibber; glibbest**) loquace; (tongue) facile, sciolto
**glide** [glaɪd] s scivolata; (aer) volo a vela, volo planato; (mus) legamento ‖ intr scivolare; (aer) librarsi, planare; **to glide away** scorrere
**glider** ['glaɪdər] s (aer) libratore m, veleggiatore m
**glimmer** ['glɪmər] s barlume m ‖ intr brillare, luccicare; tralucere
**glimmering** ['glɪmərɪŋ] adj tenue, tremulo ‖ s luce fioca; barlume m
**glimpse** [glɪmps] s occhiata; **to catch a glimpse of** intravedere ‖ tr travedere
**glint** [glɪnt] s scintillio ‖ intr scintillare
**glisten** ['glɪsən] s scintillio, luccichio ‖ intr scintillare, luccicare
**glitter** ['glɪtər] s luccichio ‖ intr rilucere, sfolgorare
**gloaming** ['glomɪŋ] s crepuscolo (vespertino)
**gloat** [glot] intr guardare con maligna soddisfazione; **to gloat over** godere di
**global** ['globəl] adj globale; universale; globulare
**globe** [glob] s globo; (with map of earth) mappamondo
**globe-trotter** ['globˌtrɑtər] s giramondo
**globule** ['glɑbjʊl] s globulo
**glockenspiel** ['glɑkənˌspil] s vibrafono
**gloom** [glum] s oscurità f; malinconia, uggia
**gloom·y** ['glumi] adj (**·ier; -iest**) lugubre, triste, tetro
**glori·fy** ['glorɪˌfaɪ] v (pret & pp **-fied**) tr glorificare; (to enhance) esaltare

**glorious** ['glorɪ·əs] *adj* glorioso; magnifico, splendido

**glo·ry** ['glorɪ] *s* (**-ries**) gloria; **to go to glory** morire ‖ *v* (*pret* & *pp* **-ried**) *intr* gloriarsi

**gloss** [glɔs] or [glɑs] *s* lucentezza, patina; (*commentary*) glossa ‖ *tr* satinare, patinare; (*to annotate*) glossare; **to gloss over** nascondere, discolpare

**glossa·ry** ['glɑsərɪ] *s* (**-ries**) glossario

**gloss·y** ['glɔsɪ] or ['glɑsɪ] *adj* (**-ier; -iest**) lucido; (*paper*) satinato

**glottal** ['glɑtəl] *adj* articolato alla glottide

**glottis** ['glɑtɪs] *s* glottide *f*

**glove** [glʌv] *s* guanto

**glove' compart'ment** *s* cassetto portaoggetti

**glow** [glo] *s* fuoco, incandescenza; splendore *m*, scintillio; calore *m*; colorito acceso ‖ *intr* essere incandescente; (*said of cheeks*) avvampare; (*said of cat's eyes*) fosforeggiare

**glower** ['glau·ər] *s* sguardo torvo ‖ *intr* guardare col viso torvo

**glowing** ['glo·ɪŋ] *adj* incandescente; acceso; entusiasta, entusiastico

**glow'worm'** *s* lucciola; lampiride *m*

**glucose** ['glukos] *s* glucosio

**glue** [glu] *s* colla, mastice *m* ‖ *tr* incollare, ingommare

**glue'pot'** *s* pentolino per la colla

**gluey** ['glu·i] *adj* (**gluier; gluiest**) attaccaticcio; (*smeared with glue*) incollato

**glum** [glʌm] *adj* (**glummer; glummest**) tetro, accigliato

**glut** [glʌt] *s* abbondanza; eccesso; **there is a glut on the market** il mercato è saturo ‖ *v* (*pret* & *pp* **glutted; ger glutting**) *tr* saziare; (*the market*) saturare; (*a channel*) otturare

**glutton** ['glʌtən] *adj* & *s* ghiottone *m*

**gluttonous** ['glʌtənəs] *adj* ghiotto

**glutton·y** ['glʌtənɪ] *s* (**-ies**) ghiottoneria, golosità *f*

**glycerine** ['glɪsərɪn] *s* glicerina

**G'-man'** *s* (**-men'**) agente *m* federale

**gnarl** [nɑrl] *s* nodo ‖ *tr* torcere ‖ *intr* ringhiare

**gnarled** [nɑrld] *adj* nodoso; (*wrinkled*) grinzoso

**gnash** [næʃ] *tr* digrignare ‖ *intr* digrignare i denti

**gnat** [næt] *s* moscerino, pappataci *m*

**gnaw** [nɔ] *tr* rosicchiare, rodere ‖ *intr* —**to gnaw at** (fig) rimordere

**gnome** [nom] *s* gnomo

**go** [go] *s* (**goes**) andata; energia; (*for traffic*) via libera; **it's a go** è un affare fatto; **it's all the go** (coll) è all'ultimo grido; **it's no go** (coll) è impossibile; **on the go** in continuo andare e venire; **to make a go of** (coll) aver successo con ‖ *v* (*pret* **went** [wɛnt]; *pp* **gone** [gɔn] or [gɑn]) *tr* (coll) sopportare; (coll) scommettere; (coll) pagare; **to go it alone** fare da sé ‖ *intr* andare; (*to operate*) camminare, funzionare; (*e.g., mad*) diventare; (*said of numbers*) entrare; **gone!** venduto!; **so it goes** così va il mondo; **to**

**be going to** + *inf* andare a + *inf*, e.g., **I am going to New York to see him** vado a New York a vederlo; (*to express futurity*) use *fut ind*, e.g., **I am going to stay home today** starò a casa oggi; **to be gone** essere andato; esser morto; **to go against** opporsi a; **to go ahead** andar avanti; tirare avanti; **to go around** andare in giro; **to go away** andarsene; **to go back** tornare; **to go by** passare per; regolarsi su; (*said of time*) passare; **to go down** discendere; (*said of a boat*) affondare; **to go fishing** andare a pescare; **to go for** vendersi per; andare a pigliare; attaccare; favorire; **to go get** andare a pigliare; **to go house hunting** andare in cerca di una casa; **to go hunting** andare a caccia; **to go in** entrare in; (*to fit in*) starci in; **to go in for** dedicarsi a; **to go into** investigare; darsi a, dedicarsi a; (*gear*) (aut) ingranare; **to go in with** associarsi con; **to go off** andarsene; aver luogo; (*said of a bomb*) esplodere; (*said of a rifle*) sparare; (*said of a trap*) scattare; **to go on** continuare, protrarsi; **to go on** + *ger* continuare a + *inf*; **to go out** uscire; passare di moda; (*said, e.g., of fire*) spegnersi; (*to strike*) mettersi in sciopero; **to go over** aver successo; leggere; esaminare; **to go over to** passare ai ranghi di; **to go skiing** andare a sciare; **to go swimming** andare a nuotare, andare al bagno; **to go through** esperimentare; (*to examine carefully*) rovistare; (*said, e.g., of a plan or a project*) aver successo; (*a fortune*) dissipare; **to go through a red light** passare la strada col semaforo rosso; **to go with** andare con, accompagnare; (*a girl*) essere l'amico di; **to go without** fare a meno di

**goad** [god] *s* pungolo ‖ *tr* pungolare; (fig) spronare

**go'-ahead'** *adj* intraprendente ‖ *s* via *m*

**goal** [gol] *s* meta; (football) gol *m*

**goalie** ['goli] *s* portiere *m*

**goal'keep'er** *s* portiere *m*

**goal' line'** *s* linea di porta

**goal' post'** *s* montante *m*

**goat** [got] *s* capra; (*male*) becco; (coll) capro espiatorio; **to get the goat of** (coll) irritare

**goatee** [go'ti] *s* barbetta, pizzo

**goat'herd'** *s* capraio

**goat'skin'** *s* pelle *f* di capra

**goat'suck'er** *s* caprimulgo

**gob** [gɑb] *s* massa informe; **gobs** (coll) mucchio, quantità *f* enorme

**gobble** ['gɑbəl] *s* gloglottio ‖ *tr* ingozzare; **to gobble up** (coll) trangugiare; (coll) impadronirsi di ‖ *intr* trangugiare; (*said of a turkey*) gloglottare

**gobbledegook** ['gɑbəldɪ‚guk] *s* linguaggio oscuro

**go'-between'** *s* intermediario; (*pander*) mezzano; (poet) pronubo

**goblet** ['gɑblɪt] *s* coppa

**goblin** ['gɑblɪn] *s* folletto

**go'-by' s**—**to give s.o. the go-by** (coll) schivare qlcu

**go'-cart'** *s* carrettino; (*walker*) girello

god [gad] *s* dio; **God forbid** Dio ci scampi; **God grant** voglia Dio; **God willing** se Dio vuole
god'child' *s* (**-chil'dren**) figlioccio
god'daugh'ter *s* figlioccia
goddess ['gadɪs] *s* dea, diva
god'fa'ther *s* padrino
God'-fear'ing *adj* timorato di Dio
God'for·sak'en *adj* miserabile; (*place*) sperduto, fuori di mano
god'head' *s* deità *f* ‖ **Godhead** *s* Ente Supremo, Dio
godless ['gadlɪs] *adj* ateo; malvagio ‖ **the godless** i senza Dio
god·ly ['gadli] *adj* (**-lier; -liest**) devoto, pio
god'moth'er *s* madrina
God's' a'cre *s* camposanto
god'send' *s* manna, provvidenza
god'son' *s* figlioccio
God'speed' *s* successo, buona fortuna
go-getter ['go ˌgɛtər] *s* (coll) persona intraprendente
goggle ['gagəl] *intr* stralunare gli occhi
goggle-eyed ['gagəl ˌaɪd] *adj* dagli occhi sporgenti
goggles ['gagəlz] *spl* occhiali *mpl* da protezione
going ['go·ɪŋ] *adj* in moto, in funzione; **going on** quasi, e.g., **it is going on seven o'clock** sono quasi le sette ‖ *s* andata; progresso
go'ings on' *s* (coll) comportamento, contegno; (coll) avvenimenti *mpl*
goiter ['gɔɪtər] *s* gozzo
gold [gold] *adj* aureo, d'oro ‖ *s* oro
gold'beat'er *s* battiloro
gold'brick' *s* imitazione, frode *f*; (slang) fannullone *m*
gold' dig'ger ['dɪgər] *s* cercatore *m* d'oro; (coll) donna unicamente interessata nel denaro
golden ['goldən] *adj* aureo, d'oro; (*gilt*) dorato; (fig) splendido
gold'en age' *s* età *f* dell'oro
gold'en calf' *s* vitello d'oro
Gold'en Fleece' *s* vello d'oro
gold'en mean' *s* aurea mediocrità
gold'en·rod' *s* (bot) verga d'oro
gold'en rule' *s* regola della carità cristiana
gold'en wed'ding *s* nozze *fpl* d'oro
gold-filled ['gold ˌfɪld] *adj* otturato in oro
gold'finch' *s* cardellino
gold'fish' *s* pesce rosso
goldilocks ['goldɪ ˌlaks] *s* bionda; (bot) ranuncolo
gold' leaf' *s* oro in foglia
gold' mine' *s* miniera d'oro
gold' plate' *s* vasellame *m* d'oro
gold'-plate' *tr* dorare
gold' rush' *s* febbre *f* dell'oro
gold'smith' *s* orefice *m*
gold' stand'ard *s* regime aureo
golf [galf] *s* golf *m* ‖ *intr* giocare a golf
golf' cart' *s* mini-auto *f* per campi da golf
golf' club' *s* mazza; associazione di giocatori di golf
golfer ['galfər] *s* giocatore *m* di golf
golf' links' *spl* campo di golf

Golgotha ['galgəθə] *s* il Golgota
gondola ['gandələ] *s* gondola
gondolier [ˌgandə'lɪr] *s* gondoliere *m*
gone [gɔn] or [gan] *adj* partito; rovinato; andato; morto; **gone on** (coll) innamorato di
gong [gɔŋ] or [gaŋ] *s* gong *m*
goo [gu] *s* (coll) sostanza appiccicaticcia
good [gud] *adj* (**better; best**) buono; **good and ...** (coll) molto, e.g., **good and cheap** molto a buon mercato; **good for** buono per; responsabile per; (*equivalent*) valido per; **to be good at** esser bravo a; **to be no good** (coll) non servire a nulla; (coll) essere un perdigiorno; **to make good** avere successo; (*one's promise*) mantenere; (*a debt*) pagare; (*damages*) indennizzare ‖ *s* bene *m*; utile *m*, profitto; **for good** per sempre; **for good and all** una volta per sempre; **goods** merce *f*, mercanzia; **the good** il bene; i buoni; **to catch with the goods** (coll) cogliere in flagrante; **to deliver the goods** (slang) mantenere le promesse; **to do good** fare del bene; **to the good** come profitto; come attivo; **what is the good of ... ?** a che serve ... ?
good' afternoon' *s* buon pomeriggio
good'-by' [ˌgud'baɪ] *s* addio ‖ *interj* addio!; arrivederci!
good' day' *s* buon giorno
good' deed' *s* buona azione
good' egg' *s* (slang) bonaccione *m*, gran brava persona
good' eve'ning *s* buona sera; buona notte
good' fel'low *s* buon ragazzo
good'-fel'low·ship' *s* cameratismo
good'-for-noth'ing *adj* inutile, senza valore ‖ *s* pelandrone *m*, inetto
Good' Fri'day *s* Venerdì Santo
good' grac'es *spl* buone grazie
good-hearted ['gud'hartɪd] *adj* di buon cuore
good'-hum'ored *adj* di buon umore
good'-look'ing *adj* bello
good' looks' *s* bellezza
good·ly ['gudli] *adj* (**-lier; -liest**) bello; di buona qualità; ampio, considerevole
good' morn'ing *s* buon giorno
good-natured ['gud'netʃərd] *adj* bonaccione, affabile
goodness ['gudnɪs] *s* bontà *f*; **for goodness sake!** per amor di Dio!; **goodness knows!** chi sa mai! ‖ *interj* Dio mio!
good' night' *s* buona notte
good'-sized' *adj* piuttosto grande
good' speed' *s* buona fortuna
good'-tem'pered *adj* di carattere mite, gioviale
good' time' *s* periodo gradevole; **to have a good time** divertirsi; **to make good time** andare di buon passo
good' turn' *s* favore *m*, servizio
good' will' *s* buona volontà; (com) reputazione; (com) clientela
good·y ['gudi] *adj* (coll) troppo buono ‖ *s* (**-ies**) (coll) santerello; **goodies**

(coll) ghiottonerie *fpl* || *interj* (coll) bene!, benissimo!

**gooey** ['gu·i] *adj* (**gooier; gooiest**) (slang) attaccaticcio

**goof** [guf] *s* (slang) sciocco || *tr* (slang) rovinare; **to goof up** (*an opportunity*) (slang) mancare || *intr* (slang) pigliare un granchio; **to goof off** (slang) battere la fiacca; **to goof up** (slang) farla grossa

**goof·y** ['gufi] *adj* (**-ier; -iest**) (slang) sciocco

**goon** [gun] *s* (slang) scemo; (coll) crumiro, gaglioffo, terrorista *m*

**goose** [gus] *s* (**geese** [gis]) oca; **the goose hangs high** tutto va per il meglio; **to cook one's goose** rompere le uova nel paniere di qlcu; **to kill the goose that lays the golden eggs** uccidere la gallina delle uova d'oro || *s* (**gooses**) ferro da stiro per sarto

**goose'ber'ry** *s* (**-ries**) uva spina; (*berry*) bacca d'uva spina

**goose' egg'** *s* (slang) zero; (*lump on the head*) (coll) bernoccolo

**goose' flesh'** *s* pelle *f* d'oca

**goose'neck'** *s* collo d'oca

**goose' pim'ples** *spl* pelle *f* d'oca

**goose' step'** *s* passo dell'oca

**gopher** ['gofər] *s* scoiattolo di terra, citillo

**gore** [gor] *s* sangue coagulato; (*in a garment*) gherone *m* || *tr* (*with a horn*) incornare; inserire gheroni in

**gorge** [gɔrdʒ] *s* gola, burrone *m*; (*meal*) mangiata || *tr* rimpinzare || *intr* rimpinzarsi

**gorgeous** ['gɔrdʒəs] *adj* splendido, magnifico

**gorilla** [gə'rɪlə] *s* gorilla *m*

**gorse** [gɔrs] *s* gineprone *m*

**gor·y** ['gori] *adj* (**-ier; -iest**) sanguinolento

**gosh** [gɑʃ] *interj* perbacco!

**goshawk** ['gɑs,hɔk] *s* sparviere *m*, astore *m*

**gospel** ['gɑspəl] *s* vangelo || **Gospel** *s* Vangelo

**gos'pel truth'** *s* santissima verità

**gossamer** ['gɑsəmər] *s* ragnatela; (*variety of gauze*) garza finissima; tessuto impermeabile finissimo

**gossip** ['gɑsɪp] *s* maldicenza; (*person*) pettegolo; **piece of gossip** maldicenza || *intr* spettegolare

**gossipy** ['gɑsɪpi] *adj* pettegolo

**Goth** [gɑθ] *s* Goto

**Gothic** ['gɑθɪk] *adj* & *s* gotico

**gouge** [gaudʒ] *s* (*cut made with a gouge*) scanalatura; (*tool*) sgorbia; (coll) truffa || *tr* sgorbiare; (coll) truffare

**goulash** ['gulaʃ] *s* gulasch *m*

**gourd** [gord] *or* [gurd] *s* zucca

**gourmand** ['gurmənd] *s* ghiottone *m*

**gourmet** ['gurme] *s* buongustaio

**gout** [gaut] *s* gotta, podagra

**gout·y** ['gauti] *adj* (**-ier; -iest**) gottoso

**govern** ['gʌvərn] *tr* governare; (gram) reggere

**governess** ['gʌvərnɪs] *s* governante *f*, istitutrice *f*

**government** ['gʌvərnmənt] *s* governo; (gram) reggenza

**governmental** [,gʌvərn'mentəl] *adj* governativo

**governor** ['gʌvərnər] *s* governatore *m*; (mach) regolatore *m*

**governorship** ['gʌvərnər,ʃɪp] *s* governatorato

**gown** [gaun] *s* (*of a woman*) vestito; (*academic*) toga; (*of a physician or patient*) gabbanella; (*of a priest*) veste *f* talare

**grab** [græb] *s* presa; **up for grabs** (coll) pronto a esser pigliato || *v* (*pret* & *pp* **grabbed;** *ger* **grabbing**) *tr* pigliare, afferrare

**grace** [gres] *s* (*charm; favor*) grazia; (*pardon*) mercé *f*; (*prayer*) benedicite *m*; (com) dilazione; **to say grace** recitare il benedicite; **with good grace** di buona voglia || *tr* adornare

**graceful** ['gresfəl] *adj* grazioso, vezzoso, leggiadro

**grace' note'** *s* (mus) appoggiatura

**gracious** ['greʃəs] *adj* grazioso; misericordioso || *interj* Dio buono!

**gradation** [gre'deʃən] *s* gradazione; (*step in a series*) passo

**grade** [gred] *s* grado; (*slope*) pendenza; (*mark in school*) voto; **to make the grade** raggiungere la meta || *tr* selezionare; (*a student*) dare un voto a; (*land*) spianare

**grade' cros'sing** *s* (rr) passaggio a livello

**grade' school'** *s* scuola elementare

**gradient** ['gredɪ·ənt] *adj* in pendenza || *s* pendenza; (phys) gradiente *m*

**gradual** ['grædʒu·əl] *adj* graduale

**graduate** ['grædʒu·ɪt] *adj* graduato; superiore; (*student*) laureato; (*candidate for degree*) laureando *m* || ['grædʒu,et] *tr* graduare; laureare, diplomare || *intr* laurearsi, diplomarsi

**grad'uate school'** *s* facoltà *f* di studi avanzati

**graduation** [,grædʒu'eʃən] *s* graduazione; laurea; cerimonia della consegna delle lauree

**graft** [græft] *or* [graft] *s* (hort) innesto; (surg) trapianto; (coll) prevaricazione || *tr* (hort) innestare; (surg) trapiantare || *intr* (coll) prevaricare

**gra'ham bread'** ['gre·əm] *s* pane *m* integrale

**grain** [gren] *s* chicco; (*of sand*) granello; (*cereal seeds*) granaglie *fpl;* (*in wood*) venatura; (*in stone*) grana; **against the grain** di cattivo verso || *tr* granulare; (*leather*) zigrinare; (*metal*) granire

**grain' el'evator** *s* elevatore *m* di grano; (*building*) deposito di cereali

**graining** ['grenɪŋ] *s* venatura

**gram** [græm] *s* grammo

**grammar** ['græmər] *s* grammatica

**grammarian** [grə'merɪ·ən] *s* grammatico

**gram'mar school'** *s* scuola elementare

**grammatical** [grə'mætɪkəl] *adj* grammatico

**gramophone** ['græmə‚fon] s (trademark) grammofono

**grana·ry** ['grænəri] s (-ries) granaio

**grand** [grænd] adj grandioso, grande, famoso

**grand'aunt'** s prozia

**grand'child'** s (-chil'dren) nipote mf

**grand'daugh'ter** s nipote f

**grand' duch'ess** s granduchessa

**grand' duke'** s granduca m

**grandee** [græn'di] s grande m

**grandeur** ['grændʒər] or ['grændʒʊr] s grande m, grandiosità f

**grand'fa'ther** s nonno; (forefather) antenato

**grand'father's clock'** s grande orologio a pendolo

**grandiose** ['grændɪ‚os] adj grandioso

**grand' ju'ry** s giuria investigativa

**grand' lar'ceny** s furto importante

**grand' lodge'** s grande oriente m

**grandma** ['grænd‚mɑ], ['græm‚mɑ] or ['græmə] s (coll) nonna

**grand'moth'er** s nonna

**grand'neph'ew** s pronipote m

**grand'niece'** s pronipote f

**grand' op'era** s opera, opera lirica

**grandpa** ['grænd‚pɑ], ['græn‚pɑ] or ['græmpə] s (coll) nonno

**grand'par'ent** s nonno, nonna

**grand' pian'o** s pianoforte m a coda

**grand'son'** s nipote m

**grand'stand'** s tribuna

**grand' to'tal** s somma totale; importo globale

**grand'un'cle** s prozio

**grand' vizier'** s gran visir m

**grange** [grendʒ] s (farm) fattoria; (organization of farmers) sindacato di agricoltori

**granite** ['grænɪt] s granito

**grant** [grænt] or [grɑnt] s concessione; (sum of money) sovvenzione; trapasso di proprietà || tr concedere; (a wish) esaudire; (a permit) rilasciare; (law) trasferire; **to take for granted** ammettere come vero; trattare con indifferenza

**grantee** [græn'ti] or [grɑn'ti] s concessionario; beneficiario

**grant'-in-aid'** s (grants'-in-aid') sussidio governativo a un ente pubblico; borsa di studio

**grantor** [græn'tɔr] or [grɑn'tɔr] s concedente m, concessore m

**granular** ['grænjələr] adj granulare

**granulate** ['grænjə‚let] tr granulare || intr diventare granulato

**gran'ulated sug'ar** s zucchero cristallizzato

**granule** ['grænjʊl] s granulo

**grape** [grep] s chicco d'uva; (vine) vite f; **grapes** uva

**grape' ar'bor** s pergolato

**grape'fruit'** s pompelmo

**grape' juice'** s succo d'uva

**grape'shot'** s mitraglia

**grape'vine'** s vite f; **by the grapevine** di bocca in bocca; (mil) attraverso la radio fante

**graph** [græf] or [grɑf] s (diagram) grafico; (gram) segno grafico

**graphic(al)** ['græfɪk(əl)] adj grafico

**graphite** ['græfaɪt] s grafite f

**graph'** pa'per s carta millimetrata

**grapnel** ['græpnəl] s uncino; (anchor) grappino

**grapple** ['græpəl] s uncino; lotta corpo a corpo || tr uncinare || intr combattere; **to grapple with** lottare con

**grap'pling i'ron** s raffio, grappino

**grasp** [græsp] or [grɑsp] s impugnatura; (power) possesso; **to have a good grasp of** sapere a fondo; **within the grasp of** nei limiti della comprensione di || tr (with hand) impugnare; (to get control of) impadronirsi di; (fig) capire || intr—**to grasp at** cercare di afferrare

**grasping** ['græspɪŋ] or ['grɑspɪŋ] adj tenace; avido, cupido

**grass** [græs] or [grɑs] s erba; (pasture land) pastura; (lawn) tappeto erboso; **to go to grass** (said of cattle) andare al pascolo; andare in vacanza; ritirarsi; andare in rovina; morire; **to not let the grass grow under one's feet** non dormire in piuma

**grass' court'** s campo da tennis d'erba

**grass'hop'per** s cavalletta

**grass'-roots'** adj popolare

**grass' seed'** s semente f d'erba

**grass' wid'ow** s donna separata dal marito

**grass·y** ['græsi] or ['grɑsi] adj (-ier; -iest) erboso

**grate** [gret] s (for cooking) griglia; (at a window) grata || tr mettere una grata a; (one's teeth) digrignare; (e.g., cheese) grattugiare || intr stridere, cigolare; **to grate on one's nerves** dare sui nervi di qlcu

**grateful** ['gretfəl] adj riconoscente; (pleasing) piacevole, gradito

**grater** ['gretər] s grattugia

**grati·fy** ['grætɪ‚faɪ] v (pret & pp -fied) tr gratificare, soddisfare

**gratifying** ['grætɪ‚faɪ·ɪŋ] adj soddisfacente, piacevole

**grating** ['gretɪŋ] adj irritante; (sound) stridente || s inferriata

**gratis** ['gretɪs] or ['grætɪs] adj gratuito || adv gratis

**gratitude** ['grætɪ‚tjud] or ['grætɪ‚tud] s gratitudine f, riconoscenza

**gratuitous** [grə'tju·ɪtəs] or [grə'tu·ɪtəs] adj gratuito

**gratui·ty** [grə'tju·ɪti] or [grə'tu·ɪti] s (-ties) mancia, regalia

**grave** [grev] adj grave || s tomba, sepolcro, fossa

**gravedigger** ['grev‚dɪgər] s becchino

**gravel** ['grævəl] s ghiaia; (pathol) renella

**grav'en im'age** ['grevən] s idolo

**grave'stone'** s pietra tombale

**grave'yard'** s cimitero, camposanto

**gravitate** ['grævɪ‚tet] intr gravitare

**gravitation** [‚grævɪ'te'ʃən] s gravitazione

**gravi·ty** ['grævɪti] s (-ties) gravità f

**gravure** [grə'vjʊr] or ['grevjʊr] s fotoincisione

**gra·vy** ['grevi] s (-vies) (juice from

*cooking meat*) sugo; (*sauce made with it*) salsa, intingolo; (slang) guadagni *mpl* facili

**gra'vy boat'** *s* salsiera

**gra'vy train'** *s* (slang) greppia, mangiatoia

**gray** [gre] *adj* grigio; (*gray-haired*) canuto || *s* grigio; cavallo grigio || *intr* incanutire

**gray'beard'** *s* vecchio

**gray-haired** ['gre͵hɛrd] *adj* canuto

**gray'hound'** *s* levriere *m*

**grayish** ['gre·ɪʃ] *adj* grigiastro

**gray' mat'ter** *s* materia grigia

**graze** [grez] *tr* (*to touch lightly*) sfiorare; (*to scratch lightly*) scalfire; (*grass*) brucare; (*cattle*) pascere, pascolare || *intr* pascere, brucare

**grease** [gris] *s* grasso, unto || [gris] or [griz] *tr* ingrassare, ungere

**grease' cup'** [gris] *s* coppa dell'olio

**grease' gun'** [gris] *s* ingrassatore *m*

**grease' lift'** [gris] *s* piattaforma di lubrificazione

**grease' paint'** [gris] *s* cerone *m*

**grease' pit'** [gris] *s* fossa di riparazione

**greas·y** ['grisi] or ['grizi] *adj* (**-ier; -iest**) grasso, unto, untuoso

**great** [gret] *adj* grande; (coll) eccellente || **the great** i grandi

**great'-aunt'** *s* prozia

**Great' Bear'** *s* Orsa Maggiore

**Great' Brit'ain** ['brɪtən] *s* la Gran Bretagna

**Great' Dane'** *s* danese *m*, alano

**Great'er New York'** *s* Nuova York e i suoi sobborghi

**great'-grand'child'** *s* (**-chil'dren**) pronipote *mf*

**great'-grand'daught'er** *s* pronipote *f*

**great'-grand'fa'ther** *s* bisnonno

**great'-grand'moth'er** *s* bisnonna

**great'-grand'par'ent** *s* bisnonno, bisnonna

**great'-grand'son'** *s* pronipote *m*

**greatly** ['gretli] *adj* molto

**great'-neph'ew** *s* pronipote *m*

**greatness** ['gretnɪs] *s* grandezza

**great'-niece'** *s* pronipote *f*

**great'-un'cle** *s* prozio

**Grecian** ['griʃən] *adj* & *s* greco

**Greece** [gris] *s* la Grecia

**greed** [grid] *s* avarizia, avidità *f*

**greediness** ['gridɪnɪs] *s* bramosia

**greed·y** ['gridi] *adj* (**-ier; -iest**) avaro; ingordo, bramoso

**Greek** [grik] *adj* & *s* greco

**green** [grin] *adj* verde; (fig) verde, inesperto || *s* verde *m*; (*lawn*) tappeto erboso; **greens** verdura, insalata

**green'back'** *s* (U.S.A.) biglietto di banca

**green' earth'** *s* verdaccio

**greener·y** ['grinəri] *s* (**-ies**) (*foliage*) vegetazione; (*hothouse*) serra

**green'-eyed'** *adj* dagli occhi verdi; (coll) geloso

**green'gage'** *s* regina claudia

**green'horn'** *s* (slang) pivello, semplicotto

**green'house'** *s* serra

**greenish** ['grinɪʃ] *adj* verdastro

**Greenland** ['grinlənd] *s* la Groenlandia

**green' light'** *s* semaforo verde; (coll) via *m*

**greenness** ['grinnɪs] *s* verdore *m*, verdezza; inesperienza

**green' pep'per** *s* peperone *m* verde

**greensward** ['grin͵swɔrd] *s* tappeto erboso

**green' thumb'** *s* abilità *f* speciale per il giardinaggio

**green' veg'etables** *spl* verdura

**green'wood'** *s* bosco verde

**greet** [grit] *tr* salutare; ricevere; (*e.g., one's ears*) offrirsi a

**greeting** ['gritɪŋ] *s* saluto; accoglienza || **greetings** *interj* saluti!

**greet'ing card'** *s* cartolina d'auguri

**gregarious** [grɪ'gɛri·əs] *adj* (*living in the midst of others*) gregario; (*sociable*) sociale

**Gregorian** [grɪ'gori·ən] *adj* gregoriano

**grenade** [grɪ'ned] *s* granata

**grenadier** [͵grɛnə'dɪr] *s* granatiere *m*

**grenadine** [͵grɛnə'din] *s* granatina

**grey** [gre] *adj*, *s* & *intr* var of **gray**

**grid** [grɪd] *s* (*network*) rete *f*; (*on map*) reticolato; (electron) griglia

**griddle** ['grɪdəl] *s* tegame *m*

**grid'dle·cake'** *s* frittella cotta in teglia, crêpe *m*

**grid'i'ron** *s* griglia; campo di football; (theat) graticcia

**grief** [grif] *s* affanno, dolore *m*; disgrazia; **to come to grief** andare in rovina

**grievance** ['grivəns] *s* lagnanza; motivo di lagnanza

**grieve** [griv] *tr* affliggere || *intr* affliggersi, dolersi; **to grieve over** soffrire per

**grievous** ['grivəs] *adj* doloroso, penoso; (*error*) grave; (*deplorable*) deplorevole

**griffin** ['grɪfɪn] *s* grifo, grifone *m*

**grill** [grɪl] *s* griglia || *tr* mettere alla griglia; (coll) interrogare insistentemente

**grille** [grɪl] *s* inferriata; (aut) mascherina, calandra

**grill'room'** *s* grill-room *m*, rosticceria

**grim** [grɪm] *adj* (**grimmer; grimmest**) (*stern*) accigliato; (*fierce*) feroce; (*sinister*) sinistro; (*unyielding*) implacabile

**grimace** ['grɪməs] or [grɪ'mes] *s* smorfia, sberleffo || *intr* fare le boccacce

**grime** [graɪm] *s* sporco; (*soot*) fuliggine *f*

**grim·y** ['graɪmi] *adj* (**-ier; -iest**) sporco; fuligginoso

**grin** [grɪn] *s* sorriso; (*malicious in intent*) ghigno || *v* (*pret* & *pp* **grinned;** *ger* **grinning**) *intr* sorridere; ghignare

**grind** [graɪnd] *s* macinata; (*laborious work*) (coll) macina; (slang) sgobbone *m* || *v* (*pret* & *pp* **ground** [graʊnd]) *tr* macinare; (*to sharpen*) molare; (*lenses*) smerigliare; (*meat*) tritare; opprimere; (*a crank*) girare; (mach) rettificare || *intr* macinare; frantumarsi; cigolare; (coll) sgobbare

**grinder** ['graɪndər] *s* (*to sharpen tools*) mola; (*to grind coffee*) macinino;

*(back tooth)* molare *m; (person)* molatore *m*

**grind'stone'** *s* mola; **to keep one's nose to the grindstone** lavorare senza posa

**grin·go** ['grɪŋgo] *s* (-gos) *(disparaging)* gringo

**grip** [grɪp] *s (grasp)* presa; *(with hand)* stretta; *(handle)* impugnatura; **to come to grips** venire alle prese ‖ *v (pret & pp* **gripped;** *ger* **gripping)** *tr* stringere; impugnare; attirare l'attenzione di

**gripe** [graɪp] *s* (coll) lamentela; (naut) rizza; **gripes** colica ‖ *intr* (coll) lamentarsi, brontolare

**grippe** [grɪp] *s* influenza

**gripping** ['grɪpɪŋ] *adj* interessantissimo, affascinante

**gris·ly** ['grɪzli] *adj* (-lier; -liest) orribile, spaventoso

**grist** [grɪst] *s (grain to be ground)* macinata; *(ground grain)* farina; (coll) mucchio; **to be grist to the mill of** (coll) fare comodo a

**gristle** ['grɪsəl] *s* cartilagine *f*

**gris·tly** ['grɪsli] *adj* (-tlier; -tliest) cartilaginoso

**grist'mill'** *s* mulino

**grit** [grɪt] *s* sabbia, arenaria; (fig) forza d'animo ‖ *v (pret & pp* **gritted;** *ger* **gritting)** *tr (one's teeth)* far stridere, digrignare

**grit·ty** ['grɪti] *adj* (-tier; -tiest) sabbioso, granuloso; (fig) forte, coraggioso

**griz·zly** ['grɪzli] *adj* (-zlier; -zliest) brizzolato, canuto ‖ *s* (-zlies) orso grigio

**groan** [gron] *s* gemito ‖ *intr* gemere; *(to be overburdened)* essere sovraccarico

**grocer** ['grosər] *s* droghiere *m;* pizzicagnolo; proprietario di negozio di generi alimentari

**grocer·y** ['grosəri] *s* (-ies) *(store selling spices, soap, etc.)* drogheria; *(store selling cheese, cold cuts, etc.)* negozio di pizzicagnolo; negozio di generi alimentari; **groceries** generi *mpl* alimentari, commestibili *mpl*

**grog** [grɑg] *s* grog *m*

**grog·gy** ['grɑgi] *adj* (-gier; -giest) (coll) groggy, intontito

**groin** [grɔɪn] *s* (anat) inguine *m;* (archit) costolone *m*

**groom** [grum] *s* mozzo di stalla; *(bridegroom)* sposo ‖ *tr* rassettare; *(horses)* rigovernare; (pol) preparare per le elezioni

**grooms'man** *s* (-men) compare *m* di nozze

**groove** [gruv] *s* scanalatura; *(of a pulley)* gola; *(of a phonograph record)* solco; (fig) routine *f* ‖ *tr* scanalare, incavare

**grope** [grop] *intr* brancicare; *(for words)* cercare; **to grope for** cercare a tastoni

**gropingly** ['gropɪŋli] *adv* a tastoni

**gross** [gros] *adj (thick)* spesso; *(coarse)* volgare; *(fat)* grosso; *(error)* mar-

chiano; *(without deductions)* lordo ‖ *s* grossa ‖ *tr* fare un incasso lordo di

**grossly** ['grosli] *adv* approssimativamente; totalmente

**gross' na'tional prod'uct** *s* reddito nazionale

**grotesque** [gro'tɛsk] *adj & s* grottesco

**grot·to** ['grɑto] *s* (-toes or -tos) grotta

**grouch** [graʊtʃ] *s* (coll) malumore *m;* (coll) persona stizzosa ‖ *intr* (coll) brontolare

**grouch·y** ['graʊtʃi] *adj* (-ier; -iest) (coll) stizzoso, brontolone

**ground** [graʊnd] *s (earth, soil, land)* terra; *(piece of land)* terreno; *(basis)* causa, fondatezza; (elec) terra, massa; (fig) occasione, motivo; **grounds** giardini *mpl,* terreno; *(of coffee)* fondi *mpl;* **on the ground of** per motivo di; **to break ground** dare la prima palata; (fig) mettere la prima pietra; **to fall to the ground** cadere al suolo; (fig) fallire; **to gain ground** guadagnar terreno; **to give ground** ceder terreno; **to lose ground** perder terreno; **to stand one's ground** non indietreggiare ‖ *tr* fondare; (elec) mettere a massa; **to be grounded** *(said of an airplane)* essere forzato di rimanere a terra; **to be well grounded** essere bene al corrente ‖ *intr* incagliarsi

**ground' connec'tion** *s* messa a terra

**ground' crew'** *s* (aer) personale *m* di servizio

**ground' floor'** *s* pianterreno

**ground' glass'** *s* vetro smerigliato

**ground' hog'** *s* marmotta americana

**ground' lead'** [lid] *s* (elec) collegamento a massa

**groundless** ['graʊndlɪs] *adj* infondato

**ground' meat'** *s* carne tritata

**ground' plan'** *s* progetto, pianta

**ground' swell'** *s* mareggiata

**ground' wire'** *s* filo di terra, filo di massa

**ground'work'** *s* fondamento, base *f*

**group** [grup] *adj* collettivo ‖ *s* gruppo; (aer) stormo ‖ *tr* raggruppare ‖ *intr* raggrupparsi

**grouse** [graʊs] *s* gallo cedrone; (slang) brontolio ‖ *intr* (slang) brontolare

**grout** [graʊt] *s* stucco ‖ *tr* stuccare

**grove** [grov] *s* boschetto

**grov·el** ['grʌvəl] or ['grɑvəl] *v (pret & pp* -eled or -elled; *ger* -eling or -elling) *intr* umiliarsi

**grow** [gro] *v (pret* **grew** [gru]; *pp* **grown** [gron])* *tr (plants)* coltivare; *(animals)* allevare; *(a beard)* farsi crescere ‖ *intr* crescere; svilupparsi; nascere; venir su; *(to become)* diventare; farsi; **to grow angry** arrabbiarsi; **to grow old** invecchiare; **to grow out of** *(fashion)* passare di; originare da; **to grow up** svilupparsi

**growing** ['gro·ɪŋ] *adj* crescente; *(pains)* di crescenza; *(child)* in crescita

**growl** [graʊl] *s* ringhio; brontolio ‖ *intr (said of animals)* ringhiare; brontolare

**grown'-up'** *adj* adulto, grande || *s* (**grown-ups**) adulto

**growth** [groθ] *s* crescita, sviluppo; aumento; (pathol) escrescenza

**growth' stock'** *s* azione *f* che promette di aumentare di valore

**grub** [grʌb] *s* (*drudge*) sgobbone *m*; larva di coleottero; (coll) mangiare *m* || *v* (*pret & pp* **grubbed**; *ger* **grubbing**) *tr* scavare, zappare, dissodare || *intr* cercare assiduamente; scavare; sgobbare

**grub·by** ['grʌbi] *adj* (**-bier; -biest**) sporco; bacato; infestato di larve

**grudge** [grʌdʒ] *s* rancore *m;* **to have a grudge against** nutrire rancore contro || *tr* (*to spend unwillingly*) lesinare; invidiare

**grudgingly** ['grʌdʒɪŋli] *adv* di cattiva voglia

**gru·el** ['gru·əl] *s* farinata d'avena || *v* (*pret & pp* **-eled** or **-elled**; *ger* **-eling** or **-elling**) *tr* estenuare

**gruesome** ['grusəm] *adj* raccapricciante

**gruff** [grʌf] *adj* brusco, burbero; (*voice*) rauco, roco

**grumble** ['grʌmbəl] *s* brontolio || *intr* brontolare, borbottare

**grump·y** ['grʌmpi] *adj* (**-ier; -iest**) di cattivo umore, scontroso

**grunt** [grʌnt] *s* grugnito || *intr* grugnire

**G-string** ['dʒi,strɪŋ] *s* (*loincloth*) perizoma *m*; (*worn by a female entertainer*) triangolino di stoffa; (mus) corda di sol

**guarantee** [,gærən'ti] *s* garanzia; (*guarantor*) garante *mf* || *tr* garantire

**guarantor** ['gærən,tɔr] *s* garante *mf*

**guaran·ty** ['gærənti] *s* (**-ties**) garanzia || *v* (*pret & pp* **-tied**) *tr* garantire

**guard** [gɑrd] *s* guardia; (*safeguard*) protezione; (*in a prison*) guardia carceraria; (*of a sword*) guardamano; (football) mediano; **off guard** alla sprovvista; **on guard** in guardia; di fazione; **to mount a guard** montare la guardia; **under guard** ben custodito || *tr* guardare || *intr* fare la sentinella; **to guard against** guardarsi da

**guarded** ['gɑrdɪd] *adj* (*remark*) prudente

**guard'house'** *s* locale *m* di detenzione; (mil) corpo di guardia

**guardian** ['gɑrdɪ·ən] *adj* tutelare || *s* guardiano; (law) tutore *m*

**guard'ian an'gel** *s* angelo custode

**guardianship** ['gɑrdɪ·ən,ʃɪp] *s* protezione; (law) tutela

**guard'rail'** *s* guardavia *m;* (naut) parapetto

**guard'room'** *s* (mil) corpo di guardia

**guards'man** *s* (**-men**) guardia

**guerrilla** [gə'rɪlə] *s* guerrigliero

**guerril'la war'fare** *s* guerriglia

**guess** [ges] *s* congettura, supposizione || *tr & intr* congetturare, supporre; (*to estimate correctly*) indovinare; (coll) credere; **I guess so** credo di sì

**guess'work'** *s* congettura

**guest** [gest] *s* invitato, ospite *m;* (*of a hotel*) cliente *mf;* (*of a boarding house*) pensionante *mf*

**guest' book'** *s* albo d'onore; (*in a hotel*) registro

**guffaw** [gə'fɔ] *s* sghignazzata || *intr* sghignazzare

**Guiana** [gɪ'ɑnə] or [gɪ'ænə] *s* la Guayana

**guidance** ['gaɪdəns] *s* guida, governo; **for your guidance** per Sua norma

**guide** [gaɪd] *s* guida || *tr* guidare

**guide'board'** *s* indicatore *m* stradale

**guide'book'** *s* guida

**guid'ed mis'sile** ['gaɪdɪd] *s* telearma, teleproietto, missile teleguidato

**guide' dog'** *s* cane *m* conduttore di un cieco

**guide'line'** *s* falsariga; corda fissa; linea di condotta, direttiva

**guide'post'** *s* indicatore *m* stradale

**guide' word'** *s* esponente *m* in testa di pagina

**guidon** ['gaɪdən] *s* guidone *m*

**guild** [gɪld] *s* associazione mutua; (hist) gilda

**guild'hall'** *s* palazzo delle corporazioni

**guile** [gaɪl] *s* astuzia, frode *f*

**guileful** ['gaɪlfəl] *adj* astuto, insidioso

**guileless** ['gaɪllɪs] *adj* sincero, innocente

**guillotine** ['gɪlə,tin] *s* ghigliottina || [,gɪlə'tin] *tr* ghigliottinare

**guilt** [gɪlt] *s* colpa, reità *f*

**guiltless** ['gɪltlɪs] *adj* innocente

**guilt·y** ['gɪlti] *adj* (**-ier; -iest**) colpevole, reo

**guimpe** [gɪmp] or [gæmp] *s* sprone *m*

**guinea** ['gɪni] *s* ghinea; gallina faraona || **Guinea** *s* la Guinea

**guin'ea fowl'** *s* gallina faraona

**guin'ea pig'** *s* porcellino d'India, cavia; (fig) cavia

**guise** [gaɪz] *s* aspetto; veste *f;* **under the guise of** in guisa di

**guitar** [gɪ'tɑr] *s* chitarra

**guitarist** [gɪ'tɑrɪst] *s* chitarrista *mf*

**gulch** [gʌltʃ] *s* burrone *m*

**gulf** [gʌlf] *s* golfo; abisso

**Gulf' Stream'** *s* corrente *f* del Golfo

**gull** [gʌl] *s* gabbiano; (coll) credulone *m* || *tr* darla da bere a

**gullet** ['gʌlɪt] *s* gargarozzo; esofago

**gullible** ['gʌlɪbəl] *adj* credulone

**gul·ly** ['gʌli] *s* (**-lies**) borro, zanella

**gulp** [gʌlp] *s* sorsata || *tr*—**to gulp down** (*food*) ingoiare; (*drink*) tracannare; (fig) ingoiare, tranguggiare

**gum** [gʌm] *s* gomma; (*mucus on eyelids*) cispa; (anat) gengive *fpl* || *v* (*pret & pp* **gummed**; *ger* **gumming**) *tr* ingommare; **to gum up** (slang) guastare || *intr* secernere gomma

**gum' ar'abic** *s* gomma arabica

**gum'boil'** *s* flemmone *m* gengivale

**gum' boot'** *s* stivale *m* da palude

**gum'drop'** *s* caramella alla gelatina di frutta, pasticca di gomma, drop *m*

**gum·my** ['gʌmi] *adj* (**-mier; -miest**) gommoso, vischioso; (*eyelid*) cisposo

**gumption** ['gʌmpʃən] *s* (coll) iniziativa; (coll) coraggio, fegato

**gum'shoe'** *s* caloscia; (slang) poliziotto || *v* (*pret & pp* **-shoed**; *ger* **-shoeing**)

*intr* (slang) camminare silenziosa-mente
**gun** [gʌn] *s* (*rifle*) fucile *m*; (*revolver*) revolver *m*; (*pistol*) rivoltella; (*e.g.*, *for spraying*) rivoltella; **to stick to one's guns** tener duro ‖ *v* (*pret & pp* **gunned; ger gunning**) *tr* far fuoco su, freddare; (*a motor*) (slang) accelerare rapidamente ‖ *intr* andare a caccia; sparare; **to gun for** andare a caccia di
**gun'boat'** *s* cannoniera, esploratore *m*
**gun' car'riage** *s* affusto
**gun'cot'ton** *s* fulmicotone *m*
**gun'fire'** *s* fuoco, tiro
**gun'man** *s* (**-men**) bandito, sicario
**gun' met'al** *s* bronzo da cannoni; acciaio brunito
**gunnel** ['gʌnəl] *s* (naut) frisata
**gunner** ['gʌnər] *s* artigliere *m*, servente *m*
**gunnery** ['gʌnəri] *s* àrtiglieria, tiro
**gunnysack** ['gʌni ˌsæk] *s* sacco di tela greggia
**gunpoint** ['gʌn ˌpɔint] *s* mirino; **at gunpoint** a mano armata, e.g., **he was held up at gunpoint** subì una rapina a mano armata
**gun'pow'der** *s* polvere nera or pirica
**gun'run'ner** *s* contrabbandiere *m* di armi da fuoco
**gun'shot'** *s* schioppettata; revolverata; **within gunshot** a tiro di schioppo
**gun'shot' wound'** *s* schioppettata
**gun'smith'** *s* armaiolo
**gun'stock'** *s* cassa del fucile
**gunwale** ['gʌnəl] *s* frisata
**gup•py** ['gʌpi] *s* (**-pies**) lebiste *m*
**gurgle** ['gʌrgəl] *s* gorgoglio, borboglio ‖ *intr* gorgogliare, borbogliare; (*said of a human being*) barbugliare
**gush** [gʌʃ] *s* getto, fiotto ‖ *intr* zampillare, sgorgare; (coll) dare in effusioni
**gusher** ['gʌʃər] *s* pozzo di petrolio; (coll) persona espansiva
**gushing** ['gʌʃɪŋ] *adj* zampillante, sgorgante; (coll) espansivo ‖ *s* zampillo; (coll) espansione, effusione

**gush•y** ['gʌʃi] *adj* (**-ier; -iest**) (coll) espansivo, effusivo
**gusset** ['gʌsɪt] *s* gherone *m*
**gust** [gʌst] *s* (*of wind*) raffica; (*of smoke*) ondata, zaffata; (*of noise*) esplosione; (*of anger*) sfuriata
**gusto** ['gʌsto] *s* gusto; entusiasmo
**gust•y** ['gʌsti] *adj* (**-ier; -iest**) a raffiche, burrascoso
**gut** [gʌt] *s* budello; **guts** budello; (slang) fegato, coraggio ‖ *v* (*pret & pp* **gutted; ger gutting**) *tr* sparare, spanciare; distruggere l'interno di
**gutta-percha** ['gʌtə'pʌrtʃə] *s* guttaperca
**gutter** ['gʌtər] *s* (*on side of road*) cunetta; (*in street*) rigagnolo; (*of roof*) doccia, grondaia; (fig) bassifondi *mpl*
**gut'ter•snipe'** *s* monello
**guttural** ['gʌtərəl] *adj & s* gutturale *f*
**guy** [gaɪ] *s* cavo di sicurezza; (coll) tipo, tizio ‖ *tr* burlarsi di
**guzzle** ['gʌzəl] *tr & intr* trincare, bere a garganella
**guzzler** ['gʌzlər] *s* ubriacone *m*
**gym** [dʒɪm] *s* (coll) palestra
**gymnasi•um** [dʒɪm'nɛzɪ-əm] *s* (**-ums** or **-a** [ə]) palestra
**gymnast** ['dʒɪmnæst] *s* ginnasta *mf*
**gymnastic** [dʒɪm'næstɪk] *adj* ginnastico ‖ **gymnastics** *spl* ginnastica
**gynecologist** [ ˌgaɪnə'kɑlədʒɪst], [ ˌdʒaɪnə'kɑlədʒɪst] or [ ˌdʒɪnə'kɑlədʒɪst] *s* ginecologo
**gyp** [dʒɪp] *s* (coll) imbroglio; (*person*) (coll) imbroglione *m* ‖ *v* (*pret & pp* **gypped; ger gypping**) *tr* imbrogliare
**gypsum** ['dʒɪpsəm] *s* gesso
**gyp•sy** ['dʒɪpsi] *adj* zingaresco, zingaro ‖ *s* (**-sies**) zingaro ‖ **Gypsy** *s* (*language*) zingaresco
**gypsyish** ['dʒɪpsɪ-ɪʃ] *adj* zingaresco
**gyrate** ['dʒaɪret] *intr* turbinare
**gyrocompass** ['dʒaɪro ˌkʌmpəs] *s* girobussola
**gyroscope** ['dʒaɪrə ˌskop] *s* giroscopio

## H

**H, h** [etʃ] *s* ottava lettera dell'alfabeto inglese
**haberdasher** ['hæbər ˌdæʃər] *s* camiciaio; (*dealer in notions*) merciaio
**haberdasher•y** ['hæbər ˌdæʃəri] *s* (**-ies**) camiceria; merceria
**habit** ['hæbɪt] *s* abitudine *f*; (*addiction*) vizio; (*garb*) saio; **to be in the habit of** aver l'usanza di
**habitat** ['hæbɪ ˌtæt] *s* habitat *m*
**habitation** [ ˌhæbɪ'teʃən] *s* abitazione
**habit-forming** ['hæbɪt ˌfɔrmɪŋ] *adj* (*e.g., drugs*) stupefacente; (*e.g., T.V.*) assuefacente, che fa venire il vizio
**habitual** [hə'bɪtʃu-əl] *adj* abituale
**habitué** [hə ˌbɪtʃu'e] *s* habitué *m*

**hack** [hæk] *s* (*cut*) taglio; (*notch*) tacca; (*cough*) tosse secca; cavallo da nolo; vettura di piazza; (*nag*) ronzino; (*poor writer*) scribacchino ‖ *tr* tagliare; stagliare
**hack'man** *s* (**-men**) vetturino
**hackney** ['hækni] *s* cavallo da sella; vettura di piazza
**hackneyed** ['hæknid] *adj* banale, trito
**hack'saw'** *s* seghetto per metalli
**haddock** ['hædək] *s* eglefino
**haft** [hæft] or [hɑft] *s* impugnatura
**hag** [hæg] *s* (*ugly old woman*) megera; (*witch*) strega
**haggard** ['hægərd] *adj* sparuto, macilento; (*wild-looking*) stralunato

**haggle** ['hægəl] *intr* mercanteggiare
**hagiographer** [ˌhægi'agrəfər] or [ˌhedʒi'agrəfər] *s* agiografo
**hagiography** [ˌhægi'agrəfi] or [ˌhedʒi-'agrəfi] *s* agiografia
**Hague, The** [heg] *s* L'Aia *f*
**hail** [hel] *s* (*precipitation*) grandine *f*; (*greeting*) saluto; **within hail** a portata di voce ‖ *tr* salutare; accogliere; chiamare; (*e.g.*, *blows*) far cadere ‖ *intr* grandinare; **to hail from** venire da ‖ *interj* salute!; **salve!**
**hail'-fel'low** *adj* gioviale
**Hail' Mar'y** *s* Ave Maria, avemaria
**hail'stone'** *s* chicco di grandine
**hail'storm'** *s* grandinata
**hair** [her] *s* capelli *mpl;* (*of animals*) pelame *m* or pelo; **a hair** (*a single filament*) un capello or un pelo; **to a hair** a perfezione; **to get in one's hair** (slang) dare sui nervi a qlcu; **to let one's hair down** (slang) parlare francamente; (slang) comportarsi alla buona; **to make one's hair stand on end** far rizzare i capelli a qlcu; **to not turn a hair** non scomporsi; **to split hairs** cercare il pelo nell'uovo
**hair'breadth'** *s* spessore *m* di un capello; **to escape by a hairbreadth** scamparla per un pelo
**hair'brush'** *s* spazzola per i capelli
**hair'cloth'** *s* cilicio
**hair'cut'** *s* taglio dei capelli; **to get a haircut** farsi tagliare i capelli
**hair'do'** *s* (**-dos**) acconciatura
**hair'dress'er** *s* parrucchiere *m* per signora; pettinatrice *f*
**hair' dri'er** *s* asciugacapelli *m*
**hair' dye'** *s* tintura per i capelli
**hairless** ['herlɪs] *adj* pelato, calvo
**hair' net'** *s* rete *f* per i capelli
**hair'pin'** *s* forcella, forcina, molletta
**hair-raising** ['herˌrezɪŋ] *adj* orripilante
**hair' re•mov'er** *s* depilatorio
**hair' restor'er** [rɪ'storər] *s* rigeneratore *m* per i capelli
**hair' rib'bon** *s* nastro per i capelli
**hairsplitting** ['herˌsplɪtɪŋ] *adj* meticoloso, pignolo
**hair'spring'** *s* spirale *f*
**hair' styl'ing** *s* pettinatura per signora
**hair•y** ['heri] *adj* (**-ier; -iest**) peloso, villoso, irsuto
**hake** [hek] *s* merluzzo, nasello
**halberd** ['hælbərd] *s* alabarda
**halberdier** [ˌhælbər'dɪr] *s* alabardiere *m*
**halcyon** ['hælsɪ•ən] *adj* calmo, pacifico
**hale** [hel] *adj* sano, robusto ‖ *tr* trascinare a viva forza
**half** [hæf] or [haf] *adj* mezzo; **a half** or **half a** mezzo; **half the** la metà di ‖ *s* (**halves** [hævz] or [havz]) metà *f;* (*arith*) mezzo; **in half** a metà; **to go halves** fare a metà ‖ *adv* mezzo, e.g., **half asleep** mezzo addormentato; a metà, e.g., **half finished** a metà finito; **half past** e mezzo or e mezza, e.g., **half past three** le tre e mezzo or le tre e mezza; **half . . . half** metà . . . metà
**half'-and-half'** *adj* mezzo e mezzo ‖ *s* mezza crema e mezzo latte; mezza

birra chiara e mezza scura ‖ *adv* a metà, in parti uguali
**half'back'** *s* (football) mediano; (soccer) laterale *m*
**half-baked** ['hæf ˌbekt] or ['haf ˌbekt] *adj* mezzo cotto; (*ideas*) infondato, inesperto
**half' bind'ing** *s* rilegatura in mezza pelle
**half'-blood'** *s* meticcio; fratellastro; sorellastra
**half'-breed'** *s* meticcio
**half' broth'er** *s* fratellastro
**half-cocked** ['hæf ˌkakt] or ['haf ˌkakt] *adj* immaturo, precipitato ‖ *adv* (coll) precipitatamente
**half' fare'** *s* mezza corsa
**half'-full'** *adj* mezzo pieno
**half-hearted** ['hæf ˌhartɪd] or ['haf-ˌhartɪd] *adj* indifferente, freddo
**half'-hol'iday** *s* mezza festa
**half' hose'** *s* calzini *mpl* corti
**half'-hour'** *s* mezz'ora; **on the half-hour** ogni trenta minuti allo scoccare dell'ora e della mezz'ora
**half'-length'** *adj* a mezzo busto ‖ *s* ritratto a mezzo busto
**half'life'** *s* (phys) vita media
**half'-mast'** *s*—**at half-mast** a mezz'asta
**half'moon'** *s* mezzaluna
**half' mourn'ing** *s* mezzo lutto
**half' note'** *s* (mus) minima
**half' pay'** *s* mezza paga
**halfpen•ny** ['hepəni] or ['hepni] *s* (**-nies**) mezzo penny
**half' pint'** *s* mezza pinta; (slang) mezza cartuccia, mezza calzetta
**half'-seas o'ver** *adj*—**to be half-seas over** (slang) essere sbronzato
**half' shell'** *s*—**on the half shell** in conchiglia
**half' sis'ter** *s* sorellastra
**half' sole'** *s* mezza suola
**half'-sole'** *tr* mettere la mezza suola a
**half'-staff'** *s*—**at half-staff** a mezz'asta
**half-timbered** ['hæf ˌtɪmbərd] or ['haf-ˌtɪmbərd] *adj* in legno e muratura
**half' ti'tle** *s* occhiello, occhietto
**half'tone'** *s* mezzatinta
**half'-track'** *s* semicingolato
**half'truth'** *s* mezza verità, mezza bugia
**half'way'** *adj* a metà strada; parziale, mezzo ‖ *adv* a metà strada; **halfway through** nel mezzo di; **to meet halfway** fare concessioni mutue
**half-witted** ['hæf ˌwɪtɪd] or ['haf-ˌwɪtɪd] *adj* mezzo scemo
**halibut** ['hælɪbət] *s* ippoglosso
**halide** ['hælaɪd] or ['helaɪd] *s* alogenuro
**halitosis** [ˌhælɪ'tosɪs] *s* alito cattivo, fiato puzzolente
**hall** [hɔl] *s* (*passageway*) corridoio; (*entranceway*) vestibolo; (*large meeting room*) salone *m;* (*assembly room of a university*) aula magna; (*building of a university*) edificio
**halleluiah** or **hallelujah** [ˌhælɪ'lujə] *s* alleluia *m* ‖ *interj* alleluia!
**hall'mark'** *s* punzone *m* di garanzia; (fig) contrassegno, caratteristica
**hal•lo** [hə'lo] *s* (**-los**) grido ‖ *interj* ehi!
**hallow** ['hælo] *tr* santificare

**hallowed** ['hælod] *adj* consacrato
**Halloween** or **Hallowe'en** [ ,hælo'in] *s* vigilia di Ognissanti
**hallucination** [hə ,lusɪ'neʃən] *s* allucinazione
**hall'way'** *s* corridoio; entrata
**ha·lo** ['helo] *s* (**-los** or **-loes**) alone *m*
**halogen** ['hælədʒən] *s* alogeno
**halt** [hɔlt] *adj* zoppicante || *s* fermata; **to call a halt** dare ordine di fermarsi; **to come to a halt** fermarsi || *tr* fermare || *intr* fermarsi, esitare || *interj* altolà!
**halter** ['hɔltər] *s* (*for leading horse*) cavezza; (*noose*) capestro; (*hanging*) impiccagione; corpino bagno di sole
**halting** ['hɔltɪŋ] *adj* zoppicante; esitante
**halve** [hæv] or [hɑv] *tr* dimezzare
**halyard** ['hæljərd] *s* (naut) drizza
**ham** [hæm] *s* (*part of leg behind knee*) polpaccio; (*thigh and buttock*) coscia; (*cured meat from hog's hind leg*) prosciutto; (slang) istrione *m*; (slang) radioamatore *m*; **hams** natiche *fpl*
**ham' and eggs'** *spl* uova *fpl* col prosciutto
**hamburger** ['hæm ,bʌrgər] *s* hamburger *m*
**hamlet** ['hæmlɪt] *s* frazione, paese *m* || **Hamlet** *s* Amleto
**hammer** ['hæmər] *s* martello; (*of gun*) cane *m*; (*of piano*) martelletto; **under the hammer** all'asta pubblica || *tr* martellare; **to hammer out** battere; portare a fine faticosamente || *intr* martellare; **to hammer away** lavorare accanitamente
**hammock** ['hæmək] *s* amaca
**hamper** ['hæmpər] *s* cesta || *tr* imbarazzare, intralciare
**hamster** ['hæmstər] *s* criceto
**ham·string** ['hæm ,strɪŋ] *v* (*pret & pp* **-strung**) *tr* azzoppare; tagliare i garretti a; (fig) impastoiare
**hand** [hænd] *adj* manuale; fatto a mano || *s* mano *f*; (*workman*) garzone *m*, operaio; (*way of writing*) scrittura; (*signature*) firma; (*clapping of hands*) applauso; (*of clock or watch*) lancetta; (*all the cards in one's hand*) gioco; (*a round of play*) smazzata, mano *f*; (*player*) giocatore *m*; (*skill*) destrezza; (*side*) lato; **all hands** (naut) tutto l'equipaggio; (coll) tutti *mpl*; **at first hand** direttamente; **at hand** a portata di mano; **hand in glove** in perfetta unione; **hand in hand** tenendosi per mano; **hands up!** le mani in alto!; **hand to hand** corpo a corpo; **in hand** tra le mani; **in his own hand** di proprio pugno; **on hand** disponibile; **on hands and knees** (*crawling*) a gattoni; (*beseeching*) in ginocchio; **on the one hand** da un canto; **on the other hand** per contro; **to change hands** cambiare di mano; **to clap hands** battere le mani; **to eat out of one's hand** essere sottomesso a qlcu; **to get out of hand** diventare incontrollabile; **to have a hand in** prender parte a; **to have one's hands**

**full** essere occupatissimo; **to hold hands** tenersi per mano; **to hold up one's hands** (*as a sign of surrender*) alzare le mani; **to join hands** darsi la mano; **to keep one's hands off** non mettere il naso in; **to lend a hand** dare una mano; **to live from hand to mouth** vivere alla giornata; **to not lift a hand** non alzare un dito; **to play into the hands of** fare il gioco di; **to shake hands** darsi la mano; **to show one's hand** scoprire il proprio gioco; **to take in hand** prendere in mano; (*a matter*) prendere in esame; **to throw up one's hands** darsi per vinto; **to try one's hand** mettere la propria abilità alla prova; **to turn one's hand to** dedicarsi a; **to wash one's hands of** lavarsi le mani di; **under my hand** di mia firma autografa; **under the hand and seal of** firmato di pugno da || *tr* dare, porgere; **to hand down** tramandare; **to hand in** consegnare; **to hand on** trasmettere; **to hand out** distribuire
**hand'bag'** *s* borsetta
**hand' bag'gage** *s* valigie *fpl* a mano
**hand'ball'** *s* palla a mano
**hand'bill'** *s* manifestino, foglio volante
**hand'book'** *s* manuale *m*; guida; (*of a particular field*) prontuario
**hand'breadth'** *s* palmo
**hand'car'** *s* (rr) carrello a mano
**hand'cart'** *s* carretto a mano
**hand'cuffs'** *spl* manette *fpl* || *tr* mettere le manette a
**handful** ['hænd ,fʊl] *s* manata, manciata
**hand' glass'** *s* lente *f* di ingrandimento; specchietto
**hand' grenade'** *s* bomba a mano
**handi·cap** ['hændɪ ,kæp] *s* svantaggio; (sports) handicap *m* || *v* (*pret & pp* **-capped**; *ger* **-capping**) *tr* andicappare
**handicraft** ['hændɪ ,kræft] or ['hændɪ ,krɑft] *s* destrezza manuale; artigianato
**handiwork** ['hændɪ ,wʌrk] *s* lavoro fatto a mano; opera, lavoro
**handkerchief** ['hæŋkərtʃɪf] or ['hæŋkər ,tʃif] *s* fazzoletto
**handle** ['hændəl] *s* manico; (*of a sword*) impugnatura; (*of a door*) maniglia; (*of a drawer*) pomolo; (*of a hand organ*) manovella; espediente *m*; **to fly off the handle** (slang) uscire dai gangheri || *tr* maneggiare; manovrare, dirigere; commerciare in || *intr* comportarsi
**handle'bar'** *s* manubrio
**handler** ['hændlər] *s* (sports) allenatore *m*
**hand'made'** *adj* fatto a mano
**hand'maid'** or **hand'maid'en** *s* domestica, serva; (fig) ancella
**hand'-me-down'** *adj* smesso || *s* vestito smesso or di seconda mano
**hand' or'gan** *s* organetto, organino, organetto di Barberia
**hand'out'** *s* elemosina di cibo; articolo distribuito gratis; comunicato stampa
**hand-picked** ['hænd ,pɪkt] *adj* colto a mano; scelto specialmente

**hand'rail'** s guardamano, passamano

**hand'saw'** s sega a mano

**hand'set'** s microtelefono

**hand'shake'** s stretta di mano

**handsome** ['hænsəm] *adj* bello; considerevole; generoso

**hand'spring'** s capriola, salto mortale fatto toccando il terreno con le mani

**hand'-to-hand'** *adj* corpo a corpo

**hand'-to-mouth'** *adj* precario, da un giorno all'altro

**hand'work'** s lavoro fatto a mano

**hand'writ'ing** s scrittura

**hand'wrought'** *adj* lavorato a mano

**hand·y** ['hændi] *adj* (-ier; -iest) (*easy to handle*) maneggevole; (*within easy reach*) vicino; (*skillful*) destro, abile; **to come in handy** tornare utile

**hand'y·man'** s (-men') factotum *m*

**hang** [hæŋ] s maniera di cadere; **to get the hang of** (coll) imparare a adoperare; **to not give a hang** (coll) non importare un fico a || *v* (*pret & pp* **hung** [hʌŋ]) *tr* sospendere; (*laundry*) stendere; (*to attach*) attaccare; (*a door or window*) mettere sui cardini; (*one's head*) abbassare; **hang it!** (coll) al diavolo!; **to hang up** appendere; sospendere il progresso di || *intr* pendere, penzolare; esitare; essere sospeso; essere attaccato; **to hang around** ciondolare, oziare, gironzolare; **to hang on** essere sospeso a; dipendere da; persistere; (*s.o.'s words*) pendere; **to hang out** sporgersi; (slang) raccogliersi; (slang) vivere; **to hang over** esser sospeso; (*to threaten*) minacciare; **to hang together** mantenersi uniti; **to hang up** (telp) riattaccare || *v* (*pret* **hanged** or **hung**) *tr* (*to execute*) impiccare || *intr* impiccarsi

**hangar** ['hæŋər] or ['hæŋɡɑr] s rimessa; (aer) aviorimessa, hangar *m*

**hanger** ['hæŋər] s gancio, uncino; (*for clothes*) attaccapanni *m*

**hang'er-on'** s (hangers-on) seguace *mf;* seccatore *m;* (*sponger*) parassita *m*

**hanging** ['hæŋɪŋ] *adj* pendente, pensile || s impiccagione; **hangings** parati *mpl*

**hang'man** s (-men) boia *m*

**hang'nail'** s pipita delle unghie

**hang'out'** s (coll) ritrovo abituale

**hang'o'ver** s mal *m* di testa dopo una sbornia

**hank** [hæŋk] s matassa

**hanker** ['hæŋkər] *intr* agognare

**Hannibal** ['hænɪbəl] s Annibale *m*

**haphazard** [ˌhæp'hæzərd] *adj* fortuito, a caso || *adv* a caso; alla carlona

**hapless** ['hæplɪs] *adj* sfortunato

**happen** ['hæpən] *intr* succedere; **to happen along** sopravvenire; **to happen on** incontrarsi per caso con; **to happen to** + *inf* per caso + *ind,* e.g., **I happened to see her at the theater** l'ho incontrata per caso a teatro

**happening** ['hæpənɪŋ] s avvenimento, fatto

**happily** ['hæpɪli] *adv* felicemente; fortunatamente

**happiness** ['hæpɪnɪs] s felicità *f;* gioia, piacere *m*

**hap·py** ['hæpi] *adj* (-pier; -piest) lieto, felice, contento; **to be happy to** avere il piacere di

**hap'py-go-luck'y** *adj* spensierato

**hap'py me'dium** s giusto mezzo

**Hap'py New Year'** *interj* buon anno!, felice anno nuovo!

**harangue** [hə'ræŋ] s arringa, concione || *tr & intr* arringare

**harass** ['hærəs] or [hə'ræs] *tr* bersagliare; tartassare, tormentare

**harbinger** ['hɑrbɪndʒər] s foriero; annunzio || *tr* annunziare

**harbor** ['hɑrbər] *adj* di porto, portuario || s porto || *tr* albergare; (*love or hatred*) nutrire; (*e.g., a criminal*) dare ricetto a

**har'bor mas'ter** s capitano di porto

**hard** [hɑrd] *adj* duro; (*difficult*) difficile; (*work*) improbo; (*solder*) forte; (*hearing or breathing*) grosso; (*drinker*) impenitente; (*liquor*) fortemente alcolico; **to be hard on** essere severo con; (*to wear out fast*) logorare rapidamente || *adv* duro; forte; molto; **hard upon** subito dopo

**hard'-and-fast'** *adj* inflessibile

**hard-bitten** ['hɑrd'bɪtən] *adj* duro, incallito

**hard-boiled** ['hɑrd'bɔɪld] *adj* (*egg*) sodo; (coll) duro

**hard' can'dy** s caramelle *fpl;* **piece of hard candy** caramella

**hard' cash'** s denaro contante

**hard' ci'der** s sidro fermentato

**hard' coal'** s antracite *f*

**hard'-earned'** *adj* guadagnato a stento

**harden** ['hɑrdən] *tr* indurire || *intr* indurirsi

**hardening** ['hɑrdənɪŋ] s indurimento; (metallurgy) tempra

**hard' facts'** *spl* realtà *f*

**hard-fought** ['hɑrd'fɔt] *adj* accanito

**hard-headed** ['hɑrd'hɛdɪd] *adj* astuto; ostinato, caparbio

**hard-hearted** ['hɑrd'hɑrtɪd] *adj* dal cuore duro

**hardihood** ['hɑrdɪˌhʊd] s forza, coraggio; insolenza

**hardiness** ['hɑrdɪnɪs] s ardire *m;* vigore *m,* robustezza fisica

**hard' la'bor** s lavori forzati

**hard' luck'** s mala sorte

**hard'-luck' sto'ry** s storia delle proprie disgrazie

**hardly** ['hɑrdli] *adv* appena, quasi no; (*with great difficulty*) a malapena, a fatica; **hardly ever** quasi mai

**hardness** ['hɑrdnɪs] s durezza

**hard'-of-hear'ing** *adj* duro d'orecchio

**hard-pressed** ['hɑrd'prɛst] *adj* oppresso; **to be hard-pressed for** essere a corto di

**hard' rub'ber** s ebanite *f*

**hard' sauce'** s miscela di burro e zucchero

**hard'-shell crab'** s granchio con la corazza

**hardship** ['hɑrdʃɪp] s pena, privazione; **hardships** privazioni *fpl,* strettezze *fpl*

**hard'tack'** s galletta

**hard' times'** spl strettezze fpl

**hard' to please'** adj di difficile contentatura

**hard' up'** adj (coll) in urgente bisogno; **to be hard up for** (coll) essere a corto di

**hard'ware'** s ferramenta fpl; macchinario

**hard'ware store'** s negozio di ferramenta

**hard-won** ['hɑrd‚wʌn'] adj (victory, battle) conquistato con molti sforzi; (money) acquistato con molti sforzi

**hard'wood'** s legno forte

**hard'wood floor'** s pavimento di legno, parquet m

**har•dy** ['hɑrdi] adj (-dier; -diest) forte, resistente; (rash) temerario; (hort) resistente al freddo

**hare** [hɛr] s lepre f

**harebrained** ['hɛr‚brend] adj scervellato, sventato

**hare'lip'** s labbro leporino

**harem** ['hɛrəm] s arem m

**hark** [hɑrk] intr ascoltare; **to hark back** (said of hounds) ritornare sulla pista; riandare col pensiero || interj ascolta!

**harken** ['hɑrkən] intr ascoltare

**harlequin** ['hɑrləkwɪn] s arlecchino

**harlot** ['hɑrlət] s meretrice f, baldracca

**harm** [hɑrm] s danno || tr rovinare; nuocere (with dat), fare del male (with dat)

**harmful** ['hɑrmfəl] adj nocivo

**harmless** ['hɑrmlɪs] adj innocuo

**harmonic** [hɑr'mɑnɪk] adj armonico || s (phys) armonica || **harmonics** ssg armonica; spl suoni armonici

**harmonica** [hɑr'mɑnɪkə] s armonica a bocca

**harmonious** [hɑr'moni•əs] adj armonioso

**harmonize** ['hɑrmə‚naɪz] tr intonare; (mus) armonizzare || intr intonarsi; (mus) cantare all'unisono

**harmo•ny** ['hɑrməni] s (-nies) armonia

**harness** ['hɑrnɪs] s bardatura, finimenti mpl; (fig) routine f; **to die in the harness** morire sulla breccia || tr bardare, imbrigliare; (a waterfall) captare

**har'ness mak'er** s sellaio

**har'ness race'** s corsa al trotto, corsa di cavalli col sulky

**harp** [hɑrp] s arpa || intr—**to harp on** ripetere ostinatamente

**harpist** ['hɑrpɪst] s arpista mf

**harpoon** [hɑr'pun] s rampone m || tr & intr arpionare

**harpsichord** ['hɑrpsɪ‚kɔrd] s arpicordo, clavicembalo

**har•py** ['hɑrpi] s (-pies) arpia

**harrow** ['hæro] s erpice m || tr (agr) erpicare; (fig) tormentare

**harrowing** ['hæro•ɪŋ] adj straziante

**har•ry** ['hæri] v (pret & pp -ried) tr saccheggiare; tormentare

**harsh** [hɑrʃ] adj (to touch) ruvido; (to taste or hearing) aspro; inclemente

**harshness** ['hɑrʃnɪs] s ruvidezza; asprezza; inclemenza

**hart** [hɑrt] s cervo

**harum-scarum** ['hɛrəm'skɛrəm] adj & s scervellato

**harvest** ['hɑrvɪst] s raccolta, mietitura || tr raccogliere, mietere

**harvester** ['hɑrvɪstər] s (person) mietitore m; (machine) mietitrice f

**har'vest home'** s fine f della mietitura; festa dei mietitori; canzone f dei mietitori

**har'vest moon'** s luna di settembre

**has-been** ['hæz‚bɪn] s (person) fallito; (thing) anticaglia

**hash** [hæʃ] s polpettone m || tr tritare

**hash' house'** s osteria di terz'ordine

**hashish** ['hæʃiʃ] s ascisc m

**hasp** [hæsp] or [hɑsp] s boncinello

**hassle** ['hæsəl] s (coll) rissa, disputa

**hassock** ['hæsək] s cuscino poggiapiedi

**haste** [hest] s premura; **in haste** di premura; **to make haste** fare presto

**hasten** ['hesən] tr affrettare || intr affrettarsi

**hast•y** ['hesti] adj (-ier; -iest) frettoloso; precipitato

**hat** [hæt] s cappello; **to keep under one's hat** (coll) mantenere il segreto su; **to throw one's hat in the ring** (coll) dichiarare la propria candidatura

**hat'band'** s nastro del cappello

**hat' block'** s forma da cappelli

**hat'box'** s cappelliera

**hatch** [hætʃ] s (brood) nidiata; (shading line) tratteggio; (trap door) porta a ribalta; (lower half of door) mezza porta; (naut) boccaporto || tr (eggs) covare; (a drawing) tratteggiare; complottare, tramare || intr schiudersi

**hat'check' girl'** s guardarobiera

**hatchet** ['hætʃɪt] s accetta; **to bury the hatchet** fare la pace

**hatch'way'** s (trap door) porta a ribalta; (naut) boccaporto

**hate** [het] s odio || tr & intr odiare

**hateful** ['hetfəl] adj odioso

**hat'pin'** s spillone m

**hat'rack'** s attaccapanni m

**hatred** ['hetrɪd] s odio, livore m

**hatter** ['hætər] s cappellaio

**haughtiness** ['hɔtɪnɪs] s superbia

**haugh•ty** ['hɔti] adj (-tier; -tiest) superbo, sprezzante

**haul** [hɔl] s (tug) tiro; (amount caught) retata; (distance transported) percorso, pezzo || tr trasportare; tirare; (naut) alare

**haunch** [hɔntʃ] or [hɑntʃ] s fianco; anca; (hind quarter of an animal) coscia; (same used for food) sciotto

**haunt** [hɔnt] or [hɑnt] s ritrovo, nido || tr frequentare assiduamente; perseguitare

**haunt'ed house'** s casa frequentata dai fantasmi

**haute couture** [ot ku'tyr] s alta moda

**have** [hæv] s—**the haves and the have-nots** gli abbienti e i nullatenenti || v (*pret & pp* **had** [hæd]) *tr* avere; (*a dream*) fare; (*to get, take*) prendere, ottenere, ricevere; **to have got** (coll) avere; **to have got to** + *inf* (coll) dovere + *inf;* **to have it in for** (coll) serbar rancore per; **to have it out with** avere a che dire con; **to have on** portare; **to have (s.th) to do with** avere (qlco) a che fare con, e.g., I don't want to have anything to do with him non voglio aver nulla a che fare con lui; **to have** + *inf* fare + *inf*, e.g., I had him pay the bill gli ho fatto pagare il conto; **to have** + *pp* fare + *inf*, e.g., I had my watch repaired ho fatto aggiustare l'orologio || *intr*—**to have at** attaccare, mettersi di buzzo buono con; **to have to** + *inf* dovere + *inf;* **to have to do with** avere a che fare con; trattare di, e.g., this book has to do with superstition questo libro tratta di superstizione || *v aux* avere, e.g., he has studied his lesson ha studiato la sua lezione

**havelock** [ˈhævlɑk] *s* coprinuca *m*

**haven** [ˈhevən] *s* porto; asilo

**haversack** [ˈhævərˌsæk] *s* bisaccia; (mil) zaino

**havoc** [ˈhævək] *s* rovina; **to play havoc with** rovinare; scompigliare

**haw** [hɔ] *s* (*of hawthorn*) bacca; (*in speech*) esitazione || *intr* voltare a sinistra || *interj* voltare a sinistra!

**hawk** [hɔk] *s* falco; (*mortarboard*) sparviere *m;* (coll) persona rapace || *tr* imbonire; (*newspapers*) strillare; **to hawk up** sputare raschiandosi la gola || *intr* fare il merciaiolo ambulante; schiarirsi la gola

**hawker** [ˈhɔkər] *s* merciaiolo ambulante

**hawse** [hɔz] *s* (naut) cubia; (*hole*) (naut) occhio di cubia; (naut) altezza di cubia

**hawse'hole'** *s* occhio di cubia

**hawser** [ˈhɔzər] *s* cavo, gomena

**haw'thorn'** *s* biancospino

**hay** [he] *s* fieno; **to hit the hay** (slang) andare a letto; **to make hay while the sun shines** battere il ferro fin ch'è caldo

**hay' fe'ver** *s* febbre *f* da fieno, raffreddore *m* da fieno

**hay'field'** *s* prato seminato a fieno

**hay'fork'** *s* forcone *m;* (mach) rastrello

**hay'loft'** *s* fienile *m*

**haymow** [ˈheˌmaʊ] *s* fienile *m*

**hay'rack'** *s* rastrelliera

**hay'ride'** *s* gita notturna in carro da fieno

**hay'seed'** *s* semente *f* d'erba; (coll) semplicione *m*, campagnolo

**hay'stack'** *s* meta, pagliaio

**hay'wire'** *adj* (coll) disordinato, in confusione; (coll) impazzito || *s* filo per legare il fieno

**hazard** [ˈhæzərd] *s* pericolo; (*chance*) rischio; (golf) ostacolo || *tr* rischiare; (*an opinion*) arrischiare

**hazardous** [ˈhæzərdəs] *adj* pericoloso

**haze** [hez] *s* foschia; (fig) confusione || *tr* far la matricola a

**hazel** [ˈhezəl] *adj* nocciola || *s* (*tree*) nocciolo; (*fruit*) nocciola

**ha'zel·nut'** *s* nocciola

**hazing** [ˈhezɪŋ] *s* vessazione, angheria; (*at university*) matricola

**ha·zy** [ˈhezi] *adj* (**-zier; -ziest**) nebbioso; confuso

**H-bomb** [ˈetʃˌbɑm] *s* bomba H

**he** [hi] *s* (**hes**) maschio || *pron pers* (**they**) lui, egli, esso

**head** [hɛd] *s* testa, capo; (*of bed*) testiera; (*caption*) testata; (*of a nail*) cappello; (*on a glass of beer*) schiuma; (*of a boil*) punta purulenta; (*e.g., of cattle*) capo; **at the head of** a capo di; **from head to foot** da capo a piedi; **head over heels** a gambe levate; completamente; **heads or tails** testa o croce; **over one's head** al di sopra della capacità intellettuale di qlcu; (*going to a higher authority*) al di sopra di qlcu; **to be out of one's head** (coll) esser matto; **to bring to a head** far giungere alla crisi; **to come into one's head** passar per la mente a qlcu; **to go to one's head** dare al cervello a qlcu; **to keep one's head** non perdere la testa; **to keep one's head above water** arrivare a sbarcare il lunario; **to not make head or tail of** non riuscire a raccappezzarsi su || *tr* dirigere, comandare; essere alla testa di || *intr*—**to head towards** dirigersi verso

**head'ache'** *s* mal di capo, emicrania

**head'band'** *s* fascia sul capo; (bb) capitello; (typ) filetto

**head'board'** *s* testiera del letto

**head' cheese'** *s* salame *m* di testa

**head'dress'** *s* acconciatura

**header** [ˈhɛdər] *s*—**to take a header** (coll) gettarsi a capofitto

**head'first'** *adv* a capofitto

**head'gear'** *s* copricapo; (*for protection*) casco

**head'hunt'er** *s* cacciatore *m* di teste

**heading** [ˈhɛdɪŋ] *s* intestazione; (*of a chapter of a book*) titolo; (journ) testata, capopagina *m*

**headland** [ˈhɛdlənd] *s* promontorio

**headless** [ˈhɛdlɪs] *adj* senza testa

**head'light'** *s* (naut, rr) fanale *m;* (aut) faro

**head'line'** *s* (*of a page of a book*) titolo; (journ) testata || *tr* intestare; fare pubblicità a

**head'lin'er** *s* (slang) attrazione principale

**head'long'** *adj* precipitoso || *adv* a precipizio; a capofitto

**head'man** *s* (**-men**) capo; giustizere *m*

**head'mas'ter** *s* direttore *m* di un collegio per ragazzi

**head'most'** *adj* primo, più avanzato

**head' of'fice** *s* sede *f* centrale

**head' of hair'** *s* capigliatura

**head'-on'** *adj* frontale || *adv* di fronte, frontalmente

**head'phones'** *spl* cuffia

**head'piece'** *s* (*any covering for the head*) copricapo; (*helmet*) elmo; (*brains, judgment*) testa; (*of bed*)

spalliera; (*headset*) cuffia; (typ) testata
**head'quar'ters** *s* sede *f* centrale, direzione; (mil) quartier *m* generale
**head'rest'** *s* poggiatesta *m*, testiera
**head'set'** *s* cuffia
**head'ship'** *s* direzione
**head'stone'** *s* pietra angolare; (*on a grave*) pietra tombale
**head'stream'** *s* affluente *m* principale
**head'strong'** *adj* testardo, ostinato
**head'wait'er** *s* capocameriere *m*
**head'wa'ters** *spl* fonti *fpl* or sorgenti *fpl* d'un fiume
**head'way'** *s* progresso; **to make headway** progredire
**head'wear'** *s* copricapo
**head'wind'** *s* vento di prua
**head'work'** *s* lavoro intellettuale
**head·y** ['hɛdi] *adj* (-**ier**; -**iest**) eccitante; impetuoso; violento; (*clever*) astuto; intossicante
**heal** [hil] *tr* sanare, guarire; **purificare**
‖ *intr* risanarsi, guarire; (*said of a wound*) rimarginare
**healer** ['hilər] *s* guaritore *m*
**health** [hɛlθ] *s* salute *f;* **to radiate health** sprizzare salute da tutti i pori; **to your health!** alla Sua salute!
**health' depart'ment** *s* sanità *f*
**healthful** ['hɛlθfəl] *adj* salutare
**health' insur'ance** *s* assicurazione malattia
**health·y** ['hɛlθi] *adj* (-**ier**; -**iest**) sano; salubre
**heap** [hip] *s* mucchio; (coll) insalata, mare *m* ‖ *tr* ammucchiare; **to heap s.th upon s.o.** colmare qlcu di qlco; **to heap with** colmare di
**hear** [hɪr] *v* (*pret & pp* **heard** [hʌrd]) *tr* udire; **to hear it said** sentirlo dire ‖ *intr* udire; **hear!, hear!** bravo!; **to hear about** sentir parlare di; **to hear from** aver notizie di; **to hear of** sentir parlare di; **to hear that** sentir dire che
**hearer** ['hɪrər] *s* ascoltatore *m*
**hearing** ['hɪrɪŋ] *s* (*sense*) udito, orecchio; (*act*) udienza; **in the hearing of** in presenza di; **within hearing** a portata d'orecchio
**hear'ing aid'** *s* uditofono
**hear'say'** *s* diceria; **by hearsay** per sentito dire
**hearse** [hʌrs] *s* carro, carrozzone *m*, or furgone *m* funebre
**heart** [hɑrt] *s* cuore *m;* (*e.g., of lettuce*) grumolo; **after one's heart** di gusto di qlcu; **by heart** a memoria; **heart and soul** di tutto cuore; **to break the heart of** spezzare il cuore di; **to die of a broken heart** morire di crepacuore; **to eat one's heart out** piangere silenziosamente; **to get to the heart of** sviscerare il nocciolo di; **to have one's heart in one's work** lavorare di buzzo buono; **to have one's heart in the right place** avere buone intenzioni; **to lose heart** scoraggiarsi; **to open one's heart to** aprire il cuore a; **to take heart** prender coraggio; **to take to heart** prendersi a cuore; **to**

**wear one's heart on one's sleeve** parlare a cuore aperto; **with one's heart in one's mouth** col cuore in bocca
**heart'ache'** *s* angustia, angoscia
**heart' attack'** *s* attacco cardiaco
**heart'beat'** *s* battito del cuore
**heart'break'** *s* angoscia straziante
**heart'break'er** *s* rubacuori *m*
**heartbroken** ['hɑrt,brokən] *adj* col cuore spezzato
**heart'burn'** *s* bruciore *m* di stomaco
**heart' disease'** *s* mal *m* di cuore
**hearten** ['hɑrtən] *tr* rincuorare
**heart' fail'ure** *s* (*death*) arresto cardiaco; collasso cardiaco
**heartfelt** ['hɑrt,fɛlt] *adj* sentito
**hearth** [hɑrθ] *s* focolare *m*
**hearth'stone'** *s* pietra del focolare
**heartily** ['hɑrtɪli] *adv* di cuore, cordialmente; saporitamente
**heartless** ['hɑrtlɪs] *adj* senza cuore, insensibile
**heart' mur'mur** *s* soffio al cuore
**heart-rending** ['hɑrt,rɛndɪŋ] *adj* da far male al cuore
**heart'sick'** *adj* afflitto, sconsolato
**heart'strings'** *spl* precordi *mpl*
**heart'-to-heart'** *adj* cuore a cuore
**heart' trans'plant** *s* trapianto cardiaco
**heart'wood'** *s* cuore *m* del legno
**heart·y** ['hɑrti] *adj* (-**ier**; -**iest**) cordiale, di cuore; abbondante; (*eater*) grande
**heat** [hit] *adj* termico ‖ *s* calore *m;* (*of room, house, etc.*) riscaldamento; (zool) fregola; (sports) batteria; (fig) fervore *m;* **in heat** (zool) in amore ‖ *tr* scaldare, riscaldare; (fig) eccitare ‖ *intr* riscaldarsi; (fig) accalorarsi
**heated** ['hitɪd] *adj* accalorato
**heater** ['hitər] *s* riscaldatore *m;* (*for central heating*) calorifero; (*to heat hands or bed*) scaldino; (*to heat water in tub*) scaldabagno
**heath** [hiθ] *s* (*shrub*) brugo, erica; (*tract of land*) brughiera
**hea·then** ['hiðən] *adj* pagano; irreligioso ‖ *s* (-**then** or -**thens**) pagano
**heathendom** ['hiðəndəm] *s* (*worship*) paganesimo; (*land*) pagania
**heather** ['hɛðər] *s* erica, brugo
**heating** ['hitɪŋ] *adj* di riscaldamento ‖ *s* riscaldamento
**heat'ing pad'** *s* termoforo
**heat' light'ning** *s* lampo di caldo
**heat' shield'** *s* (rok) scudo termico
**heat'stroke'** *s* colpo di calore
**heat' wave'** *s* ondata di caldo
**heave** [hiv] *s* sollevamento, sforzo; **heaves** (vet) bolsaggine *f* ‖ *v* (*pret & pp* **heaved** or **hove** [hov]) *tr* sollevare, alzare; rigettare; (*a sigh*) emettere ‖ *intr* alzarsi e abbassarsi; (*said of one's chest*) palpitare; avere conati di vomito
**heaven** ['hɛvən] *s* cielo; **for heaven's sake!** or **good heavens!** per amor del cielo!; **heavens** (*firmament*) cielo ‖ Heaven *s* cielo
**heavenly** ['hɛvənli] *adj* celeste
**heav'enly bod'y** *s* corpo celeste
**heav·y** ['hɛvi] *adj* (-**ier**; -**iest**) (*of great*

weight) pesante; (liquid) denso, (cloth, sea) grosso; (traffic) forte; (serious) grave; (crop) abbondante; (rain) dirotto; (features) grossolano; (heart) stretto; (ponderous) macchinoso; (industry) grande; (stock market) abbattuto || adv (coll) pesantemente; **to hang heavy** (said of time) passar lentamente

**heav'y-du'ty** adj extraforte

**heavy-hearted** [ 'hɛvɪ 'hɑrtɪd] adj afflitto, triste

**heav'y•set'** adj forte, corpulento

**heav'y•weight'** s peso massimo

**Hebrew** [ 'hibru] adj & s ebreo; (language) ebraico

**hecatomb** [ 'hɛkə ,tom] or [ 'hɛkə ,tum] s ecatombe f

**heckle** [ 'hɛkəl] tr interrompere con domande imbarazzanti

**hectic** [ 'hɛktɪk] adj febbrile

**hedge** [hɛdʒ] s barriera; (of bushes) siepe f; (in stock market) operazione controbilanciante || tr circondare con siepe; **to hedge in** circondare || intr evitare di compromettersi; (com) coprirsi

**hedge'hog'** s (zool) riccio; (porcupine) (zool) porcospino

**hedge'hop'** v (pret & pp -hopped; ger hopping) intr volare a volo radente

**hedgehopping** [ 'hɛdʒ ,hɑpɪŋ] s volo radente

**hedge'row'** [ro] s siepe f

**heed** [hid] s attenzione; **to take heed** fare attenzione || tr badare a || intr fare attenzione, badare

**heedless** [hidlɪs] adj sbadato

**heehaw** [ 'hi ,hɔ] s (of donkey) raglio d'asino; risata || intr ragliare; ridere fragorosamente

**heel** [hil] s (of shoe, of foot) calcagno, tallone m; (of stocking or shoe) tallone m; (raised part of shoe below heel) tacco; (coll) farabutto; **down at the heel** mal ridotto; **to cool one's heels** aspettare a lungo; **to kick up one's heels** darsi alla pazza gioia; **to show a clean pair of heels** or **to take to one's heels** battere i tacchi

**heeler** [ 'hilər] s politicante mf

**heft•y** [ 'hɛfti] adj (-ier; -iest) (heavy) pesante; (strong) forte

**hegemon•y** [hɪ 'dʒɛmənɪ] or [ 'hɛdʒɪ ,moni] s (-ies) egemonia

**hegira** [hɪ 'dʒaɪrə] or [ 'hɛdʒɪrə] s fuga

**heifer** [ 'hɛfər] s manza, giovenca

**height** [haɪt] s altezza; (of a person) altezza, statura; (e.g., of folly) colmo

**heighten** [ 'haɪtən] tr innalzare; (to increase the amount of) accrescere, aumentare || intr aumentare

**heinous** [ 'henəs] adj nefando, odioso

**heir** [er] s erede m

**heir' appar'ent** s (heirs' appar'ent) erede necessario

**heirdom** [ 'erdəm] s eredità f

**heiress** [ 'ɛrɪs] s ereditiera, erede f

**heirloom** [ 'er ,lum] s cimelio di famiglia

**Helen** [ 'hɛlən] s Elena

**helicopter** [ 'hɛlɪ ,kɑptər] s elicottero

**heliport** [ 'hɛlɪ ,port] s eliporto

**helium** [ 'hili•əm] s elio

**helix** [ 'hiliks] s (helixes or helices [ 'hɛlɪ ,siz]) spirale f; (geom) elica

**hell** [hɛl] s inferno

**hell-bent** [ 'hɛl 'bɛnt] adj (coll) risoluto; **to be hell-bent on** (coll) avere un chiodo in testa di

**hell'cat'** s arpia, megera

**hellebore** [ 'hɛlɪ ,bor] s elleboro

**Hellene** [ 'hɛlin] s greco

**Hellenic** [hɛ 'lɛnɪk] or [hɛ 'linɪk] adj ellenico

**hell'fire'** s fuoco dell'inferno

**hellish** [ 'hɛlɪʃ] adj infernale

**hel•lo** [hɛ 'lo] s saluto || interj ciao!; (on telephone) pronto!

**helm** [hɛlm] s barra del timone; ruota del timone; timone m || tr dirigere

**helmet** [ 'hɛlmɪt] s (mil) elmetto; (sports) casco; (hist) elmo

**helms'man** s (-men) timoniere m

**help** [hɛlp] s aiuto; (relief) rimedio, e.g., **there's no help for it** non c'è rimedio; servitù f; impiegati mpl; operai mpl; **to come to the help of** venire in aiuto di || tr aiutare; soccorrere, mitigare; (to wait on) servire; **it can't be helped** non c'è rimedio; **so help me God!** Dio mi sia testimonio!; **to help down** aiutare a scendere; **to help s.o. with his coat** aiutare qlcu a mettersi il cappotto; **to help oneself** servirsi da solo; **to help up** aiutare a salire; aiutare ad alzarsi; **to not be able to help** + ger non poter fare a meno di + inf, e.g., **he can't help laughing** non può fare a meno di ridere || intr aiutare || interj aiuto!

**helper** [ 'hɛlpər] s aiutante m; (in a shop) garzone m, lavorante m

**helpful** [ 'hɛlpfəl] adj utile, servizievole

**helping** [ 'hɛlpɪŋ] s (of food) razione

**helpless** [ 'hɛlplɪs] adj (weak) debole; (powerless) impotente; senza risorse; (confused) perplesso; (situation) irrimediabile

**help'mate'** s compagno; (wife) compagna

**helter-skelter** [ 'hɛltər 'skɛltər] adj & adv in fretta e furia; alla rinfusa

**hem** [hɛm] s (any edge) orlo; (of skirt) basta, pedana; (of suit) falda || v (pret & pp hemmed; ger hemming) tr orlare, bordare; **to hem in** insaccare || intr esitare; **to hem and haw** esitare; essere evasivo

**hemisphere** [ 'hɛmɪ ,sfɪr] s emisfero

**hemistich** [ 'hɛmɪ ,stɪk] s emistichio

**hem'line'** s orlo della gonna

**hem'lock'** s (herb and poison) cicuta; (Tsuga canadensis) abete m del Canada

**hemoglobin** [ ,hɛmə 'globɪn] or [ ,himə 'globɪn] s emoglobina

**hemophilia** [ ,hɛmə 'fɪlɪ•ə] or [ ,himə 'fɪlɪ•ə] s emofilia

**hemorrhage** [ 'hɛmərɪdʒ] s emorragia

**hemorrhoids** [ 'hɛmə ,rɔɪdz] spl emorroidi fpl

**hemostat** [ 'hɛmə ,stæt] or [ 'himə ,stæt] s pinza emostatica

**hemp** [hɛmp] s canapa

**hemstitch** ['hɛm ‚stɪtʃ] s orlo a giorno || tr & intr orlare a giorno

**hen** [hɛn] s gallina

**hence** [hɛns] adv di qui; da ora; quindi; di qui a, e.g., **three weeks hence** di qui a tre settimane

**hence'forth'** adv d'ora innanzi

**hench·man** ['hɛntʃmən] s (-men [mən]) accolito; politicante m

**hen'house'** s pollaio

**henna** ['hɛnə] s henna || tr tingere con la henna

**hen'peck'** tr (a husband) trovare a ridire con

**hen'pecked' hus'band** s marito dominato dalla moglie

**her** [hʌr] adj poss suo, il suo || pron pers la, lei; **to her** le, a lei

**herald** ['hɛrəld] s araldo; annunziatore m || tr annunziare

**heraldic** [hɛ'rældɪk] adj araldico

**herald·ry** ['hɛrəldri] s (-ries) (office) consulta araldica; (science) araldica; (coat of arms) blasone m

**herb** [ʌrb] or [hʌrb] s erba; erba medicinale

**herbaceous** [hʌr'beʃəs] adj erbaceo

**herbage** ['ʌrbɪdʒ] or ['hʌrbɪdʒ] s erba; (law) erbatico

**herbalist** ['hʌrbəlɪst] or ['ʌrbəlɪst] s erborista mf

**herbari·um** [hʌr'bɛrɪ·əm] s (-ums or -a [ə]) erbario

**herb' doc'tor** s erborista mf

**herculean** [hʌr'kjulɪ·ən] or [ ‚hʌrkju'li·ən] adj erculeo

**herd** [hʌrd] s (of sheep) gregge m; (of cattle) mandria; (of men) torma || tr & intr imbrancare

**herds'man** s (-men) (of cattle) mandriano, vaccaio; (of sheep) pastore m

**here** [hɪr] adj presente || s—**the here and the hereafter** la vita presente e l'aldilà || adv qui, qua; **here and there** qua e là; **here is** or **here are** ecco; **that's neither here not there** ciò non ha nulla a che vedere || interj presente!

**hereabouts** ['hɪrə ‚bauts] adv qua vicino

**here·af'ter** s aldilà m || adv d'ora innanzi; nel futuro

**here·by'** adv con la presente

**hereditary** [hɪ'rɛdɪ ‚tɛri] adj ereditario

**heredi·ty** [hɪ'rɛdɪti] s (-ties) eredità f

**here·in'** adv qui; in questo posto

**here·of'** adv di questo

**here·on'** adv in questo; su questo

**here·sy** ['hɛrəsi] s (-sies) eresia

**heretic** ['hɛrətɪk] adj & s eretico

**heretical** [hɪ'rɛtɪkəl] adj eretico

**heretofore** [ ‚hɪrtʊ'for] adv sinora

**here·u·pon'** adv su questo; in questo; immediatamente dopo

**here·with'** adv accluso; con la presente

**heritage** ['hɛrɪtɪdʒ] s eredità f

**hermetic(al)** [hʌr'mɛtɪk(əl)] adj ermetico

**hermit** ['hʌrmɪt] s eremita m

**hermitage** ['hʌrmɪtɪdʒ] s eremitaggio

**herni·a** ['hʌrnɪ·ə] s (-as or -ae [ ‚i]) ernia

**he·ro** ['hɪro] s (-roes) eroe m

**heroic** [hɪ'ro·ɪk] adj eroico || **heroics** spl linguaggio altisonante

**heroin** ['hɛro·ɪn] s (pharm) eroina

**heroine** ['hɛro·ɪn] s eroina

**heroism** ['hɛro ‚ɪzəm] s eroismo

**heron** ['hɛrən] s airone m

**herring** ['hɛrɪŋ] s aringa

**her'ring·bone'** s (in fabrics) spina di pesce; (in hardwood floors) spiga

**hers** [hʌrz] pron poss il suo; **of hers** suo

**herself** [hʌr'sɛlf] pron pers lei stessa; sé stessa; si, e.g., **she enjoyed herself** si divertì; **with herself** con sé

**hertz** [hʌrts] s hertz m

**hesitan·cy** ['hɛzɪtənsi] s (-cies) titubanza, esitanza

**hesitant** ['hɛzɪtənt] adj esitante

**hesitate** ['hɛzɪ ‚tet] intr esitare, titubare; (to stutter) balbettare

**hesitation** [ ‚hɛzɪ'te/ən] s esitazione

**heterodox** ['hɛtərə ‚dɑks] adj eterodosso

**heterodyne** ['hɛtərə ‚daɪn] s eterodina

**heterogeneous** [ ‚hɛtərə'dʒɪni·əs] adj eterogeneo

**hew** [hju] v (pret **hewed**; pp **hewed** or **hewn**) tr tagliare; (a passage) aprirsi; (a statue) abbozzare; **to hew down** abbattere || intr—**to hew close to the line** (coll) filare diritto

**hex** [hɛks] s strega; incantesimo || tr stregare, incantare

**hexameter** [hɛks'æmɪtər] s esametro

**hey** [he] interj ehi!

**hey'day'** s apogeo

**hia·tus** [haɪ'etəs] s (-tuses or -tus) (gap) lacuna; (gram) iato

**hibernate** ['haɪbər ‚net] intr ibernare; (said of people) svernare

**hibiscus** [hɪ'bɪskəs] or [haɪ'bɪskəs] s ibisco

**hic·cup** ['hɪkəp] s singhiozzo || v (pret & pp -cuped or -cupped; ger -cuping or -cupping) intr singhiozzare

**hick** [hɪk] adj & s (coll) rustico

**hicko·ry** ['hɪkəri] s (-ries) hickory m

**hidden** ['hɪdən] adj nascosto

**hide** [haɪd] s cuoio, pelle f; **hides** cuoio; **neither hide nor hair** nemmeno una traccia; **to tan s.o.'s hide** (coll) dargliele sode a qlcu || v (pret **hid** [hɪd]; pp **hid** or **hidden** ['hɪdən]) tr nascondere || intr nascondersi; **to hide out** (coll) rintanarsi

**hide'-and-seek'** s rimpiattino; **to play hide-and-seek** giocare a rimpiattino or a nascondino

**hide'bound'** adj retrogrado, conservatore

**hideous** ['hɪdɪ·əs] adj orribile, brutto

**hide'out'** s nascondiglio

**hiding** ['haɪdɪŋ] s nascondere m; (place) nascondiglio; **in hiding** nascosto

**hid'ing place'** s nascondiglio

**hie** [haɪ] v (pret & pp **hied**; ger **hieing** or **hying**) tr—**hie thee home** affrettati a tornare a casa || intr affrettarsi

**hierar·chy** ['haɪ·ə ‚rɑrki] s (-chies) gerarchia

**hieroglyphic** [ ‚haɪ·ərə'glɪfɪk] adj & s geroglifico

**hi-fi** ['haɪ'faɪ] *adj* di alta fedeltà || *s* alta fedeltà

**higgledy-piggledy** ['hɪgəldɪ'pɪgəldɪ] *adj* confuso || *adv* alla rinfusa

**high** [haɪ] *adj* alto; (*color*) forte; (*merry*) allegro; (*luxurious*) lussuoso; (coll) ubriaco; (culin) frollo; **high and dry** abbandonato; **high and mighty** (coll) arrogante || *adv* molto; riccamente; **to aim high** mirare in alto; **to come high** essere caro || *s* (aut) quarta, diretta; **on high** in cielo

**high' al'tar** *s* altare *m* maggiore

**high'ball'** *s* whiskey con ghiaccio e gazosa || *intr* (slang) andare di carriera

**high' blood' pres'sure** *s* ipertensione

**high'born'** *adj* di nobile lignaggio

**high'boy'** *s* cassettone alto

**high'brow'** *s* intellettuale *mf;* (coll) intellettualoide *mf*

**high'chair'** *s* seggiolino per bambini

**high' command'** *s* comando supremo

**high' cost' of liv'ing** *s* carovita *m*, caroviveri *m*

**high'er educa'tion** *s* insegnamento universitario, istruzione superiore

**higher-up** [,haɪ·ər'ʌp] *s* (coll) superiore *m*

**high' explo'sive** *s* esplosivo ad alta potenza

**highfalutin** [,haɪfə'lutən] *adj* (coll) pomposo, pretenzioso

**high' fidel'ity** *s* high fidelity, alta fedeltà

**high'-fre'quency** *adj* ad alta frequenza

**high' gear'** *s* (aut) presa diretta

**high'-grade'** *adj* di qualità superiore

**high-handed** ['haɪ'hændɪd] *adj* arbitrario

**high' hat'** *s* cappello a cilindro

**high'-hat'** *adj* (coll) snob *m* || *v* (*pret & pp* **-hatted;** *ger* **-hatting**) *tr* (coll) snobbare

**high'-heeled' shoe'** ['haɪ,hild] *s* scarpa coi tacchi alti

**high' horse'** *s* comportamento arrogante; **to get up on one's high horse** darsi le grandi arie

**high' jinks'** [dʒɪŋks] *s* (slang) pagliacciata, gazzarra

**high' jump'** *s* salto in altezza

**highland** ['haɪlənd] *adj* montagnoso || **highlands** *spl* regione montagnosa

**high' life'** *s* high-life *f*, alta società

**high'light'** *s* punto culminante || *tr* mettere in risalto

**highly** ['haɪlɪ] *adv* altamente, molto; (*paid*) profumatamente; **to speak highly of** parlar molto bene di

**High' Mass'** *s* messa cantata

**high-minded** ['haɪ'maɪndɪd] *adj* magnanimo

**highness** ['haɪnɪs] *s* altezza || **Highness** *s* Altezza

**high' noon'** *s* mezzogiorno in punto; (fig) sommo

**high-pitched** ['haɪ'pɪtʃt] *adj* acuto; intenso, emozionante

**high-powered** ['haɪ'pau·ərd] *adj* ad alta potenza; (*binoculars*) ad alto ingrandimento

**high'pres'sure** *adj* ad alta pressione || *tr* sollecitare con insistenza

**high-priced** ['haɪ'praɪst] *adj* caro, di alto prezzo

**high' priest'** *s* sommo sacerdote

**high' rise'** *s* edificio di molti piani

**high'road'** *s* strada principale

**high'school'** *s* scuola media; (*in Italy*) liceo

**high' sea'** *s* alto mare; **high seas** alto mare

**high' soci'ety** *s* l'alta società

**high'-sound'ing** *adj* altisonante

**high'-speed'** *adj* ad alta velocità

**high-spirited** ['haɪ'spɪrɪtɪd] *adj* fiero, vivace, focoso

**high' spir'its** *spl* allegria, vivacità *f*

**high-strung** ['haɪ'strʌŋ] *adj* teso, nervoso

**high'-test' fuel'** *s* supercarburante *m*

**high' tide'** *s* alta marea; punto culminante

**high' time'** *s* ora, e.g., **it is high time for you to go** è proprio ora che Lei se ne vada; (coll) baldoria

**high' trea'son** *s* (*against the sovereign*) lesa maestà; (*against the state*) alto tradimento

**high' wa'ter** *s* alta marea; (*in a river*) straripamento

**high'way'** *adj* autostradale || *s* autostrada

**high'way'man** *s* (**-men**) grassatore *m*

**hijack** ['haɪ,dʒæk] *tr* rubare; (*e.g., an airplane*) dirottare || *intr* effettuare un dirottamento

**hijacker** ['haɪ,dʒækər] *s* ladro a mano armata; (*e.g., of an airplane*) dirottatore *m*

**hijacking** ['haɪ,dʒækɪŋ] *s* furto a mano armata; dirottamento

**hike** [haɪk] *s* (*for pleasure*) gita, camminata; (*increase*) aumento; (mil) marcia || *tr* tirar su; aumentare || *intr* fare una gita; (mil) fare una marcia

**hiker** ['haɪkər] *s* camminatore *m*

**hilarious** [hɪ'lerɪ·əs] or [haɪ'lerɪ·əs] *adj* ilare; (*e.g., joke*) allegro, divertente

**hill** [hɪl] *s* collina || *tr* rincalzare

**hillbil·ly** ['hɪl,bɪlɪ] *s* (**-lies**) (coll) montanaro rustico

**hillock** ['hɪlək] *s* poggio, collinetta

**hill'side'** *s* pendio

**hill'top'** *s* cima

**hill·y** ['hɪlɪ] *adj* (**-ier; -iest**) collinoso; ripido

**hilt** [hɪlt] *s* impugnatura, elsa; **up to the hilt** completamente

**him** [hɪm] *pron pers* lo; lui; **to him** gli, a lui

**himself** [hɪm'self] *pron pers* lui stesso; sé stesso; si, e.g., **he enjoyed himself** si è divertito; **with himself** con sé

**hind** [haɪnd] *adj* posteriore, di dietro || *s* cerva

**hinder** ['hɪndər] *tr* ostacolare, impedire

**hindmost** ['haɪnd,most] *adj* ultimo

**hind'quar'ter** *s* quarto posteriore

**hindrance** ['hɪndrəns] *s* ostacolo, impedimento

**hind'sight'** s senno di poi
**Hindu** ['hɪndu] adj & s indù mf
**hinge** [hɪndʒ] s cardine m; (bb) cerniera; (philately) listello gommato; punto principale ‖ tr munire di cardini ‖ intr—**to hinge on** dipendere da
**hin·ny** ['hɪnɪ] s (-nies) bardotto
**hint** [hɪnt] s insinuazione; **to take the hint** capire l'antifona ‖ tr & intr insinuare; **to hint at** alludere a
**hinterland** ['hɪntər‚lænd] s retroterra m, entroterra m
**hip** [hɪp] adj—**to be hip to** (slang) essere al corrente di ‖ s anca, fianco; (of a roof) spigolo
**hip'bone'** s ileo, osso iliaco
**hipped** [hɪpt] adj (livestock) zoppicante; (roof) a padiglione; **hipped on** (coll) ossessionato per
**hippie** ['hɪpɪ] s capellone m
**hip·po** ['hɪpo] s (-pos) (coll) ippopotamo
**hippodrome** ['hɪpə‚drom] s ippodromo
**hippopota·mus** [‚hɪpə'pɑtəməs] s (-muses or -mi [‚maɪ]) ippopotamo
**hip' roof'** s tetto a padiglione
**hire** [haɪr] s paga, salario; nolo; **for hire** a nolo ‖ tr (help) impiegare; (a conveyance) noleggiare ‖ intr—**to hire out** mettersi a servizio
**hired' girl'** s lavorante f di campagna
**hired' hand'** s lavorante mf
**hired' man'** s (men') lavorante m di campagna
**hireling** ['haɪrlɪŋ] adj venale ‖ s persona prezzolata
**his** [hɪz] adj poss suo, il suo ‖ pron poss il suo
**Hispanic** [hɪs'pænɪk] adj ispano
**Hispanist** ['hɪspənɪst] s ispanista mf
**hiss** [hɪs] s (of fire, wind, serpent, etc.) sibilo; (of disapproval) fischio, zittio ‖ tr zittire ‖ intr zittire; sibilare; (said of a kettle) fischiare
**histology** [hɪs'tɑlədʒɪ] s istologia
**historian** [hɪs'tɔrɪ‚ən] s storico
**historic(al)** [hɪs'tɑrɪk(əl)] or [hɪs'tɔrɪk(əl)] adj storico
**histo·ry** ['hɪstərɪ] s (-ries) storia
**histrionic** [‚hɪstrɪ'ɑnɪk] adj teatrale; (artificial, affected) istrionico, teatrale ‖ **histrionics** s istrionismo, teatralità f
**hit** [hɪt] s colpo; successo; (sarcastic remark) frecciata; **to be a hit** far furore; **to make a hit with** fare ottima impressione con ‖ v (pret & pp hit; ger hitting) tr colpire; (to bump) cozzare; (the target) toccare, imbroccare, infilare; (with a car) metter sotto; (a certain speed) andare a ‖ intr battere; **to hit on** (s.th new) imbroccare; **to hit out at** attaccare
**hit'-and-run'** adj (driver) colpevole di mancato soccorso
**hit'-and-run' driv'er** s pirata m della strada
**hitch** [hɪtʃ] s (jerk) strattone m; (knot) nodo; difficoltà f, ostacolo; ‖ tr (to tie) attaccare; (oxen) aggiogare; (slang) sposare
**hitch'hike'** intr fare l'autostop

**hitch'hik'er** s autostoppista mf
**hitch'ing post'** s palo per attaccare un cavallo
**hither** ['hɪðər] adv qua, qui; **hither and thither** qua e là
**hith'er·to'** adv sinora
**hit'-or-miss'** adj fatto alla carlona
**hit' rec'ord** s disco di grande successo
**hive** [haɪv] s (box for bees) alveare m; (swarm) sciame m; **hives** orticaria ‖ tr (bees) raccogliere
**hoard** [hord] s cumulo; (of money) gruzzolo ‖ tr & intr custodire gelosamente; tesaurizzare
**hoarding** ['hordɪŋ] s ammassamento, tesaurizzazione
**hoarfrost** ['hor‚frɔst] s brina
**hoarse** [hors] adj rauco, svociato
**hoarseness** ['horsnɪs] s raucedine f
**hoar·y** ['horɪ] adj (-ier; -iest) canuto, incanutito
**hoax** [hoks] s mistificazione ‖ tr mistificare
**hob** [hɑb] s mensola del focolare; **to play hob with** (coll) mettere a soqquadro
**hobble** ['hɑbəl] s zoppicamento; (to tie legs of animal) pastoia ‖ tr far zoppicare; imbarazzare; mettere le pastoie a ‖ intr zoppicare
**hob·by** ['hɑbɪ] s (-bies) svago, passatempo; **to ride a hobby** dedicarsi troppo alla propria occupazione favorita
**hob'by-horse'** s cavallo a dondolo
**hob'gob'lin** s folletto
**hob'nail'** s brocca, bulletta
**hob·nob** ['hɑb‚nɑb] v (pret & pp -nobbed; ger -nobbing) intr essere amiconi; **to hobnob with** essere intimo di
**ho·bo** ['hobo] s (-bos or -boes) girovago, vagabondo
**Hob'son's choice'** ['hɑbsənz] s scelta fra quanto viene offerto o niente
**hock** [hɑk] s garretto; (coll) pegno; **in hock** (coll) impegnato, al monte di pietà ‖ tr tagliare i garretti a; (coll) impegnare
**hockey** ['hɑkɪ] s hockey m
**hock'ey play'er** s hockeista m, discatore m
**hock'shop'** s (coll) negozio di prestiti su pegno
**hocus-pocus** ['hokəs'pokəs] s (meaningless formula) abracadabra m; gherminella
**hod** [hɑd] s vassoio; secchio per il carbone
**hod' car'rier** s manovale m
**hodgepodge** ['hɑdʒ‚pɑdʒ] s farragine f
**hoe** [ho] s marra, zappa ‖ tr & intr zappare
**hog** [hɑg] or [hɔg] s suino, porco, maiale m ‖ v (pret & pp hogged; ger hogging) tr (slang) mangiarsi il meglio di
**hoggish** ['hɑgɪʃ] or ['hɔgɪʃ] adj maialesco; egoista
**hogs'head'** s barilozzo di sessantatré galloni
**hog'wash'** s broda da maiali

**hoist** [hɔɪst] *s* montacarichi *m; (lift)* spinta ǁ *tr* alzare, rizzare; *(a flag)* inastare; *(naut)* issare

**hoity-toity** ['hɔɪti'tɔɪti] *adj* arrogante, altezzoso

**hokum** ['hokəm] *s* (coll) fandonie *fpl;* (coll) sentimentalismo volgare

**hold** [hold] *s* presa, piglio; *(handle)* impugnatura; autorità *f*, ascendente *m;* (wrestling) presa; (aer) cabina bagagli; (mus) corona; (naut) cala, stiva; **to take hold of** afferrare; impossessarsi di ǁ *v (pret & pp* **held** [held]) *tr* tenere; *(to hold up)* sostenere; *(e.g., with a pin)* assicurare; *(a rank)* rivestire; contenere; *(a meeting)* avere; *(a note)* (mus) filare; **to hold back** trattenere; **to hold in** trattenere; **to hold one's own** non perdere terreno; **to hold over** differire; **to hold up** reggere, sostenere; *(to rob)* (coll) derubare, rapinare ǁ *intr* stare; *(to cling)* reggere; restare valido; **hold on!** un momento!; **to hold back** frenarsi; **to hold forth** fare un discorso; **to hold off** astenersi; mantenersi a distanza; **to hold on** continuare; **to hold on to** attaccarsi a; **to hold out** tener duro, resistere; **to hold out for** mantenersi fermo per

**holder** ['holdər] *s* possessore *m*, detentore *m; (e.g., for a cigar)* bocchino; *(e.g., for a pot)* manico, impugnatura

**holding** ['holdɪŋ] *s* possesso; **holdings** valori *mpl*, patrimonio

**hold'ing com'pany** *s* società finanziaria

**hold'up'** *s (delay)* interruzione; (coll) rapina a mano armata; (fig) furto

**hold'up man'** *s* grassatore *m*

**hole** [hol] *s* buco; *(in cheese)* occhio; *(in a road)* buca; *(den)* tana; *(burrow)* fossa; **in a hole** in grane, in difficoltà; **to burn a hole in one's pocket** *(said of money)* scorrere attraverso le mani bucate di qlcu; **to pick holes in** trovare a ridire su ǁ *intr*—**to hole up** (coll) imbucarsi

**holiday** ['halɪˌde] *s* giorno festivo, festa; vacanza

**holiness** ['holɪnɪs] *s* santità *f;* **his Holiness** sua Santità

**Holland** ['haland] *s* l'Olanda *f*

**Hollander** ['haləndər] *s* olandese *mf*

**hollow** ['halo] *adj* vuoto; *(sound)* sordo; *(eyes, cheeks)* infossato; vano, futile ǁ *s* buca, cavità *f; (small valley)* valletta ǁ *adv*—**to beat all hollow** (coll) battere completamente ǁ *tr* scavare

**hol•ly** ['hali] *s* (-lies) agrifoglio

**holly'hock'** *s* altea, malvone *m*

**holm' oak'** [hom] *s* leccio

**holocaust** ['haləˌkɔst] *s* olocausto

**holster** ['holstər] *s* fondina

**ho•ly** ['holi] *adj* (-lier; -liest) santo; *(writing)* sacro; *(water)* benedetto

**Ho'ly Ghost'** *s* Spirito Santo

**ho'ly or'ders** *spl* ordini sacri; **to take holy orders** entrare in un ordine religioso

**Ho'ly Rood'** [rud] *s* Santa Croce

**Ho'ly Scrip'ture** *s* Sacra Scrittura

**Ho'ly See'** *s* Santa Sede

**Ho'ly Sep'ulcher** *s* Santo Sepolcro

**Ho'ly Thurs'day** *s* l'Ascensione; il giovedì santo

**ho'ly wa'ter** *s* acqua benedetta, acquasanta

**Ho'ly Writ'** *s* Sacra Scrittura

**homage** ['hamɪdʒ] or ['amɪdʒ] *s* omaggio

**homburg** ['hambʌrg] *s* lobbia *m & f*

**home** [hom] *adj* casalingo, domestico; nazionale ǁ *s* casa, dimora; *(fatherland)* patria; *(for the sick, aged, etc.)* ricovero; (sports) meta, traguardo; **at home** a casa; *(at ease)* a proprio agio; (sports) nel proprio campo; **away from home** fuori di casa; **make yourself at home** stia comodo; **to be at home** *(to receive callers)* ricevere ǁ *adv* a casa; **to see home** accompagnare a casa; **to strike home** toccare nel vivo

**home'bod'y** *s* (-ies) persona casalinga

**homebred** ['homˌbred] *adj* domestico; rozzo; semplice

**home'brew'** *s* bevanda fatta in casa

**home-coming** ['homˌkʌmɪŋ] *s* ritorno a casa

**home' coun'try** *s* paese *m* natale

**home' deliv'ery** *s* trasporto a domicilio

**home' front'** *s* fronte domestico

**home'land'** *s* paese natio

**homeless** ['homlɪs] *adj* senza tetto

**home' life'** *s* vita familiare

**home-loving** ['homˌlʌvɪŋ] *adj* casalingo

**home•ly** ['homli] *adj* (-lier; -liest) *(not goodlooking)* brutto; *(not elegant)* semplice, scialbo

**homemade** ['homˈmed] *adj* fatto in casa

**homemaker** ['homˌmekər] *s* casalinga

**home' of'fice** *s* sede *f* centrale ǁ **Home Office** *s* (Brit) ministero degli interni

**homeopath** ['homɪ•əˌpæθ] or ['hamɪ•əˌpæθ] *s* omeopatico

**home' plate'** *s* casa base

**home' port'** *s* porto d'iscrizione (nel registro marittimo)

**home' rule'** *s* autogoverno

**home' run'** *s* colpo che permette al battitore di percorrere tutte le basi del diamante fino alla casa base

**home'sick'** *adj* nostalgico; **to be homesick for** sentire la nostalgia per

**home'sick'ness** *s* nostalgia

**homespun** ['homˌspʌn] *adj* filato a casa; semplice

**home'stead** *s* casa e terreno

**home'stretch'** *s* (sports) dirittura d'arrivo; (fig) fase *f* finale

**home'town'** *s* città *f* natale

**homeward** ['homwərd] *adj* di ritorno ǁ *adv* verso casa; verso la patria

**home'work'** *s* lavoro a domicilio; *(of a student)* dovere *m*, esercizio

**homey** ['homi] *adj* (homier; homiest) intimo, comodo

**homicidal** [ˌhamɪˈsaɪdəl] *adj* omicida

**homicide** ['hamɪˌsaɪd] *s (act)* omicidio; *(person)* omicida *mf*

**homi•ly** ['hamɪli] *s* (-lies) omelia

**homing** ['homɪŋ] *adj* (*pigeon*) viaggiatore; (*weapon*) cercatore del bersaglio

**hominy** ['hɑmɪnɪ] *s* granturco macinato

**homogenei·ty** [ˌhomədʒɪˈni·ɪtɪ] or [ˌhɑmədʒɪˈni·ɪtɪ] *s* (**-ties**) omogeneità *f*

**homogeneous** [ˌhomə'dʒɪnɪ·əs] or [ˌhɑmə'dʒɪnɪ·əs] *adj* omogeneo

**homogenize** [hə'mɑdʒəˌnaɪz] *tr* omogeneizzare

**homonym** ['hɑmənɪm] *s* omonimo

**homonymous** [hə'mɑnɪməs] *adj* omonimo

**homosexual** [ˌhomə'sekʃu·əl] *adj* & *s* omosessuale *mf*

**hone** [hon] *s* cote *f* ‖ *tr* affilare

**honest** ['ɑnɪst] *adj* onesto; guadagnato onestamente; integro, schietto

**honesty** ['ɑnɪstɪ] *s* onestà *f*; (bot) lunaria

**hon·ey** ['hʌni] *adj* melato, dolce ‖ *s* miele *m;* nettare *m;* (coll) caro ‖ *v* (*pret* & *pp* **-eyed** or **-ied**) *tr* dire parole melate a

**hon'ey·bee'** *s* ape domestica

**hon'ey·comb'** *s* favo ‖ *tr* crivellare

**honeyed** ['hʌnid] *adj* melato

**hon'eydew mel'on** *s* melone *m* dolce dalla scorza liscia

**hon'ey lo'cust** *s* acacia a tre spine

**hon'ey·moon'** *s* luna di miele ‖ *intr* andare in viaggio di nozze

**honeysuckle** ['hʌniˌsʌkəl] *s* caprifoglio

**honk** [hɑŋk] or [hɔŋk] *s* (*of wild goose*) schiamazzo; (*of automobile horn*) suono del clacson ‖ *tr* (aut) suonare ‖ *intr* schiamazzare; (aut) suonare

**honkytonk** ['hɑŋkiˌtɑŋk] or ['hɔŋkiˌtɔŋk] *s* (coll) locale notturno rumoroso

**honor** ['ɑnər] *s* onore *m* ‖ *tr* onorare; (com) accettare e pagare

**honorable** ['ɑnərəbəl] *adj* (*upright*) onorato; (*bringing honor; worthy of honor*) onorevole

**honorari·um** [ˌɑnəˈrerɪ·əm] *s* (**-ums** or **-a** [ə]) onorario

**honorary** ['ɑnəˌreri] *adj* onorario

**honorific** [ˌɑnə'rɪfɪk] *adj* onorifico ‖ *s* titolo onorifico; formula di gentilezza

**hon'or sys'tem** *s* sistema scolastico basato sulla parola d'onore

**hood** [hud] *s* cappuccio; cappuccio di toga universitaria; (*of carriage*) soffietto; (aut) cofano; (slang) gangster *m* ‖ *tr* incappucciare

**hoodlum** ['hudləm] *s* (slang) facinoroso, gangster *m*, teppista *m*

**hoodoo** ['hudu] *s* (*body of primitive rites*) vuduismo; (*bad luck*) iettatura; (*person who brings bad luck*) iettatore *m* ‖ *tr* iettare

**hood'wink'** *tr* turlupinare, imbrogliare

**hooey** ['hu·i] *s* (coll) sciocchezze *fpl*

**hoof** [huf] or [huf] *s* zoccolo, unghia; **on the hoof** (*cattle*) vivo ‖ *tr*—**to hoof it** (slang) camminare; ballare

**hoof'beat'** *s* rumore *m* degli zoccoli

**hook** [huk] *s* gancio; (*for fishing*) amo; (*to join two things*) agganciamento; (*for pulling*) raffio, rampino; (*curve*) curva; (*of hook and eye*) uncinello; (boxing) hook *m*, gancio; **by hook or by crook** di riffa o di raffa; to swallow the hook abboccare all'amo ‖ *tr* agganciare; (*to bend*) curvare; (*fish*) pigliare; (*to wound with the horns*) incornare; **to hook up** agganciare; (*e.g., a loudspeaking system*) montare ‖ *intr* agganciarsi; curvarsi

**hookah** ['hukə] *s* narghilè *m*

**hook' and eye'** *s* uncinello e occhiello

**hook' and lad'der** *s* autoscala

**hooked' rug'** *s* tappeto fatto all'uncinetto

**hook'nose'** *s* naso gobbo

**hook'up'** *s* (electron) diagramma *m*, schema *m* di montaggio; (rad, telv) rete *f*

**hook'worm'** *s* anchilostoma *m*

**hooky** ['huki] *s*—**to play hooky** marinare la scuola

**hooligan** ['huligən] *s* teppista *m*

**hooliganism** ['huligənˌɪzəm] *s* teppismo

**hoop** [hup] or [hup] *s* cerchio ‖ *tr* cerchiare

**hoop' skirt'** *s* crinolina

**hoot** [hut] *s* grido della civetta; grido di derisione ‖ *tr* zittire ‖ *intr* stridere; **to hoot at** fischiare

**hoot' owl'** *s* allocco

**hop** [hɑp] *s* salto, saltello; (aer) breve volo; (bot) luppolo; (coll) corsa; **hops** (*dried flowers of hop vine*) luppolo ‖ *v* (*pret* & *pp* **hopped;** *ger* **hopping**) *tr* saltare su; (aer) trasvolare ‖ *intr* saltellare; saltellare su un piede; **to hop over** saltare su; fare una corsa a

**hope** [hop] *s* speranza ‖ *tr* & *intr* sperare; **to hope for** sperare

**hope' chest'** *s* corredo da sposa

**hopeful** ['hopfəl] *adj* (*feeling hope*) fiducioso; (*giving hope*) promettente

**hopeless** ['hoplɪs] *adj* disperato

**hopper** ['hɑpər] *s* tramoggia

**hop'scotch'** *s* gioco del mondo

**horde** [hord] *s* orda

**horehound** ['horˌhaund] *s* marrubio; pastiglie *fpl* per la tosse al marrubio

**horizon** [hə'raɪzən] *s* orizzonte *m*

**horizontal** [ˌhɑrɪ'zɑntəl] or [ˌhɑrɪ'zɑntəl] *adj* & *s* orizzontale *f*

**hormone** ['hɔrmon] *s* ormone *m*

**horn** [hɔrn] *s* corno; (aut) clacson *m*, avvisatore acustico; (mus) corno; (*trumpet*) tromba; (slang) tromba; **to blow one's horn** cantare le proprie lodi; **to lock horns** lottare, disputare; **to pull in one's horns** battere in ritirata ‖ *intr*—**to horn in** (slang) intromettersi (in)

**horned' owl'** ['hɔrned] *s* allocco

**hornet** ['hɔrnɪt] *s* calabrone *m*

**hor'net's nest'** *s* vespaio; **to stir up a hornet's nest** suscitare un vespaio

**horn' of plen'ty** *s* corno dell'abbondanza

**horn'pipe'** *s* clarinetto contadinesco inglese fatto di corno di bue

**horn'-rimmed glass'es** ['hɔrn'rɪmd] *spl* occhiali cerchiati di corno or con la montatura di corno

**horn·y** ['hɔrni] *adj* (**-ier; -iest**) corneo; (*callous*) calloso; (*having hornlike projections*) cornuto; (slang) preso da desiderio lussurioso

**horoscope** ['harə͵skop] or ['hɔrə͵skop] *s* oroscopo

**horrible** ['harɪbəl] or ['hɔrɪbəl] *adj* orrendo, orribile

**horrid** ['harɪd] or ['hɔrɪd] *adj* orrido, orribile

**horri·fy** ['harɪ͵faɪ] or ['hɔrɪ͵faɪ] *v* (*pret & pp* **-fied**) *tr* inorridire

**horror** ['harər] or ['hɔrər] *s* orrore *m*; **to have a horror of** provare orrore per

**hors d'oeuvre** [ɔr 'dʌrv] *s* (**hors d'oeuvres** [ɔr 'dʌrvz]) *s* antipasto

**horse** [hɔrs] *s* cavallo; (*of carpenter*) cavalletto; **hold your horses!** (coll) aspetti un momento!; **to back the wrong horse** (coll) puntare sul perdente; **to be a horse of another color** (coll) essere un altro paio di maniche ‖ *intr*—**to horse around** (slang) giocherellare; (slang) fare tiri burloni

**horse'back'** *s*—**on horseback** a cavallo ‖ *adv*—**to ride horseback** montare a cavallo

**horse' block'** *s* montatoio

**horse'break'er** *s* domatore *m* di cavalli

**horse'car'** *s* tram *m* a cavalli

**horse' chest'nut** *s* (*tree*) ippocastano; (*nut*) castagna d'India

**horse' deal'er** *s* mercante *m* di cavalli

**horse' doc'tor** *s* veterinario

**horse'fly'** *s* (**-flies**) tafano

**horse'hair'** *s* crine *m* di cavallo; (*fabric*) cilicio

**horse'hide'** *s* cuoio di cavallo

**horse'laugh'** *s* risataccia

**horse'man** *s* (**-men**) cavallerizzo

**horsemanship** ['hɔrsmən͵ʃɪp] *s* equitazione, maneggio

**horse' meat'** *s* carne equina

**horse' op'era** *s* western *m*

**horse' pis'tol** *s* pistola da sella

**horse'play'** *s* gioco violento, tiro burlone

**horse'pow'er** *s* cavallo vapore inglese

**horse' race'** *s* corsa ippica

**horse'rad'ish** *s* cren *m*, barbaforte *m*

**horse' sense'** *s* (coll) senso comune

**horse'shoe'** *s* ferro di cavallo

**horse'shoe mag'net** *s* calamita a ferro di cavallo

**horse'shoe nail'** *s* chiodo da cavallo

**horse' show'** *s* concorso ippico

**horse' thief'** *s* ladro di cavalli

**horse'-trade'** *intr* trafficare

**horse'whip'** *s* staffile *m* ‖ *v* (*pret & pp* **-whipped; ger -whipping**) *tr* staffilare

**horse'wom'an** *s* (**-wom'en**) amazzone *f*

**hors·y** ['hɔrsi] *adj* (**-ier; -iest**) equestre; (*interested in horses*) appassionato ai cavalli; (coll) goffo

**horticulture** ['hɔrtɪ͵kʌltʃər] *s* orticoltura

**horticulturist** [͵hɔrtɪ'kʌltʃərɪst] *s* orticoltore *m*

**hose** [hoz] *s* (*stocking*) calza; (*sock*) calzino corto; (*flexible tube*) manica ‖ **hose** *spl* calze *fpl*

**hosier** ['hoʒər] *s* calzettaio

**hosiery** ['hoʒəri] *s* calze *fpl;* calzificio

**hospice** ['haspɪs] *s* ospizio

**hospitable** ['haspɪtəbəl] or [has'pɪtəbəl] *adj* ospitale

**hospital** ['haspɪtəl] *s* ospedale *m*

**hospitali·ty** [͵haspɪ'tælɪti] *s* (**-ties**) ospitalità *f*

**hospitalize** ['haspɪtə͵laɪz] *tr* ospedalizzare

**host** [host] s ospite *m; (at an inn)* oste *m; (army)* milizia; (*crowd*) folla ‖ **Host** *s* (eccl) ostia

**hostage** ['hɑstɪdʒ] *s* ostaggio

**hostel** ['hɑstəl] *s* ostello della gioventù

**hostel·ry** ['hɑstəlri] *s* (**-ries**) albergo

**hostess** ['hostɪs] *s* ospite *f*, padrona di casa; (*e.g., on a bus*) accompagnatrice *f*, guida *f;* (aer) assistente *f* di volo

**hostile** ['hɑstɪl] *adj* ostile

**hostili·ty** [hɑs'tɪlɪti] *s* (**-ties**) ostilità *f*

**hostler** ['hɑslər] or ['ɑslər] *s* stalliere *m*

**hot** [hɑt] *adj* (**hotter; hottest**) caldo; (*reception*) caloroso; (*e.g., pepper*) piccante; (*fresh*) fresco; (*pursuit*) impetuoso; (*in rut*) in calore; (coll) radioattivo; **to be hot** (said of a person) aver caldo; (said of the weather) fare caldo; **to make it hot for** (coll) dare del filo da torcere a

**hot' air'** *s* aria calda; (slang) fumo

**hot'-air fur'nace** *s* impianto di riscaldamento ad aria calda

**hot' baths'** *spl* terme *fpl*

**hot'bed'** *s* (*e.g., of revolt*) focolaio; (hort) semenzaio, letto caldo

**hot'-blood'ed** *adj* ardente; impetuoso

**hot' cake'** *s* frittella; **to sell like hot cakes** vendersi come se fosse regalato

**hot' dog'** *s* Frankfurter *m*, Würstel *m*

**hotel** [ho'tel] *adj* alberghiero ‖ *s* albergo

**ho·tel'keep'er** *s* albergatore *m*

**hot'head'** *s* testa calda

**hotheaded** ['hɑt͵hedɪd] *adj* esaltato, scalmanato

**hot'house'** *s* serra

**hot' plate'** *s* fornello elettrico, scaldavivande *m*

**hot' springs'** *spl* terme *fpl*

**hot-tempered** ['hɑt'tempərd] *adj* impulsivo, irascibile

**hot' wa'ter** *s*—**to be in hot water** (coll) essere nei guai

**hot'-wa'ter boil'er** *s* caldaia del termosifone

**hot'-wa'ter bot'tle** *s* borsa dell'acqua calda

**hot'-wa'ter heat'er** *s* scaldabagno

**hot'-wa'ter heat'ing** *s* riscaldamento a circolazione di acqua calda

**hound** [haund] *s* bracco; **to follow the hounds** or **to ride to hounds** andare a caccia alla volpe ‖ *tr* perseguitare

**hour** [aur] *s* ora; **by the hour** a ore; **in an evil hour** in un brutto momento; **on the hour** ogni ora al suonar del-

l'ora; **to keep late hours** andare a letto tardi
**hour'glass'** s clessidra
**hour' hand'** s lancetta delle ore
**hourly** ['aʊrlɪ] adj orario ǁ adv ogni ora; spesso
**house** [haʊs] s (**houses** ['haʊzɪz]) casa; (legislative body) camera; (size of audience) concorso di pubblico; teatro; **to keep house** fare le faccende domestiche; **to put one's house in order** migliorare il proprio comportamento; accomodare le proprie faccende ǁ [haʊz] tr allogare
**house' arrest'** s arresto a domicilio
**house'boat'** s casa galleggiante
**house'break'er** s scassinatore m
**housebreaking** ['haʊs ˌbrekɪŋ] s violazione di domicilio, scasso
**housebroken** ['haʊs ˌbrokən] adj (e.g., cat) che è stato addestrato a tenersi pulito
**house'clean'ing** s pulizia della casa; (fig) pulizia, repulisti m
**house'coat'** s vestaglia da casa
**house' cur'rent** s corrente f da rete
**house'fly'** s (-flies) mosca domestica
**houseful** ['haʊs ˌfʊl] s casa piena
**house' fur'nishings** spl arredi domestici
**house'hold'** adj domestico ǁ s famiglia
**house'hold'er** s capo della famiglia
**house'-hunt'** intr—**to go house-hunting** andare in cerca di casa
**house'keep'er** s governante f
**house'keep'ing** s faccende domestiche; **to set up housekeeping** metter su casa
**house'keeping apart'ment** s appartamentino
**house'maid'** s domestica
**house' me'ter** s contatore domestico
**house'moth'er** s maestra in pensionato per studenti
**house' of cards'** s castello di carte
**house' of ill' repute'** s casa di malaffare
**house' paint'er** s imbianchino
**house' physi'cian** s medico residente
**house'top'** s tetto; **to shout from the housetops** proclamare ai quattro venti
**housewarming** ['haʊs ˌwɔrmɪŋ] s festa per l'inaugurazione di una casa
**house'wife'** s (-wives') donna di casa
**house'work'** s faccende domestiche
**housing** ['haʊzɪŋ] s (of a horse) gualdrappa; (dwelling) abitazioni fpl; (carp) alloggiamento; (mach) gabbia, custodia; (aut) coppa; (of transmission) (aut) scatola
**hous'ing short'age** s crisi f degli alloggi
**hovel** ['hʌvəl] or ['hɑvəl] s catapecchia, stamberga; (shed) baracca
**hover** ['hʌvər] or ['hɑvər] intr librarsi; (on the lips) trapelare; (fig) ondeggiare, esitare
**how** [haʊ] adv come; (at what price) a quanto; **how early** quando, a che ora; **how else** in che altro modo; **how far** fino a dove; quanto, e.g., **how far is it to the station?** quanto c'è da qui alla stazione?; **how long** quanto tempo; **how many** quanti; **how much**

quanto; **how often** quante volte; **how old are you?** quanti anni ha?; **how soon** quando, a che ora; **how + adj** quanto + adj, e.g., **how beautiful she is!** quanto è bella!
**how·ev'er** adv comunque; in qualunque modo; per quanto . . . , e.g., **however wrong he may be** per quanto torto possa avere ǁ conj come, e.g., **do it however you want** lo faccia come vuole
**howitzer** ['haʊ·ɪtsər] s obice m
**howl** [haʊl] s ululato, urlo; scoppio di risa ǁ tr gridare; **to howl down** sopraffare a grida; ǁ intr ululare, urlare
**howler** ['haʊlər] s urlatore m; (coll) strafalcione m, topica
**hoyden** ['hɔɪdən] s ragazzaccia
**hub** [hʌb] s mozzo; (fig) centro
**hubbub** ['hʌbəb] s putiferio, fracasso
**hub'cap'** s (aut) calotta della ruota
**huckleber·ry** ['hʌkəl ˌberi] s (-ries) mirtillo
**huckster** ['hʌkstər] s venditore m ambulante; trafficante m
**huddle** ['hʌdəl] s conferenza segreta ǁ intr affollarsi, accalcarsi
**hue** [hju] s tono, tinta; **hue and cry** grido d'indignazione
**huff** [hʌf] s stizza; **in a huff** di cattivo umore ǁ tr (checkers) buffare
**hug** [hʌg] s abbraccio ǁ v (pret & pp **hugged**; ger **hugging**) tr abbracciare; (e.g., a wall) costeggiare ǁ intr abbracciarsi
**huge** [hjudʒ] adj smisurato, immane
**huh** [hʌ] interj eh!
**hulk** [hʌlk] s scafo, carcassa; (unwieldy object) trabiccolo
**hulking** ['hʌlkɪŋ] adj grosso e goffo
**hull** [hʌl] s (of ship or hydroplane) scafo; (of dirigible) intelaiatura; (of airplane) fusoliera; (e.g., of a nut) guscio ǁ tr sgusciare; (rice) brillare
**hullabaloo** ['hʌləbə ˌlu] or [ ˌhʌləbə'lu] s fracasso, baccano
**hum** [hʌm] s canterellio; (of bee, machine, etc.) ronzio ǁ v (pret & pp **hummed**; ger **humming**) tr canterellare ǁ intr canterellare; (to buzz) ronzare; (coll) vibrare, essere attivo
**human** ['hjumən] adj umano
**hu'man be'ing** s essere umano
**humane** [hju'men] adj umano; compassionevole
**humanist** ['hjumənɪst] adj umanistico ǁ s umanista mf
**humanitarian** [hju ˌmænɪ'terɪ·ən] adj & s umanitario
**humani·ty** [hju'mænɪti] s (-ties) umanità f; **humanities** (of Greece and Rome) studi umanistici; (literature, art, philosophy) scienze umanistiche
**hu'man·kind'** s genere umano
**humble** ['hʌmbəl] or ['ʌmbəl] adj umile ǁ tr umiliare
**hum'ble pie'** s—**to eat humble pie** accettare un'umiliazione
**hum'bug'** s frottola; (person) impostore m ǁ v (pret & pp **-bugged**; ger

**-bugging)** *tr* imbrogliare ‖ *intr* fare l'imbroglione
**hum'drum'** *adj* noioso, monotono
**humer·us** ['hjumərəs] *s* (-**i** [,aɪ]) omero
**humid** ['hjumɪd] *adj* umido
**humidifier** [hju'mɪdɪ,faɪ·ər] *s* evaporatore *m*
**humidi·fy** [hju'mɪdɪ,faɪ] *v* (*pret* & *pp* -**fied**) *tr* inumidire
**humidity** [hju'mɪdɪti] *s* umidità *f*
**humiliate** [hju'mɪlɪ,et] *tr* umiliare
**humiliating** [hju'mɪlɪ,etɪŋ] *adj* umiliante
**humility** [hju'mɪlɪti] *s* umiltà *f*
**hummingbird** ['hʌmɪŋ,bʌrd] *s* colibrì *m*
**humor** ['hjumər] or ['jumər] *s* umore *m;* umorismo; **out of humor** di cattivo umore ‖ *tr* adattarsi alle fisime di, assecondare
**humorist** ['hjumərɪst] or ['jumərɪst] *s* umorista *mf*
**humorous** ['hjumərəs] or ['jumərəs] *adj* umoristico
**hump** [hʌmp] *s* gobba; (*in the ground*) monticello
**hump'back'** *s* gobba; (*person*) gobbo
**humus** ['hjuməs] *s* humus *m*
**hunch** [hʌntʃ] *s* gobba; (*premonition*) (coll) sospetto ‖ *tr* piegare ‖ *intr* accovacciarsi
**hunch'back'** *s* gobba; (*person*) gobbo
**hundred** ['hʌndrəd] *adj, s* & *pron* cento; **a hundred** or **one hundred** cento; **by the hundreds** a centinaia
**hundredth** ['hʌndrədθ] *adj, s* & *pron* centesimo
**hun'dred·weight'** *s* cento libbre
**Hungarian** [hʌŋ'gerɪ·ən] *adj* & *s* ungherese *mf*
**Hungary** ['hʌŋgəri] *s* l'Ungheria *f*
**hunger** ['hʌŋgər] *s* fame *f* ‖ *intr* aver fame; **to hunger for** aver un desiderio ardente di, agognare
**hun'ger strike'** *s* sciopero della fame
**hun·gry** ['hʌŋgri] *adj* (-**grier**; -**griest**) affamato; **to be hungry** aver fame; **to go hungry** andare digiuno
**hunk** [hʌŋk] *s* (coll) bel pezzo
**hunt** [hʌnt] *s* caccia; **on the hunt for** a caccia di ‖ *tr* cacciare; (*to look for*) cercare ‖ *intr* andare a caccia; **to go hunting** andare a caccia; **to hunt for** cercare
**hunter** ['hʌntər] *s* cacciatore *m;* (*dog*) cane *m* da caccia
**hunting** ['hʌntɪŋ] *adj* da caccia ‖ *s* caccia
**hunt'ing box'** *s* capanno
**hunt'ing dog'** *s* cane *m* da caccia
**hunt'ing ground'** *s* terreno di caccia
**hunt'ing horn'** *s* corno da caccia
**hunt'ing jack'et** *s* cacciatora
**hunt'ing lodge'** *s* (*hut*) capanno; villino da caccia
**hunt'ing sea'son** *s* stagione della caccia
**huntress** ['hʌntrɪs] *s* cacciatrice *f*
**hunts'man** *s* (-**men**) cacciatore *m*
**hurdle** ['hʌrdəl] *s* (*hedge*) siepe *f;* (*wooden frame*) barriera; (sports, fig) ostacolo; **hurdles** corsa ad ostacoli ‖ *tr* saltare, superare

**hur'dle race'** *s* corsa agli ostacoli
**hurl** [hʌrl] *s* lancio ‖ *tr* lanciare; **to hurl back** respingere
**hurrah** [hʊ'rɑ] or **hurray** [hʊ're] *s* viva *m* ‖ *tr* applaudire ‖ *intr* gridare urrà ‖ *interj* evviva!, urrà!; **hurrah for . . .!** viva **. . .!**
**hurricane** ['hʌrɪ,ken] *s* uragano
**hurried** ['hʌrid] *adj* frettoloso
**hur·ry** ['hʌri] *s* (-**ries**) fretta; **to be in a hurry** avere fretta ‖ *v* (*pret* & *pp* -**ried**) *tr* affrettare, sollecitare ‖ *intr* affrettarsi; **to hurry after** correr dietro a; **to hurry away** andarsene di furia; **to hurry back** ritornare presto; **to hurry up** spicciarsi
**hurt** [hʌrt] *adj* (*injured*) ferito; (*offended*) risentito ‖ *s* (*harm*) danno; (*injury*) ferita; (*pain*) dolore *m* ‖ *v* (*pret* & *pp* **hurt**) *tr* (*to harm*) fare male a; (*to injure*) ferire; (*to offend*) offendere; (*to pain*) dolere (with *dat*) ‖ *intr* fare male, dolere; aver male, e.g., **my head hurts** ho male alla testa
**hurtle** ['hʌrtəl] *intr* sferrarsi, scagliarsi, precipitarsi
**husband** ['hʌzbənd] *s* marito ‖ *tr* amministrare con economia
**hus'band·man** *s* (-**men**) agricoltore *m*
**husbandry** ['hʌzbəndri] *s* agricoltura; (*management of domestic affairs*) governo, economia domestica
**hush** [hʌʃ] *s* silenzio ‖ *tr* far tacere; **to hush up** (*a scandal*) soffocare ‖ *intr* tacere ‖ *interj* zitto!
**hushaby** ['hʌʃə,baɪ] *interj* fa' la nanna!
**hush'-hush'** *adj* segretissimo
**hush' mon'ey** *s* prezzo del silenzio
**husk** [hʌsk] *s* guscio; (*of corn*) spoglia ‖ *tr* sgusciare; (*rice*) brillare; (*corn*) scartocciare, spogliare
**husk·y** ['hʌski] *adj* (-**ier**; -**iest**) forte; (*voice*) rauco
**hus·sy** ['hʌzi] or ['hʌsi] *s* (-**sies**) poca di buono; ragazza impudente
**hustle** ['hʌsəl] *s* vigore *m;* (slang) traffico ‖ *tr* forzare, spingere ‖ *intr* affrettarsi, scalmanarsi; (slang) trafficare; (*said of a prostitute*) (slang) accostare un cliente
**hustler** ['hʌslər] *s* (*go-getter*) persona intraprendente; (slang) trafficone *m*, imbroglione *m;* (slang) passeggiatrice *f*
**hut** [hʌt] *s* casolare *m*, casupola
**hyacinth** ['haɪ·əsɪnθ] *s* giacinto
**hybrid** ['haɪbrɪd] *adj* & *s* ibrido
**hybridize** ['haɪbrɪ,daɪz] *tr* & *intr* ibridare
**hy·dra** ['haɪdrə] *s* (-**dras** or -**drae** [dri]) idra
**hydrant** ['haɪdrənt] *s* idrante *m;* (*water faucet*) rubinetto
**hydrate** ['haɪdret] *s* idrato ‖ *tr* idratare ‖ *intr* idratarsi
**hydraulic** [haɪ'drɔlɪk] *adj* idraulico ‖ **hydraulics** *s* idraulica
**hydrau'lic ram'** *s* pompa idraulica
**hydriodic** [,haɪdrɪ'ɑdɪk] *adj* iodidrico
**hydrobromic** [,haɪdrə'bromɪk] *adj* bromidrico

**hydrocarbon** [ˌhaɪdrəˈkɑrbən] s idrocarburo
**hydrochloric** [ˌhaɪdrəˈklorɪk] adj cloridrico
**hydroelectric** [ˌhaɪdro·ɪˈlɛktrɪk] adj idroelettrico
**hydrofluoric** [ˌhaɪdrəfluˈɑrɪk] or [ˌhaɪdrəfluˈɔrɪk] adj fluoridrico
**hydrofoil** [ˈhaɪdrəˌfɔɪl] s superificie idrodinamica; (winglike member) aletta idrodinamica; (vessel) aliscafo, idroplano
**hydrogen** [ˈhaɪdrədʒən] s idrogeno
**hy'drogen bomb'** s bomba all'idrogeno
**hy'drogen perox'ide** s perossido d'idrogeno, acqua ossigenata
**hy'drogen sul'fide** s solfuro d'idrogeno
**hydrometer** [haɪˈdrɑmɪtər] s areometro
**hydrophobia** [ˌhaɪdrəˈfobɪ·ə] s idrofobia
**hydroplane** [ˈhaɪdrəˌplen] s (aer) idrovolante m; (naut) idroscivolante m, idroplano
**hydroxide** [haɪˈdrɑksaɪd] s idrossido
**hyena** [haɪˈinə] s iena
**hygiene** [ˈhaɪdʒin] or [ˈhaɪdʒɪˌin] s igiene f
**hygienic** [ˌhaɪdʒɪˈɛnɪk] or [haɪˈdʒɪnɪk] adj igienico
**hymn** [hɪm] s inno
**hymnal** [ˈhɪmnəl] s innario
**hyperacidity** [ˌhaɪpərəˈsɪdɪti] s iperacidità f
**hyperbola** [haɪˈpʌrbələ] s (geom) iperbole f
**hyperbole** [haɪˈpʌrbəli] s (rhet) iperbole f

**hyperbolic** [ˌhaɪpərˈbɑlɪk] adj iperbolico
**hypersensitive** [ˌhaɪpərˈsɛnsɪtɪv] adj ipersensibile
**hypertension** [ˌhaɪpərˈtɛnʃən] s ipertensione
**hyphen** [ˈhaɪfən] s trattino
**hyphenate** [ˈhaɪfəˌnet] tr unire con trattino; scrivere con trattino
**hypno·sis** [hɪpˈnosɪs] s (-ses [siz]) ipnosi f
**hypnotic** [hɪpˈnɑtɪk] adj & s ipnotico
**hypnotism** [ˈhɪpnəˌtɪzəm] s ipnotismo
**hypnotize** [ˈhɪpnəˌtaɪz] tr ipnotizzare
**hypochondriac** [ˌhaɪpəˈkɑndrɪˌæk] or [ˌhɪpəˈkɑndrɪˌæk] s ipocondriaco
**hypocri·sy** [hɪˈpɑkrəsi] s (-sies) ipocrisia
**hypocrite** [ˈhɪpəkrɪt] s ipocrita mf
**hypocritical** [ˌhɪpəˈkrɪtɪkəl] adj ipocrita
**hypodermic** [ˌhaɪpəˈdʌrmɪk] adj ipodermico
**hyposulfite** [ˌhaɪpəˈsʌlfaɪt] s iposolfito
**hypotenuse** [haɪˈpɑtɪˌnus] or [haɪˈpɑtɪˌnjus] s ipotenusa
**hypothesis** [haɪˈpɑθɪsɪs] s (-ses [ˌsiz]) ipotesi f
**hypothesize** [haɪˈpɑθɪˌsaɪz] tr ipotizzare
**hypothetic(al)** [ˌhaɪpəˈθɛtɪk(əl)] adj ipotetico
**hyssop** [ˈhɪsəp] s issopo
**hysteria** [hɪsˈtɪrɪ·ə] s isterismo
**hysteric** [hɪsˈtɛrɪk] adj isterico || **hysterics** s isterismo
**hysterical** [hɪsˈtɛrɪkəl] adj isterico

# I

**I, i** [aɪ] s nona lettera dell'alfabeto inglese
**I** [aɪ] pron pers (we [wi]) io; **it is I** sono io
**iambic** [aɪˈæmbɪk] adj giambico
**iam·bus** [aɪˈæmbəs] s (-bi [baɪ]) giambo
**I'-beam'** s putrella
**Iberian** [aɪˈbɪrɪ·ən] adj iberico || s abitante mf dell'Iberia; lingua iberica
**ibex** [ˈaɪbɛks] s (ibexes or ibices [ˈɪbɪˌsiz]) stambecco
**ice** [aɪs] s ghiaccio; **to break the ice** rompere il ghiaccio; **to cut no ice** (coll) non avere importanza; **to skate on thin ice** cacciarsi in una situazione delicata || tr gelare; (to cover with icing) glassare || intr gelarsi
**ice' age'** s epoca glaciale
**ice' bag'** s borsa di ghiaccio
**iceberg** [ˈaɪsˌbʌrg] s borgognone m, montagna di ghiaccio
**ice'boat'** s slitta a vela; (icebreaker) rompighiaccio
**icebound** [ˈaɪsˌbaʊnd] adj chiuso dal ghiaccio
**ice'box'** s ghiacciaia
**ice'break'er** s rompighiaccio

**ice' buck'et** s secchiello da ghiaccio
**ice'cap'** s calotta glaciale
**ice'-cold'** adj gelido, ghiacciato
**ice' cream'** s gelato, sorbetto
**ice'-cream cone'** s cono gelato
**ice'-cream freez'er** s gelatiera
**ice'-cream par'lor** s gelateria
**ice' cube'** s cubetto di ghiaccio
**ice' hock'ey** s hockey m su ghiaccio
**Iceland** [ˈaɪslənd] s l'Islanda f
**Icelander** [ˈaɪsˌlændər] or [ˈaɪsləndər] s islandese mf
**Icelandic** [aɪsˈlændɪk] adj islandese || s (language) islandese m
**ice'man'** s (-men') venditore m di ghiaccio
**ice' pack'** s banco di ghiaccio; (ice bag) borsa di ghiaccio
**ice' pick'** s rompighiaccio
**ice' shelf'** s tavolato di ghiaccio
**ice' skate'** s pattino da ghiaccio
**ice' wa'ter** s acqua gelata
**ichthyology** [ˌɪkθɪˈɑlədʒi] s ittiologia
**icicle** [ˈaɪsɪkəl] s ghiacciolo
**icing** [ˈaɪsɪŋ] s glassa; (meteor) gelo
**iconoclast** [aɪˈkɑnəˌklæst] s iconoclasta mf

**iconoscope** [aɪ'kɑnə‚skop] *s* (trademark) iconoscopio

**icy** ['aɪsi] *adj* (**icier; iciest**) ghiacciato; (*e.g., wind, hands*) gelido; (fig) glaciale

**idea** [aɪ'di·ə] *s* idea

**ideal** [aɪ'di·əl] *adj & s* ideale *m*

**idealist** [aɪ'di·əlɪst] *adj & s* idealista *mf*

**idealistic** [aɪ‚dɪ·əl'ɪstɪk] *adj* idealistico

**idealize** [aɪ'di·ə‚laɪz] *tr* idealizzare

**identic(al)** [aɪ'dɛntɪk(əl)] *adj* identico

**identification** [aɪ‚dɛntɪfɪ'keʃən] *s* identificazione, riconoscimento

**identifica'tion card'** *s* carta d'identità

**identifica'tion tag'** *s* piastrina

**identi·fy** [aɪ'dɛntɪ‚faɪ] *v* (*pret & pp* **-fied**) *tr* identificare

**identi·ty** [aɪ'dɛntɪti] *s* (**-ties**) identità *f*

**ideolo·gy** [‚aɪdɪ'ɑlədʒi] or [‚ɪdɪ'ɑlədʒi] *s* (**-gies**) ideologia

**ides** [aɪdz] *spl* idi *mpl & fpl*

**idio·cy** ['ɪdɪ·əsi] *s* (**-cies**) idiozia

**idiom** ['ɪdɪ·əm] *s* (*expression that is contrary to the usual patterns of the language*) locuzione idiomatica, idiotismo; (*style of language*) lingua, idioma *m*; (*style of an author*) stile *m*; (*character of a language*) indole *f*

**idiomatic** [‚ɪdɪ·ə'mætɪk] *adj* idiomatico

**idiosyncra·sy** [‚ɪdɪ·ə'sɪnkrəsi] *s* (**-sies**) eccentricità *f*, originalità *f*; (med) idiosincrasia

**idiot** ['ɪdɪ·ət] *s* idiota *mf*

**idiotic** [‚ɪdɪ'ɑtɪk] *adj* idiota

**idle** ['aɪdəl] *adj* (*unemployed*) disoccupato; (*machine*) fermo; (*capital*) giacente; (*time*) perso; (*talk*) vano; (*lazy*) fannullone, ozioso; **to run idle** girare a vuoto ‖ *tr*—**to idle away** (*time*) sprecare ‖ *intr* poltrire, fare il fannullone; (aut) girare al minimo

**idleness** ['aɪdəlnɪs] *s* ozio

**idler** ['aɪdlər] *s* fannullone *m*

**idling** ['aɪdlɪŋ] *s* (*of motor*) minimo

**idol** ['aɪdəl] *s* idolo

**idola·try** [aɪ'dɑlətri] *s* (**-tries**) idolatria

**idolize** ['aɪdə‚laɪz] *tr* idolatrare

**idyll** ['aɪdəl] *s* idillio

**idyllic** [aɪ'dɪlɪk] *adj* idilliaco

**if** [ɪf] *conj* se; **as if** come se; **even if** anche se; **if so** se è così; **if true** se è vero

**ignis fatuus** ['ɪgnɪs'fætʃu·əs] *s* (**ignes fatui** ['ɪgniz'fætʃu‚aɪ]) fuoco fatuo

**ignite** [ɪg'naɪt] *tr* infiammare ‖ *intr* infiammarsi

**ignition** [ɪg'nɪʃən] *s* ignizione; (aut) accensione

**igni'tion switch'** *s* (aut) chiavetta dell'accensione

**igni'tion sys'tem** *s* (aut) apparecchiatura d'accensione

**ignoble** [ɪg'nobəl] *adj* ignobile

**ignominious** [‚ɪgnə'mɪnɪ·əs] *adj* ignominioso

**ignoramus** [‚ɪgnə'reməs] *s* ignorante *mf*

**ignorance** ['ɪgnərəns] *s* ignoranza

**ignorant** ['ɪgnərənt] *adj* ignorante; **to be ignorant of** ignorare

**ignore** [ɪg'nor] *tr* (*a person; a person's kindness*) ignorare

**ill** [ɪl] *adj* (**worse** [wʌrs]; **worst** [wʌrst]) malato; **to take ill** cadere malato ‖ *adv* male; **to take ill** prendere in mala parte

**ill-advised** ['ɪləd'vaɪzd] *adj* inconsulto, sconsiderato

**ill'-at-ease'** *adj* imbarazzato, spaesato

**ill-bred** ['ɪl'brɛd] *adj* maleducato

**ill-considered** ['ɪlkən'sɪdərd] *adj* sconsiderato

**ill-disposed** ['ɪldɪs'pozd] *adj* maldisposto, malintenzionato

**illegal** [ɪ'ligəl] *adj* illegale

**illegible** [ɪ'lɛdʒɪbəl] *adj* illeggibile

**illegitimate** [‚ɪlɪ'dʒɪtɪmɪt] *adj* illegittimo

**ill' fame'** *s* pessima fama

**ill-fated** ['ɪl'fetɪd] *adj* infausto

**ill-gotten** ['ɪl'gɑtən] *adj* male acquistato

**ill-humored** ['ɪl'hjumərd] *adj* di cattivo umore

**illicit** [ɪ'lɪsɪt] *adj* illecito

**illitera·cy** [ɪ'lɪtərəsi] *s* (**-cies**) analfabetismo; (*mistake*) solecismo; ignoranza

**illiterate** [ɪ'lɪtərɪt] *adj* (*uneducated*) illetterato; (*unable to read or write*) analfabeta ‖ *s* analfabeta *mf*

**ill-mannered** ['ɪl'mænərd] *adj* screanzato, ineducato

**illness** ['ɪlnɪs] *s* malattia

**illogical** [ɪ'lɑdʒɪkəl] *adj* illogico

**ill-spent** ['ɪl'spɛnt] *adj* sprecato

**ill-starred** ['ɪl'stɑrd] *adj* nato sotto una cattiva stella; sfortunato, funesto

**ill-tempered** ['ɪl'tɛmpərd] *adj* di cattivo umore

**ill-timed** ['ɪl'taɪmd] *adj* inopportuno

**ill'-treat'** *tr* maltrattare, tartassare

**illuminate** [ɪ'lumɪ‚net] *tr* illuminare; (*a manuscript*) miniare

**illumination** [ɪ‚lumɪ'neʃən] *s* illuminazione; (*in manuscript*) miniatura

**illusion** [ɪ'luʒən] *s* illusione

**illusive** [ɪ'lusɪv] *adj* illusorio

**illusory** [ɪ'lusəri] *adj* illusorio

**illustrate** ['ɪləs‚tret] or [ɪ'lʌstret] *tr* illustrare

**illustration** [‚ɪləs'treʃən] *s* illustrazione

**illustrator** ['ɪləs‚tretər] *s* illustratore *m*

**illustrious** [ɪ'lʌstrɪ·əs] *adj* illustre

**ill' will'** *s* astio, ruggine *f*, malevolenza

**image** ['ɪmɪdʒ] *s* immagine *f*; **the very image of** il ritratto parlante di

**image·ry** ['ɪmɪdʒri] or ['ɪmɪdʒəri] *s* (**-ries**) (*mental images*) fantasia; (*images collectively*) immagini *fpl*; (rhet) linguaggio figurato

**imaginary** [ɪ'mædʒɪ‚nɛri] *adj* immaginario

**imagination** [ɪ‚mædʒɪ'neʃən] *s* immaginazione

**imagine** [ɪ'mædʒɪn] *tr & intr* immaginare; (*to conjecture*) immaginarsi; **imagine!** si figuri!

**imbalance** [ɪm'bæləns] *s* scompenso

**imbecile** ['ɪmbɪsɪl] *adj & s* imbecille *mf*

**imbecili·ty** [ˌɪmbɪˈsɪlɪti] s (**-ties**) imbecillità f, imbecillaggine f
**imbibe** [ɪmˈbaɪb] tr (to drink) bere; assorbire ‖ intr bere
**imbue** [ɪmˈbju] tr imbevere
**imitate** [ˈɪmɪˌtet] tr imitare
**imitation** [ˌɪmɪˈteʃən] adj (e.g., jewelry) falso ‖ s imitazione
**imitator** [ˈɪmɪˌtetər] s imitatore m
**immaculate** [ɪˈmækjəlɪt] adj immacolato
**immaterial** [ˌɪməˈtɪrɪ·əl] adj immateriale; poco importante; **it's immaterial to me** a me fa lo stesso
**immature** [ˌɪməˈtjʊr] or [ˌɪməˈtʊr] adj immaturo
**immeasurable** [ɪˈmeʒərəbəl] adj incommensurabile, smisurato
**immediacy** [ɪˈmidɪ·əsi] s immediatezza
**immediate** [ɪˈmidɪ·ɪt] adj immediato
**immediately** [ɪˈmidɪ·ɪtli] adv immediatamente
**immemorial** [ˌɪmɪˈmorɪ·əl] adj immemorabile
**immense** [ɪˈmɛns] adj immenso
**immerge** [ɪˈmʌrdʒ] intr sommergersi
**immerse** [ɪˈmʌrs] tr immergere
**immersion** [ɪˈmʌrʃən] or [ɪˈmʌrʒən] s immersione
**immigrant** [ˈɪmɪgrənt] adj & s immigrante mf
**immigrate** [ˈɪmɪˌgret] intr immigrare
**immigration** [ˌɪmɪˈgreʃən] s immigrazione
**imminent** [ˈɪmɪnənt] adj imminente
**immobile** [ɪˈmobɪl] or [ɪˈmobɪl] adj immobile
**immobilize** [ɪˈmobɪˌlaɪz] tr immobilizzare
**immoderate** [ɪˈmɑdərɪt] adj smodato, sregolato
**immodest** [ɪˈmɑdɪst] adj immodesto
**immoral** [ɪˈmɑrəl] or [ɪˈmɔrəl] adj immorale
**immortal** [ɪˈmɔrtəl] adj & s immortale mf
**immortalize** [ɪˈmɔrtəˌlaɪz] tr eternare, immortalare
**immune** [ɪˈmjun] adj immune
**immunize** [ˈɪmjəˌnaɪz] or [ɪˈmjunaɪz] tr immunizzare
**imp** [ɪmp] s diavoletto; (child) frugolo
**impact** [ˈɪmpækt] s impatto
**impair** [ɪmˈper] tr danneggiare; (to weaken) indebolire
**impan·el** [ɪmˈpænəl] v (pret & pp **-eled** or **-elled**; ger **-eling** or **-elling**) tr iscrivere nella lista dei giurati; (a jury) selezionare
**impart** [ɪmˈpɑrt] tr (a secret) far conoscere; (knowledge) impartire; (motion) imprimere
**impartial** [ɪmˈpɑrʃəl] adj imparziale
**impassable** [ɪmˈpæsəbəl] or [ɪmˈpɑsəbəl] adj impraticabile, intransitabile
**impasse** [ɪmˈpæs] or [ˈɪmpæs] s vicolo cieco, impasse f
**impassible** [ɪmˈpæsɪbəl] adj impassibile
**impassioned** [ɪmˈpæʃənd] adj caloroso, veemente
**impassive** [ɪmˈpæsɪv] adj impassibile

**impatience** [ɪmˈpeʃəns] s impazienza
**impatient** [ɪmˈpeʃənt] adj impaziente
**impeach** [ɪmˈpitʃ] tr accusare; (a public official) sottoporre a un'inchiesta; (a statement) mettere in dubbio
**impeachment** [ɪmˈpitʃmənt] s accusa; inchiesta
**impeccable** [ɪmˈpɛkəbəl] adj impeccabile
**impecunious** [ˌɪmpɪˈkjunɪ·əs] adj indigente
**impedance** [ɪmˈpidəns] s impedenza
**impede** [ɪmˈpid] tr impedire, intralciare
**impediment** [ɪmˈpɛdɪmənt] s impedimento; ostacolo
**im·pel** [ɪmˈpɛl] v (pret & pp **-peled** or **-pelled**; ger **-peling** or **-pelling**) tr spingere, forzare
**impending** [ɪmˈpɛndɪŋ] adj imminente, incombente
**impenetrable** [ɪmˈpɛnətrəbəl] adj impenetrabile
**impenitent** [ɪmˈpɛnɪtənt] adj impenitente ‖ s persona impenitente
**imperative** [ɪmˈpɛrɪtɪv] adj (commanding) imperativo; (urgent) imperioso ‖ s imperativo
**imperceptible** [ˌɪmpərˈsɛptɪbəl] adj impercettibile
**imperfect** [ɪmˈpʌrfɪkt] adj & s imperfetto
**imperfection** [ˌɪmpərˈfɛkʃən] s imperfezione
**imperial** [ɪmˈpɪrɪ·əl] adj imperiale ‖ s (goatee) barbetta, mosca; (top of coach) imperiale m
**imperialist** [ɪmˈpɪrɪ·əlɪst] adj & s imperialista mf
**imper·il** [ɪmˈpɛrɪl] v (pret & pp **-iled** or **-illed**; ger **-iling** or **-illing**) tr mettere in pericolo
**imperious** [ɪmˈpɪrɪ·əs] adj imperioso
**imperishable** [ɪmˈpɛrɪʃəbəl] adj imperituro, duraturo
**impersonate** [ɪmˈpʌrsəˌnet] tr (to pretend to be) spacciarsi per; (on the stage) impersonare
**impertinence** [ɪmˈpʌrtɪnəns] s impertinenza
**impertinent** [ɪmˈpʌrtɪnənt] adj impertinente
**impetuous** [ɪmˈpɛtʃʊ·əs] adj impetuoso
**impetus** [ˈɪmpɪtəs] s impeto, foga
**impie·ty** [ɪmˈpaɪ·əti] s (**-ties**) empietà f
**impinge** [ɪmˈpɪndʒ] intr—to impinge on or upon violare; (said, e.g., of the sun) ferire; (the imagination) colpire
**impious** [ˈɪmpɪ·əs] adj empio
**impish** [ˈɪmpɪʃ] adj indiavolato
**implant** [ɪmˈplænt] tr innestare; instillare, istillare
**implement** [ˈɪmplɪmənt] s utensile m, strumento ‖ [ˈɪmplɪˌment] tr completare, mettere in opera; (to provide with implements) attrezzare
**implicate** [ˈɪmplɪˌket] tr implicare
**implicit** [ɪmˈplɪsɪt] adj implicito; (unquestioning) assoluto, cieco
**implied** [ɪmˈplaɪd] adj implicito
**implore** [ɪmˈplor] tr (a person; pardon)

implorare; (to entreat) raccomandarsi a

im·ply [ɪm'plaɪ] v (pret & pp -plied) tr voler dire, significare; implicare, sottintendere

impolite [ˌɪmpə'laɪt] adj scortese

import ['ɪmport] s importazione; articolo d'importazione; importanza || [ɪm'port] or ['ɪmport] tr importare; significare || intr importare

importance [ɪm'pɔrtəns] s importanza

important [ɪm'pɔrtənt] adj importante

importation [ˌɪmpɔr'teʃən] s importazione

importer [ɪm'pɔrtər] s importatore m

importunate [ɪm'pɔrtʃənɪt] adj importuno

importune [ˌɪmpɔr'tjun] or [ˌɪmpɔr'tun] tr importunare

impose [ɪm'poz] tr imporre || intr—to impose on or upon abusare di; abusare della gentilezza di

imposing [ɪm'pozɪŋ] adj imponente

imposition [ˌɪmpə'zɪʃən] s imposizione; abuso; abuso della gentilezza; inganno

impossible [ɪm'pɑsɪbəl] adj impossibile

impostor [ɪm'pɑstər] s impostore m

imposture [ɪm'pɑstʃər] s impostura

impotence ['ɪmpətəns] s impotenza

impotent ['ɪmpətənt] adj impotente

impound [ɪm'paʊnd] tr rinchiudere, recintare; (water) raccogliere; (law) sequestrare, confiscare

impoverish [ɪm'pɑvərɪʃ] tr impoverire

impracticable [ɪm'præktɪkəbəl] adj impraticabile; (intractable) intrattabile

impractical [ɪm'præktɪkəl] adj poco pratico

impregnable [ɪm'prɛgnəbəl] adj inespugnabile, imprendibile

impregnate [ɪm'prɛgnet] tr impregnare

impresari·o [ˌɪmprɪ'sɑri ˌo] s (-os) impresario

impress [ɪm'prɛs] tr (to affect in mind or feelings) impressionare; (to produce by pressure; to fix on s.o.'s mind) imprimere; (mil) arruolare

impression [ɪm'prɛʃən] s impressione

impressionable [ɪm'prɛʃənəbəl] adj impressionabile

impressive [ɪm'prɛsɪv] adj impressionante, imponente

imprint ['ɪmprɪnt] s impronta; (typ) indicazione dell'editore || [ɪm'prɪnt] tr imprimere

imprison [ɪm'prɪzən] tr imprigionare

imprisonment [ɪm'prɪzənmənt] s prigione, prigionia

improbable [ɪm'prɑbəbəl] adj improbabile

impromptu [ɪm'prɑmptju] or [ɪm'prɑmptu] adj improvvisato || s improvvisazione; (mus) impromptu m || adv all'improvviso

improper [ɪm'prɑpər] adj (erroneous) improprio; (inappropriate; unseemly) scorretto; (math) improprio

improve [ɪm'pruv] tr migliorare; (an opportunity) approfittare di || intr migliorare; to improve on or upon perfezionare

improvement [ɪm'pruvmənt] s miglioramento, perfezionamento; (in real estate) miglioria; (e.g., of time) buon uso

improvident [ɪm'prɑvɪdənt] adj improvvido, imprevidente

improvise ['ɪmprə ˌvaɪz] tr & intr improvvisare

imprudence [ɪm'prudəns] s imprudenza

imprudent [ɪm'prudənt] adj imprudente

impudence ['ɪmpjədəns] s impudenza, sfrontatezza, sfacciataggine f

impudent ['ɪmpjədənt] adj sfrontato, sfacciato, spudorato

impugn [ɪm'pjun] tr impugnare

impulse ['ɪmpʌls] s impulso

impulsive [ɪm'pʌlsɪv] adj impulsivo

impunity [ɪm'pjunɪti] s impunità f

impure [ɪm'pjur] adj impuro

impuri·ty [ɪm'pjurɪti] s (-ties) impurità f

impute [ɪm'pjut] tr imputare

in [ɪn] adj interno; (coll) moderno, alla moda || s relazione; the ins and outs tutti i dettagli || adv dentro; a casa; in ufficio; in here qui dentro; in there lì dentro; to be in essere a casa; to be in for essere destinato a; to be in with essere in intimità con || prep in; (within) dentro a; (over, through) per; di, e.g., the best in the class il migliore della classe; dressed in vestito di; in so far as per quanto; in that per quanto, dato che

inability [ˌɪnə'bɪlɪti] s inabilità f

inaccessible [ˌɪnæk'sɛsɪbəl] adj inaccessibile

inaccura·cy [ɪn'ækjərəsi] s (-cies) inesattezza, imprecisione

inaccurate [ɪn'ækjərɪt] adj inesatto

inaction [ɪn'ækʃən] s inazione

inactive [ɪn'æktɪv] adj inattivo

inadequate [ɪn'ædɪkwɪt] adj inadeguato, inadatto

inadvertent [ˌɪnəd'vʌrtənt] adj disattento; inavvertito

inadvisable [ˌɪnəd'vaɪzəbəl] adj poco consigliabile

inane [ɪn'en] adj insensato, assurdo

inanimate [ɪn'ænɪmɪt] adj inanimato

inappreciable [ˌɪnə'priʃɪ·əbəl] adj inapprezzabile

inappropriate [ˌɪnə'propri·ɪt] adj non appropriato, improprio

inarticulate [ˌɪnɑr'tɪkjəlɪt] adj (sounds, words) inarticolato; (person) incapace di esprimersi

inasmuch as [ˌɪnəs'mʌtʃ ˌæz] conj dato che, visto che, in quanto che

inattentive [ˌɪnə'tɛntɪv] adj disattento

inaugural [ɪn'ɔgjərəl] adj inaugurale || s discorso inaugurale

inaugurate [ɪn'ɔgjə ˌret] tr inaugurare

inauguration [ɪn ˌɔgjə'reʃən] s inaugurazione; (investiture of a head of government) assunzione dei poteri

inborn ['ɪn ˌbɔrn] adj innato, ingenito

inbreeding ['ɪn ˌbridɪŋ] s incrocio fra animali o piante affini

incandescent [ˌɪnkən'dɛsənt] adj incandescente

**incapable** [ɪn'kepəbəl] *adj* incapace
**incapacitate** [ˌɪnkə'pæsɪ ˌtet] *tr* inabilitare; (law) interdire
**incapaci·ty** [ˌɪnkə'pæsɪti] *s* (**-ties**) incapacità *f*
**incarcerate** [ɪn'kɑrsə ˌret] *tr* incarcerare
**incarnate** [ɪn'kɑrnɪt] or [ɪn'kɑrnet] *adj* incarnato ‖ [ɪn'kɑrnet] *tr* incarnare
**incarnation** [ˌɪnkɑr'neʃən] *s* incarnazione
**incendiarism** [ɪn'sendɪ·ə ˌrɪzəm] *s* incendio doloso; (*agitation*) sobillazione
**incendiar·y** [ɪn'sendɪ ˌeri] *adj* incendiario ‖ *s* (**-ies**) incendiario; (fig) sobillatore *m*
**incense** ['ɪnsens] *s* incenso ‖ *tr* (*to burn incense for*) incensare ‖ [ɪn'sens] *tr* irritare, esasperare
**in'cense burn'er** *s* (*person*) incensatore *m;* (*vessel*) incensiere *m*
**incentive** [ɪn'sentɪv] *adj* & *s* incentivo
**inception** [ɪn'sepʃən] *s* principio
**incertitude** [ɪn'sʌrtɪ ˌtjud] or [ɪn'sʌrtɪ ˌtud] *s* incertezza
**incest** ['ɪnsest] *s* incesto
**incestuous** [ɪn'sestʃʊ·əs] *adj* incestuoso
**inch** [ɪntʃ] *s* pollice *m;* **to be within an inch of** essere a due dita da ‖ *intr* **to inch ahead** spingersi avanti poco a poco
**incidence** ['ɪnsɪdəns] *s* incidenza
**incident** ['ɪnsɪdənt] *adj* incidente, incidentale ‖ *s* incidente *m*
**incidental** [ˌɪnsɪ'dentəl] *adj* incidentale ‖ *s* elemento incidentale; **incidentals** piccole spese
**incidentally** [ˌɪnsɪ'dentəli] *adv* incidentalmente, per inciso; a proposito
**incinerator** [ɪn'sɪnə ˌretər] *s* inceneritore *m*
**incision** [ɪn'sɪʒən] *s* incisione
**incisive** [ɪn'saɪsɪv] *adj* incisivo
**incite** [ɪn'saɪt] *tr* incitare, stimulare
**inclemen·cy** [ɪn'klemənsi] *s* (**-cies**) inclemenza
**inclination** [ˌɪnklɪ'neʃən] *s* inclinazione
**incline** ['ɪnklaɪn] or [ɪn'klaɪn] *s* declivio ‖ [ɪn'klaɪn] *tr* inclinare ‖ *intr* inclinarsi
**inclose** [ɪn'kloz] *tr* includere, accludere; **to inclose herewith** accludere alla presente
**inclosure** [ɪn'kloʒər] *s* (*land surrounded by fence*) recinto; (*e.g., letter*) allegato
**include** [ɪn'klud] *tr* includere; **including** incluso, e.g., **three books including the grammar** tre libri inclusa la grammatica
**inclusive** [ɪn'klusɪv] *adj* incluso, e.g., **until next Friday inclusive** fino a venerdì prossimo incluso; **inclusive of** inclusivo di, e.g., **price inclusive of freight** prezzo inclusivo delle spese di trasporto
**incogni·to** [ɪn'kɑgnɪ ˌto] *adj* incognito ‖ *s* (**-tos**) incognito ‖ *adv* in incognito

**incoherent** [ˌɪnko'hɪrənt] *adj* incoerente
**incombustible** [ˌɪnkəm'bʌstɪbəl] *adj* incombustibile
**income** ['ɪnkʌm] *s* reddito, provento
**in'come tax'** *s* imposta sul reddito
**incoming** ['ɪn ˌkʌmɪŋ] *adj* entrante; futuro; (*tide*) ascendente ‖ *s* entrata
**incomparable** [ɪn'kɑmpərəbəl] *adj* incomparabile, impareggiabile
**incompatible** [ˌɪnkəm'pætɪbəl] *adj* incompatibile
**incomplete** [ˌɪnkəm'plit] *adj* incompleto, tronco, scompleto
**incomprehensible** [ˌɪnkɑmprɪ'hensɪbəl] *adj* incomprensibile
**inconceivable** [ˌɪnkən'sivəbəl] *adj* inconcepibile
**inconclusive** [ˌɪnkən'klusɪv] *adj* inconcludente
**incongruous** [ɪn'kɑŋgru·əs] *adj* incongruo
**inconsequential** [ɪn ˌkɑnsɪ'kwenʃəl] *adj* (*lacking proper sequence of thought or speech*) inconseguente; (*trivial*) di poca importanza
**inconsiderate** [ˌɪnkən'sɪdərɪt] *adj* inconsiderato, sconsiderato
**inconsisten·cy** [ˌɪnkən'sɪstənsi] *s* (**-cies**) inconsistenza
**inconsistent** [ˌɪnkən'sɪstənt] *adj* inconsistente, inconseguente
**inconsolable** [ˌɪnkən'soləbəl] *adj* inconsolabile, sconsolato
**inconspicuous** [ˌɪnkən'spɪkju·əs] *adj* poco appariscente, poco apparente
**inconstant** [ɪn'kɑnstənt] *adj* incostante
**incontinence** [ɪn'kɑntɪnəns] *s* incontinenza
**incontrovertible** [ˌɪnkɑntrə'vʌrtɪbəl] *adj* incontrovertibile
**inconvenience** [ˌɪnkən'vini·əns] *s* scomodo, incomodo ‖ *tr* scomodare
**inconvenient** [ˌɪnkən'vini·ənt] *adj* incomodo, inconveniente
**incorporate** [ɪn'kɔrpə ˌret] *tr* incorporare; costituire in società anonima ‖ *intr* incorporarsi; costituirsi in società anonima
**incorrect** [ˌɪnkə'rekt] *adj* scorretto
**increase** ['ɪnkris] *s* aumento; crescita; **to be on the increase** essere in aumento ‖ [ɪn'kris] *tr* aumentare; (*by propagation*) moltiplicare ‖ *intr* aumentarsi; moltiplicarsi
**increasingly** [ɪn'krisɪŋli] *adv* sempre più
**incredible** [ɪn'kredɪbəl] *adj* incredibile
**incredulous** [ɪn'kredʒələs] *adj* incredulo
**increment** ['ɪnkrɪmənt] *s* aumento, incremento
**incriminate** [ɪn'krɪmɪ ˌnet] *tr* incriminare
**incrust** [ɪn'krʌst] *tr* incrostare
**incubate** ['ɪnkjə ˌbet] *tr* incubare ‖ *intr* essere in incubazione; (*said, e.g., of a hen*) covare; (fig) covare
**incubator** ['ɪnkjə ˌbetər] *s* incubatrice *f*
**inculcate** [ɪn'kʌlket] or ['ɪnkʌl ˌket] *tr* inculcare

**incumben·cy** [ɪn'kʌmbənsi] *s* **(-cies)** incombenza

**incumbent** [ɪn'kʌmbənt] *adj*—**to be incumbent on** incombere a, spettare a ‖ *s* titolare *mf*

**incunabula** [ˌɪnkjuˈnæbjələ] *spl (beginnings)* origini *fpl; (early printed books)* incunaboli *mpl*

**in·cur** [ɪn'kʌr] *v (pret & pp* **-curred;** *ger* **-curring)** *tr* incorrere in; *(a debt)* assumere, contrarre

**incurable** [ɪn'kjurəbəl] *adj & s* incurabile *mf*

**incursion** [ɪn'kʌrʒən] or [ɪn'kʌrʃən] *s* incursione, scorreria

**indebted** [ɪn'dɛtɪd] *adj* indebitato; obbligato

**indecen·cy** [ɪn'disənsi] *s* **(-cies)** indecenza, sconcezza

**indecent** [ɪn'disənt] *adj* indecente, sconveniente

**indecisive** [ˌɪndɪ'saɪsɪv] *adj* indeciso; *(e.g., event)* non decisivo

**indeed** [ɪn'did] *adv* difatti, infatti ‖ *interj* davvero!

**indefatigable** [ˌɪndɪ'fætɪgəbəl] *adj* indefesso, infaticabile

**indefensible** [ˌɪndɪ'fɛnsɪbəl] *adj* indifendibile, insostenibile

**indefinable** [ɪndɪ'faɪnəbəl] *adj* indefinibile

**indefinite** [ɪn'dɛfɪnɪt] *adj* indefinito

**indelible** [ɪn'dɛlɪbəl] *adj* indelebile

**indemnification** [ɪnˌdɛmnɪfɪ'keʃən] *s* indennità *f*, indennizzo

**indemni·fy** [ɪn'dɛmnɪˌfaɪ] *v (pret & pp* **-fied)** *tr* indennizzare

**indemni·ty** [ɪn'dɛmnɪti] *s* **(-ties)** indennità *f*, indennizzo

**indent** [ɪn'dɛnt] *tr* frastagliare, dentellare; *(typ)* far rientrare

**indentation** [ˌɪndɛn'teʃən] *s* frastaglio, dentellatura; *(typ)* accapo

**indenture** [ɪn'dɛntʃər] *s* scrittura pubblica; contratto di apprendista ‖ *tr* obbligare per contratto

**independence** [ˌɪndɪ'pɛndəns] *s* indipendenza

**independent** [ˌɪndɪ'pɛndənt] *adj & s* indipendente *mf*

**indescribable** [ˌɪndɪ'skraɪbəbəl] *adj* indescrivibile

**indestructible** [ˌɪndɪ'strʌktɪbəl] *adj* indistruttibile

**indeterminate** [ˌɪndɪ'tʌrmɪnɪt] *adj* indeterminato

**index** ['ɪndɛks] *s* **(indexes or indices** ['ɪndɪˌsiz]) indice *m; (typ)* indice *m* indicatore ‖ *tr* mettere un indice a; mettere all'indice ‖ **Index** *s* Indice *m*

**in'dex card'** *s* scheda di catalogo

**in'dex fin'ger** *s* dito indice

**India** ['ɪndɪ·ə] *s* l'India *f*

**In'dia ink'** *s* inchiostro di china

**Indian** ['ɪndɪ·ən] *adj & s* indiano

**In'dian club'** *s* clava di ginnastica

**In'dian corn'** *s* granoturco

**In'dian file'** *s* fila indiana ‖ *adv* in fila indiana

**In'dian O'cean** *s* Oceano Indiano

**In'dian sum'mer** *s* estate *f* di San Martino

**In'dian wres'tling** *s* braccio di ferro

**In'dia pa'per** *s* carta bibbia, carta d'India

**In'dia rub'ber** *s* caucciù *m*

**indicate** ['ɪndɪˌket] *tr* indicare

**indication** [ˌɪndɪ'keʃən] *s* indicazione

**indicative** [ɪn'dɪkətɪv] *adj & s* indicativo

**indicator** ['ɪndɪˌketər] *s* indicatore *m*, indice *m*

**indict** [ɪn'daɪt] *tr* accusare

**indictment** [ɪn'daɪtmənt] *s* accusa, atto d'accusa

**indifferent** [ɪn'dɪfərənt] *adj* indifferente; *(not particularly good)* passabile

**indigenous** [ɪn'dɪdʒɪnəs] *adj* indigeno

**indigent** ['ɪndɪdʒənt] *adj* indigente ‖ **the indigent** gli indigenti

**indigestion** [ˌɪndɪ'dʒɛstʃən] *s* indigestione

**indignant** [ɪn'dɪgnənt] *adj* indignato

**indignation** [ˌɪndɪg'neʃən] *s* indignazione

**indigni·ty** [ɪn'dɪgnɪti] *s* **(-ties)** indignità *f*

**indi·go** ['ɪndɪˌgo] *adj* indaco ‖ *s* **(-gos** or **-goes)** indaco

**indirect** [ˌɪndɪ'rɛkt] or [ˌɪndaɪ'rɛkt] *adj* indiretto

**in'direct dis'course** *s* discorso indiretto

**indiscernible** [ˌɪndɪ'zʌrnɪbəl] or [ˌɪndɪ'sʌrnɪbəl] *adj* indiscernibile

**indiscreet** [ˌɪndɪs'krit] *adj* indiscreto

**indispensable** [ˌɪndɪs'pɛnsəbəl] *adj* indispensabile, imprescindibile

**indispose** [ˌɪndɪs'poz] *tr* indisporre

**indisposed** [ˌɪndɪs'pozd] *adj (disinclined)* mal disposto; *(slightly ill)* indisposto

**indissoluble** [ˌɪndɪ'saljəbəl] *adj* indissolubile

**indistinct** [ˌɪndɪ'stɪŋkt] *adj* indistinto

**indite** [ɪn'daɪt] *tr* redigere

**individual** [ˌɪndɪ'vɪdʒʊ·əl] *adj* individuale ‖ *s* individuo

**individuali·ty** [ˌɪndɪˌvɪdʒʊ'ælɪti] *s* **(-ties)** individualità *f; (person of distinctive character)* individuo

**Indochina** ['ɪndo'tʃaɪnə] *s* l'Indocina *f*

**Indo-Chi·nese** ['ɪndot/aɪ'niz] *adj* indocinese ‖ *s* **(-nese)** indocinese *mf*

**Indo-European** ['ɪndoˌjurə'pi·ən] *adj & s* indoeuropeo

**indolent** ['ɪndələnt] *adj* indolente

**Indonesia** [ˌɪndo'niʃə] or [ˌɪndo'niʒə] *s* l'Indonesia *f*

**Indonesian** [ˌɪndo'niʃən] or [ˌɪndo'niʒən] *adj & s* indonesiano

**indoor** ['ɪnˌdor] *adj* situato in casa; da farsi in casa

**indoors** ['ɪn'dorz] *adv* dentro, a casa, al coperto

**indorse** [ɪn'dors] *tr* (com) girare; (fig) appoggiare, approvare

**indorsee** [ˌɪndor'si] *s* giratario

**indorsement** [ɪn'dorsmənt] *s* (com) girata; (fig) appoggio, approvazione

**indorser** [ɪn'dorsər] *s* girante *mf*

**induce** [ɪn'djus] or [ɪn'dus] *tr* indurre

**inducement** [ɪn'djusmənt] or [ɪn'dusmənt] *s* stimolo, incentivo

**induct** [ɪn'dʌkt] *tr* installare; iniziare; (mil) arruolare

**induction** [ɪn'dʌkʃən] *s* iniziazione; (elec & log) induzione; (mil) arruolamento

**indulge** [ɪn'dʌldʒ] *tr* indulgere (with *dat*) || *intr* cedere, lasciarsi andare; **to indulge in** abbandonarsi a; permettersi il lusso di

**indulgence** [ɪn'dʌldʒəns] *s* compiacenza; intemperanza, abbandono; (*leniency*) indulgenza

**indulgent** [ɪn'dʌldʒənt] *adj* indulgente

**industrial** [ɪn'dʌstrɪ·əl] *adj* industriale

**industrialist** [ɪn'dʌstrɪ·əlɪst] *s* industriale *m*

**industrialize** [ɪn'dʌstrɪ·ə‚laɪz] *tr* industrializzare

**industrious** [ɪn'dʌstrɪ·əs] *adj* industrioso, laborioso

**indus·try** ['ɪndʌstri] *s* (**-tries**) industria

**inebriation** [ɪn‚ibrɪ'eʃən] *s* ubriachezza

**inedible** [ɪn'ɛdɪbəl] *adj* immangiabile

**ineffable** [ɪn'ɛfəbəl] *adj* ineffabile

**ineffective** [‚ɪnɪ'fɛktɪv] *adj* inefficace; (*person*) incapace

**ineffectual** [‚ɪnɪ'fɛktʃʊ·əl] *adj* inefficace

**inefficient** [‚ɪnɪ'fɪʃənt] *adj* inefficiente

**ineligible** [ɪn'ɛlɪdʒɪbəl] *adj* ineleggibile

**inequali·ty** [‚ɪnɪ'kwɑlɪti] *s* (**-ties**) disuguaglianza

**inequi·ty** [ɪn'ɛkwɪti] *s* (**-ties**) ingiustizia

**ineradicable** [‚ɪnɪ'rædɪkəbəl] *adj* inestirpabile

**inertia** [ɪn'ʌrʃe] *s* inerzia

**inescapable** [‚ɪnɛs'kepəbəl] *adj* ineluttabile, inderogabile

**inevitable** [ɪn'ɛvɪtəbəl] *adj* inevitabile

**inexact** [‚ɪnɛg'zækt] *adj* inesatto

**inexcusable** [‚ɪnɛks'kjuzəbəl] *adj* inescusabile

**inexhaustible** [‚ɪnɛg'zɔstɪbəl] *adj* inesauribile

**inexorable** [ɪn'ɛksərəbəl] *adj* inesorabile

**inexpedient** [‚ɪnɛk'spidɪ·ənt] *adj* inopportuno

**inexpensive** [‚ɪnɛk'spɛnsɪv] *adj* poco costoso, a buon mercato

**inexperience** [‚ɪnɛk'spɪrɪ·əns] *s* inesperienza

**inexplicable** [ɪn'ɛksplɪkəbəl] *adj* inesplicabile

**inexpressible** [‚ɪnɛk'sprɛsɪbəl] *adj* indicibile, inesprimibile

**infallible** [ɪn'fælɪbəl] *adj* infallibile

**infamous** ['ɪnfəməs] *adj* infame

**infa·my** ['ɪnfəmi] *s* (**-mies**) infamia

**infan·cy** ['ɪnfənsi] *s* (**-cies**) infanzia

**infant** ['ɪnfənt] *adj* infantile; (*in the earliest stage*) (fig) nascente || *s* neonato, bebè *m*

**infantile** ['ɪnfən‚taɪl] *or* ['ɪnfəntɪl] *adj* infantile

**infan·try** ['ɪnfəntri] *s* (**-tries**) fanteria

**in'fantry·man** *s* (**-men**) fante *m*

**infatuated** [ɪn'fætʃʊ‚etɪd] *adj* infatuato

**infect** [ɪn'fɛkt] *tr* infettare

**infection** [ɪn'fɛkʃən] *s* infezione

**infectious** [ɪn'fɛkʃəs] *adj* infettivo

**in·fer** [ɪn'fʌr] *v* (*pret & pp* **-ferred;** *ger* **-ferring**) *tr* inferire; (coll) dedurre, supporre

**inferior** [ɪn'fɪrɪ·ər] *adj & s* inferiore *m*

**inferiority** [ɪn‚fɪrɪ'ɑrɪti] *s* inferiorità *f*

**inferior'ity com'plex** *s* complesso di inferiorità

**infernal** [ɪn'fʌrnəl] *adj* infernale

**infest** [ɪn'fɛst] *tr* infestare

**infidel** ['ɪnfɪdəl] *adj & s* infedele *mf*

**infideli·ty** [‚ɪnfɪ'dɛlɪti] *s* (**-ties**) infedeltà *f*

**in'field'** *s* campo interno, diamante *m*

**infiltrate** [ɪn'fɪltret] *or* ['ɪnfɪl‚tret] *tr* infiltrarsi in || *intr* infiltrarsi

**infinite** ['ɪnfɪnɪt] *adj & s* infinito

**infinitive** [ɪn'fɪnɪtɪv] *adj* infinitivo || *s* infinito

**infini·ty** [ɪn'fɪnɪti] *s* (**-ties**) infinità *f*; (math) infinito

**infirm** [ɪn'fʌrm] *adj* infermo; (*not firm*) debole

**infirma·ry** [ɪn'fʌrməri] *s* (**-ries**) infermeria

**infirmi·ty** [ɪn'fʌrmɪti] *s* (**-ties**) infermità *f*

**inflame** [ɪn'flem] *tr* infiammare || *intr* infiammarsi

**inflammable** [ɪn'flæməbəl] *adj* infiammabile

**inflammation** [‚ɪnflə'meʃən] *s* infiammazione

**inflate** [ɪn'flet] *tr* gonfiare; (*currency, prices*) inflazionare || *intr* gonfiarsi

**inflation** [ɪn'fleʃən] *s* inflazione; (*of a tire*) gonfiatura

**inflect** [ɪn'flɛkt] *tr* curvare; (*voice*) modulare; (gram) flettere

**inflection** [ɪn'flɛkʃən] *s* inflessione; (gram) flessione

**inflexible** [ɪn'flɛksɪbəl] *adj* inflessibile

**inflict** [ɪn'flɪkt] *tr* infliggere, inferire

**influence** ['ɪnflu·əns] *s* influenza || *tr* influire su, influenzare

**influential** [‚ɪnflu'ɛnʃəl] *adj* influente

**influenza** [‚ɪnflu'ɛnzə] *s* influenza

**inform** [ɪn'fɔrm] *tr* informare || *intr* dare informazioni; **to inform on** denunziare, fare la spia contro

**informal** [ɪn'fɔrməl] *adj* non ufficiale, ufficioso; (*unceremonious*) alla buona, familiare

**informant** [ɪn'fɔrmənt] *s* informatore *m*; (*informer*) delatore *m*; (ling) fonte *f* orale, informatore *m*

**information** [‚ɪnfər'meʃən] *s* informazioni *fpl*; conoscenze *fpl*

**informational** [‚ɪnfər'meʃənəl] *adj* informativo

**informed' sour'ces** *spl* fonti *fpl* attendibili

**informer** [ɪn'fɔrmər] *s* (*informant*) informatore *m*; (*spy*) delatore *m*

**infraction** [ɪn'frækʃən] *s* infrazione

**infrared** [‚ɪnfrə'rɛd] *adj & s* infrarosso

**infrequent** [ɪn'frikwənt] *adj* infrequente

**infringe** [ɪn'frɪndʒ] *tr* violare || *intr* **to infringe on** *or* **upon** violare, contravvenire a

**infringement** [ɪn'frɪndʒmənt] *s* infrazione

**infuriate** [ɪnˈfjʊrɪ ˌet] *tr* infuriare
**infuse** [ɪnˈfjuz] *tr* infondere
**infusion** [ɪnˈfjuʒən] *s* infusione
**ingenious** [ɪnˈdʒinjəs] *adj* ingegnoso
**ingenui·ty** [ ˌɪndʒɪˈnu·ɪti] or [ ˌɪndʒɪ-ˈnju·ɪti] *s* (**-ties**) ingegnosità *f*
**ingenuous** [ɪnˈdʒɛnjʊ·əs] *adj* ingenuo
**ingenuousness** [ɪnˈdʒɛnjʊ·əsnɪs] *s* ingenuità *f*
**ingest** [ɪnˈdʒɛst] *tr* ingerire
**ingoing** [ˈɪn ˌɡoɪŋ] *adj* entrante
**ingot** [ˈɪŋɡət] *s* lingotto, massello
**ingraft** [ɪnˈɡræft] or [ɪnˈɡrɑft] *tr* (hort & surg) innestare; (fig) inculcare
**ingrate** [ˈɪŋɡret] *s* ingrato
**ingratiate** [ɪnˈɡreʃɪ ˌet] *tr*—**to ingratiate oneself with** ingraziarsi
**ingratiating** [ɪnˈɡreʃɪ ˌetɪŋ] *adj* attraente, affascinante, insinuante
**ingratitude** [ɪnˈɡrætɪ ˌtjud] or [ɪn-ˈɡrætɪ ˌtud] *s* ingratitudine *f*
**ingredient** [ɪnˈɡridɪ·ənt] *s* ingrediente *m*
**in'grown nail'** [ˈɪŋɡron] *s* unghia incarnita
**ingulf** [ɪnˈɡʌlf] *tr* sommergere, inondare
**inhabit** [ɪnˈhæbɪt] *tr* abitare, popolare
**inhabitant** [ɪnˈhæbɪtənt] *s* abitante *mf*
**inhale** [ɪnˈhel] *tr* & *intr* inspirare
**inherent** [ɪnˈhɪrənt] *adj* inerente
**inherit** [ɪnˈhɛrɪt] *tr* & *intr* ereditare
**inheritance** [ɪnˈhɛrɪtəns] *s* eredità *f*
**inheritor** [ɪnˈhɛrɪtər] *s* erede *mf*
**inhibit** [ɪnˈhɪbɪt] *tr* inibire
**inhospitable** [ɪnˈhɑspɪtəbəl] or [ ˌɪn-hɑsˈpɪtəbəl] *adj* inospitale
**inhuman** [ɪnˈhjumən] *adj* inumano
**inhumane** [ ˌɪnhjuˈmen] *adj* inumano
**inimical** [ɪˈnɪmɪkəl] *adj* nemico
**iniqui·ty** [ɪˈnɪkwɪti] *s* (**-ties**) iniquità *f*
**ini·tial** [ɪˈnɪʃəl] *adj* & *s* iniziale *f* ‖ *v* (*pret* **-tialed** or **-tialled**; *ger* **-tialing** or **-tialling**) *tr* siglare
**initiate** [ɪˈnɪʃɪ ˌet] *tr* iniziare
**initiation** [ɪ ˌnɪʃɪˈeʃən] *s* iniziazione
**initiative** [ɪˈnɪʃɪ·ətɪv] or [ɪˈnɪʃətɪv] *s* iniziativa
**inject** [ɪnˈdʒɛkt] *tr* iniettare; introdurre
**injection** [ɪnˈdʒɛkʃən] *s* iniezione
**injudicious** [ ˌɪndʒuˈdɪʃəs] *adj* avventato, sconsiderato
**injunction** [ɪnˈdʒʌŋkʃən] *s* ingiunzione
**injure** [ˈɪndʒər] *tr* (*to harm*) danneggiare; (*to wound*) ferire; (*to offend*) offendere, ingiuriare
**injurious** [ɪnˈdʒʊrɪ·əs] *adj* dannoso; offensivo, ingiurioso
**inju·ry** [ˈɪndʒəri] *s* (**-ries**) (*harm*) danno; (*wound*) ferita, lesione; offesa, ingiuria
**injustice** [ɪnˈdʒʌstɪs] *s* ingiustizia
**ink** [ɪŋk] *s* inchiostro ‖ *tr* inchiostrare
**inkling** [ˈɪŋklɪŋ] *s* sentore *m*, indizio
**ink'stand'** *s* (*container*) calamaio; (*stand*) calamaiera
**ink'well'** *s* calamaio
**ink·y** [ˈɪŋki] *adj* (**-ier; -iest**) nero come l'inchiostro; nero d'inchiostro
**inlaid** [ˈɪn ˌled] or [ ˌɪnˈled] *adj* intarsiato, incrostato

**inland** [ˈɪnlənd] *adj* & *s* interno ‖ *adv* verso l'interno
**in'-law'** *s* affine *mf*
**in·lay** [ˈɪn ˌle] *s* intarsio, tassello ‖ [ɪnˈle] or [ˈɪn ˌle] *v* (*pret* & *pp* **-laid**) *tr* intarsiare
**in'let** *s* (*of the shore*) insenatura; (*entrance*) ammissione
**in'mate'** *s* (*patient, e.g., in an insane asylum*) internato; (*in a jail*) prigioniero
**inn** [ɪn] *s* taverna, osteria
**innate** [ɪˈnet] or [ˈɪnet] *adj* innato
**inner** [ˈɪnər] *adj* interno, interiore; intimo, profondo
**in'ner·spring' mat'tress** *s* materasso a molle
**in'ner tube'** *s* camera d'aria
**inning** [ˈɪnɪŋ] *s* (baseball) turno
**inn'keep'er** *s* locandiere *m*, oste *m*
**innocence** [ˈɪnəsəns] *s* innocenza
**innocent** [ˈɪnəsənt] *adj* & *s* innocente *mf*
**innovate** [ˈɪnə ˌvet] *tr* innovare
**innovation** [ ˌɪnəˈveʃən] *s* innovazione
**innuen·do** [ ˌɪnjuˈɛndo] *s* (**-does**) sottinteso, insinuazione
**innumerable** [ɪˈnjumərəbəl] or [ɪˈnumərəbəl] *adj* innumerevole
**inoculate** [ɪnˈɑkjə ˌlet] *tr* inoculare; (*e.g., with hatred*) inoculare; permeare
**inoculation** [ɪn ˌɑkjəˈleʃən] *s* inoculazione
**inoffensive** [ ˌɪnəˈfɛnsɪv] *adj* inoffensivo
**inopportune** [ɪn ˌɑpərˈtjun] or [ɪn-ˌɑpərˈtun] *adj* inopportuno
**inordinate** [ɪnˈɔrdɪnɪt] *adj* smoderato
**inorganic** [ ˌɪnɔrˈɡænɪk] *adj* inorganico
**in'pa'tient** *s* degente *mf*
**in'put'** *s* entrata; (elec, mach) energia immessa
**inquest** [ˈɪnkwɛst] *s* inchiesta
**inquire** [ɪnˈkwaɪr] *tr* domandare, chiedere ‖ *intr*—**to inquire about, after,** or **for** chiedere di; **to inquire into** investigare
**inquir·y** [ɪnˈkwaɪri] or [ˈɪnkwɪri] *s* (**-ies**) indagine *f*, inchiesta
**inquisition** [ ˌɪnkwɪˈzɪʃən] *s* inquisizione
**inquisitive** [ɪnˈkwɪzɪtɪv] *adj* indagatore, curioso
**in'road'** *s* incursione, invasione
**insane** [ɪnˈsen] *adj* pazzo, matto
**insane' asy'lum** *s* manicomio
**insani·ty** [ɪnˈsænɪti] *s* (**-ties**) pazzia, follia, demenza
**insatiable** [ɪnˈseʃəbəl] *adj* insaziabile
**inscribe** [ɪnˈskraɪb] *tr* iscrivere; (*a book*) dedicare; (geom) inscrivere
**inscription** [ɪnˈskrɪpʃən] *s* scritta, iscrizione; (*of a book*) dedica
**inscrutable** [ɪnˈskrutəbəl] *adj* imperscrutabile
**insect** [ˈɪnsɛkt] *s* insetto
**insecticide** [ɪnˈsɛktɪ ˌsaɪd] *adj* & *s* insetticida *m*
**insecure** [ ˌɪnsɪˈkjʊr] *adj* malsicuro
**inseparable** [ɪnˈsɛpərəbəl] *adj* inseparabile

**insert** ['ɪnsʌrt] *s* inserzione; (*circular*) inserto || [ɪn'sʌrt] *tr* inserire

**insertion** [ɪn'sʌrʃən] *s* inserzione; (*in lunar orbit*) immissione; (*of lace*) tramezzo

**in·set** ['ɪn ˌsɛt] *s* intercalazione || [ɪn-'sɛt] or ['ɪn ˌsɛt] *v* (*pret & pp* **-set;** *ger* **-setting**) *tr* intercalare

**in'shore'** *adj & adv* vicino alla spiaggia

**in'side'** *adj* interno; privato, confidenziale || *s* interno; **insides** (coll) interiora *fpl;* **to be on the inside** avere informazioni confidenziali || *adv* dentro; all'interno; **inside of** dentro, dentro a, dentro di; **to turn inside out** rovesciare, voltare il diritto al rovescio || *prep* dentro, dentro a

**in'side flap'** *s* (bb) risvolto

**insider** [ˌɪn'saɪdər] *s* persona informata

**in'side track'** *s* (racing) steccato; **to have the inside track** (coll) trovarsi in una situazione vantaggiosa

**insidious** [ɪn'sɪdɪ·əs] *adj* insidioso

**in'sight'** *s* intuito, penetrazione

**insigni·a** [ɪn'sɪgnɪ·ə] *s* (-a or -as) distintivo; (*distinguishing sign*) segno

**insignificant** [ˌɪnsɪg'nɪfɪkənt] *adj* insignificante

**insincere** [ˌɪnsɪn'sɪr] *adj* insincero

**insinuate** [ɪn'sɪnju ˌet] *tr* insinuare

**insist** [ɪn'sɪst] *intr* insistere

**insofar as** [ˌɪnso'fɑr ˌæz] *conj* per quanto

**insolence** ['ɪnsələns] *s* insolenza

**insolent** ['ɪnsələnt] *adj* insolente

**insoluble** [ɪn'sɑljəbəl] *adj* insolubile

**insolven·cy** [ɪn'sɑlvənsi] *s* (-cies) insolvenza

**insomnia** [ɪn'sɑmnɪ·ə] *s* insonnia

**insomuch** [ˌɪnso'mʌtʃ] *adv* fino al punto; **insomuch as** giacché, visto che; **insomuch that** fino al punto che

**inspect** [ɪn'spɛkt] *tr* ispezionare

**inspection** [ɪn'spɛkʃən] *s* ispezione

**inspector** [ɪn'spɛktər] *s* ispettore *m*

**inspiration** [ˌɪnspɪ'reʃən] *s* ispirazione

**inspire** [ɪn'spaɪr] *tr & intr* ispirare

**install** [ɪn'stɔl] *tr* istallare

**installment** [ɪn'stɔlmənt] *s* rata; (*of a book*) dispensa; **in installments** a rate

**install'ment plan'** *s* pagamento rateale; **on the installment plan** con facilitazioni di pagamento

**instance** ['ɪnstəns] *s* esempio; (law) istanza; **for instance** per esempio

**instant** ['ɪnstənt] *adj* istantaneo || *s* istante *m;* mese *m* corrente

**instantaneous** [ˌɪnstən'tenɪ·əs] *adj* istantaneo

**instantly** ['ɪnstəntli] *adv* immediatamente, istantaneamente

**instead** [ɪn'stɛd] *adv* invece; **instead of** invece di

**in'step'** *s* collo del piede

**instigate** ['ɪnstɪ ˌget] *tr* istigare

**instigation** [ˌɪnstɪ'geʃən] *s* istigazione

**in·still'** *tr* instillare, istillare

**instinct** ['ɪnstɪŋkt] *s* istinto

**instinctive** [ɪn'stɪŋktɪv] *adj* istintivo

**institute** ['ɪnstɪ ˌtjut] or ['ɪnstɪ ˌtut] *s* istituto || *tr* istituire

**institution** [ˌɪnstɪ'tjuʃən] or [ˌɪnstɪ-'tuʃən] *s* istituzione

**institutionalize** [ˌɪnstɪ'tjuʃənə ˌlaɪz] or [ˌɪnstɪ'tuʃənə ˌlaɪz] *tr* istituzionalizzare

**instruct** [ɪn'strʌkt] *tr* istruire

**instruction** [ɪn'strʌkʃən] *s* istruzione

**instructive** [ɪn'strʌktɪv] *adj* istruttivo

**instructor** [ɪn'strʌktər] *s* istruttore *m*

**instrument** ['ɪnstrəmənt] *s* strumento; (law) istrumento || ['ɪnstrə ˌmɛnt] *tr* strumentare

**instrumental** [ˌɪnstrə'mɛntəl] *adj* strumentale; **to be instrumental in** contribuire a

**instrumentalist** [ˌɪnstrə'mɛntəlɪst] *s* strumentista *mf*

**instrumentali·ty** [ˌɪnstrəmən'tælɪti] *s* (-ties) mediazione, aiuto

**in'strument fly'ing** *s* volo strumentale

**in'strument pan'el** *s* (aut) cruscotto

**insubordinate** [ˌɪnsə'bɔrdɪnɪt] *adj* insubordinato

**insufferable** [ɪn'sʌfərəbəl] *adj* insoffribile

**insufficient** [ˌɪnsə'fɪʃənt] *adj* insufficiente

**insular** ['ɪnsələr] or ['ɪnsjʊlər] *adj* insulare; (*e.g., attitude*) gretto

**insulate** ['ɪnsə ˌlet] *tr* isolare

**in'sulating tape'** ['ɪnsəletɪŋ] *s* nastro isolante

**insulation** [ˌɪnsə'leʃən] *s* isolamento

**insulator** ['ɪnsə ˌletər] *s* isolatore *m*

**insulin** ['ɪnsəlɪn] *s* insulina

**insult** ['ɪnsʌlt] *s* insulto || [ɪn'sʌlt] *tr* insultare, insolentire

**insulting** [ɪn'sʌltɪŋ] *adj* insultante

**insurance** [ɪn'ʃʊrəns] *s* assicurazione

**insure** [ɪn'ʃʊr] *tr* assicurare

**insurer** [ɪn'ʃʊrər] *s* assicuratore *m*

**insurgent** [ɪn'sʌrdʒənt] *adj & s* insorgente *mf*

**insurmountable** [ˌɪnsər'maʊntəbəl] *adj* insormontabile

**insurrection** [ˌɪnsə'rɛkʃən] *s* insurrezione

**insusceptible** [ˌɪnsə'sɛptɪbəl] *adj* non suscettibile

**intact** [ɪn'tækt] *adj* intatto, integro

**in'take'** *s* (*place of taking in*) entrata; (*act of taking in*) ammissione; (mach) presa, immissione, aspirazione

**in'take man'ifold'** *s* collettore *m* d'ammissione

**intangible** [ɪn'tændʒɪbəl] *adj* intangibile; (fig) vago, inafferrabile

**integer** ['ɪntɪdʒər] *s* numero intero

**integral** ['ɪntɪgrəl] *adj* integrale; (*part of a whole*) integrante || *s* (math) integrale *m*

**integration** [ˌɪntɪ'greʃən] *s* integrazione

**integrity** [ɪn'tɛgrɪti] *s* integrità *f*

**intellect** ['ɪntə ˌlɛkt] *s* intelletto

**intellectual** [ˌɪntə'lɛktʃʊ·əl] *adj & s* intellettuale *mf*

**intelligence** [ɪn'tɛlɪdʒəns] *s* intelligenza; informazione, conoscenza

**intel'ligence bu'reau** *s* ufficio spionaggi

**intel'ligence quo'tient** *s* quoziente *m* d'intelligenza

**intelligent** [ɪn'telɪdʒənt] *adj* intelligente

**intelligentsia** [ɪn‚telɪ'dʒentsɪ·ə] *or* [ɪn‚telɪ'gentsɪ·ə] *s* intellighenzia, intellettualità *f*

**intelligible** [ɪn'telɪdʒɪbəl] *adj* intelligibile, comprensibile

**intemperance** [ɪn'tempərəns] *s* intemperanza, sregolatezza

**intemperate** [ɪn'tempərɪt] *adj* intemperante; (*climate*) rigoroso

**intend** [ɪn'tend] *tr* intendere, prefiggersi; (*to mean for a particular purpose*) destinare; (*to signify*) voler dire

**intendance** [ɪn'tendəns] *s* intendenza

**intendant** [ɪn'tendənt] *s* intendente *m*

**intended** [ɪn'tendɪd] *adj & s* (coll) promesso, promessa

**intense** [ɪn'tens] *adj* intenso

**intensi·fy** [ɪn'tensɪ·faɪ] *v* (*pret & pp* -fied) *tr* intensificare, rinforzare; (phot) rinforzare ‖ *intr* intensificarsi, rinforzarsi

**intensi·ty** [ɪn'tensɪti] *s* (-ties) intensità *f*

**intensive** [ɪn'tensɪv] *adj* intensivo

**intent** [ɪn'tent] *adj* intento, attento; **intent on** deciso a ‖ *s* (*purpose*) intento, scopo; (*meaning*) significato; **to all intents and purposes** virtualmente, in realtà

**intention** [ɪn'tenʃən] *s* intenzione

**intentional** [ɪn'tenʃənəl] *adj* intenzionale, deliberato

**intentionally** [ɪn'tenʃənəli] *adv* apposta, deliberatamente

**in·ter** [ɪn'tʌr] *v* (*pret & pp* -terred; *ger* -terring) *tr* interrare, inumare

**interact** [‚ɪntər'ækt] *intr* esercitare un'azione reciproca

**interaction** [‚ɪntər'ækʃən] *s* azione reciproca

**inter·breed** [‚ɪntər'brid] *s* (*pret & pp* -bred** [‚ɪntər'bred]) *tr* incrociare ‖ *intr* incrociarsi

**intercalate** [ɪn'tʌrkə‚let] *tr* intercalare

**intercede** [‚ɪntər'sid] *intr* intercedere

**intercept** [‚ɪntər'sept] *tr* intercettare

**interceptor** [‚ɪntər'septər] *s* (*person*) intercettatore *m*; (aer) intercettore *m*

**interchange** ['ɪntər‚tʃendʒ] *s* interscambio; (*on a highway*) svincolo autostradale ‖ [‚ɪntər'tʃendʒ] *tr* scambiare ‖ *intr* scambiarsi

**intercollegiate** [‚ɪntərkə'lidʒɪ·ɪt] *adj* interscolastico, fra università

**intercom** ['ɪntər‚kɑm] *s* citofono

**intercourse** ['ɪntər‚kors] *s* comunicazione; (*of products, ideas, etc.*) scambio; (*copulation*) copula, coito; **to have intercourse** accoppiarsi sessualmente

**intercross** [‚ɪntər'krɔs] *or* [‚ɪntər'krɑs] *tr* incrociare ‖ *intr* incrociarsi

**interdict** ['ɪntər‚dɪkt] *s* interdetto ‖ [‚ɪntər'dɪkt] *tr* interdire; **to interdict s.o. from** + *ger* interdire a qlcu di + *ger*

**interest** ['ɪntərɪst] *or* ['ɪntrɪst] *s* interesse *m;* **the interests** i potenti ‖ ['ɪntərɪst], ['ɪntrɪst] *or* ['ɪntə‚rest] *tr* interessare

**interested** ['ɪntrɪstɪd] *or* ['ɪntə‚restɪd] *adj* interessato

**interesting** ['ɪntrɪstɪŋ] *or* ['ɪntə‚restɪŋ] *adj* interessante

**interfere** [‚ɪntər'fɪr] *intr* interferire; (sports) ostacolare l'azione; **to interfere with** interferire in

**interference** [‚ɪntər'fɪrəns] *s* interferenza

**interim** ['ɪntərɪm] *adj* interino ‖ *s* interim *m;* **in the interim** frattanto

**interior** [ɪn'tɪrɪ·ər] *adj & s* interno

**interject** [‚ɪntər'dʒekt] *tr* interporre ‖ *intr* interporsi

**interjection** [‚ɪntər'dʒekʃən] *s* interposizione; esclamazione; (gram) interiezione

**interlard** [‚ɪntər'lɑrd] *tr* infiorare, lardellare

**interline** [‚ɪntər'laɪn] *tr* scrivere nell'interlinea di; (*a garment*) foderare con ovattina

**interlining** ['ɪntər‚laɪnɪŋ] *s* soppanno

**interlink** [‚ɪntər'lɪŋk] *tr* concatenare

**interlock** [‚ɪntər'lɑk] *tr* connettere ‖ *intr* connettersi

**interlope** [‚ɪntər'lop] *intr* intromettersi; trafficare senza permesso

**interloper** [‚ɪntər'lopər] *s* intruso

**interlude** ['ɪntər‚lud] *s* interludio; (theat) intermezzo

**intermarriage** [‚ɪntər‚mærɪdʒ] *s* matrimonio tra consanguinei; matrimonio fra membri di razze diverse

**intermediar·y** [‚ɪntər'midɪ‚eri] *adj* intermediario ‖ (-ies) *s* intermediario

**intermediate** [‚ɪntər'midɪ·ɪt] *adj* intermedio

**interment** [ɪn'tʌrmənt] *s* inumazione

**intermingle** [‚ɪntər'mɪŋgəl] *tr* mescolare ‖ *intr* mescolarsi

**intermission** [‚ɪntər'mɪʃən] *s* interruzione; (theat) intervallo

**intermittent** [‚ɪntər'mɪtənt] *adj* intermittente

**intermix** [‚ɪntər'mɪks] *tr* mescolare ‖ *intr* mescolarsi

**intern** ['ɪntʌrn] *s* interno ‖ [ɪn'tʌrn] *tr* internare

**internal** [ɪn'tʌrnəl] *adj* interno

**inter'nal-combus'tion en'gine** *s* motore *m* a combustione interna, motore *m* a scoppio

**inter'nal rev'enue** *s* fisco

**international** [‚ɪntər'næʃənəl] *adj* internazionale

**in'terna'tional date' line'** *s* linea del cambiamento di data

**internationalize** [‚ɪntər'næʃənə‚laɪz] *tr* internazionalizzare

**internecine** [‚ɪntər'nisɪn] *adj* micidiale, sanguinario

**internee** [‚ɪntʌr'ni] *s* internato

**internist** [ɪn'tʌrnɪst] *s* internista *mf*

**internment** [ɪn'tʌrnmənt] *s* internamento

**internship** ['ɪntʌrn‚ʃɪp] *s* tirocinio in un ospedale, internato

**interpellate** [ ˌɪntərˈpɛlet] or [ɪnˈtʌrpɪˌlet] *tr* interpellare

**interplanetary** [ ˌɪntərˈplænəˌteri] *adj* interplanetario

**interplay** [ˈɪntərˌple] *s* azione reciproca

**interpolate** [ɪnˈtʌrpəˌlet] *tr* interpolare

**interpose** [ ˌɪntərˈpoz] *tr* frapporre

**interpret** [ɪnˈtʌrprɪt] *tr* interpretare

**interpreter** [ɪnˈtʌrprətər] *s* interprete *mf*

**interrogate** [ɪnˈtɛrəˌget] *tr & intr* interrogare

**interrogation** [ɪnˌtɛrəˈgeʃən] *s* interrogazione

**interroga'tion mark'** or **point'** *s* punto interrogativo

**interrupt** [ ˌɪntəˈrʌpt] *tr* interrompere

**interruption** [ ˌɪntəˈrʌpʃən] *s* interruzione

**interscholastic** [ ˌɪntərskəˈlæstɪk] *adj* interscolastico

**intersect** [ ˌɪntərˈsɛkt] *tr* intersecare || *intr* intersecarsi

**intersection** [ ˌɪntərˈsɛkʃən] *s* (*of streets, roads, etc.*) crocevia *m;* (geom) intersezione

**intersperse** [ ˌɪntərˈspʌrs] *tr* cospargere, inframezzare

**interstellar** [ ˌɪntərˈstɛlər] *adj* interstellare

**interstice** [ɪnˈtʌrstɪs] *s* interstizio

**intertwine** [ ˌɪntərˈtwaɪn] *tr* intrecciare || *intr* intrecciarsi

**interval** [ˈɪntərvəl] *s* intervallo; **at intervals** a intervalli; di tanto in tanto

**intervene** [ ˌɪntərˈvin] *intr* intervenire; (*to happen*) succedere

**intervening** [ ˌɪntərˈvinɪŋ] *adj*—**in the intervening time** nel frattempo

**intervention** [ ˌɪntərˈvɛnʃən] *s* intervenzione

**interview** [ˈɪntərˌvju] *s* intervista || *tr* intervistare

**inter·weave** [ ˌɪntərˈwiv] *v* (*pret* -**wove** [ˈwov] or -**weaved;** *pp* -**wove, -woven** or -**weaved**) *tr* intessere

**intestate** [ɪnˈtɛstet] or [ɪnˈtɛstɪt] *adj* intestato

**intestine** [ɪnˈtɛstɪn] *s* intestino

**inthrall** [ɪnˈθrɔl] *tr* affascinare, incantare; (*to subjugate*) asservire, soggiogare

**inthrone** [ɪnˈθron] *tr* mettere sul trono, intronizzare; esaltare, innalzare

**intima·cy** [ˈɪntɪməsi] *s* (-**cies**) intimità *f*

**intimate** [ˈɪntɪmɪt] *adj & s* intimo || [ˈɪntɪˌmet] *tr* insinuare

**intimation** [ ˌɪntɪˈmeʃən] *s* insinuazione

**intimidate** [ɪnˈtɪmɪˌdet] *tr* intimidire

**into** [ˈɪntu] or [ˈɪntʊ] *prep* in; verso; contro

**intolerant** [ɪnˈtɑlərənt] *adj & s* intollerante *mf*, insofferente *mf*

**intomb** [ɪnˈtum] *tr* inumare, seppellire

**intombment** [ɪnˈtummənt] *s* sepoltura

**intonation** [ ˌɪntoˈneʃən] *s* intonazione

**intone** [ɪnˈton] *tr* intonare || *intr* salmodiare

**intoxicant** [ɪnˈtɑksɪkənt] *s* bevanda alcoolica

**intoxicate** [ɪnˈtɑksɪˌket] *tr* ubriacare; esilarare; (*to poison*) avvelenare, intossicare

**intoxication** [ɪnˌtɑksɪˈkeʃən] *s* ubriachezza; ebbrezza, allegria; (*poisoning*) avvelenamento, intossicazione

**intractable** [ɪnˈtræktəbəl] *adj* intrattabile

**intransigent** [ɪnˈtrænsɪdʒənt] *adj & s* intransigente *mf*

**intransitive** [ɪnˈtrænsɪtɪv] *adj* intransitivo

**intravenous** [ ˌɪntrəˈvinəs] *adj* intravenoso, endovenoso

**intrench** [ɪnˈtrɛntʃ] *tr & intr* var of **entrench**

**intrepid** [ɪnˈtrɛpɪd] *adj* intrepido

**intrepidity** [ ˌɪntrɪˈpɪdɪti] *s* intrepidezza

**intricate** [ˈɪntrɪkɪt] *adj* intricato

**intrigue** [ɪnˈtrig] or [ˈɪntrig] *s* intrigo; tresca, intrigo amoroso; (theat) intreccio || [ɪnˈtrig] *tr* incuriosire || *intr* intrigare; trescare

**intrinsic(al)** [ɪnˈtrɪnsɪk(əl)] *adj* intrinseco

**introduce** [ ˌɪntrəˈdjus] or [ ˌɪntrəˈdus] *tr* introdurre; (*a product*) lanciare; (*a person*) presentare

**introduction** [ ˌɪntrəˈdʌkʃən] *s* introduzione; presentazione

**introductory** [ ˌɪntrəˈdʌktəri] *adj* introduttivo

**introit** [ˈɪntroˌɪt] *s* (eccl) introito

**introspective** [ ˌɪntrəˈspɛktɪv] *adj* introspettivo

**introvert** [ˈɪntrəˌvʌrt] *adj & s* introverso

**intrude** [ɪnˈtrud] *intr* intrudersi, intrufolarsi

**intruder** [ɪnˈtrudər] *s* intruso; importuno

**intrusion** [ɪnˈtruʒən] *s* intrusione

**intrusive** [ɪnˈtrusɪv] *adj* invadente

**intrust** [ɪnˈtrʌst] *tr* affidare, confidare

**intuition** [ ˌɪntuˈɪʃən] or [ ˌɪntjuˈɪʃən] *s* intuizione, intuito

**inundate** [ˈɪnənˌdet] *tr* inondare

**inundation** [ ˌɪnənˈdeʃən] *s* inondazione

**inure** [ɪnˈjʊr] *tr* indurire, assuefare || *intr* entrare in vigore; **to inure to** ridondare in favore di

**invade** [ɪnˈved] *tr* invadere

**invader** [ɪnˈvedər] *s* invasore *m*

**invalid** [ɪnˈvælɪd] *adj* (*non valid*) invalido || [ˈɪnvəlɪd] *adj* (*person*) invalido; (*thing*) povero; (*diet*) per malati || [ˈɪnvəlɪd] *s* invalido

**invalidate** [ɪnˈvælɪˌdet] *tr* invalidare

**invalidity** [ ˌɪnvəˈlɪdɪti] *s* invalidità *f*

**invaluable** [ɪnˈvælju·əbəl] *adj* inestimabile, inapprezzabile

**invariable** [ɪnˈvɛrɪ·əbəl] *adj* invariabile

**invasion** [ɪnˈveʒən] *s* invasione

**invective** [ɪnˈvɛktɪv] *s* invettiva

**inveigh** [ɪnˈve] *intr*—**to inveigh against** inveire contro

**inveigle** [ɪnˈvegəl] or [ɪnˈvigəl] *tr* sedurre, abbindolare

**invent** [ɪnˈvɛnt] *tr* inventare

**invention** [ɪnˈvɛnʃən] *s* invenzione

**inventiveness** [ɪn'vɛntɪvnɪs] *s* inventiva
**inventor** [ɪn'vɛntər] *s* inventore *m*
**invento·ry** ['ɪnvən,tori] *s* (-ries) inventario ‖ *v* (*pret & pp* -ried) *tr* inventariare
**inverse** [ɪn'vʌrs] *adj & s* inverso
**inversion** [ɪn'vʌrʒən] or [ɪn'vʌrʃən] *s* inversione
**invert** ['ɪnvʌrt] *s* invertito ‖ [ɪn'vʌrt] *tr* invertire
**invertebrate** [ɪn'vʌrtɪ,bret] or [ɪn'vʌrtɪbrɪt] *adj & s* invertebrato
**invest** [ɪn'vɛst] *tr* investire ‖ *intr* fare un investimento; fare investimenti
**investigate** [ɪn'vɛstɪ,get] *tr* investigare
**investigation** [ɪn,vɛstɪ'geʃən] *s* investigazione
**investigator** [ɪn'vɛstɪ,getər] *s* investigatore *m*
**investment** [ɪn'vɛstmənt] *s* (*of money*) investimento; (*e.g., with an office*) investitura; (*siege*) assedio
**investor** [ɪn'vɛstər] *s* investitore *m*
**inveterate** [ɪn'vɛtərɪt] *adj* inveterato
**invidious** [ɪn'vɪdɪ·əs] *adj* irritante, odioso
**invigorate** [ɪn'vɪgə,ret] *tr* invigorire
**invigorating** [ɪn'vɪgə,retɪŋ] *adj* ritemprante, ricostituente, rinforzante
**invincible** [ɪn'vɪnsɪbəl] *adj* invincibile
**invisible** [ɪn'vɪzɪbəl] *adj* invisibile
**invis'ible ink'** *s* inchiostro simpatico
**invitation** [,ɪnvɪ'teʃən] *s* invito
**invite** [ɪn'vaɪt] *tr* invitare
**inviting** [ɪn'vaɪtɪŋ] *adj* invitante, attrattivo; (*food*) appetitoso; accogliente
**invoice** ['ɪnvɔɪs] *s* fattura; **as per invoice** secondo fattura ‖ *tr* fatturare
**invoke** [ɪn'vok] *tr* invocare; (*a spirit*) evocare
**involuntary** [ɪn'vɑlən,tɛri] *adj* involontario
**involve** [ɪn'vɑlv] *tr* involvere, includere; occupare; (*to bring unpleasantness upon*) implicare, coinvolgere; complicare
**invulnerable** [ɪn'vʌlnərəbəl] *adj* invulnerabile
**inward** ['ɪnwərd] *adj* interno ‖ *adv* al di dentro, verso l'interno
**iodide** ['aɪ·ə,daɪd] *s* ioduro
**iodine** ['aɪ·ə,dɪn] *s* iodio ‖ ['aɪ·ə,daɪn] *s* tintura di iodio
**ion** ['aɪ·ən] or ['aɪ·ɑn] *s* ione *m*
**ionize** ['aɪ·ə,naɪz] *tr* ionizzare
**IOU** ['aɪ,o'ju] *s* (letterword) (**I owe you**) cambiale *f*, pagherò *m*
**I.Q.** ['aɪ'kju] *s* (letterword) (**intelligence quotient**) quoziente *m* d'intelligenza
**Iranian** [aɪ'renɪ·ən] *adj & s* iraniano
**Ira·qi** [ɪ'rɑki] *adj* iracheno ‖ *s* (-qis) iracheno
**irate** ['aɪret] or [aɪ'ret] *adj* irato
**ire** [aɪr] *s* ira, collera
**Ireland** ['aɪrlənd] *s* l'Irlanda *f*
**iris** ['aɪrɪs] *s* iride *f*
**I'rish·man** *s* (-men) irlandese *m*
**I'rish stew'** *s* stufato all'irlandese
**I'rish·wom'an** *s* (-wom'en) irlandese *f*
**irk** [ʌrk] *tr* infastidire, annoiare

**irksome** ['ʌrksəm] *adj* fastidioso
**iron** ['aɪ·ərn] *adj* ferreo; *s* ferro; (*to press clothes*) ferro da stiro; **irons** ferri *mpl;* **strike while the iron is hot** batti il ferro fin ch'è caldo ‖ *tr* (*clothes*) stirare; **to iron out** (*a difficulty*) (coll) appianare
**i'ron·bound'** *adj* ferrato; (*unyielding*) ferreo, inflessibile; (*rock-bound*) roccioso, scabroso
**ironclad** ['aɪ·ərn,klæd] *adj* corazzato, blindato; inflessibile, ferreo
**i'ron constitu'tion** *s* salute *f* di ferro
**i'ron cur'tain** *s* cortina di ferro
**i'ron horse'** *s* locomotiva a vapore
**ironic(al)** [aɪ'rɑnɪk(əl)] *adj* ironico
**ironing** ['aɪ·ərnɪŋ] *s* stiratura; roba stirata; roba da stirare
**i'roning board'** *s* tavolo or asse *m* da stiro
**i'ron lung'** *s* polmone *m* d'acciaio
**i'ron·ware'** *s* ferrame *m*
**i'ron will'** *s* volontà *f* di ferro
**i'ron·work'** *s* lavoro in ferro; **ironworks** *ssg* ferriera
**i'ron-work'er** *s* ferraio; metalmeccanico, siderurgico
**iro·ny** ['aɪrəni] *s* (-nies) ironia
**irradiate** [ɪ'redɪ,et] *tr* irradiare ‖ *intr* irradiare, irradiarsi
**irrational** [ɪ'ræʃənəl] *adj* irrazionale
**irrecoverable** [,ɪrɪ'kʌvərəbəl] *adj* irrecuperabile
**irredeemable** [,ɪrɪ'diməbəl] *adj* irredimibile
**irrefutable** [,ɪrɪ'fjutəbəl] *adj* irrefutabile
**irregular** [ɪ'rɛgjələr] *adj* irregolare ‖ *s* (mil) irregolare *m*
**irrelevance** [ɪ'rɛləvəns] *s* irrilevanza
**irrelevant** [ɪ'rɛləvənt] *adj* irrilevante
**irreligious** [,ɪrɪ'lɪdʒəs] *adj* irreligioso
**irremediable** [,ɪrɪ'midɪ·əbəl] *adj* irrimediabile
**irremovable** [,ɪrɪ'muvəbəl] *adj* irremovibile, inamovibile
**irreplaceable** [,ɪrɪ'plesəbəl] *adj* insostituibile
**irrepressible** [,ɪrɪ'prɛsɪbəl] *adj* irreprimibile, incontenibile
**irreproachable** [,ɪrɪ'protʃəbəl] *adj* irreprensibile
**irresistible** [,ɪrɪ'zɪstɪbəl] *adj* irresistibile
**irrespective** [,ɪrɪ'spɛktɪv] *adj—***irrespective of** senza riguardo a
**irresponsible** [,ɪrɪ'spɑnsɪbəl] *adj* irresponsabile
**irretrievable** [,ɪrɪ'trivəbəl] *adj* irrecuperabile
**irreverent** [ɪ'rɛvərənt] *adj* irriverente
**irrevocable** [ɪ'rɛvəkəbəl] *adj* irrevocabile
**irrigate** ['ɪrɪ,get] *tr* irrigare
**irrigation** [,ɪrɪ'geʃən] *s* irrigazione
**irritant** ['ɪrɪtənt] *adj & s* irritante *m*
**irritate** ['ɪrɪ,tet] *tr* irritare
**irritation** [,ɪrɪ'teʃən] *s* irritazione
**irruption** [ɪ'rʌpʃən] *s* irruzione
**isinglass** ['aɪzɪŋ,glæs] or ['aɪzɪŋ,glɑs] *s* (*gelatine*) colla di pesce; mica
**Islam** ['ɪsləm] or [ɪs'lɑm] *s* l'Islam *m*

**island** ['aɪlənd] *adj* isolano ‖ *s* isola; (*for safety of pedestrians*) salvagente *m*
**islander** ['aɪləndər] *s* isolano
**isle** [aɪl] *s* isoletta
**isolate** ['aɪsə,let] *or* ['ɪsə,let] *tr* isolare
**isolation** [ ,aɪsə'leʃən] *or* [ ,ɪsə'leʃən] *s* isolamento
**isolationist** [ ,aɪsə'leʃənɪst] *or* [ ,ɪsə'leʃənɪst] *s* isolazionista *mf*
**isosceles** [aɪ'sɑsə,liz] *adj* isoscele
**isotope** ['aɪsə,top] *s* isotopo
**Israel** ['ɪzrɪ-əl] *s* l'Israele *m*
**Israe·li** [ɪz'reli] *adj* israeliano ‖ *s* (**-lis** [liz]) israeliano
**Israelite** ['ɪzrɪ-ə,laɪt] *adj & s* israelita *mf*
**issuance** ['ɪʃʊ-əns] *s* (*of stamps, stocks, bonds, etc.*) emissione; (*e.g., of clothes*) distribuzione; (*of a law*) emanazione
**issue** ['ɪʃʊ] *s* (*outlet*) uscita; distribuzione; (*result*) conseguenza; (*offspring*) prole *f;* (*of a magazine*) puntata, fascicolo; (*of a bond*) emissione; (*yield*) prodotto; (*of a law*) promulgazione; (pathol) flusso; **at issue** in discussione; **to face the issue** affrontare la situazione; **to force the issue** forzare la soluzione; **to take issue with** non essere d'accordo con, dissentire da ‖ *tr* (*e.g., a book*) pubblicare; (*bonds, orders*) emettere; (*a communiqué*) diramare; (*e.g., food*) distribuire ‖ *intr* uscire; **to issue from** provenire da
**isthmus** ['ɪsməs] *s* istmo
**it** [ɪt] *pron pers* esso, essa; lo, la; **it is**

**I** sono io; **it is raining** piove; **it is four o'clock** sono le quattro
**Italian** [ɪ'tæljən] *adj & s* italiano
**Ital'ian-speak'ing** *adj* italofono
**italic** [ɪ'tælɪk] *adj* (typ) corsivo ‖ **italics** *s* (typ) corsivo ‖ **Italic** *adj* italico
**italicize** [ɪ'tælɪ,saɪz] *tr* stampare in carattere corsivo; sottolineare
**Italy** ['ɪtəli] *s* l'Italia *f*
**itch** [ɪtʃ] *s* prurito; (pathol) rogna; (*eagerness*) (fig) pizzicore *m* ‖ *tr* prudere, e.g., **his foot itches him** gli prude il piede ‖ *intr* (*said of a part of body*) prudere; (*said of a person*) avere il prurito; **to itch to** avere il pizzicore di
**itch·y** ['ɪtʃi] *adj* (**-ier; -iest**) che prude; (pathol) rognoso
**item** ['aɪtəm] *s* articolo; notizia; (*on the agenda*) questione; (slang) notizia scottante
**itemize** ['aɪtə,maɪz] *tr* dettagliare, specificare
**itinerant** [aɪ'tɪnərənt] *or* [ɪ'tɪnərənt] *adj* itinerante, ambulante ‖ *s* viaggiatore *m*, viandante *m*
**itinerar·y** [aɪ'tɪnə,reri] *or* [ɪ'tɪnə,reri] *adj* itinerario ‖ *s* (**-ies**) itinerario
**its** [ɪts] *adj & pron poss* il suo
**itself** [ɪt'self] *pron pers* sé stesso; si, e.g., **it opened itself** si è aperto
**ivied** ['aɪvid] *adj* coperto di edera
**ivo·ry** ['aɪvəri] *adj* d'avorio ‖ *s* (**-ries**) avorio; **ivories** (slang) tasti *mpl* del piano; (slang) palle *fpl* da bigliardo; (*dice*) (slang) dadi *mpl;* (slang) denti *mpl*
**i'vory tow'er** *s* torre *f* d'avorio
**ivy** ['aɪvi] *s* (**ivies**) edera

# J

**J, j** [dʒe] *s* decima lettera dell'alfabeto inglese
**jab** [dʒæb] *s* puntata; (*prick*) puntura; (*with elbow*) gomitata ‖ *v* (*pret & pp* **jabbed;** *ger* **jabbing**) *tr* pugnalare; pungere; dare una gomitata a ‖ *intr* dare colpi
**jabber** ['dʒæbər] *s* borbottamento, ciarla ‖ *tr & intr* borbottare, ciarlare
**jack** [dʒæk] *s* (*for lifting heavy objects*) cricco, martinetto; (*jackass*) asino; (*device for turning a spit*) girarrosto; (*to remove a boot*) cavastivali *m;* (cards) fante *m;* (bowling) pallino; (rad & telv) jack *m;* (elec) presa; (slang) soldi *mpl;* **every man jack** ognuno, tutti *mpl* ‖ **Jack** *s* marinaio; (coll) buonuomo ‖ *tr*—**to jack up** alzare col cricco; (*prices*) (coll) alzare
**jackal** ['dʒækəl] *s* sciacallo
**jack'ass'** *s* asino
**jack'daw'** *s* cornacchia
**jacket** ['dʒækɪt] *s* giacca; (*of boiled*

*potatoes*) buccia; (*of book*) soprac-coperta; (*metal casing*) camicia
**jack'ham'mer** *s* martello perforatore
**jack'-in-the-box'** *s* scatola a sorpresa
**jack'knife'** *s* (**-knives**) coltello a serra-manico; (sports) salto a pesce
**jack'-of-all'-trades'** *s* factotum *m*
**jack-o'-lantern** ['dʒækə,læntərn] *s* lanterna a forma di testa umana fatta con una zucca; fuoco fatuo
**jack'pot'** *s* monte *m* premi; **to hit the jackpot** (slang) vincere un terno al lotto
**jack' rab'bit** *s* lepre nordamericana di taglia grande
**jack'screw'** *s* cricco a verme
**jack'-tar'** *s* (coll) marinaio
**jade** [dʒed] *adj* di giada, come la giada ‖ *s* (*ornamental stone*) giada; (*worn-out horse*) ronzino; (*disreputable woman*) donnaccia ‖ *tr* logorare
**jad'ed** ['dʒedɪd] *adj* logoro, stanco; (*appetite*) stucco
**jag** [dʒæg] *s* slabbratura; **to have a jag on** (slang) avere la sbornia

**jagged** ['dʒægɪd] *adj* dentato, slabbrato

**jaguar** ['dʒægwɑr] *s* giaguaro

**jail** [dʒel] *s* prigione *f;* **to break jail** evadere dal carcere ‖ *tr* carcerare

**jail'bird'** *s* galeotto, remo di galera

**jail'break'** *s* evasione *f* dal carcere

**jailer** ['dʒelər] *s* carceriere *m*

**jalop·y** [dʒə'lɑpi] *s* (**-ies**) carcassa, trespolo, trabiccolo

**jam** [dʒæm] *s* stretta, compressione; (*in traffic*) imbottigliamento; (*preserve*) marmellata, confettura; (*difficult situation*) (coll) pasticcio ‖ *v* (*pret & pp* **jammed;** *ger* **jamming**) *tr* stipare; (*e.g., one's finger*) schiacciare, schiacciarsi; (rad) disturbare; **to jam on the brakes** bloccare i freni ‖ *intr* schiacciarsi; (*said of firearms*) incepparsi; (mach) grippare

**jamb** [dʒæm] *s* stipite *m*

**jamboree** [ˌdʒæmbə'ri] *s* riunione nazionale di giovani esploratori; (coll) riunione

**James** [dʒemz] *s* Giacomo

**jamming** ['dʒæmɪŋ] *s* radiodisturbo

**jam-packed** ['dʒæm'pækt] *adj* gremito, pieno fino all'orlo

**jangle** ['dʒæŋɡəl] *s* suono stridente; (*quarrel*) baruffa ‖ *tr* fare suoni stridenti con ‖ *intr* stridere; litigare

**janitor** ['dʒænɪtər] *s* portiere *m*

**janitress** ['dʒænɪtrɪs] *s* portinaia

**January** ['dʒænju̇ˌɛri] *s* gennaio

**ja·pan** [dʒə'pæn] *s* lacca giapponese; oggetto di lacca ‖ *v* (*pret & pp* **-panned;** *ger* **-panning**) *tr* laccare ‖ **Japan** *s* il Giappone

**Japa·nese** [ˌdʒæpə'niz] *adj* giapponese ‖ *s* (**-nese**) giapponese *mf*

**Jap'anese bee'tle** *s* scarabeo giapponese

**Jap'anese lan'tern** *s* lampioncino alla veneziana

**Jap'anese persim'mon** *s* cachi *m*

**jar** [dʒɑr] *s* barattolo; (*earthenware container*) orcio, giara; discordanza; (*jolt*) scossa; (fig) brutta sorpresa; **on the jar** (*said of a door*) socchiuso ‖ *v* (*pret & pp* **jarred;** *ger* **jarring**) *tr* scuotere; far stridere ‖ *intr* vibrare; stridere; essere in conflitto; **to jar on** irritare

**jardiniere** [ˌdʒɑrdɪ'nɪr] *s* (*pot*) vaso da fiori; giardiniera

**jargon** ['dʒɑrɡən] *s* gergo

**jasmine** ['dʒæsmɪn] *or* ['dʒæzmɪn] *s* gelsomino

**jasper** ['dʒæspər] *s* diaspro

**jaundice** ['dʒɔndɪs] *or* ['dʒɑndɪs] *s* itterizia; (fig) invidia

**jaundiced** ['dʒɔndɪst] *or* ['dʒɑndɪst] *adj* itterico; (fig) invidioso

**jaunt** [dʒɔnt] *or* [dʒɑnt] *s* passeggiata, gita

**jaun·ty** ['dʒɔnti] *or* ['dʒɑnti] *adj* (**-tier; -tiest**) disinvolto; elegante

**Java·nese** [ˌdʒævə'niz] *adj* giavanese ‖ *s* (**-nese**) giavanese *m*

**javelin** ['dʒævlɪn] *or* ['dʒævəlɪn] *s* giavellotto

**jaw** [dʒɔ] *s* mascella, mandibola; (mach) ganascia; **jaws** fauci *fpl;* gola, stretta ‖ *tr* (slang) rimproverare ‖ *intr* (slang) chiacchierare; (slang) fare la predica

**jaw'bone'** *s* mascella, mandibola

**jaw'break'er** *s* (coll) parola difficile da pronunciare; (coll) caramella durissima; (mach) frantoio a mascelle

**jay** [dʒe] *s* (orn) ghiandaia; (coll) sempliciotto

**jay'walk'** *intr* attraversare la strada contro la luce rossa del semaforo

**jay'walk'er** *s* (coll) pedone distratto che attraversa la strada contro la luce rossa del semaforo

**jazz** [dʒæz] *s* jazz *m;* (slang) spirito ‖ *tr*—**to jazz up** (slang) dar vita a

**jazz' band'** *s* orchestra jazz

**jealous** ['dʒɛləs] *adj* geloso; (*envious*) invidioso; vigilante

**jealous·y** ['dʒɛləsi] *s* (**-ies**) gelosia; invidia; vigilanza

**jean** [dʒin] *s* tela cruda; **jeans** pantaloni *mpl* di tela cruda

**jeep** [dʒip] *s* gip *f,* jeep *f*

**jeer** [dʒɪr] *s* beffa ‖ *tr* beffare ‖ *intr* beffarsi; **to jeer at** motteggiare

**Jeho'vah's Wit'nesses** [dʒɪ'hovəs] *spl* Testimoni *mpl* di Geova

**jell** [dʒel] *s* gelatina ‖ *intr* (*to congeal*) gelatinizzarsi; (*to become substantial*) cristallizzarsi

**jel·ly** ['dʒeli] *s* (**-lies**) gelatina ‖ *v* (*pret & pp* **-lied**) *tr* gelatinizzare ‖ *intr* gelatinizzarsi

**jel'ly·fish'** *s* medusa; (*weak person*) (coll) fiaccone *m*

**jeopardize** ['dʒepər ˌdaɪz] *tr* compromettere, mettere a repentaglio

**jeopardy** ['dʒepərdi] *s* pericolo, repentaglio

**jeremiad** [ˌdʒerɪ'maɪˌæd] *s* geremiade *f*

**Jericho** ['dʒerɪˌko] *s* Gerico *f*

**jerk** [dʒʌrk] *s* strattone *m,* scatto; tic *m;* (*stupid person*) scempio, sciocco; **by jerks** a scatti ‖ *tr* tirare a strattoni; (*meat*) essiccare ‖ *intr* sobbalzare

**jerked' beef'** *s* fetta di carne di bue essiccata

**jerkin** ['dʒʌrkɪn] *s* giubbetto

**jerk'wa'ter** *adj* di scarsa importanza

**jerk·y** ['dʒʌrki] *adj* (**-ier; -iest**) sussultante; (*style*) disuguale

**Jerome** [dʒə'rom] *s* Gerolamo

**jersey** ['dʒʌrzi] *s* jersey *m,* maglione *m*

**Jerusalem** [dʒɪ'rusələm] *s* Gerusalemme *f*

**jest** [dʒest] *s* scherzo, burla; **in jest** per celia ‖ *intr* scherzare

**jester** ['dʒestər] *s* motteggiatore *m,* burlone *m;* (hist) buffone *m*

**Jesuit** ['dʒeʒu̇ˌɪt] *or* ['dʒezju̇ˌɪt] *adj & s* gesuita *m*

**Jesuitic(al)** [ˌdʒeʒu̇'ɪtɪk(əl)] *or* [ˌdʒezju̇'ɪtɪk(əl)] *adj* gesuitico

**Jesus** ['dʒizəs] *s* Gesù *m*

**Je'sus Christ'** *s* Gesù *m* Cristo

**jet** [dʒet] *adj* di giaietto ‖ *s* (*of a fountain*) zampillo; (*stream shooting forth from nozzle*) getto; (*mineral; lustrous black*) giaietto; (aer) aereo a getto ‖ *v* (*pret & pp* **jetted;** *ger* **jetting**) *tr* spruzzare || *intr* zampillare; volare in aereo a getto

**jet′ age′** *s* era dell'aviogetto

**jet′-black′** *adj* nero come il carbone

**jet′ bomb′er** *s* bombardiere *m* a reazione

**jet′ coal′** *s* carbone *m* a lunga fiamma

**jet′ en′gine** *s* motore *m* a reazione

**jet′ fight′er** *s* caccia *m* a reazione

**jet′lin′er** *s* aviogetto da trasporto passeggeri

**jet′ plane′** *s* aviogetto

**jet′ propul′sion** *s* gettopropulsione

**jetsam** ['dʒɛtsəm] *s* relitto

**jet′ stream′** *s* corrente *f* a getto; scappamento di motore a razzo

**jettison** ['dʒɛtɪsən] *s* (naut) alleggerimento || *tr* (naut) alleggerirsi di; (fig) disfarsi di

**jet·ty** ['dʒɛti] *s* (**-ties**) gettata; (*wharf*) molo, imbarcadero

**Jew** [dʒu] *s* giudeo

**jewel** ['dʒu·əl] *s* pietra preziosa; (*valuable personal ornament*) gioia, gioiello; (*of a watch*) rubino; (*costume jewelry*) gioia finta; (fig) valore *m*, gioiello

**jew′el case′** *s* scrigno, portagioie *m*

**jeweler** or **jeweller** ['dʒu·ələr] *s* gioielliere *m*, orefice *m*

**jewelry** ['dʒu·əlri] *s* gioielli *mpl*

**jew′elry shop′** *s* gioielleria

**Jewess** ['dʒu·ɪs] *s* giudea

**Jewish** ['dʒu·ɪʃ] *adj* giudeo

**jews′-harp** or **jew′s-harp** ['dʒuz ‚hɑrp] *s* scacciapensieri *m*

**jib** [dʒɪb] *s* (*of a crane*) (mach) braccio (di gru); (naut) fiocco, vela Marconi

**jib′ boom′** *s* asta di fiocco

**jibe** [dʒaɪb] *s* burla, beffa || *intr* beffarsi; accordarsi; **to jibe at** beffarsi di

**jif·fy** ['dʒɪfi] *s*—**in a jiffy** (coll) in men che non si dica

**jig** [dʒɪg] *s* (*dance*) giga; **the jig is up** (slang) tutto è perduto

**jigger** ['dʒɪgər] *s* bicchierino di liquore d'un'oncia e mezza; (*flea*) pulce *f* tropicale; (*gadget*) (coll) aggeggio; (naut) bozzello; (min) crivello

**jiggle** ['dʒɪgəl] *s* scossa || *tr* scuotere, agitare || *intr* scuotersi

**jig′ saw′** *s* sega da traforo

**jig′saw puz′zle** *s* gioco di pazienza, rompicapo

**jilt** [dʒɪlt] *tr* piantare

**jim·my** ['dʒɪmi] *s* (**-mies**) piccolo piede di porco || *v* (*pret & pp* **-mied**) *tr* scassinare; **to jimmy open** scassinare

**jingle** ['dʒɪŋgəl] *s* sonaglio, bubbolo; (*sound*) rumore *m* di sonagliera; cantilena, rima infantile || *tr* far suonare || *intr* tintinnare

**jin·go** ['dʒɪŋgo] *adj* sciovinista || *s* (**-goes**) sciovinista *mf*; **by jingo!** perbacco!

**jingoism** ['dʒɪŋgo‚ɪzəm] *s* sciovinismo

**jinx** [dʒɪŋks] *s* iettatura; (*person*) iettatore *m* || *tr* portare la iettatura a

**jitters** ['dʒɪtərz] *spl* (coll) nervosismo; **to have the jitters** (coll) essere nervoso

**jittery** ['dʒɪtəri] *adj* nervoso

**job** [dʒab] *s* (*piece of work*) lavoro; (*task*) mansione; (*employment*) posto, impiego; (slang) furto; **by the job** a cottimo; **on the job** (slang) attento, sollecito; **to be out of a job** essere disoccupato; **to lie down on the job** (slang) dormire sul lavoro

**job′ anal′ysis** *s* valutazione delle mansioni

**jobber** ['dʒabər] *s* grossista *mf*; (*pieceworker*) lavoratore *m* a cottimo; funzionario disonesto

**job′hold′er** *s* impiegato; (*in the government*) burocrate *m*

**jobless** ['dʒablɪs] *adj* disoccupato

**job′ lot′** *s* (com) saldo

**job′ print′er** *s* piccolo tipografo non specializzato

**job′ print′ing** *s* piccolo lavoro tipografico

**jockey** ['dʒaki] *s* fantino || *tr* (*a horse*) montare; manovrare; (*to trick*) abbindolare

**jockstrap** ['dʒak‚stræp] *s* sospensorio

**jocose** ['dʒo'kos] *adj* giocoso

**jocular** ['dʒakjələr] *adj* scherzoso

**jog** [dʒag] *s* spinta; piccolo trotto || *v* (*pret & pp* **jogged**; *ger* **jogging**) *tr* spingere leggermente; (*the memory*) rinfrescare || *intr* barcarellare; **to jog along** continuare col solito tran tran

**jog′ trot′** *s* piccolo trotto; (fig) tran tran *m*

**John** [dʒan] *s* Giovanni *m*

**John′ Bull′** *s* il tipico inglese; gli inglesi, il popolo inglese

**John′ Han′cock** ['hænkak] *s* (coll) la firma

**johnnycake** ['dʒani‚kek] *s* pane *m* di granturco

**John′ny-come′-late′ly** *s* (coll) ultimo arrivato

**John′ny-jump′-up′** *s* violetta, viola del pensiero

**John′ny-on-the-spot′** *s* (coll) persona sempre pronta

**John′ the Bap′tist** *s* San Giovanni Battista

**join** [dʒɔɪn] *tr* giungere, congiungere; associarsi a; unire; (*e.g., a party*) farsi membro di; (*the army*) arruolarsi in; (*battle*) ingaggiare; (*to empty into*) sfociare in || *intr* congiungersi, unirsi; (*said, e.g., of two rivers*) confluire

**joiner** ['dʒɔɪnər] *s* falegname *m*; membro di molte società

**joint** [dʒɔɪnt] *adj* congiunto || *s* (*in a pipe*) giuntura; (*of bones*) giuntura, articolazione; (*hinge of book*) brachetta; (*in woodwork*) incastro, commettitura; (*of meat*) taglio; (mach) snodo; (*gambling den*) (slang) bisca; (elec) innesto; (slang) bettola; **out of joint** slogato; (fig) fuori luogo; **to throw** (*e.g., one's arm*) **out of joint** slogarsi

**joint′ account′** *s* conto in comune

**joint′ commit′tee** *s* commissione mista

**jointly** ['dʒɔɪntli] *adv* unitamente

**joint′ own′er** *s* condomino

**joint′-stock′ com′pany** *s* società *f* per azioni a responsabilità illimitata

**joist** [dʒɔɪst] *s* trave *f*

**joke** [dʒok] *s* burla, barzelletta; (*trifling matter*) cosa da nulla; (*person laughed at*) zimbello; **to tell a joke** raccontare una barzelletta; **to play a joke on** fare uno scherzo a || *tr*—**to joke one's way into** ottenere dicendo barzellette || *intr* burlare, dire storielle; **joking aside** senza scherzi

**joker** ['dʒokər] *s* burlone *m*, fumista *m*; (*wise guy*) saputello; (*hidden provision*) clausola ingannatrice; (*cards*) matta

**jol·ly** ['dʒali] *adj* (**-lier; -liest**) allegro, gaio || *adv* (coll) molto || *v* (*pret & pp* **-lied**) *tr* (coll) prendersi gioco di

**jolt** [dʒolt] *s* scossa || *tr* scuotere || *intr* sobbalzare

**Jonah** ['dʒonə] *s* Giona; (fig) uccello di mal augurio

**jongleur** ['dʒaŋglər] *s* giullare *m*

**jonquil** ['dʒaŋkwɪl] *s* giunchiglia

**Jordan** ['dʒɔrdən] *s* (*country*) la Giordania; (*river*) Giordano

**Jordanian** [dʒɔr'denɪ·ən] *adj & s* giordano

**josh** [dʒaʃ] *tr & intr* (coll) canzonare

**jostle** ['dʒasəl] *s* spintone *m* || *tr* spingere || *intr* scontrarsi; farsi strada a gomitate

**jot** [dʒat] *s*—**I don't care a jot for** non mi importa un fico di || *v* (*pret & pp* **jotted**; *ger* **jotting**) *tr*—**to jot down** notare, gettar giù

**jounce** [dʒauns] *s* scossa || *tr* scuotere || *intr* sobbalzare

**journal** ['dʒarnəl] *s* (*newspaper*) giornale *m*; (*magazine*) rivista; (*daily record*) diario; (com) giornale *m*; (*mach*) perno; (naut) giornale *m* di bordo

**journalese** [ˌdʒarnə'liz] *s* linguaggio giornalistico

**journalism** ['dʒarnə ˌlɪzəm] *s* giornalismo

**journalist** ['dʒarnəlɪst] *s* giornalista *mf*

**journey** ['dʒarni] *s* viaggio || *intr* viaggiare

**jour'ney·man** *s* (**-men**) operaio specializzato

**joust** [dʒast] *or* [dʒust] *or* [dʒaust] *s* giostra || *intr* giostrare

**jovial** ['dʒovɪ·əl] *adj* gioviale

**jowl** [dʒaul] *s* (*cheek*) guancia; (*jawbone*) mascella; (*of cattle*) giogaia; (*of fowl*) bargiglio; (*of fat person*) pappagorgia

**joy** [dʒɔɪ] *s* gioia, allegria; **to leap with joy** ballare dalla gioia

**joyful** ['dʒɔɪfəl] *adj* gioioso, festoso; **joyful over** lieto di

**joyless** ['dʒɔɪlɪs] *adj* senza gioia

**joyous** ['dʒɔɪ·əs] *adj* gioioso

**joy' ride'** *s* (coll) gita in auto; (coll) gita all'impazzata in auto

**jubilant** ['dʒubɪlənt] *adj* esultante

**jubilation** [ˌdʒubɪ'leʃən] *s* giubilo

**jubilee** ['dʒubɪ ˌli] *s* (*jubilation*) giubilo; (eccl) giubileo

**Judaism** ['dʒude ˌɪzəm] *s* giudaismo

**judge** [dʒadʒ] *s* giudice *m* || *tr & intr* giudicare; **judging by** a giudicare da

**judge' ad'vocate** *s* avvocato militare; avvocato della marina da guerra

**judgeship** ['dʒadʒʃɪp] *s* carica di giudice

**judgment** ['dʒadʒmənt] *s* giudizio; (*legal decision*) sentenza

**judg'ment day'** *s* giorno del giudizio

**judg'ment seat'** *s* banco dei giudici; tribunale *m*

**judicature** ['dʒudɪkətʃər] *s* carica di giudice

**judicial** [dʒu'dɪʃəl] *adj* giudiziario; (*becoming a judge*) giudizioso

**judiciar·y** [dʒu'dɪʃɪ ˌeri] *adj* giudiziario || *s* (**-ies**) (*judges collectively*) magistratura; (*judicial branch*) potere giudiziario

**judicious** [dʒu'dɪʃəs] *adj* giudizioso

**jug** [dʒag] *s* brocca, boccale *m*; (*narrow-necked vessel*) orcio; (*jail*) (slang) prigione

**juggle** ['dʒagəl] *s* gioco di prestigio || *tr* fare il giocoliere con; (*documents, facts*) alterare frodolentemente; **to juggle away** ghermire, trafugare || *intr* fare il giocoliere; fare l'imbroglione

**juggler** ['dʒaglər] *s* giocoliere *m*, prestigiatore *m*; impostore *m*

**juggling** ['dʒaglɪŋ] *s* giochi *mpl* di prestigio

**Jugoslav** ['jugo'slav] *adj & s* iugoslavo, jugoslavo

**Jugoslavia** ['jugo'slavɪ·ə] *s* la Iugoslavia, la Jugoslavia

**jugular** ['dʒagjələr] *or* ['dʒugjələr] *adj & s* giugulare *f*

**juice** [dʒus] *s* sugo; (*natural fluid of an animal body*) succo; (slang) elettricità *f*; (slang) benzina; **to stew in one's own juice** (coll) annegarsi nel proprio sugo

**juic·y** ['dʒusi] *adj* (**-ier; -iest**) sugoso, succoso; (*spicy*) piccante

**jukebox** ['dʒuk ˌbaks] *s* grammofono a gettone, juke-box *m*

**julep** ['dʒulɪp] *s* bibita di menta col ghiaccio; (pharm) giulebbe *m*

**julienne** [ˌdʒuli'en] *s* giuliana

**July** [dʒu'laɪ] *s* luglio

**jumble** ['dʒambəl] *s* intrico, garbuglio || *tr* ingarbugliare

**jum·bo** ['dʒambo] *adj* (coll) enorme || *s* (**-bos**) (*person*) (coll) elefante *m*; (*thing*) (coll) oggetto enorme

**jump** [dʒamp] *s* salto; (*in a parachute*) lancio; (*of prices*) sbalzo; (*start*) soprassalto; **on the jump** in moto; **to get or to have the jump on** (coll) avere il vantaggio su || *tr* saltare; (*a horse*) far saltare; (*prices*) alzare; uscire da, e.g., **the train jumped the track** il treno uscì dalle rotaie; (*to attack*) (coll) balzare su; (*checkers*) suffiare || *intr* saltare; (*from surprise*) trasalire; (*said of prices*) salire; (*in a parachute*) lanciarsi; **to jump at** (*e.g., an offer*) afferrare; **to jump on** saltare su; (coll) sgridare, arrabbiarsi con; **to jump over** oltrepassare; (*a page*) saltare; **to jump to a conclusion** arrivare precipitosamente a una conclusione

**jumper** ['dʒampər] *s* saltatore *m*; camiciotto; **jumpers** tuta da bambini

**jump'ing jack'** ['dʒʌmpɪŋ] *s* marionetta
**jump'ing-off' place'** *s* fine *f* del mondo; (fig) trampolino, punto di partenza
**jump' seat'** *s* strapuntino
**jump' spark'** *s* scintilla elettrica; (*of induction coil*) (elec) scintilla d'intraferro
**jump' wire'** *s* filo elettrico di contatto
**jump·y** ['dʒʌmpi] *adj* (**-ier; -iest**) nervoso, eccitato
**junction** ['dʒʌŋktʃən] *s* congiunzione; (*of two rivers*) confluenza; (carp) commettitura; (rr) raccordo ferroviario
**juncture** ['dʒʌŋktʃər] *s* giuntura; (*occasion*) congiuntura; (*moment*) momento
**June** [dʒun] *s* giugno
**jungle** ['dʒʌŋgəl] *s* giungla
**junglegym** ['dʒʌŋgəl,dʒɪm] *s* (trademark) castello
**junior** ['dʒunjər] *adj* minore, di minore età; giovane; (*in American university*) del penultimo anno; figlio, e.g., **John H. Smith, Junior** Giovanni H. Smith, figlio || *s* minore *m;* socio secondario; studente *m* del penultimo anno
**jun'ior col'lege** *s* scuola universitaria unicamente di primo biennio
**jun'ior high' school'** *s* scuola media; ginnasio
**juniper** ['dʒunɪpər] *s* ginepro
**ju'niper ber'ry** *s* coccola di ginepro
**junk** [dʒʌŋk] *s* roba vecchia, ferro vecchio; (*Chinese ship*) giunca; (naut) carne salata || *tr* (slang) gettar via
**junk' deal'er** *s* robivecchi *m*
**junket** ['dʒʌŋkɪt] *s* budino di giuncata; (*outing*) viaggio di piacere; viaggio pagato a spese del tesoro || *intr* far un viaggio di piacere; far un viaggio a spese del tesoro
**junk'man'** *s* (**-men'**) ferravecchio; rigattiere *m*
**junk' room'** *s* ripostiglio

**junk' shop'** *s* negozio di robivecchi
**junk'yard'** *s* cantiere *m* di ferravecchio
**juridical** [dʒu'rɪdɪkəl] *adj* giuridico
**jurisdiction** [,dʒurɪs'dɪkʃən] *s* giurisdizione
**jurisprudence** [,dʒurɪs'prudəns] *s* giurisprudenza
**jurist** ['dʒurɪst] *s* giurista *mf*
**juror** ['dʒurər] *s* giurato
**ju·ry** ['dʒuri] *s* (**-ries**) giuria
**ju'ry box'** *s* banco della giuria
**ju'ry·man** *s* (**-men**) giurato
**just** [dʒʌst] *adj* giusto || *adv* giusta·mente, giusto; appena; proprio; **just as** come, proprio come; **just beyond** un po' più in là (di); **just now** poco fa, or ora; **just out** appena uscito, appena pubblicato
**justice** ['dʒʌstɪs] *s* giustizia; (*judge*) giudice *m;* **to bring to justice** arrestare e condannare; **to do justice to** render giustizia a; apprezzare bastantemente
**jus'tice of the peace'** *s* giudice *m* conciliatore
**justifiable** ['dʒʌstɪ,faɪ·əbəl] *adj* giustificabile
**justi·fy** ['dʒʌstɪ,faɪ] *v* (*pret & pp* **-fied**) *tr* giustificare; (typ) giustificare
**justly** ['dʒʌstli] *adj* giustamente
**jut** [dʒʌt] *v* (*pret & pp* **jutted; ger jutting**) *intr*—**to jut out** strapiombare, sporgere
**jute** [dʒut] *s* iuta || **Jute** *s* Juto
**juvenile** ['dʒuvənɪl] or ['dʒuvə,naɪl] *adj* giovanile; minorile || *s* giovane *mf;* libro per la gioventù; (theat) amoroso
**ju'venile court'** *s* tribunale *m* per i minorenni
**ju'venile delin'quency** *s* delinquenza minorile
**juvenilia** [,dʒuvə'nɪlɪ·ə] *spl* opere *fpl* giovanili; libri *mpl* per ragazzi
**juxtapose** [,dʒʌkstə'poz] *tr* giustapporre

# K

**K, k** [ke] *s* undicesima lettera dell'alfabeto inglese
**kale** [kel] *s* verza; (slang) cocuzza, soldi *mpl*
**kaleidoscope** [kə'laɪdə,skop] *s* caleidoscopio
**kangaroo** [,kæŋgə'ru] *s* canguro
**katydid** ['ketidɪd] *s* grossa cavalletta verde nordamericana
**kedge** [kɛdʒ] *s* (naut) ancorotto
**keel** [kil] *s* chiglia || *intr*—**to keel over** (naut) abbattersi in carena, capovolgersi; (fig) svenire
**keelson** ['kɛlsən] or ['kɪlsən] *s* (naut) controchiglia
**keen** [kin] *adj* (*sharpened*) affilato; (*wind; wit*) tagliente, mordente; (*eyes*) penetrante; (*ears; mind*) acuto,

fine; (*eager*) entusiasta; intenso, vivo; (slang) meraviglioso; **to be keen on** essere appassionato per
**keep** [kip] *s* mantenimento; (*of medieval castle*) torrione *m*, maschio; **for keeps** (coll) seriamente; (coll) per sempre; **to earn one's keep** guadagnarsi la vita || *v* (*pret & pp* **kept** [kɛpt]) *tr* mantenere; (*watch*) fare; (*one's word*) mantenere; (*to withhold*) trattenere; (*accounts*) tenere; (*servants, guests*) avere; (*a garden*) coltivare; (*a business*) esercitare; (*a holiday*) festeggiare; (*to support*) sostentare; (*a secret; one's seat*) serbare; (*to decide to purchase*) prendere **to keep away** tener lontano; **to keep back** trattenere; (*a secret*) man-

tenere; **to keep down** reprimere; (*expenses*) ridurre al minimo; **to keep s.o. from** + *ger* impedire a qlcu di + *inf;* **to keep in** tener chiuso; **to keep off** tenere a distanza; (*e.g., moisture*) non lasciar penetrare; **to keep s.o. informed about s.th** tenere qlcu al corrente di qlco; **to keep s.o. waiting** fare aspettare qlcu; **to keep up** mantenere, sostenere ‖ *intr* **to keep** + *ger* continuare a + *inf;* **to keep away** tenersi lontano; **to keep from** + *ger* evitare di + *inf;* **to keep informed (about)** tenersi al corrente (di); **to keep in with** (coll) stare nelle buone grazie di; **to keep off** stare lontano (da); (*the grass*) non calpestare; **to keep on** + *ger* seguitare a + *inf;* **to keep out** star fuori, non entrare; **to keep out of** non entrare in; (*danger*) stare lontano da; non immischiarsi in; **to keep quiet** stare tranquillo; **to keep to** (*left or right*) tenere; **to keep to oneself** stare in disparte; **to keep up** continuare; **to keep up with** stare alla pari con; (*e.g., the news*) tenersi al corrente di

**keeper** ['kipər] *s* (*of a shop*) tenitore *m;* guardiano; (*of a game preserve*) guardacaccia *m;* (*of a magnet*) ancora

**keeping** ['kipɪŋ] *s* custodia; (*of a holiday*) celebrazione; **in keeping with** in armonia con; **in safe keeping** in luogo sicuro; **out of keeping with** in cattivo accordo con

**keep'sake'** *s* ricordo

**keg** [kɛg] *s* barilotto, botticella

**ken** [kɛn] *s* portata; **beyond the ken of** al di là dell'ambito di

**kennel** ['kɛnəl] *s* canile *m*

**kep·i** ['kepi] or ['kepi] *s* (-is) chepì *m*

**kept' wo'man** [kɛpt] *s* (**wom'en**) mantenuta

**kerchief** ['kʌrtʃɪf] *s* fisciù *m*

**kernel** ['kʌrnəl] *s* (*of a nut*) gheriglio; (*of wheat*) chicco; (fig) nucleo

**kerosene** ['kɛrə‚sin] or [‚kɛrə'sin] *s* cherosene *m,* petrolio da illuminazione

**kerplunk** [kər'plʌŋk] *interj* patapum!

**ketchup** ['ketʃəp] *s* salsa piccante di pomodoro, ketchup *m*

**kettle** ['ketəl] *s* marmitta, paiolo; (*teakettle*) bricco, teiera

**ket'tle·drum'** *s* timpano

**key** [ki] *adj* a chiave; chiave ‖ *s* chiave *f;* (*of piano, typewriter, etc.*) tasto; (*cotter pin*) chiavetta, coppiglia; (*reef*) isolotto; (*tone of voice*) tono; (fig, mus) chiave *f;* (bot) samara; (telg) tasto trasmettitore, manipolatore *m;* **off key** stonato ‖ *tr* aggiustare; inchiavardare; **to key up** eccitare, portare al parossismo

**key'board'** *s* tastiera

**key'hole'** *s* toppa, buco della serratura; (*of a clock*) buco della chiave

**key'note'** *s* (mus) tono; (fig) principio informatore

**key'note address'** *s* discorso d'apertura

**key'punch op'era'tor** *s* perforatore *m*

**key' ring'** *s* portachiavi *m*

**key'stone'** *s* chiave *f* di volta

**key' word'** *s* parola chiave

**kha·ki** ['kɑki] or ['kæki] *adj* cachi ‖ *s* (-kis) cachi *m*

**khedive** [kə'div] *s* kedivè *m*

**kibitz** ['kɪbɪts] *intr* (coll) dare consigli non richiesti

**kibitzer** ['kɪbɪtsər] *s* (*at a card game*) (coll) consigliere *m* importuno; (coll) ficcanaso *mf*

**kibosh** ['kaɪbɑʃ] or [kɪ'bɑʃ] *s* (coll) sciocchezza; **to put the kibosh on** (coll) impossibilitare

**kick** [kɪk] *s* calcio, pedata; (*of a gun*) rinculo; (*complaint*) (slang) protesta; (*of liquor*) (slang) forza; **to get a kick out of** (slang) pigliar piacere da ‖ *tr* prendere a calci; (*a ball*) calciare; (*one's feet*) battere; **to kick out** (coll) sbatter fuori a pedate; **to kick up a row** scatenare un putiferio ‖ *intr* calciare; (*said of an animal*) scalciare, trarre; (*said of a firearm*) rinculare; (coll) lamentarsi; **to kick against the pricks** dar calci al vento; **to kick off** (football) dare il calcio d'inizio

**kick'back'** *s* (coll) contraccolpo; (coll) intrallazzo, bustarella

**kick'off'** *s* calcio d'inizio

**kid** [kɪd] *s* capretto; (coll) piccolo; **kids** guanti *mpl* or scarpe *fpl* di capretto ‖ *v* (*pret & pp* **kidded**) *ger* **kidding**) *tr* (coll) prendere in giro; **to kid oneself** (coll) farsi illusioni ‖ *intr* (coll) dirlo per scherzo

**kidder** ['kɪdər] *s* (coll) burlone *m*

**kid' gloves'** *spl* guanti *mpl* di capretto; **to handle with kid gloves** trattare con la massima cautela

**kid'nap'** *v* (*pret & pp* **-naped** or **-napped**; *ger* **-naping** or **-napping**) *tr* rapire, sequestrare

**kidnaper** or **kidnapper** ['kɪd‚næpər] *s* rapitore *m* a scopo d'estorsione

**kidnaping** or **kidnapping** ['kɪd‚næpɪŋ] *s* rapimento a scopo di estorsione

**kidney** ['kɪdni] *s* rene *m;* (culin) rognone *m;* (*temperament*) carattere *m;* (*kind*) tipo

**kid'ney bean'** *s* fagiolo

**kid'ney stone'** *s* calcolo renale

**kill** [kɪl] *s* uccisione; (*game killed*) cacciagione; (coll) fiumicello; **for the kill** per il colpo finale ‖ *tr* uccidere; eliminare; (*a bill*) bocciare; (fig) opprimere

**killer** ['kɪlər] *s* uccisore *m*

**kill'er whale'** *s* orca

**killing** ['kɪlɪŋ] *adj* mortale; (*exhausting*) opprimente; (coll) molto divertente ‖ *s* uccisione; (*game killed*) cacciagione; (coll) fortuna; **to make a killing** (coll) fare una fortuna da un giorno all'altro

**kill'-joy'** *s* guastafeste *mf*

**kiln** [kɪl] or [kɪln] *s* forno, fornace *f*

**kil·o** ['kɪlo] or ['kilo] *s* (-os) chilogrammo; chilometro

**kilocycle** ['kɪlə‚saɪkəl] *s* chilociclo

**kilogram** ['kɪlə‚græm] *s* chilogrammo

**kilo·hertz** ['kɪlə‚hʌrts] *s* (-hertz) chilohertz

**kilometer** ['kɪlə,mitər] or [kɪ'lɑmɪtər] s chilometro

**kilowatt** ['kɪlə,wɑt] s kilowatt m, chilowatt m

**kilowatt-hour** ['kɪlə,wɑt'aʊr] s (**kilowatt-hours**) chilowattora m

**kilt** [kɪlt] s gonnellino

**kilter** ['kɪltər] s—**to be out of kilter** (coll) essere fuori squadra

**kimo·no** [kɪ'monə] or [kɪ'mono] s (**-nos**) chimono

**kin** [kɪn] s (family relationship) parentela; (relatives) parenti mpl; **of kin** parente, affine; **the next of kin** il parente più prossimo, i parenti più prossimi

**kind** [kaɪnd] adj gentile; **kind to** buono con || s genere m, specie f; **a kind of** una specie di; **all kinds of** (coll) ogni sorta di; **in kind** in natura; **kind of** (coll) quasi, piuttosto; **of a kind** dello stesso stampo; (mediocre) di poco valore

**kindergarten** ['kɪndər,gɑrtən] s scuola materna, giardino d'infanzia

**kindergartner** ['kɪndər,gɑrtnər] s allievo della scuola d'infanzia; (teacher) maestra giardiniera

**kind-hearted** ['kaɪnd'hɑrtɪd] adj gentile, di buon cuore

**kindle** ['kɪndəl] tr accendere || intr accendersi

**kindling** ['kɪndlɪŋ] s accensione; legna minuta

**kin'dling wood'** s legna minuta per accendere il fuoco

**kind·ly** ['kaɪndli] adj (**-lier; -liest**) gentile; (climate) benigno; favorevole || adv gentilmente; cordialmente; per gentilezza; **to not take kindly to** non accettare di buon grado

**kindness** ['kaɪndnɪs] s gentilezza; **have the kindness to** abbia la bontà di

**kindred** ['kɪndrɪd] adj imparentato; affine || s parentela; affinità f

**kinescope** ['kɪnɪ,skop] s (trademark) cinescopio

**kinetic** [kɪ'nɛtɪk] or [kaɪ'nɛtɪk] adj cinetico || **kinetics** s cinetica

**kinet'ic en'ergy** s forza viva, energia cinetica

**king** [kɪŋ] s re m; (checkers) dama; (cards, chess) re m

**king'bolt'** s perno

**kingdom** ['kɪŋdəm] s regno

**king'fish'er** s martin pescatore m

**king·ly** ['kɪŋli] adj (**-lier; -liest**) reale; (stately) maestoso || adv regalmente

**king'pin'** s birillo centrale; (aut) perno dello sterzo; (fig) figura principale

**king' post'** s (archit) ometto, monaco

**king's' e'vil** s scrofola

**kingship** ['kɪŋʃɪp] s regalità f

**king'-size'** adj extra-grande

**king's' ran'som** s ricchezza di Creso

**kink** [kɪŋk] s (in a rope) arricciatura; (in hair) crespatura; (soreness in neck) torcicollo; (flaw) ostacolo; (mental twist) ghiribizzo || tr attorcigliare || intr attorcigliarsi

**kink·y** ['kɪŋki] adj (**-ier; -iest**) attorcigliato; (hair) crespo

**kinsfolk** ['kɪnz,fok] s parentado

**kinship** ['kɪnʃɪp] s parentela; affinità f

**kins'man** s (**-men**) parente m

**kins'wom'an** s (**-wom'en**) parente f

**kipper** ['kɪpər] s aringa affumicata || tr (herring or salmon) affumicare

**kiss** [kɪs] s bacio; (billiards) rimpallo leggerissimo; (confection) meringa || tr baciare; **to kiss away** (tears) asciugare con baci || intr baciare, baciarsi; (billiards) rimpallare leggermente

**kit** [kɪt] s (case) cassetta dei ferri; (tools) ferri mpl del mestiere; (set of supplies) corredo; (of small tools) astuccio; (of a traveler) borsa da viaggio; (pail) secchio; **the whole kit and caboodle** (coll) tutti quanti

**kitchen** ['kɪtʃən] s cucina

**kitchenette** [,kɪtʃə'nɛt] s cucinetta

**kitch'en gar'den** s orto

**kitch'en·maid'** s sguattera

**kitch'en police'** s (mil) corvè f di cucina

**kitch'en range'** s cucina economica

**kitch'en sink'** s acquaio

**kitch'en·ware'** s utensili mpl di cucina

**kite** [kaɪt] s cervo volante, aquilone m; (orn) nibbio

**kith' and kin'** [kɪθ] spl amici mpl e parenti mpl

**kitten** ['kɪtən] s gattino

**kittenish** ['kɪtənɪʃ] adj giocattolone; civettuolo

**kit·ty** ['kɪti] s (**-ties**) gattino; (cards) piatto || interj micio!

**kleptomaniac** [,klɛptə'menɪ,æk] s cleptomane mf

**knack** [næk] s abilità f, destrezza

**knapsack** ['næp,sæk] s zaino

**knave** [nev] s furfante m; (cards) fante m

**knaver·y** ['nevəri] s (**-ies**) furfanteria

**knead** [nid] tr maneggiare, intridere; (a muscle) massaggiare

**knee** [ni] s ginocchio; (of trousers) ginocchiera; (mach) gomito; **to bring s.o. to his knees** ridurre qlcu all'obbedienza; **to go down on one's knees (to)** gettarsi in ginocchio (davanti a)

**knee' breech'es** [,brɪtʃ/ɪz] spl calzoni mpl al ginocchio

**knee'cap'** s rotula, patella; (protective covering) ginocchiera

**knee'-deep'** adj fino al ginocchio

**knee'-high'** adj fino al ginocchio

**knee' jerk'** s riflesso patellare

**kneel** [nil] v (pret & pp **knelt** [nɛlt] or **kneeled**) intr inginocchiarsi

**knee'pad'** s ginocchiera

**knee'pan'** s rotula, patella

**knell** [nɛl] s rintocco funebre, campana a morto; **to toll the knell of** annunciare la morte di || intr suonare a morte

**knickers** ['nɪkərz] spl knickerbockers mpl, calzoni mpl alla zuava

**knickknack** ['nɪk,næk] s soprammobile m; gingillo, ninnolo

**knife** [naɪf] s (**knives** [naɪvz]) coltello; (of a paper cutter) mannaia; (of a milling machine) fresa; **to go under the knife** essere sulla tavola operatoria || tr accoltellare; mettere il coltello nella schiena di

**knife' sharp'ener** s affilatoio

**knife' switch'** *s* (elec) coltella
**knight** [naɪt] *s* cavaliere *m;* (chess) cavallo ‖ *tr* armare cavaliere
**knight-errant** ['naɪt'ɛrənt] *s* (**knights-errant**) cavaliere *m* errante
**knighthood** ['naɪt·hud] *s* cavalleria
**knightly** ['naɪtli] *adj* cavalleresco
**knit** [nɪt] *v* (*pret & pp* **knitted** or **knit;** *ger* **knitting**) *tr* lavorare a maglia; (*to join*) unire; (*e.g., the brow*) corrugare ‖ *intr* lavorare a maglia; fare la calza; unirsi; (*said of a bone*) saldarsi
**knitting** ['nɪtɪŋ] *s* maglia, lavoro a maglia
**knit'ting machine'** *s* macchina per maglieria
**knit'ting mill'** *s* maglieria
**knit'ting nee·dle** *s* ferro da calza
**knit'wear'** *s* maglieria
**knit'wear store'** *s* maglieria
**knob** [nɑb] *s* (*lump*) bozza, protuberanza; (*of a door*) maniglia; (*on furniture*) pomolo; (*hill*) collinetta rotondeggiante; (rad, telv) manopola, pulsante *m*
**knock** [nɑk] *s* colpo; (*on a door*) tocco; (slang) attacco, critica ‖ *tr* battere; (*repeatedly*) sbatacchiare; (slang) attaccare, criticare; **to knock down** (*with a punch*) stendere a terra; (*a wall*) diroccare; (*to the highest bidder*) aggiudicare; (*e.g., a machine*) smontare; **to knock off** (*work*) (slang) sospendere; (slang) terminare; (slang) uccidere; **to knock out** mettere fuori combattimento ‖ *intr* battere; (aut) battere in testa; (slang) criticare; **to knock about** (slang) gironzolare; **to knock against** urtare contro; **to knock at** (*e.g., a door*) battere a, bussare a; **to knock off** (slang) cessare di lavorare
**knock'down'** *adj* (*blow*) knock down, che atterra; (*dismountable*) smontabile ‖ *s* (*blow*) colpo che atterra; (*discount*) sconto
**knocker** ['nɑkər] *s* (*on a door*) battaglio, bussatoio; (coll) criticone *m*
**knock-kneed** ['nɑk ˌnid] *adj* con le gambe a **X** [ɪks]
**knock'out'** *s* pugno che mette fuori combattimento; fuori combattimento; (coll) pezzo di giovane
**knock'out drops'** *spl* (slang) narcotico
**knoll** [nol] *s* poggio, rialzo
**knot** [nɑt] *s* nodo; (*worn as an ornament*) fiocco; (*in wood*) nocchio; gruppo; protuberanza; (*tie*) nodo;

(naut) nodo; **to tie the knot** (coll) sposarsi ‖ *v* (*pret & pp* **knotted;** *ger* **knotting**) *tr* annodare; (*the brow*) corrugare ‖ *intr* annodarsi
**knot'hole'** *s* buco lasciato da un nodo (nel legno)
**knot·ty** ['nɑti] *adj* (**-tier; -tiest**) nodoso; (fig) spinoso
**know** [no] *s*—**to be in the know** (coll) essere al corrente ‖ *v* (*pret* **knew** [nju] or [nu]; *pp* **known**) *tr & intr* (*by reasoning or learning*) sapere; (*by the senses or by perception; through acquaintance or recognition*) conoscere; **as far as I know** per quanto io ne sappia; **to know about** essere al corrente di; **to know best** essere il miglior giudice; **to know how to** + *inf* sapere + *inf;* **to know it all** (coll) sapere tutto; **to know what's what** (coll) saperla lunga; **you ought to know better** dovresti vergognarti
**knowable** ['no·əbəl] *adj* conoscibile
**know'-how'** *s* sapere *m*, abilità *f*
**knowingly** ['no·ɪŋli] *adv* con conoscenza di causa; (*on purpose*) apposta
**know'-it-all'** *adj & s* (coll) saputello
**knowledge** ['nɑlɪdʒ] *s* (*faculty*) scibile *m*, sapere *m*, sapienza; (*awareness, acquaintance, familiarity*) conoscenza; **to have a thorough knowledge of** conoscere a fondo; **to my knowledge** per quanto io ne sappia; **with full knowledge** con conoscenza di causa; **without my knowledge** a mia insaputa
**knowledgeable** ['nɑlɪdʒəbəl] *adj* intelligente, bene informato
**knuckle** ['nʌkəl] *s* nocca; foro del cardine, cardine *m;* **knuckles** pugno di ferro ‖ *intr*—**to knuckle down** (coll) lavorare di impegno; **to knuckle under** (coll) darsi per vinto
**knurl** [nʌrl] *s* granitura ‖ *tr* godranare, zigrinare
**Koran** [ko'rɑn] or [ko'ræn] *s* Corano
**Korea** [ko'ri·ə] *s* la Corea
**Korean** [ko'ri·ən] *adj & s* coreano
**kosher** ['koʃər] *adj* kasher, casher, puro secondo la legge giudaica; (coll) autentico
**kowtow** ['kau'tau] or ['ko'tau] *intr* inchinarsi servilmente
**Kremlin** ['krɛmlɪn] *s* Cremlino
**Kremlinology** [ˌkrɛmlɪ'nɑlədʒi] *s* Cremlinologia
**kudos** ['kjudɑs] or ['kudɑs] *s* (coll) gloria, fama, approvazione

## L

**L, l** [ɛl] *s* dodicesima lettera dell'alfabeto inglese
**la·bel** ['lebəl] *s* marca, etichetta; (*descriptive word*) qualifica ‖ *v* (*pret & pp* **-beled** or **-belled;** *ger* **-beling** or **-belling**) *tr* etichettare; qualificare
**labial** ['lebɪ·əl] *adj & s* labiale *f*

**labor** ['lebər] *adj* operaio ‖ *s* lavoro; (*toil*) fatica; (*childbirth*) parto; (*body of wage earners*) manodopera; (*class as contrasted with management*) prestatori *mpl* d'opera, lavoro; **labors** fatiche *fpl;* **to be in labor** avere le doglie ‖ *intr* lavorare; (*to exert one-*

*self*) travagliare; (*said of a ship*) rollare e beccheggiare; **to labor for** lottare per; **to labor under** soffrire di
**laborato·ry** ['læbərə‚tori] *s* (**-ries**) laboratorio
**la'bor dispute'** *s* vertenza sindacale
**labored** ['lebərd] *adj* elaborato, artificiale; penoso, difficile
**laborer** ['lebərər] *s* lavoratore *m;* (*unskilled worker*) bracciante *m,* manovale *m,* uomo di fatica
**laborious** [lə'bori·əs] *adj* laborioso
**la'bor un'ion** *s* sindacato
**Labourite** ['lebə‚raɪt] *s* laburista *mf*
**labyrinth** ['læbɪrɪnθ] *s* labirinto
**lace** [les] *s* (*cord or string*) strínga; (*netlike ornament*) trina, merletto; (*braid*) gallone *m* ‖ *tr* stringare; merlettare; (coll) fustigare
**lace'work'** *s* trina, merletto, pizzo
**lachrymose** ['lækrɪ ‚mos] *adj* lacrimoso
**lacing** ['lesɪŋ] *s* stringa, cordone *m;* gallone *m;* (coll) battuta, frustata
**lack** [læk] *s* mancanza, scarsezza, difetto ‖ *tr* mancare di, scarseggiare di ‖ *intr* mancare, scarseggiare, difettare
**lackadaisical** [‚lækə'dezɪkəl] *adj* letargico, indifferente
**lackey** ['læki] *s* lacchè *m*
**lacking** ['lækɪŋ] *prep* privo di
**lack'lus'ter** *adj* smorto, spento
**laconic** [lə'kɑnɪk] *adj* laconico
**lacquer** ['lækər] *s* lacca ‖ *tr* laccare
**lac'quer spray'** *s* lacca spray
**lac'quer ware'** *s* oggetti *mpl* laccati
**lacu·na** [le'kjunə] *s* (**-nas** or **-nae** [ní]) lacuna
**lac·y** ['lesi] *adj* (**-ier; -iest**) simile al merletto
**lad** [læd] *s* ragazzo, fanciullo
**ladder** ['lædər] *s* scala; (*stepladder hinged on top*) scaleo; (*stepping stone*) (fig) scalino
**lad'der truck'** *s* autocarro di pompieri munito di scale
**la'dies' man'** *s* beato fra le donne
**la'dies' room'** *s* gabinetto per signore
**ladle** ['ledəl] *s* ramaiolo, mestolo; (*of tinsmith*) cucchiaio ‖ *tr* scodellare
**la·dy** ['ledi] *s* (**-dies**) signora, dama
**la'dy·bug'** *s* coccinella
**la'dy·fin'ger** *s* savoiardo, lingua di gatto
**la'dy-in-wait'ing** *s* (**ladies-in-waiting**) dama di corte
**la'dy-kil'ler** *s* rubacuori *m*
**la'dy·like'** *adj* signorile; **to be ladylike** comportarsi come una signora
**la'dy·love'** *s* amata
**la'dy of the house'** *s* padrona di casa
**ladyship** ['ledi ‚ʃɪp] *s* signoria
**la'dy's maid'** *s* cameriera personale della signora
**lag** [læg] *s* ritardo ‖ *v* (*pret & pp* **lagged;** *ger* **lagging**) *intr* ritardare; **to lag behind** rimanere indietro
**la'ger beer'** ['lagər] *s* birra invecchiata
**laggard** ['lægərd] *s* tardo, pigro
**lagoon** [lə'gun] *s* laguna
**laid' pa'per** ['led] *s* carta vergata
**laid' up'** *adj* messo da parte; (naut) disarmato; (coll) costretto a letto

**lair** [lɛr] *s* tana, covo
**laity** ['le·ɪti] *s* laicato
**lake** [lek] *adj* lacustre ‖ *s* lago
**lamb** [læm] *s* agnello
**lambaste** [læm'best] *tr* (*to thrash*) sferzare; (*to reprimand*) riprovare
**lamb' chop'** *s* cotoletta d'agnello
**lambkin** ['læmkɪn] *s* agnellino; (fig) innocente *mf*
**lamb'skin'** *s* (*leather*) pelle *f* d'agnello; (*skin with its wool*) agnello
**lame** [lem] *adj* zoppo; difettoso; (*disabled*) invalido; (*excuse*) debole ‖ *tr* azzoppare
**lament** [lə'mɛnt] *s* lamento; lamento funebre ‖ *tr* lamentare ‖ *intr* lamentarsi
**lamentable** ['læməntəbəl] or [lə'mɛntəbəl] *adj* lamentevole
**lamentation** [ ‚læmən'teʃən] *s* lamentazione
**laminate** ['læmɪ ‚net] *tr* laminare
**lamp** [læmp] *s* lampada
**lamp'black'** *s* nerofumo
**lamp' chim'ney** *s* tubo di vetro di lampada a petrolio
**lamp'light'** *s* luce *f* di lampada
**lamp'light'er** *s* lampionaio
**lampoon** [læm'pun] *s* satira ‖ *tr* satireggiare
**lamp'post'** *s* colonna del lampione
**lamp'shade'** *s* paralume *m,* ventola
**lamp'wick'** *s* lucignolo
**lance** [læns] or [lɑns] *s* lancia; (surg) lancetta ‖ *tr* (*with an oxygen lance*) tagliare col cannello ossidrico; (surg) sbrigliare, incidere col bisturi
**lance' rest'** *s* resta
**lancet** ['lænsɪt] or ['lɑnsɪt] *s* (surg) lancetta
**land** [lænd] *adj* terrestre; (*wind*) di terra ‖ *s* terra; **on land, on sea, and in the air** per mare, per terra e nel cielo; **to make land** toccare terra; **to see how the land lies** tastare terreno ‖ *tr* sbarcare; (aer) fare atterrare; (coll) pigliare ‖ *intr* sbarcare; (*to come to rest*) andare a finire; (naut) toccar terra; (aer) atterrare; **to land on one's feet** cadere in piedi; **to land on one's head** andare a gambe all'aria; **to land on the moon** allunare; **to land on the water** ammarare
**land' breeze'** *s* vento di terra
**landed** ['lændɪd] *adj* (*owning land*) terriero; (*real estate*) immobile
**land'fall'** *s* (*sighting land*) avvistamento; terra avvistata; (*landslide*) frana
**land' grant'** *s* terreno ricevuto in dono dallo stato
**land'hold'er** *s* proprietario terriero
**landing** ['lændɪŋ] *s* (*of passengers*) sbarco; (*place where passengers and goods are landed*) imbarcadero; (*of stairway*) pianerottolo; (aer, naut) atterraggio
**land'ing bea'con** *s* radiofaro d'atterraggio
**land'ing card'** *s* cartoncino di sbarco
**land'ing craft'** *s* imbarcazione da sbarco
**land'ing field'** *s* campo d'atterraggio

**land'ing flap'** *s* (aer) iposostentatore *m*
**land'ing gear'** *s* (aer) carrello d'atterraggio
**land'ing strip'** *s* (aer) pista d'atterraggio
**land'la'dy** *s* (**-dies**) (*of an apartment*) padrona di casa; (*of a lodging house*) affittacamere *f*; (*of an inn*) ostessa
**landlocked** ['lænd ,lɑkt] *adj* circondato da terra
**land'lord'** *s* (*of an apartment*) padrone *m* di casa; (*of a lodging house*) affittacamere *m*; (*of an inn*) oste *m*
**land·lubber** ['lænd ,lʌbər] *s* marinaio d'acqua dolce
**land'mark'** *s* (*boundary stone*) pietra di confine; (*distinguishing landscape feature*) punto di riferimento; (fig) pietra miliare
**land' of'fice** *s* ufficio del catasto
**land'-office busi'ness** *s* (coll) sacco d'affari
**land'own'er** *s* proprietario terriero
**landscape** ['lænd ,skep] *s* paesaggio || *tr* abbellire
**land'scape gar'dener** *s* giardiniere *m* ornamentale
**land'scape paint'er** *s* paesista *mf*
**landscapist** ['lænd ,skepɪst] *s* paesista *mf*
**land'slide'** *s* frana; (fig) vittoria strepitosa
**landward** ['lændwərd] *adv* verso terra, verso la costa
**land' wind'** *s* vento di terra
**lane** [len] *s* (*narrow street*) vicolo, viuzza; (*of a highway*) corsia; (naut) rotta; (aer) corridoio
**langsyne** [ ,læŋ'saɪn] *s* (Scotch) tempo passato || *adv* (Scotch) molto tempo fa
**language** ['læŋgwɪdʒ] *s* lingua; (*style of language*) linguaggio; (*of a special group of people*) gergo
**lan'guage lab'oratory** *s* laboratorio linguistico
**languid** ['læŋgwɪd] *adj* languido
**languish** ['læŋgwɪʃ] *intr* languire; affettare languore
**languor** ['læŋgər] *s* languore *m*
**languorous** ['læŋgərəs] *adj* languido; (*causing languor*) snervante
**lank** [læŋk] *adj* scarnito, sparuto
**lank·y** ['læŋki] *adj* (**-ier; -iest**) scarnito, sparuto
**lantern** ['læntərn] *s* lanterna
**lan'tern slide'** *s* diapositiva
**lanyard** ['lænjərd] *s* (naut) drizza; (mil) aghetto, cordellina
**lap** [læp] *s* (*of human body or clothing*) grembo; (*with the tongue*) leccata; (*of the waves*) sciacquio; (sports) giro, tappa; **in the lap of** in mezzo a, e.g., **in the lap of luxury** in mezzo alle delicatezze || *v* (*pret & pp* **lapped;** *ger* **lapping**) *tr* lappare; (*said, e.g., of waves*) lambire; (*to fold*) piegare; (*to overlap*) sovrapporre; **to lap up** lappare; (coll) accettare con entusiasmo || *intr* sovrapporsi; **to lap against** (*said of the waves*) lambire; **to lap over** traboccare

**lap'board'** *s* tavolino da lavoro da tenersi sulle ginocchia
**lap' dissolve'** *s* (mov) dissolvenza incrociata
**lap' dog'** *s* cagnolino da salotto
**lapel** [lə'pel] *s* risvolto
**Lap'land'** *s* la Lapponia
**Laplander** ['læp ,lændər] *s* lappone *mf*
**Lapp** [læp] *s* lappone *mf*; (*language*) lappone *m*
**lap' robe'** *s* coperta da viaggio
**lapse** [læps] *s* (*interval*) spazio di tempo; (*fall, decline*) caduta; (*of memory*) perdita; errore *m*; (ins) risoluzione; (law) decadenza || *intr* cadere, ricadere; cadere in disuso; (*said of time*) passare; (ins) risolversi; (law) decadere
**lap'wing'** *s* pavoncella
**larce·ny** ['lɑrsəni] *s* (**-nies**) furto
**larch** [lɑrtʃ] *s* larice *m*
**lard** [lɑrd] *s* strutto || *tr* lardellare
**larder** ['lɑrdər] *s* dispensa
**large** [lɑrdʒ] *adj* grande, grosso || *s—* **at large** in libertà
**large' intes'tine** *s* intestino crasso
**largely** ['lɑrdʒli] *adv* in gran parte
**large'-scale'** *adj* su larga scala
**lariat** ['lærɪ·ət] *s* lazo, laccio
**lark** [lɑrk] *s* allodola; (coll) burla; **to go on a lark** (coll) far festa
**lark'spur'** *s* (*rocket larkspur*) sprone *m* di cavaliere; (*field larkspur*) consolida reale
**lar·va** ['lɑrvə] *s* (**-vae** [vi]) larva
**laryngitis** [ ,lærɪn'dʒaɪtɪs] *s* laringite *f*
**laryngoscope** [lə'rɪŋgə ,skop] *s* laringoscopio
**larynx** ['lærɪŋks] *s* (**larynxes** or **larynges** [lə'rɪndʒiz]) laringe *f*
**lascivious** [lə'sɪvɪ·əs] *adj* lascivo
**lasciviousness** [lə'sɪvɪ·əsnɪs] *s* lascivia
**laser** ['lesər] *s* (acronym) (*light amplification by stimulated emission of radiation*) laser *m*
**lash** [læʃ] *s* (*cord on end of whip*) sverzino; (*blow with whip; scolding*) staffilata; (*of animal's tail*) colpo; (*eyelash*) ciglio; (fig) assalto || *tr* (*to whip*) frustare; (*to bind*) legare; (*to shake*) agitare; (*to attack with words*) staffilare || *intr* lanciarsi; **to lash out at** attaccare violentemente
**lashing** ['læʃɪŋ] *s* legatura; (*severe scolding*) staffilata; (*fastening with a rope*) (naut) rizza
**lass** [læs] *s* ragazza, giovane *f*; innamorata
**las·so** ['læso] or [læ'su] *s* (**-sos** or **-soes**) lasso, lazo || *tr* pigliare col lasso
**last** [læst] or [lɑst] *adj* ultimo, passato; (*most recent*) scorso; **before last** ierlaltro, e.g., **the night before last** ierlaltro notte; **every last one** tutti senza eccezione; **last but one** penultimo || *s* ultima persona; ultima cosa; fine *f*; (*for holding shoes*) forma; **at last** alla fine; **at long last!** finalmente!; **stick to your last!** fa' il mestiere tuo!; **the last of the month** alla fine del mese; **to breathe one's last** dare l'ultimo sospiro; **to see the last of s.o.** vedere qlcu per l'ultima

volta; **to the last** fino alla fine ‖ *adv* ultimo, per ultimo, alla fine ‖ *intr* durare, continuare

**lasting** [ˈlæstɪŋ] or [ˈlɑstɪŋ] *adj* duraturo, durevole

**lastly** [ˈlæstli] or [ˈlɑstli] *adv* finalmente, in conclusione

**last'-min'ute news'** *s* notizie *fpl* dell'ultima ora

**last' name'** *s* cognome *m*

**last' night'** *adv* ieri sera; la notte scorsa

**last' quar'ter** *s* ultimo quarto

**last' sleep'** *s* ultimo sonno

**last' straw'** *s* ultima, colmo

**Last' Sup'per** *s* Ultima Cena

**last will' and tes'tament** *s* ultime volontà *fpl*

**last' word'** *s* ultima parola; (*latest style*) ultima novità, ultimo grido

**latch** [lætʃ] *s* saliscendi *m;* (*wooden*) nottola ‖ *tr* chiudere col saliscendi

**latch'key'** *s* chiave *f* per saliscendi

**latch'string'** *s*—**the latchstring is out** faccia come fosse a casa Sua

**late** [let] *adj* (*happening after the usual time*) tardo; (*person*) in ritardo; (*hour of the night*) avanzato; (*news*) dell'ultima ora, recente; (*incumbent of an office*) predecessore, ex, passato; (*coming toward the end of a period*) tardivo; (*deceased*) defunto, fu; **in the late 30's, 40's, etc.** verso la fine del decennio che va dal 1930, 1940, etc. al 1940, 1950, etc.; **of late** recentemente; **to be late** + *ger* essere in ritardo a + *inf;* **to grow late** farsi tardi; **to keep late hours** fare le ore piccole ‖ *adv* tardi; in ritardo; **late in** (*the week, the month, etc.*) alla fine di; **late in life** a un'età avanzata

**latecomer** [ˈlet ˌkʌmər] *s* ritardatario

**lateen' sail'** [læˈtin] *s* vela latina

**lately** [ˈletli] *adv* recentemente

**latent** [ˈletənt] *adj* latente

**later** [ˈletər] *adj comp* più tardi; (*event*) susseguente; **later than** posteriore a ‖ *adv comp* più tardi; **later on** più tardi; **see you later** (coll) arrivederci, a ben presto

**lateral** [ˈlætərəl] *adj* laterale

**lath** [læθ] or [lɑθ] *s* listello, striscia di legno ‖ *tr* mettere listelli su

**lathe** [leð] *s* tornio

**lather** [ˈlæðər] *s* schiuma di sapone; schiuma ‖ *tr* insaponare; (coll) bastonare ‖ *intr* schiumare

**lathery** [ˈlæðəri] *adj* schiumoso

**lathing** [ˈlæθɪŋ] or [ˈlɑθɪŋ] *s* costruzione con listelli

**Latin** [ˈlætɪn] or [ˈlætən] *adj & s* latino

**Lat'in Amer'ica** *s* l'America latina

**Lat'in-Amer'ican** *adj* dell'America latina

**Lat'in Amer'ican** *s* abitante *mf* dell'America latina

**latitude** [ˈlætɪ ˌtjud] or [ˈlætɪ ˌtud] *s* latitudine *f*

**latrine** [ləˈtrin] *s* latrina militare

**latter** [ˈlætər] *adj* (*more recent*) posteriore; (*of two*) secondo; **the latter** questo; **the latter part of** la fine di

**lattice** [ˈlætɪs] *s* graticcio ‖ *tr* munire di graticcio, graticciare

**lat'tice gird'er** *s* trave *f* a traliccio

**lat'tice-work'** *s* graticcio, traliccio

**Latvia** [ˈlætvɪ·ə] *s* la Lettonia

**laud** [lɔd] *tr* lodare

**laudable** [ˈlɔdəbəl] *adj* lodevole

**laudanum** [ˈlɔdənəm] or [ˈlɔdnəm] *s* laudano

**laudatory** [ˈlɔdə ˌtori] *adj* lodativo

**laugh** [læf] or [lɑf] *s* riso ‖ *tr*—**to laugh away** dissipare ridendo; **to laugh off** prendere sotto gamba, non dare importanza a ‖ *intr* ridere, ridersi; **to laugh at** ridersi di; **to laugh up one's sleeve** ridere sotto i baffi

**laughable** [ˈlæfəbəl] or [ˈlɑfəbəl] *adj* risibile

**laughing** [ˈlæfɪŋ] or [ˈlɑfɪŋ] *adj* che ride; **to be no laughing matter** non esserci niente da ridere ‖ *s* riso

**laugh'ing gas'** *s* gas *m* esilarante

**laugh'ing-stock'** *s* ludibrio, zimbello

**laughter** [ˈlæftər] or [ˈlɑftər] *s* riso

**launch** [lɔntʃ] or [lɑntʃ] *s* (*of a ship*) varo; (*of a rocket*) lancio; (naut) lancia, scialuppa ‖ *tr* (*to throw; to send forth*) lanciare; (naut) varare ‖ *intr* lanciarsi

**launching** [ˈlɔntʃɪŋ] or [ˈlɑntʃɪŋ] *s* lancio; (*of a ship*) varo

**launch'ing pad'** *s* piattaforma di lancio

**launder** [ˈlɔndər] or [ˈlɑndər] *tr* lavare e stirare ‖ *intr* riuscire dopo il lavaggio

**launderer** [ˈlɔndərər] or [ˈlɑndərər] *s* lavandaio stiratore *m*

**laundress** [ˈlɔndrɪs] or [ˈlɑndrɪs] *s* lavandaia stiratrice *f*

**laundromat** [ˈlɔndrə ˌmæt] or [ˈlɑndrə ˌmæt] *s* (trademark) lavanderia a gettone

**laun·dry** [ˈlɔndri] or [ˈlɑndri] *s* (**-dries**) lavanderia; (*clothing*) bucato

**laun'dry·man'** *s* (**-men'**) lavandaio

**laun'dry·wom'an** *s* (**-wom'en**) lavandaia

**laureate** [ˈlɔrɪ·ɪt] *adj* laureato ‖ *s* laureato; poeta laureato

**lau·rel** [ˈlɔrəl] or [ˈlɑrəl] *s* lauro, alloro; **laurels** (fig) alloro; **to rest** or **sleep on one's laurels** dormire sugli allori ‖ *v* (*pret & pp* **-reled** or **-relled;** *ger* **-reling** or **-relling**) *tr* laureare

**lava** [ˈlɑvə] or [ˈlævə] *s* lava

**lavato·ry** [ˈlævə ˌtori] *s* (**-ries**) (*room*) gabinetto da bagno; (*bowl*) lavabo; (*toilet*) gabinetto di decenza, cesso

**lavender** [ˈlævəndər] *s* lavanda

**lavish** [ˈlævɪʃ] *adj* prodigo ‖ *tr* prodigare, profondere

**law** [lɔ] *s* (*of man, of nature, of science*) legge *f;* (*study, profession of law*) diritto; **to enter the law** farsi avvocato; **to go to law** ricorrere alla legge; **to lay down the law** dettar legge; **to maintain law and order** mantenere la pace interna; **to practice law** fare l'avvocato

**law-abiding** [ˈlɔ·ə ˌbaɪdɪŋ] *adj* osservante della legge

**law'break'er** *s* violatore *m* della legge

**law' court'** *s* tribunale *m* di giustizia

**lawful** ['lɔfəl] *adj* legale, legittimo

**lawless** ['lɔlɪs] *adj* illegale; *(unbridled)* sfrenato

**law'mak'er** *s* legislatore *m*

**lawn** [lɔn] *s* tappeto erboso; *(fabric)* batista

**lawn' mow'er** *s* tosatrice *f*

**law' of'fice** *s* ufficio d'avvocato

**law' of na'tions** *s* diritto delle genti

**law' of the jun'gle** *s* legge *f* della giungla

**law' stu'dent** *s* studente *m* di legge

**law'suit'** *s* causa, lite *f*, processo

**lawyer** ['lɔjər] *s* avvocato, legale *m*

**lax** [læks] *adj (in morals)* lasso, rilassato; *(rope)* lento; *(negligent)* trascurato; vago, indeterminato

**laxative** ['læksətɪv] *adj* purgativo ‖ *s* purga, purgante *m*

**lay** [le] *adj (not belonging to the clergy)* laico; *(not having special training)* non dotto, profano ‖ *s* configurazione, disposizione ‖ *v (pret & pp laid [led]) tr* mettere, collocare; *(snares)* tendere; *(one's eyes; a stone)* porre; *(blame)* dare, gettare; *(a bet)* fare; *(for consideration)* presentare; *(the table)* imbandire; *(said of a hen)* deporre; *(plans)* impostare; *(to locate)* disporre; **to be laid in** *(said of a scene)* aver luogo in; **to lay aside** mettere da parte; **to lay down** dichiarare; *(one's life)* dare; *(one's arms)* deporre; **to lay low** abbattere; uccidere; **to lay off** *(workers)* licenziare; *(to measure)* marcare; *(slang)* lasciare in pace; **to lay open** rivelare; *(to a danger)* esporre; **to lay out** estendere; preparare, disporre; *(a corpse)* comporre; *(money)* *(coll)* sborsare; **to lay over** posporre; **to lay up** mettere da parte; obbligare a letto; *(naut)* disarmare ‖ *intr (said of a hen)* fare le uova; **to lay about** dar botte da orbi; **to lay for** *(slang)* attendere al varco; **to lay off** *(coll)* cessare di lavorare; **to lay over** trattenersi, fermarsi; **to lay to** *(naut)* navigare alla cappa

**lay' broth'er** *s* frate *m* secolare; converso

**lay' day'** *s (com)* stallia

**layer** ['le·ər] *s (of paint)* mano *f;* *(of bricks)* testa; *(e.g., of rocks)* strato, falda; *(anat)* pannicolo; *(hort)* propaggine *f* ‖ *tr (hort)* propagginare

**lay'er cake'** *s* dolce *m* a strati

**layette** [le'ɛt] *s* corredino

**lay' fig'ure** *s* manichino

**laying** ['le·ɪŋ] *s* posa; *(of eggs)* deporre *m;* *(of a wire)* tendere *m*

**lay'man** *s* (-**men**) *(member of the laity)* laico, secolare *m;* *(not a member of a special profession)* laico, profano

**lay'off'** *s (dismissal of workers)* licenziamento; *(period of unemployment)* disoccupazione

**lay' of the land'** *s* andamento generale

**lay'out'** *s* piano; *(sketch)* tracciato; *(of tools)* armamentario; *(coll)* residenza; *(typ)* menabò *m;* *(coll)* banchetto, festino

**lay'o'ver** *s* fermata in un viaggio

**lay' sis'ter** *s* suora al secolo; conversa

**laziness** ['lezɪnɪs] *s* pigrizia

**la·zy** ['lezi] *adj* (-**zier; -ziest**) pigro

**la'zy·bones'** *s (coll)* poltrone *m*

**lea** [li] *s (fallow land)* maggese *m;* *(meadow)* prato

**lead** [lɛd] *adj* plumbeo ‖ *s* piombo; *(of lead pencil)* mina; *(for sounding depth)* (naut) scandaglio; (typ) interlinea ‖ *v (pret & pp leaded; ger leading) tr* impiombare; (typ) interlineare ‖ [lid] *s (foremost place)* primato; *(guidance)* guida, direzione; *(leash)* guinzaglio; (journ) testata; (cards) mano *f*, prima mano; (elec) conduttore *m;* (mach) passo; (min) filone *m;* (rad, telv) filo d'entrata; (theat) ruolo principale; (theat) primo attore; (theat) prima attrice; **to take the lead** prendere il comando ‖ [lid] *v (pret & pp led* [led]) *tr* condurre, portare; *(to command)* comandare, essere alla testa di; *(an orchestra)* dirigere; *(a good or bad life)* fare; *(s.o. into vice)* trascinare; *(cards)* cominciare a giocare; *(elec, mach)* anticipare; **to lead astray** forviare ‖ *intr* essere in testa, guidare; prendere l'offensiva; *(said of a road)* condurre; *(cards)* cominciare a giocare; **to lead to** risultare in; **to lead up to** andare a condurre a

**leaden** ['lɛdən] *adj (of lead; like lead)* plumbeo; *(sluggish)* tardo; *(with sleep)* carico; triste

**leader** ['lidər] *s* capo, comandante *m;* *(ringleader)* capobanda *m;* *(of an orchestra)* direttore *m;* *(among animals)* guidaiolo; *(in a dance)* ballerino guidaiolo; *(sports)* capintesta *m;* (journ) articolo di fondo

**lead'er dog'** *s* cane *m* guida di ciechi

**leadership** ['lidər ˌʃɪp] *s* comando, direzione; doti *fpl* di comando

**leading** ['lidɪŋ] *adj* principale; primo; dirigente, preeminente

**lead'ing ar'ticle** *s* articolo di fondo

**lead'ing edge'** *s* (aer) bordo d'attacco

**lead'ing la'dy** *s* prima attrice

**lead'ing man'** *s* (**men'**) primo attore

**lead'ing ques'tion** *s* domanda suggestiva, domanda orientatrice

**lead'ing strings'** *spl* dande *fpl*

**lead'-in wire'** ['lid ˌɪn] *s* filo d'antenna

**lead' pen'cil** [lɛd] *s* lapis *m*, matita

**leaf** [lif] *s* (**leaves** [livz]) *(of plant)* foglia; *(of vine)* pampino; *(of paper)* foglio; *(of double door)* battente *m;* *(of table)* asse *m* a ribalta; **to turn over a new leaf** ricominciare una nuova vita ‖ *intr* fogliare; **to leaf through** sfogliare

**leafless** ['liflɪs] *adj* senza foglie

**leaflet** ['liflɪt] *s* manifestino, volantino; *(of plant)* foglietta

**leaf' spring'** *s* molla a balestra

**leaf'stalk'** *s* picciolo

**leaf·y** ['lifi] *adj* (-**ier; -iest**) foglioso, frondoso

**league** [lig] *s* lega ‖ *tr* associare ‖ *intr* associarsi

**League'** of **Na'tions** s Società f delle Nazioni

**leak** [lik] s (in a roof) stillicidio; (in a ship) falla; (of water, gas, steam) fuga; (of electricity) dispersione; buco, fessura; (of news) filtrazione; **to spring a leak** avere una perdita; (naut) cominciare a far acqua || tr (gas, liquids) perdere, lasciar scappare; (news) lasciar trapelare || intr (said of water, gas etc.,) scappare; (said of a barrel) spillare; (naut) fare acqua; **to leak away** (said of money) andarsene; **to leak out** (said of news) trapelare

**leakage** ['likɪdʒ] s perdita, fuoruscita, fuga; (elec) dispersione; (com) colaggio

**leak·y** ['liki] adj (-ier; -iest) che perde; (naut) che fa acqua; (coll) indiscreto

**lean** [lin] adj magro, secco; (gasoline mixture) povero || v (pret & pp **leaned** or **leant** [lɛnt]) tr inclinare; appoggiare || intr pendere, inclinarsi; (fig) inclinare, tendere; **to lean against** appoggiarsi a, addossarsi a; **to lean back** sdraiarsi; **to lean on** appoggiarsi su; **to lean out (of)** sporgersi (da); **to lean over backwards** fare di tutto; **to lean toward** (fig) tendere a, avere un'inclinazione per

**leaning** ['linɪŋ] adj inclinato, pendente || s inclinazione

**lean'ing tow'er** s torre f pendente

**lean'-to'** s (-tos) tetto a una falda

**leap** [lip] s salto, balzo; **by leaps and bounds** a passi da gigante; **leap in the dark** salto nel vuoto || v (pret & pp **leaped** or **leapt** [lɛpt]) tr saltare || intr saltare; (said of one's heart) balzare

**leap'frog'** s cavallina; **to play leapfrog** giocare alla cavallina

**leap' year'** s anno bisestile

**learn** [lʌrn] s (pret & pp **learned** or **learnt** [lʌrnt]) tr imparare; imparare a memoria; (news) apprendere || intr istruirsi, apprendere

**learned** ['lʌrnɪd] adj dotto; (word) colto

**learn'ed jour'nal** s rivista scientifica

**learn'ed soci'ety** s associazione di eruditi

**learn'ed word'** s parola dotta

**learn'ed world'** s mondo di dotti

**learner** ['lʌrnər] s apprendista mf; studente m; (beginner) principiante mf

**learning** ['lʌrnɪŋ] s istruzione; (scholarship) erudizione

**lease** [lis] s locazione, contratto d'affitto; **a new lease on life** nuove prospettive di felicità; vita nuova (dopo una malattia) || tr locare; prendere in affitto || intr affittare

**lease'hold'** adj affittato || s beni mpl sotto locazione

**leash** [liʃ] s guinzaglio; **to strain at the leash** mordere il freno || tr frenare, controllare

**least** [list] adj minore, menomo, minimo || s (il) meno; **at least** or **at the least** per lo meno, quanto meno;

**not in the least** nient'affatto || adv meno

**leather** ['lɛðər] s cuoio

**leath'er·back tur'tle** s tartaruga di mare

**leath'er goods' store'** s pelletteria

**leathery** ['lɛðəri] adj coriaceo

**leave** [liv] s (permission) permesso; (permission to be absent) licenza; (farewell) commiato; **on leave** in licenza; **to take French leave** andarsene all'inglese; **to take leave (of)** prender congedo (da) || v (pret & pp **left** [lɛft]) tr (to go away from) lasciare, uscire da; (to let stay) lasciare; (to bequeath) lasciare in testamento; **leave it to me!** lasciami fare!; **to be left** restare, e.g., **the door was left open** la porta restò aperta; esserci, e.g., **there is no bread left** non c'è più pane; **to leave alone** lasciare in pace; **to leave no stone unturned** cercare ogni possibilità; **to leave off** abbandonare, lasciare; **to leave out** omettere; **to leave things as they are** lasciar stare le cose || intr andarsene; (said of a conveyance) partire

**leaven** ['lɛvən] s lievito || tr lievitare; (fig) impregnare, permeare

**leavening** ['lɛvənɪŋ] s lievito

**leave' of ab'sence** s licenza; (without pay) aspettativa

**leave'-tak'ing** s commiato

**leavings** ['livɪŋz] spl rifiuti mpl

**Leba·nese** [ˌlɛbəˈniz] adj libanese || s (-nese) libanese mf

**Lebanon** ['lɛbənən] s il Libano

**lecher** ['lɛtʃər] s libertino

**lecherous** ['lɛtʃərəs] adj libidinoso

**lechery** ['lɛtʃəri] s lussuria

**lectern** ['lɛktərn] s leggio

**lecture** ['lɛktʃər] s conferenza; (tedious reprimand) pistolotto || tr dare una conferenza a; sermoneggiare || intr fare una conferenza; sermoneggiare

**lecturer** ['lɛktʃərər] s conferenziere m

**ledge** [lɛdʒ] s cornice f, cornicione m

**ledger** ['lɛdʒər] s (com) libro mastro

**ledg'er line'** s (mus) rigo supplementare

**lee** [li] s (shelter) rifugio; (naut) parte f sottovento; **lees** feccia

**leech** [litʃ] s mignatta, sanguisuga; **to stick like a leech** attaccarsi come una sanguisuga

**leek** [lik] s porro

**leer** [lɪr] s occhiata lussuriosa or maligna || intr—**to leer at** guardare di sbieco, sbirciare

**leer·y** ['lɪri] adj (-ier; -iest) sospettoso

**leeward** ['liwərd] or ['lu·ərd] adj di sottovento || s sottovento, poggia || adv sottovento

**lee'way'** s (aer, naut) deriva, scarroccio; (in time) (coll) tolleranza; (coll) libertà f d'azione

**left** [lɛft] adj sinistro; (pol) di sinistra || s sinistra; (boxing) sinistro || adv alla sinistra

**left' field'** s fuoricampo di sinistra

**left'-hand' drive'** s guida a sinistra

**left-handed** ['lɛftˈhændɪd] adj (individual) mancino; (awkward) goffo;

(*compliment*) ambiguo; (mach) sinistrorso

**leftish** [ˈlɛftɪʃ] *adj* sinistrista

**leftist** [ˈlɛftɪst] *adj* di sinistra ‖ *s* membro della sinistra

**left′o′ver** *adj* & *s* rimanente *m;* **left-overs** resti *mpl*

**left′-wing′** *adj* di sinistra

**left-winger** [ˈlɛftˈwɪŋər] *s* (coll) membro dell'estrema sinistra; (coll) membro della sinistra

**leg** [lɛg] *s* (*of man, animal, table, chair; of trousers*) gamba; (*of fowl; of lamb*) coscia; (*of boot*) gambale *m;* (*of a journey*) tappa; **to be on one's last legs** essere agli estremi, essere ridotto alla disperazione; **to not have a leg to stand on** (coll) non avere la minima giustificazione; **to pull the leg of** (coll) prendere in giro, burlarsi di; **to shake a leg** (coll) affrettarsi; (*to dance*) (coll) ballare; **to stretch one's legs** sgranchirsi le gambe

**lega·cy** [ˈlɛgəsɪ] *s* (-cies) legato

**legal** [ˈligəl] *adj* legale

**legali·ty** [lɪˈgælɪtɪ] *s* (-ties) legalità *f*

**legalize** [ˈligə ˌlaɪz] *tr* legalizzare

**le′gal ten′der** *s* denaro a corso legale

**legate** [ˈlɛgɪt] *s* legato

**legatee** [ ˌlɛgəˈti] *s* legatario

**legation** [lɪˈgeʃən] *s* legazione

**legend** [ˈlɛdʒənd] *s* leggenda

**legendary** [ˈlɛdʒən ˌdɛrɪ] *adj* leggendario

**legerdemain** [ ˌlɛdʒərdɪˈmen] *s* gioco di prestigio; (*trickery*) imbroglio

**legging** [ˈlɛgɪŋ] *s* gambale *m*

**leg·gy** [ˈlɛgɪ] *adj* (-gier; -giest) dalle gambe lunghe

**leg′horn′** *s* cappello di paglia di Firenze; gallina bianca livornese ‖ **Leghorn** *s* Livorno

**legible** [ˈlɛdʒɪbəl] *adj* leggibile

**legion** [ˈlidʒən] *s* legione *f*

**legislate** [ˈlɛdʒɪs ˌlet] *tr* ordinare per mezzo di legge ‖ *intr* legiferare

**legislation** [ ˌlɛdʒɪsˈleʃən] *s* legislazione

**legislative** [ˈlɛdʒɪs ˌletɪv] *adj* legislativo

**legislator** [ˈlɛdʒɪs ˌletər] *s* legislatore *m*

**legislature** [ˈlɛdʒɪs ˌletʃər] *s* legislatura; corpo legislativo

**legitimacy** [lɪˈdʒɪtɪməsɪ] *s* legittimità *f*

**legitimate** [lɪˈdʒɪtɪmɪt] *adj* legittimo ‖ [lɪˈdʒɪtɪ ˌmet] *tr* legittimare

**legit′imate dra′ma** *s* teatro serio

**legitimize** [lɪˈdʒɪtɪ ˌmaɪz] *tr* legittimare

**leg′ of lamb′** *s* cosciotto d'agnello

**legume** [ˈlɛgjum] or [lɪˈgjum] *s* (*pod*) legume *m;* (*table vegetables*) legumi *mpl;* (bot) leguminose *fpl*

**leg′work′** *s* lavoro che involve molto cammino

**leisure** [ˈliʒər] or [ˈlɛʒər] *s* ozio; **at leisure** senza fretta; disoccupato; **at one's leisure** quando si abbia un po' di tempo libero

**lei′sure class′** *s* gente agiata

**lei′sure hours′** *spl* ore *fpl* d'ozio

**leisurely** [ˈliʒərlɪ] or [ˈlɛʒərlɪ] *adj* lento ‖ *adv* lentamente, a tempo perso

**lei′sure time′** *s* tempo libero

**lemon** [ˈlɛmən] *s* limone *m;* (*car*) (coll) catorcio

**lemonade** [ ˌlɛməˈned] *s* limonata

**lem′on squeez′er** *s* spremilimoni *m*

**lend** [lɛnd] *s* (*pret & pp* **lent** [lɛnt]) *tr* prestare; (*a hand*) dare

**lender** [ˈlɛndər] *s* prestatore *m*

**lend′ing li′brary** *s* biblioteca circolante

**length** [lɛŋθ] *s* lunghezza; (*of time*) durata; **at length** finalmente; **to go to any lengths** fare quanto è possibile; essere disposto a tutto; **to keep at arm's length** (*someone else*) tenere a distanza (qlcu); (*said of oneself*) tenere la distanza

**lengthen** [ˈlɛŋθən] *tr* allungare ‖ *intr* allungarsi

**length′wise′** *adj* longitudinale ‖ *adv* per il lungo

**length·y** [ˈlɛŋθɪ] *adj* (-ier; -iest) lungo, prolungato

**lenien·cy** [ˈlinɪ·ənsɪ] *s* (-cies) indulgenza

**lenient** [ˈlinɪ·ənt] *adj* indulgente, clemente

**lens** [lɛnz] *s* lente *f;* (*of the eye*) cristallino

**Lent** [lɛnt] *s* quaresima

**Lenten** [ˈlɛntən] *adj* quaresimale

**lentil** [ˈlɛntəl] *s* lenticchia

**Leo** [ˈli·o] *s* (astr) il Leone

**leopard** [ˈlɛpərd] *s* leopardo

**leotard** [ˈli·ə ˌtɑrd] *s* calzamaglia

**leper** [ˈlɛpər] *s* lebbroso

**leprosy** [ˈlɛprəsɪ] *s* lebbra

**leprous** [ˈlɛprəs] *adj* lebbroso; (*of an animal or plant*) squamoso

**Lesbian** [ˈlɛzbɪ·ən] *adj* lesbico ‖ *s* lesbico; (*female homosexual*) lesbica

**lesbianism** [ˈlɛzbɪ·ə ˌnɪzəm] *s* lesbismo

**lese majesty** [ˈliz ˈmædʒɪstɪ] *s* delitto di lesa maestà

**lesion** [ˈliʒən] *s* lesione

**less** [lɛs] *adj* minore ‖ *adv* meno; **less and less** sempre meno; **less than** meno che; (*followed by numeral or personal pron*) meno di; (*followed by verb*) meno di quanto ‖ *s* meno

**lessee** [lɛsˈi] *s* locatario; (*of business establishment*) concessionario

**lessen** [ˈlɛsən] *tr* diminuire, ridurre ‖ *intr* diminuire, ridursi

**lesser** [ˈlɛsər] *adj comp* minore

**lesson** [ˈlɛsən] *s* lezione

**lessor** [ˈlɛsər] *s* locatore *m*

**lest** [lɛst] *conj* per paura che

**let** [lɛt] *v* (*pret & pp* **let;** *ger* **letting**) *tr* permettere; (*to rent*) affittare; **let** + *inf* che + *subj*, e.g., **let him go** che vada; **let alone** tanto meno; senza menzionare; **let good enough alone** essere contento dell'onesto; **let us** + *inf* = *1st pl impv*, e.g., **let us sing** cantiamo; **to let da affittare; to let alone** lasciare in pace; **to let be** lasciar stare; **to let by** lasciar passare; **to let down** far scendere; deludere; tradire; abbandonare; **to let fly** (*insults*) lanciare; **to let go** lasciar libero; vendere; **to let in** fare entrare; **to let it go at that** non parlarne più; **to let know** far sapere; **to**

**let loose** sciogliere; **to let out** lasciar uscire; (*a secret*) divulgare; (*a scream*) lasciarsi scappare; (*to enlarge*) allargare; affittare; **to let through** lasciar passare; **to let up** lasciar salire; lasciar alzare ‖ *intr* affittare; **to let down** diminuire gli sforzi; **to let go of** disfarsi di; **to let on** (coll) fare finta; **to not let on** (coll) non lasciar trapelare; **to let out** (*said, e.g., of school*) terminare; **to let up** (coll) cessare; (coll) diminuire

**let'down'** *s* diminuzione; smacco, umiliazione; delusione

**lethal** ['liθəl] *adj* letale

**lethargic** [lɪ'θɑrdʒɪk] *adj* letargico

**lethar•gy** ['lɛθərdʒi] *s* (**-gies**) letargo

**Lett** [lɛt] *s* lettone *mf;* (*language*) lettone *m*

**letter** ['lɛtər] *s* lettera; **letters** (*literature*) lettere *fpl*, letteratura; **to the letter** alla lettera ‖ *tr* marcare con lettere

**let'ter box'** *s* cassetta delle lettere

**let'ter car'rier** *s* postino

**let'ter drop'** *s* buca delle lettere

**let'ter•head'** *s* capolettera *m;* (*paper with printed heading*) carta da lettera intestata

**lettering** ['lɛtərɪŋ] *s* iscrizione; lettere *fpl*

**let'ter of cred'it** *s* lettera di credito

**let'ter o'pener** ['opənər] *s* tagliacarte *m*

**let'ter pa'per** *s* carta da lettere

**let'ter-per'fect** *adj* alla lettera; che sa alla perfezione

**let'ter•press'** *s* stampato in tipografia ‖ *adv* a stampa tipografica

**let'ter scales'** *spl* pesalettere *m*

**let'ter•word'** *s* sigla

**Lettish** ['lɛtɪʃ] *adj & s* lettone *m*

**lettuce** ['lɛtɪs] *s* lattuga

**let'up'** *s* (coll) pausa, sosta; (coll) tregua; **without letup** (coll) senza posa

**leucorrhea** [ˌlukə'ri•ə] *s* leucorrea

**leukemia** [lu'kimi•ə] *s* leucemia

**Levant** [lɪ'vænt] *s* levante *m*

**levee** ['lɛvi] *s* (*embankment*) argine *m;* (*reception*) ricevimento

**lev•el** ['lɛvəl] *adj* piano; livellato; equilibrato; **level with** a livello di; **one's level best** (coll) il proprio meglio ‖ *s* (*instrument*) livella; (*degree of elevation*) livello; (*flat surface*) spianata, pianura; **on the level** (slang) onesto; onestamente; **to find one's level** trovare il proprio ambiente ‖ *v* (*pret & pp* **-eled** or **-elled;** *ger* **-eling** or **-elling**) *tr* livellare; (*to flatten out*) spianare; (*e.g., prices*) pareggiare, ragguagliare; (*a gun*) puntare; (coll) gettare a terra; (fig) dirigere ‖ *intr—* **to level off** (aer) volare orizzontalmente

**level-headed** ['lɛvəl'hɛdɪd] *adj* equilibrato

**lev'eling rod'** *s* stadia

**lever** ['livər] or ['lɛvər] *s* leva ‖ *tr* far leva su ‖ *intr* far leva

**leverage** ['livərɪdʒ] or ['lɛvərɪdʒ] *s* azione di una leva; (fig) potere *m*

**leviathan** [lɪ'vaɪ•əθən] *s* leviatano

**levitation** [ˌlɛvɪ'teʃən] *s* levitazione

**levi•ty** ['lɛvɪti] *s* (**-ties**) leggerezza

**lev•y** ['lɛvi] *s* (**-ies**) (*of taxes*) esazione; (*of money*) tributo; (*of troops*) leva ‖ *v* (*pret & pp* **-ied**) *tr* (*a tax*) imporre; (*soldiers*) reclutare; (*war*) fare

**lewd** [lud] *adj* (*lustful*) lascivo; osceno

**lexical** ['lɛksɪkəl] *adj* lessicale

**lexicographer** [ˌlɛksɪ'kɑgrəfər] *s* lessicografo

**lexicographic(al)** [ˌlɛksɪko'græfɪk(əl)] *adj* lessicografico

**lexicography** [ˌlɛksɪ'kɑgrəfi] *s* lessicografia

**lexicology** [ˌlɛksɪ'kɑlədʒi] *s* lessicologia

**lexicon** ['lɛksɪkən] *s* lessico

**liabili•ty** [ˌlaɪ•ə'bɪlɪti] *s* (**-ties**) svantaggio; responsabilità *f;* (*e.g., to disease*) tendenza; (com) passivo; **liabilities** debiti *mpl;* (com) passivo

**liabil'ity insur'ance** *s* assicurazione sulla responsabilità civile

**liable** ['laɪ•əbəl] *adj* (*e.g., to disease; e.g., to make mistakes*) soggetto; responsabile; probabile; (*e.g., to a fine*) passibile

**liaison** ['li•ə ˌzɑn] or [li'ezən] *s* legame *m;* relazione illecita; (mil, nav) collegamento; (phonet) legamento

**li'aison of'ficer** *s* ufficiale *m* di collegamento

**liar** ['laɪ•ər] *s* bugiardo, mentitore *m*

**libation** [laɪ'beʃən] *s* (joc) libazione, bevuta

**li•bel** ['laɪbəl] *s* diffamazione; (*defamatory writing*) libello ‖ *v* (*pret & pp* **-beled** or **-belled;** *ger* **-beling** or **-belling**) *tr* diffamare

**libelous** ['laɪbələs] *adj* diffamatorio

**liberal** ['lɪbərəl] *adj* liberale; (*translation*) libero ‖ *s* liberale *mf*

**liberali•ty** [ˌlɪbə'rælɪti] *s* (**-ties**) liberalità *f;* (*breadth of mind*) ampiezza di vedute

**liberal-minded** ['lɪbərəl'maɪndɪd] *adj* liberale, tollerante

**liberate** ['lɪbə ˌret] *tr* liberare

**liberation** [ˌlɪbə're[ʃ]ən] *s* liberazione

**liberator** ['lɪbə ˌretər] *s* liberatore *m*

**libertine** ['lɪbər ˌtin] *adj & s* libertino

**liber•ty** ['lɪbərti] *s* (**-ties**) libertà *f;* **to take the liberty to** permettersi di

**liberty•loving** ['lɪbərti'lʌvɪŋ] *adj* amante della libertà

**libidinous** [lɪ'bɪdɪnəs] *adj* libidinoso

**libido** [lɪ'bido] or [lɪ'baɪdo] *s* libidine *f;* (psychoanal) libido *f*

**Libra** ['lɪbrə] or ['laɪbrə] *s* (astr) Bilancia

**librarian** [laɪ'brɛrɪ•ən] *s* bibliotecario

**librar•y** ['laɪ ˌbrɛri] or ['laɪbrəri] *s* (**-ies**) biblioteca; (*room in a house; collection of books*) libreria

**li'brary num'ber** *s* segnatura

**li'brary sci'ence** *s* biblioteconomia

**libret•to** [lɪ'breto] *s* (**-tos**) (mus) libretto

**Libya** ['lɪbɪ•ə] *s* la Libia

**license** ['laɪsəns] *s* licenza; (aut) patente *f* ‖ *tr* dare la licenza a

**li'cense num'ber** _s_ numero di targa di circolazione

**li'cense plate'** or **tag'** _s_ targa di circolazione

**licentious** [laɪ'senʃəs] _adj_ licenzioso

**lichen** ['laɪkən] _s_ lichene _m_

**lick** [lɪk] _s_ leccata, leccatura; (coll) esplosione di energia; (coll) velocità _f;_ (coll) battitura; (coll) ripulita; **to give a lick and a promise to** (coll) fare rapidamente e con poca attenzione ‖ _tr_ leccare; (_said of waves, flames, etc._) lambire; (_to defeat_) (_coll_) battere, vincere; (_e.g., with a stick_) (coll) bastonare

**licorice** ['lɪkərɪs] _s_ liquirizia

**lid** [lɪd] _s_ coperchio; (_eyelid_) palpebra; (_curb_) (coll) restrizione, freno; (_hat_) (slang) cappello

**lie** [laɪ] _s_ menzogna; **to catch in a lie** pigliare in castagna; **to give the lie to** smentire ‖ _v_ (_pret & pp_ **lied**; _ger_ **lying**) _tr_—**to lie oneself out of** or **to lie one's way out of** trarsi fuori da (_un impaccio_) con una menzogna ‖ _intr_ mentire ‖ _v_ (_pret_ **lay** [le]; _pp_ **lain** [len]; _ger_ **lying**) _intr_ essere sdraiato; trovarsi; (_in the grave_) giacere; **to lie down** sdraiarsi

**lie' detec'tor** _s_ macchina della verità

**lien** [lin] or ['li·ən] _s_ diritto di pegno, diritto di garanzia

**lieu** [lu] _s_—**in lieu of** in luogo di

**lieutenant** [lu'tɛnənt] _s_ luogotenente _m;_ (mil) tenente _m;_ (nav) tenente _m_ di vascello

**lieuten'ant colo'nel** _s_ (mil) tenente _m_ colonnello

**lieuten'ant command'er** _s_ (nav) capitano di corvetta

**lieuten'ant gen'eral** _s_ (mil) generale _m_ di corpo d'armata

**lieuten'ant gov'ernor** _s_ (USA) vicegovernatore _m_

**lieuten'ant jun'ior grade'** _s_ (nav) sottotenente _m_ di vascello

**life** [laɪf] _adj_ (_animate_) vitale; (_lifelong_) perpetuo; (_annuity_) vitalizio; (_working from nature_) dal vero ‖ _s_ (**lives** [laɪvz]) vita; (_of an insurance policy_) forza; **for life** a vita; **for the life of me** per quanto io provi; **the life and soul of** (_e.g., the party_) l'anima di; **to come to life** tornare a sé; riprender vita; **to depart this life** passar a miglior vita; **to run for one's life** scappare a tutta corsa

**life' annu'ity** _s_ rendita vitalizia

**life' belt'** _s_ cintura di salvataggio

**life'boat'** _s_ imbarcazione di salvataggio, lancia di salvataggio

**life' buoy'** _s_ salvagente _m_

**life' float'** _s_ zattera di salvataggio

**life'guard'** _s_ bagnino

**life' impris'onment** _s_ ergastolo

**life' insur'ance** _s_ assicurazione sulla vita

**life' jack'et** _s_ cintura or giubbotto di salvataggio

**lifeless** ['laɪflɪs] _adj_ inanimato; (_in a faint_) esanime; senza vita

**life'like'** _adj_ (_e.g., portrait_) parlante; naturale

**life' line'** _s_ sagola di salvataggio; (fig) linea di comunicazione vitale

**life'long'** _adj_ perpetuo, a vita

**life' of Ri'ley** ['raɪli] _s_ vita del michelaccio

**life' of the par'ty** _s_ anima della festa

**life' preserv'er** [prɪ'zʌrvər] _s_ salvagente _m_

**lifer** ['laɪfər] _s_ (slang) ergastolano

**life' raft'** _s_ zattera di salvataggio

**life'sav'er** _s_ salvatore _m_ della vita; (_something that saves from a predicament_) ancora di salvezza

**life' sen'tence** _s_ condanna all'ergastolo

**life'-size** _adj_ in grandezza naturale

**life'time'** _adj_ vitalizio ‖ _s_ corso della vita

**life' vest'** _s_ (air, naut) giubbotto salvagente or di salvataggio

**life'work'** _s_ lavoro di tutta una vita

**lift** [lɪft] _s_ sollevamento; (_act of helping_) aiuto; (_ride_) passaggio; (_apparatus_) elevatore _m;_ (aer) portanza ‖ _tr_ sollevare, alzare; (_one's hat_) levarsi; rimuovere; (coll) plagiare; (coll) rubare; (fire) (mil) sospendere ‖ _intr_ sollevare, sollevarsi; (_said, e.g., of fog_) dissiparsi

**lift'-off'** _s_ (aer) decollo verticale

**lift' truck'** _s_ carrello elevatore

**ligament** ['lɪgəmənt] _s_ legamento

**ligature** ['lɪgətʃər] _s_ legatura

**light** [laɪt] _adj_ (_in weight_) leggero; (_hair_) biondo; (_complexion_) chiaro; (_oil_) fluido; (_naut_) con poco carico; (_room_) chiaro, illuminato; (_beer_) chiaro; **light in the head** (_dizzy_) allegro; (_silly_) scimunito; **to make light of** prendere sotto gamba ‖ _s_ luce _f;_ (_to light a cigarette_) fuoco; (_to control traffic_) segnale _m;_ (_shining example_) luminare _m;_ (_lighthouse_) faro; (_window_) luce _f;_ **according to one's lights** secondo l'intelligenza che il buon Dio gli (le) ha dato; **against the light** controluce; **in this light** sotto questo punto di vista; **lights** esempio; (_of sheep_) polmone _m;_ **to come to light** venire alla luce; **to shed** or **throw light on** mettere in luce; **to strike a light** accendere un fiammifero ‖ _v_ (_pret & pp_ **lighted** or **lit** [lɪt] _tr_ (_to furnish with illumination_) illuminare; (_to ignite_) accendere; **to light up** illuminare ‖ _intr_ illuminarsi; accendersi; (_said, e.g., of a bird_) posarsi; (_from a car_) scendere; **to light into** (coll) gettarsi contro; **to light out** (slang) darsela a gambe; **to light upon** imbattersi in ‖ _adv_ senza bagagli; senza carico

**light' bulb'** _s_ lampadina

**light-complexioned** ['laɪtkəm'plɛkʃənd] _adj_ dal colorito chiaro

**lighten** ['laɪtən] _tr_ alleggerire, sgravare; illuminare; (_to cheer up_) rallegrare ‖ _intr_ alleggerirsi; (_to become less dark_) illuminarsi; (_to give off flashes of lightning_) lampeggiare

**lighter** ['laɪtər] _s_ accenditore _m;_ (naut) burchio

**light-fingered** ['laɪt'fɪŋgərd] _adj_ svelto di mano, con le mani lunghe

**light-footed** ['laɪt'fʊtɪd] *adj* agile
**light-headed** ['laɪt'hedɪd] *adj* (*dizzy*) allegro; (*simple*) scemo
**light-hearted** ['laɪt'hɑrtɪd] *adj* allegro
**light'house'** *s* faro
**lighting** ['laɪtɪŋ] *s* illuminazione
**lightly** ['laɪtli] *adv* alla leggera
**light' me'ter** *s* esposimetro
**lightness** ['laɪtnɪs] *s* (*in weight*) leggerezza; (*in illumination*) chiarezza
**light•ning** ['laɪtnɪŋ] *s* lampo, fulmine *m* ‖ *v* (*ger* **-ning**) *intr* lampeggiare
**light'ning arrest'er** [ə'rɛstər] *s* scaricatore *m*
**light'ning bug'** *s* lucciola
**light'ning rod'** *s* parafulmine *m*
**light' op'era** *s* operetta
**light'ship'** *s* battello faro
**light-struck** ['laɪt,strʌk] *adj* che ha preso luce
**light'weight'** *adj* leggero; da mezza stagione, e.g., **lightweight coat** cappotto da mezza stagione
**light'-year'** *s* anno luce
**likable** ['laɪkəbəl] *adj* simpatico
**like** [laɪk] *adj* uguale, simile; uguale a, simile a, e.g., **this hat is like mine** questo cappello è simile al mio; (*elec*) di segno uguale; **like father like son** tale il padre quale il figlio; **to feel like** + *ger* aver voglia di + *inf*; **to look like** assomigliare a; sembrare, e.g., **it looks like rain** sembra che pioverà ‖ *s* (*liking*) preferenza; (*fellow man*) simile *m*; **and the like** e cose dello stesso genere; **to give like for like** rendere pane per focaccia ‖ *adv* come; **like enough** (coll) probabilmente ‖ *prep* come ‖ *conj* (coll) come; come se; (coll) che, e.g., **it seems like he is afraid** sembra che abbia paura ‖ *tr* voler bene (with *dat*), e.g., **I like her very much** le voglio molto bene; trovar piacere in, e.g., **I like music** trovo piacere nella musica; piacere (with *dat*), e.g., **John likes apples** le mele piacciono a Giovanni; **to like best** or **better** preferire; **to like it in** trovarsi a proprio agio in; **to like to** + *inf* piacere (with *dat*) + *inf*, e.g., **she likes to dance** le piace ballare; gradire che + *subj*, e.g., **I should like him to pay a visit to my parents** gradirei che facesse una visita ai miei genitori ‖ *intr* volere, desiderare, e.g., **as you like** come desidera; **if you like** se vuole
**likelihood** ['laɪklɪ,hʊd] *s* probabilità *f*
**like•ly** ['laɪkli] *adj* (**-lier; -liest**) probabile; verosimile; a proposito; promettente; **to be likely to** + *inf* essere probabile che + *fut*, e.g., **Mary is likely to get married in the spring** è probabile che Maria si sposerà in primavera ‖ *adv* probabilmente
**like-minded** ['laɪk'maɪndɪd] *adj* dello stesso parere, della stessa opinione
**liken** ['laɪkən] *tr* paragonare
**likeness** ['laɪknɪs] *s* (*picture*) ritratto; (*similarity*) rassomiglianza; apparenza
**like'wise'** *adv* ugualmente; inoltre; **to do likewise** fare lo stesso

**liking** ['laɪkɪŋ] *s* simpatia; **to be to the liking of** essere di gusto di; **to have a liking for** (*things*) prendere gusto per; (*people*) affezionarsi a
**lilac** ['laɪlək] *adj* & *s* lilla *m*
**Lilliputian** [,lɪlɪ'pjuʃən] *adj* & *s* lilliputiano
**lilt** [lɪlt] *s* canzone *f* a cadenza; movimento a cadenza; (*in verse*) cadenza
**lil•y** ['lɪli] *s* (**-ies**) giglio; **to gild the lily** cercare di migliorare quanto è già perfetto
**lil'y of the val'ley** *s* mughetto
**li'ma bean'** ['laɪmə] *s* fagiolo bianco
**limb** [lɪm] *s* (*of body*) membro, arto; (*of tree*) ramo; (*of cross*) braccio; **to be out on a limb** (coll) essere nei guai
**limber** ['lɪmbər] *adj* agile ‖ *intr*—**to limber up** sciogliersi i muscoli, sgranchirsi le gambe
**lim•bo** ['lɪmbo] *s* (**-bos**) esilio; dimenticatoio; (theol) limbo
**lime** [laɪm] *s* (*calcium oxide*) calce *f*; (*Citrus aurantifolia*) limetta agra; (*linden tree*) tiglio ‖ *tr* gessare
**lime'kiln'** *s* fornace *f* da calce
**lime'light'** *s*—**to be in the limelight** essere in vista
**limerick** ['lɪmərɪk] *s* canzoncina umoristica di cinque versi
**lime'stone'** *s* calcare *m*
**limit** ['lɪmɪt] *s* limite *m*; (coll) colmo; **to go to the limit** andare agli estremi ‖ *tr* limitare
**limitation** [,lɪmɪ'teʃən] *s* limitazione
**lim'ited-ac'cess high'way** ['lɪmɪtɪd] *s* autostrada, strada con corsia d'accesso
**lim'ited com'pany** *s* società *f* a responsabilità limitata
**lim'ited mon'archy** *s* monarchia costituzionale
**limitless** ['lɪmɪtlɪs] *adj* illimitato
**limousine** ['lɪmə,zin] or [,lɪmə'zin] *s* berlina
**limp** [lɪmp] *adj* floscio; debole ‖ *s* zoppicatura ‖ *intr* zoppicare
**limpid** ['lɪmpɪd] *adj* limpido
**linage** ['laɪnɪdʒ] *s* (typ) numero di linee
**linchpin** ['lɪntʃ,pɪn] *s* acciarino
**linden** ['lɪndən] *s* tiglio
**line** [laɪn] *s* linea; (*e.g., of people*) fila; (*of trees*) filare *m*; (*for fishing*) lenza; (*written or printed*) rigo, riga; (*wrinkle*) ruga; (*of goods*) ramo; (naut) gherlino; **all along the line** su tutta la linea; **in line** allineato; sotto controllo; **in line with** secondo; **out of line** fuori d'allineamento; (slang) in disaccordo; **to bring into line** far filare; **to draw the line at** fermarsi a; stabilire il limite a; **to fall in line** conformarsi; allinearsi; **to have a line on** (coll) aver informazioni su; **to read between the lines** leggere fra le righe; **to stand in line** fare la coda; **to toe the line** filare diritto; **to wait in line** fare la fila ‖ *tr* rigare; (*e.g., the street*) schierare lungo; (*a suit*) foderare; (*a brake*) rivestire; **to line up** allineare; trovare, scovare ‖ *intr*

**—to line up** mettersi in fila; fare la coda
**lineage** ['lɪnɪ·ɪdʒ] s lignaggio
**lineaments** ['lɪnɪ·əmənts] spl lineamenti mpl
**linear** ['lɪnɪ·ər] adj lineare
**line'man** s (-men) (elec) guardafili m; (sports) guardalinee m; (surv) assistente geometra m
**linen** ['lɪnən] adj di tela di lino || s (fabric) tela di lino, lino; (yarn) filo di lino; biancheria
**lin'en clos'et** s guardaroba m per la biancheria
**line' of fire'** s (mil) linea di tiro
**line' of least' resist'ance** s principio del minimo sforzo; **to follow the line of least resistance** prendere la via più facile
**line' of sight'** s visuale f; (mil) linea di mira
**liner** ['laɪnər] s transatlantico
**line'-up'** s disposizione; (of prisoners) allineamento; (sports) formazione
**linger** ['lɪŋgər] intr indugiare, soffermarsi; (to be tardy) tardare; rimanere in vita; **to linger over** contemplare
**lingerie** [,lænʒə'ri] s biancheria intima
**lingering** ['lɪŋgərɪŋ] adj prolungato
**lingual** ['lɪŋgwəl] adj linguale || s suono linguale
**linguist** ['lɪŋgwɪst] s poliglotto; (specialist in linguistics) glottologo
**linguistic** [lɪŋ'gwɪstɪk] adj linguistico || **linguistics** s linguistica, glottologia
**lining** ['laɪnɪŋ] s (of a coat) fodera; (of auto brake) guarnizione; (of a furnace) rivestimento interno; (of wall) rivestimento
**link** [lɪŋk] s anello, maglia; unione; (of sausage) nocco; **links** campo di golf || tr connettere || intr connettersi
**linnet** ['lɪnɪt] s fanello
**linotype** ['laɪnə,taɪp] s linotype f || tr comporre in linotipia
**lin'otype op'erator** s linotipista mf
**linseed** ['lɪn,sid] s linosa
**lin'seed oil'** s olio di lino
**lint** [lɪnt] s peluria, sfilacciatura; (for dressing wounds) filaccia
**lintel** ['lɪntəl] s architrave m
**lion** ['laɪ·ən] s leone m; celebrità f; **to beard the lion in his den** affrontare l'avversario a casa sua; **to put one's head in the lion's mouth** cacciarsi nei pericoli
**lioness** ['laɪ·ənɪs] s leonessa
**lion-hearted** ['laɪ·ən,hɑrtɪd] adj cuor di leone, coraggioso
**lionize** ['laɪ·ə,naɪz] tr festeggiare come una celebrità
**li'ons' den'** s fossa dei leoni
**li'on's share'** s parte f del leone
**lip** [lɪp] s labbro; (of a jar) beccuccio; (slang) linguaggio insolente; **to smack one's lips** leccarsi le labbra
**lip'read'** v (pret & pp -read [,red]) tr leggere le labbra di || intr leggere le labbra
**lip' read'ing** s labiolettura
**lip' serv'ice** s omaggio non sentito

**lip'stick'** s rossetto per le labbra, matita per le labbra
**lique·fy** ['lɪkwɪ,faɪ] v (pret & pp -fied) tr & intr liquefare
**liqueur** [lɪ'kʌr] s liquore m
**liquid** ['lɪkwɪd] adj liquido || s liquido; (phonet) liquida
**liquidate** ['lɪkwɪ,det] tr & intr liquidare
**liquidity** [lɪ'kwɪdɪti] s liquidità f
**liq'uid meas'ure** s misura di capacità per liquidi
**liquor** ['lɪkər] s distillato alcolico, bevanda alcolica; (broth) brodo
**Lisbon** ['lɪzbən] s Lisbona
**lisp** [lɪsp] s pronuncia blesa || intr parlare bleso
**lissome** ['lɪsəm] adj flessibile, agile
**list** [lɪst] s lista, elenco; (border) orlo; (selvage) cimossa, vivagno; (naut) sbandamento; **lists** lizza; **to enter the lists** entrare in lizza || tr elencare, listare || intr (naut) sbandare, andare alla banda
**listen** ['lɪsən] intr ascoltare; obbedire; **to listen in** ascoltare una conversazione; (rad) captare una comunicazione; **to listen to** ascoltare; obbedire a, prestare attenzione a; **to listen to reason** intendere ragione
**listener** ['lɪsənər] s ascoltatore m; radioascoltatore m
**lis'tening post'** s (mil) posto di ascolto
**listless** ['lɪstlɪs] adj svogliato
**list' price'** s prezzo di catalogo
**lita·ny** ['lɪtəni] s (-nies) litania
**liter** ['litər] s litro
**literacy** ['lɪtərəsi] s abilità f di leggere e scrivere; istruzione
**literal** ['lɪtərəl] adj letterale
**literary** ['lɪtə,reri] adj letterario; (individual) letterato
**literate** ['lɪtərɪt] adj che sa leggere e scrivere; (educated) istruito; (well-read) letterato || s persona che sa leggere e scrivere; letterato
**literature** ['lɪtərət∫ər] s letteratura; (printed matter) opuscoli pubblicitari
**lithe** [laɪθ] adj flessibile, agile
**lithium** ['lɪθɪ·əm] s litio
**lithograph** ['lɪθə,græf] or ['lɪθə,grɑf] s litografia || tr litografare
**lithographer** [lɪ'θɑgrəfər] s litografo
**lithography** [lɪ'θɑgrəfi] s litografia
**Lithuania** [,lɪθu'enɪ·ə] s la Lituania
**Lithuanian** [,lɪθu'enɪ·ən] adj & s lituano
**litigant** ['lɪtɪgənt] adj & s litigante mf
**litigate** ['lɪtɪ,get] tr & intr litigare
**litigation** [,lɪtɪ'geʃən] s litigio; (lawsuit) lite f, causa
**litmus** ['lɪtməs] s tornasole m
**lit'mus pa'per** s cartina al tornasole
**litter** ['lɪtər] s disordine m; (scattered rubbish) pattume m; (young brought forth at one birth) figliata; (of puppies) cucciolata; (bedding for animals) strame m; (stretcher; bed carried by men or animals) lettiga, portantina || tr mettere in disordine; spargere rifiuti per; coprire di strame || intr partorire

**lit′ter·bug′** *s* sparpagliatore *m* di rifiuti
**littering** [′lɪtərɪŋ] *s*—**no littering** vietato gettare rifiuti
**little** [′lɪtəl] *adj* (*in size*) piccolo; (*in amount*) poco, e.g., **little salt** poco sale; **a little un po′ di,** e.g., **a little salt un po′ di sale; the little ones** i piccini ‖ *s* poco; **a little un po′; to make little of** farsi gioco di; non pigliar sul serio; **to think little of** non tener di conto ‖ *adv* poco; **little by little** poco a poco, mano a mano
**Lit′tle Bear′** *s* Orsa minore
**Lit′tle Dip′per** *s* Piccolo Carro
**lit′tle fin′ger** *s* mignolo; **to twist around one′s little finger** maneggiare come un fantoccio
**lit′tle·neck** *s* piccola vongola (*Venus mercenaria*)
**lit′tle owl′** *s* civetta
**lit′tle peo′ple** *spl* fate *fpl;* folletti *mpl*
**Lit′tle Red Rid′inghood′** [′raɪdɪŋ ,hʊd] *s* Cappuccetto Rosso
**lit′tle slam′** *s* (bridge) piccolo slam
**liturgic(al)** [lɪ′tʌrdʒɪk(əl)] *adj* liturgico
**litur·gy** [′lɪtərdʒi] *s* (**-gies**) liturgia
**livable** [′lɪvəbəl] *adj* abitabile; socievole; tollerabile
**live** [laɪv] *adj* vivo; (*flame*) ardente; di attualità; (elec) sotto tensione; (telv) in diretta ‖ [lɪv] *tr* vivere; **to live down** (*one′s past*) far dimenticare; **to live it up** (coll) darsi alla bella vita, scialare; **to live out** (*e.g., a war*) sopravvivere (**with** *dat*) ‖ *intr* vivere; **to live from hand to mouth** vivere alla giornata; **to live high** darsi alla bella vita; **to live on** continuare a vivere; (*e.g., vegetables*) vivere di; vivere alle spalle di; **to live up to** (*one′s promises*) compiere; (*one′s earnings*) spendere
**live′ coal′** [laɪv] *s* brace *f*
**livelihood** [′laɪvlɪ ,hʊd] *s* vita; **to earn one′s livelihood** guadagnarsi la vita
**livelong** [′lɪv ,lɔŋ] or [′lɪv ,lɑŋ] *adj*— **all the livelong day** tutto il santo giorno
**live·ly** [′laɪvli] *adj* (**-lier; -liest**) vivo, vivace; (*color*) vivido; (*resilient*) elastico; (*tune*) brioso
**liven** [′laɪvən] *tr* animare ‖ *intr* animarsi, rianimarsi
**liver** [′lɪvər] *s* abitante *mf;* (anat) fegato
**liver·y** [′lɪvəri] *s* (**-ies**) livrea
**liv′ery·man** [-mən] *s* (**-men**) stalliere *m*
**liv′ery sta′ble** *s* stallaggio
**livestock** [′laɪv ,stɑk] *adj* zootecnico ‖ *s* bestiame *m*
**live′ wire′** [laɪv] *s* (elec) filo carico di corrente; (slang) persona energica
**livid** [′lɪvɪd] *adj* livido; (*with anger*) incollerito
**living** [′lɪvɪŋ] *adj* vivo; (*conditions*) abitativo ‖ *s* vivere *m;* **to earn a living** guadagnarsi la vita
**liv′ing quar′ters** *spl* abitazione, alloggio
**liv′ing room′** *s* stanza di soggiorno
**liv′ing wage′** *s* salario sufficiente per vivere
**lizard** [′lɪzərd] *s* lucertola

**load** [lod] *s* peso, carico; **loads of** (coll) un mucchio di; **to get a load of** (slang) stare a vedere; (slang) stare a sentire; **to have a load on** (slang) essere ubriaco ‖ *tr* caricare ‖ *intr* caricarsi
**loaded** [′lodɪd] *adj* caricato; (slang) ubriaco fradicio; (slang) ricchissimo
**load′ed dice′** *spl* dadi truccati
**load′stone′** *s* magnetite *f;* (fig) calamita
**loaf** [lof] *s* (**loaves** [lovz]) pane *m;* (*molded mass*) forma; (*of sugar*) pane *m;* (*long and thin loaf*) filone *m* ‖ *intr* batter fiacca, oziare
**loafer** [′lofər] *s* fannullone *m*
**loam** [lom] *s* ricca argilla sabbiosa; terra da fonderia
**loan** [lon] *s* prestito; **to hit for a loan** (coll) dare una stoccata a ‖ *tr* prestare
**loan′ shark′** *s* (coll) strozzino
**loan′ word′** *s* (ling) prestito
**loath** [loθ] *adj* poco disposto; **nothing loath** molto volentieri
**loathe** [loð] *tr* detestare, aborrire
**loathsome** [′loðsəm] *adj* abominevole, disgustoso
**lob** [lɑb] *s* (tennis) pallonetto ‖ *v* (*pret & pp* **lobbed;** *ger* **lobbing**) *tr* (tennis) dare un pallonetto a
**lob·by** [′lɑbi] *s* (**-bies**) anticamera, vestibolo; sollecitazione di voti ‖ *v* (*pret & pp* **-bied**) *intr* sollecitare voti, influenzare il voto dietro le quinte
**lobbyist** [′lɑbɪ·ɪst] *s* politicante *m* che cerca di influenzare il voto dietro le quinte
**lobe** [lob] *s* lobo
**lobster** [′lɑbstər] *s* (*Palinurus vulgaris*) aragosta; (*Hommarus vulgaris*) astice *m*
**lob′ster pot′** *s* nassa per aragoste
**local** [′lokəl] *adj* locale ‖ *s* treno accelerato; notizia di interesse locale; (*of a union*) sezione
**locale** [lo′kæl] *s* località *f*
**locali·ty** [lo′kælɪti] *s* (**-ties**) località *f*
**localize** [′lokə ,laɪz] *tr* localizzare
**lo′cal op′tion** *s* referendum *m* locale sulla vendita di alcolici
**locate** [′lo′ket] or [′loket] *tr* (*to discover the location of*) localizzare; (*to place, settle*) situare, stabilire; (*to ascribe a location to*) individuare ‖ *intr* stabilirsi
**location** [lo′keʃən] *s* localizzazione; posizione; sito; **on location** (mov) in esterno
**lock** [lɑk] *s* serratura; (*of a canal*) chiusa; (*of hair*) ciocca; (*of a firearm*) percussore *m;* (mach) freno; **lock, stock, and barrel** (coll) completamente; **under lock and key** sotto chiave ‖ *tr* chiudere a chiave; serrare; (*a boat*) far passare per una chiusa; unire; abbracciare; **to lock in** chiudere sotto chiave; **to lock out** chiudere fuori; (*workers*) sbarrare dal lavoro; **to lock up** chiudere a chiave; incarcerare
**locker** [′lɑkər] *s* armadietto a chiave; (*in the form of a chest*) bauletto

**lock′er room′** s spogliatoio
**locket** [′lakɪt] s medaglione m
**lock′jaw′** s tetano, trisma m
**lock′ nut′** s controdado
**lock′out′** s serrata
**lock′smith′** s magnano, fabbro
**lock′ step′** s—**to march in lock step** marciare a passo serrato
**lock′ stitch′** s punto a filo doppio
**lock′ ten′der** s guardiano di chiusa
**lock′up′** s prigione; (typ) messa in forma
**lock′ wash′er** s rondella di sicurezza
**locomotive** [ˌlokə′motɪv] s locomotiva
**lo·cus** [′lokəs] s (**-ci** [saɪ]) luogo
**locust** [′lokəst] s (ent) locusta; (*cicada*) (ent) cicala; (bot) robinia
**lode** [lod] s filone m, vena
**lode′star′** s stella polare; guida
**lodge** [ladʒ] s casetta; padiglione m da caccia; albergo; (*e.g., of Masons*) loggia ‖ tr alloggiare, ospitare; depositare; contenere; (*a complaint*) sporgere ‖ intr alloggiare; essere contenuto, trovarsi; andar a finire
**lodger** [′ladʒər] s inquilino
**lodging** [′ladʒɪŋ] s alloggio
**loft** [lɔft] or [laft] s (*attic*) solaio; (*hayloft*) fienile m; (*in theater or church*) galleria
**loft·y** [′lɔfti] or [′lafti] adj (**-ier; -iest**) alto, elevato; (*haughty*) orgoglioso
**log** [lɔg] or [lag] s ceppo, ciocco; (naut) solcometro; (aer, naut) giornale m di bordo; **to sleep like a log** dormire della grossa ‖ v (*pret & pp* **logged; ger logging**) tr registrare; (*a speed*) fare; (*a distance*) percorrere
**logarithm** [′logəˌrɪðəm] or [′logəˌrɪðəm] s logaritmo
**log′book′** s (aer, naut) libro di bordo
**log′ cab′in** s capanna di tronchi
**log′ chip′** s (naut) barchetta
**log′ driv′er** s zatteriere m
**log′ driv′ing** [′draɪvɪŋ] s fluitazione
**logger** [′lɔgər] or [′lagər] s taglialegna m; trattore m per trasporto tronchi
**log′ger·head′** s testone m; **at loggerheads** in lite
**loggia** [′lodʒə] s loggia
**logic** [′ladʒɪk] s logica
**logical** [′ladʒɪkəl] adj logico
**logician** [lo′dʒɪ/ən] s logico
**logistic(al)** [lo′dʒɪstɪk(əl)] adj logistico
**logistics** [lo′dʒɪstɪks] s logistica
**log′jam′** s ingorgo fluviale dovuto a ammasso di tronchi; (fig) ristagno
**log′ line′** s (naut) sagola
**log′roll′** intr barattare favori politici
**log′wood′** s campeggio
**loin** [lɔɪn] s lombo; **to gird up one's loins** prepararsi per l'azione
**loin′cloth′** s perizoma m, copripudende m
**loiter** [′lɔɪtər] tr—**to loiter away** (*time*) sprecare in ozio ‖ intr bighellonare, trastullarsi
**loiterer** [′lɔɪtərər] s perdigiorno
**loll** [lal] intr sdraiarsi pigramente, adagiarsi pigramente; pendere
**lollipop** [′lali ˌpap] s caramella sullo stecchetto, lecca-lecca m

**Lombard** [′lambard] or [′lambərd] adj & s lombardo; (hist) longobardo
**Lom′bardy pop′lar** s pioppo italico
**London** [′lʌndən] adj londinese ‖ s Londra
**Londoner** [′lʌndənər] s londinese mf
**lone** [lon] adj solo; solitario
**loneliness** [′lonlɪnɪs] s solitudine f
**lone·ly** [′lonli] adj (**-lier; -liest**) solingo, solo, solitario
**lonesome** [′lonsəm] adj solitario
**lone′ wolf′** s (coll) orso, solitario
**long** [lɔŋ] or [laŋ] (**longer** [′lɔŋgər] or [′laŋgər]; **longest** [′lɔŋgɪst] or [′laŋgɪst]) adj lungo; **three meters long** lungo tre metri ‖ adv molto, molto tempo; **as long as** mentre; (*provided*) fin tanto che; (*inasmuch as*) dato che; **before long** fra poco; **how long?** quanto?; **long ago** molto tempo fa; **long before** molto prima; **long since** molto tempo fa; **no longer** non più; **so long!** (coll) ciao!, arrivederci!; **so long as** fino a che, finché ‖ intr anelare; **to long for** sviscerarsi per, sospirare per
**long′boat′** s (naut) lancia
**long′-dis′tance** adj (telp) interurbano, intercomunale; (sports) di fondo; (aer) a distanza
**long′-drawn′-out′** adj prolungato
**longeron** [′landʒərən] s longherone m
**longevity** [lan′dʒevɪti] s longevità f
**long′ face′** s (coll) faccia triste, muso lungo
**long′hair′** adj & s (coll) intellettuale mf; (coll) musicomane mf
**long′hand′** adj (scritto) a mano ‖ s scrittura a mano; **in longhand** scritto a mano
**longing** [′lɔŋɪŋ] or [′laŋɪŋ] adj bramoso, anelante ‖ s brama, anelito
**longitude** [′landʒɪˌtjud] or [′landʒɪˌtud] s longitudine f
**long-lived** [′lɔŋ′laɪvd], [′lɔŋ′lɪvd], [′laŋ′laɪvd] or [′laŋ′lɪvd] adj (*person*) longevo, di lunga vita; (*e.g., rumor*) di lunga durata
**long′-play′ing rec′ord** s disco di grande durata
**long′-range′** adj a lunga portata
**long′shore′man** s (**-men**) portuale m, scaricatore m
**long′stand′ing** adj vecchio, che esiste da lungo tempo
**long′-suf′fering** adj paziente, longanime
**long′ suit′** s (cards) serie lunga; (fig) forte m
**long′-term′** adj a lunga scadenza
**long′-wind′ed** adj verboso; (*speech*) chilometrico
**look** [lʊk] s (*appearance*) aspetto; (*glance*) sguardo; (*search*) ricerca; **looks** aspetto, apparenza; **to take a look at** dare un'occhiata a ‖ tr guardare; (*one's age*) mostrare; **to look daggers at** fulminare con lo sguardo; **to look up** (*e.g., in a dictionary*) cercare; andare a visitare; venire a visitare ‖ intr guardare; cercare; parere; **look out!** attenzione!; **to look after** badare a; occuparsi di; **to look at** guardare; **to look back** riguardare;

(fig) guardare al passato; **to look down on s.o.** guardare qlcu dall'alto in basso; **to look for** cercare; aspettarsi; **to look forward to** anticipare il piacere di; **to look ill** avere una brutta cera; **to look in on** passare per la casa di; **to look into** esaminare a fondo; **to look like** sembrare, parere; **to look out** fare attenzione; **to look out for** aver cura di; **to look out of** guardare da; **to look out on** dare su; **to look through** guardare per; (*a book*) sfogliare; **to look toward** dare su; **to look up to** ammirare, guardare con ammirazione; **to look well** avere una buona cera; fare figura

**looker-on** [ˌlukərˈɑn] or [ ˌlukərˈɔn] *s* (**lookers-on**) astante *m*

**look'ing glass'** [ˈlukɪŋ] *s* specchio

**look'out'** *s* guardia; (*person; watch kept; place from which a watch is kept*) vedetta; (*concern*) (coll) affare *m;* **to be on the lookout** stare in guardia; **to be on the lookout for** essere in cerca di

**loom** [lum] *s* telaio ‖ *intr* apparire indistintamente; pararsi dinanzi; apparire

**loon** [lun] *s* scemo; fannullone *m;* (orn) (*Gavia*) strolaga

**loon·y** [ˈluni] *adj* (**-ier; -iest**) (slang) pazzo ‖ *s* (**-ies**) (slang) pazzo

**loop** [lup] *s* cappio; (*e.g., of a road*) tortuosità *f;* (*for fastening a button*) occhiello; (aer) cerchio or giro della morte; (phys) ventre *m;* ‖ *tr* fare cappi in; annodare; **to loop the loop** (aer) fare il giro della morte ‖ *intr* avanzare tortuosamente, girare

**loop'hole'** *s* (*narrow opening*) feritoia; (*means of evasion*) scappatoia

**loose** [lus] *adj* libero, sciolto; (*available*) disponibile; (*not firm*) rilasciato; (*tooth*) che balla; (*unchaste*) facile; (*garment*) ampio; (*soil*) smosso; (*translation*) libero; (*rein*) lento; **to become loose** sciogliersi; **to break loose** mettersi in libertà; **to have loose bowels** avere la diarrea; **to turn loose** liberare ‖ *s*—**to be on the loose** (coll) essere in libertà; (coll) correre la cavallina ‖ *tr* sciogliere; slegare; lanciare

**loose' change'** *s* spiccioli *mpl*

**loose' end'** *s* capo sciolto; **at loose ends** indeciso; disoccupato, senza nulla da fare

**loose'-leaf'** *adj* a fogli mobili

**loosen** [ˈlusən] *tr* snodare; rilasciare; smuovere; allentare; (*the bowels*) liberare dalla stitichezza ‖ *intr* snodarsi; rilasciarsi; smuoversi; allentarsi

**looseness** [ˈlusnɪs] *s* scioltezza; (*in morals*) rilassamento

**loose-tongued** [ˈlusˈtʌŋd] *adj* sciolto di lingua; linguacciuto, maldicente

**loot** [lut] *s* bottino ‖ *tr* saccheggiare

**lop** [lɑp] *v* (*pret & pp* **lopped;** *ger* **lopping**) *tr* lasciar cadere, lasciar penzolare; **to lop off** mozzare; (*a tree*) potare; (*a vine*) stralciare ‖ *intr* penzolare

**lopsided** [ˈlɑpˈsaɪdɪd] *adj* che pende da una parte; asimmetrico, sproporzionato

**loquacious** [loˈkweʃəs] *adj* loquace

**lord** [lɔrd] *s* signore *m;* (Brit) lord *m* ‖ *tr*—**to lord it over** signoreggiare su

**lord·ly** [ˈlɔrdli] *adj* (**-lier; -liest**) signorile, magnifico; altero, disdegnoso, arrogante

**Lord's' Day'**, **the** la domenica, il giorno del Signore

**lordship** [ˈlɔrdʃɪp] *s* signoria

**Lord's' Prayer'** *s* paternostro

**Lord's' Sup'per** *s* Eucarestia; Ultima Cena

**lore** [lor] *s* tradizioni *fpl* popolari; cognizioni *fpl*

**lorgnette** [lɔrnˈjɛt] *s* occhialetto, lorgnette *f;* binocolo da teatro col manico

**lor·ry** [ˈlɑri] or [ˈlɔri] *s* (**-ries**) (rr) vagoncino; (Brit) camion *m*

**lose** [luz] *v* (*pret & pp* **lost** [lɔst] or [lɑst]) *tr* perdere; (*said of a physician*) non riuscire a salvare; **to lose heart** perdersi d'animo; **to lose oneself** perdersi, smarrirsi ‖ *intr* perdere; (*said of a watch*) ritardare; **to lose out** rimetterci

**loser** [ˈluzər] *s* perdente *mf*

**losing** [ˈluzɪŋ] *adj* perdente ‖ **losings** *spl* perdite *fpl*

**loss** [lɔs] or [lɑs] *s* perdita; **to be at a loss** essere perplesso; **to be at a loss to** + *inf* non saper come + *inf;* **to sell at a loss** vendere in perdita

**loss' of face'** *s* perdita di faccia

**lost** [lɔst] or [lɑst] *adj* perduto; **lost in thought** assorto in sè stesso; **lost to** perso per; insensibile a

**lost'-and-found' depart'ment** *s* ufficio degli oggetti smarriti

**lost' sheep'** *s* percorella smarrita

**lot** [lɑt] *s* (*for building*) lotto; (*fate*) sorte *f;* (*parcel, portion*) partita; (*of people*) gruppo; (coll) grande quantità *f;* (coll) tipo, soggetto; **a lot (of)** or **lots of** (coll) molto, molti; **to cast** or **to throw in one's lot with** condividere la sorte di; **to draw** or **to cast lots** tirare a sorte

**lotion** [ˈloʃən] *s* lozione

**lotter·y** [ˈlɑtəri] *s* (**-ies**) lotteria, riffa

**lotto** [ˈlɑto] *s* tombola, lotto

**lotus** [ˈlotəs] *s* loto

**loud** [laud] *adj* forte; (*noisy*) rumoroso; (*voice*) alto; (*garish*) sgargiante, chiassoso, appariscente; (*foul-smelling*) puzzolente ‖ *adv* a voce alta; rumorosamente

**loud-mouthed** [ˈlaudˌmauθt] or [ˈlaudˌmauðd] *adj* chiassone

**loud'speak'er** *s* altoparlante *m*

**lounge** [laundʒ] *s* divano, sofà *m;* sala soggiorno; ridotto ‖ *intr* oziare, star senza far niente; bighellonare; **to lounge around** bighellonare

**lounge' liz'ard** *s* (slang) damerino, bellimbusto, gagà *m*

**louse** [laus] *s* (**lice** [laɪs]) pidocchio ‖ *tr*—**to louse up** (slang) rovinare

**lous·y** [ˈlauzi] *adj* (**-ier; -iest**) pidocchioso; (*mean; bungling*) (coll) schi-

foso; (*filthy*) (coll) sporco; **lousy with** (*e.g., money*) (slang) pieno di
**lout** [laut] *s* gaglioffo, tanghero
**louver** ['luvər] *s* sportello girevole di persiana; (aut) feritoia per ventilazione
**lovable** ['lʌvəbəl] *adj* amabile
**love** [lʌv] *s* amore *m;* (tennis) zero; **not for love nor money** a nessun prezzo; **to be in love (with)** essere innamorato (di); **to make love to** fare l'amore con ‖ *tr* amare; voler bene a; piacere (with *dat*), e.g., **she loves short skirts** le piacciono le sottane corte
**love' affair'** *s* passione, amori *mpl*
**love'bird'** *s* (orn) inseparabile *m;* **love-birds** (slang) amanti appassionati
**love' child'** *s* figlio naturale
**love' feast'** *s* agape *f*
**loveless** ['lʌvlɪs] *adj* senza amore
**lovelorn** ['lʌv ,lɔrn] *adj* abbandonato dalla persona amata
**love·ly** ['lʌvli] *adj* (**-lier; -liest**) bello; (coll) delizioso
**love' match'** *s* matrimonio d'amore
**love' po'tion** *s* filtro d'amore
**lover** ['lʌvər] *s* amante *m;* (*e.g., of music*) amico, appassionato
**love' seat'** *s* amorino
**love'sick'** *adj* malato d'amore
**love'sick'ness** *s* mal *m* d'amore
**love' song'** *s* canzone *f* d'amore
**loving** ['lʌvɪŋ] *adj* affezionato, amoroso; **your loving son** il vostro affezionato figlio
**lov'ing-kind'ness** *s* tenera sollecitudine
**low** [lo] *adj* basso; (*deep*) profondo; (*diet*) magro; (*visibility*) cattivo; (*dress*) scollato; (*dejected*) abbattuto; (*fire*) lento; (*flame; speed*) piccolo; **to lay low** ammazzare; abbattere; **to lie low** rimanere nascosto; attendere ‖ *s* punto basso; prezzo minimo; (*of cow*) muggito; (aut) prima velocità; (meteor) depressione ‖ *adv* basso, a basso, in basso ‖ *intr* (*said of a cow*) muggire
**low'born'** *adj* di umili origini
**low'boy'** *s* cassettone basso con le gambe corte
**low'brow'** *adj & s* (coll) ignorante *mf*
**low'-cost hous'ing** *s* case *fpl* popolari
**Low' Coun'tries, the** i Paesi Bassi
**low'-down'** *adj* (coll) basso, vile ‖ **low'-down'** *s* (coll) semplice verità *f,* notizie *fpl* confidenziali
**lower** ['lo·ər] *adj* inferiore, disotto ‖ *tr* abbassare; (*prices*) ribassare ‖ *intr* diminuire; discendere ‖ ['lau·ər] *intr* aggrottare le ciglia; (*said of the weather*) imbronciarsi
**low'er berth'** ['lo·ər] *s* cuccetta inferiore
**low'er case'** ['lo·ər] *s* (typ) cassa inferiore
**lower-case** ['lo·ər ,kes] *adj* (typ) minuscolo
**low'er mid'dle class'** ['lo·ər] *s* piccola borghesia
**lowermost** ['lo·ər ,most] *adj* (il) più basso, (l') infimo
**low'-fre'quency** *adj* a bassa frequenza

**low' gear'** *s* prima velocità, prima
**lowland** ['loland] *s* pianura ‖ **Lowlands** *spl* Scozia meridionale, bassa Scozia
**low·ly** ['loli] *adj* (**-lier; -liest**) umile
**Low' Mass'** *s* messa bassa
**low-minded** ['lo'maɪndɪd] *adj* vile, basso
**low-necked** ['lo'nɛkt] *adj* scollato
**low-pitched** ['lo'pɪt∫t] *adj* (*sound*) basso, grave; (*roof*) poco inclinato
**low'-pres'sure** *adj* a bassa pressione
**low-priced** ['lo'praɪst] *adj* a buon mercato, a basso prezzo
**low' shoe'** *s* scarpa bassa
**low'-speed'** *adj* di piccola velocità
**low-spirited** ['lo'spɪrɪtɪd] *adj* depresso
**low' tide'** *s* bassa marea; (fig) punto più basso
**low' visibil'ity** *s* scarsa visibilità
**low' wa'ter** *s* (*low tide*) bassa marea; (*of a river*) magra
**loyal** ['lɔɪ·əl] *adj* leale
**loyalist** ['lɔɪ·əlɪst] *s* lealista *mf*
**loyal·ty** ['lɔɪ·əlti] *s* (**-ties**) lealtà *f*
**lozenge** ['lɑzɪndʒ] *s* losanga; (*candy cough drop*) pasticca, pastiglia
**LP** ['ɛl'pi] *s* (letterword) (trademark) disco di grande durata
**lubricant** ['lubrɪkənt] *adj & s* lubrificante *m*
**lubricate** ['lubrɪ ,ket] *tr* lubrificare; (*e.g., one's hands*) ungersi
**lubrication** [ ,lubrɪ'ke∫ən] *s* lubrificazione
**lubricous** ['lubrɪkəs] *adj* lubrico; incerto, incostante
**lucerne** [lu'sʌrn] *s* erba medica
**lucid** ['lusɪd] *adj* lucido
**Lucifer** ['lusɪfər] *s* Lucifero
**luck** [lʌk] *s* (*good or bad*) sorte *f;* (*good*) sorte *f,* fortuna; **down on one's luck** in cattive condizioni; **in luck** fortunato; **out of luck** sfortunato; **to bring luck** portare (buona) fortuna; **to try one's luck** tentare la sorte; **worse luck** disgraziatamente
**luckily** ['lʌkɪli] *adv* fortunatamente
**luckless** ['lʌklɪs] *adj* sfortunato
**luck·y** ['lʌki] *adj* (**-ier; -iest**) fortunato; (*supposed to bring luck*) portafortuna; (*foretelling good luck*) di buon augurio; **to be lucky** aver fortuna
**luck'y hit'** *s* (coll) colpo di fortuna
**lucrative** ['lukrətɪv] *adj* lucrativo
**ludicrous** ['ludɪkrəs] *adj* ridicolo
**lug** [lʌg] *s* manico; (*pull*) tiro; **to put the lug on s.o.** (slang) batter cassa a qlcu ‖ *v* (*pret & pp* **lugged**; *ger* **lugging**) *tr* tirarsi dietro; (coll) introdurre a sproposito
**luggage** ['lʌgɪdʒ] *s* (*used in traveling*) bagaglio; (*found in a store*) valigeria
**lug'gage store'** *s* valigeria
**lugubrious** [lu'gubrɪ·əs] or [lu'gjubrɪ·əs] *adj* lugubre
**lukewarm** ['luk ,wɔrm] *adj* tiepido
**lull** [lʌl] *s* momento di calma, calma ‖ *tr* calmare, pacificare; addormentare
**lulla·by** ['lʌlə ,baɪ] *s* (**-bies**) ninna-nanna
**lumbago** [lʌm'bego] *s* lombaggine *f*

**lumber** [ˈlʌmbər] s legname m, legno da costruzione; cianfrusaglie fpl ‖ intr muoversi pesantemente
**lum'ber·jack'** s boscaiolo
**lum'ber jack'et** s giaccone m
**lum'ber·man** s (-men) (dealer) commerciante m in legname; (man who cuts down lumber) boscaiolo
**lum'ber room'** s ripostiglio
**lum'ber·yard'** s deposito legnami
**luminar·y** [ˈlumɪ ˌneri] s (-ies) luminare m
**luminous** [ˈlumɪnəs] adj luminoso
**lummox** [ˈlʌməks] s (coll) scimunito
**lump** [lʌmp] s grumo; mucchio; cumulo; (swelling) bernoccolo; (of sugar) zolletta; (in one's throat) groppo; (coll) stupidone m; **in the lump** in blocco; nell'insieme ‖ tr mescolare; (to make into lumps) raggrumare; **to lump it** (coll) mandarla giù
**lumpish** [ˈlʌmpɪʃ] adj grumoso; goffo; balordo
**lump' sum'** s ammontare unico, somma globale
**lump·y** [ˈlʌmpi] adj (-ier; -iest) grumoso; (person) pesante, ottuso; (sea) agitato
**luna·cy** [ˈlunəsi] s (-cies) pazzia
**lunar** [ˈlunər] adj lunare
**lu'nar land'ing** s allunaggio
**lu'nar mod'ule** s modulo lunare
**lu'nar rov'er** s auto f lunare
**lunatic** [ˈlunətɪk] adj & s demente mf
**lu'natic asy'lum** s manicomio
**lu'natic fringe'** s estremisti mpl fanatici
**lunch** [lʌntʃ] s (regular midday meal) seconda colazione; (light meal) spuntino, merenda ‖ intr fare colazione; fare uno spuntino
**lunch' bas'ket** s portavivande m
**luncheon** [ˈlʌntʃən] s seconda colazione; pranzo ufficiale
**luncheonette** [ ˌlʌntʃəˈnet] s tavola calda
**lunch'eon meat'** s insaccati mpl
**lunch'room'** s tavola calda
**lung** [lʌŋ] s polmone m
**lunge** [lʌndʒ] s slancio; (fencing) affondo ‖ intr slanciarsi
**lurch** [lʌrtʃ] s barcollamento; (at close of a game) cappotto; (naut) sbandata; **to leave in the lurch** piantare in asso ‖ intr barcollare; (naut) sbandare
**lure** [lur] s esca; (fig) insidie fpl ‖ tr adescare; **to lure away** distogliere, sviare
**lurid** [ˈlurɪd] adj (fiery) ardente, acceso; sensazionale; (gruesome) orripilante
**lurk** [lʌrk] intr stare in agguato, nascondersi; (fig) essere latente
**luscious** [ˈlʌʃəs] adj delizioso; lussuoso, lussureggiante; voluttuoso
**lush** [lʌʃ] adj lussureggiante, lussuoso
**lust** [lʌst] s desiderio sfrenato; libidine f, lussuria ‖ intr—**to lust after** or **for** aver sete di
**luster** [ˈlʌstər] s (gloss) lustro, lucentezza; (glory) lustro, onore m
**lus'ter·ware'** s ceramiche smaltate
**lustful** [ˈlʌstfəl] adj lussurioso
**lustrous** [ˈlʌstrəs] adj lucido
**lust·y** [ˈlʌsti] adj (-ier; -iest) vigoroso, gagliardo
**lute** [lut] s (mus) liuto; (chem) luto
**Lutheran** [ˈluθərən] adj & s luterano
**luxuriance** [lʌgˈʒurɪ·əns] s rigoglio
**luxuriant** [lʌgˈʒurɪ·ənt] adj lussureggiante; (imagery) ridondante
**luxuriate** [lʌgˈʒurɪ ˌet] or [lʌkˈʃurɪ ˌet] intr lussureggiare; trovare piacere
**luxurious** [lʌgˈʒurɪ·əs] or [lʌkˈʃurɪ·əs] adj lussuoso, fastoso
**luxu·ry** [ˈlʌkʃəri] or [ˈlʌgʒəri] s (-ries) lusso, sfarzo
**lye** [laɪ] s ranno, liscivia
**lying** [ˈlaɪ·ɪŋ] adj menzognero ‖ s il mentire
**ly'ing-in' hos'pital** s clinica ostetrica, maternità f
**lymph** [lɪmf] s linfa
**lymphatic** [lɪmˈfætɪk] adj linfatico
**lynch** [lɪntʃ] tr linciare
**lynching** [ˈlɪntʃɪŋ] s linciaggio
**lynx** [lɪŋks] s lince f
**lynx-eyed** [ˈlɪŋks ˌaɪd] adj dagli occhi di lince
**lyonnaise** [ ˌlaɪ·əˈnez] adj (culin) alla maniera di Lione
**lyre** [laɪr] s lira
**lyric** [ˈlɪrɪk] adj lirico ‖ s lirica; (words of a song) parole fpl
**lyrical** [ˈlɪrɪkəl] adj lirico
**lyricism** [ˈlɪrɪ ˌsɪzəm] s lirismo
**lyricist** [ˈlɪrɪsɪst] s (writer of words for songs) paroliere m; (poet) lirico

# M

**M, m** [em] s tredicesima lettera dell'alfabeto inglese
**ma'am** [mæm] or [mɑm] s (coll) signora
**macadam** [məˈkædəm] s macadàm m
**macadamize** [məˈkædə ˌmaɪz] tr macadamizzare
**macaroni** [ ˌmækəˈroni] s maccheroni mpl
**macaroon** [ ˌmækəˈrun] s amaretto
**macaw** [məˈkɔ] s ara
**mace** [mes] s mazza; (spice) macis m & f
**mace' bear'er** s mazziere m
**machination** [ ˌmækɪˈneʃən] s macchinazione, macchina
**machine** [məˈʃin] s macchina ‖ tr fare a macchina
**machine' gun'** s mitragliatrice f
**machine'-gun'** v (pret & pp -gunned; ger -gunning) tr mitragliare
**machine'-made'** adj fatto a macchina

**machiner·y** [mə'ʃinəri] *s* (**-ies**) macchinario, meccanismo
**machine' screw'** *s* vite *f* per metallo
**machine' shop'** *s* officina meccanica
**machine' tool'** *s* macchina utensile
**machinist** [mə'ʃinɪst] *s* meccanico; (nav) secondo macchinista
**mackerel** ['mækərəl] *s* maccarello
**mack'erel sky'** *s* cielo a pecorelle
**mackintosh** ['mækɪn‚taʃ] *s* impermeabile *m*
**mad** [mæd] *adj* (**madder; maddest**) (*angry; rabid*) arrabbiato; (*insane; foolish*) pazzo, folle; furioso; **to be mad about** (coll) andar pazzo per; **to drive mad** far impazzire; **to go mad** impazzire; (*said of a dog*) diventare idrofobo
**madam** ['mædəm] *s* signora
**mad'cap'** *s* mattoide *m*, rompicollo
**madden** ['mædən] *tr* (*to make angry*) inferocire; (*to make insane*) fare impazzire
**made-to-order** ['medtə'ɔrdər] *adj* fatto apposta; (*clothing*) fatto su misura
**made'-up'** *adj* inventato; (*using cosmetics*) truccato
**mad'house'** *s* manicomio
**mad'man'** *s* (**-men'**) pazzo
**madness** ['mædnɪs] *s* rabbia; pazzia
**Madonna lily** [mə'dɑnə] *s* giglio
**maelstrom** ['melstrəm] *s* vortice *m*
**magazine** ['mægə‚zin] or [‚mægə'zin] *s* (*periodical*) rivista, giornale *m*; (*warehouse*) magazzino; (*for cartridges*) caricatore *m*; (*for powder*) polveriera; (naut) santabarbara; (phot) magazzino
**maggot** ['mægət] *s* larva di dittero
**Magi** ['medʒaɪ] *spl* Re Magi
**magic** ['mædʒɪk] *adj* magico ‖ *s* magia; illusionismo; **as if by magic** come per incanto
**magician** [mə'dʒɪʃən] *s* (*entertainer*) illusionista *mf*; (*sorcerer*) mago
**magistrate** ['mædʒɪs‚tret] *s* magistrato
**magnanimous** [mæg'nænɪməs] *adj* magnanimo
**magnesium** [mæg'niʃɪ·əm] or [mæg-'niʒɪ·əm] *s* magnesio
**magnet** ['mægnɪt] *s* calamita, magnete *m*
**magnetic** [mæg'nɛtɪk] *adj* magnetico
**magnetism** ['mægnɪ‚tɪzəm] *s* magnetismo
**magnetize** ['mægnɪ‚taɪz] *tr* calamitare, magnetizzare
**magne·to** [mæg'nito] *s* (**-tos**) magnete *m*
**magnificent** [mæg'nɪfɪsənt] *adj* magnifico
**magni·fy** ['mægnɪ‚faɪ] *v* (*pret & pp* **-fied**) *tr* ingrandire; (*to exaggerate*) magnificare
**mag'nifying glass'** *s* lente *f* d'ingrandimento
**magnitude** ['mægnɪ‚tjud] or ['mægnɪ‚tud] *s* grandezza
**magpie** ['mæg‚paɪ] *s* gazza
**mahlstick** ['mɑl‚stɪk] or ['mɔl‚stɪk] *s* appoggiamano
**mahoga·ny** [mə'hɑgəni] *s* (**-nies**) mogano

**Mahomet** [mə'hɑmɪt] *s* Maometto
**maid** [med] *s* (*girl*) ragazza; (*servant*) cameriera, domestica
**maiden** ['medən] *s* pulzella
**maid'en·hair'** *s* (bot) capelvenere *m*
**maid'en·head'** *s* imene *m*
**maidenhood** ['medən‚hud] *s* verginità *f*
**maid'en la'dy** *s* zitella
**maid'en name'** *s* nome *m* da signorina
**maid'en voy'age** *s* viaggio inaugurale
**maid'-in-wait'ing** *s* (**maids-in-waiting**) (*of a princess*) damigella d'onore; (*of a queen*) dama d'onore
**maid' of hon'or** *s* (*attendant at a wedding; attendant of a princess*) damigella d'onore; (*attendant of a queen*) dama d'onore
**maid'serv'ant** *s* domestica, ancella
**mail** [mel] *s* posta; (*of armor*) maglia; **by return mail** a volta di corriere ‖ *tr* impostare
**mail'bag'** *s* sacco postale
**mail'boat'** *s* battello postale
**mail'box'** *s* cassetta or buca delle lettere
**mail' car'** *s* vagone *m* postale
**mail' car'rier** *s* postino, portalettere *m*
**mail'ing list'** *s* indirizzario
**mail'ing per'mit** *s* abbonamento postale
**mail'man'** *s* (**-men'**) portalettere *m*
**mail' or'der** *s* ordinazione per corrispondenza
**mail'-order house'** *s* ditta che fa affari unicamente per corrispondenza
**mail'plane'** *s* areoplano postale
**mail' train'** *s* treno postale
**maim** [mem] *tr* mutilare
**main** [men] *adj* principale, maggiore ‖ *s* condotta principale; **in the main** principalmente, per lo più
**main' clause'** *s* proposizione principale
**main' course'** *s* piatto forte
**main' deck'** *s* ponte *m* principale
**mainland** ['men‚lænd] or ['menlənd] *s* terra ferma, continente *m*
**main' line'** *s* (rr) linea principale
**mainly** ['menli] *adv* principalmente
**mainmast** ['menməst], ['men‚mæst] or ['men‚mɑst] *s* albero maestro
**mainsail** ['mensəl] or ['men‚sel] *s* vela maestra
**main'spring'** *s* molla motrice; (fig) molla
**main'stay'** *s* (naut) strallo di maestra; (fig) cardine *m*
**main' street'** *s* strada principale
**maintain** [men'ten] *tr* mantenere
**maintenance** ['mentɪnəns] *s* mantenimento; (*upkeep*) manutenzione
**maître d'hôtel** [‚metər do'tɛl] *s* (*butler*) maggiordomo; (*headwaiter*) capocameriere *m*
**maize** [mez] *s* mais *m*
**majestic** [mə'dʒɛstɪk] *adj* maestoso
**majes·ty** ['mædʒɪsti] *s* (**-ties**) maestà *f*
**major** ['medʒər] *adj* maggiore ‖ *s* (educ) specializzazione; (mil) maggiore *m* ‖ *intr* (educ) specializzarsi
**major·do·mo** [‚medʒər'domo] *s* (**-mos**) maggiordomo
**ma'jor gen'eral** *s* generale *m* di divisione

**majori•ty** [mə'dʒɑrıtı] or [mə'dʒɔrıtı]
*adj* maggioritario ‖ *s* (**-ties**) (*being
of full age*) maggiore età *f;* (*larger
number or part*) maggioranza; (mil)
grado di maggiore
**make** [mek] *s* (*brand*) marca; (*form*)
stile *m;* produzione; **on the make**
(slang) tirando l'acqua al proprio
mulino ‖ *v* (*pret & pp* **made** [med])
*tr* fare; (*a train*) pigliare; (*a circuit*)
chiudere; essere, e.g., **she will make
a good typist** sarà una buona dattilo-
grafa; **to make** + *inf* fare + *inf*, e.g.,
**she made him study** lo fece studiare;
**to make into** trasformare in; **to make
known** far sapere; **to make of** pensare di; **to make oneself known**
darsi a conoscere; **to make out** decifrare; (*a prescription*) scrivere, preparare; (*a check*) riempire; **to make
over** convertire; (com) trasferire; **to
make up** preparare, comporre; (*a
story*) inventare; (*lost time*) riguadagnare; (typ) impaginare; (theat) truccare ‖ *intr* essere fatto; **to make
away with** rubare; disfarsi di; **to
make believe that** + *ind* far finta di +
*inf*, e.g., **he made believe (that) he
was sleeping** fece finta di dormire;
**to make for** avvicinarsi a; attaccare;
(*better relations*) contribuire a cementare; **to make much of** (coll)
fare le feste a; **to make off** andarsene; **to make off with** svignarsela
con; **to make out** (coll) farcela; **to
make toward** incamminarsi verso; **to
make up** truccarsi; fare la pace; **to
make up for** compensare per, supplire a; **to make up to** (coll) ingraziarsi; (coll) fare la corte a
**make'-be•lieve'** *adj* immaginario ‖ *s*
finzione, sembianza
**maker** ['mekər] *s* fabbricante *mf*, costruttore *m* ‖ **Maker** *s* Fattore *m*
**make'shift'** *adj* improvvisato, di fortuna ‖ *s* espediente *m*, ripiego; (*person*) tappabuchi *mf*
**make'-up'** *s* composizione, costituzione;
truccatura, cosmetico; (typ) impagi-
nazione; (journ) caratteristica
**make'-up man'** *s* truccatore *m*
**make'-up test'** *s* esame *m* di riparazione
**make'weight'** *s* giunta, contentino; (fig)
supplemento, di più *m*
**making** ['mekıŋ] *s* fabbricazione; costituzione; causa del successo; **mak•
ings** materiale *m;* (*potential*) stoffa
**maladjusted** [ˌmælə'dʒʌstıd] *adj* spostato
**mala•dy** ['mælədi] *s* (**-dies**) malattia
**malaise** [mæ'lez] *s* malessere *m*
**malapropos** [ˌmæləprə'po] *adj* inopportuno ‖ *adv* a sproposito
**malaria** [mə'lɛrɪ•ə] *s* malaria
**Malay** ['mele] or [mə'le] *adj & s*
malese *mf*
**malcontent** ['mælkən ˌtɛnt] *adj & s*
malcontento
**male** [mel] *adj & s* maschio
**malediction** [ˌmælı'dıkʃən] *s* maledi-
zione
**malefactor** ['mælı ˌfæktər] *s* malfattore
*m*

**male' nurse'** *s* infermiere *m*
**malevolent** [mə'lɛvələnt] *adj* malevolo
**malfeasance** [mæl'fizəns] *s* reato di
pubblico funzionario
**malice** ['mælıs] *s* malizia; (law) dolo;
**to bear malice** serbar rancore; **with
malice prepense** (law) con premeditazione
**malicious** [mə'lıʃəs] *adj* malizioso,
maligno
**malign** [mə'laın] *adj* maligno ‖ *tr*
calunniare
**malignan•cy** [mə'lıgnənsi] *s* (**-cies**)
malignità *f;* (pathol) malignità *f*
**malignant** [mə'lıgnənt] *adj* maligno
**maligni•ty** [mə'lıgnıti] *s* (**-ties**) malignità *f*
**malinger** [mə'lıŋgər] *intr* fingersi ammalato, darsi malato (per sottrarsi al
proprio dovere)
**mall** [mɔl] or [mæl] *s* viale *m;* (*strip
of land in a boulevard*) aiola
**mallet** ['mælıt] *s* maglio; (*of a stone
cutter*) mazzuolo
**mallow** ['mælo] *s* malva
**malnutrition** [ˌmælnju'trıʃən] or
[ˌmælnu'trıʃən] *s* malnutrizione
**malodorous** [mæl'odərəs] *adj* puzzolente
**malpractice** [mæl'præktıs] *s* incuria,
negligenza; (*of physician or lawyer*)
negligenza colposa
**malt** [mɔlt] *s* malto
**maltreat** [mæl'trit] *tr* maltrattare
**mamma** [ˈmɑmə] or [mə'mɑ] *s* (coll)
mamma
**mammal** ['mæməl] *s* mammifero
**mammalian** [mæ'melɪ•ən] *adj & s*
mammifero
**mammoth** ['mæməθ] *adj* mastodontico
‖ *s* mammut *m*
**man** [mæn] *s* (**men** [mɛn]) uomo; (*in
chess*) pedina; (*in checkers*) pezzo; **a
man** uno, e.g., **a man can get lost in
this town** uno può perdersi in questa
città; **as one man** come un sol uomo;
**man alive!** accidenti!; **man and wife**
marito e moglie; **to be one's own
man** essere completamente indipendente ‖ *v* (*pret & pp* **manned;** *ger*
**manning**) *tr* (*a boat*) equipaggiare; (*a
fortress*) guarnire; (*a cannon*) maneggiare
**man' about town'** *s* vitaiolo
**manacle** ['mænəkəl] *s*—**manacles** manette *fpl* ‖ *tr* ammanettare
**manage** ['mænıdʒ] *tr* (*a business*) gestire; (*e.g., a tool*) maneggiare ‖
*intr* sbrogliarsela; **to manage to** fare
in modo di; ingegnarsi a; **to manage
to get along** barcamenarsi
**manageable** ['mænıdʒəbəl] *adj* maneggevole
**management** ['mænıdʒmənt] *s* direzione, gestione; (*executives collectively*) classe *f* dirigente; direzione;
(*college course*) economia aziendale
**manager** ['mænədʒər] *s* direttore *m*,
gerente *mf;* (theat) impresario;
(sports) procuratore *m*, manager *m*
**managerial** [ˌmænə'dʒırı•əl] *adj* diret-
toriale, imprenditoriale

**man'aging ed'itor** s gerente m responsabile, redattore m in capo

**mandate** ['mændet] s mandato ‖ tr dare in mandato a

**mandatory** ['mændə,tori] adj obbligatorio

**mandolin** ['mændəlɪn] s mandolino

**mandrake** ['mændrek] s mandragola

**mandrel** ['mændrəl] s (mach) mandrino

**mane** [men] s criniera

**maneuver** [mə'nuvər] s manovra ‖ tr manovrare ‖ intr manovrare; (aer, nav) evoluire; (fig) intrigare

**manful** ['mænfəl] adj maschile, risoluto

**manganese** ['mæŋgə,nis] or ['mæŋgə,niz] s manganese m

**mange** [mendʒ] s rogna

**manger** ['mendʒər] s presepio

**mangle** ['mæŋgəl] tr straziare, lacerare

**man·gy** ['mendʒi] adj (-gier; -giest) rognoso; (squalid) misero

**man'han'dle** tr malmenare, maltrattare

**man'hole'** s passo d'uomo, pozzetto

**manhood** ['mænhʊd] s virilità f; uomini mpl, umanità f

**man'hunt'** s caccia all'uomo

**mania** ['meni·ə] s mania

**maniac** ['meni,æk] adj & s maniaco

**manicure** ['mæni,kjur] s (treatment) manicure f; (manicurist) manicure mf ‖ tr (a person) curare le mani di; (the hands) curare

**manicurist** ['mæni,kjurɪst] s manicurista mf, manicure mf

**manifest** ['mæni,fɛst] adj manifesto ‖ s (naut) manifesto di carico ‖ tr manifestare

**manifes·to** [,mæni'fɛsto] s (-toes) manifesto

**manifold** ['mæni,fold] adj molteplice ‖ s copia; carta velina; (aut, mach) collettore m

**manikin** ['mænikɪn] s manichino; (dwarf) nano

**man' in the moon'** s faccia di uomo che appare nella luna piena

**man' in the street'** s uomo qualunque, uomo della strada

**manipulate** [mə'nɪpjə,let] tr manipolare

**man'kind'** s genere umano ‖ **man'kind'** s il sesso maschile

**manliness** ['mænlɪnɪs] s virilità f

**man·ly** ['mænli] adj (-lier; -liest) maschio, virile

**manned' space'ship** s astronave pilotata

**mannequin** ['mænikɪn] s (figure) manichino; (person) indossatrice f

**manner** ['mænər] s maniera; **by all manner of means** in tutti i modi; **in a manner of speaking** in una certa maniera; **in the manner of** alla moda di; **manners** maniere, fpl, educazione; **to the manner born** avvezzo sin dalla nascita

**mannish** ['mænɪʃ] adj maschile; (woman) mascolino

**man' of God'** s santo; profeta m; (priest) uomo al servizio di Dio

**man' of let'ters** s letterato

**man' of means'** s uomo danaroso

**man' of parts'** s uomo di talento

**man' of straw'** s uomo di paglia

**man' of the world'** s uomo di mondo

**man-of-war** [,mænəv'wɔr] s (men-of-war [,mɛnəv'wɔr] nave f da guerra

**manor** ['mænər] s maniero; feudo

**man'or house'** s maniero, palazzo

**man' o'verboard** interj uomo in mare!

**man'pow'er** s manodopera; (mil) effettivo

**mansard** ['mænsɑrd] s mansarda

**man'serv'ant** s (men'serv'ants) servo, servitore m

**mansion** ['mænʃən] s palazzo, palazzina; (manor house) maniero

**man'slaugh'ter** s omicidio colposo

**mantel** ['mæntəl] s parte f anteriore dei pilastri del camino; (shelf above it) mensola

**man'tel·piece'** s mensola del camino

**man'tis shrimp'** ['mæntɪs] s canocchia

**mantle** ['mæntəl] s mantello, cappa ‖ tr ammantare; (to conceal) nascondere ‖ intr (to blush) arrossire

**manual** ['mænjʊ·əl] adj manuale ‖ s (book) manuale m; (mil) esercizio; (mus) tastiera d'organo

**man'ual train'ing** s istruzione nelle arti e mestieri

**manufacture** [,mænjə'fæktjər] s fabbricazione; (thing manufactured) manufatto ‖ tr fabbricare

**manufacturer** [,mænjə'fæktjərər] s fabbricante mf, industriale m

**manure** [mə'njur] or [mə'nur] s letame m ‖ tr concimare

**manuscript** ['mænjə,skrɪpt] adj & s manoscritto

**many** ['mɛni] adj & pron molti; **a good many** or **a great many** un buon numero; **as many . . . as** tanti . . . quanti; **as many as** fino a, e.g., **they sell as many as five thousand dozen** vendono fino a cinquemila dozzine; **how many** quanti; **many a** molti, e.g., **many a day** molti giorni; **many another** molti altri; **many more** molti di più; **so many** tanti; **too many** troppi; **twice as many** altrettanti, il doppio

**many-sided** ['mɛni,saɪdɪd] adj multilaterale; versatile

**map** [mæp] s mappa; (of a city) piano ‖ v (pret & pp mapped; ger mapping) tr tracciare la mappa di; mostrare sulla mappa; **to map out** fare il piano di

**maple** ['mepəl] s acero

**maquette** [mɑ'ket] s plastico

**mar** [mɑr] v (pret & pp marred; ger marring) tr deturpare, sfigurare

**maraud** [mə'rɔd] tr & intr predare

**marauder** [mə'rɔdər] s predone m

**marble** ['mɑrbəl] adj marmoreo ‖ s marmo; (little ball of glass) bilia; **marbles** bilie fpl; **to lose one's marbles** (slang) mancare una rotella a qlcu ‖ tr marmorizzare

**march** [mɑrtʃ] s marcia; (hist) marca; **to steal a march on** guadagnare il vantaggio su ‖ *tr* far marciare ‖ *intr* marciare ‖ **March** *s* marzo

**marchioness** [ˈmɑrʃənɪs] *s* marchesa

**mare** [mɛr] *s (female horse)* cavalla; *(female donkey)* asina

**margarine** [ˈmɑrdʒərɪn] *s* margarina

**margin** [ˈmɑrdʒɪn] *s* margine *m;* (econ) scoperto

**mar'gin stop'** *s* marginatore *m*

**marigold** [ˈmæri ˌgold] *s* fiorrancio

**marihuana** or **marijuana** [ ˌmɑri-ˈhwɑnə] *s* marijuana

**marina** [məˈrinə] *s* porto turistico di imbarcazioni, porticciolo turistico

**marinate** [ˈmæri ˌnet] *tr* marinare

**marine** [məˈrin] *adj* marino, marittimo ‖ *s* marina; soldato di fanteria da sbarco; **marines** fanteria da sbarco; **tell that to the marines!** (coll) va a raccontarlo ai frati!

**mariner** [ˈmærɪnər] *s* marinaio

**marionette** [ ˌmæri-əˈnɛt] *s* marionetta

**mar'ital sta'tus** [ˈmærɪtəl] *s* stato civile

**maritime** [ˈmærɪ ˌtaɪm] *adj* marittimo

**marjoram** [ˈmɑrdʒərəm] *s* origano; *(sweet marjoram)* maggiorana

**mark** [mɑrk] *s* segno; *(brand)* marca; *(of punctuation)* punto; *(in an examination)* voto; *(sign made by illiterate person)* croce *f; (landmark)* segnale *m; (target)* bersaglio; *(spot)* macchia; *(starting point in a race)* linea di partenza; *(of confidence)* voto; *(coin)* marco; impronta; **to be beside the mark** essere fuori del seminato; **to hit the mark** colpire il bersaglio; **to leave one's mark** lasciare la propria impronta; **to make one's mark** raggiungere il successo; **to miss the mark** fallire il colpo; **to toe the mark** mettersi in fila; filare diritto ‖ *tr* marcare, segnare, contrassegnare; *(a student)* dar il voto a; *(a test)* esaminare; improntare; notare, avvertire; **to mark down** mettere in iscritto; ribassare il prezzo di

**mark'down'** *s* riduzione di prezzo

**market** [ˈmɑrkɪt] *s* mercato; **to bear the market** giocare al ribasso; **to bull the market** giocare al rialzo; **to play the market** giocare in borsa; **to put on the market** lanciare sul mercato ‖ *tr* mettere sul mercato

**marketable** [ˈmɑrkɪtəbəl] *adj* commerciabile, vendibile

**marketing** [ˈmɑrkɪtɪŋ] *s* compravendita; marketing *m*

**mar'ket•place'** *s* piazza del mercato

**mar'ket price'** *s* prezzo corrente

**mark'ing gauge'** [ˈmɑrkɪŋ] *s* graffietto

**marks'man** *s* (-men) tiratore *m;* **a good marksman** un tiratore scelto

**marksmanship** [ˈmɑrksmən ˌʃɪp] *s* qualità *f* di tiratore scelto

**mark'up'** *s* margine *m* di rivendita

**marl** [mɑrl] *s* marna ‖ *tr* marnare

**marmalade** [ˈmɑrmə ˌled] *s* marmellata d'arance

**marmot** [ˈmɑrmət] *s* marmotta

**maroon** [məˈrun] *adj* & *s* marrone *m* ‖ *tr* abbandonare *(in un luogo deserto)*

**marquee** [mɑrˈki] *s* pensilina

**marquess** [ˈmɑrkwɪs] *s* marchese *m*

**marque•try** [ˈmɑrkətri] *s* (-tries) intarsio

**marquis** [ˈmɑrkwɪs] *s* marchese *m*

**marquise** [mɑrˈkiz] *s* marchesa; (Brit) pensilina

**marriage** [ˈmærɪdʒ] *s* matrimonio

**marriageable** [ˈmærɪdʒəbəl] *adj* adatto al matrimonio; *(woman)* nubile

**mar'riage por'tion** *s* dote *f*

**mar'riage rate'** *s* nuzialità *f*

**mar'ried life'** *s* vita coniugale

**marrow** [ˈmæro] *s* midollo

**mar•ry** [ˈmæri] *v (pret & pp -ried) tr* sposare; **to get married to** sposarsi con ‖ *intr* sposarsi; **to marry into** *(e.g., a noble family)* imparentarsi con; **to marry the second time** risposarsi

**Mars** [mɑrz] *s* Marte *m*

**Marseilles** [mɑrˈselz] *s* Marsiglia

**marsh** [mɑrʃ] *s* palude *f*, lama

**mar•shal** [ˈmɑrʃəl] *s* direttore *m* di una sfilata; maestro di cerimonie; (mil) maresciallo; (U.S.A.) ufficiale *m* di giustizia ‖ *v (pret & pp -shaled or -shalled; ger -shaling or -shalling) tr* introdurre cerimoniosamente; mettere in buon ordine

**marsh' mal'low** *s* (bot) altea

**marsh'mal'low** *s* dolce *m* di gelatina e zucchero

**marsh•y** [ˈmɑrʃi] *adj* (-ier; -iest) paludoso, palustre

**marten** [ˈmɑrtən] *s (Martes martes)* martora; *(Martes zibellina)* zibellino

**martial** [ˈmɑrʃəl] *adj* marziale

**mar'tial law'** *s* legge *f* marziale

**Martian** [ˈmɑrʃən] *adj* & *s* marziano

**martin** [ˈmɑrtɪn] *s* rondicchio

**martinet** [ ˌmɑrtɪˈnɛt] or [ˈmɑrtɪ ˌnɛt] *s* pignolo

**martyr** [ˈmɑrtər] *s* martire *mf*

**martyrdom** [ˈmɑrtərdəm] *s* martirio

**mar•vel** [ˈmɑrvəl] *s* meraviglia ‖ *v (pret & pp -veled or -velled; ger -veling or -velling) intr* meravigliarsi; **to marvel at** stupirsi di, meravigliarsi di

**marvelous** [ˈmɑrvələs] *adj* meraviglioso

**Marxist** [ˈmɑrksɪst] *adj* & *s* marxista *mf*

**mascara** [mæsˈkærə] *s* bistro, rimmel *m*

**mascot** [ˈmæskət] *s* mascotte *f*

**masculine** [ˈmæskjəlɪn] *adj* & *s* maschile *m*

**mash** [mæʃ] *s (crushed mass)* poltiglia; *(to form wort)* decotto d'orzo germinato; *(e.g., for poultry)* intriso ‖ *tr* schiacciare; impastare

**mashed' pota'toes** *spl* purè *m* di patate

**masher** [ˈmæʃər] *s* utensile *m* per schiacciare; (slang) pappagallo

**mask** [mæsk] or [mɑsk] *s* maschera; (phot) mascherina ‖ *tr* mascherare; (phot) mettere una mascherina a ‖ *intr* mascherarsi

**masked' ball'** *s* ballo in maschera

**mason** [ˈmesən] *s* muratore *m* ‖ **Mason** *s* massone *m*

**mason•ry** [ˈmesənri] *s* (-ries) arte *f* del

muratore; muratura ‖ **Masonry** *s* massoneria

**masquerade** [ˌmæskəˈred] or [ˌmɑskəˈred] *s* mascherata; *(disguise)* maschera; *(pretense)* finzione ‖ *intr* mascherarsi; **to masquerade as** mascherarsi da; farsi passare per

**mass** [mæs] *s* massa; *(celebration of the Eucharist)* messa; **in the mass** nell'insieme; **the masses** le masse ‖ *tr* ammassare ‖ *intr* ammassarsi, accumularsi

**massacre** [ˈmæsəkər] *s* massacro, strage *f* ‖ *tr* massacrare, trucidare

**massage** [məˈsɑʒ] *s* massaggio ‖ *tr* massaggiare

**masseur** [mæˈsœr] *s* massaggiatore *m*

**masseuse** [mæˈsœz] *s* massaggiatrice *f*

**massive** [ˈmæsɪv] *adj* massiccio; *(e.g., dose)* massivo; solido

**mass′ me′dia** [ˈmidɪ·ə] *s* mezzi *mpl* di comunicazione di massa

**mass′ meet′ing** *s* assemblea popolare; adunanza in massa

**mass′ produc′tion** *s* produzione in serie

**mast** [mæst] or [mɑst] *s* *(post)* palo; (agr) ghiande *fpl*, faggiole *fpl;* (naut) albero; **before the mast** come marinaio semplice

**master** [ˈmæstər] or [ˈmɑstər] *s* *(employer)* padrone *m*; *(male head of household)* capo di casa; *(man who possesses some special skill)* maestro; *(title of respect for a boy)* signorino; (naut) capitano ‖ *tr* dominare; *(a language)* possedere

**mas′ter bed′room** *s* camera da letto padronale

**mas′ter blade′** *s* foglia maestra (di una balestra)

**mas′ter build′er** *s* capomastro

**masterful** [ˈmæstərfəl] or [ˈmɑstərfəl] *adj* autoritario; provetto, magistrale

**mas′ter key′** *s* chiave maestra

**masterly** [ˈmæstərli] or [ˈmɑstərli] *adj* magistrale ‖ *adv* magistralmente

**mas′ter mechan′ic** *s* mastro meccanico

**mas′ter·mind′** *s* mente direttiva ‖ *tr* organizzare, dirigere

**mas′ter of cer′emonies** *s* maestro di cerimonia; *(in a night club, radio, etc.)* presentatore *m*

**mas′ter·piece′** *s* capolavoro

**mas′ter ser′geant** *s* (mil) sergente *m* maggiore

**mas′ter stroke′** *s* colpo da maestro

**mas′ter·work′** *s* capolavoro

**master·y** [ˈmæstəri] or [ˈmɑstəri] *s* (-ies) *(command of a subject)* dominio; *(skill)* maestria

**mast′head′** *s* (journ) titolo; (naut) testa d'albero

**masticate** [ˈmæstɪˌket] *tr* masticare

**mastiff** [ˈmæstɪf] or [ˈmɑstɪf] *s* mastino

**masturbate** [ˈmæstərˌbet] *tr* masturbare ‖ *intr* masturbarsi

**mat** [mæt] *s* *(for floor)* tappeto, stuoia; *(under a dish)* tondo, sottocoppa, centrino; *(before a door)* stoino, zerbino; *(around a picture)* bordo di cartone; (sports) materas-

síno; (typ) flan *m;* flano ‖ *v (pret & pp* **matted;** *ger* **matting)** *tr* coprire di stuoie; arruffare ‖ *intr* arruffarsi

**match** [mætʃ] *s (counterpart)* uguale *m;* *(suitably associated pair)* paio; *(light)* fiammifero; *(wick)* miccia; *(prospective mate)* partito; (sports) partita, gara; **to be a match for** essere pari a, fare fronte a; **to meet one's match** trovare un degno rivale ‖ *tr* uguagliare, pareggiare; *(colors)* combinare; *(in pairs)* appaiare; giocarsi, e.g., **to match s.o. for the drinks** giocarsi le bevande con qlcu ‖ *intr* corrispondersi, fare il paio

**match′box′** *s* scatola di fiammiferi; *(of wax matches)* scatola di cerini

**matchless** [ˈmætʃlɪs] *adj* incomparabile, senza pari

**match′mak′er** *s* paraninfo

**mate** [met] *s* compagno; *(husband or wife)* consorte *mf*; *(to a female)* maschio; *(to a male)* femmina; (chess) scacco matto; (naut) primo ufficiale ‖ *tr* appaiare; (chess) dar scacco matto a; **to be well mated** esser ben appaiato ‖ *intr* accoppiarsi

**material** [məˈtɪrɪ·əl] *adj* materiale; importante ‖ *s* materiale *m*, materia; *(cloth, fabric)* tela, stoffa; **materials** occorrente *m*

**materialist** [məˈtɪrɪ·əlɪst] *s* materialista *mf*

**materialize** [məˈtɪrɪ·əˌlaɪz] *intr* materializzarsi

**matériel** [məˌtɪrɪˈel] *s* materiale *m;* materiale bellico

**maternal** [məˈtʌrnəl] *adj* materno

**maternity** [məˈtʌrnɪti] *s* maternità *f*

**mater′nity ward′** *s* maternità *f*

**mathematical** [ˌmæθɪˈmætɪkəl] *adj* matematico

**mathematician** [ˌmæθɪməˈtɪʃən] *s* matematico

**mathematics** [ˌmæθɪˈmætɪks] *s* matematica

**matinée** [ˌmætɪˈne] *s* mattinata, diurna

**mat′ing sea′son** *s* calore *m*

**matins** [ˈmætɪnz] *spl* mattutino

**matriarch** [ˈmetrɪˌɑrk] *s* matrona dignitosa; donna che possiede l'autorità matriarcale

**matricidal** [ˌmetrɪˈsaɪdəl] or [ˌmætrɪˈsaɪdəl] *adj* matricida

**matricide** [ˈmetrɪˌsaɪd] or [ˈmætrɪˌsaɪd] *s* *(act)* matricidio; *(person)* matricida *mf*

**matriculate** [məˈtrɪkjəˌlet] *tr* immatricolare ‖ *intr* immatricolarsi

**matriculation** [məˌtrɪkjəˈleʃən] *s* immatricolazione, iscrizione

**matrimonial** [ˌmætrɪˈmoni·əl] *adj* matrimoniale

**matrimo·ny** [ˈmætrɪˌmoni] *s* (-nies) matrimonio

**ma·trix** [ˈmetrɪks] or [ˈmætrɪks] *s* (-trices[ trɪˌsiz] or -trixes) matrice *f*

**matron** [ˈmetrən] *s* matrona; direttrice *f;* guardiana

**matronly** [ˈmetrənli] *adj* matronale

**matter** [ˈmætər] *s (physical substance)* materia; *(pus)* materia; *(affair, busi-*

*ness*) faccenda; (*material of a book*) contenuto; (*reason*) motivo; (*copy for printer*) manoscritto; (*printed material*) stampati *mpl;* **a matter of** un caso di; **for that matter** per quanto riguarda ciò; **in the matter** al soggetto; **no matter** non importa; **no matter how** non importa come; **no matter when** non importa quando; **no matter where** non importa dove; **what is the matter?** cosa succede?; **what is the matter with you?** cosa ha? || *intr* importare

**mat′ter of course′** *s*—**as a matter of course** come se nulla fosse, come se fosse una cosa naturale

**mat′ter of fact′** *s*—**as a matter of fact** in realtà, a onor del vero

**matter-of-fact** [ˈmætərəvˌfækt] *adj* prosaico, pratico

**mattock** [ˈmætək] *s* piccone *m*

**mattress** [ˈmætrɪs] *s* materasso

**mature** [məˈtʃʊr] *or* [məˈtʊr] *adj* maturo; (*due*) scaduto || *tr* maturare || *intr* maturare; (*com*) scadere

**maturity** [məˈtʃʊrɪti] *or* [məˈtʊrɪti] *s* maturità *f;* (*com*) scadenza

**maudlin** [ˈmɔdlɪn] *adj* sentimentale, lagrimoso; piagnucoloso e ubriaco

**maul** [mɔl] *tr* maltrattare, bistrattare

**maulstick** [ˈmɔlˌstɪk] *s* appoggiamano

**maundy** [ˈmɔndi] *s* lavanda

**Maun′dy Thurs′day** *s* giovedì santo

**mausole·um** [ˌmɔsəˈli·əm] *s* (**-ums** *or* **-a** [ə]) mausoleo

**maw** [mɔ] *s* (*e.g., of a hog*) stomaco; (*of carnivorous mammal*) fauci *fpl;* (*of fowl*) gozzo; (fig) bocca, fauci *fpl*

**mawkish** [ˈmɔkɪʃ] *adj* (*sickening*) nauseante; (*sentimental*) svenevole

**maxim** [ˈmæksɪm] *s* massima

**maximum** [ˈmæksɪməm] *adj* & *s* massimo

**may** [me] *v aux*—**it may be** può essere; **may I come in?** si può?; **may you be happy!** possa tu essere felice! || **May** *s* maggio

**maybe** [ˈmebi] *adv* forse

**May′ Day′** *s* primo maggio; festa della primavera; (hist) calendimaggio (*in Florence*)

**mayhem** [ˈmehɛm] *or* [ˈme·əm] *s* mutilazione dolosa

**mayonnaise** [ˌme·əˈnez] *s* maionese *f*

**mayor** [ˈme·ər] *or* [mɛr] *s* sindaco

**mayoress** [ˈme·ərɪs] *or* [ˈmɛrɪs] *s* donna sindaco

**May′pole′** *s* maio, maggio, palo per le danze di calendimaggio

**May′pole dance′** *s* ballo figurato con nastri per la festa di primavera

**May′ queen′** *s* reginetta di maggio

**maze** [mez] *s* dedalo, labirinto

**me** [mi] *pron* me; mi; **to me** mi; **a me**

**meadow** [ˈmɛdo] *s* prato

**mead′ow·land′** *s* prateria

**meager** [ˈmigər] *adj* magro

**meal** [mil] *s* (*food*) pasto; (*unbolted grain*) farina

**meal′time′** *s* ora del pasto

**mean** [min] *adj* (*intermediate*) medio;

(*low in rank*) basso, umile; (*shabby*) misero; (*of poor quality*) inferiore; (*stingy*) taccagno; (*nasty*) villano; (*vicious, as a horse*) intrattabile; (coll) indisposto; (coll) vergognoso; (slang) splendido; **no mean** eccellente || *s* media, termine medio; **by all means** certamente, senza dubbio; **by means of** per mezzo di; **by no means** in nessuna maniera; **means** beni *mpl;* (*agency*) mezzo, maniera; **to live on one's means** vivere di rendita || *v* (*pret* & *pp* **meant** [mɛnt]) *tr* significare, voler dire; **to mean to** pensare || *intr*—**to mean well** aver buone intenzioni

**meander** [mɪˈændər] *s* meandro || *intr* serpeggiare, vagare

**meaning** [ˈminɪŋ] *s* senso, significato

**meaningful** [ˈminɪŋfəl] *adj* significativo

**meaningless** [ˈminɪŋlɪs] *adj* senza senso, senza significato

**meanness** [ˈminnɪs] *s* viltà *f*, bassezza; (*stinginess*) meschinità *f;* (*lowliness*) umiltà *f*, povertà *f*

**mean′time′** *s*—**in the meantime** nel frattempo || *adv* frattanto, intanto

**mean′while′** *s* & *adv* var of **meantime**

**measles** [ˈmizəlz] *s* morbillo; (*German measles*) rosolia

**mea·sly** [ˈmizli] *adj* (**-slier; -sliest**) col morbillo; (coll) miserabile

**measurable** [ˈmɛʒərəbəl] *adj* misurabile

**measure** [ˈmɛʒər] *s* misura; (*legislative bill*) progetto di legge; (mus) battuta; **in a measure** in un certo senso; **to take the measure of** prendere le misure di; giudicare accuratamente || *tr* misurare; (*a distance*) percorrere; **to measure out** somministrare || *intr* misurare; **to measure up to** essere all'altezza di

**measurement** [ˈmɛʒərmənt] *s* misura; **to take s.o.'s measurements** prendere le misure di qlcu

**meas′uring cup′** *s* vetro graduato

**meat** [mit] *s* carne *f;* (*food in general*) cibo; (*of nut*) gheriglio; (fig) sostanza, midollo

**meat′ball′** *s* polpetta

**meat′ grind′er** *s* tritacarne *m*

**meat′ loaf′** *s* polpettone *m*

**meat′ mar′ket** *s* macelleria

**meat·y** [ˈmiti] *adj* (**-ier; -iest**) carnoso, polputo; (fig) sostanzioso

**Mecca** [ˈmɛkə] *s* la Mecca; **the Mecca** (fig) la Mecca

**mechanic** [mɪˈkænɪk] *s* meccanico; (aut) motorista *m*

**mechanical** [mɪˈkænɪkəl] *adj* meccanico; (*machinelike*) (fig) macchinale

**mechan′ical engineer′ing** *s* ingegneria meccanica

**mechan′ical pen′cil** *s* matita automatica

**mechanics** [mɪˈkænɪks] *s* meccanica

**mechanism** [ˈmɛkəˌnɪzəm] *s* meccanismo, congegno

**mechanize** [ˈmɛkəˌnaɪz] *tr* meccanizzare

**medal** [ˈmɛdəl] *s* medaglia

**medallion** [mɪˈdæljən] *s* medaglione *m*

**meddle** ['mɛdəl] *intr* intromettersi

**meddler** ['mɛdlər] *s* ficcanaso

**meddlesome** ['mɛdəlsəm] *adj* invadente, indiscreto

**median** ['midɪ·ən] *adj* medio, mediano || *s* punto medio, numero medio

**me′dian strip′** *s* spartitraffico

**mediate** ['midɪˌet] *tr* (*a dispute*) comporre; (*parties*) pacificare || *intr* (*to be in the middle*) mediare; fare da paciere

**mediation** [ˌmidɪ'eʃən] *s* mediazione

**mediator** ['midɪˌetər] *s* mediatore *m*

**medical** ['mɛdɪkəl] *adj* medico; (*student*) di medicina

**medicinal** [mə'dɪsɪnəl] *adj* medicinale

**medicine** ['mɛdɪsɪn] *s* medicina

**med′icine cab′inet** *s* armadietto farmaceutico

**med′icine kit′** *s* cassetta farmaceutica

**med′icine man′** *s* (**men′**) stregone indiano

**medieval** [ˌmidɪ'ivəl] *or* [ˌmɛdɪ'ivəl] *adj* medievale

**medievalist** [ˌmidɪ'ivəlɪst] *or* [ˌmɛdɪ'ivəlɪst] *s* medievalista *mf*

**mediocre** ['midɪˌokər] *or* [ˌmidɪ'okər] *adj* mediocre

**mediocri·ty** [ˌmidɪ'ɑkrɪti] *s* (**-ties**) mediocrità *f*

**meditate** ['mɛdɪˌtet] *tr & intr* meditare

**meditation** [ˌmɛdɪ'teʃən] *s* meditazione

**Mediterranean** [ˌmɛdɪtə'renɪ·ən] *adj & s* Mediterraneo

**medi·um** ['midɪ·əm] *adj* medio; (*heat*) moderato; (*meat*) cotto moderatamente || *s* (**-ums** *or* **-a** [ə]) (*middle state; mean*) media; mezzo; (*in spiritualism*) medium *m*; **media** (*of communication*) media *mpl*; **through the medium of** per mezzo di

**medlar** ['mɛdlər] *s* (*tree*) nespolo; (*fruit*) nespola

**medley** ['mɛdli] *s* farragine *f*, mescolanza; (*mus*) pot-pourri *m*

**medul·la** [mɪ'dʌlə] *s* (**-lae** [li]) midollo

**meek** [mik] *adj* mansueto, umile

**meekness** ['miknɪs] *s* mansuetudine *f*

**meerschaum** ['mɪrʃəm] *or* ['mɪrʃɑm] *s* schiuma; pipa di schiuma

**meet** [mit] *adj* conveniente || *s* incontro || *v* (*pret & pp* **met** [mɛt]) *tr* incontrare, incontrarsi con; (*to become acquainted with*) fare la conoscenza di; riunirsi con; (*to cope with*) sopperire a; (*said of a public carrier*) fare coincidenza con; andar incontro a; (*one's obligations*) far fronte a; (*bad luck*) avere; **to meet the eyes of** presentarsi agli occhi di || *intr* incontrarsi; riunirsi; conoscersi; **till we meet again** arrivederci; **to meet with** incontrare, incontrarsi con; (*an accident*) avere; (*said of a public carrier*) fare coincidenza con

**meeting** ['mitɪŋ] *s* riunione, ritrovo; seduta, convegno; (*political*) comizio; (*e.g., of two rivers*) confluenza; duello

**meet′ing of the minds′** *s* accordo, consonanza di voleri

**meet′ing place′** *s* luogo di riunione

**megacycle** ['mɛgəˌsaɪkəl] *s* megaciclo

**megaphone** ['mɛgəˌfon] *s* megafono, portavoce *m*

**megohm** ['mɛgˌom] *s* megaohm *m*

**melancholia** [ˌmɛlən'kolɪ·ə] *s* melanconia, malinconia

**melanchol·y** ['mɛlənˌkɑli] *adj* malinconico || *s* (**-ies**) malinconia

**melee** ['mele] *or* ['mɛle] *s* (*fight*) mischia; confusione

**mellow** ['mɛlo] *adj* (*fruit*) maturo; (*wine*) pastoso; (*voice*) soave, melodioso || *tr* raddolcire || *intr* raddolcirsi

**melodic** [mɪ'lɑdɪk] *adj* melodico

**melodious** [mɪ'lodɪ·əs] *adj* melodioso

**melodramatic** [ˌmɛlədrə'mætɪk] *adj* melodrammatico

**melo·dy** ['mɛlədi] *s* (**-dies**) melodia

**melon** ['mɛlən] *s* melone *m*, popone *m*

**melt** [mɛlt] *tr* sciogliere; (*metals*) fondere; (*fig*) intenerire || *intr* sciogliersi; fondersi; (*fig*) intenerirsi; **to melt away** svanire; **to melt into** convertirsi in, diventare; (*tears*) struggersi in

**melt′ing pot′** *s* crogiolo

**member** ['mɛmbər] *s* membro

**membership** ['mɛmbərˌʃɪp] *s* associazione; numero di membri

**membrane** ['mɛmbren] *s* membrana

**memen·to** [mɪ'mɛnto] *s* (**-tos** *or* **-toes**) oggetto ricordo

**mem·o** ['mɛmo] *s* (**-os**) (coll) memorandum *m*

**memoir** ['mɛmwɑr] *s* memoria, memoriale *m*; biografia; **memoirs** memorie *fpl*

**memoran·dum** [ˌmɛmə'rændəm] *s* (**-dums** *or* **-da** [də]) memorandum *m*

**memorial** [mɪ'morɪ·əl] *adj* commemorativo || *s* sacrario; (*petition*) memoriale *m*

**Memo′rial Day′** *s* giorno dei caduti

**memorialize** [mɪ'morɪ·əˌlaɪz] *tr* commemorare

**memorize** ['mɛməˌraɪz] *tr* imparare a memoria

**memo·ry** ['mɛməri] *s* (**-ries**) memoria; **to commit to memory** imparare a memoria

**menace** ['mɛnɪs] *s* minaccia || *tr & intr* minacciare

**ménage** [me'nɑʒ] *s* casa; (*housekeeping*) economia domestica

**menagerie** [mə'næʒəri] *or* [mə'nædʒəri] *s* serraglio

**mend** [mɛnd] *s* riparo; **to be on the mend** migliorare || *tr* (*to repair*) raccomodare, riparare; (*to patch*) rammendare; (fig) correggere || *intr* correggersi

**mendacious** [mɛn'deʃəs] *adj* mendace

**mendicant** ['mɛndɪkənt] *adj & s* mendicante *mf*

**menfolk** ['mɛnˌfok] *spl* uomini *mpl*

**menial** ['minɪ·əl] *adj* basso, servile || *s* servitore *m*, servo

**menses** ['mɛnsiz] *spl* mestruazione, mestrui *mpl*

**men′s′ fur′nishings** *spl* articoli *mpl* d'abbigliamento maschile

**men′s′ room′** *s* gabinetto per signori

**menstruate** ['mɛnstrʊ ,et] *intr* avere le mestruazioni

**men'tal arith'metic** ['mɛntəl] *s* calcolo mentale

**men'tal hos'pital** *s* manicomio

**men'tal ill'ness** *s* malattia mentale

**men'tal reserva'tion** *s* riserva mentale

**men'tal test'** *s* test *m* mentale

**mention** ['mɛnʃən] *s* menzione ‖ *tr* menzionare; **don't mention it** non c'è di che

**menu** ['mɛnju] or ['menju] *s* menu *m*, lista

**meow** [mɪ'aʊ] *s* miagolio ‖ *intr* miagolare

**Mephistophelian** [ ,mɛfɪstə'fili·ən] *adj* mefistofelico

**mercantile** ['mʌrkən ,til] or ['mʌrkən ,taɪl] *adj* mercantile

**mercenar·y** ['mʌrsə ,neri] *adj* mercenario ‖ *s* (**-ies**) mercenario

**merchandise** ['mʌrtʃən ,daɪz] *s* mercanzia, merce *f*

**merchant** ['mʌrtʃənt] *adj* mercantile ‖ *s* mercante *m*, commerciante *mf*

**mer'chant·man** *s* (**-men**) mercantile *m*

**mer'chant marine'** *s* marina mercantile

**merciful** ['mʌrsɪfəl] *adj* misericordioso

**merciless** ['mʌrsɪlɪs] *adj* spietato

**mercu·ry** ['mʌrkjəri] *s* (**-ries**) mercurio ‖ **Mercury** *s* Mercurio

**mer·cy** ['mʌrsi] *s* (**-cies**) misericordia; **at the mercy of** alla mercé di

**mere** [mɪr] *adj* mero, puro

**meretricious** [ ,mɛrɪ'trɪʃəs] *adj* vistoso, chiassoso, sgargiante; artificiale, falso, finto

**merge** [mʌrdʒ] *tr* fondere ‖ *intr* fondersi; (*said of two roads*) convergere; **to merge into** convertirsi lentamente in

**merger** ['mʌrdʒər] *s* fusione

**meridian** [mə'rɪdi·ən] *adj* meridiano; culminante ‖ *s* meridiano; apogeo

**meringue** [mə'ræŋ] *s* meringa

**merit** ['mɛrɪt] *s* merito ‖ *tr* meritare

**meritorious** [ ,mɛrɪ'tɔri·əs] *adj* meritorio

**merlon** ['mʌrlən] *s* merlo

**mermaid** ['mʌr ,med] *s* sirena

**mer'man'** *s* (**-men'**) tritone *m*

**merriment** ['mɛrɪmənt] *s* allegria

**mer·ry** ['mɛri] *adj* (**-rier; -riest**) allegro, giocondo; **to make merry** divertirsi

**Mer'ry Christ'mas** *interj* Buon Natale!

**mer'ry-go-round'** *s* giostra, carosello; (*of parties*) serie ininterrotta

**mer'ry·mak'er** *s* festaiolo

**mesh** [mɛʃ] *s* (*network*) rete *f*; (*each open space of net*) maglia; (*mach*) ingranaggio; **meshes** rete *f* ‖ *tr* irretire; (*mach*) ingranare ‖ *intr* irretirsi; (*mach*) ingranarsi

**mess** [mɛs] *s* (*dirty condition*) disordine *m*; (*meal for a group of people*) mensa, rancio; porzione; **to get into a mess** mettersi nei pasticci; **to make a mess of** rovinare ‖ *tr* sporcare; disordinare; rovinare ‖ *intr* mangiare in comune; **to mess around** (coll) perdersi in cose inutili

**message** ['mɛsɪdʒ] *s* messaggio

**messenger** ['mɛsəndʒər] *s* messaggero; (*person who goes on an errand*) fattorino; (mil) portaordini *m*

**mess' hall'** *s* mensa

**Messiah** [mə'saɪ·ə] *s* Messia *m*

**mess' kit'** *s* gavetta, gamella

**mess'mate'** *s* compagno di rancio

**mess' of pot'tage** ['pɑtɪdʒ] *s* (Bib & fig) piatto di lenticchie

**Messrs.** ['mɛsərz] *pl* of **Mr.**

**mess·y** ['mɛsi] *adj* (**-ier; -iest**) disordinato; sporco

**metal** ['mɛtəl] *adj* metallico ‖ *s* metallo

**metallic** [mɪ'tælɪk] *adj* metallico

**metallurgy** ['mɛtə ,lʌrdʒi] *s* metallurgia

**met'al pol'ish** *s* lucido per metalli

**met'al·work'** *s* lavoro di metallo

**metamorpho·sis** [ ,mɛtə'mɔrfəsɪs] *s* (**-ses** [ ,siz]) metamorfosi *f*

**metaphony** [mə'tæfəni] *s* metafonia, metafonesi *f*

**metaphor** ['mɛtəfər] or ['mɛtə ,fɔr] *s* metafora

**metaphorical** [ ,mɛtə'fɑrɪkəl] or [ ,mɛtə'fɔrɪkəl] *adj* metaforico

**metathe·sis** [mɪ'tæθɪsɪs] *s* (**-ses** [ ,siz]) metatesi *f*

**mete** [mit] *tr*—**to mete out** distribuire

**meteor** ['mitɪ·ər] *s* meteora

**meteoric** [ ,mitɪ'ɑrɪk] or [ ,mitɪ'ɔrɪk] *adj* meteorico; (fig) rapidissimo, folgorante

**meteorite** ['mitɪ·ə ,raɪt] *s* meteorite *m* & *f*

**meteorology** [ ,mitɪ·ə'rɑlədʒi] *s* meteorologia

**meter** ['mitər] *s* (*unit of length; verse*) metro; (*instrument for measuring gas, water, etc.*) contatore *m*; (mus) tempo ‖ *tr* misurare col contatore

**me'ter read'er** *s* lettore *m*, letturista *m*

**methane** ['mɛθen] *s* metano

**method** ['mɛθəd] *s* metodo

**methodic(al)** [mɪ'θɑdɪk(əl)] *adj* metodico

**Methodist** ['mɛθədɪst] *adj* & *s* metodista *mf*

**Methuselah** [mɪ'θuzələ] *s* Matusalemme *m*

**meticulous** [mɪ'tɪkjələs] *adj* meticoloso

**metric(al)** ['mɛtrɪk(əl)] *adj* metrico

**metronome** ['mɛtrə ,nom] *s* metronomo

**metropolis** [mɪ'trɑpəlɪs] *s* metropoli *f*

**metropolitan** [ ,mɛtrə'pɑlɪtən] *adj* & *s* metropolitano

**mettle** ['mɛtəl] *s* disposizione, temperamento; brio, animo; **to be on one's mettle** impegnarsi a fondo

**mettlesome** ['mɛtəlsəm] *adj* brioso

**mew** [mju] *s* miagolio; (orn) gabbiano; **mews** scuderie *fpl*

**Mexican** ['mɛksɪkən] *adj* & *s* messicano

**Mexico** ['mɛksɪ ,ko] *s* il Messico

**mezzanine** ['mɛzə ,nin] *s* mezzanino

**mica** ['maɪkə] *s* mica

**microbe** ['maɪkrob] *s* microbio

**microbiology** [ ,maɪkrəbaɪ'alədʒi] *s* microbiologia

**microcard** ['maɪkrə ,kard] *s* microscheda

**microfarad** [ˌmaɪkrəˈfæræd] *s* microfarad *m*

**microfilm** [ˈmaɪkrəˌfɪlm] *s* microfilm *m* ‖ *tr* microfilmare

**microgroove** [ˈmaɪkrəˌgruv] *adj* microsolco ‖ *s* microsolco; disco microsolco

**microphone** [ˈmaɪkrəˌfon] *s* microfono

**microscope** [ˈmaɪkrəˌskop] *s* microscopio

**microscopic** [ˌmaɪkrəˈskɑpɪk] *adj* microscopico

**microwave** [ˈmaɪkrəˌwev] *s* microonda

**mid** [mɪd] *adj* mezzo, la metà di, e.g., **mid October** la metà di ottobre

**mid′day′** *adj* di mezzogiorno ‖ *s* mezzogiorno

**middle** [ˈmɪdəl] *adj* medio, mezzo ‖ *s* mezzo, metà *f*; (*of human body*) cintura; **about the middle of** verso la metà di; **in the middle of** nel mezzo di

**mid′dle age′** *s* mezza età ‖ **Middle Ages** *spl* Medio Evo

**mid′dle class′** *s* ceto medio, borghesia

**Mid′dle East′** *s* Medio Oriente

**Mid′dle Eng′lish** *s* inglese *m* medievale parlato fra il 1150 e il 1500

**mid′dle fin′ger** *s* dito medio

**mid′dle-man′** *s* (-men′) intermediario

**middling** [ˈmɪdlɪŋ] *adj* mediocre, passabile ‖ *s* (*coarsely ground wheat*) farina grossa integrale; **middlings** articoli *mpl* di qualità mediocre ‖ *adv* moderatamente

**mid·dy** [ˈmɪdi] *s* (-dies) aspirante *m* di marina

**mid′dy blouse′** *s* marinara

**midget** [ˈmɪdʒɪt] *s* nano

**midland** [ˈmɪdlənd] *adj* centrale, interno ‖ *s* regione centrale

**mid′night′** *adj* di mezzanotte; **to burn the midnight oil** studiare a lume di candela ‖ *s* mezzanotte *f*

**midriff** [ˈmɪdrɪf] *s* diaframma *m*; (*middle part of body*) cintura, vita

**mid′ship′man** *s* (-men) aspirante *m* di marina

**midst** [mɪdst] *s* mezzo, centro; **in the midst of** in mezzo a

**mid′stream′** *s*—**in midstream** in mezzo al fiume

**mid′sum′mer** *s* cuore *m* dell'estate

**mid′way′** *adj* situato a metà strada ‖ *s* metà strada; viale *m* principale di un' esposizione ‖ *adv* a metà strada

**mid′week′** *s* mezzo della settimana

**mid′wife′** *s* (-wives′) levatrice *f*

**mid′win′ter** *s* cuore *m* dell'inverno

**mid′year′** *adj* nel mezzo dell'anno ‖ *s* mezzo dell'anno; **midyears** (coll) esami *mpl* nel mezzo dell'anno scolastico

**mien** [min] *s* aspetto, portamento

**miff** [mɪf] *s* (coll) battibecco ‖ *tr* (coll) offendere

**might** [maɪt] *s* forza, potenza; **with might and main** a tutta forza ‖ *v aux* used to form the potential, e.g., **he might change his mind** è possibile che cambi opinione

**might·y** [ˈmaɪti] *adj* (-ier; -iest) po-

tente; (*huge*) grandissimo ‖ *adv* (coll) moltissimo, grandemente

**migraine** [ˈmaɪgren] *s* emicrania

**migrate** [ˈmaɪgret] *intr* migrare

**migratory** [ˈmaɪgrəˌtori] *adj* migratore

**milch** [mɪltʃ] *adj* lattifero

**mild** [maɪld] *adj* dolce, mite, gentile; (*disease*) leggero

**mildew** [ˈmɪlˌdju] *or* [ˈmɪlˌdu] *s* (*mold*) muffa; (*plant disease*) peronospora

**mile** [maɪl] *s* miglio terrestre; miglio marino

**mileage** [ˈmaɪlɪdʒ] *s* distanza in miglia

**mile′age tick′et** *s* biglietto calcolato in miglia simile al biglietto chilometraggio

**mile′post′** *s* colonnina miliare

**mile′stone′** *s* pietra miliare

**milieu** [mɪlˈju] *s* ambiente *m*

**militancy** [ˈmɪlɪtənsi] *s* bellicismo; spirito militante

**militant** [ˈmɪlɪtənt] *adj* & *s* militante *mf*

**militarism** [ˈmɪlɪtəˌrɪzəm] *s* militarismo

**militarist** [ˈmɪlɪtərɪst] *adj* & *s* militarista *mf*

**militarize** [ˈmɪlɪtəˌraɪz] *tr* militarizzare

**military** [ˈmɪlɪˌteri] *adj* militare ‖ *s*—**the military** le forze armate

**mil′itary acad′emy** *s* scuola allievi ufficiali, accademia militare

**mil′itary police′** *s* polizia militare

**militate** [ˈmɪlɪˌtet] *intr* militare

**militia** [mɪˈlɪʃə] *s* milizia

**mili′tia·man** *s* (-men) miliziano

**milk** [mɪlk] *adj* lattifero; di latte; **al latte** ‖ *s* latte *m* ‖ *tr* mungere; (fig) spillare ‖ *intr* dare latte

**milk′ can′** *s* bidone *m* per il latte

**milk′ choc′olate** *s* cioccolato al latte

**milk′ diet′** *s* regime latteo

**milking** [ˈmɪlkɪŋ] *s* mungitura

**milk′maid′** *s* lattaia

**milk′man′** *s* (-men′) lattaio

**milk′ of hu′man kind′ness** *s* grande compassione

**milk′ pail′** *s* secchio da latte

**milk′ shake′** *s* frappé *m or* frullato di latte

**milk′sop′** *s* effeminato

**milk′weed′** *s* vincetossico

**milk·y** [ˈmɪlki] *adj* (-ier; -iest) latteo; (*whitish*) lattiginoso

**Milk′y Way′** *s* Via Lattea

**mill** [mɪl] *s* (*for grinding grain*) mulino; (*for making fabrics*) filanda; (*for cutting wood*) segheria; (*for refining sugar*) zuccherificio; (*for producing steel*) acciaieria; (*to grind coffee*) macinino; (*part of a dollar*) millesimo; **to put through the mill** mettere a dura prova ‖ *tr* (*grains*) macinare; (*coins*) zigrinare; (*steel*) laminare; (*ore*) frantumare; (*with a milling machine*) fresare; (*chocolate*) frullare ‖ *intr*—**to mill about** *or* **around** girare intorno

**millennial** [mɪˈlɛnɪˌəl] *adj* millenario

**milleni·um** [mɪ'lɛnɪ·əm] s (-ums or -a [ə]) millennio

**miller** ['mɪlər] s mugnaio; (ent) tignola notturna

**millet** ['mɪlɪt] s panico, miglio

**milliampere** [ ,mɪlɪ'æmpɪr] s milliampere m

**milliard** ['mɪljərd] or ['mɪljɑrd] s (Brit) miliardo, bilione m

**milligram** ['mɪlɪ ,græm] s milligrammo

**millimeter** ['mɪlɪ ,mitər] s millimetro

**milliner** ['mɪlɪnər] s modista

**milliner·y** ['mɪlɪ ,nɛri] or ['mɪlɪnərɪ] s (-ies) cappelli mpl per signora; modisteria; articoli mpl di modisteria

**mil'linery shop'** s modisteria

**milling** ['mɪlɪŋ] s (of grain) macina· tura; (of coins) granitura; (mach) fresatura

**mill'ing machine'** s fresatrice f

**million** ['mɪljən] adj milione di, mi· lioni di || s milione m

**millionaire** [ ,mɪljən'ɛr] s milionario

**millionth** ['mɪljənθ] adj, s & pron mi· lionesimo

**millivolt** ['mɪlɪ ,volt] s millivolt m

**mill'pond'** s gora

**mill'race'** s corrente f che aziona il mulino; canale m di presa

**mill'stone'** s mola, macina, palmento; (fig) peso, gravame m

**mill' wheel'** s ruota del mulino

**mill'work'** s lavoro di falegnameria; lavoro di falegnameria fatto a mac· china

**mime** [maɪm] s mimo || tr mimare

**mimeograph** ['mɪmɪ·ə ,græf] or ['mɪmɪə ,grɑf] s (trademark) ciclo· stile m || tr ciclostilare

**mim·ic** ['mɪmɪk] s mimo, imitatore m || v (pret & pp -icked; ger -icking) tr imitare, scimmiottare

**mimic·ry** ['mɪmɪkrɪ] s (-ries) mimica; (biol) mimetismo

**minaret** [ ,mɪnə'rɛt] or ['mɪnə ,rɛt] s minareto

**mince** [mɪns] tr tagliuzzare, triturare; (words) pronunziare con affettazione; **to not mince one's words** non aver peli sulla lingua

**mince'meat'** s carne tritata; **to make mincemeat of** annientare completa· mente

**mince' pie'** s torta di frutta secca e carne tritata

**mind** [maɪnd] s mente f; opinione; **to bear in mind** tener presente; **to be not in one's right mind** essere fuori di senno; **to be of one mind** essere d'accordo; **to be out of one's mind** essere impazzito; **to change one's mind** cambiare d'opinione; **to go out of one's mind** impazzire; **to have a mind to** aver voglia di; **to have in mind to** pensare a; **to have on one's mind** avere in mente; **to lose one's mind** uscire di mente; **to make up one's mind** decidersi; **to my mind** a mio modo di vedere; **to say whatever comes to one's mind** dire quanto salta in testa, e.g., **John always says whatever comes to his mind** Gio·

vanni dice sempre quanto gli salta in testa; **to set one's mind on** risolversi a; **to slip one's mind** scappare di mente (with dat), e.g., **it slipped his mind** gli è scappato di mente; **to speak one's mind** dire la propria opinione; **with one mind** unanima· mente || tr (to take care of) occu· parsi di; obbedire (with dat); **do you mind the smoke?** Le disturba il fumo?; **mind your own business** si occupi degli affari Suoi || intr osser· vare, fare attenzione; rincrescere, e.g., **do you mind if I go?** Le rin· cresce se vado?; **never mind** non si preoccupi

**mindful** ['maɪndfəl] adj memore

**mind' read'er** s lettore m del pensiero

**mind' read'ing** s lettura del pensiero

**mine** [maɪn] s (e.g., of coal) miniera; (mil & nav) mina || pron poss il mio; mio || tr minare; (earth) scavare; (ore) estrarre || intr lavorare una miniera; (mil & nav) minare

**mine' detec'tor** s rivelatore m di mine

**mine'field'** s campo minato

**mine'lay'er** s posamine m

**miner** ['maɪnər] s minatore m

**mineral** ['mɪnərəl] adj & s minerale m

**mineralogy** [ ,mɪnə'rælədʒɪ] s minera· logia

**min'eral wool'** s cotone m or lana minerale

**mine' sweep'er** s dragamine m

**mingle** ['mɪŋgəl] tr mescolare; unire || intr mescolarsi, associarsi

**miniature** ['mɪnɪ·ət/ər] or ['mɪnɪt/ər] s miniatura; **to paint in miniature** miniare, dipingere in miniatura

**min'iature golf'** s minigolf m

**miniaturization** [ ,mɪnɪ·ət/ərɪ'ze/ən] or [ ,mɪnɪt/ərɪ'ze/ən] s miniaturizza· zione

**minimal** ['mɪnɪməl] adj minimo

**minimize** ['mɪnɪ ,maɪz] tr minimizzare

**minimum** ['mɪnɪməm] adj & s minimo

**min'imum wage'** s salario minimo

**mining** ['maɪnɪŋ] adj minerario || s estrazione di minerali; (nav) posa di mine

**minion** ['mɪnjən] s servo; favorito, be· niamino

**min'ion of the law'** s poliziotto

**miniskirt** ['mɪnɪ ,skʌrt] s minigonna

**minister** ['mɪnɪstər] s ministro; pastore m protestante || tr & intr ministrare

**ministerial** [ ,mɪnɪs'tɪrɪ·əl] adj mini· steriale

**minis·try** ['mɪnɪstrɪ] s (-tries) mini· stero; sacerdozio

**mink** [mɪŋk] s visone m

**minnow** ['mɪno] s pesciolino; (ichth) ciprino

**minor** ['maɪnər] adj minore || s minore m, minorenne mf; (educ) corso se· condario

**minori·ty** [mɪ'nɑrɪtɪ] or [mɪ'nɔrɪtɪ] adj minoritario || s (-ties) (smaller number or part; group differing in race, etc., from majority) minoranza; (under legal age) minorità f

**minstrel** ['mɪnstrəl] s (hist) mene·

strello; (U.S.A.) comico vestito da nero

**minstrel·sy** ['mɪnstrəlsi] *s* (**-sies**) giulleria; poesia giullaresca

**mint** [mɪnt] *s* zecca; (*plant*) menta; (*losenge*) mentina; (fig) miniera d'oro ‖ *tr* coniare

**minuet** [‚mɪnjʊ'ɛt] *s* minuetto

**minus** ['maɪnəs] *adj* meno ‖ *s* meno, perdita ‖ *prep* meno, senza

**minute** [maɪ'njut] or [maɪ'nut] *adj* minuto ‖ ['mɪnɪt] *adj* fatto in un minuto ‖ *s* minuto; momento; **minutes** processo verbale; **to write up the minutes** tenere i verbali; **up to the minute** al corrente; dell'ultima ora

**min'ute hand'** ['mɪnɪt] *s* sfera or lancetta dei minuti

**minutiae** [mɪ'njuʃɪ‚i] or [mɪ'nuʃɪ‚i] *spl* minuzie *fpl*

**minx** [mɪŋks] *s* sfacciata, civetta

**miracle** ['mɪrəkəl] *s* miracolo

**mir'acle play'** *s* sacra rappresentazione

**miraculous** [mɪ'rækjələs] *adj* miracoloso

**mirage** [mɪ'rɑʒ] *s* miraggio

**mire** [maɪr] *s* limo, mota

**mirror** ['mɪrər] *s* specchio ‖ *tr* specchiare, riflettere

**mirth** [mʌrθ] *s* allegria, gioia

**mir·y** ['maɪri] *adj* (**-ier; -iest**) fangoso, limaccioso

**misadventure** [‚mɪsəd'vɛntʃər] *s* disavventura, contrattempo

**misanthrope** ['mɪsən‚θrop] *s* misantropo

**misanthropy** [mɪs'ænθrəpi] *s* misantropia

**misapprehension** [‚mɪsæprɪ'hɛnʃən] *s* malinteso

**misappropriation** [‚mɪsə‚proprɪ'eʃən] *s* malversazione

**misbehave** [‚mɪsbɪ'hev] *intr* comportarsi male

**misbehavior** [‚mɪsbɪ'hevɪ·ər] *s* cattiva condotta

**miscalculation** [‚mɪskælkjə'leʃən] *s* calcolo errato

**miscarriage** [mɪs'kærɪdʒ] *s* (*of justice*) errore *m;* (*of a letter*) disguido; (pathol) aborto

**miscar·ry** [mɪs'kæri] *v* (*pret & pp* **-ried**) *intr* (*said of a project*) fallire; (*said of a letter*) smarrirsi; (pathol) abortire

**miscellaneous** [‚mɪsə'lenɪ·əs] *adj* miscellaneo

**miscella·ny** ['mɪsə‚leni] *s* (**-nies**) miscellanea

**mischief** ['mɪstʃɪf] *s* (*harm*) danno; (*disposition to annoy*) malizia; (*prankishness*) birichinata

**mis'chief·mak'er** *s* mettimale *mf*

**mischievous** ['mɪstʃɪvəs] *adj* dannoso; malizioso; birichino

**misconception** [‚mɪskən'sɛpʃən] *s* concetto erroneo, fraintendimento

**misconduct** [mɪs'kɑndəkt] *s* cattiva condotta; (*of a public official*) malgoverno ‖ [‚mɪskən'dʌkt] *tr* male amministrare; **to misconduct oneself** comportarsi male

**misconstrue** [‚mɪskən'stru] or [mɪs'kɑnstru] *tr* fraintendere

**miscount** [mɪs'kaʊnt] *s* conteggio erroneo ‖ *tr & intr* contare male

**miscue** [mɪs'kju] *s* sbaglio; (*in billiards*) stecca ‖ *intr* steccare; (theat) sbagliarsi di battuta

**mis·deal** [mɪs‚dil] *s* distribuzione sbagliata ‖ [mɪs'dil] *v* (*pret & pp* **-dealt** [dɛlt]) *tr & intr* distribuire erroneamente

**misdeed** [mɪs'did] or ['mɪs‚did] *s* misfatto, malfatto

**misdemeanor** [‚mɪsdɪ'minər] *s* cattiva condotta; (law) delitto colposo

**misdirect** [‚mɪsdɪ'rɛkt] or [‚mɪsdaɪ'rɛkt] *tr* dare un indirizzo sbagliato a; (*a letter*) mettere un indirizzo sbagliato su

**misdoing** [mɪs'du·ɪŋ] *s* misfatto

**miser** ['maɪzər] *s* avaro, spilorcio

**miserable** ['mɪzərəbəl] *adj* miserabile, miserevole; (coll) malissimo; (coll) schifoso

**miserly** ['maɪzərli] *adj* spilorcio

**miser·y** ['mɪzəri] *s* (**-ies**) miseria

**misfeasance** [mɪs'fizəns] *s* infrazione della legge; abuso di autorità commesso da pubblico funzionario

**misfire** [mɪs'faɪr] *s* difetto di esplosione; (aut) difetto d'accensione ‖ *intr* (*said of a gun*) fare cilecca; (aut) dare accensione irregolare; (fig) fallire

**mis·fit** ['mɪs‚fɪt] *s* vestito che non va bene; (*person*) spostato, pesce *m* fuor d'acqua ‖ [mɪs'fɪt] *v* (*pret & pp* **-fitted**); *ger* **-fitting**) *intr* andar male

**misfortune** [mɪs'fɔrtʃən] *s* disgrazia

**misgiving** [mɪs'gɪvɪŋ] *s* dubbio, timore *m*, cattivo presentimento

**misgovern** [mɪs'gʌvərn] *tr* amministrare male

**misguided** [mɪs'gaɪdɪd] *adj* fuorviato; (*e.g., kindness*) sconsigliato

**mishap** ['mɪshæp] or [mɪs'hæp] *s* accidente *m*, infortunio

**misinform** [‚mɪsɪn'fɔrm] *tr* dare informazioni errate a

**misinterpret** [‚mɪsɪn'tɛrprɪt] *tr* interpretare male, trasfigurare

**misjudge** [mɪs'dʒʌdʒ] *tr & intr* giudicare male

**mis·lay** [mɪs'le] *v* (*pret & pp* **-laid** [‚led]) *tr* (*e.g., tile*) applicare in maniera sbagliata; (*e.g., papers*) smarrire, mettere al posto sbagliato

**mis·lead** [mɪs'lid] *v* (*pret & pp* **-led** [‚led]) *tr* sviare, traviare

**misleading** [mɪs'lidɪŋ] *adj* ingannatore

**mismanagement** [mɪs'mænɪdʒmənt] *s* malgoverno

**misnomer** [mɪs'nomər] *s* termine improprio

**misplace** [mɪs'ples] *tr* mettere fuori di posto; (*trust*) riporre erroneamente

**misprint** ['mɪs‚prɪnt] *s* errore *m* di stampa, refuso ‖ [mɪs'prɪnt] *tr* stampare erroneamente

**mispronounce** [‚mɪsprə'naʊns] *tr* pronunciare in modo erroneo

**mispronunciation** [‚mɪsprə‚nʌnsɪ-

'eʃən] or [ˌmɪsprəˌnʌnʃɪ'eʃən] *s* errore *m* di pronuncia

**misquote** [mɪs'kwot] *tr* citare incorrettamente

**misrepresent** [ˌmɪsreprɪ'zent] *tr* travisare, snaturare; (pol) rappresentare slealmente

**miss** [mɪs] *s* sbaglio, omissione; tiro fuori bersaglio; signorina || *tr* (*a train, an opportunity*) perdere; (*the target*) fallire; (*an appointment*) mancare; (*the point*) non vedere, non capire; per poco, e.g., **the car missed hitting him** l'automobile non l'ha investito per poco || *intr* sbagliare, fallire; mancare il bersaglio || **Miss** *s* signorina, la signorina

**missal** ['mɪsəl] *s* messale *m*

**misshapen** [mɪs'ʃepən] *adj* deforme, malfatto

**missile** ['mɪsɪl] *adj* missilistico || *s* missile *m*

**mis'sile launch'er** *s* lanciamissili *m*

**missing** ['mɪsɪŋ] *adj* mancante; assente; (*in action*) disperso

**mis'sing link'** *s* anello di congiunzione

**miss'ing per'son** *s* disperso

**mission** ['mɪʃən] *s* missione

**missionar·y** ['mɪʃənˌerɪ] *adj* missionario || *s* (**-ies**) (eccl) missionario; (dipl) incaricato in missione

**missive** ['mɪsɪv] *s* missiva

**mis·spell** [mɪs'spel] *v* (*pret & pp* **-spelled** or **-spelt** ['spelt]) *tr & intr* scrivere male

**misspelling** [mɪs'spelɪŋ] *s* errore *m* di ortografia

**misspent** [mɪs'spent] *adj* sprecato

**misstatement** [mɪs'stetmənt] *s* dichiarazione inesatta

**misstep** [mɪs'step] *s* passo falso

**miss·y** ['mɪsi] *s* (**-ies**) (coll) signorina

**mist** [mɪst] *s* caligine *f*, foschia; (*of tears*) velo; (*of smoke, vapors, etc.*) nuvola

**mis·take** [mɪs'tek] *s* errore *m*, sbaglio; **and no mistake** (coll) di sicuro; **by mistake** per sbaglio; **to make a mistake** sbagliarsi || *v* (*pret* **-took** ['tʊk]; *pp* **-taken**) *tr* fraintendere; **to be mistaken for** essere preso per; **to mistake for** pigliare per

**mistaken** [mɪs'tekən] *adj* errato, sbagliato; **to be mistaken** essere in errore, sbagliarsi

**mister** ['mɪstər] *s* (mil, nav) signore *m*; (coll) marito || *interj* (coll) signore!; (coll) Lei!; (coll) buonuomo! || **Mister** *s* Signore *m*

**mistletoe** ['mɪsəlˌto] *s* vischio

**mistreat** [mɪs'trit] *tr* maltrattare

**mistreatment** [mɪs'tritmənt] *s* maltrattamento

**mistress** ['mɪstrɪs] *s* (*of a household*) signora, padrona; (*paramour*) amante *f*, ganza; (Brit) maestra di scuola

**mistrial** [mɪs'traɪ·əl] *s* processo viziato da errore giudiziario

**mistrust** [mɪs'trʌst] *s* diffidenza || *tr* diffidare di || *intr* diffidarsi

**mistrustful** [mɪs'trʌstfəl] *adj* diffidente

**mist·y** ['mɪsti] *adj* (**-ier; -iest**) fosco, brumoso; (fig) vago, confuso

**misunder·stand** [ˌmɪsʌndər'stænd] *v* (*pret & pp* **-stood** ['stʊd]) *tr* fraintendere, equivocare

**misunderstanding** [ˌmɪsʌndər'stændɪŋ] *s* malinteso

**misuse** [mɪs'jus] *s* abuso; (*of funds*) malversazione || [mɪs'juz] *tr* abusare di; (*funds*) malversare

**misword** [mɪs'wʌrd] *tr* comporre male

**mite** [maɪt] *s* obolo; (ent) acaro

**miter** ['maɪtər] *s* (carp) ugnatura; (carp) giunto a quartabuono; (eccl) mitra || *tr* tagliare a quartabuono, ugnare; giungere a quartabuono

**mi'ter box'** *s* cassetta per ugnature

**mi'ter joint'** *s* giunto a quartabuono

**mitigate** ['mɪtɪˌget] *tr* mitigare

**mitten** ['mɪtən] *s* manopola, muffola

**mix** [mɪks] *tr* mescolare; (*colors*) mesticare; (*dough*) impastare; (*salad*) condire; **to mix up** confondere || *intr* confondersi, mescolarsi

**mixed** [mɪkst] *adj* misto; (*candy*) assortito; (coll) confuso

**mixed' com'pany** *s* riunione *f* di ambo i sessi

**mixed' drink'** *s* miscela di liquori diversi

**mixed' feel'ing** *s* sentimento ambivalente

**mixed' met'aphor** *s* metafora incongruente

**mixer** ['mɪksər] *s* (mach) mescolatrice *f*; **to be a good mixer** essere socievole

**mixture** ['mɪkstʃər] *s* mistura, mescolanza; (aut) miscela, carburazione

**mix'-up'** *s* confusione; (coll) baruffa

**mizzen** ['mɪzən] *s* mezzana

**moan** [mon] *s* gemito || *intr* gemere

**moat** [mot] *s* fosso, fossato

**mob** [mɑb] *s* turba || *v* (*pret & pp* **mobbed**; *ger* **mobbing**) *tr* assaltare; affollarsi intorno a; (*a place*) affollare

**mobile** ['mobɪl] or ['mobɪl] *adj* mobile

**mo'bile home'** *s* caravan *m*, roulotte *f*

**mobility** [mo'bɪlɪti] *s* mobilità *f*

**mobilization** [ˌmobɪlɪ'zeʃən] *s* mobilitazione

**mobilize** ['mobɪˌlaɪz] *tr & intr* mobilitare

**mob' rule'** *s* legge *f* della teppa

**mobster** ['mɑbstər] *s* gangster *m*

**moccasin** ['mɑkəsɪn] *s* mocassino

**Mo'cha cof'fee** ['mokə] *s* caffè *m* moca

**mock** [mɑk] *adj* finto, imitato || *s* dileggio, burla || *tr* deridere, canzonare; ingannare || *intr* motteggiare; **to mock at** farsi gioco di

**mocker·y** ['mɑkəri] *s* (**-ies**) dileggio, scherno; (*subject of derision*) zimbello; (*poor imitation*) contraffazione

**mock'-hero'ic** *adj* eroicomico

**mockingbird** ['mɑkɪŋˌbɑrd] *s* mimo

**mock' or'ange** *s* gelsomino selvatico

**mock' tur'tle soup'** *s* finto brodo di tartaruga

**mock'-up'** *s* modello dimostrativo

**mode** [mod] *s* modo, maniera; (*fashion*) moda; (gram) modo

**mod·el** ['mɑdəl] *adj* modello, e.g., **model student** studente modello || *s* modello; (*woman serving as subject for artists*) modello *f*; (*woman wearing clothes at fashion show*) indossatrice *f* ‖ *v* (*pret & pp* **-eled** or **-elled**; *ger* **-eling** or **-elling**) *tr* modellare ‖ *intr* modellarsi; fare il manichino

**mod'el air'plane** *s* aeromodello

**mo'del-air'plane build'er** *s* aeromodellista *mf*

**mod'eling clay'** *s* plastilina

**moderate** ['madərɪt] *adj* moderato ‖ ['madə‚ret] *tr* moderare; (*a meeting*) presiedere a ‖ *intr* moderarsi

**moderator** ['madə‚retər] *s* moderatore *m*; (*mediator*) arbitro; (*phys*) moderatore *m*

**modern** ['madərn] *adj* moderno

**modernize** ['madər‚naɪz] *tr* modernizzare, rimodernare

**modest** ['madɪst] *adj* modesto

**modes·ty** ['madɪsti] *s* (**-ties**) modestia

**modicum** ['madɪkəm] *s* piccola quantità

**modi·fy** ['madɪ‚faɪ] *v* (*pret & pp* **-fied**) *tr* modificare; (*gram*) determinare

**modish** ['madɪʃ] *adj* alla moda

**modulate** ['madʒə‚let] *tr & intr* modulare

**modulation** [‚madʒə'leʃən] *s* modulazione

**mohair** ['mo‚her] *s* mohair *m*

**Mohammedan** [mo'hæmɪdən] *adj & s* maomettano

**Mohammedanism** [mo'hæmɪdə‚nɪzəm] *s* maomettismo

**moist** [mɔɪst] *adj* umido; lacrimoso

**moisten** ['mɔɪsən] *tr* inumidire ‖ *intr* inumidirsi

**moisture** ['mɔɪstʃər] *s* umidità *f*

**molar** ['molər] *s* molare *m*

**molasses** [mə'læsɪz] *s* melassa

**mold** [mold] *s* stampo, forma; (*fungus*) muffa; humus *m*; (*fig*) indole *f* ‖ *tr* plasmare, conformare; (*to make moldy*) fare ammuffire ‖ *intr* ammuffire

**molder** ['moldər] *s* modellatore *m* ‖ *intr* sgretolarsi; polverizzarsi

**molding** ['moldɪŋ] *s* modellato; (*archit, carp*) modanatura

**mold·y** ['moldi] *adj* (**-ier**; **-iest**) ammuffito

**mole** [mol] *s* (*pier*) molo; (*harbor*) darsena; (*spot on skin*) neo; (*small mammal*) talpa

**molecule** ['malɪ‚kjul] *s* molecola

**mole'hill'** *s* mucchio di terra sopra la tana di talpe

**mole'skin'** *s* pelle *f* di talpa; (*fabric*) fustagno di prima qualità

**molest** [mə'lɛst] *tr* molestare; fare proposte disoneste a

**moll** [mal] *s* (slang) ragazza della malavita; (slang) puttana

**molli·fy** ['malɪ‚faɪ] *v* (*pret & pp* **-fied**) *tr* pacificare, placare

**mollusk** ['maləsk] *s* mollusco

**mollycoddle** ['malɪ‚kadəl] *s* effeminato ‖ *tr* viziare, coccolare

**Mo'lotov cock'tail** ['malə‚tɔf] *s* bottiglia Molotov

**molt** [molt] *s* muda ‖ *intr* andare in muda

**molten** ['moltən] *adj* fuso

**molybdenum** [mə'lɪbdɪnəm] or [‚malɪb'dinəm] *s* molibdeno

**moment** ['moment] *s* momento; **at any moment** da un momento all'altro

**momentary** ['momen‚teri] *adj* momentaneo

**momentous** [mo'mentəs] *adj* grave, importante

**momen·tum** [mo'mentəm] *s* (**-tums** or **-ta** [tə]) slancio; (mech) momento

**monarch** ['manərk] *s* monarca *m*

**monarchic(al)** [mə'narkɪk(əl)] *adj* monarchico

**monarchist** ['manərkɪst] *adj & s* monarchico

**monar·chy** ['manərki] *s* (**-chies**) monarchia

**monaster·y** ['manəs‚teri] *s* (**-ies**) monastero

**monastic** [mə'næstɪk] *adj* monastico, monacale

**monasticism** [mə'næstɪ‚sɪzəm] *s* monachesimo

**Monday** ['mʌndi] *s* lunedì *m*

**monetary** ['manɪ‚teri] *adj* monetario; pecuniario

**money** ['mʌni] *s* denaro; **to be in the money** esser carico di soldi; **to make money** far quattrini

**mon'ey·bag'** *s* borsa per denaro; **moneybags** (coll) riccone sfondato

**moneychanger** ['mʌnɪ‚tʃendʒər] *s* cambiavalute *m*

**moneyed** ['mʌnid] *adj* danaroso

**moneylender** ['mʌni‚lendər] *s* prestatore *m* di denaro

**mon'ey·mak'er** *s* capitalista *mf*; affare vantaggioso

**mon'ey or'der** *s* vaglia *m*

**Mongolian** [maŋ'golɪ‚ən] *adj & s* mongolo

**mon·goose** ['maŋgus] *s* (**-gooses**) mangusta

**mongrel** ['mʌŋgrəl] or ['maŋgrəl] *adj* ibrido ‖ *s* ibrido; cane bastardo

**monitor** ['manɪtər] *s* (educ) capoclasse *mf*; (rad, telv) monitore *m* ‖ *tr* osservare; (*a signal*) controllare; (*a broadcast*) ascoltare

**monk** [mʌŋk] *s* monaco

**monkey** ['mʌŋki] *s* scimmia; **to make a monkey of** farsi gioco di ‖ *intr*—**to monkey around** (coll) oziare; **to monkey around with** (coll) giocherellare con

**mon'key·shines'** *spl* (slang) monellerie *fpl*, pagliacciate *fpl*

**mon'key wrench'** *s* chiave *f* inglese

**monkhood** ['mʌŋkhʊd] *s* monacato

**monkshood** [mʌŋks‚hʊd] *s* (bot) aconito

**monocle** ['manəkəl] *s* monocolo

**monogamy** [mə'nagəmi] *s* monogamia

**monogram** ['manə‚græm] *s* monogramma *m*

**monograph** ['manə‚græf] or ['manə‚graf] *s* monografia

**monolithic** [‚manə'lɪθɪk] *adj* monolitico

**monologue** [ˈmɑnəˌlɔg] or [ˈmɑnə‑ ˌlɑg] s monologo
**monomania** [ˌmɑnəˈmenɪ·ə] s monomania
**monomial** [məˈnomɪ·əl] s monomio
**monopolize** [məˈnɑpəˌlaɪz] tr monopolizzare, accaparrare
**monopo·ly** [məˈnɑpəli] s (**-lies**) monopolio, privativa
**monorail** [ˈmɑnəˌrel] s monorotaia
**monosyllable** [ˈmɑnəˌsɪləbəl] s monosillabo
**monotheist** [ˈmɑnəˌθi·ɪst] adj & s monoteista mf
**monotonous** [məˈnɑtənəs] adj monotono
**monotype** [ˈmɑnəˌtaɪp] s (method) monotipia; (typ) monotipo
**monoxide** [məˈnɑksaɪd] s monossido
**monseigneur** [ˌmɑnsenˈjœr] s monsignore m
**monsignor** [mɑnˈsinjər] s (**-monsignors** or **monsignori** [ˌmɑnsiˈnjori]) (eccl) monsignore m
**monsoon** [mɑnˈsun] s monsone m
**monster** [ˈmɑnstər] adj mostruoso ‖ s mostro
**monstrance** [ˈmɑnstrəns] s ostensorio
**monstrosi·ty** [mɑnˈstrɑsɪti] s (**-ties**) mostruosità f
**monstrous** [ˈmɑnstrəs] adj mostruoso
**month** [mʌnθ] s mese m
**month·ly** [ˈmʌnθli] adj mensile ‖ s (**-lies**) rivista mensile; **monthlies** (coll) mestruazione ‖ adv mensilmente
**monument** [ˈmɑnjəmənt] s monumento
**moo** [mu] s muggito ‖ intr muggire
**mood** [mud] s umore m, vena; (gram) modo; **moods** luna, malumore m
**mood·y** [ˈmudi] adj (**-ier; -iest**) triste, malinconico; lunatico, capriccioso
**moon** [mun] s luna; **once in a blue moon** ad ogni morte di papa ‖ tr—**to moon away** (time) (coll) sprecare ‖ intr—**to moon about** (coll) gingillarsi, baloccarsi; (to daydream about) (coll) sognarsi di
**moon′beam′** s raggio di luna
**moon′light′** s chiaro m di luna
**moon′light′ing** s secondo lavoro notturno
**moon′shine′** s chiaro di luna; (coll) chiacchiere fpl, balle fpl; (coll) whisky m distillato illegalmente
**moon′shot′** s lancio alla luna
**moon′stone′** s lunaria
**moor** [mur] s brughiera, landa ‖ tr ormeggiare ‖ intr ormeggiarsi ‖ **Moor** s moro
**Moorish** [ˈmurɪʃ] adj moresco
**moor′land′** s brughiera, landa
**moose** [mus] s (**moose**) alce americano
**moot** [mut] adj controverso, discutibile
**mop** [mɑp] s scopa di filacce; (naut) redazza; (of hair) zazzera ‖ v (pret & pp **mopped**; ger **mopping**) tr (a floor) pulire, asciugare; (one's brow) asciugarsi; **to mop up** rastrellare
**mope** [mop] intr andare rattristato
**mopish** [ˈmopɪʃ] adj triste, avvilito

**moral** [ˈmɑrəl] or [ˈmɔrəl] adj morale ‖ s (of a fable) morale f; **morals** (ethics) morale f; (modes of conduct) costumi mpl
**morale** [məˈræl] or [məˈrɑl] s morale m
**morali·ty** [məˈrælɪti] s (**-ties**) moralità f
**mor′als charge′** s accusa di oltraggio al pudore
**morass** [məˈræs] s palude f
**moratori·um** [ˌmɑrəˈtorɪ·əm] or [ˌmɑrəˈtɔrɪ·əm] s (**-ums** or **-a** [ə]) moratoria
**morbid** [ˈmɔrbɪd] adj (gruesome) orribile; (feelings; curiosity; pertaining to disease; pathologic) morboso
**mordacious** [mɔrˈdeʃəs] adj mordace
**mordant** [ˈmɔrdənt] adj & s mordente m
**more** [mor] adj & s più m ‖ adv più; **more and more** sempre più; **more than** più di; (followed by verb) più di quanto; **the more . . . the less** tanto più . . . quanto meno
**more·o′er** adv per di più, inoltre
**Moresque** [moˈrɛsk] adj moresco
**morgue** [mɔrg] s deposito, obitorio; (journ) archivio di un giornale, frigorifero
**moribund** [ˈmɔrɪˌbʌnd] or [ˈmɑrɪˌbʌnd] adj moribondo
**morning** [ˈmɔrnɪŋ] adj mattiniero ‖ s mattina, mattino; **good morning** buon giorno; **in the morning** di mattina
**morn′ing coat′** s giacca nera a code
**morn′ing-glo′ry** s (**-ries**) convolvolo; (Ipomea) campanella; (Convolvulus tricolor) bella di giorno
**morn′ing sick′ness** s vomito di gravidanza
**morn′ing star′** s Lucifero, stella del mattino
**Moroccan** [məˈrɑkən] adj & s maroccchino
**morocco** [məˈrɑko] s (leather) maroccchino ‖ **Morocco** s il Marocco
**moron** [ˈmɔrɑn] s deficiente mf
**morose** [məˈros] adj tetro, imbronciato
**morphine** [ˈmɔrfin] s morfina
**morphology** [mɔrˈfɑlədʒi] s morfologia
**morrow** [ˈmɑro] or [ˈmɔro] s—**on the morrow** l'indomani, il giorno seguente; domani
**morsel** [ˈmɔrsəl] s boccone m, bocconcino; pezzetto
**mortal** [ˈmɔrtəl] adj & s mortale m
**mortality** [mɔrˈtælɪti] s mortalità f; (death or destruction on a large scale) moria
**mortar** [ˈmɔrtər] s (mixture of lime or cement) malta, calcina; (bowl) mortaio; (mil) mortaio, lanciabombe m
**mor′tar·board′** s sparviere m; (cap) tocco accademico
**mortgage** [ˈmɔrgɪdʒ] s ipoteca ‖ tr ipotecare
**mortgagee** [ˌmɔrgɪˈdʒi] s creditore m ipotecario
**mortgagor** [ˈmɔrgɪdʒər] s debitore m ipotecario

**mortician** [mɔr'tɪʃən] *s* impresario di pompe funebri

**morti·fy** ['mɔrtɪ,faɪ] *v* (*pret* & *pp* **-fied**) *tr* mortificare; **to be mortified** vergognarsi

**mortise** ['mɔrtɪs] *s* intaccatura, inca- stro || *tr* incassare, incastrare

**mor'tise lock'** *s* serratura incastrata

**mortuar·y** ['mɔrtʃʊ,ɛri] *adj* mortuario || *s* (**-ies**) camera mortuaria

**mosaic** [mo'ze·ɪk] *s* mosaico

**Moscow** ['mɑskaʊ] *or* ['mɑsko] *s* Mosca

**Moses** ['mozɪz] *or* ['mozɪs] *s* Mosè *m*

**Mos·lem** ['mɑzləm] *or* ['mɑsləm] *adj* musulmano || *s* (**-lems** *or* **-lem**) mu- sulmano

**mosque** [mɑsk] *s* moschea

**mosqui·to** [məs'kito] *s* (**-toes** *or* **-tos**) zanzara

**mosqui'to net'** *s* zanzariera

**moss** [mɔs] *or* [mɑs] *s* musco

**moss'back'** *s* (coll) ultraconservatore *m*, fossile *m*

**moss·y** ['mɔsi] *or* ['mɑsi] *adj* (**-ier;** **-iest**) muscoso

**most** [most] *adj* il più di, la maggior parte di || *s* la maggioranza, i più; **most of** la maggior parte di; **to make the most of** trarre il massimo da || *adv* più, maggiormente, al massimo

**mostly** ['mostli] *adv* per lo più, mag- giormente, al massimo

**motel** [mo'tɛl] *s* motel *m*, autostello

**moth** [mɔθ] *or* [mɑθ] *s* falena; (*clothes moth*) tarma

**moth'ball'** *s* pallina antitarmica

**moth-eaten** ['mɔθ,itən] *or* ['mɑθ,itən] *adj* tarmato; antiquato

**mother** ['mʌðər] *adj* (*love, tongue*) materno; (*country*) natio; (*church, company*) madre || *s* madre *f*; (*elderly woman*) (coll) zia || *tr* fare da madre a; creare; procreare; assu- mere la maternità di

**moth'er coun'try** *s* madrepatria

**Moth'er Goose'** *s* supposta autrice di una raccolta di favole infantili

**motherhood** ['mʌðər,hʊd] *s* maternità *f*

**moth'er-in-law'** *s* (**moth'ers-in-law'**) suocera

**moth'er·land'** *s* madrepatria

**motherless** ['mʌðərlɪs] *adj* orfano di madre, senza madre

**mother-of-pearl** ['mʌðərəv'pʌrl] *adj* madreperlaceo || *s* madreperla

**motherly** ['mʌðərli] *adj* materno

**Moth'er's Day'** *s* giorno della madre, festa della mamma

**moth'er supe'rior** *s* madre superiora

**moth'er tongue'** *s* madrelingua; (*lan- guage from which another language is derived*) lingua madre

**moth'er wit'** *s* intelligenza nativa

**moth' hole'** *s* tarlatura

**moth·y** ['mɔθi] *or* ['mɑθi] *adj* (**-ier;** **-iest**) tarmato

**motif** [mo'tif] *s* motivo

**motion** ['moʃən] *s* movimento; (*e.g., of a dancer*) movenza, mossa; (*in par- liamentary procedure*) mozione; **in motion** in moto || *intr* fare cenno

**motionless** ['moʃənlɪs] *adj* immobile

**mo'tion pic'ture** *s* pellicola cinemato- grafica; **motion pictures** cinemato- grafia

**mo'tion-picture'** *adj* cinematografico

**motivate** ['motɪ,vet] *tr* animare, inci- tare

**motive** ['motɪv] *adj* motivo; (*produc- ing motion*) motore || *s* motivo; (*in- centive*) movente *m*

**mo'tive pow'er** *s* forza motrice; im- pianto motore; (rr) insieme *m* di locomotive

**motley** ['mɑtli] *adj* eterogeneo; va- riato, variopinto

**motor** ['motər] *adj* motore; (*operated by motor*) motorizzato; (*pertaining to motor vehicles*) motoristico || *s* mo- tore *m*; (aut) macchina || *intr* viag- giare in macchina

**mo'tor·boat'** *s* motobarca, motoscafo

**mo'tor·bus'** *s* torpedone *m*; autobus *m*

**motorcade** ['motər,ked] *s* carovana di automobili

**mo'tor·car'** *s* automobile *f*

**mo'tor·cy'le** *s* motocicletta

**motorist** ['motərɪst] *s* automobilista *mf*

**motorize** ['motə,raɪz] *tr* motorizzare

**mo'torman** *s* (**-men**) guidatore *m* di tram; guidatore *m* di locomotore

**mo'tor sail'er** *s* motoveliero

**mo'tor scoot'er** *s* motoretta

**mot'or ship'** *s* motonave *f*

**mo'tor truck'** *s* autocarro, camion *m*

**mo'tor ve'hicle** *s* motoveicolo

**mottle** ['mɑtəl] *tr* chiazzare, screziare

**mot·to** ['mɑto] *s* (**-toes** *or* **-tos**) motto, divisa

**mould** [mold] *s*, *tr*, & *intr* var of **mold**

**mound** [maʊnd] *s* monticello, colli- netta

**mount** [maʊnt] *s* monte *m*, montagna; (*horse for riding*) cavalcatura, monta; (*setting for a jewel*) monta- tura; supporto; (*for a picture*) incor- niciatura || *tr* montare; (*a wall*) sca- lare; (theat) allestire || *intr* montare; (*to climb*) salire

**mountain** ['maʊntən] *s* montagna; **to make a mountain out of a molehill** fare di un bruscolo una trave, fare d'una mosca un elefante

**moun'tain climb'ing** *s* alpinismo

**mountaineer** [,maʊntə'nɪr] *s* monta- naro

**mountainous** ['maʊntənəs] *adj* monta- gnoso

**moun'tain rail'road** *s* ferrovia a den- tiera

**moun'tain range'** *s* catena di montagne

**moun'tain sick'ness** *s* mal *m* di mon- tagna

**mountebank** ['maʊntɪ,bæŋk] *s* ciarla- tano

**mounting** ['maʊntɪŋ] *s* (*act*) il mon- tare, montaggio; (*setting*) montatura; (mach) supporto

**mourn** [morn] *tr* (*the loss of s.o.*) piangere; (*a misfortune*) lamentare || *intr* piangere; vestire a lutto

**mourner** ['mornər] *s* persona in lutto; (*penitent sinner*) penitente *mf*;

(*woman hired to attend a funeral or funerals*) prefica

**mourn'er's bench'** *s* banco dei penitenti

**mournful** ['mornfəl] *adj* luttuoso, funesto; (*gloomy*) lugubre

**mourning** ['mornɪŋ] *s* lutto; **to be in mourning** portare il lutto

**mourn'ing band'** *s* bracciale *m* a lutto

**mouse** [maʊs] *s* (**mice** [maɪs]) topo, sorcio

**mouse'hole'** *s* topaia; piccolo buco

**mouser** ['maʊzər] *s* cacciatore *m* di topi

**mouse'trap'** *s* trappola per topi

**moustache** [məs'tæʃ] or [məs'taʃ] *s* baffi *mpl*, mustacchi *mpl*

**mouth** [maʊθ] *s* (**mouths** [maʊðz]) bocca; **by mouth** per via orale; **to be born with a silver spoon in one's mouth** essere nato con la camicia; **to make one's mouth water** fare venire a qlcu l'acquolina in bocca

**mouthful** ['maʊθ ˌfʊl] *s* boccata

**mouth' or'gan** *s* armonica a bocca

**mouth'piece'** *s* (*of wind instrument*) bocchetta; (*of bridle*) imboccatura; (*of megaphone*) boccaglio; (*of cigarette*) bocchino; (*of telephone*) imboccatura; (*spokesman*) portavoce *m*

**mouth'wash'** *s* sciacquo, risciacquo

**movable** ['muvəbəl] *adj* mobile, mobile; (law) mobiliare

**move** [muv] *s* movimento; (*change of residence*) trasloco; (*step*) passo; (*e.g., in chess*) mossa; **on the move** in moto, in movimento; **to get a move on** (coll) affrettarsi || *tr* muovere; (*the bowels*) provocare l'evacuazione di; (*to prompt*) spingere; (*to stir the feelings of*) emozionare, commuovere; (law) proporre; (com) svendere; **to move up** (*a date*) anticipare || *intr* muoversi; passare; (*to another house*) traslocare; (*to another city*) trasferirsi; (*said of goods*) avere una vendita; (*said of the bowels*) evacuare; procedere; (law) presentare una mozione; (coll) andarsene; **to move away** andarsene; trasferirsi; **to move back** tirarsi indietro; **to move in** avanzare; (*society*) frequentare; **to move off** allontanarsi

**movement** ['muvmənt] *s* movimento; (*of a watch*) meccanismo; (*of the bowels*) evacuazione; (mus) movimento, tempo

**movie** ['muvi] *s* (coll) film *m*, pellicola

**movie·goer** ['muvi ˌgoˌər] *s* frequentatore *m* del cinema

**mov'ie house'** *s* (coll) cinematografo

**mov'ie·land'** *s* (coll) cinelandia

**moving** ['muvɪŋ] *adj* commovente, emozionante || *s* trasporto; (*from one house to another*) trasloco

**mov'ing pic'ture** *s* film *m*, pellicola

**mov'ing stair'case'** *s* scala mobile

**mow** [mo] *v* (*pret* **mowed;** *pp* **mowed** or **mown**) *tr* & *intr* falciare

**mower** ['moˌər] *s* falciatore *m;* (mach) falciatrice *f*

**Mr.** ['mɪstər] *s* (**Messrs.** ['mesərz]) Signore *m*

**Mrs.** ['mɪsɪz] *s* Signora

**much** [mʌtʃ] *adj* & *pron* molto; **as much . . . as** tanto . . . quanto; **too much** troppo || *adv* molto; **however much** per quanto; **how much** quanto; **too much** troppo; **very much** moltissimo

**mucilage** ['mjusɪlɪdʒ] *s* colla; (*gummy secretion in plants*) mucillagine *f*

**muck** [mʌk] *s* letame *m;* (*dirt*) sudiciume *m;* (min) materiale *m* di scoria

**muck'rake'** *intr* (coll) sollevare scandali

**mucous** ['mjukəs] *adj* mucoso

**mucus** ['mjukəs] *s* muco

**mud** [mʌd] *s* fango, melma, limo; **to sling mud at** calunniare

**muddle** ['mʌdəl] *s* confusione, guazzabuglio || *tr* confondere, intorbidire || *intr*—**to muddle through** arrangiarsi; cavarsela alla meno peggio in

**mud'dle·head'** *s* (coll) semplicione *m*

**mud·dy** ['mʌdi] *adj* (**-dier; -diest**) fangoso, melmoso; (*obscure*) torbido || *v* (*pret* & *pp* **-died**) *tr* turbare, intorbidare; (*to soil with mud*) infangare

**mud'guard'** *s* parafango

**mud'hole'** *s* pozzanghera, fangaia

**mud' slide'** *s* smottamento

**mudslinger** ['mʌd ˌslɪŋgər] *s* calunniatore *m*

**muff** [mʌf] *s* manicotto || *tr* (coll) mancare; (*to handle badly*) (coll) abborracciare; (sports) mancare di pigliare

**muffin** ['mʌfɪn] *s* panino soffice

**muffle** ['mʌfəl] *tr* infagottare, imbacuccare; (*a sound*) velare, smorzare

**muffler** ['mʌflər] *s* sciarpa; (aut) silenziatore *m*, marmitta

**mufti** ['mʌfti] *s*—**in mufti** in borghese

**mug** [mʌg] *s* tazzona; (slang) muso, grugno || *v* (*pret* & *pp* **mugged;** *ger* **mugging**) *tr* (slang) fotografare; (slang) attaccare proditoriamente || *intr* fare le smorfie

**mug·gy** ['mʌgi] *adj* (**-gier; -giest**) afoso, opprimente

**mulat·to** [mju'læto] or [mə'læto] *s* (**-toes**) mulatto

**mulber·ry** ['mʌl ˌberi] *s* (**-ries**) (*tree*) gelso; (*fruit*) mora di gelso

**mulct** [mʌlkt] *tr* defraudare

**mule** [mjul] *s* mulo; (*slipper*) pianella

**muleteer** [ ˌmjulə'tɪr] *s* mulattiere *m*

**mulish** ['mjulɪʃ] *adj* testardo

**mull** [mʌl] *tr* (*wine*) scaldare aggiungendo spezie || *intr*—**to mull over** pensarci sopra, rinvangare

**mulled' wine'** *s* vino caldo

**mullion** ['mʌljən] *s* colonnina che divide una bifora

**multigraph** ['mʌltɪ ˌgræf] or ['mʌltɪ ˌgraf] *s* (trademark) poligrafo || *tr* poligrafare

**multilateral** [ ˌmʌltɪ'lætərəl] *adj* multilaterale

**multimotor** [ ˌmʌltɪ'motər] *s* plurimotore *m*

**multiple** ['mʌltɪpəl] *adj* & *s* multiplo

**multiplici·ty** [ ˌmʌltɪ'plɪsɪti] *s* (**-ties**) molteplicità *f*

**multi·ply** ['mʌltɪ ˌplaɪ] *v* (*pret* & *pp* **-plied**) *tr* moltiplicare || *intr* moltiplicarsi

**multistage** ['mʌltɪ ˌstedʒ] *adj* (rok) pluristadio

**multitude** ['mʌltɪ ˌtjud] or ['mʌltɪˌtud] s moltitudine *f*

**mum** [mʌm] *adj* zitto; **mum's the word!** acqua in bocca!; **to keep mum** stare zitto ‖ *interj* zitto!

**mumble** ['mʌmbəl] *tr* biascicare ‖ *intr* farfugliare

**mummer·y** ['mʌməri] *s* (**-ies**) buffonata, mascherata

**mum·my** ['mʌmi] *s* (**-mies**) mummia

**mumps** [mʌmps] *s* orecchioni *mpl*

**munch** [mʌntʃ] *tr* sgranocchiare

**mundane** ['mʌnden] *adj* mondano

**municipal** [mju'nɪsɪpəl] *adj* municipale

**municipali·ty** [mju ˌnɪsɪ'pælɪti] *s* (**-ties**) municipio

**munificent** [mju'nɪfɪsənt] *adj* munifico

**munition** [mju'nɪʃən] *s* munizione ‖ *tr* fornire di munizioni

**muni'tion dump'** *s* deposito munizioni

**mural** ['mjurəl] *adj* murale ‖ *s* pittura murale

**murder** ['mʌrdər] *s* omicidio ‖ *tr* assassinare

**murderer** ['mʌrdərər] *s* omicida *m*

**murderess** ['mʌrdərɪs] *s* omicida *f*

**murderous** ['mʌrdərəs] *adj* omicida, crudele, sanguinario

**murk·y** ['mʌrki] *adj* (**-ier; -iest**) fosco, tenebroso; brumoso, nebbioso

**murmur** ['mʌrmər] *s* mormorio ‖ *tr & intr* mormorare

**Mur'phy bed'** ['mʌrfi] *s* letto a scomparsa

**muscle** ['mʌsəl] *s* muscolo

**muscular** ['mʌskjələr] *adj* muscolare; (*having well-developed muscles*) muscoloso

**muse** [mjuz] *s* musa; **the Muses** le Muse ‖ *intr* meditare, rimuginare

**museum** [mju'zi·əm] *s* museo

**mush** [mʌʃ] *s* pappa, polentina; (fig) leziosaggine *f*, sdolcinatura

**mush'room** *s* fungo ‖ *intr* venir su come i funghi; **to mushroom into** diventare rapidamente

**mush'room cloud'** *s* fungo atomico

**mush·y** ['mʌʃi] *adj* (**-ier; -iest**) polposo, spappolato; (fig) sdolcinato, sentimentale

**music** ['mjuzɪk] *s* musica; **to face the music** (coll) affrontare le conseguenze; **to set to music** mettere in musica

**musical** ['mjuzɪkəl] *adj* musicale

**mu'sical com'edy** *s* operetta, commedia musicale

**musicale** [ˌmjuzɪ'kæl] *s* serata musicale

**mu'sic box'** *s* scatola armonica

**mu'sic cab'inet** *s* scaffaletto per la musica

**mu'sic hall'** *s* salone *m* da concerti; (Brit) teatro di varietà, music-hall *m*

**musician** [mju'zɪʃən] *s* musicista *mf*

**musicianship** [mju'zɪʃən ˌʃɪp] *s* abilità *f* musicale, virtuosismo

**musicologist** [ˌmjuzɪ'kalədʒɪst] *s* musicologo

**musicology** [ˌmjuzɪ'kalədʒi] *s* musicologia

**mu'sic stand'** *s* portamusica *m*

**musk** [mʌsk] *s* muschio

**musk' deer'** *s* mosco

**musket** ['mʌskɪt] *s* moschetto

**musketeer** [ˌmʌskɪ'tɪr] *s* moschettiere *m*

**musk'mel'on** *s* melone *m*

**musk' ox'** *s* bue muschiato

**musk'rat'** *s* ondatra, topo muschiato

**muslin** ['mʌzlɪn] *s* mussolina

**muss** [mʌs] *tr* (*the hair*) scompigliare, arruffare; (*clothing*) (coll) sciupare

**mussel** ['mʌsəl] *s* mussolo

**Mussulman** ['mʌsəlmən] *adj & s* musulmano

**muss·y** ['mʌsi] *adj* (**-ier; -iest**) (coll) arruffato, scompigliato

**must** [mʌst] *s* (*new wine*) mosto; (*mold*) muffa; (coll) cosa assolutamente indispensabile ‖ *v aux*—**I must go now** devo andarmene ora; **it must be Ann** deve essere Anna; **she must be ill** dev'essere malata; **they must have known it** devono averlo saputo

**mustache** [məs'tæʃ], [məs'taʃ] or ['mʌstæʃ] *s* baffi *mpl*, mustacchi *mpl*

**mustard** ['mʌstərd] *s* mostarda

**mus'tard plas'ter** *s* senapismo

**muster** ['mʌstər] *s* adunata, rivista; **to pass muster** passar ispezione ‖ *tr* chiamare a raccolta; riunire; **to muster in** arruolare; **to muster out** congedare; **to muster up courage** prendere coraggio a quattro mani

**mus'ter roll'** *s* ruolo; (naut) appello

**mus·ty** ['mʌsti] *adj* (**-tier; -tiest**) (*moldy*) ammuffito; (*stale*) stantio; (fig) ammuffito, stantio

**mutation** [mju'teʃən] *s* mutazione

**mute** [mjut] *adj & s* muto ‖ *tr* mettere la sordina a

**mutilate** ['mjutɪ ˌlet] *tr* mutilare

**mutineer** [ˌmjutɪ'nɪr] *s* ammutinato

**mutinous** ['mjutɪnəs] *adj* ammutinato

**muti·ny** ['mjutɪni] *s* (**-nies**) ammutinamento ‖ *v* (*pret & pp* **-nied**) *intr* ammutinarsi

**mutt** [mʌt] *s* (slang) cane bastardo; (slang) scemo

**mutter** ['mʌtər] *tr & intr* borbottare

**mutton** ['mʌtən] *s* montone *m*

**mut'ton chop'** *s* cotoletta di montone

**mutual** ['mutʃu·əl] *adj* mutuo, vicendevole

**mu'tual aid'** *s* mutualità *f*

**mu'tual fund'** *s* fondo comune di investimento

**muzzle** ['mʌzəl] *s* (*of animal*) muso; (*device to keep animal from biting*) museruola; (*of firearm*) bocca ‖ *tr* mettere la museruola a; (fig) imbavagliare

**my** [maɪ] *adj poss* mio, il mio ‖ *interj* (coll) corbezzoli!

**myriad** ['mɪrɪ·əd] *s* miriade *f*

**myrrh** [mʌr] *s* mirra

**myrtle** ['mʌrtəl] *s* mirto, mortella

**myself** [maɪ'self] *pron pers* io stesso; me, me stesso; mi, e.g., **I hurt myself** mi sono fatto male

**mysterious** [mɪs'tɪrɪ·əs] *adj* misterioso
**myster·y** ['mɪstəri] *s* (-ies) mistero
**mystic** ['mɪstɪk] *adj* & *s* mistico
**mystical** ['mɪstɪkəl] *adj* mistico
**mysticism** ['mɪstɪ‚sɪzəm] *s* misticismo
**mystification** [‚mɪstɪfɪ'keʃən] *s* mistificazione
**mysti·fy** ['mɪstɪ‚faɪ] *v* (*pret* & *pp*

**-fied**) *tr* avvolgere nel mistero; (*to hoax*) mistificare
**myth** [mɪθ] *s* mito
**mythical** ['mɪθɪkəl] *adj* mitico
**mythological** [‚mɪθə'ladʒɪkəl] *adj* mitologico
**mytholo·gy** [mɪ'θalədʒi] *s* (-gies) mitologia

# N

**N, n** [ɛn] *s* quattordicesima lettera dell'alfabeto inglese
**nab** [næb] *v* (*pret* & *pp* **nabbed;** *ger* **nabbing**) *tr* (slang) afferrare, agguantare
**nag** [næg] *s* ronzino ‖ *v* (*pret* & *pp* **nagged;** *ger* **nagging**) *tr* & *intr* tormentare, infastidire
**naiad** ['ne·æd] or ['naɪ·æd] *s* naiade *f*
**nail** [nel] *s* (*of finger or toe*) unghia; (*of metal*) chiodo; **to hit the nail on the head** cogliere nel giusto ‖ *tr* inchiodare
**nail'brush'** spazzolino per le unghie
**nail' file'** *s* lima per le unghie
**nail' pol'ish** *s* smalto per le unghie
**nail' set'** *s* punzone *m*
**naïve** [na'iv] *adj* candido, ingenuo
**naked** ['nekɪd] *adj* nudo, ignudo; **to strip naked** denudare; denudarsi; **with the naked eye** a occhio nudo
**name** [nem] *s* nome *m*; (*first name*) nome *m*; (*last name*) cognome *m*; fama, reputazione; titolo; lignaggio; **in the name of** nel nome di; **to call s.o. names** coprire qlco di ingiurie; **to go by the name of** essere conosciuto sotto il nome di; **to make a name for oneself** farsi un nome; **what is your name?** come si chiama Lei? ‖ *tr* nominare; menzionare; battezzare; (*a price*) fissare
**name' day'** *s* onomastico
**nameless** ['nemlɪs] *adj* senza nome, anonimo
**namely** ['nemli] *adv* cioè, vale a dire
**name'plate'** *s* targa, targhetta
**namesake** ['nem‚sek] *s* omonimo; persona chiamata in onore di qualcun altro
**nan'ny goat'** ['næni] *s* capra
**nap** [næp] *s* lanugine *f;* (*pile*) pelo; pisolino, sonnellino; **to take a nap** schiacciare un sonnellino ‖ *v* (*pret* & *pp* **napped;** *ger* **napping**) *intr* sonnecchiare; **to catch napping** cogliere alla sprovvista
**napalm** ['nepam] *s* napalm *m*
**nape** [nep] *s* nuca
**naphtha** ['næfθə] *s* nafta
**napkin** ['næpkɪn] *s* tovagliolo
**nap'kin ring'** *s* portatovagliolo
**Naples** ['nepləz] *s* Napoli *f*
**Napoleonic** [nə‚poli'anɪk] *adj* napoleonico
**narcissus** [nar'sɪsəs] *s* narciso
**narcotic** [nar'katɪk] *adj* & *s* narcotico
**narrate** [næ'ret] *tr* narrare

**narration** [næ'reʃən] *s* narrazione
**narrative** ['nærətɪv] *adj* narrativo ‖ *s* narrazione; (*genre*) narrativa
**narrator** [næ'retər] *s* narratore *m*
**narrow** ['næro] *adj* stretto; limitato; (*illiberal*) meschino, ristretto ‖ **narrows** *spl* stretti *mpl* ‖ *tr* limitare, restringere ‖ *intr* limitarsi, restringersi
**nar'row escape'** *s*—**to have a narrow escape** scamparla bella
**nar'row-gauge'** *adj* a scartamento ridotto
**narrow-minded** ['næro'maɪndɪd] *adj* gretto, ristretto d'idee
**nasal** ['nezəl] *adj* & *s* nasale *f*
**nasturtium** [nə'stʌrʃəm] *s* nasturzio
**nas·ty** ['næsti] or ['nasti] *adj* (-tier; -tiest) brutto, cattivo; sgradevole, orribile; sudicio; (*foul*) perfido
**natatorium** [‚netə'torɪ·əm] *s* piscina
**nation** ['neʃən] *s* nazione
**national** ['næʃənəl] *adj* & *s* nazionale *mf*
**na'tional an'them** *s* inno nazionale
**na'tional debt'** *s* debito pubblico
**na'tional hol'iday** *s* festa nazionale
**nationalism** ['næʃənə‚lɪzəm] *s* nazionalismo
**national·ty** [‚næʃən'ælɪti] *s* (-ties) nazionalità *f*
**nationalize** ['næʃənə‚laɪz] *tr* nazionalizzare
**na'tion·wide'** *adj* su scala nazionale
**native** ['netɪv] *adj* nativo, indigeno, oriundo; (*language*) materno ‖ *s* indigeno, nativo
**na'tive land'** *s* patria, paese natio
**nativi·ty** [nə'tɪvɪti] *s* (-ties) nascita, natività *f* ‖ **Nativity** *s* Natività *f*
**Nato** ['neto] *s* (acronym) (**North Atlantic Treaty Organization**) la N.A.T.O.
**nat·ty** ['næti] *adj* (-tier; -tiest) accurato, elegante
**natural** ['nætʃərəl] *adj* naturale ‖ *s* imbecille *mf;* (mus) bequadro; (mus) tono naturale; (mus) tasto bianco; **a natural** (coll) proprio quello che ci vuole
**naturalism** ['nætʃərə‚lɪzəm] *s* naturalismo
**naturalist** ['nætʃərəlɪst] *s* naturalista *mf*
**naturalization** [‚nætʃərəlɪ'zeʃən] *s* naturalizzazione
**nat'uraliza'tion pa'pers** *spl* documenti *mpl* di naturalizzazione

**naturalize** ['næt∫ərə ,laız] *tr* naturalizzare

**naturally** ['næt∫ərəli] *adv* naturalmente

**nature** ['net∫ər] *s* natura; **from nature** dal vero

**naught** [nɔt] *s* niente *m;* zero; **to come to naught** ridursi al nulla; **to set at naught** disprezzare

**naugh·ty** ['nɔti] *adj* (**-tier; -tiest**) cattivo, disubbidiente; (*joke*) di cattivo genere

**nausea** ['nɔ∫ı·ə] or ['nɔsı·ə] *s* nausea

**nauseate** ['nɔ∫ı ,et] or ['nɔsı ,et] *tr* nauseare ‖ *intr* essere nauseato

**nauseating** ['nɔ∫ı ,etıŋ] or ['nɔsı ,etıŋ] *adj* nauseabondo, stomachevole

**nauseous** ['nɔ∫ı·əs] or ['nɔsı·əs] *adj* nauseabondo

**nautical** ['nɔtıkəl] *adj* nautico, marittimo, marino

**naval** ['nevəl] *adj* navale

**na'val acad'emy** *s* accademia navale

**na'val of'ficer** *s* ufficiale *m* di marina

**na'val sta'tion** *s* base *f* navale

**nave** [nev] *s* navata centrale; (*of a wheel*) mozzo

**navel** ['nevəl] *s* ombelico

**na'vel or'ange** *s* arancia (con depressione alla sommità)

**navigability** [ ,nævıgə'bılıti] *s* navigabilità *f;* (*of a ship*) manovrabilità *f*

**navigable** ['nævıgəbəl] *adj* (*river*) navigabile; (*ship*) manovrabile

**navigate** ['nævı ,get] *tr & intr* navigare

**navigation** [ ,nævı 'ge∫ən] *s* navigazione

**navigator** ['nævı ,getər] *s* navigatore *m;* (*in charge of navigating ship or plane*) ufficiale *m* di rotta

**na·vy** ['nevi] *adj* blu marino ‖ *s* (**-vies**) marina (da guerra)

**na'vy bean'** *s* fagiolo secco

**na'vy blue'** *s* blu marino

**na'vy yard'** *s* arsenale *m*

**nay** [ne] *s* no; voto negativo ‖ *adv* no; anzi

**Nazarene** [ ,næzə'rin] *adj & s* nazzareno; **the Nazarene** il Nazzareno

**Nazi** ['nɑtsi] or ['nætsi] *adj & s* nazista *mf*

**N-bomb** ['ɛn ,bɑm] *s* bomba al neutrone

**Neapolitan** [ ,ni·ə'pɑlıtən] *adj & s* napoletano

**neap' tide'** [nip] *s* marea di quadratura

**near** [nır] *adj* vicino, prossimo; intimo; esatto ‖ *adv* vicino, da vicino ‖ *prep* vicino a, accanto a; **to come near** avvicinarsi a ‖ *tr* avvicinarsi a ‖ *intr* avvicinarsi

**nearby** ['nır ,baı] *adj* vicino ‖ *adv* vicino, qui vicino

**Near' East'** *s* Medio Oriente

**nearly** ['nırli] *adv* quasi; (*a little more or less*) press'a poco; per poco non, e.g., **he nearly died** per poco non morì

**near-sighted** ['nır'saıtıd] *adj* miope

**near'-sight'ed·ness** *s* miopia

**neat** [nit] *adj* netto, pulito; elegante, accurato; puro

**neat's'-foot oil'** *s* olio di piede di bue

**Nebuchadnezzar** [ ,nɛbjəkəd'nɛzər] *s* Nabucodonosor *m*

**nebu·la** ['nɛbjələ] *s* (**-lae** [ ,li] or **-las**) nebulosa

**nebular** ['nɛbjələr] *adj* nebulare

**nebulous** ['nɛbjələs] *adj* nebuloso

**necessary** ['nɛsı ,seri] *adj* necessario

**necessitate** [nı'sɛsı ,tet] *tr* necessitare, esigere

**necessitous** [nı'sɛsıtəs] *adj* bisognoso

**necessi·ty** [nı'sɛsıti] *s* (**-ties**) necessità *f*

**neck** [nɛk] *s* collo; (*of a horse*) incollatura; (*of violin*) manico; (*of mountain*) gola, passo; **neck and neck** testa a testa; **to stick one's neck out** (coll) esporsi al pericolo; **to win by a neck** vincere per una corta testa ‖ *intr* (slang) abbracciarsi, sbaciucchiarsi

**neck'band'** *s* colletto

**neckerchief** ['nɛkər ,t∫ıf] *s* fazzoletto da collo

**necklace** ['nɛklıs] *s* collana

**neck'line'** *s* giro collo, scollatura

**necktie** ['nɛk ,taı] *s* cravatta

**neck'tie pin'** *s* spilla da cravatta

**necrolo·gy** [nɛ'krɑlədʒi] *s* (**-gies**) necrologia

**necromancy** ['nɛkrə ,mænsi] *s* necromanzia

**nectar** ['nɛktər] *s* nettare *m*

**née** or **nee** [ne] *adj* nata

**need** [nid] *s* necessità *f*, bisogno; povertà *f;* **if need be** se ci fosse bisogno; **in need** in strettezze ‖ *tr* aver bisogno di ‖ *intr* necessitare, essere in necessità ‖ *v aux*—**to need (to)** + *inf* dovere + *inf*

**needful** ['nidfəl] *adj* necessario

**needle** ['nidəl] *s* ago; (*of phonograph*) puntina; **to look for a needle in a haystack** cercare l'ago nel pagliaio ‖ *tr* cucire; (fig) aguzzare, eccitare

**nee'dle bath'** *s* bagno a doccia filiforme

**nee'dle·case'** *s* agoraio

**nee'dle·point'** *s* merletto; ricamo su canovaccio

**needless** ['nidlıs] *adj* inutile

**nee'dle·work'** *s* lavoro di cucito; (*embroidery*) ricamo; (*needlepoint*) merletto

**needs** [nidz] *adv* necessariamente; **it must needs be** dev'essere proprio così

**need·y** [nidi] *adj* (**-ier; -iest**) bisognoso, indigente ‖ **the needy** i bisognosi

**ne'er-do-well** ['nɛrdu ,wɛl] *adj & s* buono a nulla

**negate** ['nɛget] or [nı'get] *tr* invalidare; negare

**negation** [nı'ge∫ən] *s* negazione

**negative** ['nɛgətıv] *adj* negativo ‖ *s* negativa; (elec) polo negativo; (gram) negazione ‖ *tr* respingere, votare contro; neutralizzare

**neglect** [nı'glɛkt] *s* negligenza, trascuratezza ‖ *tr* trascurare; **to neglect to** trascurare di; dimenticarsi di

**neglectful** [nı'glɛktfəl] *adj* negligente, trascurato

**négligée** or **negligee** [ ,nɛglı'ʒe] *s* veste *f* da camera or vestaglia per signora

**negligence** ['nɛglıdʒəns] *s* negligenza, trascuratezza

**negligent** ['nɛglɪdʒənt] *adj* negligente, trascurato

**negligible** ['nɛglɪdʒɪbəl] *adj* trascurabile, insignificante

**negotiable** [nɪ'goʃɪ·əbəl] *adj* negoziabile; (*security*) al portatore; (*road*) transitabile

**negotiate** [nɪ'goʃɪ‚et] *tr* negoziare; (*to overcome*) superare ‖ *intr* negoziare

**negotiation** [nɪ‚goʃɪ'eʃən] *s* negoziazione, negoziato

**Ne·gro** ['nigro] *adj* negro ‖ *s* (**-groes**) negro, nero

**neigh** [ne] *s* nitrito ‖ *intr* nitrire

**neighbor** ['nebər] *adj* vicino, adiacente ‖ *s* vicino; (*fellow man*) prossimo ‖ *tr* essere vicino a ‖ *intr* essere vicino

**neighborhood** ['nebər‚hud] *s* vicinanza, vicinato; **in the neighborhood of** nei pressi di; (coll) a un dipresso, all'incirca

**neighboring** ['nebərɪŋ] *adj* vicino, attiguo; (*country*) limitrofo

**neighborly** ['nebərli] *adj* da buon vicino, socievole

**neither** ['niðər] or ['naɪðər] *adj indef* nessuno dei due, e.g., **neither boy** nessuno dei due ragazzi ‖ *pron indef* nessuno dei due, nè l'uno nè l'altro ‖ *conj* neppure, nemmeno, e.g., **neither do I** nemmeno io; **neither . . . nor** nè . . . nè

**neme·sis** ['nɛmɪsɪs] *s* (**-ses** [‚siz]) nemesi *f* ‖ **Nemesis** *s* Nemesi *f*

**neologism** [ni'alə‚dʒɪzəm] *s* neologismo

**neomycin** [‚ni·ə'maɪsɪn] *s* neomicina

**ne'on lamp'** ['ni·an] *s* lampada al neon

**neophyte** ['ni·ə‚faɪt] *s* neofita *mf*

**nepenthe** [nɪ'pɛnθi] *s* nepente *f*

**nephew** ['nɛfju] or ['nɛvju] *s* nipote *m*

**Nepos** ['nipas] or ['nɛpas] *s* Nipote *m*

**Neptune** ['nɛptʃun] or ['nɛptjun] *s* Nettuno

**neptunium** [nɛp't'juni·əm] or [nɛp-'tjuni·əm] *s* (chem) nettunio

**Nero** ['nɪro] *s* Nerone *m*

**nerve** [nʌrv] *adj* nervoso ‖ *s* nervo; (*courage*) coraggio; (*boldness*) (coll) faccia tosta; **to get on one's nerves** dare ai nervi di qlcu; **to lose one's nerve** perdere le staffe

**nerve-racking** ['nʌrv‚rækɪŋ] *adj* irritante, esasperante

**nervous** ['nʌrvəs] *adj* nervoso

**nerv'ous break'down** *s* esaurimento nervoso

**nervousness** ['nʌrvəsnɪs] *s* nervosismo

**nerv·y** ['nʌrvi] *adj* (**-ier; -iest**) (*strong*) forte, vigoroso; audace; (coll) insolente, sfacciato

**nest** [nɛst] *s* nido; (*of hen*) cova; (*retreat*) rifugio; (*hangout*) tana; (*brood*) nidiata; **to feather one's nest** farsi il gruzzolo ‖ *tr* (e.g., *tables*) mettere l'uno nell'altro ‖ *intr* nidificare

**nest' egg'** *s* endice *m;* (fig) gruzzolo

**nestle** ['nɛsəl] *tr* annidare ‖ *intr* annidarsi, nidificare; (*to cuddle up*) rannicchiarsi

**net** [nɛt] *adj* netto ‖ *s* rete *f;* (*snare*) laccio, trappola; guadagno netto ‖ *tr* prendere con la rete; (*a sum of money*) fare un guadagno netto di

**nether** ['nɛðər] *adj* inferiore, infero

**Netherlander** ['nɛðər‚lændər] or ['nɛð-ərləndər] *s* olandese *mf*

**Netherlands, The** ['nɛðərləndz] *spl* i Paesi Bassi

**netting** ['nɛtɪŋ] *s* rete *f*

**nettle** ['nɛtəl] *s* ortica ‖ *tr* irritare, provocare

**net'work'** *s* rete *f*

**neuralgia** [nju'rældʒə] or [nu'rældʒə] *s* nevralgia

**neurology** [nju'ralədʒi] or [nu'ralədʒi] *s* neurologia

**neuro·sis** [nju'rosɪs] or [nu'rosɪs] (**-ses** [siz]) *s* neurosi *f*

**neurotic** [nju'ratɪk] or [nu'ratɪk] *adj & s* neurotico

**neuter** ['njutər] or ['nutər] *adj* neutro ‖ *s* genere neutro

**neutral** ['njutrəl] or ['nutrəl] *adj* neutro; (*not aligned*) neutrale ‖ *s* neutrale *m;* (mach) folle *m*

**neutralist** ['njutrəlɪst] or ['nutrəlɪst] *adj & s* neutralista *mf*

**neutrality** [nju'trælɪti] or [nu'trælɪti] *s* neutralità *f*

**neutralize** ['njutrə‚laɪz] or ['nutrə‚laɪz] *tr* neutralizzare

**neutron** ['njutran] or ['nutran] *s* neutrone *m*

**neu'tron bomb'** *s* bomba al neutrone

**never** ['nɛvər] *adv* mai, giammai; non . . . mai; **never mind** non importa

**nev'er·more'** *adv* mai più

**nevertheless** [‚nɛvərðə'lɛs] *adv* ciò nonostante, ciò nondimeno, tuttavia

**new** [nju] or [nu] *adj* nuovo; **what's new?** che c'è di nuovo?

**new' arri'val** *s* nuovo venuto; (*baby*) neonato

**new'born'** *adj* neonato; (e.g., *faith*) rinato

**New'cas'tle** *s*—**to carry coals to Newcastle** portare l'acqua al mare, portare vasi a Samo

**newcomer** ['nju‚kʌmər] or ['nu‚kʌmər] *s* nuovo venuto

**New' Eng'land** *s* la Nuova Inghilterra

**newfangled** ['nju‚fæŋgəld] or ['nu‚fæŋgəld] *adj* all'ultima moda; di nuovo conio, di nuova invenzione

**Newfoundland** ['njufənd‚lænd] or ['nufənd‚lænd] *s* la Terranova ‖ [nju'faundlənd] or [nu'faundlənd] *s* (*dog*) terranova *m*

**newly** ['njuli] or ['nuli] *adv* di recente, di fresco

**new'ly·wed'** *s* sposino or sposina; **the newlyweds** gli sposi

**new' moon'** *s* luna nuova, novilunio

**news** [njuz] or [nuz] *s* notizie *fpl;* **a news item** una notizia; **a piece of news** una notizia

**news' a'gency** *s* agenzia d'informazioni

**news'beat'** *s* colpo giornalistico

**news'boy'** *s* strillone *m*

**news'cast'** *s* notiziario

**news'cast'er** *s* annunziatore *m*, radiocommentatore *m*, telecommentatore *m*

**news' con'ference** *s* conferenza stampa

**news′ cov′erage** *s* reportaggio
**news′deal′er** *s* venditore *m* di giornali
**news′man′** *s* (-men′) (*reporter*) giornalista *m;* giornalaio
**newsmonger** [′njuz ˌmʌŋgər] *or* [′nuz ˌmʌŋgər] *s* persona pettegola, gazzettino
**news′pa′per** *adj* giornalistico ‖ *s* giornale *m*
**news′pa′per•man′** *s* (-men′) giornalista *m*
**news′print′** *s* carta da giornale
**news′reel′** *s* cinegiornale *m*
**news′stand′** *s* chiosco, edicola
**news′week′ly** *s* (-lies) settimanale *m* d'informazione
**news′wor′thy** *adj* degno d'essere pubblicato, di viva attualità
**news•y** [′njuzi] *or* [′nuzi] *adj* (-ier; -iest) (coll) informativo
**New′ Tes′tament** *s* Nuovo Testamento
**New′ Year′s′ card′** *s* cartolina d'auguri di capodanno
**New′ Year′s′ Day′** *s* il capo d'anno, il capodanno
**New′ Year′s′ Eve′** *s* la vigilia di capodanno, la sera di San Silvestro
**New′ York′** [jɔrk] *adj* nuovayorchese ‖ *s* New York *f,* Nuova York
**New′ York′er** [′jɔrkər] *s* nuovayorchese *mf*
**New′ Zea′land** [′zilənd] *adj* neozelandese ‖ *s* la Nuova Zelanda
**New′ Zea′lander** [′ziləndər] *s* neozelandese *mf*
**next** [nɛkst] *adj* prossimo, seguente; (*month*) prossimo, entrante ‖ *adv* la prossima volta; dopo, in seguito; **next to** vicino a; **next to nothing** quasi nulla; **to come next** essere il prossimo
**next′-door′** *adj* della casa vicina ‖ **next′-door′** *adv* nella casa vicina
**next′ of kin′** *s* (next′ of kin′) parente più prossimo
**niacin** [′naɪ•əsɪn] *s* niacina
**Niag′ara Falls′** [naɪ′ægərə] *spl* le Cascate del Niagara
**nib** [nɪb] *s* becco; punta; **his nibs** (slang & pej) sua eccellenza
**nibble** [′nɪbəl] *s* piccolo morso ‖ *tr & intr* mordicchiare, sbocconcellare; (*said of a fish*) abboccare
**nice** [naɪs] *adj* (*pleasant*) simpatico, gentile; (*requiring skill*) buono, bello; (*fine*) sottile; (*refined*) raffinato, per bene; (*fussy*) esigente, difficile; rispettabile; (*weather*) bello; (*attractive*) bello; **nice . . . and** (coll) bello, e.g., **it is nice and warm** fa un bel caldo
**nice-looking** [′naɪs′lʊkɪŋ] *adj* bello, attraente
**nicely** [′naɪsli] *adv* precisamente, esattamente; (coll) benissimo
**nice•ty** [′naɪsəti] *s* (-ties) esattezza, precisione; **to a nicety** con la massima precisione
**niche** [nɪtʃ] *s* nicchia
**Nicholas** [′nɪkələs] *s* Nicola *m*
**nick** [nɪk] *s* intaccatura; (*of a dish*) slabbratura; **in the nick of time** al

momento giusto ‖ *tr* intaccare; (*to cut*) tagliare; (*a dish*) slabbrare
**nickel** [′nɪkəl] *s* nichel *m;* moneta americana di cinque cents ‖ *tr* nichelare
**nick′el plate′** *s* nichelatura
**nick′el-plate′** *tr* nichelare
**nicknack** [′nɪk ˌnæk] *s* soprammobile *m;* gingillo, ninnolo
**nick′name′** *s* nomignolo, soprannome *m* ‖ *tr* soprannominare
**nicotine** [′nɪkə ˌtin] *s* nicotina
**niece** [nis] *s* nipote *f*
**nif•ty** [′nɪfti] *adj* (-tier; -tiest) (coll) elegante; (coll) eccellente
**niggard** [′nɪgərd] *adj & s* spilorcio
**night** [naɪt] *adj* notturno ‖ *s* notte *f;* **at or by night** di notte; **the night before last** l'altra notte; **to make a night of it** (coll) fare le ore piccole
**night′cap′** *s* berretto da notte; bicchierino di liquore che si beve prima di coricarsi
**night′ club′** *s* night-club *m*
**night′ driv′ing** *s* il guidare di notte
**night′fall′** *s* crepuscolo; **at nightfall** sul cader della notte, all'imbrunire
**night′gown′** *s* camicia da notte
**nightingale** [′naɪtən ˌgel] *s* usignolo
**night′ latch′** *s* serratura a molla
**night′ let′ter** *s* telegramma notturno
**night′long′** *adj* di tutta la notte ‖ *adv* tutta la notte
**nightly** [′naɪtli] *adj* di notte; di ogni notte ‖ *adv* di notte; ogni notte
**night′mare′** *s* incubo
**nightmarish** [′naɪt ˌmɛrɪʃ] *adj* raccapricciante
**night′ owl′** *s* (coll) nottambulo
**night′ school′** *s* scuola serale
**night′shirt′** *s* camicia da notte
**night′time′** *s* notte *f*
**night′walk′er** *s* nottambulo; vagabondo notturno; (*prostitute*) passeggiatrice *f*
**night′ watch′** *s* guardia notturna
**night′ watch′man** *s* (-men) guardiano notturno
**nihilist** [′naɪ•ɪlɪst] *s* nichilista *mf*
**nil** [nɪl] *s* nulla *m,* niente *m*
**Nile** [naɪl] *s* Nilo
**nimble** [′nɪmbəl] *adj* agile, svelto
**Nimrod** [′nɪmrɑd] *s* Nembrod *m*
**nincompoop** [′nɪnkəm ˌpup] *s* babbeo, tonto, semplicione *m*
**nine** [naɪn] *adj & pron* nove ‖ *s* nove *m;* **nine o' clock** le nove
**nine′ hun′dred** *adj, s & pron* novecento
**nineteen** [′naɪn′tin] *adj, s & pron* diciannove *m*
**nineteenth** [′naɪn′tinθ] *adj & s* diciannovesimo; (*century*) decimonono ‖ *s* (*in dates*) diciannove *m* ‖ *pron* diciannovesimo
**ninetieth** [′naɪntɪ•ɪθ] *adj, s & pron* novantesimo
**nine•ty** [′naɪnti] *adj & pron* novanta ‖ *s* (-ties) novanta *m;* **the gay nineties** il decennio scapestrato dal 1890 al 1900
**ninth** [naɪnθ] *adj, s & pron* nono ‖ *s* (*in dates*) nove *m*
**nip** [nɪp] *s* morso, pizzicotto; freddo pungente; (*of liquor*) bicchierino,

sorso; **nip and tuck** testa a testa ‖ *v* (*pret & pp* **nipped; *ger* nipping**) *tr* pizzicare, mordere; (*to squeeze*) spremere; (*to freeze*) gelare; (*liquor*) sorseggiare; **to nip in the bud** arrestare di bel principio ‖ *intr* bere a sorsi

**nipple** ['nɪpəl] *s* capezzolo; (*of rubber*) tettarella; (*mach*) corto tubo filettato a entrambe le estremità, manicotto, cappuccio

**Nippon** [nɪ'pɑn] or ['nɪpɑn] *s* il Giappone

**Nippon·ese** [ˌnɪpə'niz] *adj* nipponico ‖ *s* (**-ese**) Giapponese *mf*

**nip·py** ['nɪpi] *adj* (**-pier; -piest**) mordente, pizzicante; gelato

**nirvana** [nɪr'vɑnə] *s* il nirvana

**nit** [nɪt] *s* lendine *m;* pidocchio

**niter** ['naɪtər] *s* nitro

**nit'-pick'** *intr* (coll) cercare il pelo nell'uovo

**nitrate** ['naɪtret] *s* nitrato; (agr) nitrato di soda; (agr) nitrato di potassio

**ni'tric ac'id** ['naɪtrɪk] *s* acido nitrico

**nitride** ['naɪtraɪd] *s* azoturo, nitruro

**nitrogen** ['naɪtrədʒən] *s* azoto

**nitroglycerin** [ˌnaɪtrə'glɪsərɪn] *s* nitroglicerina

**ni'trous ox'ide** ['naɪtrəs] *s* ossidulo di azoto

**nitwit** ['nɪtˌwɪt] *s* (slang) baggiano

**no** [no] *adj* nessuno; **no admittance** vietato l'ingresso; **no doubt** senza dubbio; **no matter** non importa; **no parking** divieto di sosta; **no smoking** vietato fumare; **no thoroughfare** divieto di transito; **no use** inutilmente; **with no** senza ‖ *s* no; voto negativo ‖ *adv* no; non; **no longer** non . . . più; **no sooner** non appena

**Noah** ['no·ə] *s* Noè *m*

**nob·by** ['nɑbi] *adj* (**-bier; -biest**) (slang) elegante; (slang) eccellente

**nobili·ty** [no'bɪlɪti] *s* (**-ties**) nobiltà *f*

**noble** ['nobəl] *adj & s* nobile *m*

**no'ble·man** *s* (**-men**) nobile *m*, nobiluomo

**no'ble·wom'an** *s* (**-wom'en**) nobile *f*, nobildonna

**nobod·y** ['noˌbɑdi] or ['nobədi] *s* (**-ies**) nessuno, illustre sconosciuto ‖ *pron indef* nessuno; **nobody but** nessun altro che; **nobody else** nessun altro

**nocturnal** [nɑk'tʌrnəl] *adj* notturno

**nod** [nɑd] *s* cenno d'assenso, cenno del capo; (*of person going to sleep*) crollo del capo ‖ *v* (*pret & pp* **nodded; *ger* nodding**) *tr* (*one's head*) inclinare; **to nod assent** fare cenno di sì ‖ *intr* inclinare il capo; (*to drowse*) assopirsi

**node** [nod] *s* nodo; protuberanza; (phys) nodo

**no'-good'** *adj & s* (coll) buono a nulla

**nohow** ['noˌhaʊ] *adv* (coll) in nessuna maniera

**noise** [nɔɪz] *s* rumore *m* ‖ *tr* divulgare

**noiseless** ['nɔɪzlɪs] *adj* silenzioso

**nois·y** ['nɔɪzi] *adj* (**-ier; -iest**) rumoroso, chiassoso

**nomad** ['nomæd] *adj & s* nomade *m*

**no' man's' land'** *s* terra di nessuno

**nominal** ['nɑmɪnəl] *adj* nominale; simbolico

**nominate** ['nɑmɪˌnet] *tr* presentare la candidatura di; (*to appoint*) nominare, designare

**nomination** [ˌnɑmɪ'neʃən] *s* candidatura; nomina

**nominative** ['nɑmɪnətɪv] *adj & s* nominativo

**nominee** [ˌnɑmɪ'ni] *s* candidato designato

**nonbelligerent** [ˌnɑnbə'lɪdʒərənt] *adj & s* non belligerante *m*

**nonbreakable** [nɑn'brekəbəl] *adj* infrangibile

**nonce** [nɑns] *s*—**for the nonce** per l'occasione

**nonchalance** ['nɑnʃələns] or [ˌnɑnʃə'lɑns] *s* disinvoltura, indifferenza

**nonchalant** ['nɑnʃələnt] or [ˌnɑnʃə'lɑnt] *adj* disinvolto, indifferente

**noncom** ['nɑnˌkɑm] *s* (coll) sottufficiale *m*

**noncombatant** [nɑn'kɑmbətənt] *adj* non combattente ‖ *s* persona non combattente

**non'commis'sioned of'ficer** [ˌnɑnkə'mɪʃənd] *s* sottufficiale *m*

**noncommittal** [ˌnɑnkə'mɪtəl] *adj* ambiguo, evasivo

**non compos mentis** ['nɑn'kɑmpəs'mentɪs] *adj* pazzo; (law) incapace

**nonconformist** [ˌnɑnkən'fɔrmɪst] *s* anticonformista *mf*, nonconformista *mf*

**nondelivery** [ˌnɑndɪ'lɪvəri] *s* mancata consegna

**nondescript** ['nɑndɪˌskrɪpt] *adj* indefinibile, inclassificabile

**none** [nʌn] *pron indef* nessuno; **none of** nessuno di; **none other** nessun altro ‖ *adv* non; affatto, niente affatto; **none the less** ciò nonostante, nondimeno

**nonenti·ty** [nɑn'entɪti] *s* (**-ties**) inesistenza; (*person*) nullità *f*

**nonfiction** [nɑn'fɪkʃən] *s* letteratura non romanzesca

**nonfulfillment** [ˌnɑnfʊl'fɪlmənt] *s* mancanza di esecuzione

**nonintervention** [ˌnɑnɪntər'venʃən] *s* non intervento

**nonmetal** ['nɑnˌmetəl] *s* metalloide *m*

**nonpayment** [nɑn'pemənt] *s* mancato pagamento

**non·plus** ['nɑnplʌs] or [nɑn'plʌs] *s* perplessità *f* ‖ *v* (*pret & pp* **-plussed** or **plused; *ger* -plussing** or **-plusing**) *tr* lasciare perplesso

**nonprofit** [nɑn'prɑfɪt] *adj* senza scopo lucrativo

**nonrefillable** [ˌnɑnrɪ'fɪləbəl] *adj* (*prescription*) non ripetibile; (*e.g., bottle*) non ricaricabile

**nonresident** [nɑn'rezɪdənt] *s* persona di passaggio, non residente *mf*

**nonresidential** [nɑnˌrezɪ'denʃəl] *adj* commerciale, non residenziale

**nonscientific** [nɑnˌsaɪ·ən'tɪfɪk] *adj* non scientifico

**nonsectarian** [ ‚nɑnsek'tɛrɪ·ən] *adj* che non segue nessuna confessione religiosa

**nonsense** ['nɑnsɛns] *s* sciocchezza, assurdità *f*, nonsenso

**nonsensical** [nɑn'sɛnsɪkəl] *adj* sciocco, assurdo, illogico

**nonskid** ['nɑn'skɪd] *adj* antiderapante

**nonstop** ['nɑn'stɑp] *adj* & *adv* senza scalo

**nonsupport** [ ‚nɑnsə'pɔrt] *s* mancato pagamento degli alimenti

**noodle** ['nudəl] *s* (slang) scemo; (slang) testa; **noodles** tagliatelle *fpl*

**noo'dle soup'** *s* tagliatelle *fpl* in brodo

**nook** [nʊk] *s* angolo, cantuccio

**noon** [nun] *s* mezzogiorno; **at high noon** a mezzogiorno in punto

**no one** or **no-one** ['no ‚wʌn] *pron indef* nessuno; **no one else** nessun altro

**noontime** ['nun ‚taɪm] *s* mezzogiorno

**noose** [nus] *s* laccio, nodo scorsoio

**nor** [nɔr] *conj* nè

**Nordic** ['nɔrdɪk] *adj* nordico

**norm** [nɔrm] *s* norma, media, tipo

**normal** ['nɔrməl] *adj* normale ‖ *s* condizione normale; norma; (geom) normale *f*

**Norman** ['nɔrmən] *adj* & *s* normanno

**Normandy** ['nɔrməndi] *s* la Normandia

**Norse** [nɔrs] *adj* norvegese; scandinavo ‖ *s* (*ancient Scandinavian language*) scandinavo; (*language of Norway*) norvegese *m;* **the Norse** gli scandinavi; i norvegesi

**Norse'man** *s* (-men) normanno

**north** [nɔrθ] *adj* del nord, settentrionale ‖ *s* nord *m* ‖ *adv* al nord, verso il nord

**North' Amer'ica** *s* l'America del Nord

**North' Amer'ican** *adj* & *s* nordamericano

**north'east'** *adj* di nord-est ‖ *s* nord-est *m* ‖ *adv* al nord-est

**north'east'er** *s* vento di nord-est

**northern** ['nɔrðərn] *adj* settentrionale; (*Hemisphere*) boreale

**North' Kore'a** *s* la Corea del Nord

**North' Pole'** *s* polo nord

**northward** ['nɔrθwərd] *adv* verso il nord

**north'west'** *adj* di nord-ovest ‖ *s* nord-ovest *m* ‖ *adv* al nord-ovest

**north' wind'** *s* vento del nord, aquilone *m*

**Norway** ['nɔrwe] *s* la Norvegia

**Norwegian** [nɔr'widʒən] *adj* & *s* norvegese *mf* ‖ *s* (*language*) norvegese *m*

**nose** [noz] *s* naso; (*of missile*) testata; **to blow one's nose** soffiarsi il naso; **to count noses** contare il numero dei presenti; **to follow one's nose** andare a lume di naso; **to lead by the nose** menare per il naso; **to look down one's nose at** (coll) guardare dall'alto in basso; **to pay through the nose** pagare un occhio della testa; **to pick one's nose** mettersi le dita nel naso; **to speak through the nose** parlare nel naso; **to thumb one's nose at** fare marameo a; **to turn up one's nose at** guardare dall'alto in basso, guardare

con disprezzo ‖ *tr* fiutare; **to nose out** vincere per un pelo ‖ *intr* fiutare; **to nose about** curiosare

**nose' bag'** *s* musetta

**nose'band'** *s* museruola di cavallo

**nose'bleed'** *s* sangue *m* dal naso

**nose' cone'** *s* ogiva

**nose' dive'** *s* (*of prices*) subita discesa; (aer) discesa in picchiata

**nose'-dive'** *intr* discendere in picchiata

**nosegay** ['noz ‚ge] *s* mazzolino di fiori

**nose' glass'es** *spl* occhiali *mpl* a stringinaso

**nose' ring'** *s* nasiera

**nose'wheel'** *s* (aer) ruota del carrello anteriore

**no'-show'** *s* (coll) passeggero che si è prenotato e non parte

**nostalgia** [nɑ'stældʒə] *s* nostalgia

**nostalgic** [nɑ'stældʒɪk] *adj* nostalgico

**nostril** ['nɑstrɪl] *s* narice *f*

**nos·y** ['nozi] *adj* (**-ier; -iest**) (coll) curioso

**not** [nɑt] *adv* no; non; **not at all** niente affatto; **not yet** non ancora; **to think not** credere di no; **why not?** come no?

**notable** ['notəbəl] *adj* notevole, notabile ‖ *s* notabile *m*

**notarize** ['notə ‚raɪz] *tr* munire di fede notarile

**nota·ry** ['notəri] *s* (**-ries**) notaio

**notch** [nɑtʃ] *s* tacca; (*in mountain*) passo; (coll) tantino; **notches** (coll) di gran lunga, e.g., **notches above** di gran lunga migliore ‖ *tr* intaccare

**note** [not] *s* nota, annotazione; (*currency*) banconota; (*communication*) memorandum *m;* (*of bird*) canto; (*tone of voice*) tono; (*reputation*) riguardo; (*short letter*) biglietto, letterina; (mus) nota; (com) cambiale *f* ‖ *tr* notare, annotare; osservare

**note'book'** *s* (*for school*) quaderno; taccuino, notes *m*

**noted** ['notɪd] *adj* ben noto, eminente

**note' pa'per** *s* carta da lettera

**note'wor'thy** *adj* notevole

**nothing** ['nʌθɪŋ] *s* niente *m*, nulla; **for nothing** gratis; inutilmente; **next to nothing** quasi niente ‖ *pron indef* niente, nulla, non . . . niente, non . . . nulla; **nothing else** nient'altro; **to make nothing of it** non farne caso ‖ *adv* per nulla; **nothing less** non meno

**notice** ['notɪs] *s* attenzione; notizia, notifica; annunzio, preavviso; (*in newspaper*) trafiletto; (law) disdetta; **on short notice** senza preavviso; (com) a breve scadenza; **to escape the notice of** passare inavvertito a; **to serve notice to** far sapere a, far constatare a ‖ *tr* osservare, notare, prendere nota di

**noticeable** ['notɪsəbəl] *adj* notevole; (*e.g., difference*) percettibile

**noti·fy** ['notɪ ‚faɪ] *v* (*pret* & *pp* **-fied**) *tr* informare, far sapere

**notion** ['noʃən] *s* nozione; (*whim*) capriccio; **notions** mercerie *fpl;* **to have a notion to** aver voglia di

**notorie·ty** [ ‚notə'raɪ·ɪti] *s* (**-ties**) (*state*

*of being well known*) notorietà *f;* cattiva fama

**notorious** [noˈtorɪ·əs] *adj* (*generally known*) notorio; (*unfavorably known*) famigerato

**no′-trump′** *adj & s* senza atout *m*

**notwithstanding** [ˌnɑtwɪðˈstændɪŋ] or [ˌnɑtwɪθˈstændɪŋ] *adv* ciò nonostante ‖ *prep* malgrado ‖ *conj* sebbene

**nougat** [ˈnugət] *s* torrone *m*

**noun** [naʊn] *s* nome *m,* sostantivo

**nourish** [ˈnʌrɪʃ] *tr* nutrire

**nourishing** [ˈnʌrɪʃɪŋ] *adj* nutriente

**nourishment** [ˈnʌrɪʃmənt] *s* nutrimento

**novel** [ˈnɑvəl] *adj* nuovo, novello, insolito, originale ‖ *s* romanzo

**novelist** [ˈnɑvəlɪst] *s* romanziere *m*

**novel·ty** [ˈnɑvəlti] *s* (**-ties**) novità *f;* novelties chincaglierie *fpl*

**November** [noˈvɛmbər] *s* novembre *m*

**novice** [ˈnɑvɪs] *s* novizio

**novitiate** [noˈvɪʃɪ·ɪt] *s* noviziato

**novocaine** [ˈnovə‚ken] *s* novocaina

**now** [naʊ] *s* presente *m* ‖ *adv* adesso; **from now on** d'ora in poi; **just now** un momento fa; **now and then** di tempo in tempo; **now that** visto che ‖ *conj* visto che, dato che

**nowadays** [ˈnaʊ·ə‚dez] *adv* al giorno d'oggi, oggidì

**no′way′** *adv* in nessun modo; nient'affatto

**no′where′** *adv* da nessuna parte; **nowhere else** da nessun'altra parte, in nessun altro luogo

**noxious** [ˈnɑkʃəs] *adj* nocivo

**nozzle** [ˈnɑzəl] *s* (*of hose or pipe*) boccaglio; (*of tea pot, gas burner*) becco; (*of gun*) bocca; (*of sprinkling can*) bocchetta; (aut, mach) becco; (slang) naso

**nth** [enθ] *adj* ennesimo; **to the nth degree** all'ennesima potenza

**nuance** [njuˈɑns] or [ˈnju·ɑns] *s* sfumatura

**nub** [nʌb] *s* protuberanza; (*of coal*) pezzo; (coll) nocciolo, cuore *m*

**nuclear** [ˈnjuklɪ·ər] or [ˈnuklɪ·ər] *adj* nucleare

**nu′clear fis′sion** *s* fissione nucleare

**nu′clear fu′sion** *s* fusione nucleare

**nu′clear test′ ban′** *s* accordo per la tregua atomica

**nucle·us** [ˈnjuklɪ·əs] or [ˈnuklɪ·əs] *s* (**-i** [‚aɪ] or **-uses**) nucleo

**nude** [njud] or [nud] *adj* nudo ‖ *s*—**in the nude** nudo

**nudge** [nʌdʒ] *s* gomitina ‖ *tr* dare di gomito a

**nudist** [ˈnjudɪst] or [ˈnudɪst] *adj & s* nudista *mf*

**nudi·ty** [ˈnjudɪti] or [ˈnudɪti] *s* (**-ties**) nudità *f*

**nugget** [ˈnʌgɪt] *s* pepita

**nuisance** [ˈnjusəns] or [ˈnusəns] *s* noia, seccatura; (*person*) seccatore *m,* pittima *mf*

**null** [nʌl] *adj* nullo; **null and void** invalido

**nulli·fy** [ˈnʌlɪ‚faɪ] *v* (*pret & pp* **-fied**) *tr* annullare, invalidare

**nulli·ty** [ˈnʌlɪti] *s* (**-ties**) nullità *f*

**numb** [nʌm] *adj* intorpidito; (*from cold*) intirizzito; **to become numb** intorpidirsi ‖ *tr* intorpidire

**number** [ˈnʌmbər] *s* numero; (*for sale*) articolo di vendita; (*publication*) fascicolo; (*of a serial*) dispensa, puntata; **a number of** parecchi; **beyond or without number** senza numero, infiniti ‖ *tr* numerare, contare; **his days are numbered** i suoi giorni sono contati ‖ *intr*—**to number among** essere tra

**numberless** [ˈnʌmbərlɪs] *adj* innumerevole

**numeral** [ˈnjumərəl] or [ˈnumərəl] *adj* numerale ‖ *s* numero

**numerical** [njuˈmɛrɪkəl] or [nuˈmɛrɪkəl] *adj* numerico

**numerous** [ˈnjumərəs] or [ˈnumərəs] *adj* numeroso

**numskull** [ˈnʌm‚skʌl] *s* (coll) stupido

**nun** [nʌn] *s* monaca, religiosa

**nuptial** [ˈnʌpʃəl] *adj* nuziale ‖ **nuptials** *spl* nozze *fpl*

**nurse** [nʌrs] *s* infermiera; (*to suckle a child*) nutrice *f;* (*to take care of a child*) bambinaia ‖ *tr* (*to minister to*) curare; allattare; allevare; (*e.g., hatred*) covare ‖ *intr* fare l'infermiera

**nurser·y** [ˈnʌrsəri] *s* (**-ies**) stanza dei bambini; (*shelter for children*) asilo infantile; (hort) vivaio

**nurs′ery·man** *s* (**-men**) orticoltore *m*

**nurs′ery rhyme′** *s* canzoncina per i più piccini

**nurs′ery school′** *s* scuola materna

**nursing** [ˈnʌrsɪŋ] *adj* infermieristico ‖ *s* allattamento; professione d'infermiera

**nurs′ing bot′tle** *s* biberon *m,* poppatoio

**nurs′ing home′** *s* convalescenziario; ospizio dei vecchi, gerontocomio

**nurture** [ˈnʌrtʃər] *s* allevamento; nutrimento ‖ *tr* allevare; alimentare; (*e.g., hope*) accarezzare

**nut** [nʌt] *s* noce *f;* (*eccentric*) (slang) esaltato, pazzoide *m;* (mus) capotasto; (mach) madrevite *f,* dado; **a hard nut to crack** un osso duro da rodere; **to be nuts for** (coll) essere pazzo per

**nut′crack′er** *s* schiaccianoci *m*

**nutmeg** [ˈnʌt‚mɛg] *s* noce moscata

**nutrition** [njuˈtrɪʃən] or [nuˈtrɪʃən] *s* (*process*) nutrizione; (*food*) nutrimento

**nutritious** [njuˈtrɪʃəs] or [nuˈtrɪʃəs] *adj* nutriente

**nut′shell′** *s* guscio di noce; **in a nutshell** in breve, in poche parole

**nut·ty** [ˈnʌti] *adj* (**-tier; -tiest**) che sa di noci; (slang) pazzo; **nutty about** (slang) pazzo per

**nuzzle** [ˈnʌzəl] *tr* toccare col muso, ammusare ‖ *intr* (*said of swine*) grufolare; (*said of other animals*) stare muso a muso, ammusare; (*to snuggle*) rannicchiarsi

**nylon** [ˈnaɪlɑn] *s* nailon *m*

**nymph** [nɪmf] *s* ninfa

# O

**O, o** [o] *s* quindicesima lettera del-l'alfabeto inglese

**O** *interj* o!, oh!

**oaf** [of] *s* balordo, scemo, imbecille *mf*

**oak** [ok] *s* quercia

**oaken** ['okən] *adj* di quercia, quercino

**oakum** ['okəm] *s* stoppa incatramata

**oar** [or] *s* remo; **to lie or rest on one's oars** dormire sugli allori; non lavorare più ‖ *tr* spingere coi remi ‖ *intr* remare

**oar'lock'** *s* scalmo

**oars'man** *s* (-men) rematore *m*

**oa·sis** [o'esɪs] *s* (-ses [siz]) oasi *f*

**oat** [ot] *s* avena; **oats** (*seeds*) avena; **to feel one's oats** (coll) essere pieno di vita; (coll) sentirsi importante; **to sow one's wild oats** correre la cavallina

**oath** [oθ] *s* giuramento; **on oath** sotto giuramento; **to take an oath** giurare, prestar giuramento

**oat'meal'** *s* (*breakfast food*) fiocchi *mpl* d'avena; farina d'avena

**obdurate** ['abdjərɪt] *adj* indurito, inesorabile; impenitente, incallito

**obedience** [o'bidɪ·əns] *s* obbedienza, ubbidienza

**obedient** [o'bidɪ·ənt] *adj* ubbidiente

**obeisance** [o'besəns] or [o'bisəns] *s* saluto rispettoso; omaggio

**obelisk** ['abəlɪsk] *s* obelisco

**obese** [o'bis] *adj* obeso

**obesity** [o'bisɪti] *s* obesità *f*

**obey** ['obe] *tr* ubbidire (with *dat*), ubbidire ‖ *intr* ubbidire

**obfuscate** [ab'fʌsket] or ['abfəs ,ket] *tr* offuscare

**obituar·y** [o'bɪtʃʊ ,ɛri] *adj* necrologico ‖ *s* (-ies) necrologia

**object** ['abdʒɪkt] *s* oggetto ‖ [ab-'dʒɛkt] *tr* obiettare ‖ *intr* fare obiezioni, obiettare

**objection** [ab'dʒɛkʃən] *s* obiezione

**objectionable** [ab'dʒɛkʃənəbəl] *adj* reprensibile; (*e.g., odor*) sgradevole; offensivo

**objective** [ab'dʒɛktɪv] *adj & s* obiettivo

**obligate** ['ablɪ ,get] *tr* obbligare

**obligation** [ ,ablɪ'geʃən] *s* obbligo, obbligazione

**oblige** [ə'blaɪdʒ] *tr* obbligare; favorire; **much obliged** obbligatissimo

**obliging** [ə'blaɪdʒɪŋ] *adj* compiacente, accomodante, servizievole

**oblique** [ə'blik] *adj* obliquo; indiretto

**obliterate** [ə'blɪtə ,ret] *tr* obliterare; spegnere, distruggere

**oblivion** [ə'blɪvɪ·ən] *s* oblio

**oblivious** [ə'blɪvɪ·əs] *adj* (*forgetful*) dimentico; (*unaware*) ignaro

**oblong** ['ablɔŋ] or ['ablaŋ] *adj* oblungo

**obnoxious** [ab'nakʃəs] *adj* detestabile

**oboe** ['obo] *s* oboe *m*

**oboist** ['obo·ɪst] *s* oboista *mf*

**obscene** [ab'sin] *adj* osceno

**obsceni·ty** [ab'sɛnɪti] or [ab'sinɪti] *s* (-ties) oscenità *f*, scenezza

**obscure** [əb'skjʊr] *adj* oscuro ‖ *tr* oscurare

**obscuri·ty** [əb'skjʊrɪti] *s* (-ties) oscurità *f*

**obsequies** ['absɪkwiz] *spl* esequie *fpl*

**obsequious** [əb'sikwɪ·əs] *adj* ossequioso, servile

**observance** [əb'zʌrvəns] *s* osservanza; **observances** pratiche *fpl*; cerimonie *fpl*

**observation** [ ,abzər've ʃən] *s* osservazione; osservanza

**observa'tion car'** *s* (rr) vettura belvedere

**observato·ry** [əb'zʌrvə ,tori] *s* (-ries) osservatorio

**observe** [əb'zʌrv] *tr* osservare

**observer** [əb'zʌrvər] *s* osservatore *m*

**obsess** [əb'sɛs] *tr* ossessionare

**obsession** [əb'sɛʃən] *s* ossessione

**obsolescent** [ ,absə'lɛsənt] *adj* che sta cadendo in disuso

**obsolete** ['absə ,lit] *adj* disusato

**obstacle** ['abstəkəl] *s* ostacolo

**obstetrical** [ab'stɛtrɪkəl] *adj* ostetrico

**obstetrics** [ab'stɛtrɪks] *s* ostetricia

**obstina·cy** ['abstɪnəsi] *s* (-cies) ostinazione

**obstinate** ['abstɪnɪt] *adj* ostinato

**obstreperous** [əb'strɛpərəs] *adj* turbolento; rumoroso

**obstruct** [əb'strʌkt] *tr* ostruire

**obstruction** [əb'strʌkʃən] *s* ostruzione

**obtain** [əb'ten] *tr* ottenere ‖ *intr* prevalere, essere in voga

**obtrusive** [əb'trusɪv] *adj* intruso, importuno; sporgente

**obtuse** [əb'tjus] or [əb'tus] *adj* ottuso

**obviate** ['abvɪ ,et] *tr* ovviare (with *dat*)

**obvious** ['abvɪ·əs] *adj* ovvio, palmare

**occasion** [ə'keʒən] *s* occasione; **on occasion** di quando in quando ‖ *tr* occasionare

**occasional** [ə'keʒənəl] *adj* saltuario; (*e.g., verses*) d'occasione

**occasionally** [ə'keʒənəli] *adv* occasionalmente, di tanto in tanto

**occident** ['aksɪdənt] *s* occidente *m*

**occidental** [ ,aksɪ'dɛntəl] *adj & s* occidentale *mf*

**occlud'ed front'** [ə'kludɪd] *s* fronte occluso

**occlusion** [ə'kluʒən] *s* occlusione

**occlusive** [ə'klusɪv] *adj* occlusivo ‖ *s* occlusiva

**occult** [ə'kʌlt] or ['akʌlt] *adj* occulto

**occupancy** ['akjəpənsi] *s* occupazione, presa di possesso; (*tenancy*) locazione

**occupant** ['akjəpənt] *s* occupante *m*; (*tenant*) inquilino

**occupation** [ ,akjə'peʃən] *s* occupazione

**occupational** [ ,akjə'peʃənəl] *adj* occupazionale; (*e.g., disease*) professionale, del lavoro

**occu·py** ['akjə ,paɪ] *v* (*pret & pp -pied*) *tr* occupare; (*to dwell in*) abitare

**oc·cur** [ə'kʌr] *v* (*pret & pp -curred*;

ger **-curring**) *intr* accadere, succedere; incontrarsi; (*to come to mind*)
venir in mente, e.g., **it occurs to me**
mi viene in mente

**occurrence** [ə'kʌrəns] *s* evento, avvenimento; apparizione

**ocean** ['oʃən] *s* oceano

**o'cean lin'er** *s* transatlantico

**o'clock** [ə'klɑk] *adv* secondo l'orologio; **it is one o'clock** è la una; **it is
two o'clock** sono le due

**octane** ['ɑkten] *adj* ottanico || *s* ottano

**octave** ['ɑktɪv] *or* ['ɑktev] *s* ottava

**Octavian** [ɑk'tevɪ·ən] *s* Ottaviano

**October** [ɑk'tobər] *s* ottobre *m*

**octo·pus** ['ɑktəpəs] *s* (**-puses** *or* **-pi**
['paɪ]) (*small*) polpo; (*large*) piovra;
(fig) piovra

**ocular** ['ɑkjələr] *adj & s* oculare *m*

**oculist** ['ɑkjəlɪst] *s* oculista *mf*

**odd** [ɑd] *adj* (*number*) dispari;
strambo, bizzarro; (*not matching*)
scompagnato, spaiato; strano; e rotti,
e.g., **three hundred odd** tre cento e
rotti || **odds** *ssg or spl* probabilità *f;*
(*advantage*) vantaggio, superiorità *f;*
**at odds** in disaccordo; **by all odds**
senza dubbio; **it makes no odds** fa lo
stesso; **the odds are** la quota è; **to
set at odds** seminare zizzania fra

**odd·i·ty** ['ɑdɪti] *s* (**-ties**) stranezza

**odd' jobs'** *spl* lavori saltuari

**odd' lot'** *s* (fin) compravendita di meno
di cento unità

**odds' and ends'** *spl* un po' di tutto

**odious** ['odɪ·əs] *adj* odioso

**odor** ['odər] *s* odore *m;* **to be in bad
odor** aver cattiva fama

**odorless** ['odərlɪs] *adj* inodoro

**odorous** ['odərəs] *adj* odoroso

**Odysseus** [o'dɪsjus] *or* [o'dɪsɪ·əs] *s*
Odisseo

**Odyssey** ['ɑdɪsi] *s* Odissea

**Oedipus** ['ɛdɪpəs] *or* ['idɪpəs] *s* Edipo

**of** [ʌv] *or* [əv] *prep* di, e.g., **the lead
of the pencil** la mina della matita; a,
e.g., **to think of** pensare a; meno,
e.g., **a quarter of ten** le dieci meno
un quarto

**off** [ɔf] *or* [ɑf] *adj* (*wrong*) sbagliato;
(*slightly abnormal*) matto, pazzo; inferiore; (*electricity*) tagliato; (*agreement*) sospeso; libero, in libertà; di-
stante; destro; (*season*) morto || *adv*
via; fuori, lontano, distante; **to be
off** mettersi in marcia || *prep* da;
fuori da; al disotto di; lontano da;
distolto da, e.g., **his eyes were off the
target** i suoi occhi erano distolti dal
bersaglio; (naut) al largo di

**offal** ['ɑfəl] *or* ['ɔfəl] *s* (*of butchered
animal*) frattaglie *fpl;* rifiuti *mpl*

**off' and on'** *adv* di tempo in tempo

**off'beat'** *adj* insolito, originale

**off' chance'** *s* possibilità remota

**off'-col'or** *adj* scolorito; indisposto;
(*joke*) di dubbio gusto

**offend** [ə'fɛnd] *tr & intr* offendere

**offender** [ə'fɛndər] *s* offensore *m*

**offense** [ə'fɛns] *s* offesa; **to take offense
(at)** offendersi (di)

**offensive** [ə'fɛnsɪv] *adj* offensivo || *s*
offensiva

**offer** ['ɔfər] *or* ['ɑfər] *s* offerta || *tr*
offrire; (*thanks*) porgere; (*resistance*)
opporre || *intr* offrirsi

**offering** ['ɔfərɪŋ] *or* ['ɑfərɪŋ] *s* offerta

**off'hand'** *adj* fatto all'improvviso; sbri-
gativo, alla buona || *adv* all'improv-
viso; bruscamente

**office** ['ɔfɪs] *or* ['ɑfɪs] *s* ufficio; funzione, incombenza; (*of a doctor*) gabinetto; (*of a lawyer*) studio; (eccl)
uffizio; **through the good offices of**
per tramite di

**of'fice boy'** *s* fattorino

**of'fice·hold'er** *s* pubblico funzionario

**of'fice hours'** *spl* orario d'ufficio

**officer** ['ɔfɪsər] *or* ['ɑfɪsər] *s* (*in a
corporation*) funzionario; (*policeman*) agente *m;* (mil, nav, naut)
ufficiale *m;* **officer of the day** (mil)
ufficiale *m* di giornata

**of'fice seek'er** ['sikər] *s* aspirante *m* a
un ufficio pubblico

**of'fice supplies'** *spl* articoli *mpl* di
cancelleria

**official** [ə'fɪʃəl] *adj* ufficiale || *s* fun-
zionario, ufficiale *m*

**officiate** [ə'fɪʃɪ·ˌet] *intr* ufficiare

**officious** [ə'fɪʃəs] *adj* invadente, infra-
mettente; **to be officious** essere un
impiccione

**offing** ['ɔfɪŋ] *or* ['ɑfɪŋ] *s—***in the
offing** al largo; (fig) in preparazione,
probabile

**off'-lim'its** *adj* proibito; **off-limits to**
ingresso proibito a

**off'-peak' heat'er** *s* (elec) scaldabagno
azionato unicamente in periodi di
consumo minimo

**off'-peak' load'** *s* (elec) carico di consumo minimo

**off'print'** *s* estratto

**off'set'** *s* compensazione; (typ) offset *m*
|| **off'set'** *v* (*pret & pp* **-set;** *ger*
**-setting**) *tr* compensare; stampare in
offset

**off'shoot'** *s* (*of plant*) germoglio; (*of
family or race*) discendente *mf;*
(*branch*) ramo; (fig) conseguenza

**off'shore'** *adj* (*wind*) di terra; (*fishing*)
vicino alla costa; (*island*) costiero ||
*adv* al largo

**off'side'** *adv* (sports) fuori gioco

**off'spring'** *s* discendente *m;* prole *f;*
figlio; figli *mpl*

**off'stage'** *adv* tra le quinte

**off'-the-rec'ord** *adj* confidenziale || *adv*
confidenzialmente

**often** ['ɔfən] *or* ['ɑfən] *adv* sovente,
spesso; **how often?** quante volte?;
**once too often** una volta di troppo

**ogive** ['odʒaɪv] *or* [o'dʒaɪv] *s* ogiva

**ogle** ['ogəl] *tr* adocchiare, occhieggiare

**ogre** ['ogər] *s* orco

**ohm** [om] *s* ohm *m*

**oil** [ɔɪl] *adj* (*pertaining to edible oil*)
oleario; (*e.g., well*) di petrolio; (*e.g.,
lamp*) a olio; (*tanker*) petroliero;
(*field*) petrolifero || *s* olio; petrolio;
**to burn the midnight oil** studiare a
lume di candela; **to pour oil on troubled waters** pacificare; **to strike oil**
trovare petrolio || *tr* oliare; lubrifi-

care; ungere ‖ *intr* (*said of a motor-ship*) fare petrolio

**oil′ burn′er** *s* bruciatore *m* a gasolio

**oil′can′** *s* oliatore *m*

**oil′cloth′** *s* incerata, tela cerata

**oil′ field′** *s* giacimento petrolifero

**oil′ lamp′** *s* lampada a petrolio

**oil′man** *s* (**-men**) (*retailer*) mercante *m* di petrolio; (*operator*) petroliere *m*

**oil′ paint′ing** *s* quadro a olio

**oil′ slick′** *s* macchia d'olio

**oil′ tank′er** *s* petroliera

**oil′ well′** *s* pozzo di petrolio

**oil•y** [ˈɔɪli] *adj* (**-ier; -iest**) oleoso; untuoso

**ointment** [ˈɔɪntmənt] *s* unguento

**O.K.** [ˈoˈke] *adj* (coll) corretto ‖ *s* (coll) approvazione ‖ *adv* (coll) benissimo, d'accordo ‖ *v* (*pret & pp* **O.K.'d**; *ger* **O.K.'ing**) *tr* (coll) dare l'approvazione a ‖ *interj* benissimo!

**okra** [ˈokrə] *s* (bot) ibisco esculento; (bot) baccello dell'ibisco esculento

**old** [old] *adj* vecchio; antico, vetusto; **how old is . . . ?** quanti anni ha . . . ?; **of old** anticamente; **to be . . . years old** avere . . . anni

**old′ age′** *s* vecchiaia

**old′ boy′** *s* vecchietto arzillo; (Brit) vecchio mio

**old′-clothes′man′** *s* (**-men′**) rigattiere *m*

**old′ coun′try** *s* madre patria

**old-fashioned** [ˈoldˈfæʃənd] *adj* all'antica; fuori moda

**old′ fo′gey** or **old′ fo′gy** [ˈfogi] *s* (**-gies**) uomo di idee antiquate, reazionario

**Old′ Glo′ry** *s* la bandiera degli Stati Uniti

**Old′ Guard′** *s* (U.S.A.) parte *f* più conservatrice di un partito

**old′ hand′** *s* vecchio del mestiere

**old′ maid′** *s* zitella

**old′ mas′ter** *s* grande maestro; quadro di un gran maestro

**old′ moon′** *s* luna calante

**old′ salt′** *s* lupo di mare

**old′ school′** *s* gente *f* all'antica

**old′ school′ tie′** *s* (Brit) cravatta coi colori della propria scuola; (fig) tradizionalismo

**Old′ Tes′tament** *s* Antico Testamento

**old′-time′** *adj* all'antica; del tempo antico

**old-timer** [ˈoldˈtaɪmər] *s* (coll) veterano; (coll) vecchio

**old′ wives″ tale′** *s* superstizione da donnicciole; racconto di vecchie comari

**Old′ World′** *s* mondo antico

**oleander** [ˌoliˈændər] *s* oleandro

**oligar•chy** [ˈɑliˌgɑrki] *s* (**-chies**) oligarchia

**olive** [ˈɑlɪv] *adj* oleario; (*color*) olivastro ‖ *s* (*tree*) olivo; (*fruit*) oliva

**ol′ive branch′** *s* ramoscello d'olivo

**ol′ive grove′** *s* oliveto

**ol′ive oil′** *s* olio d'oliva

**Oliver** [ˈɑlɪvər] *s* Oliviero

**ol′ive tree′** *s* olivo

**Olympiad** [oˈlɪmpɪˌæd] *s* olimpiade *f*

**Olympian** [oˈlɪmpɪən] *adj* olimpico ‖ *s* deità olimpica; giocatore olimpico

**Olympic** [oˈlɪmpɪk] *adj* olimpico, olimpionico

**omelet** or **omelette** [ˈɑməlɪt] or [ˈɑmlɪt] *s* frittata, omelette *f*

**omen** [ˈomən] *s* augurio

**ominous** [ˈɑmɪnəs] *adj* infausto, ominoso

**omission** [oˈmɪʃən] *s* omissione

**omit** [oˈmɪt] *v* (*pret & pp* **omitted**; *ger* **omitting**) *tr* omettere

**omnibus** [ˈɑmnɪˌbʌs] or [ˈɑmnɪbəs] *adj* di interesse generale ‖ *s* bus *m*; volume collettivo

**omnipotent** [ɑmˈnɪpətənt] *adj* onnipotente

**omniscient** [ɑmˈnɪʃənt] *adj* onnisciente

**omnivorous** [ɑmˈnɪvərəs] *adj* onnivoro

**on** [ɑn] or [ɔn] *adj* addosso, e.g., **with his hat on** col cappello addosso; in uso, in funzione; (*light*) acceso; (*deal*) fatto, concluso; (*e.g., game*) già cominciato; **what is on at the theater?** che cosa si dà al teatro? ‖ *adv* su; avanti; dietro, e.g., **to drag on** tirarsi dietro; **and so on** e così via; **come on!** va via!; **farther on** più in là; **later on** più tardi; **to be on to s.o.** (coll) scoprire il gioco di qlcu; **to have on** avere addosso; **to . . . on** continuare a, e.g., **the band played on** la banda continuò a suonare; **to put on** mettersi ‖ *prep* su, sopra; a, e.g., **on foot** a piedi; **on his arrival** al suo arrivo; sotto, e.g., **on my responsibility** sotto la mia responsabilità; contro, e.g., **an attack on the government** un attacco contro il governo; da, e.g., **on good authority** da buona fonte; su, e.g., **on all sides** da tutte le parti; verso, e.g., **to march on the capital** marciare verso la capitale; dopo, e.g., **victory on victory** vittoria dopo vittoria

**on′ and on′** *adv* senza cessa

**once** [wʌns] *s* una volta; volta, e.g., **this once** questa volta ‖ *adv* una volta; mai, e.g., **if this once becomes known** se questo si risapesse mai; **all at once** repentinamente; **at once** subito; allo stesso tempo; **for once** almeno una volta; **once and again** ripetutamente; **once in a blue moon** ad ogni morte di papa; **once in a while** di tanto in tanto; **once upon a time there was** c'era una volta ‖ *conj* se appena; una volta che

**once′-o′ver** *s* (coll) occhiata rapida; **to give s.th the once-over** (coll) esaminare qlco rapidamente; (coll) pulire qlco superficialmente

**one** [wʌn] *adj* uno; un certo, e.g., **one Smith** un certo Smith; unico e.g., **one price** prezzo unico ‖ *s* uno ‖ *pron* uno, e.g., **how can one live here?** come è possibile che uno viva qui?; si, e.g., **how does one go to the museum?** come si va al museo?; **I for one** per lo meno io; **it's all one and the same to me** per me fa lo stesso; **my little one** piccolo mio; **one and all** tutti; **one another** si, e.g., **they wrote one another** si scrissero;

l'un(o) l'altro, e.g., **they looked at one another** si guardarono l'un l'altro; **one o'clock** la una; **one's** il suo, il proprio; **the blue hat and the red one** il cappello blu e quello rosso; **the one and only l'unico; the one that** chi, quello che; **this one** questo; **that one** quello; **to make one** unire

**one'-eyed'** *adj* monocolo

**one'-horse'** *adj* a un solo cavallo; (coll) da nulla, poco importante

**one'-man' show'** *s* personale *f*

**onerous** ['anərəs] *adj* oneroso

**one·self'** *pron* sé stesso; se; si; **to be oneself** essere normale; comportarsi normalmente

**one-sided** ['wʌn'saɪdɪd] *adj* unilaterale; ingiusto, parziale

**one'-track'** *adj* a un solo binario; (coll) unilaterale, limitato

**one'-way'** *adj* a senso unico; (*ticket*) semplice, d'andata

**onion** ['ʌnjən] *s* cipolla; **to know one's onions** (coll) conoscere i propri polli

**on'ion·skin'** *s* carta pelle aglio, carta velina

**on'look'er** *s* presente *m*, spettatore *m*

**only** ['onlɪ] *adj* solo, unico || *adv* solo, soltanto, non . . . più di; **not only . . . but also** non solo . . . ma anche || *conj* ma; se non che

**on'set'** *s* attacco; (*beginning*) inizio; **at the onset** dapprincipio

**onslaught** ['an,slɔt] or ['ɔn,slɔt] *s* attacco

**on'to** *prep* su, sopra a; **to be onto** (coll) rendersi conto del gioco di

**onward** ['anwərd] or **onwards** ['anwərdz] *adv* avanti, più avanti

**onyx** ['anɪks] *s* onice *m*

**ooze** [uz] *s* trasudazione; liquido per concia || *tr* sudare || *intr* trasudare; (*said, e.g., of blood*) stillare; (*said, e.g., of air*) filtrare; (fig) trapelare

**opal** ['opəl] *s* opale *m*

**opaque** [o'pek] *adj* opaco; (*writer's style*) oscuro; stupido

**open** ['opən] *adj* aperto, scoperto; (*job*) vacante; (*time*) libero; (*hunting season*) legale; indeciso; manifesto; (*hand*) liberale; (*needlework*) a giorno; **to break** or **to crack open** forzare; **to throw open** aprire completamente || *s* apertura; (*in the woods*) radura; **in the open** all'aperto; all'aria aperta; in alto mare; apertamente || *tr* aprire; (*an account*) impostare; **to open up** spalancare; (*one's eyes*) sbarrare || *intr* aprire, aprirsi; (theat) esordire; **to open into** sboccare in; **to open on** dare su; **to open up** sbottonarsi

**o'pen-air'** *adj* all'aria aperta

**open-eyed** ['opən,aɪd] *adj* con gli occhi aperti; meravigliato; fatto con piena conoscenza

**open-handed** ['opən'hændɪd] *adj* generoso, liberale

**open-hearted** ['opən'hartɪd] *adj* franco, sincero; gentile

**o'pen house'** *s* tavola imbandita; **to keep open house** aver sempre ospiti

**opening** ['opənɪŋ] *s* apertura; (*of dress*) giro collo; (*e.g., of sewer*) imbocco; (*in the woods*) radura; (*vacancy*) posto vacante; (*beginning*) inizio; (*chance to say something*) occasione

**o'pening night'** *s* debutto, prima

**o'pening num'ber** *s* primo numero

**o'pening price'** *s* prezzo d'apertura

**open-minded** ['opən'maɪndɪd] *adj* di larghe vedute; imparziale

**o'pen se'cret** *s* segreto di Pulcinella

**o'pen shop'** *s* officina che impiega chi non è membro del sindacato

**o'pen·work'** *s* traforo

**opera** ['apərə] *s* opera

**op'era glass'es** *spl* binocolo da teatro

**op'era hat'** *s* gibus m

**op'era house'** *s* teatro dell'opera

**operate** ['apə,ret] *tr* (*a machine*) far funzionare; (*a shop*) gestire; operare || *intr* funzionare; operare; **to operate on** (surg) operare

**operatic** [,apə'rætɪk] *adj* operistico

**op'erating expens'es** *spl* spese *fpl* di ordinaria amministrazione

**op'erating room'** *s* sala operatoria

**op'erating ta'ble** *s* tavola operatoria

**operation** [,apə're/ən] *s* operazione; funzionamento, marcia

**opera'tions research'** *s* ricerca operativa

**operator** ['apə,retər] *s* operatore *m*; (*of a conveyance*) conduttore *m*, conducente *mf*; (com) gestore *m*; (telp) telefonista *mf*; (surg) chirurgo operatore; (slang) faccendiere *m*

**opiate** ['opɪ·ɪt] or ['opɪ,et] *adj* & *s* oppiato

**opinion** [ə'pɪnjən] *s* opinione; **in my opinion** a mio modo di vedere; **to have a high opinion of** avere una grande stima di

**opinionated** [ə'pɪnjə,netɪd] *adj* ostinato, testardo, dogmatico

**opium** ['opɪ·əm] *s* oppio

**o'pium den'** *s* fumeria d'oppio

**opossum** [ə'pasəm] *s* opossum *m*

**opponent** [ə'ponənt] *s* avversario

**opportune** [,apər'tjun] or [,apər'tun] *adj* opportuno

**opportunist** [,apər'tjunɪst] or [,apər'tunɪst] *s* opportunista *mf*

**opportuni·ty** [,apər'tjunɪti] or [,apər'tunɪti] *s* (**-ties**) opportunità *f*, occasione

**oppose** [ə'poz] *tr* opporsi a

**opposite** ['apəsɪt] *adj* opposto; di rimpetto, e.g., **the house opposite** la casa di rimpetto || *s* contrario || *prep* di faccia a, di rimpetto a

**op'posite num'ber** *s* persona di grado corrispondente

**opposition** [,apə'zɪ/ən] *s* opposizione

**oppress** [ə'prɛs] *tr* opprimere

**oppressive** [ə'prɛsɪv] *adj* oppressivo; opprimente, soffocante

**oppressor** [ə'prɛsər] *s* oppressore *m*

**opprobrious** [ə'probrɪ·əs] *adj* obbrobrioso

**opprobrium** [ə'prɒbrɪ‧əm] *s* obbrobrio
**optic** ['ɒptɪk] *adj* ottico ‖ **optics** *ssg* ottica
**optical** ['ɒptɪkəl] *adj* ottico
**optician** [ɒp'tɪʃən] *s* ottico, occhialaio
**optimism** ['ɒptɪ ˌmɪzəm] *s* ottimismo
**optimist** ['ɒptɪmɪst] *s* ottimista *mf*
**optimistic** [ ˌɒptɪ'mɪstɪk] *adj* ottimistico
**option** ['ɒpʃən] *s* opzione
**optional** ['ɒpʃənəl] *adj* facoltativo
**optometrist** [ɒp'tɒmɪtrɪst] *s* optometrista *mf*
**opulent** ['ɒpjələnt] *adj* opulento
**or** [ɔr] *conj* o; (*or else*) oppure
**oracle** ['ɒrəkəl] or ['ɔrəkəl] *s* oracolo
**oracular** [o'rækjələr] *adj* profetico; ambiguo; misterioso; sentenzioso
**oral** ['ɔrəl] *adj* orale
**orange** ['ɒrɪndʒ] or ['ɔrɪndʒ] *adj* di arance; arancio ‖ *s* arancia
**orangeade** [ ˌɒrɪndʒ'ed] or [ ˌɔrɪndʒ-'ed] *s* aranciata
**or'ange blos'som** *s* zagara
**or'ange grove'** *s* aranceto
**or'ange juice'** *s* sugo d'arancia
**or'ange squeez'er** *s* spremiagrumi *m*
**or'ange tree'** *s* arancio
**orang-outang** [o'ræŋʊ ˌtæŋ] *s* orango
**oration** [o're ʃən] *s* orazione, discorso
**orator** ['ɒrətər] or ['ɔrətər] *s* oratore *m*
**oratorical** [ ˌɒrə'tɒrɪkəl] or [ ˌɔrə'tɒrɪkəl] *adj* oratorio
**oratori‧o** [ ˌɒrə'tɒrɪ ˌo] or [ ˌɔrə'tɒrɪ ˌo] *s* (*-os*) (mus) oratorio
**orato‧ry** ['ɒrə ˌtori] or ['ɔrə ˌtori] *s* (*-ries*) oratoria; (eccl) oratorio
**orb** [ɔrb] *s* orbe *m*
**orbit** ['ɔrbɪt] *s* orbita; **to go into orbit** entrare in orbita ‖ *tr* mettere in orbita; orbitare intorno a ‖ *intr* orbitare
**or'biting sta'tion** *s* stazione orbitale
**orchard** ['ɔrtʃərd] *s* frutteto
**orchestra** ['ɔrkɪstrə] *s* orchestra; (*parquet*) platea
**orchestral** [ɔr'kestrəl] *adj* orchestrale
**or'chestra pit'** *s* golfo mistico
**or'chestra seat'** *s* poltrona di platea
**orchestrate** ['ɔrkɪs ˌtret] *tr* orchestrare
**orchid** ['ɔrkɪd] *s* orchidea
**ordain** [ɔr'den] *tr* predestinare; decretare; (eccl) ordinare
**ordeal** [ɔr'dil] or [ɔr'di‧əl] *s* sfacchinata; (hist) ordalia
**order** ['ɔrdər] *s* ordine *m*; compito, e.g., **a big order** un compito difficile; (com) commessa, ordinazione; (mil) consegna; **in order that** affinché; **in order to** + *inf* per + *inf*; **made to order** fatto su misura; **to get out of order** guastarsi; **to give an order** dare un ordine; (com) fare una commessa ‖ *tr* (*e.g., a drink*) ordinare; (*a person*) ordinare (with *dat*); (*e.g., a suit of clothes*) far fare; **to order around** mandare attorno; **to order s.o. away** mandar via qlcu
**or'der blank'** *s* cedola d'ordinazione
**order‧ly** ['ɔrdərli] *adj* ordinato; disciplinato ‖ *s* (*-lies*) (*in a hospital*) in-

serviente *mf*; (mil) ordinanza, attendente *m*
**ordinal** ['ɔrdɪnəl] *adj* & *s* ordinale *m*
**ordinance** ['ɔrdɪnəns] *s* ordinanza
**ordinary** ['ɔrdɪ ˌneri] *adj* ordinario
**ordnance** ['ɔrdnəns] *s* artiglieria; bocche *fpl* da fuoco; munizionamento
**ore** [or] *s* minerale *m* (metallifero)
**organ** ['ɔrgən] *s* organo
**organ‧dy** ['ɔrgəndi] *s* (*-dies*) organdì *m*
**or'gan grind'er** *s* suonatore *m* d'organetto
**organic** [ɔr'gænɪk] *adj* organico
**organism** ['ɔrgə ˌnɪzəm] *s* organismo
**organist** ['ɔrgənɪst] *s* organista *mf*
**organization** [ ˌɔrgənɪ'zeʃən] *s* organizzazione
**organize** ['ɔrgə ˌnaɪz] *tr* organizzare
**organizer** ['ɔrgə ˌnaɪzər] *s* organizzatore *m*
**or'gan loft'** *s* palco, galleria per l'organo
**orgasm** ['ɔrgæzəm] *s* orgasmo
**or‧gy** ['ɔrdʒi] *s* (*-gies*) orgia
**orient** ['ɔrɪ‧ənt] *s* oriente *m* ‖ **Orient** *s* Oriente *m* ‖ **orient** ['ɔrɪ ˌent] *tr* orientare, orizzontare
**oriental** [ ˌɔrɪ'entəl] *adj* orientale ‖ **Oriental** *s* orientale *mf*
**orifice** ['ɒrɪfɪs] or ['ɔrɪfɪs] *s* orifizio
**origin** ['ɒrɪdʒɪn] or ['ɔrɪdʒɪn] *s* origine *f*, provenienza
**original** [ə'rɪdʒɪnəl] *adj* & *s* originale *mf*
**originate** [ə'rɪdʒɪ ˌnet] *tr* originare ‖ *intr* originare, originarsi
**oriole** ['ɔrɪ ˌol] *s* oriolo, rigogolo
**Ork'ney Is'lands** ['ɔrkni] *spl* Orcadi *fpl*
**ormolu** ['ɔrmə ˌlu] *s* (*alloy*) similoro; (*gold powder*) polvere *f* d'oro; (*gilded metal*) bronzo dorato
**ornament** ['ɔrnəmənt] *s* ornamento ‖ ['ɔrnə ˌment] *tr* ornamentare
**ornamental** [ ˌɔrnə'mentəl] *adj* ornamentale
**ornate** [ɔr'net] or ['ɔrnet] *adj* ornato; (*style*) elaborato
**ornithologist** [ ˌɔrnɪ'θɒlədʒɪst] *s* ornitologo
**orphan** ['ɔrfən] *adj* & *s* orfano ‖ *tr* rendere orfano
**orphanage** ['ɔrfənɪdʒ] *s* (*institution*) orfanotrofio; (*condition*) orfanezza
**Orpheus** ['ɔrfjus] or ['ɔrfɪ‧əs] *s* Orfeo
**orthodox** ['ɔrθə ˌdɑks] *adj* ortodosso
**orthogra‧phy** [ɔr'θɑgrəfi] *s* (*-phies*) ortografia
**oscillate** ['ɑsɪ ˌlet] *intr* oscillare
**osier** ['oʒər] *s* vimine *m*; (bot) vinco
**osmosis** [ɑz'mosɪs] or [ɑs'mosɪs] *s* osmosi *f*
**osprey** ['ɑspri] *s* falco pescatore
**ossi‧fy** ['ɑsɪ ˌfaɪ] *v* (*pret* & *pp* **-fied**) *tr* ossificare ‖ *intr* ossificarsi
**ostensible** [ɑs'tensɪbəl] *adj* apparente, preteso
**ostentatious** [ ˌɑsten'teʃəs] *adj* ostentato
**osteopathy** [ ˌɑstɪ'ɑpəθi] *s* osteopatia
**ostracism** ['ɑstrə ˌsɪzəm] *s* ostracismo

**ostracize** ['ɑstrə‚saɪz] *tr* dare l'ostracismo a, ostracizzare

**ostrich** ['ɑstrɪtʃ] *s* struzzo

**Othello** [o'θelo] or [ə'θelo] *s* Otello

**other** ['ʌðər] *adj* & *pron indef* altro ‖ *adv*—**other than** diversamente che

**otherwise** ['ʌðər‚waɪz] *adv* altrimenti; differentemente

**otter** ['ɑtər] *s* lontra

**ottoman** ['ɑtəmən] *s* (*fabric*) ottomano; (*sofa*) ottomana; cuscino per i piedi ‖ **Ottoman** *adj* & *s* ottomano

**ouch** [autʃ] *interj* ahi!

**ought** [ɔt] *s* qualcosa; zero; **for ought I know** per quanto io sappia ‖ *v aux* is rendered in Italian by the conditional of *dovere*, e.g., **you ought to be ashamed** dovresti vergognarti

**ounce** [auns] *s* oncia

**our** [aur] *adj poss* nostro, il nostro

**ours** [aurz] *pron poss* il nostro

**ourselves** [aur'selvz] *pron pers* noi stessi; ci, e.g., **we enjoyed ourselves** ci siamo divertiti

**oust** [aust] *tr* espellere; (*a tenant*) sfrattare

**out** [aut] *adj* erroneo; esterno; fuori pratica; svenuto; ubriaco; finito; (*book*) pubblicato; (*lights*) spento; fuori moda; introvabile; palmare; di permesso, e.g., **my night out** la mia serata di permesso; (*e.g., at the knees*) frusto; (sports) fuori gioco ‖ *s* via d'uscita; **to be on the outs or at outs with** (coll) essere in disaccordo con ‖ *adv* fuori, all'infuori; all'aria libera; **out for** in cerca di; **out of** fuori, fuori di; di; da; (*e.g., money*) a corto di, senza; su, e.g., **two students out of three** due studenti su tre ‖ *prep* fuori di; per, lungo ‖ *interj* fuori!

**out' and away'** *adv* di gran lunga

**out'-and-out'** *adj* perfetto, completo ‖ *adv* perfettamente, completamente

**out'bid'** *v* (*pret* -bid; *pp* -bid or -bidden; *ger* -bidding) *tr* fare un'offerta migliore di; (bridge) fare una dichiarazione più alta di

**out'board mo'tor** *s* fuoribordo, motore *m* fuoribordo

**out'break'** *s* insurrezione; (*of hives*) eruzione; (*of anger; of war*) scoppio

**out'build'ing** *s* dipendenza

**out'burst'** *s* (*of tears; of laughter*) scoppio; (*of energy*) impeto, slancio

**out'cast'** *s* vagabondo reietto

**out'come'** *s* risultato

**out'cry'** *s* (-cries) grido, chiasso

**out'dat'ed** *adj* fuori moda

**out'dis'tance** *tr* distanziare

**out'do'** *v* (*pret* -did; *pp* -done) *tr* sorpassare; **to outdo oneself** sorpassare sé stesso

**out'door'** *adj* all'aria aperta

**out'doors'** *s* aria libera, aperta campagna ‖ *adv* all'aria aperta, fuori di casa

**out'er space'** ['autər] *s* spazio cosmico

**out'field'** *s* (baseball) campo esterno

**out'field'er** *s* (baseball) esterno

**out'fit'** *s* equipaggiamento; (*female cos-*tume) insieme *m;* (*of bride*) corredo; (*group*) (coll) corpo; (com) compagnia ‖ *v* (*pret* & *pp* -fitted; *ger* -fitting) *tr* equipaggiare

**out'flow'** *s* efflusso

**out'go'ing** *adj* in partenza; (*tide*) decrescente; (*character*) espansivo ‖ *s* efflusso

**out'grow'** *v* (*pret* -grew; *pp* -grown) *tr* essere troppo grande per; sorpassare in statura; perdere l'interesse per ‖ *intr* protrudere

**out'growth'** *s* risultato, conseguenza; crescita

**outing** ['autɪŋ] *s* gita, scampagnata

**outlandish** [aut'lændɪʃ] *adj* strano, bizzarro; dall'aspetto straniero; (*remote, far away*) in capo al mondo

**out'last'** *tr* sopravvivere (with *dat*)

**out'law'** *s* fuorilegge *mf* ‖ *tr* proscrivere; dichiarare illegale

**out'lay'** *s* disborso ‖ **out-lay'** *v* (*pret* & *pp* -laid) *tr* sborsare

**out'let** *s* uscita; (*e.g., of river*) sbocco; (com) mercato; (elec) presa di corrente; (fig) sfogo

**out'line'** *s* contorno; traccia, tracciato; sagoma, profilo; prospetto ‖ *tr* delineare; tracciare, tratteggiare; sagomare, profilare; prospettare

**out'live'** *tr* sopravvivere (with *dat*)

**out'look'** *s* prospettiva; (*watch*) guardia; (*mental view*) modo di vedere, opinione

**out'ly'ing** *adj* lontano, fuori di mano; periferico

**outmoded** [‚aut'modɪd] *adj* fuori moda, antiquato

**out'num'ber** *tr* superare in numero

**out'-of-date'** *adj* fuori moda

**out'-of-door'** *adj* all'aria aperta

**out'-of-doors'** *adj* all'aria aperta ‖ *s* aria aperta ‖ *adv* all'aria aperta; fuori di casa

**out'-of-print'** *adj* esaurito

**out'-of-the-way'** *adj* appartato, fuori mano; inusitato, strano

**out' of tune'** *adj* stonato ‖ *adv* fuori di tono

**out' of work'** *adj* disoccupato

**out'pa'tient** *s* paziente *mf* esterno

**out'post'** *s* (mil) posto avanzato

**out'put'** *s* produzione; (elec) uscita; (mach) rendimento, potenza utile

**out'rage'** *s* oltraggio, indecenza ‖ *tr* oltraggiare; (*a woman*) violare

**outrageous** [aut'redʒəs] *adj* oltraggioso; (*excessive*) eccessivo; atroce, feroce

**out'rank'** *tr* superare in grado

**out'rid'er** *s* battistrada *m*

**out'right'** *adj* completo, intero ‖ *adv* completamente; apertamente; sul colpo, sull'istante

**out'set'** *s* inizio, principio

**out'side'** *adj* esterno; (*unlikely*) improbabile; (*price*) massimo ‖ *s* esterno, di fuori *m;* aspetto esteriore; vita fuori del carcere ‖ *adv* fuori, di fuori; **outside of** fuori di ‖ *prep* fuori di; (coll) all'infuori di

**outsider** [ ,aut'saɪdər] *s* estraneo, intruso; (sports) outsider *m*

**out'skirts'** *spl* sobborghi *mpl*, periferia

**out'spo'ken** *adj* franco, esplicito

**out'stand'ing** *adj* saliente, eminente; (*debt*) arretrato, non pagato

**outward** ['aʊtwərd] *adj* esterno, superficiale ‖ *adv* al di fuori

**out'weigh'** *tr* pesare più di; eccedere in importanza

**out'wit'** *v* (*pret & pp* **-witted;** *ger* **-witting**) *tr* farla in barba di; (*a pursuer*) far perdere la traccia or la pista a

**oval** ['ovəl] *adj & s* ovale *m*

**ova·ry** ['ovəri] *s* (**-ries**) ovaia

**ovation** [o've/ən] *s* ovazione

**oven** ['ʌvən] *s* forno

**over** ['ovər] *adj* superiore; esterno; finito, concluso ‖ *adv* su, sopra; dall'altra parte; dall'altra sponda; al rovescio; di nuovo; (*at the bottom of a page*) continua; qui, e.g., **hand over the money** dammi qui il denaro; **over again** di nuovo; **over against** contro; **over and over** ripetutamente; **over here** qui; **over there** là ‖ *prep* su, sopra; dall'altra parte di; attraverso, per; (*a certain number*) più di; a causa di; **over and above** in eccesso di

**o'ver·all'** *adj* completo, totale ‖ **overalls** *spl* tuta

**o'ver·bear'ing** *adj* arrogante, prepotente

**o'ver·board'** *adv* in acqua; **man overboard!** uomo in mare!; **to go overboard** andare agli estremi

**o'ver·cast'** *adj* annuvolato ‖ *s* cielo annuvolato ‖ *v* (*pret & pp* **-cast**) *tr* coprire, annuvolare

**o'ver·charge'** *s* prezzo eccessivo; sovraccarico; (elec) carica eccessiva ‖ **o'ver·charge'** *tr* far pagare eccessivamente; sovraccaricare

**o'ver·coat'** *s* soprabito, pastrano

**o'ver·come'** *v* (*pret* **-came;** *pp* **-come**) *tr* vincere, sopraffare; (*e.g., passions*) frenare; opprimere

**o'vercon'fidence** *s* sicumera

**o'ver·crowd'** *tr* gremire

**o'ver·do'** *v* (*pret* **-did;** *pp* **-done**) *tr* esagerare; strafare; esaurire; (*meat*) stracuocere ‖ *intr* esaurirsi

**o'ver·dose'** *s* dose eccessiva

**o'ver·draft'** *s* assegno allo scoperto

**o'ver·draw'** *v* (*pret* **-drew;** *pp* **-drawn**) *tr* (*a check*) emettere allo scoperto; (*a character*) esagerare la descrizione di

**o'ver·due'** *adj* in ritardo; (com) in sofferenza, scaduto

**o'ver·eat'** *v* (*pret* **-ate;** *pp* **-eaten**) *tr & intr* mangiare troppo

**o'ver·exer'tion** *s* sforzo eccessivo

**o'ver·expose'** *tr* sovresporre

**o'ver·expo'sure** *s* sovresposizione

**o'ver·flow'** *s* (*of a river*) piena, straripamento; (*excess*) sovrabbondanza; (*e.g., of a fountain*) trabocco; (*outlet*) tubo di troppopieno ‖ **o'ver·flow'** *intr* (*said of a river*) straripare; (*said of a container*) traboccare

**o'ver·fly'** *v* (*pret* **-flew;** *pp* **-flown**) *tr* sorvolare; (*a target*) oltrepassare

**o'ver·grown'** *adj* cresciuto troppo; coperto, denso

**o'ver·hang'** *s* strapiombo ‖ **o'ver·hang'** *v* (*pret & pp* **-hung**) *tr* sovrastare (with *dat*); sovrastare; (*to threaten*) minacciare; pervadere, permeare ‖ *intr* sovrastare, strapiombare

**o'ver·haul'** *s* riparazione; esame *m*, revisione ‖ *tr* riparare; esaminare, ripassare, rivedere; raggiungere, mettersi alla pari con

**o'ver·head'** *adj* in alto, sopra la testa; aereo; elevato, pensile; generale ‖ **o'ver·head'** *adv* in alto, di sopra ‖ **o'ver·head'** *s* spese *fpl* generali

**o'ver·head projec'tor** *s* lavagna luminosa

**o'ver·head valve'** *s* valvola in testa

**o'ver·hear'** *v* (*pret & pp* **-heard**) *tr* sentire per caso, udire per caso

**o'ver·heat'** *tr* surriscaldare ‖ *intr* surriscaldarsi; eccitarsi

**overjoyed** [ ,ovər'dʒɔɪd] *adj* felicissimo; **to be overjoyed** non stare in sé dalla contentezza

**overland** ['ovər ,lænd] or ['ovərlənd] *adj & adv* per via di terra

**o'ver·lap'** *v* (*pret & pp* **-lapped;** *ger* **-lapping**) *tr* sovrapporre, estendersi sopra ‖ *intr* sovrapporsi, estendersi; coincidere parzialmente

**o'ver·load'** *s* sovraccarico ‖ **o'ver·load'** *tr* sovraccaricare, stracaricare

**o'ver·look'** *tr* sovrastare su, dominare; ispezionare, sorvegliare; passare sopra, trascurare; dare su, e.g., **the window overlooks the street** la finestra dà sulla strada

**o'ver·lord'** *s* dominatore *m* ‖ *tr* dominare despoticamente

**overly** ['ovərli] *adv* eccessivamente

**o'ver·night'** *adj* per la notte, per solo una notte ‖ **o'ver·night'** *adv* durante la notte; la notte prima

**o'vernight bag'** *s* astuccio di toletta per la notte

**o'ver·pass'** *s* cavalcavia, viadotto

**o'ver·pop'ulate'** *tr* sovrappopolare

**o'ver·pow'er** *tr* sopraffare

**o'ver·pow'ering** *adj* schiacciante

**o'ver·produc'tion** *s* sovrapproduzione

**o'ver·rate'** *tr* sopravvalutare

**o'ver·run'** *v* (*pret* **-ran;** *pp* **-run;** *ger* **-running**) *tr* invadere, infestare; inondare; (*one's time*) oltrepassare, eccedere

**o'ver·sea'** or **o'ver·seas'** *adj* di oltremare ‖ **o'ver·sea'** or **o'ver·seas'** *adv* oltremare, al di là dei mari

**o'ver·see'** *v* (*pret* **-saw;** *pp* **-seen**) *tr* sorvegliare

**o'ver·seer'** *s* sorvegliante *mf*

**o'ver·shad'ow** *tr* oscurare, eclissare

**o'ver·shoe'** *s* soprascarpa

**o'ver·shoot'** *v* (*pret & pp* **-shot**) *tr* (*the target*) oltrepassare; (*said of water*) scorrere sopra; (*said of a fountain*) trabocco; **to overshoot oneself** andare troppo in là ‖ *intr* (aer) atterrare lungo e richiamare

**o'ver·sight'** *s* sbadataggine *f*, svista; sorveglianza, supervisione o'ver·sleep' v (pret & pp -slept) tr (a certain hour) dormire oltre ‖ intr dormire troppo a lungo

o'ver·step' v (pret & pp -stepped; ger -stepping) tr eccedere, oltrepassare

o'ver·stock' tr riempire eccessivamente

o'ver·sup·ply' s (-plies) fornitura superiore alla richiesta ‖ o'ver·sup·ply' v (pret & pp -plied) tr fornire in quantità superiore alla richiesta

overt ['ovərt] or [o'vʌrt] adj palmare, chiaro, manifesto

o'ver·take' v (pret -took; pp -taken) tr raggiungere, sorpassare; sorprendere

o'ver-the-count'er adj (securities) venduto direttamente al compratore

o'ver·throw' s rovesciamento; disfatta ‖ o'ver·throw' s (pret -threw; pp -thrown) tr rovesciare, sconfiggere

o'ver·time' adj supplementare, fuori orario ‖ s straordinario; (sports) tempo supplementare ‖ adv fuori orario

o'ver·tone' s (mus) suono armonico; (fig) sottinteso

o'ver·trump' s taglio con atout più alto ‖ o'ver·trump' tr & intr tagliare con atout più alto

overture ['ovərtʃər] s apertura; (mus) preludio, sinfonia

o'ver·turn' s rovesciamento ‖ o'ver·turn' tr rovesciare, travolgere ‖ intr rovesciarsi, ribaltarsi

overweening [,ovər'winɪŋ] adj presuntuoso, vanitoso; esagerato, eccessivo

o'ver·weight' adj troppo grasso; oltrepassante i limiti di peso ‖ o'ver·weight' s sovraccarico; preponderanza; eccesso di peso

overwhelm [,ovər'hwɛlm] tr schiacciare, debellare; coprire; (e.g., with kindness) colmare, ricolmare

o'ver·work' s lavoro straordinario; superlavoro ‖ o'ver·work' tr far lavorare eccessivamente ‖ intr lavorare eccessivamente

Ovid ['avɪd] s Ovidio

ow [au] interj ahi!

owe [o] tr dovere ‖ intr essere in debito

owing ['o·ɪŋ] adj dovuto; owing to a causa di

owl [aul] s gufo, barbagianni m

own [on] adj proprio, e.g., my own brother il mio proprio fratello ‖ s il proprio; on one's own (coll) per proprio conto; (without anybody's advice) di testa propria; to come into one's own entrare in possesso del proprio; essere riconosciuto per quanto si vale; to hold one's own non perdere terreno; essere pari ‖ tr possedere; riconoscere ‖ intr—to own up to confessare

owner ['onər] s padrone m, proprietario, titolare m

ownership ['onər,ʃɪp] s proprietà f

own'er's li'cence s permesso di circolazione

ox [aks] s (oxen ['aksən]) bue m

ox'cart' s carro tirato da buoi

oxide ['aksaɪd] s ossido

oxidize ['aksɪ,daɪz] tr ossidare ‖ intr ossidarsi

oxygen ['aksɪdʒən] s ossigeno

ox'ygen mask' s maschera respiratoria

ox'ygen tent' s tenda ad ossigeno

oxytone ['aksɪ,ton] adj tronco, ossitono ‖ s ossitono

oyster ['ɔɪstər] adj di ostriche ‖ s ostrica

oys'ter bed' s ostricaio, banco di ostriche

oys'ter cock'tail s ostriche fpl servite in valva

oys'ter fork' s forchettina da ostriche

oys'ter·house' s ristorante m per la vendita delle ostriche

oys'ter·knife' s coltello per aprire le ostriche

oys'ter·man s (-men) ostricaio

oys'ter shell' s conchiglia d'ostrica

oys'ter stew' s brodetto d'ostriche

ozone ['ozon] s ozono

# P

P, p [pi] s sedicesima lettera dell'alfabeto inglese

pace [pes] s passo, andatura; (of a horse) ambio; to keep pace with andare di pari passo con; to put s.o. through his paces mettere qlcu a dura prova; to set the pace for fare l'andatura per; dare l'esempio a ‖ tr misurare a passi, percorrere; to pace the floor andare avanti e indietro per la stanza ‖ intr camminare lentamente; andare al passo; (said of a horse) ambiare

pace'mak'er s battistrada m; (in races) chi stabilisce il passo; (med) pacemaker m

pacific [pə'sɪfɪk] adj pacifico ‖ Pacific adj & s Pacifico

pacifier ['pæsɪ,faɪ·ər] s paciere m; (teething ring) succhietto, tettarella

pacifism ['pæsɪ,fɪzəm] s pacifismo

pacifist ['pæsɪfɪst] adj & s pacifista mf

paci·fy ['pæsɪ,faɪ] v (pret & pp -fied) tr pacificare

pack [pæk] s fardello, pacco; (of merchandise) balla; (of lies) mucchio; (of cards) mazzo; (of thieves) banda; (of dogs) muta; (of animals) branco; (of birds) stormo; (of cigarettes) pacchetto; (of ice) banchiglia; (of people) turba ‖ tr affardellare, impaccare; (to wrap) imballare; ammucchiare; (in cans) mettere in conserva; (people) stipare; (a trunk) fare; to pack in stipare; to pack off mandare via ‖ intr ammucchiarsi, pigiarsi, accalcarsi; **to pack up** fare il baule

**package** ['pækɪdʒ] s pacco, collo; (small) pacchetto ‖ tr impacchettare

**pack' an'imal** s bestia da soma

**packer** ['pækər] s imballatore m; (of canned goods) proprietario (di fabbrica di conserve alimentari)

**packet** ['pækɪt] s pacchetto; (boat) vapore m postale

**packing** ['pækɪŋ] s imballaggio; (on shoulders of suit) spallina; (mach) stoppa; (ring) (mach) guarnizione

**pack'ing box'** or **case'** s cassa d'imballaggio

**pack'ing house'** s fabbrica di conserve alimentari; fabbrica di carne in conserva

**pack'ing slip'** s foglio d'imballaggio

**pack'sad'dle** s basto

**pack'thread'** s spago d'imballaggio

**pack'train'** s fila di animali da soma

**pact** [pækt] s patto

**pad** [pæd] s cuscinetto, tampone m; imbottitura; (of writing paper) blocco da annotazioni; (of an animal) superficie f plantare, zampa; (of a water lily) foglia; (rok) piattaforma ‖ v (pret & pp padded) ger padding) tr imbottire, ovattare; (e.g., a speech) infarcire ‖ intr camminare pesantemente

**pad'ding** s imbottitura

**paddle** ['pædəl] s pagaia; (of waterwheel) pala ‖ tr remare; (to spank) bastonare ‖ intr remare; (to splash) diguazzare

**pad'dle wheei'** s ruota a pale

**paddock** ['pædək] s prato d'allenamento, paddock m

**pad'lock'** s lucchetto ‖ tr chiudere col lucchetto

**pagan** ['pegən] adj & s pagano

**paganism** ['pegə,nɪzəm] s paganesimo

**page** [pedʒ] s (of a book) pagina; (at court) paggio; (in hotels) fattorino, valletto ‖ tr impaginare; (in hotels) chiamare, far chiamare

**pageant** ['pædʒənt] s parata, corteo, spettacolo

**pageant·ry** ['pædʒəntri] s (-ries) pompa, fasto

**paginate** ['pædʒɪ,net] tr impaginare

**pail** [pel] s secchio

**pain** [pen] s dolore m; **on pain of** sotto pena di; **to take pains to** prendersi cura di; **to take pains not to** guardarsi da ‖ tr & intr dolere

**painful** ['penfəl] adj doloroso, penoso

**pain'kill'er** s (coll) analgesico

**painless** ['penlɪs] adj indolore

**painstaking** ['penz,tekɪŋ] adj meticoloso

**paint** [pent] s (for pictures) colore m; (for a house) vernice f; (make-up) trucco ‖ tr dipingere; (a house) verniciare, tinteggiare ‖ intr (with make-up) dipingersi; essere pittore

**paint'box'** s scatola da colori

**paint'brush'** s pennello

**painter** ['pentər] s (of pictures) pittore m; (of a house) verniciatore m; (naut) barbetta

**painting** ['pentɪŋ] s pittura, dipinto

**paint' remov'er** [rɪ'muvər] s solvente m per levar la vernice

**paint' thin'ner** s diluente m

**pair** [pɛr] s paio; (of people) coppia ‖ tr appaiare, accoppiare ‖ intr appaiarsi, accoppiarsi

**pair' of scis'sors** s forbici fpl

**pair' of trou'sers** s calzoni mpl

**pajamas** [pə'dʒɑməz] or [pə'dʒæməz] spl pigiama m

**Pakistan** [,pɑkɪ'stɑn] s il Pakistan

**Pakistani** [,pɑkɪ'stɑni] adj & s pachistano

**pal** [pæl] s (coll) compagno ‖ v (pret & pp palled; ger palling) intr (coll) essere compagni

**palace** ['pælɪs] s palazzo

**palatable** ['pælətəbəl] adj gustoso, appetitoso; accettabile

**palatal** ['pælətəl] adj & s palatale f

**palate** ['pælɪt] s palato

**pale** [pel] adj pallido ‖ s palo; (enclosure) recinto; (fig) ambito ‖ intr impallidire

**pale'face'** s faccia pallida

**palette** ['pælɪt] s tavolozza

**palfrey** ['pɔlfri] s palafreno

**palisade** [,pælɪ'sed] s palizzata; (line of cliffs) dirupo

**pall** [pɔl] s panno mortuario; (of smoke) cappa ‖ tr saziare, infastidire ‖ intr saziarsi, perdere l'appetito

**pall'bear'er** s chi accompagna il feretro; chi porta il feretro

**palliate** ['pælɪ,et] tr attenuare, alleviare

**pallid** ['pælɪd] adj pallido

**pallor** ['pælər] s pallore m

**palm** [pɑm] s (tree and leaf) palma; (of hand; measure) palmo; **to carry off the palm** riportare la palma; **to grease the palm of** ungere le ruote a ‖ tr far sparire nella mano; nascondere; **to palm off s.th on s.o.** rifilare qlco a qlcu

**palmet·to** [pæl'mɛto] s (-tos or -toes) palmeto

**palmist** ['pɑmɪst] s chiromante mf

**palmistry** ['pɑmɪstri] s chiromanzia

**palm' leaf'** s palma, foglia di palma

**palm' oil'** s olio di palma

**Palm' Sun'day** s Domenica delle Palme

**palpable** ['pælpəbəl] adj palpabile

**palpitate** ['pælpɪ,tet] intr palpitare

**pal·sy** ['pɔlzi] s (-sies) paralisi f ‖ v (pret & pp -sied) tr paralizzare

**pal·try** ['pɔltri] adj (-trier; -triest) vile, meschino, irrisorio

**pamper** ['pæmpər] tr viziare; (the appetite) saziare

**pamphlet** ['pæmflɪt] s opuscolo, libello

**pan** [pæn] s padella, casseruola; (of a balance) coppa, piatto; (phot) bacinella ‖ v (pret & pp panned) ger panning) tr friggere; (gold) vagliare in padella; (salt) estrarre in salina; (coll) criticare ‖ intr essere estratto; **to pan out** (coll) riuscire ‖ **Pan** s Pan m

**panacea** [,pænə'si·ə] s panacea

**Pan'ama Canal'** ['pænə,mɑ] s Canale m di Panama

**Pan'ama hat'** *s* panama *m*
**Panamanian** [ˌpænəˈmɛnɪ·ən] or
[ˌpænəˈmɑnɪ·ən] *adj* & *s* panamegno
**pan'cake'** *s* frittella ‖ *intr* (aer) atterrare a piatto
**pan'cake land'ing** *s* atterraggio a piatto
**pancreas** [ˈpænkrɪ·əs] *s* pancreas *m*
**pander** [ˈpændər] *s* mezzano ‖ *intr* ruffianeggiare; **to pander to** favorire, assecondare i desideri di
**pane** [pen] *s* pannello, vetro di finestra
**pan·el** [ˈpænəl] *s* pannello; gruppo che discute in faccia al pubblico, telequiz *m;* discussione pubblica; (*of door or window*) specchio; (law) lista di giurati ‖ *v* (*pret* & *pp* -**eled** or -**elled; ger** -**eling** or -**elling**) *tr* coprire di pannelli
**pan'el discus'sion** *s* colloquio di esperti in faccia al pubblico
**panelist** [ˈpænəlɪst] *s* partecipante *mf* a una discussione in faccia al pubblico
**pan'el lights'** *spl* luci *fpl* del cruscotto
**pan'el truck'** *s* camioncino
**pang** [pæŋ] *s* (*sharp pain*) spasimo; (*of remorse*) tormento
**pan'han'dle** *s* manico della padella ‖ *intr* accattare, mendicare
**pan·ic** [ˈpænɪk] *adj* & *s* panico ‖ *v* (*pret* & *pp* -**icked; ger** -**icking**) *tr* riempire di panico ‖ *intr* essere colto dal panico
**pan'ic·strick'en** *adj* morto di paura, in preda al panico
**pano·ply** [ˈpænəpli] *s* (-**plies**) panoplia; abbigliamento in pompa magna
**panorama** [ˌpænəˈræmə] or [ˌpænəˈrɑmə] *s* panorama *m*
**pan·sy** [ˈpænzi] *s* (-**sies**) viola del pensiero
**pant** [pænt] *s* anelito, affanno; **pants** pantaloni *mpl*, calzoni *mpl;* **to wear the pants** portare i calzoni ‖ *intr* ansare; (*said of heart*) palpitare
**pantheism** [ˈpænθɪ·ɪzəm] *s* panteismo
**pantheon** [ˈpænθɪ·ɑn] or [ˈpænθɪ·ən] *s* panteon *m*, pantheon *m*
**panther** [ˈpænθər] *s* pantera
**panties** [ˈpæntiz] *spl* mutandine *fpl*
**pantomime** [ˈpæntəˌmaɪm] *s* pantomima
**pan·try** [ˈpæntri] *s* (-**tries**) dispensa
**pap** [pæp] *s* pappa
**papa·cy** [ˈpepəsi] *s* (-**cies**) papato
**Pa'pal States'** [ˈpepəl] *spl* Stati *mpl* pontifici
**paper** [ˈpepər] *adj* di carta, cartaceo ‖ *s* carta; (*newspaper*) giornale *m;* (*of a student*) tema *m*, saggio; (*of a scholar*) dissertazione; **on paper** per iscritto ‖ *tr* (*a wall*) tappezzare
**pa'per·back'** *s* libro in brossura
**pa'per·boy'** *s* giornalaio, strillone *m*
**pa'per clip'** *s* fermaglio per le carte, clip *m*
**pa'per cone'** *s* cartoccio
**pa'per cut'ter** *s* rifilatrice *f*
**pa'per doll'** *s* pupazzetto di carta
**pa'per·hang'er** *s* tappezziere *m*
**pa'per knife'** *s* tagliacarte *m*
**pa'per mill'** *s* cartiera
**pa'per mon'ey** *s* carta moneta

**pa'per prof'its** *spl* guadagni *mpl* non realizzati su valori non venduti
**pa'per tape'** *s* (*of teletype*) nastro di carta; (*of computer*) nastro perforato
**pa'per·weight'** *s* fermacarte *m*
**pa'per work'** *s* lavoro a tavolino
**papier-mâché** [ˌpepərməˈʃe] *s* cartapesta
**paprika** [pæˈprikə] or [ˈpæprɪkə] *s* paprica
**papy·rus** [pəˈpaɪrəs] *s* (-**ri** [raɪ]) papiro
**par** [pɑr] *adj* alla pari, nominale; normale ‖ *s* parità *f*, valore *m* nominale; **at par** alla pari
**parable** [ˈpærəbəl] *s* parabola
**parabola** [pəˈræbələ] *s* parabola
**parachute** [ˈpærəˌʃut] *s* paracadute *m* ‖ *intr* lanciarsi col paracadute
**par'a·chute jump'** *s* lancio col paracadute
**parachutist** [ˈpærəˌʃutɪst] *s* paracadutista *mf*
**parade** [pəˈred] *s* parata, sfilata; ostentazione, sfoggio ‖ *tr* ostentare, sfoggiare; disporre in parata ‖ *intr* fare mostra di sé; (mil) sfilare
**paradise** [ˈpærəˌdaɪs] *s* paradiso
**paradox** [ˈpærəˌdɑks] *s* paradosso
**paradoxical** [ˌpærəˈdɑksɪkəl] *adj* paradossale
**paraffin** [ˈpærəfɪn] *s* paraffina
**paragon** [ˈpærəˌgɑn] *s* paragone *m*
**paragraph** [ˈpærəˌgræf] or [ˈpærəˌgrɑf] *s* paragrafo, capoverso; (*in a newspaper*) trafiletto; (*of law*) comma *m*
**parakeet** [ˈpærəˌkit] *s* parrocchetto
**paral·lel** [ˈpærəˌlɛl] *adj* parallelo ‖ *s* (geog, fig) parallelo; (geom) parallela; **parallels** (typ) sbarrette *fpl* verticali ‖ *v* (*pret* & *pp* -**leled** or -**lelled; ger** -**leling** or -**lelling**) *tr* collocare parallelamente; correre parallelo a; confrontare
**par'allel bars'** *spl* parallele *fpl*
**paraly·sis** [pəˈrælɪsɪs] *s* (-**ses** [ˌsiz]) paralisi *f*
**paralytic** [ˌpærəˈlɪtɪk] *adj* & *s* paralitico
**paralyze** [ˈpærəˌlaɪz] *tr* paralizzare
**paramount** [ˈpærəˌmaʊnt] *adj* capitale, supremo
**paramour** [ˈpærəˌmʊr] *s* amante *mf*
**paranoiac** [ˌpærəˈnɔɪˌæk] *adj* & *s* paranoico
**parapet** [ˈpærəˌpɛt] *s* parapetto
**paraphernalia** [ˌpærəfərˈnɛlɪ·ə] *spl* roba, cose *fpl;* attrezzi *mpl*, aggeggi *mpl*
**parasite** [ˈpærəˌsaɪt] *s* parassita *m*
**parasitic(al)** [ˌpærəˈsɪtɪk(əl)] *adj* parassitico, parassitario
**parasol** [ˈpærəˌsɔl] or [ˈpærəˌsɑl] *s* parasole *m*, ombrellino da sole
**par'a·troop'er** *s* paracadutista *m*
**par'a·troops'** *spl* truppe *fpl* paracadutiste
**parboil** [ˈpɑrˌbɔɪl] *tr* bollire parzialmente; (fig) far bollire
**parcel** [ˈpɑrsəl] *s* pacchetto; (*of land*) appezzamento ‖ *v* (*pret* & *pp* -**celed** or -**celled; ger** -**celing** or -**celling**) *tr*

impacchettare; **to parcel out** dividere, distribuire

**par'cel post'** s servizio pacchi postali

**parch** [pɑrtʃ] tr bruciare; (land) inaridire; (e.g., beans) essiccare; **to be parched** bruciare dalla sete || intr arrostirsi; inaridire

**parchment** ['pɑrtʃmənt] s pergamena

**pardon** ['pɑrdən] s perdono, grazia; **I beg your pardon** scusi || tr perdonare; (an offense) graziare

**pardonable** ['pɑrdənəbəl] adj perdonabile, veniale

**par'don board'** s ufficio per la decisione delle grazie

**pare** [per] tr (fruit, potatoes) sbucciare, pelare; (nails) tagliare; (expenses) ridurre

**parent** ['perənt] adj madre, principale || s genitore m or genitrice f; (fig) origine f; **parents** genitori mpl

**parentage** ['perəntɪdʒ] s discendenza, lignaggio

**parenthesis** [pə'renθɪsɪs] s (-ses [ˌsiz]) parentesi f; **in parenthesis** tra parentesi

**parenthetically** [ˌpærən'θɛtɪkəli] adv tra parentesi

**parenthood** ['perənt ˌhʊd] s paternità f or maternità f

**pariah** [pə'raɪ-ə] or ['pɑrɪ-ə] s paria m

**pari-mutuel** ['pærɪ 'mjutʃʊ-əl] s totalizzatore m

**par'ing knife'** ['perɪŋ] s coltello per sbucciare

**Paris** ['pærɪs] s Parigi f

**parish** ['pærɪʃ] s parrocchia

**parishioner** [pə'rɪʃənər] s parrocchiano

**Parisian** [pə'rɪʒən] adj & s parigino

**parity** ['pærɪti] s parità f

**park** [pɑrk] s parco || tr parcare, parcheggiare || intr parcare, parcheggiare, stazionare

**parking** ['pɑrkɪŋ] s posteggio, parcheggio; **no parking** divieto di parcheggio

**park'ing lights'** spl luci fpl di posizione

**park'ing lot'** s posteggio, parcheggio

**park'ing me'ter** s parchimetro

**park'ing tick'et** s contravvenzione per parcheggio abusivo

**park'way'** s boulevard m

**parlay** ['pɑrli] or [pɑr'le] tr rigiocare

**parley** ['pɑrli] s trattativa, conferenza || tr parlamentare

**parliament** ['pɑrlɪmənt] s parlamento

**parlor** ['pɑrlər] s salotto; (of beautician or undertaker) salone m; (of convent) parlatorio

**par'lor car'** s vettura salone

**par'lor game'** s gioco di società

**par'lor pol'itics** s politica da caffè

**Parmesan** [ˌpɑrmɪ'zæn] adj & s parmigiano

**Parnassus** [pɑr'næsəs] s (poetry; poets) parnaso; il Parnaso

**parochial** [pə'rokɪ-əl] adj parrocchiale; ristretto, limitato; (school) confessionale

**paro-dy** ['pærədi] s (-dies) parodia || v (pret & pp -died) tr parodiare

**parole** [pə'rol] s parola d'onore; libertà f condizionale, condizionale f || tr mettere in libertà condizionale

**paroxytone** [pær'ɑksɪ ˌton] adj parossitono || s parola parossitona

**par·quet** [pɑr'ke] s pavimento di legno tassellato, tassellato; (theat) platea || v (pret & pp -queted ['ked]; ger -queting ['ke·ɪŋ]) tr pavimentare in legno tassellato

**par'quet cir'cle** s poltroncine fpl

**parricide** ['pærɪ ˌsaɪd] s (act) patricidio, parricidio; (person) patricida mf, parricida mf

**parrot** ['pærət] s pappagallo || tr scimmiottare, fare il pappagallo a

**par·ry** ['pæri] s (-ries) parata || v (pret & pp -ried) tr parare; (fig) evitare

**parse** [pɑrs] tr (gram) analizzare grammaticalmente

**parsimonious** [ˌpɑrsɪ'moni-əs] adj parsimonioso

**parsley** ['pɑrsli] s prezzemolo

**parsnip** ['pɑrsnɪp] s pastinaca

**parson** ['pɑrsən] s parroco; pastore m protestante

**part** [pɑrt] s parte f; (of a machine) pezzo, organo; (of hair) riga; **for my part** per parte mia; **on the part of** da parte di; **part and parcel** parte f integrante; **parts** abilità f, dote f; regione f, paesi mpl; **to do one's part** fare il proprio dovere || adv parzialmente, in parte || tr dividere, separare; **to part company** separarsi; **to part one's hair** farsi la riga || intr separarsi; **to part from** separarsi da, dividersi da; **to part with** rinunciare a

**par·take** [pɑr'tek] v (pret -took ['tʊk]; pp -taken) tr condividere || intr—to **partake in** partecipare a; **to partake of** condividere

**parterre** [pɑr'ter] s aiola; (theat) platea

**Parthenon** ['pɑrθɪ ˌnɑn] s Partenone m

**partial** ['pɑrʃəl] adj parziale

**participate** [pɑr'tɪsɪ ˌpet] intr partecipare; **to participate in** partecipare a

**participation** [pɑr ˌtɪsɪ'peʃən] s partecipazione

**participle** ['pɑrtɪ ˌsɪpəl] s participio

**particle** ['pɑrtɪkəl] s particella

**particular** [pər'tɪkjələr] adj (belonging to a single person) particolare; (exacting) esigente, fastidioso || s particolare m; **in particular** specialmente, particolarmente

**part'ing** adj (words) di commiato; (last) ultimo || s commiato; separazione

**partisan** ['pɑrtɪzən] adj & s partigiano

**partition** [pɑr'tɪʃən] s partizione, divisione; (of house) tramezzo || tr dividere; tramezzare

**partner** ['pɑrtnər] s (in sports) compagno; (in dancing) cavaliere m, dama; (husband or wife) consorte mf; (com) socio

**partnership** ['pɑrtnər ˌʃɪp] s associazione; (com) società f

**part' of speech'** s parte f del discorso

**partridge** ['pɑrtrɪdʒ] s pernice f

**part'-time'** adj a orario ridotto, a ore

**par·ty** ['pɑrti] adj comune; di gala || s (-ties) festa, ricevimento, trattenimento; (of people) gruppo; (indi-

*vidual*) persona; (pol) partito; (law) contraente *mf*; (mil) distaccamento; **to be a party to** prendere parte a; essere complice di

**par'ty girl'** *s* ragazza che fa la vita

**par'ty-go'er** *s* frequentatore *m* di trattenimenti

**part'y line'** *s* (*boundary*) linea di confine; (*of Communist party*) politica del partito; (telp) linea in coutenza

**pass** [pæs] or [pɑs] *s* passaggio; (*state*) stato, situazione; (*free ticket*) ingresso gratuito; (*leave of absence given to a soldier*) congedo, permesso; (*of a hypnotist*) gesto; (*between mountains*) passo; (slang) tentativo d'abbraccio; **a pretty pass** (coll) un bell'affare ‖ *tr* (*a course in school*) passare; (*to promote*) promuovere; (*a law*) approvare; (*a sentence*) pronunciare; (*an opinion*) esprimere, avanzare; (*to excrete*) evacuare; far muovere; **to pass by** non fare attenzione a; **to pass off** (*e.g., bogus money*) azzeccare; **to pass on** trasmettere; **to pass out** distribuire; **to pass over** omettere ‖ *intr* (*to go*) passare; (*said of a law*) essere approvato; (*said of a student*) essere promosso; (*to be accepted*) farsi passare; (*said, e.g., of two trains*) incrociarsi; **to come to pass** accadere, succedere; **to pass as** passare per; **to pass away** morire; **to pass out** (slang) svenire; **to pass over** or **through** attraversare, passare per

**passable** ['pæsəbəl] or ['pɑsəbəl] *adj* praticabile; (*by boat*) navigabile; (*adequate*) passabile; (law) promulgabile

**passage** ['pæsɪdʒ] *s* passaggio; (*of a law*) approvazione; (*ticket*) biglietto di passaggio; (*of the bowels*) evacuazione

**pass'book'** *s* libretto di banca; libretto della cassa di risparmio

**passenger** ['pæsəndʒər] *s* passeggero

**passer-by** ['pæsər'baɪ] or ['pɑsər'baɪ] *s* (**passers-by**) passante *mf*

**passing** ['pæsɪŋ] or ['pɑsɪŋ] *adj* (*fleeting*) fuggente; (*casual*) incidentale; (*grade*) che concede la promozione ‖ *s* passaggio; (*death*) morte *f*; promozione

**passion** ['pæʃən] *s* passione

**passionate** ['pæʃənɪt] *adj* appassionato; (*hot-tempered*) collerico, veemente, ardente

**passive** ['pæsɪv] *adj* & *s* passivo

**pass'key'** *s* chiave maestra; (*for use of hotel help*) comunella

**Pass'o'ver** *s* Pasqua ebraica

**pass'port** *s* passaporto

**pass'word'** *s* parola d'ordine

**past** [pæst] or [pɑst] *adj* passato, scorso; ex, e.g., **past president** ex presidente ‖ *s* passato ‖ *adv* oltre; al di fuori; al di là ‖ *prep* oltre; al di là di; dopo (di); **past belief** incredibile; **past cure** incurabile; **past hope** senza speranza; **past recovery** incurabile; **past three o'clock** le tre passate

**paste** [pest] *s* (*dough*) pasta; (*adhesive*) colla; diamante *m* artificiale ‖ *tr* incollare; (slang) dare pugni a

**paste'board'** *s* cartone *m*

**pastel** [pæs'tɛl] *adj* & *s* pastello

**pasteurize** ['pæstə‚raɪz] *tr* pastorizzare

**pastime** ['pæs‚taɪm] or ['pɑs‚taɪm] *s* diversione, passatempo

**pastor** ['pæstər] or ['pɑstər] *s* pastore *m*, sacerdote *m*

**pastoral** ['pæstərəl] or ['pɑstərəl] *adj* pastorale ‖ *s* (*poem, letter*) pastorale *f*; (*crosier*) pastorale *m*

**pas•try** ['pestri] *s* (**-tries**) pasticceria

**pas'try cook'** *s* pasticciere *m*

**pas'try shop'** *s* pasticceria

**pasture** ['pæstʃər] or ['pɑstʃər] *s* pastura, pascolo ‖ *tr* condurre al pascolo ‖ *intr* brucare

**past•y** ['pesti] *adj* (**-ier; -iest**) pastoso; flaccido

**pat** [pæt] *s* colpetto; (*of butter*) panetto ‖ *v* (*pret & pp* **patted;** *ger* **patting**) *tr* accarezzare leggermente; battere leggermente; **to pat on the back** elogiare, incoraggiare battendo sulla spalla

**patch** [pætʃ] *s* (*on a suit or shoes*) toppa; (*in a tire*) pezza; (*on wound*) benda; (*of ground*) appezzamento; (*small area*) lembo ‖ *tr* rammendare; **to patch up** (*an argument*) comporre; (*to produce crudely*) raffazzonare

**patent** ['petənt] *adj* patente, palmare ‖ ['pætənt] *adj* brevettato ‖ *s* (*of invention*) brevetto; (*sole right*) privativa ‖ *tr* brevettare

**pat'ent leath'er** ['pætənt] *s* copale *m* & *f*, pelle *f* di vernice

**pat'ent med'icine** ['pætent] *s* specialità *f* medicinale

**pat'ent right'** ['pætent] *s* proprietà brevettata

**paternal** [pə'tʌrnəl] *adj* paterno

**paternity** [pə'tʌrnɪti] *s* paternità *f*

**path** [pæθ] or [pɑθ] *s* via battuta, sentiero; (fig) via

**pathetic** [pə'θɛtɪk] *adj* patetico

**path'find'er** *s* esploratore *m*

**pathology** [pə'θɑlədʒi] *s* patologia

**pathos** ['peθɑs] *s* patos *m*, pathos *m*

**path'way'** *s* sentiero, cammino

**patience** ['peʃəns] *s* pazienza

**patient** ['peʃənt] *adj* & *s* paziente *mf*

**patriarch** ['petri‚ɑrk] *s* patriarca *m*

**patrician** [pə'trɪʃən] *adj* & *s* patrizio

**patricide** ['pætri‚saɪd] *s* (*act*) parricidio; (*person*) parricida *mf*

**Patrick** ['pætrɪk] *s* Patrizio

**patrimo•ny** ['pætri‚moni] *s* (**-nies**) patrimonio

**patriot** ['petri•ət] or ['pætri•ət] *s* patriota *mf*

**patriotic** [‚petri'ɑtɪk] or [‚pætri'ɑtɪk] *adj* patriottico

**patriotism** ['petri•ə‚tɪzəm] or ['pætri•ə‚tɪzəm] *s* patriottismo

**pa•trol** [pə'trol] *s* (*group*) pattuglia; (*individual*) soldato or agente *m* di pattuglia ‖ *v* (*pret & pp* **-trolled;** *ger* **-trolling**) *tr* & *intr* pattugliare

**patrol'man** *s* (**-men**) agente *m*, poliziotto

**patrol' wag'on** s carrozzone m cellulare, cellulare m

**patron** ['petrən] or ['pætrən] s patrono, sostenitore m; (customer) cliente mf

**patronize** ['petrə͵naɪz] or ['pætrə͵naɪz] tr (to support) sostenere; trattare con condiscendenza; essere cliente abituale di

**pa'tron saint'** s patrono

**patter** ['pætər] s (e.g., of rain) battito; (of feet) scalpiccio; (speech) chiacchierio ‖ intr battere, picchiettare; chiaccherare

**pattern** ['pætərn] s modello; disegno; (of flight) procedura ‖ tr modellare

**pat·ty** ['pæti] s (-ties) pasticcino; (meat cake) polpetta

**paucity** ['pɔsɪti] s pochezza, scarsità f, insufficienza

**Paul** [pɔl] s Paolo

**paunch** [pɔntʃ] s pancia

**paunch·y** ['pɔntʃi] adj (-ier; -iest) panciuto

**pauper** ['pɔpər] s povero, indigente mf

**pause** [pɔz] s pausa; (of a tape recorder) arresto momentaneo; **to give pause (to)** dar di che pensare (a) ‖ intr far pausa, fermarsi; (to hesitate) esitare, vacillare

**pave** [pev] tr pavimentare, lastricare; **to pave the way (for)** aprire il cammino (a)

**pavement** ['pevmənt] s pavimentazione, lastricato; (sidewalk) marciapiede m

**pavilion** [pə'vɪljən] s padiglione m; (of circus) tendone m

**paw** [pɔ] s zampa ‖ tr (to touch with paws) dar zampate a; (to handle clumsily) maneggiare goffamente; (coll) palpeggiare ‖ intr zampare

**pawn** [pɔn] s (security) pegno; (tool of another person) pedina; (chess) pedina, pedone m; (fig) ostaggio ‖ tr dare in pegno, impegnare

**pawn'bro'ker** s prestatore m su pegno

**pawn'shop'** s agenzia di prestiti su pegno, monte m di pietà

**pawn' tick'et** s ricevuta di pegno, polizza del monte di pietà

**pay** [pe] s pagamento; (wages) paga, salario; (mil) soldo ‖ v (pret & pp **paid** [ped]) tr pagare; (wages) conguagliare; (one's respects) presentare; (a visit) fare; (a bill) saldare; (attention) fare, presentare; **to pay back** ripagare; (fig) pagare pan per focaccia a; **to pay for** pagare; **to pay off** liquidare; (in order to discharge) pagare e licenziare; **to pay up** saldare ‖ intr pagare; valere la pena; **pay as you enter** pagare all'ingresso; **pay as you go** pagare le tasse per trattenuta; **pay as you leave** pagare all'uscita

**payable** ['pe·əbəl] adj pagabile

**pay' boost'** s aumento di salario

**pay'check'** s assegno in pagamento del salario; salario, paga

**pay'day'** s giorno di paga

**payee** [pe'i] s beneficiario

**pay' en'velope** s bustapaga

**payer** ['pe·ər] s pagatore m

**pay'load'** s peso utile

**pay'mas'ter** s ufficiale m pagatore

**payment** ['pemənt] s pagamento

**pay'off'** s pagamento, regolamento; (coll) conclusione

**pay' phone'** s telefono a moneta

**pay'roll'** s lista degli impiegati; libro paga

**pay' sta'tion** s telefono pubblico

**pea** [pi] s pisello

**peace** [pis] s pace f; **to hold one's peace** tacere, stare zitto

**peaceable** ['pisəbəl] adj pacifico

**peaceful** ['pisfəl] adj pacifico

**peace'mak'er** s paciere m

**peace' of mind'** s serenità f d'animo

**peace' pipe'** s calumet m della pace

**peach** [pitʃ] s pesca; (coll) persona or cosa stupenda

**peach' tree'** s pesco

**peach·y** ['pitʃi] adj (-ier; -iest) (coll) stupendo

**pea'cock'** s pavone m

**peak** [pik] s picco; (of traffic) punta; (of one's career) sommo

**peak' hour'** s ora di punta

**peak' load'** s carico delle ore di punta, carico massimo

**peal** [pil] s (of bells) squillo; (of gun) rombo; (of laughter) scoppio; (of thunder) scroscio ‖ intr scampanare, squillare

**pea'nut'** s nocciolina americana; (plant) arachide f

**pea'nut but'ter** s pasta d'arachidi

**pear** [per] s (fruit) pera; (tree) pero

**pearl** [pʌrl] s perla; (mother-of-pearl) madreperla; colore perlaceo

**pearl' oys'ter** s ostrica perlifera

**pear' tree'** s pero

**peasant** ['pɛzənt] adj & s contadino

**pea'shoot'er** s cerbottana

**pea' soup'** s minestra di piselli; (coll) nebbione m

**peat** [pit] s torba

**pebble** ['pɛbəl] s ciottolo

**peck** [pɛk] s beccata; misura di due galloni; **a peck of trouble** un mare di guai ‖ tr beccare ‖ intr beccare; **to peck at** beccucciare

**peculation** [͵pɛkjə'leʃən] s malversazione, peculato

**peculiar** [pɪ'kjuljər] adj peculiare; (odd) strano

**pedagogue** ['pɛdə͵gag] s pedagogo

**pedagogy** ['pɛdə͵godʒi] or ['pɛdə͵gadʒi] s pedagogia

**ped·al** ['pɛdəl] s pedale m ‖ v (pret & pp **-aled** or **-alled**; ger **-aling** or **-alling**) tr spingere coi pedali ‖ intr pedalare

**pedant** ['pɛdənt] s pedante mf

**pedantic** [pɪ'dæntɪk] adj pedantesco

**pedant·ry** ['pɛdəntri] s (-ries) pedanteria

**peddle** ['pɛdəl] tr vendere di porta in porta ‖ intr fare il venditore ambulante

**peddler** ['pɛdlər] s venditore m or merciaiolo ambulante

**pedestal** ['pɛdɪstəl] s piedistallo
**pedestrian** [pɪ'destrɪ·ən] adj pedestre || s pedone m
**pediatrics** [ ,pidɪ'ætrɪks] or [ ,pɛdɪ'ætrɪks] s pediatria
**pedigree** ['pɛdɪ ,gri] s albero genealogico; discendenza, lignaggio
**pediment** ['pɛdɪmənt] s frontone m
**peek** [pik] s sbirciata || intr sbirciare
**peel** [pil] s scorza, buccia; (of baker) pala || tr sbucciare; **to keep one's eyes peeled** (slang) tenere gli occhi aperti || intr pelarsi
**peep** [pip] s sbirciata; (sound) pigolio || intr guardare attraverso una fessura; (said of birds) pigolare; (to begin to appear) fare capolino
**peep'hole'** s spioncino
**Peep'ing Tom'** s guardone m
**peep' show'** s cosmorama m
**peer** [pɪr] s pari m, uguale m; (Brit) pari m || intr guardare da vicino
**peerless** ['pɪrlɪs] adj senza pari
**peeve** [piv] s (coll) seccatura, irritazione || tr (coll) seccare, irritare
**peevish** ['pivɪʃ] adj irritabile
**peg** [pɛg] s (to plug holes) zipolo; (pin) cavicchio; (mus) bischero; (coll) grado; **to take down a peg** (coll) fare abbassare la testa a || v (pret & pp pegged; ger pegging) tr fissare con cavicchi; (prices) stabilizzare || intr—**to peg away** lavorare di lena
**peg' leg'** s gamba di legno
**Peking** ['pi'kɪŋ] s Pechino f
**Peking·ese** [ ,piki'niz] adj pechinese || s (-ese) pechinese mf
**pelf** [pɛlf] s (pej) denaro rubacchiato, maltolto
**pelican** ['pɛlɪkən] s pellicano
**pellet** ['pɛlɪt] s pallottola; (for shotgun) pallino; (pill) pillola
**pell-mell** ['pɛl'mɛl] adj confuso, disordinato || adv alla rinfusa
**Peloponnesian** [ ,pɛləpə'niʃən] adj & s peloponnesiaco
**pelt** [pɛlt] s pelle grezza; (blow) colpo || tr scagliare contro; (to beat) battere violentemente || intr battere, scrosciare
**pen** [pɛn] s (enclosure) recinto; (for writing) penna; (pen point) pennino || v (pret & pp penned; ger penning) tr scrivere a penna; (to compose) redigere || v (pret & pp penned or pent; ger penning) tr recintare
**penalize** ['pina ,laɪz] tr punire; (sports) penalizzare
**penal·ty** ['pɛnəlti] s (-ties) punizione; (fine) multa; (for late payment) penale f; **under penalty of** sotto pena di
**pen'alty goal'** s calcio di rigore
**penance** ['pɛnəns] s penitenza
**penchant** ['pɛnʃənt] s propensione
**pen·cil** ['pɛnsəl] s matita; (of rays) fascio || v (pret & pp -ciled or -cilled; ger -ciling or -cilling) tr scrivere a matita; (med) pennellare
**pen'cil sharp'ener** s temperalapis m
**pendent** ['pɛndənt] adj pendente, sospeso || s pendente m, ciondolo

**pending** ['pɛndɪŋ] adj imminente; in sospeso || prep durante; fino a
**pendulum** ['pɛndʒələm] s pendolo
**pen'dulum bob'** s lente f
**penetrate** ['pɛnɪ ,tret] tr & intr penetrare
**penguin** ['pɛŋgwɪn] s pinguino
**pen'hold'er** s portapenne m
**penicillin** [ ,pɛnɪ'sɪlɪn] s penicillina
**peninsula** [pɛ'nɪnsələ] s penisola
**peninsular** [pə'nɪnsələr] adj & s peninsulare
**penitence** ['pɛnɪtəns] s penitenza
**penitent** ['pɛnɪtənt] adj & s penitente mf
**pen'knife'** s (-knives) temperino
**penmanship** ['pɛnmən ,ʃɪp] s calligrafia
**pen' name'** s nome m di penna, pseudonimo
**pennant** ['pɛnənt] s pennone m
**penniless** ['pɛnɪlɪs] adj povero in canna, senza un soldo
**pennon** ['pɛnən] s pennone m
**pen·ny** ['pɛni] s (-nies) (U.S.A.) centesimo || s (pence [pɛns]) (Brit) penny m
**pen'ny pinch'er** ['pɪntʃər] s spilorcio
**pen' pal'** s amico corrispondente
**pen'point'** s pennino; (of ball-point pen) punta
**pension** ['pɛnʃən] s pensione || tr pensionare, mettere in pensione
**pensioner** ['pɛnʃənər] s pensionato
**pensive** ['pɛnsɪv] adj pensieroso
**Pentecost** ['pɛntɪ ,kɔst] or ['pɛntɪ ,kɑst] s la Pentecoste
**penthouse** ['pɛnt ,haʊs] s appartamento di lusso sul tetto; tettoia
**pent-up** ['pɛnt ,ʌp] adj represso
**penult** ['pinʌlt] s penultima
**penum·bra** [pɪ'nʌmbrə] s (-brae [bri] or -bras) penombra
**penurious** [pɪ'nʊrɪ·əs] adj taccagno, meschino; indigente
**penury** ['pɛnjəri] s taccagneria; estrema povertà, miseria
**pen'wip'er** s nettapenne m
**people** ['pipəl] spl popolo, gente f; (relatives) famiglia; gente f del popolo; si, e.g., **people say** si dice || ssg (peoples) nazione, popolazione || tr popolare
**pep** [pɛp] s (coll) animo, brio || v (pret & pp pepped; ger pepping) tr— **to pep up** (coll) dar animo a
**pepper** ['pɛpər] s pepe m || tr pepare; (to pelt) tempestare
**pep'per·box'** s pepaiola
**pep'per·mint'** s menta piperita
**per** [pʌr] prep per; (for each) il, e.g., **three dollars per meter** tre dollari il metro; **as per** secondo
**perambulator** [pər'æmbjə ,letər] s carrozzella, carrozzino
**per capita** [pər 'kæpɪtə] per persona, a testa
**perceive** [pər'siv] tr percepire
**percent** [pər'sɛnt] s percento, per cento
**percentage** [pər'sɛntɪdʒ] s percento, percentuale f; (coll) vantaggio
**perception** [pər'sɛpʃən] s percezione

**perch** [pʌrtʃ] s (roost) posatoio; (horizontal rod) ballatoio; (ichth) pesce persico ‖ intr appollaiarsi

**percolator** ['pʌrkə,letər] s caffettiera filtro a circolazione

**percus'sion cap'** [pər'kʌʃən] s capsula di percussione

**per diem** [pər 'daɪ·əm] s assegno giornaliero

**perdition** [pər'dɪʃən] s perdizione

**perennial** [pə'rɛnɪ·əl] adj perenne ‖ s pianta perenne

**perfect** ['pʌrfɪkt] adj & s perfetto ‖ [pər'fɛkt] tr perfezionare

**perfidious** [pər'fɪdɪ·əs] adj perfido

**perfi·dy** ['pʌrfɪdɪ] s (-dies) perfidia

**perforate** ['pʌrfə,ret] tr perforare

**perforation** [,pʌrfə'reʃən] s perforazione; (of postage stamp) dentellatura

**perforce** [pər'fɔrs] adv per forza, necessariamente

**perform** [pər'fɔrm] tr (a task) eseguire; (a promise) adempiere; (to enact) rappresentare ‖ intr recitare; (said, e.g., of a machine) funzionare

**performance** [pər'fɔrməns] s esecuzione; (of a machine) funzionamento; (deed) atto di prodezza; (theat) rappresentazione

**performer** [pər'fɔrmər] s esecutore m; attore m; acrobata mf

**perform'ing arts'** spl arti fpl dello spettacolo

**perfume** ['pʌrfjum] s profumo ‖ [pər'fjum] tr profumare

**perfumer·y** [pər'fjuməri] s (-ies) profumeria

**perfunctory** [pər'fʌŋktəri] adj superficiale, pro forma; indifferente

**perhaps** [pər'hæps] adv forse

**per·il** ['pɛrəl] s pericolo ‖ v (pret & pp -iled or -illed; ger -iling or -illing) tr mettere in pericolo

**perilous** ['pɛrɪləs] adj pericoloso

**period** ['pɪrɪ·əd] s periodo; mestruazione; (in school) ora; (sports) tempo; (gram) punto

**pe'riod cos'tume** s costume m dell'epoca

**periodic** [,pɪrɪ'ɑdɪk] adj periodico

**periodical** [,pɪrɪ'ɑdɪkəl] adj & s periodico

**peripher·y** [pə'rɪfəri] s (-ies) periferia

**periscope** ['pɛrɪ,skop] s periscopio

**perish** ['pɛrɪʃ] intr perire

**perishable** ['pɛrɪʃəbəl] adj deteriorabile

**periwig** ['pɛrɪ,wɪg] s parrucca

**perjure** ['pʌrdʒər] tr—**to perjure oneself** spergiurare, giurare il falso

**perju·ry** ['pʌrdʒəri] s (-ries) spergiuro

**perk** [pʌrk] tr (the head, the ears) alzare; **to perk oneself up** agghindarsi ‖ intr—**to perk up** ringalluzzirsi

**permanence** ['pʌrmənəns] s permanenza

**permanen·cy** ['pʌrmənənsi] s (-cies) permanenza

**permanent** ['pʌrmənənt] adj permanente ‖ s permanente f, ondulazione permanente

**per'manent fix'ture** s cosa or persona permanente

**per'manent ten'ure** s inamovibilità f

**per'manent way'** s (rr) sede f stradale ed armamento

**permeate** ['pʌrmɪ,et] tr permeare ‖ intr permearsi

**permissible** [pər'mɪsɪbəl] adj permissibile

**permission** [pər'mɪʃən] s permesso

**per·mit** ['pʌrmɪt] s permesso; patente f, licenza ‖ [pər'mɪt] v (pret & pp -mitted; ger -mitting) tr permettere

**permute** [pər'mjut] tr permutare

**pernicious** [pər'nɪʃəs] adj pernicioso

**pernickety** [pər'nɪkɪti] adj (coll) incontentabile, meticoloso

**perorate** ['pɛrə,ret] intr perorare

**peroxide** [pər'ɑksaɪd] s perossido; perossido d'idrogeno

**perox'ide blonde'** s bionda ossigenata

**perpendicular** [,pʌrpən'dɪkjələr] adj & s perpendicolare f

**perpetrate** ['pʌrpɪ,tret] tr (a crime) perpetrare; (a blunder) commettere

**perpetual** [pər'pɛtʃʊ·əl] adj perpetuo

**perpetuate** [pər'pɛtʃʊ,et] tr perpetuare

**perplex** [pər'plɛks] tr lasciare perplesso

**perplexed** [pər'plɛkst] adj perplesso

**perplexi·ty** [pər'plɛksɪti] s (-ties) perplessità f

**per se** [pər 'si] di per se

**persecute** ['pʌrsɪ,kjut] tr perseguitare

**persevere** [,pʌrsɪ'vɪr] intr perseverare

**Persian** ['pʌrʒən] adj & s persiano

**Per'sian Gulf'** s Golfo Persico

**persimmon** [pər'sɪmən] s diospiro virginiano; cachi m

**persist** [pər'sɪst] or [pər'zɪst] intr persistere

**persistent** [pər'sɪstənt] or [pər'zɪstənt] adj persistente

**person** ['pʌrsən] s persona; **no person** nessuno

**personage** ['pʌrsənɪdʒ] s personaggio; persona

**personal** ['pʌrsənəl] adj personale; (goods) mobile ‖ s inserzione personale; trafiletto di società

**personali·ty** [,pʌrsə'nælɪti] s (-ties) personalità f; offesa personale

**personal'ity cult'** s culto della personalità

**per'sonal prop'erty** s beni mpl mobili

**personi·fy** [pər'sɑnɪ,faɪ] v (pret & pp -fied) tr personificare

**personnel** [,pʌrsə'nɛl] s personale m

**per'son-to-per'son call'** s (telp) chiamata con preavviso

**perspective** [pər'spɛktɪv] s prospettiva

**perspicacious** [,pʌrspɪ'keʃəs] adj perspicace

**perspire** [pər'spaɪr] intr sudare

**persuade** [pər'swed] tr persuadere

**persuasion** [pər'sweʒən] s persuasione; fede religiosa

**pert** [pʌrt] adj impertinente, sfacciato; vivace

**pertain** [pər'ten] intr appartenere; (to have reference) riferirsi

**pertinacious** [,pʌrtɪ'neʃəs] adj pertinace

**pertinent** ['pʌrtɪnənt] *adj* pertinente
**perturb** [pər'tʌrb] *tr* perturbare
**Peru** [pə'ru] *s* il Perù
**perusal** [pə'ruzəl] *s* attenta lettura
**peruse** [pə'ruz] *tr* leggere attentamente
**pervade** [pər'ved] *tr* pervadere
**perverse** [pər'vʌrs] *adj* perverso; (*obstinate*) ostinato
**perversion** [pər'vʌrʒən] *s* perversione
**perversi•ty** [pər'vʌrsɪti] *s* (**-ties**) perversità *f*; contrarietà *f*
**pervert** ['pʌrvərt] *s* pervertito, degenerato || [pər'vʌrt] *tr* pervertire, degenerare
**pes•ky** ['pɛski] *adj* (**-kier; -kiest**) (coll) noioso, molesto
**pessimism** ['pɛsɪ ˌmɪzəm] *s* pessimismo
**pessimist** ['pɛsɪmɪst] *s* pessimista *mf*
**pessimistic** [ˌpɛsɪ'mɪstɪk] *adj* pessimistico
**pest** [pɛst] *s* peste *f*, pestilenza; insetto; animale nocivo; (*person*) peste *f*, seccatore *m*
**pester** ['pɛstər] *tr* seccare, annoiare
**pest'house'** *s* lazzaretto
**pesticide** ['pɛstɪ ˌsaɪd] *s* insetticida *m*
**pestiferous** [pɛs'tɪfərəs] *adj* pestifero
**pestilence** ['pɛstɪləns] *s* pestilenza
**pestle** ['pɛsəl] *s* pestello
**pet** [pɛt] *s* animale favorito; beniamino || *v* (*pret & pp* **petted;** *ger* **petting**) *tr* accarezzare || *intr* (coll) pomiciare
**petal** ['pɛtəl] *s* petalo
**petard** [pɪ'tard] *s* petardo
**pet'cock'** *s* chiavetta
**Peter** ['pitər] *s* Pietro; **to rob Peter to pay Paul** fare un buco per tapparne un altro || *intr*—**to peter out** (coll) affievolirsi
**petition** [pɪ'tɪʃən] *s* petizione || *tr* rivolgere un'istanza a
**pet' name'** *s* nomignolo vezzeggiativo
**Petrarch** ['pitrark] *s* Petrarca *m*
**petri•fy** ['petrɪ ˌfaɪ] *v* (*pret & pp* **-fied**) *tr* pietrificare || *intr* pietrificarsi
**petrol** ['petrəl] *s* (Brit) benzina
**petroleum** [pɪ'trolɪ•əm] *s* petrolio
**pet' shop'** *s* negozio di animali domestici
**petticoat** ['pɛtɪ ˌkot] *s* sottoveste *f*; (coll) sottana, gonnella
**pet•ty** ['pɛti] *adj* (**-tier; -tiest**) insignificante, minore; meschino
**pet'ty cash'** *s* cassa delle piccole spese
**pet'ty lar'ceny** *s* furterello
**pet'ty of'ficer** *s* (nav) sottufficiale *m* di marina
**petulant** ['pɛtjələnt] *adj* stizzoso, irritabile
**pew** [pju] *s* banco di chiesa
**pewter** ['pjutər] *s* peltro; oggetti *mpl* di peltro
**phalanx** ['felæŋks] *or* ['fælæŋks] *s* falange *f*
**phantasm** ['fæntæzəm] *s* fantasma *m*
**phantom** ['fæntəm] *s* fantasma *m*
**Pharaoh** ['fero] *s* Faraone *m*
**pharisee** ['færɪ ˌsi] *s* fariseo || **Pharisee** *s* fariseo
**pharmaceutical** [ˌfɑrmə'sutɪkəl] *adj* farmaceutico

**pharmacist** ['fɑrməsɪst] *s* farmacista *mf*
**pharma•cy** ['fɑrməsi] *s* (**-cies**) farmacia
**pharynx** ['færɪŋks] *s* faringe *f*
**phase** [fez] *s* fase *f* || *tr* mettere in fase; sincronizzare; **to phase in** mettere in operazione gradualmente; **to phase out** eliminare gradualmente
**pheasant** ['fɛzənt] *s* fagiano
**phenobarbital** [ˌfino'bɑrbɪ ˌtæl] *s* acido fenil-etilbarbiturico, barbiturato
**phenomenal** [fɪ'nɑmɪnəl] *adj* fenomenale
**phenome•non** [fɪ'nɑmɪ ˌnɑn] *s* (**-na** [nə]) fenomeno
**phial** ['faɪ•əl] *s* fiala
**philanderer** [fɪ'lændərər] *s* donnaiolo
**philanthropist** [fɪ'lænθrəpiist] *s* filantropo
**philanthro•py** [fɪ'lænθrəpi] *s* (**-pies**) filantropia
**philatelist** [fɪ'lætəlɪst] *s* filatelico
**philately** [fɪ'lætəli] *s* filatelia
**Philip** ['fɪlɪp] *s* Filippo
**Philippine** ['fɪlɪ ˌpin] *adj* filippino || **Philippines** *spl* isole *fpl* Filippine
**Philistine** [fɪ'lɪstin], ['fɪlɪ ˌstin] *or* ['fɪlɪ ˌstaɪn] *adj & s* filisteo
**philologist** [fɪ'lɑlədʒɪst] *s* filologo
**philology** [fɪ'lɑlədʒi] *s* filologia
**philosopher** [fɪ'lɑsəfər] *s* filosofo
**philosophic(al)** [ˌfɪlə'sɑfɪk(əl)] *adj* filosofico
**philoso•phy** [fɪ'lɑsəfi] *s* (**-phies**) filosofia
**philter** ['fɪltər] *s* filtro
**phlebitis** [flɪ'baɪtɪs] *s* flebite *f*
**phlegm** [flɛm] *s* (*secretion*) muco, catarro; (*self-possession*) flemma; apatia
**phlegmatic(al)** [flɛg'mætɪk(əl)] *adj* flemmatico
**Phoebus** ['fibəs] *s* Febo
**Phoenician** [fɪ'nɪ/ən] *or* [fɪ'nɪ/ən] *adj & s* fenicio
**phoenix** ['finɪks] *s* fenice *f*
**phone** [fon] *s* (coll) telefono || *tr & intr* (coll) telefonare
**phone' call'** *s* chiamata telefonica
**phonetic** [fo'nɛtɪk] *adj* fonetico || **phonetics** *s* fonetica
**phonograph** ['fonə ˌgræf] *or* ['fonə ˌgraf] *s* fonografo
**phonology** [fə'nɑlədʒi] *s* fonologia
**pho•ny** ['foni] *adj* (**-nier; -niest**) (coll) falso || *s* (**-nies**) (coll) frode *f*; (*person*) (coll) impostore *m*
**phosphate** ['fɑsfet] *s* fosfato
**phosphorescent** [ˌfɑsfə'rɛsənt] *adj* fosforescente
**phospho•rus** ['fɑsfərəs] *s* (**-ri** [ˌraɪ]) fosforo
**pho•to** ['foto] *s* (**-tos**) (coll) foto *f*
**photo•cop•y** ['fotə ˌkɑpi] *s* (**-ies**) fotocopia || *tr* fotocopiare
**pho'toelec'tric cell'** [ˌfoto•ɪ'lɛktrɪk] *s* cellula fotoelettrica
**photoengraving** [ˌfoto•ɛn'grevɪŋ] *s* fotoincisione
**pho'to fin'ish** *s* photofinish *m*, arrivo con fotografia

**photogenic** [ˌfotoˈdʒɛnɪk] *adj* fotogenico

**photograph** [ˈfotəˌgræf] or [ˈfotəˌgraf] *s* fotografia ‖ *tr* fotografare ‖ *intr*—**to photograph well** riuscire in fotografia

**photographer** [fəˈtɑgrəfər] *s* fotografo

**photography** [fəˈtɑgrəfi] *s* fotografia

**photojournalism** [ˌfotəˈdʒʌrnəˌlɪzəm] *s* giornalismo fotografico

**pho·to·play** *s* dramma adattato per il cinematografo

**photostat** [ˈfotəˌstæt] *s* (trademark) copia fotostatica ‖ *tr* riprodurre fotostaticamente

**phototube** [ˈfotəˌtjub] or [ˈfotəˌtub] *s* fototubo

**phrase** [frez] *s* (gram) locuzione; (mus) frase *f* ‖ *tr* esprimere, formulare ‖ *intr* (mus) fraseggiare

**phrenology** [frɪˈnɑlədʒi] *s* frenologia

**Phyllis** [ˈfɪlɪs] *s* Fillide *f*

**phy·lum** [ˈfaɪləm] *s* (**-la** [lə]) phylum *m*, tipo

**phys·ic** [ˈfɪzɪk] *s* purgante *m* ‖ *v* (*pret & pp* **-icked**; *ger* **-icking**) *tr* dare il purgante a, purgare

**physical** [ˈfɪzɪkəl] *adj* fisico

**physician** [fɪˈzɪʃən] *s* medico

**physicist** [ˈfɪzɪsɪst] *s* fisico

**physics** [ˈfɪzɪks] *s* fisica

**physiognomy** [ˌfɪziˈɑgnəmi] or [ˌfɪziˈɑnəmi] *s* fisionomia

**physiological** [ˌfɪziəˈlɑdʒɪkəl] *adj* fisiologico

**physiology** [ˌfɪziˈɑlədʒi] *s* fisiologia

**physique** [fɪˈzik] *s* fisico

**pi** [paɪ] *s* (math) pi greco; (typ) tipi scartati ‖ *v* (*pret & pp* **pied**; *ger* **piing**) *tr* (typ) scompaginare, scomporre

**pian·o** [pɪˈæno] *s* (**-os**) piano

**picaresque** [ˌpɪkəˈrɛsk] *adj* picaresco

**picayune** [ˌpɪkəˈjun] *adj* meschino, minore, di poca importanza

**picco·lo** [ˈpɪkəˌlo] *s* (**-los**) ottavino

**pick** [pɪk] *s* (*tool*) piccone *m*; (*choice*) scelta; (*the best*) fiore *m*; (mus) plettro ‖ *tr* scavare; (*to scratch at*) grattare; (*to gather*) cogliere; (*to pluck*) spennare; (*to pull apart*) separare; (*one's teeth*) stuzzicarsi; (*a bone*) rosicchiare; (*to choose*) scegliere; (*a lock*) scassinare; (*a pocket*) tagliare, rubare; (mus) pizzicare; **to pick a fight** attaccare briga; **to pick faults** trovare a ridire; **to pick out** scegliere; distinguere; discriminare; **to pick s.o. to pieces** (coll) tagliare i panni addosso a qlcu; **to pick up** sollevare; (*to find*) trovare; (*to learn*) arrivare a sapere; (*a radio signal*) captare; (*speed*) acquistare ‖ *intr* usare il piccone; **to pick at** (*food*) spilluzzicare; (coll) criticare; **to pick on** (coll) scegliere; (coll) criticare; **to pick up** (coll) migliorarsi

**pick·ax** *s* piccone *m*

**picket** [ˈpɪkɪt] *s* picchetto ‖ *tr* rinchiudere con palizzata; (*to hitch*) legare; (*to post*) (mil) mettere di picchetto; (*e.g., a factory*) picchettare

**pick·et fence·** *s* steccato

**pick·et line·** *s* corteo di scioperanti; corteo di dimostranti

**pickle** [ˈpɪkəl] *s* salamoia, sottaceto; (*cucumber*) cetriolo sottaceto; **to get into a pickle** (coll) cacciarsi in un imbroglio ‖ *tr* mettere sottaceto; (metallurgy) decapare

**pick-me-up** [ˈpɪkmiˌʌp] *s* (coll) spuntino; (coll) bevanda stimulante

**pick·pock·et** *s* borseggiatore *m*, borsaiolo

**pick·up·** *s* sollevamento; (*in speed*) accelerazione; (*of phonograph*) pick-up *m*, fonorivelatore *m*; (aut) camioncino; (coll) persona conosciuta per caso; (coll) miglioramento

**pick·-up-sticks·** *spl* sciangai *m*

**pic·nic** [ˈpɪknɪk] *s* picnic *m* ‖ *v* (*pret & pp* **-nicked**; *ger* **-nicking**) *intr* fare merenda all'aperto

**pictorial** [pɪkˈtorɪəl] *adj* pittorico; illustrato; vivido ‖ *s* rivista illustrata

**picture** [ˈpɪktʃər] *s* illustrazione, disegno; (*painting*) quadro, dipinto; (*of a person*) ritratto; fotografia; film *m*, pellicola ‖ *tr* fare il ritratto di; disegnare; dipingere; fotografare; descrivere; immaginare, immaginarsi

**pic·ture frame·** *s* cornice *f*

**pic·ture gal·lery** *s* pinacoteca, galleria di quadri, quadreria

**pic·ture post·card·** *s* cartolina illustrata

**pic·ture show·** *s* cinematografo; mostra di quadri

**picturesque** [ˌpɪktʃəˈrɛsk] *adj* pittoresco

**pic·ture tube·** *s* tubo televisivo

**pic·ture win·dow** *s* finestra panoramica

**piddling** [ˈpɪdlɪŋ] *adj* insignificante

**pie** [paɪ] *s* (*with fruit*) torta; (*with meat*) timballo; (orn) pica ‖ *v* (*pret & pp* **pied**; *ger* **pieing**) *tr* (typ) scompaginare, scomporre

**piece** [pis] *s* pezzo; (*e.g., of cloth*) pezza; **a piece of advice** un consiglio; **a piece of baggage** un collo; **a piece of furniture** un mobile *m;* **a piece of news** una notizia; **by the piece** a cottimo; **to break to pieces** frantumare; frantumarsi; **to cut to pieces** fare a pezzi; **to fall to pieces** cadere a pezzi; **to fly to pieces** rompersi in mille pezzi; **to give s.o. a piece of one's mind** dirne a qlcu di tutti i colori; **to go to pieces** perdere il controllo di sé stesso; **to take to pieces** confutare punto per punto ‖ *tr* rappezzare, mettere insieme ‖ *intr* (coll) mangiucchiare

**piece·meal·** *adv* poco a poco

**piece·work·** *s* lavoro a cottimo

**piece·work·er** *s* cottimista *mf*

**pier** [pɪr] *s* (*of a bridge*) pila; (*over water*) molo; (archit) pilastro, pilone *m*

**pierce** [pɪrs] *tr* forare, bucare; penetrare; (*to stab*) trapassare ‖ *intr* penetrare

**piercing** [ˈpɪrsɪŋ] *adj* acuto; (*eyes*) penetrante; (*pain*) lancinante

**pier' glass'** *s* specchiera

**pie·ty** ['paɪ·əti] *s* (**-ties**) pietà *f*

**piffle** ['pɪfəl] *s* (coll) fesserie *fpl*

**pig** [pɪg] *s* maiale *m*, porco; (metallurgy) lingotto, massello; **to buy a pig in the poke** comprare il gatto nel sacco

**pigeon** ['pɪdʒən] *s* piccione *m*

**pi'geon·hole'** *s* nicchia nella piccionaia; (*for filing*) casella || *tr* (*to lay aside for later time*) archiviare; (*to shelve, e.g., an application*) insabbiare

**pi'geon house'** *s* colombaia, piccionaia

**piggish** ['pɪgɪʃ] *adj* porcino, maialesco

**pig'gy·back'** ['pɪgɪˌbæk] *adv* sulle spalle, sulla schiena; (rr) su carrello stradale per trasporto carri

**pig'head'ed** *adj* ostinato, cocciuto

**pig' i'ron** *s* ghisa, ferro grezzo

**pigment** ['pɪgmənt] *s* pigmento || *tr* pigmentare || *intr* pigmentarsi

**pig'pen'** *s* porcile *m*

**pig'skin'** *s* pelle *f* di maiale; (coll) pallone *m* da football, sfera di cuoio

**pig'sty'** *s* (**-sties**) porcile *m*

**pig'tail'** *s* codino; (*of girl*) treccia; treccia di tabacco

**pike** [paɪk] *s* (*weapon*) picca; (*road*) autostrada; (ichth) luccio

**piker** ['paɪkər] *s* (coll) uomo piccino

**pile** [paɪl] *s* (*heap*) pila; (*for burning a corpse*) pira; (*large building*) mole *f*; (*beam*) palo; (*of carpet*) pelo; (*of money*) (slang) gruzzolo; (coll) mucchio; **piles** emorroidi *fpl* || *tr* ammucchiare, accumulare; **to pile up** ammonticchiare || *intr* accumularsi; **to pile into** pigiarsi in; **to pile up** accumularsi

**pile' driv'er** *s* battipalo, berta

**pilfer** ['pɪlfər] *tr & intr* rubacchiare

**pilgrim** ['pɪlgrɪm] *s* pellegrino

**pilgrimage** ['pɪlgrɪmɪdʒ] *s* pellegrinaggio

**pill** [pɪl] *s* pillola; amara pillola; (coll) rompiscatole *mf*; **to sugar-coat the pill** addolcire la pillola

**pillage** ['pɪlɪdʒ] *s* saccheggio, rapina || *tr & intr* saccheggiare, rapinare

**pillar** ['pɪlər] *s* pilastro, colonna; **from pillar to post** da Erode a Pilato

**pill'box'** *s* scatoletta per le pillole; (mil) casamatta

**pillo·ry** ['pɪləri] *s* (**-ries**) gogna, berlina || *v* (*pret & pp* **-ried**) *tr* mettere alla berlina

**pillow** ['pɪlo] *s* cuscino, guanciale *m*

**pil'low·case'** *s* federa

**pilot** ['paɪlət] *adj* pilota || *s* pilota *m*; (*of locomotive*) respingente *m* || *tr* pilotare

**pi'lot light'** *s* fiammella automatica

**pimp** [pɪmp] *s* ruffiano, lenone *m*

**pimple** ['pɪmpəl] *s* bitorzolo

**pim·ply** ['pɪmpli] *adj* (**-plier; -pliest**) bitorzoluto

**pin** [pɪn] *s* (*of metal*) spillo; (*peg*) caviglia; (*adornment*) spilla; (*linchpin*) acciarino; (*of key*) mappa; (*clothespin*) molletta; (*bowling pin*) birillo; **to be on pins and needles** stare sulle spine || *tr* appuntare; (*to hold*) immobilizzare; **to pin s.o. down** forzare qlcu a rivelare i propri piani **to pin s.th on s.o.** (coll) dare la colpa a qlcu per qlco

**pinafore** ['pɪnəˌfor] *s* grembiulino

**pinaster** [paɪ'næstər] *s* pino marittimo

**pin'ball machine'** *s* biliardino

**pince-nez** ['pæns ˌne] *s* occhiali *mpl* a stringinaso

**pincers** ['pɪnsərz] *ssg or spl* tenaglie *fpl*; (zool) pinze *fpl*

**pinch** [pɪntʃ] *s* (*squeeze*) pizzicotto; (*of tobacco*) presa; (*of salt*) pizzico; (*hardship*) strettoia; **in a pinch** in caso di necessità || *tr* stringere, pizzicare; (*to press*) comprimere; ridurre alle strettezze; (slang) rubare; (slang) arrestare || *intr* stringere; (*to be stingy*) fare l'avaro

**pin'cush'ion** *s* puntaspilli *m*

**pine** [paɪn] *s* pino || *intr*—**to pine away** struggersi; **to pine for** spasimare per

**pine'ap'ple** *s* ananas *m*

**pine' cone'** *s* pigna

**pine' nee'dle** *s* ago del pino

**ping** [pɪŋ] *s* rumore secco; rumore metallico || *intr* fare un rumore secco or metallico

**pin'head'** *s* capocchia di spillo; (slang) testa quadra

**pin'hole'** *s* forellino

**pink** [pɪŋk] *adj* rosa || *s* color *m* rosa; condizione perfetta; (bot) garofano || *tr* orlare a zig-zag; (*to stab*) perforare

**pin' mon'ey** *s* denaro per le piccole spese

**pinnacle** ['pɪnəkəl] *s* pinnacolo

**pin'point'** *adj* di precisione || *s* punta di spillo || *tr* mettere in rilievo

**pin'prick'** *s* puntura di spillo

**pint** [paɪnt] *s* pinta

**pintle** ['pɪntəl] *s* maschietto

**pin'up'** *s* pin-up-girl *f*

**pin'wheel'** *s* girandola

**pioneer** [ˌpaɪ·ə'nɪr] *s* pioniere *m* || *tr* aprire la via a || *intr* fare il pioniere

**pioneering** [ˌpaɪ·ə'nɪrɪŋ] *adj* pionieristico

**pious** ['paɪ·əs] *adj* pio, devoto

**pip** [pɪp] *s* (*seed*) seme *m*; (vet) pipita

**pipe** [paɪp] *s* tubo, canna; (*of stove*) cannone *m*; (*for smoking*) pipa; (mus) legno; (mus) cornamusa || *tr* suonare; cantare ad alta voce; fischiare; condurre in una tubatura; munire di tubatura || *intr* suonare la zampogna; **to pipe down** (slang) stare zitto

**pipe' clean'er** *s* scovolino

**pipe' dream'** *s* castello in aria

**pipe' line'** *s* oleodotto; (fig) fonte *f* (d'informazioni)

**pipe' or'gan** *s* organo a canne

**piper** ['paɪpər] *s* zampognaro; **to pay the piper** pagare lo scotto

**pipe' wrench'** *s* chiave *f* per tubi

**piping** ['paɪpɪŋ] *adj* (*voice*) acuto; (*sound*) acuto; (mus) cornamusa || *s* tubatura; suono di cornamuse; suono acuto; (*on cakes*) fregio; (*on garments*) cor-

doncino ornamentale ‖ *adv*—**piping
hot** scottante, bollente
**pippin** ['pɪpɪn] *s* mela renetta; (*seed*)
seme *m;* (fig) gran brava persona
**piquant** ['pikənt] *adj* piccante
**pique** [pik] *s* picca, ripicco ‖ *tr* offendere, eccitare
**pira·cy** ['paɪrəsi] *s* (**-cies**) pirateria
**pirate** ['paɪrɪt] *s* pirata *mf* ‖ *tr* derubare; (*a book*) svaligiare, pubblicare
illegalmente ‖ *intr* pirateggiare
**pirouette** [,pɪru'ɛt] *s* piroetta ‖ *intr*
piroettare
**Pisces** ['paɪsiz] or ['pɪsiz] *s* (astr)
Pesci *mpl*
**pistol** ['pɪstəl] *s* pistola
**piston** ['pɪstən] *s* pistone *m*
**pis'ton displace'ment** *s* cilindrata
**pis'ton ring'** *s* segmento elastico
**pis'ton rod'** *s* (*of a steam engine*) biella
d'accoppiamento; (*of a motor*) asta
del pistone, biella
**pis'ton stroke'** *s* corsa dello stantuffo
**pit** [pɪt] *s* (*in the ground*) buca; (*trap*)
trappola; (*of fruit*) nocciolo; (*of
stomach*) bocca; (*scar*) buttero; (*in
exchange*) recinto delle grida; (*for
fights*) arena; (theat) platea; (min)
miniera; (aut) fossa di riparazione ‖
*v* (*pret & pp* **pitted;** *ger* **pitting**) *tr*
infossare; butterare; opporre; (*to remove pits from*) snocciolare
**pitch** [pɪtʃ] *s* (*black sticky substance*)
pece *f;* (*throw*) lancio; (*of a roof*)
pendenza, inclinazione; (*of a boat*)
beccheggio; (*of a screw*) passo; (*of
sound*) altezza ‖ *tr* lanciare; (*a tent*)
rizzare ‖ *intr* beccheggiare; **to pitch
in** (coll) mettersi al lavoro; (coll)
cominciare a mangiare
**pitch' ac'cent** *s* accento di altezza
**pitch' at'titude** *s* assetto longitudinale
**pitch'-dark'** *adj* nero come la pece
**pitched' bat'tle** *s* battaglia campale
**pitcher** ['pɪtʃər] *s* brocca; (baseball)
lanciatore *m*
**pitch'fork'** *s* forca, tridente *m;* **to rain
pitchforks** (coll) piovere a dirotto
**pitch' pipe'** *s* (mus) corista *m*
**pit'fall'** *s* trappola, trabocchetto
**pith** [pɪθ] *s* midollo; (*strength*) (fig)
forza; (fig) succo, essenza
**pith·y** ['piθi] *adj* (**-ier; -iest**) midolloso;
succoso, essenziale
**pitiful** ['pɪtɪfəl] *adj* pietoso
**pitiless** ['pɪtɪlɪs] *adj* spietato
**pit·y** ['pɪti] *s* (**-ies**) pietà *f;* **it is a pity
that** è un peccato che; **what a pity!**
che peccato! ‖ *v* (*pret & pp* **-ied**) *tr*
aver pietà di
**Pius** ['paɪ·əs] *s* Pio
**pivot** ['pɪvət] *s* asse *m,* perno; (fig)
asse *m* ‖ *tr* imperniare ‖ *intr* imper-
niarsi; **to pivot on** fare perno su; dipendere da
**placard** ['plækɑrd] *s* manifesto, affisso
‖ *tr* affiggere
**place** [ples] *s* luogo; locale *m;* (*court*)
piazzetta; (*short street*) vicolo; residenza; sito, luogo, località *f;* (*point*)
punto; (*space occupied*) posto;
(*office*) posto, impiego; **in no place**

da nessuna parte; **in place** a posto;
**in place of** al posto di, invece di; **in
the first place** in primo luogo; **in the
next place** in secondo luogo; **to know
one's place** saper stare al proprio
posto; **to take place** aver luogo ‖ *tr*
piazzare, mettere; (*to find employment for*) collocare; (*to identify*) ravvisare ‖ *intr* (sports) piazzarsi
**place·bo** [plə'sibo] *s* (**-bos** or **-boes**)
rimedio fittizio
**place' card'** *s* segnaposto
**placement** ['plesmənt] *s* (*e.g., of furniture*) collocazione; (*employment*) collocamento
**place' name'** *s* toponimo
**place' of busi'ness** *s* ufficio, negozio
**placid** ['plæsɪd] *adj* placido
**plagiarism** ['pledʒə,rɪzəm] *s* plagio
**plagiarize** ['pledʒə,raɪz] *tr* plagiare
**plague** [pleg] *s* peste bubbonica; (*widespread affliction*) piaga, flagello ‖ *tr*
infestare, appestare; tormentare
**plaid** [plæd] *s* tessuto scozzese
**plain** [plen] *adj* piano; aperto; evidente, esplicito; semplice; (*undyed*)
naturale; comune, ordinario; **in plain
English** senz'ambagi; **in plain view**
di fronte a tutti ‖ *s* pianura
**plain'-clothes' man'** *s* (**-men'**) agente *m*
in borghese
**plains'man** *s* (**-men**) abitante *m* della
pianura
**plaintiff** ['plentɪf] *s* querelante *mf*
**plaintive** ['plentɪv] *adj* lamentevole
**plan** [plæn] *s* piano, progetto ‖ *v* (*pret
& pp* **planned;** *ger* **planning**) *tr & intr*
progettare
**plane** [plen] *adj* piano ‖ *m* piano;
(*tool*) pialla; (aer) aeroplano; (aer)
ala d'aeroplano; (bot) platano ‖ *tr*
piallare ‖ *intr* andare in aeroplano
**plane' sick'ness** *s* male *m* d'aria
**planet** ['plænɪt] *s* pianeta *m*
**plane' tree'** *s* platano
**plan'ing mill'** *s* officina di piallatura
**plank** [plæŋk] *s* tavola, asse *m;* (*of
political party*) piattaforma ‖ *tr* coprire d'assi; cucinare sulla graticola e
servire sul tagliere; **to plank down**
(*e.g., money*) (coll) snocciolare
**plant** [plænt] or [plɑnt] *s* (*factory*)
impianto, stabilimento; (*e.g., of a
college*) complesso di edifici; (bot)
pianta; (mach) apparato motore;
(slang) trappola ‖ *tr* (*e.g., a tree*)
piantare; (*seeds*) seminare; (*to stock*)
fornire
**plantation** [plæn'teʃən] *s* piantagione
**planter** ['plæntər] *s* piantatore *m;*
(mach) piantatrice *f*
**plaster** ['plæstər] or ['plɑstər] *s* (*gypsum*) gesso; (*mixture to cover walls*)
intonaco, malta; (*poultice*) impiastro
‖ *tr* ingessare; intonacare; impiastrare; (*with posters*) affiggere, ricoprire
**plas'ter·board'** *s* cartone *m* di gesso
**plas'ter cast'** *s* (sculp) gesso; (surg) ingessatura
**plas'ter of Par'is** *s* gesso, stucco
**plastic** ['plæstɪk] *adj & s* plastico

**plate** [plet] *s* (*dish*) piatto; (*sheet of metal*) placca, piastra; (*thin sheet of metal*) lamina; (*of vacuum tube*) placca; (*of auto license*) targa; (*of condenser*) armatura; (*tableware*) vasellame *m* d'argento, vasellame *m* d'oro; dentiera; (*baseball*) casa base; (phot) lastra; (typ) cliché *m* ‖ *tr* (*with gold or silver*) placcare; (*with armor*) blindare, corazzare

**plateau** [plæ'to] *s* altipiano

**plate' glass'** *s* lastrone *m*

**platen** ['plætən] *s* rullo

**platform** ['plæt‚fɔrm] *s* piattaforma; (*for speaker*) tribuna, palco; (*for passengers*) (rr) marciapiede *m;* (*at end of car*) (rr) piattaforma

**plat'form car'** *s* (rr) pianale *m*

**platinum** ['plætɪnəm] *s* platino

**plat'inum blonde'** *s* bionda platinata

**platitude** ['plætɪ‚tjud] or ['plætɪ‚tud] *s* trivialità *f*, banalità *f*

**Plato** ['pleto] *s* Platone *m*

**platoon** [plə'tun] *s* plotone *m*

**platter** ['plætər] *s* piatto di portata; (slang) disco di grammofono

**plausible** ['plɔzɪbəl] *adj* plausibile; (*person*) credibile, attendibile

**play** [ple] *s* gioco; libertà *f* d'azione; recreazione; turno, volta; (theat) dramma *m;* (mach) gioco ‖ *tr* giocare; giocare contro; causare, produrre; (*a drama*) rappresentare; (*a character*) fare la parte di; (*to wield*) esercitare; (mus) suonare; **to play back** (*e.g., a tape*) riprodurre; **to play down** diminuire l'importanza di; **to play one off against another** mettere uno contro l'altro; **to play up** dare importanza a ‖ *intr* giocare; (*to act*) giocare, comportarsi; (theat) recitare; (mus) suonare; (mach) aver gioco; **to play on** continuare a giocare; continuare a suonare; valersi di; **to play safe** non prendere rischi; **to play sick** fare il malato; **to play up to** fare la corte a

**play'back'** *s* riproduzione; apparechiatura di riproduzione

**play'bill'** *s* (theat) programma *m*

**play'boy'** *s* playboy *m*, gaudente *m*

**player** ['pleər] *s* giocatore *m;* (theat) attore *m;* (mus) suonatore *m*

**play'er pian'o** *s* pianola

**playful** ['plefəl] *adj* giocoso

**playgoer** ['ple‚go·ər] *s* frequentatore *m* del teatro

**play'ground'** *s* parco di ricreazione; (*resort*) posto di villeggiatura

**play'house'** *s* teatro; casa di bambole

**play'ing card'** ['ple·ɪŋ] *s* carta da gioco

**play'ing field'** *s* campo da gioco

**play'mate'** *s* compagno di gioco

**play'-off'** *s* (sports) spareggio

**play'pen'** *s* recinto, box *m*

**play'thing'** *s* giocattolo

**play'time'** *s* ricreazione

**playwright** ['ple‚raɪt] *s* drammaturgo, commediografo

**play'writ'ing** *s* drammaturgia

**plaza** ['plæzə] or ['plɑzə] *s* piazzale *m*

**plea** [pli] *s* scusa; richiesta, domanda; (law) dichiarazione

**plead** [plid] *v* (*pret & pp* **pleaded** or **pled** [plɛd]) *tr* (*ignorance*) dichiarare; (*a case*) perorare ‖ *intr* supplicare; argomentare; **to plead guilty** dichiararsi colpevole

**pleasant** ['plɛzənt] *adj* piacevole; (*person*) simpatico

**pleasant·ry** ['plɛzəntri] *s* (**-ries**) facezia, motto

**please** [pliz] *tr* piacere (with *dat*) ‖ *intr* piacere; **as you please** come vuole; **if you please** per favore; **please per cortesia; to be pleased to** avere il piacere di; **to be pleased with** essere soddisfatto con; **to do as one pleases** fare come par e piace

**pleasing** ['plizɪŋ] *adj* piacevole

**pleasure** ['plɛʒər] *s* piacere *m;* desiderio; **what is your pleasure?** cosa desidera?

**pleas'ure car'** *s* vettura da turismo

**pleat** [plit] *s* piega ‖ *tr* piegare, pieghettare

**plebeian** [plɪ'bi·ən] *adj & s* plebeo

**plebiscite** ['plɛbɪ‚saɪt] *s* plebiscito

**pledge** [plɛdʒ] *s* pegno; promessa; voto; (*person*) ostaggio; (*toast*) brindisi *m;* **as a pledge** in pegno; **to take the pledge** giurare d'astenersi dal bere ‖ *tr* dare in pegno; (*to bind*) far promettere a

**plentiful** ['plɛntɪfəl] *adj* abbondante

**plenty** ['plɛnti] *s* abbondanza ‖ *adv* (coll) abbastanza

**pleurisy** ['plʊrɪsi] *s* pleurite *f*

**pliable** ['plaɪ·əbəl] *adj* flessibile, pieghevole; docile

**pliers** ['plaɪ·ərz] *ssg* or *spl* pinze *fpl*

**plight** [plaɪt] *s* condizione or situazione precaria ‖ *tr*—**to plight one's troth** fidanzarsi

**plod** [plɑd] *v* (*pret & pp* **plodded;** *ger* **plodding**) *tr* percorrere pesantemente ‖ *intr* camminare pesantemente; (*to drudge*) sgobbare

**plot** [plɑt] *s* (*of ground*) appezzamento; (*of a play*) trama, intreccio; (*evil scheme*) cospirazione, trama ‖ *v* (*pret & pp* **plotted;** *ger* **plotting**) *tr* fare il piano di; macchinare; preparare la trama di; (aer, naut) fare il punto di ‖ *intr* tramare, cospirare

**plover** ['plʌvər] or ['plovər] *s* piviere *m*

**plow** [plau] *s* aratro; (*for snow*) spazzaneve *m* ‖ *tr* arare; (*e.g., water*) solcare; (*snow*) spazzare; **to plow back** reinvestire ‖ *intr* arare; aprirsi la via; camminare pesantemente

**plow'man** *s* (**-men**) aratore *m;* contadino

**plow'share'** *s* vomere *m*

**pluck** [plʌk] *s* strattone *m;* coraggio; (*giblets*) frattaglie *fpl* ‖ *tr* (*to snatch*) tirare; (*e.g., fruit*) svellere; (*a fowl*) spennare; (mus) pizzicare ‖ *intr* tirare; **to pluck up** farsi coraggio

**pluck·y** ['plʌki] *adj* (**-ier; -iest**) coraggioso

**plug** [plʌg] *s* tappo, zaffo; tavoletta di

tabacco; bocca da incendi; (elec) spina; (*horse*) (slang) ronzino; (slang) raccomandazione ‖ v (*pret & pp* **plugged**) *ger* **plugging** *tr* tappare, otturare; colpire; inserire; (slang) fare la pubblicità di; **to plug in** (elec) innestare, connettere ‖ *intr* (coll) sgobbare

**plum** [plʌm] *s* (*fruit*) susina; (*tree*) susino; (slang) cosa bellissima; (slang) colpo di fortuna

**plumage** ['plumɪdʒ] *s* piumaggio

**plumb** [plʌm] *adj* appiombo ‖ *s* piombino ‖ *adv* appiombo; (coll) completamente ‖ *tr* determinare la verticale col piombino; assodare

**plumb' bob'** *s* piombino

**plumber** ['plʌmər] *s* installatore *m*, idraulico

**plumbing** ['plʌmɪŋ] *s* impianto idraulico; mestiere *m* d'idraulico; sondaggio

**plumb'ing fix'tures** *spl* rubinetteria, impianti *mpl* sanitari

**plumb' line'** *s* filo a piombo

**plum' cake'** *s* panfrutto

**plume** [plum] *s* piuma; (*tuft of feathers*) pennacchio ‖ *tr* coprire di piume; **to plume oneself on** piccarsi di; **to plume one's feathers** pulirsi le penne

**plummet** ['plʌmɪt] *s* piombino ‖ *intr* cadere a piombo

**plump** [plʌmp] *adj* grassoccio, paffuto; franco ‖ *s* caduta ‖ *adv* francamente ‖ *intr* cadere a piombo

**plum' pud'ding** *s* budino con uva passa

**plum' tree'** *s* susino

**plunder** ['plʌndər] *s* (*act*) saccheggio; (*loot*) bottino ‖ *tr & intr* saccheggiare

**plunge** [plʌndʒ] *s* (*fall*) caduta; (*dive*) nuotata, tuffo ‖ *tr* gettare; tuffare; (*e.g., a knife*) configgere ‖ *intr* (*to rush*) precipitarsi; (*to gamble*) (coll) darsi al gioco; (fig) ripiombare

**plunger** ['plʌndʒər] *s* tuffatore *m*; (*for clearing clogged drains*) sturalavandini *m*; (mach) stantuffo; (coll) giocatore temerario

**plunk** [plʌŋk] *adv* (coll) proprio; (coll) con un colpo secco ‖ *tr* (coll) gettare; lasciar cadere; (mus) pizzicare ‖ *intr* (coll) lasciarsi cadere

**plural** ['plurəl] *adj & s* plurale *m*

**plus** [plʌs] *adj* superiore; (elec) positivo; (coll) con lode ‖ *s* più *m*; soprappiù *m* ‖ *prep* più

**plush** [plʌʃ] *adj* di lusso ‖ *s* peluche *f*, felpa

**Plutarch** ['plutɑrk] *s* Plutarco

**Pluto** ['pluto] *s* Plutone *m*

**plutonium** [plu'tonɪ·əm] *s* plutonio

**ply** [plaɪ] *s* (**plies**) spessore *m*; (*layer*) strato; (*of rope*) legnolo ‖ *v* (*pret & pp* **plied**) *tr* (*a trade*) esercitare; (*a tool*) maneggiare; (*to assail*) premere, incalzare ‖ *intr* lavorare assiduamente; **to ply between** fare la spola tra

**ply'wood'** *s* legno compensato

**pneumatic** [nju'mætɪk] or [nu'mætɪk] *adj* pneumatico

**pneumat'ic drill'** *s* martello perforatore or pneumatico

**pneumonia** [nju'monɪ·ə] or [nu'monɪ·ə] *s* polmonite *f*

**poach** [potʃ] *tr* (*eggs*) affogare ‖ *intr* cacciare or pescare di frodo

**poacher** ['potʃər] *s* bracconiere *m*; pescatore *m* di frodo

**pock** [pak] *s* buttero

**pocket** ['pakɪt] *adj* tascabile ‖ *s* tasca; (billiards) buca; (aer) vuoto; (min) deposito ‖ *tr* intascare; (*e.g., one's pride*) ingoiare

**pock'et·book'** *s* portafoglio; (*woman's purse*) borsetta

**pock'et book'** *s* libro tascabile

**pock'et-hand'kerchief** *s* fazzoletto

**pock'et-knife'** *s* (**-knives**) temperino

**pock'et mon'ey** *s* spiccioli *mpl*

**pock'mark'** *s* buttero

**pod** [pad] *s* baccello; (aer) contenitore *m*

**poem** ['po·ɪm] *s* poesia; (*of some length*) poema *m*

**poet** ['po·ɪt] *s* poeta *m*

**poetess** ['po·ɪtɪs] *s* poetessa

**poetic** [po'etɪk] *adj* poetico ‖ **poetics** *ssg* poetica

**poetry** ['po·ɪtri] *s* poesia

**pogrom** ['pogrəm] *s* pogrom *m*

**poignancy** ['pɔɪnjənsi] or ['pɔɪnənsi] *s* strazio; intensità *f*

**poignant** ['pɔɪnjənt] or ['pɔɪnənt] *adj* straziante; intenso

**point** [pɔɪnt] *s* (*sharp end*) punta; (*something essential*) essenziale *m*; (*hint*) suggerimento; (*dot, decimal point, spot, degree, instant, position of compass*) punto; (coll) costrutto; **beside the point** fuori del seminato; **in point of** per quanto concerne; **to come to the point** venire al sodo; **to get the point** capire l'antifona; **to make a point of** dar importanza a; insistere di; **to stretch a point** fare un'eccezione, fare uno strappo alla regola; **to the point** a proposito ‖ *tr* (*e.g., a weapon*) puntare; (*to sharpen*) aguzzare; (*to dot*) punteggiare; (*to give force to*) dare enfasi a; (*with mortar*) rinzaffare ‖ *intr* puntare; **to point at** puntare il dito a; **to point to** mostrare a dito

**point'blank'** *adj & adv* a bruciapelo

**pointed** ['pɔɪntɪd] *adj* appuntito; personale, diretto, acuto

**pointer** ['pɔɪntər] *s* (*rod*) bacchetta; indice *m*, indicatore *m*; cane *m* da punta, pointer *m*; (coll) direttiva

**poise** [pɔɪz] *s* equilibrio, stabilità *f*; dignità *f* ‖ *tr* equilibrare ‖ *intr* equilibrarsi, stare in equilibrio

**poison** ['pɔɪzən] *s* veleno ‖ *tr* avvelenare

**poi'son i'vy** *s* edera del Canada, tossicodendro

**poisonous** ['pɔɪzənəs] *adj* velenoso

**poke** [pok] *s* spinta, urto; (*with elbow*) gomitata; (slang) polentone *m* ‖ *tr* (*to prod*) spingere, urtare; (*the head*) sporgere; (*the fire*) attizzare; **to poke fun at** burlarsi di; **to poke one's nose into** ficcare il naso in ‖ *intr* (*to jab*) urtare; (*to thrust oneself*) ficcarsi; (*to pry*) ficcare il naso; **to poke around** gironzolare; **to poke out** spuntare, protrudere

**poker** ['pokər] *s* (*game*) poker *m;* (*bar*) attizzatoio

**pok'er face'** *s* faccia impassibile

**pok·y** ['poki] *adj* (**-ier; -iest**) (coll) lento; (coll) meschino, modesto ‖ (**-ies**) *s* (slang) gattabuia

**Poland** ['polənd] *s* la Polonia

**po'lar bear'** ['polər] *s* orso bianco

**polarize** ['polə‚raɪz] *tr* polarizzare

**pole** [pol] *s* palo; (*long rod*) pertica; (*of wagon*) timone *m;* (*for jumping*) asta; (astr, biol, elec, geog, math) polo ‖ *tr* (*a boat*) spingere con un palo ‖ *intr* spingere una barca con un palo ‖ **Pole** *s* polacco

**pole'cat'** *s* puzzola

**pole' lamp'** *s* lampada a stelo

**pole'star'** *s* stella polare

**pole' vault'** *s* salto coll'asta

**police** [pə'lis] *s* polizia ‖ *tr* vigilare, proteggere; (mil) pulire

**police'man** *s* (**-men**) agente *m* di polizia, vigile urbano

**police' state'** *s* governo poliziesco

**police' sta'tion** *s* commissariato di polizia

**poli·cy** ['polɪsi] *s* (**-cies**) politica; (ins) polizza

**polio** ['polɪ‚o] *s* (coll) polio *f*

**polish** ['polɪʃ] *s* lustro, lucentezza; (*for shoes or furniture*) cera; (fig) raffinatezza, eleganza ‖ *tr* pulire; (*e.g., a stone*) levigare; **to polish off** (slang) finire; **to polish up** (slang) migliorare ‖ *intr* pulirsi; diventar lucido ‖ **Polish** ['polɪʃ] *adj & s* polacco

**polisher** ['polɪʃər] *s* lucidatore *m;* (mach) lucidatrice *f*

**polite** [pə'laɪt] *adj* raffinato, cortese

**politeness** [pə'laɪtnɪs] *s* cortesia

**politic** ['polɪtɪk] *adj* prudente; (*expedient*) diplomatico

**political** [pə'lɪtɪkəl] *adj* politico

**politician** [‚polɪ'tɪʃən] *s* politico; (pej) politicante *m*, politicastro

**politics** ['polɪtɪks] *ssg or spl* politica

**poll** [pol] *s* votazione; (*registering of votes*) scrutinio; lista elettorale; (*analysis of public opinion*) referendum *m*, sondaggio; (*head*) testa; **to go to the polls** andare alle urne; **to take a poll** fare un'inchiesta ‖ *tr* ricevere i voti di; contare i voti di; (*a tree*) potare; fare un'inchiesta di

**pollen** ['polən] *s* polline *m*

**pollinate** ['polɪ‚net] *tr* fecondare col polline

**poll'ing booth'** ['polɪŋ] *s* cabina elettorale

**polliwog** ['polɪ‚wag] *s* girino

**poll' tax'** *s* capitazione

**pollute** [pə'lut] *tr* insudiciare; (*to defile*) desecrare, profanare; (*e.g., the environment*) inquinare, contaminare

**pollution** [pə'luʃən] *s* inquinamento, contaminazione

**poll' watch'er** *s* rappresentante *m* di lista

**polo** ['polo] *s* polo

**po'lo play'er** *s* giocatore *m* di polo, polista *m*

**po'lo shirt'** *s* maglietta, polo

**polygamist** [pə'lɪgəmɪst] *s* poligamo

**polygamous** [pə'lɪgəməs] *adj* poligamo

**polyglot** ['polɪ‚glat] *adj & s* poliglotto

**polygon** ['polɪ‚gan] *s* poligono

**polynomial** [‚polɪ'nomɪ‚əl] *adj* polinomiale ‖ *s* polinomio

**polyp** ['polɪp] *s* (pathol, zool) polipo

**polytheist** ['polɪ‚θi·ɪst] *s* politeista *mf*

**polytheistic** [‚polɪθi'ɪstɪk] *adj* politeistico

**pomade** [pə'med] *or* [pə'mɑd] *s* pomata

**pomegranate** ['pom‚grænɪt] *s* (*shrub*) melograno; (*fruit*) melagrana

**pom·mel** ['pʌməl] *or* ['poməl] *s* (*of sword*) pomello; (*of saddle*) arcione *m* ‖ *v* (*pret & pp* **-meled** *or* **-melled; ger** **-meling** *or* **-melling**) *tr* prendere a pugni

**pomp** [pomp] *s* pompa

**pompadour** ['pompə‚dor] *or* ['pompə‚dur] *s* acconciatura a ciuffo

**pompous** ['pompəs] *adj* pomposo

**pon·cho** ['pontʃo] *s* (**-chos**) poncho

**pond** [pond] *s* stagno

**ponder** ['pondər] *tr & intr* ponderare; **to ponder over** pensare sopra

**ponderous** ['pondərəs] *adj* ponderoso

**poniard** ['ponjərd] *s* pugnale *m*

**pontiff** ['pontɪf] *s* pontefice *m*

**pontifical** [pon'tɪfɪkəl] *adj* pontificale

**pontoon** [pon'tun] *s* (*boat*) chiatta, pontone *m;* (aer) galleggiante *m*

**po·ny** ['poni] *s* (**-nies**) pony *m;* (*glass and drink*) bicchierino; (*for cheating*) (slang) bigino

**poodle** ['pudəl] *s* barbone *m*, cane *m* barbone

**pool** [pul] *s* (*pond*) stagno; (*puddle*) pozza; (*for swimming*) piscina; (*game*) biliardo; (com) cartello, consorzio; (com) fondo comune ‖ *tr* mettere in un fondo comune ‖ *intr* formare un cartello or un consorzio

**pool'room'** *s* sala da biliardo

**pool' ta'ble** *s* tavolo da biliardo

**poop** [pup] *s* poppa; (*deck*) casseretto

**poor** [pur] *adj* povero; (*inferior*) scadente ‖ **the poor** *spl* i poveri

**poor' box'** *s* cassetta per l'elemosina

**poor'house'** *s* asilo dei poveri

**poorly** ['purli] *adv* male

**pop** [pap] *s* scoppio; (*soda*) gazzosa ‖ *v* (*pret & pp* **popped; ger** **popping**) *tr* far scoppiare; **to pop the question** (coll) fare la domanda di matrimonio ‖ *intr* esplodere con fragore; **to pop in** fare una capatina; entrare all'improvviso

**pop'corn'** *s* pop-corn *m*

**pope** [pop] *s* papa *m*

**popeyed** ['pop‚aɪd] *adj* con gli occhi sporgenti; con gli occhi fuori dalle orbite

**pop'gun'** *s* fucile *m* ad aria compressa

**poplar** ['poplər] *s* pioppo

**pop·py** ['popi] *s* (**-pies**) papavero

**pop'py·cock'** *s* (coll) scemenza

**popsicle** [ˈpɑpsɪkəl] s (trademark) gelato da passeggio
**populace** [ˈpɑpjəlɪs] s gente f, popolino
**popular** [ˈpɑpjələr] adj popolare
**popularize** [ˈpɑpjələˌraɪz] tr divulgare, volgarizzare
**populate** [ˈpɑpjəˌlet] tr popolare
**population** [ˌpɑpjəˈleʃən] s popolazione
**populous** [ˈpɑpjələs] adj popoloso
**porcelain** [ˈpɔrsəlɪn] or [ˈpɔrslɪn] s porcellana
**porch** [pɔrtʃ] s portico
**porcupine** [ˈpɔrkjəˈpaɪn] s (Hystrix cristata) istrice m & f, porcospino; (Erethizon dorsatum) ursone m, porcospino americano
**pore** [por] s poro ‖ intr—to pore over studiare minutamente
**pork** [pork] s carne f di maiale
**pork' butch'er shop'** s salumeria
**pork'chop'** s cotoletta di maiale
**porous** [ˈporəs] adj poroso
**po'rous plas'ter** s cataplasma m
**porphy·ry** [ˈpɔrfɪri] s (-ries) porfido
**porpoise** [ˈpɔrpəs] s focena; (dolphin) delfino
**porridge** [ˈpɑrɪdʒ] or [ˈpɔrɪdʒ] s pappa, farinata
**port** [port] adj portuario ‖ s (harbor; wine) porto; (naut) babordo, sinistra; (opening in side of ship) portello; (round opening) (naut) oblò m
**portable** [ˈportəbəl] adj portabile
**portal** [ˈportəl] s portale m
**portend** [porˈtend] tr presagire
**portent** [ˈportent] s presagio
**portentous** [porˈtentəs] adj sinistro, funesto, premonitore; (amazing) portentoso
**porter** [ˈportər] s (doorman) portiere m; (man who carries luggage) facchino; (of a sleeper) conduttore m; (in a store) inserviente mf; (beverage) birra scura e amara
**portfoli·o** [portˈfoliˌo] s (-os) cartella; (office; holdings) portafoglio
**port'hole'** s (opening in side of ship) portello; (round opening) (naut) oblò m
**porti·co** [ˈportɪˌko] s (-cos or -coes) portico
**portion** [ˈporʃən] s porzione; (dowry) dote f ‖ tr—to portion out dividere, ripartire
**port·ly** [ˈportli] adj (-lier; -liest) obeso, corpulento
**port' of call'** s scalo
**portrait** [ˈportret] or [ˈportrɪt] s ritratto
**portray** [porˈtre] tr ritrarre
**portrayal** [porˈtre·əl] s delineazione; ritratto
**Portugal** [ˈportʃəgəl] s il Portogallo
**Portu·guese** [ˈportʃəˌgiz] adj portoghese ‖ s (-guese) portoghese mf
**pose** [poz] s posa ‖ tr (a question) avanzare; (a model) mettere in posa ‖ intr posare; **to pose as** posare a, atteggiarsi a
**posh** [pɑʃ] adj (coll) di lusso
**position** [pəˈzɪʃən] s posizione; rango;

impiego, posto; **to be in a position to** essere in grado di
**positive** [ˈpɑzɪtɪv] adj positivo ‖ s positivo; (phot) positiva
**possess** [pəˈzɛs] tr possedere
**possession** [pəˈzɛʃən] s possedimento; (of mental faculties) possesso; **possessions** (wealth) beni mpl
**possessive** [pəˈzɛsɪv] adj possessivo; (e.g., mother) opprimente, soffocante
**possible** [ˈpɑsɪbəl] adj possibile
**possum** [ˈpɑsəm] s opossum m; **to play possum** (coll) fare il morto
**post** [post] s (mail) posta; (pole) palo; (in horse racing) linea di partenza; posizione, rango; (job) posto; (mil) presidio ‖ tr mettere in una lista; impostare; tenere al corrente; **post no bills** divieto d'affissione
**postage** [ˈpostɪdʒ] s affrancatura
**post'age me'ter** s affrancatrice f
**post'age stamp'** s francobollo
**postal** [ˈpostəl] adj postale
**post'al card'** s cartolina postale
**pos'tal per'mit** s abbonamento postale
**post'al sav'ings bank'** s cassa di risparmio postale
**post'al scale'** s pesalettere m
**post' card'** s cartolina illustrata; cartolina postale
**post'date'** tr postdatare
**poster** [ˈpostər] s cartellone m, manifesto pubblicitario
**posterity** [pɑsˈtɛrɪti] s posterità f
**postern** [ˈpostərn] adj posteriore ‖ s postierla
**post' exchange'** s spaccio militare
**post'haste'** adv al più presto possibile
**posthumous** [ˈpɑstʃuməs] adj postumo
**post'man** s (-men) portalettere m
**post'mark'** s bollo, timbro postale ‖ tr bollare, timbrare
**post'mas'ter** s ricevitore m postale
**post'master gen'eral** s (postmasters general) ministro delle poste
**post-mortem** [ˈpostˈmortəm] adj postumo ‖ s autopsia
**post' of'fice** s ufficio postale
**post'-office box'** s casella postale
**postpaid** [ˈpostˌped] adj franco di porto
**postpone** [postˈpon] tr differire, posporre
**postscript** [ˈpostˌskrɪpt] s poscritto
**postulant** [ˈpostʃələnt] s postulatore m, postulante mf
**posture** [ˈpɑstʃər] s portamento; posa ‖ intr posare
**post'war'** s del dopoguerra
**po·sy** [ˈpozi] s (-sies) fiore m; (nosegay) mazzolino di fiori
**pot** [pɑt] s pentola, pignatta; pitale m, orinale m; (in gambling) (coll) piatto; **to go to pot** andare a gambe all'aria
**potash** [ˈpɑtˌæʃ] s potassa
**potassium** [pəˈtæsɪ·əm] s potassio
**pota·to** [pəˈteto] s (-toes) patata
**pota'to om'elet** s omelette f con patate
**potbellied** [ˈpɑtˌbelɪd] adj panciuto
**poten·cy** [ˈpotənsi] s (-cies) potenza
**potent** [ˈpotənt] adj potente

**potentate** ['potən‚tet] *s* potentato
**potential** [pə'tɛnʃəl] *adj & s* potenziale *m*
**pot'hold'er** *s* patta, presa
**pot'hook'** *s* uncino
**potion** ['poʃən] *s* pozione
**pot'luck'** *s*—**to take potluck** mangiare quello che passa il convento
**pot' shot'** *s* colpo sparato a casaccio
**potter** ['patər] *s* vasaio
**pot'ter's clay'** *s* argilla per stoviglie
**pot'ter's field'** *s* cimitero dei poveri
**potter·y** ['patəri] *s* (**-ies**) vasellame *m;* fabbrica di vasellame; ceramica
**pouch** [pautʃ] *s* sacchetto, borsa; (*of kangaroo*) borsa
**poultice** ['poltɪs] *s* cataplasma *m*
**poultry** ['poltri] *s* pollame *m*
**poul'try·man** *s* (**-men**) pollivendolo
**pounce** [pauns] *intr*—**to pounce on** balzare su
**pound** ['paund] *s* libbra; lira sterlina; (*for stray animals*) recinto ‖ *tr* battere, picchiare; tempestare di colpi; (*to crush*) polverizzare ‖ *intr* battere
**pound' cake'** *s* dolce *m* fatto con una libbra di burro, una di zucchero ed una di farina
**pound' ster'ling** *s* lira sterlina
**pour** [por] *tr* versare; (*e.g., tea*) servire; (*wine*) mescere; (*stones upon an enemy*) far piovere ‖ *intr* fluire; (*to rain*) diluviare; **to pour in** affluire; **to pour out** uscire in massa
**pout** [paut] *s* broncio ‖ *intr* tenere il broncio
**poverty** ['pavərti] *s* povertà *f*
**POW** ['pi'o'dʌbl‚ju] *s* (letterword) (**prisoner of war**) prigioniero di guerra
**powder** ['paudər] *s* polvere *f;* (*for the face*) cipria; (med) polverina ‖ *tr* incipriare; (*to sprinkle with powder*) spolverizzare
**pow'dered sug'ar** *s* zucchero in polvere
**pow'der puff'** *s* piumino
**pow'der room'** *s* toletta
**powdery** ['paudəri] *adj* polveroso; fragile; (*snow*) farinoso
**power** ['pau·ər] *s* (*ability, authority*) potere *m;* forza, energia; (*nation*) potenza; (math, phys) potenza; **in power** al potere; **the powers that be** i potenti ‖ *tr* azionare
**pow'er·boat'** *s* barca a motore
**pow'er brake'** *s* (aut) servofreno
**pow'er com'pany** *s* compagnia di elettricità
**pow'er drive'** *s* picchiata
**powerful** ['pau·ərfəl] *adj* poderoso
**pow'er·house'** *s* centrale elettrica
**powerless** ['pau·ərlɪs] *adj* impotente
**pow'er line'** *s* elettrodotto
**pow'er mow'er** *s* motofalciatrice *f*
**pow'er of attor'ney** *s* procura legale
**pow'er plant'** *s* stazione *f* generatrice; (aut) gruppo motore
**pow'er steer'ing** *s* servosterzo
**pow'er tool'** *s* apparecchiatura a motore
**pow'er vac'uum** *s* vuoto di potere
**practical** ['præktɪkəl] *adj* pratico

**prac'tical joke'** *s* scherzo da prete
**practically** ['præktɪkəli] *adv* (*in a practical manner; virtually, really*) praticamente; più o meno, quasi
**practice** ['præktɪs] *s* pratica; (*of a profession*) esercizio; (*e.g., of a doctor*) clientela; (*process of doing something*) prassi *f;* (*habitual performance*) abitudine *f* ‖ *tr* praticare, esercitare ‖ *intr* esercitarsi, praticare; (*to be active in a profession*) esercitare; **to practice as** esercitare la professione di
**practitioner** [præk'tɪʃənər] *s* professionista *mf*
**Prague** [prag] or [preg] *s* Praga
**prairie** ['prɛri] *s* prateria
**prai'rie dog'** *s* cinomio
**prai'rie wolf'** *s* coyote *m*
**praise** [prez] *s* lode *f,* elogio ‖ *tr* lodare, elogiare; **to praise to the skies** levare alle stelle
**praise'wor'thy** *adj* lodevole
**pram** [præm] *s* (coll) carrozzella
**prance** [præns] or [prans] *s* caracollo ‖ *intr* caracollare; (*to caper*) ballonzolare
**prank** [præŋk] *s* burla, tiro
**prate** [pret] *intr* cianciare
**prattle** ['prætəl] *s* ciancia, chiacchierio ‖ *intr* cianciare, parlare a vanvera
**pray** [pre] *tr & intr* pregare
**prayer** [prɛr] *s* preghiera
**prayer' book'** *s* libro di preghiere
**preach** [pritʃ] *tr & intr* predicare
**preacher** ['pritʃər] *s* predicatore *m*
**preamble** ['pri‚æmbəl] *s* preambolo
**precarious** [prɪ'kɛrɪ·əs] *adj* precario
**precaution** [prɪ'kɔʃən] *s* precauzione
**precede** [prɪ'sid] *tr & intr* precedere
**precedent** ['prɛsɪdənt] *s* precedente *m*
**precept** ['prisɛpt] *s* precetto
**precinct** ['prisɪŋkt] *s* distretto; circoscrizione elettorale; **precincts** dintorni *mpl*
**precious** ['prɛʃəs] *adj* prezioso ‖ *adv*—**precious little** (coll) molto poco
**precipice** ['prɛsɪpɪs] *s* precipizio
**precipitate** [prɪ'sɪpɪ‚tet] *adj* precipitoso ‖ *s* precipitato ‖ *tr & intr* precipitare
**precipitous** [prɪ'sɪpɪtəs] *adj* precipitoso, a precipizio
**precise** [prɪ'saɪs] *adj* preciso
**precision** [prɪ'sɪʒən] *s* precisione
**preclude** [prɪ'klud] *tr* precludere; escludere
**precocious** [prɪ'koʃəs] *adj* precoce
**predatory** ['prɛdə‚tori] *adj* da preda, predatore
**predicament** [prɪ'dɪkəmənt] *s* situazione critica or imbarazzante
**predict** [prɪ'dɪkt] *tr* predire
**prediction** [prɪ'dɪkʃən] *s* predizione
**predispose** [‚pridɪs'poz] *tr* predisporre
**predominant** [prɪ'damɪnənt] *adj* predominante
**preeminent** [prɪ'ɛmɪnənt] *adj* preminente
**preempt** [prɪ'ɛmpt] *tr* occupare or acquistare in precedenza
**preen** [prin] *tr* (*feathers, fur*) lisciarsi;

**to preen oneself** agghindarsi, attillarsi

**prefabricate** [pri'fæbrɪ‚ket] *tr* prefabbricare

**preface** ['prɛfɪs] *s* prefazione || *tr* prefazionare; essere la prefazione di

**pre·fer** [prɪ'fʌr] *v* (*pret* & *pp* **-ferred;** *ger* **-ferring**) *tr* preferire; (*to advance*) promuovere; (*law*) presentare, avanzare

**preferable** ['prɛfərəbəl] *adj* preferibile

**preference** ['prɛfərəns] *s* preferenza

**preferred' stock'** *s* azioni *fpl* privilegiate

**prefix** ['prifɪks] *s* prefisso || *tr* prefiggere

**pregnan·cy** ['prɛgnənsi] *s* (**-cies**) gravidanza

**pregnant** ['prɛgnənt] *adj* incinta, gravida; (fig) gravido

**prehistoric** [‚prihɪs'tɑrɪk] or [‚prihɪs-'tɔrɪk] *adj* preistorico

**prejudice** ['prɛdʒədɪs] *s* pregiudizio; preconcetto; **without prejudice** senza detrimento || *tr* (*to harm*) pregiudicare; predisporre; **to prejudice against** prevenire contro

**prejudicial** ['prɛdʒə'dɪʃəl] *adj* pregiudizievole

**prelate** ['prɛlɪt] *s* prelato

**preliminar·y** [prɪ'lɪmɪ‚nɛri] *adj* preliminare || *s* (**-ies**) preliminare *m*

**prelude** ['prɛljud] or ['prɪlud] *s* preludio || *tr* preludere a || *intr* preludere

**premeditate** [prɪ'mɛdɪ‚tet] *tr* premeditare

**premier** [prɪ'mɪr] or ['primɪ‚ər] *s* primo ministro, presidente *m* del consiglio

**premiere** [prə'mjɛr or [prɪ'mɪr] *s* prima; prima attrice

**premise** ['prɛmɪs] *s* premessa; **on the premises** nella proprietà, sul luogo; **premises** proprietà *f*

**premium** ['primɪ‚əm] *s* premio; **at a premium** in gran richiesta; a prezzo altissimo

**premonition** [‚primə'nɪʃən] *s* presentimento; indizio

**preoccupation** [pri‚ɑkjə'peʃən] *s* preoccupazione

**preoccu·py** [pri'ɑkjə‚paɪ] *v* (*pret* & *pp* **-pied**) *tr* preoccupare; (*to occupy beforehand*) occupare prima

**prepaid** [pri'ped] *adj* pagato in anticipo; franco di porto

**preparation** [‚prɛpə'reʃən] *s* preparazione; (*for a trip*) preparativo; (pharm) preparato

**preparatory** [prɪ'pærə‚tori] *adj* preparatorio

**prepare** [prɪ'per] *tr* preparare || *intr* prepararsi

**preparedness** [prɪ'pɛrɪdnəs] or [prɪ-'pɛrdnɪs] *s* preparazione; preparazione militare

**pre·pay** [pri'pe] *v* (*pret* & *pp* **-paid**) *tr* pagare anticipatamente

**preponderant** [prɪ'pɑndərənt] *adj* preponderante

**preposition** [‚prɛpə'zɪʃən] *s* preposizione

**prepossessing** [‚pripə'zɛsɪŋ] *adj* simpatico, attraente, piacevole

**preposterous** [prɪ'pɑstərəs] *adj* assurdo, ridicolo

**prep' school'** [prɛp] *s* (coll) scuola preparatoria

**prerecorded** [‚priri'kɔrdɪd] *adj* (rad & telv) a registrazione differita

**prerequisite** [pri'rɛkwɪzɪt] *s* requisito

**prerogative** [prɪ'rɑgətɪv] *s* prerogativa

**presage** ['prɛsɪdʒ] *s* presagio || [prɪ-'sɛdʒ] *tr* presagire

**Presbyterian** [‚prɛzbɪ'tɪri·ən] *adj* & *s* presbiteriano; Presbiteriano

**prescribe** [prɪ'skraɪb] *tr* & *intr* prescrivere

**prescription** [prɪ'skrɪpʃən] *s* prescrizione; (pharm) ricetta

**presence** ['prɛzəns] *s* presenza; **in the presence of** alla presenza di

**present** ['prɛzənt] *adj* presente || *s* presente *m*, regalo || [prɪ'zɛnt] *tr* presentare; **present arms!** presentat'arm!; **to present s.o. with s.th** regalare qlco a qlcu

**presentable** [prɪ'zɛntəbəl] *adj* presentabile

**presentation** [‚prɛzən'teʃən] or [‚prizən'teʃən] *s* presentazione; (theat) rappresentazione

**presenta'tion cop'y** *s* copia d'omaggio

**presentiment** [prɪ'zɛntɪmənt] *s* presentimento

**presently** ['prɛzəntli] *adv* fra poco; attualmente

**preserve** [prɪ'zʌrv] *s* (*for hunting*) riserva; **preserves** conserva, marmellata || *tr* preservare; conservare

**preserved' fruit'** *s* frutta in conserva

**preside** [prɪ'zaɪd] *intr* presiedere; **to preside over** presiedere, presiedere a

**presiden·cy** ['prɛzɪdənsi] *s* (**-cies**) presidenza

**president** ['prɛzɪdənt] *s* presidente *m*; (*of a university*) rettore *m*

**press** [prɛs] *s* pressione; (*crowd*) folla; (*closet*) armadio; (mach) pressa; (typ) stampa; **to go to press** andare in macchina || *tr* (*to push*) spingere, premere; (*to squeeze*) spremere; (*to embrace*) abbracciare; forzare; costringere; urgere, sollecitare; (*to iron*) stirare || *intr* premere; avanzare

**press' a'gent** *s* agente pubblicitario

**press' con'ference** *s* conferenza stampa

**pressing** ['prɛsɪŋ] *adj* pressante, urgente || *s* (*of records*) incisione

**press' release'** *s* comunicato stampa

**pressure** ['prɛʃər] *s* pressione; tensione, urgenza || *tr* pressare, incalzare con insistenza

**pres'sure cook'er** ['kʊkər] *s* pentola a pressione

**pressurize** ['prɛʃə‚raɪz] *tr* pressurizzare

**prestige** [prɛs'tiʒ] or ['prɛstɪdʒ] *s* prestigio

**prestigious** [prɛ'stɪdʒɪ·əs] or [prɛ-'stɪdʒəs] *adj* onorato, stimato

**presumably** [prɪ'zuməbli] or [prɪ'zjuməbli] *adv* presumibilmente

**presume** [prɪ'zum] or [prɪ'zjum] *tr* presumere; **to presume to** prendersi la libertà di ‖ *intr* assumere; **to presume on** or **upon** abusare di

**presumption** [prɪ'zʌmpʃən] *s* presunzione; supposizione

**presumptuous** [prɪ'zʌmptʃʊ·əs] *adj* presuntuoso

**presuppose** [‚prisə'poz] *tr* presupporre

**pretend** [prɪ'tɛnd] *tr* fingere, fare finta di ‖ *intr* fingere; **to pretend to** (*e.g., the throne*) pretendere a

**pretender** [prɪ'tɛndər] *s* pretendente *mf*; impostore *m*

**pretense** [prɪ'tɛns] or ['pritɛns] *s* pretesa; finzione; **under false pretenses** allegando ragioni false; **under pretense of** sotto l'apparenza di

**pretentious** [prɪ'tɛnʃəs] *adj* pretenzioso

**preterit** ['prɛtərɪt] *adj* passato, preterito ‖ *s* passato remoto, preterito

**pretext** ['pritɛkst] *s* pretesto

**pretonic** [prɪ'tɑnɪk] *adj* pretonico

**pret·ty** ['prɪti] *adj* (**-tier; -tiest**) grazioso, carino; (*e.g.*, *sum of money*) (coll) bello ‖ *adv* abbastanza; molto; **sitting pretty** (slang) ben messo

**prevail** [prɪ'vel] *intr* prevalere; **to prevail on** or **upon** persuadere

**prevailing** [prɪ'velɪŋ] *adj* prevalente

**prevalent** ['prɛvələnt] *adj* comune

**prevaricate** [prɪ'værɪ‚ket] *intr* mentire

**prevent** [prɪ'vɛnt] *tr* impedire; **to prevent from** + *ger* impedire (with *dat*) di + *inf* or che + *subj*

**prevention** [prɪ'vɛnʃən] *s* prevenzione

**preventive** [prɪ'vɛntɪv] *adj* preventivo ‖ *s* rimedio preventivo

**preview** ['pri‚vju] *s* indizio; (*private showing*) (mov) anteprima; (*showing of brief scenes for advertising*) (mov) scene *fpl* di prossima programmazione

**previous** ['privɪ·əs] *adj* previo, precedente ‖ *adv* precedentemente; **previous to** prima di

**prewar** ['pri‚wɔr] *adj* anteguerra

**prey** [pre] *s* preda; **to be prey to** essere preda di ‖ *intr* predare; **to prey on** or **upon** predare, sfruttare; preoccupare

**price** [praɪs] *s* prezzo; **at any price** a qualunque costo ‖ *tr* chiedere il prezzo di; fissare il prezzo di

**price' control'** *s* calmiere *m*

**price' cut'ting** *s* riduzione di prezzo

**price' fix'ing** *s* regolamento dei prezzi

**price' freez'ing** *s* congelamento dei prezzi

**priceless** ['praɪslɪs] *adj* inestimabile; (coll) molto divertente

**price' list'** *s* listino prezzi

**price' tag'** *s* cartellino del prezzo

**price' war'** *s* guerra dei prezzi

**prick** [prɪk] *s* punta; puntura; **to kick against the pricks** tirare calci al vento ‖ *tr* bucare, forare; pungere; (*to goad*) spronare; (*the ears*) ergere; (*said, e.g., of the conscience*) rimordere (with *dat*)

**prick·ly** ['prɪkli] *adj* (**-lier; -liest**) spinoso, pungente

**prick'ly heat'** *s* sudamina

**prick'ly pear'** *s* ficodindia *m*

**pride** [praɪd] *s* orgoglio; arroganza; **the**

**pride of** il fiore di ‖ *tr*—**to pride oneself on** or **upon** inorgoglirsi di

**priest** [prist] *s* prete *m*, sacerdote *m*

**priesthood** ['prist·hʊd] *s* sacerdozio

**priest·ly** ['pristli] *adj* (**-lier; -liest**) sacerdotale

**prig** [prɪg] *s* pedante *mf*, moralista *mf*

**prim** [prɪm] *adj* (**primmer; primmest**) formale, corretto, compito

**prima·ry** ['praɪ‚mɛri] or ['praɪmɛri] *adj* primario ‖ *s* (**-ries**) elezione preferenziale; (elec) bobina primaria; (elec) primario

**prime** [praɪm] *adj* primo; originale; di prima qualità ‖ *s* (*earliest part*) inizio; (*best period*) fiore *m*; (*choicest part*) fior fiore *m*; (math) numero primo; (*mark*) (math) primo ‖ *tr* preparare; (*a pump*) adescare; (*a firearm*) innescare; (*a canvas*) mesticare; (*a wall*) dare la prima mano a; (*to supply with information*) istruire

**prime' min'ister** *s* primo ministro

**primer** ['prɪmər] *s* sillabario, abbecedario ‖ ['praɪmər] *s* innesco, detonatore *m*

**primeval** [praɪ'mivəl] *adj* primordiale

**primitive** ['prɪmɪtɪv] *adj* primitivo

**primp** [prɪmp] *tr* agghindare ‖ *intr* agghindarsi

**prim'rose'** *s* primula

**prim'rose path'** *s* sentiero dei piaceri

**prince** [prɪns] *s* principe *m*; **to live like a prince** vivere da principe

**prince' roy'al** *s* principe ereditario

**princess** ['prɪnsɪs] *s* principessa

**principal** ['prɪnsɪpəl] *adj* principale ‖ *s* (*chief*) padrone *m*, principale *m*; (*of school*) direttore *m*, preside *m*; (*actor*) primo attore; (com) capitale *m*; (law) mandante *mf*

**principle** ['prɪnsɪpəl] *s* principio; **on principle** per principio

**print** [prɪnt] *s* stampa; (*cloth*) tessuto stampato; (*printed matter*) stampato; (*newsprint*) giornale *m*; (*mark made by one's thumb*) impronta; (phot) positiva; **in print** stampato; disponibile; **out of print** esaurito ‖ *tr* stampare, tirare; (*to write in print*) scrivere in stampatello; (*in the memory*) imprimere

**print'ed cir'cuit** *s* circuito stampato

**print'ed mat'ter** *s* stampati *mpl*

**printer** ['prɪntər] *s* stampatore *m*; (*of computer*) tabulatrice *f*

**print'er's dev'il** *s* apprendista *m* tipografo

**print'er's ink'** *s* inchiostro da stampa

**printing** ['prɪntɪŋ] *s* stampa; stampato; tiratura, edizione; (*writing in printed letters*) stampatello

**prior** ['praɪ·ər] *adj* anteriore, precedente ‖ *s* priore *m* ‖ *adv* prima; **prior to** prima di

**priori·ty** [praɪ'ɑriti] or [praɪ'ɔriti] *s* (**-ties**) priorità *f*

**prism** ['prɪzəm] *s* prisma *m*

**prison** ['prɪzən] *s* prigione, carcere *m*

**prisoner** ['prɪzənər] or ['prɪznər] *s* prigioniero

**pris'on van'** *s* furgone *m* cellulare

**pris·sy** ['prɪsi] *adj* (**-sier; -siest**) smanceroso, smorfioso

**priva·cy** ['praɪvəsi] *s* (**-cies**) ritiro; segreto; **to have no privacy** non esser mai lasciato in pace

**private** ['praɪvɪt] *adj* privato, personale || *s* soldato semplice; **in private** privatamente; **privates** pudende *fpl*

**pri'vate eye'** *s* poliziotto privato

**pri'vate first' class'** *s* soldato scelto

**pri'vate hos'pital** *s* clinica

**priv'ate view'ing** *s* (mov) anteprima; (painting) vernice *f*

**privet** ['prɪvɪt] *s* ligustro

**privilege** ['prɪvɪlɪdʒ] *s* privilegio

**priv·y** ['prɪvi] *adj* privato; **privy to** segretamente a conoscenza di || *s* (**-ies**) latrina

**prize** [praɪz] *s* premio; (nav) preda || *tr* valutare, stimare

**prize' fight'** *s* incontro di pugilato

**prize' fight'er** *s* pugile *m*, pugilista *m*

**prize' ring'** *s* ring *m*, quadrato

**pro** [pro] *s* (**pros**) pro; voto favorevole; argomento favorevole; (coll) professionista *m*; **the pros and the cons** il pro e il contro

**probabili·ty** [‚prɑbə'bɪlɪti] *s* (**-ties**) probabilità *f*

**probable** ['prɑbəbəl] *adj* probabile

**probate** ['probet] *s* omologazione di un testamento; copia autentica di un testamento || *tr* (*a will*) omologare

**probation** [pro'beʃən] *s* prova; periodo di prova; (law) condizionale *f*, libertà vigilata; (educ) provvedimento disciplinare

**probe** [prob] *s* inchiesta; (surg) sonda || *tr* indagare; sondare

**problem** ['prɑbləm] *s* problema *m*

**procedure** [pro'sidʒər] *s* procedura

**proceed** ['prosid] *s*—**proceeds** provento || [pro'sid] *intr* procedere

**proceeding** [pro'sidɪŋ] *s* procedimento; **proceedings** atti *mpl*; (law) procedimenti *mpl*

**process** ['proses] *s* processo; **in the process of time** in processo di tempo || *tr* trattare

**procession** [pro'seʃən] *s* processione

**proc'ess serv'er** *s* ufficiale giudiziario

**proclaim** [pro'klem] *tr* proclamare

**proclitic** [pro'klɪtɪk] *adj* proclitico || *s* parola proclitica

**procrastinate** [pro'kræstɪ‚net] *tr & intr* procrastinare

**procure** [pro'kjur] *tr* ottenere || *intr* ruffianeggiare

**prod** [prɑd] *s* pungolo, stimolo || *v* (*pret & pp* **prodded;** *ger* **prodding**) *tr* stimulare, pungolare, incitare

**prodigal** ['prɑdɪgəl] *adj & s* prodigo

**prodigious** [pro'dɪdʒəs] *adj* prodigioso

**prodi·gy** ['prɑdɪdʒi] *s* (**-gies**) prodigio

**produce** ['prodjus] or ['produs] *s* produzione; prodotti *mpl* agricoli || [pro'djus] or [pro'dus] *tr* produrre; (theat) presentare

**producer** [pro'djusər] or [pro'dusər] *s* produttore *m*; (*of a play*) impresario; (mov) produttore *m*

**product** ['prɑdəkt] *s* prodotto

**production** [pro'dʌkʃən] *s* produzione

**profane** [pro'fen] *adj* profano; blasfemo || *tr* profanare

**profani·ty** [pro'fænɪti] *s* (**-ties**) bestemmia

**profess** [pro'fɛs] *tr & intr* professare

**profession** [pro'fɛʃən] *s* professione

**professor** [pro'fesər] *s* professore *m*

**proffer** ['prɑfər] *s* offerta || *tr* offrire

**proficient** [pro'fɪʃənt] *adj* abile, competente

**profile** ['profaɪl] *s* profilo || *tr* profilare

**profit** ['prɑfɪt] *s* profitto; vantaggio; **at a profit** con guadagno || *tr* avvantaggiare; giovare (with *dat*) || *intr* avvantaggiarsi; **to profit by** approfittare di

**profitable** ['prɑfɪtəbəl] *adj* vantaggioso

**prof'it and loss'** *s* profitti *mpl* e perdite *fpl*

**profiteer** [‚prɑfɪ'tɪr] *s* profittatore *m* || *intr* fare il profittatore

**prof'it shar'ing** *s* cointeressenza, partecipazione agli utili

**prof'it tak'ing** *s* realizzo

**profligate** ['prɑflɪgɪt] *adj & s* dissoluto; prodigo

**pro for'ma in'voice** ['fɔrmə] *s* fattura fittizia

**profound** [pro'faund] *adj* profondo

**profuse** [prə'fjus] *adj* profuso, abbondante; **profuse in** prodigo di

**proge·ny** ['prɑdʒəni] *s* (**-nies**) prole *f*

**progno·sis** [prɑg'nosɪs] *s* (**-ses** [siz]) prognosi *f*

**prognostic** [prɑg'nɑstɪk] *s* pronostico

**prognosticate** [prɑg'nɑstɪ‚ket] *tr* pronosticare

**pro·gram** ['progræm] *s* programma *m* || *v* (*pret & pp* **-gramed** or **-grammed;** *ger* **-graming** or **-gramming**) *tr* programmare

**programmer** ['progræmər] *s* pannellista *mf*, programmatore *m*

**progress** ['prɑgres] *s* progresso; **in progress** in corso; **to make progress** fare dei progressi || [prə'gres] *intr* progredire; migliorare

**progressive** [prə'gresɪv] *adj* (*proceeding step by step*) progressivo; progressista || *s* progressista *mf*

**prohibit** [pro'hɪbɪt] *tr* proibire

**prohibition** [‚pro·ə'bɪʃən] *s* proibizione; (hist) proibizionismo

**project** ['prɑdʒekt] *s* progetto || [prə'dʒekt] *tr* (*to propose, plan*) progettare; (*light, a shadow, etc.*) proiettare || *intr* sporgere, protrudere

**projectile** [prə'dʒektɪl] *s* proiettile *m*

**projection** [prə'dʒekʃən] *s* proiezione, sporgenza

**projector** [prə'dʒektər] *s* (*apparatus*) proiettore *m*; (*person*) progettista *mf*

**proletarian** [‚prolɪ'terɪ·ən] *adj & s* proletario

**proliferate** [prə'lɪfə‚ret] *intr* proliferare

**prolific** [prə'lɪfɪk] *adj* prolifico

**prolix** ['prolɪks] or [pro'lɪks] *adj* prolisso

**prologue** ['prolɔg] or ['prolɑg] *s* prologo

**prolong** [pro'lɔŋ] or pro'laŋ] *tr* prolungare

**promenade** [ˌpramɪ'ned] or [ˌpramɪ'nad] *s* passeggiata; ballo di gala || *tr & intr* passeggiare

**promenade' deck'** *s* ponte *m* passeggiata

**prominent** ['pramɪnənt] *adj* prominente

**promise** ['pramɪs] *s* promessa || *tr & intr* promettere

**prom'ising young' man'** *s* giovane *m* di belle speranze

**prom'issory note'** ['pramɪˌsori] *s* cambiale *f*, pagherò *m*

**promonto·ry** ['pramən ˌtori] *s* (**-ries**) promontorio

**promote** [prə'mot] *tr* promuovere

**promotion** [prə'moʃən] *s* promozione

**prompt** [prampt] *adj* pronto || *tr* incitare, istigare; (theat) suggerire

**prompter** ['pramptər] *s* suggeritore *m*, rammentatore *m*

**prompt'er's box'** *s* buca del suggeritore

**promptness** ['pramptnɪs] *s* prontezza

**promulgate** ['praməlˌget] or [pro'mʌlget] *tr* promulgare

**prone** [pron] *adj* prono

**prong** [prɔŋ] or [praŋ] *s* punta; (*of fork*) dente *m*; (*of pitchfork*) rebbio

**pronoun** ['pronaun] *s* pronome *m*

**pronounce** [prə'nauns] *tr* pronunziare

**pronounced** [prə'naunst] *adj* pronunziato, marcato

**pronouncement** [prə'naunsmənt] *s* dichiarazione ufficiale

**pronunciamen·to** [prə ˌnʌnsɪ·ə'mento] *s* (**-tos**) pronunciamento

**pronunciation** [prə ˌnʌnsɪ'eʃən] or [prə ˌnʌnʃɪ'eʃən] *s* pronunzia

**proof** [pruf] *adj*—**proof against** a prova di || *s* prova; (*of alcoholic beverages*) gradazione; (typ) bozza

**proof'read'er** *s* correttore *m* di bozze

**prop** [prap] *s* sostegno, puntello; (*pole*) palo; **props** attrezzi *mpl* teatrali || *v* (*pret & pp* **propped; *ger* propping**) *tr* sostenere, puntellare

**propaganda** [ˌprapə'gændə] *s* propaganda

**propagate** ['prapəˌget] *tr* propagare || *intr* propagarsi

**pro·pel** [prə'pel] *v* (*pret & pp* **-pelled; *ger* -pelling**) *tr* propulsare, spingere, azionare; (*a rocket*) propellere

**propeller** [prə'pelər] *s* elica

**propensi·ty** [prə'pensɪti] *s* (**-ties**) propensione

**proper** ['prapər] *adj* appropriato, corretto; decente, convenevole; (gram) proprio; **proper to** proprio di

**proper·ty** ['prapərti] *s* (**-ties**) proprietà *f*; **properties** attrezzi *mpl* teatrali

**prop'erty man'** *s* trovarobe *m*, attrezzista *m*

**prop'erty own'er** *s* proprietario fondiario

**prophe·cy** ['prafɪsi] *s* (**-cies**) profezia

**prophe·sy** ['prafɪˌsai] *v* (*pret & pp* **-sied**) *tr* profetizzare

**prophet** ['prafɪt] *s* profeta *m*

**prophetess** ['prafɪtɪs] *s* profetessa

**prophylactic** [ˌprafɪ'læktɪk] *adj* profilattico || *s* rimedio profilattico; preservativo

**propitiate** [prə'pɪʃɪˌet] *tr* propiziare

**propitious** [prə'pɪʃəs] *adj* propizio

**prop'jet'** *s* turboelica *m*

**proportion** [prə'porʃən] *s* proporzione; **in proportion as** a misura che; **in proportion to** in proporzione a; **out of proportion** sproporzionato || *tr* proporzionare, commensurare

**proportionate** [prə'porʃənɪt] *adj* proporzionato

**proposal** [prə'pozəl] *s* proposta; proposta di matrimonio

**propose** [prə'poz] *tr* proporre || *intr* fare una proposta di matrimonio; **to propose to** chiedere la mano di; **proporsi di** + *inf*

**proposition** [ˌprapə'zɪʃən] *s* proposizione, proposta; (coll) progetto || *tr* fare delle proposte indecenti a

**propound** [prə'paund] *tr* proporre

**proprietary** [prə'praɪ·ə ˌteri] *adj* padronale; esclusivo, patentato

**proprietor** [prə'praɪ·ətər] *s* proprietario

**proprietress** [prə'praɪ·ətrɪs] *s* proprietaria

**proprie·ty** [prə'praɪ·əti] *s* (**-ties**) correttezza, decoro; **proprieties** convenzioni *fpl* sociali

**propulsion** [prə'pʌlʃən] *s* propulsione

**prorate** [pro'ret] *tr* rateizzare

**prosaic** [pro'ze·ɪk] *adj* prosaico

**proscribe** [pro'skraɪb] *tr* proscrivere

**prose** [proz] *adj* prosaico || *s* prosa

**prosecute** ['prasɪˌkjut] *tr* eseguire; (law) processare

**prosecutor** ['prasɪˌkjutər] *s* esecutore *m*; (law) querelante *m*; (law) avvocato d'accusa

**proselyte** ['prasɪˌlait] *s* proselito

**prose' writ'er** *s* prosatore *m*

**prosody** ['prasədi] *s* prosodia, metrica

**prospect** ['praspekt] *s* vista; prospettiva; candidato; probabile cliente *m*; **prospects** speranze *fpl* || *intr* fare il cercatore; **to prospect for** fare il cercatore di

**prospectus** [prə'spektəs] *s* prospetto

**prosper** ['praspər] *tr & intr* prosperare

**prosperi·ty** [pras'perɪti] *s* (**-ties**) prosperità *f*, benessere *m*

**prosperous** ['praspərəs] *adj* prospero

**prostitute** ['prastɪˌtjut] or ['prastɪˌtut] *s* prostituta || *tr* prostituire

**prostrate** ['prastret] *adj* prostrato || *tr* prostrare

**prostration** [pras'treʃən] *s* prostrazione

**protagonist** [pro'tægənɪst] *s* protagonista *mf*

**protect** [prə'tekt] *tr* proteggere

**protection** [prə'tekʃən] *s* protezione

**protégé** ['protəˌʒe] *s* protetto, favorito

**protégée** ['protəˌʒe] *s* protetta, favorita

**protein** ['proti·ɪn] or ['protin] *s* proteina

**pro tempore** [pro'tempəˌri] *adj* provvisorio, interinale

**protest** ['protest] *s* protesta; (com)

protesto ‖ [pro'test] *tr & intr* protestare

**Protestant** ['pratɪstənt] *adj & s* protestante *mf*

**protester** [prə'testər] *s* protestatario

**prothonotar·y** [pro'θanə,teri] *s* (**-ies**) (law) cancelliere *m* capo

**protocol** ['protə,kal] *s* protocollo

**protoplasm** ['protə,plæzəm] *s* protoplasma *m*

**prototype** ['protə,taɪp] *s* prototipo

**proto·zoon** [,protə'zo·an] *s* (**-zoa** ['zo·ə]) protozoo

**protract** [pro'trækt] *tr* prolungare

**protractor** [pro'træktər] *s* rapportatore *m*

**protrude** [pro'trud] *intr* sporgere

**proud** [praud] *adj* fiero; arrogante; maestoso, magnifico

**proud' flesh'** *s* tessuto di granulazione

**prove** [pruv] *v* (*pret* **proved**; *pp* **proved** or **proven**) *tr* provare; (*ore*) analizzare; (law) omologare; (math) fare la prova di ‖ *intr* risultare

**proverb** ['pravərb] *s* proverbio

**provide** [prə'vaɪd] *tr* provvedere ‖ *intr*—**to provide for** provvedere a; (*to be ready for*) prepararsi a

**provided** [prə'vaɪdɪd] *conj* a condizione che, purché; **provided that** a condizione che, purché

**providence** ['pravɪdəns] *s* provvidenza

**providential** [,pravɪ'dɛn/əl] *adj* provvidenziale

**providing** [prə'vaɪdɪŋ] *conj* var of **provided**

**province** ['pravɪns] *s* provincia; (fig) pertinenza, competenza

**provision** [prə'vɪʒən] *s* provvedimento; clausola; **provisions** viveri *mpl*

**provi·so** [prə'vaɪzo] *s* (**-sos** or **-soes**) stipulazione, clausola

**provoke** [prə'vok] *tr* provocare; contrariare, irritare

**prow** [prau] *s* prora, prua

**prowess** ['prau·ɪs] *s* prodezza; maestria

**prowl** [praul] *intr* andare in cerca di preda; vagabondare

**prowler** ['praulər] *s* vagabondo; ladro

**proximity** [prak'sɪmɪti] *s* prossimità *f*

**prox·y** ['praksi] *s* (**-ies**) procura; (*person*) procuratore *m*

**prude** [prud] *s* pudibondo

**prudence** ['prudəns] *s* prudenza

**prudent** ['prudənt] *adj* prudente

**pruder·y** ['prudəri] *s* (**-ies**) attitudine pudibonda

**prudish** ['prudɪ/] *adj* pudibondo

**prune** [prun] *s* prugna secca ‖ *tr* potare

**pry** [praɪ] *v* (*pret & pp* **pried**) *tr*—**to pry open** forzare con una leva; **to pry s.th out of s.o.** strappare qlco a qlcu ‖ *intr* intromettersi, cacciarsi

**psalm** [sam] *s* salmo

**pseudo** ['sudo] or ['sjudo] *adj* falso, finto, sedicente

**pseudonym** ['sudənɪm] or ['sjudənɪm] *s* pseudonimo

**psychiatrist** [saɪ'kaɪ·ətrɪst] *s* psichiatra *mf*

**psychiatry** [saɪ'kaɪ·ətri] *s* psichiatria

**psychic** ['saɪkɪk] *adj* psichico ‖ *s* medium *mf*

**psychoanalysis** [,saɪko·ə'nælɪsɪs] *s* psicanalisi *f*

**psychoanalyze** [,saɪko'ænə,laɪz] *tr* psicanalizzare

**psychologic(al)** [,saɪko'ladʒɪk(əl)] *adj* psicologico

**psychologist** [saɪ'kalədʒɪst] *s* psicologo

**psycholo·gy** [saɪ'kalədʒi] *s* (**-gies**) psicologia

**psychopath** ['saɪkə,pæθ] *s* psicopatico

**psycho·sis** [saɪ'kosɪs] *s* (**-ses** [siz]) psicosi *f*

**psychotic** [saɪ'katɪk] *adj* psicotico

**pub** [pʌb] *s* (Brit) taverna, bar *m*

**puberty** ['pjubərti] *s* pubertà *f*

**public** ['pʌblɪk] *adj & s* pubblico

**pub'lic-address' sys'tem** *s* sistema *m* d'amplificazione per discorsi in pubblico

**publication** [,pʌblɪ'ke/ən] *s* pubblicazione

**pub'lic convey'ance** *s* veicolo di servizi pubblici

**publicity** [pʌb'lɪsɪti] *s* pubblicità *f*

**publicize** ['pʌblɪ,saɪz] *tr* pubblicare, divulgare

**pub'lic li'brary** *s* biblioteca comunale

**pub'lic-opin'ion poll'** *s* sondaggio d'opinioni

**pub'lic pros'ecutor** *s* pubblico ministero

**pub'lic school'** *s* (U.S.A.) scuola dell'obbligo; (Brit) scuola privata, collegio

**pub'lic serv'ant** *s* funzionario pubblico

**pub'lic speak'ing** *s* oratoria

**pub'lic spir'it** *s* civismo

**pub'lic toi'let** *s* gabinetto pubblico

**pub'lic util'ity** *s* impresa di servizio pubblico; **public utilities** azioni emesse da imprese di servizi pubblici

**publish** ['pʌblɪ/] *tr* pubblicare

**publisher** ['pʌblɪ/ər] *s* editore *m*; (journ) direttore *m* responsabile

**pub'lishing house'** *s* casa editrice

**pucker** ['pʌkər] *s* grinza ‖ *tr* raggrinzire ‖ *intr* raggrinzirsi

**pudding** ['pudɪŋ] *s* budino, torta

**puddle** ['pʌdəl] *s* pozza, pozzanghera ‖ *intr* diguazzare

**pudg·y** ['pʌdʒi] *adj* (**-ier**; **-iest**) grassoccio

**puerile** ['pju·ərɪl] *adj* puerile

**Puerto Rican** ['pwerto'rikən] *adj & s* portoricano

**puff** [pʌf] *s* soffio, sbuffo; (*e.g., of cigar*) boccata; (*pad*) piumino; (*exaggerated praise*) pistolotto; (culin) bigné *m* ‖ *tr* sbuffare; gonfiare; adulare ‖ *intr* soffiare, sbuffare; (*to breathe heavily*) ansimare, ansare; gonfiarsi; tirare boccate

**puff' paste'** *s* pasta sfoglia

**pugilist** ['pjudʒɪlɪst] *s* pugile *m*

**pug-nosed** ['pʌg,nozd] *adj* camuso

**puke** [pjuk] *tr & intr* (slang) vomitare

**pull** [pul] *s* tiro; (*act of drawing in*) tirata; (*handle*) maniglia *m*; (slang) influenza, appoggi *mpl* ‖ *tr* tirare; (*a tooth*) cavare; (*a muscle*) strappare;

(*a punch*) (coll) limitare la forza di; **to pull apart** fare a pezzi; **to pull down** abbattere; degradare; **to pull on** (*e.g., one's pants*) infilarsi; **to pull oneself together** ricomporsi; **to pull s.o.'s leg** beffarsi di qlcu || *intr* tirare; **to pull apart** andare a pezzi; **to pull at** tirare; **to pull away** andarsene; **to pull for** (coll) fare il tifo per; **to pull in** (*said of a train*) arrivare, entrare in stazione; **to pull out** (*said of a train*) partire; **to pull through** guarire, riuscire a cavarsela; **to pull up** to avanzare fino a

**pullet** ['pulɪt] *s* pollastra

**pulley** ['puli] *s* puleggia, carrucola

**pulp** [pʌlp] *s* polpa; (*for making paper*) pasta

**pulpit** ['pulpɪt] *s* pulpito

**pulsate** ['pʌlset] *intr* pulsare

**pulsation** [pʌl'seʃən] *s* pulsazione

**pulse** [pʌls] *s* polso; **to feel** or **take the pulse of** tastare il polso a

**pulverize** ['pʌlvə‚raɪz] *tr* polverizzare

**pum'ice stone'** *s* ['pʌmɪs] *s* pomice *f*, pietra pomice

**pum·mel** ['pʌməl] *v* (*pret & pp* -**meled** or -**melled;** *ger* -**meling** or -**melling**) *tr* prendere a pugni

**pump** [pʌmp] *s* pompa; (*slipper*) scarpina || *tr* pompare; (coll) cavare un segreto a; **to pump up** pompare

**pumpkin** ['pʌmpkɪn] or ['puŋkɪn] *s* zucca

**pump-priming** ['pʌmp‚praɪmɪŋ] *s* stimolo governativo per sostenere l'economia

**pun** [pʌn] *s* gioco di parole || *v* (*pret & pp* **punned;** *ger* **punning**) *intr* fare giochi di parole

**punch** [pʌntʃ] *s* pugno; (*tool*) punteruolo, punzone *m;* (*drink*) ponce *m;* (coll) forza || *tr* dare un pugno a; (*metal*) punzonare; (*a ticket*) perforare || **Punch** *s* Pulcinella *m;* **pleased as Punch** soddisfattissimo

**punch' bowl'** *s* vaso per il ponce

**punch' card'** *s* scheda perforata

**punch' clock'** *s* orologio di controllo

**punch'-drunk'** *adj* stordito

**punched' tape'** *s* nastro perforato

**punch'ing bag'** *s* sacco

**punch' line'** *s* perfinire *m*, motto finale

**punctilious** [pʌŋk'tɪlɪ·əs] *adj* cerimonioso, pignolo

**punctual** ['pʌŋktʃu·əl] *adj* puntuale

**punctuate** ['pʌŋktʃu‚et] *tr* punteggiare

**punctuation** [‚pʌŋktʃu'eʃən] *s* punteggiatura

**punctua'tion mark'** *s* segno d'interpunzione

**puncture** ['pʌŋktʃər] *s* puntura; (*hole*) bucatura; **to have a puncture** avere una gomma a terra || *tr* bucare, perforare || *intr* essere bucato

**punct'ure-proof'** *adj* antiperforante

**pundit** ['pʌndɪt] *s* esperto, autorità *f*

**pungent** ['pʌndʒənt] *adj* pungente

**punish** ['pʌnɪʃ] *tr* punire

**punishment** ['pʌnɪʃmənt] *s* punizione, castigo

**punk** [pʌŋk] *adj* (slang) di pessima

qualità || *s* esca; (*decayed wood*) legno marcio; (slang) malandrino

**punster** ['pʌnstər] *s* freddurista *mf*

**punt** [pʌnt] *s* (football) calcio dato al pallone prima che tocchi il terreno

**pu·ny** ['pjuni] *adj* (-**nier; -niest**) insignificante, meschino; (*weak*) debole

**pup** [pʌp] *s* cucciolo

**pupil** ['pjupəl] *s* allievo, scolaro; (anat) pupilla

**puppet** ['pʌpɪt] *s* marionetta, burattino; (fig) fantoccio

**puppeteer** [‚pʌpɪ'tɪr] *s* burattinaio

**pup'pet gov'ernment** *s* governo fantoccio or pupazzo

**pup'pet show'** *s* spettacolo di marionette

**pup·py** ['pʌpi] *s* (-**pies**) cucciolo

**pup'py love'** *s* amore *m* giovanile

**purchase** ['pʌrtʃəs] *s* compra, acquisto; (*grip*) presa, leva || *tr* comprare, acquistare

**pur'chasing pow'er** *s* potere *m* d'acquisto

**pure** [pjur] *adj* puro

**purgative** ['pʌrgətɪv] *adj* purgativo || *s* purga

**purge** [pʌrdʒ] *s* purga || *tr* purgare

**puri·fy** ['pjurɪ‚faɪ] *v* (*pret & pp* **-fied**) *tr* purificare || *intr* purificarsi

**puritan** ['pjurɪtən] *adj & s* puritano || **Puritan** *adj & s* puritano

**purity** ['pjurɪti] *s* purezza

**purloin** [pər'lɔɪn] *tr & intr* rubare

**purple** ['pʌrpəl] *adj* purpureo || *s* porpora

**purport** ['pʌrport] *s* senso, significato || [pər'port] *tr* significare; **to purport to** + *inf* pretendere di + *inf*

**purpose** ['pʌrpəs] *s* scopo, fine *m;* **on purpose** apposta; **to good purpose** con buoni risultati; **to no purpose** inutilmente; **to serve one's purpose** fare al caso proprio

**purposely** ['pʌrpəsli] *adv* a bella posta, apposta

**purr** [pʌr] *s* ronfare *m* || *intr* fare le fusa

**purse** [pʌrs] *s* borsa; (*woman's handbag*) borsetta; (*for men*) borsetto || *tr* (*one's lips*) arricciare

**purser** ['pʌrsər] *s* commissario di bordo

**purse' snatch'er** ['snætʃər] *s* borsaiolo

**purse' strings'** *spl* cordini *mpl* della borsa; **to hold the purse strings** controllare le spese

**purslane** ['pʌrslen] or ['pʌrslɪn] *s* (bot) porcellana

**pursue** [pər'su] or [pər'sju] *tr* perseguire; (*to harass*) perseguitare; (*a career*) proseguire

**pursuit** [pər'sut] or [pər'sjut] *s* inseguimento, caccia; occupazione, esercizio

**pursuit' plane'** *s* caccia *m*

**purvey** [pər've] *tr* provvedere, fornire

**pus** [pʌs] *s* pus *m*

**push** [puʃ] *s* spinta; (*advance*) avanzata; (coll) impulso, energia || *tr* premere, spingere; (*a product*) promuovere la vendita di; dare impulso a; (*narcotics*) (slang) spacciare; **to**

**push around** (coll) dare spintoni a; (fig) fare pressione su; **to push back** ricacciare ‖ *intr* spingere; **to push ahead** avanzarsi a spintoni, avanzarsi; **to push on** avanzare
**push' but'ton** *s* pulsante *m*, bottone *m*
**push'-button con'trol** *s* controllo a pulsanti
**push'cart'** *s* carretto a mano
**pusher** ['puʃər] *adj* spingente; (aer) propulsivo ‖ *s* spingitore *m;* (aer) aeroplano a elica propulsiva; (slang) spacciatore *m* di stupefacenti
**pushing** ['puʃɪŋ] *adj* aggressivo, intraprendente
**puss** [pus] *s* micio
**puss' in the cor'ner** *s* gioco dei quattro cantoni
**puss·y** ['pusi] *s* (-ies) micio
**puss'y wil'low** *s* salice americano a gattini
**pustule** ['pʌstʃul] *s* pustola
**put** [put] *v* (*pret & pp* put; *ger* putting) *tr* mettere; (*to estimate*) stimare; (*a question*) rivolgere; (*to throw*) lanciare; imporre; **to put across** (slang) far accettare; **to put aside, away or by** mettere da parte; **to put down** annotare; (*to suppress*) reprimere; **to put off** differire; evadere; **to put on** (*clothes*) mettersi; (*a brake*) azionare; (*to assume*) fingere; (*airs*) darsi; **to put out** spegnere; imbarazzare; incomodare; deludere; annoiare, irritare; (*of a game*) espellere; **to put it over on s.o.** fargliela a qlcu; **to put off** rinviare; **to put over** mandare ad effetto; **to put to flight** mettere in fuga; **to put to shame** svergognare; **to put through** portare a

termine; **to put up** offrire; mettere in conserva; alloggiare; costruire; (*money*) contribuire; (coll) incitare ‖ *intr* dirigersi; **to put to sea** mettersi in mare; **to put up** prendere alloggio; **to put up with** tollerare
**put'-out'** *adj* sconcertato, seccato
**putrid** ['pjutrɪd] *adj* putrido
**Putsch** [putʃ] *s* tentativo di sollevazione, sollevazione
**putter** ['pʌtər] *intr* occuparsi di inezie; **to putter about** andare avanti e indietro
**put·ty** ['pʌti] *s* (-ties) stucco, mastice *m* ‖ *v* (*pret & pp* -tied) *tr* stuccare
**put'ty knife'** *s* spatola
**put'-up'** *adj* (coll) complottato
**puzzle** ['pʌzəl] *s* enigma *m;* (*toy*) indovinello ‖ *tr* rendere perplesso, confondere; **to puzzle out** decifrare ‖ *intr* essere perplesso
**puzzler** ['pʌzlər] *s* enigma *m*
**puzzling** ['pʌzlɪŋ] *adj* enigmatico
**pyg·my** ['pɪgmi] *s* (-mies) pigmeo
**pylon** *s* pilone *m*
**pyramid** ['pɪrəmɪd] *s* piramide *f* ‖ *tr* (*e.g., costs*) aumentare gradualmente; (*one's money*) aumentare giocando in margine
**pyre** [paɪr] *s* pira
**Pyrenees** ['pɪrɪ ˌniz] *spl* Pirenei *mpl*
**pyrites** [paɪ'raɪtiz] or ['paɪraɪts] *s* pirite *f*
**pyrotechnics** [ˌpaɪrə'tɛknɪks] *spl* pirotecnica
**python** ['paɪθɑn] or ['paɪθən] *s* pitone *m*
**pythoness** ['paɪθənɪs] *s* pitonessa
**pyx** [pɪks] *s* (eccl) pisside *f*

# Q

**Q, q** [kju] *s* diciassettesima lettera dell'alfabeto inglese
**quack** [kwæk] *adj* falso ‖ *s* medicastro; ciarlatano; qua qua *m* ‖ *intr* (*said of a duck*) fare qua qua
**quacker·y** ['kwækəri] *s* (-ies) ciarlataneria
**quadrangle** ['kwɑd ˌræŋgəl] *s* quadrangolo
**quadrant** ['kwɑdrənt] *s* quadrante *m*
**quadruped** ['kwɑdru ˌpɛd] *adj & s* quadrupede *m*
**quadruple** ['kwɑdrupəl] or [kwɑ'drupəl] *adj* quadruplo; (*alliance*) quadruplice ‖ *s* quadruplo ‖ *tr* quadruplicare ‖ *intr* quadruplicarsi
**quaff** [kwɑf] or [kwæf] *s* lungo sorso ‖ *tr & intr* bere a lunghi sorsi
**quail** [kwel] *s* quaglia ‖ *intr* sgomentarsi
**quaint** [kwent] *adj* strano, strambo, originale; all'antica ma bello
**quake** [kwek] *s* terremoto ‖ *intr* tremare, sussultare
**Quaker** ['kwekər] *adj & s* quacchero, quacquero

**Quak'er meet'ing** *s* riunione di quaccheri; (coll) riunione in cui si parla poco
**quali·fy** ['kwɑlɪ ˌfaɪ] *v* (*pret & pp* -fied) *tr* qualificare; (*for a profession*) abilitare ‖ *intr* qualificarsi; abilitarsi
**quali·ty** ['kwɑlɪti] *s* (-ties) qualità *f;* (*of a sound*) timbro
**qualm** [kwɑm] *s* scrupolo di coscienza; preoccupazione; nausea
**quanda·ry** ['kwɑndəri] *s* (-ries) incertezza, perplessità *f*
**quanti·ty** ['kwɑntɪti] *s* (-ties) quantità *f*
**quan·tum** ['kwɑntəm] *adj* quantistico ‖ *s* (-ta [tə]) quanto
**quarantine** ['kwɑrən ˌtin] or ['kwɔrən ˌtin] *s* quarantena ‖ *tr* mettere in quarantena
**quar·rel** ['kwɑrəl] or ['kwɔrəl] *s* litigio, diverbio; **to have no quarrel with** non essere in disaccordo con; **to pick a quarrel with** venire a diverbio con ‖ *v* (*pret & pp* -reled or -relled; *ger* -reling or -relling) *intr* litigare

**quarrelsome** ['kwɑrəlsəm] or ['kwɔrəl-səm] *adj* litigioso, rissoso

**quar·ry** ['kwɑri] or ['kwɔri] *s* (**-ries**) cava; (*game*) selvaggina, cacciagione || *v* (*pret & pp* **-ried**) *tr* cavare

**quart** [kwɔrt] *s* quarto di gallone

**quarter** ['kwɔrtər] *adj* quarto || *s* quarto; moneta di un quarto di dollaro; (*three months*) trimestre *m*; (*of town*) quartiere *m*; **a quarter after one** l'una e un quarto; **a quarter of an hour** un quarto d'ora; **a quarter to one** l'una meno un quarto; **at close quarters** corpo a corpo; **quarters** quartiere *m* || *tr* squartare; (*soldiers*) accasermare

**quar'ter-deck'** *s* cassero

**quar'ter-hour'** *s* quarto d'ora; **on the quarter-hour** ogni quindici minuti allo scoccare del quarto d'ora

**quarter·ly** ['kwɔrtərli] *adj* trimestrale || *s* (**-lies**) pubblicazione trimestrale || *adv* trimestralmente

**quar'ter·mas'ter** *s* (mil) intendente *m* militare; (nav) secondo capo

**quartet** [kwɔr'tɛt] *s* quartetto

**quartz** [kwɔrts] *s* quarzo

**quasar** ['kwesɑr] *s* (astr) radiostella

**quash** [kwɑʃ] *tr* sopprimere; annullare

**quaver** ['kwevər] *s* tremito; (mus) tremolo; (mus) croma || *intr* tremare

**quay** [ki] *s* molo

**queen** [kwin] *s* regina; (*in cards*) donna; (chess) regina

**queen' bee'** *s* ape regina; (fig) basilessa

**queen' dow'ager** *s* regina vedova

**queen·ly** ['kwinli] *adj* (**-lier; -liest**) da regina; regio

**queen' moth'er** *s* regina madre

**queen' post'** *s* monaco

**queen's' Eng'lish** *s* inglese corretto

**queer** [kwɪr] *adj* strano, curioso; poco bene, indisposto; falso; (slang) omosessuale || *s* (slang) finocchio || *tr* rovinare, mettere in pericolo

**quell** [kwɛl] *tr* soffocare, domare; (*pain*) calmare

**quench** [kwɛntʃ] *tr* (*fire, thirst*) spegnere, estinguere; (*rebellion*) soffocare; (elec) ammortizzare

**que·ry** ['kwɪri] *s* (**-ries**) domanda; punto interrogativo; dubbio || *v* (*pret & pp* **-ried**) *tr* interrogare; (typ) apporre punto interrogativo a

**quest** [kwɛst] *s* ricerca; **in quest of** in cerca di

**question** ['kwɛstʃən] *s* domanda; problema *m*, quesito; (*matter*) questione; **beyond question** senza dubbio; **out of the question** impossibile; **this is beside the question** questo non c'entra; **to ask a question** fare una domanda; **to be a question of** trattarsi di; **to call in** or **into question** mettere in dubbio; **without question** senza dubbio || *tr* interrogare; mettere in dubbio; (pol) interpellare

**questionable** ['kwɛstʃənəbəl] *adj* discutibile

**ques'tion mark'** *s* punto interrogativo

**questionnaire** [ ,kwɛstʃən'ɛr] *s* questionario

**queue** [kju] *s* (*of hair*) codino; (*of people*) coda || *intr* fare la coda

**quibble** ['kwɪbəl] *intr* sottilizzare

**quick** [kwɪk] *adj* pronto, sollecito; sbrigativo; veloce, rapido; vivo || *s*— **the quick and the dead** i vivi e i morti; **to cut to the quick** toccare nel vivo

**quicken** ['kwɪkən] *tr* sveltire; animare; ravvivare

**quick'lime'** *s* calce viva

**quick' lunch'** *s* tavola calda

**quickly** ['kwɪkli] *adv* svelto, alla svelta; presto

**quick'sand'** *s* sabbia mobile

**quick'-set'ting** *adj* a presa rapida

**quick'sil'ver** *s* argento vivo

**quick'work'** *s* (naut) opera viva

**quiet** ['kwaɪ·ət] *adj* quieto; silenzioso; (com) calmo; **to keep quiet** stare zitto || *s* quiete *f*, tranquillità *f*; pace *f*, calma || *tr* quietare; calmare || *intr*— **to quiet down** quietarsi, calmarsi

**quill** [kwɪl] *s* penna d'oca; (*basal part of feather*) calamo; (*e.g., of porcupine*) aculeo

**quilt** [kwɪlt] *s* trapunta, imbottita || *tr* trapuntare

**quince** [kwɪns] *s* cotogna; (*tree*) cotogno

**quinine** ['kwaɪnaɪn] *s* (*alkaloid*) chinina; (*salt of the alkaloid*) chinino

**quinsy** ['kwɪnzi] *s* angina

**quintessence** [kwɪn'tɛsəns] *s* quintessenza

**quintet** [kwɪn'tɛt] *s* quintetto

**quintuplet** [kwɪn'tjuplɛt] or [kwɪn-'tuplɛt] *s* gemello nato da un parto quintuplice

**quip** [kwɪp] *s* frizzo, uscita || *v* (*pret & pp* **quipped;** *ger* **quipping**) *tr & intr* uscire a dire, dire come battuta

**quire** [kwaɪr] *s* ventiquattro fogli; (bb) quinterno

**quirk** [kwʌrk] *s* stranezza, manierismo; (*quibble*) cavillo; (*sudden turn*) mutamento improvviso

**quit** [kwɪt] *adj* libero; **to be quits** esser pari; **to call it quits** finirla, farla finita || *v* (*pret & pp* **quit** or **quitted;** *ger* **quitting**) *tr* abbandonare || *intr* andarsene; abbandonare l'impiego; smettere (di + *inf*)

**quite** [kwaɪt] *adv* completamente; molto, del tutto

**quitter** ['kwɪtər] *s* persona che abbandona facilmente

**quiver** ['kwɪvər] *s* fremito; (*to hold arrows*) faretra, turcasso || *intr* fremere, tremare

**quixotic** [kwɪks'ɑtɪk] *adj* donchisciottesco

**quiz** [kwɪz] *s* (**quizzes**) esame *m*; interrogatorio || *v* (*pret & pp* **quizzed;** *ger* **quizzing**) *tr* esaminare; interrogare

**quiz' game'** *s* quiz *m*

**quiz' pro'gram** *s* programma *m* di quiz

**quiz' sec'tion** *s* (educ) classe *f* a base di esercizi (e non di conferenze)

**quizzical** ['kwɪzɪkəl] *adj* strano, curioso; (*derisive*) canzonatore

**quoin** [kɔɪn] or [kwɔɪn] *s* cantone *m*,

pietra angolare; (*piece of wood*) zeppa; (typ) serraforme *m* ‖ *tr* fissare con serraforme

**quoit** [kwɔɪt] or [kɔɪt] *s* anello di corda o di metallo da lanciarsi come gioco; **quoits** *ssg* gioco consistente nel lancio di anelli su di un piolo

**quondam** ['kwɑndæm] *adj* quondam

**quorum** ['kwɔrəm] *s* quorum *m*

**quota** ['kwotə] *s* (*share*) quota; (*of*

imports) contingentamento; (*of persons*) contingente *m*

**quotation** [kwo'teʃən] *s* (*from a book*) citazione; (*of prices*) quotazione

**quota'tion mark'** *s* doppia virgola, virgoletta

**quote** [kwot] *s* citazione, richiamo ‖ *tr* & *intr* citare, richiamare; (com) quotare; **quote** cito

**quotient** ['kwoʃənt] *s* quoziente *m*

# R

**R, r** [ɑr] *s* diciottesima lettera dell'alfabeto inglese

**rabbet** ['ræbɪt] *s* scanalatura, incastro ‖ *tr* scanalare, incastrare

**rab·bi** ['ræbaɪ] *s* (-bis) rabbino

**rabbit** ['ræbɪt] *s* coniglio

**rab'bit ears'** *spl* (telv) doppia antenna a stilo

**rabble** ['ræbəl] *s* gentaglia, marmaglia

**rab'ble-rous'er** ['rauzər] *s* arruffapopoli *m*

**rabies** ['rebiz] or ['rebɪ͵iz] *s* rabbia

**raccoon** [ræ'kun] *s* procione *m*

**race** [res] *s* (*branch of human stock*) razza; (*contest in speed*) corsa; (*contest of any kind*) gara; (*channel*) canale *m* di adduzione ‖ *tr* far correre; gareggiare (in velocità) con; (*a motor*) imballare ‖ *intr* correre; fare le corse; (*said of a motor*) imballarsi; (naut) fare le regate

**race' horse'** *s* cavallo da corsa

**race' ri'ot** *s* contestazione di razza

**race' track'** *s* pista

**racial** ['reʃəl] *adj* razziale

**rac'ing car'** *s* automobile *f* da corsa

**rack** [ræk] *s* (*to hang clothes*) attaccapanni *m*; (*framework to hold fodder, baggage, guns, etc.*) rastrelliera; (mach) cremagliera; **to go to rack and ruin** andare a rotoli ‖ *tr* tormentare, torturare; **to rack off** (*wine*) travasare; **to rack one's brains** rompersi il capo, lambiccarsi il cervello

**racket** ['rækɪt] *s* racchetta; (*noise*) chiasso, gazzarra; (coll) racket *m*; **to raise a racket** fare gazzarra

**racketeer** [͵rækɪ'tɪr] *s* chi è nel racket; (*engaged in extortion*) ricattatore *m* ‖ *intr* essere nel racket; fare il ricattatore

**rack' rail'way** *s* ferrovia a cremagliera

**rac·y** ['resi] *adj* (-ier; -iest) pungente, vigoroso; piccante

**radar** ['redɑr] *s* radar *m*

**radiant** ['redɪ·ənt] *adj* raggiante, radioso

**radiate** ['redɪ͵et] *tr* irradiare ‖ *intr* irradiarsi

**radiation** [͵redɪ'eʃən] *s* radiazione

**radia'tion sick'ness** *s* malattia causata da radiazione atomica

**radiator** ['redɪ͵etər] *s* radiatore *m*

**ra'diator cap'** *s* tappo del radiatore

**radical** ['rædɪkəl] *adj* radicale ‖ *s*

radicale *mf*; (chem, math) radicale *m*

**radi·o** ['redɪ͵o] *s* (-os) radio *f*; radiogramma *m* ‖ *tr* radiotrasmettere

**radioactive** [͵redɪ·o'æktɪv] *adj* radioattivo

**ra'dio am'ateur** *s* radioamatore *m*

**ra'dio announc'er** *s* radioannunciatore *m*

**ra'dio bea'con** *s* radiofaro

**ra'dio·broad'cast** *s* radiodiffusione ‖ *tr* radiodiffondere

**ra'dio com'pass** *s* radiobussola

**ra'dio·fre'quency** *s* radiofrequenza

**ra'dio lis'tener** *s* radioascoltatore *m*

**radiology** [͵redɪ'ɑlədʒɪ] *s* radiologia

**ra'dio net'work** *s* rete *f*

**ra'dio news'caster** *s* radiocronista *mf*

**ra'dio·pho'to** *s* (-tos) (coll) radiofoto *f*

**ra'dio set'** *s* radioricevente *f*

**ra'dio sta'tion** *s* stazione radio

**radish** ['rædɪʃ] *s* ravanello

**radium** ['redɪ·əm] *s* radio

**radi·us** ['redɪ·əs] *s* (-i [͵aɪ] or -uses) (anat) radio; (fig, geom) raggio; **within a radius of** entro un raggio di

**raffle** ['ræfəl] *s* riffa ‖ *tr* sorteggiare

**raft** [ræft] or [rɑft] *s* zattera; (coll) mucchio

**rafter** ['ræftər] or ['rɑftər] *s* puntone *m*

**rag** [ræg] *s* straccio; **to chew the rag** (slang) chiacchierare

**ragamuffin** ['rægə͵mʌfɪn] *s* straccione *m*

**rag' doll'** *s* bambola di pezza

**rage** [redʒ] *s* rabbia; **to be all the rage** furoreggiare; **to fly into a rage** montare in bestia ‖ *intr* infuriare

**ragged** ['rægɪd] *adj* cencioso; (*torn*) stracciato; (*edge*) rozzo, scabroso

**ragpicker** ['ræg͵pɪkər] *s* cenciaiolo, straccivendolo

**rag'weed'** *s* (bot) ambrosia

**raid** [red] *s* irruzione, razzia ‖ *tr* scorrere ‖ *intr* scorrazzare

**rail** [rel] *s* (*of fence*) stecca, traversa; (*fence*) stecconata; (*railing*) ringhiera; (rr) rotaia; **by rail** per ferrovia; **rails** titoli *mpl* ferroviari ‖ *intr* inveire; **to rail at** inveire contro

**rail'car'** *s* automotrice *f*

**rail' fence'** *s* stecconata fatta di traverse piallate alla buona

**rail'head'** *s* fine *f* della linea ferroviaria
**railing** ['relɪŋ] *s* ringhiera
**rail'road'** *adj* ferroviario || *s* ferrovia || *tr* trasportare in ferrovia; (*a bill*) far passare precipitosamente; (coll) imprigionare falsamente
**rail'road cros'sing** *s* passaggio a livello
**rail'road'er** *s* ferroviere *m*
**rail'way'** *s* ferrovia, strada ferrata
**raiment** ['remənt] *s* (lit) abbigliamento
**rain** [ren] *s* pioggia; **rain or shine** con qualunque tempo || *tr* fare piovere; (lit) piovere; **to rain cats and dogs** piovere a catinelle; **to rain out** far sospendere per via della pioggia || *intr* piovere
**rainbow** ['ren‚bo] *s* arcobaleno
**rain'coat'** *s* impermeabile *m*
**rain'fall'** *s* acquazzone *m*; piovosità *f*
**rain‑y** ['reni] *adj* (**‑ier; ‑iest**) piovoso, piovano
**rain'y day'** *s* giorno piovoso; (fig) tempi *mpl* difficili
**raise** [rez] *s* aumento || *tr* levare, rialzare; (*children, animals*) allevare; (*to build*) tirare su; (*a question*) sollevare; (*the dead*) risollevare; (*to increase*) aumentare; (*money*) raccogliere; (*a siege*) togliere; (*at cards*) rilanciare; (*anchor*) salpare; (math) elevare
**raisin** ['rezən] *s* grano d'uva passa, grano d'uva secca; **raisins** uva passa, uva secca
**rake** [rek] *s* rastrello; (*person*) porcaccione *m*, libertino || *tr* rastrellare; **to rake in money** far soldoni
**rake'‑off'** *s* (coll) compenso illecito, bustarella; (coll) sconto
**rakish** ['rekɪʃ] *adj* libertino; brioso, vivace; **to wear one's hat at a rakish angle** portare il cappello sulle ventitré
**ral‑ly** ['ræli] *s* (**‑lies**) riunione, comizio; adunata; ricupero || *v* (*pret & pp* **‑lied**) *tr* riunire, chiamare a raccolta; rianimare || *intr* riunirsi; rianimarsi; (*said of stock prices*) rialzarsi; rimettersi in forze; **to rally to the side of** correre all'aiuto di
**ram** [ræm] *s* (*male sheep*) montone *m*; (mil) ariete *m*; (nav) sperone *m*; (mach) maglio del battipalo || *v* (*pret & pp* **rammed**; *ger* **ramming**) *tr* battere, sbattere contro; cacciare, conficcare; forzare; (nav) speronare || *intr*—**to ram into** sbattere contro
**ramble** ['ræmbəl] *s* girata || *intr* (*to wander around*) gironzolare; vagare; (*said of a vine*) crescere disordinatamente; (*said, e.g., of a river*) serpeggiare; (fig) scorrazzare, divagare
**rami‑fy** ['ræmɪ‚faɪ] *v* (*pret & pp* **‑fied**) *tr* ramificare || *intr* ramificarsi
**ram'jet en'gine** *s* statoreattore *m*
**ramp** [ræmp] *s* rampa
**rampage** ['ræmpedʒ] *s* stato d'eccitazione; **to go on a rampage** infierire, comportarsi furiosamente
**rampart** ['ræmpɑrt] *s* baluardo, muraglione *m*

**ram'rod'** *s* (*for ramming*) (mil) bacchetta; (*for cleaning*) (mil) scovolo
**ram'shack'le** *adj* cadente, in rovina
**ranch** [ræntʃ] *s* fattoria agricola
**rancid** ['rænsɪd] *adj* rancido
**rancor** ['ræŋkər] *s* rancore *m*
**random** ['rændəm] *adj* fortuito; **at random** alla rinfusa, a casaccio
**range** [rendʒ] *s* (*row*) fila; (*rank*) classe *f*; (*distance*) portata; campo di tiro a segno; raggio d'azione; (*scope*) gamma; (*for grazing*) pascolo; (*stove*) fornello, cucina economica; **within range of** alla portata di || *tr* allineare; ordinare; passare attraverso; mandare al pascolo || *intr* variare, fluttuare; estendersi; trovarsi; (mil) portare; **to range over** percorrere; (fig) trattare
**range' find'er** *s* telemetro
**rank** [ræŋk] *adj* esuberante; grossolano; denso, spesso; puzzolente; eccessivo; completo, assoluto || *s* rango, grado; (*row*) fila, schiera; **ranks** truppe *fpl*, ranghi *mpl* || *tr* arrangiare, allineare; classificare; avere rango superiore a || *intr* avere il massimo rango; **to rank high** avere un'alta posizione; **to rank low** avere una posizione bassa; **to rank with** essere allo stesso livello di
**rank' and file'** *s* truppa; massa
**rankle** ['ræŋkəl] *tr* irritare || *intr* inasprirsi
**ransack** ['rænsak] *tr* (*to search thoroughly*) frugare, rovistare; (*to pillage*) svaligiare, saccheggiare
**ransom** ['rænsəm] *s* taglia, riscatto || *tr* riscattare
**rant** [rænt] *intr* farneticare, parlare a vanvera
**rap** [ræp] *s* colpo, colpetto; **I don't care a rap** non m'importa un fico; **to take the rap** (slang) prendersi la colpa || *v* (*pret & pp* **rapped**; *ger* **rapping**) *tr* dare colpi a; battere; **to rap out** (*e.g., a command*) lanciare || *intr* dare colpi, bussare
**rapacious** [rə'peʃəs] *adj* rapace
**rape** [rep] *s* rapimento; (*of a woman*) stupro; (bot) ravizzone *m* || *tr* rapire; forzare, violentare
**rapid** ['ræpɪd] *adj* rapido || **rapids** *spl* rapide *fpl*
**rap'id‑fire'** *adj* a tiro rapido
**rapidity** [rə'pɪdəti] *s* rapidità *f*
**rapier** ['repɪ‑ər] *s* spada, stocco
**rapt** [ræpt] *adj* assorto; estatico
**rapture** ['ræptʃər] *s* rapimento, estasi *f*
**rare** [rer] *adj* raro; (*thinly distributed*) rado; (*gas*) rarefatto; (*meat*) al sangue; (*gem*) prezioso
**rare'‑earth' met'al** *s* metallo delle terre rare
**rare‑fy** ['rerɪ‚faɪ] *v* (*pret & pp* **‑fied**) *tr* rarefare || *intr* rarefarsi
**rarely** ['rerli] *adv* di rado, raramente
**rascal** ['ræskəl] *s* briccone *m*, birbante *m*
**rash** [ræʃ] *adj* temerario, precipitato || *s* eruzione; (fig) mucchio
**rasp** [ræsp] *or* [rɑsp] *s* raspa; rumore

*m* di raspa ‖ *tr* raspare; irritare; dire con voce roca ‖ *intr* fare rumore raspante

**raspber·ry** ['ræz‚beri] *or* ['rɑz‚beri] *s* (**-ries**) lampone *m;* (slang) pernacchia

**rat** [ræt] *s* ratto; (*to give fullness to hair*) posticcio; (slang) traditore *m;* **to smell a rat** (coll) subodorare un inganno

**ratchet** ['ræt∫ɪt] *s* nottolino

**rate** [ret] *s* (*of interest*) saggio, tasso; prezzo; costo; velocità *f;* (*degree of action*) ragione; tariffa; **at any rate** ad ogni modo; **at the rate of** in ragione di ‖ *tr* valutare, classificare ‖ *intr* essere considerato; essere classificato

**rate' of exchange'** *s* corso del cambio

**rather** ['ræðər] *or* ['rɑðər] *adv* piuttosto; a preferenza; per meglio dire; bensì; discretamente; **rather than** piuttosto di ‖ *interj* e come!

**rati·fy** ['rætɪ‚faɪ] *v* (*pret & pp* **-fied**) *tr* ratificare, sancire

**rating** ['retɪŋ] *s* classifica; (nav) grado; (com) valutazione

**ra·tio** ['re∫o] *or* ['re∫ɪ‚o] *s* (**-tios**) ragione, rapporto; proporzione

**ration** ['re∫ən] *or* ['ræ∫ən] *s* razione ‖ *tr* razionare

**rational** ['ræ∫ənəl] *adj* razionale

**ra'tion book'** *s* tessera di razionamento

**rat' poi'son** *s* veleno per i topi

**rat' race'** *s* (coll) corsa dei barbieri

**rattle** ['rætəl] *s* (*sharp sounds*) fracasso; (*child's toy*) sonaglio; (*noise-making device*) raganella; (*in throat*) rantolo ‖ *tr* scuotere; (*to confuse*) sconcertare; **to rattle off** dire rapidamente, snocciolare ‖ *intr* risuonare; scuotersi; cianciare

**rat'tle·snake'** *s* serpente *m* a sonagli

**rat'trap'** *s* trappola per topi; (*hovel*) topaia; (*jam*) (fig) frangente *m*

**raucous** ['rɔkəs] *adj* rauco

**ravage** ['rævɪdʒ] *s* distruzione; **ravages** (*of time*) oltraggio ‖ *tr* distruggere, disfare

**rave** [rev] *intr* farneticare, delirare; infuriare; andare in estasi; **to rave about** levare alle stelle

**raven** ['revən] *s* corvo

**ravenous** ['rævənəs] *adj* famelico

**ravine** [rə'vin] *s* canalone *m*, burrone *m*

**ravish** ['rævɪ∫] *tr* incantare, entusiasmare; rapire; (*a woman*) stuprare

**raw** [rɔ] *adj* crudo; (*e.g., silk*) grezzo; (*flesh*) vivo; inesperto

**raw' deal'** *s* trattamento brutale e ingiusto

**raw'hide'** *s* pelle greggia

**raw' mate'rial** *s* materia prima

**ray** [re] *s* raggio; (*fish*) razza

**rayon** ['re·ɑn] *s* raion *m*

**raze** [rez] *tr* radere al suolo

**razor** ['rezər] *s* rasoio

**ra'zor blade'** *s* lametta

**ra'zor strop'** *s* coramella

**razz** [ræz] *s* (slang) pernacchia ‖ *tr* (slang) prendere in giro

**reach** [rit∫] *s* portata; estensione; **out of reach (of)** fuori della portata (di); oltre alle possibilità (di); fuori tiro (di); **within reach of** alla portata di ‖ *tr* raggiungere; toccare; (*customers*) guadagnare ‖ *intr* estendere la mano; **to reach for** cercare di raggiungere

**react** [rɪ'ækt] *intr* reagire

**reaction** [rɪ'æk∫ən] *s* reazione

**reactionar·y** [rɪ'æk∫ə‚neri] *adj* reazionario ‖ *s* (**-ies**) reazionario

**reactor** [rɪ'æktər] *s* reattore *m*

**read** [rid] *v* (*pret & pp* **read** [red]) *tr* leggere; (*s.o.'s thoughts*) leggere in; **to read over** ripassare ‖ *intr* leggere; saper leggere; essere concepito, e.g., **your cable reads thus** il vostro telegramma è concepito così; leggersi, e.g., **this books reads easily** questo libro si legge facilmente; **to read on** continuare a leggere

**reader** ['ridər] *s* lettore *m;* libro di lettura, sillabo

**readily** ['rɛdɪli] *adv* velocemente; facilmente; di buona voglia

**reading** ['ridɪŋ] *s* lettura; dizione

**read'ing desk'** *s* leggio

**read'ing glass'** *s* lente *f* d'ingrandimento; **reading glasses** occhiali *mpl* per la lettura

**read'ing lamp'** *s* lampada da scrittoio

**read'ing room'** *s* sala di lettura

**read·y** ['rɛdi] *adj* (**-ier; -iest**) pronto; disponibile; **to make ready** preparare; prepararsi ‖ *v* (*pret & pp* **-ied**) *tr* preparare ‖ *intr* prepararsi

**read'y cash'** *s* denaro contante

**read'y-made cloth'ing** *s* confezioni *fpl*

**read'y-made suit'** *s* vestito già fatto

**reaffirm** [‚ri·ə'fʌrm] *tr* riaffermare

**reagent** [rɪ'edʒənt] *s* reagente *m*

**real** ['ri·əl] *adj* effettivo, reale

**re'al estate'** *s* beni *mpl* immobili, proprietà *f* immobiliare

**re'al-estate'** *adj* immobiliare, fondiario

**realism** ['ri·ə‚lɪzəm] *s* realismo

**realist** ['ri·əlɪst] *s* realista *mf*

**realistic** [‚ri·ə'lɪstɪk] *adj* realistico

**reali·ty** [rɪ'ælɪti] *s* (**-ties**) realtà *f*

**realize** ['ri·ə‚laɪz] *tr* rendersi conto di; concretare; realizzare ‖ *intr* convertire proprietà in contanti

**realm** [rɛlm] *s* regno

**realtor** ['ri·əl‚tɔr] *or* ['ri·əltər] *s* (trademark) agente *m* d'immobili membro dell'associazione nazionale

**realty** ['ri·əlti] *s* proprietà *f* immobiliare

**ream** [rim] *s* risma; **reams** pagine *fpl* e pagine ‖ *tr* alesare

**reamer** ['rimər] *s* (mach) alesatore *m;* (dentistry) fresa

**reap** [rip] *tr & intr* (*to cut*) mietere; (*to gather*) raccogliere

**reaper** ['ripər] *s* (*person*) mietitore *m;* (mach) mietitrice *f*

**reappear** [‚ri·ə'pɪr] *intr* ricomparire, riapparire

**reappearance** [‚ri·ə'pɪrəns] *s* riapparizione, ricomparsa

**reapportionment** [‚ri·ə'pɔr∫ənmənt] *s* ridistribuzione

**rear** [rɪr] *adj* posteriore, di dietro ‖ *s*

retro, di dietro; posteriore *m;* (mil) retroguardia ‖ *tr* alzare, elevare; allevare, educare ‖ *intr* (*said of a horse*) impennarsi

**rear' ad'miral** *s* contrammiraglio

**rear' drive'** *s* trazione posteriore

**rear' end'** *s* retro, di dietro; (coll) posteriore *m;* (aut) retrotreno

**rearmament** [ri'ɑrməmənt] *s* riarmo

**rear'-view mir'ror** *s* specchietto retrovisivo

**rear' win'dow** *s* (aut) lunetta posteriore

**reason** ['rizən] *s* ragione; **by reason of** per causa di; **to bring s.o. to reason** indurre qlcu alla ragione; **to stand to reason** esser logico ‖ *tr & intr* ragionare

**reasonable** ['rizənəbəl] *adj* ragionevole

**reassessment** [ ,ri·ə'sɛsmənt] *s* rivalutazione

**reassure** [ ,ri·ə'ʃur] *tr* rassicurare, riassicurare

**reawaken** [ ,ri·ə'wekən] *tr* risvegliare ‖ *intr* risvegliarsi

**rebate** ['ribet] or [ri'bet] *s* ribasso ‖ *tr* ribassare

**rebel** ['rɛbəl] *adj & s* ribelle *mf* ‖ **re·bel** [ri'bɛl] *v* (*pret & pp* -**belled;** *ger* -**belling**) *intr* ribellarsi

**rebellion** [ri'bɛljən] *s* ribellione

**rebellious** [ri'bɛljəs] *adj* ribelle

**re·bind** [ri'baind] *v* (*pret & pp* - **bound** ['baund]) *tr* rifasciare; (bb) rilegare

**rebirth** ['ribʌrθ] or [ri'bʌrθ] *s* rinascita

**rebore** [ri'bor] *tr* rialesare, rettificare

**rebound** ['ri ,baund] or [ri'baund] *s* rimbalzo ‖ [ri'baund] *intr* rimbalzare

**rebroad'casting sta'tion** *s* stazione ripetitrice

**rebuff** [ri'bʌf] *s* rifiuto ‖ *tr* respingere, rifiutare

**rebuild** [ri'bild] *v* (*pret & pp* -**built** ['bilt]) *tr* ricostruire, riedificare

**rebuke** [ri'bjuk] *s* rabbuffo ‖ *tr* rabbuffare

**re·but** [ri'bʌt] *v* (*pret & pp* -**butted;** *ger* -**butting**) *tr* confutare

**rebuttal** [ri'bʌtəl] *s* confutazione

**recall** [ri'kɔl] or ['rikɔl] *s* richiamo; revoca ‖ [ri'kɔl] *tr* richiamare; ricordare, ricordarsi di; richiamare alla memoria

**recant** [ri'kænt] *tr* ritrattare ‖ *intr* ritrattarsi

**re·cap** ['ri ,kæp] or [ri'kæp] *v* (*pret & pp* -**capped;** *ger* -**capping**) *tr* ricapitolare, riepilogare; (*a tire*) rifare il battistrada a

**recapitulation** [ ,rikə ,pitʃə'leʃən] *s* ricapitolazione, riepilogo

**re·cast** ['ri ,kæst] or ['ri ,kɑst] *s* rifusione ‖ [ri'kæst] or [ri'kɑst] *v* (*pret & pp* -**cast**) *tr* rifondere

**recede** [ri'sid] *intr* ritirarsi, allontanarsi; recedere, retrocedere; (*said, e.g., of chin*) sfuggire

**receipt** [ri'sit] *s* ricevimento; (*acknowledgment of payment*) ricevuta; (*recipe*) ricetta; **receipts** incasso, introito ‖ *tr* quietanzare

**receive** [ri'siv] *tr* ricevere; (*stolen goods*) ricettare; (*to have inflicted upon one*) subire ‖ *intr* ricevere

**receiver** [ri'sivər] *s* ricevitore *m;* ricettatore *m;* (law) curatore *m* fallimentare; (telp) auricolare *m*

**receiv'ing set'** *s* apparecchio radioricevente

**receiv'ing tell'er** *s* cassiere *m* incaricato delle riscossioni

**recent** ['risənt] *adj* recente

**recently** ['risəntli] *adv* recentemente, di recente

**receptacle** [ri'sɛptəkəl] *s* recipiente *m;* (elec) presa

**reception** [ri'sɛpʃən] *s* accoglienza; (*function*) ricevimento

**recep'tion desk'** *s* ufficio informazioni, bureau *m*

**receptionist** [ri'sɛpʃənist] *s* accoglitrice *f;* (*male*) usciere *m*

**receptive** [ri'sɛptiv] *adj* ricettivo

**recess** [ri'sɛs] or ['rises] *s* intermezzo, interludio; ora di ricreazione; (*in a line*) rientranza; (*in a wall*) nicchia, alcova; (fig) recesso ‖ [ri'sɛs] *tr* aggiornare, dare vacanza a; incassare, mettere in una nicchia ‖ *intr* aggiornarsi, prendersi vacanza

**recession** [ri'sɛʃən] *s* ritirata; processione finale; (com) recessione

**recipe** ['rɛsi ,pi] *s* ricetta

**reciprocal** [ri'siprəkəl] *adj* reciproco

**reciprocity** [ ,rɛsi'prɑsiti] *s* reciprocità *f*

**recital** [ri'saitəl] *s* narrazione; (*of music or poetry*) recital *m*

**recite** [ri'sait] *tr* raccontare; (*music or poetry*) recitare

**reckless** ['rɛklis] *adj* temerario, spericolato

**reckon** ['rɛkən] *tr* calcolare; considerare; (coll) supporre ‖ *intr* contare; **to reckon with** prevedere, tener conto di

**reclaim** [ri'klem] *tr* (*land*) sanare, prosciugare; (*substances*) rigenerare; (fig) rigenerare

**recline** [ri'klain] *tr* reclinare ‖ *intr* reclinarsi, adagiarsi

**recluse** [ri'klus] or ['rɛklus] *adj & s* recluso

**recognition** [ ,rɛkəg'niʃən] *s* riconoscimento

**recognize** ['rɛkəg ,naiz] *tr* riconoscere

**recoil** [ri'kɔil] *s* indietreggiamento; (*of a firearm*) rinculo ‖ *intr* indietreggiare; rinculare

**recollect** [ ,rɛkə'lɛkt] *tr & intr* ricordare

**recollection** [ ,rɛkə'lɛkʃən] *s* ricordo

**recommend** [ ,rɛkə'mɛnd] *tr* raccomandare

**recompense** ['rɛkəm ,pɛns] *s* ricompensa ‖ *tr* ricompensare

**reconcile** ['rɛkən ,sail] *tr* riconciliare; **to reconcile oneself** rassegnarsi

**reconnaissance** [ri'kɑnisəns] *s* ricognizione

**reconnoiter** [ ,rɛkə'nɔitər] or [ ,rikə- 'nɔitər] *tr & intr* perlustrare

**reconsider** [ ,rikən'sidər] *tr* riconsiderare

**reconstruct** [ ˌrikən'strʌkt] *tr* ricostruire

**reconversion** [ ˌrikən'vʌrʒən] *s* riconversione

**record** ['rɛkərd] *s* registrazione; annotazione; (*official report*) verbale *m*, protocollo; (*criminal*) fedina sporca; (*of a phonograph*) disco; (educ) documenti *mpl* scolastici; (sports) record *m*, primato; **off the record** confidenziale; confidenzialmente; **records** annali *mpl*, documenti *mpl*; **to break a record** battere un record || [rɪ'kɔrd] *tr* registrare; mettere a verbale; (*e.g., a song*) incidere

**rec'ord break'er** *s* (sports) primatista *mf*

**rec'ord chang'er** ['tʃendʒər] *s* cambiadischi *m*

**recorder** [rɪ'kɔrdər] *s* (*apparatus*) registratore *m*; (law) cancelliere *m*; (mus) flauto a imboccatura a tubo

**rec'ord hold'er** *s* (sports) primatista *mf*

**recording** [rɪ'kɔrdɪŋ] *s* registrazione; (*of a record*) incisione; (*record*) disco

**record'ing sec'retary** *s* cancelliere *m*

**rec'ord play'er** *s* giradischi *m*

**recount** ['ri ˌkaʊnt] *s* nuovo conteggio || [ri'kaʊnt] *tr* (*to count again*) ricontare || [rɪ'kaʊnt] *tr* (*to narrate*) raccontare

**recourse** [rɪ'kors] or ['rikors] *s* ricorso; (com) rivalsa; **to have recourse to** ricorrere a

**recover** [rɪ'kʌvər] *tr* ricuperare, riacquistare; (*a substance*) rigenerare; **to recover consciousness** riaversi, riprendere conoscenza || *intr* rimettersi; guadagnare una causa

**recover·y** [rɪ'kʌvəri] *s* (**-ies**) ricupero; guarigione; **past recovery** incurabile

**recreant** ['rɛkrɪ·ənt] *adj* & *s* codardo; traditore *m*

**recreation** [ ˌrɛkrɪ'eʃən] *s* ricreazione

**recruit** [rɪ'krut] *s* recluta || *tr* & *intr* reclutare

**rectangle** ['rɛk ˌtæŋgəl] *s* rettangolo

**rectifier** ['rɛktə ˌfaɪ·ər] *s* rettificatore *m*; (elec) raddrizzatore *m*

**recti·fy** ['rɛktɪ ˌfaɪ] *v* (*pret* & *pp* **-fied**) *tr* rettificare; (elec) raddrizzare

**rectitude** ['rɛktɪ ˌtud] or ['rɛktɪ ˌtjud] *s* rettitudine *f*

**rec·tum** ['rɛktəm] *s* (**-tums** or **-ta** [tə]) retto

**recumbent** [rɪ'kʌmbənt] *adj* sdraiato

**recuperate** [rɪ'kjupə ˌret] *tr* ricuperare || *intr* ristabilirsi, rimettersi

**re·cur** [rɪ'kʌr] *v* (*pret* & *pp* **-curred**; *ger* **-curring**) *intr* ricorrere; ritornare; tornare a mente

**recurrent** [rɪ'kʌrənt] *adj* ricorrente

**recycle** [ri'saɪkəl] *tr* riconvertire; (*e.g., in chemical industry*) riciclare

**red** [rɛd] *adj* (**redder; reddest**) rosso || *s* rosso; **in the red** in debito , in rosso || **Red** *adj* & *s* (*Communist*) rosso

**red'bait'** *tr* dare del comunista a

**red'bird'** *s* cardinale *m*

**red-blooded** ['rɛd ˌblʌdɪd] *adj* sanguigno; vigoroso

**red'breast'** *s* pettirosso

**red'bud'** *s* siliquastro

**red'cap'** *s* (Brit) poliziotto militare; (U.S.A.) facchino

**red' cell'** *s* globulo rosso

**red' cent'** *s*—**to not have a red cent** (coll) non avere il becco di un quattrino

**Red' Cross'** *s* Croce Rossa

**redden** ['rɛdən] *tr* arrossare || *intr* arrossire

**redeem** [rɪ'dim] *tr* redimere; (*a promise*) disimpegnare

**redeemer** [rɪ'dimər] *s* redentore *m*

**redemption** [rɪ'dɛmpʃən] *s* redenzione; disimpegno

**red-handed** ['rɛd'hændɪd] *adj*—**to be caught red-handed** esser colto sul fatto or con le mani nel sacco

**red'head'** *s* persona dai capelli rossi

**red' her'ring** *s* argomento usato per sviare l'attenzione; aringa affumicata

**red'-hot'** *adj* rovente, incandescente; fresco fresco, appena uscito

**rediscover** [ ˌridɪs'kʌvər] *tr* riscoprire

**red'-let'ter** *adj* memorabile

**red'-light' dis'trict** *s* quartiere *m* delle case di tolleranza

**red' man'** *s* pellerossa *m*

**re·do** ['ri'du] *v* (*pret* **-did** ['dɪd]; *pp* **-done** ['dʌn]) *tr* rifare

**redolent** ['rɛdələnt] *adj* fragrante, profumato; **redolent of** che sa di

**redoubt** [rɪ'daʊt] *s* (mil) ridotta

**redound** [rɪ'daʊnd] *intr* ridondare

**red' pep'per** *s* pepe *m* di Caienna

**redress** [rɪ'drɛs] or ['ridrɛs] *s* riparazione, risarcimento || [rɪ'drɛs] *tr* riparare, risarcire

**red'skin'** *s* pellerossa *mf*

**red' tape'** *s* trafila, burocrazia

**reduce** [rɪ'djus] or [rɪ'dus] *tr* ridurre; diluire; (mil) retrocedere; (*a hernia*) (surg) sbrigliare || *intr* ridursi; (*to lose weight*) dimagrire

**reducing** [rɪ'djusɪŋ] or [rɪ'dusɪŋ] *adj* dimagrante; (chem) riducente

**reduction** [rɪ'dʌkʃən] *s* riduzione

**redundant** [rɪ'dʌndənt] *adj* ridondante

**red'wood'** *s* sequoia

**reed** [rid] *s* (*stalk*) calamo; (*plant*) canna; (mus) linguetta; (mus) strumento a linguetta

**reedit** [ri'ɛdɪt] *tr* rifondere

**reef** [rif] *s* scoglio, barriera; (naut) terzarolo; (min) vena, filone *m* || *tr* (*sail*) imbrogliare

**reefer** ['rifər] *s* giacchetta a doppio petto; (slang) sigaretta di marijuana

**reek** [rik] *intr* puzzare; sudare, evaporare, fumare

**reel** [ril] *s* (*spool*) bobina; (*sway*) vacillamento; (*for fishing*) mulinello; **off the reel** senza esitazione || *tr* bobinare; **to reel off** rifilare || *intr* barcollare

**reelection** [ ˌri·ɪ'lɛkʃən] *s* rielezione

**reenlist** [ ˌri·ɛn'lɪst] *tr* arruolare di nuovo || *intr* arruolarsi di nuovo

**reen·try** [rɪ'ɛntri] *s* (**-tries**) rientro

**reexamination** [ ˌri·ɛg ˌzæmɪ'neʃən] *s* riesame *m*

**re·fer** [rɪ'fʌr] v (pret & pp **-ferred;** ger **-ferring**) tr riferire || intr riferirsi
**referee** [ ,rɛfə'ri] s arbitro || tr & intr arbitrare
**reference** ['rɛfərəns] s riferimento; (testimonial) referenza; (e.g., in a book) rinvio, rimando
**ref'erence book'** s libro di consultazione
**referen·dum** [ ,rɛfə'rɛndəm] s (**-dums** or **-da** [də]) referendum m
**refill** ['rifɪl] s ricambio || [rɪ'fɪl] tr riempire di nuovo
**refine** [rɪ'faɪn] tr raffinare
**refinement** [rɪ'faɪnmənt] s raffinatezza; (of oil) raffinatura
**refiner·y** [rɪ'faɪnəri] s (**-ies**) raffineria
**reflect** [rɪ'flɛkt] tr riflettere || intr riflettere, riflettersi
**reflection** [rɪ'flɛkʃən] s riflessione
**reflex** ['riflɛks] adj riflesso || s riflesso; (camera) reflex m
**reflexive** [rɪ'flɛksɪv] adj riflessivo
**reforestation** [ ,rifɔrɪs'teʃən] or [ ,rifɔrɪs'teʃən] s rimboschimento
**reform** [rɪ'fɔrm] s riforma || tr riformare || intr correggersi
**reformation** [ ,rɛfər'meʃən] s riforma || **Reformation** s—**the Reformation** la Riforma
**reformato·ry** [rɪ'fɔrmə ,tori] adj riformativo || s (**-ries**) riformatorio
**reformer** [rɪ'fɔrmər] s riformatore m
**reform' school'** s riformatorio
**refraction** [rɪ'frækʃən] s rifrazione
**refrain** [rɪ'fren] s ritornello, intercalare m || intr astenersi
**refresh** [rɪ'frɛʃ] tr rinfrescare; ristorare || intr ristorarsi
**refreshing** [rɪ'frɛʃɪŋ] adj rinfrescante; ristoratore; ricreativo
**refreshment** [rɪ'frɛʃmənt] s rinfresco
**refrigerate** [rɪ'frɪdʒə ,ret] tr refrigerare
**refrigerator** [rɪ'frɪdʒə ,retər] s refrigerante m, frigorifero
**refrig'erator car'** s vagone frigorifero
**re·fuel** [ri'fjul] v (pret & pp **-fueled** or **-fuelled;** ger **-fueling** or **-fuelling**) tr rifornire di carburante || intr rifornirsi di carburante
**refuge** ['rɛfjudʒ] s rifugio; scampo; **to take refuge (in)** rifugiarsi (in)
**refugee** [ ,rɛfju'dʒi] s rifugiato
**refund** ['rifʌnd] s rifusione || [rɪ'fʌnd] tr (to repay) rifondere || [rɪ'fʌnd] tr (bonds) consolidare; (to fund anew) rifondere
**refurnish** [ri'fʌrnɪʃ] tr riammobiliare
**refusal** [rɪ'fjuzəl] s rifiuto
**refuse** ['rɛfjus] s rifiuto, spazzatura || [rɪ'fjuz] tr rifiutare; **to refuse to** rifiutarsi di
**refute** [rɪ'fjut] tr smentire, confutare
**regain** [rɪ'gen] tr riguadagnare; **to regain consciousness** tornare in sé
**regal** ['rigəl] adj reale, regale
**regale** [rɪ'gel] tr intrattenere, rallegrare
**regalia** [rɪ'gelɪ·ə] spl (of royalty) prerogative fpl reali; alta uniforme
**regard** [rɪ'gard] s riguardo; (look)

sguardo; (esteem) rispetto; **in regard to** rispetto a; **regards** rispetti mpl; **warm regards** cordiali saluti mpl; **without regard to** senza considerare || tr considerare; osservare; concernere; **as regards** per quanto concerne
**regarding** [rɪ'gardɪŋ] prep per quanto concerne
**regardless** [rɪ'gardlɪs] adj incurante || adv ciò nonostante; costi quello che costi; **regardless of** malgrado
**regatta** [rɪ'gætə] s regata
**regen·cy** ['ridʒənsi] s (**-cies**) reggenza
**regenerate** [rɪ'dʒɛnə ,ret] tr rigenerare || intr rigenerarsi
**regent** ['ridʒənt] s reggente mf
**regicide** ['rɛdʒɪ ,saɪd] s (act) regicidio; (person) regicida mf
**regiment** ['rɛdʒɪmənt] s reggimento || ['rɛdʒɪ ,mɛnt] tr irregimentare
**regimental** [ ,rɛdʒɪ'mɛntəl] adj reggimentale || **regimentals** spl uniforme f reggimentale
**region** ['ridʒən] s regione
**register** ['rɛdʒɪstər] s registro; (for controlling the flow of air) regolatore m dell'aria || tr registrare; (e.g., a student) iscrivere; (e.g., anger) dimostrare; (a letter) raccomandare || intr registrarsi; iscriversi; fare impressione
**reg'istered let'ter** s raccomandata
**reg'istered nurse'** s infermiera diplomata
**registrar** ['rɛdʒɪs ,trar] s registratore m, archivista mf; (of deeds) ricevitore m
**registration** [ ,rɛdʒɪs'treʃən] s registrazione; (e.g., of a student) iscrizione; (of mail) raccomandazione
**registra'tion fee'** s diritto di segreteria
**re·gret** [rɪ'grɛt] s pentimento, rammarico; **regrets** scuse fpl || v (pret & pp **-gretted;** ger **-gretting**) tr rimpiangere; **to regret to** essere spiacente di
**regrettable** [rɪ'grɛtəbəl] adj deplorevole
**regular** ['rɛgjələr] adj regolare; (life) regolato; (coll) vero || s cliente m abituale; (mil) effettivo
**regularity** [ ,rɛgju'lærɪti] s regolarità f
**regu!arize** ['rɛgjələ ,raɪz] tr regolarizzare
**regulate** ['rɛgjə ,let] tr regolare
**regulation** [ ,rɛgjə'leʃən] s regolazione; (rule) regolamento
**rehabilitate** [ ,rihə'bɪlɪ ,tet] tr riabilitare
**rehearsal** [rɪ'hʌrsəl] s prova
**rehearse** [rɪ'hʌrs] tr provare || intr fare le prove
**rehiring** [ri'haɪrɪŋ] s riassunzione
**reign** [ren] s regno || intr regnare
**reimburse** [ ,ri·ɪm'bʌrs] tr rimborsare
**rein** [ren] s redine f; **to give full rein to** dare briglia sciolta a || tr guidare con le redini; frenare
**reincarnation** [ ,ri·ɪnkar'neʃən] s reincarnazione
**reindeer** ['ren ,dɪr] s renna
**reinforce** [ ,ri·ɪn'fors] tr rinforzare; (a wall) armare
**re'inforced con'crete** s cemento armato

**reinforcement** [,ri·in'forsmənt] *s* rinforzo

**reinstate** [,ri·in'stet] *tr* reintegrare

**reiterate** [ri'itə,ret] *tr* reiterare

**reject** ['ridʒɛkt] *s* rigetto, rifiuto; **rejects** scarti *mpl* ‖ [ri'dʒɛkt] *tr* rigettare; (*to refuse*) rifiutare

**rejection** [ri'dʒɛkʃən] *s* rigetto; rifiuto

**rejoice** [ri'dʒɔis] *intr* rallegrarsi

**rejoin** [ri'dʒɔin] *tr* raggiungere; (*to reunite*) riunire; (*to reply*) rispondere

**rejoinder** [ri'dʒɔindər] *s* risposta; (law) controreplica

**rejuvenation** [ri,dʒuvi'neʃən] *s* ringiovanimento

**rekindle** [ri'kindəl] *tr* riaccendere

**relapse** [ri'læps] *s* ricaduta ‖ *intr* ricadere

**relate** [ri'let] *tr* mettere in relazione; (*to tell*) narrare

**relation** [ri'leʃən] *s* relazione; (*account*) resoconto; (*relative*) parente *mf*; (*kinship*) parentela; **in relation to** or **with** in relazione a

**relationship** [ri'leʃən,ʃip] *s* rapporto, relazione; (*kinship*) parentela

**relative** ['rɛlətiv] *adj* relativo ‖ *s* congiunto, parente *mf*

**relativity** [,rɛlə'tiviti] *s* relatività *f*

**relax** [ri'læks] *tr* rilasciare, rilassare ‖ *intr* rilasciarsi, rilassarsi

**relaxation** [,rilæks'eʃən] *s* distensione; (*entertainment*) ricreazione

**relaxa'tion of ten'sion** *s* distensione

**relaxing** [ri'læksiŋ] *adj* rilassante; divertente

**relay** ['rile] or [ri'le] *s* (elec) relè *m*; (rad) ripetitore *m*; (mil, sports) staffetta; (sports) corsa a staffetta ‖ *v* (*pret & pp* **-layed**) *tr* trasmettere, ritrasmettere ‖ [ri'le] *v* (*pret & pp* **-laid**) *tr* rimettere, porre di nuovo

**re'lay race'** *s* corsa a staffetta

**release** [ri'lis] *s* (*e.g., from jail*) liberazione; (*from obligation*) disimpegno; (*for publication*) autorizzazione; (mov) distribuzione; (journ) comunicato; (aer) lancio; (mach) scappamento ‖ *tr* liberare; disimpegnare; autorizzare la pubblicazione di; (mov) distribuire; (*a bomb*) (aer) lanciare; **to release s.o. from a debt** rimettere un debito a qlcu

**relent** [ri'lɛnt] *intr* placarsi

**relentless** [ri'lɛntlis] *adj* implacabile

**relevant** ['rɛlivənt] *adj* pertinente

**reliable** [ri'lai·əbəl] *adj* (*person*) fidato; (*source*) attendibile

**reliance** [ri'lai·əns] *s* fiducia, fede *f*

**relic** ['rɛlik] *s* reliquia

**relief** [ri'lif] *s* sollievo; sussidio; (*prominence; projection*) rilievo; (mil) cambio; **in relief** in rilievo; **on relief** sotto sussidio

**relieve** [ri'liv] *tr* (*e.g., pain*) alleviare; (*e.g., a load*) sgravare; (mil) rilevare

**religion** [ri'lidʒən] *s* religione

**religious** [ri'lidʒəs] *adj* religioso

**relinquish** [ri'liŋkwiʃ] *tr* abbandonare

**relish** ['rɛliʃ] *s* piacere *m*, gusto; sapore *m*, aroma *m*; (culin) condimento ‖ *tr* gustare, apprezzare; dare gusto a

**reluctance** [ri'lʌktəns] *s* riluttanza

**reluctant** [ri'lʌktənt] *adj* riluttante

**re·ly** [ri'lai] *v* (*pret & pp* **-lied**) *intr* fare assegnamento; **to rely on** fidarsi di, fondarsi su

**remain** [ri'men] *s—***remains** resti *mpl;* resti *mpl* mortali ‖ *intr* restare, rimanere

**remainder** [ri'mendər] *s* resto, restante *m*; (*unsold books*) fondi *mpl* di libreria ‖ *tr* vendere come rimanenza

**re·make** [ri'mek] *v* (*pret & pp* **-made** ['med]) *tr* rifare

**remark** [ri'mark] *s* osservazione, rimarco ‖ *tr & intr* osservare; **to remark on** fare osservazioni su

**remarkable** [ri'markəbəl] *adj* notevole

**remar·ry** [ri'mæri] *v* (*pret & pp* **-ried**) *intr* riprendere moglie, risposarsi

**reme·dy** ['rɛmidi] *s* (**-dies**) rimedio ‖ *v* (*pret & pp* **-died**) *tr* rimediare (with *dat*)

**remember** [ri'mɛmbər] *tr* ricordarsi di; (*to send greetings to*) ricordare ‖ *intr* ricordare, ricordarsi

**remembrance** [ri'mɛmbrəns] *s* rimembranza, ricordo

**remind** [ri'maind] *tr* rammentare

**reminder** [ri'maindər] *s* promemoria

**reminisce** [,rɛmi'nis] *intr* ricordare il passato

**reminiscence** [,rɛmi'nisəns] *s* reminiscenza

**remiss** [ri'mis] *adj* negligente

**re·mit** [ri'mit] *v* (*pret & pp* **-mitted;** *ger* **-mitting**) *tr* rimettere; (*to a lower court*) (law) rinviare

**remittance** [ri'mitəns] *s* rimessa

**remnant** ['rɛmnənt] *s* (*remaining quantity*) rimanente *m*; (*of cloth*) scampolo; vestigio; **remnants** (*of merchandise*) rimanenze *fpl*, fondi *mpl* di magazzino

**remod·el** [ri'madəl] *v* (*pret & pp* **-eled** or **-elled;** *ger* **-eling** or **-elling**) *tr* rimodellare; ricostruire

**remonstrance** [ri'manstrəns] *s* rimostranza

**remonstrate** [ri'manstret] *intr* protestare, rimostrare; **to remonstrate with** rimostrare a

**remorse** [ri'mɔrs] *s* rimorso

**remorseful** [ri'mɔrsfəl] *adj* tormentato dal rimorso, pentito

**remote** [ri'mot] *adj* remoto

**remote' control'** *s* telecomando

**removable** [ri'muvəbəl] *adj* amovibile

**removal** [ri'muvəl] *s* rimozione; trasferimento; (*dismissal*) destituzione

**remove** [ri'muv] *tr* rimuovere; (*one's jacket*) togliersi, cavarsi; (*from office*) destituire; eliminare ‖ *intr* trasferirsi; andarsene

**remuneration** [ri,mjunə'reʃən] *s* rimunerazione

**renaissance** [,rɛnə'sans] or [ri'nesəns] *s* rinascimento, rinascita ‖ **Renaissance** *s* Rinascimento

**rend** [rɛnd] *v* (*pret & pp* **rent** [rɛnt]) *tr* (*to tear*) stracciare; (*to split*) fendere, squarciare

**render** ['rɛndər] *tr* (*justice*) rendere;

(*a service*) fare; (*aid*) prestare; (*a bill*) presentare; (*to translate*) tradurre; (*a piece of music*) interpretare; (*e.g., fat*) struggere

**rendez·vous** ['rɑndə,vu] *s* (**-vous** [,vuz]) appuntamento; (*in space*) incontro ‖ *v* (*pret & pp* **-voused** [,vud]; *ger* **-vousing** [,vu·ɪŋ]) *intr* incontrarsi

**rendition** [rɛn'dɪʃən] *s* restituzione, resa; traduzione; interpretazione

**renege** [rɪ'nɪg] *s* rifiuto ‖ *intr* rifiutare; (coll) venire meno

**renew** [rɪ'nju] or [rɪ'nu] *tr* rinnovare ‖ *intr* rinnovarsi

**renewal** [rɪ'nju·əl] or [rɪ'nu·əl] *s* rinnovo, rinnovamento

**renounce** [rɪ'naʊns] *tr* rinunziare (with *dat*); ripudiare

**renovate** ['rɛnə,vet] *tr* rinnovare; (*a building*) restaurare; (*a room*) rimettere a nuovo

**renown** [rɪ'naʊn] *s* rinomanza

**renowned** [rɪ'naʊnd] *adj* rinomato

**rent** [rɛnt] *adj* scisso ‖ *s* fitto, pigione; (*tear*) squarcio ‖ *tr* locare, dare a pigione ‖ *intr* prendere a pigione

**rental** ['rɛntəl] *s* affitto

**renter** ['rɛntər] *s* affittuario, locatario

**renunciation** [rɪ,nʌnsɪ'eʃən] or [rɪ-,nʌnʃɪ'eʃən] *s* rinunzia

**reopen** [ri'opən] *tr* riaprire ‖ *intr* riaprirsi

**reopening** [ri'opənɪŋ] *s* riapertura

**reorganize** [ri'ɔrgə,naɪz] *tr* riorganizzare ‖ *intr* riorganizzarsi

**repair** [rɪ'pɛr] *s* riparazione; **in good repair** in buono stato ‖ *tr* riparare ‖ *intr* riparare, dirigersi

**repair'man'** *s* (**-men'**) aggiustatore *m*

**repaper** [ri'pepər] *tr* ritappezzare

**reparation** [,rɛpə'reʃən] *s* riparazione

**repartee** [,rɛpɑr'ti] *s* replica arguta, rimando

**repast** [rɪ'pæst] or [rɪ'pɑst] *s* pasto

**repatriate** [ri'petrɪ,et] *tr* rimpatriare

**re·pay** [rɪ'pe] *v* (*pret & pp* **-paid** ['ped]) *tr* ripagare

**repayment** [rɪ'pemənt] *s* rimborso; risarcimento, compensazione

**repeal** [rɪ'pil] *s* revoca, abrogazione ‖ *tr* revocare, abrogare

**repeat** [rɪ'pit] *s* ripetizione ‖ *tr* ripetere ‖ *intr* ripetere; (*said of food*) tornare a gola

**re·pel** [rɪ'pɛl] *v* (*pret & pp* **-pelled; ger -pelling**) *tr* respingere, ricacciare; ripugnare (with *dat*)

**repent** [rɪ'pɛnt] *tr* pentirsi di ‖ *intr* pentirsi, ravvedersi

**repentance** [rɪ'pɛntəns] *s* pentimento

**repentant** [rɪ'pɛntənt] *adj* pentito

**repercussion** [,rɪpər'kʌʃən] *s* ripercussione

**reperto·ry** ['rɛpər,tori] *s* (**-ries**) (com) magazzino; (theat) repertorio

**repetition** [,rɛpɪ'tɪʃən] *s* ripetizione

**repine** [rɪ'paɪn] *intr* lamentarsi

**replace** [rɪ'ples] *tr* (*to put back*) rimettere; (*to take the place of*) rimpiazzare

**replaceable** [rɪ'plesəbəl] *adj* sostituibile

**replacement** [rɪ'plesmənt] *s* rimpiazzo, sostituzione; **as a replacement for** al posto di

**replenish** [rɪ'plɛnɪʃ] *tr* rifornire

**replete** [rɪ'plit] *adj* pieno zeppo

**replica** ['rɛplɪkə] *s* replica

**re·ply** [rɪ'plaɪ] *s* (**-plies**) risposta ‖ *v* (*pret & pp* **-plied**) *tr & intr* rispondere

**report** [rɪ'port] *s* rapporto, informazione; voce *f*, rumore *m*; (*of a physician*) responso; (*of a firearm*) detonazione ‖ *tr* riportare, rapportare; denunziare ‖ *intr* fare un rapporto; fare il cronista; presentarsi; **to report sick** (mil) marcare visita

**report' card'** *s* pagella

**reportedly** [rɪ'portɪdli] *adv* secondo la voce comune

**reporter** [rɪ'portər] *s* cronista *mf*, reporter *m*

**reporting** [rɪ'portɪŋ] *s* reportage *m*

**repose** [rɪ'poz] *s* riposo ‖ *tr* posare, riporre ‖ *intr* riposare

**reprehend** [,rɛprɪ'hɛnd] *tr* riprovare, rimproverare

**represent** [,rɛprɪ'zɛnt] *tr* rappresentare

**representation** [,rɛprɪsɛn'teʃən] *s* rappresentazione; protesta; **representations** dichiarazioni *fpl*

**representative** [,rɛprɪ'zɛntətɪv] *adj* rappresentativo ‖ *s* rappresentante *mf*; (pol) deputato

**repress** [rɪ'prɛs] *tr* reprimere

**repression** [rɪ'prɛʃən] *s* repressione

**reprieve** [rɪ'priv] *s* tregua temporanea; sospensione della pena capitale ‖ *tr* accordare una tregua a; sospendere l'esecuzione di

**reprimand** ['rɛprɪ,mænd] or ['rɛprɪ-,mɑnd] *s* sgridata, ramanzina ‖ *tr* sgridare, rimproverare

**reprint** ['ri,prɪnt] *s* ristampa; (*off-print*) estratto ‖ [ri'prɪnt] *tr* ristampare

**reprisal** [rɪ'praɪzəl] *s* rappresaglia

**reproach** [rɪ'protʃ] *s* rimprovero; vituperio ‖ *tr* rimproverare; **to reproach s.o. for s.th** rimproverare qlcu di qlco, rimproverare qlco a qlcu

**reproduce** [,riprə'djus] or [,riprə-'dus] *tr* riprodurre ‖ *intr* riprodursi

**reproduction** [,riprə'dʌkʃən] *s* riproduzione

**reproof** [rɪ'pruf] *s* rimprovero

**reprove** [rɪ'pruv] *tr* rimproverare; disapprovare

**reptile** ['rɛptɪl] *s* rettile *m*

**republic** [rɪ'pʌblɪk] *s* repubblica

**republican** [rɪ'pʌblɪkən] *adj & s* repubblicano

**repudiate** [rɪ'pjudɪ,et] *tr* ripudiare; rinnegare

**repugnant** [rɪ'pʌgnənt] *adj* ripugnante

**repulse** [rɪ'pʌls] *s* rifiuto; sconfitta ‖ *tr* rifiutare; (*e.g., an enemy*) sconfiggere

**repulsive** [rɪ'pʌlsɪv] *adj* ripulsivo

**reputation** [,rɛpjə'teʃən] *s* reputazione

**repute** [rɪ'pjut] *s* reputazione, fama ‖ *tr* reputare

**reputedly** [rɪ'pjutɪdlɪ] *adv* secondo l'opinione corrente

**request** [rɪ'kwɛst] *s* domanda, richiesta; **at the request of** su domanda di ‖ *tr* richiedere

**Requiem** ['rikwɪ ,ɛm] *or* ['rɛkwɪ ,ɛm] *adj* di Requiem ‖ *s* Requiem *m & f;* Messa di Requiem

**require** [rɪ'kwaɪr] *tr* richiedere

**requirement** [rɪ'kwaɪrmənt] *s* requisito; richiesta, fabbisogno

**requisite** ['rɛkwɪzɪt] *adj* requisito, richiesto ‖ *s* requisito

**requisition** [ ,rɛkwɪ'zɪʃən] *s* requisizione

**requital** [rɪ'kwaɪtəl] *s* contraccambio

**requite** [rɪ'kwaɪt] *tr* (*e.g., an injury*) contraccambiare; (*a person*) contraccambiare (with *dat*)

**re·read** [ri'rid] *v* (*pret & pp* **-read** ['rɛd]) *tr* rileggere

**resale** ['ri ,sɛl] *or* [ri'sɛl] *s* rivendita

**rescind** [rɪ'sɪnd] *tr* annullare, cancellare; (law) rescindere

**rescue** ['rɛskju] *s* salvataggio, liberazione; **to go to the rescue of** andare al soccorso di ‖ *tr* salvare, liberare, soccorrere

**research** [rɪ'sʌrtʃ] *or* ['risʌrtʃ] *s* ricerca, indagine *f* ‖ *intr* investigare

**re·sell** [ri'sɛl] *v* (*pret & pp* **-sold** ['sold]) *tr* rivendere

**resemblance** [rɪ'zɛmbləns] *s* somiglianza

**resemble** [rɪ'zɛmbəl] *tr* somigliare (with *dat*), rassomigliare (with *dat*); **to resemble one another** rassomigliarsi

**resent** [rɪ'zɛnt] *tr* (*a remark*) risentirsi per; (*a person*) risentirsi con

**resentful** [rɪ'zɛntfəl] *adj* risentito

**resentment** [rɪ'zɛntmənt] *s* risentimento

**reservation** [ ,rɛzər'veʃən] *s* riserva; (*e.g., for a room*) prenotazione

**reserve** [rɪ'zʌrv] *s* riserva; (*self-restraint*) riserbo, contegno ‖ *tr* riservare; prenotare

**reservist** [rɪ'zʌrvɪst] *s* riservista *m*

**reservoir** ['rɛzər ,vwɑr] *s* serbatoio, cisterna; (*large storage place for supplying community with water*) bacino di riserva; (fig) pozzo

**re·set** [ri'sɛt] *v* (*pret & pp* **-set**; *ger* **-setting**) *tr* rimettere a posto; (*a watch*) regolare; (*a gem*) incastonare di nuovo; (*a machine*) rimontare

**re·ship** [ri'ʃɪp] *v* (*pret & pp* **-shipped**; *ger* **-shipping**) *tr* rispedire; (*on a ship*) reimbarcare ‖ *intr* reimbarcarsi

**reshipment** [ri'ʃɪpmənt] *s* rispedizione; (*on a ship*) reimbarco

**reside** [rɪ'zaɪd] *intr* risiedere

**residence** ['rɛzɪdəns] *s* residenza

**resident** ['rɛzɪdənt] *adj & s* residente *mf*

**residential** [ ,rɛzɪ'dɛnʃəl] *adj* residenziale

**residue** ['rɛzɪ ,dju] *or* ['rɛsɪ ,du] *s* residuo

**resign** [rɪ'zaɪn] *tr* rassegnare, abbandonare; **to be resigned to** rassegnarsi a ‖ *intr* dimettersi, rassegnare le dimissioni

**resignation** [ ,rɛzɪg'neʃən] *s* (*from a job*) dimissione; (*submission*) rassegnazione

**resin** ['rɛzɪn] *s* resina

**resist** [rɪ'zɪst] *tr* resistere (with *dat*) ‖ *intr* resistere

**resistance** [rɪ'zɪstəns] *s* resistenza

**resole** [ri'sol] *tr* risolare

**resolute** ['rɛzə ,lut] *adj* risoluto

**resolution** [ ,rɛzə'luʃən] *s* risoluzione; **good resolutions** buoni propositi

**resolve** [rɪ'zɒlv] *s* risoluzione ‖ *tr* risolvere ‖ *intr* risolversi

**resonance** ['rɛzənəns] *s* risonanza

**resort** [rɪ'zɔrt] *s* (*appeal*) ricorso; (*for vacation*) centro di villeggiatura ‖ *intr* ricorrere

**resound** [rɪ'zaʊnd] *intr* risonare

**resounding** [rɪ'zaʊndɪŋ] *adj* risonante; (*success*) strepitoso

**resource** [rɪ'sɔrs] *or* ['risɔrs] *s* risorsa

**resourceful** [rɪ'sɔrsfəl] *adj* ingegnoso

**respect** [rɪ'spɛkt] *s* rispetto; **respects** rispetti *mpl*, ossequi *mpl;* **with respect to** rispetto a ‖ *tr* rispettare

**respectable** [rɪ'spɛktəbəl] *adj* rispettabile; onesto, per bene

**respectful** [rɪ'spɛktfəl] *adj* rispettoso

**respecting** [rɪ'spɛktɪŋ] *prep* rispetto a

**respective** [rɪ'spɛktɪv] *adj* rispettivo

**respiratory** ['rɛspɪrə ,torɪ] *or* [rɪ'spaɪrə ,torɪ] *adj* respiratorio

**respire** [rɪ'spaɪr] *tr & intr* respirare

**respite** ['rɛspɪt] *s* tregua, requie *f;* (*reprieve*) proroga, dilazione

**resplendent** [rɪ'splɛndənt] *adj* risplendente

**respond** [rɪ'spɒnd] *intr* rispondere

**response** [rɪ'spɒns] *s* risposta

**responsibil·ty** [rɪ ,spɒnsɪ'bɪlɪtɪ] *s* (-ties) responsibilità *f*

**responsible** [rɪ'spɒnsɪbəl] *adj* responsabile; (*job*) di fiducia; **responsible for** responsabile di

**responsive** [rɪ'spɒnsɪv] *adj* rispondente; (*e.g., to affection*) sensibile; (*e.g., motor*) che risponde

**rest** [rɛst] *s* riposo; (*what remains*) resto; (mus) pausa; **at rest** in riposo; tranquillo, in pace; (*dead*) morto; **the rest** il resto, gli altri; **to come to rest** andare a finire; **to lay to rest** sotterrare ‖ *tr* riposare; (*to direct one's eyes*) dirigere; (*faith*) porre ‖ *intr* riposarsi, riposare; appoggiarsi; **to rest assured (that)** esser sicuro (che); **to rest on** aver fiducia in; basarsi su; (*one's laurels*) dormire su

**restaurant** ['rɛstərənt] *or* ['rɛstə ,rɑnt] *s* ristorante *m*

**restful** ['rɛstfəl] *adj* riposante, tranquillo

**rest' home'** *s* casa di riposo

**rest'ing place'** *s* luogo di riposo; (*of a staircase*) pianerottolo; (*of the dead*) ultima dimora

**restitution** [ ,rɛstɪ'tjuʃən] *or* [ ,rɛstɪ'tuʃən] *s* restituzione

**restive** ['restɪv] *adj* irrequieto; *(e.g., horse)* recalcitrante

**restless** ['restlɪs] *adj* irrequieto; *(night)* insonne, in bianco

**restock** [ri'stɑk] *tr* rifornire; *(e.g., with fish)* ripopolare

**restoration** [ˌrestə'reʃən] *s* restaurazione

**restore** [rɪ'stor] *tr* restaurare, ripristinare

**restrain** [rɪ'stren] *tr* ritenere, frenare; limitare

**restraint** [rɪ'strent] *s* restrizione; controllo, ritegno; detenzione

**restrict** [rɪ'strɪkt] *tr* restingere, limitare

**restriction** [rɪ'strɪkʃən] *s* restrizione

**rest' room'** *s* toletta; gabinetto di decenza

**restructuring** [rɪ'strʌktʃərɪŋ] *s* ristrutturazione

**result** [rɪ'zʌlt] *s* risultato || *intr* risultare; **to result in** risolversi in, concludersi con

**resume** [rɪ'zum] *or* [rɪ'zjum] *tr* riprendere || *intr* ricominciare

**résumé** [ˌrezu'me] *or* [ˌrezju'me] *s* sunto, riassunto

**resumption** [rɪ'zʌmpʃən] *s* ripresa

**resurface** [ri'sʌrfɪs] *tr* mettere copertura nuova a || *intr* riemergere

**resurrect** [ˌrezə'rekt] *tr & intr* risuscitare

**resurrection** [ˌrezə'rekʃən] *s* risurrezione

**resuscitate** [rɪ'sʌsɪˌtet] *tr* rendere alla vita

**retail** ['ritel] *adj & adv* al dettaglio, al minuto || *s* dettaglio || *tr* dettagliare, vendere al minuto || *intr* vendere or vendersi al minuto

**retailer** ['ritelər] *s* dettagliante *mf*

**retain** [rɪ'ten] *tr* ritenere; *(a lawyer)* assicurarsi i servizi di

**retaliate** [rɪ'tælɪˌet] *intr* fare rappresaglie; **to retaliate for** ricambiare

**retaliation** [rɪˌtælɪ'eʃən] *s* rappresaglia

**retard** [rɪ'tɑrd] *s* ritardo || *tr* ritardare

**retch** [retʃ] *intr* avere sforzi di vomito

**reticence** ['retɪsəns] *s* riservatezza

**reticent** ['retɪsənt] *adj* riservato, taciturno

**retina** ['retɪnə] *s* retina

**retinue** ['retɪˌnju] *or* ['retɪˌnu] *s* seguito, corteggio

**retire** [rɪ'taɪr] *tr* ritirare; *(an employee)* giubilare, mettere a riposo || *intr* ritirarsi; andare a riposo; *(to go to bed)* andare a letto

**retired** [rɪ'taɪrd] *adj (employee)* in pensione; *(officer)* a riposo

**retirement** [rɪ'taɪrmənt] *s* ritiro; *(of an employee)* pensionamento, quiescenza

**retort** [rɪ'tɔrt] *s* risposta per le rime; controreplica; *(chem)* storta || *tr* rispondere per le rime a || *intr* rispondere per le rime

**retouch** [ri'tʌtʃ] *tr* ritoccare

**retrace** [rɪ'tres] *tr* ripercorrere; **to retrace one's steps** ritornare sui propri passi

**retract** [rɪ'trækt] *tr* ritrattare, disdire || *intr* disdirsi

**re-tread** ['ri ˌtred] *s* pneumatico col copertone ricostruito || [ri'tred] *v (pret & pp* **-treaded***) tr* ricostruire il copertone di || *v (pret* **-trod** ['trɑd]; *pp* **-trod** *or* **-trodden***) tr* ripercorrere || *intr* rimettere il piede

**retreat** [rɪ'trit] *s (seclusion)* ritiro; (mil) ritirata; (eccl) esercizio spirituale; **to beat a retreat** battere in ritirata || *intr* ritirarsi

**retrench** [rɪ'trentʃ] *tr* ridurre, tagliare; (mil) trincerare || *intr* ridurre le spese; (mil) trincerarsi

**retribution** [ˌretrɪ'bjuʃən] *s* ricompensa; (theol) giudizio finale

**retributive** [rɪ'trɪbjətɪv] *adj* retributivo

**retrieve** [rɪ'triv] *tr* riguadagnare, riconquistare; *(to repair)* risarcire; (hunt) riportare || *intr* riportare la presa

**retriever** [rɪ'trivər] *s* cane *m* da presa

**retroactive** [ˌretro'æktɪv] *adj* retroattivo

**retrofiring** [ˌretro'faɪrɪŋ] *s* accensione dei retrorazzi

**retrogress** ['retrəˌgres] *intr* regredire; retrocedere

**retrorocket** [ˌretro'rɑkɪt] *s* retrorazzo

**retrospect** ['retrəˌspekt] *s* esame retrospettivo; **in retrospect** retrospettivamente

**retrospective** [ˌretrə'spektɪv] *adj* retrospettivo

**re-try** [ri'traɪ] *v (pret & pp* **-tried***) tr (a person)* riprocessare; *(a case)* ritentare

**return** [rɪ'tʌrn] *adj* di ritorno; ripetuto || *s* restituzione; ritorno; profitto; *(of income tax)* dichiarazione; risposta; rapporto ufficiale; *(of an election)* responso; (sports) rimando, rimessa; **in return (for)** in cambio (di); **many happy returns of the day!** cento di questi giorni!; **returns** *(of an election)* responso, risultato || *tr* tornare, ritornare restituire; *(a favor)* contraccambiare; *(a profit)* dare; *(thanks; a decision)* rendere; (sports) ribattere || *intr* tornare; rispondere

**return' ad'dress** *s* indirizzo del mittente

**return' bout'** *s* (boxing) rivincita

**return' mail'** *s—by return mail* a volta di corriere, a giro di posta

**return' tick'et** *s* biglietto di ritorno; (Brit) biglietto di andata e ritorno

**reunification** [riˌjunɪfɪ'keʃən] *s* riunione, unificazione

**reunion** [ri'junjən] *s* riunione

**reunite** [ˌriju'naɪt] *tr* riunire || *intr* riunirsi

**rev** [rev] *s* (coll) giro || *v (pret & pp* **revved***; ger* **revving***) tr*—**to rev up** (coll) imballare || *intr* (coll) accelerare, imballarsi

**revamp** [ri'væmp] *tr* rinnovare, rappezzare

**reveal** [rɪ'vil] *tr* rivelare, svelare

**reveille** ['revəli] *s* sveglia, levata

**rev·el** ['revəl] *s* baldoria || *v (pret &*

*pp* **-eled** or **-elled;** *ger* **-eling** or **-elling**) *intr* gozzovigliare; bearsi
**revelation** [ˌrɛvəˈleʃən] *s* rivelazione || **Revelation** *s* (Bib) Apocalisse *f*
**revel·ry** [ˈrɛvəlri] *s* (**-ries**) baldoria
**revenge** [rɪˈvɛndʒ] *s* vendetta || *tr* vendicare
**revengeful** [rɪˈvɛndʒfəl] *adj* vendicativo
**revenue** [ˈrɛvəˌnju] or [ˈrɛvəˌnu] *s* entrata, profitto; (*government income*) entrate *fpl* erariali
**rev'enue cut'ter** *s* motobarca della guardia di finanza
**rev'enue stamp'** *s* marca da bollo
**reverberate** [rɪˈvʌrbəˌret] *intr* riverberarsi; (*said, e.g., of sound*) ripercuotersi, risonare; (*said of an echo*) rimbalzare
**revere** [rɪˈvɪr] *tr* venerare, riverire
**reverence** [ˈrɛvərəns] *s* riverenza || *tr* ossequiare
**reverend** [ˈrɛvərənd] *adj* & *s* reverendo
**reverent** [ˈrɛvərənt] *adj* reverente
**reverie** [ˈrɛvəri] *s* sogno, fantasticheria
**reversal** [rɪˈvʌrsəl] *s* inversione, cambio; (*law*) annullamento
**reverse** [rɪˈvʌrs] *adj* rovescio, contrario; (mach) di retromarcia || *s* contrario; (*rear*) dietro; (*misfortune*) side of a coin not bearing principal design) rovescio; (mach) retromarcia || *tr* invertire; rovesciare; mettere in marcia indietro; **to reverse oneself** cambiare d'opinione; **to reverse the charges** far pagare al destinatario; (telp) far pagare al numero chiamato || *intr* invertirsi
**revert** [rɪˈvʌrt] *intr* ritornare
**review** [rɪˈvju] *s* (*critical article*) recensione; (*magazine*) rivista; (educ) ripasso, ripetizione; (mil) rivista || *tr* recensire; rivedere; (*a lesson*) ripassare; (mil) passare in rassegna
**revile** [rɪˈvaɪl] *tr* insultare, offendere
**revise** [rɪˈvaɪz] *s* revisione; (typ) seconda bozza || *tr* rivedere; correggere
**revision** [rɪˈvɪʒən] *s* revisione
**revisionism** [rɪˈvɪʒəˌnɪzəm] *s* revisionismo
**revival** [rɪˈvaɪvəl] *s* ripresa delle forze; (*restoration*) ripristino; (*of learning*) rinascimento; risveglio religioso; (theat, mov) ripresa
**revive** [rɪˈvaɪv] *tr* ravvivare; (*a custom*) ripristinare; (theat) dare la ripresa di || *intr* ravvivarsi; risorgere
**revoke** [rɪˈvok] *tr* revocare
**revolt** [rɪˈvolt] *s* rivolta || *tr* rivoltare || *intr* rivoltarsi
**revolting** [rɪˈvoltɪŋ] *adj* rivoltante
**revolution** [ˌrɛvəˈluʃən] *s* rivoluzione
**revolutionar·y** [ˌrɛvəˈluʃəˌnɛri] *adj* rivoluzionario || *s* (**-ies**) rivoluzionario
**revolve** [rɪˈvalv] *tr* far rotare; (*in one's mind*) rivolgere || *intr* girare, rotare
**revolver** [rɪˈvalvər] *s* rivoltella
**revolv'ing book'case** *s* scaffale *m* girevole
**revolv'ing cred'it** *s* credito rotativo
**revolv'ing door'** *s* porta girevole

**revolv'ing fund'** *s* fondo rotativo
**revue** [rɪˈvju] *s* rivista
**revulsion** [rɪˈvʌlʃən] *s* ripugnanza, avversione; (med) revulsione
**reward** [rɪˈwɔrd] *s* premio, ricompensa; (*money offered for capture*) taglia; (*for return of articles lost*) mancia competente || *tr* premiare, ricompensare
**rewarding** [rɪˈwɔrdɪŋ] *adj* rimunerativo; gradevole
**re·wind** [rɪˈwaɪnd] *s* (*of a tape*) ribobinazione || *v* (*pret* & *pp* **-wound** [waʊnd]) *tr* ribobinare
**re·write** [rɪˈraɪt] *v* (*pret* **-wrote** [ˈrot]; *pp* **-written** [ˈrɪtən]) *tr* riscrivere; (*news*) rimaneggiare, correggere
**rhapso·dy** [ˈræpsədi] *s* (**-dies**) rapsodia
**rheostat** [ˈriːəˌstæt] *s* reostato
**rhesus** [ˈrisəs] *s* reso
**rhetoric** [ˈretərɪk] *s* retorica
**rhetorical** [rɪˈtɑrɪkəl] or [rɪˈtɔrɪkəl] *adj* retorico
**rheumatic** [ruˈmætɪk] *adj* & *s* reumatico
**rheumatism** [ˈruməˌtɪzəm] *s* reumatismo
**Rhine** [raɪn] *s* Reno
**Rhineland** [ˈraɪnˌlænd] *s* la Renania
**rhine'stone'** *s* gemma artificiale
**rhinoceros** [raɪˈnɑsərəs] *s* rinoceronte *m*
**Rhodes** [rodz] *s* Rodi *f*
**Rhone** [ron] *s* Rodano
**rhubarb** [ˈrubarb] *s* rabarbaro; (*slang*) baruffa
**rhyme** [raɪm] *s* rima; **without rhyme or reason** senza capo né coda || *tr* & *intr* rimare
**rhythm** [ˈrɪðəm] *s* ritmo
**rhythmic(al)** [ˈrɪðmɪk(əl)] *adj* ritmico
**rial·to** [rɪˈælto] *s* (**-tos**) mercato || **the Rialto** il ponte di Rialto; il centro teatrale di New York
**rib** [rɪb] *s* costola; (*cut of meat*) costata; (*of umbrella*) stecca; (*of leaf*) nervatura; (aer, archit) centina; (naut) costa || (*pret* & *pp* **ribbed;** *ger* **ribbing**) *tr* (*slang*) prendersi gioco di
**ribald** [ˈrɪbəld] *adj* volgare, indecente
**ribbon** [ˈrɪbən] *s* nastro; (*decoration*) nastrino; **ribbons** (*shreds*) brandelli *mpl*
**rice** [raɪs] *s* riso
**rich** [rɪtʃ] *adj* ricco; (*food*) nutrito, grasso; (*wine*) generoso; (*voice*) caldo; (*color*) vivo; (*odor*) forte; (coll) divertente; (coll) assurdo; **to strike it rich** trovare la miniera d'oro || **riches** *spl* ricchezze *fpl*; **the rich i** ricchi
**rickets** [ˈrɪkɪts] *s* rachitismo
**rickety** [ˈrɪkɪti] *adj* (*object*) sgangherato; (*person*) vacillante; (*suffering from rickets*) rachitico
**rid** [rɪd] *v* (*pret* & *pp* **rid;** *ger* **ridding**) *tr* liberare, sbarazzare; **to get rid of** liberarsi di, sbarazzarsi di
**riddance** [ˈrɪdəns] *s* liberazione; **good riddance!** che sollievo!
**riddle** [ˈrɪdəl] *s* enigma *m*, indovi-

nello; (*sieve*) crivello ‖ *tr* crivellare; (*to sift*) vagliare; (*s.o.'s reputation*) rovinare; **to riddle with** crivellare di
**ride** [raɪd] *s* scarrozzata; cavalcata; gita ‖ *v* (*pret* **rode** [rod]; *pp* **ridden** [ˈrɪdən]) *tr* cavalcare, montare, montare su; (*e.g., a bus*) andare in; (*the waves*) galleggiare su; attraversare; tiranneggiare; farsi gioco di; **to ride down** travolgere; sorpassare; **to ride out** uscire felicemente da ‖ *intr* cavalcare; fare una passeggiata, fare una gita; (*to float*) galleggiare; **to let ride** lasciar correre; **to ride on** dipendere da
**rider** [ˈraɪdər] *s* cavallerizzo; ciclista *mf;* viaggiatore *m*, passeggero
**ridge** [rɪdʒ] *s* (*of mountains*) crinale *m*, dorsale *f;* (*of roof*) displuvio; (agr) porca
**ridge'pole'** *s* trave maestra, colmo
**ridicule** [ˈrɪdɪˌkjul] *s* ridicolo; **to expose to ridicule** porre in ridicolo ‖ *tr* ridicolizzare
**ridiculous** [rɪˈdɪkjələs] *adj* ridicolo
**rid'ing boot'** *s* stivalone *m* d'equitazione
**rid'ing school'** *s* maneggio
**rife** [raɪf] *adj* comune, prevalente; **rife with** pieno di
**riffraff** [ˈrɪfˌræf] *s* gentaglia
**rifle** [ˈraɪfəl] *s* fucile *m;* cannone rigato ‖ *tr* (*a place*) svaligiare; (*a person*) derubare; (*a gun*) rigare
**rifle' range'** *s* tiro a segno
**rift** [rɪft] *s* crepa, fessura; disaccordo
**rig** [rɪg] *s* attrezzatura, equipaggio; impianto di sondaggio (per il petrolio); (*outfit*) tenuta ‖ *v* (*pret & pp* **rigged;** *ger* **rigging**) *tr* attrezzare, equipaggiare; guarnire; abbigliare in maniera strana
**rigging** [ˈrɪgɪŋ] *s* (naut) padiglione *m;* (*tackle*) (naut) rizza; (coll) vestiti *mpl*
**right** [raɪt] *adj* giusto; corretto; (*mind*) sano; destro, diritto; (geom) retto; (geom) perpendicolare; **right or wrong** a torto o a ragione; **to be all right** star bene di salute; **to be right** aver ragione ‖ *s* diritto; quanto è giusto, (il) giusto; (*in a company*) interessenza; (*right hand*) destra; (*turn*) giro a destra; (boxing) diritto; (tex) dritto; (pol) destra; **by right** in giustizia; **on the right** alla destra; **to be in the right** aver ragione ‖ *adv* direttamente; completamente; immediatamente; proprio, precisamente; correttamente, giustamente; bene; alla destra; (coll) molto; **all right** benissimo ‖ *tr* drizzare; correggere; rimettere a posto ‖ *intr* drizzarsi
**righteous** [ˈraɪtʃəs] *adj* retto; virtuoso
**right' field'** *s* (baseball) campo destro
**rightful** [ˈraɪtfəl] *adj* giusto; legittimo
**right'-hand drive'** *s* guida a destra
**right-handed** [ˈraɪtˈhændɪd] *adj* che usa la destra; destrorso
**right'-hand man'** *s* braccio destro
**rightist** [ˈraɪtɪst] *adj* conservatore ‖ *s* conservatore *m*, membro della destra

**rightly** [ˈraɪtli] *adv* correttamente; giustamente; **rightly or wrongly** a torto o a ragione
**right' mind'** *s*—**in one's right mind** nel pieno possesso delle proprie facoltà, con la testa a posto
**right' of way'** *s* precedenza; (law) servitù *f* di passaggio; (rr) sede *f*
**rights' of man'** *s* diritti *mpl* dell'uomo
**right'-wing'** *adj* della destra
**right-winger** [ˈraɪtˈwɪŋər] *s* membro della destra, conservatore *m*
**rigid** [ˈrɪdʒɪd] *adj* rigido
**rigmarole** [ˈrɪgməˌrol] *s* sproloquio
**rigorous** [ˈrɪgərəs] *adj* rigoroso
**rile** [raɪl] *tr* irritare, esasperare
**rill** [rɪl] *s* rigagnolo
**rim** [rɪm] *s* orlo, bordo; (*of a wheel*) cerchione *m*
**rime** [raɪm] *s* brina; (*in verse*) rima ‖ *tr* brinare; rimare ‖ *intr* rimare
**rind** [raɪnd] *s* (*of animals*) cotenna; (*of fruit or cheese*) scorza
**ring** [rɪŋ] *s* (*for finger*) anello; (*anything round*) cerchio; (*circular course*) pista; (*of people*) crocchio; (*of evildoers*) combriccola; (*of anchor*) anello; (*sound of bell*) squillo; (*loud sound of bell*) scampanellata; (*of small bell; of glassware*) tintinnio; (*act of ringing*) sonata; (telp) chiamata; (fig) suono; (boxing) quadrato; (mach) ghiera; (fig, taur) arena; **to run rings around** essere molto migliore di ‖ *v* (*pret & pp* **ringed**) *tr* accerchiare; mettere un anello a ‖ *intr* formare cerchi ‖ *v* (*pret* **rang** [ræŋ]; *pp* **rung** [rʌŋ]) *tr* sonare; squillare; tintinnare; chiamare al telefono; **to ring up** chiamare al telefono; (*a sale*) battere sul registratore di cassa ‖ *intr* sonare; squillare; tintinnare; chiamare; (*said of one's ears*) fischiare; **to ring for** chiamare col campanello; **to ring off** terminare una conversazione telefonica; **to ring up** chiamare al telefono
**ring-around-a-rosy** [ˈrɪŋəˌraʊndəˈrozi] *s* girotondo
**ringing** [ˈrɪŋɪŋ] *adj* alto, sonoro ‖ *s* accerchiamento; squillo; tintinnio; (*in the ears*) fischio
**ring'lead'er** *s* capobanda *m*
**ringlet** [ˈrɪŋlɪt] *s* anellino
**ring'mas'ter** *s* direttore *m* di circo equestre
**ring'side'** *s* posto vicino al quadrato
**ring'worm'** *s* tigna
**rink** [rɪŋk] *s* pattinatoio
**rinse** [rɪns] *s* risciacquatura ‖ *tr* risciacquare
**riot** [ˈraɪət] *s* sommossa, tumulto; profusione; **to be a riot** (coll) essere divertentissimo; **to run riot** sfrenarsi; (*said of plants*) crescere disordinatamente ‖ *intr* tumultuare; darsi alle gozzoviglie
**rioter** [ˈraɪətər] *s* rivoltoso
**rip** [rɪp] *s* sdrucitura; (*open seam*) scucitura ‖ *v* (*pret & pp* **ripped;** *ger* **ripping**) *tr* sdrucire; (*to open the*

seam of) scucire ‖ intr sdrucirsi; scucirsi; **to rip out with insults** (coll) prorompere in improperi

**ripe** [raɪp] adj maturo; (lips) turgido; (cheese) stagionato; pronto

**ripen** [ˈraɪpən] tr & intr maturare

**ripple** [ˈrɪpəl] s increspatura; (sound) mormorio ‖ tr increspare ‖ intr incresparsi; mormorare

**rise** [raɪz] s (of prices, temperature) aumento; (of a road) salita; (of ground) elevazione; (of a heavenly body) levata; (in rank) ascesa; (of a step) alzata; (of a stream) sorgente f; (of water) crescita; **to get a rise out of** (coll) farsi rispondere per le rime da; **to give rise to** dar origine a ‖ v (pret **rose** [roz]; pp **risen** [ˈrɪzən]) intr (said of the sun) sorgere; rialzarsi; (said of plants) crescere; (said of the wind) alzarsi; (said of a building) ergersi; (to return from the dead) risorgere; (to increase) aumentare; **to rise above** alzarsi al di sopra di; essere al di sopra di; **to rise to** sorgere all'altezza di

**riser** [ˈraɪzər] s (of step) alzata; (upright) montante m; **early riser** persona mattiniera; **late riser** dormiglione m

**risk** [rɪsk] s rischio; **to run or take a risk** correre un rischio ‖ tr rischiare

**risk·y** [ˈrɪski] adj (-ier; -iest) rischioso

**risqué** [rɪsˈke] adj audace, spinto

**rite** [raɪt] s rito; **last rites** riti mpl funebri

**ritual** [ˈrɪtʃuˑəl] adj & s rituale m

**ri·val** [ˈraɪvəl] s rivale mf ‖ v (pret & pp **-valed** or **-valled**; ger **-valing** or **-valling**) tr rivaleggiare con

**rival·ry** [ˈraɪvəlri] s (-ries) rivalità f

**river** [ˈrɪvər] s fiume m; **down the river** a valle; **up the river** a monte

**riv'er ba'sin** s bacino fluviale

**riv'er·bed'** s letto di fiume

**riv'er front'** s riva di fiume

**riv'er·head'** s sorgente f di fiume

**riv'er·side'** adj rivierasco ‖ s riva del fiume

**rivet** [ˈrɪvɪt] s ribattino; (of scissors) perno ‖ tr ribadire; (s.o.'s attention) concentrare

**roach** [rotʃ] s scarafaggio

**road** [rod] adj stradale ‖ s strada; via; (naut) rada; **to be in the road of** ostacolare il cammino a; **to burn up the road** divorare la strada; **to get out of the road** togliersi di mezzo

**roadability** [ˌrodəˈbɪlɪti] s tenuta di strada

**road'bed'** s (of highway) piattaforma; (rr) massicciata, infrastruttura

**road'block'** s (mil) barricata; (fig) impedimento

**road'house'** s taverna su autostrada

**road' la'borer** s cantoniere m

**road' map'** s carta stradale

**road' roll'er** s compressore m stradale, rullo compressore

**road' serv'ice** s servizio di assistenza stradale

**road'side'** s bordo della strada

**road'side inn'** s taverna posta su autostrada

**road' sign'** s indicatore m stradale

**road'stead'** s rada

**road'way'** s carreggiata; strada

**roam** [rom] s vagabondaggio ‖ tr girovagare per ‖ intr girovagare

**roar** [ror] s ruggito, muggito; boato, fragore m ‖ intr muggire; **to roar with laughter** fare una risata

**roast** [rost] s arrosto; torrefazione ‖ tr arrostire; (coffee) tostare, torrefare; (coll) farsi beffe di ‖ intr arrostirsi

**roast' beef'** s rosbif m

**roast'ed pea'nut** s nocciolina americana abbrustolita

**roast' pork'** s arrosto di maiale

**rob** [rab] v (pret & pp **robbed**; ger **robbing**) tr & intr derubare

**robber** [ˈrabər] s ladro, malandrino

**robber·y** [ˈrabəri] s (-ies) furto

**robe** [rob] s (of a woman) vestito; (of a professor) toga; (of a priest) abito talare; (dressing gown) vestaglia; (for lap) coperta da viaggio; **robes** vestiti mpl ‖ tr vestire ‖ intr vestirsi

**robin** [ˈrabɪn] s pettirosso

**robot** [ˈrobat] s robot m

**robust** [roˈbʌst] adj robusto

**rock** [rak] s roccia; (any stone) pietra; (sticking out of water) scoglio; (one that is thrown) sasso; (hill) rocca; (slang) pietra preziosa; **on the rocks** (coll) in rovina; (coll) al verde; (said, e.g., of whiskey) sul ghiaccio ‖ tr far vacillare; dondolare ‖ intr vacillare; dondolare

**rock'-bot'tom** adj (l') ultimo; (il) minimo

**rock' can'dy** s zucchero candito

**rock' crys'tal** s cristallo di rocca

**rocker** [ˈrakər] s (curved piece at bottom of rocking chair) dondolo; sedia a dondolo; (mach) bilanciere m; **off one's rocker** (slang) matto

**rocket** [ˈrakɪt] s razzo ‖ intr partire come un razzo

**rock'et launch'er** [ˈlɔntʃər] or [ˈlɑntʃər] s lanciarazzo

**rock' gar'den** s giardino piantato fra le rocce

**rock'ing chair'** s sedia a dondolo

**rock'ing horse'** s cavallo a dondolo

**rock' salt'** s salgemma m

**rock' wool'** s cotone m or lana minerale

**rock·y** [ˈraki] adj (-ier; -iest) roccioso; traballante; (coll) debole

**rod** [rad] s verga, bacchetta; scettro; punizione; (bar) asta; (for fishing) canna da pesca; (anat, biol) bastoncino; (mach) biella; (surv) biffa; (Bib) razza, tribù f; (slang) pistola; **spare the rod and spoil the child** la madre pietosa fa la piaga cancrenosa

**rodent** [ˈrodənt] adj & s roditore m

**rod'man** s (-men) s aiutante m geometra

**roe** [ro] s capriolo; (of fish) uova fpl

**rogue** [rog] s furfante m; (scamp) picaro

**rogues'' gal'lery** *s* collezione di fotografie di malviventi

**rôle** or **role** [rol] *s* ruolo, parte *f;* **to
play a role** fare la parte

**roll** [rol] *s (of film, paper, etc.*) rotolo,
bobina; (*of fat*) strato; (*roller*) rotella; (*of bread*) panino; ondulazione; (*noise*) rullio, rullo; (*of a
boat*) rollio; (*of thunder*) rombo;
(*list*) ruolo; (*of money*) (slang)
fascio; **to call the roll** fare la chiama
|| *tr* far rotolare; (*one's r's*) arrotare;
(*one's eyes*) stralunare; (*e.g., dough*)
spianare; (*steel*) laminare; (*to wrap*)
arrotolare; (*a drum*) rullare; **to roll
back** (*prices*) ridurre; **to roll out** spianare; srotolare; **to roll up** (*one's
sleeves*) arrotolarsi; accumulare; au-
mentare || *intr* rotolare; rullare; ar-
rotolarsi; raggomitolarsi; **to roll on**
passare; **to roll out** srotolarsi; (*to get
out of bed*) (slang) alzarsi

**roll' call'** *s* chiama, appello

**roller** ['rolər] *s* rotella; (*for hair*) bigodino; rotolo; (*wave*) ondata lunga

**roll'er bear'ing** *s* cuscinetto a rotola-
mento

**roll'er coast'er** *s* montagne russe

**roll'er skate'** *s* pattino a rotelle

**roll'er-skate'** *intr* pattinare coi pattini a
rotelle

**roll'er tow'el** *s* bandinella

**roll'ing mill'** ['rolɪŋ] *s* laminatoio

**roll'ing pin'** *s* matterello

**roll'ing stock'** *s* (rr) materiale *m* rota-
bile

**roll'-top desk'** *s* scrivania a piano scorrevole

**roly-poly** ['roli'poli] *adj* grassoccio

**roman** ['romən] *adj* (typ) romano,
tondo || *s* (typ) carattere romano,
tondo || **Roman** *adj & s* romano

**Ro'man can'dle** *s* candela romana

**Ro'man Cath'olic Church'** *s* Chiesa
Cattolica Apostolica Romana

**romance** [ro'mæns] or ['romæns] *s*
romanzo; sentimentalità *f;* idillio,
intrigo amoroso; (mus) romanza ||
[ro'mæns] *intr* scrivere romanzi;
raccontare romanzi; fare il roman-
tico || **Romance** ['romæns] or [ro-
'mæns] *adj* romanzo, neolatino

**Ro'man Em'pire** *s* Impero Romano

**romanesque** [,romən'esk] *adj* roman-
tico || **Romanesque** *adj & s* romanico

**Ro'man nose'** *s* naso aquilino

**romantic** [ro'mæntɪk] *adj* romantico

**romanticism** [ro'mæntɪ,sɪzəm] *s* romanticismo

**romanticist** [ro'mæntɪsɪst] *s* romantico

**romp** [romp] *intr* ruzzare

**rompers** ['rompərz] *spl* pagliaccetto

**roof** [ruf] or [ruf] *s (of house*) tetto;
(*of heaven*) volta; (*of car*) tetto,
padiglione *m;* **to hit the roof** (slang)
andare fuori dai gangheri; **to raise
the roof** (slang) fare molto chiasso;
(slang) protestare violentemente || *tr*
ricoprire con tetto

**roofer** ['rufər] or ['rufər] *s* conciatetti
*m*

**roof' gar'den** *s* giardino pensile

**rook** [ruk] *s (bird*) cornacchia; (*in
chess*) torre *f* || *tr* truffare

**rookie** ['ruki] *s* novizio; (mil) recluta

**room** [rum] or [rum] *s* stanza, camera; vano, locale *m;* posto, spazio;
opportunità *f;* **to make room** far
luogo || *intr* alloggiare

**room' and board'** *s* vitto e alloggio

**room' clerk'** *s* impiegato d'albergo assegnato alle prenotazioni

**roomer** ['rumər] or ['rumər] *s* inquilino

**room'ing house'** *s* casa con camere
d'affittare

**room'mate'** *s* compagno di stanza

**room·y** ['rumi] or ['rumi] *adj* (**-ier;**
**-iest**) ampio, spazioso

**roost** [rust] *s (perch*) ballatoio; (*house
for chickens*) pollaio; (*place for rest-
ing*) posto di riposo; **to rule the roost**
essere il gallo del pollaio || *intr*
appollaiarsi; andare a dormire

**rooster** ['rustər] *s* gallo

**root** [rut] or [rut] *s* radice *f;* **to get to
the root of** andare al fondo di; **to
take root** metter radici || *tr* inchio-
dare, piantare || *intr* radicare; (*said
of swine*) grufolare; **to root for** fare
il tifo per

**rooter** ['rutər] or ['rutər] *s* tifoso

**rope** [rop] *s* fune *f,* corda; (*of a hangman*) capestro; laccio, lasso; **to know
the ropes** (coll) conoscere la fac-
cenda a fondo, saperla lunga || *tr*
legare con fune; prendere al laccio;
**to rope in** (slang) imbrogliare

**rope'danc'er** or **rope'walk'er** *s* funam-
bolo

**rosa·ry** ['rozəri] *s* (**-ries**) rosario

**rose** [roz] *adj & s* rosa

**rose'bud'** *s* bottoncino di rosa

**rose'bush'** *s* rosaio

**rose'-col'ored** *adj* color di rosa

**rose'-colored glass'es** *spl* occhiali *mpl*
rosa

**rose' gar'den** *s* roseto

**rosemar·y** ['roz,meri] *s* (**-ies**) rosmarino

**rose' of Shar'on** ['ʃerən] *s* altea

**rosette** [ro'zet] *s* rosetta; (archit) rosone *m*

**rose' win'dow** *s* rosone *m*

**rose'wood'** *s* palissandro

**rosin** ['razɪn] *s* colofonia

**roster** ['rostər] *s* ruolino; orario scolastico

**rostrum** ['rostrəm] *s* tribuna

**ros·y** ['rozi] *adj* (**-ier; -iest**) rosa, roseo

**rot** [rat] *s* marcio; (coll) stupidaggine
*f* || *v* (*pret & pp* **rotted;** *ger* **rotting**)
*tr & intr* imputridire

**ro'tary en'gine** ['rotəri] *s* motore rotativo

**ro'tary press'** *s* rotativa

**rotate** ['rotet] or [ro'tet] *tr & intr*
rotare

**rotation** [ro'teʃən] *s* rotazione; **in rotation** in successione, a turno

**rote** [rot] *s* ripetizione macchinale; **by
rote** a memoria

**rot'gut'** *s* (slang) acquavite *f* di infima
qualità

**rotisserie** [ro'tɪsəri] *s* girarrosto a motore

**rotten** ['rɑtən] *adj* marcio, fradicio; corrotto

**rotund** [ro'tʌnd] *adj* (*plump*) rotondetto; (*voice*) profondo; (*speech*) enfatico

**rouge** [ruʒ] *s* belletto, rossetto || *tr* dare il belletto a || *intr* darsi il belletto

**rough** [rʌf] *adj* scabroso; (*sea*) agitato; (*crude*) rozzo, rude; (*road*) accidentato; approssimativo || *tr*—**to rough it** vivere primitivamente; **to rough up** malmenare

**rough'cast'** *s* intonaco; modello disgrossato || *v* (*pret & pp* -**cast**) *tr* (*a wall*) intonacare; disgrossare, dirozzare

**rough' cop'y** *s* brutta copia

**rough-hew** ['rʌf'hju] *tr* digrossare, dirozzare

**roughly** ['rʌfli] *adv* aspramente; rozzamente; approssimativamente

**round** [raund] *adj* rotondo || *s* tondo; (*of applause*) salva; (*of guns*) salva; (*of a single gun*) colpo, tiro; (*of a chair*) piolo; (*of a doctor*) giro; (*of a policeman*) ronda; serie *f*; (*of golf*) partita; (*e.g., of bridge*) mano *f*; cerchio; (*boxing*) ripresa || *adv* intorno; dal principio alla fine || *prep* intorno a; attraverso || *tr* (*to make round*) arrotondare; circondare; (*a corner*) scantonare; **to round off** arrotondare; completare, perfezionare; **to round up** raccogliere; (*cattle*) condurre

**roundabout** ['raundə,baut] *adj* indiretto || *s* giacca attillata; via traversa; giro di parole; (Brit) giostra; (Brit) anello stradale

**round'house'** *s* rimessa per locomotive

**round-shouldered** ['raund'ʃoldərd] *adj* dalle spalle spioventi

**round'-trip tick'et** *s* biglietto d'andata e ritorno

**round'up'** *s* (*of cattle*) riunione; (*of criminals*) retata; (*of facts*) riassunto

**rouse** [rauz] *tr* svegliare; suscitare; (*game*) scovare || *intr* svegliarsi

**rout** [raut] *s* sconfitta, rotta || *tr* sconfiggere, mettere in rotta || *intr* grufolare

**route** [rut] or [raut] *s* via, rotta; itinerario || *tr* istradare

**routine** [ru'tin] *adj* ordinario || *s* trafila, routine *f*

**rove** [rov] *intr* vagabondare, vagare

**rover** ['rovər] *s* vagabondo

**row** [rau] *s* piazzata, scenata; (*clamor*) (coll) baccano; **to raise a row** (coll) fare baccano || [ro] *s* fila; (*of figures*) finca; (*e.g., of trees*) filare *m*; **in a row** in continuazione, di seguito || *tr* vogare || *intr* remare, vogare

**rowboat** ['ro,bot] *s* barca a remi

**row·dy** ['raudi] *adj* (-**dier**; -**diest**) turbolento || *s* (-**dies**) attaccabrighe *mf*

**rower** ['ro·ər] *s* rematore *m*

**rowing** ['ro·ɪŋ] *s* (*action*) voga; (*sport*) canottaggio

**royal** ['rɔɪ·əl] *adj* reale, regio

**royalist** ['rɔɪ·əlɪst] *adj* sostenitore del re || *s* realista *mf*

**royal·ty** ['rɔɪ·əlti] *s* (-**ties**) regalità *f*; membro della famiglia reale; nobiltà *f*; diritto d'autore; diritto d'inventore; percentuale *f* sugli utili

**rub** [rʌb] *s* frizione; difficile *m*; **here's the rub** qui sta il busillis || *v* (*pret & pp* **rubbed**; *ger* **rubbing**) *tr* fregare; **to rub elbows with** stare giunto a gomiti con; **to rub out** cancellare con la gomma; (slang) togliere di mezzo || *intr* sfregare; **to rub off** venir via sfregando; cancellarsi

**rubber** ['rʌbər] *s* gomma, caucciù *m*; gomma da cancellare; (*overshoe*) caloscia; (*in cards*) rubber *m*; (sports) bella

**rub'ber band'** *s* elastico

**rub'ber·neck'** *s* (coll) ficcanaso; (coll) turista curioso || *intr* (coll) allungare il collo

**rub'ber plant'** *s* albero del caucciù

**rub'ber stamp'** *s* timbro di gomma; (coll) persona che approva inconsultamente

**rub'ber-stamp'** *tr* timbrare; (coll) approvare inconsultamente

**rubbish** ['rʌbɪʃ] *s* spazzatura; immondizia; (fig) detrito; (coll) sciocchezza

**rubble** ['rʌbəl] *s* (*broken stone*) pietrisco; (*masonry*) mistura di malta e pietrame; (*broken bits*) calcinacci *mpl*

**rub'down'** *s* fregagione

**rube** [rub] *s* (slang) contadino gonzo

**ru·by** ['rubi] *adj* vermiglio || (-**bies**) *s* rubino

**rudder** ['rʌdər] *s* timone *m*; (aer) timone *m* di direzione

**rud·dy** ['rʌdi] *adj* (-**dier**; -**diest**) rubicondo

**rude** [rud] *adj* rude, sgarbato

**rudiment** ['rudɪmənt] *s* rudimento

**rue** [ru] *tr* lamentare, rimpiangere

**rueful** ['rufəl] *adj* lamentevole; triste

**ruffian** ['rʌfɪ·ən] *s* ribaldo

**ruffle** ['rʌfəl] *s* increspatura; (*of drum*) rullo; (sew) gala, crespa || *tr* increspare; arruffare; irritare; (*a drum*) far rullare; (sew) guarnire di gala or crespa

**rug** [rʌg] *s* tappeto

**rugged** ['rʌgɪd] *adj* aspro, irregolare; rugoso; rozzo; forte; tempestuoso

**ruin** ['ru·ɪn] *s* rovina || *tr* rovinare, mandare in rovina

**rule** [rul] *s* regola; dominazione; (*reign*) regno; (law) ordinanza; (typ) filetto; **as a rule** in generale || *tr* governare; dominare; (*with lines*) rigare; (law) deliberare; **to rule out** escludere || *intr* governare; regnare; **to rule over** governare

**rule' of thumb'** *s* regola basata sull'esperienza; **by rule of thumb** secondo la propria esperienza

**ruler** ['rulər] *s* governante *m*, dominatore *m*; (*for ruling lines*) riga, regolo

**ruling** ['rulɪŋ] *adj* dirigente || *s* (*ruled lines*) rigatura; (law) decisione

**rum** [rʌm] *s* rum *m*; (*any alcoholic drink*) acquavite *f*

**Rumanian** [ru'menɪ·ən] *adj & s* rumeno

**rumble** ['rʌmbəl] *s* rimbombo; (*of the intestines*) gorgoglio; (*slang*) rissa fra ganghe rivali ‖ *intr* rimbombare; gorgogliare

**ruminate** ['rumɪ ˌnet] *tr & intr* ruminare

**rummage** ['rʌmɪdʒ] *tr & intr* rovistare, frugare

**rum'mage sale'** *s* vendita di cianfrusaglie

**rumor** ['rumər] *s* voce *f*, diceria ‖ *tr* vociferare; **it is rumored that** corre voce che

**rump** [rʌmp] *s* anca; posteriore *m*; (*of beef*) quarto posteriore

**rumple** ['rʌmpəl] *s* piega ‖ *tr* spiegazzare, sgualcire ‖ *intr* sgualcirsi

**rumpus** ['rʌmpəs] *s* tumulto; rissa; **to raise a rumpus** fare baccano

**run** [rʌn] *s* corsa; percorso; produzione; (*e.g., in a stocking*) smagliatura; direzione; (*spell*) serie *f*; (*in cards*) scala; (*of goods*) richiesta; (*on a bank*) afflusso; **in the long run** a lungo andare; **on the run** (coll) di corsa; in fuga; **the common run of men** la media della gente; **to give s.o. a run for his money** dare a qlcu del filo da torcere; essere denaro ben speso per qlcu, e.g., **that sweater gave me a run for my money** quello sweater è stato denaro ben speso per me; **to have a long run** tenere il cartellone per lungo tempo; **to have the run of** avere la libertà di andare e venire ‖ *v* (*pret* ran [ræn]; *pp* run; *ger* running) *tr* muovere; (*a horse*) far correre; (*the street*) vivere liberamente in; (*game*) inseguire; trasportare; (*a machine*) far camminare; (*a store*) esercire; (*a candidate*) portare; (*a risk*) correre; (*a blockade*) violare; mettere, ficcare; (*a line*) tirare; **to run down** cacciare; esaminare, trovare; (*a pedestrian*) investire; denigrare, criticare; **to run in** (*a machine*) rodare; (slang) schiaffare in prigione; **to run off** creare di getto; cacciare; (typ) tirare; **to run up** ammassare ‖ *intr* correre; scappare; (*in a race*) arrivare; (*said of a candidate*) portarsi; passare; (*said of knitted material*) smagliarsi; (*said of a liquid*) scorrere; (*said of a color*) sbavare; (*said of fish*) migrare; funzionare; (*to become*) diventare; (*to be worded*) essere del tenore; (com) decorrere; (theat, mov) durare in cartellone; **to run across** imbattersi in; **to run aground** incagliarsi; **to run away** fuggire; (*said of a horse*) prendere la mano; **to run down** (*said of a liquid*) scorrere; (*said of a battery, a watch*) scaricarsi; (*in health*) sciuparsi; **to run for** presentarsi candidato per; **to run in the family** essere una caratteristica familiare; **to run into** imbattersi in; ammontare a; (*to follow*) succedersi a; **to run off the track** (rr) uscire dalle rotaie; **to run out** aver termine; scadere; esaurirsi;

**to run out of** rimanere senza; **to run over** oltrepassare; (*e.g., with a car*) investire; **to run through** trapassare; (*a fortune*) dilapidare; esaminare rapidamente

**run'a·way'** *adj* fuggiasco; (*horse*) che ha preso la mano ‖ *s* fuggiasco; cavallo che ha preso la mano; fuga

**run'-down'** *adj* esausto; negletto, cadente; (*watch, battery*) scarico

**rung** [rʌŋ] *s* (*of chair or ladder*) piolo

**runner** ['rʌnər] *s* corridore *m*; messaggero; fattorino, messo; (*of sleigh*) pattino; (*of ice skate*) lama; (*rug*) guida; (*on a table*) striscia di pizzo; (*in stocking*) smagliatura

**run'ner-up'** *s* (**runners-up**) finalista *mf* secondo

**running** ['rʌnɪŋ] *adj* in corsa; da corsa; (*water*) corrente; (*vine*) rampicante; (*knot*) scorsoio; (*sore*) purulento; (*writing*) corsivo; consecutivo; (*start*) (sports) lanciato ‖ *s* corsa; (*of a business*) esercizio; direzione; funzionamento; **to be in the running** avere possibilità di vittoria

**run'ning board'** *s* (aut) pedana

**run'ning head'** *s* titolo corrente

**run·ny** ['rʌni] *adj* (-nier; -niest) (*liquid*) scorrevole; (*color*) sbavante; **to have a runny nose** avere la goccia al naso

**run'off'** *s* ballottaggio

**run-of-the-mill** ['rʌnəvðə'mɪl] *adj* ordinario, corrente

**run'proof'** *adj* indemagliabile

**runt** [rʌnt] *s* nanerottolo; animale deperito

**run'way'** *s* pista; (*of a stream*) letto; (*for animals*) chiusa; (aut) corsia

**rupture** ['rʌptʃər] *s* rottura; (pathol) ernia ‖ *tr* rompere; causare un'ernia a ‖ *intr* rompersi; soffrire di ernia

**ru'ral free' deliv'ery** ['rurəl] *s* distribuzione postale campestre

**ruse** [ruz] *s* astuzia, stratagemma *m*

**rush** [rʌʃ] *adj* urgente ‖ *s* fretta; slancio, corsa; (*of blood*) ondata; (*rushing of persons to a new mine*) febbre *f*; (bot) giunco; **in a rush** in fretta e furia ‖ *tr* affrettare; portare di fretta; spingere; (coll) fare la corte a; **to rush through** fare di fretta; (*e.g., a bill through Congress*) far approvare di fretta ‖ *intr* lanciarsi; affrettarsi; passare velocemente; **to rush through** (*a book*) leggere velocemente; (*one's work*) fare in fretta; (*a town*) attraversare velocemente

**rush'-bot'tomed chair'** *s* sedia di giunchi

**rush' can'dle** *s* lumicino con lo stoppino fatto di midollo di giunco

**rush' hour'** *s* ora di punta

**russet** ['rʌsɪt] *adj* color cannella

**Russia** ['rʌʃə] *s* la Russia

**Russian** ['rʌʃən] *adj & s* russo

**rust** [rʌst] *s* ruggine *f*; (fig) torpore *m* ‖ *tr* arrugginire ‖ *intr* arrugginirsi

**rustic** ['rʌstɪk] *adj & s* rustico

**rustle** ['rʌsəl] *s* fruscio; (*of leaves*) stormire *m* ‖ *tr* far frusciare; far stormire; (*cattle*) (coll) rubare || *intr* frusciare; stormire; (coll) lavorare di buzzo buono

**rust•y** ['rʌsti] *adj* (**-ier; -iest**) rugginoso; color ruggine; fuori pratica

**rut** [rʌt] *s* (*track*) solco, carrareccia; (*of animals*) fregola; (il) solito tran tran

**ruthless** ['ruθlɪs] *adj* spietato

**rye** [raɪ] *s* segala; whiskey *m* di segala

## S

**S, s** [ɛs] *s* diciannovesima lettera dell'alfabeto inglese

**Sabbath** ['sæbəθ] *s* (*of Jews*) sabato; (*of Christians*) domenica; **to keep the Sabbath** osservare il riposo domenicale

**sabbat'ical year'** [sə'bætɪkəl] *s* anno di congedo; (Bib) anno sabbatico

**saber** ['sebər] *s* sciabola

**sa'ber rat'tling** *s* minacce *fpl* di guerra

**sable** ['sebəl] *adj* nero || *s* zibellino; **sables** vestiti di lutto

**sabotage** ['sæbə‚taʒ] *s* sabotaggio || *tr & intr* sabotare

**saccharin** ['sækərɪn] *s* saccarina

**sachet** ['sæʃe] or [sæ'ʃe] *s* sacchetto profumato (per la biancheria)

**sack** [sæk] *s* sacco; (*of an employee*) (slang) licenziamento; (slang) letto || *tr* insaccare; (*to lay waste*) saccheggiare, mettere a sacco; (slang) licenziare

**sack'cloth'** *s* tela di sacco; (*for penitence*) sacco, cilicio; **in sackcloth and ashes** pentito e contrito

**sacrament** ['sækrəmənt] *s* sacramento

**sacramental** [‚sækrə'mentəl] *adj* sacramentale

**sacred** ['sekrəd] *adj* sacro

**sacrifice** ['sækrɪ‚faɪs] *s* sacrificio; **at a sacrifice** in perdita || *tr* sacrificare; (com) svendere

**sacrilege** ['sækrɪlɪdʒ] *s* sacrilegio

**sacrilegious** [‚sækrɪ'lɪdʒəs] or [‚sækrɪ'lidʒəs] *adj* sacrilego

**sacristan** ['sækrɪstən] *s* sagrestano

**sacris•ty** ['sækrɪsti] *s* (**-ties**) sagrestia

**sad** [sæd] *adj* (**sadder; saddest**) triste; (*bad*) cattivo; (*color*) tetro

**sadden** ['sædən] *tr* rattristare || *intr* rattristarsi

**saddle** ['sædəl] *s* sella || *tr* insellare; **to saddle with** gravare di

**saddle'bag'** *s* fonda

**saddlebow** ['sædəl‚bo] *s* arcione *m* anteriore

**sad'dle•cloth'** *s* gualdrappa

**saddler** ['sædlər] *s* sellaio

**sad'dle•tree'** *s* arcione *m*

**sadist** ['sædɪst] or ['sedɪst] *s* sadico

**sadistic** [sæ'dɪstɪk] or [se'dɪstɪk] *adj* sadico

**sadness** ['sædnɪs] *s* tristezza

**sad' sack'** *s* (coll) marmittone *m*

**safe** [sef] *adj* sicuro; cauto; (*distance*) rispettoso; **safe and sound** sano e salvo || *s* cassaforte *f*

**safe'-con'duct** *s* salvacondotto

**safe'-depos'it box'** *s* cassetta di sicurezza

**safe'guard'** *s* salvaguardia || *tr* salvaguardare

**safe•ty** ['sefti] *adj* di sicurezza || *s* (**-ties**) sicurezza; (*of a gun*) sicura; **to reach safety** mettersi in salvo

**safe'ty belt'** *s* (*of a worker*) imbraca; (aer, aut) cintura di sicurezza; (naut) cintura di salvataggio

**safe'ty glass'** *s* vetro infrangibile

**safe'ty is'land** *s* salvagente *m*

**safe'ty match'** *s* fiammifero svedese

**safe'ty pin'** *s* spillo di sicurezza

**safe'ty ra'zor** *s* rasoio di sicurezza

**safe'ty valve'** *s* valvola di sicurezza

**saffron** ['sæfrən] *s* zafferano

**sag** [sæg] *s* cedimento; depressione; (*of a rope*) allentamento || *v* (*pret & pp* **sagged;** *ger* **sagging**) *intr* curvarsi; cedere, afflosciarsi; allentarsi; (*said of prices*) calare

**sagacious** [sə'geʃəs] *adj* sagace

**sage** [sedʒ] *adj* saggio, savio || *s* saggio, savio; (bot) salvia

**sage'brush'** *s* artemisia

**Sagittarius** [‚sædʒɪ'teri•əs] *s* Sagittario

**sail** [sel] *s* vela; (*of windmill*) ala; gita a vela; **to set sail** far vela; **under full sail** a piena velatura || *tr* veleggiare, navigare; (*a boat*) far navigare || *intr* veleggiare, navigare; far vela; volare; (*said of a vessel*) partire; **to sail into** (coll) attaccare

**sail'boat'** *s* nave *f* a vela, veliero

**sail'cloth'** *s* tela di olona

**sailing** ['selɪŋ] *adj* in partenza || *s* partenza; navigazione; navigazione a vela

**sail'ing ship'** *s* veliero

**sail'mak'er** *s* velaio

**sailor** ['selər] *s* marinaio

**saint** [sent] *adj & s* santo || *tr* santificare, canonizzare

**saint'hood** *s* santità *f*

**saintliness** ['sentlɪnɪs] *s* santità *f*

**Saint' Vi'tus's dance'** ['vaɪtəsəz] *s* (pathol) ballo di San Vito

**sake** [sek] *s* causa, interesse *m*; **for the sake of** per il bene di, per l'amor di

**salaam** [sə'lɑm] *s* salamelecco || *tr* fare salamelecchi a

**salable** ['seləbəl] *adj* vendibile

**salacious** [sə'leʃəs] *adj* salace

**salad** ['sæləd] *s* insalata

**sal'ad bowl'** *s* insalatiera

**sal'ad oil'** *s* olio da tavola

**sala•ry** ['sæləri] *s* (**-ries**) stipendio

**sale** [sel] *s* vendita; (*at reduced prices*) svendita, saldo; **for sale** in vendita; si vende, si vendono

**sales'clerk'** *s* commesso, impiegato

**sales′la′dy** *s* **(-dies)** commessa, impiegata

**sales′man** *s* **(-men)** venditore *m;* commesso; *(traveling)* piazzista *m*

**sales′man·ship′** *s* arte *f* di vendere

**sales′ promo′tion** *s* promozione delle vendite, promotion *f*

**sales′room′** *s* sala di esposizione; sala vendite

**sales′ talk′** *s* discorso da venditore; *(e.g., of a barker)* imbonimento

**sales′ tax′** *s* imposta sulle vendite

**saliva** [sə′laɪvə] *s* saliva

**sallow** [′sælo] *adj* giallastro, olivastro

**sal·ly** [′sæli] *s* **(-lies)** escursione, gita; *(outburst)* esplosione; *(witty remark)* uscita; (mil) sortita ‖ *v pret & pp* **-lied** *intr* fare una sortita; **to sally forth** balzar fuori

**salmon** [′sæmən] *s* salmone *m*

**salon** [sæ′lɑn] *s* salone *m*

**saloon** [sə′lun] *s* taverna; *(on a passenger vessel)* salone *m*

**saloon′ keep′er** *s* taverniere *m*

**salt** [sɔlt] *s* sale *m;* **to be worth one's salt** valere il pane che si mangia ‖ *tr* salare; *(cattle)* dare sale a; **to salt away** (coll) metter via, conservare

**salt′ bed′** *s* salina

**salt′cel′lar** *s* saliera

**saltine** [sɔl′tin] *s* galletta salata

**saltish** [′sɔltɪʃ] *adj* salmastro

**salt′pe′ter** *s* *(potassium nitrate)* salnitro; *(sodium nitrate)* nitro del Cile

**salt′ shak′er** *s* saliera

**salt·y** [′sɔlti] *adj* **(-ier; -iest)** salato

**salubrious** [sə′lubrɪ·əs] *adj* salubre

**salutation** [ ,sæljə′te/ən] *s* saluto

**salute** [sə′lut] *s* saluto ‖ *tr* salutare

**salvage** [′sælvɪdʒ] *s* ricupero ‖ *tr* ricuperare

**salvation** [sæl′veʃən] *s* salvezza

**Salva′tion Ar′my** *s* Esercito della Salvezza

**salve** [sæv] or [sɑv] *s* unguento ‖ *tr* lenire, alleviare

**sal·vo** [′sælvo] *s* **(-vos** or **-voes)** salva

**Samaritan** [sə′mærɪtən] *adj & s* samaritano

**same** [sem] *adj & pron indef* medesimo, stesso; **it's all the same to me** a me fa lo stesso; **just the same** lo stesso, ugualmente; ciò nonostante; **same . . . as** lo stesso . . . che

**sameness** [′semnɪs] *s* uniformità *f;* monotonia

**sample** [′sæmpəl] *s* campione *m,* saggio ‖ *tr (to take a sample of)* campionare; *(to taste)* assaggiare; provare

**sam′ple cop′y** *s* esemplare *m* di campione

**sancti·fy** [′sæŋktɪ ,faɪ] *v (pret & pp* **-fied)** *tr* santificare

**sanctimonious** [ ,sæŋktɪ′moni·əs] *adj* che affetta devozione ipocrita

**sanction** [′sæŋk/ən] *s* sanzione ‖ *tr* sanzionare

**sanctuar·y** [′sæŋkt/ʊ ,ɛri] *s* **(-ies)** santuario; **to take sanctuary** prendere asilo, rifugiarsi

**sand** [sænd] *s* sabbia ‖ *tr* insabbiare;

*(to polish)* smerigliare; cospergere di sabbia

**sandal** [′sændəl] *s* sandalo

**san′dal·wood′** *s* sandalo

**sand′bag′** *s* sacchetto a terra

**sand′bank′** *s* banco di sabbia

**sand′ bar′** *s* cordone *m* litorale, banco di sabbia

**sand′blast′** *s* sabbiatura ‖ *tr* pulire con sabbiatura, sabbiare

**sand′box′** *s* cassone *m* pieno di sabbia; (rr) sabbiera

**sand′glass′** *s* orologio a polvere or a sabbia

**sand′pa′per** *s* carta vetrata ‖ *tr* pulire con carta vetrata

**sand′stone′** *s* arenaria

**sandwich** [′sændwɪ/] *s* panino imbottito, tramezzino ‖ *tr* inserire

**sand′wich man′** *s* tramezzino, uomo sandwich

**sand·y** [′sændi] *adj* **(-ier; -iest)** sabbioso; *(hair)* biondo rossiccio

**sane** [sen] *adj* sensato

**sanguinary** [′sæŋgwɪn ,ɛri] *adj* sanguinario

**sanguine** [′sæŋgwɪn] *adj* fiducioso; *(complexion)* sanguigno

**sanitary** [′sænɪ ,tɛri] *adj* sanitario

**san′itary nap′kin** *s* pannolino igienico

**sanitation** [ ,sænɪ′te/ən] *s* sanità *f*

**sanity** [′sænɪti] *s* sanità *f* di mente

**Santa Claus** [′sæntə ,klɔz] *s* Babbo Natale

**sap** [sæp] *s* linfa, succhio; (mil) trincea; (coll) scemo ‖ *v (pret & pp* **sapped;** *ger* **sapping)** *tr* scavare; insidiare, minare; *(to weaken)* indebolire

**sapling** [′sæplɪŋ] *s* alberello; *(youth)* giovanetto

**sapphire** [′sæfaɪr] *s* zaffiro

**Saracen** [′særesən] *adj & s* saraceno

**sarcasm** [′sɑrkæzəm] *s* sarcasmo

**sarcastic** [sɑr′kæstɪk] *adj* sarcastico

**sardine** [sɑr′din] *s* sardina; **packed in like sardines** pigiati come le acciughe

**Sardinia** [sɑr′dɪnɪ·ə] *s* la Sardegna

**Sardinian** [sɑr′dɪnɪ·ən] *adj & s* sardo

**sarsaparilla** [ ,sɑrsəpə′rɪlə] *s* salsapariglia

**sash** [sæʃ] *s* sciarpa; *(around one's waist)* fusciacca; *(of window)* telaio

**sash′ win′dow** *s* finestra a ghigliottina

**sas·sy** [′sæsi] *adj* **(-ier; -iest)** (coll) impertinente; *(pert)* (coll) vivace

**satchel** [′sæt/əl] *s* sacca; *(of schoolboy)* cartella

**sateen** [sæ′tin] *s* satin *m*

**satellite** [′sætə ,laɪt] *s* satellite *m*

**satiate** [′se/ɪ ,et] *tr* saziare

**satin** [′sætən] *s* raso

**satire** [′sætaɪr] *s* satira

**satiric(al)** [sə′tɪrɪk(əl)] *adj* satirico

**satirist** [′sætɪrɪst] *s* satirico

**satirize** [′sætɪ ,raɪz] *tr* satireggiare

**satisfaction** [ ,sætɪs′fæk/ən] *s* soddisfazione

**satisfactory** [ ,sætɪs′fæktəri] *adj* soddisfacente

**satis·fy** [′sætɪs ,faɪ] *v (pret & pp* **-fied)** *tr & intr* soddisfare

**saturate** [′sæt/ə ,ret] *tr* saturare

**Saturday** ['sætərdi] *s* sabato
**Saturn** ['sætərn] *s* (astr) Saturno
**sauce** [sɔs] *s* salsa; (*of fruit*) conserva; (*of chocolate*) crema; (coll) insolenza, impertinenza ‖ *tr* condire; rendere piccante ‖ [sɔs] or [sæs] *tr* (coll) rispondere con impertinenza a
**sauce'pan'** *s* casseruola
**saucer** ['sɔsər] *s* piattino
**sau·cy** ['sɔsi] *adj* (-cier; -ciest) impertinente; (*pert*) vivace
**sauerkraut** ['saʊr‚kraʊt] *s* sarcrauti *mpl*, crauti *mpl*
**saunter** ['sɔntər] *s* giro, bighellonata ‖ *intr* girandolare, bighellonare
**sausage** ['sɔsɪdʒ] *s* salsiccia
**savage** ['sævɪdʒ] *adj* & *s* selvaggio
**savant** ['sævənt] *s* erudito
**save** [sev] *prep* tranne, salvo ‖ *tr* salvare; (*money*) risparmiare; (*to set apart*) serbare; **to save face** salvare le apparenze ‖ *intr* fare economia
**saving** ['sevɪŋ] *adj* economico; che redime ‖ **savings** *spl* risparmi *mpl*, economie *fpl* ‖ **saving** *prep* eccetto, salvo
**sav'ings account'** *s* conto di risparmio
**sav'ings and loan' associa'tion** *s* cassa di risparmio che concede mutui
**sav'ings bank'** *s* cassa di risparmio
**savior** ['sevjər] *s* salvatore *m*
**Saviour** ['sevjər] *s* Salvatore *m*
**savor** ['sevər] *s* sapore *m* ‖ *tr* assaporare; (*to flavor*) saporire ‖ *intr* odorare; **to savor of** sapere di; odorare di
**savor·y** ['sevəri] *adj* (-ier; -iest) saporoso; piccante; delizioso ‖ *s* (-ies) (bot) santoreggia
**saw** [sɔ] *s* (*tool*) sega; detto, proverbio ‖ *tr* segare
**saw'buck'** *s* cavalletto
**saw'dust'** *s* segatura
**saw'horse'** *s* cavalletto
**saw'mill'** *s* segheria
**Saxon** ['sæksən] *adj* & *s* sassone *m*
**saxophone** ['sæksə‚fon] *s* sassofono
**say** [se] *s* dire *m*; **to have no say** non aver voce in capitolo; **to have one's say** esprimere la propria opinione; **to have the say** avere l'ultima parola ‖ *v* (*pret* & *pp* **said** [sed]) *tr* dire; **I should say so!** certamente!; **it is said** si dice; **no sooner said than done** detto fatto; **that is to say** vale a dire; **to go without saying** essere ovvio
**saying** ['se·ɪŋ] *s* detto, proverbio
**scab** [skæb] *s* crosta; (*strikebreaker*) crumiro
**scabbard** ['skæbərd] *s* guaina, fodero
**scab·by** ['skæbi] *adj* (-bier; -biest) crostoso; (*animal*) rognoso; (slang) vile
**scabrous** ['skæbrəs] *adj* scabroso
**scads** [skædz] *spl* (slang) un mucchio
**scaffold** ['skæfəld] *s* impalcatura; (*to execute a criminal*) patibolo
**scaffolding** ['skæfəldɪŋ] *s* incastellatura, ponteggio
**scald** [skɔld] *tr* scottare; (*e.g., milk*) cuocere al disotto del punto d'ebollizione
**scale** [skel] *s* (*e.g., of map*) scala;

piatto della bilancia; (*of fish*) squama; **on a large scale** in grande scala; **scales** bilancia; **to tip the scales** far inclinare la bilancia ‖ *tr* squamare; (*to incrust*) incrostare; (*to weigh*) pesare; scalare; graduare; ridurre a scala ‖ *intr* squamarsi; scrostarsi
**scallion** ['skæljən] *s* scalogno
**scallop** ['skɑləp] or ['skæləp] *s* (*for cooking*) conchiglia; (*mollusk*) pettine *m*; (*slice of meat*) scaloppina; (*on edge of cloth*) dentello, smerlo ‖ *tr* (*fish*) cuocere in conchiglia; dentellare, smerlare
**scalp** [skælp] *s* cuoio capelluto ‖ *tr* scotennare; (*tickets*) fare il bagarinaggio di
**scalpel** ['skælpəl] *s* scalpello
**scalper** ['skælpər] *s* bagarino
**scal·y** ['skeli] *adj* (-ier; -iest) squamoso; scrostato
**scamp** [skæmp] *s* cattivo soggetto, briccone *m*
**scamper** ['skæmpər] *intr* sgambettare; **to scamper away** darsela a gambe
**scan** [skæn] *v* (*pret* & *pp* **scanned;** *ger* **scanning**) *tr* scrutare; dare un'occhiata a; (*verse*) scandire; (telv) analizzare, scandire, esplorare
**scandal** ['skændəl] *s* scandalo
**scandalize** ['skændə‚laɪz] *tr* scandalizzare
**scandalous** ['skændələs] *adj* scandaloso
**Scandinavian** [‚skændɪ'nevɪ·ən] *adj* & *s* scandinavo
**scanning** ['skænɪŋ] *s* (telv) esplorazione
**scan'ning line'** *s* (telv) riga di analisi
**scant** [skænt] *adj* scarso; corto ‖ *tr* diminuire; lesinare
**scant·y** ['skænti] *adj* (-ier; -iest) appena sufficiente; povero, magro; (*clothing*) succinto
**scapegoat** ['skep‚got] *s* capro espiatorio
**scar** [skɑr] *s* cicatrice *f*; (fig) sfregio ‖ *v* (*pret* & *pp* **scarred;** *ger* **scarring**) *tr* segnare, marcare; sfregiare ‖ *intr* cicatrizzarsi
**scarce** [skers] *adj* scarso, raro; **to make oneself scarce** (coll) non farsi vedere
**scarcely** ['skersli] *adv* appena; a mala pena; non . . . affatto; **scarcely ever** raramente; non . . . affatto
**scarci·ty** ['skersɪti] *s* (-ties) scarsità *f*, scarsezza; carestia
**scare** [sker] *s* spavento ‖ *tr* spaventare, impaurire; **to scare away** fare scappare per lo spavento; **to scare up** (*money*) (coll) metter insieme
**scare'crow'** *s* spaventapasseri *m*
**scarf** [skɑrf] *s* (**scarfs** or **scarves** [skɑrvz]) sciarpa; cravattone *m*; (*cover for table*) centro, striscia
**scarf'pin'** *s* spilla da cravatta
**scarlet** ['skɑrlɪt] *adj* scarlatto
**scar'let fe'ver** *s* scarlattina
**scar·y** ['skeri] *adj* (-ier; -iest) (*timid*) (coll) fifone; (*causing fright*) (coll) spaventevole

**scathing** ['skeðɪŋ] *adj* severo, bruciante

**scatter** ['skætər] *tr* disperdere, sparpagliare || *intr* disperdersi, sparpagliarsi

**scatterbrained** ['skætər‚brend] *adj* scervellato, stordito

**scenari•o** [sɪ'nɛrɪ‚o] or [sɪ'nɑrɪ‚o] *s* (-os) scenario

**scenarist** [sɪ'nɛrɪst] or [sɪ'nɑrɪst] *s* scenarista *mf*, sceneggiatore *m*

**scene** [sin] *s* (*view*) paesaggio; (*place*) scena; (*theat*) scena, quadro; **behind the scenes** dietro le quinte; **to make a scene** fare una scenata

**scener•y** ['sinəri] *s* (-ies) paesaggio; (*theat*) scenario

**scenic** ['sinɪk] or ['sɛnɪk] *adj* pittoresco; (*pertaining to the stage*) scenico

**scent** [sɛnt] *s* odore *m;* profumo; (*sense of smell*) fiuto, odorato; (*trail*) traccia, pista || *tr* profumare; (*to detect*) fiutare, annusare

**scepter** ['sɛptər] *s* scettro

**sceptic** ['skɛptɪk] *adj & s* scettico

**sceptical** ['skɛptɪkəl] *adj* scettico

**scepticism** ['skɛptɪ‚sɪzəm] *s* scetticismo

**schedule** ['skɛdjul] *s* lista; programma *m;* (*of trains, planes, etc.*) orario || *tr* programmare; mettere in orario

**scheme** [skim] *s* schema *m;* piano, progetto; (*plot*) trama || *tr* progettare; tramare

**schemer** ['skimər] *s* progettista *mf;* (*underhanded*) manipolatore *m*, concertatore *m*

**scheming** ['skimɪŋ] *adj* intrigante, scaltro

**schism** ['sɪzəm] *s* scisma *m*

**schist** [ʃɪst] *s* scisto

**scholar** ['skɑlər] *s* (*pupil*) alunno; detentore *m* di una borsa di studio; (*learned person*) dotto, studioso

**scholarly** ['skɑlərli] *adj* erudito, studioso

**scholarship** ['skɑlər‚ʃɪp] *s* erudizione; (*money*) borsa di studio

**scholasticism** [skə'læstɪ‚sɪzəm] *s* scolastica

**school** [skul] *s* scuola; (*of a university*) facoltà *f;* (*of fish*) banco || *tr* istruire, insegnare

**school' age'** *s* età scolastica

**school'bag'** *s* cartella

**school' board'** *s* comitato scolastico

**school'boy'** *s* alunno, scolaro

**school' bus'** *s* scuolabus *m*

**school' day'** *s* giorno di scuola; durata della giornata scolastica

**school'girl'** *s* alunna, scolara

**school'house'** *s* scuola, edificio scolastico

**schooling** ['skulɪŋ] *s* istruzione

**school'mas'ter** *s* maestro di scuola; direttore scolastico

**school'mate'** *s* compagno di scuola, condiscepolo

**school'room'** *s* aula scolastica

**school'teach'er** *s* maestro

**school' year'** *s* anno scolastico

**schooner** ['skunər] *s* goletta

**sciatica** [saɪ'ætɪkə] *s* (pathol) sciatica

**science** ['saɪ‚əns] *s* scienza

**sci'ence fic'tion** *s* fantascienza

**sci'ence-fic'tion** *adj* fantascientifico

**scientific** [‚saɪ‚ən'tɪfɪk] *adj* scientifico

**scientist** ['saɪ‚əntɪst] *s* scienziato

**scimitar** ['sɪmɪtər] *s* scimitarra

**scintillate** ['sɪntɪ‚let] *intr* scintillare

**scion** ['saɪ‚ən] *s* rampollo, discendente *m*

**scissors** ['sɪzərz] *ssg* or *spl* forbici *fpl*

**scoff** [skɔf] or [skɑf] *s* dileggio, beffa || *intr* burlarsi; **to scoff at** burlarsi di, dileggiare

**scold** [skold] *s* megera || *tr & intr* sgridare, rimproverare

**scoop** [skup] *s* (*ladlelike utensil*) paletta; (*kitchen utensil*) cucchiaio, cucchiaione *m;* cucchiaiata; palettata; (*of dredge*) benna; (*hollow*) buco; (*naut*) gottazza; (*journ*) primizia, esclusiva; (*coll*) colpo || *tr* vuotare a cucchiaiate; (*journ*) battere; (*naut*) gottare; **to scoop out** (*e.g., sand*) scavare; (*soup*) scodellare

**scoot** [skut] *s* (*coll*) corsa || *intr* (*coll*) correre precipitosamente

**scooter** ['skutər] *s* monopattino

**scope** [skop] *s* ampiezza; lunghezza; **to give full scope to** dare piena libertà d'azione a

**scorch** [skɔrtʃ] *s* scottatura || *tr* bruciacchiare; bruciare, inaridire; (fig) ferire || *intr* bruciarsi

**scorching** ['skɔrtʃɪŋ] *adj* bruciante

**score** [skor] *s* (*in a game*) punteggio; (*in an examination*) nota; linea, segno, marca; (*twenty*) ventina; (*mus*) partitura; **scores** un mucchio; **to keep score** segnare il punteggio; **to settle a score** (fig) saldare un conto || *tr* raggiungere il punteggio di, fare; marcare; guadagnare; (*to censure*) sgridare, rimproverare; (*mus*) orchestrare

**score'board'** *s* quadro del punteggio

**score'keep'er** *s* segnapunti *m*

**scorn** [skɔrn] *s* disdegno, disprezzo || *tr & intr* disdegnare, disprezzare

**scornful** ['skɔrnfəl] *adj* disdegnoso

**Scorpio** ['skɔrpi‚o] *s* Scorpione *m*

**scorpion** ['skɔrpi‚ən] *s* scorpione *m*

**Scot** [skɑt] *s* scozzese *mf*

**Scotch** [skɑtʃ] *adj* scozzese || *s* scozzese *m;* whisky *m* scozzese; **the Scotch** gli scozzesi

**Scotch'man** *s* (-men) scozzese *m*

**Scotch' pine'** *s* pino silvestre

**Scotch' tape'** *s* (trademark) nastro autoadesivo Scotch

**scot'-free'** *adj* impune; **to get off scot-free** farla franca

**Scotland** ['skɑtlənd] *s* la Scozia

**Scottish** ['skɑtɪʃ] *adj* scozzese || *s* scozzese *mf;* **the Scottish** gli scozzesi

**scoundrel** ['skaundrəl] *s* birbante *m*, farabutto, manigoldo

**scour** [skaur] *tr* sgrassare fregando, pulire fregando; (*the countryside*) battere

**scourge** [skʌrdʒ] *s* sferza; (fig) flagello || *tr* sferzare

**scout** [skaʊt] s esplorazione; giovane esploratore m; giovane esploratrice f; (mil) ricognitore m; (nav) esploratore m; (slang) tipo || tr esplorare, riconoscere; cercar di trovare; disdegnare

**scouting** ['skaʊtɪŋ] s scoutismo

**scowl** [skaʊl] s cipiglio || intr aggrottare le ciglia; guardare torvamente

**scram** [skræm] v (pret & pp **scrammed;** ger **scramming**) intr (coll) tagliare la corda; **scram!** (coll) vattene!, (coll) escimi di tra i piedi!

**scramble** ['skræmbəl] s ruffa, gara || tr (to grab up) arraffare; confondere, mescolare; (eggs) strapazzare || intr arrampicarsi; (to struggle) azzuffarsi

**scram'bled eggs'** spl uova strapazzate

**scrap** [skræp] s pezzetto, frammento; ritaglio, rottame m; (coll) baruffa; **scraps** avanzi mpl; || v (pret & pp **scrapped;** ger **scrapping**) tr scartare || intr (coll) fare baruffa

**scrap'book'** s album m di ritagli (di giornale o fotografie)

**scrape** [skrep] s impiccio, imbroglio; baruffa || tr raschiare, graffiare; **to scrape together** racimolare || intr raschiare; **to scrape along** vivacchiare; **to scrape through** passare per il rotto della cuffia

**scraper** ['skrepər] s raschietto

**scrap' i'ron** s rottami mpl di ferro

**scrap' pa'per** s carta straccia; carta da appunti

**scratch** [skrætʃ] s graffio, scalfittura; scarabocchio; (billiards) punto perduto; (sports) linea di partenza; **from scratch** dal bel principio; dal niente; **up to scratch** soddisfacente || tr graffiare, grattare; (e.g., a horse) cancellare || intr graffiare; (said of a chicken) raspare; (said of a pen) grattare

**scratch' pad'** s quaderno per appunti

**scratch' pa'per** s carta da appunti

**scrawl** [skrɔl] s scarabocchio || tr & intr scarabocchiare

**scraw·ny** ['skrɔni] adj (-nier; -niest) ossuto, scarno

**scream** [skrim] s grido, strillo; cosa divertentissima; persona divertentissima || intr gridare, strillare

**screech** [skritʃ] s stridio || intr stridere

**screech' owl'** s gufo; (barn owl) barbagianni m

**screen** [skrin] s (movable partition) paravento; (in front of fire) parafuoco; rete metallica; (sieve) vaglio; (mov; phys) schermo; (telv) teleschermo || tr schermare; riparare, proteggere; (to sieve) vagliare; (a film) proiettare; (to adapt) (mov) sceneggiare

**screen' grid'** s (rad, telv) griglia schermo

**screen' test'** s provino

**screw** [skru] s vite f; giro di vite; (of a boat) elica; **to have a screw loose** (slang) avere una rotella fuori di posto; **to put the screws on** far pressione su || tr avvitare; (to twist)

torcere; **to screw up** (slang) rovinare; **to screw up one's courage** prendere il coraggio a quattro mani || intr avvitarsi

**screw'ball'** s (slang) pazzoide m, svitato

**screw'driv'er** s cacciavite m

**screw' eye'** s occhiello a vite

**screw' jack'** s martinetto a vite

**screw' propel'ler** s elica

**screw·y** ['skru·i] adj (-ier; -iest) (slang) pazzo; (slang) fuori di posto, strano

**scribble** ['skrɪbəl] s scarabocchio || tr & intr scribacchiare

**scribe** [skraɪb] s (Jewish scholar) scriba m; copista mf || tr tracciare, incidere

**scrimmage** ['skrɪmɪdʒ] s ruffa; (football) azione

**scrimp** [skrɪmp] tr & intr lesinare

**script** [skrɪpt] s scrittura, scrittura a mano; manoscritto; testo; (e.g., of a play) copione m; (typ) carattere m inglese

**scriptural** ['skrɪptʃərəl] adj scritturale, biblico

**scripture** ['skrɪptʃər] s scrittura || **Scripture** s Scrittura

**script'writ'er** s soggettista mf

**scrofula** ['skrɑfjələ] s scrofola

**scroll** [skrol] s rotolo di carta, rotolo di pergamena; (of violin) riccio; (archit) voluta, cartoccio

**scroll'work'** s ornamentazione a voluta

**scro·tum** ['skrotəm] s (-ta [tə] or -tums) scroto

**scrub** [skrʌb] s boscaglia; alberelli mpl; animale bastardo; persona di poco conto; (act of scrubbing) fregata; (sports) giocatore m di riserva || v (pret & pp **scrubbed;** ger **scrubbing**) tr pulire, fregare

**scrub' oak'** s rovere basso

**scrub'wom'an** s (-wom'en) lavatrice f, donna a giornata

**scruff** [skrʌf] s nuca, collottola

**scruple** ['skrupəl] s scrupolo

**scrupulous** ['skrupjələs] adj scrupoloso

**scrutinize** ['skrutɪ͵naɪz] tr scrutare, disaminare

**scruti·ny** ['skrutɪni] s (-nies) attento esame, disamina

**scuff** [skʌf] s graffio, logorio || tr logorare, graffiare

**scuffle** ['skʌfəl] s zuffa, rissa || intr azzuffarsi, colluttare

**scull** [skʌl] s (oar) remo a bratto; (boat) canotto || tr spingere a bratto || intr vogare a bratto

**scul·ler·y** ['skʌləri] s (-ies) retrocucina

**scul'lery maid'** s sguattera

**scullion** ['skʌljən] s sguattero

**sculptor** ['skʌlptər] s scultore m

**sculptress** ['skʌlptrɪs] s scultrice f

**sculpture** ['skʌlptʃər] s scultura || tr & intr scolpire

**scum** [skʌm] s schiuma; (slag) scoria; (rabble) feccia, gentaglia || v (pret & pp **scummed;** ger **scumming**) tr & intr schiumare

**scum·my** ['skʌmi] *adj* (**-mier; -miest**) spumoso; (coll) vile, schifoso

**scurf** [skʌrf] *s* (*shed by the skin*) squama; incrostazione

**scurrilous** ['skʌrɪləs] *adj* scurrile

**scur·ry** ['skʌri] *v* (*pret & pp* **-ried**) *intr* affrettarsi; **to scurry around** dimenarsi

**scur·vy** ['skʌrvi] *adj* (**-vier; -viest**) spregevole, meschino ‖ *s* scorbuto

**scuttle** ['skʌtəl] *s* (*for coal*) secchio; (*trap door*) botola; corsa, fuga; (*naut*) boccaporto ‖ *tr* aprire una falla in, affondare ‖ *intr* affrettarsi, darsi alla corsa

**scut'tle·butt'** *s* (naut) barilozzo dell'acqua; (coll) rumore *m*, diceria

**scuttling** ['skʌtlɪŋ] *s* autoaffondamento

**Scylla** ['sɪlə] *s* Scilla; **between Scylla and Charybdis** fra Scilla e Cariddi

**scythe** [saɪð] *s* falce *f*

**sea** [si] *s* mare *m;* (*wave*) maroso; **at sea** in alto mare; **by the sea** a mare, sulla costa; **to follow the sea** farsi marinaio; **to put to sea** prendere il largo

**sea'board'** *adj* costiero ‖ *s* litorale *m*

**sea' breeze'** *s* brezza marina

**sea'coast'** *s* costa, litorale *m*

**sea' dog'** *s* (*seal*) foca; (*sailor*) lupo di mare

**seafarer** ['si,fɛrər] *s* marinaio; viaggiatore marittimo

**sea'food'** *s* pesce *m;* (*shellfish*) frutti *mpl* di mare

**seagoing** ['si,go·ɪŋ] *adj* di alto mare

**sea' gull'** *s* gabbiano

**seal** [sil] *s* sigillo; (*sea animal*) foca; (fig) suggello ‖ *tr* sigillare, apporre i sigilli a; (fig) suggellare

**sea' legs'** *spl*—**to have good sea legs** avere piede marino

**sea' lev'el** *s* livello del mare

**seal'ing wax'** *s* ceralacca

**seal'skin'** *s* pelle *f* di foca

**seam** [sim] *s* (*abutting of edges*) giuntura; (*stitches*) costura, cucitura; (*scar*) cicatrice *f;* (*wrinkle*) ruga; (in metal) commettitura; (min) filone *m*, vena

**sea'man** *s* (**-men**) marinaio

**sea' mile'** *s* miglio marino

**seamless** ['simlɪs] *adj* senza giuntura; (*stockings*) senza cucitura

**seamstress** ['simstrɪs] *s* cucitrice *f*

**seam·y** ['simi] *adj* (**-ier; -iest**) pieno di cuciture; basso, sordido; (*unpleasant*) spiacevole

**séance** ['se·ɑns] *s* seduta spiritica

**sea'plane'** *s* idrovolante *m*

**sea'port'** *s* porto di mare

**sea' pow'er** *s* potenza navale

**sear** [sɪr] *adj* secco ‖ *s* scottatura ‖ *tr* scottare, bruciare; (*to brand*) marcare a fuoco; inaridire; (fig) indurire

**search** [sʌrtʃ] *s* ricerca, investigazione; (*frisking a person*) perquisizione; **in search of** in cerca di ‖ *tr* cercare, investigare; perquisire, frugare ‖ *intr* investigare; **to search for** cercare; **to search into** investigare

**searching** ['sʌrtʃɪŋ] *adj* (e.g., inspec-

tion) profondo; (*e.g., glance*) indagatore, penetrante

**search'light'** *s* proiettore *m*, riflettore *m;* (mil) fotoelettrica

**search' war'rant** *s* mandato di perquisizione

**sea'scape'** *s* vista del mare; (*painting*) marina

**sea' shell'** *s* conchiglia

**sea'shore'** *s* costa, marina, mare *m*

**sea'sick'** *adj*—**to be seasick** aver mal di mare

**sea'sick'ness** *s* mal *m* di mare

**sea'side'** *s* costa, riviera, marina

**season** ['sizən] *s* stagione; **in season** di stagione; **in season and out of season** sempre, continuamente; **out of season** fuori stagione ‖ *tr* (*food*) condire; (*to mature*) stagionare; (*e.g., wood*) stagionare

**seasonal** ['sizənəl] *adj* stagionale

**seasoning** ['sizənɪŋ] *s* condimento; (*of wood*) stagionamento

**sea'son's greet'ings** *spl* migliori auguri *mpl* per le feste natalizie

**sea'son tick'et** *s* biglietto d'abbonamento

**seat** [sit] *s* sedia; (*part of chair*) sedile *m;* (*of human body*) sedere *m;* (*of pants*) fondo; sito, posto; (e.g., of government) sede *f;* (*in parliament*) seggio; (*e.g., of learning*) centro; (rr, theat) posto ‖ *tr* far sedere; aver posti per; (*a chair*) mettere il sedile a; (*pants*) mettere il fondo a; (*an official*) insediare; (mach) installare; **to be seated** essere seduto; **to seat oneself** sedersi

**seat' belt'** *s* cintura di sicurezza

**seat' cov'er** *s* guaina, foderina

**seat'ing room'** *s* posti *mpl* a sedere

**sea' wall'** *s* diga

**sea'way'** *s* via marittima; alto mare; mare grosso; rotta percorsa; via di fiume accessibile a navi da trasporto

**sea'weed'** *s* alga marina; pianta marina

**sea'wor'thy** *adj* atto a tenere il mare

**secede** [sɪ'sid] *intr* separarsi, distaccarsi

**secession** [sɪ'sɛʃən] *s* secessione

**seclude** [sɪ'klud] *tr* appartare; isolare

**seclusion** [sɪ'kluʒən] *s* reclusione; solitudine *f*, intimità *f*

**second** ['sɛkənd] *adj & pron* secondo; **to be second to none** non cederla a nessuno ‖ *s* secondo; (*in a duel*) padrino; (*in dates*) due *m;* (aut, mus) seconda; **seconds** (com) articoli *mpl* di seconda qualità; **to have seconds** on servirsi una seconda volta di ‖ *tr* assecondare; (*a motion*) appoggiare ‖ *adv* in secondo luogo

**secondar·y** ['sɛkən,deri] *adj* secondario ‖ *s* (**-ies**) (elec) secondario

**sec'ond-best'** *adj* (il) migliore dopo il primo; **to come off second-best** arrivare secondo

**sec'-ond-class'** *adj* di seconda qualità; (aer, naut, rr) di seconda classe

**sec'ond hand'** *s* lancetta dei secondi

**sec'ond·hand'** *adj* di seconda mano, d'occasione

**sec'ond lieuten'ant** s sottotenente m
**sec'ond-rate'** adj di seconda categoria;
  (inferior) da strapazzo
**sec'ond sight'** s chiaroveggenza
**sec'ond wind'** [wind] s—to get one's
  second wind riprendere fiato
**secre·cy** ['sikrəsi] s (-cies) segretezza;
  in secrecy in segreto
**secret** ['sikrit] adj & s segreto; in
  secret in segreto
**secretar·y** ['sɛkrɪ,tɛri] s (-ies) segretario; (desk) scrittoio
**se'cret bal'lot** s scrutinio segreto
**secrete** [sɪ'krit] tr nascondere;
  (physiol) secernere
**secretive** ['sikrɪtɪv] or [sɪ'kritɪv] adj
  riservato, poco comunicativo
**sect** [sɛkt] s setta
**sectarian** [sɛk'tɛrɪ·ən] adj & s settario
**section** ['sɛkt/ən] s sezione; (of city)
  rione m; (of fruit) spicchio; (of
  highway) tronco; (rr) tratta ‖ tr sezionare
**sectional** ['sɛk/ənəl] adj (e.g., bookcase) componibile; sezionale; locale,
  regionale
**secular** ['sɛkjələr] adj & s secolare m
**secularism** ['sɛkjələ,rɪzəm] s laicismo
**secure** [sɪ'kjur] adj salvo, sicuro ‖ tr
  ottenere; assicurare; fissare; (law)
  garantire
**securi·ty** [sɪ'kjurɪti] s (-ties) sicurezza; protezione; garanzia; (person)
  garante m; securities valori mpl,
  titoli mpl
**sedan** [sɪ'dæn] s (aut) berlina
**sedan' chair'** s bussola, portantina
**sedate** [sɪ'det] adj calmo, posato
**sedation** [sɪ'de/ən] s ritorno alla
  calma; stato di calma mentale
**sedative** ['sɛdətɪv] adj & s sedativo
**sedentary** ['sɛdən,tɛri] adj sedentario
**sedge** [sɛdʒ] s carice m
**sediment** ['sɛdɪmənt] s sedimento
**sedition** [sɪ'dɪ/ən] s sedizione
**seditious** [sɪ'dɪ/əs] adj sedizioso
**seduce** [sɪ'djus] or [sɪ'dus] tr sedurre
**seducer** [sɪ'djusər] or [sɪ'dusər] s seduttore m, corruttore m
**seduction** [sɪ'dʌk/ən] s seduzione
**seductive** [sɪ'dʌktɪv] adj seduttore
**sedulous** ['sɛdjələs] adj diligente
**see** [si] s (eccl) sede f ‖ v (pret saw
  [sɔ]; pp seen [sin]) tr vedere; to
  see off andare ad accompagnare; to
  see through portare a termine ‖ intr
  vedere; see here! faccia attenzione!;
  to see after prender cura di; to see
  through conoscere il gioco di
**seed** [sid] s seme m, semenza; to go to
  seed andare in semenza; deteriorarsi
  ‖ tr seminare; (fruit) togliere i semi
  da ‖ intr seminare; produrre semi
**seed'bed'** s semenzaio; (fig) vivaio
**seeder** ['sidər] s (person) seminatore
  m; (machine) seminatrice f
**seedling** ['sidlɪŋ] s piantina da trapianto
**seed·y** ['sidi] adj (-ier; -iest) pieno di
  semi; (unkempt) malmesso, malvestito
**seeing** ['si·ɪŋ] conj visto che, dato che

**See'ing Eye' dog'** s cane m guida per
  ciechi
**seek** [sik] v (pret & pp sought [sɔt]) tr
  cercare, ricercare; to be sought after
  essere ricercato; to seek to cercare di
**seem** [sim] intr parere, sembrare
**seemingly** ['simɪŋli] adv apparente-
  mente
**seem·ly** ['simli] adj (-lier; -liest) decoroso; appropriato
**seep** [sip] intr colare, filtrare
**seer** [sɪr] s profeta m, veggente m
**see'saw'** s altalena; (motion) viavai m
  ‖ intr altalenare
**seethe** [sið] intr bollire
**segment** ['sɛgmənt] s segmento
**segregate** ['sɛgrɪ,get] tr segregare
**segregation** [,sɛgrɪ'ge/ən] s segregazione
**segregationist** [,sɛgrɪ'ge/ənɪst] s segre-
  gazionista mf
**Seine** [sen] s Senna
**seismograph** ['saɪzmə,græf] or ['saɪzmə,graf] s sismografo
**seismology** [saɪz'malədʒi] s sismologia
**seize** [siz] tr afferrare; impossessarsi
  di; (with one's clenched fist) impugnare; comprendere; (law) sequestrare, confiscare
**seizure** ['siʒər] s conquista, cattura;
  (of an illness) attacco; (law) sequestro, pignoramento
**seldom** ['sɛldəm] adj di raro, raramente
**select** [sɪ'lɛkt] adj scelto, selezionato
  ‖ tr prescegliere, selezionare
**selectee** [sɪ,lɛk'ti] s (mil) recluta
**selection** [sɪ'lɛk/ən] s selezione, scelta
**selective** [sɪ'lɛktɪv] adj selettivo
**self** [sɛlf] adj stesso ‖ s (selves [sɛlvz])
  sé stesso; io, personalità f; all by
  one's self senza aiuto altrui ‖ pron
  sé stesso
**self'-abuse'** s abuso delle proprie forze;
  masturbazione
**self'-addressed'** adj col nome e l'indirizzo del mittente
**self'-cen'tered** adj egocentrico
**self'-con'scious** adj imbarazzato, vergognoso, timido
**self'-control'** s padronanza di sé stesso,
  autocontrollo
**self'-defense'** s autodifesa; in self-
  defense in legittima difesa
**self'-deni'al** s abnegazione
**self'-deter'mina'tion** s autodetermina-
  zione
**self'-dis'cipline** s autodisciplina
**self'-ed'ucat'ed** adj autodidatta
**self'-employed'** adj che lavora in proprio
**self'-ev'i·dent** adj evidente, lampante
**self'-ex·plan'a·tor'y** adj ovvio, che si
  spiega da sé
**self'-gov'ernment** s autogoverno; controllo sopra sé stesso
**self'-im·por'tant** adj presuntuoso
**self'-in·dul'gence** s intemperanza
**self'-in'terest** s egoismo, interesse m
**selfish** ['sɛlfɪ/] adj egoista
**selfishness** ['sɛlfɪ/nɪs] s egoismo

**selfless** ['sɛlflɪs] *adj* disinteressato; altruista

**self'-liq'ui·dat'ing** *adj* autoammortizzabile

**self'-love'** *s* amor proprio

**self'-made'** *adj* che si è fatto da sé

**self'-por'trait** *s* autoritratto

**self'-pos·sessed'** *adj* calmo, padrone di sé

**self'-pres'er·va'tion** *s* conservazione

**self'-pro·pelled'** *adj* semovente

**self'-re·li'ant** *adj* pieno di fiducia in sé stesso

**self'-re·spect'** *s* rispetto di sé stesso

**self'-right'eous** *adj* che si considera più morale degli altri, ipocrita

**self'-sac'ri·fice'** *s* sacrificio di sé, spirito di sacrifico

**self'-same'** *adj* stesso e medesimo

**self'-sat'is·fied'** *adj* contento di sé

**self'-seek'ing** *adj* egoista ‖ *s* egoismo

**self'-serv'ice** *s* autoservizio

**self'-start'er** *s* motorino d'avviamento

**self'-styled'** *adj* sedicente

**self'-support'** *s* indipendenza economica

**self'-tap'ping screw'** *s* vite *f* autofilettante

**self'-taught'** *adj* autodidatta

**self'-threading** ['sɛlf'θrɛdɪŋ] *adj* autofilettante

**self'-willed'** *adj* ostinato, caparbio

**self'-wind'ing** *adj* a carica automatica

**sell** [sɛl] *v* (*pret & pp* **sold** [sold]) *tr* vendere; (*an idea*) fare accettare; **to sell off** svendere, liquidare; **to sell out** smerciare; vendere a stralcio; (coll) tradire ‖ *intr* vendere, vendersi; fare il venditore; **to sell off** (*said of the stock market*) essere in ribasso; **to sell out** vendere a stralcio; vendersi

**seller** ['sɛlər] *s* venditore *m*

**Selt'zer wa'ter** ['sɛltsər] *s* selz *m*

**selvage** ['sɛlvɪdʒ] *s* cimosa, vivagno

**semantic** [sɪ'mæntɪk] *adj* semantico ‖ **semantics** *s* semantica

**semaphore** ['sɛmə ˌfor] *s* semaforo

**semblance** ['sɛmbləns] *s* apparenza, specie *f*; apparizione

**semen** ['simɛn] *s* sperma *m*

**semester** [sɪ'mɛstər] *adj* semestrale ‖ *s* semestre *m*

**semicircle** ['sɛmɪ ˌsʌrkəl] *s* semicircolo

**semicolon** ['sɛmɪ ˌkolən] *s* punto e virgola

**semiconductor** [ ˌsɛmikən'dʌktər] *s* semiconduttore *m*

**semiconscious** [ ˌsɛmi'kɑnʃəs] *adj* mezzo cosciente

**semifinal** [ ˌsɛmi'faɪnəl] *s* semifinale *f*

**semilearned** [ ˌsɛmi'lʌrnɪd] *adj* semidotto

**semimonth·ly** [ ˌsɛmi'mʌnθli] or [ ˌsɛmaɪ'mʌnθli] *adj* quindicinale ‖ *s* (-lies) rivista quindicinale

**seminar** ['sɛmɪ ˌnɑr] or [ ˌsɛmɪ'nɑr] *s* seminario

**seminar·y** ['sɛmɪ ˌnɛri] *s* (-ies) seminario

**Semite** ['sɛmaɪt] or ['simaɪt] *s* semita *mf*

**Semitic** [sɪ'mɪtɪk] *adj* semitico ‖ *s* lingua semitica; (*family of languages*) semitico

**semitrailer** ['sɛmɪ ˌtrelər] *s* semirimorchio

**semiweek·ly** [ ˌsɛmi'wikli] or [ ˌsɛmaɪ'wikli] *adj* bisettimanale ‖ *s* (-lies) periodico bisettimanale

**semiyearly** [ ˌsɛmi'jɪrli] or [ ˌsɛmaɪ'jɪrli] *adj* semestrale ‖ *adv* due volte all'anno

**senate** ['sɛnɪt] *s* senato

**senator** ['sɛnətər] *s* senatore *m*

**send** [sɛnd] *v* (*pret & pp* **sent** [sɛnt]) *tr* inviare, mandare; spedire; (*e.g., a punch*) lanciare; **to send back** rimandare; **to send forth** emettere; **to send packing** licenziare su due piedi ‖ *intr* (rad) trasmettere; **to send for** mandare a chiamare, far venire

**sender** ['sɛndər] *s* speditore *m*, mittente *m*; (telg) trasmettitore *m*

**send'-off'** *s* (coll) addio affettuoso; (coll) lancio

**senility** [sɪ'nɪlɪti] *s* (pathol) senilismo

**senior** ['sinjər] *adj* maggiore, più anziano; seniore, di grado più elevato; dell'ultimo anno, laureando; senior, il vecchio ‖ *s* maggiore *m*; seniore *m*, persona di grado più elevato; studente *m* dell'ultimo anno, laureando

**sen'ior cit'izen** *s* vecchio, pensionato

**seniority** [sin'jɑrɪti] or [sin'jɔrɪti] *s* anzianità *f*

**sensation** [sɛn'seʃən] *s* sensazione

**sensational** [sɛn'seʃənəl] *adj* sensazionale

**sense** [sɛns] *s* senso; **in a sense** in un certo senso; **to come to one's senses** riprendere il giudizio; **to make sense out of** arrivare a capire; **to take leave of one's senses** perdere il ben dell'intelletto ‖ *tr* intuire; comprendere

**senseless** ['sɛnslɪs] *adj* (*unconscious*) privo di sensi; (*meaningless*) insensato, privo di senso

**sense' or'gan** *s* organo di senso

**sensibili·ty** [ ˌsɛnsɪ'bɪlɪti] *s* (-ties) sensibilità *f*; **sensibilities** suscettibilità *f*

**sensible** ['sɛnsɪbəl] *adj* sensato; (*keenly aware*) sensibile; cosciente

**sensitive** ['sɛnsɪtɪv] *adj* sensitivo, sensibile; delicato

**sensitize** ['sɛnsɪ ˌtaɪz] *tr* sensibilizzare

**sensory** ['sɛnsəri] *adj* sensorio

**sensual** ['sɛnʃʊ·əl] *adj* sensuale

**sensuous** ['sɛnʃʊ·əs] *adj* sensuale

**sentence** ['sɛntəns] *s* (gram) frase; (law) sentenza, condanna ‖ *tr* sentenziare, condannare

**sentiment** ['sɛntɪmənt] *s* sentimento

**sentimental** [ ˌsɛntɪ'mɛntəl] *adj* sentimentale

**sentimentalism** [ ˌsɛntɪ'mɛntəl ˌɪzəm] *s* sentimentalismo

**sentinel** ['sɛntɪnəl] *s* sentinella; **to stand sentinel** montare di sentinella

**sen·try** ['sɛntri] *s* (-tries) sentinella

**sen'try box'** *s* garitta, casotto

**separate** ['sɛpərɪt] *adj* separato ‖

['sepə‚ret] *tr* separare ‖ *intr* separarsi

**separation** [‚sepə'reʃən] *s* separazione
**Sephardic** [sɪ'fɑrdɪk] *adj* sefardita
**September** [sep'tembər] *s* settembre *m*
**septic** ['septɪk] *adj* settico
**sep'tic tank'** *s* fossa settica
**sepulcher** ['sepəlkər] *s* sepolcro
**sequel** ['sikwəl] *s* seguito
**sequence** ['sikwəns] *s* serie *f*, sequenza, successione; conseguenza; (cards, eccl, mov) sequenza; (gram) correlazione
**sequester** [sɪ'kwestər] *tr* isolare, appartare; (law) sequestrare
**sequin** ['sikwɪn] *s* lustrino
**ser·aph** ['serəf] *s* (**-aphs** or **-aphim** [əfɪm]) serafino
**Serbian** ['sʌrbɪ·ən] *adj & s* serbo
**Serbo-Croatian** [‚sʌrbokro'eʃən] *adj & s* serbocroato
**sere** [sɪr] *adj* secco, appassito
**serenade** [‚serə'ned] *s* serenata ‖ *tr* fare la serenata a ‖ *intr* fare la serenata
**serene** [sɪ'rin] *adj* sereno
**serenity** [sɪ'renɪti] *s* serenità *f*
**serf** [sʌrf] *s* servo della gleba
**serfdom** ['sʌrfdəm] *s* servitù *f* della gleba
**serge** [sʌrdʒ] *s* saia
**sergeant** ['sɑrdʒənt] *s* sergente *m*
**ser'geant at arms'** *s* (**ser'geants at arms'**) ufficiale *m* delegato a mantenere l'ordine
**ser'geant ma'jor** *s* (**sergeants major** or **sergeant majors**) (in U.S. Army) sergente *m* maggiore; (in Italian Army) maresciallo
**serial** ['sɪrɪ·əl] *adj* a puntate, a dispense ‖ *s* periodico; romanzo a puntate; programma *m* a serie
**se'rial num'ber** *s* matricola; (of a book) segnatura; (aut) matricola di telaio
**se·ries** ['sɪrɪz] *s* (**-ries**) serie *f*; (works dealing with the same topic) collana; **in series** (elec) in serie
**serious** ['sɪrɪ·əs] *adj* serio
**seriousness** ['sɪrɪ·əsnɪs] *s* serietà *f*; **in all seriousness** molto sul serio
**sermon** ['sʌrmən] *s* sermone *m*
**sermonize** ['sʌrmə‚naɪz] *tr & intr* sermonare
**serpent** ['sʌrpənt] *s* serpente *m*
**se·rum** ['sɪrəm] *s* (**-rums** or **-ra** [rə]) siero
**servant** ['sʌrvənt] *s* servo, domestico; (civil servant) funzionario; (fig) servitore *m*
**serv'ant girl'** *s* serva, domestica
**serv'ant prob'lem** *s* crisi *f* ancillare
**serve** [sʌrv] *s* (in tennis) servizio ‖ *tr* servire; (a sentence) espiare; (to suffice) bastare (with dat); (a writ) notificare; **to serve s.o. right** stare bene (with dat), e.g., **it serves him right** gli sta bene ‖ *intr* servire; **to serve as** fare da
**service** ['sʌrvɪs] *s* servizio; (of a writ) notifica; (branch of the armed forces) arma; **at your service** per servirLa ‖ *tr* rifornire, riparare

**serviceable** ['sʌrvɪsəbəl] *adj* utile; durevole; pratico; riparabile
**serv'ice club'** *s* casa del soldato
**serv'ice·man'** *s* (**-men'**) militare *m;* riparatore *m*, aggiustatore *m*
**serv'ice mod'ule** *s* modulo di servizio
**serv'ice rec'ord** *s* stato di servizio
**serv'ice sta'tion** *s* stazione di servizio or di rifornimento
**serv'ice-sta'tion attend'ant** *s* benzinaio
**serv'ice stripe'** *s* gallone *m*
**servile** ['sʌrvɪl] *adj* servile
**servitude** ['sʌrvɪ‚tjud] or ['sʌrvɪ‚tud] *s* servitù *f*; lavori forzati
**sesame** ['sesəmi] *s* sesamo; **open sesame** apriti sesamo
**session** ['seʃən] *s* sessione *f*, seduta
**set** [set] *adj* determinato, preordinato; abituale; fisso, rigido; (ready) pronto; meditato, studiato ‖ *s* (e.g., of books) collezione, serie *f*; (e.g., of chess) gioco; set *m*, insieme *m*, completo; (of tires) treno; (of horses) pariglia; (of tennis) partita; (of dishes) servizio; (of kitchen utensils) batteria; posizione, atteggiamento; (of a garment) linea; (e.g., of cement) presa; (of people) gruppo; (of thieves) genia; (of sails) muta; (of lines) (geom) fascio; (rad, telv) apparato; (theat, mov) set *m* ‖ *v* (pret & pp **set;** ger **setting**) *tr* porre, deporre; mettere; (fire) dare; (the table) imbandire; (a watch) regolare; (s.o. a certain number of tricks) far cadere di; (a price) fissare; (a gem) incastonare; (a fracture) mettere a posto; (a saw) allicciare; (a trap) tendere; (hair) acconciare; stabilire; insediare; (to plant) piantare; (a sail) tendere; (e.g., milk) rapprendere; calibrare, tarare; (cement) solidificare; (typ) comporre; **to set back** ritardare; (a clock) mettere indietro; **to set forth** descrivere; **to set one's heart on** desiderare ardentemente; **to set store by** tenere in gran conto; **to set up** metter su; impiantare; (drinks) (slang) pagare ‖ *intr* (said, e.g., of the sun) tramontare; (said of a liquid) solidificarsi; (said of cement) fare presa; (said of milk) rapprendersi; (said of a hen) covare; (said of a garment) cascare; (said of hair) prendere la piega; **to set about** mettersi a; **to set out** porsi in cammino; **to set out to** mettersi a; **to set to work** mettersi a lavorare; **to set upon** attaccare
**set'back'** *s* rovescio, contrarietà *f*
**set'screw'** *s* vite *f* di pressione
**setting** ['setɪŋ] *s* (environment) ambiente *m;* (of a gem) montatura; (of cement) presa; (e.g., of the sun) tramonto; (theat) scenario; (mus) arrangiamento
**set'ting-up' ex'ercises** *spl* ginnastica da camera
**settle** ['setəl] *tr* determinare, risolvere; sistemare, regolare; (a bill) liquidare; installarsi in, colonizzare; calmare; (a liquid) far depositare; (law)

conciliare || *intr* mettersi d'accordo;
saldare un conto; stanziarsi, domici-
liarsi; fermarsi, posare; (*said of a
liquid*) depositare, calmarsi; solidificarsi; **to settle down to work** mettersi
a lavorare di buzzo buono; **to settle
on** scegliere, fissare

**settlement** ['sɛtəlmənt] *s* stabilimento;
sistemazione, regolamento; colonia;
comunità *f;* (*of a building*) infossa-
mento; agenzia di beneficenza

**settler** ['sɛtlər] *s* fondatore *m;* colono;
conciliatore *m*

**set'up'** *s* portamento; (*e.g., of tools*)
disposizione; quanto è necessario per
mescolare una bibita alcolica; (coll)
incontro truccato

**seven** ['sɛvən] *adj & pron* sette || *s*
sette *m;* **seven o'clock** le sette

**sev'en hun'dred** *adj, s & pron* settecento

**seventeen** ['sɛvən'tin] *adj, s & pron*
diciassette *m*

**seventeenth** ['sɛvən'tinθ] *adj, s & pron*
diciassettesimo || *s* (*in dates*) dicias-
sette *m*

**seventh** ['sɛvənθ] *adj, s & pron* settimo
|| *s* (*in dates*) sette *m*

**seventieth** ['sɛvəntɪ·ɪθ] *adj, s & pron*
settantesimo

**seven·ty** ['sɛvənti] *adj & pron* settanta
|| *s* (**-ties**) settanta *m;* **the seventies**
gli anni settanta

**sever** ['sɛvər] *tr* tagliare, mozzare; (*re-
lations*) troncare || *intr* separarsi

**several** ['sɛvərəl] *adj* parecchi, vari;
rispettivi || *spl* parecchi *mpl*

**sev'erance pay'** ['sɛvərəns] *s* buonuscita, indennità *f* di licenziamento

**severe** [sɪ'vɪr] *adj* severo; (*weather*)
rigido; (*pain*) acuto; (*illness*) grave

**sew** [so] *v* (*pret* **sewed;** *pp* **sewed or
sewn**) *tr & intr* cucire

**sewage** ['su·ɪdʒ] *or* ['sju·ɪdʒ] *s* acque
*fpl* di scolo or di rifiuto

**sewer** ['su·ər] *or* ['sju·ər] *s* fogna,
chiavica

**sewerage** ['su·ərɪdʒ] *or* ['sju·ərɪdʒ] *s*
fognatura; drenaggio, rimozione delle
acque di rifiuto

**sew'ing machine'** ['so·ɪŋ] *s* macchina
da cucire

**sex** [sɛks] *s* sesso

**sex' appeal'** *s* attrattiva fisica, sex appeal *m*

**sextant** ['sɛkstənt] *s* sestante *m*

**sextet** [sɛks'tɛt] *s* sestetto

**sexton** ['sɛkstən] *s* sagrestano

**sexual** ['sɛkʃʊ·əl] *adj* sessuale

**sex·y** ['sɛksi] *adj* (**-ier; -iest**) (coll)
erotico; (coll) procace

**shab·by** ['ʃæbi] *adj* (**-bier; -biest**)
(*clothes*) frusto; (*house*) malandato;
(*person*) malvestito; (*deal*) cattivo

**shack** [ʃæk] *s* baracca

**shackle** ['ʃækəl] *s* ceppo; (*to tie an
animal*) pastoia; (fig) ostacolo;
**shackles** ceppi *mpl*, manette *fpl* || *tr*
mettere in ceppi; (fig) inceppare

**shad** [ʃæd] *s* alosa

**shade** [ʃed] *s* ombra; (*of lamp*) paralume *m;* (*of window*) tendina; (*for

*the eyes*) visiera; (*hue*) tinta, sfumatura; **a shade of** un po' di; **shades**
tenebre *fpl;* ombre *fpl* || *tr* ombreg-
giare; sfumare, digradare; (*a price*)
ribassare leggermente

**shadow** ['ʃædo] *s* ombra || *tr* ombreg-
giare; (*to follow*) pedinare; **to
shadow forth** adombrare, preannun-
ciare

**shadowy** ['ʃædo·ɪ] *adj* ombroso, om-
breggiato; illusorio, chimerico

**shad·y** ['ʃedi] *adj* (**-ier; -iest**) ombroso;
spettrale; (coll) losco; **to keep shady**
(slang) starsene lontano

**shaft** [ʃæft] *or* [ʃɑft] *s* (*of arrow*)
asta; (*of feather*) rachide *f;* (*of light*)
raggio; (*handle*) manico; (*of wagon*)
stanga, timone *m;* (*of motor*) albero;
(*of column*) fusto; (*of elevator*)
pozzo; (*in a mountain*) camino;
(min) fornello; (fig) frecciata

**shag·gy** ['ʃægi] *adj* (**-gier; -giest**) peloso, irsuto; (*unkempt*) trasandato;
(*cloth*) ruvido

**shag'gy dog' sto'ry** *s* storiella senza
capo né coda

**shake** [ʃek] *s* scossa; stretta di mano;
momento, istante *m;* **the shakes** la
tremarella || *v* (*pret* **shook** [ʃuk];
*pp* **shaken**) *tr* scuotere; scrollare;
(*s.o.'s hands*) serrare; (*e.g., with a
mixer*) sbattere; agitare, perturbare;
eludere, disfarsi di || *intr* tremare;
(*to totter*) traballare, tentennare;
scuotere; darsi la mano

**shake'down'** *s* estorsione, concussione;
(*bed*) lettuccio di fortuna

**shake'down' cruise'** *s* (naut) viaggio di
prova

**shaker** ['ʃekər] *s* (*e.g., for sugar*) spolverino; (*for cocktails*) sbattighiaccio,
shaker *m*

**shake'-up'** *s* cambiamento completo,
riorganizzazione, rimaneggiamento

**shak·y** ['ʃeki] *adj* (**-ier; -iest**) treme-
bondo; traballante, zoppicante

**shall** [ʃæl] *v* (*cond* **should** [ʃud]) *v
aux* si usa per formare (1) il futuro
dell'indicativo, per es., **I shall do
it** lo farò; (2) il futuro perfetto del-
l'indicativo, per es., **I shall have done
it** l'avrò fatto; (3) espressioni di obbligo o necessità, per es., **what shall
I do?** che devo fare?, che vuole che
faccia?

**shallow** ['ʃælo] *adj* basso, poco profondo; leggero, superficiale

**sham** [ʃæm] *adj* falso, finto || *s* frode
*f,* contraffazione || *v* (*pret & pp*
**shammed;** *ger* **shamming**) *tr & intr*
fingere

**sham' bat'tle** *s* finta battaglia

**shambles** ['ʃæmbəlz] *s* macello; confusione, disordine

**shame** [ʃem] *s* vergogna; **shame on
you!** vergogna!; **what a shame!** che
peccato! || *tr* svergognare, disonorare

**shame'faced'** *adj* timido, vergognoso

**shameful** ['ʃemfəl] *adj* vergognoso

**shameless** ['ʃemlɪs] *adj* sfrontato, impudente, svergognato

**shampoo** [ʃæm'pu] s shampoo m ‖ tr fare lo shampoo a
**shamrock** ['ʃæmrɑk] s trifoglio irlandese
**shanghai** ['ʃæŋhaɪ] or [ʃæŋ'haɪ] tr imbarcare a viva forza ‖ **Shanghai** s Sciangai f
**shank** [ʃæŋk] s fusto; (of tool) codolo; (stem) gambo; (of bird) zampa; (of anchor) fuso; (coll) principio; (coll) fine f; **to ride shank's mare** andare col cavallo di San Francesco
**shan·ty** ['ʃænti] s (-ties) bicocca
**shan'ty·town'** s bidonville f
**shape** [ʃep] s forma; **in bad shape** in cattive condizioni; **out of shape** sformato ‖ tr formare, foggiare; plasmare, conformare ‖ intr formarsi; **to take shape** prender forma
**shapeless** ['ʃeplɪs] adj informe
**shape·ly** ['ʃepli] adj (-lier; -liest) ben fatto, formoso
**share** [ʃɛr] s parte f; interesse m; (of stock) azione f; (of plow) suola; **to go shares** dividere in parti eguali ‖ tr (to enjoy jointly) condividere; (to apportion) ripartire ‖ intr partecipare, prender parte
**sharecropper** ['ʃɛr,krɑpər] s mezzadro
**share'hold'er** s azionista mf
**shark** [ʃɑrk] s pescecane m; (schemer) piovra; (slang) esperto
**sharp** [ʃɑrp] adj affilato, acuto; angoloso; (e.g., curve) forte; distinto, ben delineato; (taste) pungente, salato; (pain) vivo; (words) mordace; (slang) elegante ‖ s (mus) diesis m ‖ adv acutamente; in punto, e.g., **at seven o'clock sharp** alle sette in punto
**sharpen** ['ʃɑrpən] tr affilare; (a pencil) fare la punta a ‖ intr affilarsi
**sharpener** ['ʃɑrpənər] s (person) affilatore m; (machine) affilatrice f
**sharper** ['ʃɑrpər] s gabbamondo
**sharp'shoot'er** s tiratore scelto
**shatter** ['ʃætər] tr frantumare; sfracellare; (health) rovinare; (nerves) sconvolgere; distruggere ‖ intr frantumarsi, andare in pezzi
**shat'ter·proof'** adj infrangibile
**shave** [ʃev] s rasatura; **to have a close shave** scapparla or scamparla bella ‖ tr (the face) radere, sbarbare; (wood) piallare; (to scrape) sfiorare; (prices) ridurre; (a lawn) tosare ‖ intr rasarsi
**shaving** ['ʃevɪŋ] adj da barba, per barba, e.g., **shaving cream** crema da or per barba ‖ s rasatura; **shavings** trucioli mpl
**shav'ing brush'** s pennello da barba
**shav'ing soap'** s sapone m per la barba
**shawl** [ʃɔl] s scialle m
**she** [ʃi] s (shes) femmina f ‖ pron pers (they) essa, lei
**sheaf** [ʃif] s (sheaves [ʃivz]) covone m; (of paper) fascio
**shear** [ʃɪr] s lama di cesoia; tagliatura; **shears** cesoie fpl ‖ v (pret **sheared**; pp **sheared** or **shorn** [ʃɔrn]) tr (sheep) tosare; (cloth) tagliare; **to shear s.o. of** privare qlcu di

**sheath** [ʃiθ] s (sheaths [ʃiðz]) guaina, coperta; (of a sword) fodero
**sheathe** [ʃið] tr rinfoderare, inguainare
**shed** [ʃɛd] s portico, tettoia; (geog) spartiacque m, versante m ‖ v (pret & pp **shed**; ger **shedding**) tr (e.g., blood) spargere, versare; (light) dare, fare; (feathers) spogliarsi di, lasciar cadere
**sheen** [ʃin] s lucentezza
**sheep** [ʃip] s (sheep) pecora; **sheep's eyes** occhio di triglia; **to separate the sheep from the goats** separare i buoni dai cattivi
**sheep'dog'** s cane m da pastore
**sheepish** ['ʃipɪʃ] adj timido, goffo; pecoresco, pedissequo
**sheep'skin'** s pelle f di pecora; (parchment) cartapecora; (bb) bazzana; (coll) diploma m
**sheer** [ʃɪr] adj trasparente, fino, velato; puro; (cliff) stagliato ‖ adv completamente ‖ intr deviare
**sheet** [ʃit] s (for bed) lenzuolo; (of paper) foglio; (of metal) lamina; (of water) specchio; (naut) scotta
**sheet' light'ning** s lampeggio all'orizzonte
**sheet' met'al** s lamiera
**sheet' mu'sic** s spartito non rilegato
**sheik** [ʃik] s sceicco; (great lover) (slang) rubacuori m
**shelf** [ʃɛlf] s (shelves [ʃɛlvz]) scaffale m, scansia; (ledge) terrazzo, ripiano; banco di sabbia; **on the shelf** in disparte, dimenticato
**shell** [ʃɛl] s (of egg or crustacean) guscio; (of mollusk) conchiglia; (of vegetable) baccello; proietto, proiettile m; (cartridge) cartuccia; (of a cartridge) bossolo; (framework) armatura; (of boiler) involucro; imbarcazione da regata, schifo, iole f ‖ tr (vegetables) sgranare; bombardare, cannoneggiare; **to shell out** (slang) tirar fuori
**shel·lac** [ʃə'læk] s gomma lacca ‖ v (pret & pp **-lacked**; ger **-lacking**) tr verniciare con gomma lacca; (slang) dare una batosta a
**shell'fish'** ssg (-fish) frutto di mare; crostaceo; spl frutti mpl di mare; crostacei mpl
**shell' hole'** s cratere m
**shell' shock'** s psicosi traumatica bellica
**shelter** ['ʃɛltər] s rifugio, ricovero; **to take shelter** rifugiarsi ‖ tr raccogliere, ospitare, dare rifugio a
**shelve** [ʃɛlv] tr mettere sullo scaffale; (a bill) insabbiare; mettere a riposo
**shepherd** ['ʃɛpərd] s pastore m ‖ tr guardare, curarsi di
**shep'herd dog'** s cane m da pastore
**shepherdess** ['ʃɛpərdɪs] s pastora
**sherbet** ['ʃʌrbət] s sorbetto
**sheriff** ['ʃɛrɪf] s sceriffo
**sher·ry** ['ʃɛri] s (-ries) xeres m
**shield** [ʃild] s scudo; (for armpit) sottoascella m; (badge) scudetto; (elec) schermo ‖ tr proteggere; (elec) schermare
**shift** [ʃɪft] s cambio, cambiamento;

(*period of work*) turno; (*group of workmen*) operai *mpl* di turno, squadra di lavoro; espediente *m*, sotterfugio || *tr* cambiare; spostare; (*blame*) riversare; || *intr* cambiare; spostarsi; fare da sé; vivere di espedienti; (rr) manovrare; (aut) cambiare marcia

**shift' key'** *s* tasto maiuscole

**shiftless** ['ʃɪftlɪs] *adj* pigro, ozioso

**shift·y** ['ʃɪfti] *adj* (**-ier; -iest**) astuto; evasivo; pieno d'espedienti; (*glance*) sfuggente

**shilling** ['ʃɪlɪŋ] *s* scellino

**shimmer** ['ʃɪmər] *s* luccichio || *intr* luccicare, mandare bagliori

**shim·my** ['ʃɪmi] *s* (**-mies**) (*dance*) shimmy *m;* (aut) farfallamento delle ruote, shimmy *m* || *intr* ballare lo shimmy; vibrare

**shin** [ʃɪn] *s* stinco; (*of cattle*) cannone *m* || *v* (*pret & pp* **shinned;** *ger* **shinning**) *tr* arrampicarsi su || *intr* arrampicarsi

**shin'bone'** *s* stinco, tibia

**shine** [ʃaɪn] *s* splendore *m;* luce *f;* bel tempo; lucidatura, lucido; **to take a shine to** (coll) prender simpatia per || *v* (*pret & pp* **shined**) *tr* pulire, lucidare || *v* (*pret & pp* **shone** [ʃon]) *tr* (*e.g., a flashlight*) dirigere i raggi di || *intr* brillare, luccicare, risplendere; (*to excel*) essere brillante, eccellere

**shiner** ['ʃaɪnər] *s* (slang) occhio pesto

**shingle** ['ʃɪŋɡəl] *s* assicella di copertura; (*to cover a wall*) mattoncino di rivestimento; (Brit) greto ciottoloso; (coll) capelli *mpl* alla bebé; **shingles** (pathol) erpete *m*, zona; **to hang out one's shingle** (coll) aprire un ufficio professionale || *tr* coprire di assicelle or mattoncini; (*hair*) tagliare alla bebé

**shining** ['ʃaɪnɪŋ] *adj* brillante, lucente

**shin·y** ['ʃaɪni] *adj* (**-ier; -iest**) lucente, lucido; (*paper*) patinato

**ship** [ʃɪp] *s* nave *f*, bastimento; aeronave *f;* aeroplano; (*crew*) equipaggio || *v* (*pret & pp* **shipped;** *ger* **shipping**) *tr* imbarcare; mandare, spedire; (*oars*) disarmare; (*water*) imbarcare || *intr* imbarcarsi

**ship'board'** *s*—**on shipboard** a bordo

**ship'build'er** *s* costruttore *m* navale

**ship'build'ing** *s* architettura navale

**ship'mate'** *s* compagno di bordo

**shipment** ['ʃɪpmənt] *s* invio, spedizione

**ship'own'er** *s* armatore *m*

**shipper** ['ʃɪpər] *s* speditore *m*, spedizioniere *m*, mittente *m*

**shipping** ['ʃɪpɪŋ] *s* imbarco; spedizione; (naut) trasporto marittimo

**ship'ping clerk'** *s* speditore *m*

**ship'ping room'** *s* ufficio impaccatura

**ship'shape'** *adj & adv* in perfette condizioni

**ship'side'** *s* molo

**ship's' pa'pers** *spl* documenti *mpl* di bordo

**ship'wreck'** *s* naufragio; (*remains*) relitto || *tr* far naufragare || *intr* naufragare

**ship'yard'** *s* cantiere *m* navale

**shirk** [ʃʌrk] *tr* (*work*) evitare; (*responsibility*) sottrarsi a || *intr* imboscarsi

**shirt** [ʃʌrt] *s* camicia; **to keep one's shirt on** (slang) non perdere la calma; **to lose one's shirt** (slang) perdere la camicia

**shirt' front'** *s* sparato

**shirt' sleeve'** *s* manica di camicia

**shirt'tail'** *s* falda della camicia

**shirt'waist'** *s* blusa da donna

**shiver** ['ʃɪvər] *s* brivido || *intr* rabbrividire, battere i denti

**shoal** [ʃol] *s* secca, banco di sabbia

**shock** [ʃɑk] *s* urto, collisione; scossa; scossa elettrica; (pathol) shock *m* || *tr* scuotere; (*to strike against*) urtare; scandalizzare, indignare; dare la scossa elettrica a; (fig) scioccare

**shock' absorb'er** [æb'sɔrbər] *s* ammortizzatore *m* di colpi

**shocking** ['ʃɑkɪŋ] *adj* disgustoso, scandalizzante

**shock' ther'apy** *s* terapia d'urto

**shock' troops'** *spl* truppe *fpl* d'assalto

**shod·dy** ['ʃɑdi] *adj* (**-dier; -diest**) scadente, falso

**shoe** [ʃu] *s* scarpa; (*horseshoe*) ferro da cavallo; (*of a tire*) copertone *m;* (*of brake*) ganascia, ceppo || *v* (*pret & pp* **shod** [ʃɑd]) *tr* calzare; (*a horse*) ferrare

**shoe'black'** *s* lustrascarpe *m*

**shoe'horn'** *s* corno da scarpe, calzatoio

**shoe'lace'** *s* laccio delle scarpe

**shoe'mak'er** *s* calzolaio

**shoe' pol'ish** *s* crema or cera da scarpe

**shoe'shine'** *s* lucidatura, lustramento di scarpe

**shoe' store'** *s* calzoleria

**shoe'string'** *s* laccio delle scarpe; **on a shoestring** con quattro soldi

**shoe'tree'** *s* tendiscarpe *m*

**shoo** [ʃu] *tr* fare sció a || *intr* fare sció

**shoot** [ʃut] *s* (*e.g., with a firearm*) tiro; gara di tiro; (*chute*) scivolo; (rok) lancio; (bot) getto, virgulto || *v* (*pret & pp* **shot** [ʃɑt]) *tr* (*any missile*) tirare; (*a bullet*) sparare; (*to execute with a bullet*) fucilare; (*to fling*) lanciare; (*the sun*) prendere l'altezza di; (*dice*) gettare; (mov, telv) girare, riprendere; **to shoot down** (*a plane*) abbattere; **to shoot up** (coll) terrorizzare sparando a casaccio || *intr* tirare, sparare; passare rapidamente; nascere; (*said of pain*) dare fitte; (mov) cinematografare; **to shoot at** tirare a; (coll) cercare di ottenere

**shoot'ing gal'lery** *s* tiro a segno

**shoot'ing match'** *s* gara di tiro a segno; (slang) tutto, ogni cosa

**shoot'ing star'** *s* stella cadente

**shop** [ʃɑp] *s* (*store*) negozio, rivendita; (*workshop*) officina; **to talk shop** parlare del proprio lavoro || *v* (*pret & pp* **shopped;** *ger* **shopping**) *intr* fare la spesa; **to go shopping** andare a fare la spesa; **to shop around** cercare un'occasione di negozio in negozio

**shop'girl'** *s* venditrice *f*

**shop'keep'er** s negoziante mf

**shoplifter** ['ʃɑp͵lɪftər] s taccheggiatore m

**shopper** ['ʃɑpər] s compratore m

**shopping** ['ʃɑpɪŋ] s compra; (purchases) compre fpl, shopping m

**shop'ping bag'** s sporta, shopping m

**shop'ping cen'ter** s centro d'acquisto, ipermercato

**shop'ping dis'trict** s zona commerciale

**shop'win'dow** s vetrina

**shop'worn'** adj sciupato, usato

**shore** [ʃor] s costa, riva; spiaggia, lido; (fig) regione; (support) sostegno, puntello || tr puntellare

**shore' din'ner** s pranzo di pesce

**shore' leave'** s (naut) franchigia

**shore'line'** s frangia costiera

**shore' patrol'** s polizia della marina

**short** [ʃort] adj (in stature) piccolo, basso; (in space, time) breve; (scanty) scarso; succinto; (in quantity) poco, piccolo; (rude) brusco; in a short time in breve; in short per farla breve; on short notice senza preavviso; short of breath corto di fiato; to be short of scarseggiare di || s (elec) cortocircuito; (mov) cortometraggio; shorts (underwear) mutande fpl; (sports attire) calzoncini mpl, shorts mpl || adv brevemente; bruscamente; (com) allo scoperto, e.g., to sell short vendere allo scoperto; to run short of essere a corto di; to stop short fermarsi di colpo || tr (elec) causare un cortocircuito in || intr (elec) andare in cortocircuito

**shortage** ['ʃortɪdʒ] s mancanza; (of food) carestia; (from pilfering) ammanco

**short'cake'** s torta di pasta frolla; torta ricoperta di frutta fresca

**short'-change'** tr non dare il cambio giusto a; (coll) imbrogliare

**short' cir'cuit** s (elec) cortocircuito

**short'-cir'cuit** tr mandare in cortocircuito; (coll) rovinare || intr andare in cortocircuito

**short'com'ing** s difetto, manchevolezza

**short'cut'** s scorciatoia

**shorten** ['ʃortən] tr raccorciare, abbreviare || intr raccorciarsi, abbreviarsi

**shortening** ['ʃortənɪŋ] s raccorciamento; (culin) grasso, strutto

**short'hand'** adj stenografico || s stenografia; to take shorthand stenografare

**short'hand' typ'ist** s stenodattilografo

**short-lived** ['ʃort'laɪvd] or ['ʃort'lɪvd] adj effimero, di breve vita

**shortly** ['ʃortli] adv in breve, brevemente; fra poco; bruscamente; shortly after poco dopo

**short'-range'** adj di corta portata

**short' sale'** s vendita allo scoperto

**short-sighted** ['ʃort'saɪtɪd] adj miope; (fig) miope

**short'stop'** s (baseball) interbase m

**short' sto'ry** s novella

**short-tempered** ['ʃort'tempərd] adj irascibile

**short'-term'** adj a breve scadenza

**short'wave'** adj alle onde corte || s onda corta

**short' weight'** s—**to give short weight** rubare sul peso

**shot** [ʃat] s tiro, sparo; (cartridge) cartuccia; (for cannon) palla; (pellets of lead) pallini mpl; (person) tiratore m; (hypodermic injection) iniezione; (of liquor) bicchierino; (phot) istantanea; (sports) peso; (mov) inquadratura; **not by a long shot** nemmeno a pensarci; **to start like a shot** partire come una palla da cannone; **to take a shot at** tirare un colpo a; (to attempt to) provarsi a

**shot'gun'** s schioppo, fucile m da caccia

**shot' put'** s lancio del peso

**should** [ʃud] v aux si usa nelle seguenti situazioni: 1) per formare il condizionale presente, per es., **if I should wait for him, I should miss the train** se lo aspettassi, perderei il treno; 2) per formare il perfetto del condizionale, per es., **if I had waited for him, I should have missed the train** se lo avessi aspettato, avrei perso il treno; 3) per indicare la necessità di un'azione, per es., **he should go at once** dovrebbe andare immediatamente; **he should have gone immediately** sarebbe dovuto andare immediatamente

**shoulder** ['ʃoldər] s spalla; (of highway) banchina; **across the shoulder** a bandoliera; **to put one's shoulders to the wheel** mettersi a lavorare di buzzo buono; **to turn a cold shoulder to** volgere le spalle a || tr portare sulle spalle; (a responsibility) addossarsi; spingere con le spalle

**shoul'der blade'** s scapola

**shoul'der strap'** s spallina; (mil) tracolla

**shout** [ʃaut] s urlo, grido || tr urlare, gridare; **to shout down** far tacere a forza di strilli || intr gridare

**shove** [ʃʌv] s spintone m || tr spingere || intr spingere, dare spintoni; **to shove off** allontanarsi dalla riva; (slang) andarsene

**shov·el** ['ʃʌvəl] s pala || v (pret & pp -eled or -elled; ger -eling or -elling) tr spalare || intr lavorare di pala

**show** [ʃo] s mostra; apparenza; (mov, telv, theat) spettacolo; **to make a show of** dar spettacolo di; **to steal the show from** ricevere tutti gli applausi invece di || tr mostrare, esporre; (a movie) presentare; dimostrare, insegnare; provare; (to register) segnare; (one's feelings) manifestare; (to the door) accompagnare; **to show in** fare entrare; **to show off** mettere in mostra || intr mostrarsi; presentarsi, apparire; (said of a horse) (sports) arrivare terzo, piazzarsi; **to show off** mettersi in mostra; **to show up** (coll) mostrarsi; (coll) farsi vedere

**show' bill'** s cartellone m

**show'boat'** s battello per spettacoli teatrali

**show' busi'ness** *s* industria dello spettacolo

**show'case'** *s* bacheca, vetrina

**show'down'** *s* carte scoperte; chiarificazione

**shower** ['ʃaυ·ər] *s (of rain)* acquazzone *m; (shower bath)* doccia; *(e.g., for a bride)* ricevimento cui i partecipanti devono portare un regalo; (fig) pioggia ‖ *tr* inaffiare; **to shower with** colmare di ‖ *intr* diluviare; fare la doccia

**show'er bath'** *s* doccia

**show' girl'** *s* ballerina, girl *f*

**show'man** *s* (-men) impresario teatrale; persona che ha molta scena

**show'-off'** *s* reclamista *m*, strombazzatore *m*

**show'piece'** *s* capolavoro, oggetto d'arte

**show'place'** *s* luogo celebre; **to be a showplace** *(said, e.g., of a house)* essere arredato perfettamente

**show'room'** *s* sala di mostra

**show' win'dow** *s* vetrina

**show·y** ['ʃo·i] *adj* (-ier; -iest) vistoso, sgargiante

**shrapnel** ['ʃræpnəl] *s* shrapnel *m*

**shred** [ʃrɛd] *s* brano, brandello; ritaglio; (fig) granello; **to cut to shreds** fare a brandelli ‖ *v (pret & pp* **shredded** or **shred;** *ger* **shredding)** *tr* fare a brandelli; *(paper)* tagliuzzare

**shrew** [ʃru] *s (woman)* bisbetica; *(animal)* toporagno

**shrewd** [ʃrud] *adj* astuto, scaltro

**shriek** [ʃrik] *s* strido; strillo; risata stridula ‖ *intr* stridere; strillare

**shrill** [ʃrɪl] *adj* stridulo, squillante

**shrimp** [ʃrɪmp] *s* gamberetto; *(person)* omiciattolo, nanerottolo

**shrine** [ʃraɪn] *s* santuario, sacrario

**shrink** [ʃrɪŋk] *v (pret* **shrank** [ʃræŋk] or **shrunk** [ʃrʌŋk]; *pp* **shrunk** or **shrunken)** *tr* contrarre, restringere ‖ *intr* contrarsi, restringersi; ritirarsi

**shrinkage** ['ʃrɪŋkɪdʒ] *s* restringimento; *(in weight)* calo

**shriv·el** ['ʃrɪvəl] *v (pret & pp* **-eled** or **-elled;** *ger* **-eling** or **-elling)** *tr* raggrinzire; *(from heat)* raccartocciare; *(to wither)* avvizzire ‖ *intr* raggrinzirsi; accartocciarsi; avvizzire; **to shrivel up** incartapecorire

**shroud** [ʃraυd] *s* sudario, lenzuolo funebre; (fig) cappa ‖ *tr* avvolgere

**Shrove' Tues'day** [ʃrov] *s* martedì grasso

**shrub** [ʃrʌb] *s* arbusto

**shrubber·y** ['ʃrʌbəri] *s* (-ies) arbusti *mpl*, cespugli *mpl*

**shrug** [ʃrʌg] *s* scrollata di spalle ‖ *v (pret & pp* **shrugged;** *ger* **shrugging)** *tr* scrollare; **to shrug one's shoulders** scrollare le spalle ‖ *intr* fare spallucce

**shudder** ['ʃʌdər] *s* brivido, fremito ‖ *intr* rabbrividire, fremere

**shuffle** ['ʃʌfəl] *s (of cards)* mescolata; turno di fare il mazzo; *(of feet)* strascichio; evasione ‖ *tr* mescolare; strisciare, strascicare ‖ *intr* fare il

mazzo; scalpicciare; ballare di striscio; **to shuffle off** strascicarsi, scalpicciare; **to shuffle out of** evadere da

**shun** [ʃʌn] *v (pret & pp* **shunned;** *ger* **shunning)** *tr* evitare, schivare

**shunt** [ʃʌnt] *tr* sviare; (elec) shuntare; (rr) deviare

**shut** [ʃʌt] *adj* chiuso ‖ *v (pret & pp* **shut;** *ger* **shutting)** *tr* chiudere, serrare; **to shut in** rinchiudere; **to shut off** *(e.g., gas)* tagliare; **to shut up** tappare; imprigionare; (coll) fare star zitto ‖ *intr* chiudersi; **to shut up** (coll) stare zitto, tacere

**shut'down'** *s* chiusura

**shutter** ['ʃʌtər] *s (outside a window)* persiana, gelosia; *(outside a store window)* serranda, saracinesca; (phot) otturatore *m*

**shuttle** ['ʃʌtəl] *s* spola, navetta ‖ *intr* fare la spola

**shut'tle·cock'** *s* volano, volante *m*

**shut'tle train'** *s* treno che fa la spola fra due stazioni

**shy** [ʃaɪ] *adj* (**shyer** or **shier; shyest** or **shiest)** timido; *(fearful)* schivo, ritroso; corto, a corto, e.g., **he is shy of funds** è a corto di denaro ‖ *v (pret & pp* **shied)** *intr* ritirarsi; schivarsi; *(said of a horse)* adombrarsi; **to shy away** tenersi discosto

**shyster** ['ʃaɪstər] *s* (coll) azzeccagarbugli *m*

**Sia·mese** [ˌsaɪ·ə'miz] *adj* siamese ‖ *s* (-mese) siamese *mf*

**Si'amese twins'** *spl* fratelli *mpl* siamesi

**Siberian** [saɪ'bɪrɪ·ən] *adj & s* siberiano

**sibilant** ['sɪbɪlənt] *adj & s* sibilante *f*

**sibyl** ['sɪbɪl] *s* sibilla

**sic** [sɪk] *adv* sic ‖ [sɪk] *v (pret & pp* **sicked;** *ger* **sicking)** *tr* aizzare; **sick 'em!** va!; **to sick on** aizzare contro

**Sicilian** [sɪ'sɪljən] *adj & s* siciliano

**Sicily** ['sɪsɪli] *s* la Sicilia

**sick** [sɪk] *adj* ammalato; nauseato; *(bored)* stucco; **sick at heart** con una spina nel cuore; **to be sick and tired** averne sin sopra i capelli; **to be sick at one's stomach** avere la nausea; **to take sick** cader malato ‖ *tr (a dog)* aizzare

**sick'bed'** *s* letto d'ammalato

**sicken** ['sɪkən] *tr* ammalare; disgustare ‖ *intr* ammalarsi

**sickening** ['sɪkənɪŋ] *adj* stomachevole

**sick' head'ache** *s* emicrania accompagnata da nausea

**sickle** ['sɪkəl] *s* falce messoria, falcetto

**sick' leave'** *s* congedo per motivi di salute

**sick·ly** ['sɪkli] *adj* (-lier; -liest) cagionevole, malaticcio

**sickness** ['sɪknɪs] *s* malattia; nausea

**side** [saɪd] *adj* laterale ‖ *s* parte *f*, lato; *(e.g., of a coin)* faccia; *(slope)* versante *m; (of human body, of a ship)* fianco; **to take sides** parteggiare ‖ *intr* parteggiare; **to side with** schierarsi dalla parte di

**side'board'** *s* credenza

**side'burns'** *spl* basette *fpl*, favoriti *mpl*

**side'car'** *s* motocarrozzetta; carrozzino laterale (di motocarrozzetta)

**side' dish'** *s* portata extra

**side' door'** *s* porta laterale

**side' effect'** *s* effetto secondario

**side'-glance'** *s* occhiata di sbieco

**side' is'sue** *s* questione secondaria

**side'line'** *s* linea laterale; impiego secondario; attività secondaria

**sidereal** [saɪ'dɪrɪ·əl] *adj* siderale

**side'sad'dle** *adv* all'amazzone

**side' show'** *s* spettacolo secondario di baraccone; affare secondario

**side'slip'** *intr* (aer) scivolare d'ala

**side'split'ting** *adj* che fa sbellicare dalle risa

**side' step'** *s* passo laterale; scartata

**side'-step'** *v* (*pret & pp* **-stepped;** *ger* **-stepping**) *tr* evitare ‖ *intr* farsi da parte; fare una scartata

**side'track'** *s* binario morto di smistamento ‖ *tr* sviare; (rr) smistare

**side' view'** *s* vista di profilo

**side'walk'** *s* marciapiede *m*

**side'walk café'** *s* caffè *m* con tavolini all'aperto

**sideward** ['saɪdwərd] *adj* obliquo, a sghembo ‖ *adv* verso un lato; di sghembo

**side'ways'** *adj* sghembo ‖ *adv* di sghembo; di fianco

**side' whisk'ers** *spl* favoriti *mpl*

**siding** ['saɪdɪŋ] *s* (rr) diramazione, binario morto, raccordo ferroviario

**sidle** ['saɪdəl] *intr* andare al lato; muoversi furtivamente

**siege** [sidʒ] *s* assedio; (*of illness*) ricorrenza d'attacchi; **to lay siege to** cingere d'assedio, assediare

**siesta** [si'estə] *s* siesta; **to take a siesta** fare la siesta

**sieve** [sɪv] *s* vaglio, setaccio ‖ *tr* vagliare, setacciare

**sift** [sɪft] *tr* (*flour*) abburattare; setacciare; (*to scatter with a sieve*) spolverare; (fig) vagliare

**sigh** [saɪ] *s* sospiro ‖ *tr* mormorare sospirando ‖ *intr* sospirare; **to sigh for** sospirare

**sight** [saɪt] *s* vista, visione; spettacolo, veduta, (opt) mira, traguardo; (mil) mirino, tacca di mira; (coll) mucchio; **a sight of** (coll) molto; **at first sight a** prima vista; **at sight** ad apertura di libro; (com) a vista; **out of sight** fuori di vista; lontano dagli occhi; (*prices*) astronomico; **sights** luoghi *mpl* interessanti; **sight unseen** senza averlo visto prima, a occhi chiusi; **to be a sight** (coll) essere un orrore; **to catch sight of** arrivare a intravedere; **to know by sight** conoscere di vista; **to not be able to stand the sight of s.o.** not poter vedere qlcu nemmeno dipinto ‖ *tr* avvistare; (*a weapon*) mirare ‖ *intr* mirare, prendere di mira; osservare attentamente

**sight' draft'** *s* (com) tratta a vista

**sight'-read'** *v* (*pret & pp* **-read** [ˌrɛd]) *tr & intr* leggere a libro aperto

**sight'see'ing** *adj* turistico ‖ *s* turismo, visite *fpl* turistiche

**sightseer** ['saɪtˌsi·ər] *s* turista *mf*

**sign** [saɪn] *s* segno; segnale *m;* (*e.g., on a store*) insegna, cartello; **signs** tracce *fpl* ‖ *tr* firmare; ingaggiare; indicare, segnalare ‖ *intr* firmare; fare segno; **to sign off** (rad, telv) terminare la trasmissione; **to sign up** iscriversi

**sig·nal** ['sɪgnəl] *adj* insigne, segnalato ‖ *s* segnale *m* ‖ *v* (*pret & pp* **-naled** or **-nalled;** *ger* **-naling** or **-nalling**) *tr* segnalare ‖ *intr* fare segnalazioni

**sig'nal corps'** *s* (mil) armi *fpl* di trasmissione

**sig'nal tow'er** *s* (rr) posto di blocco

**signato·ry** ['sɪgnɪˌtori] *s* (**-ries**) firmatario

**signature** ['sɪgnətʃər] *s* firma; segno musicale; (typ) segnatura

**sign'board'** *s* cartellone *m*

**signer** ['saɪnər] *s* firmatario

**sig'net ring'** ['sɪgnɪt] *s* anello col sigillo

**significance** [sɪg'nɪfɪkəns] *s* importanza; (*meaning*) significato

**significant** [sɪg'nɪfɪkənt] *adj* importante

**signi·fy** ['sɪgnɪˌfaɪ] *v* (*pret & pp* **-fied**) *tr* significare

**sign'post'** *s* palo indicatore

**silence** ['saɪləns] *s* silenzio ‖ *tr* far tacere; (mil) ridurre al silenzio

**silent** ['saɪlənt] *adj* silenzioso, tacito

**si'lent mov'ie** *s* cinema muto

**silhouette** [ˌsɪlu'ɛt] *s* silhouette *f*, siluetta

**silicon** ['sɪlɪkən] *s* silicio

**silicone** ['sɪlɪˌkon] *s* silicone *m*

**silk** [sɪlk] *adj* di seta ‖ *s* seta; **to hit the silk** (slang) gettarsi col paracadute

**silken** ['sɪlkən] *adj* serico, di seta

**silk' hat'** *s* cappello a cilindro

**silk'screen proc'ess** *s* serigrafia

**silk'-stock'ing** *adj & s* aristocratico

**silk'worm'** *s* baco da seta, filugello

**silk·y** ['sɪlki] *adj* (**-ier; -iest**) di seta; come la seta

**sill** [sɪl] *s* basamento; (*of a door*) soglia; (*of a window*) davanzale *m*

**sil·ly** ['sɪli] *adj* (**-lier; -liest**) sciocco, scemo

**si·lo** ['saɪlo] *s* (**-los**) silo ‖ *tr* insilare

**silt** [sɪlt] *s* sedimento

**silver** ['sɪlvər] *adj* d'argento; (*voice*) argentino; (*plated with silver*) argentato ‖ *s* argento ‖ *tr* inargentare

**sil'ver·fish'** *s* (ent) lepisma

**sil'ver foil'** *s* foglia d'argento

**sil'ver fox'** *s* volpe argentata

**sil'ver lin'ing** *s* spiraglio di speranza

**sil'ver plate'** *s* vasellame *m* d'argento; argentatura

**sil'ver screen'** *s* (mov) schermo

**sil'ver·smith'** *s* argentiere *m*

**sil'ver spoon'** *s* ricchezza ereditata; **to be born with a silver spoon in one's mouth** esser nato con la camicia

**sil'ver·ware'** *s* argenteria

**sil'ver·ware' chest'** *s* portaposate *m*

**similar** ['sɪmɪlər] *adj* simile

**similari·ty** [ˌsɪmɪ'lærɪti] *s* (**-ties**) similarità *f*, somiglianza

**simile** ['sɪmɪli] *s* similitudine *f*

**simmer** ['sɪmər] *tr* cuocere a fuoco lento ǁ *intr* cuocere a fuoco lento; (fig) ribollire; **to simmer down** (slang) calmarsi

**simper** ['sɪmpər] *s* sorriso scemo ǁ *intr* fare un sorriso scemo

**simple** ['sɪmpəl] *adj* semplice

**simple-minded** ['sɪmpəl'maɪndɪd] *adj* semplicione, scemo

**simpleton** ['sɪmpəltən] *s* semplicione *m*

**simulate** ['sɪmjə‚let] *tr* simulare

**simultaneous** [‚saɪməl'tenɪ‧əs] or [‚sɪməl'tenɪ‧əs] *adj* simultaneo

**sin** [sɪn] *s* peccato ǁ *v* (*pret & pp* **sinned; ger sinning**) *intr* peccare

**since** [sɪns] *adv* da allora, da allora in poi; da tempo fa ǁ *prep* da ǁ *conj* dacché; poiché, dato che

**sincere** [sɪn'sɪr] *adj* sincero

**sincerity** [sɪn'serɪti] *s* sincerità *f*

**sine** [saɪn] *s* (math) seno

**sinecure** ['saɪnɪ‚kjur] or ['sɪnɪ‚kjur] *s* sinecura

**sinew** ['sɪnju] *s* tendine *m;* (fig) nerbo

**sinful** ['sɪnfəl] *adj* (*person*) peccatore; (*act, intention, etc.*) peccaminoso

**sing** [sɪŋ] *v* (*pret* **sang** [sæŋ] or **sung** [sʌŋ]; *pp* **sung**) *tr* cantare; **to sing to sleep** ninnare ǁ *intr* cantare; (*said, e.g., of the ears*) fischiare

**singe** [sɪndʒ] *v* (*ger* **singeing**) *tr* strinare, bruciacchiare

**singer** ['sɪŋər] *s* cantante *mf;* (*in night club*) canzonettista *mf*

**single** ['sɪŋgəl] *adj* unico, solo; (*room*) a un letto; (*bed*) a una piazza; (*man*) celibe; (*woman*) nubile; (*combat*) corpo a corpo; semplice, sincero ǁ **singles** *ssg* singolare *m* ǁ *tr* scegliere; **to single out** individuare

**single-breasted** ['sɪŋgəl'brestɪd] *adj* a un petto, monopetto

**sin'gle entry'** *s* partita semplice

**sin'gle file'** *s* fila indiana

**single-handed** ['sɪŋgəl'hændɪd] *adj* da solo, senza aiuto altrui

**sin'gle-phase'** *adj* (elec) monofase

**sin'gle room'** *s* camera a un letto

**sin'gle-track'** *adj* (rr) a binario semplice; (fig) di corte vedute

**sing'song'** *adj* monotono ǁ *s* cantilena

**singular** ['sɪŋgjələr] *adj & s* singolare *m*

**sinister** ['sɪnɪstər] *adj* sinistro

**sink** [sɪŋk] *s* acquaio; (*sewer*) scolo, fogna; (fig) sentina ǁ *v* (*pret* **sank** [sæŋk] or **sunk** [sʌŋk]; *pp* **sunk**) *tr* sprofondare; infiggere; (*a well*) scavare; (*in tone*) abbassare; (*a boat*) mandare a picco; rovinare; investire; perdere ǁ *intr* sprofondarsi; abbassarsi; (*said, of the sun, prices, etc.*) calare; andare a picco; lasciarsi cadere; (*in vice*) impantanarsi; (*said of one's cheeks*) infossarsi; (*in thought*) perdersi; **to sink down** sedersi; **to sink in** penetrare

**sink'ing fund'** *s* fondo d'ammortamento

**sinner** ['sɪnər] *s* peccatore *m*

**Sinology** [si'nɑlədʒi] *s* sinologia

**sinuous** ['sɪnju‧əs] *adj* sinuoso

**sinus** ['saɪnəs] *s* seno

**sip** [sɪp] *s* sorso ǁ *v* (*pret & pp* **sipped; ger sipping**) *tr* sorbire, sorseggiare

**siphon** ['saɪfən] *s* sifone *m* ǁ *tr* travasare con un sifone

**si'phon bot'tle** *s* sifone *m*

**sir** [sʌr] *s* signore *m;* (Brit) **sir** *m;* **Dear Sir** Illustrissimo signore; (com) Egregio signore

**sire** [saɪr] *s* (*king*) sire *m;* padre *m,* stallone *m* ǁ *tr* generare

**siren** ['saɪrən] *s* sirena

**sirloin** ['sʌrlɔɪn] *s* lombata, lombo

**sirup** ['sɪrəp] or ['sʌrəp] *tr* sciroppo

**sis‧sy** ['sɪsi] *s* (**-sies**) effemminato

**sister** ['sɪstər] *adj* (*ship*) gemello; (*language*) sorella; (*corporation*) consorella ǁ *s* sorella; (*nun*) suora, monaca

**sis'ter-in-law'** *s* (**sis'ters-in-law'**) cognata

**Sis'tine Chap'el** ['sɪstin] *s* Cappella Sistina

**sit** [sɪt] *v* (*pret & pp* **sat** [sæt]; *ger* **sitting**) *intr* sedere; posare; (*said of a hen*) covare; (*said of a jacket*) stare; essere in sessione; **to sit down** sedersi; **to sit in on** partecipare a; assistere a; **to sit still** stare tranquillo; **to sit up** alzarsi; (coll) essere sorpreso

**sit'-down strike'** *s* sciopero bianco

**site** [saɪt] *s* sito, luogo, posizione

**sitting** ['sɪtɪŋ] *s* seduta; (*of a court*) sessione; (*of a hen*) covata; (*serving of a meal*) turno

**sit'ting duck'** *s* (slang) facile bersaglio

**sit'ting room'** *s* soggiorno

**situate** ['sɪtʃu‚et] *tr* situare

**situation** [‚sɪtʃu'eʃən] *s* situazione, posizione; posto

**sitz' bath'** [sɪts] *s* semicupio

**six** [sɪks] *adj & pron* sei ǁ *s* sei *m;* **at sixes and sevens** in disordine; **six o'clock** le sei

**six' hun'dred** *adj, s & pron* seicento

**sixteen** ['sɪks'tin] *adj, s & pron* sedici *m*

**sixteenth** ['sɪks'tinθ] *adj, s & pron* sedicesimo ǁ *s* (*in dates*) sedici *m*

**sixth** [sɪksθ] *adj, s & pron* sesto ǁ *s* (*in dates*) sei *m*

**sixtieth** ['sɪkstɪ‧ɪθ] *adj, s & pron* sessantesimo

**six‧ty** ['sɪksti] *adj & pron* sessanta ǁ *s* (**-ies**) sessanta *m;* **the sixties** gli anni sessanta

**sizable** ['saɪzəbəl] *adj* considerevole

**size** [saɪz] *s* grandezza; quantità *f;* (*of person or garment*) taglia; (*of shoes*) numero; (*of hat*) giro; (*of a pipe*) diametro; (*for gilding*) colla; (fig) situazione ǁ *tr* misurare, classificare secondo grandezza; incollare; **to size up** (coll) stimare, giudicare

**sizzle** ['sɪzəl] *s* sfrigolio ǁ *intr* sfriggere

**skate** [sket] *s* pattino; (slang) tipo ǁ *intr* pattinare; **to skate on thin ice** andare in cerca di disgrazie

**skat'ing rink'** *s* pattinatoio

**skein** [sken] *s* gomitolo, matassa

**skeleton** ['skelɪtən] *adj* scheletrico ǁ *s* scheletro

**skel'eton key'** *s* chiave maestra

**skeptic** ['skeptɪk] *adj & s* scettico

**skeptical** ['skɛptɪkəl] *adj* scettico
**sketch** [skɛtʃ] *s* schizzo, disegno; abbozzo, bozzetto; (theat) scenetta || *tr* schizzare, disegnare; abbozzare
**sketch'book'** *s* album *m* di schizzi; quaderno per abbozzi
**skew** [skju] *adj* obliquo || *s* movimento obliquo; (*chisel*) scalpello a taglio obliquo || *tr* tagliare di sghembo || *intr* (*to swerve*) deviare; (*to look obliquely*) guardare di sghembo
**skew' chis'el** *s* scalpello a taglio obliquo
**skewer** ['skju·ər] *s* spiedino || *tr* mettere allo spiedo
**ski** [ski] *s* (**skis** or **ski**) sci *m* || *intr* sciare
**ski' boot'** *s* scarpa da sci
**skid** [skɪd] *s* (*device to check a wheel*) scarpa; (*skidding forward*) slittamento; (*skidding sideway*) sbandamento; (aer, mach) pattino || *v* (*pret & pp* **skidded;** *ger* **skidding**) *tr* frenare || *intr* (*forward*) slittare; (*sideways*) sbandare
**skid' row'** [ro] *s* quartiere malfamato
**skier** ['ski·ər] *s* sciatore *m*
**skiff** [skɪf] *s* skiff *m*, singolo
**skiing** ['ski·ɪŋ] *s* sci *m*
**ski' jump'** *s* salto con gli sci; trampolino di salto
**ski' lift'** *s* sciovia
**skill** [skɪl] *s* destrezza, perizia
**skilled** [skɪld] *adj* abile, esperto
**skilled' la'bor** *s* manodopera qualificata
**skillet** ['skɪlɪt] *s* padella
**skilful** ['skɪlfəl] *adj* destro, abile
**skim** [skɪm] *v* (*pret & pp* **skimmed;** *ger* **skimming**) *tr* (*milk*) scremare; (e.g., *broth*) sgrassare; (*to graze*) sfiorare; (*the ground*) radere; (*a page*) trascorrere || *intr* sfiorare; **to skim over** scorrere
**ski' mask'** *s* passamontagna *m*
**skimmer** ['skɪmər] *s* schiumaiola; (*hat*) canottiera
**skim' milk'** *s* latte scremato or magro
**skimp** [skɪmp] *tr* lesinare || *intr* economizzare, risparmiare
**skimp·y** ['skɪmpi] *adj* (**-ier; -iest**) corto, scarso; taccagno
**skin** [skɪn] *s* pelle *f*; (*rind*) scorza; (*of onion*) spoglia; **by the skin of one's teeth** (coll) per il rotto della cuffia; **soaked to the skin** bagnato fino alle ossa; **to have a thin skin** offendersi facilmente || *v* (*pret & pp* **skinned;** *ger* **skinning**) *tr* pelare, spellare; (e.g., *one's knee*) spellarsi; (slang) tosare; **to skin alive** (slang) scotennare; (slang) battere in pieno
**skin'-deep'** *adj* a fior di pelle
**skin'-div'er** *s* nuotatore subacqueo, sub *m*; (mil) sommozzatore *m*
**skin'flint'** *s* avaro
**skin' game'** *s* truffa
**skin·ny** ['skɪni] *adj* (**-nier; -niest**) magro, scarno
**skin' test'** *s* cutireazione
**skip** [skɪp] *s* salto || *v* (*pret & pp*

**skipped;** *ger* **skipping**) *tr* (*a fence; a meal*) saltare; (*a subject*) sorvolare; (*school*) (coll) marinare || *intr* saltare, salterellare; (*said of typewriter*) saltare uno spazio; (coll) svignarsela
**ski' pole'** *s* racchetta da sci
**skipper** ['skɪpər] *s* capitano, comandante *m*
**skirmish** ['skʌrmɪʃ] *s* scaramuccia || *intr* battersi in una scaramuccia
**skirt** [skʌrt] *s* sottana, gonna; (*edge*) orlo; (*woman*) (slang) gonnella || *tr* orlare; costeggiare; (*a subject*) evitare
**ski' run'** *s* pista da sci
**skit** [skɪt] *s* (theat) quadretto comico
**skittish** ['skɪtɪʃ] *adj* bizzarro, balzano; timido; (*horse*) ombroso
**skulduggery** [skʌl'dʌgəri] *s* trucco disonesto
**skull** [skʌl] *s* cranio, teschio
**skull' and cross'bones** *s* due tibie incrociate ed un teschio
**skull'cap'** *s* papalina
**skunk** [skʌŋk] *s* puzzola, moffetta; (coll) puzzone *m*
**sky** [skaɪ] *s* (**skies**) cielo; firmamento; **to praise to the skies** portare al cielo
**sky'div'er** *s* paracadutista *mf*
**sky'jack'er** *s* pirata *m* dell'aria
**sky'lark'** *s* allodola || *intr* (coll) darsi alla pazza gioia
**sky'light'** *s* lucernario
**sky'line'** *s* linea dell'orizzonte; (*of city*) profilo
**sky'rock'et** *s* razzo || *intr* salire come un razzo
**sky'scrap'er** *s* grattacielo
**sky'writ'ing** *s* scrittura pubblicitaria aerea
**slab** [slæb] *s* (*of stone*) lastra, lastrone *m*; (*of wood*) tavola; (*slice*) fetta
**slack** [slæk] *adj* lento, allentato; negligente, indolente; (fig) fiacco, morto || *s* lentezza; negligenza; stagione morta, inattività *f*; **slacks** pantaloni *mpl* da donna; pantaloni sciolti || *tr* allentare; trascurare; (*lime*) spegnere || *intr* rilasciarsi; essere negligente; **to slack up** rallentare
**slacker** ['slækər] *s* fannullone *m*; (mil) imboscato
**slag** [slæg] *s* scoria
**slake** [slek] *tr* spegnere
**slalom** ['slɑləm] *s* slalom *m*
**slam** [slæm] *s* colpo; (*of door*) sbatacchiamento; (*in cards*) cappotto; (coll) strapazzata || *v* (*pret & pp* **slammed;** *ger* **slamming**) *tr* sbattere, sbatacchiare; (coll) strapazzare || *intr* sbattere, sbatacchiare
**slam'bang'** *adv* (coll) con gran rumore, precipitosamente
**slander** ['slændər] *s* calunnia, maldicenza || *tr* calunniare, diffamare
**slanderous** ['slændərəs] *adj* calunnioso, diffamatorio
**slang** [slæŋ] *s* gergo
**slant** [slænt] *s* inclinazione; punto di vista || *tr* inclinare; (*news*) snaturare || *intr* inclinarsi; deviare

**slap** [slæp] *s* manata; (*in the face*) schiaffo, ceffone *m*; (*noise*) rumore *m*; insulto ‖ *v* (*pret & pp* **slapped;** *ger* **slapping**) *tr* dare una manata a; schiaffeggiare

**slap'dash'** *adj* raffazzonato, fatto a casaccio ‖ *adv* a casaccio

**slap'hap'py** *adj* (*punch-drunk*) stordito; (*giddy*) allegro, brillo

**slap'stick'** *adj* buffonesco ‖ *s* bastone *m* d'Arlecchino; buffonata

**slash** [slæʃ] *s* sfregio; (*of prices*) riduzione ‖ *tr* sfregiare; (*cloth*) tagliare; (*prices*) ridurre

**slat** [slæt] *s* travicello, regolo; (*for bed*) traversa; (*of shutter*) stecca

**slate** [slet] *s* ardesia, lavagna; lista elettorale; **clean slate** buon certificato ‖ *tr* coprire con tegole d'ardesia; proporre la nomina di; (*to schedule*) mettere in cantiere

**slate' roof'** *s* tetto d'ardesia

**slattern** ['slætərn] *s* (*slovenly woman*) sciamannona; (*harlot*) puttana

**slaughter** ['slɔtər] *s* eccidio, carneficina ‖ *tr* sgozzare, scannare

**slaugh'ter·house'** *s* macello, scannatoio

**Slav** [slɑv] *or* [slæv] *adj & s* slavo

**slave** [slev] *adj & s* schiavo ‖ *intr* lavorare come uno schiavo

**slave' driv'er** *s* negriere *m*

**slavery** ['slevəri] *s* schiavitù *f*

**slave' trade'** *s* tratta degli schiavi

**Slavic** ['slɑvɪk] *or* ['slævɪk] *adj & s* slavo

**slay** [sle] *v* (*pret* **slew** [slu]; *pp* **slain** [slen]) *tr* scannare, uccidere

**slayer** ['sle·ər] *s* uccisore *m*

**sled** [slɛd] *s* slittino, slitta ‖ *v* (*pret & pp* **sledded;** *ger* **sledding**) *intr* slittare

**sledge' ham'mer** *s* [slɛdʒ] *s* mazza

**sleek** [slik] *adj* liscio, lustro; elegante ‖ *tr* lisciare, ammorbidire

**sleep** [slip] *s* sonno; **to go to sleep** addormentarsi; **to put to sleep** addormentare; uccidere con un anestetico ‖ *v* (*pret & pp* **slept** [slɛpt]) *tr* dormire; aver posto a dormire per; **to sleep it over** dormirci sopra; **to sleep off a hangover** smaltire una sbornia dormendo ‖ *intr* dormire; **to sleep in** dormire fino a tardi; passare la notte a casa; **to sleep out** passare la notte fuori di casa

**sleeper** ['slipər] *s* (*person*) dormiente *mf*; (*beam, timber*) trave *f*

**sleep'ing bag'** *s* sacco a pelo

**sleep'ing car'** *s* vettura letto

**sleep'ing pill'** *s* sonnifero

**sleepless** ['slipləs] *adj* insonne; (*night*) bianco

**sleep'walk'er** *s* sonnambulo

**sleep·y** ['slipi] *adj* (-**ier;** -**iest**) insonnolito, sonnolento; **to be sleepy** aver sonno

**sleep'y-head'** *s* dormiglione *m*

**sleet** [slit] *s* nevischio ‖ *impers* **it is sleeting** cade il nevischio

**sleeve** [sliv] *s* manica; (*of phonograph record*) busta; (*mach*) manicotto; **to laugh in** *or* **up one's sleeve** ridere sotto i baffi

**sleigh** [sle] *s* slitta ‖ *intr* andare in slitta

**sleigh' bells'** *spl* bubboli *mpl* da slitta, sonagliera da slitta

**sleigh' ride'** *s* passeggiata in slitta

**sleight' of hand'** [slaɪt] *s* gioco di prestigio

**slender** ['slɛndər] *adj* smilzo, snello; esiguo, esile

**sleuth** [sluθ] *s* segugio

**slew** [slu] *s* (coll) mucchio

**slice** [slaɪs] *s* fetta; (*of an orange*) spicchio ‖ *tr* tagliare a fette; (fig) fendere

**slick** [slɪk] *adj* liscio, lustro; scivoloso; astuto; (slang) ottimo ‖ *s* posto scivoloso; (coll) rivista stampata su carta patinata ‖ *tr* lisciare, lustrare; **to slick up** (coll) acconciare

**slicker** ['slɪkər] *s* impermeabile *m* di tela cerata; (coll) furbo di tre cotte

**slide** [slaɪd] *s* scivolata, scivolone *m*; (*chute*) scivolo; (*landslide*) frana; (*for projection*) diapositiva; (*of a microscope*) vetrino; (mach) guida; (*of a slide rule*) (mach) cursore *m* ‖ *v* (*pret & pp* **slid** [slɪd]) *tr* far scivolare ‖ *intr* sdrucciolare, scivolare; (*said of a car*) pattinare, slittare; **to let slide** lasciar correre

**slide' fas'tener** *s* chiusura lampo

**slide' projec'tor** *s* diascopio

**slide' rule'** *s* regolo calcolatore

**slide' valve'** *s* (mach) cassetto di distribuzione

**slid'ing door'** *s* porta scorrevole

**slid'ing scale'** *s* scala mobile

**slight** [slaɪt] *adj* leggero, lieve; delicato ‖ *s* noncuranza, disattenzione; affronto ‖ *tr* fare con negligenza; (*to snub*) trattare con noncuranza, snobbare

**slim** [slɪm] *adj* (**slimmer; slimmest**) sottile; magro

**slime** [slaɪm] *s* melma; (*e.g., of a snail*) bava

**slim·y** ['slaɪmi] *adj* (-**ier;** -**iest**) melmoso; bavoso; sudicio

**sling** [slɪŋ] *s* (*to shoot stones*) fionda; (naut) braca; **in a sling** (*arm*) al collo ‖ *v* (*pret & pp* **slung** [slʌŋ]) *tr* gettare; lanciare; (*freight*) imbracare; sospendere; mettere a bandoliera

**sling'shot'** *s* fionda

**slink** [slɪŋk] *v* (*pret & pp* **slunk** [slʌŋk]) *intr* andare furtivamente; **to slink away** eclissarsi

**slip** [slɪp] *s* scivolone *m*; svista, errore *m*; (*in prices*) discesa; (*underdress*) sottoveste *f*; (*pillowcase*) federa; (*of paper*) pezzo; (*space between two wharves*) darsena, imbarcatoio; (*form*) modulo; personcina; (*inclined plane*) (naut) scalo d'alaggio; (bot) innesto; **to give the slip to** eludere ‖ *v* (*pret & pp* **slipped;** *ger* **slipping**) *tr* infilare; liberare; liberarsi da; omettere; **to slip off** togliersi; **to slip on** mettersi; **to slip one's mind** dimenticarsi di, e.g., **it slipped my mind** me ne sono dimenticato ‖ *intr* scivolare,

scorrere; sdrucciolare; sbagliare; peggiorare; **to let slip** lasciarsi sfuggire; **to slip away** svignarsela; **to slip by** (*said of time*) passare, fuggire; **to slip out of s.o.'s hands** sgusciare dalle mani di qlcu; **to slip up** sbagliarsi
**slip'cov'er** *s* fodera
**slip'knot'** *s* nodo scorsoio
**slip' of the tongue'** *s* errore *m* nel parlare
**slipper** ['slɪpər] *s* pantofola
**slippery** ['slɪpəri] *adj* sdrucciolevole, scivoloso; evasivo; incerto
**slip'shod'** *adj* trasandato, mal fatto
**slip'-up'** *s* (coll) sbaglio
**slit** [slɪt] *s* taglio, fenditura ‖ *v* (*pret & pp* **slit;** *ger* **slitting**) *tr* tagliare, fendere; **to slit the throat of** sgozzare
**slob** [slɑb] *s* (slang) rozzo, villanzone *m*
**slobber** ['slɑbər] *s* bava; sdolcinatura ‖ *intr* sbavare; parlare sdolcinatamente
**sloe** [slo] *s* (*shrub*) prugnolo; (*fruit*) prugnola
**slogan** ['slogən] *s* slogan *m*
**sloop** [slup] *s* cutter *m*
**slop** [slɑp] *s* pastone *m;* (slang) sbobba ‖ *v* (*pret & pp* **slopped;** *ger* **slopping**) *tr* versare, imbrodare ‖ *intr* rovesciarsi, scorrere; (slang) perdersi in smancerie
**slope** [slop] *s* costa, pendice *f;* (*of mountain or roof*) spiovente *m* ‖ *tr* inclinare ‖ *intr* digradare, scendere
**slop•py** ['slɑpi] *adj* (**-pier; -piest**) fangoso; bagnato; (*slovenly*) sciatto; (*done badly*) abborracciato
**slot** [slɑt] *s* scanalatura; (*for letters*) buca; (*e.g., on a broadcasting schedule*) posizione
**sloth** [sloθ] *or* [slɔθ] *s* pigrizia; (zool) bradipo, poltrone *m*
**slot' machine'** *s* macchina a gettone
**slouch** [slautʃ] *s* postura goffa; persona goffa; (coll) poltrone *m* ‖ *intr* muoversi goffamente; **to slouch in a chair** sdraiarsi
**slouch' hat'** *s* cappello floscio
**slough** [slau] *s* pantano; (fig) abisso ‖ [slʌf] *s* (*of snake*) spoglia; (pathol) crosta ‖ *tr*—**to slough off** spogliarsi di ‖ *intr* sbucciarsi, cadere
**Slovak** ['slovæk] *or* [slo'væk] *adj & s* slovacco
**sloven•ly** ['slʌvənli] *adj* (**-lier; -liest**) sciatto, trasandato
**slow** [slo] *adj* lento; (*sluggish*) tardo; (*clock*) indietro, in ritardo; (*in understanding*) tardivo ‖ *adv* piano ‖ *tr* rallentare ‖ *intr* rallentarsi; (*said of a watch*) ritardare
**slow'down'** *s* sciopero pignolo
**slow' mo'tion** *s*—**in slow motion** al rallentatore
**slow'-motion projec'tor** *s* rallentatore *m*
**slow'poke'** *s* (coll) poltrone *m*
**slug** [slʌg] *s* (*heavy piece of metal*) lingotto; (*metal disk*) gettone *m;* (fig) poltrone *m;* (zool) lumaca; (coll) colpo, mazzata ‖ *v* (*pret & pp*

**slugged;** *ger* **slugging**) *tr* picchiare sodo
**sluggard** ['slʌgərd] *s* poltrone *m*
**sluggish** ['slʌgɪʃ] *adj* pigro, indolente; lento, fiacco
**sluice** [slus] *s* canale *m;* stramazzo
**sluice' gate'** *s* paratoia
**slum** [slʌm] *s* bassifondi *mpl* ‖ *v* (*pret & pp* **slummed;** *ger* **slumming**) *intr* visitare i bassifondi
**slumber** ['slʌmbər] *s* dormiveglia *m,* sonnellino ‖ *intr* dormire, dormicchiare
**slump** [slʌmp] *s* depressione, crisi *f;* (*in prices*) ribasso, calo ‖ *intr* impantanarsi; peggiorare; (*said of prices*) ribassare, calare
**slur** [slʌr] *s* insulto, macchia; critica; (mus) legatura ‖ *v* (*pret & pp* **slurred;** *ger* **slurring**) *tr* pronunziare indistintamente; (*a subject*) sorvolare; insultare, calunniare; (mus) legare
**slush** [slʌʃ] *s* poltiglia di neve; fanghiglia; (fig) sdolcinatezza
**slut** [slʌt] *s* cagna; (*slovenly woman*) sciamannona; troia, puttana
**sly** [slaɪ] *adj* (**slyer** *or* **slier; slyest** *or* **sliest**) furbo; insidioso; (*hiding one's true feelings*) sornione; **on the sly** furtivamente
**smack** [smæk] *s* schiaffo; (*of whip or lips*) schiocco; (*taste*) traccia, sapore *m;* (coll) bacio collo schiocco ‖ *adv* di colpo, direttamente ‖ *tr* dare uno schiaffo a; colpire; (*the whip or one's lips*) schioccare; schioccare un bacio a ‖ *intr*—**to smack of** sapere di
**small** [smɔl] *adj* piccolo; povero; basso, umile; (*change*) spicciolo; (typ) minuscolo
**small' arms'** *spl* armi *fpl* portatili
**small' busi'ness** *s* piccolo commercio
**small' cap'ital** *s* (typ) maiuscoletto
**small' change'** *s* spiccioli *mpl*
**small' fry'** *s* minutaglia; bambini *mpl;* gente *f* di poca importanza
**small' hours'** *spl* ore *fpl* piccole
**small' intes'tine** *s* intestino tenue
**small-minded** ['smɔl'maɪndɪd] *adj* di corte vedute, gretto
**small' of the back'** *s* fine *f* della schiena, reni *fpl*
**smallpox** ['smɔl,pɑks] *s* vaiolo
**small' talk'** *s* conversazione futile
**small'-time'** *adj* di poca importanza
**small'-town'** *adj* di provincia
**smart** [smɑrt] *adj* intelligente; scaltro, furbo; (*pain*) acuto; (*in appearance*) elegante; (pert) impertinente; (coll) grande, abbondante ‖ *s* dolore acuto, sofferenza ‖ *intr* bruciare; dolere; soffrire
**smart' al'eck** ['ælɪk] *s* saputello
**smart' set'** *s* bel mondo
**smash** [smæʃ] *s* sconquasso; colpo; collisione; rovina, fallimento; (tennis) smash *m,* schiacciata ‖ *tr* sconquassare; sfracellare; rovinare; (tennis) schiacciare ‖ *intr* sconquassarsi; sfracellarsi; andare in rovina; **to smash into** scontrarsi con
**smash' hit'** *s* successone *m*

**smash'-up'** *s* sconquasso

**smattering** ['smætərɪŋ] *s* infarinatura, spolvero

**smear** [smɪr] *s* macchia, imbrattatura; calunnia; (bact) striscio || *tr* imbrattare; spalmare; calunniare

**smear' campaign'** *s* campagna di vilipendio

**smell** [smɛl] *s* odore *m;* (*sense*) olfatto, odorato; profumo || *v* (*pret & pp* **smelled** or **smelt**) *tr* fiutare, odorare || *intr* odorare; (*to stink*) puzzare; profumare; **to smell of** odorare di; puzzare di

**smell'ing salts'** *spl* sali aromatici

**smell·y** ['smɛli] *adj* (**-ier; -iest**) puzzolente

**smelt** [smɛlt] *s* (ichth) eperlano || *tr & intr* fondere

**smile** [smaɪl] *s* sorriso || *intr* sorridere

**smiling** ['smaɪlɪŋ] *adj* sorridente

**smirk** [smʌrk] *s* ghigno || *intr* ghignare

**smite** [smaɪt] *v* (*pret* **smote** [smot]; *pp* **smitten** ['smɪtən] or **smit** [smɪt]) *tr* colpire; percuotere; affliggere, castigare

**smith** [smɪθ] *s* fabbro

**smith·y** ['smɪθi] *s* (**-ies**) fucina

**smit'ten** *adj* afflitto; innamorato

**smock** [smɑk] *s* camice *m;* (*of mechanic*) camiciotto

**smock' frock'** *s* blusa da lavoro

**smog** [smɑg] *s* foschia, smog *m*

**smoke** [smok] *s* fumo; **to go up in smoke** andare in cenere || *tr* affumicare; (*tobacco*) fumare; **to smoke out** cacciare col fumo; scoprire || *intr* fumare; (*said, e.g., of the earth*) fumigare

**smoke'-filled room'** *s* stanza da riunioni piena di fumo

**smoke'less pow'der** ['smoklɪs] *s* polvere *f* senza fumo

**smoker** ['smokər] *s* fumatore *m;* salone *m* fumatori; (rr) vagone *m* fumatori

**smoke' rings'** *spl* anelli *mpl* di fumo

**smoke' screen'** *s* cortina di fumo

**smoke'stack'** *s* fumaiolo

**smoking** ['smokɪŋ] *s* (il) fumare; **no smoking** vietato fumare

**smok'ing car'** *s* vagone *m* fumatori

**smok'ing jack'et** *s* giacca da casa

**smok'ing room'** *s* stanza per fumatori

**smok·y** ['smoki] *adj* (**-ier; -iest**) fumoso

**smolder** ['smoldər] *s* fumo derivante da fuoco che cova || *intr* (*said of fire or passion*) covare; (*said of s.o.'s eyes*) ardere

**smooch** [smutʃ] *intr* (coll) baciarsi, baciucchiarsi

**smooth** [smuð] *adj* liscio, levigato; (*face*) glabro; di consistenza uniforme; (*flat*) piano; senza interruzioni; tranquillo; elegante; (*sound*) armonioso; (*taste*) gradevole; (*wine*) abboccato; (*sea*) calmo; (*style*) fluido || *tr* lisciare, levigare; appianare, facilitare; calmare; **to smooth away** appianare

**smooth-faced** ['smuð ˌfest] *adj* (*beardless*) glabro; liscio

**smooth-spoken** ['smuðˌspokən] *adj* mellifluo

**smooth·y** ['smuði] *s* (**-ies**) galante *m*

**smother** ['smʌðər] *tr* affoggare, soffocare

**smudge** [smʌdʒ] *s* macchia, imbrattatura || *tr* macchiare, imbrattare; (*a garden*) affumicare

**smudge' pot'** *s* apparecchiatura per affumicare

**smug** [smʌg] *adj* (**smugger; smuggest**) pieno di sé stesso; liscio, lisciato

**smuggle** ['smʌgəl] *tr* contrabbandare || *intr* praticare il contrabbando

**smuggler** ['smʌglər] *s* contrabbandiere *m*

**smuggling** ['smʌglɪŋ] *s* contrabbando

**smut** [smʌt] *s* sudiciume *m;* oscenità *f;* (agr) volpe *f,* golpe *f*

**smut·ty** ['smʌti] *adj* (**-tier; -tiest**) sudicio; osceno; (agr) malato di volpe

**snack** [snæk] *s* spuntino, merenda; porzione

**snack' bar'** *s* tavola calda

**snag** [snæg] *s* tronco sommerso; protuberanza, sporgenza; (*tooth*) dente rotto; (fig) intoppo, ostacolo; **to hit a snag** incontrare un ostacolo || *v* (*pret & pp* **snagged;** *ger* **snagging**) *tr* fare uno straccio a; (fig) ostacolare

**snail** [snel] *s* chiocciola, lumaca; **at a snail's pace** come una lumaca

**snake** [snek] *s* serpente *m;* (*nonvenomous*) biscia

**snake' in the grass'** *s* pericolo nascosto; (*person*) serpe *f* in seno

**snap** [snæp] *s* (*sharp sound*) schiocco; (*bite*) morso; (*fastener*) bottone automatico; (*of cold weather*) breve periodo; (*manner of speaking*) tono tagliente; (phot) istantanea; (coll) vigore *m;* (coll) cosa da nulla || *v* (*pret & pp* **snapped;** *ger* **snapping**) *tr* schioccare; chiudere di colpo; spezzare di colpo; (*a picture*) scattare; **to snap one's fingers at** infischiarsi di; **to snap up** afferrare; (*a person*) tagliare la parola a || *intr* schioccare; (*to crack*) rompersi di colpo; **to snap at** cercare di mordere; (*a bargain*) cercare di afferrare; **to snap out of it** (coll) riprendersi; **to snap shut** chiudersi di colpo

**snap'drag'on** *s* (bot) bocca di leone

**snap' fas'tener** *s* bottone automatico

**snap' judg'ment** *s* decisione presa senza riflessione

**snap·py** ['snæpi] *adj* (**-pier; -piest**) mordente, mordace; (coll) vivo, vivace; (coll) elegante; **to make it snappy** (slang) sbrigarsi

**snap'shot'** *s* istantanea

**snare** [sner] *s* laccio, lacciolo; (*of a drum*) corda

**snare' drum'** *s* cassa rullante

**snarl** [snɑrl] *s* (*of a dog*) ringhio; groviglio; (*of traffic*) ingorgo; (fig) confusione || *tr* urlare con un ringhio; (*to tangle*) aggrovigliare; complicare || *intr* ringhiare; aggrovigliarsi; complicarsi

**snatch** [snætʃ] *s* strappo, strappone *m;* presa; pezzetto; momentino || *tr &*

*intr* strappare; **to snatch at** cercare di afferrare; **to snatch from** strappare a

**sneak** [snik] *s* furfante *m* ‖ *tr* mettere di nascosto; pigliare di nascosto ‖ *intr*—**to sneak in** entrare di nascosto; **to sneak out** svignarsela

**sneaker** ['snikər] *s* furfante *m; scarpetta da ginnastica

**sneak' thief'** *s* ladro, topo

**sneak·y** ['sniki] *adj* (**-ier; -iest**) furtivo

**sneer** [snɪr] *s* ghigno ‖ *intr* sogghignare; **to sneer at** beffarsi si

**sneeze** [sniz] *s* starnuto ‖ *intr* starnutare; **not to be sneezed at** (coll) non essere disprezzabile

**snicker** ['snɪkər] *s* risatina ‖ *intr* fare una risatina

**snide** [snaɪd] *adj* malizioso

**sniff** [snɪf] *s* fiuto, fiutata; (*scent*) odore *m* ‖ *tr* fiutare ‖ *intr* aspirare rumorosamente; (*with emotion*) moccicare; **to sniff at** annusare; mostrare disprezzo per

**sniffle** ['snɪfəl] *s* moccio; **to have the sniffles** moccicare ‖ *intr* moccicare

**snip** [snɪp] *s* taglio; pezzetto; (*person*) (coll) mezza cartuccia ‖ *v* (*pret & pp* **snipped;** *ger* **snipping**) *tr* tagliuzzare

**snipe** [snaɪp] *s* tiro di nascosto; (orn) beccaccino ‖ *intr* sparare in appostamento; attaccare da lontano

**sniper** ['snaɪpər] *s* franco tiratore, cecchino

**snippet** ['snɪpɪt] *s* ritaglio, frammento; (fig) mezza cartuccia

**snip·py** ['snɪpi] *adj* (**-pier; -piest**) frammentario; (coll) corto, brusco; (coll) arrogante

**snitch** [snɪtʃ] *tr & intr* (coll) graffignare, sgraffignare

**sniv·el** ['snɪvəl] *s* moccio; singhiozzo, piagnisteo; falsa commozione ‖ *v* (*pret & pp* **-eled** or **-elled;** *ger* **-eling** or **-elling**) *intr* singhiozzare, piagnucolare; (*to have a runny nose*) moccicare, avere il moccio

**snob** [snɑb] *s* snob *mf*

**snobbery** ['snɑbəri] *s* snobismo

**snobbish** ['snɑbɪʃ] *adj* snobistico

**snoop** [snup] *s* (coll) ficcanaso ‖ *intr* (coll) ficcare il naso

**snoop·y** ['snupi] *adj* (**-ier; -iest**) (coll) curioso, invadente

**snoot** [snut] *s* (slang) naso

**snoot·y** ['snuti] *adj* (**-ier; -iest**) (coll) snobistico

**snooze** [snuz] *s* (coll) sonnellino ‖ *intr* (coll) fare un sonnellino

**snore** [snor] *s* russamento ‖ *intr* russare

**snort** [snɔrt] *s* sbuffo ‖ *intr* sbuffare

**snot** [snɑt] *s* (slang) moccio

**snot·ty** ['snɑti] *adj* (**-tier; -tiest**) (coll) snobistico; (coll) arrogante; (slang) moccioso

**snout** [snaʊt] *s* muso; (*of pig*) grugno; (*of person*) muso, grugno

**snow** [sno] *s* neve *f* ‖ *intr* nevicare

**snow'ball'** *s* palla di neve ‖ *tr* gettare palle di neve a ‖ *intr* aumentare come una palla di neve

**snow'blind'** *adj* accecato dalla neve

**snow'bound'** *adj* prigioniero della neve

**snow-capped** ['sno ˌkæpt] *adj* coperto di neve

**snow'drift'** *s* banco di neve

**snow'fall'** *s* nevicata

**snow' fence'** *s* barriera contro la neve

**snow'flake'** *s* fiocco di neve

**snow' flur'ry** *s* neve portata da raffiche

**snow' line'** *s* limite *m* delle nevi perenni

**snow'man'** *s* (**-men'**) uomo di neve

**snow'plow'** *s* spazzaneve *m*

**snow'shoe'** *s* racchetta da neve

**snow'slide'** *s* valanga

**snow'storm'** *s* bufera di neve

**snow' tire'** *s* gomma da neve, pneumatico da neve

**snow'-white'** *adj* bianco come la neve

**snow·y** ['sno·i] *adj* (**-ier; -iest**) nevoso

**snub** [snʌb] *s* affronto ‖ *v* (*pret & pp* **snubbed;** *ger* **snubbing**) *tr* snobbare

**snub-by** ['snʌbi] *adj* (**-bier; -biest**) camuso, rincagnato

**snuff** [snʌf] *s* fiutata; tabacco da fiuto; (*of a candlewick*) moccolo; **up to snuff** (coll) soddisfacente; (coll) bene ‖ *tr* fiutare; tabaccare; (*a candle*) smoccolare; **to snuff out** spegnere; (fig) soffocare

**snuff'box'** *s* tabacchiera

**snuffers** ['snʌfərz] *spl* smoccolatoio

**snug** [snʌg] *adj* (**snugger; snuggest**) comodo; (*dress*) attillato; compatto; (*well-off*) agiato; (*sum*) discreto; (*sheltered*) ben protetto; (*well-hidden*) nascosto

**snuggle** ['snʌgəl] *intr* rannicchiarsi; **to snuggle up to** stringersi a

**so** [so] *adv* così; così or tanto + *adj* or *adv;* per quanto; **and so** certamente; pure; **and so on** e così via; **or so** più o meno; **to think so** credere di sì; **so as to** + *inf* per + *inf;* **so far** sinora, finora; **so long!** arrivederci!; **so many** tanti; **so much** tanto; **so so** così così; **so that** in maniera che, di modo che; **so to speak** per così dire ‖ *conj* cosicché ‖ *interj* bene!; basta!; così!

**soak** [sok] *s* bagnata; (*toper*) (slang) ubriacone *m* ‖ *tr* bagnare, inzuppare; imbevere; (coll) ubriacare; (slang) far pagare un prezzo esorbitante a; **to soak up** assorbire; **soaked to the skin** bagnato fino alle ossa ‖ *intr* stare a molle, macerare; inzupparsi

**so'-and-so'** *s* (**-sos**) tal *m* dei tali; tal cosa

**soap** [sop] *s* sapone *m* ‖ *tr* insaponare

**soap'box'** *s* cassa di sapone; tribuna improvvisata

**soap'box or'ator** *s* oratore *m* che parla da una tribuna improvvisata

**soap' bub'ble** *s* bolla di sapone

**soap' dish'** *s* portasapone *m*

**soap' flakes'** *spl* sapone *m* a scaglie

**soap' op'era** *s* (coll) trasmissione radiofonica o televisiva lacrimogena

**soap' pow'der** *s* sapone *m* in polvere

**soap'stone'** *s* pietra da sarto

**soap'suds'** *spl* saponata

**soap·y** ['sopi] *adj* (**-ier; -iest**) saponoso

**soar** [sor] *intr* spaziare, slanciarsi; (aer) librarsi

**sob** [sab] *s* singhiozzo || *v* (*pret & pp* **sobbed;** *ger* **sobbing**) *tr* dire a singhiozzi || *intr* singhiozzare

**sober** ['sobər] *adj* sobrio; non ubriaco || *intr* smaltire la sbornia; **to sober down** calmarsi; **to sober up** smaltire la sbornia

**sobriety** [so'braɪ·əti] *s* sobrietà *f*

**sobriquet** ['sobrɪ‚ke] *s* nomignolo

**sob' sis'ter** *s* giornalista lacrimogeno

**sob' sto'ry** *s* storia lacrimogena

**so'-called'** *adj* cosiddetto

**soccer** ['sakər] *s* calcio, football *m*

**sociable** ['soʃəbəl] *adj* sociale, socievole

**social** ['soʃəl] *adj* sociale || *s* riunione sociale

**so'cial climb'er** ['klaɪmər] *s* arrampicatore *m* sociale

**so'cial con'tract** *s* patto sociale

**socialism** ['soʃə‚lɪzəm] *s* socialismo

**socialist** ['soʃəlɪst] *s* socialista *mf*

**socialite** ['soʃə‚laɪt] *s* persona che appartiene all'alta società

**So'cial Reg'ister** *s* (trademark) annuario dell'alta società

**so'cial secu'rity** *s* sicurezza sociale

**so'cial work'er** *s* visitatrice *f*, assistente *mf* sociale

**socie·ty** [sə'saɪ·əti] *s* (**-ties**) società *f;* (*companionship or company*) compagnia

**soci'ety ed'itor** *s* cronista mondano

**sociology** [‚sosɪ'alədʒi] or [‚soʃɪ-'alədʒi] *s* sociologia

**sock** [sak] *s* calzino; (slang) colpo forte; (slang) attore *m* di prim'ordine; (slang) spettacolo eccezionale || *tr* (slang) dare un forte colpo a

**socket** ['sakɪt] *s* (*of eye*) occhiaia; (*of tooth*) alveolo; (*of candlestick*) bocciolo; (*wall socket*) (elec) presa di corrente; (elec) portalampada *m*

**sock'et wrench'** *s* chiave *f* a tubo

**sod** [sad] *s* zolla; terreno erboso || *v* (*pret & pp* **sodded;** *ger* **sodding**) *tr* piotare

**soda** ['sodə] *s* soda

**so'da crack'er** *s* galletta fatta al bicarbonato

**so'da wa'ter** *s* soda, gazosa

**sodium** ['sodɪ·əm] *adj* sodico || *s* sodio

**sofa** ['sofə] *s* sofà *m*, divano

**so'fa bed'** *s* sofà *m* letto

**soft** [sɔft] or [saft] *adj* molle; (*smooth*) morbido; (*iron*) dolce; (*hat*) floscio; (*person*) rammollito; (coll) facile

**soft'-boiled' egg'** ['sɔft'bɔɪld] or ['saft'bɔɪld] *s* uovo alla coque

**soft' coal'** *s* carbone bituminoso

**soft' drink'** *s* bibita

**soften** ['sɔfən] or ['safən] *tr* mollificare, rammollire; (fig) intenerire || *intr* intenerirsi

**softener** ['sɔfənər] or ['safənər] *s* ammorbidente *m*

**soft' land'ing** *s* allunaggio morbido

**soft'-ped'al** *v* (*pret & pp* **-aled** or **-alled;** *ger* **-aling** or **-alling**) *tr* mettere in sordina; (coll) moderare

**soft'-shell crab'** *s* mollecca

**soft' soap'** *s* sapone *m* molle; (coll) adulazione

**soft'-soap'** *tr* (coll) insaponare

**sog·gy** ['sagi] *adj* (**-gier; -giest**) rammollito, inzuppato

**soil** [sɔɪl] *s* suolo, terreno; territorio; (*spot*) macchia; (*filth*) porcheria, lordura || *tr* sporcare, macchiare || *intr* sporcarsi, macchiarsi

**soil' pipe'** *s* tubo di scarico

**soiree** or **soirée** [swa're] *s* serata

**sojourn** ['sodʒʌrn] *s* soggiorno || ['sodʒʌrn] or [so'dʒʌrn] *intr* soggiornare

**solace** ['salɪs] *s* conforto || *tr* confortare, consolare

**solar** ['solər] *adj* solare

**so'lar bat'tery** *s* batteria solare

**solder** ['sadər] *s* saldatura; lega per saldatura || *tr* saldare

**sol'dering i'ron** *s* saldatoio

**soldier** ['soldʒər] *s* (*man of rank and file*) soldato; (*man in military service*) militare *m* || *intr* fare il soldato

**sol'dier of for'tune** *s* soldato di ventura

**soldier·y** ['soldʒəri] *s* (**-ies**) soldatesca

**sold-out** ['sold ‚aut] *adj* esaurito; (*e.g., theater*) completo

**sole** [sol] *adj* solo, unico; esclusivo || *s* (*of foot*) pianta; (*of stocking*) soletta; (*of shoe*) suola; (*fish*) sfoglia || *tr* solare

**solely** ['solli] *adv* solamente

**solemn** ['saləm] *adj* solenne

**solicit** [sə'lɪsɪt] *tr* sollecitare; adescare, accostare

**solicitor** [sə'lɪsɪtər] *s* sollecitatore *m;* agente *m;* (law) procuratore *m*

**solicitous** [sə'lɪsɪtəs] *adj* sollecito

**solicitude** [sə'lɪsɪ‚tjud] or [sə'lɪsɪ-‚tud] *s* sollecitudine *f*

**solid** ['salɪd] *adj* solido; (*not hollow*) sodo; (*e.g., clouds*) denso; (*wall*) pieno, massiccio; (*word*) con grafia unita; intero; unanime, solidale; (*good*) buono; (*e.g., gold*) puro, massiccio

**solidity** [sə'lɪdɪti] *s* solidità *f*

**sol'id-state'** *adj* transistorizzato, senza valvole

**solilo·quy** [sə'lɪləkwi] *s* (**-quies**) soliloquio

**solitaire** ['salɪ‚ter] *s* solitario

**solitar·y** ['salɪ‚teri] *adj* solitario; unico || *s* (**-ies**) persona solitaria

**sol'itary confine'ment** *s* segregazione cellulare

**solitude** ['salɪ‚tjud] or ['salɪ‚tud] *s* solitudine *f*

**so·lo** ['solo] *adj* solo, solitario; (mus) solista || *s* (**-los**) (mus) solo

**soloist** ['solo·ɪst] *s* solista *mf*

**so' long'** *interj* (coll) ciao!; (coll) addio!; (coll) arrivederci!

**solstice** ['salstɪs] *s* solstizio

**soluble** ['saljəbəl] *adj* solubile

**solution** [sə'luʃən] *s* soluzione *f*

**solvable** ['salvəbəl] *adj* risolvibile

**solve** [salv] *tr* risolvere, sciogliere

**solvency** ['sɑlvənsi] *s* solvenza
**solvent** ['sɑlvənt] *adj & s* solvente *m*
**somber** ['sɑmbər] *adj* tetro
**some** [sʌm] *adj indef* qualche; di + *art*, e.g., **some apples** delle mele; (coll) forte, grande || *pron indef* alcuni, taluni; ne, e.g., **I have some** ne ho
**some'bod'y** *pron indef* taluno, qualcuno; **somebody else** qualcun altro || *s* (-ies) (coll) qualcuno
**some'day'** *adv* qualche giorno
**some'how'** *adv* in qualche modo; **somehow or other** in un modo o nell'altro
**some'one'** *pron indef* qualcuno, taluno; **someone else** qualcun altro
**somersault** ['sʌmər,sɔlt] *s* salto mortale || *intr* fare un salto mortale
**something** ['sʌmθɪŋ] *pron indef* qualcosa; **something else** qualcos'altro || *adv* un po'; (coll) molto, moltissimo
**some'time'** *adj* antico, di un tempo || *adv* un giorno o l'altro, uno di questi giorni
**some'times'** *adv* talora, talvolta
**some'way'** *adv* in qualche modo
**some'what'** *s* qualcosa || *adv* piuttosto, un po'
**some'where'** *adv* in qualche luogo, da qualche parte; a qualche momento; **somewhere else** altrove
**somnambulist** [sɑm'næmbjəlɪst] *s* sonnambulo
**somnolent** ['sɑmnələnt] *adj* sonnolento
**son** [sʌn] *s* figlio
**sonar** ['sonɑr] *s* ecogoniometro, sonar *m*
**song** [sɔŋ] or [sɑŋ] *s* canto, canzone *f*; **for a song** per un soldo
**song'bird'** *s* uccello canoro
**Song' of Songs'** *s* Cantico dei Cantici
**songster** ['sɔŋgstər] *s* cantante *m*, canzonettista *m*
**songstress** ['sɔŋgstrɪs] *s* cantante *f*, canzonettista *f*
**song'writ'er** *s* canzoniere *m*
**son'ic boom'** ['sɑnɪk] *s* boato sonico
**son'-in-law'** *s* (sons'-in-law') genero
**sonnet** ['sɑnɪt] *s* sonetto
**son•ny** ['sʌni] *s* (-nies) figliolo
**sonori•ty** [sə'nɑrɪti] or [sə'nɔrɪti] *s* (-ties) sonorità *f*
**soon** [sun] *adv* in breve, ben presto; subito, presto; **as soon as** non appena, quanto prima; **as soon as possible** quanto prima; **I had sooner** preferirei; **how soon?** quando?; **soon after** poco dopo; **sooner or later** prima o poi, tosto o tardi
**soot** [sʊt] or [sut] *s* fuliggine *f*
**soothe** [suð] *tr* calmare, lenire
**soothsayer** ['suθ,se·ər] *s* indovino
**soot•y** ['suti] or ['suti] *adj* (-ier; -iest) fuligginoso
**sop** [sɑp] *s* (*soaked food*) zuppa; (*bribe*) dono, offa || *v* (*pret & pp* **sopped**; *ger* **sopping**) *tr* intingere, inzuppare; **to sop up** assorbire
**sophisticated** [sə'fɪstɪ,ketɪd] *adj* sofisticato, smaliziato
**sophistication** [sə,fɪstɪ'keʃən] *s* eccessiva ricercatezza; gusti *mpl* raffinati

**sophomore** ['sɑfə,mor] *s* studente *m* del secondo anno, fagiolo
**sophomoric** [,sɑfə'mɑrɪk] *adj* saputello, presuntuoso; ingenuo, imberbe
**sopping** ['sɑpɪŋ] *adv*—**sopping wet** inzuppato
**sopran•o** [sə'præno] or [sə'prano] *adj* per soprano, da soprano || *s* (-os) soprano *mf*
**sorcerer** ['sɔrsərər] *s* mago, stregone *m*
**sorceress** ['sɔrsərɪs] *s* maga, strega
**sorcer•y** ['sɔrsəri] *s* (-ies) stregoneria
**sordid** ['sɔrdɪd] *adj* sordido
**sore** [sor] *adj* irritato; indolenzito; estremo, grave; **to be sore at** (coll) aversela con || *s* piaga, ulcera; dolore *m*, afflizione; **to open an old sore** riaprire una ferita
**sorely** ['sorli] *adv* penosamente; gravemente, urgentemente
**soreness** ['sornɪs] *s* dolore *m*, afflizione
**sore' spot'** *s* (fig) piaga
**sore' throat'** *s* mal *m* di gola
**sorori•ty** [sə'rarɪti] or [sə'rɔrɪti] *s* (-ties) associazione femminile universitaria
**sorrel** ['sɑrəl] or ['sɔrəl] *adj* sauro
**sorrow** ['sɑro] or ['sɔro] *s* dolore *m*, cordoglio || *intr* affliggersi, provar cordoglio; **to sorrow for** rimpiangere
**sorrowful** ['sɑrəfəl] or ['sɔrəfəl] *adj* doloroso
**sor•ry** ['sɑri] or ['sɔri] *adj* (-rier; -riest) spiacente, desolato, dolente; povero, cattivo; **to be sorry** dolersi; dispiacere a, e.g., **he is sorry** gli dispiace || *interj* mi dispiace!, scusi!
**sort** [sɔrt] *s* tipo, specie *f*; maniera; **a sort of** una specie di; **out of sorts** depresso; ammalato; di mal umore; **sort of** (coll) piuttosto; (coll) un certo, e.g., **sort of a headache** un certo mal di testa || *tr* assortire; (*mail*) smistare
**so'-so'** *adj* passabile || *adv* così così
**sot** [sɑt] *s* ubriacone *m*
**soubrette** [su'brɛt] *s* (theat) soubrette *f*
**soul** [sol] *s* anima; **upon my soul!** sulla mia parola!
**sound** [saʊnd] *adj* sano; solido, forte; valido, buono; (*sleep*) profondo; valido, legale; onesto || *s* suono; rumore *m*; (*of an animal*) verso; (*passage of water*) stretto; (surg) sonda; (ichth) vescica natatoria; **within sound of** alla portata di || *adv* profondamente || *tr* (*an instrument*) sonare; pronunciare; (*e.g., s.o.'s chest*) auscultare; (*praises*) cantare; (*to measure*) sondare || *intr* sonare; parere, sembrare; fare uno scandaglio; **to sound like** avere il suono di; dare l'impressione di, parere
**sound' bar'rier** *s* muro del suono
**sound' film'** *s* pellicola sonora
**soundly** ['saʊndli] *adv* solidamente; profondamente; completamente
**sound'proof'** *adj* a prova di suono || *tr* insonorizzare

**sound' track'** s (mov) sonoro, colonna sonora

**sound' truck'** s autoveicolo con impianto sonoro

**sound' wave'** s onda sonora

**soup** [sup] s zuppa, minestra

**soup' dish'** s piatto fondo

**soup' kitch'en** s asilo dei poveri che serve zuppa gratuitamente

**soup'spoon'** s cucchiaio (da minestra)

**sour** [saʊr] adj acido; (fruit) acerbo || tr inacidire || intr inacidirsi

**source** [sors] s fonte f, sorgente f

**source' lan'guage** s lingua di partenza

**source' mate'rial** s fonti fpl originali

**sour' cher'ry** s (fruit) amarena; (tree) amareno

**sour' grapes'** interj l'uva è verde!

**south** [saʊθ] adj meridionale, del sud || s sud m, meridione m || adv verso il sud

**South' Amer'ica** s l'America f del Sud

**South' Amer'ican** adj & s sudamericano

**southeast** [ˌsaʊθˈist] adj di sud-est || s sud-est || adv al sud-est

**southern** [ˈsʌðərn] adj meridionale

**South'ern Cross'** s Croce f del Sud

**southerner** [ˈsʌðərnər] s meridionale mf

**South' Kore'a** s la Corea del Sud

**south'paw'** adj & s (coll) mancino

**South' Pole'** s Polo sud

**South' Vietnam•ese'** [vɪˌɛtnəˈmiz] adj vietnamita del sud || s (-ese) vietnamita mf del sud

**southward** [ˈsaʊθwərd] adv verso il sud

**south'west'** adj di sud-ovest || s sud-ovest m || adv al sud-ovest

**souvenir** [ˌsuvəˈnɪr] or [ˈsuvəˌnɪr] s ricordo, memoria

**sovereign** [ˈsavrɪn] or [ˈsʌvrɪn] adj sovrano || s (king) sovrano; (queen; coin) sovrana

**sovereign•ty** [ˈsavrɪnti] or [ˈsʌvrɪnti] s (-ties) sovranità f

**soviet** [ˈsovɪˌɛt] or [ˌsovɪˈɛt] adj sovietico || s soviet m

**So'viet Rus'sia** s la Russia Sovietica

**sow** [saʊ] s porca, troia || [so] v (pret sowed; pp sown or sowed) tr seminare

**soybean** [ˈsɔɪˌbin] s soia; seme m di soia

**spa** [spa] s terme fpl

**space** [spes] adj spaziale || s spazio; periodo; **after a space** dopo un po' || tr spaziare; **to space out** diradare

**space' bar'** s barra spaziatrice, spaziatrice f

**space' cen'ter** s cosmodromo

**space'craft'** s astronave f

**space' flight'** s volo spaziale

**space'man'** s (-men') navigatore m spaziale

**spacer** [ˈspesər] s spaziatrice f, barra spaziatrice

**space'ship'** s astronave f

**space'suit'** s scafandro astronautico, tuta spaziale

**spacious** [ˈspeʃəs] adj spazioso

**spade** [sped] s vanga; (cards) picca; **to call a spade a spade** dire pane al pane, vino al vino || tr vangare

**spade'work'** s lavoro preliminare

**spaghetti** [spəˈgeti] s spaghetti mpl

**Spain** [spen] s la Spagna

**span** [spæn] s (of the hand) spanna; (of time) tratto; (of a bridge) campata, luce f; (of horses) paio; (aer) apertura || v (pret & pp spanned; ger spanning) tr misurare a spanne; attraversare, oltrepassare; (said of time) abbracciare

**spangle** [ˈspæŋgəl] s lustrino || tr tempestare di lustrini; (with bright objects) stellare || intr brillare

**Spaniard** [ˈspænjərd] s spagnolo

**Spanish** [ˈspænɪʃ] adj & s spagnolo; **the Spanish** gli spagnoli

**Span'ish-Amer'ican** adj & s ispanoamericano

**Span'ish broom'** s ginestra

**Span'ish fly'** mosca cantaride

**Span'ish om'elet** s frittata di pomodori, cipolle e peperoni

**Span'ish-speak'ing** adj di lingua spagnola

**spank** [spæŋk] tr sculacciare

**spanking** [ˈspæŋkɪŋ] adj rapido; forte; (coll) eccellente, straordinario || s sculacciata

**spar** [spar] s (mineral) spato; (naut) asta, pennone m; (aer) longherone m || v (pret & pp sparred; ger sparring) intr fare la box

**spare** [spɛr] adj di riserva; libero, in eccesso; (e.g., diet) frugale; (lean) magro || tr salvare, risparmiare; perdonare; (to do without) fare a meno di, privarsi di; **to have . . . to spare** aver . . . d'avanzo; **to spare oneself** risparmiarsi

**spare' parts'** s pezzi mpl di ricambio

**spare' room'** s camera per gli ospiti

**spare' tire'** s ruota di scorta, pneumatico di scorta

**spare' wheel'** s ruota di scorta

**sparing** [ˈspɛrɪŋ] adj economico; (scanty) scarso

**spark** [spark] s scintilla; traccia || tr (coll) rianimare; (coll) corteggiare || intr scintillare

**spark' coil'** s bobina d'accensione

**spark' gap'** s (elec) traferro, intraferro

**sparkle** [ˈsparkəl] s scintilla; (luster) scintillio; allegria, vivacità f || intr scintillare; (said, e.g., of eyes) brillare, luccicare; (said of wine) frizzare, spumeggiare

**sparkling** [ˈsparklɪŋ] adj scintillante; (wine) frizzante, spumeggiante; (water) gassoso

**spark' plug'** s candela

**sparrow** [ˈspæro] s passero

**sparse** [spars] adj rado

**Spartan** [ˈspartən] adj & s spartano

**spasm** [ˈspæzəm] s spasmo; sprazzo d'energia

**spasmodic** [spæzˈmɑdɪk] adj spasmodico; intermittente, a sprazzi

**spastic** [ˈspæstɪk] adj & s spastico

**spat** [spæt] s litigio, battibecco; **spats**

ghette *fpl* || *v (pret & pp* **spatted; ger spatting)** *intr* avere un battibecco

**spatial** ['speʃəl] *adj* spaziale

**spatter** ['spætər] *tr* schizzare, spruzzare || *intr* gocciolare

**spatula** ['spætʃələ] *s* spatola

**spawn** [spɔn] *s* prole *f*, progenie *f;* risultato || *tr* produrre, generare || *intr* (ichth) deporre le uova

**spay** [spe] *tr* asportare le ovaie a

**speak** [spik] *v (pret* **spoke** [spok]; *pp* **spoken)** *tr (a language)* parlare; *(the truth)* dire || *intr* parlare; **so to speak** per così dire; **speaking!** al telefono!; **to speak of** importante, che valga parlarne; **to speak out** dire la propria opinione

**speak'-eas'y** *s* (-ies) bar clandestino

**speaker** ['spikər] *s* conferenziere *m*, oratore *m; (of a language)* parlante *mf;* (pol) presidente *m;* (rad) altoparlante *m*

**speaking** ['spikɪŋ] *adj* parlante; **to be on speaking terms** parlarsi || *s* parlare *m*, discorso

**speak'ing tube'** *s* tubo acustico

**spear** [spɪr] *s* lancia; *(for fishing)* arpione *m; (of grass)* stelo || *tr* trafiggere con la lancia

**spear' gun'** *s* fucile subacqueo

**spear'head'** *s* punta di lancia || *tr* condurre, dirigere

**spear'mint'** *s* menta romana spicata

**special** ['speʃəl] *adj* speciale || *s* prezzo speciale; treno speciale

**spe'cial deliv'ery** *s* espresso

**spe'cial draw'ing rights'** *spl* (econ) diritti *mpl* speciali di prelievo

**specialist** ['speʃəlɪst] *s* specialista *mf*

**specialize** ['speʃə,laɪz] *tr* specializzare || *intr* specializzarsi

**spe'cial part'ner** *s* accomandante *mf*

**special·ty** ['speʃəlti] *s* (-ties) specialità *f*

**spe·cies** ['spisiz] *s* (-cies) specie *f*

**specific** [spɪ'sɪfɪk] *adj & s* specifico

**specification** [,spesɪfɪ'keʃən] *s* specifica; (com) capitolato

**specif'ic grav'ity** *s* peso specifico

**speci·fy** ['spesɪ,faɪ] *v (pret & pp* **-fied)** *tr* specificare

**specimen** ['spesɪmən] *s* esemplare *m;* (coll) tipo

**specious** ['spiʃəs] *adj* specioso

**speck** [spek] *s* macchiolina; *(of dust)* granello; *(of hope)* filo || *tr* ⸱ ⸱ ⸱chiettare

**speckle** ['spekəl] *s* macchiolina || *tr* macchiettare, picchiettare

**spectacle** ['spektəkəl] *s* spettacolo; **spectacles** occhiali *mpl*

**spectator** ['spektetər] *or* [spek'tetər] *s* spettatore *m*

**specter** ['spektər] *s* spettro

**spec·trum** ['spektrəm] *s* (-tra [trə] *or* -trums) spettro; (fig) gamma

**speculate** ['spekjə,let] *intr* speculare

**speech** [spitʃ] *s* parola, parlata; *(before an audience)* discorso; *(of an actor)* elocuzione; **in speech** oralmente

**speech' clin'ic** *s* clinica per la correzione dei difetti del linguaggio

**speechless** ['spitʃlɪs] *adj* senza parole, muto

**speed** [spid] *s* velocità *f;* (aut) marcia || *tr* accelerare, affrettare || *intr* accelerare, affrettarsi; guidare oltre la velocità massima

**speed'boat'** *s* motoscafo da corsa

**speeding** ['spidɪŋ] *s* eccesso di velocità

**speed' king'** *s* asso del volante

**speed' lim'it** *s* limite *m* di velocità

**speedometer** [spi'damɪtər] *s* tachimetro; *(to record the distance covered)* contachilometri *m*

**speed'-up'** *s* accelerazione

**speed'way'** *s (highway)* autostrada; *(for races)* pista

**speed·y** ['spidi] *adj* (-ier; -iest) veloce, rapido

**spell** [spel] *s* malia, incantesimo; fascino; turno; attacco; periodo di tempo; **to cast a spell on** incantare || *v (pret & pp* **spelled** *or* **spelt** [spelt]) *tr* compitare; scrivere in tutte lettere; voler dire; **to spell out** (coll) spiegare dettagliatamente || *intr* scrivere, sillabare || *v (pret & pp* **spelled)** *tr* rimpiazzare

**spell'bind'** *v (pret & pp* **-bound)** *tr* affascinare

**spell'bind'er** *s* oratore *m* abbagliante

**spelling** ['spelɪŋ] *adj* ortografico || *s (act)* compitazione; *(way a word is spelled)* grafia; *(subject of study)* ortografia

**spell'ing bee'** *s* gara di ortografia

**spelunker** [spɪ'lʌŋkər] *s* esploratore *m* di caverne

**spend** [spend] *v (pret & pp* **spent** [spent]) *tr* spendere; *(time)* passare

**spender** ['spendər] *s* spenditore *m*

**spend'ing mon'ey** *s* denaro per le piccole spese personali

**spend'thrift'** *s* sprecone *m*, spendaccione *m*

**sperm** [spʌrm] *s* sperma *m*

**sperm' whale'** *s* capodoglio

**spew** [spju] *tr & intr* vomitare

**sphere** [sfɪr] *s* sfera

**spherical** ['sferɪkəl] *adj* sferico

**sphinx** [sfɪŋks] *s* (**sphinxes** *or* **sphinges** ['sfɪndʒiz]) sfinge *f*

**spice** [spaɪs] *s* droga; spezie *fpl;* (fig) gusto, sapore *m* || *tr* drogare; dare gusto a, rendere piccante

**spick-and-span** ['spɪkənd'spæn] *adj* ordinato e pulito

**spic·y** ['spaɪsi] *adj* (-ier; -iest) drogato; piccante

**spider** ['spaɪdər] *s* ragno

**spi'der·web'** *s* ragnatela

**spiff·y** ['spɪfi] *adj* (-ier; -iest) (slang) elegante, bello

**spigot** ['spɪgət] *s (peg)* zipolo; *(faucet)* rubinetto

**spike** [spaɪk] *s* chiodo, chiodone *m; (sharp-pointed piece)* spuntone *m;* (rr) arpione *m;* (bot) spiga || *tr* inchiodare; mettere chiodi a; *(a rumor)* porre fine a; (coll) alcolizzare

**spill** [spɪl] *s* rovesciamento; liquido rovesciato; (coll) caduta || *v (pret & pp* **spilled** *or* **spilt** [spɪlt]) *tr* rovesciare, spandere; versare; (naut) sventare; (coll) far cadere; (slang) snocciolare ‖ *intr* rovesciarsi; versarsi

**spill'way'** *s* sfioratore *m*, stramazzo

**spin** [spɪn] *s* giro; *(twirl)* mulinello; corsa; **to go into a spin** (aer) cadere a vite ‖ *v* *(pret & pp* **spun** [spʌn]; *ger* **spinning)** *tr* far girare; *(e.g., thread)* filare; **to spin out** prolungare; **to spin a yarn** raccontare una storia ‖ *intr* girare; *(said of a top)* prillare; filare

**spinach** ['spɪnɪtʃ] *or* ['spɪnɪdʒ] *s* spinacio; *(leaves used as food)* spinaci *mpl*

**spi'nal col'umn** ['spaɪnəl] *s* spina dorsale, colonna vertebrale

**spi'nal cord'** *s* midollo spinale

**spindle** ['spɪndəl] *s* *(rounded rod)* fuso; *(shaft, axle)* asse *m;* balaustro

**spine** [spaɪn] *s* spina; spina dorsale; (bb) costola; (fig) forza, carattere *m*

**spineless** ['spaɪnlɪs] *adj* senza spine; senza carattere

**spinet** ['spɪnɪt] *s* spinetta

**spinner** ['spɪnər] *s* filatore *m;* *(machine)* filatrice *f*

**spinning** ['spɪnɪŋ] *adj* filante ‖ *s* filatura; rotazione

**spin'ning mill'** *s* filanda

**spin'ning wheel'** *s* filatoio

**spinster** ['spɪnstər] *s* zitella

**spi·ral** ['spaɪrəl] *adj & s* spirale *f* ‖ *v* *(pret & pp* **-raled** *or* **-ralled;** *ger* **-raling** *or* **-ralling)** *intr* muoversi lungo una spirale

**spi'ral stair'case** *s* scala a chiocciola

**spire** [spaɪr] *s* *(of a steeple)* guglia, freccia; *(of grass)* foglia; *(spiral)* spirale *f*

**spirit** ['spɪrɪt] *s* spirito; valore *m*, vigore *m;* bevanda spiritosa; **out of spirits** giù di morale ‖ *tr*—**to spirit away** portar via misteriosamente

**spirited** ['spɪrɪtɪd] *adj* brioso; *(horse)* superbo, vivace

**spir'it lamp'** *s* lampada a spirito

**spiritless** ['spɪrɪtlɪs] *adj* senza anima, senza vita

**spir'it lev'el** *s* livella a bolla d'aria

**spiritual** ['spɪrɪtʃʊ·əl] *adj* spirituale; *(séance)* spiritico

**spiritualism** ['spɪrɪtʃʊə‚lɪzəm] *s* spiritismo; (philos) spiritualismo

**spiritualist** ['spɪrɪtʃʊ·əlɪst] *s* spiritista *mf;* (philos) spiritualista *mf*

**spirituous** ['spɪrɪtʃʊ·əs] *adj* alcolico

**spit** [spɪt] *s* sputo; *(for roasting)* spiedo, schidione *m;* punta; **the spit and image of** (coll) il ritratto parlante di ‖ *v* *(pret & pp* **spat** [spæt] *or* **spit;** *ger* **spitting)** *tr & intr* sputare

**spite** [spaɪt] *s* dispetto, ripicco; **in spite of** a dispetto di, a onta di; **out of spite** per picca ‖ *tr* far dispetto a; offendere; contrariare

**spiteful** ['spaɪtfəl] *adj* dispettoso

**spit'fire'** *s* persona collerica; *(woman)* bisbetica

**spit'ting im'age** *s* (coll) ritratto parlante

**spittoon** [spɪ'tun] *s* sputacchiera

**splash** [splæʃ] *s* schizzo, spruzzo; *(of mud)* zacchera; *(sound)* tonfo; **to make a splash** fare molto sci-sci ‖ *tr & intr* sguazzare

**splash'down'** *s* (rok) ammaraggio, urto con l'acqua

**spleen** [splin] *s* cattivo umore, bile *f;* (anat) milza, splene *m*

**splendid** ['splendɪd] *adj* splendido; ottimo, magnifico

**splendor** ['splendər] *s* splendore *m*

**splice** [splaɪs] *s* giuntura ‖ *tr* giuntare

**splint** [splɪnt] *s* stecca ‖ *tr* steccare

**splinter** ['splɪntər] *s* scheggia ‖ *tr* scheggiare ‖ *intr* scheggiarsi

**splin'ter group'** *s* gruppo dissidente

**split** [splɪt] *adj* spaccato; diviso ‖ *s* spaccatura; fessura; rottura, divisione; **splits** (sports) spaccato ‖ *v* *(pret & pp* **split;** *ger* **splitting)** *tr* spaccare; dividere; **to split one's sides with laughter** scoppiare dalle risa ‖ *intr* scindersi, dividersi; **to split up** separarsi

**split' personal'ity** *s* sdoppiamento della personalità

**splitting** ['splɪtɪŋ] *adj* che fende; che si fende; violento, fortissimo ‖ *s*— **splittings** frammenti *mpl*

**splotch** [splɑtʃ] *s* macchia, chiazza ‖ *tr* macchiare, chiazzare

**splurge** [splʌrdʒ] *s* ostentazione ‖ *intr* fare ostentazione; fare una spesa matta

**splutter** ['splʌtər] *s* crepitio; *(utterance)* barbugliamento ‖ *tr* barbugliare ‖ *intr* crepitare; barbugliare

**spoil** [spɔɪl] *s* spoglia, bottino; **spoils** (mil) spoglie *fpl;* (pol) profitto, vantaggio ‖ *v* *(pret & pp* **spoiled** *or* **spoilt** [spɔɪlt]) *tr* rovinare, sciupare; *(a child)* viziare; *(food)* deteriorare ‖ *intr* guastarsi, andare a male

**spoilage** ['spɔɪlɪdʒ] *s* deterioramento

**spoiled** [spɔɪld] *adj* *(child)* viziato; *(food)* andato a male, passato

**spoils' sys'tem** *s* sistema politico secondo il quale le cariche vanno al partito vincitore

**spoke** [spok] *s* *(of a wheel)* raggio; *(of a ladder)* piolo

**spokes'man** *s* (-men) portavoce *m*

**sponge** [spʌndʒ] *s* spugna; **to throw in the sponge** (slang) gettare la spugna ‖ *tr* pulire con spugna; assorbire; (coll) scroccare ‖ *intr* assorbire; **to sponge off** (coll) vivere alle spalle di

**sponge' bath'** *s* spugnatura

**sponge' cake'** *s* pan *m* di Spagna

**sponger** ['spʌndʒər] *s* scroccatore *m*

**sponge' rub'ber** *s* gommapiuma

**spon·gy** ['spʌndʒi] *adj* (-gier; -giest) spugnoso

**sponsor** ['spɑnsər] *s* patrocinatore *m;* *(of a charitable institution)* patrono; *(godfather)* padrino; *(godmother)* madrina ‖ *tr* patrocinare; (rad, telv) offrire

**sponsorship** ['spɑnsər‚ʃɪp] *s* patrocinio

**spontaneous** [spɑn'tenɪ·əs] *adj* spontaneo

**spoof** [spuf] *s* mistificazione; parodia || *tr* mistificare; parodiare || *intr* mistificare; fare una parodia ,

**spook** [spuk] *s* (coll) spettro

**spook‧y** [ˈspuki] *adj* (**-ier; -iest**) (coll) spettrale; (*horse*) (coll) nervoso

**spool** [spul] *s* spola, rocchetto

**spoon** [spun] *s* cucchiaio; (*lure*) cucchiaino; **born with a silver spoon in one's mouth** nato con la camicia || *tr* servire col cucchiaio || *intr* (coll) limonare

**spoonerism** [ˈspunəˌrɪzəm] *s* papera

**spoon'-feed'** *v* (*pret & pp* **-fed**) *tr* nutrire col cucchiaino; (fig) coccolare

**spoonful** [ˈspunˌfʊl] *s* cucchiaiata

**spoon‧y** [ˈspuni] *adj* (**-ier; -iest**) (coll) svenevole

**sporadic(al)** [spəˈrædɪk(əl)] *adj* sporadico

**spore** [spor] *s* spora

**sport** [sport] *adj* sportivo || *s* sport *m;* gioco; (*laughingstock*) zimbello; (*gambler*) (coll) giocatore *m;* (*person who behaves in a sportsmanlike manner*) (coll) spirito sportivo; (*flashy fellow*) (coll) tipo fino; (biol) mutazione; **to make sport of** farsi gioco di || *tr* (coll) sfoggiare; **to sport away** dissipare || *intr* divertirsi; giocare; farsi beffe

**sport' clothes'** *spl* vestiti *mpl* sport

**sport'ing chance'** *s* pari opportunità *f* di vincere

**sport'ing goods'** *spl* articoli *mpl* sportivi

**sport'ing house'** *s* (coll) bordello

**sports'cast'er** *s* annunziatore sportivo

**sports' fan'** *s* appassionato agli spettacoli sportivi, tifoso

**sports'man** *s* (**-men**) sportivo

**sports'man‧ship'** *s* sportività *f,* spirito sportivo

**sports' news'** *s* notiziario sportivo

**sports'wear'** *s* articoli *mpl* d'abbigliamento sportivo

**sports'writ'er** *s* cronista sportivo

**sport‧y** [ˈsporti] *adj* (**-ier; -iest**) (coll) elegante; (coll) sportivo; (coll) appariscente

**spot** [spɑt] *s* macchia; luogo, punto, posto; (*e.g., of tea*) goccia; **spots** locali *mpl;* **on the spot** sul posto; (*right now*) seduta stante; (slang) in difficoltà; **to hit the spot** (slang) soddisfare completamente || *v* (*pret & pp* **spotted;** *ger* **spotting**) *tr* macchiare; spargere; (coll) riconoscere || *intr* macchiare; macchiarsi

**spot' cash'** *s* pronta cassa

**spot'-check'** *tr* fare un breve sondaggio di; controllare rapidamente

**spot' check'** *s* breve sondaggio; rapido controllo

**spotless** [ˈspɑtlɪs] *adj* immacolato, senza macchia

**spot'light'** *s* riflettore *m;* (aut) proiettore *m;* **to be in the spotlight** (fig) essere al centro d'attenzione

**spot' remov'er** [rɪˈmuvər] *s* smacchiatore *m*

**spot' weld'ing** *s* saldatura per punti

**spouse** [spauz] *or* [spaus] *s* consorte *mf*

**spout** [spaut] *s* (*to carry water from roof*) doccia; (*of jar, pitcher, etc.*) becco, beccuccio; (*jet*) zampillo, getto || *tr & intr* sprizzare, zampillare; (coll) declamare

**sprain** [spren] *s* distorsione || *tr* distorcere, distorcersi

**sprawl** [sprɔl] *intr* sdraiarsi

**spray** [spre] *s* spruzzo; (*of the sea*) schiuma; (*device*) spruzzatore *m;* (*twig*) ramoscello || *tr & intr* spruzzare

**sprayer** [ˈspreər] *s* spruzzatore *m,* schizzetto, vaporizzatore *m;* (hort) irroratrice *f*

**spray' gun'** *s* pistola a spruzzo; (hort) irroratrice *f*

**spray' paint'** *s* vernice *f* a spruzzo

**spread** [spred] *s* espansione; diffusione; differenza; tappeto, coperta; elasticità *f;* (*of the wings of bird or airplane*) apertura; (coll) cibo da spalmare; (coll) festino; (journ) articolo di fondo *or* pubblicitario su varie colonne || *v* (*pret & pp* **spread**) *tr* tendere, estendere; (*one's legs*) divaricare; (*wings*) spiegare; spargere, cospargere; (*the table*) preparare; (*butter*) spalmare; diffondere || *intr* estendersi; spiegarsi; spargersi; spalmarsi; diffondersi

**spree** [spri] *s* baldoria, bisboccia; **to go on a spree** darsi alla pazza gioia

**sprig** [sprɪg] *s* ramoscello

**spright‧ly** [ˈspraɪtli] *adj* (**-lier; -liest**) brioso, vivace

**spring** [sprɪŋ] *adj* primaverile; sorgivo; a molla || *s* (*season*) primavera; (*issue of water from earth*) fonte *f,* polla; (*elastic device*) molla; elasticità *f;* (*leap*) salto; (*crack*) fenditura; (aut) balestra || *v* (*pret* **sprang** [spræŋ] *or* **sprung** [sprʌŋ]) *pp* **sprung**) *tr* (*e.g., a lock*) far scattare; (*a leak*) aprire; (*a mine*) far brillare || *intr* saltare; (*said of a metal spring*) scattare; scaturire; zampillare; nascere, derivare; esplodere; **to spring forth** *or* **up** sorgere

**spring'board'** *s* pedana, trampolino

**spring' chick'en** *s* pollo giovanissimo; (slang) ragazzina

**spring' fe'ver** *s* indolenza primaverile

**spring' mat'tress** *s* materasso a molle

**spring' tide'** *s* marea di sizigia

**spring'time'** *s* primavera

**sprinkle** [ˈsprɪŋkəl] *s* spruzzo, spruzzatina; (*small amount*) pizzico || *tr* spruzzare; (*e.g., sugar*) spolverizzare || *intr* sprizzare; piovigginare

**sprinkler** [ˈsprɪŋklər] *s* annaffiatoio; (*person*) annaffiatore *m*

**sprinkling** [ˈsprɪŋklɪŋ] *s* spruzzo, spruzzo; (*with holy water*) aspersione; (*with powder*) spolverizzamento; (*e.g., of knowledge*) spolvero, spolveratura; (*of people*) piccolo numero

**sprin'kling can'** *s* annaffiatoio

**sprint** [sprɪnt] s (sports) scatto, volata || intr (sports) scattare
**sprite** [spraɪt] s spirito folletto
**sprocket** ['sprɑkɪt] s moltiplica; (phot) trasportatore m
**sprout** [spraut] s germoglio || intr germogliare; crescere rapidamente
**spruce** [sprus] adj elegante, attillato || s abete rosso || tr attillare, azzimare || intr attillarsi, azzimarsi
**spry** [spraɪ] adj (**spryer** or **sprier; spryest** or **spriest**) vegeto
**spud** [spʌd] s vanghetto, tagliaradici m; (coll) patata
**spun' glass'** s lana di vetro
**spunk** [spʌŋk] s (coll) coraggio, fegato
**spur** [spʌr] s sperone m; (rr) raccordo ferroviario; (fig) pungolo; **on the spur of the moment** lì per lì || v (pret & pp **spurred**; ger **spurring**) tr spronare; **to spur on** spronare, incitare
**spurious** ['spjurɪ·əs] adj spurio
**spurn** [spʌrn] s disprezzo, sdegno; rifiuto || tr disprezzare, sdegnare; rifiutare
**spurt** [spʌrt] s spruzzo, zampillo; (sudden burst) scatto repentino || intr sprizzare, zampillare; scattare
**sputter** ['spʌtər] s barbugliamento; (sizzling) crepitio || tr barbugliare || intr barbugliare; crepitare
**spu·tum** ['spjutəm] s (-ta [tə]) sputo
**spy** [spaɪ] s (**spies**) spia || v (pret & pp **spied**) tr spiare; osservare || intr fare la spia; **to spy on** spiare
**spy'glass'** s cannocchiale m
**spying** ['spaɪ·ɪŋ] s spionaggio
**squabble** ['skwɑbəl] s battibecco || intr litigare
**squad** [skwɑd] s squadra
**squadron** ['skwɑdrən] s (of cavalry) squadrone m; (aer, nav) squadriglia; (mil) squadra
**squalid** ['skwɑlɪd] adj sordido; squallido, misero
**squall** [skwɔl] s groppo, turbine m; urlo || intr gridare, urlare
**squalor** ['skwɑlər] s sordidezza; squallore m, miseria
**squander** ['skwɑndər] tr scialacquare, dilapidare, sperperare
**square** [skwer] adj quadrato, e.g., **two square miles** due miglia quadrate; di . . . di lato, e.g., **two miles square** di due miglia di lato; ad angolo retto; solido; saldato; (coll) onesto; (coll) diretto; (coll) sostanzioso; (slang) all'antica; **to get square with** (coll) fargliela pagare a || s quadrato; (small square, e.g., of checkerboard) quadretto; (city block) isolato; (open area in city) piazza, piazzale m; (of carpenter) squadra; **on the square** ad angolo retto; (coll) onesto || adv ad angolo retto; (coll) onestamente || tr squadrare; dividere in quadretti; elevare al quadrato; quadrare; (a debt) saldare; **to square with** adattare a || intr quadrare; **to square off** prepararsi, mettersi in posizione difensiva

**square' dance'** s danza figurata americana
**square' meal'** s (coll) pasto abbondante
**square' root'** s radice quadrata
**square' shoot'er** ['ʃutər] s (coll) persona onesta
**squash** [skwɑʃ] s spappolamento; (bot) zucca; (sports) squash m || tr spappolare; spiaciccare; (e.g., a rumor) sopprimere; (a person) (coll) ridurre al silenzio || intr spiaciccarsi
**squash·y** ['skwɑʃi] adj (-ier; -iest) tenero; (ground) fangoso, pantanoso; (fruit) maturo
**squat** [skwɑt] adj tozzo || v (pret & pp **squatted**; ger **squatting**) intr accoccolarsi; stabilirsi illegalmente su territorio altrui; stabilirsi su terreno pubblico per ottenerne titolo
**squatter** ['skwɑtər] s intruso
**squaw** [skwɔ] s squaw f; (coll) donna
**squawk** [skwɔk] s schiamazzo; (slang) lamento stridulo || intr schiamazzare; (slang) lamentarsi strillando
**squaw' man'** s bianco sposato con una pellerossa
**squeak** [skwik] s strido; cigolio || intr stridere; cigolare; (said of a mouse) squittire; **to squeak through** farcela per il rotto della cuffia
**squeal** [skwil] s strido || intr **stridere;** (slang) cantare, fare il delatore
**squealer** ['skwilər] s (slang) delatore m
**squeamish** ['skwimɪʃ] adj pudibondo; scrupoloso; (easily nauseated) schifiltoso, schizzinoso
**squeeze** [skwiz] s spremuta; stretta, abbraccio; **to put the squeeze on** (coll) far pressione su || tr premere; spremere, pigiare; stringere || intr stringere; **to squeeze through** aprirsi il passo attraverso; (fig) farcela a pena
**squeezer** ['skwizər] s spremifrutta m
**squelch** [skwɛltʃ] s osservazione schiacciante || tr schiacciare
**squid** [skwɪd] s calamaro, totano
**squint** [skwɪnt] s tendenza losca; (coll) occhiata; (pathol) strabismo || tr (one's eyes) socchiudere || intr socchiudere gli occhi; guardare furtivamente
**squint-eyed** ['skwɪnt ˌaɪd] adj guercio, losco; malevolo
**squire** [skwaɪr] s (of a lady) cavalier m servente; (Brit) proprietario terriero; (U.S.A.) giudice m conciliatore || tr (a woman) accompagnare
**squirm** [skwʌrm] s contorsione || intr contorcersi; mostrare imbarazzo; **to squirm out of** cavarsela da
**squirrel** ['skwʌrəl] s scoiattolo
**squirt** [skwʌrt] s schizzo; (instrument) schizzetto; (coll) saputello || tr & intr schizzare
**stab** [stæb] s pugnalata; (of pain) fitta; **to make a stab at** (coll) provare || v (pret & pp **stabbed**; ger **stabbing**) tr pugnalare, trafiggere || intr pugnalare
**stabilize** ['stebəlˌaɪz] tr stabilizzare
**stab' in the back'** s pugnalata nella schiena or alle spalle

**stable** ['stebəl] *adj* stabile ‖ *s* stalla; (*of race horses*) scuderia

**sta'ble·boy'** *s* stalliere *m*

**stack** [stæk] *s* pila; (*of hay or straw*) pagliaio; (*of firewood*) catasta; (*of books*) scaffale *m;* camino; (coll) mucchio, sacco ‖ *tr* ammonticchiare, accatastare

**stadi·um** ['stedɪ·əm] *s* (**-ums** or **-a** [ə]) stadio

**staff** [stæf] or [staf] *s* bastone *m;* asta, albero; personale *m,* corpo; (mil) stato maggiore; (mus) rigo, pentagramma *m* ‖ *tr* dotare di personale

**staff' of'ficer** *s* ufficiale *m* di stato maggiore

**stag** [stæg] *adj* per signori soli ‖ *s* (*deer*) cervo; maschio; (coll) signore *m* ‖ *adv* senza compagna

**stage** [stedʒ] *s* fase *f,* stadio; tappa, giornata; (*coach*) diligenza; teatro; piattaforma; (*of microscope*) piatto portaoggetti; (theat) scena, palcoscenico; **by easy stages** poco a poco; **to go on the stage** diventare attore ‖ *tr* mettere in scena; organizzare

**stage'coach'** *s* diligenza

**stage'craft'** *s* scenotecnica

**stage' door'** *s* (theat) ingresso degli artisti

**stage' fright'** *s* tremarella

**stage'hand'** *s* macchinista *m*

**stage' left'** *s* (theat) la sinistra della scena guardando il pubblico

**stage' man'ager** *s* direttore *m* di scena

**stage' right'** *s* (theat) la destra della scena guardando il pubblico

**stage'-struck'** *adj* innamorato del teatro

**stage' whis'per** *s* a parte *m*

**stagger** ['stægər] *tr* far traballare; impressionare; (*troops; hours*) scaglionare ‖ *intr* traballare

**stag'gering** *adj* traballante; impressionante, stupefacente

**staging** ['stedʒɪŋ] *s* impalcatura; (theat) messa in scena

**stagnant** ['stægnənt] *adj* stagnante

**staid** [sted] *adj* serio, grave

**stain** [sten] *s* macchia; tinta; colorante *m* ‖ *tr* macchiare; tingere; colorare ‖ *intr* macchiarsi

**stained' glass'** *s* vetro colorato

**stained'-glass win'dow'** *s* vetrata a colori

**stainless** ['stenlɪs] *adj* immacolato; (*steel*) inossidabile

**stair** [stɛr] *s* scala

**stair'case'** *s* scala

**stair'way'** *s* scala

**stair'well'** *s* tromba delle scale

**stake** [stek] *s* picchetto; (*e.g., of cart*) staggio; (*to support a plant*) puntello; (*in gambling*) puglia, giocata; **at stake** in gioco; **to die at the stake** morire sul rogo; **to pull up stakes** (coll) andarsene, traslocare ‖ *tr* picchettare; puntellare; attaccare a un palo; arrischiare; (coll) aiutare; **to stake out** picchettare; (slang) tenere sotto sorveglianza; **to stake out a claim** avanzare una pretesa

**stale** [stel] *adj* stantio; (*air*) viziato; (fig) ritrito

**stale'mate'** *s* (chess) stallo; **to reach a**

**stalemate** essere in una posizione di stallo ‖ *tr* mettere in una posizione di stallo

**stalk** [stɔk] *s* stelo; (*of corn*) stocco; (*of salad*) piede *m* ‖ *tr* braccare ‖ *intr* avanzare furtivamente; camminare con andatura maestosa

**stall** [stɔl] *s* (*in a stable*) posta; (*booth in a market*) bancarella; (*seat*) stallo; (*space in a parking lot*) spazio per il parcheggio ‖ *tr* (*an animal*) stallare; (*a car*) parcheggiare; (*a motor*) far fermare; **to stall off** eludere, tenere a bada ‖ *intr* impantanarsi; stare nella posta; (*said of a motor*) fermarsi; (*to temporize*) menare il can per l'aia

**stallion** ['stæljən] *s* stallone *m*

**stalwart** ['stɔlwərt] *adj* forte, gagliardo ‖ *s* sostenitore *m*

**stamen** ['stemən] *s* stame *m*

**stamina** ['stæmɪnə] *s* forza, vigore *m*

**stammer** ['stæmər] *s* balbuzie *f* ‖ *tr* & *intr* balbettare

**stammerer** ['stæmərər] *s* balbuziente *mf*

**stamp** [stæmp] *s* (*postage stamp*) francobollo; (*device to show that a fee has been paid*) timbro, bollo; impressione; carattere *m;* sigillo; (*tool for stamping coins*) conio; (*tool for crushing ore*) maglio ‖ *tr* timbrare, stampigliare, bollare; sigillare; coniare; (*one's foot*) battere, pestare; imprimere; caratterizzare; (mach) stampare; **to stamp out** spegnere; sopprimere ‖ *intr* battere il piede; (*said of a horse*) zampare

**stampede** [stæm'pid] *s* fuga precipitosa ‖ *tr* precipitarsi verso; far fuggire precipitosamente ‖ *intr* precipitarsi

**stamp'ing ground'** *s* (coll) luogo di ritrovo abituale

**stamp' pad'** *s* tampone *m*

**stamp'-vend'ing machine'** *s* distributore automatico di francobolli

**stance** [stæns] *s* posizione

**stanch** [stantʃ] *adj* leale; forte; a tenuta d'acqua ‖ *s* chiusa ‖ *tr* arrestare il flusso da; (*blood*) stagnare

**stand** [stænd] *s* posizione; resistenza, difesa; tribuna, palco; sostegno, supporto; (*booth in market*) posteggio; posto di sosta ‖ *v* (*pret & pp* **stood** [stud]) *tr* mettere in piedi; reggere, sostenere; sopportare, tollerare; (*one's ground*) mantenere; (*a chance*) avere; (*watch*) fare; (coll) pagare; **to stand off** tenere a distanza ‖ *intr* stare; essere alto; fermarsi; stare in piedi; trovarsi; aver forza; essere; (*e.g., apart*) tenersi; **to stand back of** spalleggiare; **to stand by** appoggiare; **to stand for** rappresentare, voler dire; appoggiare, favorire; tenere a battesimo; (coll) tollerare; **to stand in line** fare la fila or la coda; **to stand in with** (coll) essere nelle buone grazie di; **to stand out** stagliarsi, distaccarsi, risaltare; **to stand up** tenersi in piedi; resistere, durare; **to stand up to** affrontare

**standard** ['stændərd] *adj* (*usual*) normale; uniforme, standard; *(language)* corretto, preferito ‖ *s* standard *m;* *(model)* modello, campione *m;* *(flag)* stendardo

**stand'ard•bear'er** *s* portabandiera *m*

**standardize** ['stændər ˌdaɪz] *tr* standardizzare

**stand'ard of liv'ing** *s* tenore *m* di vita

**stand'ard time'** *s* ora ufficiale, ora legale

**standee** [stæn'di] *s* passeggero in piedi; spettatore *m* in piedi

**stand'-in'** *s* (mov) controfigura; **to have a stand-in with** (coll) essere nelle buone grazie di

**standing** ['stændɪŋ] *adj (jump)* da fermo; in piedi; fermo; *(water)* stagnante; vigente, permanente; *(idle)* fuori uso ‖ *s* posizione, rango, situazione; classifica; **in good standing** riconosciuto da tutti; **of long standing** vecchio, da lungo tempo

**stand'ing ar'my** *s* esercito permanente

**stand'ing room'** *s* posto in piedi

**standpatter** ['stænd'pætər] *s* (coll) seguace *mf* dell'immobilismo

**stand'point'** *s* punto di vista

**stand'still'** *s* fermata; riposo; **to come to a standstill** fermarsi

**stanza** ['stænzə] *s* stanza

**staple** ['stepəl] *adj* principale ‖ *s* articolo di prima necessità; elemento indispensabile; *(e.g., to hold wire)* cavallottino, cambretta; *(to fasten papers)* grappetta; fibra tessile ‖ *tr* aggraffare

**stapler** ['steplər] *s* cucitrice *f* a grappe

**star** [star] *s (any heavenly body, except the moon, appearing in the sky)* astro; *(heavenly body radiating self-produced energy)* stella; *(actor)* divo; *(actress)* diva, stella *(athlete)* asso; (fig, mov) stella; (typ) stelletta; **to thank one's lucky stars** ringraziare la propria stella ‖ *v (pret & pp* **starred;** *ger* **starring)** *tr* costellare, stellare; presentare come stella; (typ) marcare con stelletta ‖ *intr* primeggiare

**starboard** ['starbərd] *or* ['star ˌbord] *adj* di dritta, di tribordo ‖ *s* dritta, tribordo ‖ *adv* a dritta, a tribordo

**starch** [startʃ] *s* amido, fecola; *(in laundering)* salda; (coll) forza ‖ *tr* inamidare

**starch•y** ['startʃi] *adj* **(-ier; -iest)** amidaceo; *(e.g., collar)* inamidato; *(manner)* sostenuto, contegnoso

**star' dust'** *s* polveri *fpl* meteoriche; (fig) polvere *f* di stelle

**stare** [ster] *s* sguardo fisso ‖ *intr* rimirare; **to stare at** fissare gli occhi addosso a

**star'fish'** *s* stella di mare

**star'gaze'** *intr* guardare le stelle; sognare ad occhi aperti

**stark** [stark] *adj* completo; desolato; severo, serio; duro, rigido ‖ *adv* completamente

**stark'-na'ked** *adj* nudo e crudo

**starlet** ['starlɪt] *s* stellina, divetta

**star'light'** *s* lume *f* delle stelle

**starling** ['starlɪŋ] *s* storno, stornello

**Stars' and Stripes'** *s* bandiera stellata

**Star'-Spangled Ban'ner** *s* bandiera stellata

**star' sys'tem** *s* (mov) divismo

**start** [start] *s* inizio, principio; partenza; linea di partenza; *(sudden jerk)* sussulto, soprassalto; *(advantage)* vantaggio; *(spurt)* scatto ‖ *tr* iniziare, principiare; mettere in moto; dare il via a; *(a conversation)* intavolare; *(game)* stanare ‖ *intr* iniziare, principiare; mettersi in moto; incamminarsi; *(to be startled)* trasalire, sussultare; **to start + ger** mettersi a + *inf;* **to start + ger + again** rimettersi a + *inf;* **to start after** andare in cerca di

**starter** ['startər] *s (of a venture)* iniziatore *m;* partente *m;* (aut) motorino d'avviamento; (sports) mossiere *m*

**starting** ['startɪŋ] *adj* di partenza ‖ *s* messa in marcia

**start'ing crank'** *s* manovella d'avviamento

**start'ing point'** *s* punto di partenza

**startle** ['startəl] *tr* far trasalire ‖ *intr* trasalire, sussultare

**startling** ['startlɪŋ] *adj* allarmante, sorprendente

**starvation** [star'veʃən] *s* fame *f*, inedia, inanizione

**starva'tion wag'es** *spl* paga da fame

**starve** [starv] *tr* affamare; far morire di fame; **to starve out** prendere per fame ‖ *intr* essere affamato; morire di fame

**starving** ['starvɪŋ] *adj* famelico

**state** [stet] *adj* statale; ufficiale; di gala, di lusso ‖ *s* condizione; stato; gala, pompa; **to lie in state** essere esposto in camera ardente; **to live in state** vivere sfarzosamente ‖ *tr* dichiarare, affermare; *(a problem)* impostare

**stateless** ['stetlɪs] *adj* apolide

**state•ly** ['stetli] *adj* **(-lier; -liest)** maestoso, imponente

**statement** ['stetmənt] *s* dichiarazione, affermazione; comunicazione; (com) estratto conto

**state' of mind'** *s* stato d'animo

**state'room'** *s* cabina; (rr) compartimento privato

**states'man** *s* **(-men)** statista *m*, uomo di stato

**static** ['stætɪk] *adj* statico; (rad) atmosferico ‖ *s* disturbi *mpl* atmosferici

**station** ['steʃən] *s* stazione; rango, condizione ‖ *tr* stazionare

**sta'tion a'gent** *s* capostazione *m*

**stationary** ['steʃən ˌeri] *adj* stazionario

**sta'tion break'** *s* (rad, telv) intervallo

**stationer** ['steʃənər] *s* cartolaio

**stationery** ['steʃən ˌeri] *s (writing paper)* carta da lettere; *(writing materials)* cancelleria

**sta'tionery store'** *s* cartoleria

**sta'tion house'** *s* posto di polizia

**sta'tion•mas'ter** *s* capostazione *m*

**sta'tion wag'on** *s* giardinetta

**statistical** [stə'tɪstɪkəl] *adj* statistico

**statistician** [ˌstætɪs'tɪʃən] *s* statistico

**statistics** [stə'tɪstɪks] *ssg (science)* statistica; *spl (data)* statistiche *fpl*
**statue** ['stætʃu] *s* statua
**statuesque** [ˌstætʃu'esk] *adj* statuario
**stature** ['stætʃər] *s* statura
**status** ['stetəs] *s* stato, condizione; condizione sociale
**sta'tus sym'bol** *s* simbolo della posizione sociale
**statute** ['stætʃut] *s* legge *f;* regolamento
**stat'ute of limita'tions** *s* legge *f* che governa la prescrizione
**statutory** ['stætʃu ˌtori] *adj* legale
**staunch** [stɔntʃ] or [stɑntʃ] *adj, s &* *tr* var of **stanch**
**stave** [stev] *s (of barrel)* doga; *(of ladder)* piolo; *(mus)* rigo, pentagramma *m* ‖ *v (pret & pp* **staved** or **stove** [stov]) *tr* bucare; *(to smash)* sfondare; **to stave off** tenere a bada
**stay** [ste] *s* permanenza, soggiorno; *(brace)* staggio; *(of corset)* stecca di balena; sostegno; *(law)* sospensione; *(naut)* strallo ‖ *tr* fermare; sospendere; poner freno a ‖ *intr* stare; mantenersi; restare, rimanere; *(at a hotel)* sostare; **to stay up** stare alzato
**stay'-at-home'** *adj* casalingo ‖ *s* persona casalinga
**stead** [sted] *s* posto; **in his stead** in suo luogo; **to stand in good stead** esser utile
**stead'fast'** *adj* fermo, risoluto
**stead·y** ['stedi] *adj (*-ier; -iest)* stabile, fermo; regolare, costante; abituale; calmo, sicuro ‖ *v (pret & pp* -ied)* rinforzare; calmare ‖ *intr* rinforzarsi; calmarsi
**steak** [stek] *s* bistecca
**steal** [stil] *s (coll)* furto ‖ *v (pret* **stole** [stol]; *pp* **stolen**) *tr* rubare; involare; *(the attention)* cattivare ‖ *intr* rubare; **to steal away** svignarsela; **to steal out** uscire di soppiatto; **to steal upon** approssimarsi silenziosamente a
**stealth** [stelθ] *s* clandestinità *f;* **by stealth** di straforo, di soppiatto
**steam** [stim] *adj* a vapore ‖ *s* vapore *m;* fumo; **to get up steam** aumentare la pressione; **to let off steam** scaricare la pressione; (slang) sfogarsi ‖ *tr (a steamship)* guidare; esalare; esporre al vapore; *(e.g., glasses)* appannare ‖ *intr* dar vapore, fumigare; bollire; *(to become clouded)* appannarsi; andare a vapore; **to steam ahead** avanzare a tutto vapore
**steam'boat'** *s* vapore *m*
**steam' en'gine** *s* macchina a vapore
**steamer** ['stimər] *s* vapore *m*
**steam'er rug'** *s* coperta da viaggio
**steam'er trunk'** *s* bauletto da cabina
**steam' heat'** *s* riscaldamento a vapore
**steam' roll'er** *s* rullo compressore; (fig) rullo compressore
**steam'ship'** *s* piroscafo, vapore *m*
**steam' shov'el** *s* escavatore *m* a vapore
**steam' ta'ble** *s* tavola riscaldata a vapore per mantenere calde le vivande
**steed** [stid] *s* destriere *m*

**steel** [stil] *adj* d'acciaio; *(industry)* siderurgico ‖ *s* acciaio; *(bar)* stecca d'acciaio; *(for sharpening knives)* affilacoltelli *m;* (fig) spada, brando ‖ *tr* acciaiare; **to steel oneself** corazzarsi, indurirsi; armarsi di coraggio
**steel' wool'** *s* paglia di ferro
**steel'works'** *spl* acciaieria
**steelyard** ['stil ˌjard] or ['stiljərd] *s* stadera
**steep** [stip] *adj* erto, scosceso, ripido; *(price)* alto ‖ *tr* immergere, saturare, imbevere
**steeple** ['stipəl] *s* campanile *m; (spire)* cuspide *f,* guglia
**stee'ple·chase'** *s* corsa ad ostacoli
**stee'ple·jack'** *s* aggiustatore *m* di campanili
**steer** [stɪr] *s* bue *m,* manzo ‖ *tr* governare, guidare; *(aer)* pilotare ‖ *intr* governare; **to steer clear of** evitare
**steerage** ['stɪrɪdʒ] *s* (naut) alloggio passeggeri di terza classe
**steer'ing wheel'** *s (aut)* volante *m,* sterzo; (naut) ruota del timone
**stellar** ['stelər] *adj* stellare; *(role)* da stella
**stem** [stem] *s (of pipe, of key)* cannello; *(of goblet)* gambo; *(of column)* fusto; *(of spoon)* manico; *(of watch)* corona; *(of a word)* tema *m; (of note)* (mus) gamba; (bot) peduncolo, stelo; (bot) gambo; **from stem to stern** da poppa a prua ‖ *v (pret & pp* **stemmed;** *ger* **stemming)** *tr* togliere il gambo a; *(to check)* arrestare; *(to dam up)* arginare; *(to plug)* otturare; *(the tide)* risalire, andare contro ‖ *intr* originare, derivare
**stem'-win'der** *s* orologio a corona
**stench** [stentʃ] *s* tanfo, fetore *m*
**sten·cil** ['stensəl] *s* stampo, stampino; parole *fpl* a stampo ‖ *v (pret & pp* **-ciled** or **-cilled;** *ger* **-ciling** or **-cilling)** *tr* stampinare
**stenographer** [stə'nɑgrəfər] *s* stenografo
**stenography** [stə'nɑgrəfi] *s* stenografia
**step** [step] *s* passo; *(footprint)* orma, impronta; *(of ladder)* piolo; *(of staircase)* gradino; *(of carriage)* montatoio; **step by step** passo passo; **to watch one's step** fare molta attenzione ‖ *v (pret & pp* **stepped;** *ger* **stepping)** *tr* scaglionare; **to step off** misurare a passi ‖ *intr* camminare, andare a passi; mettere il piede; **to step aside** scostarsi; **to step back** indietreggiare; **to step on it** (slang) fare presto; **to step on the gas** (coll) accelerare; **to step on the starter** avviare il motore
**step'broth'er** *s* fratellastro, fratello consanguineo
**step'child'** *s (*-children [ˌtʃɪldrən])* figliastro
**step'daugh'ter** *s* figliastra
**step'fa'ther** *s* patrigno
**step'lad'der** *s* scala a gradini or a libretto
**step'moth'er** *s* matrigna
**steppe** [step] *s* steppa

**step'ping stone'** *s* passatoio, pietra per guadare; (fig) gradino

**step'sis'ter** *s* sorellastra

**step'son'** *s* figliastro

**stere·o** ['sterɪ ,o] or ['stɪrɪ ,o] *adj* stereofonico; stereoscopico ‖ *s* (**-os**) musica stereofonica; sistema stereofonico; fotografia stereoscopica

**stereotyped** ['sterɪ·ə,taɪpt] or ['stɪrɪ·ə-,taɪpt] *adj* stereotipato

**sterile** ['sterɪl] *adj* sterile

**sterilize** ['sterɪ ,laɪz] *tr* sterilizzare

**sterling** ['stɑrlɪŋ] *adj* di lira sterlina; d'argento; puro; eccellente ‖ *s* argento .925; vasellame *m* d'argento puro

**stern** [stʌrn] *adj* severo ‖ *s* poppa

**stet** [stet] *v* (*pret & pp* **stetted; ger stetting**) *tr* marcare con la parola "vive"

**stethoscope** ['stɛθə ,skop] *s* stetoscopio

**stevedore** ['stivə ,dor] *s* stivatore *m*

**stew** [stju] or [stu] *s* stufato, guazzetto ‖ *tr* stufare ‖ *intr* cuocere a fuoco lento; (coll) preoccuparsi

**steward** ['stju·ərd] or ['stu·ərd] *s* amministratore *m*, agente *m;* maggiordomo; (aer, naut) cambusiere *m*, cameriere *m*

**stewardess** ['stju·ərdɪs] or ['stu·ərdɪs] *s* (naut) cameriera; (aer) hostess *f*, assistente *f* di volo

**stewed' fruit'** *s* composta di frutta

**stewed' toma'toes** *spl* pomodori *mpl* in umido

**stick** [stɪk] *s* stecco; legno; bacchetta; bastone *m;* (*e.g., of candy*) cannello; (naut) albero; (typ) compositoio; **in the sticks** (coll) in casa del diavolo ‖ *v* (*pret & pp* **stuck** [stʌk]) *tr* pungere; ficcare, infiggere; attaccare; confondere; **to be stuck** essere insabbiato; essere attaccato; (fig) essere confuso; **to stick out** (*the head*) sporgere; (*the tongue*) cacciare; **to stick up** (slang) assaltare a mano armata, rapinare ‖ *intr* rimanere attaccato; persistere; (*said of glue*) appiccicarsi; (*to one opinion*) tenersi; stare; **to stick out** sporgere; **to stick together** rimanere unito; **to stick up** risaltare; (*said, e.g., of quills*) rizzarsi; **to stick up for** (coll) stare dalla parte di

**sticker** ['stɪkər] *s* etichetta gommata; spina; persona zelante; (coll) busillis

**stick'ing plas'ter** *s* cerotto

**stick'pin'** *s* spilla da cravatta

**stick'up'** *s* (slang) grassazione

**stick·y** ['stɪki] *adj* (**-ier; -iest**) attaccaticcio; vischioso; (*weather*) afoso, soffocante; (fig) difficile

**stiff** [stɪf] *adj* rigido, duro; forte; (*price*) alto; denso ‖ *s* (slang) cadavere *m;* **poor stiff** (slang) povero diavolo

**stiff' col'lar** *s* colletto duro

**stiffen** ['stɪfən] *tr* irrigidire ‖ *intr* irrigidirsi

**stiff' neck'** *s* torcicollo; ostinazione

**stiff'-necked'** *adj* testardo

**stiff' shirt'** *s* camicia inamidata

**stifle** ['staɪfəl] *tr* soffocare

**stigma** ['stɪgmə] *s* (**-mas** or **-mata** [mətə]) stigma *m*

**stigmatize** ['stɪgmə ,taɪz] *tr* stigmatizzare

**still** [stɪl] *adj* fermo, tranquillo; silenzioso; (*wine*) non spumante ‖ *s* calma; distillatore *m;* distilleria; (phot) fotografia singola ‖ *adv* ancora; tuttora ‖ *conj* tuttavia ‖ *tr* calmare ‖ *intr* calmarsi

**still'birth'** *s* parto di infante nato morto

**still'born'** *adj* nato morto

**still' life'** *s* (**lifes'**) natura morta

**stilt** [stɪlt] *s* trampolo; (*in water*) palafitta; (orn) trampoliere *m*

**stilted** ['stɪltɪd] *adj* elevato; pomposo

**stimulant** ['stɪmjələnt] *adj & s* stimulante *m*, eccitante *m*

**stimulate** ['stɪmjə ,let] *tr* stimulare

**stimu·lus** ['stɪmjələs] *s* (**-li** [ ,laɪ]) stimolo

**sting** [stɪŋ] *s* puntura; (*of insect*) pungiglione; (fig) scottatura ‖ *v* (*pret & pp* **stung** [stʌŋ]) *tr & intr* pungere

**stin·gy** ['stɪndʒi] *adj* (**-gier; -giest**) tirchio, taccagno

**stink** [stɪŋk] *s* puzza ‖ *v* (*pret* **stank** [stæŋk] or **stunk** [stʌŋk]; *pp* **stunk**) *tr* far puzzare ‖ *intr* puzzare; **to stink of money** (slang) aver soldi a palate

**stinker** ['stɪŋkər] *s* (slang) puzzone *m*

**stint** [stɪnt] *s* limite *m;* lavoro assegnato, compito ‖ *intr* lesinarsi

**stipend** ['staɪpənd] *s* stipendio; assegno di studio, presalario

**stipulate** ['stɪpjə ,let] *tr* stipulare

**stir** [stʌr] *s* agitazione, movimento; (*poke*) spinta; **to create a stir** creare una sensazione ‖ *v* (*pret & pp* **stirred; ger stirring**) *tr* mescolare; muovere; (*fire*) ravvivare; (*pity*) fare; **to stir up** eccitare, svegliare; (*to rebellion*) sommuovere ‖ *intr* muoversi, agitarsi

**stirring** ['stʌrɪŋ] *adj* commovente

**stirrup** ['stʌrəp] or ['stɪrəp] *s* staffa

**stitch** [stɪtʃ] *s* punto; maglia; (*pain*) fitta; (*bit*) poco, po' *m;* **to be in stitches** (coll) sbellicarsi dalle risa ‖ *tr* cucire; aggraffare ‖ *intr* cucire

**stock** [stɑk] *adj* regolare, comune; banale, ordinario; di bestiame; borsistico; azionario; (aut) di serie; (theat) stabile ‖ *s* provvista, scorta; capitale *m* sociale; azione *f;* azioni *fpl*, titoli *mpl;* (*of tree*) tronco; (*of family; of anchor; of anvil*) ceppo; razza, famiglia; materia prima; (*of rifle*) cassa; (*broth*) brodo; (*handle*) manico; (*livestock*) bestiame *m;* (theat) compagnia stabile; **in stock** in magazzino, disponibile; **out of stock** esaurito; **stocks** gogna, berlina; **to take stock** fare l'inventario; **to take stock in** (coll) aver fede in ‖ *tr* fornire; fornire di bestiame; fornire di pesci ‖ *intr*—**to stock up** fare rifornimenti

**stockade** [stɑ'ked] *s* staccionata

**stock'breed'er** *s* allevatore *m* di bestiame

**stock'bro'ker** s agente m di cambio

**stock' car'** s automobile f di serie; (rr) carro bestiame

**stock' com'pany** s (theat) compagnia stabile; (com) società anonima

**stock' div'idend** s dividendo pagato in azioni

**stock' exchange'** s borsa valori

**stock'fish'** s stoccafisso

**stock'hold'er** s azionista mf

**stock'holder of rec'ord** s azionista mf registrato nei libri della compagnia

**Stockholm** ['stakhom] s Stoccolma

**stocking** ['stakɪŋ] s calza

**stock' in trade'** s stock m; ferri mpl del mestiere

**stock' mar'ket** s borsa valori

**stock'pile'** s riserva, scorta || tr mettere in riserva || intr mettere in riserva materie prime

**stock' rais'ing** s allevamento bestiame

**stock'room'** s magazzino, deposito

**stock·y** ['staki] adj (-ier; -iest) tozzo, tarchiato

**stock'yard'** s chiuso per il bestiame

**stoic** ['sto·ɪk] adj & s stoico

**stoicism** ['sto·ɪ‚sɪzəm] s stoicismo

**stoke** [stok] tr (fire) attizzare; (a furnace) caricare

**stoker** ['stokər] s fochista m

**stolid** ['stalɪd] adj impassibile

**stomach** ['stʌmək] s stomaco || tr (fig) digerire

**stone** [ston] s sasso, pietra; (of fruit) osso; (pathol) calcolo || tr lapidare; affilare con la pietra; (fruit) snocciolare

**stone'-broke'** adj (coll) senza un soldo, senza il becco di un quattrino

**stone'-deaf'** adj sordo come una campana

**stone'ma'son** s tagliapietra m

**stone' quar'ry** s cava di pietra

**stone's' throw'** s tiro di sasso; **within a stone's throw** a un tiro di schioppo

**ston·y** ['stoni] adj (-ier; -iest) di sasso, sassoso, pietroso

**stooge** [studʒ] s (theat) spalla; (slang) complice mf

**stool** [stul] s sgabello, seggiolino; gabinetto; (mass evacuated) feci fpl

**stool' pi'geon** s piccione m di richiamo; (slang) spia

**stoop** [stup] s curvatura, inclinazione; scalini mpl d'ingresso || intr inclinarsi, piegarsi; degnarsi, umiliarsi

**stoop-shouldered** ['stup'ʃoldərd] adj con le spalle cadenti

**stop** [stap] s fermata, sosta; arresto; otturazione, blocco; cessazione; ostacolo; (of a check) fermo; (restraint) freno; (of organ) registro; **to come to a stop** fermarsi; cessare; **to put a stop** to metter fine a || v (pret & pp stopped; ger stopping) tr fermare, cessare; arrestare, sospendere; tappare, otturare; (a check) mettere il fermo a; **to stop up** tappare, otturare || intr fermarsi; arrestarsi; (said of a ship) fare scalo; (at an hotel) scendere; **to stop + ger** smettere di or cessare di + inf

**stop'cock'** s rubinetto di arresto

**stop'gap'** adj provvisorio || s soluzione provvisoria; (person) tappabuchi m

**stop'light'** s (traffic light) semaforo; (aut) luce f di stop

**stop'o'ver** s fermata intermedia

**stoppage** ['stapɪdʒ] s fermata, arresto; (of work, wages, etc.) sospensione

**stopper** ['stapər] s tappo, turacciolo

**stop' sign'** s segnale m di fermata

**stop'watch'** s cronometro a scatto

**storage** ['storɪdʒ] s magazzinaggio; (place for storing) magazzino; (of a computer) memoria

**stor'age bat'tery** s (elec) accumulatore m

**store** [stor] s negozio; magazzino; (supply) scorta; **in store** in serbo; **to set store by** dare molta importanza a || tr immagazzinare; **to store away** accumulare

**store'house'** s magazzino, deposito; (of knowledge) miniera

**store'keep'er** s negoziante m

**store'room'** s magazzino; (naut) dispensa

**stork** [stɔrk] s cicogna

**storm** [stɔrm] s tempesta, temporale m; (on the Beaufort scale) burrasca; (mil) assalto; (fig) scoppio || tr assaltare || intr tempestare; imperversare; (mil) andare all'attacco

**storm' cloud'** s nuvolone m

**storm' door'** s controporta

**storm' sash'** s controfinestra

**storm' troops'** spl truppe fpl d'assalto

**storm' win'dow** s controfinestra

**storm·y** ['stɔrmi] adj (-ier; -iest) tempestoso, burrascoso; (fig) inquieto, violento

**sto·ry** ['stori] s (-ries) storia, racconto; romanzo; (plot) trama; (level) piano; (coll) storia, menzogna || v (pret & pp -ried) tr istoriare

**sto'ry·tell'er** s narratore m, novelliere m; (coll) mentitore m

**stoup** [stup] s (eccl) acquasantiera

**stout** [staut] adj grasso, obeso; forte, robusto; leale; coraggioso || s birra nera forte

**stout-hearted** ['staut‚hartɪd] adj coraggioso

**stove** [stov] s (for warmth) stufa; (for cooking) fornello, cucina economica

**stove'pipe'** s tubo della stufa, cannone m; (hat) (coll) tuba

**stow** [sto] tr mettere in riserva; riempire; (naut) stivare || intr—**to stow away** imbarcarsi clandestinamente

**stowage** ['sto·ɪdʒ] s stivaggio; (place) stiva

**stow'a·way'** s passeggero clandestino

**straddle** ['strædəl] s divaricamento || tr (a horse) cavalcare; (the legs) divaricare; favorire entrambe le parti in || intr cavalcare; stare a gambe divaricate; (coll) tenere il piede tra due staffe

**strafe** [straf] or [stref] s attacco violento || tr attaccare violentemente con fuoco aereo; bombardare violentemente; (slang) punire

**straggle** ['strægəl] *intr* sbandarsi, sviarsi; sparpagliarsi, essere sparpagliato

**straggler** ['stræglər] *s* ritardatario

**straight** [stret] *adj* diritto, ritto; (*e.g., shoulders*) quadro; candido, franco; (*honest, upright*) retto; inalterato; (*hair; whiskey*) liscio; **to set s.o. straight** mettere qlcu sulla retta via; mostrare la verità a qlcu || *s* rettilinea; (*cards*) scala || *adv* dritto; sinceramente; rettamente; **straight ahead** sempre diritto; **straight away** immediatamente; **to go straight** vivere onestamente

**straighten** ['stretən] *tr* ordinare; raddrizzare || *intr* raddrizzarsi

**straight' face'** *s* faccia seria

**straight' flush'** *s* (cards) scala reale

**straight'for'ward** *adj* diretto; onesto

**straight' man'** *s* (theat) spalla

**straight' ra'zor** *s* rasoio a mano libera

**straight'way'** *adv* immediatamente

**strain** [stren] *s* sforzo; fatica eccessiva; tensione, pressione; strappo muscolare; tono, stile *m*; (*family*) famiglia; tendenza, vena; (coll) lavoro severo; (mus) aria, melodia || *tr* passare, colare; (*e.g., a rope*) tirare al massimo; (*one's ear*) tendere; (*a muscle*) strappare; (*the ankle*) slogare; (*e.g., words*) storcere, forzare || *intr* colare, filtrare; tendersi, tirare; sforzarsi; fare resistenza; **to strain at** tirare; resistere a

**strained** [strend] *adj* (*smile*) stentato; (*relations*) teso

**strainer** ['strenər] *s* scolatoio

**strait** [stret] *s* stretto; **straits** stretto; (fig) strettezze *fpl*; **to be in dire straits** essere nei frangenti

**strait' jack'et** *s* camicia di forza

**strait'-laced'** *adj* puritano, pudibondo

**strand** [strænd] *s* sponda, lido; (*of metal cable*) trefolo; (*of rope*) legnolo; (*of pearls*) filo || *tr* sfilare; (*e.g., a rope*) ritorcere, intrecciare; (*e.g., a boat*) lasciare incagliato; **to be stranded** trovarsi incagliato

**stranded** ['strændɪd] *adj* (*ship*) incagliato, arenato; (*e.g., rope*) ritorto, intrecciato

**strange** [strendʒ] *adj* strano; straniero; non abituato; inusitato

**stranger** ['strendʒər] *s* forestiero; nuovo venuto, intruso

**strangle** ['stræŋgəl] *tr* strangolare; soffocare || *intr* strangolarsi; soffocarsi

**strap** [stræp] *s* (*of leather*) correggia; (*for holding things together*) tirante *m*; (*shoulder strap*) bretella; (*for passengers to hold on to*) manopola; (*to hold a sandal*) guiggia; (*to hold a baby*) falda; (*strop*) coramella || *v* (*pret & pp* **strapped**; *ger* **strapping**) *tr* legare con correggia or tirante; (*a razor*) affilare

**strap'hang'er** *s* (coll) passeggero senza posto a sedere

**strapping** ['stræpɪŋ] *adj* robusto; (coll) grande, enorme

**stratagem** ['strætedʒəm] *s* stratagemma *m*

**strategic(al)** [strə'tidʒɪk(əl)] *adj* strategico

**strategist** ['strætɪdʒɪst] *s* stratego

**strate·gy** ['strætɪdʒi] *s* (*-gies*) strategia

**strati·fy** ['strætɪ,faɪ] *v* (*pret & pp -fied*) *tr* stratificare || *intr* stratificarsi

**stratosphere** ['strætə,sfɪr] or ['stretə,sfɪr] *s* stratosfera

**stra·tum** ['stretəm] or ['strætəm] *s* (*-ta* [tə] or *-tums*) strato

**straw** [strɔ] *adj* di paglia; di nessun valore; falso, fittizio || *s* paglia; (*for drinking*) cannuccia; **I don't care a straw** non mi importa un fico; **to be the last straw** essere il colmo

**straw'ber·ry** *s* (*-ries*) fragola

**straw'hat'** *s* cappello di paglia; (*with hard crown*) paglietta

**straw' man'** *s* (*figurehead*) uomo di paglia; (*scarecrow*) spaventapasseri *m*

**straw' mat'tress** *s* pagliericcio

**straw' vote'** *s* votazione esplorativa

**stray** [stre] *adj* sbandato, randagio; casuale, fortuito || *s* animale randagio || *intr* sviarsi; (fig) sbandarsi

**streak** [strik] *s* stria; (*of light*) raggio; (*of madness*) ramo, vena; (*of luck*) (coll) periodo; **like a streak** (coll) come un lampo || *tr* striare, venare || *intr* striarsi, venarsi; andare come un lampo

**stream** [strim] *s* corrente *f*; (*of light*) raggio; (*of people*) fiumana, torrente *m*; (*of cars*) fila || *intr* colare; filtrare, penetrare; (*said of a flag*) fluttuare

**streamer** ['strimər] *s* pennone *m*; nastro; raggio di luce

**streamlined** ['strim,laɪnd] *adj* aerodinamico; (aer) carenato

**stream'lin'er** *s* treno dal profilo aerodinamico

**street** [strit] *adj* stradale || *s* via, strada

**street'car'** *s* tram *m*

**street' clean'er** *s* spazzino; (mach) spazzatrice *f*

**street' clothes'** *spl* vestiti *mpl* da passeggio; vestito da passeggio

**street' floor'** *s* pianterreno

**street'light'** *s* lampione *m*

**street' map'** *s* pianta della città; stradario

**street' sign'** *s* segnale *m* stradale

**street' sprin'kler** *s* carro annaffiatoio

**street' walk'er** *s* passeggiatrice *f*

**strength** [strɛŋθ] *s* forza; resistenza; (*of spirituous liquors*) gradazione; (com) tendenza al rialzo; (mil) numero; **on the strength of** basandosi su

**strengthen** ['strɛŋθən] *tr* rinforzare; (fig) convalidare, rinsaldare || *intr* rinforzarsi, ingagliardirsi

**strenuous** ['strɛnju·əs] *adj* vigoroso; strenuo

**stress** [strɛs] *s* enfasi *f*, importanza; spinta; tensione, preoccupazione; accento; (mech) sollecitazione; **to lay**

**stress on** mettere in rilievo ‖ *tr (a word)* accentare, accentuare; *(to emphasize)* accentuare; *(mech)* sollecitare

**stress' ac'cent** *s* accento di intensità

**stretch** [strɛtʃ] *s* tiro, tirata; *(in time or space)* periodo; *(of road)* tratto, percorrenza; *(of imagination)* sforzo; *(rr)* tratta; *(slang)* periodo di detenzione; **at a stretch** di un tiro ‖ *tr* tirare; tendere, distendere; *(the imagination)* forzare; *(facts)* esagerare; *(money)* stiracchiare; *(one's legs)* sgranchirsi; *(the truth)* esagerare; **to stretch oneself** sdraiarsi ‖ *intr* estendersi; stiracchiarsi; distendersi; **to stretch out** sdraiarsi

**stretcher** ['strɛtʃər] *s (for a painting)* telaio; *(tool)* tenditore *m*, tenditoio; *(to carry wounded)* barella, lettiga

**stretch'er-bear'er** *s* portantino

**strew** [stru] *v (pret* **strewed;** *pp* **strewed** or **strewn)** *tr* spargere, cospargere; disseminare

**stricken** ['strɪkən] *adj* afflitto; ferito; danneggiato

**strict** [strɪkt] *adj* stretto, severo

**stricture** ['strɪktʃər] *s* aspra critica; *(pathol)* stenosi *f*

**stride** [straɪd] *s* passo; andatura; **rapid strides** grandi passi *mpl*; **to hit one's stride** avanzare a andatura regolare; **to take s.th in one's stride** fare qlco senza sforzi ‖ *v (pret* **strode** [strod]; *pp* **stridden** ['strɪdən]) *tr* attraversare a grandi passi; attraversare di un salto ‖ *intr* camminare a grandi passi; *(majestically)* incedere

**strident** ['straɪdənt] *adj* stridente

**strife** [straɪf] *s* discordia; concorrenza

**strike** [straɪk] *s (blow)* colpo; *(stopping of work)* sciopero; *(discovery of oil, ore, etc.)* scoperta; *(of fish)* abboccatura; colpo di fortuna ‖ *v (pret & pp* **struck** [strʌk]) *tr* colpire, percuotere; infiggere; *(a match)* strofinare; *(fire)* accendere; fare impressione su; incontrare improvvisamente; *(e.g., ore)* scoprire; *(roots)* mettere; *(a coin)* coniare; andare in sciopero contro; arrivare a; *(a posture)* prendere; *(the hour)* scoccare; cancellare, eliminare; *(sails)* calare; *(attention)* richiamare; **to strike it rich** scoprire una miniera; avere un colpo di fortuna ‖ *intr* dare un colpo; cadere; *(said of a bell)* suonare; accendersi; scioperare; *(mil)* attaccare; **to strike out** mettersi in marcia; *(to fail)* (fig) fallire, venir meno

**strike'break'er** *s* crumiro

**striker** ['straɪkər] *s* battitore *m;* *(clapper in clock)* martelletto; *(worker)* scioperante *m*

**striking** ['straɪkɪŋ] *adj* impressionante, sorprendente; notevole; scioperante

**strik'ing pow'er** *s* potere *m* d'assalto

**string** [strɪŋ] *s* spago, cordicella; *(e.g., of apron)* laccio; *(of pearls)* filo; *(of onions; of lies)* filza; *(row)* fila, infilata; *(mus)* corda; **no strings attached** (coll) senza condizioni;

**strings** strumenti *mpl* a corda; (coll) condizioni *fpl;* **to pull strings** usare influenza ‖ *v (pret & pp* **strung** [strʌŋ]) *tr* legare; allacciare; infilare; infilzare; *(a racket)* munire de corde; *(to stretch)* tendere; *(a musical instrument)* mettere le corde a; (slang) ingannare; **to string along** (slang) menare per il naso; **to string up** impiccare ‖ *intr*—**to string along with** (slang) andare d'accordo con

**string' bean'** *s* fagiolino

**stringed' in'strument** *s* strumento a corda

**stringent** ['strɪndʒənt] *adj* stringente; urgente; severo

**string' quartet'** *s* quartetto d'archi

**strip** [strɪp] *s* striscia; *(of metal)* lamina; *(of land)* lingua ‖ *v (pret & pp* **stripped;** *ger* **stripping)** *tr* spogliare; denudare; *(a fruit)* pelare; *(a ship)* sguarnire; *(tobacco)* togliere le nervature da; scortecciare; *(thread)* spanare; **to strip of** spogliare di ‖ *intr* spogliarsi; denudarsi; fare lo spogliarello

**stripe** [straɪp] *s* stria, striscia, riga, lista; tipo, qualità *f;* (mil) gallone *m* ‖ *tr* striare, filettare, rigare

**strip' min'ing** *s* sfruttamento minerario a cielo aperto

**strip'tease'** *s* spogliarello

**stripteaser** ['strɪp,tizər] *s* spogliarellista

**strive** [straɪv] *v (pret* **strove** [strov]; *pp* **striven** ['strɪvən]) *intr* sforzarsi; lottare; **to strive to** sforzarsi di

**stroke** [strok] *s* colpo; *(of bell or clock)* rintocco; *(of pen)* tratto, frego; *(of brush)* pennellata; *(of arms in swimming)* bracciata; colpo apoplettico; *(caress)* carezza; *(with oar)* vogata; *(of oar or paddle)* palata; *(of a master)* tocco; *(of a piston)* corsa; *(keystroke)* battuta; *(of genius)* lampo; *(of the hour)* scocco; **to not do a stroke of work** non muovere un dito ‖ *tr* accarezzare

**stroll** [strol] *s* passeggiata; **to take a stroll** fare una passeggiata ‖ *intr* fare una passeggiata, andare a zonzo; errare

**stroller** ['strolər] *s* girovago; carrozzella; *(itinerant performer)* (theat) guitto

**strong** [strɔŋ] or [straŋ] *adj* forte, vigoroso; valido; acceso, zelante; *(butter)* rancido; *(cheese)* piccante; (com) sostenuto

**strong'box'** *s* cassaforte *f*

**strong' drink'** *s* bevanda alcolica

**strong'hold'** *s* piazzaforte *f*

**strong' man'** *s (in a circus)* maciste *m;* *(leader)* anima; dittatore *m*

**strong-minded** ['strɔŋ,maɪndɪd] **or** ['straŋ,maɪndɪd] *adj* volitivo

**strong'point'** *s* luogo fortificato

**strontium** ['strɑnʃɪəm] *s* stronzio

**strop** [strɑp] *s* coramella, affilarasoio ‖ *v (pret & pp* **stropped;** *ger* **stropping)** *tr* affilare

**strophe** ['strofi] *s* strofa, strofe *f*

**struc'tural steel'** [ˈstrʌktʃərəl] *s* profilato di acciaio

**structure** [ˈstrʌktʃər] *s* struttura; edificio ‖ *tr* strutturare

**struggle** [ˈstrʌgəl] *s* lotta; sforzo ‖ *intr* lottare; sforzare, dibattersi

**strum** [strʌm] *v* (*pret & pp* **strummed;** *ger* **strummed**) *tr & intr* strimpellare

**strumpet** [ˈstrʌmpɪt] *s* sgualdrina, puttana

**strut** [strʌt] *s* controvento, puntello, saettone *m;* incedere impettito; (aer) montante ‖ *v* (*pret & pp* **strutted;** *ger* **strutting**) *intr* pavoneggiarsi, fare la ruota

**strychnine** [ˈstrɪknaɪn] or [ˈstrɪknɪn] *s* stricnina

**stub** [stʌb] *s* (*of tree*) coppo; (*e.g., of cigar*) mozzicone *m;* (*of a check*) matrice *f*, madre *f* ‖ *v* (*pret & pp* **stubbed;** *ger* **stubbing**) *tr* sradicare; **to stub one's toe** inciampare

**stubble** [ˈstʌbəl] *s* (*of beard*) pelo ispido; **stubbles** stoppie *fpl*

**stubborn** [ˈstʌbərn] *adj* (*headstrong*) testardo; (*resolute*) accanito; (*e.g., resistance*) ostinato; (*e.g., illness*) ribelle; (*soil*) ingrato

**stuc·co** [ˈstʌko] *s* (**-coes** or **-cos**) stucco ‖ *tr* stuccare

**stuck** [stʌk] *adj* infisso; attaccato; (*glued*) incollato; (*unable to continue*) in panna; **stuck on** (slang) invaghito di

**stuck'-up'** *adj* (coll) presuntuoso, arrogante

**stud** [stʌd] *s* (*in upholstery*) borchia; bottone *m* da sparato; (*of walls*) montante *m;* (*stallion*) stallone *m;* (*for mares*) monta; (archit) bugna, bugnato ‖ *v* (*pret & pp* **studded;** *ger* **studding**) *tr* cospergere; (*with stars*) costellare; (*with jewels*) incastonare, ingioiellare

**stud' bolt'** *s* prigioniero

**stud'book'** *s* registro della genealogia

**student** [ˈstjudənt] or [ˈstudənt] *adj* studentesco ‖ *s* studente *m;* scolaro; (*investigator*) studioso

**stu'dent bod'y** *s* scolaresca

**stud'horse'** *s* stallone *m*

**studied** [ˈstʌdid] *adj* premeditato; (*affected*) studiato

**studi·o** [ˈstudɪˌo] or [ˈstjudɪˌo] *s* (**-os**) studio

**studious** [ˈstjudɪ·əs] or [ˈstudɪ·əs] *adj* studioso; assiduo, zelante

**stud·y** [ˈstʌdi] *s* (**-ies**) studio ‖ *v* (*pret & pp* **-ied**) *tr & intr* studiare

**stuff** [stʌf] *s* roba, cosa; stoffa; materiale *m;* (*nonsense*) scemenze *fpl;* medicina; (coll) mestiere *m* ‖ *tr* riempire, inzeppare; (*one's stomach*) rimpinzare; (*e.g., poultry*) farcire; (*e.g., salami*) insaccare; (*a dead animal*) impagliare; **to stuff up** intasare ‖ *intr* rimpinzarsi

**stuffed' shirt'** *s* persona altezzosa

**stuffing** [ˈstʌfɪŋ] *s* ripieno

**stuff·y** [ˈstʌfi] *adj* (**-ier; -iest**) soffocante, opprimente; (*nose*) chiuso; pedante

**stumble** [ˈstʌmbəl] *intr* incespicare, inciampare; sbagliare, impaperarsi; **to stumble on** or **upon** intoparsi in

**stum'bling block'** *s* inciampo, scoglio

**stump** [stʌmp] *s* (*of tree*) toppo, ceppo; (*e.g., of arm*) moncherino, moncone *m;* (*of cigar, candle*) mozzicone *m;* dente rotto; tribuna popolare; (*for drawing*) sfumino; **up a stump** (coll) completamente perplesso ‖ *tr* mozzare; lasciare perplesso; (coll) fare discorsi politici in

**stump' speech'** *s* discorso politico

**stun** [stʌn] *v* (*pret & pp* **stunned;** *ger* **stunning**) *tr* tramortire; (fig) sbalordire

**stunning** [ˈstʌnɪŋ] *adj* (*blow*) che stordisce; sbalorditivo, magnifico

**stunt** [stʌnt] *s* atrofia; creatura striminzita; bravata, prodezza; (*for publicity*) montatura ‖ *tr* striminzire; arrestare la crescita di ‖ *intr* fare delle acrobazie

**stunt'ed** *adj* striminzito

**stunt' fly'ing** *s* acrobazia aerea

**stunt' man'** *s* (mov) controfigura

**stupe·fy** [ˈstjupɪˌfaɪ] or [ˈstupɪˌfaɪ] *v* (*pret & pp* **-fied**) *tr* istupidire, intontire

**stupendous** [stjuˈpɛndəs] or [stuˈpɛndəs] *adj* stupendo

**stupid** [ˈstjupɪd] or [ˈstupɪd] *adj* stupido, ebete, scemo

**stupor** [ˈstjupər] or [ˈstupər] *s* torpore *m*, stupore *m*

**stur·dy** [ˈstʌrdi] *adj* (**-dier; -diest**) forte; (*robust*) tarchiato; risoluto

**sturgeon** [ˈstʌrdʒən] *s* storione *m*

**stutter** [ˈstʌtər] *s* tartagliamento ‖ *tr & intr* tartagliare

**sty** [staɪ] *s* (**sties**) porcile *m;* (pathol) orzaiolo

**style** [staɪl] *s* stile *m;* tono; (*mode of living*) treno ‖ *tr* chiamare col nome di

**stylish** [ˈstaɪlɪʃ] *adj* alla moda, di tono

**sty·mie** [ˈstaɪmi] *v* (*pret & pp* **-mied;** *ger* **-mieing**) *tr* ostacolare, contrastare

**styp'tic pen'cil** [ˈstɪptɪk] *s* matita emostatica

**Styx** [stɪks] *s* Stige *m*

**suave** [swɑv] or [swev] *adj* soave

**subaltern** [səbˈɔltərn] *adj & s* subalterno

**subcommittee** [ˈsʌbkə ˌmɪti] *s* sottocommissione

**subconscious** [səbˈkɑnʃəs] *adj & s* subcosciente *m*

**subconsciousness** [səbˈkɑnʃəsnɪs] *s* subcosciente *m*, subcoscienza

**sub'deb'** *s* (coll) signorina più giovane di una debuttante

**subdivide** [ˈsʌbdɪ ˌvaɪd] or [ ˌsʌbdɪˈvaɪd] *tr* suddividere ‖ *intr* suddividersi

**subdue** [səbˈdju] or [səbˈdu] *tr* soggiogare, sottomettere; (*color, voice*) attenuare

**subdued** [səbˈdjud] or [səbˈdud] *adj* (*voice*) sommesso; (*light*) tenue

**subheading** ['sʌb‚hedɪŋ] *s* sottotitolo; (journ) sommario

**subject** ['sʌbdʒɪkt] *adj* soggetto; **subject to** (*e.g., a cold*) soggetto a; (*e.g., a fine*) passibile di || *s* soggetto, materia, proposito; (*of a ruler*) suddito; (gram, med, philos) soggetto || [səb-'dʒɛkt] *tr* sottomettere

**sub'ject cat'alogue** *s* catalogo per materie

**sub'ject in'dex** *s* indice *m* per materie

**subjection** [səb'dʒɛkʃən] *s* soggezione

**subjective** [səb'dʒɛktɪv] *adj* soggettivo

**sub'ject mat'ter** *s* soggetto

**subjugate** ['sʌbdʒə‚get] *tr* soggiogare

**subjunctive** [səb'dʒʌŋktɪv] *adj & s* congiuntivo

**sublease** ['sʌb‚lis] *s* subaffitto || [‚sʌb-'lis] *tr* subaffittare

**sub·let** [sʌb'lɛt] or ['sʌb‚lɛt] *v* (*pret & pp* **-let; *ger* -letting**) *tr* subaffittare

**sub·machine' gun'** [‚sʌbmə'ʃin] *s* mitra *m*

**submarine** ['sʌbmə‚rin] *adj & s* sottomarino

**sub'marine chas'er** ['tʃesər] *s* cacciasommergibili *m*

**submerge** [səb'mʌrdʒ] *tr* sommergere || *intr* sommergersi

**submersion** [səb'mʌrʒən] or [səb-'mʌrʃən] *s* sommersione

**submission** [səb'mɪʃən] *s* sottomissione

**submissive** [səb'mɪsɪv] *adj* sottomesso

**sub·mit** [səb'mɪt] *v* (*pret & pp* **-mitted**; *ger* **-mitting**) *tr* sottomettere; presentare, deferire; osservare rispettosamente || *intr* sottomettersi

**subordinate** [səb'ɔrdɪnɪt] *adj & s* subordinato || [səb'ɔrdɪ‚net] *tr* subordinare

**suborna'tion of per'jury** [‚sʌbər'neʃən] *s* subornazione

**subplot** ['sʌb‚plɑt] *s* intreccio secondario

**subpoena** or **subpena** [sʌb'pinə] or [sə-'pinə] *s* mandato di comparizione || *tr* citare

**sub rosa** [sʌb'rozə] *adv* in segreto

**subscribe** [səb'skraɪb] *tr* sottoscrivere || *intr* sottoscrivere; **to subscribe to** sottoscrivere a; (*a magazine*) abbonarsi a; (*an opinion*) approvare

**subscriber** [səb'skraɪbər] *s* sottoscrittore *m*; abbonato

**subscription** [sʌb'skrɪpʃən] *s* sottoscrizione; (*e.g., to a newspaper*) abbonamento; (*e.g., to club*) quota

**subsequent** ['sʌbsɪkwənt] *adj* susseguente, posteriore

**subservient** [səb'sʌrvɪ‚ənt] *adj* subordinato; ossequioso, servile

**subside** [səb'saɪd] *intr* calmarsi; (*said of water*) decrescere

**subsidiar·y** [səb'sɪdɪ‚ɛri] *adj* sussidiario || *s* (**-ies**) sussidiario

**subsidize** ['sʌbsɪ‚daɪz] *tr* sussidiare, sovvenzionare; (*by bribery*) subornare

**subsi·dy** ['sʌbsɪdi] *s* (**-dies**) sussidio, sovvenzione

**subsist** [səb'sɪst] *intr* sussistere

**subsistence** [səb'sɪstəns] *s* sussistenza

**subsoil** ['sʌb‚sɔɪl] *s* sottosuolo

**substance** ['sʌbstəns] *s* sostanza

**substandard** [sʌb'stændərd] *adj* inferiore al livello normale

**substantial** [səb'stænʃəl] *adj* considerevole; ricco, influente; (*food*) sostanzioso; (*e.g., reason*) sostanziale

**substantiate** [səb'stænʃɪ‚et] *tr* provare, verificare; dare prova di, sostanziare

**substantive** ['sʌbstəntɪv] *adj & s* sostantivo

**substation** ['sʌb‚steʃən] *s* ufficio postale secondario; (elec) sottostazione

**substitute** ['sʌbstɪ‚tjut] or ['sʌbstɪ‚tut] *adj* provvisorio, interino || *s* (*thing*) sostituto, surrogato; (*person*) sostituto, supplente *mf*; **beware of substitutes** guardarsi dalle contraffazioni || *tr*—**to substitute for** sostituire (*qlco* or *qlcu*) a || *intr*—**to substitute for** sostituire, rimpiazzare, e.g., **he substituted for the teacher** sostituì il maestro

**substitution** [‚sʌbstɪ'tjuʃən] or [‚sʌbstɪ'tuʃən] *s* sostituzione; (*by fraud*) contraffazione

**substra·tum** [sʌb'stretəm] *s* (**-ta** [tə]) sostrato, substrato

**subterfuge** ['sʌbtər‚fjudʒ] *s* sotterfugio

**subterranean** [‚sʌbtə'renɪ‚ən] *adj & s* sotterraneo

**subtitle** ['sʌb‚taɪtəl] *s* sottotitolo; (journ) titolo corrente; (mov) didascalia || *tr* dare una didascalia a

**subtle** ['sʌtəl] *adj* sottile

**subtle·ty** ['sʌtəlti] *s* (**-ties**) sottigliezza

**subtract** [səb'trækt] *tr* sottrarre

**subtraction** [sʌb'trækʃən] *s* sottrazione

**suburb** ['sʌbʌrb] *s* suburbio, sobborgo; **the suburbs** la periferia

**suburban** [sə'bʌrbən] *adj* suburbano

**suburbanite** [sə'bʌrbə‚naɪt] *s* abitante *mf* dei suburbi

**subvention** [səb'vɛnʃən] *s* sovvenzione || *tr* sovvenzionare

**subversive** [səb'vʌrsɪv] *adj & s* sovversivo

**subvert** [səb'vʌrt] *tr* sovvertire

**subway** ['sʌb‚we] *s* sotterranea, metropolitana, metrovia; sottopassaggio

**sub'way sta'tion** *s* stazione della metropolitana

**succeed** [sək'sid] *tr* succedere (with *dat*), subentrare (with *dat*) || *intr* riuscire; **to succeed to** (*the throne*) succedere a

**success** [sək'sɛs] *s* successo, riuscita

**successful** [sək'sɛsfəl] *adj* felice, fortunato; che ha avuto successo

**succession** [sək'sɛʃən] *s* successione; **in succession** in seguito, uno dopo l'altro

**successive** [sək'sɛsɪv] *adj* successivo

**succor** ['sʌkər] *s* soccorso || *tr* soccorrere

**succotash** ['sʌkə‚tæʃ] *s* verdura di fagioli e granturco

**succumb** [sə'kʌm] *intr* soccombere

**such** [sʌtʃ] *adj & pron indef* tale, simile; **such a** un simile, un tale; **such**

a + *adj* tanto + *adj*, e.g., **such a beautiful story** una storia tanto bella; **such as** tale quale, come
**suck** [sʌk] *s* succhio ‖ *tr* succhiare; (*air*) aspirare; **to suck in** (slang) ingannare
**sucker** [ˈsʌkər] *s* lattante *mf*; (bot) succhione *m*; (mach) pistone *m*; (coll) fesso, pollo, minchione *m*
**suckle** [ˈsʌkəl] *tr* allattare; nutrire ‖ *intr* poppare
**suck′ling pig′** [ˈsʌklɪŋ] *s* maiale *m* di latte
**suction** [ˈsʌkʃən] *s* aspirazione
**suc′tion cup′** *s* ventosa
**suc′tion pump′** *s* pompa aspirante
**sudden** [ˈsʌdən] *adj* subito, improvviso; **all of a sudden** all'improvviso
**suddenly** [ˈsʌdənli] *adv* all'improvviso
**suds** [sʌdz] *spl* saponata; schiuma; (coll) birra
**sue** [su] or [sju] *tr* querelare ‖ *intr* querelarsi; **to sue for damages** chiedere i danni; **to sue for peace** chiedere la pace
**suede** [swed] *s* pelle scamosciata
**suet** [ˈsu·ɪt] or [ˈsju·ɪt] *s* grasso, sego
**suffer** [ˈsʌfər] *tr* soffrire; (e.g., *heavy losses*) subire ‖ *intr* soffrire, patire
**sufferance** [ˈsʌfərəns] *s* tolleranza
**suffering** [ˈsʌfərɪŋ] *adj* sofferente ‖ *s* sofferenza, strazio, patimento
**suffice** [səˈfaɪs] *intr* bastare
**sufficient** [səˈfɪʃənt] *adj* sufficiente
**suffix** [ˈsʌfɪks] *s* suffisso
**suffocate** [ˈsʌfəˌket] *tr & intr* soffocare
**suffrage** [ˈsʌfrɪdʒ] *s* suffragio
**suffragette** [ˌsʌfrəˈdʒɛt] *s* suffragetta
**suffuse** [səˈfjuz] *tr* soffondere
**sugar** [ˈʃugər] *adj* (*water*) zuccherato; (*industry*) zuccheriero ‖ *s* zucchero ‖ *tr* zuccherare
**sug′ar beet′** *s* barbabietola da zucchero
**sug′ar bowl′** *s* zuccheriera
**sug′ar cane′** *s* canna da zucchero
**sug′ar-coat′** *tr* inzuccherare; (e.g., *the pill*) addolcire
**sug′ar ma′ple** *s* acero
**sug′ar·plum′** *s* zuccherino
**sug′ar spoon′** *s* cucchiaino per lo zucchero
**sug′ar tongs′** *spl* mollette *fpl* per lo zucchero
**sugary** [ˈʃugəri] *adj* zuccherino, zuccheroso
**suggest** [səgˈdʒɛst] *tr* suggerire
**suggestion** [səgˈdʒɛstʃən] *s* suggerimento; (psychol) suggestione; ombra, traccia
**suggestive** [səgˈdʒɛstɪv] *adj* suggestivo; (*risqué*) scabroso
**suicidal** [ˌsu·ɪˈsaɪdəl] or [ˌsju·ɪˈsaɪdəl] *adj* suicida
**suicide** [ˈsu·ɪˌsaɪd] or [ˈsju·ɪˌsaɪd] *s* (*person*) suicida *mf*; (*act*) suicidio; **to commit suicide** suicidarsi
**suit** [sut] or [sjut] *s* vestito da uomo; (*of a lady*) tailleur *m*; (*of cards*) seme *m*, colore *m*; (*for bathing*) costume *m*; corte *f*, corteggiamento; domanda, supplica; (law) causa; **to follow suit** seguire l'esempio; (cards)

rispondere a colore ‖ *tr* adattarsi (with *dat*); convenire (with *dat*); **suit yourself** faccia come vuole ‖ *intr* convenire, andare a proposito
**suitable** [ˈsutəbəl] or [ˈsjutəbəl] *adj* indicato, conveniente
**suit′case′** *s* valigia
**suite** [swit] *s* gruppo, serie *f*; serie *f* di stanze; (*of furniture*) mobilia; (*retinue*) seguito; (mus) suite *f*
**suiting** [ˈsutɪŋ] or [ˈsjutɪŋ] *s* taglio d'abito
**suit′ of clothes′** *s* completo maschile
**suitor** [ˈsutər] or [ˈsjutər] *s* pretendente *m*; (law) querelante *mf*
**sul′fa drugs′** [ˈsʌlfə] *spl* sulfamidici *mpl*
**sulfate** [ˈsʌlfet] *s* solfato
**sulfide** [ˈsʌlfaɪd] *s* solfuro
**sulfite** [ˈsʌlfaɪt] *s* solfito
**sulfur** [ˈsʌlfər] *adj* solfiero ‖ *s* zolfo; color *m* zolfo
**sulfuric** [sʌlˈfjurɪk] *adj* solforico
**sul′fur mine′** *s* solfara
**sulfurous** [ˈsʌlfərəs] *adj* solforoso
**sulk** [sʌlk] *s* broncio ‖ *intr* imbronciarsi
**sulk·y** [ˈsʌlki] *adj* (**-ier; -iest**) imbronciato ‖ *s* (**-ies**) (*in horse racing*) sediolo, sulky *m*
**sullen** [ˈsʌlən] *adj* bieco, triste, tetro
**sul·ly** [ˈsʌli] *v* (*pret & pp* **-lied**) *tr* insudiciare, insozzare
**sulphur** [ˈsʌlfər] *adj & s* var of **sulfur**
**sultan** [ˈsʌltən] *s* sultano
**sul·try** [ˈsʌltri] *adj* (**-trier; -triest**) soffocante; infocato, appassionato
**sum** [sʌm] *s* somma; sommario; problema *m* di aritmetica ‖ *v* (*pret & pp* **summed**; *ger* **summing**) *tr* sommare; **to sum up** riepilogare
**sumac** or **sumach** [ˈumæk] or [ˈsumæk] *s* (bot) sommacco
**summarize** [ˈsʌməˌraɪz] *tr* riassumere
**summa·ry** [ˈsʌməri] *adj* sommario ‖ *s* (**-ries**) sommario, sunto
**summer** [ˈsʌmər] *adj* estivo ‖ *s* estate *f* ‖ *intr* passare l'estate
**sum′mer resort′** *s* stazione estiva
**summersault** [ˈsʌmərˌsɔlt] *s & intr* var of **somersault**
**sum′mer school′** *s* scuola estiva
**summery** [ˈsʌməri] *adj* estivo
**summit** [ˈsʌmɪt] *s* sommità *f*
**sum′mit con′ference** *s* riunione al vertice
**summon** [ˈsʌmən] *tr* convocare, invitare; evocare; (law) compulsare
**summons** [ˈsʌmənz] *s* ordine *m*, comando; (law) citazione ‖ *tr* (law) citare
**sumptuous** [ˈsʌmptʃu·əs] *adj* sontuoso
**sun** [sʌn] *s* sole *m*; **place in the sun** posto al sole ‖ *v* (*pret & pp* **sunned**; *ger* **sunning**) *tr* esporre al sole ‖ *intr* prendere il sole
**sun′ bath′** *s* bagno di sole
**sun′beam′** *s* raggio di sole
**sun′burn′** *s* abbronzatura ‖ *v* (*pret & pp* **-burned** or **-burnt**) *tr* abbronzare ‖ *intr* abbronzarsi

**sundae** ['sʌndi] *s* gelato con sciroppo, frutta o noci
**Sunday** ['sʌndi] *adj* domenicale ‖ *s* domenica
**Sun'day best'** *s* (coll) vestito da festa
**Sun'day's child'** *s* bambino nato con la camicia
**Sun'day school'** *s* scuola domenicale della dottrina
**sunder** ['sʌndər] *tr* separare
**sun'di'al** *s* meridiana
**sun'down'** *s* tramonto
**sundries** ['sʌndriz] *spl* generi *mpl* diversi
**sundry** ['sʌndri] *adj* vari, diversi
**sun'fish'** *s* pesce *m* mola, pesce *m* luna
**sun'flow'er** *s* girasole *m*
**sun'glass'es** *spl* occhiali *mpl* da sole
**sunken** ['sʌŋkən] *adj* affondato, sommerso; (hollow) incavato
**sun' lamp'** *s* sole *m* artificiale
**sun'light'** *s* luce *f* del sole
**sun'lit'** *adj* illuminato dal sole
**sun·ny** ['sʌni] *adj* (-nier; -niest) solatio, soleggiato; allegro, ridente; **it is sunny** fa sole
**sun'ny side'** *s* parte soleggiata; lato buono; **on the sunny side of** (*e.g.*, *thirty*) al disotto dei . . . anni
**sun' porch'** *s* veranda a solatio
**sun'rise'** *s* sorgere *m* del sole; **from sunrise to sunset** dall'alba al tramonto
**sun'set'** *s* tramonto
**sun'shade'** *s* tenda; parasole *m*
**sun'shine'** *s* sole *m*, luce *f* del sole; **in the sunshine** al sole
**sun'spot'** *s* macchia solare
**sun'stroke'** *s* insolazione
**sun' tan'** *s* tintarella
**sun'tan lo'tion** *s* pomata antisole, abbronzante *m*
**sun'up'** *s* sorgere *m*, levare *m* del sole
**sun' vi'sor** *s* (aut) aletta parasole, parasole *m*
**sup** [sʌp] *v* (*pret & pp* **supped; ger supping**) *intr* cenare
**super** ['supər] *adj* (coll) superficiale; (coll) di prim'ordine, super ‖ *s* (coll) sovrintendente *m*; (coll) articolo di prim'ordine, super *m*
**superabundant** [,supərə'bʌndənt] *adj* sovrabbondante
**superannuated** [,super'ænju,etıd] *adj* giubilato, pensionato; messo a riposo per limiti di età; antiquato
**superb** [su'pʌrb] *or* [sə'pʌrb] *adj* superbo
**supercar·go** ['supər,kargo] *s* (-goes) (naut) sopraccarico
**supercharge** [,supər't/ardʒ] *tr* sovralimentare
**supercilious** [,supər'sılı·əs] *adj* altero, arrogante
**superficial** [,supər'fı/əl] *adj* superficiale
**superfluous** [su'pʌrflu·əs] *adj* superfluo
**su'per·high'way** *s* autostrada
**superhuman** [,supər'hjumən] *adj* sovrumano
**superimpose** [,supərim'poz] *tr* sovrapporre

**superintendent** [,supərin'tendənt] *s* soprintendente *m*; (*of schools*) provveditore *m*
**superior** [sə'pırı·ər] *or* [su'pırı·ər] *adj* superiore; di superiorità; (typ) esponente ‖ *s* superiore *m*
**superiority** [sə'pırı'arıti] *or* [su,pırı'arıti] *s* superiorità *f*
**superlative** [sə'pʌrlətıv] *or* [su'pʌrlətıv] *adj & s* superlativo
**su'per·man'** *s* (-men') superuomo
**supermarket** ['supər,markıt] *s* supermercato
**supernatural** [,supər'næt/ərəl] *adj* soprannaturale
**superpose** [,supər'poz] *tr* sovrapporre
**supersede** [,supər'sid] *tr* rimpiazzare, sostituire
**supersensitive** [,supər'sensıtıv] *adj* ipersensibile
**supersonic** [,supər'sanık] *adj* supersonico
**superstition** [,supər'stı/ən] *s* superstizione
**superstitious** [,supər'stı/əs] *adj* superstizioso
**supervene** [,supər'vin] *intr* sopravvenire
**supervise** ['supər,vaız] *tr* sorvegliare, dirigere
**supervision** [,supər'vı/ən] *s* supervisione, sorveglianza, direzione
**supervisor** ['supər,vaızər] *s* supervisore *m*, sorvegliante *mf*; ispettore *m*
**supper** ['sʌpər] *s* cena
**sup'per·time'** *s* ora di cena
**supplant** [sə'plænt] *tr* rimpiazzare
**supple** ['sʌpəl] *adj* flessibile; docile
**supplement** ['sʌplımənt] *s* supplemento ‖ ['sʌplı,ment] *tr* completare, supplire (with *dat*)
**suppliant** ['sʌplı·ənt] *adj & s* supplicante *mf*
**supplicant** ['sʌplıkənt] *s* supplicante *mf*
**supplication** [,sʌplı'ke/ən] *s* supplica
**supplier** [sʌ'plaı·ər] *s* fornitore *m*
**sup·ply** [sə'plaı] *s* (-plies) rifornimento, fornitura; provvista, scorta; (com) offerta; **supplies** rifornimenti *mpl*, vettovaglie *fpl* ‖ *v* (*pret & pp* -plied) *tr* fornire, provvedere; (*food*) vettovagliare
**supply' and demand'** *s* domanda ed offerta
**support** [sə'port] *s* sostegno, appoggio; puntello, rincalzo; mantenimento ‖ *tr* sostenere, appoggiare; puntellare; (*a cause*) caldeggiare; mantenere
**supporter** [sə'portər] *s* fautore *m*, sostenitore *m*; (*jockstrap*) sospensorio; giarrettiera; fascia elastica
**suppose** [sə'poz] *tr* supporre; ammettere; **suppose we take a walk?** che ne dice se facessimo una passeggiata?; **to be supposed to be** aver fama di essere; **to suppose so** credere di sì
**supposed** [sə'pozd] *adj* presunto
**supposition** [,sʌpə'zı/ən] *s* supposizione
**supposito·ry** [sə'pazı,tori] *s* (-ries) suppositorio, supposta
**suppress** [sə'pres] *tr* sopprimere

**suppression** [sə'prɛʃən] *s* soppressione
**suppurate** ['sʌpjə‚ret] *intr* suppurare
**supreme** [sə'prim] or [su'prim] *adj* supremo, sommo
**Supreme' Court'** *s* (*in Italy*) Corte *f* di Cassazione; (*in U.S.A.*) tribunale *m* di ultima istanza
**surcharge** ['sʌr‚tʃɑrdʒ] *s* soprapprezzo; soprattassa; sovraccarico; (philately) sovrastampa ‖ [‚sʌr-'tʃɑrdʒ] or ['sʌr‚tʃɑrdʒ] *tr* sovraccaricare
**sure** [ʃur] *adj* sicuro; **to be sure!** certamente!, senza dubbio! ‖ *interj* (coll) certamente!; **sure enough!** (coll) difatti
**sure-footed** ['ʃjur'futɪd] *adj* dal piede sicuro
**sure' thing'** *s* (coll) successo garantito ‖ *adv* (coll) certamente ‖ *interj* (coll) di sicuro!
**sure·ty** ['ʃurti] or ['ʃuriti] *s* (-ties) malleveria
**surf** [sʌrf] *s* frangente *m*
**surface** ['sʌrfɪs] *adj* superficiale ‖ *s* superficie *f* ‖ *tr* rifinire; spianare; ricoprire ‖ *intr* emergere
**sur'face mail'** *s* posta ordinaria
**surf'board'** *s* tavola per il surfing
**surfeit** ['sʌrfɪt] *s* eccesso; sazietà *f* ‖ *tr* saziare, rimpinzare ‖ *intr* saziarsi, rimpinzarsi
**surf'ing** *s* surfing *m*
**surge** [sʌrdʒ] *s* ondata; fiotto; (elec) sovratensione ‖ *intr* ondeggiare, fluttuare; (*said*, *e.g.*, *of a crowd*) affluire
**surgeon** ['sʌrdʒən] *s* (medico) chirurgo
**surger·y** ['sʌrdʒəri] *s* (-ies) chirurgia; sala operatoria
**surgical** ['sʌrdʒɪkəl] *adj* chirurgico
**sur·ly** ['sʌrli] *adj* (-lier; -liest) arcigno, imbronciato
**surmise** [sʌr'maɪz] or ['sʌrmaɪz] *s* congettura, supposizione ‖ [sʌr-'maɪz] *tr* & *intr* congetturare, supporre
**surmount** [sʌr'maunt] *tr* sormontare; coronare
**surname** ['sʌr‚nem] *s* cognome *m*; (*added name*) soprannome *m* ‖ *tr* dare il cognome a; soprannominare
**surpass** [sʌr'pæs] or [sʌr'pɑs] *tr* sorpassare, superare
**surplice** ['sʌrplɪs] *s* cotta
**surplus** ['sʌrplʌs] *adj* eccedente ‖ *s* sopravanzo, eccedenza
**surprise** [sʌr'praɪz] *adj* insperato, improvviso ‖ *s* sorpresa ‖ *tr* sorprendere
**surprise' par'ty** *s* improvvisata
**surprising** [sʌr'praɪzɪŋ] *adj* sorprendente
**surrender** [sə'rɛndər] *s* resa ‖ *tr* arrendere ‖ *intr* arrendersi
**surren'der val'ue** *s* (ins) valore *m* di riscatto
**surreptitious** [‚sʌrɛp'tɪʃəs] *adj* clandestino, nascosto, furtivo
**surround** [sə'raund] *tr* circondare, contornare; (mil) aggirare
**surrounding** [sə'raundɪŋ] *adj* circostante, circonvicino ‖ **surroundings** *spl* dintorni *mpl*; ambiente *m*

**surtax** ['sʌr‚tæks] *s* sovrimposta, soprattassa; imposta complementare
**surveillance** [sʌr'veləns] or [sər-'veljəns] *s* sorveglianza, vigilanza
**survey** ['sʌrve] *s* quadro generale, schizzo; indagine *f*; (*of opinion*) sondaggio; rapporto; rilievo topografico; perizia ‖ [sʌr've] or ['sʌrve] *tr* fare un'indagine di; sondare; rilevare; misurare ‖ *intr* fare un rilievo
**sur'vey course'** *s* corso di rassegna generale
**surveyor** [sʌr've·ər] *s* livellatore *m*, geometra *m*
**survival** [sʌr'vaɪvəl] *s* sopravvivenza
**survive** [sər'vaɪv] *tr* sopravvivere (with *dat*) ‖ *intr* sopravvivere
**surviving** [sər'vaɪvɪŋ] *adj* superstite
**survivor** [sər'vaɪvər] *s* sopravvissuto, superstite *mf*
**survivorship** [sər'vaɪvər‚ʃɪp] *s* (law) sopravvivenza
**susceptible** [sə'sɛptɪbəl] *adj* suscettibile, ricettivo; impressionabile; **susceptible to** (*e.g.*, *colds*) soggetto a
**suspect** ['sʌspɛkt] or [səs'pɛkt] *adj* sospetto ‖ ['sʌspɛkt] *s* sospetto ‖ [səs'pɛkt] *tr* sospettare
**suspend** [səs'pɛnd] *tr* sospendere ‖ *intr* essere sospeso; fermarsi; fermare i pagamenti
**suspenders** [səs'pɛndərz] *spl* bretelle *fpl*
**suspense** [səs'pɛns] *s* sospensione; sospeso; **in suspense** in sospeso
**suspen'sion bridge'** [səs'pɛnʃən] *s* ponte sospeso
**suspicion** [səs'pɪʃən] *s* sospetto
**suspicious** [səs'pɪʃəs] *adj* (*subject to suspicion*) sospetto; (*inclined to suspect*) sospettoso
**sustain** [səs'ten] *tr* sostenere, sorreggere; (*with food*) sostentare; (*a conversation*) mantenere; (*a loss*) soffrire; (law) confermare
**sustenance** ['sʌstɪnəns] *s* sostentamento
**sutler** ['sʌtlər] *s* (mil) vivandiere *m*
**swab** [swɑb] *s* (mil) scovolo; (naut) redazza; (surg) batufolo di cotone ‖ *v* (*pret* & *pp* **swabbed**; *ger* **swabbing**) *tr* pulire con la redazza; spugnare; assorbire col cotone
**swaddle** ['swɑdəl] *tr* fasciare
**swad'dling clothes'** *spl* fasce *fpl* del neonato
**swagger** ['swægər] *s* spavalderia ‖ *intr* fare lo spavaldo
**swain** [swen] *s* innamorato; (*lad*) contadinotto
**swallow** ['swɑlo] *s* (*of liquid*) sorso; (*of food*) boccone *m*; (orn) rondine *f* ‖ *tr* & *intr* tranguggiare, inghiottire
**swal'low-tailed coat'** ['swɑlo‚teld] *s* frac *m*, marsina, abito a coda di rondine
**swal'low·wort'** *s* vincetossico
**swamp** [swɑmp] *s* pantano, palude *f* ‖ *tr* inondare, sommergere
**swamp·y** ['swɑmpi] *adj* (-ier; -iest) paludoso, pantanoso
**swan** [swɑn] *s* cigno
**swan' dive'** *s* volo dell'angelo

swank [swæŋk] *adj* (coll) elegante, vistoso ‖ *s* (coll) eleganza vistosa

swan's-down ['swɑnz,daʊn] *s* piuma di cigno, piumino; mollettone *m*

swan' song' *s* canto del cigno

swap [swɑp] *s* scambio, baratto ‖ *v* (*pret & pp* swapped; *ger* swapping) *tr & intr* scambiare, barattare

swarm [swɔrm] *s* sciame *m* ‖ *intr* sciamare; (fig) formicolare

swarth·y ['swɔrði] or ['swɔrθi] *adj* (-ier; -iest) olivastro, abbronzato

swashbuckler ['swɑʃ,bʌklər] *s* spadaccino, rodomonte *m*

swat [swɑt] *s* colpo ‖ *v* (*pret & pp* swatted; *ger* swatting) *tr* colpire; (*a fly*) schiacciare

sway [swe] *s* dondolio, ondeggiamento; dominio ‖ *tr* dondolare, fare oscillare; influenzare; dominare ‖ *intr* dondolarsi, ondulare; oscillare

swear [swer] *v* (*pret* swore [swor]; *pp* sworn [sworn]) *tr* giurare; (*to secrecy*) fare giurare; to swear in fare prestar giuramento a; to swear off giurare di rinunziare a; to swear out a warrant ottenere un atto di accusa sotto giuramento ‖ *intr* giurare; (*to blaspheme*) bestemmiare; to swear at maledire; to swear by giurare su, avere certezza di; to swear to dichiarare sotto giuramento; giurare di + *inf*

swear'word' *s* bestemmia, parolaccia

sweat [swɛt] *s* sudata; sudore *m* ‖ *v* (*pret & pp* sweat or sweated) *tr* sudare; far sudare; to sweat it out (slang) farcela fino alla fine; to sweat off (*weight*) perdere sudando ‖ *intr* sudare

sweater ['swɛtər] *s* maglione *m*, golf *m*, sweater *m*

sweat' shirt' *s* maglione *m* da ginnastica

sweat·y ['swɛti] *adj* (-ier; -iest) sudato; che fa sudare

Swede [swid] *s* svedese *mf*

Sweden ['swidən] *s* la Svezia

Swedish ['swidɪʃ] *adj & s* svedese *m*

sweep [swip] *s* scopata; movimento circolare; estensione; curva; (*of wind*) soffio; (*of well*) mazzacavallo; to make a clean sweep of far piazza pulita di ‖ *v* (*pret & pp* swept [swɛpt]) *tr* spazzare, scopare; percorrere con lo sguardo; (*eyes*) dirigere; travolgere ‖ *intr* scopare; passare; estendersi; dragare

sweeper ['swipər] *s* spazzino; (*machine*) spazzatrice *f*; (nav) dragamine *m*

sweeping ['swipɪŋ] *adj* esteso; travolgente, decisivo ‖ sweepings *spl* spazzatura

sweep'-sec'ond *s* lancetta dei secondi a perno centrale

sweep'stakes' *ssg* or *spl* lotteria abbinata alle corse dei cavalli

sweet [swit] *adj* dolce; (*butter*) senza sale; (*cider*) analcolico; to be sweet on (coll) essere innamorato di ‖

sweets *spl* dolci *mpl*; (coll) patate *fpl* dolci ‖ *adv* dolcemente; to smell sweet saper di buono

sweet'bread' *s* animella

sweet'bri'er *s* eglantina

sweeten ['switən] *tr* inzuccherare; raddolcire; purificare ‖ *intr* raddolcirsi; purificarsi

sweet'heart' *s* innamorato; innamorata; caro, amore *m*

sweet' mar'joram *s* maggiorana

sweet'meats' *spl* dolci *mpl*, confetti *mpl*

sweet' pea' *s* pisello odoroso

sweet' pota'to *s* batata, patata americana; (mus) ocarina

sweet-scented ['swit,sɛntɪd] *adj* odoroso, profumato

sweet' tooth' *s* debole *m* per i dolci

sweet-toothed ['swit,tuθt] *adj* goloso

sweet' wil'liam *s* garofano barbuto

swell [swɛl] *adj* (slang) elegante; (slang) eccellente, di prim'ordine ‖ *s* gonfiore *m*; onda, ondata; aumento; (mus) crescendo; (slang) elegantone *m* ‖ *v* (*pret* swelled; *pp* swelled or swollen ['swolən]) *tr* gonfiare, ingrossare; aumentare ‖ *intr* gonfiare, ingrossarsi; aumentare; (*said of the sea*) alzarsi; (*with pride*) montarsi

swelled' head' *s* borioso; to have a swelled head montarsi, essere pieno di sé

swelter ['swɛltər] *intr* soffocare dal caldo

swept'back wing' *s* ala a freccia

swerve [swʌrv] *s* scarto, sbandamento ‖ *tr* sviare ‖ *intr* scartare, sbandare

swift [swɪft] *adj* rapido ‖ *s* rondone *m* ‖ *adv* rapidamente

swig [swɪg] *s* (coll) sorso ‖ *v* (*pret & pp* swigged; *ger* swigging) *tr & intr* (coll) bere a grandi sorsi

swill [swɪl] *s* imbratto; risciacquatura ‖ *tr* tracannare, trincare ‖ *intr* bere a lunghi sorsi

swim [swɪm] *s* nuoto; the swim (*in social activities*) la corrente ‖ *v* (*pret* swam [swæm]; *pp* swum [swʌm]; *ger* swimming) *tr* traversare a nuoto ‖ *intr* nuotare; essere inondato; (*said of one's head*) girare, e.g., her head is swimming le gira la testa

swimmer ['swɪmər] *s* nuotatore *m*

swimming ['swɪmɪŋ] *s* nuoto

swim'ming pool' *s* piscina

swim'ming trunks' *spl* mutandine *fpl* da bagno

swim'suit' *s* costume *m* da bagno

swindle ['swɪndəl] *s* truffa, imbroglio ‖ *tr* truffare, imbrogliare

swine [swaɪn] *s* suino, maiale *m*, porco; swine *spl* suini *mpl*

swing [swɪŋ] *s* oscillazione; dondolio; curva; (*suspended seat*) altalena; alternarsi *m*; piena attività; (boxing) sventola; (mus) swing *m*; free swing libertà *f* d'azione; in full swing (coll) in piena attività ‖ *v* (*pret & pp* swung [swʌŋ]) *tr* (e.g., *one's arms*) dondolare, oscillare; (*a weapon*) brandire; (*e.g., a club*) rotare; far girare; appendere; (*a deal*) (coll) riuscire ad ottenere || *intr* dondolare, dondolarsi, oscillare; girare; essere sospeso; cambiare; (boxing) dare una sventola; **to swing open** aprirsi di colpo

**swing'ing door'** ['swɪŋɪŋ] *s* porta oscillante

**swinish** ['swaɪnɪʃ] *adj* porcino

**swipe** [swaɪp] *s* (coll) colpo forte || *tr* (coll) dare un forte colpo a; (slang) portare via, rubare

**swirl** [swʌrl] *s* turbine *m*, vortice *m* || *tr* far girare || *intr* turbinare

**swirling** ['swʌrlɪŋ] *adj* vorticoso

**swish** [swɪʃ] *s* (*of whip*) schiocco; (*of silk*) fruscio || *tr* (*a whip*) schioccare; || *intr* schioccare; frusciare

**Swiss** [swɪs] *adj* svizzero || *s* svizzero; **the Swiss** gli svizzeri

**Swiss' chard'** [tʃard] *s* bietola

**Swiss' cheese'** *s* groviera

**Swiss' Guards'** *spl* guardie *fpl* svizzere

**switch** [swɪtʃ] *s* verga; vergata; (*false hair*) posticcio; cambio, trapasso; (elec) interruttore *m*; (rr) scambio || *tr* battere, frustare; (elec) commutare; (rr) deviare; (fig) girare; **to switch off** (*light, radio, etc.*) spegnere; **to switch on** (*light, radio, etc.*) accendere || *intr* fustigare; cambiare; (rr) deviare

**switch'back'** *s* strada a zigzag; (rr) tracciato a zigzag

**switch'blade knife'** *s* coltello a serramanico

**switch'board'** *s* quadro

**switch'board op'erator** *s* centralinista *mf*

**switch'ing en'gine** *s* locomotiva da manovra

**switch'man** *s* (-men) deviatore *m*

**switch'yard'** *s* stazione smistamento

**Switzerland** ['swɪtsərlənd] *s* la Svizzera

**swiv·el** ['swɪvəl] *s* perno, gancio girevole || *v* (*pret & pp* -eled or -elled; *ger* -eling or -elling) *intr* girare

**swiv'el chair'** *s* sedia girevole

**swoon** [swun] *s* deliquio, svenimento || *intr* svenire

**swoop** [swup] *s* calata a piombo || *intr* calare a piombo, piombare

**sword** [sord] *s* spada; **at swords' points** pronti a incrociare le spade; **to put to the sword** passare a fil di spada

**sword' belt'** *s* cinturone *m*

**sword' cane'** *s* bastone animato

**sword'fish'** *s* pesce *m* spada

**swords'man** *s* (-men) spadaccino

**sword' swal'lower** ['swalo·ər] *s* giocoliere *m* che ingoia spade

**sword' thrust'** *s* stoccata

**sworn** [sworn] *adj* giurato

**sycophant** ['sɪkəfənt] *s* adulatore *m*; parassita *mf*

**syllable** ['sɪləbəl] *s* sillaba

**sylla·bus** ['sɪləbəs] *s* (-bi [ˌbaɪ]) sillabo, sommario scolastico

**syllogism** ['sɪləˌdʒɪzəm] *s* sillogismo

**sylph** [sɪlf] *s* silfo; silfide *f*; (fig) silfide *f*

**sylvan** ['sɪlvən] *adj* silvano

**symbol** ['sɪmbəl] *s* simbolo

**symbolic(al)** [sɪm'balɪk(əl)] *adj* simbolico

**symbolism** ['sɪmbəˌlɪzəm] *s* simbolismo

**symbolize** ['sɪmbəˌlaɪz] *tr* simboleggiare

**symmetric(al)** [sɪ'metrɪk(əl)] *adj* simmetrico

**symme·try** ['sɪmɪtri] *s* (-tries) simmetria

**sympathetic** [ˌsɪmpə'θetɪk] *adj* simpatico; ben disposto

**sympathize** ['sɪmpəˌθaɪz] *intr*—**to sympathize with** aver compassione di; mostrar comprensione per; (*to be in accord with*) simpatizzare con

**sympa·thy** ['sɪmpəθi] *s* (-thies) compassione, commiserazione; **to be in sympathy with** essere d'accordo con; **to extend one's sympathy to** fare le condoglianze a

**sym'pathy strike'** *s* sciopero di solidarietà

**symphonic** [sɪm'fanɪk] *adj* sinfonico

**sympho·ny** ['sɪmfəni] *s* (-nies) sinfonia

**symposi·um** [sɪm'pozɪ·əm] *s* (-a [ə]) simposio, colloquio

**symptom** ['sɪmptəm] *s* sintomo

**synagogue** ['sɪnəˌgag] or ['sɪnəˌgag] *s* sinagoga

**synchronize** ['sɪŋkrəˌnaɪz] *tr & intr* sincronizzare

**synchronous** ['sɪŋkrənəs] *adj* sincrono

**sincopation** [ˌsɪŋkə'peʃən] *s* sincope *f*

**syncope** ['sɪŋkəˌpi] *s* (phonet) sincope *f*

**syndicate** ['sɪndɪkɪt] *s* sindacato || ['sɪndɪˌket] *tr* organizzare in un sindacato

**synonym** ['sɪnənɪm] *s* sinonimo

**synonymous** [sɪ'nanɪməs] *adj* sinonimo

**synop·sis** [sɪ'napsɪs] *s* (-ses [siz]) sinossi *f*; (mov) sinopsi *f*

**synoptic(al)** [sɪ'naptɪk(əl)] *adj* sinottico

**syntax** ['sɪntæks] *s* sintassi *f*

**synthe·sis** ['sɪnθɪsɪs] *s* (-ses [ˌsiz]) sintesi *f*

**synthesize** ['sɪnθɪˌsaɪz] *tr* sintetizzare

**synthetic(al)** [sɪn'θetɪk(əl)] *adj* sintetico

**syphilis** ['sɪfɪlɪs] *s* sifilide *f*

**Syria** ['sɪrɪ·ə] *s* la Siria

**Syrian** ['sɪrɪ·ən] *adj & s* siriano

**syringe** [sɪ'rɪndʒ] or ['sɪrɪndʒ] *s* (*fountain syringe*) schizzetto; (*for hypodermic injections*) siringa || *tr* schizzettare; iniettare

**syrup** ['sɪrəp] or ['sʌrəp] *s* sciroppo

**system** ['sɪstəm] *s* sistema *m*

**systematic(al)** [ˌsɪstə'mætɪk(əl)] *adj* sistematico

**systematize** ['sɪstəməˌtaɪz] *tr* ridurre a sistema

**systole** ['sɪstəli] *s* sistole *f*

# T

**T, t** [ti] *s* ventesima lettera dell'alfabeto inglese; **to fit to a T** calzare come un guanto

**tab** [tæb] *s* (*strap*) linguetta; (*of a pocket*) patta; targa; (*label*) etichetta; **to keep tabs on** (coll) sorvegliare; **to pick up the tab** (coll) pagare il conto

**tab·by** ['tæbi] *s* (**-bies**) gatto tigrato; gatta; (*spinster*) zitella; vecchia pettegola

**tabernacle** ['tæbər‚nækəl] *s* tabernacolo

**table** ['tebəl] *s* tavola; (*food*) mensa; (*people at a table*) tavolata; (*synopsis*) quadro, prospetto; (*list or catalogue*) indice *m;* **to turn the tables** rovesciare la posizione; **under the table** ubriaco fradicio ‖ *tr* aggiornare, rinviare

**tab·leau** ['tæblo] *s* (**-leaus** or **-leaux** [loz]) quadro vivente

**ta'ble·cloth'** *s* tovaglia

**table d'hôte** ['tɑbəl'dot] *s* pasto a prezzo fisso

**tableful** ['tebəl‚fʊl] *s* (*persons*) tavolata; (*food*) tavola apparecchiata

**ta'ble·land'** *s* tavoliere *m*

**ta'ble lin'en** *s* biancheria da tavola

**ta'ble man'ners** *spl* maniere *fpl* a tavola

**ta'ble of con'tents** *s* indice *m* delle materie

**ta'ble·spoon'** *s* cucchiaio

**tablespoonful** ['tebəl‚spun‚fʊl] *s* cucchiaiata

**tablet** ['tæblɪt] *s* (*writing pad*) blocco; (*slab*) lapide *f;* (*flat rigid sheet*) tabella, tavoletta; (pharm) disco, pastiglia

**ta'ble talk'** *s* conversazione familiare a tavola

**ta'ble ten'nis** *s* ping-pong *m*, tennis *m* da tavolo

**ta'ble·ware'** *s* servizio da tavola

**ta'ble wine'** *s* vino da pasto

**tabloid** ['tæblɔɪd] *s* giornale *m* a carattere sensazionale

**taboo** [tə'bu] *adj* & *s* tabù *m* ‖ *tr* proibire assolutamente

**tabulate** ['tæbjə‚let] *tr* tabulare

**tabulator** ['tæbjə‚letər] *s* tabulatore *m*, incolonnatore *m*

**tachometer** [tə'kɑmɪtər] *s* tachimetro

**tacit** ['tæsɪt] *adj* tacito

**taciturn** ['tæsɪ‚tʌrn] *adj* taciturno

**tack** [tæk] *s* bulletta; cambio di direzione; (naut) virata; (sew) imbastitura ‖ *tr* imbullettare; attaccare; (naut) bordeggiare; (sew) imbastire ‖ *intr* virare; mutare di direzione

**tackle** ['tækəl] *s* attrezzatura; (mach) taglia, paranco; (*gear*) (naut) padiglione *m* ‖ *tr* attaccare, affrontare; (sports) placcare, bloccare

**tack·y** ['tæki] *adj* (**-ier; -iest**) appiccicaticcio; (coll) trasandato

**tact** [tækt] *s* tatto

**tactful** ['tæktfəl] *adj* pieno di tatto

**tactical** ['tæktɪkəl] *adj* tattico

**tactician** [tæk'tɪʃən] *s* tattico

**tactics** ['tæktɪks] *ssg* (mil) tattica ‖ *spl* tattica

**tactless** ['tæktlɪs] *adj* che non ha tatto, indiscreto

**tadpole** ['tæd‚pol] *s* girino

**taffeta** ['tæfɪtə] *s* taffettà *m*

**taffy** ['tæfi] *s* caramella, zucchero d'orzo; (coll) lisciata

**tag** [tæg] *s* etichetta; (*on a shoelace*) punta dell'aghetto; conclusione; (*last words of speech*) pistolotto finale; epiteto; frase fatta; (*of hair*) ciocca; (*in writing*) ghirigoro; (*game*) toccaferro ‖ *v* (*pret* & *pp* **tagged;** *ger* **tagging**) *tr* etichettare; (*to fine*) multare; aggiungere; soprannominare; accusare; stabilire il prezzo di; (coll) pedinare ‖ *intr* seguire da presso

**tag' end'** *s* (*e.g., of day*) fine *f;* estremità logorata; avanzo

**tail** [tel] *adj* di coda ‖ *s* coda; fine *f;* (*of coin*) croce *f;* **tails** falde *fpl*, frac *m;* **to turn tails** darsela a gambe ‖ *tr* attaccare; finire; (coll) pedinare

**tail' assem'bly** *s* (aer) impennaggio

**tail' end'** *s* coda, fine *f*

**tail'light'** *s* fanale *m* di coda

**tailor** ['telər] *s* sarto ‖ *tr* (*a suit*) tagliare, confezionare; (*one's conduct*) adattare ‖ *intr* fare il sarto

**tailoring** ['telərɪŋ] *s* sartoria

**tai'lor-made'** *adj* fatto su misura

**tai'lor shop'** *s* sartoria

**tail'piece'** *s* coda, estremità *f;* (mus) cordiera; (typ) fusello finale

**tail'race'** *s* canale *m* di scarico

**tail'spin'** *s* avvitamento

**tail'wind'** *s* (aer) vento di coda; (naut) vento in poppa

**taint** [tent] *s* macchia; infezione ‖ *tr* macchiare, infettare, corrompere

**take** [tek] *s* presa; (*of fish*) retata; (mov) presa; ripresa; (slang) incasso ‖ *v* (*pret* **took** [tʊk]; *pp* **taken**) *tr* prendere, pigliare; ricevere, accettare; portare; (*to get by force*) portar via; (*a nap*) schiacciare; (*a bath*) fare; (*a joke*) stare a; (*an examination*) sostenere; (*one's own life*) togliersi; (*to deduct*) cavare; (*a purchase*) comprare; (*to convey*) portare; (*time*) impiegare; (*a step, a walk*) fare; (*a subject*) studiare; (*a responsibility, role, etc.*) assumere; (*an oath*) prestare; (*root*) mettere; (*exception*) sollevare; credere; (*e.g., a photograph*) fare, scattare; (slang) fregare; **it takes** ci vuole, ci vogliono; **to take amiss** prendere a male; **to take apart** scomporre; smontare; **to take back** riprendere; **to take down** abbassare; smontare; prender nota di; **to take for** prendere per; **to take from** portar via a; **to take in** (*to admit*) ammettere, ricevere; (*to encompass*) includere; (*a dress*) restringere; (*to cheat*) ingannare; (*water*) fare; (*a point of inter-*

*est*) visitare; **to take it** accettare, ammettere; (slang) resistere; **to take off** (*e.g., one's coat*) togliersi; portar via; scontare, defalcare; (slang) imitare; **to take on** ingaggiare; assumere; intraprendere; accettare la sfida di; **to take out** cavare, togliere; (*e.g., a girl*) portar fuori; (*e.g., a patent*) ottenere; **to take over** rilevare; (slang) imbrogliare; **to take place** aver luogo; **to take s.o.'s eye** attrarre l'attenzione di qlcu; **to take the place of** sottentrare a; **to take up** cominciare a studiare; sollevare, tirar su; (*a duty*) assumere; (*time, space*) occupare || *intr* prendere; scattare; darsi; diventare; **to take after** rassomigliare a; **to take off** (coll) partire, andarsene; (aer) decollare, involare; **to take up with** (coll) fare amicizia con; (coll) vivere con; **to take well** riuscire bene in fotografia
**take'off'** *s* parodia; (aer) decollaggio; (mach) presa di forza
**tal'cum pow'der** [ˈtælkəm] *s* talco
**tale** [tel] *s* storia, racconto; favola, fiaba; (*lie*) bugia, frottola; (*piece of gossip*) maldicenza
**tale'bear'er** *s* pettegolo
**talent** [ˈtælənt] *s* talento; persona di talento; gente *f* di talento
**talented** [ˈtæləntɪd] *adj* dotato di talento, dotato d'ingegno
**tal'ent scout'** *s* scopritore *m* di talenti
**talk** [tɔk] *s* chiacchierata; discorso, conferenza; (*language*) parlata; (*gossip*) pettegolezzo; **to cause talk** originare pettegolezzi || *tr* parlare; convincere parlando; **to talk up** elogiare || *intr* parlare; discutere; **to talk on** discutere; continuare a parlare; **to talk up** parlare apertamente
**talkative** [ˈtɔkətɪv] *adj* loquace
**talker** [ˈtɔkər] *s* parlatore *m*
**talkie** [ˈtɔki] *s* (coll) parlato
**talk'ing machine'** *s* grammofono
**talk'ing pic'ture** *s* film parlato
**tall** [tɔl] *adj* alto; (coll) stravagante, esagerato
**tallow** [ˈtælo] *s* sego
**tal·ly** [ˈtæli] *s* (-**lies**) tacca, taglia || *v* (*pret & pp* -**lied**) *tr* contare, registrare || *intr* riscontrare
**tal'ly sheet'** *s* foglio di spunta
**talon** [ˈtælən] *s* artiglio
**tambourine** [ˌtæmbəˈrin] *s* tamburello
**tame** [tem] *adj* addomesticato; docile, mansueto; mite || *tr* addomesticare; domare; (*water power*) captare
**tamp** [tæmp] *tr* pigiare, comprimere; (*e.g., ground*) costipare
**tamper** [ˈtæmpər] *s* (*person*) pigiatore *m*; (*tool*) mazzeranga || *intr* intrigare; **to tamper with** (*a lock*) forzare; (*a document*) manomettere; (*a witness*) corrompere
**tampon** [ˈtæmpɑn] *s* (surg) tampone *m* || *tr* (surg) tamponare
**tan** [tæn] *adj* marrone; (*by sun*) abbronzato || *v* (*pret & pp* **tanned;** *ger* **tanning**) *tr* (*leather*) conciare; ab-

bronzare; (coll) picchiare, sculacciare
**tandem** [ˈtændəm] *adj & adv* in tandem || *s* tandem *m*
**tang** [tæŋ] *s* sapore *m* piccante; odore *m* forte; traccia; (*of knife*) tallone *m;* (*sound*) tintinnio
**tangent** [ˈtændʒənt] *adj* tangente || *s* tangente *f;* **to fly off at a tangent** cambiare improvvisamente d'idea
**tangerine** [ˌtændʒəˈrin] *s* mandarino
**tangible** [ˈtændʒɪbəl] *adj* tangibile
**Tangier** [tænˈdʒɪr] *s* Tangeri *f*
**tangle** [ˈtæŋgəl] *s* intrico; (coll) litigio || *tr* intricare || *intr* intricarsi; (coll) litigare
**tank** [tæŋk] *s* conserva, serbatoio; (mil) carro armato
**tankard** [ˈtæŋkərd] *s* boccale *m*
**tank' car'** *s* (rr) carro botte
**tanker** [ˈtæŋkər] *s* petroliera; (aer) aerocisterna
**tank' farm'ing** *s* idroponica
**tank' truck'** *s* autocisterna
**tanner** [ˈtænər] *s* conciapelli *m*
**tanner·y** [ˈtænəri] *s* (**-ies**) conceria
**tantalize** [ˈtæntəˌlaɪz] *tr* stuzzicare con vane promesse
**tantamount** [ˈtæntəˌmaʊnt] *adj* equivalente
**tantrum** [ˈtæntrəm] *s* bizze *fpl*
**tap** [tæp] *s* colpetto, buffetto; (*in a keg*) spina, cannella; (*faucet*) rubinetto; (elec) presa; (mach) maschio; **on tap** alla spina; (coll) disponibile; **taps** (mil) silenzio || *v* (*pret & pp* **tapped;** *ger* **tapping**) *tr* battere; picchiare, picchiettare; (*from a barrel*) spillare; mettere il cannello a; (*resources*) usare; (*a telephone*) intercettare; (*water, electricity*) derivare; (mach) maschiare || *intr* picchiare
**tap' dance'** *s* tip tap *m*
**tap'-dance'** *intr* ballare il tip tap
**tape** [tep] *s* nastro; (sports) striscione *m* del traguardo || *tr* legare con nastro; misurare col metro a nastro; registrare su nastro magnetico
**tape' meas'ure** *s* metro a nastro; nastro per misurare
**tape' play'er** *s* riproduttore *m* a nastro magnetico
**taper** [ˈtepər] *s* cerino || *tr* affusolare || *intr* affusolarsi; **to taper off** rastremarsi; diminuire in intensità; diminuire a poco a poco
**tape'-re·cord'** *tr* registrare su nastro magnetico
**tape' record'er** *s* magnetofono, registratore *m* a nastro
**tapes·try** [ˈtæpɪstri] *s* (**-tries**) tappezzeria || *v* (*pret & pp* **-tried**) *tr* tappezzare
**tape'worm'** *s* verme solitario, tenia
**tappet** [ˈtæpɪt] *s* (aut) punteria
**tap'room'** *s* taverna, osteria
**tap'root'** *s* radice *f* a fittone
**tap' wa'ter** *s* acqua corrente
**tap' wrench'** *s* giramaschio
**tar** [tɑr] *s* catrame *m* || *v* (*pret & pp* **tarred;** *ger* **tarring**) *tr* incatramare

**tar·dy** ['tɑrdi] *adj* (**-dier; -diest**) in ritardo; lento

**tare** [ter] *s* tara ‖ *tr* tarare

**target** ['tɑrgɪt] *s* segno, bersaglio

**tar'get date'** *s* data progettata

**tar'get lan'guage** *s* lingua obbiettivo, lingua di arrivo

**tar'get prac'tice** *s* esercizio di tiro a segno

**tariff** ['tærɪf] *s* (*duties*) tariffa doganale; (*charge or fare*) tariffa

**tarnish** ['tɑrnɪʃ] *s* ossidazione; (fig) macchia ‖ *tr* appannare ‖ *intr* appannarsi, perdere il lustro

**tar'pa'per** *s* carta catramata

**tarpaulin** [tɑr'pɔlɪn] *s* telone *m* impermeabile incatramato

**tarragon** ['tærəgən] *s* dragoncello

**tar·ry** ['tɑri] *adj* incatramato ‖ ['tæri] *v* (*pret & pp* **-ried**) *intr* rimanere; ritardare

**tart** [tɑrt] *adj* acido, pungente ‖ *s* torta; (slang) puttana

**tartar** ['tɑrtər] *s* tartaro; cremore *m* di tartaro; (*shrew*) megera; **to catch a tartar** imbattersi in un muso duro

**Tartarus** ['tɑrtərəs] *s* Tartaro

**task** [tæsk] or [tɑsk] *s* compito, incarico; **to take to task** rimproverare

**task' force'** *s* gruppo formato per una missione speciale

**task'mas'ter** *s* sorvegliante *m;* sorvegliante severo

**tassel** ['tæsəl] *s* nappa; (bot) ciuffo

**taste** [test] *s* gusto, sapore *m;* buon gusto; (*sampling, e.g., of wine*) assaggio; esperienza; **to one's taste** a genio di qlcu ‖ *tr* gustare, assaggiare ‖ *intr* sentire, sapere; **to taste of** degustare; sapere di

**tasteless** ['testlɪs] *adj* insipido; di cattivo gusto

**tast·y** ['testi] *adj* (**-ier; -iest**) saporito; (coll) di buon gusto

**tatter** ['tætər] *s* brandello, sbrendolo ‖ *tr* sbrindellare

**tattered** ['tætərd] *adj* sbrindellato

**tattle** ['tætəl] *s* chiacchiera; (*gossip*) pettegolezzo ‖ *intr* chiacchierare; spettegolare

**tat'tle·tale'** *adj* rivelatore ‖ *s* gazzetta, chiacchierone *m*

**tattoo** [tæ'tu] *s* tatuaggio; (mil) ritirata ‖ *tr* tatuare

**taunt** [tɔnt] or [tɑnt] *s* rimprovero sarcastico, insulto ‖ *tr* rimproverare sarcasticamente, insultare

**Taurus** ['tɔrəs] *s* (astr) Toro

**taut** [tɔt] *adj* teso, tirato

**tavern** ['tævərn] *s* osteria

**taw·dry** ['tɔdri] *adj* (**-drier; -driest**) vistoso, sgargiante, pacchiano

**taw·ny** ['tɔni] *adj* (**-nier; -niest**) falbo, fulvo

**tax** [tæks] *s* tassa, imposta ‖ *tr* tassare; (*s.o.'s patience*) mettere a dura prova

**taxable** ['tæksəbəl] *adj* tassabile

**tax'able in'come** *s* imponibile *m*

**taxation** [tæk'seʃən] *s* imposizione, tassazione, contribuzione

**tax' collec'tor** *s* esattore *m* delle imposte

**tax' deduc'tion** *s* detrazione

**tax'-ex·empt'** *adj* esente da tasse

**tax' evad'er** [ɪ'vedər] *s* evasore *m*

**tax·i** ['tæksi] *s* (**-is**) tassì *m* ‖ *v* (*pret & pp* **-ied;** *ger* **-iing** or **-ying**) *tr* far rullare ‖ *intr* andare in tassì; (aer) rullare

**tax'i·cab'** *s* tassì *m*

**tax'i driv'er** *s* tassista *m*

**tax'i·plane'** *s* aeroplano da noleggio, aerotassì *m*

**taxi' stand'** *s* posteggio di tassì

**tax'pay'er** *s* contribuente *mf*

**tax' rate'** *s* imponibilità *f*

**tea** [ti] *s* tè *m;* (*medicinal infusion*) tisana; (*beef broth*) brodo di carne

**tea' bag'** *s* sacchetto di tè

**tea' ball'** *s* uovo da tè

**tea'cart'** *s* servitore *m*

**teach** [titʃ] *v* (*pret & pp* **taught** [tɔt]) *tr & intr* insegnare

**teacher** ['titʃər] *s* maestro, insegnante *mf*

**teach'ers col'lege** *s* scuola magistrale

**teach'er's pet'** *s* beniamino del maestro

**teaching** ['titʃɪŋ] *adj* insegnante ‖ *s* insegnamento, dottrina

**teach'ing aids'** *spl* sussidi *mpl* didattici

**teach'ing staff'** *s* corpo insegnante

**tea'cup'** *s* tazza da tè

**tea' dance'** *s* tè *m* danzante

**teak** [tik] *s* tek *m*

**tea'ket'tle** *s* bricco del tè

**team** [tim] *s* (*e.g., of horses*) pariglia; (sports) squadra, equipaggio ‖ *tr* apparigliare; tirare or trasportare con pariglia ‖ *intr*—**to team up** unirsi, associarsi

**team'mate'** *s* compagno di squadra

**teamster** ['timstər] *s* (*of horses*) carrettiere *m;* (*of truck*) camionista *m*, autotrenista *m*

**team'work'** *s* affiatamento, collaborazione

**tea'pot'** *s* teiera

**tear** [tɪr] *s* lacrima; **to hold back one's tears** ingoiare le lacrime; **to laugh away one's tears** cambiare dal pianto al riso ‖ [ter] *s* strappo ‖ [ter] *v* (*pret* **tore** [tor]; *pp* **torn** [torn]) *tr* strappare; stracciare; (*one's heart*) squarciare; (*to wound*) sbranare; (*one's hair*) strapparsi; **to tear apart** rompere in due; separare; **to tear down** demolire; (*a piece of equipment*) smontare; **to tear off** staccare; **to tear to pieces** dilaniare; fare a pezzi; **to tear up** (*a piece of paper*) stracciare; (*a street*) scavare ‖ *intr* strapparsi, stracciarsi; **to tear along** precipitarsi; correre all'impazzata

**tear' bomb'** [tɪr] *s* bomba lacrimogena

**tearful** ['tɪrfəl] *adj* lacrimoso

**tear' gas'** [tɪr] *s* gas lacrimogeno

**tear-jerker** ['tɪr ˌdʒʌrkər] *s* (coll) storia lacrimogena

**tear-off** ['ter ˌɔf] *adj* da staccarsi, perforato

**tea'room'** *s* sala da tè

**tear' sheet'** [ter] *s* copia di annuncio pubblicitario

**tease** [tiz] *tr* stuzzicare, molestare;

(*hair*) accotonare; (*e.g., wool*) cardare

**tea'spoon'** *s* cucchiaino

**teaspoonful** ['ti ,spun ,fʊl] *s* cucchiaino

**teat** [tit] *s* capezzolo

**tea'time'** *s* l'ora del tè

**tea' wag'on** *s* servitore *m*

**technical** ['tɛknɪkəl] *adj* tecnico

**technicali·ty** [ ,tɛknɪ'kælɪti] *s* (**-ties**) tecnicismo; dettaglio tecnico

**technician** [tɛk'nɪʃən] *s* tecnico

**technics** ['tɛknɪks] *ssg* or *spl* tecnica

**technique** [tɛk'nik] *s* tecnica

**ted'dy bear'** ['tɛdi] *s* orsacchiotto

**tedious** ['tidɪ·əs] or ['tidʒəs] *adj* tedioso, noioso

**tee** [ti] *adj* fatto a T ‖ *s* giunto a tre vie; (*golf*) piazzola di partenza ‖ *tr—* **to tee off** (slang) cominciare ‖ *intr—* **to be teed off** (slang) essere arrabbiato; **to tee off** (golf) colpire la palla dalla piazzola di partenza; **to tee off on** (slang) rimproverare severamente

**teem** [tim] *intr* brulicare; piovere a dirotto; **to teem with** abbondare di

**teeming** ['timɪŋ] *adj* brulicante; (*rain*) torrenziale

**teen-ager** ['tin ,edʒər] *s* giovane *mf* dai 13 ai 19 anni

**teens** [tinz] *spl* numeri inglesi che finiscono in **-teen** (dal 13 al 19); **to be in one's teens** avere dai 13 ai 19 anni

**tee·ny** ['tini] *adj* (**-nier; -niest**) (coll) piccolo, piccolissimo

**teeter** ['titər] *s* altalena, dondolio ‖ *intr* dondolarsi, oscillare

**teethe** [tið] *intr* mettere i denti

**teething** ['tiðɪŋ] *s* dentizione

**teeth'ing ring'** *s* dentaruolo

**teetotaler** [ti'totələr] *s* astemio

**tele·cast** ['tɛlɪ ,kæst] or ['tɛlɪ ,kɑst] *s* teletrasmissione ‖ *v* (*pret & pp* **-cast** or **-casted**) *tr & intr* teletrasmettere

**telegram** ['tɛlɪ ,græm] *s* telegramma *m*

**telegraph** ['tɛlɪ ,græf] or ['tɛlɪ ,grɑf] *s* telegrafo ‖ *tr & intr* telegrafare

**tel'egraph pole'** *s* palo del telegrafo

**Telemachus** [tɪ'lɛməkəs] *s* Telemaco

**telemeter** [tɪ'lɛmɪtər] *s* telemetro ‖ *tr* misurare col telemetro

**telepathy** [tɪ'lɛpəθi] *s* telepatia

**telephone** ['tɛlɪ ,fon] *s* telefono ‖ *tr & intr* telefonare

**tel'ephone book'** *s* elenco or guida dei telefoni

**tel'ephone booth'** *s* cabina telefonica

**tel'ephone call'** *s* chiamata telefonica, colpo di telefono

**tel'ephone direc'tory** *s* elenco or guida dei telefoni

**tel'ephone exchange'** *s* centrale telefonica

**tel'ephone op'erator** *s* centralinista *mf*, telefonista *mf*

**tel'ephone receiv'er** *s* ricevitore *m*

**tel'ephoto lens'** ['tɛlɪ ,foto] *s* teleobbiettivo

**teleplay** ['tɛlɪ ,ple] *s* teledramma *m*

**teleprinter** ['tɛlɪ ,prɪntər] *s* telescrivente *f*

**telescope** ['tɛlɪ ,skop] *s* telescopio ‖ *tr*

snodare; condensare ‖ *intr* essere snodabile; (*in a collision*) incastrarsi

**teletype** ['tɛlɪ ,taɪp] *s* telescrivente *f* ‖ *tr & intr* trasmettere per telescrivente

**teleview** ['tɛlɪ ,vju] *tr* telericevere

**televiewer** ['tɛlɪ ,vju·ər] *s* telespettatore *m*

**televise** ['tɛlɪ ,vaɪz] *tr* teletrasmettere

**television** ['tɛlɪ ,vɪʒən] *adj* televisivo ‖ *s* televisione

**tel'evision screen'** *s* teleschermo

**tel'evision set'** *s* televisore *m*

**tell** [tɛl] *v* (*pret & pp* **told** [told]) *tr* dire; (*to narrate*) raccontare; (*to count*) contare; distinguere; **I told you so!** te l'avevo detto!; **to tell off** (coll) dire il fatto suo a ‖ *intr* dire; prevedere; avere effetto; **to tell on** (*s.o.'s health*) pesare a, e.g., **age was telling on his health** l'età pesava alla sua salute; (coll) denunciare

**teller** ['tɛlər] *s* narratore *m*; (*of bank*) cassiere *m*; (*of votes*) scrutatore *m*

**temper** ['tɛmpər] *s* indole *f*, temperamento; umore *m*; calma; (metallurgy) tempra; **to keep one's temper** mantenersi calmo; **to lose one's temper** perdere la pazienza ‖ *tr* temprare ‖ *intr* temprarsi

**temperament** ['tɛmpərəmənt] *s* indole *f*, temperamento, carattere *m*

**temperamental** [ ,tɛmpərə'mɛntəl] *adj* emotivo, capriccioso

**temperance** ['tɛmpərəns] *s* (*self-restraint in action*) temperanza; (*abstinence from alcoholic beverages*) sobrietà *f*

**temperate** ['tɛmpərɪt] *adj* temperato

**temperature** ['tɛmpərətʃər] *s* temperatura

**tempest** ['tɛmpɪst] *s* tempesta; **tempest in a teapot** tempesta in un bicchier d'acqua

**tempestuous** [tɛm'pɛstʃʊ·əs] *adj* tempestoso

**temple** ['tɛmpəl] *s* (*place of worship*) tempio; (*of spectacles*) susta, stanghetta; (anat) tempia

**tem·po** ['tɛmpo] *s* (**-pos** or **-pi** [pi]) (mus) tempo; (fig) ritmo

**temporal** ['tɛmpərəl] *adj* temporale

**temporary** ['tɛmpə ,rɛri] *adj* temporaneo, provvisorio, transitorio, interino

**temporize** ['tɛmpə ,raɪz] *intr* temporeggiare

**tempt** [tɛmpt] *tr* tentare

**temptation** [tɛmp'teʃən] *s* tentazione

**tempter** ['tɛmptər] *s* tentatore *m*

**tempting** ['tɛmptɪŋ] *adj* tentatore

**ten** [tɛn] *adj & pron* dieci ‖ *s* dieci *m*; **ten o'clock** le dieci

**tenable** ['tɛnəbəl] *adj* difendibile

**tenacious** [tɪ'neʃəs] *adj* tenace

**tenant** ['tɛnənt] *s* inquilino, pigionante *mf*; (*of land*) fittavolo

**tend** [tɛnd] *tr* riguardare, governare; accudire (with *dat*), e.g., **he tends the fire** accudisce al fuoco ‖ *intr* tendere; **to tend to** propendere verso; (*e.g., one's own business*) attendere a; **to tend to + *inf*** tendere a + *inf*

**tenden·cy** ['tɛndənsi] *s* (**-cies**) tendenza, propensione

**tender** ['tɛndər] *adj* tenero; sensibile, dolorante ‖ *s* offerta; (naut) nave *f* rifornimento; (naut) lancia; (rr) carboniera ‖ *tr* offrire

**tender-hearted** ['tɛndər ,hɑrtɪd] *adj* dal cuore tenero

**ten'der·loin'** *s* filetto ‖ **Tenderloin** *s* rione *m* della mala vita

**tenderness** ['tɛndərnɪs] *s* tenerezza

**tendon** ['tɛndən] *s* tendine *m*

**tendril** ['tɛndrɪl] *s* viticcio

**tenement** ['tɛnɪmənt] *s* appartamento; casa; casamento

**ten'ement house'** *s* casamento

**tenet** ['tɛnɪt] *s* dogma *m*, dottrina

**tennis** ['tɛnɪs] *s* tennis *m*

**ten'nis court'** *s* campo da tennis

**ten'nis play'er** *s* tennista *mf*

**tenor** ['tɛnər] *s* tenore *m*

**tense** [tɛns] *adj* teso ‖ *s* (gram) tempo

**tension** ['tɛn/ən] *s* tensione *f*

**tent** [tɛnt] *s* tenda; (*of circus*) tendone *m*

**tentacle** ['tɛntəkəl] *s* tentacolo

**tentative** ['tɛntətɪv] *adj* a titolo di prova; (*smile*) esile

**tenth** [tɛnθ] *adj, s & pron* decimo ‖ *s* (*in dates*) dieci *m*

**tenuous** ['tɛnjʊ·əs] *adj* tenue

**tenure** ['tɛnjər] *s* (*in office*) rafferma; (*permanency of employment*) inamovibilità *f*; (law) possesso

**tepid** ['tɛpɪd] *adj* tiepido

**tercet** ['tʌrsɪt] *s* terzina

**term** [tʌrm] *s* vocabolo, voce *f*; periodo, durata; termine *m*; (com) scadenza; **terms** condizioni *fpl*; **to be on good terms** essere in buone relazioni; **to come to terms** venire a patti ‖ *tr* chiamare, definire

**termagant** ['tʌrməgənt] *s* megera

**terminal** ['tʌrmɪnəl] *adj* terminale ‖ *s* (*end or extremity*) terminale *m*; (elec) morsetto; (rr) capolinea *m*

**terminate** ['tʌrmɪ ,net] *tr & intr* terminare

**terminus** ['tʌrmɪnəs] *s* termine *m*, fine *m*; (rr) capolinea *m*

**termite** ['tʌrmaɪt] *s* termite *f*

**terrace** ['tɛrəs] *s* terrazza, terrazzo; (agr) gradino, scaglione *m*

**terra firma** ['tɛrə 'fʌrmə] *s* terra ferma

**terrain** [tɛ'ren] *s* terreno

**terrestrial** [tə'rɛstrɪ·əl] *adj* terrestre

**terrific** [tə'rɪfɪk] *adj* terrificante; (coll) tremendo

**terri·fy** ['tɛrɪ ,faɪ] *v* (*pret & pp* -**fied**) *tr* terrificare, inorridire

**territo·ry** ['tɛrɪ ,tori] *s* (-ries) territorio

**terror** ['tɛrər] *s* terrore *m*

**terrorize** ['tɛrə ,raɪz] *tr* terrorizzare; dominare col terrore

**ter'ry cloth'** ['tɛri] *s* tessuto a spugna

**terse** [tʌrs] *adj* conciso, terso

**tertiary** ['tʌr/ɪ ,ɛri] or ['tʌr/əri] *adj* terziario

**test** [tɛst] *s* prova, saggio; esame *m* ‖ *tr* provare, saggiare; esaminare; (*e.g., a machine*) collaudare

**testament** ['tɛstəmənt] *s* testamento ‖ **Testament** *s* Testamento Nuovo

**test' ban'** *s* interdizione degli esperimenti nucleari

**test' flight'** *s* volo di prova

**testicle** ['tɛstɪkəl] *s* testicolo

**testi·fy** ['tɛstɪ ,faɪ] *v* (*pret & pp* -**fied**) *tr & intr* testimoniare

**testimonial** [ ,tɛstɪ'monɪ·əl] *s* (*certificate*) benservito, referenza; (*expression of esteem*) segno di gratitudine

**testimo·ny** ['tɛstɪ ,moni] *s* (-**nies**) testimonianza

**test' pat'tern** *s* (telv) monoscopio

**test' pi'lot** *s* pilota *m* collaudatore

**test' tube'** *s* provetta

**tetanus** ['tɛtənəs] *s* tetano

**tether** ['tɛðər] *s* cavezza, pastoia; **at the end of one's tether** al limite delle proprie risorse ‖ *tr* legare; incavezzare, impastoiare

**tetter** ['tɛtər] *s* eczema *m*, impetigine *f*

**text** [tɛkst] *s* testo; tema *m*

**text'book'** *s* libro di testo

**textile** ['tɛkstɪl] or ['tɛkstaɪl] *adj & s* tessile *m*

**textual** ['tɛkst/ʊ·əl] *adj* testuale

**texture** ['tɛkst/ər] *s* (*of cloth*) trama; caratteristica, proprietà *f*

**Thai** ['tɑ·i] or ['taɪ] *adj & s* tailandese *mf*

**Thailand** ['taɪlənd] *s* la Tailandia

**Thames** [tɛmz] *s* Tamigi *m*

**than** [ðæn] *conj* di, e.g., **he is faster than you** è più veloce di te; (*before a verb*) di quanto, e.g., **he is smarter than I thought** è più intelligente di quanto pensavo; che, e.g., **he had barely begun to eat than it was time to leave** non aveva appena cominciato a mangiare che era ora di andarsene

**thank** [θæŋk] *s*—**thanks** ringraziamenti *mpl*; **thanks to** grazie a, in grazia di ‖ *tr* ringraziare ‖ **thanks** *interj* grazie!

**thankful** ['θæŋkfəl] *adj* grato

**thankless** ['θæŋklɪs] *adj* ingrato

**Thanksgiv'ing Day'** [ ,θæŋks'gɪvɪŋ] *s* giorno del Ringraziamento

**that** [ðæt] *adj dem* (**those**) quel; codesto; **that one** quello, quello là ‖ *pron dem* (**those**) quello; codesto ‖ *pron rel* che, quello che, il quale; **that is** cioè; **that's that** (coll) ecco fatto, ecco tutto ‖ *adv* (coll) tanto, così; **that far** così lontano; **that many** tanti; **that much** tanto ‖ *conj* che

**thatch** [θæt/] *s* paglia, copertura di paglia; (*hair*) capigliatura ‖ *tr* coprire di paglia

**thaw** [θɔ] *s* sgelo ‖ *tr* sgelare ‖ *intr* sgelarsi

**the** [ðə], [ðɪ], or [ði] *art def* il; al, e.g., **one dollar the dozen** un dollaro alla dozzina ‖ *adv*—**so much the worse for him** tanto peggio per lui; **the more . . . the more** quanto più . . . tanto più

**theater** ['θi·ətər] *s* teatro

**the'ater-go'er** *s* frequentatore *m* abituale del teatro

**the'ater news'** *s* cronaca teatrale

**theatrical** [θɪ'ætrɪkəl] *adj* teatrale

**Thebes** [θibz] *s* Tebe *f*

**thee** [ði] *pron pers* (Bib; poet) ti; te

**theft** [θɛft] *s* furto, ruberia

**their** [ðɛr] *adj poss* il loro, loro

**theirs** [ðɛrz] *pron poss* il loro

**them** [ðɛm] *pron pers* li; loro; **to them** loro

**theme** [θim] *s* tema *m*, soggetto; saggio; (mus) tema *m*

**theme' song'** *s* (mus) tema *m* centrale; (rad) sigla musicale

**them·selves'** *pron pers* essi stessi, loro stessi; si, e.g., **they enjoyed themselves** si divertirono

**then** [ðɛn] *adj* allora, di allora ‖ *s* quel tempo; **by then** a quell'epoca; **from then on** da quel giorno in poi ‖ *adv* allora; indi; poi; **then and there** a quel momento

**thence** [ðɛns] *adv* indi, quindi; da lì; da allora in poi

**thence'forth'** *adv* da allora in poi

**theolo·gy** [θiˈɑlədʒi] *s* (-**gies**) telogia

**theorem** [ˈθiˑərəm] *s* teorema *m*

**theoretical** [ˌθiˑəˈrɛtɪkəl] *adj* teoretico ‖ **theoretics** *ssg* teoretica

**theo·ry** [ˈθiˑəri] *s* (-**ries**) teoria

**therapeutic** [ˌθɛrəˈpjutɪk] *adj* terapeutico ‖ **therapeutics** *ssg* terapeutica

**thera·py** [ˈθɛrəpi] *s* (-**pies**) terapia

**there** [ðɛr] *adv* lì, là; **there are** ci sono; **there is** c'è; ecco, e.g., **there it is** eccolo

**there'abouts'** *adv* circa, approssimativamente, giù di lì

**there'af'ter** *adv* in seguito, dipoi

**there'by'** *adv* quindi, perciò, così

**therefore** [ˈðɛrfor] *adv* per questo, quindi, dunque

**there'in'** *adv* lì; in quel rispetto

**there'of'** *adv* di ciò, da ciò

**Theresa** [təˈrisə] *or* [təˈrɛsə] *s* Teresa

**there'upon'** *adv* su questo; a quel momento; come conseguenza

**thermal** [ˈθʌrməl] *adj* (water) termale; (capacity) termico

**thermistor** [θərˈmɪstər] *s* (elec) termistore *m*

**thermocouple** [ˈθʌrmo ˌkʌpəl] *s* termocoppia

**thermodynamic** [ˌθʌrmodaɪˈnæmɪk] *adj* termodinamico ‖ **thermodynamics** *ssg* termodinamica

**thermometer** [θərˈmɑmɪtər] *s* termometro

**thermonuclear** [ˌθʌrmoˈnjuklɪˑər] *or* [ˌθʌrmoˈnuklɪˑər] *adj* termonucleare

**ther'mos bot'tle** [ˈθʌrməs] *s* termos *m*

**thermostat** [ˈθʌrməˌstæt] *s* termostato

**thesau·rus** [θɪˈsɔrəs] *s* (-**ri** [raɪ] *or* -**ruses**) tesoro, lessico, compendio

**these** [ðiz] *pl* of **this**

**the·sis** [ˈθisɪs] *s* (-**ses** [siz]) tesi *f*

**Thespis** [ˈθɛspɪs] *s* Tespi *m*

**they** [ðe] *pron pers* essi, loro

**thick** [θɪk] *adj* spesso, grosso; folto, denso; pieno, coperto; viscoso; stupido; (coll) intimo ‖ *s* spessore *m*; **in the thick of** nel folto di; **through thick and thin** nei tempi buoni e cattivi

**thicken** [ˈθɪkən] *tr* ispessire; ingrossare; infoltire ‖ *intr* ispessirsi; ingrossarsi; (said of a plot) complicarsi

**thicket** [ˈθɪkɪt] *s* boscaglia, macchia

**thick-headed** [ˈθɪk ˌhɛdɪd] *adj* indietro, stupido

**thick'set'** *adj* tarchiato; (hedge) fitto, denso

**thief** [θif] *s* (**thieves** [θivz]) ladro

**thieve** [θiv] *intr* rubare

**thiever·y** [ˈθivəri] *s* (-**ies**) furto

**thigh** [θaɪ] *s* coscia

**thigh'bone'** *s* femore *m*

**thimble** [ˈθɪmbəl] *s* ditale *m*

**thin** [θɪn] *adj* (**thinner; thinnest**) (paper, ice) sottile; (lean) magro, smilzo; (e.g., hair) rado; (air) fine; (excuse) tenue; (voice) esile; (wine) leggero, annacquato ‖ *v* (pret & pp **thinned**; ger **thinning**) *tr* assottigliare; (paint) diluire ‖ *intr* assottigliarsi; **to thin out** (said of a crowd; one's hair) diradarsi

**thine** [ðaɪn] *adj* & *pron poss* (Bib & poet) tuo, il tuo

**thing** [θɪŋ] *s* cosa; **not to get a thing out of** non riuscire a capire; non cavare un briciolo d'informazione da; **of all things!** che cosa!; che sorpresa!; **the thing** l'ultima moda; **things** roba; **to see things** avere allucinazioni

**think** [θɪŋk] *v* (pret & pp **thought** [θɔt]) *tr* pensare; credere; **to think it over** ripensarci; **to think nothing of** non darci la minima importanza; **to think of** (to have as an opinion of) pensare di, e.g., **what do you think of that doctor?** cosa ne pensa di quel medico?; **to think out** decifrare; **to think up** immaginare ‖ *intr* pensare; **to think not** credere di no; **to think of** (to turn one's thoughts to) pensare a, e.g., **he is thinking of the future** pensa al futuro; (to imagine) immaginare; **to think so** credere di sì; **to think well of** avere una buona opinione di

**thinkable** [ˈθɪŋkəbəl] *adj* pensabile

**thinker** [ˈθɪŋkər] *s* pensatore *m*

**third** [θʌrd] *adj*, *s* & *pron* terzo ‖ *s* terzo; (in dates) tre *m*; (aut) terza

**third' degree'** *s* interrogatorio di terzo grado

**third' rail'** *s* (rr) rotaia elettrificata di contatto

**third'-rate'** *adj* di terz'ordine

**Third' World'** *s* Terzo Mondo

**thirst** [θʌrst] *s* sete *f* ‖ *intr* aver sete; **to thirst for** aver sete di

**thirst·y** [ˈθʌrsti] *adj* (-**ier; -iest**) assetato, sitibondo; **to be thirsty** avere sete

**thirteen** [ˈθʌrˈtin] *adj*, *s* & *pron* tredici *m*

**thirteenth** [ˈθʌrˈtinθ] *adj*, *s* & *pron* tredicesimo ‖ *s* (in dates) tredici *m*

**thirtieth** [ˈθʌrtɪˑθ] *adj*, *s* & *pron* trentesimo ‖ *s* (in dates) trenta *m*

**thir·ty** [ˈθʌrti] *adj* & *pron* trenta ‖ *s* (-**ties**) trenta *m*; **the thirties** gli anni trenta

**this** [ðɪs] *adj dem* (**these**) questo; **this one** questo, questo qui ‖ *pron dem* (**these**) questo, questo qui ‖ *adv* (coll) tanto, così

**thistle** [ˈθɪsəl] *s* cardo

**thither** [ˈθɪðər] *or* [ˈðɪðər] *adv* là, da quella parte

**Thomas** ['tɑməs] s Tommaso
**thong** [θɔŋ] or [θɑŋ] s coreggia
**thorax** ['θoræks] s (**-raxes** or **-races** [rə ͵siz]) torace m
**thorn** [θɔrn] s spina
**thorn·y** ['θɔrni] adj (**-ier; -iest**) spinoso
**thorough** ['θʌro] adj completo, esauriente
**thor'ough·bred'** adj di razza; (horse) purosangue ‖ s individuo di razza; (horse) purosangue mf
**thor'ough·fare'** s passaggio; **no thoroughfare** divieto di passaggio
**thor'ough·go'ing** adj completo, esauriente
**thoroughly** ['θʌroli] adv a fondo
**those** [ðoz] pl of **that**
**thou** [ðaʊ] pron pers (Bib; poet) tu ‖ tr dare del tu a
**though** [ðo] adv tuttavia ‖ conj malgrado, sebbene; **as though** come se
**thought** [θɔt] s pensiero; **perish the thought!** (coll) nemmeno a pensarci!
**thoughtful** ['θɔtfəl] adj pensieroso, riflessivo; (considerate) sollecito
**thoughtless** ['θɔtlɪs] adj irriflessivo; sconsiderato; (reckless) incurante
**thought' transfer'ence** s trasmissione del pensiero
**thousand** ['θaʊzənd] adj, s & pron mille m; **a thousand** or **one thousand** mille m
**thousandth** ['θaʊzəndθ] adj, s & pron millesimo
**thralldom** ['θrɔldəm] s schiavitù f
**thrash** [θræʃ] tr battere; (agr) trebbiare; **to thrash out** discutere a fondo ‖ intr agitarsi, dibattersi
**thread** [θrɛd] s filo; (mach) filetto, verme m; **to lose the thread of** perdere il filo di ‖ tr infilare; (fig) pervadere; (mach) filettare, impanare; **to thread one's way through** aprirsi il passaggio attraverso
**thread'bare'** adj frusto, logoro
**threat** [θrɛt] s minaccia
**threaten** ['θrɛtən] tr & intr minacciare
**threatening** ['θrɛtənɪŋ] adj minaccioso; (e.g., letter) minatorio
**three** [θri] adj & pron tre ‖ s tre m; **three o'clock** le tre
**three'-cor'nered** adj triangolare; (hat) a tre punte
**three' hun'dred** adj, s & pron trecento
**threepenny** ['θrɛpəni] or ['θrɪpəni] adj del valore di tre penny; di nessun valore
**three'-phase'** adj trifase
**three'-ply'** adj a tre spessori
**three' R's'** [ɑrz] spl lettura, scrittura e aritmetica
**three'score'** adj sessanta
**three' thou'sand** adj, s & pron tre mila mpl
**threno·dy** ['θrɛnədi] s (**-dies**) trenodia
**thresh** [θrɛʃ] tr (agr) trebbiare; **to thresh out** discutere a fondo ‖ intr trebbiare; battere
**thresh'ing machine'** s trebbiatrice f
**threshold** ['θrɛʃold] s soglia
**thrice** [θraɪs] adv tre volte; molto
**thrift** [θrɪft] s economia
**thrift·y** ['θrɪfti] adj (**-ier; -iest**) eco-

nomo, economico; vigoroso; prospero
**thrill** [θrɪl] s fremito d'emozione; esperienza emozionante ‖ tr emozionare ‖ intr emozionarsi; vibrare
**thriller** ['θrɪlər] s (coll) thrilling m
**thrilling** ['θrɪlɪŋ] adj emozionante, thrilling
**thrive** [θraɪv] v (pret **thrived** or **throve** [θrov]; pp **thrived** or **thriven** ['θrɪvən]) intr prosperare, fiorire
**throat** [θrot] s gola; **to clear one's throat** schiarirsi la voce
**throb** [θrɑb] s battito, palpito, tuffo ‖ v (pret & pp **throbbed**; ger **throbbing**) intr palpitare, pulsare
**throe** [θro] s agonia, travaglio, spasimo; **in the throes of** nel travaglio di; (e.g., battle) nel momento più penoso di
**throne** [θron] s trono
**throng** [θrɔŋ] or [θrɑŋ] s folla, stuolo ‖ intr affollarsi
**throttle** ['θrɑtəl] s (of locomotive) leva di comando; (of motorcycle) manetta; (of car) acceleratore m; (mach) valvola di controllo ‖ tr soffocare; (mach) regolare
**through** [θru] adj diretto, senza fermate; **to be through** aver finito; **to be through with** farla finita con ‖ adv attraverso; da una parte all'altra; completamente; ‖ prep attraverso, per; durante; fino alla fine di; per mezzo di
**through·out'** adv completamente, da un capo all'altro; dappertutto ‖ prep durante tutto, e.g., **throughout the afternoon** durante tutto il pomeriggio; per tutto, e.g., **throughout the house** per tutta la casa
**throw** [θro] s getto, tiro, lancio; gettata; coperta leggera ‖ v (pret **threw** [θru]; pp **thrown**) tr gettare, tirare, lanciare; (a shadow) proiettare; (the current) connettere; (said of a horse) disarcionare; (wrestling) gettare a terra; (a game) perdere intenzionalmente; (coll) stupire; **to throw away** gettar via; perdere; **to throw back** rigettare; ritardare; **to throw in** (the clutch) innestare; (coll) aggiungere; **to throw oneself into** darsi a; **to throw out** sbatter fuori; (the clutch) disinnestare; **to throw over** abbandonare ‖ intr gettare, tirare, lanciare; **to throw up** vomitare
**thrum** [θrʌm] v (pret & pp **thrummed**; ger **thrumming**) intr tambureggiare; (mus) far scorrere la mano sulle corde di uno strumento
**thrush** [θrʌʃ] s tordo
**thrust** [θrʌst] s (push) spinta; botta; (with dagger) pugnalata; (with sword) stoccata ‖ v (pret & pp **thrust**) tr spingere; conficcare, configgere; **to thrust oneself** (e.g., into a conversation) ficcarsi
**thru'way'** s autostrada
**thud** [θʌd] s tonfo ‖ v (pret & pp **thudded**; ger **thudding**) intr fare un rumore sordo
**thug** [θʌg] s fascinoroso

**thumb** [θʌm] *s* pollice *m;* **all thumbs** maldestro, goffo; **thumbs down** pollice verso; **to twiddle one's thumbs** girare i pollici, essere ozioso; **under the thumb of** sotto l'influenza di ‖ *tr* sporcare con le dita; (*a book*) sfogliare; **to thumb a ride** chiedere l'autostop; **to thumb one's nose (at)** fare marameo (a)

**thumb′ in′dex** *s* margine *m* a scaletta

**thumb′nail′** *adj* breve, conciso ‖ *s* unghia del pollice

**thumb′screw′** *s* vite *f* ad aletta

**thumb′tack′** *s* puntina

**thump** [θʌmp] *s* tonfo ‖ *tr* battere, percuotere ‖ *intr* battere; cadere con un tonfo; camminare a passi pesanti (*said of the heart*) palpitare violentemente

**thumping** ['θʌmpɪŋ] *adj* (coll) straordinario, eccezionale; (coll) grande

**thunder** ['θʌndər] *s* tuono; (*of applause*) scroscio; (*of a cannon*) rombo ‖ *tr* lanciare ‖ *intr* tonare, rombare; (fig) scrosciare

**thun′der•bolt′** *s* folgore *f*, fulmine *m*

**thun′der•clap′** *s* scroscio di tuono

**thunderous** ['θʌndərəs] *adj* fragoroso

**thun′der•show′er** *s* acquazzone *m* accompagnato da tuoni

**thun′der•storm′** *s* temporale *m*

**thun′der•struck′** *adj* attonito

**Thursday** ['θʌrsdɪ] *s* giovedì *m*

**thus** [ðʌs] *adv* così; **thus far** sino qui

**thwack** [θwæk] *s* colpo ‖ *tr* colpire

**thwart** [θwɔrt] *adj* obliquo ‖ *adv* di traverso ‖ *tr* contrariare, sventare

**thy** [ðaɪ] *adj poss* (Bib; poet) tuo, il tuo

**thyme** [taɪm] *s* timo

**thy′roid gland′** ['θaɪrɔɪd] *s* tiroide *f*

**thyself** [ðaɪ'sɛlf] *pron* (Bib; poet) te stesso; te, ti

**tiara** [taɪ'ɑrə] *or* [taɪ'ɛrə] *s* (*female adornment*) diadema *m;* (eccl) tiara

**tick** [tɪk] *s* (*of pillow*) fodera; (*of mattress*) guscio; (*of clock*) ticchettio; (*dot*) punto; (ent) zecca; **on tick** (coll) a credito ‖ *intr* fare ticchettio; **to make s.o. tick** mandare avanti qlcu

**ticker** ['tɪkər] *s* telescrivente *f;* (slang) orologio; (slang) cuore *m*

**tick′er tape′** *s* nastro della telescrivente

**ticket** ['tɪkɪt] *s* biglietto; (*e.g., of pawnbroker*) polizza; (*slip of paper or identifying tag*) bolletta, bollettino; (*summons*) verbale *m;* (*e.g., to indicate price*) etichetta; lista dei candidati; **that's the ticket** (coll) questo è quello che fa

**tick′et a′gent** *s* bigliettaio

**tick′et of′fice** *s* biglietteria

**tick′et scalp′er** ['skælpər] *s* bagarino

**tick′et win′dow** *s* sportello

**ticking** ['tɪkɪŋ] *s* traliccio

**tickle** ['tɪkəl] *s* solletico ‖ *tr* solleticare; divertire ‖ *intr* avere il solletico

**ticklish** ['tɪklɪʃ] *adj* sensibile al solletico; delicato; permaloso; **to be ticklish** soffrire il solletico

**tick-tock** ['tɪk ˌtɑk] *s* tic tac *m*

**tid′al wave′** ['taɪdəl] *s* onda di marea; (fig) ondata

**tidbit** ['tɪd ˌbɪt] *s* bocconcino

**tiddlywinks** ['tɪdli ˌwɪŋks] *s* gioco della pulce

**tide** [taɪd] *s* marea; **to go against the tide** andare contro la corrente; **to stem the tide** fermare la corrente ‖ *tr* portare sulla cresta delle onde; **to tide over** aiutare; (*a difficulty*) sormontare

**tide′wa′ter** *s* marea; costa marina

**tidings** ['taɪdɪŋz] *spl* notizie *fpl*

**ti•dy** ['taɪdi] *adj* (**-dier; -diest**) pulito, ordinato ‖ *s* (**-dies**) cofanetto, astuccio; appoggiacapo ‖ *v* (*pret & pp* **-died**) *tr* rassettare, mettere in ordine ‖ *intr* rassettarsi

**tie** [taɪ] *s* laccio, nodo, vincolo; (*in games*) patta; (*necktie*) cravatta; (archit) traversa; (rr) traversina; (mus) legatura ‖ *v* (*pret & pp* **tied;** *ger* **tying**) *tr* allacciare, annodare; legare; confinare; (*a game*) impattare; (*a person*) impattarla con; **to be tied up** essere occupato; **to tie down** confinare, limitare; **to tie up** legare; impedire; (*e.g., traffic*) intasare ‖ *intr* allacciare; (*in games*) impattare

**tie′ beam′** *s* catena

**tie′pin′** *s* spilla da cravatta

**tier** [tɪr] *s* gradinata; ordine *m*, livello

**tiff** [tɪf] *s* screzio, litigio

**tiger** ['taɪgər] *s* tigre *f*

**ti′ger lil′y** *s* giglio cinese

**tight** [taɪt] *adj* teso; stretto; compatto; impermeabile, ermetico; pieno; (*game*) (coll) serrato; (coll) tirato; (slang) ubriaco ‖ **tights** *spl* calzamaglia ‖ *adv* strettamente; **to hold tight** tenere stretto

**tighten** ['taɪtən] *tr* (*e.g., one's belt*) tirare; (*e.g., a screw*) stringere ‖ *intr* tirarsi; stringersi

**tight-fisted** ['taɪt'fɪstɪd] *adj* taccagno

**tight′-fit′ting** *adj* attillato

**tight′rope′** *s* corda tesa

**tight′ squeeze′** *s*—**to be in a tight squeeze** (coll) essere alle strette

**tight′wad′** *s* (coll) spilorcio

**tigress** ['taɪgrɪs] *s* tigre femmina

**tile** [taɪl] *s* mattonella; (*for floor*) piastrella; (*for roof*) tegola, coppo ‖ *tr* coprire di mattonelle; coprire di piastrelle; coprire di coppi

**tile′ roof′** *s* tetto di tegole

**till** [tɪl] *s* cassetto dei soldi ‖ *prep* fino a ‖ *conj* fino a che . . . non, fino a che, sinché . . . non, sinché ‖ *tr* lavorare, coltivare

**tilt** [tɪlt] *s* inclinazione; giostra, torneo; **full tilt** di gran carriera; a tutta forza ‖ *tr* inclinare; (*a lance*) mettere in resta; attaccare ‖ *intr* inclinarsi; giostrare; **to tilt at** combattere con

**timber** ['tɪmbər] *s* legno, legname *m* da costruzione; alberi *mpl;* (fig) tempra

**tim′ber•land′** *s* bosco destinato a produrre legname

**tim′ber line′** *s* linea della vegetazione

**timbre** ['tɪmbər] *s* (phonet & phys) timbro

**time** [taɪm] *s* tempo; ora, e.g., **what time is it?** che ora è?; volta, e.g., **three times** tre volte; giorni *mpl*, e.g., **in our time** ai giorni nostri; momento; ultima ora; ore *fpl* lavorative; periodo, e.g., **Xmas time** periodo natalizio; **for a long time** da lungo; **for the time being** per ora, per il momento; **in time** presto; col tempo; **on time** a tempo; a rate; (*said*, e.g., *of a bus*) in orario; **times** volte, e.g., **seven times seven** sette volte sette; **to bide one's time** aspettare l'ora propizia; **to do time** (coll) essere in prigione; **to have a good time** divertirsi; **to have no time for** non poter sopportare; **to lose time** (*said of a watch*) ritardare; **to make time** avanzare rapidamente; guadagnare terreno; **to pass the time of day** fare una chiacchierata; salutarsi; **to take one's time** fare le cose senza fretta; **to tell time** leggere l'orologio ‖ *tr* fissare il momento di; calcolare il tempo di; (sports) cronometrare

**time' bomb'** *s* bomba a orologeria
**time'card'** *s* cartellino di presenza
**time' clock'** *s* orologio di controllo (delle presenze)
**time' expo'sure** *s* (phot) posa
**time' fuse'** *s* spoletta a tempo
**time'keep'er** *s* marcatempo; orologio; (sports) cronometrista *mf*
**timeless** ['taɪmlɪs] *adj* senza fine, eterno
**time·ly** ['taɪmli] *adj* (**-lier; -liest**) opportuno, tempestivo
**time'piece'** *s* orologio; cronometro
**time' sig'nal** *s* segnale orario
**time'ta'ble** *s* orario; tabella di marcia
**time'work'** *s* lavoro a ore
**time'worn'** *adj* logorato dal tempo
**time' zone'** *s* fuso orario
**timid** ['tɪmɪd] *adj* timido, pavido
**tim'ing gears'** ['taɪmɪŋ] *spl* ingranaggi *mpl* di distribuzione
**timorous** ['tɪmərəs] *adj* timoroso
**tin** [tɪn] *s* (*element*) stagno; (*tin plate; can*) latta ‖ *v* (*pret & pp* **tinned;** *ger* **tinning**) *tr* stagnare
**tin' can'** *s* latta
**tincture** ['tɪŋktʃər] *s* tintura
**tin' cup'** *s* tazzina metallica
**tinder** ['tɪndər] *s* esca
**tin'der·box'** *s* cassetta con l'esca e l'acciarino; persona eccitabile; (fig) polveriera
**tin' foil'** *s* stagnola
**ting-a-ling** ['tɪŋə‚lɪŋ] *s* dindìn *m*
**tinge** [tɪndʒ] *s* sfumatura; pizzico, punta ‖ *v* (*ger* **tingeing** or **tinging**) *tr* sfumare; dare una traccia di sapore a
**tingle** ['tɪŋɡəl] *s* formicolio, pizzicore *m* ‖ *intr* informicolirsi, pizzicare; (*said of the ears*) ronzare; (*with enthusiasm*) fremere
**tin' hat'** *s* (slang) elmetto
**tinker** ['tɪŋkər] *s* calderaio, ramaio ‖ *intr* armeggiare
**tinkle** ['tɪŋkəl] *s* tintinnio ‖ *tr* far tintinnare ‖ *intr* tintinnare

**tin' plate'** *s* latta
**tin' roof'** *s* tetto di lamiera di latta
**tinsel** ['tɪnsəl] *s* orpello, lustrino
**tin'smith'** *s* lattoniere *m*, stagnino
**tin' sol'dier** *s* soldatino di piombo
**tint** [tɪnt] *s* tinta, sfumatura ‖ *tr* tinteggiare
**tin'ware'** *s* articoli *mpl* di latta
**ti·ny** ['taɪni] *adj* (**-nier; -niest**) piccino
**tip** [tɪp] *s* punta; (*of mountain*) vetta; (*of umbrella*) gorbia; (*of shoe*) mascherina; (*of cigarette*) bocchino; (*of shoestring*) aghetto; colpetto; (*fee*) mancia; informazione confidenziale; inclinazione ‖ *v* (*pret & pp* **tipped;** *ger* **tipping**) *tr* mettere la punta a; inclinare, rovesciare; (*one's hat*) levarsi; dare la mancia a; toccare, battere; (*the scales*) far traboccare; **to tip in** (bb) inserire fuori testo; **to tip off** (coll) dare informazioni confidenziali a ‖ *intr* inclinarsi; dare la mancia
**tip'cart'** *s* carro ribaltabile
**tip'-off'** *s* (coll) avvertimento confidenziale
**tipped'-in'** *adj* (bb) fuori testo
**tipple** ['tɪpəl] *intr* sbevucchiare
**tip'staff'** *s* usciere *m*
**tip·sy** ['tɪpsi] *adj* (**-sier; -siest**) brillo
**tip'toe'** *s* punta di piedi ‖ *v* (*pret & pp* **-toed;** *ger* **-toeing**) *intr* camminare in punta di piedi
**tirade** ['taɪred] *s* tirata
**tire** [taɪr] *s* gomma, pneumatico; (*of metal*) cerchione *m* ‖ *tr* stancare ‖ *intr* stancarsi; infastidirsi
**tire' chain'** *s* catena antineve
**tired** [taɪrd] *adj* stanco, stracco
**tire' gauge'** *s* manometro della pressione delle gomme
**tireless** ['taɪrlɪs] *adj* infaticabile
**tire' pres'sure** *s* pressione (delle gomme)
**tire' pump'** *s* pompa (per i pneumatici)
**tiresome** ['taɪrsəm] *adj* faticoso; (*boring*) noioso
**tissue** ['tɪsjʊ] *s* tessuto; tessuto finissimo, velina
**tis'sue pa'per** *s* carta velina
**titanium** [taɪ'tɛnɪ·əm] or [tɪ'tɛnɪ·əm] *s* titanio
**tithe** [taɪð] *s* decima ‖ *tr* imporre la decima su; pagare la decima di
**Titian** ['tɪʃən] *adj* tizianesco ‖ *s* Tiziano
**title** ['taɪtəl] *s* titolo; (sports) campionato ‖ *tr* intitolare
**ti'tle deed'** *s* titolo di proprietà
**ti'tle·hold'er** *s* campione *m*, primatista *mf*
**ti'tle page'** *s* frontespizio
**ti'tle role'** *s* (theat) ruolo principale
**tit'mouse'** *s* (**-mice**) (orn) cincia
**titter** ['tɪtər] *s* risatina ‖ *intr* ridacchiare
**titular** ['tɪtʃələr] *adj* titolare
**TNT** ['ti‚ɛn'ti] *s* (letterword) tritolo
**to** [tu], [tʊ] or [tə] *adv*—**to and fro** da una parte all'altra, avanti e indietro; **to come to** tornare in sè ‖ *prep* a, e.g., **he is going to Rome** va a Roma; **he gave a kiss to his mother**

diede un bacio a sua madre; **she is learning to sew** impara a cucire; per, e.g., **he has been a true friend to me** è stato un vero amico per me; da, e.g., **there is still a lot of work to do** c'è ancora molto lavoro da fare; con, e.g., **she was very kind to me** è stata molto gentile con me; in, e.g., **we went to church** siamo andati in chiesa; fino a, e.g., **to see s.o. to the station** accompagnare qlcu fino alla stazione; in confronto di, e.g., **the accounts are nothing to what really happened** le storie non sono nulla, in confronto di quanto è realmente successo; meno, e.g., **ten minutes to seven** le sette meno dieci

**toad** [tod] *s* rospo

**toad'stool'** *s* agarico, fungo velenoso

**to-and-fro** [tu-ənd'fro] *adj* avanti e indietro

**toast** [tost] *s* pane tostato; (*drink to s.o.'s health*) brindisi *m;* **a piece of toast** una fetta di pane tostato ‖ *tr* tostare; brindare alla salute di ‖ *intr* tostarsi; brindare

**toaster** ['tostər] *s* (*of bread*) tostapane *m;* persona che fa un brindisi

**toast'mas'ter** *s* persona che annuncia i brindisi, maestro di cerimonie

**tobac•co** [tə'bæko] *s* (-cos) tabacco

**tobacconist** [tə'bækənɪst] *s* tabaccaio

**tobac'co pouch'** *s* borsa da tabacco

**toboggan** [tə'bɑgən] *s* toboga *m*

**tocsin** ['tɑksɪn] *s* campana a martello; scampanata d'allarme

**today** [tu'de] *s & adv* oggi *m*

**toddle** ['tɑdəl] *s* passo vacillante ‖ *intr* traballare, trotterellare

**tod•dy** ['tɑdi] *s* (-dies) ponce *m*

**to-do** [tə'du] *s* (-dos) (coll) daffare *m*, rumore *m*

**toe** [to] *s* dito del piede; (*of shoe*) punta ‖ *v* (*pret & pp* toed; *ger* toeing) *tr*—**to toe the line** filare diritto

**toe'nail'** *s* unghia del piede

**together** [tu'gɛðər] *adv* insieme; **to bring together** riunire; riconciliare; **to call together** chiamare a raccolta; **to stick together** (coll) rimanere uniti, stare insieme

**togs** [tɑgz] *spl* vestiti *mpl*

**toil** [tɔɪl] *s* travaglio, sfacchinata; **toils** reti *fpl*, lacci *mpl* ‖ *intr* travagliare, sfacchinare

**toilet** ['tɔɪlɪt] *s* toletta; gabinetto, ritirata; **to make one's toilet** farsi la toletta

**toi'let pa'per** *s* carta igienica

**toi'let pow'der** *s* polvere *f* di talco

**toi'let soap'** *s* sapone *m* da toletta

**toi'let wa'ter** *s* acqua da toletta

**token** ['tokən] *s* segno, marca; ricordo; (*used as money*) gettone *m;* **by the same token** per di più; **in token of** in segno di, come prova di

**tolerance** ['tɑlərəns] *s* tolleranza

**tolerate** ['tɑlə‚ret] *tr* tollerare

**toll** [tol] *s* (*of bell*) rintocco; (*e.g., for passage over bridge*) pedaggio; (*tax*) dazio; (*compensation for grinding grains*) molenda; (*number of victims*) perdite *fpl;* (telp) tariffa inter-

urbana ‖ *tr* (*a bell*) sonare a morto; (*the faithful*) chiamare a raccolta ‖ *intr* sonare a morto

**toll' bridge'** *s* ponte *m* a pedaggio

**toll' call'** *s* (telp) chiamata interurbana

**toll'gate'** *s* barriera di pedaggio; (*in a turnpike*) casello

**toma•to** [tə'meto] *or* [tə'mɑto] *s* (-toes) pomodoro

**toma'to juice'** *s* sugo di pomodoro

**tomb** [tum] *s* tomba

**tomboy** ['tɑm‚bɔɪ] *s* maschietta

**tomb'stone'** *s* pietra tombale, lapide *f*

**tomcat** ['tɑm‚kæt] *s* gatto maschio

**tome** [tom] *s* tomo

**tomorrow** [tu'mɑro] *or* [tu'mɔro] *s* domani *m;* **the day after tomorrow** dopodomani *m* ‖ *adv* domani

**tom-tom** ['tɑm‚tɑm] *s* tam-tam *m*

**ton** [tʌn] *s* tonnellata; **tons** (coll) montagne *fpl*

**tone** [ton] *s* tono; (fig) tenore *m* ‖ *tr* intonare; **to tone down** (*colors*) smorzare; (*sounds*) sfumare ‖ *intr* intonarsi; **to tone down** moderarsi; **to tone up** rinforzarsi

**tone' po'em** *s* poema sinfonico

**tongs** [tɔŋz] *or* [tɑŋz] *spl* tenaglie *fpl;* (*e.g., for sugar*) molle *fpl*

**tongue** [tʌŋ] *s* (*language*) lingua; (*of bell*) battaglio; (*of shoe*) linguetta; (*of wagon*) timone *m;* (anat) lingua; (carp) maschio; **tongue in cheek** poco sinceramente; **to hold one's tongue** mordersi la lingua; **to speak with forked tongue** essere di due lingue

**tongue' depres'sor** *s* abbassalingua *m*

**tongue'-lash'ing** *s* sgridata

**tongue' twist'er** *s* scioglilingua *m*

**tonic** ['tɑnɪk] *adj & s* tonico

**tonight** [tu'naɪt] *s* questa sera, questa notte ‖ *adv* stasera; stanotte

**tonnage** ['tʌnɪdʒ] *s* tonnellaggio, stazza

**tonsil** ['tɑnsəl] *s* tonsilla

**ton•y** ['toni] *adj* (-ier; -iest) (slang) elegante, di lusso

**too** [tu] *adv* (*also*) anche, pure; (*more than enough*) troppo; **too bad!** peccato!; **too many** troppi; **too much** troppo

**tool** [tul] *s* utensile *m*, attrezzo; (*person*) strumento; (*of lathe*) punta ‖ *tr* lavorare; (bb) decorare

**tool' bag'** *s* borsa degli attrezzi

**tool'box'** *s* cassetta attrezzi

**tool'mak'er** *s* attrezzista *m*

**tool'shed'** *s* barchessa

**toot** [tut] *s* (*of horn*) suono; (*of locomotive*) fischio; (*of car's horn*) colpo; (coll) gazzarra ‖ *tr* strombettare; **to toot one's own horn** strombazzare i propri meriti ‖ *intr* strombettare

**tooth** [tuθ] *s* (teeth [tiθ]) dente *m*

**tooth'ache'** *s* mal *m* di denti

**tooth'brush'** *s* spazzolino da denti

**toothless** ['tuθlɪs] *adj* sdentato

**tooth'paste'** *s* pasta dentifricia

**tooth'pick'** *s* stuzzicadenti *m*

**tooth' pow'der** *s* polvere dentifricia

**top** [tɑp] *s* cima, sommo, vertice *m;* (*upper part of anything*) disopra *m;*

(*of mountain, tree*) vetta; (*of box*) coperchio; (*beginning*) principio; (*of bottle*) imboccatura; (*of a bridle*) testata; (*of wagon*) mantice *m;* (*of car*) tetto; (*of wall*) coronamento; (*toy*) trottola; (naut) gabbia; **at the top of one's voice** a perdifiato; **from top to bottom** daccapo a piedi, dal principio alla fine; **on top of** in cima di; subito dopo; **the tops** (coll) il migliore, il fiore; **to blow one's top** (slang) dare in escandescenze; **to sleep like a top** dormire come un ghiro ‖ *v* (*pret & pp* **topped;** *ger* **topping**) *tr* (*a tree*) svettare; coronare; superare

**topaz** ['topæz] *s* topazio

**top' bil'ling** *s*—**to get top billing** essere artista di cartello; (journ) ricevere il posto più importante

**top' boot'** *s* stivale *m* a tromba

**top'coat'** *s* soprabito di mezza stagione

**toper** ['topər] *s* ubriacone *m*

**topgal'lant sail'** [ ,tap'gælənt] *s* (naut) pappafico, veletta

**top' hat'** *s* cappello a staio o a cilindro

**top'-heav'y** *adj* troppo pesante in cima, sovraccarico in cima

**topic** ['tapık] *s* topica, tema *m*

**top'knot'** *s* crocchia

**topless** ['taplıs] *adj* (*mountain*) di cui non si vede la vetta, eccelso; (*bathing suit*) topless

**top'mast'** *s* (naut) alberetto

**top'most'** *adj* il più alto

**topogra·phy** [tə'pagrəfi] *s* (**-phies**) topografia

**topple** ['tapəl] *tr* abbattere, rovesciare ‖ *intr* rovesciarsi, cadere

**top' prior'ity** *s* priorità massima

**topsail** ['tapsəl] *or* ['tap ,sel] *s* (naut) gabbia

**top'-se'cret** *adj* segretissimo

**top'soil'** *s* strato superiore del terreno

**topsy-turvy** ['tapsı'tʌrvi] *adj* rovesciato; confuso ‖ *s* soqquadro ‖ *adv* a soqquadro

**torch** [tortʃ] *s* fiaccola, torcia; **to carry the torch for** (slang) amare disperatamente

**torch'bear'er** *s* portatore *m* di fiaccola; (fig) capo, guida *m*

**torch'light'** *s* luce *f* di fiaccola

**torch' song'** *s* canzone *f* triste d'amore non corrisposto

**torment** ['torment] *s* tormento ‖ [tor-'ment] *tr* tormentare

**torna·do** [tor'nedo] *s* (**-dos** *or* **-does**) tornado, tromba d'aria

**torpe·do** [tor'pido] *s* (**-does**) siluro ‖ *tr* silurare

**torpe'do boat'** *s* motosilurante *f*

**torpe'do-boat destroy'er** *s* torpediniera

**torrent** ['tarənt] *or* ['torənt] *s* torrente *m*

**torrid** ['tarıd] *or* ['torıd] *adj* torrido

**torsion** ['torʃən] *s* torsione

**tor'sion bar'** *s* barra di torsione

**tor·so** ['torso] *s* (**-sos**) torso

**tortoise** ['tortəs] *s* tartaruga

**tor'toise shell'** *s* tartaruga

**torture** ['tortʃər] *s* tortura ‖ *tr* torturare

**toss** [tos] *or* [tas] *s* lancio, getto ‖ *tr* lanciare, gettare; (*to fling about*) sballottare; (*one's head*) alzare sdegnosamente; agitare; rivoltare; (*an opinion*) avventare; **to toss off** fare rapidamente; (*e.g., a drink*) buttar giù; **to toss up** (*a coin*) gettar in aria, gettare a testa e croce; (coll) rigettare ‖ *intr* agitarsi, dimenarsi; **to toss and turn** (*in bed*) girarsi; **to toss up** giocare a testa e croce

**toss'up'** *s* testa e croce; (coll) eguale probabilità *f*

**tot** [tat] *s* bambino, piccolo

**to·tal** ['totəl] *adj* totale; (*e.g., loss*) completo ‖ *s* totale *m* ‖ *v* (*pret & pp* **-taled** *or* **-talled;** *ger* **-taling** *or* **-talling**) *tr* ammontare a; (*to make a total of*) sommare

**totalitarian** [to ,tælı'terı·ən] *adj* totalitario ‖ *s* aderente *mf* al totalitarismo

**totter** ['tatər] *s* vacillamento ‖ *intr* vacillare

**touch** [tʌtʃ] *s* (*act*) tocco; (*sense*) tatto; (*of an illness*) leggero attacco; (*slight amount*) punta; (*for money*) (slang) stoccata; **to get in touch with** mettersi in contatto con; **to lose one's touch** perdere il tocco personale ‖ *tr* toccare; raggiungere; riguardare; (*for a loan*) (slang) dare una stoccata a; **to touch on** menzionare; **to touch up** ritoccare ‖ *intr* toccare; **to touch down** (aer) atterrare

**touching** ['tʌtʃıŋ] *adj* toccante, commovente ‖ *prep* riguardo a

**touch'stone'** *s* pietra di paragone

**touch' type'writing** *s* dattilografia a tatto

**touch·y** ['tʌtʃi] *adj* (**-ier; -iest**) suscettibile, permaloso; delicato, precario, rischioso

**tough** [tʌf] *adj* duro; forte; (*luck*) cattivo; violento ‖ *s* malvivente *m*

**toughen** ['tʌfən] *tr* indurire ‖ *intr* indurirsi

**tough' luck'** *s* disdetta, sfortuna

**tour** [tur] *s* gita, viaggio; (sports) giro; (mil) turno; (theat) tournée *f* ‖ *tr* girare; (theat) portare in tournée ‖ *intr* girare; (theat) andare in tournée

**tour'ing car'** ['turıŋ] *s* automobile *f* da turismo

**tourist** ['turıst] *adj* turistico ‖ *s* turista *mf*

**tournament** ['turnəmənt] *or* ['tʌrnəmənt] *s* torneo

**tourney** ['turni] *or* ['tʌrni] *s* torneo ‖ *intr* giostrare

**tourniquet** ['turnı ,ket] *or* ['tʌrnı ,ke] *s* laccio emostatico

**tousle** ['tauzəl] *tr* spettinare

**tow** [to] *s* rimorchio; (*e.g., of hemp*) stoppa; **to take in tow** prendere a rimorchio ‖ *tr* rimorchiare

**towards** [tord(z)] *or* [tə'word(z)] *prep* (*in the direction of*) verso; (*in respect to*) per; (*near*) vicino a; (*a certain hour*) su, verso

**tow'boat'** *s* rimorchiatore *m*

**tow' car'** *s* rimorchiatore *m*

**tow·el** ['tau·əl] *s* asciugamano; (*of paper*) salvietta; **to throw in the**

**towel** (slang) gettare la spugna ‖ *v* (*pret & pp* **-eled** or **-elled; ger -eling** or **-elling**) *tr* asciugare

**tow'el rack'** *s* portaasciugamani *m*

**tower** ['tau·ər] *s* torre *f* ‖ *intr* torreggiare

**towering** ['tau·ərɪŋ] *adj* torreggiante; gigantesco; eccessivo

**towline** ['to,laɪn] *s* cavo di rimorchio

**town** [taun] *s* città *f;* (*townspeople*) cittadinanza; **in town** in città

**town' clerk'** *s* segretario municipale

**town' coun'cil** *s* consiglio comunale

**town' cri'er** *s* banditore *m* municipale

**town' hall'** *s* municipio

**township** ['taunʃɪp] *s* suddivisione di contea

**towns'man** *s* (**-men**) cittadino; concittadino

**towns'peo'ple** *spl* cittadini *mpl;* gente *f* di città

**town' talk'** *s* dicerie *fpl,* pettegolezzi *mpl*

**tow'path'** *s* strada d'alaggio

**tow'rope'** *s* corda da rimorchio

**tow' truck'** *s* autogru *f*

**toxic** ['taksɪk] *adj & s* tossico

**toy** [tɔɪ] *adj* giocattolo; di giocattoli ‖ *s* giocattolo; (*trifle*) nonnulla *m;* (*trinket*) gingillo ‖ *intr* giocare; **to toy with** (*to play with*) giocare con; (*to trifle, e.g., with food*) baloccarsi con; (*an idea*) accarezzare; (*to flirt with*) flirtare con

**toy' bank'** *s* salvadanaio

**toy' sol'dier** *s* soldatino di piombo

**trace** [tres] *s* traccia, vestigio; (*tracing*) tracciato; (*of harness*) tirella; (fig) ombra ‖ *tr* tracciare; (*e.g., s.o.'s ancestry*) rintracciare; (*a pattern*) lucidare

**trac'er bul'let** ['tresər] *s* pallottola tracciante

**trache·a** ['trekɪ·ə] *s* (**-ae** [,i]) trachea

**tracing** ['tresɪŋ] *s* tracciato

**track** [træk] *s* (*of foot*) traccia, pesta; (*rut*) solco, rotaia; (*of boat*) scia; corso; (*course followed by boat*) rotta; (*of tape recorder*) pista; (*of tractor*) cingolo; (*of ideas*) successione; (*width of a vehicle measured from wheel to wheel*) (aut) carreggiata; (rr) binario; (*track and field*) (sports) atletica leggera; (*for horses*) (sports) galoppatoio; (*for running*) (sports) pista, corsia; **to keep track of** non perder di vista; **to lose track of** perder di vista; **to make tracks** (coll) affrettarsi; **to stop in one's tracks** (coll) fermarsi di colpo ‖ *tr* rintracciare, seguire le tracce di; lasciare tracce su; **to track down** rintracciare

**track'ing sta'tion** ['trækɪŋ] *s* (rok) stazione di avvistamento

**track'less trol'ley** ['træklɪs] *s* filobus *m*

**track' meet'** *s* incontro di atletica leggera

**track'walk'er** *s* (rr) guardialinee *m*

**tract** [trækt] *s* tratto, opuscolo, trattatello; (anat) tubo, canale *m*

**traction** ['trækʃən] *s* trazione

**trac'tion com'pany** *s* società *f* di trasporti urbani

**tractor** ['træktər] *s* trattore *m;* (*of a tractor-trailer*) motrice *f*

**trac'tor-trail'er** *s* treno stradale

**trade** [tred] *s* commercio; affare *m;* occupazione, mestiere *m;* (*people*) commercianti *mpl,* professionisti *mpl;* mercato; (*customers*) clientela; (*in slaves*) tratta ‖ *tr* mercanteggiare; cambiare; **to trade in** dare come pagamento parziale ‖ *intr* trafficare, commerciare; comprare; **to trade in** lavorare in; **to trade on** approfittarsi di

**trade'mark'** *s* marca or marchio di fabbrica

**trade' name'** *s* ragione sociale

**trader** ['tredər] *s* trafficante *m*

**trade' school'** *s* scuola d'avviamento professionale, scuola d'arti e mestieri

**trades'man** *s* (**-men**) commerciante *m;* artigiano

**trade' un'ion** *s* sindacato di lavoratori

**trade' un'ionist** *s* sindacalista *mf*

**trade' winds'** *spl* alisei *mpl*

**trad'ing post'** *s* centro di scambi commerciali; (*in stock exchange*) posto delle compravendite

**trad'ing stamp'** *s* buono premio

**tradition** [trə'dɪʃən] *s* tradizione

**traditional** [trə'dɪʃənəl] *adj* tradizionale

**traduce** [trə'djus] or [trə'dus] *tr* calunniare

**traf·fic** ['træfɪk] *s* traffico, circolazione; commercio; comunicazione ‖ *v* (*pret & pp* **-ficked; ger -ficking**) *intr* trafficare

**traf'fic cir'cle** *s* raccordo a circolazione rotatoria

**traf'fic court'** *s* tribunale *m* della polizia stradale

**traf'fic is'land** *s* isola spartitraffico

**traf'fic jam'** *s* intralcio del traffico, ingorgo stradale

**traf'fic light'** *s* semaforo

**traf'fic man'ager** *s* dirigente *m* del traffico; (rr) gestore *m* di stazione

**traf'fic sign'** *s* segnale *m* di circolazione stradale, cartello indicatore

**traf'fic tick'et** *s* contravvenzione per violazione del traffico

**tragedian** [trə'dʒidɪ·ən] *s* tragico

**trage·dy** ['trædʒɪdi] *s* (**-dies**) tragedia

**tragic** ['trædʒɪk] *adj* tragico

**trail** [trel] *s* sentiero; (*track*) traccia, pista; (*of robe*) strascico, coda; (*of smoke*) pennacchio; (*left by an airplane*) striscia; (*of people*) codazzo ‖ *tr* strascicare; essere sulla fatta di; (*e.g., dust on the road*) sollevare; (*mud*) lasciar cadere ‖ *intr* strascicare; (*said, e.g., of a snake*) strisciare; (*said of a plant*) arrampicarsi; **to trail off** mutare; (*to weaken*) affievolirsi

**trailer** ['trelər] *s* traino; (*to haul freight*) semirimorchio; (*for living*) carovana, roulotte *f;* (bot) rampicante *m*

**train** [tren] *s* (*of vehicles*) convoglio; (*of robe*) strascico; (*of thought*) ordine *m;* (*of people*) coda; (rr) treno ‖ *tr* addestrare, impratichire; (*a weapon*) puntare, rivolgere; (*a horse*) scozzonare; (*e.g., a dog*) ammaestrare; (*a plant*) far crescere; (sports) allenare ‖ *intr* addestrarsi; ammaestrarsi; (sports) allenarsi

**trained' nurse'** *s* infermiera diplomata

**trainer** ['trenər] *s* allenatore *m*

**training** ['trenɪŋ] *s* esercizio, esercitazione; (sports) allenamento

**train'ing camp'** *s* campo addestramento

**train'ing school'** *s* scuola di addestramento professionale; riformatorio

**train'ing ship'** *s* nave *f* scuola

**trait** [tret] *s* tratto, caratteristica

**traitor** ['tretər] *s* traditore *m*

**traitress** ['tretrɪs] *s* traditrice *f*

**trajecto·ry** [trə'dʒɛktəri] *s* (**-ries**) traiettoria

**tramp** [træmp] *s* lunga camminata; vagabondo; (*hussy*) sgualdrina ‖ *tr* attraversare; calpestare ‖ *intr* camminare a passi fermi; fare il vagabondo

**trample** ['træmpəl] *tr* calpestare; (fig) conculcare ‖ *intr*—**to trample on** or **upon** calpestare

**trampoline** ['træmpə ‚lin] *s* trampolino di olona per salti mortali

**tramp' steam'er** *s* carretta

**trance** [træns] or [trɑns] *s* trance *f;* (*dazed condition*) estasi *f*

**tranquil** ['træŋkwɪl] *adj* tranquillo

**tranquilize** ['træŋkwɪ ‚laɪz] *tr* tranquillizzare ‖ *intr* tranquillizzarsi

**tranquilizer** ['træŋkwɪ ‚laɪzər] *s* tranquillante *m*

**tranquillity** [træn'kwɪlɪti] *s* tranquillità *f*

**transact** [træn'zækt] or [træns'ækt] *tr* sbrigare, trattare

**transaction** [træn'zækʃən] or [træns'ækʃən] *s* disbrigo, operazione

**transatlantic** [ ‚trænsət'læntɪk] *adj* & *s* transatlantico

**transcend** [træn'sɛnd] *tr* trascendere, sorpassare ‖ *intr* eccellere

**transcribe** [træn'skraɪb] *tr* trascrivere

**transcript** ['trænskrɪpt] *s* copia; traduzione; (educ) copia ufficiale del certificato di studi

**transcription** [træn'skrɪpʃən] *s* trascrizione

**transept** ['trænsept] *s* transetto

**trans·fer** ['trænsfər] *s* trasferimento; passaggio; (*pattern*) rapporto; (*of funds*) giro; (*of real estate*) compravendita; (law) voltura ‖ [træns'fʌr] or ['trænsfər] *v* (*pret* & *pp* **-ferred;** *ger* **-ferring**) *tr* trasferire, trasportare; (*funds*) stornare; (*a design*) rapportare; (*real estate*) compravendere ‖ *intr* trasferirsi; cambiare di treno

**trans'fer tax'** *s* tassa di successione; tassa sulla compravendita

**transfix** [træns'fɪks] *tr* trafiggere; paralizzare, inchiodare

**transform** [træns'fɔrm] *tr* trasformare; (elec) trasformare ‖ *intr* trasformarsi

**transforma'tional gram'mar** [ ‚trænsfər-'meʃənəl] *s* grammatica trasformativa

**transformer** [træns'fɔrmər] *s* trasformatore *m*

**transfusion** [træns'fjuʃən] *s* trasfusione

**transgress** [træns'grɛs] *tr* trasgredire; (*a limit or boundry*) oltrepassare ‖ *intr* peccare

**transgression** [træns'grɛʃən] *s* trasgressione; peccato

**transient** ['trænʃənt] *adj* passeggero, temporaneo; di passaggio ‖ *s* ospite *mf* di passaggio

**transistor** [træn'zɪstər] *s* transistore *m*

**transit** ['trænsɪt] or ['trænzɪt] *s* transito

**transition** [træn'zɪʃən] *s* transizione

**transitional** [træn'zɪʃənəl] *adj* di transizione

**transitive** ['trænsɪtɪv] *adj* transitivo ‖ *s* verbo transitivo

**transitory** ['trænsɪ ‚tori] *adj* transitorio

**translate** [træns'let] or ['trænslet] *tr* tradurre; convertire; (*to transfer*) trasportare ‖ *intr* tradursi

**translation** [træns'leʃən] *s* traduzione; trasformazione; (telg) ritrasmissione

**translator** [træns'letər] *s* traduttore *m*

**transliterate** [træns'lɪtə ‚ret] *tr* traslitterare

**translucent** [træns'lusənt] *adj* traslucido; (fig) chiaro

**transmission** [træns'mɪʃən] *s* trasmissione; (aut) trasmissione

**trans·mit** [træns'mɪt] *v* (*pret* & *pp* **-mitted;** *ger* **-mitting**) *tr* & *intr* trasmettere

**transmitter** [træns'mɪtər] *s* trasmettitore *m*

**transmit'ting set'** *s* emittente *f*

**transmit'ting sta'tion** *s* stazione trasmettitrice

**transmute** [træns'mjut] *tr* & *intr* trasmutare

**transom** ['trænsəm] *s* (*crosspiece*) traversa; (*window over door*) vasistas *m;* (naut) specchio di poppa

**transparen·cy** ['træns'pɛrənsi] *s* (**-cies**) trasparenza; (*design on a translucent substance*) trasparente *m;* (phot) diapositiva

**transparent** [træns'pɛrənt] *adj* trasparente

**transpire** [træns'paɪr] *intr* (*to happen*) avvenire; (*to perspire*) traspirare; (*to become known*) trapelare

**transplant** [træns'plænt] or [træns'plɑnt] *tr* trapiantare ‖ *intr* trapiantarsi

**transport** ['trænsport] *s* trasporto; mezzo di trasporto ‖ [træns'port] *tr* trasportare

**transportation** [ ‚trænspor'teʃən] *s* trasporto; trasporti *mpl,* locomozione; biglietto di trasporto

**trans'port work'er** *s* ferrotranviere *m*

**transpose** [træns'poz] *tr* trasporre; (mus) trasportare

**trans·ship** [træns'ʃɪp] *v* (*pret* & *pp* **-shipped;** *ger* **-shipping**) *tr* trasbordare

**trap** [træp] *s* trappola, tranello;

(*double-curved pipe*) sifone *m;* (slang) bocca; (sports) congegno lanciapiattelli || *v* (*pret & pp* **trapped;** *ger* **trapping**) *tr* intrappolare, accalappiare

**trap' door'** *s* trabocchetto, botola; (theat) ribalta

**trapeze** [trə'piz] *s* (sports) trapezio

**trapezoid** ['træpɪ‚zɔɪd] *s* (geom) trapezio, trapezoide *m*

**trapper** ['træpər] *s* cacciatore *m* di animali da pelliccia con trappole

**trappings** ['træpɪŋz] *spl* ornamenti *mpl;* (*for a horse*) gualdrappa

**trap'shoot'ing** *s* tiro al piattello

**trash** [træʃ] *s* immondizia, spazzatura; (*nonsense*) sciocchezze *fpl;* (*junk*) ciarpame *m;* (*worthless people*) gentaglia

**trash' can'** *s* portaimmondizie *m*

**travail** ['trævel] or [trə'vel] *s* travaglio; travaglio di parto

**trav·el** ['trævəl] *s* viaggio; traffico; (mach) corsa || *v* (*pret & pp* **-eled** or **-elled;** *ger* **-eling** or **-elling**) *tr* viaggiare per, percorrere || *intr* viaggiare; muoversi; (coll) andare

**trav'el a'gency** *s* ufficio turistico

**traveler** ['trævələr] *s* viaggiatore *m*

**trav'eler's check'** *s* assegno viaggiatori

**trav'eling bag'** *s* sacca da viaggio

**trav'eling expens'es** *spl* spese *fpl* di viaggio; (*per diem*) trasferta

**trav'eling sales'man** *s* (**-men**) commesso viaggiatore

**traverse** ['trævərs] or [trə'vʌrs] *tr* attraversare

**traves·ty** ['trævɪsti] *s* (**-ties**) parodia || *v* (*pret & pp* **-tied**) *tr* parodiare

**trawl** [trɔl] *s* (*fishing net*) rete *f* a strascico; (*fishing line*) lenza al traino || *tr & intr* pescare con la rete a strascico; pescare con la lenza al traino

**trawling** ['trɔlɪŋ] *s* pesca con la rete a strascico; pesca con la lenza al traino

**tray** [tre] *s* guantiera, vassoio; (chem, phot) bacinella

**treacherous** ['tretʃərəs] *adj* traditore, subdolo; incerto, pericoloso

**treacher·y** ['tretʃəri] *s* (**-ies**) tradimento

**tread** [trɛd] *s* (*step*) passo; (*of shoe*) suola; (*of tire*) battistrada *m;* (*of stairs*) pedata || *v* (*pret* **trod** [trɑd], *pp* **trodden** ['trɑdən] or **trod**) *tr* calpestare; (*the boards*) calcare; accoppiarsi con || *intr* camminare; **to tread on** calpestare

**treadle** ['trɛdəl] *s* pedale *m*

**tread'mill'** *s* ruota azionata col camminare; (fig) lavoro ingrato

**treason** ['trizən] *s* tradimento

**treasonable** ['trizənəbəl] *adj* traditore

**treasure** ['trɛʒər] *s* tesoro || *tr* far tesoro di

**treasurer** ['trɛʒərər] *s* tesoriere *m*

**treas'ure hunt'** *s* caccia al tesoro

**treasur·y** ['trɛʒəri] *s* (**-ies**) tesoreria; tesoro, erario

**treat** [trit] *s* trattenimento; (*something affording pleasure*) piacere *m,* diletto || *tr* trattare; (*to cure*) curare, medi-

care; offrire un trattenimento a || *intr* trattare; pagare per il trattenimento

**treatise** ['tritɪs] *s* trattato

**treatment** ['tritmənt] *s* trattamento; (*of a theme*) trattazione

**trea·ty** ['triti] *s* (**-ties**) trattato

**treble** ['trɛbəl] *adj* (*threefold*) triplo; (mus) soprano || *s* (*person*) soprano *mf;* (*voice*) soprano || *tr* triplicare || *intr* triplicarsi

**tree** [tri] *s* albero

**tree' farm'** *s* bosco ceduo

**tree' frog'** *s* raganella

**treeless** ['trilɪs] *adj* spoglio, senza alberi

**tree'top'** *s* cima dell'albero

**trellis** ['trɛlɪs] *s* traliccio, graticcio

**tremble** ['trɛmbəl] *s* tremito || *intr* tremare

**tremendous** [trɪ'mɛndəs] *adj* tremendo

**tremor** ['trɛmər] or ['trimər] *s* tremito; (*of earth*) scossa

**trench** [trɛntʃ] *s* fosso, canale *m;* (mil) trincea

**trenchant** ['trɛntʃənt] *adj* mordace, caustico; vigoroso; incisivo

**trench' coat'** *s* trench *m*

**trench' mor'tar** *s* lanciabombe *m*

**trend** [trɛnd] *s* tendenza, orientamento || *intr* tendere, dirigersi

**Trent** [trɛnt] *s* Trento *f*

**trespass** ['trɛspəs] *s* (law) intrusione, violazione di proprietà || *intr* entrare senza diritto, intrudersi; peccare; **no trespassing** divieto di passaggio; **to trespass against** peccare contro; **to trespass on** entrare abusivamente in; (*e.g., s.o.'s time*) abusare di; violare

**tress** [trɛs] *s* treccia

**trestle** ['trɛsəl] *s* cavalletto; viadotto a cavalletti; ponte *m* a cavalletti

**trial** ['traɪ·əl] *s* tentativo, prova; tribolazione, croce *f;* (law) giudizio, processo; **on trial** in prova; (law) sotto processo; **to bring to trial** sottoporre a processo

**tri'al and er'ror** *s* metodo per tentativo; **by trial and error** a tastoni

**tri'al balloon'** *s* pallone *m* sonda

**tri'al by ju'ry** *s* processo con giuria

**tri'al ju'ry** *s* giuria civile or processuale

**tri'al or'der** *s* (com) ordine *m* di prova

**tri'al run'** *s* viaggio di prova

**triangle** ['traɪ‚æŋgəl] *s* triangolo; (*in drafting*) quartabuono

**tribe** [traɪb] *s* tribù *f*

**tribunal** [trɪ'bjunəl] or [traɪ'bjunəl] *s* tribunale *m*

**tribune** ['trɪbjun] *s* tribuna

**tributar·y** ['trɪbjə‚tɛri] *adj* tributario || *s* (**-ies**) tributario

**tribute** ['trɪbjut] *s* tributo; **to pay tribute to** (*e.g., beauty*) rendere omaggio a

**trice** [traɪs] *s* momento, istante *m;* **in a trice** in un batter d'occhio

**trick** [trɪk] *s* gherminella, inganno; trucco, tiro, scherzo; (*knack*) abilità *f;* (*feat*) atto; (*set of cards won*) presa; turno; (coll) piccola; **to be up to one's old tricks** farne una delle sue; **to play a dirty trick on** fare un brutto tiro a‖ *tr* giocare, ingannare

**tricker·y** ['trɪkəri] *s* (**-ies**) gherminella, inganno

**trickle** ['trɪkəl] *s* gocciolio, filo ‖ *intr* gocciolare; (*said of people*) andare or venire alla spicciolata; (*said of news*) trapelare

**trickster** ['trɪkstər] *s* imbroglione *m*

**trick·y** ['trɪki] *adj* (**-ier; -iest**) ingannatore; (*machine*) complicato; (*ticklish to deal with*) delicato

**tried** [traɪd] *adj* fedele, provato

**trifle** ['traɪfəl] *s* bazzecola, bagatella; (*small amount of money*) piccolezza, miseria; **a trifle** un po' ‖ *tr*—**to trifle away** sprecare ‖ *intr* gingillarsi; **to trifle with** giocherellare con; scherzare con; divertirsi con

**trifling** ['traɪflɪŋ] *adj* futile; insignificante, trascurabile

**trifocal** [traɪ'fokəl] *adj* trifocale ‖ **trifocals** *spl* occhiali *mpl* trifocali

**trigger** ['trɪgər] *s* (*of a firearm*) grilletto; (*of any device*) leva di sgancio ‖ *tr* (*a gun*) far sparare; (fig) scatenare

**trigonometry** [,trɪgə'nɑmɪtri] *s* trigonometria

**trill** [trɪl] *s* trillo, gorgheggio; vibrazione; (*speech sound*) (phonet) vibrante *f* ‖ *tr* gorgheggiare; pronunziare con vibrazione ‖ *intr* trillare, gorgheggiare

**trillion** ['trɪljən] *s* trilione *m*

**trilo·gy** ['trɪlədʒi] *s* (**-gies**) trilogia

**trim** [trɪm] *adj* (**trimmer; trimmest**) lindo, azzimato ‖ *s* condizione; buona condizione; (*dress*) vestito; (*of hair*) taglio, sfumatura; decorazione, ornamento; (*of sails*) orientamento; (aut) attrezzatura della carrozzeria ‖ *v* (*pret & pp* **trimmed;** *ger* **trimming**) *tr* tagliare; (*an edge*) rifilare; adattare; arrangiare; (*Christmas tree*) decorare; (*hair*) sfumare; (*a tree*) potare; ordinare, assettare; (*a sail*) orientare; (aer) equilibrare; (mach) sbavare; (coll) rimproverare; (coll) bastonare; (*to defeat* (coll) battere, vincere

**trimming** ['trɪmɪŋ] *s* ornamento, guarnizione; (coll) battitura, batosta; **trimmings** guarnizioni *mpl;* (mach) sbavatura; (mach) rifilatura

**trini·ty** ['trɪnɪti] *s* (**-ties**) (*group of three*) triade *f* ‖ **Trinity** *s* Trinità *f*

**trinket** ['trɪŋkɪt] *s* (*small ornament*) ninnolo, gingillo; **trinkets** (*trivial objects*) paccottiglia

**tri·o** ['tri·o] *s* (**-os**) terzetto

**trip** [trɪp] *s* viaggio; corsa; (*stumble*) inciampata; (*act of causing s.o. to stumble*) sgambetto; (*error*) passo falso; passo agile ‖ *v* (*pret & pp* **tripped;** *ger* **tripping**) *tr* far inciampare, far cadere; fare lo sgambetto a; cogliere in fallo; (mach) far scattare ‖ *intr* inciampare; fare un passo falso; avanzare saltellando, saltellare; **to trip over** inciampare in

**tripartite** [traɪ'pɑrtaɪt] *adj* tripartito

**tripe** [traɪp] *s* trippa; (slang) sciocchezze *fpl*

**trip'ham'mer** *s* maglio meccanico

**triphthong** ['trɪfθɔŋ] or ['trɪfθɑŋ] *s* trittongo

**triple** ['trɪpəl] *adj & s* triplo ‖ *tr* triplicare ‖ *intr* triplicarsi

**triplet** ['trɪplɪt] *s* (*offspring*) nato da un parto trigemino; (mus, poet) terzina

**triplicate** ['trɪplɪkɪt] *adj* triplicato ‖ *s* triplice copia ‖ ['trɪplɪ ,ket] *tr* triplicare

**tripod** ['traɪpɑd] *s* (*e.g., for a camera*) treppiede *m;* (*stool with three legs*) tripode *m*

**triptych** ['trɪptɪk] *s* trittico

**trite** [traɪt] *adj* trito, ritrito

**triumph** ['traɪ·əmf] *s* trionfo ‖ *intr* trionfare

**trium'phal arch'** [traɪ'ʌmfəl] *s* arco trionfale

**trivia** ['trɪvɪ·ə] *spl* banalità *f*, futilità *f*

**trivial** ['trɪvɪ·əl] *adj* insignificante, futile, banale

**Trojan** ['trodʒən] *adj & s* troiano

**Tro'jan Horse'** *s* cavallo di Troia

**Tro'jan War'** *s* guerra troiana

**troll** [trol] *tr & intr* pescare con la lenza al traino, pescare con il cucchiaino

**trolley** ['trɑli] *s* asta di presa, trolley *m;* carrozza tranviaria, tram *m*

**trol'ley bus'** *s* filobus *m*

**trol'ley car'** *s* vettura tranviaria, tram *m*

**trol'ley pole'** *s* trolley *m*

**trollop** ['trɑləp] *s* (*slovenly woman*) sciattona; (*hussy*) sgualdrina

**trombone** ['trɑmbon] *s* trombone *m*

**troop** [trup] *s* truppa, gruppo; (*of animals*) branco; (*of cavalry*) squadrone *m;* **troops** soldati *mpl* ‖ *intr* raggrupparsi; marciare insieme

**trooper** ['trupər] *s* soldato di cavalleria; poliziotto a cavallo; **to swear like a trooper** bestemmiare come un turco

**tro·phy** ['trofi] *s* (**-phies**) trofeo; (*any memento*) ricordo

**tropic** ['trɑpɪk] *adj* tropicale ‖ *s* tropico; **tropics** zona tropicale

**tropical** ['trɑpɪkəl] *adj* tropicale

**troposphere** ['trɑpə ,sfɪr] *s* troposfera

**trot** [trɑt] *s* trotto ‖ *v* (*pret & pp* **trotted;** *ger* **trotting**) *tr* far trottare; **to trot out** (coll) squadernare, esibire ‖ *intr* trottare

**troth** [troθ] or [troθ] *s* promessa di matrimonio; **by my troth** affé di Dio; **in troth** in verità; **to plight one's troth** impegnarsi; dare la parola

**troubadour** ['trubə ,dor] or ['trubə ,dʊr] *s* trovatore *m*

**trouble** ['trʌbəl] *s* disturbo, fastidio; inconveniente *m*, grattacapo; disordine *m*, conflitto; (*of a mechanical nature*) panna, guasto; **not to be worth the trouble** non valere la pena; **that's the trouble** questo è il male; **the trouble is that** il guaio è che; **to be in trouble** essere nei guai; **to be**

looking for trouble andare a cercarsi le grane; **to get into trouble** mettersi nei pasticci; **to have trouble in** + *ger* durar fatica a + *inf;* **to take the trouble** incomodarsi ‖ *tr* molestare, disturbare; *(e.g., water)* intorbidare; dar del filo da torcere a; **to be troubled with** soffrire di; **to trouble oneself** scomodarsi

**trouble′ light′** *s* lampada di soccorso

**trou′ble·mak′er** *s* mettimale *mf*

**troubleshooter** [′trʌbəl·ʃutər] *s* localizzatore *m* di guasti; *(in disputes)* paciere *m,* conciliatore *m*

**troubleshooting** [′trʌbəl·ʃutɪŋ] *s* localizzazione dei guasti; *(of disputes)* composizione

**troublesome** [′trʌbəlsəm] *adj* molesto; difficile

**trouble′ spot′** *s* luogo di disordini, polveriera

**trough** [trɔf] *or* [trɔf] *s (to knead bread)* madia; *(for feeding pigs)* trogolo; *(for feeding animals)* mangiatoia; *(for watering animals)* abbeveratoio; *(gutter)* doccia; *(between two waves)* cavo

**troupe** [trup] *s* troupe *f*

**trouper** [′trupər] *s* membro della troupe; vecchio attore; tipo di cui ci si può fidare

**trousers** [′trauzərz] *spl* pantaloni *mpl*

**trousseau** [tru′so] *or* [′truso] *s* (**-seaux** *or* **-seaus**) corredo da sposa

**trout** [traut] *s* trota

**trouvère** [tru′vɛr] *s* troviero

**trowel** [′trau·əl] *s* cazzuola, mestola

**Troy** [trɔɪ] *s* Troia

**truant** [′tru·ənt] *s* fannullone *m;* **to play truant** marinare la scuola

**truce** [trus] *s* tregua

**truck** [trʌk] *s* autocarro, camion *m; (tractor-trailer)* autotreno; *(van)* furgone *m; (to be moved by hand)* carretto; verdura per il mercato; *(mach, rr)* carrello; *(coll)* robaccia; *(coll)* relazioni *fpl* ‖ *tr* trasportare per autocarro, autotrasportare

**truck′driv′er** *s* camionista *m*

**truck′ farm′** *s* fattoria agricola per la produzione degli ortaggi

**truculent** [′trʌkjələnt] *or* [′trukjələnt] *adj* truculento

**trudge** [trʌdʒ] *intr* camminare; **to trudge along** camminare laboriosamente, scarpinare

**true** [tru] *adj* vero; esatto, conforme; legittimo; infallibile; a livello; **to come true** verificarsi; **true to life** conforme alla realtà

**true′ cop′y** *s* copia conforme

**true-hearted** [′tru ˌhɑrtɪd] *adj* fedele

**true′love knot′** *s* nodo d'amore

**truffle** [′trʌfəl] *or* [′trufəl] *s* tartufo

**truism** [′tru·ɪzəm] *s* truismo

**truly** [′truli] *adv* veramente; correttamente; **yours truly** distinti saluti

**trump** [trʌmp] *s* (cards) atout *m;* (Italian cards) briscola; **no trump** senza atout ‖ *tr* superare; (cards) pigliare con un atout o con una briscola; **to**

**trump up** inventare, fabbricare ‖ *intr* giocare un atout or una briscola

**trumpet** [′trʌmpɪt] *s* tromba; *(toy)* trombetta; **to blow one's own trumpet** cantare le proprie lodi ‖ *tr* strombazzare ‖ *intr* sonar la tromba; strombazzare; *(said of an elephant)* barrire

**truncheon** [′trʌntʃən] *s* bastone *m* del comando; (Brit) manganello

**trunk** [trʌŋk] *s (of living body, tree, family, railroad)* tronco; *(for clothes)* baule *m; (of elephant)* tromba; *(aut)* bagagliaio; *(archit)* fusto; *(telp)* linea principale; **trunks** pantaloncini *mpl*

**trunk′ hose′** *s* (hist) brache *fpl*

**truss** [trʌs] *s (to support a roof)* capriata, incavallatura; *(based on cantilever system)* intralicciatura; *(for reducing a hernia)* cinto, brachiere *m;* (bot) infiorescenza ‖ *tr* legare, assicurare

**trust** [trʌst] *s* fede *f;* speranza; fiducia, custodia; (com) trust *m,* cartello; (law) fedecommesso; **in trust** in deposito; come fedecommesso; **on trust** a credito ‖ *tr* fidarsi di; credere (with *dat*); *(to entrust)* dare in deposito a; dare a credito a ‖ *intr* credere; fidarsi, prestar fede; **to trust in** *(e.g., a friend)* fidarsi di; *(God)* aver fede in

**trust′ com′pany** *s* compagnia fedecommissaria; banca di deposito

**trustee** [trʌs′ti] *s* amministratore *m;* fiduciario; *(of a university)* curatore *m; (of an estate)* fedecommissario

**trusteeship** [trʌs′ti/ɪp] *s* amministrazione; (law) fedecommesso; (pol) amministrazione fiduciaria

**trustful** [′trʌstfəl] *adj* fiducioso

**trust′wor′thy** *adj* fidato, di fiducia

**trust·y** [′trʌsti] *adj* (**-ier; -iest**) fidato ‖ *s* (**-ies**) carcerato degno di fiducia

**truth** [truθ] *s* verità *f;* **in truth** in verità

**truthful** [′truθfəl] *adj* verace, veritiero

**try** [traɪ] *s* (**tries**) tentativo, prova ‖ *v* (*pret & pp* **tried**) *tr* provare; *(s.o.'s patience)* mettere a dura prova; *(a person)* (law) processare; *(a case)* (law) giudicare; **to try on** *(clothes)* provare; **to try out** provare; esperimentare ‖ *intr* cercare, tentare; **to try out for** cercare di ottenere il posto di; (sports) cercare di farsi accettare in; **to try to** cercare di

**trying** [′traɪ·ɪŋ] *adj* duro, penoso, difficile

**tryst** [trɪst] *or* [traɪst] *s* appuntamento

**T′-shirt′** *s* maglietta

**tub** [tʌb] *s* tino, bigoncia; vasca da bagno; *(clumsy boat)* (slang) carretta; *(fat person)* (slang) bombolo

**tube** [tjub] *or* [tub] *s* tubo; *(e.g., for toothpaste)* tubetto; *(of tire)* camera d'aria; (anat) tuba, tromba; (coll) ferrovia sotterranea

**tuber** [′tjubər] *or* [′tubər] *s* tubero

**tubercle** [′tjubərkəl] *or* [′tubərkəl] *s* tubercolo

**tuberculosis** [tju͵bɑrkjə'losɪs] or [tu-͵bɑrkjə'losɪs] s tubercolosi f

**tuck** [tʌk] s basta ‖ tr ripiegare; **to tuck away** nascondere; (slang) fare una scorpacciata di; **to tuck in** rincalzare; **to tuck up** rimboccare

**tucker** ['tʌkər] s collarino di merletto ‖ tr—**to tucker out** (coll) stancare

**Tuesday** ['tjuzdɪ] or ['tuzdɪ] s martedì m

**tuft** [tʌft] s (of feathers) pennacchio; (of hair) cernecchio; (of flowers) cespo; (fluffy threads) fiocco, nappa ‖ tr impuntire; adornare di fiocchi ‖ intr crescere a cernecchio

**tug** [tʌg] s strattone m, strappata; (struggle) lotta; (boat) rimorchiatore m ‖ v (pret & pp **tugged**) ger **tugging**) tr tirare; (a boat) rimorchiare ‖ intr tirare con forza; lottare

**tug'boat'** s rimorchiatore m

**tug' of war'** s tiro alla fune

**tuition** [tju'ɪʃən] or [tu'ɪʃən] s (instruction) insegnamento; tassa scolastica

**tulip** ['tjulɪp] or ['tulɪp] s tulipano

**tumble** ['tʌmbəl] s rotolone m, ruzzolone m; (somersault) salto mortale; caduta; disordine m, confusione; (confused heap) mucchio ‖ intr rotolare, ruzzolare; cadere, capitombolare; gettarsi; rigirarsi; **to tumble down** cadere in rovina; **to tumble to** (coll) rendersi conto di

**tum'ble-down'** adj dilapidato

**tumbler** ['tʌmblər] s (acrobat) saltimbanco; (glass) bicchiere m; (in a lock) levetta; (toy) misirizzi m

**tumor** ['tjumər] or ['tumər] s tumore m

**tumult** ['tjumʌlt] or ['tumʌlt] s tumulto

**tun** [tʌn] s botte f, barile m

**tuna** ['tunə] s tonno

**tune** [tjun] or [tun] s (air) aria; (manner of speaking) tono; **in tune** intonato; **out of tune** stonato; **to change one's tune** cambiare di tono ‖ tr intonare; **to tune in** (rad) sintonizzare; **to tune out** (rad) interrompere la sintonizzazione di; **to tune up** (a motor) mettere a punto; (mus) intonare

**tuner** ['tunər] or ['tjunər] s (rad) sintonizzatore m; (mus) accordatore m

**tungsten** ['tʌŋstən] s tungsteno

**tunic** ['tjunɪk] or ['tunɪk] s tunica

**tun'ing coil'** ['tunɪŋ] or ['tjunɪŋ] s bobina di sintonia

**tun'ing fork'** s diapason m, corista m

**Tunis** ['tjunɪs] or ['tunɪs] s Tunisi f

**Tunisia** [tju'nɪʒə] or [tu'nɪʒə] s la Tunisia

**Tunisian** [tju'nɪʒən] or [tu'nɪʒən] adj & s tunisino

**tun·nel** ['tʌnəl] s tunnel m, traforo, galleria; (min) galleria ‖ v (pret & pp **-neled** or **-nelled**; ger **-neling** or **-nelling**) tr costruire un passaggio attraverso or sotto a

**turban** ['tʌrbən] s turbante m

**turbid** ['tʌrbɪd] adj turbido

**turbine** ['tʌrbɪn] or ['tʌrbaɪn] s turbina

**turbojet** ['tʌrbo͵dʒɛt] s turboreattore m

**turboprop** ['tʌrbo͵prɑp] s turboelica m

**turbulent** ['tʌrbjələnt] adj turbolento

**tureen** [tu'rin] or [tju'rin] s terrina

**turf** [tʌrf] s zolla erbosa; (peat) torba; **the turf** il campo delle corse; **le corse**, il turf

**turf'man** s (-men) amatore m delle corse ippiche

**Turk** [tʌrk] s turco

**turkey** ['tʌrki] s tacchino ‖ **Turkey** s la Turchia

**turk'ey vul'ture** s (Cathartes aura) avvoltoio americano

**Turkish** ['tʌrkɪʃ] adj & s turco

**Turk'ish tow'el** s asciugamano spugna

**turmoil** ['tʌrmɔɪl] s subbuglio

**turn** [tʌrn] s giro; (time for action) turno, volta; (change of direction) voltata; (bend) svolta, curva; (of events) piega; servizio; inclinazione, attitudine f; (of key) mandata; (of coil) spira; (coll) colpo, sussulto; (aer, naut) virata; **at every turn** a ogni piè sospinto; **in turn** a tua (Sua, vostra, etc.) volta; **to be one's turn** toccare a qlcu, e.g., **it's your turn** tocca a Lei; **to take turns** fare a turno ‖ tr girare, voltare; (soil) rovesciare; cambiare; (to make sour) coagulare; (to translate) tradurre; (e.g., ten years) raggiungere; (e.g., one's eyes) volgere; (on a lathe) tornire; (e.g., a coat) rivoltare; (to twist) torcere; (the wheel) (aut) sterzare; **to turn against** mettere su contro; **to turn around** rigirare; (s.o.'s words) ritorcere; **to turn aside** sviare; **to turn away** cacciare via; **to turn back** ricacciare; restituire; (the clock) ritardare; **to turn down** ripiegare; (the light) abbassare; (an offer) rifiutare; **to turn in** ripiegare; denunziare; rassegnare; **to turn off** (e.g., light) spegnere, smorzare; (gas, water, etc.) tagliare; (e.g., a faucet) chiudere; **to turn on** (e.g., light, radio, etc.) accendere; (e.g., a faucet) aprire; **to turn out** mettere alla porta; (animals) fare uscire dalla stalla; rivoltare; (light) spegnere; produrre, fabbricare; **to turn up** ripiegare in su, rimboccare; (on a lathe) tornire; tirar su; (a card) scoprire; trovare; (e.g., the radio) alzare ‖ intr girare; svoltare, e.g., **turn left at the corner** svolti a sinistra all'angolo; girarsi; cambiare; fermentare; cambiare di colore; diventare; (naut) virare; **to turn against** voltarsi contro; inimicarsi con; **to turn around** fare una giravolta; **to turn aside** or **away** sviarsi; **to turn back** ritornare; retrocedere; **to turn down** piegarsi in giù; rovesciarsi; **to turn in** piegarsi, ripiegarsi; tornare a casa; (coll) andare a dormire; **to turn into** sfogare in; trasformarsi in; **to turn on** voltarsi contro; girarsi su; dipendere da; occuparsi di; **to turn**

**out** riuscire; **to turn out to be** manifestarsi; riuscire ad essere; **to turn over** rotolarsi; rovesciarsi; **to turn up** voltarsi all'insù; alzarsi; apparire, farsi vedere

**turn'buck'le** *s* tenditore *m*

**turn'coat'** *s* voltagabbana *mf;* **to become a turncoat** voltar gabbano

**turn'down'** *adj* (*collar*) rovesciato ‖ *s* rifiuto

**turn'ing point'** *s* punto decisivo

**turnip** ['tʌrnɪp] *s* rapa

**turn'key'** *s* secondino, carceriere *m*

**turn' of life'** *s* menopausa

**turn' of mind'** *s* disposizione naturale

**turn'out'** *s* (*gathering of people*) concorso; (*crowd*) folla; produzione; (*outfit*) vestito; stile *m*, moda; (*in a road*) slargo, piazzola; (*horse and carriage*) equipaggio; (rr) binario laterale

**turn'over'** *s* (*upset*) rovesciamento, ribaltamento; (*of customers*) movimento di clienti; (*of business*) giro d'affari; rotazione di lavoratori; (com) ciclo operativo

**turn'pike'** *s* autostrada a pedaggio

**turn' sig'nal** *s* (aut) indicatore *m* di direzione, lampeggiatore *m*

**turnstile** ['tʌrn ˌstaɪl] *s* tornello

**turn'ta'ble** *s* (*of phonograph*) piatto rotante; (rr) piattaforma girevole

**turpentine** ['tʌrpən ˌtaɪn] *s* trementina

**turpitude** ['tʌrpɪ ˌtjud] or ['tʌrpɪ ˌtud] *s* turpitudine *f*

**turquoise** ['tʌrkɔɪz] or ['tʌrkwɔɪz] *s* turchese *m*

**turret** ['tʌrɪt] *s* torretta

**turtle** ['tʌrtəl] *s* tartaruga; **to turn turtle** rovesciarsi, capovolgersi

**tur'tle-dove'** *s* tortora

**Tuscan** ['tʌskən] *adj & s* toscano

**Tuscany** ['tʌskəni] *s* la Toscana

**tusk** [tʌsk] *s* zanna

**tussle** ['tʌsəl] *s* lotta, zuffa ‖ *intr* lottare, azzuffarsi

**tutor** ['tjutər] or ['tutər] *s* istitutore privato, ripetitore *m;* (*guardian*) tutore *m* ‖ *tr* dare ripetizione a ‖ *intr* dare ripetizioni; studiare con un ripetitore

**tuxe·do** [tʌk'sido] *s* (-dos) smoking *m*

**twaddle** ['twɑdəl] *s* sciocchezze *fpl* ‖ *intr* dire sciocchezze

**twang** [twæŋ] *s* (*of musical instrument*) suono vibrato; (*of voice*) timbro nasale ‖ *tr* pizzicare; dire con un timbro nasale ‖ *intr* parlare con voce nasale

**twang·y** [twæŋi] *adj* (-ier; -iest) (*tone*) metallico; (*voice*) nasale

**tweed** [twid] *s* tweed *m;* **tweeds** abito di tweed

**tweet** [twit] *s* pigolio ‖ *intr* pigolare

**tweeter** ['twitər] *s* altoparlante *m* per alte audiofrequenze, tweeter *m*

**tweezers** ['twizərz] *spl* pinzette *fpl*

**twelfth** [twelfθ] *adj, s & pron* dodicesimo ‖ *s* (*in dates*) dodici *m*

**Twelfth'-night'** *s* vigilia dell'Epifania; sera dell'Epifania

**twelve** [twɛlv] *adj & pron* dodici ‖ *s* dodici *m;* **twelve o'clock** le dodici

**twentieth** ['twɛntɪ·ɪθ] *adj, s & pron* ventesimo ‖ *s* (*in dates*) venti *m*

**twen·ty** ['twɛnti] *adj & pron* venti ‖ *s* (-ties) venti *m;* **the twenties** gli anni venti

**twice** [twaɪs] *adv* due volte

**twice'-told'** *adj* detto più di una volta; detto e ridetto

**twiddle** ['twɪdəl] *tr*—**to twiddle one's thumbs** rigirare i pollici, oziare

**twig** [twɪg] *s* ramoscello; **twigs** sterpi *mpl*

**twilight** ['twaɪ ˌlaɪt] *adj* crepuscolare ‖ *s* crepuscolo

**twill** [twɪl] *s* diagonale *m* ‖ *tr* tessere in diagonale

**twin** [twɪn] *adj & s* gemello

**twine** [twaɪn] *s* spago ‖ *tr* intrecciare ‖ *intr* intrecciarsi

**twinge** [twɪndʒ] *s* punta, dolore acuto

**twinkle** ['twɪŋkəl] *s* scintillio; batter *m* d'occhio ‖ *intr* scintillare

**twin'-screw'** *adj* a due eliche

**twirl** [twʌrl] *s* giro, mulinello ‖ *tr* girare; (slang) lanciare ‖ *intr* girare rapidamente, frullare

**twist** [twɪst] *s* curva; giro; viluppo, intreccio; tendenza, inclinazione; (*yarn*) ritorno; (*e.g., of lemon*) fettina; (*dance*) twist *m* ‖ *tr* intrecciare; torcere; (*e.g., the face*) contorcere; (*the meaning*) stravolgere, stiracchiare; girare ‖ *intr* intrecciarsi; torcersi, divincolarsi; girare; serpeggiare; **to twist and turn** (*in bed*) girarsi e rigirarsi

**twister** ['twɪstər] *s* (coll) tromba d'aria

**twit** [twɪt] *v* (*pret & pp* **twitted;** *ger* **twitting**) *tr* ridicolizzare

**twitch** [twɪtʃ] *s* tic *m;* (*jerk*) strattone *m;* (*to restrain a horse*) torcinaso ‖ *intr* contrarsi; tremare; **to twitch at** tirare

**twitter** ['twɪtər] *s* garrito, cinguettio; (*chatter*) chiacchierio; ansia, agitazione ‖ *intr* garrire, cinguettare; chiacchierare; tremare d'ansia

**two** [tu] *adj & pron* due ‖ *s* due *m;* **to put two and two together** arrivare alle logiche conclusioni; **two o'clock** le due

**two'-cy'cle** *adj* a due tempi

**two'-cyl'inder** *adj* a due cilindri

**two-edged** ['tu ˌɛdʒd] *adj* a doppio filo

**two'fold'** *adj* duplice, doppio

**two' hun'dred** *adj, s & pron* duecento

**twosome** ['tusəm] *s* coppia

**two'-time'** *tr* (slang) fare le corna a

**two'-way ra'dio** *s* ricetrasmettitore *m*

**tycoon** [taɪ'kun] *s* magnate *m*

**type** [taɪp] *s* tipo; (typ) carattere *m;* (*pieces collectively*) (typ) caratteri *mpl* ‖ *tr* scrivere a macchina; simbolizzare ‖ *intr* scrivere a macchina

**type'face'** *s* stile *m* di carattere

**type'script'** *s* dattiloscritto

**typesetter** ['taɪp ˌsɛtər] *s* (*person*) compositore *m;* (*machine*) compositrice *f*

**type'write'** v (pret **-wrote;** pp **-written**) tr & intr dattilografare, scrivere a macchina

**type'writ'er** s (machine) macchina da scrivere; (typist) dattilografo

**type'writ'ing** s dattilografia, scrittura a macchina; lavoro battuto a macchina

**ty'phoid fe'ver** ['taɪfɔɪd] s febbre f tifoide

**typhoon** [taɪ'fun] s tifone m

**typical** ['tɪpɪkəl] adj tipico

**typi·fy** ['tɪpɪ͵faɪ] v (pret & pp **-fied**) tr simbolizzare

**typist** ['taɪpɪst] s dattilografo

**typographic(al)** [͵taɪpə'græfɪk(əl)] adj tipografico

**typograph'ical er'ror** s errore m di stampa

**typography** [taɪ'pɑgrəfi] s tipografía

**tyrannic(al)** [tɪ'rænɪk(əl)] or [taɪ-'rænɪk(əl)] adj tirannico

**tyrannous** ['tɪrənəs] adj tiranno

**tyrant** ['taɪrənt] s tiranno

**ty·ro** ['taɪro] s (**-ros**) principiante m

**Tyrrhe'nian Sea'** [tɪ'rinɪ·ən] s Mare Tirreno

# U

**U, u** [ju] s ventunesima lettera dell'alfabeto inglese

**ubiquitous** [ju'bɪkwɪtəs] adj ubiquo

**udder** ['ʌdər] s mammella

**ugliness** ['ʌglɪnɪs] s bruttezza

**ug·ly** ['ʌgli] adj (**-lier; -liest**) brutto

**Ukraine, the** ['jukren] or [ju'kren] s l'Ucraina f

**Ukrainian** [ju'krenɪ·ən] adj & s ucraino

**ulcer** ['ʌlsər] s piaga, ulcera; (corrupting element) (fig) piaga

**ulcerate** ['ʌlsə͵ret] tr ulcerare ‖ intr ulcerarsi

**ulterior** [ʌl'tɪrɪ·ər] adj ulteriore; (motive) nascosto, secondo

**ultimate** ['ʌltɪmɪt] adj ultimo

**ultima·tum** [͵ʌltɪ'metəm] s (**-tums** or **-ta** [tə]) ultimato

**ultimo** ['ʌltɪ͵mo] adv del mese scorso

**ul'tra·high fre'quency** ['ʌltrə'haɪ] s frequenza ultraelevata

**ultrashort** [͵ʌltrə'ʃɔrt] adj ultracorto

**ultraviolet** [͵ʌltrə'vaɪ·əlɪt] adj & s ultravioletto

**umbil'ical cord'** [ʌm'bɪlɪkəl] s cordone m ombelicale

**umbrage** ['ʌmbrɪdʒ] s—**to take umbrage at** adombrarsi per

**umbrella** [ʌm'brɛlə] s ombrello, paracqua m; (mil) ombrello

**umbrel'la stand'** s portaombrelli m

**Umbrian** ['ʌmbrɪ·ən] adj & s umbro

**umlaut** ['umlaut] s metafonesi f; (mark) dieresi f ‖ tr cambiare il timbro di; scrivere con dieresi

**umpire** ['ʌmpaɪr] s arbitro ‖ tr arbitrare ‖ intr fare l'arbitro

**UN** ['ju'ɛn] s (letterword) (**United Nations**) ONU f

**unable** [ʌn'ebəl] adj incapace; **to be unable to** essere impossibilitato a, non potere

**unabridged** [͵ʌnə'brɪdʒd] adj integrale, non abbreviato

**unaccented** [ʌn'æksɛntɪd] or [͵ʌnæk-'sɛntɪd] adj non accentato, atono

**unacceptable** [͵ʌnək'sɛptəbəl] adj inaccettabile

**unaccountable** [͵ʌnə'kauntəbəl] adj irresponsabile; inesplicabile

**unaccounted-for** [͵ʌnə'kauntɪd͵fɔr]

adj (e.g., failure) inesplicato; (e.g., soldier) irreperibile, mancante

**unaccustomed** [͵ʌnə'kʌstəmd] adj (unusual) insolito; non abituato

**unafraid** [͵ʌnə'fred] adj impavido

**unaligned** [ʌnə'laɪnd] adj non impegnato

**unanimity** [͵junə'nɪmɪti] s unanimità f

**unanimous** [ju'nænɪməs] adj unanime

**unanswerable** [ʌn'ænsərəbəl] adj per cui non vi è risposta; (argument) irrefutabile, incontestabile

**unappreciative** [͵ʌnə'priʃɪ͵etɪv] adj sconoscente, ingrato

**unapproachable** [͵ʌnə'protʃəbəl] adj inabbordabile; incomparabile

**unarmed** [ʌn'ɑrmd] adj disarmato, inerme

**unascertainable** [ʌn͵æsər'tenəbəl] adj non verificabile

**unassailable** [͵ʌnə'seləbəl] adj inattaccabile

**unassembled** [͵ʌnə'sɛmbəld] adj smontato

**unassuming** [͵ʌnə'sumɪŋ] or [͵ʌnə-'sjumɪŋ] adj modesto, semplice

**unattached** [͵ʌnə'tætʃt] adj indipendente; (loose) sciolto; non sposato; non fidanzato

**unattainable** [͵ʌnə'tenəbəl] adj inarrivabile, irraggiungibile

**unattractive** [͵ʌnə'træktɪv] adj poco attraente

**unavailable** [͵ʌnə'veləbəl] adj non disponibile

**unavailing** [͵ʌnə'velɪŋ] adj futile

**unavoidable** [͵ʌnə'vɔɪdəbəl] adj inevitabile, ineluttabile

**unaware** [͵ʌnə'wɛr] adj inconsapevole, ignaro ‖ adv inaspettatamente; (unknowingly) inavvertitamente

**unawares** [͵ʌnə'wɛrz] adv inaspettatamente; (unknowingly) inavvertitamente

**unbalanced** [ʌn'bælənst] adj sbilanciato, squilibrato

**unbandage** [ʌn'bændɪdʒ] tr sbendare

**un·bar** [ʌn'bɑr] v (pret & pp **-barred;** ger **-barring**) tr disserrare il chiavistello di

**unbearable** [ʌn'bɛrəbəl] adj insopportabile, insostenibile

**unbeatable** [ʌn'bitəbəl] *adj* imbattibile

**unbecoming** [ˌʌnbɪ'kʌmɪŋ] *adj* sconveniente, indegno; (*e.g.*, *hat*) disadatto, che non sta bene

**unbelievable** [ˌʌnbɪ'livəbəl] *adj* incredibile

**unbeliever** [ˌʌnbɪ'livər] *s* miscredente *mf*

**unbending** [ʌn'bendɪŋ] *adj* inflessibile

**unbiased** [ʌn'baɪ·əst] *adj* imparziale, spassionato

**un·bind** [ʌn'baɪnd] *v* (*pret & pp* **-bound** ['baʊnd]) *tr* slegare

**unbleached** [ʌn'blit/t] *adj* non candeggiato, al colore naturale

**unbolt** [ʌn'bolt] *tr* (*a door*) togliere il chiavistello a; sbullonare

**unborn** [ʌn'bɔrn] *adj* nascituro

**unbosom** [ʌn'bʊzəm] *tr* (*a secret*) rivelare; **to unbosom oneself** aprire il proprio animo, sfogarsi

**unbound** [ʌn'baʊnd] *adj* sciolto, libero; (*book*) non rilegato

**unbreakable** [ʌn'brekəbəl] *adj* infrangibile

**unbridle** [ʌn'braɪdəl] *tr* sbrigliare

**unbuckle** [ʌn'bʌkəl] *tr* sfibbiare

**unburden** [ʌn'bʌrdən] *tr* scaricare; **to unburden oneself (of)** vuotare il sacco (di)

**unburied** [ʌn'berid] *adj* insepolto

**unbutton** [ʌn'bʌtən] *tr* sbottonare

**uncalled-for** [ʌn'kɔld ˌfɔr] *adj* superfluo, gratuito; fuori di posto, sconveniente

**uncanny** [ʌn'kæni] *adj* misterioso, straordinario

**uncared-for** [ʌn'kerd ˌfɔr] *adj* negletto, trascurato

**unceasing** [ʌn'sisɪŋ] *adj* incessante

**unceremonious** [ˌʌnserɪ'moni·əs] *adj* senza cerimonie

**uncertain** [ʌn'sʌrtən] *adj* incerto

**uncertain·ty** [ʌn'sʌrtənti] *s* (**-ties**) incertezza

**unchain** [ʌn't/en] *tr* scatenare, sferrare

**unchangeable** [ʌn't/endʒəbəl] *adj* immutabile

**uncharted** [ʌn't/ɑrtɪd] *adj* inesplorato

**unchecked** [ʌn't/ɛkt] *adj* incontrollato

**uncivilized** [ʌn'sɪvɪ ˌlaɪzd] *adj* incivile

**unclad** [ʌn'klæd] *adj* svestito

**unclaimed** [ʌn'klemd] *adj* non reclamato; (*letter*) giacente

**unclasp** [ʌn'klæsp] or [ʌn'klɑsp] *tr* sfibbiare

**unclassified** [ʌn'klæsɪ ˌfaɪd] *adj* non classificato; non secreto

**uncle** ['ʌŋkəl] *s* zio

**unclean** [ʌn'klin] *adj* immondo

**un·clog** [ʌn'klɑg] *v* (*pret & pp* **-clogged;** *ger* **-clogging**) *tr* disintasare

**unclouded** [ʌn'klaʊdɪd] *adj* sereno, senza nubi

**uncollectible** [ˌʌnkə'lɛktɪbəl] *adj* inesigibile

**uncomfortable** [ʌn'kʌmfərtəbəl] *adj* scomodo, disagevole

**uncommitted** [ˌʌnkə'mɪtɪd] *adj* non impegnato

**uncommon** [ʌn'kɑmən] *adj* raro, straordinario

**uncompromising** [ʌn'kɑmprə ˌmaɪzɪŋ] *adj* intransigente

**unconcerned** [ˌʌnkən'sʌrnd] *adj* indifferente, noncurante

**unconditional** [ˌʌnkən'dɪ/ənəl] *adj* incondizionato

**uncongenial** [ˌʌnkən'dʒɪnɪ·əl] *adj* antipatico, sgradito

**unconquerable** [ʌn'kɑŋkərəbəl] *adj* inconquistabile, inespugnabile

**unconscionable** [ʌn'kɑn/ənəbəl] *adj* senza scrupoli; eccessivo

**unconscious** [ʌn'kɑn/əs] *adj* (*without awareness*) inconscio, inconsapevole; (*temporarily devoid of consciousness*) incosciente; (*unintentional*) involontario

**unconsciousness** [ʌn'kɑn/əsnɪs] *s* incoscienza

**unconstitutional** [ˌʌnkɑnstɪ'tju/ənəl] or [ˌʌnkɑnstɪ'tu/ənəl] *adj* incostituzionale

**uncontrollable** [ˌʌnkən'troləbəl] *adj* incontrollabile, ingovernabile

**unconventional** [ˌʌnkən'vɛn/ənəl] *adj* non convenzionale, anticonformista

**uncork** [ʌn'kɔrk] *tr* stappare

**uncouple** [ʌn'kʌpəl] *tr* sganciare, disconnettere

**uncouth** [ʌn'kuθ] *adj* zotico, incivile, pacchiano

**uncover** [ʌn'kʌvər] *tr* scoprire

**unction** ['ʌŋk/ən] *s* unzione; (fig) untuosità *f*

**unctuous** ['ʌŋkt/u·əs] *adj* untuoso

**uncultivated** [ʌn'kʌltɪ ˌvetɪd] *adj* incolto

**uncultured** [ʌn'kʌlt/ərd] *adj* incolto, rozzo

**uncut** [ʌn'kʌt] *adj* non tagliato; (*book*) intonso

**undamaged** [ʌn'dæmɪdʒd] *adj* indenne, illeso

**undaunted** [ʌn'dɔntɪd] *adj* imperterrito, impavido

**undeceive** [ˌʌndɪ'siv] *tr* disingannare

**undecided** [ˌʌndɪ'saɪdɪd] *adj* indeciso

**undefeated** [ˌʌndɪ'fitɪd] *adj* invitto

**undefended** [ˌʌndɪ'fɛndɪd] *adj* indifeso

**undefensible** [ˌʌndɪ'fɛnsɪbəl] *adj* insostenibile

**undefiled** [ˌʌndɪ'faɪld] *adj* puro, immacolato

**undeniable** [ˌʌndɪ'naɪ·əbəl] *adj* innegabile, indubitato

**under** ['ʌndər] *adj* di sotto; (*lower*) inferiore; (*clothing*) intimo, personale ‖ *adv* sotto; più sotto; **to go under** affondare; cedere; (coll) fallire ‖ *prep* sotto; sotto a; (*e.g.*, *20 years old*) meno di; **under full sail** a vele spiegate; **under lock and key** sotto chiave; **under oath** sotto giuramento; **under penalty of death** sotto pena di morte; **under sail** a vela; **under separate cover** in plico separato; **under steam** sotto pressione; **under the hand and seal of** firmato di pugno di; **under the weather** (coll) un po' indisposto; **under way** già iniziato

**un'der·age'** *adj* minorenne

**un'der-arm' pad'** *s* sottoascella *m*

**un'der·bid'** v (pret & pp **-bid; ger -bidding**) tr fare un'offerta inferiore a quella di

**un'der·brush'** s sottobosco

**un'der·car'riage** s (aut) telaio; (aer) carrello d'atterraggio

**un'der·clothes'** spl biancheria intima

**un'der·consump'tion** s sottoconsumo

**un'der·cov'er** adj segreto

**un'der·cur'rent** s (of water) corrente subacquea; (of air) corrente f inferiore; (fig) controcorrente f

**underdeveloped** [ˌʌndərdɪ'vɛləpt] adj sottosviluppato

**un'der·dog'** s chi è destinato ad avere la peggio; vittima; **the underdogs** i diseredati

**un'der·done'** adj non cotto abbastanza

**un'der·es'timate'** tr sottovalutare

**un'der·gar'ment** s indumento intimo

**un'der·go'** v (pret **-went;** pp **-gone**) tr (a test) passare, sottostare (with dat); (surgery) subire, sottoporsi a; soffrire

**un'der·grad'uate** adj (student) non ancora laureato; (course) per studenti non ancora laureati || s studente universitario che non ha ancora ricevuto il primo diploma

**un'der·ground'** adj sotterraneo; segreto || s regione sotterranea; macchia, resistenza || adv sottoterra; alla macchia, segretamente

**un'der·growth'** s sterpaglia

**underhanded** ['ʌndər'hændəd] adj subdolo, di sottomano

**un'der·line'** or **un'der·line'** tr sottolineare

**underling** ['ʌndərlɪŋ] s tirapiedi m

**un'der·mine'** tr scalzare, minare

**underneath** [ˌʌndər'niθ] adj inferiore || s disotto || adv sotto, di sotto || prep sotto a, sotto

**undernourished** [ˌʌndər'nʌrɪʃt] adj denutrito, malnutrito

**un'der·pass'** s sottopassaggio

**un'der·pay'** s (pret & pp **-paid**) tr & intr pagare insufficientemente

**un'der·pin'** v (pret & pp **-pinned; ger -pinning**) tr rincalzare

**underprivileged** [ˌʌndər'prɪvɪlɪdʒd] adj derelitto, diseredato

**un'der·rate'** tr sottovalutare

**un'der·score'** tr sottolineare

**un'der·sea'** adj sottomarino || adv sotto il mare

**un'der·seas'** adv sotto il mare

**un'der·sec'retar'y** s (-ies) sottosegretario

**un'der·sell'** v (pret & pp **-sold**) tr vendere a prezzo minore di; (to sell for less than actual value) svendere

**un'der·shirt'** s camiciola, canottiera

**undersigned** ['ʌndər ˌsaɪnd] adj sottoscritto

**un'der·skirt'** s sottogonna

**un'der·stand'** v (pret & pp **-stood**) tr capire, comprendere; sottintendere; (to accept as true) constare, e.g., **he understands that you are wrong** gli consta che Lei ha torto || intr capire, comprendere

**understandable** [ˌʌndər'stændəbəl] adj comprensibile

**understanding** [ˌʌndər'stændɪŋ] adj comprensivo, tollerante || s (mind) intelletto; (knowledge) conoscenza; comprensione, intendimento; (agreement) intesa, accordo

**understatement** [ˌʌndər'stetmənt] s sottovalutazione

**un'der·stud'y** s (-ies) (theat) doppio, sostituto || v (-ied) tr (an actor) fare il doppio di

**un'der·take'** v (pret **-took;** ger **-taken**) tr intraprendere; (to promise) promettere

**undertaker** [ˌʌndər'tekər] or ['ʌndərˌtekər] s impresario || ['ʌndərˌtekər] s impresario di pompe funebri

**undertaking** [ˌʌndər'tekɪŋ] s (task) impresa; (promise) promessa || ['ʌndərˌtekɪŋ] s impresa di pompe funebri

**un'der·tone'** s bassa voce; (background sound) ronzio di fondo; tono; colore smorzato

**un'der·tow'** s (on the beach) risacca; (countercurrent below surface) controcorrente f

**un'der·wa'ter** adj subacqueo || adv sottacqua

**un'der·wear'** s biancheria intima

**un'der·world'** s (criminal world) malavita, teppa; (abode of spirits) ade m, averno; mondo sotterraneo; mondo sottomarino; antipodi mpl

**un'der·write'** v (pret **-wrote;** pp **-written**) tr sottoscrivere; (to insure) assicurare

**un'der·writ'er** s sottoscrittore m; (ins) assicuratore m

**undeserved** [ˌʌndɪ'zʌrvd] adj immeritato

**undesirable** [ˌʌndɪ'zaɪrəbəl] adj & s indesiderabile mf

**undetachable** [ˌʌndɪ'tætʃəbəl] adj non movibile

**undeveloped** [ˌʌndɪ'vɛləpt] adj (land) non sfruttato; (country) sottosviluppato

**undigested** [ˌʌndɪ'dʒɛstɪd] adj non digerito

**undignified** [ʌn'dɪgnɪˌfaɪd] adj poco decoroso

**undiscernible** [ˌʌndɪ'zʌrnɪbəl] or [ˌʌndɪ'sʌrnɪbəl] adj impercettibile

**undisputed** [ˌʌndɪ'spjutəd] adj indiscusso, incontrastato

**un·do** [ʌn'du] v (pret **-did;** pp **-done**) tr sfare, disfare; rovinare; (a package) aprire; (a knot) sciogliere

**undoing** [ʌn'duˌɪŋ] s rovina

**undone** [ʌn'dʌn] adj non finito; **to come undone** disfarsi; **to leave nothing undone** non tralasciare di fare nulla

**undoubtedly** [ʌn'daʊtɪdli] adv indubbiamente, senza dubbio

**undress** ['ʌnˌdrɛs] or [ʌn'drɛs] s vestaglia; vestito da ogni giorno || [ʌn'drɛs] tr spogliare, svestire; (a *wound*) sbendare ‖ *intr* spogliarsi, svestirsi

**undrinkable** [ʌn'drɪŋkəbəl] *adj* imbevibile, non potabile

**undue** [ʌn'dju] or [ʌn'du] *adj* indebito; immeritato; eccessivo

**undulate** ['ʌndjə ˌlet] *intr* ondulare

**unduly** [ʌn'djuli] or [ʌn'duli] *adv* indebitamente, eccessivamente

**unearned** [ʌn'ʌrnd] *adj* non guadagnato col lavoro; immeritato; non ancora guadagnato

**un'earned in'crement** *s* plusvalenza

**unearth** [ʌn'ʌrθ] *tr* dissotterrare

**unearthly** [ʌn'ʌrθli] *adj* ultraterreno; spettrale; impossibile, straordinario

**uneasy** [ʌn'izi] *adj* (*worried*) preoccupato; (*constrained*) scomodo; (*not conducive to ease*) inquietante, a disagio

**uneatable** [ʌn'itəbəl] *adj* immangiabile

**uneconomic(al)** [ˌʌnikə'nɑmɪk(əl)] or [ˌʌnɛkə'nɑmɪk(əl)] *adj* antieconomico

**uneducated** [ʌn'ɛdjə ˌketɪd] *adj* ineducato

**unemployed** [ˌʌnɛm'plɔɪd] *adj* disoccupato, incollocato; improduttivo ‖ **the unemployed** i disoccupati

**unemployment** [ˌʌnɛm'plɔɪmənt] *s* disimpiego, disoccupazione

**unemploy'ment compensa'tion** *s* sussidio di disoccupazione

**unending** [ʌn'ɛndɪŋ] *adj* interminabile

**unequal** [ʌn'ikwəl] *adj* disuguale, impari; **to be unequal to** (*a task*) non essere all'altezza di

**unequaled** or **unequalled** [ʌn'ikwəld] *adj* ineguagliato

**unerring** [ʌn'ʌrɪŋ] or [ʌn'ɛrɪŋ] *adj* infallibile; corretto, preciso

**unessential** [ˌʌnɛ'sɛnfəl] *adj* non essenziale

**uneven** [ʌn'ivən] *adj* disuguale, ineguale; (*number*) dispari

**uneventful** [ˌʌnɪ'vɛntfəl] *adj* senza avvenimenti importanti; (*life*) tranquillo

**unexceptionable** [ˌʌnɛk'sɛpfənəbəl] *adj* ineccepibile, irreprensibile

**unexpected** [ˌʌnɛk'spɛktɪd] *adj* inospettato, imprevisto

**unexplained** [ˌʌnɛk'splend] *adj* inesplicato

**unexplored** [ˌʌnɛk'splord] *adj* inesplorato

**unexposed** [ˌʌnɛk'spozd] *adj* (phot) non esposto alla luce

**unfading** [ʌn'fedɪŋ] *adj* immarcescibile; imperituro

**unfailing** [ʌn'felɪŋ] *adj* immancabile, infallibile; (*inexhaustible*) inesauribile; (*dependable*) sicuro

**unfair** [ʌn'fɛr] *adj* ingiusto; disonesto, sleale

**unfaithful** [ʌn'feθfəl] *adj* infedele

**unfamiliar** [ˌʌnfə'mɪljər] *adj* poco pratico; poco abituale, strano; non conosciuto

**unfasten** [ʌn'fæsən] or [ʌn'fasən] *tr* sfibbiare, sciogliere

**unfathomable** [ʌn'fæðəməbəl] *adj* insondabile

**unfavorable** [ʌn'fevərəbəl] *adj* sfavorevole

**unfeeling** [ʌn'filɪŋ] *adj* insensibile

**unfetter** [ʌn'fɛtər] *tr* sciogliere dalle catene

**unfinished** [ʌn'fɪnɪʃt] *adj* incompiuto; grezzo, non rifinito; (*business*) inevaso

**unfit** [ʌn'fɪt] *adj* disadatto; inabile

**unfledged** [ʌn'flɛdʒd] *adj* implume

**unfold** [ʌn'fold] *tr* schiudere; (*e.g., a newspaper*) spiegare ‖ *intr* schiudersi; svolgersi

**unforeseeable** [ˌʌnfor'si·əbəl] *adj* imprevedibile

**unforeseen** [ˌʌnfor'sin] *adj* imprevisto

**unforgettable** [ˌʌnfər'gɛtəbəl] *adj* indimenticabile

**unforgivable** [ˌʌnfər'gɪvəbəl] *adj* imperdonabile

**unfortunate** [ʌn'fɔrtjənɪt] *adj & s* disgraziato, sfortunato

**unfounded** [ʌn'faundɪd] *adj* infondato

**un-freeze** [ʌn'friz] *v* (*pret* **-froze;** *pp* **-frozen**) *tr* disgelare; (*credit*) sbloccare

**unfriend-ly** [ʌn'frɛndli] *adj* (**-lier; -liest**) *adj* mal disposto, ostile; sfavorevole

**unfruitful** [ʌn'frutfəl] *adj* infruttuoso

**unfulfilled** [ˌʌnfəl'fɪld] *adj* incompiuto

**unfurl** [ʌn'fʌrl] *tr* spiegare, dispiegare

**unfurnished** [ʌn'fʌrnɪʃt] *adj* smobiliato

**ungainly** [ʌn'genli] *adj* sgraziato, maldestro

**ungentlemanly** [ʌn'dʒɛntəlmənli] *adj* indegno di un gentleman

**ungird** [ʌn'gʌrd] *tr* discingere

**ungodly** [ʌn'gɑdli] *adj* irreligioso, empio; (*dreadful*) (coll) atroce

**ungracious** [ʌn'greʃəs] *adj* rude, scortese; (*task*) sgradevole

**ungrammatical** [ˌʌngrə'mætɪkəl] *adj* sgrammaticato

**ungrateful** [ʌn'gretfəl] *adj* ingrato

**ungrudgingly** [ʌn'grʌdʒɪŋli] *adv* di buon grado, volentieri

**unguarded** [ʌn'gardɪd] *adj* incustodito, indifeso; incauto, imprudente

**unguent** ['ʌŋgwənt] *s* unguento

**unhappiness** [ʌn'hæpɪnɪs] *s* infelicità *f*

**unhap-py** [ʌn'hæpi] *adj* (**-pier; -piest**) infelice, sfortunato

**unharmed** [ʌn'harmd] *adj* illeso

**unharness** [ʌn'harnɪs] *tr* togliere i finimenti a

**unhealth-y** [ʌn'hɛlθi] *adj* (**-ier; -iest**) malsano

**unheard-of** [ʌn'hʌrd ˌɑv] *adj* (*unknown*) sconosciuto; inaudito

**unhinge** [ʌn'hɪndʒ] *tr* sgangherare; (fig) sconvolgere

**unhitch** [ʌn'hɪtʃ] *tr* sganciare; (*a horse*) staccare

**unho-ly** [ʌn'holi] *adj* (**-lier; -liest**) empio; terribile, atroce

**unhook** [ʌn'huk] *tr* sganciare

**unhoped-for** [ʌn'hopt ˌfɔr] *adj* insperato

**unhorse** [ʌn'hɔrs] *tr* disarcionare

unhurt [ʌn'hʌrt] *adj* incolume, illeso
unicorn ['junɪ,kɔrn] *s* unicorno
unification [,junɪfɪ'keʃən] *s* unificazione
uniform ['junɪ,fɔrm] *adj* & *s* uniforme *f* || *tr* uniformare
uni·fy ['junɪ,faɪ] *v* (*pret* & *pp* -fied) *tr* unificare
unilateral [,junɪ'lætərəl] *adj* unilaterale
unimpeachable [,ʌnɪm'pitʃəbəl] *adj* irrefutabile; irreprensibile
unimportant [,ʌnɪm'pɔrtənt] *adj* poco importante
uninhabited [,ʌnɪn'hæbɪtɪd] *adj* inabitato, disabitato
uninspired [,ʌnɪn'spaɪrd] *adj* senza ispirazione, prosaico
unintelligent [,ʌnɪn'tɛlɪdʒənt] *adj* non intelligente; stupido
unintelligible [,ʌnɪn'tɛlɪdʒɪbəl] *adj* inintelligibile
uninterested [ʌn'ɪntrɪstɪd] or [ʌn-'ɪntə,rɛstɪd] *adj* non interessato
uninteresting [ʌn'ɪntrɪstɪŋ] or [ʌn-'ɪntə,rɛstɪŋ] *adj* poco interessante
uninterrupted [,ʌnɪntə'rʌptɪd] *adj* ininterrotto
union ['junjən] *s* unione; unione matrimoniale; (*of workers*) sindacato
unionize ['junjə,naɪz] *tr* organizzare in un sindacato || *intr* organizzarsi in un sindacato
un'ion shop' *s* fabbrica che assume solo sindacalisti
un'ion suit' *s* combinazione
unique [ju'nik] *adj* unico
unison ['junɪsən] or ['junɪzən] *s* unisono; in unison all'unisono
unit ['junɪt] *adj* unitario || *s* unità *f*; (mach, elec) gruppo
unite [ju'naɪt] *tr* unire || *intr* unirsi
united [ju'naɪtɪd] *adj* unito
Unit'ed King'dom *s* Regno Unito
Unit'ed Na'tions *spl* Organizzazione delle Nazioni Unite
Unit'ed States' *adj* statunitense || the United States *ssg* gli Stati Uniti
uni·ty ['junɪti] *s* (-ties) unità *f*
universal [,junɪ'vʌrsəl] *adj* universale
u'niver'sal joint' *s* giunto cardanico
universe ['junɪ,vʌrs] *s* universo
universi·ty [,junɪ'vʌrsɪti] *adj* universitario || *s* (-ties) università *f*
unjust [ʌn'dʒʌst] *adj* ingiusto
unjustified [ʌn'dʒʌstɪ,faɪd] *adj* ingiustificato
unkempt [ʌn'kɛmpt] *adj* spettinato; trascurato
unkind [ʌn'kaɪnd] *adj* scortese; duro, crudele
unknowable [ʌn'no·əbəl] *adj* inconoscibile
unknowingly [ʌn'no·ɪŋli] *adv* inconsapevolmente
unknown [ʌn'non] *adj* sconosciuto || *s* incognito; (math) incognita
Un'known Sol'dier *s* Milite Ignoto
unlace [ʌn'les] *tr* slacciare
unlatch [ʌn'lætʃ] *tr* tirare il saliscendi a
unlawful [ʌn'lɔfəl] *adj* illegale

unleash [ʌn'liʃ] *tr* sguinzagliare; (fig) scatenare
unleavened [ʌn'lɛvənd] *adj* azzimo
unless [ʌn'lɛs] *conj* se non che, salvo che
unlettered [ʌn'lɛtərd] *adj* ignorante; (*illiterate*) analfabeta
unlike [ʌn'laɪk] *adj* dissimile, differente; dissimile da, e.g., **a copy unlike the original** una copia dissimile dall'originale; (elec) di segno contrario || *prep* diversamente da, a differenza di; **it was unlike him to arrive late** non era cosa normale per lui arrivare in ritardo
unlikely [ʌn'laɪkli] *adj* improbabile
unlimber [ʌn'lɪmbər] *tr* mettere in batteria || *intr* prepararsi a fare fuoco; (fig) prepararsi
unlimited [ʌn'lɪmɪtɪd] *adj* illimitato
unlined [ʌn'laɪnd] *adj* (*e.g., coat*) non foderato; (*paper*) non rigato
unload [ʌn'lod] *tr* scaricare; (*passengers*) sbarcare; (*to get rid of*) liberarsi di || *intr* scaricare; sbarcare
unloading [ʌn'lodɪŋ] *s* discarica; sbarco
unlock [ʌn'lak] *tr* aprire
unloose [ʌn'lus] *tr* rilasciare; sciogliere
unloved [ʌn'lʌvd] *adj* poco amato
unlovely [ʌn'lʌvli] *adj* poco attraente
unluck·y [ʌn'lʌki] *adj* (-ier; -iest) sfortunato, disgraziato
un·make [ʌn'mek] *v* (*pret* & *pp* -made ['med]) *tr* disfare; deporre
unmanageable [ʌn'mænɪdʒəbəl] *adj* incontrollabile
unmanly [ʌn'mænli] *adj* non virile, effeminato; codardo
unmannerly [ʌn'mænərli] *adj* scortese
unmarketable [ʌn'markɪtəbəl] *adj* invendibile
unmarriageable [ʌn'mærɪdʒəbəl] *adj* che non si può sposare; non adatto al matrimonio
unmarried [ʌn'mærɪd] *adj* scapolo; (*female*) nubile
unmask [ʌn'mæsk] or [ʌn'mask] *tr* smascherare || *intr* smascherarsi
unmatchable [ʌn'mætʃəbəl] *adj* impareggiabile
unmatched [ʌn'mætʃd] *adj* impareggiabile; (*unpaired*) sparigliato
unmentionable [ʌn'mɛnʃənəbəl] *adj* innominabile
unmerciful [ʌn'mʌrsɪfəl] *adj* spietato
unmesh [ʌn'mɛʃ] *tr* disingranare || *intr* disingranarsi
unmindful [ʌn'maɪndfəl] *adj* immemore; incurante
unmistakable [,ʌnmɪs'tekəbəl] *adj* inconfondibile
unmitigated [ʌn'mɪtɪ,getɪd] *adj* completo; assoluto, perfetto
unmixed [ʌn'mɪkst] *adj* puro
unmoor [ʌn'mur] *tr* disormeggiare
unmoved [ʌn'muvd] *adj* immoto; fisso, immobile; (fig) impassibile
unmuzzle [ʌn'mʌzəl] *tr* togliere la museruola a
unnamed [ʌn'nemd] *adj* innominato
unnatural [ʌn'nætʃərəl] *adj* contro natura, snaturato; innaturale, affettato

**unnecessary** [ʌn'nɛsə‚sɛri] *adj* inutile

**unnerve** [ʌn'nʌrv] *tr* snervare

**unnoticeable** [ʌn'notɪsəbəl] *adj* impercettibile

**unnoticed** [ʌn'notɪst] *adj* inosservato

**unobserved** [‚ʌnəb'zʌrvd] *adj* inosservato

**unobtainable** [‚ʌnəb'tenəbəl] *adj* non ottenibile, irraggiungibile

**unobtrusive** [‚ʌnəb'trusɪv] *adj* discreto, riservato

**unoccupied** [ʌn'akjə‚paɪd] *adj* libero, disponibile; (*not busy*) disoccupato

**unofficial** [‚ʌnə'fɪʃəl] *adj* non ufficiale, ufficioso

**unopened** [ʌn'opənd] *adj* non aperto, chiuso; (*letter*) non dissuggellato; (*book*) intonso

**unorthodox** [ʌn'ɔrθə‚daks] *adj* non ortodosso

**unpack** [ʌn'pæk] *tr* spaccare, sballare

**unpalatable** [ʌn'pælətəbəl] *adj* di gusto spiacevole

**unparalleled** [ʌn'pærə‚lɛld] *adj* incomparabile, senza pari

**unpardonable** [ʌn'pardənəbəl] *adj* imperdonabile

**unpatriotic** [‚ʌnpetri'atɪk] or [‚ʌnpætri'atɪk] *adj* antipatriottico

**unperceived** [‚ʌnpər'sivd] *adj* inosservato

**unperturbable** [‚ʌnpər'tʌrbəbəl] *adj* imperterrito, imperturbato

**unpleasant** [ʌn'plɛsənt] *adj* spiacevole; (*person*) antipatico

**unpopular** [ʌn'papjələr] *adj* impopolare

**unpopularity** [ʌn‚papjə'lærɪti] *s* impopolarità *f*

**unprecedented** [ʌn'prɛsɪ‚dɛntɪd] *adj* senza precedenti, inaudito

**unprejudiced** [ʌn'prɛdʒədɪst] *adj* senza pregiudizio, imparziale

**unpremeditated** [‚ʌnpri'mɛdɪ‚tɛtɪd] *adj* impremeditato

**unprepared** [‚ʌnprɪ'pɛrd] *adj* impreparato

**unprepossessing** [‚ʌnpripə'zɛsɪŋ] *adj* poco attraente, antipatico

**unpresentable** [‚ʌnprɪ'zɛntəbəl] *adj* impresentabile

**unpretentious** [‚ʌnprɪ'tɛnʃəs] *adj* modesto, senza pretese

**unprincipled** [ʌn'prɪnsɪpəld] *adj* senza principi

**unproductive** [‚ʌnprə'dʌktɪv] *adj* improduttivo

**unprofitable** [ʌn'prafɪtəbəl] *adj* infruttuoso

**unpronounceable** [‚ʌnprə'naunsəbəl] *adj* impronunziabile

**unpropitious** [‚ʌnprə'pɪʃəs] *adj* inauspicato

**unpublished** [ʌn'pʌblɪʃt] *adj* inedito

**unpunished** [ʌn'pʌnɪʃt] *adj* impunito

**unqualified** [ʌn'kwalɪ‚faɪd] *adj* inabile, inidoneo; assoluto, completo

**unquenchable** [ʌn'kwɛntʃəbəl] *adj* inappagabile, inestinguibile

**unquestionable** [ʌn'kwɛstʃənəbəl] *adj* indiscutibile

**unrav·el** [ʌn'rævəl] *v* (*pret & pp* **-eled**

or **-elled**; *ger* **-eling** or **-elling**) *tr* dipanare ‖ *intr* districarsi; chiarirsi

**unreachable** [ʌn'ritʃəbəl] *adj* irraggiungibile

**unreal** [ʌn'ri·əl] *adj* irreale

**unreali·ty** [‚ʌnrɪ'ælɪti] *s* (**-ties**) irrealità *f*

**unreasonable** [ʌn'rizənəbəl] *adj* irragionevole

**unrecognizable** [ʌn'rɛkəg‚naɪzəbəl] *adj* irriconoscibile

**unreel** [ʌn'ril] *tr* svolgere, srotolare ‖ *intr* srotolarsi

**unrefined** [‚ʌnrɪ'faɪnd] *adj* non raffinato, greggio; volgare, ordinario

**unrelenting** [‚ʌnrɪ'lɛntɪŋ] *adj* inesorabile, inflessibile; indefesso

**unreliable** [‚ʌnrɪ'laɪ·əbəl] *adj* malfido; (*news*) inattendibile

**unremitting** [‚ʌnrɪ'mɪtɪŋ] *adj* incessante, costante

**unrented** [ʌn'rɛntɪd] *adj* da affittare

**unrepeatable** [‚ʌnrɪpitəbəl] *adj* irripetibile

**unrepentant** [‚ʌnrɪ'pɛntənt] *adj* impenitente

**un'requit'ed love'** [‚ʌnrɪ'kwaɪtɪd] *s* amore non corrisposto

**unresponsive** [‚ʌnrɪ'spansɪv] *adj* apatico, insensibile

**unrest** [ʌn'rɛst] *s* agitazione

**un·rig** [ʌn'rɪg] *v* (*pret & pp* **-rigged**; *ger* **-rigging**) *tr* (naut) disarmare

**unrighteous** [ʌn'raɪtʃəs] *adj* ingiusto

**unripe** [ʌn'raɪp] *adj* immaturo

**unrivaled** or **unrivalled** [ʌn'raɪvəld] *adj* senza pari

**unroll** [ʌn'rol] *tr* srotolare

**unromantic** [‚ʌnro'mæntɪk] *adj* poco romantico

**unruffled** [ʌn'rʌfəld] *adj* calmo, imperturbabile

**unruly** [ʌn'ruli] *adj* turbolento; indisciplinato, insubordinato

**unsaddle** [ʌn'sædəl] *tr* (*a horse*) dissellare; (*a rider*) scavalcare

**unsafe** [ʌn'sef] *adj* malsicuro, pericolante

**unsaid** [ʌn'sɛd] *adj* non detto, taciuto; **to leave unsaid** passare sotto silenzio

**unsalable** [ʌn'seləbəl] *adj* invendibile

**unsanitary** [ʌn'sænɪ‚tɛri] *adj* antigienico

**unsatisfactory** [ʌn‚sætɪs'fæktəri] *adj* poco soddisfacente

**unsatisfied** [ʌn'sætɪs‚faɪd] *adj* insoddisfatto, inappagato

**unsavory** [ʌn'sevəri] *adj* insipido; (fig) disgustoso, nauseabondo

**un·say** [ʌn'se] *v* (*pret & pp* **-said** [sɛd']) *tr* disdire

**unscathed** [ʌn'skeðd] *adj* incolume

**unscheduled** [ʌn'skɛdjuld] *adj* non in elenco; (*event*) fuori programma; (*e.g., flight*) fuori orario; (*phase of production*) non programmato

**unscientific** [‚ʌnsaɪ·ən'tɪfɪk] *adj* poco scientifico

**unscrew** [ʌn'skru] *tr* svitare ‖ *intr* svitarsi

**unscrupulous** [ʌn'skrupjələs] *adj* senza scrupoli

**unseal** [ʌn'sil] *tr* dissigillare

**unseasonable** [ʌn'sizənəbəl] *adj* fuori stagione; inopportuno

**unseasoned** [ʌn'sizənd] *adj* scondito; (*crop*) immaturo; (*crew*) inesperto

**unseat** [ʌn'sit] *tr* (*a rider*) scavalcare, disarcionare; (*e.g., a congressman*) far perdere il seggio a, defenestrare

**unseemly** [ʌn'simli] *adj* disdicevole, sconveniente

**unseen** [ʌn'sin] *adj* non visto, inosservato; nascosto, occulto; invisibile

**unselfish** [ʌn'sɛlfɪʃ] *adj* disinteressato

**unsettled** [ʌn'sɛtəld] *adj* disabitato; disorganizzato; disordinato, erratico; indeciso; (*bill*) da pagare

**unshackle** [ʌn'ʃækəl] *tr* liberare

**unshaken** [ʌn'ʃekən] *adj* inconcusso

**unshapely** [ʌn'ʃepli] *adj* senza forma, deforme

**unshaven** [ʌn'ʃevən] *adj* non rasato

**unshatterable** [ʌn'ʃætərəbəl] *adj* infrangibile

**unsheathe** [ʌn'ʃið] *tr* sguainare

**unshod** [ʌn'ʃad] *adj* scalzo; (*horse*) sferrato

**unshrinkable** [ʌn'ʃrɪŋkəbəl] *adj* irrestringibile

**unsightly** [ʌn'saitli] *adj* ripugnante, brutto

**unsinkable** [ʌn'sɪŋkəbəl] *adj* insommergibile

**unskilled** [ʌn'skɪld] *adj* inesperto

**un'skilled la'bor** *s* lavoro manuale; mano d'opera non specializzata

**unskillful** [ʌn'skɪlfəl] *adj* maldestro

**unsnarl** [ʌn'snarl] *tr* sbrogliare

**unsociable** [ʌn'soʃəbəl] *adj* insocievole

**unsold** [ʌn'sold] *adj* invenduto

**unsolder** [ʌn'sadər] *tr* dissaldare

**unsophisticated** [ˌʌnsə'fɪstɪˌketɪd] *adj* semplice, puro

**unsound** [ʌn'saund] *adj* malsano, malato; (*decayed*) guasto, imputridito; falso, fallace; (*sleep*) leggero

**unsown** [ʌn'son] *adj* incolto, non seminato

**unspeakable** [ʌn'spikəbəl] *adj* indicibile; (*atrocious*) innominabile, inqualificabile

**unsportsmanlike** [ʌn'sportsmən ˌlaik] *adj* antisportivo

**unstable** [ʌn'stebəl] *adj* instabile

**unsteady** [ʌn'stɛdi] *adj* malfermo; incostante; irregolare

**unstinted** [ʌn'stɪntɪd] *adj* generoso, senza limiti

**unstitch** [ʌn'stɪtʃ] *tr* scucire

**un-stop** [ʌn'stap] *v* (*pret & pp* -stopped; *ger* -stopping) *tr* stasare

**unstressed** [ʌn'strɛst] *adj* non accentuato; (*e.g., syllable*) non accentato

**unstrung** [ʌn'strʌŋ] *adj* (*beads*) sfilato; (*instrument*) allentato; (*person*) snervato

**unsuccessful** [ˌʌnsək'sɛsfəl] *adj* (*person*) sfortunato; (*deal*) mancato; **to be unsuccessful** fallire

**unsuitable** [ʌn'sutəbəl] or [ʌn'sjutəbəl] *adj* inappropriato

**unsurpassable** [ʌnsər'pæsəbəl] or [ˌʌnsər'pasəbəl] *adj* insuperabile

**unsuspected** [ˌʌnsəs'pɛktɪd] *adj* insospettato

**unswerving** [ʌn'swʌrvɪŋ] *adj* diritto, fermo, costante

**unsympathetic** [ˌʌnsɪmpə'θɛtɪk] *adj* indifferente, che non mostra comprensione

**unsystematic(al)** [ˌʌnsɪstə'mætɪk(əl)] *adj* senza sistema

**untactful** [ʌn'tæktfəl] *adj* senza tatto

**untamed** [ʌn'temd] *adj* indomito

**untangle** [ʌn'tæŋgəl] *tr* sgrovigliare

**unteachable** [ʌn'titʃəbəl] *adj* indocile; refrattario agli studi

**untenable** [ʌn'tɛnəbəl] *adj* insostenibile

**unthankful** [ʌn'θæŋkfəl] *adj* ingrato

**unthinkable** [ʌn'θɪŋkəbəl] *adj* impensabile

**unthinking** [ʌn'θɪŋkɪŋ] *adj* irriflessivo

**untidy** [ʌn'taidi] *adj* disordinato

**un-tie** [ʌn'tai] *v* (*pret & pp* -tied; *ger* -tying) *tr* sciogliere; (*a knot*) slacciare, snodare ǁ *intr* sciogliersi

**until** [ʌn'tɪl] *prep* fino, fino a ǁ *conj* fino a che, finché

**untillable** [ʌn'tɪləbəl] *adj* incoltivabile

**untimely** [ʌn'taimli] *adj* intempestivo; (*death*) prematuro

**untiring** [ʌn'tairɪŋ] *adj* instancabile

**untold** [ʌn'told] *adj* non detto, non raccontato; incalcolabile; (*inexpressable*) indicibile

**untouchable** [ʌn'tʌtʃəbəl] *adj & s* intoccabile *mf*

**untouched** [ʌn'tʌtʃt] *adj* intatto; insensibile; non menzionato

**untoward** [ʌn'tord] *adj* sfavorevole; sconveniente, disdicevole

**untrammeled** or **untrammelled** [ʌn'træməld] *adj* non inceppato

**untried** [ʌn'traid] *adj* non provato

**untroubled** [ʌn'trʌbləd] *adj* tranquillo

**untrue** [ʌn'tru] *adj* falso

**untrustworthy** [ʌn'trʌstˌwʌrði] *adj* infido, malfido

**untruth** [ʌn'truθ] *s* falsità *f*, menzogna

**untruthful** [ʌn'truθfəl] *adj* falso, menzognero

**untwist** [ʌn'twist] *tr* districare ǁ *intr* districarsi

**unusable** [ʌn'juzəbəl] *adj* inservibile

**unused** [ʌn'juzd] *adj* inutilizzato; **unused to** [ʌn'justu] disavvezzo a

**unusual** [ʌn'juʒuəl] *adj* insolito

**unutterable** [ʌn'ʌtərəbəl] *adj* impronunciabile; indicibile

**unvanquished** [ʌn'væŋkwɪʃt] *adj* invitto

**unvarnished** [ʌn'varnɪʃt] *adj* non verniciato; puro, semplice

**unveil** [ʌn'vel] *tr* svelare; (*a statue*) scoprire, inaugurare ǁ *intr* scoprirsi

**unveiling** [ˌʌn'velɪŋ] *s* scoprimento

**unvoiced** [ʌn'vɔist] *adj* non espresso; (*phonet*) sordo

**unwanted** [ʌn'wantɪd] *adj* non desiderato

**unwarranted** [ʌn'warəntɪd] *adj* ingiustificato

**unwary** [ʌn'wɛri] *adj* incauto

**unwavering** [ʌn'wevərɪŋ] *adj* fermo, incrollabile

**unwelcome** [ʌn'wɛlkəm] *adj* malaccetto, sgradito

**unwell** [ʌn'wɛl] *adj* poco bene; **to be**

**unwell** (*said of a woman*) (coll) avere le mestruazioni

**unwholesome** [ʌn'holsəm] *adj* malsano

**unwieldy** [ʌn'wildi] *adj* ingombrante

**unwilling** [ʌn'wɪlɪŋ] *adj* riluttante

**unwillingly** [ʌn'wɪlɪŋli] *adv* a malincuore, a controvoglia

**un·wind** [ʌn'waɪnd] *v* (*pret & pp* -wound ['waʊnd]) *tr* svolgere || *intr* svolgersi; (*said of a watch*) scaricarsi; (*said of a person*) rilasciarsi

**unwise** [ʌn'waɪz] *adj* malaccorto

**unwished-for** [ʌn'wɪʃt‚fɔr] *adj* indesiderato, non augurato

**unwitting** [ʌn'wɪtɪŋ] *adj* involontario

**unwonted** [ʌn'wʌntɪd] *adj* insolito

**unworldly** [ʌn'wʌrdli] *adj* (*not of this world*) non terrestre; (*not interested in things of this world*) non mondano; (*naive*) semplice

**unworthy** [ʌn'wʌrði] *adj* indegno

**un·wrap** [ʌn'ræp] *v* (*pret & pp* -wrapped; *ger* -wrapping) *tr* scartare, svolgere, scartocciare

**unwrinkled** [ʌn'rɪŋkəld] *adj* senza una grinza

**unwritten** [ʌn'rɪtən] *adj* orale; non scritto; (*blank*) in bianco

**unyielding** [ʌn'jildɪŋ] *adj* inflessibile

**unyoke** [ʌn'jok] *tr* liberare dal giogo

**up** [ʌp] *adj* che va verso la città; diretto al nord; al corrente; finito, terminato; su; (sports) pari; **to be up and about** essere in piedi || *s* salita; vantaggio; aumento; **ups and downs** alti e bassi *mpl* || *adv* su; in alto; alla pari; **to be up** essere alzato; (*in sports or games*) essere avanti; **to be up in arms** essere in armi; essere indignato; **to be up to a person** toccare a una persona; **to get up** alzarsi; **to go up** salire; **to keep up** mantenere; continuare; **to keep up with** mantenersi alla pari con; **up above** lassù; **up against** (coll) contro; **up against it** (coll) in una strettoia; **up to** fino a; (*capable of*) (coll) all'altezza di; (*scheming*) (coll) tramando; **what's up?** che succede? || *prep* su; sopra; fino a; **to go up a river** risalire un fiume

**up-and-coming** ['ʌpən'kʌmɪŋ] *adj* promettente

**up-and-doing** ['ʌpən'du·ɪŋ] *adj* (coll) intraprendente; (coll) attivo

**up-and-up** ['ʌpən'ʌp] *s*—**on the up-and-up** (coll) aperto; (coll) apertamente; (coll) in ascesa

**up·braid'** *tr* rimproverare, strapazzare

**upbringing** ['ʌp‚brɪŋɪŋ] *s* educazione

**up'coun'try** *adj* all'interno || *s* interno || *adv* verso l'interno

**up·date'** *tr* aggiornare

**upheaval** [ʌp'hivəl] *s* sommovimento; (geol) sconvolgimento tellurico

**up'hill'** *adj* erto, scosceso; arduo, faticoso || *adv* in salita, all'insù

**up·hold'** *v* (*pret & pp* -held) *tr* alzare; sostenere; difendere

**upholster** [ʌp'holstər] *tr* tappezzare

**upholsterer** [ʌp'holstərər] *s* tappezziere *m*

**upholster·y** [ʌp'holstəri] *s* (-ies) tap-

pezzeria; (*e.g., of cushions*) imbottitura; (aut) selleria

**up'keep'** *s* manutenzione; **spese** *fpl* **di** manutenzione

**upland** ['ʌplənd] or ['ʌplænd] *adj* alto, elevato || *s* terreno elevato

**up'lift'** *s* elevazione; miglioramento sociale; edificazione || **up'lift'** *tr* elevare

**upon** [ʌ'pɑn] *prep* su, sopra, in; **upon** + *ger* non appena + *pp*, e.g., **upon arising** non appena alzato; **upon my word!** sulla mia parola!

**upper** ['ʌpər] *adj* superiore, disopra; (*town*) soprano; (*river*) alto || *s* disopra *m*; (*of shoe*) tomaia; (rr) (coll) cuccetta; **on one's uppers** ridotto al verde

**up'per berth'** *s* cuccetta superiore

**up'per case'** *s* (typ) cassa delle maiuscole, cassa superiore

**up'per-case'** *adj* (typ) maiuscolo

**up'per classes'** *spl* classi *fpl* elevate

**up'per hand'** *s* vantaggio; **to have the upper hand** prendere il disopra

**up'per·most'** *adj* (il) più alto; principale || *adv* principalmente, in primo luogo

**uppish** ['ʌpɪʃ] *adj* (coll) arrogante, snob

**up·raise'** *tr* alzare, tirare su

**up'right'** *adj* ritto, verticale; dabbene, onesto || *s* staggio, montante *m* || *adv* verticalmente

**uprising** [ʌp'raɪzɪŋ] or ['ʌp‚raɪzɪŋ] *s* sollevazione, insurrezione

**up'roar'** *s* gazzarra, cagnara, fracasso

**uproarious** [ʌp'rori·əs] *adj* tumultuoso; (*noisy*) rumoroso; (*funny*) comico

**up·root'** *tr* sradicare

**up·set'** *adj* rovesciato; scompigliato; (*emotionally*) scombussolato; (*stomach*) imbarazzato || **up'set'** *s* (*overturn*) rovesciamento; (*defeat*) rovescio; (*disorder*) scompiglio; (*illness*) imbarazzo, disturbo || **up·set'** *v* (*pret & pp* -set; *ger* -setting) *tr* rovesciare; scompigliare; indisporre || *intr* rovesciarsi, ribaltarsi

**upset' price'** *s* prezzo minimo di vendita di un oggetto all'asta

**upsetting** [ʌp'sɛtɪŋ] *adj* sconcertante

**up'shot'** *s* conclusione; essenziale *m*

**up'side'** *s* disopra *m*

**up'side down'** *adv* alla rovescia; **a gambe all'aria;** a soqquadro

**up'stage'** *adj* al fondo della scena; altiero, arrogante || *adv* al fondo della scena || *tr* trattare altezzosamente; (theat) rubare la scena a

**up'stairs'** *adj* del piano di sopra || *s* piano di sopra || *adv* su, al piano di sopra

**upstanding** [ʌp'stændɪŋ] *adj* diritto; forte; onorevole

**up'start'** *s* arrivato, nuovo ricco

**up'stream'** *adv* a monte, controcorrente

**up'stroke'** *s* (*in handwriting*) tratto ascendente; (mach) corsa ascendente

**up'swing'** *s* (*in prices*) ascesa; miglioramento; **to be on the upswing** migliorare

**up'-to-date'** *adj* recentissimo; moderno; dell'ultima ora

**up'town'** *adj* della parte più alta della città || *adv* nella parte più alta della città

**up'trend'** *s* tendenza al rialzo

**up'turn'** *s* rivolta; (com) rialzo

**upturned** [ˌʌpˈtʌrnd] *adj* rivolto all'insù; (*upside down*) capovolto

**upward** [ˈʌpwərd] *adj* ascendente || *adv* all'insù; **upward of** più di

**U'ral Moun'tains** [ˈjʊrəl] *spl* Urali *mpl*

**uranium** [jʊˈrenɪ·əm] *s* uranio

**urban** [ˈʌrbən] *adj* urbano

**urbane** [ʌrˈben] *adj* urbano

**urbanite** [ˈʌrbəˌnaɪt] *s* abitante *mf* di una città

**urbanity** [ʌrˈbænɪti] *s* urbanità *f*

**urbanize** [ˈʌrbəˌnaɪz] *tr* urbanizzare

**ur'ban renew'al** *s* ricostruzione urbanistica

**urchin** [ˈʌrtʃɪn] *s* monello, birichino

**ure·thra** [jʊˈriθrə] *s* (**-thras** or **-thrae** [θri]) uretra

**urge** [ʌrdʒ] *s* stimolo || *tr* urgere, sollecitare, spronare; (*to endeavor to persuade*) esortare; (*an enterprise*) accelerare || *intr*—**to urge against** opporsi a

**urgen·cy** [ˈʌrdʒənsi] *s* (**-cies**) urgenza

**urgent** [ˈʌrdʒənt] *adj* urgente; (*desire*) prepotente

**urinal** [ˈjʊrɪnəl] *s* (*receptacle*) orinale *m*; (*for a bedridden person*) pappagallo; (*place*) orinatoio, vespasiano

**urinary** [ˈjʊrɪˌnɛri] *adj* urinario

**urinate** [ˈjʊrɪˌnet] *tr & intr* orinare

**urine** [ˈjʊrɪn] *s* urina

**urn** [ʌrn] *s* urna; (*for making coffee*) caffettiera; (*for making tea*) samovar *m*

**urology** [jʊˈrɑlədʒi] *s* urologia

**Uruguay** [ˈjʊrəˌgwe] or [ˈjʊrəˌgwaɪ] *s* l'Uruguai *m*

**Uruguayan** [ˌjʊrəˈgwe·ən] or [ˌjʊrəˈgwaɪ·ən] *adj & s* uruguaiano

**us** [ʌs] *pron pers* ci; noi; **to us** ci, a noi, per noi

**U.S.A.** [ˈjuˈɛsˈe] *s* (letterword) (**United States of America**) S.U.A. *mpl*

**usable** [ˈjuzəbəl] *adj* servibile, adoperabile

**usage** [ˈjusɪdʒ] or [ˈjuzɪdʒ] *s* uso, usanza; (*of a language*) uso

**use** [jus] *s* uso, impiego, usanza; **in use** in uso, in servizio; **it's no use** non giova; **out of use** disusato; **to be of no use** non servire a nulla; **to have**

**no use for** non aver bisogno di; non poter soffrire; **to make use of** servirsi di; **what's the use?** a che pro? || [juz] *tr* usare, impiegare, servirsi di; **to use badly** maltrattare; **to use up** consumare, esaurire || *intr*—**used to** translated in Italian in three ways: (1) by the imperfect indicative, e.g., **he used to go to church at seven o'clock** andava in chiesa alle sette; (2) by the imperfect indicative of **solere**, e.g., **he used to smoke all day** soleva fumare tutto il giorno; (3) by the imperfect indicative of **avere l'abitudine di**, e.g., **he used to go to the shore** aveva l'abitudine di andare alla spiaggia

**used** [juzd] *adj* uso, usato; **to get used to** [ˈjuzdtʊ] or [ˈjustʊ] fare la mano a, abituarsi a

**useful** [ˈjusfəl] *adj* utile

**usefulness** [ˈjusfəlnɪs] *s* utilità *f*

**useless** [ˈjuslɪs] *adj* inutile, inservibile

**user** [ˈjuzər] *s* utente *mf*

**usher** [ˈʌʃər] *s* (*doorkeeper*) portiere *m*; (hist) cerimoniere *m*; (theat) maschera; (mov) lucciola || *tr* introdurre; **to usher in** annunciare, introdurre

**U.S.S.R.** [ˈjuˈɛsˈɛsˈɑr] *s* (letterword) (**Union of Soviet Socialist Republics**) U.R.S.S. *f*

**usual** [ˈjuʒʊ·əl] *adj* usuale, abituale; **as usual** come il solito

**usually** [ˈjuʒʊ·əli] *adj* usualmente

**usurp** [jʊˈzʌrp] *tr* usurpare

**usu·ry** [ˈjuʒəri] *s* (**-ries**) usura

**utensil** [jʊˈtɛnsɪl] *s* utensile *m*

**uter·us** [ˈjutərəs] *s* (**-i** [ˌaɪ]) utero

**utilitarian** [ˌjutɪlɪˈtɛri·ən] *adj* utilitario

**utili·ty** [jʊˈtɪlɪti] *s* (**-ties**) utilità *f*; compagnia di servizi pubblici

**utilize** [ˈjutɪˌlaɪz] *tr* utilizzare

**utmost** [ˈʌtˌmost] *adj* sommo; estremo; massimo || *s*—**the utmost** il massimo; **to do one's utmost** fare tutto il possibile; **to the utmost** al massimo limite

**utopia** [juˈtopɪ·ə] *s* utopia

**utopian** [juˈtopɪ·ən] *adj* utopistico || *s* utopista *mf*

**utter** [ˈʌtər] *adj* completo, totale || *tr* proferire, pronunziare; (*a sigh*) dare, fare

**utterly** [ˈʌtərli] *adj* completamente

**uxoricide** [ʌkˈsorɪˌsaɪd] *s* (*husband*) uxoricida *m*; (*act*) uxoricidio

**uxorious** [ʌkˈsorɪ·əs] *adj* eccessivamente innamorato della propria moglie; dominato dalla moglie

# V

**V, v** [vi] *s* ventiduesima lettera dell'alfabeto inglese

**vacan·cy** [ˈvekənsi] *s* (**-cies**) (*emptiness*) vuoto; (*unfilled position*) vacanza; (*unfilled job*) posto vacante; (*in a building*) appartamento libero;

(*in a hotel*) camera libera; **no vacancy** completo

**vacant** [ˈvekənt] *adj* (*empty*) vuoto; (*position*) vacante; (*expression of the face*) vago

**vacate** [ˈveket] *tr* sgombrare; (*a posi-*

*tion*) ritirarsi da; (law) annullare; **to vacate one's mind of worries** liberarsi dalle preoccupazioni ‖ *intr* sloggiare; (coll) andarsene

**vacation** [ve'keʃən] *s* vacanza, villeggiatura; **vacanze** *fpl* ‖ *intr* estivare, villeggiare

**vacationer** [ve'keʃənər] *s* villeggiante *mf*, vacanziere *m*

**vacationist** [ve'keʃənɪst] *s* villeggiante *mf*, vacanziere *m*

**vaca'tion with pay'** *s* vacanze *fpl* pagate

**vaccinate** ['væksɪ,net] *tr* vaccinare

**vaccination** [,væksɪ'neʃən] *s* vaccinazione

**vaccine** [væk'sin] *s* vaccino

**vacillate** ['væsɪ,let] *intr* vacillare

**vacillating** ['væsɪ,letɪŋ] *adj* vacillante

**vacui·ty** [væ'kjuˑɪti] *s* (-ties) vacuità *f*

**vacu·um** ['vækjuˑəm] *s* (-ums or -a [ə]) vuoto; **in a vacuum** sotto vuoto ‖ *tr* pulire con l'aspirapolvere

**vac'uum clean'er** *s* aspirapolvere *m*

**vac'uum-pack'ed** *adj* confezionato sotto vuoto

**vac'uum tube'** *s* tubo elettronico

**vagabond** ['vægə,bɑnd] *adj* & *s* vagabondo

**vagar·y** [və'gɛri] *s* (-ies) capriccio

**vagran·cy** ['vegrənsi] *s* (-cies) vagabondaggio

**vagrant** ['vegrənt] *adj* & *s* vagabondo

**vague** [veg] *adj* vago

**va'gus nerve'** ['vegəs] *s* (anat) vago

**vain** [ven] *adj* vano; (*conceited*) vanitoso; **in vain** in vano

**vainglorious** [ven'glɔrɪˑəs] *adj* vanaglorioso

**valance** ['væləns] *s* balza, mantovana

**vale** [vel] *s* valle *f*

**valedictorian** [,vælɪdɪk'tɔrɪˑən] *s* studente *m* che pronuncia il discorso di commiato

**valence** ['veləns] *s* (chem) valenza

**valentine** ['vælən,taɪn] *s* (*sweetheart*) valentino; (*card*) cartolina di San Valentino

**valet** ['vælɪt] or ['væle] *s* valletto

**valiant** ['væljənt] *adj* valoroso

**valid** ['vælɪd] *adj* valido

**validate** ['vælɪ,det] *tr* convalidare, vidimare; (sports) omologare

**validation** [,vælɪ'deʃən] *s* convalida, vidimazione; (sports) omologazione

**validi·ty** [və'lɪdɪti] *s* (-ties) validità *f*

**valise** [və'lis] *s* valigetta

**valley** ['væli] *s* valle *f*, vallata; (*of roof*) linea di compluvio

**valor** ['vælər] *s* valore *m*, coraggio

**valorous** ['vælərəs] *adj* valoroso

**valuable** ['væljuˑəbəl] or ['væljəbəl] *adj* (*having monetary worth*) prezioso; pregevole, pregiato ‖ **valuables** *spl* valori *mpl*

**value** ['vælju] *s* valore *m;* importanza; (com) valuta, valore *m;* **an excellent value** un acquisto eccellente ‖ *tr* stimare, valutare

**value'-added tax'** *s* imposta sul valore aggiunto

**valueless** ['væljulɪs] *adj* senza valore

**valve** [vælv] *s* (anat, mach, rad, telv)

valvola; (bot, zool) valva; (mus) pistone *m*

**valve' gears'** *spl* meccanismo di distribuzione

**valve'-in-head' en'gine** *s* motore *m* a valvole in testa

**valve' lift'er** ['lɪftər] *s* alzavalvole *m*

**valve' seat'** *s* sede *f* della valvola

**valve' spring'** *s* molla di valvola

**valve' stem'** *s* stelo di comando della valvola

**vamp** [væmp] *s* parte *f* anteriore della tomaia; (*patchwork*) rabberciatura; (*female*) vamp *f* ‖ *tr* (*a shoe*) rimontare; rabberciare; (*to concoct*) inventare, raffazzonare; (*an accompaniment*) improvvisare; (*said of a female*) sedurre

**vampire** ['væmpaɪr] *s* vampiro; (*female*) vamp *f*

**van** [væn] *s* camionetta, autofurgone *m;* (mil & fig) avanguardia

**vanadium** [və'nedɪˑəm] *s* vanadio

**vandal** ['vændəl] *adj* & *s* vandalo ‖ **Vandal** *adj* & *s* Vandalo

**vandalism** ['vændə,lɪzəm] *s* vandalismo

**vane** [ven] *s* (*weathervane*) banderuola; (*of windmill, of turbine*) pala; (*of feather*) barba

**vanguard** ['væn,gɑrd] *s* avanguardia; **in the vanguard** all'avanguardia

**vanilla** [və'nɪlə] *s* vaniglia

**vanish** ['vænɪʃ] *intr* svanire

**van'ishing cream'** ['vænɪʃɪŋ] *s* crema evanescente

**vani·ty** ['vænɪti] *s* (-ties) vanità *f;* (*table*) toletta; (*case*) astuccio di toletta

**vanquish** ['væŋkwɪʃ] *tr* superare, vincere

**van'tage ground'** ['væntɪdʒ] *s* posizione favorevole

**vapid** ['væpɪd] *adj* insipido

**vapor** ['vepər] *s* vapore *m;* (*visible vapor*) vapori *mpl*

**vaporize** ['vepə,raɪz] *tr* vaporizzare ‖ *intr* vaporizzarsi

**va'por lock'** *s* tampone *m* di vapore

**vaporous** ['vepərəs] *adj* vaporoso

**va'por trail'** *s* scia di condensazione

**variable** ['vɛrɪˑəbəl] *adj* & *s* variabile *f*

**variance** ['vɛrɪˑəns] *s* divario, differenza; **at variance with** (*a thing*) differente da; differentemente da; (*a person*) in disaccordo con

**variant** ['vɛrɪˑənt] *adj* & *s* variante *f*

**variation** [,vɛrɪ'eʃən] *s* variazione

**varicose** ['vɛrɪ,kos] *adj* varicoso

**varied** ['vɛrɪd] *adj* vario, svariato

**variegated** ['vɛrɪˑə,getɪd] or ['vɛrɪ,getɪd] *adj* variegato, screziato

**varie·ty** [və'raɪˑɪti] *s* (-ties) varietà *f*

**vari'ety show'** *s* spettacolo di varietà

**varnish** ['vɑrnɪʃ] *s* vernice *f* ‖ *tr* verniciare; (fig) dare la vernice a

**variola** [və'raɪˑələ] *s* (pathol) vaiolo

**various** ['vɛrɪˑəs] *adj* vari; (*vari-colored*) vario, variegato

**varsi·ty** ['vɑrsɪti] *adj* (sports) universitario ‖ *s* (-ties) (sports) squadra numero uno

**var·y** ['vεri] v (pret & pp -ied) tr & intr variare

**vase** [ves] or [vez] s vaso

**vaseline** ['væsə,lin] s (trademark) vaselina

**vassal** ['væsəl] adj & s vassallo

**vast** [væst] or [vɑst] adj vasto

**vastly** ['væstli] or ['vɑstli] adv enormemente

**vastness** ['væstnɪs] or ['vɑstnɪs] s vastità f

**vat** [væt] s tino, bigoncia

**Vatican** ['vætɪkən] adj vaticano || s Vaticano

**Vat'ican Cit'y** s Città f del Vaticano

**vaudeville** ['vodvɪl] or ['vɔdəvɪl] s spettacolo di varietà; (theatrical piece) vaudeville m, commedia musicale

**vault** [vɔlt] s volta; (underground chamber) cantina; (of a bank) camera di sicurezza; (burial chamber) cripta; (of heaven) cappa; (leap) salto || tr formare a mo' di volta; saltare || intr saltare

**vaunt** [vɔnt] or [vɑnt] s vanto, vanteria || tr vantarsi di || intr vantarsi

**veal** [vil] s vitello

**veal' chop'** s scaloppa, cotoletta di vitello

**veal' cut'let** s scaloppina

**vedette** [vɪ'dεt] s (nav) vedetta; (mil) sentinella avanzata

**veer** [vɪr] s virata || tr far cambiare di direzione a || intr virare; (said of the wind) cambiare di direzione

**vegetable** ['vεdʒɪtəbəl] adj vegetale || s (plant) vegetale m; (edible plant) ortaggio; **vegetables** verdura, erbe fpl, erbaggi mpl, ortaggi mpl

**veg'etable gar'den** s orto

**veg'etable soup'** s minestra di verdura

**vegetarian** [,vεdʒɪ'tεrɪ·ən] adj & s vegetariano

**vegetate** ['vεdʒɪ,tet] intr vegetare

**vehemence** ['vi·ɪməns] s veemenza

**vehement** ['vi·ɪmənt] adj veemente

**vehicle** ['vi·ɪkəl] s veicolo

**vehic'ular traf'fic** [vɪ'hɪkjələr] s circolazione stradale

**veil** [vel] s velo; **to take the veil** prendere il velo || tr velare

**vein** [ven] s vena; (streak) venatura; (of ore) filone m || tr venare

**velar** ['vilər] adj & s velare f

**vellum** ['vεləm] s pergamena

**veloci·ty** [vɪ'lɑsɪti] s (-ties) velocità f

**velvet** ['vεlvɪt] adj di velluto || s velluto; (slang) guadagno al gioco; (coll) situazione all'acqua di rose

**velveteen** [,vεlvɪ'tin] s vellutino di cotone

**velvety** ['vεlvɪti] adj vellutato

**vend** [vεnd] tr vendere; (to peddle) fare il venditore ambulante di

**vend'ing machine'** s distributore automatico

**vendor** ['vεndər] s venditore m

**veneer** [və'nɪr] s impiallacciatura, piallaccio; (fig) vernice f || tr impiallacciare

**venerable** ['vεnərəbəl] adj venerabile

**venerate** ['vεnə,ret] tr venerare

**venereal** [vɪ'nɪrɪ·əl] adj venereo

**Venetia** [vɪ'niʃɪ·ə] or [vɪ'niʃə] s (province) Venezia

**Venetian** [vɪ'niʃən] adj & s veneziano

**Vene'tian blind'** s veneziana, persiana avvolgibile

**Venezuelan** [,vεnɪ'zwilən] adj & s venezolano

**vengeance** ['vεndʒəns] s vendetta; **with a vengeance** violentemente; eccessivamente

**vengeful** ['vεndʒfəl] adj vendicativo

**Venice** ['vεnɪs] s Venezia

**venire·man** [vɪ'naɪrimən] s (-men) membro di un collegio di giurati

**venison** ['vεnɪsən] or ['vεnɪzən] s carne f di cervo

**venom** ['vεnəm] s veleno

**venomous** ['vεnəməs] adj velenoso

**vent** [vεnt] s sfiatatoio; (of jacket) spacco; **to give vent to** dare sfogo a || tr sfogare, sfuriare; mettere uno sfiatatoio a; **to vent one's spleen** sfogare la bile

**vent' hole'** s apertura di sfogo

**ventilate** ['vεntɪ,let] tr ventilare

**ventilator** ['vεntɪ,letər] s ventilatore m

**ventricle** ['vεntrɪkəl] s ventricolo

**ventriloquist** [vεn'trɪləkwɪst] s ventriloquo

**venture** ['vεntʃər] s azzardo, avventura rischiosa; **at a venture** alla ventura || tr avventurare || intr avventurarsi, arrischiarsi

**venturesome** ['vεntʃərsəm] adj (risky) rischioso; (daring) avventuroso

**venturous** ['vεntʃərəs] adj avventuroso

**vent' win'dow** s (aut) deflettore m

**venue** ['vεnju] s (law) posto dove ha avuto luogo il reato; (law) luogo dove si riunisce la corte; **change of venue** cambio di giurisdizione

**Venus** ['vinəs] s (very beautiful woman) venere f; (astr) Venere m; (myth) Venere f

**veracious** [vɪ'reʃəs] adj verace

**veraci·ty** [vɪ'ræsɪti] s (-ties) veridicità f

**veranda** or **verandah** [və'rændə] s veranda

**verb** [vʌrb] adj verbale || s verbo

**verbalize** ['vʌrbə,laɪz] tr esprimere con parole; (gram) convertire in forma verbale || intr essere verboso

**verbatim** [vər'betɪm] adj letterale || adv parola per parola, testualmente

**verbena** [vər'binə] s (bot) verbena

**verbiage** ['vʌrbɪ·ɪdʒ] s verbosità f; (style of wording) espressione

**verbose** [vər'bos] adj verboso

**verdant** ['vʌrdənt] adj verde, verdeggiante

**verdict** ['vʌrdɪkt] s verdetto

**verdigris** ['vʌrdɪ,gris] s verderame m

**verdure** ['vʌrdʒər] s verde m

**verge** [vʌrdʒ] s orlo, limite m; bordo; (of a column) fusto; **on the verge of** al punto di; all'orlo di || intr—**to verge on** costeggiare, rasentare

**verification** [,vεrɪfɪ'keʃən] s verifica

**veri·fy** ['vɛrɪ ˌfaɪ] v (pret & pp **-fied**) tr verificare, confermare

**verily** ['vɛrɪli] adv in verità

**veritable** ['vɛrɪtəbəl] adj vero

**vermilion** [vər'mɪljən] adj & s vermiglio

**vermin** ['vʌrmɪn] ssg (person) persona abominevole ‖ spl (animals or persons) insetti mpl

**vermouth** [vər'muθ] or ['vʌrmuθ] s vermut m

**vernacular** [vər'nækjələr] adj volgare ‖ s volgare m, vernacolo; (language peculiar to a class or profession) gergo

**versatile** ['vʌrsətɪl] adj (person) versatile; (tool or device) a vari usi

**verse** [vʌrs] s verso; (Bib) versetto

**versed** [vʌrst] adj versato

**versification** [ ˌvʌrsɪfɪ'keʃən] s versificazione

**versi·fy** ['vʌrsɪ ˌfaɪ] v (pret & pp **-fied**) tr & intr versificare

**version** ['vʌrʒən] s versione

**ver·so** ['vʌrso] s (**-sos**) (of coin) rovescio; (of page) verso

**versus** ['vʌrsəs] prep contro; in confronto a

**verte·bra** ['vʌrtɪbrə] s (**-brae** [ ˌbri] or **-bras**) vertebra

**vertebrate** ['vʌrtə ˌbret] adj & s vertebrato

**ver·tex** ['vʌrtɛks] s (**-texes** or **-tices** [tɪ ˌsiz]) vertice m

**vertical** ['vʌrtɪkəl] adj & s verticale f

**ver'tical hold'** s (telv) regolatore m del sincronismo verticale

**ver'tical sta'bilizer** s (aer) deriva

**verti·go** ['vʌrtɪ ˌgo] s (**-goes** or **-gos**) vertigine f

**verve** [vʌrv] s verve f, brio

**very** ['vʌri] adj (utter) grande, completo; (precise) vero e proprio; (mere) stesso, e.g., **his very brother** suo fratello stesso ‖ adv molto, e.g., **to be very rich** essere molto ricco

**vesicle** ['vesɪkəl] s vescichetta

**vesper** ['vespər] s vespro; **vespers** vespri mpl ‖ **Vesper** s Vespero

**ves'per bell'** s campana a vespro

**vessel** ['vesəl] s (ship) nave f, vascello; (container) vaso; (anat) vaso; (fig) vasello

**vest** [vest] s (of man's suit) panciotto, gilè m; (of woman's garment) corpino ‖ tr vestire; **to vest** (authority) in concedere a; **to vest with** investire di ‖ intr vestirsi; **to vest in** passare a

**vest'ed in'terest** s interesse acquisito

**vestibule** ['vestɪ ˌbjul] s vestibolo

**vestige** ['vestɪdʒ] s vestigio

**vestment** ['vestmənt] s (eccl) paramento

**vest'-pock'et** adj da tasca, tascabile

**ves·try** ['vestri] s (**-tries**) sagrestia; (chapel) cappella; giunta esecutiva della chiesa episcopaliana

**ves'try·man** s (**-men**) membro della giunta esecutiva della chiesa episcopaliana

**Vesuvius** [vɪ'suvɪ·əs] or [vɪ'sjuvɪ·əs] s il Vesuvio

**vetch** [vetʃ] s veccia; (grass pea) cicerchia

**veteran** ['vetərən] adj & s veterano

**veterinarian** [ ˌvetərɪ'nɛrɪ·ən] s veterinario

**veterinar·y** ['vetərɪ ˌnɛri] adj veterinario ‖ s (**-ies**) veterinario

**ve·to** ['vito] s (**-toes**) veto ‖ tr porre il veto a

**vex** [veks] tr irritare, tormentare

**vexation** [vek'seʃən] s fastidio, contrarietà f

**vexatious** [vek'seʃəs] adj irritante, fastidioso; (law) vessatorio

**vexing** ['veksɪŋ] adj noioso, fastidioso, irritante

**via** ['vaɪ·ə] prep via, per via di

**viaduct** ['vaɪ·ə ˌdʌkt] s viadotto

**vial** ['vaɪ·əl] s fiala, boccetta

**viand** ['vaɪ·ənd] s vivanda, manicaretto

**viati·cum** [vaɪ'ætɪkəm] s (**-cums** or **-ca** [kə]) (eccl) viatico

**vibrate** ['vaɪbret] tr & intr vibrare

**vibration** [vaɪ'breʃən] s vibrazione

**vicar** ['vɪkər] s vicario

**vicarage** ['vɪkərɪdʒ] s residenza del vicario; (office; duties) vicariato

**vicarious** [vaɪ'kerɪ·əs] or [vɪ'kerɪ·əs] adj sostituto; (punishment) ricevuto in vece di altra persona; (power) delegato; (enjoyment) di riflesso

**vice** [vaɪs] s vizio

**vice'-ad'miral** s viceammiraglio, ammiraglio di squadra

**vice'-pres'ident** s vicepresidente m

**viceroy** ['vaɪsrɔɪ] s viceré m

**vice versa** ['vaɪsi 'vʌrsə] or ['vaɪsə 'vʌrsə] adv viceversa

**vicini·ty** [vɪ'sɪnɪti] s (**-ties**) vicinanze fpl, paraggi mpl

**vicious** ['vɪʃəs] adj vizioso; maligno, malvagio; (dog) cattivo, che morde; (horse) selvaggio; (headache) tremendo; (reasoning; circle) vizioso

**victim** ['vɪktɪm] s vittima

**victimize** ['vɪktɪ ˌmaɪz] tr fare una vittima di; ingannare; (hist) sacrificare

**victor** ['vɪktər] s vincitore m

**victorious** [vɪk'torɪ·əs] adj vittorioso

**victo·ry** ['vɪktəri] s (**-ries**) vittoria

**victuals** ['vɪtəlz] spl vettovaglie fpl

**vid'eo cassette'** ['vɪdɪ ˌo] s videocassetta

**vid'eo sig'nal** s segnale m video

**vid'eo tape'** s nastro televisivo

**vie** [vaɪ] v (pret & pp **vied**; ger **vying**) intr gareggiare; **to vie for** disputarsi

**Vien·nese** [ ˌvi·ə'niz] adj viennese ‖ s (**-nese**) viennese mf

**Vietnam** [ ˌviet'nɑm] s il Vietnam

**Vietnam·ese** [vɪ ˌɛtnə'miz] adj vietnamita ‖ s (**-ese**) vietnamita mf; (language) vietnamita m

**view** [vju] s vista; (picture) veduta; prospetto; esame m; punto di vista; **to be on view** (said of a corpse) essere esposto; **to keep in view** non perdere di vista; **to take a dim view of** avere un'opinione scettica di; **with a view to** con lo scopo di ‖ tr guardare, osservare; considerare

**viewer** ['vju·ər] *s* spettatore *m;* (telv) telespettatore *m;* (phot) visore *m;* (phot) proiettore *m* di diapositive

**view'find'er** *s* (phot) traguardo, visore *m*

**view'point'** *s* punto di vista

**vigil** ['vɪdʒɪl] *s* vigilia; **to keep vigil** vegliare

**vigilance** ['vɪdʒɪləns] *s* vigilanza

**vigilant** ['vɪdʒɪlənt] *adj* vigilante

**vignette** [vɪn'jet] *s* vignetta

**vigor** ['vɪgər] *s* vigore *m*, gagliardia

**vigorous** ['vɪgərəs] *adj* vigoroso

**Viking** ['vaɪkɪŋ] *s* vichingo

**vile** [vaɪl] *adj* vile, malvagio; (*wretchedly bad*) orribile; disgustoso, ripugnante; (*filthy*) sporco; (*poor*) povero, basso

**vili·fy** ['vɪlɪ,faɪ] *v* (*pret & pp* **-fied**) *tr* vilificare

**villa** ['vɪlə] *s* villa

**village** ['vɪlɪdʒ] *s* villaggio, paese *m*

**villager** ['vɪlɪdʒər] *s* paesano

**villain** ['vɪlən] *s* scellerato; (*of a play*) cattivo, anima nera

**villainous** ['vɪlənəs] *adj* vile, infame

**villain·y** ['vɪləni] *s* (**-ies**) scelleratezza, malvagità *f*

**vim** [vɪm] *s* vigore *m*, brio

**vinaigrette** [,vɪnə'gret] *s* boccetta dell'aceto aromatico

**vinaigrette' sauce'** *s* salsa verde

**vindicate** ['vɪndɪ,ket] *tr* scolpare; difendere, sostenere; (*e.g., a claim*) rivendicare

**vindictive** [vɪn'dɪktɪv] *adj* vendicativo

**vine** [vaɪn] *s* (*climber*) rampicante *f;* (*grape plant*) vite *f*

**vine'dress'er** *s* vignaiolo

**vinegar** ['vɪnɪgər] *s* aceto

**vinegarish** ['vɪnɪgərɪʃ] *adj* acetoso; (fig) acre, mordace

**vinegary** ['vɪnɪgəri] *adj* acetoso; (fig) irritabile, irascibile

**vineyard** ['vɪnjərd] *s* vigna, vigneto

**vintage** ['vɪntɪdʒ] *s* vendemmia; vino di annata eccezionale; (fig) edizione

**vintager** ['vɪntɪdʒər] *s* vendemmiatore *m*

**vin'tage wine'** *s* vino di marca

**vin'tage year'** *s* buona annata

**vintner** ['vɪntnər] *s* produttore *m* di vino; vinaio

**vinyl** ['vaɪnɪl] or ['vɪnɪl] *s* vinile *m*

**violate** ['vaɪ·ə,let] *tr* violare

**violation** [,vaɪ·ə'leʃən] *s* violazione

**violence** ['vaɪ·ələns] *s* violenza

**violent** ['vaɪ·ələnt] *adj* violento

**violet** ['vaɪ,əlɪt] *adj* violetto || *s* (*color*) violetto, viola; (bot) violetta; (*Viola odorata*) viola mammola

**violin** [,vaɪ·ə'lɪn] *s* violino

**violinist** [,vaɪ·ə'lɪnɪst] *s* violinista *mf*

**violoncellist** [,vaɪ·ələn'tʃɛlɪst] or [,vi·ələn'tʃɛlɪst] *s* violoncellista *mf*

**violoncel·lo** [,vaɪ·ələn'tʃɛlo] or [,vi·ələn'tʃɛlo] *s* (**-los**) violoncello

**VIP** ['vi·aɪ'pi] *s* (letterword) (**Very Important Person**) persona di maggiore riguardo

**viper** ['vaɪpər] *s* vipera; (*any snake*) serpe *f;* (*spiteful person*) vipera

**vira·go** [vɪ'rego] *s* (**-goes** or **-gos**) megera, donna dal caratteraccio impossibile

**virgin** ['vʌrdʒɪn] *adj & s* vergine *f* || **Virgin** *s* Vergine *f*

**vir'gin birth'** *s* parto verginale della Madonna; (zool) partenogenesi *f*

**Virgin'ia creep'er** [vər'dʒɪnɪ·ə] *s* vite *f* del Canada

**virginity** [vər'dʒɪnɪti] *s* virginità *f*

**Virgo** ['vʌrgo] *s* (astr) Vergine *f*

**virility** [vɪ'rɪlɪti] *s* virilità *f*

**virology** [vaɪ'rɑlədʒi] *s* virologia

**virtual** ['vʌrtʃu·əl] *adj* virtuale

**virtue** ['vʌrtʃu] *s* virtù *f*

**virtuosi·ty** [,vʌrtʃu'ɑsɪti] *s* (**-ties**) virtuosità *f*, virtuosismo

**virtuo·so** [,vʌrtʃu'oso] *s* (**-sos** or **-si** [si]) virtuoso

**virtuous** ['vʌrtʃu·əs] *adj* virtuoso

**virulence** ['vɪrjələns] *s* virulenza

**virulent** ['vɪrjələnt] *adj* virulento

**virus** ['vaɪrəs] *s* virus *m*

**visa** ['vizə] *s* visto || *tr* vistare

**visage** ['vɪzɪdʒ] *s* faccia; apparenza

**vis-à-vis** [,vizə'vi] *adj* l'uno di fronte all'altro || *adv* vis-à-vis || *prep* di fronte a

**viscera** ['vɪsərə] *spl* visceri *mpl*, viscere *fpl*

**viscount** ['vaɪkaunt] *s* visconte *m*

**viscountess** ['vaɪkauntɪs] *s* viscontessa

**viscous** ['vɪskəs] *adj* viscoso

**vise** [vaɪs] *s* morsa

**visé** ['vize] or [vi'ze] *s & tr* var of **visa**

**visible** ['vɪzɪbəl] *adj* visibile

**Visigoth** ['vɪzɪ,gɑθ] *s* visigoto

**vision** ['vɪʒən] *s* visione; (*sense*) vista

**visionar·y** ['vɪʒə,neri] *adj* visionario || *s* (**-ies**) visionario

**visit** ['vɪzɪt] *tr* visitare; affliggere, colpire; (*a punishment*) far ricadere || *intr* visitare; (*to chat*) fare un chiacchierata

**visitation** [,vɪzɪ'teʃən] *s* visitazione; punizione divina, visita del Signore

**vis'iting card'** *s* biglietto da visita

**vis'iting hours'** *spl* orario delle visite

**vis'iting nurse'** *s* infermiera che visita i pazienti a domicilio

**visitor** ['vɪzɪtər] *s* visitatore *m*

**visor** ['vaɪzər] *s* visiera; (fig) maschera

**vista** ['vɪstə] *s* vista, prospettiva

**visual** ['vɪʒu·əl] *adj* visivo, visuale

**vis'ual acu'ity** *s* acutezza visiva

**visualize** ['vɪʒu·ə,laɪz] *tr* formare l'immagine mentale di; (*to make visible*) visualizzare

**vital** ['vaɪtəl] *adj* vitale; (*deadly*) mortale || **vitals** *spl* organi vitali

**vitality** [vaɪ'tælɪti] *s* vitalità *f*

**vitalize** ['vaɪtə,laɪz] *tr* animare, infondere vita a

**vi'tal statis'tics** *spl* statistiche *fpl* anagrafiche

**vitamin** ['vaɪtəmɪn] *s* vitamina

**vitiate** ['vɪʃɪ,et] *tr* viziare

**vitreous** ['vɪtrɪ·əs] *adj* vitreo, vetroso

**vitriolic** [,vɪtrɪ'ɑlɪk] *adj* di vetriolo; (fig) caustico

**vituperate** [vaɪ'tupə,ret] or [vaɪ'tjupə,ret] *tr* vituperare

**viva** ['vivə] *s* evviva || *interj* viva!
**vivacious** [vɪ'veʃəs] *or* [vaɪ've ʃəs] *adj* vivace
**vivaci·ty** [vɪ'væsɪti] *or* [vaɪ'væsɪti] *s* (**-ties**) vivacità *f*, gaiezza
**viva voce** ['vaɪvə 'vosi] *adv* a viva voce
**vivid** ['vɪvɪd] *adj* vivido
**vivi·fy** ['vɪvɪ ˌfaɪ] *v* (*pret* & *pp* **-fied**) *tr* vivificare
**vivisection** [ ˌvɪvɪ'sɛkʃən] *s* vivisezione
**vixen** ['vɪksən] *s* volpe femmina; (*ill-tempered woman*) megera
**vizier** [vɪ'zɪr] *or* ['vɪzjər] *s* visir *m*
**vocabular·y** [vo'kæbjə ˌlɛri] *s* (**-ies**) vocabolario
**vocal** ['vokəl] *adj* vocale; (*inclined to express oneself freely*) che si fa sentire, loquace; (*e.g., outburst*) verbale
**vocalist** ['vokəlɪst] *s* cantante *mf*; (*of jazz*) vocalist *mf*
**vocalize** ['vokə ˌlaɪz] *tr* vocalizzare || *intr* vocalizzarsi
**vocation** [vo'keʃən] *s* vocazione; professione, impiego
**voca'tional educa'tion** *s* istruzione professionale
**vocative** ['vɑkətɪv] *s* vocativo
**vociferate** [vo'sɪfə ˌret] *intr* vociferare
**vociferous** [vo'sɪfərəs] *adj* rumoroso, vociferante
**vogue** [vog] *s* voga, moda; **in vogue** in voga, di moda
**voice** [vɔɪs] *s* voce *f*; (*of animals*) verso; **in a loud voice** a voce alta; **in a low voice** a voce bassa; **to give voice to** esprimere; **with one voice** con una sola voce || *tr* esprimere; (*phonet*) sonorizzare || *intr* sonorizzarsi
**voiced** [vɔɪst] *adj* (phonet) sonoro
**voiceless** ['vɔɪslɪs] *adj* senza voce; muto; (phonet) sordo, duro
**void** [vɔɪd] *adj* (*useless*) inutile; (*empty*) vuoto; (*law*) invalido, nullo; **void of** sprovvisto di || *s* vuoto; (*gap*) buco || *tr* vuotare; (*the bowels*) evacuare; annullare || *intr* andare di corpo
**volatile** ['vɑlətɪl] *adj* volatile; instabile; (*disposition*) volubile, incostante
**volatilize** ['vɑlətɪ ˌlaɪz] *tr* volatilizzare || *intr* volatilizzarsi
**volcanic** [vɑl'kænɪk] *adj* vulcanico
**volca·no** [vɑl'keno] *s* (**-noes** *or* **-nos**) vulcano
**volition** [və'lɪʃən] *s* volontà *f*; **of one's own volition** di propria volontà
**volley** ['vɑli] *s* (*e.g., of bullets*) scarica, sventagliata; (*tennis*) volata || *tr* colpire a volo || *intr* colpire la palla a volo
**vol'ley-ball'** *s* pallavolo *f*
**volplane** ['vɑl ˌplen] *s* planata || *intr* planare
**volt** [volt] *s* volt *m*
**voltage** ['voltɪdʒ] *s* voltaggio
**volt'age divid'er** [dɪ'vaɪdər] *s* divisore *m* del voltaggio
**voltaic** [vɑl'te·ɪk] *adj* voltaico
**volte-face** [vɔlt'fɑs] *s* voltafaccia *m*

**volt'me'ter** *s* voltmetro
**voluble** ['vɑljəbəl] *adj* locuace
**volume** ['vɑljəm] *s* volume *m*; **to speak volumes** avere molta importanza; essere molto espressivo
**voluminous** [və'lumɪnəs] *adj* voluminoso
**voluntar·y** ['vɑlən ˌtɛri] *adj* volontario || *s* (**-ies**) assolo di organo
**volunteer** [ ˌvɑlən'tɪr] *adj* & *s* volontario || *tr* dare *or* dire volontariamente || *intr* offrirsi; arruolarsi come volontario; **to volunteer to** + *inf* offrirsi di + *inf*
**voluptuar·y** [və'lʌptʃu ˌɛri] *adj* voluttuoso || *s* (**-ies**) sibarita *m*, epicureo
**voluptuous** [və'lʌptʃu·əs] *adj* voluttuoso
**volute** [və'lut] *s* voluta
**vomit** ['vɑmɪt] *s* vomito || *tr* & *intr* vomitare, rigettare
**voodoo** ['vudu] *adj* di vudù || *s* (*practice*) vudù *m*; (*person*) vuduista *mf*
**voracious** [və're ʃəs] *adj* vorace
**voracity** [və'ræsɪti] *s* voracità *f*
**vor·tex** ['vɔrtəks] *s* (**-texes** *or* **-tices** [tɪ ˌsiz]) vortice *m*
**vota·ry** ['votəri] *s* (**-ries**) persona legata da un voto; amante *mf*, appassionato
**vote** [vot] *s* voto; **to put to the vote** mettere ai voti; **to tally the votes** procedere allo scrutinio dei voti || *tr* votare; dichiarare; **to vote down** respingere; **to vote in** eleggere; **to vote out** scacciare || *intr* votare
**vote' get'ter** ['gɛtər] *s* accaparratore *m* di voti; slogan *m* che conquista voti
**voter** ['votər] *s* elettore *m*
**vot'ing machine'** ['votɪŋ] *s* macchina per registrare lo scrutinio dei voti
**votive** ['votɪv] *adj* votivo
**vo'tive of'fering** *s* voto, ex voto, offerta votiva
**vouch** [vautʃ] *tr* garantire || *intr*—**to vouch for** (*s.th*) garantire; (*s.o.*) rendersi garante per, garantire per
**voucher** ['vautʃər] *s* garante *mf*; (*certificate*) ricevuta, pezza d'appoggio
**vouch·safe'** *tr* concedere, accordare || *intr*—**to vouchsafe to** + *inf* degnarsi di + *inf*
**voussoir** [vu'swar] *s* cuneo
**vow** [vau] *s* voto; **to take vows** pronunciare i voti || *tr* promettere; (*vengeance*) giurare || *intr* fare un voto
**vowel** ['vau·əl] *s* vocale *f*
**voyage** ['vɔɪ·ɪdʒ] *s* viaggio; (*by sea*) traversata || *tr* attraversare || *intr* viaggiare
**voyager** ['vɔɪ·ɪdʒər] *s* viaggiatore *m*, passeggero
**vulcanize** ['vʌlkə ˌnaɪz] *tr* vulcanizzare
**vulgar** ['vʌlgər] *adj* volgare; comune, popolare
**vulgari·ty** [vʌl'gærɪti] *s* (**-ties**) volgarità *f*
**Vul'gar Lat'in** *s* latino volgare
**Vulgate** ['vʌlget] *s* Vulgata
**vulnerable** ['vʌlnərəbəl] *adj* vulnerabile
**vulture** ['vʌltʃər] *s* avvoltoio

# W

**W, w** ['dʌbəl ˌju] *s* ventitreesima lettera dell'alfabeto inglese

**wad** [wɑd] *s* (*of cotton*) batuffolo, bioccolo; (*of money*) mazzetta, rotolo; (*of tobacco*) pallottola; (*in a gun*) stoppaccio ‖ *v* (*pret & pp* **wadded;** *ger* **wadding**) *tr* arrotolare; (*shot*) comprimere; (fig) imbottire

**waddle** ['wɑdəl] *s* andatura a mo' di anitra ‖ *intr* sculettare

**wade** [wed] *tr* guadare ‖ *intr* guadare; avanzare faticosamente; sguazzare; **to wade into** (coll) attaccare violentemente; **to wade through** procedere a stento per; leggere con difficoltà

**wad'ing bird'** ['wedɪŋ] *s* trampoliere *m*

**wafer** ['wefər] *s* disco adesivo di carta per chiudere lettere; (*cake*) wafer *m*, cialda; (eccl, med) ostia

**waffle** ['wɑfəl] *s* cialda

**waf'fle i'ron** *s* schiacce *fpl*

**waft** [wæft] or [wɑft] *tr* portare leggermente or a volo ‖ *intr* librarsi, spandersi

**wag** [wæg] *s* (*of head*) cenno; (*of tail*) scodinzolio; (*person*) burlone *m* ‖ *v* (*pret & pp* **wagged;** *ger* **wagging**) *tr* (*the head*) scuotere; (*the tail*) dimenare ‖ *intr* scodinzolare

**wage** [wedʒ] *s* salario, paga; **wages** salario, paga; ricompensa; prezzo, e.g., **the wages of sin is death** la morte è il prezzo del peccato ‖ *tr* (*war*) fare

**wage' earn'er** ['ˌʌrnər] *s* salariato

**wager** ['wedʒər] *s* scommessa; **to lay a wager** fare una scommessa ‖ *tr & intr* scommettere

**wage'work'er** *s* lavoratore salariato

**waggish** ['wægɪʃ] *adj* scherzoso, comico, burlone

**Wagnerian** [vɑgˈnɪrɪ·ən] *adj & s* wagneriano

**wagon** ['wægən] *s* carro, carretto; (*e.g., Conestoga wagon*) carriaggio; furgone *m*; carrozzone *m*; **to be on the wagon** (slang) astenersi dal bere; **to hitch one's wagon to a star** avere altissime ambizioni

**wag'tail'** *s* (orn) ballerina, cutrettola

**waif** [wef] *s* (*foundling*) trovatello; abbandonato; animale smarrito

**wail** [wel] *s* gemito, lamento ‖ *intr* gemere, lamentarsi

**wain·scot** ['wenskət] or ['wenskɑt] *s* pannello per rivestimenti ‖ *v* (*pret & pp* **-scoted** or **-scotted;** *ger* **-scoting** or **-scotting**) *tr* rivestire di pannelli di legno

**waist** [west] *s* vita, cintura; blusa, camicetta, corpetto

**waist'band'** *s* cintola

**waist'cloth'** *s* perizoma *m*

**waistcoat** ['west ˌkot] or ['westkət] *s* corpetto, gilè *m*

**waist'line'** *s* vita, cintura; **to keep or watch one's waistline** conservare la linea

**wait** [wet] *s* attesa; **to lie in wait** attendere al varco ‖ *tr* (*one's turn*) attendere ‖ *intr* attendere, aspettare; **to wait for** attendere, aspettare; **to wait on** servire; **to wait up for** (coll) aspettare alzato

**wait'-and-see' pol'icy** *s* attendismo

**waiter** ['wetər] *s* cameriere *m*; (*tray*) vassoio

**wait'ing list'** *s* lista di aspettativa

**wait'ing room'** *s* sala d'aspetto

**waitress** ['wetrɪs] *s* cameriera

**waive** [wev] *tr* (*one's rights*) rinunciare (with *dat*); differire; mettere da parte

**waiver** ['wevər] *s* rinuncia

**wake** [wek] *s* (*any watch*) veglia; (*watch by a dead body*) veglia funebre; (*of a boat*) solco, scia; **in the wake of** come risultato di; nelle orme di ‖ *v* (*pret* **waked** or **woke** [wok]; *pp* **waked**) *tr* svegliare ‖ *intr* svegliarsi; **to wake to** darsi conto di; **to wake up** svegliarsi

**wakeful** ['wekfəl] *adj* sveglio; insonne

**waken** ['wekən] *tr* svegliare ‖ *intr* svegliarsi

**wale** [wel] *s* segno lasciato da una frustata, vescica; (*in fabric*) riga, costa

**Wales** [welz] *s* la Galles

**walk** [wɔk] *s* (*act*) camminata; (*distance*) cammino; (*for pleasure*) passeggiata; (*gait*) andatura; (*line of work*) attività *f*, mestiere *m*; (*sidewalk*) marciapiede *m*; (*in a garden*) sentiero; (*yard for domestic animals to exercise in*) recinto; (sports) marcia; **to go for a walk** andare a fare una passeggiata ‖ *tr* (*a street*) percorrere; (*a horse*) passeggiare; (*a patient*) far camminare; (*a heavy piece of furniture*) abbambinare; **to walk off** (*a headache*) far passare camminando ‖ *intr* camminare; passeggiare; (*said of a horse*) andare al passo; (sports) marciare; **to walk away from** andarsene a piedi da; **to walk off with** rubare; vincere con facilità; **to walk out** uscire in segno di protesta; (coll) mettersi in sciopero; **to walk out on** (coll) piantare in asso

**walkaway** ['wɔkəˌwe] *s* facile vittoria

**walker** ['wɔkər] *s* camminatore *m*; (*to teach a baby to walk*) girello

**walkie-talkie** ['wɔkiˈtɔki] *s* trasmettitore-ricevitore *m* portatile

**walk'ing pa'pers** *spl*—**to give s.o. his walking papers** (coll) dare gli otto giorni a qlcu

**walk'-in refrig'erator** *s* cella frigorifera

**walk'ing stick'** *s* bastone *m* da passeggio

**walk'-on'** *s* (*actor*) figurante *m*, comparsa; (*role*) particina

**walk'out'** *s* sciopero

**walk'o'ver** *s* facile vittoria, passeggiata

**wall** [wɔl] *s* muro; (*between rooms; of a vein*) parete *f*; (*rampart*) muraglia; **to drive to the wall** ridurre alla disperazione; **to go to the wall** perdere; fare fallimento ‖ *tr* murare; **to wall up** circondare con muro

**wall'board'** *s* pannello da costruzione

**wallet** ['wɑlɪt] *s* portafoglio

**wall'flow'er** *s* violacciocca gialla; **to be a wallflower** fare tappezzeria

**Walloon** [wɑ'lun] *adj & s* vallone *mf*

**wallop** ['wɑləp] *s* (coll) colpo violento; (coll) effetto ‖ *tr* (coll) dare un colpo violento a; (coll) battere completamente

**wallow** ['wɑlo] *s* diguazzamento; (*place*) brago, pantano ‖ *intr* diguazzare; (*in wealth*) nuotare

**wall'pa'per** *s* tappezzeria ‖ *tr* tappezzare

**walnut** ['wɔlnət] *s* (*tree; wood*) noce *m;* (*fruit*) noce *f*

**walrus** ['wɔlrəs] or ['wɑlrəs] *s* tricheco

**Walter** ['wɔltər] *s* Gualtiero

**waltz** [wɔlts] *s* valzer *m* ‖ *tr* ballare il valzer con; (coll) condurre con disinvoltura ‖ *intr* ballare il valzer

**wan** [wɑn] *adj* (**wanner; wannest**) (*face*) smunto, sparuto, smorto; (*light*) debole

**wand** [wɑnd] *s* bacchetta

**wander** ['wɑndər] *tr* vagare per ‖ *intr* vagare, vagabondare; errare

**wanderer** ['wɑndərər] *s* vagabondo; pellegrino

**Wan'dering Jew'** *s* ebreo errante

**wan'der·lust'** *s* passione del vagabondaggio

**wane** [wen] *s* decadenza, declino; calare *m* della luna; **on the wane** in declino; (*moon*) calante ‖ *intr* decadere, declinare; (*said of the moon*) calare

**wangle** ['wæŋgəl] *tr* (coll) ottenere con l'astuzia, rimediare; (coll) falsificare; **to wangle one's way out of** (coll) tirarsi fuori da . . . con l'astuzia ‖ *intr* (coll) arrangiarsi

**want** [wɑnt] or [wɔnt] *s* bisogno, necessità *f;* domanda; miseria; **for want of** a causa della mancanza di; **to be in want** essere in miseria; **to be in want of** aver bisogno di ‖ *tr* volere, desiderare; mancare; aver bisogno di ‖ *intr* desiderare; **to be wanting** mancare, e.g., **three cards are wanting** mancano tre carte; **to want for** aver bisogno di

**want' ad'** *s* annunzio economico

**wanton** ['wɑntən] *adj* di proposito, deliberato; arbitrario; licenzioso, sfrenato; (*archaic*) lussureggiante

**war** [wɔr] *s* guerra; **to go to war** entrare in guerra; (*said of a soldier*) andare in guerra; **to wage war** fare la guerra ‖ *v* (*pret & pp* **warred;** *ger* **warring**) *intr* guerreggiare; **to war on** fare la guerra a

**warble** ['wɔrbəl] *s* gorgheggio ‖ *intr* gorgheggiare

**warbler** ['wɔrblər] *s* canterino; uccello canoro; (orn) beccafico

**war' cloud'** *s* minaccia di guerra

**ward** [wɔrd] *s* (*of city*) distretto; (*division of hospital*) corsia; (*separate building in hospital*) padiglione *m;*

(*guardianship*) tutela; (*minor*) pupillo; (*of lock*) scontro ‖ *tr*—**to ward off** stornare, schermirsi da

**warden** ['wɔrdən] *s* guardiano; (*of jail*) direttore *m;* (*in wartime*) capofabbricato

**ward' heel'er** *s* politicantuccio

**ward'robe** *s* guardaroba *m*

**ward'robe trunk'** *s* baule *m* armadio

**ward'room'** *s* (nav) quadrato

**ware** [wer] *s* vasellame *m;* **wares** merce *f*

**war' ef'fort** *s* sforzo bellico

**ware'house'** *s* deposito, magazzino

**ware'house'man** *s* (-**men**) magazziniere *m*

**war'fare'** *s* guerra

**war'head'** *s* (mil) testa

**war'horse'** *s* cavallo di battaglia; (coll) veterano

**warily** ['werɪli] *adv* con cautela

**wariness** ['werɪnɪs] *s* cautela

**war'like'** *adj* guerresco, guerriero

**war' loan'** *s* prestito di guerra

**war' lord'** *s* generalissimo

**warm** [wɔrm] *adj* caldo; (*lukewarm*) tiepido; (*clothes*) che tiene caldo; (*with anger*) acceso; **to be warm** (*said of a person*) avere caldo; (*said of the weather*) fare caldo ‖ *tr* scaldare, riscaldare; (*s.o.'s heart*) slargare; **to warm up** riscaldare ‖ *intr* scaldarsi, riscaldarsi; **to warm up** (*said, e.g., of a room*) riscaldarsi; (*with emotion*) eccitarsi, accalorarsi; **to warm up to** prender simpatia per

**warm-blooded** ['wɔrm'blʌdɪd] *adj* (*animal*) a sangue caldo; impetuoso, ardente

**war' memo'rial** *s* monumento ai caduti

**warmer** ['wɔrmər] *s* scaldino

**warm-hearted** ['wɔrm'hɑrtɪd] *adj* caloroso, cordiale

**warm'ing pan'** *s* scaldaletto

**warmonger** ['wɔr,mʌŋgər] *s* guerrafondaio

**war' moth'er** *s* madrina di guerra

**warmth** [wɔrmθ] *s* calore *m*, tepore *m;* foga, entusiasmo

**warm'up'** *s* preparazione; (*of radio, engine, etc.*) riscaldamento

**warn** [wɔrn] *tr* avvertire, mettere in guardia; (*to admonish*) ammonire; informare; **to warn off** intimare di allontanarsi (da)

**warn'ing** *adj* di avvertimento ‖ *s* avvertimento, ammonimento; (law) diffida

**war' nose'** *s* acciarino, testa

**war' of nerves'** *s* guerra dei nervi

**War' of the Roses'** *s* Guerra delle due Rose

**warp** [wɔrp] *s* (*of a fabric*) ordito; (*of a board*) svergolamento, curvatura; aberrazione mentale; (naut) gherlino ‖ *tr* curvare, svergolare; (*a fabric*) ordire; falsare, alterare; (naut) tirare col gherlino ‖ *intr* curvarsi; falsarsi, alterarsi; (naut) alare

**war'path'** *s*—**to be on the warpath** essere sul sentiero della guerra, prepararsi alla guerra; (*to be angry*) essere arrabiato, essere di cattivo umore

**war'plane'** *s* aeroplano da guerra

**war' prof'iteer** *s* pescecane *m*

**warrant** ['warənt] *or* ['wɔrənt] *s* garanzia; certificato; ricevuta; (com) nota di pegno; (law) ordine *m*, mandato ‖ *tr* garantire; autorizzare

**warrantable** ['warəntəbəl] *or* ['wɔrəntəbəl] *adj* giustificabile, legittimo

**war'rant of'ficer** *s* sottufficiale *m*

**warran·ty** ['warənti] *or* ['wɔrənti] *s* (-ties) garanzia; autorizzazione

**warren** ['warən] *or* ['wɔrən] *s* conigliera; (fig) formicaio

**warrior** ['wɔrjər] *or* ['wɑrjər] *s* guerriero

**Warsaw** ['wɔrsɔ] *s* Varsavia

**war'ship'** *s* nave *f* da guerra

**wart** [wɔrt] *s* verruca

**war'time'** *s* tempo di guerra

**war'-torn'** *adj* devastato dalla guerra

**war' to the death'** *s* guerra a morte

**war·y** ['weri] *adj* (-ier; -iest) guardingo

**wash** [waʃ] *or* [wɔʃ] *s* lavata; (*clothes washed or to be washed*) bucato; (*rushing movement of water*) sciacquio; (*dirty water*) lavatura; (*painting*) mano *f* di colore; (aer, naut) scia ‖ *tr* lavare; (*dishes*) rigovernare; (*said of sea or river*) bagnare; **to be washed up** essere finito; **to wash away** (*soil of river bank*) dilavare; portar via ‖ *intr* lavarsi; fare il bucato; essere lavabile; (*said of waves*) battere

**washable** ['waʃəbəl] *or* ['wɔʃəbəl] *adj* lavabile

**wash'-and-wear'** *adj* non-stiro

**wash'ba'sin** *s* conca, catinella

**wash'bas'ket** *s* cesto del bucato

**wash'board'** *s* asse *m* da lavanda; (*baseboard*) battiscopa *m*

**wash'bowl'** *s* conca, catinella

**wash'cloth'** *s* pezzuola per lavarsi

**wash'day'** *s* giorno del bucato

**washed-out** ['waʃt,aut] *or* ['wɔʃt,aut] *adj* slavato; (coll) stanco; (coll) abbattuto, accasciato

**washed-up** ['waʃt'ʌp] *or* ['wɔʃt'ʌp] *adj* (coll) finito

**washer** ['waʃər] *or* ['wɔʃər] *s* (*person*) lavatore *m*; (*machine*) lavatrice *f*; (*under head of bolt*) rondella, rosetta; (*ring to prevent leakage*) guarnizione

**wash'er·man** *s* (-men) lavatore *m*

**wash'er·wom'an** *s* (-wom'en) lavatrice *f*, lavandaia

**wash' goods'** *spl* tessuti *mpl* lavabili

**washing** ['waʃɪŋ] *or* ['wɔʃɪŋ] *s* lavata, lavaggio, lavanda; (*of clothes*) bucato; **washings** lavaggio

**wash'ing machine'** *s* lavabiancheria, lavatrice *f*

**wash'ing so'da** *s* soda da lavare

**wash'out'** *s* erosione; (aer) svergolamento negativo; (coll) rovina completa

**wash'rag'** *s* pezzuola per lavarsi; straccio di cucina

**wash'room'** *s* gabinetto, toletta

**wash'stand'** *s* lavabo, lavamano

**wash'tub'** *s* mastello, lavatoio

**wash' wa'ter** *s* lavatura

**wasp** [wasp] *s* vespa

**waste** [west] *s* spreco; (*refuse*) scarico, rifiuto; (*desolate country*) landa; (*excess material*) scarto; (*for wiping machinery*) cascame *m* di cotone; **to go to waste** essere sciupato; **to lay waste** devastare ‖ *tr* perdere, sciupare, sprecare ‖ *intr*—**to waste away** intristire, consumarsi

**waste'bas'ket** *s* cestino della carta straccia

**wasteful** ['westfəl] *adj* dispendioso; distruttivo

**waste'pa'per** *s* cartastraccia

**waste' pipe'** *s* tubo di scarico

**waste' prod'uct** *s* scarto; (*body excretion*) escremento

**wastrel** ['westrəl] *s* sciupone *m;* spendaccione *m*, prodigo

**watch** [watʃ] *s* orologio; (*lookout*) guardia; (mil) guardia; (naut) turno; **to be on the watch for** essere all'erta per; **to keep watch over** vegliare su ‖ *tr* (*to look at*) osservare; (*to oversee*) vigilare; guardare; fare attenzione a ‖ *intr* guardare; (*to keep awake*) vegliare; **to watch for** fare attenzione a; **to watch out** fare attenzione; **to watch out for** fare attenzione a; essere all'erta per; **to watch over** sorvegliare; **watch out!** attenzione!

**watch'band'** *s* cinturino dell'orologio

**watch'case'** *s* cassa dell'orologio

**watch' charm'** *s* ciondolo dell'orologio

**watch' crys'tal** *s* cristallo dell'orologio

**watch'dog'** *s* cane *m* da guardia; (fig) guardiano

**watch'dog' commit'tee** *s* comitato di sorveglianza

**watchful** ['watʃfəl] *adj* vigile

**watchfulness** ['watʃfəlnɪs] *s* vigilanza

**watch'mak'er** *s* orologiaio

**watch'man** *s* (-men) guardiano, sorvegliante *m;* (*at night*) guardia notturna, metronotte *m*

**watch' night'** *s* notte *f* di San Silvestro; ufficio religioso della vigilia di Capodanno

**watch' pock'et** *s* taschino dell'orologio

**watch'tow'er** *s* torre *f* d'osservazione

**watch'word'** *s* parola d'ordine, consegna; slogan *m*

**water** ['wɔtər] *or* ['watər] *s* acqua; **of the first water** di prim'ordine; (*e.g., a thief*) della più bell'acqua; **to back water** retrocedere; **to be in deep water** essere in cattive acque; **to fish in troubled waters** pescare nel torbido; **to hold water** aver fondamento; **to keep above water** (fig) tenersi a galla; **to make water** (*to urinate*) urinare; (naut) fare acqua; **to throw cold water on** scoraggiare ‖ *tr* bagnare; dare acqua a; (*cattle*) abbeverare; (*wine*) annacquare ‖ *intr* abbeverarsi; (*said of the mouth*) aver l'acquolina; (*said, e.g., of a ship*) fare acqua; (*said of the eyes*) lacrimare

wa'ter bug' *s* bacherozzolo
wa'ter car'rier *s* acquaiolo
wa'ter·col'or *s* acquerello
wa'ter-cooled' *adj* a raffreddamento ad acqua
wa'ter·course' *s* corso d'acqua
wa'ter·cress' *s* crescione *m*
wa'ter cure' *s* cura delle acque
wa'ter·fall' *s* cascata
wa'ter·front' *s* riva, banchina
wa'ter gap' *s* gola, passo
wa'ter ham'mer *s* colpo d'ariete
wa'ter heat'er *s* scaldabagno, scalda·acqua *m*
wa'ter ice' *s* granita
wa'tering can' *s* annaffiatoio
wa'tering place' *s* stabilimento bal·neare; stazione termale; (*drinking place*) abbeveratoio
wa'tering pot' *s* annaffiatoio
wa'tering trough' *s* abbeveratoio
wa'ter jack'et *s* camicia d'acqua
wa'ter lil'y *s* nenufaro
wa'ter line' *s* linea di galleggiamento or d'acqua; linea di livello
wa'ter main' *s* tubo di flusso principale
wa'ter·mark' *s* linea di livello massimo; (*in paper*) filigrana
wa'ter·mel'on *s* cocomero, anguria
wa'ter me'ter *s* contatore *m* dell'acqua
wa'ter mill' *s* mulino ad acqua
wa'ter pipe' *s* tubo dell'acqua
wa'ter po'lo *s* pallanuoto *f*
wa'ter pow'er *s* forza idrica
wa'ter·proof' *adj & s* impermeabile *m*
wa'ter·repel'lent *adj* idroripellente
wa'ter·shed' *s* spartiacque *m*, displuvio
wa'ter ski' *s* idrosci *m*
wa'ter sof'tener *s* decalcificatore *m*
wa'ter·spout' *s* (*to carry water from roof*) pluviale *m*; (meteor) tromba marina
wa'ter sys'tem *s* (*of a river*) sistema *m* fluviale; (*of city*) conduttura dell'acqua, impianto idrico
wa'ter·tight' *adj* stagno, ermetico; (fig) perfetto, inconfutabile
wa'ter tow'er *s* torre *f* serbatoio
wa'ter wag'on *s* (mil) carro dell'acqua; **to be on the water wagon** (slang) astenersi dal bere
wa'ter·way' *s* via d'acqua, idrovia
wa'ter wheel' *s* ruota or turbina idrau·lica; (*of steamboat*) ruota a pale
wa'ter wings' *spl* galleggiante *m* per nuotare
wa'ter·works' *s* impianto idrico; (*pumping station*) impianto di pom·paggio
watery ['wɔtəri] or ['wɑtəri] *adj* ac·quoso; lacrimoso; povero, insipido; umido, acquitrinoso
watt [wɑt] *s* watt *m*
watt'-hour' *s* (-hours) wattora *m*
wattle ['wɑtəl] *s* (*of bird*) bargiglio
watt'me'ter *s* wattmetro
wave [wev] *s* onda; (*of cold; of feel·ing*) ondata; (*of the hand*) cenno; (*of hair*) onda, ondulazione ‖ *tr* (*a flag*) sventolare; (*the hair*) ondulare; (*the hand*) fare cenno con; **to wave aside** fare cenno di allontanarsi a; (*e.g., a*

proposal*) rifiutare ‖ *intr* ondeggiare; fare cenni con la mano
wave'length' *s* lunghezza d'onda
wave' mo'tion *s* movimento ondula·torio
waver ['wevər] *intr* ondeggiare, oscil·lare; (*to hesitate*) titubare, tenten·nare; (*to totter*) pencolare
wav·y ['wevi] *adj* (-ier; -iest) (sea) on·doso; (*hair*) ondulato
wax [wæks] *s* cera; (fig) fantoccio ‖ *tr* incerare; (*a recording*) (coll) regi·strare ‖ *intr* aumentare; diventare; (*said of the moon*) crescere; **to wax indignant** indignarsi
wax' pa'per *s* carta cerata, carta oleata
wax'works' *s* museo di statue di cera
way [we] *s* maniera, modo; via; condi·zione; **across the way** di fronte; **a good way** un buon tratto; **all the way** fino alla fine della strada; completa·mente; **all the way to** fino a; **any way** ad ogni modo; **by the way** a propo·sito; **in a way** in un certo modo; fino a un certo punto; **in every way** per ogni verso; **in this way** in questa maniera; **one way** senso unico; **on the way** to andando a; **on the way out** uscendo; diminuendo, sparendo; **out of the way** eliminato; fuori mano; strano; irregolare; **that way** in quella direzione; per di lì; in quella maniera; **this way** in questa direzione; per di qui; in questa ma·niera; **to be in the way** essere d'im·paccio; **to feel one's way** avanzare a tentoni; **to force one's way** aprirsi il passo a viva forza; **to get out of the way** togliersi di mezzo; **to give way** ritirarsi, cedere; (*said of a rope*) rompersi; **to give way to** cedere a, darsi a; **to go out of one's way** darsi da fare, disturbarsi; **to have one's way** vincerla; **to keep out of the way** stare fuori dai piedi; **to know one's way around** conoscere bene la via; (fig) sapere il fatto proprio; **to know one's way to** sapere andare a; **to lead the way** guidare, fare da guida; pren·dere l'iniziativa; **to lose one's way** perdersi; **to make one's way** avan·zare; fare carriera; **to make way for** far largo a; **to mend one's ways** met·tere la testa a partito; **to not know which way to turn** non sapere a che santo votarsi; **to put out of the way** togliere di mezzo; **to see one's way to** vedere la possibilità di; **to take one's way** andarsene; **to wind one's way through** andare a zig zag per; **to wing one's way** andare a volo; **under way** in moto; in cammino, avviato; **way in** entrata; **way out** uscita; **ways** modi *mpl*, maniere *fpl*; (naut) scalo; **which way?** da che parte?; in che modo?, per dove?
way'bill' *s* lettera di vettura
wayfarer ['we ˌferər] *s* viandante *m*
way'lay' *v* (*pret & pp* -laid) *tr* tendere un agguato a; fermare improvvisa·mente
way' of life' *s* tenore *m* di vita

**way'side'** *s* bordo della strada; **to fall by the wayside** cadere per istrada; (fig) fare fiasco

**way' sta'tion** *s* stazione con fermata facoltativa

**way' train'** *s* treno omnibus

**wayward** ['wewərd] *adj* indocile, caparbio; irregolare; capriccioso

**we** [wi] *pron pers* noi; noialtri, e.g., **we Italians** noialtri italiani

**weak** [wik] *adj* debole

**weaken** ['wikən] *tr* indebolire, infiacchire ‖ *intr* indebolirsi, infiacchirsi

**weakling** ['wiklɪŋ] *s* debolino, rammollito

**weak-minded** ['wik'maɪndɪd] *adj* irresoluto; scemo

**weakness** ['wiknɪs] *s* debolezza, fiacchezza; (*liking*) debole *m*

**wealth** [wɛlθ] *s* ricchezza

**wealth·y** ['wɛlθi] *adj* (**-ier; -iest**) ricco

**wean** [win] *tr* svezzare, slattare; **to wean away from** disavvezzare da

**weanling** ['winlɪŋ] *adj* appena svezzato ‖ *s* bambino or animale appena svezzato

**weapon** ['wepən] *s* arma

**weaponry** ['wepənri] *s* armi *fpl*, armamento

**wear** [wer] *s* uso, servizio; (*clothing*) vestiti *mpl*, indumenti *mpl*; (*wasting away from use*) consumo, logorio; (*lasting quality*) durata, durabilità *f*; **for everyday wear** per ogni giorno ‖ *v* (*pret* **wore** [wor]; *pp* **worn** [worn]) *tr* portare, avere indosso; (*to cause to deteriorate*) logorare, consumare; (*to tire*) stancare; **to wear out** logorare, strusciare; (*a horse*) sfiancare; (*one's patience*) esaurire; (*s.o.'s hospitality*) abusare di ‖ *intr* logorarsi, consumarsi; **to wear off** diminuire, sparire; **to wear out** logorarsi; stancarsi; esaurirsi; **to wear well** essere di ottima durata

**wear' and tear'** [ter] *s* logorio

**weariness** ['wɪrɪnɪs] *s* fatica, stanchezza

**wear'ing appar'el** ['werɪŋ] *s* abbigliamento, articoli *mpl* d'abbigliamento

**wearisome** ['wɪrɪsəm] *adj* affaticante; (*tedious*) noioso

**wea·ry** ['wɪri] *adj* (**-ier; -iest**) stanco ‖ *v* (*pret & pp* **-ried**) *tr* stancare ‖ *intr* stancarsi

**weasel** ['wizəl] *s* donnola

**wea'sel words'** *spl* parole *fpl* ambigue

**weather** ['wɛðər] *s* tempo; maltempo; **to be under the weather** (coll) non sentirsi bene; (*to be slightly drunk*) (coll) essere alticcio ‖ *tr* (*lumber*) stagionare; (*adversities*) superare, resistere (with *dat*)

**weather-beaten** ['wɛðər‚bitən] *adj* segnato dalle intemperie

**weath'er bu'reau** *s* servizio metereologico

**weath'er·cock'** *s* banderuola

**weath'er fore'cast** *s* previsioni *fpl* del tempo, bollettino metereologico

**weath'er·man'** *s* (**-men'**) metereologo

**weath'er report'** *s* bollettino metereologico

**weath'er strip'ping** ['strɪpɪŋ] *s* guarnizione a nastro per inzeppare

**weath'er vane'** *s* banderuola, ventarola

**weave** [wiv] *s* tessitura ‖ *v* (*pret* **wove** [wov] or **weaved**; *pp* **wove** or **woven** ['wovən]) *tr* tessere; (fig) inserire; **to weave one's way** aprirsi un varco serpeggiando ‖ *intr* tessere; serpeggiare

**weaver** ['wivər] *s* tessitore *m*

**web** [wɛb] *s* tessuto; (*of spider*) tela; (*of rail*) anima, gambo; (zool) membrana; (fig) rete *f*, maglia

**web-footed** ['wɛb‚fʊtɪd] *adj* palmipede

**wed** [wɛd] *v* (*pret & pp* **wed** or **wedded**; *ger* **wedding**) *tr* sposare; (*said of the groom*) impalmare; (*said of the bride*) andare in sposa a ‖ *intr* sposarsi

**wedding** ['wɛdɪŋ] *adj* nuziale ‖ *s* sposalizio, nozze *fpl*, matrimonio

**wed'ding cake'** *s* torta nuziale

**wed'ding day'** *s* giorno di nozze

**wed'ding invita'tion** *s* invito a nozze

**wed'ding march'** *s* marcia nuziale

**wed'ding ring'** *s* fede *f*, vera

**wedge** [wɛdʒ] *s* cuneo; (*of pie*) spicchio; (*to split wood*) bietta; (*to hold a wheel*) scarpa ‖ *tr* incuneare

**wed'lock** *s* matrimonio

**Wednesday** ['wɛnzdi] *s* mercoledì *m*

**wee** [wi] *adj* piccolo piccolo

**weed** [wid] *s* malerba, erbaccia; (coll) sigaretta; (slang) marijuana; **weeds** vestito da lutto, gramaglie *fpl* ‖ *tr* sarchiare, mondare

**weeder** ['widər] *s* (agr) estirpatore *m*

**weed'ing hoe'** *s* sarchio, zappa

**weed'-kill'er** *s* diserbante *m*

**week** [wik] *s* settimana; **week in, week out** una settimana dopo l'altra

**week'day'** *s* giorno feriale

**week'end'** *s* fine-settimana *m*, fine *f* di settimana, week-end *m* ‖ *intr* passare il fine-settimana

**week·ly** ['wikli] *adj* settimanale ‖ *s* (**-lies**) settimanale *m* ‖ *adv* settimanalmente

**weep** [wip] *v* (*pret & pp* **wept** [wɛpt]) *tr* piangere; **to weep oneself to sleep** addormentarsi piangendo; **to weep one's eyes out** piangere a calde lacrime ‖ *intr* piangere; **to weep for joy** piangere di gioia

**weeper** ['wipər] *s* piagnone *m*; (*hired mourner*) prefica

**weep'ing wil'low** *s* salice *m* piangente

**weep·y** ['wipi] *adj* (**-ier; -iest**) piangente, lacrimoso

**weevil** ['wivəl] *s* curculione *m*

**weft** [wɛft] *s* (*yarns running across warp*) trama; (*fabric*) tela, tessuto

**weigh** [we] *tr* pesare; (*anchor*) levare; (*to make heavy*) appesantire; (fig) soppesare, ponderare; **to weigh down** piegare ‖ *intr* pesare; gravitare; **to weigh in** (sports) pesarsi; **to weigh upon** gravare a

**weigh'bridge'** *s* stadera

**weight** [wet] *s* peso; (fig) peso; **to carry weight** aver del peso; **to lose weight** diminuire di peso; **to put on weight** crescere di peso; **to throw**

**one's weight around** far sentire la propria importanza || *tr* appesantire; (*statistically*) ponderare, dare un certo peso a

**weightless** ['wetlɪs] *adj* senza peso, imponderabile

**weightlessness** ['wetlɪsnɪs] *s* imponderabilità *f*

**weight•y** ['weti] *adj* (**-ier; -iest**) pesante; importante

**weir** [wɪr] *s* sbarramento; (*for catching fish*) pescaia

**weird** [wɪrd] *adj* soprannaturale, misterioso; strano, bizzarro

**welcome** ['welkəm] *adj* benvenuto; gradito; **you are welcome** (*i.e., gladly received*) sia il benvenuto; (*in answer to thanks*) prego; **you are welcome to it** è a Sua disposizione; **you are welcome to your opinion** pensi come la vuole || *s* benvenuto || *tr* dare il benvenuto a; accettare; gradire || *interj* benvenuto!

**weld** [weld] *s* saldatura autogena; (bot) guaderella || *tr* saldare || *intr* saldarsi

**welder** ['weldər] *s* saldatore *m*; (*machine*) saldatrice *f*

**welding** ['weldɪŋ] *s* saldatura autogena

**wel'fare'** *s* benessere *m*; (*effort to improve living conditions*) beneficenza, assistenza; **to be on welfare** ricevere assistenza pubblica

**wel'fare state'** *s* stato sociale or assistenziale

**well** [wel] *adj* bene; in buona salute || *s* pozzo; (*for ink*) pozzetto, serbatoio; (*spring*) sorgente *f*; (*shaft for stairs*) tromba || *adv* bene; **as well** pure; **as well . . . as** tanto . . . come; **as well as** tanto come, non meno che || *intr* —**to well up** sgorgare || *interj* behl; bene!; alloral, dunque!

**well-appointed** ['welə'pɔɪntɪd] *adj* ben ammobiliato

**well-attended** ['welə'tendɪd] *adj* molto frequentato

**well-behaved** ['welbɪ'hevd] *adj* beneducato; **to be well-behaved** comportarsi bene

**well'-be'ing** *s* benessere *m*

**well'born'** *adj* bennato

**well-bred** ['wel'bred] *adj* educato, costumato

**well-disposed** ['weldɪs'pozd] *adj* bendisposto

**well-done** ['wel'dʌn] *adj* benfatto; (*meat*) ben cotto

**well-fixed** ['wel'fɪkst] *adj* (coll) agiato, abbiente

**well-formed** ['wel'fɔrmd] *adj* benfatto

**well-founded** ['wel'faundɪd] *adj* fondato

**well-groomed** ['wel'grumd] *adj* (*person*) curato; (*horse*) ben governato

**well-heeled** ['wel'hild] *adj* (coll) agiato, benestante

**well-informed** ['welɪn'fɔrmd] *adj* bene informato

**well-intentioned** ['welɪn'tenʃənd] *adj* benintenzionato

**well'-kept'** *adj* ben conservato; (*person*) benportante; (*secret*) ben mantenuto

**well-known** ['wel'non] *adj* notorio, ben noto

**well-meaning** ['wel'minɪŋ] *adj* benevolo, benintenzionato

**well-nigh** ['wel'naɪ] *adv* quasi

**well'-off'** *adj* agiato, benestante

**well-preserved** ['welprɪ'zʌrvd] *adj* ben conservato; (*person*) benportante

**well-read** ['wel'red] *adj* colto, che ha letto molto

**well-spoken** ['wel'spokən] *adj* (*person*) raffinato nel parlare; (*word*) a proposito

**well'spring'** *s* sorgente *f*

**well' sweep'** *s* mazzacavallo del pozzo

**well-tempered** ['wel'tempərd] *adj* ben temperato

**well-thought-of** ['wel'θɔt ˌɑv] *adj* tenuto in alta considerazione

**well-timed** ['wel'taɪmd] *adj* opportuno

**well-to-do** ['weltə'du] *adj* benestante

**well-wisher** ['wel'wɪʃər] *s* amico, sostenitore *m*

**well-worn** ['wel'worn] *adj* (*clothing*) liso, consunto, trito; (*argument*) logoro, banale; portato con eleganza

**welsh** [welʃ] *intr*—**to welsh on** (*a promise*) (slang) mancare a; (*a person*) (slang) fregare || **Welsh** *adj & s* gallese *mf*; **the Welsh** i gallesi

**Welsh'man** *s* (**-men**) gallese *m*

**Welsh' rab'bit** or **rare'bit** ['rerbɪt] *s* fonduta fatta con la birra servita su pane abbrustolito

**welt** [welt] *s* (*finish along a seam*) costa; (*of shoe*) guardolo; (*wale from a blow*) riga, sferzata

**welter** ['weltər] *s* guazzabuglio; confusione; (*a tumbling about*) rotolio || *intr* rotolarsi, guazzare

**wel'ter•weight'** *s* (boxing) peso welter, peso medio-leggero

**wench** [wentʃ] *s* ragazza, giovane *f*

**wend** [wend] *tr*—**to wend one's way** dirigere i propri passi

**werewolf** ['wɪr ˌwulf] *s* lupo mannaro

**west** [west] *adj* occidentale || *s* ovest *m*, occidente *m* || *adv* verso l'ovest

**western** ['westərn] *adj* occidentale || *s* western *m*

**West' In'dies** ['ɪndiz] *spl* Indie *fpl* Occidentali

**westward** ['westwərd] *adv* verso l'ovest

**wet** [wet] *adj* (**wetter; wettest**) bagnato; (*paint*) fresco; (*damp*) umido; (*rainy*) piovoso; che permette la vendita delle bevande alcoliche || *s* umidità *f*; antiproibizionista *mf* || *v* (*pret* & *pp* **wet** or **wetted**; *ger* **wetting**) *tr* bagnare || *intr* bagnarsi

**wet' blan'ket** *s* guastafeste *mf*

**wether** ['weðər] *s* castrone *m*

**wet' nurse'** *s* nutrice *f*, balia

**whack** [hwæk] *s* (slang) colpo, percossa; (slang) prova, tentativo || *tr* (slang) percuotere

**whale** [hwel] *s* balena; **a whale of** (slang) gigantesco, e.g., **a whale of a lie** una bugia gigantesca; enorme, e.g., **a whale of a difference** una differenza enorme || *tr* (coll) battere || *intr* pescare balene

**whale'bone'** *s* osso di balena, fanone *m*

**wharf** [hwɔrf] s (**wharves** [hwɔrvz] or **wharfs**) molo

**what** [hwɑt] adj interr che; quale || adj rel quello . . . che; il . . . che, e.g., **wear what tie you prefer** mettiti la cravatta che preferisci || pron interr che; quale; **what else?** che altro?; **what if . . . ?** e se . . . ?; **what of it?** e che me ne importa? || pron rel quello che; **what's what** (coll) tutta la situazione || interj **what a . . . !** che . . . !, e.g., **what a beautiful day!** che splendida giornata!

**what·ev'er** adj qualsiasi; qualunque || pron quanto; che; quello che

**what'not'** s scaffaletto

**wheal** [hwil] s vescichetta

**wheat** [hwit] s grano, frumento

**wheedle** ['hwidǝl] tr adulare; persuadere con lusinghe; (money) spillare

**wheel** [hwil] s ruota; (of cheese) forma; (coll) bicicletta; **at the wheel** al volante; in controllo || tr roteare; portare in carrozzella || intr girare

**wheelbarrow** ['hwil ˌbæro] s carriola

**wheel'base'** s passo

**wheel'chair'** s carrozzella

**wheel' col'umn** s (aut) piantone m di guida

**wheeler-dealer** ['hwilǝr'dilǝr] s (slang) grande affarista m

**wheel' horse'** s cavallo di timone; lavoratore m di fiducia

**wheelwright** ['hwil ˌraɪt] s carradore m

**wheeze** [hwiz] s affanno; (pathol) rantolo || intr respirare affannosamente; (pathol) rantolare

**whelp** [hwelp] s cucciolo || tr & intr figliare, partorire

**when** [hwen] adv & conj quando

**whence** [hwens] adv donde, di dove || conj donde; per che ragione

**when·ev'er** conj ogniqualvolta, qualora

**where** [hwer] adv & conj dove

**whereabouts** ['hwɛrǝ ˌbauts] s luogo dove uno si trova || adv & conj dove

**whereas** [hwer'æz] conj mentre; visto che, considerato che

**where·by'** adv per cui, col quale

**wherever** [hwer'evǝr] adv dove mai || conj dovunque

**wherefore** ['hwerfor] s perché m || adv perché || conj per cui, percome

**where·from'** adv donde

**where·in'** adv dove; in che modo || conj dove; nel quale

**where·of'** adv di che || conj di che; del quale

**where'upon'** adv sul che; laonde, dopodiché

**wherewithal** ['hwɛrwɪð ˌɔl] s mezzi mpl

**whet** [hwet] v (pret & pp **whetted**; ger **whetting**) tr affilare; (the appetite) aguzzare

**whether** ['weðǝr] conj se; **whether or no** ad ogni modo, in ogni caso; **whether or not** che . . . o che non

**whet'stone'** s pietra da affilare

**whey** [hwe] s scotta

**which** [hwɪt∫] adj interr quale || adj rel il (la, etc.) quale || pron interr che; quale; **which is which** qual'è l'uno e qual'è l'altro || pron rel che; il quale; quello che

**which·ev'er** adj & pron rel qualunque

**whiff** [hwɪf] s (of air) soffio; fiutata; (trace of odor) zaffata; **to get a whiff of** sentire l'odore di || intr soffiare; (said of a smoker) dare boccate

**while** [hwaɪl] s tempo; **a long while** un bel pezzo; **a while ago** un tratto fa; **to be worth one's while** valere la pena || conj mentre || tr—**to while away** passare piacevolmente

**whim** [hwɪm] s capriccio, estro

**whimper** ['hwɪmpǝr] s piagnucolio || tr & intr piagnucolare

**whimsical** ['hwɪmzɪkǝl] adj capriccioso, estroso, stravagante

**whine** [hwaɪn] s (of dog) guaito; (of person) piagnucolio || intr (said of a dog) guaire, uggiolare; (said of a person) piagnucolare

**whin·ny** ['hwɪni] s (-nies) nitrito || v (pret & pp -nied) intr nitrire

**whip** [hwɪp] s frusta; uova fpl sbattute con frutta || v (pret & pp **whipped** or **whipt**; ger **whipping**) tr frustare, battere; (eggs) frullare; (coll) vincere, sconfiggere; **to whip off** (coll) buttar giù; **to whip out** tirar fuori rapidamente; **to whip up** (coll) preparare in quattro e quattr'otto; (coll) eccitare, incitare

**whip'cord'** s cordino della frusta; (fabric) saia a diagonale

**whip' hand'** s mano che tiene la frusta; vantaggio, posizione vantaggiosa

**whip'lash'** s scudisciata

**whipped' cream'** s panna montata

**whipper-snapper** ['hwɪpǝr ˌsnæpǝr] s pivello

**whippet** ['hwɪpɪt] s piccolo levriere

**whip'ping boy'** ['hwɪpɪŋ] s testa di turco

**whip'ping post'** s palo per la fustigazione

**whippoorwill** [ ˌhwɪpǝr'wɪl] s caprimulgo, succiacapre m

**whir** [hwʌr] s ronzio || v (pret & pp **whirred**; ger **whirring**) intr ronzare; volare ronzando

**whirl** [hwʌrl] s giro improvviso; corsa; mulinello; (fig) successione || tr & intr mulinare; **my head whirls** mi gira la testa

**whirligig** ['hwʌrli ˌgɪg] s turbine m; (carrousel) giostra; (toy) girandola; (ent) ragno d'acqua

**whirl'pool'** s risucchio, mulinello

**whirl'wind'** s turbine m, tromba d'aria

**whirlybird** ['hwʌrli ˌbʌrd] s (coll) elicottero

**whish** [hwɪ∫] s fruscio || intr frusciare

**whisk** [hwɪsk] s scopatina || tr scopare, spolverare; (eggs) sbattere; **to whisk out of sight** far sparire || intr guizzare

**whisk' broom'** s scopetta per i vestiti, spolverino

**whiskers** ['hwɪskǝrz] spl barba; (on side of man's face) basette fpl; (of cat) baffi mpl

**whiskey** ['hwɪski] s whisky m

**whisper** ['hwɪspər] *s* sussurro, bisbiglio, mormorio; **in a whisper** in un sussurro || *tr* & *intr* sussurrare, bisbigliare, mormorare

**whisperer** ['hwɪspərər] *s* sussurrone *m*

**whispering** ['hwɪspərɪŋ] *adj* di maldicenze || *s* sussurro; maldicenza

**whistle** ['hwɪsəl] *s* fischio; **to wet one's whistle** (coll) bagnarsi l'ugola || *tr* fischiare || *intr* fischiare, zufolare; **to whistle for** chiamare con un fischio; (*money*) aspettare in vano

**whis'tle stop'** *s* stazioncina, paesetto

**whit** [hwɪt] *s*—**not a whit** niente affatto

**white** [hwaɪt] *adj* bianco || *s* bianco; **whites** (pathol) leucorrea

**white'cap'** *s* frangente *m*, cavallone *m*, onda crespa

**white' coal'** *s* carbone bianco

**white'-col'lar** *adj* impiegatizio

**white' feath'er** *s*—**to show the white feather** mostrarsi vile

**white' goods'** *spl* biancheria da casa; articoli *mpl* di cotone; apparecchi *mpl* elettrodomestici

**white-haired** ['hwaɪt,herd] *adj* dai capelli bianchi; (coll) favorito

**white' heat'** *s* calor bianco

**white' lead'** [led] *s* biacca

**white' lie'** *s* bugia innocente

**white' meat'** *s* bianco; carne *f* del petto

**whiten** ['hwaɪtən] *tr* imbiancare, sbiancare || *intr* imbiancarsi, sbiancarsi; impallidire

**whiteness** ['hwaɪtnɪs] *s* bianchezza

**white' plague'** *s* tubercolosi *f*

**white' slav'ery** *s* tratta delle bianche

**white' tie'** *s* cravatta da frac; marsina, abito da cerimonia

**white'wash'** *s* imbiancatura; (fig) copertura || *tr* imbiancare, intonacare; (fig) coprire

**white' wa'ter lil'y** *s* ninfea

**whither** ['hwɪðər] *adv* dove, a che luogo || *conj* dove

**whiting** ['hwaɪtɪŋ] *s* (ichth) nasello; (ichth) merlango

**whitish** ['hwaɪtɪʃ] *adj* biancastro

**whitlow** ['hwɪtlo] *s* patereccio

**Whitsuntide** ['hwɪtsən,taɪd] *s* settimana di Pentecoste

**whittle** ['hwɪtəl] *tr* digrossare; **to whittle away or down** ridurre gradualmente

**whiz or whizz** [hwɪz] *s* sibilo; (coll) asso || *v* (*pret* & *pp* **whizzed**; *ger* **whizzing**) *intr*—**to whiz by** passare sibilando; passare come una freccia

**who** [hu] *pron interr* chi; **who else?** chi altri?; **who goes there?** (mil) chi va là?; **who's who** chi è l'uno e chi è l'altro; chi è la gente importante || *pron rel* chi; il quale

**whoa** [hwo] or [wo] *interj* fermo!

**who·ev'er** *pron rel* chiunque

**whole** [hol] *adj* tutto, intero; sano, intatto; **made out of the whole cloth** completamente immaginario || *s* tutto; **as a whole** nell'insieme; **on the whole** in generale

**wholehearted** ['hol,hɑrtɪd] *adj* molto sincero, generoso

**whole' note'** *s* (mus) semibreve *f*

**whole'sale'** *adj* & *adv* all'ingrosso || *s* ingrosso || *tr* vendere all'ingrosso || *intr* vendersi all'ingrosso

**wholesaler** ['hol,selər] *s* grossista *mf*

**wholesome** ['holsəm] *adj* (*beneficial*) salutare; (*in good health*) sano

**wholly** ['holi] *adv* interamente

**whom** [hum] *pron interr* chi || *pron rel* che; il quale

**whom·ev'er** *pron rel* chiunque

**whoop** [hup] or [hwup] *s* urlo; (pathol) urlo della pertosse; **to not be worth a whoop** (coll) non valere un fico secco || *tr*—**to whoop it up** (slang) fare il diavolo a quattro || *intr* urlare

**whoop'ing cough'** ['hupɪŋ] or ['hwup-ɪŋ] *s* pertosse *f*

**whopper** ['hwɑpər] *s* (coll) enormità *f;* (coll) fandonia, bugia enorme

**whopping** ['hwɑpɪŋ] *adj* (coll) enorme

**whore** [hor] *s* puttana || *intr*—**to whore around** puttaneggiare; andare a puttane

**whortleber·ry** ['hwʌrtəl,beri] *s* (-ries) mirtillo

**whose** [huz] *pron interr* di chi || *pron rel* di chi; del quale; di cui

**why** [hwaɪ] *s* (whys) perché *m;* **the whys and the wherefores** il perché e il percome || *adv* perché || *interj* diamine!; **why, certainly!** certamente!; **why, yes!** evidentemente!

**wick** [wɪk] *s* stoppino, lucignolo

**wicked** ['wɪkɪd] *adj* malvagio; (*mischievous*) cattivo; (*dreadful*) terribile, bestiale

**wicker** ['wɪkər] *adj* di vimini || *s* vimine *m*

**wicket** ['wɪkɪt] *s* (*small door*) portello; (*ticket window*) sportello; (*of a canal*) chiusa; (cricket) porta; (croquet) archetto

**wide** [waɪd] *adj* largo; esteso; (*eyes*) aperto; (*sense of a word*) lato || *adv* largamente; completamente; lontano; **wide of the mark** lontano dal bersaglio

**wide'-an'gle** *adj* grandangolare

**wide'-awake'** *adj* sveglio

**widen** ['waɪdən] *tr* slargare, estendere || *intr* slargarsi, estendersi

**wide'-o'pen** *adj* spalancato; (*to a gambler*) accessibile

**wide'-spread'** *adj* (e.g., *arms*) aperto; diffuso

**widow** ['wɪdo] *s* vedova; (cards) morto || *tr* lasciar vedova

**widower** ['wɪdo·ər] *s* vedovo

**widowhood** ['wɪdo,hud] *s* vedovanza

**wid'ow's mite'** *s* obolo della vedova

**wid'ow's weeds'** *spl* gramaglie *fpl* vedovili

**width** [wɪdθ] *s* larghezza

**wield** [wild] *tr* (e.g., *a sword*) brandire; (e.g., *a hammer*) maneggiare; (*power*) esercitare

**wife** [waɪf] *s* (**wives** [waɪvz]) moglie *f*

**wig** [wɪg] *s* parrucca

**wiggle** ['wɪgəl] *s* dimenio; (*of fish*)

guizzo || *tr* dimenare || *intr* dime-narsi; guizzare

**wig'wag'** *s* segnalazione con bandierine || *v* (*pret* & *pp* **-wagged;** *ger* **-wagging**) *tr* & *intr* segnalare con bandierine

**wigwam** ['wɪgwɑm] *s* tenda a cupola dei pellirosse, wigwam *m*

**wild** [waɪld] *adj* (*animal*) feroce; (*e.g.*, *berry*) selvatico; (*barbarous*) selvaggio; (*violent*) furioso; (*mad*) pazzo; (*unruly*) discolo, indisciplinato; (*extravagant*) pazzesco; (*shot or throw*) lanciato all'impazzata; **wild about** pazzo per || *s* regione deserta; **the wild** la foresta; **wilds** regioni selvagge || *adv* pazzamente; **to go wild** andare in delirio; **to run wild** crescere all'impazzata; correre senza freno

**wild' boar'** *s* cinghiale *m*

**wild' card'** *s* matta

**wild'cat'** *s* gatto selvatico; lince *f;* impresa arrischiata || *v* (*pret* & *pp* **-catted;** *ger* **-catting**) *tr* & *intr* esplorare per conto proprio

**wild'cat strike'** *s* sciopero non autorizzato dal sindacato

**wilderness** ['wɪldərnɪs] *s* deserto

**wild-eyed** ['waɪld,aɪd] *adj* stralunato; (*scheme*) pazzesco

**wild'fire'** *s* fuoco greco; fuoco fatuo; **to spread like wildfire** crescere come la gramigna; (*said of news*) spargersi come il baleno

**wild' flow'er** *s* fiore *m* di campo

**wild' goose'** *s* oca selvatica

**wild'-goose' chase'** *s* ricerca della luna nel pozzo

**wild'life'** *s* animali *spl* selvatici

**wild' oat'** *s* avena selvatica; **to sow one's wild oats** correre la cavallina

**wild' ol'ive** *s* olivastro, oleastro

**wile** [waɪl] *s* stratagemma *m*, inganno; (*cunning*) astuzia || *tr* allettare; **to wile away** passare piacevolmente

**will** [wɪl] *s* volontà *f*, volere *m;* (*law*) testamento; **at will** a volontà || *tr* volere; (*law*) legare || *intr* volere; **do as you will** faccia come vuole || *v* (*pret* & *cond* **would**) *aux* **she will leave tomorrow** partirà domani; **a cactus plant will live two months without water** una pianta grassa può vivere due mesi senz'acqua

**willful** ['wɪlfəl] *adj* volontario; ostinato

**willfulness** ['wɪlfəlnɪs] *s* volontarietà *f;* ostinatezza

**William** ['wɪljəm] *s* Guglielmo

**willing** ['wɪlɪŋ] *adj* volonteroso; **to be willing** essere disposto

**willingly** ['wɪlɪŋli] *adv* di buon grado, volentieri

**willingness** ['wɪlɪŋnɪs] *s* buona voglia, propensione

**will-o'-the-wisp** ['wɪləðə'wɪsp] *s* fuoco fatuo; (*fig*) illusione, chimera

**willow** ['wɪlo] *s* salice *m*

**willowy** ['wɪlo·i] *adj* pieghevole; (*slender*) snello; pieno di giunchi

**will' pow'er** *s* forza di volontà

**willy-nilly** ['wɪlɪ'nɪli] *adv* volente o nolente

**wilt** [wɪlt] *tr* far appassire || *intr* appassire, avvizzire

**wil·y** ['waɪli] *adj* (**-ier; -iest**) astuto, scaltro

**wimple** ['wɪmpəl] *s* soggolo

**win** [wɪn] *s* vittoria, vincita || *v* (*pret* & *pp* **won** [wʌn]; *ger* **winning**) *tr* & *intr* guadagnare; **to win out** vincere, aver successo

**wince** [wɪns] *s* sussulto || *intr* sussultare

**winch** [wɪntʃ] *s* verricello; (*handle*) manovella; (naut) molinello

**wind** [wɪnd] *s* vento; (*gas in intestines*) vento; (*breath*) fiato, tenuta; **to break wind** scoreggiare; **to get wind of** subodorare; **to sail close to the wind** (naut) andare all'orza; **to take the wind out of the sails of** sconcertare; **winds** (mus) fiati *mpl* || *tr* far perdere il fiato a || [waɪnd] *v* (*pret* & *pp* **wound** [waʊnd]) *tr* (*to wrap up*) arrotolare; (*thread, wool*) dipanare, aggomitolare; (*a clock*) caricare; (*a handle*) far girare; **to wind one's way through** serpeggiare per; **to wind up** arrotolare; eccitare; finire, portare a termine || *intr* serpeggiare, snodarsi

**windbag** ['wɪnd,bæg] *s* (*of a bagpipe*) otre *m;* (fig) parolaio, otre *m* di vento

**windbreak** ['wɪnd,brek] *s* frangivento

**wind' cone'** [wɪnd] *s* manica a vento

**winded** ['wɪndɪd] *adj* senza fiato

**windfall** ['wɪnd,fɔl] *s* frutta abbattuta dal vento; provvidenza, manna del cielo

**wind'ing sheet'** ['waɪndɪŋ] *s* lenzuolo funebre

**wind'ing stairs'** ['waɪndɪŋ] *spl* scala a chiocciola

**wind' in'strument** [wɪnd] *s* (mus) strumento a fiato

**windlass** ['wɪndləs] *s* verricello

**windmill** ['wɪnd,mɪl] *s* mulino a vento; (*air turbine*) aeromotore *m;* **to tilt at windmills** combattere i mulini a vento

**window** ['wɪndo] *s* finestra; (*of ticket office*) sportello; (*of car or coach*) finestrino

**win'dow dress'er** *s* vetrinista *mf*

**win'dow dress'ing** *s* vetrinistica; (fig) facciata, apparenza

**win'dow en'velope** *s* busta a finestrella

**win'dow frame'** *s* intelaiatura della finestra

**win'dow·pane'** *s* vetro, invetriata

**win'dow sash'** *s* intelaiatura della finestra

**win'dow screen'** *s* zanzariera

**win'dow shade'** *s* tendina avvolgibile

**win'dow-shop'** *v* (*pret* & *pp* **-shopped;** *ger* **-shopping**) *intr* guardare nelle vetrine senza comprare

**win'dow sill'** *s* davanzale *m* della finestra

**windpipe** ['wɪnd,paɪp] *s* trachea

**windproof** ['wɪnd,pruf] *adj* resistente al vento

**windshield** ['wɪnd,ʃild] *s* parabrezza *m*

**wind'shield wash'er** *s* lavacristallo

**wind'shield wip'er** *s* tergicristallo
**windsock** ['wɪnd ˌsɑk] *s* (aer) manica a vento
**windstorm** ['wɪnd ˌstɔrm] *s* bufera di vento
**wind' tun'nel** [wɪnd] *s* (aer) galleria aerodinamica
**wind-up** ['waɪnd ˌʌp] *s* conclusione
**windward** ['wɪndwərd] *s* orza, sopravvento; **to turn to windward** mettersi al sopravvento
**Wind'ward Is'lands** *spl* Isole *fpl* Sopravvento
**wind·y** ['wɪndi] *adj* (**-ier; -iest**) ventoso; verboso, ampolloso; **it is windy** fa vento
**wine** [waɪn] *s* vino || *tr* offrire vino a || *intr* bere del vino
**wine' cel'lar** *s* cantina
**wine'glass'** *s* bicchiere da vino
**winegrower** ['waɪn ˌgro·ər] *s* vinificatore *m*, viticoltore *m*
**wine' press'** *s* torchio per l'uva
**winer·y** ['waɪnəri] *s* (**-ies**) stabilimento vinicolo
**wine'shop'** *s* fiaschetteria
**wine'skin'** *s* otre *m*
**wine' stew'ard** *s* sommelier *m*
**winetaster** ['waɪn ˌtestər] *s* degustatore *m* di vini
**wing** [wɪŋ] *s* ala; (*unit of air force*) aerobrigata; (theat) quinta; **to take wing** levarsi a volo; **under one's wing** sotto la protezione di qlcu || *tr* ferire nell'ala; **to wing one's way** volare, portarsi a volo
**wing' chair'** *s* poltrona a orecchioni
**wing' col'lar** *s* colletto per marsina
**wing' nut'** *s* (mach) galletto
**wing'span'** *s* (*of airplane*) apertura alare
**wing'spread'** *s* (*of bird*) apertura alare
**wink** [wɪŋk] *s* ammicco; **in a wink** in un batter d'occhio; **to not sleep a wink** non chiudere occhio; **to take forty winks** (coll) schiacciare un pisolino || *tr* (*the eye*) strizzare || *intr* ammiccare, strizzare l'occhio; (*to blink*) battere le ciglia; **to wink at** ammiccare a; far finta di non vedere
**winner** ['wɪnər] *s* vincitore *m*
**winning** ['wɪnɪŋ] *adj* vincente, vincitore; attraente, simpatico || **winnings** *spl* vincita
**winnow** ['wɪno] *tr* ventilare, brezzare; (fig) vagliare || *intr* svolazzare
**winsome** ['wɪnsəm] *adj* attraente
**winter** ['wɪntər] *adj* invernale || *s* inverno || *intr* svernare
**win'ter·green'** *s* tè *m* del Canadà; olio di gaulteria
**win·try** ['wɪntri] *adj* (**-trier; -triest**) invernale; freddo
**wipe** [waɪp] *tr* forbire, detergere; (*to dry*) asciugare; **to wipe away** (*tears*) asciugare; **to wipe off** pulire, forbire; **to wipe out** distruggere completamente; (coll) eliminare
**wiper** ['waɪpər] *s* strofinaccio; (mach) camma; (elec) contatto scorrevole
**wire** [waɪr] *s* filo metallico; telegramma *m*; (coll) telegrafo; **to pull wires** manovrare di dietro le quinte

|| *tr* legare con filo metallico; attrezzare l'elettricità in; (coll) mandare per telegrafo; (coll) telegrafare || *intr* (coll) telegrafare
**wire' cut'ter** *s* pinza tagliafili
**wire' entan'glement** *s* reticolato di filo spinato
**wire' gauge'** *s* calibro da fili
**wire-haired** ['waɪr ˌherd] *adj* a pelo ruvido
**wireless** ['waɪrlɪs] *adj* senza fili || *s* telegrafo senza fili; telegrafia senza fili
**wire' nail'** *s* chiodo da falegname
**wirepulling** ['waɪr ˌpulɪŋ] *s* manovra dietro alle quinte
**wire' record'er** *s* magnetofono a filo
**wire' screen'** *s* rete metallica
**wire'tap'** *v* (*pret & pp* **-tapped; ger -tapping**) *tr* (*a conversation*) intercettare
**wiring** ['waɪrɪŋ] *s* sistema *m* di fili elettrici
**wir·y** ['waɪri] *adj* (**-ier; -iest**) fatto di filo; (*hair*) ispido; (*tone*) metallico, vibrante; (*sinewy*) segaligno
**wisdom** ['wɪzdəm] *s* senno, sapienza, saggezza
**wis'dom tooth'** *s* dente *m* del giudizio
**wise** [waɪz] *adj* saggio, sapiente; (*decision*) giudizioso; **to be wise to** (slang) accorgersi del gioco di; **to get wise** (slang) mangiare la foglia; (slang) diventare impertinente || *s* modo, maniera; **in no wise** in nessun modo || *tr*—**to wise up** (slang) avvertire || *intr*—**to wise up** (slang) accorgersi
**wiseacre** ['waɪz ˌekər] *s* sapientone *m*
**wise'crack'** *s* (coll) spiritosaggine *f* || *intr* (coll) dire spiritosaggini
**wise' guy'** *s* (slang) sputasentenze *m*
**wish** [wɪʃ] *s* desiderio; augurio; **to make a wish** formulare un desiderio || *tr* desiderare; augurare; **to wish s.o. a good day** dare il buon giorno a qlcu || *intr* desiderare; **to wish for** desiderare
**wish'bone'** *s* forcella
**wishful** ['wɪʃfəl] *adj* desideroso
**wish'ful think'ing** *s* pio desiderio
**wistful** ['wɪstfəl] *adj* melanconico, pensoso, meditabondo
**wit** [wɪt] *s* spirito; (*person*) bellospirito; (*understanding*) senso; **to be at one's wits' end** non sapere a che santo votarsi; **to have one's wits about one** avere presenza di spirito; **to live by one's wits** vivere di espedienti
**witch** [wɪtʃ] *s* strega
**witch'craft'** *s* stregoneria
**witch' doc'tor** *s* stregone *m*
**witch'es' Sab'bath** *s* sabba *m*
**witch' ha'zel** *s* (*shrub*) amamelide *f*; (*liquid*) estratto di amamelide
**witch' hunt'** *s* caccia alle streghe
**with** [wɪð] or [wɪθ] *prep* con; a, e.g., **with open arms** a braccia aperte; di, e.g., **covered with silk** coperto di seta; **to be satisfied with the performance** essere contento della rappresentazione; da, e.g., **with the In-**

dians dagli indiani; **to part with** separarsi da

**with·draw'** *v* (*pret* **-drew;** *pp* **-drawn**) *tr* ritirare || *intr* ritirarsi

**withdrawal** [wɪð'drɔ·əl] or [wɪθ'drɔ·əl] *s* ritiro, ritirata; (*of funds*) prelevamento

**wither** ['wɪðər] *tr* intisichire; (*with a glance*) incenerire || *intr* avvizzire, intisichire

**with·hold'** *v* (*pret & pp* **-held**) *tr* trattenere; (*information*) sottacere; (*payment*) defalcare; (*permission*) negare

**withhold'ing tax'** *s* imposta trattenuta

**with·in'** *adv* dentro, didentro || *prep* entro, entro di, dentro a, dentro di; fra; in; (*a time period*) nel giro di

**with·out'** *adv* fuori || *prep* senza; fuori, fuori di; **to do without** fare a meno di; **without** + *ger* senza + *inf*, e.g., **without saying a word** senza dire una parola; senza che + *subj*, e.g., **she fell without anyone helping her** cadde senza che nessuno l'aiutasse

**with·stand'** *v* (*pret & pp* **-stood**) *tr* resistere (with *dat*), reggere (with *dat*)

**witness** ['wɪtnɪs] *s* testimone *mf;* **in witness whereof** in fé di che; **to bear witness** far fede || *tr* (*to be present at*) presenziare; (*to attest*) testimoniare, firmare come testimone

**wit'ness stand'** *s* banco dei testimoni

**witticism** ['wɪtɪ ˌsɪzəm] *s* motto, battuta spiritosa, spiritosaggine *f*

**wittingly** ['wɪtɪŋli] *adv* consapevolmente

**wit·ty** ['wɪti] *adj* (**-tier; -tiest**) spiritoso, divertente

**wizard** ['wɪzərd] *s* mago

**wizardry** ['wɪzərdri] *s* magia

**wizened** ['wɪzənd] *adj* raggrinzito

**woad** [wod] *s* (bot) guado

**wobble** ['wabəl] *s* oscillazione, dondolio || *intr* oscillare, dondolare; (*said of a chair*) zoppicare; (fig) titubare

**wob·bly** ['wabli] *adj* (**-blier; -bliest**) oscillante, zoppo, malfermo

**woe** [wo] *s* disgrazia, afflizione, sventura; || *interj*—**woe is me!** ahimè!

**woebegone** ['wobɪ ˌgɔn] or ['wobɪ ˌgan] *adj* triste, abbattuto

**woeful** ['wofəl] *adj* sfortunato, disgraziato; (*of poor quality*) orribile

**wolf** [wʊlf] *s* (**wolves** [wʊlvz]) lupo; (coll) dongiovanni *m;* **to cry wolf** gridare al lupo; **to keep the wolf from the door** tener lontana la miseria || *tr & intr* mangiare come un lupo

**wolf'hound'** *s* cane *m* da pastore alsaziano

**wolfram** ['wʊlfrəm] *s* wolframio

**wolf's-bane** or **wolfsbane** ['wʊlfs ˌben] *s* (bot) aconito

**wolverine** [ ˌwʊlvə'rin] *s* (zool) ghiottone *m*

**woman** ['wʊmən] *s* (**women** ['wɪmɪn]) donna

**womanhood** ['wʊmən ˌhʊd] *s* (*quality*) femminilità *f;* (*women collectively*) donne *fpl*, sesso femminile

**womanish** ['wʊmənɪʃ] *adj* femminile; (*effeminate*) effeminato

**wom'an·kind'** *s* sesso femminile

**womanly** ['wʊmənli] *adj* (**-lier; -liest**) femminile, muliebre

**wom'an suf'frage** *s* suffragio alle donne

**woman-suffragist** ['wʊmən'sʌfrədʒɪst] *s* suffragista *mf*

**womb** [wʊm] *s* utero; (fig) seno

**womenfolk** ['wɪmɪn ˌfok] *spl* le donne

**wonder** ['wʌndər] *s* (*something strange and surprising*) meraviglia; (*feeling*) ammirazione; (*miracle*) prodigio, miracolo; **for a wonder** cosa strana; **no wonder that** non fa meraviglia che; **to work wonders** fare miracoli || *tr*—**to wonder that** meravigliarsi che; **to wonder how, if, when, where, who, why** domandarsi or chiedersi come, se, quando, dove, chi, perché || *intr* meravigliarsi; chiedersi; **to wonder at** ammirare

**won'der drug'** *s* medicina miracolosa

**wonderful** ['wʌndərfəl] *adj* meraviglioso

**won'der·land'** *s* paese *m* delle meraviglie

**wonderment** ['wʌndərmənt] *s* sorpresa, meraviglia, stupore *m*

**won'der-work'er** *s* taumaturgo

**wont** [wʌnt] or [wɔnt] *adj* abituato, solito || *s* abitudine *f*, costume *m*

**wonted** ['wʌntɪd] or ['wɔntɪd] *adj* solito, abituale

**woo** [wu] *tr* (*a woman*) corteggiare; (*to seek to win*) allettare; (*good or bad consequences*) andare in cerca di

**wood** [wʊd] *s* legno; (*firewood*) legna; (*keg*) barile *m;* **out of the woods** fuori pericolo; al sicuro; **woods** bosco, selva

**woodbine** ['wʊd ˌbaɪn] *s* (*honeysuckle*) abbracciabosco; (*Virginia creeper*) vite *f* del Canadà

**wood' carv'ing** *s* intaglio in legno, statua in legno

**wood'chuck'** *s* marmotta americana

**wood'cock'** *s* beccaccia

**wood'cut'** *s* silografia

**wood'cut'ter** *s* boscaiolo

**wooded** ['wʊdɪd] *adj* legnoso, boschivo

**wooden** ['wʊdən] *adj* di legno; duro, rigido; inespressivo

**wood' engrav'ing** *s* silografia

**wooden-headed** ['wʊdən ˌhɛdɪd] *adj* (coll) dalla testa dura

**wood'en leg'** *s* gamba di legno

**wood'en shoe'** *s* zoccolo

**wood' grouse'** *s* gallo cedrone

**woodland** ['wʊdlənd] *adj* boschivo || *s* foresta, bosco

**wood'man** *s* (**-men**) boscaiolo

**woodpecker** ['wʊd ˌpɛkər] *s* picchio

**wood'pile'** *s* legnaia

**wood' screw'** *s* vite *f* per legno

**wood'shed'** *s* legnaia

**woods'man** *s* (**-men**) abitatore *m* dei boschi; boscaiolo

**wood'wind'** *s* strumento a fiato di legno

**wood'work'** *s* lavoro in legno; parti *fpl* di legno

**wood'work'er** *s* ebanista *m*, falegname *m*

**wood'worm'** *s* tarlo

**wood·y** ['wʊdì] *adj* (**-ier; -iest**) boscoso, alberato; (*like wood*) legnoso

**wooer** ['wu·ər] *s* corteggiatore *m*

**woof** [wuf] *s* (*yarns running across warp*) trama; (*fabric*) tessuto

**woofer** ['wufər] *s* altoparlante *m* per basse audiofrequenze, woofer *m*

**wool** [wʊl] *s* lana

**woolen** ['wʊlən] *adj* di lana ‖ *s* tessuto di lana; **woolens** laneria

**woolgrower** ['wʊl‚gro·ər] *s* allevatore *m* di pecore

**wool·ly** ['wʊli] *adj* (**-ier; -liest**) di lana; lanoso; (coll) confuso

**word** [wʌrd] *s* parola; **by word of mouth** oralmente; **to be as good as one's word** essere di parola; **to have a word with** dire quattro parole a; **to have word from** aver notizie da; **to keep one's word** essere di parola; **to leave word** lasciar detto; **to send word that** mandare a dire che; **words** (*quarrel*) baruffa ‖ *tr* esprimere, formulare ‖ **Word** *s* (theol) Verbo

**word' count'** *s* conto lessicale

**word' forma'tion** *s* formazione delle parole

**wording** ['wʌrdɪŋ] *s* fraseologia, dicitura

**word' or'der** *s* disposizione delle parole in una frase

**word'stock'** *s* lessico

**word·y** ['wʌrdi] *adj* (**-ier; -iest**) verboso, parolaio

**work** [wʌrk] *s* lavoro; (*of art, fortification, etc.*) opera; **at work** al lavoro, in ufficio; (*in operation*) in servizio; **out of work** senza lavoro, disoccupato; **to give s.o. the works** (slang) trattare male; (slang) ammazzare; **to shoot the works** (slang) scialare; **works** opificio; meccanismo; (*of clock*) castello ‖ *tr* far funzionare; lavorare, maneggiare; (*e.g., a miracle*) operare; (*e.g., iron*) trattare; **to work up** preparare; stimulare, eccitare ‖ *intr* lavorare; (*said of a machine*) funzionare; (*said of a remedy*) avere effetto; **to work loose** sciogliersi; **to work out** andare a finire; (*said of a problem*) sciogliersi; (*said of a total*) ammontare; (sports) allenarsi

**workable** ['wʌrkəbəl] *adj* (*feasible*) praticabile; (*e.g., iron*) lavorabile

**work'bench'** *s* banco

**work'book'** *s* manuale *m* d'istruzioni; (*for students*) quaderno d'esercizi

**work'box'** *s* cassetta dei ferri del mestiere; (*for needlework*) cestino da lavoro

**work'day'** *adj* lavorativo; ordinario, di tutti i giorni ‖ *s* (*working day*) giorno feriale, giornata lavorativa

**worked-up** ['wʌrkt‚ʌp] *adj* sovreccitato

**worker** ['wʌrkər] *s* lavorante *m*, lavoratore *m*, operaio

**work' force'** *s* mano *f* d'opera

**work'horse'** *s* cavallo da tiro; (*tireless worker*) lavoratore indefesso

**work'house'** *s* carcere *m* con lavoro obbligatorio; (Brit) istituto dei poveri

**work'ing class'** *s* classe operaia

**work'ing condi'tions** *spl* trattamento, condizioni *fpl* di lavoro

**work'ing girl'** *s* ragazza lavoratrice

**work'ing hours'** *spl* orario di lavoro

**working'man** *s* (**-men**) lavoratore *m*

**work'ing or'der** *s* buone condizioni, efficienza

**work'ing·wom'an** *s* (**-wom'en**) operaia, lavoratrice *f*

**work'man** *s* (**-men**) lavoratore *m;* (*skilled worker*) operaio specializzato

**workmanship** ['wʌrkmən‚ʃɪp] *s* fattura; (*work executed*) opera

**work' of art'** *s* opera d'arte

**work'out'** *s* (sports) esercizio, allenamento

**work'room'** *s* (*for manual work*) officina; (*study*) gabinetto, laboratorio

**work'shop'** *s* officina

**work' stop'page** *s* sospensione del lavoro

**world** [wʌrld] *adj* mondiale ‖ *s* mondo; **a world of** un monte di; **for all the world** per tutto l'oro del mondo; **in the world** al mondo; **since the world began** da che mondo è mondo; **the other world** l'altro mondo; **to bring into the world** mettere al mondo; **to see the world** conoscere il mondo; **to think the world of** tenere in altissima considerazione

**world' affairs'** *spl* relazioni *fpl* internazionali

**world·ly** ['wʌrldli] *adj* (**-lier; -liest**) mondano, secolare

**world'ly-wise'** *adj* vissuto

**world's' fair'** *s* esposizione *f* mondiale

**world' war'** *s* guerra mondiale

**world'-wide'** *adj* mondiale

**worm** [wʌrm] *s* verme *m* ‖ *tr* liberare dai vermi; **to worm a secret out of s.o.** carpire un segreto a qlcu; **to worm one's way into** insinuarsi in

**worm-eaten** ['wʌrm‚itən] *adj* tarlato, bacato

**worm' gear'** *s* meccanismo a vite perpetua, ingranaggio elicoidale

**worm'wood'** *s* assenzio; (fig) amarezza

**worm·y** ['wʌrmi] *adj* (**-ier; -iest**) verminoso; (*worm-eaten*) bacato; (*groveling*) vile, strascicante

**worn** [worn] *adj* usato; (*look*) stanco, esausto

**worn'-out'** *adj* logoro, scalcinato; (*by illness*) consunto; (fig) trito

**worrisome** ['wʌrisəm] *adj* preoccupante; (*inclined to worry*) preoccupato

**wor·ry** ['wʌri] *s* (**-ries**) preoccupazione, inquietudine *f*; (*trouble*) fastidio ‖ *v* (*pret & pp* **-ried**) *tr* preoccupare, inquietare; **to be worried** essere impensierito ‖ *intr* preoccuparsi, inquietarsi; **don't worry!** non si preoccupi!

**worse** [wʌrs] *adj & s* peggiore *m*, peggio ‖ *adv* peggio; **worse and worse** di male in peggio

**worsen** ['wʌrsən] *tr & intr* peggiorare

**wor·ship** ['wʌrʃɪp] *s* venerazione, adorazione; servizio religioso; **your Worship** La Signoria Vostra ‖ *v* (*pret &*

**pp -shiped** or **-shipped; ger -shiping** or **-shipping)** *tr* venerare, adorare

**worshiper** or **worshipper** ['wʌrʃɪpər] *s* adoratore *m;* (*in church*) devoto, fedele *m*

**worst** [wʌrst] *adj* (il) peggiore; pessimo || *s* peggio, peggiore *m;* **at worst** alla peggio; **if worst comes to worst** alla peggio; **to get the worst** averne la peggio || *adv* peggio

**worsted** ['wustɪd] *adj* di lana pettinata || *s* tessuto di lana pettinata

**wort** [wʌrt] *s* mosto di malto; pianta, erba

**worth** [wʌrθ] *adj* che vale, da, e.g., **worth ten dollars** da dieci dollari; **to be worth** valere; essere di pregio; **to be worth** + *ger* valere la pena (di) + *inf*, e.g., **it is worth reading** vale la pena (di) leggerlo || *s* pregio, valore *m;* **a dollar's worth** un dollaro di

**worthless** ['wʌrθlɪs] *adj* senza valore; inutile; inservibile; (*person*) indegno

**worth'while'** *adj* meritevole, meritevole d'attenzione

**wor·thy** ['wʌrði] *adj* (**-thier; -thiest**) degno, meritevole || *s* (**-thies**) maggiorente *mf*

**would** [wud] *v aux* **they said they would come** dissero che sarebbero venuti; **he would buy it if he had the money** lo comprerebbe se avesse i soldi; **would you be so kind to** avrebbe la cortesia di; **he would spend every winter in Florida** passava tutti gli inverni in Florida; **would that . . . !** oh se . . . !, volesse il cielo che . . . !, magari . . . !

**would'-be'** *adj* preteso, sedicente; (*intended to be*) inteso

**wound** [wund] *s* ferita || *tr* ferire

**wounded** ['wundɪd] *adj* ferito || **the wounded** i feriti

**wow** [wau] *s* distorsione acustica di suono riprodotto; (slang) successore *m* || *tr* (slang) entusiasmare || *interj* (coll) accidenti!

**wrack** [ræk] *s* naufragio; vestigio; (*seaweed*) alghe marine gettate sulla spiaggia; **to go to wrack and ruin** andare completamente in rovina

**wraith** [reθ] *s* spettro, fantasma *m*

**wrangle** ['ræŋgəl] *s* baruffa, alterco || *intr* altercare, rissare

**wrap** [ræp] *s* sciarpa; mantello || *v* (*pret & pp* **wrapped; ger wrapping**) *tr* involgere; impaccare; **to be wrapped up in** essere assorto in; **to wrap up** avvolgere; (*in paper*) incartare; (*in clothing*) imbaccuccare; (coll) concludere || *intr*—**to wrap up** imbaccuccarsi, avvolgersi

**wrapper** ['ræpər] *s* veste *f* da camera, peignoir *m;* (*of newspaper*) fascia, fascetta; (*of cigars*) involto

**wrap'ping pa'per** ['ræpɪŋ] *s* carta d'impacco or d'imballaggio

**wrath** [ræθ] or [rɑθ] *s* ira; vendetta

**wrathful** ['ræθfəl] or ['rɑθfəl] *adj* collerico, iracondo

**wreak** [rik] *tr* (*vengeance*) infliggere; (*anger*) scaricare

**wreath** [riθ] *s* (**wreaths** [riðz]) ghirlanda; (*of laurel*) laurea; (*of smoke*) spirale *f*

**wreathe** [rið] *tr* inghirlandare; avviluppare; (*a garland*) intessere || *intr* (*said of smoke*) innalzarsi in spire

**wreck** [rek] *s* rottame *m*, relitto; naufragio; rovina; catastrofe *f*, disastro; (fig) rottame *m*, relitto || *tr* far naufragare; distruggere, rovinare; (*a train*) fare scontrare, fare deragliare; (*a building*) demolire

**wreckage** ['rekɪdʒ] *s* rottami *mpl*, relitti *mpl;* rovine *fpl*

**wrecker** ['rekər] *s* (*tow truck*) autogrù *f;* (*housewrecker*) demolitore *m*

**wreck'ing ball'** *s* martello demolitore

**wreck'ing car'** *s* autogrù *f*

**wrecking' crane'** *s* (rr) carro gru

**wren** [ren] *s* scricciolo

**wrench** [rentʃ] *s* chiave *f;* (*pull*) tiro; (*of a joint*) distorsione || *tr* torcere, distorcere; (*one's limb*) torcersi, distorcersi

**wrest** [rest] *tr* strappare, togliere a viva forza; (*to twist*) torcere

**wrestle** ['resəl] *s* lotta, combattimento || *intr* fare la lotta, lottare

**wrestler** ['restlər] *s* lottatore *m*

**wrestling** ['reslɪŋ] *s* lotta

**wretch** [retʃ] *s* disgraziato, tapino

**wretched** ['retʃɪd] *adj* (*pitiable*) misero, disgraziato, tapino; (*poor, worthless*) miserabile

**wriggle** ['rɪgəl] *s* (e.g., *of a snake*) guizzo; dondolio || *tr* dondolare, dimenare || *intr* guizzare; dimenarsi; **to wriggle out of** sgattaiolare da, divincolarsi da

**wrig·gly** ['rɪgli] *adj* (**-glier; -gliest**) che si contorce; (fig) evasivo

**wring** [rɪŋ] *v* (*pret & pp* **wrung** [rʌŋ]) *tr* torcere; (*wet clothing*) strizzare; (*one's heart*) stringersi; (e.g., *one's hands*) torcersi; **to wring the truth out of** strappare la verità a

**wringer** ['rɪŋər] *s* strizzatoio

**wrinkle** ['rɪŋkəl] *s* (*on skin*) ruga; (*on fabric*) crespa, grinza; (coll) trovata, espediente *m* || *tr* corrugare, raggrinzire; (*fabric*) increspare

**wrin'kle-proof'** *adj* antipiega, ingualcibile

**wrin·kly** ['rɪŋkli] *adj* (**-klier; -kliest**) rugoso, grinzoso

**wrist** [rɪst] *s* polso

**wrist'band'** *s* polso

**wrist' pin'** *s* spinotto

**wrist' watch'** *s* orologio da polso

**writ** [rɪt] *s* scritto; (law) ordine *m*

**write** [raɪt] *v* (*pret* **wrote** [rot]; *pp* **written** ['rɪtən]) *tr* scrivere; **to write down** mettere in iscritto; (*to disparage*) menomare; **to write off** (*a debt*) cancellare; (com) stornare; **to write up** redigere, scrivere in pieno; (*to ballyhoo*) scrivere le lodi di || *intr* scrivere; **to write back** rispondere per lettera

**write'-in-vote'** *s* voto per candidato il cui nome non è nella lista

**writer** ['raɪtər] *s* scrittore *m*

**write'-up'** s descrizione scritta, conto; stamburata, elogio; (com) valutazione eccesiva

**writhe** [raɪð] intr contorcersi, spasimare, dibattersi

**writing** ['raɪtɪŋ] s lo scrivere; (something written) scritto; (characters written) scrittura; professione di scrittore; **at this writing** scrivendo questa mia; **in one's own writing** di proprio pugno; **to put in writing** mettere in iscritto

**writ'ing desk'** s scrittoio

**writ'ing mate'rials** spl l'occorrente m per scrivere, oggetti mpl di cancelleria

**writ'ing pa'per** s carta da lettere

**writ'ten ac'cent** ['rɪtən] s accento grafico

**wrong** [rɔŋ] or [rɑŋ] adj sbagliato, erroneo; (awry) guasto; (step) falso; cattivo, ingiusto; **there is nothing wrong with him** non ha niente; **to be wrong** (mistaken) aver torto; (guilty) aver la colpa || s torto; **to**

**be in the wrong** essere in errore; **to do wrong** fare del male; commettere un'ingiustizia || adv male; (backward) alla rovescia; **to go wrong** andare alla rovescia; andare per la cattiva strada || tr far torto a, offendere, maltrattare

**wrongdoer** ['rɔŋ‚du·ər] or ['rɑŋ‚du·ər] s peccatore m, trasgressore m

**wrongdoing** ['rɔŋ‚du·ɪŋ] or ['rɑŋ‚du·ɪŋ] s peccato, offesa, trasgressione

**wrong' num'ber** s (telp) numero sbagliato; **you have the wrong number** Lei si è sbagliato di numero

**wrong' side'** s rovescio; (of street) altra parte; **to get out of bed on the wrong side** alzarsi di malumore; **wrong side out** alla rovescia

**wrought' i'ron** [rɔt] s ferro battuto

**wrought'-up'** adj sovreccitato

**wry** [raɪ] adj (wrier; wriest) sbieco, storto; pervertito, alterato; ironico

**wry'neck'** s (orn & pathol) torcicollo

# X

**X, x** [ɛks] s ventiquattresima lettera dell'alfabeto inglese

**Xanthippe** [zæn'tɪpi] s Santippe f

**Xavier** ['zævɪ·ər] or ['zevɪ·ər] s Saverio

**xebec** ['zibɛk] s (naut) sciabecco

**xenon** ['zinɑn] or ['zenɑn] s xeno

**xenophobe** ['zɛnə‚fob] s xenofobo

**Xenophon** ['zɛnəfən] s Senofonte m

**xerography** [zɪ'rɑgrəfi] s xerografia

**xerophyte** [zɪrə‚faɪt] s xerofito

**Xerxes** ['zɑrksɪs] s Serse m

**Xmas** ['krɪsməs] s Natale m

**x-ray** ['ɛks‚re] adj radiografico || s raggio X; (photograph) radiogramma m, radiografia || tr radiografare

**xylograph** ['zaɪlə‚græf] or ['zaɪlə‚grɑf] s silografia

**xylophone** ['zaɪlə‚fon] s silofono

# Y

**Y, y** [waɪ] s venticinquesima lettera dell'alfabeto inglese

**yacht** [jɑt] s yacht m, panfilo

**yacht' club'** s club m nautico, associazione velica

**yak** [jæk] s yak m || v (pret & pp **yakked;** ger **yakking**) intr (slang) ciarlare, chiacchierare

**yam** [jæm] s igname m; (sweet potato) patata dolce, batata

**yank** [jæŋk] s tiro, strattone m || tr dare uno strattone a, tirare || intr dare uno strattone, tirare

**Yankee** ['jæŋki] adj & s yankee mf

**yap** [jæp] s guaito; (slang) chiacchierio, ciancia || v (pret & pp **yapped;** ger **yapping**) intr latrare, guaire; (slang) chiacchierare, ciarlare

**yard** [jɑrd] s cortile m; recinto; yard m, iarda; (naut) pennone m; (rr) scalo smistamento

**yard'arm'** s estremità f del pennone

**yard' goods'** spl tessuti mpl in pezza

**yard'mas'ter** s (rr) capo dello scalo smistamento

**yard'stick'** s stecca di una iarda di lunghezza; (fig) metro

**yarn** [jɑrn] s filo, filato; (coll) storia

**yarrow** ['jæro] s millefoglie m

**yaw** [jɔ] s (naut) straorzata; (aer) imbardata || intr (naut) straorzare, guizzare; (aer) imbardare

**yawl** [jɔl] s barca a remi; (naut) iolla

**yawn** [jɔn] s sbadiglio || intr sbadigliare; (said, e.g., of a hole) vaneggiare, aprirsi

**yea** [je] s & adv sì m

**yean** [jin] intr (said of sheep or goat) partorire

**year** [jɪr] s anno; **to be . . . years old** avere . . . anni; **year in, year out** un anno dopo l'altro

**year'book'** s annuario

**yearling** ['jɪrlɪŋ] adj di un anno di età || s animale m di un anno di età

**yearly** ['jɪrli] *adj* annuale ‖ *adv* annualmente

**yearn** [jʌrn] *intr* smaniare, sospirare; **to yearn for** anelare per

**yearning** ['jʌrnɪŋ] *s* anelo, sospiro ardente

**yeast** [jist] *s* lievito

**yeast' cake'** *s* compressa di lievito

**yell** [jɛl] *s* urlo ‖ *tr* gridare ‖ *intr* urlare

**yellow** ['jɛlo] *adj* giallo; (*newspaper*) sensazionale; (*cowardly*) (coll) vile ‖ *s* giallo; giallo d'uovo ‖ *intr* ingiallire

**yellowish** ['jɛlo·ɪʃ] *adj* giallastro

**yel'low·jack'et** *s* vespa, calabrone *m*

**yel'low streak'** *s* (coll) vena di codardia

**yelp** [jɛlp] *s* guaito ‖ *intr* guaire

**yeoman** *s* (**-men**) (naut) sottufficiale *m*; (Brit) piccolo proprietario terriero

**yeo'man of the guard'** *s* guardia del servizio reale

**yeo'man's serv'ice** *s* lavoro onesto

**yes** [jɛs] *s* sì sì *m*; **to say yes** dire di sì ‖ *adv* sì ‖ *v* (*pret* & *pp* **yessed**; *ger* **yessing**) *tr* dire di sì a ‖ *intr* dire di sì

**yes' man'** *s* (coll) persona che approva sempre; (coll) leccapiedi *m*

**yesterday** ['jɛstərdi] *or* ['jɛstər‚de] *s* & *adv* ieri *m*

**yet** [jɛt] *adv* ancora; tuttavia; **as yet** sinora; **nor yet** nemmeno; **not yet** non ancora ‖ *conj* ma, però, pure

**yew' tree'** [ju] *s* tasso

**Yiddish** ['jɪdɪʃ] *adj* & *s* yiddish *m*

**yield** [jild] *s* rendimento, resa; (*crop*) raccolto; (com) reddito, gettito ‖ *tr* rendere, fruttare ‖ *intr* rendere, fruttare, produrre; (*to surrender*) cedere, arrendersi; sottomettersi; cedere il posto

**yodeling** *or* **yodelling** ['jodəlɪŋ] *s* tirolesa

**yoke** [jok] *s* (*contrivance*) giogo; (*pair, e.g., of oxen*) paio; (*of shirt*) sprone *m*; (naut) barra del timone; **to throw off the yoke** scuotere il giogo ‖ *tr* aggiogare

**yokel** ['jokəl] *s* zoticone *m*

**yolk** [jok] *s* tuorlo

**yonder** ['jandər] *adj* situato lassù; situato laggiù ‖ *adv* lassù; laggiù

**yore** [jor] *s*—**of yore** del tempo antico, del tempo in cui Berta filava

**you** [ju] *pron pers* Lei; tu; Le, La; te, ti; voi; vi; Loro ‖ *pron indef* si, e.g., **you eat at noon** si mangia a mezzogiorno

**young** [jʌŋ] *adj* (**younger** ['jʌŋgər]; **youngest** ['jʌŋgɪst]) giovane ‖ **the young** i giovani

**young' hope'ful** *s* giovane *m* di belle speranze

**young' la'dy** *s* giovane *f*; (*married*) giovane signora

**young' man'** *s* giovane *m*, giovanotto

**young' peo'ple** *s* i giovani

**youngster** ['jʌŋstər] *s* giovanetto; (*child*) bambino

**your** [jur] *adj* Suo, il Suo; tuo, il tuo; vostro, il vostro

**yours** [jurz] *pron poss* Suo, il Suo; tuo, il tuo; vostro, il vostro; **of yours** Suo; **very truly yours** distinti saluti

**your·self** [jur'sɛlf] *pron pers* (**-selves** ['sɛlvz]) Lei stesso; sé stesso; si, e.g., **are your enjoying yourself?** si diverte?

**youth** [juθ] *s* (**youths** [juθs] *or* [juðz]) gioventù *f*, giovinezza; (*person*) giovane *mf*; i giovani

**youthful** ['juθfəl] *adj* giovane, giovanile

**yowl** [jaul] *s* urlo ‖ *intr* urlare

**Yugoslav** ['jugo'slav] *adj* & *s* iugoslavo

**Yugoslavia** ['jugo'slavɪ·ə] *s* la Iugoslavia

**Yule** [jul] *s* il Natale; le feste natalizie

**Yule' log'** *s* ceppo

**Yuletide** ['jul‚taɪd] *s* le feste natalizie

# Z

**Z, z** [zi] *s* ventiseiesima lettera dell'alfabeto inglese

**za·ny** ['zeni] *adj* (**-nier; -niest**) comico, buffonesco ‖ *s* (**-nies**) buffone *m*, pagliaccio

**zeal** [zil] *s* zelo, entusiasmo

**zealot** ['zɛlət] *s* zelante *mf*, fanatico

**zealotry** ['zɛlətri] *s* fanatismo

**zealous** ['zɛləs] *adj* zelante, volenteroso

**zebra** ['zibrə] *s* zebra

**ze'bra cross'ing** *s* zebre *fpl*

**zebu** ['zibju] *s* zebù *m*

**zenith** ['zinɪθ] *s* zenit *m*

**zephyr** ['zɛfər] *s* zefiro

**ze·ro** ['ziro] *s* (**-roes**) zero ‖ *tr*—**to zero in** (mil) aggiustare il mirino di ‖ *intr*—**to zero in on** (mil) concentrare il fuoco su

**ze'ro grav'ity** *s* gravità *f* zero

**ze'ro hour'** *s* ora zero

**zest** [zɛst] *s* entusiasmo; (*flavor*) aroma *m*, sapore *m*

**Zeus** [zus] *s* Zeus *m*

**zig-zag** ['zɪg‚zæg] *adj* & *adv* a zigzag ‖ *s* zigzag *m*; serpentina ‖ *v* (*pret* & *pp* **-zagged**; *ger* **-zagging**) *intr* zigzagare; serpeggiare

**zinc** [zɪŋk] *s* zinco

**zinnia** ['zɪnɪ·ə] *s* zinnia

**Zionism** ['zaɪ·ə‚nɪzəm] *s* sionismo

**zip** [zɪp] *s* (coll) sibilo; (coll) energia, vigore *m* ‖ *v* (*pret* & *pp* **zipped**; *ger* **zipping**) *tr* chiudere con cerniera lampo; aprire con cerniera lampo; (coll) portare rapidamente; **to zip up** (*to add zest to*) dare gusto a ‖ *intr* aprirsi con cerniera lampo; sibilare; (coll) filare, correre; **to zip by** (coll) passare come un lampo

**zip' code'** s codice m di avviamento postale

**zipper** ['zɪpər] s cerniera or serratura lampo

**zircon** ['zʌrkɑn] s zircone m

**zirconium** [zər'konɪ·əm] s zirconio

**zither** ['zɪθər] s cetra tirolese

**zodiac** ['zodɪ ˌæk] s zodiaco

**zone** [zon] s zona; distretto postale || tr dividere in zone

**zoo** [zu] s giardino zoologico

**zoologic(al)** [ˌzo·ə'lɑdʒɪk(əl)] adj zoologico

**zoologist** [zo'ɑlədʒɪst] s zoologo

**zoology** [zo'ɑlədʒi] s zoologia

**zoom** [zum] s ronzio; (aer) cabrata, impennata; (mov, telv) zumata || tr (aer) far cabrare, fare impennare; (mov, telv) zumare || intr ronzare; (aer) cabrare, impennarsi; (mov, telv) zumare

**zoom' lens'** s (phot) transfocatore m

**zoophite** ['zo·ə ˌfaɪt] s zoofito

**Zu·lu** ['zulu] adj zulù || s (-lus) zulù mf

**Zurich** ['zurɪk] s Zurigo f